D1228128

Oxford Dictionary of National Biography

IN ASSOCIATION WITH
The British Academy

From the earliest times to the year 2000

Edited by
H. C. G. Matthew
and
Brian Harrison

Volume 34
Liston–McAlpine

OXFORD
UNIVERSITY PRESS

Great Clarendon Street, Oxford OX2 6DP

Oxford University Press is a department of the University of Oxford.
It furthers the University's objective of excellence in research, scholarship,
and education by publishing worldwide in

Oxford New York

Auckland Bangkok Buenos Aires Cape Town
Chennai Dar es Salaam Delhi Hong Kong Istanbul Karachi
Kolkata Kuala Lumpur Madrid Melbourne Mexico City Mumbai Nairobi
São Paulo Shanghai Taipei Tokyo Toronto

Oxford is a registered trade mark of Oxford University Press
in the UK and in certain other countries

Published in the United States
by Oxford University Press Inc., New York

First published 2004

British Library Cataloguing in Publication Data
Data available

Library of Congress Cataloging in Publication Data
Data available: for details see volume 1, p. iv

ISBN 0-19-861384-9 (this volume)
ISBN 0-19-861411-X (set of sixty volumes)

Text captured by Alliance Phototypesetters, Pondicherry
Illustrations reproduced and archived by
Alliance Graphics Ltd, UK
Typeset in OUP Swift by Interactive Sciences Limited, Gloucester
Printed in Great Britain on acid-free paper by
Butler and Tanner Ltd,
Frome, Somerset

LIST OF ABBREVIATIONS

1 *General abbreviations*

AB	bachelor of arts
ABC	Australian Broadcasting Corporation
ABC TV	ABC Television
act.	active
A$	Australian dollar
AD	*anno domini*
AFC	Air Force Cross
AIDS	acquired immune deficiency syndrome
AK	Alaska
AL	Alabama
A level	advanced level [examination]
ALS	associate of the Linnean Society
AM	master of arts
AMICE	associate member of the Institution of Civil Engineers
ANZAC	Australian and New Zealand Army Corps
appx *pl.* appxs	appendix(es)
AR	Arkansas
ARA	associate of the Royal Academy
ARCA	associate of the Royal College of Art
ARCM	associate of the Royal College of Music
ARCO	associate of the Royal College of Organists
ARIBA	associate of the Royal Institute of British Architects
ARP	air-raid precautions
ARRC	associate of the Royal Red Cross
ARSA	associate of the Royal Scottish Academy
art.	article / item
ASC	Army Service Corps
Asch	Austrian Schilling
ASDIC	Antisubmarine Detection Investigation Committee
ATS	Auxiliary Territorial Service
ATV	Associated Television
Aug	August
AZ	Arizona
b.	born
BA	bachelor of arts
BA (Admin.)	bachelor of arts (administration)
BAFTA	British Academy of Film and Television Arts
BAO	bachelor of arts in obstetrics
bap.	baptized
BBC	British Broadcasting Corporation / Company
BC	before Christ
BCE	before the common (*or* Christian) era
BCE	bachelor of civil engineering
BCG	bacillus of Calmette and Guérin [inoculation against tuberculosis]
BCh	bachelor of surgery
BChir	bachelor of surgery
BCL	bachelor of civil law
BCnL	bachelor of canon law
BCom	bachelor of commerce
BD	bachelor of divinity
BEd	bachelor of education
BEng	bachelor of engineering
bk *pl.* bks	book(s)
BL	bachelor of law / letters / literature
BLitt	bachelor of letters
BM	bachelor of medicine
BMus	bachelor of music
BP	before present
BP	British Petroleum
Bros.	Brothers
BS	(1) bachelor of science; (2) bachelor of surgery; (3) British standard
BSc	bachelor of science
BSc (Econ.)	bachelor of science (economics)
BSc (Eng.)	bachelor of science (engineering)
bt	baronet
BTh	bachelor of theology
bur.	buried
C.	command [identifier for published parliamentary papers]
c.	*circa*
c.	*capitulum pl. capitula*: chapter(s)
CA	California
Cantab.	Cantabrigiensis
cap.	*capitulum pl. capitula*: chapter(s)
CB	companion of the Bath
CBE	commander of the Order of the British Empire
CBS	Columbia Broadcasting System
cc	cubic centimetres
C$	Canadian dollar
CD	compact disc
Cd	command [identifier for published parliamentary papers]
CE	Common (*or* Christian) Era
cent.	century
cf.	compare
CH	Companion of Honour
chap.	chapter
ChB	bachelor of surgery
CI	Imperial Order of the Crown of India
CIA	Central Intelligence Agency
CID	Criminal Investigation Department
CIE	companion of the Order of the Indian Empire
Cie	Compagnie
CLit	companion of literature
CM	master of surgery
cm	centimetre(s)

Cmd	command [identifier for published parliamentary papers]
CMG	companion of the Order of St Michael and St George
Cmnd	command [identifier for published parliamentary papers]
CO	Colorado
Co.	company
co.	county
col. *pl.* cols.	column(s)
Corp.	corporation
CSE	certificate of secondary education
CSI	companion of the Order of the Star of India
CT	Connecticut
CVO	commander of the Royal Victorian Order
cwt	hundredweight
$	(American) dollar
d.	(1) penny (pence); (2) died
DBE	dame commander of the Order of the British Empire
DCH	diploma in child health
DCh	doctor of surgery
DCL	doctor of civil law
DCnL	doctor of canon law
DCVO	dame commander of the Royal Victorian Order
DD	doctor of divinity
DE	Delaware
Dec	December
dem.	demolished
DEng	doctor of engineering
des.	destroyed
DFC	Distinguished Flying Cross
DipEd	diploma in education
DipPsych	diploma in psychiatry
diss.	dissertation
DL	deputy lieutenant
DLitt	doctor of letters
DLittCelt	doctor of Celtic letters
DM	(1) Deutschmark; (2) doctor of medicine; (3) doctor of musical arts
DMus	doctor of music
DNA	dioxyribonucleic acid
doc.	document
DOL	doctor of oriental learning
DPH	diploma in public health
DPhil	doctor of philosophy
DPM	diploma in psychological medicine
DSC	Distinguished Service Cross
DSc	doctor of science
DSc (Econ.)	doctor of science (economics)
DSc (Eng.)	doctor of science (engineering)
DSM	Distinguished Service Medal
DSO	companion of the Distinguished Service Order
DSocSc	doctor of social science
DTech	doctor of technology
DTh	doctor of theology
DTM	diploma in tropical medicine
DTMH	diploma in tropical medicine and hygiene
DU	doctor of the university
DUniv	doctor of the university
dwt	pennyweight
EC	European Community
ed. *pl.* eds.	edited / edited by / editor(s)
Edin.	Edinburgh
edn	edition
EEC	European Economic Community
EFTA	European Free Trade Association
EICS	East India Company Service
EMI	Electrical and Musical Industries (Ltd)
Eng.	English
enl.	enlarged
ENSA	Entertainments National Service Association
ep. *pl.* epp.	*epistola(e)*
ESP	extra-sensory perception
esp.	especially
esq.	esquire
est.	estimate / estimated
EU	European Union
ex	sold by (*lit.* out of)
excl.	excludes / excluding
exh.	exhibited
exh. cat.	exhibition catalogue
f. *pl.* ff.	following [pages]
FA	Football Association
FACP	fellow of the American College of Physicians
facs.	facsimile
FANY	First Aid Nursing Yeomanry
FBA	fellow of the British Academy
FBI	Federation of British Industries
FCS	fellow of the Chemical Society
Feb	February
FEng	fellow of the Fellowship of Engineering
FFCM	fellow of the Faculty of Community Medicine
FGS	fellow of the Geological Society
fig.	figure
FIMechE	fellow of the Institution of Mechanical Engineers
FL	Florida
fl.	*floruit*
FLS	fellow of the Linnean Society
FM	frequency modulation
fol. *pl.* fols.	folio(s)
Fr	French francs
Fr.	French
FRAeS	fellow of the Royal Aeronautical Society
FRAI	fellow of the Royal Anthropological Institute
FRAM	fellow of the Royal Academy of Music
FRAS	(1) fellow of the Royal Asiatic Society; (2) fellow of the Royal Astronomical Society
FRCM	fellow of the Royal College of Music
FRCO	fellow of the Royal College of Organists
FRCOG	fellow of the Royal College of Obstetricians and Gynaecologists
FRCP(C)	fellow of the Royal College of Physicians of Canada
FRCP (Edin.)	fellow of the Royal College of Physicians of Edinburgh
FRCP (Lond.)	fellow of the Royal College of Physicians of London
FRCPath	fellow of the Royal College of Pathologists
FRCPsych	fellow of the Royal College of Psychiatrists
FRCS	fellow of the Royal College of Surgeons
FRGS	fellow of the Royal Geographical Society
FRIBA	fellow of the Royal Institute of British Architects
FRICS	fellow of the Royal Institute of Chartered Surveyors
FRS	fellow of the Royal Society
FRSA	fellow of the Royal Society of Arts

FRSCM	fellow of the Royal School of Church Music
FRSE	fellow of the Royal Society of Edinburgh
FRSL	fellow of the Royal Society of Literature
FSA	fellow of the Society of Antiquaries
ft	foot *pl.* feet
FTCL	fellow of Trinity College of Music, London
ft-lb per min.	foot-pounds per minute [unit of horsepower]
FZS	fellow of the Zoological Society
GA	Georgia
GBE	knight or dame grand cross of the Order of the British Empire
GCB	knight grand cross of the Order of the Bath
GCE	general certificate of education
GCH	knight grand cross of the Royal Guelphic Order
GCHQ	government communications headquarters
GCIE	knight grand commander of the Order of the Indian Empire
GCMG	knight or dame grand cross of the Order of St Michael and St George
GCSE	general certificate of secondary education
GCSI	knight grand commander of the Order of the Star of India
GCStJ	bailiff or dame grand cross of the order of St John of Jerusalem
GCVO	knight or dame grand cross of the Royal Victorian Order
GEC	General Electric Company
Ger.	German
GI	government (*or* general) issue
GMT	Greenwich mean time
GP	general practitioner
GPU	[Soviet special police unit]
GSO	general staff officer
Heb.	Hebrew
HEICS	Honourable East India Company Service
HI	Hawaii
HIV	human immunodeficiency virus
HK$	Hong Kong dollar
HM	his / her majesty('s)
HMAS	his / her majesty's Australian ship
HMNZS	his / her majesty's New Zealand ship
HMS	his / her majesty's ship
HMSO	His / Her Majesty's Stationery Office
HMV	His Master's Voice
Hon.	Honourable
hp	horsepower
hr	hour(s)
HRH	his / her royal highness
HTV	Harlech Television
IA	Iowa
ibid.	*ibidem*: in the same place
ICI	Imperial Chemical Industries (Ltd)
ID	Idaho
IL	Illinois
illus.	illustration
illustr.	illustrated
IN	Indiana
in.	inch(es)
Inc.	Incorporated
incl.	includes / including
IOU	I owe you
IQ	intelligence quotient
Ir£	Irish pound
IRA	Irish Republican Army
ISO	companion of the Imperial Service Order
It.	Italian
ITA	Independent Television Authority
ITV	Independent Television
Jan	January
JP	justice of the peace
jun.	junior
KB	knight of the Order of the Bath
KBE	knight commander of the Order of the British Empire
KC	king's counsel
kcal	kilocalorie
KCB	knight commander of the Order of the Bath
KCH	knight commander of the Royal Guelphic Order
KCIE	knight commander of the Order of the Indian Empire
KCMG	knight commander of the Order of St Michael and St George
KCSI	knight commander of the Order of the Star of India
KCVO	knight commander of the Royal Victorian Order
keV	kilo-electron-volt
KG	knight of the Order of the Garter
KGB	[Soviet committee of state security]
KH	knight of the Royal Guelphic Order
KLM	Koninklijke Luchtvaart Maatschappij (Royal Dutch Air Lines)
km	kilometre(s)
KP	knight of the Order of St Patrick
KS	Kansas
KT	knight of the Order of the Thistle
kt	knight
KY	Kentucky
£	pound(s) sterling
£E	Egyptian pound
L	lira *pl.* lire
l. *pl.* ll.	line(s)
LA	Lousiana
LAA	light anti-aircraft
LAH	licentiate of the Apothecaries' Hall, Dublin
Lat.	Latin
lb	pound(s), unit of weight
LDS	licence in dental surgery
lit.	literally
LittB	bachelor of letters
LittD	doctor of letters
LKQCPI	licentiate of the King and Queen's College of Physicians, Ireland
LLA	lady literate in arts
LLB	bachelor of laws
LLD	doctor of laws
LLM	master of laws
LM	licentiate in midwifery
LP	long-playing record
LRAM	licentiate of the Royal Academy of Music
LRCP	licentiate of the Royal College of Physicians
LRCPS (Glasgow)	licentiate of the Royal College of Physicians and Surgeons of Glasgow
LRCS	licentiate of the Royal College of Surgeons
LSA	licentiate of the Society of Apothecaries
LSD	lysergic acid diethylamide
LVO	lieutenant of the Royal Victorian Order
M. *pl.* MM.	Monsieur *pl.* Messieurs
m	metre(s)

m. *pl.* mm.	membrane(s)
MA	(1) Massachusetts; (2) master of arts
MAI	master of engineering
MB	bachelor of medicine
MBA	master of business administration
MBE	member of the Order of the British Empire
MC	Military Cross
MCC	Marylebone Cricket Club
MCh	master of surgery
MChir	master of surgery
MCom	master of commerce
MD	(1) doctor of medicine; (2) Maryland
MDMA	methylenedioxymethamphetamine
ME	Maine
MEd	master of education
MEng	master of engineering
MEP	member of the European parliament
MG	Morris Garages
MGM	Metro-Goldwyn-Mayer
Mgr	Monsignor
MI	(1) Michigan; (2) military intelligence
MI1c	[secret intelligence department]
MI5	[military intelligence department]
MI6	[secret intelligence department]
MI9	[secret escape service]
MICE	member of the Institution of Civil Engineers
MIEE	member of the Institution of Electrical Engineers
min.	minute(s)
Mk	mark
ML	(1) licentiate of medicine; (2) master of laws
MLitt	master of letters
Mlle	Mademoiselle
mm	millimetre(s)
Mme	Madame
MN	Minnesota
MO	Missouri
MOH	medical officer of health
MP	member of parliament
m.p.h.	miles per hour
MPhil	master of philosophy
MRCP	member of the Royal College of Physicians
MRCS	member of the Royal College of Surgeons
MRCVS	member of the Royal College of Veterinary Surgeons
MRIA	member of the Royal Irish Academy
MS	(1) master of science; (2) Mississippi
MS *pl.* MSS	manuscript(s)
MSc	master of science
MSc (Econ.)	master of science (economics)
MT	Montana
MusB	bachelor of music
MusBac	bachelor of music
MusD	doctor of music
MV	motor vessel
MVO	member of the Royal Victorian Order
n. *pl.* nn.	note(s)
NAAFI	Navy, Army, and Air Force Institutes
NASA	National Aeronautics and Space Administration
NATO	North Atlantic Treaty Organization
NBC	National Broadcasting Corporation
NC	North Carolina
NCO	non-commissioned officer
ND	North Dakota
n.d.	no date
NE	Nebraska
nem. con.	*nemine contradicente*: unanimously
new ser.	new series
NH	New Hampshire
NHS	National Health Service
NJ	New Jersey
NKVD	[Soviet people's commissariat for internal affairs]
NM	New Mexico
nm	nanometre(s)
no. *pl.* nos.	number(s)
Nov	November
n.p.	no place [of publication]
NS	new style
NV	Nevada
NY	New York
NZBS	New Zealand Broadcasting Service
OBE	officer of the Order of the British Empire
obit.	obituary
Oct	October
OCTU	officer cadets training unit
OECD	Organization for Economic Co-operation and Development
OEEC	Organization for European Economic Co-operation
OFM	order of Friars Minor [Franciscans]
OFMCap	Ordine Frati Minori Cappucini: member of the Capuchin order
OH	Ohio
OK	Oklahoma
O level	ordinary level [examination]
OM	Order of Merit
OP	order of Preachers [Dominicans]
op. *pl.* opp.	opus *pl.* opera
OPEC	Organization of Petroleum Exporting Countries
OR	Oregon
orig.	original
OS	old style
OSB	Order of St Benedict
OTC	Officers' Training Corps
OWS	Old Watercolour Society
Oxon.	Oxoniensis
p. *pl.* pp.	page(s)
PA	Pennsylvania
p.a.	per annum
para.	paragraph
PAYE	pay as you earn
pbk *pl.* pbks	paperback(s)
per.	[during the] period
PhD	doctor of philosophy
pl.	(1) plate(s); (2) plural
priv. coll.	private collection
pt *pl.* pts	part(s)
pubd	published
PVC	polyvinyl chloride
q. *pl.* qq.	(1) question(s); (2) quire(s)
QC	queen's counsel
R	rand
R.	Rex / Regina
r	recto
r.	reigned / ruled
RA	Royal Academy / Royal Academician

RAC	Royal Automobile Club
RAF	Royal Air Force
RAFVR	Royal Air Force Volunteer Reserve
RAM	[member of the] Royal Academy of Music
RAMC	Royal Army Medical Corps
RCA	Royal College of Art
RCNC	Royal Corps of Naval Constructors
RCOG	Royal College of Obstetricians and Gynaecologists
RDI	royal designer for industry
RE	Royal Engineers
repr. *pl.* reprs.	reprint(s) / reprinted
repro.	reproduced
rev.	revised / revised by / reviser / revision
Revd	Reverend
RHA	Royal Hibernian Academy
RI	(1) Rhode Island; (2) Royal Institute of Painters in Water-Colours
RIBA	Royal Institute of British Architects
RIN	Royal Indian Navy
RM	Reichsmark
RMS	Royal Mail steamer
RN	Royal Navy
RNA	ribonucleic acid
RNAS	Royal Naval Air Service
RNR	Royal Naval Reserve
RNVR	Royal Naval Volunteer Reserve
RO	Record Office
r.p.m.	revolutions per minute
RRS	royal research ship
Rs	rupees
RSA	(1) Royal Scottish Academician; (2) Royal Society of Arts
RSPCA	Royal Society for the Prevention of Cruelty to Animals
Rt Hon.	Right Honourable
Rt Revd	Right Reverend
RUC	Royal Ulster Constabulary
Russ.	Russian
RWS	Royal Watercolour Society
S4C	Sianel Pedwar Cymru
s.	shilling(s)
s.a.	*sub anno*: under the year
SABC	South African Broadcasting Corporation
SAS	Special Air Service
SC	South Carolina
ScD	doctor of science
S$	Singapore dollar
SD	South Dakota
sec.	second(s)
sel.	selected
sen.	senior
Sept	September
ser.	series
SHAPE	supreme headquarters allied powers, Europe
SIDRO	Société Internationale d'Énergie Hydro-Électrique
sig. *pl.* sigs.	signature(s)
sing.	singular
SIS	Secret Intelligence Service
SJ	Society of Jesus
Skr	Swedish krona
Span.	Spanish
SPCK	Society for Promoting Christian Knowledge
SS	(1) Santissimi; (2) Schutzstaffel; (3) steam ship
STB	bachelor of theology
STD	doctor of theology
STM	master of theology
STP	doctor of theology
supp.	supposedly
suppl. *pl.* suppls.	supplement(s)
s.v.	*sub verbo* / *sub voce*: under the word / heading
SY	steam yacht
TA	Territorial Army
TASS	[Soviet news agency]
TB	tuberculosis (*lit.* tubercle bacillus)
TD	(1) *teachtaí dála* (member of the Dáil); (2) territorial decoration
TN	Tennessee
TNT	trinitrotoluene
trans.	translated / translated by / translation / translator
TT	tourist trophy
TUC	Trades Union Congress
TX	Texas
U-boat	*Unterseeboot*: submarine
Ufa	Universum-Film AG
UMIST	University of Manchester Institute of Science and Technology
UN	United Nations
UNESCO	United Nations Educational, Scientific, and Cultural Organization
UNICEF	United Nations International Children's Emergency Fund
unpubd	unpublished
USS	United States ship
UT	Utah
v	verso
v.	versus
VA	Virginia
VAD	Voluntary Aid Detachment
VC	Victoria Cross
VE-day	victory in Europe day
Ven.	Venerable
VJ-day	victory over Japan day
vol. *pl.* vols.	volume(s)
VT	Vermont
WA	Washington [state]
WAAC	Women's Auxiliary Army Corps
WAAF	Women's Auxiliary Air Force
WEA	Workers' Educational Association
WHO	World Health Organization
WI	Wisconsin
WRAF	Women's Royal Air Force
WRNS	Women's Royal Naval Service
WV	West Virginia
WVS	Women's Voluntary Service
WY	Wyoming
¥	yen
YMCA	Young Men's Christian Association
YWCA	Young Women's Christian Association

2 *Institution abbreviations*

All Souls Oxf.	All Souls College, Oxford
AM Oxf.	Ashmolean Museum, Oxford
Balliol Oxf.	Balliol College, Oxford
BBC WAC	BBC Written Archives Centre, Reading
Beds. & Luton ARS	Bedfordshire and Luton Archives and Record Service, Bedford
Berks. RO	Berkshire Record Office, Reading
BFI	British Film Institute, London
BFI NFTVA	British Film Institute, London, National Film and Television Archive
BGS	British Geological Survey, Keyworth, Nottingham
Birm. CA	Birmingham Central Library, Birmingham City Archives
Birm. CL	Birmingham Central Library
BL	British Library, London
BL NSA	British Library, London, National Sound Archive
BL OIOC	British Library, London, Oriental and India Office Collections
BLPES	London School of Economics and Political Science, British Library of Political and Economic Science
BM	British Museum, London
Bodl. Oxf.	Bodleian Library, Oxford
Bodl. RH	Bodleian Library of Commonwealth and African Studies at Rhodes House, Oxford
Borth. Inst.	Borthwick Institute of Historical Research, University of York
Boston PL	Boston Public Library, Massachusetts
Bristol RO	Bristol Record Office
Bucks. RLSS	Buckinghamshire Records and Local Studies Service, Aylesbury
CAC Cam.	Churchill College, Cambridge, Churchill Archives Centre
Cambs. AS	Cambridgeshire Archive Service
CCC Cam.	Corpus Christi College, Cambridge
CCC Oxf.	Corpus Christi College, Oxford
Ches. & Chester ALSS	Cheshire and Chester Archives and Local Studies Service
Christ Church Oxf.	Christ Church, Oxford
Christies	Christies, London
City Westm. AC	City of Westminster Archives Centre, London
CKS	Centre for Kentish Studies, Maidstone
CLRO	Corporation of London Records Office
Coll. Arms	College of Arms, London
Col. U.	Columbia University, New York
Cornwall RO	Cornwall Record Office, Truro
Courtauld Inst.	Courtauld Institute of Art, London
CUL	Cambridge University Library
Cumbria AS	Cumbria Archive Service
Derbys. RO	Derbyshire Record Office, Matlock
Devon RO	Devon Record Office, Exeter
Dorset RO	Dorset Record Office, Dorchester
Duke U.	Duke University, Durham, North Carolina
Duke U., Perkins L.	Duke University, Durham, North Carolina, William R. Perkins Library
Durham Cath. CL	Durham Cathedral, chapter library
Durham RO	Durham Record Office
DWL	Dr Williams's Library, London
Essex RO	Essex Record Office
E. Sussex RO	East Sussex Record Office, Lewes
Eton	Eton College, Berkshire
FM Cam.	Fitzwilliam Museum, Cambridge
Folger	Folger Shakespeare Library, Washington, DC
Garr. Club	Garrick Club, London
Girton Cam.	Girton College, Cambridge
GL	Guildhall Library, London
Glos. RO	Gloucestershire Record Office, Gloucester
Gon. & Caius Cam.	Gonville and Caius College, Cambridge
Gov. Art Coll.	Government Art Collection
GS Lond.	Geological Society of London
Hants. RO	Hampshire Record Office, Winchester
Harris Man. Oxf.	Harris Manchester College, Oxford
Harvard TC	Harvard Theatre Collection, Harvard University, Cambridge, Massachusetts, Nathan Marsh Pusey Library
Harvard U.	Harvard University, Cambridge, Massachusetts
Harvard U., Houghton L.	Harvard University, Cambridge, Massachusetts, Houghton Library
Herefs. RO	Herefordshire Record Office, Hereford
Herts. ALS	Hertfordshire Archives and Local Studies, Hertford
Hist. Soc. Penn.	Historical Society of Pennsylvania, Philadelphia
HLRO	House of Lords Record Office, London
Hult. Arch.	Hulton Archive, London and New York
Hunt. L.	Huntington Library, San Marino, California
ICL	Imperial College, London
Inst. CE	Institution of Civil Engineers, London
Inst. EE	Institution of Electrical Engineers, London
IWM	Imperial War Museum, London
IWM FVA	Imperial War Museum, London, Film and Video Archive
IWM SA	Imperial War Museum, London, Sound Archive
JRL	John Rylands University Library of Manchester
King's AC Cam.	King's College Archives Centre, Cambridge
King's Cam.	King's College, Cambridge
King's Lond.	King's College, London
King's Lond., Liddell Hart C.	King's College, London, Liddell Hart Centre for Military Archives
Lancs. RO	Lancashire Record Office, Preston
L. Cong.	Library of Congress, Washington, DC
Leics. RO	Leicestershire, Leicester, and Rutland Record Office, Leicester
Lincs. Arch.	Lincolnshire Archives, Lincoln
Linn. Soc.	Linnean Society of London
LMA	London Metropolitan Archives
LPL	Lambeth Palace, London
Lpool RO	Liverpool Record Office and Local Studies Service
LUL	London University Library
Magd. Cam.	Magdalene College, Cambridge
Magd. Oxf.	Magdalen College, Oxford
Man. City Gall.	Manchester City Galleries
Man. CL	Manchester Central Library
Mass. Hist. Soc.	Massachusetts Historical Society, Boston
Merton Oxf.	Merton College, Oxford
MHS Oxf.	Museum of the History of Science, Oxford
Mitchell L., Glas.	Mitchell Library, Glasgow
Mitchell L., NSW	State Library of New South Wales, Sydney, Mitchell Library
Morgan L.	Pierpont Morgan Library, New York
NA Canada	National Archives of Canada, Ottawa
NA Ire.	National Archives of Ireland, Dublin
NAM	National Army Museum, London
NA Scot.	National Archives of Scotland, Edinburgh
News Int. RO	News International Record Office, London
NG Ire.	National Gallery of Ireland, Dublin

NG Scot.	National Gallery of Scotland, Edinburgh
NHM	Natural History Museum, London
NL Aus.	National Library of Australia, Canberra
NL Ire.	National Library of Ireland, Dublin
NL NZ	National Library of New Zealand, Wellington
NL NZ, Turnbull L.	National Library of New Zealand, Wellington, Alexander Turnbull Library
NL Scot.	National Library of Scotland, Edinburgh
NL Wales	National Library of Wales, Aberystwyth
NMG Wales	National Museum and Gallery of Wales, Cardiff
NMM	National Maritime Museum, London
Norfolk RO	Norfolk Record Office, Norwich
Northants. RO	Northamptonshire Record Office, Northampton
Northumbd RO	Northumberland Record Office
Notts. Arch.	Nottinghamshire Archives, Nottingham
NPG	National Portrait Gallery, London
NRA	National Archives, London, Historical Manuscripts Commission, National Register of Archives
Nuffield Oxf.	Nuffield College, Oxford
N. Yorks. CRO	North Yorkshire County Record Office, Northallerton
NYPL	New York Public Library
Oxf. UA	Oxford University Archives
Oxf. U. Mus. NH	Oxford University Museum of Natural History
Oxon. RO	Oxfordshire Record Office, Oxford
Pembroke Cam.	Pembroke College, Cambridge
PRO	National Archives, London, Public Record Office
PRO NIre.	Public Record Office for Northern Ireland, Belfast
Pusey Oxf.	Pusey House, Oxford
RA	Royal Academy of Arts, London
Ransom HRC	Harry Ransom Humanities Research Center, University of Texas, Austin
RAS	Royal Astronomical Society, London
RBG Kew	Royal Botanic Gardens, Kew, London
RCP Lond.	Royal College of Physicians of London
RCS Eng.	Royal College of Surgeons of England, London
RGS	Royal Geographical Society, London
RIBA	Royal Institute of British Architects, London
RIBA BAL	Royal Institute of British Architects, London, British Architectural Library
Royal Arch.	Royal Archives, Windsor Castle, Berkshire [by gracious permission of her majesty the queen]
Royal Irish Acad.	Royal Irish Academy, Dublin
Royal Scot. Acad.	Royal Scottish Academy, Edinburgh
RS	Royal Society, London
RSA	Royal Society of Arts, London
RS Friends, Lond.	Religious Society of Friends, London
St Ant. Oxf.	St Antony's College, Oxford
St John Cam.	St John's College, Cambridge
S. Antiquaries, Lond.	Society of Antiquaries of London
Sci. Mus.	Science Museum, London
Scot. NPG	Scottish National Portrait Gallery, Edinburgh
Scott Polar RI	University of Cambridge, Scott Polar Research Institute
Sheff. Arch.	Sheffield Archives
Shrops. RRC	Shropshire Records and Research Centre, Shrewsbury
SOAS	School of Oriental and African Studies, London
Som. ARS	Somerset Archive and Record Service, Taunton
Staffs. RO	Staffordshire Record Office, Stafford
Suffolk RO	Suffolk Record Office
Surrey HC	Surrey History Centre, Woking
TCD	Trinity College, Dublin
Trinity Cam.	Trinity College, Cambridge
U. Aberdeen	University of Aberdeen
U. Birm.	University of Birmingham
U. Birm. L.	University of Birmingham Library
U. Cal.	University of California
U. Cam.	University of Cambridge
UCL	University College, London
U. Durham	University of Durham
U. Durham L.	University of Durham Library
U. Edin.	University of Edinburgh
U. Edin., New Coll.	University of Edinburgh, New College
U. Edin., New Coll. L.	University of Edinburgh, New College Library
U. Edin. L.	University of Edinburgh Library
U. Glas.	University of Glasgow
U. Glas. L.	University of Glasgow Library
U. Hull	University of Hull
U. Hull, Brynmor Jones L.	University of Hull, Brynmor Jones Library
U. Leeds	University of Leeds
U. Leeds, Brotherton L.	University of Leeds, Brotherton Library
U. Lond.	University of London
U. Lpool	University of Liverpool
U. Lpool L.	University of Liverpool Library
U. Mich.	University of Michigan, Ann Arbor
U. Mich., Clements L.	University of Michigan, Ann Arbor, William L. Clements Library
U. Newcastle	University of Newcastle upon Tyne
U. Newcastle, Robinson L.	University of Newcastle upon Tyne, Robinson Library
U. Nott.	University of Nottingham
U. Nott. L.	University of Nottingham Library
U. Oxf.	University of Oxford
U. Reading	University of Reading
U. Reading L.	University of Reading Library
U. St Andr.	University of St Andrews
U. St Andr. L.	University of St Andrews Library
U. Southampton	University of Southampton
U. Southampton L.	University of Southampton Library
U. Sussex	University of Sussex, Brighton
U. Texas	University of Texas, Austin
U. Wales	University of Wales
U. Warwick Mod. RC	University of Warwick, Coventry, Modern Records Centre
V&A	Victoria and Albert Museum, London
V&A NAL	Victoria and Albert Museum, London, National Art Library
Warks. CRO	Warwickshire County Record Office, Warwick
Wellcome L.	Wellcome Library for the History and Understanding of Medicine, London
Westm. DA	Westminster Diocesan Archives, London
Wilts. & Swindon RO	Wiltshire and Swindon Record Office, Trowbridge
Worcs. RO	Worcestershire Record Office, Worcester
W. Sussex RO	West Sussex Record Office, Chichester
W. Yorks. AS	West Yorkshire Archive Service
Yale U.	Yale University, New Haven, Connecticut
Yale U., Beinecke L.	Yale University, New Haven, Connecticut, Beinecke Rare Book and Manuscript Library
Yale U. CBA	Yale University, New Haven, Connecticut, Yale Center for British Art

3 *Bibliographic abbreviations*

Adams, *Drama*	W. D. Adams, *A dictionary of the drama*, 1: *A–G* (1904); 2: *H–Z* (1956) [vol. 2 microfilm only]
AFM	J O'Donovan, ed. and trans., *Annala rioghachta Eireann / Annals of the kingdom of Ireland by the four masters*, 7 vols. (1848–51); 2nd edn (1856); 3rd edn (1990)
Allibone, *Dict.*	S. A. Allibone, *A critical dictionary of English literature and British and American authors*, 3 vols. (1859–71); suppl. by J. F. Kirk, 2 vols. (1891)
ANB	J. A. Garraty and M. C. Carnes, eds., *American national biography*, 24 vols. (1999)
Anderson, *Scot. nat.*	W. Anderson, *The Scottish nation, or, The surnames, families, literature, honours, and biographical history of the people of Scotland*, 3 vols. (1859–63)
Ann. mon.	H. R. Luard, ed., *Annales monastici*, 5 vols., Rolls Series, 36 (1864–9)
Ann. Ulster	S. Mac Airt and G. Mac Niocaill, eds., *Annals of Ulster (to AD 1131)* (1983)
APC	*Acts of the privy council of England*, new ser., 46 vols. (1890–1964)
APS	*The acts of the parliaments of Scotland*, 12 vols. in 13 (1814–75)
Arber, *Regs. Stationers*	F. Arber, ed., *A transcript of the registers of the Company of Stationers of London, 1554–1640 AD*, 5 vols. (1875–94)
ArchR	*Architectural Review*
ASC	D. Whitelock, D. C. Douglas, and S. I. Tucker, ed. and trans., *The Anglo-Saxon Chronicle: a revised translation* (1961)
AS chart.	P. H. Sawyer, *Anglo-Saxon charters: an annotated list and bibliography*, Royal Historical Society Guides and Handbooks (1968)
AusDB	D. Pike and others, eds., *Australian dictionary of biography*, 16 vols. (1966–2002)
Baker, *Serjeants*	J. H. Baker, *The order of serjeants at law*, SeldS, suppl. ser., 5 (1984)
Bale, *Cat.*	J. Bale, *Scriptorum illustrium Maioris Brytannie, quam nunc Angliam et Scotiam vocant: catalogus*, 2 vols. in 1 (Basel, 1557–9); facs. edn (1971)
Bale, *Index*	J. Bale, *Index Britanniae scriptorum*, ed. R. L. Poole and M. Bateson (1902); facs. edn (1990)
BBCS	*Bulletin of the Board of Celtic Studies*
BDMBR	J. O. Baylen and N. J. Gossman, eds., *Biographical dictionary of modern British radicals*, 3 vols. in 4 (1979–88)
Bede, *Hist. eccl.*	*Bede's Ecclesiastical history of the English people*, ed. and trans. B. Colgrave and R. A. B. Mynors, OMT (1969); repr. (1991)
Bénézit, *Dict.*	E. Bénézit, *Dictionnaire critique et documentaire des peintres, sculpteurs, dessinateurs et graveurs*, 3 vols. (Paris, 1911–23); new edn, 8 vols. (1948–66), repr. (1966); 3rd edn, rev. and enl., 10 vols. (1976); 4th edn, 14 vols. (1999)
BIHR	*Bulletin of the Institute of Historical Research*
Birch, *Seals*	W. de Birch, *Catalogue of seals in the department of manuscripts in the British Museum*, 6 vols. (1887–1900)
Bishop Burnet's History	*Bishop Burnet's History of his own time*, ed. M. J. Routh, 2nd edn, 6 vols. (1833)
Blackwood	*Blackwood's [Edinburgh] Magazine*, 328 vols. (1817–1980)
Blain, Clements & Grundy, *Feminist comp.*	V. Blain, P. Clements, and I. Grundy, eds., *The feminist companion to literature in English* (1990)
BL cat.	*The British Library general catalogue of printed books* [in 360 vols. with suppls., also CD-ROM and online]
BMJ	*British Medical Journal*
Boase & Courtney, *Bibl. Corn.*	G. C. Boase and W. P. Courtney, *Bibliotheca Cornubiensis: a catalogue of the writings … of Cornishmen*, 3 vols. (1874–82)
Boase, *Mod. Eng. biog.*	F. Boase, *Modern English biography: containing many thousand concise memoirs of persons who have died since the year 1850*, 6 vols. (privately printed, Truro, 1892–1921); repr. (1965)
Boswell, *Life*	*Boswell's Life of Johnson: together with Journal of a tour to the Hebrides and Johnson's Diary of a journey into north Wales*, ed. G. B. Hill, enl. edn, rev. L. F. Powell, 6 vols. (1934–50); 2nd edn (1964); repr. (1971)
Brown & Stratton, *Brit. mus.*	J. D. Brown and S. S. Stratton, *British musical biography* (1897)
Bryan, *Painters*	M. Bryan, *A biographical and critical dictionary of painters and engravers*, 2 vols. (1816); new edn, ed. G. Stanley (1849); new edn, ed. R. E. Graves and W. Armstrong, 2 vols. (1886–9); [4th edn], ed. G. C. Williamson, 5 vols. (1903–5) [various reprs.]
Burke, *Gen. GB*	J. Burke, *A genealogical and heraldic history of the commoners of Great Britain and Ireland*, 4 vols. (1833–8); new edn as *A genealogical and heraldic dictionary of the landed gentry of Great Britain and Ireland*, 3 vols. [1843–9] [many later edns]
Burke, *Gen. Ire.*	J. B. Burke, *A genealogical and heraldic history of the landed gentry of Ireland* (1899); 2nd edn (1904); 3rd edn (1912); 4th edn (1958); 5th edn as *Burke's Irish family records* (1976)
Burke, *Peerage*	J. Burke, *A general* [later edns *A genealogical*] *and heraldic dictionary of the peerage and baronetage of the United Kingdom* [later edns *the British empire*] (1829–)
Burney, *Hist. mus.*	C. Burney, *A general history of music, from the earliest ages to the present period*, 4 vols. (1776–89)
Burtchaell & Sadleir, *Alum. Dubl.*	G. D. Burtchaell and T. U. Sadleir, *Alumni Dublinenses: a register of the students, graduates, and provosts of Trinity College* (1924); [2nd edn], with suppl., in 2 pts (1935)
Calamy rev.	A. G. Matthews, *Calamy revised* (1934); repr. (1988)
CCI	*Calendar of confirmations and inventories granted and given up in the several commissariots of Scotland* (1876–)
CClR	*Calendar of the close rolls preserved in the Public Record Office*, 47 vols. (1892–1963)
CDS	J. Bain, ed., *Calendar of documents relating to Scotland*, 4 vols., PRO (1881–8); suppl. vol. 5, ed. G. G. Simpson and J. D. Galbraith [1986]
CEPR letters	W. H. Bliss, C. Johnson, and J. Twemlow, eds., *Calendar of entries in the papal registers relating to Great Britain and Ireland: papal letters* (1893–)
CGPLA	*Calendars of the grants of probate and letters of administration* [in 4 ser.: England & Wales, Northern Ireland, Ireland, and Éire]
Chambers, *Scots.*	R. Chambers, ed., *A biographical dictionary of eminent Scotsmen*, 4 vols. (1832–5)
Chancery records	chancery records pubd by the PRO
Chancery records (RC)	chancery records pubd by the Record Commissions

CIPM	*Calendar of inquisitions post mortem*, [20 vols.], PRO (1904–); also *Henry VII*, 3 vols. (1898–1955)
Clarendon, *Hist. rebellion*	E. Hyde, earl of Clarendon, *The history of the rebellion and civil wars in England*, 6 vols. (1888); repr. (1958) and (1992)
Cobbett, *Parl. hist.*	W. Cobbett and J. Wright, eds., *Cobbett's Parliamentary history of England*, 36 vols. (1806–1820)
Colvin, *Archs.*	H. Colvin, *A biographical dictionary of British architects, 1600–1840*, 3rd edn (1995)
Cooper, *Ath. Cantab.*	C. H. Cooper and T. Cooper, *Athenae Cantabrigienses*, 3 vols. (1858–1913); repr. (1967)
CPR	*Calendar of the patent rolls preserved in the Public Record Office* (1891–)
Crockford	*Crockford's Clerical Directory*
CS	Camden Society
CSP	*Calendar of state papers* [in 11 ser.: *domestic, Scotland, Scottish series, Ireland, colonial, Commonwealth, foreign, Spain* [at Simancas], *Rome, Milan*, and *Venice*]
CYS	Canterbury and York Society
DAB	*Dictionary of American biography*, 21 vols. (1928–36), repr. in 11 vols. (1964); 10 suppls. (1944–96)
DBB	D. J. Jeremy, ed., *Dictionary of business biography*, 5 vols. (1984–6)
DCB	G. W. Brown and others, *Dictionary of Canadian biography*, [14 vols.] (1966–)
Debrett's Peerage	*Debrett's Peerage* (1803–) [sometimes *Debrett's Illustrated peerage*]
Desmond, *Botanists*	R. Desmond, *Dictionary of British and Irish botanists and horticulturists* (1977); rev. edn (1994)
Dir. Brit. archs.	A. Felstead, J. Franklin, and L. Pinfield, eds., *Directory of British architects, 1834–1900* (1993); 2nd edn, ed. A. Brodie and others, 2 vols. (2001)
DLB	J. M. Bellamy and J. Saville, eds., *Dictionary of labour biography*, [10 vols.] (1972–)
DLitB	Dictionary of Literary Biography
DNB	*Dictionary of national biography*, 63 vols. (1885–1900), suppl., 3 vols. (1901); repr. in 22 vols. (1908–9); 10 further suppls. (1912–96); *Missing persons* (1993)
DNZB	W. H. Oliver and C. Orange, eds., *The dictionary of New Zealand biography*, 5 vols. (1990–2000)
DSAB	W. J. de Kock and others, eds., *Dictionary of South African biography*, 5 vols. (1968–87)
DSB	C. C. Gillispie and F. L. Holmes, eds., *Dictionary of scientific biography*, 16 vols. (1970–80); repr. in 8 vols. (1981); 2 vol. suppl. (1990)
DSBB	A. Slaven and S. Checkland, eds., *Dictionary of Scottish business biography, 1860–1960*, 2 vols. (1986–90)
DSCHT	N. M. de S. Cameron and others, eds., *Dictionary of Scottish church history and theology* (1993)
Dugdale, *Monasticon*	W. Dugdale, *Monasticon Anglicanum*, 3 vols. (1655–72); 2nd edn, 3 vols. (1661–82); new edn, ed. J. Caley, J. Ellis, and B. Bandinel, 6 vols. in 8 pts (1817–30); repr. (1846) and (1970)
DWB	J. E. Lloyd and others, eds., *Dictionary of Welsh biography down to 1940* (1959) [Eng. trans. of *Y bywgraffiadur Cymreig hyd 1940*, 2nd edn (1954)]
EdinR	*Edinburgh Review, or, Critical Journal*
EETS	Early English Text Society
Emden, *Cam.*	A. B. Emden, *A biographical register of the University of Cambridge to 1500* (1963)
Emden, *Oxf.*	A. B. Emden, *A biographical register of the University of Oxford to* AD *1500*, 3 vols. (1957–9); also *A biographical register of the University of Oxford,* AD *1501 to 1540* (1974)
EngHR	*English Historical Review*
Engraved Brit. ports.	F. M. O'Donoghue and H. M. Hake, *Catalogue of engraved British portraits preserved in the department of prints and drawings in the British Museum*, 6 vols. (1908–25)
ER	The English Reports, 178 vols. (1900–32)
ESTC	*English short title catalogue, 1475–1800* [CD-ROM and online]
Evelyn, *Diary*	*The diary of John Evelyn*, ed. E. S. De Beer, 6 vols. (1955); repr. (2000)
Farington, *Diary*	*The diary of Joseph Farington*, ed. K. Garlick and others, 17 vols. (1978–98)
Fasti Angl. (Hardy)	J. Le Neve, *Fasti ecclesiae Anglicanae*, ed. T. D. Hardy, 3 vols. (1854)
Fasti Angl., 1066–1300	[J. Le Neve], *Fasti ecclesiae Anglicanae, 1066–1300*, ed. D. E. Greenway and J. S. Barrow, [8 vols.] (1968–)
Fasti Angl., 1300–1541	[J. Le Neve], *Fasti ecclesiae Anglicanae, 1300–1541*, 12 vols. (1962–7)
Fasti Angl., 1541–1857	[J. Le Neve], *Fasti ecclesiae Anglicanae, 1541–1857*, ed. J. M. Horn, D. M. Smith, and D. S. Bailey, [9 vols.] (1969–)
Fasti Scot.	H. Scott, *Fasti ecclesiae Scoticanae*, 3 vols. in 6 (1871); new edn, [11 vols.] (1915–)
FO List	*Foreign Office List*
Fortescue, *Brit. army*	J. W. Fortescue, *A history of the British army*, 13 vols. (1899–1930)
Foss, *Judges*	E. Foss, *The judges of England*, 9 vols. (1848–64); repr. (1966)
Foster, *Alum. Oxon.*	J. Foster, ed., *Alumni Oxonienses: the members of the University of Oxford, 1715–1886*, 4 vols. (1887–8); later edn (1891); also *Alumni Oxonienses … 1500–1714*, 4 vols. (1891–2); 8 vol. repr. (1968) and (2000)
Fuller, *Worthies*	T. Fuller, *The history of the worthies of England*, 4 pts (1662); new edn, 2 vols., ed. J. Nichols (1811); new edn, 3 vols., ed. P. A. Nuttall (1840); repr. (1965)
GEC, *Baronetage*	G. E. Cokayne, *Complete baronetage*, 6 vols. (1900–09); repr. (1983) [microprint]
GEC, *Peerage*	G. E. C. [G. E. Cokayne], *The complete peerage of England, Scotland, Ireland, Great Britain, and the United Kingdom*, 8 vols. (1887–98); new edn, ed. V. Gibbs and others, 14 vols. in 15 (1910–98); microprint repr. (1982) and (1987)
Genest, *Eng. stage*	J. Genest, *Some account of the English stage from the Restoration in 1660 to 1830*, 10 vols. (1832); repr. [New York, 1965]
Gillow, *Lit. biog. hist.*	J. Gillow, *A literary and biographical history or bibliographical dictionary of the English Catholics, from the breach with Rome, in 1534, to the present time*, 5 vols. [1885–1902]; repr. (1961); repr. with preface by C. Gillow (1999)
Gir. Camb. opera	*Giraldi Cambrensis opera*, ed. J. S. Brewer, J. F. Dimock, and G. F. Warner, 8 vols., Rolls Series, 21 (1861–91)
GJ	*Geographical Journal*

Gladstone, *Diaries*	*The Gladstone diaries: with cabinet minutes and prime-ministerial correspondence*, ed. M. R. D. Foot and H. C. G. Matthew, 14 vols. (1968–94)
GM	*Gentleman's Magazine*
Graves, *Artists*	A. Graves, ed., *A dictionary of artists who have exhibited works in the principal London exhibitions of oil paintings from 1760 to 1880* (1884); new edn (1895); 3rd edn (1901); facs. edn (1969); repr. [1970], (1973), and (1984)
Graves, *Brit. Inst.*	A. Graves, *The British Institution, 1806–1867: a complete dictionary of contributors and their work from the foundation of the institution* (1875); facs. edn (1908); repr. (1969)
Graves, *RA exhibitors*	A. Graves, *The Royal Academy of Arts: a complete dictionary of contributors and their work from its foundation in 1769 to 1904*, 8 vols. (1905–6); repr. in 4 vols. (1970) and (1972)
Graves, *Soc. Artists*	A. Graves, *The Society of Artists of Great Britain, 1760–1791, the Free Society of Artists, 1761–1783: a complete dictionary* (1907); facs. edn (1969)
Greaves & Zaller, *BDBR*	R. L. Greaves and R. Zaller, eds., *Biographical dictionary of British radicals in the seventeenth century*, 3 vols. (1982–4)
Grove, *Dict. mus.*	G. Grove, ed., *A dictionary of music and musicians*, 5 vols. (1878–90); 2nd edn, ed. J. A. Fuller Maitland (1904–10); 3rd edn, ed. H. C. Colles (1927); 4th edn with suppl. (1940); 5th edn, ed. E. Blom, 9 vols. (1954); suppl. (1961) [see also *New Grove*]
Hall, *Dramatic ports.*	L. A. Hall, *Catalogue of dramatic portraits in the theatre collection of the Harvard College library*, 4 vols. (1930–34)
Hansard	*Hansard's parliamentary debates*, ser. 1–5 (1803–)
Highfill, Burnim & Langhans, *BDA*	P. H. Highfill, K. A. Burnim, and E. A. Langhans, *A biographical dictionary of actors, actresses, musicians, dancers, managers, and other stage personnel in London, 1660–1800*, 16 vols. (1973–93)
Hist. U. Oxf.	T. H. Aston, ed., *The history of the University of Oxford*, 8 vols. (1984–2000) [1: *The early Oxford schools*, ed. J. I. Catto (1984); 2: *Late medieval Oxford*, ed. J. I. Catto and R. Evans (1992); 3: *The collegiate university*, ed. J. McConica (1986); 4: *Seventeenth-century Oxford*, ed. N. Tyacke (1997); 5: *The eighteenth century*, ed. L. S. Sutherland and L. G. Mitchell (1986); 6–7: *Nineteenth-century Oxford*, ed. M. G. Brock and M. C. Curthoys (1997–2000); 8: *The twentieth century*, ed. B. Harrison (2000)]
HJ	*Historical Journal*
HMC	Historical Manuscripts Commission
Holdsworth, *Eng. law*	W. S. Holdsworth, *A history of English law*, ed. A. L. Goodhart and H. L. Hanbury, 17 vols. (1903–72)
HoP, *Commons*	*The history of parliament: the House of Commons* [*1386–1421*, ed. J. S. Roskell, L. Clark, and C. Rawcliffe, 4 vols. (1992); *1509–1558*, ed. S. T. Bindoff, 3 vols. (1982); *1558–1603*, ed. P. W. Hasler, 3 vols. (1981); *1660–1690*, ed. B. D. Henning, 3 vols. (1983); *1690–1715*, ed. D. W. Hayton, E. Cruickshanks, and S. Handley, 5 vols. (2002); *1715–1754*, ed. R. Sedgwick, 2 vols. (1970); *1754–1790*, ed. L. Namier and J. Brooke, 3 vols. (1964), repr. (1985); *1790–1820*, ed. R. G. Thorne, 5 vols. (1986); in draft (used with permission): *1422–1504*, *1604–1629*, *1640–1660*, and *1820–1832*]
IGI	*International Genealogical Index*, Church of Jesus Christ of the Latterday Saints
ILN	*Illustrated London News*
IMC	Irish Manuscripts Commission
Irving, *Scots.*	J. Irving, ed., *The book of Scotsmen eminent for achievements in arms and arts, church and state, law, legislation and literature, commerce, science, travel and philanthropy* (1881)
JCS	*Journal of the Chemical Society*
JHC	*Journals of the House of Commons*
JHL	*Journals of the House of Lords*
John of Worcester, *Chron.*	*The chronicle of John of Worcester*, ed. R. R. Darlington and P. McGurk, trans. J. Bray and P. McGurk, 3 vols., OMT (1995–) [vol. 1 forthcoming]
Keeler, *Long Parliament*	M. F. Keeler, *The Long Parliament, 1640–1641: a biographical study of its members* (1954)
Kelly, *Handbk*	*The upper ten thousand: an alphabetical list of all members of noble families*, 3 vols. (1875–7); continued as *Kelly's handbook of the upper ten thousand for 1878* [1879], 2 vols. (1878–9); continued as *Kelly's handbook to the titled, landed and official classes*, 94 vols. (1880–1973)
LondG	*London Gazette*
LP Henry VIII	J. S. Brewer, J. Gairdner, and R. H. Brodie, eds., *Letters and papers, foreign and domestic, of the reign of Henry VIII*, 23 vols. in 38 (1862–1932); repr. (1965)
Mallalieu, *Watercolour artists*	H. L. Mallalieu, *The dictionary of British watercolour artists up to 1820*, 3 vols. (1976–90); vol. 1, 2nd edn (1986)
Memoirs FRS	*Biographical Memoirs of Fellows of the Royal Society*
MGH	Monumenta Germaniae Historica
MT	*Musical Times*
Munk, *Roll*	W. Munk, *The roll of the Royal College of Physicians of London*, 2 vols. (1861); 2nd edn, 3 vols. (1878)
N&Q	*Notes and Queries*
New Grove	S. Sadie, ed., *The new Grove dictionary of music and musicians*, 20 vols. (1980); 2nd edn, 29 vols. (2001) [also online edn; see also Grove, *Dict. mus.*]
Nichols, *Illustrations*	J. Nichols and J. B. Nichols, *Illustrations of the literary history of the eighteenth century*, 8 vols. (1817–58)
Nichols, *Lit. anecdotes*	J. Nichols, *Literary anecdotes of the eighteenth century*, 9 vols. (1812–16); facs. edn (1966)
Obits. FRS	*Obituary Notices of Fellows of the Royal Society*
O'Byrne, *Naval biog. dict.*	W. R. O'Byrne, *A naval biographical dictionary* (1849); repr. (1990); [2nd edn], 2 vols. (1861)
OHS	Oxford Historical Society
Old Westminsters	*The record of Old Westminsters*, 1–2, ed. G. F. R. Barker and A. H. Stenning (1928); suppl. 1, ed. J. B. Whitmore and G. R. Y. Radcliffe [1938]; 3, ed. J. B. Whitmore, G. R. Y. Radcliffe, and D. C. Simpson (1963); suppl. 2, ed. F. E. Pagan (1978); 4, ed. F. E. Pagan and H. E. Pagan (1992)
OMT	Oxford Medieval Texts
Ordericus Vitalis, *Eccl. hist.*	*The ecclesiastical history of Orderic Vitalis*, ed. and trans. M. Chibnall, 6 vols., OMT (1969–80); repr. (1990)
Paris, *Chron.*	*Matthaei Parisiensis, monachi sancti Albani, chronica majora*, ed. H. R. Luard, Rolls Series, 7 vols. (1872–83)
Parl. papers	*Parliamentary papers* (1801–)
PBA	*Proceedings of the British Academy*

Pepys, *Diary*	*The diary of Samuel Pepys*, ed. R. Latham and W. Matthews, 11 vols. (1970–83); repr. (1995) and (2000)
Pevsner	N. Pevsner and others, Buildings of England series
PICE	*Proceedings of the Institution of Civil Engineers*
Pipe rolls	*The great roll of the pipe for ...*, PRSoc. (1884–)
PRO	Public Record Office
PRS	*Proceedings of the Royal Society of London*
PRSoc.	Pipe Roll Society
PTRS	*Philosophical Transactions of the Royal Society*
QR	*Quarterly Review*
RC	Record Commissions
Redgrave, *Artists*	S. Redgrave, *A dictionary of artists of the English school* (1874); rev. edn (1878); repr. (1970)
Reg. Oxf.	C. W. Boase and A. Clark, eds., *Register of the University of Oxford*, 5 vols., OHS, 1, 10–12, 14 (1885–9)
Reg. PCS	J. H. Burton and others, eds., *The register of the privy council of Scotland*, 1st ser., 14 vols. (1877–98); 2nd ser., 8 vols. (1899–1908); 3rd ser., [16 vols.] (1908–70)
Reg. RAN	H. W. C. Davis and others, eds., *Regesta regum Anglo-Normannorum, 1066–1154*, 4 vols. (1913–69)
RIBA Journal	*Journal of the Royal Institute of British Architects* [later *RIBA Journal*]
RotP	J. Strachey, ed., *Rotuli parliamentorum ut et petitiones, et placita in parliamento*, 6 vols. (1767–77)
RotS	D. Macpherson, J. Caley, and W. Illingworth, eds., *Rotuli Scotiae in Turri Londinensi et in domo capitulari Westmonasteriensi asservati*, 2 vols., RC, 14 (1814–19)
RS	Record(s) Society
Rymer, *Foedera*	T. Rymer and R. Sanderson, eds., *Foedera, conventiones, literae et cuiuscunque generis acta publica inter reges Angliae et alios quosvis imperatores, reges, pontifices, principes, vel communitates*, 20 vols. (1704–35); 2nd edn, 20 vols. (1726–35); 3rd edn, 10 vols. (1739–45), facs. edn (1967); new edn, ed. A. Clarke, J. Caley, and F. Holbrooke, 4 vols., RC, 50 (1816–30)
Sainty, *Judges*	J. Sainty, ed., *The judges of England, 1272–1990*, SeldS, suppl. ser., 10 (1993)
Sainty, *King's counsel*	J. Sainty, ed., *A list of English law officers and king's counsel*, SeldS, suppl. ser., 7 (1987)
SCH	Studies in Church History
Scots peerage	J. B. Paul, ed. *The Scots peerage, founded on Wood's edition of Sir Robert Douglas's Peerage of Scotland, containing an historical and genealogical account of the nobility of that kingdom*, 9 vols. (1904–14)
SeldS	Selden Society
SHR	*Scottish Historical Review*
State trials	T. B. Howell and T. J. Howell, eds., *Cobbett's Complete collection of state trials*, 34 vols. (1809–28)
STC, 1475–1640	A. W. Pollard, G. R. Redgrave, and others, eds., *A short-title catalogue of ... English books ... 1475–1640* (1926); 2nd edn, ed. W. A. Jackson, F. S. Ferguson, and K. F. Pantzer, 3 vols. (1976–91) [see also Wing, *STC*]
STS	Scottish Text Society
SurtS	Surtees Society
Symeon of Durham, *Opera*	*Symeonis monachi opera omnia*, ed. T. Arnold, 2 vols., Rolls Series, 75 (1882–5); repr. (1965)
Tanner, *Bibl. Brit.-Hib.*	T. Tanner, *Bibliotheca Britannico-Hibernica*, ed. D. Wilkins (1748); repr. (1963)
Thieme & Becker, *Allgemeines Lexikon*	U. Thieme, F. Becker, and H. Vollmer, eds., *Allgemeines Lexikon der bildenden Künstler von der Antike bis zur Gegenwart*, 37 vols. (Leipzig, 1907–50); repr. (1961–5), (1983), and (1992)
Thurloe, *State papers*	*A collection of the state papers of John Thurloe*, ed. T. Birch, 7 vols. (1742)
TLS	*Times Literary Supplement*
Tout, *Admin. hist.*	T. F. Tout, *Chapters in the administrative history of mediaeval England: the wardrobe, the chamber, and the small seals*, 6 vols. (1920–33); repr. (1967)
TRHS	*Transactions of the Royal Historical Society*
VCH	H. A. Doubleday and others, eds., *The Victoria history of the counties of England*, [88 vols.] (1900–)
Venn, *Alum. Cant.*	J. Venn and J. A. Venn, *Alumni Cantabrigienses: a biographical list of all known students, graduates, and holders of office at the University of Cambridge, from the earliest times to 1900*, 10 vols. (1922–54); repr. in 2 vols. (1974–8)
Vertue, *Note books*	[G. Vertue], *Note books*, ed. K. Esdaile, earl of Ilchester, and H. M. Hake, 6 vols., Walpole Society, 18, 20, 22, 24, 26, 30 (1930–55)
VF	*Vanity Fair*
Walford, *County families*	E. Walford, *The county families of the United Kingdom, or, Royal manual of the titled and untitled aristocracy of Great Britain and Ireland* (1860)
Walker rev.	A. G. Matthews, *Walker revised: being a revision of John Walker's Sufferings of the clergy during the grand rebellion, 1642–60* (1948); repr. (1988)
Walpole, *Corr.*	*The Yale edition of Horace Walpole's correspondence*, ed. W. S. Lewis, 48 vols. (1937–83)
Ward, *Men of the reign*	T. H. Ward, ed., *Men of the reign: a biographical dictionary of eminent persons of British and colonial birth who have died during the reign of Queen Victoria* (1885); repr. (Graz, 1968)
Waterhouse, *18c painters*	E. Waterhouse, *The dictionary of 18th century painters in oils and crayons* (1981); repr. as *British 18th century painters in oils and crayons* (1991), vol. 2 of *Dictionary of British art*
Watt, *Bibl. Brit.*	R. Watt, *Bibliotheca Britannica, or, A general index to British and foreign literature*, 4 vols. (1824) [many reprs.]
Wellesley index	W. E. Houghton, ed., *The Wellesley index to Victorian periodicals, 1824–1900*, 5 vols. (1966–89); new edn (1999) [CD-ROM]
Wing, *STC*	D. Wing, ed., *Short-title catalogue of ... English books ... 1641–1700*, 3 vols. (1945–51); 2nd edn (1972–88); rev. and enl. edn, ed. J. J. Morrison, C. W. Nelson, and M. Seccombe, 4 vols. (1994–8) [see also *STC, 1475–1640*]
Wisden	*John Wisden's Cricketer's Almanack*
Wood, *Ath. Oxon.*	A. Wood, *Athenae Oxonienses ... to which are added the Fasti*, 2 vols. (1691–2); 2nd edn (1721); new edn, 4 vols., ed. P. Bliss (1813–20); repr. (1967) and (1969)
Wood, *Vic. painters*	C. Wood, *Dictionary of Victorian painters* (1971); 2nd edn (1978); 3rd edn as *Victorian painters*, 2 vols. (1995), vol. 4 of *Dictionary of British art*
WW	*Who's who* (1849–)
WWBMP	M. Stenton and S. Lees, eds., *Who's who of British members of parliament*, 4 vols. (1976–81)
WWW	*Who was who* (1929–)

Liston, Henrietta, Lady Liston (1751–1828). *See under* Liston, Sir Robert (1742–1836).

Liston, Henry (1771–1836), inventor of a musical instrument and writer on music, the eldest son of Robert Liston, minister of Aberdour, Fife, was born on 30 June 1771. He matriculated at Edinburgh University in 1787 and read physics and mathematics before studying for the church. In 1793 he became minister of the parish of Ecclesmachan, Linlithgowshire, where he remained for the rest of his life. He married Margaret Ireland, the daughter of David Ireland, town clerk of Culross, on 21 October 1793. There were two sons of their marriage: Robert *Liston and David Liston, professor of oriental languages at Edinburgh. Henry Liston died suddenly at Merchiston Hall, Falkirk, on 24 February 1836.

Liston's abilities in mechanics and music led to his invention of the euharmonic organ, an acknowledged adaptation of a similar instrument by Dr Robert Smith of Trinity College, Cambridge. In Liston's instrument, built by Flight and Robson, each note of the chromatic scale was provided with a further pipe tuned to its enharmonic equivalent. Designed to give perfect intonation in each of the major and minor keys, an 'original scale' (C–C♯–D–E♭–E– F–F♯–G–G♯–A–B♭–B) was played from the manual keys, but the pipes of the 'euharmonic scale' (B♯–C♯–D♯–E♯–F♯–A♯– D♭–F♭–G♭–B♭–C♭) were made playable as required through five pedals, three 'acute' and two 'grave', which acted on the sharp and flat pitches respectively. Although complicated to operate, it was approved by Samuel Wesley, who compared it favourably with similar inventions by Hawkes and Loeschman when it was exhibited in London in 1811. In his *Essay on Perfect Intonation* (1812), Liston described his instrument and related it to the theory of acoustics and tonal music. He wrote the article 'Music' in the *Edinburgh Encyclopaedia*, and translated the sixth book of Caesar's *Gallic Wars* for use in schools. Liston also invented an improved form of plough, which was used in his district. CHRISTOPHER KENT

Sources H. Liston, *An essay on perfect intonation* (1812) · H. B. McCall, *Some old families: a contribution to the genealogical history of Scotland* (1890) · *Fasti Scot.* · 'On the major and minor semitones, and on the Rev. Mr Liston's organ', *The Harmonicon*, 6 (1828), 28–30 · *The Harmonicon*, 7 (1829), 99–103, 125–29 · matriculation records, U. Edin. L., special collections division, university archives

Liston, John (*c*.1776–1846), actor, was born in London, reputedly the son of a watchmaker or of the occupant of an inferior position in the gaming houses, or of a cook's shopkeeper, in either the parish of St James's or St Ann's, Soho, although no record of his birth appears in the registers for either parish. His death certificate gives his age as seventy in 1846. He was allegedly educated at Soho School and he later worked as an usher at the Library School in Castle Street, close to the Haymarket. He made his début as an actor at the Theatre Royal, Haymarket, on 15 August 1799, as Rawbold in George Colman's *The Iron Chest*, for Charles Kemble's benefit. He appeared in Dublin, though as little more than a spear carrier, for the winter season of 1799–1800, then from 1800 to 1801 he acted at Taunton,

John Liston (*c*.1776–1846), by George Clint, *c*.1825

Weymouth, and Exeter. He then joined Stephen Kemble's company, which performed in a circuit based on Newcastle upon Tyne, and made his first recorded appearance on the Newcastle stage on 3 August 1801. According to Anne Matthews, Liston's début on the Newcastle circuit was at Durham, during Sarah Siddons's engagement; she adds that he later revealed his comic talents to Kemble in the role of Diggory in *She Stoops to Conquer*. Apart from several months with Tate Wilkinson's York-based company in 1803, Liston remained with Stephen Kemble until May 1805; he acquired a particular reputation for his skills in low-comedy roles, for which he was regularly praised in the *Monthly Mirror* and in the Newcastle press.

On Monday 10 June 1805 Liston made his début as a low comedian at the Theatre Royal, Haymarket, playing Sheepface in *The Village Lawyer*. When the Haymarket season ended he was engaged by Covent Garden, where he remained until 1822. His Covent Garden début occurred on 15 October 1805, when he played Jacob Gawkey in *The Chapter of Accidents*. He then played Memmo in 'Monk' Lewis's *Rugantino* and Gaby Grim in Colman's *We Fly by Night*. It took several years before he established himself as a major comedian, but his reputation was considerably enhanced through summer seasons at the Haymarket, where, partnered with Charles Mathews, he appeared in a number of specially written plays by Theodore Hook, such as *Catch him who Can* (1806), *The Fortress* (1807), *Music Mad* (1807), and *Killing No Murder* (1809). He developed a skill in performing conceited and affected provincial characters, such as Apollo Belvi in the last-mentioned play, often embellished with comic dancing, which was also a feature of his Caper in *Who Wins* (1808) and his Lord

Grizzle in *Tom Thumb*, the first role for which he won particular acclaim at Covent Garden. Apart from Lord Grizzle, Liston also achieved acclaim in other burlesque roles, especially Don Whiskerandos in *The Critic* and the title role in *Bombastes furioso*. A particular contribution of Liston's to the English stage was the conceited cockney, which first surfaced in the character of Henry Augustus Mug in Colman's *The Africans* (Haymarket, 1808) and for which he achieved particular renown as Lubin Log in James Kenney's *Love, Law and Physic* (Covent Garden, 1812). Sam Swipes in Hook's *Exchange No Robbery* (Haymarket, 1820) was another successful character in this mould. Liston created many new low-comedy parts in the comedies, farces, and melodramas played at Covent Garden and the Haymarket, as well as re-creating a number of already established roles, such as Bob Acres and Sir Benjamin Backbite. His Shakespearian performances included Bottom, Sir Andrew Aguecheek, Malvolio, Pompey, Launce, Dromio, Polonius, Slender, and Cloten, while he was also the first English-speaking Figaro in Henry Bishop's Covent Garden versions of *The Marriage of Figaro* and *The Barber of Seville*. In adaptations of the novels of Sir Walter Scott he was particularly praised for his Dominie Sampson in *Guy Mannering*, Baillie Nicol Jarvie in *Rob Roy*, and Captain Dalgetty in *Montrose*. His benefits often showed him in new guises, most notoriously as Ophelia in John Poole's *Hamlet Travestie* in 1813 and as Lord Grizzle delivering an *Epilogue on an Ass* in 1818. A desire to play more serious roles emerged in his 1809 benefit, when he played Octavian in *The Mountaineers*, and in 1829, when he played Baron Wildenheim in *Lovers' Vows* for his last Haymarket benefit.

Liston left Covent Garden Theatre on 31 May 1822, on which occasion his wife, Sarah, took her professional leave of the stage. Liston had married Sarah Tyrer (1781–1854) at St Martin-in-the-Fields on 22 March 1807, and she had given birth to a son, John Terry, in 1813 and a daughter, Emma, in 1814. She had originally made her début at Drury Lane on 21 May 1801 and first appeared at the Haymarket a month later. A short, plump woman, she was first engaged at Covent Garden in 1805, where she played comic roles, such as serving maids, and was also in demand on account of her vocal powers. One of her most famous parts was Queen Dollallola in *Tom Thumb*.

By 1822 Liston had also become a popular attraction in the provinces, and often toured during the summer seasons in which he was not engaged at the Haymarket. At Covent Garden his weekly salary had never risen above £17, considerably less than he could earn on provincial tours and than the £50 he was offered to join the Drury Lane company in 1823. He made his Drury Lane début on 28 January as Tony Lumpkin, and remained there, when not fulfilling equally lucrative engagements in the provinces and at the Haymarket, until 1831. During these years he became a firm favourite of George IV and developed some of his most popular roles, such as Mawworm in *The Hypocrite*, Tristram Sappy in *Deaf as a Post*, Billy Lackaday in *Sweethearts and Wives*, and Paul Pry, described by Genest as 'a perfect piece of acting' (Genest, *Eng. Stage*, 10.318). John Poole's *Paul Pry* was first performed at the Haymarket Theatre on 13 September 1825, and had one of the most successful runs enjoyed by a play since *The Beggar's Opera* in the previous century. Liston was reputedly paid £100 per week for his performance, although it was later rumoured he was paid £50 or £60 per night when *Paul Pry* was revived. Paul Pry, with his catchphrase 'I hope I don't intrude', was a unique creation, dressed in baggy striped trousers tucked into hessian boots, tail coat, and top hat, and accompanied always by an umbrella. Likenesses soon appeared everywhere: in prints, on porcelain and toby jugs, adorning cakes and pats of butter, sewn into pocket handkerchiefs, embellishing snuff boxes, and used as insignia on carts, buses, and fairground stalls. The part itself became the *sine qua non* of the low comedian: even in the 1890s J. L. Toole was still re-creating the role in a style of dress based on Liston's original costume.

While Liston's renown was based largely on his performance in low-comedy roles, he was sometimes also praised for parts that required a quieter and more restrained style of acting, such as Adam Brock in J. R. Planché's *Charles XII* (Drury Lane, 1828). These qualities were particularly in evidence during the last six years of Liston's professional career, which were spent almost entirely at the small Olympic Theatre under the management of Madame Vestris, at a salary variously reported as £60 and £100 per week. Liston had previously appeared with Vestris, not only in *Paul Pry*, but also as a Broom Girl, in the duet *Buy a Broom*, in 1826. He made his début there on 1 October 1831 as Dominique in *Talk of the Devil*, and during the next six years created a succession of largely original roles, contributing greatly to the theatre's success. In 1835 he introduced Charles Mathews the younger to the theatrical public in *The Old and Young Stager*, and the following year played with him in Planché's *The Two Figaros*. He took his leave of the Olympic stage on 31 May 1837, and on 5 June he played in a benefit at Covent Garden for George Herbert Buonaparte Rodwell, who was married to his daughter, Emma. His last professional performance occurred on Saturday 10 June at the Lyceum Theatre for the benefit of James Vining. He then moved to his country villa at Penn, near Windsor, but spent the final years of his life at his residence in St George's Place, near Hyde Park Corner.

Liston was undoubtedly the greatest comic actor of his generation. He gave detailed, well-observed performances which emphasized such human foibles as greed, conceit, affectation, and cowardice. His deadpan style was enhanced by his extraordinary face. 'There is one face of Farley', wrote Charles Lamb, 'one of Knight, one (but what a one it is!) of Liston' (*London Magazine*, Oct 1822). His high forehead was offset by goggle eyes, a snub nose with dilated nostrils, fleshy lips, and large cheeks. Leigh Hunt noted how his mouth and chin with the throat under it 'hung like an old bag' (*Autobiography*, 186). The gravity of his face added to his comic effect. According to Hazlitt, describing his Sir Peter Pigwiggin in *Pigeons and Crows*, 'His jaws seem to ache with laughter, his eyes look out of his head with wonder, his face is unctuous all over and bathed with jests' (*Complete Works*, 15.359). Liston was 5 feet 11 inches in height, and in his younger days was considered one of the best-built men around London. As he grew older he grew fatter, and his typical posture in performance, judging from surviving prints, was a slouch with knees bent, bottom thrust out, and hands in pocket. He dressed his characters with great skill and enjoyed a very good relationship with his audiences, partly because of his powers of ad libbing. Although some critics accused him of buffoonery, many praised him for his quietness and repose, for the original and natural qualities of his performances, and for his effortlessness. 'Other actors labour to be comic. I see nothing like labour or system about Liston', wrote Boaden (2.198). He was unique in himself and also possessed the ability to merge his special talents with the character he was creating—'an outline or figure was all that was wanting to his art; he infused into it the richness of his own comic imagination'.

In his lifetime Liston embodied a number of contradictions. Solemn in private life, he was also something of a practical joker; a reader of serious literature and books on theology, he allegedly wanted to play tragedy, but his career was devoted to low comedy. He was accused by some of heavy drinking and hypochondria, but there is little firm evidence to substantiate such claims. Ludicrously dressed on stage, he was always exquisitely dressed in private life and a frequenter of such fashionable resorts as Brighton. In his last years his spirits and health declined, and he died in London, after a severe apoplectic fit, on 22 March 1846. He was buried at Kensal Green cemetery. JIM DAVIS

Sources J. Davis, *John Liston, comedian* (1985) • B. N. Webster, 'An original biographical sketch of John Liston, esq.', *The acting national drama*, 1 (1837), 5–9 • *Oxberry's Dramatic Biography*, 1/2 (1825) • *ILN* (28 March 1846) • [J. Roach], *Authentic memoirs of the green-room*, 2nd edn, 5 pts in 2 vols. (1806) • Genest, *Eng. stage* • J. Boaden, *The life of Mrs Jordan*, 2 vols. (1831) • *The complete works of William Hazlitt*, ed. P. P. Howe, 21 vols. (1930–34) • L. Hunt, *The autobiography of Leigh Hunt*, ed. J. E. Morpurgo (1949) • A. Mathews, *Tea table talk* (1844) • G. Daniel, *Cumberland's British theatre* (1829) • *GM*, 2nd ser., 25 (1846), 547, 660 • d. cert.

Archives Harvard TC • Theatre Museum, London

Likenesses S. De Wilde, oils, 1812, V&A, Theatre Museum • S. De Wilde, oils, 1812, Garr. Club • E. F. Lambert, portrait, 1823, Royal National Theatre • G. Clint, oils, *c.*1825, Garr. Club [*see illus.*] • G. Clint, group portrait, oils, exh. RA 1827, V&A, Theatre Museum • C. Brocky, chalk drawing, BM • S. De Wilde, watercolour drawings, Garr. Club • T. Marlay, watercolour drawing (as Billy Lackaday), NPG • portraits, priv. coll. • prints, BM, NPG, Harvard TC • prints, V&A, Theatre Museum • silhouette, NPG

Wealth at death property to £40,000; plate, jewels, etc. to wife; £6000 to daughter: will, *GM*

Liston, Sir Robert (1742–1836), tutor and diplomat, was born at Overtoun, Kirkliston, Linlithgowshire, on 8 October 1742, the second, and oldest surviving, son of Patrick Liston of Torbanehill (*d.* 1749) and Christian Dick (*d.* 1790). He studied for the Church of Scotland at Edinburgh University, but then was offered the post of private tutor to the sons of Sir Gilbert Elliot of Stobs. He was expected to 'perfect himself in classics, law and dancing' (*Life and Letters*, 1.91) before accompanying the boys—Gilbert, aged twelve, afterwards first earl of Minto, and Hugh, aged ten—to Paris in 1763. There he directed their studies under the general supervision of the historian David Hume, who introduced him to the retired actress Marie-Jeanne Riccoboni. Liston submitted a continuous record of activities and expenses to Elliot, which gives an insight into the life and upbringing abroad of the two young Scottish gentlemen. In 1772 he assisted Gilbert Stuart on the *London Magazine*, contributing letters compiled from the journals of his own travels, mainly in France. Between 1766 and 1782 he maintained a lively and, certainly on her side, intimate correspondence (eighty-three of her letters to 'mon cher Bob' survive) with Madame Riccoboni, who was thirty years his senior. The letters remain together among his papers in the National Library of Scotland.

When Hugh Elliot adopted a diplomatic career Liston became his private secretary, and accompanied him on missions to Munich, Regensburg, and Berlin. In March 1783 Lord Mountstewart, later first marquess of Bute, was sent to Madrid as ambassador-extraordinary, and appointed Liston as secretary to the embassy. This, at forty-one years old, was his first diplomatic appointment. He acted as chargé d'affaires in Mountstewart's absence, and succeeded him as minister-plenipotentiary at Madrid for five years. In May 1785 he was made LLD Edinburgh. From August 1788 to May 1793 he served as envoy-extraordinary at Stockholm. In 1793 he was appointed to the once lucrative position of ambassador-extraordinary to the prestigious embassy of the Sublime Porte in Constantinople during the reign of Selim III. He travelled overland with Dr John Sibthorp among others, and served there just three years. At a time of decreasing trade with the Levant Company (which paid most of his salary) Liston believed that the British in the Ottoman states 'flouted Ottoman sovreignty at every turn' (Cunningham, 85). In February 1796 he was appointed British minister to the United States of America, only thirteen years after the ending of the American War of Independence. On 27 February 1796 he married Henrietta [**Henrietta Liston**, Lady Liston (1751–1828)], botanist, daughter of Nathaniel (*d.* 1761) and Sarah Marchant of Antigua, at the episcopal chapel, Glasgow; they had no children.

Liston was not eager to accept this post at a crucial period in British–American relations, with the heavy responsibility it carried of 'clearing up the debris left behind in 1783: Indian affairs, debt questions and boundary issues' (Wright, 123). He remained at Philadelphia until December 1800, and, through his actions, the British government agreed that Britain would not intervene in west or south-west America. He acted skilfully as an intermediary between the Canadian and American governments about the upper Mississippi valley, and did much to encourage the informal system whereby Royal Navy ships convoyed American merchantmen. When he handed over, 'British-American relations were much more cordial than anyone might have foreseen five years earlier' (Wright, 127). Henrietta Liston wrote frequent frank letters home, reporting knowledgeably on life and politics in America. Her letters tell of housekeeping, Liston's observation that the planned site for Washington strongly resembled Constantinople, George Washington's favourite occupation of farming, the social life in Philadelphia, freedom of speech, and visiting Niagara Falls.

Liston was next appointed envoy-extraordinary and plenipotentiary to the Batavian republic. He arrived in The Hague in September 1802, but in June 1803 left on a mission to Copenhagen until May 1804. Then, at the age of sixty-two, he retired on a pension. The Listons built Millburn Tower near Edinburgh. Henrietta Liston created an American garden, and introduced plants from America and the West Indies and later from Constantinople. In 1811, after the renewal of diplomatic relations with Turkey, Liston was reappointed to Constantinople, taking over from Stratford Canning, who had been acting in the senior post for some time. The Listons were accompanied by a large embassy, including Brigadier-General Sir Robert Wilson (as special military commissioner), Bartholomew Frere, and William Turner. Wilson's diary of their journey (BL, Add. MS 30100) was published as the *Private Diary of Sir Robert Wilson* in 1861. The mission in Constantinople started unfavourably for, since the peace of Bucharest, the Turks were 'in a state of … extreme ill-humour with England for having *advised* the conciliation of the treaty' (*Private Diary*, 1.395). However, over the years, relations improved, and Liston departed before the start of the Greek War of Independence.

Liston is notable as one of only three commoners to hold the highest diplomatic office at this time. He was sworn of the privy council in 1812, and made GCB (civil) in 1816. He finally retired on a pension at the age of seventy-nine. He died at his residence, Millburn Tower, on 15 July 1836, at the age of ninety-three. He was an accomplished linguist in ten languages. The *Gentleman's Magazine* recorded that he was 'the father of the diplomatic body throughout Europe'. An American admirer summed him up as 'sensible—pleasant—easy—an agreeable man' (Cowan, 190). His wife, Henrietta, had died in 1828, probably at Millburn Tower. Apart from her letters home from their diplomatic appointments, she took a keen interest in botany and collected specimens for Sir Joseph Banks. Sir Robert and Lady Liston were buried near each other in Gogar churchyard. DEBORAH MANLEY

Sources E. Wright, 'Robert Liston, second British minister to the U.S.', *History Today*, 11 (1961), 118–27 • H. B. McCall, *Some old families: a contribution to the genealogical history of Scotland* (1890) • *Life and letters of Sir Gilbert Elliot, first earl of Minto, from 1751 to 1806*, ed. countess of Minto [E. E. E. Elliot-Murray-Kynynmound], 3 vols. (1874) • F. C. Green, 'Robert Liston and Mme Riccoboni, une liaison franco-écossaise' [Robert Liston and Mme R., a Franco-Scottish connection in the eighteenth century], *Revue de Littérature Comparé*, 38/4 (1964) • *London Magazine*, 41 (1772) • B. Perkins, 'A diplomat's wife in Philadelphia: letters of Henrietta Liston, 1796–1800', *William and Mary Quarterly*, 11 (1954), 592–632 • *Private diary of Sir R. Wilson* (1861), vol. 1; appx to vol. 2 • C. Taylor, ed., 'Correspondence relating to Millburn Tower and its garden, 1804–29', *Miscellany … XI*, Scottish History Society, 5th ser., 3 (1990), 329–87 • *Scots Magazine*, 58 (1828) • *GM*, 2nd ser., 6 (1836), 539 • *Corrections and additions to the Dictionary of National Biography*, Institute of Historical Research (1966) • *DNB* • A. Cunningham, *Anglo-Ottoman encounters … collected essays by Alan Cunningham*, ed. E. Ingram, 1 (1992) • C. W. Cowan, Rochester Historical Society Publications, 19 (1941)

Archives BL, letter-book and corresp., Add. MSS 36805–36806, 36811 • NL Scot., corresp. and papers | BL, corresp. with Lord Auchinlech, etc., Add. MSS 34415–34465 • BL, corresp. with Lord Auckland, etc., Add. MSS 34415–34465, *passim* • BL, letters to Francis Drake, Add. MS 46822 • BL, letters to Sir Robert Keith, Add. MSS 35510–35539, *passim* • BL, letters to fifth duke of Leeds, Add. MSS 28061–28066, 34465 • BL OIOC, letters to Sir Henry Willock, MS Eur. D 488 • CKS, corresp. with third duke of Dorset • Mount Stuart Trust Archive, Isle of Bute, letters to Lord Hastings • NL Scot., letters to Hugh Elliot • NL Scot., letters to Francis Laing, etc. • NMM, letters to Sir Samuel Hood • priv. coll., letters to Edward Walpole • PRO, corresp. with Francis Jackson, FO 353 • PRO, letters to William Pitt, PRO 30/8 • PRO NIre., corresp. with Lord Castlereagh • U. Nott. L., letters to Lord William Bentinck, etc.

Likenesses G. Stuart, oils, 1802, National Gallery of Art, Washington, DC • G. Stuart, oils, 1802 (Henrietta Liston), National Gallery of Art, Washington, DC • D. Wilkie, oils, 1811, Scot. NPG • Raeburn, portrait, Millburn Tower, Gogar, Edinburgh • D. Wilkie, engraving (after unknown artist), repro. in McCall, *Some old families*

Wealth at death estate in county of Edinburgh: McCall, *Some old families*

Liston, Robert (1794–1847), surgeon, was born on 28 October 1794 in the manse of Ecclesmachan, Linlithgowshire, the eldest child of Henry *Liston (1771–1836), the minister of the parish, and his wife, Margaret, daughter of David Ireland, town clerk of Culross. His brother David became professor of oriental languages at the University of Edinburgh. Liston spent a short time at school in Abercorn, but was chiefly educated by his father. In 1808 he entered the University of Edinburgh, where he won a prize for Latin prose composition. In 1810 he became assistant to John Barclay (1758–1826), a well-known extra-academical lecturer in anatomy and physiology. Liston continued with Barclay until 1815, eventually acting as his senior assistant and prosector. Barclay was an enthusiastic teacher, and from him Liston derived his love for anatomy. From 1814 to 1816 he became 'surgeon's clerk' (house surgeon) at Edinburgh Royal Infirmary, first to George Bell and afterwards to Dr Gillespie. He went to London in 1816, and worked under Sir William Blizard and Thomas Blizard at the London Hospital; he was also admitted a member of the Royal College of Surgeons and began to attend John Abernethy's lectures at St Bartholomew's Hospital. He then returned to Edinburgh, where he taught anatomy with James Syme. In 1818 he was made FRCS (Edinburgh) with a thesis on strictures of the urethra.

Between 1818 and 1828 Liston gained a great reputation in Edinburgh as a teacher of anatomy and as an operating surgeon. However, he quarrelled constantly with the infirmary authorities, and this led to his expulsion from the Royal Infirmary in 1822. Nevertheless, in 1827 he was appointed one of the infirmary surgeons, apparently by the exercise of private influence, and in 1828 he was made the operating surgeon. Liston was married and had six children. A daughter married a son of William Dalrymple, surgeon, and his eldest surviving son became a colonel.

Liston failed to be elected professor of clinical surgery in 1833 in succession to James Russell; Syme, his younger rival and former colleague, was appointed instead, and this failure for Liston probably determined the rest of his career. In 1834 he came to London having been appointed surgeon to the newly founded North London (University College) Hospital. In 1835 he was appointed professor of clinical surgery at London University (University College). He was a member of the council of the Royal College of Surgeons in 1840, and of the board of examiners in 1846. In May 1841 he was elected a fellow of the Royal Society.

Liston was remembered for his surgical skill and his profound knowledge of anatomy, which enabled him to operate successfully in cases from which other surgeons shrank. Mainly working at a time immediately before the introduction of anaesthetics, he attained a dexterity in the use of cutting instruments which has probably never been equalled. When anaesthetics were unknown it was of the utmost importance that surgical operations should be performed as quickly as possible. It was said of Liston that when he amputated the gleam of his knife was followed so instantaneously by the sound of sawing as to make the two actions appear almost simultaneous, and yet he perfected the method of amputating by flaps. He was 6 feet 2 inches tall and so strong that he could amputate through a thigh with only a single assistant, who held the limb. He could compress an artery with one hand while operating with the other. He excelled too in cutting for stone, and he devised a straight splint for treating dislocation of the thigh.

Liston wrote many pamphlets and case reports, and also *The Elements of Surgery* (1831–2; 2nd edn, 1840) and *Practical Surgery* (1837). He was also the first man in England to perform an operation under ether vapour, at University College Hospital on Monday 21 December 1846. He posted a notice that the operation would take place and the theatre was filled with spectators. 'Gentlemen, time me', said Liston, and the successful amputation of the mid-thigh took twenty-five seconds (Cock, 137). Stitching was done later. The frightened patient, who recovered, was Frederick Churchill, a Harley Street butler in his thirties, who on coming round asked when the operation was going to start.

Liston was not a good speaker. He was:

> a surgeon, nothing but a surgeon, having no interests, artistic, literary or scientific, except in connection with his profession; for he was in the habit of using his microscope with care and intelligence … a man exceedingly (one might say excessively) fond of all kinds of pleasure. (Bellot, 165–6)

He was popular with students, though many stories were told of his rough manners to his inferiors, his rudeness, and the retorts which followed. He was devoted to outdoor sports, especially yachting.

Liston died of an aneurysm of the arch of the aorta on 7 December 1847, at his house, 5 Clifford Street, London; after a large funeral he was buried in Highgate cemetery. His eldest son, Robert, aged fourteen or fifteen, died at Duddingston House, Edinburgh, only twelve days after his father. After Liston's death a subscription raised £700, not enough for the suggested marble statue, but enough for four busts and the Liston gold medal, which was still being awarded 150 years later. In 1850–51 his widow was awarded a government pension of £100.

D'A. POWER, *rev.* JEAN LOUDON

Sources *The Times* (9 Dec 1847) • *The Times* (20 Dec 1847) • *GM*, 2nd ser., 29 (1848), 202–4, 333 • F. W. Cock, 'The first operation under ether in Europe', *University College Hospital Magazine*, 1 (1911), 127–44 • D. J. Coltart, 'Surgery between Hunter and Lister as exemplified by the life and works of Robert Liston, 1794–1847', *Proceedings of the Royal Society of Medicine*, 65 (1972), 556–60 • *The Lancet* (11 Dec 1847), 633–4 • *The Lancet* (25 Dec 1847), 687 • *The Lancet* (1 Jan 1848), 19 • *The Lancet* (4 March 1848), 272 • *The Lancet* (25 March 1848), 351 • *The Lancet* (13 May 1848), 538 • *The Lancet* (17 June 1848), 673 • *The Lancet* (26 May 1849), 569–70 • *The Lancet* (2 June 1849), 592 • *The Lancet* (9 March 1850), 320–1 • *The Lancet* (13 July 1850), 44 • *The Lancet* (25 Jan 1851), 99 • H. H. Bellot, *University College, London, 1826–1926* (1929), 164–6 • V. G. Plarr, *Plarr's Lives of the fellows of the Royal College of Surgeons of England*, rev. D'A. Power, 2 vols. (1930) • A. H. M. Littlewood, 'Robert Liston, 1794–1847', *British Journal of Plastic Surgery*, 13 (1960), 97–101 • 'The classic reprint: closure of cleft palate by Robert Liston, MD, with commentary by F. McDowell', *Plastic and reconstructive surgery*, 48 (1971), 167–9, 366–7 • private information (1892)

Archives Wellcome L., letters to James Miller • Yale U., Beinecke L., letters to T. J. Pettigrew

Likenesses chalk drawing, *c.*1824, repro. in Coltart, 'Surgery between Hunter and Lister', 127 • M. Gauci, lithograph, pubd 1836 (after E. U. Eddis), BM, Wellcome L. • J. C. Bromley, mezzotint, pubd 1839 (after F. Grant), BM, Wellcome L. • C. Turner, mezzotint, 1839, BM, Wellcome L. • W. O. Geller, mezzotint, 1841 (after W. Bagg), Wellcome L. • T. Campbell, bust, 1850, UCL; replica, Royal Infirmary • T. Bridgford, lithograph, Wellcome L. • C. Stanfield, portrait (as a young man), Royal College of Surgeons, Edinburgh • L. Wyon, silvered glass medal, Scot. NPG • portrait, Royal College of Surgeons, Edinburgh • silhouette, Wellcome L.

Wealth at death approx. £5000: *The Lancet* (25 March 1848), 351; (17 June 1848), 673

Listowel. For this title name *see* Hare, William Francis, fifth earl of Listowel (1906–1997).

Litchfield [*née* Sylvester Hay], **Harriett** (1777–1854), actress, is said to have been born on 4 March 1777. Her father, John Sylvester Hay (*d.* 1787?), the only son of the vicar of Maldon, Essex, was surgeon of the East Indiaman *Nassau*, and afterwards head surgeon of the Royal Hospital, Calcutta, where he is stated to have died in his thirty-seventh year, leaving his daughter aged about nine. He may have been the 'Mr John Hay' who was 'proprietor and printer of the *Calcutta Gazette*', and proprietor and manager of the Calcutta theatre, who died at Fort William in April 1787 (*Gentleman's Magazine*, 2, 1787, 1024).

Miss Hay, sometimes called Miss Sylvester, made her first appearance at Richmond in the summer of 1792, as Julia in Colman's *The Surrender of Calais*. Encouraged by Dorothy Jordan's applause, she played three or four other characters. Early in 1793 she acted in Scotland and later received a letter from Robert Burns inviting her in the name of the citizens of Dumfries to revisit that town. Her next engagement, under Francis Aickin at Liverpool, proved unsatisfactory. He allowed her only two parts: Sophia in Thomas Holcroft's *The Road to Ruin* and Edward in Elizabeth Inchbald's *Everyone has his Fault*. On 27 May 1796 she appeared in London at Covent Garden 'as a young Lady' for the benefit of Mary Ann Davenport, playing her Liverpool role of Edward.

Parish records at St Paul's, Covent Garden, confirm that Harriett Sylvester Hay married John Litchfield (1774–1858) on 14 September 1796. He was a clerk of the privy council,

Harriett Litchfield (1777–1854), by Samuel Drummond, exh. RA 1799

and Gilliland in the *Dramatic Mirror* reported that he was 'a gentleman well known and admired in the literary world, and much esteemed as a private character'. He was also the author of some prologues and epilogues, and he occasionally acted. After their marriage the couple settled at 36 Bedford Street, Covent Garden. A child, the first of six, most of whom died in infancy, was born on 30 September 1796, and baptized Thomas Litchfield at St Paul's on 21 November 1796.

Harriett Litchfield had briefly left the stage upon her marriage, but reappeared in the benefit performances for Mary Ann Yates at the Haymarket on 9 February 1797 and later for other benefits at Covent Garden. Her reception on these occasions gained her an engagement for the following season, and she performed at Richmond during the summer. Engaged at £3 a week, she appeared at Covent Garden on 20 September 1797 as Marianne in Reynolds's *The Dramatist*. Her other roles that season included Catalina in *The Castle of Andalusia*, Lady Anne in *Richard III*, and Dimity in Arthur Murphy's *Three Weeks after Marriage*. In October 1797 the *Monthly Mirror* was enthusiastic in praising her performances, and it is possible that the reviews of her work in that journal were written by her husband.

On 5 December 1800 Mrs Litchfield played Lady Macbeth, making such a success that she was established as a judicious actress. The *Monthly Mirror* enthused 'the attempt was bold and hazardous, but her success in the character was complete'. After a quarrel in 1806 with her managers, she returned to the Haymarket. Richard Brinsley Peake recalled that Colman relied on her 'capability of sustaining a variety of parts'. Thereafter her name all but disappears from the theatrical record. She played for six nights at Bath in May 1810, enacting Lady Clermont in Dimond's *Adrian and Orilla* and performing in a monodrama by Matthew Gregory Lewis that had been written especially for her. On 8 October 1812 she appeared at the Haymarket as Emilia in *Othello*, one of her best characters. This was announced as her first appearance on the stage for six years; it seems also to have been her last.

The *Thespian Dictionary* (1805) complimented her skill in tragedy and in irascible characters such as Mrs Oakley in Colman's *The Jealous Wife*, and further commented 'that the animation of her performance makes ample compensation for the disadvantage of figure'. Thomas Gilliland and Anne Mathews remembered her as an esteemed and celebrated actress, and the former further recorded her cheerful and unaffected manners in private life.

Harriett Litchfield and her husband survived another four decades. She died, probably in London, on 11 January 1854. The *Gentleman's Magazine* (July 1858) reported John Litchfield's death as having occurred on 30 May 1858, at the age of eighty-four, at the home of his only surviving daughter, Mrs Harriet Sarah Abraham, of Mountfield House, Harrow Road, London. K. A. CROUCH

Sources Highfill, Burnim & Langhans, *BDA*, vols. 9, 15 • C. B. Hogan, ed., *The London stage, 1660–1800*, pt 5: *1776–1800* (1968) • T. Gilliland, *The dramatic mirror, containing the history of the stage from the earliest period, to the present time*, 2 vols. (1808) • *The thespian dictionary, or, Dramatic biography of the present age*, 2nd edn (1805) • *Monthly Mirror* (Oct 1797) • *Monthly Mirror* (Jan 1801) • *GM*, 3rd ser., 5 (1858), 92 • R. B. Peake, *Memoirs of the Colman family*, 2 vols. (1841) • A. Mathews, *Memoirs of Charles Mathews, comedian*, 4 vols. (1838)

Archives Theatre Museum, London, Enthoven collection, letters

Likenesses S. Drummond, oils, exh. RA 1799, Garr. Club [*see illus.*] • W. Say, mezzotint, pubd 1816 (after G. H. Harlow), BM, NPG • Chapman, engraving (as Belvidera in *Venice preserved*; after Moses), repro. in R. Cumberland, ed., *The British drama*, 14 vols. (1817) • S. De Wilde, portrait (as Ophelia in *Hamlet*) • S. De Wilde, watercolour (as Susan in *Follies of the day*), Harvard TC • W. Ridley, stipple (after C. Allingham), repro. in *Monthly Mirror* (1802) • engraving (as Imoinda in *Oroonoko*), repro. in R. Cumberland, ed., *The British drama*, 14 vols. (1817) • engraving (as Zara in *The mourning bride*), repro. in R. Cumberland, ed., *The British drama*, 14 vols. (1817) • five prints, Harvard TC

Liter, Monia (**1905–1988**), pianist and composer, was born in Odessa, southern Russia, on 27 January 1905. Having studied the piano at the Imperial School of Music in Odessa, he went after the revolution with his father to Harbin in northern China. He began to earn his living as pianist in a cinema in Shanghai and played in the Shanghai Symphony Orchestra. From there he travelled widely in the Near and Far East; he went to the Malay States, and while resident in Singapore became a naturalized British subject. For seven years he played in a dance band led by Jimmy Lequime, going with the band in 1925 to Calcutta and in 1926 to the Raffles Hotel in Singapore, where he took over as leader. The singer and guitarist Al Bowlly was playing in the band in 1927, and Liter, recognizing his potential, persuaded him that he ought to make his way to

Europe. Bowlly's first move in that direction took him to Germany, where he made his first recordings, and eventually he went to London to join the Fred Elizalde band. Monia Liter left the East and went to London in 1933 and accompanied Bowlly on his first stage appearance at the Holborn Empire on 11 September 1933. Bowlly was a great success, but much praise was reserved for the 'Sensational Accompaniments by New Pianistic Discovery' and 'Pianist Par Excellence', the *Melody Maker* saying (apropos Bowlly's first 'solo' appearance):

> Solo is perhaps the wrong word, as it would do less than justice to Al's brilliant accompanist, a young man from Singapore by the name of Monia Liter, a pianist of exceptional all-round ability. Liter comes from a poor family and is in many respects a self-taught musician. Not only does he play the piano with the ability of a concert virtuoso, but in some way or other he has acquired a rhythm style seemingly every bit as futuristic as Fred Elizalde's … an accompanist of no mean order. It is said that Liter is also a fine arranger, and it seems quite evident that we shall be hearing a great deal more about him in the near future. (Pallett, 62)

Liter accompanied Bowlly on most of his Decca recordings. They were together for many years in the Lew Stone band and teamed up for a trip to the USA in 1935.

Monia Liter was always in demand in London, and played and recorded with the New Mayfair Dance Orchestra led by Ray Noble (1932–3), and also with bands led by Nat Gonella (1935), Jack Hylton (1936–7), and Harry Roy (1939–40). He served for six months in the Royal Army Service Corps in 1941 and during the following war years played with Billy Ternent's BBC Radio Orchestra and toured with Larry Adler entertaining the troops. He led his own 20th Century Orchestra and did solo broadcasts, toured with Sophie Tucker, and played with Maurice Winnick, Victor Silvester, and Harry Roy again in 1949. Most notably, he played with the Lew Stone Orchestra (on and off for recordings and other engagements at various periods between 1933 and 1949), where for a time he duetted in partnership with Stanley Black. When given a chance to shine with Stone he continued to reveal a very advanced piano style, which Albert McCarthy described as being almost 'Thelonious Monkish'. He was a prolific composer of light music, writing the score for a London revue *SS Sunshine* (1933) and composing music for a number of films, including Robert Wyler's and Carol Reed's *It Happened in Paris* (1935). From 1944 he was closely associated with the BBC as composer, conductor, and arranger and led a popular broadcasting group known as the Twentieth Century Serenaders. He was responsible for many of the orchestras that broadcast in the late forties and early fifties. After playing with the Harry Robbins Quartet in 1951 he joined the staff of Boosey and Hawkes and later became head of the light music department; he retired in 1977. He was married to (Nina) Betty Doreen, a harpist. The couple lived at 23 Warren Court, Euston Road, London; but Liter died of a heart attack in a nursing home at 52 Friern Barnet Road, Friern Barnet, London, on 5 October 1988 at the age of eighty-three. PETER GAMMOND

Sources P. Gammond, *The Oxford companion to popular music* (1991) · J. Chilton, *Who's who of British jazz* (1997) · S. Colin and T. Staveacre, *Al Bowlly* (1979) · d. cert. · *CGPLA Eng. & Wales* (1989) · R. Pallett, *Goodnight sweetheart: life and times of Al Bowlly* (1986)

Wealth at death under £70,000: probate, 7 Feb 1989, *CGPLA Eng. & Wales*

Lithgow family (*per. c.*1870–1952), shipbuilders and industrialists, came to prominence with **William Todd Lithgow** (1854–1908), shipbuilder, and his sons, James and Henry. Born at Port Glasgow, William Todd Lithgow was the second son of James Lithgow (*d.* 1870), a cotton yarn merchant, and his wife, Margaret MacNicol (*d.* 1861). His father had moved from Glasgow to Greenock before setting up in Port Glasgow in 1856. Lithgow became a premium apprentice with the old-established Port Glasgow shipbuilder John Reid & Co., and he was trained as a ship's draughtsman just at the time when the River Clyde was emerging as the main seat of iron and steam shipbuilding in Britain.

The young William Todd Lithgow had little opportunity to draw on family support in developing his career: his mother died when he was only seven, and his father died in 1870 when William was still only sixteen and had barely begun his apprenticeship. By 1874 he was acting draughtsman for John Reid & Co. and he had invested his £1000 patrimony in a new partnership with an experienced shipbuilder, Joseph Russell, and another young man, Anderson Rodger. The firm of Russell & Co. had a capital of £7000—£5000 from Russell with £1000 each from the two young men. The new firm did not try to rival the emerging metal and steam shipyards which required large capitals, but concentrated on exploiting the opportunity of the depression years of 1874–9 by building large, simple, iron-hulled sailing ships, designed for long hauls of bulk commodities which did not have to meet urgent delivery deadlines. From the outset Lithgow influenced the company in designing semi-standard bulk cargo sailing vessels with interchangeable components and crew-saving devices, and the company also helped to sell its ships by taking shares with the shipowners. The formula was simple, but effective.

The new company leased its shipyard, the Bay Yard, and by 1879, as the depression eased, extended its capacity by leasing a second yard, the Cartsdyke Yard at Port Glasgow. Two years later in 1881 it purchased the site of what was to be its main yard, the Kingston Yard, establishing there a new yard with six berths. Between 1874 and 1881 William Todd Lithgow's investment of £1000 had grown to £4893, and he had also withdrawn £7830 from the business, of which £4951 had been reinvested in ships. As Lithgow's fortune prospered, in 1879 he married; his wife was Agnes Birkmyre, daughter of Henry Birkmyre, rope manufacturer, whose family owned the Gourock Rope Company and were also substantial shipowners. The couple had two sons. The elder, **Sir James Lithgow**, first baronet (1883–1952), was born on 27 January 1883 at Huntly Bank, Port Glasgow. The same year his parents established the family home at Drums, at Langbank, overlooking the Clyde, where his brother, **Henry Lithgow** (1886–1948), was born on 23 December 1886.

The 1880s were a busy period for the firm of Russell & Co., in which Lithgow acted as the chief designer. While the relationships between Lithgow and the older partner, Joseph Russell, were amicable, that with Anderson Rodger was strained and Lithgow indicated a desire to leave the partnership in 1889. He was dissuaded from doing so by Russell, who offered to withdraw himself from the partnership to leave Lithgow in control; matters, however, deteriorated and in 1891, with Rodger ill, Lithgow again sought to leave the partnership; it was dissolved by mutual agreement on 30 November 1891, leaving Lithgow as sole proprietor of Russell & Co. operating from the Cartsdyke and Kingston yards; Rodger retained the Bay Yard and continued to build independently. That Joseph Russell was close to William Lithgow is clear in the terms of the settlement. Russell lent Lithgow £122,965 to buy out Rodger and set up his own operations; Russell also continued to act as a bookkeeper for Lithgow and as an adviser on the purchasing of timber. By 1891 Lithgow's capital in the business had grown to £159,386. In addition, since 1874 he had withdrawn capital of £67,940, of which £40,681 was reinvested in ships. Russell's judgement of Lithgow was that he was 'very clever, sharp, light headed but strong willed'. This had been amply borne out by Lithgow's rapid progress in business.

Under Lithgow's sole control the firm of Russell & Co. prospered, and by the mid-1890s was transferring its formula of constructing standard cargo ships to a new generation of through-deck tramp steamers, of between 4000 and 5000 gross registered tons. He also began concentrating more on steamship construction and the last sailing vessel was launched in 1894. Profitability remained strong in these years, rising from £15,500 in 1899 to £123,601 by 1901, the year in which William Todd Lithgow brought his elder son, James, into the business as an apprentice. With an eye to diversifying and securing his personal wealth, William Todd Lithgow ceased investing in shipping and transferred into equities, purchasing almost £200,000 worth of stock between 1901 and 1903, while at the same time buying a country estate, Ormsary, in Knapdale, Argyll, in 1902. Large capitals of £313,304 were withdrawn from the business between 1903 and 1906, most of this being transferred as *inter vivos* gifts to his sons; the younger son, Henry, took up his apprenticeship in 1905.

Even as the family business grew in wealth and prosperity, William Todd Lithgow declined, his health breaking early in 1907. Before the end of the year he had undergone surgery for stomach cancer and in November 1907 he brought his two sons into full partnership, while his long-time friend Joseph Russell came out of retirement to help the young men run the business. The founder of the family business and fortune died from cancer on 7 June 1908 at Drums, at the early age of fifty-three. His business career had lasted only twenty-six years, in which he had turned his £1000 investment into a fortune of about £2.2 million; his personal estate at death was valued at £1,000,237, of which £102,000 was invested in shipping, but he had also made cumulative drawings of nearly £1,240,000 from the business during his working life. His sons inherited the leading cargo construction yard on the Clyde, but they themselves were only twenty-five and twenty-two, with little experience of the business.

At the time of their father's death the two brothers still lived at Drums; they had been schooled together by private tutor before both going to Glasgow Academy and then serving their apprenticeships. They were remarkably close, sharing a staunch Presbyterian upbringing and outlook, and were deeply attached to the attractions of the grouse and deer shoots on the family estate at Ormsary. They were a complementary team, James taking the lead as the elder, while Henry supported and followed in his path, although later correspondence shows that once Henry had made up his mind his elder brother often recognized that he could not be persuaded to another course of action. Where James could be abrupt and forceful, Henry was a man who liked to take time to think over a problem and in this he was a moderating influence on his brother. It is clear that they trusted each other completely and that in business no important matter was ever entered into that did not have both brothers' full support and approval.

In the six years between their father's death and the beginning of the First World War James and Henry Lithgow quickly grew into the control of their family business, and began to lay the foundations for expansion. In 1911 the original yard of Russell & Co., the Bay Yard, was acquired on the death of Anderson Rodger; this added to the Lithgow capacity while ensuring that no newcomer could set up business in the Lithgow domain at Port Glasgow. At the same time, James Lithgow took a first step into wider industry affairs, becoming vice-president of the Clyde Shipbuilders' Association; he was its president in 1912–13. It was there that he met and formed a friendship with Andrew Rae *Duncan, an industrial lawyer who became secretary of the Shipbuilding Employers' Federation, then a director and industrial adviser to the Bank of England and chairman of the Central Electricity Generating Board. He was to be greatly influential in bringing James Lithgow into public affairs and involving him in industrial reconstruction in the 1930s. Before the war, the only other involvement that James Lithgow had outside the business was in the volunteer force of the Port Glasgow company of the first Renfrew and Dumbarton Royal Garrison Artillery. He had been involved in this since 1905 and was commissioned as a second lieutenant. When the volunteer force became the Territorial Army in 1908, James Lithgow was promoted to the rank of captain. This involvement was a deliberate choice of the two brothers; the elder took on the public responsibility in case of war, while the younger Henry was to concentrate on the shipyard management. Consequently when war did come James spent the first year and a half manning the river defence unit at Fort Matilda in Greenock. In summer 1915 he and his men were sent to Plymouth and then to Lydd in Kent to train with new howitzers. The battery finally sailed for France in February 1916 and James Lithgow spent the next fifteen months at the western front, gained the Military Cross, and advanced to the rank of brevet colonel.

In contrast Henry kept control in the Port Glasgow yards and proved to be a tough and capable manager, maintaining production under difficult conditions while being forcefully critical of the way the government squandered effort and resources in ship construction. During these years, with the agreement of his brother, Henry took the chance to expand the business. In 1915 the Lithgows took over the local yard of Robert Duncan & Co., and in 1917 bought into David Rowan & Co., marine engineers at Govan in Glasgow.

From letters written to Henry it is clear that James Lithgow ultimately came to regard his time at the front as a waste of his talent; after the battle of the Somme he wrote in November 1916:

> The authorities can claim what they like for military service: three of the four juniors who came out with us are now considered fit to do my job here and the supply of such fellows is ample. I am therefore forced to the conclusion that I would be more useful helping you in our own business than messing about out here.

However, James Lithgow's desire to return to his shipbuilding business and employ his talents more effectively in aid of the war effort were not to be quickly answered. Not until May 1917, when Sir Eric Campbell Geddes was appointed controller of merchant shipbuilding, was James Lithgow finally recalled from the front to take up a new position of director of merchant shipbuilding with the responsibility of ensuring that the merchant yards met the country's needs for new tonnage. Quite suddenly he was enmeshed in a network of influence, forming working relationships with men who were to be useful contacts in his later career, notably through his work with Lord Pirrie, controller of Harland and Woolf, and Lord Weir of Eastwood.

James Lithgow was able to return to Port Glasgow to join his brother early in 1919, and at this time the name of the business was at last changed from Russell & Co. to Lithgows Ltd and the brothers changed the partnership to a private limited company. This was a prelude to much expansion and merger activity, encouraged by the buoyancy of demand for new tonnage at the end of the war. The Lithgows widened their own control of the local industry, acquiring another two yards in 1919, those of Dunlop Bremner & Co. and William Hamilton & Co. The Clydeside industry was then also reshaping itself in order to secure its supplies of steel, and the Lithgows integrated into coal, iron, and steel with the acquisition of James Dunlop & Co. Consequently, by 1920 the two brothers presided over a much enlarged business empire, which was vertically integrated with interests in coal, iron and steel making, marine engineering, and shipbuilding, and in shipowning and ship operation.

With both brothers now at home in Port Glasgow, the pattern of management reshaped itself, with James based in his office in the old William Hamilton's yard and Henry in the East Yard, purchased from Duncan & Co., while the Kingston site was the base for their manager, John Muirhead. The three worked closely together and on this foundation the Lithgow yards sustained a high level of activity during the difficult years of the 1920s and 1930s. Between 1920 and 1939 the Lithgow group launched 1.017 million tons of merchant ships, making them the third yard by rank in Britain behind Swan Hunter and Harland and Woolf. During this period they launched nearly twice as much tonnage as the next ranked Clyde yard of Barclay Curle & Co.

In the period following the First World War Henry Lithgow and John Muirhead were closely concerned with the day-to-day management of the yards while James Lithgow was soon sucked into public affairs. In 1920 James Lithgow became president of the Shipbuilding Employers' Federation; this re-established his wartime contacts with Lord Weir of Eastwood who was then president of the National Confederation of Employers' Organisations, and James Lithgow became vice-president of that body in 1922, representing the employers at the International Labour Organization in Geneva between 1922 and 1927. There he met Horace Wilson, permanent secretary of the Ministry of Labour, who was to become industrial adviser to the government and ultimately head of the civil service.

Even as his public career was opening up, James Lithgow began to enjoy a different style of life: in 1924, at the age of forty-one, he married Gwendolyn Amy Harrison, daughter of John Robinson Harrison, a former Clyde shipowner. The couple had a son and two daughters. He then also built his own home, Gleddoch House at Langbank, finally moving out of Drums, leaving his brother Henry to live at home with his mother. Henry then purchased another house of his own at Ormsary where he could entertain his own guests. Like James he was passionately fond of country pursuits, and at the same time he purchased a grouse moor at Duchal in the Renfrewshire hills behind the shipyards, where he built a 7 mile long light railway to carry him and his guests on the shoots. Henry Lithgow remained unmarried. This busy period also saw the Lithgows again extend their industrial empire by acquiring the engine works of Rankine and Blackmore in 1923. James Lithgow's public involvement brought him a baronetcy from Stanley Baldwin in 1923.

The Lithgow brothers had very strong views on the post-war condition of British industry, and James was their joint spokesman. They both believed that competitiveness could only be regained through reducing costs, and by organized labour delivering a fair day's work for fair wages. They were openly critical of the attitude of organized labour to wages and to manning arrangements, and believed that labour was obstructive to their efforts to introduce labour-saving machinery which could have improved productivity. They also feared that the excessive wartime expansion of capacity, costs, and wages would have to be paid for, and this was borne out in the difficulties of the later 1920s and early 1930s. Both James and Henry Lithgow were ultimately to be converted to the view that a fundamental readjustment of industry was required which involved the rationalization of capacity, bringing with it a loss of jobs and the closure of redundant capacity.

Sir James Lithgow took a leading role in preparing the shipbuilding industry for this experience, being the main spokesman in designing the industry rationalization scheme. At this point his friendship with Andrew Duncan made it possible for him to bring his proposal to the attention of Montagu Norman, governor of the Bank of England, who was committed to the concept of rationalization, as well as seeing it as a measure to untangle the morass of debt which bore down on the banks and heavy industry by the end of the 1920s. The Bank of England agreed to underwrite the shipbuilding industry's scheme, which created the rationalization company National Shipbuilders' Security Ltd (NSS) in November 1930. Lithgow was not only the major industry spokesman for this purpose but became chairman of NSS in 1930 and at the same time president of the Federation of British Industry. In the same year he showed his commitment to industrial regeneration by becoming chairman of the Scottish National Development Council executive committee.

Under Lithgow's guidance NSS successfully purchased and closed about one-third of shipbuilding industry capacity between 1930 and 1939. James Lithgow defended this action and the loss of jobs as necessary to put the industry on a firm and competitive footing which would allow it to re-employ men as business regained momentum. He also believed it was necessary for industries to put their own house in order so that the government would not be drawn in. The first great casualty of NSS was the huge Beardmore Yard at Dalmuir on the Clyde, in which the Bank of England held considerable debt. Lithgow's role in relieving the Bank of England of this responsibility was not unconnected with the terms on which, in 1934, the Lithgow brothers were able to purchase Beardmore debentures from the Bank of England in order to take control of that great iron and steel company.

The steel industry was also subject to rationalization at this time and the Lithgow ownership of James Dunlop & Co. involved them in the rationalization of Scottish steelmaking capacity. The main player here was John *Craig of the Colville group; in discussion with Craig the Lithgows agreed to merge their Dunlop holdings with the Colvilles in 1931, as a consequence of which both brothers joined the board of the Colville companies. Later in 1934 the Bank of England accepted the advice of their steel rationalizer J. Bruce Gardner to help the Lithgow brothers buy the shares of the Steel Company of Scotland. Their ownership of these shares posed a threat to the growing monopoly of the Colville group in supplying the shipbuilding market, and encouraged the Colville group also to incorporate the Steel Company of Scotland in its rationalization scheme. When the Colvilles purchased the Steel Company of Scotland from the Lithgows in 1936 they paid £951,750, while the Lithgows had purchased the company for £672,975; the profit, however, was donated by the two brothers to the Church of Scotland.

Henry and James Lithgow consequently played a significant role in the creation of the new Scottish steel industry in the 1930s, as well as securing their own interests in shipbuilding. Their involvement with Montagu Norman and Andrew Duncan again placed them in the position to acquire the shares of the troubled Fairfield yard after it was involved in the insolvency of the Anchor Line. Norman and Duncan made it possible for the Lithgows to acquire Fairfields and bring that great but ailing yard within the Lithgow group in 1935.

The Lithgows led by James Lithgow emerged as leading players in Scottish industrial politics and policy in the 1930s. While James took the public role, he was enabled to do so because Henry took the brunt of the responsibility of the day-to-day industrial management of their expanding business empire. James Lithgow also emerged as the leading spokesman for new industrial development in Scotland and he was much involved with the Scottish Economic Committee and its labours to attract new lighter industry to the economy in these years. Henry supported James's efforts in this regard because both brothers shared a highly moral philosophy on business responsibility. They believed that 'those who had made their money in Scotland have an obligation to keep it there and to use their best endeavours to develop and keep the health of the industry to which they owe their own prosperity'.

This same commitment to their industry and their country set the pattern for their roles in the Second World War. Sir James was almost automatically called to London by Winston Churchill in 1940 to become controller of merchant shipbuilding and repairs. He also became one of the lords of the Admiralty, was briefly controller of tanks, and also acted as deputy chairman of the industrial capacity committee of the production council, working there with Harold MacMillan as chairman. He was also president of the Iron and Steel Federation between 1943 and 1945, while retaining his chairmanship of both Beardmores and Fairfields. The public pressure on James Lithgow was obvious and intense, but the private pressure on his brother Henry was unremitting. Henry now lived alone at Drums after his mother's death, and his sole family life came from his attachment to his brother's family. He carried most of the burden of wartime management of the Lithgow yards, and he was usually there in the yards seven days each week unless James was home from London and they could snatch a little shared leisure together.

At the end of the war James returned eagerly to Port Glasgow to rejoin his brother and his family, but neither brother was long to survive the wartime pressures. Henry had never been robust and his health deteriorated abruptly in 1947; he died at home at Drums on 28 May 1948. Except for wartime duty the two brothers had never lived more than a few miles apart and had always depended heavily on each other. Henry's death faced the Lithgows with death duties of £2 million, which Sir James paid within a week of receiving the statement. Henry's death was a bitter blow to James, for the demands for new tonnage were unceasing and the post-war scarcities made it difficult for yards to meet all the demands made upon them. James, however, was not to have the opportunity to cope effectively with the post-war condition of the industry, for four months after his brother's death he suffered a serious thrombosis while shooting on his estate at Ormsary. He fought the consequences of his stroke for three years but never fully recovered, dying on 23 February 1952 at Gleddoch House, Langbank. He was buried at Ormsary, Argyll. He was survived by his wife.

With the death of the two brothers, Sir James's son William inherited the baronetcy and also the largest private shipbuilding concern in the world. The two brothers had been given early control of a substantial shipbuilding and shipping business when their father died, and during the next forty years extended this business into Scotland's leading industrial dynasty. They did so through re-investing heavily in their own operations and through long hours of hard work in the yards and in public service, sustained throughout by a strong sense of duty and a desire to give back to others what life had delivered to them. They were both staunch supporters of the Church of Scotland, which benefited greatly from their donations. They were also continuous benefactors of their industrial community and especially of the town of Port Glasgow, which honoured Sir James in 1951 by creating him the first honorary citizen of the burgh. The driving force behind the Lithgows was a desire to serve and give value for money. Henry made his contribution in the yards and on the boards of the companies in the Lithgow group, while James extended his service to the industry and to the country at large, emerging as an industrial statesman of rare quality.

Between 1874 and 1952 the Lithgow family created an industrial empire unrivalled in Scotland's economic history. Little of consequence was achieved in Scotland's industrial economy between the 1920s and the 1940s that did not in significant measure owe something to the contribution, the drive, the energy, and the leadership of the Lithgows of Port Glasgow. ANTHONY SLAVEN

Sources 'Extracts from the diaries and papers of Joseph Russell, 1834–1917', ed. B. Fyfe, U. Glas., Archives and Business Records Centre, Lithgows Ltd records • *DSBB*, vol. 1 • M. Moss, 'William Todd Lithgow: founder of a fortune', *SHR*, 62 (1983), 47–72 • J. M. Reid, *James Lithgow, master of work* (1964) • C. A. Oakley, *Our illustrious forebears* (1980) • P. L. Payne, *Colvilles and the Scottish steel industry* (1979) • J. Shields, *Clyde built: a history of ship-building on the River Clyde* (1949) • H. C. Whitley, *Laughter in heaven* (1962) • *WWW* • m. cert. [William Todd Lithgow] • d. cert. [William Todd Lithgow] • b. cert. [James Lithgow] • d. cert. [James Lithgow] • b. cert. [Henry Lithgow] • d. cert. [Henry Lithgow]

Archives U. Glas., records of Lithgows Ltd | NL Scot., Reid MSS

Likenesses W. Stoneman, photograph, NPG

Wealth at death £1,000,237 5*s*. 5*d*.—William Todd Lithgow: confirmation, 11 July 1908, *CCI* • £436,961 6*s*. 8*d*.—James Lithgow: confirmation, 7 Aug 1952, *CCI* • £1,960,034 18*s*. 10*d*.—Henry Lithgow: confirmation, 2 Feb 1949, *CCI*

Lithgow, Henry (1886–1948). *See under* Lithgow family (*per. c.*1870–1952).

Lithgow, Sir James, first baronet (1883–1952). *See under* Lithgow family (*per. c.*1870–1952).

Lithgow, William (*b.* 1582, *d.* in or after 1645), traveller, was born at Lanark, the eldest of three known children of James Lithgow (*d.* 1623), a wealthy burgess, and Alison Graham (*d.* 1603), possibly a relation of the earls of Montrose who were later Lithgow's patrons. He was educated at Lanark grammar school. An unlikely tradition that he was intended to become a tailor seems to derive from the appointment of a tailor, James Lithgow (relationship unknown), as an overseer of his mother's will. The provisions of the will included a bequest of 200 marks to William Lithgow.

The early travels of Lugless Will Some time before he was twenty-one Lithgow was savagely maltreated by the brothers of a woman with whom he was involved—he described the incident thirty years later as 'foure blood-shedding wolves' devouring 'one silly stragling lambe' (Lithgow, *Totall Discourse*, 6). Tradition affirms (there is no contemporary evidence) that the family's name was Lockhart and that the brothers cut off or mutilated Lithgow's ears so that he became known as Cutlugged Willie or Lugless Will. He says that the authorities made him submit at the time to 'arbitrement, satisfaction and reconciliation', but that as he grew in years and understood 'the unallowable redresses, and the hainousnesse of the offence; I choosed rather … to seclude my selfe from my soyle … then to have a quotidian occular inspection' (ibid., 7). Among the other reasons he gave for embracing a life of difficult travel is that 'the science of the world', which is superior to other branches of knowledge, is 'acquisted … above all, and principally by Travellers, and Voyagers in divers Regions, and remote places, whose experience confirmeth the true Science therof' (ibid., 301).

While still in 'the stripling age of my adolescency' (Lithgow, *Totall Discourse*, 9) Lithgow twice visited Orkney and Shetland, the abundance of which he was later to contrast with the relative barrenness of the Aegean Islands. By the early summer of 1609 he had also toured extensively, doubtless, as later, on foot, in Germany, Bohemia, Switzerland, and the Low Countries. He spent ten months in Paris before setting off, in March 1610, on a forty-day walk to Rome. There he inspected the antiquities, violently disapproved of Roman Catholic rites, and was, he claims, harried by the Inquisition. After encountering the 'ignorant devotion' of pilgrims to Loreto (ibid., 25) he sailed from Ancona to Venice. His companion until Venice was James Arthur, a Scottish gentleman who long remained his friend. Lithgow continued, via Zara and Ragusa, to Corfu and the Greek mainland. 'In all this countrey of Greece' he observes:

> I could find nothing, to answer the famous relations, given by Auncient Authors, of the excellency of that land, but the name onely; the barbarousnesse of Turkes and Time, having defeated all the Monuments of Antiquity: No shew of honour, no habitat of men in an honest fashion … But rather prisoners shut up in prisons, or addicted slaves to cruell and tyrrannicall Maisters. (ibid., 65)

At Khania in Crete, Lithgow says, he rescued a French protestant condemned to the Venetian galleys by getting his keeper drunk and smuggling him away disguised as a woman. After other adventures, including shipwreck on Chios, he saw what was then believed to be the remains of Troy and, surviving a beating by four French 'runnagates' on the quayside, landed in Constantinople, where he remained until the early summer of 1611. He stayed for three months with the ambassador, Sir Thomas Glover, and studied Turkish customs, religion, and society.

Among the many other places Lithgow now visited were Smyrna, Rhodes, Cyprus, and Aleppo. In the spring of 1612 he left Aleppo with a caravan of Armenians and Turks, travelling via Damascus to Galilee and eventually, on Palm Sunday, Jerusalem. During the journey marauding Arabs had to be fought off or paid off, an ambush was narrowly avoided, and Lithgow's Turkish conductor had to be palliated continually with money and tobacco. Once in the city Lithgow looked askance at the rites and observances of his Franciscan hosts but was prepared on the whole to take more seriously the sights at the holy sepulchre, where he spent Easter. With a caravan including six German protestants he made the hard desert journey to Cairo in May 1612. Three of the Germans died on the journey and the other three soon after their arrival. Lithgow claims that he inherited from the Germans some 942 sequins (about £400). From Cairo, 'Microcosmus of the greater World' (Lithgow, *Totall Discourse*, 274), he saw the pyramids and sphinx before sailing, by way of Malta, to Sicily. There, he claims, he narrowly escaped capture by Moorish slavers, raised the alarm, and, on the slavers' arrest, was feasted and richly rewarded by local people. He accompanied the earl of Bothwell and Captain George Hepburn to Rome, travelled fairly rapidly to the Alps, was saved from murder near Fréjus partly by his pilgrim's patent, and went to Montpellier, Barcelona, Pau, Bordeaux, and Paris, where ended 'my first, my painefull, and Pedestriall Pilgrimage' (ibid., 298).

The 'delectable' and 'totall' discourses Soon afterwards Lithgow returned to Britain. In London he presented to King James a hunting rod which he had cut from a turpentine tree by the River Jordan and to Queen Anne some medicinal white earth from the cave in Bethlehem and a girdle and garters 'all richly wrought in silke and gold' and inscribed 'Sancto Sepulchro, and the word Jerusalem, &c.' (Lithgow, *Totall Discourse*, 247). He also sought the favour of the earl and countess of Somerset, initially dedicating to him, with verses to her, *A Most Delectable and True Discourse, of an Admired and Painefull Peregrination* (1614, reissued 1616). At the Somersets' fall a dedication to 'all Noble-minded Gentlemen, and Heroicke Spirits' was substituted.

The 1614 account was much expanded, and supplemented by accounts of the two later 'peregrinations', in the new edition of 1623 (also extensively selected for *Purchas his Pilgrimes … the Second Part*, 1625) and *The totall discourse of the rare adventures and painefull peregrinations of long nineteene yeares travayles* (1632). Already in 1614, however, many of the distinctive features of Lithgow's writing were in place: the anti-Catholicism (varied by and on occasion linked to anti-Muslim sentiments); the action-filled narrative (doubtless exaggerated at times; usually there is no way of telling which incidents, if any, are actually invented); the accounts of charges, expenses, thefts, and counter-balancing gifts and rewards; the often colourful 'aureate' style and vocabulary.

Lithgow departed for his second round of peregrinations in September 1614 'upon some distaste' (Lithgow, *Totall Discourse*, 298). In the Netherlands he was received equally by the opposing generals Spinola and Prince Maurice. He sailed up the Rhine to Heidelberg and 'saluted the Princesse Palatine [Elizabeth of Bohemia] with certayne rare Relickes of the Holy land' (ibid., 305). At Pistoia he was (allegedly) unjustly arrested and condemned to the galleys by the corrupt Bargello but freed by the governor and given 50 Florentine gold crowns in compensation. But the most famous or infamous (conceivably untrue) incident of the second journey took place in Sicily, where, coming upon the bodies of two noblemen who had killed each other, he stole and concealed their rings and money, alerted the townspeople to the deaths, retrieved the booty, left Sicily for Malta as soon as possible, and later vaunted the deed in print—'there is aye some fortune falleth by accident, whether lawfull or not, I will not question'. From Malta he sailed to Tunis, visiting the Christian renegade John Ward in his magnificent palace. He went with Ward's safe conduct to 'the theevish Towne of Algier' (ibid., 317) and on to Fez, whose free sexual practices he abhorred but whose palaces, mosques, colleges, hospitals, and palatial taverns he admired. After an unsuccessful attempt to strike south through the desert he returned to Sicily. In September 1615, at Syracuse, he arranged the burial of the renegade Sir Francis Verney, whom he had met six weeks earlier in Palermo. The rest of the second journey continued, amid the usual vicissitudes, through Italy to Vienna, Hungary, Moldavia, Cracow, Danzig (where he was for a time seriously ill), Elsinore, Stockholm (where the illness seemed to be returning), and, from Elsinore again, to England.

Before beginning his third expedition Lithgow published his poem 'The Pilgrimes Farewell, to his Native Country of Scotland' (1618). This was printed at the author's own expense, but one of its aims was clearly to attract finance for the journey. Among the many dignitaries saluted is John Graham, fourth earl of Montrose, probably already a patron, as apparently was his father, John, third earl (*d.* 1606). (The epistle dedicatory of Lithgow's religious poem 'The Gushing Teares of Godly Sorrow', 1640, asks the fifth earl to continue the favour extended to him by his father and grandfather.) The motivation of the journey was to see the remaining parts of Europe, including Ireland and much of Spain, and to press further into Africa to the realm of Prester John. Lithgow was in Ireland between August 1619 and February 1620 and reported much ignorance, misery, irreligion, and water. From Youghal he sailed to St Malo and proceeded to Portugal and Spain through France (where the traveller is advised to avoid lodging near 'palludiat Ditches, least the vehemency of chirking frogs, vexe the wish'd for Repose of his fatigated body, and cast him in a vigilant perplexity'; Lithgow, *Totall Discourse*, 382).

The attack at Malaga Lithgow's account of what happened to him in Malaga in the autumn of 1620 needs to be treated—like his other encounters with Roman Catholics—with a degree of caution, especially since it was first published in the virulently anti-Spanish context of 1623. He was waiting for a boat bound for Alexandria, he says, when he was seized and secretly imprisoned in the governor's palace. He was suspected of spying for the English ships which had come against the pirates of Algiers and with the crews of which he had been happily fraternizing. Kept in irons, he was taken in late December to be tortured at a vine-pressing house a league from the town. His terrible sufferings included six hours on the rack. When he failed to confess to spying—this is where the details become arguably less convincing—he was charged instead with heresy, tortured again, and told that he would be burnt at the stake unless he recanted within eight days. But at this point a Flemish servant told the English consul about Lithgow's plight. The consul alerted the ambassador in Madrid, who was able to arrange Lithgow's release on Easter Sunday 1621.

When Lithgow landed in England he was taken on a feather bed to Theobalds to show his 'martyrd anatomy' to the king and court. Clearly his injuries were severe, whether or not they were inflicted in exactly the way he claims. At James's expense he twice took the cure at Bath and largely recovered his health and strength, although his left arm remained badly damaged, but he found it more difficult to achieve redress from the Spaniards. The ambassador in London, Gondomar, promised compensation in June 1621, but it was not forthcoming. In April 1622 he confronted Gondomar and as a result was committed to the Marshalsea prison for nine weeks. In September the council asked for him to be admitted to the Charterhouse Hospital at the first vacancy, but in February 1623 he was committed again, for unknown reasons, this time to the Gatehouse. In January 1624 his bond in £200 for good behaviour was required. Nevertheless, he continued to pursue his case. He preferred a bill of grievance to the House of Lords in 1626, returning to Scotland only after the dissolution of parliament in 1627.

In 1628 Lithgow visited the marquess of Hamilton on Arran. He spent the winter of 1628–9 in northern Scotland before crossing to Orkney, which he found well governed and notable for 'the stately and magnifick Church of St. Magnus built by the Danes' in Kirkwall (Lithgow, *Totall Discourse*, 437), and Shetland, contrastingly badly administered, a victim of recent 'deoccular' (ibid., 438)—absentee—government. (By now, he claims at the end of the *Totall Discourse*, he had travelled 36,000 miles.) He says that he 'perfected' but had not yet published 'Lithgowes Surveigh of Scotland'. It has not survived, but something of its tenor, and perhaps the difficulty in publishing, are indicated in his long poem 'Scotland's Welcome to her Native Sonne, and Soveraigne Lord, King Charles' (1633). The king is asked to redress the many ills of Scotland, where trade, agriculture, seaports and defences, learning, law and order, and morality suffer while the nobility and gentry are at court trying out strange fashions and wasting money. They should 'spend their rents, where growes their graine' (*Poetical Remains*, B4). Lithgow's anger was perhaps fuelled not only by Scotland's wrongs but by a further spell in the Gatehouse apparently resulting from the outspoken anti-Spanish material in the comprehensive 1632 version of his travels.

Lithgow's last journeys Lithgow's last known foreign journey was to witness the siege of Breda in the summer of 1637. (He had intended originally to sail to Russia.) *A True and Experimentall Discourse … of the Siege of Breda* (1637), pithier than his other writings, was composed as he lay on cold straw amid the clangour of military preparations and draws on personal observation and conversations with officers and men. His remaining works are more polemical in intention but share this 'experimentall'—experientially grounded—emphasis. For example, in 'A briefe and summarie discourse upon that lamentable and dreadfull disaster at Dunglasse' (1641), Lithgow, investigating the explosion which killed sixty people in August 1640, has:

> search'd, and tryde, and seen the place,
> And spoke with some alive.
> (*Poetical Remains*, A4v)

He was in London in 1643, walking 'eighteen Kentish miles' around the perimeter of the city to inspect its impressive fortifications and telling anyone who would listen that the Scots will come to their aid now if the citizens will completely give up their 'popish observances' (Lithgow, *Present Surveigh*, B4v, C2v). He was at the siege of Newcastle and wrote about it in *An Experimentall Relation upon that Famous Siege of Newcastle* (1645).

Nothing more is heard of Lithgow after 1645. According to tradition he died at Lanark and was buried in the churchyard of St Kentigern's. His late works chronicle the rapidly changing political and military situation while retaining something of the exotic style of the *Rare Adventures* and much of their anti-Catholicism. He is convinced that in England there is no real dispute between king and parliament—rather 'the quarrell dependeth only and absolutely betweene the Papists and Protestants' (Lithgow, *Present Surveigh*, C2v); still at Marston Moor the enemy are 'Romish Butchers' (Lithgow, *Experimentall Relation*, 6). It was mostly, however, as the hero of his own travels (prominent in various guises and plights in the accompanying woodcuts) that he continued to appeal to readers. There were editions of his travels in 1640, 1682, 1692, 1770, 1814, and 1906, and a chapbook version published in Glasgow (1816?). Some nineteenth-century readers found his style 'inflated and obscure' (*Poetical Remains*, vii), but many later readers have relished its baroque richness and exaggeration. MARTIN GARRETT

Sources W. Lithgow, *The totall discourse of the rare adventures and painefull peregrinations* (1906) · *DNB* · *The poetical remains of William Lithgow, the Scottish traveller*, ed. J. M. Maidment (1863) · *CSP dom., 1619–23*, p. 129, no. 378, p. 133, no. 445; *1631–3*, p. 229, nos. 479–80 · W. Lithgow, *A true and experimentall discourse … of the siege of Breda* (1637) · W. Lithgow, *The present surveigh of London and Englands state* (1643) · W. Lithgow, *An experimentall relation upon that famous siege of Newcastle* (1645) · will, 16 April 1603

Likenesses woodcut (in Oriental dress), BM, NPG; repro. in W. Lithgow, *Totall discourse* (1632) • woodcut (after woodcut, 1618), BM, NPG

Lithgow, William Todd (1854–1908). *See under* Lithgow family (*per. c.*1870–1952).

Litlyngton [Litlington], **Nicholas** (*b.* before 1315, *d.* 1386), abbot of Westminster, claimed to be a member of the Despenser family, a claim corroborated by his familiarity with Bishop Henry Despenser of Norwich (*d.* 1406), who ate three times at his table in the period October 1371 – July 1372, and with Sir Edward Despenser (*d.* 1375), for whom he was attorney during the latter's absence in France in 1373–4, and from whom he received a legacy of a gilt hanaper in 1375. His parents, for whom he founded anniversaries at Hurley Priory and Great Malvern Priory, were named Hugh and Joan. They cannot now be further identified, but their marriage can probably be inferred from the fact that Litlyngton used the Despenser arms without any mark of illegitimacy. The toponym by which he was known in the monastery may derive from Littleton, or Litlyngton, Middlesex, where the abbey purchased land, as part of Billets manor, during his abbacy.

Litlyngton entered the monastery in or, quite possibly, before 1333. Aristocratic recruits were rare at Westminster, but high birth did not speed his progress through the monastic *cursus honorum*. Although he had already served the monastery in external affairs at important junctures, he was twice passed over for the priorship in 1349, and became prior only when the office again fell vacant in 1350. The convent was perhaps wary of the pride of family that would inspire Litlyngton, when abbot, to place his monogram—the initials N. L., surmounted by a coronet—on sets of plate given by him to the refectory and misericord, and to acquiesce in, if he did not initiate, the use of this device and the Despenser arms on bosses in the cloister, on tiles on the refectory floor, and in other strategic places.

Yet Litlyngton was no blinkered snob in monk's clothing, but a competent and energetic man of business who, after he became abbot in 1362, completed the rehabilitation of the monastery begun by his predecessor, Simon Langham, following the crushing blow delivered to its numbers and income by the black death of 1348–9. Langham, who became successively bishop of Ely and archbishop of Canterbury, maintained a stream of benefactions to the abbey until his death in 1376, and enabled Litlyngton, who enjoyed his confidence and was an executor of his will, to spend on a large scale. The rebuilding of the cloister, long in hand, was completed; work on the nave of the abbey church resumed after the lapse of a century; and new quarters, including a new infirmary, provided for some major departments. Litlyngton himself contributed to these works on a relatively generous scale. What the prior and convent long remembered, however, was his failure to pay them for lead from the old nave which was used to roof the abbot's new house in the precinct; this was built in the 1370s. Even so, he spent about £450 on this house from abbatial funds and also paid for the new house which he had built earlier, in the 1360s, at Denham, Buckinghamshire. If the new buildings served to glorify the abbot, they also raised the morale of his monks and probably assisted the recruitment of novices. The total number of monks climbed into the mid-forties—a remarkable achievement, since the number before the black death had probably not exceeded fifty. The missal, now known as the Litlyngton missal, that he gave to the high altar, and in which his monogram and arms are frequently displayed, was produced in the monastery in 1383/4 at a total cost to Litlyngton of £34 4*s.* 7*d.* The scribe, Thomas Preston, subsequently entered the community as a monk. The illumination was the work of two artists, now unknown.

Litlyngton itinerated less extensively than most of his predecessors. He normally attended parliament if it met at Westminster, and when he did so was named as a trier of petitions. In October 1378, however, in the tense aftermath of the murder of Robert Hawley in Westminster Abbey, he attended parliament at Gloucester, to answer the council's charge that in admitting Hawley, a debtor and alleged traitor, to sanctuary he had obstructed royal justice. Outwitting his opponents, Litlyngton took the initiative in addressing the Commons in defence of the abbey's liberties before they heard John Wyclif, who had been summoned by the council to speak against them. Writing about fifty years later, John Flete praises Litlyngton's zeal for the interests of the monastery both in this controversy, and in the long-running dispute with the dean and canons of St Stephen's Chapel, Westminster, over jurisdiction in the Palace of Westminster. In the late summer of 1386 the threat of a French invasion enabled Litlyngton to demonstrate a different kind of patriotism, and he and two other senior monks equipped themselves for service against the French, should they invade. The hauberks, cuirass, and other items of military equipment found among his chattels at his death, and given by his executors to his successor, William Colchester, were presumably purchased on this occasion. However, the bows and arrows mentioned in the same list had probably been used on hunting parties, for Litlyngton kept hounds.

Unusual, perhaps, in his martial zeal, Litlyngton was in many other respects the epitome of the successful Benedictine prelate in late medieval England: unembarrassed by wealth and a largely secularized mode of life, a good man of business, a great builder, and courageous in defence of monastic privilege. He died at La Neyte, his house in present-day Pimlico, on 29 November 1386 and was buried on 17 December in the chapel of St Blaise in the abbey church. BARBARA F. HARVEY

Sources household accounts, Westminster Abbey Muniments, 24261, 24510–24536 • partial list of chattels at death, Westminster Abbey Muniments, 5446 • diet account, 1371–2, PRO, SC6/1261/6 • J. Flete, *The history of Westminster Abbey*, ed. J. A. Robinson (1909), 135–8 • V. H. Galbraith, ed., *The Anonimalle chronicle, 1333 to 1381* (1927) • E. H. Pearce, *The monks of Westminster* (1916), 84–6 • J. A. Robinson and M. R. James, *The manuscripts of Westminster Abbey* (1909) • B. Harvey, *The obedientiaries of Westminster Abbey and their financial records, c.1275 to 1540* (2002) • B. Harvey, *Westminster Abbey and its estates in the middle ages* (1977) • J. A. Robinson, *The abbot's house at Westminster* (1911), 9–12, 16–22 • private information (2004)

Archives Westminster Abbey Muniments, household accounts, WAM 24261, 24510–24536 | PRO, diet account, SC6/1261/6
Likenesses illuminated initial (Nicholas Litlyngton?), Westminster Abbey, Litlyngton missal, fol. 164
Wealth at death chattels: Westminster Abbey Muniments, 5446

Litster, Geoffrey. *See* Lister, Geoffrey (*d.* 1381).

Little [*née* Bewicke], **Alicia Ellen Neve** [*known as* Mrs Archibald Little] (**1845–1926**), author and campaigner against foot-binding, was born in Madeira, the youngest of the three daughters and three sons of Calverley Bewicke (1816–1864), a landowner, of Hallaton Hall, Leicestershire, and his wife, Mary Amelia, youngest daughter of the Revd Nathaniel John Hollingworth. She was educated at home in Madeira (1850–65). For twenty years, until 1886, she lived in England, but she travelled widely. Her novels, written in her twenties and thirties, reveal her impatience with the marriage market of the English 'season'. *Miss Standish* (1883), about a feminist spinster with passionate humanitarian convictions who finally achieves a marriage of true minds, seems clearly autobiographical and over a century later is still of interest to students of nineteenth-century British women's history. She also wrote a story, *Mother Darling* (1885), in support of the Married Women's Property Act, out of indignation at a woman's vulnerability in law if a blackguard husband sought to take their children and her property away. Allegedly she was fired by the plight of her own eldest sister.

On 2 November 1886 Alicia Bewicke married the merchant, Sinologist, and practical dreamer Archibald John Little (1838–1908), who first opened the waters of the Yangtze (Yangzi) River to steam navigation; he was the son of William John *Little, physician. Together they went to live in the far west of China at Chungking (Chongqing) in Szechwan (Sichuan) province. After dogged persistence Alicia Little managed to out-face the crowd's astonishment at the sight of a European woman and to walk the streets of Chungking unmolested. But travelling in the wilds was more difficult; both she and her husband were sometimes pelted by foreigner-hating locals and at other times she had to try to pass for a male to be allowed shelter overnight. In 1900 they succeeded in reaching the frontier of Tibet.

Alicia Little was admiring of many aspects of Chinese culture, although deeply upset by the extreme poverty of the people. The routine infliction of torture to induce false confessions, she wrote, 'made one's blood boil' (Little, *The Land of the Blue Gown*, 193). What she found intolerable, however, was the continued, widespread foot-binding of Chinese girls as the traditional symbol of the girl's desire to please a future husband. She saw countless lame girls hobbling with sticks, dark lines under their sad eyes, their pale faces rouged to look healthy; she heard many gruesome accounts of gangrenous limbs, mortification, and amputations; she saw ladies having to be helped by their (unbound) women slaves to cross a room; she saw women carried on the backs of men like sacks because they could not walk, and knew that many died or committed suicide in civil wars because they could not flee; she learned from doctors of the lifelong injury done to Chinese women's internal organs from the necessity to throw the balance of their whole bodies on to their heels; and in the west of China she noted how poor women even tracked boats:

Alicia Ellen Neve Little (1845–1926), by Tze-Yung-Ming & Co., 1894 [with her husband, Archibald John Little]

> with bound, hoof-like feet, besides carrying water, whilst in the north the unfortunate working women do field work, often kneeling on the heavy clay soil, because they are incapable of standing. It is only at Canton that bound feet are in any sense a mark of gentility, though in Shanghai and many other parts they are a sign of respectability.
> (ibid., 343)

Alicia Little knew that a few missionaries had already campaigned against foot-binding, forbidding the practice to their own schoolgirls and even finding husbands willing to have them. But she also knew that this handful of Christians could have little influence on Confucian China, and that any reform movement she started must be quite separate from religious evangelizing. Therefore, in April 1895 she started the Tianzuhui or Natural Feet Society, first asking European ladies in Shanghai—the wives of consuls and merchants—for support. Full of trepidation—for 'what were we to fight against centuries and millions?' (Little, *Intimate China*, 151)—they published poems on the subject by two Chinese ladies and then medical tracts. They then reprinted and circulated the influential Suifu appeal by an eminent Chinese official: 'no pain [is] more injurious than the breaking of the bones and sinews … It makes the daughters cry day and night, aching with pain … I do not think much of such respect for ancestors'. Other learned, scholarly tracts followed in classical Chinese with great authority, including one by a descendant of Confucius himself, and were posted as placards by her society all over China (ibid., 154–60).

With the moral support of her husband and his invaluable Chinese network of important contacts, including viceroys, Alicia Little then braced herself to make personal lecture tours throughout the cities of southern China as well as in Hong Kong and Macao. She used the recently invented Röntgen X-ray slides as well as medical photographs to prove the crippling damage done to girls' growing bones. She spoke to businessmen, high officials, women's drawing-room meetings (with many hundreds of girls and women present), and assemblies of secondary-school boys—who pledged themselves only to marry an unbound girl. She was immensely heartened by the founding of the first girls' high school in China in 1898—all of whose pupils had to be unbound—and she did not disdain the influence of a supportive inscription on her fan by the aged and much feared viceroy of Canton (Guangzhou), Lord Li Hongzhang.

For ten years (1896–1906) Alicia Little was the vigorous and eloquent leader of the anti-foot-binding movement. She 'played a more active public role than any of her European contemporaries' (Croll, 23), and 'she, more than any one person, was responsible for the abolition of foot-binding in China' (Hoe, 19). She was even called the second Chinese goddess of mercy by the *taotai* of Foochow (Fuzhou). After her departure Chinese men and women carried on the movement and eventually it triumphed over the whole of China. She returned to England in 1908, after her husband's death, and lived first at Falmouth, Cornwall, and from 1909 in London. There she supported the British women's suffrage movement, which she had earlier championed in *Miss Standish*. Her written records and photographs of China at the end of the nineteenth century became a historical source for Western students of Chinese history. She died a childless but beloved, eccentric aunt at her home, 34 Stamford Road, Kensington, London, on 31 July 1926. SYBIL OLDFIELD

Sources Mrs Archibald Little, *Intimate China* (1899) • Mrs Archibald Little, *The land of the blue gown* (1902) • *The Times* (6 Aug 1926) • *Daily Telegraph* (21 Dec 1954) • E. Croll, *Wise daughters from foreign lands* (1989) • S. Hoe, *Chinese footprints* (1996) • F. Hong, *Footbinding, feminism and freedom: the liberation of women's bodies in modern China* (1997) • Walford, *County families* • Burke, *Gen. GB* (1858) • *WWW* • *CGPLA Eng. & Wales* (1927)

Likenesses Tze-Yung-Ming & Co., photograph, 1894, NPG [*see illus.*] • photographs, *c*.1900, repro. in Little, *Land of the blue gown*, pp. 136, 187

Wealth at death £4275 7*s*. 9*d*.: probate, 15 Feb 1927, *CGPLA Eng. & Wales*

Little, Andrew George (1863–1945), historian, was born at Marsh Gibbon, Buckinghamshire, on 28 September 1863, the second of the three sons of the Revd Thomas Little, curate, who in 1864 became rector of Princes Risborough, and his wife, Ann Wright, of Chalfont St Giles. Thomas Little, who was of Scottish birth, was the eldest of eleven children. One of these, David Little, a distinguished ophthalmic surgeon in Manchester, provided a home for Andrew and his brothers after the death of their father and mother in 1876 until his own death in 1902. Andrew owed much to his parents and uncle and to the latter's young wife, all of whom were widely loved and respected.

Andrew George Little (1863–1945), by Walter Stoneman, 1923

Little was educated at a preparatory school at Folkestone and then went to Clifton College in 1878. At Clifton he was deeply influenced by Charles Edwyn Vaughan, who became a lifelong friend. Little edited Vaughan's fine *Studies in the History of Political Philosophy: before and after Rousseau* in two volumes in 1925, three years after Vaughan's death. In 1882 Little entered Balliol College, Oxford, and there formed another permanent friendship, with his tutor A. L. Smith. After obtaining a first class in modern history in 1886 he studied in Dresden and Göttingen until the spring of 1888. At Göttingen, although he failed to make much headway with the problems of Domesday Book, upon which he had embarked, he was introduced by Ludwig Weiland to 'the principles and practices of the critical examination of original historical documents', a discipline for which he remained grateful throughout his life. He deserted Domesday Book for ecclesiastical and academic history, making the Franciscans or Greyfriars the centre of his studies.

After four years of private investigation in London and

Oxford, Little was appointed the first independent lecturer in history in the University College of South Wales at Cardiff in 1892. Vaughan, who since 1889 had been professor of English and history, relinquished the teaching of history to his former pupil. Little married, in 1893, Alice Jane, daughter of William Hart, of Fingrith Hall, Blackmore, Essex. In 1898 Little was given a professorial chair at Cardiff, but resigned in 1901 on account of the poor health of his wife, and he settled at Sevenoaks. He had been a successful professor and had done much for the new University of Wales, but apart from a visiting lectureship (from 1920 a readership) in palaeography in the University of Manchester (1903–28), an engagement most fruitful in results, he undertook no regular teaching work and devoted himself to writing history and to promoting, in every way open to him, educational and learned enterprises.

Although Little did not write the big book which he planned on the history of the Greyfriars in England, he wrote much. A bibliography may be found in a little volume presented to him on 14 June 1938 by more than two hundred friends, and, for the years 1938–45, in the memoir published in the *Proceedings of the British Academy*. His first book, *The Grey Friars in Oxford* (1892), was of the first importance, not only for Little's thorough treatment of his subject, but also because he gave a fresh and influential impetus to the study of academic history in England. Moreover, it led to wider investigations and friendly co-operation with foreign scholars. Paul Sabatier's famous book on St Francis happened to follow close on Little's volume, and the two scholars became friends and allies. In July 1901 Sabatier established a society of Franciscan studies: in September 1902 Little founded a British branch of this society. In order to emphasize the need for the publication of texts, the British branch in 1907 was reconstituted on an independent basis as the British Society of Franciscan Studies. Little was chairman and honorary general editor of the new society but Sabatier was retained as honorary president until his death in 1928. While its publications were mainly texts and studies relating to the English friars, the society never took a narrow view of its opportunities and one of Little's most important publications—a new edition (based on Sabatier's papers, but containing a great deal of his own original work) of Sabatier's edition of *Speculum perfectionis* (2 vols., 1928–31)—was issued by the society. Before it was dissolved in 1936–7, the society published twenty-two volumes.

Little's own works express his twofold interest in local history and medieval life and thought as a whole. On the one hand is the long series of studies, many of them contributed to the Victoria History of the Counties of England, on Franciscan and other houses of friars in the British Isles, culminating in his Ford's lectures, *Studies in English Franciscan History* (1917), which he had delivered at Oxford in 1916; on the other hand are the *Initia operum Latinorum quae saeculis xiii., xiv., xv. attribuuntur* (1904), his edition of Eccleston's *Tractatus de adventu Fratrum Minorum in Angliam* (1909), his various papers on Roger Bacon, his important paper on the Franciscan school at Oxford (*Archivum Franciscanum historicum*, 19, 1926), his contributions to the *Proceedings of the British Academy*, and, most notable of all, the volume prepared in co-operation with his friend Father Franz Pelster SJ, *Oxford Theology and Theologians, c.* A.D. *1282–1302* (1934). Little—with a profound knowledge of manuscripts at home and abroad, and in close touch with colleagues in England, France, Belgium, and Italy—illuminated in his numerous writings nearly every side of medieval life and thought.

Little was anything but a recluse. He welcomed every opportunity to assist historical movements and to guide the studies of younger scholars. At Cardiff he prepared popular lectures on Welsh history, which grew into a little book, *Mediaeval Wales* (1902). From Sevenoaks he exerted a quiet and continuous influence which penetrated far. His physique was not robust, but he rode regularly until 1918, and in his youth rode to hounds. He did much to encourage the study of local history and to maintain a knowledge of current historical literature among the members of the Historical Association, over which he presided from 1926 to 1929. He chaired a committee which prepared for the Institute of Historical Research a report on how to edit documents. In Pelster's words, 'he maintained with vigour the old principle that history is to be founded in facts and not on reveries … He will remain in my mind as a sincere, upright and gifted man of unselfish kindness' (letter, 9 Dec 1946). Many who knew him well observed in him something of the spirit of St Francis.

Little was elected a fellow of the British Academy in 1922. He received honorary degrees from the universities of Oxford (1928) and Manchester (1935). He gave his collection of manuscripts to the Bodleian Library and left his interleaved and annotated copy of his *Initia operum* to the Institute of Historical Research. He died at his home, Risborough, 26 Vine Court Road, Sevenoaks, Kent, on 22 October 1945. F. M. Powicke, *rev.* Mark Pottle

Sources F. M. Powicke, 'Andrew George Little, 1863–1945', *PBA*, 31 (1945), 335–56 · J. R. H. Moorman, 'A. G. Little: Franciscan historian', *Church Quarterly Review*, 144 (1947), 17–27 · *An address presented to Andrew George Little, with a bibliography of his writings* (1938) · *The Times* (23 Oct 1945) · personal knowledge (1959) · private information (1959) · *CGPLA Eng. & Wales* (1946)

Archives Bodl. Oxf., notes and collections relating to Franciscans in England · Greyfriars Priory, Oxford, corresp. and notes relating to Franciscans in Britain | BL, letters to J. P. Gilson, Add. MS 47687

Likenesses W. Stoneman, photograph, 1923, NPG [*see illus.*]

Wealth at death £36,248 9*s.* 11*d.*: probate, 31 Jan 1946, *CGPLA Eng. & Wales*

Little, Sir Charles James Colebrooke (1882–1973), naval officer, was born at Shanghai on 14 June 1882, the son of Louis Stromeyer Little, surgeon, and his wife, Rosetta Annie Miller. He joined HMS *Britannia* in 1897 and after service in battleships as midshipman and sub-lieutenant volunteered for the infant submarine branch in 1903. In 1908 Little married Rothes Beatrix (*d.* 1939), daughter of Colonel Sir Charles Leslie, seventh baronet; they had one daughter.

At the outbreak of the First World War Little commanded the *Arrogant* and the submarine flotilla attached to the Dover patrol, and in 1915 was selected as assistant to the commodore (submarines) at the headquarters at Gosport. He took over command of the *Fearless* and the submarines attached to the Grand Fleet in 1916, the flotilla consisting of the new steam-driven K-class submarines designed to operate tactically with the Grand Fleet in battle. He remained in this appointment until the end of the war, being promoted captain in 1917 and appointed CB (civil). Immediately after the war he commanded the cruiser *Cleopatra* in the abortive Baltic operations against the Russian communists, for which service he was appointed CB (military, 1919).

In 1920 Little went to the Admiralty as director of the trade division of the naval staff and, while holding that appointment, was a member of the British delegation to the Washington naval conference of 1921 on the limitation of naval armaments. He was captain of the fleet in the Mediterranean in 1922 and returned home in 1924 to become senior staff officer of the Royal Naval War College. He commanded the *Iron Duke* in 1926–7 and was then selected as director of the Royal Naval Staff College, Greenwich. On promotion to rear-admiral in 1930 he was appointed in command of the 2nd battle squadron of the Home Fleet and as second in command of the fleet. In 1931 he returned to his first naval love as rear-admiral (submarines), responsible for the well-being and efficiency of the entire submarine branch.

Little's wide experience, both afloat and at the Admiralty, had already marked him for high command and in 1932 he joined the Board of Admiralty as deputy chief of the naval staff, remaining in the appointment for the three years which saw the beginning of naval rearmament and the conclusion of the Anglo-German naval treaty, in both of which he played a considerable part. He was promoted vice-admiral in 1933 and appointed KCB in 1935. The following year he became commander-in-chief of the China station, an appointment which corresponded in time with the Japanese attack on China. Little found himself responsible for the protection of British nationals in China, particularly at Shanghai which was the centre of much of the fighting, an anxious and strenuous duty in particularly difficult circumstances which he performed with skill and complete success. His promotion to admiral came in 1937 while he was still in China.

Little returned to the Admiralty in 1938 as second sea lord, responsible for the personnel of the navy. There were few by then who thought that war with Germany could be averted and within a few weeks of taking up his appointment Little found himself responsible for the mobilization of the fleet ordered as a result of the crisis which preceded the Munich conference. Although the result of the conference averted the immediate danger of war, this mobilization provided invaluable experience for that of eleven months later when war against Germany was declared. Again the responsibility for the smooth running of the machine fell entirely on Little, and that full mobilization was achieved with speed and precision was due largely to his administrative skill. The next two years saw the huge expansion of personnel which the war demanded, again the responsibility of the second sea lord.

In 1941 Little was appointed to Washington as head of the British Admiralty delegation and it was during his tenure of that appointment that the United States entered the war. As head of the delegation, Little was the British Admiralty's representative on the joint chiefs of staff committee in Washington, a task calling for diplomacy and fortitude in his dealings with Admiral Ernest King, the American chief of naval operations and a noted Anglophobe. On his relief in 1942 by Admiral Sir Andrew Cunningham he was appointed GBE.

Little returned to England from Washington to become commander-in-chief at Portsmouth, an appointment he held until the end of the war in 1945. In May 1943 he was ordered to act as the naval commander-in-chief designate for the invasion of Europe during the absence of Admiral Sir Bertram Ramsay who had originally been selected for the post, and as such became deeply involved with the operational planning for the forthcoming assault. This appointment lapsed on Ramsay's return after the successful invasion of Sicily and Italy, though Little still had many duties directly linked with the invasion, being responsible for the provision of training areas and the organization of exercises for the vast armada collected for the operation, as well as for accommodation for all the crews and the supply of stores, ammunition, and fuel.

At the end of the war Little was placed on the retired list after forty-eight years of continuous service and was advanced to GCB (1945). He held the bronze medal of the Royal Humane Society for life-saving and among many foreign orders he was made a grand officer of the Légion d'honneur (France) and commander of the Legion of Merit (USA) and was awarded the grand cross of the order of Orange Nassau (Netherlands) and the order of St Olaf (Norway). During his retirement he was president of the British Legion (southern area) and a vice-president of the Navy Records Society and the Royal United Services Institution. In 1940 he married his cousin Mary Elizabeth (Bessy), daughter of Ernest Muirhead Little FRCS. Little died on 20 June 1973 at 46 Shelley Road, Worthing, Sussex. PETER KEMP, *rev.*

Sources *The Times* (22 June 1973) • private information (1986) • personal knowledge (1986) • *WWW* • S. W. Roskill, *The war at sea, 1939–1945*, 3 vols. in 4 (1954–61) • *CGPLA Eng. & Wales* (1974) • Burke, *Peerage* (1980) • b. cert. • d. cert.

Archives FILM IWM FVA, actuality footage

Likenesses W. Stoneman, photograph, 1935, NPG

Wealth at death £158,746: probate, 16 Jan 1974, *CGPLA Eng. & Wales*

Little, Sir Ernest Gordon Graham Graham- (1867–1950), physician, was born at Monghyr, Bengal, on 8 February 1867, the only child of Michael Little, of the Indian Civil Service, and his wife, Anna, daughter of Alexander English, of Cape Town. His mother died when he was four years old and he was taken to South Africa where his uncle

F. A. English, a friend of Cecil Rhodes, became his guardian. He was educated at the South African College and in 1887 graduated BA in the University of the Cape of Good Hope, heading the honours list in literature and philosophy, thereby becoming a university scholar. In the same year he was awarded the Porter studentship which took him to London University where he studied medicine, his hospitals being Guy's and St George's. Little graduated with honours in 1893 and later went to the Rotunda Hospital, Dublin, and the University of Paris. In later years he stated that throughout his student career he maintained himself by scholarships and prizes.

In 1895 Little was appointed physician to the East London Hospital for Children where in 1925 he was to become consulting physician. In 1902 he decided to make skin diseases his speciality, when he was appointed physician to the skin department of St Mary's Hospital and lecturer in dermatology in its medical school. In 1934 he became consulting physician and maintained his connection with the hospital until he died. He established a worldwide reputation in dermatology, on which he published widely, and became a corresponding or honorary member of many learned societies at home and abroad. He was honorary president of the International Dermatological Congress held in Budapest in 1935. He was a pioneer in the use of carbon dioxide and crude coal tar in the treatment of skin conditions. In 1923 he was the first to describe fully a disorder which became known as benign superficial epithelioma of Graham-Little.

From 1906 to 1950 Little served on the senate of the University of London. He was chairman of the external council (1922–46), a member of the court from its inception, and served on fifteen of the university committees. He regarded the university as a great Commonwealth link, and never wavered from the fundamental principle upon which it was founded: equality of opportunity, independent of race, sex, or class. He was mainly instrumental in securing recognition of the West London Hospital as an institution for the admission of women medical students to the university, and successfully resisted an effort to impose on the university official co-operation with the conjoint board in its final MB examinations which, in his judgement, would have lowered the standard of the London medical degree.

In 1911 he married Sarah Helen, daughter of Maurice Kendall. She was a constant support to him throughout his life which was not without its sorrows, for their only daughter was drowned while bathing in 1932 and their only son was killed while flying on active service in 1942.

The general election of 1924 coincided with an important issue for London University. The Haldane scheme of reform was thought by many to jeopardize the external side of the university. The graduates' association opposed the plan, and Little was adopted by them as an independent candidate (originally for a by-election in the university which was cancelled when the general election supervened) in opposition to the candidates for the three main parties, all of whom supported the scheme. His election by a majority of 389 had a decisive influence on the act of 1926 under which representation of both graduates and teachers on the senate was retained intact. He continued to hold the seat. Towards the end of his life his majority declined, and in 1945 he came within a few votes of being beaten by Mary Stocks, principal of Westfield College. The new University of London Society criticized the graduates' association as a front operating only to secure his re-election; it argued for more active involvement of graduates in the affairs of the university. Little held the seat until the university franchise was abolished in 1950. He was knighted in 1931 when he assumed the surname of Graham-Little.

In parliament Graham-Little was a convincing, although not a fluent, speaker; he spoke only on subjects he knew thoroughly. He was the founder and first chairman of the university members' committee, which functioned only under his leadership. He resisted any concession to unqualified medical practitioners, fought for professional secrecy for doctors' evidence in law courts, and opposed the compulsory notification of venereal disease. From the first he was an implacable opponent of the National Health Service which he maintained would ruin the art of medicine. He was one of the few members of parliament who voted against the Yalta agreement. Although a strong anti-socialist, his views were in some respects progressive. He pleaded unceasingly for equality of opportunity for the sexes, for pure food, pasteurized milk, and wholewheat bread. School buildings, teachers' pay, and milk in schools were matters of great interest to him. He was the first member to press for tests for driving licences for motorists. A strong supporter of the Society of Individualists, he was a persistent controversialist, a formidable pamphleteer, a scholar, a linguist, an enthusiastic player of chess—and a kind and gentle friend. His house in Wimpole Street, which contained priceless art treasures, was destroyed by enemy action during the Second World War. Graham-Little moved to Epsom, Surrey, where he died at 201 Manor Green Road on 6 October 1950. HENRY MORRIS-JONES, *rev.* VIRGINIA BERRIDGE

Sources *The Times* (10 Oct 1950) • *BMJ* (14 Oct 1950), 894–5 • *The Lancet* (11 Nov 1950), 543 • N. B. Harte, *The University of London, 1836–1986: an illustrated history* (1986) • J. Stewart Cook, *Convocation: a study in academic democracy* (1939) • private information (1959) • private information (2004) • personal knowledge (1959) • d. cert.

Archives LUL, papers

Likenesses portrait, repro. in *BMJ* • portrait, repro. in *The Lancet* • print, NPG

Wealth at death £8073 7s. 6d.: probate, 14 March 1952, *CGPLA Eng. & Wales*

Little [*married name* Richmond], **Janet** (1759–1813), poet, was born in Nether Bogside, Dumfriesshire, the daughter of George Little; though her exact birth date is unknown, she was baptized on 13 August 1759. Very little is known about her childhood, although her earliest biographer stated—possibly on the evidence of her later career as a poet—that 'she was early distinguished for her superior capacity and love of reading' (Paterson, 79). She went into service when still very young, perhaps acquiring some education while with an early employer, the Revd Mr Johnstone. In 1788 she sought a place with Frances Dunlop of Dunlop, one of the patrons and correspondents of Robert Burns. Little was sent to Loudoun Castle, which had been rented in 1789 by Susan Henrie, one of Mrs Dunlop's daughters, where she was responsible for supervising the dairy. She had presumably become interested in the work of Burns while with Mrs Dunlop and, in 1789, she sent him some of her poems. Burns was slow and cool in his response, apparently choosing to send his reply to Mrs Dunlop rather than Little herself. (If he did write directly to Little, the letter has been lost.) Hilton Brown has explained this coolness by suggesting that Burns might have found Little's writing a somewhat 'disquieting imitation' of his own work (Brown, 15); certainly Little herself saw Burns as both a model and an inspiration. She apparently called on him in January 1791—unluckily arriving just before Burns was brought home with a broken arm following a riding accident—and then commemorated the occasion in a rather breathless poem:

Is't true? or does some magic spell
My wondr'ing eyes beguile?
Is this the place where deigns to dwell
The honour of our isle?
(Little, 111)

There is no independent reference to Little's presence in Burns's household on that day, however, and at least one critic has 'speculate[d that] the encounter may be imagined' (Bold, 25).

Little published a collection of her poems in 1792, describing herself in the title as the Scotch Milkmaid. Dedicated to the eleven-year-old countess of Loudoun, the volume was published by subscription and seems to have been moderately successful, reportedly earning the author £50. According to the subscription list Little sold nearly 800 copies to just over 650 subscribers, among whom were Burns and James Boswell. In a poetic dedication Little described herself as '[a] rustic damsel' who hopes that 'public candour' will rescue her work from the attacks of 'snarling critic[s]' (Little, 25–6). She experimented with a variety of poetic forms and wrote in both Scots and standard English; she tended to adhere rather more closely to conventional eighteenth-century subjects ('To Hope', 'To Happiness') in her English verse than she did when writing in Scots. The volume also gives some evidence of her reading; in addition to the tributes to Burns there is a poem on the letters of Lady Mary Wortley Montagu and Elizabeth Rowe, in which Little imagines 'MONTAGUE bright' praising Rowe for transcending her in 'virtue and wit' (Little, 154). In another, 'To a Lady', on the works of David Siller, a working-class poet for whom Little had nothing but contempt, she writes:

[L]est with such dunces as these I be number'd,
Tho' pen, ink and paper, are by me in store
O madam excuse, for I ne'er shall write more.
(Little, 207)

Despite this proclamation, in the last lines of Little's only published collection of verse, she did write more; in 1840 James Paterson concluded his brief account of her life by reprinting some poems which had remained in manuscript until then.

After Mrs Henrie left Loudoun Castle, Little stayed on, continuing to run the dairy; on 14 December 1792 she married John Richmond (*c.*1741–1819), a widower with five children. Paterson describes Richmond as a labourer on the Loudoun estate; little else is known about either Richmond or the marriage, except that Little is said to have been a kind stepmother. Paterson preserves a few anecdotes about her later life, related by a Mr Blackwood, the dissenting minister whose church she attended. According to Blackwood, Little's memory was so remarkable that she was able to point out a skipped sentence when she heard, for the second time, a sermon which he had read at another church a few weeks earlier. More generally, he remembered her as being 'greatly beloved in the neighbourhood, and enjoy[ing] a high character for piety and rectitude of conduct' (Paterson, 88). Little remained at Loudoun Castle until her death from 'a cramp in the stomach' on 15 March 1813; she was buried in the cemetery at Loudoun kirk (Paterson, 89). Her association with Burns has prevented her work from being forgotten as completely as that of some of her contemporaries, such as the Aberdeen poet Christian Milne, but she was rarely seen as anything more than a footnote in Burns studies during the nineteenth, and most of the twentieth, centuries. Hilton Brown, for example, writing about her in 1950, thought the best that could be said of her writing was that it 'could have been … much worse' (Brown, 17). In the 1990s, however, renewed interest in working-class writing led to some re-evaluations of her work; in addition, one critic has argued strongly that reading Little only through Burns obscures the range of her work and that she ought to be read in the larger Scots 'vernacular tradition of Ramsay and Ferguson' (Bold, 21). PAM PERKINS

Sources J. Paterson, *The contemporaries of Burns and the more recent poets of Ayrshire* (1840) • V. Bold, 'Janet Little, "the Scotch Milkmaid" and "peasant poetry"', *Scottish Literary Journal*, 20/2 (1993), 21–30 • H. Brown, 'Burns and the Scottish Milkmaid', *Burns Chronicle*, 2nd ser., 25 (1950), 15–20 • M. Lindsay, *The Burns encyclopedia*, 3rd edn (1980) • J. Little, *Poetical works* (1792) • bap. reg. Scot. • m. reg. Scot.

Little, Kenneth Lindsay (1908–1991), anthropologist, was born at 97 Priory Road, West Derby, Liverpool, on 19 September 1908, the son of Harold Muir Little, a ship broker, and his wife, Annie, *née* Livesey. Little was educated at Liverpool College and at Selwyn College, Cambridge, as a mature student in the late 1930s, having previously worked in a repertory theatre. His interest was in physical anthropology, and when the lecturer was called up for military service, Little left the students' benches for the lecturer's rostrum and finished off the course. Declared medically unfit for the armed forces, he was appointed William Wyse student at Trinity College, Cambridge, and an assistant in the Duckworth laboratory. In this capacity he travelled to Cardiff in the summer vacation of 1940 to study the stature of what he called, in the terminology of the time, the 'Anglo-negroid cross'. It was a kind of research that led into a dead end, but while in Cardiff Little became interested in the social aspects of black–white interaction and racial discrimination—then referred to as the colour bar. His London PhD thesis (supervised by Raymond Firth and published in 1948 as *Negroes in Britain*) brought together elements from the British tradition of social surveys with lessons from the Chicago school of sociology and the Lynds' *Middletown*. Balancing this with a history of racial attitudes, Little developed a novel theory that 'colour-class-consciousness' underlay racial discrimination in Britain. By the time the book was published, Little was in Sierra Leone conducting an ethnographic study of the Mende which, in addition to its careful examination of rice farming, paid much more attention to social change than did other contemporary ethnographies. He returned to an appointment at the London School of Economics as lecturer in anthropology, with special reference to race relations.

Moving to head the department of social anthropology at the University of Edinburgh in 1950 (first as reader, then from 1965 as professor and from 1971 as professor of African urban studies, becoming emeritus in 1978), Little started a programme of research into British racial relations and then another into the changes associated with urbanization in west Africa. He travelled extensively, both to teach and to study. His early invitation to Fisk University (Nashville, Tennessee) and his other visits to US universities meant a lot to him, but he was particularly proud of having established the department of social anthropology at the University of Sudan in Khartoum while on leave from Edinburgh. More than most Europeans of his generation, Little struck up easy personal relations with members of the new African élite, male and female, and wrote about their parts in the changes their societies were undergoing. This was not the kind of research that builds prestige in universities. It could invoke no intellectual tradition and it challenged the prevailing demarcation of social anthropology and sociology. Its pursuit required a measure of courage as well as independence of mind, but by his pioneering work Little made it easier for his junior colleagues to take up such studies.

In 1968 Little was appointed the first chairman of the home secretary's advisory committee on race relations research, but cerebral malaria—contracted on a visit to Ghana—prevented him from exploiting the new research opportunities that were opening in this field and occasioned his move sideways within the university. After *The Mende of Sierra Leone* (1951) and the UNESCO booklet *Race and Society* (1952) he went on to author *West African Urbanization* (1967), *African Women in Towns* (1973), *Urbanization as a Social Process* (1974), and *The Sociology of Urban Women's Image in African Literature* (1980). On 28 August 1939 he had married Birte Hoeck; they had a daughter, Katherine, and a son, John. After the dissolution of this marriage he was married from 2 June 1956 to 1979 to Iris Mary Buchanan, *née* Cadogan, a nursing sister. He died at the Royal Victoria Hospital, Edinburgh, on 28 February 1991.

MICHAEL BANTON

Sources *WW* (1991) • *Directory*, Association of Social Anthropologists • personal knowledge (2004) • *The Scotsman* (4 March 1991) • b. cert. • m. cert. [Birte Hoeck] • m. cert. [Iris Buchanan] • d. cert.
Archives U. Edin. L., corresp., notebooks, and papers

Little, William John (1810–1894), orthopaedic surgeon, was born on 7 August 1810 at the Red Lion inn, Red Lion Street, Whitechapel, London, the only son and eldest of three children of John Little, proprietor of the Red Lion inn, and his wife, Hannah. The family were related to the Littles who for many generations lived in Carbrooke, Norfolk. At the age of two Little developed a club foot, presumed to be due to poliomyelitis. After schooling at Goodman's Fields, London, and St Margaret's, Dover, he was, from the age of thirteen, educated at the Jesuit college of St Omer, France, winning the laurel wreath for French studies. After being apprenticed to Mr James Sequeira in 1826, his indenture was cancelled in 1828 and he began five years as an apprentice apothecary with the Apothecaries' Company of London. He studied at the London Hospital and the Aldersgate school of medicine. He became MRCS (1832) and MRCP (1837).

In 1834 Little went to study with Johannes Müller at the University of Berlin in order to discover what could be done to correct his club-foot, which English surgeons refused to treat, leaving it to the bone-setters. During the course of dissections of cadaver club-feet, Little recognized the role of muscles and tendons rather than bones in this deformity. In 1836 Dr Louis Stromeyer of Hanover successfully undertook Achilles tendon division for Little's club-foot. Little received a doctorate from the University of Berlin in 1837 for his work on the nature of club-foot. During the same year he married Elizabeth ('Isa'), daughter of Thomas Roff Tamplin, brewer, of Horsted Keynes, Sussex, and brother of R. W. Tamplin, surgeon to the Royal Orthopaedic Hospital. They had four sons and seven daughters, only seven of whom reached maturity. His fourth son, Edward Muirhead Little, became a well-known orthopaedic surgeon on the staff of the Royal National Orthopaedic Hospital. His grandson was Admiral Sir Charles Little.

From 1837 Little began to introduce the Stromeyer technique of tenotomy into England. The operation involved anterior division of the Achilles tendon just above the ankle, without anaesthetic, followed by splintage and manipulation. Little's *Treatise on the Nature of Club-Foot and Analogous Distortions* (1839) recognized the association between fever and club-foot, and came close to describing foot deformity secondary to poliomyelitis. In 1839 Little was elected assistant physician at the London Hospital.

In 1840 Little founded the Orthopaedic Institution in Bloomsbury, an infirmary for the cure of club-foot and other distortions, and for the study of orthopaedics. In so doing he played an important part in the development of modern British orthopaedics. The Orthopaedic Institution became the Royal Orthopaedic Hospital in 1845, but Little had resigned in 1844. In the following year he was appointed physician to the London Hospital, and he held this position until he resigned in 1863. In 1854 the Revd Andrew Reed, a friend of Little's, established the Royal Hospital for Incurables, and Little became medical examiner and a member of the governing board.

Little continued his pioneering work throughout his

William John Little (1810–1894), by Elliott & Fry

career. In 1843, in a series of lectures at the Orthopaedic Institution (published in 1855 as *Lectures on the Deformities of the Human Frame*), he described what became known as 'Little's disease', a spastic paralysis of both lower limbs secondary to infantile cerebral palsy. Little recognized that the cause was an abnormal birth which produced brain damage and secondary spasticity of the limbs. In 1843 he published *On ankylosis or stiff joint: a practical treatise on the contractions and deformities resulting from diseases of joints*. In 1847 he described two boys with what was obviously pseudo-hypertrophic muscular dystrophy, itself described twenty-one years later by Guillaume Duchenne. *On the Nature and Treatment of the Deformities of the Human Frame* appeared in 1853, and *Spinal Weakness and Spinal Curvature* was published in 1868.

In 1877 Little was elected FRCP, a rare honour for a surgeon. He visited North America in 1878, and was elected honorary member of the American Orthopaedic Association in 1890. Little died at home in Ryarsh, West Malling, near Maidstone, Kent, on 7 July 1894, and was buried there. GEORGE BENTLEY

Sources J. Schleichkorn, *The sometime physician: William John Little, pioneer in treatment of cerebral palsy and orthopaedic surgery* (1987) · W. A. M. Smart, *London Hospital Gazette*, 47 (1944), 84–7 · A. R. Jones, 'William John Little', *Journal of Bone and Joint Surgery* (Feb 1949), 123–6 · P. F. Smith, 'William John Little, 1810–1894', *Health Libraries Review*, 3 (1986), 193–4 · T. A. Cholmeley, *History of the Royal National Orthopaedic Hospital* (1985)

Likenesses F. Schappes, lithograph, 1854, Wellcome L. · Boning & Small, photograph, Wellcome L. · Elliott & Fry, photograph, Wellcome L. [*see illus.*]

Wealth at death £8173 1s. od.: probate, 7 Sept 1894, *CGPLA Eng. & Wales*

Little, William John Knox- (1839–1918), Church of England clergyman, the sixth son of John Little JP of Stewartstown, co. Tyrone, and his wife, Emily Kyle, was born at Stewartstown on 1 December 1839. He was educated, as were several of his nine brothers, at the Royal Grammar School, Lancaster, from where he proceeded to Trinity College, Cambridge. He graduated BA with a third class in the classical tripos of 1862, and proceeded MA in 1865. He was ordained deacon in 1863, priest in 1864, and was an assistant master at his old school and curate of Christ Church, Lancaster, in 1863–4. He was next an assistant master at Sherborne School from 1864 to 1870. In 1866 he married Annette (Annie), eldest daughter of Henry Gregson of Moorlands, Lancashire; they had six sons and four daughters.

In 1870 Little became curate-in-charge of Turweston, Buckinghamshire, a parish of 330 inhabitants. Here he worked devotedly as a parish priest, and discovered, it is said, by chance his powers as a preacher when he was required to preach extempore when standing in for a neighbour.

In January 1874 Knox-Little (he transferred his third Christian name, Knox, to his surname at this time) took part in a general mission in London as missioner at St Thomas's, Regent Street, and became curate there to the Revd W. J. Richardson. His mission preaching made him famous, and in 1875 the dean of Manchester, Dr Cowie, persuaded him to accept the benefice of St Alban's, Cheetwood, Manchester, a parish of 15,000 people. Here he worked zealously, and his church rapidly became an important religious centre. In January 1877 he took Manchester itself by storm as preacher at the cathedral in a general mission; the effects were thought comparable with those produced by the Wesleys and Whitefield, and the services at the cathedral had to be duplicated.

Knox-Little was an uncompromising high-churchman, and insisted frankly on the benefit of sacramental confession—at that time a practice unacceptable to most Anglicans. Knox-Little's ritualism consequently became the centre of controversy, both in Britain and in the USA. He conducted remarkable missions at Leeds parish church in 1883 and at St Paul's Cathedral in 1884; at St Paul's he was for some years the preacher at the Passiontide services and drew vast congregations.

In 1881 Knox-Little was appointed by the crown to the residentiary canonry in Worcester Cathedral vacated by George Granville Bradley. He at once intervened in the row about the imprisoned ritualist priest S. F. Green; the intervention led Gladstone to expect his resignation, but Knox-Little did not resign from his canonry. He resigned St Alban's, Cheetwood, in 1885 and accepted the vicarage of Hoar Cross, Staffordshire, which he held until 1907, henceforth living in Worcester, where he was subdean from 1902 and proctor in convocation for the chapter from 1888 to 1911. Despite his age Knox-Little served as a chaplain for part of the Second South African War (1899–1902), first with the brigade of guards, later with the

Household Cavalry. Ignoring gunfire, he carried the sacrament to soldiers in the field, being mentioned in dispatches and receiving the queen's medal and clasp. On their return he marched with the guards through London. He recorded his experiences in *Sketches and Studies in South Africa* (1899). For many years the cathedral at Worcester was crowded when he preached. Latterly his health, always delicate, broke; his voice began to fail, and he preached written sermons.

Between 1877 and 1891 Knox-Little published nine volumes of sermons and two short stories, *The Broken Vow* (1887) and *The Child of Stafferton* (1888); in 1893 he addressed to his old friend, W. J. Butler, dean of Lincoln, a controversial work, *Sacerdotalism, if rightly understood, the teaching of the Church of England: a letter in four parts*. In 1905 he published an interesting book entitled *The Conflict of Ideals in the Church of England*.

Knox-Little was one of the leading preachers of the later nineteenth century, though in the view of his obituarist in *The Times* there was, despite the drama of his preaching, 'a certain meagreness about the result … the mere ease with which words came to him tended to deprive his utterances of any permanent grip on men's minds'. 'He had a thoughtful Irish face with the mouth of an orator. In appearance he was of middle height with broad shoulders and a pronounced stoop. His slight Irish accent added to the attraction of his low but most agreeable voice' (*DNB*). He was also a pianist and a good linguist, preaching fluently in French as well as English.

Knox-Little died at 10 The College, Worcester, on 3 February 1918, and is buried at Turweston. He was survived by his wife and seven of their children.

H. C. G. MATTHEW

Sources *DNB* · *The Times* (4 Feb 1918) · *Fountain* (7 July 1881) · *Yorkshire Post* (6 Feb 1883) · *Court and Society* (30 Sept 1886) · Crockford (1880–1920) · *Clergy List* (1860–1918) · Venn, *Alum. Cant.* · Gladstone, *Diaries*

Archives BL, corresp. with W. E. Gladstone, Add. MSS 44454–44524 · Notts. Arch., letters to Harry Cowgill

Wealth at death £2020 15s. 2d.: probate, 26 Aug 1918, *CGPLA Eng. & Wales*

Littledale, Sir Joseph (1767–1842), judge, was the eldest son of Henry Littledale of Eton House, Lancashire, who came from a Cumberland family, and his wife, Mary, daughter of Isaac Wilkinson of Whitehaven. He was educated at St John's College, Cambridge, where he was senior wrangler and Smith's prizeman, and graduated BA in 1787, proceeding to an MA in 1790. He entered Gray's Inn, and practised as a special pleader until he was called to the bar on 28 June 1798. Asked about his politics, he is said to have given the reply, which became a *bon mot* in legal circles: 'My politics are the politics of a special pleader'. He joined the northern circuit, attending the Chester sessions, and in 1813 was appointed counsel to the University of Cambridge. It was during this period, in 1821, that he edited Skelton's *Magnyfycence, an Interlude* for the Roxburghe Club.

On 30 April 1824 Littledale succeeded Mr Justice Best as judge in the court of king's bench, although he had never been made a king's counsel or sat in parliament. Nor did he find any government patronage, beyond being appointed to assist in government prosecutions in Scotland in 1822. He was knighted on 9 June 1824.

Littledale resigned because of poor health on 31 January 1841. He was sworn of the privy council, but died shortly afterwards at his house in Bedford Square on 26 June 1842. He left a daughter, Elizabeth, who afterwards married Thomas Coventry, a barrister. Details of his wife are not known.

J. A. HAMILTON, *rev.* HUGH MOONEY

Sources *The Times* (20 June 1842) · E. Foss, *Biographia juridica: a biographical dictionary of the judges of England … 1066–1870* (1870), 410 · *GM*, 2nd ser., 18 (1842), 319 · *Annual Register* (1842) · J. Arnould, *Memoir of Thomas, first Lord Denman*, 2 vols. (1873)

Likenesses T. Phillips, oils, Gray's Inn, London

Wealth at death under £250,000: *DNB*

Littledale, Richard Frederick (1833–1890), Church of England clergyman and religious controversialist, the fourth son of John Littledale, auctioneer of Dublin, was born there on 14 September 1833. On 15 October 1850 he entered Trinity College, Dublin, as a foundation scholar, graduated BA as a first class in classics, and in 1855 obtained the senior Berkeley gold medal and the first divinity prize. He proceeded at Dublin MA in 1858, and LLB and LLD in 1862, and at Oxford on 5 July 1862 DCL *comitatis causa*. He was curate of St Matthew in Thorpe Hamlet, Norfolk, from 1856 to 1857, and from 1857 to 1861 curate of St Mary the Virgin, Crown Street, Soho, London, where he took a great interest in the House of Charity. For the rest of his life he suffered from chronic ill health, performed few parochial duties, and devoted himself mainly to writing.

Littledale was a significant controversialist, becoming a leading exponent of ritualism in the Church of England in the 1860s and 1870s. In a series of pamphlets and lectures he argued that the Tractarian movement was ripe for a further advance, specifically in terms of ceremonial practice. In pamphlets such as *The Real Presence* (n.d.) and *The Christian Sacrifice* (n.d.) he asserted that Tractarian eucharistic doctrine had reached a point where its visible expression in ceremonial had become essential. In *The Law of Ritual* (n.d.) he further claimed a legal basis for this, arguing that all pre-Reformation uses were legal unless specifically repealed. In *The North Side of the Altar* (1865) legalistic complexity led him into a detailed examination of the precise meaning of such terms as 'side' and 'end' of the communion table. A further line of argument developed from his long association with John Mason Neale (1818–1866), namely that the restoration of church buildings led inevitably to a desire for a more elaborate ceremonial, a point he first made in *On the Application of Colour to the Decoration of Churches* (1857) and repeated in *Ritualists not Romanists* (1876).

Yet despite Littledale's claim that the ritualists were the inheritors of the Tractarians, he never gained the support of all the clergy of that older generation. Some of them, such as William Gresley, William Butler, and Thomas Stevens, were deeply concerned that country parishioners were unprepared for such elaborate ceremonial. The parishes most influenced by Littledale's theories were mainly in London and other urban centres with more sophisticated congregations. As ritualistic practices spread among them, so the controversy they aroused extended throughout the Church of England and beyond, leading to royal commissions sitting from 1867, and finally to the Public Worship Regulation Act of 1874 and the prosecution of ritualist clergy that followed.

Another area of controversy in which Littledale engaged was the defence of Anglicanism against the claims of Rome following the declaration of papal infallibility in 1870. His arguments were elaborated in a series of works such as *An Inner View of the Vatican Council* (1877), *Why Ritualists do not Become Roman Catholics* (1878), *Plain Reasons for not Joining the Church of Rome* (1880), *Words for Truth: Replies to Roman Cavils Against the Church of England* (1888), and *The Petrine Claims: a Critical Inquiry* (1889). For Littledale the revival of Catholic doctrine and ceremonial in the Church of England, combined with what he saw as unauthorized additions to the faith by Rome, made conversion both unnecessary and morally dubious.

Littledale also collaborated with other authors, most notably John Mason Neale in the *Liturgy of SS Mark, James, Clement, Chrysostom, Basil* (1868–9), and after Neale's death in 1866 he completed the *Commentary on the Psalms from Primitive and Mediaeval Writers* (vols. 2, 3, and 4, 1868–74), and later re-edited two other editions of the entire work. With James Edward Vaux he wrote *The Priest's Prayer Book* (1864), *The People's Hymnal* (1867), *The Christian Passover* (1873), and *The Altar Manual* (n.d.). Littledale was also a noted confessor, and it was claimed that he had heard more confessions than any other priest in the Church of England apart from Pusey.

Littledale died on 11 January 1890, at his home, 9 Red Lion Square, London. A reredos to his memory was erected in the chapel at St Katherine's, 32 Queen Square, London, in March 1891. GEORGE HERRING

Sources G. W. Herring, 'Tractarianism to ritualism: a study of some aspects of tractarianism outside Oxford, from the time of Newman's conversion in 1845 until the first Ritual Commission in 1867', DPhil diss., U. Oxf., 1984, pt 3, 284–348 · N. Green-Armytage, *Dr Littledale's place in the Catholic revival* (1890) · O. C. H. King, *Character of Dr Littledale as a controversialist* (1888) · *The Times* (14 Feb 1890), 9 · *Church Portrait Journal*, new ser., 3 (1882), 85–8 · *Guardian* (15 Jan 1890), 84 · *CGPLA Eng. & Wales* (1890)

Likenesses portrait, repro. in *Church Portrait Journal* · portrait, repro. in *London Figaro* (1 Feb 1890), 9

Wealth at death £3916 4*s*. 6*d*.: probate, 22 Feb 1890, *CGPLA Eng. & Wales*

Littlejohn, Sir Henry Duncan (1826–1914), medical officer of health and expert in forensic medicine, was born on 8 May 1826 at the family home, 33 Leith Street, Edinburgh, the seventh of the nine children of Thomas Littlejohn, master baker and a burgess of Edinburgh, and his wife, Isabella Duncan, daughter of Henry Duncan, merchant of Edinburgh. He received a general education at Perth Academy and then attended Edinburgh high school from 1838 until 1841, after which he entered upon the study of medicine; he graduated MD at Edinburgh University in 1847, and in the same year became a licentiate of the Royal College of Surgeons of Edinburgh. His postgraduate training included a period as house surgeon at Edinburgh Royal Infirmary (1847–8) and then a year spent in Paris, Vienna, and Berlin, with his lifelong friend John Smith, founder of the Edinburgh Dental Dispensary. Littlejohn then returned to the Edinburgh Royal Infirmary as assistant pathologist. There followed a brief spell of general practice in Selkirk, specializing in obstetrics, until he returned to Edinburgh in 1853. He took his examinations for the fellowship of the Royal College of Surgeons in 1854.

Sir Henry Duncan Littlejohn (1826–1914), by Sir George Reid

Littlejohn is acclaimed equally by historians both of public health and of legal medicine. Certainly his role in public health is more evident, owing perhaps to the larger number of published reports and articles. Nevertheless, his career began and ended in forensic medicine, running concurrently with his employment in public health. In August 1854 he was elected by Edinburgh town council to the part-time salaried position of police surgeon in place of Dr George Glover, who had been dismissed owing to his overzealous pursuit of public health infractions. Ironically, Littlejohn himself was destined to become one of Scotland's leading sanitarians. By coincidence he was related to the then lord provost of Edinburgh, a fact commented upon by Littlejohn's rivals.

Littlejohn's medico-legal career began with appearances in the summary courts immediately following his appointment as police surgeon. His high-court career began in 1855, when he appeared in a variety of criminal cases, including culpable homicide resulting from a railway accident with twenty deaths, an assault with intent to ravish, a wife murder, and three cases of child murder. In one of the last category, the drowning of a newborn child in Duddingston Loch by the mother, Littlejohn's cogent medical report drew a note of commendation from the bench which assured his rise.

By 1858 Littlejohn was appearing as a crown medical examiner in the Edinburgh justiciary courts. In 1856 he began lecturing on forensic medicine at Surgeons' Hall, the extramural school at which he had attended undergraduate classes. Perhaps spurred by Littlejohn's medico-legal ability, the Board of Supervision for the relief of the poor (all of whose members were lawyers), the central Scottish public health authority, first appointed under the 1856 Nuisance Removal (Scotland) Act, commissioned Littlejohn in 1859 to investigate the sanitary condition of Wick; it was the board's first report under the act. The accuracy of this and subsequent reports earned Littlejohn the permanent salaried post of medical adviser to the board in 1873.

In 1862 Littlejohn was also appointed as Edinburgh's first medical officer of health, under the terms of the 1862 General Police Act (Scotland). Thus he simultaneously filled no less than five part-time posts in public and legal medicine. He had no private practice and derived his income from two sources: the permanent salaried posts of Edinburgh's medical officer of health and police surgeon, and medical adviser to the Board of Supervision; he also received fees obtained from the posts of extramural lecturer and crown medical examiner.

In 1855 the *Edinburgh Medical Journal* was launched to replace the *Edinburgh Medical and Surgical Journal* and the *Edinburgh Monthly Journal of Medical Science*, and Littlejohn became its first editor. He remained in the post until 1860. During that time and throughout his career he used the *Journal* to report interesting forensic cases, to air medico-legal differences with colleagues, and to publish texts of his extramural lectures. He found no time, however, to write a textbook similar to John Glaister's *Text-Book of Medical Jurisprudence and Toxicology and Public Health* (1902).

Littlejohn's cases included deaths by firearms, poisoning, stabbing, and strangling. Like Glaister he considered himself a medical detective, who used fingerprints, bite marks, and photography as evidence to solve criminal mysteries. He became an expert in all theatres of death, appearing in more than a hundred capital charges and many culpable homicide and assault cases. He shared the limelight with Douglas Maclagan in the notorious poisoning cases of Dr Pritchard, for the murder of his wife and mother-in-law (Glasgow, 1865), and of Eugene Marie Chantrelle, for the murder of his wife (Edinburgh, 1878). In 1893 Littlejohn gave crown medical evidence during the trial of Arthur Monson for the murder, by shooting, of his aristocratic pupil Cecil Hamborough, with Matthew Hay giving evidence for the defence.

Littlejohn lectured without notes, using his accumulating forensic cases and skills to illustrate his lectures. His extramural lecture course was extremely well attended, at times attracting more than 250 students, possibly to the detriment of Douglas Maclagan's university course. Littlejohn counted some of the foremost future medical figures among his students, including Joseph Bell, thought to be model for Conan Doyle's master sleuth, Sherlock Holmes. Littlejohn himself has been described as providing the author with authentic High Court examples.

In 1897, at the age of seventy-one, Littlejohn succeeded to the Edinburgh chair of forensic medicine and public health, on the retirement of Sir Douglas Maclagan. Taking the opportunity provided by the changeover, Edinburgh University recognized the growing importance of public health and established a separate, endowed, chair of public health; Littlejohn therefore became professor solely of forensic medicine. He retired from the chair in 1906 and was succeeded by his only son, Harvey Littlejohn. In 1907 Littlejohn senior was presented with his portrait by Sir George Reid at a packed ceremony in Surgeons' Hall.

In sanitary matters Littlejohn did much to prod the social conscience of ratepayers and local councils to further the improvement of Scottish public health in general and of Edinburgh in particular. His services to the Board of Supervision and the Local Government Board are charted in their annual reports. Littlejohn's *Report on the Sanitary Condition of Edinburgh* (1865) pinpointed the capital's sanitary inadequacies and their sequelae, which led to a death rate of 24 per thousand: this had reduced to 14 per thousand by 1908, when Littlejohn retired as medical officer of health. He was deeply involved with William Chambers in the building of Victorian Edinburgh and in the provision of a municipal fever hospital. In strictly medical matters Littlejohn invoked the wrath of most of the local profession during his campaign for compulsory notification of infectious diseases, accomplished in clause 208 of the 1879 Edinburgh Municipal Police Act. Significantly, the clause placed the onus of notification squarely on the shoulders of the attending doctor rather than the householder. Scotland achieved compulsory notification of infectious diseases under the 1897 Public Health (Scotland) Act.

Littlejohn was elected president of the Royal College of Surgeons of Edinburgh in 1875, and from 1883 until 1885 he was president of the Edinburgh Medico-Chirurgical Society. The University of Edinburgh conferred upon him its honorary degree of LLD in 1893 and he was president of the Royal Institute of Public Health in the same year. He was knighted in 1895. Littlejohn's interests were many. He was an unpaid director of the Sick Children's Hospital, manager of the Edinburgh Royal Infirmary, and chairman of the Scottish Society for the Prevention of Cruelty to Children and of other medical and charitable institutions. He was also a founder member of the Scottish Burial Reform and Cremation Society in 1888.

A 'well-kent' Edinburgh figure in his frock coat and top hat, Littlejohn enjoyed being seen to board moving tram cars, whose drivers knew not to stop. He was an elder of St Giles's Church and attended daily services there, and was once mistaken for an official guide, whose task he duly performed before being recognized, much to his chagrin, by a passing colleague. A glimpse of Littlejohn's pawky humour is caught in his story that although he had been rejected for life insurance by three medical referees, it had been his doleful duty to attend the funerals of all three doctors. Littlejohn was married to Isabella Jane, daughter of H. Harvey; she predeceased him. In addition to their son they had at least one daughter. A medical giant who bestrode Edinburgh public life for half a century, Littlejohn died at his country house, Benreoch, Arrochar, Dunbartonshire, on 30 September 1914. He was cremated at the Glasgow crematorium and his ashes were then taken to the Dean cemetery, Edinburgh.

BRENDA M. WHITE

Sources *The Lancet* (10 Oct 1914) · *BMJ* (10 Oct 1914), 648–50 · *Edinburgh Medical Journal*, 3rd ser., 13 (1914), 404–9 · *Scots Law Times: News* (17 Oct 1914) · *The Times* (2 Oct 1914) · *Annual report of the local government board* (1908), cd 4679 · *BMJ* (16 April 1907), 653 · H. MacDonald, 'Public health legislation and problems in Victorian Edinburgh with special reference to the work of Dr Littlejohn', PhD diss., U. Edin., 1975 · H. P. Tait, *A doctor and two policemen* (1974) · H. P. Tait, 'Sir Henry Duncan Littlejohn, great Scottish sanitarian and medical jurist', *The Medical Officer* (21 Sept 1962), 183–9 [lists most of Littlejohn's publications] · I. Levitt, 'Henry Littlejohn and Scottish health policy', *Scottish Archives*, 2 (1997), 63–77 [lists Littlejohn's reports, papers, and inquiries etc., for the board of supervision and the Scottish local government board 1859–1908] · B. M. White, 'Training medical policemen', *Legal medicine in history*, ed. M. Clark and C. Crawford (1994), 145–63 · B. M. White, 'The police surgeon as medical officer of health in Scotland, 1862–1897', *The Police Surgeon*, 35 (May 1989), 29–37 · G. A. Gibson, *Life of Sir William Tennant Gairdner* (1912) · Royal College of Physicians of Edinburgh, Sir Sydney Smith MSS, box 33, file 254 · 'Who is Sherlock Holmes? Dr Joseph Bell or Sir Henry Littlejohn?', *Edinburgh Magazine*, 1 (1903–4), 210–11 · minute book of the Scottish Burial Reform and Cremation Society, 6 Aug 1888, priv. coll. · minute books of Edinburgh Watch Committee, 1855–1908, vol. 12, 524–5 · minute books of Edinburgh Watch Committee, 1855–1908, vol. 4, 300–31 · NA Scot., JC 9, JC 26, LA 14, LA 15 · d. cert. · *WWW* · *CGPLA Eng. & Wales* (1914)
Archives NA Scot. · U. Edin. L. · Wellcome L.
Likenesses G. Reid, oils, Scot. NPG [*see illus.*] · photograph, Wellcome L.
Wealth at death £26,624 0s. 11d.: confirmation, 30 Nov 1914, *CCI* · £1016 14s.: additional estate, 19 Dec 1916, *CCI*

Littlejohn, James (1921–1988), social anthropologist, was born on 20 April 1921 at Clydevale, Clydesdale Street, Hamilton, Lanarkshire, the second of three sons and a daughter of James Argentine Littlejohn, schoolteacher, and his wife, Ann Robertson, *née* Shanks. From Hamilton Academy (1933–9) he went with a Kitchener bursary to the University of Glasgow, where he matriculated in the faculty of arts in 1939 and studied English literature, history, and philosophy. Before he graduated he was called up in 1941 into the Cameron Highlanders. After officer training at Poona, he was posted to the 14th Punjabi regiment and was in action in the Burma campaign. After the war he was with the Black Watch before being discharged in 1947. It was in India that he met his future wife, Isabella (Ann) Anderson.

James Littlejohn's academic career was spent entirely in the service of the University of Edinburgh. In 1948, after completing a postgraduate diploma in anthropology at the London School of Economics, he was appointed to the department of social anthropology of the university. In 1971 he succeeded Professor Kenneth Little to the chair of social anthropology. When he retired in 1983 he was elected emeritus professor and university fellow. For his doctorate Littlejohn conducted ethnographic field work in the parish of Eskdalemuir, in the Scottish borders, between 1949 and 1951. The results were presented in 1955 in a thesis entitled 'The social structure of a Scottish rural community'. The rather prosaic title conceals an intellectually ambitious project which has come to be recognized as an outstanding success. Littlejohn showed how contemporary social and cultural differentiation in the parish was the outcome of a relatively recent historical process transforming a locally determined agrarian community into one organized by a class structure embedded in the wider national social system of the United Kingdom. He also sought to find out how far anthropological techniques of research could be used effectively in the study of modern society. In this respect his research was the first study in Britain of social class by an anthropologist. The effectiveness of such techniques is evidenced in his pioneering analysis of the relationship of men and women to the class system. The thesis was published in 1963 as *Westrigg: the Sociology of a Cheviot Parish*.

Littlejohn then became part of a major multidisciplinary research project into industrialization and urbanization in Africa. The focus of this research was the mining town of Lunsar in Sierra Leone. Littlejohn's particular objective was to provide ethnographic data about a world defined in terms of magical relations changing into one of technical and rational relations. Field research among Temne-speaking people began in April 1959 and continued until March 1960. As in the earlier work in Scotland, Littlejohn set about investigating, through anthropological research into everyday life at a local level, historical processes of great generality. However, he was now attempting to document and explain something much more problematical: a human trajectory which Max Weber had called 'the disenchantment of the world'. In a series of articles, of which the best-known is 'The Temne house', first published in 1960 and reprinted in *Mythology and Symbolism*, edited by John Middleton (1967), he attempted to elucidate forms of knowledge and modes of thought in 'a world from which the gods have not yet departed'. In 1977 he returned to Sierra Leone and carried out further research with Temne diviners. Some of the results were presented in his unpublished Frazer lecture 'Magic boughs', at the University of Oxford on 30 November 1978. In all this work he became increasingly aware that notions such as that of 'sign', 'system', or 'metaphor' as organizing principles of knowledge were inextricably contaminated with their own European history and, while they could not provide him with concepts adequate to the larger task he had set himself, they were, as a result, subject to searching critical analysis.

Jimmy Littlejohn (as he was widely known) died at his home, 14 Merchiston Avenue, Edinburgh, on 17 October 1988 after a short illness. His funeral took place at Mortonhall crematorium, Edinburgh. He is remembered by his students, many of whom now enjoy academic distinction themselves, as an inspiring teacher and intellectual, but also as a reserved and rather private man.

CHARLES JĘDREJ

Sources minutes of the senatus academicus, 30 Nov 1983, U. Edin., pp. 71–2, appx III, special minute, Professor James Littlejohn, APDA, PhD • calendars, 1948–83, U. Edin. • b. cert. • d. cert. • personal knowledge (2004)
Archives U. Edin. L., papers

Littler, Sir John Hunter (1783–1856), army officer in the East India Company, eldest son of Thomas Littler and his wife, Diana, daughter of John Hunter, a director of the East India Company, was born on 6 January 1783 at Tarvin, Cheshire, where his family had been established for many generations. He was educated under the Revd Dr Devonport at the grammar school at Acton, near Nantwich. On 19 August 1800 he was appointed ensign in the 10th Bengal native infantry, and in that regiment became lieutenant on 29 November the same year, captain on 16 December 1812, and major on 22 September 1824. He went out to India in the Indiaman *Kent*, which was captured by a French privateer in the Bay of Bengal. The passengers were set adrift in a pinnace, but arrived safely at their destination. Littler served with his regiment in the campaigns under Lord Lake in 1804–5 and at the reduction of Java in 1811, returning to India in 1816. He then served as sub-assistant commissary-general in the marquess of Hastings's army, continuing in the post until 1824. Littler had previously been married, and on 25 June 1827 married, at Benares, Helen Olympia (*d.* 12 Jan 1885), only daughter of Lieutenant-Colonel Henry Stewart, a claimant of the Orkney peerage; they had four daughters. After his death, in 1858 she married Thomas Aston Cokayne.

Littler became lieutenant-colonel of the 14th Bengal native infantry in 1828, and colonel of the 36th Bengal native infantry in 1839, the colonelcy of which he retained until his death. In 1841 he was promoted major-general, and in 1843 was appointed to command the Agra division of the Bengal army. He commanded a division of Sir Hugh Gough's army at the defeat of the Gwalior army at Maharajpur on 29 December 1843, where he was slightly wounded and had two horses killed under him. He received for his services the thanks of parliament and the Gwalior star, and was made KCB on 2 May 1844. At the outbreak of the First Anglo-Sikh War in 1845 he was in command of the Ferozepore division. Leaving half his troops to protect the cantonment, he marched with the rest to meet the Sikhs when they first crossed the Sutlej on 11 December, but they declined the challenge, although they considerably outnumbered Littler's force, and turned aside to Ferozeshahr. Littler effected a junction with Gough's army on 21 December 1845, and at the battle of Ferozeshahr on 21–2 December commanded a division, and again had a horse killed under him, receiving once more the thanks of parliament. At the close of the campaign he was appointed to command at Lahore. In 1848 he was appointed to the supreme council of India, and was made GCB and deputy governor of Bengal. Littler returned home, with the rank of lieutenant-general, in 1851. The remainder of his life was passed in retirement at his seat, Bigaden, Buckfastleigh, near Totnes, Devon, where he died on 18 February 1856. He was buried at Tarvin, Cheshire.

H. M. CHICHESTER, *rev.* JAMES FALKNER

Sources *East-India Register* • *Indian Army List* • R. G. Burton, *The First and Second Sikh wars* (1911) • G. Bruce, *Six battles for India: the Anglo-Sikh wars, 1845–6, 1848–9* (1969) • *GM*, 2nd ser., 45 (1856), 423 • Kelly, *Handbk* • Walford, *County families* • V. C. P. Hodson, *List of officers of the Bengal army, 1758–1834*, 3 (1946)
Archives BL OIOC, letter-book, MS Eur. 32 | NA Scot., letters to Lord Dalhousie
Likenesses Roods of Calcutta, oils, *c.*1845, priv. coll.; Sothebys, 1 Feb 1960 • wood-engraving, NPG; repro. in *ILN* (1845–6)

Littler, Prince Frank (1901–1973), theatre proprietor and manager, was born on 25 July 1901, at Ramsgate, Kent, the elder son of Frank R. Littler and his wife, Agnes, who were at the time the lessees of the Royal Artillery Theatre at Woolwich. Prince had an elder sister, Blanche, and a younger brother, Emile, who also went into theatrical management. Educated privately at Stratford upon Avon, Prince started his theatrical career in 1927 with his sister, Blanche, sending out small-scale regional tours and becoming resident manager of his parents' theatre in Woolwich.

In 1931 Prince bought his first two theatres, both in Leicester. On 17 November 1932 he married a widow, Annie Leonora Maclachlan, *née* Delaney (the actress Norah Delaney; *b.* 1893/4). During the rest of the thirties he acquired further theatres in Manchester and Norwich, and by the end of the decade he was also touring George Robey (whom Blanche soon married, as his second wife) in *The Bing Boys are Here*. His first London ventures were pantomimes at the Coliseum, the Prince's, and Drury Lane, but in 1939 he scored his first great West End success with Ivor Novello's long-running operetta *Glamorous Night*.

With the coming of the Second World War Prince Littler was appointed chairman and managing director of first the Stoll (later Stoll Moss) and then the Associated Theatres chains, which effectively left him as resident manager of the Globe Theatre and (until it was bombed) the Queen's Theatre on Shaftesbury Avenue as well as the Theatre Royal, Drury Lane, which in 1946 Littler reopened after its wartime occupation by the Entertainments National Service Association, with Noël Coward's *Pacific 1860*. This was not a great success, and already it was becoming clear that, unlike his brother Emile, Littler had no special affection for plays or players individually; his interest was the business of showbusiness, and he remained throughout the rest of his life, despite a long and happy marriage, primarily a money-man, interested only in bricks and mortar and in the profits that could be made, either in London or on the road, with the right—that is, long-running and star-led—attractions. He was always a landlord and a manager, seldom a producer in the creative sense.

By 1947 Littler was chairman of Moss Empires and a director of the Howard and Wyndham chain, a double responsibility which gave him unique powers as a landlord in London and the regions; he was also one of the first to import tried-and-tested Broadway hits, so that his post-war shows included such musicals as *Carousel*, *Guys and Dolls*, and *Can-Can*, as well as two straight plays which had also been great Broadway hits, *Teahouse of the August Moon* and *No Time for Sergeants*. He was a reasonably fair and decent landlord, and the case against him was principally that he felt no interest in investing in the unknown or in fostering local talent when his theatres could be filled with pre-existing hits of one transatlantic kind or another; he always played safe, but fought several prolonged board-room battles to protect and preserve his empire and of course his Empires. In 1960 he fought successfully a takeover attempt for Stoll by a formidable team which included Bernard Delfont and the property millionaires Jack Cotton and Charles Clore; later that year he merged Stoll with Moss Empires, thereby gaining control of sixteen London theatres, including the Palladium and the Victoria Palace, as well as a major shareholding in one of the founding ITV companies in Britain, Associated Television. As with the Grade organization, this concentration of showbusiness power led to several legal actions (in one of which he fought his own brother Emile, though privately the brothers remained on good terms) as rival managers tried to chip away at the Littler holdings.

A passionate breeder of Guernsey dairy cattle in his spare time, Prince Littler always refused the limelight. He gave only one major press interview in 1961, in which he announced: 'I am not in the theatre for fun, but merely to keep my shareholders happy', and that was indeed always his credo. If a show failed to make money or pay its rent, Littler would close it as swiftly as possible and go in search of a more profitable tenant for his stages. He was, however, a chairman of the Denville Hall home for elderly thespians, a vice-president of the Variety Artists Benevolent Fund, and a member of both the South Bank Theatre and Opera House boards. His last three shows, *The Black and White Minstrel Show*, *There's a Girl in my Soup*, and *Fiddler on the Roof* (all 1966) were considerable hits, and when he died seven years later, after a peaceful retirement, they dimmed all the West End theatre lights in tribute to one of its most dominant and successful landlords.

Littler was made a CBE in 1957. He died on 13 September 1973 at his home, Chestham Park, Henfield, Sussex. After his death, one last legal battle was fought to clarify a complex series of bequests arising from two apparently contradictory wills; the estate had been valued at just over £1 million, and there were no children.

SHERIDAN MORLEY

Sources *The Times* (14 Sept 1973) • *WWW* • *Who's who in the theatre* • personal knowledge (2004) • private information (2004) • m. cert. • d. cert.

Archives SOUND BL NSA, current affairs recordings • BL NSA, documentary recordings • BL NSA, oral history interview • BL NSA, performance recordings

Wealth at death over £1,000,000

Littler, Sir Ralph Daniel Makinson (1835–1908), barrister, second son of Robert Littler, and his wife, Sarah, was born on 2 October 1835 at Matlock Bath, Derbyshire, where his father was minister of the Lady Huntingdon Chapel. His mother was the daughter of Daniel Makinson, cotton spinner and borough reeve of Bolton-le-Moors, Lancashire. His father was a cousin of Sir John Hunter Littler, a lieutenant-general in the Indian army. Littler was educated at University College School and University College, London, where he graduated BA in 1854. Admitted to the Inner Temple on 14 November 1854, he was called to the bar on 6 June 1857.

Littler went on the northern and afterwards the north-eastern circuit, but developing no large practice, he was appointed a revising barrister for Northumberland in 1868. He published a work on evidence in matrimonial cases in 1860. In 1866 he contributed a chapter on engineering and a digest of the reports made by the referees to a treatise by John Henry Fawcett entitled *The Court of Referees in Parliament*. He returned to London, obtaining work in the field of public law. His interest in engineering proved useful to him as counsel for the railway companies, and he became an associate of the Institution of Civil Engineers in 1877. He took silk in 1873. He was made a bencher of the Middle Temple (to which he had been admitted *ad eundem* on 28 April 1870) on 24 November 1882, and was treasurer 1900–01. He was created CB in 1890 and was knighted in 1902.

From 1889 until his death Littler was chairman of the Middlesex sessions. As a justice, he was renowned in the contemporary press for his stiff sentencing practices and, at the time of his death, he was taking proceedings for libel against *Reynolds's Newspaper* and *Vanity Fair*. In 1899 he published *The Rights and Duties of Justices*, written jointly with Arthur Hutton. He was chairman of the Middlesex county council from 1889. As a freemason he attained the rank of past deputy grand registrar and past provincial grand senior warden for Middlesex. He died on 23 November 1908 at his residence, 89 Oakwood Court, Kensington, and was buried at Hampstead.

C. E. A. BEDWELL, *rev.* ERIC METCALFE

Sources *Law Journal* (28 Nov 1908) • J. Foster, *Men-at-the-bar: a biographical hand-list of the members of the various inns of court*, 2nd edn (1885) • catalogue [BM] • private information (1912) • *CGPLA Eng. & Wales* (1909)

Likenesses H. von Herkomer, after 1889; The Guildhall, Westminster, 1912 • B. O. Offer, after 1889; The Guildhall, Westminster, 1912

Wealth at death £29,827 5*s*. 8*d*.: administration with will, 18 Jan 1909, *CGPLA Eng. & Wales*

Little Tich. *See* Relph, Harry (1867–1928).

Littleton, Adam (1627–1694), Church of England clergyman and philologist, was born on 2 November 1627 at Halesowen, which was then in Shropshire, the sixth son of Thomas Littleton, the vicar there. He claimed to descend from the ancient Littleton/Westcote family of Worcestershire, which included the fifteenth-century jurist

Sir Thomas Littleton. Having been educated under Richard Busby at Westminster School, in 1644 he was admitted to Christ Church, Oxford. By 1647 he was a stipendiary student at Christ Church, but he was ejected in 1648 by parliamentary visitors. He might have written the single sheet *Tragi-Comoedia Oxoniensis, a Latin Poem on the Mad Proceedings of the Parliamentary Visitors* (1648), but this is doubtful.

Soon afterwards Littleton became usher under Busby at Westminster School, where he was later (1658) appointed second master; he also taught at other places. His fame as a grammarian dates from this time. He wrote *Pasor metricus, sive, Voces* (a Greek and Latin grammar printed in 1658 with *Diatriba in octo tractatus distributa*) and *Elementa religionis, sive, Quatuor capita catechetica totiden linguis descripter, in usum scholarum* (supposedly printed in 1658 with *Complicatio radicum in primaevô Hebraeorum linguâ*). By 1657, when his first child was born, he had married his first wife, Elizabeth, but having given birth to a second child in 1659, she died that year and was buried in St Paul's, Covent Garden.

During the 1660s Littleton was appointed a chaplain in ordinary to Charles II, who at some point also granted him the reversion of Busby's post, although the ageing master in the event outlived him. In 1662 he published *Solomon's Gate, or, An Entrance into the Church*, ostensibly commemorating the north gate of Westminster Abbey, but, in fact, a sort of catechism 'of the grounds of religion conteined in … the Lord's prayer, the Apostles creed, the Ten commandments, the sacraments'. On 24 January 1667 Littleton married his second wife, Susan Rich of West Ham, Essex. Two years later Littleton obtained the rectory of St Luke's in Chelsea, where he may already have done some teaching, and also in 1669 delivered the funeral sermon for Lady Jane Cheyne, wife of Charles Cheyne, later Viscount Newhaven, also of Chelsea and perhaps his patron. The same year he became a prebend at Westminster and some time later was subdean. On 12 July 1670 he received a DD, 'without taking any in arts, on account of his extraordinary merit', because letters from Humfrey Henchman, bishop of London, recommended him for his humanity, manners, genius, 'and ready faculty in preaching' (Nichols, *Lit. anecdotes*, 2.58–60n.). Increasingly this talent was exhibited in occasional sermons at, among other places, Guildhall, Westminster, and Whitehall, before the royal family; he may have been chaplain to the prince Palatine. Many of his sermons were published in three large folio volumes, entitled *Sixty One Sermons Preached Mostly upon Publick Occasions* (1680). They emphasized the ceremonies and uniqueness of Anglicanism, 'having stood intirely (*sic*) upon her own Bottom' (2.sig. B[3]), and being neither Calvinist nor Lutheran. He repeatedly attacked 'the foolish and outragious zeal and odd practises of our fanatick brethren' (1.172) and reminded dissenters of their obligation to authority. Indeed, loyalty and a distrust of nonconformity were his watchwords. Even during the Popish Plot scare, when he delivered *A sermon at a solemn meeting of the natives of the city and county of Worcester, in the church of St Mary le Bow* (1680), he hoped 'that neither Popery nor Schism may ever prevail over' us and recommended charity for 'the old Cavaliers', who 'have since the Kings happy Restauration been too too much neglected' (p. 34).

Alongside his active preaching schedule, Littleton maintained his philological research and in 1678 published *Linguae Latinae liber dictionarius quadripartitus*, a huge Latin dictionary, which was published at least four times by his death, and several more times in the eighteenth century before it was superseded by later dictionaries. He was working on a Greek lexicon at the end of his life and read and annotated pieces in Hebrew, Chaldee, and Arabic. His skill in languages allowed him to publish an edition of Cicero in 1681 and translate from Greek a life of Themistocles, which appeared in an edition of Plutarch's *Lives* (1683). The same year, adopting the pen-name Redman Westcote in evocation of his Worcestershire ancestors, he published as *Tracts Written by John Selden* a translation of the latter's *Jani Anglorum facies altera*. He also composed some commendatory verses to his friend, Baldwin Hamey, which he published appended to Hamey's posthumous *Dissertatio epistolaris de juramento medicorum* (1693) (Greek and Latin texts of the Hippocratic oath), and several other pieces. He purchased so many books and manuscripts from Europe, Asia, and Africa that he might have exhausted his income, because his successor at Chelsea, John King, claimed he died insolvent and left his widow, his third wife, the daughter of Richard Guildford of Chelsea, in distressed circumstances even though she had brought her husband some wealth. Neither the Greek lexicon nor his pieces on 'mystical numeration' (Nichols, *Lit. anecdotes*, 2.60n.) survive.

Littleton retained the Chelsea living to the end of his life. He may also have held the rectory of Overton, Hampshire, from 1683, and he was minister of St Botolph, Aldersgate, London, from about 1685 until about 1691, when he resigned, perhaps because of ill health. He died at Chelsea on 30 June 1694 at the age of sixty-seven and was buried at St Luke's, Chelsea, where a tablet to his memory was placed. A catalogue of his library, *Bibliotheca Littletoniana* was printed the next year and his books dispersed. His widow died in 1698 and was buried at Chelsea on 14 November. NEWTON E. KEY

Sources Nichols, *Lit. anecdotes*, vol. 2 • J. Spurr, *The Restoration Church of England, 1646–1689* (1991) • D. Lysons, *The environs of London*, 2nd edn, 2 (1811) • *Walker rev.* • Wood, *Ath. Oxon.*, new edn, 4.403 • J. Welch, *The list of the queen's scholars of St Peter's College, Westminster*, ed. [C. B. Phillimore], new edn (1852) • Foster, *Alum. Oxon.* • J. Bullord, ed., *Bibliotheca Littletoniana: the library of … Adam Littleton* (1695) [sale catalogue, J. Bullord, London, 15 April 1695; sale catalogue, 'Tom's coffee house', London, 15 April 1695] • Wing, *STC* • *BL cat.*
Archives BL, Add. MS (Cole), 5875, fol. 6b

Littleton, Edward, **Baron Littleton** (1589–1645), judge and politician, came from a prodigious legal background. His family were descendants of the younger son of the famous fifteenth-century judge and writer on tenures, Sir Thomas Littleton. Born at Mounslow, Shropshire, in 1589, Edward was the eldest son of Sir Edward Littleton of Henley, chief justice of north Wales, and Mary, daughter of

Edward Littleton, Baron Littleton (1589–1645), by R. Williams (after Sir Anthony Van Dyck, *c.*1640–41)

Edmund Walter, chief justice of south Wales. After entering Oxford as a gentleman commoner of Christ Church on 28 November 1606, he took a BA degree on 28 April 1609. Admitted to the Inner Temple in London in 1608 he was called to the bar there in 1617. Littleton was a close friend of the famous jurist John Selden, and was said by Clarendon to have taken 'great pains in the hardest and most knotty part of the law' (Clarendon, *Hist. rebellion*, 5.§204), suggesting that he was expert in records as well as book learning. Among lawyers in his generation he was widely regarded as 'the best antiquary of the profession who gave himself to practice' (ibid.).

Littleton's early public career was associated with Wales and the border counties, where he also maintained personal as well as political connections. In 1614 he was returned to the Addled Parliament by Bishop's Castle, Shropshire. He became a justice of the peace in Shropshire and was appointed second judge for the northern circuit of the court of great sessions in 1622. Made a member of the council in the marches in 1623, he also served as recorder of Bridgnorth from 1624 until 1640. After the death of his first wife, Anne, the daughter of John Lyttelton of Frankley, Worcestershire, he married (before 1625) Sidney, the daughter of the judge Sir William Jones of Castellmarch, and the widow of both Richard Wynn of Glasinfryn, and Sir George Calverley, of Ley, Cheshire. Returned to parliament for both Leominster and Caernarfon borough in 1625, he vacated the Welsh seat in favour of his brother-in-law, Robert Jones. He was elected again for the same places to the next two parliaments and sat in 1626 for Leominster and in 1628 for Caernarfon. Though he was apparently sometimes absent from the house while away on circuit, Littleton gradually made an increasingly significant impact. He sat on a few committees in 1625, but was quite active both as a speaker and committee man in 1626. A participant in the attack on the king's favourite, the duke of Buckingham, Littleton none the less advised that while common fame constituted sufficient grounds on which to accuse the duke, it was not sufficient evidence on which to condemn him. He was also involved in drafting a remonstrance for presentation to the king in which the house responded to the arrest of Elliot and Digges by asserting its claim to freedom of speech in discussing all business that concerned the commonwealth.

Littleton emerged as a leading figure in the parliament of 1628 which condemned the forced loan and pushed forward the petition of right in the wake of the arrest by the council, and detention without bail, of the five knights who had refused to pay the loan. He spoke frequently and was appointed to forty-six committees. The chairman of that on liberty and property, he guided the inquiry into the use of martial law and the detested practice of billeting soldiers on the country. Making a report from the committee on 3 April he stressed that it was 'an ancient and undoubted right of every free man that he hath a full and absolute propriety in his goods and estate' (Johnson, 2.278). Presenting the Commons' case against arbitrary arrest to the Lords less than a week later, he used Magna Carta and other statutes to demonstrate how 'due process of law', including the right to bail and trial by peers, was 'lex terrae', the law of the land, and that it applied to those arrested by the crown and council in just the same way as it did in ordinary cases (ibid., 2.334ff.). When the goods of John Rolle, a member of the house, were seized for his refusal to pay tonnage and poundage Littleton moved, on 22 January 1629, that those responsible for the breach of parliamentary privilege should be sent for. Later on in the same session he stated that no canon made by the convocation of the church could have any authority unless it had the approval of the state, expressed in parliament.

Acting as counsel for Selden in the case of the MPs arrested on the king's orders for causing a disturbance at the end of the 1629 session, Littleton referred several times to the petition of right in arguing that they should be granted bail. Early in 1631 he acted for defendants who had refused to compound for the recently introduced knighthood fines, although he appears to have accepted that the king had the substantive right to impose the measure. Like several other leading lawyers of the 1620s who had been critical of royal policy he was in any case advanced as a servant of the crown in the course of the 1630s. On the recommendation of King Charles the City of London made him its recorder on 7 December 1631, and in the same year he was appointed counsel to the University of Oxford. Nominated autumn reader at the Inner Temple in 1632 he lectured on the statute 27 Ed. III c. 17 (Merchant Strangers), a topic that gave him the opportunity to quote the works of the Dutch jurist Hugo Grotius and reflect on a subject of some importance at the time, the sovereignty of the seas. The diarist Sir Richard Hutton thought that Littleton was the first choice of William Noy to succeed him in the post of attorney-general, but when Noy died in 1634 John Bankes was promoted instead. Littleton replaced Bankes as solicitor-general on 17 October 1634, and he was knighted in October 1635. Although he was a member of the court of high commission from 1633 and a commissioner for searching out defective titles to land, Littleton's role in the formulation and execution of Caroline financial measures is unclear, but in 1637, when the legality of ship money was tested in court, he spoke for three days in response to the case made for John Hampden against the king. Invoking the words of Sir Edward Coke, who had said that court records were a much better guide to legal history than chronicles, Littleton elaborated his case with a 'beadroll of examples and precedents' (*State trials*, 3.926) from before the conquest to the time of the forced loan, but since Hampden's lawyers had not yet questioned the claim that the levy was made in response to an emergency his principal point was also based on the law of nature and reason. The defence of the realm was more important than the law of property; indeed, individual property could not be safe if the commonwealth was in danger.

> Salus populi suprema lex … And truly it is a strange imposture, that the law should so provide, that the king by his writ can give us a remedy for white-acre and black-acre, for a clod of earth, and not be able to give a writ to defend the kingdom when it is in imminent danger. (ibid.)

Between 1634 and 1638 Littleton served as treasurer of the Inner Temple. Having been made a serjeant-at-law just a few days earlier, on 27 January 1640 he became chief justice of the court of common pleas. This was the most lucrative position in the legal system, and the one which Littleton had always described as his highest ambition, but his tenure was short, and he was soon enveloped in the growing political storms of the next couple of years. Having been appointed a privy councillor on the advice of Archbishop William Laud and the earl of Strafford, on 18 January 1641 he was removed from common pleas and made lord keeper of the great seal after the previous holder, Sir John Finch, had fled into exile. A month later he was created Baron Littleton of Mounslow, with the probable intention that he should use his position in the House of Lords to help deflect the growing attack on the earl of Strafford. At this point, however, Littleton suffered a serious illness that incapacitated him until after Strafford's trial, and which, according to Clarendon, took a permanent toll on his 'natural vigour and vivacity' (Clarendon, *Hist. rebellion*, 5.§203).

On 18 May 1641 Littleton was placed at the head of a commission to execute the office of lord high treasurer. When, on 16 August, the parliamentary commissioners were about to proceed to Edinburgh to treat with the Scottish parliament Littleton refused to pass their commission under the great seal in the absence of directions from the king, but thereafter his actions began to lead King Charles seriously to question his loyalty. He firmly refused to put the great seal to the proclamation for the arrest of the five members in January 1642, and some reports suggest that he asked to be allowed to resign his position. In April and May he lent his weight to the view that it was legal for the houses to commission lord lieutenants, and he also spoke for, and voted in favour of, the militia ordinance, perhaps hoping that the measures would help stop the king from declaring war. In a private conversation reported by Clarendon, Littleton claimed that he feigned complicity with the houses because he feared that they would otherwise take the great seal into their own custody, but the king, now in York, remained dissatisfied. Charles sent a messenger to collect the seal, and after handing it over Littleton took advantage of a weekend break in the parliamentary proceedings to depart from London on 23 May. Soon afterwards he informed the Lords that the king had ordered him not to leave his presence; after giving him warning a year later that he would lose his place if he did not return the seal, the two houses passed an ordinance for creating a new one on 10 November 1643.

Evidently depressed at what he saw as the inevitability of war, Littleton displayed a 'visible dejectedness' (Clarendon, *Hist. rebellion*, 5.§203) when he arrived at York which did little to restore Charles's confidence in him; for some time afterwards the great seal was kept in the king's bedchamber. Though he possessed a 'grave and comely' presence (ibid., 3.§81), Littleton's manner and legal learning appear not to have made him a very effective councillor, but he was present when Charles received the parliamentary peace proposals at Oxford in early 1643. In May of the same year he was again appointed a commissioner of the treasury, and on 21 May 1644 he was given a commission as colonel to raise a regiment of foot from among the gentlemen of the inns of court and chancery in London. Along with other royalists he was granted a DCL degree from Oxford University on 31 January 1643, and it was probably when he was with the king in Oxford that he began working on a major jurisprudential treatise, which he seems to have intended for publication and which he entitled, with reference to his distinguished ancestor, 'The newe Littleton'. Although only parts of the manuscript survive (now at Harvard law school, MS 2106), it demonstrates his vast learning not only in English legal sources, but also in a very wide selection of continental works ranging from the *Corpus juris civilis* to Italian and especially French treatises of the sixteenth century. Organized on an alphabetical basis the treatise was intended to be an encyclopaedic comparative work that would cover international and ecclesiastical as well as private and constitutional law.

Littleton died at Oxford on 27 August 1645 and was buried in Christ Church Cathedral, where his daughter erected a monument to his memory. When parliament ordered in the following September that his books and manuscripts in London should be seized they were put into the hands of Bulstrode Whitelocke, but were evidently disbursed thereafter. A volume of law reports published under Littleton's name in 1683 may have been owned by him, but he is unlikely to have been the author.

CHRISTOPHER W. BROOKS

Sources *DNB* · 'Littleton, Sir Edward', HoP, *Commons, 1604–29* [draft] · Clarendon, *Hist. rebellion* · J. H. Baker, *The legal profession and* *the common law* (1986), chap. 5 • *State trials*, vol. 3 • R. C. Johnson and others, eds., *Commons debates, 1628*, 6 vols. (1977–83) • CUL, MS Mm 6.62, fol. 90ff. • B. Whitelocke, *Memorials of the English affairs*, new edn (1732) • *CSP dom., 1626–45* • *The diary of Sir Richard Hutton, 1614–1639*, ed. W. R. Prest, SeldS, suppl. ser., 9 (1991) • W. R. Williams, *The history of the great sessions in Wales, 1542–1830* (privately printed, Brecon, 1899) • C. Russell, *The fall of the British monarchies, 1637–1642* (1991) • K. Sharpe, *The personal rule of Charles I* (1992) • Baker, *Serjeants* • Reading on 27 Ed., III, c. 17, Merchant Strangers, BL, Hargrave MS 372, fols. 90ff. • will, PRO, PROB 11/210, sig. 165

Archives CUL, MSS

Likenesses A. Van Dyck, portrait, *c*.1640–1641, priv. coll. • W. Faithorne, line engraving (after A. Van Dyck), BM, NPG • R. Williams, mezzotint (after A. Van Dyck, *c*.1640–1641), BM, NPG [*see illus.*] • oils (after A. Van Dyck), NPG

Wealth at death wealthy; landed estate at Henley, Shropshire: will, PRO, PROB 11/210, sig. 165

Littleton, Edward (*bap.* **1625**, *d.* **1702**), planter and judge in Barbados, was baptized on 21 December 1625 in Stoke St Milborough, Shropshire, the son of Sir Adam Littleton (*d.* 1647), son of Thomas Littleton, and his wife Frances Lutley. His mother was Audrey (*d.* 1648), daughter of Thomas Poyntz of North Ockendon, Essex, and his wife, Jane Peryam. He attended Westminster School (according to Anthony Wood) before becoming a commoner in St Mary Hall, Oxford, matriculating on 2 April 1641. He graduated BA on 6 July 1644, was elected a fellow of All Souls in 1646, and proceeded MA on 14 December 1648. He was admitted to Lincoln's Inn on 24 April 1649, but seems to have remained in Oxford for several years, as he was senior proctor in 1656. He was incorporated MA at Cambridge in 1657, but resigned his Oxford fellowship in 1663 and was called to the bar in 1664. Two years later he sailed to Barbados to serve both as secretary to William, sixth Baron Willoughby of Parham, the governor, and as king's attorney for the island colony. About 1669, while living on Barbados, Littleton married Dorothy, widow of Edward Harrison of Barbados and daughter of John Booth, of Glossop, Derbyshire. The Littletons had no children.

By 1673 Littleton had become one of the largest landowners on Barbados, with 600 acres. Although he soon sold much of the land, the census of 1679 reveals that he remained one of the leading planters on the island. He had 205 acres in St James parish with 120 slaves and three servants. Littleton served for several years as a judge of the Holetown court of common pleas, and for six years from 1674 he represented St James parish in the house of assembly, twice serving as speaker of that body. In these positions he became a staunch advocate for the interests of the planter class. When a new governor, Sir Richard Dutton, arrived in 1680, Littleton led the opposition to Dutton's efforts to force planters into compliance with imperial rule. Early in 1682 Dutton reported that he had dissolved the assembly and dismissed all his detractors from civil and military positions including Littleton. The latter was vindicated when a newly elected assembly selected him as speaker.

In 1683 Littleton returned to England, where he spent the rest of his life. He remained an opponent of Dutton, appearing as a witness against him before the lords of trade in autumn 1683. He also published an impassioned defence of his fellow planters in a pamphlet entitled *The groans of the plantations, or, A true account of their grievous and extreme sufferings by the heavy impositions upon sugar, and other hardships relating more particularly to the island of Barbados* (1689). In it he charged that his fellow sugar planters had been brought to the brink of ruin by heavy customs duties, the requirement that they purchase all imports from within the empire, and their dependence upon the Royal African Company for slaves. The Barbados assembly not only sent a letter of thanks to Littleton; they hired him to serve as their agent. For a decade beginning in 1691 he lobbied successfully with William III and the House of Commons on behalf of his fellow sugar planters. His efforts contributed to the repeal of an imperial sugar tax imposed in 1685 and the withdrawal from the Royal African Company of its monopoly permitting new traders to enter the slave trade—a circumstance that rapidly doubled the number of slaves delivered to the island. Although Littleton published several other pamphlets dealing largely with imperial, diplomatic, and economic issues, his significance derives from *The Groans of the Plantations* and his other activities on behalf of Barbados sugar planters. He is last recorded as agent for Barbados in 1701, and was buried at Greenwich, Kent, on 9 February 1702.

LARRY GRAGG

Sources *CSP col.*, vols. 7–19 • Wood, *Ath. Oxon.*, new edn, vol. 4 • Wood, *Ath. Oxon.: Fasti* (1820) • E. Littleton, *The groans of the plantations, or, A true account of their grievous and extreme sufferings by the heavy impositions upon sugar, and other hardships relating more particularly to the island of Barbados* (1689), 11 • *IGI* • J. C. Hotten, *The original lists of persons of quality, emigrants, religious exiles, political rebels, serving men sold for a term of years, apprentices, children stolen, maidens pressed, and others who went from Great Britain to the American plantations, 1600–1700* (1874) • *Old Westminsters* • W. P. Baildon, ed., *The records of the Honorable Society of Lincoln's Inn: admissions*, 1 (1896), 260 • All Souls Oxf.

Wealth at death 205 acres, 120 slaves, three servants: 1679 census for St James parish, Barbados; *CSP col. 1669–74*, 496–7; Hotten, *Original lists of persons … 1600–1700*

Littleton, Edward (*bap.* **1698**, *d.* **1733**), Church of England clergyman and poet, was baptized at Stoke St Milborough, Shropshire, on 16 February 1698, the son of John Littleton and his wife, Ann. He was educated upon the royal foundation at Eton College under Dr Snape. In 1717 he was elected to a scholarship at King's College, Cambridge, where he graduated BA in 1721, MA in 1724, and LLD in 1728.

In 1720 Littleton was appointed an assistant master at Eton. He was ordained deacon in April 1724, and priest the following month. In 1726 he was elected a fellow of Eton and presented to the vicarage of Mapledurham, Oxfordshire. Littleton married Frances, daughter of Barnham Goode, under-master of Eton, and they had three children.

While an undergraduate Littleton composed a humorous poem entitled 'A Letter from Cambridge to Master Henry Archer, a Young Gentleman at Eton School'. This first appeared posthumously in the *Gentleman's Magazine* in 1738. His more celebrated poem 'On a Spider' appeared in James Ralph's collection of *Miscellaneous Poems* (1729). Both pieces were reprinted in Robert Dodsley's popular anthology, *A Collection of Poems* (1748–58), and there were a number of later editions. Littleton also wrote a pastoral elegy on the death of Ralph Banks, a scholar of King's College, but only a few fragments of this have been preserved. On 30 January 1730 he preached a sermon before the House of Commons at St Margaret's, Westminster, and on 9 June 1730 he was appointed one of the king's chaplains. Littleton died of a fever on 16 November 1733, and was buried at his church at Mapledurham. His wife subsequently married John Burton (1696–1771), Littleton's successor in the living at Mapledurham.

Two volumes of Littleton's *Sermons upon Several Practical Subjects*, dedicated to Queen Caroline, were published by subscription in 1735, for the benefit of his family. A third edition, with a memoir of Littleton by Thomas Morell, appeared in 1749.

THOMPSON COOPER, *rev.* ROBERT BROWN

Sources R. A. Austen-Leigh, ed., *The Eton College register, 1698–1752* (1927) • [R. Dodsley and I. Reed], eds., *A collection of poems by several hands*, new edn, 6 vols. (1782); facs. edn with introduction by M. F. Suarez (1997) • A. Chalmers, ed., *The general biographical dictionary*, new edn, 32 vols. (1812–17) • E. Littleton, *Sermons upon several practical subjects … to which is prefixed an account of the author*, ed. F. Littleton (1749) • Nichols, *Lit. anecdotes* • Venn, *Alum. Cant.* • W. P. Courtney, *Dodsley's collection of poetry, its contents and contributors: … the history of English literature in the eighteenth century* (privately printed, London, 1910) • *GM*, 1st ser., 8 (1738) • *IGI*

Archives U. Nott. L., Cavendish-Bentinck MSS

Littleton [*formerly* Walhouse], **Edward John, first Baron Hatherton** (**1791–1863**), politician, was born in London on 18 March 1791; he was the only son of Moreton Walhouse of Hatherton in the parish of Wolverhampton, Staffordshire, and his wife, Anne Cracroft, daughter of Abraham Portal, goldsmith and dramatist. He entered Rugby School at midsummer 1806, and matriculated from Brasenose College, Oxford, on 27 January 1809, and was created a DCL on 18 June 1817. He was admitted a student of Lincoln's Inn on 17 November 1810, but took his name off the books on 6 November 1812. In compliance with the will of his great-uncle, Sir Edward Littleton, bt (a lineal descendant of Sir Thomas Littleton KB, author of the *Treatise of Tenures*), he assumed the surname of Littleton in lieu of Walhouse on 23 July 1812, and on attaining the age of twenty-four succeeded to the family estates in Worcestershire and Staffordshire and to £18,000 p.a. At a by-election in June 1812, occasioned by his great-uncle's death in the previous month, he was returned unopposed as MP for Staffordshire, holding the seat until 1832. He applied for the baronetcy but decided the request compromised his political independence, and withdrew it.

On 21 December 1812 Littleton joined the Canningite camp by marrying Hyacinthe Mary (1789?–1849), illegitimate daughter of Richard, first Marquess Wellesley, and Hyacinthe Gabrielle, daughter of Pierre Roland, a Frenchman. After 'early prepossessions' of toryism, his 'feelings were with the more liberal party' and he supported Catholic emancipation; however, he supported the property tax in 1816. He seconded Manners Sutton's nomination for

Edward John Littleton, first Baron Hatherton (1791–1863), by Sir George Hayter, 1834

the speakership on 2 June 1817 and supported Mackintosh's motion for a select committee on the criminal laws on 2 March 1819, serving on the subsequent committee. He sat on many other committees (finance, Windsor's establishment, the Bank of England). From 1817 until 1862 he kept a journal which has been much used by historians, and was partly published in A. Aspinall's edition of extracts from three such works (1952). He supported radical poor-law reform. On 22 April 1825 he introduced his Elective Franchise in Ireland Bill, a buttress to Burdett's Roman Catholic Relief Bill; both bills failed. It reflected his increasing whiggery, which, after the death of Canning in 1827, became overt. In 1828 he supported parliamentary reform; in 1830 he represented the views of Huskissonites to the tory leadership, pressing for reform; in 1831 the whig government appointed him to superintend and report on the boundary commissioners.

In 1832 Littleton was elected unopposed for South Staffordshire. Annoyed by the cabinet's decision to continue Manners Sutton as speaker, the radicals nominated Littleton (proposed by Joseph Hume, seconded by Daniel O'Connell); but he declared himself 'unwilling' and the motion was lost. In May 1833 he was appointed chief secretary to Ireland and was re-elected by 439 votes to 6 for South Staffordshire (his only contested election); in June he was sworn of the privy council. His position as chief secretary was, to say the least, awkward. The Liberal section of the cabinet pressed for a more radical policy towards the Irish church and for an accommodation with O'Connell. Littleton got on good terms with O'Connell and used the Irish secret service funds to secure a good press in Ireland. But O'Connell took him by surprise on 13 February 1834 by introducing a motion for a select committee on Baron Smith. Littleton accepted O'Connell's motion which was passed but was then reversed, the debate seriously weakening the government. On 20 February Littleton carried a motion for the commutation of existing tithes into a land tax and on 2 May introduced his Tithe Bill. On 6 May Russell, without consultation, announced that Irish church revenues were unnecessarily large and that the surplus should be appropriated. The crisis over appropriation, as a result of which Stanley and Graham resigned, merged with that over coercion a month later, when Lord Wellesley (the lord lieutenant and Littleton's father-in-law), who had hitherto advised renewal of the meetings' clauses, changed his advice in response to an appeal from Littleton, who recommended their abandonment on 21 June. Littleton, who had written to Wellesley at Brougham's instigation, then saw O'Connell and gave him the strong but erroneous impression that the Liberals in cabinet had carried the day. When it was clear that Grey had in fact overruled the Liberals, O'Connell revealed to the Commons his private dealings with Littleton, who in turn admitted 'a gross indiscretion'. The episode led to the resignations of Grey and Althorp and the premiership of Melbourne. Littleton's tenure of the chief secretaryship was thus the occasion for a string of resignations which affected British politics for a generation. These were not altogether Littleton's fault, but his amiable character did not equip him to bring a tense situation under control. On 16 July 1834, recognizing that he had been 'the main cause of Lord Grey's resignation', Littleton offered his resignation to Melbourne but agreed to stay on when Althrop, who had resigned over the same matter, withdrew his resignation. He passed his Coercion Bill (the court-martial and meetings' clauses being omitted) but his Tithe Bill was rejected by the Lords. He resigned on Melbourne's dismissal in November 1834.

Littleton was again unopposed in South Staffordshire in January 1835, but his hopes of the speakership were denied by the government's support for Abercromby. He was never appointed to any other ministerial office. He was created Baron Hatherton of Hatherton on 11 May 1835 and took his seat in the Lords on 1 June. In his maiden speech the next day he caused a short but excited discussion by applying the word 'sectarian' to the established church in Ireland (*Hansard* 3, 28, 1835, 355–8). He supported the repeal of the corn laws in 1846 and was appointed lord lieutenant of Staffordshire on 8 June 1854.

Hatherton's first wife died on 4 January 1849, aged fifty-nine, leaving him with one son, Edward Richard, who succeeded to the title, and three daughters. On 11 February 1852 he married Caroline Anne, widow of Edward Davies Davenport of Capesthorne, Macclesfield, and daughter of Richard Hurt of Wirksworth, Derbyshire; they had no children and she died aged eighty-eight at Worthing on 16 May 1897.

Hatherton spoke for the last time in the Lords on 23 May 1862. He died on 4 May 1863 at his seat, Teddesley, near Penkridge, Staffordshire (demolished in 1954); he was buried in Penkridge church on 12 May. Hatherton was a man of moderate abilities and little tact who at the vital moment of his career found himself the superficial cause of a split in the whig party, which was in fact of long-standing causation, though he compounded it by an overestimation of his capacity to manage the strong personalities around him; when warned against O'Connell he is reported to have said: 'Oh! leave me to manage Dan' (*Greville Memoirs*). He had not the will or the ability to recover from the blame consequently attached to him.

G. F. R. Barker, *rev.* H. C. G. Matthew

Sources A. Aspinall, ed., *Three early nineteenth-century diaries* (1952) [extracts from Le Marchant, E. J. Littleton, Baron Hatherton, and E. Law, earl of Ellenborough] · A. D. Macintyre, *The Liberator: Daniel O'Connell and the Irish party, 1830–1847* (1965) · *Lord Hatherton's memoir and correspondence relating to political occurrences in June and July 1834*, ed. H. Reeve (1872) · *GM* (1863) · GEC, *Peerage* · *The Times* (5 May 1863) · *Staffordshire Advertiser* (9 May 1863) · *Staffordshire Advertiser* (16 May 1863) · *The Greville memoirs, 1814–1860*, ed. L. Strachey and R. Fulford, 8 vols. (1938)

Archives Staffs. RO, corresp. and papers | Birm. CA, letters to Boulton family · BL, corresp. with William Huskisson, Add. MSS 38751–38758 · BL, corresp. with Sir Robert Peel, Add. MSS 40314–40606, *passim* · BL, Spencer MSS · BL, corresp. with Lord Wellesley, Add. MSS 37306–37416 · Derbys. RO, corresp. with Sir R. J. Wilmot-Horton · Durham RO, letters to Lord Londonderry and Lady Londonderry · Herts. ALS, corresp. with Lord Lytton · Institution of Mechanical Engineers, London, corresp. with John S. Rutter, Wolverhampton solicitor, relating to Staffordshire & Worcestershire Canal Co. · Keele University Library, letters to Ralph Sneyde · Lpool RO, letters to Lord Stanley · NL Scot., corresp. with Edward Ellice sen. · PRO NIre., corresp. with first Marquess Anglesey · U. Durham L., letters to second Earl Grey [copies] · W. Sussex RO, letters to duke of Richmond

Likenesses G. Hayter, oils, 1834, NPG [*see illus.*] · Cosway, miniature; formerly in possession of Lord Hatherton, 1892 · G. Hayter, group portrait, oils (*The House of Commons, 1833*), NPG · Lauder, portrait; formerly in possession of Lord Hatherton, 1892 · Lewis, stipple (after J. Slater; *Grillion's Club* series), BM, NPG · Pickersgill, portrait; formerly in possession of Lord Hatherton, 1892

Wealth at death under £30,000: probate, 1 July 1863, *CGPLA Eng. & Wales*

Littleton, Henry (1823–1888), music publisher, was born in London on 7 January (Krummel and Sadie give 2 January) 1823, the son of James and Elizabeth Littleton. About 1837 he began working for the music-sellers and publishers George and Manby of Fleet Street, and was later employed by the music and musical instrument sellers and publishers Monro and May in Holborn. In 1841 he entered the music publishing house of Novello (then at 69 Dean Street, Soho) as a 'collector', when his job was to go round the publishing houses to obtain ordered copies of works not issued by the firm. In 1846 he became manager, in 1861 a partner, and in 1866 sole proprietor. However, J. Alfred Novello had ceased to be personally involved in the day-to-day running of the firm from 1857, when he moved to Italy, and Littleton had effectively been in charge since then. He was evidently a great businessman, and many of the transactions which gained the firm a name for enterprise are attributable to him. The company expanded rapidly, and the development of the English taste for choral music during the period was owing largely to Novello's cheap publications. This was Alfred Novello's idea but it was Littleton who executed it. One of his earliest publications was Novello's *Parish Choir Book*, and the first edition of *Hymns Ancient and Modern* appeared in 1861. The business of Ewer was acquired in 1867, and the firm subsequently began to publish more secular and orchestral music and entered into concert promotion.

Littleton promoted many well-known composers, including Verdi and Dvořák, as well as publishing editions of works by Purcell. It was partly on his invitation that Liszt visited England in 1886, after an absence of nearly fifty years, when he was Littleton's guest at his home, Westwood House, Sydenham, Kent. When Littleton retired in 1887 the business was the largest of its kind in the world. Both his sons, Alfred Henry (1845–1914) and Augustus James (1854–1942), became chairmen of the company in turn. (His daughter had died in 1885.) He died on 11 May 1888 at Westwood House, and was buried on 16 May at Lee cemetery, Kent. His residence in London was at 1 Berners Street, where the business was located until the end of 1906, and where his sons also resided.

Littleton's portrait reveals a man of heavy build with a long beard and moustache. His 'singleness of purpose and integrity of action' is commented on in *A Short History of Cheap Music* (p. 142), and an obituary (written by Joseph Bennett) remarked that

> under the mask of the man of business—which was all that the general public saw—lay a most affectionate and tender nature … For proof I need only refer to the kindness he showed to young composers, in several cases going so far as to bear the expense of their education at home and abroad. (*Musical Times*, 29, 332)

J. C. Hadden, *rev.* David J. Golby

Sources J. Bennett, *MT*, 29 (1888), 329–32 • [J. Bennett], *A short history of cheap music, as exemplified in the records of the house of Novello, Ewer & Co.* (1887) • D. W. Krummel and S. Sadie, eds., *Music printing and publishing* (1990), 352–3 • C. Humphries and W. C. Smith, *Music publishing in the British Isles, from the beginning until the middle of the nineteenth century: a dictionary of engravers, printers, publishers, and music sellers*, 2nd edn (1970), 246–7 • 'Liszt in London, 1886', *MT*, 27 (1886), 253–9, esp. 253 • *CGPLA Eng. & Wales* (1888)

Likenesses portrait, repro. in Bennett, *A short history of cheap music*, 73

Wealth at death £8650 2s. 8d.: probate, 29 Sept 1888, *CGPLA Eng. & Wales*

Littleton, James (*bap.* **1668**, *d.* **1723**), naval officer, was baptized on 29 October 1668, the fourth son of James Littleton of Lingfield, Surrey, and Susanna White (*née* Medlicot). He was the grandnephew of Sir Thomas Littleton, speaker of the House of Commons and treasurer of the navy, whom he succeeded to the estate of North Ockenden, Essex, in 1714. He became first lieutenant of the *Dreadnought* in the battle of La Hogue in May 1692. On 27 February 1693 he was promoted captain of the *Swift Prize* (24 guns); subsequently he commanded the *Dover* and the *Winchelsea*. In 1696 he commanded the *Portland* (48 guns) in the channel, and also escorted the annual convoy from Newfoundland to Cadiz and the Mediterranean; he returned to England in May 1697. For the rest of 1697 and throughout 1698 the *Portland* was employed on the home station.

In 1699 Littleton went out to the East Indies in the *Anglesea*, one of a small squadron under Commodore George Warren, which had been ordered to act against the pirates of Madagascar. Warren died in November, and the command passed to Littleton. Several of the pirate ships were destroyed and, after proclamations of pardon had broken up the other crews, Littleton returned to England. From 1702 to 1705 he commanded the *Medway* in the channel, and in January 1705 he was commodore of a small squadron which captured the *Auguste*, a large French privateer, when her consort, the *Jason*, commanded by the celebrated René Duguay-Trouin, escaped with difficulty. In 1706 he commanded the *Cambridge* under Sir John Leake at the relief of Barcelona and the capture of Alicante, where he is said to have been landed in command of a battalion of seamen.

In 1709 Littleton was captain of the *Somerset* in the West Indies; and in July 1710 he was appointed commodore and commander-in-chief of the squadron going to Jamaica, with his broad pennant in the *Defence*. He arrived there in November, and in the following July put to sea on intelligence of a Spanish fleet of twelve large ships being assembled at Cartagena. He arrived on the coast of New Spain with five two-decked ships on 26 July, and drove five large vessels in under the guns of the castle of Boca-Chica, the entrance to the harbour of Cartagena. The next day, 27 July, four others were sighted and chased. At about 6 p.m. the headmost ships, *Salisbury* and *Salisbury Prize*, came up with the rearmost, which, after a sharp combat, struck flag on the approach of the *Defence*. The *Jersey* captured another; the other two escaped. Afterwards Littleton, with his squadron, cruised off Havana, in order to intercept Admiral Jean-Baptiste Du Casse, who was expected there. He then drew back to cover Jamaica on receiving intelligence that a fleet of eighteen French warships was gathering at Martinique, presumably for an attack on that island. The information proved to be false; but Du Casse, taking advantage of Littleton's absence, got into Havana.

In July 1712 Littleton was relieved by Sir Hovenden Walker and returned to England. In November 1714 he was appointed resident commissioner and commander-in-chief at Chatham, a post he held until 1722. On 1 February 1716 he was promoted rear-admiral of the red, and on 15 March 1717 vice-admiral of the blue, after which he served as second-in-command to Sir George Byng in the Baltic before returning home in June. In the spring of 1719 he was for a few weeks first captain to the earl of Berkeley, first lord of the Admiralty, specially authorized to fly the flag of lord high admiral.

Littleton married Jane, daughter of Richard Bunch MD; they had one son and two daughters. Elected MP for Weymouth in 1710, despite being in the Caribbean, he was unseated on petition both then and after the subsequent by-election in 1711. He was returned successfully at Weymouth in 1713, and served as a whig until 1715; after a break from parliament he had a brief term as MP for Queenborough, serving from 24 March 1722 until his death on 3 February 1723.

J. K. Laughton, *rev.* J. D. Davies

Sources HoP, *Commons, 1690–1715* [draft] • R. R. Sedgwick, 'Littleton, James', HoP, *Commons, 1715–54* • J. Charnock, ed., *Biographia navalis*, 3 (1795), 37–45 • W. L. Clowes, *The Royal Navy: a history from the earliest times to the present*, 7 vols. (1897–1903), vol. 2, pp. 499, 526, 529–30 • PRO, ADM/6/424, ADM/7/549 • NMM, Sergison MSS, SER/136
Archives NMM • PRO

Littleton [Lyttleton], **Sir Thomas** (*b.* before **1417**, *d.* **1481**), justice and legal writer, was the eldest son of Thomas Westcote and Elizabeth Littleton, daughter and heir of Thomas Littleton (*d.* 1422). It is known that he was born before 1417, since by that date his mother had a second husband, Thomas Heuster, chief protonotary of the common pleas. It is supposed that he assumed his mother's surname and arms under the terms of her first marriage settlement, as heir to the Littletons' manor of Frankley in Worcestershire.

Lawyer and judge In the 1430s, perhaps under his stepfather's influence, Littleton went to London to study law, and he was admitted to the Inner Temple. Sir Edward Coke's claim that Littleton was a member of the inn was long doubted, but it is corroborated by manuscript evidence that he attended readings there after he became a serjeant. Coke also said he had seen Littleton's own reading on the Statute of Westminster II c. 1, *De donis* (concerning entails); this would have been given in the 1440s, and if it could be found would be the earliest named reading. By the end of the 1440s Littleton was an established lawyer, and he was elected recorder of Coventry in 1449. In 1453, when probably not out of his thirties, he was created serjeant-at-law, and two years later he was appointed king's serjeant. His clients included the earl of Wiltshire, the duke of Buckingham, Lord Clinton, Sir William Trussel, and the duchy of Lancaster. In 1466 he was raised to the bench, and from then until his death he sat as a justice of the common pleas. As an assize justice he was sent at first on the northern circuit, but in 1471 he changed to the midland. In company with Chief Justice Bryan he was made a knight of the Bath at Whitsun 1475.

Marriage In January 1444 Littleton married Jane (*d.* 1505), the young widow of Sir Philip Chetwynd. She brought him estates at Grendon and Dordon in Warwickshire, and Ingestre in Staffordshire, which she claimed as her jointure but which were the subject of litigation with the Chetwynd family for over thirty years. Fifteen years later, she inherited other lands in Shropshire and Staffordshire from her father, William Burley (*d.* 1459), a Shropshire apprentice of the law and sometime speaker of the Commons. Littleton bought further property in those counties, as well as in his home county of Worcestershire, and also rented a London house on the north side of St Sepulchre's Church in Holborn.

***Littleton*: its history and reputation** The justice's professional immortality derives not so much from his learning as displayed in the year-books, which report many of his arguments and opinions, as from his celebrated treatise on tenures. The treatise, known simply as *Littleton*, was printed anonymously and without title by John Lettou and William Machlinia within a year of his death in 1481: it was the first law book printed in England. Since it purported to have been written for the instruction of one of the author's sons, it probably dates from about ten years earlier. A few fifteenth-century manuscripts survive, though none can be positively dated before the first printed edition, and it therefore seems possible that the text was indeed private to the Littleton family until the justice's death. Littleton's modesty might have deprived posterity of a masterpiece. It proved to be the most successful law book ever written in England, enjoying over ninety editions, some of them (after 1525) translated from the original law French into English. (There is an earlier English translation in manuscript.) It was already an established authority by the early sixteenth century, and its propositions were cited as 'maxims' and 'grounds' of the law of property. Chief Justice Mountague asserted in 1550 that it was 'the true and most sure register of the foundations and principles of our law' (*Les commentaries*, fol. 58*r–v*), and in 1600 William Fulbecke went so far as to say that 'Littleton is not now the name of a lawyer, but of the law itself' (*Direction*, fol. 27*v*).

Until Victorian times, *Littleton* was one of the first books placed in the hands of a law student. Copies were often interleaved for heavy annotation, and the contents laboriously digested into commonplaces. An anonymous Jacobean commentary was printed in 1829, but the best-known commentary was that by Sir Edward Coke. *Coke on Littleton* (1628) took the form of a massive gloss piled around the words of Littleton, in the continental manner, emphasizing the almost oracular authority of the original text. Coke, outraged by the ill-judged censures of the French civil lawyer François Hotman, lauded the text as 'the most perfect and absolute work that ever was written in any human science' (Coke, *Le Second Parte des Reportes*, fol. 67). Littleton himself made no such claim to infallibility, and in the epilogue expressly denied it, stating that his object was to communicate an elementary understanding of legal reasoning, and warning that some of what he wrote might not be law. The key to the book's success lay in the clarity of its style and the simplicity of its propositions. Littleton sensed more keenly than most lawyers of his time the need for a distinction between the theoretical and the vocational stages of legal education. He knew the finer points of pleading and practice as well as anyone, but kept them from cluttering his exposition of first principles. He cited few cases, mentioned few controversies, and passed over modern developments (such as uses or trusts of land) which might have confused the beginner. Instead, the underlying axioms of the land law were revealed in easy stages, with examples and reasoned explanations—the law was more praiseworthy, according to the concluding Latin motto, when it could be proved by reason: 'Lex plus laudatur quando ratione probatur' (Coke, *Institutes*, fol. 395). The work shows a coherence in common-law thought which the year-books of the same period largely conceal from the modern reader.

The treatise is divided into three books. The second book alone deals with tenures, the author having decided first to describe the system of estates in land. The first begins with a definition of fee simple, which is still found in textbooks on real property. These first two books, according to a note at the end, were intended to explain the *Old Tenures*, a fourteenth-century primer which Littleton's *New Tenures* virtually supplanted. The third book is three times longer than the first two together, and covers a series of topics relating to title. The further division of the treatise into 749 sections was made by the Tudor printers, who also interpolated some apocrypha—including a few references to cases—about 1530. A translation into modern French, by the Norman lawyer Houard, was published at Rouen in 1766. William Jones (*d.* 1794) prepared a new law-French text in 1776, but abandoned his plan for a new edition on learning that Hargrave was working on a new edition of *Coke on Littleton*. The last French edition was printed in 1841, and the last English reprint was published in Washington, DC in 1903.

Death and succession Littleton died on 23 August 1481 and was buried in Worcester Cathedral, where he founded a chantry for his parents and for William Burley and Sir Philip Chetwynd. His tomb chest, bearing the indent of a figure in judicial robes, is still to be seen in the nave; the brass was stolen during the civil war. There was formerly a portrait in scarlet gown and coif, kneeling at a prie-dieu, in the windows of Frankley church, where at the time of his marriage he had founded for his domestic use a chapel of the Holy Trinity; there was a similar figure at Halesowen in Shropshire. The Frankley window was probably the basis of the engraving executed by Robert Vaughan for the 1629 edition of *Coke on Littleton*. The Inner Temple has a more fanciful full-length painting, attributed to Cornelis Janssens, which was given by Coke's daughter in 1662; for over 250 years it hung in hall with a companion portrait of Coke. Littleton's will, dated the day before his death, does not list his law books but mentions a number of others, including a *Catholicon* and *Polychronicon*, Lyndwode's *Provinciale*, *De gestis Romanorum*, *Fasciculus morum*, *Medulla grammatica*, and an obscure 'grete English boke'. He appointed as its overseer John Alcock, then bishop of Worcester.

The justice's eldest son, Sir William (1450–1507), knighted after the battle of Stoke, and his second son, Richard (*d.* 1517), were both members of the Inner Temple; a third son, Thomas (*d.* 1524), was admitted to Lincoln's Inn in 1476 and kept chambers there for many years. He also had two daughters, Ellen and Alice, who died unmarried. Only Richard—who represented Ludlow in the 1491 parliament—seems to have practised law, and his father left him the town house near Newgate; he became a bencher of the Inner Temple, where he gave an important reading on the law of felony (Westminster II cc. 12–14) in 1493. Richard Littleton was seated at Pillatonhall in Staffordshire, where his male line continued until 1812; there is a portrait of him incised on stone in Penkridge church. From William Littleton descended the lords Lyttleton of Frankley (now represented by Viscount Cobham), and from Thomas descended Edward Lyttelton (*d.* 1645), lord keeper to Charles I, who became Lord Lyttelton of Mounslow. J. H. Baker

Sources *Littleton's tenures*, ed. E. Wambaugh (1903) • Holdsworth, *Eng. law*, vol. 2 • P. Winfield, *Chief sources of English legal history* (1925), 309–14 • C. Carpenter, *Locality and polity: a study of Warwickshire landed society, 1401–1499* (1992) • Baker, *Serjeants* • J. H. Baker and J. S. Ringrose, *A catalogue of English legal manuscripts in Cambridge University Library* (1996) • *The reports of Sir John Spelman*, ed. J. H. Baker, 2, SeldS, 94 (1978) • E. Coke, *First part of the institutes* (1628) • H. Cary, *A commentary on the tenures of Littleton* (1829) • B. Willis, *A survey of the cathedrals of York, Durham, Carlisle … Bristol*, 2 vols. (1727) • BL, Harley MSS 965, fol. 193 • F. H. Inderwick and L. Field, *Report on the paintings of Littleton and Coke in the Inner Temple* (1894) • *Les commentaries, ou, Les reportes de Edmunde Plowden* (1571)

Archives priv. coll.

Likenesses R. Vaughan, engraving, 1629 • C. Janssens, painting, *c.*1635, Inner Temple, London • line engraving (after a plate by R. Vaughan), BM, NPG; repro. in E. Coke, *The first part of the institutes of the laws of England*, 9th edn (1684) • portraits, Inner Temple, London

Littleton, Sir Thomas, second baronet (1619/20?–1681), politician, was the eldest of the four sons of Sir Adam Littleton (created baronet 1642, *d.* 1647) of Stoke St Milborough, Shropshire, and his wife, Etheldreda Poyntz (*d.* 1648), the heir of North Ockendon, Essex. Educated at the Inner Temple (1636) and Jesus College, Oxford (1638), he married in October 1637, when he was said to be seventeen, his cousin Anne (1623–1705), daughter and heir of Sir Edward Littleton, the lord keeper, with whom he had four sons. He was returned for Much Wenlock, where his father was recorder, at both elections of 1640, and called to the bar in 1642, though he never practised.

Littleton left Westminster early in the civil war, and was disabled from sitting in the Commons on 5 February 1644. Probably protected by the able and influential clerk of the parliament, John Browne, he was 'never sequestered nor judicially impeached of delinquency' (PRO, SP 23/217/15); but when Browne lost office on the abolition of the House of Lords, Littleton thought fit 'for his future quiettnes to discover himselfe to be guilty of … adhering to the forces raysed against the Parliament' (ibid.) and was fined £307. He took no part in royalist activity during the interregnum, and in obedience to the last ordinance of the Long Parliament he did not stand in 1660.

Littleton regained his seat at Wenlock in 1661 and at once became prominent in the parliamentary opposition to the administration of Clarendon, disliking its intolerant and absolutist tendencies. Exceptionally among the parliament men of his day, he can be regarded as a full-time politician, whether in or out of office, and resided in London all the year round. The bulk of his income came from City property, which he improved on borrowed money by buying in leases and rebuilding. He planned careers in trade for his younger sons, like their uncle James Littleton, a partner in the victualling business controlled by the leading City dissenters Thomas Papillon and Sir Josiah Child.

Despite his ineradicable mistrust of Charles II, Littleton was not long in securing office after the fall of Clarendon. Attaching himself to the earl of Arlington (Henry Bennet), he served on the trade commission, and on 5 November 1668 he was appointed, jointly with Sir Thomas Osborne, to execute the office of treasurer of the navy on the handsome salary of £1250 a year. In a pamphlet, *The Alarum* (1669), he was described as 'that angry man against the Court, till he was silenced by a good place' (Cruickshanks, 2.750). But he had to resign after his brother, 'a very bold, villainous fellow' (*CSP dom.*, *1671*, 255), misused the funds at his disposal in the navy pay office to finance the all but successful attempt of Thomas Blood to steal the crown jewels. He was allowed to join with Papillon and Child in the naval victualling contract until Osborne, now Lord Treasurer Danby, ousted him from this in 1673.

Back in opposition Littleton worked closely with Henry Powle to plan the sessions, as his next-door neighbour Gilbert Burnet had good opportunity to observe: 'Littleton was the ablest and vehementest arguer of them all, … speaking with a strain of conviction and sincerity that was not easily resisted' (*Burnet's History*, 2.82). Strongly Francophobe in public, Littleton accepted £500 from the French embassy for his part in the overthrow of Danby. In other respects he took a moderate line, regarding legislation to exclude the duke of York from the succession to the throne as 'the most impracticable thing imaginable' (Grey, 6.255).

Defeated at the next general election, and unable to find a constituency for the second Exclusion Parliament, Littleton was appointed to the Admiralty commission on 19 February 1681 and elected to the Oxford parliament for a safe government borough. Here he distinguished himself by presenting the only plausible alternative to exclusion, proposing that on the king's death the royal power should be invested in the princess of Orange as regent for her father 'to ensure the administration of the Government in Protestant hands' (Grey, 8.117). He died only a few days later, on 12 April 1681, and was buried on 16 April at North Ockendon. He was succeeded as third baronet by his eldest surviving son, also Sir Thomas *Littleton (1647–1709).

Littleton's appearance in the pages of Pepys and Burnet, for whom 'he had generally the character of the ablest Parliament man of his time' (*Burnet's History*, 1.403), should have secured his reputation for posterity. But he left no correspondence or memoirs, and when this branch of the family became extinct he was soon forgotten.

John Ferris

Sources E. Cruickshanks, 'Littleton, Sir Thomas', HoP, *Commons*, *1660–90* • GEC, *Baronetage*, vol. 2 • Keeler, *Long Parliament* • *Bishop Burnet's History of his own time: with the suppressed passages of the first volume*, ed. M. J. Routh, 6 vols. (1823), vols. 1–2 • A. Grey, ed., *Debates of the House of Commons, from the year 1667 to the year 1694*, 10 vols. (1763) • A. Browning, *Thomas Osborne, earl of Danby and duke of Leeds, 1632–1712*, 3 vols. (1944–51) • *CSP dom.*, *1648–9*, 338; *1671*, 255 • Pepys, *Diary*, vols. 7–9 • D. T. Witcombe, *Charles II and the cavalier House of Commons* (1966) • P. Morant, *Essex* (1768), vol. 2, pp. 102–3 • PRO, SP 23/217/15 • E. R. Foster, *The House of Lords, 1603–1649* (1983), 48 • P. Seaward, *The Cavalier Parliament and the reconstruction of the old regime* (1989) • J. Milward, *Diary* (1938) • *English historical documents*, 8, ed. A. Browning (1953), 235 • *Survey of London*, 5.75 • W. A. Shaw, ed., *Calendars of treasury books*, 2–6, PRO (1905–13) • *The diaries and papers of Sir Edward Dering, second baronet, 1644 to 1684*, ed. M. F. Bond (1976)

Littleton, Sir Thomas, third baronet (1647–1709), speaker of the House of Commons, was born on 3 April 1647, the second but eldest surviving son of Sir Thomas *Littleton, second baronet (1619/20?–1681), of Stoke St Milborough, Shropshire, and North Ockenden, Essex, and his wife, the Hon. Anne (1623–1705), daughter and heir of Edward Littleton, first Baron Lyttleton of Mounslow. As a younger son Littleton was apprenticed to a City merchant, but on the death of his elder brother, Edward, he was sent to Oxford where he matriculated at St Edmund Hall in April 1665. He entered the Inner Temple the following year and was called to the bar in 1671. On his father's death, on 14 April 1681, he succeeded to the baronetcy, and on 6 September 1682 he married Anne (*bap.* 21 Aug 1663, *d.* 1714), daughter and heir of Benjamin Baun of Westcote, Gloucestershire; they had no children.

Littleton was elected to the convention of 1689 for Woodstock, Oxfordshire, through the interest of his kinsman Sir Littleton Osbaldeston, first baronet, and continued to represent the town until 1702. His whiggish outlook had been moulded against the background of his father's prominence as a presbyterian spokesman in Charles II's Cavalier Parliament, although as an adult he had also imbibed lessons from his father's bitter experiences of factional politics. Moderation, pragmatism, and good sense were always Littleton's chief strengths, and his even and agreeable temper made him a great advocate of restraint and conciliation. The irony of Littleton's career was that these sterling abilities, coupled with a flair for financial administration, should make him a compliant tool from the early 1690s of the Junto whigs.

Littleton soon made his mark in parliament as a diligent spokesman for the court. He was made a commissioner of prizes in June 1689 in recognition of his efforts in the promotion of measures to ensure the stability of the revolution settlement; promotion to the clerkship of the ordnance followed in 1690. His association with the Junto group began during their embryonic phase early in William III's reign, and it was highly significant that Littleton should be chosen in 1693 to succeed one of them, Sir John Somers, as chairman of the committees of supply and ways and means. In this demanding role Littleton was responsible for supervising the court's financial measures through the House of Commons. It also involved him in the informal processes of managing the court's supporters and he regularly briefed them on government measures at meetings of the backbench Rose Club. In March 1695 Littleton was put forward as the Junto's choice for the speaker's chair following the disgrace of Sir John Trevor, but on this occasion the favoured candidate was Paul Foley. Littleton's rising importance to the Junto dominated ministry was acknowledged in his appointment in April 1696 to a place on the Treasury board. In this new capacity Littleton worked closely with his Junto friend Charles Montagu, the chancellor of the exchequer, in ensuring the survival of the newly established Bank of England, and in the execution of a broad programme of financial reconstruction.

Following the 1698 general election Littleton was elected speaker of the House of Commons without challenge. In May the following year, at his own request, he was transferred from the Treasury board to the more profitable treasurership of the navy. However, Littleton's term as speaker proved brief and stormy. The Junto ministry grew unpopular and was subject to increasing opposition in the Commons. Littleton's efforts to appear impartial while doing his best to serve his Junto masters weakened his authority. Worse still an aggravated bladder problem, necessitating frequent exits from proceedings, made him a laughing stock. When parliament returned after the next election in January 1701 he was replaced by Robert Harley. Littleton was now able to devote much fuller attention to the Navy Office. Despite the appointment of a mainly tory administration at the accession of Queen Anne in 1702 he retained the treasurership, and was to do so for the rest of his life. Through a series of far-reaching reforms he was able to rationalize the office's chaotic accounting procedures, thereby leaving a legacy which remained in force for much of the eighteenth century.

Littleton lost his safe electoral haven at Woodstock in 1702, but was MP for Castle Rising in Norfolk, 1702–5, for Chichester in Sussex, 1705–8, and for Portsmouth from 1708 until his death. His links with the junto whigs largely ceased in these later years. He remained a government supporter, and in debates on major questions was always particularly attentive to the defence of procedural form. Commanding the respect due to a former speaker he 'often diverted the House of Commons with a pleasant story which was always apropos' (newsletter, 3 Jan 1710, BL, Add. MS 70421). He died on 31 December 1709, his baronetcy becoming extinct, and was buried at his home parish of North Ockenden in Essex. A. A. HANHAM

Sources E. Cruickshanks, 'Littleton, *alias* Poyntz, Sir Thomas, 2nd bt', HoP, *Commons, 1660–90*, 2.748–51 • L. Naylor and G. Jagger, 'Littleton *alias* Poyntz, Sir Thomas, 3rd bt', HoP, *Commons, 1660–90*, 2.751–3 • 'Littleton, Sir Thomas, 3rd bt', HoP, *Commons, 1690–1715* [draft] • will, PRO, PROB 11/513, sig. 24 • GEC, *Baronetage* • *IGI* • Foster, *Alum. Oxon.* • F. A. Inderwick and R. A. Roberts, eds., *A calendar of the Inner Temple records*, 3 (1901), 39, 79
Likenesses J. Simon, mezzotint (after T. Forster, 1700), BM

Littlewood, Dudley Ernest (1903–1979), mathematician, was born on 7 September 1903 at 289 Kennington Road, London, the only child of Harry Bramley Littlewood, a solicitor's clerk, and his wife, Ada Piper. He was educated at Tottenham county school, Middlesex, and Trinity College, Cambridge, supported by a state scholarship and a major open entrance scholarship. He was in the first class in part one, and graduated in 1925 as a wrangler with distinction, having earlier been awarded college prizes and a share of the Yeats prize. After one unproductive year of research in Cambridge working in analysis, he was forced, mainly for financial reasons, to seek employment. After a number of temporary positions as a schoolteacher he was appointed in 1928 as a temporary part-time lecturer at University College, Swansea. Except for a short period as an assistant at University College, Dundee, he remained at Swansea until 1947, first as assistant lecturer (from 1930) and as lecturer from 1934. He was then appointed university lecturer at Cambridge, but after a short period returned to Wales, in 1948, to the chair of mathematics at the University College of North Wales, Bangor, where he remained until his retirement in 1970. In 1930 he married Muriel Doris Dyson (1901–1989); their only son was born in 1935.

At Swansea Littlewood found that Archibald Read Richardson (1881–1954), the professor of mathematics, who had a considerable reputation as an algebraist, was 'bursting with problems' (Barker and Brown); he immediately set to work on these, producing a series of papers, but this early work did not truly fire his imagination—indeed, it had little long term impact. In the meantime, again at the instigation of Richardson, Littlewood studied the work of the leading German algebraists Ferdinand Georg Frobenius (1849–1917) and Issai Schur (1875–1941). This resulted in his joint paper with Richardson, 'Group characters and algebras' (*PTRS*, 233A, 1934, 99–141), which laid the foundation for his life's work. In it they introduced the 'immanant' of a matrix (a generalization of the determinant and permanent) and its relationship with a class of symmetric functions, which they christened S-functions (or Schur functions). Above all, this paper is renowned for its statement of a rule for multiplying S-functions, now universally called the Littlewood–Richardson rule (this had to wait a further thirty-five years for a rigorous proof). There followed in quick succession a number of papers in which Littlewood developed these ideas and discovered a number of fascinating combinatorial formulae involving S-functions. This led to his monograph, *The Theory of Group Characters and Matrix Representations of Groups* (1940). He continued to be a prolific author, applying S-functions skilfully to classical invariant theory. As a by-product he obtained a new purely combinatorial definition of S-functions in terms of tableaux and introduced his new multiplication of S-functions which he called 'plethysm'. His many original ideas had to wait for almost half a century before they were taken up in the modern area of algebraic combinatorics.

There were other major contributions; for example, Littlewood introduced some of the basic combinatorial ideas on the modular representations of the symmetric groups. His last major acknowledged contribution was a generalization of his beloved S-functions, now called the Hall–Littlewood functions (named after him and Phillip Hall, his Trinity contemporary). His elegant combinatorial definition of these laid the foundation for a new area of research with applications on a broad front.

Littlewood also had a passionate interest in the fundamental problems of theoretical physics with a belief that S-functions could be used profitably in this context. In the early sixties he was left bitter and despondent when his proposed unified field theory was rejected by the Royal Society. His Trinity tutor J. E. Littlewood's comment that 'his has always been an unusual type of mind' (private information) was truly perceptive and could explain the lack of recognition during his lifetime. His style was reminiscent of an earlier generation but in some respects he could be regarded as a man before his time.

Littlewood did not appreciate mathematical rigour—he had a strong intuitive grasp of formal mathematics—and when he felt a result to be true he could be perfunctory about its proof. He had little direct contact with his contemporaries, felt isolated, and later became quite depressed by the absence of interest in his work. Towards the end of his life he was gratified with the growing interest in his ideas; he would have been overwhelmed by their impact later—he has come to be regarded as a master of the usable formula.

Littlewood also had a profound interest in philosophy and religion, which he regarded as 'subjects far more worthy of investigation than mathematics' (private information). On his retirement in 1970 he wrote up his ideas in an unpublished manuscript, 'In search of wisdom'. He was an avid reader of science fiction, shy and retiring by nature, always with a friendly smile; kind, caring, and supportive in an unobtrusive way. Littlewood died suddenly at his home, Melrose, Queens Road, Llandudno, on 6 October 1979, a few weeks after breaking a leg. He was buried in Llan-rhos, Llandudno. A. O. MORRIS

Sources A. O. Morris and C. C. H. Barker, *Bulletin of the London Mathematical Society*, 15 (1983), 56–9 · C. C. H. Barker and R. Brown, *University College of North Wales, Bangor, Gazette*, 19 (1980), 11–12 · personal knowledge (2004) · private information (2004) · b. cert. · d. cert. · m. cert.

Likenesses photograph, repro. in Morris and Barker, *Bulletin of the London Mathematical Society*, 57

Wealth at death £73,750: probate, 8 Jan 1980, *CGPLA Eng. & Wales*

Littlewood, John Edensor (1885–1977), mathematician, was born on 9 June 1885, at 4 Clevedon Terrace, Roebuck Lane, Rochester, Kent, the eldest of three children of Edward Thornton Littlewood (1859–1941), schoolmaster, and Sylvia Maud Ackland. Littlewood's mother was part Irish, but his father was from old English stock—a Littlewood fought at Agincourt. Littlewood's grandfather, the writer the Revd William Edensor Littlewood (1831–1886), had been educated at Pembroke College, Cambridge, and graduated thirty-fifth wrangler in the mathematical tripos. Littlewood's father went to Peterhouse, Cambridge, and was ninth wrangler; in 1892 he accepted the headmastership of a school at Wynberg, near Cape Town. Littlewood spent eight years of his childhood in South Africa, attending school and some classes at Cape Town University. Then, at the age of fourteen, he was sent by his father to St Paul's School, London where, under F. S. Macaulay, he acquired an excellent grounding in mathematics.

In 1903 Littlewood proceeded to Trinity College, Cambridge. There was cut-throat competition to do well in the Order of Merit (abolished in 1910), but, as he wrote later, 'the game we were playing came easily to me' (Littlewood, *Littlewood's Miscellany*, 84), and in 1905 he was senior wrangler, bracketed with J. Mercer who had previously graduated at Manchester. In his third year he took part two of the mathematical tripos: this was much less of a sporting event and contained much genuine mathematics.

In the long vacation of 1906 Littlewood started research under E. W. Barnes (later bishop of Birmingham). His first topic was integral functions of zero order. Littlewood 'rather luckily struck oil at once by switching to more "elementary" methods' (Littlewood, *Littlewood's Miscellany*, 88). The next problem was rather different: 'prove the Riemann hypothesis'—the 1860 conjecture of the great German mathematician Bernhard Riemann that all 'non-trivial' zeros of the [Riemann] zeta-function are on the 'critical line', an assertion closely related to the distribution of prime numbers. Most mathematicians now consider the Riemann hypothesis the most famous problem in mathematics, whose solution seems far away despite many powerful attacks. It is a clear proof of the isolated and backward state of British mathematics at the beginning of the twentieth century that Barnes should have thought it suitable for a research student. Nevertheless, Littlewood attacked the hypothesis and even benefited from it. This led him to try hard problems because if one fails to solve them something else will be proved.

Between 1907 and 1910 Littlewood was Richardson lecturer at Manchester University. In 1908 he won a Smith's prize, and was elected into a prize (research) fellowship in Trinity College, returning to Cambridge two years later to succeed A. N. Whitehead on the Trinity mathematics staff. His reading at this time of Landau's newly published *Primzahlen* marked the end of his education. Soon he wrote his first important paper (on the converse of Abel's theorem) and started his collaboration with his Trinity colleague G. H. Hardy (1877–1947). The pattern was set for his professional life: in 1912 he moved into a spacious set of rooms in Nevile's Court; with the exception of the First World War, he occupied these rooms for the next sixty-five years, until his death.

The Hardy–Littlewood collaboration, the greatest collaboration in all of mathematics, continued for thirty-five years, their last paper being published a year after Hardy's death. In a hundred joint works they made fundamental contributions to summability, inequalities, function theory, Diophantine approximation, Fourier series, and, above all, number theory. They worked on the theory of the Riemann zeta-function, proving the first major results about the zeros of the zeta-function on the critical line. In their series of papers entitled *Partitio numerorum* they developed the powerful Hardy–Littlewood circle method to overcome formidable technical difficulties, so creating a research area that is still very active. Hardy and Littlewood also greatly extended earlier results of David Hilbert concerning Waring's problem. Landau expressed a widely held view when he said that 'The mathematician Hardy-Littlewood was the best in the world, with Littlewood the more original genius, and Hardy the better journalist'. Their habit of communicating via letters meant that, when Hardy left Cambridge during 1919–1931 for a chair at Oxford, their collaboration rose to new heights rather than withered. In 1926 they wrote a highly original paper on rearrangements of sequences, and in 1930 they proved their very influential 'maximal theorem'.

As related by their Danish colleague Harald Bohr:

> when they planned and began their far-reaching and intensive team work, they still had some misgivings about it because they feared that it might encroach on their personal freedom, so vitally important to them. Therefore … they

> amused themselves by formulating four so-called 'axioms' for their mutual collaboration. The first of them said that, when one wrote to the other … it was completely indifferent whether what they wrote was right or wrong. … The second axiom was to the effect that, when one received a letter from the other, he was under no obligation whatsoever to read it, let alone to answer it. … And they really observed this axiom to the fullest extent. When Hardy once stayed with me in Copenhagen, thick mathematical letters arrived from Littlewood, who was obviously very much in the mood for work, and I have seen Hardy calmly throw the letters into a corner of the room, saying: 'I suppose I shall want to read them some day'. The third axiom was to the effect that, although it did not really matter if they both thought about the same detail, still, it was preferable that they should not do so. And, finally, the fourth, and perhaps most important axiom stated that it was quite indifferent if one of them had not contributed the least bit to the contents of a paper under their common name; otherwise there would constantly arise quarrels and difficulties in that now one, and now the other, would oppose being named co-author. I think one may safely say that seldom—or ever—was such an important and harmonious collaboration founded on such apparently negative axioms. (Littlewood, *Littlewood's Miscellany*, 9–11)

In 1914 Littlewood published his famous result concerning the error term in the prime number theorem, which asserts that the 'logarithmic integral' li(x) is a good approximation of $\zeta(x)$, the number of primes up to the number x. Empirical evidence suggests that $\zeta(x)$ is less than li(x), but Littlewood proved the surprising result that $\zeta(x) - \text{li}(x)$ changes sign infinitely often, giving bounds for the difference that are essentially best to this day. This result was instrumental in his election to the Royal Society in 1916.

From 1914 to 1918 Littlewood served in the Royal Garrison Artillery, working on the somewhat utilitarian mathematics of gunnery. It was at this time that the Indian genius Srinivasa Ramanujan (1877–1920) went to Cambridge on the invitation of Hardy. Littlewood's absence during the war meant that his contact with Ramanujan was never more than slight. In 1928 Littlewood was elected to the newly established Rouse Ball chair of mathematics, founded by a benefaction of his former tutor. From then on, he had no college teaching and could give lectures on topics of his choice. His reputation was well established and the quality of his mathematical output was very high. In 1934 he published *Inequalities* with Hardy and G. Pólya: it became an instant bestseller and is still popular. From 1928 he held a weekly conversation class in his rooms for advanced students (he had close on thirty research students in all); on Hardy's return from Oxford in 1931 this metamorphosed into a larger gathering run by Hardy, and became known as the 'Hardy–Littlewood conversation class at which Littlewood is never present'.

It was not only with Hardy that Littlewood did much important collaborative work. With his outstanding student R. C. A. Paley he developed powerful ideas to tackle problems in harmonic analysis, but this highly successful collaboration was cut short by Paley's untimely death. From the late 1930s Littlewood and A. C. Offord investigated the distribution of zeros of random polynomials and entire functions. Among many other results, they discovered the curious phenomenon of 'pits effect' that Littlewood continued to study until 1970. Their original work on random algebraic objects was decades ahead of its time.

For the last forty years of his life, from just before the Second World War, Littlewood took a great interest in ordinary differential equations. It began when a Radio Research Board memorandum asked for help with differential equations connected to radio oscillators and thermionic valves (vacuum tubes). M. L. Cartwright took up the challenge and fired Littlewood's own interest in the problems. They began to study the behaviour of the stable periodic solutions of Balthasar van der Pol's equation. Littlewood later recalled that for something to do they went on and on with no prospect of 'results', but suddenly the entire vista of the dramatic fine structure of solutions stared them in the face. The twelve-year collaboration of Littlewood and Cartwright produced three joint papers and several others published under one or other name only, including Littlewood's enormous 1957 paper that he called 'the monster', saying of it 'I should never have read it had I not written it myself' (Littlewood, *Littlewood's Miscellany*, 16). Littlewood and Cartwright were among the first to recognize the combined power of topological and analytical methods to tackle deep problems in differential equations, discovering the phenomenon now known as 'chaos', although this had already been hinted at by Poincaré.

Littlewood abhorred administration and official position of any kind—later in life he was proud to say that he had never been chairman or secretary of any body. However, he was president of the London Mathematical Society from 1941 to 1943, and was also happy to be a foreign member of various academies and to receive honorary doctorates from several universities, including one from Cambridge in 1965. He received the royal (1929), Sylvester (1943), and Copley (1958) medals of the Royal Society, and the De Morgan medal (1938) and senior Berwick prize (1960) of the London Mathematical Society. He retired from his chair in 1950, but he continued publishing and went on several lecture tours to the USA. In 1953 he published *A Mathematician's Miscellany*, a delightful book of essays about his education, mathematics, and academic life; twenty-six years later a considerably expanded version of it was published as *Littlewood's Miscellany*.

Littlewood was below average in height but was strongly built and athletic. In school he was a good gymnast and batsman; later he was a keen swimmer and rock climber. He took up skiing in Switzerland in 1924, and went on skiing well into his seventies. He must have thought of himself when he wrote: 'Mathematics is very hard work, and dons tend to be above the average in health and vigour. Below a certain threshold a man cracks up, but above it hard work makes for health and vigour' (Littlewood, *Littlewood's Miscellany*, 195). However, he suffered from bouts of depression, occasionally in his youth but more intensely in later years. It was an enormous relief to him when in 1960 his illness responded to newly discovered drugs.

Littlewood spent most of his summer vacations on the Cornish coast, swimming, walking, and climbing. He never married, but had a son, Philip Streatfeild, and a daughter, Ann Streatfeild, with whom he spent all his time away from Cambridge. He read voraciously, not only classical literature but also science fiction and thrillers, and he listened to records of Bach, Beethoven, and Mozart many hours a day. His range of conversation was exceptional and his presence enlivened every gathering. He died on 6 September 1977 in the Evelyn Nursing Home, Cambridge, having suffered heart failure after a bad fall in his room.

Littlewood was undoubtedly one of the greatest English mathematicians of the first half of the twentieth century—together with Hardy he created a school of pure mathematics second to none. Hardy considered him the finest mathematician he ever knew: 'He was the man most likely to storm and smash a really deep and formidable problem; there was no one else who could command such a combination of insight, technique and power' (Littlewood, *Littlewood's Miscellany*, 22).

BÉLA BOLLOBÁS

Sources M. L. Cartwright, 'Later Hardy and Littlewood manuscripts', *Bulletin of the London Mathematical Society*, 17 (1985), 318–390 · *Collected papers of G. H. Hardy: including joint papers with J. E. Littlewood and others*, ed. London Mathematical Society, 7 vols. (1966–79) · G. H. Hardy, J. E. Littlewood, and G. Pólya, *Inequalities* (1988) · E. Landau, *Handbuch der Lehre von der Verteilung der Primzahlen*, 1–2 (1909) · J. E. Littlewood, *A mathematician's miscellany* (1953) · J. E. Littlewood, *Collected papers of J. E. Littlewood*, 2 vols. (1982) · J. E. Littlewood, *Littlewood's miscellany*, ed. B. Bollobás (1986) · S. L. McMurran and J. J. Tattersall, 'The mathematical collaboration of M. L. Cartwright and J. E. Littlewood', *American Mathematical Monthly*, 103 (1996), 833–45 · R. C. Vaughan, *The Hardy–Littlewood method*, 2nd edn (1997) · H. Bohr, *Collected mathematical works*, ed. E. Folner and B. Hessen, 1 (1952), xxvii–xxviii · b. cert. · d. cert. · J. C. Burkill, *Memoirs FRS*, 24 (1978), 323–67

Archives Bodl. Oxf., autobiographical papers · CUL, papers on Waring's problem · Trinity Cam., papers | McMaster University, Hamilton, Ontario, corresp. with Bertrand Russell · Trinity Cam., corresp. with A. E. Ingham

Likenesses W. Stoneman, photograph, 1932, NPG · R. Brill, pen-and-ink and sepia drawing, 1933, Trinity Cam. · G. Bollobás, bronze bust, 1973, Trinity Cam. · G. Bollobás, bust, Institution of Mathematics and its Applications, Southend-on-Sea, Essex · photograph, repro. in Burkill, *Memoirs FRS*, facing p. 323 · photograph, repro. in Littlewood, *Collected papers*

Wealth at death £16,895: probate, 12 Dec 1977, *CGPLA Eng. & Wales*

Littlewood, Sir Sydney Charles Thomas (1895–1967), lawyer, was born in Bournemouth on 15 December 1895, the elder son of Charles Sydney Littlewood (1872–1940), of Southampton, and his wife, Sarah Ann Harris. His father from 1892 devoted his life to the service of the Hampshire police force, retiring in 1920 as a much respected superintendent to live in Bromley, Kent.

On leaving school Littlewood worked first as an office boy with a firm of country solicitors and after that for a year as a constable in the same police force as his father. Then the First World War changed the course of his life. Serving with the Loyal North Lancashire regiment he won his subaltern's commission on 21 September 1915. Soon he transferred to the Royal Flying Corps and joined 35 squadron, British expeditionary force, as a flying officer. On 1 June 1916 he was shot down behind the enemy lines near Armentières and was captured. Until the end of 1918 he was held a prisoner at various camps, where his extensive range of reading included the classics, law, politics, and Egyptology. On demobilization in 1919 he chose the legal profession as his career and after two years in articles was, in May 1922, admitted as a solicitor. He joined the Territorial Army in 1926 and became a captain in the 6th East Surrey regiment.

Littlewood's first marriage, in 1919, to Evelyn Myrtle Prior (1897–1989), a farmer's daughter, was childless and ended in divorce; his second, patently happy, on 7 February 1934, was to Barbara (Bill; 1909–1995), daughter of Dr Langdon-Down, herself a solicitor who practised in Guildford and was a magistrate. In due course she became president of the Surrey Law Society, president of the International Federation of Business and Professional Women, and a lay member of the Press Council; her combination of charm and calm ability provided her husband with notable support and wise counsel in testing times. Their son Paul, born in 1936, also became a solicitor.

By 1932 (when he resigned his commission) Littlewood was making his mark in his profession, after setting up in 1928 in a partnership with Messrs Wilkinson, Howlett & Co. of Kingston-on-Thames, Surrey, which lasted for thirty years. His talent for advocacy was being exercised mainly in magistrates' courts; later, to an increasing extent, it served him well in the specialized field of town planning inquiries. In 1940, aged forty-five, he was elected to the council of the Law Society which in 1944 nominated him for appointment by Lord Simon to the Committee on Legal Aid chaired by Lord Rushcliffe. The existing poor persons procedure had depended on lawyers giving their services without charge, and had already come under strain before the war. Wartime conditions had led to a number of new initiatives to provide legal assistance to those without means, such as the services divorce department, run by the Law Society, and a scheme under which Citizens' Advice Bureaux could refer clients to solicitors who would act for reduced fees. The committee's unanimous and historic report (1945) proposed a radical reform of the existing arrangements, to be controlled 'by the lawyers themselves'. This guarded against interference in the profession by central or local government and helped to get lawyers to accept the scheme.

The government adopted the basic scheme recommended in that report, and decided to place its control in the hands of the Law Society with its large secretariat. To draft in detail the scheme itself and the statutory instruments needed to implement the provisions of the proposed bill, a legal aid committee was constituted consisting of twelve members of the council of the Law Society, all of whom later became presidents, three members of the Bar Council, each of whom became a High Court judge, and one of the lord chancellor's staff. Littlewood was aptly selected to be its chairman, and presided with whole-hearted enthusiasm and conspicuous success over its meetings, many of which called for his compound of fairness, common sense, and legal acumen.

The scheme was enacted through the Legal Aid and Advice Act 1949, which came into partial effect in 1950. It covered matters which might or did become the subject of proceedings in courts of civil jurisdiction, the grant and control of legal aid in criminal cases being administered under a quite different system. Eligibility was determined by a means test, which had been the subject of criticism from the Haldane Society and others on the left, and by a test of the merits of the case. Lawyers were paid from a legal aid fund, made up partly from a grant by central government, and partly from contributions by assisted litigants. It had originally been intended that the scheme would extend to virtually all courts and tribunals in which barristers and solicitors were entitled to appear, and that it should include legal advice. Unfortunately, because of financial pressures, legal aid was not made available for county court proceedings until 1956 and was not extended to appeals in the House of Lords until 1960. Magistrates' courts were not covered until 1961, and legal advice did not become available until 1959, when a somewhat different scheme was introduced from that originally envisaged. Tribunals were altogether excluded for fear of swamping the system, which was a particularly serious defect, since they handled many of the legal matters of most concern to the underprivileged.

In spite of these deficiencies, which were not the fault of the scheme's framers, nearly 50,000 applications were received in the first full year of operation. It has been said that the scheme was 'at its inception … at least as comprehensive as any in the developed world and arguably the most advanced then in existence' (Morgan, 73). A review by the Commons select committee on estimates found that 'the Scheme is well run and … proper regard is shown for economy' (*Parl. papers*, 1955–6, 7). The failure to provide for adjusting eligibility levels in line with inflation was addressed by the Legal Aid Act 1960, which had an immediate effect in nearly doubling the number of certificates granted. However, in the changed political climate of the late 1960s and 1970s, the scheme attracted significant criticism, such as that voiced in the pamphlet *Justice for All* by the Society of Labour Lawyers in 1968. In later years it was radically modified to meet evolving social, political, and economic conditions, but this does not detract from Littlewood's achievement in establishing the scheme despite substantial opposition from within the legal profession.

For his successful work Littlewood was knighted in June 1951. He continued with unabated zest to take a leading part in the administration of the scheme for the rest of his life. In 1959 he became, in addition, president of the Law Society and was generally regarded as being an outstanding holder of that office. His presidential address, on the keynote of 'friendship', included many innovative ideas, especially in the field of professional training.

Littlewood's notable activities were not confined to his work for that society. His impressive stature, his keen and common-sense approach to new problems, and his patent integrity led to his being in demand in several spheres. Within that of the law, he had been president of the Justices' Clerks' Society in 1944–5. A little later his specialized experience in town and country planning matters often led to his being briefed at inquiries as a leading advocate instead of a QC; and in 1956 he became legal member of the Town Planning Institute, an appointment in which he took pride.

Because of Littlewood's interest in medical matters he became a member of the South-West Metropolitan Regional Hospital Board in 1952, chairman of the Council of Professions Supplementary to Medicine in 1961, and chairman of the departmental committee on experiments on animals, whose deliberations in 1963–4 resulted in much needed control of laboratories and protection for the animals used there. His flair for finance led to his joining the commission that de-cartelized the Krupp organization in Germany and to his chairing the Westminster Fire Office, an insurance company.

It was, however, Littlewood's presidency of the London rent assessment panel from 1965 to 1967 (an appointment by Richard Crossman on the recommendation of Dame Evelyn Sharp) that brought him most into the public eye. He thus became, as was intended, the leading authority on those provisions of the Rent Act of 1965 which set up tribunals to determine 'fair rents'. Crossman thought him 'superbly solid' and highly effective in establishing an objective measure of 'fairness' which was intended to take private rents out of politics. But Labour backbenchers, mainly but not exclusively on the left of the party, attacked him for not invariably reducing the current rents, and regarded him as a 'reactionary solicitor' (Crossman, *Diaries*, 1.346, 589). Littlewood forcefully criticized them for failing to understand what the word 'fair' meant in the act they had just passed. Their much headlined threats to call for his resignation subsided in due course.

Littlewood's classically impressive presence—'Olympian', to quote a close colleague—and his strong personality tended on initial acquaintance to obscure the warmth and humanity of his character. Fond of the company of his fellow men, he took pleasure in his membership of the Garrick Club, the Company of Basketmakers, and his dining clubs. His leisure interests included extensive reading, shooting, and gardening. His death at King Edward VII Hospital, near Midhurst, Sussex, on 9 September 1967 closed the career of a man of all-round knowledge and great ability who would have made an admirable High Court judge had that office then been open to solicitors.

ERIC SACHS, *rev.* SHEILA DOYLE

Sources Ministry of Defence records • personal knowledge (1981, 2004) • private information (1981, 2004) • *The Times* (11 Sept 1967) • *The Times* (14 Sept 1967) • R. I. Morgan, 'The introduction of civil legal aid in England and Wales, 1914–1949', *Twentieth Century British History*, 5/1 (1994), 38–76 • *Law Society's Gazette* (Nov 1959), 735–44 • *WWW, 1961–70* • *WWW, 1991–5* • R. H. S. Crossman, *The diaries of a cabinet minister*, 1 (1975) • *The Times* (1939–68) • Burke, *Peerage* (1967)

Archives PRO, series LC 02, LC 04, LC 032, LC 033 | University of Strathclyde, Glasgow, corresp. with Sir George L. Pepler
Likenesses W. Bird, photograph, 1962, NPG · photograph, repro. in *The Times* (11 July 1959), 6 · photograph, repro. in *The Times* (11 Sept 1967), 10 · photograph, repro. in *Law Society's Gazette* (Aug 1959)
Wealth at death £26,544: probate, 28 Nov 1967, *CGPLA Eng. & Wales*

Littlewood, William Edensor (1831–1886), writer, was born at London on 2 August 1831, the only son of George Littlewood, a London printer and engraver, and Catherine, his wife. He was educated at Merchant Taylors' School (from 1840) and at Pembroke College, Cambridge, which he entered on 12 June 1850. In 1851 he was awarded the chancellor's medal for an English poem on Gustavus Adolphus, later printed in *A Complete Collection of English Poems*, (1859). He graduated BA in 1854, taking a third class in classics and being bracketed thirty-fifth wrangler. He proceeded MA in 1860, was ordained deacon in 1857, and priest in 1858. In the same year he married Laetitia Thornton, the third daughter of T. Thornton of London. Littlewood was curate of St John's, Wakefield, from 1857 to 1861; headmaster of Hipperholme grammar school, Halifax, Yorkshire, from 1861 to 1868; perpetual curate of Southall, Middlesex, from 1868 to 1870, and vicar of Ironville, Derbyshire, from 1870 to 1872. From 1872 to 1881 he was vicar of St James's, Bath, and served as minister-in-charge of St Thomas's, Finsbury Park, Middlesex, from 1881 to 1886.

Besides various contributions to the *Sunday at Home*, Littlewood's publications were numerous. Among his religious works were *A Garland from the Parables* (1858), being a volume of religious verse, *Essentials of New Testament Study* (1872), and *Bible Biographies, or, Stories from the Old Testament* (1878). His historical interests found expression in *Essentials of English History* (1862), *An Elementary History of Britain* in Cassell's Primary Series (1869), and *England at home: being a familiar description of the principal physical, social, commercial, and topographical features of England and Wales* (1870). He also published *The Visitation of the Poor: a Practical Manual for District Visitors* (1876). Littlewood died on 3 September 1886 at Rushend vicarage, Hatfield, Broad Oak, Essex. He was survived by his wife and two sons.

J. M. Rigg, *rev.* Nilanjana Banerji

Sources Venn, *Alum. Cant.* · C. J. Robinson, ed., *A register of the scholars admitted into Merchant Taylors' School, from AD 1562 to 1874*, 2 (1883) · *The Record* (10 Sept 1886) · Boase, *Mod. Eng. biog.*
Wealth at death £2052 6s. 4d.: probate, 5 Nov 1886, *CGPLA Eng. & Wales*

Littlington, William of. *See* Ludlington, William (*d. c.*1310x12).

Littman, Joseph Aaron (1898–1953), property investor, was born in Russia into a peasant family. Poverty deprived him of an education and in later life he could still hardly sign his name. However, as Edward Erdman later recalled, 'he knew how to deal with people' (Erdman, 54). Furthermore he had an incredible memory for figures and details, which proved extremely useful in the career that he eventually adopted.

After migrating to New York with his family, Joe Littman, as he was popularly known, moved to London in the early 1920s. He married at a comparatively young age but his wife's name is not known; they had seven children. In 1935 he became a British subject. Littman, who had no previous experience of the business, began his property career while he was working as the manager of Poppy's, a ladies' hat shop owned by his wife's family, at 248 High Road, Kilburn, London. From there he began to purchase property in Kilburn High Road, gradually assembling what was to become a massive property empire. He specialized in shop property, taking advantage of the 1930s' boom in high street retailing, a period in which the multiple chains rapidly displaced local traders.

Littman had negligible capital to fund his activities; his success was based on institutional finance. His property purchases were initially funded via a bank loan and he was later able to obtain mortgage finance from the Royal Liver Friendly Society. Littman's key innovation, however, was in pioneering one of the most important financial techniques used by property speculators, investors, and developers—the sale and leaseback arrangement. This involved his selling property to a financial institution which would simultaneously lease it back to him on a long (99- or 999-year) lease. He could then sub-let it to an occupier on a short lease and thus accrue the benefits from any future appreciation in market rents. Littman used this method, which became known in the trade as the 'Littman cocktail' to expand his business at a very rapid rate. A key advantage of sale and leaseback was that it did not require Littman to commit any of his own funds, and he was able to obtain financial backing from the Alliance Building Society and the Legal and General Insurance Company.

Littman initially acquired properties in Kilburn, later concentrating on the West End (particularly Oxford Street) as the scope of his activities expanded. Despite the fact that he concentrated on property investment rather than development he ranked as one of the most important property entrepreneurs of the 1930s, 1940s, and early 1950s. Littman is said to have sustained heavy losses during the Second World War, although his business activities made a strong recovery after 1945 and by the late 1940s his companies had a rent roll of £375,000 a year. However, from the late 1940s Littman suffered from ill health. He died of lung cancer on 21 August 1953 at the age of fifty-five, at the Palace Court Hotel, Bournemouth. He was survived by his wife. His estate was valued at over £3 million.

Peter Scott

Sources O. Marriott, *The property boom* (1967) · E. L. Erdman, *People and property* (1982) · B. P. Whitehouse, *Partners in property* (1964) · *The Times* (27 Aug 1953) · d. cert. · *CGPLA Eng. & Wales* (1953)
Wealth at death £3,264,167 6s. 5d.: administration, 21 Nov 1953, *CGPLA Eng. & Wales*

Litton, Edward Arthur (1813–1897), writer on theology, was born at 14 Holles Street, Dublin, on 12 August 1813 and was baptized privately by his uncle, the Revd John Letablère. He was the eldest of the eight children of Edward Litton (1787–1870) of Altmore, and his wife, Sophia (*née*

Stewart); his father was master of the Irish court of chancery (1843–70) and MP for Coleraine. Educated at Winchester College (1830–31) and expected to study for the bar, he was enrolled as a student of Gray's Inn in 1829; ten years later he transferred his membership to Lincoln's Inn, although by then his career had moved away from jurisprudence. He matriculated in April 1832 from Balliol College, Oxford, and in 1835 graduated BA with a double first. Noted for his exemplary conduct and for his Calvinistic views which were said, in a testimonial from Frederick Oakeley, his tutor at Balliol, to have undergone a change, he was in 1836 elected a fellow of Oriel College, Oxford. Having proceeded MA in 1840, he was granted the same degree at Durham in the following year. Ordained as a priest, he served until 1843 as a curate of St Ebbe's in Oxford. He then was dean of Oriel until the end of 1844, when he relinquished his fellowship because of his marriage a year earlier on 28 December 1843. His wife Anne (*d.* 1901) was the youngest daughter of the Revd William Carus Wilson of Casterton Hall, Westmorland, whose school at Cowan Bridge was attended by the Brontë sisters, and who is unfairly portrayed as Brocklehurst in *Jane Eyre*. In April 1844 Litton's sister Mary was married to his brother-in-law, William Carus Wilson junior. In 1850 Litton was described as the incumbent of Wilderspool, near Warrington, a living he had held since 1845.

Although, when a fellow of Oriel in 1842, Litton was described by A. H. Clough as 'exceedingly grave, silent and almost bashful' (*Correspondence*, 1.117), he had been aware of at least some of the developments in John Henry Newman's theological thinking. His rejection of the Tractarian emphasis on apostolic succession in his *The Church of Christ in its Idea, Attitudes and Ministry* (1851) marked Litton out as an evangelical leader at Oxford. It may also have contributed to his being chosen to succeed the evangelical John Hill as vice-principal of St Edmund Hall, Oxford, in 1851, but the Tractarian John Barrow was appointed principal in 1853 and Litton resigned in the following year.

With the institution in 1850 of a royal commission to investigate the state of the university at Oxford, Litton published a letter to Lord John Russell on university reform in 1851. When the subsequent Oxford University Act (1854) abolished the imposition of religious tests for members of the university and encouraged the establishment of private halls, licensed by the vice-chancellor, Litton was associated with the creation in 1855 of an evangelical hall at Oxford of which he was the master. However, Litton Hall never attracted many students and he closed it in 1860. The growing influence of liberalism in the university meant that his opposition to Tractarianism was something of an asset, and Litton was one of three evangelicals nominated during the 1850s to deliver the Bampton lectures, his subject being *The Mosaic Dispensation Considered as Introductory to Christianity* (1856). In the same year he was appointed an examining chaplain to the bishop of Durham—a position which he retained under successive bishops until 1870.

From 1858 to early 1861 Litton was rector of St Clement's in Oxford, Newman's old parish church, but in 1861 he left Oxford on his appointment as rector of Naunton in Gloucestershire. It was there that he wrote his *Introduction to Dogmatic Theology* (2 vols., 1882, 1892), a magisterial work, more Lutheran than Calvinist and greatly valued by twentieth-century evangelical Anglicans, who have republished it several times. Litton died on 27 August 1897 at Kingstown, near Dublin. TIMOTHY C. F. STUNT

Sources Boase, *Mod. Eng. biog.* • G. C. Richards and C. L. Shadwell, *The provosts and fellows of Oriel College, Oxford* (1922), 73 • J. S. Reynolds, *The evangelicals at Oxford, 1735–1871: a record of an unchronicled movement*, [2nd edn] (1975), pt 1., 127–8, 130, 175–6; pt 2., 29–30; 86–7 • C. W. Holgate, ed., *Winchester commoners, 1800–1835* (1893) • Burke, *Gen. GB* (1906) • Burke, *Gen. Ire.* (1904) • J. M. Ewbank, *Life and works of William Carus Wilson, 1791–1859* (1960) • *Correspondence of A. H. Clough*, ed. F. L. Mulhauser, 2 vols. (1957) • m. cert. • *Clergy List* (1850) • private information (2004) [archivist, Winchester School]
Archives Oriel College, Oxford, details of birth and parentage

Litton, Marie [*real name* Maria Lowe] (**1847–1884**), actress and theatre manager, was born of unknown parentage in Derbyshire. She made her first appearance on the stage in London, at the Princess's Theatre on 23 March 1868, as Effie Deans in a revised version by Boucicault of *The Trial of Effie Deans*, his adaptation from Scott's *The Heart of Midlothian*. It was a performance of much promise. On the opening of the Gaiety on 21 December 1868 she played Mrs Cureton in *On the Cards*, an adaptation by Alfred Thompson from *L'Escamoteur*. In December of the next year she understudied Lilian Adelaide Neilson in H. J. Byron's *Uncle Dick's Darling*, but was prevented by the recent birth of her baby from taking the leading role when Miss Neilson was incapacitated by a falling piece of scenery. (Her husband was William Wybrow Robertson.) She was later connected with the Brighton theatre.

On 25 January 1871 Marie Litton undertook the management of the Court Theatre in Sloane Square, London (designs by Walter Emden), and opened with *Randall's Thumb* by W. S. Gilbert. She retained the theatre until 13 March 1874 and put on very many plays; comments were made on the grace of manner of her acting. She took secondary roles in her own theatre and at the same time appeared at the Haymarket. By 24 April 1875 she was playing the original Caroline Effingham in Gilbert's *Tom Cobb* at the St James's, and from there went on to the Prince of Wales's. She then took the Royal Aquarium Theatre (renamed the Imperial) and, with a strong company, which included Samuel Phelps nearing the end of his career, began a series of revivals of 'old comedy', taking many leading roles, including Lady Teazle and Lydia Languish, herself. Her Miss Hardcastle played for 137 nights at the Imperial and her Rosalind for 100 nights at the same house before transferring to Drury Lane. There she acted with a distinguished cast which included Hermann Vezin, William Farren, and Sylvia Hodson; her Rosalind was much admired. In 1879 she managed the matinées at the Gaiety and was seen to even greater advantage as Peggy in a modification of Garrick's *The Country Girl*. She then went north to manage the new Theatre Royal in Glasgow, but by August 1881 was back at Drury Lane as Eve de Malvoisie in *Youth* by Paul Meritt and Augustus Harris. After this she played at the Globe and was the original Vere Herbert in

Henry Hamilton's adaptation of Ouida's novel *Moths*, in which role she gave an excellent interpretation.

However, signs of serious illness intervened and Marie Litton was compelled to quit the stage. She retired with her husband and two children to Ascot, where her health continued to fail. She died after a long illness at her town house, 6 Alfred Place, Thurloe Square, South Kensington, on 1 April 1884. JOSEPH KNIGHT, *rev.* J. GILLILAND

Sources *The life and reminiscences of E. L. Blanchard, with notes from the diary of Wm. Blanchard*, ed. C. W. Scott and C. Howard, 2 vols. (1891) · J. Hollingshead, *Gaiety chronicles* (1898) · W. M. Phelps, *The life and work of Samuel Phelps* (1886) · Boase, *Mod. Eng. biog.* · E. Stirling, *Old Drury Lane*, 2 vols. (1881) · D. Cook, *Nights at the play* (1883) · C. Scott, *The drama of yesterday and today*, 2 vols. (1899) · C. E. Pascoe, ed., *The dramatic list*, 2nd edn (1880) · A. Davies and E. Kilmurray, *Dictionary of British portraiture*, 4 vols. (1979–81) · Hall, *Dramatic ports.* · *The Era* (5 April 1884) · personal knowledge (1892) · *CGPLA Eng. & Wales* (1884)

Likenesses woodburytype photograph, *c.*1880, NPG · E. Matthews, lithograph, NPG; repro. in *The New Era* (8 June 1878) · photograph, Harvard TC · photograph, repro. in Hollingshead, *The Gaiety chronicles*, 117 · photograph, repro. in Scott, *The drama of yesterday and today*

Wealth at death £329 10*s.* 9*d.*: administration, 21 April 1884, *CGPLA Eng. & Wales*

Liulf. *See* Ligulf (*d.* 1080).

Liveing, George Downing (1827–1924), chemist and university administrator, was born on 21 December 1827 at Nayland, Suffolk, the eldest son of Edward Liveing, surgeon, and his wife, Catherine, the only daughter of George Downing, of Lincoln's Inn, barrister. He entered St John's College, Cambridge, in 1847, and graduated as eleventh wrangler in the 1850 mathematical tripos. The following year he read for the natural sciences tripos, the first year of its establishment, during which he studied line spectra under J. J. Griffin. He was the first of six successful candidates, with distinction in chemistry and mineralogy. Next he studied with A. W. Hofmann at the Royal College of Chemistry before working with Karl Rammelsberg at Berlin. In 1852 he returned to Cambridge where he started the first course of practical chemistry for medical students in a primitive laboratory fitted up, at his own expense, in a cottage in Corn Exchange Street.

Liveing was elected a fellow of St John's in 1853, and the college founded a lectureship in chemistry and built a laboratory for him. That he was an active and courageous junior fellow is clear from a pamphlet which he printed in 1857, attacking the existing system of government of the college and advocating measures of reform which foreshadow those put into effect many years later. He was a friend of many of the supporters of science education reform in Cambridge, including J. D. Hooker, with whom, according to W. J. Pope, he visited Charles Darwin to encourage him to hasten publication of *The Origin of Species* (1859).

On 14 August 1860 Liveing married Catherine, second daughter of Rowland Ingram, rector of Little Ellingham, Norfolk. They had no children and she died in 1888. By his marriage he vacated his fellowship at St John's, but retained his lectureship until 1865. In 1860 he also became

George Downing Liveing (1827–1924), by Olive Edis, 1923

professor of chemistry at the Staff College, Camberley, and at the Royal Military College, Sandhurst. In 1889 he returned to St John's as a professorial fellow; he was re-elected a fellow in 1908 and in 1911 became president, an office corresponding to that of vice-master.

Following the death in 1861 of James Cumming, professor of chemistry at Cambridge, Liveing, who had deputized for him since 1859, succeeded to the chair. The salary was about £100 a year (though this was later increased to £500), and the material provision made by the university for the subject was meagre, consisting of one lecture room, which Liveing had to share with the professor of botany and the Jacksonian professor of natural philosophy, and two small empty rooms which might be used for other purposes. In 1863, after much controversy, the university began building laboratories, thus initiating the development in experimental science which transformed Cambridge. The first buildings were raised on land which, acquired in 1762, had been used as a botanic garden. During 1864 and 1865 accommodation was provided successively for zoology, anatomy, chemistry, mineralogy, and botany. In 1865 Liveing began to give regular experimental courses in chemistry (and, until 1871, on heat) at the university laboratory.

In 1875 the chemist James Dewar was elected Jacksonian professor of experimental natural philosophy and came into close association with Liveing. C. T. Heycock wrote in 1925: 'Liveing and Dewar were men of widely different temperaments and widely different ideals, and they were both quick-tempered. Nevertheless, a close lifelong friendship was formed between them' (Heycock, *PRS*, xxvii). In 1878 they began a series of spectroscopic investigations which continued until 1900. Some of this work was undertaken to disprove some of Norman Lockyer's speculations concerning dissociation of elements in the sun. Their earlier work was concerned with the reversal of emission lines into dark absorption lines by which the chemical composition of the stars could be ascertained. After publishing in 1882 some work on the spectrum of carbon, in turn they studied ultraviolet spectra, sunspot spectra, the spectra of gaseous explosions, the effect of pressure on spectra, the spectra of liquefied gases, the absorption spectra of solutions, and, finally, the spectra at the anode and cathode when an electric discharge is passed through gases. Their seventy-eight joint papers were published as a single volume in 1915.

Liveing's only book was a thin volume entitled *Chemical Equilibrium the Result of the Dissipation of Energy*, which appeared in 1885. This early recognition of the importance of thermodynamics to chemistry clearly showed his insight into the fundamental principles of chemistry. He returned to this subject in his last paper, 'The recuperation of energy in the universe', read to the Cambridge Philosophical Society on 7 May 1923.

During the 1880s and early 1890s Liveing delivered lectures both to elementary and to advanced students. To the former he taught general chemistry and to the latter, principles of chemistry and spectroscopy. The rest of the teaching was shared among an increasing staff, both in the university laboratory and in several college laboratories. His elementary lectures were attended by men conspicuous more for light-heartedness than love of learning. The lectures were illustrated with experiments and his impatience with laboratory attendants when experiments went wrong was eagerly watched for by his youthful class. His advanced students found him somewhat difficult to approach, but when the approach was made he took great trouble and gave them individual attention. By 1885 the number of students and staff had made the university laboratory quite inadequate. In 1888 a new laboratory was begun in Pembroke Street which was expanded in the ensuing decades. Liveing took endless trouble over the plans, and the success of the building was largely due to his examination of other laboratories and careful studies of the whole problem. However, he continued, until his retirement, to maintain the laboratory out of his private means. Also in 1888 he arranged a course of lectures on agricultural chemistry, thus inaugurating what ultimately developed into the Cambridge school of agriculture. For many years that school owed much to Liveing's help and support.

Elected a fellow of the Chemical Society in 1853, Liveing was vice-president in 1883–6 and 1898–1901. In 1882 he was president of the chemical section of the British Association. He was elected a fellow of the Royal Society in 1879, and served on its council in 1891–2 and 1903–4. He was awarded the society's Davy medal in 1901. In 1904 he played a leading role in the society's radium investigation advisory committee.

For many years Liveing acted as the Cambridge correspondent of the dukes of Devonshire as chancellors of the university. He took a prominent part in revising the statutes of the university in the early 1880s. In 1896 he was appointed, together with Herbert Warren, to inspect the university colleges in Britain. He also took part in local affairs, working as a county and borough magistrate, and was a member of the rifle corps.

Liveing retired from the professorship of chemistry in 1908 and was given the degree of ScD. He continued to live a busy life between his house and garden at The Pightle, Newnham, the laboratory, and St John's College. He remained to the end of his life in touch with research, working, in the last years of his life, on the absorption of radiant energy by dense substances. His memories of days long past were of historic interest, both to chemists and to other members of the university. In 1923 he gave up his house at Newnham, and, after a short stay at the University Arms Hotel, moved to 10 Maid's Causeway. On 11 October 1924, while walking to the laboratory, he was knocked down by a bicyclist and on 26 December he died at home of his injuries. He was buried at Cambridge on 31 December. W. C. D. DAMPIER, *rev.* FRANK A. J. L. JAMES

Sources W. J. Pope, *Nature*, 115 (1925), 127–9 · *The Times* (27 Dec 1925) · G. K. Roberts, 'The liberally-educated chemist: chemistry in the Cambridge natural sciences tripos', *Historical Studies in the Physical Sciences*, 11 (1980–81), 157–83 · C. T. H. [C. T. Heycock], *PRS*, 109A (1925), xxvii–xxix · Venn, *Alum. Cant.* · W. McGucken, *Nineteenth-century spectroscopy: development of the understanding of spectra, 1802–1897* (1969) · C. T. Heycock, *JCS*, 127 (1925), 2982–4 · *CGPLA Eng. & Wales* (1925)

Archives RS, collections | Air Force Research Laboratories, Cambridge, Massachusetts, Strutt MSS · CUL, letters to Sir George Stokes · King's AC Cam., letters to Oscar Browning · Royal Institution of Great Britain, London, Dewar MSS

Likenesses E. Bateson, bronze bust, 1901–2, U. Cam., department of organic and inorganic chemistry · O. Edis, photographs, 1923, priv. coll. [*see illus.*] · G. Reid, oils, St John Cam. · two photographs, RS

Wealth at death £19,908 12*s.* 2*d.*: resworn probate, 30 April 1925, *CGPLA Eng. & Wales*

Lively, Edward (*c.*1545–1605), Hebraist, was a scholar and later fellow of Trinity College, Cambridge, whence he graduated BA in 1569 and MA in 1572. He was taught Hebrew by the eminent John Drusius, a former student of the trilingual college at Louvain and one of several religious refugees who promoted the study of Semitics in sixteenth-century England. He succeeded Thomas Wakefield as regius professor of Hebrew in 1575, but resigned from his college fellowship when he married Katherine Lorkin on 14 June 1578, with whom he had eleven children. In 1602 he was collated to a prebend of Peterborough, and in 1604 he was presented by the king to the living of Purleigh. He was among the learned men appointed by James I to be responsible for the Authorized Version of the Bible, but died before the work got under way. He was buried at St Edward's, Cambridge, on 7 May 1605; his wife predeceased him, dying on 8 April 1599.

In the course of a distinguished career Lively proved to be a competent teacher and an able scholar. The letters which passed between James Ussher, later archbishop of

Armagh, and his friends early in the seventeenth century testify to the respect in which he was held as a Hebraist by biblical scholars of his own day. His funeral oration, delivered by Thomas Playfere, Lady Margaret professor of divinity at Cambridge, demonstrates how successfully he had communicated his love of Semitics, and in particular his interest in and appreciation of rabbinic literature, to his contemporaries. Referring to Hebrew, Playfere says:

> Which tongue, howsoever some account of it, yet ought to be preferred above all the rest. For it is the ancientest, the shortest, the plainest of all … The rabbis themselves, though they have no small number of fables and lies in them, yet diverse things they have notwithstanding fit for the opening of the Old Testament. Therefore though a man cannot read the rabbis, yet unless he can understand handsomely well the Hebrew text, he is counted but a maimed, or as it were half a divine, especially in this learned age. (Playfere, 1.57)

Although three of Lively's works are extant in manuscript, as far as is known he is the author of only two books. The first was a series of notes on five of the minor prophets, originally published in London in 1587 and later printed in Pearson's *Critici sacri* of 1660. The second was his commentary on the seventy weeks mentioned in Daniel 9: 24–7, that 'dismal swamp of Old Testament criticism' which engendered fierce debate among sixteenth-century theologians. Entitled *A true chronologie of the times of the Persian monarchy and after to the destruction of Jerusalem by the Romans* (1597), the book runs to 250 octavo pages, and offers ample evidence of the author's breadth of scholarship and of his attitude towards the Hebraic tradition of exegesis. As the title-page states, his intention is to expound 'the Angel Gabriel's message to Daniel … against the frivolous conceits of Matthew Beroald', a French protestant; but after refuting other opinions, he presents a well-ordered and logical case for his own understanding of the passage. His exegetical principles, on which he expands in a lengthy introduction, are twofold: 'the one is a just account of the times; the other, a true interpretation of the words in the original tongue'. If the commentator fails in either of these, 'there is no hope to know what Daniel meant by his weeks' (*A True Chronologie*, 27). In his search for the true interpretation he has constant recourse to the 'judgment of cunning linguists and sound divines' (ibid., 44). The result is that the comments of classical authors, church fathers, and Jewish exegetes are harnessed to the task of biblical interpretation.

It is this blending of three quite distinct sources in his exposition of the text that renders Lively's scholarship exceptional for the age in which he lived. Classical learning, in which he himself was steeped, is recommended to all those aspiring to understand scripture. He stresses the contribution made by such non-Christian writers as Pliny, Horace, Homer, and Herodotus, to the understanding of the Bible: 'For many parts of Scripture they are diligently to be sought unto, and not as some rash brains imagine, to be cast away as unprofitable in the Lord's schoolhouse; but especially for Daniel above all' (*A True Chronologie*, 22). It was this reliance on classical texts for help in difficult places that displeased Richard Simon and led him to criticize Lively for parading his learning and 'adorning his discourse with unnecessary authorities' (Simon, 3.110). Simon represents a later generation of biblical scholars who rarely illustrated any points by referring to classical authors, and certainly did not accept them as authoritative. But in Lively's opinion these 'profane writers' were important sources for the illumination of the word of God.

The second source of information was the church fathers, who should be respected by the exegete because they had the weight of tradition. Jerome, Eusebius, Theodoret, and Tertullian feature prominently throughout the exposition of the seventy weeks. Clement of Alexandria should be a constant source of reference because of his great knowledge, while Sulpicius Severus's comments on Daniel are invaluable because they are more illuminating than those of any other ancient writer.

Lively's third and constant court of appeal as he wrestles with the angel Gabriel's message is the work of post-biblical Jewish exegetes, lexicographers, grammarians, and historians. As well as Targum and Talmud, and the principal commentators of the late middle ages, he makes use of two significant lexicographical works, David Kimchi's *Book of Roots* and the *Tisbi* of Elias Levita. On matters related to Jewish history and chronology he introduces us to two sources not previously used by Christians: Abraham ibn Daud's *Book of Tradition*, a survey of Jewish history from 300 BCE to 1100 CE, and the *Seder Òlam*, a history of the Jews from Adam to Bar Kochba written in the second century CE. A notable omission in Lively's list of Jewish authors is Isaac Abravanel, one of medieval Jewry's most illustrious sons, whose commentary on Daniel (*The Wells of Salvation*) was published in 1497 and again in 1551. In the whole of *A True Chronologie* there is not one explicit reference to it. This is all the more surprising when we remember the interest which Abravanel's writings generated among Christians. In all probability he is omitted from the list of rabbinic sources because of his spirited defence of Judaism and his refutation of the Christian interpretation of crucial passages. On the whole, however, Lively is favourably disposed towards post-biblical Jewish works, and states categorically that they are of value for the Christian biblical scholar: 'The Church of God … is much beholding to the Hebrew rabbis, being great helps unto us for understanding holy scripture in many places, as well of the New Testament as the Old' (*A True Chronologie*, 35).

By his linguistic expertise and his appreciation of rabbinic sources, Cambridge's second regius professor of Hebrew played a leading role in furthering Hebrew studies in Elizabethan England. Lively's only major published work reflects controversies about the interpretation of scripture current in the sixteenth century. In defence of his views he made extensive use of post-biblical Jewish sources, and on the whole adopted an unbiased attitude towards the Jews. G. LLOYD JONES

Sources E. I. J. Rosenthal, 'Edward Lively: Cambridge Hebraist', *Essays and studies presented to Stanley Arthur Cook*, ed. D. W. Thomas

(1950), 95–112 • Cooper, *Ath. Cantab.*, 2.407ff. • T. Playfere, *Collection of tracts*, 1 (1609), 57 • C. Anderson, *Annals of the English Bible*, 2 (1845), 375 • G. Lloyd Jones, *The discovery of Hebrew in Tudor England: a third language* (1983), 195–9, 205, 269–70 • R. Simon, *A critical history of the Old Testament*, trans. H. D. [H. Dickinson] (1682), 3.110 [Fr. orig. *Histoire critique du Vieux Testament*]
Archives CUL, papers

Lively, John Frederick [Jack] (**1930–1998**), political scientist, was born on 15 June 1930 at the Princess Mary Maternity Hospital, Newcastle upon Tyne, the son of James William Lively (*d.* *c.*1973), a clerical worker, and his wife, Gladys, *née* Peel (*d.* *c.*1990). He was a working-class boy whose rise up the educational ladder began when he won a scholarship to the Royal Grammar School, Newcastle. From there he went, after national service, to St John's College, Cambridge, to read history (1950–53), gaining a first in both parts of the tripos. He was then awarded a research fellowship at St Antony's College, Oxford (1956–8). At Oxford he met and on 27 June 1957 married Penelope Margaret Low (*b.* 1933), a writer (as Penelope Lively), and daughter of Roger Low. They had two children, Josephine, who became a professional oboist, and Adam, who became a writer and with his father edited *Democracy in Britain: a Reader* (1994) for the British Council.

From 1958 to 1962 Jack Lively was a lecturer in political theory and government at University College, Swansea. He was lecturer in politics at the University of Sussex from 1962 to 1965. In 1965 he moved to St Peter's College, Oxford, as fellow and tutor in politics. He stayed there until his appointment as professor of politics at the University of Warwick in 1975. He retired in 1989.

Lively was an intellectual descendant of the liberal Enlightenment. In his influential edited collection, *The Enlightenment* (1966), he cited a definition of 'enlightened' from the *Oxford English Dictionary*: 'Possessed of mental light; instructed, well-informed; free from superstition and prejudice'. This perfectly captured Lively himself. What he admired in the Enlightenment was its preference for the systematic spirit over the spirit of system. This also implied that he inherited the sceptical aspects of the Enlightenment rather than its certainties.

It is perhaps indicative of Lively's commitment to Enlightenment values of objectivity as he perceived them that he should devote so much of his scholarly production to two major critics of the Enlightenment. The substantial introductory essay to his translation and selection, *The Works of Joseph de Maistre* (1965), offered a remarkably sympathetic understanding of an author with whom he must have had little political affinity. In *The Social and Political Thought of Alexis de Tocqueville* (1962) Lively examined a writer with a more complex attitude to the Enlightenment. While he acknowledged Tocqueville's scepticism towards Enlightenment rationalism, he also stressed his uncommitted, critical disposition which made him an outstanding political observer. The leitmotif of Lively's study is Tocqueville's role as a liberal who saw no necessary contradiction between negative liberty and political participation. His attack on apathy as the breeding ground of despotism, his belief in the moralizing value of the act of participation, his advocacy of decentralization as a means of promoting activism—all these resonated with Lively's own views on liberalism, democracy, and the fundamental importance of politics itself.

The form of democratic participation was also the underlying theme of the magisterial and balanced introduction which Lively co-wrote with John Rees to an edition of James Mill's *Essay on Government* along with Macaulay's critique, published as *Utilitarian Logic and Politics* (1978). All these elements in Lively's work came together in his most widely read book, *Democracy* (1975), in which he identified the most significant ends that democracy might promote as the general interest, the common good, liberty, and participation. In retrospect these can be seen as the values Lively sought to explore and explain throughout his work.

Lively had the strongest sense for the academic vocation and for the values of intellectual autonomy which, he feared, were under threat in the conditions of modern British universities. He was a formidable debater at academic seminars. As a teacher he ranged widely, reflecting an education and training before the era of academic specialization. This breadth made him an appropriate editor of *Political Studies*, the journal of the Political Studies Association of the United Kingdom, from 1982 to 1988. His sense of academic citizenship led him to take on a major role as external examiner, in adult education and as a head of department. He set an example of the enduring values of the academy in his work and his life. His marriage to Penelope was extremely happy and he watched with pride her own growing international celebrity as a novelist, including her winning the Booker prize for *Moon Tiger* in 1987. During his time at Warwick and up to his death his principal residence was Duck End, Great Rollright, Oxfordshire, where he and Penelope developed a fine garden. He died on 27 October 1998 of carcinoma of the oesophagus at Edenhall Nursing Home, 11 Lyndhurst Gardens, Camden, London, and was cremated at St Marylebone crematorium on 4 November 1998. He was survived by his wife and their two children.

GERAINT PARRY

Sources *The Independent* (30 Oct 1998) • *St Peter's College Record* (2000) • *St Antony's College Journal* (1999) • records, St John Cam. • records, U. Sussex • private information (2004) [P. Lively, widow] • personal knowledge (2004) • b. cert. • m. cert. • d. cert.
Likenesses photograph, priv. coll.; repro. in *The Independent*
Wealth at death £719,239—gross; £716,519—net: probate, 15 Feb 1999, *CGPLA Eng. & Wales*

Livens, William Howard (**1889–1964**), army officer and inventor of oil and gas weapons, was born at Lincoln on 28 March 1889, the only son of Frederick Howard Livens, chief engineer of the firm which became Ruston and Hornsby, and his wife, Priscilla Mary Abbott. He was educated at Oundle School and Christ's College, Cambridge, where he took the natural sciences tripos and graduated in 1911. He was an outstanding games player and rifle shot and was a member of the English shooting eight in 1910. Writing was another of his interests, and on going down from Cambridge he worked for *Country Life*.

Livens was commissioned in the Royal Engineers in September 1914. After a spell as brigade signals officer he went to Chatham where he was in charge of motorcyclists. It was here in the spring of 1915, after the first German gas attack on the western front that, on his own initiative, he began to experiment with weapons for trench warfare. Soon he was asked to select recruits for the special companies of the Royal Engineers, then being formed in France by Colonel C. H. Foulkes for the purpose of retaliating with gas. He himself later went to France and became one of the company commanders.

Gas was at that time discharged by cylinders and metal piping and blown by the wind in the direction of the enemy. Livens appreciated that this system was too cumbrous and vulnerable. With the help of his father he substituted garden hose for the unwieldy pipes; it withstood both the chemical action of the gas and the pressure to which it might be subjected; and he designed simple connections instead of the metal joints which, if they leaked, incapacitated the operators. After an encouraging trial of this equipment at Loos in September 1915 Livens was sent to England to get more apparatus made as quickly as possible. When ready, he commissioned a Pullman coach for the rail journey to France. At Boulogne he persuaded the quartermaster-general to send twenty lorries to collect the equipment. On 13 October the new appliances were used effectively against the Hohenzollern redoubt covering the mining villages north of Loos.

Meanwhile the Germans had begun to use portable flamethrowers. Livens, who had already designed his own version at Chatham, took charge of a special flamethrower company and developed a model which was simple to produce and easy to handle. As it only had a limited range it had to be installed as far forward as possible. As an alternative Livens hit on the idea of using oil drums as mortars, digging them into the ground just behind the forward trenches. Lubricating oil cans served as bombs being fired by a small powder charge. Although of crude construction, the mortars had twice the range of their German counterparts and, when fired in salvos, saturated a wide area with pools of burning oil. They were used successfully during the battle of the Somme and were made safe to operate by the introduction of a simple time fuse.

Reinforcing the drums with steel and devising improved fuses enabled Livens to experiment with gas-filled bombs which, when concentrated against a target area, would be far more deadly than gas clouds blown by the wind. Moreover, the factor of surprise would be introduced. Livens found a quantity of waste steel tubing which was made up into 8 inch projectors. Their range was just under a mile. The projector and bomb charged with lethal phosgene gas were first used at Beaumont Hamel on 13 November 1916 against a system of deep dugouts. The gas saturated the enemy shelters, inflicting many casualties and showing what could be done by firing salvos. Increased production of the new weapon made a much larger operation possible at Vimy Ridge on 4 April 1917. Livens observed from an aircraft 2000 detonated electrically and saw the gas travel 7 kilometres behind the German front line.

Projectors became the principal allied gas weapon until the introduction of longer ranged shells charged with mustard and phosgene gas. They were greatly feared by the Germans who, in due course, made more accurate copies of Livens's invention with a longer range but only capable of discharging half the weight of gas. They had failed to grasp the fundamental and important principle of quantity.

Livens later became a member of the trench warfare committee in the Ministry of Munitions. In that capacity he continued to improve his projector and design other weapons for trench warfare, some of which were useful, others not; but he was never put off if a weapon failed to come up to expectation. He was awarded the MC, appointed to the DSO, and mentioned in dispatches.

Livens's career after the First World War was uneventful. Having independent means, he no longer had any incentive to produce new inventions. In 1916 he had married Elizabeth Price (1886/7–1934); they had three daughters. He returned to work on gas projects in the Ministry of Supply in September 1939. But the advent of airborne gas weapons enabled either side to retaliate instantly and gas warfare was never resorted to in the Second World War.

Livens died in the General Hospital, Hampstead, London, on 1 February 1964, and was survived by his three daughters. GUY HARTCUP

Sources PRO, WO 188/143, R8/A • PRO, T 173/330 • PRO, T 173/702, RCA 1 • L. F. Haber, *The poisonous cloud: chemical warfare in the First World War* (1986) • C. H. Foulkes, *'Gas!' The story of the special brigade* (1934) • H. Hartley, 'Historical sketch of gas warfare by Germany', CAC Cam., Hartley MSS, 261 Hart, Box 34 • G. Hartcup, *The war of invention: scientific developments, 1914–18* (1988) • *DNB* • *The Times* (5 Feb 1964) • *The Times* (6 Feb 1964) • *The Times* (11 Feb 1964) • *CGPLA Eng. & Wales* (1964) • m. cert.

Archives PRO, awards to inventors, T 173/330 | CAC Cam., Sir Harold Hartley MSS

Likenesses H. Kidman, oils, priv. coll. • A. G. Walker, oils, priv. coll.

Wealth at death £82,561: probate, 19 June 1964, *CGPLA Eng. & Wales*

Livermore, Samuel (1732–1803), judge and politician in the United States of America, was born on 25 May 1732 in Waltham, Massachusetts, the third son and fourth child of Samuel Livermore, a farmer and local politician, and his wife, Hannah, the daughter of Deacon William Brown of Waltham. All that is known of his early education is that he was teaching in Chelsea, Massachusetts, at the age of eighteen, and that in 1751 he entered the College of New Jersey, where he took his degree one year later. Livermore returned to Massachusetts and studied law under Edmund Trowbridge, and in 1756 was admitted to the bar.

In 1757 Samuel Livermore moved to Portsmouth, New Hampshire, and mingled with the leading families of the area, including the Wentworths. Two years later on 23 September 1759 he married Jane, the daughter of the Revd Arthur Browne, a Church of England clergyman. They had five children. After developing his reputation as an aggressive but most competent lawyer, Livermore was elected in 1768 to represent the township of Londonderry in the New Hampshire general assembly, but was recalled to Portsmouth and in 1769 was appointed by Governor John Wentworth as judge-advocate in the admiralty court and attorney-general. In 1774 he returned to Londonderry, and a year later moved further north into Holderness, where he maintained his main residence until his death. He established himself as the primary landholder in Holderness, building a large estate, farm, and church.

In 1776, after the outbreak of the American War of Independence, Samuel Livermore was re-elected as attorney-general; he was formally appointed in 1778. In 1779 he was elected by the general court to act as commissioner to the continental congress to represent New Hampshire in its dispute with New York over territory that was to become Vermont. The general court also appointed him five times to serve as a New Hampshire representative to the continental congress. He also was present and active at the 1779 and 1791 state constitutional conventions, presiding over the latter. In 1789 and 1791 he was chosen and elected to serve as a New Hampshire representative to the United States congress, and he was appointed in 1793 and again in 1799 as a US senator. As a member of the New Hampshire convention to ratify the US constitution in 1788, Livermore did much to bring about a positive vote. Because New Hampshire was the ninth state to do so, its vote assured final ratification. While holding federal positions, Samuel Livermore also held state offices, the most important of those being chief justice of the superior court (1782–90).

Throughout the twenty-five years of Samuel Livermore's life as a leading early US national political figure and state politician, he maintained a balanced view of the relationship between centralized federal government and a belief in the rights of states. He was much respected for his judiciousness and practical even-handedness, and thus abstained from lending active support to either the federalist or anti-federalist (early republican) political parties. Before he retired in 1801 from the senate, his colleagues in the senate had chosen him as their president *pro tempore* in 1797 and 1799. After retiring, Livermore spent two years at home in Holderness before dying there, much respected by his many friends and close family, on 18 May 1803. He was buried in the cemetery at Holderness's Trinity Church. MURNEY GERLACH

Sources E. V. Moffett, 'Livermore, Samuel', *DAB* • J. R. Daniell, 'Livermore, Samuel', *ANB* • C. R. Coming, *Address before the Grafton and Coos Bar Association* (1888) • C. H. Bell, *Bench and bar of New Hampshire* (1894), 34–8 • F. M. Colby, 'Holderness and the Livermore', *Granite Monthly*, 4 (Feb 1881), 175–81 • G. Hodges, *Holderness: an account of the beginnings of a New Hampshire town* (1907) • N. Bouton and others, eds., *Provincial and state papers: documents and records relating to the province of New Hampshire*, 40 vols. (1867–1943), vols. 7–8, 10–12 • E. Bennett, ed., *Letters of the members of the continental congress*, 5–8 (1931–6) • J. R. Daniell, *Experiment in republicanism: New Hampshire politics and the American Revolution* (1970) • L. W. Turner, *The ninth state: New Hampshire's formative years* (1983) • J. R. Daniell, 'Frontier and constitution: why Grafton county delegates voted 10–1 for ratification', *Historical New Hampshire*, 45/3 (autumn 1990), 207–29

Archives New Hampshire Historical Society, Concord, family papers and other collections

Likenesses J. Trumbull, oils, State Library, Concord, New Hampshire

Liverpool. For this title name *see* Jenkinson, Charles, first earl of Liverpool (1729–1808); Jenkinson, Robert Banks, second earl of Liverpool (1770–1828); Jenkinson, Charles Cecil Cope, third earl of Liverpool (1784–1851).

Liverseege, Henry (1803–1832), painter, was born on 4 September 1803 at Manchester, where his father was employed in a cotton mill; he had at least one sister. Neglected by his father, he owed his early education to his uncle, Mr Green, a wealthy mill owner who encouraged him to pursue the profession of artist, for which he showed an early inclination at school. He was initially self-taught, copying in order to learn. His earliest attempts at painting were in portraiture, for which he received instruction from Mr Knowles; these included miniatures, silhouettes, and inn signs, but he soon devoted himself to genre painting including subjects from works by Sir Walter Scott, Shakespeare, and Cervantes. He also excelled as an amateur actor. Liverseege exhibited three small pictures of 'Banditti' at the Royal Manchester Institution in 1827 which attracted attention, and at the end of that year he went to London to study at the British Museum, and also to copy the works of old masters at the British Institution. He visited Thomas Lawrence's collection of paintings and Lawrence offered him an introductory letter to the Royal Academy. Through some informality in his application he failed to gain admission and returned to Manchester in 1828 where he resumed portrait painting. He visited London again in 1829, but in 1830 returned to Manchester, where his mother died early the next year. He paid one more visit to London, where the duke of Devonshire purchased his *Sir Piercie Shafton and Mysie Happer* (exh. RA, 1831; Chatsworth, Derbyshire). In four years he exhibited eighteen works in London, between the Royal Academy, British Institution, and Suffolk Street. He also showed works in exhibition at Birmingham, Liverpool, Leeds, and Norwich.

Liverseege was considered to be a painter of some promise. His *The Recruit* (exh. RA, 1832; Whitworth Art Gallery, Manchester) shows the influence, in both subject and treatment, of works by Sir David Wilkie. His works were published in mezzotint in twelve parts under the title *Recollections of Liverseege* (1832–5) and a set of thirty-five mezzotint engravings from his pictures was published in 1875, with a portrait engraved from a painting by his friend William Bradley. Many of his works are now in Manchester City Galleries.

Liverseege suffered throughout his life from a collapsed lung and as a result was often tired and melancholic. After he returned to Manchester in 1831 his health broke down completely, and he died of a lung disease on 13 January 1832; he was buried on 19 January in St Luke's churchyard,

Manchester. He was unmarried. Liverseege was 5 feet tall, slightly built, with deformed shoulders and a pale complexion. L. H. CUST, *rev.* L. R. HOULISTON

Sources C. Swain, *Memoir of Henry Liverseege* (1835) · A. Cunningham, *The lives of the most eminent British painters*, rev. Mrs C. Heaton, 3 (1880) · R. Edwards, 'The pictures of Henry Liverseege (1803–1832)', *Apollo*, 20 (1934), 25–8 · Bryan, *Painters* · J. Turner, ed., *The dictionary of art*, 34 vols. (1996) · T. Fawcett, *The rise of English provincial art: artist, patron and institution outside London, 1800–1830* (1974) · Redgrave, *Artists* · M. Arnold, *Library of the Fine Arts*, 3 (1832) · D. Child, *Painters in the northern counties of England and Wales* (1994) · *Concise catalogue of British paintings*, Man. City Gall., 1 (1976) · G. Richardson, *Works of Henry Liverseege with a memoir* (1875) · Graves, *RA exhibitors*

Likenesses W. Bradley, charcoal sketch, 1832, BM · W. Bradley, oils, 1832?, Royal Museum and Art Galleries, Salford · Parry, stipple, 1832 (after C. Hawthorn), BM, NPG; repro. in *Library of the Fine Arts* (1832) · J. Stephens, bust, 1832, repro. in J. Johnson, *R.B.A. Exhibition Catalogue, 1826–1893* (1975) · W. Bradley, mezzotint, pubd 1835 (after H. Cousins), BM, NPG · H. Cousins, mezzotint (after W. Bradley), BM, NPG; repro. in G. Richardson, *Works* · H. Liverseege, oils?, priv. coll.; Christies, 12 Nov 1948, lot 50

Liversidge, Archibald (1846–1927), chemist and promoter of science in Australia, was born on 17 November 1846, at Turnham Green, Middlesex, the fourth son and eighth of nine children of John Liversidge (1810–1887), wheelwright and coachbuilder, and his wife, Caroline Sophia Jarratt (1813–1865), of Sussex. Ever moving to be near the highway traffic of London, the family finally settled in Hackney, where the elder brothers prospered in small business, light engineering, and commerce. As the youngest son, and thus freed from the family business, Liversidge was privately educated. He soon acquired the contemporary fascination for natural history. In the tradition of the Microscopical and Natural History Society of Hackney, 'habitual observation' became his motto. An enquiring mind led him from classes at the Anglican-inspired City of London College in Leadenhall Street (a precursor of the City University) to the popular lectures of the Royal Polytechnic Institution. In 1867 he won a royal exhibition to the Royal School of Mines (RSM) and Royal College of Chemistry; his teachers there included Edward Frankland, T. H. Huxley, and Warrington Smyth.

In 1868 Liversidge became an assistant in Frankland's laboratory, where he learned analytical methods, taught chemistry at the Royal School of Naval Architecture and published his first scientific note (*Chemical News*, 17, 1868, 49). Encouraged by the example of Frankland and Smyth, he showed equal proficiency in microscopy, spectroscopy, mineralogy, and mineral analysis. In 1870, with several analytical papers to his credit, he was awarded the associateship of the RSM; he was also among the first to win a Bunting exhibition (of £50) created by Christ's College, Cambridge, for men reading for the natural sciences tripos.

Liversidge matriculated at Christ's in 1870 and was soon enlisted as a temporary demonstrator in chemistry. He started the Cambridge University Natural Sciences Club, and published papers in physiological biochemistry. His interests remained eclectic. In 1873, during his third undergraduate year but before he could take the tripos, he was appointed as reader in geology and assistant in the chemical laboratory at the University of Sydney—a preferment secured by the patronage of the RSM.

Archibald Liversidge (1846–1927), by Maull & Fox

At Sydney, Liversidge was one of only four teaching staff. He had an ill-equipped laboratory and museum that occupied two rooms in a splendid neo-Gothic building, on a hill overlooking the commercial city, where fifteen students toiled for a BA degree that included experimental science. His challenge was to create a scientific metropolis at the periphery. Within a year he issued a manifesto calling for a school of science, and welcomed the introduction of secondary science as a university matriculation subject. In 1874 he became professor of geology and mineralogy; in 1882 geology was separated, and he became professor of mineralogy and chemistry. From the university, his influence radiated in all directions.

In addition to teaching undergraduates, Liversidge was a 'public scientist', a participant in the transit of Venus observations, a leading analyst of water supply and fossil remains, a consultant to the mines department, and a trustee of the Australian Museum. He was also joint honorary secretary of the Royal Society of New South Wales, which he virtually re-established, and served three times as its president (in 1886, 1890, and 1901); he edited its *Journal and Proceedings* from 1874 to 1885. In 1878 he helped represent New South Wales at the Paris Universal Exhibition, and produced a report on European museums and technical schools that guided colonial policy for the next fifty years. The following year he was a guiding force behind the international exhibition (the 'Garden Palace') in Sydney. The same year Sydney University followed London in creating a faculty of science, and Liversidge was its first (and almost perpetual) dean between 1880 and 1907. From the late 1870s he helped establish science at the new University of Adelaide, and frequently exercised his patronage in the appointment of chemists to government departments and museums in New South Wales. In the mid-1880s, as the colony approached the centenary of European settlement, he turned to the improvement of intercolonial scientific co-operation. Building upon visits to New Zealand, and professional friendships with Victorians, Queenslanders, and South Australians, he launched at Sydney in 1888 the Australasian Association for the Advancement of Science (later ANZAAS). He was its honorary secretary until 1907, and president at its second Sydney congress in 1898.

A bachelor, Liversidge lived for his friends and his work. He was a member of five clubs in London and Sydney and, until he moved to a generous house with sweeping gardens on salubrious Darling Point, a resident of the Union Club. By 1921, he had published over 120 scientific papers, and 22 colonial government reports, plus 16 other notes and articles. He was best known overseas for his studies of the geochemistry of gold, and was among the first to detect rare minerals in meteorites. In 1894 he helped establish the School of Mines at Sydney University. A devoted empirical analyst, he personified the 'inventory sciences' and refrained from speculation on contemporary theories of the earth. He published a chemical 'audit', *The Minerals of New South Wales* (1876), which was enlarged in 1882 and 1888.

Liversidge attracted few research students, but did count Douglas Mawson (1882–1968) among them. He belonged to twenty-six learned societies in Britain, Australasia, and the United States, but considered his election to the Royal Society in 1882 as the most important honour of his life. An avid collector of minerals and artefacts, Liversidge exhibited at several intercolonial and international exhibitions. He presented specimens of Australian minerals to a number of museums in the northern hemisphere; his own crystal collection went to the Australian Museum.

Liversidge promoted degrees for women, and compulsory European languages, in lieu of the classics, for all undergraduates. Among his achievements was the appointment of T. W. Edgeworth David to Sydney's chair of geology in 1891. A dedicated empire man, Liversidge repeatedly sought ways to bring the ethos of South Kensington to Sydney. As a member of the board of technical education and trustee of the Museum of Applied Arts and Sciences (later the Powerhouse Museum), he advocated technical training, the metric system, and the industrial application of science, along lines he had seen argued in England. Thus he encouraged Sydney pupils to take the City and Guilds examinations, and founded in Sydney a section of the (UK) Society of Chemical Industry. He also helped form the New South Wales branch of the British Science Guild in 1907. In 1896, on the occasion of Kelvin's jubilee, Glasgow University awarded him an honorary LLD. Liversidge also contributed to colonial nationalism—he promoted the idea of an Australasian equivalent of *Nature* and an Australian Academy of Science half a century before either was realized.

Liversidge retired, exhausted, from Sydney in 1907. He returned to England to live in some state at Fieldhead, Kingston Hill, Surrey, where he kept three domestic staff, and entertained visiting colleagues, nephews, and nieces. For the next twenty years he enjoyed a second career as a visiting researcher in the Davy–Faraday Laboratory of the Royal Institution. Liversidge never returned to Australia, despite advocating the first (and only) Australian visit of the British Association in 1914, but between 1910 and 1917, as vice-president of the Chemical Society, and as a member of the overseas branch committee of the Institute of Chemistry, he was active in promoting the cause of colonial scientists. During the First World War his advice was sought by the Admiralty on magnesium alloys used in German airships. For the British Science Guild he drafted recommendations for post-war government funding of science in the British universities. Peace brought a renewal of his private research at the Royal Institution where, as a mineralogist and crystallographer, he shared in the general fascination with the new technology of X-ray diffraction. He died, unmarried, of a heart attack, in his sleep, at home in Kingston on 26 September 1927, and was buried the following day at Putney Vale cemetery.

Internationally known by entries in ten biographical directories, Liversidge received twenty-one obituary notices and several retrospective tributes. His will specified legacies of £500 to the Chemical Society, the Royal Society of New South Wales, and the AAAS, and to the chemistry department of the University of Sydney; and £500 to Christ's College, Cambridge, for a 'Lecturer alternately in chemistry and on the English language' with special reference to 'possible improvements in its grammar and spelling'. A portrait, by John Collier RA, was completed after Liversidge returned to England, and hangs in the Great Hall of Sydney University. Striking a pose similar to that of T. H. Huxley in Collier's famous painting, Liversidge is shown in academic dress, lecturing on the processes of reducing gold from its ores—an image by which generations would remember him, long after his scientific statesmanship was forgotten. ROY M. MACLEOD

Sources Liversidge MSS, University of Sydney Archives · Archives of the Royal Society of New South Wales · Archives of the Australian Museum, Sydney · ICL, Archives of the Royal School of Mines · private information (2004)

Archives Archives of the Royal Society of New South Wales, Sydney, lecture notes · University of Sydney, archives, corresp. and papers | Mitchell L., NSW, corresp. with W. B. Clarke

Likenesses J. Collier, oils, 1910, University of Sydney · Maull & Fox, photograph, NPG [*see illus.*]

Wealth at death £46,128 6*s*. 7*d*.: probate, 30 Nov 1927, *CGPLA Eng. & Wales*

Livesay [Livesey], **Sir Michael, first baronet** (**1614–1665?**), politician and regicide, was the only surviving son of Gabriel Livesay (*d*. 1622) of Hollingborne, Kent, and his second wife, Anne, daughter of Sir Michael Sondes, of Throwley.

Although often portrayed as an upstart family, the Livesays were in fact established members of the gentry. Sir Michael's grandfather had been sheriff of Surrey, and although his father was the first member of the family to settle in Kent he soon established himself as a figure of influence in the community, and served as sheriff in 1618. Their status was reflected in the baronetcy granted to Michael Livesay in 1627, by which time he was settled at Eastchurch on the Isle of Sheppey. By 1637 he was a justice of the peace, and in 1640 he emerged as one of the most prominent puritan firebrands in the county. He presented information against recusants to the Long Parliament in November 1640, and was one of the ringleaders of the Kentish petition of grievances in February 1642. In November 1642 he was one of only two Kentish parliamentarians excluded from pardon by Charles I.

During the first civil war Livesay commanded a Kentish regiment, and in addition to fighting throughout the southern counties he was active against malignants in his own county, an enthusiastic member of the county committee, and sheriff in 1643. Depicted as ruthless by royalist enemies, he was also regarded with suspicion by fellow parliamentarians. The accusations of cowardice levelled against him by a disgruntled and paranoid junior officer, Colonel Anthony Weldon, were probably without substance, and were contradicted by other commanders. However, Livesay was clearly one of a number of local military commanders who challenged the authority of Sir William Waller in the summer of 1644. Their disagreement was brought before the committee of both kingdoms in July 1644, and by the following September the two appear to have reached an uneasy reconciliation. Livesay's troops rejoined Waller's army until the spring of 1645, and although there were fresh accusations of mutinous behaviour, he went unpunished. He refused to serve in the New Model Army, and his place was taken by Henry Ireton.

Livesay was elected to parliament on 15 September 1645 as a recruiter for Queenborough, where he had been a freeman since 1641. He quickly emerged as a supporter of the independents and the army interest, and appears to have worked closely with the most radical members of the Commons. This was particularly clear during the counter-revolution of 1647, when he was one of the members who fled to the safety of the army in the face of presbyterian inspired riots in Westminster in July. When royalist riots broke out in Kent in December 1647 he returned to the county to quell the trouble, and spent much of the spring and summer of 1648 in service against royalists both there and in Surrey and Sussex. In August he was granted a commission of martial law in order to punish royalist spies in the region, and advocated harsh treatment for offenders. Once again, his troops were accused of disorder and plunder, and he had to be warned to keep them under control, for fear of disaffecting the community further. It seems likely that his men had become radicalized, and they certainly expressed approval of Pride's Purge in December 1648.

During a brief spell in parliament in April 1648 Livesay had opposed reopening talks with the king and indicated his republican credentials by refusing to commit himself to a constitution which included a monarchical element. He was an obvious candidate to serve on the high court of justice to try Charles I, and attended every day of the trial prior to signing the death warrant [*see also* Regicides]. During the republic Livesay's troops were disbanded, leaving him able to concentrate on parliament, where he remained a controversial figure. His hardline views on the constitution led to a determination to defend the Commons against the council of state as the locus of sovereign power. He probably grew disillusioned by the drift of political events in 1653, and almost certainly opposed the protectorate established in 1654. During the mid-1650s he confined his activity to local affairs, serving as sheriff of Kent in both 1655 and 1656.

Like many republicans Livesay returned to Westminster when the Rump was recalled in May 1659, although illness delayed his appearance. Thereafter he supported civilian rule rather than the army faction based at Wallingford House. Upon the Restoration, however, he was forced to flee to the continent, and his lands were forfeited to the crown. Although there were reports that he had been murdered by a royalist mob in the Low Countries in October 1660, he was at Hanau in early 1662, and in the following year was allegedly involved in plotting against Charles II. In October 1663 he was rumoured to have returned to England in order to further such plans, although in June 1665 he was at Rotterdam, where he probably died shortly afterwards. When administration of his wife's estate was granted to one of their daughters in February 1666 Elizabeth Livesay (*d.* 1665) was described as a widow.

J. T. Peacey

Sources *JHC* · *CSP dom.*, *1644–64* · *Fifth report*, HMC, 4 (1876) · *Sixth report*, HMC, 5 (1877–8) · *Seventh report*, HMC, 6 (1879) · C. H. Firth and R. S. Rait, eds., *Acts and ordinances of the interregnum, 1642–1660*, 3 vols. (1911) · D. Underdown, *Pride's Purge: politics in the puritan revolution* (1971) · *The Clarke Papers*, ed. C. H. Firth, 2, CS, new ser., 54 (1894) · J. Rushworth, *Historical collections*, new edn, 8 vols. (1721–2) · A. Everitt, *The community of Kent and the great rebellion, 1640–60* (1966) · *Calendar of the Clarendon state papers preserved in the Bodleian Library*, ed. O. Ogle and others, 5 vols. (1869–1970) · *The manuscripts of his grace the duke of Portland*, 10 vols., HMC, 29 (1891–1931), vol. 1 · *To the parliament of England and army: the declaration of Colonel Anthony Weldon* (1649) · R. H. Dickson, 'Eastchurch', *Archaeologia Cantiana*, 26 (1904), 326–7

Likenesses oils, *c.*1650, NMM

Livesay, Richard (1750–1826), painter and engraver, was born on 8 December 1750. Of his parents, nothing is known. He entered the Royal Academy Schools on 21 March 1774, as a draughtsman. He exhibited for the first time at the Royal Academy in 1776. Between 1777 and 1785 he lodged with William Hogarth's widow in Leicester Fields, and executed for her a series of facsimiles of drawings by Hogarth, among them the seven illustrating the well-known tour, *An account of what seemed most remarkable in the five days' peregrination of the following five persons, viz. Messieurs Tothall, Scott, Hogarth, Thornhill and F. Begun on Saturday, May 27, 1732, and finished on the 31st of the same month*, by E. F. (Ebenezer Forrest), published in 1782. He also made engravings after Hogarth's paintings. He was engaged by Benjamin West, of whom he was a pupil, to copy pictures at Windsor Castle. Livesay went to reside there about 1790, and gave lessons in drawing to some of the royal children. While at Windsor he executed many portraits of young Etonians, generally small whole-lengths, many of which were exhibited at the Royal Academy. His large unfinished picture of *Eton Boys Going to Montem* hangs in Eton College.

Livesay exhibited sixty-nine pictures in total at the Royal Academy between 1776 and 1821. On 8 October 1793, Joseph Farington recorded Livesay as being one of the candidates for the election of two associates. In 1796 he was appointed drawing-master to the Royal Naval Academy (later College) at Portsmouth and so moved to Portsea. On an address card which he issued at that time he described himself as 'Portrait, Landscape, and Marine Painter, Drawing-Master to the Royal Academy, Portsmouth, 61 Hanover Street, Portsea.' He painted some of the English warships and their French prizes, and in 1800 published a set of four plates of the reviews of the Isle of Wight Volunteers, aquatinted by Wells. Archibald noted his 'impressive picture of a review of the Worcestershire Regiment with a background of Portsmouth harbour and shipping' (Archibald, 148). Livesay's large picture *The Grand Review of Troops at Hatfield by King George III on June 13, 1800*, is in the collection at Hatfield House. It was engraved by J. C. Stadler. He also made engravings after marine subjects. His portrait of James Caulfeild, first earl of Charlemont, is in the National Portrait Gallery, London. Several of Livesay's portraits have been engraved. Livesay was succeeded at the Royal Naval College in 1811 by John Schetky and then returned to London. He was in Winchester in 1821 but when he wrote his will in January 1826 he was resident in Bath. He died at Southsea, Hampshire, in November 1826. The sole legatee, his nephew John Livesay of Penny Street, Portsmouth, renounced his claim when it became apparent that his uncle's debts were likely to exceed his assets.

F. M. O'Donoghue, *rev.* Jill Springall

Sources S. C. Hutchison, 'The Royal Academy Schools, 1768–1830', *Walpole Society*, 38 (1960–62), 123–91, esp. 140 · B. Stewart and M. Cutten, *The dictionary of portrait painters in Britain up to 1920* (1997) · Graves, *RA exhibitors* · Redgrave, *Artists*, 2nd edn · Farington, *Diary*, 1.69 · J. McConnell, *Treasures of Eton* (1976) · E. Auerbach and C. Kingsley Adams, *Paintings and sculpture at Hatfield House* (1971) · J. H. Anderdon, *Royal Academy catalogues in the British Museum*, 4, no. 1556 · L. Cust, *Eton College portraits* (1910) · E. H. H. Archibald, *Dictionary of sea painters*, 2nd edn (1989) · *Bath Chronicle* (6 Dec 1826) · limited administration of estate, 11 May 1831, PRO, PROB 7/32, fols. 174r–179r

Wealth at death died in debt: will, 1826, PRO, PROB 22/46; limited administration, 1831, PRO, PROB 7/32, fols. 174r–179r

Livesey, Sir George Thomas (1834–1908), gas engineer and industrialist, was born on 8 April 1834 at Canonbury Terrace, Islington, London, the eldest of the three children of Thomas Livesey (1807–1871), company manager, and his wife, Ellen, *née* Hewes (1806–1886). His family was already active in the developing gas industry: his great-uncle, also Thomas Livesey, was from 1813 to 1840 the deputy governor of the Gas Light and Coke Company, established in Brick Lane, Shoreditch, in 1812; and his father was a clerk with the same company from 1821 until 1839, when he joined the South Metropolitan Gas Company. In that business the father became a notably successful general manager, improving efficiency and profitability; he also introduced a workmen's contributory sick fund in 1842, a superannuation fund in 1855, and a week's holiday with pay in 1860. George's younger brother, Frank (1844–1899), was also a gas engineer with South Metropolitan. In 1859 Livesey married Harriet Howard (*d.* 1909), daughter of George Howard; they had no children.

In 1848, at the age of fourteen, George Livesey joined South Metropolitan as his father's assistant and soon showed a marked talent for engineering. He helped to reconstruct the company's Old Kent Road works, which became the most efficient in London; and he later built the East Greenwich works. He introduced new techniques for gas purification, and pioneered the building of very large gasholders, which cut the cost of storage by two-thirds. He was president of the British Association of Gas Managers in 1873–4, and was the first recipient in 1882 of the association's Birmingham medal for research; he was also a member of the Institution of Civil Engineers and the Institution of Mechanical Engineers. He was much in demand as a consultant on gasworks design.

Livesey was made assistant manager of the South Metropolitan in 1857 and engineer in 1862; and on his father's death in October 1871 he was appointed to the dual post of engineer and secretary. He became a director of the company in 1882 and its chairman in 1885. Under Livesey's long and energetic control the company prospered greatly. Between 1862 and Livesey's death in 1908, the annual gas output of the company rose from 350 million to 12,520 million cubic feet, making it second only to the Gas Light and Coke Company in volume of output; by that date South Metropolitan had absorbed almost all the London gas companies south of the Thames and had 6000 employees.

However, it was to be through his role in altering the commercial organization of the business that Livesey made his main contribution to the gas industry. He saw that statutory regulation of gas prices and share dividends gave companies little incentive to improve efficiency and pass the benefits on to customers. In the early 1870s, therefore, he proposed that dividends and prices should be linked: as prices fell, dividends could be raised, and vice versa. At first the idea had few supporters, but it was soon implemented by the major London companies and over the next quarter of a century the sliding scale was widely adopted, being seen as fair to producers and customers alike.

Livesey was also quick to seize on promising ideas both to develop new markets and to exploit them vigorously. The most notable example was the provision at the company's expense of gas in homes previously without a supply. Customers were provided with a full lighting installation and a cooker at no direct cost. A prepayment meter gave security for payment and the initial costs were recovered through a surcharge on the price of gas over succeeding years. In 1892 South Metropolitan was the first major company to adopt the scheme, which became enormously successful throughout the country. Gas, previously the preserve of the better-off, now appeared in working-class homes, and the use of gas for cooking became commonplace.

Despite his real engineering skills and commercial acumen, Livesey became known less for his professional achievements than for his part in defeating a strike by gas stokers. In 1889 the newly established Gas Workers' Union, under the redoubtable Will Thorne, threatened strike action: the union had won an eight-hour day for gas stokers and then attempted to establish a closed shop. Livesey was determined to resist any diminution of management authority, and contingency plans to recruit new stokers were made. However, he attempted to defuse the crisis by proposing a workmen's profit-sharing scheme and offering the security of three- or twelve-month contracts of employment. Ironically this offer precipitated the strike, when three stokers applied to join the scheme. The union demanded their dismissal and Livesey refused; the strike started a week later when the men had worked out their notice. Being prepared, the company was able to maintain gas supplies through the bitter two-month strike and the union was finally forced to concede defeat.

With the strike out of the way, Livesey's ideas progressed from profit-sharing to 'co-partnership'. This may have been 'a management strategy of labour discipline' (Matthews, 461), but Livesey perceived it differently—as a compact between manager and employee to recognize their common interests. He declared that 'co-partnership is Christianity in business' (*DBB*). Co-partnership was to be expressed through fair employment practices, consultation, and ultimately through elected worker-directors (from 1898 in South Metropolitan's case) and the encouragement of thrift. The innovation was fully justified by its success. In 1906 a record bonus of 9.34 per cent was paid on wages and salaries; by 1910 nearly 5500 employees had more than £340,000 invested in the company, and there were three employees on the board. A portion of the bonus, left invested in the company at 4 per cent interest, was channelled into home loans via the Metrogas Building Society, founded in 1884. Many gas companies subsequently introduced similar co-partnership schemes, which contributed to good labour relations in the gas industry over the following half century.

From the 1870s rivalry developed between the South Metropolitan and Gas Light and Coke companies. Livesey not only resisted Gas Light and Coke's attempts to expand south of the Thames, but also mounted fierce public attacks on the competence of its management—its prices were considerably higher than those of its neighbours. Forthrightness occasionally degenerated into obstinacy. In 1882, just after he joined the board of South Metropolitan, Livesey arranged an exhibition on behalf of the Gas Managers' Association. Complaints were made that he favoured an old friend at the expense of a trade rival; the ensuing row precipitated a schism in the professional body which remained unhealed for several years.

A complex and forceful character, Livesey was the outstanding gas industry engineer of his generation, and was knighted in 1902. An industrialist with great technical talent, he was also endowed with strong commercial sense and paternalist views. He was a lifelong member of the Church of England, and served as a Sunday school teacher at Christ Church, in the Old Kent Road. A teetotaller and a member of the Band of Hope, he was a generous benefactor to religious and philanthropic causes. He erected the first public library in Camberwell and bought land for a public recreation ground off the Old Kent Road. In his private life he was a keen cyclist and walker, and an early and enthusiastic motorist. Following his death on 4 October 1908 from cancer, at his home, Shagbrook, Buckland Road, Reigate, Surrey, thousands lined the streets from Old Kent Road to Nunhead cemetery as the funeral cortège passed. Livesey left estate valued at £157,063, and his wife survived him by a year. As his memorial the gas industry endowed the Livesey professorship of coal gas and fuel industries at the University of Leeds.

FRANCIS GOODALL

Sources M. Mills, 'Profit sharing in the South Metropolitan Gas Company, 1889–1920', MPhil diss., Thames Polytechnic, 1983 • M. Mills, 'George Livesey', *London's Industrial Archaeology*, 4 (1989), 41–8 • D. Matthews, 'The British experience of profit-sharing', *Economic History Review*, 2nd ser., 42 (1989), 439–64 • F. Goodall, 'The British gas appliance industry, 1875–1939', PhD diss., U. Lond., 1992 • W. T. K. Braunholtz, *The Institution of Gas Engineers: the first hundred years, 1863–1963* (1963) • S. Everard, *The history of the Gas Light and Coke Company, 1812–1949* (1949) • T. I. Williams, *A history of the British gas industry* (1981) • W. T. Layton, *The early years of the South Metropolitan Gas Company, 1853–71* (1920) • *Gas World* (10–17 Oct 1908) • *Journal of Gas Lighting* (6–13 Oct 1908) • *Gas World* (1875–) • *Journal of Gas Lighting* (1875–) • F. Goodall, 'Livesey, Sir George Thomas', *DBB* • 'Royal commission on labour: minutes of evidence, group C', *Parl. papers* (1893–4), vol. 34, C. 6894-IX • 'Select committee on metropolitan gas companies', *Parl. papers* (1899), 10.19, no. 294 • d. cert.

Archives Southwark Local Studies Library, London, papers

Likenesses W. M. Palin, oils, *c.*1890, British Gas, Old Kent Road, London • S. March, bronze bust, 1909, Ferens Art Gallery, Kingston upon Hull • F. W. Pomeroy, bronze statue, 1910, British Gas, Old Kent Road, London • A. Bryan, pen-and-ink drawing, NPG

Wealth at death £157,063 3*s.* 10*d.*: probate, 11 Dec 1908, *CGPLA Eng. & Wales*

Livesey, James (1626–1682), Church of England clergyman, was born in Heape, in the parish of Bury, Lancashire, on 1 January 1626, the son of Robert Livesey (1591?–1675), yeoman. He was educated locally and on 9 May 1645 was admitted to Christ's College, Cambridge. He did not complete his studies and on 26 February 1647 he was admitted sizar at St John's College, Cambridge, where he graduated MA. He returned to Lancashire and was appointed minister at Turton, near Bolton, by the Bury classis on 23 October 1650. Here he married, probably in 1652, Elizabeth Chetham, daughter of George Chetham of Turton Tower (nephew of the philanthropist Humphrey Chetham). They had five sons and two daughters.

On 28 June 1652 Livesey became minister at the chapel at Atherton or Chowbent, in the neighbouring parish of

Leigh, then in the patronage of the godly magistrate John Atherton. Here he established a reputation as a zealous presbyterian, and published *Enchiridion judicum … a Sermon before the Judges … at Lancaster, March 26, 1655*, a lengthy exposition upon the alliance of magistracy and ministry, together with *Catastrophe magnatum … a Sermon … at the Funeral of … John Atherton* (1657). In 1657, following Atherton's death, the dean and chapter of Christ Church, Oxford, appointed him minister of the largely puritan-inclined parish of Great Budworth, Cheshire. In 1662 he initially failed to subscribe to the canons, but later reluctantly conformed and remained minister at Great Budworth. Nevertheless, he remained familiar with local nonconformists, especially the ejected minister Adam Martindale, and preached the funeral sermon for Martindale's son in 1680. His own son, Robert, became schoolmaster within his parish. Until his death he remained a zealous preacher and three further sermons were published in 1674. He died suddenly at Great Budworth on 7 February 1682. He was survived by his wife and clearly mourned by his parishioners, as shown by this excerpt from a poem penned by Thomas Bradshaw, rector of Lymm, for Livesey's funeral on 10 February, before burial at the church there:

Great Budworth's faithfull pastour now is gone
And left his congregation here alone.
How desolate is she: well may she weep
Her learned Livesey now in Christ doth sleep.
(Shaw, *Minutes of Bury Presbyterian Classis*, 2.247–50)

S. J. Guscott

Sources W. A. Shaw, ed., *Minutes of the Bury presbyterian classis, 1647–1657*, 2 vols., Chetham Society, new ser., 36, 41 (1896–8), 109–12, 247–50 · will and probate inventory, 1682, Ches. & Chester ALSS · W. A. Shaw, ed., *Minutes of the committee for the relief of plundered ministers and of the trustees for the maintenance of ministers … 1643–1660*, 1, Lancashire and Cheshire RS, 28 (1893), 119, 123, 231–2 · *The life of Adam Martindale*, ed. R. Parkinson, Chetham Society, 4 (1845), 219–21 · H. Hodson, *Cheshire, 1660–1780: Restoration to industrial revolution* (1978), 29–49 · *VCH Cheshire*, 3.36–48 · *DNB* · *The registers of the parish church of Bury in the county of Lancaster: christenings, burials and weddings*, 2: *1617–1646*, ed. W. J. Lowenberg and H. Brierley, Lancashire Parish Register Society, 10 (1901) · Venn, *Alum. Cant.*, 1/3.93 · W. J. Shiels, ed., *Restoration exhibit books and the northern clergy, 1662–1664*, Borthwick Texts and Calendars (1987), 44 · parish register, Great Budworth, Ches. & Chester ALSS

Wealth at death £252 19*s*. incl. £80 in bonds and £80 in debts: will and probate inventory, 1682, Ches. & Chester ALSS

Livesey, James (1833–1925), civil engineer, was born at Preston, Lancashire, the youngest of three sons of Joseph *Livesey (1794–1884) and his wife, Jane, *née* Williams (*d.* 1869). Livesey was a precocious, innovative child, endowed with an enquiring mind. He demonstrated an early flair for engineering, an aptitude that was recognized and encouraged by his father, sometime proprietor of the *Preston Guardian* and a leading light in the local temperance movement. He was educated at Mr Isherwood's day school in Preston and apprenticed at the age of fourteen to Isaac Dodds, working on the Caledonian Railway. At the age of sixteen he entered the engineering works of Musgrave & Co., Bolton, specialists in agricultural equipment. Subsequently, he worked at the famous Manchester locomotive firm, Beyer, Peacock & Co. and served as a railway engineer in Spain on the Isabel II Railway, before establishing in Manchester in 1862 his own business, manufacturing newspaper-folding machinery. While in Spain he may have married a Spanish woman. A son, Fernando Harry, was born in 1860. He had at least two other sons, and two daughters. Later he practised as an engineering consultant, and it was in this capacity that he became associated with the Buenos Ayres Great Southern Railway Company, of which he became chief engineer, and thereafter several other British-owned South American railways, many of which were promoted by Alexander Henderson, first Baron Faringdon. He was a member of the Institution of Civil Engineers and the Iron and Steel Institute, and was director of the Costa Rica Markets Company Limited.

Livesey is credited with several inventions, including newspaper-folding and -cutting machinery (he presented a mechanically folded newspaper to Queen Victoria at the Great Exhibition in 1851), cast-iron railway sleepers (laid experimentally in Britain and Argentina), grain elevators, and domestic sanitation systems, but his career is most closely associated with the engineering consultancy business that he founded, successively James Livesey, James Livesey & Son, Livesey, Son, and Henderson, and, ultimately, Livesey and Henderson. His early ventures were backed by his father; subsequently he obtained financial support from W. Owen, iron manufacturers and equipment makers of Rotherham, and from Alexander Henderson. In 1885 his son, Fernando Harry (later Sir Harry) Livesey (1860–1932), joined the consultancy business, followed in 1891 by Henderson's brother, Brodie Haldane Henderson. Brodie Henderson became senior partner in 1893 when Livesey retired, and at this point the firm was known as Livesey and Henderson. Associated with railway engineering at a relatively early stage in the history of the industry, Livesey was from time to time connected with several prominent figures, including Thomas Brassey the contractor, Andrew Carnegie the American steel magnate, Sir Sandford Fleming, promoter of Canadian Railways, and George Hudson, the railway king. Besides working in Spain, he cultivated business contacts in France and Scandinavia and travelled extensively in the Americas, from Canada to Argentina. Touring in the USA and Canada, he familiarized himself with the distinct techniques of railway building in North America, and worked briefly as a railway engineer in Canada. Subsequently, he spent lengthy periods in the River Plate region, where he supervised work on a number of pioneer lines, including the Central Uruguay, the Buenos Ayres and Rosario, and the Entre Ríos, in addition to the Buenos Ayres Great Southern. Under his direction, the partnership was also concerned with railway construction in Brazil, Chile, Peru, and Venezuela. Later the firm developed an extensive contract business in Africa.

After a colourful life, several times having been involved in serious railway accidents, Livesey died of pneumonia at his London residence, 4 Whitehall Court, Westminster, on 3 February 1925, at the age of ninety-two. He was buried at

Rotherfield, his estate in Sussex, on 6 February. He was survived by three sons and two married daughters. In addition to an estate valued at over £300,000, he left property in Sussex, and houses in France and Norway.

COLIN M. LEWIS

Sources D. H. E. Wainwright, 'Livesey, James', *DBB* • *The Times* (11 Feb 1925) • *DNB* • *Bradshaw's General Railway Directory and Shareholders' Guide* (1847–1923) [various issues; title varies] • *PICE*, 50 (1869–70) • C. Wood, 'Iron permanent way', *PICE*, 67 (1881–2), 1–26 [see also discussion, 27–68] • d. cert. • *CGPLA Eng. & Wales* (1925)
Archives NRA, priv. coll., memoirs
Wealth at death £302,210 12*s*. 5*d*.: probate, 6 April 1925, *CGPLA Eng. & Wales*

Livesey, Joseph (1794–1884), temperance advocate, was born on 5 March 1794 at Walton, near Preston, Lancashire. His parents, John Livesey and Jennette Ainsworth, died of consumption in 1801, and William, his only sibling, died early. Joseph's paternal grandfather, a small farmer also named Joseph, took responsibility for Joseph and for John's hand-loom weaving business, which failed. In a damp cellar, the young Joseph educated himself while working at the loom. Influenced by the Portlock family, he became a Scotch Baptist, was baptized (*c*.1811) in a Baptist chapel, and in 1815 married a Scotch Baptist, Jane Williams (*d*. 1869), the daughter of a Liverpool master rigger. The marriage was happy; the couple had ten sons (including the civil engineer James *Livesey) and three daughters, but lost four children in infancy.

In 1816 Livesey moved from Walton to Preston and became a prosperous cheese factor, henceforth his lifelong occupation. Self-denying and economical with time, he was an exemplar of self-help. Acknowledging no barrier between middle and working class, he concentrated on making recruits for respectability and on harmonizing employer with employee. He was active in local government, championing municipal reform and public health with all the early-Victorian radical's angry energy, defending Preston's hand-loom weavers, and helping to fend off local application of the reformed poor law. Sharing the Quakers' distaste for formalities, he attacked privilege in religion as in everything else—once deliberately sitting on a tasselled Bible cushion before beginning a sermon. But there was a gentler side: he loved children, and in repudiating Anglican and aristocratic values he was discriminating and not vindictive. His religion was unsectarian and practical, his daily life founded on the New Testament.

There were many early-Victorian Liveseys. Joseph was distinctive for acting upon his belief that economic progress required moral reform. He, above all others, pushed the temperance movement into abandoning beer as well as spirits, thus transforming it into an exhilarating crusade against the entire drink trade. This required courage, if only because beer then seemed essential to health. Yet Livesey was a teetotaller from early in 1831, and on 1 September 1832 joined six Preston men in taking a pledge to abstain experimentally from beer for one year. A temperance 'reformation' seemed imminent, and he publicly walked arm-in-arm with drunkards ripe for reclamation.

A resourceful propagandist and courageous lecturer, Livesey gave teetotalism its doctrinal foundation with his populist, closely argued, widely delivered, and oft-reprinted *Malt Lecture*, complete with scientific demonstrations that then seemed exciting but now seem flawed. Teetotalism also benefited from the avalanche of his publications, weapons in a lifelong quest to improve the world. His monthly *Moral Reformer* (January 1831 – December 1833) became the *Preston Temperance Advocate* (January 1834 – December 1837), the first teetotal periodical. Its cheap woodcuts, plain speaking, and diverse approaches to its subject aimed at the millions. Likewise his widely circulated weekly, *The Struggle* (235 numbers from 1842 to 1846), helped render the Anti-Corn Law League popular. From there he moved easily into general journalism, and from 1844 to 1859 he and his sons managed the *Preston Guardian*, a leading Liberal weekly. Livesey published many more teetotal periodicals and tracts, as well as his autobiography (1867–82).

Yet by the 1850s teetotalism had lost momentum, and with others Livesey turned to prohibition, promoted from 1853 by the United Kingdom Alliance. Drink was, after all, a trade where his free-trade principles clearly did not apply. Characteristically, he soon questioned the new orthodoxy, seeing prohibitionists' political preoccupations as divisive and as downgrading the reclamation and visitation of drunkards which he prized. Controversy resulted, old friends were disappointed, and Livesey's later writings breathe an air of disillusioned nostalgia for the teetotallers' pioneering days. As an old man he was revered as the founder of a movement which now seems somewhat sectarian. It was an ironic outcome, for he had aimed, not at a movement, but at a reformation, nor had temperance ever been his sole enthusiasm. He died on 2 September 1884 at Bank Parade, Preston, and was buried in the nonconformist section of Preston cemetery.

BRIAN HARRISON

Sources J. Pearce, *The life and teachings of Joseph Livesey*, 2nd edn (1887) • B. Harrison, *Drink and the Victorians: the temperance question in England, 1815–1872*, 2nd edn (1994) • *CGPLA Eng. & Wales* (1884)
Archives University of Central Lancashire, Preston, temperance collection
Likenesses group portrait, line engraving, 1838 (*The family of Joseph and Jane Livesey*), BM • two portraits, 1864–*c*.1882, repro. in Pearce, *Life and teachings of Joseph Livesey*
Wealth at death £9399 9*s*. 3*d*.: resworn probate, Sept 1885, *CGPLA Eng. & Wales* (1884)

Livesey, Sir Michael. *See* Livesay, Sir Michael, first baronet (1614–1665?).

Livesey, Roger (1906–1976), actor, was born on 25 June 1906 at 138 Holton Road, Barry, south Wales, the son of Joseph Livesey and his wife, Mary Catherine Edwards. His father, known as Sam, was an actor, and the young Roger Livesey was to make his first stage appearance at the age of seven, alongside his father, as an office boy in *Loyalty* at the St James's Theatre. Educated in London, he attended the Westminster City School and the Italia Conti School, which prepared its pupils for a career in the theatre, and between 1920 and 1926 he was playing juvenile roles in the

West End theatre, including an appearance at the Aldwych Theatre in a farce by Ben Travers. This was followed by a period of touring in the West Indies and South Africa, where he played two seasons. On his return he appeared in a cast which included John Gielgud in the try-out of Ronald MacKenzie's *Musical Chairs*, subsequently taking over a role in the play from his brother Jack in 1932. Further association with Gielgud, in the try-out of *Richard of Bordeaux* by Gordon Daviot, brought him to the attention of Harcourt Williams, who engaged him for a season at the Old Vic Theatre; from September 1932 to May 1934 he stayed a member of the Old Vic Company, where the most eminent actors of the day appeared in Shakespearian and other roles. Under the direction of Tyrone Guthrie he played the Duke in *Measure for Measure* (with Flora Robson as Isabella), and Caliban (with Charles Laughton as Prospero) in *The Tempest*. William Congreve's *Love for Love* saw him appearing in a cast which included his brother as well as his father.

By now established as a promising young actor whose rugged good looks seemed to conceal a shrewd, humorous intelligence, Livesey was rarely out of work, and he tackled demanding roles both on stage and, a little later, in film. He continued to make appearances on the Old Vic and West End stages during the early years of the war, before making a tour of the Middle and Far East for ENSA (the Entertainments National Service Association, the wartime agency which brought performances to serving troops). He starred in a number of films by Michael Powell and Emeric Pressburger, giving a sympathetic portrayal of the seemingly blinkered military mind in *The Life and Death of Colonel Blimp* (1943), as well as playing major roles in *I know where I'm going* (1945) and *A Matter of Life and Death* (1946), the film selected for the first royal command film performance in 1946. During and after the war he appeared in a number of plays with his wife, Ursula Jeans (who predeceased him in 1973), and when the Old Vic reopened in 1953 they were both members of the company. They appeared together in *Twelfth Night*, *The Merry Wives of Windsor*, and George Bernard Shaw's *Captain Brassbound's Conversion*, and they toured Australia and New Zealand together between 1956 and 1958 in West End successes including William Douglas Home's *The Reluctant Debutante*.

On television Livesey appeared in Terence Rattigan's *The Winslow Boy*, Jean Giraudoux's *Amphitryon 38*, Ibsen's *The Master Builder*, and Dürrenmatt's *The Physicists*; he also played Archie Rice's father in John Osborne's *The Entertainer* (in the film version of which he played the same part) and the Duke of St Bungay in the BBC serialization of Trollope's novels presented under the title *The Pallisers*. By the 1960s his appearance and husky voice were used to advantage in a number of elderly roles, including Captain Shotover in Shaw's *Heartbreak House* (which transferred from the Oxford Playhouse to Wyndham's Theatre in 1961), Chebutykin in Chekhov's *The Three Sisters* (Oxford Playhouse, 1964), and the earl of Caversham in Oscar Wilde's *An Ideal Husband* (1965). In 1969 he doubled as the First Player and the Gravedigger in a production of *Hamlet* which opened at the Round House in London in 1969 and was presented at the Lunt-Fontanne Theater, New York, later in the same year. He toured South Africa in 1970. He died in the General Hospital, Watford, on 4 February 1976. MICHAEL ANDERSON

Sources *The Times* (6 Feb 1976) · I. Herbert, ed., *Who's who in the theatre*, 16th edn (1977) · *WWW* · b. cert. · d. cert. · *CGPLA Eng. & Wales* (1976)

Archives FILM BFI NFTVA, news footage · BFI NFTVA, performance footage | SOUND BL NSA, performance recordings

Likenesses photograph, Hult. Arch.

Wealth at death £62,298: probate, 10 May 1976, *CGPLA Eng. & Wales*

Living. *See* Lyfing (*d.* 1046).

Living, Elfstan. *See* Lyfing (*d.* 1020).

Livingston, Sir Alexander, of Callendar (*b. c.*1375, *d.* in or before 1456), courtier and administrator, was the eldest of four sons of the first marriage of Sir John Livingston of Callendar (*fl.* 1371–1402) to a daughter of John Menteith of Kerse. It is likely that Alexander was born in Stirlingshire about 1375 at the latest as Sir John's second marriage occurred in 1381. The family's principal estate was Callendar, near Falkirk. Alexander was probably knighted on the return of James I from captivity in England in 1424, but neither he nor any son of his acted as a hostage for the king's ransom, as happened with many Scottish barons. Although he played little part in political life under James I, the assassination in 1437 of King James (succeeded by the six-year-old James II) and the subsequent deaths of various senior members of the Scottish nobility opened the way for hitherto little-known men to make their mark. Livingston was apparently so enraged by the queen mother's marriage to Sir James Stewart of Lorne less than a month after the death of Archibald Douglas, fifth earl of Douglas, the lieutenant-general of the realm, in June 1439, that he arrested her and imprisoned Stewart and his brother in Stirling Castle. Despite the severity of the act, in September 1439 a settlement was concluded between the Livingstons and the queen mother, with the approval of the three estates, whereby the king was to reside in Stirling Castle under Livingston's guardianship until his majority. The possession of the king was a crucial gain.

The chancellor, Sir William Crichton (*d.* 1454), was now Livingston's only real rival at court. Together, however, they engineered the execution of the sixth earl of Douglas on 24 November 1440. There can be no doubt that they worked with the connivance of Douglas's great-uncle James Douglas, earl of Avondale (*d.* 1443), already a significant court figure. He became seventh earl of Douglas and acted to improve the lot of his own sons, including William, eighth earl of Douglas (*d.* 1452), who began to ally himself with Livingston. The replacement of Crichton as chancellor by James Bruce, bishop of Dunkeld, in 1444 removed the last check on the Livingstons, notwithstanding the presence of the eighth earl of Douglas. Their power can be clearly seen in the distribution of offices acquired during the 1440s, many of which would have brought pensions to their holders. Sir Alexander was justiciar from about 1444 and sheriff of Stirlingshire by 1448. His son and heir, James, was captain of Stirling Castle by May 1442, keeper of the king's person by March 1445, and chamberlain by June 1448. Other family members held the posts of constable of Stirling Castle, captain of Methven and Doune castles, Perthshire, sheriff of Fife, and king's comptroller (the financial officer responsible for the maintenance of the royal household). Beyond the immediate family, the custumar of Dumbarton burghs, the keepers of the castles of Dumbarton, Dunoon in Argyll, Restalrig in Edinburghshire, and Kildrummy in Aberdeenshire, and the master of the king's household were Livingston associates or relatives.

This stranglehold on government, particularly in central Scotland, came to a dramatic end in 1449. James Livingston and three others were arrested on 23 September, and Sir Alexander and Robert Livingston, the comptroller, soon afterwards. After a trial in parliament in January 1450 Robert and Sir Alexander's second son, Alexander, were executed. Sir Alexander, who may later have been expelled from Scotland, and James Dundas of Dundas, probably his brother-in-law, were imprisoned in Dumbarton Castle. The terms of a remission in 1452 suggest a plot against the persons of the king or queen, although there has also been speculation that the Livingstons abused their power for financial gain.

Sir Alexander Livingston's death is usually dated about 1451, but as his son is not styled of 'Callendar' in a Scottish source until September 1456 a date in mid-1456 is preferable. He is said to have married a daughter of Dundas of Dundas and had two sons, James and Alexander, and four daughters. Of the daughters, Janet married James *Hamilton of Cadzow [*see under* Hamilton family] and Joanna married Sir John Sibbald of Balgonie, master of the king's household. Livingston had attempted to found a collegiate church at Falkirk, obtaining papal approval in 1449, but following his family's loss of power the project foundered.

Sir Alexander's eldest son, **James Livingston**, first Lord Livingston (*c.*1400–1467), courtier and administrator, who may never have been knighted, was first brought to prominence at court by his father. After the fall of the family in 1449 he was imprisoned in Holyrood, only to escape and associate himself with his son-in-law, the lord of the Isles, in attacking royal castles in the north in 1451. His reward was the keepership of the nominally royal castles of Inverness and Urquhart, Inverness-shire. The Livingstons nevertheless received a general remission of rancour from the crown in August 1452, James II being now engaged in his struggle with the Douglases. James's rehabilitation was marked by his reappointment as chamberlain by March 1454; while he continued in office until his death, it seems that before the 1460s he entrusted the conduct of chamberlain ayres to deputes because he was constantly at court. He was sheriff of Stirlingshire by mid-1455 and master of the king's household from at the latest October 1455, both posts held until the end of 1460.

It is surprising that only in March 1458 (not in 1455 as traditionally stated) was he created Lord Livingston, especially given the Livingston dominance in the 1440s when many Scottish families adopted a peerage style. In April 1458 the free barony of Callendar was created for Lord Livingston by consolidation of his estates in Stirlingshire, Lanarkshire, and Perthshire. After the king's death in August 1460 Livingston is seldom found at court, although he remained chamberlain and was appointed ambassador on occasion. His exclusion may have resulted from the personal animosity towards him of the queen mother, Mary of Gueldres. If this is true it may help explain the fall of his family in 1449, three months after the arrival of the queen in Scotland.

James Livingston died about August 1467. He is known to have married Marion (*d.* between June and October 1478), daughter of Thomas Berwick, a burgess and custumar of Edinburgh. She had apparently married first Sir John Oliphant of Aberdalgie (*d.* 1446) and may therefore have been Livingston's second spouse. His children included James, second Lord Livingston, whose idiocy prevented the family from returning to prominence in the remainder of the century, and Elizabeth, who married John MacDonald, earl of Ross and lord of the Isles.

ALAN R. BORTHWICK

Sources J. B. Paul, ed., *Registrum magnisigilli regum scottorum, AD 1424–1513* (1882) • *APS*, 1424–1567 • *The Asloan manuscript*, ed. W. A. Craigie, 2 vols., STS, new ser., 14, 16 (1923–5) • G. Burnett and others, eds., *The exchequer rolls of Scotland*, 4–7 (1880–84) • various collections of manuscript estate and other papers in archive offices and in private hands in Scotland and England • *CDS*, vol. 4 • *RotS*, vol. 2 • A. I. Dunlop, ed., *Calendar of Scottish supplications to Rome*, 4: 1433–1447, ed. D. MacLauchlan (1983) • J. Kirk, R. J. Tanner, and A. I. Dunlop, eds., *Calendar of Scottish supplications to Rome*, 5: 1447–1471 (1997) • E. B. Livingston, *The lords Livingston of Callendar* (1920), 50 • NA Scot., GD 97/2/24 • *Scots peerage*, 5.430 • M. Brown, *The Black Douglases* (2000)

Archives priv. coll. | NA Scot., GD 97/2/24

Livingston, Alexander. *See* Livingstone, Alexander, first earl of Linlithgow (*d.* 1621).

Livingston, Anne. *See* Shippen, Anne (1763–1841).

Livingston, Lady Elizabeth. *See* Delaval, Lady Elizabeth (1648?–1717).

Livingston, James, first Lord Livingston (*c.*1400–1467). *See under* Livingston, Sir Alexander, of Callendar (*b. c.*1375, *d.* in or before 1456).

Livingston [Livingstone]**, James, first earl of Callendar** (*d.* **1674**), army officer, was the third son of Alexander Livingston, first earl of Linlithgow (*d.* 1621), and Helen Hay, daughter of Andrew Hay, earl of Erroll.

Early career Livingston was probably born in the 1590s, and enlisted in the Dutch service, being lieutenant of a company commanded by his elder brother, Sir Henry Livingston, in 1618. He was promoted lieutenant-colonel of one of the three regiments of the Scottish brigade in the Netherlands in 1629, and colonel in 1633. That his

James Livingston, first earl of Callendar (*d.* 1674), by R. S., pubd 1647

early career also saw service to the British crown is indicated by the facts that he was granted a pension by James VI and that by 1628 he had been knighted, being referred to by Charles I as one who 'has been soe long abroad in our service beyond sea' (C. Rogers, ed., *The Earl of Stirling's Register of Royal Letters*, 2 vols., 1885, 1.326). The following year he is mentioned as a gentleman of the king's privy chamber, and when Charles I visited Scotland in 1633 he was created Lord Livingston of Almond (Amont) on 19 June.

The bishops' wars Lord Almond was one of those sent to Scotland in 1638 by Charles I to encourage opposition to the covenanters; he was admitted to the privy council there on 2 July, but his loyalties proved uncertain. Almond signed the 'king's covenant', intended to rival the national covenant, on 22 September, but in December joined others in declaring that he understood it as upholding presbyterianism, the opposite of the king's intention. In the first bishops' war of 1639 the covenanters expected that Almond would accept appointment as second in command of their forces, but 'in the tyme of our most need, the grievousness of his gravell, or the pretence of it, made him goe to France to be cutted' (*Letters and Journals of Robert Baillie*, 1.212). He had sought treatment for the stone previously, at Harrogate in 1637, but suspicion that his illness was a pretext to avoid having to take sides in the conflict was heightened when, after he found that he did not need to be 'cut', he proceeded to Holland to take command of his regiment there instead of returning to Scotland. However, the covenanters having been successful in their defiance of the king in 1639, Almond agreed to serve as their lieutenant-general in the second bishops' war of 1640. He played a leading role in the Scottish army's advance into England, which led to victory at the battle of Newburn and the occupation of Newcastle, but just before the campaign had begun he had signed the Cumbernauld bond with the earl of Montrose and others, indicating opposition to the policies of the earl of Argyll and other covenanting leaders. In spite of the discovery of the bond and the denunciation of its signatories Almond retained his military command, as the covenanters did not want to emphasize division in their ranks, and perhaps because Argyll remained 'to that man a most speciall friend' (*Letters and Journals of Robert Baillie*, 1.390).

Support for the covenanters lost Almond his Dutch command for, evidently at the request of Charles I, he was replaced as colonel of his regiment on 5 November 1640. When Charles was negotiating a settlement with the covenanters in 1641 he still had sufficient hopes of Almond's loyalty to propose his appointment as treasurer of Scotland, but Argyll took a lead in blocking the proposal, indicating that public good came before private friendship. That the covenanters' doubts about Almond's reliability were justified was confirmed in October by 'the Incident', a plot whereby a group of royalist officers planned a *coup d'état*. Proposals to arrest the earl of Argyll and the marquess of Hamilton were alleged to have been made in Almond's house, and he was said to have been assigned a leading part in seizing the two nobles. However, the matter was not investigated too closely, as both king and covenanters were determined not to let the affair prevent them reaching an agreement. As part of the settlement Almond was created earl of Callendar on 6 October 1641.

Service in Scotland and England, 1643–1647: divided loyalties In spite of Callendar's flirtations with royalists in 1640–41 the new earl's military reputation was sufficient for the covenanters to offer him the position of lieutenant-general again in 1643, when they were moving towards alliance with the English parliament against the king in the English civil war, even though some still doubted his commitment to the cause. Early in 1644 he was involved in the plottings of royalists with malcontent army officers for risings in favour of the king. According to James Turner he 'persuaded me in his oune house of Callendar, and upon a Lords day [Sunday] too, that he would faithfullie serve the King', and swore oaths to that effect (Turner, 36). But on 16 May he accepted a commission to serve the covenanters as lieutenant-general, commanding in chief all forces being raised in Scotland. This meant that the marquess of Argyll, who was to command an expedition being sent north against the royalist rising led by Sir John Gordon of Haddo, came technically under Callendar's command. Callendar's insistence on this arrangement may not have been merely a squabble about rank, but a reflection of hopes of his that having Argyll, the covenanters' political leader, under his military command could help him to divert the new army from fighting against to fighting for the king. Certainly he continued to assure Turner of his loyalty to Charles I, and that high rank among the covenanters would increase his ability to help him. However, his manoeuvrings look more like the fumblings of an ambitious man seeking to keep open the option of changing sides if events made that expedient than those of a man of firm loyalty to any cause.

Callendar's forces were first used to police the border, to prevent incursions of royalists from the north of England, such as that led by Montrose in April 1644. However, when it turned out that the main Scottish army in England, engaged in the siege of York, was unable to suppress the activities of Montrose and other royalists in northern England, Callendar was sent into England with his army, 7000 to 10,000 strong, on 25 June. He reasserted Scottish military control of the north-east, and was joined in the siege of Newcastle by the main Scottish army in England in August. On the victory of Montrose at Tippermuir, near Perth, on 1 September, Callendar's army was at first ordered to return to Scotland, but the covenanters' determination to give priority to the war in England led to the orders being countermanded. Callendar was then offered command of another new army being raised in Scotland, to pursue Montrose, but chose to remain in England, where he took part in the storming of Newcastle on 19 October.

In January 1646 there were renewed demands that Callendar return to Scotland to direct action against the royalists in the north, and thus take up the duties envisaged in his 1644 commission as commander of the forces within the country, but his demands for authority over all other commanders were rejected on this occasion, and he was left without employment. As before, his motives are hard to fathom, perhaps belief in his own indispensability mingling with thoughts of gaining as much military authority as possible for political ends. Like several other senior Scottish officers in England he had had secret meetings with royalists in 1645, and he visited Charles I when he was being held prisoner by the Scottish army in Newcastle in 1646. In March 1647 Callendar's tendency to overprice himself when attempting to sell his services again revealed itself. As civil war in Britain seemed to have ended he proposed to raise a regiment to serve the king of France—provided that he was made a brigadier-general (thus outranking the French officer who commanded all Scottish troops in French service) and captain of the horse of the king's household. The offer was refused (Fotheringham, 2.30).

The engagement and the battle of Preston Callendar played an active part in the making of the engagement treaty between Scottish commissioners and the king, then imprisoned at Carisbrooke Castle, in December 1647, and was rewarded with appointments as sheriff of Stirling and keeper of Stirling Castle. When the engagers raised an army in 1648 Callendar had hopes of being appointed general, but his refusal to serve against Montrose in Scotland in 1644–6, his tendency to harbour grievances, and doubts as to his trustworthiness counted against him. Instead he was commissioned to his old position of lieutenant-general, with the duke of Hamilton as general. The appointment was politically expedient, for to get the engagement accepted by the Scottish parliament the votes of a group of royalists who were suspicious of the sincerity of Hamilton's commitment to the king, and were led by Callendar, was essential. But Callendar's commission gave the engagers' army a second in command who was notoriously difficult to work with and who deeply distrusted his commander.

The disastrous decisions that led the engagers' invasion of England to defeat at Preston in August 1648 owed much to the unfortunate combination of Callendar, ever ready with ill-judged advice, and Hamilton, uncertain in military matters and ready to accept the opinions of the overbearing professional soldier he was supposed to command. By 17 August the Scottish cavalry had reached Wigan, and Hamilton ordered his infantry to follow it by crossing the River Ribble at Preston. However, news arrived that an English royalist force under Sir Marmaduke Langdale, which was moving to join Hamilton, had come under attack by Cromwell. Hamilton therefore cancelled his orders for the advance over the Ribble so that his infantry could support Langdale. But Callendar argued that the Scottish infantry could not resist Cromwell without cavalry support. The infantry should after all cross the Ribble, to put the river between them and Cromwell until the cavalry could be recalled from Wigan. Hamilton agreed, and only he, with Callendar and a few Scottish horsemen, went to Langdale's support. The royalists were quickly crushed by Cromwell. Hamilton and Callendar, with the remnants of the royalist force, escaped across the Ribble, and it was proposed to make a stand on the river. Callendar again intervened, arguing in favour of a withdrawal southwards under cover of darkness in an attempt to link up with the Scots cavalry. Hamilton again gave way to Callendar, but with the infantry already demoralized and bewildered by a confusion of orders and counter-orders, planned retreat quickly turned to precipitate flight, and the Scottish army disintegrated. Callendar's final contribution to the campaign was to advise the infantry to surrender at Warrington. Hamilton surrendered with the remaining cavalry at Uttoxeter, while Callendar fled to Holland, and was rumoured to be the only man in the whole army to succeed in escaping to the continent.

Unemployment and imprisonment Callendar returned to Scotland in May 1650, but was forced to leave immediately because of his role in the engagement. However, disaster at the battle of Dunbar (3 September 1650) and the English occupation of southern Scotland led to a relaxing of attitudes, and he was soon allowed to return. On 23 April 1651 the kirk accepted his declarations of repentance for his part in the engagement. It was even proposed that he yet again be made lieutenant-general, and when his reluctance to fight Montrose in 1644–6 was cited as showing he was 'not worthy of trust' (T. M'Crie, ed., *The Life of Mr. Robert*

Blair, Wodrow Society, 11, 1848, 170–71) he argued that he had refused because Montrose had held a royal commission—a declaration of royalism that suited the atmosphere of royalist revival in 1651 but failed to explain why he had been ready to fight those holding the king's commissions in England. Callendar was refused a military command but was appointed a member of the committee of estates, and he was present when the remnants of the committee were captured by the English at Alyth on 28 August 1651, though he managed to escape. He surrendered to General Monck in November 1651, but by December 1653 was reported to be 'lurking in some parts of the North' awaiting an opportunity to join the royalist rebels there (Firth, *Scotland and the Commonwealth*, 305). He soon did so, a move that worried the English because of 'the dangerousnesse of his principles and spiritt' (Firth, *Scotland and the Protectorate*, 47). However, he was arrested in February 1654, and spent some time as a prisoner in Edinburgh Castle, his estates being confiscated. In 1655 he went to London and after having 'kissed the Lord Protecteur his hands' (*Correspondence of Sir Robert Kerr, First Earl of Ancram, and his Son William, Third Earl of Lothian*, ed. D. Laing, 2 vols., 1875, 2.391) obtained the restoration of his lands. On his return to Scotland he gave General Monck, the commander-in-chief there, his word as a gentleman that he would not act against Cromwell or the government. However, in August 1659 he refused to sign an undertaking, imposed by the collapsing republican regime, not to act against it or in favour of the exiled Charles II, and orders were given for his imprisonment in Stirling (*The Clarke Papers*, ed. C. H. Firth, 4 vols., CS, new ser., vols. 49, 54, 61, 62, 1891–1901, 4.41).

Rehabilitation After the Restoration Callendar's refusal to serve against Montrose in the 1640s at last brought praise instead of suspicion, and on 11 May 1661 he was one of the fourteen earls who carried Montrose's coffin in the elaborate procession through Edinburgh which preceded his burial. Glimpses at personal life behind the public facade of the shifty professional soldier are rare. In 1633 he had married Margaret Hay (*c*.1592–1659), daughter of Lord Yester and widow of the first earl of Dunfermline. They had no children, though Callendar had two illegitimate children. In 1640 he founded a hospital for four aged and infirm persons at Falkirk. Nothing is known of his final years; he died at Callendar House and was buried at Falkirk on 25 March 1674. He was succeeded as earl by his nephew Alexander, the second surviving son of his elder brother Alexander Livingston, second earl of Linlithgow.

Lack of information about Callendar's early career makes it difficult to know what particular qualities as a soldier made Scottish regimes in 1639–48 so eager to secure his services in a senior position. What political scruples he had probably inclined him towards royalism, but ambition made him willing to serve the covenanters. He then attempted to salve his conscience by serving the covenanters against the king in England but refusing service in Scotland, earning general distrust. In the 1648 engagement he at last served the king directly, but his animosity towards Hamilton combined with ill judgement on the field of battle to bring what had once been a distinguished military career to an ignominious conclusion.

David Stevenson

Sources *DNB* • *Scots peerage* • GEC, *Peerage* • J. Turner, *Memoirs of his own life and times, 1632–1670*, ed. T. Thomson, Bannatyne Club, 28 (1829) • *The letters and journals of Robert Baillie*, ed. D. Laing, 3 vols., Bannatyne Club, 73 (1841–2) • *The memoirs of Henry Guthry, late bishop*, ed. G. Crawford, 2nd edn (1748) • D. Stevenson, *The Scottish revolution, 1637–44: the triumph of the covenanters* (1973) • D. Stevenson, *Revolution and counter-revolution in Scotland, 1644–1651*, Royal Historical Society Studies in History, 4 (1977) • *The historical works of Sir James Balfour*, ed. J. Haig, 4 vols. (1824–5) • *APS* • *Reg. PCS*, 1st ser. • *Reg. PCS*, 2nd ser. • *Reg. PCS*, 3rd ser. • C. H. Firth, ed., *Scotland and the Commonwealth: letters and papers relating to the military government of Scotland, from August 1651 to December 1653*, Scottish History Society, 18 (1895) • C. H. Firth, ed., *Scotland and the protectorate: letters and papers relating to the military government of Scotland from January 1654 to June 1659*, Scottish History Society, 31 (1899) • J. G. Fotheringham, ed., *The diplomatic correspondence of Jean de Montereul and the brothers de Bellièvre: French ambassadors in England and Scotland, 1645–1648*, 2 vols., Scottish History Society, 29–30 (1898–9)

Archives NL Scot., account book

Likenesses R. S., engraving, pubd 1647, NPG [*see illus.*] • print, BM; repro. in J. Ricraft, *A survey of England's champions* (1647)

Livingston [Livingstone], **James, of Barncloich, first Viscount Kilsyth (1616–1661)**, nobleman, was born on 25 June 1616, the younger son of Sir William Livingston of Kilsyth (*d*. 1627), a lord of session from 1609 and vice-chamberlain of Scotland from 1613, and his second wife, Margaret, daughter of Sir John Houston of Houston. On 23 April 1647 he was served heir to his brother's grandson William Livingston of Kilsyth. He suffered substantial losses during Montrose's campaign in 1645, and his house was burned and his lands plundered—apparently by both English and Scottish forces—in 1650–51. He was imprisoned in Edinburgh in 1651, excepted from Cromwell's Act of Pardon and Grace (1654), and fined £1500 (later reduced to £800). After the Restoration, in recognition of his loyalty to the crown, he was raised to the peerage, as Viscount Kilsyth and Lord Campsie, on 17 August 1661. He acted as a commissioner of supply and as commissioner to parliament for Stirlingshire in 1661. Kilsyth and his wife, Euphame, daughter of Sir David Cunningham of Robertland, whom he had married on 10 December 1639, had four children: James, second Viscount Kilsyth, died in 1706 and was succeeded by his brother, William (1650–1733), who, having engaged in the Jacobite rising of 1715, was forced to seek safety abroad and suffer forfeiture of his estates; the title died with him, in Rome. Elizabeth married Major-General Robert Montgomery, fifth son of Alexander, sixth earl of Eglinton; her sister, Anne (*b*. 1648), died unmarried. Kilsyth died in London on 9 September 1661.

T. F. Henderson, *rev*. Alison G. Muir

Sources *Scots peerage* • M. D. Young, ed., *The parliaments of Scotland: burgh and shire commissioners*, 2 (1993), 430 • *APS, 1593–1625; 1648–69* • R. Douglas, *The peerage of Scotland*, 2nd edn, ed. J. P. Wood, 2 (1813), 37–8 • G. Brunton and D. Haig, *An historical account of the senators of the college of justice, from its institution in MDXXXII* (1832), 249

Archives NL Scot., business corresp. | NA Scot., Duntreath muniments, section 2

Livingston, James, of Kinnaird, first earl of Newburgh (**1621/2–1670**), nobleman, was the only son of Sir John Livingston of Kinnaird, first baronet (*d.* 1628), groom of the bedchamber to James VI and I, and his wife, Jane (*c.*1584–1665), daughter of Richard Sproxtoune of Wakefield, steward of the Star Chamber, and widow of William Marwood of Little Burby, Yorkshire. Livingston was about six years old when his father died. On 17 December 1638 he matriculated at Merton College, Oxford, aged sixteen, and, two years after that, Sir Nathaniel Brent reported to Archbishop Laud that although the young man had recently been neglecting his books and had begun 'to haunt the town more than is fit', no one had more civil and gentle behaviour than Livingston did. Moreover, 'the remonstrances of myself and his tutor, and our recommendations to his mother to remove him in case he change not his course, have made him a new man of late' (*CSP dom.*, *1644–5*, 302).

Livingston was not always as gentle as he seemed, for in March 1645, while in Paris to continue his education, he fought the first of a long series of duels, on that occasion with Elizabeth of Bohemia's son Edward. On his return to Britain he became a staunch supporter of Charles I, and on 13 September 1647 was created Viscount Newburgh. At the end of the following year he married Katherine *Stuart (*d.* 1650), whose husband, George, seigneur d'Aubigny, had been killed at Edgehill. Their only child Elizabeth [*see* Delaval, Lady Elizabeth] became a Jacobite agent. That December he and his father-in-law, Theophilus Howard, second earl of Suffolk, devised a plan to rescue the king from his captors when Charles was taken briefly to Newburgh's house at Bagshot, but they did not put it into effect.

Newburgh and his wife fled to The Hague, where she died in 1650, leaving him with a son and a daughter. He returned to Scotland with Charles II. An intercepted letter from Scotland to his mother, requesting robes for the coronation of Charles II, resulted in the sequestration of his property. In November 1650 he was made lieutenant-colonel of the king's lifeguards. He sat in the Scottish parliament, took the covenant, and was presumably present when Charles was crowned at Scone. He fought in the royal army at the battle of Worcester on 3 September 1651, afterwards escaping back to the continent.

Newburgh's military career continued, and he was in 1656 given command of Middleton's regiment in the Low Countries. Much of Charles II's correspondence with Scottish royalists was conducted through him, and in consequence he was excluded from Cromwell's Act of Grace of 12 April 1654. After showing an interest in Anne, daughter of James Douglas, ninth earl of Morton, and being linked with Mrs Jane Lane, Charles II's rescuer after Worcester, about 1656 he married Anne (*bap.* 1637, *d.* 1692), daughter of Sir Henry Poole of Saperton, Gloucestershire.

With the Restoration, Newburgh's loyalty was well rewarded. His estates, estimated in 1656 as having a value of £411 p.a., were now restored to him, he was granted a tack of the customs of the borders, said to be worth £1000 p.a., and received a grant of £1600, arrears of the tenths of the clergy in the diocese of Lincoln. Elected MP for Cirencester, he was given the degree of MA by his old university, and became vice-admiral for Scotland. He was also made captain of the king's bodyguard and colonel of the 4th Horse Guards. On 31 December 1660 Charles II created him earl of Newburgh, viscount of Kinnaird, and Lord Livingston of Flacraig.

In 1662–3 Newburgh was associated with John, first earl of Middleton, in the king's efforts to establish episcopacy in Scotland, but by 1670 he had to retire from his military appointments because of 'corpulency and goutishness' (GEC, *Peerage*). He died on 4 December 1670, to the regret of contemporaries, who praised him as one of the finest gentlemen of the age, with untainted principles of loyalty and honour. He was buried two days later, beside his father in 'Kinges Armes Valt', at St Margaret's, Westminster. ROSALIND K. MARSHALL

Sources R. Douglas, *The peerage of Scotland*, 2nd edn, ed. J. P. Wood, 2 (1813), 308 • GEC, *Peerage*, new edn, 1.330; 9.511–14 • *CSP dom.*, *1639–40*, 510; *1644–5*, 302; *1650*, 225; *1661–2*, 27, 33; *1673–5*, 501 • M. A. E. Green, ed., *Calendar of the proceedings of the committee for compounding … 1643–1660*, 1, PRO (1889), 2983 • *Scots peerage*, 6.451 • *Report on the manuscripts of the late Reginald Rawdon Hastings*, 4 vols., HMC, 78 (1928–47), vol. 2, p. 144 • *Calendar of the manuscripts of the marquis of Bath preserved at Longleat, Wiltshire*, 5 vols., HMC, 58 (1904–80), vol. 2, pp. 130–31 • Burke, *Peerage* (1957) • Foster, *Alum. Oxon.*, *1500–1714* [James Levingston]

Likenesses W. N. Gardiner, wash drawing, AM Oxf.

Wealth at death extensive properties, mostly bequeathed to son: will, PRO, PROB 11/337, sig. 106

Livingston, Jean [*known as* Lady Warriston] (**1579–1600**), murderer, was the daughter of John Livingston, laird of Dunipace, a man of good family and fortune, and a favourite of James VI. She was married young to John Kincaid of Warriston, lands then to the north of Edinburgh. Whether or not he did, as some suggested, treat her cruelly, she came to hate him, and began to listen to Janet Murdo, her old nurse, who suggested murder as a means of revenge and escape from her marriage. Robert Weir, a young servant to Livingston, who was then in attendance on the king at Holyrood, was proposed as the man to effect it. He proved willing, and came to Warriston's house on 1 July 1600 to discuss the plan.

No time was wasted; that evening Warriston was induced to exceed his usual measure of wine and went off to bed. After midnight, Weir, who had been secreted in the house, went into Warriston's chamber, knocked him out of bed, kicked him, then strangled him as he lay on the floor. Hearing the cries, Jean Livingston leapt from her bed and with her nurse went to the hall, where Weir came to tell them that Warriston was dead. It is not known how the news reached Edinburgh, but the officers of justice came to the house next morning, found the body, and arrested Jean, her nurse, and two other women. Weir, meanwhile, had fled. The trial took place before the Edinburgh magistrates on 3 July. Jean showed no grief or remorse, was found guilty, and condemned to death by strangulation followed by burning at the stake, the nurse also to be burnt. Livingston made no effort to save his daughter's life, and the family, resenting the disgrace her deed had brought on them, urged a quick end to the matter.

While held in the Tolbooth, Jean Livingston had been visited by a Presbyterian minister whom she had treated in a very offhand fashion; after sentence was passed she summoned the minister, who now found her truly penitent and resigned to her fate. This conversion was described in a small pamphlet of the day, entitled *Memorial of the conversion of Jean Livingston (Lady Warriston), with an account of her carriage at her execution*, republished in 1827. They spent most of the day in prayer together; Jean dictated her will to the minister, and he left, to return early on the morning of 5 July 1600, the execution now changed to one of beheading by the guillotine known as 'the Maiden'. Her family wished this to take place early when few people would be about the streets, and they arranged that the nurse should be burnt at the stake on Castle Hill at four in the morning, thus attracting the attention of anyone on the streets, while Jean was taken down Canongate to the Girth Cross, the ancient boundary of the abbey sanctuary. Warriston's brother, who was present, showed sufficient humanity to kiss Jean and forgive her. The eyewitness author of the *Memorial* stated that she went as cheerfully as if to her wedding rather than her death, and that she read an address to the many spectators and continued to utter devotions until silenced by the fall of the blade.

Weir was arrested four years later, tried on 26 June 1604, and condemned to be taken to the Edinburgh scaffold and there broken on the wheel, a most unusual punishment in Scotland at that time. The cold-blooded nature of the crime was commemorated in songs variously ascribing blame to the husband, the wife, or the devil.

ANITA MCCONNELL

Sources W. Roughead, 'The doom of Lady Warriston', *Twelve Scots trials* (1913); repr. (1995), 16–40 • R. Law, *Memorialls, or, The memorable things that fell out within this island of Brittain from 1638 to 1684*, ed. C. K. Sharpe (1818), xlvii–xlix • Z. Ashford, 'The lands of Warriston', *Book of the Old Edinburgh Club*, new ser., 3 (1994), 1–24 • J. A. Fairley, 'The Old Tolbooth: with extracts from the original records', *Book of the Old Edinburgh Club*, 4 (1911), 75–144 • J. Grant, *Cassell's old and new Edinburgh*, 3 vols. [1880–83], vol. 3, pp. 98–9 • R. Pitcairn, ed., *Ancient criminal trials in Scotland*, 2, Bannatyne Club, 42 (1833), pt 2, pp. 445–50

Livingston, Mary (*d.* 1585). *See under* Queen's Maries (*act.* 1548–1567).

Livingston, Philip (1716–1778), merchant and politician in America, was born on 15 January 1716 in Albany, Albany county, New York, the fourth of nine children of Philip Livingston (1686–1749), merchant and proprietor of Livingston Manor, and his wife, Catrina, *née* Van Brugh (1689–1756). Livingston enjoyed the benefits of membership in New York's colonial élite. Having been educated at home and, from about 1733 to 1737, at Yale College, he then served a mercantile apprenticeship in Albany with his father, whose influence brought him valuable clerkships in Albany's local government. In 1740 Livingston married Christina (1718–1801), daughter of Colonel Dirck Ten Broeck, mayor of Albany. They had nine children, of whom eight survived infancy.

After several years in Albany, Livingston moved to New York city. There he became a general merchant, and made his fortune provisioning and privateering during the Anglo-French wars. He also speculated in real estate, acquiring more than 120,000 acres of unimproved rural land, along with holdings in Albany and New York city, including his residence on Duke Street in Manhattan and a country seat in Brooklyn Heights.

Livingston, now financially secure, was prominent in New York's civic and political life. He promoted education by endowing a professorship at Yale in 1746, participating in efforts to establish a college in New York, and serving as one of the original trustees of New Jersey's Queen's College in 1766. One of a circle of merchants and lawyers who about mid-century undertook an array of civic and philanthropic projects, Livingston was among the founders of the New York Society Library (1754), the St Andrew's Society (1756), the New York chamber of commerce (1768), and the New York Hospital (1771). An elder and a deacon in the Dutch Reformed church, he was also a benefactor of New York's Anglican King's College and of the local Presbyterian and Methodist congregations. Between 1754 and 1763 he served as alderman for the city's East ward.

Before the revolution Livingston's most significant political service was at the provincial level. In 1758 New Yorkers elected him to the provincial assembly, where in 1764 he helped prepare a remonstrance against the Westminster parliament's unprecedented attempt to raise revenue in America. A year later he represented New York at the Stamp Act Congress. In 1768 Livingston became the assembly's speaker, but the following year an alliance of merchants, Anglicans, and radical Sons of Liberty unseated him and many other more moderate opponents of British policies. Livingston never returned to the provincial legislature, and his party, a coalition of lawyers, landowners, and religious dissenters, remained in opposition for the remainder of the colonial era. In 1774–5, however, Livingston and his allies were prominent in the extralegal committees and congresses that organized New York's cautious resistance to British imperial policies.

From his initial election to the continental congress in 1774, Livingston increasingly devoted himself to continental politics. In his 1774 pamphlet, *The Other Side of the Question*, he staunchly opposed parliamentary taxation, but deemed American independence imprudent and undesirable. In 1776 he signed the Declaration of Independence, though, like many conservative whigs, he dreaded the 'levelling spirit' of revolution. In 1777, when he took his seat in New York's first state senate, he disparaged the abilities of his fellow legislators, many of whom he believed to lack the requisite education and experience to govern effectively.

A conscientious leader with an aristocratic sense of

social responsibility, Livingston exemplified the conservative patriotism of many revolutionary élites. He died on 12 June 1778 in York, Pennsylvania, while attending the continental congress, and was buried at York.

CYNTHIA A. KIERNER

Sources C. A. Kierner, *Traders and gentlefolk: the Livingstons of New York, 1675–1790* (1992) • C. L. Becker, *The history of political parties in the province of New York, 1760–1776* (1909) • P. U. Bonomi, *A factious people: politics and society in colonial New York* (1971) • *Historical memoirs from 16 March 1763 to 25 July 1778 of William Smith*, ed. W. H. W. Sabine, 2 vols. (1956–8) • P. H. Smith and others, eds., *Letters of delegates to congress, 1774–1789*, 26 vols. (1976–2000) • C. A. Kierner, 'Livingston, Philip', *ANB*
Archives NYPL, family MSS • NYPL, MSS
Likenesses T. McIlworth?, oils, *c*.1757–1762, Brooklyn Historical Society, New York • A. Delanoy?, oils, *c*.1771, Clermont State Historic Site, Germantown, New York
Wealth at death real and personal property: will, NYPL, Livingston family MSS

Livingston, Robert R. (1746–1813), politician in the United States of America, was born on 27 November 1746 in Manhattan, New York city, the eldest son of eleven children of Robert Robert *Livingston (1718–1775), lawyer and political leader, and his wife, Margaret (1724–1800), daughter of Colonel Henry Beekman. Livingston graduated from King's College (later Columbia) in 1765 and then studied law with William Livingston and William Smith jun. In 1768 he began practising law in New York. In 1770 Livingston married Mary (1752–1814), the daughter of John Stevens, a wealthy New Jersey landowner, with whom he had two daughters. In 1775–6 the deaths of his father, grandfather, and father-in-law made him a great landowner in his own right, as he inherited Clermont, a 13,000 acre family seat in Dutchess county, in addition to nearly 1 million acres scattered throughout New Jersey and New York.

Although Livingston was the royally appointed recorder of the city of New York from 1773 until 1775, he was increasingly drawn into revolutionary politics, serving as Dutchess county's representative in New York's provincial congress and as a delegate to both the first and second continental congresses. A cautious revolutionary, Livingston sought to postpone congress's vote on independence in July 1776. Appointed to the committee charged with drafting a declaration of independence, he did not participate in its work and, having left congress to attend New York's state constitutional convention, he never signed the finished document.

Accepting the need for independence, Livingston worked at both the state and continental levels to minimize its destabilizing effects. He helped shape New York's first state constitution, which combined modest democratic reforms with checks on popular influence, including a council of revision composed of the governor, chancellor, and supreme court justices, who were collectively empowered to veto legislation. As the state's first chancellor, Livingston sat on the council of revision, where he opposed taxes and other measures that adversely affected the economic and political interests of the landed élite. Between 1779 and 1781 he also returned to the continental congress and was its secretary of foreign affairs from 1781 until 1783. Concluding that a stronger central government might secure American diplomatic interests and counteract the democracy of the states, Livingston was a forceful advocate for the federal constitution, using his impressive oratorical skills at the New York convention in 1788 to promote ratification.

Livingston's subsequent exclusion from federal patronage, his opposition to federalist fiscal policies, and early support for the French Revolution soon led him into the ranks of Thomas Jefferson's Republican Party. When Jefferson became president in 1801, Livingston shared the fruits of victory, turning down the post of navy secretary but accepting that of minister to France. In 1803 he was the chief negotiator of the Louisiana purchase, which doubled the size of the United States.

In 1804 Livingston returned to New York where, since at least 1793 when he was co-founder and president of the state Society for the Promotion of Agriculture, Manufactures, and Useful Arts, he had been an influential proponent of experimental farming and other practical scientific projects. His best-known endeavours were experimentation with Merino sheep culture—which led to the publication of an *Essay on Sheep* in 1809—and his partnership with Robert Fulton in the steamboat business. The partners, who began regular service between New York and Albany in 1807, held a monopoly on steamboating on the Hudson and Mississippi rivers. Challenges to their monopoly, however, resulted in expensive litigation that was resolved in the partners' favour less than one year before Livingston's death. He died on 25 February 1813 at Clermont, where on 28 February he was buried in the family vault.

A republican aristocrat with wide-ranging accomplishments and interests, Livingston shared the achievements and limitations of American élites during a crucial transitional era. Unwilling to accept either democracy or full-blown capitalism, they none the less launched and strengthened a republic that came to epitomize both.

CYNTHIA A. KIERNER

Sources G. Dangerfield, *Chancellor Robert R. Livingston of New York, 1746–1813* (1960) • C. A. Kierner, *Traders and gentlefolk: the Livingstons of New York, 1675–1790* (1992) • A. F. Young, *The democratic-republicans of New York: the origins, 1763–1797* (1967) • E. Countryman, *A people in revolution: the American revolution and political society in New York, 1760–1790* (1981) • L. G. DePauw, *The eleventh pillar: New York state and the federal convention* (1966) • C. L. Becker, *The history of political parties in the province of New York, 1760–1776* (1909) • S. B. Kim, *Landlord and tenant in colonial New York: manorial society, 1664–1775* (1978) • D. M. Ellis, *Landlords and farmers in the Hudson-Mohawk region, 1790–1850* (1946) • J. M. Banner, 'Livingston, Robert R.', *ANB*
Archives New York Historical Society, Clermont account book • New York Historical Society, MSS
Likenesses C. W. Peale, oils, 1783, Independence National Historical Park, Philadelphia • J. Wright, oils, 1790, Harvard U., law school • G. Stuart, oils, *c*.1794, Clermont State Historic Site, Germantown, New York

Livingston, Robert Robert (1718–1775), landowner and politician in America, was born in August 1718 in New York city, the only child of Robert Livingston (1688–1775), merchant and later proprietor of Clermont, and his wife, Margaret, *née* Howarden (*c*.1693–1758). Livingston was educated at home and then trained as a lawyer in New York city, where he was practising law by 1742. That year he married Margaret (1724–1800), the only child of Colonel Henry Beekman of Dutchess county. The couple had eleven children, including the politician Robert R. *Livingston. Livingston's marriage made him heir to both the Livingston and Beekman fortunes: he expected to inherit some 100,000 productive acres, which he believed would make him the wealthiest man in New York.

A lifelong resident of New York's provincial capital, Livingston was prominent in the colony's civic and political life. In 1744 he was a charter member of the Society for the Promotion of Useful Knowledge, and a decade later he joined with five other leading men to found the New York Society Library. Livingston served on three successive commissions charged with establishing a boundary between New York and Massachusetts, and from 1759 until 1768 he represented Dutchess county in the provincial legislature. In 1760 he became a judge of the court of Admiralty. In 1763 Governor Robert Monckton appointed him to the provincial supreme court, a position he retained until 1775.

A steadfast champion of the landed interest in New York politics, Livingston was an outspoken critic of both tenant insurgency—which convulsed the Hudson valley manors during the 1750s and again in 1766—and a proposed tax on unimproved land. He vigorously defended New York's land tenancy system, by which he and his family profited handsomely. Livingston asserted that leaseholders, too, benefited from a land system that promoted industry and productivity, as well as from a political system that protected their civil and economic rights.

Despite his aristocratic outlook, Livingston became a leader in the fight to protect colonial liberty. Along with other leading lawyers, and members of his own extended family, he opposed attempts to augment royal control of New York's provincial judiciary in the early 1760s. Seeking to preserve judicial independence, he and his associates unsuccessfully contested the imperial directive that colonial judges serve at the king's pleasure, rather than during good behaviour. A few years later they effectively opposed the bid by acting governor Cadwallader Colden to circumvent both a jury's verdict and the supreme court's ruling by hearing an appeal in the case of *Forsey* v. *Cunningham*.

Sensitive to the dangers of encroaching prerogative power as a result of their involvement in these judicial controversies, Livingston and his allies were prominent among the opponents of the Stamp Act of 1765. Serving as both chair of New York's committee of correspondence and a member of the Stamp Act Congress, Livingston none the less opposed the Stamp Act riots in New York city, where he tried in vain to disperse plebeian protesters. Livingston's criticism of politicized urban mechanics and artisans, along with his approval of the brutal suppression of the Hudson valley's tenant insurgents in 1766, ensured the loss of his Dutchess county assembly seat in 1768. Anticipating Livingston's attempt to regain his seat, the majority party led by James DeLancey passed a bill excluding supreme court justices from the legislature. In 1769 Livingston was elected to represent Livingston Manor, but the majority refused to seat him. Although he was re-elected to the Manor seat five times in the next four years, the majority consistently refused to admit him to the lower house.

In 1774 Livingston supported the convening of the extralegal provincial and continental congresses. Had he not died in New York on 9 December 1775, he doubtless would have reluctantly accepted American independence. He was buried at Clermont, in Dutchess county. Public-spirited, aristocratic, and legalistic, Livingston typified the conservative whigs who led New York's resistance to imperial authority, even as they attempted to preserve their hierarchical privileged world.

CYNTHIA A. KIERNER

Sources C. A. Kierner, *Traders and gentlefolk: the Livingstons of New York, 1675–1790* (1992) · C. L. Becker, *The history of political parties in the province of New York, 1760–1776* (1909) · P. U. Bonomi, *A factious people: politics and society in colonial New York* (1971) · S. B. Kim, *Landlord and tenant in colonial New York: manorial society, 1664–1775* (1978) · B. McAnear, ed., 'Mr. Robert R. Livingston's reasons against a land tax', *Journal of Political Economy*, 48 (1940), 63–90 · R. Champagne, 'Family politics versus constitutional principles: the New York assembly elections of 1768 and 1769', *William and Mary Quarterly*, 20 (1963), 57–79 · M. L. Lustig, 'Livingston, Robert Robert', *ANB* · private information (2004) [B. Narramore, Clermont State Historical Site, Germantown, New York]

Archives New York Historical Society, MSS · New York Historical Society, Clermont account book | Franklin Delano Roosevelt Library, Hyde Park, New York, Livingston-Redmond MSS

Likenesses J. Wollaston?, oils, 1749–92, priv. coll.

Livingston, Thomas (1390/91–1460), titular bishop of Dunkeld and diplomat, was the illegitimate son of (almost certainly) a member of the baronial family of Livingston of Callendar in Stirlingshire, possibly Sir John Livingston (*d.* 1402). He was among the first graduates of St Andrews University (MA, 1415) and subsequently taught in the arts faculty there. Having become a Cistercian monk, he was elected abbot of Newbattle before 10 June 1422, but his claim was pre-empted at the papal court by a rival. He then went to Cologne University, matriculating in 1423 to pursue the theological studies on which he had already embarked. At Cologne he probably met Nikolaus von Kues (Cusanus), who matriculated there in 1425, the year of Livingston's inception as master of theology. On 28 July 1430 Livingston, still a monk of Newbattle and now a priest, sought papal dispensation to hold abbatial office despite his defect of birth. He was abbot of Dundrennan by 14 November 1432, when he was incorporated at the Council of Basel. Thus began an active career in the council, to which Livingston remained committed until its dissolution in 1449. Much of his early activity concerned Scottish affairs. His advice contributed to James I's decision in the summer of 1433 to send representatives to Basel, and he was part of the Scottish delegation whose other members were incorporated on 8 February 1434. When the king's ecclesiastical policies were vehemently attacked by William Croyser, archdeacon of Teviotdale, as spokesman for Pope Eugenius IV, Livingston was one of James's principal defenders. In the spring of 1436 he helped to negotiate a partial resolution of the conflict, followed by the pope's decision in July to send a legate to Scotland.

Livingston, however, also participated in the council's wider concerns, above all the issue of whether supreme authority within the church derived from the council or from the pope. At the most critical stage in conciliar relations with Eugenius—culminating in the pope's deposition—he emerged as a figure of real prominence at Basel. He seems to have been absent, perhaps in Scotland, for six months or so after September 1437 (maybe in response to the murder of James I early that year); but from the spring of 1438 he was fully involved in events in Basel and, elsewhere, in defending the council's proceedings. On 18 June 1439, with the archdeacon of Metz, Livingston delivered the five-hour report on the charges against Eugenius which preceded his deposition a week later. Livingston was one of the council's ambassadors at the imperial diet in Mainz in August and spoke in defence of the deposition. In the autumn he was among the electors appointed by the council to choose a new pope and a member of the embassy to invite Amadeus, duke of Savoy, to accept election as Felix V. The year 1440 saw Livingston actively promoting Felix's claims at episcopal synods in Bourges and in Cologne. His reward for these efforts was provision by Felix V, on 29 November 1440, to the see of Dunkeld. Though he never had effective possession as bishop, this gave Livingston a foothold in the Scottish church at a time when, during the minority of James II, his family played a leading if controversial part in a political situation in which conflict over papal allegiance was a significant element. The conciliar cause was essentially lost by the spring of 1443, but the death of Eugenius IV in February 1447 rekindled hopes. This was the context of Livingston's legatine mission to Scotland that spring on Felix's behalf, armed with powers to effect a reconciliation which (the event proved) had to await the anti-pope's resignation in 1449.

Meanwhile Livingston continued his activity in Basel and, more importantly, elsewhere on behalf of the council and of Felix. He was a member of the conciliar delegation at the imperial diet in Frankfurt am Main in the summer of 1442. In February 1446 he was one of two Basel representatives in Vienna, vainly urging Emperor Friedrich III to summon the council of the German church proposed eight months before. When the healing of the schism was at last in sight, Livingston took part in meetings for that purpose in Lyons between August and December 1447.

For some years after the council ended Livingston worked closely with Nikolaus von Kues, now a cardinal. He accompanied Kues on his important mission to promote church reform in Germany and the Netherlands between January 1451 and April 1452. Monastic renewal, in which Livingston had already been concerned at Basel, had a substantial place in this mission. By the mid-1450s he had returned to Scotland. Still 'bishop in the universal church' (a term of art indicating that he was a bishop without a see or diocese) and confessor and counsellor to James II, he had no episcopal income and depended on provision, sometimes contested, to various benefices, the last being the abbacy of Coupar Angus *in commendam*. He died in the summer of 1460, blind and in his seventieth year.

Livingston, though much of his career lay outside Scotland, was clearly one of the outstanding Scottish churchmen of his generation. His sermons and other addresses, preserved in a dozen manuscripts, employ a pervasively scriptural rhetoric which is more heavily indebted to the Old Testament prophets than to the books of the New Testament, other than the Apocalypse. What is expounded is not so much a closely argued ecclesiology as a prophetic vision of the church beset by its enemies—and above all by the heretical enemy within. At the same time this vision is inseparable from a theology of the church in which 'unfailing authority to teach' (*indefectibile magisterium*) is ascribed to a general council representing the whole body of the faithful. The council's authority is, however, judicial as well as doctrinal, and its sentence binds every member of the church, including the pope. This conciliarist doctrine contributed to a tradition of considerable importance for later Scottish thinking, a point exemplified in the work of John Ireland and John Mair. J. H. BURNS

Sources D. Shaw, 'Thomas Livingston, a conciliarist', *Records of the Scottish Church History Society*, 12 (1954–6), 120–55 • J. H. Burns, *Scottish churchmen and the Council of Basle* (1962) • [J. Haldenston], *Copiale prioratus Sanctiandree: the letter-book of James Haldenstone, prior of St Andrews, 1418–1443*, ed. J. H. Baxter, St Andrews University Publications, 31 (1930) • J. Haller, G. Beckmann, R. Wackernagel, G. Coggiola, and H. Hesse, eds., *Concilium Basiliense: Studien und Quellen zur Geschichte des Concils von Basel*, 8 vols. in 7 (Basel, 1896–1936) • J. W. Stieber, *Pope Eugenius IV, the Council of Basel, and the secular and ecclesiastical authorities in the empire* (1978) • J. H. Baxter, 'Four "new" mediaeval Scottish authors', *SHR*, 25 (1927–8), 90–97 • R. Nicholson, *Scotland: the later middle ages* (1974), vol. 2 of *The Edinburgh history of Scotland*, ed. G. Donaldson (1965–75) • A. I. Dunlop, *The life and times of James Kennedy, bishop of St Andrews*, St Andrews University Publications, 46 (1950) • E. R. Lindsay, A. I. Dunlop, and others, eds., *Calendar of Scottish supplications to Rome*, 1–2, Scottish History Society, 3rd ser., 23, 48 (1934–56); 3, Scottish History Society, 4th ser., 7 (1970); 4 (1983) • *CEPR letters*, vols. 7, 9–11 • *Deutsche Reichstagsakten unter König Albrecht II*, 14, ed. G. Beckmann (Göttingen, 1914) • *Deutsche Reichstagsakten unter Kaiser Friedrich III*, 15–16, ed. H. Herre (Göttingen, 1914–28) • E. Birk and R. Beer, eds., *Monumenta conciliorum generalium seculi decimi quinti*, 2–3 (1873–96)

Archives Österreichische Nationalbibliothek, Vienna, Cod. lat. Vind. 5116, fols. 127–31 • Balliol Oxf., MS 164, fols. 172–80 • Biblioteca Apostolica Vaticana, Vatican City, MS lat. 4191, fols 17–22 • Bibliothèque Nationale, Paris, MS Lat. 1499, fols. 141 ff. • Bodl. Oxf., MS Laud misc. 96, fols. 65–74, 85–91, 157–62

Livingston, William, sixth Lord Livingston (*d.* **1592**), nobleman, was the second son of Alexander Livingston, fifth Lord Livingston (*d.* in or before 1553), and his wife, Lady Agnes Douglas, daughter of John Douglas, second earl of Morton. His parents were guardians of Mary, queen of Scots, when she was a child, and his sister Mary Livingston became one of the queen's famous attendants, the four *Queen's Maries. The Livingston lands lay in Linlithgowshire and Stirlingshire and included Kilsyth and Falkirk, as well as Callendar House, the family's principal residence. William succeeded to these, and to his father's titles in 1553, and about that time married Agnes, daughter of Malcolm Fleming, third Lord Fleming. Their eldest son was the politician and courtier Alexander *Livingstone. Livingston was a protestant, but nevertheless when Mary, queen of Scots, returned to Scotland from France in 1561 he became one of her most loyal supporters, entertaining her at Callendar House on various occasions. On Sunday 1 July 1565, for instance, Mary was present at the christening of one of his seven children there, and although he declined to attend her mass on 2 February 1566, he was one of the few protestants to accept an invitation to the Roman Catholic baptism of her son, the future James VI and I, at Stirling on 17 December 1566.

Livingston was present during many of the dramatic events of Mary's life. He was with her in the little supper room in the palace of Holyroodhouse on the evening of 9 March 1566 when her husband, Lord Darnley, and his fellow conspirators burst in to murder her secretary, David Riccio. On 13 January 1567 Mary spent the night at Callendar House on her way from Stirling to Edinburgh with her infant son, and she was back less than a fortnight later, when she rode to Glasgow to visit Darnley, who was lying ill there. One of the notorious casket letters describes how Livingston teased her that evening. She allegedly wrote that Livingston:

> at supper sayd softly to me when I was leaning upon him and warming myself, 'You may well go and see sick folk, yet can you not be so welcome unto them as you have this day left somebody in pain'. (Henderson, 135)

The letters are generally believed to be forgeries but even so, this passage with its unpleasant innuendo was probably not a complete invention, but rather an exaggerated account of a relationship which, while entirely innocent, was indeed one of close and friendly informality.

Three days later Mary and her husband spent the night at Callendar on their way back to Kirk o'Field, just outside Edinburgh's city walls, where Darnley was to convalesce. When he was murdered shortly afterwards Mary's enemies alleged that she had deliberately lured him to his death, and she made matters worse by marrying James Hepburn, fourth earl of Bothwell, generally believed to be the principal assassin. Livingston was a guest at their wedding on 15 May 1567. He may have been unhappy with its disastrous consequences, for he was not with the queen when she surrendered to her rebellious lords at Carberry Hill. During her imprisonment in Lochleven Castle, however, Livingston was one of a deputation who went to the regent Moray to plead for her release. The request was refused, but when Mary finally managed to escape from Lochleven, Livingston rode at once with his vassals to join her at Niddrie Castle, and accompanied her to Hamilton. Present in her army at the battle of Langside in 1568, he was one of the three lords who led her away when it became obvious that her forces would be defeated, and he went with her when she escaped to England.

Livingston remained with Mary in England for almost two years, and his wife, Agnes Fleming, was allowed to join him. He was one of Mary's commissioners at her first trial in York in October 1568, and throughout her years of imprisonment he continued to be active in her cause. He was in Scotland in July 1570 on her behalf, and in 1571 he visited France, staying in Paris during the St Bartholomew's day massacre in the following year. Lady Livingston was allowed to return to Callendar House in 1572, and took the opportunity of passing on secret correspondence between the queen's various friends. As a result, she was imprisoned for two months.

Livingston was finally allowed to go home to Scotland after Edinburgh Castle fell to James VI's supporters in May 1573. He was made a member of the Scottish privy council in March 1575, but his influence had waned because of his identification with Mary's cause. He was among the lords who advised the young James VI to start ruling for himself in 1577, became a friend of James's favourite, Esmé Stewart, first duke of Lennox, and was rumoured to be a Roman Catholic in his later years. His last known public act was to serve on the jury which convicted the first earl of Gowrie of treason in 1584. Livingston's signature appears on a family charter dated 18 October 1592, but he was dead by 29 November. He was buried in the churchyard at Falkirk. ROSALIND K. MARSHALL

Sources *Scots peerage*, 5.435–42 • T. Henderson, *The casket letters and Mary, queen of Scots* (1889), letter 2 • R. Douglas, *The peerage of Scotland*, 2nd edn, ed. J. P. Wood, 2 vols. (1813) • A. Fraser, *Mary, queen of Scots* (1969) • J. M. Thomson and others, eds., *Registrum magni sigilli regum Scotorum / The register of the great seal of Scotland*, 11 vols. (1882–1914), vol. 2, p. 766, no. 3560

Livingston, William [*pseud.* the American Whig] (**1723–1790**), lawyer, political writer, and colonial governor, was born in Albany, New York, on 30 November 1723. He was the son of Catherine Van Brugh (1689–1756) and Philip Livingston (1686–1749), second lord of the Livingston Manor, one of the large landed estates created by colonial governors which possessed unique privileges, including the right to send a representative to the colonial assembly. He was the younger brother of Philip *Livingston, New York merchant and political leader. Livingston attended Yale College from 1737 to 1741, and then studied law in New York as an apprentice to two of the colony's most prominent attorneys, James Alexander and William Smith senior. He practised law, often in conjunction with two Yale colleagues, William Smith junior and John Morin Scott. The three became known as the triumvirate or, from their Anglican opponents, the Presbyterian triumvirate. On 2 March 1747 Livingston married Susannah French (1723–1789).

Livingston was fairly successful in the law, handling both civil and criminal cases and working assiduously to raise standards for admission to the bar, eliminate 'pettifoggers', and professionalize the law among those already practising. In this last respect one of the most ambitious of his efforts was the organization in 1770 of a legal debating society called the Moot, where practising attorneys debated legal issues much on the model of the English inns of court. Livingston himself was admitted to the Middle Temple, though he never attended its sessions.

A versatile and talented writer but a poor speaker, Livingston soon began writing poetry and essays. His

William Livingston (1723–1790), by John Wollaston

poem *Philosophic Solitude, or, The Choice of a Rural Life* (1747), largely imitative of Pope and representing a popular genre that praised the virtues of country living, was one of New York's earliest poetic productions, went through thirteen editions, and was widely quoted throughout the colonies. A more serious and controversial publication, *The Independent Reflector*, was begun by the triumvirate in 1752 in imitation of *The Tatler* and *The Spectator*. However, its essays on morals and manners soon turned to more serious subjects, such as the contract theory of government, limitations on monarchical power, and the rights and liberties of the people, modelled after Thomas Gordon's and John Trenchard's radical English whig journals, *Cato's Letters* and *The Independent Whig*. The *Reflector's* contents encapsulated almost perfectly the radical whig ideology expressed by American patriot leaders in their contest with Great Britain in the years immediately preceding the American War of Independence.

The *Reflector's* most serious crusade was against the attempt by New York's Anglicans to establish in the colony an Episcopalian college chartered by the crown. Livingston and his friends proposed a non-sectarian college chartered by the New York assembly. In the heated contest that followed Livingston managed to mobilize public opinion, create a vigorous exchange of articles in the press, and introduce New Yorkers to popular politics, though the triumvirate lost its battle when the governor chartered King's College along the lines advocated by the Anglicans. But it was in the course of the *Reflector*'s crusading that Livingston expressed most eloquently the principle of freedom of religion and separation of church and state, a view he maintained throughout his life. 'Matters of Religion relate to another World, and have nothing to do with the Interest of the State', he wrote in 1753 (*Independent Reflector*, 307), and he repeated the belief twenty-five years later: 'the consciences of men are not the object of human legislation' (*New-Jersey Gazette*, 18 Feb 1778).

While Livingston became a spokesman of the Livingston party in opposition to its rival, one led by the colony's lieutenant-governor and chief justice, James De Lancey, he never became a popular political leader, and was uncomfortable in crowds and unimpressive as a public speaker. His talents were instead put to use in penning anti-British essays in the press and writing petitions to the crown and parliament on behalf of the New York assembly. One other dispute in which he did take an active part was the effort in 1768 on the part of some New York Anglicans to secure appointment of a bishop for the American colonies. This led to another heated public controversy, in which Livingston took a leading role as a columnist under the pseudonym The American Whig. Both these essays and the ones in the *Reflector* made him well known among the American leadership in other colonies.

Livingston moved to New Jersey in 1772, having built a country home where he thought he could indulge in the contemplative life of which he had written years earlier in his poem *Philosophic Solitude*, but his reputation soon made him the obvious choice as leader of the revolutionary cause in New Jersey. He was elected a delegate from that colony to the first and second continental congresses, was recalled to head the New Jersey militia, and then was elected governor in 1776 under the state's new constitution, a position to which he was re-elected annually until his death in 1790.

The governor possessed very limited powers under the New Jersey constitution, and Livingston constantly fretted about his inability to provide stronger leadership for a colony that was the scene of many battles between the British and the Americans, and was adjacent to New York city, which was in British hands throughout the revolution. New Jersey was faced with frequent British invasions, tory incursions, and illegal intercourse between it and New York city. Livingston urged strong measures to mobilize the state's militia and impress supplies for George Washington's forces, but he often met with intransigence from the state's legislature. His most forceful role, however, was again played with his pen. His addresses to the legislature urged the Americans to persist in the war effort, and these addresses were often reproduced in newspapers in other colonies. He also engaged in correspondence with friends abroad, urging support for the revolutionaries, and contributed a series of essays to the New Jersey newspaper the *Gazette*, again reminding the state's residents of their obligation to contribute manpower, money, and supplies for the American cause, and to resist efforts by the British to bring about a reconciliation and a return of the colonies to the empire. His pen gave Livingston a reputation as the ablest propagandist, next to Thomas Paine, on the American side.

At the war's end Livingston complained of his countrymen's loss of public spirit, exemplified by the depreciation of the currency, quarrels between the states, and an unwillingness to grant the government adequate taxing powers under the articles of confederation. He was chosen a delegate to the constitutional convention, where he played a fairly silent role, but he praised the body's finished work and urged its ratification by New Jerseyites. The constitution represented for Livingston the kind of balanced government he had once admired in Britain, with an executive possessed of ample powers yet curbed by republican institutions such as the house of representatives.

Livingston died at Elizabethtown, New Jersey, on 25 July 1790, and was buried at the town's Presbyterian church two days later. His death came too soon for him to see the new constitution in operation. He was not forgotten at the time by his fellow Americans, who recalled his vigorous exposition of whig principles before the revolution, but his basic inclination to trust aristocratic leadership more than popular democracy made him a forgotten figure as the United States became more democratic in time. Nevertheless, as an early spokesman for whig ideology he occupies a distinctive position in American history, even if, on balance, among the American patriot leadership of the revolution he must be considered a secondary figure, albeit an important one. MILTON M. KLEIN

Sources M. M. Klein, *The American Whig: William Livingston of New York* (1993) · M. M. Klein, ed., *The Independent Reflector* (1963) · M. L. Levine, 'The transformation of a radical whig under republican government: William Livingston of New Jersey, 1776–1790', PhD diss., Rutgers University, 1975 · *The papers of William Livingston*, ed. C. Prince and others, 5 vols. (1979–88) · T. Sedgwick, jun., *A memoir of the life of William Livingston* (1833) · C. E. Prince, 'Livingston, William', *ANB* · Bible of Catherine Livingston, Mass. Hist. Soc.

Archives Franklin D. Roosevelt Library, Hyde Park, New York, Livingston–Redmond Collection · Mass. Hist. Soc. · New York State Library, Livingston family letters · NYPL, Livingston family MSS | Dartmouth College, Livingston–Wheelock MSS/corresp. · Mass. Hist. Soc., Sedgwick MSS · NYPL, William Smith MSS · South Carolina Historical Society, Laurens MSS, Livingston–Henry Laurens corresp. · Yale U., Johnson MSS, Livingston–Welles corresp.

Likenesses attrib. J. Watson, portrait (in youth), priv. coll. · J. Wollaston, portrait, Fraunces Tavern Museum, New York [*see illus.*] · portrait, repro. in P. M. Hamlin, *Legal education in colonial New York* (1939), following p. 96

Wealth at death approx. $60,000: Klein, *The American Whig*

Livingstone [*née* Stickney], **Dame Adelaide Lord** (*c*.1881–1970), peace campaigner, was born in the United States, the daughter of Charles Daniel Stickney of Fall River, Massachusetts, and his wife, Mrs Sutherland Orr. Little is known of her early life but she was educated privately in America and Europe, variously in Italy, Germany, Switzerland, and France. On 14 May 1915, while an American citizen resident in London, she married William Henry Darley Livingstone (*b*. 1876), a landowner of Belclare, Westport, co. Mayo, Ireland, the son of Henry Darley

Dame Adelaide Lord Livingstone (*c*.1881–1970), by Harold Tomlin, 1935

Livingstone; she then acquired British nationality. At the time of their marriage her husband was a lieutenant in the motor machine-gun service.

During the First World War Adelaide Livingstone worked for the Friends' Emergency Committee, set up in 1914 to counteract the mass hysteria surrounding 'enemy aliens' in England. She also worked for the International Women's Relief Committee from November 1914 to May 1915. While in Brussels she organized repatriation parties, escorting British citizens back to the UK. In May 1915 the British government appointed her a member of the committee on the treatment of British prisoners of war, of which she became honorary secretary later in 1915. She spent some time in Switzerland investigating the system of repatriating British prisoners of war from Germany. In 1917 and 1918 she was sent to Holland with the British delegation to investigate the treatment of prisoners. At the end of the war she was appointed the Army Council head of the War Office mission to trace British soldiers reported as 'missing' in France and Flanders. In this capacity she travelled widely in Europe, managing a staff of officials from both Germany and England. Between 1920 and April 1922 she was assistant director of Graves Registration and Enquiries in central Europe, with headquarters in Berlin and with the rank of lieutenant-colonel. For her wartime services she was among the first women to be created DBE in 1918.

A prominent pacifist, Livingstone joined the staff of the League of Nations Union (LNU) in 1923 and became head of special activities from 1928 to 1933. In 1934 she was seconded by the LNU to the National Declaration on the League of Nations and Armaments, which organized the national peace ballot. Between November 1934 and June 1935 half a million volunteers were organized to deliver and collect ballot forms in which the public were asked to vote on issues such as international disarmament and collective security. Over 11 million people took part in this voluntary poll, whose results were published in *The Peace Ballot: an Official History* (1935), written by Livingstone and her colleagues on the National Declaration Committee.

They revealed overwhelming support for multilateral disarmament (90 per cent) and British membership of the League of Nations (nearly 96 per cent), but the ballot was soon rendered redundant by the collapse of collective security.

From 1936 to 1940 Adelaide Livingstone was secretary of the International Peace Campaign and became a leader of the United Nations Association in 1945. She obtained a divorce from her husband in 1924; there were no children of the marriage. She died at her home, 80 Carlisle Mansions, Westminster, London, on 14 September 1970.

JANE POTTER

Sources *WW* · *WWW* · *The Times* (16 Jan 1970) · Walford, *County families* (1919) · m. cert. · d. cert. · M. Ceadel, 'The first British referendum: the Peace Ballot, 1934–35', *EngHR*, 95 (1980), 810–39 · J. Wheeler-Bennett, *Knaves, fools and heroes* (1974)
Archives BL, corresp. with Lord Cecil, Add. MS 51142 · BL, corresp. with Gilbert Murray
Likenesses H. Tomlin, photograph, 1935, NPG [*see illus.*]
Wealth at death £55,718: probate, 11 Jan 1971, *CGPLA Eng. & Wales*

Livingstone, Sir Alexander, of Callendar. *See* Livingston, Sir Alexander, of Callendar (*b. c.*1375, *d.* in or before 1456).

Livingstone [Livingston], **Alexander, first earl of Linlithgow** (*d.* **1621**), politician and courtier, was the eldest son of William *Livingston, sixth Lord Livingston (*d.* 1592), and Agnes Fleming (*fl.* 1553–1584), daughter of the third Lord Fleming, who had married about 1553. As master of Livingstone he fought with the queen's party during the civil wars of 1567–73, and was captured at the taking of Dumbarton Castle on 2 April 1571. With his father he submitted to the regents, but was not in favour until the end of the earl of Morton's regency in 1578. He accompanied the young James VI on his progress from Stirling to make his entry to Edinburgh in September–October 1579. The establishment of a more formal court followed, and on 15 October 1580 Livingstone became one of the gentlemen of the chamber. He was on the assize which on 1 June 1581 found Morton guilty of the murder of Darnley.

After the seizure of the king by the Ruthven raid of 23 August 1582, Livingstone mustered forces to oppose the raiders. On the latter's success he retreated to Glasgow with the fallen royal favourite the duke of Lennox. He eventually accompanied Lennox to France (in December), and remained with him until his death on 26 May 1583. Having returned to Scotland, he was sent back to France after the fall of the Ruthven regime in 1583 to bring Lennox's son to Scotland.

By contract dated 26 and 31 January 1584 Livingstone married Lady Eleanor Hay (*d.* 1627) [*see* Livingstone, Helen], daughter of Andrew Hay, fifth earl of Erroll. In April that year he played a leading part in suppressing the Stirling raid in which the earl of Mar and other former Ruthven raiders attempted to recover power. When the raiders fled, he and his followers took possession of Stirling Castle. In August he temporarily gained the abbey of Cambuskenneth from Adam Erskine, a Ruthven raider. However, when Mar and his pro-English faction regained power in a successful coup of 2 November 1585, Livingstone was one of those captured at Stirling. Thereafter he was temporarily in eclipse. In the turbulent early 1590s he took a generally conservative stance, but was mentioned as an associate of the fugitive earl of Bothwell in 1592. He succeeded his father as seventh Lord Livingstone about November 1592, and gained in political prominence. He was a privy councillor from May 1593 onwards. He attended council meetings only irregularly, but he did assiduously attend the frequent conventions of the nobility held in this period. He carried the towel at the baptism of Prince Henry on 23 August 1594. In 1595 he incurred the wrath of the earl of Mar when a Livingstone killed one of Mar's followers. The feud rumbled on until 1599, but the king prevented further bloodshed.

On 3 December 1596 Livingstone received a notable mark of royal trust, being appointed keeper of the infant Princess Elizabeth. This angered many leading ministers because, though he himself was at least nominally a protestant, his wife was a committed Catholic, regularly in trouble with the church. Nevertheless, Livingstone retained the princess and also gained custody of her shortlived sister Margaret (1598–1600). Unlike Mar, keeper of Prince Henry, he was on good terms with Queen Anne, whom he escorted to England with her daughter in 1603. He was created earl of Linlithgow on 25 December 1600, at the baptism of Prince Charles. It had been rumoured in November that he would refuse the honour. In a 'Catalogue' of the nobility of about 1602 he was 'estemit to be Catholique, no actor, but a peaceable nobill man, and wealthy' (Rogers, 78).

Linlithgow's direct connection with the court lapsed with the union of the crowns in 1603. He was one of the Scottish commissioners for union with England in 1604. Having been appointed in July, the commission met at court between October and December, and Linlithgow served on a subcommittee to discuss customs rates. However, he made no attempt to build a court career in England. He remained an irregular privy councillor, and served on some minor parliamentary commissions.

As keeper of the palace of Linlithgow, and of the state prison Blackness Castle, the earl was involved in the show trial of six dissident Presbyterian ministers in 1606. David Calderwood noted that his wife on this occasion was 'howbeit an obstinat papist, but now a zealous professour', who received the ministers 'verie courteouslie' (Calderwood, 6.375). Linlithgow was forced to inform the king in 1607 that the palace's north quarter had collapsed through neglect (it was eventually rebuilt in 1618).

Linlithgow attended the privy council for the last time on 30 September 1618, though he remained nominally a councillor until his death. The five articles of Perth introduced kneeling at communion in 1618, and as a councillor Linlithgow received an order to communicate kneeling at Easter 1619. He refused, citing sickness as an excuse but indicating tacit disapproval of the articles. He gave a proxy to his son-in-law the earl of Eglinton to attend the parliament of August 1621. Eglinton used it to cast Linlithgow's vote against the ratification of the articles.

Whether this accorded with Linlithgow's own views cannot be proved conclusively, but Linlithgow could have given his proxy instead to another son-in-law, the earl of Wigtown, who voted with the government. Linlithgow died at Callendar House, near Falkirk, on 24 December 1621.

JULIAN GOODARE

Sources *CSP Scot.*, *1547–1603* • J. M. Thomson and others, eds., *Registrum magni sigilli regum Scotorum / The register of the great seal of Scotland*, 11 vols. (1882–1914) • *Reg. PCS*, 1st ser. • M. Livingstone, D. Hay Fleming, and others, eds., *Registrum secreti sigilli regum Scotorum / The register of the privy seal of Scotland*, 1 (1908) • A. Hay, *Estimate of the Scottish nobility during the minority of James the Sixth*, ed. C. Rogers, Grampian Club (1873) • *Scots peerage* • D. Calderwood, *The history of the Kirk of Scotland*, ed. T. Thomson and D. Laing, 8 vols., Wodrow Society, 7 (1842–9) • K. M. Brown, *Bloodfeud in Scotland, 1573–1625* (1986)

Livingstone, Charles (1821–1873), missionary and traveller in Africa, younger brother of David *Livingstone, was born at Blantyre in Lanarkshire on 28 February 1821, the son of Neil Livingstone and his wife, Agnes Hunter. He attended the local school and worked with his brother in the cotton factory of H. Monteith & Co., from which he moved to a lace factory at Hamilton, near Glasgow. He devoted his leisure time to study, and became a Sunday school teacher. In 1840 he emigrated to the United States of America, where he became a student at Oberlin College, Ohio, a training college for missionaries. In 1847 he entered the Union Theological College in New York city, from which he took his degree in 1850. He then held ministerial posts in New York state, Vermont, and Massachusetts. On 29 January 1852 he married Harriette Cemanthia Ingram (*d.* 1900) in Plympton, Massachusetts; they had three children.

In April 1857 Livingstone went to Britain on leave of absence, and met his brother David, fresh from his discoveries in central Africa, who induced him to leave his family and his post in America, and to join the Zambezi expedition (1858–64), as 'moral agent'. Through many privations and difficulties he remained with the expedition until 1863, when he was invalided home and went to join his family in America. His health did not, however, allow him to resume his ministerial duties, and after writing out his journal he again went to meet his brother in England, to assist him in preparing a joint journal, *Narrative of an Expedition to the Zambesi* (1865). In October 1864 he accepted an appointment as her majesty's consul for the Bight of Biafra, west Africa, which was extended in 1867 to include the Bight of Benin. His time as consul was taken up largely in dealing with the ramifications for British trading interests of the crisis within the state of Bonny, which culminated in the secession of Opobo in 1869, and of the accompanying wars across the Niger delta. His actions, particularly in demanding a trade blockade, made him unpopular with British traders and he was recalled by the Foreign Office in 1873. His career as consul was dogged by ill health and he died at sea near Lagos on 28 October 1873, during his return to Britain.

R. H. VETCH, *rev.* MARTIN LYNN

Charles Livingstone (1821–1873), by unknown photographer, 1860s

Sources H. Frere, *Proceedings* [Royal Geographical Society], 18 (1873–4), 512–14 • K. O. Dike, *Trade and politics in the Niger delta, 1830–1885* (1956) • *David Livingstone: family letters, 1841–1856*, ed. I. Schapera, 2 vols. (1959) • D. Livingstone and C. Livingstone, *Narrative of an expedition to the Zambesi and its tributaries* (1865) • *CGPLA Eng. & Wales* (1874)

Archives Livingstone Museum, Zambia • National Archives of Zimbabwe, Harare, corresp. • NL Scot., corresp. • Oberlin College Archives, Ohio, journal of Zambezi expedition | PRO, FO 84/- and FO 2/- series

Likenesses photograph, 1860–69, David Livingstone Centre, Blantyre [*see illus.*] • chromolithograph (after C. Gow), NPG

Wealth at death under £1500: probate, 6 March 1874, *CGPLA Eng. & Wales*

Livingstone, David (1813–1873), explorer and missionary, was born on 19 March 1813 at Blantyre, Lanarkshire. He was the second son of Neil Livingstone (1788–1856) and his wife, Agnes (1782–1865), daughter of David Hunter. Neil's father, also Neil, had been a tenant farmer on the island of Ulva, off Mull, who in 1792 had left with his wife and seven children for the cotton mills of central Scotland, and found work in Blantyre, on the River Clyde, with H. Monteith. His sons became clerks for the firm, though Neil, the youngest, was soon apprenticed to the firm's tailor, David Hunter, whose daughter Agnes he married in 1810. The younger Neil then became a self-employed tea dealer. His first child, John, was born in Glasgow, but the family soon returned to Blantyre; they took over the one-room tenement in Shuttle Row, a block owned by Monteith's mill, in which Agnes had grown up.

Early life, 1813–1841 In that tenement David Livingstone was born. As other children arrived, the family struggled to make ends meet, and from the age of ten David was employed in the mill (as John had been) as a 'piecer', tying up broken threads on spinning jennies for twelve hours a day. Yet David and a few other children still had the energy and will-power after work to put in two hours at the village school. Such determination was to be characteristic of the grown man, but study was also a family trait. Reading, conjoined with religion, was taken seriously by both Livingstones and Hunters. Neil Livingstone, a strict teetotaller and Sunday school teacher, distributed tracts; he interested himself in missionary work and accounts of

David Livingstone (1813–1873), by Thomas Annan, 1864

foreign travel. He raised his children in the Church of Scotland, and vainly pressed religious literature on David, who preferred not only travel books but also science, which Neil distrusted as hostile to faith. Limestone quarries aroused David's interest in geology; if he feared for his soul, it was due to his fascination with the astrology embedded in Culpeper's *Herbal*, one of his aids to the collection of medicinal plants.

In 1832, at a time of crisis in the Church of Scotland, father and son both reached a spiritual turning point. David came across recent books by Thomas Dick, a minister and amateur astronomer. These gave him the assurance he had been seeking that science could be reconciled with Christian belief. Meanwhile, a sermon by a Canadian preacher prompted Neil to leave the Church of Scotland for a Congregational church in Hamilton, near Blantyre; he was soon followed by David. Both heard the Glasgow Congregationalist Ralph Wardlaw declare that atonement was not confined to a predestined elect. Both were introduced through the Hamilton church to the liberal theology of the American Charles Finney. In 1834 Neil brought home a pamphlet by Karl Gutzlaff appealing for medical missionaries for China. David seized on this to prove to his father that his own growing ambition to study medicine could serve religious ends. For the past three years he had been working as a cotton spinner, and by 1836 he had saved enough to enter Anderson's College in Glasgow as a medical student; he also took Greek classes at Glasgow University and attended divinity lectures by Wardlaw. David is likely to have been impressed at this time by the anti-slavery campaign in Glasgow, in which Wardlaw was prominent.

In 1837 the Hamilton church put David in touch with the London Missionary Society (LMS), which was in effect a Congregational body. In April 1838 the Blantyre mill refused to let David continue to earn money for college fees through vacation work, and in August he went to London for an interview. He was sent for a probationary year of scriptural studies to a clergyman in Chipping Ongar, Essex. Livingstone had hoped to be sent in due course to China, but by June 1839 this had become problematical (the First Opium War broke out in September). The LMS proposed to Livingstone that he should go to the West Indies; Livingstone preferred South Africa. The LMS continued his training, and in January 1840 he moved to London for lectures on anatomy and medicine, where his teachers included Richard Owen and James Risdon Bennett. In the same year he met Robert Moffat, on leave from the LMS outpost at Kuruman, north of the Orange River and well beyond the limits of the Cape Colony. Moffat excited Livingstone's imagination with talk of work to be done still further north. In June 1840 Livingstone attended the meeting at Exeter Hall which launched the ill-fated Niger expedition of 1841–2; he heard T. F. Buxton expound the strategy of undermining the slave trade through 'legitimate trade' in conjunction with the Christian gospel. Later in 1840 Livingstone returned to Glasgow for examinations; in November he became a licentiate of the Faculty of Physicians and Surgeons of Glasgow. Back in London he was ordained, on 20 November, in Albion Chapel, London Wall, which belonged to the Congregational Union of England and Wales.

South Africa, 1841–1852 The LMS assigned Livingstone to Kuruman, and on 8 December 1840 he sailed for South Africa. Gales forced the ship to put in at Rio de Janeiro, where Livingstone spent some time ashore; he reached Simon's Bay on 15 March 1841, having learned the rudiments of navigation from the ship's captain. He spent three weeks in Cape Town, and stayed with the veteran LMS missionary John Philip, a champion of Africans against the demands of white colonists for land and labour. Divisions among white Christians provoked Livingstone to write home, 'I would never build on another man's foundation. I shall preach the gospel beyond every other man's line of things' (*David Livingstone: Family Letters*, 1.31), a phrase that recurs in later letters. At the end of July he reached Kuruman. He was not impressed by it as a mission centre: there seemed to be far too few people. Rogers Edwards, one of the two artisan missionaries at Kuruman, had already decided to visit the Kwena, a seTswana-speaking people 250 miles to the north-east. He set off with Livingstone in October, and they were away for six weeks. They identified a site for a new mission, but Livingstone was looking still further afield: he was sure that the northern Tswana would welcome missionaries as allies at a time of growing insecurity. The region was disturbed by the advance of *trekboer* Afrikaners into the Transvaal, to the east, while the Ndebele (Matabele), though now settled far to the north, near

Bulawayo, were still feared as raiders. The scale of violence increased as traders and hunters, European and African, took firearms ever further into the interior.

In the course of 1842, Livingstone made two more long journeys northwards, and by June he was fluent in seTswana; he then worked at Kuruman as a preacher, doctor, builder, and printer, and also travelled northwards again. In December 1843 Robert Moffat returned with his family to Kuruman; in January 1844 Edwards, Livingstone, and an African teacher named Mebalwe founded a mission at Mabotsa, among the Kgatla. On 2 January 1845 at Kuruman, Livingstone married Moffat's eldest daughter, Mary (1821–1862); in January 1846 she gave birth to a son, Robert. Meanwhile, Edwards had left Mabotsa after a quarrel with Livingstone, who himself began work to the north-east at Chonuane among the Kwena, whose chief, Sechele, soon learned to read. Livingstone believed that the LMS should make more use of African evangelists, and at Kuruman in March 1847 the annual LMS district committee unanimously supported his proposal to assess the number of African converts suitable for training as teachers. However, Livingstone had a low opinion of his colleagues, apart from Moffat; he already had a more acute, and more tolerant, understanding of African custom and belief, and he sent the directors in London his views on mission strategy as well as tactics.

In May 1847 Mary gave birth to a daughter, Agnes; in July the Livingstones returned to Chonuane. The water supplies there had proved inadequate, so together with Sechele they moved west to Kolobeng, near the present Gaborone. While Mary started an infant school, David began writing a philological analysis of seTswana. In October, Livingstone made the only convert of his career: he baptized Sechele after the chief had sent away all but his senior wife. When he took back one of his rejected wives, Livingstone suspended him from communion. Drought made it likely that the Kwena would move yet again: altogether, the prospects for Livingstone's mission seemed far from promising, whether among the Kwena or among people under Boer influence to the east.

However, Livingstone now had a new field in mind. Ever since his arrival at the Cape he had been intrigued by stories of a lake in the far interior (in fact, Lake Ngami). In 1847 he had proposed going there with Moffat; in 1848 he secured as companion William Cotton Oswell, a wealthy sportsman who had visited Mabotsa in 1845. Livingstone dispatched his family (now including a second son, Thomas) to Kuruman. Oswell reached Kolobeng in May 1849, with the horses, oxen, wagons, and supplies required for a year-long expedition. The moment was propitious: not only was this the right season to cross the Kalahari, but Livingstone had just been visited by envoys from the Tawana, near the lake, who wanted a resident white man: there was also the possibility of meeting Sebituane, the Kololo chief, known to Sechele, who had recently settled north of Lake Ngami. The expedition, including a trader, J. H. Wilson, reached the Botletle River in July and followed it westward to the lake. The lake made less impression on Livingstone than the river, which was connected to rivers further north and opened out 'the prospect of a highway capable of being quickly traversed by boats to a large section of well-peopled territory' (*Livingstone's Missionary Correspondence*, 133). Since the Niger expedition had failed, Livingstone believed that of all the missionaries in Africa he now had 'the key to the Interior' (ibid., 140). Without a boat, however, it proved impossible to advance northward, and the expedition returned to Kolobeng.

Livingstone's set purpose now was to reach Sebituane. Oswell agreed to return with a boat, but before he got back from the Cape, in May 1850, Livingstone had already set off northward, this time with his family and Sechele. They reached the Botletle, where Oswell caught up with them, but two of the children fell ill, and the Livingstones got back to Kolobeng just before a second daughter was born (she lived for six weeks). This ill-conceived journey was an early example of Livingstone's erratic judgement when gripped by a powerful idea, but it only stiffened his resolve to find 'a passage to the sea, on either the Eastern or Western coasts … the Bechuana Mission was virtually shut up in a cul de sac' (*Livingstone's Missionary Correspondence*, 157). Besides, envoys of Sebituane arrived at Kolobeng with gifts of cattle for the Tswana and requests that they help the whites to visit him. Moreover, while the family were at Kuruman recovering from their ordeal, news came that Livingstone had been awarded 25 guineas by the Royal Geographical Society (RGS) for discovering Lake Ngami. This had, in truth, been a joint effort, but Livingstone had got in first with his report.

Oswell returned to Kolobeng in 1851, with fresh supplies and animals, and set out once more for the north, this time ahead of Livingstone, who had defied a plea from Mary's mother to leave his family behind. Learning that another group of white travellers were on their way to the Kololo, he risked a short cut across the desert north of the Botletle. The party nearly died of thirst, but reached the Chobe River. Livingstone and Oswell went on to meet Sebituane, who had recently conquered the Lozi kingdom on the upper Zambezi. Sebituane barely had time to express his urgent desire for guns before he died suddenly of pneumonia. None the less, Livingstone now knew that there was a great river to the north, and on 4 August 1851 he and Oswell reached the Zambezi, near Sesheke. This indeed seemed the hoped-for highway to the east coast; moreover, many people understood seTswana. These facts were the more significant since slave traders from Angola now visited the upper Zambezi. Recalling Buxton, Livingstone looked to a legitimate trade in English manufactured goods to undermine this slave trade. First, though, it would be necessary to find a more healthy site for a mission and trading station than the malarial swamps to which Sebituane had retreated for fear of Ndebele attacks. Livingstone rejoined his family and took them back south; a third son, named after Oswell, was born *en route*. The party duly reached Kolobeng but then went farther south, since Livingstone had decided to send his family to Britain while he made a fuller exploration of the Zambezi. In March 1852, helped by Oswell, the Livingstones reached

Cape Town; Mary and the children embarked for Britain, where they spent the next four years, without a settled home, dependent on handouts from the LMS.

The crossing of Africa, 1852–1856 Livingstone had other business in Cape Town. He had a troublesome uvula excised. With Oswell he composed his first direct communication to the RGS, a report on their recent journey. From the astronomer royal, Thomas Maclear, Livingstone learned how to make observations with sextant and chronometer; thereafter he regularly sent his results to Maclear. With further help from Oswell, he fitted out his new expedition and enlisted George Fleming, who had worked for Oswell, to accompany him with trade goods for buying ivory on the Zambezi. On their return to Kuruman news came of a Boer attack in August on Sechele's people, and the sacking of Livingstone's house at Kolobeng. Livingstone considered that the Kwena had been justly punished for rejecting the gospel; besides, he had already declared, 'We ought to give all if possible a chance, and not spend an age on one tribe or people' (*David Livingstone: Family Letters*, 1.14). In face of the Moffats' disapproval he turned his back on Sechele and in December started for the north. On 23 May 1853 he and Fleming reached Linyanti, the Kololo capital on the Chobe.

Livingstone's conviction that he was the favoured instrument of providence was reinforced by the welcome he received from Sekeletu, Sebituane's eighteen-year-old son and successor, to whom he gave powder and ammunition. The search for a mission site was fruitless: the upper Zambezi valley was malarial, and Livingstone himself suffered several attacks of fever. The highlands downstream sounded more promising, but were vulnerable to the Ndebele. Meanwhile, Livingstone's search for a trade route to the sea was influenced by meeting two Portuguese traders who had come from the west coast. Sekeletu was eager to co-operate: he organized an expedition under two Kololo headmen to open up trade with Luanda. In November 1853 Livingstone set off once more up the Zambezi with this party; Fleming in due course went south.

Once the expedition had left Kololo-controlled territory, Livingstone depended heavily on his African companions as interpreters, for he could no longer communicate through seTswana. Their progress was smoothed by Sekeletu's presents of oxen and beads for chiefs, but they soon had to give up travelling by canoe, and as they struck out westwards (Livingstone riding on an ox), the going was very difficult, for the rainy season had set in. The prospects for wagon traffic were further blighted by the tsetse-fly, which was liable to kill domestic animals. Slave trading in the region had raised prices, and when the expedition reached the Kwango River, on 4 April 1854, they had exhausted their trade goods and sold much of the ivory intended for the coast. Soon afterwards they reached Kasanje, a Portuguese military and trading post where Livingstone was made welcome. On the last stretch Livingstone had a severe attack of malaria; he collapsed when he reached Luanda, on 31 May, at the house of Edmund Gabriel, the local British commissioner for the suppression of the slave trade. Yet he declined a passage to England: he wished to see whether a route from the Zambezi to the east coast might be easier than that to the west. He duly set off on 20 September, with presents for Sekeletu from the government of Angola.

The return to Linyanti took almost a year—twice as long as the outward journey. Sekeletu was sufficiently impressed by the travellers' tales and presents to send another expedition with ivory to Luanda, in the care of an Arab from Zanzibar, Said b. Habib, who had already been to Benguela. (This enabled Livingstone to dispatch to one of his Portuguese hosts a model of the Crystal Palace, which he had received from his sister Agnes by way of the Ndebele king Mzilikazi, who had forwarded to the Zambezi mail brought north by Moffat in 1854.) News of the route from Zanzibar intrigued Livingstone, but he held to his intention of finding a water route to the east coast. Sekeletu was also keen on this project, and on Livingstone's behalf he fitted out a new expedition, led by Kololo; and Livingstone agreed to sell a consignment of ivory for Sekeletu.

The expedition set off for the Zambezi in November. Not far below Sesheke it came to the colossal waterfalls known locally as Mosi-oa-Tunya, 'the waters that thunder'; Livingstone named them after Queen Victoria. The party then moved away from the valley, to the plateau beyond the north bank. By the time they reached the Kafue River, Livingstone was sure that this fertile country, 'well adapted for cattle and health', was just what he sought for a mission (*Livingstone's African Journal*, 348). In December they rejoined the Zambezi not far above Zumbo, crossed the river further down, and followed the right bank down to the Portuguese settlement at Tete. As a result Livingstone failed to see the formidable cataracts of Quebrabasa, which he persuaded himself were only a 'small rapid'. They reached Tete on 2 March, and Livingstone found the governor very hospitable, as indeed most Africans had been throughout this journey. He left most of his companions at Tete, where they were given land to cultivate; Livingstone intended to accompany them home when he returned from Britain. From Tete he proceeded down river by canoe, with his chief guide and interpreter, Sekwebu, who was anxious to see Britain. In May, enfeebled by fever, they reached the seaport of Quelimane, where Livingstone left Sekeletu's ivory. In July they took ship for Mauritius, but rough seas so unbalanced Sekwebu's mind that he drowned himself. Livingstone grieved at the loss of a 'very good friend'; 'he was my right hand man and contributed greatly to my success' (*David Livingstone: Family Letters*, 2.291). In Mauritius, Livingstone recuperated before going home by way of the Red Sea. Mary met him at Southampton on 12 December 1856.

Livingstone had intended to stay only a month or two in Britain: he did not reckon with the problems of the LMS, or the effects of his own celebrity. His reports on the journeys between 1849 and 1851 to Lake Ngami and the Zambezi had been published by the RGS. Its president in 1851–2 (as in 1856–7 and between 1862 and 1871) was the geologist Sir Roderick Murchison. British exploration in Africa was currently at a low ebb, even if the German Heinrich

Barth had in 1849 gone overland to west Africa with British support. Livingstone had sent Murchison ten letters during his crossing of Africa between 1854 and 1856, and these too had been duly published. By the time news of Livingstone's arrival at Luanda reached London, Murchison had prompted the RGS, in 1855, to award Livingstone its annual gold medal. Livingstone, in turn, was acquainted with Murchison's work; at Sesheke, in October 1855, he had read Murchison's argument that the structure of Africa was basin-like, shaped by ridges near the coasts—a theory confirmed by his own laborious travels. It was thus to Murchison that Livingstone had turned when, on reaching Quelimane in May 1856, he learned that the directors of the LMS 'were restricted in their power of aiding plans connected only remotely with the spread of the Gospel'. The LMS was, as it happened, heavily in debt, and understandably reluctant to reach out into 'untried, remote, and difficult fields of labour' (*Livingstone's Missionary Correspondence*, 277). Livingstone, however, was deeply wounded by this advice, which directly challenged his own conception of mission work. On the way to Mauritius, Livingstone told Murchison that he would prefer to work in Africa as a 'private Christian' (Livingstone, *Zambezi Expedition*, ed. J. P. R. Wallis, 1956, xx). He also painted a rosy picture of the commercial prospects for British enterprise on the Zambezi, even implying the possibility of new sources of cotton to replace the slave states of the USA.

In Britain, 1856–1858 Within days of Livingstone's return to Britain in 1856 the RGS held a special meeting, on 15 December, to bestow on him its gold medal; on the next day the LMS held a reception for him, chaired by Lord Shaftesbury. Over Christmas and the new year, Livingstone visited his mother and sisters in Hamilton (his father had died in February 1856), after which he began work in London on a book to be published (through Murchison's good offices) by John Murray. In April Murchison induced the foreign secretary, Lord Clarendon, to employ Livingstone as a consul in central Africa. Livingstone himself concealed this from the LMS, even after persuading its directors (on the strength of his recent information about the Kafue plateau) to support a Zambezi mission led by himself, coupled with a mission by Moffat to the Ndebele.

Surrounded by his family Livingstone wrote his book in great haste, at first in lodgings in Sloane Street and then, from May to August, at Hadley Green, Barnet. The title, *Missionary Travels and Researches in South Africa*, evokes earlier accounts of southern Africa, notably by Philip and Moffat, but Livingstone's book stands out from these by reason of its intellectual breadth. Throughout his sixteen years in Africa, Livingstone had kept himself supplied with reading matter on religion, medicine, natural history, and physical anthropology. He had, moreover, maintained an extensive correspondence with friends made in Glasgow, Ongar, and London. And from 1851, aware of his growing reputation as an explorer, he kept a journal. Here he recorded a miscellany of ruminations and minute observation which attest to a wide-ranging curiosity about the human race and the natural world, and owe much to his medical training. When he came to write his book, he enriched a stirring narrative, told in conversational style, with insights acquired by informed eyes and ears, as well as with shafts of caustic humour.

However, Livingstone aimed to do more than instruct and amuse. Murchison (who ensured that the book was dedicated to himself) might value *Missionary Travels* as a commercial prospectus and confirmation of his own theories; Livingstone conceived it as propaganda for the campaign against the slave trade and for his own role in spreading knowledge of the Christian gospel. The book was a highly self-conscious presentation of a career which Livingstone had come to believe was divinely ordained. This coloured his reporting. He now believed that legitimate trade was a precondition for the spread of Christianity. He thus had a reason not only for noting economic resources but for exaggerating them. Besides, his lifelong fear of being 'cut out' by other travellers led him to imply that he was the first European to travel between Angola and the upper Zambezi. *Missionary Travels* fails to mention either Silva Porto or Ladislav Magyar, who did so in 1853, let alone earlier crossings of the continent by African-Portuguese or Arab traders. But these are flaws in an avowedly popular work of unusual humanity. It is untouched by the 'pseudo-scientific racism' of mid-century anthropology, and while Livingstone looked to the 'Anglo-American race' to promote liberty and progress he could also assess African behaviour in terms of environment and history, making cross-cultural comparisons to support his arguments. He concluded that Africans are 'just such a strange mixture of good and evil, as men are everywhere else' (Livingstone, *Missionary Travels*, 510).

Livingstone spent the latter part of 1857 on a speaking tour. To one listener he appeared:

> plainly and rather carelessly dressed, of middle height [he was 5 ft 8 in.], bony frame and Gaelic countenance, with short-cropped hair and moustachios … His face is deeply furrowed, and pretty well tanned … when excited, a varied expression of earnest and benevolent feeling, and remarkable enjoyment of the ludicrous … passes over it … When he speaks to you, you think him at first to be a Frenchman; but as he tells you a Scotch anecdote in the Glaswegian dialect, you make up your mind that he must be, as his face indicates, a countryman from the north.
> (G. Seaver, *David Livingstone*, 1957, 286–7)

In Dublin, Livingstone addressed the British Association for the Advancement of Science; in Manchester, the chamber of commerce. He also spoke in Glasgow, Blantyre, Edinburgh, Leeds, Liverpool, Birmingham, and Oxford—where, as in Glasgow, he received an honorary degree. In Cambridge, on 4 December, he was introduced at Senate House by William Whewell and the geologist Adam Sedgwick. A large audience cheered his concluding appeal for missionaries:

> It is a mistake to suppose that *any one*, as long as he is pious, will do for this office. Pioneers in everything should be the ablest and best qualified men … I beg to direct your attention to Africa … do you carry out the work which I have begun.
> (J. Simmons, *Livingstone and Africa*, 1955, 79)

By this time, *Missionary Travels* had appeared. The first impression, of 12,000, was sold out before publication in November, and 30,000 were sold in Britain by 1863. Livingstone had meant the book to make money; it earned him over £8500. A compelling drama of self-improvement, expanding knowledge, and non-sectarian Christian fortitude, it was admired by Charles Dickens, no friend of missionaries, whose own precarious early life had resembled Livingstone's. *Missionary Travels* quite eclipsed the austere erudition of Barth's *Travels and Discoveries in North and Central Africa* (1857–8).

Well before the end of 1857 Livingstone had become a national hero. Early in 1858 he was elected a fellow of the Royal Society and in February he had an audience with the queen. To help him get back to Africa was a matter of public concern. The travels which made him famous had been financed by well-wishers in Africa, especially Oswell and Sekeletu. His return might be assisted by public subscriptions (£2000 was raised in Glasgow), but there was pressure on the government (notably from Manchester businessmen and the British Association) to provide Livingstone with a steamship for use on the Zambezi. Although preoccupied with the Indian mutiny the prime minister, Lord Palmerston, was responsive, while Lord Clarendon had already promised Livingstone a consulate and had recently funded William Baikie's trading expedition on the Niger and supported exploration in east Africa by Richard Burton and John Hanning Speke. Late in October 1857 Livingstone clarified his own position by formally resigning from the LMS. On 1 December he sent Clarendon plans for a Zambezi expedition, which he expected to last two years; on 11 December parliament approved a grant to this end of £5000. The expedition was to include several Europeans besides Livingstone; in choosing them he was given a remarkably free hand, though Murchison ensured that they included scientists whose work could have practical results. Livingstone chose Norman Bedingfeld, whom he had met in Luanda, as steamship commander, and George Rae, from Blantyre, as engineer. Murchison chose as geologist Richard Thornton, a recent graduate of the School of Mines; as economic botanist, John Kirk, a young physician; and as artist to the expedition, Thomas Baines, who had lately worked for the RGS in Australia. Finally, and crucially, Livingstone created the nebulous post of 'moral agent' for his younger brother Charles *Livingstone, who had recently returned to Britain from the USA (he had gone there to study in 1839 and had become a pastor in New England).

The Zambezi expedition, 1858–1864 For the government the aim of the expedition was to assess the prospects for British trade up the Zambezi. This involved negotiations early in 1858 with the Portuguese, whose maps were limited and patchy but who claimed authority as far west as Zumbo and confined foreign traders to the mouth of the Zambezi. They exempted the expedition from import duties, but otherwise held firm in opposing free trade and accepted Livingstone as British consul only for Quelimane. This put in question the ultimate purpose of the expedition and Livingstone was duly angered; besides, he privately cherished the hope that the expedition might result 'in an English colony in the healthy highlands of Central Africa' (G. Seaver, *David Livingstone*, 1957, 308), albeit very different in character from the British in South Africa, of whom he was highly critical. He had in any case kept up pressure on the LMS for a Kololo mission, even though he would not take part in it; the LMS, against its better judgement, appointed its own team.

The Zambezi expedition left Birkenhead on 10 March 1858, on the steamship *Pearl*, which carried, in three sections, a steam launch which had been hastily built by Macgregor Laird. This was called the *Ma-Robert*, the African name for Mary Livingstone, who was on board with her youngest son Oswell: the other children had been left with relatives and were supported by a trust fund from their father's literary earnings. It then became clear that Mary was pregnant, and she and Oswell were left behind at Cape Town to be taken to Kuruman by her parents. The *Pearl* reached the Zambezi in mid-May but was too large to sail, as intended, through the delta and up to Tete; instead, stores had to be taken up in relays by the *Ma-Robert*. Meanwhile, Bedingfeld fell out with Livingstone and resigned. Livingstone took over the *Ma-Robert*, which often ran aground on sandbanks and also consumed a great deal of firewood. In November and December, Livingstone and Kirk investigated the Quebrabasa cataracts. Kirk realized that these were an insuperable obstacle to navigation. Livingstone refused to admit this; indeed, he asked the British government to supply a more powerful steamer, and asserted that the whole expedition expected the cataracts to be submerged when the river was in flood.

However, Livingstone now had in mind an alternative to the Zambezi as a 'highway' to the interior. This was the Shire River, which joins the Zambezi below Sena, from the north, and which was said to flow from a large lake. By 9 January 1859 Livingstone and Kirk had ascended 100 miles up the Shire; again they encountered cataracts, and again Livingstone made light of them. Moreover, Livingstone's first glimpse of the hill country above the Shire convinced him that this, as well as the Kafue plateau, was suitable both for a mission and for a cotton-exporting British colony, even if the slave trade was also on the increase here. In March and April, Livingstone, Kirk, and others reached Lake Shirwa, north of the highlands. Backbiting by Charles Livingstone caused David to dismiss Thornton in June, and Baines in July. In August the Livingstones, Kirk, and Rae, with several Kololo resident in Tete, went once again up the Shire; on 17 September they reached the south end of Lake Nyasa. There was little more that Livingstone could do to further his designs until he knew whether the government would prolong the expedition beyond its allotted two years and replace the *Ma-Robert*. He was committed to escorting the Kololo back to the upper Zambezi, but the journey would not be practicable before a new harvest in the countries upriver. Rae went home in March 1860 to advise on the construction of a steamer which could be carried in sections past the Shire cataracts and placed on Lake Nyasa. Meanwhile, Livingstone was considering yet another possible water route to the interior: the Rovuma River. This later formed the northern frontier of Mozambique; to Livingstone it appealed because it lay well beyond the sphere of the Portuguese, whom he not only saw as an obstacle to any future British trade but now believed to be implicated in the expanding slave trade of east central Africa.

In May 1860, two years later than he had originally intended, Livingstone, with Charles and Kirk, set off from Tete with those few Kololo who wished to go home. On the middle Zambezi, they found outcrops of coal, supplementing those examined (and mined) by Thornton near Tete. In August, Livingstone delivered to Sekeletu goods he had ordered in 1856, though not the sugar mill (which remained at Tete) or the rifles and ammunition. The Kololo told Livingstone of the disastrous LMS mission, which had reached Linyanti in April 1860: of the Europeans three out of four adults had died and three out of five children, while four Africans had also died. During this Zambezi journey the Livingstone brothers quarrelled bitterly; David came to think he had relied far too much on Charles. Yet neither Charles nor Kirk (who loathed Charles) thwarted David's foolhardy impulse, on the way back, to descend the uppermost Quebrabasa rapids in canoes: Kirk nearly drowned, and lost his notes, drawings, and instruments. At Tete, Livingstone found a dispatch from London extending the expedition for a further three years. This decision had not been taken lightly. Ministers were unexcited by Livingstone's visions of British colonies in tropical Africa, whether of master farmers or the urban poor, which were 'only to be reached by forcing steamers up cataracts' (G. Martelli, *Livingstone's River*, 1970, 108). Eventually, however, his shift of focus to the Shire highlands was approved, along with his proposal to explore the Rovuma, and a new steamship was sent out.

Missionaries were also coming to join him. Livingstone had tried in 1859 to interest the Church Missionary Society in the Shire highlands; he also approached the bishop of Cape Town, Robert Gray, who had already reported that Anglicans in the universities of Oxford, Cambridge, Durham, and Dublin were planning a mission to central Africa. By the end of 1860 this had been organized under the leadership of Charles Mackenzie. In December, Livingstone descended the Zambezi and abandoned the leaking *Ma-Robert* on a sandbank. In February 1861 he met the missionaries, who had just arrived from Cape Town, together with his new ship, the *Pioneer*. Livingstone insisted that Mackenzie join him on a reconnaissance of the Rovuma. This diversion proved fruitless: the *Pioneer* could get only 30 miles upriver. Its master resigned, since Livingstone would not accept him as second in command of the expedition. It was not until July that the Universities' Mission to Central Africa (UMCA) established itself in the Shire highlands, at Magomero. This was a Manganja village harassed by Yao slavers. By entrusting abandoned slaves to the mission, and burning a slavers' village, Livingstone plunged the UMCA fatefully into local politics.

Livingstone's next concern was to explore Lake Nyasa. In August, with Charles, Kirk, and an Irish seaman, John Neil, Livingstone set off northwards with a four-oared gig. Just below the lake he noted that mosquitoes 'showed … the presence of malaria', but did not guess at a causal connection, despite being aware that tsetse-flies and ticks were vectors of disease. Once on the lake he hoped to find an outlet to the Rovuma, but he followed the western shore and, delayed by equinoctial gales, turned back at Nkata Bay for want of food. The country they had seen was troubled by Arab slavers, and also by Ngoni raiders. From the lower Shire, in November, Livingstone took the *Pioneer* down to meet new arrivals. At the end of January a ship from the Cape brought Rae with the new portable steamer, *Lady Nyassa*. Livingstone had had to pay for this himself: the Admiralty considered that he 'has already discovered more country and more people than he can deal with' (G. Martelli, *Livingstone's River*, 161). There was also Mary Livingstone, who after the birth of another daughter, Anna Mary, at Kuruman in November 1858 had returned to Scotland. On this latest voyage she was escorted by James Stewart, a young Scots minister who had decided on his own initiative to assess the prospects for a Scottish mission in the Zambezi region.

It took over four months to assemble the *Lady Nyassa* at Shupanga; meanwhile news came in March of the death of Mackenzie and another missionary, and on 27 April 1862 Mary Livingstone died. (The use of quinine as prophylactic or cure for malaria was still at an experimental stage; Livingstone himself had, from at least 1853, relied much on pills combining quinine and mild purgatives.) Livingstone pressed on; the *Lady Nyassa* was launched in June, but by then the Zambezi was too low to allow ascent and instead he took the *Pioneer*, with Charles, Kirk, and Rae, back to the Rovuma, which this time they entered in sailing boats. Livingstone's determination to get the boats through every shallow forced Kirk (who in February had declared him 'always very good company') to conclude that 'Dr L. is out of his mind … he is a most unsafe leader' (*Zambesi Journal … of John Kirk*, 567, 475, 482). Livingstone himself was aware that such frantic activity was a means to keep grief at bay. After 160 miles, even he had had enough. By December they were back at Shupanga, where they met a disenchanted James Stewart on his way home.

The year 1863 was still more depressing. In January the *Pioneer* and *Lady Nyassa* went up into the Shire valley. This was now a scene of horror: there were corpses in the river and along its banks, victims of drought as well as slave raids. The river was so low that it was April before the ships reached the cataracts. It was here that Richard Thornton died (after his dismissal in 1859 he had travelled in east Africa, and in 1862 returned to the Zambezi delta, where Livingstone had reinstated him). The rest of the expedition suffered severe dysentery, and on 19 May Kirk and Charles Livingstone left for Quelimane. Livingstone himself, with Rae, began to dismantle the *Lady Nyassa* and to build a road past the cataracts, but famine threatened food supplies. At this critical juncture, on 2 July Livingstone received a letter from London recalling the expedition. The ships could not get downriver until the end of the year, so Livingstone decided to investigate the sources of the slave trade to the north-west. With Thomas Ward, a steward on the *Pioneer*, he reached Lake Nyasa at Nkhota Kota and then travelled west for 100 miles. He got back to the ships on 1 November and reached the Zambezi mouth in February 1864, after learning to his fury that the UMCA, now much depleted, had decided to withdraw. From Mozambique the *Pioneer* returned to the Cape, while Livingstone and Rae took the *Lady Nyassa* to Zanzibar. With a crew of twelve but without Rae, Livingstone sailed the little ship across to Bombay just before the monsoon broke. He left her in Bombay, where she was later sold unprofitably; he was back in London on 23 July.

In Britain, 1864–1865 This time Livingstone's reception was subdued. The Zambezi expedition had cost much more, and achieved much less, than expected. At least £30,000 had been spent on it (as much as on the Niger expedition of 1857–60). It had involved the deaths of Thornton and Mary Livingstone, and also missionaries of the LMS and UMCA, as well as several sailors. It had lasted six and a half years, though scarcely eighteen months were spent on travel above the Shire and Zambezi cataracts and on the Rovuma, due to sickness and logistical problems. The geographical and scientific results seemed hardly commensurate with the effort expended, and plans to check the slave trade had come to nothing. Stewart had identified:

> the fallacy in Livingstone's method. He meets a difficulty, overcomes it by an amount of perseverance and an expenditure of strength and money which men will put forth once or twice but which it would be ruinous to carry out as a rule.

Kirk was driven to write to Stewart in 1864, 'in him I believe all kindly feelings to be absolutely extinct' (J. P. R. Wallis, ed., *The Zambesi Journal of James Stewart*, 1952, 264, 228).

Fortunately, this was untrue. Livingstone regretted that he had seen so little of his children, and in August 1864 he rejoined his family, in Hamilton, though Robert had gone to the USA (and later that year died fighting for the north in the civil war). Livingstone then visited the west highlands, including Ulva, as the guest of the duke of Argyll. From September 1864 to April 1865 Livingstone and his elder daughter Agnes were at Newstead, in Nottinghamshire, the home of W. F. Webb, whom he had known in south Africa. Here he worked on a second book. This had originally been planned as a pamphlet in which to accuse the Portuguese of fostering the slave trade in central Africa; however, Charles made his own journal available, and David drew extensively on this. The *Narrative of an Expedition to the Zambesi and its Tributaries* (1865) shows some of the qualities of *Missionary Travels*, but it is more impersonal and much more tendentious. Given the quarrels and reverses which marred the expedition, there was much for which Livingstone could attract blame, and he sought to direct it elsewhere.

Livingstone was intent on returning to Africa. On his way home he had learned more about the Arab slave trade and had glimpsed possibilities for legitimate trade with India. He was, moreover, convinced that he could throw light on the Nile problem. In 1862 Speke had found that the White Nile flowed from Lake Victoria, but Livingstone did not believe this was the whole answer: since at least 1857 he had thought that the source of the Nile was close to that of the Zambezi. He wanted to outshine Burton as well as Speke, and by November 1864 he had agreed with Murchison that he would try to 'settle' the watersheds of central Africa, though he insisted that he remained primarily a missionary. He planned to return to the Rovuma, pass to the north of Lake Nyasa, look for the Nile headwaters, and then make for Ujiji, on Lake Tanganyika; but he still hoped to find a site for a trading mission. The expedition was to be small-scale, without a steamboat, and without other Europeans. The RGS put up £500, as did the British government; and £1000 came from James Young, a friend from Livingstone's student days in Glasgow, who had made a fortune from distilling paraffin. Livingstone was appointed to a roving consulship outside the Portuguese sphere, without salary or pension. As the time for departure approached he continued to spend much time with Agnes: a month in London, and two months in Scotland (where he attended his mother's burial in June). In August he settled Agnes in a finishing school in Paris, before taking ship from Marseilles.

The last journey, 1866–1873 In Bombay, Livingstone recruited several sepoys, and twelve Africans from mission schools, including four whom he had brought across in 1864. His host in Bombay was the governor, Sir Bartle Frere, who in January 1866 gave the party passage in a government ship to Zanzibar. Here Livingstone added ten men from the Comoro Islands. Once on the mainland the expedition soon ran into trouble. It took four months to reach Lake Nyasa, past frightful evidence of slaving, and by then the sepoys had been dismissed. Rumours of war obliged Livingstone to go round the south end of the lake, where the Comorans gave up. In January 1867, soon after crossing the Luangwa River, the chronometers were damaged, which caused persistent error in observations of longitude. Then a temporary porter made off with the medicine chest. Livingstone was aiming for Lake Bangweulu, which he believed to be linked to Lake Tanganyika (and thus, he thought, to the Nile), but it was now the rainy season, and the country in that direction was so swampy that he made directly for Lake Tanganyika, visiting the Bemba king Chitimukulu.

Henceforward, progress was repeatedly interrupted by local wars and by illness. Livingstone received much help from Arab and Swahili traders, but he suffered from pneumonia, dysentery, ulcers, and haemorrhoids. Between November 1867 and July 1868 he reached Lake Mweru and Lake Bangweulu, and visited the Lunda king Kazembe, on the Luapula. In March 1869 he got to Ujiji, where he found few of the stores he had ordered from the coast. He now thought it likely that the upper Nile was to be identified with the Lualaba River, west of Lake Tanganyika, but he did not reach this until March 1871, after receiving further supplies relayed by Kirk, now vice-consul in Zanzibar. At Nyangwe, Livingstone vainly sought canoes to explore the course of the Lualaba, and rejected Arab help after a massacre of local Manyema in July. He returned to Ujiji in October to find little left of the goods from Zanzibar funded by the British government (at Murchison's insistence). Instead, he was relieved in November by H. M. *Stanley, who had been told to 'find Livingstone' by the editor of the *New York Herald* and who traced him to Ujiji, there greeting him with the famous and premeditated salutation, 'Dr Livingstone, I presume?' (H. M. Stanley, *How I Found Livingstone*, 1872, 412). They travelled together to the north end of Lake Tanganyika and proved that it had no outlet there. They parted on 14 March 1872 at Tabora, on the caravan route to the east coast, where Livingstone waited for fresh supplies to be sent up by Stanley. These arrived in August, along with the fifty-six porters who had contracted to work for him, and the five remaining from his original team.

Livingstone resumed his quest. He was not sure that the Lualaba was the Nile, but his obsession with finding the Nile's ultimate source drove him to seek not where the Lualaba went but where it came from. Thus he went south from Tabora to the south-eastern shore of Lake Tanganyika, and returned to Lake Bangweulu. However, his attempt in 1872–3 to traverse the 'sponges' around the lake and push west was confused by the faulty longitudes of 1867–8 and was further delayed by heavy rains and by his own debility. By April 1873 he was bleeding profusely and soon had to be carried in a litter. He died during the night of 30 April at the village of Chitambo, a Lala headman. Command of the expedition was assumed by Abdullah Susi, from Shupanga, who with James Chuma, a Yao, and Edward Gardner had accompanied Livingstone continuously. The heart and viscera were buried on the spot, but Susi decided to carry Livingstone's body, duly embalmed, to the coast, along with his effects. At Tabora, Susi's expedition met a search party led by V. L. Cameron; against his advice, the team held firm to their remarkable purpose and reached Bagamoyo in February 1874. Kirk's deputy arranged for the body to be dispatched to England. On 18 April 1874 Livingstone was buried in the nave of Westminster Abbey. The pallbearers included Oswell, Kirk, Stanley, and Jacob Wainwright, one of Stanley's recruits for the final journey from Tabora. Murchison—'the best friend I ever had' (*Last Journals*, 2.205)— had died in 1871, but Robert Moffat was there, and James Stewart.

Significance and reputation In death Livingstone became once more a national hero. The Treasury paid £500 for the funeral; Gladstone awarded a pension to Livingstone's daughters; and Disraeli's subsequent ministry gave the family £3000. Although Livingstone's Nile theory had already been disproved, he was acclaimed once again as a great abolitionist: his numerous reports on the slavers' advance across Africa from the east coast were seen to have led to the treaty against the trade enforced on the sultan of Zanzibar in 1873. Missionaries soon began to realize Livingstone's vision of rivers and lakes as highways for the spiritual and social regeneration of Africa, even if his views on the commercial function of missions were sometimes more influential than his lifelong advocacy of 'native agency'. Two Scottish missions—one named Livingstonia and the other Blantyre—went out to Lake Nyasa and the Shire highlands in 1875–6. Both were crucial factors in the British occupation of what became Nyasaland and then Malawi. Meanwhile the UMCA, which had re-established itself in Zanzibar, was at work on the mainland; by 1878 the LMS was on Lake Tanganyika, and the Church Missionary Society was in Buganda, as a result of Stanley's return to east Africa. Stanley himself completed Livingstone's geographical work by reaching the Lualaba and following the Congo to the sea.

Stanley had, of course, taken the lead in reviving Livingstone's celebrity and his book, *How I Found Livingstone* (1872), presented the traveller as a genial saint. Horace Waller, who had been with the UMCA at Magomero, fastidiously edited Livingstone's *Last Journals* (1874), a poignant testimony to soul-searching, suffering, forbearance, and tenacity. These books, and their derivatives, contributed to a Livingstone legend which had begun with *Missionary Travels*. There was a peculiar romance about the lone missionary ever pressing into new country, concerned not to convert but to bear Christian witness by preaching the gospel, giving magic-lantern shows, and speaking against slavery. Livingstone became a symbol of what the British—and other Europeans—wished to believe about their motives as they took over tropical Africa in the late nineteenth century: in effect he redeemed the colonial project. In 1929 the Scottish national memorial to David Livingstone was opened at his birthplace, Blantyre, by the duchess of York; by 1963 there had been 2 million visitors. In Africa, he is still commemorated in the names of two towns: Blantyre, in Malawi, and Livingstone, in Zambia, beside the Victoria Falls.

For half a century after his death Livingstone was the subject of hagiography rather than scholarship. More realistic assessments became possible with access to the papers of Kirk and other members of the Zambezi expedition. The chief work of reappraisal, however, was achieved in Isaac Schapera's magisterial editions of Livingstone's journals and letters up to 1856. During the later twentieth century a complex character came into focus: versatile in practical skills, intellectually curious, strikingly free from religious or racial prejudice, exerting unusual charm, and inspiring at least a few to great loyalty; yet deficient in political sense, tactless, touchy, rancorous, stingy with thanks or encouragement, devious, and callous when other people's interests seemed to conflict with his duty to God. Livingstone's reputation for managing Africans, if not Europeans, rests on the expeditions of 1853–6, which were organized chiefly by Africans, and on Waller's emollient edition of his last journals. None the less, his writings have acquired new value as a rich source for the history of Africans. His pioneering cartography of eastern Angola and what became Botswana, Zambia, and Malawi was but one facet of his skill as an amateur field-scientist in an age of growing specialization. Secular knowledge and material mastery were integral to his missiology: the industrial revolution was part of a divine plan. Livingstone both embodied and transcended the nineteenth-century tension between religion and science, and it was this which accounted for the scale and complexity of his career in Africa.

A. D. ROBERTS

Sources D. Livingstone, *Missionary travels and researches in South Africa* (1857) · D. Livingstone and C. Livingstone, *Narrative of an expedition to the Zambesi and its tributaries … 1858–1864* (1865) · *The last journals of David Livingstone, in central Africa, from 1865 to his death*, ed. H. Waller, 2 vols. (1874) · W. G. Blaikie, *Personal life of David Livingstone* (1880) · *David Livingstone: family letters, 1841–1856*, ed. I. Schapera, 2 vols. (1959) · *Livingstone's missionary correspondence, 1841–1856*, ed. I. Schapera (1961) · *Livingstone's private journals, 1851–1853*, ed. I. Schapera (1960) · *Livingstone's African journal, 1853–1856*, ed. I. Schapera, 2 vols. (1963) · *David Livingstone: South African papers, 1849–1853*, ed. I. Schapera (1974) · R. C. Bridges, 'The British exploration of east Africa, 1788–1885', PhD diss., U. Lond., 1963, chaps. 5–6 · *The Zambesi journal and letters of John Kirk, 1858–63*, ed. R. Foskett (1965) · T. Jeal, *Livingstone* (1973) · G. W. Clendennen and I. C. Cunningham, *David Livingstone: a catalogue of documents* (1979); suppl. (1985) · *David Livingstone: letters and documents, 1841–1872*, ed. T. Holmes (1990) · M. Gelfand, *Livingstone the doctor* (1957)

Archives BL, letters to his wife, daughters, and others, Add. MS 50184 · Bodl. Oxf., letters · David Livingstone Centre, Blantyre, letters and notebooks · Livingstone Museum, Zambia, letters and notebooks · National Archives of Zimbabwe, Harare, corresp., diary, and papers · National Museum, Livingstone, Zambia · NL Scot., corresp. and papers · NL Scot., priv. coll. · RGS, corresp. and papers · Scottish National Memorial to David Livingstone, Blantyre, Glasgow · SOAS, corresp. and papers · University of Strathclyde Library, Glasgow, papers | BL, letters to Edmund Gabriel, Add. MS 37410 · Bodl. RH, Waller MSS · PRO, FO 2, 63, 84, 97

Likenesses S. Newell, miniature, 1840, SOAS, Archives of the Council for World Mission · Cameron, daguerreotypes, 1852, Council for World Mission, London · J. Bonomi, pencil drawing, 1857, NPG · E. Grimstone, chalk drawing, exh. RA 1857, Scot. NPG · J. E. Mayall, photograph, 1857, NPG · H. W. Phillips, oils, 1857, priv. coll. · D. J. Pound, print, pubd 1859 (after photograph by Mayall), NPG · T. Annan, photograph, 1864, Scot. NPG [*see illus.*] · Maull & Polyblank, photograph, *c.*1864, NPG · A. R. Hill, bronze statue, *c.*1869, Edinburgh; related plaster statuette, Scot. NPG · F. Havill, oils, 1874–84 (posthumous), NPG · A. B. Wyon, medal, exh. RA 1875, Royal Geographic Society, London · A. R. Paton, statue, 1876 (after A. Robertson), East Princes Street Gardens, Edinburgh · M. Stewart, oils, 1876, Glasgow Art Gallery · W. Brodie, marble bust, *c.*1878, Dundee City Art Gallery · J. G. Mossman, statue, 1879, Cathedral Square, Glasgow · W. R. Dick, statue, 1934, Victoria Falls, Zimbabwe · T. Huxley-Jones, bronze statue, 1953, Royal Geographical Society, Kensington Gore, London · H. N. King, cartes-de-visite, NPG · engravings, NPG · photographs, NPG · woodcuts, NPG

Wealth at death £1463 19*s.* 3*d.*: confirmation, 3 Oct 1874, NA Scot., SC 36/48/74/705

Livingstone [Livingston], **George, third earl of Linlithgow (1616–1690)**, army officer, was born in July 1616, the eldest son of Alexander Livingstone, from 1622 second earl of Linlithgow (*d.* 1648), and his first wife, Lady Elizabeth Gordon, second daughter of George *Gordon, first marquess of Huntly. From 1622 until his succession to the earldom George was styled Lord Livingstone. His early years were spent with his maternal grandfather, and in 1626 the king wrote to Linlithgow expressing his displeasure that the young Lord Livingstone was being brought up in the household of the Catholic Huntly: 'in regard of his [Huntly's] aversness from the religion professed within that our kingdome not giving the Church satisfaction, we doe not lyk that your sone should be bred up in such companie' (GEC, *Peerage*, 8.28). Nevertheless, there is no evidence that George as an adult deviated from the Church of Scotland in his religion, moving from presbyterian to episcopalian when the church did at the Restoration. In the summer of 1640 he attended the court of Elizabeth of Bohemia at The Hague. On 15 December 1642 he was appointed constable and keeper of Linlithgow Palace and Blackness Castle upon the resignation of his father.

The Scottish estates appointed Livingstone colonel of the Stirlingshire foot in the army of the solemn league and covenant on 26 August 1646. He also became a member of the Clackmannanshire committee of war. He served with his regiment at Marston Moor and led it in storming the Sandgate during the climax of the siege of Newcastle. Livingstone and his regiment subsequently quartered in co. Durham, then served in Leven's field army during the 1645 campaign. In November 1645 he was under investigation by the estates for communicating with royalists. In 1648 he commanded the Midlothian and Linlithgowshire horse in support of the engagement for the rescue of Charles I. He resisted the Whiggamore raid of late summer 1648. As a result of being an engager he was barred from all state offices.

Livingstone succeeded his father as earl on the latter's death between 11 June and 20 December 1648. On 30 July 1650 he married his first wife, Lady Elizabeth Maule (*d.* 1659), daughter of Patrick *Maule, first earl of Panmure, and widow of John Lyon, second earl of Kinghorn. She was the mother of all Linlithgow's children before her death at Castle Huntly in October 1659. In October 1650 Linlithgow repented as an engager, removing his incapacity for holding offices. On 4 December he was admitted to the estates, which on the 29th nominated him to command a cavalry regiment from Perthshire. In January 1651 Hartwoodburn's Horse was added to his regiment. He served in the Worcester campaign but escaped capture. By 1653 he had become a supporter of the English regime in Scotland; he was one of the few nobles not penalized in Cromwell's Act of Pardon and Grace. However, the Scottish royalists in Glencairn's rising burnt his Perthshire estates. In 1654–5 Linlithgow represented Perthshire in Oliver Cromwell's parliament, and he was again in the united parliament in 1656 and 1659. He became a JP (another sign of English favour) in 1656.

Despite his service to the protectorate, at the Restoration Linlithgow received the colonelcy of the Royal Regiment of Horse Guards, and a place on the privy council on 13 July 1661. He served on various commissions of the council and regularly attended parliament until his death. On 5 May 1663 he began a lengthy career of suppressing covenanters when the council ordered him to enforce the regime's anti-presbyterian religious policies. In the same cause the council named him one of the justiciars in the south-west on 5 December 1666. He seems to have gained additional military commands for on 9 October 1667 the council disbanded his regiment and sent his men to Lord

George Douglas's Foot in the French service. On 29 October the king commissioned him a colonel of foot with the earl of Kellie as his lieutenant-colonel and Sir James Turner as his major. Several weeks later, on 26 November, the council appointed Linlithgow commander-in-chief in Scotland during the absences of the lord chancellor. On 22 June 1671 he became colonel of the King's regiment of foot guards. In a change from state business he was noted as feuding with his stepbrother Alexander who had succeeded their uncle James *Livingston as earl of Callendar over the detention of goods bequeathed by the latter in 1674. The council appointed Linlithgow colonel of the Linlithgowshire and Peeblesshire militia on 25 February 1675. On 8 June 1676 he received command of his heir, George's, horse troop during the latter's absence. The regime's use of the earl in military affairs is further indicated by his appointment to the militia committee in 1676. Likewise his support of its authoritarian policies appears from his position as supervisor of the election for provost in Linlithgow.

In June 1677 Linlithgow married again; his second wife was Agnes Wauchope, daughter and coheir of George Wauchope, merchant and burgess of Edinburgh, and widow of Alexander Scott, goldsmith, of Edinburgh. During that year the earl became a member of the highland and public affairs committee. On 26 December the council recorded his appointment as Sir George Monro's replacement as major-general of horse and foot in Scotland—or simply commander-in-chief. His assistance in suppressing the conventicles is apparent from his appointment on the anti-covenanter committee for the west on 18 January 1678. His actions in assailing the covenanters gained him the council's thanks that April. He received and implemented additional orders to the same end. In December the council had him make the militia take the oath of allegiance and supremacy. In January 1679 he garrisoned Blackness Castle (a prison for covenanters) and imposed order in Edinburgh. In March and May the council authorized him to act against covenanters in Linlithgowshire and Fife. After the defeat of Claverhouse at Drumclog on 1 June 1679, the earl became disheartened. On 6 June he asked for English or Irish reinforcements. Meanwhile he had ordered Claverhouse to fall back to the main army at Stirling. The united royal army failed to confront the rebels, but retreated to Edinburgh where it awaited reinforcements from England. On 18 June James, earl of Monmouth, arrived with English troops and took command of the army. After Monmouth's victory at Bothwell Bridge the council sent Linlithgow and Claverhouse to London to advocate sterner measures against the rebellious areas.

On 19 September Linlithgow resigned as major-general and commander-in-chief and had his former rank abolished owing to the demobilization of the army. He again became or was reconfirmed as constable of Blackness Castle on 15 January 1680. His importance in local affairs is apparent from his appointment as convener of the Linlithgowshire excise commissioners. His military duties continued in 1681 with service in the Linlithgowshire-Peeblesshire militia and reduction of his regiment. Likewise he continued to repress dissent, this time as the imposer of the Test Act on Linlithgow, Queensferry, the regality of Ogilface, and the JPs of Linlithgowshire. On 7 January 1682 he replaced Callendar, who had refused the test, in a heritable jurisdiction in Stirlingshire. In November he became a member of the commission to proceed against the disaffected in Linlithgowshire. The following year the council named him convener of the shire's JPs and provost of Queensferry. The king made him lord justice-general on 15 July 1684. Owing to his personal expenditure in repairing Blackness Castle his royal pension rose to £200 sterling annually in December 1685. With the revolution of 1689 he lost his offices, but he accepted the convention of estates as a free and lawful assembly. In April he was named to the Linlithgowshire commission for supply. He died on 1 February 1690 and was buried at St Michael's Kirk, Linlithgow. The earl exemplified the self-interested Scots nobleman of the second half of the seventeenth century, who exchanged political and religious principles for personal aggrandizement.

Linlithgow's elder son and heir, George *Livingstone (*d.* 7 Aug 1695), was implicated in Jacobite activities in 1689. After brief imprisonment he submitted; though apparently still toying with Jacobitism, in May 1690 the new earl of Linlithgow was reported as having 'beaten the Highlanders' and in 1692 he was admitted to the privy council (GEC, *Peerage*, 8.31). The younger son Alexander (*d.* 1692), who had succeeded by entail to the earldom of Callendar in 1685, likewise was imprisoned for Jacobitism with his brother in 1689. Linlithgow's daughter Henrietta (*d.* 1683) married Robert MacGill, viscount of Oxfuird and Lord MacGill of Cousland. EDWARD M. FURGOL

Sources *Reg. PCS*, 3rd ser. • *APS, 1642–90* • *Scots peerage* • E. M. Furgol, *A regimental history of the covenanting armies, 1639–1651* (1990) • F. D. Dow, *Cromwellian Scotland, 1651–1660* (1979) • *The historical works of Sir James Balfour*, ed. J. Haig, 4 vols. (1824–5) • *Historical notices of Scotish affairs, selected from the manuscripts of Sir John Lauder of Fountainhall*, ed. D. Laing, 2 vols., Bannatyne Club, 87 (1848) • GEC, *Peerage*

Archives NL Scot., documents incl. financial papers, deeds, corresp., and commissions | BL, letters to duke of Lauderdale, Charles II, etc., Add. MSS 23114–23137, 23242–23247 • Buckminster Park, Grantham, corresp. with duke of Lauderdale

Livingstone, George, fourth earl of Linlithgow (*c.*1652–1695), army officer, was the eldest son of George *Livingston, third earl of Linlithgow (1616–1690), soldier and politician, and his first wife, Lady Elizabeth (*d.* 1659), daughter of Patrick *Maule, first earl of Panmure, and widow of John, second earl of Kinghorne. First commissioned, as captain in the Scots foot guards (the new regiment of foot guards), in September 1668, he actively assisted his father in harrying the covenanters in the aftermath of the Pentland uprising of 1666. During the covenanter rising of 1679 Lord Livingstone, as he was then titled, saw further active service at the battle of Bothwell Bridge on 22 July. During the critical point in this engagement he advanced with 300 Scots foot guards to support Theophilus Oglethorpe's troop of the Royal Dragoons, which was in danger of being cut off. His intervention swayed the balance in favour of the duke of Monmouth's army, and the covenanters were heavily defeated. On 1 May 1684 he was promoted through the patronage of the duke of York to command the troop of the Scottish life guards (the Scottish troop of horse guards) in succession to the marquess of Montrose. About this time he was created provost of Linlithgow equipped with special powers by the Scottish privy council to deal with covenanters in and around that town, where the burghal authorities had, in Livingstone's opinion, been deficient in vigour.

In September 1688 the entire Scottish army, amounting to 2946 soldiers, marched south to reinforce James II, ready to face the anticipated invasion by William of Orange. Livingstone and his men were thus present at the débâcle on Salisbury Plain during November, and retired with the royal army along the Thames valley towards London. Following the earl of Feversham's decision to disband the royal army, Livingstone, now acting commander of the Scottish forces, asked permission of William of Orange to march his troops home in formed units. William was happy to oblige as he thereby preserved the Scottish army intact and assisted the maintenance of law and order in England. Livingstone attended the Scottish convention on 14 March 1689 as representative of Linlithgow, but he was not allowed to take his seat because he was the son of a peer. When Viscount Dundee defied the convention on behalf of James II on 18 March 1689 and left for Stirling with a troop of dragoons, he spent that night at Linlithgow. Livingstone was tempted to join him but, on receipt of a visit from a herald of the Scottish estates, who ordered him to lay down his arms and appear before the convention within twenty-four hours on pain of arrest for treason, he immediately detached himself from Dundee and complied. Later in the year, accompanied by a body of horsemen, he travelled to the residence of his brother-in-law Lord Duffus in Sutherland. This was construed as an intention to join the Jacobite army in the highlands and the council summoned him to Edinburgh. Although he endured a few days' imprisonment in Edinburgh Castle, his explanations were accepted and he was among those who took advantage of the offer of indemnity before the deadline of 10 September.

Livingstone succeeded as fourth earl of Linlithgow on 1 February 1690 and continued to toy with Jacobite conspiracies, but a serious illness in 1691 presented the opportunity for reflection upon the direction of his career. He determined to abandon flirtations with Jacobitism in favour of seeking an accommodation with William III and to transfer his allegiance from episcopacy to presbyterianism. Initially the earl of Portland was sceptical of the sincerity of Linlithgow's sudden double conversion, but on receipt of a signed statement giving the reasons for his change of heart, an interview with the king was arranged. William was impressed with his personal qualities and apparent political acumen and considered making him lord chancellor of Scotland. Instead, in 1692 he was appointed to both the Scottish privy council and Treasury commission, a move sometimes seen as seeking to balance party positions within the government of Scotland, Linlithgow still being considered part of an 'episcopalian' party. On 22 July 1695 he was granted the escheat of Urquhart, part of the forfeited estate of the earl of Dunfermline. Linlithgow had married, before 1689, Lady Henrietta Sutherland, the eldest daughter of Alexander, Lord Duffus, but, as they had no children, the succession passed to his nephew James Livingstone, fourth earl of Callandar, on his death on 7 August 1695. Linlithgow was survived by his wife. He was buried in Linlithgow church.

HENRY PATON, *rev.* JOHN CHILDS

Sources GEC, *Peerage* • *Historical notices of Scotish affairs, selected from the manuscripts of Sir John Lauder of Fountainhall*, ed. D. Laing, 2 vols., Bannatyne Club, 87 (1848) • W. H. L. Melville, ed., *Leven and Melville papers: letters and state papers chiefly addressed to George, earl of Melville … 1689–1691*, Bannatyne Club, 77 (1843) • P. Hopkins, *Glencoe and the end of the highland war* (1986) • P. W. J. Riley, *William III and the Scottish politicians* (1979) • C. Dalton, ed., *The Scots army, 1661–1688* (1909)

Archives NL Scot., Livingstone family and estate MSS, MSS 9635–9639, Ch 8501–890

Livingstone [*née* Hay], **Helen**, **countess of Linlithgow** (*d.* **1627**), royal tutor, was the only daughter of Andrew Hay, eighth earl of Erroll, and Jean, his first wife. Helen and her brother's financial and marital interests were represented by the king (to whom they were said to be 'of kyn'; Pitcairn, 2.546), after her father's second marriage. In 1584 she married Alexander *Livingstone (*d.* 1621), seventh Lord Livingstone from 1592 and created earl of Linlithgow in 1600; they had five children, of whom two daughters married in 1609 and 1612.

In 1587 the 'Grieves of the Kirk', presented to James VI, described Lady Livingstone as a 'malicious papist'. Her brother Francis [*see* Hay, Francis] was an active Catholic and their family had had a resident Jesuit priest. She was cited to appear before the presbytery for failure to attend church and confess her faith in 1594 and 1596, but James VI and his wife, Anne of Denmark, entrusted her and her husband to educate their daughters, the princesses Elizabeth and Margaret, in 1596. In 1597 she was threatened with excommunication, although a deputation found that she was reading the Bible daily, and attending church. Nevertheless, the general assembly's concern, both with her recusancy and with her position of influence over the royal daughters, meant that she continued to be targeted for her religious beliefs. In 1601 they cited: 'the education of their Majesties' children [in] the company of obstinat and profest Papists sic as the Ladie Livingstoun' (*Universall Kirk*, 3.965) as a major cause 'of the deflection from the purity, zeal and practice of true religion' (ibid.). The king, despite the order to remove his daughters, did not, suggesting that religious affiliations were inconsequential, relative to his daughters' safe care. In 1602 the countess's husband gained her a stay of excommunication so long as he 'deal with her at all times carefully for her conversion' (ibid., 1004). James VI's accession to the English throne in 1603 ended Helen Livingstone's care of his daughters, which may explain the kirk's silence until 1611, when the visitation to the kirk of Linlithgow recorded her recusancy. In 1612 the presbytery called her to appear on an excommunication charge and, despite her non-appearance, enjoined their brethren to 'give her public admonition and prayer' to convert. She was described as a kind and hospitable woman by the imprisoned ministers who were lodged at Linlithgow Castle in 1606.

In 1627 Helen Livingstone's daughter, the countess of Wigtown, wrote to John Livingstone, requesting his presence at her mother's deathbed. He wrote afterwards that '[she] had been all her days a papist, but some while before had deserted that religion' (*Brief Relation*). She died in 1627 at her daughter's house in Cumbernauld.

The confession and conversion of the right honourable, most illustrious and elect lady, my lady C. of L. (1629), printed by John Livingston (no known relation), gives little flavour of individuality, being an orthodox, conventional confession of Calvinist faith and rejection of Catholicism. The countess speaks of how Catholicism 'this many years contented mee, till at last in my old dayes GOD so happily moved my heart to heare the trueth of better and sounder instructers and their warrand' (sig. B2*r*–*v*), and how she now hopes to hear 'a hundreth sermons in GOD's true Kirk' (sig. B4*r*). The confession is appended by a collection of psalms and prayers, focusing on the experience of rebirth and salvation. John Livingston claims her words were 'most joyfullie, and constantlie uttered and declared before many honourable men and women' (sig. B7*v*).

KATE AUGHTERSON

Sources H. Livingstone, *The confession and conversion of the right honourable, most illustrious and elect lady, my lady C. of L.* (1629) · G. Johnston, ed., *The confession and conversion* (1924) · D. Laing, ed., *Original letters relating to the ecclesiastical affairs of Scotland* (1859), 2.404 · *A brief relation of the life of Mr John Livingstone* (1727) · R. Pitcairn, ed., *Ancient criminal trials in Scotland*, 7 pts in 3, Bannatyne Club, 42 (1833) · *The booke of the universall kirk of Scotland*, ed. A. Peterkin (1839) · 'Livingstone, Alexander, seventh Baron Livingstone and first earl of Linlithgow', *DNB*

Livingstone, Sir James, of Barncloich. *See* Livingston, James, of Barncloich, first Viscount Kilsyth (1616–1661).

Livingstone, Sir James, of Kinnaird. *See* Livingston, James, of Kinnaird, first earl of Newburgh (1621/2–1670).

Livingstone, James. *See* Livingston, James, first earl of Callendar (*d.* 1674).

Livingstone, John (1603–1672), Presbyterian minister in the Netherlands, was born on 21 June 1603 at Monyabrock, Kilsyth, Stirlingshire, one of three sons of William Livingstone (*c.*1576–1641), minister of Kilsyth and afterwards of Lanark, and his wife, Agnes (*c.*1585–1617), daughter of Alex Livingstone, portioner of Falkirk and brother of the laird of Belstane. He was educated from 1613 at Stirling grammar school and graduated MA in 1621 after four years' study under Robert Blair at the University of Glasgow. Despite his father's wish for him to live as a country gentleman, he decided to study theology at St Andrews and was licensed to preach in 1625. He acted as assistant in the parish of Torphichen from 1626 until told by the presbytery to leave in October 1627, and was afterwards chaplain to the earl and countess of Wigtown until August 1630. He was in great demand as a preacher: famously in June 1630 his sermon at Shotts, Lanarkshire, was said to have affected five hundred people.

Despite his popularity Livingstone's steadfast refusal to promise obedience to the five articles of Perth prevented his receiving ordination in Scotland, so in 1630 he travelled to Ireland, a country with which he was to keep close links during the following two decades. Livingstone was ordained by some Scottish ministers under the presidency of Andrew Knox, bishop of Raphoe, and he became minister at Killinchy in co. Down. In May 1632 he was suspended for nonconformity by the bishop of Down, but according to his memoirs was restored in May 1634 on the intervention of the lord deputy, Viscount Wentworth. In November of the following year Livingstone was deposed again and subsequently excommunicated. He turned instead to America, leaving Ireland in September 1636 with a number of Scots and English presbyterians and independents, but this venture was soon forced to turn back because of severe weather in the Atlantic.

Livingstone often returned to Scotland during the 1630s, and in Edinburgh on 23 June 1635 he was married by his father to Janet (*d.* 1693), eldest daughter of Bartholomew Fleming, a merchant, and his wife, Marion Hamilton. Although necessity often meant they were separated in the years ahead, theirs seems to have remained a close marriage. They had eight sons and seven daughters, of whom three sons and four daughters survived childhood.

When the national covenant was signed in March 1638 Livingstone was sent to London with copies for friends at court. In July of that year he was inducted to the parish of Stranraer, where his preaching proved as popular as it had been in the 1620s. He was a member of the Glasgow general assembly of 1638, and of all subsequent assemblies until 1650 with the exception of 1640, when he travelled as the earl of Cassillis's regiment chaplain to Newcastle.

Livingstone participated most actively in national church affairs in the 1640s and 1650s. He and others who had been in Ireland formed the core of an extreme party, which demanded the abolition of some traditional forms of worship. In 1648 the general assembly sent him to try to dissuade Scottish troops in Ulster (where he had continued to officiate during summer months) from joining the army then being raised in support of the engagement. In August of that year he was translated to the parish of Ancrum, Roxburghshire.

Livingstone was one of the commissioners appointed by the church to treat with Charles II at Breda in 1650 and he received the king's oath of fidelity to the covenants before Charles was permitted to land in Scotland. Despite having performed this office, Livingstone soon afterwards joined the party who opposed the king's coronation. In October 1651 he was elected moderator of a meeting of protesters (who rejected the government's view that those who had taken part in the engagement might be allowed to serve in the army), but he withdrew from their discussions when he found he could not modify their extremist views. In

1654 Cromwell sent for Livingstone and two other protesters in an attempt to secure co-operation in introducing a new system for managing the Scottish church.

After the Restoration Livingstone was called before the privy council, on 11 December 1662, and on refusing to take the oath of allegiance was banished. In April 1663 he arrived in Rotterdam, and he spent the remainder of his life there, occasionally preaching in the Scottish church and devoting himself to theological study and correspondence with Dutch theologians. He also met other exiled presbyterian stalwarts, such as Robert McWard, John Brown, and Robert Traill. His wife and two of their younger children (one of whom died in Rotterdam) joined him in exile.

While in Rotterdam, Livingstone did not shirk involvement in religious disputes. In February 1670 the Quakers John Swinton and George Keith attempted to speak to a number of exiled ministers. Livingstone was the only one who would speak to them, though he refused to allow them to enter his house and denounced them for their lack of respect and 'blasphemous' writings. He continued to exhort his former congregation in Ancrum to avoid contact with the Quakers in a letter written from Rotterdam in October 1671, and also dipped into the debate about indulgences. He was more humble than his fellow exiles McWard and Brown, however, admitting that 'None of us who are here, and seem to be dissatisfied with some things at Home, want conviction of our own grievous miscarriages' (Livingstone, *Letter*, 15–16). Most of Livingstone's diverse writings—including his autobiography, written in Rotterdam—were gathered together and published by the Wodrow Society in 1845. A noted linguist, Livingstone worked on Latin biblical texts while in exile, but he never published them. He also assisted McWard and the Dutch theologian Matthias Nethenus with the publication of Samuel Rutherford's *Examen Arminianismi* in 1668.

Despite his continuing interest in theological debate, Livingstone was by this time clearly in poor health. He complained of gravel in the bladder from 1667 and it became so severe that he had to take a house nearer the church so that he could attend the services on Sundays. He died aged sixty-nine in Rotterdam on 9 August 1672 and was buried there five days later in the 'French Church' (probably the chapel of St Sebastian, where the Scots worshipped). His wife went back to Edinburgh; and herself a strong supporter of the presbyterian cause, in 1674 presented with others a petition to the Scottish privy council asking that nonconforming ministers should have greater liberty to preach. She returned to Rotterdam in 1679 to live with their daughter Janet (*d.* 1696), who had married the notable Rotterdam merchant Andrew Russell, and died there in 1693. Most of her children went into the merchant trade, including William (1638–1700), a merchant in Edinburgh who moved to Rotterdam in 1682 and was appointed clerk to the Edinburgh kirk sessions after the revolution of 1688, and Robert (1654–1725), an American merchant who established the merchant dynasty of Livingston Manor, New York.

Livingstone was remembered by contemporaries as a gifted presbyterian preacher and theologian. Matthias Nethenus described him as 'most learned, most industrious and most zealous in the cause of God' (S. Rutherford, *Examen Arminianismi*, 1668, preface), and Robert McWard affectionately recalled his fellow exile as a 'burning and shining light, worthy and warme' (MS, Scot Church, Rotterdam). GINNY GARDNER

Sources *Fasti Scot.*, 2.356, 2.99–100 · J. Livingstone, 'A brief historical relation of the life of Mr John Livingstone', *Select biographies*, ed. W. K. Tweedie, 1, Wodrow Society, 7/1 (1845), 127–97 · J. W. Brown, *The covenanters of the Merse* (1893) · J. Livingston, *A letter written by that famous and faithfull minister of Christ, Mr John Livingston unto his parishoners of Ancrum*, 2nd edn (1710) · *DSCHT*, 491–2 · *DNB* · G. Gardner, 'The Scottish exile community in the United Provinces, 1660–1690', DPhil diss., U. Oxf., 1998

Archives Mitchell L., Glas., autobiography · NL Scot., autobiography · Stranraer Museum, diary | NA Scot., Andrew Russell MSS · NL Scot., Wodrow MSS

Likenesses portrait (of Livingstone?), Gosford House, East Lothian; repro. in *DNB*

Livingstone, Sir Richard Winn (1880–1960), classical scholar and university administrator, was born in Liverpool on 23 January 1880, the son of the Revd Richard John Livingstone (1828–1907), vicar of Aigburth and later honorary canon of Liverpool, whose family came from Westport, co. Mayo, Ireland, and his Irish wife, Millicent Julia Allanson-Winn (*d.* 1933), daughter of Charles Allanson-Winn, third Baron Headley. A scholar of Winchester College and of New College, Oxford, Livingstone was Hertford scholar (1900), obtained first classes in honour moderations (1901) and *literae humaniores* (1903), and won the chancellor's Latin verse (1901) and the Arnold historical essay (1905) prizes. In 1904 he became fellow and tutor, and in 1905 librarian, of Corpus Christi College, where he remained until 1924, interrupted by a year (1917–18) as an assistant master at Eton College. He married in 1913 Cécile Stephanie Louise, daughter of George Maryon-Wilson, of Searles, Fletching, Sussex; they had two daughters and two sons, one of whom was killed in action in 1944.

Livingstone made a deep and lasting impression on many able pupils, for he had a power to charm and a genuine interest which brought out the best in others. Beneath a somewhat dreamy manner lay a certainty of purpose which developed with the years. As a young tutor at Oxford he had been attracted to the modernist movement in the Church of England after attending the lectures in Berlin of the German theologian Adolf Harnack. He also belonged to the group of university reformers, led by William Temple, R. H. Tawney, and A. E. Zimmern, who wished to raise standards, improve the teaching, and broaden access. Their views were publicized in a series of letters to *The Times* on 'Oxford and the nation' (1907).

Livingstone's first publication, *The Greek Genius and its Meaning to Us* (1912), showed the influence of the Hellenist revival in Edwardian Oxford, inspired by Gilbert Murray, which treated Greek thought 'as a living thing'. His scholarship was graced by the elegance with which he wrote or translated and illuminated with 'the habitual vision of greatness' of which he loved to speak. The humanism of the Greeks he saw as complementary to Judaism: 'And so when Christianity comes she finds the world in a sense prepared for her.' In *A Defence of Classical Education* (1916) he maintained that 'We study Ancient Greece as containing, with Rome, the history of our origins, and explaining much in our literature, language and ideals'; Greek was 'an introduction to modern problems: in history, thought and politics'. He pursued this theme as editor successively of *The Legacy of Greece* (1921), *The Pageant of Greece* (1923), and *The Mission of Greece* (1928). He was a member of the prime minister's committee on the position of the classics in the educational system in 1920, the year in which he became joint editor of the *Classical Review*, a position which he held until 1922.

Livingstone moved in 1924 to Belfast, where as vice-chancellor of Queen's University he was persuasive in arousing throughout the six counties a pride in the university and a sense of responsibility towards it which brought valuable financial support. Among his achievements was the establishment of a faculty of theology. He was knighted in 1931.

On returning to Oxford in 1933 as president of Corpus, Livingstone was able to exert a wider influence, his interests now extending to the whole field of the aims and methods of education. He was president of the educational section of the British Association in 1936 and Rede lecturer at Cambridge in 1944 when he gave the lecture 'Plato and modern education'. In 1937 and 1938 he was an originator of summer schools at Oxford for colonial administrators. 'Adult education for the educated' was a subject later developed in *The Future in Education* (1941), a book which included his views on part-time continued education as an alternative to a general raising of the school age, and a suggestion for residential colleges for adults on the Danish system which aroused much interest. In 1948 he had the satisfaction of opening Denman College, the Women's Institute Residential College at Marcham named after Lady Denman, which owed much to his inspiration.

Over his own college Livingstone presided with dignity and shrewdness. In 1934 he had unsuccessfully argued that the university vice-chancellorship at Oxford should be permanent and filled by merit rather than by seniority. It was perhaps unfortunate that his own period of service as vice-chancellor came at a difficult time (1944–7) to which his particular talents were not best suited. In poor health, and not an efficient administrator, he failed to gain the full confidence of the university.

In 1950 Livingstone retired but he continued much in demand as a lecturer, especially in the United States where his reputation was greater than it was at home. He was a lucid and skilful speaker, and popular as a broadcaster. He had remained active in his own field, as president of the Hellenic Society in 1938 and of the Classical Association in 1940–41. His translation of Plato, *Portrait of Socrates*, appeared in 1938 and his edition of a translation of Thucydides on the Peloponnesian War in 1943. He was also the originator and general editor of the Clarendon Greek and Latin Series, texts issued partly in the original and partly in translation, with introductions, notes, and vocabularies. He never ceased to emphasize his belief in the value of a classical education. The complete education, he maintained, must give man a philosophy of life and 'Greece and Christianity are the two supreme masters of the ethical, the spiritual life.' In *The Rainbow Bridge* (1959), a collection of essays and addresses, he was still calling for university reform: towards a more liberal education which would include some study of religion or philosophy, or both.

Livingstone received honorary degrees from ten universities and was awarded the King Haakon VII liberty cross. He was a commander of the Légion d'honneur and was made a knight commander of the order of King George I of Greece shortly before his death at the Radcliffe Infirmary, Oxford, on 26 December 1960.

H. M. Palmer, *rev.* M. C. Curthoys

Sources *The Times* (28 Dec 1960) · W. F. R. Hardie, *Oxford Magazine* (16 Feb 1961), 226–7 · D. Veale and T. Finnegan, *Pelican Record*, 33 (1959–61), 117–24 · L. Price, 'Hellas and Israel: a portrait of Sir Richard Livingstone', *Proceedings of the Massachusetts Historical Society*, 75 (1963), 66–83 · F. M. Turner, *The Greek heritage in Victorian Britain* (1981) · *Hist. U. Oxf.*, vols. 7–8 · *CGPLA Eng. & Wales* (1961)

Archives BL, corresp. with Albert Mansbridge, Add. MSS 65256–65258 · BLPES, corresp. with Lord Beveridge · Bodl. Oxf., corresp. with L. G. Curtis · Bodl. Oxf., corresp. with Gilbert Murray · U. Warwick Mod. RC, corresp. with Sir Victor Gollancz · U. Warwick Mod. RC, corresp. with A. P. Young | FILM BFI NFTVA, documentary footage · BFI NFTVA, news footage

Likenesses W. Stoneman, photograph, 1946, NPG · K. Parbury, plaster bust, *c.*1959, Women's Institute, Marcham Park, Berkshire, Denman College · E. Kennington, oils, CCC Oxf.

Wealth at death £53,587 3*s.* 7*d.*: probate, 5 May 1961, *CGPLA Eng. & Wales*

Livingstone, Thomas, Viscount Teviot (*c.*1651–1711), army officer, was born in the Netherlands, the elder of the two sons of Sir Thomas Livingstone (*d.* 1673), who was created a baronet by Charles I, and was colonel of a regiment of foot in the Dutch service. His mother, Gertrat, was the daughter of Captain Thomas Edmond. He succeeded his father as second baronet in 1673. Having followed his father into the Dutch service, he acquired military reputation as an officer in the 3rd Scottish regiment in the Anglo-Dutch brigade. By 1688 he was lieutenant-colonel of Balfour's foot regiment and went to England with William of Orange in that year. On 31 December 1688 he was appointed colonel of the Royal regiment of Scots dragoons (later the Royal Scots Greys). Livingstone was already well known in the regiment from his numerous visits to Scotland when recruiting for the Anglo-Dutch brigade. The regiment (not to be confused with the Royal regiment of Scots horse, afterwards disbanded) was in England at the time, and its colonel, Charles Murray, first earl of Dunmore, had refused to serve against King James. Livingstone served in Scotland under General Hugh Mackay, and when in command at Inverness, by forced marches with a body of horse and dragoons, surprised and completely routed the Jacobite forces under General Thomas Buchan at Cromdale, on 1 May 1690. The engagement put an end to the resistance of the clans. Livingstone succeeded General Mackay as commander-in-chief in Scotland, and was sworn of the privy council. On 1 January 1696 he became major-general on the English establishment, and on 4 December 1696 was created Viscount Teviot in the peerage of Scotland.

Livingstone married Macktellina Walrave de Nimmeguen (*d.* 1729), from whom he appears to have separated about 1701. She pursued him in the Scottish courts in November 1703 for the sum of £500, to pay her debts contracted since he left her, and alimony at the rate of £400 per annum. The lords of session 'recommended, under the circumstances of the case, to cause pay her bygone debts, and to settle somewhat upon the lady yearly with the time coming, and to treat with the viscount to that effect' (J. Lauder, Lord Fountainhall, *Decisions of the Lords of Council and Session*, 1759–61, 2.200). As a result probably of this litigation, Teviot sold the colonelcy of the Scots Greys on 7 April 1704 to Lord John Hay. In the great seal registers are charters of resignation by him of the lands of Lethington on 23 June 1702, and of the lands of Waughton on 26 July 1709. Teviot became a lieutenant-general on 1 January 1704. He died in London, aged sixty, on 14 January 1711, when, his having no male heirs, the viscountcy became extinct, and the family baronetcy devolved on his brother, Sir Alexander Livingstone, third baronet. Teviot was buried in Westminster Abbey on 24 February, where his brother is said to have erected to his memory a sumptuous monument, which no longer exists. By his will, dated 27 September 1710, he left his house and estate, known as Livingstone House, Wimbledon, Surrey, with furniture, plate, and other effects, to Lady Elizabeth Gordon, daughter of Charles Gordon, second earl of Aboyne. The lady, at this time a child, died unmarried in 1770. The remainder of his property went to his brother, Sir Alexander, except a legacy of £1000 to his cousin german John Cornelius Edmond, then residing in the Netherlands.

H. M. CHICHESTER, *rev.* TIMOTHY HARRISON PLACE

Sources *Scots peerage* • GEC, *Peerage*, new edn, vol. 12/1 • J. C. R. Childs, *Nobles, gentlemen and the profession of arms in Restoration Britain, 1660–1688: a biographical dictionary of British army officers on foreign service* (1987) • J. Carswell, *The descent on England: a study of the English revolution of 1688 and its European background* (1969) • *The prose works of Jonathan Swift*, ed. H. Davis, 5: *Miscellaneous and autobiographical pieces, fragments, and marginalia* (1962), 167 • G. Crawfurd, *The peerage of Scotland: containing an historical and genealogical account of the nobility of that kingdom* (privately printed, Edinburgh, 1716) • N. B. Leslie, *The succession of colonels of the British army from 1660 to the present day* (1974)

Archives NA Scot., letters to William Bennett, GD 205/box 31 • NA Scot., letters to Lord Melville, GO 26/9/284, 315, 335

Wealth at death left Livingstone House, Wimbledon: *DNB*; GEC

Livingstone, William. *See* Livingston, William, sixth Lord Livingston (*d.* 1592).

Livinus [St Livinus] (*supp. d.* 633?), missionary, is patron of St Lievens-Esse and St Lievens-Houtem in Belgium and is sometimes known as 'the Apostle of Brabant'. All information about him, which is late and of dubious reliability, derives from the church of St Bavo at Ghent, to where his relics were translated in 1007. These include a verse and epitaph, attributed to 'Livinus archiepiscopus' and allegedly composed for Flobert, abbot of Ghent, which are now recognized to be eleventh-century works. Livinus is named in a letter by Abbot Othelbald to Countess Otgiva (dated to between 1019 and 1024) which lists the saints buried at Ghent. His life is recounted in a *Vita sancti Livini*, composed between 1025 and 1058 (probably *c.*1050), and there is a *translatio* describing the events of 1007, composed after 1066. Finally, a number of late chronicles, especially the fourteenth-century *Annales sancti Bavonis Gandensis*, refer to Livinus.

The biographical information supplied by these Ghent sources may be summarized as follows. He was regarded as being of Irish (or perhaps Scottish) origin: 'episcopus de Scotia' or 'genere Scotus et Hiberniae archiepiscopus'. He was born during the reign of a Colmán (Cologmagnus or Calomagnus), king of the 'Scoti', to a *dux* of the 'Scoti' called Theagnius and mother Agalmia (Agalinia or Agalunia), daughter of an Irish king Ephigenius. His birth was prophesied by the Irish holy man Menalchius and he was subsequently baptized by Menalchius and by Augustine, apostle of the Anglo-Saxons. Following his education by a priest of the 'Scoti' of noble birth called Benignus (Benén), he spent a period of solitude with three disciples, called Foillanus (Faelan), Helias, and Kilianus, before travelling to the continent as a missionary. Having made a token visit to Ghent during the abbacy of Flobert, the party arrived at Esse. Eventually, Livinus was killed there by two brothers Walbertus and Meinzo (or Menizo), along with a noblewoman Chraphildis (whose blind son Livinus had previously cured) and St Brictius, 'the infant', and all three are said to have been buried at Houtem. The Ghent annals describe the saint's arrival and subsequent martyrdom *sub anno* 633. Furthermore, his relics are said to have been 'elevated' by Theodoric, bishop of Cambrai, in 842, and were formally moved to Ghent in 1007. The annals also record a *translatio prima* in 1083 by Radbod, bishop of Noyon, and Wichmann, abbot of Ghent, and a *translatio secunda* in 1171 by Gautier, bishop of Tournai.

All this information can probably be dismissed as eleventh-century Ghent ecclesiastical propaganda and tells little, if anything, about a historical personage called Livinus. Indeed, it has been noted that Livinus (Lieven or Liévin in the vernacular) shares his feast day (12 November) with the Anglo-Saxon missionary saint Lebuin (also known as Leofwine or Livinus) of Deventer in Holland. The evident similarity of their names, plus the fact that in the tenth century Count Wichmann of Hamaland (incorporating Deventer as well as Houtem and Esse) was also the Burggraf of Ghent, may even suggest that Livinus is simply a doublet of Lebuin, attached to Esse and Houtem and subsequently appropriated by Ghent, and that his Irish origin was merely inspired by the tradition of Irish *peregrini* (pilgrim monks) on the continent.

DAVID E. THORNTON

Sources Bonifacius Moguntinus, 'Vita S. Livini', *Patrologia Latina*, 87 (1851), 327–44; 89 (1850), 871–88 • 'Annales sancti Bavonis Gandensis', [*Scriptores rerum Sangallensium. Annales, chronica et historiae aevi Carolini*], MGH Scriptores [folio], 2 (Stuttgart, 1829), 186–90 • *Acta sanctorum: November*, 1 (Paris, 1887), 380–81 [poems attributed to Livinus] • A. P. V. Descamps, *La vie de S. Lieven* (1891) • O. Holder-Egger, 'Zu den Heiligengeschichten des Genter St

Bavosklosters', *Historische Aufsätze dem Andenken an Georg Waitz Gewidmet* (1886) • J. F. Kenney, *The sources for the early history of Ireland* (1929)

Livio, Tito, dei Frulovisi [Titus Livius Forojuliensis] (*fl.* **1429–1456**), humanist and historian, was born in Ferrara, probably after 1400. Educated in Venice and Padua, he became a notary but by 1429 he was running a school in Venice in the parish of San Basso and was also described as a physician. In the early 1430s he wrote three Latin comedies, which were heavily influenced by readings of the classical playwrights but which drew themes from contemporary life and raised many hackles. He left Venice in 1433–4, travelling via Florence, Rome, Capua, and Naples, where he began his *De republica*; returning to Venice in 1434–5 he once again caused outbursts by two new satirical plays. He fled to Candia (Crete) and Rhodes before coming to England, probably in 1436. He subsequently claimed to have been attracted thence by the fame of Henry V in arms and of Humphrey, duke of Gloucester, in letters, but it seems more likely that he was recommended to the latter by Piero da Monte, the papal envoy.

In the duke's service Livio assisted with formal Latin correspondence and composed Latin plays (*Peregrinatio* and *Eugenius*). In letters of denization granted at Humphrey's request on 7 March 1437, he is described as the duke's *poeta et orator*. His employment did not prove permanent; he seems to have made enemies in the duke's circle and may have been dismissed. In 1438–9 he approached the chancellor of England, John Stafford, bishop of Bath and Wells (*d.* 1452), for a post in royal service, or, failing that, for financial assistance to return to Italy. Monte secured for him a papal sub-collectorship in England but he did not take up the post, being faced with a charge of defamation by John Gele, another naturalized Englishman who held a canonry at Lübeck. His letter of *c.*1442 to fellow humanist Pier Candido Decembrio suggests that he was afterwards in Milan, which he left because he was 'nauseated by princes' (*Opera*, xiv), and then Toulouse, where he received the degrees of doctor of physic and arts, and that he had moved to Barcelona by 1442. Decembrio urged him to lead a quiet life and to earn money. By 1456 he was once more in Venice, practising as a doctor. The *De orthographia* printed in Cologne under his name in 1480 is now thought unlikely to be his work.

In addition to two plays, other compositions, all of which reveal contemporary humanist trends, are directly linked to Livio's time in England. The petition to Stafford takes the form of an encomium of sixty-three lines. Another Latin poem, the *Humfroidos*, celebrates Duke Humphrey's successes against Philip, duke of Burgundy, in 1436, and may have been commissioned by the duke or else written to please him. His most famous work, the *Vita Henrici quinti* (*c.*1438), was probably commissioned by Humphrey in order to stimulate renewed interest in the French war, particularly on the part of Henry VI, to whom the work was addressed. The *Vita* was intended to glorify the duke as well as his royal brother—it begins with a panegyric on Gloucester, and devotes much space to his military prowess during the conquest of Normandy. Livio's precise contribution to Duke Humphrey's patronage of humanism in England is unclear; he was only one of several Italians in the duke's service, and his works have not enjoyed scholarly esteem. But his *Vita Henrici quinti* still stands as an important and independent near contemporary account of Henry V's reign, being an early chronicle authority for the period from 1418 to 1422. It was undoubtedly a source for the Pseudo-Elmham chronicle, a longer work on Henry V written about 1445–6, which is also humanist in tone and connected with Gloucester's circle. The *First English Life* of Henry V, composed in 1513–14, is essentially a translation of Livio's *Vita*, with additions drawn from Monstrelet, the *Brut*, and a now lost source connected with James Butler, fourth earl of Ormond (*d.* 1452).

ANNE CURRY

Sources *Opera hactenus inedita T. Livii de Frulovisiis de Ferrara*, ed. C. Previté-Orton (1932) • *Titi Livii Foro-Juliensis vita Henrici quinti*, ed. T. Hearne (1716) • M. Borsa, 'Pier candido decembri e l'lumanesimo in lombardia', *Archivo Storico Lombardo*, 10 (1893), 5–75, 358–441 esp. 63, 428 • Rymer, *Foedera* • C. Previté-Orton, 'The earlier career of Titus Livius de Frulovisiis', *EngHR*, 30 (1915), 74–8 • R. Weiss, 'Humphrey duke of Gloucester and Tito Livio Frulovisi', *Fritz Saxl, 1890–1948: a volume of memorial essays from his friends in England*, ed. D. J. Gordon (1957), 218–27 • R. Weiss, *Humanism in England during the fifteenth century* (1941) • A. Gransden, *Historical writing in England*, 2 (1982) • C. L. Kingsford, *English historical literature in the fifteenth century* (1913) • J. H. Wylie, 'Decembri's version of the *Vita Henrici quinti* by Tito Livio', *EngHR*, 24 (1909), 84–9 • R. Sabbadini, 'Tito Livio Frulovisio umanista del sec. XV', *Giornale Storico della Letteratura Italiana*, 103 (1934) • V. Ferrari, 'Il *De Republica* di Tito Livio de Frulovisi (seculo XV)', *Studi di storia di letteratura e d'arte in onore di Naborre Campanini* (1921) • D. Rundle, 'On the difference between virtue and Weiss: humanist texts in England during the fifteenth century', *Courts, counties and the capital in the later middle ages*, ed. D. E. S. Dunn (1996)

Lizars, Daniel (**1760–1812**). *See under* Lizars, William Home (1788–1859).

Lizars, John (**1791/2–1860**), surgeon, was born in Edinburgh, the son of Daniel *Lizars (1760–1812) [*see under* Lizars, William Home], a publisher and engraver, and his wife, Margaret Home. The painter and engraver William Home *Lizars (1788–1859) was his brother. He was educated at Edinburgh high school and at Edinburgh University. He was taught surgery and surgical anatomy by John Bell, an eminent surgeon and extramural teacher, to whom he had been apprenticed. From 1810 he acted as surgeon on board a man-of-war commanded by Admiral Sir Charles Napier, and he saw active service on the Portuguese coast during the Peninsular War, under Lord Exmouth. After returning to his home city in 1814, he was elected a fellow of the Royal College of Surgeons of Edinburgh and became a partner in surgical practice with John Bell and Robert Allan. He was highly successful, first in partnership and afterwards alone, as a teacher of anatomy and surgery. In 1828 he joined the Brown Square School, and in 1831 he was appointed to succeed John Turner as professor of surgery in the Royal College of Surgeons. Lizars defeated James Syme for this post, which was the cause of lasting enmity between the two men. Lizars also became a senior operating surgeon in the Edinburgh Royal Infirmary.

A bold and accomplished operator, Lizars was the first to ligate the innominate artery for aneurysm, the first to cut the deeper branches of the Trigeminus nerve for the relief of neuralgia, and the first Scottish surgeon to excise the upper jaw. His most famous work, *A system of anatomical plates of the human body, accompanied with descriptions, and physiological, pathological, and surgical observations*, was published in five folio volumes between 1822 and 1826. The many plates, beautifully engraved by his brother William under Lizars's close direction, were intended as a practical guide to dissection and were extensively used by medical students for several decades. In 1825 Lizars published *Observations on Extraction of Diseased Ovaria*, which dealt with four cases of ovariotomy, one of which had been successful. The patient survived despite Lizars's misdiagnosis of a tumour in the abdominal cavity, when in fact the 'swelling' was due to the woman's obesity. Lizars was, nevertheless, the first British surgeon to perform an ovariotomy. His suggestion that the operation should become part of the normal repertoire of the general surgeon was, however, controversial and damaged his reputation among his surgical colleagues.

In 1838 Lizars published *A System of Practical Surgery*, which contained a bitter attack on James Syme, now professor of clinical surgery at the University of Edinburgh, accusing him of gross negligence in the course of an operation for anal fistula. Syme sued and won, albeit only with token damages. In 1839 the Royal College of Surgeons did not renew Lizars's appointment as professor of surgery, a move in which Syme's influence has been discerned. Lizars never held a public appointment again. In 1851, Lizars published a treatise on urethral stricture in which he criticized Syme's practice of external excision. Syme responded with a vehement attack on Lizars's personal and professional character. Lizars sued and lost, unfairly in the view of many contemporary observers. His private practice, already in difficulties from his bluntness of speech and considerable eccentricity of manner, declined.

Lizars, who was married to Sarah, *née* McCraken, died suddenly on 21 May 1860, at his residence, 15 South Charlotte Street, Edinburgh, possibly due to an overdose of laudanum. He was buried in the West Church burial-ground, Edinburgh, and was survived by his wife.

MALCOLM NICOLSON

Sources J. D. Comrie, *History of Scottish medicine*, 2nd edn, 2 vols. (1932) • J. A. Shepherd, *Simpson and Syme of Edinburgh* (1969) • *Edinburgh Medical Journal*, 6 (1860–61), 101–3 • *The Lancet* (26 May 1860) • S. Behrman, 'John Lizars: centenary of a forgotten pioneer of the surgery of trigeminal neuralgia', *BMJ* (3 Dec 1960), 1665–6 • *DNB* • O. Moscucci, *The science of woman: gynaecology and gender in England, 1800–1929* (1990), 136–7 • d. cert. • NA Scot., SC 70/1/105/234–40

Archives Royal College of Physicians of Edinburgh, anatomical drawings and lecture notes • U. Edin. L., lecture notes

Likenesses bust, Royal College of Surgeons, Edinburgh; repro. in Behrman, 'John Lizars'

Wealth at death £425 2*s*. 10*d*.: confirmation, 20 July 1860, NA Scot., SC 70/1/105/234–40

Lizars, William Home (1788–1859), painter and engraver, was born in Edinburgh, the son of **Daniel Lizars** (1760–1812), who worked as a printer and engraver in Edinburgh, and his wife, Margaret Home. Daniel Lizars was a student of the engraver Andrew Bell. He engraved Raeburn's portrait of Lord Braxfield, but was better known for his views of Edinburgh, including *Perspective View of South Bridge Street*, which appeared in the 1786 edition of the *Edinburgh Magazine*. Six of his works were also mentioned in the *Edinburgh Scene*, among them *View of the New Bridge of Edinburgh*.

William Home Lizars was educated at the Royal High School in Edinburgh. He was then apprenticed to his father, from whom he learned engraving, but in order to pursue his ambition to become a professional painter he entered the Trustees' Academy in Edinburgh, under John Graham. It is possible that at about this time he took painting lessons from Alexander Nasmyth. Certainly he was influenced by Nasmyth's emphasis on the importance of drawing, but his contemporary David Wilkie played a significant role in the development of his work. Indeed, Lizars's arresting portrait of an Edinburgh beggar, John Cowper (Fitzwilliam Museum, Cambridge), painted in 1808 when the artist was just twenty years old, was formerly attributed to Wilkie. Lizars's early promise was noticed, and the same year he received a commission to paint David Steuart Erskine, eleventh earl of Buchan.

Between 1808 and 1815 Lizars exhibited portraits and genre paintings in Edinburgh. In 1812 he exhibited two works at the Royal Academy in London; *Reading the will* and *A Scotch Wedding* (both National Gallery of Scotland, Edinburgh) were hung on the line, where they were much admired, and both were later engraved. They illustrate clearly Lizars's skilful observation of character and still life. His use of dramatic lighting and anecdotal detail reveal his debt to seventeenth-century Dutch artists and Adriaen Brouwer in particular, a debt that he shared with David Wilkie (as was revealed when Wilkie tackled the same subjects a few years later).

In the same year that Lizars achieved acclaim with these two works, his father died and, in spite of his recent success as a painter, he decided to concentrate on the business of engraving and copperplate printing in order to support his mother and family. With his artistic and printmaking background it is perhaps hardly surprising that Lizars proved to be a superb topographical draughtsman, etcher, and illustrator, and it is as an engraver that he subsequently became best known. The family firm, which he ran with his brother Daniel, was known variously as W. and D. Lizars or W. H. and D. Lizars. It produced a variety of printed material, including many illustrated maps, charts, anatomical plates, and Scottish scenes. Lizars perfected a method of copper-engraving which imitated the effect of wood-engraving and first used this for the frontispiece to J. G. Lockhart's *Peter's Letters to his Kinfolk* in June 1819. An important illustrative project was reproducing the design of the architect Andrew Elliot for the national monument of Scotland and, together with Andrew Geddes and John Thomson, he recorded the Scottish regalia following their rediscovery in 1818. He also illustrated news events—such as the fire in the Old Town of

Edinburgh in 1824, and engraved paintings, such as Richard Dadd's *Puck and the Fairies*. In 1826 Lizars met J. J. Audubon when he visited Edinburgh, and later he engraved the plates of his *Birds of America*. Early in their subsequently very successful careers Lizars employed two Glasgow artists, Horatio McCulloch and Daniel McNee, to hand-colour prints.

Lizars was closely involved with the founding of the Royal Scottish Academy in 1826 and that year was appointed an associate engraver. In 1832 Lizars's company was declared bankrupt and the following year Daniel Lizars emigrated to Canada. William Home Lizars married, first, Eliza, whose portrait bust of 1852 by Patrick Park RSA (1811–1855) is in the collections of Aberdeen Art Gallery, and, second, Henrietta Wilson. He died in High Town, Galashiels, on 30 March 1859, leaving a widow and family, although this may not have been Henrietta. He was buried at St Cuthbert's churchyard, Edinburgh. The Scottish National Portrait Gallery, Edinburgh, houses several intimate studies by him in chalk and pencil, including depictions of the sculptor John Flaxman, the naturalist Sir William Jardine, and the agriculturist James Smith of Deanstone. JENNIFER MELVILLE

Sources P. J. M. McEwan, *Dictionary of Scottish art and architecture* (1994) • D. Macmillan, *Scottish art, 1460–1990* (1990) • W. D. McKay, *The Scottish school of painting* (1906) • J. L. Caw, *Scottish painting past and present, 1620–1908* (1908) • D. Irwin and F. Irwin, *Scottish painters at home and abroad, 1700–1900* (1975) • *DNB* • C. B. de Laperriere, ed., *The Royal Scottish Academy exhibitors, 1826–1990*, 4 vols. (1991) • *IGI* • d. cert. • will, NA Scot., SC 70/4/65, pp. 429–55

Archives NL Scot., corresp. | National Museums of Scotland, letters to Sir William Jardine

Likenesses W. Lizars, self-portrait, chalk drawing, Scot. NPG

Wealth at death £8163 12s. 5d.: confirmation, NA Scot., SC 70/4/65/429–55

Ljungberg, Jøns Mathias (1748–1812). *See under* Industrial spies (*act.* c.1700–c.1800).

Llancarfan, Caradog of. *See* Caradog of Llancarfan (*d.* after 1138).

Llandaff. For this title name *see* Matthews, Henry, Viscount Llandaff (1826–1913).

Llanover. For this title name *see* Hall, Augusta, Lady Llanover (1802–1896); Hall, Benjamin, Baron Llanover (1802–1867).

Llanthony, Clement of (*d.* after **1169**), prior of Llanthony and theologian, seems to have been a brother, or perhaps a less close relative, of the Miles of *Gloucester (*d.* 1143) who was earl of Hereford. This Miles is buried at Llanthony in Gloucestershire. Clement was given to Llanthony Priory as a boy, received his education there, and eventually became canon, sub-prior, and then, about 1180, the fifth prior of the house. As prior he witnessed a charter of David, bishop of St David's (1147–76). He won no great praise for his conduct of the business of the monastery, although he put effort into it and made changes to the observances of his house. He won plaudits, on the other hand, for his learning (Gerald of Wales and Osbert de Clare pay him compliments). He is said to have died of a stroke, but the year of his death is unknown. The last reasonably secure reference to him is 1169 (Knowles, Brooke, and London, 172).

Clement lived and worked among other theological writers at Llanthony. He himself was the author of a number of theological works which had a wide circulation. Notable among these is a gospel harmony, *Unum et quatuor*, which Clement compiled, together with a huge if derivative commentary, for which he drew upon a good range of the then available sources. This harmony came into fairly standard use in England and further afield. It was revised by William of Nottingham before the middle of the thirteenth century. A Middle English translation of the harmony (*Oon of Foure*) is known to survive in at least nine English manuscripts, and seems to have had a readership in Lollard circles.

Clement also commented on the Acts of the Apostles, the Pauline epistles, and Revelation. The *De sex alis cherubim*, which is associated with Alain de Lille, is attributed to Clement in a group of English manuscripts. One of these, now MS Auct. D.2.1, in the Bodleian Library, Oxford, was probably written at Llanthony in the third quarter of the twelfth century. Cambridge, Corpus Christi College, MS 66, from the Cistercian abbey of Sawley, and Bodl. Oxf., MS e Museo 62, from Kingswood, *c.*1200, also give the work to Clement, as do some slightly later English manuscripts. It is not impossible that Alain de Lille used the work in writing his prologue on the vision of Isaiah, and that the confusion arose in that way. Clement is also reported to have composed a commentary on the Augustinian rule, which does not survive. G. R. EVANS

Sources A. de Lille, *Textes inédits*, ed. M. T. d' Alverny (1965), 155 • J. C. Dickinson, *The origins of the Austin canons and their introduction into England* (1950) • R. W. Hunt, 'English learning in the late twelfth century', *TRHS*, 4th ser., 19 (1936), 19–42 • L. Hodl, *Die Geschichte der scholastischen Litteratur und der Schlüsselgewalt* (1960) • P. Mandonnet, *Saint Dominique*, ed. M. H. Vicaire and R. Ladner, 2 vols. (1937) • J. Burton, *Monastic and religious orders in Britain, 1000–1300* (1994) • A. Hudson, *The premature reformation: Wycliffite texts and Lollard history* (1988) • J. E. Wells, *A manual of the writings in Middle English, 1050–1400* (1916) • D. Knowles, C. N. L. Brooke, and V. C. M. London, eds., *The heads of religious houses, England and Wales*, 1: *940–1216* (1972), 172

Archives Bodl. Oxf., MS Auct. D.2.1 • Bodl. Oxf., MS e Museo 62 • CCC Cam., MS 66

Llawdden. *See* Howell, David (1831–1903).

Llewellin, John Jestyn, Baron Llewellin (**1893–1957**), politician and governor-general of the Federation of Rhodesia and Nyasaland, was born at Chevening, near Sevenoaks, on 6 February 1893, the younger son of William Llewellin, later of Upton House, Poole, and his first wife, Frances Mary, daughter of Lewis Davis Wigan of Oakwood, Maidstone. He was educated at Eton College and at University College, Oxford (later being elected to an honorary fellowship there). In September 1914 he was commissioned into the Dorset Royal Garrison Artillery and served in France (1915–19), winning the MC in 1917 and achieving the rank of major. On his return to England he read for the bar and was called by the Inner Temple in 1921. His real interests, however, lay in the field of politics. In 1929 he gained the

Uxbridge division of Middlesex for the Conservatives and very soon made his mark in the house. He was parliamentary private secretary to the postmaster-general from September to October 1931 and to the first commissioner of works from 1931 to 1935, assistant government whip from 1935 to 1937, and civil lord of the Admiralty from 1937 to 1939.

In July 1939 Llewellin became parliamentary secretary at the Ministry of Supply, a key department which had recently inherited from the Board of Trade responsibility for the whole of the government's supplies organization, and was thus engaged in quietly making preparation against a war. In May 1940 he went as parliamentary secretary to the Ministry of Aircraft Production for which he was spokesman in the House of Commons, Lord Beaverbrook being in the upper house. Everything which could be done to produce the quality and quantity of aircraft needed to hold and defeat the Luftwaffe was done under Lord Beaverbrook's dynamic driving power, and in this historic endeavour Llewellin ably assisted him.

In May 1941 Llewellin became parliamentary secretary to the Ministry of Transport and was sworn of the privy council. He was spokesman in the house for the departments of shipping and transport which were in the process of being amalgamated as the Ministry of War Transport, of which he became joint parliamentary secretary in June. In February 1942 he attained cabinet rank as president of the Board of Trade, but in the same month was transferred back to his old department as minister of aircraft production. The need was as urgent then as it had been before and it was a great moment and a tribute to his own endeavours when in May he was able in a broadcast speech to assure the Commonwealth that British aircraft had improved 'out of all recognition' and were superior to anything which the enemy could put in the air. In November 1942 he was appointed to Washington to fill the new post of minister resident for supply, for which his recent ministerial experience particularly suited him and which he greatly enjoyed. At the end of 1943 he returned to England to succeed Lord Woolton as minister of food at a time when food problems were becoming increasingly difficult. There he remained until July 1945 and again a difficult job was well done.

In the general election of 1945 Llewellin lost his seat and in the resignation honours was created a baron. For a few years he was able to enjoy a somewhat more leisured life, although he was a regular attendant at the House of Lords and active outside parliament in his various capacities as deputy lieutenant for Dorset, chairman of Dorset quarter sessions, president of the Royal Society for the Prevention of Accidents, president of the chambers of commerce of the British empire, a member of the BBC General Advisory Council, and in many other interests such as freemasonry and the British Legion.

In September 1953 Llewellin took up his appointment as first governor-general of the newly created Federation of Rhodesia and Nyasaland in central Africa. This was an office calling for the greatest tact and skill. He had not only to advise the federal prime minister on political matters, but also to help establish relations between the federal government and the territorial governments, in particular the governors of the two colonial territories of Northern Rhodesia and Nyasaland who were answerable to the Colonial Office. The first federal elections were held in December and resulted in a sweeping victory for the Federal Party led by Sir Godfrey Huggins (later Viscount Malvern). Then followed the difficult tasks of forming a federal administration and civil service, an operation which afforded plenty of play for the part of mediator. White Rhodesians called for 'improved status' and discussions over the federal franchise occupied the political stage in Salisbury. In this Llewellin's intimate knowledge of the political temperature in Britain was of especial value.

Jay Llewellin, as he was generally called, was a warm and genial Englishman (his name was pronounced accordingly) who enjoyed wide interests and activities. He never married. A keen sportsman, he was in 'upper boats' at Eton where he also went in for athletics and football, and later rowed for the University College boat which ended up head of the river in 1914. He was a countryman at heart and an enthusiastic gardener, and always went to Upton whenever he could, even at the busiest time of his career. When tied to London he used to enjoy quick visits to Hurlingham. His sister ran Upton for him and acted as hostess both there and at the governor-general's house in Rhodesia where his facility for informal entertainment was of particular value. Perhaps because he was a bachelor he was a strong opponent of women in public life, particularly in politics. 'They are always inclined to be so bossy', he used to say, 'and the ladies in the House of Commons have a tremendous amount of bees in their bonnets'. He strongly opposed the admission of women into the House of Lords. Llewellin was appointed CBE in 1939 and GBE in 1953. He died at Government House in Salisbury on 24 January 1957. One of his last public acts was to open the arts wing, which was named after him, of the then new University College of Rhodesia and Nyasaland.

JONATHAN LEWIS, *rev.*

Sources *Manchester Guardian* (25 Jan 1957) · *The Times* (25 Jan 1957) · *Dorset Year Book* (1957–8) · G. Thomas, *Llewellin* (1961) · personal knowledge (1971) · *WWW* · *CGPLA Eng. & Wales* (1957)
Archives NRA, papers · PRO, Private Office papers, AVIA 9, AVIA 11 | Bodl. RH, corresp. with Sir R. R. Welensky · Nuffield Oxf., corresp. with Lord Cherwell
Likenesses W. Stoneman, photograph, 1945, NPG · C. J. McCall, oils, Federal Assembly building, Salisbury, Zimbabwe
Wealth at death £92,055 11*s.* 1*d.* in England: Rhodesian probate sealed in England, 31 May 1957, *CGPLA Eng. & Wales*

Llewellyn, Sir David Richard, **first baronet** (1879–1940), coal owner and financier, was born on 9 March 1879 at Bwllfa House, Aberdâr, the eldest son of Alderman Rees Llewellyn of Bwllfa House, and his wife, Elizabeth. The father was a renowned mining engineer, who had successfully reorganized the Bwllfa colliery; together with two other sons he later joined forces with David in a number of coal ventures. 'D. R.', as Llewellyn was often called, was educated at Aberdâr higher grade school and Llandovery

College. In 1900 he enrolled in a course for mining engineers at University College, Cardiff, and qualified in 1903. After two years in the USA studying mechanical mining he started the Windber colliery in 1905, aiming to work its thin seams—on which he became something of an expert—with electrically driven cutters. Between 1914 and 1916 he acquired four additional collieries, all drift mines, around Aberdâr. These became the nucleus of the company of D. R. Llewellyn & Sons Ltd, which was registered in 1920.

These initial business interests were small-scale and (relatively) mundane. What really launched Llewellyn and made him a major force in coal production in south Wales for nearly a quarter century was his involvement, especially between 1916 and the early 1920s, in a frenzy of mergers and acquisitions. Initially the central figure was D. A. Thomas, Lord Rhondda (1856–1918), but his removal by war service and his subsequent death left control increasingly with his right-hand man, H. Seymour Berry (later Lord Buckland). It was the Aberdâr connection with Berry (one of the extraordinary Berry brothers: the two others became Lord Camborne and Lord Kemsley) which brought in Llewellyn. In 1916, after Berry negotiated the purchase of the Gwaun-Cae-Gurwen Colliery Company for D. A. Thomas, Llewellyn was made chairman of this subsidiary enterprise.

The two young men (assisted by H. H. Merrett) took over a range of companies across the south Wales coalfields. Llewellyn or Berry were frequently designated chairman. The companies they controlled included Bwllfa and Merthyr Dare; D. R. Llewellyn & Sons; Graigola Merthyr Company; Gwaen-Cae-Gurwen; Cambrian Collieries; Celtic Collieries; North's Navigation; D. Davis & Son; and Welsh Navigation. One of their most spectacular acquisitions took place in 1919, when they took a controlling interest, for £4.5 million, of John Lysaght Ltd. A few months later the business was sold on to Guest, Keen and Nettlefold (GKN) with Llewellyn becoming chairman of GKN's colliery committee.

In 1930 the most important of the south Wales coal companies, namely GKN, D. R. Llewellyn & Sons, and Gueret, Llewellyn, and Merrett, collaborated to form Welsh Associated Collieries Ltd, and Llewellyn was elected chairman. In 1935 this group fused with the Powell Duffryn Steam Coal Company Ltd. The resulting group controlled some ninety pits, produced over 20 million tons of coal, and employed over 37,000 people. Llewellyn served as vice-chairman. If much of this was essentially financial engineering, the more constructive aspect of these amalgamations and rationalizations was seen in the marketing and distribution of the group's coal output. Thus when Llewellyn joined the board of Lord Melchett's Amalgamated Anthracite Company, he secured efficiencies by pooling wagons, centralizing purchases of stores, and introducing uniform systems of accounting. In much of this Llewellyn's main adviser and associate was H. H. Merrett, who in the early 1930s published a plan for the total co-ordination of selling and transport in the industry.

In 1905 Llewellyn married Magdalene Anne (*d.* 1966), the daughter of the Revd Henry Harries; they had four sons and four daughters. He and his family lived at The Court, St Fagans, Glamorgan; and there was also a London residence at 3 Whitehall Court. Despite his strong roots in south Wales, Llewellyn's involvement in local affairs was limited, especially during his last two decades. In 1920 he was (like his father before him, and his brother afterwards) chairman of Aberdâr district council and high constable of Miskin Higher. He was created a baronet in 1922. He became treasurer and, in 1924, president of University College, Cardiff, to which he had given £30,000 in 1922. He was awarded an honorary LLD by the University of Wales in 1929. He was active in the Coalowners' Association (serving as chairman in 1929), but this was more to extend his business interests.

D. R. Llewellyn died on 15 December 1940 at Tŷ Newydd, Penderyn, Aberdâr, Glamorgan, the home of his brother, W. M. Llewellyn. JOHN WILLIAMS

Sources *Cardiff Times* (21 Dec 1940) · *Western Mail* [Cardiff] (16 Dec 1940) · A. P. Barnett and D. W. Lloyd, eds., *The south Wales coalfield* (1921) · H. H. Merrett, *I fight for coal* (1932) · *The Times* (16 Dec 1940) · D. J. Davies, 'The South Wales Anthracite Industry', diss., U. Wales, 1930 · *South Wales Coal Annual* (1922) · *WWW* · *CGPLA Eng. & Wales* (1941) · b. cert.

Archives NL Wales, corresp. with Thomas Jones

Likenesses photographs, repro. in Barnett and Lloyd, eds., *The south Wales coalfield*

Wealth at death £714,130 17*s.* 7*d.*: probate, 7 June 1941, *CGPLA Eng. & Wales*

Llewellyn, Sir Henry Morton [Harry], **third baronet** (**1911–1999**), showjumper and businessman, was born on 18 July 1911 at Fairfield, near Aberdâr, Glamorgan, the second son and second child in the family of four sons and four daughters of Sir David Richard *Llewellyn, first baronet (1879–1940), landowner and businessman, and his wife, Magdalene Anne (*d.* 1966), daughter of the Revd Dr Henry Harries, of Porth-cawl, Glamorgan. His father was chairman of Welsh Associated Collieries Ltd (founded by Llewellyn's grandfather Rees Llewellyn), and was made a baronet during Lloyd George's premiership, in 1922. Among his ancestors was Sir Davy Gam, knighted at Agincourt.

As a child Llewellyn was often ill; he had double pneumonia at seven and suffered from chronic asthma. This restricted his participation in games and helped to make him highly competitive when he could play; in adult life he stressed the importance of winning. He was educated at Arlington House School, Hove, St Christopher's in Bath, Oundle School, and Trinity College, Cambridge, where he first read economics before switching to law, in which he obtained a pass degree. He did not enjoy scholastic activities and his economics tutor, Maurice Dobb, described him as 'indolent' (Llewellyn, 32). He also played a good deal of rugby until a serious elbow injury forced him to give up the game and the hopes of gaining a blue.

Llewellyn's father was a master of hounds and as a child Harry learned to ride. In his twenties he had some success, first in point-to-point races and then as an amateur steeplechase jockey, usually riding horses owned by his father, a heavy gambler. Perhaps his most notable rides were in the Grand National at Aintree, where in 1936 he piloted his father's horse Ego, a 50–1 outsider, to second place. After shedding 39 lb from his 14 stone frame, he rode Ego into fourth place the next year and might have won had not a riderless horse crossed his path, causing his mount to come to a standstill. In 1939 he led a team of British steeplechase horses and jockeys to the European amateur riders' championship in Hungary. He went on to Munich to ride in the Brown Band steeplechase for amateur riders but while there was advised—as a fellow horseman—by a high-ranking Nazi official to return to Britain as soon as possible. The next day Germany invaded Poland.

In October 1939 Llewellyn secured a commission in the Warwickshire yeomanry and during the Second World War he served with the Anglo-French force that invaded Syria and Lebanon in 1941. Later he was in north Africa, Italy, and north-west Europe. He rose to the rank of lieutenant-colonel, was twice mentioned in dispatches, and was awarded the US Legion of Merit. From November 1942 until the end of the war in Europe he was on Field Marshal Montgomery's staff, and spent part of the time as senior liaison officer at the headquarters of the Eighth Army. He was appointed OBE (military) in 1944.

On 15 April 1944, at St Margaret's, Westminster, Llewellyn married the Hon. Christine (Teeny) Saumarez (1916–1998), younger daughter of James St Vincent Broke Saumarez, fifth Baron de Saumarez; they had courted since 1938, and she had previously been the girlfriend of his elder brother, Rhys. In the winter of 1945–6 they bought Gobion Manor, an Elizabethan house 5 miles east of Abergavenny, where they brought up their sons David (Dai; *b.* 1946) and Roderic (Roddy; *b.* 1947), and daughter Anna (*b.* 1956). They later moved to Tŷ'r Nant, Llan-arth Fawr, near Raglan.

Llewellyn continued to race until 1949, by which time he had already made his name in showjumping. Although his first efforts at Olympia in 1935 had been disastrous, with a total during the week's events of ten refusals and only one fence jumped, things improved. With his horse Kilgeddin he won the Victory cup at White City in 1946 and gained victory in the Rome puissance in 1947, the first British civilian to win a post-war jumping competition abroad. In 1949 he became captain of the British showjumping team and supplied many of its horses.

Llewellyn's real fame came via the big bay thoroughbred gelding Foxhunter, which he purchased as a six-year-old in 1947 for £1500. He made his choice after studying the records of every horse registered with the British Show Jumping Association. Together they won seventy-eight international competitions, including the King George V gold cup three times—he was the only rider to win this prestigious event three times with the same horse—and the puissance competition at White City four times. Their greatest triumph came in the team contest at the 1952 Olympics in Helsinki, along with team-mates Wilf White on Nizefela and Duggie Stewart on Aherlow (also owned by Llewellyn), when Britain secured the gold medal, the only one won by Britain in any sport at those Olympic games. His final round captured the British public's imagination because of the pressure under which it was ridden. His first round had resulted in an almost disastrous 16.75 faults, caused, he believed, by his failure to warm up Foxhunter adequately. He needed fewer than five faults if Britain was to gain gold, a cause that many thought a lost one in the light of his first round only a few hours earlier. Yet he and Foxhunter went clear. Unlike the press and public, he always acknowledged the contribution of his team-mates, who each had fewer total faults than himself.

After he gave up competitive riding over fences both in the show ring and on the race course, following Foxhunter's retirement in 1955 Llewellyn devoted substantial time to equestrian administration, though he had already been involved as a member of the national hunt committee from 1946 and had served as a steward from 1948 to 1950, as well as being a director and steward of Chepstow races from 1950. He was elected a Jockey Club steward in 1969. He was *chef de mission* for all equestrian disciplines at the Rome Olympics in 1960 but felt unappreciated and resigned from the British Show Jumping Association's international affairs committee, and did not return until 1966. Subsequently he was appointed *chef d'équipe* of the showjumping and eventing team at the Mexico Olympics of 1968. He was chairman of the British Show Jumping Association between 1967 and 1969, chairman of the British Equestrian Federation in 1976–81, and president of the Royal International Horse Show from 1989 to 1991. He had two terms of office as master of the Monmouthshire hounds but gave up hunting in 1959 after a fall damaged his sight. He claimed never to have broken a bone in all his years of riding. Although a strong supporter of hunting, he did not like the ritual of 'blooding', which he felt gave the sport 'an unnecessary barbaric touch' (Llewellyn, 232).

Llewellyn's old equine partner, who died in 1959, was commemorated in the annual Foxhunter trophy for novice horses at the Horse of the Year show, which, in terms of the participants in the preliminary rounds, became the largest showjumping competition in the world. Initiated by Llewellyn in south Wales to encourage new blood, it was then taken up in London by the *Evening Standard*, before being extended nationally under the sponsorship of the *Daily Express*. By the 1980s it was attracting over 60,000 entries a year.

Llewellyn was brought up in the expectation that he would move into the coal business, and during university vacations he travelled to Spain and Canada (with his father) to learn the trade. The nationalization of Britain's coalmines in 1947—described by Llewellyn as 'legalised daylight robbery' (Llewellyn, 174)—deprived him of two successful businesses in which he had acquired half shares ten years previously: the Rhigos colliery and the coal exporters C. L. Clay & Co. He knew that there would eventually be compensation, but in the meantime he devoted himself to equestrian affairs. At the end of 1953 the colliery compensation money came through and Llewellyn turned seriously to business once again. He became chairman of the Andrew Buchanan brewery, which he renamed Rhymni and eventually sold to Whitbread in 1972. He was president of Whitbread Wales Ltd thereafter. In the late 1950s he also took up dairy and sheep farming and established the Revel stud for Welsh mountain ponies.

Llewellyn became a major figure in Welsh public and business life. He was a foundation director of Television Wales and West, elected chairman of the Institute of Directors (Wales) for 1963 and 1964, and appointed chairman of the Welsh board of the Nationwide building society. In 1963 he became chairman of Eagle Star Insurance for south-east Wales and joined the regional board of Lloyds Bank in Cardiff. Five years later he was appointed to the Welsh Tourist Board and in 1971 became chairman of the Sports Council for Wales. He also served as a JP on the Abergavenny bench for fifteen years and was high sheriff of Monmouthshire in 1965. He had been advanced to CBE in 1953 and in 1977 was knighted for his services to Wales. In the following year he succeeded to the baronetcy on the death of his older brother. He died at his home at Tŷ'r Nant on 15 November 1999. He was survived by his three children, and succeeded in the baronetcy by his elder son, Dai; his wife had died the previous year. WRAY VAMPLEW

Sources H. Llewellyn, *Passports to life* (1980) • *Daily Telegraph* (16 Nov 1999) • *The Independent* (17 Nov 1999) • *The Guardian* (17 Nov 1999) • *The Scotsman* (17 Nov 1999) • *The Times* (16 Nov 1999) • D. Williams, *Master of one* (1978) • *WWW* • Burke, *Peerage* • C. Stratton, *Encyclopaedia of showjumping* (1973) • m. cert.

Likenesses photograph, 1950, repro. in *Daily Telegraph* • photograph, *c.*1952, repro. in *The Guardian* • photograph, 1952, repro. in *The Scotsman* • photograph, 1952, repro. in *The Times* • photograph, 1953, repro. in *The Independent* • photographs, repro. in Llewellyn, *Passports*

Wealth at death £192,144—gross; £168,523—net: probate, 12 April 2000, *CGPLA Eng. & Wales*

Llewellyn, Richard. *See* Lloyd, Richard Dafydd Vivian Llewellyn (1906–1983).

Llewellyn, Sir (Samuel Henry) William (1858–1941), painter, was born on 1 December 1858 at Alma Place, Cirencester, the son of Samuel Llewellyn, a moulder, and his wife, Alice Jane Jennings. According to contemporary information, Llewellyn's decision to become an artist caused him to leave home after a bitter quarrel with his parents, without any means of support except his art. Owing to these circumstances little is known of his early years. He was trained for a number of years at the National Art Training School, South Kensington, under Edward Poynter, and afterwards at Paris in the ateliers of Fernand Cormon, Jules Lefebvre, and Gabriel Ferrier. He began exhibiting at the Royal Academy (RA) in 1884, at first with etchings as well as paintings, under the first names successively of Samuel Henry William and Samuel; after 1889 he used only the name William, and showed mainly portraits. In the 1880s he joined the New English Art Club, where he employed a characteristic impressionistic 'economy of means', depicting only the essential parts of a subject while retaining 'a regard for certain refinements of the laws of picture-making which modern art has for the most part been all too ready to despise' (*The Studio*, 155). However, by the 1890s he had severed his connections with the New English Art Club, and as a member of both the Royal Society of British Artists and the Royal Society of Portrait Painters he devoted himself to portraiture, showing at the chief galleries in London. His portraits are generally refined in colour and skilful in surface rendering, sincere and graceful rather than searching or emphatic presentations of character. His occasional landscapes, such as *Sailing at Blakeney* (Tate collection), show a delicate sense of light and atmosphere.

In 1893 Llewellyn married Marion Meates (*d.* 1926), a painter of miniatures and an exhibitor at the RA between 1896 and 1913. Their only son, David, a flying officer who made a record flight from the Cape to England in 1935, was killed in a flying accident in 1938. In 1912 Llewellyn exhibited a state portrait of Queen Mary at the RA and was elected an associate. From 1913 he was an occasional visiting professor at the RA painting school, and he also sat on committees of reorganization after the First World War. Full membership of the RA came in 1920, followed by appointments to the council in 1922 and 1923, the exhibition committee in 1922, and the finance committee in 1923–5. His diploma piece was a portrait of Sir Aston Webb.

After serving again on the RA council in 1927, Llewellyn was elected president on 10 December 1928 in succession to Sir Frank Dicksee. His greatest success as president was the negotiation and supervision of the exhibitions of Dutch, Italian, Persian, French, British, Chinese, and Scottish art which were held at the academy before the threat of war caused the abandonment of further plans for American, Japanese, German, and Indian loans exhibitions. However, the autocratic and inflexible style of his presidency precipitated the resignation of Walter Sickert from the RA in 1935 over a 'misunderstanding'. Llewellyn had refused to sign a petition to save Jacob Epstein's sculptures on the façade of Rhodesia House on the Strand in London, giving the reason that his personal action would implicate the RA, which he could not do without consulting the council. It is possible that Llewellyn agreed with the earlier campaign of the National Vigilance Society (1907), which had objected to the nudity of the statues. Llewellyn's presidency was none the less successful. He attained a record-breaking attendance of between 540,000 and 600,000 for the Italian loan exhibition. He also presided in 1931 over the innovations of introducing a modern electronic lighting system into the galleries, the use of an electronic ray security system for the treasures of the Persian exhibition, and the first loan exhibition at the RA of impressionists and post-impressionists.

Llewellyn's practical character made him an excellent chairman of committees. An entirely new departure came in with the use of the galleries of the academy for an exhibition in 1935 promoting co-operation between artists and manufacturers. Llewellyn had formulated this scheme with Prince George (later the duke of Kent) at the academy dinner in 1932, and with the assistance of the Royal Society of Arts he succeeded in showing the public how important trained artists were for the design of many products of British industry. Having, as it was believed, reached the statutory retirement age of seventy-five—for the date of his birth had always been recorded as 1863—Llewellyn could not stand again in 1938 for the annual election of president. It was later discovered, however, that he had been born in 1858. His retirement was much regretted, as his work, especially on the winter exhibitions, had won him wide respect.

Llewellyn received many honours. In 1918 he was appointed KCVO, and in 1931 he was promoted GCVO. In 1929 he was appointed grand officer of the order of Orange-Nassau, in 1930 he received the grand cross of the order of the Crown of Italy, and in 1933 he was appointed commander of the Légion d'honneur. In 1933 he received the Albert medal of the Royal Society of Arts for his encouragement of art in industry. In the same year he became a trustee of the National Gallery, and he was associated with numerous learned societies. The art historian Sidney Hutchison described him in later life as a 'good-looking Welshman' who:

> seldom expressed personal opinions but was skilful in summing up at meetings and when he did speak, it was with autocratic finality. His manner was pleasant but full of the dignity of his office. His soft, rather twisted smile was inscrutable and his demeanour imperturbable. (Hutchison, 169)

In 1940 Llewellyn's health began to fail, and he died at his home, Little Blundell House, Campden Hill, London, on 28 January 1941. After a funeral service at Westminster Abbey his ashes were deposited in the crypt of St Paul's Cathedral, alongside the remains of other artists. A memorial tablet was subsequently unveiled there by his successor at the RA, Sir Edwin Lutyens.

W. R. M. LAMB, *rev.* MATTHEW C. POTTER

Sources S. C. Hutchison, *The history of the Royal Academy, 1768–1968* (1968) • M. H. Dixon, 'The portraits of Mr. W. Llewellyn', *Lady's Realm* (Sept 1906) • *The Studio*, 41 (1907) • J. A. Kestner, *Mythology and misogyny* (Madison, 1989) • b. cert. • d. cert.

Archives RA

Likenesses W. Goscombe John, bronze bust, exh. RA 1932, RA • H. Coster, photograph, 1937, NPG • Elliott & Fry, photograph, NPG • F. W. Elwell, group portrait (*RA Selection and Hanging Committees, 1938*) • S. H. W. Llewellyn, self-portrait, priv. coll. • B. Partridge, pencil sketches, NPG; repro. in *Punch* (19 Dec 1928)

Wealth at death £32,441 16s. 2d.: probate, 19 May 1941, *CGPLA Eng. & Wales*

Llewelyn. *See also* Llywelyn.

Llewelyn, John Dillwyn (1810–1882), photographer, was born at The Willows, Swansea, on 12 January 1810, the son of the naturalist Lewis Weston *Dillwyn (1778–1855) and his wife, Mary Adams (1776–1865). Mary was the illegitimate daughter of Colonel John Llewelyn (*d.* 1817) of Ynysgerwn and Penlle'r-gaer, Glamorgan, and she retained her mother's surname. John Dillwyn succeeded to the estates of his maternal grandfather, Colonel Llewelyn, and assumed the additional surname of Llewelyn upon coming of age. He was educated privately by tutors, and at Oriel College, Oxford, from 1827. His eldest sister, Fanny

John Dillwyn Llewelyn (1810–1882), by unknown photographer, *c.*1853 [with his wet collodion equipment]

Dillwyn (1808–1894), married Matthew Moggridge; his brother, Lewis Llewelyn *Dillwyn (1814–1892), became MP for Swansea and a director of the Great Western Railway. On 18 June 1833 Llewelyn married Emma Thomasina Talbot (1808–1881), cousin of the pioneer photographer William Henry Fox Talbot and one of the sisters of Christopher Rice Mansel Talbot of Penrice and Margam. They had several children, of whom the eldest, Thereza Dillwyn Llewelyn (1834–1926), married the mineralogist Mervyn Herbert Nevil Story-Maskelyne (1823–1911); the eldest son, Sir John Talbot Dillwyn Llewelyn (1836–1927), married Caroline Julia Hicks-Beach.

Llewelyn's first photographic experiments, which preceded those of his friend and distant relative Calvert Richard Jones, took place at his house, Penlle'r-gaer, near Swansea, in February 1839 and were inspired by news of Fox Talbot's activities. His earliest surviving images are daguerreotypes from 1840 of his family and house. Not surviving, but recorded in letters, are daguerreotypes of orchids grown at Penlle'r-gaer and sent to William Hooker, the director of Kew Gardens, in January 1842, probably the first time that a photographic process was used for the identification of botanical specimens. Later in the 1840s Llewelyn worked with the daguerreotypist Antoine Claudet on some experiments in photography: no details are known, as the only references to the collaboration appear in the diaries of Lewis Weston Dillwyn. However, several daguerreotypes of Llewelyn by Claudet survive.

In 1852 Llewelyn was elected to the first council of the newly formed Photographic Society of London (now the Royal Photographic Society); he remained on the council until 5 February 1857. At a meeting on 21 December 1854 he was nominated as the first country vice-president. Llewelyn wrote a letter, dated 20 March 1854, for the society's *Journal* on the calotype process. In 1856 he announced his oxymel process, a mixture of honey and vinegar, whereby the collodion plates of the period could be prepared some time before use and developed when the photographer returned home. He claimed, in a letter to Fox Talbot, to have tried all the then known processes. In 1852 he had built an equatorial observatory at Penlle'r-gaer for his daughter Thereza and in the mid-1850s together they took collodion images of the moon. The July 1856 edition of the *Illustrated London News* hailed him 'as a gentleman to whom all photographers owe a world of thanks'.

Llewelyn exhibited regularly and successfully in the exhibitions of the Photographic Society until 1858. At the Paris Universal Exhibition of 1855 he won a silver medal of honour for four 'instantaneous' photographs. His first instantaneous image had been taken in 1853 of the waves in Caswell Bay, south Wales. One of the Paris images, *Clouds over St Catherines, Tenby*, included a cloud taken in the same exposure, probably the first time this had been achieved; the negative, which still exists, dates from mid-1854 or earlier. Other of his photographic images also appeared in *The Sunbeam*, which was edited by his friend and fellow photographer P. H. Delamotte in 1859. The *Photographic Exchange Albums* was another forum for some of his images; the publisher Joseph Cundall announced 'Pictures of Welsh scenery' by Llewelyn in 1854, in parts, but these scenes never appeared. In the 1870s Llewelyn's name appears as a council member of the Amateur Photographic Association.

In 1846 the first *Journal* of the Horticultural Society had, as its first article and illustration, an account of the Orchid House which Llewelyn had built at Penlle'r-gaer: heated by steam, the original building dated back to 1835. Specimens of his orchids were used to illustrate Samuel Curtis's *Botanical Magazine* over the course of several years. Llewelyn also created two lakes at Penlle'r-gaer, one of almost 20 acres and a man-made waterfall. It was on the lower lake that Llewelyn, in 1848, demonstrated the first boat in Britain to be propelled by an electric motor; it was constructed from a model by his friend Benjamin Hill of Clydach, who had taught electricity to William Grove.

In 1843, as a magistrate, Llewelyn was involved in the Rebecca riots in south Wales when the local farmers protested against the tolls extracted from them, allegedly for the maintenance of the road but usually ending up in the landlords' pockets. This episode ended with a major trial in Cardiff, at which Llewelyn and his brother were on the bench. A great, though unassuming, benefactor to the people and poor of the Swansea region, Llewelyn gave 42 acres of his land in 1878 to create Parc Llewelyn for the people of Swansea, at a cost of £20,000. He was a member of the Swansea school board for many years, though in 1877 he scandalized his colleagues by writing a public letter to the ratepayers of Swansea, condemning the board's waste of money.

Llewelyn was the high sheriff of Glamorgan in 1834 and 1835, and deputy lieutenant in 1836. He became a fellow of the Royal Society in 1836, a fellow of the Linnean Society in 1837, and an FRAS in 1852. For much of his life he suffered from asthma, which in later life prevented him from taking part in his public duties. From 1871 he and his wife lived at 39 Cornwall Gardens, London, and from 1879 at Atherton Grange, Somerset Road, Wimbledon, Surrey. He died at Atherton Grange on 24 August 1882 and was buried in Penlle'r-gaer church in Glamorgan.

RICHARD LESLIE MORRIS

Sources family MSS, priv. coll. • National Museum of Photography, Film, and Television, Bradford, Royal Photographic Society archives • *The Cambrian* (1817–82) • R. Morris, *John Dillwyn Llewelyn, 1810–1882: the first photographer in Wales* (1980) [exhibition catalogue, Arts Council of Great Britain] • R. Morris, 'The forgotten negatives of John Dillwyn Llewelyn', *The Photohistorian*, 109 (Oct 1995) • R. Morris, 'The oxymel process', *The Photohistorian*, 99 (winter 1992) • R. Morris, 'The oxymel process', *The Photohistorian*, 100 (spring 1993) • R. Morris, 'The orchid house at Penllergare', *Gower*, 44 (1993), 134–49 • R. Morris, 'The daguerreotype and John Dillwyn Llewelyn', *Daguerreotype Annual* (1998), 161–73 • Foster, *Alum. Oxon.*

Archives National Museum of Photography, Film and Television, Bradford, Royal Photographic Society collection, photographs • NL Wales, family papers, photographs • NMG Wales, negatives, prints and miscellaneous articles plus photographic equipment • priv. coll., family archives • V&A, photographs

Likenesses G. Delamotte, miniature, 1826–8, priv. coll. • C. R. Leslie, oils, 1830–31, priv. coll. • R. Beard, daguerreotype, 1840–49, priv. coll. • A. Claudet, daguerreotype, 1840–49, priv. coll. • J. D. Llewelyn, self-portraits, photographs, 1850–59, priv. coll. • photograph, *c.*1853, NL Wales [*see illus.*]

Wealth at death £35,597 10*s*. excl. estates entailed to son: probate, 5 Dec 1882, *CGPLA Eng. & Wales*

Llewelyn, Mary Catherine Pendrill [*née* Mary Catherine Rhys] (**1811–1874**), writer and translator, was born on 12 March 1811 at Cowbridge, Glamorgan, the daughter of Thomas Rhys (1778–1851), schoolmaster, and his first wife, Joanna (*c.*1775–1815). Educated first at home, she later attended an academy for young ladies at Swansea. She displayed early signs of a literary and artistic flair, and was influenced by Edward Williams (Iolo Morganwg), in whose company she spent many of her childhood evenings. She met her future husband, Richard Pendrill Llewelyn (1813–1891) [*see below*], while he studied in Cowbridge. The two were well matched, as they shared a deep interest in Welsh culture and both were mildly eccentric characters. Rejecting her father's wishes in the matter, she chose to marry Llewelyn, a poor curate: their clandestine marriage took place at Clifton on 25 January 1837. They lived initially at Blaen-gwrach, Glamorgan, before moving to Sussex, where their first two children were born. On returning to Glamorgan in 1841 they took up residence at Llangynwyd vicarage. This was Mary's home for the rest of her life; she had seven more children and did the bulk of her writing here. The living of Llangynwyd was meagre, and the Llewelyns had no money of their own: with the cares of raising a large family and managing a penurious household, Mary Llewelyn's literary work was done in most unfavourable circumstances.

In 1845 the Llewelyns contributed letters, signed 'R & M', to *The Cambrian* regarding their collected folklore of Llangynwyd parish, including the first appearance in writing of 'The Maid of Cefn Ydfa', which became a nationally known Welsh folk story. Mary Llewelyn published much poetry of her own, in English and Welsh, notably in *The Cambrian* and the *Cardiff and Merthyr Guardian*; she also contributed 'sacred sonnets' and hymns to the *Church of England Magazine*. Her translations were mainly of hymns and popular ballads. She published *Hymns Translated from the Welsh* (1850), chiefly those of William Williams, Pantycelyn. John Jones (Tegid) hailed her as 'one of the ... very best translators of Welsh poetry', linking her name with those of Charlotte Guest and Maria Jane Williams as women whose work would assist towards rekindling Welsh nationality and the revival of Welsh literature and music (*Archaeologia Cambrensis*, 1846, 185). Mary Llewelyn died of cancer on 19 November 1874.

Richard Pendrill Llewelyn (1813–1891), Church of England clergyman, was born on 5 August 1813 at Laleston, Glamorgan, the son of Thomas Llewelyn (*c*.1788–1818), farmer, and his wife, Jane Pendrill (1788–1872), a descendant of John Penderel of Boscobel. He was educated at the Eagle Academy of Thomas Rhys and at the Cowbridge divinity school. In 1838 he received the Lambeth degree of MA. He became vicar of Llangynwyd in 1841 and served there for fifty years. A prominent evangelical clergyman, he published historical work, notably on Samuel Jones, his seventeenth-century predecessor at Llangynwyd. He gave his wife every possible support and encouragement in all her literary endeavours. He died on 22 October 1891; both Llewelyns were buried at Llangynwyd.

D. R. L. Jones

Sources D. R. L. Jones, *Richard and Mary Pendrill Llewelyn* (1991) · R. and M. Pendrill Llewelyn, Taliesin ab Iolo letters, NL Wales, 371–84 (1839–45) · T. C. Evans, *History of Llangynwyd parish* (1887) · G. J. Williams, *Traddodiad llenyddol Morgannwg* (1948) · G. J. Williams, 'Wil Hopcyn and the maid of Cefn Ydfa', *Glamorgan Historian* [ed. S. Williams], 6 (1969), 228–51 · private information (2004)

Likenesses V. Parminter, photograph, *c*.1870, Museum of Welsh Life, St Fagans, Cardiff

Llewelyn, Richard Pendrill (1813–1891). *See under* Llewelyn, Mary Catherine Pendrill (1811–1874).

Llewelyn, Thomas (*c*.1720–1783), Particular Baptist minister, was born at Penalltau isaf, Gelli-gaer, Glamorgan, the son of a farmer, Evan Llewelyn. After embarking on the tailoring trade as a youth, he was baptized in 1738 in the Hengoed Baptist Church and trained for the Baptist ministry at Trosnant Academy, near Pontypool, in 1740, together with Morgan Edwards. He then studied at Bristol Baptist Academy under Bernard Foskett, and in London at the Independent academy under doctors Walker, Marriott, and Jennings. He was ordained at Prescott Street, Goodman's Fields, London, about 1747, but never took pastoral charge and was described as 'no preacher' (Swaine, 65). After securing financial independence through his marriage to Mary, he established an academy to train poor students for the Baptist ministry, where he taught from 1746 to 1770. He was presented with the degree of MA, and afterwards LLD, by the University of Aberdeen.

Llewelyn played a major role in the promotion and distribution of the Welsh translation of the Bible. To this end he published in 1768 *An Historical Account of the British and Welsh Versions and Editions of the Bible*, translated into Welsh in *Seren Gomer* (1815), and his *Historical and Critical Remarks on the British Tongue* (1769). His work prompted the SPCK to publish 20,000 copies (8000 more than originally intended) of the Welsh Bible in 1769. He also joined the Book Society for Promoting Religious Knowledge among the Poor in 1768 and prepared a list of congregations, of all denominations, to whom free copies of the Welsh Bible might be sent. Both of his works demonstrate his classical scholarship, and his historical research has been used by subsequent writers on the history of the Welsh Bible. Llewelyn was said to have been a descendant of Thomas Llewelyn of Rhigos, near Aberdâr, who, it was claimed by Edward Williams (Iolo Morganwg), translated a portion of the Bible into Welsh about 1540, twenty-seven years before William Salesbury's translation of the New Testament was printed (B. H. Malkin, *The Scenery, Antiquities, and Biography of South Wales*, 2nd edn., 2 vols., 1807, 1.297).

In 1776 Llewelyn took a prominent part in the establishment of a Baptist mission for north Wales. He was one of the first members of the Gwyneddigion Society of London, and was its president in 1775. He was also a great supporter of the School for Welsh Girls, subsequently located at Ashford in Middlesex. He lived for many years in Queen Square, Bloomsbury, but died in Castleton, Monmouthshire, on 7 August 1783. He was buried in Bunhill Fields. He gave generously to education, and in particular to the Baptist college in Rhode Island and to Bristol Baptist college, to which he left his library, valued at his death at £1500.

D. L. Thomas, *rev.* Karen E. Smith

Sources *DWB*, 568–9 · D. M. Lewis, ed., *The Blackwell dictionary of evangelical biography, 1730–1860*, 2 vols. (1995) · W. Richards, *The Welsh nonconformists' memorial*, ed. J. Evans (1820), 278–86 · T. R. Roberts, *Eminent Welshmen: a short biographical dictionary* (1908), 307–18 · T. M. Bassett, *The Welsh Baptists* (1977) · S. A. Swaine, *Faithful men, or, Memorials of Bristol Baptist College* (1884), 65–7 · H. M. Davies, *Transatlantic brethren: Rev. Samuel Jones (1735–1814) and his friends* (1995), 109 · J. Rippon, ed., *The Baptist Annual Register*, 1 (1793), 185 · J. Thomas, *A history of the Baptist Association in Wales* (1795), 52, 66, 69 · *Trafodion Cymdeithas Hanes y Bedyddwyr* (1907–8), 7ff. · W. Roberts, 'Hanes bywyd Thomas Llewelyn', *Seren Gomer* (1885), 385–9, 433–9 · S. Gummer, 'Trosnant Academy', *Baptist Quarterly*, 9 (1938–9), 417–23

Wealth at death see will, *Trafodion Cymdeithas Hanes*, 19–22

Llewelyn-Davies. For this title name *see* Davies, Richard Llewelyn, Baron Llewelyn-Davies (1912–1981); Davies, Annie Patricia Llewelyn-, Baroness Llewelyn-Davies of Hastoe (1915–1997).

Lloyd. *See also* Llwyd, Loyd.

Lloyd, Albert Bushnell (1871–1946), missionary in Uganda and Church of England clergyman, was born at home, in Bosworth Terrace, King Richard's Road, Leicester, on 22 February 1871, the son of Thomas Howard Lloyd, a druggist, and his wife, Elizabeth, *née* Bushnell. Both his parents were devout Christians, and he had at least one sibling, his sister Elsie. An adventure-loving boy, he read all the African travelogues he could and trained as an

Albert Bushnell Lloyd (1871–1946), by unknown photographer, pubd 1899

engineer to equip himself as an explorer. At the age of eighteen he experienced an evangelical conversion and determined to become a missionary instead.

Accepted by the Church Missionary Society in 1892, Lloyd left for Uganda in 1894 and arrived in March 1895 having walked from the coast through German East Africa. In 1896 he was sent to the western Ugandan Bantu kingdom of Toro, recently restored under its king, Kasagama, by the British authorities. There, as later in Bunyoro, he was friendly with the African ruler and chiefs. During his time in Toro he visited the mission outpost of Mboga (afterwards Boga) in the Belgian Congo where he first met the saintly Ugandan missionary to the Bambuti pygmies, Apolo Kivebulaya. He travelled home on leave via the Congo in 1898. On 15 August 1899 he married Mary Ethel Masters, the daughter of Henry Masters, a draper, at St Mark's Church in New Milverton, Warwickshire; they returned to Uganda together in 1899. Also in 1899 Lloyd published *In Dwarf Land and Cannibal Country*; a substantial account of his travels and of Uganda, spiced with adventures with lion and elephant, it was reprinted several times.

On his second tour of service Lloyd worked first in the kingdom of Bunyoro. Then in 1904 he pioneered his mission's first venture into a non-Bantu area of Uganda, going to the Acholi who lived north and east of the Nile. Lloyd himself was the instigator, believing the Acholi to be hungering for the gospel. This proved to be a misapprehension, largely fostered by Bunyoro Christians who reworded enquiries to make them more attractive to the missionaries. Lloyd's account of an exploratory journey to the Acholi in 1903, of what he could learn of the people and their history, and the beginnings of mission work with the Acholi, are among the most valuable sections of *Uganda to Khartoum* (1906), another exciting read.

By the end of 1907 it was clear that a series of calamities and the opposition of the Acholi had made the mission untenable. It was temporarily abandoned, and the Lloyds were re-posted to Bunyoro on their return from leave in 1907. Lloyd was ordained deacon and priest in 1909, and the following year he returned to Toro. There he settled down to steady pastoral and administrative church work, including oversight of Mboga where Canon Apolo Kivebulaya worked. Lloyd was made rural dean of Toro in 1916 and archdeacon of western Uganda in 1922, and he remained in Toro until he left Uganda in 1926 to join the mission's home staff.

Lloyd retired in 1930 to become vicar of Combe Down, Bath; from 1936 he was vicar of Stanstead Abbots, Hertfordshire; and finally he became rector of Ladbroke-with-Radbourne, Rugby, in 1938. His ties with Uganda continued: in 1926 he was appointed bishop's commissary of the newly established diocese of the upper Nile, and in 1933–4 he returned to Africa briefly to Mboga after the death of Apolo Kivebulaya. Lloyd's later writings were slight, but they kept Kivebulaya's memory alive until the work of the biographer Anne Luck was published in 1963. Lloyd produced *Dayspring in Uganda* in 1921 and three short works about Kivebulaya in 1923, 1928, and 1934; *A Life's Thrills*, a brief memoir, was published posthumously in 1948; it comprised mainly a retelling of his earlier works.

Lloyd was an uncritical admirer of British colonialism and believed in the civilizing agency of mission and empire. Like most of his contemporaries he saw his call as one to save Africans from depravity and heathen darkness. Yet he liked and respected his African colleagues and acquaintances, and could not quite square his experience with this stereotype. He found himself profoundly moved, for instance, when a heathen diviner prayed for his safe passage on a dangerous river crossing, and could not believe that these prayers would be unheard by the Christian God (Lloyd, *Uganda to Khartoum*, 103–4). Lloyd died of a brain haemorrhage at his home, 7 Eastnor Grove, Leamington Spa, on 13 December 1946.

M. Louise Pirouet

Sources A. B. Lloyd, *In dwarf land and cannibal country* (1899) • A. B. Lloyd, *Uganda to Khartoum* (1906) • A. B. Lloyd, *A life's thrills* (1948) • Church Missionary Society, *Intelligencer* (1894–1906) • *Mengo Notes* [CMS, Uganda mission] (1900–02) • *Uganda Notes*, 3–13 (1902–12); *Uganda Notes and Diocesan Gazette*, 13 (1913) • E. Stock, *The history of the Church Missionary Society: its environment, its men and its work*, 3 (1899) • E. Stock, *The history of the Church Missionary Society: its environment, its men and its work*, 4 (1916) • G. Hewitt, *The problems of success: a history of the Church Missionary Society, 1910–1942*, 1 (1971) • A. Luck, *African saint: the story of Apolo Kivebulaya* (1963) • M. L. Pirouet, *Black evangelists: the spread of Christianity in Uganda, 1891–1914* (1978), 144–

68 • A. R. Tucker, *Eighteen years in Uganda and east Africa*, 2 vols. (1908) • A. Cook, *Uganda memories* (1945) • *Register of missionaries … from 1804 to 1904*, Church Missionary Society (privately printed, c.1905) • Crockford (1947) • m. cert. • b. cert.

Likenesses photograph, repro. in Lloyd, *In dwarf land*, frontispiece [*see illus.*] • photograph, repro. in Lloyd, *A life's thrills*, frontispiece

Wealth at death £4129 5*s*. 8*d*.: probate, 3 March 1947, *CGPLA Eng. & Wales*

Lloyd, Albert Lancaster (1908–1982), ethnomusicologist and radio and television broadcaster, was born on 29 February 1908 at 136A Trevelyan Road, off Tooting High Street, London, the son of Ernest Lancaster Lloyd, a draper's packer, and his wife, Mabel Emily Barrett. His father was an accountant's son from Islington, his mother a printer's daughter from Battersea. Details of his early life are sketchy; he lived in both London and Sussex and attended Hornsey grammar school, where he began his lifelong involvement with languages. At the age of sixteen, with his mother dead and his father, a war invalid, unable to look after him, Lloyd went to Australia as an assisted migrant.

In Australia Lloyd worked as a farm-hand and shepherd and had what was probably his first significant encounter with traditional songs. He began to jot these down in notebooks in order to remember what he encountered—not, in any sense, as a folk-song collector. It was in his teenage years that Lloyd made use of library postal loans to continue his education. He also listened extensively to Western classical music on borrowed 78 r.p.m. records.

Lloyd returned to England in the early 1930s and lived near King's Cross, London. In a short space of time he encountered unemployment, the British Library reading room, a group of left-wing intellectuals including Dylan Thomas, Jack Lindsay, George Rudé, and A. L. Morton, and, via this group, the Communist Party. He remained a loyal member for the rest of his life. He worked for a time in Foyles foreign book department and started writing translations (including editions of Lorca's poems) and criticism. In 1937 and 1938 he worked as a labourer on a whaling ship and as a merchant seaman.

In 1940 Lloyd obtained a job as a journalist with *Picture Post*, which (with some interruption for military service) lasted for about ten years. His regular partner on the magazine was the celebrated photojournalist Bert Hardy, and 'the two Berts' created many acclaimed features. Lloyd's language skills enabled him to travel widely. He purposely suggested stories in parts of the world that he knew were 'musically lively' and thus acquainted himself directly with a diversity of foreign folk musics. In the end Lloyd fell out with the owners of *Picture Post*, who had become uneasy about Lloyd's political views in the growing cold war atmosphere. The proprietor, Edward Hulton, fired the editor, Tom Hopkinson, over the printing of a story felt to be 'politically too hot'. Lloyd resigned in sympathy with Hopkinson, and resolved to make a living as a freelance writer and collector. During his period at *Picture Post*, on 13 April 1946 he married Charlotte Maria Ohly (*b*. 1912/13), daughter of Jean Adam, an assistant bank manager; they had a daughter.

Lloyd's Communist Party connections were important in establishing him as a freelance. In the cold war atmosphere of the 1950s he had easy access, where others were denied, and was welcomed in eastern Europe. It is reported that he caused no little resentment among Soviet bloc folklorists because of the way in which he was able to obtain privileged access to their hard-won sources. Another important connection that sustained Lloyd was with the BBC. He had done some work in the late 1930s with producer Lawrence Gilliam on *The Voice of the Seaman*, a revolutionary piece of radio that made use of actuality, not actors. Soon after, he worked on *Shadow of the Swastika*, a drama documentary on the rise of Hitler. Lloyd's left-wing enthusiasms worried some at the BBC and his contract was not renewed. In spite of continuing suspicion, Lloyd produced many scripts in the post-war period, ranging from ethnomusicological work for the Third Programme to twenty-minute scripts for schools' broadcasts. A significant number of BBC personnel realized the uniqueness of his talents and made extensive use of him. In the 1970s he made a number of highly acclaimed television programmes with the film-maker Barry Gavin.

Lloyd was instrumental in the creation of the British folk music revival of the post-war period as both a writer and a performer. His pamphlet *The Singing Englishman* (1944), produced under wartime conditions, laid the foundation for his mature work, *Folk Song in England* (1967). In this book Lloyd combines the tradition of English folk-song scholarship, largely derived from Cecil Sharp, with the radical historiography of such people as A. L. Morton and E. P. Thompson. This is further fleshed out with understandings derived from American and eastern European folk music scholars. It is a heady concoction that fitted well with the spirit of the time; a seminal work which tried to unite disparate and perhaps incompatible elements. Perhaps Lloyd's most significant contribution was to map out the territory of what he called 'industrial folk song', the work of mainly mining and cloth making communities who continued producing songs into the earlier phases of industrialization. The book has attracted much scholarly criticism, sometimes mixed with deep admiration, since the time of its publication. Lloyd had a way of side-stepping questions which were inconvenient or did not fit with his particular perceptions of the world. He could always draw on a rich store of esoteric knowledge to confound his opponents.

Lloyd, together with Ewan MacColl, the Scottish actor turned singer, was the most important influence on the post-war British folk-song revival in the 1950s and 1960s. Some people objected to the way in which he altered and adapted traditional material, collating variants and creating versions that some thought were 'too good to be true'. Numerous people attest to his generosity with his time and material, and to the encouragement he gave younger performers and scholars who were just beginning to discover the riches of traditional music. He bridged the gap between the first and second folk-song revivals in collaborating with Ralph Vaughan Williams on *The Penguin Book of English Folk Song* (1959), a classic collection which drew extensively on the work of pre-1914 collectors.

It is as a presenter and performer that many people remember Lloyd. He had an extensive repertory of English and Australian songs. The early experiences of hearing him sing could be likened to the opening of a door on to a fascinating, strange, and yet familiar country. His performances were characterized by his total involvement with the song. He often bore a wry smile. His voice took unexpected turns as he explored a song. His pitching was occasionally approximate, but many found his performances deeply satisfying. Most of all, he communicated his obvious delight in the songs he so valued and did so much to popularize. Lloyd died on 29 September 1982 at his home, 16 Crooms Hill, Greenwich, from pneumonia and heart failure, and was cremated. He was survived by his wife. VIC GAMMON

Sources I. Russell, ed., *Singer, song and scholar* (1986) • *The Times* (1 Oct 1982) • W. Ward, 'Profile: A. L. Lloyd—in a conversation with Wally Ward', Workers' Music Association duplicated paper, Jan 1978, Goldsmiths' College, London, A. L. Lloyd archive • D. Arthur, 'A. L. Lloyd, a brief biography', *Classic A. L. Lloyd: traditional songs* (Fellside FECD98, 1994) [CD booklet] • B. Hardy, *My life* (1985) • miscellaneous notebooks and papers, Goldsmiths' College, London, A. L. Lloyd archive • personal knowledge (2004) • *CGPLA Eng. & Wales* (1982) • private information (2004) • b. cert. • m. cert. • d. cert.

Archives Goldsmiths' College, London • Vaughan Williams Memorial Library, London | FILM BFI NFTVA | SOUND BL NSA • Topic Records, London • Vaughan Williams Memorial Library, London

Likenesses B. Shad, photographs

Wealth at death £70,500: probate, 8 Nov 1982, *CGPLA Eng. & Wales*

Lloyd [*née* Parsons], **Anna Shatford** (1837–1912), school principal, was born on 22 January 1837, the younger daughter of the Revd Benjamin *Parsons (1797–1855) and his wife, Amelia Parsons (*née* Fry), in Ebley, near Stroud, Gloucestershire. Her father, minister of the Congregational church in Ebley, was notable for the schools he opened and ran, and for his advocacy of education for women as much as for men. Anna Parsons was educated in her father's school in the family home. At the age of twenty, in 1857, she married Thomas Lloyd (1823–1885), her father's successor in Ebley, who was also a supporter of education for women. She and her husband had three daughters and a son.

In 1861 Thomas and Anna Lloyd moved to the Independent (Congregational) church at St Ives in Huntingdonshire. Soon after their arrival the church was rebuilt in co-operation with the Baptists, and was henceforward known as the Free Church. Anna Lloyd, a quiet, gentle person who was always happy to be active, was involved with many of the outreach activities of the church, such as the mothers' meeting, the temperance association, and the coal and clothing club. The whole family were lifelong supporters of the London Missionary Society.

When a local girls' school hitherto owned by Anglicans, Slepe Hall (on the site of which Oliver Cromwell had once lived), was put on the market in 1877 the Lloyds, anxious that it should not be bought by some Roman Catholics who had expressed interest, persuaded nonconformists in the town to help them to raise sufficient money to purchase it. The Lloyd family moved to the hall, and Anna Lloyd became principal of the Ladies' School, Slepe Hall, which was both a day and a boarding-school, with Christian nonconformist principles as the guiding ethos. As her daughters reached adulthood they too became teachers in the school, alongside other female relatives; none had formal qualifications, but they shared an enthusiasm and support for the work of the school. Visiting teachers came from Cambridge, Bedford, and London. It was a small, friendly school with a family atmosphere, the pupils, aged between five and seventeen, coming mostly from the surrounding county, usually from nonconformist families; there were special scholarships for the daughters of Congregational ministers and missionaries. Boys were admitted to the youngest classes. After the death of Thomas Lloyd in 1885 Anna Lloyd and her family continued to live and work in Slepe Hall.

As Anna Lloyd grew older, her unmarried daughter **Martha Lloyd** (1860–1943) took more share in the running of the school and eventually became co-principal. When Anna Lloyd died at Slepe Hall on 17 November 1912 and was buried in the St Ives cemetery on 20 November after a funeral in the Free Church, Martha Lloyd assumed complete responsibility for the school until her retirement in 1928. She was born in Ebley on 7 February 1860, but after the family move to St Ives in 1861 lived the rest of her life in Huntingdonshire. After being educated at home she had had ambitions to go to Girton College, but it was only her brother who went to Cambridge; finances were limited and her mother needed help in the school. At some point, however, she studied in France and Germany, and acquired a knowledge of Old English. She was very well known in the county, being active on the county education committee and in the Free Church, and for many years was a director of the London Missionary Society. She was a keen mountaineer, one of the earliest members of the Ladies' Alpine Club, and the first woman to climb the Sudlenspitze. She died at The Priory, St Ives, on 24 October 1943; her remains were cremated in Cambridge. Slepe Hall continued for another two decades, but was closed in 1965. ELAINE KAYE

Sources Lloyd family folder, Norris Museum, St Ives • *Huntingdonshire County News* (22 Nov 1912) • *Huntingdonshire County Post* (4 Nov 1943) • M. Wagner, *Not an easy church: a history of the Free Church of St Ives, 1672–1981* (1982) • private information (2004) • C. Binfield, *Belmont's Portias: Victorian non-conformists and middle-class education for girls* (1981) • *Congregational Year Book* (1886) • box of documents relating to Slepe Hall, Norris Museum, St Ives • d. cert. • b. cert. [Martha Lloyd] • d. cert. [Martha Lloyd]

Likenesses P. Clarke, photograph, Slepe Hall Hotel, St Ives, Cambridgeshire • P. Clarke, photograph (Martha Lloyd), Slepe Hall Hotel, St Ives, Cambridgeshire

Wealth at death £13,322 15*s.* 5*d.*: probate, 30 Jan 1913, *CGPLA Eng. & Wales* • £14,644 14*s.* 1*d.*—Martha Lloyd: probate, 8 Feb 1944, *CGPLA Eng. & Wales*

Lloyd, Bartholomew (1772–1837), college head, born at New Ross, co. Wexford, on 5 February 1772, was descended

Bartholomew Lloyd (1772–1837), by Campanile

from a Welsh family which, about the end of the seventeenth century, settled in co. Wexford. He was the eldest son of Humphrey Lloyd (1735–1786), himself the son of the Revd Bartholomew Lloyd of the Abbey House of New Ross. His father died while he was still a boy, and an uncle, the Revd John Lloyd, rector of Ferns and Kilbride, to whose care he had been committed, did not long survive, so that he was left to struggle for himself. He entered Trinity College, Dublin, in 1787 as a pensioner. In 1790 he gained first scholarship, in 1792 graduated BA, and in 1796 obtained a junior fellowship on passing a remarkably high examination. He graduated MA in the same year, BD in 1805, and DD in 1808. In July 1799 he married Eleanor, daughter of Patrick McLaughlin of Dublin, and had a family of four sons and six daughters.

In 1813 Lloyd was appointed Erasmus Smith's professor of mathematics at Trinity College, Dublin, on the resignation of William Magee, afterwards archbishop of Dublin. In 1822 came a further appointment, as Erasmus Smith's professor of natural and experimental philosophy in succession to William Davenport. His publications, *A Treatise on Analytic Geometry* (1819) and *An Elementary Treatise of Mechanical Philosophy* (1826), were not the result of original work. In both his chairs, however, he introduced radical change into the methods of teaching. Immediately after his appointment to the mathematics chair, he began to bring in the new analytical methods of French mathematics. In revolutionizing the curriculum, he has been reckoned 'the founder of the distinguished Dublin mathematical school of the nineteenth century' (McDowell and Webb, 159). His versatility and the wide range of his attainments are shown by the facts that in 1821 and again in 1823 and 1825 he was elected regius professor of Greek in the university, and in 1823 and again in 1827 Archbishop King's lecturer in divinity. His *Discourses, Chiefly Doctrinal, Delivered in the Chapel of Trinity College, Dublin* were published in 1822.

In 1831 Lloyd was elected provost of the college, in succession to Samuel Kyle. He embarked on a programme of academic reform including the foundation of new chairs, and alterations in the tenure of existing chairs to allow holders more opportunity to undertake advanced teaching and original work. A new undergraduate course in logic and ethics was introduced. His reorganization of the academic year and establishment of a division between pass and honours courses lasted for over a century.

The magnetic observatory of the college was founded through Lloyd's influence. In 1835 he was appointed president of the Royal Irish Academy, in the affairs of which he took an active interest; and in the same year he acted as president of the British Association meeting at Dublin. His inaugural address dealt mainly with 'the correspondence of the objects of science with divine revelation'. His house in Dublin was a meeting place for men of science. Lloyd died suddenly in Dublin of apoplexy on 24 November 1837, and was buried in the chapel of his college. The Lloyd exhibitions were founded by subscription in 1839 in his memory. His eldest son, Humphrey *Lloyd, became provost of Trinity College, Dublin, in 1867.

THOMAS HAMILTON, *rev.* M. C. CURTHOYS

Sources J. H. Singer, *Proceedings of the Royal Irish Academy*, 1 (1836–40), 121–6 • *Dublin University Magazine*, 11 (1838), 111–21 • *GM*, 2nd ser., 9 (1838), 208–9 • Burke, *Gen. Ire.* • Burtchaell & Sadleir, *Alum. Dubl.* • R. B. McDowell and D. A. Webb, *Trinity College, Dublin, 1592–1952: an academic history* (1982)

Archives TCD, corresp. with Beresford

Likenesses T. Kirk, marble bust, *c.*1830–1837, NG Ire. • C. Turner, mezzotint, pubd 1838 (after drawing by H. O'Neill), BM, NG Ire. • Campanile, oils, TCD [*see illus.*] • M. Cregan, oils, Royal Irish Acad. • T. Kirk, marble bust, TCD

Lloyd [Floyd], **Sir Charles** (*c.***1602–1661**), royalist army officer, was the son of Sergeant-major Brochwel Lloyd of Moel-y-garth, Montgomeryshire, and his wife, Honoria, daughter of Sir Stephen *Procter. He served in the Dutch army in the 1630s, where he showed his skill as a map maker and military engineer, and was an ensign by 1632. His abilities as an engineer were such that in April 1639 he was appointed engineer-in-chief and quartermaster-general for life of all fortifications in the British Isles, at 13*s.* 4*d.* per day. He was employed to repair the fortifications of Berwick upon Tweed in the winter of 1639–40 and served as a captain in the earl of Northumberland's regiment in the second bishops' war.

In December 1641 parliament appointed Lloyd chief engineer and quartermaster-general with the army to serve in Ireland, at £1 10*s.* per day. He went to Ireland, but when the civil war began returned to England and joined the royalist army. Oxford's fortifications were constructed under his direction in spring 1643 and he supervised the setting out of the camp at Culham in May. Lloyd took command of Sir Thomas Salusbury's regiment following his death in the summer of 1643. This was raised in Denbighshire and Flintshire and was then the largest of the king's foot regiments. It was part of the army during the campaign in 1643 which saw the capture of Bristol, the siege of Gloucester, and the first battle of Newbury. In October 1643 Lloyd was directed to supervise the fortification of Newport Pagnell, Buckinghamshire. He took part in the campaign in the west country in 1644 and on the army's return was appointed governor of Devizes in Wiltshire. He was knighted in Oxford on 8 December 1644.

Lloyd was an active garrison commander, leading a raid on parliamentarian forces at Aldbourne, Wiltshire, in August 1645 and attempting to make Devizes more secure by firing or wrecking country houses nearby, including Bromham House. He was, however, wary of the reactions of local people. On 15 September 1645 Oliver Cromwell arrived with a detachment of the New Model Army and quickly occupied the town, forcing Lloyd and the garrison, which was said to number 300 men, to retire to the castle gatehouse. This was bombarded by Cromwell's artillery and Lloyd surrendered on 23 September 1645, attracting criticism from Sir Edward Walker for not having made a longer defence. He was given the use of three carriages to take his belongings to Worcester.

In October 1654 Lloyd arrived at The Hague from England. He returned to England after the Restoration and petitioned for the resumption of the pay of 13*s*. 4*d*. per day granted him by Charles I. He was appointed chief engineer in 1660, but did not receive his salary and was forced to borrow money. Lloyd made his will on 8 March 1661 and died, apparently unmarried, at some point between then and 14 March when he was buried at St Margaret's, Westminster. His sister Blanch was his executor and residuary legatee and both she and his mother petitioned after his death for his arrears of pay. He was succeeded as chief engineer by his brother Sir Godfrey *Lloyd.

STEPHEN PORTER

Sources *DWB*, 572 • N. Tucker, *Royalist officers of north Wales, 1642–1660* (1961), 37 • I. Roy, ed., *The royalist ordnance papers, 1642–1646*, 1, Oxfordshire RS, 43 (1964), 187, 222; 2, Oxfordshire RS, 49 (1975), 444, 469, 477, 480, 484, 486 • H. F. Westlake and L. E. Tanner, eds., *The register of St Margaret's, Westminster, London, 1660–1675*, Harleian Society, register section, 64 (1935), 187 • will, City Westm. AC, filed wills 122 • will, PRO, PROB 11/307/51 [will of Blanch Lloyd, sister] • *Diary of the marches of the royal army during the great civil war, kept by Richard Symonds*, ed. C. E. Long, CS, old ser., 74 (1859); repr. with new introduction by I. Roy as *Richard Symonds' diary of the marches of the royal army* (1997), 161 • *CSP Ire., 1633–47*, 782 • E. Walker, *Historical collections of several important transactions relating to the late rebellion and civil wars of England* (1707), 134 • *The Nicholas papers*, ed. G. F. Warner, 2, CS, new ser., 50 (1892), 114 • *CSP dom., 1660–1*, 302; *1661–2*, 223 • R. Norton, *A letter concerning the storming and delivering up of the castle of the Devises* (1645) [Thomason tract E 303(2)] • *The Weekly Account, Containing Certain Speciall and Remarkable Passages* (4–11 July 1645) [Thomason tract E 288(2)] • *JHC*, 2 (1640–42), 349

Lloyd, Charles (1735–1773), politician and pamphleteer, was born in Westminster, the second son of Philip Lloyd (*d*. 1735) of Grosvenor Street, Westminster, and Catherine Cade (*d*. in or after 1773). His father, who eloped with his mother, an heiress with a fortune of £5000, in 1724, had represented Saltash since 1723 on the duke of Wharton's interest. By 1727, however, Lloyd had changed his political allegiance and was a firm friend of Sir Robert Walpole, a friendship which secured for him in 1730 the position of equerry to George II. Educated at Westminster School as a king's scholar, Charles Lloyd later graduated from Christ Church, Oxford (BA, 1758; MA, 1761). Through his elder brother, Philip *Lloyd, who was tutor to George Grenville's sons, he entered the Grenville circle and gained early preferment.

Lloyd was given the sinecure as receiver-general and paymaster of the band of gentlemen pensioners in March 1762 and a clerkship in the Treasury. He became George Grenville's private secretary in April 1763, and was soon entrusted with the patronage of the new administration, thereby establishing himself as Grenville's man of business. Rewarded with a further sinecure as the receiver of Gibraltar, he also became a member of the corporation of the Treasury borough of Orford, Suffolk. There can be little doubt that if Grenville had remained in power he would have found Lloyd a safe seat in the Commons. Lloyd also proved to be adept as a polemic administration penman and he attacked William Pitt's attempt to replace Grenville in *The Anatomy of a Late Negotiation*, published in September 1763. He also defended Grenville's actions over the prosecution of John Wilkes and the question of general warrants in *A Defense of the Majority in the House of Commons on the Question Relating to General Warrants* (September 1764), in answer to Charles Townshend's pamphlet *A Defense of the Minority in the House of Commons*, published the previous month. Removed from his sinecures by Lord Rockingham following Grenville's surprising fall from office in July 1765, Lloyd became a successful and prolific political pamphleteer.

In opposition Lloyd gave full vent to the Grenvillite suspicion that Lord Bute had brought down the administration in his pamphlet *An Honest Man's Reasons for Declining to Take any Part in the New Administration* (July 1765), and when Grey Cooper defended Rockingham in September 1765 Lloyd answered with his *A Critical Review of the New Administration* (December 1765). After Rockingham's own short-lived ministry fell in the summer of 1766, Lloyd elaborated upon the view that Lord Bute remained the puppet-master behind the throne in *The History of the Late Minority Exhibiting the Conduct, Principles, and Views of that Party* (July 1766), a work which gave great offence to George III. When William Pitt succeeded Rockingham, and also accepted a peerage as the earl of Chatham, Lloyd reflected Grenville's own anger in the vicious *An examination of the principles and boasted disinterestedness of a late right honourable gentleman* (August 1766), a pamphlet which portrayed Chatham as both corrupt and dictatorial.

Eager to defend the measures of the Rockingham administration, Edmund Burke published a pamphlet in August 1766, which immediately provoked a response from Lloyd, *A True History of a Late Short Administration*, and prompted him to research, with Grenville's help, a much longer defence of Grenville's colonial policy. Published in December 1766, *The Conduct of the Late Administration Examined* remains one of the best works justifying the Stamp Act. Portraying Grenville as one of the few senior politicians who was above party, the work also damned Rockingham for repealing the Stamp Act, a political blunder,

Lloyd argued, that would only increase American disobedience.

The opposition intention of creating a united front against the Chatham–Grafton ministry was weakened in 1767 by Grenville's continued hostility towards Rockingham, and all hope of overthrowing the administration died when the followers of the duke of Bedford negotiated terms for their inclusion in the ministry in November 1767. Lloyd himself had tired of opposition and left Grenville's service that year to accept a government place as deputy teller of the exchequer. This did not prevent him, however, from publishing a passing shot at the Bedfordites in the *Political Register*, 'A word of parting to the grace the d(uke) of B(edford)' (December 1767), a work which greatly offended the duke.

Whether Lloyd continued secretly to publish articles in the *Political Register* throughout 1768 remains unknown, but he did remain close to Grenville and until the latter's death in 1770 continued to correspond with him on many of the political issues which would appear in that journal. After a long illness, Lloyd died in St Martin's parish, Westminster, on 22 January 1773. Unmarried, he left his estate, which was administered by his brother Philip, to his mother, Catherine Lloyd. RORY T. CORNISH

Sources R. T. Cornish, *George Grenville, 1717–1770: a bibliography* (1992) • L. B. Namier, *The structure of politics at the accession of George III*, 2 vols. (1929) • R. R. Rea, *The English press in politics, 1760–1774* (1963) • E. Cruickshanks, 'Lloyd, Philip', HoP, *Commons, 1715–54* • J. Almon, *Biographical, literary, and political anecdotes*, 3 vols. (1797), vol. 3 • *DNB*

Archives BL, corresp. with George Grenville, Add. MS 57818 • BL, corresp. with Charles Jenkinson, Add. MSS 38197–38207, 38304, 38458, 38469–38470, *passim*

Wealth at death see administration, PRO, PROB 6/149, fol. 134r

Lloyd, Charles (1748–1828), banker and philanthropist, was born in Edgbaston Street, Birmingham, on 22 August 1748, the second son of Sampson Lloyd (1727–1807) of Birmingham, iron manufacturer and banker and a member of the Society of Friends, and his second wife, Rachel (1712–1756), daughter of Nehemiah Champion of Bristol. He was at a school in Worcester run by a member of the society, Ephraim Goodere, and then entered the family manufacturing and banking business. His chief, and eventually only, concern was banking, as a partner in Taylors and Lloyds Bank (a forerunner of Lloyds Bank). On 13 May 1774 he married Mary (*d.* 1821), daughter of James Farmer of Birmingham, with whom he had fifteen children. His eldest son, Charles *Lloyd (1775–1839), was a poet associated with Samuel Taylor Coleridge and with Charles Lamb.

Though his principles as a member of the Society of Friends debarred him from holding public office Lloyd was active in public activities in Birmingham, was a member of the board of commissioners, then responsible for local government, and helped to found the Birmingham General Hospital, where he served as treasurer for fifty years. In a wider field he went to London in 1775 to meet Benjamin Franklin, in the vain hope of persuading him to avoid war, and was actively concerned with the campaign to abolish the slave trade, his brother John Lloyd being a founder member of the Abolition Committee.

Having studied the classics, in his spare time Lloyd composed verse translations of Homer and Horace, some of which were published. Inspired by Virgil's *Georgics* he bought a farm at Olton, just outside Birmingham, and for thirty years he devoted one day a week to farming, which 'contributed, in conjunction with temperance and cheerfulness, to keep a naturally delicate constitution in health and vigour to a late period of his life' (*GM*). He died on 16 January 1828 at his residence, Bingley House, Birmingham, and was buried at the Quaker burial-ground at Bull Lane in the city. CHRISTOPHER FYFE

Sources H. Lloyd, *The Quaker Lloyds in the industrial revolution* (1975) • *GM*, 1st ser., 98/1 (1828), 281 • J. A. Langford, ed., *A century of Birmingham life … 1741–1841* (1868)

Archives Friends' House Library, Lloyd MSS

Likenesses P. Hollins, bust, *c.*1831, Birmingham General Hospital • stipple, NPG

Wealth at death see Lloyd, *The Quaker Lloyds*, 249

Lloyd, Charles (1766–1829), dissenting minister and schoolmaster, was born at Llwynrhydowen, Cardiganshire, on 18 December 1766. He was the third son and fourth child of five born to David Lloyd (1724–1779), Presbyterian minister there, and his second wife, Letitia Lloyd of Llanfechan; a sister had been born in the first marriage. On his father's death his education for the ministry was undertaken by his uncle John Lloyd of Coedlannau. His uncle, however, provided only for his schooling in 1779–84 under David Davis (1745–1827), who had been his father's colleague; Lloyd thought Davis the superior of any teacher of classics who came after.

In the autumn of 1784 Lloyd entered (with an exhibition of £10) the Presbyterian academy best known as Carmarthen but then at Swansea under Solomon Harries (1726–1785). Lloyd developed an aversion to Hebrew, which was Harries's principal interest, but believed that he profited from his instruction in mathematics. Harries was succeeded in 1785 by Josiah Rees (1749–1804), father of Thomas Rees (1777–1864), and Thomas Lloyd, son of Charles Lloyd's uncle John. William Howell (1740–1822) became theological tutor in 1786, and the other tutors established a grammar school preparatory to the academy, in which Charles Lloyd was appointed afternoon teacher. Among his fellow students was Lewis Loyd (1767–1858), who left the ministry for a highly successful career in banking and who was the father of Samuel Jones Loyd, first Baron Overstone.

After leaving the academy in 1788 in ill health, Charles Lloyd went to Hotwells, near Bristol, where he received much kindness from John Wright MD (*d.* 1794), and his brother Thomas Wright (*d.* 1797), Presbyterian minister at Lewin's Mead, Bristol, who are among the few whom Lloyd, in his singular autobiography, exempts from censure.

Through the influence of Nathaniel Philipps (1757?–1842), Presbyterian minister at Derby, Lloyd was elected minister, in August 1788, of the Oat Street congregation, Evesham, Worcestershire, with a stipend of £40. He was at this time a 'moderately high Arian'. He started a Sunday school and an evening service and increased his congregation from 40 to 200. He wished, however, to administer the sacraments without being ordained—ordination was a matter of serious disagreement among Presbyterians and Unitarians at that time. When the congregation objected he consulted Joseph Priestley, then at Birmingham, who, to his surprise, urged him to be ordained. At length the congregation yielded, persuaded by the expense attending an ordination. Shortly afterwards Lloyd began to have doubts about infant baptism, and on 3 April 1790 proposed to omit this rite or resign; his resignation was at once accepted.

Through Joshua Toulmin he was put in charge of a General Baptist congregation at Ditchling, Sussex, at a stipend of 60 guineas. There he received adult baptism, but refused to submit to the additional rite of imposition of hands, then usual among General Baptists; he also again declined ordination. He cultivated extempore preaching. At the beginning of 1792 he started a boarding-school and married in the following summer. Early in 1793 he left the ministry and moved his school to Exeter, where it flourished. His first pupil was John Kenrick, who described Lloyd as 'a good classical scholar, [who] grounded his pupils well … interesting them by his remarks on the authors. … But his temper was warm, and he corrected passionately. He was sensitive, and suspicious of affront.'

Lloyd then turned farmer in 1799 on the small estate of Coedlannau Fawr, Cardiganshire, inherited from his brother Richard, who died on 27 September 1797 aged thirty-seven. His agricultural experiment, caught in the price instability of the war years, exhausted all his savings. By then he had abandoned his Arian position for Unitarianism and would have been glad to act as colleague in the congregation at Llwynrhydowen, which had been his father's, but the pastor, his old schoolmaster David Davis, opposed the election of a Socinian Baptist. By this time, however, he had rejected the rite of baptism in any form, as an institution necessary only in the apostolic age. A secession from the chapel in 1801 resulted in the founding of two small chapels at Capel-y-groes (with a membership of eighty) and Pantydefaid (with a membership of sixty); they chose Lloyd as their minister. His stay in Cardiganshire did not last long. Leaving his congregations to the care of John James (1779–1864), he settled in 1803 in Palgrave, Suffolk, undertaking a school and the charge of a Presbyterian congregation, which he held from 5 April 1803 to 4 October 1811. In 1809 he received the degree of LLD from the University of Glasgow. His first wife, Letty, with whom he had several children, died at Palgrave on 11 December 1808. From a second marriage, to Sara Maria Smith, he had a son, Francis Vaughan (*b.* 1811).

From Palgrave Lloyd moved to London, where for many years he kept a school in Keppel Street, Russell Square. He died on a visit to relatives near Lampeter, Cardiganshire, on 23 May 1829, and was buried at Llanwenog.

Lloyd published relatively little: *Two Sermons on Christian Zeal* (1808), *Observations on the Choice of a School* (1812), *Travels at Home* (1814), and a version of the epistles of St Paul and St James 'by Philalethes', identified by John Kentish as Lloyd. Even as a controversialist, he put little in print. One dispute is the overlong exchange in the *Monthly Repository* at the end of 1813 and the beginning of 1814, over the translation of Acts 20: 28, between Lloyd and John Jones (1766?–1827); Lloyd is said to have played cards with Jones and quarrelled with him every evening. In *The 'Monthly Repository' Extraordinaire* (1819) he took Robert Aspland to task for his attack on Thomas Paine's *Age of Reason*, which had just been republished by Richard Carlile, though Aspland had conceded Carlile's right to publish.

Lloyd's fame will rest on his anonymous autobiography, *Particulars of the Life of a Dissenting Minister … Written by Himself* (1813), an edition with only a few surviving copies because Lloyd subsequently tried to suppress it; but the book was reprinted in 1911, with marginal identifications by the Revd R. T. Jenkins of some of the nameless targets of Lloyd's abuse. Alexander Gordon (*DNB*) refers to the impression given by the book of 'an acute and honest, though jaundiced mind', while Robert Brook Aspland, commenting on Lloyd's unsparing characterization of the Evesham congregation, refers to his 'sickness of heart and a temper soured by disappointment' (*Christian Reformer*, new ser., 8, 1852, 618). Some of the portraits with which the book ends are harsh beyond any deserving, notably of Timothy Kenrick (1759–1804) and John Jones. Yet the book abounds in insights and offers a pathetic, even tragic, depiction of failure.

ALEXANDER GORDON, *rev.* R. K. WEBB

Sources [C. Lloyd], *Particulars of the life of a dissenting minister … written by himself* [1813]; repr. (1911) · *DNB* · *DWB* · [R. B. Aspland], 'A brief history of the Presbyterian congregation at Evesham', *Christian Reformer, or, Unitarian Magazine and Review*, new ser., 8 (1852), 607–21, esp. 618–9 · *Monthly Repository*, 8 (1813), 521–3, 595–600, 660–68 · *Monthly Repository*, 9 (1814), 38–44, 120–25 · *Monthly Repository*, new ser., 3 (1829), 443 · *Christian Reformer, or, Unitarian Magazine and Review*, new ser., 5 (1849), 359n · A. M. Hill, 'The death of ordination in the Unitarian tradition', *Transactions of the Unitarian Historical Society*, 14/4 (1967–70), 190–208

Archives NL Wales, letters

Lloyd, Charles (1775–1839), poet, was born in Birmingham, on 12 February 1775, the eldest son of Charles *Lloyd (1748–1828), the Quaker banker and philanthropist, and his wife, Mary Farmer (1751?–1821). He was educated privately, and was intended to have entered his father's bank, but he found this unpalatable, as he did the medical studies he briefly attempted at Edinburgh. His first published volume of poems appeared in Carlisle in 1795, and in the following year he met Coleridge when the latter visited Birmingham to enlist subscribers to his newspaper, *The Watchman*. He was so attracted by Coleridge's conversation that he offered to pay him £80 a year, in return for staying with him and having the benefit of his conversation. They lived together in Kingsdown, Bristol, and Lloyd came to know others in radical and literary circles in that city, including Robert Southey and Joseph Cottle. At the close of 1796 Lloyd accompanied Coleridge and his wife to Nether Stowey. Coleridge's sonnet 'To a Friend', on the birth of his son Hartley, and his lines 'To a Young Man of Fortune', are probably addressed to Lloyd.

The latter had already printed at Bristol, for publication in London, a volume of elegiac verse to the memory of his grandmother Priscilla Farmer, with an introductory sonnet by Coleridge, and concluded by 'The Grandam' of Charles Lamb, to whom Lloyd had been introduced by Coleridge. Almost immediately after his arrival at Nether Stowey, Lloyd was attacked by fits, the precursors of his subsequent depressive illness. He remained with the Coleridges until the summer of 1797, and in the autumn of that year all the poems which he wanted to preserve were added by Cottle, along with poems by Charles Lamb, to a second edition of Coleridge's poems. But Coleridge did not think well of this publication, and ridiculed its contents in sonnets signed Nehemiah Higginbottom in the *Monthly Magazine* (November 1797).

In the turbulent political climate prevailing in the aftermath of the French Revolution, Lloyd's association with a notable radical like Coleridge made him the object of attacks by conservative publicists—understandably, when one of the blank-verse poems that he published with Lamb in 1798 celebrated

> the promis'd time ... when equal man
> Shall deem the world his temple
> (*Blank Verse*, 1798, 12–13)

He and Lamb figure in Gillray's famous cartoon illustrating Canning's satire on revolutionary sympathizers, *The New Morality*, appearing there as a toad and a frog. Lloyd was anxious to rid himself of this reputation, and defended his respectability in a *Letter to the Anti-Jacobin Reviewers*. He reinforced this, in 1799, with some *Lines Suggested by the Fast ... February 27th 1799*, where he censured the modern 'spirit of insubordination', and helpfully included in a footnote a quotation from a similar satire by Lamb. Partly with the same purpose, and with Southey's encouragement, he had published in the previous year an epistolary novel, *Edmund Oliver*, a polemic against William Godwin's radical views on marriage, and on the rule of reason over the passions. Although poor as a novel, it gives some insight into contemporary moral and political controversies. It also draws on Coleridge's experiences as a private soldier in a way that Coleridge felt was a betrayal of confidence. This, and Lloyd's resentment at the Higginbottom sonnets, led to an estrangement.

In 1798 Lloyd was admitted to Gonville and Caius College, Cambridge, and made the acquaintance of Thomas Manning, who was giving private tuition in mathematics. On 24 April 1799 he married Sophia Pemberton. They lived for a time at Barnwell, near Cambridge, but in late November 1800 moved into Old Brathay, a house near Ambleside, where they saw much of the Wordsworths, Southey, and (later) Thomas De Quincey. At first he appeared enviably happy, with no financial anxieties thanks to his wealthy father, and a growing number of children (eventually five sons and four daughters). Sophia herself, De Quincey maintained, was 'as a wife and mother unsurpassed by anybody I have known in either of those characters' (De Quincey, 259). But from 1811 Lloyd began to suffer from distressing auditory illusions, and a serious illness occurred in July 1813.

For some years Lloyd was engaged in translating Ovid's *Metamorphoses*, and in 1815 published a translation of Alfieri's plays, a project which De Quincey suggests he undertook to divert his mind from the threat of the onset of insanity. He also wrote, and printed privately at Ulverston, a novel, entitled *Isabel*, which was published in 1820; it has remained almost unknown. Meanwhile he was removed to the Quaker psychiatric hospital in York. If De Quincey is to be believed, he was not well treated there, and he escaped some time in 1818, and found his way back to De Quincey's cottage in Grasmere.

Lloyd now entered on a period of relative health. He himself attributed this to the healing effect of a performance by W. C. Macready in a stage adaptation of Scott's *Rob Roy*, which moved him in a way that recalls the emotional release described by John Stuart Mill in his account of recovery from depression. He became quite productive, publishing a collection of his poems under the title of *Nugae canorae* (1819); *Desultory Thoughts in London* (1821); *Poetical Essays on the Character of Pope* (1821); *The Duke d'Ormond* (1822), a tragedy published with *Beritola*, a metrical tale; and a small volume of poems (1823). But from this time he was silent, and evidently his disabling depression returned. He eventually went to France, and died in a *maison de santé* at Chaillot, near Versailles, on 16 January 1839. His wife had predeceased him on 7 August 1830.

Although Lloyd's life touched several of the older generation of English Romantic writers, his own work is mainly of historical interest. Lamb thought his poetry obscure ('not to be understood reading on one leg') but '*sinuous*, and to be won with wrestling' (*Letters of Charles Lamb*, 2.402, autumn 1823). As for De Quincey, whose account of Lloyd in *Recollections of the Lake Poets* is the fullest contemporary assessment that we have, he declared that Lloyd was 'amongst the most interesting men I have known' (p. 258). But this is hardly apparent from Lloyd's published writings. RICHARD GARNETT, *rev.* GEOFFREY CARNALL

Sources E. V. Lucas, ed., *Charles Lamb and the Lloyds* (1898) • F. L. Beaty, ed., *The Lloyd–Manning letters* (1957) • T. De Quincey, *Recollections of the Lake poets*, ed. E. Sackville-West (1948) • *Macready's reminiscences, and selections from his diaries and letters*, ed. F. Pollock, new edn (1876) • D. H. Reiman, introduction, in C. Lloyd, *Desultory thoughts in London* (1977); *Nugae canorae* (1977); *Poems on various subjects* (1978) • B. R. Pollin, 'Charles Lamb and Charles Lloyd as Jacobins and anti-Jacobins', *Studies in Romanticism*, 12 (1973) • *The letters of Charles Lamb: to which are added those of his sister, Mary Lamb*, ed. E. V. Lucas, 3 vols. (1935) • H. Lloyd, *The Quaker Lloyds in the industrial revolution* (1975)

Archives Harvard U., Houghton L., notebooks • JRL, letters • RS Friends, Lond., MSS • U. Leeds, letters

Likenesses J. Constable, oils, 1806, repro. in Lucas, ed., *Charles Lamb* • J. Ireland, watercolour stipple drawing, BM

Lloyd, Charles (1784–1829), bishop of Oxford, was born at West Wycombe, Buckinghamshire, on 26 September 1784, the second son and third of seven children of Thomas Lloyd (1745–1815), a clergyman and schoolmaster, and his wife, Elizabeth (1760–1814), an illegitimate daughter of Nathaniel *Ryder, first Baron Harrowby [*see under* Ryder, Sir Dudley (1691–1756)]. His father, who had been nominated by Ryder to the rectory of Aston-sub-Edge,

Charles Lloyd (1784–1829), by Frederick Christian Lewis senior (after Benjamin Rawlinson Faulkner, *c.*1822)

Gloucestershire, ran a successful private school at Peterley House, Great Missenden, the seat of Lord Dormer. After tuition by his father, Charles went to Eton College in 1800 as a colleger, supported by foundation scholarships to pay tuition and board. In 1803 he matriculated from Christ Church, Oxford, where he was nominated to a studentship by the dean, Cyril Jackson, who exerted a strong influence on Lloyd's early career.

After gaining first place in the Oxford honours list in 1806 (graduating BA in 1806, MA in 1809, BD in 1818, and DD in 1821), Lloyd left Oxford to serve as private tutor to the children of Lord Elgin at Dunfermline, but within a year was summoned back to Oxford by Dean Jackson, who needed a mathematics tutor. One of Lloyd's first assignments was to prepare Robert Peel for his examinations; Peel attributed his double first to the teaching of Lloyd, who was in later life 'a friend and counsellor', corresponding with him on various political matters and probably influencing his views on currency. Daily correspondence of another Christ Church undergraduate, G. R. Chinnery, suggests that Lloyd was an extraordinarily attentive and effective tutor. He served for several years as librarian and censor of Christ Church, but his most important contribution was a pedagogical zeal which helped to extricate Oxford from the slough of 'port and prejudice' denounced by Gibbon.

Ordained in 1808, Lloyd held the curacies of Drayton (1810) and Binsey (1818), both near Oxford. In June 1819 he was appointed under Peel's influence to the preachership of Lincoln's Inn, which he held until February 1822 when, on the nomination of Lord Liverpool, he was appointed to the regius professorship of divinity at Oxford, to which was attached a canonry at Christ Church and the rectory of Ewelme. On 15 August 1822 he married Mary Harriet (*d.* 1857), daughter of Colonel John Stapleton of Thorpe Lee, Surrey, and within four years they had a family of one son and three daughters.

As regius professor Lloyd revived theological studies in the university and was regarded as: 'if not the founder of a new school, at least the infuser of a new and more energetic spirit' (*GM*, 561). He supplemented his statutory public lectures with private classes attended by graduates, who included R. H. Froude, J. H. Newman, Frederick Oakeley, and E. B. Pusey (it was on Lloyd's suggestion that Pusey went to Germany to study its theology). Lloyd's revelation of the ancient roots and historical development of the Anglican liturgy and dogma influenced a generation of Oxford theologians, many of his liturgical notes being incorporated into William Palmer's *Origines liturgicae* (1832). An abstract of his lectures was later published in E. S. Ffoukes's *A History of the Church of S. Mary, Oxford* (1892). Short, stocky, and prematurely bald, Lloyd was remembered for informally bantering with, and occasionally bullying, the attenders at his private lectures. For a wider clerical readership he published a collection of *Formularies of Faith Put Forth by Authority during the Reign of Henry VIII* (1825).

On 4 March 1827 Lloyd was consecrated bishop of Oxford, to which position he had been nominated through Peel's influence. He retained his professorship, continuing to deliver lectures while coping with the considerable problems of pluralism and non-residence in the diocese of Oxford. As a member of the House of Lords Lloyd was confronted with the contentious question of Catholic emancipation. Although he held traditional high-church views hostile to Catholic civil liberties, he had given a favourable assessment of Roman Catholic doctrines in an essay for the *British Critic* (October 1825). Admitting that some Roman Catholics practised idolatry, he insisted that none of Rome's historical documents or public formularies supported the worship of images. By 1829, however, the Catholic question turned on practical politics rather than religious principles, and he joined Peel in supporting Catholic relief, though he mishandled Peel's unsuccessful candidature for re-election to the Oxford seat (February 1829). During the Lords' debates on emancipation he delivered an important speech in favour of reform (2 April 1829), a stand which made him a favourite scapegoat of defeated conservatives. Shortly afterwards George IV snubbed him at a public function.

Mentally distressed and physically fatigued, Lloyd attended an anniversary dinner at the Royal Academy at Somerset House, where he caught a cold that lingered and worsened. He died of pneumonia on 31 May 1829 at the house in Whitehall Place, London, which he had rented for the summer season. Two days later he was given a private funeral in Lincoln's Inn chapel, and was interred in the Benchers' vault.

Of all the posthumous accolades, J. H. Newman's comment was most heartfelt and appropriate: 'He brought me forward, made me known, spoke well of me, and gave me confidence in myself' (*Letters and Correspondence*, 1.209).

Later interest in Lloyd has been stimulated as studies of Peel, Tractarianism, and of the revival of liturgical and ecclesiological scholarship have come to show his importance in the academic life of early nineteenth century Oxford. WILLIAM J. BAKER

Sources W. J. Baker, *Beyond port and prejudice: Charles Lloyd of Oxford, 1784–1829* (1981) • *GM*, 1st ser., 99/1 (1829), 560–63 • *Letters and correspondence of John Henry Newman during his life in the English church*, ed. A. Mozley, 2 vols. (1891) • C. S. Parker, ed., *Sir Robert Peel: from his private papers*, 3 vols. (1891–9) • parish registers, Bucks. RLSS, DAT 197, West Wycombe, Bucks. • *Jackson's Oxford Journal* (24 Aug 1822) • Shrewsbury School, Letters of Edward Copleston and J. E. Devison • W. F. Lloyd to Edward Burton, 2 June 1829, Shrewsbury School, Burton MSS

Archives BL, corresp. with Robert Peel, Add. MSS 40342–40343 • Bodl. Oxf., Oxford Diocesan MSS • Christ Church Oxf., Chinnery MSS • Houton Castle, Dublin, corresp. with Thomas Gaisford • Pusey Oxf., corresp. with E. B. Pusey • Shrewsbury School, Burton MSS

Likenesses B. R. Faulkner, oils, Christ Church Oxf. • F. C. Lewis senior, mezzotint (after B. R. Faulkner, *c*.1822), BM, NPG [*see illus.*]

Lloyd, Charles Dalton Clifford (1844–1891), magistrate and diplomatist, was born in Portsmouth on 13 January 1844, the eldest son of Colonel Robert Clifford Lloyd (1809–1863) of the 68th Durham light infantry, and his wife, Annie Savage (*d.* 1908). Both his grandfather, Bartholomew *Lloyd, and his uncle, Humphrey Lloyd, had been provosts of Trinity College, Dublin.

Lloyd was educated at the Royal Military College, Sandhurst and, in 1862, entered the police force in British Burma, where he rose through the ranks as assistant, deputy commissioner, and finally inspector-general of registration. On 30 April 1867 he married Isabel Henrietta Browne; they returned to Britain in 1872. On 3 July 1872 he entered Lincoln's Inn, London, and on 16 February 1874 he was appointed resident magistrate for co. Down, in Ireland. He was called to the bar in Trinity term, 1875.

The battle conducted by the Land League on behalf of tenant farmers against rack rents and extortion by landlords resulted in non-payment of rent, riots, and agrarian crime throughout the country. W. E. Forster (then Irish secretary) quickly moved Lloyd from co. Down to the south of the country. Lloyd managed to restore order during riots in Longford and was seen by his supporters as having displayed energy and discretion in his role. His detractors, however, saw him as being 'cruel and despotic' (Townshend, 138–40).

Lloyd began a campaign to break the resistance of tenants to payment of rent in the counties of Cork and Limerick. This he did by extending both his powers and those of the Royal Irish Constabulary, ostensibly within the bounds of the ordinary law. He was a staunch unionist and favoured the decentralization of the Irish administrative system. He was opposed to the use of emergency measures since he felt these would undermine the authority of the union. He therefore extended the interpretation of the Riot Act so far that people could be arrested on the merest suspicion of criminality. On 20 May 1881, amid mass hysteria, he arrested Father Sheehy and other members of the league under the Protection of Person and Property Act.

Ireland under Forster was divided into five regions, each governed by a special resident magistrate with executive powers. With such executive freedom Lloyd was able to request an increase in the number of troops in Ireland, until by the end of 1881 they numbered over 25,000. He also gradually infused the Royal Irish Constabulary with a military element until by the end of the same year it was composed almost entirely of military personnel, with officers sent from divisional police headquarters to avoid using local forces. He organized an extensive patrolling network, involving 'flying columns', and so intensified security arrangements that they became tantamount to martial law. As a result, over sixteen parliamentary questions were lodged about Lloyd's conduct in 1881–2. Allegations were made to the effect that he refused to accept bail, dispensed summary justice in his own house, and dispersed crowds under the Riot Act with threats that they would be shot. In 1883 he eventually resigned and moved to Egypt, where he was to serve under the khedive as inspector-general of reforms and, subsequently, as under-secretary at the Home Office.

In Egypt Lloyd's career was again tainted by controversy. He threw himself with zeal into sanitation schemes and judicial reform. However, in his attempted reform of the prison system he met with much resistance from the mudirs, members of the Egyptian ruling class who occupied much the same position as special resident magistrates did in Ireland. Under the existing judicial system an individual could be arrested and convicted without even a written order. Prisons were overcrowded and bribes, torture, false imprisonment, and false convictions were rife.

Lloyd set about reforming the police force so that it would be answerable to local authorities but could also report to central government. No arrest could be made without a written order. Those who opposed reform were removed from office and replaced by Egyptians from the central administration. The reforms had initial support from Sir Evelyn Baring, but eventually the Egyptian minister Nubar Pasha threatened to resign on the grounds that the proposed reforms deprived the mudirs of all authority and gave their executive powers to the police. There were also allegations that torture in prisons had not been completely eradicated. Despite Lloyd's best efforts he again had to resign, but later he defended his plan of reform in letters to *The Times* (30 June; 7 and 10 July 1884; 29 Sept 1888).

In 1885 Lloyd resumed his post as resident magistrate in Ireland, this time in Londonderry. However, in the winter of that year he left for Mauritius, where he had been appointed lieutenant-governor and colonial secretary. This appointment was short-lived, as he could not see eye to eye with the then governor, Sir John Pope Hennessy, recently elected nationalist MP for co. Kilkenny. Lloyd was then transferred to the Seychelles, in August 1886 (to a post which he never took up), and he eventually resigned in 1887. During his subsequent period of unemployment he published memoirs of his time in Ireland under the title, *Ireland under the Land League: a Narrative of Personal*

Experiences. Finally, on 15 September 1889, he was appointed consul for Kurdistan, where his attempts to promote the Armenian cause were appreciated by Sir William White, the English ambassador at Constantinople. Lloyd died of pneumonia at Erzurum, Kurdistan, on 7 January 1891; his wife survived him.

J. M. RIGG, *rev.* SINÉAD AGNEW

Sources Boase, *Mod. Eng. biog.* • Burke, *Gen. Ire.* • W. P. Baildon, ed., *The records of the Honorable Society of Lincoln's Inn: admissions*, 2 (1896), 353 • *The Times* (30 June 1884), 8 • *The Times* (7 July 1884), 10 • *The Times* (10 July 1884), 8 • *The Times* (29 Sept 1888), 8 • *The Times* (8 Jan 1891), 6 • *The Times* (10 Jan 1891), 7 • C. D. Clifford, *Ireland under the Land League* (1892), preface • P. Bew, *Land and the national question in Ireland, 1858–82* (1978), 169, 177, 212–13 • C. Townshend, *Political violence in Ireland* (1983), 72, 137–40, 141, 193 • *Annual Register* (1891) • *The Times* (18–19 Sept 1883) • *The Times* (27 Sept 1883) • *The Times* (22 March 1884) • *The Times* (27 March 1884) • *The Times* (7–10 April 1884) • *The Times* (21 Feb 1885) • *The Times* (7 March 1885) • *The Times* (14 March 1885) • *The Times* (21 Aug 1885) • *The Times* (25 Aug 1886) • *The Times* (20 May 1887) • *The Times* (16 June 1887) • *The Times* (28 Dec 1887) • *The Times* (26 Nov 1888) • *The Times* (18 March 1889) • *The Times* (15 Sept 1889) • *The Times* (8 Nov 1889) • *Dublin Gazette* (Feb 1874) • *Dublin Gazette* (March 1885) • *LondG* (Nov 1885) • *FO List* (1890) • 'Correspondence respecting the affairs of Egypt', *Parl. papers* (1884), vol. 88, no. 1, p. 73, C. 3844; vol. 88, no. 5, pp. 16–19, C. 3852; vol. 89, no. 18, p. 27, C. 4001; vol. 89, no. 25, pp. 38–42, 94–103, C. 4100 • 'Despatch on … the affairs of the colony of Mauritius', *Parl. papers* (1887), 58.347, C. 5101 • Gladstone, *Diaries* • *CGPLA Eng. & Wales* (1891)

Likenesses S. P. Hall, double portrait, pencil drawing, 1888–9 (with Lord Leighton), NPG • portrait, repro. in *The Graphic*, 25 (1882) • wood-engraving (after photograph by Lafayette of Dublin), NPG; repro. in *ILN* (6 Oct 1883), 333

Wealth at death £4372 19*s*. 0*d*.: administration with will, 4 July 1891, *CGPLA Eng. & Wales*

Lloyd, David. *See* Yale, David (*d.* 1626), *under* Yale, Thomas (1525/6–1577).

Lloyd, David (1597–1663), poet and dean of St Asaph, was born in Berth-lwyd, in the parish of Llanidloes, Montgomeryshire, the son of David Lloyd. His uncle was a fellow of All Souls College, Oxford, and held the post of dean of Hereford from 1617 until his death in 1625 at the age of fifty-four. There is also record of a brother called Oliver (*d.* 1662), a doctor of law, who was also a fellow of All Souls, and who, like his brother, suffered deprivation during the interregnum. Lloyd entered Hart Hall, Oxford, on 30 October 1612, graduating BA on 22 June 1615. He was elected a fellow of All Souls in 1618, obtaining a BCL in 1622 (probably in May) and a DCL on 26 March 1628, having been incorporated at Cambridge in 1616.

Lloyd is chiefly notable for his bawdy mock epic poem, *The Legend of Captain Jones* (1631), which is his only surviving literary work, although Anthony Wood suggests that he also wrote songs, sonnets, and elegies, 'some of which are printed in several books' (Wood, *Ath. Oxon.*, 3.653). These have not been discovered. *The Legend* tells the story of a famous Elizabethan sailor who performed many spectacular feats of military prowess with his sword, Kyl-zadog. He killed the mighty giant Asdriasdust and fought off the eleven kings who sought to bar his progress, before being captured by the king of Spain, who lost 6000 warriors in the process. He was immediately ransomed by his loyal countrymen. Andrew Marvell refers to this burlesque poem in *The Rehearsal Transprosed* (1672–3), suggesting that forty years after its first publication it had become a byword for ridiculous and comic exaggeration. Certainly the existence of separate and revised editions in 1636, 1648, 1656 (containing a frontispiece of Jones on horseback confronting an Indian king mounted on an elephant), and 1659 indicates considerable popularity, and imitations and sequels were published in the eighteenth century.

The Legend is almost certainly not based on a real figure but may refer to various Elizabethan soldiers such as Sir John Norris or Sir Thomas Arundell. It is undoubtedly a pastiche or parody of a Welsh poem, *Awdl foliant Rhisiart Siôn o Fuellt* ('Ode in Praise of Rhisiart Siôn of Buellt') by Siôn Tudur, a prominent Welsh bard who later lived in Lloyd's diocese of St Asaph. It is also likely that the poem satirizes the boastful and legendary autobiographical accounts of Captain John Smith's exploits in the Americas, which were published in the 1620s and 1630s. The expanded version of Lloyd's poem published in 1656 makes the satirical relationship clearer, probably because Smith died in 1632 and Lloyd felt less constrained in his parodic intentions.

In 1639 Lloyd became chaplain to William Stanley, sixth earl of Derby, and also controller of his household. He was made a canon of Chester the same year before becoming rector of Trefdraeth, Anglesey, on 2 December 1641. He was subsequently made vicar of Llangynhafal, and, on 21 December of the same year, vicar of Llanfair Dyffryn Clwyd. He also became warden of Ruthin, Denbighshire, in 1642. During the civil war he was deprived of his offices and imprisoned for a time by the Long Parliament. He was reinstated after the Restoration and promoted to the deanery of St Asaph, and then presented to one of the two comportions of Llansannan in 1662. Lloyd's plea to the king for his reinstatement, dated August 1660, claims that he did all he could for the king and church, having entertained princes Rupert and Maurice and Charles I himself on one occasion. He also claims that he was robbed as well as imprisoned by the parliamentary forces. Another letter, dated 16 October 1660, signifies the election of George Griffith to the see of St Asaph, after the death of Dr John Owen. Lloyd died on 7 September 1663 at Ruthin, although no monument remains. A humorous epitaph represents him as running into debt through his love of eating:

This is the epigraph,
Of the dean of St. Asaph,
Who by keeping a table,
Better than he was able,
Run into debt
Which is not paid yet.
(Wood, *Ath. Oxon.*, 3.653)

ANDREW HADFIELD

Sources Wood, *Ath. Oxon.*, new edn, 3.652–3 • *Willis' survey of St Asaph, considerably enlarged and brought down to the present time*, ed. E. Edwards, 2 vols. (1801) • *CSP dom.*, *1660–61*, 219, 314 • W. C. Hazlitt, *Hand-book to the popular, poetical and dramatic literature of Great Britain* (1867), 338 • R. Williams, *Enwogion Cymru: a biographical dictionary of* *eminent Welshmen* (1852), 280 • M. Burrows, *Worthies of All Souls* (1874), 307–8 • J. Walker, *An attempt towards recovering an account of the numbers and sufferings of the clergy of the Church of England*, pt 2 (1714), 1 • W. T. Lowndes, *The bibliographer's manual of English literature*, ed. H. G. Bohn, [new edn], 3 (1864), 1375–6 • H. Blackwell, 'Dictionary of Welsh biography', 1928, NL Wales, MS 9265 • *DNB* • Foster, *Alum. Oxon.* • E. Roberts, ed., *Gwaith Siôn Tudur*, 2 vols. (1980), 1.458–63; 2.441–7 • A. T. Vaughan, 'John Smith satirized: *The legend of Captain Jones*', *William and Mary Quarterly*, 45 (1988), 712–32

Archives PRO, corresp. | PRO, SP Dom Car. II, vol. 12, no. 4, vol. 18, no. 104

Lloyd, David [*pseud.* Oliver Foulis] (**1635–1692**), biographer, son of Hugh Lloyd, was born at Pant Mawr, in the parish of Trawsfynydd, Merioneth, on 28 September 1635, and was educated in the free school of Ruthin in Denbighshire. In 1653 he became a servitor of Merton College, Oxford, and graduated BA on 30 January 1657 from Oriel College. The warden and fellows of Merton College presented him to the rectory of Ibstone, Buckinghamshire, in May 1658, and he proceeded MA on 4 July 1659.

Resigning his rectory in 1659, Lloyd went to London and was appointed reader in the Charterhouse under Timothy Thurscross. Around 1663 he suffered six months' imprisonment at the suit of the earl of Bridgewater, who resented Lloyd's publication of *The Countess of Bridgewater's Ghost* (1663), describing the late countess's virtues. Subsequently he became chaplain to Isaac Barrow, bishop of St Asaph, who gave him several preferments in that diocese and collated him to a canonry.

The majority of Lloyd's published writings belong to the 1660s and are distinguished by a fervent royalism: he was what Robert Watt called 'a loyal biographer and historian' (2.612). Two such works appeared in the year of the Restoration itself, *Modern policy completed, or, The publick actions and councels, both civil and military, of … General Monck, under the general revolutions since 1639 to 1660* (1660)—otherwise known as *Modern Policy, the Second Part*—and *Eikon basilike, or, The True Portraicture of his Sacred Majesty Charles the II* (1660), which incorporated biographies of the dukes of York and of Gloucester. In choosing the latter title, Lloyd was referring to the far better known book attributed to Charles I. In 1664, Lloyd published, under the pseudonym Oliver Foulis, *Cabala, or, The history of conventicles unvail'd: in an historical account of the principles and practices of the nonconformists* (1664), listing 120 plots alleged to have been perpetrated against the present government. Here Lloyd accused the dissenters of continued disloyalty to the monarchy and the Church of England, and of clinging on to ideas of popular resistance inherited from the civil wars and republic.

Perhaps Lloyd's most famous works are *The Statesmen and Favourites of England since the Reformation* (1665), reissued in 1670, and *Memoires of the lives, actions, sufferings, and deaths of those noble, reverend, and excellent personages, that suffered by death, sequestration, decimation, or otherwise, for the protestant religion, and the great principle thereof, allegiance to their sovereigne, in our late intestine wars, from the year 1637, to the year 1660* (1668), reprinted with a new title in 1677. The *Memoires* included 'the life and martyrdom of King Charles I', which conformed entirely to the contemporary royalist Anglican view of Charles as a saint and martyr for the establishment in church and state. In 1766 Charles Whitworth reissued *The Statesmen and Favourites of England* in two volumes, under the title *State Worthies*, in which he balanced the royalist bias of Lloyd's original by additions of his own and added a biographical sketch of Lloyd.

Anthony Wood says of the *Memoires*—which included material already used in *The Statesmen and Favourites of England*—that there 'are almost as many errors as lines', and Lloyd gained something of a reputation not only as 'a most impudent plagiary, but a false writer and mere scribbler'. Bishop Humphreys relates that in later years Lloyd himself 'would express no great esteem of his youthful performances' (Wood, *Ath. Oxon.*, 4.349, 352n.). Yet for all the errors of detail, Lloyd's writings provide an insight into the beliefs and opinions of the Anglican and royalist clergy in the first decades of the Restoration.

On 14 August 1671 Lloyd was instituted to the vicarage of Abergele, Denbighshire, which he exchanged in 1672 for that of Northop, Flintshire, where he was also master of the free school. He was also rector of Llanddulas, Denbighshire, in 1672. When his health failed some time after 1673, he retired to his birth place, Pant Mawr, where he died on 16 February 1692. He was buried at Trawsfynydd.

THOMPSON COOPER, *rev.* ANDREW LACEY

Sources D. Lloyd, *State worthies*, ed. C. Whitworth, 2 vols. (1766) • Wood, *Ath. Oxon.*, new edn, 4.348–53 • *The life and times of Anthony Wood*, ed. A. Clark, 5 vols., OHS, 19, 21, 26, 30, 40 (1891–1900) • Watt, *Bibl. Brit.*, 2.612 • *Fasti Angl.* (Hardy), 1.86 • *Remarks and collections of Thomas Hearne*, ed. C. E. Doble and others, 2, OHS, 7 (1886), 73, 263, 331–2 • W. T. Lowndes, *Bibliographer's manual*, ed. H. G. Bohm, [new edn], 1 (1864), 1376 • Foster, *Alum. Oxon.* • F. F. Madan, *A new bibliography of the Eikon basilike of King Charles the First* (1950), 112 • E. Brydges, *Censura literaria: containing titles, abstracts, and opinions of old English books*, 2nd edn, 4 (1815), 194–7

Lloyd, David (1642/3–1723), naval officer, was born at Ffosybleiddiaid, Cardiganshire, the second of three sons of Oliver Lloyd (1610–1668) and Jane, daughter of John Lloyd of Llanllŷr. He was entered as a volunteer on the *Phoenix* on 2 November 1671 and, later, as an able seaman. In June 1672 he was promoted to lieutenant and appointed to the *Henry*. Discharged at the end of the Third Anglo-Dutch War, in 1674, he was appointed a cornet in the earl of Oxford's regiment, from which he was given leave to take up the captaincy of the *Mermaid* in September 1677. He served in the North Sea with Sir John Holmes, who later accused him of having insolently claimed that 'the only difference between us was the flag' (Bodl. Oxf., MS Rawl. A191, fol. 99). Lloyd escorted William and Mary back to the Netherlands, following their marriage. When he returned to England he found himself in trouble with Pepys for leaving the *Mermaid*, without permission, in the Downs but, despite their earlier dispute, Holmes took Lloyd's side. Lloyd was appointed captain of the *Reserve* in June 1678 and, shortly before he sailed for Tangier, he provided Samuel Atkins, Pepys's clerk, with an alibi (that they had been in an alehouse) when Atkins was accused of being involved in the murder of Sir Edmundbury Godfrey.

It was probably because of this alibi that Pepys had Lloyd appointed captain of the *Dover* in June 1679 and sent as convoy to Newfoundland. Lloyd returned to England in March 1680, when he was dismissed, but in November 1680 he was appointed captain of the *Crown* and served in the Mediterranean under Arthur Herbert (1680–83). When Atkins arrived in Tangier in 1681 he asked to serve under Lloyd, whom he regarded as 'the best governed, soberest, reasonable man my conversation ever fell with' (Bodl. Oxf., MS Rawl. A183). In December 1681 Lloyd helped to capture a large Algerian ship, the *Golden Rose*, after a long fight. When Herbert returned to England in June 1683 Lloyd remained with Cloudesley Shovell. The *Crown*'s leaks 'being so low not to be stopt otherwise' (PRO, ADM 106/376, fol. 492), Shovell ordered Lloyd back to England. When George Legge, Baron Dartmouth, arrived in 1683 to demolish Tangier he learned that Lloyd was on his way back to England and promptly recalled him. While in Tangier Pepys discovered that Lloyd was 'a very good artist and curious in it above any gentleman captain' (*Tangier Papers*, 134).

Lloyd was appointed a groom of the bedchamber to James II in May 1685. In May 1687 he was appointed captain of the *Sedgemoor* and took James Fitzjames, the king's illegitimate son, with him as a volunteer. The *Sedgemoor* was part of the fleet commanded by Henry, duke of Grafton, that escorted the new queen of Portugal to Lisbon and then sailed into the Mediterranean to make sure the peace treaty negotiated with Algiers, Tunis, and Tripoli remained intact. When Grafton returned to England in 1687 Lloyd remained in the Mediterranean with Shovell; he did not return to England until mid-December 1688, by which time the invasion of William of Orange was accomplished. Lloyd followed James into exile in 1689 and was appointed a groom of the bedchamber, whereupon the House of Commons proclaimed him a traitor. After William and Mary had been crowned James, 'inveighing, with tears, against his daughters', told Lloyd that the behaviour of his younger daughter, Anne, was worse than Mary's. Lloyd, 'who had turned impatiently away, put his head round the door to remark "Both bitches, by God!"' (H. W. Chapman, *Mary II Queen of England*, 172).

Lloyd became an active secret agent for James, travelling back and forth between England and St Germain. He was in England in 1691, sounding out Edward Russell and John Churchill about helping James to return, and carried back Lord Dartmouth's 'proffer of service' (Clarke, 2.446–7, 450). While in England Lloyd drew up a 'Memorandum of persons well inclined to his Mjies interest' (Lloyd, vol. 3, pt 3, no. 232). He was also named as the possible commander-in-chief of any invasion fleet. He returned to England in 1692 'with instructions to the King's friends' (Clarke, 2.477). He met Edward Russell several times in connection with bringing the English fleet over to James, but in vain. Lloyd was again declared a traitor but he managed to avoid capture and he returned to St Germain with a letter from Princess Anne to her father.

Lloyd was in England again in March 1694, when he met John Churchill again and held further meetings with Russell. He continued to act as a go-between for James and his supporters in England and gave naval advice to Louis XIV, for which he was paid 'some 3000 livres a year' (Hilton Jones, *Mainstream of Jacobitism*, 41) until 1701, when, following James's death, he seems to have retired and lived in France. In 1703 he was among the 'friends indefinite' left a mourning ring by Samuel Pepys (*Private Correspondence*, 2.318). He appears to have returned to England some time before 1708; there he was 'living very cautiously' when Charles, earl of Middleton, wrote to assure him that his son would be looked after. Lloyd died, aged eighty, on 4 January 1723, while drinking a dish of chocolate at the Cocoa Tree in Pall Mall. His son having died before him, administration of his estate was granted, on 19 February 1723, to his only daughter, Briany. PETER LE FEVRE

Sources J. D. Davies, 'Wales and Mr Pepys's navy', *Maritime Wales*, 12 (1988), 27–8 • *The historical register*, 8 (1723), chronological diary section, p. 6 • PRO, Admiralty papers, letters to navy board, ADM 106/326 'L', 335 'L', 336 'L', 344 'L', 357 'L', 362 'L', 376 'L' • Bodl. Oxf., MS Rawl. A. 183, fol. 190 • Bodl. Oxf., MS Rawl. A. 191, fol. 99 • S. Pepys, letters, Magd. Cam., Pepys Library, Pepys MS 2854 • *Phoenix* paybook, PRO, ADM 33/1112 • PRO, ADM 10/15, p. 83 • *The Tangier papers of Samuel Pepys*, ed. E. Chappell, Navy RS, 73 (1935) • *Private correspondence and miscellaneous papers of Samuel Pepys, 1679–1703*, ed. J. R. Tanner, 2 (1926) • the *Sedgemoor*, captain's log, PRO, ADM 51/957/1 • D. Lloyd, memorandum, Westm. DA, Old Brotherhood papers, vol. 3 • E. Grew and M. S. Grew, *English court in exile: James II at St Germain* (1911) • *The life of James the Second, king of England*, ed. J. S. Clarke, 2 vols. (1816) • PRO, PROB 6/99, fol. 31 [Admon of David Lloyd, 19/2/1723] • G. Hilton Jones, *The mainstream of Jacobitism* (1954), 41 • G. Hilton Jones, *Charles Middleton: the life and times of a Restoration politician* (1967), 285

Archives Magd. Cam., Pepys letters • PRO, Admiralty papers, navy board letters

Lloyd, David (1656–1731), lawyer and politician in America, was born at Manafon, Montgomeryshire, the son of Thomas *Lloyd (1640–1694). Having left grammar school in the 1670s he trained under the infamous George Jeffreys. From the 1680s he was legal adviser to William Penn, at that time managing the colony of Pennsylvania, and he converted to Quakerism in 1692. Under Penn he was responsible for drawing up deeds, warrants, and sundry documents for the colony's purchasers. Having moved to Pennsylvania in 1686 he became the colony's first attorney-general. Although he held other offices throughout his career—for instance as a member of the assembly and of the provincial council, and as clerk of the Philadelphia county court—it was his superb legal abilities that were his making and his undoing. His aim to increase Pennsylvanian autonomy brought him into conflict with its deputy governors and, finally, with Penn.

Although Lloyd remained in Pennsylvania for the rest of his life his prominence in the colony's politics involved him in imperial affairs. Elected to the general assembly in 1693, when the proprietorship of Pennsylvania was taken over by Benjamin Fletcher, he played a significant role in the review and negotiations to bring the colony's laws in line with English law. He was also at the forefront in writing a petition to William III protesting against Anglican attempts at overthrowing Quaker hegemony. In 1698 he emerged as the ablest defender against charges made by the surveyor-general, Edmund Randolph, that Pennsylvania was not enforcing the navigation laws and was, as a result, colluding with smuggling. Moreover he was accused by the vice-Admiralty judge Robert Quary of defying the order of the crown in open court and of having 'affronted his Majty in their open Court' by ridiculing the king's picture (*Papers of William Penn*, 3.572). This last incident resulted in an order from the Board of Trade demanding the removal of the colony's deputy governor, William Markham, a justice of the peace, Anthony Morris, and particularly David Lloyd 'not only from the place of Attorney General, but from all public Imployments whatsoever' (ibid., 3.576–7). His removal embittered him against Penn, whom he blamed for not defending his fellow Quakers against the likes of Randolph and Quary. Earlier Lloyd had been responsible, as an assemblyman, for drafting a petition demanding changes in the land policy and the regulation of drinking-houses. He also drafted the new frame of government (1696) in an effort to diminish the power of the Philadelphia merchants, who were seen as a conduit for British control. However, from 1698 all Lloyd's efforts were directed against Penn, whom he accused of lying and of undermining the government of the colony, and he opposed Penn's efforts to sell the right of government to the crown. His opposition to Penn did not deter his re-election to the assembly, his election as its speaker, or his appointment as recorder for Philadelphia. His fight against Penn was given an added boost when he was recruited by the Ford family as their agent in their suit against the proprietor. The appointment gave Lloyd power to prohibit Penn from selling land and collecting quitrents, thus weakening the proprietor's bargaining position with the crown.

Lloyd's fortunes changed when the 1710 elections resulted in his removal from government. Though he was elected to subsequent assemblies he no longer played as powerful a role in politics. Nevertheless he continued to promote Pennsylvania's government over British law. In 1725 he issued *A Vindication of the Legislative Power*, in which he criticized proprietary attempts to revive the role of the provincial council as a second chamber. It was also part of an ongoing attack against Penn's agent, James Logan, who condemned the unicameral assembly conceded by Penn in 1701. Logan accused Lloyd of being hypocritical in his legal judgments. He was not above compromising his defence of the colonial rights when he negotiated the passage of the Affirmation Act through the assembly. In doing so he introduced English statutes enacting the death penalty for minor crimes. In turn Lloyd denounced Logan as 'an Evil Minister, and ungrateful Servant' (*Papers of William Penn*, 3.502).

Though Lloyd intended to retire from politics the feud with Logan and the critical issue of paper money saw him stand for office and returned as member for Chester county in 1725. By this time he was in his sixties. His last years were spent in a number of roles. He remained chief justice of Pennsylvania (to which he had been appointed in 1717) and participated in the state supreme court. At the same time he acted as recorder of Chester county. He kept his ties with the Society of Friends as an archivist for the Philadelphia yearly meeting, where he collected historical records. He also edited and promoted the publication of books from Europe. His encouragement in the literary sphere was recognized by the Baptist minister Abel Morgan, who dedicated the first Welsh concordance of the Bible to him. Lloyd, who died at Chester, Pennsylvania, on 6 April 1731, was twice married. Details of his first wife, Sarah (*b.* *c.*1661), are unknown; his second wife, Grace Growdon, whom he married in 1697, survived him.

MARY K. GEITER

Sources C. W. Horle, 'Lloyd, David', *Lawmaking and legislators in Pennsylvania: a biographical dictionary*, ed. C. W. Horle and others, 1 (Philadelphia, 1991), 490–503 · R. N. Lokken, *David Lloyd: colonial lawmaker* (Washington, 1959) · *The papers of William Penn*, ed. M. M. Dunn, R. S. Dunn, and others, 5 vols. (1981–7)

Archives Hist. Soc. Penn., manuscript book · Hist. Soc. Penn., notebook

Wealth at death estate valued at £1175; library valued at £150; livestock valued at £148; ten slaves valued at £340: Horle and Wokeck, *Lawmakers and legislators in Pennsylvania*; C. Horle, minutes of the provincial council of Pennsylvania, Philadelphia, 1852

Lloyd, David (1752–1838), Church of England clergyman and writer, was born on 12 May 1752 at Croes Cynon (Croscunnon), Llanbister, Radnorshire, the only son of Thomas Lloyd, a farmer of Trefodig, and his wife, Mary, daughter of David James of Little Croscunnon. Although as a boy he had to work on his father's farm a lot of the time, he received a sporadic education in Latin and mathematics from local schools, as well as teaching himself Greek and developing an appreciation of 'Druidical' and Welsh poetry. In 1771 at the age of nineteen he opened a small school in Llanbister. While teaching he prepared himself for holy orders and was ordained priest in 1778. He married Mary (1747–1836), daughter of John Griffiths of Leehall, Llangunllo, Radnorshire, in 1779, and they had one son, John, who died in childhood. Lloyd was curate at Putley, Herefordshire, between 1785 and 1789, before returning to be vicar of Llanbister, one of the largest parishes in Radnorshire, where he remained for the rest of his life.

In 1792 Lloyd published *The Voyage of Life*, a religious poem in nine volumes. A new and enlarged second edition was published in 1812; renamed *Characteristics of Men, Manners and Sentiments, or, The Voyage of Life*, it contained an additional (tenth) volume to the original as well as some miscellaneous poems. His other main work was *Horae theologicae, or, A series of essays on subjects interesting and important; embracing physics, morals and theology*, published in 1823. The thirty-seven essays, which include such titles as 'The authenticity of the scriptures', 'The nature and effects of sin', and 'The fall of our parents and its effects', are in fact entirely theological, and provide a brief exposition of the faith of the Anglican church, designed for the 'improvement in Divine knowledge, and confirmation of faith, in readers of all ranks' (preface). His only other published works were a sermon, *England's Privileges* (1797), and an undated march entitled *The Loyal Cambrian Volunteers*. Of the many pieces of his music, the latter was the only one to be published. Lloyd's wife died in 1836 aged eighty-nine, and he died at Llanbister two years later, on 3 March.

JONATHAN HERAPATH

Sources *DWB* · *DNB* · R. Williams, *Enwogion Cymru: a biographical dictionary of eminent Welshmen* (1852) · J. Williams, *The history of Radnorshire* (1999)

Wealth at death £500 (?): *DNB*

Lloyd, Dennis, Baron Lloyd of Hampstead (1915–1992), jurist, was born on 22 October 1915 in London, the second son and second child of Isaac Lloyd (*b.* 1891), company director, and Betty Jaffa. He was educated at University College School, at University College, London (LLB, 1935), and at Gonville and Caius College, Cambridge (BA, 1937; MA, 1941; LLD, 1956). He was called to the bar by Inner Temple in 1936. He was appointed reader in English law at University College, London, in 1947 and held the Quain professorship in the University of London from 1956 until his retirement, in 1981. He was head of the department of laws in University College, London, from 1969 to 1981. He married Ruth Emma Cecilia Przytulla (*b.* 1920/21) on 15 September 1940. They had two daughters, and celebrated fifty-two years of happy marriage.

Dennis Lloyd was a man who played many parts. He was a distinguished jurist, a prominent barrister (made a QC in 1975), a minor but influential politician, a law reformer (it was for his political activity and law reform work that the Labour government in 1965 made him a life peer, as Baron Lloyd of Hampstead—in fact he spent most of his time in the House of Lords on the cross-benches), a passionate supporter of the British film industry, and much else besides. In an age of increasing specialism he belonged to a dying breed of polymaths: a man of culture and erudition, at home in different disciplines (his jurisprudential writing is characterized by this), at ease with different worlds.

Lloyd's academic interests and scholarly abilities were demonstrated early. His *Unincorporated Associations*, for which he had been awarded the Yorke prize at Cambridge, was published as a monograph in 1938. His work on rent control saw him produce a book that went through two editions and enabled him to become one of the architects of the Rent Act of 1965. He helped to frame the concept of the 'fair rent', which guaranteed sensible levels of rent and gave security of tenure to long-term tenants. Both these books showed Lloyd the analytical lawyer. *Public Policy: a Comparative Study in English and French Law*, published in 1953, saw him at his more reflective. The book remains a model of how comparative law should be undertaken.

The two sides of Lloyd's academic thinking were brought together in his scholarly but popular *The Idea of Law*, published as a Pelican book in 1964. Lloyd's 'idea' of law was functionalist and consensus-based. He had a vision of law as competent to solve any problem, whether it was concerned with the right to work (the subject of his inaugural lecture as Quain professor), homosexual behaviour, or the control of outer space. He believed that the idea of law that would prevail would be 'one which emphasises not so much the self-contained character of law, but rather its function as an instrument of social cohesion and social progress'. With most of his academic life spent (almost literally) in the shadow of Bentham it is difficult to ignore the great utilitarian philosopher's influence—and Bentham would have applauded Lloyd's stand against the incorporation of the European Convention on Human Rights into UK law—but in *The Idea of Law* and elsewhere it is the influence of twentieth-century American legal thought that is the more apparent. For Lloyd law was not so much 'logic' as 'experience'. He was no formalist, and he readily appreciated the social, economic, and political context of law. In *The Idea of Law* the influences of Llewellyn's functionalism and Roscoe Pound's jural postulates, and his view of law as 'social engineering', are manifest. Lloyd insisted that 'the idea of law must not confine itself to grappling with the technical problem of giving effect to human values through legal machinery'. The idea of law that we find in Lloyd's jurisprudence is a vision consonant with Lloyd the man: a liberal in the best sense of that tradition, a believer in the importance of rights (though he was happy to rely on a common-law formulation of them), in the value of the rule of law, in the value of law as the 'essential guarantee for all those freedoms which are looked upon as vital to the good life in a social democracy'. He saw law as a building block of civilization.

There is less of Lloyd the man in his magisterial *Introduction to Jurisprudence*, but it is this by which generations of law students will remember him. First published in 1959, when jurisprudence was not as central to law studies as it is now (Hart's *Concept of Law* had not yet been published), it had gone through seven editions by 2001. Lloyd himself did not play a major part in the preparation of any edition after the second (in 1965) but he took a keen interest in the book, and was offering assistance and often valuable insights right up to his death. The significance of the publication of the *Introduction* in 1959 cannot be underestimated. It introduced law students in much of the English-speaking world to the writings of Kelsen, Olivercrona, Savigny, and Gény, as well as to more obvious English classics. The recipe of insightful text and suitably chosen extract remains a model guide to the study of legal thought. To the text he brought his own philosophical training—he was proud to have studied with Wittgenstein—his culture, and his erudition. The *Introduction* has its detractors but it remains the standard student text on the subject.

Throughout his life Lloyd grappled with the problems of modernity and the conflicts of contemporary civilization. He was interested in the place of the individual within collectivist states, in the power of the press, in the role of the judiciary, in industrial relations. He wrote on all these subjects, and in law-reform bodies (he was a member of the Law Reform Committee for twenty-one years) and in the Lords he played an active part in engineering change (and, as in the case of human rights legislation, in resisting it where he strongly disapproved).

Lloyd enjoyed films, and to a lesser extent music. He was a keen painter: his paintings graced the faculty of laws during his headship, and his home in Hampstead Garden Suburb. He chaired the committee that planned the National Film School, and was the chairman of the British Film Institute from 1973 to 1976. He spent the last years of his life in Hove, and remained active (indeed was studying modern Greek) right up to his death, in King's College Hospital, London, on 31 December 1992. Though of Jewish descent Lloyd was not a religious or practising Jew. He was cremated at Golders Green crematorium in January 1993.

M. D. A. FREEMAN

Sources M. Freeman, *The Independent* (8 Jan 1993) · *The Times* (14 Jan 1993) · *The Guardian* (13 Jan 1993) · *Daily Telegraph* (6 Jan 1993) · *WWW* · Burke, *Peerage* (1999) · m. cert. · personal knowledge (2004) · d. cert.

Likenesses photograph, repro. in *The Independent* · photograph, repro. in *The Times*

Lloyd, Dorothy Jordan (1889–1946), biochemist, was born in Birmingham on 1 May 1889, the daughter of George Jordan Lloyd, surgeon and later professor of surgery at the University of Birmingham, and his wife, Marian Hampson Simpson. One of four children, she was educated at the King Edward VI High School, Birmingham, and entered Newnham College, Cambridge, in 1908. She was placed in the first class in part one of the natural sciences tripos in 1910 and in part two (zoology) in 1912, was a Bathurst student, and became the third Newnham fellow (1914–21). She worked for a time at Cambridge on problems of regeneration and osmotic phenomena in muscle, and this led her to a study of osmotic phenomena in simpler nonliving colloidal systems. Her researches were interrupted by the First World War when she investigated—for the Medical Research Committee (later Council)—substitute culture media for bacteriology, and the causes and prevention of ropiness in bread.

Dorothy Jordan Lloyd felt keenly that women could do valuable work as scientists, and she was well aware of the need for the application of science to industry which had been revealed by the war. She therefore accepted an invitation from R. H. Pickard in 1921 to join the newly formed British Leather Manufacturers' Research Association. While maintaining her interest in fundamental research (particularly into the behaviour of protein fibres in aqueous systems), she rapidly acquired an insight into the art of leather manufacture, and introduced many methods of control which have since become normal tannery practice. In 1927 she succeeded Pickard as director, and was, until her death, the only woman leading such an association for industrial research. In spite of many set-backs, including the destruction of new laboratories by German bombing in 1940, support for the association increased under her directorship, and it was recognized as an integral part of the industry.

Dorothy Jordan Lloyd served on the councils and committees of many societies, including the executive committee of the International Society of Leather Trades' Chemists. In 1939 she was awarded the Fraser Muir Moffat medal by the Tanners' Council of America for her contributions to leather chemistry. She was also vice-president of the Royal Institute of Chemistry (1943–6) and a member of the Chemical Council.

Besides many contributions to scientific journals, Dorothy Jordan Lloyd was the author of *The Chemistry of the Proteins* (1926; 2nd edn, with Agnes Shore, 1938), and planned and contributed to *Progress in Leather Science, 1920–45* (3 vols., 1946–8), which became one of the world's foremost textbooks on leather technology.

A keen mountaineer, in 1928 Dorothy Jordan Lloyd achieved the distinction of making the first ascent and descent in one day of the Mittellegi Ridge of the Eiger. Her other recreation was riding and she competed at the Richmond Royal and the international horse shows. Her contemporaries gained much from her stimulating personality and her gift for friendship. She died, unmarried, at Kenilworth Lodge, Great Bookham, Surrey, on 21 November 1946.

HENRY PHILLIPS, *rev.*

Sources records of the British Leather Manufacturers' Research Association · personal knowledge (1959) · *CGPLA Eng. & Wales* (1947)

Likenesses photograph, British Leather Manufacturers' Research Association, Northampton

Wealth at death £34,933 0s. 11d.: probate, 27 May 1947, *CGPLA Eng. & Wales*

Lloyd, Edward (*c.*1648–1713), coffee house keeper, publisher, and eponymist of 'Lloyd's insurance', was probably born about 1648, but nothing is known of his origins. He was the proprietor of a London coffee house licensed some time between March 1685 and 1687. This was almost certainly 'Mr Edward Lloyd's Coffee House in Tower Street', referred to in an advertisement in the *London Gazette* (18–21 February 1688). Edward Lloyd and his wife, Abigail, had previously lived in the parish of All Hallows Barking, but by September 1682 they were living elsewhere in Tower Street ward, though Lloyd's occupation at that time is unknown. In 1691 he moved to premises in Lombard Street, at the corner of Abchurch Lane, where Lloyd's Coffee House became the recognized centre of shipbroking and marine insurance business. Previously, the chief meeting-place of the brokers and shipowners had been a coffee house known as John's, in Birchin Lane; the well-known Garraway's also had considerable popularity among customers with maritime connections.

Lloyd appears to have been a man of great intelligence and enterprise. Already by January 1692 he was publishing the first series of a weekly news-sheet, which came out on Saturdays; it was succeeded in September 1699 by a Friday publication, which continued until at least March 1704. The running title for these single-sheet serial publications was *Ships Arrived at, and Departed from several Ports of England, as I have Account of them in London … [and] An Account of what English Shipping and Foreign Ships for England, I hear of in Foreign Ports*. In September 1696 Lloyd also started the newspaper *Lloyd's News*, a shipping and commercial chronicle which lasted until 1698, but *Ships Arrived* has a better claim, on grounds of similarity of marine intelligence content, to be the predecessor of *Lloyd's List*, reputedly the second-oldest continuously published newspaper in the world. Under this title, *Lloyd's List* dates from about 1734, some twenty years after Edward Lloyd's death, but rather than being a new enterprise, it is possible that this twice-weekly paper was a further development of the earlier news-sheet associated with Lloyd's Coffee House. If so, Edward Lloyd deserves recognition as an even more significant figure than the association of his name with marine insurance suggests.

Another publication associated with marine insurance, which originated in Lloyd's Coffee House, was *Lloyd's Register of Shipping*, first published in 1764. The earliest extant issue of Edward Lloyd's *Ships Arrived* was dated 22 December 1696 and that of *Lloyd's List*, 2 January 1740.

In 1693 the Hudson's Bay Company looked to 'Mr Lloyd the Coffee Man for his Intelligence of the Compies Shipps', and by 1700 a poem which professed to follow the daily movements of 'The wealthy shopkeeper, or charitable Christian,' contained the lines:

Then to Lloyd's Coffee-house he never fails
To read the letters and attend the sales.

During the next decade Lloyd's Coffee House prospered continuously. Steele mentioned it in the *Tatler* (25 December 1710), and Addison described the manners of its frequenters in *The Spectator* (23 April 1711). The merchants and underwriters used it as a free place of meeting, without rules or organization.

In 1769 John Julius Angerstein and other City merchants started an association of underwriters, under the name of New Lloyd's, with its headquarters in Pope's Head Alley, Cornhill. Various improvements in marine insurance were introduced. The adjective 'new' was soon dropped, and the offices were moved to the Royal Exchange. This association, improved and reorganized, was incorporated in 1870. At first the contest between the original informal group at Lloyd's Coffee House and New Lloyd's was reflected in rival newspapers, but in due course *Lloyd's List* became established as a Committee of Lloyd's publication. In 1884 *Lloyd's List* merged with the *Shipping and Mercantile Gazette*; later, in 1914, responsibility for the publication reverted to the Corporation of Lloyd's and it resumed the title *Lloyd's List*.

Apart from a break (1838–44) at the South Sea House while rebuilding took place following a fire, Lloyd's remained at the Royal Exchange until 1928 when it moved to a larger new building in Leadenhall Street. In 1958 it expanded further into a second building in Lime Street and in 1986 yet another new Lloyd's opened on the site of the earlier Leadenhall building.

Edward and Abigail Lloyd had at least nine children of whom four daughters survived to adulthood. The youngest, Handy, married William Newton, the coffee house head waiter, with whom—and subsequently with her second husband, Samuel Sheppard—she managed the business after her father's death. Abigail died in 1698, and in the same year Lloyd married Elizabeth Mashbourne (*d.* 1712). His third wife was Martha Denham, whom he married in 1712. Lloyd died in London on 15 February 1713, and was buried at St Mary Woolnoth in the City of London.

SARAH PALMER

Sources C. Wright and C. E. Fayle, *A history of Lloyd's from the founding of Lloyd's Coffee House to the present day* (1928) • J. J. McCusker, *European bills of entry and marine lists: early commercial publications and the origins of the business press* (1985) • V. Harding and P. Metcalf, *Lloyd's at home* (1986) • W. R. Dawson, 'The London coffee houses and the beginning of Lloyd's', *Journal of the British Archaeological Association*, new ser., 40 (1934), 104–34 • R. Flower and M. W. Jones, *Lloyd's of London: an illustrated history* (1974) • F. W. Martin, *The history of Lloyd's and of marine insurance in Great Britain* (1876) • *Annals of Lloyd's Register: being a sketch of the origin, constitution, and progress of Lloyd's Register of British and Foreign Shipping* (1884) • D. T. Barriskill, *A guide to the Lloyd's marine collection and related marine sources at the Guildhall Library* (1994)

Archives BL, letters to John Ellis, Add. MSS 28877–28894 • GL, Lloyd's Marine Collection

Lloyd, Edward (*bap.* **1666**, *d.* **1715**), antiquary, was baptized on 18 April 1666, at Whittington, near Oswestry in Shropshire, the son of Marmaduke Lloyd (*bap.* 1647) and his wife, Penelope (*d.* 1713), of Drenewydd in the parish of Whittington. He was distantly related to the Oxford scholar and antiquary Edward Lhuyd (*d.* 1709). Educated in the law, he spent some years while a young man living in London, although his name has not been traced on the admission lists of the inns of court. While in London he studied antiquarian history, transcribing material from public records in the Tower, and was acquainted with John Le Neve and the circle of antiquaries who met at the Fountain tavern by Temple Bar. On returning to Shropshire he began work on a history of the county. According to the Shropshire topographer John Blakeway, Lloyd 'devoted a very large portion of his time to the pursuit of our provincial antiquities' (Bodl. Oxf., MS Blakeway 8, fol. 1). From his notes Lloyd compiled a large folio volume titled 'The antiquities of Shropshire with the state of that county down to the present times'. Blakeway described it as 'a very creditable outline: but not much more. From his collections, however, it is evident that Mr. Lloyds design was of a very comprehensive nature' (ibid.). Lloyd died, apparently unmarried, in 1715 without having published his 'Antiquities'.

About 1730 Lloyd's brother Charles passed his papers on to a neighbouring antiquary, **William Mytton** (1693–1746), who was also interested in writing a county history. Mytton was born at Halston by Oswestry, Shropshire, on 19 December 1693, the third surviving son of Richard Mytton of Halston and his wife, Arabella or Sarah, the daughter of Sir John Halston. Educated at Wadham College, Oxford, whence he matriculated on 8 May 1711 and graduated BA (1715) and MA (1717), Mytton was originally destined for a career in the church, but imbibing what Blakeway called 'principles of Jacobitism' (Bodl. Oxf., MS Blakeway 8, fol. 18) he became a wine merchant, the trade of two of his brothers. Until at least 1729 he spent much of his time on the continent, probably on business chiefly in Spain. He made inscriptions of antiquities in Rome, Naples, and other parts of Italy, and was learned in classical languages as well as French, Italian, and Spanish. On returning to England he changed his career to the law, settling in Shrewsbury. Between 1732 and 1736 he travelled widely in Shropshire and collected antiquarian material, assisted by James Bowen (1718–1774), 'a young man possessed of talents exactly suited to this purpose' (ibid.). He also visited London, where he studied the records in the Tower, and in 1733 was in Oxford, examining Dugdale's manuscripts. About 1735 he met and became good friends with the antiquary Charles Lyttelton. The antiquary Browne Willis corresponded with Mytton on the subject of Shropshire churches in 1740 and 1741, by which time Mytton was circulating proposals for a general history and 'Actual survey' of the county. Lyttelton's correspondence with Mytton, however, reveals the latter's declining health from about 1740. He complained of deafness and a 'distemper' or 'rheumatick complaint', and retired to his brother's house in Chester (ibid., fol. 22). He decided to abandon the law and enter the church, becoming rector of Habberley in Shropshire.

Mytton's declining health prevented him from completing his history of Shropshire antiquities, and he died at Habberley on 3 September 1746. It does not appear that he ever married. His assistant Bowen's materials, however, were probably used by Bowen's son John Bowen (1754–1832) whose researches were published in Thomas Phillips's *History and Antiquities of Shrewsbury* (1779), while Lloyd's manuscript was extensively used by Thomas Farmer Dukes for his *Antiquities of Shropshire* (1844).

DAVID BOYD HAYCOCK

Sources Bodl. Oxf., MS Blakeway 8, fols. 1–3, 9–25 • C. R. J. Currie and C. P. Lewis, eds., *English county histories: a guide* (1994) • Foster, *Alum. Oxon.* • *IGI*

Archives BL, notes, papers, and collections relating to Shropshire history, Add. MSS 21019–21023, 30324–30331 • Bodl. Oxf., Shropshire antiquities, MS Top. Salop c. 1–2 • Shrops. RRC | Bodl. Oxf., MS Blakeway 8

Lloyd, Edward (1671–1719), planter and politician in America, was born on 7 February 1671 at Wye House, Talbot county, Maryland, the eldest of the three sons and seven daughters of Colonel Philemon Lloyd (1645/6–1685), planter, merchant, and politician, and his wife, Henrietta Maria (1647–1697), widow of Richard Bennett and daughter of James Neale and his wife, Ann. His father was born in Virginia but moved to Maryland in 1649; his mother was born in England and emigrated to Maryland in 1660. Lloyd was well educated, but there is no evidence as to the manner of his education. His father's will, written when Lloyd was nine, included a bequest to 'my children's schoolmaster'. Because Lloyd's grandfather Edward Lloyd was then living in London, and because Lloyd was made his principal Maryland heir, it is possible that Lloyd was sent to England in the care of his grandfather for some of his schooling.

Upon his father's death in 1685, Lloyd inherited his 'White House and Woolman Neck land' (acreage unspecified). In 1696 his grandfather left him the family's Wye River residence and its associated land, as well as uncultivated land in a nearby county. Lloyd received an additional 250 acres the following year from his mother's estate. These lands, and others Lloyd subsequently acquired on his own, he devoted to the production of tobacco, Maryland's staple crop. Like his father and grandfather before him, Lloyd exported his own and neighbours' tobacco to England, and imported English goods for sale in the colony. He also traded with Barbados, where markets existed for his livestock and grains.

Lloyd was also the third generation of his family to play an extensive political role at both the county and provincial levels. He was named a justice of the Talbot county court in October 1694 and served on the bench until August 1701. By 1698 he was a colonel in the county militia, a position he held until 1707, when he was named major-general of the Eastern Shore militia, an 'extraordinary title' (Land, 124). In March 1698 Talbot voters elected Lloyd to the general assembly's lower house, where he served until 1701, when he received an appointment to the governor's council, or upper house. Lloyd remained a member of that body until 1716. On 1 February 1704 he married Sarah (1683–1755), daughter of Nehemiah Covington and his wife, Rebecca Denwood, of Somerset county. Lloyd was raised as an Anglican, though his mother was a devout Roman Catholic; his wife was a Quaker, but their children were also raised as Anglicans. Lloyd and his wife had five sons, the third being Edward *Lloyd (1711–1770), and one daughter, all but one of whom survived their father.

When Governor John Seymour died in 1709, Lloyd, as president of the council, served as acting governor until the arrival of the new governor, John Hart, in 1714. Lloyd is credited with making a strong, albeit often unsuccessful, effort during his tenure to defend the royal prerogative against determined local interests which found their voice in the lower house. Lloyd and the council attempted to maintain Seymour's policies, but the lower house eventually prevailed on issues such as judicial procedures and regulation of the tobacco trade, the latter in particular a matter of great importance to the colony's planters. The lower house accused Lloyd in 1716 of having taken a double salary as both councillor and acting governor, but dropped the charge after his death in deference to his widow. Despite the accusation against Lloyd, in a letter of March 1719 the lord proprietor directed Governor Hart that if Hart were absent from the province or died, Lloyd was to be the keeper of Maryland's great seal and was to administer the government. Perhaps Lord Baltimore hoped that Lloyd would defend his prerogative as diligently as he had defended the queen's.

Lloyd died on 20 March 1719 at Wye House and was buried in the family burial-ground there. He left an estate of at least 7000 acres of land in four Maryland counties, personal property valued at £8846 7*s.* 7*d.* current money of Maryland, and 108,283 pounds of tobacco. The personalty included seventeen indentured servants, thirty slaves, two vessels, and £1765 in credits on accounts with London merchants. Lloyd had inherited extensive lands, substantial wealth, and social and political prominence from his grandfather and father, and he greatly augmented all of those inheritances before passing them on to the next generation.

JEAN B. RUSSO

Sources E. C. Papenfuse and others, eds., *A biographical dictionary of the Maryland legislature, 1635–1789*, 2 (1985), 534 • C. Johnston, 'Lloyd family', *Maryland Historical Magazine*, 7 (1912), 420–30 • A. C. Land, *Colonial Maryland: a history* (1981) • O. Tilghman, 'The Lloyds of Wye', *History of Talbot county, Maryland, 1661–1861*, 1 (1915), 132–228 • J. D. Warfield, *The founders of Anne Arundel and Howard counties, Maryland* (1905–73), 203

Archives Maryland Historical Society, Baltimore, papers

Wealth at death approx. 7000 acres of land; £8846 7*s*. 7*d*. current money of Maryland; 108,283 pounds of tobacco; seventeen servants and thirty slaves; brigantine and sloop; £1765 15*s*. 4*d*. in hands of London merchants; 33,465 pounds of tobacco produced on five plantations in 1719: Papenfuse and others, *Biographical dictionary*, vol. 2, p. 535

Lloyd, Edward (*fl.* **1703–1736**), printer and bookseller, is earliest referred to in 1703, when he moved from London and settled at the Oxmantown Coffee House, Church Street, Dublin; details of his parentage and upbringing are unknown. Soon afterwards he and his business partner, Richard Pue, published their first newspaper, *Impartial Occurrences*, with issue 1 dated 25 December 1703. The title was published regularly, priced at 8*s*. including postage, and was regarded as 'excellent value'. Lloyd was described as the author in the paper for 6 January 1705, but by February 1712 the title had changed to *Pue's Occurrences*, marking the transition to Richard Pue's sole ownership.

In May 1705 Lloyd opened a second coffee house, the Golden Ball at Cole's Alley, off Castle Street. Through his friendship with Jonathan Swift he was able to sell at both his premises Swift's controversial satire on abuses in religion and learning, *A Tale of a Tub* (4th edn, 1704). Gaining in confidence as a publisher, Lloyd in the same year offered readers a series of 'ingenious and entertaining pamphlets upon everything of moment', which gave rise to his *Dublin Courant, or, Diverting Post*. Alongside this venture Lloyd began a range of trading initiatives, including the import of 'one hundred curious statues, cut in allabaster, many of which are fit for placing in gardens' (*Impartial Occurrences*, quoted in Pollard, 367–8).

By 1707 Lloyd had established his own publishing company, the New Post Office Printing House, in Essex Street at the corner of Sycamore Alley. However, on 29 July the Irish House of Lords ordered his arrest for printing a *Postscript to Mr Higgins's Sermon*, a seditious and libellous tract (attributed to the nonjuror Charles Leslie) which defended Francis Higgins's earlier anti-whig polemic. Lloyd promptly disappeared and left his trading interest in the hands of his wife, of whom further details are unknown. However, he was back in business in 1709, and on 12 March, with help from his friend the printer and publisher Francis Dickson, he was able to rent the Union (hereafter Lloyd's) Coffee House, Cork Hill, and subsequently relinquished his ownership of another premises on Bridge Street.

In 1711 Lloyd visited Cork to dispose of copies of his single-sheet *Memorial of the Church of England*, which had appeared earlier that year and remained largely unsold. He was soon in trouble, and on 12 September Cork magistrates published a *Presentment of the grand jury of the city of Cork against Edward Lloyd, for publishing several libels* (1711), which argued that the bookseller intended to 'make the way easier for a popish pretender to possess the throne'. A year later he was in dire trouble for publishing the *Memoirs of Chevalier de St George* and for issuing proposals for printing an abridgement of William Dicconson's life of James II. The magistrates at once ordered the seizure of Lloyd's book and identified him at his prosecution for treasonable libel, recorded in the Armagh diocesan papers, as the architect of a plan to promote the Pretender (James Stuart). Lloyd fled to England, and his petition to the duke of Ormond was referred to the tory lord chancellor of Ireland, Sir Constantine Phipps. Ormond ordered a stop to the legal proceedings on 18 June 1713 and Phipps interposed with a warrant for a *nolle prosequi*, to the anger of Dublin whigs. Unbowed by recent events, Lloyd began a new title, *Lloyd's Newsletter*, a vehemently anti-whig periodical. The whigs, victorious in the general election of autumn 1713, immediately threatened Phipps with impeachment for his defence of Lloyd, who had now returned to Dublin, if only for a brief period. In May 1714 he and his family gave up the Cork Hill coffee house and left Ireland for London.

The situation faced by Lloyd and Phipps was temporarily eased with the dissolution of parliament following the death of Queen Anne in August 1714. However, on 30 September Phipps was relieved of his responsibilities in Ireland and also returned to London, which he entered in October attended by a train of thirty horses, with Lloyd at the head of the procession. Thereafter Lloyd disappeared into obscurity until he published his *Description of the City of Dublin* (1732), in which he identified himself as a 'citizen and silk-thrower of London' who had 'lived nearly twenty years in Ireland', suggesting that he had lived some ten years in Ireland between 1714 and 1732. In the same year as his account of Dublin he published a *Description of Cork* and a work on the Irish mercantile economy, *Thoughts on Trade*, in 1736. He then disappeared once more; details of his date and place of death remain unknown. D. BEN REES

Sources R. Munter, *A dictionary of the print trade in Ireland, 1550–1775* (New York, 1988) • M. Pollard, *A dictionary of members of the Dublin book trade 1550–1800* (2000) • Scaramuccio [W. J. Lawrence], *Irish Life*, 7 (1913–14), 469–70 • J. W. Phillips, *Printing and bookselling in Dublin, 1670–1800* (1998) • *A long history of a certain session of a certain parliament* (1714)

Lloyd, Edward (1711–1770), planter and politician in America, was born on 8 May 1711 at Wye House, Talbot county, Maryland, the third child of Edward *Lloyd (1671–1719), planter, merchant, and politician, and his wife, Sarah (1683–1755), daughter of Nehemiah Covington and Rebecca Denwood. Lloyd had two older and two younger brothers and a younger sister, as well as two half-brothers and one half-sister by his mother's second marriage, to James Hollyday (1696–1747). Lloyd was well educated, but further details are unknown. In his own will, written in 1750 when his children were still quite young, he requested that his sons be sent to England at the age of twelve to study, and it is possible that he himself received some of his schooling abroad. Lloyd's mother was a Quaker but his Anglican father reared his children in that faith. Lloyd served two terms as vestryman, in 1734 and 1766, for St Michael's parish.

Lloyd inherited 1900 acres of land, mostly in Talbot county, when his father died in 1719, and an additional 1500 acres with the death of his older brother Philemon in 1729. Over the next twenty years Lloyd continued to augment his estate through patents and purchases, but the most dramatic increase in his wealth came in 1749 with the death of his father's half-brother, Richard Bennett. 'Supposed to be the richest man on the Continent' (*Maryland Gazette*, 8 Nov 1749), Bennett named Lloyd as his executor and, 'as he died without issue … left the Bulk of his Estate to his Executor'. Lloyd inherited outright nearly 9000 acres, and controlled another 3000 acres for his daughter, in addition to substantial personalty. Lloyd acknowledged the generosity of his benefactor by naming his next child Richard Bennett Lloyd.

Talbot voters elected Lloyd as their representative to the lower house for the assemblies of 1738 and 1739–41. Before the 1744 session he was appointed to the upper house, where he served until 1769. For three decades Lloyd also held a number of important proprietary offices. He served on the governor's council from February 1744 until ill health necessitated his resignation in November 1769. From October 1747 until his resignation in 1766 he was treasurer of the colony's eastern shore, and from November 1747 until 1754 he was naval officer for the Oxford (Talbot county) customs district. In March 1753 he assumed the post of western shore rent-roll keeper, responsible for overseeing collection of proprietary quit-rents, a position he occupied until 1768. In October 1753 he was sworn in as agent and receiver-general for all proprietary revenues, a post he held until 1768. Thus, for a period of about fifteen years he filled simultaneously three of the major offices of profit at the proprietor's disposal.

While Lloyd's tenure was undoubtedly profitable to himself, it was of less benefit to the lords Baltimore: 'A correspondent of the Hanburys of London, and the greatest merchant in the province, Lloyd was too busy to do his job [as agent and receiver-general] properly and too important to offend' (Owings, 167). As early as the mid-1750s his administration of the office was in disarray. The proprietary establishment adopted various measures to improve Lloyd's performance, but with little benefit. Lloyd was finally prevailed upon to resign in March 1768, though his successor proved to be even less effective.

Lloyd's mercantile business operated as a partnership between himself, his brother Richard, and his brother-in-law William Anderson, a London merchant. The firm's ships traded cargoes of Maryland tobacco, wheat, and meat to England, the West Indies, and New England. In addition to stores on the eastern shore, Lloyd also operated grist and fulling mills in nearby Queen Anne's county.

Edward Lloyd married Anne (1721–1769), the daughter of John Rousby (1685–1744) and his second wife, on 26 March 1739; they had two sons and two daughters, three of whom survived to adulthood.

Lloyd died at Wye House on 27 January 1770 and was buried in the family graveyard. His estate included about 43,000 acres of land in five counties; £23,000 current money in personal property; some £8000 sterling and 33,000 pounds of tobacco in the hands of London merchants; and £17,500 sterling, £12,000 current money, and 12,000 pounds of tobacco in debts receivable. While Lloyd may not have managed the affairs of the proprietor with diligence, it was during his lifetime that his family became pre-eminent in wealth and power among the eastern shore gentry. JEAN B. RUSSO

Sources E. C. Papenfuse and others, eds., *A biographical dictionary of the Maryland legislature, 1635–1789*, 2 (1985), 535–7 · D. M. Owings, *His lordship's patronage: offices of profit in colonial Maryland* (1953) · C. A. Barker, *The background of the revolution in Maryland*, another edn (1967), 258–67 · C. Johnston, 'Lloyd family', *Maryland Historical Magazine*, 7 (1912), 420–30 · O. Tilghman, 'The Lloyds of Wye', *History of Talbot county, Maryland, 1661–1861*, 1 (1915), 132–228

Archives Maryland Historical Society, Baltimore, papers

Wealth at death livestock, slaves, and personal property on seven plantations, inventoried at approx. £23,000 current money; assets in the hands of English merchants, £8200 sterling; debts valued at £17,500 sterling, £12,000 current money, and 12,000 pounds of tobacco; 33,000 pounds of tobacco shipped to England; *c*.43,000 acres of land in five Maryland counties: Papenfuse and others, eds., *Biographical dictionary*, 2.537; ledger, 1770–1774, fol. 230. MS. 2001, Lloyd papers

Lloyd, Edward (*d*. 1847), colonist in the Gambia, came from the Lloyd family of Beechmount, near Limerick, who, according to *Burke's Peerage*, were a branch of the family of Lloyd of Castle Lloyd, co. Limerick. Lloyd obtained an ensigncy in the 54th foot division in 1799, and served with the regiment in Egypt in 1801. In 1803 he became lieutenant in the 58th foot, and in 1804 received a company without purchase in the Royal African Colonial Corps, then re-formed. He retired from the army in July 1812. An Edward Lloyd, presumably the same person, had set up in trade at Goree, then British occupied, in 1806, with other traders subsequently transferred to Bathurst, and commanded the Royal Gambia militia. Edward Lloyd (of this article) was regarded as a founder of the Gambia River settlement, where he died, after forty-three years' residence, on 16 March 1847.

Major Richard Lloyd, an officer mentioned by the African traveller Mungo Park, was, like Edward Lloyd, in the Royal African Corps, and was killed as lieutenant-colonel commanding the 2nd battalion, 84th foot, at the battle of the Nive in December 1813.

H. M. CHICHESTER, *rev.* LYNN MILNE

Sources *Army List* · *Annual Register* (1847) · Burke, *Gen. GB* (1868) · J. M. Gray, *A history of the Gambia* (1940) · C. W. Newbury, ed., *British policy towards west Africa: select documents*, 2 vols. (1965–71); repr. (1992)

Lloyd, Edward (1815–1890), publisher and newspaper proprietor, was born on 16 February 1815 in Thornton Heath, Surrey, the son of a Welsh labourer who died in Lloyd's infancy. After a brief elementary education, he worked in a solicitor's office and studied shorthand at the London Mechanics' Institution, winning a silver pen for being first in his class. By the time he was eighteen he had written

Lloyd's Stenography (1833) and opened shops in London selling comic valentines and penny story books.

Beginning with *The Calendar of Horrors* (1835), Lloyd launched himself into a career as a leading publisher of cheap and mostly sensational literature aimed at the working class. Among these were a series of plagiarisms of the work of Charles Dickens that included *Nikelas Nickelbery* (1838), *Oliver Twiss* (1838–9), and *The Penny Pickwick* (1837–9); the latter apparently enjoyed sales of 50,000 copies. He also started a series of periodicals mainly containing popular fiction which included *Lloyd's Penny Weekly Miscellany* (1842–7) and *Lloyd's Penny Atlas* (1842–5). In addition, he published songbooks and treatises on domestic economy. In September 1843 he moved his offices to 12 Salisbury Square, near Fleet Street, which became the centre of his 'penny dreadful' publishing industry. He was responsible for stories such as James Malcolm Rymer's *Varney the Vampire* (1845) and 'The String of Pearls' (1846) (published in Lloyd's *People's Periodical and Family Library* and usually attributed to Thomas Peckett Prest), which introduced the character of Sweeney Todd. G. A. Sala remembered that Lloyd's instructions to his illustrators were 'there must be more blood—much more blood' (G. A. Sala, *The Life and Adventures of George Augustus Sala*, 1875, 1.209).

Lloyd also moved into journalism, publishing *Lloyd's Illustrated London Newspaper* for a penny in September 1842 as a rival to the *Illustrated London News*. The paper was originally unstamped but was compelled by the stamp office to pay the duty, as the paper contained news. It was then relaunched on 27 November price 2*d*. In 1843 the paper became *Lloyd's Weekly London Newspaper*, which was to last until 1931, one of the most successful newspapers of the Victorian period and the first of the cheap Sunday newspapers aimed at the working class. By 1850 the paper was selling 49,000 copies a week. The politics of the paper were Liberal to radical, though not as extreme as those of a number of its competitors. Lloyd became increasingly concerned about the respectability of his publications, a move signalled by his abandonment of 'penny dreadfuls' in the early 1850s and the appointment in 1852 of the popular writer Douglas Jerrold (1803–1857) as editor of *Lloyd's Weekly Newspaper*. Circulation rose thereafter. By 1853 the paper was selling 90,000 copies to a lower-middle-class and working-class readership, particularly in London, although the paper was distributed throughout the country and abroad; it enjoyed a strong following among women and small property owners. The abolition of the stamp and paper duties allowed for a reduction in price to 1*d*. in 1861. By 1872 the paper was selling half a million copies. Lloyd was devoted to publicity, scouring the country for hoardings to advertise his paper. At one time, he paid his staff with coins on which his newspaper's name was embossed so that they would enter the currency; he was only stopped by government intervention.

To sustain his popular publications, Lloyd was active in promoting new publishing techniques. In 1856 he introduced Hoe's rotary press into Britain and the web press in 1873. He established a paper mill at Bow in 1861 and a second in 1877 at Sittingbourne in Kent. To supply his mills, he leased 100,000 acres in Algeria to grow esparto grass. Lloyd found himself supplying other newspapers as well as his own with paper and became the owner of a lucrative stationery business.

In 1876 Lloyd purchased the *Daily Chronicle* (formerly the *Clerkenwell News*) for £30,000, on which he spent £150,000, transforming it from a suburban paper into a leading London daily paper with special correspondents all over the world. The paper in particular advocated the unification of London local government to restore order to its affairs. Circulation soon increased from 8000 to 140,000 copies.

Lloyd was a leading Liberal, elected to the Reform Club and a promoter of the National Liberal Club. *Lloyd's Weekly Newspaper* mainly supported Liberal causes, such as the extension of the suffrage in 1867. Although it opposed home rule in 1886, it tended to support Gladstone. The paper's politics were always moderate, which meant that it was often disliked by radicals. Such was its appeal that when a young singer called Matilda Alice Victoria Wood sought a memorable stage name she called herself Marie Lloyd. By the time of Lloyd's death in 1890 the paper was in sight of achieving sales of 1 million, a feat it accomplished on 16 February 1896, the first paper ever to do so.

Lloyd was married twice, the second time to Maria Martins. He had nineteen children in total, among them Frank Lloyd (1854–1927), who became chairman and managing director of his father's company on his death. Edward Lloyd died on 8 April 1890 at his home, 17 Delahay Street, Westminster. The cause of death was heart disease, apparently brought on by the strain of revamping his newspaper. He was buried in Highgate cemetery on 11 April, and a plaque was placed in St Margaret's Church, Westminster. One of the leading figures in the expansion of mass publishing in the Victorian period, Lloyd's career is important because of its promotion of the cheap press, new techniques in publishing, and the basic formulae which came to be associated with popular fiction and journalism (with its taste for the sensational).

ROHAN MCWILLIAM

Sources V. S. Berridge, 'Popular journalism and working-class attitudes, 1854–1886: a study of *Reynolds's Newspaper*, *Lloyd's Weekly Newspaper* and *The Weekly Times*', DPhil diss., U. Lond., 1976 · T. Catling, *My life's pilgrimage* (1911) · J. Medcraft, *A bibliography of the penny bloods of Edward Lloyd* (1911) · *Daily Chronicle* [London] (9 April 1890), 5 · *Lloyd's Weekly London Newspaper* (13 April 1890), 7 · *British and Colonial Printer and Stationer* (17 April 1890), 1–2 · *The Times* (9 April 1890), 5 · [E. Lloyd], *A glimpse into papermaking and journalism* (1895) · T. Frost, *Forty years' recollections* (1880) · J. Hatton, *Journalistic London* (1882) · P. R. Hoggart, 'Edward Lloyd, the father of the cheap press', *The Dickensian*, 80 (1984), 33–8 · L. James, *Fiction for the working man, 1830–1850* (1963)

Likenesses T. Fall of Baker Street, photograph, repro. in *ILN* (19 April 1890), 486 · Fradelle and Young, photograph, repro. in *British and Colonial Printer and Stationer*, 1

Wealth at death £565,240 1*s*. 6*d*.: resworn probate, Aug 1891, *CGPLA Eng. & Wales* (1890)

Lloyd, Edward Mayow Hastings (1889–1968), civil servant and internationalist, was born on 30 November 1889 at Hartley Wintney, Hampshire, the fourth son of Edward

Wynell Mayow Lloyd (1864–1928), headmaster, of Hartford House preparatory school, and his wife, Eleanor Elizabeth Hastings. He was educated at Rugby School and Corpus Christi College, Oxford, where he obtained second classes in classical honour moderations (1910) and *literae humaniores* (1912). After Oxford Lloyd joined the home civil service in 1913 and was posted to the Inland Revenue. When war broke out, he moved to the War Office contracts department, where he worked with Edward Frank Wise on the requisitioning of raw materials and control of prices. Wise and Lloyd had already met at Toynbee Hall on the eve of war, and it was their joint work at the War Office contracts department and, after 1917, at the new Ministry of Food that made them lifelong friends and allies for the cause of international government and economic controls.

Lloyd's work at the Ministry of Food between 1917 and 1919 proved formative in his development as an internationalist thinker and administrator. His primary responsibility was the control of meat, milk, oils, and fats. It brought him into intimate contact with the international dimension of food control and distribution; his later thinking was shaped by this experience of the network of controls developed by the allies. In September 1918 he was among a small group of British civil servants, including John Maynard Keynes, Robert Henry Brand, and Alfred Eckhard Zimmern, who called for an extension of allied controls into a supreme economic council after the war. For Lloyd the war highlighted the failure of the competitive market system in conditions of scarcity or monopoly; the growing number of trusts in the food trades, such as the meat trade, pointed to the need for more, not fewer, international controls.

Lloyd married on 18 December 1918 Margaret Frances (*b.* 1894), daughter of (Francis Albert) Rollo *Russell and granddaughter of Lord John Russell; they had two sons and one daughter. Educated at Bedales and the London School of Economics, she had undertaken war work at the Ministry of Labour, done relief work with immigrants, belonged to the Independent Labour Party and the Women's International League, and during the 1920s became secretary to the North Kensington women's welfare centre, which offered birth-control advice.

While Britain underwent 'decontrol', Lloyd moved to the economic and financial section at the League of Nations secretariat (1919–21). His hope of turning the league into an organ of economic co-ordination became apparent in spring 1920. If the league was to become successful in removing the causes of international conflict, Lloyd argued, it had to concern itself with private international monopolies and national monopolies and the controls of imports and exports by governments. Emboldened by British commercial car users' protests at profiteering by international trusts, he urged the general secretary to put on the agenda the international control of essential raw materials such as wheat, coal, and petroleum; the general secretary had to remind Lloyd that such initiatives had to come from national governments. In October 1920 Lloyd confessed his disillusionment with the 'self-complacent and dreary old men' he met at the financial conference who, to him, proved 'the complete intellectual bankruptcy of capitalism' (Lloyd papers, 7/16, Lloyd to E. F. Wise, 20 Oct 1920). Next to economic controls, the new global order required men like Lloyd: public-minded experts who would displace diplomats concerned with national interests.

Lloyd played an important part in analysing the weakness of nineteenth-century political economy and in using the experience of commodity controls during the First World War as a model for an alternative system of co-ordination and stabilization suited for a twentieth-century world. After his return to Britain in 1921 Lloyd pursued this vision through two spheres of activity: his everyday life in Whitehall and his political advocacy as a progressive writer and adviser to the Independent Labour Party. The first took him to the Ministry of Agriculture, then in 1926 to the newly created Empire Marketing Board, and in 1933 to the market supply committee as its secretary. The second saw him write *Stabilisation: an Economic Policy for Producers and Consumers* (1923), *Experiments in State Control* (1924) for the Carnegie endowment, and a string of (sometimes anonymous) articles for the *Nation and Athenaeum*, the *New Statesmen*, the *Daily News*, and other papers. It was the second set of activities that established Lloyd as a leading internationalist. *Experiments in State Control*, in particular, which documented the benefits to state and society from wartime controls, was greeted as a blueprint for future ways of efficiently controlling international food supplies.

Lloyd saw price fluctuations in food as a principal source of domestic and international instability. At the global level the rise of private trusts had distorted market conditions and put small producers and consumers alike at risk from uncertainty and profiteering. At the domestic level fluctuations in food prices undermined stable wages and thus eroded the foundations of industrial peace and political stability. Free trade, the panacea of pre-war days, could no longer automatically guarantee the interests of consumers and civil society. The future lay with controls. The public had a choice, Lloyd argued, between control by trusts and control by democratic governments. Wartime experiments with co-ordinating supply and distribution, such as the wheat executive and bulk purchases, proved the potential for controls as sources of more stable and efficient social and international relations.

Within Whitehall and outside, Lloyd became a key advocate of a more organized form of capitalism. He supported a state monopoly import board for wheat as a way to improve domestic efficiency and as a stepping-stone towards greater imperial co-ordination. Already in the early 1920s his call for food controls was complemented by support for the public regulation of the money supply, as he disseminated new monetary theories among the left. His vision of food control as a way of social, economic, and international reconstruction left its mark on the Independent Labour Party's *Living Wage* (1926). Lloyd and his wife were in close touch with H. N. Brailsford, Arnold Toynbee, Norman Angell, Leonard Woolf, Frank Wise, and

Thomas Jones. In the late 1920s his expertise also brought him into contact with a small circle studying the prospects of imperial co-operation, which included Conservatives such as Leo Amery and Walter Elliott. Like many progressives Lloyd had come to accept trade regulation as superior to free trade for inducing rationalization and facilitating trading arrangements, though he questioned the relative merits of tariffs as the best instruments for doing so.

Britain's departure from the gold standard and free trade in 1931 introduced new possibilities for regulation, but under a Conservative-dominated government geared towards protection and assisting producers, as well as nationalist resurgence elsewhere, Lloyd's ambitious ideas for international co-ordination had little prospect of becoming official policy. It was through the growing concern over nutrition that Lloyd regained influence on the domestic and international debate. What had earlier been discussed in terms of surplus and scarcities, price fluctuation and stabilizing demand, now became linked to a broader view of food as a basis of welfare and human rights, in which nutritional imperatives pointed towards an international commitment to more equitable distribution of basic foodstuffs. At the market supply committee Lloyd directed research into food consumption levels and nutritional data. In a cabinet paper of 1935, Lloyd presented food policy as the sheet anchor of national health and welfare, capable of erasing social division and malnourishment. Internationally, too, the idea of stabilizing commodity markets became part of a more expansionist programme attacking poor nutrition in western societies and starvation elsewhere. Lloyd assisted John Boyd Orr in his studies of nutrition and poverty in the mid-1930s. He also came into contact with the group around the Australians Stanley Melbourne Bruce and Frank Lidgett McDougall, who were largely responsible for the League of Nations report on the *Relation of Nutrition, Agriculture and Economic Policy* (1937), the most popular of all League reports, which initiated the establishment of national nutrition committees.

In 1936 Lloyd moved as assistant director to the food (defence plans) department set up to prepare for the possibility of war. Here his experience of the First World War paid important dividends. Assisted by outside experts and businessmen, he helped develop the commodity schemes in 1938. When the Second World War broke out, Lloyd returned to the re-established Ministry of Food as principal assistant secretary. He also wrote more academically on the nature of rationing. While in theory rationing might avoid the need for price controls, in practice they best worked together, Lloyd argued. Personal difficulties with Henry Leon French, the director of the food (defence plans) department, rooted as much in a clash of personalities as in different administrative mentalities, led in 1942 to Lloyd's posting as economic adviser to the minister of state in the Middle East, which was suffering from inflation and food shortages.

During the war Lloyd gave his support to the idea of extending the Atlantic charter to include a minimum standard of nutrition, though he was less happy about ideas tying this to wage standards. He urged Britain and America jointly to pursue a global nutritional programme, buttressed by a food charter for the United Nations. He argued for an international relief fund to distribute dried milk. In general he urged a shift of global production from grain to dairy products and high protein foods. Ironically, it was at the very time when his domestic career was entering a difficult path because of personal tensions, that ideas for international food co-ordination and nutritional rights returned to the centre stage of global politics, with the Hot Springs conference on food and agriculture in May 1943. Like Orr, Bruce, and McDougall, who had helped to push the American president Roosevelt to calling the conference, Lloyd had been an important voice promoting the new internationalism and the nutritional campaign of the inter-war years. At the Hot Springs conference, however, which led to the establishment of the UN Food and Agriculture Organization (FAO), Lloyd was not included in the British delegation. Only in 1946 did he join the FAO, after a short term as economic and financial adviser to the Balkans for the United Nations Relief and Rehabilitation Administration. While at UNRRA he also concerned himself with ways of combating European inflation, arguing that price control and rationing needed to be supplemented by indirect taxes and direct taxes on accumulated wealth.

In 1947 Lloyd returned to the Ministry of Food as under-secretary. After retiring in 1953 he published a third book, *Food and Inflation in the Middle East, 1940–45* (1956). He became president of the Agricultural Economics Society in 1956. From 1958 to 1964 he was a consultant to Political and Economic Planning, focusing on the problems for food and agriculture arising from the EEC. He was appointed CMG in 1945 and CB in 1952. He died in a London hospital on 27 January 1968. FRANK TRENTMANN

Sources *The Times* (29 Jan 1968) • *DNB* • F. Trentmann, 'The strange death of free trade: the erosion of "liberal consensus" in Great Britain, *c.*1903–32', *Citizenship and community: liberals, radicals and collective identities in the British Isles, 1865–1931*, ed. E. F. Biagini (1996), 219–50 • Burke, *Peerage* (1999) [Russell] • *CGPLA Eng. & Wales* (1968) • BLPES, Lloyd MSS • A. Salter, *Allied shipping control* (1921) • A. F. Wilt, *Food for war: agriculture and rearmament in Britain before the second world war* (2001)

Archives BLPES, corresp. and MSS of him and his wife • League of Nations Archive, Geneva • U. Lond., Institute of Commonwealth Studies, MSS relating to visit to Malaya, Ceylon, and Java, with under-secretary of state for the colonies | Bodl. Oxf., Zimmern papers • CUL, corresp. with Sir E. L. Spears

Wealth at death £20,677: probate, 2 May 1968, *CGPLA Eng. & Wales*

Lloyd, Evan (1734–1776), poet, was baptized on 15 April 1734 at Llanycil, Merioneth, the younger son of John Lloyd (1693–1774), gentleman, of Fron-dderw, Bala, and his wife, Bridget Bevan (*d.* 1746).

Lloyd was educated at Ruthin School, Denbighshire, and at Jesus College, Oxford, where he matriculated as a scholar on 22 March 1751; he took his BA in 1754 and MA in 1757, but failed to obtain a hoped-for fellowship. Nothing is known of his life over the next four years. He was ordained, probably in November 1761, and became curate of St Mary's, Redriff (Rotherhithe), London, while continuing to haunt the theatres and coffee houses of Westminster. On 27 October 1763, through the influence of Henry Bilson Legge, former chancellor of the exchequer, Lloyd was instituted as vicar of Llanfair Dyffryn Clwyd, near Ruthin, but he employed a curate there and remained in Redriff and London, his tithes and other dues being forwarded via his father. He made frequent visits to Wales, but stayed with his father at Fron-dderw, rather than with his parishioners in Llanfair.

Occasional poems by Lloyd appeared in journals before he published three substantial verse satires in 1766. *The Powers of the Pen*, in octosyllabic couplets, follows Charles Churchill in attacking critics and ridiculing Warburton and Johnson. *The Curate*, in heroic couplets, on the miserable lot of all the curates in England and Wales, includes some particularly scathing lines on the venality of bishops. *The Methodist*, nearly 1000 lines long, in octosyllabic couplets, and again indebted to Churchill, expresses Lloyd's detestation of Methodism, but is perhaps more strongly motivated by a venomous unexplained personal feud: the character Libidinoso in this poem is a wildly slanderous representation of William Price, former high sheriff of Merioneth, the Lloyds' powerful neighbour in Bala.

Price sued for libel. Lloyd was tried on 2 May 1768, was imprisoned for two weeks in the king's bench prison, and, on 16 May, was fined £50; to add to his troubles his brother Robert died in September, aged thirty-six. On the other hand Lloyd made two valuable friendships that year: with David Garrick, on whom he called in February, and with John Wilkes, who by chance was a fellow gaolbird in the king's bench prison. Meanwhile Lloyd published *Conversation* (1767), an inoffensive satire in heroic couplets, followed in 1768 by a second, enlarged edition of *The Powers of the Pen* and an abortive plan to publish his poems by subscription. He also wrote anonymous anti-government squibs in newspapers.

In September 1769 Lloyd asked Garrick and Wilkes to help him obtain a nominal chaplaincy to a nobleman, as a device to evade a prosecution threatened by William Price for his non-residence at Llanfair. It is not known whether a chaplaincy or a prosecution ensued, but Lloyd never resided at Llanfair. He became a chaplain, but only to a sheriff of London, Watkin Lewes, during his year of office, 1772–3.

In 1770 and 1772 Garrick unsuccessfully sought further church preferment for Lloyd, but the bishop of St Asaph, Jonathan Shipley, declared that Lloyd had to 'perform quarantine' for his satires. Reporting this, Garrick's friend Mrs Sarah Wilmot wondered if Lloyd was 'too lively for his cloth' (*Private Correspondence*, 2.357). Garrick's friendship was repaid in Lloyd's fulsome *Epistle to David Garrick* (1773), which was promptly and deservedly ridiculed in William Kenrick's *A Whipping for the Welsh Parson* (1773).

Lloyd was a lover of conviviality in London. During his annual visits to Wales he 'buried his talents in Ale, and at last, in consequence of sottishness, brought on consumption' (Fenton). He was also afflicted by gout and rheumatism from 1769. He died unmarried on 26 January 1776 at Fron-dderw and was buried in Llanycil churchyard; his epitaph in the church was written by Wilkes.

James Sambrook

Sources C. Price, 'The unpublished letters of Evan Lloyd', *National Library of Wales Journal*, 8 (1953–4), 264–305, 426–48 • R. Jones, 'Two Welsh correspondents of John Wilkes', *Y Cymmrodor*, 29 (1919), 110–39 • C. J. L. Price, *A man of genius, and a Welch man* (1963) • *The letters of David Garrick*, ed. D. M. Little and G. M. Kahrl, 3 vols. (1963) • R. Fenton, *Tours in Wales*, ed. J. Fisher (1917), 92 • *The private correspondence of David Garrick*, ed. J. Boaden, 2 (1832), 357 • parish register, Llanycil, Merioneth, 15 April 1734 [baptism] • parish register, Llanycil, Merioneth, 22 Aug 1746 [burial, Bridget Lloyd] • Lloyd monument, Llanycil parish church • episcopal register, Bangor diocese, NL Wales, MS B/BR/4 • parish registers, Llanfair Dyffryn Clwyd • *GM*, 1st ser., 46 (1776), 94 • C. Price, 'David Garrick and Evan Lloyd', *Review of English Studies*, new ser., 3 (1952), 28–38, esp. 36–7 • *DWB* • H. W. Pedicord, 'Mr and Mrs Garrick: some unpublished correspondence', *Publications of the Modern Language Association of America*, 60 (1945), 779–80 • *European Magazine and London Review*, 18 (1790), 168 • *The Methodist*, Augustan Reprint Society (1972) [with introduction by R. Bentman] • *The journal of the Rev. John Wesley*, 3 (1906), 318 [23 Feb 1768] • *GM*, 1st ser., 52 (1782), 495

Archives NL Wales, poems and family corresp. | BL, letters to John Wilkes, Add. MSS 30870–30871, 30875 • NL Wales, letters to H. Davies and R. Wynne and Mrs Wynne, Peniarth 418D, fols. 68b–71b • NL Wales, letters to father J. Lloyd, MSS 9664, 12294 • V&A, letters to Garrick, Garrick corresp., vol. xxxix, fols. 103–6, 209

Likenesses portrait, repro. in Jones, 'Two Welsh correspondents', facing p. 110; formerly in possession of Mrs Anwyl of Bala in 1919

Lloyd, Gamaliel (1744–1817), merchant and political reformer, was born on 26 May 1744 at Hulme Hall near Manchester, the second son of four children of George Lloyd (*bap.* 1708, *d.* 1783), merchant and manufacturer, and his second wife, Susannah Horton (*bap.* 1718, *d.* 1783), daughter of Thomas Horton of Chadderton, Lancashire. The Lloyds had been successful merchants even before the family moved from Mattersey, Nottinghamshire, to Lancashire in the late seventeenth century. George Lloyd, who had taken an MB at Cambridge in 1731 and had been elected a fellow of the Royal Society in 1737, moved to Barrowby Hall, near Leeds, some time after 1760, though his son John with his first wife, Eleanor, *née* Wright (*d.* 1735), continued to reside at Hulme Hall. He became a deputy lieutenant for the West Riding of Yorkshire. Gamaliel and his brother Thomas (1750–1828) were apprenticed in the woollen industry at Leeds, and his other brother, George, became a barrister. His sister, Susannah, married the Revd Henry Wray.

In 1764 Gamaliel Lloyd formed a partnership in a dyeing enterprise with the Gautier family in Leeds. The business eventually failed, and in 1776 he entered a partnership with an Italian merchant, Horace Cattaneo, to export woollen cloth. Although Lloyd was fined in 1777 for 'reeling false and short yarn', Lloyd, Cattaneo & Co. proved profitable, the firm's gross profits totalling £35,000 in 1782. Indeed, Lloyd was one of the half-dozen wealthiest merchants of Leeds. With his profits he purchased a country estate, Stockton Hall, near York. Lloyd became involved in local politics as his business career prospered. He was elected to the Leeds corporation and the common council in 1771, became alderman in 1775, and served as lord mayor for 1778–9. He married in 1780 Elizabeth, daughter of James Attwood of Bristol. They had three children: two daughters and a son.

Beginning in March 1780, Lloyd became an active member of Christopher Wyvill's extra-parliamentary Yorkshire Association. Wyvill and the association movement, which was dominated by the merchant gentry, favoured moderate reforms of parliament. Particularly interested in the association's promotion of shorter parliaments and reform of the civil list and sinecures, Lloyd collected signatures on association petitions and solicited support from the sympathetic county MP, Sir George Savile. He wrote to Savile on 15 May 1780 expressing gratitude for Savile's vote in favour of John Sawbridge's unsuccessful Commons motion for triennial parliaments. Lloyd remained optimistic: 'This has very much raised our Spirits … the Whigs united upon truly Whiggish and Constitutional Grounds, will be an over-match for their Opposers' (Wyvill, 1.253). He further expressed support for John Dunning's resolution in the Commons citing the growing 'influence of the Crown' and lamented the 'still greater and more unconstitutional influence of Lords and other great Men by their property in the Boroughs: an influence very dangerous … as it is the greatest support of the influence of the Crown' (ibid., 1.261). Parliamentary reform, he asserted, would ensure a shift in political influence to the 'wise, honest, able and incorruptible' independent merchants and gentry (ibid., 1.260–61). His association colleague William Strickland requested that Lloyd encourage participation from fellow merchants in Manchester, Liverpool, Norwich, Birmingham, and Exeter. The association petition circulated by Lloyd obtained an impressive 318 signatures by December 1782.

Upon the failure of the association's petitioning campaign and parliamentary reform, Lloyd became less active politically. He moved in 1789 to Bury St Edmunds, Suffolk, and also later acquired a residence at Hampstead, near London. Continuing his interest in reform, however, he made the acquaintance of Capel Lofft, a disciple of John Jebb and leader in Jebb's Society for Constitutional Information. Yet he wrote to Wyvill in 1793 or 1794 that he was alarmed at the increasingly radical nature of Lofft's ideas. Thereafter he lived in quiet retirement until his death by natural causes in Great Ormond Street, London, on 31 August 1817. Although the value of Lloyd's real properties must have been large, the exact figure cannot be determined. DANIEL WEBSTER HOLLIS, III

Sources D. W. Hollis, 'Lloyd, Gamaliel', *BDMBR*, vol. 1 • C. Wyvill, ed., *Political papers*, 6 vols. [1794–1804] • R. G. Wilson, *Gentlemen merchants: the merchant community in Leeds, 1700–1830* (1971) • I. R. Christie, 'The Yorkshire Association, 1780–4: a study in political organization', *HJ*, 3 (1960), 144–61 • Burke, *Gen. GB* (1952) • W. B. Crump, 'The Leeds woollen industry, 1780–1820', *Thoresby Society Publications*, 32 (1931), 1–58 • 'Extracts from the *Leeds Intelligencer* and the *Leeds Mercury*, 1777–82', *Thoresby Society Publications*, 40 (1947), 1–247 • G. D. Lamb, 'Extracts from the *Leeds Intelligencer* and the *Leeds Mercury*, 1769–76', *Thoresby Society Publications*, 38 (1938) • J. Wardell, *The municipal history of the borough of Leeds* (1846) • R. V. Taylor, ed., *The biographia Leodiensis, or, Biographical sketches of the worthies of Leeds* (1865) • *GM*, 1st ser., 87/2 (1817), 377 • *IGI*
Archives N. Yorks. CRO, corresp. with Christopher Wyvill
Wealth at death over £10,000

Lloyd, George (1560/61–1615), bishop of Chester, was the sixth son of Meredith Lloyd of Llanelian-yn-Rhos, Denbighshire, and Janet, daughter of Hugh Conway, both from old gentry families. He may have settled in Chester as early as 1566: in October 1613 he said he had 'known' the city 'these forty-seven years' (BL, Harleian MS 2103, fol. 8*v*). Certainly he attended the King's School, Chester, from 1575 to 1579, before entering Jesus College, Cambridge, where he graduated BA in 1582. He became a fellow of Magdalene College, Cambridge, in 1585 and proceeded BD in 1593 and DD in 1598. In 1594 Lloyd was elected to the divinity lectureship in Chester Cathedral, during the mayoralty of his eldest brother David Lloyd, a wealthy merchant. Three years later he became rector of Heswall, Cheshire, and he held the parish for the next seventeen years; during that time he and his wife, Anne (*d.* 1648), daughter of John Wilkinson, probably of Northwich, Cheshire (given as Norwich in BL, Lansdowne MS 879), had at least seven children, the eldest of whom, John, was baptized at Heswall in October 1599. On 23 December 1599 Lloyd was presented to the bishopric of Sodor and Man, by the queen rather than the earl of Derby, there being no dean or chapter in the diocese of Man by which any election might be made. His consecration may have been at Chester, not York. Little is known of his activities on Man but the extent and promptness of the reforms introduced five years later by his successor, John Phillips, suggest that there was pressing need for them after Lloyd was translated to Chester, in succession to Richard Vaughan.

Lloyd was presented to the bishopric of Chester on 18 December 1604 and the royal assent followed on 9 January 1605. He was attentive to his administrative duties in his new see but his mildness of manner encouraged laxity among his officials. Visitations were held regularly, but with limited results. He deprived two ministers in 1606, and occasionally rejected others unwilling to conform to the terms of the 1604 canons, but puritan clergy in general were dealt with leniently. In the aftermath of the Gunpowder Plot he treated Roman Catholics with moderation and even diffidence, at times seeking guidance from the privy council. Relations between the city and the cathedral grew fractious during Lloyd's episcopate, however, and in two sermons preached in the cathedral in 1614 he seemed to reflect adversely on the outgoing mayor, Robert Whitby, the puritanical clerk of the pentice and client of Lord Keeper Ellesmere, and his son Edward Whitby, the new recorder. Lloyd's family associations with the late recorder, Thomas Gamull, prompted the accusation that he had been 'an earnest labourer' for a rival candidate (Harleian MS 2103, fol. 11*r*). Lloyd, a skilful preacher, held firmly Calvinist convictions nevertheless; Sir John Harington noted how Prince Henry 'heard him Preach often, and very well', although none of his sermons was published (Harington). Twice, in 1605 and 1609, Lloyd was invited to deliver a Lenten sermon at court, but on each occasion Martin Heton, bishop of Ely, deputized.

At the time of his appointment to Sodor and Man, Lloyd claimed his finances would not bear a journey to York; however, as bishop of Chester he had the benefit of Marian improvements to the see and held, in addition first to Heswall and then to Bangor (the living favoured by bishops of Chester) which he exchanged for Heswall in 1613, the substantial livings of Thornton, Waverton, Childwall, and Cartmel in Lancashire, while in 1608 his wife and sons leased Shotwick, Cheshire, from the dean and chapter of Chester. Like Vaughan, Lloyd struggled with the deaneries, in 1615 giving up his attempt to control those in the archdeaconry of Richmond, and granting leases of seven rural deaneries to the commissaries there. Financially there remained much for his successor, John Bridgeman, to do. Lloyd died in his rectory at Thornton on 1 August 1615 in his fifty-fifth year, and was buried 'swiftly' (Burne, 95) five days later in Chester Cathedral. A brass plate set up in his memory has since disappeared, but the text of its inscription has survived.

BRIAN QUINTRELL

Sources BL, R. Whitby to Lord Keeper Ellesmere, 1614, Harleian MS 2103 [fols. 7r–11r] · *CSP dom.*, *1598–1618* · Ches. & Chester ALSS, Chester diocesan records, EDA 1/4, EDA 2/2, EDC 1/33, 35, EDV 1/14, 15, 17, 19 · *Calendar of the manuscripts of the most hon. the marquis of Salisbury*, 24 vols., HMC, 9 (1883–1976), vols. 17–19 · F. Sanders, 'George Lloyd, DD, bishop of Chester, 1605–1616', *Journal of the Architectural, Archaeological, and Historic Society for the County and City of Chester and North Wales*, new ser., 10 (1904), 86–100 · Lloyd pedigree, BL, Lansdowne MS 879 · S. J. Lander, 'The diocese of Chester, 1540–1660', *VCH Cheshire*, 3.12–36 · K. Fincham, *Prelate as pastor: the episcopate of James I* (1990) · C. Haigh, 'Finance and administration in a new diocese: Chester, 1541–1641', *Continuity and change: personnel and administration of the Church of England, 1500–1642*, ed. R. O'Day and F. Heal (1976), 145–66 · R. V. H. Burne, *Chester Cathedral: from its founding by Henry VIII to the accession of Queen Victoria* (1958) · K. Fincham, ed., *Visitation articles and injunctions of the early Stuart church*, 1 (1994) · J. Harington, *A briefe view of the state of the Church of England* (1653) [to 1608] · P. E. McCullough, *Sermons at court: politics and religion in Elizabethan and Jacobean preaching* (1998) [incl. CD-ROM] · W. Harrison, *An account of the diocese of Sodor and Man*, Manx Society, 29 (1879) · *DNB*

Lloyd, George Ambrose, **first Baron Lloyd** (1879–1941), politician and colonial administrator, was born on 19 September 1879 at Olton Hall, near Solihull, Warwickshire, the third son and youngest of the six children of Sampson Samuel Lloyd (1846–1899), a Birmingham industrialist, and his wife, Jane Emelia Lloyd (*d.* 1899). The family was of Welsh descent, and his grandfathers were directors of Lloyds Bank.

Early life Educated at home until 1891, Lloyd enjoyed seven years at Eton College and from 1898 read history at Trinity College, Cambridge, where he coxed the crew which won the university boat race in 1899 and 1900. Unsettled by his parents' deaths, he left Cambridge in 1900 without taking a degree to tour India. He sought big game but found much more: a fascination with the East, a love of the wilderness, and a strong sense of purpose.

George Ambrose Lloyd, first Baron Lloyd (1879–1941), by Sir Cecil Beaton

Amid the ruins of the Lucknow residency, the heroic ideal of British imperialism fired his imagination. Curzon, the viceroy, became a role model, as did Joseph Chamberlain.

Lloyd worked for the family firm of steel-tube makers, Lloyd and Lloyd (later Stewart and Lloyd), but he had a private income of £2000 per year and a keen desire to gain expert knowledge of some aspect of imperial or foreign affairs. Consequently in 1905 he became an honorary attaché at the British embassy in Constantinople, alongside Aubrey Herbert (a friend) and Mark Sykes (a rival). Although prone to stomach upsets, he traversed the Ottoman empire comprehensively and wrote a 249-page report on trade in the Persian Gulf, which was well received in 1908. He contributed articles to *The Times* during the Young Turk revolution and frequently revisited the region.

In January 1910 Lloyd entered the House of Commons as Liberal Unionist (later Conservative) member for West Staffordshire. He spoke regularly on imperial issues, but the petty politicking of Westminster disgusted him and he contemplated emigrating to east Africa. Friends were surprised when, on 13 November 1911, he married Blanche Isabella Lascelles (1880–1969), maid of honour to Queen Alexandra and daughter of Frederick Canning Lascelles, for his attitude to women was generally disparaging. Blanche proved a faithful helpmeet, and their only child, David, arrived in September 1912. Lloyd's obvious preference for male companionship still gave rise to whispered speculation of a flimsy sort.

First World War On 1 August 1914 Lloyd joined Leo Amery in lobbying Conservative leaders to press for an immediate declaration of war. Already an officer in the Warwickshire yeomanry, he yearned to go to France; but his grasp of Turkish meant that he was seconded in November 1914 to the intelligence department of the general staff in Egypt. Often frustrated, he relished facing fire at Gallipoli in 1915. Special missions took him to Petrograd to improve Anglo-Russian liaison, to Basrah to update his study of gulf commerce, and to Mecca to help plan the Arab revolt. Back in Cairo with the Arab bureau in 1917, he supported Arab aspirations.

Captain Lloyd returned to London in January 1918 and served as secretary to the British delegation to the financial committee of the inter-allied war council. Though unhappy that the war had offered him few opportunities for bravery, he welcomed the chance to renew political contacts, especially with Austen Chamberlain, and he collaborated with Edward Wood (Lord Halifax) on *The Great Opportunity*, a small book whose earnest platitudes went down well in November 1918. Lloyd did not seek re-election himself, having secured a colonial governorship, accompanied by a knighthood (GCIE).

Bombay Sir George Lloyd took up his duties in December 1918 as governor of the Bombay presidency, a province which comprised the western coast of India between Karachi and Goa. He at once made his mark by dealing with a rash of strikes and then turned his mind to the Montagu–Chelmsford reforms, intended to permit a limited measure of self-government. At the time he considered these concessions expedient, but he soon concluded that Indians would be unfit for more self-government until equal to white men in character, education, and standard of life. Because Bombay was a stronghold of Indian nationalism, Lloyd faced serious public order problems, which he handled with a blend of strictness and discretion. In 1921 he finally insisted on the arrest of Gandhi (who received a six-year prison sentence for sedition).

Horrified by overcrowded slums, Lloyd instigated the Back Bay land reclamation scheme to make room in Bombay for a further quarter of a million citizens. A dam on the Indus to irrigate 6 million acres of Sind had been discussed for sixty years: it took the energy of Sir George to raise finance for the Sukkur barrage (constructed between 1923 and 1935). He excelled at practical management of this kind, preferring to deal directly with the man at the top and the man on the spot. When responsibility for relations with the princely states was transferred from Bombay to Delhi in 1923, he took it as a personal affront.

Late to bed and early to rise, Lloyd was ever a compulsive overworker, who would not suffer fools, slackness, or contradiction. That said, subordinates who passed the test found him loyal and generous. His excellency held rigid views on the deference due to the king's representative, and he always cut a figure—with his clipped moustache, brilliantined black hair, and faultless attire. His manner was so masterful as to seem artificial, yet he could charm as well as bully. Few were allowed to see his sensitive side. At the close of the day, with his aides-de-camp, he would sip a whisky and soda, play popular songs on the piano, and give way to boyish good humour—or sometimes to anguished soul-searching. This devout Anglo-Catholic felt an onerous obligation to fight for the right on every occasion.

Lloyd left India in 1924, at the end of his five-year term, with a reputation for brusque efficiency. Honoured with a privy councillorship and made GCSI, he could not however expect a fresh appointment from the new Labour government, so he accepted working directorships at Lloyds Bank and Shell. His tendency to spend to the limit of his income rendered him liable to money worries.

Cairo Lloyd returned to the House of Commons in October 1924, having agreed to fill a late vacancy at Eastbourne on the understanding that a Conservative government would send him abroad again soon. The offer of Kenya offended him. Egypt was acceptable. He arrived in Cairo in October 1925 as first Baron Lloyd of Dolobran (the ancestral home at Meifod, Montgomeryshire) after insisting on a peerage to impress the Egyptians.

The high commissioner for Egypt and the Sudan was technically a diplomat rather than an imperial administrator, for the British had granted Egypt nominal independence in 1922 while preserving (by unilateral declaration backed by a military presence) their supremacy in relation to four 'reserved points': the Suez Canal, defence, foreign interests, and the Sudan. The British Foreign Office hoped to keep its intervention in domestic politics to a minimum and to negotiate a treaty with the Egyptian government, enshrining these special rights in international law.

It gradually became apparent that Lloyd diverged from the Foreign Office in his estimate of the level of political intervention needed to guard British interests. He repeatedly advocated taking a firmer line with Egyptian ministers and he often won his point—by mobilizing robust imperialists in the British cabinet, like Amery and Churchill, to overcome the caution of the foreign secretary, Austen Chamberlain. Every summer he wanted to summon a gunboat to Alexandria to help him prevail in the latest Anglo-Egyptian dispute. In 1926 he needed to dissuade the nationalist Saʿd Zaghlul from assuming the premiership; in 1927 control of the Egyptian army was at stake; in 1928 a damaging assemblies bill had to be stopped.

As many observers rightly inferred, Lloyd thought that conceding independence had been a bad mistake. His clear-cut mind disapproved of an arrangement which left Britain power without authority and responsibility without control. It was wrong to let Egyptians be misgoverned by a crafty king and a handful of semi-westernized lawyers and journalists. If the British desired the strategic benefits of ultimate hegemony over Egypt, they had a duty and a need to provide it with good administration.

In 1927 Chamberlain began negotiating with the Egyptian premier about a treaty—without informing Lloyd, who had warned that it would be pointless to seek recognition of Britain's rights while nationalists in the Egyptian parliament remained obdurate. Eight months later Egypt rejected the treaty, exactly as he had predicted. Senior advisers in the Foreign Office, Sir William Tyrrell among them, suspected Lloyd of undermining the project and endeavoured to turn Chamberlain against his former protégé. Some individuals at the Cairo residency were happy to tell tales of his viceregal airs, propensity to dramatize, and occasional tactless remarks, but he survived so long as he retained support in cabinet. Then Labour won the 1929 election. Arthur Henderson, the new foreign secretary, intended another attempt at an Anglo-Egyptian treaty. He recalled the high commissioner to London and compelled him to resign on 24 July 1929. That Lord Lloyd had been fundamentally out of sympathy with Foreign Office thinking is undeniable. That he had wilfully misinterpreted and misapplied government policy—as Henderson publicly alleged—is more debatable. Lloyd, jealous of his honour, felt betrayed when Baldwin and Chamberlain did not defend him, and a supportive speech from Churchill merely exposed the extent of tory disarray. Lloyd later published his two-volume justification, *Egypt since Cromer* (1933–4).

Tory rebel Viewed as a maverick, Lloyd plunged into pressure-group politics. As president of the Navy League from 1930, he called strenuously for rearmament, and his debunking of collective security turned him into the bugbear of idealistic internationalists. As chairman of the Empire Economic Union, meanwhile, he campaigned for imperial preference (though unwilling to ally himself with Beaverbrook). He was best known, however, for opposing greater self-government for India. The inapplicability of western-style institutions to oriental peoples appeared to him so obvious that he doubted the sincerity of British politicians who suggested otherwise: these cynics were using liberal cant to cloak a craven policy of 'cut and run'. He formed the India Defence League in 1933.

Lloyd's concerns amounted to a sweeping critique of the National Government. His mission was to reinvigorate a nation perilously demoralized by Baldwinism and female suffrage. Relishing combat, he delivered thirty or forty speeches per year, often recalling how ancient Rome had lost faith in itself once it began to call home the legions. Was the present generation going to dissipate the British imperial legacy, perhaps with like consequences for human progress? His earnestness could impress, despite his harsh voice and too rapid delivery, yet his appeal never stretched far beyond his natural constituency of die-hard *Morning Post* readers. Perhaps he had been overseas so long that he did not realize how Britain had changed since 1914. The left painted him as a would-be dictator, what with his hard and fast views on everything and his sympathy for Mussolini and Franco (though never for Hitler, whose paganism repelled him). In truth, he remained committed to British democracy and could not bring himself to break with the Conservative Party, whose drift to the left he aspired to reverse.

Directorships of International Wagon Lits and the British South Africa Company helped Lloyd to support a grand home in Portman Square, a sports car, a yacht, and a busy social life. Friends included Noël Coward and T. E. Lawrence. His restlessness was proverbial. He would shift in his chair, fiddle with his monocle, and race from one topic of conversation to the next. A confessed travel addict who loved hot climates, he went abroad every couple of months. His wife desired a quieter existence, and in 1935 he bought the old vicarage (renamed Clouds Hill) at Offley, near Hitchin, Hertfordshire. With Blanche usually resident there, Lloyd grew closer to his son. He learnt to fly at fifty-four, and, when made an honorary air-commodore, insisted on truly qualifying as a military pilot.

Lloyd initially welcomed the premiership of Neville Chamberlain and endorsed appeasement of Italy. This facilitated his return to official circles as chairman of the British Council in July 1937. In three years he expanded its network of lecturers, widened its range of activities, doubled and redoubled its funding, safeguarded its independence, and won permanent recognition for the role of cultural propaganda.

Second World War Since 1936, Lloyd had been wholly convinced that Nazi Germany was a menace to European peace which had to be countered by an Anglo-French alliance. He would have preferred war to the dismemberment of Czechoslovakia in October 1938, when he denounced the Munich agreement as a shameful surrender.

The defence of Christian civilization against atheistic totalitarianism was how Lloyd characterized the Second World War to neutrals, as he journeyed around Europe as a kind of roving ambassador on the pretext of British Council business. He was overjoyed when Churchill appointed him secretary of state for the colonies on 11 May 1940. At last he knew that the British were realizing the greatness of their destiny. He would not hear of an early peace, and the cabinet sent him to Bordeaux in June to make the final appeal to the French to fight on. The fate of the French colonies and the Italian threat in Africa demanded Lloyd's attention. There was no real opportunity for him to pursue his long-cherished schemes for imperial union, though he still jibbed at Zionism and Indian constitutional reform. The destroyers-for-bases deal with the USA also perturbed him.

On 7 January 1941, at his own prompting, Lloyd assumed additional duties as leader of the House of Lords. Soon afterwards he asked for a few days' rest. What was first diagnosed as German measles turned out to be myeloma, an uncommon form of leukaemia. He died at a clinic in Marylebone on 4 February 1941 and was buried in the village graveyard at St Ippollitts, Hertfordshire.

Some people said that George Lloyd seemed un-English—in looks and in mentality—to which he would lightly reply that he was wholly Welsh. A driven man, highly self-conscious, he combined exceptional ambition with a horror of careerism. He needed to convince himself that he sought preferment solely to advance a transcendent cause: namely, British imperialism as

God's chosen instrument. This made him sound arrogant to those not privy to his moods of doubt and self-reproach. So intense a personality beneath a dapper exterior variously inspired and disconcerted. A romantic, who idealized the Elizabethan spirit, he embodied a Kiplingesque brand of patriotism no longer universally admired. Perhaps the timing of his death was fitting, for he abhorred the USSR and despised the USA, both shortly to enter the war. He had once told his wife that if the British empire suffered eclipse his heart would find solace only in the next world.

A well-known figure in the 1930s, Lloyd faded rapidly from popular recollection, inevitably overshadowed by Churchill in histories of the decade. His achievement at the British Council commanded great respect within that institution, but post-war Britain had generally no wish to remember him while transforming its empire into a Commonwealth. Fifty years on, however, Lloyd may appear to have been more prescient (or more honest) than many of his contemporaries—in his Cassandra-like prognoses for British global power, if not in his prescriptions.

JASON TOMES

Sources J. Charmley, *Lord Lloyd and the decline of the British empire* (1987) • C. F. Adam, *The life of Lord Lloyd* (1948) • F. Donaldson, *The British Council: the first fifty years* (1984) • J. Lees-Milne, *Another self* (1970) • L. Grafftey-Smith, *Bright Levant* (1970) • G. A. Lloyd, *Egypt since Cromer*, 2 vols. (1933–4) • *Hansard 5C* • *Hansard 5L* • G. A. Lloyd, *The British case* (1939) • G. A. Lloyd, *Leadership in democracy* (1939) • G. A. Lloyd and E. Wood, *The great opportunity* (1918) • B. Westrate, *The Arab bureau: British policy in the Middle East, 1916–1920* (1992) • *WWW*, 1941–50 • *DNB* • Burke, *Peerage*

Archives CAC Cam., corresp. and papers • PRO, reports on tours to Europe and Middle East, BW 2/222–226 | BL, corresp. with Sir Roger Keyes • BL OIOC, letters to Lord Halifax, MS Eur. B 158 • BL OIOC, letters to second earl of Lytton, MS Eur. F 160 • BL OIOC, letters to Lord Reading, MSS Eur. E 238, F 118 • Bodl. Oxf., letters to Lady Milner • Bodl. Oxf., corresp. with Lord Monckton • CAC Cam., corresp. with Sir Henry Page Croft • Nuffield Oxf., corresp. with Lord Cherwell • PRO, Foreign Office general correspondence, FO 371 • Som. ARS, corresp. with Aubrey Herbert • St Ant. Oxf., Middle East Centre, letters to his sister, Mrs Gwen Carleton, and papers • U. Birm. L., corresp. with Austen Chamberlain; letters to Joseph Chamberlain • U. Durham L., letters to Sir Harold MacMichael • U. Edin. L., corresp. with Charles Sarolea • U. Hull, Brynmor Jones L., letters to Irene Forbes Adam | FILM BFI NFTVA, news footage • BFI NFTVA, party political footage

Likenesses O. Birley, oils, 1926–9, priv. coll. • S. Morse-Brown, chalk drawing, *c*.1938, NMG Wales • C. Beaton, photograph, NPG [*see illus.*] • photographs, priv. coll.; repro. in Charmley, *Lord Lloyd*

Wealth at death £56,967 9*s*. 5*d*.: probate, 12 March 1941, *CGPLA Eng. & Wales*

Lloyd, George Walter Selwyn (1913–1998), composer, was born at St Ives, Cornwall, on 28 June 1913, the son of William Alexander Charles Lloyd (1885–1951), gentleman, and his wife, Constance Priestley, *née* Rawson (1889–1985). Chronic rheumatic fever meant that he was denied a conventional education. However, he spent his childhood in a house overlooking St Ives' Bay, where the arts, and especially music, were highly prized and often practised. Each weekend musicians would come to a big artist's studio in the house and play chamber works. Lloyd's father had the musical and literary tastes of a connoisseur and a particularly advanced knowledge of Italian opera. The education Lloyd had at home was probably better than he would have acquired at most public schools of the time: it equipped him with a wide knowledge of literature, the classics, history, and the arts that would inform his career as a composer.

Lloyd showed a precocious talent for music that his enlightened parents were keen to develop. He was playing the violin by the age of five, and by the time he was ten had started to compose. William Lloyd would, as an exercise, give his son short scenes from English plays for him to set to music. If he found it difficult, his father would show him what Bellini or Verdi had done in such a situation. As a consequence, Lloyd had a deep understanding of Italian operatic method at a very early age. In his teens his father arranged for him to have violin lessons with Albert Sammons and counterpoint lessons from C. H. Kitson, and to learn composition from Harry Farjeon at the Royal Academy of Music. This training paid off, for Lloyd's music is distinguished by bright orchestration that betrays the composer's deep understanding of the capabilities of every instrument. His writing for brass was particularly fine, and later in life he wrote many pieces for brass band. This intensive musical education, and a love of the Romantics, especially Verdi and Brahms, led to Lloyd's writing his first symphony at the age of nineteen. It was given its première by the Bournemouth Symphony Orchestra in 1933, thanks to the patronage of the orchestra's conductor, Sir Dan Godfrey.

Unlike his exact contemporary Benjamin Britten, Lloyd was motivated to write beautiful tunes for their own sake rather than to produce music as a result of intense intellectualization, experiment, or—in the pre-war years—turbulent emotional experiences. This attachment to the musical forms of the nineteenth century would, in time, cause him to be viewed as an anachronism by those responsible for programming music for concerts and for broadcasting; but until 1939 he enjoyed popularity, success, and celebrity. No sooner had his first symphony been launched than he wrote an opera, *Iernin*, with a libretto by his father based on a Cornish legend. Frank Howes, the music critic of *The Times*, happened to be on holiday in Cornwall and saw a performance at Penzance in November 1934. He wrote an enthusiastic review, saying that 'Lloyd showed the rarest of all qualities in a British composer, an almost unerring perception of what the stage requires' (*The Times*, 7 Nov 1934).

This encomium resulted in the opera's being staged at the Lyceum in London in June the following year. Its three-week run was the third longest in English operatic history, and it closed only because a heatwave made the theatre intolerable. No less a master than Ralph Vaughan Williams told Lloyd: 'It isn't fair. I've been trying to write operas like that all my life and here you are, a youth of 21, and you do it first time' (*Daily Telegraph*, 6 July 1998). Lloyd was already at work on a second opera, *The Serf*. It was performed at Covent Garden in 1938, this time thanks partly to the admiration Sir Thomas Beecham had for the work of the young composer. His second symphony, like the third (written contemporaneously with the first), was first performed at Eastbourne in 1935. The third was taken up by the BBC Symphony Orchestra on the recommendation of John Ireland, another admirer of *Iernin*, and a man who became something of a mentor to Lloyd. Its première was in a BBC concert of contemporary music in London in November 1935, conducted by the 22-year-old composer. The BBC Scottish Symphony Orchestra offered Lloyd the post of conductor, but his father dissuaded him, counselling instead that his future lay in composition. The following year, on holiday in Switzerland, he met Nancy Kathleen Juvet (1913–2000), whom he married on 22 January 1937. In the course of their sixty-one-year marriage, Nancy Lloyd provided support for her husband and his work that was literally vital.

The advent of the Second World War put a brake on Lloyd's meteoric career and almost ended it. A deeply patriotic man, he did not hesitate to enlist in the Royal Marines, and he played the cornet in a military band. On active service, this meant he doubled up as a gunner. In 1942 he served on the Arctic convoys on HMS *Trinidad*. She was badly damaged after one of her own torpedoes executed a U-turn and hit her. Lloyd was rescued, though only after seeing many of his fellow gunners drown in oil. His lungs were damaged by oil, and a combination of severe shell-shock and trauma, on top of his weak constitution, caused a complete mental and physical collapse. His doctors told his wife he might have to be institutionalized for the rest of his life. She refused to believe it, and resolved to nurse him back to health. Slowly, she succeeded. His recovery advanced when, at the end of the war, the couple were able to go to Switzerland. He began to write music again, usually only for half an hour early each morning before the strain overcame him.

Lloyd's first post-war work was his epic fourth symphony, finished in 1946. Regarded by many aficionados as his masterpiece, it begins in great gloom that suggests the Arctic convoys, but ends with the triumph of life over death. A fifth symphony followed in 1948, though neither received a performance at the time. None the less, Lloyd and his father were commissioned by the Arts Council to write an opera for the 1951 Festival of Britain. The result was *John Socman*, about a Wiltshire soldier returning from Agincourt. The production toured round England with the Carl Rosa Company but was a disaster, mainly because of artistic differences between director and conductor. Lloyd, still emotionally fragile after his war experiences, lacked the strength to confront and overcome this disappointment. He decided with his wife to abandon music as a way of life. In 1949 they had bought a market garden at Folke, near Sherborne in Dorset, and this became their home and their life for more than twenty years.

Lloyd continued to write music, rising at 4.30 a.m. for three hours' composition before the start of his day's work growing carnations and mushrooms. Although his horticultural business was a success and soon expanded, nothing happened to alleviate his gloom about his music. Manuscripts sent to the BBC in the hope of performance were returned unread. Impresarios were uninterested. Musical opinion was by then in fee to serialism and atonality, modes Lloyd completely rejected. 'I never wrote 12-tone music because I didn't like the theory', he later said. 'I studied the blessed thing in the 1930s and thought it was a cock-eyed idea that produced horrible sounds. It made composers forget how to sing' (*The Times*, 6 July 1998). Sir William Glock, the BBC's music director, drew up a blacklist of composers whose works failed to match his own modernist tastes, and Lloyd's name was on it. At the time, such a refusal of patronage created a formidable hurdle.

In 1973, both aged sixty, Lloyd and his wife sold their horticultural business and moved back to London. Lloyd had a soundproofed room built in his flat near Marylebone Station in which he could embark on a new era of composition—a bold step which was in part the result of a slight upturn in his artistic fortunes. Two conductors, Sir Charles Groves and Sir Edward Downes, had in the 1960s launched a rearguard action on Lloyd's behalf. Most successful of all, however, was the pianist John Ogdon. In recognition of Ogdon's friendship, Lloyd had earlier written a piano concerto, *Scapegoat*, for him, which the dedicatee performed with the Royal Liverpool Philharmonic Orchestra under Groves in 1964. Five years later Ogdon showed the BBC the score of Lloyd's eighth symphony without revealing the name of the composer. It was accepted, though the BBC waited until 1977 to perform it. After the eighth's première, which was a great popular success, the BBC Philharmonic Orchestra under Sir Edward Downes set about championing Lloyd's music. In terms of his personal renaissance, 1981 was an *annus mirabilis* for him. His sixth symphony was included in the Proms, to great acclaim, and Lyrita Records recorded, under Downes, the fourth, fifth, and eighth symphonies. A relay from the Cheltenham festival of the fourth symphony—its first performance, ecstatically received, thirty-five years after it was written—seemed to set the seal not just on Lloyd's cultural rehabilitation but on his status as a considerable composer. A prodigious Indian summer followed. This was due in part to Peter Kermani, an American industrialist and sponsor of the Albany Symphony Orchestra in New York state. The orchestra recorded all of Lloyd's main works, and many minor ones, between the mid-1980s and the composer's death. A huge new audience in America led to better promotion of his music in Britain. This not only expanded the audience for Lloyd's music, and brought him, in his early eighties, an income from his work: it also forced a critical reappraisal of his output that was, on the whole, positive.

The Indian summer also inspired Lloyd to a prodigious output of music in the last fifteen years of his life, though it unquestionably put strains on his ever-delicate health. In all he wrote twelve symphonies, the last two receiving performances in 1986 and 1990 respectively. He turned increasingly to choral music in his last years. There were four notable works in this genre: *The Vigil of Venus*, whose first performance was at the Festival Hall in 1989; the *Symphonic Mass*, which the composer conducted at the Brighton festival in 1993; *A Litany*, settings of John Donne first performed at the Festival Hall in March 1996; and his Requiem, the posthumous première of which took place in Oxford in April 2000. Despite his advancing years and his and his wife's increasing frailty, both of them travelled around the world to give performances of and record his music; they made frequent trips to America and to the Far East when Lloyd was well into his eighties.

Lloyd was a generous, modest, immensely likeable man of utter artistic integrity. He eschewed fashion because it did not chime with the convictions that motivated his art, and the neglect he endured as a result was something he bore with great moral courage. One critical assessment of him after his death had it that, 'though the idiom of his music was totally traditional, consistently tonal and lyrical in a late romantic way, it was only rarely imitative … his music had its own distinctive flavour' (*The Guardian*, 8 July 1998). His genial and gentle exterior, which projected a remarkable youthfulness well into his old age, concealed fiercely held views. A committed free-marketeer, he deplored composers who demanded public subsidies to write music, for he felt it was a sure way to give the public what it did not want. He believed he could earn a living by giving audiences what they did want and, though it took him most of his life to achieve this, in the end he did. 'Composers cannot go on despising their audiences', he once observed. 'I like the same sort of thing the average person likes. I write what pleases me' (*Daily Telegraph*, 6 July 1998).

Lloyd died at University College Hospital, Marylebone, London, on 3 July 1998 after a year of increasing heart trouble, and was cremated at Golders Green crematorium on 10 July. He completed his last work, appropriately enough the Requiem, three weeks before he died. He was survived by his wife; there were no children of the marriage. SIMON HEFFER

Sources personal knowledge (2004) · private information (2004) · *The Times* (6 July 1998) · *The Independent* (7 July 1998) · *Daily Telegraph* (6 July 1998) · *The Guardian* (8 July 1998) · *The Times* (7 Nov 1934) · *WWW*

Archives priv. coll., MSS | SOUND BBC Sound Archives

Likenesses W. Dudeney, bust, 1935, priv. coll. · A. Crowley, photograph, 1990–98, repro. in *Daily Telegraph* · K. Saunders, photograph, repro. in *The Guardian* · photograph, repro. in *The Times* · studio portraits, priv. coll.

Wealth at death £200,000: probate, 1998, *CGPLA Eng. & Wales*

Lloyd, Sir Godfrey (*b.* after **1608**, *d.* **1671**?), military engineer, was the son of Sergeant-Major Brochwel Lloyd of Leighton and Moel-y-Garth, Montgomeryshire, and his wife, Honoria, daughter of Sir Stephen *Procter. Godfrey was a younger brother of Sir Charles *Lloyd (*c.*1602–1661), also a military engineer.

Much of Lloyd's early career was focused on military service abroad. Lloyd, like his father and elder brother, probably served in the Dutch army in the years before the English civil war. Between 1642 and 1644 he was a colonel in the king's northern army commanded by the earl of Newcastle. During the Commonwealth he was a captain of a company of foot in the Dutch service. He is believed to be the Captain Lloyd recalled by James II in his military memoirs as 'a stout choleric Welshman … bred up under the Prince of Orange' and mentioned as the engineer in charge of the approach trenches at the French siege of Condé (Clarke, 1.253). Lloyd, proscribed as a conspirator by the English authorities, was knighted at Brussels by the exiled Charles II in 1657.

Following the Restoration Lloyd was appointed 'chief engineer of all forts, castles and fortifications etc in England and Wales' in succession to his brother on 27 December 1661, with a fee of £240 (*CSP dom., 1661–2*, 129). His petition in 1666 for arrears of pay (£360) mentions that he had left the service of the duke of Lüneburg in order to follow the king's service.

On 12 May 1666 Lloyd was commissioned captain of a company of foot guards in Portsmouth. In the following month he was superintendent of the fortification of Portsmouth Dockyard being built to the designs of Sir Bernard de Gomme. Lloyd was engaged more widely, as on 2 October that year he requested the usual allowance for thirty-nine days' service in the Isle of Wight viewing the forts, castles, and such and making a map of Yarmouth on the isle. Back in the garrison at Portsmouth in December he was again petitioning the king for arrears of pay. In April 1667 he continued to be involved with the fortification of Portsmouth Dockyard as superintendent of the works. In June he reported to the earl of Arlington that the French fleet was said to be in the channel and heading towards Guernsey and Jersey.

In the aftermath of the Dutch raid on the Medway in June 1667 Lloyd was consulted by the king, together with Sir Bernard de Gomme, as the leading military engineers, in respect of the defences of the kingdom. By August he had become involved with the fortification of Sheerness. In that month Robert Slater reported to the navy commissioners that, having gone to Sheerness to survey the ground, the fortifications, and the laying out of the navy yard in order to present them with a 'plot', he was denied permission by Sir Godfrey Lloyd to do so without the king's special order, Lloyd 'having the command of that affair but said he would do it himself and send the first draft to His Majesty' (*CSP dom., 1667*, 387). Lloyd himself was fallible: in July he had confessed to Arlington that in his haste to wait on Prince Rupert at Sheerness he had forgotten to tell the ordnance commissioners that 590 palisades were needed for the fort at West Tilbury, with further timbers required to secure the magazine at Gravesend.

On 17 December 1667 Lloyd was sent £150 towards his travelling charges relating to the fortifications at Portsmouth and Sheerness over the period 24 March to 7 October 1667. He was ordered on 22 January 1668 to prepare an estimate for finishing the fortifications at Sheerness, which he produced a month later. Sir Godfrey Lloyd, 'one of His Majeties Principal Engineers', was by then named as one of the commissioners responsible for managing the works at Sheerness. Shortly afterwards, however, he was dismissed. Charles II, commenting to Pepys on the lack of English-bred engineers, remarked that

> he never remembering any but two in all his time viz. Sir Charles (I think) Floud and Sir Godfrey Floud, the former of whom he said [was] worth very little and the latter … [was]

entrusted with the designing and managing the work at Sheerness, where after spending £2000 the king said he was forced to undo all that he had done and put it into the hand of Sir Bernard Degum. (*Samuel Pepys's Naval Minutes*, 28)

On 2 April 1668 Sir Godfrey was given leave to accept the offer of the post of quartermaster-general to the States and was licensed to pass to the Netherlands and remain there for six months: he was still holding the position of quartermaster-general to the United Provinces when he made his will on 20 January 1670. He maintained his captaincy in a foot company in Colonel John Russell's regiment of guards during 1669, but in February of the following year he was succeeded in the post by Captain Arthur Broughton. During 1670 he was claiming that he had spent £600 of his own money in the king's service since he had left Germany and £480 of his fees as chief engineer were still due to him.

Lloyd appears to have died in 1671 since £360 that were due to him were then paid to his executors. There is a mention that Sir Godfrey Lloyd's lady passed 'by one of our packet boats for Holland on 25 July 1672'. His will (translated from Low Dutch) shows him married to a widow, Catherine Smith, previously married to a Thomas Claypole with whom she had a son, also named Thomas Claypole. The will was witnessed by Adriaen Ruysenaers and Peter Adriaenson Block, lidermen of the lordship of Dongen. ANDREW SAUNDERS

Sources *DNB* • *CSP dom., 1605–6; 1661–2; 1666–72* • *The life of James the Second, king of England*, ed. J. S. Clarke, 2 (1816) • *Le Neve's Pedigrees of the knights*, ed. G. W. Marshall, Harleian Society, 8 (1873), 40 • Pepys, *Diary* • *Samuel Pepys's naval minutes*, ed. J. R. Tanner, Navy Records Society, 60 (1926) • H. C. Tomlinson, *Guns and government* (1979) • W. Porter, *History of the corps of royal engineers*, 2 vols. (1889) • *DWB*, 572 • P. R. Newman, *Royalist officers in England and Wales, 1642–1660: a biographical dictionary* (1981) • will, PRO, PROB 11/339, sig. 78 • ordnance office, estimates relating to Sheerness, PRO, WO 49/180 • ordnance office, entry book, 1660–1668, PRO, WO 55/425

Wealth at death see will, PRO, PROB 11/339, sig. 78

Lloyd, Hannibal Evans (1771–1847), philologist and translator, was born in London, the son of Henry Humphrey Evans *Lloyd (*c*.1718–1783) and his wife, the sister of the Chevalier James de Johnstone. His parents died in his youth, but he was carefully brought up by some near relations, and thrived on a strict programme of studies and activities. He had an extraordinary memory, and was a lover not only of the arts, but of mathematics and science. He visited Europe, and in the spring of 1800 settled at Hamburg. He suffered severely from the hardships that Hamburg endured during its occupation by the French army, and joined the inhabitants in taking up arms in its defence. He eventually escaped, but lost most of his property. On his arrival in England in July 1813 he published, at the suggestion of Lord Bathurst, the foreign secretary, a volume based on his experiences, entitled *Hamburgh, or, A particular account of the transactions which took place in that city during the first six months of 1813*. About the same time he received an appointment in the Foreign Office, the duties of which had previously been divided among several clerks, but Lloyd's competence in continental languages enabled him to discharge them single-handed. He retained the post until his death. Lloyd married a Miss Von Schwartzkopff of Hamburg, who bore him a son and several daughters, including Elizabeth [*see* Thompson, Elizabeth Maria Bowen]. A friend of Klopstock, Lloyd translated under his auspices a large part of *The Messiah*, but did not publish his version. His excellent memory and varied acquirements made him a delightful companion. He wrote elegant Italian verse and corresponded with many eminent travellers and men of science.

Throughout his career in the Foreign Office Lloyd continued to produce many works of a varied nature. He enjoyed biography and historical works, and, capitalizing on his knowledge of European countries, published such works as *Alexander I, Emperor of Russia* (1826), and *Descriptive and Historical Illustrations*, in English and French, accompanying J. Coney's *Architectural Beauties of Continental Europe* (1831–4). Lloyd's linguistic studies were also important: his *Theoretisch-praktische englische Sprachlehre für Deutsche* (1828) ran to four editions, and was long the standard grammar in several German universities. In 1829 he edited a German–English dictionary, and edited or revised several such works during his lifetime. Chief among his own great number of translations are many works of travel literature rendered into English, including Saabye's *Greenland* (1818), Prince Wied-Neuwied's *Travels in Brazil* (1820), Von Kotzebue's *Voyage of Discovery into the South Sea and Beerings Straits* (1821), Timkovsky's *Travels of the Russian Mission through Mongolia to China* (1827), Wolff and Doering's *German Tourist* (1837), Count Bjornstjerna's *British Empire in the East* (1840), Prince Wied-Neuwied's *Travels in the Interior of North America* (1843), and Tam's *Visit to the Portuguese Possessions in South-Western Africa* (1845).

Lloyd was a constant contributor to the *Literary Gazette* from its commencement in 1817, chiefly on foreign archaeology and the fine arts. During the last sixteen months of his life he suffered repeated attacks of 'congestion of the brain' (*GM*), and died at St Germain's Place, Blackheath, Kent, on 14 July 1847.

GORDON GOODWIN, *rev.* JOHN D. HAIGH

Sources *GM*, 2nd ser., 28 (1847), 324–6 • d. cert.

Lloyd, Henry Humphrey Evans (*c*.1718–1783), army officer and military writer, was born the son of a clergyman at Cwm Bychan Farm, in the parish of Llanbedr, Merioneth. He was educated at Jesus College, Oxford. Lloyd hoped to pursue a military career but could not afford to purchase a commission. In 1744 he went to France, where he also failed to secure an officer's posting. Disappointed, he entered a Jesuit college as a lay brother tutoring military officers in geography and field engineering. A year later he left to accompany the French army on an invasion of the Austrian Netherlands during the War of the Austrian Succession (1740–48). Lloyd's sketches of the battlefield of Fontenoy (1745) attracted the attention of the French commanding engineer, and Lloyd received a commission as a junior officer in the engineer corps. With a captain's rank, he then accompanied the forces of Charles Stuart, the Young Pretender, on the ill-fated Jacobite expedition to Scotland (1745–6). Lloyd left the prince's army on a secret mission carrying dispatches to rebel supporters in Wales. Later, disguised as a clergyman, he reconnoitred the south English coast in anticipation of a possible French invasion. Lloyd was arrested (probably under an assumed name since there is no official record of his imprisonment) as a suspected spy and transported to London. His friend John Drummond obtained Lloyd's release and they returned to France. Promoted major, Lloyd distinguished himself in a subsequent French campaign in the Low Countries as an engineer officer at the siege of the Dutch fortress at Bergen op Zoom (1747). Later he entered the Prussian army, but then offered his skills to Marshal Charles Louis Auguste Fouquet de Belle-Isle, returning to French service in 1754. He collected information on the various armies of Europe, subsequently published as *Capt. Lloyd's Lists* (1760). Lloyd then travelled to England disguised as a merchant and conducted another reconnaissance of the British coast for a proposed French landing. When Drummond met him in London in 1756, however, Lloyd claimed to be receiving a pension from the British government of £500 a year (he was never commissioned in the British army; if true, these funds were most likely from secret service moneys).

On his return to the continent Lloyd joined the Austrian army with the rank of lieutenant-colonel. He served as a quartermaster officer on Field Marshal F. M. Lacy's staff in the first campaigns of the Seven Years' War (1756–63). Having achieved the rank of major-general, in 1760 he commanded a reconnaissance force tracking the movements of the Prussian army. That same year Lloyd changed sides and entered the Prussian service under Ferdinand, duke of Brunswick. After the war in Germany ended he attempted to obtain a position with Count Wilhelm Schaumburg-Lippe, who was preparing to defend Portugal against a Spanish invasion. Hostilities ended before Lloyd entered the Portuguese service and instead he returned to England, where he began an intermittent writing career. Colonel David Graeme of Grothy allegedly employed Lloyd in negotiating the marriage of Queen Charlotte and George III. In 1768 Lloyd was again serving the British, conducting a secret mission to Italy to organize supplies for the defence of Corsica. In 1773–4 he commanded a Russian division in combat against the Turks and distinguished himself at the siege of Silistria (1773). He later commanded a Russian force opposing the Swedish. He allegedly quit Russian service after he was refused the order of St Anne because of his common birth. His travels then took him to Italy, Spain, and Gibraltar. Lloyd married a sister of the Chevalier James de Johnstone, details of whom are unknown; they had one son, Hannibal Evans *Lloyd, the philologist and translator.

Lloyd is best remembered as a writer on military strategy. His books include *A Rhapsody of the Present System of French Politics* (1779), in which he set out ways to frustrate a French invasion of Great Britain. After Lloyd's death, British agents allegedly searched his house and removed confidential papers. Lloyd's heirs were later paid by the British government not to publish further editions of his work. Subsequent editions did appear, however, under a different title, *A Political and Military Rhapsody on the Invasion and Defence of Great Britain*, during the invasion scares of 1794 and 1798. Lloyd's most enduring and influential work remains *The history of the late war in Germany between the king of Prussia and the empress of Germany and her allies* (1766). His 'Reflections on the principles of the art of war', also known as 'Political and military memoirs', was added for the second edition (1781). The *History* was translated into at least five German and three French editions, the most famous by Georg Fredrich von Templehoff (1783). A second volume of the work, compiled from Lloyd's papers after his death, was published in 1784. In these works rests Lloyd's reputation as the father of the principles of modern warfare. It was his belief that 'this [military] art, like all others is founded on certain fixed principles which are by their nature invariable' (Alger, 19). Lloyd's military principles referred mainly to the organization of armies and the conduct of operations, many of which he based on mathematical calculations. His enunciation of the principles of war reflected the French military school, particularly the writings of Field Marshal Maurice de Saxe (under whom Lloyd had served in 1745), and the philosophy of the Enlightenment which advocated that rational, scientific rules could be derived to predict human behaviour. Among his acquaintances, Lloyd served for a period (1759) with a well-known Milanese exponent of Enlightenment philosophy, Pietro Verri, and the two thinkers undoubtedly influenced one another. Lloyd's other works included *An Essay on the English Constitution* (1770), an elaboration on the balance of power between monarchy, aristocracy, and democracy (another manuscript on this subject, 'Essai philosophique sur les governments', remained unpublished), and *An Essay on the Theory of Money* (1771), a defence of the use of paper money.

Henry Lloyd had significant influence on military leaders and theorists in Europe and in colonial America. General George Washington, commander of the colonial army during the American War of Independence, had a well-read copy of *Political and Military Rhapsody* in his library. While Napoleon called Lloyd's military theories absurd, Antoine-Henri de Jomini, the best-known contemporary analyst of Napoleon's campaigns, credited Lloyd in his *Traité de grande tactique* (1803), and plagiarized much of Lloyd's work in the text. Carl von Clausewitz, in his major work *Vom Kriege* (1832–7), rejected Lloyd's dogmatic approach to military operations for a more comprehensive theory of warfare emphasizing the interplay between the state, politics, chance, individual action, and military affairs.

In the twentieth century Lloyd's theories were influential on the writings of Colonel J. F. C. Fuller. Fuller, reflecting on the military disasters of trench warfare in the First World War, believed that reviving Lloyd's principles might be instructive to future military leaders. The American Second World War general George S. Patton, who led the US Third Army during the allied campaign in Europe (1944–5), retained a dog-eared copy of Lloyd's *History* in his extensive professional library. Although the notion of fixed, inviolable principles of war has long gone out of fashion in Western armies, many still retain principles of war in their doctrine as broad guidelines for the conduct of warfare. Lloyd died at The Hague on 19 June 1783. JAMES JAY CARAFANO

Sources A. Gat, *The origins of military thought* (1989) • F. Venturi, 'Le avventure del generale Henry Lloyd', *Rivista Storia Italiana*, 91 (1979), 369–433 • T. R. Roberts, *Eminent Welshmen: a short biographical dictionary* (1908) • J. Alger, *The quest for victory: the history of the principles of war* (1982) • J. Eltins, 'Jomini: disciple of Napoleon', *Military Affairs*, 28 (spring 1964), 17–26 • S. E. Dietrich, 'The professional readings of General George S. Patton jr', *Journal of Military History*, 53 (Oct 1989), 387–418 • B. Holden Reid, 'Colonel J. F. C. Fuller and the revival of classical military thinking in Britain, 1918–1926', *Military Affairs*, 49 (Oct 1985), 192–7 • O. L. Spaulding, 'The military studies of George Washington', *American Historical Review*, 29 (1923–4), 675–80
Archives FM Cam.

Lloyd, Sir Herbert, first baronet (**1720–1769**), politician and landowner, born on 22 July 1720 at Peterwell, Lampeter, Cardiganshire, was the third of five surviving children of Walter Lloyd (1678?–1747) and his wife, Elizabeth Evans (*d.* 1743), daughter of Daniel Evans of Peterwell, a wealthy landowner. His father, a whig supporter, was appointed the local law officer of the crown after the Hanoverian succession, and served as MP for Cardiganshire from 1734 to 1742. Educated initially at home, Lloyd studied at Jesus College, Oxford (1738–40), and proceeded to the Inner Temple. He was called to the bar in 1742. He married in 1742 Elizabeth Bragge of Essex, who died the following year. In 1745 he married Ann (1702–1778), daughter of William Powell of Nanteos, Cardiganshire, and widow of Richard Stedman of Great Abbey, Strata Florida. They took up residence at Foelallt, Llanddewibrefi. Although an Anglican Lloyd had some early sympathy with the Methodists and was friendly with Howel Harris, one of the founders of Welsh Methodism. On the death of his brother John, MP for Cardiganshire, in 1755, he inherited the Peterwell and Llechwedd Dderi estates. Together with Foelallt, this made him a substantial landowner.

Herbert Lloyd became notorious for his irascible nature and oppressive behaviour. Appointed a JP at an early age, he soon acquired a reputation for harshness. Lloyd's intemperate behaviour led to his being struck out of the commission of the peace in 1755, and his treatment of Ann, his second wife, caused her to leave him. He is associated with falsely accusing Siôn Philip, a freeholder, of stealing his prized black ram and of securing his execution at Cardigan in order to acquire his land. He harboured political ambitions but was persuaded by the Newcastle administration to stand aside, in favour of another, in the contest to succeed his brother as MP in 1755. At that time his rival, Wilmot Vaugham, wrote to Newcastle that 'The views of the present Mr Lloyd of Peterwell are so very extensive, his principles so little fixed, and his whole character so unstable' (HoP, *Commons, 1754–90*, 47). However, Lloyd was finally elected to parliament in 1761 as member for the Cardigan Boroughs. He sought to ingratiate himself with the prime minister, the duke of Newcastle, and with his successor, the earl of Bute, and was granted a baronetcy in January 1763. The title served to increase his unpopularity among the Cardiganshire gentry and they began to refer to him as the Vulture Knight.

Lloyd's parliamentary career was inauspicious, but he was one of those members who favoured the ending of the Seven Years' War. Lloyd approved of the expulsion of John Wilkes from parliament in 1764; but he was listed by the marquess of Rockingham as 'doubtful' in July 1765. On 22 February 1766 he voted against the administration's bill to repeal the Stamp Act. He nevertheless seems to have supported the administration of William Pitt the elder. Having alienated his local political allies due to his erratic behaviour, Lloyd declined to contest the 1768 election. Following the death of the successful member, however, Lloyd again offered himself as a candidate in the by-election held in January 1769, but was defeated. He challenged the result, but unsuccessfully petitioned the committee of privileges and elections to have it overturned. Having spent vast sums of money on his mansion at Peterwell, and with his political career now in ruins, he faced increasing financial problems. Allied to this, his excesses over the years had greatly affected his health. He frequently visited the gaming tables in London in vain attempts to recoup his losses. During one of these visits, shortly before his death, Lloyd bigamously married a Mrs Bacon of Bishop Auckland. There were also regular visits to take the waters at Bath.

On one of these journeys Sir Herbert was taken ill and died *en route* for Bath on 20 August 1769. His body was returned to Peterwell and he was interred with due pomp at midnight on 3 September 1769 in the family vault at St Peter's Church, Lampeter. It appears that he died of natural causes and there is no foundation to the tradition that he committed suicide in London. As Lloyd had no children, Peterwell passed to his nephew, John Adams of Whitland. The estate had been heavily mortgaged to the sum of £54,000 and it was sold on 24 September 1781 to Albany Wallis, a London lawyer. BETHAN PHILLIPS

Sources B. Phillips, *Peterwell, the history of a mansion and its infamous squire* (1983) • HoP, *Commons, 1754–90* • HoP, *Commons, 1715–54* • parish register, Lampeter, NL Wales • Foster, *Alum. Oxon.* • P. D. G. Thomas, 'Society, government and politics', *Wales in the eighteenth century*, ed. D. Moore (1976) • P. D. G. Thomas, 'Eighteenth century elections in the Cardigan Boroughs constituency', *Ceredigion* [Cardiganshire Antiquarian Society], 5 (1967), 402–21 • NL Wales, Gogerddan papers • incriptions, Strata Florida church
Archives BL, Newcastle MSS, Add. MS 32855, fol. 346 • NL Wales, Dolaucothi MSS • NL Wales, Falcondale MSS, 15–19 • NL Wales, Peterwell MSS • NL Wales, Powis Castle MSS, 2995, 3189, 3246 • NL Wales, Trevecka letters, 572
Likenesses A. Ramsay, oils, Yale U. CBA, Paul Mellon collection • J. Zoffany, oils, National Trust collection
Wealth at death estate mortgaged to sum of £54,000: NL Wales, Gogerddan papers

Lloyd [*née* Shufflebotham], **Dame Hilda Nora** (**1891–1982**), gynaecologist and obstetrician, was born on 11 August 1891 at 170 Moseley Road, Balsall Heath, Birmingham, the younger daughter of John Shufflebotham (*d.* 1937), a master grocer, and his wife, Emma Amelia Jenkins. She was a foundation scholar at King Edward VI High School for

Girls, Birmingham, where she was educated from 1902 to 1910 before graduating BSc (1914) and MB, BCh (1916) at Birmingham University. Further postgraduate training at the London Hospital brought her the conjoint diploma of MRCP and LRCP (1918). Hilda Shufflebotham returned to Birmingham as a resident in obstetrics and gynaecology. She became FRCS (1920) and consultant and senior surgeon on the staff of the Maternity and Women's hospitals in Birmingham. Kind to junior colleagues and patients, she displayed skilful dexterity, speed, and energy both in private and in hospital practice. On 27 December 1930 she married Bertram Arthur Lloyd (1884–1948), a former captain in the Royal Army Medical Corps (1915–19) and professor of forensic medicine at Birmingham University (1932–42), the son of Walter John Lloyd; there were no children from the marriage.

Hilda Lloyd pioneered an obstetrical flying squad, which saved many mothers and babies in Birmingham, and understood the dangers of poverty, venereal disease, and illegal abortion. Her interests were clinical and practical, but she believed that innovations should be shared in her profession, and was a founder member of the Women's Visiting Gynaecological Club (1936). Her published papers included 'Observations on 380 cases of induction of labour' (*Journal of the Obstetricians and Gynaecologists of the British Empire*, 37, 1930, 860) and 'The management of the third stage of labour and haemorrhage therein' (ibid., 55, 1948; *Proceedings of the Royal Society of Medicine*, 4.370–76). She became university lecturer at Birmingham in 1934, professor in 1944, and was chair of obstetrics and gynaecology from 1946 to 1951. In 1948 Hilda Lloyd became president of the obstetrical and gynaecological section of the Royal Society of Medicine, serving on the board of governors of the united Birmingham hospitals and medical advisory committee attached. In the National Health Service (NHS) she was a member of the maternity committee of the regional board (midlands area), the planning, cancer and radiotherapy, and transfusion regional boards, and was on the advisory board of the Royal College of Nursing, work which greatly interested her.

As fellow of the Royal College of Obstetricians and Gynaecologists (1936) Hilda Lloyd served as council member and examiner for the college. In 1949 she was elected first woman president of the college. Her tact won over the opposition, and two subsequent re-elections were unanimous. A slender, fair woman, she presided gracefully at political and social occasions, including the presentation of Princess Elizabeth as honorary fellow (1951). Among her achievements was a new and more widely circulated journal (1950). In 1952 she led opposition to the separation of obstetrics and gynaecology in the NHS and their under-representation on regional boards, and developed the idea of midwifery committees in each region to unify services. Dame Hilda, as she became in 1951, arranged a compromise on remuneration involving the joint consultants' committee and the Whitley Council, ensuring that the Royal College had a representative on the General Medical Council (GMC) and examining boards in Britain. Nominated as first representative of the GMC by the Royal College, she lost a battle to ensure that obstetrics should follow after the pre-registration year of hospital appointments (1951).

Widowed in 1948, Hilda Lloyd married a widower surgical colleague, Baron Theodore Rose (1892–1978), in the following year. They retired to Herefordshire to enjoy country pursuits. Dame Hilda lectured for the Medical Women's Federation on domiciliary midwifery, and for the Royal Sanitary Institute on the need to offer contraceptive advice in post-natal clinics to mothers who 'live in fear' (*Liverpool Echo*, 27 April 1954). She was a vice-president of the Family Planning Association (1949) and opposed its becoming part of the NHS on grounds of patient confidentiality. As a member of the Medico-Legal Society she was concerned at attacks on some fertility treatments and early pregnancy diagnosis, advising on cervical smears and the contraceptive pill. She was a member of the medical manpower committee (1955–6). She received doctorates in law from Birmingham and Leeds universities, but she declared the presentation made to her by the Medical Women's Federation 'The greatest pleasure' of her professional life (*BMJ*, 10 Nov 1951). Baron Rose died in 1978 and Dame Hilda moved to Broome House, Clent, Worcestershire, where she died on 18 July 1982 after a stroke. A funeral service was held at Broome church on 20 July 1982 after which her body was cremated; she had been a regular churchgoer. Substantial legacies to the Medical Women's Federation, the NSPCC, and RSPCA indicated her concerns. Her outstanding career in medicine was a successful struggle to reverse the disadvantages under which women suffered, and was commemorated in 1985 by a memorial plaque at the Birmingham hospitals.

V. E. Chancellor

Sources J. Peel, *The lives of the fellows of the Royal College of Obstetricians and Gynaecologists, 1929–1969* (1976) • *Golden jubilee year, 1929–1979*, Royal College of Obstetricians and Gynaecologists (1980) • J. M. M. Kerr, R. W. Johnstone, and M. H. Phillips, *Historical review of British obstetrics and gynaecology, 1800–1950* (1954) • D'A. Power and W. R. Le Fanu, *Lives of the fellows of the Royal College of Surgeons of England, 1930–1951* (1953) • E. H. Cornelius and S. F. Taylor, *Lives of the fellows of the Royal College of Surgeons of England, 1974–1982* (1988) • J. Barnes, 'Personal memoir of Hilda Nora Lloyd', *Women in Medicine*, 2/1 (1983), 28–9 • *BMJ* (10 Nov 1951), 1146 • *BMJ* (7 Aug 1982), 449 • *Journal of the Obstetricians and Gynaecologists of the British Empire*, 36 (1930) • *Journal of the Obstetricians and Gynaecologists of the British Empire*, 40 (1933) • *Journal of the Obstetricians and Gynaecologists of the British Empire*, 55 (1948) • *Medical Women's Federation Quarterly Review* (1935–42), esp. (Oct. 1941), 38–9 • *The Lancet* (7 Aug 1982) • *Birmingham Evening Mail* (12 Aug 1985) • *Sandwell Evening Mail* (8 Aug 1985) • S. Coetzee, *Birmingham Post* (2 Aug 1982) • *The Times* (21 July 1982) • *Hereford Times* (31 Dec 1982) • *The Phoenix* [magazine of King Edward VI High School for Girls, Birmingham] (1953–5) • W. F. Shaw, *Twenty-five years: the story of the Royal College of Obstetricians and Gynaecologists, 1929–1954* (1954) • *Liverpool Echo* (27 April 1954) • b. cert. • m. cert.

Archives Royal College of Obstetricians and Gynaecologists, London, corresp. and MSS • Wellcome L., MSS relating to the Women's Medical Federation, C114, J4/1, A 14/142, F 4/2 | King Edward VI Foundation, Birmingham, archive • U. Birm. L., special collections department

Likenesses A. Devas, oils, 1952, Royal Society of Obstetricians and Gynaecologists, London; copy, Women's Medical Federation •

J. Epstein, bronze bust, U. Birm., medical school • photographs, repro. in *Golden Jubilee year book*, Royal College of Obstetricians and Gynaecologists, p. 12 • photographs, Women's Medical Federation

Wealth at death £836,225: probate; *Hereford Times* (31 Dec 1982)

Lloyd, Hugh (1546–1601), headmaster, was born in Llŷn, Caernarvonshire. Nothing is known of his parents but there were at least two other sons and a daughter of the marriage. He was elected a scholar of Winchester College in 1560, as was his brother John in 1574. They were only two of numerous Welshmen who entered the college in Elizabeth's reign, an upsurge perhaps resulting from the Act of Union in 1536. He proceeded to New College, Oxford, in 1562, becoming a fellow in 1564. He graduated BA in 1566, BCL in 1570, and DCL in 1588. He married at an unknown date; nothing is known of his wife except that she survived him. He resigned his fellowship in 1578 on his appointment as chancellor of Rochester.

In 1579 Lloyd became vicar of Charlbury, Oxfordshire, and was elected headmaster of Winchester College. In the latter case he had attracted the support of Ambrose Dudley, earl of Warwick, who wrote to the warden and fellows of Winchester that his recommendation was hardly needed when Lloyd was 'so well known unto you all for his lyfe, religion, and learninge' (Winchester College muniment 23443). As headmaster his teaching of classics seems to have had a certain breadth: one of his pupils was John Owen, the noted writer of epigrams, and another was the poet and wit John Hoskins (whom Lloyd remembered in his will). Lloyd himself compiled *Phrases elegantiores ex Caesaris commentariis Cicerone, aliisque, in usum scholae Winton*, although this was not published until 1654.

In 1584 Lloyd was made a prebendary of St Paul's and in 1588 he resigned as headmaster on becoming rector of Islip, near Oxford. There he maintained his intellectual interests through contact with a number of academics, particularly from St John's College and New College. Two of them—Ralph Hutchinson, the biblical scholar, and Anthony Ayleworth, regius professor of medicine—were made his executors. Lloyd died on 17 October 1601 and was buried in the outer chapel of New College.

R. D. H. Custance

Sources Foster, *Alum. Oxon.* • A. F. Leach, *A history of Winchester College* (1899) • will, PRO, PROB 11/98, sig. 86 • Winchester College Archives, WCM 23443 • *DNB*

Wealth at death approx. £120 in money; plus silver and books: will, PRO, PROB 11/98, sig. 86

Lloyd, Hugh (1588/9–1667), bishop of Llandaff, was born in Cardiganshire; his parents have not been identified. Having matriculated as a servitor of Oriel College, Oxford, in 1607, he graduated BA on 12 November 1611 and proceeded MA on 30 June 1614, by which time he had been ordained. He was elected to a fellowship of Jesus College, Oxford, and proceeded BD in 1624 and DD in 1638. He became rector of St Andrews, Glamorgan, in 1617 and rector of St Nicholas in the same county in 1628. He was presented to the sinecure rectory of Denbigh in 1637 and to the rectory of Hirnant, Montgomeryshire, in 1638. He was appointed a canon and archdeacon of St David's on 19 October 1644.

There is scant trace of Lloyd during the civil wars and interregnum. Walker claimed that his benefices were sequestered and that he was allowed the customary fifth of his income for some years, but Matthews does not record him as a 'sufferer'. In 1660 Lloyd was appointed to the see of Llandaff, perhaps principally because of his long-standing connection with the diocese and because the political situation needed appointees of such uncontroversial 'obscurity' (Green, 95–6). Lloyd was also restored to the archdeaconry of St David's, which he held *in commendam*, and to his livings in Glamorgan and Montgomeryshire; he became a prebendary of Llandaff in 1660 and rector of Llangattock, Brecknockshire, in 1661. As bishop Lloyd left little mark. In October 1662 he wrote to his clergy urging them to manifest their religious zeal and their political loyalty in supporting free schools. White Kennett records some signs of Lloyd's concern to reconcile nonconforming clergy, such as Samuel Jones, former fellow of Jesus College and minister of Llangynwyd, and of his leniency. Lloyd allowed Richard Hawes, ejected minister of Leintwardine, to preach in public without subscription. Lloyd died in Llandaff at the age of seventy-eight on 7 June 1667 and was buried in the dilapidated Llandaff Cathedral.

John Spurr

Sources Foster, *Alum. Oxon.* • *Calamy rev.*, 253 • Wood, *Ath. Oxon.*, new edn, 4.834–6 • *Fasti Angl.* (Hardy), 1.309; 2.26, 254 • W. Kennett, *A register and chronicle ecclesiastical and civil* (1728), 315–16, 815, 816 • I. M. Green, *The re-establishment of the Church of England, 1660–1663* (1978) • G. Williams, ed., *Glamorgan county history*, 4: *Early modern Glamorgan* (1974)

Lloyd, Sir Hugh Pughe (1894–1981), air force officer, was born on 12 December 1894 at Leigh, Worcestershire, the third of the four sons and third of the six children of Lewis Thomas Lloyd, a schoolmaster of Leigh, and his wife, Anne Pughe. From King's School, Worcester, he went to Peterhouse, Cambridge, in 1913 and studied law before enlisting as a private in the Royal Engineers in February 1915.

On the western front Lloyd served as a dispatch rider and was wounded three times before being commissioned in the Royal Flying Corps in April 1917. From January 1918 he was a bomber reconnaissance pilot with 52 squadron. He soon distinguished himself, and in quick succession won the MC, the Croix de Guerre, and the DFC. In August 1919 he was granted a permanent commission in the Royal Air Force. The following month he married Kathleen (*d.* 1976), the daughter of Major Robert Thornton Meadows DSO, an army doctor. At the end of the year he was posted to India, where the only child of the marriage, a daughter, was born.

After four years mainly as a flight commander with 28 squadron, Lloyd returned home in 1924. During the next five years he flew with 16 squadron, passed through the RAF Staff College, and served for three years on the staff of a training group (23). Promoted squadron leader, he was then for nearly a year chief flying instructor at 2 flying training school. Clearly marked out for senior posts, he was next sent out to take the Staff College course at Quetta (1931–2). Three years on the air staff at headquarters 1 Indian group at Peshawar followed. His two spells in India brought him operational experience on the north-west frontier and mentions in dispatches.

Back in England, Lloyd became senior RAF instructor at the Staff College, Camberley (1936–8), and then commanded 9 (bomber) squadron. Soon after the outbreak of war he was given command, as a group captain, of the bomber station at Marham, but he was quickly summoned to air staff duties at the headquarters of Bomber Command. On 20 May 1940 he became senior air staff officer at 2 (bomber) group, where he organized many strikes against German shipping. This made him an ideal choice for his next post. On 1 June 1941, with the rank of air vice-marshal, he took over command of RAF Mediterranean at Malta. Its resources were pitifully small, and reinforcement appallingly difficult, but Lloyd's determination to maintain an offensive never faltered. Despite all the Italian and German bombing, which by June 1942 brought the island to the verge of starvation, Malta remained unsubdued. Throughout it all Lloyd kept the island in use as a staging post for bombers reinforcing RAF Middle East, and—except briefly during the very worst of the German air assault—he kept up attacks on the axis shipping lanes across the Mediterranean. The result, in conjunction with the work of the submarines, was the denial of vital supplies to the axis forces in north Africa and an easier task for the British Eighth Army. Of these experiences, Lloyd left a vivid account in his book *Briefed to Attack* (1949).

Lloyd left his Malta command on 15 July 1942 to become senior air staff officer at RAF Middle East and then, from March 1943, commanded the newly formed north-west African coastal air forces. In this role he again waged a successful offensive against axis shipping. For his work from 1941 onwards he received many honours. He was appointed CBE in 1941, CB and KBE in 1942, officer of the French Légion d'honneur in 1943 (commander in 1945), and officer of the American Legion of Merit in 1944. After the war he received an honorary degree from the University of Wales.

At the end of 1944 Lloyd returned to England. In July 1945 he was appointed, as acting air marshal, to command Tiger Force, the long-range RAF bomber group intended to join the Americans in their air assault on Japan. The dropping of the two atomic bombs, however, obviated the need for this. For two years Lloyd was then RAF instructor at the Imperial Defence College before being sent out to command the RAF in the Far East (1947–9). Finally, in 1950, he was entrusted with Bomber Command, which benefited greatly from his drive. He was appointed air chief marshal and KCB in 1951 and retired in 1953.

Following his retirement Lloyd reared pigs and poultry on a small farm in Buckinghamshire. His chief recreations were sailing and riding. Among voluntary activities he was for more than twenty-five years a very active president of the Polish Air Force Association and of the RAF Association, Wales.

In manner, Lloyd had something of the air of an attractive buccaneer. His intensely light blue eyes had a normally smiling look but could fix an offender with a laser-like probe. He had the great gift of making people feel that they were the sole subject of his attention. He was popular—he was known throughout the service as Hugh Pughe or Hughie Pughie—and extremely brave and tough. His humour, virility, and outgoing character to some extent masked his more intellectual qualities: in the 1920s he had gained high awards in the RAF's most prestigious essay competitions, and he was a respected instructor at the staff colleges. He died on 13 July 1981 at Cheltenham.

DENIS RICHARDS, *rev.*

Sources H. P. Lloyd, *Briefed to attack* (1949) • *The Times* (15 July 1981) • personal knowledge (1990) • private information (1990)
Archives Royal Air Force Museum, Hendon, papers | FILM IWM FVA, actuality footage | SOUND IWM SA, oral history interview
Wealth at death £174,713: probate, 30 Dec 1981, *CGPLA Eng. & Wales*

Lloyd, Humphrey (1610–1689), bishop of Bangor, was born in July or August 1610 at Bod-y-fudden in the parish of Trawsfynydd, Merioneth, the third son of Richard Lloyd DD (1573/4–1647?), vicar of Ruabon, Denbighshire, and his wife, Jane (*d.* in or after 1648), daughter of Rhydderch Hughes, another cleric. He matriculated from Jesus College, Oxford, on 25 January 1628, but it was from Oriel College that he graduated BA on 23 January 1630. In 1631 he became a fellow of Oriel, where he remained a tutor for many years, and proceeded MA on 12 May 1635.

When parliament's lord lieutenant of Oxfordshire, Lord Saye, visited Oxford in September 1642 Lloyd was 'kept as a prisoner at *the Starre*, for some words uttered by him to this effect that "if he was able he had rather lend the king a thousand pound than one penny to the parliament"' (*Life and Times of Anthony Wood*, 1.62). Lloyd was chaplain to John Williams, archbishop of York, who, on 9 April 1644, presented him to the prebend of Ampleforth, but his installation was prevented by the advance of the Scottish army. On 10 June 1647 the House of Lords ordered that he be installed as vicar of Ruabon following the death of the previous incumbent, possibly his father, 'he taking the National League and Covenant' (*JHL*, 9.252). Presumably Lloyd did not in the event take the covenant because he either did not take possession of Ruabon or else he was deprived of it soon afterwards.

At some point following the death of Edward Brereton in 1644, and before 1650 or 1651 when a son was born, Lloyd married his widow, Jane (*d.* 1689), daughter of John Griffith of Cefnamwlch, Caernarvonshire. They had at least three sons, John, Francis, and Richard. His stepson was Edward Brereton, MP for Denbigh Boroughs between 1689 and 1705. Following the Restoration Lloyd returned to Ruabon. In a petition of 1660 he sought confirmation for his prebend at York and also for the archdeaconry of Nottingham. He was presented by the king to the prebend of Ampleforth on 30 July 1660, and installed on 22 September. In another petition of 1660 he enlisted the support of Gilbert Sheldon to ask for the deanery of Bangor, which was not in fact vacant. On 12 September 1661 Lloyd was created DD. In the same year he became vicar of Northop, Flintshire (which he resigned in December 1664) and cursal canon of St Asaph. He was collated dean of St Asaph on 14 December 1663.

In 1673 Lloyd left Ruabon to succeed his brother, Samuel, at Gresford, Denbighshire. On 10 September 1673 a warrant for a *congé d'élire* was issued to elect Lloyd bishop of Bangor. On 23 October he was granted permission to hold the archdeaconries of Bangor and Anglesey, the vicarage of Gresford, and the prebend of Ampleforth together with his bishopric. He was enthroned by proxy on 5 January 1674, and the following day a writ was issued summoning him to sit in the House of Lords. He voted by proxy on 20 November 1675 against addressing the king to dissolve parliament. In 1676 he became a canon of Bangor.

In 1685 Lloyd procured the archdeaconries of Bangor and Anglesey and the sinecure of Llanraeadr-yng-Nghinmeirch, Denbighshire, to be annexed to the bishopric. Lloyd's episcopate was marked by his firm maintenance of the rights of the Church of England and his unbending hostility to dissent. He distrusted the missionary activities in Wales of the presbyterian Thomas Gouge, whose attempts to dispel popular ignorance and spread the protestant word in the dark corners of the land were supported by both nonconformists and moderate Anglicans, and who had sought Lloyd's support for his Welsh edition of the Bible. To Lloyd Gouge was using his preaching tours to sow sedition and religious disaffection in the minds of the gentry and of the 'credulous common people' (Jenkins, 184). Lloyd made his will, 'sick and weake in body', on 22 December 1686, adding a codicil on 9 January 1689. He died on 18 January 1689 and was buried in Bangor Cathedral. STUART HANDLEY

Sources Wood, *Ath. Oxon.*, new edn, 4.873–4 • Foster, *Alum. Oxon.* • *Fasti Angl., 1541–1857*, [York] • *Fasti Angl.* (Hardy), vol. 1 • *CSP dom., 1660–73* • *The life and times of Anthony Wood*, ed. A. Clark, 5 vols., OHS, 19, 21, 26, 30, 40 (1891–1900) • J. E. Griffith, *Pedigrees of Anglesey and Carnarvonshire families* (privately printed, Horncastle, 1914), 7 • PRO, PROB 11/394, sig. 28, fols. 221v–222v • *JHL*, 9 (1646–7), 252 • R. Davis, 'The "presbyterian" opposition and the emergence of party in the House of Lords', *Party and management in parliament, 1660–1784*, ed. C. Jones (1984), 1–35 • G. H. Jenkins, *The foundations of modern Wales, 1642–1780* (1993)

Lloyd, Humphrey (1800–1881), physicist and university administrator, was born on 16 April 1800, at Dublin, the eldest son of the Revd Bartholomew *Lloyd (1772–1837), later provost of Trinity College, Dublin, and his wife, Eleanor McLaughlin. Having received his early education at Mr White's school, Dublin, he entered Trinity College, Dublin, in 1815, gaining first prize, out of sixty-three competitors, at the entrance examination, then entirely classical. He profited greatly from the renaissance in mathematical education initiated at the college by his father. Following a brilliant undergraduate career, during which he obtained a scholarship in 1818, he graduated BA in 1819, taking first place and the gold medal for science, and proceeded MA in 1827, and DD in 1840. He became a junior fellow in 1824 and a senior fellow in 1843. He devoted himself especially to scientific studies and in 1831 succeeded his father as Erasmus Smith's professor of natural and experimental philosophy. During his tenure of this chair he sought successfully to improve the position of physical science in the university. Following the abolition of celibacy rules for fellows, he married, in July 1840, Dorothea, only daughter of the Revd James Bulwer, rector of Hunworth-cum-Stody, Norfolk. They had no children.

In physical optics Lloyd made a number of noteworthy contributions. The first of these, in December 1832, was the experimental proof of existence of conical refraction in a crystal of aragonite following a prediction arising from a mathematical investigation of the Fresnel wave surface in biaxial crystals by his colleague William Rowan Hamilton. He demonstrated two species of conical refraction and established the law governing the polarization of the rays. Of significance also was the preparation of a substantial report, 'The progress and present state of physical optics' (*Report of the British Association for the Advancement of Science*, 1834). Another success followed shortly afterwards (published 1837) when he demonstrated the interference of light passing directly from a luminous source with that coming from the same source but reflected at an angle of incidence of nearly 90° from a plane surface. This variation of Fresnel's famous twin-mirror experiment was regarded as further proof of the correctness of the wave theory of light of which Lloyd was an ardent supporter. He also investigated the phenomena of light incident on thin plates. In 1841 he submitted a communication on the subject to the British Association and in 1859 he described his complete investigation of the phenomena to the Royal Irish Academy.

Investigation of the earth's magnetic field was Lloyd's primary research interest from the mid-1830s. Working under the aegis of the British Association he achieved prominence in the field of instrumentation. Having devised a method for measuring dip and relative intensity with a single instrument, he carried out, in collaboration with Edward Sabine and James Clerk Ross, a magnetic survey of Ireland in 1834 and 1835. In the two following years this work was extended to Scotland, England, and Wales. At the end of 1835 he established contact with Carl Friedrich Gauss of Göttingen, who, in developing the theory and technique of absolute measurement of the earth's field, had established geomagnetic investigation on a new foundation.

Lloyd resolved to join the organization of observing stations established by the Hanoverian mathematician over the northern hemisphere. An observatory was built at Trinity College, Dublin, in 1837–8 and fitted out with instruments of Lloyd's design, operating on Gaussian principles and constructed for the most part by Thomas Grubb of Dublin. This became the prototype for a series of similar observatories in Britain and the colonies, established, on the recommendation of the Royal Society, by the government and the East India Company. These, like the Antarctic expedition (1839–43) led by Ross, were provided with instruments similar to those of Lloyd, and the observers received practical training from him at Dublin.

This worldwide network of observing stations superseded Gauss's earlier organization and many continental stations joined the association. In all thirty-three observatories were established or re-equipped with instruments of Lloyd's design and the work was continued for nine years (1839–48). For the Arctic expeditions of Sir John Franklin in 1845 and of Sir John Richardson and Sir James Ross in 1848 Lloyd designed an instrument to be used by travelling observers and by mariners.

Many papers which Lloyd wrote on these and other subjects, such as meteorology, are to be found in the *Reports* of the British Association and in the *Transactions* and *Proceedings* of the Royal Irish Academy. Of the latter body he was president from 1846 to 1851, and in 1862 he was awarded its Cunningham gold medal. He resigned his chair of natural philosophy in 1843, on his accession to a senior fellowship in Trinity College. In 1862 he became vice-provost, and in 1867 provost of the college. He was president of the British Association in 1857, when it met in Dublin, a fellow of the Royal societies of London and Edinburgh, and an honorary member of many other learned societies of Europe and America. In 1855 the University of Oxford conferred on him the degree of DCL.

Lloyd journeyed on at least four occasions to the continent. Accompanied by Sabine, he visited Berlin, Leipzig, and Göttingen in the autumn of 1839, and met important scientists such as Gauss, Wilhelm Weber, and Alexander von Humboldt. Following his marriage in the second week of July 1840 Lloyd and his wife travelled through Switzerland, northern Italy, Tyrol, and Bavaria. They visited observatories at Milan and Munich, and joined the meeting of the Italian Physical Society at Turin in September before reaching the Brussels observatory about 24 October. In the summer of 1841 he travelled with his wife to Paris to study the French system of training engineers. On a further tour with his wife he visited Berlin in early October 1849 as president of the Royal Irish Academy and was received there by von Humboldt. In 1874 the emperor of Germany awarded him the Order of Merit.

In university administration, and in educational and ecclesiastical policy, Lloyd was a man of firm principle who was open to reform and innovation. In 1860 he published anonymously a pamphlet entitled *Is it a Sin?* in which—diverging from the majority view held by his fellow Irish Anglicans—he advocated participation, at least in principle, of the Irish church in the national education board that was concerned with the organization of primary education in Ireland. This led to an invitation in the same year for him to join the board but he declined. The biggest issue he had to face as provost of Trinity College was the political pressure for change in its status following the enactment of Gladstone's Irish Church Act of 1869 (effective, 1 January 1871) that disestablished the episcopal Church of Ireland. It was evident to him that the educational advantages hitherto enjoyed by members of his church would have to be shared by protestant dissenters and the majority Roman Catholic population. He welcomed the passing of the University of Dublin Tests Act in 1873, which abolished remaining religious tests in the college, in preference to legislation that might have partitioned the endowments of the college among several denominational colleges and transferred its university powers to a nominated senate.

Lloyd was a leading member of the general synod of the disestablished Church of Ireland and he contributed in the 1870s to debate on the revision of the church prayer book, particularly on the issue of absolution. His views on this subject, published in pamphlets entitled *Doctrine of Absolution* (anonymous, 1871), and *The Power of the Keys* (1873), were close to those of the evangelical, anti-sacerdotal wing of the church.

Lloyd, like his father, may be regarded as a progressive educator of the nineteenth century. His scientific philosophy was firmly Baconian and his commitment to the scientific method and the central role of experiment was already evident in his *Two Introductory Lectures on Physical and Mechanical Science* of 1834. He was primarily responsible, in 1850, for the introduction of the first science moderatorship (equivalent to Cambridge tripos) in experimental physics and was the founder of a tradition of scientific research, particularly in physics, within the University of Dublin. He contributed to the advancement of science and engineering education in the university, was instrumental in the establishment of the school of engineering that opened in November 1841, and helped to create chairs of geology and mineralogy and of applied chemistry. His mature philosophy of education is revealed in a pamphlet, *Brief Suggestions in Reference to the Undergraduate Curriculum in Trinity College*, published anonymously in 1869, in which he stressed the importance of mental training, of preparation for professional life, and of a broad and varied curriculum combined with a freedom of choice for advanced students. He advocated that English language and literature, and the sciences, should occupy a more prominent place at the expense of mathematics and classics that had previously dominated undergraduate studies.

Lloyd died at his residence, Provost's House, Trinity College, on 17 January 1881. He published, in addition to a circular for directors of magnetic observatories and university addresses and lectures, a total of eight textbooks or monographs and sixty-four papers (three jointly with others) on scientific topics (including reports to the British Association). A translation of his 'The progress and present state of physical optics' (*Report of the British Association for the Advancement of Science*, 1834) was published in Berlin (1836). His more important publications include *A Treatise on Light and Vision* (1831), *The Elements of Optics* (1849), and *Treatise on Magnetism, General and Terrestrial* (1874).

James G. O'Hara

Sources *DNB* • J. G. O'Hara, 'Humphrey Lloyd (1800–1881) and the Dublin mathematical school of the nineteenth century', PhD diss., University of Manchester Institute of Science and Technology, 1979 • T. D. Spearman, 'Humphrey Lloyd, 1800–1881', *Hermathena*, 130 (1981), 37–52 • T. D. Spearman, 'Mathematics and theoretical physics', *The Royal Irish Academy: a bicentennial history, 1785–1985*, ed. T. Ó Raifeartaigh (1985), 201–39 • J. G. O'Hara, 'The prediction and discovery of conical refraction by William Rowan Hamilton and

Humphrey Lloyd, 1832–1833', *Proceedings of the Royal Irish Academy*, 82A (1982), 231–57 • J. G. O'Hara, 'Gauss and the Royal Society: the reception of his ideas on magnetism in Britain (1832–1842)', *Notes and Records of the Royal Society*, 38 (1983–4), 17–78 • J. G. O'Hara, 'Gauβ's method for measuring the terrestrial magnetic force in absolute measure: its invention and introduction in geomagnetic research', *Centaurus*, 27 (1984), 121–47 • J. G. O'Hara, 'Humphrey Lloyd: ambassador of Irish science and technology', *Science in Ireland, 1800–1930: tradition and reform*, ed. J. R. Nudds and others (1988), 124–40 • Burtchaell & Sadleir, *Alum. Dubl.* • *Dublin University Calendar* • *PRS*, 31 (1880–81), xxi–xxvi • T. W. Moody and others, eds., *A new history of Ireland*, 8: *A chronology of Irish history to 1976* (1982) • A. J. McConnell, 'The Dublin mathematical school in the first half of the nineteenth century', *Proceedings of the Royal Irish Academy*, 50A (1944–5), 75–88 • T. L. Hankins, *Sir William Rowan Hamilton* (1980) • R. P. Graves, *Life of Sir William Rowan Hamilton*, 3 vols. (1882–9)

Archives RS • TCD, corresp. and papers | CUL, Royal Greenwich Observatory archives • CUL, letters to Sir George Stokes • PRO, letters to Lord Cairns, PRO 30/51 • PRO, letters to Sir Edward Sabine, BJ 3 • RS, corresp. with Sir John Herschel • RS, corresp. with Sir Edward Sabine, etc. • TCD, corresp. with Sir William Hamilton • U. St Andr. L., corresp. with James David Forbes

Likenesses A. B. Joy, bust, repro. in G. Sarton, 'Discovery of conical refraction, etc.', *Isis*, 17 (1932), 154 • A. B. Joy, marble bust, TCD • C. J. Ovenden, portrait, TCD; repro. in T. O'Raifeartaigh, *The Royal Irish Academy: a bicentennial history, 1785–1985* (1985), 215 • drawing, RS; repro. in J. Morrell and A. Thackray, *Gentlemen of science* (1982), following p. 296 • wood-engraving (after photograph by Chancellor & Son of Dublin), NPG; repro. in *ILN* (5 Feb 1881)

Wealth at death under £14,000: probate, 16 March 1881, *CGPLA Eng. & Wales*

Lloyd [*formerly* Hinde], **Jacob Youde William** (1816–1887), antiquary, was the eldest son of Jacob William Hinde (*d.* 1868) of Ulverston, Lancashire, afterwards of Langham Hall, Essex, and Harriet, younger daughter and coheir of the Revd Thomas Youde of Clochfaen, Montgomeryshire, Plas Madog, Denbighshire, and Rowley's Mansion, Shrewsbury. He was educated at Wadham College, Oxford (BA 1839, MA 1874), and was ordained deacon in December 1839. He became curate of Llandinam, Montgomeryshire. Between October 1841 and December 1842, he converted to Roman Catholicism, and then served in the pontifical Zouaves. In 1870 Pius IX conferred upon him the knighthood of the order of St Gregory. He was also a knight of the Saviour of Greece.

On the death of his aunt in 1857 he succeeded to the estates at Clochfaen and Plas Madog, and in 1868 he changed his name from Hinde to Lloyd, the old name of the Clochfaen family, and assumed the Lloyd coat of arms. He was a generous landlord, and although a Catholic he restored the parish church of Llangurig at a cost of £10,000. He also gave financial support to Catholic causes. However, about 1875—possibly in the wake of promulgation of papal infallibility—Lloyd renounced the title of chevalier, to which his membership of the order of St Gregory entitled him, and gradually became estranged from the Roman Catholic church.

Lloyd was a keen antiquary and published several genealogical works, the chief of which is *The history of the princes, the lords marcher, and the ancient nobility of Powys Fadog, the ancient lords of Arwystli, Cedewen, and Meirionydd, and many of the descendants of the fifteen noble tribes of Gwynedd* (6 vols., 1881–7). He also contributed to the *Archaeologia Cambriensis* and the *Montgomeryshire Collections*. Lloyd died unmarried on 14 October 1887 at Rock Cottage, Belgrave Road, Ventnor, on the Isle of Wight.

THOMPSON COOPER, *rev.* MICHAEL ERBEN

Sources *DWB* • *The Times* (25 Oct 1887) • *Clergy List* (1841–50) • Walford, *County families* (1874) • Foster, *Alum. Oxon.* • *A catalogue of all graduates … in the University of Oxford, between … 1659 and … 1850* (1851) • *CGPLA Eng. & Wales* (1887)

Wealth at death £3311 4s. 10d.: probate, 18 Nov 1887, *CGPLA Eng. & Wales*

Lloyd [Flude], **John** (*c.*1475–1523), musician, is of unknown parentage and upbringing; the terms of his will and his early circumstances connect him with Caerleon and the Bristol region. By 1498–9 he was already sufficiently well connected to petition successfully for conferment of a corrody of Thetford Priory. From 1504 to 1508 he was employed by Edward, duke of Buckingham, as director of an ensemble of men and boy singers for his private entertainment. During 1509 he was admitted a gentleman of Henry VIII's Chapel Royal, an appointment held until death.

In 1512 he obtained a corrody of St Augustine's Abbey, Bristol, and following the death of the abbot in June 1515 saw fit to foment dissension among the canons. Richard Fox, bishop of Winchester, wrote of 'the inordinat, hedye and unreligiose dealyng' of a troublesome clique, and claimed that 'Lloyd of the Kynges chapell is auctor of much of this busynesse' (*Letters*, 79–80); Lloyd hoped to influence the choice of a new abbot and so earn himself a large fee in gratitude. Perhaps an unfavourable outcome left him stricken with contrition, since by January 1519, when he made his will, he had resolved to go on pilgrimage to the Holy Land. Having visited the tomb of Christ in Jerusalem, he returned in time to join the Chapel Royal at the Field of Cloth of Gold (1520).

Lloyd's tombstone (minutely described by Strype) represented him as bachelor of music, though his award is recorded at neither English university. As 'Flude in armonia graduatus' he was the composer of three items surviving in a songbook of *c.*1520 from the court of Henry VIII. All exhibit technical ingenuity. One is a straightforward vocal canon, three parts in one. Each of the others is a brief textless fantasia whose three written-out voices are all but self-sufficient, to which a fourth voice can be added through the solution of an encrypted instruction. Dart's attribution to Lloyd of the magnificent mass *O quam suavis est* and its associated antiphon *Ave regina celorum* seems unconvincing. Their pairing in a single presentation manuscript appears to constitute a submission for a doctoral degree, which Lloyd did not possess, and consideration of the encrypted attribution seems to point more convincingly toward Dr George Newton. Lloyd died on 3 April 1523, and was buried in the chapel of the Savoy Hospital, London.

ROGER BOWERS

Sources archives, household of Henry VIII, PRO • archives, household of Henry VIII, BL • archival details of the household of Edward Stafford, third duke of Buckingham, Longleat House, Wiltshire • papers of the household of Edward Stafford, third duke of Buckingham, Staffs. RO • archives, household of Edward

Stafford, third duke of Buckingham, PRO • archives, household of Edward Stafford, third duke of Buckingham, BL • J. Stow, *A survey of the cities of London and Westminster and the borough of Southwark*, new edn, ed. J. Strype, 2 (1720), 109–10 • *Letters of Richard Fox, 1486–1527*, ed. P. S. Allen and H. M. Allen (1929), 79–80 • J. Stevens, ed., *Music at the court of Henry VIII*, Musica Britannica, 18 (1962), nos. 21, 26, 74 • R. T. Dart, 'Cambrian Eupompus', *The Listener* (17 March 1955), 497 • J. Stevens, 'Rounds and canons from an early Tudor songbook', *Music and Letters*, 32 (1951), 29–37 • A. Ashbee and D. Lasocki, eds., *A biographical dictionary of English court musicians, 1485–1714*, 2 (1998), 729–30 [incl. abstract of will] • R. Bowers, 'University Library, MS Nn.vi.46', *Cambridge music manuscripts, 900–1700*, ed. I. A. Fenlon (1982), 118–21 [exhibition catalogue, Fitzwilliam Museum, Cambridge, 1982]

Wealth at death modest: will

Lloyd, John (*c.*1558–1603). *See under* Llwyd, Humphrey (1527–1568).

Lloyd, John [St John Lloyd] (*c.*1630–1679), Roman Catholic priest, was born in Brecon, the son of Walter Lloyd. He was a brother of William Lloyd, archdeacon of south Wales, and is believed to be the brother of Mother Margaret Bruno Lloyd of Paris. On 16 October 1649 he entered the English College at Valladolid after studying humanities at Ghent and on 7 June 1653 was ordained a secular priest. On 17 April 1654, after the completion of his studies in philosophy and theology, he was sent to conduct missionary work in south Wales and served various Catholic communities on the Glamorgan–Monmouthshire border. From this period he lived at the home of Walter James, a Roman Catholic from 'Treivor' in St Maughan's parish, Monmouthshire, and was also associated with the Turberville family of Pen-llin in Glamorgan, the Carne family of Nash in the same county, and the Williams family of Llanffwyst, Monmouthshire.

With the persecution of Catholics as a result of the Popish Plot accusations Lloyd was arrested at the house of his patron, John Turberville of Pen-llin Castle, near Cowbridge, on 20 November 1678. He was imprisoned in Cardiff and brought before Judge Richard Bassett of Beaupre and charged with saying mass at Llandeilo Gresynni, Pen-Rhos, and Treivor. He was then committed to gaol, possibly in the Black Tower of Cardiff Castle where, shortly afterwards, he was joined by the Jesuit Philip Evans. His persecutors had to wait several months before they found witnesses willing to testify against him or produce any evidence of his being a priest. The gaol calendar for May 1679 names Samuel Hancorne of Colwinston, Benjamin Browne of Cardiff, and Margaret and John Nicholls as those who came forward to testify against him, the witnesses in the original recognizances taken at Monk Nash on 7 April being excused from presenting evidence. It has been conjectured that 'a friend of Lloyd had paid their forfeits of £20 each in the hope of saving the priest's life' (Lewis, 63). In May 1679 Lloyd and Evans were brought before the spring assizes in the shire hall in Cardiff and both were found guilty of high treason as seminary priests under the statute of 27 Eliz. I.

The execution of Lloyd and Evans was delayed until 22 July 1679, during which time both men were allowed out of prison, and it was believed that they would be reprieved. On 28 May the privy council had nevertheless issued an order to execute all condemned priests, though the two were not informed until 21 July. Consequently on 22 July the two priests were put in a cart and with their arms tied behind them were taken to the gallows field in Cardiff. When the two men arrived at their place of execution they knelt down, kissed the post, and cited a prayer from St Andrew: 'Welcome good Cross' (*Short Memorandums*, 5). Evans was the first to be executed and Lloyd shortly afterwards. During the proceedings he 'stood by with as much constancy and cheerfulness as any man could have' and before his execution he addressed the crowd and briefly explained the reason why he was prepared to suffer for his religious beliefs: 'I believe in the Holy Catholick Church, and those three Virtues, Faith, Hope and Charity: I forgive all those that have offended me; and if I have offended any body I am heartily sorry for it, and ask them forgiveness' (*Short Memorandums*, 5–6). After this speech he was, like Evans, hanged, disembowelled while still conscious, decapitated, and quartered.

The executions were to have a significant impact upon the Catholic community in south Wales and 'the total disruption of Catholic life that the persecution caused, was to inflict a grievous blow upon the Church from which it was to take nearly a century to recover' (Lewis, 62). Shortly after the executions *Short Memorandums*, about Evans and Lloyd, was published at London. On 25 October 1970 Pope Paul VI canonized Lloyd as one of the forty martyr saints of England and Wales. RICHARD C. ALLEN

Sources M. Tanner, *Brevis relatio felicis agonis* (1683) • [J. Keynes and T. Stapleton], *Florus Anglo-Bavaricus* (Liège, 1685) • main papers 321, papist returns, 1680, House of Lords • transcript of PRO Glamorgan plea rolls, Cardiff Central Library, David Jones Wallington Collection, trans. MS 2. 1148, vol. 9, p. 15 • *Short memorandums upon the deaths of Mr Philip Evans, and Mr John Lloyd, both priests, who were executed at Cardiff in Glams, the 22nd day of July, 1679* (1679) • J. H. Canning, 'The Titus Oates plot in south Wales and the marches', *St Peter's Magazine*, 3 (1923), 38–47 • J. H. Canning, 'The Cardiff martyrs: the venerables Philip Evans, SJ and John Lloyd', *St Peter's Magazine*, 3 (1923), 62–74 • H. Foley, ed., *Records of the English province of the Society of Jesus*, 5 (1879), 96, 868–931 • M. R. Lewis, *From darkness to light: the Catholics of Breconshire, 1536–1851* (1992), 60–67 • Gillow, *Lit. biog. hist.*, 4.289–90 • M. M. C. O'Keefe, 'The Popish Plot in south Wales and the marches of Gloucester and Hereford', MA diss., National University of Ireland (University College, Galway), 1970 • M. C. O'Keeffe, *Four martyrs of south Wales and the marches* (1970), 32–55 • T. P. Ellis, *The Catholic martyrs of Wales, 1535–1680* (1933), 123–5 • J. Warner, *The history of English persecution of Catholics and the presbyterian plot*, ed. T. A. Birrell, trans. J. Bligh, 2 vols., Catholic RS, 47–8 (1953), 296–7

Lloyd, John (1641/2–1687), college head and bishop of St David's, was born at 'Pentaine' (possibly Pendine/Pentywyn), Carmarthenshire, the son of Morgan Lloyd. He matriculated at Merton College, Oxford, aged fifteen, on 10 March 1657, graduating BA on 12 October 1659 and proceeding MA in 1662, the year in which he became a fellow of Jesus College, Oxford. He was presented to the living of Llan-dawg, Carmarthenshire, in 1668 (which he retained until 1687) and proceeded BD on 15 March 1670. He was made rector of the Pembrokeshire livings of Llangwm in 1671 and Burton in 1672. On 9 April 1672 he was chosen precentor of Llandaff. Lloyd was elected principal of Jesus College, Oxford, on 24 April 1673, probably on the recommendation of his predecessor, Sir Leoline Jenkins. He added to his clutch of degrees and preferments by proceeding DD in 1674 and by becoming treasurer of Llandaff on 10 May 1679.

Lloyd served as vice-chancellor of the University of Oxford from 1682 to 1685. Anthony Wood was not overly impressed, describing him as 'a clown, pedag[ogue], sot, not speak Latin' (*Life and Times of Anthony Wood*, 3.27). Humphrey Prideaux also expressed reservations: 'I doubt how he may acquit himself of it; he is an honest good man, but of a temper too mild for a governor' (*Letters of Humphrey Prideaux*, 133). Nevertheless Lloyd, who could look to the support of Jenkins (now secretary of state), was thought to be a good man to strengthen the authority of the tory university over the town's whig magistracy. He undoubtedly played a crucial part in the assertion of loyalist Anglican values within and by the university. He urged the composition, and presided over the promulgation, of the much publicized decree of convocation of July 1683 which upheld the subject's duty of obedience to lawful authority, and whose condemnation of dissident opinions was followed by the public burning of offending books—among them Hobbes's *Leviathan* and books by Richard Baxter, John Owen, John Milton, and Cardinal Bellarmine.

Lloyd's loyalty to the Stuart regime was rewarded when he was consecrated bishop of St David's on 17 October 1686, in company with bishops Cartwright of Chester and Parker of Oxford. However, he returned to Oxford sick, and died of a 'dropsy' in the principal's lodgings at Jesus College on 13 February 1687 (*Life and Times of Anthony Wood*, 3.212); he was buried in the college chapel two days later. Evidently unmarried, his will divided his estate between his two executors, both members of Jesus College, William Bevan MA and John Laugharne BA, who became tory MP for Haverfordwest between 1702 and 1715.

STUART HANDLEY

Sources Foster, *Alum. Oxon.* • Wood, *Ath. Oxon.*, new edn, 4.870 • *DWB* • *The life and times of Anthony Wood*, ed. A. Clark, 3, OHS, 26 (1894) • R. A. Beddard, 'Tory Oxford', *Hist. U. Oxf.* 4: *17th-cent. Oxf.*, 863–906, esp. 871, 889, 892, 896–9 • R. A. Beddard, 'James II and the Catholic challenge', *Hist. U. Oxf.* 4: *17th-cent. Oxf.*, 907–54, esp. 909, 915 • will, PRO, PROB 11/386, sig. 40, fol. 311 • *Fasti Angl.* (Hardy), 2.261, 263 • *The diary of Thomas Cartwright, bishop of Chester*, ed. J. Hunter, CS, 22 (1843), 3–6 • *Letters of Humphrey Prideaux … to John Ellis*, ed. E. M. Thompson, CS, new ser., 15 (1875), 133

Lloyd [Floyd], **John** (1643/4–1682), poet, born in Wonston, near Winchester, Hampshire, was the son of George Lloyd, or Floyd (1597/8–1658?), rector of Wonston, and the younger brother of Nicholas *Lloyd (1630?–1680). His family was of Welsh origin and besides Nicholas he had two other brothers (George and Edward) and three sisters. Three of his siblings died before him and it appears that his brother Nicholas only just managed to survive the smallpox which was raging while John was a student at Oxford.

Lloyd entered Wadham College, Oxford (under the name Floyd), on 13 November 1662 aged eighteen, was fully admitted on 30 September 1663, received his BA in 1666, and graduated MA on 18 February 1669. On 20 May 1675 he was appointed vicar of Holyrood, Southampton.

Despite his being ordained, Lloyd's real calling seems to have been poetry and music and he is reported to have 'shared the friendship and esteem of Addison' (Rose, 297). Lloyd achieved modest fame with his translation of *The Song of Songs*, which first appeared in 1681 in an allegedly plagiarized version. Apparently the author at first did not want the translation to be published: as Lloyd informs his readers in a foreword, the work was handed to a friend in London privately and was 'not intended to trouble the press', but was rather mysteriously 'borrowed … by a stranger, and printed without my leave … and not only so, but owned by that same person … for a thing of his own composure' (Lloyd, *Shir ha shirim, or, The Song of Songs; being a Paraphrase upon the most Excellent Canticles of Solomon in a Pindarick Poem*, 1682). This affront induced Lloyd to set matters right and the volume was published in 1682 under its proper author's name with a dedication to Lady Ann Newland, wife of Sir Benjamin Newland. There are several dedications to the author, including one signed 'Thomas Butler A.M.' as well as one by the author's brother George. The second edition of 1682 comprises Lloyd's translation *The Hymn on the Works of the Six Days*, dated 1681. This seems to be the only other work Lloyd ever published. He died at Southampton on 31 August 1682.

ARTEMIS GAUSE-STAMBOULOPOULOU

Sources H. J. Rose, *A new general biographical dictionary*, ed. H. J. Rose and T. Wright, 12 vols. (1848), vol. 9, p. 297 • Wood, *Ath. Oxon.*, new edn, 4.736 • S. A. Allibone, *A critical dictionary of English literature and British and American authors*, [another edn], 1 (1877), 1111 • Watt, *Bibl. Brit.*, 2.611 • *DNB* • Foster, *Alum. Oxon.*, *1500–1714*, 3.926

Lloyd, John Augustus (1800–1854), engineer and surveyor, the youngest son of John Lloyd of King's Lynn, Norfolk, was born in London on 1 May 1800. He was educated successively at private schools at Tooting and at Winchester, where he was taught some basic science. On a visit to Derbyshire he carried out a survey of the Wirksworth mines. The peace of 1815 prevented his obtaining a commission in the army as he had wanted, and he was sent out to his elder brother, who was king's counsel at Tortola (Virgin Islands). There John spent his time surveying and learning Spanish and French. After crossing to South America he presented an introduction, which had been given him by Sir Robert Ker Porter, artist and sometime British consul in Venezuela, to Simón Bolívar, the liberator of Colombia; he served for some years on Bolívar's staff as a captain of engineers, and ultimately attained the rank of lieutenant-colonel. In November 1827 Lloyd and Captain Maurice Falmarc, a Swedish officer in the Colombian military service, were granted permission by a rather reluctant Bolívar to survey the Isthmus of Panama and report on the best means of inter-oceanic communication. Bolívar was keen to encourage commerce among Central and South American countries, having in 1826 visited Panama as convenor of a conference which, among other things, promoted such trade; but, although he approved in theory of inter-oceanic communication, in practice he was not persuaded by any proposed schemes.

Work on the survey began in May 1828, but their progress was arrested by disturbances at Cartagena, where in helping to restore order Lloyd was severely wounded and narrowly escaped death. The survey was ultimately completed under immense difficulties, including heavy rain, dense forests, and attacks by the followers of General Sarda, the enemy of Bolívar. Lloyd and Falmarc recommended using the rivers and constructing a railway and canal to link the oceans. Theirs was the first canal proposed to suggest Limón Bay as the Atlantic terminus, a plan included in most subsequent schemes and finally carried out with the building of the present canal. Lloyd suggested the use of British convicts to construct the link. Soon afterwards he appears to have returned to England. His report on his survey appeared in *Philosophical Transactions of the Royal Society* (1830, 59–68), with supplementary information in the *Journal of the Royal Geographical Society* (1, 1830, 69–101). On 11 March 1830 he was elected a fellow of the Royal Society. He was then employed, under the joint direction of the Board of Admiralty and the Royal Society, in determining the difference of level in the Thames between London Bridge and the sea. His report appeared in *Philosophical Transactions of the Royal Society* (1831, 167–98).

In 1831 Lloyd went out to Mauritius, where he was appointed colonial civil engineer and surveyor-general. He arrived at Port Louis on 31 August 1831, and soon afterwards made a daring ascent of the Peter Botte (Pieter Both) Mountain, which was 823 metres high and previously regarded as unassailable. He recounted the adventure later in the *Journal of the Royal Geographical Society*, volume 3. During his twenty years' service in Mauritius he carried out many useful public works, including a breakwater for the inner harbour, the custom house, a patent slip for vessels of 600 tons, the colonial observatory, iron bridges, district churches, hundreds of miles of macadamized roads, and a trigonometrical survey of the island and the adjoining islets. He also compiled a new map of Madagascar, with a memoir, published in the *Journal of the Royal Geographical Society*, volume 20. He left the island on 4 April 1849, and reached Europe by way of Ceylon. He made his way to Norway, and afterwards travelled through Poland, where he was temporarily detained by the Russian authorities at Cracow. On his release he visited the Carpathians, Vienna, the Tyrol, and France, and inspected the observatories *en route*.

Lloyd became an associate of the Institution of Civil Engineers in 1849, and served on the council. His paper on the 'Facilities for a ship canal between the Atlantic and Pacific' (*PICE*, 9, 1849–50, 58ff.) was awarded the Telford medal. 'There was nothing', he wrote, 'but the climate and the expense to prevent a canal being cut from one sea to the other of sufficient depth to float the largest ship in her majesty's navy' (ibid., 60).

In 1851 Lloyd was special commissioner charged with organizing displays of manufacturing and industrial products for the Great Exhibition. He performed his work with indefatigable industry and by way of reward was appointed British chargé d'affaires to Bolivia on 4 December 1851. A paper which he wrote there on the mines of Copiapó, Chile, was published in the *Journal of the Royal Geographical Society* (1853, 23, 196–212).

After the outbreak of war with Russia, Lloyd started on a mission to persuade the Circassians to support the British side. He was detained in the Crimea after the battle of the Alma to collect information, and died at Therapia of cholera on 10 October 1854. He left a widow, Fanny Drummond Lloyd (*d.* 28 Sept 1856), and family. Two of his sons were officers in the British army.

Lloyd was a man of immense energy and of much scientific aptitude. He published several papers, including those on Panama (*Journal of the Royal Geographical Society*, 1, 1931, 69–100); and on Mauritius (*Astronomical Society's Monthly Notices*, 3, 1833–6, 186–94; *Geological Society's Proceedings*, 3, 1842, 317–18; *Procès Verbaux, Société d'Histoire Naturelle, Mauritius*, 1846, 155–6). His *Papers relating to proposals for establishing colleges of arts and manufactures for the industrial classes* was published privately in 1851. He made many drawings of Madagascar, and charts, mostly of South America. H. M. CHICHESTER, *rev.* ELIZABETH BAIGENT

Sources *PICE*, 14 (1854–5), 161–5 • *Journal of the Royal Geographical Society*, 25 (1855), 91–2 • *ILN* (28 June 1851), 623–4 • G. Mack, *The land divided* (1944) • Boase, *Mod. Eng. biog.*
Archives RGS, travel and survey papers • RS, papers
Likenesses portrait, repro. in *ILN*

Lloyd, Sir John Edward (1861–1947), historian, was born in Liverpool on 5 May 1861. His parents—Edward Lloyd JP, a draper, and his wife, Margaret Jones—both came from northern Montgomeryshire and kept a house there; throughout his life Lloyd was very proud of his roots in the old principality of Powys. He was educated at the recently established University College of Wales, Aberystwyth, before proceeding to Lincoln College, Oxford, where he secured first-class honours in both classical moderations (1883) and modern history (1885). He returned to Aberystwyth as lecturer in history and Welsh in 1885, and was sufficiently confident of his abilities and standing to apply for the post of principal of the college in 1891. In the next year he left for Bangor, where a new university college had been founded in 1884, and was to remain there for the rest of his life. He was registrar of the college for almost thirty years (until 1919) and played a key role in developing and shaping the college (including its library, of which he had charge until 1926). From 1899 he was also professor of history and held that post until his retirement in 1930. In 1893 he married one of his former Aberystwyth students, Clementina Clunes (*d.* 1951), daughter of John Clunes Millar of Aberdeen, with whom he had a son and daughter.

Lloyd's early career was shaped at a momentous period in the history of modern Wales; these were years of remarkable literary renaissance and political assertiveness. One of the manifestations of this newly found self-confidence was a fascination with the history and character of Wales as a country, manifested for example in John Rhys and Brynmor Jones, *The Welsh People* (1900) and O. M.

Edwards, *Wales* (1901). Lloyd himself was a product and promoter of this revival. As early as 1884 he had won the prize at the national eisteddfod in his native Liverpool for a handbook (in Welsh) on the history of Wales to 1282. It set the agenda for the rest of his life. Between 1893 and 1912 he served an invaluable apprenticeship as a young historian by contributing over 120 entries on Welsh subjects to the *Dictionary of National Biography*.

The appearance of Lloyd's two-volume work *A History of Wales from the Earliest Times to the Edwardian Conquest* (1911; 3rd edn, 1939) may be said, without exaggeration, to inaugurate the history of Wales as a modern academic subject. It was to be followed in 1931 by his classic biography *Owen Glendower, Owain Glyn Dŵr*, based on the Ford lectures delivered at Oxford in 1920. As well as those two masterpieces, Lloyd produced a steady flow of articles and associated papers. Among the most influential was his fundamental analysis of the various redactions and likely provenance of *Brut y tywysogyon* (*The Chronicle of the Princes*), the primary narrative source for the study of medieval Wales. He was also the editor of, and substantial contributor to, the two-volume *History of Carmarthenshire* (1935–9) and wrote single-handedly *The Story of Ceredigion, 400–1277* (1937).

All Lloyd's *œuvre* shared the same broad characteristics. He was the most meticulous of scholars, weighing each item of evidence with the greatest care and, in his own words, 'clearing away a good deal of the undergrowth of legend and error' (*Owen Glendower, Owain Glyn Dŵr*, Preface). In terms of the sources he used and the approach he adopted, his was work which would never need to be done again. He had an exceptional command of the topography and toponomy of Wales and the ability to reconstruct the historical personality of each of the country's regions (as he showed in the remarkable eighth chapter of his *History*). Having first secured the scholarly foundations of his subject matter, he then wove the disparate histories of the fragmented polities of medieval Wales into a single whole and constructed a compelling historical narrative in the grand manner—and not without the occasional rhetorical flourish—out of them.

Lloyd's forte lay in narrative political history; he was less successful in analysing and depicting the social and economic forces which transformed medieval Wales after the coming of the Normans. Even on the political front his anxiety to construct a single, dramatic political story did less than justice to the plurality of Wales and, arguably, over-privileged the history of *pura Wallia* (the area of Wales under native control until 1282) in general and of Gwynedd in particular. But by any standard the scale of his achievement was monumental: he was the father of the modern academic historiography of medieval Wales. In that respect he stands shoulder to shoulder with two of his other famous contemporaries: Sir John Morris Jones, the pioneer student of the study of Welsh grammar, and Sir Ifor Williams, the founder of the modern study of medieval Welsh literature and language. Furthermore, he set scholarly standards which those who worked on the later, post-medieval, study of the history of Wales would be expected to follow.

Lloyd never shirked his public responsibilities in Wales. He was a lifelong lay preacher, and no honour gave him greater pleasure than the chairmanship of the Union of Welsh Congregationalists from 1934 to 1935. Throughout his long life he played an active part in the cultural and historical institutions of Wales, notably as a member of the councils of the National Museum and National Library, the Royal Commission on the Ancient and Historical Monuments of Wales, and the Cambrian Archaeological Association (of which he was twice president and whose summer tours he regularly addressed). His organizing skills and vision were critical in launching two projects which were cardinal to the literary and historical life of twentieth-century Wales. It was he who prepared the draft constitution of the Board of Celtic Studies, served as its first chairman (1919–40), and oversaw the appearance of its *Bulletin* and of its various series of publications. He was also the original editor of *The Dictionary of Welsh Biography*, eventually published (originally in Welsh) in 1953; he had completed sixty-two articles to it before his death. He received honorary degrees from the universities of Wales and Manchester, was elected a fellow of the British Academy in 1930, knighted in 1934, and given the freedom of his adopted city of Bangor in 1941.

Sir John Lloyd had been brought up in the Victorian era and there was a certain Victorian formality about his character. He had a tidy, well-ordered mind; the deliberateness of his judgements and grasp of detail made him an outstanding chairman and promoter of causes at a critical stage in the development of Welsh scholarship. His patriotism was natural and unchallengeable, rather than showy; as he himself said in the Preface to his *History*, he had 'not written in support of any special theory or to urge any preconceived opinion on the reader'. He was active in the Welsh Language Society and wrote three handbooks on the history of Wales in Welsh. Publicly rather aloof, he had a puckish sense of humour, as his closest friends acknowledged and as his correspondence reveals. He died at the Caernarvonshire and Anglesey Infirmary, Bangor, on 20 June 1947 and was buried at Llandysilio, on the Menai Strait. R. R. Davies

Sources J. G. Edwards, 'Sir John Edward Lloyd', *PBA*, 41 (1955), 319–27 · R. T. Jenkins and T. Richards, *Y Llenor*, 26 (1947), 67–87 · R. Richards, 'Sir John Edward Lloyd', *Archaeologia Cambrensis*, 99 (1946–7), 302–3 · 'A bibliography of J. E. Lloyd's writings', *BBCS*, 12 (1946–8), 96–105 · [R. T. Jenkins, E. D. Jones, and W. L. Davies], eds., *Y bywgraffiadur Cymreig, 1941–1950* (1970), 40–42 · E. L. Ellis, *The University College of Wales, Aberystwyth, 1872–1972* (1972) · J. G. Williams, *The University College of North Wales: foundations 1884–1927* (1985) · *CGPLA Eng. & Wales* (1947)

Archives NL Wales, corresp. · U. Wales, Bangor | Gwynedd Archives Service, Caernarfon, W. G. Williams MSS · NL Wales, W. J. Gruffydd MSS

Likenesses W. Stoneman, photograph, 1932, NPG · E. J. Walters, oils, 1937, NL Wales · R. Dobson, portrait, priv. coll. · photographs, repro. in Richards, 312

Wealth at death £31,832 18*s*. 9*d*.: probate, 10 Sept 1947, *CGPLA Eng. & Wales*

Lloyd, John Horatio (1798–1884), barrister, was born on 1 September 1798 at Stockport, Cheshire, the son of John Lloyd, banker and town clerk, and his wife, Mary, daughter of James Watson of Swinton, Lancashire. He attended Stockport grammar school before going to Queen's College, Oxford, in 1818 to study classics and mathematics and then becoming a fellow of Brasenose College, Oxford. A period of legal studies in the Inner Temple, London, led to his admission to the bar in 1826, and in September of that year he married Caroline (*d.* 1875), daughter of Holland Watson, a magistrate of Cheshire. They had eight children, five of whom, including all four sons, predeceased him. His granddaughter, Constance Mary Lloyd, married Oscar Wilde in 1884.

After establishing a successful practice on the north Wales circuit, Lloyd was elected as whig MP for Stockport, 1832–4. His efforts in the 1830s both in and out of parliament were frequently directed towards the cause of legal reform, including support for less severe sentences for some types of felony, such as arson.

Lloyd's reputation largely rests on his contribution to legal and financial aspects of the development of the railway network. He acted as counsel for many railway companies, but above all is known as the originator in the early 1860s of Lloyd's bonds. An explanation of the nature and use of this form of security in railway construction appears in the evidence which he gave to a House of Lords' select committee in 1864: the bonds were a formal acknowledgement of a debt, usually to a contractor, by companies which could not issue more shares and had exhausted their borrowing powers; the debt had eventually to be repaid, but meanwhile construction continued because bonds could be exchanged for a banker's loan. No legal limit existed on the extent to which Lloyd's bonds could be issued, and their indiscriminate use in relation to railways undoubtedly contributed to the speculation which terminated in the financial crisis of 1866. Nevertheless, the lines promoted by many small companies would not have been constructed without them and they were still in use at the end of the nineteenth century.

Lloyd was the co-author of several volumes of reports on law cases, and in 1860, because of his contributions to legal aspects of railway contracts, arbitration, and engineering, he became an associate of the Institution of Civil Engineers. Lloyd died in his home, 100 Lancaster Gate, Hyde Park, London, on 18 July 1884 and was buried at Hendon, Middlesex, on 23 July. DAVID BROOKE

Sources *PICE*, 78 (1883–4), 450–54 • 'Select committee … on railway companies' borrowing powers', *Parl. papers* (1864), 11.43, no. 518 • Boase, *Mod. Eng. biog.* • *The Times* (22 July 1884) • will of J. H. Lloyd, 1884, Probate Office, fol. 795 • election proposal form, 1860, Inst. CE • d. cert.

Likenesses oils; bequeathed to his daughter Emily Frances Lloyd

Wealth at death £92,392 4*s*. 1*d*.: probate, 15 Oct 1884, *CGPLA Eng. & Wales*

Lloyd, Julius (1830–1892), Church of England clergyman and author, eldest son of Francis Lloyd, manufacturer, of Norbiton, Kingston upon Thames, Surrey, was born on 10 September 1830 and was educated at the New Proprietary School, Blackheath. He was admitted as a pensioner to Trinity College, Cambridge, on 11 May 1848, and elected a scholar on 3 May 1851, graduating BA in 1852 as 22nd wrangler. In 1853 he was placed in the first class of the moral science tripos. On 30 May 1850 he was admitted to the Inner Temple, and in 1853 was president of the Cambridge Union. In 1855 he proceeded MA. He was ordained deacon in 1855 and priest in 1856 by the bishop of Rochester.

Lloyd served curacies in succession at Brentwood, Essex (1855–7), St Peter, Wolverhampton (1858–62), Trysull, Staffordshire (1862–6), and St Peter, Pimlico (1866–8). In 1868 he became vicar of High Cross, Hertfordshire, and in 1871 incumbent of St John, Greenock. In 1880 he was presented by Bishop Fraser to the rectory of St Ann, Manchester, and in 1886 became vicar of Leesfield, Lancashire, rural dean of Oldham, and honorary canon of Manchester. Finally, in 1891, Lloyd was appointed by Bishop Moorhouse as canon residentiary of Manchester and rector of St Philip, Salford, where he was elected a member of the Salford school board. Bishop Fraser appointed him his examining chaplain in 1881, to which post he was reappointed in 1886 by Bishop Moorhouse.

Lloyd was an effective preacher and a hard-working parish priest, of pronounced liberal views. In 1865 he was appointed select preacher at Cambridge, and published a collection of sermons, *The Unity of God in Revelation* (1866).

Lloyd also published other of his sermons; sketches of church history in Germany, Scotland, Africa, and France; and a history of the English church in biographical sketches. In 1877 he published *Christian Politics: a Study of the Principles of Politics According to the New Testament*, which put his views on the contemporary church in a historical context. In it he presented the moral principles of the church as the moral principles of the nation. He argued against disestablishment, holding that the title of Church of England helped to hold disparate elements together. Lloyd died at his home, Moorfield, Kersal, Manchester, on 27 May 1892 after addressing a Church Day Schools Association meeting in Manchester Town Hall. He left a widow, Caroline Fanny.

GORDON GOODWIN, *rev.* ELLIE CLEWLOW

Sources Venn, *Alum. Cant.* • *The Times* (28 May 1892) • Boase, *Mod. Eng. biog.* • Crockford (1892) • *CGPLA Eng. & Wales* (1892)

Wealth at death £2657 7*s*. 9*d*.: probate, 21 July 1892, *CGPLA Eng. & Wales*

Lloyd, Lodowick [Ludovic] (*fl.* **1573–1607**), writer and courtier, was the fifth son of Oliver Lloyd, lord of the manor of Marrington, and Gwenllian, daughter of Griffith ap Howel ab Ieuan Blayney of Gregynog. Nothing is known of his early life, but his works suggest that he was highly educated, being able to write in Latin and having a wide range of reference to numerous classical and biblical authorities. A number of Lloyd's early works are dedicated to Sir Christopher Hatton, including one of his most significant efforts, *The Pilgrimage of Princes* (1573), a long advice book for princes, which is prefaced by an elaborate acrostic poem to Hatton. It is possible that Hatton may have been Lloyd's patron and helped to launch his career at court. Lloyd refers to himself as an 'old servant' of Hatton's in *The First Part of the Diall of Daies* (1590). Lloyd also refers to himself as 'her Maiesties Seargeant at arms' in *The Stratagems of Jerusalem* (1602), and evidently kept this post after James I ascended the throne.

Lloyd appears to have been a notable figure at court. He was friendly with the printer and poet John Lane, who claims that Lloyd paid for the funeral expenses of Edmund Spenser, a story which seems unlikely and cannot be corroborated. He wrote an epitaph on Sir Edward Saunders in 1576, which was published as a broadsheet and included in a collection of poetry, *The Paradise of Dainty Devices* (1576). He wrote prefatory verses, as Lodowick Flood, for Humphrey Llwyd's *Breviary of Britain*, translated by Thomas Twyne (1573), and William Blandy's *The Castle, or, Picture of Pollicy* (1581), a work dedicated to Sir Philip Sidney. Edward Grant and Thomas Churchyard wrote prefatory verses to *The Pilgrimage of Princes*. Lloyd's works were all dedicated to Elizabeth, James, Prince Henry (*The Jublie of Britaine*, 1607), and Queen Anne (*The Choyce of Jewels*, 1607), or to prominent courtiers such as Sir Robert Cecil (*The Stratagems of Jerusalem*, 1602), and John Whitgift, archbishop of Canterbury (*The Consent of Time*, 1590). Whether this indicates Lloyd's success in gaining influence in the highest circles in the land, or simply a hopeful ambition, is unclear.

Most of Lloyd's works are collections of moralistic advice to princes, governors, and courtiers, relying heavily on classical and biblical examples (often the same ones). Lloyd exhibits a strongly protestant bias and warns of the dangers of Catholicism, notably in his poem, *Certaine Englishe Verses, Presented unto the Queenes most Excellent Maiestie, by a Courtier* (1586), written after the exposure of the Babington plot. The most substantial of his compositions are *The Pilgrimage of Princes* and *The Consent of Time*, a huge comparative history of the Jews, Egyptians, Greeks, Romans, French, Spanish, and other peoples, concluding with a history of the martyrs of the early church. Other of his works are clearly based on the substantial scholarship of these two books. Lloyd's output appears to have been erratic. After his first two works he published little until the early 1590s, and then nothing more until the early 1600s, culminating in five works published in 1607. This may indicate a busy career or other duties at court apart from his writing.

A stationer, also called Lodowick Lloyd, kept a shop in Pope's Head Alley, Lombard Street, London, possibly a son or relative of the above. With Henry Crips he published the first London edition of Robert Burton's *Anatomy of Melancholy* (1652) and, after moving to the Castle in Cornhill, published Matthew Stevenson's *Poems* (1665).

ANDREW HADFIELD

Sources Wood, *Ath. Oxon.*, new edn • W. C. Hazlitt, *Collections and notes, 1867–1876* (1876) • W. T. Lowndes, *The bibliographer's manual of English literature*, ed. H. G. Bohn, [new edn], 6 vols. (1890) • J. Ritson, *Bibliographia poetica* (1802) • W. C. Hazlitt, *Hand-book to the popular, poetical and dramatic literature of Great Britain* (1867) • *The complete works in verse and prose of Edmund Spenser*, ed. A. B. Grosart, 9 vols. (1882–4) • Tanner, *Bibl. Brit.-Hib.* • H. Lemoine, *Typographical antiquities* (1865) • *DNB* • *CSP dom.*, 1651–2 • BL, Harleian MS 1982, fol. 134v

Lloyd, Lucy Catherine (1834–1914). *See under* Bleek, Wilhelm Heinrich Immanuel (1827–1875).

Lloyd, Marie [*real name* Matilda Alice Victoria Wood] (**1870–1922**), music-hall entertainer, was born on 12 February 1870 at 36 Plumber Street, Hoxton, London, the eldest of nine children born to Matilda Mary Caroline *née* Archer and her husband, John Wood, an artificial flower maker and part-time waiter at the Eagle public house on City Road. Through her father's influence she studied artistes and finally performed at the Grecian Music-Hall attached to the Eagle at the age of fourteen, under the name Bella Delmere, in the same week that Jenny Hill appeared there.

Marie herself dated her career from her first appearance as Marie Lloyd, at the Falstaff Music-Hall on 22 June 1884, when she was spotted by George Belmont. Within six weeks she was fourth on the bill at the Star Palace of Varieties in Bermondsey, singing 'The boy I love is up in the gallery', a song which became something of a trademark although originally written for Nelly Power. By 1886, still only sixteen, she was earning £100 per week and in a position to buy her own songs. The following year, on 12 November, she married Percy Charles Courtenay, a racecourse tout; they had one daughter, Marie. The marriage rapidly proved difficult, but professionally she went from strength to strength; the regard in which she was held is made clear by the invitations to perform in pantomime at Drury Lane in 1891, 1892, and 1893. Lloyd, however, found the restrictions of a script unsuited to her talent, remarking of her performance, 'Bloody awful, eh?' (Farson, 46). Music-hall offered greater scope for the apposite and bawdy ad-libs that created a framework for her songs, and its format was well suited to her unique delivery. Shaw praised her perfect sense of pitch and rhythm, and the precision of her diction is apparent in the feeblest archive recordings. This vocal accuracy allowed a complex relationship with her material. She could play out the contrast between the persona of a song and her own stage presence: as a cockney child in the country, giggling as a bull 'wagged 'is apparatus', she wiped her nose on her sleeve and kicked aimlessly, dressed in one of the elaborate gowns she loved; she could add a top-spin of lewdness to the most innocent lyric and slip into amused contemplation of her own naughtiness; the title of one of her first commissioned songs, 'When you wink the other eye', symbolized her stage presence—the sense of sharing a secret with her audience rather than simply a smutty joke.

Lloyd articulated disappointments of working-class life, especially those of women. Some of her most famous songs were grounded in the realities of poverty: 'My old man', despite its jolly chorus, is about the disorientation of a wife forced yet again to do a moonlight flit because there is no money for the rent. 'Off went the cart with me home packed in it', she sang confidingly, and the audience understood the desolation that sets the wife drinking until she can't remember her new address. The violence that underlay many marriages underscored the song 'It's a bit of a ruin that Cromwell knocked about a bit', the story of a woman who loses her money after 'sitting in the grass with a commercial traveller'. Lloyd favoured these poignant vignettes increasingly as her career progressed, giving rise to an image that her friend Naomi Jacob describes with some indignation in her biography: 'Realising that she was growing old, [she] determined … to show herself to her public as she really was … an old, grey-faced, tired woman' (Jacob, 199). Lloyd loved clothes, designing luxurious stagewear as well as painstakingly detailed costumes for numbers like these. It was not fading looks that prompted her interest, but rather a pride in versatility. Nor were her 'drabs' always downtrodden: in Lloyd's most quoted song, an old woman whose husband fancies a fortnight on his own is told:

> If that's your blooming gime, I intend to do the sime
> 'Cos a little of what you fancy does yer good.

This insistence on women's right to pleasure brought Lloyd into frequent collisions with censorship, most famously in her clash with Laura Ormiston Chant of the Social Purity Alliance. In 1894 Chant campaigned against the 'ladies of the promenade' who used the Empire Theatre as a marketplace. She succeeded in prompting the London county council to erect screens around the promenade, only to have them torn down by an outraged public (Winston Churchill used the occasion to make his first political speech). She went on to make a public protest when Lloyd was singing at the Empire, and Lloyd was called before the council's theatres and music-halls committee with a view to changing some of her songs. The story goes that she sang 'Johnny Jones', a child's-eye view of the facts of life, in tones of angelic purity; she then performed 'Come into the garden, Maud', larded with leers and nudges, provocatively nibbling her pearls to point up each innuendo, finally arguing 'it's all in the mind'.

The episode has passed into legend, and this masks the real tragedy—that Lloyd and Chant were constructed by the press of their time as natural enemies, and have continued to be read as such. In fact they often shared a political position. If Lloyd asserted female desire, Chant was as concerned with the right to resist marital rape. Her concern for censorship arose out of the Contagious Diseases Act, which sought to stop the spread of venereal infection by allowing the police to subject any woman on the streets to forcible examination; she fought to prevent men excited by the sensual patter of the halls gaining access to prostitutes and infecting their wives. Chant frequently spoke out against domestic violence: in the same year as the battle of the promenade Lloyd was threatened by her estranged husband, Percy Courtenay. Chant was preoccupied by the low wages of music-hall performers: in 1907 Lloyd supported a strike by the Variety Artistes' Federation against an attempt by Stoll-Moss to create a monopoly and limit the freedom of performers; she was appalled by contractual loopholes permitting managements to extract unpaid matinées from exhausted performers, gave generously to the strike fund, and picketed theatres using non-union labour.

Lloyd's popularity substantially aided federation victory but in a few years she encountered both political and personal difficulties. In 1896 she had met the singer Alexander (Alec) Hurley (1870/71–1913) but, denied a divorce until May 1905, did not marry him until 27 October 1906. Their marriage crumbled in 1910 as she became infatuated with Bernard Dillon (*c*.1888–1941), the jockey who rode Lemberg to Derby victory in that year. They lived together openly, although she did not pursue her intended divorce, and from the outset the partnership was fraught with problems; Dillon lost his jockey's licence and turned to drink. Meanwhile Lloyd was snubbed by Oswald Stoll when he organized the royal command performance in 1912. It seems likely that this was an act of revenge for the strike, although Stoll may also have seen Lloyd's exclusion

Marie Lloyd (1870–1922), by Schloss, 1890

as illustrating his policy of making music-hall respectable. He published a manifesto in *The Era* on the day of the performance: 'Coarseness and vulgarity etc are not allowed … this intimation is rendered necessary only by a few artists' (Jacob, 93).

Lloyd's response was to stage her own show at the London Pavilion, under a banner proclaiming every one of her performances a 'command performance by order of the British public'. Her departure for America in 1913 was a further attempt to recover from the snub, but on landing she and Dillon were threatened with deportation and sent back to Ellis Island. Dillon was charged under the White Slave Act with 'taking to the country a woman who is not his wife' and Lloyd with being a 'passive agent'. Lloyd was outspoken on the subject of American hypocrisy; pointing to the Statue of Liberty she remarked 'I love your sense of humour'. The Washington board of enquiry reversed the decision as Lloyd was boarding the *Olympic* to sail back; Lloyd and Dillon were allowed to stay on surety of £300 each if they would undertake to live apart in the USA. Lloyd agreed, and performed to enthusiastic houses. Hurley died during the tour, and Lloyd and Dillon married at the British consulate in Portland, Oregon, on 21 February 1914.

Throughout the First World War Lloyd toured factories and gave special concerts for soldiers, but she did not receive any official recognition for her work. Her post-war years were marked by the increasing violence of Dillon, and she continued to work out of financial necessity; their marriage ended in separation in 1920. She died from heart and kidney failure on 7 October 1922 at her home, 37 Woodstock Road, Golders Green, Middlesex, having been taken ill on the stage of the Alhambra, and was buried in Hampstead cemetery. Descriptions of her at the end of her career range from assurances of her continuing greatness to accounts of performances marred by drunkenness and depression. Sentiment, perhaps, colours both these images. What is clear, however, is that the nation's grief at Marie Lloyd's death was also grief for the death of the music-hall that had shaped her. FRANCES GRAY

Sources M. Gillies, *Marie Lloyd: the one and only* (1999) · D. Farson, *Marie Lloyd and music hall* (1972) · N. Jacob, *Our Marie* (1936) · H. C. Newton, *Idols of the halls* (1975) · T. S. Eliot, *Selected essays*, 3rd edn (1951) · M. Banks and A. Swift, *The joke's on us* (1987) · F. Gray, *Women and laughter* (1994) · *DNB* · b. cert. · m. certs.

Archives FILM BFI NFTVA, performance footage; actuality footage; documentary footage; news footage | SOUND BL NSA, 'Marie Lloyd: a heart as big as Waterloo Station', H716/03 · BL NSA, documentary recordings · BL NSA, performance recordings

Likenesses Schloss, photograph, 1890, NPG [*see illus.*] · Rotary Photo, postcard, *c*.1905, NPG

Wealth at death £7334 2*s*.: probate, 11 Nov 1922, *CGPLA Eng. & Wales*

Lloyd, Martha (1860–1943). *See under* Lloyd, Anna Shatford (1837–1912).

Lloyd [*née* Honeychurch]**, Mary** (1795–1865), slavery abolitionist, was born on 12 March 1795 in Falmouth, the younger of the two daughters of Joseph Honeychurch (1735?–1818), a cooper, and his wife, Jane (1753?–1803), daughter of Samuel and Elizabeth Treffry of Beerferris, Devon. Her parents were Quakers and her mother was a minister in the Society of Friends.

Mary's mother died when she was only eight, and a few years later her father became ill and she spent ten lonely years nursing him. After her father's death she stayed with a succession of relatives (at Camp Hill near Birmingham, Neath in Wales, and then Plymouth) before her marriage on 12 November 1823 to Samuel Lloyd (1795–1862). Samuel was a member of a prominent midlands Quaker family and was head of the firm of Lloyds, Foster & Co., which owned an iron foundry and a colliery at Wednesbury in Staffordshire. The couple initially lived at The Crescent, Birmingham, but soon settled in Wood Green, near Wednesbury. Mary Lloyd gave birth to nine children between 1824 and 1839, of whom one died aged only thirteen.

Mary Lloyd is best known as co-secretary of the first women's anti-slavery society in Britain. Women's contributions to the anti-slavery movement in Britain received little attention from historians until the late 1980s, being generally dismissed as small in scale, local in impact, and merely supportive in function, but since this date studies have demonstrated the distinctiveness and national significance of the activities of female anti-slavery societies. The Ladies Society for the Relief of Negro Slaves (later the Female Society for Birmingham [etc.] for the Relief of British Negro Slaves, then the Ladies' Negro's Friend Society) was founded on 8 April 1825 and Mary Lloyd joined her friend Lucy Townsend (*d*. 1847) as joint secretary of the new society. The society was from its foundation independent of both the national Anti-Slavery Society and of the local men's anti-slavery society, in which Mary's husband, Samuel, was involved. It acted as the hub of a developing national network of female anti-slavery societies, rather than as a local auxiliary. It also had important international connections, and, through links with Benjamin Lundy, editor of the *Genius of Universal Emancipation*, it influenced the formation of the first female anti-slavery societies in America. Under Mary Lloyd's and Lucy Townsend's leadership, the society developed the distinctive forms of female anti-slavery activity, involving an emphasis on the sufferings of women under slavery, systematic promotion of abstention from slave-grown sugar through door-to-door canvassing, and the production of innovative forms of propaganda, such as albums containing anti-slavery poems, engravings, and tracts, and work bags embroidered with anti-slavery emblems. The society was at the height of its influence during the 1823–33 campaign against British colonial slavery. From 1839 it aligned itself with the newly formed British and Foreign Anti-Slavery Society and combined support for the universal abolition movement with support for educational work among freed slaves. The society continued to be active until 1919, at which time its secretary was Mary Lloyd's daughter Sara Wilson Sturge.

Mary Lloyd maintained her commitment to the anti-slavery cause until her death, acting as secretary of the society into the 1830s, and as treasurer from the 1840s to 1861, and continuing to collect funds and preside at annual meetings until her death. She was also active in many other organizations. She set up a benevolent society, a mothers' meeting, and a provident society to help the local poor, and in 1834 she and Lucy Townsend set up a Juvenile Association in Aid of Uninstructed Deaf Mutes. In 1841 she was recorded as a minister in the Society of Friends and over the next twenty years she travelled to Quaker meetings throughout the United Kingdom as well as addressing local public meetings.

Supported emotionally and financially by her husband, Mary Lloyd thus successfully combined raising a large family with demanding religious and philanthropic commitments requiring leadership qualities, organizational skills, and a facility for public speaking. A portrait of her in her forties shows a woman with angular facial features wearing typical Quaker attire and holding a book inscribed 'The Chain is broken Africa is free Aug 21st 1839'. Mary Lloyd died on 25 January 1865 at Wood Green, near Wednesbury, Staffordshire, and she was buried on 1 February in Birmingham. CLARE MIDGLEY

Sources S. W. Sturge, *Memoir of Mary Lloyd of Wednesbury* (privately printed, 1921) • *Annual Monitor* (1866), 72–85 • C. Midgley, *Women against slavery: the British campaigns, 1780–1870* (1992) • *Ladies' Society for the Relief of Negro Slaves: at a meeting of ladies, held in West-Bromwich on the 8th of April, 1825, the following resolutions were read and approved* [1825] • *Annual Report* [The Female Society for Birmingham … and their Respective Neighbourhoods, for the Relief of British Negro Slaves], 1–3, 5 (1826–30) • *Report of the Ladies' Negro's Friend Society for Birmingham, West Bromwich, Wednesbury, Walsall, and their Respective Neighbourhoods*, 7–9 (1832–4); 11 (1836); 20–26 (1845–51); 28–30 (1853–5); 36 (1861); 39–40 (1864–5) • *Digest registers of births, marriages and burials for England and Wales, c.1650–1837* [1992] [Cornwall quarterly meeting, births digests; Devon quarterly meeting, marriages digest; microfilm] • 'Digest of deaths, 1837–1961', *Digest registers of births, marriages and burials in the custody of the library of the Society of Friends* (1987) [microfilm] • L. Mott, *Slavery and 'the woman question': Lucretia Mott's diary of her visit to Great Britain to attend the world's anti-slavery convention of 1840*, ed. F. B. Tolles (1952), 18 • d. cert.
Archives Birm. CL
Likenesses painting, *c.*1839, repro. in Sturge, *Memoir of Mary Lloyd of Wednesbury*
Wealth at death under £2000: probate, 26 June 1865, *CGPLA Eng. & Wales*

Lloyd, Sir Nathaniel (**1669–1741**), college head, was born in the Savoy, London, on 29 November 1669, the eldest son of **Sir Richard Lloyd** (*c.*1634–1686), judge, and his wife, Elizabeth, daughter of John Jones, an apothecary. Richard Lloyd was the fourth son of the parliamentary colonel Andrew Lloyd (*d.* 1663) of Aston, Shropshire, and Margaret Powell of Whittington Park, Shropshire. Having been educated in Shrewsbury he was admitted to Gray's Inn in 1655 and became an advocate at Doctors' Commons in 1664. As a fellow of All Souls, Oxford, he proceeded BCL (1659) and DCL (1662). He was Admiralty advocate (1674–85) and chancellor of the dioceses of Lichfield and of Durham. A tory and an Anglican, he sat as MP for Durham city in the parliaments of 1679–81, 1681, and 1685; he was knighted on 16 January 1677. He was dean of the arches in 1684 and a judge of the high court of Admiralty in 1685–6. He died on 28 June 1686 and was buried in the church of St Benet Paul's Wharf, London.

The eldest of eight sons, Nathaniel Lloyd was educated at St Paul's School and at Trinity College, Oxford, whence he matriculated on 9 April 1685. He was elected fellow of All Souls in 1689, graduated BCL on 22 June 1691, and proceeded DCL on 30 June 1696, in which year he was admitted a member of the College of Advocates on 21 November. He was appointed deputy Admiralty advocate, during the absence of Dr Henry Newton, on 15 November 1704 and was king's advocate from 1715 to 1727.

Lloyd was knighted on 29 May 1710, and in the same year was incorporated at Cambridge University and admitted, on 20 June, master of Trinity Hall; he served as vice-chancellor of the university in 1710–11. Under his mastership the college chapel was remodelled and the principal court transformed by the addition of Palladian doorways, sash windows, and new dormers. Lloyd, who remained unmarried, was an aloof figure in college, and in later years lived mainly in his rooms in Doctors' Commons or in his house in Sunbury-on-Thames. He resigned as master on 1 October 1735. He died at Sunbury on 10 March 1741, and was buried on 8 April in Trinity Hall chapel, where a marble monument, bearing an inscription composed by him six years earlier, was erected in his memory. He bequeathed £3000 to rebuild the hall in a classical style, and £1000 to All Souls to complete the building of the Codrington Library. J. M. RIGG, *rev.* S. J. SKEDD

Sources Foster, *Alum. Oxon.* • C. Crawley, *Trinity Hall: the history of a Cambridge college, 1350–1975* (1976) • [C. Coote], *Sketches of the lives and characters of eminent English civilians, with an historical introduction relative to the College of Advocates* (1804) • G. Hampson, 'Lloyd, Sir Richard II', HoP, *Commons, 1660–90* • will, PRO, PROB 11/709, sig. 96; PROB 11/710, sig. 182 [Richard Lloyd]
Likenesses T. Gibson, oils, 1734, All Souls Oxf. • J. Cheese, bronzed plaster bust, All Souls Oxf. • T. Hudson, portrait, All Souls Oxf. • oils, Trinity Hall, Cambridge; repro. in Crawley, *Trinity Hall*, pl. 9
Wealth at death bequests of several thousands of pounds: will, PRO, PROB 11/709, sig. 96, fols. 2*v*–4*r*

Lloyd [Floyd], **Nicholas** (**1630?–1680**), Church of England clergyman and scholar, was born, according to his own statement, at the parsonage house, Wonston, near Winchester, Hampshire, on 28 May 1630, and baptized the Sunday following, 30 May, the son of the Revd George Lloyd (Floyd; 1597/8–1658?). It has since been stated that he was born in 1634 at Holton, Flintshire, Wales. Lloyd's family was indeed Welsh in origin (George Lloyd's father, David Lloyd, was of Merioneth, Wales). Lloyd had at least three brothers (the poet John *Lloyd, George, and Edward) and three sisters. His familial affections were strong, judging from his commonplace book, dated 1656, which contains Latin verses on the deaths of two sisters and, in 1655, his brother Edward. In April 1657 he himself may have narrowly escaped death from smallpox.

Educated at home by his father until 1643, Lloyd was admitted scholar of Winchester College on 3 September 1644. He left on 26 September 1651 and matriculated at Oxford University, entering Hart Hall on 13 May 1652. On 20 October 1653 he was admitted scholar of Wadham College, where he had a distinguished career and lived, it appears, in the 'Second Middle Chamber from the Chapel' (Gardiner, 198). He proceeded BA on 16 January 1656 and

MA on 6 July 1658 and held many offices at Wadham, including bursar, catechist, humanity lecturer (1659), university rhetoric reader (1665), and sub-warden (1666, 1670). He was also rector of St Martin Carfax, Oxford (1665–70). In 1665 Dr Walter Blandford, bishop of Oxford and subsequently of Worcester, appointed Lloyd his chaplain, and Lloyd accompanied him to Worcester in the early 1670s.

A modest man, who respected and encouraged the scholarship of others, Lloyd was 'a deare and intimate acquaintance' of Oxford historiographer and antiquarian Anthony Wood (*Life and Times*, 2.197). Between November 1669 and June 1670 the two were frequently together at Oxford taverns and coffee houses such as Pont's, Pinnock's, Mother Jeanses', the Fleur-de-lis, and the Crown. During this period Wood recorded over thirty shared evenings with Lloyd, many in company with William Thornton. To Lloyd, who highly praised the work, Wood submitted the manuscript of his history of the city and university of Oxford (first published in Latin translation, 1674). Unhappily for both men, and especially embarrassing for Lloyd, who personally extended the invitation to his friend, the warden of Wadham College, Gilbert Ironside, invited them to supper on 29 October 1674 and in the course of the evening toasted Lloyd in claret and proceeded to insult Wood and metaphorically roast Wood's book (*Life and Times*, 2.296–7).

In 1670 Lloyd published a revision and enlargement of Charles Estienne's compendious *Dictionarium historicum, geographicum, poeticum*; this was the product of twenty years of Lloyd's labour, for which he drew on classical sources, the church fathers, and modern authors on geography and pagan antiquity. He 'made it quite another thing, by adding thereunto, from his great reading, almost as much more matter as there was before, with many corrections, &c.' (Wood, *Ath. Oxon.*, 3.1259). The first edition having quickly sold, Lloyd continued to revise and expand the work. Though appointed rector of St Mary Newington, Newington Butts, Surrey, on 28 April 1673, he did not live there until 23 August 1677. He died from what his doctors described as 'a dropsy in the stomack' on 27 November 1680, the parish register recording that he and Herbert Rogers, parish clerk, 'both lay dead and unburied at the same time, Dec. 1, 1680' (Bodl. Oxf., MS Rawl. D32, fol. 22*r*; Burn, 112). Lloyd was buried in the chancel with no memorial, 'leaving then behind him, among those that well knew him, the character of an harmless quiet man, and of an excellent philologist' (Wood, *Ath. Oxon.*, 3.1259). His unpublished writings, chiefly commentaries and translations, were 'retrieved from being made Waste Paper' after his brother John's death (Aubrey, 5.140). Posthumously, in 1686, Lloyd's second edition of Estienne's dictionary (completed only shortly before Lloyd's death) was published. His extensive private library, consisting of 1088 volumes (159 theology, 428 philology and history, 18 medical, and 483 'English') and 297 pamphlets, fell under a London auction hammer on 4 July 1681. PAGE LIFE

Sources Wood, *Ath. Oxon.*, new edn, 1.xxxii, lxvii, clxii; 3.233, 920, 1258–60 • Wood, *Ath. Oxon.: Fasti* (1820), 186–7, 213–14, 388 • *The life and times of Anthony Wood*, ed. A. Clark, 2, OHS, 21 (1892) • J. Aubrey, *The natural history and antiquities of the county of Surrey*, 5 (1719); repr. (1975), 140–41 • R. B. Gardiner, ed., *The registers of Wadham College, Oxford*, 1 (1889), 198, 228, 482 • *Catalogus librorum bibliothecae reverendi Nicolai Lloydii* (1681) [sale catalogue, London, 4 July 1681] • J. S. Burn, *The history of parish registers in England*, 2nd edn (1862), 112 • *The universal historical bibliotheque, or, An account of most of the considerable books printed in all languages in the month of March, 1686* (1687), 149–50 • Foster, *Alum. Oxon.*, 1500–1714, 3.927 • J. Hunter, *Chorus vatum Anglicanorum: collection concerning the poets and verse-writers of the English nation*, 6 (1854), 219–20 • J. Jefferson, 'Nicholas Floyd?', *GM*, 1st ser., 73 (1803), 896 • R. Williams, *Enwogion Cymru: a biographical dictionary of eminent Welshmen* (1852) • [C. B. Heberden], ed., *Brasenose College register, 1509–1909*, 2 vols., OHS, 55 (1909) • Bodl. Oxf., MS Rawl. D. 32, fol. 22*r*

Archives Bodl. Oxf., family papers, MSS Rawl. | Bodl. Oxf., letters to Anthony Wood

Wealth at death library (1088 volumes, 297 pamphlets) sold at auction, 4 July 1681

Lloyd, Philip (1728/9–1790), dean of Norwich, was the son of Philip Lloyd of Greenwich, gentleman. He matriculated at Christ Church, Oxford, on 15 May 1746; he graduated BA (1749) and proceeded MA (1752) and DD (1763), and was elected a student. He was tutor, at Stowe in Buckinghamshire, to the family of the first Earl Temple, and remained close to his pupils, the future second earl and his brother, William Grenville. He and his wife, Joyce (1722/3–1801), were childless.

Lloyd was appointed a prebendary of Westminster in 1763, and resigned in 1765 on being presented to the rectory of Puddletown in Dorset and the deanery of Norwich. He owed his preferment chiefly to the Grenvilles, and gossip had it that 'A recommendation from any of the Temple family would do everything with him' (*Neville*, 308). He was reckoned to be 'the commanding officer' of the diocese of Norwich in Bishop Yonge's time, and a person of great influence (ibid.).

Lloyd proved an energetic dean. Within three months of his installation a major renovation of the cathedral was agreed by the dean and chapter, to be paid for from their own funds, at the rate of £300 a year for three years. Thomas Pitt, who had previously worked for the Grenvilles at Stowe, advised, and the architect was probably Thomas Ivory of Norwich. The medieval choir stalls were renovated, the screen which had been put across the apse was removed, and the window at the east end, blocked when the lady chapel was demolished, was opened and glazed. Other major repairs undertaken during Lloyd's time included overhauling the turrets on the transepts and strengthening the spire. A programme was put in hand for repairing the lead roofs and repointing and replacing decayed stone. A 'moving scaffold' was constructed to clean the vaults.

In 1776 painted glass, given to the chapter by Norwich corporation, was fitted in windows at the east end of the choir, and in 1777 Joyce Lloyd designed a painted window for the choir clerestory; in 1780 she designed another window based on Raphael's *Transfiguration*.

Lloyd had a technical interest in the building. The reason for reopening the blocked east window was to create a through draught which, he said, would 'keep the church free from damp' (memoranda book, Norfolk RO, DCN 118/1). In 1770 he consulted the Royal Society about installing a lightning conductor on the spire. He was concerned for the quality of music at cathedral services, securing the assent of the chapter to the appointment of an additional counter-tenor to the choir. He also ensured that daily prayers should continue in the cathedral undisturbed by workmen during the restoration of the choir. He was a careful administrator, and personally maintained a record of the repairs to the cathedral and its properties, along with careful notes on the administration of the estates managed by the dean and chapter. He also had the accounts of the cathedral priory arranged in chronological order from 1274 to 1537, noting that: 'from them might be extracted a *Chronicon Pretionum* which would include not only the price of every kind of Grain (which the Bailiffs bought and sold) but of almost every article of consumption and the wages of every kind of Workman' (ibid.).

Lloyd died on 31 May 1790, and was buried in the choir of Norwich Cathedral, where he is commemorated by a wall monument by John Ivory. His wife died on 4 April 1801, aged seventy-eight.

At his death the *Norfolk Chronicle* noted:

> If an inflexible firmness of mind in resisting the importunities of the powerful, when inconsistent with the most refined attention to the interest of the body over which he presided can endear this good man to posterity, we can assure ourselves of the justest tribute of applause to his memory.

W. M. Jacob

Sources Foster, *Alum. Oxon.* • P. Browne, *An account and description of the cathedral church of the Holy Trinity Norwich and its precincts* (1807) • cathedral chapter book, 1733–94, Norfolk RO, DCN 24/5 • memoranda book, Norfolk RO, DCN 118/1 • repairs to dean and chapter properties, 1767–91, Norfolk RO, DCN 58/1 • *The diary of Sylas Neville, 1767–1788*, ed. B. Cozens-Hardy (1950) • *Norwich Mercury* (5 June 1790) • *Norfolk Chronicle* (5 June 1790) • gravestone, Norwich Cathedral [Joyce Lloyd]

Archives Norfolk RO, corresp., letter-books, memoranda, MS account of the benefices of dean and chapter, papers, and travel diary | BL, corresp. with earl of Liverpool, Add. MSS 38203–38223, 38307–38309, 38457–38458, 38471, *passim*

Lloyd, Rachel (1722–1803), housekeeper, was born on 10 January 1722 in Carmarthenshire, the eldest child of John Lloyd (1702–1728), landowner, of Dan-yr-allt, Llangadog, Carmarthenshire, and his wife, Mary (*bap.* 1701, *d.* 1764), only child of William Lloyd of Alltycadno, also a Carmarthenshire estate. She survived three brothers and a sister, none of whom married. In 1737 her mother was living in Duke Street, Westminster, and on her remarriage in 1740 she allegedly brought a dowry of £30,000 to Thomas Corbett, MP for Saltash and secretary of the Admiralty, with whom she had a daughter. In 1745 Rachel received most of her father's bequest of £3000. Her mother lived at Pallingswick, Hammersmith, purchased by Corbett, until 1754.

On her mother's death Rachel Lloyd, as sole beneficiary and sometime companion to Lady Bolingbroke, embarked on a genteel lifelong career as housekeeper at Kensington Palace, in succession to Lady Mary Churchill, Horace Walpole's sister. Unlike George II, George III disliked the palace where, once installed in October 1764, Rachel became a society favourite. Her nominal salary was £100 a year but she supplemented this through her skill at cards, and she attended or hosted many parties where half-crown loo, quinze, and cribbage were played. Her friend Lady Mary Coke reported in 1767 that her attractive apartment overlooking the garden included royal furniture salvaged during removal of the contents to St James's. In 1766, accompanying Charles Fitzroy and his wife to Paris, she met Madame du Deffand, who took to her, once inured to her hearty handshake; on Rachel's return to Paris in 1767 she made her presents of Sèvres porcelain and entrusted her as emissary to Horace Walpole, who dubbed her 'the Virgin'. During this second visit to Paris Rachel accompanied Lord and Lady Pembroke and Lord Spencer. Undeterred by gossip that she was a mere concierge, she prolonged her stay and returned to London in September 1768, after three months with the Pembrokes at Spa.

In May 1770 Rachel Lloyd became a member of a new club for both sexes at Almack's, promoted by several fashionable ladies. In December 1771 Horace Walpole complained that it languished in her absence. In August 1770 she had discovered a hoard of William III's correspondence in a palace cabinet and lent it to Lady Mary Coke. It was used by the historian John Dalrymple and eventually found its way into the Public Record Office (class SP 8). Her readiness to act as housekeeper outside Kensington Palace enabled her to frequent stately homes; in September 1770 she was at Ragley, while Lord Hertford was lodging at Kensington Palace as lord chamberlain, and at Trentham. She was at Kensington Palace in June 1773, when the duke of Gloucester and retinue rode over the palace grounds uninvited; her friends discouraged her from protesting and no royal intrusion recurred. That year Oliver Goldsmith caricatured her as Rachel Buckskin in *She Stoops to Conquer*. Reproved by one of her friends, he was persuaded to change the character's name from Rachel to Biddy. By 1774 she was visiting the Spencers at Althorp, and she later provided them with Horace Walpole's corrections to their picture catalogue. She again visited the Netherlands, where she ogled the Austrian emperor at Brussels in June 1782 before proceeding to Spa with Lady Clermont. Still gadding about, she returned often to Trentham, and stayed at Wilton. The duchess of Devonshire related in 1784 that Miss Lloyd, caught up in a metropolitan mob, had nearly been toppled by a drunken clergyman. By 1792 she was staider, critical of revolutionary Parisiennes, and became a guest at Lambeth Palace. By 1793 she was hosting public breakfasts at Kensington twice a year, to which she invited over 300 people.

Rachel Lloyd died at her home, 32 Mount Street, Grosvenor Square, London, on 10 April 1803, after a short illness and was buried at St Paul's, Hammersmith. Charles Grey informed his wife (7 April) that she had recently boasted of her good health to the French ambassador, adding 'et cependant j'ai mené une très mauvaise vie' (Earl Grey

MSS). Remembering relatives and servants, she left her manuscripts to the dowager Countess Spencer, with remainder to Lavinia, Countess Spencer, and keepsakes to her friends, including Lady Diana Beauclerk.

ROLAND THORNE

Sources F. Jones, 'Lloyd of Danyrallt', *Transactions of the Honourable Society of Cymmrodorion* (1970), 221–49 • Carmarthen RO, Cynghordy MSS • F. Green, 'Lloyd of Danyrallt', *West Wales Records* [ed. F. Green], 8, 209–20 • Walpole, *Corr.*, vols. 3–4, 7, 15, 31–3, 38–9, 43 • *GM*, 1st ser., 73 (1803), 390 • U. Durham L., archives and special collections, Grey of Howick collection • will, Sept 1803, Carmarthen RO, Cynghordy MSS • *The letters and journals of Lady Mary Coke*, ed. J. A. Home, 4 vols. (1889–96) • *The letter-journal of George Canning, 1793–1795*, ed. P. Jupp, CS, 4th ser., 41 (1991), 35, 117, 266 • *Georgiana: extracts from the correspondence of Georgiana, duchess of Devonshire*, ed. E. Ponsonby, earl of Bessborough [1955], 27, 94, 110 • Duke of Argyll, ed., *Intimate society letters of the eighteenth century*, 1 [1910], 272 • *The diaries of Sylvester Douglas (Lord Glenbervie)*, ed. F. Bickley, 1 (1928), 274

Archives Carmarthenshire Archives Service, Carmarthen, Cynghordy (Lloyd) MSS, family papers

Likenesses E. Seeman, oils, *c*.1740, Cynghordy, Carmarthenshire

Wealth at death small property in Carmarthenshire: will, proved Sept 1803, Carmarthenshire RO, Cynghordy MSS

Lloyd, Richard (1594/5–1659), Church of England clergyman, was the youngest of the five sons of David Lloyd, or Dafydd Llwyd (*d.* 1619), of Henblas, Anglesey, and his (second?) wife, Catherine, daughter of Richard Owen Tudor of Penmynydd. His father was a biblical scholar, linguist, and poet, and his mother was also an accomplished poet. He and his brothers were educated by their parents at home. He matriculated from Oriel College, Oxford, on 3 April 1612, aged seventeen, and 'took degrees in arts' (Wood, *Ath. Oxon.*, 3.472) before he proceeded BD on 7 May 1628. Like two of his brothers he became a clergyman, and, at an unknown date, minister of Sonning and of Tilehurst, Berkshire. At some point he married Joan Wickins; their elder son, Richard, may have been the Richard Lloyd baptized at Tilehurst on 28 August 1625; their younger son, William *Lloyd (1627–1717), the future bishop, was born at Tilehurst on 18 August 1627; they also had three daughters, who later married clergymen. When his sons matriculated at Oxford in March 1639, Lloyd was described as of Sonning, 'sacerd'. At an unknown date he remarried, but no details of his second wife are known.

Anthony Wood says that during the civil war Lloyd was imprisoned four or five times because of 'the great affection and zeal he had for king Charles' (Wood, *Ath. Oxon.*, 3.472). He was imprisoned as a delinquent as early as February 1641. A Denbighshire nominee to the Westminster assembly on 25 April 1643, he was not included on the final list. At some unspecified date in the 1640s he spent a period in hiding in woods near Tilehurst to escape the attentions of parliamentary soldiers. During that decade he was sequestered and retired to Oxford where he taught a private school for several years in the parish of St Peter-le-Bailey; in December 1651 he was described as 'late of Englefield'. He published *An English Grammar* (1652), *Artis poeticae* (1652), and *The Latine Grammar* (1653), and in 1654 he produced a combined English and Latin grammar entitled *The Schoole-Masters Auxilaries*. In March 1656, described as 'of Maidenhead', he was lodging at the Queens Arms at Holborn Bridge, London, but he left London for Oxford on 1 April. He died in 1659 and was buried at St Peter-le-Bailey, Oxford, in June that year.

JASON M^C^ ELLIGOTT

Sources Foster, *Alum. Oxon.* • Wood, *Ath. Oxon.*, new edn, 3.472–3 • Wood, *Ath. Oxon.: Fasti*, new edn • *Walker rev.* • *DWB* • *IGI* • *JHC*, 2 (1640–42), 89

Likenesses line engraving, pubd 1793, BM, NPG

Lloyd, Sir Richard (1606–1676), lawyer and politician, was born on 23 February 1606, the first son of Evan Lloyd (*d.* 1626) of Dulasau, Penmachno, Caernarvonshire, and Janet (*fl.* 1585–1630), daughter of Roderick ab Ieuan of Pennarth, Llanystumdwy, in the same county. He is probably the man of that name who entered Gray's Inn in 1618, matriculated from Wadham College, Oxford, in 1624, was called to the bar in 1635, and was made reader of Barnard's Inn in 1639. Having married Margaret (*d.* in or after 1650), daughter of Ralph Sneyd of Keele, Staffordshire, on 4 September 1632, he was employed on missions abroad in 1635–6, after which the young lawyer seated himself at Esclusham near Wrexham in Denbighshire.

In the late 1630s Lloyd was granted the reversion to the office of prothonotary and clerk to the crown in Denbighshire and Montgomeryshire. After attending Charles I during the first bishops' war he was appointed attorney-general for north Wales and sat for Newcastle under Lyme in the short parliament. It was in this capacity that he was called on by the earl of Bridgewater, lord president of Wales, for assistance in defending the council in the marches of Wales from the attacks of the House of Commons. Lloyd duly wrote treatises defending the council, including one against its proposed abolition.

In 1642 Lloyd was forward in organizing support for Charles I in north Wales, assuring the king of the 'loyal professions' of the principality (*CSP dom.*, *1641–3*, 336). He was appointed a commissioner of array for Denbighshire and Radnorshire, and entertained the king at his house in Wrexham on 27 September and 7 October, receiving a knighthood on the latter occasion. An active commissioner of array in north Wales, he wrote in early 1643 of his desire to assist the royalists of Chester against those 'poisoned by the industry of the factious and seditious preachers' (Tucker, 56–7). About this time he was also raising a regiment for the king, probably of dragoons.

For a time after 1643 Lloyd is inconspicuous in records, but regains prominence after his appointment as governor of Holt Castle in Denbighshire by April 1645. He and his garrison were obdurate in their resistance to parliament's advances, but were eventually forced to capitulate, surrendering the castle on 13 January 1647. Under the articles of agreement he received very favourable terms, being allowed to go into exile and having his estate of £300 per annum granted to his wife and children, though he was excluded from the pardon. Lloyd apparently settled in Calais, and does not appear to have troubled the interregnum governments.

At the Restoration Lloyd became chief justice of the

Brecon circuit, which helps account for his election as member for Radnorshire in 1661. Although not a prominent member, he continued to advocate the cause of the council in the marches, presenting a memorandum in 1661 calling for its re-establishment. He died on 5 May 1676 and was buried in Wrexham parish church, where a memorial was erected in his memory. As he died intestate his estate was subject to litigation between his daughters and his grandson, Richard, Esclus Hall eventually falling to the heirs of his son-in-law Sir Henry Conway.

LLOYD BOWEN

Sources B. E. Howells, ed., *A calendar of letters relating to north Wales, 1533–c.1700* (1967) · N. Tucker, *Denbighshire officers in the civil war* (1964) · W. Phillips, ed., 'Sir Francis Ottley's papers', *Shropshire Arch. and Nat. Hist. Soc.*, 2nd ser., 6–8 (1894–6) · Hunt. L., Ellesmere MSS 7539–7559; 7466 · J. P. Ferris, 'Lloyd (Floyd), Sir Richard I', HoP, *Commons, 1660–90*, 2.755–6 · *CSP dom.*, 1636–62 · *The letter books of Sir William Brereton*, ed. R. N. Dore, 2 vols., Lancashire and Cheshire RS, 123, 128 (1984–90) · *The letter books of Sir William Brereton*, ed. R. N. Dore, 2, Lancashire and Cheshire RS, 128 (1990) · Evelyn, *Diary* · PRO, PROB, 11/150, fols. 133v–134r; 11/355 · W. W. E. Wynne, 'Old monument in Wrexham church', *Archaeologia Cambrensis*, 4th ser., 6 (1875), 266–8 · R. J. Fletcher, ed., *The pension book of Gray's Inn*, 1 (1901) · A. H. Dodd, *Studies in Stuart Wales*, 2nd edn (1971) · H. S. Grazebrook, ed., 'The heraldic visitations of Staffordshire … in 1614 and … 1663 and 1664', *Collections for a history of Staffordshire*, William Salt Archaeological Society, 5/2 (1884) · *DNB* · PRO, C142/426/91 · *DWB* · *JHC*, 5 (1646–8)

Wealth at death £300 p.a. in 1647, estate granted to wife and children: *JHC*, 5 (1646–8), 24; *CSP dom.*, 1645–7, 338, 515

Lloyd, Sir Richard (*c.*1634–1686). *See under* Lloyd, Sir Nathaniel (1669–1741).

Lloyd, Sir Richard (1696/7–1761), judge, was baptized on 31 May 1697 at St Mary's Church, Lichfield, the elder son of Talbot Lloyd of Lichfield, a professional soldier who died a prisoner of war in France, and his wife, Elizabeth Savage, natural daughter of his commanding officer, Lord Rivers. He attended Lichfield grammar school, where four contemporary judges, William Noel, Sir Thomas Parker, Sir John Eardley Wilmot, and Sir John Willes, were also educated. From Lichfield he went at the age of sixteen, in 1713, to St John's College, Cambridge, where he was elected a fellow in 1718. The fellowship lasted until 1723, the year of his call to the bar by the Middle Temple, after which he devoted his time to the law.

During the 1720s Lloyd married Elizabeth (*d.* 1788), daughter of William Field (or Feild) of St Osyth's Priory and of Crustwic Manor in Weeley, Essex, and Arabella Savage, another natural daughter of General Lord Rivers. The couple had two sons and two daughters, and they settled close to Elizabeth's home region, probably at Ipswich. Their eldest son was born there in 1730 and about this time Lloyd acted as deputy recorder of Harwich. He held in due course the recorderships of Harwich, Orford, and Ipswich, and in 1738 he was appointed king's counsel and elected a bencher of his inn. With others of his rank, he was knighted on the occasion of the loyal address after the Jacobite rising of 1745. The year 1745 also brought him great good fortune when the dowager countess of Winchilsea, aged ninety, inexplicably left him her entire estate. This legacy enabled him immediately to enter parliament, as member for St Michael; and he remained in parliament until he became a judge, representing Malden from 1747 and Totnes from 1754. It also enabled him in 1747 to buy Hintlesham Hall, near Ipswich, which had recently been rebuilt by Richard Powys (*d.* 1743), member of parliament for Orford, who had died heavily in debt, and in 1752 to acquire the Powys estates in Hadleigh. The total outlay for these properties was more than £35,000. Lloyd also maintained a London residence in Queen Square.

In 1754 Lloyd succeeded William Murray as solicitor-general, an office he held for five years. Although he expected to follow him as attorney-general, when this was discussed in 1754 the duke of Newcastle wrote to Lord Hardwicke that his character would not support him and that he would be 'a very improper one' (Yorke, 2.315). The duke said he would not oppose Lloyd's appointment as chief justice of Chester, though he correctly predicted that he would not take it, 'as I doubt the circuits would be incompatible with his views of the chair' (ibid.). Two years later Lloyd expected promotion in the alterations after the death of Chief Justice Ryder, but was opposed by Newcastle, who appointed Sir Robert Henley as attorney-general. Newcastle reported a 'very unpleasant conversation' (ibid.) with Lloyd touching his expectations, and Hardwicke replied, 'my wish is the same as yours, that he may be let fall gently' (ibid., 317). Since Lloyd was unwilling to serve under Henley, he resigned and had to content himself for three years with the bare expectation of a judicial appointment, looking now even to Chester if it should become available.

The first vacancy went to William Noel, much to Lloyd's disappointment, but Noel was plagued by illness and Lloyd had high hopes of succeeding him. In February 1759, when Noel's successor was under consideration, Hardwicke wrote to Newcastle:

> I really think Sir Richard Lloyd has the best pretension of any body; [he] has served the King a great many years, and once in an eminent Station, with great steadiness; and behaved extremely well the last Session of Parliament. The King promised to do something for him, and can do nothing so easily as this. If this should become vacant, and he should be disappointed of it, after all his other disappointments, especially a late one, He will despair, and I shall despair for Him. (BL, Add. MS 32888, fol. 260)

Newcastle submitted his name to the king, but Noel survived, and in November 1759 Lloyd was 'let fall' into the seat in the court of exchequer vacated by the death of Mr Baron Legge. On this occasion Lord Keeper Henley wrote to Hardwicke that there had been no other applications and that 'I think both of Sir R.'s abilities and behavior to the king's government are such as to render him as proper an object of his majesty's favor on this occasion as any I could name to him' (BL, Add. MS 35596, fol. 9). Lloyd's judicial career lasted less than two years, for on 6 September 1761 he died at Northallerton, Yorkshire, while returning from the northern circuit. He was buried at Hintlesham, where an inscribed stone was later removed from his monument and placed in the churchyard. His wife survived him, and his eldest son, Richard Savage Lloyd (1730–1810), succeeded to the estates at Crustwic and Hintlesham, and also followed his father as member of parliament for Totnes. J. H. BAKER

Sources E. Cruickshanks, 'Lloyd, Richard', HoP, *Commons, 1715–54* • BL, Yorke corresp., Add. MSS 35594–35596, 35635 • BL, Newcastle corresp., Add. MS 32888 • Sainty, *King's counsel* • Sainty, *Judges* • Foss, *Judges* • Suffolk RO, Ipswich, MS HA/167/3050/53 • C. P. [C. Partridge], 'Lloyd of Hintlesham', *East Anglian Miscellany*, 26 (1932), 20–21, 65, 79, 81, 82–3, 87–91 • *GM*, 1st ser., 31 (1761), 430 • W. A. Copinger, *The manors of Suffolk*, 7 vols. (1905–11), vol. 6, p. 56 • H. A. C. Sturgess, ed., *Register of admissions to the Honourable Society of the Middle Temple, from the fifteenth century to the year 1944*, 3 vols. (1949) • P. Morant, *The history and antiquities of the county of Essex*, 2 vols. (1765) • *IGI* • monumental inscription, Hintlesham churchyard, near Ipswich, Suffolk • G. Harris, *The life of Lord Chancellor Hardwicke*, 3 vols. (1847) • *Manuscripts of the earl of Egmont: diary of Viscount Percival, afterwards first earl of Egmont*, 3 vols., HMC, 63 (1920–23) • P. C. Yorke, *The life and correspondence of Philip Yorke, earl of Hardwicke*, 3 vols. (1913)

Likenesses T. Gainsborough?, oils, NMG Wales

Lloyd, Richard (1764/5–1834), Church of England clergyman, was the younger son of John Lloyd, rector of Thorpe, Derbyshire, and curate of Wrexham, Denbighshire, and his wife, Mary. After attending Wrexham grammar school, he was admitted pensioner to Magdalene College, Cambridge, on 26 June 1783, aged eighteen. He graduated BA as fourth junior optime in 1787, proceeded MA in 1790, and was elected a fellow. He was ordained deacon by the bishop of London on 18 May 1788, and priest on 4 July 1790. For some time he acted as assistant to the evangelical Revd Richard Cecil of St John's Chapel, Bedford Row. In 1797 he became vicar of Midhurst, Sussex, and on 12 December 1805 vicar of St Dunstan-in-the-West, Fleet Street.

Lloyd was author of a treatise entitled *Christian Theology, or, An Inquiry into the Nature and General Character of Revelation* (2nd edn 1804) and a *Memoir* of his evangelical brother, the Revd Thomas Lloyd (1830). He also published sermons, and pamphlets on the Catholic claims, the duties of the clergy, education, and on the attempt in 1817 to institute an auxiliary to the British and Foreign Bible Society at Midhurst, engaging in a controversy with Edward Cooper concerning the Bible Society and the Church Missionary Society. Lloyd died at Peckham Rye, Surrey, in 1834.

GORDON GOODWIN, *rev.* ELLIE CLEWLOW

Sources [J. Watkins and F. Shoberl], *A biographical dictionary of the living authors of Great Britain and Ireland* (1816) • Venn, *Alum. Cant.*

Lloyd, Richard Dafydd Vivian Llewellyn [*pseud.* Richard Llewellyn] (**1906–1983**), novelist, was born Richard Herbert Vivian Lloyd on 8 December 1906 at 28 Belton Road, Hendon, Willesden, Middlesex, the second child and only son of William Llewellyn Lloyd (*d.* 1942) of Tongwynlais, Glamorgan, a former army officer working in hotel management, and his wife, Sarah Anne, daughter of Richard Darog Thomas, baker, of St David's, Pembrokeshire. His father's work as restaurant manager took the family to various places in London and Cardiff, but it is not known where Richard received his early education, which may have been frequently interrupted for this reason. At the

Richard Dafydd Vivian Llewellyn Lloyd (1906–1983), by Howard Coster, 1939

age of fifteen he was washing dishes at Claridges in preparation, or so his father imagined, for a career in catering, after which he spent less than a year working as a waiter in Italy. After falling out with his domineering father in 1926 he joined the army, serving in India and Hong Kong, but returned to London six years later. He found employment as a film reporter with *Cinema Express*, and then in various menial capacities within the British film industry. Encouraged by the public response to his play *Poison Pen*, which had a successful run in the Shaftesbury Theatre in 1938, he decided on a career as a writer. In October of that year he moved to Llangollen, in Denbighshire, there to assist Lord Howard de Walden (Evelyn Scott-Ellis) in his unsuccessful attempt to establish a Welsh national theatre.

Richard Lloyd took with him a draft of a novel, provisionally entitled 'Slag' or 'Land of my fathers', on which he had been working since his years in India, and which he completed in Pembrokeshire. The book was published under his pseudonym, Richard Llewellyn, as *How Green was my Valley* on 2 October 1939. This novel, set in a south Wales mining community in late Victorian and early Edwardian times (the timescale was deliberately left vague), brought him instant celebrity and an assured income for the rest of his life. Filmed in Hollywood by John Ford in 1940, the novel soon became a best-seller, was translated into some two dozen languages, and has never since been out of print. It is the most famous book ever written about south Wales and one of the most enduringly popular novels in English of the twentieth century.

The setting is sometimes said to be the mining village of Gilfach-goch in the valley of the Ogwr Fach, just over the hill from the Rhondda Fawr, but whether the author ever worked as a collier there, as he often claimed, remains uncertain; it is more likely that he visited the village while finishing his novel and based it, in part, on the memories of a former miner named Joseph Griffiths. In any case, the novel describes an unspecific, idealized community, and is less concerned with historical accuracy than with the creation of a myth, not unlike the American myth of the west, in which the hard work and communal solidarity of the valley's first settlers is spoiled by greed, on the part of both owners and workers, and by confrontation between the old Liberalism and the new militancy of the labour movement. It has nevertheless remained a powerful stereotype of industrial Wales, despite its detractors among Welsh critics, just as Dylan Thomas's play *Under Milk Wood* (1954) is still widely considered to depict life in seaside Wales.

Of the author's career after the publication of his most famous novel, only a sketchy account is possible, such was Richard Llewellyn's circumspection and peripatetic life in Europe, South America, Africa, and Israel. He was granted a commission as lieutenant in the Welsh Guards in 1940, promoted acting captain in 1942, and was released with the honorary rank of captain in 1946; he spent most of the war as a non-combatant at Sandown Park at Esher, in Surrey, and briefly with the Ministry of Economic Warfare, but saw a little action with the regiment's 3rd battalion in Italy. His second novel, *None but the Lonely Heart*, set in the East End of London, was published in 1943. He married Nona Theresa Sonsteby of Chicago in 1952; this marriage was dissolved in 1968. His second wife was Susan Frances Heimann (*b*. 1940) of New York, a publisher's editor whom he married on 29 March 1974 at Marylebone register office in London. There were no children to either of these marriages.

Richard Llewellyn was to publish another twenty-one novels, though none brought him the worldwide fame and financial reward which he enjoyed as author of *How Green was my Valley*. Perhaps the best of them are *A Few Flowers for Shiner* (1950), *A Flame for Doubting Thomas* (1953), *Mr Hamish Gleave* (1956), *Chez Pavan* (1956), *A Man in a Mirror* (1961), *Sweet Morn of Judas' Day* (1965), *Bride of Israel, my Love* (1973), and *A Hill of many Dreams* (1974). In an attempt to recapture the lyrical charm of his masterpiece he wrote three sequels which deal with the subsequent life of Huw Morgan, its central character: *Up, into the Singing Mountain* (1963), *Down where the Moon is Small* (1966), and *Green, Green my Valley now* (1975), but these are rather slick and implausible works, written in a pastiche of his earlier style. Unaffected by fashionable ideas about the novel and contemporary society, to which he was profoundly indifferent, the novels reveal little of their author, except his interest in the foreign countries in which he lived temporarily while engaged in researching or writing them. Those who met him in later life usually remarked on his military bearing, somewhat brusque manner, illiberal opinions, and carefully cultivated image of being a loner. He claimed to be Roman Catholic in religion and Welsh nationalist in politics, though he struck many of his compatriots as an untypical, Anglicized Welshman with only a romantic appreciation of the realities of life in Wales. These claims, like others he made at various times throughout his life, may be taken with a pinch of salt; he was certainly not a member of Plaid Cymru or a practising Catholic.

In 1974 Richard Llewellyn and his second wife went to live in Dublin; he claimed to be a tax exile who was not willing to pay any more of his substantial royalties to the Inland Revenue. He died of a heart attack at his home in Burleigh Court, Burlington Road, Dublin, on 30 November 1983, and was cremated; in his will he had expressed the wish that he should have no grave. There is no monument to him, but his reputed association with Gilfach-goch is marked by a plaque on the ruins of the Six Bells public house in the village. MEIC STEPHENS

Sources J. Harris, '"A hallelujah of a book": *How green was my valley* as bestseller', *Welsh writing in English: a yearbook of critical essays*, ed. T. Brown, 3 (1997) · J. Harris, 'Not only a place in Wales', *Planet*, 73 (Feb–March 1989) · M. Stephens, 'Afterword', in R. Llewellyn, *How green was my valley* (1997) · M. Felton, 'Lloyd, Richard Dafydd Vivian Llewellyn', *British novelists, 1930–1959*, ed. B. Oldsey, DLitB, 15/1 (1983) · J. Osmond, 'How false was his valley', *Western Mail* (25 April 1992) · personal knowledge (2004) [Mrs Susan Lloyd, wife] · personal knowledge (2004) · b. cert. · m. cert.

Archives NL Wales, business papers · NL Wales, corresp. and literary MSS, incl. of unpublished works · NL Wales, letters · Ransom HRC, MSS | FILM BBC Wales 2, film produced by John Osmond (1992) · *How green was my valley* film, produced by John Ford (1940) · *How green was my valley* TV films (1960, 1976)

Likenesses H. Coster, photograph, 1939, NPG [*see illus.*] · F. Mott, photograph, 1974, Hult. Arch.

Lloyd, Ridgway Robert Syers Christian Codner (1842–1884), physician and antiquary, born at Devonport on 20 December 1842, was the son of Francis Brown Lloyd, a west country doctor, who afterwards took orders, and his wife, Margaret, daughter of George Christian. He was educated at Bristol and Stratford upon Avon grammar schools, and proceeded to Guy's Hospital, where he became MRCS and LSA in 1866. He was house surgeon in the Peterborough Infirmary for three years, and in 1870 he bought a practice at St Albans. He was married to Catherine Rosa Scheriman Lloyd; they had at least one child. Lloyd died from typhoid fever at his house, Boroughfield, St Albans, on 1 June 1884, and was buried in the abbey churchyard there; his wife and one son survived him.

Lloyd was a successful physician and a diligent antiquary. He studied the history of the abbey of St Albans, and was consulted by Henry Hucks Gibbs as to the restoration of the screen. He published *An Account of the Altars, Monuments, and Tombs in St. Albans Abbey* (1873). He also wrote many papers on archaeological subjects, of which *The Shrines of St. Albans and St. Amphibalus* (1872) and *The Paintings on the Choir Ceiling of St. Albans Abbey* (1876) were published separately. He also contributed to *The Lancet* and the *British Medical Journal*.

W. A. J. ARCHBOLD, *rev.* H. C. G. MATTHEW

Sources *Medical Directory* (1884) · *Medical Directory* (1885) · *BMJ* (21 June 1884), 1233 · *N&Q*, 6th ser., 9 (1884), 480 · *CGPLA Eng. & Wales* (1884)

Wealth at death £1869 17s. 7d.: probate, 27 June 1884, *CGPLA Eng. & Wales*

Lloyd, Robert (*d.* *c.*1655), translator and Church of England clergyman, was born at Dolfonddu, Llanwrin, Montgomeryshire. His mother may have been Jane Pugh, daughter of Richard ap Hugh of Mathafarn, and his father David Lloyd of Machynlleth (NL Wales, MS 872D, fol. 273): it is just possible, therefore, that it was his baptism, as 'Robt. ap David Lloyd', that was recorded in Mallwyd parish register on 26 May 1573, since Dolfonddu had lands in the parishes of Mallwyd and Cemais as well as Llanwrin. Nothing is known of Robert Lloyd's education, but he must have attended a grammar school and may have gone to university, although it was stated in a Star Chamber action in 1619, admittedly by an opponent, that he was 'noe graduate' (PRO, St. Ch. 8, Jas. I, 25/8).

Early in the seventeenth century Lloyd married Elin (*d.* 1642), whose surname was perhaps Oliver. She had family connections with the parish of Chirk in Denbighshire, which may indicate that Lloyd was already serving the church, perhaps as a curate, in that vicinity. At least four children were born to them: John (who followed his father into the Anglican ministry and married well), Robert (who matriculated from Jesus College, Oxford, in 1626), Æthelstan (who apparently became a merchant of some kind), and Jane (who was buried at Llandysul, Montgomeryshire, on 21 September 1633). In 1611 Lloyd was collated to the vicarage of Chirk, where he remained until 1650, apart from an unexplained interlude as vicar of Llanasa (possibly as a vicar-choral of St Asaph's Cathedral) during 1613–14. In 1625 the sinecure rectory of Llandysul, Montgomeryshire, was added to him. Lloyd's position at Chirk was not easy, since he was caught up in the clash between the puritanically minded Sir Thomas Myddelton, owner of Chirk Castle and lay rector of the parish since 1595, and John Edwards of Plas Newydd, head of a notable recusant family. There is evidence, however, that Lloyd was a conscientious and effective parish priest and preacher in the puritan mould (see particularly the Star Chamber action cited above).

Lloyd wrote little original Welsh prose and is remembered for his notable translations of two classic pieces of popular English religious writing by the puritan Arthur Dent, *A Sermon of Repentaunce* (1582) and *The Plaine Mans Path-Way to Heaven* (1601). The first translation appeared as *Pregeth dduwiol yn traethu am iawn ddull ac agwedd gwir edifeirwch* in 1629, the second as *Llwybr hyffordd yn cyfarwyddo yr anghyfarwydd i'r nefoedd* in 1630 (this latter was translated at the instigation of Lloyd's bishop, John Hanmer). Dent was a precursor of Bunyan in his use of racy colloquial English and vivid characterization, and in both respects Lloyd proved himself fully equal to the task of translating him, thus introducing a new element into early modern Welsh prose. Among the early Anglican translators of popular English and Latin works into Welsh, perhaps no more than three or four are worthy of comparison with him.

It is often stated that Lloyd was expelled from his vicarage in 1650 by the commissioners for north Wales under the Act for the Propagation of the Gospel in Wales, but this has never been explained, and it is perhaps more likely that the commissioners simply retired him, on a pension of £20 per annum, due to old age; his son John may have succeeded him for a time. Lloyd probably died about the year 1655; his wife had died thirteen years earlier. R. Geraint Gruffydd

Sources R. G. Gruffydd, 'Religious prose in Welsh from the beginning of the reign of Elizabeth to the Restoration', DPhil diss., U. Oxf., 1953, 253–80 · B. H. Jarvis, 'Arolwg o ryddiaith Gymraeg, 1547–1634', MA diss., U. Wales, Aberystwyth, 1969, 85–96 · G. H. Hughes, 'Dau gyfieithiad', *Y Llenor*, 27 (1948), 63–71 · T. Richards, *A history of the puritan movement in Wales … 1639 to … 1653* (1926), 10, 117, 139 · [J. H. Davies], ed., *An act for the propagation of the gospel in Wales* (1908), 26 · 'Parochial registers … Mallwyd registers', *Collections historical and archaeological relating to Montgomeryshire*, 30 (1897–8), 319–40 · W. M. Myddelton, ed., *Chirk Castle accounts, A.D. 1605–1666* (1908) · W. M. Myddelton, ed., *Chirk Castle accounts, A.D. 1666–1733* (1931) · BL, Add. MS 9864, fol. 52v · BL, Add. MS 9865, fol. 70r · NL Wales, MS 872D, fol. 273 · PRO, St. Ch. 8, Jas. I, 25/8

Archives NL Wales, Chirk Castle MSS

Lloyd, Robert (*bap.* 1733, *d.* 1764), poet and playwright, was baptized on 7 May 1733 at St John, Smith Square, Westminster, London, the son of Pierson Lloyd DD (1704–1781) and his wife, Anne, daughter of the Revd John Maximilian De L'Angle, rector of Croughton, Northamptonshire. Pierson Lloyd, son of a Westminster victualler, was educated at Westminster School and Trinity College, Cambridge. On leaving Cambridge in 1726 he became an usher at Westminster School; in 1749 he was appointed under-master. He retired with a Lambeth DD in 1771. Forty-five years of schoolmastering did not prevent him from pursuing a successful career in the church. Ordained priest in 1730, he succeeded his father-in-law as rector of Croughton (1732–79), and held the first part of the rectory of Waddesdon, Buckinghamshire, from 1733 until his death. He published a volume of sermons in 1765. Long-standing connections with the archdiocese of York led to his appointment as prebendary in 1777 and chancellor in 1780.

His son Robert was a Westminster schoolboy of brilliant promise: king's scholar, captain of the school in 1750, elected head to Trinity College, Cambridge, in 1751; his friend George Colman (1732–1794) was elected head of those proceeding to Christ Church, Oxford, in the same year. Despite a passion for literature rather than the mathematics and natural philosophy then dominant at Cambridge, Lloyd negotiated his years in college successfully, taking his BA in 1755 (MA, 1758). He remained in Cambridge for two years. His father would have urged Robert to enter the church, and to do so by winning a college fellowship. But Robert's real interest was poetry; as early as 1754 his Westminster friend William Cowper had hailed him as

sole heir, and single,
Of dear Mat Prior's easy jingle.
('Epistle to Robert Lloyd')

Lloyd returned to London in 1757. His father then secured for him an appointment as usher at Westminster School. Teaching the rudiments of Latin verse to schoolboys was repugnant to him, however, and in 1760 he gave it up in order to devote himself to writing. He thus cut himself off successively from the two professions in which his father could assist him.

Lloyd's fortunes as a literary man were bound up with those of his friend Colman. While still at Oxford, Colman had joined with a slightly older Westminster contemporary, Bonnell Thornton (1724–1768), in conducting a successful essay periodical, *The Connoisseur* (weekly; 31 January 1754–30 September 1756); five numbers contain poems by Lloyd (67, 72, 90, 125, 135). When all three had returned to London in the later 1750s they formed the Nonsense Club, an association of seven old Westminsters. The other members were William Cowper, James Bensley, and Chase Price; the identity of the seventh is uncertain. The club's interests were literary; its characteristic activity was burlesque. Two examples survive. Lloyd and Colman collaborated on parodies of the learned Pindaric odes of Thomas Gray (1757) and the vapid efforts of William Mason (1756). In 1760, to draw attention to their fledgeling careers, they retrieved these burlesques and published them anonymously in a quarto entitled *Two Odes*.

The friends' ambition was to become associated with David Garrick and write regularly for Drury Lane. While Colman began to write plays, Lloyd published a poetical epistle, *The Actor* (1760), nominally addressed to Thornton, but in reality an extended panegyric of Garrick as exemplar nonpareil of the actor's art. The poem was popular, reaching a fourth edition in 1764. Its graceful pentameter couplets express the mid-century fascination with theatrical performance, and particularly with Garrick's powers in both tragedy and comedy. Garrick's ability to make the audience feel with him leads Lloyd to mock those conventions of the theatre intended to act directly on the spectators, but he recognizes that the price a great actor pays for his intensity is impermanence; unlike the poet, he takes his art to the grave. George II died on 25 October 1760, and to mark the reopening of the theatres on 17 November Garrick substituted for the usual afterpiece a musical ode, *The Tears and Triumphs of Parnassus*, written by Lloyd. Apollo and the muses lament the death of the old king and then elegantly rejoice in the accession of George III. Colman's first play, *Polly Honeycomb*, was produced in December 1760; his second, *The Jealous Wife*, on 12 February 1761, with a prologue by Lloyd, spoken by Garrick. So far, Lloyd and Colman were establishing themselves satisfactorily in the theatre.

Lloyd next sought regular literary employment. In April 1761 he took charge of the poetry section of *The Library, or, Moral and Critical Magazine*, a periodical edited by Andrew Kippis. He was assisted by his old Westminster friend Charles Churchill, who was now living in London. Kippis was on the staff of the *Monthly Review*, and it was probably through him that Lloyd became poetry reviewer for the *Monthly*. His first assignment, in May 1761, was to review Churchill's *Apology. Addressed to the Critical Reviewers* (24.340–42). Churchill had achieved a huge success in March with *The Rosciad*, which combined high praise of Garrick with severe personal attacks on Garrick's rivals and enemies. A crucial role in the narrative is played by a young hero identified as Lloyd (191–232). Churchill was unknown as a writer, *The Rosciad* was published anonymously, and the *Critical Review* surmised that the poem had been written by some combination of Colman, Thornton, and Lloyd. Colman and Lloyd issued denials. Churchill published a second edition with his name, and scarified the *Critical's* reviewer in the *Apology*. In his review Lloyd admired Churchill's genius for poetry, but regretted Churchill's penchant for satire and personal attacks. In two poems published in July, *Genius, Envy, and Time*, addressed to Hogarth, and *An Epistle to C. Churchill*, Lloyd defended his friend and the idea of genius unfettered by conventional restrictions with which Churchill justified his satire.

Lloyd's employment by the *Monthly Review* lasted only six months. In the autumn he wrote another lyrical afterpiece for Drury Lane: *Arcadia, or, The Shepherd's Wedding*, performed on 27 October 1761 in compliment to the king and queen on their nuptials. It received six further performances over the next month. It was to be his last theatrical venture for three years. In November 1761 Churchill published *Night*, an epistle addressed to Lloyd, a spirited defence of their shared devotion to late hours, imprudence, and unconventional opinions. It marks a shift of emphasis in Lloyd's literary and personal alliances, Colman and the theatre giving way to Churchill and dissipation.

Churchill, who had not long since been in such financial straits that Pierson Lloyd had intervened to broker a composition with his creditors, was now showing that poetry could be profitable. Lloyd, seeking to realize some money from his writing as well as to establish a reputation, prepared a collected edition of his poems which appeared in 1762 as *Poems. By Robert Lloyd, A. M.* He assembled a splendid list of subscribers, including fifty peers, two bishops, many fellows of Oxford and Cambridge colleges, and numerous old Westminsters, as well as Garrick, Hogarth, Johnson, Macpherson, Reynolds, Thomas Sheridan, Sterne, and the Warton brothers. His father's assistance is evident in the presence of the archbishop of York and a large number of names associated with York and the archdiocese. After the 'Author's apology', the poems are arranged chronologically, except that the Latin poems are grouped at the end. The Latin poems include exercises and ceremonial pieces from the Cambridge years, and a virtuoso rendering of Gray's *Elegy*. The collection offers pleasant reading, for Lloyd had a real gift for elegant verse, but as the gathering of a decade's output it underlines the slenderness of his talent and his debilitating preoccupation with his status as a poet. As Thomas Lockwood has written, he projects a 'feeling of contempt for the world in which he finds himself, characteristically intermingled with a certain determined sense of his own inferiority' (Lockwood, 63).

Kippis's *The Library* ceased publication in May 1762. In September Lloyd was engaged as founder editor of a new periodical, the *St James's Magazine*, intended to repeat the success with which Garrick, Colman, Thornton, and others had launched a newspaper, the *St James's Chronicle*, the year before. No doubt his friends saw this as a way of assuring him an income. For his part, Lloyd hoped, not entirely in vain, that his literary friends would supply him with contributions. The drudgery of editorship wore him down, however, proving as inimical to poetry as schoolmastering had been. He undertook a number of anonymous translations: the first book of Voltaire's *Henriade* for the edition by Smollett and Francklin (1762); Klopstock's *The Death of Adam* (1763); Marmontel's *Moral Tales* (3 vols., 1764–6, the third probably by his associate on the *St James's Magazine* Charles Dennis).

By 1762 Churchill was increasingly associated with John Wilkes. The appearance of Lloyd's 'The Poetry Professors' in Wilkes's *North Briton* (October–November 1762) and the mildly obscene verse tale *The New-River Head* dedicated to Wilkes (1763) placed him also firmly in Wilkes's circle. There was as yet no breach with older friends. When James Boswell called on Thornton on 24 May 1763, he met there Wilkes, Churchill, and Lloyd, 'so that I was just got into the middle of the London Geniuses' (*Boswell's London Journal*, 266). Boswell subsequently wrote verses on Lloyd's nose as sign of his intemperance.

The *St James's Magazine* was not profitable, and in March 1764 Lloyd passed the editorship to William Kenrick. In April he was arrested for debt, and confined to the Fleet prison. Churchill gave him 1 guinea a week and paid for a maidservant while he was imprisoned, but other friends proved less helpful, and there was a complete breach with Thornton. Wilkes was now a fugitive in France, and political differences may have helped to isolate Lloyd. Churchill, on a visit to France to see Wilkes, died unexpectedly on 4 November 1764. The tale of Lloyd's taking to his bed with the words 'I shall follow poor Charles', never to rise again, is a sentimental misrepresentation. Rather, his prospects were improving. On 20 November he wrote to Wilkes about his editing of the second volume of Churchill's collected poems. On 28 November his comic opera *The Capricious Lovers* was produced at Drury Lane with considerable success; it ran for nine nights, and Lloyd's text was highly praised in newspaper reviews. The profits of the third, sixth, and ninth nights went to the composer George Rush, but Lloyd's name was once again before the public. The play was published on 1 December with a dedication to Colman, who had arranged for its performance. Then, on 15 December 1764, Lloyd died of a fever in the Fleet prison. He was buried in St Bride's churchyard on 19 December. JOHN D. BAIRD

Sources *Old Westminsters* • C. Ryskamp, *William Cowper of the Inner Temple, esq.: a study of his life and works to the year 1768* (1959) • L. Bertelsen, *The Nonsense Club: literature and popular culture, 1749–1764* (1986) • E. R. Page, *George Colman the elder* (1935) • *Poems. By Robert Lloyd, A. M.* (1762) • G. W. Stone, ed., *The London stage, 1660–1800*, pt 4: 1747–1776 (1962) • Venn, *Alum. Cant.*, 1/3 • G. Colman and B. Thornton, eds., *The Connoisseur* (1754–6) • B. C. Nangle, *The Monthly Review, first series, 1749–1789: indexes of contributors and articles* (1934) • *British Museum general catalogue of printed books … to 1955*, BM, 263 vols. (1959–66) • *St James's Chronicle* (1764) • *London Chronicle*, 14–15 (1764) • *Public Advertiser* (1764) • *The poetical works of Robert Lloyd, A. M.*, ed. W. Kenrick, 2 vols. (1774) • W. C. Brown, *Charles Churchill: poet, rake, and rebel* (1953) • *The poems of William Cowper*, ed. V. D. Baird and C. Ryskamp, 3 vols. (1980–95) • *The letters of William Cowper*, ed. J. Kiup and C. Ryskamp, 5 vols. (1979–86) • T. Lockwood, *Post-Augustan satire* (1979) • *Boswell's London journal, 1762–63*, ed. F. A. Pottle (1950), vol. 1 of *The Yale editions of the private papers of James Boswell*, trade edn (1950–89) • *IGI*

Archives BL, letters and MSS

Likenesses engraving, *c.*1763, repro. in Ryskamp, *William Cowper* • engraving, repro. in *Poetical works of Robert Lloyd*, ed. Kenrick

Wealth at death imprisoned debtor

Lloyd, Robert Wylie (1868–1958), collector and mountaineer, was born at Grove House, Oswaldtwistle, Blackburn, Lancashire, the only son of John Lloyd, a calico printer, and his wife, Rachel Wylie (1844–1890). His grandfather was Nathaniel Lloyd, a successful calico printer at Church, Accrington. His father and mother separated, and he was brought up by his mother in reduced circumstances at Clapham. He started work as a clerk in Mincing Lane in the City of London, and by ruthless determination became a rich businessman, not only as managing director of his own company, Nathaniel Lloyd Ltd, colour printers and paper manufacturers, but also as a director of Druce & Co. Ltd, Chadwicks (Manchester) Ltd, cotton piece finishers, and Christie, Manson, and Woods Ltd.

It was at Clapham that Lloyd first started to collect beetles and butterflies, of which he made an important collection, and it was in pursuit of his entomological interests that he climbed the hills of Norway, and there discovered the fascination of mountains. Lloyd made important ascents in the Valais, the Matterhorn, and Mont Blanc, accounts of which appeared in the *Alpine Journal*. He travelled in the old style, with one or two first-rate guides, but after a serious operation had put an end to his own climbs he devoted his energies to raising funds for the expeditions of others, including the celebrated Mount Everest expedition of 1953. It was said that his assiduity in raising funds was matched only by his extreme reluctance to part with them.

Lloyd was a fellow of the Royal Entomological Society of London from 1885 and a member of the Alpine Club from 1901. He was scrupulously honest but at the same time had a dour strain and a vein of ruthlessness in his character. He never married. He died in his chambers at 15 The Albany, Piccadilly, London, on 29 April 1958, and was buried, at his express wish, in his mother's grave in the necropolis, Glasgow.

Lloyd's substantial collections of alpine books were left to the National Library of Scotland, his Swiss topographical prints and drawings and his Turner drawings to the British Museum, as were his Japanese swords and Chinese red lacquer. His entomological collections are at Manchester University. He was also a collector of Napoleonica—he bequeathed a portrait of the emperor to the museums of France—and he was known to express regret that Wellington had won at Waterloo. The variety of his collections provoked the opinion that he was essentially a collector of collections. ALEX M. CAIN

Sources [A. M. Cain, A. E. H. Wood, and J. Bowles], eds., *Mountaineering: catalogue of the Graham Brown and Lloyd collections in the National Library of Scotland* (1994) • *The Times* (30 April 1958) • T. S. Blakeney, A. Martin, and T. G. Brown, 'In memoriam: Robert Wylie Lloyd', *Alpine Journal*, 63 (1958), 232–8 • *GJ*, 124 (1958), 422–3 • b. cert. • d. cert. • *CGPLA Eng. & Wales* (1958) • gravestone (Rachel Lloyd), Glasgow necropolis, Lanarkshire
Archives BM, R. W. Lloyd bequest of drawings • BM, R. W. Lloyd bequest of Swiss prints and drawings • BM, R. W. Lloyd Collection, Japanese swords, Chinese red laquer • NL Scot. | Alpine Club Library, London, letters in the Herbert MSS
Likenesses photograph, repro. in *Alpine Journal*, 54 (1943–4), 208
Wealth at death £983,953 16*s*. 5*d*.: probate, 21 July 1958, *CGPLA Eng. & Wales*

Lloyd, Sampson (1699–1779), iron manufacturer and banker, was born in Birmingham on 15 July 1699, the second son and second child in the family of two sons and one daughter of Sampson Lloyd (1664–1725), a Quaker ironmonger, and his second wife, Mary, sister of Sir Ambrose *Crowley (1658–1713) and daughter of Ambrose Crowley of Stourbridge, another Quaker ironmonger and nailer. There were also four daughters from the first marriage. Sampson Lloyd the father came from a family of rural Welsh minor gentry, and was drawn to the iron trade partly through the example of his father-in-law. In Birmingham he was a wholesale supplier of bar iron, rods, and other metals to nearby manufacturers, particularly nail and hardware makers.

The younger Lloyd was apprenticed in 1717 to Thomas Sharp at a brass-wire firm in Bristol, but ill health led him to go home in 1720. He then began to convert his father's quiet business into something much more ambitious, integrating backwards into slitting mills, forges, and ultimately furnaces. By his first, brief, marriage in 1727 to Sarah Parkes (1699–1729), a local Quaker heiress, Lloyd had one son. By his second marriage, on 17 September 1731, to Rachel (1712–1756), daughter of Nehemiah Champion, a Bristol Quaker merchant with metallurgical interests, he had three more sons and two daughters. In 1757 his daughter Mary married Osgood Hanbury, a great Quaker Chesapeake merchant of London; in 1767 his other daughter, Rachel, married David Barclay, a leading Quaker merchant, banker, and brewer of London.

Lloyd's iron business prospered during the Seven Years' War, but the peace in 1763 posed a challenge, as did the need to provide careers for his four sons. The war had made many businessmen conscious of the need and opportunities for private banks in both London and the provinces. Perceiving this, in 1765 Lloyd joined with a rich Unitarian neighbour, John Taylor (*c*.1711–1775) to found the first real bank in Birmingham, Taylors and Lloyds; the four (equal) partners were Taylor, Taylor's son John, Sampson Lloyd, and his eldest son, also called Sampson. Shortly afterwards, in 1770, Lloyd's son-in-law Osgood Hanbury founded a bank in London—Hanbury, Taylor, Lloyd, and Bowman—in which both Lloyd's son Sampson and John Taylor junior, of the Birmingham bank were partners. This became the necessary London correspondent and support of the quite prosperous Taylors and Lloyds.

In his lifetime, and by his will, Lloyd provided his three eldest sons with partnerships in both the Lloyd iron firm and the Birmingham bank. His fourth son, John, was placed in London where he became a partner in the Hanbury tobacco concern in 1772 and in the Hanbury bank in 1790. In the next century, Lloyd's descendants abandoned the iron business, but not the bank. After the withdrawal of the Taylors in 1852, the Lloyd family bank was converted into a joint-stock company in 1865. The affiliated Hanbury bank in London merged in 1864 with another London bank of Quaker origins, Barnett, Hoare & Co.; the new Barnetts, Hoares, Hanburys, and Lloyd merged in turn with the main Lloyd bank of Birmingham in 1884, bringing under one corporate roof connections that had their origins in the marriages more than a century before of the children of Sampson Lloyd. He died on 30 November 1779 in Birmingham, and was buried in the Quaker burial-ground, Bull Lane, Birmingham.

JACOB M. PRICE, *rev.*

Sources H. Lloyd, *The Quaker Lloyds in the industrial revolution* (1975) • R. S. Sayers, *Lloyds Bank in the history of English banking* (1957)
Archives Lloyds TSB, London, archives of Lloyds Bank plc

Lloyd, (John) Selwyn Brooke, Baron Selwyn-Lloyd (1904–1978), speaker of the House of Commons, was born on 28 July 1904 at Red Bank, West Kirby, Wirral, the third of four children, and only son, of John Wesley (Jack) Lloyd (1865–1954), a doctor and dentist of West Kirby and Liverpool, and his wife, Mary Rachel Warhurst (1872–1959), daughter of William T. Warhurst (1838–1888) of Crosby, north Liverpool, and his wife, Amelia, *née* French (1838–1893), daughter of John French (1797–1878), and a kinswoman of the family of Sir John French, later first earl of Ypres.

Early years and education Lloyd was born into the Edwardian age with its illusory certainties. His family, of Welsh extraction, was of the solid professional class and had settled in the Wirral, where his father had a medical practice. His childhood was comfortable and assured. His father was prominent in the local Methodist church in Westbourne Road, where Selwyn Lloyd was baptized on 9 October 1904, and the values of his nonconformist upbringing remained with him throughout his life. He was brought up to understand that nothing was achieved without hard work and his childhood could have been an exemplary passage from Samuel Smiles's *Self Help*. Life had its ordered rituals, in which church attendance loomed large. He was educated at the Leas School, a local preparatory school overlooking the links of the Royal Liverpool Golf Club, of which he was captain in its centenary year in 1969. Golf was to become one of his principal recreations. He was an imaginative child, widely read in the middlebrow books of the period and with an enthusiasm for collecting toy soldiers. His interest in military history led him

(John) Selwyn Brooke Lloyd, Baron Selwyn-Lloyd (1904–1978), by Elliott & Fry, 1952

to arrange mock battles in his fort and to write up the campaigns in notebooks. In 1918 he won a scholarship to Fettes College, Edinburgh, an institution for which he always retained affection, despite the harshness of the initial regime he experienced. The school motto, 'Industria', could have been Lloyd's own. From Fettes he won a scholarship to Magdalene College, Cambridge, where he became president of the union in 1927. He took seconds in classics and history, and a third in the second part of the law tripos. Initially a Lloyd George Liberal, he was adopted as Liberal parliamentary candidate for Macclesfield at the age of twenty-two. At Cricieth in Caernarvonshire, where the family took their annual holiday, he became a political associate of Megan Lloyd George, and an assiduous attender of Liberal summer schools. After his failure to win Macclesfield at the 1929 general election he concentrated on his legal career on the northern circuit, where he established a successful common-law practice. He had been admitted to Gray's Inn in 1926 and was called to the bar in 1930.

Pre-war career In the Liverpool legal world Lloyd was a conscientious and dependable advocate. Although his bread and butter was in the law, he did not apply himself in the way that he would have done if his ambition had been to become a High Court judge. He could be sharp and even disrespectful to the bench. One Holy Week, as a case was almost finished, the judge asked the court exceptionally to reconvene on the Friday morning. The idea was dropped when Lloyd pointed out that the last judge to have sat on Good Friday was Pontius Pilate. His legal experience, in which he preferred to act for the defence, gave him a concern for the underdog and he was a consistent opponent of the death penalty. His ultimate goal, however, was always political and he gained a pragmatic apprenticeship by serving for ten years on the Hoylake urban district council, at a time when local government enjoyed a considerable autonomy; he became chairman at the age of thirty-two. Nationally, he broke with the Liberals over the 1931 financial crisis. He was disappointed by the failure of the new party in 1930–31 to establish a middle way. Convinced of the necessity for a protective tariff, and pessimistic about the long-term electoral prospects of the National Liberals, he voted thereafter for the Conservatives.

Wartime service In January 1939, certain that war was inevitable, Lloyd was one of the principal organizers in raising a second line unit of the Royal Horse Artillery, in which he was commissioned as a second lieutenant. On the outbreak of war he went to the Staff College, Camberley, where one of his instructors was Brian Horrocks. Thereafter he rose steadily through the military ranks. He was a lieutenant-colonel on the general staff by 1942. In the spring of 1943 he was posted to the newly formed Second Army. As a result he was a close observer of General Bernard Montgomery during the preparations for D-day, in which he had important logistical planning duties. As deputy chief of staff, Second Army, Lloyd sailed with his commander, lieutenant-general Miles Dempsey for France on D-day. His respect for Dempsey was profound. 'Of nothing in my life am I prouder', he wrote on the occasion of Dempsey's death, 'than that I served under him during great events and that he was my friend' (SELO 443/8). Lloyd was promoted brigadier in March 1945 and was with the first allied forces to enter Belsen. He was made a military OBE in 1943, a CBE in 1945, and was twice mentioned in dispatches. One of his last duties before returning to Britain to fight the 1945 general election was to identify the body of Heinrich Himmler, shortly after his suicide. His rise from adjutant to brigadier in six years was to be a microcosm of his entire career.

In opposition In October 1944 Lloyd, even though he was not formally a member of the Conservative Party, had received an invitation from the Wirral Conservative Association to stand for the parliamentary candidacy, as the sitting MP was not seeking re-election after the war. In his formal letter of application he acknowledged his Liberal antecedents, adding, 'I have however for the last ten years considered myself as a Conservative, and was about to take a more active part when war broke out' (SELO 272/1). In January 1945, on leave from Germany, he was unanimously adopted as Conservative candidate for the Wirral. In the Labour landslide of July 1945 Selwyn Lloyd was elected (by a majority of 16,625) as MP for the Wirral, a constituency that was to return him uninterruptedly to parliament for the next thirty-one years and from which he was eventually to take his title. He had five years' start on most of his contemporaries and was the first of his generation to attain one of the 'great' offices of state, when he became foreign secretary in December 1955.

The 1945 parliament was an unparalleled period of opportunity for the articulate and ambitious tory backbencher and Lloyd took full advantage, as the Conservative whips sought new talent among their diminished numbers. His maiden speech in February 1946 broke convention in that he spoke not on his own constituency matters but on a contentious issue, the Trades Disputes and Trade Union Bill. The leaders of the Conservative Party were also accessible in a way they would not have been in office and in six years of opposition Lloyd worked closely with Anthony Eden and R. A. Butler, both of whom sought his services when the Conservatives returned to power in October 1951. His most significant contribution in opposition, however, was as the dissenting voice in the Beveridge broadcasting committee, his minority report of 1949 on the BBC's monopoly making him in many eyes 'the father of commercial television'. He believed it should not be in the power of a single body to provide broadcasting and that competition would raise standards. As competition in broadcasting proved to be for popular ratings, he later acknowledged that he was disappointed by the results of commercial television, which began in 1955 under the next Conservative government.

At this time Lloyd also picked up the threads of his legal career, taking silk in 1947 and becoming recorder of Wigan from 1948 to 1951. His legal and political experience, coupled with his deep convictions on the subject, made him a notable figure in the contentious debates on capital punishment at the time of the Criminal Justice Bill in July 1948. As a result he developed important cross-party friendships with figures such as Sidney Silverman. These ties were to be an important factor in his later speakership.

In March 1951, at the age of forty-six, Lloyd married his secretary at Westminster, Elizabeth (*b.* 1928), known as Bae, daughter of Roland Marshall, solicitor. Her family, also established in the Wirral, had long been close to the Lloyds. The age difference (his wife was twenty-three years his junior) sadly proved insuperable and they were divorced in 1957. There was a daughter of the marriage, Joanna, to whom Lloyd was devoted.

First years in office In October 1951 the Conservatives were returned with a majority of seventeen seats. Lloyd was surprised, on being summoned to Chartwell by Winston Churchill, to be offered the post of minister of state at the Foreign Office, a promotion he owed to the advocacy of Anthony Eden. 'I think there must be some mistake', he told the prime minister. 'I've never been to a foreign country, I don't speak any foreign languages, I don't like foreigners.' 'Young man', replied Churchill, 'these all seem to be positive advantages' (Lloyd, *Suez*, 4).

As minister of state Lloyd worked for three years on disarmament questions at the United Nations. The issue of Sudanese self-determination also occupied much of his time. A treaty was signed in February 1953 which gave Sudan self-government for a period of three years, at the end of which the country would decide on full independence. Lloyd's subsequent visit to Sudan was the most dramatic of his overseas missions as minister of state. Riots broke out when he was staying at the governor-general's residence, on the site where General Gordon had been murdered, leading to fears that history might repeat itself. Nevertheless, Lloyd's contribution was vital in paving the way for full independence. 'It is futile to try and outstay one's welcome' (SELO 15/4), he wrote, an attitude he maintained also over the Suez Canal base treaty of 1954, though he would have preferred a less precipitate withdrawal from Egypt. Subsequently he served as minister of supply from October 1954, where he worked hard at mastering the technicalities as a sponsoring minister. In April 1955 he entered Eden's cabinet as minister of defence, always an important post psychologically in Conservative administrations. Because of his short spell at the ministry he missed the key period in the year which saw the preparation of the annual defence white paper and the defence debate. However, it was a significant promotion as it established him as a front-rank minister and proved one of the first examples of his ability to get *une idée en marche*. For an old free-trade Liberal, Lloyd was quite a centralist at heart and he took the first steps on long-term defence expenditure planning.

During these four years in office Lloyd developed useful working relationships with Churchill and Eden and owing to the intermittent illnesses of both men was able to gain valuable political experience beyond his initial brief. He attended more than 100 cabinet meetings before becoming minister of defence in April 1955. His rapid promotion to the Foreign Office in December 1955, which Lloyd later conceded was not in his best long-term interests, was seen by some observers as a sign that Eden, in promoting a younger colleague, wished to conduct his own foreign policy after the independent initiatives of Harold Macmillan, with whom Eden had an uneasy relationship, an impression in some ways confirmed by the subsequent Suez crisis.

The Suez crisis As foreign secretary and a key member of the cabinet's Egypt committee, Lloyd was at the eye of the storm that followed the nationalization by President Nasser of Egypt of the Suez Canal on 26 July 1956, after the withdrawal of the offer of American and British money for the building of the Aswan High Dam. Lloyd never wavered from his belief that, although this action presented a serious threat to oil supplies to Western nations, a solution should be sought through negotiation, rather than by the military action Eden favoured, and over which Lloyd, with his Second Army experience of logistical planning, continued to pose awkward questions as options were considered.

Lloyd dealt directly with the American secretary of state, John Foster Dulles, on his many visits to London. The main outcome of Dulles's initial visit was the first London conference of twenty-two countries from 16 to 23 August 1956, which Lloyd chaired. From this conference emerged a formula for a new convention, giving Egypt a place on the board of a mixed operating company and increased revenues. A mission, headed by the Australian prime minister, Sir Robert Menzies, was sent to Cairo to negotiate with Nasser. Its failure in September was a disappointment to Lloyd, who continued work on a series of suggestions by Dulles for an alternative basis for negotiation, one of which, the creation of a Suez Canal users' association, led to a second London conference from 19 to 21 September.

By now Eden was impatient for military action and preparations to that end were difficult to hold in check. Lloyd urged Eden first to exhaust whatever possibilities might exist of a solution through the United Nations. While in New York from 5 to 15 September preparing for a meeting of the Security Council, Lloyd met Dr Fawzi and Christian Pineau, the foreign ministers of Egypt and France. Lloyd developed the formula of the first London conference into a statement of six principles, which at first Fawzi considered worthy of exploration; but, with Soviet support, Fawzi shied away from the proposition that the canal should be isolated from the politics of any one country. Had Lloyd's negotiations succeeded, some cabinet colleagues, notably Lord Home, Commonwealth secretary, felt the situation might have been saved and force avoided. Nevertheless, Lloyd thought they had established what he called 'a good preamble to a missing treaty' (Robertson, 144). But on 15 October Eden suddenly summoned him back to London.

The meeting at Sèvres Events had moved on in Lloyd's absence and a French initiative of 14 October over military co-operation with Israel was to undermine all his work. He went with Eden to Paris on 16 October for talks with their opposite numbers, Guy Mollet and Pineau, who developed their plan for the United Kingdom to join the French in intervening to 'separate the forces' after an agreed Israeli invasion of Egypt. This was the *casus belli* for which Eden had been waiting and through which he hoped to recover the canal. Six days later Eden dispatched Lloyd to France, where in conditions of great secrecy he met the French and Israelis at a villa at Sèvres outside Paris on 22 October, accompanied by his private secretary, Donald Logan. Lloyd's instructions from Eden were to make clear that any British involvement in such a plan must not be regarded as a response to a request from Israel. After initial briefing by Pineau at the villa, Lloyd met the Israeli delegation, headed by prime minister David Ben-Gurion. The Israelis and French were disappointed by Lloyd's lack of enthusiasm for military action; he explained that a week earlier he had been on the verge of a negotiated settlement. The meeting was tortuous and involved, particularly over timings. Ben-Gurion wanted a definite commitment from Britain over use of its RAF Canberra bombers from Cyprus against Egyptian airfields, before any troop movements. Lloyd could only agree to report back to the cabinet over what he later laconically described as 'the plan for which I did not care' (SELO 129/1). At a subsequent meeting at the villa two days later, held while Lloyd had commitments in the House of Commons, the so-called 'protocol of Sèvres' was signed, recording the agreements made by the three governments.

The invasion of Egypt On 29 October Israeli forces duly entered Egypt and British and French action 'to separate the forces' began. When Sir Anthony Nutting, minister of state, resigned on 2 November, Lloyd, though understanding Nutting's dilemma, remained loyal to Eden, and feeling tied by collective cabinet responsibility remained so subsequently, as the operation came under political attack. By 5 November British and French forces had succeeded in capturing 23 miles of the canal, but at this stage it became clear how mistaken was the assumption that American preoccupation with the presidential election on 6 November—what Eden's press secretary William Clark called 'the quadrennial winter of the western world' ('Notes on 1956', Bodl. Oxf., MS Eng. 4814)—would ensure a benign US attitude. President Eisenhower condemned the intervention and resultant pressure on the pound led to a cease-fire within twenty-four hours. In the cabinet discussions that followed, Lloyd drew on his experience in the Second Army and as minister of defence in asking awkward military and political questions, and after the withdrawal of British troops he tried hard, though unsuccessfully, to secure a role for British services in clearing the canal. This disappointment led Lloyd to offer his resignation on 28 November, but it was refused.

With Eden convalescing in Jamaica, Lloyd somewhat unfairly bore the brunt of the opposition's wrath and the buffeting he received in the House of Commons during the next six weeks was one of the most bruising experiences of his political career. Lloyd was unapologetic about his role. 'Whatever was done then', he wrote in his unpublished memoirs, 'was done in what was genuinely believed to be the national interest' (SELO 237/3).

Years in Macmillan's cabinet Lloyd was retained as foreign secretary by Harold Macmillan, who regarded one head on a charger as enough, and the next three years saw him acting with greater autonomy with the resolution of the Cyprus question, largely owing to his initiative over sovereign bases, and the seemingly intractable Formosa Strait dispute. As Sancho Panza to Macmillan's mercurial Quixote, Lloyd also played an important steadying role when accompanying the prime minister to international summits in Bermuda, Moscow, and Paris. 'He was the ideal second', recorded the British ambassador in Moscow, Sir Patrick Reilly, of the 1959 visit, 'always at hand but careful to leave the limelight to the Prime Minister: solicitous and anxious to lighten his burden: ready to take on all the disagreeable jobs' (memorandum, 'Visit of the prime minister and foreign secretary to the Soviet Union', 1959, Sir Patrick Reilly MSS, priv. coll.). His position in the upper echelons of the cabinet was seemingly assured. Macmillan was at home with his dependable presence, and, though privately referring to him as 'a middle class lawyer from Liverpool' (Thorpe, 1), even encouraged Lloyd to consider himself a future candidate for the party leadership. Macmillan made Chequers available to him on a long-term basis and this gave Lloyd a false sense of security. But there was an edge to their complex political relationship that Lloyd's antennae did not always detect and its fracturing was to be one of the most dramatic of post-war political episodes.

In July 1960 Macmillan, whose economic thinking had been conditioned by his pre-war experiences as MP for Stockton, transferred Lloyd to the Treasury. Lloyd warned Macmillan on his appointment that he would be an orthodox chancellor on taxation and public expenditure. In fact, he was to prove highly innovative in other areas, but he was soon caught up in the battle between Stocktonian Keynesianism on the one hand and Treasury orthodoxy on the other. In a rerun of many of the issues from 1931, Lloyd thought Macmillan's gravest political misjudgement was 'thinking unemployment a worse enemy than uncontrolled inflation'. Lloyd's years as chancellor of the exchequer were marked by several important initiatives. With Macmillan's support in the face of a divided and sceptical cabinet, he set up the National Economic Development Council in 1962, a tripartite organization for government, employers, and trade unions, which survived many changes in the political landscape until June 1992. He made the first steps towards an incomes policy and (as at the Ministry of Defence) encouraged the concept of long-term expenditure planning by drawing on the lessons of the French Commissariat du Plan. At a time when the arts lobby expected few favours, he provided government funding for the National Theatre on the South Bank. In the first of his two budgets in April 1961 he introduced the 'regulator', which allowed the government to vary taxes by 10 per cent (a variation on the percentage of the current rate, not a 10 per cent change in the tax itself) without recourse to a budget, an example of his willingness to try new ideas, what he termed—in acknowledgement of an earlier Macmillan initiative—the 'premium bond' factor. Of his time at the Treasury, it was pointed out in Whitehall that 'a subtler person would have seen more difficulties and snags and not accomplished as much, so curious are the workings of human chemistry' (Brittan, 208).

Lloyd's chancellorship was to founder on the cumulative political difficulties that arose in the spring of 1962 and his less than convincing performance on television in putting across the government's case. His second and last budget that April was altered on the eve of its delivery, when the cabinet refused to endorse his plans for the abolition of the old Schedule A tax on owner occupation. But he carried the raising of the surtax starting point on earned income from £2000 to £5000. However, the 'pay pause' (a freeze in wages) he had introduced in the sharply deflationary July measures of 1961 was particularly unpopular with nurses and teachers, who had a large measure of public support, and contributed to a series of by-election reverses for the government.

On 13 July 1962 Macmillan moved with uncharacteristic haste and dismissed seven cabinet ministers, including the chancellor, in what became known as the Night of the Long Knives. The former prime minister Anthony Eden, now earl of Avon, publicly declared that Lloyd had been harshly treated. The episode was to prove more damaging in the long run to Harold Macmillan. Privately Lloyd decided that 'a bitter resentment against Macmillan would destroy my peace of mind' (SELO 180/4), and he found in forgiveness the best form of revenge. Although Lloyd now received the offer of many City posts, including the chairmanship of Martin's Bank, his eyes were already fixed on a political comeback. He therefore refused Macmillan's offer of a peerage. At the last moment he was added to the list of companions of honour. Lloyd felt that such a decoration, traditionally associated with music, literature, and the sciences, should not be handed out as compensation to superannuated politicians, but he was advised by friends that it was impossible for him to refuse.

Rehabilitation As a senior back-bencher, Lloyd loyally undertook in the severe winter of 1962–3 an inquiry into the Conservative Party Organization, an important report that never received appropriate acknowledgement as its publication coincided with the resignation of the war minister, John Profumo, in June 1963. His recommendations on proper provision for agents, especially in marginal seats, did not fall on stony ground and contributed to the surprise victory of the Conservatives in the 1970 election, when ten crucial seats were won in his native north-west. The Selwyn Lloyd report marked the beginning of his rehabilitation in the senior ranks of the party; among back-benchers there had always been admiration for his stoical conduct after Macmillan's purge.

When Macmillan resigned because of ill health from the premiership on the eve of the Conservative Party conference in Blackpool in October 1963, Lloyd played a key part in influencing the succession in favour of Lord Home. He was a pivotal figure in three ways. He was prominent among those who pressed Home to stand; after his work on the party report, he had influence with the rank and file representatives; and the chief whip, Martin Redmayne, respected his opinions. On 11 October Redmayne and Lloyd were accosted during an afternoon walk along the seafront at Blackpool by an old-age pensioner, who told them that his socialist household recognized in Home the qualities to lead the nation. Lloyd later referred to this as 'the gnarled voice of truth' (Thorpe, 375). After Home became prime minister, it was no surprise when Lloyd was recalled to the cabinet as lord privy seal and leader of the House of Commons. As a lawyer he had always seen both sides of the question and the leader of the house needs such open-mindedness. He mollified the unruly elements (a growing band at that time) and was on good terms with the opposition parties. When heckled about his sacking by Macmillan in a debate on education funding (19 November 1963), he calmly replied, 'Whatever may have happened, I am back again now' (Thorpe, 385), a reply greeted with acclamation on both sides of the house. His success in this role, in one of the happiest years of his life, paved the way for his election to the speakership of the House of Commons in January 1971.

After the Conservative defeat in the general election of October 1964, Lloyd continued to serve in the shadow cabinet, first under Sir Alec Douglas-Home, and from July 1965 under Edward Heath. In the Conservative leadership election of that month (the first under the new Douglas-Home rules) he voted for Reginald Maudling, his successor as chancellor of the exchequer. As shadow Commonwealth spokesman he visited Australia and New Zealand in 1965, and also Rhodesia in 1966, following Ian Smith's unilateral declaration of independence. On this latter fact-finding mission, Lloyd had representative meetings with over 300 people, including 60 Africans. He emphasized to all, including Ian Smith, that a white minority could not for ever rule a black majority many times its size. Although his visit brought the Conservative Party a deeper understanding of the ferocity of the entrenched positions, a ferocity that was mirrored by the obloquy heaped on him at home on his return from both extremes of the political divide, it was not the happiest of assignments on which to end his time as Commonwealth opposition spokesman.

After fifteen years of front-bench responsibility, Lloyd returned, at his own request, to the back benches in the summer of 1966. He continued to work loyally for the party, especially in the north-west at election times, and served on many Commons committees. When Heath won the 1970 election, Lloyd was sounded for, but declined, the Washington embassy. As in 1962, he did not wish to abandon the camaraderie and cut and thrust of the Commons. Also, in the opinion of many of his friends, he had set his sights on the speakership. His nomination as speaker in January 1971 was contested by many back-benchers, who believed that he was an agreed nominee of the two front benches, and that a former cabinet minister, with a controversial past, should not be chosen. He was elected by 294 votes to 55. It was very much to his credit that he subsequently overcame such misgivings.

Speakership and last years In the historic office of speaker of the House of Commons, Lloyd was respected for his inherent fairness and his concern for the back-bencher, attitudes that were redolent of his legal practice on the northern circuit forty years earlier. 'All parts of the orchestra must be heard', he used to say, 'not just the violins, but also the so-and-so who plays the triangle' (Thorpe, 420). In a skilful way he traded on the fact that ambitious and influential people did not like getting across with the speaker. He increased the number of deputy speakers to three, remembering what the long hours had done for the health of his two immediate predecessors. He believed that the greatest mistake a speaker could make was 'to be firm against his better judgment for fear of being thought weak' (SELO 129/2). As a result he applied selective deafness from time to time and defused ugly situations with appropriate put-downs, as on the occasion when a body of MPs massed before the mace and he said, 'This is as boring as a standing ovation' (quoted by Lord Home at Lloyd's funeral, private information). He retired from the speakership on 3 February 1976. From March 1976 until his death he sat on the cross benches of the House of Lords, to which he had been elevated as Baron Selwyn-Lloyd of the Wirral, after changing his name by deed poll so as to avoid confusion with other Lord Lloyds.

In a busy retirement, centred on his house at Preston Crowmarsh, Oxfordshire, Selwyn-Lloyd was a generous host (he always had a great disdain for what he called 'a two sardine barbecue') and encouraged the younger political generations, many from the Oxford University Conservative Association. He did much charitable work for the young and old, and wrote widely on political and contemporary issues. He published two books, *Mr Speaker, Sir* (1976) and *Suez 1956: a Personal View*, which came out posthumously in 1978. In this latter work he revealed some, but not all, details of the British involvement in the Sèvres negotiations. His hopes of completing his memoirs, early chapters of which he had drafted under the title 'A middle class lawyer from Liverpool', were not to be fulfilled. Many honours came his way. He became deputy lieutenant of his county and in 1972 was granted the freedom of Ellesmere Port, a part of his former constituency that was always important to him. He received honorary degrees from the universities of Cambridge, Liverpool, Oxford, and Sheffield, and became an honorary fellow of his old college, Magdalene. In 1971 he was made deputy high steward of Cambridge University.

Selwyn-Lloyd had an intuitive feeling about the nature of his last illness, which came upon him in the spring of 1978. The brain tumour that was diagnosed proved incurable. He faced the last months of his life with determination. When news came of the date of his admission to hospital, friends offered to help with the packing. Taking his father's copy of the Bible down from a shelf, Lloyd said, 'This is the only luggage I'll need' (Thorpe, 434). He died at his home, Lower Farm House, Preston Crowmarsh, Oxfordshire, on 17 May 1978, two months short of his seventy-fourth birthday. He was buried on 25 May in Grange cemetery, West Kirby.

The man and his career Selwyn Lloyd was underestimated by his contemporaries. However, the many ways in which he touched public life show that he need not fear the condescension of history or the irrelevance of Macmillan's epithet. Few, if any, have held, as he did, three of the highest posts in government and speaker in addition. He owed this to his capacity for diligent assessment of any situation and his ability to master a brief with forward vision unobscured by detail. Lacking the fashionable quality of charisma, he achieved his ends by more solid nonconformist virtues. R. A. Butler wrote that 'Selwyn is probity and sense itself' (*The Art of the Possible*, 1973, 233). Lloyd's natural modesty inhibited him from the show of assurance of some of his contemporaries, and a certain reticence in his initial relationship with individuals led him to be thought brusque by some, particularly civil servants used to a smoother style. There were many paradoxes in his career. At times he appeared the political staff officer, yet at others he proved innovative and independent, especially over broadcasting policy and the National Economic Development Council. Shy in public, he was wittily gregarious in private, especially with a wide circle of trusted friends at all levels of society who appreciated his kindness and humanity, though after the failure of his marriage he remained essentially a loner who guarded his emotional privacy. Nevertheless, he was a man to be taken seriously in everything he did, who was concerned to play a constructive part in his country's welfare, and who left a significant legacy in unexpected areas of public life.

D. R. THORPE

Sources CAC Cam., Selwyn Lloyd MSS (SELO) • S. Lloyd, *Suez 1956: a personal view* (1978) • S. Lloyd, *Mr Speaker, sir* (1976) • D. R. Thorpe, *Selwyn Lloyd* (1989) • *The Times* (18 May 1978) • D. Logan, Suez: meetings at Sèvres 1956; narrative (1986); addition (1997), Bodl. Oxf., MS Eng. c. 6168 • A. Shlaim, 'The protocol of Sèvres, 1956: anatomy of a war plot', *International Affairs*, 73/3 (1997), 509–30 • K. Kyle, *Suez* (1991) • S. Brittan, *The Treasury under the tories, 1951–1964* (1964) • A. Horne, *Macmillan*, 2 vols. (1988–9) • T. Robertson, *Crisis: the inside story of the Suez conspiracy* (1965) • baptismal record, Westbourne Road Methodist Church, West Kirby • family gravestone, Grange cemetery, West Kirby

Archives CAC Cam., papers (SELO) | BLPES, corresp. with Lady Rhys Williams • Bodl. Oxf., William Clark papers • Bodl. Oxf., Stockton papers • Bodl. Oxf., corresp. with Lord Woolton • PRO, Foreign Office corresp., diaries, and papers, FO 800/691–746 • Trinity Cam., Butler papers • U. Birm. L., corresp. with Lord Avon and Lady Avon | FILM BBC WAC • BFI NFTVA, *This week*, 25 Sept 1956 • BFI NFTVA, *This week*, 12 April 1962 • BFI NFTVA, documentary footage • BFI NFTVA, party political footage | SOUND BL NSA, documentary recordings • BL NSA, news recordings • priv. coll., recorded talk, 19 July 1962

Likenesses Elliott & Fry, photograph, 1952, NPG [*see illus.*] • M. Fresco, photograph, 1955, Hult. Arch. • W. H. Alden, photograph, 1962, Hult. Arch. • M. Noakes, oils, 1976, Palace of Westminster, London • K. Green, portrait, Gray's Inn, London

Wealth at death £154,169: probate, 16 June 1978, *CGPLA Eng. & Wales*

Lloyd, Simon (1756–1836), Methodist preacher and Church of England clergyman, was the son of Simon Lloyd (1730–1764) of Plas-yn-dre, Bala, and Sarah (1727–1807), daughter of Thomas Bowen of Tyddyn, near Llanidloes, Montgomeryshire. His mother had joined the 'Family', or religious community, established by Howel Harris in 1752 at Trefeca. However, it is believed that most of her property was restored to her on her marriage, on 17 August 1755, to Simon Lloyd the elder, who was himself a gentleman of means and the representative of an old Merioneth family.

After leaving Queen Elizabeth's School in Carmarthen, the young Simon entered Jesus College, Oxford, on 8 April 1775, and graduated BA in 1779. He entered holy orders, and obtained the curacies of Olveston, and then Bryneglwys and Llandegla in Denbighshire. He lost Bryneglwys in October 1783 for aligning himself too closely with the Methodists, in particular with his friend Thomas Charles of Bala, whose presence aroused a storm of indignation in the parish. He retained Llandegla until 1788 and was later curate of Llanycil until 1800, but for the remainder of his days he associated himself with the Calvinistic Methodist movement. In 1800 he was invited to become curate of Llanuwchllyn, and although the patron, Sir Watkin Williams-Wynn, eventually agreed, Bishop Horsley refused to sanction his nomination on the grounds of previous irregularities.

Lloyd was already married by 1789. His wife was Bridget Price, of Rhydcolomennod, Cardiganshire, with whom he had eight children. Up to 1811 Lloyd was one of the three episcopally ordained priests in north Wales (Thomas Charles of Bala and William Lloyd of Caernarfon were the other two), who were allowed to administer the sacraments among the Methodists. After Charles's death in 1814, Lloyd edited two volumes of the Welsh magazine called *Y Drysorfa*. He died at his residence, Plas-yn-dre, Bala, on 6 November 1836, and was buried in the family vault at Llanycil church, Merioneth. Although not a great preacher, Lloyd was among the foremost of the Methodists in north Wales. He was considered a good classical and biblical scholar, and was the author of a biblical chronology entitled *Amseryddiaeth ysgrythyrol* (1817), said to be the result of thirty years' study, and *Esboniad byr ar y Dadguddiad* (1828), a commentary on the Apocalypse of St John, which reached a second edition.

D. L. THOMAS, *rev.* DYLAN FOSTER EVANS

Sources D. E. Jenkin, *The life of Thomas Charles, BA, of Bala* (1908) • *DWB*, 588–9 • J. E. Griffith, *Pedigrees of Anglesey and Carnarvonshire families* (privately printed, Horncastle, 1914), 383 • 'Marriage agreement of Simon Lloyd, Bala, and Sarah Bowen, Trevecka', *Cylchgrawn Cymdeithas Hanes y Methodistiaid Calfinaidd*, 10 (1925), 30–33 • R. Bennett, 'Teulu'r Tyddyn', *Cylchgrawn Cymdeithas Hanes y Methodistiaid Calfinaidd*, 8 (1923), 57–62 • Foster, *Alum. Oxon.*

Archives NL Wales, Edwards MSS • NL Wales, Calvinistic Methodists archive

Likenesses half-tone reprint, repro. in *Y Drysorfa*, old ser., 101 (1931), 1 • photograph, half-tone reprint, repro. in J. M. Jones and W. Morgan, *Y Tadau Methodistaidd*, 2 (1897), 304

Lloyd, Sylvester (*b.* in or after 1680, *d.* 1747), Roman Catholic bishop of Waterford and Lismore and Jacobite sympathizer, was born probably in co. Tipperary, although co. Kilkenny is also claimed as his birthplace. It is probable that he was baptized as Lewis and that he later acquired the name Sylvester when he joined the Hieronymite order. His father is believed to have been an Anglican minister, Edward Lloyd (*fl.* 1663–1680), who married twice and had two daughters and probably a son with his first wife. His second wife may have been Elizabeth Tailor, who married an Edward Lloyd at Cashel, co. Tipperary, in January 1680, and Sylvester Lloyd may have been the only child of this second marriage. No information has been traced as to his early education.

Lloyd joined William III's army while still a youth and appears to have been serving on the continent when he was overtaken by remorse on killing one of the enemy. An ensuing crisis of conscience resulted not only in his defection from the army but also in his conversion to Roman Catholicism about 1698. He is believed to have spent some time in St Bonaventure's College, the English Franciscan college, at Douai, and later to have returned to Ireland before joining, about 1703, the Hieronymite order in Lisbon, where he was ordained priest in May 1711. A year later he transferred to the Irish Franciscans and spent six months in their college, St Isidore's, in Rome before being posted to their convent in Cook Street, Dublin, in 1713. He translated into English the monumental Montpellier catechism, a project which, because of alleged Jansenist tendencies, eventually caused him to fall foul of Rome. In January 1725 his translation was placed on the Vatican index of prohibited books.

In February 1726 Lloyd began a long correspondence with the exiled Stuart court with an extended report on the state of Ireland. A Catholic address in July 1727 to George II, on his succession to the throne, was fiercely attacked by Lloyd, who was the moving spirit behind a hostile pamphlet that followed the rhetorical question format used so effectively by George Berkeley in *The Querist*. Lloyd also opposed efforts to draft an oath of loyalty to the king which would be acceptable to Catholics. His unwavering loyalty to the Pretender, who had in his gift the nomination of bishops to Irish sees, was to pay dividends when he was appointed bishop of Killaloe in 1729. His initial spurt of visitations of the diocese was cut short by eye trouble as well as by government accusations that he and other bishops were engaged in collecting funds for the Pretender.

For a number of years from 1732 Lloyd based himself in Dublin, occasionally visiting his diocese but also travelling across Britain to the continent, particularly to Brussels where the nuncio with responsibility for British and Irish affairs held court. In some forty extant letters and reports he kept the Stuart court informed about the situation in Ireland, and sometimes provided information about the situation in Britain and on the continent as well. He was hopeful to the very last that the Jacobite cause would triumph and that James would be restored to the throne. He was translated to the diocese of Waterford and Lismore in 1739, but a widespread persecution of Catholics in 1744 found him, with his known Jacobite sympathies, more vulnerable than most and he had to flee the country in some haste to France, where he died in Paris in 1747. He was buried in Paris on 26 July OS / 6 August NS 1747.

According to contemporaries, Lloyd possessed a charm of speech and a pleasant manner, with an absence of the gravitas expected in a bishop. He was a gregarious man of considerable learning, a linguist who was well informed about international affairs, and a lively raconteur who could hold his own in any company. However, his influence on the Irish scene was negative in the sense that his persistent support for the Pretender and his consequent opposition to any moves towards a *rapprochement* with the Hanoverian regime stifled any move towards an amelioration of the penal laws against Catholics.

PATRICK FAGAN

Sources P. Fagan, *An Irish bishop in penal times: the chequered career of Sylvester Lloyd OFM, 1680–1747* (1993) · C. Giblin, ed., 'Catalogue of material of Irish interest in the collection *Nunziatura di Fiandra*, Vatican archives', *Collectanea Hibernica*, 1 (1958), 7–134; 3 (1960), 7–144; 4 (1961), 7–137; 5 (1962), 7–130; 9 (1966), 7–70; 10 (1967), 72–138; 11 (1968), 53–90; 12 (1969), 62–101; 13 (1970), 61–99; 14 (1971), 36–81; 15 (1972), 7–55 · P. Fagan, ed., *Ireland in the Stuart papers*, 2 vols. (1995) · I. Murphy, *The diocese of Killaloe in the eighteenth century* (1991) · H. Fenning, *The undoing of the friars of Ireland* (1972) · A. Faulkner, ed., *Liber Dubliniensis: chapter documents of Irish Franciscans, 1719–1875* (1978) · Joannes a San Antonio, *Bibliotecha universa Franciscana*, 2 (1732), 305 · F. Grannell, 'The strange story of Sylvester Lloyd OFM', *Clare Champion* (15 Jan 1972) · W. Carrigan, 'Dr Sylvester Lloyd', *Journal of the Waterford and South-East of Ireland Archaeological Society*, 3 (1897), 38–9 · Gillow, *Lit. biog. hist.*
Archives Royal Arch., Stuart MSS, letters and reports

Lloyd, Thomas (1640–1694), politician in Pennsylvania, was born in February 1640 and baptized on the 17th at Dolobran, Montgomeryshire, the son of Charles Lloyd (1613–1657), a gentleman, and his wife, Elizabeth Stanley. He studied medicine and law at Jesus College, Oxford, from 1658, but jeopardized his social position by adopting Quakerism. He obtained the release from prison of his eldest brother, Charles, and other Quakers, but was himself gaoled in 1665 for rejecting the oath of allegiance. He lived and practised medicine near Welshpool, and married a Friend, Mary Jones (*d.* 1683), in 1665. He became a prominent Quaker lobbyist to end religious persecution and disputed publicly with Anglican clergy.

In 1683 Lloyd emigrated to Pennsylvania, which William Penn had recently founded as a haven for Quakers and experiment in religious and ethnic harmony. Mary Lloyd, in tenuous health before the voyage, died soon after they arrived in Philadelphia. Lloyd married the Quaker Patience Wilson (Gardiner) Story (*d.* 1724) of New York city a year later. He was an active Friend, serving frequently on Philadelphia yearly meeting committees that wrote formal epistles to the London yearly meeting. He acquired lands totalling more than 7000 acres.

Lloyd quickly became the most influential political figure in Pennsylvania, despite acceding for several years to his wife's desire to live in New York. His penchant for dispute contributed to the young colony's turmoil, as he guarded and enhanced the power of his various offices and curtailed the autonomy of the Lower Counties (now Delaware). Throughout his career he remained loyal to Penn, though relations became strained when Lloyd opposed some of the proprietor's decisions and forced from office his ill-chosen governor, John Blackwell. Like William Penn, he negotiated an uneasy path between the prerogatives of upper-class status and Quaker restraint in seeking power and material rewards. In the proprietor's absence he exerted the authority in Pennsylvania that he could have claimed in Montgomeryshire had he not become a Friend.

Within months of Lloyd's arrival in Pennsylvania the proprietor appointed him master of the rolls, which gave him responsibility for enrolling official documents, including laws, deeds, and commissions. In March 1684 he was elected to the provincial council. When Penn left the province five months later he designated Lloyd president of the council—effectively the colony's governor—and keeper of the great seal. In 1687, when Penn attempted to undercut Lloyd's power by changing the form of government, the council president and his supporters ignored the new commission. A major showdown occurred the next year, when the proprietor appointed a brash soldier and non-Quaker, John Blackwell, as governor. As keeper of the great seal, Lloyd refused to seal Blackwell's new commission for county justices, which he said violated Pennsylvania law. At first abandoned by his fellow council members, he argued that the 'duty of my place is to advise, and with you to Endeavour that nothing be attempted … to the Subvertion of the Frame of Governm[en]t' (Horle and Haugaard, 511). Blackwell commanded him to surrender the great seal and charged him with sedition. When the governor refused to seat Lloyd and two other councillors elected in March 1689, opposition to the governor swelled. Lloyd published *A Seasonable Advertisement to the Freemen of this Province*, in which he warned voters that Blackwell threatened their 'Power of making Laws, erecting Courts of Justice, Raising of Monies' (ibid., 512). When Blackwell resigned in 1689, Lloyd served as president of the council in 1690 and as deputy governor in 1691–3. He survived the religious–political Keithian schism, in which the Scottish Quaker George Keith and his followers claimed that Quaker magistrates like Lloyd violated their faith by wielding authority. He lost the deputy governorship in 1693, however, when the crown forced Penn to surrender the province and appointed Benjamin Fletcher as royal governor. Lloyd again refused to seal documents, but had become estranged from the proprietor and resigned from government. He died in Philadelphia on 10 September 1694 of a fever, leaving his wife, Patience, and seven children. He ordered that his five slaves Mingo, Wissen, Julious, Marria, and Sarah be hired out and their wages paid to his wife and children, one of whom was the lawyer and politician David *Lloyd (1656–1731). JEAN R. SODERLUND

Sources D. Haugaard, 'Thomas Lloyd', *Lawmaking and legislators in Pennsylvania: a biographical dictionary*, ed. C. W. Horle and others, 1 (Philadelphia, 1991), 505–15, 505–17 • *The papers of William Penn*, ed. M. M. Dunn, R. S. Dunn, and others, 2–3 (1982–6) • G. B. Nash, 'Lloyd, Thomas', *ANB* • G. B. Nash, *Quakers and politics: Pennsylvania, 1681–1726* (1968) • Philadelphia yearly meeting, men's meeting, minutes, 1684–94, Swarthmore College, Swarthmore, Pennsylvania, Friends Historical Library • will, Hist. Soc. Penn., Philadelphia county wills, book A, 105 [photostat]
Archives Hist. Soc. Penn., Penn MSS
Wealth at death see will, Philadelphia county wills, Hist. Soc. Penn., book A, 105 [photostat]

Lloyd, Thomas (1784–1813), army officer, was the third son of Thomas Lloyd of Gloucester, King's county, Ireland, MP for King's county (1768–90), and his wife, Jane, youngest daughter and coheir of Thomas Le Hunte. On 1 August 1797 he was appointed ensign in the 54th foot in Ireland, and was promoted lieutenant on 6 May 1799. He served with the 54th at Ferrol, in the Egyptian campaign of 1801, and at Gibraltar in 1802, during the mutiny there, when the steadiness of the 54th gained high praise from the duke of Kent. He became captain in the 6th battalion of the reserve in 1803, and in 1804 was transferred to the 43rd light infantry, then training under Sir John Moore at Shorncliffe. He served with the 43rd at Copenhagen, and throughout the Peninsular campaigns of 1808–10. Romantic stories of his daring at the outposts were current in the army. On 8 October 1810 he was promoted major in the Old 94th, and became lieutenant-colonel of it on 17 August 1812. He commanded the 94th at the battle of Vitoria, and fell at its head at the battle of the Nivelle on 10 November 1813.

Lloyd appears to have been much loved by his men (Donaldson, 185–6, 193–5). The historian, Sir William Napier, wrote of him:

> In him were combined mental and bodily powers of no ordinary kind. Graceful symmetry, herculean strength, a countenance frank and majestic, gave a true indication of his nature, for his capacity was great and exceeding, and his military knowledge extensive, both from experience and study. Of his mirth and wit, well known in the army, it need only be said that he used the latter without offence, but so as to increase his ascendency … for though gentle, he was ambitious, valiant, and conscious of his fitness for great exploits. (Napier, 5.383–4)

H. M. CHICHESTER, *rev.* ROGER T. STEARN

Sources Burke, *Gen. GB* (1886) • *Army List* • W. F. P. Napier, *History of the war in the Peninsula and in the south of France*, rev. edn, 6 vols. (1851) • *The dispatches of … the duke of Wellington … from 1799 to 1818*, ed. J. Gurwood, 13 vols. in 12 (1834–9), vol. 4 • J. Donaldson, *Eventful life of a soldier* (1855)

Lloyd, Thomas (1803–1875), naval architect and engineer, was born at Portsea, Hampshire, on 29 October 1803 and educated at Portsmouth grammar school. He became an apprentice shipwright at Portsmouth and in 1819 passed the entry examination for the School of Naval Architecture, where his father was an instructor. After graduation in 1826 he worked at Portsmouth for four years, rated as a shipwright though he seems to have been employed on design work, before going to sea as trials officer for six months in the corvette *Columbine*. On completion of the trials he was appointed to the surveyor's office in Somerset House but was sent on a course to study steam machinery.

In 1831 Lloyd took charge of Marc Brunel's block making machinery at Portsmouth before moving to the Woolwich steam factory as inspector of steam machinery in 1833. He remained at Woolwich until 1847, with a brief seagoing appointment in 1837, rising through various posts and becoming chief engineer of the factory in 1842. The growing importance of machinery was marked by an increase in the salary of this post to £650 and the provision of a house. This period spanned the navy's industrial revolution, seeing the introduction of steam fighting ships, iron hulls, and the screw propeller. The steam factory was set up to maintain the engines of the rapidly increasing number of steamships in the navy but it soon became much more. The training of apprentices produced many good engineers, some of whom set up their own engine factories on the Thames. The Woolwich steam factory was also the navy's engineering development centre.

In 1840 Lloyd, together with a Captain Chappell, was in charge of the trials of Petit Smith's original screw steamer, *Archimedes*. As a result of Lloyd and Chappell's enthusiastic report the Admiralty decided to build a prototype screw warship—completed in 1844 as the *Rattler*. Lloyd was fully involved in the design and was instrumental in getting the stern lines lengthened to improve the flow into the propeller. This caused a short dispute with

I. K. Brunel, who had a similar idea and accused Lloyd of plagiarism, but they soon became friends, and Lloyd assisted in the trials of Brunel's *Great Britain*. Lloyd also arranged for a thrust meter to be inserted into the propeller shaft of the *Rattler* so that performance could be quantified. The trials of the *Rattler* were most successful, and well before they were complete the Admiralty ordered many large screw steamers and was planning the first screw battleships.

Lloyd retained his interest in the effect of flow into the propeller and in 1846 he carried out trials on the tender *Dwarf* in which wooden packing was added to the fine stern, reducing the original speed of 9 knots to 3 knots with a bluff stern. As chief engineer at Woolwich, Lloyd was also chief adviser to the Admiralty on engineering matters. In 1847 he became the first chief engineer of the Royal Navy, with an office in Somerset House and a staff of four. In 1850 the comptroller of steam machinery retired; the post was abolished and Lloyd was appointed chief engineer and inspector of steam machinery.

The first steam battleships had gone to sea in 1846, but they were crude conversions. Even so, the report of their performance in the manoeuvres of 1850 said that it was unlikely that the navy would ever again fight under sail. In 1851 the surveyor with Lloyd and Isaac Watts, the chief constructor, visited France and their report added urgency to the building of the first British steam battleship, the *Agamemnon*. There were many problems to be solved, particularly in finding a stern gland which would remain watertight under the rubbing and vibration of the propelled shaft.

During the Crimean War, Lloyd was shown, on a visit to Paris, the drawings of the French armoured screw-propelled batteries for attacking forts. At that time the proposed protection consisted of boxes of cannon balls, but at Lloyd's suggestion this was changed to 100 mm rolled iron plates.

In the reorganization of 1859 Lloyd moved to Whitehall at a salary of £900 and worked with Watts on the *Warrior*. Seemingly these two great engineers had mutual respect but their relationship was not warm.

Lloyd was always interested in new developments and was involved in early trials of the compound engine, but the technology of the day was inadequate. In 1866 he tried, again unsuccessfully, the use of oil fuel. He was involved in the design of the machinery to lay the first trans-Atlantic cable in 1858. It is a great tribute to Dr Inman, the principal of the School of Naval Architecture, that so many of his graduates achieved fame in areas far removed from the wooden sailing ships on which their education was focused.

Lloyd served on many important committees, notably that of 1871 which reviewed ship design after the loss of the *Captain*, and was frequently consulted by commercial engine builders. Lloyd became a member of the Institution of Civil Engineers in 1841. He was a founder in 1851 of the Royal Navy Engineers' Club in Portsmouth, which for fifty years was a centre for technical discussion. He was one of the original vice-presidents of the Institution of Naval Architects in 1860. Though he joined in debates he published no paper of his own outside the Admiralty. Within it his importance was recognized by that great surveyor Spencer Robinson, who wrote on Lloyd's retirement that there was no public servant who had so largely contributed to the advance of practical science, pointing out that the Royal Navy's lead in screw propulsion was largely due to Lloyd.

Lloyd was made a CB in 1868, and retired the following year. He never married and died at his home at 84 Finchley Road, Hampstead, London, on 23 March 1875.

DAVID K. BROWN

Sources A. F. Smith, 'Thomas Lloyd', *Journal of Naval Engineering*, 1 (1947), 1 • D. K. Brown, 'Thomas Lloyd CB', *Warship*, 20 (Oct 1981) • D. K. Brown, *Before the ironclad* (1990) • Boase, *Mod. Eng. biog.*

Wealth at death under £12,000: administration, 20 April 1875, *CGPLA Eng. & Wales*

Lloyd, Sir Thomas Ingram Kynaston (1896–1968), civil servant, was born at Shifnal, Shropshire, on 19 June 1896, the eldest of three sons of John Charles Lloyd, corn merchant, and his wife, Henrietta Elizabeth Brown. He went to Rossall School and left in 1915 with an open scholarship in mathematics to Gonville and Caius College, Cambridge. Owing to the war, however, he entered the Royal Military Academy, Woolwich, was commissioned second lieutenant in the Royal Engineers in 1916 and was promoted lieutenant in 1917. He served in Egypt and Palestine and was mentioned in dispatches. In 1919 he went for a year to Caius where he read history but took no examination.

Lloyd entered the civil service in 1920 and was posted to the Ministry of Health. In 1921 he was lent to the Colonial Office, to which he was permanently transferred the following year. Lloyd married, in 1922, Bessie Nora, daughter of G. J. Mason, of Penn, Staffordshire, who owned a chain of grocery shops. They had two sons.

Lloyd's first posting was to the Nigeria department, but in 1926 he moved to the Middle East department, where he served until, in 1929, he was appointed private secretary to the permanent under-secretary of state, Sir Samuel Wilson. In 1929 he was promoted principal and later in the year was selected to be secretary of the Palestine commission, an assignment for which his service in the Middle East department specially fitted him and which he discharged with great ability. From 1930 to 1938 he worked in the colonial service department, where he was especially concerned with the personal records and careers of members of the colonial civil service. He made a particular point of meeting as many of them as he could, and thus acquired an unrivalled knowledge of their qualities for promotion.

In 1938 Lloyd was appointed secretary of the royal commission on the West Indies under the chairmanship of Lord Moyne, who later paid tribute to his 'really remarkable efficiency and devotion to duty'. The commission's report led to the enactment in 1940 of the first Colonial Development and Welfare Act. In 1939 Lloyd was promoted assistant secretary and in 1940, following the collapse of France, took charge of a new department dealing specially with relations with the French colonies. In 1942 he was made head of the defence department. In 1943 he became assistant under-secretary of state, supervising the west African and eastern departments. In this year he was appointed CMG. In 1947 he succeeded Sir George Gater as permanent under-secretary of state and was appointed KCMG, followed by KCB in 1949 and GCMG in 1951. He retired in 1956.

In nine years as permanent under-secretary, Lloyd served four secretaries of state. This was a period of economic and social expansion, notably in the development of university colleges, made possible by colonial development and welfare funds. The territorial responsibilities and the strength of the office and colonial service were at their maximum and many improvements in organization and training were introduced. Lloyd devoted great care to planning coherent sequences of promotions and transfers. Despite an endless series of political problems, such as the Malayan emergency, Mau Mau in Kenya, terrorism in Cyprus, and the deposition of the Kabaka in Uganda, significant constitutional changes were introduced, including ministerial self-government in the Gold Coast, the West Indies Federation, the Federation of the Rhodesias and Nyasaland, and the Federation of Nigeria. The foundations were laid for the independence of Ghana and Malaya in 1957.

This would have been an indigestible menu for any permanent under-secretary. Lloyd's orderly mind enabled him to delegate without losing control of essentials, concentrating his effort where it was most needed from time to time. His advice was always shrewd and well informed, and was expressed with masterly precision and economy of words. His qualities were well summed up in *The Memoirs of Lord Chandos* (1962):

> Tom Lloyd was an example of the best in the Civil Service, wise and salty in his judgements, never in a panic or a hurry, enlightened and broad-minded on colonial policy, a good judge of men, insistent that humour must be among their qualifications. It is certainly amongst his. Some said that he did not allow his imagination to walk abroad, but only took it out on a lead for a short time. If this were true I should be far from saying that it was a fault in the permanent head of a department. A little deflation from time to time is as good a thing for Ministers as it is for monetary policy. With all this, he had perhaps too much loyalty for some of his particular swans who had turned, in the stress of colonial affairs or under the erosive influence of Government Houses, into geese. (Chandos, 347)

Lloyd did not seek further government employment after retirement. He accepted a directorship with Harrisons and Crosfield Ltd, and he was a governor and member of Rossall School council from 1956 until his death. He very rarely missed a meeting and his wisdom and experience were of very great value. But for the most part he devoted himself to his family and his grandchildren, and to his personal hobbies, particularly gardening and philately, to both of which he applied himself with expert knowledge and enthusiasm. His garden at Faggots End, Radlett, was described in *Country Life* as probably the most beautiful in Hertfordshire.

Lloyd died at Faggots End on 9 December 1968. The elder of his two sons, G. P. Lloyd, entered the colonial service in 1951. HILTON POYNTON, *rev.*

Sources *The Times* (11 Dec 1968) · *WWW* · *CGPLA Eng. & Wales* (1969) · Lord Chandos [O. Lyttleton, first Viscount Chandos], *The memoirs of Lord Chandos: an unexpected view from the summit* (1962)
Archives PRO, corresp. and papers, CO 967/169–238
Likenesses W. Stoneman, photograph, 1948, NPG
Wealth at death £50,090: probate, 28 Jan 1969, *CGPLA Eng. & Wales*

Lloyd, William (1627–1717), bishop of Worcester, was the son of Richard *Lloyd (1594/5–1659), rector of Tilehurst and vicar of Sonning, Berkshire, and his wife, Joan, *née* Wicken; Richard Lloyd's family were of an ancient distinguished Welsh lineage. William Lloyd was born in Tilehurst rectory on 18 August 1627 and baptized on the 26th of that month.

Education and early career Lloyd was taught Latin, Greek, and Hebrew by his father at home and he entered Richard Lloyd's Oxford college, Oriel, at the age of eleven, where he matriculated on 25 March 1639, moving to Jesus College in 1640 and graduating BA on 25 October 1642. He then left Oxford, which was occupied by the king's forces in the civil war, and seems to have returned to Berkshire. When Oxford surrendered to parliament Lloyd returned there and graduated MA from Jesus College, of which he was a fellow, on 9 December 1646. In 1648 he was episcopally ordained deacon in Oxford, went back to Berkshire to act as tutor in a gentry family, may have paid visits to the royal court in Paris in 1651 and 1653, and was presented to the rectory of Bradfield in Berkshire. In 1653 he married a woman whose maiden name may have been Cheney and who died in 1654. By December 1654 he had resigned his claim to the Bradfield living rather than face a contest for it with a Cromwellian claimant. He was ordained priest, again episcopally, in 1656 and took up a private tutoring post in Oxford until 1659. In that year an apparent oddity in Lloyd's career—given that his father was an ardent royalist, that he had undergone episcopal ordination and that he had reputedly paid homage to the exiled court—arose: in an attempt 'to impose upon the royalists' (Wood, *Ath. Oxon.*, 1.xxxviii), Lloyd choreographed a fraud in which a London merchant was disguised as a patriarch of the Greek Orthodox church, to whom Oxford sympathizers were prevailed upon to do reverence. However, leading Oxford presbyterians were also gulled by this fraud into discussing with the suppositious patriarch a 'modell' (ibid.) of church government and this may have been part of the reason that, although in the short term Lloyd had to flee presbyterian wrath in Oxford, upon the Restoration his career prospered.

In 1660 Lloyd was nominated for a prebend in Ripon; he took up the office in person, after a protracted spell of ill health, on 3 June 1663, and in July 1666 was made a chaplain-in-ordinary to the king. In 1667 Lloyd added BD and DD to his Oxford degrees and began a career as an anti-Catholic publicist with a work calling into question the contribution that recusants had made to the royal cause during the civil wars, *The Late 'Apology in behalf of the*

William Lloyd (1627–1717), by unknown artist, *c.*1710–15

Papists', ... Answered. A rapid series of ecclesiastical promotions now followed: vicar of St Mary's, Reading, in 1668 (until 1676) and in the same year a string of appointments appropriate to his Welsh ancestry—vicar of Llan-fawr in Merioneth, archdeacon of Merioneth, and rector of Llandudno, Caernarvonshire. His prospects steadily improving, he cemented his clerical alliances on 3 December 1668 with a marriage to Anne Jones (1646–1719), daughter of the subdean of Westminster. He consolidated his Welsh preferments with the deanery of Bangor in 1672, published three anti-Catholic works including *A Seasonable Discourse ... in Opposition to Popery* in 1673, extended his holdings to London with the acquisition of the prebend of Caddington Minor in St Paul's in the same year, was made canon residentiary of Salisbury in 1674, and gave up his St Paul's prebend in favour of the vicarage of St Martin-in-the-Fields, the hugely overpopulated Westminster parish, where he was inducted on 6 December 1676 and served as a conscientious incumbent. In the year of his appointment, in *Considerations Touching their True Way to Suppress Popery*, he argued that toleration given to Catholics who would abjure the pope's infallibility and deposing power would weaken the English Romanists by dividing them. The proposal for selective indulgence for those Catholics won the approval of the Catholic duke of York. Deeply unpopular with fellow clerics as a court protégé, between November 1677 and January 1678 Lloyd served as leading chaplain in the Netherlands to York's daughter Mary, following her marriage to the prince of Orange.

The alleged murder by Catholic extremists of the St Martin's parishioner Sir Edmund Berry Godfrey on or after 12 October 1678 allowed Lloyd as vicar to deliver, on the 31st of the month, a funeral sermon of uncompromising anti-popery: 'God keep England from your bloody religion' (Tindal Hart, 29); he subsequently played an active part in the prosecution of the alleged murder, attended one of those accused of the crime, Berry, to his execution, and has been convincingly identified by his leading biographer, Tindal Hart, as Charles II's confidential intermediary in the follow-up to the Godfrey affair, possibly keeping back features of Berry's confessions that might have embarrassed the court. The conferment on him of further Welsh benefices, a prebend at Llandaff, in March 1679, and the vicarage of Llanefydd in 1680, might fit such speculations. It seems likely that in order to protect his reputation for protestantism he refrained from coming forward to discredit the evidence, as he had the knowledge to do, of the informer Turberville against the accused Catholic peer Lord Stafford in 1680: the Stafford execution redounded to the benefit of the crown by identifying Shaftesbury and the whigs with blood lust. Lloyd, who in August 1680 was commissioned by the secretary of state with espionage against subversives in Reading, put his foot on the first rung of the episcopal ladder with his elevation to the bishopric of St Asaph on 3 October 1680, taking up residence, after attending the House of Lords over the winter, on April 1681. A series of Welsh livings newly acquired in the 1680s compensated the new bishop for the modest St Asaph stipend in return for which he had surrendered all his other benefices.

Ambitious careerist as he clearly was, Lloyd had already shown in his tenure at St Martin's that he could apply himself conscientiously to his clerical duties. In impoverished St Asaph, which had had an easy-going episcopal regime under the previous diocesan, he was determined on sweeping reforms, including the recovery of the diocese's alienated real estate. He announced his intention of holding his confirmations using the Welsh language and constantly sought improvements from his clergy, carrying out ordinations regularly, aiming to raise depressed stipends and improve educational levels, and to secure attendance on parsons' duties in person and exact record keeping of the conditions of their parishes, as well as requiring strict standards of sobriety, honesty in the charging of fees from the laity, administration of the sacraments, and rigour in the use of excommunication and of sabbath observance.

With religious repression in the tory reaction rising in England from the time of Lloyd's taking up his duties in St Asaph he used discussion with, rather than repression of, dissenters in his diocese—with Quakers on 22 September 1681 and 6 August 1682, and with presbyterians on 27 September 1681 and 28 August 1682. His preferred policy was one of public disputation and private conference to win dissenters back to the communion of the Church of England, while he established relations of real respect with individual figures such as the Quaker Richard Davies and the presbyterian Philip Henry. However, by 1682 he was assuring Archbishop Sancroft that he was energetically prosecuting religious dissidents, and in the repressive royalist and tory mood of the reaction to the whig Rye House plot in 1683 adopted the full-throated language of anti-nonconformity, demanding the rigorous enforcement of the penal laws. Amid all his storm of activity as a bishop, Lloyd the scholar found the time to complete for publication in 1684 his *History of the government of the church as it was in Great Britain, when they first received the Christian religion*, a defence of the episcopal governance of the early British church.

The seven bishops The accession of James II, who distrusted Lloyd for his prosecution of those implicated in the Popish Plot, put his career on standby, though in 1685–6 he canvassed all vacancies, impending and actual, on the bench of bishops. James's switch to the adoption of religious toleration in 1687 presented the bishop of St Asaph with a dilemma. As he showed when he cordially welcomed French protestant refugees into his bishopric in the wake of the revocation of the edict of Nantes in 1685—filling up his ordination lists with the names of their clergy and bestirring his own priests into contributing to the relief of the exiles—he could be eirenic in his attitude to protestants, but the toleration of recusants which loomed so large in James II's two declarations of indulgence, of 1687 and 1688, was beyond consideration for the anti-Catholic Lloyd. A meeting of opponents of the second, April 1688, declaration chaired by Sancroft on 12 May 1688 identified Lloyd as one of the bishops to be called to London to take part in the petition to the king against the enforced reading by the clergy of the Church of England of the toleration manifesto: he speedily arrived in the capital—at the home of the tory Anglican leader, the earl of Clarendon—on the 16th and rapidly joined the opposition to the king's plans. He was, after Sancroft, the second of the seven bishops to sign the petition that was delivered in person to James on 18 May and, in the archbishop's absence from the actual delegation, he took a leading role in the presentation, handing it to the king and attempting to deflect James's wrathful accusation that the petition hoisted the standard of rebellion with the protest, 'We have adventured our lives for your Majesty, and would loose the last drop of our blood rather than lift up a finger against you' (Tindal Hart, 99). He went on to argue with the king by pointing out that the dispensing power, the constitutional foundation on which the declaration rested, had been declared illegal by parliament under both Charles II and James himself. Though Bishop Compton of London rather than he was probably responsible for leaking the petition to the printers, it may have been Lloyd who followed up the confrontation with the king with a letter advising all ministers of the Church of England to abstain from reading the declaration. James's decision to imprison and prosecute the bishops was implicit in the interview of the evening of 18 May.

Having returned to St Asaph, Lloyd had to come back to London for an appearance before the privy council on 6 June and again took a defiant stand towards the king, insisting on the bishops' common law right not to incriminate themselves and boldly refusing James's command that the accused accept bail, which 'may be prejudicial to us' (Tindal Hart, 105–6): of all the bishops, it was Lloyd's attitude that made it impossible to maintain the claim put forward in the petition composed by Sancroft that they proceeded from no 'want of duty and obedience to your majesty' (Tindal Hart, 97). Indeed, by the time of his imprisonment in the Tower, which he shared with his brethren from 8 June, Lloyd may already having been looking towards an Orange regime—with an overthrow of popery, church reform, and an overture to the protestant dissenters. London's popular anti-popery unerringly centred on Lloyd as its chief hero among the bishops, singling him out for acclamation when the seven were bailed on 5 June. Regularly linking up with Clarendon in London, Lloyd followed the acquittal of the bishops in king's bench on 30 June by returning to his diocese.

The revolution By 7 October Lloyd was back in the capital, conferring with Clarendon but having kept away from discussions between James and the other bishops which were intended to produce concessions on James's part in the light of Orange's impending invasion. In November, though, he was active in promoting a petition to James to summon a free parliament, a plea that the king found unacceptable. The day after James's departure on 10 December, Lloyd was a signatory to an address drawn up at the London Guildhall and appealing to Orange to 'rescue the nation' (Tindal Hart, 115), and in December 1688 (when he was acting as an intermediary between Orange and the bishops) and January 1689, increasingly under the influence of Gilbert Burnet, he was becoming convinced that, in departing, James had forfeited his throne. Even so, he seems to have been absent from the vote in the Lords on 29 January on whether to confer the crown or a regency on James's behalf on William and Mary of Orange. He was hedging his bets in the early weeks of the year, but by mid-February he was commenting on Orange as a kind of acceptable usurper; he soon took the oaths of allegiance to the new sovereigns and began to commend them vigorously to other clergy. Lloyd attended the coronation and performed the absent Sancroft's primatial task of announcing Mary as queen to the congregation. His appointment as lord high almoner to Mary put him in charge of dispensing her charity to claimants, especially the still long queue of civil war victims. He went on to honour his standing commitment to an understanding with the nonconformists by helping to prepare a bill of comprehension (which was aborted). If Lloyd had had any reservations about an Orange settlement, he overcame them decisively once it was achieved and, although late in 1689 and early in 1690 he was trying to find a formula to keep the nonjuring clergy in post, he represented one of the polarized wings in a now politically much divided Church of England. Although into the early 1690s he continued to try to persuade colleagues to accept the new king and queen his participation in the consecration on 31 May 1691 of John Tillotson in succession to the displaced nonjuror Sancroft confirmed his breach with the elements of the church that distrusted James's policies but acknowledged him as their irremovable king. He shored up his rejection of James by an absolute disbelief in the legitimacy of his son, born in June 1688.

Lloyd's many services to the king and queen, which included the publication of *A Discourse of God's Ways of Disposing of Kingdoms* (1691), a defence of the revolution, and of sermons which underlined the king's role as an agent of godly reformation, merited him appointment to the vacant see of Coventry and Lichfield, to which his appointment was confirmed in October 1692. He left St Asaph in a thoroughly reformed condition and applied to Coventry and Lichfield policies of friendship to dissenters but also, it was alleged, extreme, arbitrary, divisive, and bureaucratized discipline within the clergy and of litigious behaviour to the laity. And, whatever Lloyd's preference for using methods of persuasion and argument towards dissenters, he was acutely aware of the weakness of the established church's position after the Toleration Act. What was to be done where parishioners took their infants to be baptized by nonconformist ministers, he complained to his colleague Bishop Stillingfleet of Worcester. How was he to deal with the ministers? 'For to punish those Parishioners would be to drive them from the Church & so to fill their Congregations' (Rose, 172–3).

In April 1695 Lloyd was appointed to a new commission to advise William on crown appointments in the church and from 1697 (when he refused ordination to the future high tory tribune William Sacheverell) he took a leading part in the investigation of irregularities alleged against his successor at St Asaph, Thomas Jones, suspended from office in 1701. The deprivation from St David's of the opponent of the revolution Thomas Watson (1637–1717) for alleged gross misconduct into which Lloyd had helped conduct enquiries, preceded by a few days Lloyd's own formal induction into his new see of Worcester on 8 August 1699.

Bishop of Worcester While the acquisition of wealthy Worcester (with remission of first fruits to the crown conceded by William III) represented the pinnacle of Lloyd's life as a clerical careerist, it was not necessarily the most suitable bishopric for him to serve. The new bishop may not have had insuperable problems with the dissenters of Worcestershire, who were especially entrenched in the county town, but he was less well adapted to the county's quite numerous Catholics, whose numbers were growing through conversions in the early eighteenth century. Even more ominously, Worcestershire, and especially its clergy, had marked high tory, and indeed Jacobite, leanings from which they were inclined to regard Lloyd—despite his characteristically close attention to the physical, moral, and educational state of the diocese—as a Williamite time-server and as one of the false brethren who betrayed the church to revolution principles. From his very entry into the diocese a lay inspirer of repudiation of him was the tory knight of the shire in parliament, Sir John Packington, who helped in the distribution of a bitter pamphlet attack on Lloyd. The latter retaliated in 1701 by co-ordinating a mass address of Worcestershire signatories pledging to eject Packington at the next general election. In 1702 it was reported that Lloyd 'charges his Clergy in his visitation every where, upon theyr canonicall obedience, not to give theyr votes for Sr J Pak' (Holmes, *British Politics*, 29), but the campaign, in the altered party political circumstances of the new reign of Anne, rebounded back on the bishop when the Commons denounced his 'malicious, unchristian and arbitrary' interference in the election and successfully demanded his dismissal from the position of lord almoner.

Lloyd continued to campaign in Worcestershire elections, for example in 1707, while in 1710 he ordered his clergy to refrain from ringing church bells to mark the triumphant progress in the shire of Sacheverell (whom he came to fear would succeed him), but he was increasingly immersed in his long-standing study of biblical chronology and prophecy, relating texts of Daniel and Revelation to events taking place, and to be expected, in his own day. By that time this kind of speculation seemed an old-fashioned intellectual pursuit which tended to be ridiculed as 'but his dotages' and he as 'Old Mysterio', a crazed, obsessed, and fanatical seer (Tindal Hart, 236). Nevertheless Lloyd was both a profound scholar himself and an encourager of learning in others, as well as an active diocesan bishop and regular preacher. He died at Hartlebury Castle, Worcestershire, on 30 August 1717 and was buried on 10 September at the church of Fladbury, of which his son William was the incumbent.

MICHAEL MULLETT

Sources A. Tindal Hart, *William Lloyd, 1627–1717: bishop, politician, author and prophet* (1952) • Foster, *Alum. Oxon.* • Wood, *Ath. Oxon.*, new edn • G. S. Holmes, *British politics in the age of Anne*, rev. edn (1987) • C. Rose, *England in the 1690s: revolution, religion and war* (1999) • A. Claydon, *William III and the godly revolution* (1996)

Archives BM, MSS • Bodl. Oxf., theological commonplace books • Glos. RO, corresp. and papers • NL Wales, chronological tables and indexes • Worcs. RO, diary kept by his secretary | BM, Lambeth MSS • Bodl. Oxf., letters to Henry Dodwell [copies] • TCD, corresp. with William King • U. Wales, Bangor, corresp. with Thomas Mostyn

Likenesses G. Bower, silver medal, 1688, NPG • oils, *c.*1710–1715, LPL [*see illus.*] • G. Vertue, line print, 1714 (after F. Weideman), BM, NPG • D. Loggan, line print, BM, NPG • E. Seman, portrait, repro. in Tindal Hart, *William Lloyd*; priv. coll. • Sturt, engraving • G. Vertue, line print (after T. Forster), BM, NPG • engraving, priv. coll. • group portrait, oils (*The seven bishops committed to the Tower in 1688*), NPG • oils, CCC Oxf. • portrait, priv. coll.

Lloyd, William (1636/7–1710), bishop of Norwich and nonjuror, was born at Bala, Merioneth, the son of Edward Lloyd (*d.* 1685?), rector of Llangower, Merioneth. He was educated at Ruthin School for two years under Mr Chaloner, and was admitted to St John's College, Cambridge, on 23 February 1655, aged eighteen, graduating BA in 1659 and proceeding MA in 1662.

John Evelyn, attending his parish church at Deptford, Kent, in August 1662, heard Lloyd preach a sermon and in August 1663 described him as 'our curate' (Evelyn, 3.361). Lloyd then spent some time ministering to the English factory at Lisbon, for in June 1670 the king asked that Lloyd, a 'chaplain in ordinary', be created DD by royal mandate, 'although wanting two years of his full standing, he having taken great pains' in Lisbon and being set to return to Portugal (*CSP dom.*, *1670*, 292). This was duly granted and in July he was described by Evelyn as 'preacher at Gray's Inn'.

In December 1670 Evelyn described him as 'chaplain to his Majesty' (Evelyn, 3.552, 565).

On 4 May 1672 Lloyd was collated a prebendary of St Paul's, and in February 1673 Evelyn described him as 'my Lord Treasurer's chaplain' (Evelyn, 4.3), a reference to Thomas Clifford, Lord Clifford. In March Henry Coventry, secretary of state, intimated that 'Dr. Lloyd of Battersea' (*CSP dom.*, *1675*, 472) would succeed to the vacant bishopric of Llandaff, and he was duly confirmed as such on 18 April 1675, the last Welsh-speaker to hold the diocese for two hundred years. In April a warrant was issued for Lloyd to hold his prebend in St Paul's and the rectory of St Andrew's, Llandaff, *in commendam*, but a successor was collated to his prebend in March 1676. As a bishop Lloyd proved to be a rigorous supporter of the Restoration church settlement, in both church and secular affairs. In 1676 he was instrumental in securing the dismissal from the Monmouthshire bench of a justice who was also a recusant. He was also tough on refractory clergy and diocesan officials, at one point imposing a sentence of greater excommunication on the principal registrar of the consistory court. By this date Lloyd had married his wife, Anne (*d.* 1708), for matriculation records at Cambridge in 1691 suggest that their son John was born in this period.

Lloyd was translated to the bishopric of Peterborough, being elected on 10 April 1679, and enthroned on 12 July. He was resident for at least part of the year at Acton, Middlesex, for two of his children were baptized there, a son, Edward, on 20 April 1680, and a daughter, Hannah, on 25 July 1682. In the House of Lords, Lloyd was a supporter of the court, voting on 23 November 1680 against moves for a joint committee with the Commons to debate the safety of the kingdom. Moreover Lloyd proved to be an energetic diocesan: in the four years 1679–83 he confirmed 7864 people and ordained 47 priests and deacons. He also suppressed conventicles with the aid of the local JPs, and threatened to present those not receiving the sacrament, thereby boosting the number of communicants.

Lloyd was translated to Norwich, being elected on 11 June 1685, and enthroned (by proxy) on 23 July 1685. Lloyd was loyal to James II's government, attempting to persuade those dismissed from the commission of the peace to co-operate with the regime early in 1688. Nevertheless his firm commitment to the Church of England was such that only absence from London prevented Lloyd joining the seven bishops in their petition to James II to withdraw the declaration of indulgence. Upon his arrival in London he signed the petition and helped to organize their legal defence, even paying £5 towards their legal costs.

Lloyd was one of the peers who petitioned James II in mid-November 1688 to allow parliament to meet. He opposed the revolution of 1688, voting in the Convention Parliament on 29 January 1689 for a regency. In February he brought the problems of loyalists into sharp relief with his acknowledgement that he was willing to pray for the royal family in general, but could not do so if he had to name King William and Queen Mary. Consequently he refused the oaths to the new monarchs, stopped attending the house of Lords, and in August 1689 was suspended from his diocese. As the date for the deprivation of those bishops who would not take the oaths drew nearer he remained close to Sancroft, no doubt endorsing the archbishop's refusal to make a move towards the government. He was deprived on 1 February 1690, although no successor was appointed for over a year. Lloyd was clearly popular with his clergy, even those taking the oaths, for in Norwich diocese they petitioned for the removal of penalties from the nonjuring bishops. Following the naval defeat at Beachy Head in June 1690, and consequent fears of invasion, on 4 August a mob attacked Lloyd's house in Old Street, London, forcing him to take his family into the Temple to find refuge.

On 9 February 1692 Archbishop Sancroft signed a commission bestowing upon Lloyd full primatical authority. Thus, when Sancroft died in November 1693 Lloyd was his acknowledged successor. This proved to be important when there were disagreements over whether the nonjurors should perpetuate the split with the official church of England by consecrating their own bishops. Lloyd took part in the consecration of two new bishops (George Hickes and Thomas Wagstaffe) on 24 February 1694. In July 1695 he signed a letter supporting John Kettlewell's scheme for the relief of the suffering nonjuring clergy. In 1700 he opposed Bishop Thomas Ken's initiative to Archbishop Thomas Tenison to end the split in the church, writing that he was in favour of peace, 'but without quitting my principles for I'm persuaded that the principles for which I suffer are just and true, being founded upon the authority of the scriptures and the practice of the church' (Yould, 370). In 1703, when Bishop Ken decided to resign his diocese of Bath and Wells to George Hooper, who had been appointed to the see following the death of Richard Kidder, Lloyd chastised Ken for acting on his own, and angry letters were exchanged between the two men.

Lloyd remained intransigent in his opposition to a reunification of the church once the deprived bishops had died or, in Ken's case, resigned their sees. Lloyd's wife was buried at Hammersmith on 19 June 1708. Lloyd died on 1 January 1710 after a fall and was buried at Hammersmith four days later. As the last of the deprived bishops, apart from Ken, his death allowed some prominent nonjurors, such as Henry Dodwell, Robert Nelson, and Francis Brokesby, to rejoin the national church. Lloyd's daughter, Hannah, survived him and was the recipient of some insurance money. STUART HANDLEY

Sources G. M. Yould, 'Two nonjurors', *Norfolk Archaeology*, 35 (1970–73), 364–74 • Venn, *Alum. Cant.* • *Fasti Angl., 1541–1857*, [St Paul's, London], 24 • *Fasti Angl., 1541–1857*, [Bristol], 116 • *Fasti Angl., 1541–1857*, [Ely], 39 • *DWB* • D. Lysons, *The environs of London*, 4 vols. (1792–6), vol. 2, pp. 16, 415 • J. H. Overton, *The nonjurors: their lives, principles, and writings* (1902), 38–46 • J. E. Griffith, *Pedigrees of Anglesey and Carnarvonshire families* (privately printed, Horncastle, 1914), 252 • J. Spurr, *The Restoration Church of England, 1646–1689* (1991) • Evelyn, *Diary*, 3.334–5, 361, 552, 565; 4.3, 86–7, 369 • *CSP dom.*, 1670, 292; 1675–6, 69, 472 • F. Blomefield and C. Parkin, *An essay towards a topographical history of the county of Norfolk*, [2nd edn], 11 vols. (1805–

10), 3.588 • T. Lathbury, *A history of the nonjurors* (1845) • L. K. J. Glassey, *Politics and the appointment of justices of the peace, 1675–1720* (1979), 38, 87, 94 • R. H. Mason, *The history of the county of Norfolk* (1884), 424–6 • *The diary and autobiography of Edmund Bohun*, ed. S. W. Rix (1853), 74–5, 88 • *The correspondence of Henry Hyde, earl of Clarendon, and of his brother Lawrence Hyde, earl of Rochester*, ed. S. W. Singer, 2 (1828) • J. Gutch, *Collectanea curiosa*, 2 vols. (1781), 2.342, 358
Archives BL, commonplace book, Add. MS 40160 • Bodl. Oxf., corresp. • Bucks. RLSS, letters • LPL, corresp. and papers • St John Cam., collection of MSS | BL, letters to Lord Danby, Add. MSS 28051, 28053; Egerton MSS 3331, 3334, 3384, *passim* • BL, letters to Lord Hatton, Add. MS 29584 • Bodl. Oxf., 'An account of the present state of the bishoprick of Peterborough … 1683', MS Rawl. D 1163
Likenesses oils, bishop's palace, Peterborough

Lloyd, William Forster (1794–1852), political economist, was the son of Thomas Lloyd (*d.* 1815), rector of Aston-sub-Edge, Gloucestershire, and his wife, Elizabeth (*d.* 1814). He was the younger brother of Charles *Lloyd (1784–1829), bishop of Oxford. Educated at Westminster School (captain in 1811), he was elected to Christ Church, Oxford, in 1812. He graduated BA in 1815, with a first class in mathematics and a second in classics. He proceeded MA in 1818. He was Greek reader in 1823, mathematical lecturer at Christ Church until the end of 1824, and filled the Drummond chair of political economy in 1832–7. He published *Prices of Corn in Oxford in the Beginning of the Fourteenth Century* (1830), and several books of his Oxford lectures, of which *Lectures on Population, Value, Poor-Laws and Rent* (1837) was the most widely known.

The subjects of his lectures were unusually pertinent to what were the current issues of the day in the world outside Oxford. A recent historian describes his work as 'a distinguished technical contribution' to economic analysis, and sees him as exemplifying a distinct Oxford approach to political economy (Hilton, 47, 50). He was elected fellow of the Royal Society in 1834. Although in holy orders, he held no preferment, but lived on his property, Prestwood, Missenden, Buckinghamshire, where he died on 2 June 1852. A. M. CLERKE, *rev.* ALAN YOSHIOKA

Sources J. Welch, *The list of the queen's scholars of St Peter's College, Westminster*, ed. [C. B. Phillimore], new edn (1852) • election certificate, RS • 'Lloyd, Charles (1784–1829)', *DNB* • B. Hilton, *The age of atonement: the influence of evangelicalism on social and economic thought, 1785–1865*, [2nd edn] (1991) • Foster, *Alum. Oxon.*

Lloyd, William Watkiss (1813–1893), classical and literary scholar, the second son of David Lloyd of Newcastle under Lyme, was born at Homerton, Middlesex, on 11 March 1813. He was educated at the grammar school in Newcastle under Lyme, and made so much progress that the master, the Revd John Anderton, offered to contribute towards the fees of a university course. At the age of fifteen, however, he was placed in the counting-house of his cousins' tobacco manufacturing firm, Messrs John and Francis Lloyd, at 77 Snow Hill, London, where he stayed, rising to become a partner, until he retired from business in 1864. For a period of thirty-six years his days were devoted to uncongenial duties and his nights to books. At one time he lived at Snow Hill, and for many years never left London. With an inborn love for learning he added to a solid basis of Greek and Latin a wide knowledge of modern languages and literatures, as well as of ancient art, history, and archaeology. To these pursuits every leisure hour, even to the close of his life, was applied. The first-fruit of his studies was a historical and mythological essay entitled 'The Xanthian marbles: the Nereid monument' (1845), followed by other contributions on subjects of Greek antiquities, some printed in the *Classical Museum*. In 1854 he supplied certain 'Arguments' to Owen Jones's *Apology for the Colouring of the Greek Court in the Crystal Palace*. In the same year he was elected a member of the Society of Dilettanti, chiefly through the friendly offices of Monckton Milnes (afterwards Lord Houghton). Until his death he 'was one of the principal guides and advisers of the Dilettanti in their archaeological undertakings' (Cust, 187, 206), and acted temporarily as secretary and treasurer in 1888 and 1889.

As a labour of love Lloyd supplied essays on the life and plays of Shakespeare to S. W. Singer's edition of the poet published in 1856 (2nd edn, 1875). The essays show acute criticism and thorough knowledge of Elizabethan literature, and were collected by the author in a private reprint (1858, and reissued without the life in 1875 and 1888). A memoir on the system of proportion employed in the design of ancient Greek temples was added by him to C. R. Cockerell's *Temples of Jupiter Panhellenius at Aegina and of Apollo Epicurius*, published in 1860. The subject was also treated in *A general theory of proportion in architectural design and its exemplification in detail in the Parthenon, with illustrative engravings* (1863), a lecture delivered before the Royal Institute of British Architects on 13 June 1859, and his most original work. His literary interests then turned in a different direction, and he published *The Moses of Michael Angelo: a Study of Art, History, and Legend* (1863), followed by *Christianity in the Cartoons, Referred to Artistic Treatment and Historic Fact* (1865), in which artistic criticism is coupled with a free treatment of religious matters, and *Philosophy, Theology, and Poetry in the Age and Art of Rafael* (1866). In 1868 he married Ellen Brooker (*d.* 1900), second daughter of Lionel John Beale, and sister of Lionel Smith Beale. Ancient Greek history and art were the subjects of his next two publications: *The History of Sicily to the Athenian War, with Elucidations of the Sicilian Odes of Pindar* (1872), and *The Age of Pericles: a History of the Politics and Arts of Greece from the Persian to the Peloponnesian War* (1875), the second a complete conception of the social life and art of Greece at its highest point. In 1882 he delivered four lectures on the *Iliad* and *Odyssey* at the Royal Institution, of which he acted as one of the managers from 1879 to 1881. He was elected a member of the Athenaeum in 1875, and for many years was an active member of the committee of the London Library. He was a correspondent of the archaeological societies of Rome and Palermo.

Lloyd died at 43 Upper Gloucester Place, Regent's Park, on 22 December 1893 in his eighty-first year, survived by his wife, a son, and a daughter. Watkiss Lloyd was a remarkable instance of a lifelong devotion to learning, stamped by disinterested self-denial. Without a university training, and never recognized by any academic body, he had the strong qualities and some of the weaknesses of the self-taught. His books manifest conscientious industry, originality, and sound scholarship; but while his judgement was solid and his thought clear, he was not endowed with the faculty of expressing his ideas in attractive literary form. Power of condensation and artistic arrangement of materials were wanting. One half of his life was passed in solitude, but during the last half he mixed in the world, and the angularities of the student became softened. He was a charming talker, modest, unpedantic, and a staunch friend. In personal appearance he was tall and impressive; even to the end he was strikingly upright in carriage, and showed few outward signs of his advanced age. Lloyd produced a large number of other publications, including books and articles on ancient and modern architecture, Homer, Pindar, and Shakespeare (all of whose plays he believed were written in blank verse). He also left a large number of unpublished manuscripts, several of which he bequeathed to the British Museum. H. R. TEDDER, *rev.* RICHARD SMAIL

Sources *The Times* (27 Dec 1893) · *The Athenaeum* (30 Dec 1893), 916 · *The Architect* (23 Dec 1893) · *Publishers' Circular* (30 Dec 1893) · Allibone, *Dict.* · L. Cust and S. Colvin, eds., *History of the Society of Dilettanti* (1898) · S. Beale, 'Memoir', in W. W. Lloyd, *Elijah Fenton: his poetry and friends* (1894) · *CGPLA Eng. & Wales* (1894)

Archives BL, letters to Edward Falkener, Add. MS 43458 · CUL, letters to Joseph Bonomi

Likenesses E. M. Bush, oils, Brooks's Club, London, Society of Dilettanti · W. Richmond, portrait; in family possession, 1901 · H. Watkins, carte-de-visite, NPG · photograph, carte-de-visite, NPG · photogravure photograph, repro. in W. W. Lloyd, *Elijah Fenton: his poetry and friends* (1894)

Wealth at death £6675 18*s.* 8*d.*: probate, 21 Feb 1894, *CGPLA Eng. & Wales*

Lloyd-George. For this title name *see* George, David Lloyd, first Earl Lloyd-George of Dwyfor (1863–1945); George, Frances Louise Lloyd, Countess Lloyd-George of Dwyfor (1888–1972).

Lluelyn, Martin (1616–1682), poet and physician, was born on 12 December 1616 in London, the ninth child (and eighth son) of Martin Lluelyn, whose wife's name is unrecorded. Perhaps the father was the Marten Lewellen, steward of St Bartholomew's Hospital, who in 1609 owed £52 10*s.* to John Harvey. Harvey's famous brother Dr William Harvey facilitated the repayment of the loan, although the steward continued to struggle with debt (Keynes, 60–61).

Martin Lluelyn was baptized on 22 December 1616 in St Bartholomew-the-Less, West Smithfield, the church associated with the hospital. Like so many poets of the age, he attended Westminster School. On 25 July 1636 he matriculated from Christ Church, Oxford. There he belonged to a circle of 'the choicest wits in the University, as Mr. *Cartwright*, Dr. *Lluelin*, Mr. *Gregory*, Mr. *Waring*, &c.' (Lloyd, 598–9). The patron of those scholars and poets was Brian Duppa, dean of the college and chaplain to Archbishop Laud; they all retained powerful royalist and high-church sympathies. From 1637 until 1643 Lluelyn contributed verses to several of the Oxford miscellanies commemorating royal occasions and extolling important personages. He graduated BA in 1640 and MA in 1643.

During the civil war Lluelyn joined the royalist army, attaining the rank of captain by 1646, the year his *Men-miracles, with other Poemes* was published. Prefacing the collection were seven commendatory poems, including ones by his fellow Oxonians John Fell and John Birkenhead. Four of the poems compliment Lluelyn by comparing him with his friend the poet William Cartwright, who had died in 1643.

The burlesque poem 'Men-miracles', a contemporary recalled, 'came forth into the World with great applause' (W. Winstanley, *Lives of the … Poets*, 1687, 201). Laced with mock pedantry and satire directed at presbyterians and parliamentarians, its 395 hudibrastic couplets present 22 kinds of monsters such as fantastic travellers' tales describe. 'Men-miracles' was said to have been 'written on purpose to please the Duke [James, Duke of York] into learning' (Lloyd, 598).

The collection of 1646 also contains fifty-six shorter poems—lyric, satiric, occasional. Lluelyn's five carols 'sung to His Majesty' have received particular scrutiny and praise (Wallerstein, 102–10; Loxley, 178–80). Other poems survive, in seventeenth-century manuscripts, with musical settings by John Wilson and others. A song beginning 'I felt my heart and found a Chillnesse coole' has appeared, without attribution, in collections of John Wesley's hymns (Wesley, 2.10). Lluelyn's short poems have been reprinted sporadically in anthologies, beginning with the 1650 edition of *Wit's Recreations.*

Also in 1646 a play, *The Witney Wake*, was presented at Oxford, the last such cavalier entertainment before the city's surrender to parliamentary troops in June. A description of the play with texts of the songs, published that year, gives the author as 'Mr. Loyd, Student of Christ Church in Oxford, and a Captaine of that Garison'; Lluelyn's authorship was established only in 1968 (Cutts, '*Wickham wakened*', 448–56). Perhaps it was the same play that the war-depleted university hoped to present before the new king in July 1661, 'made by Dr. Llewellyn, but they are so in want of actors, that they fear being obliged to make use of the Red Bull players, now at Oxford' (*CSP dom.*, *1661–2*, 32).

Ejected from the university by the parliamentary visitors in 1648, Lluelyn practised medicine in London, applying 'his genius as much to physic, as before he had to poetry', his acquaintance Anthony Wood remarked (Wood, *Ath. Oxon.*, 4.42). The political situation notwithstanding, Lluelyn was granted the DM degree from Oxford on 15 July 1653. On 24 September he was admitted a candidate of the College of Physicians; he was made a fellow on 27 May 1659. By the 1650s he had married, though his wife's name is unknown. They had a son Martin (1652–1729), who became an army officer, and a daughter Lettice.

During the interregnum Lluelyn continued to write poetry, including commendatory poems for the posthumous Latin works of his old Oxford friend John Gregory (1650), for the posthumous plays and poems of Cartwright (1651), for William Harvey's *Anatomical Exercitations* (1653), and for Richard Whitlock's *Zoötomia* (1654). At the Restoration, an event on which he published a 130-line panegyric, Lluelyn was appointed physician to the king, as well as principal of St Mary's Hall and a visitor of the University of Oxford.

Lluelyn married Martha, daughter of George Long of Penn, Buckinghamshire, on 5 August 1662. In 1664 the family moved from Oxford to Buckinghamshire—first, apparently, to Amersham, where a son, George (1668–1739), was born; he became a musician and clergyman. Then the family lived in High Wycombe, where a son, Richard, was born (about 1672), later referred to as 'Dr Richard Lluellyn' (Greaves, 276). Other children of that marriage were named Maurice, Martha, and Mary. In Wycombe, Lluelyn continued to practise medicine. On 9 September 1671 he was sworn burgess and alderman, and on 28 September he was elected mayor, a position that he occupied for only a year. According to Wood he 'behaved himself severe against the fanatics' (Wood, *Ath. Oxon.*, 4.43). Lluelyn published a satire, *Wickham Wakened* (1672), 'in Rime Dogrell', in response to his controversy with a Quaker faction. He was chosen to deliver an address to the king on behalf of Wycombe on 24 August 1681.

A memoir of his Wycombe friend Isaac Milles, probably written by Milles's son John, characterized Lluelyn as 'an eminent and very learned Physitian … universally esteem'd by all that knew him … A Man of singular Integrity of Life and Manners, and of the most comely and decent Gravity and Deportment' (Milles, 43–4). Lluelyn died in Wycombe on 17 March 1682 and was buried there in the north aisle of the church; his long epitaph in Latin was written by Isaac Milles. CHARLES CLAY DOYLE

Sources Wood, *Ath. Oxon.*, new edn • J. P. Cutts, 'The dramatic writing of Martin Llewellyn', *Philological Quarterly*, 47 (1968), 16–29 • R. Greaves, ed., *First ledger book of High Wycombe* (1956) • G. Keynes, *The life of William Harvey* (1966) • J. Milles (?), *Account of the life and conversation of the reverend…[Isaac] Milles* (1721) • *CSP dom.*, 1661–2 • R. Wallerstein, 'Martin Lluelyn, cavalier and "metaphysical"', *Journal of English and Germanic Philology*, 35 (1936), 94–111 • J. Loxley, *Royalism and poetry in the English civil wars* (1997) • J. Wesley and C. Wesley, *Poetical works*, ed. G. Osborn, 13 vols. (1868–72) • Foster, *Alum. Oxon.* • *DNB* • C. C. Doyle, '"To my ingenious freind Captaine LL": an attribution', *N&Q*, 217 (1972), 173–4 • J. P. Cutts, 'Martin Llewellyn and *Wickham wakened*', *Neuphilologische Mitteilungen*, 76 (1975), 448–56 • J. P. Cutts, 'Seventeenth-century lyrics: Oxford, Bodleian, MS, Mus. b.1', *Musica Disciplina*, 10 (1956), 142–209 • J. P. Cutts, 'Seventeenth-century songs and lyrics in Edinburgh University Library, Music MS, Dc.1.69', *Musica Disciplina*, 13 (1959), 169–94 • J. P. Cutts, 'Drexel manuscript 4041 … a treasure-house of early seventeenth-century song and dramatic lyric', *Musica Disciplina*, 18 (1964), 151–202 • M. Crum, 'A manuscript of John Wilson's songs', *The Library*, 5th ser., 10 (1955), 55–7 • C. Bentley, 'The rational physician: Richard Whitlock's medical satires', *Journal of the History of Medicine and Allied Sciences*, 29 (1974), 180–95 • M. Burrows, ed., *The register of the visitors of the University of Oxford, from AD 1647 to AD 1658*, CS, new ser., 29 (1881) • Burney, *Hist. mus.*, new edn • J. Welch, *The list of the queen's scholars of St Peter's College, Westminster*, ed. [C. B. Phillimore], new edn (1852) • D. Lloyd, *Memoires of the lives … of those … personages that suffered … for the protestant religion* (1668), 598–9

Llwyd, Gruffydd. *See* Gruffudd Llwyd (*fl.* 1380–1420).

Llwyd, Humphrey (1527–1568), antiquary and map maker, was born in Denbigh, the only child of Robert Lloyd and Joan, daughter of Lewis Piggott. He could claim descent through his father from Harry Rossendale, a henchman and grantee of the earl of Lincoln in the late thirteenth century. Llwyd was educated at Oxford, graduating BA in 1547–8 and proceeding MA from Brasenose College in 1551. In 1553 he entered the service of Henry Fitzalan, twelfth earl of Arundel, remaining as a member of his household for the rest of his life. (One tradition, probably dating from Anthony Wood, maintained that Llwyd was physician to Arundel: this is now disputed.) Probably through the earl's influence, he represented East Grinstead in Elizabeth's first parliament of 1559 and sat for the Denbigh boroughs from 1563 to 1567. Llwyd married Barbara (*d.* 1609?), sister to John, the last Lord Lumley, Arundel's son-in-law, a man of wealth and culture, and had with her four sons and two daughters.

Humphrey Llwyd (1527–1568), by unknown artist, 1561

By 1563 Llwyd was probably living most of the time in Denbigh, within the walls of the castle, and was elected one of the two borough aldermen. For a year between early spring 1566 and late spring 1567 he was with Arundel in Italy, having travelled via Antwerp, Brussels, Augsburg, and Milan to Padua, with a visit to Venice. It was in Antwerp, on the return journey, that Richard Gough of Denbigh, Sir Thomas Gresham's agent in Antwerp, introduced Llwyd to Abraham Ortelius, the map maker, who invited him to assist in examining old place names and who sought Llwyd's advice on a map of Britain: it was a propitious meeting.

Llwyd inherited a respect for the distinguished literary traditions of his native locality together with the humanist thinking and antiquarian interests that had penetrated there. Oxford had brought him into firsthand contact with new modes of thought and, although his religious persuasion remains uncertain, the protestant theory of the distinction of the early British church was certainly to his liking: John Bale, William Salesbury, and Llwyd were among the first to elaborate upon this. His close association with Arundel and Lumley opened up the world of books and manuscripts to him. Llwyd was the possessor of an impressive library of broad interest, representing the most up-to-date and best continental scholarship: together with the collections of Arundel and Lumley it was to be bought by James I for his son Henry and was to form the basis of the Royal Collection now in the British Library.

No copy exists of the earliest of Llwyd's works: it is known only from a reference in a letter written by Robert Davies to Anthony Wood (Bodl. Oxf., MS Wood F41, fol. 46), in 1690, 'An Almanacke and Kalender, conteynynge, the daye houre, and mynute of the change of the Moone for ever, and the sygne that she is in for these thre yeares, with the natures of the sygnes and Planetes'. No copy exists, either, of Llwyd's translation into English of *De auguriis* by the Italian Renaissance author Agostino Nifo: it was in manuscript in Lumley's library in 1609. Of greater impact was the *Cronica Walliae a Rege Cadwalader ad annum 1294* which Llwyd completed on 17 July 1559. This was an English adaptation of *Brut y tywysogyon* ('The chronicle of the princes'), the consummation of medieval Welsh historiography based on the *annales* kept by ecclesiastics and religious since the eighth century. Llwyd's work opens with a description of Wales by Sir John Price: this work and the rest of the *Cronica* are amplified by Llwyd from manuscript and printed sources (among them Matthew Paris and Nicholas Trevet) together with oral traditions and Llwyd's own glosses. Sir Henry Sidney, lord president of the council of Wales, encouraged his chaplain Dr David Powel of Ruabon to prepare an adaptation of the *Cronica* which existed in manuscript. Powel's work appeared in 1584 under the title *Historie of Cambria, now Called Wales* and although he recognized in his introduction that Llwyd's text contained 'imperfections, not onelie in the phrase, but also in the matter and substance of the historie', it remained the standard work on the history of Wales down to 1282 until Sir John Edward Lloyd's *History* was published in 1911.

Llwyd published a number of other significant works. *De Mona druidum insula … epistola* was the letter sent by Llwyd to Ortelius, dated 5 April 1568, and published by Ortelius in his atlas *Theatrum orbis terrarum* (1570). The work, according to Llwyd, was derived from reading, experience, travel and a knowledge of the Welsh tongue. Llwyd also wrote the *Commentarioli Britannicae descriptionis fragmentum*, a short historical and geographical description of Britain which he dispatched to Ortelius on 3 August 1568; it was published in Cologne in 1572 and is dedicated to Ortelius. It was translated by Thomas Twyne under the title *The Breviary of Britayne* and published in 1573. It was the first attempt to compile a *chorographia* of Britain as a whole. Central themes of Llwyd's work are his defence of Geoffrey of Monmouth (particularly countering the attacks of Polydore Vergil), and his belief in the integrity of the early British church.

Llwyd was also noted as a map maker. *Cambriae typus* was the map of Wales that Llwyd sent to Ortelius with the *Commentarioli … fragmentum*, acknowledging that it was 'not beutifully set forth in all poynctes, yet truly depeinted'; it was printed for Ortelius as a supplement to the 1573 edition of his *Theatrum orbis terrarum*. *Cambriae typus* has many inaccuracies but it was a great improvement on earlier maps. Llwyd's map was printed fifty times between 1573 and George Horn's *Accuratissima orbis delineatio* of 1741. At the same time Llwyd had dispatched to Ortelius his map of England and Wales, and this too was published by Ortelius in the *Additamentum* of 1573 under the title *Angliae regni florentissimi nova descriptio*. Here, despite inaccuracies, the main features are extremely well delineated.

In addition, Llwyd left two works in Welsh. One was a copy made by the poet Gruffudd Hiraethog of a pedigree of Llwyd's kinsman Foulk Lloyd of Foxhall, tracing him back to Harry Rossendale and declaring with pride: 'nid wyf yn kredv vod llawer yngwynedd allan ddangos mor vath sikrwydd am i bonedd ir yr amser hwnnw' ('I do not believe that many in Gwynedd can declare such certainty of their gentility since that time'). The other was a treatise on heraldry in the hand of Hiraethog's pupil Wiliam Llŷn who claims that Llwyd had compiled it 'o gymvlliad [*sic*] wmffre llwyd o dref ddinbych ai Tynnodd o ffrangec ac ieithoedd eraill' ('from the compilation of Humphrey Llwyd of Denbigh town who translated it from French and other languages').

Llwyd died on 21 August 1568, having contracted a fever before returning home from the continent, and was buried in the north aisle of Llanfarchell, Denbigh's old parish church. He had made his will on 5 August 1568: in it, he expresses deep concern for the well-being of his children. His books were to be kept safe 'tyll they or some one of theim come to yeares of discretion to Judge what a treasure they have lefte theym …'; but there is no evidence that his children were to pursue their father's scholarly interests. Llwyd's widow married William Williams of Cochwillan, Caernarvonshire: they had five children. Later, a monument of alabaster was placed in Llanfarchell bearing an epitaph 'of Humfrey Lloid Mr of arte. A famus worthy wight'. He is portrayed kneeling; there is a prayer desk covered with a carpet and a book before him and a sword at his side with three lines of musical notation below.

The poet Gruffudd Hiraethog composed a Welsh eulogy noting Llwyd's industry, his learning, and the essential part he played in easing the passage through the parliament of 1563 of the act that enabled the translation of the Bible into Welsh. Elegies were composed by two of Hiraethog's pupils, Lewis ab Edward and Wiliam Cynwal. Early in 1566 the Welsh humanist scholar and translator William Salesbury spoke of Llwyd as being 'the most famous *Antiquarius* of all our countrey'. On the basis of information collected for his *Athenae Oxonienses* of 1691–2,

Anthony Wood describes him as 'a well bred Gentleman. He was a passing right Antiquary, and a Person of great skill and knowledge in *British* affairs'. A portrait of Llwyd at the age of thirty-four, dated 1561, shows him to be a handsome man with a pointed beard wearing a black doublet, with a gold chain around his neck and holding a prayer book. It includes his coat of arms and his motto, which reads *Hwy pery klod na golyd* ('Fame lasts longer than wealth').

A near relative of Llwyd, according to Wood, was **John Lloyd** (*c.*1558–1603), classical scholar, born in Denbigh and educated at Winchester College and New College, Oxford, of which he was admitted perpetual fellow in 1579. He graduated BA (1581), MA (1584–5), BTh (1592), and DTh (1595). He married Isabell, daughter of Richard King of the parish of St Sepulchre, London. He became vicar of Writtle in Essex, a New College living, and died there in 1603. He was distinguished on account of the quality of his preaching and the distinction of his scholarship. He published *Interpretatio Latina, cum scholiis in fluv. Josephum de Maccabaeis, seu, De rationis imperio* at Oxford in 1590 and also *Barlaamus de papae Principatu, Graecè & Latinè*, again at Oxford, in 1592. He was brother of Hugh Lloyd, headmaster of Winchester College from 1580 to 1587.

R. Brinley Jones

Sources R. G. Gruffydd, 'Humphrey Llwyd of Denbigh: some documents and a catalogue', *Transactions of the Denbighshire Historical Society*, 17 (1968), 54–107 • R. G. Gruffydd, 'Humphrey Llwyd: dyneiddiwr', *Efrydiau Athronyddol*, 33 (1970), 57–74 • I. M. Williams, 'Ysgolheictod hanesyddol yr unfed ganrif ar bymtheg', *Llên Cymru*, 2 (1952–3), 111–24, 209–23 • D. J. Bowen, 'Cywyddau Gruffudd Hiraethog i dri o awduron y dadeni', *Transactions of the Honourable Society of Cymmrodorion* (1974–5), 103–31 • S. Lewis, 'Damcaniaeth eglwysig Brotestannaidd', *Efrydiau Catholig*, 2 (1947), 36–55 • D. H. Owen, *Early printed maps of Wales* (1996) • F. J. North, 'Humphrey Lhuyd's maps of England and of Wales', *Archaeologia Cambrensis*, 92 (1937), 11–63 • G. Williams, *The Welsh and their religion* (1991) • J. Steegman, *North Wales* (1957), vol. 1 of *Portraits in Welsh houses* • *Clwyd*, Pevsner (1986) • Wood, *Ath. Oxon.*, 1st edn • Foster, *Alum. Oxon.*, 1500–1714 [Humfry Lloyd] • I. Roberts and M. Roberts, 'De Mona druidum insula', *Abraham Ortelius and the first atlas: essays commemorating the quadricentennial of his death, 1598–1998*, ed. M. van den Broecke, P. van der Krogt, and P. Meurer (1998), 347–61 • I. M. Williams, ed., *Cronica Walliae, Humphrey Llwyd* (2002)

Archives NL Wales, letter to Otelius, MS 13187

Likenesses Rhiwlas, portrait, 1561, NMG Wales • portrait, 1561, NL Wales [*see illus.*] • R. Clamp, stipple, BM, NPG; repro. in S. Harding, *The biographical mirrour* (1795) • J. Faber, mezzotint, BM, NPG

Wealth at death see will, NL Wales, St Asaph register of wills, 1565–8, p. 116

Llwyd, Huw [Hugh] (*c.*1568–*c.*1630), Welsh-language poet and soldier, was the third son of eight children born to Dafydd Llwyd ap Howel and his wife, Catrin. According to an elegy by Huw Machno the father died in 1623, and by then Huw Llwyd was his heir. Huw Llwyd is almost invariably associated with Cynfal Fawr, a farmhouse in the parish of Maentwrog in Merioneth. He served in a regiment in the English army, probably under the command of Roger Williams. He composed an *englyn* (a four-line strict-metre verse) describing the victuals he tasted in England, France, and the Netherlands. Machno's elegy suggests that Llwyd settled in Cynfal after campaigning overseas.

Llwyd married the daughter of Hendre Mur (also referred to as Mur Castell), a farmhouse within 1 mile of Cynfal. Morgan *Llwyd (1619–1659), a famous Welsh author, may have been Llwyd's grandson, or even his son. Llwyd probably built part of the house that is today known as Cynfal Fawr. He mentions one peculiarity of the house, namely that water flowed 'brightly' (Bodl. Oxf., MS Welsh e10, 8) through its parlour.

In a poem of 1630 Huw Machno describes Huw Llwyd's Cynfal. He refers to Llwyd's dividing the house more skilfully and turning the water through the parlour. The poem also gives a fascinating insight into Huw Llwyd's interests by listing the contents of his room. There he had his books, his ointment boxes, his 'doctor's gear', his buckler and sword, his yew bow and quiver of arrows, cage, gun, flask, fishing rod, hunting horn and hunting staff, nets, his spying glass, and chess and draughts sets (Davies, xviii). The soldier's accoutrements are here, clearly enough. Then there are his ointment boxes and doctor's gear: add to this his work on 'old natural remedies' (NL Wales, Peniarth MS 123) and it can be understood why he had a reputation as a sorcerer and why stories about his 'magic' powers are found to this day in his locality.

Then there is Llwyd's hunting and fishing gear. It comes as no surprise to learn that Huw Llwyd composed a number of poems related to hunting. There is his poem in response to *englynion* composed by Morys Berwyn on behalf of Owen Elis to ask for two hounds, and his poem addressed to Thomas Prys of Plas Iolyn asking for a couple of hounds:

> which draw in the sweet air
> through their jowls as the fair babble of beautiful bells.
> (NL Wales, MS 12731, 53–4)

His best-known poems are two that he composed to 'The Fox'. In the first of these the poet addresses the fox, describes him, and is then advised by him about the way of the world. The advice given is cynical, pessimistic, and Machiavellian:

> and today, he who lives an honest life
> is, in the world's reckoning, a fool.
> (Parry, 242–3)

He explains that it is only by doing evil that a man may prosper. Llwyd's second poem to the same fox is a very different poem. By now the fox is old and weary, and is plagued by a bad conscience. He tells the poet that the best treasure of all is a 'good conscience' (NL Wales, Llanstephan 133, 243a).

It is unfortunate that these two poems cannot be dated, but the second was obviously composed later than the first. Does that indicate that Llwyd had attained some kind of religious conviction? Or were the two poems, by original intent, meant for moral instruction? It is interesting to note that one of Morgan Llwyd's constant obsessions was man's good conscience: is the fact that his father, or grandfather, also felt, probably later on in his life, that nothing could be compared to a good conscience mere coincidence? Not many poems are attributed to Llwyd, but most of the other—short—poems that he may have composed are meditations on death, and man's service to God. It appears as if Llwyd's early exuberance as a poet later gave way to a more meditative and religious turn of mind. GWYN THOMAS

Sources G. Thomas, 'Dau Lwyd o Gynfal', ed. J. E. Caerwyn Williams, *Ysgrifau Beirniadol*, 5 (1970) • G. Thomas, 'Changes in the tradition of Welsh poetry in north Wales in the seventeenth century', DPhil diss., U. Oxf., 1966 • *DWB* • *Gwethiau Morgan Llwyd o Wynedd*, 2, ed. J. H. Davies (1908) • T. Parry, ed., *The Oxford book of Welsh verse* (1962)

Llwyd, Morgan (1619–1659), Independent minister and mystic, was born at Cynfal, a farmstead in Maentwrog parish, Merioneth, of a family of small squires renowned for literary prowess. A near relative, Huw *Llwyd (*c.*1568–*c.*1630) who, some claim, may have been Morgan's father or grandfather, served as a professional soldier in the Low Countries before returning to provide a focus at Cynfal for the efforts of strict-metre poets who celebrated the hospitality and traditional hunting skills of its lord.

Early life and civil war Little definite is known of Morgan Llwyd's parentage and upbringing, beyond the fact that his mother's first name was Mary and that she lived until 1680. It is suggested that he was educated at Wrexham, to account for his coming under the influence of Walter Cradock, curate there from 1634. It was certainly in Denbighshire, according to his own account, that he was converted, possibly at Bromfield, and there are sufficient grounds to be confident that he followed Cradock to Llanfair Waterdine, Shropshire, although no certain link between Llwyd and the Harley family, patrons of godly ministers there, can be traced. It is not known when, or indeed if, Llwyd was ordained, but it is likely that he obtained some clerical appointment at Llanfair. Having moved with Cradock thence to Monmouthshire, Llwyd was married, to Ann, probably the sister of the wife of Edward Herbert of Magor, later MP for that county; and there he became associated in some way, on the eve of the civil war, with the Independent congregation at Llanfaches.

We rely heavily on Llwyd's autobiography in verse, 'Hanes rhyw Gymro', for what may have been his military postings, rather than wanderings, during the civil war. With the other Welsh Independent ministers of south-east Wales, Cradock and Henry Walter, Llwyd left the county in the face of the mobilizing royalist forces, and saw something of Glamorgan, Gloucester, and Somerset. It is impossible to ascribe precise dates to his movements, but his appearances in Portsmouth, London, Kent, and Pembrokeshire tell us that he accompanied the forces of parliament, and that he must have sailed to south-west Wales early in 1644. It cannot be shown that he was ever formally a chaplain, but he was probably among the Welsh ministers at Portsmouth who petitioned parliament in July 1644; Llwyd tells us that he was in southern England for a second time. From this point, he probably became attached to the force of Sir Thomas Myddelton, which had been formed to reduce north Wales to the will of parliament. The House of Commons, with the approval of the Westminster assembly of divines, sent Llwyd and Ambrose Mostyn to Myddelton as approved Welsh-language preachers, and it was by means of this service that Llwyd returned to Denbighshire, to minister at Wrexham, Myddelton's headquarters, in 1647. Before this, however, he may have been acquiring a reputation for preaching an egalitarian message. The 'Floyd' who preached to the troop of Major Robert Huntingdon, in the New Model horse regiment of Oliver Cromwell at Aston Rowant, Oxfordshire, in June 1646, sounds like Morgan Llwyd.

Ministry and spirituality Wrexham was home to Llwyd from 1647, and he held a state-provided stipend there from 1656, but always ministered as if to a gathered congregation. He did not confine himself solely to pastoral duties, and in the summer of 1651, with fellow preachers Jenkin Jones and Vavasor Powell, rode north with troops they had raised to contribute to the war of the Commonwealth against the Scots. This brief return to military activity, co-ordinated by Colonel Thomas Harrison, represented the high point of Llwyd's millenarian convictions. To combat the Scots, he broke off from his duties as an approving minister under the act of February 1650 for the Propagation of the Gospel in Wales. Llwyd's field of evangelistic activity was all over north Wales, as far west from Wrexham as the Llŷn peninsula, where, he tells us, he lost his voice in preaching. These itinerant duties were undertaken in tandem with his work at Wrexham. After the Propagation Act was not renewed beyond April 1653, and in the early years of the Cromwellian protectorate, puritan clerical opinion in Wales divided between those in support of the principles and policies of the government, including the principle of state maintenance, and those against, who either moved towards the Quaker movement or who stayed within more formal theology as Independents or Baptists. Llwyd was courted by both sides; his name appeared on *A Word for God*, the petition hostile to Cromwell and mainly inspired by Vavasor Powell, but his marginal comments on a copy of the petition were critical of the certainties of Powell's denunciations. Although there was a hint of contempt for Llwyd in the account by George Fox of how he had reduced him ('the priest') to tears by his testimony, the Wrexham minister was in fact attracted to what he called 'the book in every man', the 'fountain which springs' in everyone, the quietist possibilities of interpreting the Saints' disappointments. These tendencies alienated Llwyd both from his former ally, Powell, and from the naturally less sympathetic Richard Baxter. Although he did not sign it, Llwyd was more in tune with the counter-petition, *The Humble Representation and Address*, orchestrated by his former mentor, Cradock, and endorsed by his brother-in-law, Edward Herbert. In May 1656 both Colonel Philip Jones and Colonel John Jones were keen to see Llwyd properly maintained at Wrexham, and the minister did indeed accept state maintenance, proof that his shared perspectives with the Quakers were not without limitations. Llwyd's ministry was to last only another three years; his health evidently gave him concern in May 1658, when he made his will, and he died a little over a year later, on 3 June 1659, at Wrexham, where he was buried at Rhos-ddu burial-ground.

In his theology Llwyd was always a radical protestant, but his early association with Cradock suggests that in his early ministry he was preaching an orthodox message. By 1648 he was evidently much affected by millenarian perspectives on public affairs, deepened by his own military service, which inclined him towards a particularly hostile view of Charles I:

> The law was ever above kings
> and kings above the law
> unhappy Charles provokt the lambe
> to dust he must withdraw.
> (*Gweithiau Morgan Llwyd*, ed. Ellis and Davies, 1.55)

This interest in Fifth Monarchist ideas distanced him from Cradock, who rejected the combativeness of Vavasor Powell, as well as that of Llwyd. In the early 1650s he was forced by the disappointments of the scheme for propagating the gospel, and the failure of the nominated assembly of 1653, to adopt gradually a more cautious view of the potentialities of state power for ushering in the kingdom of Christ. His writings provide evidence that he was attracted to internalized notions of spirituality from at least as early as 1653–4, and in the later 1650s such notions became more prominent in his thought. They found expression both in his flirtation with Quaker theology and in the rich but often obscure lexicon of images he drew from the German mystic Jakob Boehme. Cradock was no more in sympathy with these developments, antinomian though he was, than he had been with his former pupil's millenarian phase, and others, including Colonel John Jones and Richard Baxter, cautioned him about his glorying in impenetrable imagery or complex theology beyond the grasp of his audience or readership. By the time of his death Llwyd was rather isolated in the context of the Welsh ministry, but his correspondence with thinkers as diverse as Samuel Hartlib, Peter Sterry, and Richard Baxter ensured that he never became cut off from religious and intellectual developments of his day.

Writings Llwyd was a prolific writer in both English and Welsh, although the works published in his own lifetime did not include any of the extensive free-metre verse, much of it on millenarian themes, which remained in manuscript in his papers. Of his verse, only the work on astrology for a popular audience, *Gwyddor uchod* (1657), was published. In general, Llwyd preferred the English language for his thoughts on public themes, such as the significance of the execution of Charles I, which he celebrated in the verses he called (old style) '1648'. These short stanzas, comparable in form with metrical versions of the Psalms, and thus suitable to be set to simple tunes, dwelt on the need for godly 'differing brethren' to seek reconciliation. In them, Llwyd saw the recasting of the British nations after 1649, the abolition of the monarchy, and setbacks suffered by the Catholic powers of Europe all as evidence of the impending kingdom of Christ. He relied heavily on ideas of inversion in these stanzas; the commission for the propagation of the gospel in Wales was proof that a once spiritually barren and politically and socially unsophisticated people were now instruments of God's will: 'the last is first' (*Gweithiau Morgan Llwyd*, ed. Ellis and Davies, 1.28). Llwyd's Welsh poetry is generally more reflective and more spiritual. He uses a range of metres, including the traditional *englyn* and *cywydd*, to a greater range of effects than his English verse achieves. Public themes are largely eschewed in favour of subtle paraphrases of scripture and spiritual reflections, in which the ballad form predominates.

It is on Morgan Llwyd's prose works, however, that his modern reputation rests. He used Welsh for his prose addresses to the Welsh people. They are marked by a sense of urgency and a deep sympathy for the common people of the country, whom he considered, with other contemporary puritan commentators, to be 'asleep' and needing an awakening to spiritual life. He made his publishing début in 1653–4 with three of these, *Llythur ir Cymru cariadus*, *Gwaedd ynghymru yn wyneb pob cydwybod*, and most famously, *Dirgelwch i rai iw ddeall ac i eraill iw watwar*, which Llwyd shortened to *Arwydd i annerch y Cymru* ('A sign to address the Welsh people'), but which is better known today as *Llyfr y tri aderyn* ('The book of the three birds'). *Llyfr y tri aderyn* is the most inventive and persuasive of them: ten editions of it appeared between 1714 and 1898, and several, under the auspices of the University of Wales Press, have been published in the twentieth century. The book takes the form of an allegorical, tripartite discussion between three birds, the raven, the dove, and the eagle, who meet after the flood. For Llwyd, as for Boehme, whose writings may have supplied him with the idea, Noah's ark was a type of Christ and the true church. In the allegory, the raven represents formalism in religion, the dove the true (gathered) church, and the eagle state power or, more specifically, the godly prince or magistrate, from which the true church can expect protection. The raven of formalism is protean: 'I can turn about with every wind, and I scent my prey afar off … whatsoever opinions the high and mighty ones may hold, I can approve them, if only I get peace in my eyrie' (Llwyd, 'Book of the Three Birds', 198). The eagle of state authority advocates teaching before coercion: 'The gimlet of instruction must precede the hammer of rule and regulation lest the wood be split, or the nail be bent' (ibid., 201). The work foreshadows the author's later flirtations with the ideas of the Quakers: 'The law of nature teacheth men to follow the light that is in them' (ibid., 211). Llwyd is unable to sustain the central, original, three-sided discussion, which he abandons midway through the book in favour of a more familiar catechistic format. Part of this loss of imaginative confidence may be attributed to the uncertainties of political power in early 1654, the date to which the book might best be ascribed. Nevertheless, *Llyfr y tri aderyn* provided the Welsh reading public with a volume as compelling, passionate, and accessible as the work in English of John Bunyan was to be. Llwyd adapts the theory of Geoffrey of Monmouth on the special relationship between the British Isles and the early church for Wales and his own times:

> This is the island which first received the gospel in the time of Lles, the son of Coel. Here, some say, was born Helen and

her son Constantine. The Welsh, others say, were the first to discover America. Britons have been steadfast unto death in behalf of the true faith. (ibid., 213)

A recurrent theme in this and Llwyd's prose and poetry works was that the Welsh had a special part to play in the dawning golden age of the gospel: 'The dawn has broken, and the sun is rising on you. The birds are singing: wake (O Welshman) wake' ('Gwaedd ynghymru', *Gweithiau Morgan Llwyd*, ed. Ellis and Davies, 1.128). Llwyd went on to translate two works of Boehme's for the Welsh-language reading public: *Yr ymroddiad* (translated 1654 and published in 1657) and *Y discybl ai athraw o newydd* (translated 1655 and also published in 1657).

Of Llwyd's two published English prose works, which appeared in 1655, *An Honest Discourse* is the most interesting. Like *Llyfr y tri aderyn*, it is structured as a dialogue, this time between three men: citizens past, present, and future. It has a greater sense of political immediacy, and in effect establishes a dialogue with the content of Vavasor Powell's intemperate *A Word for God* about the nature of the protectorate of Oliver Cromwell. *An Honest Discourse* also resumes themes left unexplored in *Llyfr y tri aderyn*. None of Llwyd's English prose works, including the unpublished 'Where is Christ?', has any particular literary distinction in format or language, however, in contrast to his Welsh prose, in which a range of images, drawn from nature, and especially from the changing seasons, combines with Llwyd's emphasis on the spiritual complexities of relationships between the Trinity and the individual soul of man. His attempts to explain and explore these mysteries take him well beyond the orthodox Calvinism of his age and have given him the label 'mystic'. Had he lived beyond 1659 he might have found eventually a natural spiritual home among the Quakers, although there was nothing simple, and much that was deeply intellectual and theologically avant-garde, in his thought.

A number of Morgan Llwyd's Welsh prose works were republished in the following century to satisfy the needs of a Welsh reading public stimulated by Methodism. At the end of the nineteenth century his published work, and much of his unpublished writing in manuscript, was brought together in two volumes of *Gweithiau*, published by the University of Wales and intended for the new class of readers brought into existence by the curriculum of the new university colleges. Llwyd's work, or at least *Llyfr y tri aderyn*, has since become a staple of undergraduate Welsh studies. A third volume of his writings was published by the University of Wales Press in 1994, making available, in particular, manuscripts among the Plas Iolyn collection housed at the National Library of Wales.

STEPHEN K. ROBERTS

Sources *Gweithiau Morgan Llywd o Wynedd*, 1–2, ed. T. E. Ellis and J. H. Davies (1899–1908) · *Gweithiau Morgan Llywd o Wynedd*, 3, ed. J. G. Jones and G. W. Owen (1994) · M. Llwyd, 'The book of the three birds', trans. L. J. Parry, *Cofnodion cyfansoddiadau buddugol, eisteddfod Llandudno, 1896* (1898) · M. W. Thomas, *Morgan Llwyd* (1984) · G. F. Nuttall, *The Welsh saints, 1640–1660* (1957) · J. W. Jones and E. L. Evans, eds., *Coffa Morgan Llwyd* (1952) · E. L. Evans, *Morgan Llwyd: ymchwil i rai o'r prif ddylanwadau a fu arno* (1930) · H. Bevan, *Morgan Llwyd y llenor* (1954) · T. Richards, *A history of the puritan movement in Wales* (1920) · T. Richards, *Religious developments in Wales, 1654–1662* (1923) · G. H. Jenkins, *Protestant dissenters in Wales, 1639–1689* (1992) · A. N. Palmer, *A history of the town and parish of Wrexham*, 3: *A history of the older nonconformity of Wrexham* [1888] · T. Richards, 'Eglwys Llanfaches', *Transactions of the Honourable Society of Cymmrodorion* (1941), 150–84

Archives Cardiff City Library, MSS · NL Wales, corresp., drafts of tracts and verses, and papers

Likenesses imagined likeness, memorial window, Ffestiniog church, Merioneth

Llwyd, Richard (1752–1835), poet, was born at the King's Head, Beaumaris, Anglesey, the son of John Llwyd, a small coast trader, and his wife, Alice. The early death of his father from smallpox left the family in financial difficulties, and so, after an education of nine months at the free school at Beaumaris, at twelve years of age Llwyd entered the domestic service of a gentleman in the neighbourhood. He used every spare moment, however, for his self-improvement. By 1780 he was entrusted with the duties of steward and secretary to a Mr Griffith of Caerhun, near Conwy, then the only acting magistrate in that district.

Llwyd finally acquired a competency, retired to Beaumaris, and published there his best-known poem, *Beaumaris Bay* (1800), with many historical and genealogical notes. 'He came to be considered an authority on Welsh heraldry and genealogy' (*DWB*), and as a result was received into many aristocratic households. Through these connections, he managed to secure Royal Literary Fund grants for Richard Robert Jones (Dic Aberdaron) and David Thomas (Daffyd Ddu Eryri), among others. His other productions were *Gayton Wake, or, Mary Dod; and her List of Merits* (1804) and *Poems, Tales, Odes, Sonnets, Translations from the British* (2 vols., 1804). He became known as the Bard of Snowdon as a result of his literary pursuits.

Early in 1807 Llwyd moved to Chester, and in 1808 he visited London, where he made the acquaintance of Owen Jones, William Owen Pughe, and others. He returned to Chester, and in May 1814 married Ann (*d.* 1834), daughter of Alderman Bingley of that town. Llwyd was a strong Welsh patriot, and in 1824 was made a member of the Honourable Society of Cymmrodorion. Llwyd died at his home, Bank Place, in Chester, on 29 December 1835, and was buried at St John's Church. On the south side of the church wall a tablet was placed to his memory. A collected edition of his works, with a memoir and portrait, was published in 1837.

D. L. THOMAS, *rev.* M. CLARE LOUGHLIN-CHOW

Sources *DWB* · E. Parry, 'Memoir', in *The poetical works of Richard Llwyd, the Bard of Snowdon* (1837) · R. Williams, *Enwogion Cymru: a biographical dictionary of eminent Welshmen* (1852), 294–5

Archives NL Wales, corresp. and literary MSS · NL Wales, notes

Likenesses portrait, repro. in Parry, 'Memoir'

Llygad Gŵr (*fl.* 1230–1295). *See under* Gogynfeirdd (*act. c.*1080–1285).

Llywarch ap Llywelyn [*called* Prydydd y Moch] (*fl. c.*1180–*c.*1220), poet, was the chief court poet of Gwynedd. He held lands and a mill, probably by Llywelyn ab Iorwerth's gift, in Rhos is Dulas. His father was presumably named Llywelyn, but nothing more is known of his family history; he himself hints that his forebears were not poets.

The sobriquet attributed to him resulted from a daring reference to casting pearls before swine in a poem rebuking Gruffudd ap Cynan; however, doubt has been cast on the identification of Llywarch with Prydydd y Moch. Of Llywarch's poetic output thirty works survive, a total of 1780 lines. His earliest extant poems (probably of *c.*1180) were addressed to Dafydd and Rhodri ab Owain Gwynedd. His chief patron, however, was Llywelyn ab Iorwerth, for whom nine poems survive, tracing the fortunes of that redoubtable prince from *c.*1183 to *c.*1220. Others of his poems are addressed to some of Llywelyn's client princelings. Llywarch also composed an intriguing poem to the ordeal by fire, and a light-hearted *awdl*, which purports to be that of an ardent lover, for Gwenllïan ferch Hywel of Gwynllŵg. R. GERAINT GRUFFYDD

Sources *Gwaith Llywarch ap Llywelyn, 'Prydydd y Moch'*, ed. E. M. Jones and N. A. Jones (1991) • A. D. Carr, 'Prydydd y Moch': ymateb hanesydd', *Transactions of the Honourable Society of Cymmrodorion* (1989), 161–80 • D. Johnston, 'Gwaith Prydydd y Moch', *Llên Cymru*, 17 (1992–3), 304–14
Archives NL Wales, MS 6680B

Llywarch Hen [Llywarch ab Elidir Lydanwyn] (*supp. fl.* **late 6th cent.**), legendary hero, the subject of an important cycle of early Welsh saga poetry, is known from the Welsh genealogies as one of the 'men of the north' (*gwŷr y gogledd*), from an unspecified British kingdom among those not yet under Anglian domination. He was a descendant of Coel Hen, and first cousin on the male side to the important historical and saga figure *Urien Rheged. Hagiographical and pseudo-historical traditions from pre-Norman Brycheiniog make the men first cousins twice over, with both their mothers said to be the daughters of the eponymous Brychan Brycheiniog. Llywarch's epithet, Hen ('the Aged'), may have had dynastic significance, but in literature he is treated as the archetype of the querulous old man. The main body of the cycle of poetry, once accompanied by a lost narrative, probably dates from the ninth century, although antiquarian additions were made to the end of the middle ages.

In the early modern period Llywarch was believed to be the author of all of the poetry of this type, and information extracted from it is responsible for the fantastical biography of Richard Thomas, followed in other sources, which gave Llywarch a lifespan of over 150 years. Modern scholarship, chiefly that of Ifor Williams, has restored Llywarch to his proper role as subject of part of the poetry. Events in the poetry follow the downfall of Urien Rheged in the north, but the main part, concerning the loss in battle of all of Llywarch's twenty-four sons, is set in Wales, perhaps originally in Brycheiniog. Llywarch is therefore an example of a northern figure whose legend has been transferred to Wales, and there is no evidence that the poetry preserves any genuine historical traditions.

The earlier genealogies of the northern heroes generally end about Llywarch's generation. Later antiquarian collections sought to codify the list of Llywarch's sons, drawing names from various sources apart from the poetry, and reaching a total of well over thirty. Even the sons named in the earliest poetry must be suspect as possible inventions. Several families in Wales claimed descent from one or another of Llywarch's sons, most notably that of Merfyn Frych who became king of Gwynedd *c.*836 from an outside base of power. This has led to various theories about Merfyn's dynasty and the Llywarch Hen poetry. It has been argued that Llywarch was a figure created by Merfyn's 'propagandists' in order to link him with the famous Urien Rheged, or that Merfyn's family had a special role in the genesis, dissemination, and preservation of the poetry, again because it stressed the family's close ties to Urien. However, there is no evidence that this genealogical link was made at an early date; the son involved is not prominent in the surviving poetry, and there is no overt political gain to be seen from the connection. The vagueness of traditions about Llywarch's enormous family of heroes allowed for much grafting onto his family. The Gwynedd link appears to be only one of many made in medieval Wales in a spirit of antiquarian speculation, and for the glory of making a claim on a character famed in literary story, and for his northern ancestry. JENNY ROWLAND

Sources I. Williams, ed., *Canu Llywarch Hen* (1935) • P. C. Bartrum, ed., *Early Welsh genealogical tracts* (1966) • J. Rowland, *Early Welsh saga poetry* (1990) • P. Sims-Williams, 'The provenance of the Llywarch Hen poems: a case for Llan-gors, Brycheiniog', *Cambrian Medieval Celtic Studies*, 26 (1993), 27–63 • P. Sims-Williams, 'Historical need and literary narrative: a caveat from ninth-century Wales', *Welsh History Review / Cylchgrawn Hanes Cymru*, 17 (1994–5), 1–40

Llywelyn ab Iorwerth [*called* Llywelyn Fawr] (*c.***1173–1240**), prince of Gwynedd, was the son of Iorwerth Drwyndwn (Iorwerth Flatnose; *d.* *c.*1174), son of *Owain Gwynedd (*d.* 1170), and his cousin Marared, daughter of *Madog ap Maredudd (*d.* 1160), king of Powys; according to one tradition Iorwerth was excluded from the succession to the kingship of Gwynedd because of a physical disability.

Early life Llywelyn was born *c.*1173, possibly at Dolwyddelan in Nant Conwy, and may have been brought up in Powys. According to Gerald of Wales he had begun to challenge his uncles *Dafydd ab Owain Gwynnedd and *Rhodri ab Owain Gwynedd [*see under* Hywel ab Owain Gwynedd] at the time of Gerald's journey through Wales in 1188, when Llywelyn would have been about fifteen (although Gerald describes him as being 'about twelve years old'); the poet Prydydd y Moch suggested that his military career had begun when he was no more than ten.

In 1194, according to the Welsh chronicle *Brut y tywysogyon*, Llywelyn joined Rhodri and his cousins, the sons of Cynan ab Owain Gwynedd, in a successful bid to expel Dafydd from the eastern half of Gwynedd, leaving Dafydd with only three castles. Two poets refer to a battle near Aberconwy in which Llywelyn appears to have defeated Dafydd and in which Rhodri was also involved; this action was followed by the ejection of Rhodri from Anglesey and Prydydd y Moch mentions Llywelyn's victories at Porthaethwy and Coedana on the island. Gerald saw his success as a divine judgment, since Dafydd and Rhodri were considered by the church to be the offspring of an

Llywelyn ab Iorwerth (*c.*1173–1240), by Matthew Paris, in or before 1259 [manuscript drawing; left, with his sons Gruffudd and Dafydd]

incestuous marriage. In 1197 Llywelyn captured Dafydd; his release was negotiated by the justiciar, Hubert Walter, and he died in exile in England in 1203.

On 6 January 1199 the castle of Mold was captured from the earl of Chester's seneschal and on the same day, according to Prydydd y Moch, Llywelyn won a victory in Arfon, almost certainly over his cousin Gruffudd ap Cynan ab Owain Gwynedd; it may be significant that Llywelyn's two charters to the Cistercian abbey of Aberconwy were dated two days later. In these charters he styled himself 'Prince of all north Wales' and dated them in the tenth year of his principate, although a recent study has suggested that they are not contemporary. Gruffudd took the Cistercian habit in the abbey and died there in 1200; in 1201 his brother Maredudd was ejected from Llŷn and Eifionydd 'because of his treachery' (*Brut: Hergest*), thereby completing Llywelyn's conquest of Gwynedd.

Llywelyn and King John In September 1199 *John, the new king of England, took Llywelyn under his protection and confirmed him in the possession of his lands. John was seeking to secure a balance of power between Llywelyn and Gwenwynwyn (*d.* 1216?) of southern Powys, who had succeeded his father, Owain Cyfeiliog, in 1197; as lord of Glamorgan in right of his wife, John understood Welsh politics. In December 1199 he also took Gwenwynwyn and Gruffudd ap Cynan under his protection, although the latter's political career may have been over by that time; as Llywelyn's power increased, however, there seems to have been a desire to reach an accommodation and after negotiations a treaty was concluded on 11 July 1201. This was the first written treaty between a Welsh ruler and the king of England and in it Llywelyn and the magnates of Wales swore fealty to John and undertook to do homage to him on his return from France; the prince would retain his territorial gains and would have the choice of English or Welsh law to settle disputes over land.

Llywelyn and Gwenwynwyn clashed for the first time in August 1202 when the former invaded Powys with a large army. War was averted by the intervention of mediators; the *History of Fouke le Fitz Waryn* credits Fulk (III) Fitzwarine with bringing hostilities to an end after the prince had seized Mechain and Mochnant. Llywelyn did homage to John on the latter's return from France in the summer of 1204, and it was probably in the following spring that he received a sign of royal favour when he married the king's illegitimate daughter *Joan. With an earlier partner, Tangwystl, the daughter of Llywarch Goch, he had had a son, *Gruffudd ap Llywelyn (*d.* 1244), and a daughter, Gwenllian, but this relationship was not recognized by the church as a valid marriage. He was certainly seeking a politically advantageous match at this time; in April 1203 he had received a papal dispensation to marry the widow of his uncle Rhodri, a daughter of the Manx king, Ragnvald (*d.* 1229), but that marriage did not take place, nor is there any evidence to corroborate the statement in one of Innocent III's letters that he had been married to a sister of the earl of Chester. The marriage to Joan was a dynastic opportunity not to be missed; their children would be part of the European royal and aristocratic network, which would in turn elevate the Gwynedd dynasty to a higher status than the other Welsh ruling houses. John presented his son-in-law with the manor of Ellesmere, Shropshire, previously given by Henry II to Dafydd on his marriage to Emma of Anjou in 1174.

Llywelyn's opportunity to assert his mastery beyond Gwynedd came in 1208 when the lands of Gwenwynwyn, prince of southern Powys, were confiscated by the king on the pretext that Gwenwynwyn had attacked the lands of one of his marcher neighbours. Llywelyn promptly moved into Powys. He then entered Ceredigion, attacking Maelgwn ap Rhys (*d.* 1231), the member of the Deheubarth lineage who was an ally of Gwenwynwyn. In spite of his opposition Llywelyn installed Maelgwn's nephews in part of the territory. Llywelyn was demonstrating his capacity to exploit the misfortunes of other Welsh dynasties and the fissures within their ranks for his own purposes. John took an indulgent view of these activities and in 1209 Llywelyn joined his campaign against William the Lion of Scotland and was at Norham on 4 August when William submitted; this was the only occasion on which a ruler of Gwynedd joined a king of England on a military expedition outside Wales.

By 1210 Llywelyn was the dominant figure in Wales, but

his relations with the king now deteriorated; it is possible that William (V) de Briouze had persuaded him to take advantage of John's absence in Ireland between June and August 1210, but, if so, this was an error of judgement. An army commanded by the earl of Chester invaded Gwynedd and the castle at Deganwy, demolished by Llywelyn, was rebuilt by the earl. John's triumphant return from Ireland seems to have been followed by a decision to move against the prince; in November 1210 Gwenwynwyn's lands were restored to him and the following spring all the other Welsh rulers were summoned to Chester. This involvement may have reflected an increasing fear and suspicion of Llywelyn's power of which John was able to take advantage. The first royal expedition entered north Wales in May 1211. Llywelyn fell back on the natural fortress of Snowdonia; the royal army, faced with a lack of supplies, was forced to withdraw to Chester, but in July a further expedition set out from Oswestry and in a lightning campaign swept into Gwynedd, capturing the bishop of Bangor in his own cathedral, holding him to ransom, and burning the town. Joan's intercession secured terms for Llywelyn and on 11 August 1211 he submitted to the king. He had to surrender the Four Cantrefs (the land between the Conwy and the Dee), along with the commote of Edeirnion, to hand over hostages, including his son Gruffudd, and to pay a heavy tribute of cattle and horses. He also agreed that if he and Joan had no heir his lands would pass to the crown, which suggests that their son *Dafydd ap Llywelyn (*d.* 1246) had not yet been born.

This was the nadir of Llywelyn's career, but he soon recovered. The other Welsh rulers had seen John as the defender of their independence but he soon showed that he had every intention of retaining a presence in Wales by building castles. Llywelyn and Joan spent Easter 1212 with him, but by the end of June war had broken out again and now most of the Welsh rulers, including Gwenwynwyn, were on the prince's side. The Four Cantrefs, apart from the castles of Deganwy and Rhuddlan, were reconquered. John now planned a major campaign to deal with Llywelyn once and for all; he had been preparing an expedition to recover Normandy and Anjou, lost to the French in 1204, and had built up a system of alliances, including the emperor Otto IV, but this was now postponed and an army was assembled at Chester in August. Nothing came of this project, however; the king was warned, by Joan according to some sources, of a baronial plot to hand him over to the Welsh or to kidnap him. The campaign was abandoned, although some Welsh hostages were executed and there was an attempt to persuade the sons of Dafydd and Rhodri to claim lands in Gwynedd.

The planned expedition to France gave this war a European dimension. Philip Augustus of France was in close touch with the pope, Innocent III, who, from his dealings with Gerald of Wales earlier in the century, knew something of Welsh affairs. Philip offered Llywelyn an alliance, sealing his letter with his golden seal, a particular mark of respect; Llywelyn's dignified answer, in which he spoke for all the Welsh rulers and undertook not to make any treaty with the English without Philip's agreement, survives in Paris. Innocent absolved Llywelyn, Gwenwynwyn, and Maelgwn ap Rhys of Deheubarth from their oaths of fealty to John, urged them to make war on him and released their lands from the interdict imposed on the English church in 1208. John's enemies saw the advantage of backing the Welsh cause.

The capture of Deganwy and Rhuddlan in 1213 completed the conquest of the Four Cantrefs. Then, on 15 May 1213, John made his peace with the papacy and became a papal vassal; this meant that the Welsh no longer enjoyed papal support but on Innocent's instructions a truce was arranged which lasted through 1214. After his defeat at Bouvines on 27 July John was faced in England with growing baronial discontent and this led to attempts to secure the support of the Welsh leaders. But when civil war broke out in 1215 Llywelyn joined the barons and in May took Shrewsbury; the key figure in this alliance may have been Giles de Briouze, the bishop of Hereford, whose brother Reginald was to marry the prince's daughter Gwladus. On 15 June 1215 John was forced by the barons to grant Magna Carta, three articles of which related to Wales; these concerned the resolution of territorial disputes, the release of Welsh hostages, including Llywelyn's son Gruffudd, and the restoration of the charters given by the Welsh in 1211 as security for peace.

The grant of the charter was followed by the renewal of hostilities, the excommunication of the king's opponents, and the baronial invitation to Philip Augustus's son Louis to take over the English throne. In December 1215 Llywelyn, accompanied by most of the Welsh rulers, invaded south-west Wales, taking Carmarthen, Cardigan, and several other castles. At an assembly of Welsh rulers at Aberdyfi in 1216 he shared out the reconquered lands among various members of the Deheubarth dynasty; this event marked his emergence as prince of Wales to all intents and purposes and the other rulers may have done homage to him. The same year saw the defection of Gwenwynwyn, persuaded by John to change sides, despite his recent homage and written pledges of loyalty; he was expelled from Powys by Llywelyn and died in exile later the same year.

Pursuit of a settlement, 1216–1230 The death of John on 15 October 1216 and the accession of the young Henry III marked the beginning of the end of the English civil war and the gradual desertion of Llywelyn's allies as they made their peace. The baronial leaders had invited him and Alexander II of Scotland to a meeting at Northampton to choose a new king, but there was no response; both rulers probably understood the potential implications of their attendance. In the summer of 1217 Llywelyn led a further invasion of south Wales which resulted in the surrender of Swansea; Haverfordwest was saved from attack by the intervention of the bishop of St David's. The civil war ended with the treaty of Lambeth on 11 September 1217; the Welsh were offered inclusion in its terms, but as these involved the surrender of all their territorial gains they were unacceptable. Further negotiations followed and at Worcester in March 1218 Llywelyn did homage to the king and his gains were confirmed; he was given the custody of Carmarthen and Cardigan until the king came of age and of southern Powys during the minority of Gwenwynwyn's sons. In the same year he made his peace with the earl of Chester.

The peace of Worcester was a cessation of hostilities rather than a treaty, but it underlined Llywelyn's supremacy; he did homage on his own on behalf of all the Welsh rulers and this symbolized his main objective for the rest of his reign. He had imposed his overlordship on the other rulers; now he sought to have this overlordship recognized by the English crown in a formal treaty. He would do homage on behalf of all the rulers and they would do homage to him. When he died his successor would inherit this position and thus a treaty would create a single Welsh principality recognized by the crown.

Llywelyn's other objective was to secure the undisputed succession of his and Joan's son, Dafydd. At a council at Shrewsbury in May 1220, attended by Pandulf (*d.* 1226), the papal legate, Hubert de Burgh (*d.* 1243), the justiciar, and the archbishop of Canterbury, Stephen Langton (*d.* 1228), Dafydd was recognized as his heir. This was confirmed by the pope in the summer of 1222; Llywelyn had informed Honorius III that he wished to abolish the Welsh custom whereby an illegitimate son was entitled to a share of the inheritance and that he had therefore ordained that Dafydd, his son born in wedlock, would succeed him. This meant the disinheriting of Gruffudd, but the fact that Dafydd was related through his mother to so many royal and aristocratic houses made him the natural choice. Honorius strengthened Dafydd's position further in April 1226 when he declared Joan legitimate, probably at the instance of her half-brother Henry III; in the same year the other Welsh rulers swore fealty to Dafydd and at Michaelmas 1229 he went to London and did homage to the king as his father's heir.

Llywelyn was on friendly terms with Ranulf (III), earl of Chester, and in 1222 his daughter Elen married the earl's nephew and heir, *John the Scot. But his position was not unchallenged; the regent William (I) Marshal, earl of Pembroke, had died in 1219 and his son was making life difficult for his Welsh neighbours around his lordship of Pembroke. In August 1220 Llywelyn led an army into south Wales, ostensibly to remove local Welsh rulers from marcher lands; having done this he marched into what is now Pembrokeshire, destroyed two castles, and burned Haverfordwest. There was no immediate response, but on 15 April 1223 the earl of Pembroke returned from Ireland and took Cardigan and Carmarthen. Llywelyn sent his son Gruffudd to deal with the earl, but a battle near Carmarthen was inconclusive and Gruffudd, short of supplies, returned to Gwynedd. In September Llywelyn besieged Builth after attempts at reconciliation with the earl had failed. Hubert de Burgh now assembled an army, advanced into Wales, and began work on a new castle at Montgomery; Llywelyn raised the siege of Builth, and in October 1223 he and the other rulers submitted to the king and he agreed to relinquish the lands in Shropshire that he had occupied earlier that year.

When Falkes de Bréauté, one of John's old henchmen, defied the king in July 1224 he sought the aid of the earl of Chester and of Llywelyn. Henry III ordered Llywelyn not to receive Bréauté and in a dignified reply the prince informed the king that, as an independent ruler, he could, like the king of Scotland, receive anyone he liked in his own lands (although he had undertaken at Worcester not to receive the king's enemies). But his relations with the crown at this time were generally good and there seems to have been some attempt to conclude a permanent agreement; Llywelyn and Henry met at Shrewsbury in September 1224 and again in August 1226, although both meetings were inconclusive. The legitimization of Joan may have been a sign of royal goodwill.

On 27 April 1228 the castle and lordship of Montgomery were granted to Hubert de Burgh, who began to clear the nearby forests. The Welsh response was to besiege the castle. In August the king and Hubert set out to relieve it; Joan met Henry at Shrewsbury and arranged a truce, but at the same time some of the leading marcher lords had been summoned to Montgomery. Hubert began building a castle in Ceri; this was a threat to Llywelyn's control of the adjacent cantref of Arwystli and he moved swiftly. The royal campaign was an ignominious failure; the army had to withdraw and Henry undertook to demolish the castle in Ceri, for which Llywelyn agreed to pay him £2000. One of the leading marcher lords, William (V) de Briouze, had been captured by the Welsh and a ransom of £2000 was negotiated; he was released early in 1229, having agreed with Llywelyn that his daughter Isabella should marry Dafydd and that Builth should be her dowry. Llywelyn was now in an even stronger position and in 1230 he began to style himself prince of Aberffraw and lord of Snowdon, rather than prince of north Wales; the first surviving record of the use of this title is in a charter dated 1 May 1230 (Aberffraw in Anglesey was the principal seat of the kings of Gwynedd). He may have been reluctant to call himself prince of Wales until that title had been confirmed by the crown in a formal treaty.

War and negotiation, 1230–1240 In the spring of 1230 William de Briouze visited Llywelyn's court to make the final arrangements for the marriage. During his earlier captivity there he appears to have had an affair with Joan and they were now discovered by Llywelyn. Both were imprisoned; the king knew of this by 20 April, when he ordered Briouze's castles to be secured. On 2 May, Briouze was hanged at Crogen near Bala; Llywelyn informed his widow and his brother-in-law that 'the magnates of the land' had insisted on the execution. There were no repercussions; Llywelyn's relations with the crown and with his marcher neighbours were unaffected and the marriage went ahead. It may have been generally felt that Briouze had received his just deserts for his abuse of Llywelyn's hospitality.

The war that came in 1231 stemmed from the ambition of Hubert de Burgh, who had built up an extensive accumulation of lordships in south Wales, including Cardigan and Carmarthen, granted to him in 1229, the overlordship of Gower, and the custody of the lands of Gilbert de Clare, earl of Gloucester, who died in 1230. On the death of Wiliam de Briouze's brother-in-law the earl of Pembroke in April 1231, de Burgh was given custody of all the Briouze lands. This made him the virtual ruler of south Wales and it was regarded by Llywelyn as a serious threat. War was expected; on 20 May 1231 the sheriffs of the border counties and some marcher lords were ordered to see that no food or arms were supplied to the Welsh. On 27 May Llywelyn's representatives met the king at Worcester, but at the beginning of June war broke out, precipitated, according to one chronicler, by the execution of some Welsh prisoners. In the ensuing campaign Llywelyn burned Montgomery, Radnor, Hay, and Brecon and took the castles of Neath and Kidwelly; the Deheubarth lords Maelgwn Fychan (*d.* 1257) and Rhys Gryg (*d.* 1231) burned Cardigan and captured the castle. In late July Henry III led an army into Wales and rebuilt the castle of Painscastle, but at the beginning of winter he withdrew and on 30 November a year's truce was agreed. On 30 September the justiciar of Ireland had been ordered to summon the magnates there to join the campaign and to land in Anglesey the following summer but nothing came of this.

The year 1232 saw the fall of Hubert de Burgh and the rise of Peter de Rivallis, who acquired most of Hubert's Welsh lands; the same year saw the death of Ranulf of Chester, who was succeeded by Llywelyn's son-in-law John the Scot. Another son-in-law, John de Briouze, died the same year and Peter de Rivallis was granted the custody of his lordship of Gower. In 1233 Richard Marshal, earl of Pembroke, clashed with the new regime in England and resorted to arms; Llywelyn joined him and attacked Brecon, while early in 1234 the Deheubarth lords mounted an unsuccessful attack on Carmarthen. But there were pressures for peace, led by Edmund Rich, the new archbishop of Canterbury, and on 6 March 1234 a truce was agreed at Brocton in Shropshire. This was followed by the fall of Peter de Rivallis and the rehabilitation of Pembroke who, however, died on 15 April. The pact of Middle, agreed at the Shropshire village of that name on 21 June, was a truce for two years and a return to the situation at the outbreak of the war. The truce was renewed annually until Llywelyn's death, so that while he lived there was no further war with the king.

Llywelyn was still anxious to secure a permanent settlement; from 1232 onwards there is a considerable body of correspondence relating to Anglo-Welsh relations but, despite various expressions of goodwill on both sides, substantive negotiations never took place. Henry seems to have been determined not to recognize Llywelyn as prince of Wales in a formal treaty. Llywelyn was also faced with the problem of Gruffudd, who had been excluded from the succession. This was a long-standing problem; father and son had clashed in 1221, when they came close to war, and this had led to the confiscation of Meirionydd and Ardudwy, which Gruffudd had held. Relations had improved by 1223 when Gruffudd was given command of the army that faced the earl marshal's challenge, but in 1228 he was imprisoned in Deganwy, where he remained until 1234. Llywelyn appears to have granted him southern Powys, the patrimony of Gwenwynwyn, possibly to be held as an apanage; he granted lands there to the Cistercian monks of Strata Marcella in 1226.

The year 1237 was particularly difficult for Llywelyn. On 2 February Joan died at Aber; she was buried at Llan-faes in Anglesey, where her husband founded a Franciscan friary in her memory. Joan had been a great support and strength to Llywelyn, especially in his dealings with her father and her half-brother. A further blow was the death in the same year of the earl of Chester, John the Scot, without an heir; according to Matthew Paris, John was poisoned by his wife, Llywelyn's daughter Elen, but there is no other evidence of this. The political implications were serious; Chester reverted to the crown, which meant that a reliable ally on Llywelyn's eastern border was replaced by the king. Matthew Paris has two other pieces of information about Llywelyn in 1237; in that year the prince suffered a stroke and he also approached Henry III to secure a treaty. Negotiations took place and Llywelyn even promised military service and to put his lands under the king's protection. His interest in such a settlement was attributed by Paris to the rivalry of Gruffudd and Dafydd, which was threatening the stability of the principality. There is no other evidence of such an offer, but there was some talk of negotiations in 1237 between the king and Dafydd, to lead to a possible settlement.

By now all parties were contemplating a Wales without Llywelyn. In spring 1238 the prince summoned the other rulers to do homage to Dafydd. This came to the king's attention and on 7 March letters were sent to the rulers and to Llywelyn and Dafydd forbidding this; at the same time several leading marcher lords were summoned to meet Henry at Oxford to discuss the matter. A meeting was eventually held at the Cistercian abbey of Strata Florida on 19 October 1238 and here the assembled rulers did fealty to Dafydd but not homage; this assembly might have been the occasion of Llywelyn's effective abdication and the investiture of Dafydd as his successor, the object being to strengthen Dafydd's position in the face of an increasing threat from Gruffudd and his supporters. According to *Brut y tywysogyon* Dafydd took Powys from his brother immediately after the Strata Florida meeting; the same source claims that he imprisoned him in 1239, although Matthew Paris states that this happened after Llywelyn's death.

Death and legacy Llywelyn ab Iorwerth died at Aberconwy Abbey on 11 April 1240, having taken the Cistercian habit on his deathbed; he was buried in the abbey. He stands out as one of the greatest rulers of independent Wales and he is remembered as Llywelyn Fawr or Llywelyn the Great; the title seems first to have been used by Matthew Paris. Having started from nothing, he ended his days as prince of Wales in all but name, having achieved this position entirely through his political and military ability. His reign saw great changes in Gwynedd, particularly in the field of native law; these were aimed at strengthening the position of the prince. The relationship of the prince of Gwynedd with the other Welsh rulers was permanently transformed; in future the only choice open to them was to be the vassals of the prince or of the king of England. The military needs of Llywelyn led to the building of castles to defend the borders of Gwynedd and the heartland of Snowdonia at Castell y Bere, Cricieth, Dolbadarn, Deganwy, and Ewloe. To provide an army for his campaigns grants of land to be held by military service were made to faithful servants, particularly to his steward *Ednyfed Fychan [*see under* Tudor family, forebears of (*per.* *c.*1215–1404)]. He was a generous patron to the church; the Cistercians of Aberconwy, Basingwerk, and Cymer benefited from his munificence and he was instrumental in refounding some native monastic communities as houses of Augustinian canons. He was also generous to the poets; the leading Gwynedd court poet, Prydydd y Moch (Llywarch ap Llywelyn, *fl.* 1180–1220), composed nine poems to him and the greatest of these, the *Canu mawr* ('Great Song'), was probably composed in 1213 to celebrate his victories, particularly the final reconquest of the Four Cantrefs. Other poets who sang to him included Cynddelw Brydydd Mawr (*fl.* 1155–1195) and Dafydd Benfras.

There is little information about Llywelyn himself, though the antiquary Edward Lhwyd, writing at the end of the seventeenth century, referred to a biography of Llywelyn and Dafydd in the library of Corpus Christi College, Cambridge; its fate is unknown. Prydydd y Moch referred to his stature, but this may have been no more than one of the attributes of the ideal ruler. The same poet suggested that he cared nothing for fine clothes or gold or silver, but this could be intended to emphasize his generosity. Other poems refer to battles or campaigns for which no other evidence survives, but which must have been familiar to the poet's audience. The fate of William de Briouze suggests the response of a man who had trusted and depended on his wife.

Llywelyn and Joan had one son, Dafydd, and at least four daughters. Three of the daughters married into marcher families; Gwladus's first husband was Reginald de Briouze, the father of William; after Reginald's death in 1227 or 1228 she married Ralph Mortimer (*d.* 1246) and it is through her that the modern English royal family traces its descent from Llywelyn. Elen married John the Scot, and Margaret, or Marared, married first John de Briouze, lord of Gower, and, after his death in 1232, Walter Clifford (*d.* 1263). The fourth daughter, Susanna, does not appear in the pedigrees; in November 1228 she was put by the king in the care of Nicholas de Verdon and his wife and that is the only reference to her. Tangwystl's daughter, Gwenllian, married William de Lacy and survived until 1281. According to the *History of Fouke le Fitz Waryn* and the Chester annals, Llywelyn married again some eighteen months before his death, his wife being Eva, the daughter of Fulk (III) Fitzwarine, but this is unconfirmed elsewhere. The marriages of his daughters suggest a consistent policy of creating close ties with some of his marcher neighbours in the interests of stability.

Llywelyn's two aims were to secure the undisputed succession of Dafydd and to have his predominance in Wales recognized by Henry III in a formal treaty, but in both he was finally unsuccessful. Gruffudd never seems to have been reconciled to being passed over for the succession and many may have supported him as *mab y Gymraes* ('the Welshwoman's son'); there may have been some hostility to Joan as a daughter of the king of England, and it may be significant that she is not mentioned by any contemporary poet. Although he had brought most of native Wales under his control, everything he had achieved depended in the end on the force of his personality and the strength of his arm. There was no institutional framework to sustain it, with the result that within a month of his death Dafydd was summoned to Gloucester and forced to concede the homage of the other Welsh lords to the king. Henry III could do nothing while Llywelyn lived because of the position he had attained, but he would not allow this position to be inherited by Dafydd, nor would he recognize its permanence by treaty. In the short term Llywelyn, despite his achievements, might be said to have failed; nevertheless, his career showed what could be done by an able and ambitious Welsh ruler and he made a single Welsh principality a political possibility. During his life and largely through his efforts native Wales had changed beyond recognition. A. D. CARR

Sources T. Jones, ed. and trans., *Brut y tywysogyon, or, The chronicle of the princes: Red Book of Hergest* (1955) • J. Williams ab Ithel, ed., *Annales Cambriae*, Rolls Series, 20 (1860) • J. G. Edwards, *Calendar of ancient correspondence concerning Wales* (1935) • Paris, *Chron.*, vols. 3–4 • T. D. Hardy, ed., *Rotuli litterarum patentium*, RC (1835) • T. D. Hardy, ed., *Rotuli litterarum clausarum*, 2 vols., RC (1833–4) • *CPR, 1216–1247* • *Close rolls of the reign of Henry III*, 1–4, PRO (1902–11) • *Gwaith Llywarch ap Llywelyn, 'Prydydd y Moch'*, ed. E. M. Jones and N. A. Jones (1991) • J. E. Lloyd, *A history of Wales from the earliest times to the Edwardian conquest*, 3rd edn, 2 vols. (1939); repr. (1988) • J. B. Smith, *Llywelyn ap Gruffudd, tywysog Cymru* (1986) [trans.: *Llywelyn ap Gruffudd, prince of Wales* (1998)] • G. A. Williams, 'The succession to Gwynedd, 1238–47', *BBCS*, 20 (1962–4), 393–413 • J. B. Smith, 'Magna Carta and the charters of the Welsh princes', *EngHR*, 99 (1984), 344–62 • D. Stephenson, *The governance of Gwynedd* (1984) • R. R. Davies, *Conquest, coexistence, and change: Wales, 1063–1415*, History of Wales, 2 (1987)

Likenesses M. Paris, manuscript drawing, in or before 1259, CCC Cam., MS 16, fol. 132r [*see illus.*] • stone head, NMG Wales

Llywelyn ab Owain (*fl.* 1275–1283). *See under* Gruffudd ap Rhys (*d.* 1201).

Llywelyn ap Gruffudd (*d.* 1282), prince of Wales, was the second of four sons of *Gruffudd ap Llywelyn (*d.* 1244) and his wife, Senana, and grandson of *Llywelyn ab Iorwerth (*c.*1173–1240). Llywelyn ab Iorwerth was succeeded as prince of Gwynedd by his younger and legitimate son *Dafydd ap Llywelyn who, in response to the challenge presented by his elder and bastard brother, Gruffudd ap Llywelyn, immediately placed him in prison. Owain, Gruffudd's eldest son, shared his father's captivity. The younger sons *Dafydd ap Gruffudd and Rhodri, who were not yet of age, were placed in the custody of Henry III as sureties for their mother's good faith in an agreement made with the king by which she sought to secure her husband's release from Dafydd ap Llywelyn's prison. Llywelyn, who was probably now aged about nineteen, is not mentioned in the record of Senana's negotiations with the king, and he appears to have acted independently at this time. By a charter probably given in the summer of 1241, when his father and Owain were transferred to Henry's custody, Llywelyn ceded all claim upon the Mortimer lordships of Maelienydd and Gwrtheyrnion in eastern central Wales, an indication that Ralph Mortimer already recognized the young man's capability and considered it prudent to obtain the release. Llywelyn established lordship in Dyffryn Clwyd, one of the Four Cantrefs of Perfeddwlad, that part of Gwynedd which lay east of the Conwy. When in 1244 war broke out between Dafydd ap Llywelyn and Henry III, Llywelyn soon identified himself with his uncle's cause. He was thus placed in a strong position when, on 25 February 1246, Dafydd died without an heir. Owain returned from England, but he could do no more than agree to a division of the patrimony between Llywelyn and himself, an arrangement confirmed by Henry III in the treaty of Woodstock on 30 April 1247.

Mastery over Gwynedd and supremacy over Wales Owain and Llywelyn were confined to Gwynedd Uwch Conwy, the land centred on Snowdonia west of the Conwy, yielding Perfeddwlad to the king. By 1253 their brother Dafydd ap Gruffudd was asserting his right to a share of the inheritance. Henry took his fealty and urged his elder brothers to provide for him 'according to the custom of Wales'. Owain may have been prepared to accept the adjustment, but Llywelyn was determined to resist a further partition. He made certain proposals to the king 'concerning his brothers', possibly urging that provision be made for Dafydd, and perhaps Rhodri, in Perfeddwlad. No solution was found by negotiation and the issue was resolved by armed conflict in June 1255 when Owain and Dafydd were defeated by Llywelyn at the battle of Bryn Derwin. The vanquished brothers were imprisoned, and Llywelyn consolidated his hold upon Gwynedd Uwch Conwy in its entirety. In November 1256, after a pause of sixteen months, Llywelyn extended his power over the whole of Perfeddwlad except for the two castles of Diserth and Deganwy. Aided by the support of the inhabitants, who nurtured grievances against the officers who had served the king and the Lord Edward, Llywelyn was able to liberate the land by a swift campaign. Henry, insufficiently attentive both to the dynastic problems of Gwynedd and the difficulties confronting the communities of the Four Cantrefs, and unable to appreciate the possibility of a link between them, found his entire settlement of north Wales undermined. With his annexation of Meirionydd immediately afterwards Llywelyn completed the reintegration of the patrimony of his grandfather. Owain would spend another twenty years in confinement, but Dafydd, released before the advance into Perfeddwlad, was given an estate in that area, to be held as a tenant of his brother.

Llywelyn moved without delay to establish a broad supremacy over the lands of other Welsh rulers, endeavouring to do so less by armed might than by drawing the rulers into a military alliance that he then sought to transform into a political association. Advancing southward to Deheubarth (south-west Wales) he won support in Ceredigion with the adherence of Maredudd ab Owain. In Ystrad Tywi he was already assured of the goodwill of Maredudd ap Rhys Gryg, who had joined him for the advance into Perfeddwlad. Together they secured possession of Ystrad Tywi to the exclusion of Maredudd's kinsman and adversary, Rhys Fychan. Rhys, however, quickly repaired to Llywelyn, leaving a royal army brought to his aid by Stephen Bauzan in June 1257 to suffer defeat at Cymerau, and he was reinstated in his portion of Ystrad Tywi. Maredudd thereupon transferred his loyalty to the crown and, after a return to Llywelyn's allegiance and a second defection, he was convicted of infidelity before the prince's council in 1259. Thereafter he acknowledged Llywelyn's supremacy only with the greatest reluctance. The prince was able to withstand Henry's campaign in the summer of 1257, when the king advanced to Deganwy and then withdrew, and improved his position when Gruffudd ap Madog of Powys Fadog (northern Powys) adhered to him. In Powys Wenwynwyn (southern Powys) Gruffudd ap Gwenwynwyn remained loyal to the crown, leaving his lands exposed to annexation by Llywelyn. The Welsh rulers, with very few exceptions, were leagued with him, and Matthew Paris was among English observers deeply impressed by the new unity established in Wales under the inspired leadership of Llywelyn ap Gruffudd.

The Welsh chronicle *Brut y tywysogyon* records that early in 1258 Llywelyn held an assembly of the magnates of Wales who swore an oath of allegiance to him. It is likely that each of them did homage to Llywelyn and that he thereby established a formal bond with the great majority of those who exercised lordship in the several parts of Powys and Deheubarth. The agreements had the support of the bishops of Bangor and St Asaph, who consented to apply ecclesiastical censure in the event of a breach of faith. In an agreement with a group of Scottish nobles in 1258 Llywelyn used the style 'prince of Wales', and although it would be some time before he used the title on a regular basis its use in that year reflects the emergence, from the initial military alliance, of a new political entity in the prince's lands.

Dominance in the march In the period 1258–62 Llywelyn concentrated upon a quest for a peace treaty by which the king would recognize the political relationships that had now been created in Wales. The central issue was Llywelyn's plea that the homages of the Welsh princes, which historically had belonged to the king of England, should be granted to himself, and that he alone should do homage to the king. With Henry confronted in 1258 by a baronial opposition whose demands were reflected in the provisions of Oxford, the time might have seemed propitious for a Welsh diplomatic initiative and envoys were sent to the Oxford parliament. But there was little prospect of securing a settlement favourable to the prince, not least because marcher lords—several of whom had been victims of Llywelyn's aggression—held powerful positions in the royal council. Twice in 1260 Llywelyn launched an attack upon the royal castle of Builth to coincide with renewed diplomatic initiatives. He created consternation in the king's council and secured an extension of the truce first arranged at Oxford, but the peace treaty on which he set his mind remained elusive. After Henry reasserted his authority in 1261 their exchanges became more cordial and Llywelyn, commended for his restraint at the time of turmoil in the realm, was given some reason to believe that the king was serious in his declared readiness to discuss peace terms as well as a truce. The king's position is revealed more clearly, however, in letters written during his stay in France in July 1262 when, upon hearing rumour of the prince's death, he indicated his resolve to terminate the hegemony established by the prince of Gwynedd, and to restore the traditional and direct relationship between the crown and each of the lords of Wales. Llywelyn evidently sensed the king's true feelings. By the end of 1262 he had resumed armed conflict with a series of forceful campaigns in the Welsh march calculated to promote his continuing quest for a definitive peace treaty. It was at this time that he began to use regularly the style 'prince of Wales and lord of Snowdon'.

Llywelyn's movements were concentrated first on Roger (III) Mortimer's lordship of Maelienydd, and then upon the lordship of Brecon and its environs as far as Abergavenny. While he intended a military response Henry indicated his readiness for negotiation, but the prospect of a peace settlement diminished in the spring of 1263 when Edward, upon his return from Gascony, intervened in the march in association with the prince's implacable opponent, Roger (III) Mortimer. No major campaign materialized even so, and the only tangible result of Edward's activity was an agreement with Dafydd ap Gruffudd upon his defection from Llywelyn. The summer saw considerable turmoil in the march. The prince's forces were engaged in a new offensive in the western portion of the lordship of Clun (that is, Tempsiter or Dyffryn Tefeidiad) about the time of Simon de *Montfort's return from France. For a brief period Montfort supporters with territories in the Welsh march, including Roger de Clifford and Hamon L'Estrange, attacked royalist positions in the area. Gruffudd ap Gwenwynwyn, lord of Powys Wenwynwyn, seized the opportunity created by the disorder to resolve a dispute with Thomas Corbet over possession of the area known as Gorddwr on the right bank of the upper Severn. But, when Montfort's transitory adherents returned to the king's allegiance, Gruffudd was left bereft of marcher allies and negotiated an agreement with Llywelyn formalized by an act of homage and fealty on 12 December 1263.

Overt collaboration between the forces of Llywelyn and Montfort is indicated from the early months of 1264 with a joint attack on Mortimer's castle of Radnor. Llywelyn provided valuable aid upon Montfort's advances to Montgomery in July and to Worcester in December, when the presence of the prince's forces west of the Severn forced their opponents into submission. There is, however, no indication that any formal agreement of a political nature was made in the period when Montfort controlled the government of the realm. A treaty was made only in June 1265, and by then Montfort's power was crumbling. Envoys of Montfort, who was at Hereford, and those of Llywelyn, encamped at Pipton in the lordship of Brecon, negotiated an agreement sealed by Llywelyn on 17 June and issued in the king's name three days later. For a fine of £20,000 Henry granted Llywelyn the lordship of all the barons of Wales, and the principality of Wales, to be held by the prince of Wales and the heirs of his body. Several of Llywelyn's annexations in the march were conceded to him. He may have been sceptical, however, that anything of permanent value would come of the agreement, and he may have endorsed the terms only as a basis for a treaty to be made when the king was able to act of his free will. Within days of the completion of the agreement, ordered government under Montfort's direction ceased. Though the earl moved to the Welsh march, there is no indication that he attempted to link up with Llywelyn's forces and, turning back to cross the Severn, he went to meet his death at Evesham.

The treaty of Montgomery, 1267 Agreement between Llywelyn and the king would need to form part of a broader settlement of the problems that confronted the realm of England following civil war. Cardinal Ottobuono, the papal legate, found his mediation made difficult by deeply discordant views among the magnates over the treatment of the Montfortians. It was only when this issue had been resolved, following Gilbert de Clare's armed intervention in London on behalf of the 'disinherited', that Henry, on 24 July 1267, indicated his wish to open negotiations with Llywelyn. Envoys of king and prince were at work at Shrewsbury by late August, but after three weeks, when conduct of the negotiations was entrusted to Ottobuono, no treaty had been made. Agreement was finally reached on 25 September and four days later Llywelyn did homage to Henry at Rhydwhiman, the ford on the Severn that marked the frontier in the neighbourhood of Montgomery. By the treaty of Montgomery (29 September 1267) Henry granted Llywelyn and his successors by hereditary right the principality of Wales and the right to be called prince of Wales. He was granted the homage of all the Welsh lords of Wales, with the single exception of Maredudd ap Rhys Gryg. Llywelyn was required to pay 25,000 marks for the treaty, and a further 5000 marks if the king were ever to concede Maredudd's homage; 5000 marks were due immediately or by Christmas and the remainder in instalments of 3000 marks a year. Possession of Gwynedd was implicit in the king's grant, and the inclusion of the Four Cantrefs of Perfeddwlad was specifically stated. The homage of the Welsh lords, the key clause of the treaty, conveyed to Llywelyn overlordship of the several lands of the former principalities of Powys and Deheubarth. Llywelyn was required to cede his conquests, except that he was permitted to hold Gwrtheyrnion, Builth, Brecon, Ceri, Cedewain, and Whittington, lands which together represented a considerable extension of his authority into the march of Wales. He would be allowed Maelienydd if he could establish his right to it, and both the lands granted to him and others to which he laid claim could be made subject to legal process according to the custom of the march. Within his principality he was required, by a clause 'specially ordained', to provide for Dafydd ap Gruffudd, either by restoring what he had held before his defection or by making further provision in accordance with the decision of named magnates of Wales, or, if necessary, by doing justice according to the laws and customs of Wales in the presence of men who would inform the king of the decision. The treaty contained several clauses that were potentially contentious, but Ottobuono felt able to commend it as an honourable settlement which brought hope of an enduring peace between two peoples who had been in prolonged conflict.

Prince of Wales, marcher lords, and Edward I Only ten years after Llywelyn won formal recognition as prince of Wales the principality was dismembered, leaving him to make peace with Edward I on humiliating terms. Historians have often sought to explain the reversal in his fortunes by emphasizing the prince's intransigent attitude to the crown after Edward's accession at the end of 1272. Edward, however, left the kingdom upon a crusade in August 1270 and was away until August 1274, a four-year period which saw a marked deterioration in Llywelyn's relations with the royal government. Problems arose in the march, partly the result of Llywelyn's intervention with armed force in Gilbert de Clare's lordship of Glamorgan. His claim to the homage of Gruffudd ap Rhys of Senghennydd was emphatically rejected by Clare, who rightly held that Gruffudd was a mesne tenant of his marcher dominion. Clare was incensed at a decision by Edward to endorse Llywelyn's parallel claim to the homage of Maredudd ap Gruffudd, who held his lands as a tenant of Clare in the lordship of Caerleon. Clare embarked on the construction of Caerphilly Castle in 1268 and, upon Edward's departure for the crusade, seized the opportunity to resolve the problems in Caerleon and Senghennydd unilaterally. By 1272 Llywelyn had been forced to withdraw from Glamorgan with nothing to show for a prolonged and costly enterprise. To the north of Glamorgan lay the lordship of Brecon where Humphrey (VI) de Bohun sought to reassert authority in a land formally conceded to the prince in 1267, and Llywelyn had to take stern measures to retain the fidelity of some of his Welsh tenants there. With Roger Mortimer now a regent of the realm, Llywelyn feared that Bohun and other marchers would gain the support of the king's council in their attempts to reassert their position. Exchanges over Llywelyn's building of the castle of Dolforwyn in his lordship of Cedewain, and over Mortimer's work at Cefnllys in Maelienydd, reveal the animosity between the two men.

Llywelyn's failure to appear at the ford of Montgomery to swear fealty to the king in January 1273 may have been less a discourtesy to Edward than a reflection of his distrust of those who were then representing the English king's authority. Llywelyn's failure to meet his financial obligations under the treaty of Montgomery became a matter of concern even before Edward's accession. Late and piecemeal delivery of the sum due at the end of 1270 may point less to a refusal to pay as a matter of principle than to an inability to meet the required payments. There is some indication that Llywelyn's financial resources were inadequate to meet the demands made upon them, particularly the costs incurred by the needs of war, which included castle building at Dolforwyn and Ewloe. Evidence assembled after his death points to the severity of his rule over the communities of his patrimony of Gwynedd, upon whose resources he was very largely dependent. Complaints made by the bishop of St Asaph similarly suggest rigorous financial exaction on the part of the prince, and relations between them were strained. Both Canterbury and the papal court, particularly in the time of Gregory X, were made aware of the internal conflicts of the principality of Wales. The most threatening occurrence was a conspiracy on the part of Dafydd ap Gruffudd and Gruffudd ap Gwenwynwyn to kill the prince. During April 1274, in proceedings before the prince's council at Dolforwyn, Gruffudd ap Gwenwynwyn was convicted of infidelity. His lands were forfeited but were in large part promptly restored by the prince's grace, and it is not certain that Llywelyn at that stage knew the full extent of the conspiracy, unless he was anxious to avoid any open admission of the seriousness of the threat he had encountered. The full story may not have emerged until much later in the year when Owain, son of Gruffudd ap Gwenwynwyn, held as a hostage for his father's good faith, made a full confession. It was only then that Dafydd came to be questioned, but before proceedings were initiated against him both he and Gruffudd fled to England. Edward had by then returned to England, and his decision to give the fugitives refuge in his realm had far-reaching implications in Anglo-Welsh relations.

Llywelyn was invited to Edward's coronation in August 1274 but did not attend. Of more consequence would be his response to a summons to do homage to the king, a call to Shrewsbury by 2 December 1274. He was given only a month's notice and the date was then brought forward by a week before Edward, on account of an abscess, cancelled the arrangement at very short notice. His inability to fulfil the engagement, which leaves unresolved the question of Llywelyn's willingness to attend, certainly caused a fateful postponement. Within days full knowledge of the conspiracy had been revealed, and before the end of 1274 Edward had given the plotters the shelter of his realm and a base from which they harried the prince. Llywelyn thus received his second summons, to come to Chester by 22 August 1275, at a time of greatly increased tension. The Welsh chronicle records that Llywelyn refused to meet Edward because the king was maintaining the two fugitives who had conspired to kill him. Llywelyn was close by the frontier while Edward was at Chester, and messengers passed between them. But no meeting took place and, at Treuddyn on 11 September, Llywelyn made a statement of his position in a letter to Pope Gregory. The essential issue was Edward's decision to provide sanctuary for his two faithless vassals, linked with the fact that he was summoned to do homage at a place to which it was unsafe for him to go, among men who had plotted his death. He was prepared to come to a safe place, as long as the king abided by the terms of the treaty of 1267 and ensured that breaches of the truce were corrected. There would be three more summonses to do homage, but the issues that would lead to war in 1277 were, with one exception, already formulated: Llywelyn had failed to fulfil his duties to the king, and he had not met his obligations under the treaty of 1267; he made war in the marches to the damage of the king's realm. The remaining issue was Llywelyn's decision to marry *Eleanor de Montfort (*d.* 1282). Negotiations, in which Welsh Dominicans played a key part, led to a marriage by proxy before Eleanor left the convent at Montargis for her voyage to Wales in December 1275. She sailed with her brother Amaury, but her ships were intercepted on the high seas, probably near the Isles of Scilly. Edward attributed the capture to divine providence, but it may have reflected the surveillance of the Montforts that Edward had initiated following the murder of Henry of Almain by Simon de Montfort's sons at Viterbo in 1271. In letters to the pope Edward emphasized the dangers that the marriage created for the security of England. There can be little doubt that Llywelyn arranged the marriage in the immediate aftermath of Edward's decision to receive the conspirators, and that he did so in retaliation against the king's action.

War and the treaty of Aberconwy, 1277 Formal condemnation of Llywelyn was made by king and council on 11 November 1276 when Llywelyn's proposals were rejected. Archbishop Kilwardby, who had attempted to engage the prince in discussions during the summer, withheld sentence of excommunication to give Llywelyn an opportunity to make his submission to the king. Llywelyn is known to have presented further proposals on two occasions early in 1277, but to no effect. By the spring, excommunication had been pronounced, and military operations were set in train in the march and in Powys and Deheubarth, where Edward was able to wean the Welsh lords from their loyalty to Llywelyn. The king launched the main offensive against Gwynedd in late July, with the declared objective of appropriating the prince's entire patrimony and sharing its possession between Owain ap Gruffudd, Dafydd ap Gruffudd, and himself. The main royal army advanced to the Conwy and another force occupied Anglesey. Llywelyn, despite some defections from among the men of Gwynedd, prepared for a long siege. From September, however, the forces confronting the prince were gradually reduced and a settlement was negotiated. Edward made provision for Dafydd in Perfeddwlad, and at the beginning of November a document was drawn up by which Llywelyn acknowledged Dafydd's hereditary right in Gwynedd Uwch Conwy, while Edward declared his willingness to allow Llywelyn to hold the land for his lifetime. These key agreements were embodied in the treaty of Aberconwy on 9 November 1277. Llywelyn was allowed to retain the style prince of Wales, with the homage of five minor lords. His broader principality was destroyed without its mention in the treaty, and he ceded the Four Cantrefs. Owain ap Gruffudd was released from prison and given land in Llŷn, and financial provision was made for Rhodri. Neither was accorded the concern shown for Dafydd, who would succeed to his share of the patrimony at Llywelyn's death. A fine of 50,000 marks by which Llywelyn secured the king's grace was immediately remitted, but the prince was held to his outstanding obligations under the terms of the treaty of Montgomery and his annual payment for Anglesey. Llywelyn swore fealty at Rhuddlan on 11 November. Before Christmas he went to London where he did homage and attended to matters of detail arising from the treaty. Edward and Llywelyn met again at Rhuddlan in September 1278, and final arrangements were made for the celebration of Llywelyn's marriage to Eleanor de Montfort at Worcester on 13 October. Edward gave the bride in marriage and provided the wedding feast.

Conflict of law and renewed warfare Early in 1278 Llywelyn initiated proceedings before royal justices to claim against Gruffudd ap Gwenwynwyn the cantref of Arwystli and part of Cyfeiliog, lands he had retained following the legal process against Gruffudd in 1274 and then ceded in war. Llywelyn, acting in accordance with the terms of the treaty of Aberconwy, which allowed for the use of Welsh or marcher law as appropriate, wished to proceed by Welsh law while Gruffudd preferred English law. After deliberations in council in 1279–80 Edward indicated that actions arising in Wales would be determined in accordance with the practice of his predecessors. Though Llywelyn pressed for a clear indication of the king's intentions, and Archbishop Pecham offered a highly critical estimate of Welsh law, Edward refrained from any elaboration. Llywelyn appears to have sought a procedure by which the case would be resolved by the judgment of Welsh judges (*ynaid, iudices*). Unwilling to consent to a procedure which would in effect take judgment away from his justices, Edward was at the same time reluctant to expose himself to the political repercussions of an explicit rejection of Llywelyn's demands. Llywelyn had placed the king in a difficult dilemma, but it is by no means certain that he was using the proceedings over Arwystli as a pretext for renewed conflict. An agreement with Roger Mortimer on 9 October 1281, by which the old adversaries set aside their differences, does not suggest impending conflict but indicates Llywelyn's wish, in the event of a successful outcome of the Arwystli case, to accommodate Mortimer's claims to lands that bordered on the cantref. Edward's anger at Llywelyn's recent action in reopening the Arwystli case is suggested in November 1281 by his more clearly declared support for Gruffudd ap Gwenwynwyn, and a hardening of his attitude is at the same time indicated in his appointment of Reynold de Grey as justice of Chester, an office that carried responsibility for Perfeddwlad. Signs of greatly increased anxiety may be recognized in letters of Llywelyn and Eleanor early in 1282.

Renewed conflict, which broke out with Dafydd's attack on Hawarden Castle on Palm Sunday (22 March) 1282, is best understood, however, as the outcome of the grievances not of Llywelyn but of Dafydd, along with those of other princes, and the discontent of communities who had a vexed experience of royal administration in Perfeddwlad. In a statement to Pecham late in 1282 Llywelyn said that he had no knowledge of the intention of those who went to war. But, he told the archbishop, after reciting the suffering endured by his people, no one should marvel that he had given his consent to those who began the war. It is not certain that Llywelyn joined the resistance at an early date, and he may not have committed himself to the conflict for some weeks, possibly not before Eleanor died giving birth to their daughter, Gwenllian, on 19 June. Even so, the record of Pecham's intervention in November, designed to persuade Llywelyn to submit to the king's will, establishes the prince's unquestioned leadership of the forces in rebellion by then. He was already besieged in Snowdonia, with Anglesey and Perfeddwlad lost, and his position was desperate. But in written statements made in anticipation of Pecham's coming, Llywelyn provided a reasoned account of the considerations that had brought his people to war, and rejected the archbishop's pleas that he submit himself to the king's will. He supplied Pecham with a substantial dossier embodying his complaints and those of his fellow princes and several communities.

Pecham, who found the king unwilling to countenance these submissions, made his way into Snowdonia for discussions with Llywelyn, probably at the prince's court at Aber or in its environs. He returned to find Edward still bent upon securing an unconditional surrender and he could do no more than secure a statement of the proposals that the magnates would put to the king if Llywelyn were prepared to submit. Nothing would be conceded concerning Anglesey or Perfeddwlad; Llywelyn and his people would be treated mercifully and the prince would be offered honourable maintenance, in fact an earldom, in England. In rejecting the proposals Llywelyn referred to his distant predecessors the Trojan founders of Britain, and emphasized both his ancient inheritance and the status accorded him by the mediation of the papacy in 1267. He would not renounce his responsibility to his people and leave them exposed to the rule of a king in whom they had no confidence. Even as the archbishop conducted his discussions with the magnates upon his return from Llywelyn the English army in Anglesey made an unsuccessful attempt to force a crossing of the Menai Strait and, when the archbishop terminated his mediation with a vigorous denunciation of those in rebellion, preparations were made for a new offensive.

Llywelyn's death and its aftermath Llywelyn's decision to depart from Gwynedd and take an army to the march of Wales has left historians perplexed. Already besieged in his redoubt in Snowdonia there were, however, military reasons for a major diversion of his opponents' resources. But there is a possibility that Llywelyn was drawn to the march by subterfuge. The continuation of *Brut y tywysogyon* records, in a statement that precedes its account of Llywelyn's departure, that 'then there was effected the betrayal of Llywelyn in the belfry at Bangor by his own men' (*Brut: Peniarth MS 20*, 120). The precise meaning of the statement is uncertain, but the circumstances in which he met his death strongly suggest that he was lured to Cilmeri, in the neighbourhood of Builth, by a ruse in which Edmund Mortimer played a key role. Llywelyn's movements were closely monitored by English field commanders, and there can be no doubt that securing his death was a prime object of their endeavours. The account of Walter of Guisborough, describing a battle in which the Welsh, defending a bridge, were attacked upon their flank by a force that had forced the river upstream, does not carry conviction. The Welsh chronicle and several English chronicles, among which that of the Premonstratensian house of Hagnaby is particularly informative, point to Llywelyn's coming at Mortimer's behest to take the homage of his men, and then a fierce and prolonged battle in which the prince was separated from his forces and killed. He died on 11 December 1282. A report by John Pecham, carrying an intriguing reference to a treasonable letter disguised by false names found on Llywelyn's person, strongly suggests conspiracy among the marcher barons.

Llywelyn was decapitated and his head was sent to Edward and displayed to his troops before it was taken to London and, crowned with ivy, placed upon a pole at the Tower. The statement in the chronicle of Bury St Edmunds that his body was buried in the Cistercian abbey of Cwmhir is not corroborated by any other writer but, given Pecham's keen inquiry into the truth of a report to that effect, is probably correct. His daughter, Gwenllian, was removed to the Gilbertine nunnery at Sempringham where, made a nun against her will according to the Welsh chronicler, she spent her days. She died at the nunnery in 1337. After Llywelyn's death his brother Dafydd ap Gruffudd assumed the title 'prince of Wales and lord of Snowdon', and maintained the struggle until his capture in the summer of 1283. Llywelyn's triumphs were celebrated by the poets Dafydd Benfras and Llygad Gŵr, and his death inspired elegies of great eloquence by Bleddyn Fardd and Gruffudd ab yr Ynad Coch. The text of the chronicle *Brenhinedd y Saesson* relates that after the death of Llywelyn 'all Wales was cast to the ground' (*Brut: Saeson*, 259). His death, and the virtual extinction in the war of 1282–3 of the princely lineages, brought an era in the history of Wales to a close.

Historical remembrance Llywelyn ap Gruffudd was not to be accorded extensive historical remembrance in the centuries following his death. Although there are occasional allusions to him in the poetry of the later middle ages, the profound sense of loss expressed in the elegies was not to be sustained. Gwenllian was his only child and consequently the prince left no lineage that might have stimulated the interest of the genealogists. More telling still was the fact that, with the extinction of the princes at the conquest, the historical writing represented by *Brut y tywysogyon* came to an end. Thereafter it was Geoffrey of Monmouth's *History of the Kings of Britain* that prevailed in the nation's awareness, and the distant figures of legendary history tended to excite greater interest than the historical persons of a more recent past. The work of Humphrey Llwyd and David Powel in the sixteenth century ensured that the memory of the princes was restored, and these scholars were the founders of a new tradition in Welsh historical writing. Their work, which accorded an appropriate place to Llywelyn ap Gruffudd's achievement, greatly influenced later writers, but in the eighteenth century Theophilus Evans and William Williams of

Llandygái still expressed their regret that the princes were not better remembered. Fuller historical discussion came with the work of William Warrington in English, and Thomas Price and Gweirydd ap Rhys in Welsh; Llywelyn was also commemorated in epic poetry and in patriotic verse set to music. Even so, he was never to share the fame enjoyed by Owain Glyn Dŵr, and efforts to raise by public subscription a memorial at Cilmeri, close by the place where he fell, came to nothing. An obelisk was eventually raised by the generosity of an Englishman, Stanley Bligh, squire of a neighbouring estate.

Authoritative discussion came with the publication of J. E. Lloyd's *History of Wales* (1911), but the descriptive nature of the work meant that Llywelyn's achievement in realigning the princes' allegiance so as to create a new political unity in Wales, and his unique success in establishing a relationship with the crown of England which reflected that change, remained largely unexplained. Moreover, the fact that Lloyd's narrative was in effect cut short at 1277 deprived his work of the advantage of being derived from the evidence relating both to the subsequent disputes over Welsh law, and to the considerations that led to renewed conflict in 1282, sources that contribute quite significantly to a study of the manner in which Welsh national identity was given political expression in this period. Modern historical investigation owes a great deal to the discussion embodied in the introduction by J. G. Edwards to *Littere Wallie* (1940), in which Llywelyn's activities were regarded as an attempt to overcome the problems caused by the 'chronic decentralization' characteristic of government in thirteenth-century Wales. The contractual relationships that Llywelyn established with the princes of Powys and Deheubarth were portrayed as a means of achieving a measure of coherence in Welsh political affairs never previously attained. Llywelyn's image as a warrior prince, so beloved by generations of historians, now receded as he emerged as an architect of the nation's political institutions, though a prince whose political judgement was still subject to close scrutiny.

A subsequent broadening of the range of studies of thirteenth-century Wales, with attention given to law texts and poetry, military organization and castle building, the economy of the prince's dominion and his relations with those whom he ruled, has led to a sharpened historical awareness both of the extent of the change in Welsh politics and society, and of the predicament in which Llywelyn found himself in his relations not only with his royal and marcher opponents but also with the princes and communities of his own nation. The exultation and denunciation characteristic of earlier interpretations have by now been moderated in favour of a critical assessment of his efforts to bring a cohesive influence to bear upon a highly fractionized country, and of his ability, albeit for a brief period, to comprehend the territories under Welsh lordship in the unifying political structure represented by the principality of Wales. J. B. SMITH

Sources PRO • *Chancery records* • J. E. Lloyd, *A history of Wales from the earliest times to the Edwardian conquest*, 2 vols. (1911) • J. B. Smith, *Llywelyn ap Gruffudd, prince of Wales* (1998) • R. R. Davies, *Conquest, coexistence and change: Wales, 1063–1415* (1987) • J. G. Edwards, *Littere Wallie* (1940) • L. B. Smith, 'The death of Llywelyn ap Gruffydd: the narratives reconsidered', *Welsh History Review / Cylchgrawn Hanes Cymru*, 11 (1982–3), 200–13 • Ll. B. Smith, 'The gravamina of the community of Gwynedd against Llywelyn ap Gruffudd', *BBCS*, 31 (1984), 158–76 • Ll. B. Smith, 'Llywelyn ap Gruffudd and the Welsh historical consciousness', *Welsh History Review / Cylchgrawn Hanes Cymru*, 12 (1984–5), 1–28 • F. M. Powicke, *King Henry III and the Lord Edward: the community of the realm in the thirteenth century*, 2 vols. (1947) • D. Stephenson, *The governance of Gwynedd* (1984) • H. Pryce, *Native law and the church in medieval Wales* (1993) • *Gwaith Bleddyn Fardd ac eraill o feirdd ail hanner y drydedd ganrif ar ddeg*, ed. R. Andrews and others (1996) • *Registrum epistolarum fratris Johannis Peckham, archiepiscopi Cantuariensis*, ed. C. T. Martin, 3 vols., Rolls Series, 77 (1882–5) • T. Jones, ed. and trans., *Brut y tywysogyon, or, The chronicle of the princes: Red Book of Hergest* (1955) • T. Jones, ed. and trans., *Brenhinedd y Saesson, or, The kings of the Saxons* (1971) [another version of *Brut y tywysogyon*] • T. Jones, ed. and trans., *Brut y tywysogyon, or, The chronicle of the princes: Peniarth MS 20* (1952)

Likenesses H. Pegram, statue, 1916, City Hall, Cardiff

Llywelyn ap Rhisiart [*pseud.* Lewis Morgannwg] (*fl.* **1520–1565**), poet, was born in Tir Iarll, Glamorgan, the son of Rhisiart ap Rhys Brydydd (*fl. c.*1480–1520), and lived either in Llantwit Major or, more probably, in Cowbridge. He was instructed in the bardic craft by his father, by Iorwerth Fynglwyd (*fl. c.*1480–1527), the greatest of all the Glamorgan bards who sang on the *cywydd* metre, and, most important of all, by Tudur Aled (*fl. c.*1480–1526), one of the supreme northern figures among the 'poets of the gentry'.

After Tudur Aled's death Lewis Morgannwg became the most important master-poet (*pencerdd*) in the whole of Wales and the only Glamorgan bard regarded as a national figure. From *c.*1530 to 1560 he was the head of the bardic order throughout the whole of Wales. One of the chief heraldic bards of his day, his advice was sought by John Leland (*c.*1506–1552) during the latter's itinerary in Wales *c.*1536–1539.

As an itinerant bard Lewis Morgannwg visited many of the noble families in both north and south Wales. Early in his career he seems to have been a sort of family bard to Sir Edward Stradling (*d.* 1535) of St Donats, and he was also an *habitué* of the court of Sir Rhys ap Thomas (1449–1525). More than 100 of his compositions are preserved in various manuscripts. Apart from some religious and amatory poems the greater part of his work consists of eulogies and elegies addressed to his patrons. His real merit as a poet is to be found in the accomplished artistry of his panegyric verses, while his sure command of *cynghanedd* reflects the influence of his great northern master.

Lewis Morgannwg sang during a critical period, when far-reaching changes occurred in society, religion, and law. The poems he addressed to the influential Herbert family reflect the attraction which London and the royal court had during this period for many of the Welsh gentry, whose political allegiance was partly determined by prospects of personal advancement and material gain.

The new political climate probably accounts for Lewis Morgannwg's own marked change of religious allegiance. Whereas some of the verses he composed in the early part of his career reflect his Catholic sympathies and allegiance, his later work testifies to his admiration for the religious changes introduced by Henry VIII. This striking change of attitude can probably be attributed to the fact that several of his important patrons were staunch supporters of the new political dispensation, from which they had derived substantial benefits. Moreover, the poet himself seems to have been regarded as a kind of semi-official royal bard by state officials in south Wales, who may have rewarded him for composing those verses which expressed support for the official standpoint on some vital contemporary issues. Although the elegy he sang to Rhys ap Siôn of Aberpergwm contains a faint suggestion of opposition to the alien influences that were penetrating into Glamorgan and Gwent during this period, his work, on the whole, does not castigate contemporary social evils. The 'exemplifying ode' he sang on each of the twenty-four strict metres to Lleision ap Thomas, the last abbot of Neath, testifies to his interest in Welsh metrics. He undoubtedly wrote on certain features of Welsh prosody, for although the work itself is no longer extant his observations on one of the Welsh metres are quoted by Siôn Dafydd Rhys (1534–*c.*1619) in his famous grammar (1592).

Lewis Morgannwg died in Cowbridge, Glamorgan; the date is unknown. In view of the exalted status he enjoyed among the bardic fraternity it is surprising that no elegy to him survives, apart from the elegiac quotations composed by the talented literary forger Edward Williams (Iolo Morganwg; 1747–1826) and claimed by him to be extracts from elegies which he attributed to the late sixteenth-century Glamorgan bards Meurig Dafydd and Dafydd Benwyn, both of whom were Lewis Morgannwg's bardic disciples. C. W. LEWIS

Sources E. J. Saunders, 'Gweithiau Lewys Morgannwg', MA diss., U. Wales, 1922 • G. J. Williams, *Traddodiad llenyddol Morgannwg* (1948), 62–71 [also references in the index] • C. W. Lewis, 'The literary tradition of Morgannwg down to the middle of the sixteenth century', *Glamorgan county history*, ed. G. Williams, 3: *The middle ages*, ed. T. B. Pugh (1971), 449–554, esp. 515–20 • G. Williams, *The Welsh church from conquest to Reformation* (1962) • L. J. Hopkin-James and Cadrawd [T. C. Evans], *Hen gwndidau, carolau, a chywyddau* (1910), 155–9 • *The itinerary of John Leland in or about the years 1535–1543*, ed. L. Toulmin Smith, 3: *The itinerary in Wales* (1906), 51–2 • S. D. Rhys, *Cambrobrytannicae Cymraecaeve linguae institutiones et rudimenta* (1592), 165, 239–42 • G. J. Williams, *Iolo Morganwg a chywyddau'r ychwanegiad* (1926), 75–6, 79, 86, 108–9, 122–4, 131–3, 137, 150–51, 169, 196–9, 202, 204 • *Gwaith Tudur Aled*, ed. J. G. Jones, 2 vols. (1926), vol. 2, pp. 737–9 • D. Rhys Phillips, *The history of the Vale of Neath* (1925), 521–2 • S. Rhydderch, *Grammadeg Cymraeg* (1728), 148–51 • D. W. Jones, *Hanes Morganwg* (1874), 501–5 • *Efrydiau Catholig*, 5 (1951), 44–5 • J. Morris-Jones, *Cerdd dafod, sef, Celfyddyd barddoniaeth Gymraeg* (1925); repr. (1980), 365–6 • *Heraldic visitations of Wales and part of the marches … by Lewys Dwnn*, ed. S. R. Meyrick, 1 (1846), 331 • D. J. Bowen, *Gruffudd Hiraethog a'i oes* (1958), 12–13, 18–19, 61 • *Trysorfa Gwybodaeth* (1770), 69–71 • *Report on manuscripts in the Welsh language*, 2 vols. in 7, HMC, 48 (1898–1910), vol. 1, pp. 822, 833, 1021–3; vol. 2. pp. 830ff • NL Wales, Peniarth MSS 60, 64, 66, 76, 77, 80, 83, 96, 97, 99, 100, 101, 103, 112, 114, 119, 121, 132 • NL Wales, Mostyn MSS 129, 145, 146, 148 • NL Wales, Llanstephan MSS 6, 7, 30, 35, 40, 47, 55, 122–124, 133–135, 148, 163–165 • Cardiff MSS 7, 18, 19, 20, 26, 27, 63, 83, 84 • Cardiff MS 3.464, 173 • Cardiff MS 4.213 • NL Wales, Peniarth MSS 133, 192; 194, 447.11 • NL Wales, Panton MS 22 • NL Wales, Llanover MSS C9, 239; C21, 203; 67, 122; E4, 47 • Jesus College, Oxford, MSS 12, 15, 17

Llywelyn ap Seisyll (*d.* **1023**). *See under* Gruffudd ap Llywelyn (*d.* 1063).

Llywelyn Bren [Llywelyn ap Gruffudd ap Rhys] (*d.* **1318**), rebel leader, was a man of large possessions and great influence in Glamorgan, where he held lands in Senghennydd and Meisgyn; his name may be translated as Llywelyn of the Wood. The earls of Gloucester were lords of Glamorgan, and were accustomed to rule their dominions with the help of the local lords, whether Welsh or English. Llywelyn's family had periodically resisted the earls, and his father, Gruffudd ap Rhys, had also supported Llywelyn ap Gruffudd, prince of Wales, in the 1260s. After the death of Gilbert, the last Clare earl of Gloucester, at Bannockburn in 1314, Glamorgan fell to the king as the guardian of the three sisters and heiresses of the deceased earl. Edward II's appointment of custodians of the lordship caused resentment, especially at a time of great famine; although Bartholomew Badlesmere (*d.* 1322) was conciliatory and returned some of Llywelyn Bren's ancestral lands and allowed his son to take office in Glamorgan, Payn Trubleville of Coety, one of the English lords of the Vale of Glamorgan, was appointed in July 1315 and acted harshly. Trubleville at once removed Llywelyn Bren and other officials to make way for his friends. Llywelyn angrily denounced Trubleville, who thereupon accused him before the king of sedition. Against the advice of his wife, Lleucu, Llywelyn went to the king's court, seeking reconciliation. But Edward II, who also faced Scottish intervention in Ireland, rejected his complaints and issued threats. Llywelyn was formally summoned to appear before the parliament at Lincoln, which assembled on 27 January 1316, but instead he returned to his own country, and, having taken counsel with his friends, rose in revolt. The quarrel was partly local, but it was also part of the longer struggle between English conquerors and Welsh lords. It reflected too the determination of the crown to curb the special privileges of the marches; the ending of Clare rule offered an opportunity to do this in Glamorgan.

Llywelyn began his revolt on 28 January 1316 with an attempt to surprise Caerphilly Castle while the constable was holding his court outside the walls. Llywelyn took the constable prisoner, and burnt the town, but failed to capture the main works of the castle. A large force of Welsh from the hills joined Llywelyn and six of his sons. Trubleville had no means of resisting such a force as the Vale of Glamorgan and several towns, including Cardiff, were devastated; an enormous booty was conveyed to the mountains. Edward was now at Lincoln, where, owing to Llywelyn's revolt, many of the most important magnates were absent from the parliament and little business was done there. Edward appointed Humphrey (VII) de Bohun, earl of Hereford and lord of the neighbouring marcher lordship of Brecon, to be captain of an army to put down the revolt. Hereford soon gathered together an overwhelming force. The neighbouring marchers, including

Roger Mortimer of Wigmore and his uncle, Roger Mortimer of Chirk, Henry, duke of Lancaster, William Montagu, and the husbands of two of the Clare heiresses, Hugh Audley and Roger Damory, joined him with forces from the border shires, Cheshire, and north Wales, and even some Welsh soldiers came from west Wales. The armies converged on Caerphilly from Brecon, Cardiff, and Monmouth in March. Llywelyn, despairing of further resistance, offered to submit if his life, limbs, and property were spared. However Hereford would accept nothing but unconditional surrender, though he agreed to plead Llywelyn's case with the king. When the English army approached the mountain fastnesses of the rebels, Llywelyn told his followers that he had been the cause of the revolt, and that it was right therefore that he should perish rather than they. He therefore went down from the hills, and at Ystradfellte (18 March) surrendered himself and two of his sons to Hereford, who sent him to the king.

By early May 1316 Llywelyn, his wife, and five sons were imprisoned in the Tower of London. A commission of inquiry and punishment was already at work in Cardiff on 4 April, when Payn Trubleville was confirmed as custodian of Glamorgan and authorized to dispossess Welsh tenantry. But later in the month more conciliatory counsels prevailed; he was replaced by John Giffard, and many rebels were received into the king's peace. Hereford and the Mortimers urged that Llywelyn should not be too severely dealt with, and it was afterwards alleged that the king had agreed to act upon their advice. On 21 May Llywelyn's lordship of Senghennydd was granted to a loyal Welshman, Runus Bwl. Large herds of 1700 cattle belonging to the rebels—more than half Llywelyn's—were rounded up, and Llywelyn's personal possessions (including his archives and several books, three of them in Welsh) were seized in Llandaff Cathedral where they had been deposited. But the Despensers were becoming all-powerful with King Edward, and the younger Despenser, as the husband of one of the Gloucester coheiresses, hoped for the renewal of the Gloucester earldom in his favour; in November 1317 he secured the lordship of Glamorgan. He seized Llywelyn's estates, carried off Llywelyn to Cardiff Castle, and caused him to be tried, condemned, hanged, drawn, and quartered in 1318; he was buried in the Grey Friars at Cardiff. In the charges brought against the Despensers at the time of their first fall in 1321, the judicial murder of Llywelyn Bren takes a conspicuous place, and it was evidently resented by marcher lords like Hereford. The sons of Llywelyn were taken into Hereford's service in 1321–2, but they remained excluded from their father's inheritance until the disturbances in south Wales that attended the final fall of the Despensers and the deposition of Edward II. They then were released and resumed possession (1326). Their names were Gruffudd, Ieuan, Meurig, Roger, William, and Llywelyn. On 11 February 1327 the government of Isabella and Mortimer formally restored to them their father's lands, 'of which they had been fraudulently dispossessed by the younger Hugh le Despenser' (*CPR, 1327–30*, 39–40). Their mother, Lleucu, received an allowance from the earl of Hereford at Brecon until 12 April 1349.

T. F. Tout, *rev.* R. A. Griffiths

Sources G. Williams, ed., *Glamorgan county history*, 3: *The middle ages*, ed. T. B. Pugh (1971), 72–86 · R. A. Griffiths, *Conquerors and conquered in medieval Wales* (1994), 84–91 · N. Denholm-Young, ed. and trans., *Vita Edwardi secundi* (1957) · *Chancery records* · PRO · J. H. Matthews, ed., *Cardiff records: being materials for a history of the county borough from the earliest times*, 6 vols. (1898–1911), vol. 4 · W. Rees, ed., *Calendar of ancient petitions relating to Wales* (1975) · J. G. Edwards, *Calendar of ancient correspondence concerning Wales* (1935), 68–9 · H. R. Luard, ed., *Flores historiarum*, 3 vols., Rolls Series, 95 (1890), vol. 3 · *Johannis de Trokelowe et Henrici de Blaneforde … chronica et annales*, ed. H. T. Riley, pt 3 of *Chronica monasterii S. Albani*, Rolls Series, 28 (1866) · A. Luders and others, eds., *Statutes of the realm*, 11 vols. in 12, RC (1810–28), vol. 1 · R. Merrick, *Morganiae archaiographia*, ed. B. L. James (1983)

Llywelyn Siôn [Llywelyn of Llangewydd] (*c.*1540–*c.*1615), Welsh-language poet and copyist, was born to unknown parents at Llangewydd, in Laleston, near Bridgend, Glamorgan. He was a pupil of Thomas Llywelyn of Y Rhigos, Glamorgan, and possibly of Morgan Powell, a priest at Laleston. Llywelyn Siôn went on to play an active role in contemporary Catholic life as poet, copyist, and recusant, for which he was summoned before the courts at least six times between 1587 and 1593. As a poet, he composed in the fixed and free metres of Welsh verse, but left only fourteen poems, the quality of which compares unfavourably with that of earlier Glamorgan poetry. Known to have undergone formal instruction in the art of copying, he became one of the foremost Welsh scribes of his age and transcribed manuscripts for members of the Glamorgan gentry, having access to many major libraries. Thirteen of his manuscripts are extant: eight are collections of poetry, four of prose, and one of genealogies. The one now known as Llanover B 9 (Aberystwyth, NL Wales) is a compendium of religious verse, much of which was published in two volumes entitled *Hen gwndidau* (1914) and *Hopkiniaid Morganwg* (1909). Three characteristically long, narrow books, known as the Long Book of Shrewsbury, the Long Book of Llywarch Reynolds, and the Long Book of Llanharan, represent his most important writings. He preserved a number of important medieval texts and also copied the sole surviving complete version of the anonymous Y Drych Cristianogawl, the most valuable Welsh Roman Catholic text of the Tudor age. Although very industrious, he was not the most meticulous of copyists, and his work contains many errors. He was, however, responsible for preserving much of Glamorgan's medieval and sixteenth-century literary heritage, which was probably what led Edward Williams (Iolo Morganwg) to depict him as one of the principal shapers of Iolo's mythical Glamorgan. Llywelyn Siôn died about 1615.

Glanmor Williams

Sources *DWB* · G. J. Williams, *Iolo Morganwg a chywyddau'r ychwanegiad* (1926) · G. J. Williams, *Traddodiad llenyddol Morgannwg* (1948) · G. J. Williams, *Iolo Morganwg* (1956) · C. W. Lewis, 'The literary tradition of Morgannwg down to the middle of the sixteenth century', *Glamorgan county history*, ed. G. Williams, 3: *The middle ages*, ed. T. B. Pugh (1971), 449–554 · C. W. Lewis, 'The literary history of Glamorgan from 1550 to 1770', *Glamorgan county history*, ed.

G. Williams, 4: *Early modern Glamorgan* (1974), 535–639 · C. W. Lewis, *Iolo Morganwg* (1995) · F. H. Pugh, 'Glamorgan recusants in the reigns of Elizabeth I and James I', *South Wales and Monmouth Record Society*, 4 (1957), 49–67 · L. J. Hopkin-James and T. C. Evans, eds., *Hen gwndidau carolau a chywyddau* (1914) · L. J. Hopkin-James, ed., *Hopkiniaid Morganwg* (1909) · T. Parry, *A history of Welsh literature*, trans. H. I. Bell (1955)

Archives BL, Harley MS 2414 · NL Wales, Cardiff MS 5.44 · NL Wales, Hafod MSS 4, 20 · NL Wales, Llanover MSS B 9, B 17, B 18 · NL Wales, Llansteffan MSS 47, 48, 134 · NL Wales, MSS 6511, 970

Lo, Kenneth Hsiao Chien [Lo Xiaojan] (**1913–1995**), restaurateur and tennis player, was born on 12 September 1913 in Fuzhou, southern China, the second of the three sons of Lo Tsung Hien (Lo Zong Xian), a diplomatist, and his wife, Wei Ying. His family were distinguished Anglophiles: his Cambridge-educated father and his grandfather (who received an honorary knighthood) both held diplomatic posts in London. In 1919 the family moved to England, where Lo acquired the name Kenneth; the Hampstead doctor who treated the family during the great influenza epidemic was unable to distinguish between the Chinese names of the three boys, and labelled their medicine bottles Charles, Kenneth, and Walter. The names stuck, despite the unflattering meaning of Kenneth when rendered in their native Fukienese. Life in Hampstead was modest compared to the grandeur of Lo Lodge, the Victorian mansion his father bought on Nantai Island when the family returned to China in 1922. Though he learned a good deal about eating, including an appreciation of the local delicacies of Fuzhou oysters and red wine sediment paste, Lo's position as 'little young master two' did not allow him to learn much about cooking. Indeed, nothing in his background intended him to be the person to popularize Chinese food in Britain.

Lo gained a BA degree in technology, physics, and English literature from Yenching (Yanjing) University, Peking (Beijing), before returning to Britain to read English at Cambridge University in 1936. He had a passion for tennis, which he played extensively at university, both in Peking (becoming north China champion) and at Cambridge (where he was a tennis blue). In 1946 he represented China in the Davis cup. He played until well into his seventies, and was proud of his many later triumphs in the veteran doubles of Britain (before 1984), and in the world superveteran championships (between 1981 and 1986).

Lo's first career followed his family's diplomatic tradition: he was student consul in Liverpool (1942–6) and vice-consul in Manchester (1946–9). In 1949 he abandoned the diplomatic service, borrowed £50 from a friend, and opened a shop selling Chinese greeting cards. Soon he was importing Chinese ceramics and high-quality craftwork for his two shops in Hampstead and South Kensington; but he was overstretched by his leases and the business eventually collapsed. On 14 May 1953 he married Anne Philippe Hempsted Brown (*b*. 1928/9), a farmer's daughter from Hertfordshire; they had two sons and two daughters. His career in food initially developed alongside his other business interests. In 1954 he accepted a commission for £50 in cash to write a Chinese cookery book for an East End publisher. He had no experience of writing or testing

Kenneth Hsiao Chien Lo (1913–1995), by Graham Wood, 1975

recipes, and cobbled the book together by translating published recipes. Many of the ingredients were not available in Britain, and Lo was a little optimistic in his recommendations for substitutes, and cavalier about Chinese cooking techniques. Nevertheless, *Cooking the Chinese Way* (1955) sold 10,000 copies in hardback. It was the first of about forty cookery books he wrote, including the classic *Chinese Food* (1963) and *Kenneth Lo's New Chinese Cookery Course* (1985), which remained in print into the twenty-first century. Kenneth Lo also became a restaurant inspector for Egon Ronay and for *The Good Food Guide*.

In 1980 Lo opened his first restaurant, Kenneth Lo's Memories of China, in Belgravia, with half the capital subscribed by friends and members of the Chinese Gourmet Club, which he had founded in 1975. The restaurant set new standards for Chinese eateries. Londoners had come to expect Chinese food and the places in which they consumed it to be cheap and, at best, cheerful, with brusque waiters and an indecipherable bill on which everything except the total was written in Chinese characters. The etched glass windows, well-designed furnishings, additional private room, friendly waiters, and all-English menu and reckoning at Memories of China were revelations—but so was the size of the bill, the equivalent of that in any posh London restaurant.

By the end of Kenneth Lo's life he and his wife had three restaurants (two in London, one in the Algarve) in which they served eclectic Chinese food, mixing dishes from the various regions of China and even using some ingredients unpopular in China, such as lamb, simply because of their high quality locally. In 1981 he opened Ken Lo's Kitchen, a contender for the title of first Chinese cookery school in Europe, where he sometimes taught personally. In 1980 Lo revisited China for the first time since the revolution. There he was reunited with his younger brother, Walter, who had survived a visit from the red guards. He was initially shocked by the changes in his homeland, but recovered quickly, and subsequently visited China often, sometimes leading food tours for clients and friends. He published a lively autobiography, *The Feast of my Life*, in 1993. He died in the Chelsea and Westminster Hospital, Chelsea, on 11 August 1995, and was survived by his wife.

Paul Levy

Sources personal knowledge (2004) • *The Guardian* (14 Aug 1995) • K. H. C. Lo, *The feast of my life* (1993) • *WW* (1993) • *The Independent* (16 Aug 1995) • *The Times* (14 Aug 1995) • *WWW, 1897–1915* • *FO List* (1921) • m. cert. • d. cert. • *Daily Telegraph* (12 Aug 1995)
Likenesses G. Wood, photograph, 1975, Hult. Arch. [*see illus.*] • photograph, repro. in *The Times*
Wealth at death under £145,000: administration with will, 30 April 1996, *CGPLA Eng. & Wales*

Loane, Alice Eliza (1863–1922). *See under* Loane, Martha Jane (1852–1933).

Loane, Martha Jane (1852–1933), nurse and social commentator, was born on 7 February 1852 at 8 North Place, Eldad, Plymouth, Devon, to Jabez Loane (*c.*1821–1895), a master in the Royal Navy, and Jane, *née* Cooley (*d.* 1852). Her father remarried on 10 November 1852 and his second wife, Harriet, *née* Kiddle (1824–1864), spinster daughter of John Kiddle RN, bore a further five children, three boys and two girls. Harriet Loane died suddenly on 7 November 1864, leaving Jabez, then a staff commander, and his six young children devastated by their loss. The family had moved to Southsea by 1863, and the following year Martha began her elementary education as a boarder at the Royal Naval School for Females, St Margaret's, Isleworth, Middlesex. Her formal education was completed in 1870. No details of her whereabouts for the next fifteen years have come to light, though it is possible that she spent time travelling in Europe.

In 1885 Loane decided to take up nursing, a profession which had recently acquired a new respectability, largely owing to the influence of Florence Nightingale. She trained at Charing Cross Hospital, London, and then, under the title of Sister Agnes, worked there as a ward sister, moving in 1888 to Shropshire and becoming a sister-in-charge at the Shrewsbury Royal Infirmary in late 1889. In 1893 she gave up hospital nursing in favour of district nursing. This branch of the profession was conducted largely under the auspices of Queen Victoria's Jubilee Institute for Nurses, a charitable organization founded in 1887, whose objectives included training nurses to care for the sick poor in their own homes. Once qualified, having attended the institute's central training school in Bloomsbury (1893–4), and having gained a midwifery qualification in 1893 from the Obstetrical Society of London, Martha worked as a queen's nurse in Buxton, Derbyshire, for two years before being promoted, in 1897, to the position of superintendent of queen's nurses for the Borough of Portsmouth Association for Nursing the Sick Poor. Martha became a highly respected figure, and was renowned for her efficiency and concern for the poor. Her enforced retirement from nursing in October 1905, following life-threatening appendicitis, was a great loss to the local community and the institute, which considered her to be an outstanding superintendent.

Loane's retirement from nursing did not affect her well-established career as a writer on nursing and social topics. Encouraged by Florence Nightingale in 1895, she made contributions to reviews, journals, and the national press (notably 35 articles in *Nursing Notes*, 1897–1907; 23 articles in the *Evening News*, 1907–10; and 13 articles in *The Spectator*, 1910–11). She also produced six nursing handbooks (*The District Nurse as Health Missioner, The Duties of a Superintendent in a Small Home for District Nurses, The Incidental Opportunities of District Nursing, Outlines of Routine in District Nursing*, 1904; *Simple Sanitation*, 1905; *Simple Introductory Lessons in Midwifery*, 1906). But of greatest significance were her six popular social commentaries (*The Queen's Poor*, 1905; *The Next Street but One*, 1907; *From their Point of View*, 1908; *Neighbours and Friends*, 1909; *An Englishman's Castle*, 1910; *The Common Growth*, 1911), which earned her a reputation as a leading authority on the condition of the working-class poor in Britain. Studies of poverty in Britain owed much to the pioneering, largely quantitative, surveys undertaken by Charles Booth in London and J. Seebohm Rowntree in York. But Loane's commentaries were significant in two major respects: not only were they, uniquely, based on the first-hand experiences of a distinguished queen's nurse who had made repeated and extensive visits to the homes of the poor, but they concentrated on revealing intimate details about the quality of working-class life.

Loane's apparently subjective doorstep accounts provided a penetrating insight into the thoughts and beliefs, emotions, and culture of the 'respectable poor'—those who kept 'even the most painfully poor and crowded home together' (*The Queen's Poor*, 1905, 27). Infancy and childhood, youth and education, health and welfare, domestic arrangements, courtship, marriage, parenthood and old age, work and play, religion, and the meaning of life and death were all addressed. Loane commented upon legislation which affected the lives of the poor and debated the numerous social problems of the day. Although the solutions which she offered to these did not always meet with unequivocal approval, she was successful in raising public awareness and in highlighting the complex nature of these issues.

What no one ever suspected was that the well-known queen's nurse was, in fact, party to a literary deception that remained undetected during and beyond her lifetime. Direct and indirect references to Martha's nursing career reinforced the popular belief that she was totally responsible for the articles and the social commentaries, but she was evidently only partly responsible. Authorship was attributed variously to M. Loane, M. J. Loane, Martha Loane, and M. E. Loane: although Martha's professional experiences provided the material and thus the credibility for the work, it was her younger half-sister, Alice Eliza Loane [*see below*], who compiled much of the work and who was posthumously credited with writing the books.

No pictures of Martha Loane have apparently survived: the only personal detail that has emerged concerns her conversion to Roman Catholicism in 1910, an event that ultimately ruptured her relationship with Alice. Martha died at her home at 22 Woodland Terrace, Lipson, Plymouth, on 16 October 1933, aged eighty-one, and was buried in the Plymouth corporation cemetery, Efford, on 19 October. The sole beneficiaries of her estate, which amounted to £463 8*s.* 3*d.*, were the Catholic Education Council and the Hospital for Women, Soho, London.

Alice Eliza Loane (1863–1922), author, was born on 23

October 1863 at 2 Exbury Place, Green Road, Southsea, Hampshire. The youngest child of Jabez Loane and his second wife, she received her elementary education at the Royal Naval School for Females (1874–81). She published one book under her own name, *Shipmates* (1912), in addition to her work published under the name M. Loane. From late 1912 she was an active member of the Bristol Civic League, an organization which dealt with the problems of poverty. She died at 22 Elmdale Road, Clifton, Bristol, on 23 February 1922. Her sister, Beatrice Mary Loane, was her sole beneficiary, but the will was unsigned, and remained unproven until 18 January 1939, four years after Beatrice's death. Probate was then granted to Lloyds Bank; the value of the estate amounted to £2363 5*s*. 8*d*.

SUSAN L. COHEN

Sources S. Cohen, 'The life and works of M. Loane', MPhil diss., Middlesex University, 1997 • roll of queen's nurses III, Wellcome L., fol. 80, SA/QNI/J3/3 • letter of Martha Loane to Florence Nightingale, 30 July 1895, BL, Nightingale MSS, Add. MS 45813, fol. 92 • *Annual Report of the Borough of Portsmouth Association for Nursing the Sick Poor* (1897–1905) • Hodder Headline Plc, London, Edward Arnold archives • register of licence to receive catechumens, Plymouth Cathedral, 22 March 1910, Plymouth Catholic Archives • Royal Naval School for Females archives, Haslemere, Surrey • M. Baly, *A history of the Queen's Nursing Institute: 100 years, 1887–1987* (1987) • b. cert. • d. cert. • d. cert. [J. Loane] • *Western Morning News* (18 Oct 1933), 1 • b. cert. [A. E. Loane] • d. cert. [H. Loane] • d. cert. [A. E. Loane]

Wealth at death £463 8*s*. 3*d*.: probate, 15 Dec 1933, *CGPLA Eng. & Wales* • £2363 5*s*. 8*d*.—Alice Eliza Loane: probate, 18 Jan 1939, *CGPLA Eng. & Wales*

Loat, Lily (1879/80–1958), anti-vaccination activist, was the daughter of John Loat. Her ancestors were Dutch weavers who moved to London at some time in the seventeenth century; Loats Road in Clapham Park, London, is named after them. Lily Loat attended Tiffin Girls' School in Surrey and became head pupil. The exact dates of her school attendance are unknown, but she joined the staff of the National Anti-Vaccination League in London shortly after leaving, in January 1898. The league had been formed two years before; the secretary answered an advertisement placed by Loat's shorthand teacher, and employed her to assist in answering correspondence. Loat did not oppose vaccination when taken on, but was quickly converted to the cause. The secretary resigned in 1908, and Loat was appointed titular secretary in January 1909; in the following month the council unanimously appointed her secretary.

Loat proceeded to dedicate herself wholeheartedly to the anti-vaccination cause and acquired a vast knowledge of the subject. Besides writing many of the league's pamphlets and leaflets, she edited its journal, the *Vaccination Inquirer and Health Review*, from 1932, and published a small book, *The Truth about Vaccination and Immunization*, in 1951. Her prose was concise, intelligent, and forcefully argued; she did not shrink from criticism but welcomed it, often engaging in correspondence with opponents. In addition to giving speeches at numerous British anti-vaccination meetings throughout her life (and addressing crowds in Hyde Park), she was invited several times to speak at meetings in Europe and America in the 1920s and 1930s. It is not known what caused Loat originally to alter her opinion about vaccination, but she employed a variety of arguments against treatment throughout her career. The most prominent of these were that vaccination caused disease—either those diseases it intended to prevent, or others—and that it was unsafe, ineffective, or unnecessary, and that to be forced by law to submit to it violated 'medical freedom'.

Other objections expressed by Loat reveal her interest in related movements. She became an ardent anti-vivisectionist and animal welfare activist, and frequently condemned the cruelty involved in the production of lymph, and the testing of vaccines and inoculations on animals, in the pages of the league's journal and in speeches to anti-vivisection meetings. She also supported alternative medical treatments, particularly naturopathy; she believed that all illnesses were nature's attempt to rid the body of 'impurities' which had accumulated as a result of heredity, bad habits, or environmental pollution. Hence she advocated sanitation as a way of preventing disease, and credited any statistical decrease in disease to public-health reforms. To her mind, vaccination failed to address the true causes of disease, and so was no defence against it; further, vaccination was offensive because it introduced impurities into a healthy body. Loat also opposed war, and wrote in 1932 that vaccination, vivisection, and war were inspired by the same 'motives'.

Loat was indefatigable; memoirists recalled her prodigious memory, intellectual abilities, and devotion to the cause. She was also remembered for her warm personality and friendliness. She was in effect the public voice of the movement: a contemporary explained that 'when one thought of the Anti-Vaccination cause the name of Lily Loat automatically arose in one's mind' (Beddow-Bayly). She never married, and remained secretary of the league and editor of its journal until her death in 1958, continuing to work even when hospitalized by her last illness. Indeed, the centrality of Loat's role was such that a search for a replacement proved fruitless, which was said to have caused her great distress. She died in St Philip's Hospital, Westminster, London, on 16 August 1958, aged seventy-eight. The National Anti-Vaccination League published the last issue of its journal in the autumn of 1972.

MOLLY BAER KRAMER

Sources *Animals' Champion and Medical Freedom Advocate* [World Coalition against Vivisection] (Dec 1933–Feb 1934), 9 • E. D. Hume, *The mind-changers* (1939), 195 • M. Beddow-Bayly, *Vaccination Inquirer and Health Review* [National Anti-Vaccination League], 80 (1958), 66–75, esp. 66–8 • *Vaccination Inquirer and Health Review* [National Anti-Vaccination League], 30 (1908–9), 136 • *Vaccination Inquirer and Health Review* [National Anti-Vaccination League], 30 (1908–9), 204 • *Vaccination Inquirer and Health Review* [National Anti-Vaccination League], 54 (1932), 67 • L. Loat, *The truth about vaccination and immunization* (1951) • L. Loat, letter to F. Madan, 19 Jan 1915, Bodl. Oxf., bound with pamphlet RSL 1561.e42 • L. Loat, *To members of parliament: the BBC charter* [n.d.] • *Vaccination Inquirer and Health Review* [National Anti-Vaccination League], 93 (1971), 75 • *IGI* • d. cert.

Archives Bodl. Oxf., letter to F. Madan, bound with subject's pamphlet, 'Anti-Typhoid Vaccines. A reply to the pamphlet by the Research Defense Society'

Likenesses group portrait, photograph, 1909, repro. in *Vaccination Inquirer and Health Review*, 31 (1909), supplement • photograph, repro. in *Vaccination Inquirer and Health Review*, 80 (1958), cover • photograph, repro. in *Animals' Champion and Medical Freedom Advocate*, 9

Wealth at death £4782 12s. 2d.: probate, 15 Sept 1958, *CGPLA Eng. & Wales*

Loates, Thomas (1867–1910), jockey, was born at 53 Agard Street, Derby, on 6 October 1867, a younger son in the family of eight children of Archibald Loates, a journeyman shoemaker and later hotel keeper there, and his wife, Louisa Cooper. Two of his brothers, Charles (generally known as Ben) and Samuel (who, after he gave up riding, became a trainer of horses at Newmarket), were also professional jockeys. Tom Loates was apprenticed to Joseph Cannon (training at that time for Lord Rosebery at Primrose House, Newmarket) and was fifteen when, in 1883, he rode his first winner, a filly belonging to Lord Rosebery, at Newmarket. Six years later he was victorious for the first time in a classic race, winning the Derby on the duke of Portland's Donovan. That year he headed the list of jockeys by riding 167 winners. He again occupied first place in 1890, and, after a two years' retirement, for a third time in 1893, his most successful season, with 222 winning mounts; he was the second jockey ever to top the double century mark. That year he rode Isinglass for Harry McCalmont when he won the 'triple crown' (the Two Thousand Guineas, Derby, and St Leger), the Ascot Cup, and other valuable races. In 1893 he also won the One Thousand Guineas on Sir Blundell Maple's Siffleuse, and rode Red Eyes in the dead heat with Cypria for the Cesarewitch. Having accepted a retainer from Leopold de Rothschild, he rode St Frusquin in 1896, when that horse won the Two Thousand Guineas, and again when it was beaten in the Derby by a neck by the prince of Wales's Persimmon. He rode sixteen seasons, had 7140 mounts, was placed first 1425 times, second 1145 times, and third 920 times. In all, Loates rode eight times in the Two Thousand Guineas; he twice won in that race as well as the One Thousand Guineas and the Derby. He won the St Leger once.

Loates, who was short-legged, sometimes had difficulty in coaxing the best out of bigger horses, but he was a resourceful rider who was quick to take advantage of openings that presented themselves during a race. Towards the end of his career he followed the lead of visiting American jockeys and hitched up his leathers, a style suited to his physique. In 1896 he had three nasty riding accidents, in one of which he broke his thigh, though he continued to ride until 1900 when, after having trouble with his eyes, he relinquished his jockey's licence at the end of the season and retired into private life.

For some years Loates lived at Newmarket, nearly always in bad health possibly associated with his drinking problem. In 1909 he married a nurse, Isabella Dale, daughter of Charles Simpson Watt of Perth. The year previously she had nursed him through alcoholism, but she left him when he again took up the bottle. They had no children. Loates died in a convulsive fit at York Cottage, Aldbourne, near Brighton, on 28 September 1910. He was buried at Brighton. Unlike many working-class professional sportsmen of the time, he hung on to the money he had made and left one of the largest fortunes accumulated by a jockey, more than £74,000.

Edward Moorhouse, *rev.* Wray Vamplew

Sources F. Collingwood, 'The tragedy of Thomas Loates', *British Racehorse* (Oct 1967), 427–8 • R. Mortimer, R. Onslow, and P. Willett, *Biographical encyclopedia of British flat racing* (1978) • M. Tanner and G. Cranham, *Great jockeys of the flat* (1992) • *Sporting Life* (29 Sept 1910) • b. cert. • *CGPLA Eng. & Wales* (1911)

Likenesses Spy [L. Ward], chromolithograph cartoon, NPG; repro. in *VF* (4 Oct 1890)

Wealth at death £74,342 9s. 1d.: probate, 10 Feb 1911, *CGPLA Eng. & Wales*

Lobb, Betsy (1868–1956). *See under* Lobb, John (1829–1895).

Lobb, Emmanuel [*alias* Joseph Simons] (1594–1671), Jesuit and playwright, was born at Portsmouth and at the age of eleven was sent to Portugal to learn the language with a view to mercantile life. There he was converted to the Catholic faith by the Jesuit Henry Floyd. After a while he was sent to the college of the English Jesuits at St Omer, and on 13 October 1616 he entered the English College at Rome under the assumed name of Joseph Simons by which he became generally known; his father was noted as dead but his mother was still alive. Having received minor orders in 1617 he left Rome for the Spanish Netherlands on 14 September 1619, was received into the Society of Jesus at Liège, and was professed of the four vows on 25 January 1633. After professing rhetoric and *belles-lettres* in the English College at St Omer for five years he became professor of theology, philosophy, and sacred scripture in the English theologate of the Society of Jesus at Liège. Between 1642 and 1644 he was involved in the foundation of the convent of the English canonesses at Liège, subsequently giving them financial help in 1668 and 1669. In 1647 he was appointed rector of the English College at Rome, and in 1650 rector of the theologate at Liège. He was also instructor of the tertian fathers at Ghent. Being subsequently sent to the English mission he was at one period rector of the college of St Ignatius. In 1667 he became the English provincial. When living in London in 1669 he was consulted by the duke of York, whom he afterwards reconciled to the Roman Catholic church. He died in London on 24 July 1671.

Simons was author of the following tragedies, all of which are in five acts and in verse. They were all first performed at the English College, St Omer, as follows: *Vitus* (13 May 1623), *Mercia* (7 February 1624), *Theoctistus* (8 August 1624), *Leo Armenus* (between 1624 and 1629), *Zeno* (7 August 1631). *Zeno* and *Mercia* were first printed at Rome in 1648 and *Theoctistus* at Liège in 1653; Simons's collected plays were published later as *Tragoediae quinque* (first edition Liège, 1656; reprinted 1657, 1680, and 1697). The tragedies were frequently acted on the continent in Simons's lifetime, and are perhaps the most distinguished contribution made by a seventeenth-century English author to the genre of Jesuit drama. Also speculatively attributable to him are *S. Damianus*, acted at St Omer on 13 February 1626 and preserved together with *Leo Armenus* and *Zeno* in two manuscripts, and a lost play on King Robert of Sicily, performed at St Omer on 19 June 1623. *An Answer to Doctor Pierce's Sermon* (1663) is attributed to Simons by a contemporary, Thomas Blount, and in the *Short-Title Catalogue*, though this work has sometimes been assigned to John Sergeant. A manuscript treatise on penitence, dated 1642 (Bodl. Oxf., MS Rawl. D. 1355), may also be Simons's.

THOMPSON COOPER, *rev.* ALISON SHELL

Sources A. Kenny, ed., *The responsa scholarum of the English College, Rome*, 1, Catholic RS, 54 (1962), 298–9 • W. H. McCabe, *An introduction to the Jesuit theater*, ed. L. J. Oldani (1983), pt 3 • A. Harbage, *Annals of English drama, 975–1700*, rev. S. Schoenbaum, 3rd edn, rev. S. S. Wagonheim (1989), 368 • H. Foley, ed., *Records of the English province of the Society of Jesus*, 1 (1877), 272–3 • W. Kelly, ed., *Liber ruber venerabilis collegii Anglorum de urbe*, 1, Catholic RS, 37 (1940), 180 • R. Trappes-Lomax, ed., 'Records of the English canonesses of the Holy Sepulchre of Liège, now at New Hall, 1652–1793', *Miscellanea*, X, Catholic RS, 17 (1915), 1–247, esp. 36–7, 102–4 • J. Miller, *James II: a study in kingship* (1978), chap. 5 • F. Brettonneau, *An abridgement of the life of James II … extracted from an English manuscript of the Reverend Father Francis Sanders of the Society of Jesus, and confessor to his late majesty* (1703), 13 • C. Dodd [H. Tootell], *The church history of England, from the year 1500, to the year 1688*, 3 (1742), 317 • J. Simons, foreword, *Jesuit theater Englished: five tragedies of Joseph Simons*, ed. L. J. Oldani and P. C. Fischer (1989) • Wing, *STC* • *The correspondence of Thomas Blount (1618–1679), a recusant antiquary*, ed. T. Bongaerts (1978), 116, 237

Lobb, John (1829–1895), maker of bespoke boots and shoes, was born on 27 December 1829, at Tywardreath, near Fowey, Cornwall, where his father was a farmworker. John would probably have followed him, had he not suffered an accident which broke his leg in several places. The leg was badly set and he was left with a permanent limp. Thus barred from agricultural labour, he was apprenticed to a local shoemaker with whom over the next five years he acquired considerable skill. He then decided to try his luck in London, where he may have had relatives, and, shod in a stout pair of his own boots, walked the distance of over 200 miles. He made his way to the shop of a Mr Thomas, most eminent of the high-class bootmakers of St James's, and demanded to see the proprietor, with the intention of being hired. This brusque approach had the opposite effect: amid shouting on both sides Lobb was swiftly ordered out. At this time, however, London was buzzing with news of the recent gold strikes in Australia and Lobb immediately decided to take passage in the first available ship bound for Sydney, New South Wales.

On his arrival Lobb made for the Turon River valley and pitched his tent among the wild and lawless encampments of the prospectors and their followers. As the only bootmaker in the district, he found many customers willing to pay in gold for hard-wearing footgear. He also designed a boot with a hollow heel which slid away from the sole to reveal a compartment in which gold could be secreted. Before long he was able to take his own hard-earned gold to Sydney, cash it in, and buy himself a shop in George Street, in the main shopping area. Business flourished: workmen were employed, Lobb became one of Sydney's leading tradesmen, and dark good looks and prosperity enabled him to marry in 1857 Caroline Victoria, daughter of Thomas Richards, the Sydney harbourmaster. A son, John, was born in 1858 and two daughters, Caroline Victoria in 1859 and Mary Aline in 1861. In 1863 John took as his first apprentice his wife's younger brother, Frederick Moses Richards (*c.*1849–1907), the first step in training a man who was to be the mainstay of the firm for many years to come.

Although there was no shortage of customers at his shop in Sydney, Lobb's sights were still set on London. He submitted a range of footwear to the 1862 Exhibition in London, securing the one gold medal awarded to an Australian entry, and this convinced him that the time had come to return. First, by some devious means which he never revealed, he obtained the foot measurements of the prince of Wales and made a fine pair of riding boots which he dispatched with a request to be appointed bootmaker to the prince. His bold approach was successful: a royal warrant was issued on 12 October 1863 and John packed up the tools of his trade, sold his shop, and sailed with his young apprentice, leaving his wife and children in Sydney for the time being. He took premises at 296 Regent Street, opened for business in 1866, and when the upper floors had been furnished, sent for his family. Two more sons were born, William Hunter Lobb [*see below*] in 1870 and Frederick Lobb in 1871, and a daughter who died in infancy, but the marriage was effectively at an end and Caroline left him to live in Paris, where she later died. Lobb was far from downcast by her departure; if anything, he gained a reputation as a gay dog and bon viveur. While his numerous outworkers toiled to make up his orders, and his children and Frederick Richards, now promoted to manager, attended to the shop, John returned frequently to his Cornish village, where he had a reputation as a local philanthropist, and went on holiday to North America. The business prospered and he continued to win medals at the various international exhibitions: Paris in 1867, Vienna in 1873, Philadelphia in 1876, Paris in 1878 and 1889, and Chicago in 1893. In 1880 he opened a second shop, at 29 St James's Street, a few doors along from that of Thomas, from which he had been ejected so many years before. Richards was installed there as manager, while John remained at 296 Regent Street where he died, still firmly in command, on 17 January 1895.

John Lobb junior did not succeed to the business, having some years previously been cast out by his father for dishonesty. He married a chorus girl and retired to Margate, discreetly supported by his brother, where in later years he and his wife were much loved and visited by the Lobb children. **William Hunter Lobb** (1870–1916) was born on 3 June 1870 at 296 Regent Street, educated at the Philological School in Marylebone, and subsequently trained as a bootmaker. The machinery which had replaced the craftsmen in many shoe- and bootmaking establishments found no place at Lobbs, where everything, from last-making to cutting, closing, and stitching, was still done by hand. William took charge of an expanding business which catered to the royalty and nobility of many countries, the upper echelons of the military, the simply rich, and increasingly, to members of the theatrical and artistic professions. In 1901 William opened a shop in Paris which after a faltering start brought in excellent returns. His acquisition of a second premises in Regent Street in 1904 was, on the other hand, unprofitable, and it coincided with an agreement with the bootmakers' union for increased rates of pay, which, taken together, sharply reduced his income.

At the height of his prosperity, on 14 January 1901 William married Betsy Smerdon [**Betsy Lobb** (1868–1956)], daughter of John Smerdon and his wife, Ellen, *née* Callard, Devon farmers, born on 15 November 1868 at Forder Farm, South Brent, Devon. Lobb swept her off on a grand European tour, before settling in at 105 Alexandra Road, St John's Wood. Betsy had previously been the manageress of a London hotel and her business abilities were to be her family's mainstay in later years. Their first son, John Hunter Lobb (*b.* 1901), died in infancy. The next three, William (*b.* 1902), Victor (*b.* 1905), and Eric (*b.* 1907), all reached maturity. Before then, however, William, after two years' illness, died of empyema at 35 Adamson Road, Swiss Cottage, on 26 August 1916.

In the middle years of the First World War, Betsy Lobb was left a reduced income, eroded by falling sales in the London and Paris shops, and three boys to educate. She handed the St John's Wood house to her sisters-in-law and moved her own family into furnished rooms in Brighton, appointing as interim manager of the business Tom Moore, who had been hired as a shop-boy by old John Lobb. After the war Betsy and her family returned to their house, now shared by three Lobb families. Her careful handling of money raised her capital account from the £7500 which she inherited to nearly £17,000 in 1922.

Young William received a good education at University College School and Brighton College before absorbing the practical side of bootmaking, studying accountancy, and spending seven years in the Paris shop. Victor, on the other hand, was less of a scholar and not keen to become a bootmaker. Eventually he opted to farm in Devon. Eric also attended Brighton College and University College School and was the first of his family to go to Oxford University where he obtained in 1926 a degree in agriculture. Lobbs, meanwhile, was once more heading for insolvency, with Betsy taking in paying guests to pay Eric's fees and keep the firm afloat. After several footloose and impecunious years, Eric too returned to the family firm, in time for it to be immersed in another war. William was summoned to the Ministry of Information and Eric was about to be called to military service when it was decided, perhaps by some influential wearer of Lobb shoes, that he should continue in civilian life. Once more the declaration of peace brought renewed trade, and with Lobbs in the hands of competent management it survived in family hands. Betsy later moved to Newlands, 43 Watford Road, Radlett, Hertfordshire, where she died on 9 December 1956.

ANITA MCCONNELL

Sources B. Dobbs, *The last shall be first: the colourful story of John Lobb, the St James's bootmakers* (1972) • *CGPLA Eng. & Wales* (1895) [John Lobb] • *CGPLA Eng. & Wales* (1916) [William Hunter Lobb] • *CGPLA Eng. & Wales* (1957) [Betsy Lobb] • b. cert. [W. H. Lobb] • b. cert. [Betsy Lobb] • m. cert. [W. H. and Betsy Lobb] • d. cert. [John Lobb] • d. cert. [Betsy Lobb]

Archives City Westm. AC, business archive

Likenesses group portrait (with family) • photographs, repro. in Dobbs, *The last shall be first*

Wealth at death £19,319 11*s.* 5*d.*: probate, 18 Feb 1895, *CGPLA Eng. & Wales* • £11,066 17*s.* 8*d.*—William Hunter Lobb: probate, 4 Oct 1916, *CGPLA Eng. & Wales* • £14,655 19*s.* 10*d.*—Betsy Lobb: probate, 8 March 1957, *CGPLA Eng. & Wales*

Lobb, Stephen (*d.* 1699), nonconformist minister, was the son of Richard Lobb (*fl.* 1652–1672) of Liskeard, Mill Park, Warleggan, and St Neots, Cornwall, high sheriff of the county in 1652 and MP for St Michael in 1659. His early years are obscure but on 16 April 1672 Lobb received a licence as a presbyterian under the declaration of indulgence to preach in his father's houses at Kenwyn, near Truro, and Mylor, near Falmouth. He married Elizabeth (*d.* 1691), daughter of the Independent minister Theophilus *Polwhele of Tiverton, Devon, and his wife, the daughter of the Independent pastor William Benn. (It is possible that Elizabeth was the playwright E. *Polewheele.) Their children included Stephen (*d.* 1720), who conformed and became chaplain of Penzance Castle; Theophilus *Lobb (1678–1763), who began his ministerial career at Guildford, Surrey, and later became a physician and fellow of the Royal Society; Samuel (*d.* 1760), rector of Farleigh Hungerford, Somerset; and a daughter who married John Greene, Independent pastor at Great Baddow, Essex. Lobb's brother Peter (*d.* 1718) was also an Independent minister.

About late 1678 Lobb wrote a lengthy letter to Richard Baxter concerning justification by Christ's imputed righteousness, a position Baxter generally found agreeable, but on 13 January 1679 he defended himself against Lobb's charge that he was insensitive to the 'tolerable weaknesses' of others (Keeble and Nuttall, 2.202). Although Baxter responded favourably to the suggestion of Samuel Annesley and Thomas Vincent that he accept Lobb as his assistant, this proved unworkable when the latter omitted the creed, the Lord's prayer, and the decalogue in the service.

In the early 1680s Lobb published his first works, including a refutation of antinomians, *The Glory of Free-Grace Display'd* (1680), to which John Owen contributed a preface. Responding to Edward Stillingfleet's *The Mischief of Separation* (1680), Lobb and the presbyterian John Humfrey wrote *An Answer to Dr. Stillingfleet's Sermon* (1680), insisting that dissenters were not schismatics and proposing that gathered congregations be comprehended in the Church of England. Samuel Thomas came to Stillingfleet's defence in *The Charge of Schism Renewed* (1680), but Lobb and Humfrey held their ground in *A Reply to the Defence of Dr. Stillingfleet* (1681), averring that differences among protestants were minor. When Stillingfleet insisted in *The Unreasonableness of Separation* (1681) that dissenters conform, Humfrey and Lobb replied in *A Modest and Peaceable Inquiry* (1682), arguing that it was 'unreasonable to beat the Drum, or sound the Trumpet for a Protestant Civil-wordy-

War' (p. 1). Appealing to the sanctity of conscience, Lobb called for comprehension or indulgence in *The Harmony between the Old and Present Non-Conformists* (1682).

After being ordained by Independents and presbyterians in the spring of 1681, Lobb was elected pastor of the Independent church to which Thomas Goodwin and Thankful Owen had ministered. He was convicted of preaching at conventicles in the summer of 1682, yet in October he participated in meetings in London to resolve cases of conscience. JPs and constables raided his meeting-house near Swallow Street, Piccadilly, in December 1682, destroying its furnishings, and again in January 1683, when they arrested two fellow ministers, William Pearse and Marmaduke Roberts.

As the government investigated the Rye House plot in the summer of 1683 the conspirator Zachary Bourne confessed that he had approached Lobb to help recruit men in the London area, but that the latter was concerned that too many were cowardly and would not rebel. Nevertheless, he allegedly promised to seek the release of two members of his congregation who would be helpful in recruiting. On 6 July the privy council ordered his arrest, but he was not captured until early August. Two others with ties to the conspirators, Edward Massey and Norwich Salisbury, implicated Lobb in the scheme to enthrone Monmouth, and the duke himself confessed that 'all the considerable Nonconformist Ministers knew of the Conspiracy', including John Owen (PRO, SP 29/434/98). Lobb also knew William Carstares, one of the Scots discussing a co-ordinated insurrection in Scotland on Argyll's behalf. Although Lobb probably knew consideration was being given to an uprising on Monmouth's behalf, the government opted not to prosecute, presumably because it doubted the credibility of Massey and Salisbury. Lobb was released, but the government ordered his rearrest as a dangerous person in October 1683, on suspicion of treason in April and May 1684, and again as a dangerous person in October 1684. His troubles inspired the anonymous satire, *A Dreadful Oration Deliver'd by … Stephen Lobb*.

Lobb was probably the person who corresponded with Baxter between March and June 1684 about occasional conformity and ecclesiastical polity, and he may have written *Bellarminus junior enervatus* (1684), defending Owen from Baxter's attack. In *The True Dissenter* (1685) he offered a plan for protestant union based on a national church, with oaths of supremacy (excluding liturgy and polity) and allegiance; liberty of conscience; a role for bishops as officers of the crown; and a provision allowing people opposed to oaths to post bonds. After Charles Morton emigrated to New England in 1685, Lobb, Francis Glascock, and William Wickins taught the students in his nonconformist academy. Following Lobb's pardon for treasonable offences in December 1686 he became so close to James II that he was called 'the Jacobite Independent'. On 30 April 1687 he and other Independents gave the king a statement of thanks for the declaration of indulgence, and the following January James, seeking nonconformist support, had him circulate a report that Anglicans had offered to suspend the penal laws and the test for Catholics as long as they remained in force for protestant dissenters. In May Lobb and William Penn unsuccessfully attempted to persuade nonconformists to submit another declaration of thanks for the indulgence's renewal. Lobb preached before the lord mayor at Grocers' Hall in September.

In 1690 Lobb helped found the Common Fund to assist needy ministers and train new ones, and in March 1691 he helped establish the Happy Union of Presbyterians and Independents in the London area, hoping to end 'our Pernitious, shamefull strifes' (Keeble and Nuttall, 2.326). From the outset, the union experienced internal strife, partly because of the controversy triggered by republication of Tobias Crisp's antinomian sermons in 1690. Daniel Williams issued a critique in *Gospel-Truth Stated* (1692), and the following year Lobb published *A Peaceable Enquiry*, profusely citing church historians, Reformation authors (especially Luther), and John Owen to repudiate antinomianism and Socinianism. When Williams was removed from the Pinners' Hall lectures and other Presbyterians resigned in protest, Lobb was appointed to one of the vacancies in February 1695. Williams blamed him for the rupture, especially for misrepresenting his views in a critique commissioned by London Independents. When John Humfrey commented on Lobb's manuscript, Williams retorted in *An Answer to Mr. J. Humphrey's Second Printed Letter* (1695). The crux of the debate was whether Christ became sinful for the sins of others, as Lobb asserted. He replied to Williams in *A Letter to Doctor Bates* (1695) and more generally in *A Report of the Present State of the Differences*, accusing his opponents of Socinianism. This elicited refutations from Vincent Alsop, *A Faithful Rebuke* (1697), and Williams, *An Answer to the Report* (1698); the latter castigated Lobb's *Report* as a '*grand peice of Art and Misrepresentation*' (sig. A3*v*). Lobb responded to Alsop in *A Defence of the Report* (1698) and *A Further Defence of the Report* (1698). Both sides appealed to Stillingfleet and Jonathan Edwards, both of whom responded by defending Williams. Accused of antinomianism, Lobb and his colleagues asserted their orthodoxy in *A Declaration of the Congregational Ministers* (1699). Responding to Lobb's plea to view the *Declaration* favourably, Williams wrote *An End to Discord* (1699), finding further debate inexcusable. However, the Independent Isaac Chauncy came to the defence of Lobb in *Alexipharmacon* (1700), which castigated Stillingfleet's criticism of him.

Lobb, who was living in Middlesex prior to his death, died of a seizure at the London house of the Independent George Griffith on 3 June 1699. In his funeral sermon Thomas Goodwin of Pinner praised him as 'a Man of a discerning, penetrating Spirit, of great strength of mind' (Goodwin, 28). RICHARD L. GREAVES

Sources PRO, SP 29/427/114; 29/430/40, 111, 120, 157; 29/431/76, 99, 103, 108; 29/434/98; 44/337, fol. 165 · BL, Add. MSS 28875, fol. 261*r*; 38847, fol. 116*r* · *CSP dom.*, 1671–2, 332–3; *1682*, 521; *July–Sept 1683*; *1683–4*, 393; *1684–5*, 28; *1686–7*, 326 · *Calendar of the correspondence of Richard Baxter*, ed. N. H. Keeble and G. F. Nuttall, 2 vols. (1991) · [T. Sprat], *Copies of the informations and original papers relating to the* *proof of the horrid conspiracy against the late king, his present majesty and the government*, 3rd edn (1685) • A. Gordon, ed., *Freedom after ejection: a review (1690–1692) of presbyterian and congregational nonconformity in England and Wales* (1917) • G. L. Turner, ed., *Original records of early nonconformity under persecution and indulgence*, 3 vols. (1911–14), vol. 2, p. 1191; vol. 3, p. 243 • R. Morrice, 'Ent'ring book, being an historical register of occurrences from April, anno 1677 to April 1691', DWL, 1.348, 352, 407, 444, 657; 2.227 • T. Goodwin, *A sermon on occasion of the death of … Stephen Lobb* (1699) • J. Jones, *The great duty of conformity* (1684), 92 • R. L. Greaves, 'The Rye House plotting, nonconformist clergy, and Calvin's resistance theory', *Later Calvinism: international perspectives*, ed. W. F. Graham (1994), 505–24 • D. R. Lacey, *Dissent and parliamentary politics in England, 1661–1689* (1969) • W. Wilson, *The history and antiquities of the dissenting churches and meeting houses in London, Westminster and Southwark*, 4 vols. (1808–14), vol. 3, pp. 436–46 • administration, GL, MS 9168/28, fol. 171*v*

Archives BL, Add. MSS 28875, fol. 261*r*; 38847, fol. 116*r* • DWL, Baxter papers • DWL, R. Morrice, 'Entr'ing Book' • PRO, state papers, domestic, SP 29/427, 430, 431, 434; 44/337 • U. Nott., Portland MSS, PwV 95, fol. 300

Wealth at death see administration, GL, MS 9168/28, fol. 171*v*

Lobb, Theophilus (1678–1763), physician and nonconformist minister, born in London on 17 August 1678, was the son of the nonconformist divine Stephen *Lobb (*d.* 1699), and his wife, Elizabeth (*d.* 1691), the daughter of Theophilus *Polwhele (*d.* 1689), nonconformist minister at Tiverton, Devon. Despite an early interest in medicine he was educated for the ministry under the Revd Thomas Goodwin (1650–1716), at Pinner, Middlesex. In 1702 he settled as a nonconformist minister at Guildford, Surrey, and there received some medical instruction from a local physician. About 1706 Lobb moved to Shaftesbury, Dorset, and began to practise as a physician. Seven years later he settled at Yeovil, Somerset, and established a successful medical practice, although he still continued to act as a minister. Dissensions in his congregation at Yeovil induced him in 1722 to move to Witham, Essex. On 26 June of that year he was created MD by the University of Glasgow, and was admitted FRS on 13 March 1729. In 1732 Lobb received a call from the congregation at Haberdashers' Hall, London, but, as his ministry did not prove acceptable, he appears to have decided about 1736 to devote himself to medicine. However, he continued to publish religious works concerning morals and portents. These include *A brief defence of the Christian religion, or, The testimony of God to the truth of the Christian religion* (1726); *Sacred declarations, or, A letter to the inhabitants of London, Westminster, and all other parts of Great Britain on the account of those sins which provoked God to send and continue the mortal sickness among the cattle, and to signify by the late awful earthquakes that his anger is not turned away* (published anonymously, 1750); and *Letters on the Sacred Predictions (with a Letter upon the Public Reading of the Scriptures)* (1761).

On 30 September 1740 Lobb was admitted a licentiate of the Royal College of Physicians, and then practised only in London. On 21 May 1762 a patent was granted to him 'for a tincture to preserve the blood from diziness, and a saline scorbutic acrimony'. Lobb's medical writings ranged from treatises on ailments in particular to the practice of physic in general. They include *A Treatise of the Small-Pox* (1731); *Rational Methods of Curing Fevers* (1734); and *Letters Concerning the Plague, Shewing the Means to Preserve People from Infection* (1745).

Lobb first married, on 28 January 1702 at Egham, Surrey, Frances (*d.* 1722), daughter of James Cooke, physician, of Shepton Mallet, Somerset, and second, in 1723, 'a lady', who died on 2 February 1760. No children survived him. He died in the parish of Christ Church, London, on 19 May 1763, and was buried in Bunhill Fields. The profit from the sale of the tincture he left to his niece Elizabeth Buckland. In 1767 the Revd John Greene of Chelmsford, Essex, his brother-in-law, published *The Power of Faith and Godliness Exemplified in some Memoirs of Theophilus Lobb*, consisting principally of extracts from Lobb's diary.

GORDON GOODWIN, *rev.* LYNDA STEPHENSON PAYNE

Sources Munk, *Roll* • W. Wilson, *The history and antiquities of the dissenting churches and meeting houses in London, Westminster and Southwark*, 4 vols. (1808–14) • Watt, *Bibl. Brit.* • Boase & Courtney, *Bibl. Corn.* • G. C. Boase, *Collectanea Cornubiensia: a collection of biographical and topographical notes relating to the county of Cornwall* (1890) • will, PRO, PROB 11/889, sig. 291 • *IGI*

Archives BL, letters to Thomas Birch, Add. MS 4312 • BL, letters to M. Folkes, Add. MS 4438

Likenesses J. Hulett, line engraving, 1767 (after N. Brown), BM, NPG; repro. in R. Burgess, *Portraits of doctors and scientists in the Wellcome Institute* (1973), no. 1791. 1

Wealth at death monies from patent for relief of scurvy to niece: will, PRO, PROB 11/889, sig. 291

Lobb, William Hunter (1870–1916). *See under* Lobb, John (1829–1895).

Lobel, Edgar (1888–1982), Greek scholar, was the elder son (there were no daughters) of Arthur Lobel, a shipowner who underwent several marked changes of fortune, and his wife, Amelia. His date of birth is given as 12 December 1888 in the Manchester grammar school records, and 24 December 1888 by the time he attended Oxford. He himself celebrated 24 December as the date. When he matriculated at Oxford he stated his place of birth to have been Jassy in Romania. He went to Kersal School and then Manchester grammar school, where he was well taught by Harold Williamson and others, became head of school, and in 1906 won a scholarship to Balliol College, Oxford. At that time his father lost most of his money and took his family to America, but Lobel remained behind in order to go up to Balliol, boarding with his former teacher during the vacations. He matriculated in 1907, and was taught by A. D. Lindsay, Cyril Bailey, and J. A. Smith, but the tutor most congenial to him was A. W. Pickard-Cambridge. Lobel flourished in the exhilarating atmosphere of the Balliol of that time, which contained so many undergraduates who were not only gifted scholars but witty and agreeable people, and he retained many of its characteristics, both superficial and serious, throughout his life. He had a highly successful undergraduate career, obtaining first classes in classical honour moderations (1909) and *literae humaniores* (1911), the Gaisford prize for Greek verse, and Craven and Derby scholarships.

After a year as assistant in humanity at Edinburgh University (1911–12), Lobel returned to Oxford as Craven fellow, and took up the study of papyri. He visited Paris, Lille,

Bonn, and Dublin, and for some months worked in Berlin under Wilhelm Schubart. In 1914 he was elected to a research studentship at the Queen's College, Oxford, the college of B. P. Grenfell and A. S. Hunt, the finders and for the first years the editors of the great hoard of papyri from Oxyrhynchus in Upper Egypt.

When the First World War broke out, Lobel was rejected for military service on account of his short sight, a deficiency which is sometimes compatible, as in his case, with keen sight if an object is held close to the eyes. After teaching briefly at Repton and at Downside schools he worked in military intelligence, first in the Admiralty and later in the War Office. The loss of so many of his contemporaries caused him deep distress, and for the remainder of his life he never wore a tie that was not black.

After the war Lobel combined his research studentship at Queen's with a sub-librarianship in the Bodleian Library (1919–34); to this side of his activity belong his authoritative studies of the medieval Latin version of Aristotle's *Poetics* and of Cardinal Pole's manuscripts (both in *Proceedings of the British Academy*, 17, 1931) and of the Greek manuscripts of the *Poetics* (*Supplement to Transactions of the Bibliographical Society*, 9, 1933). In this monograph he displayed an extraordinary skill in identifying the hands of Renaissance copyists. Another product of that same skill was an archive of specimen photographs of Greek hands of that period, which eventually served as an important ingredient of the first and second volumes of the reference work entitled *Repertorium der grieschen Kopisten*. But he continued to work on papyri, and produced two masterly editions of Sappho (1925) and Alcaeus (1927), whose introductions form a continuous essay on the textual history, language, and metre of the two poets, and whose texts were later subsumed in *Poetarum Lesbiorum fragmenta* (1955), in which Lobel collaborated with Denys Page. Important fragments of these poets which had been published from papyri had in many editions been defaced by ill-judged conjectural supplements, and by castigating these Lobel managed to arrest this tendency. In 1927 he assisted Hunt in the publication of important fragments of Callimachus in part 17 of the Oxyrhynchus papyri; in the same year he became a supernumerary fellow of Queen's College. Also in 1927 he married Mary Doreen Rogers (1900–1993), later editor of the Victoria county history of Oxfordshire (vols. 3–8) and of maps and plans of historic towns in the British Isles. She was the daughter of Frederick William Rogers, director of a company dealing in asphalt, of Bristol. After a short stay in St Giles' they moved to 16 Merton Street. They had no children.

In 1931 Lobel became keeper of Western manuscripts in the Bodleian Library, but in 1934 he succeeded Hunt as editor of the literary papyri in the Oxyrhynchus series, becoming reader in papyrology in the university from July 1936. In 1938 he resigned from the Bodleian, being at the same time elected a senior research fellow of Queen's. These appointments he retained until his retirement at the age of seventy in 1959, his tenure having been specially extended five years earlier. But retirement made little difference to his activities, since he did not cease to work at the papyri from Oxyrhynchus. After 1972 he was not again responsible for an entire volume in the series, but he continued work and intellectual activity until not long before his death.

Between part 18 of the series, published in 1941, and part 39, published in 1972, by far the greatest part of the literary papyri were published by Lobel, and in exemplary fashion. In the piecing together and reading of the papyri he showed unique palaeographical skill, and in the identification and interpretation of the texts contained in them he showed unique knowledge of and feeling for the Greek language and literature. Lobel had little use for speculation, his aim being, as he put it, 'to attain the measure of certainty possible in these studies'. But he made certain supplements in many places, including some where no other scholar would have thought of them, and his concise notes, restricted as they were by the limits which he set himself, show an astonishing familiarity with all the relevant material and the keenest critical intelligence.

Apart from Sappho and Alcaeus, it fell to Lobel to edit texts of Hesiod, Archilochus, Alcman, Stesichorus, Anacreon, Simonides, Pindar, and Bacchylides; of Aeschylus and Sophocles; of Callimachus, Antimachus, Rhianus, and Euphorion; and also many unidentified fragments. Euripides and Menander he left to others, but he handled all with equal mastery; Paul Maas, who had known all the leading Hellenists of his time and whose respect for his own teacher Wilamowitz was very great, held that Lobel knew Greek better than any of them.

Tall, erect, and distinguished in appearance, Lobel had a memorable presence. As a young man he acquired a reputation for being formidable that never quite left him: he did not suffer fools gladly, and had no use for teaching, academic gatherings, or anything else that might have distracted him from what he regarded as his proper work. He travelled widely in Britain and in Europe during vacations, and was remarkably well informed not only about European literature but about a whole range of topics, including wine, botany, and topography. His wit, though not without a sardonic edge, was highly entertaining, but at the same time his old-fashioned courtesy and consideration for others preserved something of the old Oxford collegiate atmosphere. Those who met him in his own college and in the few places where he could be persuaded to dine out found him a most agreeable companion.

Lobel scorned academic honours (he refused fellowship of the British Academy), but accepted the honorary degree of LittD from Cambridge (1954), and became an honorary fellow of Balliol College (1959) and of Queen's College (1959). He died at 16 Merton Street, Oxford, on 7 July 1982.

HUGH LLOYD-JONES, *rev.*

Sources E. G. Turner, *Gnomon*, 55 (1983), 175–80 · B. F. McGuinness, *Balliol Record* (1983), 12–16 · personal knowledge (1990) · private information (1990) · matriculation records, Oxf. UA · *CGPLA Eng. & Wales* (1982)

Likenesses photograph, repro. in Turner, *Gnomon*, facing p. 176

Wealth at death £159,068: probate, 23 Sept 1982, *CGPLA Eng. & Wales*

L'Obel, Mathias de (1538–1616), botanist, was born at Lille (then in Burgundian Flanders), the son of Jean de L'Obel, a lawyer in that city. After a schooling which left him with a poor command of both Flemish and Latin he probably first studied medicine at the University of Louvain, then before 1554 attended Luca Ghini's renowned botanical course at the University of Pisa. Extensive travel in west and central Europe followed, with intermittent returns to Flanders. Lengthy stays at Padua and Bologna can be inferred from his later writings, suggesting further study at their universities, but only his matriculation at Montpellier in the spring of 1565 is certain. There he became friendly with a Provençal student, Pierre Pena. L'Obel's knowledge and zeal so impressed the botany professor, Guillaume Rondelet, that he took the two on herbarizing excursions and on his death the next year bequeathed to L'Obel some of his manuscripts.

Deprived of their teacher, and with Flanders newly embroiled in the Dutch revolt, the two friends moved to England, probably late in 1567. There L'Obel established himself as a physician in Bristol, made botanizing trips which extended to Scotland and even Ireland, and with Pena compiled a herbal, *Stirpium adversaria nova*. Published in London in 1571, this had notes on some 1300 plants observed by them on their European travels and introduced L'Obel's improvement on the rudimentary natural classification earlier developed by Dodoens; this used leaf-breadth to separate flowering plants into two groups, but was nevertheless much inferior to that of L'Obel's contemporary, Cesalpino. Poorly illustrated and thin on new herbs, the book lacked popular appeal and sold badly.

With career hopes in England dashed, Pena went to Paris and L'Obel to Antwerp (where he probably had family connections) to practise medicine. There the publisher Christophe Plantin, having bought the unsold stock of the *Adversaria*, cunningly married its text, hastily revised by L'Obel, to a large collection of excellent woodcuts made earlier for some herbals by Dodoens but never used. Issued in 1576 as an ostensibly new work under the title *Plantarum seu stirpium historia*, but better known by its first part, *Stirpium observationes*, this proved a commercial success. Emboldened, Plantin followed it up in 1581 with two more works by L'Obel, his *Kruytboeck* and *Stirpium icones*, each again illustrated extensively.

With three of the most beautiful botanical publications of the Renaissance to his name, L'Obel had quickly gained an international reputation and on the strength of that by 1578 was appointed court physician to the prince of Orange, William the Silent, in Delft. The assassination of his patron in July 1584 abruptly reversed his fortunes and L'Obel resorted to medicine in Middelburg, in Zeeland. This was the home town of his wife, the sister of an apothecary, Pasduyn, with whom he had at least two sons and three daughters.

About 1590 L'Obel returned to England, perhaps under duress, for his writings hint at sympathy with the protestant cause. Taken on by the rising diplomat Edward, Lord Zouche, as superintendent of his well-stocked garden in Hackney, and presumably as his domestic physician as well, in 1592 and again in 1598 L'Obel accompanied his patron on missions to the court of Denmark and extended his botanical experience there and in Norway. Collaboration with Gerard led to his cataloguing the latter's physic garden in Holborn. However, the London climate did not suit L'Obel's wife, forcing him back to Middelburg for several prolonged visits while she recovered her health. Though he took a medical post locally, he could not make it pay and by 1604 they had to return to London.

Now elderly, L'Obel was still robust and resumed practice in England with apparent success, attending several patients of distinction. He quickly induced his original publisher, Thomas Purfoot, to reissue the *Adversaria* (1605), and in the same year, probably thanks to Lord Zouche to whom it was dedicated, to bring out his belated exposition of Rondelet's *Methodica pharmaceutica*. To Zouche he no doubt owed his appointment in 1607 as botanographer (responsible for describing plants) to the court of James I. Meanwhile he continued to botanize actively, exploring the Welsh mountains when over seventy. By that time, following the death of his wife in July 1605, he had made a late second marriage to an elderly widow, the mother of a London apothecary, Abraham Hugobert; there is evidence that she shared his interest in botany and also spoke habitually in French, which could indicate that she was a fellow immigrant. She lived to help bear his distress in 1615 when his son Paul was tried on a far-fetched charge of causing a death by poisoning.

L'Obel died only a few months after that upsetting episode, on 3 March 1616. Though his death occurred in the parish of St Michael Cornhill (not at Highgate, as traditionally stated), he was buried at St Dionis Backchurch. To the botanically inclined husband of his daughter Louise, James Cole (or Coel), nephew of the Antwerp cartographer Ortelius and an affluent silk importer, he bequeathed his manuscripts, including that of a further herbal on which he was engaged up to the end. Some of this material was later made available to John Parkinson for his *Theatrum botanicum* (1640), an avowed compilation, but not in such quantity or manner to warrant William How's fierce accusation of plagiarism, when How in turn used part of the material and published it in L'Obel's name in 1655 under the title *Stirpium illustrationes*. From that and other sources it has been calculated that the first records of more than eighty British wild plants stand to L'Obel's credit. It is true that he was fortunate to have had hardly any predecessors in that line of investigation, and also that there were no competing herbals published in the period during which he wrote. An aggressiveness detectable in those writings perhaps sprang from a sense that his scientific reputation was assailable for being too shallowly based. His only known portrait, though, dating from the end of his life, conveys a wholly benign appearance. The name *Lobelia* was first given to a genus of plants by Plumier in 1702 in his honour, but was later applied by Linnaeus to the different, appropriately cosmopolitan one that has borne it ever since. D. E. Allen

Sources A. Louis, *Mathieu de l'Obel, 1538–1616: épisode de l'histoire de la botanique* (1980) · E. L. Greene, *Landmarks of botanical history*, ed.

F. N. Egerton, 2 (1983), 877–937 • H. Wille, 'The botanical works of R. Dodoens, C. Clusius and M. Lobelius', *Botany in the Low Countries, end of the 15th century–ca. 1650*, ed. F. de Nave and D. Imhof (1993), 121–2 • B. Henrey, *British botanical and horticultural literature before 1800*, 1 (1975), 26–31 • R. T. Gunther, *Early British botanists and their gardens* (1922), 245–53 • C. E. Raven, *English naturalists from Neckam to Ray: a study of the making of the modern world* (1947), 235–9 • A. G. Morton, *History of botanical science* (1980), 140, 161 • A. Arber, *Herbals: their origin and evolution*, 2nd edn (1938) • Desmond, *Botanists*, rev. edn • G. A. Lindeboom, *Dutch medical biography* (1984), 1211

Archives BL, Stowe MS 1069 • Magd. Oxf., botanical notes

Likenesses F. Delaram, engraving, 1615, BM; repro. in Arber, *Herbals*

Lobengula Khumalo (*c.*1835–1893/4?), king of the Ndebele, was born in Mkwahla, a tiny settlement lying between the Marico and Crocodile rivers in what later became the Transvaal. He was one of eight sons acknowledged by Mzilikazi, ruler of the Ndebele (Matabele). Lobengula's mother, Fulata Tshabalala, a member of the Swazi royal family, was killed in the early 1840s. After Mzilikazi's death on 8 September 1868 the Ndebele kingdom was racked by civil war. Although Lobengula was widely recognized as Mzilikazi's successor in September of the following year, his claim to the throne was never entirely certain. Chronic unrest lasted until 1871/2, and thereafter persistent divisions within the Ndebele state limited Lobengula's room for manoeuvre on the increasingly crowded southern African stage.

While descriptions of Lobengula by white traders and resident missionaries vary according to prejudice, most accounts agree with an 1889 record of him as 'over six foot three inches … and very broad in proportion. He definitely had a commanding and dignified presence, and dominated the company he was in. … He was accustomed to being obeyed by everyone, and showed it' (Vaughan-Williams, 105). No authenticated photograph of Lobengula has survived. According to the leading historian of this period, Lobengula took to wife at least fifty women 'and possibly double that number' (Cobbing, 282). Probably his first wife was *Lozikeyi (*d.* 1919). A number of marriages were undertaken for diplomatic purposes, most notably in 1879 with Xwalile, daughter of the Gaza king, Mzila. Only seven of Lobengula's sons lived beyond the early 1890s, one of whom, Nyamanda, was marked out for the succession.

Lobengula's reign witnessed the balance of power in central and southern Africa tilt decisively against the Ndebele. To the east, formerly tributory Shona-speaking peoples were arming themselves with guns bought from Portuguese trading posts on the Zambezi River, while to the south the threat posed by the Boers and by the British loomed ever larger. Both cast covetous eyes on the land across the Limpopo. In 1887 Lobengula sought to contain Boer expansion by concluding a treaty of friendship with Kruger's South African Republic, and in February 1888 assented to Matabeleland becoming a British sphere of influence. This was the so-called Moffat treaty, negotiated by John Moffat, son of Robert Moffat whose friendship with Mzilikazi had resulted in a long-standing if utterly ineffectual missionary presence among the Ndebele. This was followed by the Rudd concession in October 1888 whereby Lobengula granted 'all metals and minerals situated and contained in my kingdom … together with full power to do all things that they may deem necessary to win and procure the same' (Samkange, 78–9) to a group of British concession seekers headed by Cecil Rhodes and his partner Charles Rudd. The concessionaires agreed to pay Lobengula a monthly cash income and to supply 1000 Martini-Henry rifles, ammunition, and an armed steamboat on the Zambezi. Presumably Lobengula agreed to the concession hoping to decisively strengthen his kingdom.

Considerable controversy surrounds the Rudd concession. Was Lobengula tricked into putting his mark to a document which omitted certain crucial clauses—'not more than ten white men to enter Lobengula's kingdom'; 'they would fight for the King if called upon to do so' (Samkange, 78–9)? Or did Lobengula and his trusted advisers know very well what they were doing, hoping thereby to secure their own shaky position against dissident elements? In either event, Lobengula repudiated the concession in April 1889—and ordered the killing of Lotje, the *induna* who had advised in favour of the concession, and his family and household—but by then it was too late. The concession, enormously strengthened by the judicious amalgamation of competing commercial interests and the prudent assembly of a prestigious board of directors, was accepted as the basis for a royal charter for Rhodes's British South Africa Company in October 1889. Anxious to placate Cape colonial interests and further British supremacy in the context of subcontinental rivalries transformed by the discovery of gold on the Rand three years previously, Salisbury's government backed Rhodes. His British South Africa Company was empowered to make treaties and promulgate laws, as well as to maintain a police force and undertake public works. By September 1890 it had established itself in Mashonaland, ostensibly within the terms of the concession, but actually beyond the area of effective Ndebele control. 'Did you ever see a chameleon catch a fly?' asked Lobengula:

> The chameleon gets behind the fly and remains motionless for some time, then he advances very slowly and gently, first putting forward one leg and then another. At last, when well within reach, he darts his tongue and the fly disappears. England is the chameleon and I am that fly. (Mason, 105)

A period of uneasy coexistence followed. The British South Africa Company set about enforcing its rule over the Shona, all the while encroaching on Matabeleland proper as white prospectors fanned out over the countryside in search of gold. With the Ndebele state riven with factions, Lobengula toyed with the idea of escaping company pressure by the wholesale removal of his kingdom across the Zambezi. To this end, raiding parties were dispatched northwards to probe Lozi defences. At the same time occasional forays continued against neighbouring Shona chiefdoms. In July 1893 an Ndebele impi (regiment) attacked villages in the vicinity of Fort Victoria, in the process bringing the settler mining and trading community to a standstill. Encouraged by the fact that Ndebele raiders near the town were easily dispersed by a small band of mounted men, the company administrator, Leander Starr Jameson, advised Rhodes: 'we have the excuse for a row over murdered women and children now and the getting Matabeleland open would give us a tremendous lift in shares and everything else' (Glass, 272).

Lobengula tried hard to avoid the coming war. 'I thought you came to dig gold, but it seems that you have come not only to dig the gold but to rob me of my people and country as well', he complained to the British South Africa Company. 'Tell your … [officer in command] he is like some of my young men; he has no holes in his ears, and cannot or will not hear' (Mason, 170). Despite enormous pressure from his own 'war party', Lobengula made it clear in repeated messages to the high commissioner in Cape Town that he would 'certainly not fight unless forced and all depends on action of … [the British] Government' (Keppel-Jones, 253). But the company's version of events eventually won the day—'Matabele assembling on border … in regiments' (Glass, 166)—and in October 1893 two company columns converged on Matabeleland. With a section of the Ndebele army incapacitated by smallpox contracted on the campaign against the Lozi, the invaders experienced little difficulty in breaking through to Bulawayo, Lobengula's capital. At the battles of Bembesi and Shangani, Ndebele warriors were mown down by machine-gun fire. As the company forces advanced, Lobengula withdrew northwards. No one other than his immediate entourage ever saw him again. It is believed that he died after taking poison, in either December 1893 or January 1894. IAN PHIMISTER

Sources J. R. D. Cobbing, 'The Ndebele under the Khumabs, 1820–1896', PhD diss., University of Lancaster, 1976 · S. Glass, *The Matabele war* (1968) · N. Bhebe, *Christianity and traditional religion in western Zimbabwe, 1859–1923* (1979) · M. Stocker, 'The Rudd concession', *Zimbabwean history*, 10 (1979), 1–20 · S. Samkange, *Origins of Rhodesia* (1968) · R. Brown, 'Aspects of the scramble for Matabeleland', *The Zambesian past*, ed. E. Stokes and R. Brown (1966) · A. Keppel-Jones, *Rhodes and Rhodesia: the white conquest of Zimbabwe, 1884–1902* (1983) · H. Vaughan-Williams, *A visit to Lobengula in 1889* (1947) · P. Mason, *The birth of a dilemma: the conquest and settlement of Rhodesia* (1958) · G. Preller, *Lobengula* (1963) · W. A. Wills and L. T. Collingridge, *The downfall of Lobengula: the cause, history and effect of the Matabeli War* (1894) · H. M. Hole, *Lobengula* (1929)

Archives National Archives of Zimbabwe, Harare, corresp. and MSS, concessions | National Archives of Zimbabwe, Harare, CT corresp., Matabele War · National Archives of Zimbabwe, Harare, CT [British South Africa Company, Cape Town office] corresp., Matabeleland · National Archives of Zimbabwe, Harare, James Dawson, corresp. and diary, 1890 · National Archives of Zimbabwe, Harare, John Smith Moffat, corresp., and diaries, 1862–92.

Likenesses T. Baines, coloured drawings, 1870–79, NHM · E. A. Maund, sketch, 1885, National Archives of Zimbabwe, Harare · J. Hammond, photograph, repro. in J. H. Hammond, *The autobiography of John Hays Hammond*, 1 (1935) · H. M. Hole, sketch (after sketch by L. Décle), repro. in Hole, *Lobengula*, frontispiece

Loch, Sir Charles Stewart (1849–1923), social worker, was born on 4 September 1849 at Bhagalpur, Bengal, the fifth son of George Loch, judge of the high court, Calcutta, and his first wife, Louisa Gordon, who died when he was born. He was brought up in England by friends of the family. He was educated at Trinity College, Glenalmond, and proceeded to Balliol College, Oxford, in 1869. Asthma, which

Sir Charles Stewart Loch (1849–1923), by John Singer Sargent, 1900

had interrupted his work at school, continued to handicap him at the university. He obtained a third class in classical moderations in 1870 and a second class in the final school of modern history in 1873. His tutors were Edwin Palmer and Thomas Hill Green. Loch was profoundly influenced by Green's character and philosophy, and the two men remained close friends until Green's early death in 1882. Loch was influenced by Green's sense of individual moral integrity and autonomy, whereas most of his pupils took from him a wider ambiance. Loch's chief friends at Balliol were Andrew Bradley, Bernard Bosanquet, and A. L. Smith. In 1874, during a period of residence at Oxford, while employed in London, he formed one of the gang of university men who constructed the 'Ruskin road' from Ferry Hinksey to Botley.

Loch's asthma prevented his entry to the Indian Civil Service, his first choice of career, and he rejected thoughts of ordination. Influenced by Green and Arnold Toynbee, he looked instead to social service. He decided to settle in London and from 1873 to 1875 he was clerk to the Royal College of Surgeons. He took up voluntary work for the newly founded (1869) Charity Organization Society (COS), serving on the executive committee of the Islington district committee in 1874 and becoming honorary secretary of the COS in November 1875, an office he held until 1914. In 1876 he married Sophia Emma (*d.* 1934) (daughter of Edward Peters of the Indian Civil Service), whom he had met in the context of COS work; they had a son and a daughter.

'Before long, Loch and the C.O.S. were almost interchangeable terms' wrote C. L. Mowat (Mowat, 63); but they were not wholly interchangeable, for Loch represented the COS in its sternest form. The COS saw itself as both a co-ordinator of charities and the guardian of the values which it believed essential to the efficient working of charity in the minimal-state society of which many of its members, and certainly Loch, approved. The poor law, even with its spirit of deterence, was by its existence, Loch believed, 'a permanent obstacle to thrift and self-reliance' (ibid., 68). He thought that 'degraded pauperism' had been a significant cause of the decline of the Roman empire. Loch's secretaryship coincided with a gradual national rejection of the schematic application of such views, and much of his life was something of a rearguard defence of them. The COS council, though not necessarily all its branches, thus found itself the public embodiment of reaction much more than the fertile co-ordinator of charitable activity. Loch was a hard and effective administrator. His frequent reports were presented as if they were government papers; indeed the COS foreshadowed the work and form of influence of much later 'think tanks'. Loch was not merely an effective publicist. He successfully involved public figures in the making of COS reports and thus assisted their legitimacy and reception. His most effective practical innovation was the introduction of hospital almoners, anticipated in his article 'The confusion of medical charities', *Nineteenth Century* (August 1892); he saw the almoners as a revival of a medieval tradition. This widely adopted office typified the best aspects of Loch. He aimed at 'a church of charity' (paper of 1903, Mowat, 81), which by 'scientific, religious charity' would rise above class and achieve the sort of moral autonomous society adumbrated earlier in the nineteenth century by Thomas Chalmers.

State action was therefore, for Loch, a corrupt form of intervention. His ideas found a more fertile soil in the USA (which Loch visited in 1896) than in the UK. By the 1880s the need for a partnership between charities and the state was being urged by some COS members, including Canon Barnett, and in the 1890s Alfred Marshall, also a prominent member, criticized the COS's oligarchic character. Loch took some of these criticisms personally, and felt that the best bastion against social decay was being eroded from within. He vigorously opposed state relief of unemployment and the various schemes for some form of old age pension. Loch's hostility to state action has somewhat masked his positive contribution to the complex question of charitable action in a modern society. His stress on face-to-face and one-to-one social work and the relationship of this to his view of citizenship, with the middle-class 'giver' and the working-class 'receiver', were of continuing interest and importance.

Despite its increasing alienation from the public mood, the COS continued to be well represented on official inquiries, partly because Loch was so effective a lobbyist. He was a member of the royal commission on the aged poor (1893–5), the feeble-minded (1904–8), and on the poor law (1905–9). The poor-law commission—one of the most extensive such inquiries ever undertaken—gave the COS an important forum. Loch was accompanied on it by six other COS members, including Octavia Hill. Loch condemned the Conservatives' Unemployed Workmen Act (passed just as the commission was appointed) as a 'new pseudo-industrial system of remuneration' (Harris, 174), and in a series of letters to *The Times* he repeated traditional COS views on disfranchisement as a penalty for poor relief and the like. However, faced with Beatrice Webb's attempt to portray the COS as no more than the guardian of the principles of the 1834 poor law, Loch and the other COS members of the commission led the way in the writing of its majority report which, while retaining the poor law (though changing its name to public assistance), modified its structure and governance and recommended a variety of practical reforms, while still retaining the COS tradition of voluntary action. The majority report influenced the Local Government Act (1929) and the Poor Law Act (1930). Loch criticized the National Insurance Act of 1911, which owed something to the minority report.

Loch was secretary to a committee (1908–9) on COS organization which reasserted COS principles and methods. From 1904 until 1908 he was Tooke professor of economic science at King's College, London. In 1905 Oxford University gave him an honorary DCL.

Though known for strong and increasingly unfashionable views, Loch was personally tolerant and moved in a wide circle of friends. His study of art under Ruskin in his Oxford days gave him a lifelong interest in painting. His chief published works were *How to Help Cases of Distress* (1883) and *Charity and the Social Life* (1910), an extension of his long article 'Charity and charities' in *Encyclopaedia Britannica* (10th edn, 1902). Loch had sharp features and always sported a large moustache. He suffered a stroke in the summer of 1913 and resigned the secretaryship in 1914; he declined the society's pension. He was knighted in 1915, but was unable to receive the honour in person. He lingered on until his death at his home, Drylaw Cottage, Little Bookham, Surrey, on 23 January 1923. He published his poems as *Things Within* (1922). His articles and addresses were edited by Sir Arthur Clay as *A Great Ideal and its Champion* (1923). Loch's daughter, Mary, married the historian Robert Balmain *Mowat.

Loch's views were unfashionable for much of the twentieth century, but at the end of it interest in them revived as more pluralist solutions to social welfare questions were sought. Loch kept an extensive diary, but he awaits a biography. H. C. G. MATTHEW

Sources *DNB* • C. L. Mowat, *The Charity Organisation Society, 1869–1913* (1961) • J. Harris, *Unemployment and politics* (1972) • D. E. Owen, *English philanthropy, 1660–1960* (1964) • K. Woodroofe, *From charity to social work in England and in the United States* (1962) • B. Webb, *My apprenticeship* (1926) • B. Webb, *Our partnership*, ed. B. Drake and M. I. Cole (1948) • H. Bosanquet, *Social work in London, 1869–1912* (1914) • Lord Beveridge [W. H. Beveridge], *Voluntary action* (1948) • A. Marshall, *The official papers of Alfred Marshall* (1996)

Archives LUL, diaries [extracts]

Likenesses J. S. Sargent, oils, 1900, Family Welfare Association, London [*see illus.*] • J. S. Sargent, oils, priv. coll.

Wealth at death £19,716 3*s*. 2*d*.: probate, 21 March 1923, *CGPLA Eng. & Wales*

Loch, David (*d.* 1780), shipowner and writer, is a figure about whose early life nothing is known. He graduated from being a shipmaster to become one of the leading merchants at the port of Leith, claiming to have sent, in the course of his career, some hundreds of ships to the Baltic and to the continent. He had, therefore, considerable firsthand knowledge of Scotland's trade, which he put to good effect.

In the 1770s Loch wrote a series of well-argued pamphlets which, reworked with additions, he gathered into a three-volume work, *Essays on the Trade, Commerce, Manufactures and Fisheries of Scotland* (1778). This covers a wide range of topics from British trade in general to the need to complete the Forth and Clyde Canal, then stalled for want of the necessary finance. The work provides a sympathetic account of Ireland's trade and of the penalties under which Irish traders laboured, and a supplement on what Loch called 'the unhappy dispute with the American Colonies' (Loch, 1.xli). In addition Loch describes the state of fishing in the highlands and islands, based on personal reconnaissance, and the condition of east coast fishing towns, which he knew from having made a tour of inspection in August and September 1778.

In the second volume the 'Tour through the trading villages of Scotland' provides a thorough account of the manufacturing being carried on in some 140 Scottish towns and burghs, from Alloa to Whitburn. Loch sought out statistical detail as to the value of output and the numbers employed in the leading trades, his work in many respects anticipating that of Sir John Sinclair's *Statistical Account of Scotland* (1791–9). Dundee, for example, he describes as having a population of about 14,000, of whom 2800 were linen weavers; the town had three tanneries, a large thread manufacture, and a thriving economy. Loch's 'Tour', however, is no mere accounting exercise: his descriptions are enlivened by a keen eye for the social consequences of economic growth. The prosperity of Paisley, for example, he finds reflected in the maidservants' being allowed free time every Thursday evening to go dancing: 'this practice promotes matrimony and contributes much to inspire in the minds of the people a desire to be neat and clean in their dress. The men marry here when they are twenty, the girls at seventeen' (Loch, 2.52).

The issue which most concerned Loch in all his writings, however, was the need to encourage Scotland's woollen industry, at a time when much official help was being given to the linen manufacturers. He pointed out how much flax had to be imported from either Holland or the Baltic, which made the linen industry, in his words, both 'exotic' and 'precarious'. Loch was all too aware of the risks of the trade, having been taken prisoner by a French privateer on one of his voyages back from the Baltic during the Seven Years' War. By contrast, he argued, Scotland could provide all the raw wool it needed for manufacture from domestic sources, were more attention given to improving the home supply by way of prizes for sheep-breeding. The force of his arguments and of his expertise were recognized in 1776 when the Edinburgh-based board of trustees appointed him their chief inspector for both fisheries and woollen manufactures, a position he held until his death. In July of the same year the Convention of Royal Burghs, in which Loch served for several years as member for the fishing town of Dunbar, underscored his worth by passing a special motion thanking him for his zeal in promoting the manufactures of Scotland. He died on 14 February 1780 at St Anne's Yards, Holyrood, Edinburgh. ALASTAIR J. DURIE

Sources D. Loch, *Essays on the trade, commerce, manufactures and fisheries of Scotland* (1778) · J. D. Marwick, ed., *Records of the convention of the royal burghs of Scotland*, [7 vols.] (1870–1918), 1759–1779 · *DNB* · Bank of Scotland, Edinburgh, British Linen Company MSS, Scottish letter-books

Archives Bank of Scotland, Edinburgh, British Linen Company MSS

Loch, Granville Gower (1813–1853), naval officer, born on 28 February 1813, was the second son of James *Loch (1780–1855) of Drylaw in Midlothian and his first wife, Ann (*d.* 1842), youngest daughter of Patrick Orr; he was the brother of George Loch and of Henry Brougham *Loch, first Baron Loch. He entered the navy in February 1826, passed his examination in 1832, and was promoted lieutenant on 23 October 1833. After serving on the home station and in the Mediterranean he was promoted commander 28 February 1837. From 1838 to 1840 he commanded the *Fly* (18 guns) on the South American and Pacific stations, and in 1841 the steamer *Vesuvius* in the Mediterranean. He was promoted captain on 26 August 1841, then went to China as a volunteer, and at the capture of Chinkiang Foo (Zhenjiang Fu) served as an aide-de-camp to General Sir Hugh Gough. He afterwards published his journal as *The Closing Events of the Campaign in China* (1843).

From 1846 to 1849 Loch commanded the frigate *Alarm* (26 guns) in the West Indies; in February 1848 he was sent to the coast of Nicaragua to demand and enforce redress for certain outrages, and to obtain the release of two British subjects who had been carried off from San Juan by the military commandant. The government at the time seemed to be in the hands of the army, and, without delay, Loch proceeded up the river in the boats of the *Alarm* and the sloop *Vixen*, with a total force of 260 men. The enemy had occupied a strong position at Serapaqui, defended not only by the nature of the ground and built obstructions, but by a 5 knot current which kept the boats under fire for an hour and a half before the men could land. The fort was then captured and demolished, the guns destroyed, and the ammunition thrown into the river. The British demands were conceded and a treaty was arranged: on Palmerston's recommendation Loch was made a CB on 30 May 1848.

In 1852 Loch commissioned the frigate *Winchester* (50 guns) to relieve the *Hastings* as flagship in China and the East Indies. It was the time of the Second Anglo-Burmese War. Shortly after arriving at Rangoon, Admiral Austen died of cholera; the commodore was off the coast, and command on the Irawaddy devolved on Loch. His task principally involved keeping the river clear and driving the Burmese out of positions they occupied on its banks. At the beginning of 1853 a dacoit chief, Nya-Myat-Toon, had brought together a strong force, stockaded a formidable position at Donabew, stopped the traffic, and repelled an attempt to drive him away. Loch in person led a joint naval and military expedition against him, landed, and threaded his way by a narrow path through thick jungle. They found the stockade on the farther bank of a steep ravine, in attempting to cross which they were repulsed with heavy losses. On 4 February Loch was shot through the body and he died two days later. He was buried at Rangoon, beneath a stone erected by the officers and men of the *Winchester*. A monument was erected to his memory in St Paul's Cathedral. He was unmarried.

J. K. LAUGHTON, *rev.* ANDREW LAMBERT

Sources G. S. Graham, *The China station: war and diplomacy, 1830–1860* (1978) · G. Bruce, *The Burma Wars, 1824–1886* (1973) · *Annual Register* (1853) · *GM*, 2nd ser., 39 (1853), 545–6 · private information (1893) · Boase, *Mod. Eng. biog.*
Archives NA Scot., corresp.

Loch, Henry Brougham, **first Baron Loch of Drylaw** (**1827–1900**), colonial administrator, born on 23 May 1827 at Drylaw, Midlothian, Scotland, was the son of James *Loch MP (1780–1855), of Drylaw, and his wife, Ann (*d.* 1842), the daughter of Patrick Orr. He entered the Royal Navy in 1840, but left it as a midshipman in 1842 and was gazetted to the 3rd Bengal cavalry in 1844. Although he was only seventeen, he was chosen by Lord Gough as his aide-de-camp, and in that capacity served through the Sutlej campaign of 1845. In 1850 he was appointed adjutant of the famous irregular corps Skinner's Horse. On the outbreak of the Crimean War his gift for managing Asian soldiers led to his being selected in 1854 to assist in organizing the Turkish horse in Bulgaria. He served throughout the war, and at its close was singled out for the employment which was destined to close his military career. In 1857 James Bruce, eighth earl of Elgin, was dispatched on a special embassy to China to arrange the final terms of settlement of the Second Opium War, then in progress, and Captain Loch was attached to his staff. He was present at the taking of Canton (Guangzhou) on 28 December and the seizure of Commissioner Ye, and he subsequently proceeded with Lord Elgin on his mission to Japan. In 1858 he was sent back to England with the treaty of Yeddo, concluded by Great Britain with that country. In 1860 the failure to obtain the ratification of the treaty of Tientsin (Tianjin) with China led to Lord Elgin being again sent out as minister-plenipotentiary. Mindful of Loch's services, he took him with him as private secretary. In conjunction with Harry Smith Parkes, Loch conducted the negotiations which led to the surrender of the Taku (Dagu) forts and he shared in the advance on Peking (Beijing).

On 18 September Loch formed one of the small party which was seized by Chinese officials on returning from Tungchow (Tongzhou), where they had been to arrange the preliminaries of peace. Loch had actually made his way through the enemy's lines to the British camp and had given warning of the intended arrests, but he chivalrously returned in order to try to save his comrades. For three weeks he endured the most terrible imprisonment, loaded with chains, tortured by the gaolers, and herded with the worst felons in the common prison. His situation was the more deplorable as he could not speak Chinese with any fluency. Fortunately the loyalty and determination of his fellow prisoner Parkes led first to the amelioration of his condition, and eventually to their joint release, only ten minutes before the arrival of an order from the emperor commanding their execution. On 8 October they rejoined the British camp, but, with the exception of a few Indian troopers, the rest of the party—French, British, and native—died in prison from maltreatment, and Loch himself never fully recovered his health. In 1869 he published his *Personal Narrative of Occurrences during Lord Elgin's Second Embassy to China*.

Henry Brougham Loch, first Baron Loch of Drylaw (1827–1900), by Camille Silvy, 1861

In 1860 Loch was sent home in charge of the treaty of Tientsin. The following year he finally left the army and was appointed private secretary to Sir George Grey, who was then secretary of state at the Home Office. On 7 May 1862 he married Elizabeth Villiers (1841–1938), the niece of the fourth earl of Clarendon; they had two daughters and a son. In 1863 Loch was made governor of the Isle of Man, a post which he occupied until 1882. In 1880 he was appointed KCB. He was transferred in 1882 to a commissionership of woods and forests and land revenue, and his career outside the somewhat narrow bounds of the British civil service seemed at an end. In 1884, however, Gladstone sent him to Australia, as governor of Victoria. He was made a GCMG on 24 May 1887. During his five years' tenure of this post his kindness and tact endeared him to the population, and he left a legacy of philanthropic and cultural projects behind him when in 1889 the marquess of Salisbury, the Conservative prime minister, chose him to succeed Sir Hercules Robinson, who had just completed his first term of office as governor of the Cape and high commissioner in South Africa.

It was during Loch's residence at the Cape that Anglo-Boer hostility first began to assume the threatening proportions which led to the war of 1899. In the Cape Colony itself matters were peaceful enough, owing to the temporary combination of Cecil Rhodes with the Afrikaner-Bond Party. There were few constitutional difficulties, and Loch found himself generally in accord with his constitutional advisers and able to work with them with little friction. Outside the borders, however, the elements of unrest were beginning to ferment, and Loch had inadequate knowledge of South African problems to enable him to master the situation. He was impressed, however, with the scale of Rhodes's conceptions, and with the danger to British paramountcy that would inevitably attend any expansion of the Transvaal republic. He therefore assisted the expeditions which led to the occupation of Mashonaland and Matabeleland, and he allowed the Bechuanaland police force to be sent up to threaten the Matabele (Ndebele) from the west on the outbreak of the war of 1893. One of his major objects was to bring Rhodes's British South Africa Company under greater imperial control, but in this he was largely unsuccessful. In 1891 he did, however, help to establish the separate existence of the Bechuanaland protectorate, which later evolved into Botswana.

A striking episode in Loch's South African career was his mission to Pretoria, in 1894, to interfere on behalf of the British subjects who had been commandeered by the Boers in their operations against Mmalabôhô or Malaboch, the Xananwa chieftain. He was successful in obtaining the abandonment of the claim of the Boer government; but it was thought he had not pressed the British case with sufficient vigour. It was the rough treatment accorded to President Kruger at Johannesburg on this occasion, in contrast with the enthusiastic reception accorded to the high commissioner, which persuaded Loch that a *coup d'état* by British Transvaalers, with subsequent imperial military backing, was feasible. The Colonial Office vetoed this secret project, but it reappeared in modified form, after Loch's departure, as the Jameson raid.

Earlier in his term of office Loch had succeeded in putting strong pressure on President Kruger to prevent the incursions to the north and west of immigrant Boer trekkers and roving filibusters. During negotiations on Swaziland he had, however, made to the Transvaal government an offer of access to the sea coast on condition that the president should moderate his attitude of hostility and join the Cape customs union, which Kruger refused.

Loch's Transvaal policy failed locally to create the impression of any great strength or decision. Fortunately his term of office expired at the beginning of 1895, and he left South Africa before the disasters of the Jameson raid. In spite of his bearded, patriarchal appearance, his fiery cavalryman's temperament would probably have let him down in circumstances that required a cool head.

On his return to England he was raised to the peerage in July 1895 as Baron Loch of Drylaw, but he took small part in politics, though he did vote with the Liberal Unionists. When, in December 1899, the reverses to the British army in Natal and Cape Colony at the hands of the Boers gave rise to the call for volunteers from Britain, Loch threw himself heartily into the movement, and took a leading share in raising and equipping a body of mounted men who were called, after him, Loch's Horse. He lived to hear of the occupation of Pretoria, but his health had been failing, and he died of heart disease after a short illness, at his home, 23 Lowndes Square, London, on 20 June 1900. He was buried on 25 June at Stoke by Clare, Suffolk.

His son, Edward Douglas, second baron, entered the Grenadier Guards and served with distinction in the Nile expedition of 1898 and in the Second South African War; he received a severe wound in the latter campaign. He also served throughout the First World War, during which he became major-general and was awarded several decorations. J. B. Atlay, *rev.* John Benyon

Sources H. B. Loch, *Personal narrative of occurrences during Lord Elgin's second embassy to China* (1869) • *The Times* (21 June 1900) • A. Keppel-Jones, *Rhodes and Rhodesia: the white conquest of Zimbabwe, 1884–1902* (1983) • J. A. Benyon, *Proconsul and paramountcy in South Africa: the high commission, British supremacy and the sub-continent, 1806–1910* (1980) • N. G. Garson, 'The Swaziland question and a road to the sea', *Archives year book for South African history*, 2 (1957) • E. A. Walker, *Lord de Villiers and his times: South Africa, 1842–1914* (1925) • *The Australian encyclopaedia*, 5 (1958), 356 • R. Robinson, J. Gallagher, and A. Denny, *Africa and the Victorians* (1961) • A. Sillery, *Founding a protectorate* (1965) • GEC, *Peerage* • *CGPLA Eng. & Wales* (1900)

Archives Borth. Inst., papers as high commissioner in South Africa • NA Scot., corresp. and papers • National Archives of Zimbabwe, Harare, diary • Rhodes University, Grahamstown, South Africa, Cory Library for Historical Research, corresp. with John Gordon Sprigg • State Library of Victoria, Melbourne, addresses | BL, Ripon MSS • BL, letters to Lord Carnarvon, Add. MS 60801 • Bodl. Oxf., corresp. with Sir William Harcourt • Bodl. RH, corresp. with Sir Godfrey Lagden • National Archives of South Africa, Pretoria, Transvaal archives depot, Series Staatsekretaris • NL Aus., letters to Alfred Deakin • PRO, CO confidential print 'Africa South' • U. Birm. L., corresp. with Joseph Chamberlain

Likenesses C. Silvy, photograph, 1861, NPG [*see illus.*] • H. W. Phillips, engraving, repro. in H. B. Loch, *Narrative of occurrences during Lord Elgin's second embassy to China*, 3rd edn [originally published 1869] • photograph, National Archives of South Africa, Pretoria, Transvaal archives • portrait, National Library of South Africa, Cape Town

Wealth at death £103,294 13*s.* 8*d.*: probate, 27 Aug 1900, *CGPLA Eng. & Wales*

Loch, James (1780–1855), lawyer and estate commissioner, was born on 7 May 1780 at Drylaw, near Edinburgh, the eldest son of George Loch (1749–1788), landowner, and his wife, Mary Adam. His mother was daughter of John Adam of Blair, Kinross-shire, and sister of lord chief-commissioner William Adam, of the jury court. The Drylaw estate had to be sold in 1786, and Loch was one of seven children who were all under eight years of age when their father died. He was brought up at Blair Adam estate under the care of his uncle, where he learned most

James Loch (1780–1855), by James Posselwhite, pubd 1850 (after George Richmond, 1845)

of his knowledge about agriculture and estate administration.

Loch studied law in the rationalist milieu of Edinburgh University and was much influenced by the philosophy of Adam Smith through the teaching of Dugald Stewart. He was at the centre of a glittering circle of students and was a member of the Speculative Society in 1798 and its president in the following two years. He was admitted as advocate in Scotland in 1801 and called to the English bar in Lincoln's Inn on 15 November 1806. Abandoning law after a few years of conveyancing practice, he worked as private secretary to George Tierney at the India board. He was involved in political activity and wrote a provocative article for the *Edinburgh Review* in 1804. A vigorous and effective worker in the interest of the whig party, he was offered entrée to a political career but made a clear decision, as early as 1810, to abandon politics and follow his vocation in the management of landed estates.

In August 1812 Loch became estate commissioner of the marquess of Stafford (first duke of Sutherland in the year of his death in 1833), whose estates represented the greatest accumulation of wealth in Britain at that time. Subsequently Loch supervised the estates of the second duke, and the duchess of Sutherland. He was also auditor and adviser to Lord Francis Egerton, afterwards earl of Ellesmere; to the Bridgewater trustees; to the earl of Carlisle; to the trust estates of the earl of Dudley (from which he was discharged on account of his support for the Reform Bill); and to Viscount Keith. He was responsible for estate policies over large parts of England and Scotland, which made him remarkably influential in the improvement and modernization of agricultural and industrial property across Victorian Britain.

Loch was married first in 1810, to Ann (*d.* January 1842), youngest daughter of Patrick Orr of Bridgeton, Kincardineshire. They had nine children, including Granville Gower *Loch; his sons were involved mainly in service to the empire in India and beyond, notably Henry Brougham *Loch, who was much respected as governor of both Victoria and of the Cape and also served as high commissioner for South Africa. Loch married second, on 2 December 1847, Elizabeth Mary, widow of George Macartney Grevill, of the 38th foot, and eldest daughter of John Pearson of Tettenhall Wood, Staffordshire. His second wife predeceased him on 29 December 1849.

Loch was widely regarded as the finest barrister-auditor of his day, and he worked on almost equal terms with his aristocratic employers. The dowager duchess of Bedford was told that 'she could not possibly have a better or more able adviser' (Spring, 89). Loch's contemporary Ralph Sneyd described him as 'Loch the infallible' (ibid.). He was in great demand as an adviser on most matters. He gave evidence before the select committee on public works in Ireland in 1835. He was an expert in entail and family law. In all his administrative work he gave extraordinary attention to detail. On the Sutherland estates he regarded his task as maintaining the long-term position of the family, as opposed to short-term gains. He believed that the conservative strength of the aristocracy derived from its responsibility for the 'great sinews of improvement' (Richards, 26).

Loch's career was most publicly known for his part in the great and controversial changes implemented on the highland estates of the Sutherland family from 1812 onwards. The policy predated Loch but he gave it greater clarity and direction. He presided over some of the largest clearances and then spent much of his life in defence of the consequences. He believed that the highlands had been locked in feudal squalor and its people effectively enslaved under the old highland middlemen. They had been kept poor and were ravaged by recurrent famine. His mission was to release the resources of the highlands and open the region to trade and improvement. This meant the removal of the tacksmen, the introduction of commercial sheep-farming, and the relocation of the small tenantry to the coasts. His management of the Sutherland estate was excoriated as 'the Loch policy' for its inhumanity to the people who were ousted from the inland districts and replaced by sheep. The removals often required strong-arm methods which generated widespread opprobrium. Since Loch became the principal apologist for the Sutherland clearances he also attracted much of the public abuse. None of this was diminished by his advocacy of emigration programmes to relieve population congestion in the west highlands. He attempted to deter improvident marriage and population growth by refusing to allow the subdivision of smallholdings.

Loch was much hurt by what he regarded as the 'lies' told about the Sutherland highlanders. He was critical of the middle levels of the new highland society who gave too little leadership to the people at large. He published an account of the Sutherland policies in 1820 and a privately printed memoir of the duke of Sutherland in 1834. He travelled a great deal between the estates and visited Sutherland virtually every autumn. He centralized decision making for the estate as a whole and employed professional agents on the individual estates. Most of the evictions were over by 1830 but small evictions were still in train in the 1850s where tenants fell into arrears. Beneath Loch was an elaborate management structure with estate agents and sub-agents. They were instructed to comport themselves in a particular way since they

> must be the principal gentlemen of the district, capable of acting as a deputy Lt and JP, and be very kind and forbearing to a most worthy excellent set of poor tenants, who require to be much encouraged in their most praiseworthy exertions of improvement. (Loch to Lockhart, 24 March 1827, NL Scot., MS 926)

During the course of his lifetime Loch held many public offices. These included being a director of the English Historical Society, seal keeper of the Old Quay Navigation Company, governor of the Forth and Clyde Canal, commissioner of the Caledonian and Crinan Canal, and director of the Grand Junction Railway. In addition he was active in scientific and educational circles, being elected a fellow of the Geological, Statistical, and Zoological societies; and he was a member of the committee of the Society for the Diffusion of Useful Knowledge. One of the founders of London University, for many years he served on its council and associated bodies. He was a director of the Liverpool and Manchester Railway, and of the Birmingham and Liverpool Canal. He also served in Scotland as commissioner of highland roads and bridges and as deputy lieutenant of Sutherland.

In 1827 Loch entered parliament for St Germains in Cornwall, in the whig interest, which he held until 1830; he was then returned without opposition for the Wick burghs. There he was regularly re-elected until 1852, when he was defeated by Samuel Laing (119 to 80 votes in a climacteric election). He regarded himself as one of the architects of the Reform Bill and was close to Lord John Russell during its passage. Although he worked for committees of the house, he declined more direct involvement in politics and government.

James Loch died on 28 June 1855 at his house at 12 Albemarle Street, London, and was buried in the Brompton cemetery. The duke of Sutherland erected a monument in his memory at Uppat (overlooking Dunrobin Castle), where he spent much of his time. An inscription on it praised Loch's 'virtuous labour for the land he loved' (P. G. Loch, 254). Loch's son George (1811–1877) succeeded him in the Sutherland management. ERIC RICHARDS

Sources E. Richards, *The leviathan of wealth: the Sutherland fortune in the industrial revolution* (1973) • D. Spring, *The English landed estate in the nineteenth century: its administration* (1963) • G. Loch, *The family of Loch* (privately printed, Edinburgh, 1934) • *Brougham and his early friends: letters to James Loch, 1798–1809*, ed. R. H. M. B. Atkinson and G. A. Jackson, 3 vols. (1908) • J. Loch, *Account of the improvements on the estates of the marquess of Stafford* (1820) • T. Bakewell, *Remarks on a publication of James Loch, Esq.* (1820) • H. E. Gower, *Letters, 1810–1845*, ed. F. Leveson-Gower, 2 vols. (1894) • F. C. Mather, *After the canal duke: a study of the industrial estates administered by the trustees of the third duke of Bridgewater … 1825–1872* (1970) • [W. M. Watson], ed., *The history of the Speculative Society, 1764–1904* (1905) • Loch to Lockhart, 24 March 1827, NL Scot., MS 926 • d. cert.

Archives NA Scot., corresp. and papers, mainly relating to estate management • UCL, corresp. | BL, corresp. with William Huskisson, Add. MSS 38755, 38757–38758 • BL, corresp. with Sir Robert Peel, Add. MSS 40367–40600 • Castle Howard, Yorkshire, corresp., accounts relating to earl of Carlisle's estates • National Archives of Belgium, Brussels, letters to C. A. Aylmer • NL Scot., corresp. relating to duke of Sutherland's estates, local elections • NRA, priv. coll., letters to Comte de Flahault • Shrops. RRC, corresp. relating to duke of Sutherland's Shropshire estate • St Deiniol's Library, Hawarden, corresp. with Sir John Gladstone • Staffs. RO, corresp. relating to duke of Sutherland's estates • U. Durham L., letters to Charles, second Earl Grey • U. Durham L., letters relating to Howards of Naworth's estates • UCL, letters to Society for the Diffusion of Useful Knowledge • Blair Adam, Kinross, letters to William Adam

Likenesses J. Posselwhite, engraving, pubd 1850 (after G. Richmond, 1845), NPG [*see illus.*] • G. Hayter, group portrait, oils (*The House of Commons, 1833*), NPG

Wealth at death £41,000: Loch, *Family of Loch*

Lochée, Lewis (*d.* **1791**), military educationist, was born in Brussels, the son of John Lochée and his wife, Theresa. It is unknown when or why he moved to England, though he was living in Camberwell, Surrey, in 1767. He was possibly a political exile from Austrian rule and certainly a protestant. In 1770 he set up a military academy in a large rented house in Little Chelsea, London. By 1776 he had extended the house and in 1781 he bought the freehold. The academy, with its grounds laid out as a fortification, became an object for sightseers. By 1777 Lochée described it as the 'Royal Military Academy', Little Chelsea, doubtless because George III had granted him an annual pension to encourage his work. On 8 May 1780 he was naturalized a British subject.

No military education was needed to become a British infantry or cavalry officer and none was officially provided, although a few private academies offered some teaching. Despite initial difficulties in attracting pupils, Lochée succeeded during the 1770s and 1780s in building up a notable clientele who could afford his fees. The military authorities recognized the value of his academy in providing a military education and training both for boys too young to be commissioned and for youngsters whose commissions had already been purchased. Lochée was exceptional in providing a carefully conceived combination of theoretical and practical instruction, and set out his ideas in *An Essay on Military Education* (1773). He was ahead of his time in involving the pupils in running the academy and in attention to practical work such as manoeuvres and digging fortifications. For the pupils the months in his care must have been an earnest experience, since Lochée objected to holidays—claiming that the curriculum offered sufficient diversion—was critical of sports, and expelled even the well-connected for bad conduct. Although his alumni, of whom the most distinguished was probably Lieutenant-General Sir Thomas Picton, were few compared with the number of officers entering the army, they had learned something of military value.

Lochée, who had a keen intellect, published clear and practical books on mathematics (1776), castrametation (1778), and fortification (1780 and 1783). He achieved educational, social, and financial success. He married on 26 August 1767 Elizabeth Dubourg (1749?–1801) and had a son, John (1776–1815). The academy probably closed in 1788 or 1789, since Mrs Lochée was the ratepayer on the property from 1789. On 17 December 1789 Lochée changed abruptly from military educationist to soldier, undertaking, as Lieutenant-Colonel Lochée, to raise at his own expense the 'Belgic Legion' to take part in the Belgian revolt against Austrian rule. But his patriotic idealism ended in failure, and on 29 May 1790 he was forced to resign from the defeated Belgian army. He moved to Lille in France, where Belgian refugees gathered and exchanged recriminations, in which he joined as the author of several pamphlets. He died at Lille, the circumstances unknown, on 8 June 1791. J. E. O. SCREEN

Sources J. E. O. Screen, 'The "Royal Military Academy" of Lewis Lochée', *Journal of the Society for Army Historical Research*, 70 (1992), 143–56 • F. H. W. Sheppard, ed., *Southern Kensington: Brompton*, Survey of London, 41 (1983) • N. A. Hans, *New trends in education in the eighteenth century* (1951); repr. (1966), 103–5 • act for naturalizing Lewis Lochée, HLRO, 20 Geo. III c. 39 private • *JHC*, 37 (1778–80) • L. Lochée, 'Elements of fortification', *GM*, 1st ser., 50 (1780), 284–5 • *The Times* (29 June 1791) • L. Lochée, *Observations sur la révolution belgique* (1791) • L. Lochée, *Au président du congrès* (1790) • Berwick Place, Hatfield Peverel, Essex, Barrington MSS • Staffs. RO, Paget family papers, D603/k/9/10
Archives Berwick Place, Hatfield Peverel, Essex, Barrington MSS • Staffs. RO, Paget MSS
Wealth at death will, PRO, PROB 11/1207 • 'Royal Military Academy' and nearby property in Little Chelsea: Sheppard, ed. *South Kensington*, 41.181–2

Lochhead, Sheila Ramsay (1910–1994). *See under* MacDonald, Malcolm John (1901–1981).

Lochore, Robert (1762–1852), poet, was born at Strathaven, Lanarkshire, on 7 July 1762. He became a shoemaker at the age of thirteen, and ultimately he conducted a successful business of his own in Glasgow. On 7 June 1786 he married in Paisley Isobel Browning, a native of Ayrshire. Lochore's local interests and his literary tastes brought him into contact with Robert Burns, who became a close friend. About 1797 he published an elegiac pastoral on Burns's death entitled *Patie and Ralph*; in later life he often told of having seen Burns reproved on the cutty-stool by the Revd Auld. Generous and philanthropic, Lochore founded the Glasgow Annuity Society and assisted other institutions for the public good.

Lochore wrote verses throughout his life, and he composed in his eighty-eighth year his spirited 'Last Speech of the Auld Brig of Glasgow on being Condemned to be Taken Down'. In 1795–6 he published *Willie's Vision* and *The Foppish Taylor*, and about 1815 he published anonymously *Tales in Rhyme and Minor Pieces, in the Scottish Dialect*. His song, 'Noo, Jenny, lass, my bonny bird', has been attributed to Burns. He used the vernacular dexterously, and his poems are valuable illustrations of Scottish life and character. For a time, about 1817, he edited the *Kilmarnock Mirror* for his son. Lochore died at Glasgow on 27 April 1852, leaving unpublished an autobiography and various Scottish tales and poems. T. W. BAYNE, *rev.* JAMES HOW

Sources J. G. Wilson, ed., *The poets and poetry of Scotland*, 2 vols. in 4 (1876–7) • Irving, *Scots.* • private information (1893) • C. Rogers, *The modern Scottish minstrel, or, The songs of Scotland of the past half-century*, 6 vols. (1855–7) • J. Paterson, *Autobiographical reminiscences* (1871) • Boase, *Mod. Eng. biog.*
Archives NL Scot., literary papers

Lock. *See also* Locke.

Lock, (Graham) Anthony Richard [Tony] (1929–1995), cricketer, was born on 5 July 1929 at 36 Granville Road, Limpsfield, Surrey, the son of Frederick Ernest Lock, chauffeur and later painter, and his wife, Martha Elizabeth, *née* Lockyer. He spent his early days watching cricket on the village green, and showed a precocious talent for the game. At fourteen he captained the Limpsfield Church of England school team. In 1944 through the overtures of his headmaster he was introduced by a neighbour, the former Surrey cricketer Sir Henry Leveson Gower, to Surrey. Only a few days after his seventeenth birthday he made his début in first-class cricket. By 1949—after national service in the army—he had established himself in the side, and on 24 September that year he married, in Limpsfield parish church, Audrey May Sage (1928/9–1994), clerk, of Oxted, Surrey, daughter of Alfred Edward Sage, painter. They had two sons and adopted a daughter.

Lock played in 385 matches for Surrey between 1946 and 1963. He and Jim Laker were a crucial bowling partnership in taking the county to seven successive championships in the 1950s. He himself took 100 wickets in a season on fourteen occasions, and secured 216 (for an average of 14.39 runs) in 1955. His outstanding performance came in 1956, when he took all ten Kent wickets in an innings for 54, with a match analysis of sixteen for 83. His success lay in his ability to flight the ball, bringing its spin sharply into the batsman. This was matched by an aggression more associated with fast bowlers. When he employed his own faster ball, however, he was called by umpires for throwing. The problem emerged after he had practised his spin in indoor nets and been forced to lower his arm because of a beam. The problem (and the umpires) continued to haunt him until, in 1959, he saw a film of his action and thereafter confined himself to his slower style.

Lock made the first of forty-nine appearances for England against India in 1952. In 1953 his five for 45 against Australia in their second innings helped England to regain the 'Ashes' after twenty years. He 'never erred in length or direction' (*Wisden*, 1954, 261)—at that time a stronger weapon in his armoury than the vicious spin he developed. Three years later he was a foil to Laker, when the latter took a record nineteen wickets against Australia at Manchester. In that 1956 series the two men bowled over 500 overs between them. Against the West Indies at the Oval in 1957 Lock achieved his best performance in test cricket when he took eleven wickets for 48. New Zealand suffered at his hands both in England in 1958 and in their

(**Graham**) **Anthony Richard** [Tony] **Lock** (**1929–1995**), by J. A. Hampton, 1955

own country in 1959. On tour in India and Pakistan in 1961–2, Lock took thirty-two wickets. His 174 test match wickets were taken at an average cost of 25.58 runs each.

Surprisingly, Lock was not chosen for the MCC tour to Australia in 1962–3. Instead, he went there on his own initiative and began a second 'career' with Western Australia, initially as a player-coach. He played for Western Australia until 1971, although he returned in some English summers to represent (and captain) Leicestershire (1965–7) and to lead them to hitherto uncharted territory—the county championship. On later visits to England he coached at Mill Hill School.

Some critics believed Lock's best years were those with Western Australia, when he led the state to win the Sheffield shield in 1967–8 and became the first Western Australia bowler to take 300 wickets. He also gave himself more opportunities as a batsman. While in Perth he was associated with four district clubs and coached at Wesley College. He was recalled by England in 1968 against the West Indies in the fifth test at Georgetown. His 89—his highest score in test cricket—ensured England won the series and was 'alone worth the cost of transporting him from Australia' (*Wisden*, 1969, 815). It was also his highest score in first-class cricket, in which he made 10,342 runs at an average of 15.88 per innings and took 2844 wickets at an average cost of 19.23 runs. He was, throughout his career, an outstanding catcher, who secured 830 dismissals, a figure unsurpassed except by W. G. Grace and Frank Woolley. This, together with his ability to match his late-order batting to the needs of the moment, made him an exuberant competitor: tall, red-headed (though he thinned early), and dynamic.

The last years of Lock's life were clouded by allegations of child abuse resulting in two court cases (in each of which he was acquitted), the death of his wife, and the onset of cancer. He died in Perth on 30 March 1995 and was survived by his sons and adopted daughter. A memorial service was held in Perth Cathedral. He was, wrote one of his obituarists, 'a volatile, vulnerable man but an astonishingly durable cricketer' (*Wisden*, 1996, 1408).

GERALD M. D. HOWAT

Sources *Wisden* (1947–96) [esp. 1954 and 1996] · *The Times* (31 March 1995) · *The Independent* (31 March 1995) · R. Cashman and others, eds., *The Oxford companion to Australian cricket* (1996) · A. Lock, *For Surrey and England* (1957) · K. Ward, *Put Lock on!* (1972) · b. cert. · m. cert.

Likenesses J. A. Hampton, photograph, 1955, Hult. Arch. [*see illus.*] · photograph, 1980, repro. in *The Independent* · photograph, Surrey County Cricket Club, Kennington Oval, London · photograph, repro. in *The Times* · photographs, repro. in *Wisden* (1952–4)

Lock, Walter (**1846–1933**), theologian, was born at Dorchester, Dorset, on 14 July 1846, the second son of Henry Lock, solicitor, of Dorchester, and his wife, Susannah Ware, daughter of William May, of Bridgwater. He was educated at Marlborough College, whence he gained a scholarship at Corpus Christi College, Oxford. He was awarded a first class in classical moderations (1867) and in *literae humaniores* (1869), and won the Hertford (1867) and Craven (1870) scholarships. In 1871 he was president of the Oxford Union. In 1869 he was elected to a fellowship at Magdalen College, which he held until his marriage on 28 September 1892 to Jane Cecil, eldest daughter of Charles Heathcote Campion, rector of Westmeston, Sussex. They had one son and four daughters. In 1870 Lock was appointed to one of the first tutorships of Keble College, of which he became sub-warden in 1881 and warden in 1897. The religious and theological standpoint of this follower of the original Tractarians is revealed in his essay 'The Church' in *Lux mundi* (1889), *John Keble, a Biography* (1893), and *The Bible and Christian Life* (1905). His breadth of sympathy is best displayed in his very last published work, *Oxford Memories* (1932), a charming collection of short reminiscences, chiefly obituary notes and addresses, of friends and colleagues of every shade of theological opinion. At the end of the century Lock was appointed the first general editor of the Westminster Commentaries on the Revised Version, but his own, sometimes over-cautious, scholarship is most clearly seen in his *Critical and Exegetical Commentary on the Pastoral Epistles* (1924). He was ordained deacon in 1872 and priest in 1873, and in 1895 was appointed Dean Ireland's professor of exegesis of holy scripture. He held the chair until 1919, when his election to the Lady Margaret professorship of divinity (with a canonry at Christ Church) heralded his resignation in 1920 of the wardenship of Keble College. He retired from the Lady Margaret chair in 1927, having been elected to an honorary fellowship at Magdalen in 1897 and at Corpus Christi in 1920, and to honorary membership of the council of Keble College in the last-named year.

Walter Lock (1846–1933), by Philip Brain

Whether as a member of the hebdomadal council, on which he served from 1896 to 1919, or as chairman of the board of faculty of theology, or as a member of the council of St Hugh's Hall (later College), Oxford, Lock showed himself not unsympathetic to new ideas and new causes. He supported the higher education of women and strove successfully for the abolition of the denominational restrictions on admittance to the degrees of BD and DD. Among his contemporaries he possessed a considerable reputation as a preacher, lecturer, and organizer of seminars (in the days when seminars were a novelty). At Keble College, throughout his fifty years of service, his personal popularity, determined tactfulness, and energetic leadership contributed significantly to the shaping of the institution. He died at 13 Rawlinson Road, Oxford, on 12 August 1933.

D. C. Simpson, *rev.* Peter Hinchliff

Sources *The Times* (14 Aug 1933) • *Clock Tower* [Keble College] (Nov 1933) • *Oxford Magazine* (12 Oct 1933) • R. Morgan, ed., *The religion of the Incarnation* (1989), 136–46 • P. Hinchliff, *God and history: aspects of British theology, 1875–1914* (1992), 113–15 • S. C. Carpenter, *Church and people, 1789–1889*, 2nd edn, 3 (1959), 553–5 • C. T. Wainwright, ed., *Keeping the faith* (1989) • General Register Office for England

Likenesses C. W. Furse, oils, 1895, Keble College, Oxford • W. Stoneman, photograph, 1920, NPG • P. Brain, photograph, NPG [*see illus.*]

Wealth at death £4466 19*s.* 6*d.*: probate, 4 Sept 1933, *CGPLA Eng. & Wales*

Lock, William (1732–1810), art connoisseur and patron, is believed to have been the natural son of William Lock (*d.* 1761), MP for Grimsby, from whom he inherited considerable wealth, and Mrs Mary Wood (*d.* 1785) of Cavendish Square, London. The suggestion that he was of the same family as John Locke the philosopher is not proved. On 13 January 1767 he married Frederica Augusta (1750–1832), daughter of Sir Luke *Schaub (1690–1758). In 1749 Lock set out on the grand tour and in Venice met the landscape painter Richard Wilson, with whom he travelled to Rome. He now began to collect art: among his purchases were Claude's *Embarkation of St Ursula* (National Gallery, London), antique statuary including a bronze version of the *Discobulus* (Duncombe Park, Yorkshire), and terracotta models attributed at that time to Michelangelo.

It was, however, as a friend and patron of contemporary artists and men of letters that Lock was most respected. At Norbury Park, near Mickleham, Surrey, which he bought in 1774, the Locks were generous hosts to French émigrés, including Madame de Staël, who lived nearby at Juniper Hall; Fanny Burney, to whom Lock gave land for the building of Camilla Cottage on her marriage to M. d'Arblay, was a friend for life. So too was Thomas Lawrence, whom he introduced to the influential circle of J. J. Angerstein; his daughter Amelia married Angerstein's son John, MP for Camelford, in 1799. Lawrence first painted Lock in 1790 (Museum of Fine Arts, Boston, Massachusetts) and in 1829 he made a masterly portrait of Frederica Lock in old age (Nelson Atkins Museum, Kansas). The dining room of Lock's home, Norbury Park (which still stands), was painted with celebrated landscapes and *trompe-l'œil* effects by George Barret the elder, G. B. Cipriani, and B. Pastorini. Lock's features suggest a refined, almost ascetic character but his cellar was fine and noted for its Etna Tokay which was said to have aphrodisiac qualities. He died at Norbury on 5 October 1810.

His elder son, **William Lock** (1767–1847), artist, was born in 1767. He distinguished himself as an artist of promise in his early years. Educated at the Revd William Gilpin's school at Cheam, he was also a pupil and—like his father—a friend of Henry Fuseli, who dedicated his lectures on painting to him. He is known principally for his mannered drawings in the Fuseli style, but he produced some paintings, and his *Death of Cardinal Wolsey* was engraved in stipple by Charles Knight in 1797. Lock sold Norbury in 1819 and lived afterwards principally in Rome and Paris. He married in 1800 the beautiful Elizabeth Jennings (*c.*1781–1846), daughter of Henry Constantine (Dog) *Jennings (1731–1819), a fellow collector. There was one son, William, and a daughter, who married Joseph Blake, third Baron Wallscourt. William Lock the younger died in 1847.

His son, **William Lock** (1804–1832), army officer, served as a captain in the Life Guards and was remarkable for his personal beauty. Lock eloped with Selina (1812–1892), daughter of Admiral Tollemache; they were married soon after, in Brighton, on 7 December 1829. He published some illustrations to Byron which were lithographed by V. de Villeneuve. He was drowned in Lake Como on 14 September 1832; his daughter, Augusta Selina, married successively Ernest, Lord Burghersh; the duke of Santo Teodoro; and Thomas de Grey, sixth Baron Walsingham.

Kenneth Garlick

Sources V. Caetani, duchess of Sermoneta, *The Locks of Norbury* (1940) • *The journals and letters of Fanny Burney (Madame D'Arblay)*, ed. J. Hemlow and others, 12 vols. (1972–84) • Farington, *Diary* • *GM*, 1st ser., 80 (1810), 393 • *GM*, 1st ser., 102/2 (1832), 390 • E. W. Brayley, J. Britton, and E. W. Brayley, jun., *A topographical history of Surrey*, 5 vols. (1841–8) • J. Ingamells, ed., *A dictionary of British and Irish travellers in Italy, 1701–1800* (1997) • *DNB*

Archives Bodl. Oxf., letters to William Gilpin

Likenesses C. Townley, mezzotint, pubd 1784 (William Lock, 1764–1847; after J. Hoppner), BM • T. Lawrence, oils, 1790, Museum of Fine Arts, Boston, Massachusetts • T. Lawrence, drawing, *c.*1790–1795 (William Lock, 1764–1847), priv. coll. • T. Lawrence, drawing, *c.*1800 (with his daughter, Amelia), priv. coll. • J. Barry, group portrait, oils (*The Society for the Encouragement of Arts*), RSA • T. Lawrence, portrait (William Lock, 1804–1832; as a child) • drawing (William Lock, 1804–1832), priv. coll., Rome • photograph (William Lock, 1804–1832), Vasari, Rome

Lock, William (1767–1847). *See under* Lock, William (1732–1810).

Lock, William (1804–1832). *See under* Lock, William (1732–1810).

Locke [*née* Vaughan; *other married names* Dering, Prowse], **Anne** (*c.*1530–1590x1607), translator and religious activist, was the daughter of the merchant adventurer and government agent, Stephen *Vaughan, and his first wife, Margery Gwynneth or Guinet (*d.* 1544). Vaughan died in 1549, when Anne seems to have been in her late teens, and not long afterwards she married Henry Locke (or Lok), a mercer with interests in Antwerp and her father's neighbour in Cheapside, London. Locke came of a long line of mercers. His great-grandfather was sheriff of London in 1460 and his father, Sir William Locke, who died in 1550, was a friend of Henry VIII and as sheriff had conducted the duke of Somerset to the Tower in 1549. Another of Sir William's thirteen sons was the traveller and translator Michael *Lok, whose second wife was the mother of Sir Julius Caesar, which made Anne Locke Caesar's aunt. The Lockes were an erudite family. Henry wrote Latin in an elegant Italianate hand, and Henry's and Anne's son Henry *Lok was a prolific religious poet, author of *Sundry Christian Passions* (1593). It is clear that Anne Vaughan was herself well educated, like other privileged women of her generation, primarily in languages.

Stephen Vaughan had declared himself to be 'neither Lutheran nor yet Tyndalin' (Mozley, 207), but his second wife was Margery Brinklow, the widow of Henry Brinklow, the London mercer who had written *The Complaynt of Roderyck Mors*. So Anne may well have owed her staunch and advanced protestantism to her stepmother. In the winter of 1552–3 she was one of a group of city wives who shared the company of the Scottish reformer John Knox, who lodged with the Lockes from time to time. It was the start of a remarkable friendship, and one conducted on a basis of spiritual and intellectual parity which was rare for its time. Thirteen letters from Knox to Anne Locke survive, written between 1556 and 1562, and appear to owe their survival to the puritan propagandist John Field. In November 1556 Knox wrote from his exile in Geneva: 'Ye wryt that your desyre is ernist to sie me. Deir Sister, yf I suld expres the thrist and langoure whilk I haif had for your presence, I suld appeir to pass measure' (*Works of John Knox*, 4.237–9). On 9 December he encouraged her to join him in Geneva, describing Calvin's city, famously, as 'the maist perfyt schoole of Chryst that ever was in the erth since the dayis of the Apostillis' (ibid., 239–41). On 8 May 1557 Anne Locke, having left her husband behind in London, arrived in Geneva with two infants, Harrie, the future poet, and Anne; Anne was buried within four days of their arrival. Anne Locke spent some of her time in Geneva translating into English Calvin's sermons on the song of Hezekiah from Isaiah 38. Attached to the sermons was a metrical paraphrase of the fifty-first psalm, Knox's work, which 'was delivered me by my friend' (Locke, *A Meditation*, sig. Ai). The little book was dedicated to Anne's fellow exile Catherine Bertie, dowager duchess of Suffolk. There is no reason to suppose that Henry Locke disapproved of these unusual adventures. The copy of his wife's translation in the British Library bears the inscription: 'Liber Henrici Lock ex dono Annae uxoris suae, 1559' (BL, pressmark 696.a.40).

Back in Cheapside by the summer of 1559, Anne Locke became the main link between Knox (who was *persona non grata* to Queen Elizabeth) and the developing religious revolution in Scotland, and England, and especially with the repatriated remnants of the English congregation in Geneva. Knox's richly informative letters read like drafts for his *History of the Reformation*. He depended on Mrs Locke to loosen the purse strings of wealthy London protestants in order to sustain the faltering cause of the Scottish lords of the congregation, and to send him books. He urged her to have nothing to do with the imperfect religious settlement made in England, and indeed, if he is to be believed, Anne Locke was the very first documented protestant separatist from the Elizabethan church.

With the end of this correspondence, nothing is heard of Anne Locke for ten years. But it may almost be assumed that she was at the heart of the 'womanish brabbles' (Nicholson, 289) which sorely vexed Bishop Grindal of London in the vestiarian crisis of the mid-1560s, the beginnings of the organized puritan movement. In 1571 Henry Locke died after a lingering illness. He bequeathed all his worldly goods to Anne and made her his sole executor. No wonder that the most fiery and popular London preacher of the day, Edward *Dering (*c.*1540–1576), another Knox, should refer to her as 'a good possession'. This was in a letter of proposal, doubtless the earliest letter of its kind from a clergyman to have survived:

> Yf your affection shalbe enclyned as I doo wyshe it to be bent, the Lord's name be praised. Yf you shall better like other where, I pray God blesse you. I wyll endure my losse under thys hope: when we shall have better eies that shalbe able to se God, our faythe shall lead us both into a happye societie. (Kent Archives, MS Dering U 350, C1/2, fols. 28*v*–29*r*)

Dering promised that marriage would not be detrimental to her children's interests. Thanks to the good offices of the wife of Richard Martin, goldsmith and master of the mint, Dering's suit succeeded and they married in 1572. It was to be a short and troubled marriage. With the authorities clamping down on the London puritans, Dering included, he wrote: 'My wife hath beene I thanke God in no trouble … ; if any fall, God hath made her rich in grace and knowledge to give account of her doing' (Dering, sig. A4). But Dering himself was a consumptive, by the summer of 1575 spitting blood, and a year later he was dead.

Anne's third and last marriage was as the second wife of Richard Prowse, an Exeter draper and a substantial figure in west country affairs, mayor of Exeter three times and MP for the city in 1584. They had at least two sons. Nothing is known of the circumstances which introduced her to Prowse, and took her to Exeter. In 1583 John Knox's closest male friend, Christopher Goodman, turned up in Exeter and preached a controversial sermon in the cathedral. It is hard to believe that he was not drawn there by Knox's closest female friend. In 1590 Anne Prowse for the second time ventured into translation, rendering into English as *Of the Markes of the Children of God, and of their Comfort in Afflictions* a book by a Walloon author, Jean Taffin, originally intended for the solace of the oppressed protestants of the Netherlands. There were seven further editions. Mrs Prowse's preface, addressed to the countess of Warwick, explains:

> Everie one in his calling is bound to doo somewhat to the furtherance of the holie building, but because great things by reason of my sex I may not doo, and that which I may I ought to doo, I have according to my duetie brought my poore basket of stones to the strengthning of the walles of that Jerusalem whereof (by grace) wee are all both citizens and members. (Taffin, sigs. A2–5*v*)

She looked back on the 'halcyon daies' of gospel liberty under Elizabeth and seemed apprehensive about the future. After this Anne Prowse disappears from history, and since she evidently predeceased her husband, who died in 1607, she left no will, and the date of her death is not known. PATRICK COLLINSON

Sources P. Collinson, 'The role of women in the English Reformation illustrated by the life and friendships of Anne Locke', *Godly people: essays on English protestantism and puritanism* (1983) · P. Collinson, 'John Knox, the Church of England and the women of England', *John Knox and the British reformations*, ed. R. A. Mason (1998) · W. C. Richardson, *Stephen Vaughan, financial agent of Henry VIII: a study of financial relations with the Low Countries* [1953] · *The works of John Knox*, ed. D. Laing, 6 vols., Bannatyne Club, 112 (1846–64), vols. 3–4, 6 · P. Collinson, *A mirror of Elizabethan puritanism: the life and letters of godly Master Dering* (1964); repr. in P. Collinson, *Godly people: essays on English protestantism and puritanism* (1983), 288–324 · [J. Calvin], *Foure sermons of Iohn Caluin, vpon the song that King Ezechias made after hee had been sicke*, trans. A. L. [A. Locke] (1574) [this vol. also contains A. Locke, *A meditation*, first pubd in 1560] · J. Taffin, *Of the markes of the children of God, and of their comforts in afflictions*, trans. A. Prowse (1590) [and 1591; 1597; 1599; 1608; 1609; 1615; 1634] · CKS, MS Dering U 350 C/1, 2, fols. 28*v*–29*r* · A. Peel, 'A sermon of Christopher Goodman's in 1583', *Journal of the Presbyterian Historical Society of England*, 9 (1949) · J. F. Mozley, *William Tyndale* (1937) · W. Nicholson, ed., *The remains of Edmund Grindal*, Parker Society, 9 (1843) · E. Dering, *Workes* (1597) · HoP, *Commons*, 1558–1603, 3.256

Locke, John (1632–1704), philosopher, was born on 29 August 1632 at Wrington, Somerset, the elder of the two children of John Locke (1606–1661), attorney, and his wife, Agnes (1597–1654), daughter of Edmund Keene of Wrington.

John Locke (1632–1704), by Sylvester Brounower, *c.*1685

Early life and education, 1632–1652 Locke was born into a family of very minor—indeed marginal—gentry. His father was the eldest son of Nicholas Locke (1574–1648), a clothier who had prospered in his trade and invested his profits in land, mostly in the vicinity of Pensford, a village some 10 miles east of Locke's birthplace and 7 miles south of Bristol. It was here that Locke appears to have spent his childhood with his brother, Thomas, born on 9 August 1637. His father had not entered the cloth trade, but had become an attorney, and served as clerk to the justices of the peace for the county. He also acted as a steward for a much richer and more powerful family of local gentry, the Pophams, from whom he leased part of his land.

Locke's family had puritan sympathies, and after the outbreak of the civil war his father served as a captain in one of the parliamentary armies. The commander of his regiment was Alexander Popham, MP for Bath, who was able to reward his steward by recommending his son for a place at Westminster School. Locke entered Westminster in 1647, and was made a king's scholar in 1650; his fellow pupils included John Dryden, Robert Hooke, and Christopher Wren. The curriculum was centred almost entirely on the ancient languages, including Hebrew for the most academically proficient pupils. Locke seems not to have greatly enjoyed his schooldays. Though his father had disciplined him quite severely as a child, he had relaxed as his son grew older, and it is likely that Locke resented the flogging that was so frequent at Westminster. Forty years after leaving he alarmed the young son of Edward Clarke with accounts of what happened there, and recommended to Clarke that if his son continued to be difficult he might be sent 'to Westminster or some other very severe schoole' (*Correspondence*, 4.397) until he was more pliant and willing to learn from his tutor at home.

Christ Church, Oxford, 1652–1667 In May 1652 Locke was elected to a studentship at Christ Church, Oxford, the last in a list of six. It was a position tenable for life and was broadly equivalent to a fellowship in one of the other colleges, though it gave no part in the government of Christ Church, which was the preserve of the dean and the canons. The records at Christ Church do not indicate when he came into residence, but he matriculated on 27 November. The dean of Christ Church was John Owen; Locke's tutor was Thomas Cole, subsequently a nonconformist divine.

During the civil war Oxford had been the king's headquarters, and after its surrender the university was purged of its more open and intransigent royalists. The academic curriculum remained almost entirely unaffected by all this turmoil. Locke acquired an intense and enduring dislike of the scholastic method of disputation, and of the logical and metaphysical subtleties that went with it. He took care to fulfil the unexacting requirements for his degrees (BA, 14 February 1656; MA, 29 June 1658), but otherwise seems to have spent a good part of his time reading lighter literature—plays, romances, and letters, much of it translated from French. While still an undergraduate he contributed two poems to a volume of university poetry, *Musarum Oxoniensium Elaiophoria* (1654), his first publication.

It is unclear whether at this stage of his life Locke had any definite intention about what career to pursue. He was admitted to Gray's Inn in December 1656, but nothing seems to have come of this. Another possibility was medicine. Several of Locke's notebooks show that in the late 1650s he started taking extensive notes from a large number of medical works; the quantity and character of this material indicates something more than casual interest. He may not have decided firmly on a medical career, but he was almost certainly investigating it as an option.

The study of medicine led by an easy transition to natural philosophy. Exactly when Locke first became acquainted with the ideas of the new mechanical philosophy is not easily determined. There seems to be no evidence that he had any links with the group of innovators associated with John Wilkins at Wadham College, the nucleus of the future Royal Society, and if he had read anything by Descartes during his first years at Oxford there is no trace of it among his papers. By May 1660 he had made the acquaintance of Robert Boyle, who probably introduced him to these new ideas. Locke augmented his continuing medical studies with a thorough course of reading in mechanical philosophy, starting with Boyle's recently published *New Essays Physico-Mechanical Touching the Spring of the Air* (1660). He also read widely among Descartes's works, concentrating in particular on the physical material in the later parts of the *Principia philosophiae*, and read at least some of Gassendi's *Syntagma philosophicum*.

Locke's attention was, however, by no means held solely by medicine and natural philosophy. The rather precarious political stability achieved by Cromwell was rapidly eroded after his death in September 1658. Locke's letters to his father (*Correspondence*, 1.82–3, 136–7) express a profound disenchantment with visionary politics and a strong desire for peace and security. He welcomed the return of Charles II, and contributed a poem of fulsome flattery in another university collection, *Britannia rediviva* (1660). Unlike several of his fellow students at Christ Church, he survived—apparently without difficulty—the post-Restoration visitation of the university. In December 1660 Locke's father fell ill, and though his son returned quickly to Somerset and discussed the case with several local doctors, nothing could be done; he died on 13 February, leaving the residue of his much depleted estate to Locke and his brother. His mother had died some years earlier, on 4 October 1654; her son retained a memory of her as 'a very pious woman and affectionate mother' (Fox Bourne, 1.13).

In the last months of 1660 Locke wrote a short treatise in the form of a scholastic disputation entitled *Whether the civil magistrate can lawfully determine the use of indifferent things in reference to religious worship*. It was directed against a colleague of Christ Church, Edward Bagshaw, who had recently published a work denying the magistrate's power. Bagshaw's position was that God had left indifferent things—those neither commanded nor prohibited by divine law—to the conscience of the individual believer. Locke replied that it was because they were indifferent that they lay within the scope of the magistrate's authority. After 1667 he was to adopt a position much closer to Bagshaw's; in 1660 he seems to have been motivated above all by fear of the disorder that he was sure would result from failure to impose uniformity.

Locke added a preface in the late spring of 1661 and secured a publisher, but in the end nothing appeared; much had happened in the six months or so since the work had been started, and it was clear that the new parliament intended to restore traditional prayer book worship with only minimal changes, and to enforce compliance with it.

The tract against Bagshaw was followed in 1661–2 by two further tracts, each written in Latin and set out in disputation form. The first of these discussed and rejected the Roman Catholic position that it is necessary that the scriptures should have an infallible interpreter; the second was a more general and abstract defence of the thesis already argued against Bagshaw. These writings remained unpublished until the twentieth century; all that appeared was a contribution to another official volume of poetry, *Domiduca Oxoniensis* (1662), compiled to celebrate the arrival in England of Charles II's bride, Catherine of Braganza.

At this stage in his career Locke seems to have been well regarded by the governing body of Christ Church, and in particular by the dean, John Fell. In October 1663 Fell and two of the canons signed a certificate testifying to Locke's orthodox beliefs and moral probity. Such a testimonial was required by a candidate seeking ordination, and it appears that in the autumn of 1663 Locke was seriously considering this; he was dissuaded by his friend John Strachey, who could not see Locke as a country parson, and urged him to have confidence in his ability to make his own way in the world.

One manifestation of this official favour can be observed in Locke's appointment to a succession of teaching posts at Christ Church: praelector in Greek (1661–2), praelector in rhetoric (1663), and censor of moral philosophy (1664). Many of the duties of this last post were disciplinary, but its holder was also required to preside over scholastic disputations. One standard subject for discussion was the theory of natural law; a set of eight disputations by Locke himself survives and has been published under the title *Essays on the Law of Nature*. These disputations provide the fullest account of a topic which is central to Locke's thought, but which he never again discussed in detail. The *Essays* argue that natural law exists and is of universal and perpetual obligation, but it is neither inscribed in our hearts by God nor discoverable from human consent or tradition. Our knowledge of it is founded ultimately on the experience of our senses, which provide us with the evidence required to establish the existence of a wise and benevolent creator from the order manifest in the world.

In the spring of 1661 Locke was made a tutor at Christ Church, and for the next six years was responsible for the welfare and education of a succession of pupils, of whom twenty-two can be identified. He took charge of their money, supervised their purchases, and helped impart to them the same kind of education that he had himself received a decade earlier. Locke's pupils form an unremarkable group. With the possible exception of Sir Charles Berkeley, none rose to any great eminence in either church or state, or in the world of learning. John Alford and Sir Charles Berkeley became MPs but neither achieved much of note at Westminster. Edward Pococke continued his father's work as an orientalist, Morgan Godwyn has a place in the history of the anti-slavery movement, and Corbet Owen achieved a minor and unenduring fame as a Latin poet. The only one of his former pupils with whom Locke remained on close terms was George Walls, who looked after Locke's affairs at Christ Church in his absence, and later accompanied him on his travels in France.

Throughout this time Locke continued reading widely in medicine and natural philosophy. He took detailed notes at Thomas Willis's lectures on medicine, given at Christ Church in 1661–2, and in 1663 attended a class in chemistry given by the German chemist Peter Stahl. It was here that he attracted the attention of that acerbic chronicler of Oxford life Anthony Wood, who described him as 'a man of turbulent spirit, clamorous and never contented … while every man besides, of the club, was writing, he would be prating and troblesome' (*Life and Times*, 1.472). It is a vivid picture but one that may be coloured by later political estrangement.

In the winter of 1663–4 Locke's brother Thomas died. They seem not to have been very close (no letters between them survive), and Locke did not return to Somerset until the end of March; he paid his brother's widow £220 for the portion of the family land which Thomas had inherited. Locke himself remained single. Throughout his life he enjoyed feminine company, and during the early 1660s engaged in sentimental correspondence with several young women in Oxford, but none of his friendships seems to have come close to a proposal of marriage. A passage in the *Essay Concerning Human Understanding* (bk 2, chap. 21, section 34) reveals Locke's later opinion of the married state: '*It is better to marry than to burn*, says St. *Paul*; where we may see, what it is, that chiefly drives Men into the enjoyments of a conjugal life'. Locke seems to have been able to resist sensual temptations: perhaps the only reference to any sexual activity on his part occurs in an early but undated letter sent by a friend, Francis Atkins, to which Atkins added a postscript: 'My service to thy bedfellow, for so I think shee is at this time' (*Correspondence*, 1.40), and even this may be no more than conjecture. Locke himself gave nothing away.

After Locke had finished his term as censor of moral philosophy he occupied no further university offices, and though he remained a tutor he took no new pupils. He had steadily been rising in seniority through the ranks of students at Christ Church: from the start of 1665 he was among the twenty most senior, and as such would normally have been required to take orders; that he was able to retain his studentship without doing so suggests the continued favour of the dean, but his position remained precarious.

Towards the end of 1665 a new opportunity presented itself. Sir Walter Vane was being sent to Cleves on an embassy to the elector of Brandenburg, and Locke was offered the post of secretary. The mission left England in November and returned three months later. As a venture in diplomacy it proved unsuccessful, but it is clear from Locke's letters that he greatly enjoyed his first journey abroad. The experience of living in a community in which the members of different churches lived together without provoking disorder may also have helped change his mind about the practicability of religious toleration.

Once back in Oxford, Locke resumed his studies in chemistry and medicine. He was particularly interested in the physiology of respiration, and had for some years been closely following the work being done by Boyle, Hooke, and others. It was probably about this time that he drafted a short work on the purpose of respiration; this was written in the form of a scholastic disputation and may have been produced as part of a plan to become a bachelor of medicine. In the event it remained unused, and Locke did not obtain the degree until nearly ten years later.

In the summer of 1666 a chance meeting altered the entire course of Locke's life. Anthony Ashley Cooper, then Lord Ashley and subsequently earl of Shaftesbury, had been chancellor of the exchequer since 1661. He had come to Oxford to visit his son, an undergraduate at Trinity College. Ashley was not in good health; his physician in

Oxford was David Thomas, a fellow of New College who was Locke's chief collaborator in his chemical experiments, and it was through Thomas that they first met. Each was favourably impressed by the other, and by the time Ashley left Oxford the beginnings of an enduring friendship had been established. In the autumn Locke paid a visit to London, and with Ashley's help procured a royal dispensation permitting him to retain his studentship at Christ Church without taking orders. With his position in Oxford now at least temporarily secured, Locke was able to consider a new career. At the beginning of April 1667 he packed up his belongings and left Oxford. After a trip back to Somerset to see old friends and collect his rents he travelled to London, arriving early in May. He was given accommodation in Exeter House in the Strand, Ashley's London residence; he stayed there for the next eight years.

Exeter House, 1667–1675 Locke's earliest responsibilities as a member of Ashley's household are not known with certainty. According to the third earl of Shaftesbury, Locke acted as tutor to his father, the future second earl, who had now left Oxford (Fox Bourne, 1.203). Nothing in the young Anthony Ashley Cooper's later career suggests that he would have been a particularly rewarding pupil, and though responsibility for him would have added to Locke's educational experience, it would also have left him ample free time. Locke was closely involved in the negotiations that preceded the young man's marriage in September 1669 to Lady Dorothea Manners, daughter of the earl of Rutland. Their eldest child, the future third earl, was born in February 1671; his grandfather took control of his upbringing, and Locke was later given the task of overseeing his schooling.

Locke's activities in London remained as varied as in Oxford. He continued to read extensively in medicine, but could now supplement what had hitherto been an almost exclusively theoretical education with clinical experience. Soon after arriving at Exeter House he got to know the physician Thomas Sydenham, the author of a new and controversial account of treating infectious diseases, *Methodus curandi febres* (1666). Locke accompanied Sydenham on his rounds and kept records of his methods of treatment. Soon the two men were collaborating closely. Among the Shaftesbury papers there are two short medical essays in Locke's hand, *Anatomia* (1668) and *De arte medica* (1669); though sometimes attributed to Sydenham, they are more likely to have been written by Locke. Both works expressed a profound scepticism about our capacity to discover the nature of disease, and advocated a purely empirical approach to medical practice. Locke paid Sydenham public tribute in a Latin poem included in the second edition of *Methodus curandi febres* (1668). Years later Sydenham repaid the compliment in the preface to his *Observationes medicae* (1676) by praising Locke's acute intellect, steady judgement, and simple manners.

Locke's increasing medical knowledge was put to good use in summer 1668. Ashley's generally poor health had been growing worse, and on 12 June he underwent a novel and extremely risky operation to drain an abscess on his liver. After a period of convalescence he made a good recovery. The medical papers relating to the operation (PRO 30/24/47/2) suggest that Locke's role was primarily that of a co-ordinator and supervisor of nursing care, but the original idea for the operation may have been his, and according to Locke himself, Ashley believed that Locke had saved his life (*Correspondence*, 2.662).

Locke also continued to pursue his scientific interests. In November 1668 he was elected a fellow of the Royal Society, but though he was quickly appointed to a committee for experiments and twice served on the council (1669–70, 1672–3), he seems to have attended few meetings and to have contributed little to the work of the society. His one communication to the *Philosophical Transactions* during these years (24 May 1675) was a letter on poisonous fish sent to him by a correspondent in the Bahamas.

Just as Locke's hitherto largely theoretical approach to medicine had been broadened by his association with Sydenham, so his rather academic interest in politics was modified by the experience of living in the household of one of England's most remarkable politicians. Within a year of coming to London he had written *Essay Concerning Toleration*, in which he rejected the position he had taken in 1660 and advocated the toleration of all purely speculative opinions, giving the magistrate the right to intervene only when civil order was at risk. The work was not published until 1876, but it survives in four manuscript copies and was presumably circulated among Ashley and his associates. Locke also developed an interest, hitherto absent, in economic questions. The outcome was a treatise, *Some of the Consequences that are Like to Follow upon Lessening of Interest to 4 per cent*, begun in 1668 and further added to in 1674. Nothing was published at the time, but Locke kept the manuscript and made use of it later.

In 1669 Ashley involved Locke in the affairs of the recently founded colony of Carolina. In August of that year the first group of settlers left England, taking with them an elaborate set of laws, the 'fundamental constitutions of Carolina'. It is unlikely that Locke was the sole author of this but there is evidence that he had a hand in the original drafting, and he was certainly involved in suggesting alterations and improvements. Locke continued to serve the lords proprietors of the colony in a secretarial capacity until 1675, taking minutes at their meetings and handling much of the correspondence with the newly arrived colonists. He also had a financial interest in other colonial ventures, including the Bahamas Company and the Royal African Company.

When he went to London, Locke's annual income was usually about £100, two-thirds of which came from his land and the remainder from Christ Church. Since the autumn of 1668 Ashley had been augmenting this with a half-yearly payment of £40. Two years later an opportunity arose to shift the burden to the public revenue. Locke was appointed a registrar to the commissioners of the excise at an annual salary of £175; £60 of this went to pay a clerk, who presumably performed most of the duties required. Locke lost this useful source of income in the spring of 1675, but he was able to use the wealth he had accumulated to purchase an annuity from Shaftesbury, which yielded £100 a year. For an outlay of £700 this was a bargain, though it was to cause some friction with Shaftesbury's family after his death.

Locke saw less of Sydenham after 1670, and for the next few years spent rather less of his time reading works on medicine. He was engaged in a new set of enquiries. The origins of the *Essay Concerning Human Understanding* are described with tantalizing brevity in the epistle to the reader with which the work begins. There Locke recalls how, at an unspecified but clearly distant time in the past, he and a group of five or six friends had met in his chamber to discuss some other quite remote topic, and had rapidly found themselves entangled in a mass of wholly unanticipated perplexities. It then occurred to Locke himself that they should turn their attention to the capabilities of the human understanding; he therefore set down 'some hasty and undigested thoughts on a subject I had never before considered', which he took along to the next meeting.

Two surviving works allow these events to be dated. Locke was busy with the first of these, 'Intellectus humanus cum cognitionis certitudine et assensus firmitate', in the summer of 1671. Despite its title, the work (now generally known as draft A) is in English, and its first few pages may well be derived from the hasty and undigested thoughts taken to the meeting in his chamber. A longer and considerably more polished work, 'An essay concerning the understanding, knowledge, opinion and assent' (draft B), was begun later in the same year. Both works remained unfinished, and both left unsolved the main problems that had led to their being started. Locke seems not to have resumed systematic work on philosophy until 1676, when he was in France.

Between 1672 and 1675 much of Locke's time was spent on administrative activity of various kinds. In March 1672 Ashley was created earl of Shaftesbury, and in November was appointed lord chancellor. A considerable quantity of ecclesiastical patronage came with the office, and the work this entailed was entrusted to the secretary for presentations. Locke held this post until Shaftesbury was dismissed in November 1673. Perhaps in anticipation of this, Locke had in the previous month been made secretary to the council for trade and plantations; in December he became treasurer as well. These posts were far from sinecures, and the work they entailed added to Locke's already considerable knowledge of colonial matters. He held them until the council itself was dissolved in December 1674; the combined salary of £600 per annum was never paid.

At the beginning of 1675 Locke's position had become worryingly insecure: he had lost or was about to lose all his government employment, and his patron was out of office and out of favour. His studentship at Christ Church was irregularly held and its retention depended on a royal dispensation revocable at any time. In February Locke returned to Oxford—it seems to have been only his second visit in nearly eight years—and took the degree of bachelor of medicine; later in the year he managed to secure one of the two medical studentships that the college offered, thereby relieving himself of any obligation to take holy orders. For the time being at least his position at Christ Church was safe.

On 14 November Locke crossed to France for a visit that in the end lasted nearly three and a half years; he was accompanied by George Walls, his former pupil. Locke's ostensible motive for travelling was his health—he was already suffering from an ailment of the lungs, probably asthma and chronic bronchitis, that was to trouble him for the rest of his life—but he may have had another reason as well. At the beginning of the month an anonymous pamphlet attacking in vehement terms the policy of the king's chief minister, the earl of Danby, had appeared on sale in London. The authorship of *A Letter from a Person of quality to his Friend in the Country* has never been definitely established, but it undoubtedly came from Shaftesbury's circle, and probably from his household. In 1720 it was attributed to Locke by Pierre des Maizeaux, perhaps on the basis of information from the third earl; Locke probably had a hand in its composition, though it would not always have expressed his own opinions.

France, 1675–1679 On arriving in France, Locke began to keep a journal, a practice he continued until the end of his life. In later years the number of entries grew smaller, especially after 1689, but the well-filled volumes covering the years in France make it possible, for the first time in Locke's life, to construct an almost day-by-day account of his movements and activities. Locke's journal is not an intimate document comparable with Pepys's diary, but it does reveal many aspects of his character: a love of travellers' tales, a concern with recording minute items of factual information, and a very careful attitude towards money.

Locke travelled from Calais via Paris and Lyon, and on 4 January 1676 arrived at Montpellier, where he stayed for over a year. He quickly engaged a tutor to teach him French for one hour a day and began reading books in that language. Locke had been to France before—in the autumn of 1672 he had spent a few weeks in Paris—but though he may have acquired some ability to communicate in French, he could not yet read the language with any ease; there are no citations made before 1676 from any French books among his papers. Philosophy in France was increasingly being written in the vernacular, and by learning French, Locke gained access to philosophical debates from which he had previously been excluded. His journal shows that he was thinking hard about philosophy and about how his own views differed from those of the Cartesians.

Two fellow countrymen whom Locke met in Montpellier were Thomas Herbert, later earl of Pembroke, the future dedicatee of the *Essay Concerning Human Understanding*, and Denis Grenville, archdeacon of Durham. Grenville was a weak and unhappy man who had come to France to escape his bishop, his creditors, and his manic-depressive wife; he attached himself to Locke, who treated him with considerable forbearance and sent him letters filled with sensible advice on recreation and devotion.

Early in 1677 Locke agreed to act as tutor to Caleb, the son of Sir John Banks, a prosperous London merchant. In March he left Montpellier and travelled in a leisurely manner to Paris by way of Toulouse and Bordeaux, arriving there at the beginning of June. Initially his duties were expected to last for only a few months, but in the event he and Caleb remained in Paris until their return to England in 1679, apart from a journey together through provincial France in late summer and autumn 1678; a plan to visit Italy was reluctantly abandoned.

In France two rival versions of the new mechanical philosophy had attracted supporters. Locke seems to have been far more interested in the thought of Descartes and of later Cartesians such as Malebranche than he was in Gassendi, though in Paris he became acquainted with two of Gassendi's followers, François Bernier and Gilles de Launay, both of whom presented him with copies of their own works. He also continued working on his philosophical enquiries. One of the manuscripts that he left behind in Paris in July 1678 was a folio volume described as 'Essay de Intellectu', which cannot be either draft A or draft B. Given Locke's known techniques of composition, it is virtually certain that quite substantial sections of the published *Essay* were written while he was in France, though it can only be conjectured what they are.

Two lesser works that Locke did complete while in France were both intended for private circulation within the Shaftesbury family. In the autumn of 1676 he translated three of the essays in Pierre Nicole's *Essais de morale*; a manuscript containing these was presented to the countess after he returned to England. Locke also used the knowledge acquired during his travels to write *Observations upon the Growth and Culture of Vines and Olives*; this was dedicated to Shaftesbury himself, who had thoughts of resettling French protestant refugees in Carolina.

Other friends Locke made in France included the biblical scholar and antiquarian Nicolas Toinard and the librarian and savant Henri Justel, later a refugee in England. Many of his associates were protestants, and Locke recorded in his journal evidence of the restrictions imposed on the protestant communities by the increasingly intolerant government of Louis XIV. This experience cannot have lessened his aversion to absolute monarchy and to its supporters in England.

Return to England, 1679–1683 Locke arrived back in England at the end of April 1679. Exeter House had been vacated and then demolished while he was away, and Shaftesbury had taken a lease of Thanet House in Aldersgate Street, immediately to the north of the City. Locke lived there for about half of the next four years, but he seems not to have been as closely involved with Shaftesbury's affairs as before; he spent a good part of his time either in Oxford or at the house of his friend James Tyrrell at Oakley, Buckinghamshire. At Christ Church his association with Shaftesbury had made him an object of suspicion to the college authorities: his movements were watched and attempts were made to entrap him in conversation, but nothing was discovered. As Fell later reported, Locke 'could never be provoked to take any notice, or discover in word or look the least concern; so that I believe there is not in the world such a master of taciturnity and passion' (Fox Bourne, 1.484).

The England to which Locke returned was in a state of acute political crisis. The revelations of the Popish Plot had burst upon an already discontented nation in August 1678. The plot itself was a fabrication, but few of Locke's contemporaries were prepared entirely to discount the elaborate mendacities fabricated by Titus Oates and his associates. Locke's own views remain opaque; if he harboured any doubts, he seems to have kept them to himself. For the next four years, until his flight to the Netherlands as a refugee, Locke was to be concerned primarily, though never exclusively, with politics.

Shaftesbury's grand design was to divert the succession away from the duke of York by forcing an Exclusion Bill through parliament and then coercing the king into giving it his assent. Charles saw this as an assault on the monarchy, and was determined to resist with every means in his power. The turning point came in March 1681. Parliament had been summoned to Oxford—Locke was roused from his sickbed to arrange accommodation for Shaftesbury and his associates—but was dissolved within a week. As it became apparent that Charles had no plans to summon another parliament, the opposition split: some became inactive, or even changed sides; others, including Shaftesbury, began to think with increasing seriousness about the possibility of raising an insurrection.

Charles rightly saw Shaftesbury as his most dangerous opponent, and was determined to crush him. On 2 July 1681 Shaftesbury was arrested and sent to the Tower, charged with treason. Shaftesbury could not be tried until he had been indicted by a grand jury, drawn from panels nominated by the sheriffs of the county in which the alleged offence had been committed. In London the sheriffs were Shaftesbury's close associates, who could be relied on to select like-minded jurors; the most worrying danger to Shaftesbury was that the judges would find a way to remove these jurors and replace them by others who would bring in a different verdict. Shaftesbury's associates did everything they could to assist his defence: Locke's contribution was to write a short tract on the power of judges to alter the composition of grand juries, which survives among the Shaftesbury papers. Shaftesbury remained in prison until 24 November, when a whig-nominated grand jury failed to find sufficient evidence for a prosecution to proceed. His release was greeted with wild celebration, but his position was far from secure. In June 1682 the government secured the return of two tories as sheriffs for London, and Shaftesbury knew that once they took office he would no longer be safe. At the end of September he went into hiding; two months later, after a planned insurrection had been aborted, he fled to Amsterdam, where he died in January 1683. His body was brought back to England and buried at Wimborne St Giles; Locke was among the mourners, and composed an elegant Latin epitaph.

Shaftesbury's death denied the whigs their most determined leader, but not all his associates were disheartened. One group formed a plot to assassinate Charles and James on their way back from the races at Newmarket, at the Rye House near Hertford. No attempt was ever made, and early in June the plot was betrayed to the government; the arrests began on 21 June.

It is very unlikely that Locke was involved with the assassination plot. None of the conspirators ever named him, and his movements in the weeks after the arrests started were not those of someone attempting to hide. He was, however, a known adherent of Shaftesbury, and even if he was not himself involved in the plot, he was undeniably acquainted with people who were, such as the barrister Richard West; he had therefore some reason for believing himself to be at risk. Locke spent much of July and the first half of August in the west country, visiting friends, putting his affairs in order, and arranging for money to be sent abroad. It is not known how and when he left England, but on 7 September he was in Rotterdam.

Among the papers that Locke left behind in England were two closely related works on politics. One was an extended attack on the politics of Sir Robert Filmer. Filmer had died in 1653, but his main work, *Patriarcha*, was not published until 1680. It set out the patriarchal theory of politics in its most extreme and most vulnerable form. For Filmer we are not born free, but in a state of subjection to our parents and to the rulers whom God has set over us. Paternal and political power are ultimately the same: both descend from Adam, who had by right of fatherhood royal authority over his children, and this authority passed to his successors. Locke set out to demolish this theory not merely by severing the chain of argument at its weakest link, but by destroying every part that appeared vulnerable. He argued that Adam never possessed the kind of power that Filmer supposed, and that even if he had done, it could not have been conveyed to his posterity in any manner that could justify the titles of any of the monarchs now ruling. Filmer's theory required that Adam's power descended either by a form of primogeniture, so that at any time there was a single heir who was rightful monarch of the whole world, or to all his descendants—that is, to everyone.

The other work that Locke had written was a more general treatment of the origin, extent, and end of civil government, and formed the positive counterpart to the attack on patriarchalism: Locke saw that in order to change the way that people thought about politics, it was necessary not merely to demolish Filmer's theory but also to provide a credible alternative. Like Hobbes, Locke regarded the state as a human construction, established by an original contract, but while Hobbes saw the sovereign as possessing unlimited authority, Locke did not. Private property can be acquired in the state of nature, and property rights are not extinguished by the transition to civil society. When entering into society men agree to give up some of the powers which they had exercised in the state of nature, such as the power to punish breaches of the law of nature, but their doing this is not irrevocable. If a government attempts to exceed its powers, it breaks its trust, the government is dissolved, and its former subjects are at liberty to set up another in its place.

For Locke it was absolutely essential to distinguish political from paternal power, and both from the despotic power exercised by a master over his slaves. Absolute monarchy, though claimed by its defenders as the only legitimate form of government, is inconsistent with civil society, and so no form of civil government at all. Any ruler who attempts to exercise an arbitrary power over the people 'is to be esteemed the common Enemy and Pest of mankind; and is to be treated accordingly' (*Two Treatises of Government*, 2.230). Locke was careful to insist that he was not advocating rebellion—the true rebels were those who invaded the properties and liberties of the people, not those who defended them—but it was unmistakably a defence of a right of resistance. These were not views that could have been published openly in England during the last years of Charles II's reign, and Locke had very good reasons for keeping the existence of the treatise in which they were advocated as secret as possible.

The dates of these two works have been the subject of some controversy. The attack on Filmer cannot have been started before *Patriarcha* was published in the winter of 1679–80, and most of it was probably written soon afterwards. The second work was probably composed over a rather longer period, perhaps mostly in 1681–2, though any detailed account of its composition is necessarily speculative. Both works remained unpublished until 1689, when they appeared together as *Two Treatises on Government*.

Another polemical work dating from this period has remained unpublished. In 1680 the dean of St Paul's, Edward Stillingfleet, published a sermon directed against protestant nonconformists entitled *The Mischief of Separation*; the next year he followed this with a longer treatise, *The Unreasonableness of Separation*. Among Locke's papers (MS Locke c. 34) there survives an extended reply to both these works, partly in Locke's hand, partly in that of his manservant Sylvester Brounower, but mostly in the hand of James Tyrrell. It has generally been assumed that this work was a joint venture by Locke and Tyrrell, but recent analyses suggest that Locke was the sole author and Tyrrell was merely serving as his amanuensis while Locke was unwell.

Though he deplored the persecution of the nonconformists, Locke was never one himself. His closest sympathies seem to have been with the latitudinarian Anglicans, such as Benjamin Whichcote and John Tillotson. In his later years he is known to have taken the sacrament in order to qualify for office under the Test Act and to have at least occasionally attended the parish church at High Laver, but during the middle period of his life his attendance at any form of public worship is difficult to document, and may not have been at all frequent.

Exile in the Netherlands, 1683–1689 Once in the Netherlands, Locke travelled immediately to Amsterdam, where he remained for nearly a year. The winter of 1683–4 was exceptionally cold, and Locke spent much of his time indoors reading medicine. One victim of the cold was a lioness from the zoo; Locke attended the autopsy, and met Philippus van Limborch, professor of theology at the remonstrant seminary in Amsterdam. Limborch's religious outlook was very close to Locke's own, and like Locke he detested persecution and the cruelties that accompany it. In August and September 1684 Locke spent six weeks travelling through the more remote provinces of the Netherlands, visiting Franeker, Groningen, Deventer, and Nijmegen. Between September 1684 and May 1685 he moved frequently between Amsterdam, Leiden, and Utrecht.

Locke quickly made contact with several of the other English political exiles living in the Netherlands, and this was reported back to the English government. He was suspected of writing libellous pamphlets, and in November 1684 was expelled from his studentship at Christ Church. It is not certain that he contributed financially to the duke of Monmouth's ill-fated expedition, but he undoubtedly knew—and indeed lodged with—Thomas Dare, who was its paymaster. In the following May, a fortnight before the expedition sailed, his name was included in a list of exiles sent to the states general of the United Provinces with a request that they should be arrested. Locke went underground, and remained in hiding under a variety of aliases until May 1686. For most of this time he was in Amsterdam, but he spent part of the autumn across the border in Cleves, a town he knew well from his visit twenty years before; his presence there was reported back to London, but nothing could be done.

Since coming to the Netherlands, Locke had resumed work on the *Essay Concerning Human Understanding*, and as it took shape he sent copies to his friends in England. In April 1686 he sent an unspecified portion, probably containing books 1 and 2; book 3 followed in August, and book 4 in December. By the end of 1686 the *Essay* existed in a form fairly close to what was published in 1690.

In winter 1685–6 Locke interrupted his labours on the *Essay* to write another, shorter work. Louis XIV had revoked the edict of Nantes in October, removing the last remnants of toleration for the French protestants. The *Epistola de tolerantia* was written after Locke returned from Cleves about the beginning of November. It was addressed to Limborch, who kept the manuscript and subsequently arranged for it to be printed. The Latin text was published anonymously at Gouda in April 1689, two months after Locke had returned to England. The *Epistola* develops further the theory of toleration already put forward in the *Essay Concerning Toleration* of 1667. Locke advocated the complete separation of church and state: states exist only to preserve their members' civil goods; churches are purely voluntary societies which are allowed to exercise discipline over their members, but which anyone can leave at any time without incurring any civil disabilities. Complete toleration should be given to every religious body whose doctrines are neither incompatible with civil society nor require their adherents to give allegiance to a foreign prince.

Locke's last two years in the Netherlands were less eventful. In February 1687 he moved to Rotterdam to stay with Benjamin Furly, an English merchant of broadly Quaker beliefs who had been living there since the Restoration. Locke found Furly's company agreeable and his opinions sympathetic; a further attraction was access to the substantial library that Furly had amassed. Locke remained with Furly until his final departure for England.

An acquaintance Locke had already made in Amsterdam was another refugee with unorthodox religious views, Jean le Clerc, a colleague of Limborch in the remonstrant seminary. In 1686 he began publishing a new periodical, the *Bibliothèque Universelle et Historique*. The second volume (July) included a short piece by Locke, 'Une methode nouvelle, & facile de dresser des recueuils'; this took the form of a letter to Nicolas Toinard, and described in careful detail the method of organizing a commonplace book which Locke had been using since 1660. Apart from his poems, it was Locke's first publication: though not likely to arouse much excitement in the world of learning, it would certainly not cause any trouble. Locke also probably contributed a review of Newton's *Principia* in March 1688; its contents correspond closely to notes among Locke's own papers, and there is nothing that suggests that the reviewer possessed any advanced mathematical knowledge.

A slightly earlier number of the *Bibliothèque* (January 1688) contained Locke's first publication of real importance, 'Extrait d'un livre anglois … intitulé essai philosophique concernant l'entendement', a substantial abridgement (translated by le Clerc) of the already completed but still unpublished *Essay*. Locke arranged for the printer to produce a stock of separate copies and had them circulated among his acquaintances in both England and the Netherlands.

The revolution and afterwards, 1689–1694 The success of William of Orange's expedition and the resulting flight of James II made it safe for Locke to come home. He returned on 12 February 1689, on the same ship that conveyed Princess Mary back to England. Locke was quickly offered a diplomatic post but unhesitatingly declined, mainly on grounds of health, but also because of an incapacity for the social side of diplomacy: 'I know noe such rack in the world to draw out mens thoughts as a well managed Bottle', he wrote to Lord Mordaunt, and he thought that it would be more in the king's interest 'to send a man of equall parts that could drinke his share, than the soberest man in the Kingdom' (*Correspondence*, 3.575). Locke would probably have made a very good ambassador. After his death Pierre Coste testified to his 'obliging and benevolent manners which, supported by an easy and polite expression, a great knowledge of the world, and a vast extent of capacity, made his conversation so agreeable to all sorts of people' (*Works*, 10.168); his enemies never denied his reserve and discretion. Locke did, however, accept the post of commissioner of appeals for the excise, which involved fewer duties and which brought in £200 per annum.

Now that Locke was back in England it was not obvious where he was to live. He had lost his studentship at Christ Church, and though he drafted a petition for its restoration, he made no sustained effort to achieve this. In March he moved into the house of Mrs Rabsy Smithsby in Westminster; she was an old acquaintance who had looked after some of his books while he was in exile. Locke remained her lodger until the end of June 1690, when he moved to a nearby house occupied by Robert Pawling, a former mayor of Oxford whom he had known since the early 1680s.

In the months that followed his return to England, Locke busied himself with preparing his two chief works for publication. The manuscript (or, almost certainly, manuscripts) that contained the *Two Treatises on Government* had apparently been left in England, and a large portion of the attack on Filmer in the first treatise had been either lost or deliberately destroyed; Locke appears to have made no attempt to reconstruct it. The second treatise was probably lightly revised for the changed political situation, and a new preface praising 'our Great Restorer, Our present King William' was added. *Two Treatises* was licensed for publication on 23 August, and appeared, with the date 1690 on the title page, in October. No author's name was given, and Locke never publicly acknowledged his authorship during his lifetime.

During this period Locke was also adding final touches to the *Essay Concerning Human Understanding*. The contract with the publisher was dated 24 May, and printing finished about the end of November. Like the *Two Treatises*, the *Essay* was on sale before the beginning of its nominal year of publication. There was no name on the title page, but the dedicatory epistle was signed and Locke had no desire to conceal his authorship: he sent presentation copies to over forty of his friends and acquaintances, including Queen Mary, Newton, Huygens, and Boyle; Sydenham would have been included if he had not just died (29 December). Huygens and Newton were both recent acquaintances; Huygens soon returned to the Netherlands, but Locke kept in touch with Newton, the two corresponding mostly on problems of biblical interpretation.

The *Essay* attracted attention from the start, both favourable and unfavourable. Much of this was directed towards the most conspicuous and easily understood feature of the work, the denial of innate principles in book 1. This was unacceptable—even shocking—to many of Locke's readers, including the most profound of his early critics, Leibniz. For Locke the human understanding was initially like 'white Paper, void of all Characters' (bk 2, chap. 1, section 2): all the ideas which it subsequently contains are derived from experience, either external or internal. The account of how the mind puts together various complex ideas from the material provided by sensation and reflection occupies book 2, the longest in the *Essay*. Book 3 is on words, which have meaning only by acting as signs of ideas; book 4 is on knowledge and opinion. At the beginning of the *Essay*, Locke had announced his intention 'to search out the *Bounds* between Opinion and Knowledge; and examine by what Measures, in things, whereof we have no certain Knowledge, we ought to regulate our Assent' (bk 1, chap. 1, section 3). The second part of this was crucially important: Locke was no sceptic, but he entirely lacked the boundless intellectual optimism possessed by contemporaries such as Spinoza. He deliberately turned away from metaphysical questions about the nature of the mind and contented himself with trying to find out how it works. It is only when we have done this that we will be in a position to determine what falls within the scope of our understanding, and what does not.

Many of Locke's doctrines were far from unprecedented: the denial of innatism, the empiricist account of concept acquisition and its attendant semantic theory can all be found in earlier authors, notably Hobbes, though Locke's account was far more thoroughly worked out, and such features as the distinction in book 3 between real and nominal essences were entirely new. Perhaps the most original aspect of the *Essay* is, however, the conception of philosophy which it embodies. Locke abandoned the whole enterprise of first philosophy as practised from Aristotle to Descartes: he did not see himself as laying a metaphysical foundation on which natural philosophers could then build, but rather (as he put it in the 'Epistle to the Reader') 'as an Under-Labourer … clearing Ground a little, and removing some of the Rubbish, that lies in the way to Knowledge' (*Drafts for the Essay*, 10).

While Locke was revising the *Essay* and *Two Treatises*, and seeing them through the press, an English translation was being prepared of the *Epistola de tolerantia*. The translator was William Popple, a merchant of Unitarian views and a convinced advocate of religious toleration; Locke was friendly with Popple and had supplied him with a copy of the Latin original. Popple's translation, entitled *A Letter Concerning Toleration*, went on sale in the late autumn. It sold out quickly (a second edition appeared a few months later) and immediately aroused controversy. In April 1690 an Oxford clergyman, Jonas Proast, published a vigorous attack, *The Argument of the Letter Concerning Toleration Consider'd and Answer'd*. Locke replied later in the summer with a short *Second Letter Concerning Toleration*; he chose not to reveal his identity and wrote as a third party taking the side of the author of the original *Letter*. The *Second Letter* failed to satisfy Proast: a further attack, *A Third Letter Concerning Toleration*, appeared in February 1691, and provoked Locke into elaborating a very much longer reply. *A Third Letter for Toleration* was completed in June 1692, and appeared in November. For the time being Proast made no response, and the controversy ceased.

Shortly before Locke started work on the *Second Letter*, about April 1690, he drafted a short and untitled political tract now usually known as 'A call to the nation for unity'; it was sent to Edward Clarke, and remained among his papers. The tract was directed against those tories who were prepared to recognize William as king *de facto*, but not *de jure*. Locke saw this as an evasion: if William was not king *de jure* then he could only be a usurper, as his Jacobite opponents maintained.

While working on his replies to Proast, Locke had also been thinking again about problems in economics. His concern with these matters had been revived in the summer of 1690 by the introduction into parliament of bills to reduce the legal rate of interest, and to devalue the silver coinage by increasing its nominal value. A part of *Some considerations of the consequences of the lowering of interest, and raising the value of money* was written in 1690, but much of it was taken over almost unchanged from the unpublished tract that Locke had started in 1668. Locke continued to work on *Some Considerations* during 1691, and it was eventually published rather hurriedly in December when another bill to reduce the rate of interest was placed before the House of Commons.

In summer 1690 Locke paid an extended visit to Oates, a small moated manor house near High Laver in north Essex, the home of Sir Francis Masham; Masham's wife, Damaris, was the daughter of Ralph Cudworth, and had been a close friend and correspondent of Locke since before his departure for the Netherlands. In the early part of 1691 he was invited to stay as a permanent guest. Locke was to live at Oates for the remainder of his life, though in the 1690s he was forced to spend quite long periods in London attending to government business.

Once the *Third Letter for Toleration* was out of the way, Locke's thoughts turned to a less controversial work. While in the Netherlands he had begun sending Edward Clarke a series of letters giving detailed advice about the upbringing of Clarke's children. Most of *Some Thoughts Concerning Education* was taken from these letters, though some new material was added.

For Locke the central purpose of education was education into virtue, and this meant training in self-control: 'The Principle of all Vertue and Excellency lies in a power of denying our selves the satisfaction of our own Desires, where Reason does not authorize them' (section 38). Locke did not regard children as innately cruel or malevolent—he thought the cruelty they frequently displayed as having been learned by bad example—but he did see them as naturally wilful and selfish. This was not original sin in the traditional theological sense, but it was a long way from Rousseau's faith in the goodness of the uncorrupted human heart.

Of all Locke's works, *Some Thoughts* is perhaps the one that reveals most about its author. A reader of the *Essay* might conclude that Locke had a prosaic mind, but it is only when he was writing about the education of children that the extent of his animosity towards poetry becomes apparent: 'if he [a child] have a Poetick Vein, 'tis to me the strangest thing in the World, that the Father should desire, or suffer it to be cherished or improved. Methinks the Parents should labour to have it stifled, and suppressed, as much as may be' (section 174).

Some Thoughts was published in July 1693; it sold quickly and another virtually identical edition followed soon afterwards. A third edition, containing a substantial quantity of new material, came out two years later. This revised edition was the first work since the *Essay* to be published in Locke's own name, and it helped add to his growing reputation.

During the time that Locke was adding the final touches to *Some Thoughts* and seeing to its publication, he was also thinking about new material for a second edition of the *Essay*. John Norris had been the first author to publish any criticisms of the *Essay*, in some 'Cursory reflections', added at the end of his *Christian Blessedness* (1690). Norris was an old friend of Lady Masham, and it was through her that he became acquainted with Locke. Initially friendly, their relations turned sour when Locke came to suspect that Norris had been prying into his correspondence. The first result of this was a bad-tempered fragment, entitled 'JL answer to Mr Norris's reflection', dated 1692. This was quickly followed by two rather more substantial pieces, *Remarks upon some of Mr Norris's Books*, and *An Examination of P. Malebranche's Opinion of Seeing All Things in God*, both probably dating from early 1693; these remained unpublished until 1720 and 1706 respectively. Despite its title, the *Examination of Malebranche* began as an attack on Norris, as some passages omitted in the version published in 1706 show. At one stage Locke wondered about including some of this material in the second edition of the *Essay*, but on further reflection decided against doing so: a long polemic would have been out of place in a work that aimed quite deliberately at avoiding disputation and controversy.

Some of the other new material in the second edition arose out of Locke's much more amiable relationship with a young Irish scientist, William Molyneux. Molyneux had referred to Locke in fulsome terms in the preface to his *Dioptrica nova* (1692), and Locke, who was apt to estimate anyone else's capacity for philosophical thinking by the closeness of their ideas to his own, was most favourably impressed. A correspondence ensued which continued until Molyneux's death in 1698. Molyneux's most enduring legacy was a problem that he had originally proposed in a letter of 1688, but which Locke first mentioned in the second edition of the *Essay* (bk 2, chap. 9, section 8): if someone born blind had learned to distinguish a globe and a cube by touch alone, and was then given sight, would that person be able to determine purely by sight which one was which? Both Locke and Molyneux thought that he or she would not.

The second edition of the *Essay* was published in May 1694. Apart from the changes already mentioned, the section in the chapter 'Of power' dealing with freedom was entirely recast, and there was a new chapter, 'Of identity and diversity', in which Locke equated personal identity with continuity of consciousness, and not with continuity of any spiritual substance.

A second edition of the *Two Treatises of Government* also appeared in spring 1694. Locke tried to correct the badly printed first edition, but its successor was still worse, much to his annoyance. One reason for its unsatisfactory quality was that though Locke was on friendly terms with the printers (Awnsham and John Churchill), he was so determined to conceal his identity that he conducted all the business relating to the edition indirectly, through

Edward Clarke. A third edition, little changed from the second, appeared in 1698.

Controversy and public service, 1695–1700 Locke spent the early months of 1695 at Oates, working on two very dissimilar though not entirely unrelated projects. One concerned the liberty of the press. The Licensing Act of 1662 required periodic parliamentary renewal to remain in force, and was due to lapse in 1695. Locke thought the act pernicious and prepared a paper outlining its defects. He also provided comments on a more liberal bill for regulating printing that Edward Clarke introduced into the Commons in March; though this never became law, the Licensing Act was allowed to lapse and pre-publication censorship of the press ceased.

Locke's other project was a work of apologetics, intended to set out 'the doctrine of our Saviour and his apostles, as delivered in the Scriptures, and not as taught by the several sects of Christians' (*Works*, 7.188). *The Reasonableness of Christianity* was published anonymously near the beginning of August 1695, and at once aroused controversy. The enterprise of presenting Christianity as reasonable caused little offence, but many readers regarded the version of Christianity advocated as unduly attenuated: a simple requirement of acknowledging Jesus to be the Messiah seemed to indicate sympathy with the anti-trinitarianism of the Socinians. Locke's earliest and most indefatigable antagonist was John Edwards, in *Some Thoughts Concerning the Several Causes and Occasions of Atheism* (1695). Locke replied in a brief, anonymous *Vindication of the Reasonableness of Christianity* published in November 1695. A much longer work, the *Second Vindication*, appeared in March 1697, in reply to a second assault by Edwards, *Socinianism Unmask'd* (1696).

However intemperately expressed, Edwards's suspicions about Socinianism were probably justified. Locke certainly had a large number of Socinian books in his library, and his private notes on the Trinity and the deity of Christ (MS Locke c. 43) suggest that he rejected both doctrines. Locke's caution is understandable: anti-trinitarian sects had been explicitly excluded from the protection afforded by the Toleration Act of 1689. In public he was evasive, a stance not calculated to reassure his critics.

In 1695 Locke was again busy with economics. The deterioration of the silver currency was becoming increasingly serious, and in January a committee was set up by the House of Commons to examine proposals for reform. In February, Locke published a brief pamphlet, *Short Observations on a Printed Paper*, originally written in 1693 in reply to an anonymous broadsheet by Thomas Neale. During the summer the situation grew steadily worse, so that Locke spent much of the second half of 1695 absorbed in monetary problems. The third edition of the *Essay*, which came out about December, was almost unchanged from its predecessor. In September, Locke was chosen, along with others including Newton and Wren, to supply the government with expert advice. His recommendation of recoinage without devaluation was finally adopted as government policy early in November, though it still had to be accepted by parliament. His last publication on economics—*Further Considerations Concerning Raising the Value of Money*, a defence of these proposals—appeared towards the end of December. It was the only one of Locke's writings on money to be issued in his own name.

Locke spent the early months of 1696 resting at Oates after the exertions of the previous year. By June he was sufficiently recovered to attend the first meeting of the newly constituted Board of Trade, the successor of the council for trade and plantations to which he had been secretary in 1673–4. The secretary of the new board was the translator of the *Epistola de tolerantia*, William Popple; one of the clerks was Locke's former manservant Sylvester Brounower. The business generated by the board occupied a substantial part of Locke's time over the next four years, but it was not without its reward: the annual salary was £1000, and this time it was paid. Locke found himself dealing with problems as varied as linen manufacture in Ireland, the abortive Scottish colony in Darien, the suppression of piracy, and the affairs of the colony of Virginia. In October 1697 he presented a paper to the board on the problems of vagrancy and the reform of the poor law, advocating the suppression of begging, the setting up of workhouses, and the imposition of strict discipline on their inmates; the scheme was rejected by his fellow commissioners. Locke saw the growth of begging and vagrancy as caused by the relaxation of discipline and corruption of manners, but he was aware that at least some of the poor could not support themselves. Lady Masham reported that 'He was very charitable to the Poor except such persons as were Idle or Prophane, and spent the Sunday in the Alehouses, and went not to Church'. Locke's accounts show him frequently paying out small sums for the deserving (mostly elderly) poor.

Much of the time that Locke could spare from the affairs of the Board of Trade was spent in pursuing a lengthy controversy with Edward Stillingfleet, now bishop of Worcester. Stillingfleet had read the *Essay* soon after it first appeared, and (as he later acknowledged) had not seen it as endangering religion. It was the appearance in 1696 of John Toland's *Christianity not Mysterious* that caused him to change his mind. Toland's unrelentingly rationalist approach to theology went well beyond anything Locke advocated, but it was quite apparent to Stillingfleet that his theory of knowledge was taken over without much modification from book 4 of the *Essay*. It was this that led Stillingfleet to conclude his *Discourse in Vindication of the Doctrine of the Trinity* with a criticism of both Toland and Locke.

Stillingfleet's *Discourse* was published in November 1696. Locke immediately set to work on a reply: *A Letter to the Right Reverend Edward, Lord Bishop of Worcester* was dated 7 January 1697, and was on sale by mid-March. Stillingfleet's riposte, an *Answer to Mr. Locke's Letter*, was on sale at the beginning of May. Locke again responded quickly: *Mr Locke's Reply to the Right Reverend the Lord Bishop of Worcester's Answer to his Letter* was dated 29 June and was published by mid-September; it also contained a brief reply to another critic, Thomas Burnet. Stillingfleet responded with his *Answer to Mr. Locke's Second Letter*, which he appears to have intended as his final contribution to the controversy. Locke prepared a massive rejoinder, considerably longer than its two predecessors put together: *Mr Locke's Reply to the Right Reverend the Lord Bishop of Worcester's Answer to his Second Letter* was completed in May 1698, though not published until the end of the year. Stillingfleet was by then in no condition to respond. His health had broken down, and he died on 27 March 1699.

The exchange of letters with Stillingfleet revealed in public Locke's defects as a controversialist, already apparent in the anonymous exchanges that had followed the *Letter on Toleration* and the *Reasonableness of Christianity*. Locke admired Hooker, but did not imitate his urbanity and sense of grand strategy; instead the reader is offered page after page of close-range pummelling, interspersed with episodes of sarcasm and bad temper. Locke was aware that he was prone to anger; in his life he seems to have kept this under control, but not always in his writings.

Some of the issues raised in the controversy with Stillingfleet reappeared in the material added to the fourth edition of the *Essay*, which came out in December 1699; it was the last edition published during Locke's lifetime. Other major changes included two entirely new chapters: 'Of enthusiasm' and 'Of the association of ideas'. One planned addition, like the earlier *Examination of Malebranche*, grew too large and was turned into a separate treatise: this was *The Conduct of the Understanding*, which Locke began in April 1697. He continued adding material to it in the years that followed, and it remained unfinished at his death; his executors published it in 1706. The *Conduct* is the only one of Locke's works that shows any clear evidence of having been influenced by Francis Bacon. A less easily dateable work from about this time is *The Elements of Natural Philosophy*, a short introduction said to have been written for the use of the Mashams' son Francis, which was first published in 1720.

A French translation of the *Essay* was published at Amsterdam in 1700; the translator was a young protestant refugee, Pierre Coste, who had already translated *Some Thoughts Concerning Education* (1695) and the *Reasonableness of Christianity* (1696). Coste had come to Oates in August 1697 as tutor to Francis Masham, and he was able to discuss his translation in detail with Locke. A Latin translation by Ezekiel Burridge appeared in 1701. Both these translations helped make Locke's philosophy more widely accessible to readers abroad.

Last years, 1700–1704 In June 1700 Locke resigned from the Board of Trade. He had long suffered from a weakness of the lungs, and found the cold and smoke of London in winter unbearable. In January 1698 he had been summoned to Kensington Palace for an interview with the king, apparently in order to be offered an important (though not certainly identifiable) post. By his own account the journey nearly killed him (*Correspondence*, 6.307), and his health never fully recovered.

The last four years of Locke's life were spent quietly at Oates, his visits to London becoming less frequent and very much briefer than before. He published nothing after the fourth edition of the *Essay*, though he continued to note down minor improvements, incorporated into the posthumous fifth edition (1706). When his health allowed he worked steadily on his last major project, *Paraphrases and Notes on the Epistles of St Paul*. His intention was to publish the complete series by instalments, at three-monthly intervals; the first of these, on Galatians, was in proof by August 1704, but nothing appeared before his death. The completed parts, on Galatians, 1 and 2 Corinthians, Romans, and Ephesians, were published by his executors between 1705 and 1707. Two other works date from Locke's last years: *A Discourse of Miracles* was written in 1702; an unfinished *Fourth Letter on Toleration*, a response to a belated reopening of the old controversy by Proast, was begun during the last months of Locke's life. Both were published in 1706.

One close friend Locke made in his last years was Anthony Collins, the deist. Locke's letters to him are warm, even effusive, and Collins seems not to have made Locke aware of his own disbelief in revelation. Locke's last letter to him, delivered after his death, describes this life as 'a scene of vanity which soon passes away and affords no solid satisfaction but in the consciousness of doing well and in the hopes of an other life' (*Correspondence*, 8.419).

Early in 1704 Locke's health started to deteriorate, and by the summer he knew he might not have much longer to live. In April he drew up his will, and in September added a codicil acknowledging his authorship of the works he had published anonymously. During the summer he grew steadily weaker. He had previously enjoyed taking exercise by riding, but this was now beyond him; instead, a specially designed chaise was constructed in which he could be driven about. By October he was too frail even for this, and could only be carried out into the garden to sit in the autumn sun. His mind remained lucid until the end. He died peacefully sitting in the chair in his study on the afternoon of 28 October, as Lady Masham was reading the Psalms. Three days later he was buried in the churchyard of the parish church at High Laver.

Locke had never lived extravagantly, and he died a wealthy man. His estate included just over £12,000 in cash and easily realizable assets, some freehold land in Somerset subsequently sold for £615, and various personal effects including a library of over 4000 books and pamphlets. The main beneficiary of his will was a young lawyer who had been looking after Locke's affairs for some years, Peter King, the grandson of Locke's uncle Peter, his father's younger brother. King received the majority of the estate, including Locke's manuscripts and half his library; the other half, together with £3000, went to Francis Masham. Masham's share of the library was later dispersed, and few of the books that it contained are known to have survived. King became lord chancellor in 1725, and was raised to the peerage as Baron King of Ockham. His descendants, from 1838 earls of Lovelace, retained Locke's papers until the middle of the twentieth century; most are now in the Bodleian Library, Oxford.

Locke's works were first published in a collected edition in 1714, and were reprinted at regular intervals until the 'twelfth' (actually thirteenth) edition of 1824. There were also frequent editions of individual works, especially the *Essay Concerning Human Understanding* and *Some Thoughts Concerning Education*. Locke's philosophy was immensely influential in the eighteenth century, not least in the universities of Oxford and Cambridge, where it soon replaced the scholastic doctrines in which Locke had been educated. The burden on undergraduates, and others, was lightened by an abridgement of the *Essay* made by John Wynne of Jesus College, Oxford, in 1696, and reprinted frequently in the following century.

Locke's political writings earned him a place in the whig pantheon, along with Milton, Harrington, and Algernon Sidney, but were less intensively studied. During the half-century from the death of Queen Anne (1714) to the end of the Seven Years' War (1763) the *Two Treatises of Government* was reprinted only once, except in editions of the collected works. The rising tide of discontent in the American colonies gave the *Second Treatise* a renewed relevance; it was frequently cited in debates on both sides of the Atlantic, and was published (without the *First Treatise*) in Boston in 1773, the first American printing. Locke's account of the origin and limits of government has continued to exert a profound influence on American political thought.

The epistemological doctrines of the *Essay* were subjected to acute criticism by other philosophers from Berkeley onwards, but this did little to shake their acceptability to the educated public. Locke was seen as having given a plain unmetaphysical account of the workings of the human mind that could serve as a complement to Newton's account of the physical universe. In the early nineteenth century Locke's standing began to decline: neither his doctrines nor his literary style appealed to a romantic sensibility more attuned to deep insights emerging from Germany, while thinkers faithful to empiricism were more likely to find what they needed in Bentham or in Bacon. In the later nineteenth and earlier twentieth centuries, as philosophy in Britain became increasingly professionalized, Bacon's reputation declined, but Locke's did not greatly revive: he was generally seen as a historically important but rather dull figure, a target for the nimbler intellects of Berkeley and Hume, though in the English-speaking world at least his position in the philosophical canon was never in jeopardy. Since 1950 his standing has steadily improved, partly through the stimulus to historical enquiry caused by the recovery of his papers, but mainly because of a revival in philosophical realism.

J. R. Milton

Sources Bodl. Oxf., MSS Locke • PRO, Shaftesbury papers, PRO 30/24 • BL, Add. MSS 4222, 15640, 15642, 28273, 32554, 46470 • *The correspondence of John Locke*, ed. E. S. de Beer, 8 vols. (1976–) • *The works of John Locke*, 10 vols. (1823) • H. R. Fox Bourne, *The life of John Locke*, 2 vols. (1876) • M. Cranston, *John Locke: a biography* (1957) • P. Long, *A summary catalogue of the Lovelace collection of manuscripts of John Locke in the Bodleian Library* (1959) • J. S. Yolton, *John Locke: a descriptive bibliography* (1998) • K. H. D. Haley, *The first earl of Shaftesbury* (1968) • K. Dewhurst, *John Locke, physician and philosopher* (1963) • J. Lough, *Locke's travels in France* (1953) • J. le Clerc, *An account of the life and writings of John Locke* (1706) • P. Coste, 'The character of Mr John Locke', *A collection of several pieces of Mr. John Locke* (1720) • P. H. Kelly, ed., *Locke on money*, 2 vols. (1991) • J. Locke, *Drafts for the essay concerning human understanding and other philosophical writings*, ed. P. H. Nidditch and G. A. J. Rogers, 1 (1990) • J. Locke, *Two tracts on government*, ed. P. Abrams (1967) • J. Locke, *Two treatises of government*, ed. P. Laslett, 2nd edn (1967) • J. Harrison and P. Laslett, *The library of John Locke* (1971) • J. R. Milton, 'Locke at Oxford', *Locke's philosophy: context and content*, ed. G. A. J. Rogers (1994), 29–47 • M. Goldie, 'John Locke's circle and James II', *HJ*, 35 (1992), 557–86 • J. R. Milton and P. Milton, 'The selection of juries: a tract by John Locke', *HJ*, 40 (1997), 185–94 • R. Ashcraft, *Revolutionary politics and Locke's two treatises of government* (1986) • E. G. W. Bill, *Education at Christ Church, Oxford, 1660–1800* (1988) • J. R. Milton, 'John Locke and the fundamental constitutions of Carolina', *Locke Newsletter*, 21 (1990), 111–33 • J. Farr and C. Roberts, 'John Locke on the Glorious Revolution: a rediscovered document', *HJ*, 28 (1985), 385–98 • P. Milton, 'Denis Grenville and John Locke', *Locke Newsletter*, 27 (1996), 75–108 • J. Marshall, *John Locke: resistance, religion and responsibility* (1994) • M. Goldie, 'John Locke, Jonas Proast and religious toleration, 1688–1692', *The Church of England, 1689–1833*, ed. J. Walsh and others (1993), 143–71 • *The life and times of Anthony Wood*, ed. A. Clark, 5 vols., OHS, 19, 21, 26, 30, 40 (1891–1900) • Locke MS b. 1, fol. 283

Archives BL, account book, with medical notes, Add. MS 46470 • BL, corresp. and papers, Add. MS 4290 • BL, diary, 1679, Add. MS 15642 • BL, medical commonplace book, Add. MS 32554 • BL, medical papers, Add. MS 5714 • Bodl. Oxf., corresp. and papers | BL, letters to Sir Hans Sloane and others, Sloane MSS 3692, 4036, 4038–4039, 4059 • BL, letters to Nicholas Thoynard and papers, Add. MSS 28728, 28753, 28835–28836 • Bodl. Oxf., letters to Edward Clarke • Bodl. Oxf., letters to Benjamin Furly • PRO, Shaftesbury papers, PRO 30/24 • V&A NAL, letters to Lord Shaftesbury and Lord Ashley

Likenesses J. Greenhill, oils, *c.*1672–1676, NPG • S. Brounower, plumbago drawing, *c.*1685, NPG [*see illus.*] • S. Brounower, portrait, *c.*1685, Christ Church Oxf. • H. Verelst, oils, 1689, NPG • M. Dahl, oils, 1696, NPG • M. Dahl, oils, *c.*1696, NPG • G. Kneller, oils, 1697, Hermitage, St Petersburg • oils, 1697 (after portrait by G. Kneller, 1697), Christ Church Oxf. • J. Dassier, bronze medal, 1704, NPG • G. Kneller, oils, 1704, Virginia Museum of Fine Arts, Richmond; version, NPG • J. Simon, mezzotint, 1721 (after G. Kneller), BM, NPG • J. M. Rysbrack, marble bust, 1732, Royal Collection • P. van Gunst, line engraving (after J. Greenhill, *c.*1672–1676), BM, NPG • G. Kneller, chalk drawing, Yale U. CBA • F. Kyte, mezzotint (after G. Kneller), BM, NPG • J. Neagle, line engraving (after Chodowiechi), BM, NPG • J. M. Rysbrack, marble statue, Christ Church Oxf. • J. Simon, mezzotint (after unknown artist), BM, NPG • P. Vanderbank, engraving (after drawing by S. Brounower), repro. in J. Locke, *Essay concerning human understanding*, 2nd edn (1694) • line engraving (after J. Greenhill), NPG

Wealth at death over £12,000; debts and stock owing 29 Sept 1704 totalled £12,037; leasehold land reverted to landlord after death; freehold land sold by executor for £600 and 15 broad pieces; also various personal effects and large library: Bodl. Oxf., Locke MS b.1, fol. 283

Locke, John (1805–1880), legal writer and politician, born in London, was the only son of John Locke, surveyor, of Herne Hill, Surrey, and his wife, Alice, daughter of W. Cartwright. He was educated at Dulwich College and at Trinity College, Cambridge, graduating BA in 1829 and MA in 1832. He was called to the bar at the Inner Temple in Easter term 1833, and became a bencher of his inn in 1857. He joined the home circuit and Surrey sessions, where he enjoyed a leading practice, and from 1845 to 1857 was one of the common pleaders of the City of London. In June 1857, having ceased to practise for some years, except as counsel to the commissioners of Inland Revenue, he was appointed a queen's counsel, and in 1861 became recorder of Brighton, an office which he held until 1879. Having unsuccessfully contested Hastings as a Liberal in 1852, he was elected for Southwark in April 1857, and held the seat until his death. In parliament he was a Liberal at the fringe of the Benthamite tradition, chiefly active on questions of local government and measures for improving the condition of the working classes. He introduced and passed a bill in 1861 for the admission of witnesses in criminal cases to the same right of substituting an affirmation for an oath as in civil cases. He married in 1847 Laura Rosalie, daughter of Colonel Thomas Alexander Cobb of the East India Company's army. They had at least one son, John Henry Locke. Locke was the author of a *Treatise on the Game Laws* (1836), which went through five editions, and *The Doctrine and Practice of Foreign Attachment in the Lord Mayor's Court* (1853). He died at his residence, 63 Eaton Place, London, on 28 January 1880.

J. A. HAMILTON, *rev.* H. C. G. MATTHEW

Sources Boase, *Mod. Eng. biog.* • *Solicitors' Journal*, 24 (1879–80), 274 • *Law Times* (14 Feb 1880) • *The Times* (30 Jan 1880) • *CGPLA Eng. & Wales* (1880)

Likenesses Reutlinger, portrait (after photograph), repro. in *ILN* (11 Feb 1880), 157 • chromolithograph caricature, NPG; repro. in *VF* (12 Aug 1871) • wood-engraving (after photograph by J. Watkins), NPG; repro. in *ILN* (16 March 1857), 479

Wealth at death under £60,000: probate, 25 Feb 1880, *CGPLA Eng. & Wales*

Locke, Josef [*real name* Joseph McLaughlin] (**1917–1999**), popular singer, was born at 19 Creggan Street, Londonderry, Northern Ireland, on 23 March 1917, the son of Patrick McLaughlin, a butcher and cattle dealer, and his wife Annie Doherty; he was one of ten children. As a boy he sang in churches in the Bogside, and made his first stage appearance at the age of nine. At sixteen he enlisted, two years under age, in the Irish Guards, and later served with the Palestine police, where he rose to the rank of sergeant. After returning home in the late 1930s, he joined the Royal Ulster Constabulary and won a reputation as the 'Singing Bobby'. He took some vocal lessons in Italy and began appearing in operetta at the Gaiety Theatre, Dublin.

On the advice of the Irish tenor John McCormack, McLaughlin visited London in 1945 for an audition with the bandleader and impresario Jack Hylton. He was immediately booked to sing in the Crazy Gang's show *Together Again*. It is said that Hylton advised him to change his name to Josef Locke, a shortened form of his real name, which Hylton suggested was too long for variety bills. The next year Locke was in Blackpool, the first of his nineteen consecutive holiday seasons there. It became his adopted home; he bought a house and a garage business, and settled in the town with his wife, Carmel, and their son. He toured on the northern variety circuit of Lew and Leslie Grade and established himself as a major star with all the trappings of flamboyant celebrity: expensive clothes, sports cars, and glamorous companions.

In 1947 Locke's first records were released and included six songs associated with him throughout his career. One was 'Hear my song, Violetta', originally a German tango song, 'Hör mein Lied, Violetta' (by Klose and Lukesch), given English words by Harry S. Pepper. The others were 'The Holy City' (Weatherly and Adams), 'I'll take you home again Kathleen' (Westendorf), 'Galway Bay' (Colahan), 'Goodbye' (Stolz and Graham), and 'Come back to Sorrento' (de Curtis and Aveling). During his first year of recording he had fixed what was to be his unchanging repertory: a mixture of religious and secular ballads, operetta, and songs of Ireland. His vocal techniques included an Italianate portamento and sobbing catch in his voice, and he enjoyed decorating a melodic line, treating the tempo flexibly. The clarity of his diction was supported by variety of vocal timbre and a wide dynamic range. His tender and intimate *sotto voce* is heard to effect in the penultimate verse of his 1947 recording of 'Galway Bay'. At the other extreme, his voice could soar over his audience as he encouraged them to join in the refrain of 'Goodbye'.

The first of Locke's many radio broadcasts was in 1949, on *Happydrome*, and he appeared in many television shows, such as *All-Star Bill*, *Rooftop Rendezvous*, and *Top of the Town*. He took on singing roles in three films, beginning with *Holidays with Pay* (1948), which starred his friend the Lancashire comedian Frank Randle. He appeared in five royal variety performances, the first of them in 1952. In 1958, however, at the height of his fame, the Inland Revenue investigated his tax returns. At this time Locke could command £2000 a week, but he spent money profusely and gambled recklessly on horses. When a warrant was issued for his arrest on a charge of tax evasion, he disappeared. In the 1970s many believed he had returned to the northern clubs as the mystery tenor Mr X, who was actually an impersonator and look-alike, Eric Lieson. Locke had removed himself to co. Kildare, where he had bought a farm, a public house, and some horses.

Eventually Locke came to an arrangement with tax officers in the UK, but decided to stay in retirement, although he gave the occasional charity concert and appeared in a birthday tribute on Irish television in 1984. In 1992 he found himself the subject of Peter Chelsom's film *Hear my Song*. Ambushed on his arrival in London for the première, he agreed to participate in the television programme *This is your Life*. Interest in Locke was rekindled and a compilation album of his songs became a best-seller. However, he remained in retirement in Clane, co. Kildare, where he died on 15 October 1999. He was survived by his wife. Locke's physique was of the stocky build not uncommon in tenors, and he had dark hair, a moustache, penetrating eyes, and an open, winningly roguish smile. He was a fine song interpreter who electrified audiences and, with his emotional delivery, made them feel he meant every word. No one gave stronger assurance to Kathleen that he would take her home again and when Locke courted Mary, the Rose of Tralee, the pale moon really did seem to rise above the green mountain.

DEREK B. SCOTT

Sources *The Independent* (16 Oct 1999) · C. Larkin, ed., *The encyclopedia of popular music*, 3rd edn, 8 vols. (New York, 1998) · *The Guardian* (16 Oct 1999) · D. Valentina, disc notes, in *The Josef Locke collection*, HMV, 5222472 (2000) · disc notes, *Hear my song: Josef Locke*, ASV Living Era, CD AJA 5359 (2000) [audio CD] · b. cert.
Likenesses photographs, repro. in *The Josef Locke album: containing his life story, photographs and greatest song successes* (1950)

Locke, Joseph (**1805–1860**), railway engineer, was born at Attercliffe, near Sheffield, on 9 August 1805, the fourth and youngest son of William Locke (*b.* 1770), colliery manager, and his wife, Esther, *née* Teesdale. He was educated at Barnsley grammar school, and from 1818 to 1820 was a pupil of William Stobart of Pelaw, co. Durham, a colliery viewer. In 1823 he was articled as a pupil engineer to George Stephenson at his works in Newcastle upon Tyne, and after the expiration of his time in 1826 stayed on with Stephenson, and was appointed one of his assistants in the construction of the Liverpool and Manchester Railway. He was involved in the debate over the form of motive power to be used on the new railway, and in 1829, with Stephenson, published a pamphlet entitled *Observations on the comparative merits of locomotive and fixed engines, being a reply to the report of Mr James Walker*, which finally settled the question in favour of locomotive engines. In 1834 he married Phoebe (1811–1866), daughter of John McCreery.

Locke's first major project as a civil engineer after the completion of the Liverpool and Manchester was the first trunk railway line, the Grand Junction Railway between Birmingham and Warrington, for which he was to conduct the survey under the line's chief engineer, George Stephenson. The railway's directors were greatly impressed with Locke and indicated to him that they wished him to take sole charge of building the line, which angered Stephenson and led to a rift between the great engineer and his former pupil. A compromise of dividing work on the line between the two men was agreed; but Stephenson's tendency to delegate work to inexperienced assistants led to expensive mistakes and more ill feeling. In August 1835 Stephenson withdrew from the Grand Junction project, leaving the line's construction wholly in Locke's hands. His work on the Grand Junction established Locke's reputation for good engineering combined with economy and speed of construction, and he was soon in great demand as the pace of railway construction increased. Among the many lines he went on to construct in the British Isles the main line from London to Southampton (1836–40) stands out for its directness and fine civil engineering, while the line between Sheffield and Manchester (1838–40) and the Greenock, Paisley, and Glasgow line (1837–41), with their steep gradients, are examples of Locke at his most daring. Abroad, he constructed the line between Paris and Rouen (1841–3), and that between Rouen and Le Havre (1843), for which he was awarded the grand cross of the Légion d'honneur by Louis-Philippe. He also designed and supervised the construction of the line between Barcelona and Mattaro in Spain (1847–8) and the Dutch–Rhenish railway, completed in 1856. While working on the continent Locke took John Edward Errington into partnership in 1840, and together they constructed lines in Lancashire and north-western England, and many difficult lines in Scotland, including the Caledonian main line. They also constructed a line from Mantes to Caen and Cherbourg in 1852, for which Locke was created a chevalier of the Légion d'honneur by Napoleon III. Despite the heavy civil-engineering works on the Caledonian Railway main line its cost, including the stations, was a relatively modest £16,000 a mile. This economy resulted from the adoption of steeper gradients than had previously been thought suitable for railway locomotives, and proved that level track was not absolutely necessary to prevent a loss of power, especially given the continually improving performance of British locomotives during this period. Throughout his career Locke avoided undertaking very great and costly civil-engineering works, but he approached all his work with a dauntless determination to see the job through. He also had an unerring ability to select ideal collaborators, sub-contractors, and assistants; a notable example was Thomas Brassey, whom Locke brought with him from the Grand Junction Railway to work on the Basingstoke to Winchester section of the London to Southampton line.

In 1847 Locke purchased the manor of Honiton, Devon, and sat in parliament as a Liberal for the borough of Honiton from that date to his death. He seldom spoke in the house except on matters within his special knowledge, but engaged in many parliamentary struggles, and took part in the 'battle of the gauges', favouring Stephenson's narrower gauge over Brunel's broad gauge.

Locke died suddenly at Moffat, near Dumfries, Scotland, on 18 September 1860. He was widely mourned; a window (since removed) was installed to his memory in Westminster Abbey, and an obituary in *The Times* referred to him as having formed, with Robert Stephenson and Isambard Kingdom Brunel, the 'triumvirate of the engineering world'. Locke was always proud of his Yorkshire origins, and left a number of legacies to institutions in that county, notably Barnsley grammar school. His widow presented Locke Park to the people of Barnsley in his memory, and in 1866 his statue was erected there.

G. C. Boase, *rev.* Ralph Harrington

Sources J. Devey, *The life of Joseph Locke* (1862) · N. W. Webster, *Joseph Locke: railway revolutionary* (1970) · *The Engineer* (Sept 1860) · *The Times* (21 Sept 1860) · *PICE*, 20 (1860–61), 141–8 · C. Walker, *Joseph Locke, 1805–1860* (1975) · C. H. Ellis, *Twenty locomotive men* (1958)
Archives Inst. CE · Staffs. RO, plan and reports | Flintshire RO, Hawarden, corresp. with W. B. Buddicom
Likenesses F. Grant, oils, 1838, Inst. CE · F. Grant, oils, 1845, Inst. CE · J. Brown, stipple and line engraving, pubd 1862 (after photograph by J. E. Mayall), NPG · C. Marochetti, statue, *c.*1866, Locke Park, Barnsley · C. H. Mabey, marble bust, 1897 (after E. W. Wyon, 1862), Sci. Mus. · J. Lucas, group portrait, oils (*Conference of engineers at Britannia Bridge*), Inst. CE
Wealth at death under £350,000: probate, 29 Oct 1860, *CGPLA Eng. & Wales*

Locke [*married name* Mister], **Mary** (*bap.* **1768**), poet and children's writer, was baptized on 28 September 1768 at Chipping Norton, Oxfordshire, the youngest of the four children of John Locke, attorney, and his wife, Mary, *née*

Hanwell. She had two brothers, James (*bap.* 7 Oct 1760) and John (*bap.* 10 Oct 1762), and a sister, Clementina (*bap.* 30 July 1764).

By 1786 both of Mary Locke's parents were dead, and she had taken up residence with her uncle Edward Taylor of Hill House, Steeple Aston, Oxfordshire. Taylor, son of a clergyman and grandson of the bishop of Salisbury, had been educated at Eton College and Trinity College, Cambridge, and, after travelling in Europe, had settled to the life of a country gentleman. This was to be celebrated by Mary Locke as a mixture of 'philosophic' contemplation and unostentatious philanthropy in her poem in rhyming couplets *Eugenius, or, Virtue in Retirement* (1791). The preface to this describes the author as having led 'a Life of Retirement' and being 'young, uneducated, and inexperienced'. An autobiographical section of the poem laments an early lack of schooling and a childhood or adolescence of 'misery and tears'. She writes that she has since been 'to a soil more kind / Remov'd'. Taylor, who was in his mid-forties when she began living with him, evidently had literary interests, and might well have been the author of *Cursory Remarks on Tragedy* (1774). He probably encouraged his niece's poetic ambitions. In the same year that *Eugenius* was published she began contributing verse, particularly sonnets of a gloomy cast, to the *Gentleman's Magazine*.

Taylor died on 6 December 1797 (*GM*, 1076), leaving Mary Locke property in Steeple Aston and Middle Barton. She composed the inscription for a memorial tablet in the parish church of St Peter and St Paul, Steeple Aston, in which she calls him 'her beloved and generous Benefactor' and refers to herself as '*An Orphan*, who for eleven Years found an asylum beneath his hospitable Roof'. On 18 July 1798 she married William Mister, a surgeon and apothecary of Shipston-on-Stour, Worcestershire (the marriage settlement is dated 14 July 1798). Local historian William Wing was to refer to him as 'a Welch gentleman' (Wing, 72).

Not long after her marriage, Mary Mister sold the property that Taylor had left her, including the freehold of Hill House. Under her married name she wrote a series of books for children. She may have moved with her husband to Wales, for several of these books commend the delights of the Welsh countryside, apparently described first-hand. Her children's stories are didactic and improving, though no more so than others of the period. In what appears to have been the earliest—*Mungo, the Little Traveller* (*c.*1811)—the main narrator is a dog who has travelled through Europe, Turkey, and Africa, and who provides his readers with lessons in human nature and natural history. In *The Adventures of a Doll* (1816), the storyteller is a doll, who passes from one owner to another, moralizing on their vanities and affectations. She had some success with these collections of tales: all were reprinted, some of them more than once.

Mary Mister had at least one child, referred to in the preface to *Mungo*: 'This little work was not intended, originally, for the public eye: it was the evening employment of a mother, for the amusement of her child'. The identification of Mary Locke with Mary Mister was first made by Roger Lonsdale in his *Eighteenth-Century Women Poets: an Oxford Anthology* (1989), which reprints two sonnets published under her maiden name in the *Gentleman's Magazine*. JOHN MULLAN

Sources R. Lonsdale, ed., *Eighteenth-century women poets: an Oxford anthology* (1989) • parish register, Chipping Norton, 28 Sept 1768 [baptism] • *GM*, 1st ser., 67 (1797), 1076 • memorial tablet, church of St Peter and St Paul, Steeple Aston, Oxfordshire • M. Mister, preface, *Mungo, the little traveller* (1814) • W. Wing, *Annals of Steeple Aston* (1816) • M. Locke, preface, *Eugenius, or, Virtue in retirement* (1791) • *IGI*

Locke, Matthew (*c.*1622–1677), organist and composer, is presumed to have been born in Devon, though attempts to link him with a Locke family resident in Exeter at the time have proved inconclusive. His date of birth is inferred from the inscription 'aetat 40 anno domini 1662' on a portrait given to the Oxford music school. He was a choirboy at Exeter Cathedral, where his teachers could have included the master of the choristers, Edward Gibbons, the organist John Lugge, and William Wake, who acted as Lugge's deputy from 1635 to 1642. After his voice changed Locke remained at the cathedral as a secondary, an intermediate grade between chorister and lay vicar. In 1638 and 1641 he carved his name or initials in the stone organ screen; on 29 September 1640 he was admonished for fighting, and in the same year he was twice paid for copying music for the cathedral.

The civil war and Commonwealth Locke's activities during the civil war are unknown. Exeter initially declared for parliament, but cathedral services seem to have resumed in September 1643, when the city again came under royalist control: Charles I, Henrietta Maria, and the prince of Wales all subsequently passed through Exeter and could have encountered Locke at this time. However, Locke's name does not appear in the Exeter protestation return of February 1642, either as one of those who had taken the oath or among the minority who refused, and he may already have left the city. Later he probably joined the exiled court at The Hague, as some Italian sacred music in BL, Add. MS 31437, was copied in 1648 'when I was in the Low Countreys' (fol. 29). *The Close Hypocrite Discovered* (p. 10) describes him as 'a Papist' who had been 'in Arms amongst the Rebels in Ireland'. He had returned to England by 1651, when he composed his *Little Consort* at the request of William Wake, and about the same time began his great scorebook, BL, Add. MS 17801, in which he collected and revised his chamber music for the rest of his life.

By about 1655 Locke had married Mary (*d.* 1701), daughter of the Catholic recusant Roger Garnons of Herefordshire. At least two children must have been born in the 1650s or early 1660s: the father of Locke's grandson John, executor of his grandmother's will, and Mary, who dealt with Locke's estate in 1677. In spite of religious and political differences, Locke became friendly with one of the parliamentary sequestration commissioners for Herefordshire, Silas Taylor, an enthusiastic amateur musician who provided him with a house in Hereford. Taylor's music meetings, in which Locke took a leading part, were

Matthew Locke (*c*.1622–1677), by unknown artist

suspected of being pretexts for assemblies of 'Papists and Delinquents' (*Close Hypocrite*, 10). Much of Locke's instrumental chamber music was probably composed at this time, including the two-part consort 'For Seaverall Freinds', the bass viol duos dated 1652, and the *Consort of Four Parts*; the title of *The Flatt Consort for my Cousin Kemble* refers to a prominent Herefordshire recusant family to whom Locke may have been related by marriage. Locke's own beliefs came under investigation when on 22 March 1654 he walked to the gallows with a condemned murderer whose final action was to proclaim the Catholic faith. Five depositions concerning this event were taken at Hereford on 29 March and 3 April 1654, including that of Matthew Price, a participant in at least one of Taylor's music meetings, who alleged that about a year previously Locke had made a compromising remark in the course of an argument. Locke was accused only of being a Catholic, not of breach of the peace, and his conduct, however imprudent, seems to have been compassionate and courageous.

In the mid-1650s Locke returned to London, where he became involved in the musical dramas which were the only form of public theatre permitted under the Commonwealth. He composed some of the music for William Davenant's *The Siege of Rhodes* of September 1656 and also sang the part of the Admiral. In the same year John Playford published a revised version of the 1651 *Little Consort*, and about this time Locke may have taken up a teaching post at a girls' school in Hackney, mentioned obliquely in his book *The Present Practice of Musick Vindicated* (1673, 19). In 1659 he composed the score for a revival of James Shirley's 'Morall Representation' *Cupid and Death*, incorporating music written by Christopher Gibbons for the first performance in 1653. Locke appears to have formed friendships with a number of other musicians as well as Gibbons: he wrote a dedicatory poem for the 1659 edition of *The Division Violist* by his 'dear friend' Christopher Simpson, in which he expressed a distrust of music theory later reflected in other works, and Samuel Pepys met him with Silas Taylor and either Henry or Thomas Purcell at a coffee house in Westminster on 21 February 1660.

After the Restoration Locke's rapid advancement after the Restoration suggests that he was already highly regarded by Charles II, perhaps as a result of his activities in the 1640s. In June 1660 he was appointed composer in the private music and composer for the violins. The following year Locke wrote much of the music for Charles II's ceremonial progress through London on 22 April, the eve of his coronation. The collection of suites entitled *The First Part of the Broken Consort* and the unfinished *Second Part* must have been intended for the 'broken consort' at court, a chamber music ensemble which flourished in the early 1660s. Locke also composed anthems for the Chapel Royal and from 1662 onwards was organist of Queen Catherine's Catholic chapel, until 1671 at St James's Palace and then at Somerset House. This last appointment probably provided him with accommodation, as although he was said in 1669 to be 'of St Martin in the Fields' (Ashbee, 1.92) his name cannot be found in the rate books. In June 1664 one Margaret Pothero received 10*s*. a week for lodging 'Mr Lock, organist, and his servants' for seventeen weeks (ibid., 55), at the same time as the Catholic viol player Paul Francis Bridges and John Harford, an organ blower, were lodged elsewhere, perhaps because all three were for some reason displaced from their usual apartments.

During the plague year, 1665, Locke accompanied the court to Oxford, where several manuscripts were annotated by Edward Lowe, the professor of music. Locke's motet *Ad te levavi oculos meos* was performed at the music school on Thursday 16 November; the previous week a new prelude and Gloria had been composed, added to an existing Jubilate, copied in parts, and performed, all between noon and 3 p.m. Back at Westminster, an unfortunate incident occurred on 1 April 1666 when Locke's responses to the commandments for some reason went badly wrong in a Chapel Royal service. Although straightforward, Locke's setting departed from precedent by consisting of ten different responses instead of repetitions of the same music. After unfair criticism that the music was excessively difficult and unusual, Locke had the score printed with his comments as *Modern church-musick pre-accus'd, censur'd, and obstructed in its performance before his majesty … vindicated by the author Matt. Lock* (1666). His reaction appears unnecessarily defensive, as his reputation does not seem to have suffered, and the most ambitious of his anthems, 'Be thou exalted', was performed in the Chapel Royal with great success on the 14 August following. A comparable lack of proportion marks Locke's side of a controversy about musical notation with Thomas Salmon, whose *An Essay to the Advancement of Music by Casting Away the perplexity of Different clefs* (1672) is as inoffensive in tone as it is impractical in content. Salmon inadvertently provoked Locke by inviting him to write a commendation to his *Essay*, and Locke's published replies, *Observations upon a Late Book, Entituled, an Essay to the Advancement of Musick* (1672) and *The Present Practice of Musick Vindicated* (1673), respond to Salmon's suggestions as if they constituted a personal insult. The prefaces are respectively signed 'From my Lodgings near the Savoy' and 'From my Lodgings in the Strand', implying that Locke moved into new accommodation when the queen's chapel transferred to Somerset House.

In 1673 Locke was paid £5 for composing an ode, *Descende caelo cincta sororibus*, for the Oxford 'act', or degree ceremony. The same year also saw the publication of *Melothesia, or, Certain general rules for playing upon a continued-bass. With a choice collection of lessons for the harpsichord and organ of all sorts*, an anthology edited by Locke containing the earliest surviving printed English instructions for realizing a figured bass. Locke had remained active as a theatre composer after the Restoration, and in the 1670s contributed to three important milestones in the development of English dramatic music: Elkanah Settle's *The Empress of Morocco*, including Locke's self-contained *Masque of Orpheus and Euridice* (3 July 1673), Thomas Shadwell's version of *The Tempest* (1674), with instrumental music by Locke, and Shadwell's *Psyche* (27 February 1675), for which Locke wrote the vocal music and 'the Instrumental Therein Intermix'd'. Locke's sections of *The Tempest* and *Psyche* were published as *The English Opera* in 1675. His final venture into publication was *Tripla concordia, or, A choice collection of new airs in three parts, for treble and basse violins by several authors*, advertised in November 1676 and probably supervised by Locke.

A story related by Roger North may reflect a severe physical or mental decline suffered by Locke towards the end of his life, which may in turn explain why he did not make a will. North states that the Italian singers at the Somerset House chapel were so dissatisfied with Locke's performance that he was relegated from the great organ to a chamber organ, on which he played throughout the services, but there is no evidence of this situation in other sources, including the one surviving account book of Queen Catherine's household, from 1671/2 (Weale, xxix–xxxii). Locke died, probably in his lodgings in the Strand, London, in August 1677 and was probably buried in the Anglican churchyard at St Mary Savoy, given as his parish when probate was granted to his daughter Mary on 13 December. His widow, who renounced her right to the administration of his estate, was buried at St James's, Piccadilly, on 17 July 1701. For the last few years of her life she had occupied a property in James Street, near Golden Square, and a daughter, either Mary or another unknown child, was married to Matthew Scott of Pall Mall. These circumstances suggest that Locke's widow was financially secure, in spite of difficulties caused in his lifetime by late payment of his court salaries.

Significance Locke's importance to English music in the generation before Purcell cannot be overestimated. He composed significant works in every major genre: his *Consort of Four Parts* was regarded by North, who did not know Purcell's fantasias, as the last masterpiece of the English polyphonic tradition, and he excelled in expressive, declamatory vocal writing, which he turned to dramatic effect in his theatre works and combined with counterpoint in his anthems. His achievement was recognized by Henry Purcell in an elegy published in the second book of John Playford's *Choice Ayres* (1679), 'What hope for us remains now he is gone?', and several works survive in manuscripts copied by Purcell, Blow, and other discriminating musicians. Perhaps over-sensitive to criticism, Locke was often outspoken in defence of English music and his own works, but Lefkowitz's assessment of his character as 'vain, contentious and vindictive' (*New Grove*) has little or no support beyond the polemics against Salmon. In *Observations upon a Late Book* (p. 2) Locke expresses gratitude that the civil war interrupted his career and prevented the publication of his early music before he had 'become sensible of the vanity and impudency of it'. His autograph sources bear witness to rigorous editing and revision of mature works, and high standards of artistic, religious, and personal integrity seem to have been as prominent in his character as any more negative elements sometimes evident. ROBERT THOMPSON

Sources M. Lefkowitz, 'Locke, Matthew', *New Grove* [incl. bibliography] • R. E. M. Harding, *A thematic catalogue of the works of Matthew Locke* (1971) • A. Ashbee, ed., *Records of English court music*, 1 (1986) • A. Ashbee, ed., *Records of English court music*, 5 (1991) • A. Ashbee and D. Lasocki, eds., *A biographical dictionary of English court musicians, 1485–1714*, 2 vols. (1998) [incl. bibliography] • J. D. Shute, *Anthony à Wood and his manuscript Wood D 19 (4) at the Bodleian Library, Oxford: an annotated transcription* (1982) • administration of Locke's estate, 1677, PRO, Family Record Centre, PROB 6/52, fol. 114v • will, 1701, LMA, AM/PW/1701/Locke [Mary Locke; incl. refererence to 'my nephew Garnons', proving that this Mary was Locke's widow] • depositions against Locke as a papist, Herefs. RO, vol. 5, fols. 7–8; see also *Thirteenth report*, HMC (1892), appx pt 4, p. 343 • [S. Taylor], *Impostor magnus, or, The legerdemain of Richard Delamain* (1654) • *The close hypocrite discovered, or, A true description of the life and person of Cap. Taylor, in the city of Hereford* (1654) [copy in Yale University, Beinecke Rare Book and Manuscript Library, Brit Tracts 1654 C62] • J. Webb, *Memorials of the civil war … as it affected Herefordshire*, ed. T. W. Webb, 2 vols. (1879), vol. 2, pp. 314 • A. J. Howard, ed., *The Devon protestation returns 1641* (1973) • J. Wilson, *Roger North on music* (1959) • J. C. M. Weale, ed., *Registers of the Catholic chapels royal and of the Portuguese embassy chapel, 1662–1829*, Catholic RS, 38 (1941) • M. A. E. Green, ed., *Calendar of the proceedings of the committee for compounding … 1643–1660*, 1, PRO (1889) • M. A. E. Green, ed., *Calendar of the proceedings of the committee for compounding … 1643–1660*, 4, PRO (1892) • H. W. Shaw, *The succession of organists of the Chapel Royal and the cathedrals of England and Wales from c.1538* (1991) • parish register, St James's, Piccadilly, London [burial: Mary Locke, wife] • H. Purcell, 'What hope for us remains now he is gone', *Choice ayres and dialogues* (1679) • I. Payne, *The provision and practice of sacred music at Cambridge colleges and selected cathedrals, c.1547–c.1646* (1993) • Pepys, *Diary* • accounts of the overseers of the poor (1686–1705), City Westm. AC, D2–21

Archives BL, musical MSS and papers, Add. MSS 10444–10445, 14399, 17799, 17801, 19759, 29386–29397, 31437 • Bodl. Oxf., autograph music bound with other material, MSS Mus. c. 23, Mus. Sch. A. 641, Mus. Sch. C.44, Mus. Sch. C.138 • Christ Church Oxf., autograph music bound with other material, Mus.1188/9, 1219 • U. Nott., autograph music bound with other material, Portland MS PwV23

Likenesses J. Caldwall, engraving (after oil painting attrib. I. Fuller), repro. in J. Hawkins, *A general history of the science and practice of music* (1776) • attrib. I. Fuller, oils (*aetat 40 anno domini 1662*), faculty of music, U. Oxf. • portrait, U. Oxf., faculty of music [*see illus.*]
Wealth at death regularly deferred payment of debts, 1660–77; widow quite well off

Locke, Richard (1737–1806), agriculturist and antiquary, was born at Burnham-on-Sea, Somerset, on 6 June 1737, the son of Richard and Hannah Locke and the great-nephew of the philosopher John Locke. He described himself as 'a self-taught individual of inferior ability but possessed of a laborious turn of mind' (*Supplement*, 10). He early inherited small parcels of land in Burnham-on-Sea, to which he added considerably towards the end of his life, and he played a regular part in local administration. Locke began work as a land surveyor in 1755, producing estate maps and town maps of Burnham-on-Sea (1777) and Taunton (1782). He was later to be high constable of Bempstone Hundred and, with the purchase of land in his native parish, he became lord of the manor of Huish by Highbridge. He married three times, first on 22 March 1761, at Long Sutton, Somerset, Elizabeth Lovebond (*d.* 1762); second Joan (*d.* 1792); and last in 1792, Parnell Adams, who survived him.

Throughout his life Locke was active as a practical agriculturist and collector of information about the parishes of Somerset; he was also the founder and chief supporter of a debating and benefit society called the Burnham Society from 1772 until his death. He carried out successful experiments on poor grassland by removing earth banks formed beside the ditches, spreading the soil to make the fields level, and adding wet sand, on which beans, peas, and clover were sown in the first year and thereafter grass. Improvement was spectacular. He corresponded with members of the Bath and West of England Agricultural Society on other ways of improving meadow land. He was also an advocate of enclosure and about 1780 he produced a plan to drain the vast area of King's Sedgemoor. John Billingsley applied to him for information for his *General View of the Agriculture of the County of Somerset*, published in 1794, and recommended Locke to the board of agriculture as a correspondent.

Locke's considerable literary output covered both historical and contemporary topics. It took the form of essays in periodicals on the subjects of agricultural improvement, drainage, and the benefits of enclosure; letters; surveys; and published monographs. His monographs include *The Western Rebellion* (1782), on the uprising of the duke of Monmouth in 1685; *A Chronological Register of Events Relating to the Town of Taunton* (1782); and *The Customs of the Manor of Taunton and Taunton Deane* (1785). Three of Locke's unpublished works are: materials for a history of Berrow, a parish near Burnham-on-Sea; information on clergy and benefices in Somerset for an improved version of Ecton's *Thesaurus*; and 'A survey of Somerset' (1795–1806), which amplified and extended information given by John Collinson in his *History of Somerset*, published in 1791.

Locke died at Highbridge Cottage, Burnham-on-Sea, in October 1806 and was buried in Burnham-on-Sea church on 31 October under a stone that bears the inscription 'Never to be removed'. He left bequests totalling £4000 to six grandchildren, lands worth £500 a year to Richard, his son and heir, and four houses and land to his daughters and grandchildren. ROBERT W. DUNNING

Sources *Supplement to Collinson's History of Somerset … with Extracts from Locke's Survey with a short biography*, ed. F. M. Ward (1939) • F. W. Steer and others, *Dictionary of land surveyors and local map-makers of Great Britain and Ireland, 1530–1850*, ed. P. Eden, 2nd edn, ed. S. Bendall, 2 vols. (1997) • *IGI*
Archives Som. ARS, MSS, notes, and maps • Som. ARS, Somerset Archaeological Society deposit, DD/SAS • Som. ARS, Burnham parish deposit, D/P/bons
Wealth at death £4000 in bequests; plus four houses and land

Locke, William. *See* Lock, William (1732–1810).

Locke, William John (1863–1930), novelist, was born at Cunningsbury St George, Christ Church, Demerara, British Guiana, on 20 March 1863, the elder son of John Locke, bank clerk, of Barbados, and his wife, Sarah Elizabeth. His parents were English. In 1864 his family went to Trinidad, where he was educated at the Queen's Royal College, and won an exhibition to St John's College, Cambridge. He matriculated at Cambridge in 1881, and graduated with honours in the mathematical tripos of 1884.

After leaving Cambridge, Locke became a schoolmaster. He disliked teaching, and his reticence in after years makes it difficult to trace his career as a teacher, but he is known to have been a master at the Oxford Military College at Temple Cowley in 1889 and 1890 and at Clifton College, Bristol, in 1890; from 1891 to 1897 he was modern languages master at Trinity College, Glenalmond. In 1893 he published a school edition of *Murat*, an extract from the *Crimes célèbres* of Alexandre Dumas père (1803–1870). In 1890 he became seriously ill, and he remained tuberculous for the rest of his life. From 1897 to 1907 he was secretary of the Royal Institute of British Architects, and lived in London. He resigned this position when his writing began to afford him a substantial income.

The earliest of Locke's numerous novels, *At the Gate of Samaria*, was published in 1895. It was one of the many novels of its period to deal with sexual awakening and marital breakdown while criticizing repressive social and sexual codes and the current divorce law. The heroine, Clytie, is a young artist who has left her dreary family for a studio in the King's Road, Chelsea, where her upstairs neighbour is Kent, a misogynistic assistant keeper in the British Museum. They become friends, but her marriage to a tough and chauvinistic explorer interrupts their burgeoning romance, and when his chauvinism turns out to be accompanied by brutality and philandering she leaves him, and sets up house with Kent (who is too noble to sleep with her) until the explorer is conveniently killed abroad. Although Locke's great successes were to be more whimsical and less ponderously melodramatic, the book exhibits several typical motifs: critique of the English bourgeoisie, celebration of bohemianism and cosmopolitanism, romance outside marriage, and the triumph of the woman who has suffered a social stigma for sexual transgression. In *A Study in Shadows* (1896), set in a dull Geneva boarding-house, for instance, both hero and heroine have had extramarital intrigues before meeting, but are permitted to live happily ever after.

The hero of Locke's first popular success, *The Morals of Marcus Ordeyne* (1905), is a former schoolmaster conducting a lukewarm affair with a sympathetic woman separated from her husband, who adopts a beautiful girl who has escaped from a Turkish harem. She is seduced and abandoned by a former pupil of his, and eventually realizes she loves the schoolmaster. *The Beloved Vagabond* (1906), another of his better-known works, is the story of Paragot, a drunken philosopher, wit, travelling musician, and adopter of waifs, who turns out to be a nobleman who has abandoned the world after an unhappy love affair. The woman he loves tries to marry him when she is widowed, but he realizes he is now bohemian ingrain. Locke dramatized *The Morals of Marcus Ordeyne* and several of his other books between 1907 and 1912; their focus on modern marriage was much in fashion in plays of the time, their happy endings were satisfying to audiences, and dramatic writing was then extremely lucrative.

In January 1910 Percy John Hamilton Close petitioned successfully to divorce his wife, Aimée (*d.* 1948) (whom he had married in 1906), for adultery with Locke, who had come to live near them, outside Wallingford, Berkshire, in 1908. Mrs Close, who was born Aimée Maxwell Heath, daughter of James Theodore Heath, was an actress who had been trying to write a play with Locke's help. The decree was made absolute in August 1910, and she and Locke were married at Chelsea register office on 19 May 1911. They had no children.

From 1914 to 1918 Locke, at his own expense, converted his house at Hemel Hempstead, Hertfordshire, into a hospital for soldiers from the ranks. He was also engaged untiringly in helping Belgian refugees; for this service he was made chevalier of the Belgian order of the Crown. His health, always fragile, suffered from his overwork during these years, and in 1921 it became necessary for him to settle in the south of France, at Cannes. He regarded the remaining years of his life as years of exile in which he eagerly gathered round him a social circle of English and American visitors to the French riviera. He continued to publish novels in his old vein. A weary reviewer in the *Illustrated London News*, for example, commented of *The Tombs of Tombarel* (1930):

> We find the familiar series of adventures, half-humorous and wholly sentimental, held together by the familiar figure of an urbane and charitable Frenchman, the familiar atmosphere of gentle vagabondage and innocent Bohemianism, and mild whimsicality of French ejaculations and English morals. (*ILN*, 19 April 1930)

Locke died of cancer at 34 rue Desbordes Valmore, Paris, on 15 May 1930.

E. O'Brien, *rev.* Charlotte Mitchell

Sources *The Times* (25 Jan 1910) · *The Times* (11 Aug 1910) · *The Times* (17 May 1930) · *The Times* (19 May 1930) · *The Times* (20 May 1930) · *The Times* (21 May 1930) · *Glenalmond register* (1929) · private information (1937) · *ILN* (19 April 1930) · Venn, *Alum. Cant.* · *CGPLA Eng. & Wales* (1930) · m. cert. · d. cert.

Archives Ransom HRC, MSS and corresp. | BL, corresp. with Society of Authors, Add. MS 56738 · Ransom HRC, corresp. with John Lane

Likenesses J. M. Flagg, chalk drawing, 1909, NPG · H. Furniss, two caricatures, pen-and-ink drawings, NPG · E. O. Hoppé, photograph, NPG · G. Stevenson, watercolour drawing, Garr. Club · photograph, repro. in F. T. Cooper, *Some English story tellers* (1912), facing p. 148 · photograph, repro. in *ILN*, 692 · photograph, repro. in *ILN* (24 May 1940), 932 · photograph, NPG

Wealth at death £25,030 3*s.* 1*d.*: resworn probate, 20 June 1930, *CGPLA Eng. & Wales*

Locker, Arthur (1828–1893), novelist and journalist, was born at Greenwich Hospital on 2 July 1828, second son of Edward Hawke *Locker (1777–1849) and his wife, a daughter of the Revd Jonathan Boucher. Frederick Locker-*Lampson was his brother. He was educated at Charterhouse School and, from 1847, at Pembroke College, Oxford, where he graduated BA in 1851. After graduation he worked for a year in a mercantile office in Liverpool. In 1852 he emigrated to Victoria, Australia, searching for gold. He did not succeed, and turned to journalism, also producing some tales and plays for an Australian audience. By 1856 he was back in England, where on 15 May, he married Mary Jane Rouse, daughter of John Wood Rouse of Greenwich, a lieutenant in the Royal Navy.

Locker returned permanently to England in 1861, with the ambition of devoting himself to literature; a number of novels, set mainly in Australia, were later published, among them *Sweet Seventeen* (1866), *On a Coral Reef* (1869), and *The Village Surgeon* (1874). In order to keep himself, he wrote extensively for newspapers and magazines, and in 1863 obtained a position at *The Times*, which he kept until 1870, when he was appointed editor of the newly founded illustrated newspaper *The Graphic*, owned by William Luson Thomas. He was an efficient editor, and encouraged young writers of promise. On 5 June 1890, his first wife having died, he married Catharine Sarah Carpenter, *née* Clulioth, a widow of forty-three. In December 1891 he retired because of ill health, and, after visiting Madeira and the Isle of Wight in the vain hope of recovery, died at 19 West Hill, Highgate, on 23 June 1893.

Richard Garnett, *rev.* Joseph Coohill

Sources *The Times* (26 June 1893) · *The Graphic* (1 July 1893) · m. certs. (2)

Archives BL, letters to Royal Literary Fund, loan 96 · Bodl. Oxf., letters to Anthony Trollope · Yale U., Beinecke L., letters to Friederich Locker, Eleanor Locker, and Hannah Locker, and verses

Likenesses R. T. & Co., wood-engraving, NPG; repro. in *ILN* (19 Dec 1891) · wood-engraving (after photograph by Elliott & Fry), NPG

Wealth at death £17,477 11*s.* 7*d.*: probate, 7 July 1893, *CGPLA Eng. & Wales*

Locker, Edward Hawke (1777–1849), hospital administrator and watercolour painter, born at the parsonage house, East Malling, Kent, on 9 October 1777, was the fourth of the five surviving children of Captain William *Locker (1731–1800) and his wife, Lucy (1746/7–1780), daughter of Admiral William Parry and granddaughter of Commodore Charles Brown. Locker was named after William Locker's patron Admiral Edward Hawke. He was educated at Eton College, and on 1 June 1795 entered the navy pay office as clerk (seaman's wages), a position which he held until about 1799. In October of that year he was appointed clerk to the Board of Control for affairs in India, and then to the board of naval enquiry. In 1804 he became civil secretary to Admiral Edward Pellew, Viscount Exmouth, and was with him during his commands in the East Indies (1804–9), in the North Sea (1810), and in the Mediterranean (1811–14). During this time he was a prize agent, engaged in the distribution of prize money, from which he himself derived considerable benefit. He was elected a fellow of the Royal Society in 1811.

In 1813, with Lord John Russell, Locker visited Spain during the Peninsular War, and carried dispatches to the duke of Wellington. His account, *Views of Spain*, was published in 1824, with illustrations after his own watercolours. In May 1814 he visited Napoleon at Porto Ferraio, Elba, later described by him in *The Plain Englishman* (3.375). On 28 February 1815 he married Eleanor Mary Elizabeth (*d.* 1861), daughter of the Revd Jonathan Boucher, a former friend of George Washington. They lived at Windsor until 1819, when Locker was appointed secretary to the Royal Naval Hospital, Greenwich, where his father had ended his career as lieutenant-governor; in 1824 he became civil commissioner of the hospital. With Lord John Russell, John Wilson Croker (secretary to the Admiralty), the sculptor Sir Francis Chantrey, and Sir Thomas Lawrence, president of the Royal Academy, he was one of the twenty-four founder members of the Athenaeum and sat on its general committee. Locker was co-founder (with Charles Knight) of *The Plain Englishman* (1820–30), a periodical designed to supply its readers with 'useful information, in place of [the] infidel and disloyal publications' ('Introduction', *The Plain Englishman*, 1824); he became the journal's editor. Its purpose was largely didactic and it advocated patriotism by lauding heroic deeds, including naval ones. Locker's friend the poet laureate Robert Southey was among its contributors.

At Greenwich, Locker used his astute business sense to reform the administration of the hospital, including the lead and coal mining interests of its large Northumbrian estates, employing McAdam to construct new roads to improve communication and introducing many improvements for its tenants. In 1823 he submitted a proposal to establish in the Painted Hall in the Royal Naval Hospital 'a gallery of pictures commemorating the distinguished services of the Royal Navy of England'. This revived a scheme first put forward in 1795 by William Locker as a means of raising money for the hospital's charitable purposes, but his son's aims were predominantly didactic. The Naval Gallery received the approval of George IV: in 1824 he presented twenty-nine pictures from the Royal Collection, consisting mainly of portraits of naval commanders by Lely, Kneller, and Michael Dahl. In 1829, he added de Loutherbourg's *Battle of the 1st June, 1794* and Turner's *Battle of Trafalgar*, the only painting by Turner to have been in the Royal Collection. His support was continued by his successor, William IV, and the collection was also augmented by gifts which Locker assiduously solicited from naval families, and from the British Institution; he also encouraged commissions and presented pictures himself. The Naval Gallery was, in effect, the first gallery of national history in the country and may be seen as part of the general programme to establish national art collections and to raise the artistic reputation of the capital. Locker wrote a substantial companion to the gallery, *Memoirs of Celebrated Naval Commanders* (1832), illustrated with engravings of the collection.

In 1936 the collection passed into the care of the newly formed National Maritime Museum of which it forms a principal component, although still the property of the hospital. Locker's own collection, dispersed after his death, was displayed in his apartments there and included 'excellent specimens of Thomas Lawrence, Wilkie, Prout, Edridge, Girtin, Turner, Alexander, Chinnery, Paul Sandby, Hearne, Nicholson, Cipriani, Cozens, and Lady Farnborough' (Locker-Lampson, 73). In 1823 he contributed works from his collection to the first loan exhibition at the Old Watercolour Society. His correspondence with Robert Southey, Walter Scott, William Wilberforce, Croker, Thomas Lawrence, David Wilkie, and others reveals a many-sided interest in the events of his day, and his opinion carried weight with his contemporaries in matters of art, literature, and religion.

In 1844 Locker was forced to retire from his post at the hospital owing to 'mental failure' from which he was to suffer until his death at Iver, Buckinghamshire, on 16 October 1849. He was buried at Iver. Among his children were the poet Frederick Locker-*Lampson (1821–1895), and the novelist and journalist Arthur *Locker (1828–1893), who became editor of *The Graphic*. E. H. Locker's watercolours can be found in the Victoria and Albert Museum and the British Museum in London, the National Maritime Museum at Greenwich, and the Victoria Art Gallery, Bath. ROGER QUARM

Sources *GM*, 2nd ser., 32 (1849), 654 · *Annual Register* (1849) · *The Athenaeum* (20 Oct 1849) · *The Times* (22 Oct 1849) · E. H. Locker, *Memoirs of celebrated naval commanders illustrated by engravings from original pictures in the Naval Gallery of Greenwich Hospital* (1832) · F. Locker-Lampson, *My confidences: an autobiographical sketch addressed to my descendants*, ed. A. Birrell, 2nd edn (1896) · Greenwich Hospital minutes, PRO, ADM 67, In letters ADM 65, Out letters ADM 66 · H. Ward, *History of the Athenaeum, 1824–1925* (1926) · F. R. Cowell, *The Atheanæum: club and social life in London, 1824–1974* (1975) · P. Newell, *Greenwich Hospital, a royal foundation, 1692–1983* (1983) · K. Littlewood and B. Butler, *Of ships and stars: maritime heritage and the founding of the National Maritime Museum, Greenwich* (1998) · priv. coll. [MS memoirs, 1882, of Ellen Dobie, *née* Locker] · R. May, account of Locker in India, Yale U., Beinecke L., Locker-Lampson MSS · *IGI* · d. cert.

Archives BL, travel journal, Add. MS 60352 · Bodl. Oxf., account of visit to Elba · Hunt. L., corresp. and papers · NMM, letter-book as secretary to Pellew and account book · PRO, corresp. as commissioner, with earlier documents, PRO 30, various · Yale U., Osborne collection, Locker-Lampson MSS, vols. I–III, USA [microfiche copy at W. Sussex RO] | CKS, family corresp. with Smiths · NMM, prize account book · Northumbd RO, Newcastle upon Tyne, corresp. relating to rebuilding of Falstone church · NRA priv. coll., letters to Henry Duncan · U. Edin., New Coll. L., letters to Thomas Chalmers · Yale U., Beinecke L., corresp. with J. W. Croker and Eleanor Locker

Likenesses J. F. Rigaud, group portrait, oils, 1780; Sothebys, 10 July 1996 · H. W. Phillips, oils, *c.*1842, NMM

Locker, Frederick. *See* Lampson, Frederick Locker- (1821–1895).

Locker, John (1693–1760), barrister and literary editor, was born in London on 27 August 1693, the eldest son of Stephen Locker, one-time clerk to the Leathersellers' Company. On 12 March 1707 John was admitted to the Merchant Taylors' School, London, from the Mercers' School. He matriculated at Merton College, Oxford, on 21 April 1711, stayed at Oxford for about two years, and entered Gray's Inn on 28 March 1719. He was called to the bar in 1724. He was a commissioner of bankruptcy and became clerk of the Leathersellers' Company on 2 June 1719 and of the Clockmakers' Company in 1740. He entered into membership of the Society of Antiquaries of London on 3 March 1737 and became a friend of a fellow member, William Bowyer, the learned printer.

Locker married Elizabeth (*d*. 1759), the eldest daughter of Edward Stillingfleet, rector of Wood Norton and Swanton in Norfolk and sister of the naturalist Benjamin Stillingfleet. Elizabeth and John Locker had nine children. Their second son, William *Locker, Nelson's teacher, became lieutenant-governor of Greenwich Hospital, Kent.

Dr Johnson described Locker as 'a gentleman eminent for curiosity and literature' (Nichols, *Lit. anecdotes*, 5.372–3). Some of his poems were published in *The Constellation: Poems on Several Occasions* (1715), a miscellany of short pastorals, satires, and odes, and a translation of Virgil's first eclogue; he also translated into English part of Voltaire's history of Charles XII, which was published in 1732 as the *History of Charles XII of Sweden*. He was also renowned for his skill in Greek, particularly modern Greek, which he is reputed to have acquired from a poor Greek priest found wandering lost in the streets of London. Locker took him to his house and maintained him for some years in return for which the priest provided instruction in the Greek language.

The most notable of Locker's achievements, however, was the work he undertook with Robert Stephens, historiographer royal, on the manuscript letters of Sir Francis Bacon. When Stephens died in November 1732 his papers passed to Locker who prepared them for the press adding, in accordance with Stephens's direction, 'what else he thought fit from his Collection of Manuscripts which was more than he [Stephens] had intended at that time' (BL, Add. MS 4260, fol. 19*v*). This edition of Bacon's correspondence was published by Locker's friend Bowyer in 1734. Locker also made corrections to the fourth volume of John Blackbourne's edition of Bacon's works. These corrections, in Locker's hand, are extant in the copy of this volume housed in the British Library.

Locker died in London on 30 May 1760 and was buried at St Helen, Bishopsgate, London. His collection of manuscripts was purchased by Thomas Birch in 1764 (BL, Add. MSS 4108 and 4258–4262). PATRICIA BREWERTON

Sources H. B. Wilson, *The history of Merchant-Taylors' School*, 2 vols. (1812–14) · Foster, *Alum. Oxon.* · C. J. Robinson, ed., *A register of the scholars admitted into Merchant Taylors' School, from* AD *1562 to 1874*, 1 (1882) · J. Foster, *The register of admissions to Gray's Inn, 1521–1889, together with the register of marriages in Gray's Inn chapel, 1695–1754* (privately printed, London, 1889) · *A list of the members of the Society of Antiquaries of London from their revival in 1717, to June 19, 1796* (1798) · *GM*, 1st ser., 30 (1760), 297 · Nichols, *Lit. anecdotes* · *Francisci Bacon opera omnia*, ed. J. Blackbourne, 4 (1730) · *Letters and remains of the Lord Chancellor Bacon*, ed. R. Stephens (1734) · *The constellation: poems on several occasions* (1715) · *The works of Francis Bacon, Baron of Verulam, Viscount St Alban and lord high chancellor of England*, ed. T. Birch, R. Stephens, and J. Locker, 1 (1765) · *The letters and life of Francis Bacon*, ed. J. Spedding, 7 vols. (1861–74), vol. 1 · *DNB*

Archives BL, Add. MSS 4258–4262 | BL, manuscripts from Thomas Birch's catalogue of Lord Bacon bought at the sale of the library of John Locker in 1764, Add. MS 4108

Locker, William (1731–1800), naval officer, was born in February 1731 in the official residence attached to the Leathersellers' Hall, London, the second son of John *Locker (1693–1760), the clerk to the company, and his wife, Elizabeth (*d*. 1759), daughter of Edward Stillingfleet. He followed his father to Merchant Taylors' School and entered the navy on 9 June 1746 as captain's servant in the *Kent* with a family relation, Captain Charles Windham (or Wyndham). After the latter's death Locker was moved to the *Vainqueur* (Captain James Kirk) bound for the West Indies, and then to the *Vulture* and the *Cornwall*, flagship of Charles Knowles, and was present at the capture of Port Louis. He then rejoined Kirk in the *Elizabeth* and returned home. After the peace he made two or more voyages to India and China in the East India Company's service, but in 1755 he rejoined the navy as master's mate in the *St George*, then Admiral Sir Edward Hawke's flagship. He passed for lieutenant on 7 January 1756, and was taken by Hawke in the *Antelope* when the admiral was sent out to relieve John Byng; he was promoted lieutenant to the *Experiment* on 4 July, though Sir Edward seems to have had difficulty in having the appointment confirmed (Mackay, 155, 265), and thus he earned Locker's lifelong gratitude, expressed in the name of his youngest and best-known son, Edward Hawke *Locker.

In January 1757 John Jervis, then a lieutenant of the *Culloden*, was appointed to the temporary command of the *Experiment* during Captain John Strachan's illness, and thus for two important months Jervis was Locker's shipmate. After an indecisive engagement with a large French privateer on 16 March, Jervis returned to the *Culloden*, and Strachan resumed command of the *Experiment*. On 8 July, off Alicante, she captured the *Télémaque*, a privateer of 20 guns and 460 men. Trusting to this enormous superiority in men, the *Télémaque* endeavoured to lay the *Experiment* on board, and after two attempts partially succeeded. Only a few of the French were able to get on board, and these were immediately killed. Locker was ordered by Strachan to enter the *Télémaque*, a task which he carried out successfully. The result of this remarkable action was the loss of 235 Frenchmen killed and wounded, while the *Experiment* lost only forty-eight. Locker himself suffered a wound in the leg. At the time he thought little of it; but he never completely recovered from its effects.

In December 1758 Locker was moved, with Strachan, to

the *Sapphire* (32 guns); she was attached to the fleet off Brest through summer and autumn 1759, and Locker was present at the defeat of the French in Quiberon Bay on 20 November. He was taken by Hawke into his flagship, the *Royal George*, in March 1760 and, moving up in rotation, became first lieutenant in July 1761. On 7 April 1762 he was promoted to the command of the fireship *Roman Emperor* and so began what Edward Hawke Locker was to describe as his father's happiest period of naval service.

In 1763 Locker was appointed to the sloop *Nautilus* and was sent to withdraw the British garrison from Goree in west Africa, as the peace restored it to France. After returning the garrison to England the *Nautilus* was sent to the Jamaica station, visiting ports in the Gulf of Mexico and venturing up the Mississippi River. She paid off at Deptford on 8 March 1768, and, to indicate Admiralty approval, Locker was promoted captain on 26 May 1768. In 1770 he married Lucy, daughter of Admiral William Parry, and granddaughter of Commodore Charles Brown. She died in 1780, leaving two daughters, Lucy and Elizabeth, and three sons, William, John, and Edward Hawke. Possibly through his wife the family had interests at Addington, Kent, as well as a farm at Gillingham. From 1770 to 1773 Locker commanded the frigate *Thames* on the home station, and in 1777 he commissioned the *Lowestoft* for the West Indies. Horatio Nelson, then just promoted, was at the same time appointed one of the *Lowestoft's* lieutenants, and remained with Locker for about fifteen months; he was at this time barely nineteen, and the stamp of Locker's teaching and of his experience of Hawke had a lasting effect. More than twenty years afterwards (9 February 1799) Nelson wrote to Locker:

> I have been your scholar; it is you who taught me to board a Frenchman by your conduct when in the Experiment; it is you who always told me 'Lay a Frenchman close and you will beat him;' and my only merit in my profession is being a good scholar. Our friendship will never end but with my life, but you have always been too partial to me. (*Dispatches and Letters*, 3.260)

In 1779 Locker's health gave way and he was compelled to invalid, nor could he undertake any further active employment. In 1787, on the prospect of war with France, he was appointed to regulate the impress service at Exeter. In the Spanish armament of 1790 he commanded the *Cambridge* as flag-captain to Vice-Admiral Thomas Graves, then commander-in-chief at Plymouth; and in 1792 he was for a short time commodore and commander-in-chief at the Nore. On 15 February 1793 he was appointed lieutenant-governor of Greenwich Hospital.

Much of the interest in Locker derives from his role as a teacher, friend, and correspondent of Nelson. During his later years he compiled materials for a naval history, a task in which he was much assisted by Admiral John Forbes. Locker himself had no literary experience, and subsequently handed his material to John Charnock who used it in writing his six-volume *Biographia navalis* (1794–8). It was also at Locker's suggestion, and with prior help from him, that Charnock wrote his *Life of Nelson*. Locker died at Greenwich Hospital on 26 December 1800. He asked to be buried in the family vault at Addington where he had previously erected a memorial to his wife.

J. K. Laughton, *rev.* A. W. H. Pearsall

Sources R. F. Mackay, *Admiral Hawke* (1965) • *GM*, 1st ser., 70 (1800), 1299 • 'Biographical memoirs of Commodore William Locker, late lieutenant-govenor of Greenwich Hospital', *Naval Chronicle*, 5 (1801), 97–121 • PRO, ADM 36/633, 1023, 1027, 1627, 4454, 5729 [muster bks] • PRO, ADM 51/630 [logs] • *The dispatches and letters of Vice-Admiral Lord Viscount Nelson*, ed. N. H. Nicolas, 7 vols. (1844–6) • C. Knight and E. H. Locker, eds., *The plain Englishman*, 3 (1820–23) • will

Archives NMM, MSS?

Likenesses D. Serres, oils, 1769, Yale U. CBA • G. Stuart, oils, *c.*1785, NMM • L. F. Abbott, oils, *c.*1795, NMM • L. F. Abbott, stipple (after J. Heath), NPG

Wealth at death property at Addington, Kent, and Gillingham, Kent; only left small annuities: will

Lockey, Charles (1820–1901), singer, was born on 20 March 1820 at Thatcham, near Newbury, Berkshire, the son of Angel Lockey of Oxford. He was a chorister at Magdalen College, Oxford, from 1828 to 1836, then studied singing with Edward Harris at Bath, and in 1842 became a pupil of George Smart. Lockey sang in the choirs of St George's Chapel, Windsor, and Eton College chapel. In 1843 he became a vicar-choral of St Paul's Cathedral. His first public appearance in oratorio was in October 1842, when he sang in Rossini's *Stabat mater* for the Melophonic Society. He performed in the Ancient Concerts in 1846, at the Three Choirs festivals from 1846 to 1856, and at concerts of the Sacred Harmonic Society. He was chosen to sing the tenor aria 'Then shall the righteous' in the first performance of Mendelssohn's *Elijah*, at the Birmingham festival on 26 August 1846, which was conducted by the composer. Mendelssohn was so impressed by Lockey at rehearsals that he also assigned the aria 'If with all your hearts' to him, writing to his brother after the performance that a young English tenor sang the last aria so beautifully that he was almost unable to control his feelings and to carry on beating time steadily.

In 1848 Lockey was appointed a gentleman of the Chapel Royal. On 24 May 1853 he married Martha Williams, a contralto, who died in 1897. The couple had one son. Lockey retired in 1859 after losing his voice as a result of a throat infection and went into business at Gravesend and Dover. He retained his appointments at St Paul's and the Chapel Royal until his death, but for forty-three years Fred Walker, Joseph Barnby, and Edward Lloyd were his deputies. He died on 3 December 1901 at Hastings.

Frederick Corder, *rev.* Anne Pimlott Baker

Sources Brown & Stratton, *Brit. mus.* • Grove, *Dict. mus.* • D. Baptie, *A handbook of musical biography* (1883) • *Letters of Felix Mendelssohn Bartholdy, from 1833 to 1847*, ed. P. M. Mendelssohn Bartholdy and C. M. Mendelssohn Bartholdy, trans. Lady Wallace, new edn (1865) • *CGPLA Eng. & Wales* (1902)

Wealth at death £22,283 17*s.* 7*d.*: resworn probate, Sept 1902, *CGPLA Eng. & Wales*

Lockey, Rowland (*c.*1566–1616), painter and goldsmith, was born in London, the son of Leonard Lockey (*d.* 1613), a crossbow maker and a freeman of the Company of Armourers who lived in Fleet Lane in the parish of St

Bride, London. He was apprenticed to Nicholas Hilliard of the Goldsmiths' Company for eight years in 1581, so he was a freeman probably by 1589 and certainly before 1600, when his younger brother Nicholas began an eight-year apprenticeship with him. Rowland Lockey is commended by Richard Haydocke in the preface to *A Tracte Containing the Artes of Curious Paintinge, Carvinge & Buildinge* (1598), his translation from the original by Giovanni Lomazzo, 'for oil and limning in some measure' (Kurz, 14); he is also mentioned by Francis Meres, in his *Palladis tamia* (1598), among the eminent artists then living in England, and in Edward Norgate's *Miniatura*, in a list of artists who were competent in the use of crayons, or 'dry colours'.

Lockey married Martha Juxe of St Bride's at the parish church on 2 February 1602; her father was Thomas Juxe (or Juckes), a freeman of the Grocers' Company practising as an apothecary. Lockey and his wife baptized four children between 1602 and 1608, from the records of which it is known that they were living in the parish of St Martin-in-the-Fields in 1605 and in St Dunstan-in-the-West by 1608.

Lockey is recognized for his group portraits based on the painting *The Family of Sir Thomas More* by Hans Holbein the younger made during his first visit to England in 1526–8 (destroyed; drawing, Öffentliche Kunstsammlung Basel Kunstmuseum, Kupferstichkabinett); Lockey's painting in oils (1592), at Nostell Priory, Yorkshire, is a close copy. William Burton (1575–1645), the antiquary, wrote that at Lockey's house he:

> once saw a neat piece in oil, containing in one table the picture of Sir John More … and of his wife; and of Sir Thomas More, lord chancellor, his son, and his wife; and of all the lineal heirs male descended from them; together with each man's wife until that present year living. (Kurz, 15)

Although the women are wrongly identified this description corresponds very nearly to the painting (1593) at the National Portrait Gallery, London. It differs from Holbein's original by omitting members of the household who were not blood relatives (except Anne Cresacre, mother of the younger Thomas More) and including the descendants to emphasize their dynastic connection to the Elizabethan Mores and their continued adherence to Catholicism. A miniature of 1593–4 (V&A) shows a garden view not in the two paintings.

In 1592 Hilliard and Lockey were paid for pictures for Elizabeth, countess of Shrewsbury. After her death her son William Cavendish, first earl of Devonshire, employed Lockey from 1608 to 1613 to paint more than thirty pictures, the majority of them copies, for Hardwick Hall, Derbyshire. These may have included Bess of Hardwick; Mary, queen of Scots; and James I (Hardwick Hall). The signed portrait of Lady Margaret Beaufort (*c*.1598) at St John's College, Cambridge, is also a copy by Lockey of an earlier work. A number of miniatures in Hilliard's style have been attributed to Lockey, and he may have designed the title page of the Bishops' Bible (1602).

John Langton became Lockey's apprentice in 1607 (freeman, 1616) and Raphe Blackmore in 1612; Lockey's stepbrother James Howson (*d.* 1616) was named as an apprentice in his will. In February 1614 Lockey was taken into the livery of the Goldsmiths' Company. He spent his later years in the parish of St Dunstan-in-the-West and was among those who contributed to repairing and redecorating the church in 1615. He died within the parish in March 1616 and was buried in his old parish, St Bride's, on 26 March.

In his will dated 15 February 1616 Lockey bequeathed everything but specified legacies to his wife, Martha. He left 20s., to 'make him a Ringe', to John Davies of Hereford, who wrote a poem in his praise (epigram 258 in *The Scourge of Folly*, 1611); Lockey painted his portrait, now lost but possibly that engraved for Davies's *The Writing Schoolemaster* (1636).

He left his brother Nicholas 'all my Italian Printes and all my plasters' and the lease of the family home in Fleet Lane. In a lawsuit of 1617 Nicholas describes himself as a citizen and armourer of London but 'useinge and professinge for his livinge … the Arte and skill of lymeinge and drawinge of pictures' (Edmond, 97). A portrait (1620) of John King, bishop of London, attributed to Nicholas Lockey was engraved by Francis Delaram; there are at least eight known paintings of this type. He was still active in 1624. ARIANNE BURNETTE

Sources E. Auerbach, *Nicholas Hilliard* (1961) · M. Edmond, 'Limners and picturemakers', *Walpole Society*, 47 (1978–80), 60–242 · O. Kurz, 'Rowland Locky', *Burlington Magazine*, 99 (1957), 13–16 · R. Strong and V. J. Murrell, *Artists of the Tudor court: the portrait miniature rediscovered, 1520–1620* (1983) [exhibition catalogue, V&A, 9 July – 6 Nov 1983] · R. Strong, *The English Renaissance miniature* (1983) · K. Hearn, ed., *Dynasties: painting in Tudor and Jacobean England, 1530–1630* (1995) [exhibition catalogue, Tate Gallery, London, 12 Oct 1995 – 7 Jan 1996] · C. Foley, 'Lockey, Rowland', *The dictionary of art*, ed. J. Turner (1996) · J. Murdoch and others, *The English miniature* (1981) · R. Strong, *Tudor and Jacobean portraits*, 2 vols. (1969) · J. Rowlands, *Holbein: the paintings of Hans Holbein the younger* (1985) · S. Morison and N. Barker, *The likeness of Thomas More* (1963) · J. B. Trapp and H. Schulte Herbrüggen, *'The King's Good Servant': Sir Thomas More, 1477/8–1535* (1977) [exhibition catalogue, NPG, 25 Nov 1977 – 12 March 1978] · M. Girouard, *Hardwick Hall* (1976); rev. edn (1989) · J. Ingamells, *The English episcopal portraits, 1559–1835* (1981) · E. K. Waterhouse, *The dictionary of British 16th and 17th century painters* (1988) · *DNB* · will, PRO, PROB 11/127, sig. 26

Archives Chatsworth House, Derbyshire, account book of Elizabeth, countess of Shrewsbury, MS 7, fol. 30 · Chatsworth House, Derbyshire, account book of William Cavendish, duke of Devonshire, MS 7 · City Westm. AC, Churchwarden's accounts · GL, MSS 6537, 6536, 10342, 4107/2, 2968/2 · Goldsmiths' Company, Apprentice Book, minutes, Book P, pt 1

Lockey, Thomas (1602?–1679), librarian and Church of England clergyman, was born to unknown parents, probably in 1602. He obtained a king's scholarship at Westminster School and in 1618 was elected to Christ Church, Oxford. He contributed to the Oxford collection of verses on the death of Queen Anne in 1619. He matriculated at Christ Church on 16 March 1621, graduated BA on 18 May 1622, and proceeded MA on 20 June 1625 and BD on 12 June 1634. Lockey was vicar of East Garston, Berkshire, until 1633, and he or a namesake held the prebendal stall of Thorney in Chichester Cathedral from 1639 to 1642, but he resided at Oxford, where he was noted as a college tutor

Thomas Lockey (1602?–1679), by unknown artist

and a preacher. It was his manuscript copy of Thomas Hobbes's 'Human nature' which Francis Bowman used to print a surreptitious edition of the work in 1650. In January 1651 a sermon preached by Lockey before the university offended the parliamentary visitors, and led to a ban on his preaching and deprivation of his tutorship. He thereupon left Oxford until the Restoration.

On 21 July 1660 Lockey was made prebendary of Beminster Prima, and on 17 August of Alton Pancras, both in Salisbury Cathedral. On 28 September 1660 he was elected librarian of the Bodleian Library; two months later he proceeded DD. Lockey won the good opinion of visitors by his courtesy, but, according to Anthony Wood, was 'not altogether fit for that office' (*Life and Times*, 1.335). Thomas Hearne wrote that he designed the catalogue of John Selden's vast library (*Remarks*, 2.40). In a letter dated 15 July 1664 he wrote to Archbishop Sheldon of this 'accession of about 30,000 Authors, [that] I have by mine owne paynes disposed of in a Catalogue, to be inserted afterward in the general' (Bodl. Oxf., MS Tanner 338, fol. 180). His work was not well done or brought to completion, however, and his successor was left to employ others to catalogue the Bodleian afresh. On 8 September 1665 he received Clarendon, the chancellor of Oxford, and Clarendon's guest, the earl of Manchester, chancellor of Cambridge University, on their visit to the library, and delivered a Latin speech. This was his last function as librarian; he resigned the post on 29 November.

When abroad in 1663, Lockey had been nominated to the fifth stall of Christ Church Cathedral, but was not installed until 12 July 1665; he exchanged it for the fourth stall on 6 July 1678; he had given £100 towards the rebuilding of Wolsey's quadrangle in 1660. Lockey died of a 'surfeit of cherries' on 29 June 1679 and was buried in the north transept of Christ Church Cathedral on 7 July. His epitaph says that, 'though he had been twice to Rome, his own country ever delighted him and his own faith'. Lockey had formed a substantial collection: at his death he had 247 'pictures' (perhaps mostly prints), about eighty 'statues', a quantity of rings and medals, and a telescope 'with some other mathematicall instruments', as well as a choice library of books (valued at £200) (Philip, 'Inventory', 84), all of which he left to his executor, Henry Killigrew, prebendary of Westminster. His goods were valued at a total of £652 13*s*. 6*d*. Hearne described him as a very curious, nice man, and 'reckon'd the best in the university for classical learning' (*Remarks*, 2.40).

E. T. Bradley, *rev.* Nigel Ramsay

Sources I. G. Philip, 'Inventory of the goods of Dr Thomas Lockey', *Bodleian Library Record*, 5 (1954–6), 80–84 • I. Philip, *The Bodleian Library in the seventeenth and eighteenth centuries* (1983), 48–50 • T. Lockey, letter to G. Sheldon, Bodl. Oxf., MS Tanner 338, fol. 180 • Wood, *Ath. Oxon.*: *Fasti* (1820), 242 • *Fasti Angl.* (Hardy), 2.524, 525, 656, 657 • [G. W. Wheeler], 'A cataloguing failure', *Bodleian Quarterly Record*, 2 (1917–19), 264–5 • *The life and times of Anthony Wood*, ed. A. Clark, 1, OHS, 19 (1891), 335 • M. Burrows, ed., *The register of the visitors of the University of Oxford, from AD 1647 to AD 1658*, CS, new ser., 29 (1881), 316 • *Remarks and collections of Thomas Hearne*, ed. C. E. Doble and others, 2, OHS, 7 (1886), 40 • *Old Westminsters*, 2.586 • F. Madan, *The early Oxford press: a bibliography of printing and publishing in Oxford, 1468–1640*, OHS, 29 (1895), vol. 1 of *Oxford books: a bibliography of printed works* (1895–1931), 112 • *Hist. U. Oxf.* 4: *17th-cent. Oxf.*, 414

Likenesses oils, Bodl. Oxf. [*see illus.*]

Wealth at death £652 13*s*. 6*d*.: inventory, 3 July 1679, Philip, 'Inventory', 82–4

Lockhart, David (*d.* **1845**), botanist, who was born in Cumberland, was a gardener in the Royal Gardens, Kew. In 1816 he became the assistant of Christian Smith, the naturalist of the Congo expedition under Captain James Kingston Tuckey. Lockhart escaped with his life, but suffered much from the fever that killed Tuckey and most of his crew. Two years later he was put in charge of the Colonial Gardens at Trinidad, then under the supervision of Sir Ralph Woodford; they were much improved by him. He visited England in 1844 with the view of enriching the Trinidad gardens, but he died in 1845 soon after his return to the island. A genus of orchids was named *Lockhartia* after him by William Jackson Hooker but, being already named, was subsequently merged as *Fernandezia*.

B. D. Jackson, *rev.* Giles Hudson

Sources *Gardeners' Chronicle*, new ser., 24 (1885), 236–7 • Desmond, *Botanists*, rev. edn

Archives NHM, botanical specimens • RBG Kew, letters • RBG Kew, botanical specimens

Lockhart, George. *See* Lokert, George (*c.*1485–1547).

Lockhart, Sir George, of Carnwath, Lord Carnwath (*c.***1630–1689**), advocate and judge, seems to have been the second son of Sir James *Lockhart (1588/1599–1674) of Lee in Lanarkshire, judge, and his second wife, Martha, daughter of Sir George Douglas of Mordington. His early

Sir George Lockhart of Carnwath, Lord Carnwath (*c*.1630–1689), by Sir John Baptiste de Medina

years are obscure. He may have been the George Lockhart who assented for Lanarkshire to the tender for union in February 1652, and who signed the commission for the negotiation of union six months later, but he has frequently been confused with his brother-in-law, George Lockhart of Tarbrax, also in Lanarkshire. His first definite appearance in the record is at his admission to the bar on 8 January 1656. Perhaps at the instigation of his elder brother William *Lockhart (1621?–1675), who had married Oliver Cromwell's niece and was ambassador to France, he was appointed advocate-general to the Commonwealth in June 1658. He was also appointed sheriff of Lanark, and in 1659 he represented Lanarkshire in Richard Cromwell's parliament. After the collapse of the Cromwellian government in Scotland he spent some time in composing a compendium of the law reports of Sir Alexander Gibson of Durie, which came to be widely used by other advocates after the Restoration.

Whether Lockhart shared his brother's enthusiasm for the Commonwealth is unclear, but it was thanks to his royalist father that Charles II accepted his formal apology for serving the usurper before he was readmitted to the bar on 16 July 1661. He rapidly secured a reputation as the finest pleader of his generation. Sir George Mackenzie of Rosehaugh believed that he could be regarded as 'another Cicero', explaining that his technique was to arrange his arguments in such a way that they supported each other like the stones of an arch (*Works*, 1716, 1.7). Sir John Lauder of Fountainhall maintained that when he spoke before his colleagues in court:

> he did so chain us, and with his tongue draw us all after him by the ears, in a pleasant gaping amazement and constraint, that the wonderfull effects of Orpheus' harp in moving the stones, seemes not impossible to ane orator on the stupidest spirit. (*Historical Notices*, 1.80)

Gilbert Burnet, bishop of Salisbury, thought Lockhart 'the most learned lawyer, and the best pleader I have ever yet known in any nation' (*Bishop Burnet's History*, 1.246). More formal and material recognition of his talents followed. He was knighted in 1663 and was elected dean of the Faculty of Advocates in 1672. Involved in most of the major cases of his time, he had made enough money by 1681 to buy the estates of Braidwood, Dryden, and Carnwath, all in Lanarkshire. It was from the third estate that he took his title as a lord of session when he received the ultimate accolade of his profession on 21 December 1685, being appointed president of the college of justice in succession to Sir David Falconer of Newton.

It seems clear that Lockhart rose to the top of his profession more by virtue of his abilities than by any political manoeuvring. He had frequently appeared at the bar to defend religious dissidents, like those who had rebelled at Rullion Green in 1666 or had tried to assassinate the archbishop of St Andrews in 1668, and his performance on their behalf had always been as much fearless as eloquent and ingenious. In 1674 he had advised a client to appeal against a decision of the session to parliament. With the king's support, the affronted judges had disbarred Lockhart and his allies only to find that most of the other advocates were ready to withdraw from practice in sympathy. It had taken over a year for the deadlock to be broken and the administration of justice resumed, after which Lockhart had been admitted to the bar for the third time in his career on 28 January 1676. Three years later he had accepted a commission to appear in opposition to the government of the duke of Lauderdale before the king, and he had continued his forthright criticism of the regime as a member of parliament for Lanarkshire in 1681–2. Yet if James VII had thus been given cause to favour his promotion, he had been given less cause by Lockhart's determined defence of the earl of Argyll in 1682 and by his opposition to the toleration of Catholicism in the parliament of 1685–6. He evidently shared the commitment to the reformed faith that typified his home region, and was equally committed (though less typically among the advocates of his time) to doing his best for his clients.

At an unknown date Lockhart married Barbara Gilmour, possibly the daughter of Sir John *Gilmour of Craigmillar (*d*. 1671), president of the session. Following her death he married, on 2 September 1679, Philadelphia (*b*. 1655), daughter of Philip *Wharton, fourth Baron Wharton (1613–1696). They had three children: George *Lockhart (1681?–1731), Philip *Lockhart (1689?–1715), and a daughter. On 31 March 1689 Lockhart was emerging from an Easter day service in the church of St Giles, Edinburgh, adjacent to the parliament house in which he had spent much of his professional career, when he was approached by John Chiesly of Dalry, a disgruntled litigant. Lockhart nodded and moved on, but Chiesly produced a pistol and shot him in the back. He died within minutes. His widow subsequently married Captain John Ramsey, and died in or after 1717. J. D. FORD

Sources G. Mackenzie, *Memoirs of the affairs of Scotland* (1821) · *Historical notices of Scotish affairs, selected from the manuscripts of Sir John Lauder of Fountainhall*, ed. D. Laing, 2 vols., Bannatyne Club, 87 (1848) · *Bishop Burnet's History* · G. Brunton and D. Haig, *An historical account of the senators of the college of justice, from its institution in MDXXXII* (1832) · S. M. Lockhart, *Seven centuries: the history of the Lockharts of Lee and Carnwath* [1977] · M. D. Young, ed., *The parliaments of Scotland: burgh and shire commissioners*, 2 vols. (1992–3) · F. J. Grant, ed., *The Faculty of Advocates in Scotland, 1532–1943*, Scottish RS, 145 (1944)

Archives NA Scot., title deeds to land, GD. 247 | NA Scot., letters to first earl of Aberdeen · U. Edin., letters to duke and duchess of Lauderdale

Likenesses J. B. de Medina, portrait, repro. in Lockhart, *Seven centuries* · J. B. de Medina, portrait, Faculty of Advocates, Edinburgh [*see illus.*]

Lockhart, George, of Carnwath (1681?–1731), Jacobite politician and memoirist, was the elder of two children of Sir George *Lockhart of Carnwath (*c.*1630–1689), lord president of the court of session, and his second wife, Philadelphia (*b.* 1655, *d.* in or after 1717), daughter of Philip, fourth Baron Wharton. His father was a successful lawyer and state servant who was murdered as he left Greyfriars Kirk on 31 March 1689. Lord Wharton intervened soon afterwards to have Lockhart's episcopalian tutor removed, and sent George and his brother, Philip *Lockhart, to be educated in the household of the presbyterian marquess of Argyll, with whose sons, John (later second duke of Argyll) and Archibald (later earl of Ilay and third duke of Argyll), he formed a lifelong friendship. His mother, meanwhile, contracted a secret marriage with John Mair, a former army officer who later turned out to be a bigamist, and subsequently married John Ramsey, son of the former bishop of Orkney, who, with one of Lockhart's guardians, James Lockhart of Cleghorn, embezzled substantial sums from their ward's estate. These experiences apparently estranged him from his mother. In 1695 George exercised his right under Scottish law to choose his own guardians and effectively took control of his estate. One of his first acts was to negotiate his marriage to Euphemia Montgomery (1678?–1738), ninth child of Alexander, ninth earl of Eglinton, which was contracted on 13 April 1697. The marriage was apparently an affective one despite Euphemia's notorious pride and bad temper, and they had fifteen children, of whom eleven survived to adulthood. George managed his estates very ably and was a noted agricultural improver, as well as a modernizer of his main residence of Dryden in Edinburghshire. He also energetically exploited the coal on his estates and was one of the first Scottish mine owners to introduce a steam engine to pump water out of his coal pits. A haughty man assertive of his rights, he was neither an easy neighbour nor a popular landlord. None the less, his astute stewardship pushed the family's income up to £3750 per annum by the 1720s, placing them in the top echelon of Scotland's landed élite in terms of wealth. By 1700, if not earlier, he had also ceased to attend the kirk and become a committed episcopalian, inclining toward the anti-innovatory (later anti-usager) wing of that church.

George Lockhart of Carnwath (1681?–1731), by Sir John Baptiste de Medina, 1707

Lockhart's ideological beliefs revolved around his conception of himself as a quintessential Scottish patriot; his Jacobitism flowed from his belief that only a Stuart restoration could secure Scotland's independence and put the Scottish nation back in charity with God. Throughout his political career he correspondingly pursued both the return of the exiled dynasty and (from 1707) the restoration of Scotland's independence as though they were one. In the 1702 election he successfully stood as one of the commissioners for Edinburghshire, and was appointed a Scots privy councillor through the influence of his uncle Thomas, fifth Baron Wharton, one of the leaders of the English whig party. In spite of this he increasingly voted against the court in the Scottish parliament and aligned himself with the cavalier (Jacobite) party and the second duke of Hamilton. In December 1704 he was correspondingly dropped from the new commission of the privy council. In 1705, however, his uncle's influence secured him a place on the Scots commission nominated by Queen Anne to negotiate the treaty of Union. Lockhart only reluctantly accepted in order to supply his political allies with information on its deliberations. During the last session of the Scottish parliament he spoke and protested frequently against the Act of Union, and by November 1706 was actively involved in conspiracies to oppose it by force. When these came to nothing he retired to his estates and busied himself with horse-racing, hunting, and drafting his *Memoirs Concerning the Affairs of Scotland*, an account of Scottish politics from 1703 to 1708. Despite

Hamilton's tergiversations over the Union, Lockhart remained attached to him and was involved in the Hamilton's party's preparations for a Scottish uprising to support the abortive French invasion of 1708. When it failed he escaped imprisonment only through the intervention of Lord Wharton, by then one of Queen Anne's senior ministers.

In 1708 George successfully stood for Edinburghshire in the first elections to the British parliament and was one of only four Scottish MPs to align themselves with the tory minority at Westminster. Returned again in 1710, he was chosen by the Scots tories to represent them on the commission of accounts established by tory back-benchers in 1711 to expose graft and corruption under the previous whig ministry. Lockhart was a conscientious commissioner and fell out with several former allies as a result. He also played a leading role in lobbying English tory peers to vote in favour of the appeal by James Greenshields, an Episcopalian minister, against a sentence imposed by a kirk session in 1711, and in securing the passage of the Episcopalian Toleration and Restoration of Patronages Acts of 1712. By then Lockhart had established himself as a leader in his own right among the more extreme Jacobite Scottish tories, though he remained personally attached to the duke of Hamilton until his death. In that year Lockhart also first tried to organize an explicitly Jacobite group among the back-bench tories. Though he failed on this occasion, he was increasingly recognized as an important friend by the exiled Stuart court, and was considered for a peerage there in 1713. During the malt tax crisis of that year Lockhart, despite being threatened with imprisonment in the Tower of London by the ministry, sought to use the anger felt by Scottish MPs and peers on the issue to bring on the repeal of the Union, and led a breakaway group in attacks on government legislation in the Commons to support moves to this end in the Lords. He was eventually restrained by instructions to support the ministry from the Jacobite court. Returned again for Edinburghshire in the 1713 election, he refused to align himself with either the Oxford or the Bolingbroke factions struggling for control of the tory party in 1714, and instead tried to exploit the crisis created by the queen's declining health to bring about a Jacobite restoration. He obviously did not achieve this, but, together with Sir John Pakington, MP for Worcestershire, did succeed in drawing together an explicitly Jacobite club of politicians with this as their objective. At this point, however, Sir David Dalrymple of Hailes, a whig and long-standing political enemy, obtained a copy of Lockhart's draft *Memoirs*. George had loaned his manuscript to John Houston of Houston jun. who, without consulting him, arranged for it to be transcribed. The copyist then made an extra copy which he eventually sold to Dalrymple, who published it. Lockhart's acerbic character sketches, sedition, and indiscretions in the *Memoirs* alienated friend and foe alike, and he was shunned by his former comrades throughout the election campaign which followed the death of Queen Anne, though he was ultimately never prosecuted because of the difficulty in proving a connection between the illicit copy on which the published version was based and his original text. Facing certain defeat at the poll in 1715, he withdrew at the last minute and thereafter devoted himself to estate management, memoir writing, and Jacobite conspiracy.

Lockhart was consequently soon engaged in the preparations that preceded the 1715 rising, and, more owing to his public notoriety than his prominence in the Jacobites' plans, was one of the first to be arrested on 18 August. His friendship with the commander-in-chief in Scotland, the second duke of Argyll, secured his release on bail on 2 September, and he immediately resumed his plotting for a rising in the southern lowlands to take place when the Jacobite army at Perth advanced southwards. This resulted in his re-arrest on 13 October when William Mackintosh of Borlum's Jacobite force crossed the Forth, though Lockhart's brother Philip had by that time already led a troop of former officers, servants, and tenants out from Carnwath to join Viscount Kenmuir's rising at Moffat. George was then imprisoned in Edinburgh Castle until mid-January 1716, during which time he became seriously ill, and was released at the behest of the earl of Ilay.

Lockhart was once more involved in Jacobite plotting by the summer of 1716, but his experiences in 1715–16 and the execution of his brother after the surrender at Preston henceforth made him so cautious about undertaking further attempts without substantial foreign support that he effectively contributed to the sabotaging of the Earl Marischal's rising of 1719 and aborting the projected campaigns of 1726 and 1727. Even so, with most of the leaders of the Scottish Jacobites imprisoned or in exile, he was one of the few active élite Jacobites left, and so quickly became a recognized leader in the Jacobite underground. In 1720 he suggested that James Stuart, the Old Pretender, appoint a committee of trustees to oversee his affairs in Scotland. This was done and Lockhart became its *de facto* secretary. His main tasks were laying the groundwork for a future rising by fomenting popular discontent with the Union, for example after the Shawfield riots, and trying to keep the peace between rival Jacobite and Episcopalian factions, though he also played a leading role in Scottish tory efforts to negotiate an alliance with either the Argathelians or the squadrone to return tory candidates in the representative peers election of 1722. George tried to avoid becoming aligned with any of the numerous factions that plagued the Jacobite movement at this time, but his efforts to contain their rivalries were hampered by both their intransigence and his own gathering weariness of the twilight world of Jacobite conspiracy. This was further catalysed by Lockhart's distress at the very public quarrel between the Old Pretender and his wife, Clementina Sobieska, and correspondingly eased his passage out of active Jacobitism. This was finally occasioned by the interception of letters from the exiled court directed to him (possibly as a result of indiscretions by those opposed to him in concurrent disputes between usagers and anti-usagers in the Scottish Episcopalian community), followed by the capture of one of his couriers in March 1727.

Forewarned by whig friends of his imminent arrest, Lockhart fled to the continent. There he was invited to take up a post at the exiled court, but declined and instead effectively severed his connections with the Jacobite cause by writing a scathing critique of the Old Pretender's conduct, which he directed to him personally.

Allowed to return to Britain in 1728 at the intercession of Argyll and Ilay, Lockhart spent the next three years putting the finishing touches to his memoirs. These were written up at different times in three books: the *Memoirs Concerning the Affairs of Scotland*; the *Commentarys of George Lockhart of Carnwath*, which covers the period 1708 to 1715; and *A Register of Letters twixt the King and George Lockhart of Carnwath*, which deals with 1716 to 1728. None was intended for publication within his lifetime, and all deal sharply with the politics and many of the personalities of the period. None the less, they have been found to be surprisingly accurate in almost all respects, and thus constitute one of the best sources for the politics of the era. All three were hidden after Lockhart's death, and came to light only in the early nineteenth century when the antiquary Anthony Aufrere, the husband of one of his descendants, published them in two volumes in 1817.

Lockhart died at his house in Niddry's Wynd, in Edinburgh, on 17 December 1731 as a result of wounds received in a duel fought on or about 14 December. The cause was not publicly known and his family kept it so secret that historians have no idea of its cause or the identity of his assailant. According to his wish, he was interred in the family vault at Carnwath. Euphemia survived him by seven years, but nothing is known of her life beyond 1731. DANIEL SZECHI

Sources G. Lockhart, *The Lockhart papers: containing memoirs and commentaries upon the affairs of Scotland from 1702 to 1715*, 2 vols. (1817) • *Letters of George Lockhart of Carnwath, 1698–1732*, ed. D. Szechi, Scottish History Society, 5th ser., 2 (1989) • *'Scotland's ruine': Lockhart of Carnwath's memoirs of the union*, ed. D. Szechi, Association of Scottish Literary Studies, 25 (1995) • NL Scot., Lockhart of Lee and Carnwath MSS • *APS* • Auburn University, Auburn, Alabama, Ralph Brown Draughon Library, Stuart MSS microfilm • D. Szechi, 'Constructing a Jacobite: the social and intellectual origins of George Lockhart of Carnwath', *HJ*, 40 (1997), 977–96 • NA Scot., Clerk of Penicuik MSS, GD 18

Archives NL Scot., Lockhart of Lee and Carnwath MSS | NA Scot., corresp. with Sir John Clerk

Likenesses J. B. de Medina, oils, 1707, Scot. NPG [*see illus.*]

Wealth at death approx. £75,000: estate papers

Lockhart, Sir James, of Lee, Lord Lee (1588/1599–1674), judge, was the only son of Sir James Lockhart of Lee (*b. c.*1553, *d.* in or after 1635) and his second wife, Jane Weir (*d.* 1599), of Stonebyres, Lanarkshire; his parents married in 1588. He himself married first Elizabeth Fairlie and second, probably by 1621, Martha Douglas of Mordington. Lockhart had been knighted before 1629 when he was a gentleman of the privy chamber to Charles I.

Lockhart was first elected to the Scottish parliament for Lanarkshire in 1628. On 20 June 1633 he was made lord of the articles. The same year his pension was excepted from the act of revocation and his lairdship of Lee confirmed, although his father was still alive, being recorded in

Sir James Lockhart of Lee, Lord Lee (1588/1599–1674), attrib. Robert Walker

December 1635 as being over eighty-two years of age. In 1638 Lockhart was appointed to supervise the subscription of the national covenant in Lanarkshire. He was not elected to parliament in 1641, and his commission was rejected by parliament in June 1644 and January 1645. However, even though he was not a member he engaged in the work of parliamentary interval committees from 1643, including the committee of war. Similarly he was named to the exchequer commission on 29 July 1644. On 2 July 1646 he was made an ordinary lord of session. Lockhart was a moderate royalist who supported the engagement with Charles I, and as 'an able' debater (J. R. Young, 196), he played an important role in the power struggle in March–May 1648, which saw the duke of Hamilton's views prevail over those of the marquess of Argyll. In the engager army Lockhart commanded a regiment at the battle of Preston in August 1648. Following the Whiggamore raid and the installation of a more radical government in Edinburgh, Lockhart was deprived of office by the Act of Classes in February 1649 and banished by the Act of Estates in June 1650. His banishment was lifted in December 1650. A supporter of Charles II's invasion of England, he was surprised at Alyth in Perthshire on 28 August 1651 along with other members of the committee of estates and was carried as a captive to Broughty Castle and thence to London. He was confined in the Tower until his son, Sir William *Lockhart (1621?–1675), a Cromwellian diplomat, procured his freedom on 27 May 1653.

Following the Restoration, Lockhart was reappointed a lord of session, although his official appointment dated only from 5 April 1661. He appears to have supported the earl of Crawford's moderate presbyterianism in 1661, but he had little difficulty adapting to the new regime. In parliament he served as a lord of the articles in 1661–3 and was reputed to be one of the few sober men of the so-called drunken parliament. In 1662 he thought it unwise to eject non-episcopalian clergy when there were insufficient numbers of replacements. In 1669 he was again a lord of the articles. Lockhart was named lord justice clerk in 1671. He died on 10 March 1674.

STUART HANDLEY

Sources M. D. Young, ed., *The parliaments of Scotland: burgh and shire commissioners*, 2 (1993), 435–6 • G. Brunton and D. Haig, *An historical account of the senators of the college of justice, from its institution in MDXXXII* (1832), 319–20 • J. R. Young, *The Scottish parliament, 1639–1661: a political and constitutional analysis* (1996) • *Journals of Sir John Lauder*, ed. D. Crawford, Scottish History Society, 36 (1900) • *APS*, *1625–41* • *The historical works of Sir James Balfour*, ed. J. Haig, 4 vols. (1824–5) • *The diary of Mr John Lamont of Newton, 1649–1671*, ed. G. R. Kinloch, Maitland Club, 7 (1830), 17 • G. V. Irving and A. Murray, *The upper ward of Lanarkshire* (1864), 2.298–303 • *CSP dom.*, 1652–3, 354

Archives BL, letters to Lord Lauderdale and Charles II, Add. MSS 23114–23130, *passim*

Likenesses attrib. R. Walker, oils, priv. coll. [*see illus.*]

Lockhart, Sir James Haldane Stewart (1858–1937), colonial official and art collector, was born on 25 May 1858 in the ancestral home of Ardsheal in Argyll, Scotland, the sixth of the nine children of Miles Lockhart and his wife, Anna Rebecca Charlotte Stewart (*d.* 1902), niece and heir of the last laird of Ardsheal. He was educated at home and then at a dame-school in the Isle of Man, before entering King William's College, Isle of Man (1868–72), and then George Watson's College, Edinburgh, where he distinguished himself as captain of both cricket and rugby, as well as becoming joint dux (the senior scholar) in 1874. He studied English and Greek at the University of Edinburgh, winning the gold medal for Greek in 1876. He left the university without graduating to join the Colonial Office as a Hong Kong cadet in 1878.

Throughout 1879 Stewart Lockhart studied Chinese in London before beginning his duties in 1880 with two years language training undertaken in Canton (Guangzhou) and Hong Kong. In 1882 he took up his first official appointment in Hong Kong as clerk of councils and chief clerk in the colonial secretariat. After a few months he was moved to the registrar-general's office. In 1883 he was appointed superintendent of opium revenue, and five months later became assistant colonial secretary and assistant auditor-general. He also acted as registrar-general at times during 1884, 1885, and 1886, being appointed to the full post in 1887.

The post allowed Stewart Lockhart to work directly with the Chinese community in the colony. Most Europeans in China did not mix with the Chinese socially but Stewart Lockhart had several important Chinese friends. He was fascinated by all things Chinese, made great efforts to become fluent in the language, and was quickly recognized as a Sinologist of ability. His interests extended to Chinese society and folklore, poetry, art, and numismatics. The longer he remained in the East, the more Confucianist he became in outlook. As registrar-general he promoted the Chinese power base in Hong Kong whenever he could, strengthening the authority of important Chinese societies such as the Tung Wah Hospital Group, the district watch committee, and the Po Leung Kuk.

On 25 February 1889 Stewart Lockhart married Edith Louise Rider Hancock (1870–1950), the daughter of a Hong Kong bullion broker. Happily married for almost fifty years, they had three children: Charles (1889–1962), Mary (1894–1985) [*see* Joel, Betty], and Margaret (1903–1936). It was at the time of his marriage that he formally adopted the double surname Stewart Lockhart. Edith was a loyal supporter, encouraging her husband to follow not only his scholarly pursuits but also to indulge in his love of sport.

Having served successfully for eight years as registrar-general, Stewart Lockhart combined the post with that of colonial secretary from 1895. This made him the most important permanent official in the colony. He worked as tirelessly as ever and when in 1898 the colony was extended with the lease of the New Territories from China, it fell to Stewart Lockhart to organize the administration of the area and to delineate its boundaries. His belief that the territories would one day be returned to China and that existing Chinese systems should therefore be preserved whenever possible ensured that the New Territories retained their Chinese character and were never completely subsumed by British colonial traits. His work in the colony was rewarded in 1898 when he was appointed CMG. He also wrote articles on Chinese language and poetry and between 1895 and 1898 published three volumes on *The Currency of the Farther East*.

In 1902 Stewart Lockhart was appointed to be the first civil commissioner of Weihaiwei, a leased territory in Shandong province in north-east China. He was to remain there until he retired, despite the expectation by many that he would one day be appointed governor of Hong Kong. Weihaiwei was an economic and cultural backwater and Stewart Lockhart gradually became disillusioned with this post, despite his advancement to KCMG in 1908. He was rarely overworked during these years and spent much of his time researching aspects of Chinese culture, an interest he shared with his colleague Sir Reginald *Johnston. He also amassed a considerable collection of Chinese coins and paintings. By 1915 his coin collection was of sufficient significance to merit a further publication by him, *The Stewart Lockhart Collection of Chinese Copper Coins*, which catalogued some of the thousands of coins he owned. His scholarship was acknowledged with an honorary LLD degree from the University of Hong Kong in 1918.

In 1921 Stewart Lockhart retired to London where he served on several committees. He became a governor of the School of Oriental Studies at the University of London in 1925, was president of the London Highland Club in 1926–7, a member of the Universities China Committee from 1932, and a member of the honorary committee for the 1935 exhibition of Chinese art held in London. He continued to write book reviews and scholarly articles on a variety of Chinese-related subjects. He died at home, 6 Cresswell Gardens, London, on 26 February 1937. His remains were cremated in London and interred at St Adamnan's, Appin, Argyll.

Before his death Stewart Lockhart gave his daughter Mary his collection of 600 Chinese paintings. In 1950 Mary also inherited her father's collection of coins, photographs, and papers. She gifted these to George Watson's College, Edinburgh, in 1967. The preservation of his collection has ensured that his historical importance in maintaining traditional Chinese values in Hong Kong and, most importantly, in the New Territories has not been forgotten. SHIONA M. AIRLIE

Sources S. Airlie, *Thistle and bamboo: the life and times of Sir James Stewart Lockhart* (1989) · George Watson's College, Edinburgh, Stewart Lockhart MSS · personal knowledge (2004) · *CGPLA Eng. & Wales* (1937)

Archives George Watson's College, Edinburgh, MSS · NL Scot., corresp. and papers | Mitchell L., NSW, letters to G. E. Morrison · PRO, Weihaiwei original corresp., CO 521

Likenesses photographs, George Watson's College, Edinburgh

Wealth at death £16,097 14*s*. 5*d*.: probate, 22 April 1937, *CGPLA Eng. & Wales*

Lockhart, John Gibson (1794–1854), writer and literary editor, was born on 12 June 1794 in the manse at Cambusnethan, Lanarkshire, Scotland, the eldest of five children of Dr John Lockhart (1761–1842), minister of the parish church of Cambusnethan, and his second wife, Elizabeth (*d.* 1834), daughter of John Gibson, minister of St Cuthbert's, Edinburgh, and Margaret Mary Pringle. Lockhart had three brothers—Laurence, Richard Dickson, and Robert—and one sister, Violet; he also had a half-brother, William, by his father's first wife, Elizabeth Dinwiddie.

John Gibson Lockhart (1794–1854), by Robert Scott Lauder, *c.*1841–2

Early years and education In 1796 Dr Lockhart became minister of the college kirk of Blackfriars in Glasgow, so John Lockhart's formative years were spent in an urban and university atmosphere. He attended the high school in Glasgow, and in 1805, at the age of eleven, entered the University of Glasgow, where he excelled as a classical scholar, winning a Blackstone prize in Greek. In 1809 he was awarded a Snell exhibition to Balliol College, Oxford, and in 1813 he gained a first-class degree in classics. He mastered Greek and Latin and also learned German, Italian, Spanish, Portuguese, and French. He returned to Glasgow after taking his Oxford degree, and for two years he had no formal occupation but continued informally his voracious reading and his study of languages. During this period he wrote to his friend Jonathan Christie, several months before Scott's *Waverley* was published, that 'the Scotch character has been neglected' (Lang, 1.72) in fiction. Lockhart hoped to fill that void with his own Scottish novel. A year later he contacted the publisher Archibald Constable, in Edinburgh, to enquire about publishing his novel of Scottish manners, although his plans did not immediately come to fruition. In 1815 he went to Edinburgh University to read law, and in 1816 he became an advocate. In Edinburgh he connected with the tory literati, particularly Constable's rival publisher, William Blackwood, and Walter *Scott. On 29 April 1820 Lockhart married (Charlotte) Sophia (1799–1837), Scott's elder daughter. They had three children: John Hugh (1821–1831), Walter Scott (1826–1853), and Charlotte Harriet Jane (1828–1858).

Literary career Lockhart, who was regarded by his contemporaries as a handsome man, had thick dark hair and was of slight build, with 'Hidalgo airs' (Lang, 1.16). In his youth he had periods of illness and suffered a hearing impairment, which undoubtedly exacerbated a reserved, even shy, personality. He was a tender, compassionate, loving person, who was quick to provide for his friends in need and suffered deeply in his family losses. Yet he was also fun-loving and witty, had a brilliant sense of humour, and enjoyed an opportunity for satire. In his memoir of Scott (1832) James Hogg called Lockhart a 'mischievous Oxford puppy … drawing caricatures of every one who came in contact with him' (Hogg, 75). His intellectual acumen and satirical bent were exercised freely in the early stages of his literary career in writing and editing for *Blackwood's Edinburgh Magazine*.

Lockhart began publishing in *Blackwood's* with the first issue, in 1817. He considerably increased the scope and venom of Hogg's satire of the Edinburgh publishing industry, the 'Chaldee manuscript' (October 1817), which earned him the epithet Scorpion and resulted in a lawsuit against Blackwood. His attacks on Keats and *Endymion* (August 1818) were so strong that he soon regretted them. He was involved with John Scott, editor of the *London Magazine*, in a dispute over his role in *Blackwood's* that led to Scott's death in a duel with Lockhart's friend Jonathan

Christie. However, by far the majority of Lockhart's articles were incisive, pertinent examinations of a broad range of literary publications of the day, including Greek tragedy and poetry; the poetry of Wordsworth, Coleridge, Goethe, and Byron; the fiction of Godwin and Brockden Brown; and the art of the novel in general. He eventually set the standard in literary criticism for the period.

Lockhart's first book was a translation from the German of Frederick Schlegel, *Lectures on the History of Literature* (2 vols., 1818); this was the result of a tour in Germany sponsored by Blackwood, where Lockhart met Goethe and other German writers. Both the tour and Schlegel's lectures had a significant influence on Lockhart's own writing, especially the literary criticism in *Blackwood's* and his second book-length publication, *Peter's Letters to his Kinsfolk* (3 vols., 1819). In this work of epistolary fiction Dr Peter Morris, a Welshman, travels to Scotland and connects with the important personages of the age. Penetrating and lively character sketches are the highlights of his letters to friends and relatives in Wales. As one of the most important chronicles of early nineteenth-century life in Scotland *Peter's Letters* can be seen as the 'biography of a culture' (Hart, 46).

Lockhart served for a short time in the yeomanry, and in 1820 was called to service to confront the radical uprisings in the west of Scotland. However, even his military service became an occasion for humorous, satirical poetry; written over a period of about four years, *Songs for the Edinburgh Troop* was published in collaboration with Patrick Fraser Tytler in 1825. In 1821 Lockhart toured the northern circuit as an advocate and, as his letters to Sophia attest, collected scenes and characters for his fiction. The five years from 1821 to 1825 were among the most productive of his career. He published four new novels and revised one for a second edition, experimenting with a variety of techniques and themes; he edited, with notes and a life of Cervantes, Motteux's translation of *Don Quixote* (5 vols., 1822); he published a collection of translations of Spanish poetry (*Ancient Spanish Ballads*, 1823); he began his biography of Robert Burns, although it was not published until 1828; and he wrote more than 100 articles, review essays, and original poems for *Blackwood's*.

Lockhart's first novel, *Valerius: a Roman Story* (1821), draws heavily on his classical education. Critics such as Andrew Lang and F. R. Hart admired its vivid and realistic portrayal of ancient Rome, yet the work is much more than a successful historical novel. Set in the context of the persecution of Christians under the rule of Trajan, *Valerius* balances the good-humoured, sympathetic characters and images of classical Rome with scenes of inhumane and irrational treatment of good, well-meaning, but misunderstood Christians. The effect, though not recognized in Lockhart's time, was to offer a metaphor of reason and moderation to the early nineteenth-century covenanting debate instigated by Sir Walter Scott in *Old Mortality* and taken up by James Hogg, John Galt, and others. Lockhart's second novel, *Some Passages in the Life of Mr Adam Blair* (1822; 2nd edn, 1824), is generally regarded as his best. Based on a true story that Lockhart heard from his father, it is a bold portrayal of passion and adultery in the keeper of community virtue, the Presbyterian minister. It is also an unusual story of compassion, forgiveness, and restoration. Henry James, in *Hawthorne*, compared *Adam Blair* with *The Scarlet Letter*, noting the analogies between the two and proclaiming each the 'masterpiece' of the author (Lockhart's *Life of Scott* aside): 'Each man wrote as his turn of mind impelled him, but each expressed something more than himself'. An 'interesting and powerful little tale', Adam Blair:

> borrows a charm from the fact that [Lockhart's] vigorous, but not strongly imaginative, mind was impregnated with the reality of his subject. He did not always succeed in rendering the reality … But the reader feels that his vision was clear, and his feeling about the matter very strong and rich. (James, 112)

Reginald Dalton (1823) is Lockhart's Oxford novel; though not strictly autobiographical it draws heavily on his experiences as a student at Oxford, filtered through a decade of experience and remembering. *The History of Matthew Wald* (1824), Lockhart's most ambitious and stylistically satisfying novel, is the story of a character's psychological journey through fragments of eighteenth-century Scottish life. More than any of his works *Matthew Wald* probes the internal development of the human mind and soul as the protagonist interacts with and is influenced by the social circumstances in which he finds himself.

Editorship of the *Quarterly Review* In December 1825 Lockhart moved to London to be editor of the *Quarterly Review*, a position that he held until a year before his death. The *Quarterly* had been established by John Murray in 1809 as a tory voice to counter the whig *Edinburgh Review*. Lockhart's *Blackwood's* experience had matured him as a critic and prepared him well for his editorial duties. He was a very active editor (sometimes to the displeasure of his authors) and shaped the *Quarterly* into one of the most important periodicals of the late nineteenth century. Thomas Carlyle, who never published in the *Quarterly*, expressed his high regard for Lockhart's judgement even after *Chartism* was rejected for publication in the review:

> I consider that your decision about that wild piece … was altogether what it should have been, what on the whole I expected it to be. Fraser is printing the thing now as a separate Pamphlet. Your negative was necessary to decide me as to that step … One has an equation with more than one unknown quantity in it; eliminate the Quarterly y, there remains x = printing as a pamphlet. (*Collected Letters*, 11.230)

Lockhart was editor of the *Quarterly* during the critical periods of debate on such major political issues as the Catholic question, the Reform Bill of 1832, and corn law reform. Although many of the political articles were written by John Wilson Croker and Robert Southey, Lockhart successfully accomplished what he saw as his responsibility to keep it from falling into the hands of one tory faction or another. He enjoyed the politics of reviewing; he regularly attended parliament when it was in session and at one time even aspired to a seat in the House of Commons. In May 1830 he wrote to Scott for his advice: 'One can hardly live so continually among those gamesters as I have been doing without wishing to take a hand sometimes' (NL Scot., MS 3913, fols. 112–15). Lockhart noted that his income was £5000 per annum, which meant that he was capable of an independent voice. Although he never held public office, in 1843 he was made auditor of the duchy of Lancaster, a government patronage position that provided an annual income of £400.

Lockhart also wrote for the *Quarterly* and published an article or more in most of the issues under his twenty-eight-year editorship. He reviewed fiction and poetry, as well as historical and general interest works. In 1841 he published an article on copyright that had a significant influence on the development of copyright laws. The majority of his reviews focused on biographies, including such diverse subjects as Byron, Edmund Kean, Hannah More, David Wilkie, and Astley Cooper. He was also editor for many works published by John Murray, including all but the scientific volumes of the Family Library, for which he wrote the first number for the series, a two-volume biography of Napoleon (1829), a digest, or 'compendium', of Scott's *Life of Napoleon* (1827). He was largely responsible for editing and writing notes for Murray's seventeen-volume edition of Byron's works (1833) and oversaw the publication of the series of historical and travel volumes published by Murray in the 1840s, the Colonial and Home Library. The esteem in which Lockhart was held for his contributions to the literary achievements of the house of Murray is best expressed by Whitwell Elwin, whom John Murray asked to succeed Lockhart as editor of the *Quarterly* and who was author of a collection entitled *Lives of the Poets*. Elwin wrote to Murray: 'It might look like an attempt to bend the bow of Ulysses, or rather it would look like the assumption of being able to shoot with him' (John Murray archives).

Biography of Scott and last years Lockhart's best-known work, however, is his biography of Sir Walter Scott (7 vols., 1837–8; 2nd edn, rev., 10 vols., 1839; abridged and rev., 2 vols., 1848). From its publication it has been regarded, along with Boswell's *Life of Johnson*, as one of the most important works in the history of biography. In preparing the life of Scott, Lockhart collected personal anecdotes and letters from many of Scott's friends and acquaintances and added to them his own intimate knowledge of the man and his works to portray with the power of a successful novelist a character in vivid scenes of place and time. Though modern criticism has pointed out inaccuracies in Lockhart's details and considered his portrait of Scott idealized it is clear none the less that he attempted to present the near heroic regard in which Scott was held in his time. As Maria Edgeworth wrote to Lockhart in 1838:

> We thought it impossible any publication could raise Sir Walter Scott's talents or character in public opinion or in our private opinion more especially. And yet you certainly have done it without one word of puff or exaggeration or even full-faced eulogy. (NL Scot., MS 923, no. 57)

With his health failing and his eyesight growing weaker, Lockhart resigned the editorship of the *Quarterly Review* in 1853. He travelled to Italy in October for the winter months to try to recover his health, but he experienced only a brief revival of his energies. He had what a doctor described as not a 'distinct disease' but a 'general decadence of the vital powers' (Lochhead, 298). He had known much loss over the previous two decades: the deaths of his wife, two of his children, his sister, his parents, all his wife's siblings, and his father-in-law. He spent the last weeks of his life at Abbotsford, Selkirkshire, Sir Walter Scott's estate on the River Tweed, in Scotland, with his daughter Charlotte Hope-Scott and her family. Charlotte was the only Lockhart child to marry or have children. In 1847 she had married James Robert Hope; they lived at Abbotsford, and after the death of Sir Walter Scott's son Walter they took the name Scott, as Charlotte was the last living lineal descendant of her grandfather. Lockhart died at Abbotsford on 25 November 1854; he was buried in Dryburgh Abbey, at the feet of Sir Walter Scott, as he had wished. THOMAS C. RICHARDSON

Sources A. Lang, *The life and letters of John Gibson Lockhart*, 2 vols. (1897) · letters, NL Scot. · John Murray, London, archives · J. C. Corson, *Notes and index to Sir Herbert Grierson's edition of the letters of Sir Walter Scott* (1979) · M. Lochhead, *John Gibson Lockhart* (1954) · J. Hogg, *Memoir of the author's life, and familiar anecdotes of Sir Walter Scott*, ed. D. S. Mack (1972) · F. R. Hart, *Lockhart as Romantic biographer* (1971) · H. James, *Hawthorne* (1879) · *The collected letters of Thomas and Jane Welsh Carlyle*, 11, ed. C. R. Sanders and K. J. Fielding (1985)

Archives Hunt. L., letters · John Murray, London, archives · NL Scot., biographical papers · NL Scot., corresp. · NL Scot., corresp., diaries, and papers · NL Scot., letters · U. Mich., corresp. · University of Iowa Libraries, Iowa City, corresp. · University of Virginia, Charlottesville, corresp. · Yale U., Sterling Memorial Library, letters | Alnwick Castle, Northumberland, letters to Henry Drummond · BL, letters to W. E. Gladstone, Add. MS 44237 · BL, letters to Roderick Impey Murchison, Add. MS 46127 · BL, letters to Royal Literary Fund, loan 96 · Bodl. Oxf., letters to Mary Somerville · GS Lond., letters to Roderick Impey and Lady Charlotte Murchison · LUL, letters to Lord Brougham · Mitchell L., Glas., letters to Lady Davy · NL Scot., letters to Richard Bentley · NL Scot., corresp. with Blackwoods · NL Scot., letters to Archibald Constable & Co. · NL Scot., corresp. with John Wilson Croker · NL Scot., letters to Allan Cunningham · NL Scot., corresp. with Maria Edgeworth · NL Scot., letters to Whitwell Elwin · NL Scot., letters to Lady Gifford · NL Scot., letters to William Laidlaw · NL Scot., letters to William Home Lizars · NL Scot., letters to Sir John McNeill · NL Scot., corresp. with William Mure · NL Scot., letters to Oliver & Boyd · NL Scot., corresp. with Sir Walter Scott · NL Scot., letters to Sir Walter Scott the younger and Lady Scott · NL Scot., letters to William Scott · NL Scot., corresp. with John Smith the younger · NL Scot., letters to John Wilson · NRA, priv. coll., letters to William Adam, etc. · RS, corresp. with Sir John Herschel · Trinity Cam., letters to Lord Houghton · Trinity Cam., letters to William Whewell · U. Hull, Brynmor Jones L., corresp. with Perronet Thompson · U. Mich., Clements L., John Wilson Croker papers · U. St Andr. L., letters to James David Forbes

Likenesses H. W. Pickersgill, oils, 1830, John Murray, London · R. S. Lauder, oils, *c*.1841–1842, Scot. NPG [*see illus.*] · G. T. Doo, line engraving (after H. W. Pickersgill), NPG · F. Grant, engraving, repro. in Lang, *Life and letters*, frontispiece · F. Grant, oils, Scot. NPG · D. O. Hill, photograph, NPG · D. Maclise, drawing, repro. in *A gallery of illustrious literary characters* (1873) · D. Maclise, lithograph, BM; repro. in *Fraser's Magazine* (1830) · J. Watson-Gordon, pencil and chalk drawing, Scot. NPG · stipple (after R. S. Lauder), NPG

Lockhart, John Macgregor Bruce (1914–1995), intelligence officer, was born in Rugby on 9 May 1914, the oldest

John Macgregor Bruce Lockhart (1914–1995), by unknown photographer

of four sons of John Harold Bruce Lockhart (1889–1956), a master at Rugby School, and subsequently headmaster of Sedbergh School, and his wife, Mona (1894–1980), one of two daughters of Henry Brougham, a master at Wellington College. Two of his brothers followed their father in becoming public school headmasters and in playing rugby for Scotland. Sir Robert Hamilton Bruce *Lockhart (1887–1970), the celebrated author of *Memoirs of a British Agent* (1932), was an uncle. Bruce Lockhart was educated at Eagle House, Sandhurst, a preparatory school of which his grandfather was headmaster, then at Rugby (where he captained an unbeaten fifteen which had the unique record of never having had a try scored against it), and at St Andrews University, 1932–6, where he studied French and German and was again a remarkably successful captain of the rugby football fifteen. He returned to Rugby as a master in 1937. In 1938 he received a Territorial Army commission in the Royal Warwickshire regiment. He joined the Seaforth Highlanders after mobilization in 1939. Seconded to the intelligence corps in 1940 he joined the Secret Intelligence Service (SIS) in 1942. After service in Iraq and Egypt he was appointed in 1944, at the early age of thirty, to the direction of all SIS operations in Italy, an important job involving the supply of accurate and timely military and political intelligence in a major theatre of war.

This was the turning point of Bruce Lockhart's life and career. If this appointment had not come his way, and if he had not occupied it to the satisfaction and admiration of his colleagues, he would no doubt have returned to his family profession. As things turned out, he was offered permanent employment in the SIS in 1945. He spent the next twenty years in the service, and exercised a powerful and benign influence in its transformation from a basically military and provisional wartime organization into a permanent civilian service with an established place in Whitehall. In 1945 he was posted to the British embassy in Paris, and in 1948 to Germany, where he accomplished the major task of rationalizing the British intelligence effort. In 1951 he was selected for the uniquely delicate task of succeeding the traitor Kim Philby in Washington. In the next two years Bruce Lockhart restored the service's position in Washington and made a number of lifelong friends in the American intelligence community. Given the importance in Washington at that time of the CIA—which, unlike the state department, had resisted the malign influence of Senator McCarthy—this was a major achievement.

Between 1953, when he returned to London, and his retirement in 1965, Bruce Lockhart occupied a series of senior posts at headquarters and did much to establish the peacetime SIS. He was successively responsible for SIS operations in Europe, the Middle East (where he had to provide what intelligence support he could to the ill-fated Suez expedition in 1956, and to help to mitigate its consequences), and Africa—the latter a new field for him, and indeed for the service. He became deeply engaged in African affairs and particularly the growing conflicts in southern Africa. Committed to the establishment of multiracial societies, and by no means an admirer of white supremacist governments, he nevertheless deplored the double standards commonly applied to southern African affairs.

In 1965, at the early age of fifty-one, Bruce Lockhart chose to retire from the SIS and embark on a second career—in education. He was in charge of planning development at the new University of Warwick from 1965 to 1967. For the next four years he was head of the central staff department of Courtaulds. From 1971 to 1980 he ran the post experience programme at the City University Business School. On his retirement he was made an honorary fellow of the university. In the meantime he had been chairman of the Business Education Council from 1974 to 1980, a period that covered the introduction of the national diploma system and the harmonization and development of curricula in tertiary education, which marked a big step forward in an area which had been neglected in Britain. From 1973 to 1980 he was a member of the Schools Council and the naval educational advisory committee.

In these years Bruce Lockhart also pursued his interest in international affairs, giving special emphasis to the relationship between governments and their intelligence services. In the 1970s and 1980s he ran seminars and lectured widely on these topics at various institutions, including the Royal College of Defence Studies, the University of St Andrews, the Royal United Services Institute, the Rand Afrikaans University in South Africa, and, in the United States, the Kennedy Institute of Politics and Harvard and Georgetown universities. His advice on these matters commanded respect in the corridors of power at home and abroad. A project close to his heart was the creation of a national college to be based on the Royal College of Defence Studies but reaching more widely to Whitehall departments, the City, trade unions, and industry. But in this he was to be disappointed.

After his retirement from these varied activities Bruce Lockhart continued to concern himself with local affairs in the neighbourhood of Rye and to play golf and real tennis until the end of his life. On 14 September 1939 he had married Margaret Evelyn (*b.* 1916), the daughter of the Right Revd Campbell Richard Hone, bishop of Wakefield and biographer of John Radcliffe. There were two sons and a daughter, to whom—with their children—he remained devoted, as he did to his brothers and their families. Indeed this sense of family loyalty was one of the main motive forces of his life and extended to the institutions of which he was a member. The SIS was the beneficiary of this, and he never gave any sign of resentment at his failure to achieve the post of head of the service. If the cards had fallen differently it is not unlikely that Bruce Lockhart could have succeeded Sir Dick White, and it is not unreasonable to speculate on how the service would have fared under his direction instead of the very different style of leadership provided successively by Sir John Rennie and Sir Maurice Oldfield. Bruce Lockhart would certainly have brought more practical experience of SIS work in the field and an informed judgement of men and situations, and a remarkable warmth of personality and the power to inspire loyalty and affection. The service would have been safe in his hands; he retained until the end of his life a particular concern for the purpose, function, and control of intelligence work in a democratic society.

A large, handsome man with a marked interest in games and sports, Bruce Lockhart tended to play down his many cultural and intellectual interests. His humorous blend of modesty and confidence misled some who did not know him well. This may have partially concealed the reality of a keen mind, decisiveness, and moral courage. He enjoyed a long, happy, and successful life, even though it was denied its ultimate professional recognition. He died on 7 May 1995 at the Norwich General Hospital, following a fall, two days earlier, at the home of his daughter, Mrs Sally Creelman, Keepers Cottage, Wolterton, Norfolk. He was cremated at Ashford on 20 May. He was survived by his wife, two sons, and daughter. JOHN LONGRIGG

Sources personal knowledge (2004) • private information (2004) [family] • *The Times* (10 May 1995) • *The Independent* (13 May 1995) • *WWW*

Archives SOUND IWM SA, memoirs

Likenesses photograph, News International Syndication, London [*see illus.*] • photograph, repro. in *The Independent*

Wealth at death £17,832: probate, 28 June 1995, *CGPLA Eng. & Wales*

Lockhart, Laurence William Maxwell (1831–1882), novelist, was born in Inchinnan, Renfrewshire, the third son of the Revd Laurence Lockhart of Milton Lockhart, Lanarkshire (*b.* 1796), and his wife, Louisa, daughter of David Blair, an East India merchant of Glasgow. John Gibson Lockhart (1794–1854) was his uncle. In 1841 he was sent to school at Newington House, Edinburgh. After two or three years he returned home and was educated privately until he entered Glasgow University in 1845. He stayed there, with a year's interval, until 1850, when he entered Gonville and Caius College, Cambridge. He graduated BA in 1855 and MA in 1861.

On 9 February 1855 Lockhart received a commission as ensign in the 92nd regiment (Gordon Highlanders). He joined his regiment at Edinburgh, went with it to Gibraltar, and landed at Balaklava on 15 September 1855. He was made lieutenant on 4 October and that winter he served at the siege of Sevastopol. The regiment returned to Gibraltar in May 1856, and Lockhart went to England on sick leave in 1857 and joined the depot in Scotland. During 1859 and 1860 he held a regimental appointment at Reigate, Surrey, and afterwards at Cambridge. In 1862 he joined his regiment in India, where it had been sent in 1858. He returned with it to England in 1863 and was promoted captain on 19 January 1864. He retired from the army in 1865.

In March 1860 Lockhart had married Katherine Anne Russell (*d.* 1870), daughter of Sir James Russell, of Ashiestiel, and his wife, Mary, daughter of Sir James and Lady Helen Hall of Dunglass. They had several children. Since his retirement he had been contributing to *Blackwood's Edinburgh Magazine*, and his first novel, *Doubles and quits*, was serialized there before being republished in its entirety in 1869. It was a light-hearted military comedy of errors which received mixed reviews. Personally, Lockhart was a renowned mimic, but Frederick Locker-Lampson describes him as in appearance and bearing also 'the typical horsey dragoon' (Locker-Lampson, 314–15).

In the spring of 1870 Lockhart's wife died, and on 7 June he entered the 2nd Royal Lanark militia as major. In July he was appointed the *Times* correspondent for the Franco-Prussian War. He was with the French army at the battle of Forbach, where he was frequently arrested and once almost executed owing to the fear of spies that the French had. This eventually caused them to ban foreign correspondents from their lines. However, shortly afterwards, Colonel Pemberton was killed by a stray bullet, and Lockhart succeeded him as correspondent with the Germans in the lines before Metz and the villages around Strasbourg. During this period he continued to write fiction. His second novel, *Fair to See* (1871), and his final one, *Mine is thine* (1878), were published in the same manner as his first, and each was generally agreed to be an improvement on the one before. *The Times* (18 September 1878) called him 'humorous and thoughtful' (*The Times*, 4).

Conditions in the army were not good for Lockhart's health, and his chest was weakened. He was promoted lieutenant-colonel of the Lanark militia on 8 April 1877. From 1879 until his long-foreseen death he sought warm climates, and he died at Menton, France, on 23 March 1882. He was buried in the cemetery there.

[ANON.], *rev.* JESSICA HININGS

Sources *Blackwood*, 131 (1882), 675–80 • *The Times* (18 Sept 1878) • *The Times* (28 March 1882) • Venn, *Alum. Cant.* • F. Locker-Lampson, *My confidences: an autobiographical sketch addressed to my descendants*, ed. A. Birrell, 2nd edn (1896), 314–15 • *GM*, 3rd ser., 8 (1860) • private information (1893)

Archives NL Scot., letters to Blackwoods

Wealth at death £14,268 6*s.* 0*d.*: confirmation, 17 July 1882, *CCI*

Lockhart, Philip (1689?–1715), army officer and Jacobite sympathizer, was the younger child of Sir George *Lockhart of Carnwath (*c.*1630–1689), lord president of the court of session, and his second wife, Philadelphia (*b.* 1655, *d.* in or after 1717), daughter of Philip, fourth Baron Wharton. After his father's murder, Lord Wharton had Philip and his elder brother, George *Lockhart (1681?–1731), sent to be educated in the household of the presbyterian marquess of Argyll. His mother subsequently married Captain John Ramsey, son of the former bishop of Orkney, who, with a guardian, James Lockhart of Cleghorn, embezzled substantial sums from George's estate, and presumably Philip's too. Little more is known of Philip's life. A handsome man, though apparently unmarried, he lived with his brother and was almost certainly an episcopalian. He does not appear to have owned any extensive properties. Lockhart served in Lord Mark Ker's regiment during the War of the Spanish Succession, but no record survives of his participation in any battles or campaigns. On Queen Anne's death he retired on half pay and in the summer of 1715 aided his brother in preparations for a Jacobite rising. On 12 October he joined Kenmuir's rising with a troop of horse primarily composed of his brother's tenants and servants from Carnwath, and surrendered with the Jacobite army at Preston on 14 November. He claimed to have resigned his commission, but was court-martialled for desertion and shot on 2 December 1715. He died defiant, refusing to recognize the court that tried him or admit any guilt for his actions. DANIEL SZECHI

Sources G. Lockhart, *The Lockhart papers: containing memoirs and commentaries upon the affairs of Scotland from 1702 to 1715*, 2 vols. (1817) • NL Scot., Lockhart of Lee and Carnwath MSS 27501, 27502, 27540, 27593, 27594 • NA Scot., GD 1 [miscellaneous Jacobite MSS] • R. Patten, *The history of the rebellion in the year 1715*, 3rd edn (1745)

Archives NA Scot., Jacobite MSS, GD 1 • NL Scot., Lockhart of Lee and Carnwath MSS

Likenesses R. Graves, line engraving, BM, NPG; repro. in J. Caulfield, *Portraits, memoirs and characters of remarkable persons*, 4 vols. (1819–20) • A. Johnston, mezzotint, BM, NPG

Lockhart, Sir Robert Hamilton Bruce (1887–1970), diplomatist and writer, was born on 2 September 1887 in Anstruther, Fife, the eldest of the five sons of Robert Bruce Lockhart, headmaster of the Waid Academy, Anstruther, and his wife, Florence Stuart, daughter of John Macgregor, of Balmenach, Cromdale, Morayshire. One of his brothers, Sir Rob Lockhart (1893–1981), was a general in the Indian army. His only sister, Freda, established a considerable reputation as a film critic and journalist. Lockhart was fond of boasting that he had no English blood in his veins, and his books are full of evidence of the pride which he took in his Scottish ancestry. He won a scholarship to Fettes College in Edinburgh at the age of twelve, but devoted most of his time there to sport rather than academic study. On leaving Fettes, he was sent by his family to study in Berlin and Paris, which fostered his lifelong interest in travel and the study of languages. For three years, from 1908 to 1910, he was a rubber planter in Malaya, where his mother's family had interests, but acute malaria forced him to return to Britain where in September 1911 he took the examinations for entry into the consular service.

In January 1912 Lockhart was posted as vice-consul to Moscow, where he served as acting consul-general during the war years as a result of the illness of his chief. His lively and perceptive reports about the political and economic situation in Moscow quickly attracted attention both in the Foreign Office and at the British embassy in

Sir Robert Hamilton Bruce Lockhart (1887–1970), by Konstantin Andreyevich Somov, 1934

Petrograd. His talent for making friends with a wide range of people allowed him to develop penetrating insights into the tensions that destroyed the tsarist *ancien régime* in 1917. While in Moscow, Lockhart met and married, in 1913, Jean Haslewood, daughter of Leonard Turner, of Kinellan, Brisbane, Australia; they had one daughter, who died at birth, and one son. The two quickly became estranged, although the marriage was not ended until 1938. Lockhart was recalled home a few weeks before the Bolshevik seizure of power, apparently because of an affair with a Russian woman which was attracting unfavourable attention in Moscow.

Lockhart returned to Russia in January 1918 as head of a special mission instructed to establish relations with the new government there. The appointment was not generally welcomed at the Foreign Office, where a number of senior officials believed that he was too young and reckless to carry out such an onerous task. Lockhart himself was at first hopeful that the Soviet government could be persuaded to continue the struggle against Germany, but following the Brest Litovsk treaty of March 1918 he quickly became a supporter of allied intervention in Russia. By the summer of 1918 he was closely involved in negotiations with various groups hostile to Bolshevik rule, and was subsequently arrested at the beginning of September 1918 for his part in the so-called Lockhart plot. He was released along with other British prisoners the following month and repatriated to Britain. The account which he gave of this period in his celebrated book *Memoirs of a*

British Agent (1932) was not entirely accurate, and probably understated his involvement in the various conspiracies that were hatched against the Bolshevik government during 1918.

Lockhart was appointed commercial secretary at the British legation in Prague in November 1919, but, as he subsequently testified in his *Retreat from Glory* (1934), he found the work there very tedious. He did, however, develop a great interest in the countries and peoples of central and south-eastern Europe which continued for the rest of his life. He also displayed an astonishing capacity for developing friendships with such political figures as Edvard Beneš and Jan Masaryk. He became a familiar figure in the nightclubs of Prague during these years. His tendency to live beyond his means was partly responsible for his decision to leave the foreign service for international banking in October 1922, but he continued to spend much of his time working in central Europe. He was by his own admission not well suited to the demands of his new career, but his numerous contacts and excellent negotiating skills made him a useful asset for his employers. In 1924 he converted to Catholicism, although this did not lead him to reform his ways. In 1928 he left banking to work for the *Evening Standard* as editor of the 'Londoner's diary', and it was during these years that he began his writing career, motivated in part by the need to make money to pay off his debts. The success of his books allowed writing to become his full-time career in 1937. He spent much of the next two years travelling in Yugoslavia and Romania, a turbulent period which he later described in *Guns or Butter* (1938).

Lockhart rejoined the Foreign Office when war broke out in September 1939. In July 1940 he was appointed British representative with the provisional Czechoslovak government in exile; in July 1941, with the rank of deputy under-secretary, he took over the direction of the Political Warfare Executive, which was responsible for propaganda in enemy and occupied countries. He continued in his post until the end of the war, setting down his experiences in his book *Comes the Reckoning* (1947). He was appointed a KCMG in January 1943. In 1948 he married Frances Mary, a civil servant and elder daughter of Major-General Edward Archibald Beck, of Abercairney Cottage, Crieff, Perthshire; there were no children of this second marriage.

Lockhart was a man of great energy and charm, whose open personality allowed him to make friends easily, although he could sometimes be self-indulgent and extravagant. He instinctively chafed under the constraints imposed on him during his time at the Foreign Office, and despite his successes he was probably best suited to life as a journalist and writer. He always continued to pursue his sporting interests whatever the pressures of his working life. He was a keen angler, and his book *My Rod, my Comfort* (1949) is a classic of its genre. He also had a great love of the countryside, finding solace there at times when the depression from which he periodically suffered threatened to overwhelm him. His books provided a valuable record of life in Russia and central Europe over several decades, and included lively pen portraits of individuals ranging from Trotsky to Kaiser Wilhelm II. His style was natural and fluent, characterized by an ability to describe important historical events from a personal perspective. While his writings cannot always be relied on for factual accuracy, they provide a very useful antidote to some of the drier scholastic histories of the period. Lockhart suffered considerable ill health in his later years. He died in Hove on 27 February 1970.

MICHAEL HUGHES

Sources R. H. B. Lockhart, *Memoirs of a British agent*, 2nd edn (1937) · R. H. B. Lockhart, *Retreat from glory*, 2nd edn (1937) · R. H. B. Lockhart, *Guns or butter* (1938) · *The diaries of Sir Robert Bruce Lockhart*, ed. K. Young, 2 vols. (1973–80) · R. H. B. Lockhart, *Comes the reckoning* (1947) · R. H. B. Lockhart, *My Scottish youth* (1937) · *The Times* (28 Feb 1970) · *The Times* (5 March 1970) · *DNB* · *CGPLA Eng. & Wales* (1970)

Archives HLRO, diaries · Indiana University, Bloomington, Lilly Library, corresp. and papers · NL Scot., notebooks, cuttings, and collected papers · PRO, Foreign Office corresp. and papers, FO 800/868–86 | HLRO, corresp. with Lord Beaverbrook · PRO, corresp. with Sir Percy Loraine, FO 1011/282 · U. Birm. L., corresp. with Lord Avon

Likenesses K. A. Somov, drawing, 1934; Christies, 5 Oct 1989, lot 308 [*see illus.*] · W. Stoneman, photograph, 1943, NPG · H. Coster, photographs, NPG · photograph, repro. in *The Times* · photographs, repro. in *The Bookseller* (25 Aug 1973) · photographs, repro. in *Diaries*, ed. Young

Wealth at death £2054: probate, 24 April 1970, *CGPLA Eng. & Wales*

Lockhart, William [created Sir William Lockhart under the protectorate] (**1621?–1675**), diplomat and army officer, was the eldest son of Sir James *Lockhart of Lee (1588/1599–1674) and his second wife, Martha Douglas of Mordington. Unhappy at school at Lanark, he played truant and at the age of thirteen ran away to Leith to sail to the Netherlands and enter the Dutch army. Tall and strong for his age, he was accepted, but soon went on to Danzig, where his relative Sir George Douglas protected him until he died in 1636. Lockhart escorted Douglas's body home from Pomerania, but remained restless and, funded by his mother, travelled across Europe to gain education. Having joined the French army, he caught the queen mother's eye and became captain of horse.

When William Hamilton, earl of Lanark, raised a cavalry regiment for the covenanters in April 1644, Lockhart returned to Scotland as lieutenant-colonel. He married Margaret (*d.* in or before 1654), daughter of Sir John Hamilton of Orbiston, justice clerk; they had one son. He served against Montrose and with Leslie in England until Charles I's surrender at Newark. The captive king then knighted him unofficially and used him as his emissary to the duke of Hamilton, to request Hamilton's intervention with the Scottish government on behalf of the defeated Montrose. Lockhart was then appointed commander of a cavalry troop on 29 January 1647 and colonel of horse for Lanarkshire on 4 May, serving on the county committee of war. He fought in the army sent against England under Hamilton in 1648 in support of the engagement with Charles I. First sent to Annan to protect Carlisle from Lambert, he then rejoined Hamilton for the Preston campaign. Unhorsed at Preston, he distinguished himself protecting

William Lockhart (1621?–1675), by unknown artist

Hamilton's retreat to Wigan and was one of his three commissioners to negotiate surrender at Uttoxeter. He was sent prisoner to Hull, but secured his release a year later on payment of £1000 and did penance in Scotland for supporting the engagement. His recall to service as general of horse on Charles II's arrival proved abortive, as Argyll sought to constrain him through a joint command with Baillie and Montgomery, and he refused to serve on those terms. When Charles invaded England, he offered his services as a volunteer; rejected, he indignantly declared that 'no king on earth should treat him in this manner'.

In 1652 Lockhart threw in his lot with the English and after an interview with Cromwell in London was appointed a commissioner for justice in Scotland in May, subsequently being trusted to help negotiate the Anglo-Scottish Union. He was one of four Scots who sat in the nominated parliament of 1653 and subsequently represented Lancashire in both Oliver Cromwell's parliaments. He sat on the new commission for administering civil justice from June 1654, and was granted Kelso Abbey. His rise owed most to his surprise second marriage, to Cromwell's widowed niece Robina Sewster on 2 July 1654. There were five sons of the marriage, the eldest called Cromwell, and two daughters. Admitted to the Cromwellian élite, he was appointed to Cromwell's new Scottish council in May 1655 on a salary of £600 p.a. On 31 August he spoke 'very threatening things' to Johnston of Wariston condemning plans of the Protector leadership to promote a new covenant (*Diary of Sir Archibald Johnston*, 7). He also became JP for Fife, Kinross, and Lanarkshire, and judge of the exchequer.

Following the Anglo-French treaty of October 1655 Cromwell sought alliance with France against Spain, and on 29 February 1656 Lockhart was appointed as ambassador to France on a salary of £120 a month. His 'Instructions' required him to arrange a joint campaign in Flanders, preferably financed by France, and to secure protection of Huguenots from Catholic harassment. In France his Presbyterian background and earlier service in the country prompted suspicions about his ability to stir up subversion and he had to form a secret understanding with Mazarin to counteract the deep unpopularity of the negotiations in France, to combat 'devot' intrigue for Franco-Spanish peace, and to persuade the cardinal to surrender Dunkirk to Cromwell. Cromwell indicated his confidence by knighting him on 10 December when he reported back to London.

The treaty was signed on 3 March 1657, agreeing a joint campaign against Dunkirk with France financing it and surrendering Gravelines as security if that was recaptured first. Lockhart had to accept the free practice of Catholicism in English-controlled territory, and persuaded Cromwell that this concession was essential for their strategic aims. He duly attended the campaign, taking command of the English force when Sir John Reynolds was drowned, and pressurized the dilatory French to carry out their undertakings. Mardyke, the first conquest, was handed over to the English, but was not properly supplied until Lockhart's protests led Cromwell to threaten withdrawal. On 4 June 1658 Lockhart commanded the English army with distinction at the French victory of the Dunes, leading them in a courageous charge up a sandhill, and on Dunkirk's surrender on 15 June he became governor with his own new cavalry regiment added to the garrison. A forceful administrator, he secured local supplies and English military equipment and stopped his zealous troops harassing the Catholic inhabitants. Cromwell sought to use his continental foothold to spread protestantism, and Lockhart secured the services of preachers such as Hugh Peter to assist his chaplain, Fuller, while warning Cromwell 'as Rome was not built in a day, so it will not be pulled down'. He continued to maintain good relations with Mazarin and counteract court intrigues, helped to arrange a joint naval expedition to Italy in 1658, and protested at Huguenot sufferings as in Montauban in 1657 and Nîmes in 1658 despite Catholic resentment. He also assisted Cromwell personally in assessing the suitability of Lord Fauconberg as a husband for his daughter Mary.

Cromwell's death saw no great changes, Lockhart continuing to report to Secretary Thurloe, but Richard Cromwell's deposition weakened English power. Lockhart accepted the restored republican regime, as reported to parliament on 18 May 1659, and returned to London. Despite suspicions of his fidelity he was reappointed ambassador in July on £600 a month and was sent to St Jean de Luz to attend the Franco-Spanish peace talks, though the more reliable Major Tobias Bridge served as his deputy in Dunkirk. But England's usefulness had ceased and he was 'coldly received', at least until Booth's rebellion failed. In October the council of state recalled him. Edmund Ludlow met him by chance at Sir Henry Vane's house in

November; he 'very much lamented the divisions that were amongst us, affirming that if they had not provided an obstruction to him … we might have had what terms we could have asked for either from France or Spain'. Meeting Monck on his arrival, he was assured of the general's republicanism and back in Dunkirk ordered his officers to accept whatever arrangements parliament decided. Accordingly he refused large royalist bribes to hand Dunkirk over to Charles II, and loyally refused similar inducements from Mazarin, who purportedly promised him the title of marshal of France.

With the restoration of Charles II, Lockhart was superseded at Dunkirk by Edward Harley on 31 May 1660, but through the intercession of the earl of Middleton was not proceeded against for his activities. He retired to his Scottish estates, where he was unpopular with his neighbours on account of his Cromwellian connections, and eventually lived with his wife's relations in Huntingdonshire. John Maitland, duke of Lauderdale, secured him royal employment with appointment as a 'secret councillor' for Scotland in September 1670, and a privy counsellor in 1674. In June 1671 they secured the office of justice clerk for his aged father, whom he succeeded in 1674. Having raised 1000 men for the forthcoming campaign against Holland, in 1671 he was sent as ambassador to Brunswick and Brandenburg to secure their neutrality or co-operation, in the event unsuccessfully. According to Burnet, he was opposed to this assistance to Catholic France and served 'from a desire to be safe'. In March 1673 he was reappointed envoy to France, taking leave of the king on 1 April, and performed satisfactorily enough to be raised to full ambassadorial rank when he reported to Charles in October. His permission to draw up his own equipage and submit the bill later indicated his known probity. His return was delayed by troubles in his regiment. Back in France he funded the now exiled Clarendon. By April 1675 the duke of Monmouth was commiserating on news of his 'indisposition', and he died early in June. A later story attributed his demise to a pair of poisoned gloves, but Burnet reported that he had been 'languishing' and depressed at his mission for some time. His body was returned to Scotland on the yacht *Merlin* for burial, after long delays occasioned by bad weather. His wife survived him.

A 'gallant and sober person', according to Evelyn, adventurous in youth, and a courageous officer, Lockhart was also a skilful diplomat and a capable governor, loyal beyond expectations of personal advancement in 1660 and a lifelong promoter of international protestantism. An unapologetic careerist in developing his Cromwellian family connection, his fulsome flattery of Louis XIV and obsequious letters are also notable.

TIMOTHY VENNING

Sources Thurloe, *State papers* • M. Noble, *Memoirs of the protectoral-house of Cromwell*, 2 vols. (1787) • *Fourth report*, HMC, 3 (1874) • *CSP dom.*, 1654–60; 1664–5; 1672–6 • C. H. Firth and G. Davies, *The regimental history of Cromwell's army*, 2 vols. (1940) • C. H. Firth, ed., *Scotland and the protectorate: letters and papers relating to the military government of Scotland from January 1654 to June 1659*, Scottish History Society, 31 (1899) • Clarendon, *Hist. rebellion* • *Burnet's History of my own time*, ed. O. Airy, new edn, 2 vols. (1897–1900); suppl., ed. H. C. Foxcroft (1902) • *The memoirs of Edmund Ludlow*, ed. C. H. Firth, 2 vols. (1894) • E. M. Furgol, *A regimental history of the covenanting armies, 1639–1651* (1990) • *JHC*, 7 (1651–9) • W. A. Shaw, *The knights of England*, 2 vols. (1906) • *Diary of Sir Archibald Johnston of Wariston*, 3, ed. J. D. Ogilvie, Scottish History Society, 3rd ser., 34 (1940) • *Journals of Sir John Lauder*, ed. D. Crawford, Scottish History Society, 36 (1900) • *Reg. PCS*, 3rd ser., vol. 4 • W. Stephen, ed., *Register of the consultations of the ministers of Edinburgh*, 1, Scottish History Society, 3rd ser., 1 (1921)

Archives BL, letters to John Thurloe, Add. MSS 4157–4158 • HMC, ambassador's reports • NL Scot., ambassador's reports

Likenesses attrib. J. B. Medina, oils, Scot. NPG • oils, Haddo House, Aberdeenshire • oils, Scot. NPG [*see illus.*]

Wealth at death barony of Carstairs and Lockharthill House, Lanark; salaried position as lord justice clerk, Scotland; salaried position as ambassador to France; owned abbey of Kelso: *CSP dom.*; *Diary of Johnston of Wariston*, ed. Ogilvie; Hamilton, ed., *Description of sheriffdoms of Lanark and Renfrew*

Lockhart, William (1819–1892), Roman Catholic convert and Rosminian priest, son of the Revd Alexander Lockhart (1788–1832), rector of Stone and Hartwell, Buckinghamshire, and his wife, Martha (*d.* 1872), daughter of William *Jacob (1761/2–1851), the statistician, traveller, and politician, was born on 22 August 1819. On his father's side he was a descendant of Alexander Lockhart, Lord Covington, and a cousin of John Gibson Lockhart. After education at Bedford grammar school he matriculated from Exeter College, Oxford, on 17 May 1838, and graduated BA in 1842. While still an undergraduate he felt the attraction of the Roman Catholic church, and confided his difficulties to his mother's friend H. E. Manning, who advised him, on graduating, to join the community at Littlemore then being established by J. H. Newman. However, he continued to be unsettled, and though he had promised Newman to wait for three years before making any move, he was received into the Roman Catholic church at Loughborough on 26 August 1843. He was the first of the Tractarians who went over to Rome, and the much publicized secession prompted Newman to resign his cure at Littlemore and to deliver his valedictory sermon, 'The parting of friends', in which Lockhart is disguised under the character of Orpah.

Lockhart was received into the church by Luigi Gentili of the Institute of Charity, founded by Antonio Rosmini. He entered the same order at Ratcliffe College, Leicestershire, on 29 August 1843 and was ordained there on 19 December 1845; his mother had become a Roman Catholic earlier that year. Based at Ratcliffe until 1853, he travelled widely throughout England, Scotland, and Ireland as a missioner and retreat-giver.

In 1854 Lockhart established a permanent mission at Kingsland in north London. In 1873 he was instrumental in acquiring for his order the disused church of St Etheldreda's, Ely Place, Holborn, originally built in the thirteenth century as the domestic chapel of the bishops of Ely. He remained at St Etheldreda's as rector until his death, though from 1881 he wintered in Rome as procurator for his order. Through the connection of his father's sister, the marchesa de Riario-Sforza, he had an entrée to the Roman curia, and was frequently consulted by the pope on English affairs, but diffidence prevented him from seeking or obtaining high preferment.

While at Littlemore, Lockhart had assisted Newman in the translation of Fleury's *Ecclesiastical History* and begun the life of St Gilbert of Sempringham, later completed by J. D. Dalgairns. As a writer he is best known for his work on Rosmini, whose teaching he expounded in *A Short Sketch of Modern Philosophies* (1882). In 1886 he published the second volume of a voluminous *Life of Antonio Rosmini-Serbati*, the first volume of which, by G. S. MacWalter, had appeared in 1883. As editor of *Catholic Opinion* from 1867 to 1873, and of *The Lamp* from 1871, he was a prolific journalist. He published three works of Catholic apologetics, and at the time of Newman's death in 1890 contributed reminiscences of the cardinal to several journals, including the *Paternoster Review*. He was most influential, however, as a preacher and pastor, and was an ardent apostle of total abstinence. Lockhart died of heart failure at St Etheldreda's on 15 May 1892 and was buried at Ratcliffe College on 20 May.

G. MARTIN MURPHY

Sources [J. Hirst], *Biography of Father Lockhart* (1893) · W. Lockhart, 'Some personal reminiscences of Cardinal Manning when archbisop of Chichester', *Dublin Review*, 110 (1892), 372–9 · W. Lockhart, 'Cardinal Newman: reminiscences of fifty years since 1891', *Paternoster Review*, 1 (1890) · W. Lockhart, 'Cardinal Newman: a retrospect of fifty years', *Irish Ecclesiastical Record*, 3rd ser., 11 (1890), 865–74 · W. Ward, *W. G. Ward and the Oxford Movement* (1889), 209–10 · C. Leetham, *Luigi Gentili: a sower for the second spring* (1965), 171–9

Archives International Rosminian Centre, Stresa, Italy · St Mary's College, Wonersh, Guildford, Surrey

Likenesses engraving, St Etheldreda's, Ely Place, London

Lockhart, William Ewart (1846–1900), painter, was born on 18 February 1846 at Eaglesfield, Dumfriesshire, the illegitimate son of Ann Lockhart (*b.* 1823), a domestic servant, and Thomas Ewart (1823–1881), a farm labourer. Raised by his maternal grandparents in Annan, at the age of fourteen he enrolled at the Trustees' Academy, Edinburgh. Lockhart also attended life classes at the Royal Scottish Academy where he was a pupil of Robert Scott Lauder and John Blake MacDonald. Lockhart contracted tuberculosis in 1863 and spent eighteen months recovering in Australia, thereafter spending most winters abroad. Spain became the inspiration of some of his best work, such as *The Cid and the Five Moorish Kings* (watercolour version exh. Edinburgh International Exhibition, 1886; Perth City Art Gallery) and *The Swineherd* (oil; exh. Royal Scottish Academy, 1885; McManus Galleries, Dundee).

Lockhart settled in Edinburgh, and on 5 February 1869 married Mary Blake Will (1846–1934), his tutor's niece; they had four daughters and a son. He was a visitor at the Royal Scottish Academy, and became an associate of the academy in 1871 and a member in 1878. His reputation as a watercolourist rests mainly on his scenes of the Scottish east coast though nowhere is his expertise in this medium better seen than in *Durham* (exh. Royal Scottish Academy, 1882; priv. coll.). However, the landscape painter John MacWhirter wrote in his obituary of Lockhart that 'He excelled in nearly all branches—landscape, portraiture and semi-historical subjects. His manner was broad and daring in colour, but he could also be very minute and refined, especially in his architectural works' (MacWhirter). A number of Lockhart's works were reproduced as illustrations to editions of Scott, Burns, and Stevenson.

Lockhart executed over four hundred paintings, twenty-nine of which were exhibited at the Royal Academy. He was made a member of the Society of Painters in Water Colours in 1878, and of the Royal Society of Engravers in 1881. He was president of the Scottish Arts Club from 1883 to 1888, and was the Royal Scottish Academy's representative as a trustee of the British Institution at the time of his death. In 1884 Lockhart moved to London, but was in Edinburgh in 1886 to escort Queen Victoria around the International Exhibition, which contained three of his best Spanish works, including *Gil Blas and the Archbishop of Granada* (oil; exh. RA, 1879; NG Scot.). In 1887 the queen commissioned him to paint *The Golden Jubilee Service in Westminster Abbey* (oil; Royal Collection), his most ambitious work, measuring 92 by 120 inches and containing 278 individual portraits. It took him three years to complete, but the trials of organizing sittings and of obtaining samples of fabrics and uniforms undermined his health. The picture was reproduced in photogravure and the sketch of it was bought by the French government. It brought him popularity as a portraitist: *Speaker Peel* (oil; exh. RA, 1892), which won a medal at the Paris Salon of 1895, and *A. J. Balfour* (oil; exh. Royal Scottish Academy, 1898; Glasgow Museums and Art Galleries) were two of his most acclaimed portraits. Lockhart was bitterly disappointed that he was not knighted for his royal service. Depression led to his admittance to Bethlem Hospital, where he died of pneumonia on 9 February 1900. He was buried in Brookwood cemetery, Woking, on 14 February.

J. L. CAW, *rev.* MARGERY A. WILKINS

Sources bap. reg. Scot. · Lockhart family archives, priv. coll. · J. L. Caw, *Scottish painting past and present, 1620–1908* (1908) · O. Millar, *The Victorian pictures in the collection of her majesty the queen*, 2 vols. (1992) · P. G. Hamerton, *Man in art* (1892) · J. MacWhirter, *The Scotsman* (13 Feb 1900) · *Annual Report of the Council of the Royal Scottish Academy of Painting, Sculpture, and Architecture*, 73 (1900) · M. Hardie, *Water-colour painting in Britain*, ed. D. Snelgrove, J. Mayne, and B. Taylor, 2nd edn, 3: *The Victorian period* [1968] · J. Halsby and P. Harris, *The dictionary of Scottish painters, 1600–1960* (1990) · *The Portfolio*, 14 (1883) · *The Portfolio*, 18 (1887) · *The exhibition of the Royal Academy* (1873–99) [exhibition catalogues] · exhibition catalogues (1861–1901) [Royal Scot. Acad.] · *Dumfries and Galloway Standard and Advertiser* (26 March 1884) · *Dumfries and Galloway Standard and Advertiser* (4 June 1879) · *Annandale Observer* (16 Feb 1900) · P. J. M. McEwan, *Dictionary of Scottish art and architecture* (1994) · S. Cursiter, *Art at the close of the 19th century* (1949) · Mallalieu, *Watercolour artists* · Wood, *Vic. painters*, 2nd edn · M. Wilkins, *By royal command* (1998) · gravestone · archives, Bethlem Hospital

Archives NG Scot. · priv. coll., Lockhart family archives · PRO, LCI/513 · Royal Arch., MSS, RA Add. J, RA PP, VIC 1894/8934 · Royal Scot. Acad., MSS · Tate collection, MSS, 7122.9

Likenesses J. Pettie, painting, oils, 1881, priv. coll. · W. Crooke, photograph, 1885, RSA · W. Hodgson, pencil and wash drawing, 1891, Scot. NPG · J. Archer, oils, Scot. NPG · W. E. Lockhart, self-portrait, oils, Aberdeen Art Gallery · W. E. Lockhart, self-portrait, oils, priv. coll. · T. Rodger, photograph, RSA · four engravings (after photographs), repro. in *Strand Magazine* (1893) · photograph, Tate collection

Wealth at death £2661 2*s*. 6*d*.: probate, 27 April 1900, *CGPLA Eng. & Wales*

Lockhart, Sir William Stephen Alexander (1841–1900), army officer, was born in Milton Lockhart, Lanarkshire, on 2 September 1841, fourth son of the Revd Lawrence Lockhart of Wicketshaw and Milton Lockhart, and his first wife, Louisa, daughter of David Blair, an East India merchant, and nephew of John Gibson Lockhart. His three elder brothers were John Somerville Lockhart, Major-General David Blair Lockhart of Milton Lockhart, and Laurence William Maxwell *Lockhart, the novelist. Lockhart was educated at the University of Glasgow before starting a military career. In 1864 he married Caroline Amelia, daughter of Major-General E. Lascelles Dennys; in 1888 he married his second wife, Mary Katherine, daughter of Captain William Eccles, who survived him.

Lockhart entered the Indian army as an ensign on 4 October 1858 at the age of seventeen, joining the 44th Bengal native infantry. He was promoted lieutenant (19 June 1859), captain (16 December 1868), major (9 June 1877), lieutenant-colonel (6 April 1879), brevet colonel (6 April 1883), major-general (1 September 1891), lieutenant-general (1 April 1894), and general (9 November 1896).

Lockhart served in Oudh during the Indian mutiny with the 5th fusiliers in 1858–9, and then as adjutant of the 14th Bengal lancers in the Bhutan campaigns from 1864 to 1866. During the latter he distinguished himself on a reconnaissance to Chirung, demonstrating his skill at hill warfare, keen eye for ground, and skill at outpost and scouting duty. His services were acknowledged by the government of India.

In the Abyssinian expedition of 1867–8 Lockhart was aide-de-camp to Brigadier-General J. Merewether, commanding the cavalry brigade, and taking part in the action of Arogee and the capture of Magdala. He was mentioned in dispatches.

Lockhart was then appointed deputy assistant quartermaster-general with the Hazara field force, under Brigadier-General Alfred Thomas Wilde, during the Black Mountain expedition in 1868, for which he was mentioned in dispatches. Shortly afterwards he was awarded the bronze medal of the Royal Humane Society for rescuing two women from drowning in the Morar Lake, Gwalior, on 26 December 1869.

Lockhart served ten years on the staff and was appointed successively deputy assistant and assistant quartermaster-general in the Bengal army. He also served twice in Achin in Sumatra between 1875 and 1877, the second time as military attaché to the Dutch army, when he participated in the assault and capture of Lambadde, for which he was mentioned in dispatches, offered the Netherlands order of William, which he was not allowed to accept, and received the Dutch war medal and clasp. He contracted malaria, however, and returned to Singapore seriously ill.

Sir William Stephen Alexander Lockhart (1841–1900), by Bassano, *c*.1898

During the Second Anglo-Afghan War (1878–80) Lockhart was initially appointed road commandant in the Khyber Pass, safeguarding it from attack by the Afridis, then, in November 1879, assistant quartermaster-general at Kabul. He fought at Mir Karez, Takht-i-Shah, and around Kabul under Sir Frederick Roberts in December 1879, and was subsequently deputy adjutant and quartermaster-general to Sir Donald Stewart commanding in northern Afghanistan, returning to India through the Khyber Pass in August 1880. Lockhart was mentioned in dispatches and made a CB (military division).

Lockhart was deputy quartermaster-general in the intelligence branch at headquarters between 1880 and 1885, apart from a trip to Achin to rescue the crew of the *Nisero* in 1884. He then commanded the 24th Punjab infantry, but in June 1885 was appointed an envoy under the foreign department on a political mission to Chitral. He commanded a brigade during the pacification of Upper Burma from September 1886 to March 1887, for which he was mentioned in dispatches, thanked by the government of India, and made a KCB and a CSI.

On his return to India, Lockhart commanded a second-class district in Bengal, but a severe attack of malaria compelled him to return home. For six months he was employed at the India Office preparing an account of his explorations in central Asia, and in April 1889 was appointed assistant military secretary for Indian affairs at the

Horse Guards. Lockhart returned to India in November 1890 to command the prestigious Punjab frontier force, first as brigadier-general and then as major-general, until March 1895. He conducted a succession of punitive military expeditions against the transborder Pathan peoples inhabiting the hills bordering the Punjab, establishing a reputation as the Indian army's foremost expert on frontier warfare. Lockhart commanded the Miranzai field force in January and February 1891, the 3rd brigade of the Hazara field force in March and April, and the Miranzai field force again from April to June. He was mentioned in the governor-general's dispatch and was promoted major-general. Lockhart then commanded the Isazai field force in 1892 and the Waziristan expedition in 1894–5, was again mentioned in dispatches by the government of India, and was made a KCSI. In 1895 he was given the Punjab command.

In 1897 Lockhart was placed in command of the 40,000 strong Tirah expeditionary force, after Afridis attacked British outposts along the north-west frontier during the most serious outbreak of resistance to British rule in India since the mutiny. During the difficult extended fighting in the inaccessible mountains of Tirah, he skilfully conducted punitive operations against elusive Afridi and Orakzai fighters, armed with modern rifles. Though for the most part consisting of guerrilla warfare, the campaign also included such bitterly contested engagements as the attack at Dargai and the withdrawal of the 2nd division down the Bara valley. For his services he received the thanks of the government of India, was made a GCB, and succeeded Sir George White as commander-in-chief in India in 1898. Lockhart was plagued by ill health, however, from diseases contracted during earlier military campaigns, and finally died at his residence, the Treasury Gate, Fort William, Calcutta, from malaria, complicating gout, on 18 March 1900. He was buried the following day at Fort William military cemetery.

R. H. VETCH, *rev.* T. R. MOREMAN

Sources *Indian Army List* (1 Jan 1900) • Sir W. S. A. Lockhart biographical file, BL OIOC • *The Times* (20 March 1900) • Cadet papers of W. S. A. Lockhart, BL OIOC, L/MIL/9/246 • Ecclesiastical returns, BL OIOC, N/1/281 f.21 • D. F. Rennie, *Bhotan and the story of the Dooar War, including sketches of a three months' residence in the Himalayas* (1866) • T. J. Holland and H. Hozier, *Record of the expedition to Abyssinia*, 2 vols. (1870) • S. H. Shadbolt, ed., *The Afghan campaigns of 1878–1880*, 2 vols. (1882) • H. F. Walters, *Operations of the Tirah expeditionary force 1897–1898 under the command of Sir W. S. A. Lockhart* (1900) • L. J. Shadwell, *Lockhart's advance through Tirah* (1898) • H. D. Hutchinson, *The campaign in Tirah, 1897–1898: an account of the expedition against the Orakzais and Afridis* (1898) • C. E. Cailwell, *Tirah: 1897* (1911) • d. cert. • *CGPLA Eng. & Wales* (1900)

Archives BL OIOC, White, Elgin MSS

Likenesses Hardie, oils, 1894; in possession of Major-General D. B. Lockhart, 1901 • Bassano, photograph, *c.*1898, NPG [*see illus.*] • photograph, *c.*1900, NAM • Bassano, photographs, NPG • Spy [L. Ward], caricature, NPG; repro. in *VF* (8 Sept 1898) • portrait (after photograph by Bassano), repro. in Hutchinson, *The campaign in Tirah*, frontispiece • wood-engraving, NPG; repro. in *ILN* (20 Nov 1886)

Wealth at death £2737 8*s.* 3*d.*: probate, 23 June 1900, *CGPLA Eng. & Wales*

Lockier, Francis (*bap.* 1669, *d.* 1740), dean of Peterborough, son of William and Hannah Lockier of Norwich, was born there and baptized at St Mary-in-the-Marsh, Norwich, on 25 March 1669. He was educated at the city grammar school under John Burton, and on 9 May 1683 was admitted subsizar of Trinity College, Cambridge, graduating BA in January 1687, MA in 1690, and DD in 1717, on the occasion of the visit of George I. On his first trip to London he 'thrust himself' into Will's to see the wits, and on his second visit to the coffee house contrived by a timely illustration to ingratiate himself with Dryden, whose friendship he retained throughout life (Malone, 1.478–9).

Lockier accompanied Sir Paul Rycaut to the Hanse towns, and acted as chaplain and secretary to Lord Molesworth while he was in the Low Countries. For some years Lockier was chaplain to the English factory at Hamburg, and made an annual journey to Hanover to cultivate the acquaintance of George I. He mixed much in the world, was a good judge of character, knew the chief continental languages, and was brimful of anecdote. On the nomination of the archbishop of York, to whom the benefice had lapsed, he held (1693–1740) the valuable rectory of Handsworth, near Sheffield, and for nine years (1731–40) he was, by the gift of the earl of Holdernesse, rector of the adjoining parish of Aston. Through the personal favour of George I, to whom he was chaplain-in-ordinary, Lockier was appointed in March 1725 to the deanery of Peterborough, and he retained all his preferments until his death. When unable to reside regularly at Handsworth he engaged the services of a clerk in orders. He made some provision for the education of the poor in Handsworth, and while he was dean £600 was expended from the chapter revenues in removing the Benedictine arrangement, which extended two bays into the nave, and in fitting up the eastern section of the church as the ritual choir, leaving the lantern and transepts outside it. A further sum of £500 was spent on extensive repairs to the organ.

From 21 July 1726 Lockier was a member of the Gentlemen's Society at Spalding, and he communicated an account of Sir Isaac Newton to this antiquarian society, which was later printed in Nichols's *Literary Anecdotes* (1812–15, 6.101–2), and in Nichols's *Illustrations of Literature* (1817–58, 4.17–18). His only publication was a sermon before the House of Commons on 31 January 1726. A rhyming account of the contemporary clergymen around Sheffield speaks of him as 'debonaire and civil, well read, and made complete by travel'.

Lockier died in Peterborough on 17 July 1740 and was buried in the cathedral, where a tablet at the entry from the south choir aisle into the eastern chapel was erected. He bequeathed to Bishop Zachary Pearce his excellent library, except such books as the bishop already owned, which were given to the chapter library at Peterborough. He left a manuscript book of anecdotes which was burnt in accordance with his will, but several of his reminiscences of his friends Dryden and Pope were published in Joseph Spence's *Anecdotes, Observations, and Characters, of Books and Men* (1820, 58 ff.).

W. P. COURTNEY, *rev.* ADAM JACOB LEVIN

Sources Venn, *Alum. Cant.* • *IGI* • J. Hunter, *Hallamshire: the history and topography of the parish of Sheffield in the county of York*, new edn, ed. A. Gatty (1869), 485–9 • J. Hunter, *South Yorkshire: the history and topography of the deanery of Doncaster*, 2 (1831), 166–7 • 'Life', *The works of … Thomas Newton*, 1 (1782), 45–6 • E. Malone, 'Life of Dryden', in *The critical and miscellaneous prose works of John Dryden*, 3 vols. (1800), vol. 1, pp. 478–81 • W. Sweeting, *Churches in and around Peterborough* (1868), 49, 58 • will, PRO, PROB 11/709, sig. 129

Wealth at death over £250 bequeathed; also library bequeathed to Zachary Pearce: will, PRO, PROB 11/709, sig. 129

Lockman, John (1698–1771), author and translator, was baptized on 3 March 1698 at St Paul's, Covent Garden, the son of Gerrard Lockman (*d.* 1714) and his wife, Sarah (*d.* 1742). According to his own statement he was born and spent his infancy in Petersham, Surrey (*London Magazine*, 1735, 41), but most of his life was spent in London. It is not known where he went to school or what was his earliest occupation, but it is said that by dint of hard private study he became a tolerable scholar and learned to speak French by frequenting Slaughter's Coffee House (Hawkins, 516n.). On 11 November 1725 he married Mary Boucher at St Peter-le-Poer Church, Bishopsgate.

In 1726 Lockman published *A Description of the Temple of Venus at Cnidus*, translated from the French, and over the following years he translated works of the marquise de Lambert, La Fontaine, Desfontaines, Le Sage, Marivaux, and King Stanislaus, as well as three substantial volumes of French travel writing. It was probably owing to his translation of Voltaire's *La Henriade* (1728) that, to Johnson's irritation, he was called *'l'illustre Lockman'* in France (Boswell, *Life*, 4.6), though Lockman's *Henriade* (1732), in very flat blank verse with copious anti-Roman Catholic notes, was less successful than his translations of Voltaire's *Lettres philosophiques* (*Letters Concerning the English Nation*, 1733) and *Siècle de Louis XIV* (*An Essay on the Age of Lewis XIV*, 1739). His translation of Charles Porée's Latin *Oration* on whether the stage is a school for virtue (1734) was dedicated to Alexander Pope.

Lockman was one of the team who, for 25*s.* a sheet (£1.25 for four printed folio pages), compiled the *General Dictionary, Historical and Critical*, in ten folio volumes (1734–41), which incorporated Lockman's 'new and accurate translation' (BL, Add. MS 4254, fol. 116) of Bayle's *Dictionnaire*, as well as other articles by Lockman. Equally successful and more popular compilations by Lockman were his histories of England and of Rome in the form of question and answer, with parallel text in French and English, which were used as school books until long after their author's death: the copyright of his *History of England* was worth over £100 in 1787 and its twenty-fifth edition appeared in 1811. It was said, perhaps with some exaggeration, that Lockman translated 'with general accuracy, more books for half a century together than any man of his time' (*GM*, 314).

Between 1730 and 1767 Lockman wrote about twenty separately published occasional complimentary poems, as well as others in newspapers and magazines; also he wrote songs for the theatre, prologues, and epilogues, usually for good causes. His more substantial theatrical works were *David's Lamentation*, an oratorio with music by William Boyce (1736), and *Rosalinda*, a musical drama with music by John Christopher Smith (1740), to which was prefixed an enquiry into the rise of operas and oratorios.

Between 1756 and 1762 Lockman fruitlessly circulated proposals to publish his poems by subscription, though he assured Thomas Birch that this was 'not (Heaven be Praised) the effect of necessity' (BL, Add. MS 4312, fol. 233). Appointment as secretary to the council of the Free British Fishery, incorporated in 1750, had perhaps met Lockman's necessities: it certainly provided his motive for prose and verse pamphlets on the importance of the white herring fishery in 1750–51, and presents of verses and herrings to the future George III when he was governor of the Free British Fishery. In 1734 Lockman had complained to Birch of 'unmerited rebuffs from the world' and being 'compelled to labor day and night' (BL, Add. MS 4312, fol. 221), but, thanks, one supposes, to income from his fishery appointment and buoyant sales of the histories by question and answer, he published far less new writing after 1750 than before.

For his gentle and inoffensive manners Lockman was nicknamed the Lamb by his literary acquaintances. Nevertheless, when Thomas Cooke 'abused his poetry to his face' Lockman, 'with a quickness not natural to him, retorted, "It may be so; but, thank God! my name is not at full length in the DUNCIAD!"' (*GM*, 314). Lockman died on 2 February 1771 in Brownlow Street, Long Acre; he was survived by his wife. JAMES SAMBROOK

Sources *GM*, 1st ser., 62 (1792), 314 • D. E. Baker, *Biographia dramatica, or, A companion to the playhouse*, rev. I. Reed, new edn, rev. S. Jones, 3 vols. in 4 (1812), vol. 1, p. 458 • J. Hawkins, *The life of Samuel Johnson, LL.D.* (1787), 516n. • *London Magazine*, 4 (1735), 41 • Boswell, *Life*, vols. 4, 6 • Nichols, *Lit. anecdotes*, 5.53, 287, 8.100–01 • W. Van Lennep and others, eds., *The London stage, 1660–1800*, 5 pts in 11 vols. (1960–68) • Nichols, *Illustrations*, 2.67 • transcript of St Peter le Poer registers, Society of Genealogists library • W. H. Hunt, ed., *The registers of St Paul's Church, Covent Garden, London*, 1, Harleian Society, register section, 33 (1906), 104 • *N&Q*, 3rd ser., 2 (1862), 249 • A. Chalmers, ed., *The general biographical dictionary*, new edn, 20 (1815), 374 • J. P. Lee, 'The unexamined premise: Voltaire, John Lockman and the myth of the *English letters*', *Studies in Voltaire and the eighteenth century* (2001)

Archives BL, agreement to compile *General Dictionary*, Add. MS 4254, fol. 116 • BL, assignment of *England*, Add. MS 38730, fol. 81 • BL, receipt for work on the *General Dictionary*, Add. MS 4478C, fol. 167 | BL, letters to Thomas Birch, Add. MSS 4312, 4475, fol. 118

Lockspeiser, Sir Ben (1891–1990), engineer and government administrator, was born on 9 March 1891 at 7 President Street in the parish of St Luke's in the City of London, the eldest son and second child in the family of three sons and two daughters of Leon Lockspeiser, diamond merchant, and his wife, Rosa Gleitzman, of a devout and industrious Jewish family, recently arrived from a farming background in Lubno, south-west Poland. Benny Lockspeiser—so named in his birth certificate, though he was Ben for most of his life—spent his early years at 21 Thornby Road, Clapham. He was educated at the Grocers' School, Hackney, and, at the age of seventeen, already a gifted pianist and cellist, he won an open scholarship to Sidney Sussex College, Cambridge. After gaining a first in part one of the natural sciences tripos (1912), he transferred to the mechanical sciences tripos and obtained a second class in part two (1913). After a year at the Royal School of Mines, he immediately enlisted when the First World War began. In 1915 he sailed for Gallipoli as a private with the Royal Army Medical Corps (RAMC). There he was stricken with amoebic dysentery and invalided out to Egypt, where on his recovery he continued with the RAMC, identifying the type, causes, and treatment of that devastating malady.

After Lockspeiser came back home, having been demobilized in 1919, his MA degree in engineering gained him entry to the armaments and aerodynamics section of the Royal Aircraft Establishment (RAE) at Farnborough, Hampshire, where in 1920, on a walking holiday at Newlands in Wales, he met his future wife, Elsie, a botanist, daughter of Alfred Shuttleworth, accountant, of Shuttleworth and Haworth, Manchester. They married that year and had one son and two daughters. The young Lockspeisers set up home at Newlands, Victoria Road, Farnborough, the town in which, with one move in the 1930s to Waverley Road, they lived for the rest of their lives. Lockspeiser worked hard and also immersed himself in the social activities of the RAE, which included music, drama, and gardening, and he became a member of the local branch of the emerging Labour Party. In 1922 he founded the RAE Orchestral Society, which later became the Farnborough Symphony Orchestra and which he himself conducted until 1939.

As one of a four-man elasticity research team, Lockspeiser began pioneering work on chemical means of de-icing aircraft wings and other surfaces. This led him to study how to prevent the freezing of aircrew oxygen systems and of moisture in gas-supply mains. At the same time he worked on metal fatigue and was closely involved in the design, construction, and operation of the RAE's wind tunnel, which had a diameter of 24 feet. In 1936 he succeeded Harold Roxbee Cox as head of the RAE's air defence department. Moved to the Air Ministry in 1939 as assistant director of scientific research, and then to the new Ministry of Aircraft Production in 1940, to become deputy director (armaments) in 1941, in 1943 he became the ministry's director of scientific research, and in 1945 director-general. He visited the German research centre at Volkenrode, near Brunswick, in 1945 and, as a result of seeing the advanced German technology, cancelled the contract for a Miles M52 straight-wing supersonic project in favour of an experimental series of swept-wing, radio-controlled, and rocket-powered models. Their failure caused criticism, but this was offset by his positive, and successful, backing of Frederic Callan Williams, of Ferranti and Manchester University, in producing the first electronic computers.

In 1946 Lockspeiser was appointed chief scientist of the Ministry of Supply, and thus masterminded British research into problems of nuclear physics, supersonic flight, and guided weapons. In 1949 he was appointed to succeed Sir Edward Appleton as secretary to the committee of the privy council for scientific and industrial research. He was for seven years thereafter a formidable and beneficial influence upon British advances in science and industrial development. He was always a devastating debater and a competent administrator. Among major projects he espoused and advanced in this creative period were the Festival of Britain in 1951, the National Lending Library for Science and Technology in 1952, a major clean-up of the River Thames in 1953, Bernard Lovell's Jodrell Bank radio telescope in 1954, and the creation of CERN (the European Council for Nuclear Research), of which he was the first president in 1955–7. He retired in 1956 and became chairman of the technical advisory board of the Israeli government and a director of several companies, notably Tube Investments, Staverley, H. R. Ricardo, and Warburg's.

Lockspeiser was knighted in 1946 and appointed KCB in 1950. Elected a fellow of the Royal Society in 1949, he was also FEng (1976), FIMechE (1946), and FRAeS (1944). He was an honorary fellow of Sidney Sussex College (1953) and a life fellow of the Royal Society of Arts, and he was awarded the American medal of freedom (silver palms) in 1946. He had honorary degrees from Witwatersrand (1949), Haifa (1952), and Oxford (1954).

Lockspeiser was a chubby, gentle, kindly figure, of medium height, with a determined chin and full cheeks. He surveyed the world with a benevolent but quizzical air, through wire-rimmed spectacles, from beneath a broad forehead under a mane of white hair. His first wife died in 1964 and in 1966 he married the widow of an old friend from the RAE, Mary Alice Heywood, who died in 1983. Lockspeiser died on 18 October 1990 at his home, Birchway, 15 Waverley Road, Farnborough, five months short of his one-hundredth birthday.

PETER G. MASEFIELD, *rev.*

Sources A. P. J. Edwards, *Memoirs FRS*, 39 (1994), 245–61 · *The Times* (23 Oct 1990) · *The Independent* (3 Nov 1990) · b. cert. · private information (1996) · personal knowledge (1996) · *CGPLA Eng. & Wales* (1991)

Archives CAC Cam., corresp. with A. V. Hill · Nuffield Oxf., corresp. with Lord Cherwell · RS, corresp. with Lord Blackett

Likenesses photograph, Hult. Arch.

Wealth at death £476,851: probate, 12 April 1991, *CGPLA Eng. & Wales*

Lockwood [*formerly* Wood], **Amelius Mark Richard**, **first Baron Lambourne** (**1847–1928**), politician, was born in London on 17 August 1847. He was the eldest son of Lieutenant-General William Mark Wood (*b.* 1817) and Amelia Jane, daughter of Sir Robert Williams, ninth baronet, of Penrhyn, Caernarfon. General Wood, who served in the Crimean War, had changed his name from Lockwood in 1838 on inheriting the property of his maternal uncle, Sir Mark Wood, of Gatton, Surrey. His son reverted to the original name of Lockwood in 1876.

Lockwood was educated at Eton College. He entered the Coldstream Guards, his father's regiment, in 1866 and served as adjutant and aide-de-camp to Earl Spencer, lord lieutenant of Ireland; he retired in 1883 with the rank of lieutenant-colonel. In 1876 he married Isabella (*d.* 1923), daughter of Sir John Ralph Milbanke-Huskisson, eighth baronet; they had no children. Lockwood inherited his father's estates, which consisted in 1876 of 2300 acres in Essex, as well as 1226 acres in Glamorgan and 1440 acres in Monmouthshire. In 1892, at the age of forty-five, he entered parliament as Conservative MP for the Epping division of Essex. As late as 1905 four of the eight county divisions of Essex were represented by members whose families had held estates in the county for over 150 years, and Lockwood was one.

In the house Lockwood was for many years chairman of the kitchen committee. The standard of dinners so improved that for 2*s*. members could buy a meal 'more copious and probably better cooked than could be eaten at any public place, club or pub, between Ludgate Circus and Hyde Park Corner'—a necessary reform at a time when Irish members dined nightly in the house and Conservatives needed an inducement to stay through the dinner hour if the government were to avoid defeat on a snap division. Known as Uncle Mark, Lockwood was popular with all parties. Henry Lucy described him in 1902, 'with hands in his trousers pockets, his hat pitched back on his head at an angle more miraculous than ever, the light of hospitality literally blazing on his war-bronzed face and his home-grown carnation'. Lockwood never held office, and, as Lord Onslow recalled, 'he came to be regarded as the typical country squire member of parliament, and exercised a considerable independent influence in the House of Commons' (*DNB*). He was sworn of the privy council in 1905, and he sat on the Unionist front bench. Not that Lockwood was an entirely serious figure; at the height of the crisis over the 1909 Finance Bill he endeavoured to subvert the chancellor, Lloyd George, by taking him on a spree to the Gaiety Theatre and then to supper with what he called 'bits of muslin' at the Savoy Hotel, returning Lloyd George to Downing Street at 2.30 a.m. Next day the chancellor's temper was execrable. Lockwood retired from the House of Commons in 1917, when he was created Baron Lambourne.

Lockwood took an active interest in animal welfare. He was a member of the royal commission on vivisection (1906–12): he signed the minority report urging tighter controls on vivisection, and he twice attempted unsuccessfully to carry the commission's recommendations into law. Like many country gentlemen he saw no conflict between his dislike of vivisection and his support for country sports. As Lord Lambourne he served as chairman of the RSPCA from 1919 to 1924; he endeavoured to end the export of live worn-out horses for butchery on the continent; and in 1921 he piloted through the House of Lords the bill banning the shooting of live pigeons in traps.

At Bishops's Hall, his Essex home, Lockwood grew famous carnations for his buttonholes and made a collection of flowering shrubs. He was president of the Royal Horticultural Society. He collected china and books of county history. He was a generous host, and he played a prominent part in county affairs, becoming lord lieutenant of Essex in 1919. He raised money for the Essex county cricket team; he was president of the Territorial Association, honorary colonel of the 4th Essex regiment, president of the Essex Hunt Club, president of the Essex Automobile Club, provincial grand master of the Essex freemasons, and a JP. In 1928, recalled Lord Onslow, 'Lord Lambourne refused to support the appeal for King George's Hospital at Becontree on the ground that this was a new town created by the London County Council without consulting Essex, but he withdrew his opposition immediately at the wish of the King' (*DNB*).

Lockwood did many things, but all of them as an amateur and a country gentleman. He was a 'character', an unpaid and jovial pillar of society in Essex and at Westminster; to his contemporaries he stood for more than the bare record of his achievements. He died at Bishop's Hall, Romford, Essex, on 26 December 1928. JANE RIDLEY

Sources *The Times* (28 Dec 1928) • *Daily Telegraph* (28 Dec 1928) • *Essex County Standard* (28 Dec 1928) • A. W. Moss, *Valiant crusade: the history of the RSPCA* (1961) • *VCH Essex*, vol. 2 • H. W. Lucy, *The Balfourian parliament, 1900–1905* (1906) • *The Crawford papers: the journals of David Lindsay, twenty-seventh earl of Crawford … 1892–1940*, ed. J. Vincent (1984) • T. H. S. Escott, *Club makers and club members* (1914) • *DNB*

Archives NRA, priv. coll., papers

Likenesses W. G. de Glehn, oils, 1926, Royal Horticultural Society, London • W. R. Dick, bas-relief plaque, Royal Horticultural Society, London • Spy [L. Ward], chromolithograph caricature, NPG; repro. in *VF* (6 Sept 1894)

Wealth at death £54,794 4*s*. 9*d*.: probate, 30 April 1929, *CGPLA Eng. & Wales*

Lockwood, Sir Frank (1846–1897), lawyer and politician, the second son of Charles Day Lockwood, stone quarrier at Levitt Hagg, near Doncaster, was born at Doncaster on 15 July 1846. In 1860 the family moved to Manchester, and in 1863 Lockwood entered the grammar school (having been previously at a private school at Edenbridge) under Mr Walker, afterwards headmaster of St Paul's School. In October 1865 he proceeded to Gonville and Caius College, Cambridge, where he took a pass degree in 1869. In 1869, having abandoned the idea of ordination, he entered Lincoln's Inn and he was called to the bar in January 1872. In 1872 he briefly joined the Kendals acting troupe as Daniel Macpherson. He then joined the old midland circuit, and attended sessions at Bradford, Leeds, and other places. During his early days at the bar the habit of drawing he had learned from his father grew upon him, and his rapid sketching in court of judges, witnesses, and litigants gave him occupation and secured him notice. For some of these early sketches he appears to have found a market; but in later life, though he still continued to sketch, he tossed them carelessly away. In September 1874 he married Julia, daughter of Salis Schwabe of Glyn Garth, Anglesey. His practice steadily increased, and from 1879, when, at the request of the presiding judge, he defended the burglar and murderer, Charles Peace, his name was always prominent. He took silk in 1882.

In politics Lockwood was a Liberal. His first attempt to

Sir Frank Lockwood (1846–1897), by Sir Arthur Stockdale Cope

get into parliament, at King's Lynn, was unsuccessful, as also was his first contest at York in November 1883, when, however, he was beaten by twenty-one votes only. In October 1884 he became recorder of Sheffield, and in November 1885 he and his great friend Alfred Pease were elected for York, which city he continued to represent until his death. From 1885 to 1895 Lockwood led a very busy life both professionally and socially.

> His tall powerful frame, his fine head crowned with picturesque premature white hair, his handsome healthy face, with its sunshine of genial, not vapid good nature, made him notable everywhere. So powerful was this personality that his entrance into a room seemed to change the whole complexion of the company, and I often fancied that he could dispel a London fog by his presence. (Letter of Lord Rosebery, quoted in Birrell, 201)

In the Commons, though he took no active part in debate, Lockwood was a great figure, and his sketches depicting the occasional humours of that assembly were in much demand. During the vacation of 1894 Rosebery, to whom Lockwood was warmly attached, preferred Lockwood to R. B. Haldane for the solicitor-generalship when Sir Robert Reid became attorney-general. Lockwood was knighted on 20 November 1894. As solicitor-general, Lockwood played a central part in the prosecution of Oscar Wilde in 1895. The jury failed to reach a verdict in Wilde's first trial, and Lockwood himself led for the prosecution in the second. When Timothy Healy urged Lockwood not to proceed with the prosecution he replied 'I would not but for the abominable rumours against Rosebery' (cited in Ellman, 437). Lockwood was awkwardly placed personally in the affair, for it was his nephew by marriage Maurice Schwabe who had introduced Wilde to Alfred Taylor, the homosexual who procured rent boys for Wilde. Lockwood's final speech of prosecution, on 25 May, was a powerful indictment that helped secure the guilty verdict that imprisoned Wilde and removed the threat of further allegations being made against Rosebery. The election of 1895 restored Lord Salisbury to power, but owing to a difficulty about the scale of his successor's remuneration, Lockwood nominally remained solicitor-general until August 1895, when R. B. Finlay succeeded him. In the vacation of 1896 he accompanied Charles, Lord Russell of Killowen, the lord chief justice of England, to the United States of America. About May 1897 he became depressed, and convinced of his impending death, which exacerbated his depression. He had no other condition diagnosed. He caught influenza and died, aged fifty-one, at his house, 26 Lennox Gardens, Pont Street, Chelsea, on Sunday 19 December 1897. His wife and their two daughters survived him.

Lockwood made no pretensions to be considered a learned lawyer, nor was he a consummate advocate; but his sound sense, ready wit, good feeling, and sympathetic nature, set off as these qualities were by a commanding presence and good voice, placed him in the front ranks of the bar, and easily secured him a large business. Both outside and inside his profession he enjoyed a large and deserved popularity. He drew frequently for *Punch* and some of his sketches were published in *The Frank Lockwood Sketch Book* (1898); his lecture *The Law and Lawyers of Pickwick* was published in 1894. He had the unusual Victorian distinction of giving his name to a British island, Frank Lockwood's Island, off Mull. There are a memorial window and a tablet in York Cathedral.

AUGUSTINE BIRRELL, *rev.* H. C. G. MATTHEW

Sources A. Birrell, *Sir Frank Lockwood: a sketch* (1898) • *Law Magazine*, 4th ser., 23 (1897–8), 92–9 • H. W. Lucy, *Sixty years in the wilderness*, 2 vols. (1909–12); repr. as *Nearing Jordan* (1916) • R. Ellmann, *Oscar Wilde* (1987) • J. O. Baylen and R. L. McBath, 'A note on Oscar Wilde, Alfred Douglas and Lord Rosebery, 1897', *English Language Notes*, 23/1 (1985), 42–8 • D. G. Moore, *Sir Frank Lockwood* (privately printed, 1946) • Boase, *Mod. Eng. biog.*

Archives NL Scot., corresp., mainly with Lord Rosebery • NL Scot., Haldane MSS

Likenesses B. Stone, photograph, 1897, Birm. CL • Barraud, photograph, NPG; repro. in *Men and Women of the Day*, 4 (1891) • A. S. Cope, oils, Lincoln's Inn, London [*see illus.*] • W. & D. Downey, woodburytype photograph, NPG; repro. in W. Downey and D. Downey, *The cabinet portrait gallery* (1890), 41–3 • H. Furniss, caricature, pen-and-ink sketch, NPG • S. P. Hall, pencil drawings, NPG • F. Pegram, pencil sketch, V&A • J. Russell & Sons, cabinet photograph, NPG • Walker & Boutall, photogravure photograph (after photograph by Lockwood), NPG • portrait, repro. in *VF* (20 Aug 1887) • portrait, repro. in *ILN* (9 Jan 1886) • portrait, repro. in *ILN* (27 Oct 1894)

Wealth at death £30,508 16*s.* 6*d.*: resworn probate, Jan 1899, *CGPLA Eng. & Wales*

Lockwood, Sir John Francis (1903–1965), university administrator, was born on 6 July 1903 at Preston, Lancashire, the only son and elder child of John Lockwood, stockbroker, of Preston, and his wife, Elizabeth Speight. Lockwood was educated at Preston grammar school, where he was active in sport and mountain walking. In 1922 he was awarded a classical scholarship at Corpus Christi College, Oxford, where he obtained a first class in classical honour moderations, and a second in *literae humaniores* (1926).

After a short period as assistant lecturer in Latin at the University of Manchester in 1927, in the same year Lockwood was appointed by University College, London, as senior assistant lecturer in classics. He was lecturer in Greek there from 1930 to 1940. When the Second World War began the college's classics department moved to Aberystwyth. In 1940 Lockwood was appointed University College's tutor to arts students and a London University reader in classics. In 1945, when University College returned to London, he became professor of Latin. In this post Lockwood showed himself an excellent teacher and departmental administrator.

In 1950–51 Lockwood was dean of the faculty of arts of London University; in 1951 also he was elected chairman (until 1958) of the governing delegacy of Goldsmiths' College, where a building was later named after him. As dean of a faculty he joined the university senate committee which was administering a scheme of special relationship with colleges in Africa and the West Indies.

By now it was widely believed that Lockwood might be a successful college head. The governors of Birkbeck College, the main function of which is to provide facilities for the taking of degrees by mature students, elected him to the vacant mastership on 1 October 1951. He consequently resigned his professorship and stopped teaching, but became a member of the senate. Some people needlessly wondered whether Lockwood would understand the college fully, despite his experience of cramped working space and damage done by German air raids at University College in Gower Street, and which Birkbeck College had also suffered in Fetter Lane. But he at once grasped that Birkbeck students were maturer than those at day colleges, and that the college lacked sufficient space. Even before his mastership began he successfully insisted that the college should move at once into its internally unfinished new building alongside the Senate House in Malet Street.

From 1952 to 1955 Lockwood was London University's public orator. A lover of English and never prolix, he showed, in short speeches whereby he presented candidates for honorary degrees, a ready wit and a sense of epigram as much 'Lockwoodian' as 'classical'. From 1953 to 1955 he was also chairman of the collegiate council, in 1954–5 deputy vice-chancellor, and in 1955 became a member of the court—the controlling financial body. He was vice-chancellor from 1955 to 1958, assuming his appointment a fortnight before the installation of Queen Elizabeth, the queen mother, as chancellor of the university. At the invitation of the Inter-University Council for Higher Education Overseas, in 1954 he went with a mission led by Sir Eric Ashby to Kampala, to investigate the possibilities of making Makerere College a university centre for Kenya, Uganda, and Tanganyika. From 1956 to 1961 he was a member of the United States–United Kingdom educational commission. Lockwood's knowledge, wisdom, and gaiety endeared him to American scholars and administrators alike: he had a 'modesty, cordiality and humour that made working with him a delight'. He went to the United States several times.

In 1956, when the Ford Foundation had granted £357,000 to help students and artists who had left Hungary after the revolt, Lockwood was the British representative at the discussions in Vienna between the foundation and representatives of other countries willing to accept Hungarian students. When his vice-chancellorship ended in 1958 he became chairman of the Secondary Schools Examinations Council and joined the Inter-University Council for Higher Education Overseas, on whose policy he had a decisive influence. He also did good work for the Association of the Universities of the Commonwealth committee on universities overseas. In 1958 he became chairman of a Colonial Office working party on higher education in east Africa. With the help of his hard-worked team his report (1958–9) led to the development of a single University of East Africa, federal in structure, of which Kenya, Uganda, and Tanganyika each had a constituent college. Lockwood became a member of the East African University's provisional council and of the council of the University College at Nairobi, Kenya. His attention was then drawn to west Africa. In 1957 he led a delegation to the University College at Ibadan, and in 1958 he went to Sierra Leone and Ghana as leader of the grants committee on higher education in Ghana. He also visited Basutoland. The following year he was a member of an Anglo-American commission (chaired by Sir Eric Ashby) surveying higher education in Nigeria, whose independence celebrations he attended in 1960, the year in which the new University of Nigeria opened at Nsukka. From 1960 to 1964 Lockwood was chairman of the West African Examinations Council. In 1961 Lockwood advised against the creation of a university in Mauritius because of the difficulties of staff recruitment and finance.

Meanwhile, as chairman of the Secondary Schools Examinations Council (1958–64) Lockwood produced a report, which was accepted, recommending that a schools council for curriculum and examinations should be established before the academic year 1964/5. Lockwood's name is also associated with influential reports on sixth-form studies and the English language examination, which influenced the GCE system.

In 1961 Lockwood became senior consultant in a UNESCO and International Association of Universities study of the role which institutions of higher education in south-east Asia were playing and should play. After the requisite travels he was just able to write the preface to its summary report before his death.

In 1962, when he was knighted, Lockwood attended a conference on higher education in Madagascar and was elected chairman of the new voluntary societies' committee for service overseas, which sent trained young volunteers to developing countries. When the British share in this scheme was publicly criticized, Lockwood explained and defended the policy in some detail. He became a member of a new council of volunteers in 1964.

Two years before his death Lockwood chaired two final projects, in central Africa and Northern Ireland. After a visit to Northern Rhodesia, he recommended the establishment of a university at Lusaka (this later became the University of Zambia). In Northern Ireland he participated in the decision to site a university at Coleraine (the New University of Ulster, founded in 1965).

Meanwhile, at London University, Lockwood chaired committees and served on councils (such as those of the Medical College of St Bartholomew's Hospital, the Postgraduate Medical Federation, Westfield College, and the Royal College of Art). From 1960 to 1963 he was a member of the University of Wales commission on its own structure.

Lockwood wrote articles of merit and originality, and, in the second revision of Smith's smaller Latin–English dictionary (corrected, improved, and enlarged), he produced almost a new work.

Despite his administrative and advisory commitments overseas Lockwood spent most of each academic session in administration at Birkbeck College. His conduct as master was far from overbearing, since headstrong actions and controversial policies were distasteful to him. His anger was mild and short-lived, his forgiveness quick and permanent. At meetings his lively sense of humour was restrained under the pressure of serious business except when he was not himself presiding, but when he was host at a party he was gay and seemingly carefree. His speech was restrained and his English careful and artistic, giving rein to word play only in the concocting of Anglo-Latin and Anglo-Greek menus for certain 'classical' lunches or dinners at college. An 'arts' man, he made no fetish of the classics; in politics a moderate, he held to the principle of merit alone in appointments. He was readily accessible to all—staff, students, and strangers. A Christian, he was renowned for certain qualities displayed everywhere at home or abroad, and, some thought, shown at their best in the teamwork of committees: stamina, courage, persistence; gentleness, sympathy, bonhomie; objectivity, thoroughness, conciseness; skill, diplomacy, and leadership of a new kind.

To face growing problems at Birkbeck in 1963–5 Lockwood summoned all his powers. After 1962 the two main issues were the extent to which the college could and should admit school leavers, and the justification of its bold proposals for physical expansion. Deep and divergent were opinions among the teachers, but by hard work Lockwood held the college together. There was some opposition to his own views, but he was vindicated as time passed, although the problems remained unsolved. He could have retired in 1965 but Birkbeck's governors extended his mastership until the age of sixty-seven, an age which he did not in the event attain.

Lockwood had a happy marriage; in 1929 he had married Marjorie, daughter of William Basil Clitheroe, a primary school headmaster, and his wife, Katherine. They had a son and a daughter. He was a man of middle height and build and moved with a nimble and almost bounding walk. Clean shaven always, he kept short his light brown hair which with age did not cover all the sinciput above his forehead. He died at his home at Winchmore Hill, Middlesex, on 11 July 1965. His wife survived him.

The Inter-University Council recorded especially Lockwood's tireless energy, vision, persuasiveness, and new approach to meeting the education needs of countries in Africa, and the trust inspired among leading academics and politicians there; and stressed his generosity and hospitality at Birkbeck College. Sir Christopher Cox wrote:

> The present [1950–65] packed chapter in the story of British and American co-operation in assisting African education virtually coincides with the Lockwood period; in it no Englishman except Sir Charles Morris and Sir Eric Ashby has played so influential a part.

Sir Eric Ashby himself wrote: 'Changes in British policy about overseas universities during the ten years 1955–1965 were mostly caused by Lockwood's thinking and imagination'. E. H. Warmington, *rev.*

Sources *The Times* (12–13 July 1965) · *The Times* (16 July 1965) · *The Times* (21–2 July 1965) · *The Lodestone* [magazine of Birkbeck College] · minutes of the governors of Birkbeck College and the Senate of U. Lond. · private information (1981) · personal knowledge (1981)

Likenesses N. Hepple, double portrait, oils (with Lady Lockwood), Birkbeck College, London

Wealth at death £17,933: probate, 17 Nov 1965, *CGPLA Eng. & Wales*

Lockwood, Sir Joseph Flawith (1904–1991), businessman, was born on 14 November 1904 in Southwell, Nottinghamshire, one of the four sons of Joseph Agnew Lockwood (1883/4–1910/11), miller, and his wife, Mabel, *née* Caudwell, the daughter of his employer, the fifth generation in a long line of millers. He was educated at Newark grammar school and left in 1920 to train at his grandfather's mill, but as his two older cousins were in line to run the business he went to Chile in 1924 and became manager of a flour mill in Santiago. He returned to England in 1928 and joined Henry Simon Ltd, a company which designed and built mills, in Manchester. As technical manager of the company's operations in Brussels and Paris he worked there until 1933, when he was appointed a director. He was also made a director of Henry Simon Ltd in Buenos Aires, and chairman of the Australian subsidiary, Henry Simon (Australia) Ltd. As a result of a visit he made to Minneapolis, Henry Simon Ltd won a contract to modernize a number of mills in the United States and Canada. Just before the war Lockwood published *Provender Milling—the Manufacture of Feeding Stuffs for Livestock* (1939).

During the war Lockwood was in charge of the protection of factories, warehouses, docks, and other key installations in the north-west civil defence region, under the regional commissioner Hartley Shawcross, and from 1944 he was part of a working party planning food supplies for Europe after the war. As a civilian officer attached to the

Supreme Headquarters Allied Expeditionary Force from 1944 to 1945, Lockwood was in charge of the rehabilitation of flour mills that had been damaged during the war, and the transport of wheat in liberated Europe. He returned to Henry Simon Ltd in 1945 and was appointed chairman and managing director in 1950. He published *Flour Milling* (1945), which became a standard text, with four editions by 1960 and in several languages. While still at Henry Simon Ltd he was appointed a director of the National Research Development Corporation (1951–67).

Lockwood left Henry Simon Ltd and the milling business in 1954 to become chairman of EMI (Electrical and Musical Industries Ltd), the gramophone company formed in 1931 with the merger of HMV, Columbia, and Parlophone. EMI had been losing £0.5 million a year, in part because of a decision by the board, led by the chairman, Sir Ernest Fisk, in 1952, not to develop the long-playing record, pioneered in the United States by CBS and first made by Decca in 1950. The directors were happy with the existing 78 r.p.m. records, with a maximum playing time of 4 min. 45 sec. per side, believing that no one would want to endure the tedium of a long-playing record. They were also worried about the capital expenditure that would be involved. One of the first things Lockwood did at EMI, realizing that there was a future in long-playing records, was to reverse this decision. EMI already had a good reputation for classical music recording, thanks to Walter Legge, producer of classical music at Columbia, who had brought in such internationally famous musicians as Dietrich Fischer-Dieskau (from 1951 to 1960) and Herbert von Karajan (from 1946 to 1959). Lockwood was the first to try to persuade Legge that this was not enough, and that the classical music side must also be commercially viable. He realized that the company must also expand its popular music department in order to succeed, and he appointed George Martin, a popular music producer at Parlophone since 1950, as head of the Parlophone label in 1955. At the EMI recording studios in Abbey Road, St John's Wood, London, Martin brought in popular artists including Ruby Murray, Dickie Valentine, and the trumpeter Eddie Calvert, whose 'Oh mein Papa' in 1954 was the first EMI single to top the charts after twenty-three years of making records.

Lockwood was very much involved with the Abbey Road studios in his early days at EMI, though he was unpopular at first because of his ruthlessness. Realizing the importance of the American market, in 1955 he bought Capitol records, a small American company, which went on to record Frank Sinatra and to become the largest music company in the United States in the 1960s. Although his own preference was for classical music, especially Mozart, Lockwood encouraged the Beatles, signed up by George Martin in 1962; that decade they became the leading recording group in the world. In 1963, as 'Beatlemania' swept Britain, Lockwood entertained the Beatles to lunch at the EMI headquarters in Manchester Square in central London. He gave them an increasingly free hand, while they always respected him, affectionately calling him 'Sir Joe'. 'She Loves You' (1963) became the first single to exceed sales of 1.5 million in the United Kingdom, and in one week in 1964 the Beatles held the top five positions in the hit parade. By 1966 they had earned eleven gold LPs. The government realized their importance for Britain's balance of payments, and created them MBEs in 1965.

Despite the value of the Beatles to EMI, records were only part of the company's operations, and it was less successful in other fields. Although it had been in the forefront of developing television sets, it relinquished making HMV televisions to Thorn, and in the early 1970s EMI made a large loss in marketing the CAT (computerized axial tomography) body-scanner it had developed for use in hospitals. Lockwood retired as chairman of EMI in 1974, but remained as a non-executive director until 1979. The company was taken over by Thorn in 1980, becoming Thorn-EMI.

Lockwood served on several public bodies, including the Engineering Advisory Council of the Board of Trade in 1959, the Export Council for Europe from 1961 to 1963, the Export Credits Guarantee Advisory Council from 1963 to 1967, and the Industrial Reorganization Corporation from 1966 to 1971 (as chairman from 1969 to 1971). He was knighted in 1960. A director of several large engineering companies, including the Hawker Siddeley Group, Smiths Industries Ltd, and the Laird Group, he was also involved in racecourse management as a director of Sandown Park Ltd, United Racecourses Ltd, and Epsom Grandstand Association from 1969 to 1983.

Lockwood's great passions were ballet and the theatre, and as chairman of the Royal Ballet from 1971 to 1985 and a member of the South Bank Theatre Board from 1968 to 1984 (chairman, 1977–84), he was very influential, especially in the building of the National Theatre, which opened on the South Bank in 1976. He was also chairman of the governors of the Royal Ballet School from 1960 to 1977, chairman of the Central School of Speech and Drama from 1965 to 1968, chairman of the Young Vic Theatre Company from 1974 to 1975, and a member of the Arts Council from 1967 to 1970. As with the recording activities at EMI, Lockwood took a detailed interest in all the activities with which he was involved, visiting the institutions, attending performances, and talking to performers and students. In addition, as treasurer of the Cancer Research Campaign from 1962 to 1967, he helped to build up a £1 million reserve fund, enabling the campaign to guarantee scientists continuous funding for at least three years, instead of the previous one-year funding. He died at his home, Hatchet Wood Farm, Skirmett, Henley-on-Thames, Oxfordshire, on 6 March 1991. He was unmarried.

ANNE PIMLOTT BAKER

Sources J. Tann, 'Lockwood, Sir Joseph Flawith', *DBB* • B. Southall, *Abbey Road* (1982–97) • G. Martin, *All you need is ears* (1979) • P. Gronow and I. Saunio, *An international history of the recording industry* (1998) • J. Tobler and S. Grundy, *The record producers* (1982) • *The Times* (12 March 1991) • *The Times* (28 March 1991), 7 • *The Independent* (13 March 1991) • *WWW*, 1991–5 • *CGPLA Eng. & Wales* (1991) • b. cert. • d. cert.

Archives Central Research Laboratories, Hayes, Middlesex, EMI music archives

Likenesses group photographs, 1963–5 (with the Beatles), Hult. Arch. • group photograph (with the Beatles), repro. in *The Independent* • photograph, repro. in *The Times* (12 March 1991)
Wealth at death £5,046,108: probate, 14 Oct 1991, *CGPLA Eng. & Wales*

Lockwood, Margaret Mary (1916–1990), actress, was born on 15 September 1916 in Karachi, India, the younger child and only daughter of Henry Francis Lockwood, district traffic superintendent (later chief superintendent) on the Indian railways, and his third wife, Margaret Eveline Waugh, a Scot, who had been a nurse. She also had an older stepbrother. Mother and children set up home in Upper Norwood, London, when Margaret was three and a half, after which they saw little of her father. She attended Sydenham Girls' High School, taking dancing lessons at the Italia Conti School. These led to her appearance as a fairy in *A Midsummer Night's Dream* at the Holborn Empire when she was twelve. She left Sydenham High for the Cone School of Dancing, and did the rounds of auditions, performing in clubs, concerts, cabarets, and tea dances. In 1929 she adopted a family name, Day, for her stage name Margie Day, finally leaving school altogether at fourteen.

In 1933 Lockwood was accepted by the Royal Academy of Dramatic Art (RADA) at the age of sixteen, and showed both talent and dedication, completing the two-year course in fourteen months. Playing a leading part in the annual RADA show, she caught the attention of the London agent Herbert de Leon. He quickly secured her two brief London stage engagements and second lead in the film *Lorna Doone* (1934), directed by Basil Dean. De Leon remained her manager, adviser, and friend until his death forty-five years later.

Margaret Lockwood was immediately put under contract by British Lion film company and during the next few years made over a dozen films, many of them quota quickies, often appearing on the London stage in the evenings as well. A beautiful girl with abundant dark hair, big eyes, delicate features, a beauty spot high on her left cheekbone (which was allowed to appear for the first time in *The Wicked Lady*, 1945), natural poise, and an unaffected speaking voice, she proved a hard-working and reliable actress and was much in demand. The important Gainsborough film company promoted her as a star, and in *Bank Holiday* (1938) and in Alfred Hitchcock's *The Lady Vanishes* (1938) she achieved critical success (the latter film, in which she starred with Michael Redgrave, proved enduringly popular). Before long she was appearing in some of the best British films of the period, including *The Stars Look Down* and *Night Train to Munich*, both directed by Carol Reed.

Margaret Lockwood's career entered a new phase in 1943. Gainsborough had been acquired by J. Arthur Rank, who launched a series of frankly escapist films to cheer up the war-weary British public. These were novelettish costume melodramas, dubbed 'Gainsborough Gothics', scorned by serious critics and not especially well made but an enormous success at the box office. Lockwood afterwards was always identified with her part in the best-

Margaret Mary Lockwood (1916–1990), by Anthony Buckley, 1948

known of these, *The Wicked Lady*, in which she starred with James Mason.

Lockwood was now at the peak of her career and earning a large salary, the biggest British film star of her time although no longer taken very seriously as an actress. But her films began to decline in quality and by 1948, still only thirty-two, her great days were over. Her contract with Rank was dissolved in 1951. A woman of spirit, she returned to the stage and turned also to television. Always professional, she continued to act on the London stage and on tour for another twenty-five years. She starred in two television series, *The Flying Swan* (1965) and *Justice* (1971–4). Her last film appearance was in the fairy tale *The Slipper and the Rose*, in 1976, and her last stage part was Queen Alexandra in *Motherdear* in 1980.

Not a great emotional actress, Margaret Lockwood was a straightforward and intelligent woman who worked hard and lived quietly, earning the affection of the British public. Unpretentious, she disliked the attributes of stardom. She was nominated by the *Motion Picture Herald* as the top money-making star in Britain in 1945 and 1946, and won the *Daily Mail* film award as best actress in British films in 1946, 1947, and 1948. Later she received the *Daily Mirror* television award in 1961, and best actress award from the *Sun* in 1973 and from the *TV Times* in 1977. In 1981 she was appointed CBE.

In 1937 she married Rupert William Leon (who was not related to her agent), commercial clerk (later steel broker), the son of Emil Armand Leon, managing director of the British Iron and Steel Corporation. Her mother disapproved strongly of the marriage. Their daughter Julia, later the actress Julia Lockwood, was born in 1941 but the marriage failed soon afterwards. Margaret Lockwood wished to marry Keith Dobson, but her husband refused to give her a divorce. She then had a relationship with Theo Cowan, who was in charge of Rank's publicity. She later lived for seventeen years, apparently happily, with John Stone, a minor fellow actor considerably younger than herself, whom she met in 1959. She was afflicted by ear trouble and, after he left her in 1977, she gradually withdrew from the theatre. Two years later she was devastated by the death of her friend and mentor de Leon. For the last years of her life she lived as a recluse at 34 Upper Park Road, Kingston upon Thames. She died, a wealthy woman, of cirrhosis of the liver in the Cromwell Hospital, Kensington, on 15 July 1990. RACHAEL LOW, *rev.*

Sources *Daily Telegraph* (16–17 July 1990) • *The Independent* (17 July 1990) • *The Times* (16–17 July 1990) • *Daily Mail* (4 March 1946) • *Daily Mail* (22 June 1946) • M. Lockwood, *My life and films* (1948) • M. Lockwood, *Lucky star* (1955) • H. Tims, *Once a wicked lady* (1989) • I. Herbert, ed., *Who's who in the theatre*, 17th edn, 2 vols. (1981) • L. Halliwell, *Halliwell's film guide*, 7th edn (1989) • b. cert. [Julia Lockwood] • m. cert. • d. cert. • *CGPLA Eng. & Wales* (1990)

Likenesses A. Buckley, photograph, 1938, NPG; *see illus. in* Houston, Renée (1902–1980) • A. Buckley, photograph, 1948, NPG [*see illus.*] • photographs, Hult. Arch.

Wealth at death £433,705: probate, 16 Oct 1990, *CGPLA Eng. & Wales*

Lockwood, Richard Evison [Dicky] (**1867–1915**), rugby player, was born at Summer Hall, Crigglestone, near Wakefield, Yorkshire, on 9 November 1867, the son of Benjamin Lockwood, a general labourer and groom, and his wife, Mary Evison. He made his début as a right wing three-quarter for Dewsbury at the age of sixteen in 1884 and rapidly established himself as a sporting phenomenon. He played for Yorkshire and England at nineteen—he made the first of fourteen appearances for his country in 1887—and rose to captain the English rugby union side in 1894, the first player without a public-school background to do so.

Known as 'the Little Tyke' and 'Little Dick, the World's Wonder', partly because of his age and also because of his diminutive stature—he was only 5 feet 4½ inches tall—Lockwood was brilliant in attack and deadly in the tackle, with a knack of being in the right place at the right time. An astute tactician, he was responsible for introducing the Welsh-originated four three-quarter system into the Yorkshire county team and for popularizing the tactic of running after the ball after punting it in order to put his forwards onside.

No player was as famous in northern rugby nor so symbolized the rise of the working-class player as Lockwood. He was employed as a woollen printer in a textile factory when he married on 2 February 1889, at the Wesleyan Centenary Chapel, Dewsbury, Sarah Grace Taylor, the daughter of a blanket raiser. That year he transferred to the Heckmondwike club, who paid him, it later emerged, £1 per game, contrary to rugby's amateur regulations. Although the club was suspended for professionalism by the Yorkshire Rugby Union, he survived two investigations of the same charge, much to the relief of an adoring public, as *The Yorkshireman* (18 September 1889) magazine described: 'the news of his acquittal was received with an outburst of cheering, the gathering in all respects resembling those witnessed at an exciting political election.'

If the feelings of Lockwood's supporters were unambiguous, the same could not be said for those of the rugby union authorities. He was continuously passed over for the Yorkshire captaincy in the early 1890s. And, despite the fact that he had captained England earlier in the season, he was barred by the Rugby Football Union in 1894 from playing in a club match after he had withdrawn from the Anglo-Scottish match because he couldn't afford to take time off work. This added to calls for payments for 'broken time' to working-class players, the issue over which rugby would split in 1895. A few weeks after the 1895 rugby schism, Lockwood joined Wakefield Trinity in the Northern Union (later the Rugby League). In 1900 his career turned full circle, however, as he returned to Dewsbury, and in 1903 he retired.

Sadly, Lockwood was unable to translate his football fame into material wealth. He gave up his factory job to run the Queen's Hotel pub in Heckmondwike during the 1890s, but was declared bankrupt in 1897, and was forced to sell all his household furniture and return to manual work. On 10 November 1915 he died in Leeds Infirmary, shortly before he was due to have a second operation for cancer; he was buried in Wakefield cemetery four days later. His wife and four children survived him.

TONY COLLINS

Sources 'Chats with celebrated Yorkshire footballers', *Yorkshire Chat*, 1/13 (21 Oct 1899), 394 • *Yorkshire Evening Post* (11 Nov 1915) • *Yorkshire Post* (15 Nov 1915) • 'Athletic Jottings', *The Yorkshireman*, 23/552 (10 Feb 1887), 92 • 'Athletic notes', *The Yorkshireman*, 28/688 (18 Sept 1889), 188–9 • 'Bankruptcy of an international footballer', *Yorkshire Post* (7 Jan 1897) • F. Marshall, ed., *Football: the rugby union game* (1892) • b. cert. • m. cert. • d. cert.

Lockyer, Sir Joseph Norman (**1836–1920**), astronomer and journal editor, was born on 17 May 1836 at Rugby, the only son of Joseph Hooley Lockyer, surgeon-apothecary, and his wife, Ann, daughter of Edward Norman, squire of Cosford, Warwickshire. He was educated at private schools in Leicester and Warwickshire. In his later teens he was a student-teacher both at Kenilworth and at Weston-super-Mare.

Lockyer's mother died when he was nine years old, and his father when he was nineteen. After his father's death, and with the backing of the main landowner in the Kenilworth area, Lockyer managed to obtain a civil service post—a clerkship at the War Office. Before taking up the appointment, in 1857 he travelled on the continent in order to study French and German. He settled in Wimbledon, where he soon became involved in the formation of a village club. He made many acquaintances there, one being Thomas Hughes, the Christian socialist barrister who wrote *Tom Brown's School Days*. When it was decided in the early 1860s that the workings of the War Office must be made more efficient, Hughes was called in to examine the need for revising army regulations. Requiring a member of the War Office staff to assist him, Hughes naturally

Sir Joseph Norman Lockyer (1836–1920), by Walery, *c.*1890–97

asked for Lockyer. When, as a consequence of the investigation, an army regulation branch was set up, Lockyer was promoted to be its head, but continuing reorganization of the War Office led to his subsequent demotion at the end of the 1860s.

Lockyer married twice. His first marriage, in 1858, was to Winifred, younger daughter of William *James, railway promoter, originally of Henley in Arden, Warwickshire. Winifred was a good linguist, and assisted the family budget by translating French science books into English. They had seven sons (three of whom predeceased Lockyer) and two daughters. Winifred died in 1879. Lockyer's second marriage, on 23 May 1903, was to Thomazine Mary (1852–1943), younger daughter of Samuel Woolcott Browne, of Bridgwater and Bristol, and widow of Bernard Edward Brodhurst, surgeon. His new wife, who was sixteen years his junior, was a noted feminist and Unitarian.

Lockyer's father had been keenly interested in science, and he seems to have passed this interest on to his son. One of Lockyer's friends at Wimbledon owned a telescope made by T. Cooke and Lockyer, having tried this out, ordered an identical instrument to set up in his own garden. He initially made observations of the moon's surface. He then bought a larger refractor from Cooke, and made detailed observations of Mars when it came to opposition in 1862. This led to his first scientific paper, sent to the Royal Astronomical Society (which he had just joined) in 1863. In 1865 the Lockyers moved to West Hampstead, and there he began to make observations of the sun. The new science of astrophysics was then in its infancy: the idea of making spectroscopic observations of astronomical objects was only beginning to be considered. Perhaps influenced by his contacts with William Huggins, Lockyer acquired a spectroscope for his solar studies. There was a considerable controversy at the time concerning the nature of sunspots and Lockyer found a way of examining spot spectra in isolation, and showed that they were at a different temperature from the surrounding surface.

Eclipse observers had noted that huge bright prominences often appeared above the sun's surface. Lockyer argued that it should be possible, using a spectroscope, to discern these out of eclipse. In 1868 he used a new large spectroscope for the first time, and immediately identified the bright lines of a solar prominence. A description of the observations was dispatched to the Royal Society and to the Académie des Sciences in Paris. It was received at the latter simultaneously with a letter from P. J. C. Janssen, who had been observing a solar eclipse in India. After the eclipse, he looked for the bright lines of a prominence that he had seen during the eclipse, and obtained similar results to Lockyer. Janssen and Lockyer were hailed as codiscoverers of the new technique, and the French government struck a medal, with both of their portraits on it, to commemorate the event.

Lockyer confirmed that there was a bright atmosphere—which he called the 'chromosphere'—visible all round the sun's disc. At this stage, he had only a limited knowledge of spectra. (He started working with the eminent chemist Edward Frankland in the latter part of the 1860s, in order to learn more.) However, he became convinced that a particularly bright line in the chromospheric spectrum could not be identified with any known element. Despite the considerable doubts expressed by his peers, Lockyer claimed that this indicated the existence of a new element, which he labelled 'helium'. It was not until the 1890s that this claim was confirmed, when William Ramsay observed helium in the laboratory.

Lockyer's new-found scientific eminence helped solve the immediate problems he was experiencing at the War Office. In 1870, a royal commission on scientific instruction and the advancement of science was established under the seventh duke of Devonshire. Its membership included some of Lockyer's scientific acquaintances: when a secretary for the commission was sought from the civil service, Lockyer was appointed. The commission continued its operations into 1875, when Lockyer's secondment came to an end. His friends, especially T. H. Huxley, but also J. F. D. Donnelly, at the Department of Science and Art, then managed to have him seconded to join them at South Kensington, initially to help organize a major exhibition.

One of the recommendations of the Devonshire commission had been that a new astrophysical observatory should be founded. The idea progressed slowly, but Lockyer was encouraged to develop his solar physics work at South Kensington in conjunction with a newly appointed solar physics committee. It was not until later in the 1880s that the position became regularized, with the committee acting as an advisory body for the observatory. Meanwhile, in 1882, Lockyer was appointed to a lecturing position in astrophysics in the newly organized Normal School of Science, being promoted to a professorship a few years later. It was thus only in his mid-forties that he first held a permanent scientific appointment.

Lockyer's wide range of contacts was not solely due to his scientific prowess. His early friendship with leading Christian socialists encouraged him to take up writing about science for a general audience. He was brought into contact with Huxley and his circle, and with Alexander Macmillan. This led, in 1869, to the creation of a journal, *Nature*, to be published by Macmillan and edited by Lockyer. The journal soon became an important focus for scientific discussion. Lockyer continued as its editor for fifty years, retiring in 1919. During these years he used the journal, especially its editorials, to support causes he considered important, such as better funding for science, and the need for a greater role for science in public life. He also acted as a book editor and adviser to Macmillan, as well as writing books himself.

State support for solar physics at South Kensington resulted, at least partly, from the hope that solar research would provide a greater understanding of terrestrial meteorology. One particular area of government concern was the need to foresee famines in India. In the early 1870s there were hints of a possible connection between sunspot frequency and terrestrial weather conditions and Lockyer took up this concept enthusiastically. He investigated various possible correlations (between sunspot numbers and average rainfall, for example), but decided that more detailed sunspot studies were necessary in order to understand why such correlations were imperfect. He therefore observed sunspot spectra systematically for a number of years, detecting changes in the spectra which he thought could be linked to the total amount of heat emitted by the sun. Lockyer was a strong believer in a sunspot/weather correlation, but it was never fully accepted by his contemporaries.

Lockyer's work on spectra led him to one of his most controversial hypotheses, that of the dissociation of the elements in the sun (and stars). When he had started this work, it was believed that each element had an invariant spectrum. His comparison of spectra from different sources led him to query this belief. He proposed, instead, that atoms, when exposed to high enough temperatures, could break down into new substances with different spectra. He sought to demonstrate this by looking for coincidences in the spectral lines produced by different elements under differing conditions. With these laboratory results he sought to explain how different kinds of spectral lines appear at different heights in the sun's atmosphere. His results were, however, widely disputed: some, for example, were attributed to the presence of impurities. The turning point came towards the end of the century, when the work of A. Fowler, who became Lockyer's assistant in the 1880s, suggested a new version of dissociation (essentially what is now labelled 'ionization'). Lockyer eventually accepted this version, but caused considerable confusion by failing to distinguish it clearly from its predecessor. This mainly reflected the difficulty he experienced in dropping a cherished hypothesis.

Lockyer, who enjoyed travelling, attended several solar eclipses. He sent his assistants to others, when he was too busy to travel. Though initially he was concerned with observations of the corona, he later increasingly concentrated on the spectrum of the lower atmosphere where he hoped to obtain evidence for his dissociation hypothesis.

In attempting to understand the solar atmosphere, Lockyer came to think that it was linked to meteoritic matter falling into the sun. He also decided that comets consisted of clouds of meteorites. In the latter part of the 1870s he began to believe that cometary and meteoritic spectra could be related to those of exploding stars and nebulae. These observations led him to his 'meteoritic hypothesis', by which he tried to explain how nebulae evolved into stars, and how the stars themselves evolved, beginning from an initial swarm of meteorites. On the basis of this picture he proposed a path for stellar evolution in which large and small stars were cool, while intermediate-sized stars were hotter.

The main evidence Lockyer put forward for his meteoritic hypothesis related to a spectral line found in nebulae. He believed it could be identified with a line found in meteoritic spectra. By the end of the century, however, few agreed with him, and evidence against his hypothesis was accumulating. Lockyer, characteristically, continued to defend his approach, and felt partially vindicated when work early in the twentieth century showed that at least his proposed relationship between stellar temperatures and size was basically correct. The meteoritic hypothesis and the dissociation hypothesis reflected two of Lockyer's basic scientific beliefs—in the unity of nature and in the existence of inorganic evolution alongside organic evolution.

A trip to Greece and Turkey in 1890 triggered off a new interest for Lockyer, the possibility that ancient buildings and monuments were orientated in an astronomically significant way. Initially he investigated this question in the context of Egyptian temples and their orientation relative to the rising and setting of sun and stars. Subsequently, he turned closer to home, investigating Stonehenge and other stone monuments in the UK. He believed that he had found significant directional indicators in these various constructions, and tried to relate them to what was known of the mythology of the peoples concerned. His work was subject to considerable contemporary criticism, but it helped trigger off a type of study that became increasingly popular later in the twentieth century.

Lockyer always believed strongly in the importance of scientific education. His presidential address to the British Association at Southport in 1903 took as its theme the need for the British nation as a whole to devote more attention to science. He subsequently tried to stir the British Association into campaigning for a widespread application of science to matters of policy. Dissatisfied with the association's response he launched, in 1905, a new body—the British Science Guild—for this purpose, and was active in it up to the First World War.

By this time, Lockyer had passed the retiring age from South Kensington, though he retained the directorship of the solar physics observatory. It was obviously necessary to consider the future of the observatory. After a very lengthy debate, it was decided that the entire operation should be shifted to Cambridge University. Lockyer bitterly opposed this decision, and counter-attacked by launching an appeal for funding for a new astrophysical observatory. The Hill Observatory, as it was called, began its career near Sidmouth, Devon, in 1913. One of his sons, W. J. S. Lockyer, who had been his chief assistant at South Kensington, took charge of its operations.

Lockyer was involved in controversies of one sort or another throughout his career. To some extent this isolated him scientifically, though controversial personalities were not uncommon in science at the time. However, he also had a wide circle of friends, who appreciated his abundant energy and his wide range of interests. He was elected to the Royal Society in 1869. In 1874 he was awarded the society's Rumford medal and gave the Bakerian lecture. In the following year, he was elected a corresponding member of the Académie des Sciences in Paris, and was awarded its Janssen medal. He was made CB in 1894 and created KCB in 1897. He died on 16 August 1920 at his home by the Hill Observatory in Devon, and was buried at the church of St Peter and St Mary in Salcombe Regis. A. J. MEADOWS

Sources A. J. Meadows, *Science and controversy: a biography of Sir Norman Lockyer* (1972) • T. M. Lockyer and W. L. Lockyer, eds., *The life and work of Sir Norman Lockyer* (1928)

Archives ICL • RAS, corresp. and papers • University of Exeter Library, corresp. and papers | BL, corresp. with Macmillans, Add. MS 55218 • CUL, letters to Sir George Stokes • ICL, corresp. with Sir Thomas Huxley • RAS, letters to Royal Astronomical Society • RGS, letters to Sir David Gill

Likenesses Walery, photograph, *c*.1890–1897, NPG [*see illus.*] • Lockyer, photograph, 1917, NPG • H. Thornycroft, medallion, Norman Lockyer Observatory, Sidmouth, Devon • medallion, Salcombe Regis observatory, Devon • photographs, repro. in Meadows, *Science and controversy*

Wealth at death £60,508 3*s*. 0*d*.: certified, 1921, Edinburgh

Lockyer, Nicholas (1611–1685), Independent minister, was the son of William Lockyer of Glastonbury, Somerset. He matriculated from the notoriously puritan college of New Inn Hall, Oxford, on 4 November 1631 and graduated BA on 14 May 1633. Migrating to Emmanuel College, Cambridge, where his BA was incorporated in 1635, he proceeded MA in 1636. In June 1654 he returned to Oxford to take his BTh.

Lockyer supported parliament at the outbreak of the civil wars and held the Independent position in the debate on church government. He was popular with the Commons and was occasionally asked to preach a sermon during days of fasting; an example of his preaching can be found in his sermon of 28 October 1646, where he spoke on Isaiah 53: 10. The text, Lockyer said, was a divine promise of 'deliverance from all sorts of slavery and bondage'

Nicholas Lockyer (1611–1685), by Wenceslaus Hollar, pubd 1643

(Lockyer, *A Sermon Preached*). He counselled that patience and obedience to God's word was the key to parliamentarian success. In particular he opposed a quick settlement for the sake of an ungodly peace.

In 1649, after the execution of Charles I and the establishment of the republic, Lockyer was rewarded by Oliver Cromwell, who appointed him as one of his chaplains. He was also made a fellow of Eton College and the preacher at Windsor Castle. In 1650 he was presented to the living of Farnham Royal in Buckinghamshire. Lockyer's position as one of Cromwell's chaplains earned him political favour, and in January 1651 the council of state sent him to Scotland as a preacher to the parliamentary commissioners. He was perhaps not the most politic of choices; he caused great offence when he preached a sermon at Edinburgh in favour of congregationalism. This he published in 1652 as *A Little Stone out of the Mountain*. The Scottish presbyterians were not content to let this insult go without notice and James Wood, a professor of theology at St Andrews, replied in 1654 alleging Lockyer's ideas to be 'counterfeit'. Despite this foray into controversy the majority of Lockyer's works were uncontentious, being works of puritan pietism aimed at the 'conversion of souls' (*Nonconformist's Memorial*, 1.102).

Lockyer became one of the preachers at Whitehall during the sitting of Barebone's Parliament in 1653, and in 1655 he was chosen as one of the commissioners for the approbation of public preachers. His honours were fully realized in February 1659 when he replaced Francis Rous as provost of Eton College. He was also the preacher at the

London parishes of St Benet Sherehog and St Pancras, Soper Lane.

Lockyer benefited financially from his association with Cromwell, having appropriated dean and chapter lands settled upon him and his heirs by the council of state. He chose to take the monetary value of the lands at ten years purchase instead of the land itself and used the £2100 that he acquired from the council to purchase the manors of Hambleton and Blackwell in Worcestershire. Although the protectorate council sought to reconvey the manors back to the state, Lockyer managed to keep the property. He also acquired Irish lands in Munster and corresponded with Henry Cromwell on their administration.

As an ardent Cromwellian and Independent, Lockyer refused to conform to the royalist and Anglican Restoration and was expelled as provost of Eton in August 1660 to be replaced by General George Monck's brother, Nicholas. He took up the mantle of nonconformity and in September 1666 fled to Rotterdam to escape prosecution under the Act of Uniformity. He had returned to England by 1669 and preached at a meeting at Bell Lane in Spitalfields. In 1670 he was again forced to flee to the Netherlands, for publishing *Some Seasonable and Serious Queries upon the Late Act Against Conventicles*, a pro-toleration tract that argued that the Conventicle Act was against God's word, the constitution, and the principles of prudence and policy. Lockyer was not distracted by the threat of persecution, however, and the nonconformist minister Oliver Heywood heard him preach in St Michael Street, London, in January 1683. Despite his resolve, Lockyer's health began to fail at this time and he moved to Woodford in Essex, where he died on 13 March 1685. He was buried at St Mary, Whitechapel, Stepney. The name of his wife is unknown, but they had six children: a son, Cornelius, and five daughters, Aholiabah, Rebecca, Hannah, Elizabeth, and Abigail. E. C. VERNON

Sources *Calamy rev.*, 326 • *The nonconformist's memorial … originally written by … Edmund Calamy*, ed. S. Palmer, [3rd edn], 3 vols. (1802–3) • N. Lockyer, *A sermon preached … 28 October 1646* (1646) • N. Lockyer, *A little stone out of the mountain* (1652) • N. Lockyer, *Some seasonable and serious queries* (1670) • Wood, *Ath. Oxon.*, new edn, 4.162–5 • *JHC*, 4 (1644–6), 707; 7 (1651–9), 263, 525 • *CSP dom.*, *1650–51*; *1666*; *1669* • BL, Lansdowne MS 823/1, fol. 363 • Venn, *Alum. Cant.* • Foster, *Alum. Oxon.*

Likenesses W. Hollar, etching, BM, NPG; repro. in N. Lockyer, *Baulme for bleeding England and Ireland* (1643) [*see illus.*]

Wealth at death estates in Worcestershire and Ireland: *Calamy rev.*

Lockyer, Robert (1625/6–1649), Leveller and parliamentarian soldier, may have been the son of Mary Locker, who was a householder in the parish of St Botolph without Bishopsgate, London, in 1638. If this Robert was the same man as the future Leveller, he and his mother were rebaptized by the Particular Baptist Richard Blunt in January 1642. Lockyer joined the parliamentarian army in the same year but never advanced beyond the rank of private trooper.

Lockyer's failure to be promoted may have been the consequence of his radical politics. He was rumoured to have supported the Leveller *Agreement of the People* at the army rendezvous at Ware in November 1647. He is next heard of in April 1649 when, according to the *Moderate Intelligencer*, he was twenty-three. The volatile political situation in the capital in the wake of the king's execution prompted the New Model Army's commanders to shift some units to new quarters on the outskirts where they would be less susceptible to Leveller propaganda. Colonel Edward Whalley's regiment was already restless on account of parliament's refusal to release the four imprisoned Leveller leaders from the Tower of London. When Captain John Savage's men were assigned new quarters in Essex they baulked. Seizing the troop's colours, they barricaded themselves in The Bull inn near Bishopsgate, a radical meeting place. Captain Savage tracked them down there and demanded that they hand over the colours and return to their obedience. But the men defied him, Lockyer proclaiming that 'the colours belonged as well to them as to him, and that they had as well fought for them as he' (*A True Narrative of the Late Mutiny … in Col. Whaley's Regiment*, 7). Other officers arrived on the scene, but the men still refused to return to obedience unless a fortnight's wages and their arrears were paid to them. Colonel Whalley cut short the parley, and singled out Lockyer with an order to obey. The trooper turned for advice to his comrades, who all shouted 'No, No'. As a crowd gathered in the street, and the situation seemed on the verge of spinning out of control, the commander-in-chief himself—Sir Thomas Fairfax—arrived with Lieutenant-General Oliver Cromwell, 'furiously breathing forth nothing but death to them all' (*The Army's Martyr*, 4). Those who had not slipped away were arrested and the next day the six ringleaders were sentenced to death. All expressed contrition for their acts, but Fairfax insisted that Lockyer, deemed the most guilty, should die.

The next day (27 April) Lockyer was brought to St Paul's Churchyard to face a firing squad. That morning a hastily published letter from John Lilburne and Richard Overton accused Fairfax and his council of war of 'treason and murder', threatening popular insurrection if they executed Lockyer (*Copie of a Letter*). Lockyer's bravery and eloquence at his execution won him the admiration of many. In his speech he regretted that he should lose his life for a dispute over pay rather than for the freedom and liberties of the nation for which he had fought since 1642. Disdaining the blindfold normally tied to the heads of men who were shot to death, he stared the musketeers in the face and entreated them to spare him. When they remained impassive he uttered his last prayers and then gave the appointed signal by raising both arms. Seconds later he crumpled beneath the bullets rained on him by all six musketeers.

Lockyer's funeral on Sunday 29 April proved to be a dramatic reminder of the strength of the Leveller organization in the metropolis. Starting from Smithfield in the afternoon, the procession wound slowly through the heart of the City, and then back to Moorfields for the interment in New Churchyard. Led by six trumpeters, about 4000 people reportedly accompanied the corpse. Many wore ribbons—black for mourning and sea-green to publicize their Leveller allegiance. A company of women brought up the rear, testimony to the active female involvement in the Leveller movement. If the reports can be believed there were more mourners for Trooper Lockyer than there had been for the martyred Colonel Thomas Rainborowe the previous autumn. In New Churchyard the eulogists strove to discomfit the army grandees and their unpopular military dictatorship by expatiating on the anti-militarism of the Levellers.

Lockyer was evidently a well-liked young Londoner. According to his friends he had a good war record, and was 'honest, just and faithful' and 'beloved of many' (*The Army's Martyr*, 6–7). Between the time of his execution and the decisive defeat of the Leveller movement at Burford the following month Lockyer was its most appealing martyr. On 5 May his execution was used in *The Humble Petition of Divers Well-Affected Women* to demand the end of martial law in peacetime. The Leveller-inspired revolt under William Thompson at Banbury the same month also invoked the memory of Lockyer as a martyr (Thompson, 2).

IAN J. GENTLES

Sources I. Gentles, 'Political funerals during the English Revolution', *London and the civil war*, ed. S. Porter (1996), 205–23 • I. Gentles, *The New Model Army in England, Ireland, and Scotland, 1645–1653* (1992) • *A true narrative of the late mutiny … in Col. Whaley's regiment* (1649) [Thomason tract E 522(18)] • *The army's martyr, or, A faithful relation of the barbarous and illegal proceedings of the court-martiall at White-Hall upon Mr Robert Lockier, with his … dying speech … 27 of April, 1649* (1649) [Thomason tract E 552(11)] • *The copie of a letter … from Lieut. Col. John Lilburn, M. Richard Overton, April 27 1649* (1649), fol. 14 (23) [Thomason tract 669.f.14(23)] • Greaves & Zaller, *BDBR* • M. Tolmie, *The triumph of the saints: the separate churches of London, 1616–1649* (1977) • W. Thompson, *Englands standard advanced, or, A declaration from M. Will. Thompson and the oppressed people … in Oxfordshire* (1649) [Thomason tract E 553(2)] • *To the supreme authority … the humble petition of divers well-affected women* (1649) [Thomason tract 669.f.14(27)] • R. L., *The justice of the army against evill-doers vindicated* (1649) [Thomason tract E 558(14)] • J. Lilburne, *A preparative to an hue and cry after Sir Arthur Haslerig* [1649] [Thomason tract E 573(16)] • *Perfect Occurrences* (27 April–3 May 1649) • *England's Moderate Messenger* (23–30 April 1649) • *The Kingdomes Faithfull and Impartiall Scout* (27 April–4 May 1649) • *A Modest Narrative of Intelligence* (21–8 April 1649) • *A Modest Narrative of Intelligence* (29 April–5 May 1649) • *The Moderate* (24 April–1 May 1649) • *Mercurius Pragmaticus* (24 April–1 May 1649) • *Moderate Intelligencer* (26 April–2 May 1649) • *Impartiall Intelligencer* (25 April–2 May 1649) • *A Perfect Diurnall* (30 April–7 May 1649)

Locock, Sir Charles, first baronet (1799–1875), obstetric physician, was born at Northampton on 21 April 1799, the son of Henry Locock (*d.* 1843), medical practitioner, and his first wife, Susannah Smyth. For three years he was resident private pupil of Benjamin Brodie, the influential surgeon to St George's Hospital, London, then attended lectures at the school of medicine in Great Windmill Street, and afterwards graduated MD at Edinburgh in 1821 with a *Dissertatio medico inauguralis de cordis palpitatione*, which was published in the same year and dedicated to a new mentor, Andrew Duncan. Just prior to this he had undertaken a journey to the continent. In 1822 he was a house pupil at the Westminster Lying-in Hospital. He became a licentiate of the Royal College of Physicians the next year. Brodie recommended Locock to devote himself to the practice of midwifery, and he was fortunate in receiving the support of Robert Gooch, who was retiring from practical midwifery and referred many of his patients to Locock. From a small practice based near Oxford Street, he rapidly rose to eminence, and for many years had the largest practice in London as an accoucheur. On 5 August 1826 Locock married Amelia (*d.* 1867), youngest daughter of John Lewis of Southampton Place, Euston Square, London. In 1834–5 Locock lectured on midwifery at St Bartholomew's Hospital, and was for many years physician to the Westminster Lying-in Hospital. He was admitted a fellow of the Royal College of Physicians in 1836, and was a member of its council in 1840–42. In 1840 he was appointed first physician accoucheur to Queen Victoria, and attended at the births of all her children, using chloroform in later ones. Besides contributing seven articles to the *Cyclopaedia of Practical Medicine* and another two to the *Library of Medicine* (ed. A. Tweedie, 1840), he made a valuable contribution to medicine by the discovery of the efficacy of bromide of potassium in epilepsy, analysing fifty-two cases in *The Lancet* (1857, 1.527–8).

On his retirement in 1857 he was created a baronet, although he had declined the honour in 1840. He was president of the Royal Medical and Chirurgical Society in 1857, president of the Obstetrical Society of London, and was elected FRS in 1864, and created DCL (Oxon.) in 1864. He was a justice of the peace and deputy lieutenant for the county of Kent. He unsuccessfully contested the Isle of Wight as a Conservative in 1865. Locock was 'small in person and slight, firm and decided in manner, and to strangers undemonstrative to the extent of coldness' (*BMJ*, 151). Locock, who worried about his health to the point of hypochondria, died on 23 July 1875. Sir James Paget described him as having great power of work and devotion to duty, keen insight, and great practical knowledge of the medical profession. He made quick, clear diagnoses, and his decisive manner inspired confidence and loyalty in his many patients. He was neither a scholar nor an innovator, but had many social qualities. Thus it was as much the personal as the professional regard in which he was held, together with the loyal patronage he enjoyed from an unusually early age, which ensured his success. Locock and his wife had five sons, of whom the eldest, Charles Brodie (1827–1890), succeeded to the baronetcy, and the third, Sidney (1834–1885), was the British minister resident in Serbia from 1881 until his death on 30 August 1885.

G. T. BETTANY, *rev.* ANNE DIGBY

Sources Munk, *Roll* • *The Lancet* (31 July 1875), 184–5 • *BMJ* (31 July 1875), 151 • S. Paget, *Memoirs and letters of Sir James Paget* (1903) • N. Moore and S. Paget, *The Royal Medical and Chirurgical Society of London centenary, 1805–1905* (1905) • R. C. Maulitz, 'Metropolitan medicine and the man-midwife: the early life and letters of Charles Locock', *Medical History*, 26 (1982), 25–46 • Burke, *Peerage*

Archives Bodl. Oxf., letters to Lord and Lady Lovelace • City Westm. AC, letters to R. P. Jones • Wellcome L.

Likenesses woodcut, 1875, BM • C. Baugniet, lithograph, BM

Wealth at death under £100,000: probate, 18 Aug 1875, *CGPLA Eng. & Wales*

Loddiges, George (1786–1846), nurseryman, was born on 12 March 1786 in Hackney, Middlesex, the second of two surviving sons—he also had at least three sisters, two of whom died in childhood—of Joachim Conrad Loddiges (*c.*1738–1826), a native of Hanover and the founder of the Hackney firm of nurserymen, Conrad Loddiges & Sons, and his wife, Sarah Aldous (1740–1815).

When William and George Loddiges joined their father in the nursery it had already established an international reputation and had introduced many new plants to British gardens. The gifted and versatile George, the younger of the two, proved to be the main driving force in the decades which followed, when the nursery was without equal anywhere in the world. The total retail value of their stock during this period was estimated at £200,000.

The 15 acres of nursery were skilfully planned. In the 9 acre 'arboretum', as part of it was called, each species and variety was represented by a well-grown display specimen and a stock of smaller plants for sale. The variety was remarkable. Their 1836 catalogue listed 67 species and varieties of oak, 29 of birch, 91 of crataegus, 180 of willow, and 1549 roses. 'In this department, Messrs. Loddiges have done more than all the royal and botanic gardens put together', wrote J. C. Loudon. In 1839–40 George Loddiges laid out the arboretum at the Abney Park cemetery.

Loddiges designed the steam heating and the system of irrigation from overhead pipes for the range of hothouses which was greatly admired by visitors in the 1820s. The nursery was renowned for palms and orchids, and by 1845 there were 280 species and varieties of the former and 1916 of the latter. Loddiges found an outlet for his considerable artistic talent by illustrating plants grown in the nursery, in the publication of the nursery's periodical, the *Botanical Cabinet*, which appeared at monthly intervals between 1817 and 1833. Most of the 2000 finely coloured plates, engraved by George Cooke, were from Loddiges's drawings. The text of the *Botanical Cabinet*, combining scientific information with pious observations, reflected Loddiges's deeply held religious convictions.

Loddiges was a member of the councils of the Linnean Society and of the Horticultural Society, whose garden regularly benefited from the resources of the nursery. He was always ready to provide plants for scientific purposes, and his friend Nathaniel Ward warmly acknowledged the help he received from Loddiges in developing his Wardian cases, which greatly increased the survival rate of plants transported from distant parts of the world. They were both early members of the Microscopical Society.

It was Loddiges's unfulfilled ambition to write and illustrate a folio work devoted to hummingbirds. His collection, amounting to 200 species and recognized as outstanding throughout Europe, was acquired from a descendant by the British Museum (Natural History) in 1933, along with his notes.

Loddiges married Jane (1787–1859), daughter of the Revd James Creighton, in 1811. They had one son and two daughters. Their daughter Jane married the artist Edward William Cooke. George Loddiges died in Hackney, Middlesex, on 5 June 1846 and was buried at St John-at-Hackney.

George Loddiges (1786–1846), by John Renton

A. R. P. Hayden, *rev.*

Sources Archives, London Borough of Hackney · MSS, including diaries of E. W. Cooke (1828–79), Jane Loddiges (1839), priv. coll. · *Gardener's Magazine* (1826–43) · *Journal of the Horticultural Society* (1846), 224–5 · registers of baptisms and burials, St John's, Hackney · *Botanical Cabinet* (1817–33) · *Catalogue of plants … sold by Conrad Loddiges & Sons, nursery and seedsmen*, [another edn] (1816) [sale catalogue, Conrad Loddiges & Sons, Hackney, London] · *Catalogue of plants … sold by Conrad Loddiges & Sons, nursery and seedsmen*, 11th edn (1818) [sale catalogue, Conrad Loddiges & Sons, Hackney, London] · *Catalogue of plants … sold by Conrad Loddiges & Sons, nursery and seedsmen*, [another edn] (1836) [sale catalogue, Conrad Loddiges & Sons, Hackney, London] · *Orchidae in the collection of C. Loddiges and Sons* (1845) · P. Hayden, *Biddulph Grange, Staffordshire: a Victorian garden rediscovered* (1989)

Archives Linn. Soc., corresp. · NHM, ornithological notebooks · RBG Kew, corresp. · S. Antiquaries, Lond., nursery catalogues

Likenesses J. Renton, oils, Royal Horticultural Society, Lindley Library; repro. in P. Hayden, *Biddulph Grange* (1989) [*see illus.*]

Loder, Edward James (1813–1865), composer and conductor, one of the seven children of the violinist John David *Loder (1788–1846) and his wife, *née* Mills, was born at Bath. About 1826 he was sent to Frankfurt am Main to study with his father's old friend, Beethoven's pupil Ferdinand Ries, who after several years' residence in London had just returned to the continent. A couple of years later Loder returned to England, and in 1830 he arranged the music for a production of *Black-Eyed Susan* at the Theatre Royal, Bath. Shortly thereafter he travelled again to Germany with the intention of studying medicine, but, quickly changing his mind, he resumed his study with Ries. About 1834 he returned to London and immediately received a commission to compose music for J. S. Arnold's play *Nourjahad*, recast as an opera, for the opening of the New Theatre Royal Lyceum and English Opera House after the fire of 1830. The production took place in July 1834, and Loder's music was considered its principal attraction. Unlike the usual English operas, which were primarily a succession of songs and ballads, Loder had attempted to make *Nourjahad* a genuine musical drama, and, as such, it was well received by those contemporary critics who wished to see English composers emulating their serious German contemporaries. In little more than a year Loder produced three more works at the Lyceum, which did not, however, aspire to the same high aims; none the less *The Dice of Death*, with a libretto by John Oxenford, was moderately successful in 1835.

Meanwhile, Loder had entered into an agreement with the music publishers Dalmain & Co. to supply a weekly series of compositions, and for the same firm he wrote his *First Principles of Singing* in 1838 and *A Modern Pianoforte Tutor* in 1839. Some of the songs composed to fulfil his contract with Dalmain were strung together to make the opera *Francis I*, which was produced at Drury Lane in 1838 with limited success; one song, however, 'The Old House at Home', achieved considerable popularity. Another opera, *Little Red Riding Hood*, intended for the inauguration of the regime of the impresario Hammond at Drury Lane, was not put into production, and two other stage works, *The Foresters* and *The Deer Stalkers*, produced in 1838 and 1841, were unambitious. During this period, however, Loder was also working at more consequential compositions: a string quartet in E♭ (apparently his fourth, though no trace survives of earlier ones) was performed several times at the Society of British Musicians, three sets of songs were published in 1837–8, and around 1840 he issued a number of collections of sacred music, outstanding among which was a set of nine *Sacred Songs and Ballads* (1840) with texts by Desmond Ryan and dedicated to Sterndale Bennett.

In 1846 Loder became music director at the Princess's Theatre, and in the same year he staged his 'romantic opera' *The Night Dancers*, composed to a libretto by George Soane that was based on the same German folk-tale that had provided the plot of Adolphe Adam's ballet *Giselle*. More significant musically and dramatically than the other stage works he had written since *Nourjahad*, it was an immediate success with press and public, and within twelve months was produced in New York and Sydney. In London it was revived at the Princess's Theatre in 1850 and at Covent Garden in 1860. As well as its abundance of good melodic material, apparent in such numbers as the ballad 'Wake, my love', which was essential for a success in the English theatre, *The Night Dancers* displays the masterly orchestration and genuine dramatic instinct that enabled Loder to create something worth while when he chose to exert himself. Fuller Maitland loftily described it in 1902 as having 'merits far beyond the trivial tunes with which Balfe caught the ear of his vulgar audiences' (Fuller Maitland, 42). Many of Loder's works at this time were connected with his duties at the Princess's Theatre; he contributed music to various productions, and in 1848 composed the operetta *The Andalusian* and the ballad opera *Robin Goodfellow*, though neither of these displays the same level of commitment as *The Night Dancers* or enjoyed comparable success. He put more effort into his 'operatic masque' *The Island of Calypso*, intended for the National Concerts in 1850 but not performed until 14 April 1852, when Berlioz conducted it at Exeter Hall.

In 1851 Loder was appointed music director of the Theatre Royal, Manchester, where he spent his energies in composing, arranging, and conducting the music for the theatre's daily fare. By 1855 he had completed his opera *Raymond and Agnes*, originally announced for the Princess's Theatre for the 1849–50 season, and it was given its première in Manchester on 14 August. Despite its considerable musical and dramatic qualities, it was coolly received and sustained a run of only seven performances. A later production at St James's Theatre, London, in 1859 lasted no more than a week, despite enthusiastic reviews. The opera enjoyed an isolated revival at the Cambridge Arts Theatre, in an edition by Nicholas Temperley and Max Miradin, in 1966.

Shortly after the Manchester production of *Raymond and Agnes*, Loder fell ill with a brain disorder that made it necessary for him to relinquish his Manchester post and return to London. A subscription to assist him was advertised in the *Musical World* in 1856 and 1857, and performances of his works were facilitated by family and friends. These included the London staging of *Raymond and Agnes*; a production of his last theatrical composition, the one-act operetta *Never Judge by Appearances*, given at the Adelphi on 7 July 1859; and the 1860 revival of *The Night Dancers*. Shortly before his death, a set of *Twelve Songs Sacred and Secular* was published by subscription for his benefit. The last four years of his life were largely spent in a deep coma, and Loder, a bachelor living alone, was registered by a neighbour as having died at his lodgings, 101 Bolsover Street, London, on 5 April 1865. CLIVE BROWN

Sources D. Baptie, *Sketches of the English glee composers: historical, biographical and critical (from about 1735–1866)* [1896], 148–9 • N. Temperley, 'Raymond and Agnes', *MT*, 107 (1966), 307–10 • N. Temperley, 'The English Romantic opera', *Victorian Studies*, 9 (1965–6), 293–302, esp. 293 • H. C. Banister, *George Alexander Macfarren* (1891), 246 • B. S. Penley, *The Bath stage: a history of dramatic representations in Bath* (1892), 130 • J. A. Fuller Maitland, *Music in the XIXth century: English music* (1902), 41f., 105f. • E. Walker, *A history of music in England*, 3rd edn (1952), 308–10 • P. M. Young, *A history of British music* (1967), 473–4

Loder, George (1816–1868), conductor and composer, was born in Bath, the son of George Loder, a flautist, and his wife, Fanny Philpot, a piano teacher and the sister of the pianist Lucy Anderson. His uncle was the violinist and publisher John David Loder. In 1836 he went to the USA. After residing for some years in Baltimore, in 1844 he became principal of the New York Vocal Institute; he was also a prominent member of the Philharmonic and Vocal societies, which he had helped to establish there. He played the double bass for the Philharmonic Society for five seasons, and occasionally conducted the society's orchestra, a notable occasion being the first American performance of Beethoven's ninth symphony (20 May 1846).

In 1855 Loder went to Australia with the soprano Anna Bishop, and settled in Adelaide as conductor of Lyster's opera troupe. In 1859 he was again active in London—as organist, singer, conductor, and composer; on 11 June he conducted the revival of the opera *Raymond and Agnes* by his cousin Edward Loder. In 1861 he published *Pets of the Parterre*, a comic operetta, which had been produced at the Lyceum and Adelphi theatres, and in 1862 *The Old House at Home*, a musical entertainment staged also at the Adelphi.

Loder's music was perhaps more popular in America than in Britain. *The New York Glee Book* (1843), written for the New York Vocal Institute and reissued as *The Philadelphia and New York Glee Book* in 1864, contains many of his original partsongs. He also published *The Middle Voice, Twelve Solfeggi* (1860), and various individual songs and instrumental pieces both in England and America. Loder paid a second visit to Australia, and died, after a long illness, at Adelaide on 15 July 1868.

His sister **Kate Fanny Loder** (1825–1904), a successful pianist and composer, was born in Bath on 21 August 1825. In 1844 she became a professor of piano at the Royal Academy of Music, where she had previously studied. Among her compositions were works for the piano, notably the *Twelve Studies* of 1852, an orchestral overture (1844), a string quartet (1848), and songs. On 16 December 1851 she married the surgeon Henry *Thompson (1820–1904), with whom she had a son and two daughters. Her husband was knighted in 1867 and created a baronet in 1899. She became paralysed after 1871, in which year the first performance in England of Brahms's *German Requiem* was given at her house. She died at Headley, Surrey, on 30 August 1904. L. M. Middleton, *rev.* David J. Golby

Sources N. Temperley, 'Loder', *New Grove* • *The Era* (20 Sept 1868) • private information (1893) • N. Burton and N. Temperley, 'Loder, Kate (Fanny)', *The new Grove dictionary of women composers*, ed. J. A. Sadie and R. Samuel (1994) • Burke, *Peerage*

Wealth at death £2781 3*s*. 4*d*.—Kate Loder: probate, 1904, *CGPLA Eng. & Wales*

Loder, John David (1788–1846), violinist, was born at Bath, the son of John Loder (*d.* 1795), a musician. Loder was a member of a musical family long resident in Bath, and was himself at the head of his profession there for many years. After initially playing in concert orchestras, he appeared as the first violin in a string quartet at the New Assembly Rooms on 4 April 1800, and from 1799 to 1836 was a member, and for most of that time leader, of the orchestra of the Theatre Royal. Famous musicians from London often attended his annual benefit night at the theatre, and Angelica Catalani, the celebrated Italian soprano, appeared with him at a concert on 7 October 1821. It is reported that she returned her fee 'as a small tribute of regard for his private worth, and high professional skill' (*New Grove*). He left the theatre in 1836 after a disagreement, but returned in 1840–41.

Among other engagements Loder was leader of the Yorkshire music festival (15 September 1825, alongside Franz Cramer, Mori, and Kiesewetter), soloist at the Gloucester music festival (1826), and leader at the Three Choirs festival (1826–45). He was also, from 12 May 1817, the first Englishman to lead the orchestra at the Philharmonic Society of London, which, according to Temperley, he appears to have done at least once a year. His business as a music publisher and seller of musical instruments operated from 46 Milsom Street, Bath, from around 1820 to 1835. He subsequently resided in London and, in 1840, became professor of violin at the Royal Academy of Music. He also performed in the Ancient Concerts, succeeding Cramer as leader in 1845. His thorough knowledge of orchestral and chamber music made his services especially sought after for the performance of new and intricate works.

Loder's role as a successful teacher of the violin and viola should not be overlooked, and his *General and Comprehensive Instruction Book for the Violin* (*c.*1824) was one of the first detailed and systematic English violin methods, appearing in a revised and enlarged version as late as 1911. Other works included violin duets (1837), a treatise on bowing (1842), and various arrangements.

Loder died at Albany Street, Regent's Park, London, on 13 February 1846. He and his wife, a Miss Mills, the stepdaughter of the comic actor John *Fawcett, had five sons and two daughters. The second son, **John Fawcett Loder** (1812–1853), was a violinist and viola player, who became a successful music teacher and concert director in Bath. He was a member of various London orchestras and played viola in Blagrove and Dando's Quartet Concerts from 1842 until his death, which occurred suddenly in Hawley Crescent, London, on 16 April 1853. His younger brother Edward James *Loder (1813–1865) was a successful composer, principally of theatrical works.

David J. Golby

Sources M. B. Foster, *History of the Philharmonic Society of London: 1813–1912* (1912) • C. Humphries and W. C. Smith, *Music publishing in the British Isles, from the beginning until the middle of the nineteenth century: a dictionary of engravers, printers, publishers, and music sellers*, 2nd edn (1970), 215 • G. Dubourg, *The violin*, 4th edn (1852), 290 • 'Second Yorkshire music festival', *The Harmonicon*, 3 (1825), 174–85 • N. Temperley, 'Loder, John David', *New Grove* • Brown & Stratton, *Brit. mus.*

Likenesses J. Brandard, lithograph (after F. Salabert), BM, NPG

Loder, John Fawcett (1812–1853). *See under* Loder, John David (1788–1846).

Loder, Kate Fanny (1825–1904). *See under* Loder, George (1816–1868).

Loder, Robert (*bap.* 1589, *d.* 1638), farmer and accounts keeper, was baptized at Harwell, Berkshire, on 1 November 1589, one of three sons of John Loder (*d.* 1595) and of his wife, Elizabeth (*d.* 1608), daughter of Francis Forde of Garsington, Oxfordshire; his brothers were John and Francis. Many Loder families lived in Harwell. A Richard Loder was tenant in 1557 of Prince's Harwell manor farm, and a

John Loder was in possession, presumably by purchase, in the same year. John died in 1579, and the farm passed first to his son and then to his grandson, John (Robert's father), who died on 2 August 1595 when Robert was only five. Two uncles, John and Francis Loder, already farming in Harwell, managed the farm as trustees but allowed Robert to plant an orchard in 1605. Robert took full charge in 1610, let his land for one year 'to halves' (a cost and profit-sharing arrangement), and then farmed alone from February 1611.

Loder is notable for one surviving personal record of his life, a farming account book covering the years 1610 to 1620. He was obsessed with counting the profits from every single operation on his farm, at a time when only estate owners generally recorded expenditure and income, and never to this degree of detail. His accounts register with relentless precision each year's expenditure, receipts, and profits, together with reflections on the lessons to be drawn from the annual outcome. He kept notes from day to day, referred back to them over the years, and clearly plagued his household interminably with questions and scrutiny of their farming and domestic activities. He fretted at employing two maidservants whose routines did not show any farming profit; they dealt with malting for household beer and 'thinges that must indeed be donne' (*Robert Loder's Farm Accounts*, 71). He constantly wavered between the economies achieved by boarding harvesters in house, paying for piecework, or contracting the whole job out. His life was dominated by financial reckonings, and his ruminations on changes of policy were repetitiously debated at the end of every year. Not surprisingly he complained of unruly servants.

While Loder's unique farming record sheds light on his aspirations and explains his management decisions, his reading matter is nowhere revealed, although his concerns for certain kinds of improvement faithfully reflect advice of such contemporary authors as Hugh Platt, William Folkingham, and Gervase Markham between 1580 and 1620. The crown also set an example at this time, being an active, interventionist landlord, closely scrutinizing outlay and landed income.

Loder's main interest lay in his arable strips in common fields, probably amounting to some 150 acres, and he yearly debated the profits of wheat versus barley; he always decided that wheat paid best. He also calculated annual returns from orchards, dovecote, hops, and hay. He kept sheep and cattle, using cows for household needs only, until he started commercial dairying in 1618, possibly taking a hint from Markham. He found it very profitable. His total profit per annum fluctuated between £180 and £290.

Loder married on 11 November 1611 Mary, daughter of William Andrewes of Sutton Courtenay, the next-door parish. They had two daughters, Mary, baptized on 10 February 1613, and Lettice, baptized on 30 July 1615, and two sons, Robert, baptized on 20 May 1618 (who died childless), and John, baptized on 3 February 1622; John later moved to Balston Park and claimed a coat of arms at the heralds' visitation in 1665–6. Mary Loder died in 1624, and was buried at Harwell on 16 May. Loder held no public office, and nothing is known of his later life. He died in 1638 and was buried, also at Harwell, on 8 November.

JOAN THIRSK

Sources *Robert Loder's farm accounts, 1610–1620*, ed. G. E. Fussell, CS, 3rd ser., 53 (1936) • *VCH Berkshire*, 3.84–92 • W. H. Rylands, ed., *The four visitations of Berkshire*, 1, Harleian Society, 56 (1907), 241 • parish register, Harwell, 1 Nov 1589, Berks. RO [baptism] • parish register, Harwell, 16 May 1624, Berks. RO [burial of Mary Loder] • parish register, Harwell, 8 Nov 1638, Berks. RO [burial] • parish register, Sutton Courtenay, 11 Nov 1611, Berks. RO [marriage]
Archives Berks. RO, farm accounts, D/ELs/A8

Lodewyk, Mary (*d.* 1407). *See under* Women traders and artisans in London (*act. c.*1200–*c.*1500).

Lodge, Sir Edmund (1756–1839), herald and biographer, was born on 13 June 1756, in Poland Street, London, the only surviving son of the Revd Edmund Lodge (*c.*1729–1781), rector of Carshalton in Surrey, and his wife, Mary Garrard, the daughter and sole heir of Richard Garrard of Carshalton. Nothing is known of Lodge's early life or schooling until the age of sixteen, when, on 29 November 1771, he was commissioned as cornet in His Majesty's Own (or 3rd) regiment of dragoons under the command of the earl of Albemarle. This may have been a precipitant decision, for Lodge was not happy in the army: the regiment report records his request for 'Leave to sell out' on 3 October 1772 (troop record, PRO, WO/12/564) and his resignation, one week later, on 11 October 1772. After this setback, Lodge was slow to decide what path to follow. It was not until 22 February 1782 that he obtained the post of Bluemantle pursuivant-at-arms, one of the four lowest positions, in the College of Arms—the ancient institution which functions as the official guardian and authenticator of pedigrees and armorial bearings. He was to spend the rest of his career as a herald and a genealogist. He rose through the ranks of the College of Arms, becoming Lancaster herald on 29 October 1793 and Norroy king of arms on 11 June 1822. His career as a herald was crowned when he was promoted to Clarenceux king of arms, the second in command at the College of Arms, on 30 July 1838. On 27 April 1808 he married Jane-Anne-Elizabeth Field (*d.* 1820) at St George the Martyr, Southwark.

In keeping with his antiquarian interests, which are manifest in a herald's work of tracing ancient pedigrees, Lodge was also elected a fellow of the London Society of Antiquaries on 15 March 1787 but, in practice, he made little mark on their proceedings or publications. Instead he developed as an independent antiquarian author working with commercial publishers, such as Harding and Lepard, on a number of luxury periodical publications which combined high quality engraved portrait heads of historical figures with Lodge's authoritative, 'pleasant and lucid' accounts of their lives (*Fraser's Magazine*, 595). Due to the patriotic fashion for collecting engraved portraits of illustrious figures, most of these lives were of secondary importance to the engravings. This was true of *Imitations of Original Drawings by Hans Holbein* (1792), with prints by

Sir Edmund Lodge (1756–1839), by Lemuel Francis Abbott, *c.*1790–95

Francesco Bartolozzi, and of *Portraits of Illustrious Personages of Great Britain* (1814–34), advertised as 'an assemblage of highly furnished Engravings of the Portraits of Persons most distinguished for elevated rank or splendid talents' (*Lodge's Illustrious Portraits*, prospectus). Despite the massive cost and extent of this project, which exceeded £40,000 and amounted to forty folio parts, Lodge's 'Biographical & historical memoirs' did not go unremarked. In 1828 Sir Walter Scott praised the 'vast consequence' of 'Mr Lodge's splendid work' (*Portraits & Memoirs*, prospectus). Apart from a few literary reviews, including a preface to the works of Sir Charles Hanbury Williams, Lodge specialized in such historical memoirs, and, as one commentator explained in the 'Advertisement' to the 1849 edition of *Portraits of Illustrious Personages*: 'it is on the Biographies attached to the "portraits" that his fame chiefly rests, and on them he expended his best energies'. Although Lodge was a prolific author, he was renowned for his painstaking slowness and for missed deadlines.

As well as his formal and ceremonial duties as a herald, and his work at what he called 'book-making' (BL, Add. MS 33929, fol. 26), throughout his career he also took on private commissions to compile family trees; in 1808, for example, he completed one for the Kavenaghs at the apparently modest charge of a guinea. His generous and sociable nature, and his commitment to heraldic research, are further demonstrated by the fact that he was always willing to share his knowledge and do people favours. In a letter to Philip Bliss of 15 March 1814, he explained that: 'We of This College, are allowed, by ancient Custom, to make abstracts of Wills in the King's Office, a privilege denied to all other persons, and this fortunately, puts it into my power to save you the expence [*sic*] of a copy' (BL, Add. MS 34567, fol. 418). Another act of benevolence, which also reflects his elevated reputation in the field of genealogy, was his endorsement of the *Annual Peerage* (1827–9), which was published under Lodge's name but was actually the work of Anne, Eliza, and Maria Innes. His literary achievements and public service were honoured when, in 1832, he was appointed a knight of the Royal Guelphic Order of Hanover—an unsolicited distinction that gave Lodge great pleasure.

Lodge died on 16 January 1839 at his house, 2 Bloomsbury Square, London, and was buried at St George's, Bloomsbury, on 24 January. His wife had died in May 1820, and as they had no children most of his estate was left to his unmarried sister, Mary Charlotte Lodge. An enthusiastic bibliophile, Lodge had built up an impressive topographical and heraldic library; this was sold by S. Leigh and Sotheby on 11 March 1839 and, according to their auctioneer's records, raised the sum of £361 4*s*.6*d*. Given that his position at the College of Arms made him the protector of the ancient privileges and properties of the aristocracy, it is not surprising that his obituary in the *Gentleman's Magazine* commented on the high-tory bias that tinged all his historical writings. Nevertheless, his works were commended as original, perceptive, and an 'ornament to our literature' (*GM* [2nd ser.], 11.1, 434).

LUCY PELTZ

Sources *Catalogue of the historical, genealogical, and miscellaneous library of the late Edmund Lodge* (1839) [sale catalogue, Sothebys, 11–12 March 1839] · Allibone, *Dict.* · 'Gallery of literary characters', *Fraser's Magazine*, 14 (1836), 595 · BL, letter from Edmund Lodge to William Betham, 5/8/1808, Add. MS 23687, fol. 188; 23691, fols. 18–20 · BL, letter from Edmund Lodge to Philip Bliss, 15/3/1814, Add. MS 34567, fol. 418 · BL, letter from Edmund Lodge to Sir J. Egerton-Brydges, 11/7/1809, Add. MS 33929, fol. 26 · BL, letter from Edmund Lodge to James Graham, 27/1/1794, Add. MS 19038, fol. 52 · Walpole, *Corr.* · PRO, will, 5/1/1835, proved 27/5/1839, PROB 11/1911/307 · Nichols, *Illustrations* · *Engraved Brit. ports.* · *Lodge's illustrious portraits preparing for publication* [prospectus] · E. Lodge, *Portraits of illustrious personages of Great Britain*, [new edn], 12 vols. in 6 (1835), vol. 1, p. 8 (letter by Sir Walter Scott) · *DNB* · Troop record for regiment of his majesty's own (or 3rd) regiment of dragoons, PRO, WO/12/564 · *GM*, 1st ser., 63 (1793), 158 · *GM*, 1st ser., 70 (1800), 709–10 · *GM*, 2nd ser., 11 (1839), 433–5

Archives Coll. Arms, heraldic and genealogical collections · Yale U., Beinecke L., letters and genealogical notes | BL, letters to William Betham, Add. MSS 23687, 23691 · U. Nott. L., corresp. with fourth duke of Newcastle

Likenesses L. F. Abbott, oils, *c.*1790–1795, NPG [*see illus.*] · D. Maclise, pencil drawing, 1828, BM · W. Drummond, lithograph (after D. Maclise), repro. in *Athenaeum Portraits*, 40 (1836) · D. Maclise, etching, BM, NPG; repro. in 'Gallery of literary characters' · Smith, engraving (after Maclise), repro. in E. Lodge, *Portraits of illustrious personages of Great Britain*, new edn, 8 vols. (1849–50), frontispiece

Wealth at death see will, PRO, PROB 11/1911/307

Lodge, Eleanor Constance (1869–1936), historian and college head, was born at Hanley, Staffordshire, on 18 September 1869, the youngest child (of nine) and only daughter of Oliver Lodge (1826–1884), merchant, afterwards of Wolstanton, Staffordshire, and his wife, Grace (1826–

Eleanor Constance Lodge (1869–1936), by Sir Gerald Kelly, exh. RA 1933

1879), youngest daughter of the Revd Joseph Heath. Her eldest brother, Sir Oliver *Lodge, remembered her as being always very thin and extraordinarily energetic as a child, and this remained true in adult life. She was educated at home, and in private schools in Wolverhampton, Newcastle under Lyme, and, after she was orphaned, Oxford, where two of her brothers, Alfred and Richard *Lodge, were college fellows. By her own account she was a shy, self-conscious, and anxious child. In 1890, however, after a period of illness, she went up to Lady Margaret Hall, Oxford (LMH), which 'was simply a revelation to me of what life might be, and opened a new world of happiness' (E. C. Lodge, 41). She was a dedicated student—'I could imagine no greater misery than having to miss a lecture' (ibid., 53)—and gained a second in modern history in 1894, as well as playing hockey and tennis, rowing, cycling, and skating.

At the École des Chartes and the Écoles des Hautes Études in Paris, 1898–9, Lodge received an outstanding training as a medievalist, and embarked on research into English rule in Gascony, on which she produced several important studies, especially 'The estates of the archbishop and chapter of Saint-André of Bordeaux under English rule' in volume 3 (1912) of *Oxford Studies in Social and Legal History* and *The English Rule in Gascony* (1926). She published a number of other books and articles, and contributed to volume 5 (1926) of the *Cambridge Medieval History*. Her authoritative work was based on extensive research in French archives. She also walked and cycled frequently in France, sometimes with a companion, often alone. Her long familiarity with France stood her in good stead when in the spring of 1918 she took charge of the Oxford women's canteens for French soldiers in Champagne, shared in the retreat before German forces, and then nursed in Paris.

Eleanor Lodge was 'wild with joy' (E. C. Lodge, 83) when in 1895 Elizabeth Wordsworth, principal of LMH, asked her to return. She was appointed librarian, then from 1899 to 1921 history tutor, and vice-principal from 1906. She taught for many hours each week to supplement the small retaining fee she received, and was proud to be the first woman invited by the history board to lecture in the university, on the sources of Gascon history. She was deeply committed to women's and girls' education, and encouraged students to go into schoolteaching as well as organizing classes and lectures to help teachers study for degrees. She was active in the long campaign to persuade Oxford University to award degrees to women, finally achieved in 1920—not least as a result of the contribution her generation of academic women had made to the intellectual and institutional development of the women's colleges. With her dedication to scholarship and teaching, and her devotion to LMH, it was not surprising that she hoped to become the third principal of the college when Henrietta Jex-Blake retired in 1921; her failure to achieve this was a painful blow. She decided to move on, and applied for an assistant lecturership in history at Westfield College, London, but found herself instead being appointed principal there, in succession to Bertha Surtees Phillpotts.

During her ten years as principal of Westfield College, Eleanor Lodge oversaw major library development and the building of a chapel. She also continued to write, teach, and examine, and served on the history board, noting with appreciation the fuller integration of women into university life in London, and the treatment of women as equals by their male colleagues. In 1926, jointly with the chairman of the college council, Sir Thomas Inskip, she persuaded the commissioners responsible for drawing up new statutes for the University of London to reaffirm Westfield's standing as one of the eight component colleges of the university, a position which had been threatened by Westfield's small size. She was able to point both to Westfield's good academic record, enhanced by her insistence that students should pursue honours courses, and to the continuing demand for a residential college. She strongly believed that the college should be more than a hostel, and that academic staff should mix on a daily basis with the students. Under the new statutes she became, in 1929, the first principal of Westfield to take a place on the London University senate. With her usual energy she sustained a wide range of other responsibilities, including membership of Hampstead borough council, and her role as president of the Association of University Women Teachers.

Eleanor Lodge's personal life was enriched by her close friendship with Janet Spens, whom she met when Janet was appointed as tutor in English at LMH in 1911. Just before the First World War she spent some months with Janet in Harrogate, where she was convalescing, then they took rooms together in Headington. They 'began to hanker after a cottage of our very own' especially for the university vacations when no accommodation was available in LMH, and hired one in Steeple Aston from 1916 to 1925. They then bought 5 Fyfield Road, near LMH (where Janet Spens remained a tutor until 1936), which was Eleanor's base when not in London or France.

In 1928 Eleanor Lodge became the first woman to obtain the degree of DLitt from Oxford University, and in 1932 she was appointed CBE. She was elected an honorary fellow of LMH and of Westfield, and was awarded the honorary degree of DLitt by the University of Liverpool. She died at New Lodge Clinic, Windsor, Berkshire, after a long illness on 19 March 1936, and was buried at Wolvercote cemetery, near Oxford. Her vivid autobiography, *Terms and Vacations* (published posthumously in 1938), is an important source for understanding the experience of university women from the late nineteenth century to the mid-1930s. In its pages Eleanor Lodge is revealed as an honest, unselfconscious, almost naïve woman, of great energy and intellectual drive. She was a generous and distinguished servant of women's higher education, which had nurtured her, and a loyal friend.

FRANCES LANNON

Sources E. C. Lodge, *Terms and vacations*, ed. J. Spens (1938) · *DNB* · O. Lodge, *Past years: an autobiography* (1931) · *Lady Margaret Hall: a short history* (1923) · registers and reports, Lady Margaret Hall, Oxford · women's inter-collegiate reports, Lady Margaret Hall, Oxford, archives · J. Sondheimer, *Castle Adamant in Hampstead: a history of Westfield College, 1882–1982* (1983) · M. Lodge, *Sir Richard Lodge: a biography* (1946)

Likenesses L. L. Brooke, chalk drawing, 1916, Lady Margaret Hall, Oxford · J. B. Souter, oils, 1931, Lady Margaret Hall, Oxford · G. Kelly, oils, exh. RA 1933, Queen Mary College, London [*see illus.*] · photograph, repro. in Sondheimer, *Castle Adamant in Hampstead*, 98

Wealth at death £10,820 9*s*. 11*d*.: probate, 18 May 1936, *CGPLA Eng. & Wales*

Lodge, John (1692–1774), archivist and genealogist, was born at Bolton-le-Sands, Lancashire, the son of Edmund Lodge, a farmer. He was educated at Clapham School, Yorkshire, under Mr Ashe, and entered St John's College, Cambridge, on 26 June 1716, graduating BA in 1719 and MA in 1720. He settled in Dublin, where he issued his printed prospectus for his *Irish Peerage* in 1742. In 1744 he published *Report of the Trial in Ejectment of Campbell Craig*, from notes in his own shorthand, which continued to be a feature in his manuscripts. In 1751, then living in Abbey Street, Dublin, he was appointed deputy keeper of the records in Bermingham Tower; in 1759 he became deputy clerk and keeper of the rolls, and was subsequently deputy registrar of the court of prerogative. He married, first, Miss Hamilton, who claimed kinship with the Abercorn family; and, secondly, Edwarda Galland.

Lodge's chief work, *The Peerage of Ireland* (4 vols., 1754), is a monument of industry, accuracy, and learning. Although now superseded in practical use by the second edition of Cokayne's *Complete Peerage*, it remains a mine of detailed information about the families connected with the peerage that is not otherwise available. When Mervyn Archdall was preparing his revised edition (published 1789) from Lodge's annotated copy of the *Peerage*, he found the experts completely baffled in their attempts to read the cipher Lodge had used for his notes, and was about to give up the task in despair when his wife discovered the key.

In 1770 Lodge published anonymously *The Usage of Holding Parliaments in Ireland*, and in 1772, also without his name, a selection of state papers and historical tracts illustrating the government of Ireland during the reigns of Elizabeth I, James I, and Charles I, which he called *Desiderata curiosa Hibernica*.

Lodge died at Bath on 22 February 1774. Of his nine children, only one survived him: his son, the Revd William Lodge LLD (1742–1813), who became in 1790 chancellor of Armagh Cathedral. Since 1785 he had been the first librarian of the public library of Armagh, newly established by his munificent patron, Primate Richard Robinson, the creator of Georgian Armagh. Through him, some of John Lodge's books, with marginal notes and corrections, came into the library, but Lodge himself had earlier presented the primate with several important collections dealing with Armagh. In 1865 the librarian William Reeves, who later became bishop of Down and Connor, purchased Lodge's manuscripts from his grandson, William Robinson Lodge, rector of Killybegs. These included not only some of his grandfather's collections, but also the manuscripts he had inherited from Michael Ignatius Dugan (*d.* 1768), a Dublin broker, among them manuscripts of Sir James Ware, Bishop Anthony Dopping, and Walter Harris, which thus greatly enriched the public library.

Lodge's importance now lies principally in the abstracts and indices he made from the records in his care, which serve in some measure to replace the loss of the records in the destruction of the Public Record Office in Dublin in 1922. The most used of these collections, now in the National Archives of Ireland, were purchased by the government from Lodge's heirs in 1783, in return for annuities of £100 to his widow and £200 to his son, and a detailed catalogue was printed in *The Fifty-Fifth Report of the Deputy Keeper of the Public Records … in Ireland* in 1928. Other significant parts of his collections will be found in the National Library of Ireland, the British Library, and the College of Arms.

GORDON GOODWIN, *rev.* WILLIAM O'SULLIVAN

Sources W. Reeves, 'Memoir of the Rev. William Lodge LLD', *Ulster Journal of Archaeology*, new ser., 1 (1894–5), 87–90 · *Report of the Deputy Keeper of the Public Records in Ireland*, 55 (1928), 116–22 · J. Dean, ed., *Catalogue of manuscripts in the public library of Armagh, 1928* [1928] · P. B. Phair, ed., 'Sir William Betham's manuscripts', *Analecta Hibernica*, 27 (1972), 1–99, esp. 40–45, 49, 50, 84 · R. J. Hayes, ed., *Manuscript sources for the history of Irish civilisation*, 11 vols. (1965) · Venn, *Alum. Cant.* · *N&Q*, 2nd ser., 3 (1857), 168 · A. J. Webb, *A compendium of Irish biography* (1878), 292–3 · M. Archdall, preface, in J. Lodge, *The peerage of Ireland*, rev. M. Archdall, rev. edn, 7 vols. (1789)

Archives Armagh Public Library · BL, Add. MSS 23693–23702, 23709–23710; Egerton MSS 1783–1786 · Coll. Arms · NA Ire. · NL Ire. | BL, corresp. with Lord Egmont, Add. MSS 47007–47014

Likenesses portrait, probably priv. coll.

Lodge, Sir Oliver Joseph (1851–1940), physicist, was born at The Views, Penkhull, Staffordshire, on 12 June 1851, the eldest of the eight sons and one daughter of Oliver Lodge (1826–1884), a railway clerk and later a merchant, and his wife, Grace Heath (1826–1879). Two of his brothers, including Sir Richard *Lodge (1855–1936), and his sister, Eleanor Constance *Lodge (1869–1936), also had distinguished academic careers. The family was of professional middle-class origin but the father, one of a family of twenty-five children, had to make his own way and eventually supplied materials for pottery manufacture. After attending a local dame-school Lodge studied under somewhat Dickensian conditions at Newport grammar school, Shropshire, where he boarded from 1859 to 1863, and then for two years with his uncle at Combs, Suffolk. He worked in his father's business until 1874, but an early interest in science was stimulated by an aunt and by lectures by Professor Tyndall at the Royal Institution in the winter of 1866–7. In 1872 he passed the entrance examinations for the London University external degree, and in the following winter studied at the Royal College of Science, under Huxley, Frankland, and Guthrie. His deep interest in science was confirmed when he heard James Clerk Maxwell speak at the British Association meeting at Bradford in 1873; Lodge immediately bought Maxwell's revolutionary *Treatise on Electricity and Magnetism* (which he first read at Heidelberg three years later). He made a point of attending almost every subsequent British Association meeting for the next sixty-three years, and himself soon became one of its star attractions.

Early experiments in physics In January 1874 Lodge enrolled as a full-time student at University College, London, obtaining the BSc degree in the following year. He was made demonstrator to Professor Carey Foster, and devised a teaching model of Maxwell's dielectric medium which he presented to the British Association meeting at Glasgow in 1876, receiving encouragement from Maxwell himself. In June 1877 he was awarded the degree of DSc, and two months later, on 22 August, married Mary Fanny Alexander Marshall (1851–1929) of Newcastle under Lyme, who had trained as an artist at the Slade School. The marriage was a happy one and lasted until Mary's death; they had six sons and six daughters. In 1878 Lodge made a significant friendship with the respected Dublin physicist G. F. FitzGerald, who quickly became his scientific mentor. With FitzGerald and the reclusive engineer Oliver Heaviside, Lodge became one of the three main promoters of Maxwell's then little-regarded theory of the electromagnetic field. Lodge's late start meant that he was always a little diffident about his abilities at mathematical physics, although he did attain competence in that field. His insights relied more upon qualitative thinking, but he had strong physical imagination and made many brilliant speculations. Thus, at the British Association in August 1879, he went beyond Maxwell by predicting that waves could be directly generated from electromagnetic fields, and, in February 1880, proposed (in a notebook) to discover them by discharging a Leyden jar. FitzGerald doubted this at first, and Lodge for a time dropped the idea, but after a re-examination of the problem in 1882, FitzGerald conceded the possibility, stressing that the wavelengths would be considerably longer than those of light.

Sir Oliver Joseph Lodge (1851–1940), by Sir George Reid, *c.*1907

In June 1881 Lodge was elected professor of physics at the new University College, Liverpool, ahead of fifteen other candidates, and immediately went on a scientific tour of Europe, where he met such great physicists as Helmholtz and Hertz. A lifelong interest appeared early when he lectured on the ether at the London Institution (1882). Some of his activity at Liverpool included consultancy work of a routine practical nature, but in 1883 he discovered the electrostatic condensation of fog. This observation eventually led to the development of the commercial electrostatic precipitator. Among early contributions to experimental and theoretical physics were his recognition of the significance of the local conservation of energy in Poynting's work on the electromagnetic field (1885), his method for making the migration of ions visible and for measuring their velocities by using decolorization of an alkali indicator (1886), and his production of an electrostatic field from the motion of gold leaf in a varying magnetic field (1889).

Already Lodge was beginning to make a name for himself as a public lecturer, particularly for a brilliant presentation, 'Dust', at Montreal in 1884. He was elected FRS on 9 June 1887 and was selected to give the Mann lectures on lightning conductors at the Royal Society of Arts in March the next year. During last-minute preparation for these lectures he made his first significant discovery when he used the discharge from a Leyden jar to produce electromagnetic waves guided along wires. His lecture, making the first explicit statement in the literature that electromagnetic waves had been discovered (specifically radiowaves of 30 yards length), was published on 22 June. Another paper, on lightning conductors, was sent to the *Philosophical Magazine* in July; a footnote stated that Hertz had now found electromagnetic waves in free space. On his return from another continental tour, Lodge attended the British Association meeting in Bath, where FitzGerald promoted Hertz's work and his own was somewhat overshadowed, although Heaviside and others recognized that it was at least as significant in confirming Maxwell's theory. Lodge, however, quickly realized the practical significance of free space waves, and immediately adopted Hertz's methods, developing his spark gap oscillator into an improved transmitter which generated waves of constant frequency. At the same time he became involved in an acrimonious but publicly entertaining debate on lightning conductors and the nature of the lightning discharge with the Post Office engineer William Preece, who was a 'practical' opponent of Heaviside's theoretical work on self-inductance. Lodge, who had made significant improvements in the design of lightning conductors and lightning guards, stressed the need to consider self-inductance in an oscillatory discharge, and implied that much of Preece's official work was vitiated by his ignorance of this fact. These issues had immense consequences for the future of electromagnetic theory.

Lodge's work on lightning guards led to several important discoveries, which he demonstrated in spectacular lectures at the Royal Institution and the Institution of Electrical Engineers in 1889. These included the action of syntonic (or resonant) Leyden jars, 'tuned' to the same frequency, and the 'coherer' action between metal spheres. He experimented on the concentration of electromagnetic waves using pitch lenses, and calculated the power output of a Hertzian oscillator. His interests, however, were moving away from electromagnetic waves, towards the ether. The famous Michelson–Morley experiment (1887) had given a null result for the effect of the earth's velocity, or ether drift, on that of light, and in March 1889 FitzGerald had produced a length contraction hypothesis to explain this while sitting in the study of Lodge's own house. Lodge now devised a new experiment with rotating discs to investigate the alternative hypothesis that a moving body could drag the ether along with it. This difficult, expensive, and rather dangerous experiment was paid for by the shipping owner George Holt. Lodge's theoretical analysis included the first statement of the Sagnac effect, and was original, also, in defining the ether as an absolute frame of reference. Again it gave a negative result, and is now considered as one of the foundation experiments for Einstein's special theory of relativity. Lodge announced preliminary results in his presidential address to section A of the British Association at Cardiff in August 1891, while discussing the need for a national physical laboratory and the importance of psychic research; he also alluded to the fourth dimension, with an early model of a 'world-line'.

Radio waves and telegraphy Lodge's interest in radio waves returned after he was selected to give a memorial lecture on Hertz, who had died in January 1894. He developed two new versions of the coherer as a radio-wave receiver. One, based on earlier work by Edouard Branly, was essentially a tube of metal filings; the other used a steel spring making a loose contact with an aluminium plate. Lodge recognized that coherer action was due to electrical breakdown and changes in the oxide layer on the metal. He experimented with radio signalling at University College and at his home in Grove Park. He also made pioneering searches for the effects of an upper conducting layer in the atmosphere (the ionosphere), and for radio waves from the sun, and experimented with the effect of high-frequency radio waves on animal tissues. That summer he gave presentations of his results at the Royal Institution (1 June), Royal Society (12 June), and British Association at Oxford (14 August), which were published in several journals and as a book, *The Work of Hertz and some of his Successors*; this became the immediate stimulus to the work of many others, including Bose, Jackson, Righi, and Marconi. Using telegraphic equipment (Morse key, Morse inker, marine galvanometer), and with the co-operation of a telegraphic engineer, Alexander Muirhead, Lodge gave the first public demonstration of what is now called radio-telegraphy, using the method of signalling in Morse code via long and short pulses. Although Muirhead and Lord Rayleigh, among others, tried to persuade him to take up the method commercially, Lodge went instead on a continental tour and became preoccupied with psychical research.

In September 1896 the British Association meeting was held in Liverpool, and Lodge demonstrated his apparatus there. Preece, however, announced that the Post Office had been involved with experiments with Marconi on a non-Hertzian method of telegraphy. Although this turned out to be a Hertzian method based on Lodge's coherer, and Preece, on at least two occasions, promised to acknowledge Lodge's contribution, no such acknowledgement was ever made. In May 1897 Lodge patented his system, which included his innovations of syntony or tuning to a specific frequency, the biconical antenna, and transformer coupling, but, unlike Marconi, he was never wholly convinced of its utility. He spent considerable time investigating an alternative inductive or 'magnetic' system of telegraphy, which had been pioneered by Preece. The magnetic system failed in practical terms, but one positive result was a patent for a moving coil loudspeaker (1898).

X-rays and atoms This was a particularly exciting time in the development of physics and Lodge was quick to follow up the major discoveries then being made. Early in 1896 he lectured on X-rays to massive audiences in Liverpool, and made a pioneering medical application by locating a bullet in a boy's hand. He had long before suggested the generation of electromagnetic waves from vacuum tubes and he now speculated on X-ray diffraction and on the sun as an X-ray source. He developed new types of tube and film which greatly reduced exposure times. One of the most brilliant synthesizers of his generation, he was also significant in relating the Larmor–Lorentz theoretical concept of the electron to Thomson's newly discovered physical corpuscle. As early as March 1897 he had calculated its approximate size, or classical radius. He found that the Zeeman effect involved splitting of spectral lines as well as broadening, and he was early in stating that atoms are mostly empty space, and could be represented by planetary models (1902). He gave immediate support to the Rutherford–Soddy theory of radioactive transmutation when many people opposed it, associated radioactivity with the source of the sun's energy (1903), and discussed the fusion of elements in the formation of stars in nebulae as a reverse radioactive process (1908). Later he was involved in the naming of the proton (1920), and speculated that the particle might be composite (1922). His last purely scientific book, *Atoms and Rays* (1924), was an outstanding popular exposition of the Bohr theory.

Lodge was awarded the Rumford medal of the Royal Society in 1898, and became president of the Physical Society in 1899, a year in which he narrowly survived a bout of typhoid fever. A major career change occurred in 1900 when, at the invitation of Joseph Chamberlain, he left Liverpool to become principal of the new University of Birmingham, where he remained until his retirement in February 1919. There he laid the foundations for an institution of international stature. He was created knight bachelor in the coronation honours of June 1902. His other awards included the Albert medal of the Royal Society of Arts (1919) and the Faraday medal of the Institution of Electrical Engineers (1932), and he was president of the British Association at Birmingham in 1913.

Radio Although he had less time for research at Birmingham, it was there that Lodge at last took up the commercial exploitation of radio. The Lodge–Muirhead Syndicate was formed in 1901, and a new receiver, the wheel coherer, patented in 1902. The syndicate won a major contract with the Indian government in 1904, to link Burma and the Andaman Islands, but was never able to break the Marconi Company's commercial stranglehold. In 1911, however, Lodge's patent was extended in the law courts. This led to a settlement with Marconi, Preece acting as 'honest broker' in the transaction. The syndicate was wound up; Lodge was paid an undisclosed sum for his patents, and became a nominal consultant to Marconi. Much later, in 1943, the United States supreme court ruled that Lodge's original patent was the only valid one from the time held by the company. Though he subsequently avoided commercial involvement with radio, Lodge maintained his interest in the subject, and wrote many popular articles. He became president of the Radio Society of Great Britain and a well-known broadcaster, and in his *Talks about Wireless* (1925), made the prescient suggestion that cryogenics would improve signal-to-noise ratios. At the same time, Lodge was also involved in other technical innovations, and their commercial exploitation, mainly for the benefit of his sons. He patented an igniter for motor cars with his son Alec in 1903; this led to the creation, by Alec and his brother Brodie, of the firm of Lodge Brothers, which manufactured the well-known Lodge spark plug. A significant Lodge invention was the diode rectifier bridge circuit (1903); two years later, Lodge patented his own valve rectifier. The Agricultural Electrical Discharge Company Ltd was founded in 1909 to exploit the effect of electrical currents on plant growth, and the Lodge Fume Deposit Company Ltd, in 1913, to manufacture electrostatic precipitators.

Lodge's physics, however, with its basis in the nineteenth-century ether concept, was now being increasingly perceived as old-fashioned, despite the fact that his remarkably abstract medium had, to a certain extent, anticipated the virtual particle concept and the quantum mechanical vacuum, and even the fundamental importance of the Planck length. He believed that the ether was a source of energy even greater than that of radioactivity and speculated on its use for rocket propulsion, and was convinced that he would be vindicated by the new quantum mechanics. Although he made the first public proposal of gravitational lenses (1919), he became well known also as an opponent of the idea of relativity, and his standing among contemporary physicists was accordingly reduced. In a lecture of February 1921 he stated the gravitational refractive index formula, proposed collapsed-matter stars, and explored the full range of black holes of interest to later physicists, but these ideas gained little attention at the time. Whatever its intrinsic merits as a scientific concept, Lodge's ether became discredited, partly through its application in his later books to psychical matters and to the spiritualism with which this had become increasingly associated.

Psychical research Like many eminent men of his time, Lodge believed that spiritualism should be investigated. His lifelong interest began early, in Liverpool in 1882–3, with experiments on thought transference which involved very detailed studies of famous mediums. He pioneered the use of cards with simple designs and using the 'double blind' control method. Early in 1901 he was shaken by the death not only of his closest scientific friend, FitzGerald, but also that of his psychic mentor, Frederick Myers. He took over Myers's responsibilities, however, as president of the Society for Psychical Research. His work throughout all the intervening years attained a deeper personal importance when his youngest son, Raymond, was killed in Flanders in 1915. Lodge's belief that he had had precognition of the event, and that his son had communicated with him through mediums, was the subject of the enormously popular book *Raymond* (1916), which gave comfort to many who had suffered bereavement during the First World War. However, when Lodge arranged for his last psychic experiment to be carried out posthumously, in 1954, a panel of experts failed to identify the message he had left in a series of sealed envelopes.

In his later years Lodge wrote his autobiography, *Past Years* (1931), and his summary, *My Philosophy* (1933). He discussed the ether when he met Einstein at Oxford in June 1933 and affirmed his belief when filmed for the Institution of Electrical Engineers in December 1934. He made his last visit to the British Association at Blackpool in 1936, but carried on writing a textbook, 'Physics for everyman', which he abandoned only in 1938. Lodge was an imposing figure at 6ft 4in. in height, with a fine voice and a commanding presence. He was a popular broadcaster in the early days of the BBC and, throughout his life, gave many public lectures. He was a gifted communicator, a writer of lucid prose, and author of more than 1100 books and articles. In his time, but especially after the First World War, he was the recognized voice of scientific authority among the general public. He was selected to represent the figure of Education on the Victoria monument in Liverpool. He enjoyed golf, tennis, and other active leisure pursuits, and claimed that he had never spent an idle hour in his life. He served as president of at least ten organizations. A man of fine personal character, he was notable in promoting the interests of his assistants and giving them due credit for their part in his researches. He was a Fabian sympathizer and gave his support to worthy public causes, such as women's suffrage and universal education, often speaking publicly on political issues as well as on popular religion. He deserves, however, to be remembered most for his brilliant physical intuitions, and for his innovating contributions in the physics and technology of electromagnetic waves, radio telegraphy, and the ether. He died at his home, Normanton House, Lake, near Salisbury, on 22 August 1940, and was buried at St Michael's Church, Wilsford. PETER ROWLANDS

Sources P. Rowlands and J. P. Wilson, eds., *Oliver Lodge and the invention of radio* (1994) • O. Lodge, *Past years: an autobiography* (1931) • T. Besterman, *A bibliography of Sir Oliver Lodge* (1935) • P. Rowlands, *Oliver Lodge and the Liverpool Physical Society* (1990) • W. P. Jolly, *Sir Oliver Lodge* (1974) • H. G. J. Ailken, *Syntony and spark: the origins of radio* (1976) • G. R. M. Garratt, *The early history of radio from Faraday to Marconi* (1994) • B. J. Hunt, *The Maxwellians* (1991) • private information (2004) [Lodge family] • b. cert. • m. cert. • d. cert. • gravestones, Perkhull churchyard

Archives Incorporated Society for Psychical Research, correspondence relating to psychical research • Inst. EE, correspondence and MSS • Sci. Mus., laboratory notebook • U. Birm. L., correspondence and MSS • U. Lpool L., scientific notebooks, MSS and letters • UCL, correspondence, MS Add. 89 | BL, letters to Macmillan & Co, Add. MS 55220 • BL, correspondence mainly with the Society of Authors, Add. MS 56739 • Bodl. Oxf., correspondence with Gilbert Murray • CUL, correspondence with Lord Kelvin, MS Add. 7342 • CUL, letters to Sir J. J. Thomson, MS Add. 7654 • CUL, letters to Lord Rutherford, MS Add. 7653 • ICL, letters to H. E. Armstrong • ICL, letters to S. P. Thompson • NL Wales, letters to Benjamin Davies and MS of unpublished book • Nuffield Oxf., correspondence with Viscount Cherwell • priv. coll., letters to Lord Rayleigh • priv. coll., correspondence with the earl of Balfour • U. Birm. L., letters to E. W. W. Carlier | FILM Inst. EE | SOUND priv. coll.

Likenesses G. Reid, oils, 1903, U. Birm. • G. Reid, oils, *c.*1907, NPG [*see illus.*] • W. Rothenstein, chalk, 1916, NPG • W. Stoneman, photograph, before 1917, NPG • E. Kapp, drawings, 1919–31, Barber Institute of Fine Arts, Birmingham • photograph, *c.*1927 (with John Logie Baird), NPG • M. Beerbohm, watercolour caricature, 1932, NPG; repro. in Jolly, *Sir Oliver Lodge* • C. J. Allen, marble bust, U. Lpool • Barraud, cabinet, NPG • H. Coster, photographs, NPG • O. Edis, photographs, NPG • D. Low, cartoon, repro. in Jolly, *Sir Oliver Lodge* • J. B. Munns, oils, Birmingham Art Gallery • B. Partridge, chalk caricature, NPG • A. P. F. Ritchie, print, NPG • J. Russell & Sons, photograph, NPG • Spy [L. Ward], chromolithograph caricature, NPG; repro. in *VF* (4 Feb 1904) • Thomson, oils, Royal Institution of Great Britain, London • crayon, U. Lpool • oils, Inst. EE

Wealth at death £27,899 14*s.* 5*d.*: probate, 7 Dec 1940, *CGPLA Eng. & Wales*

Lodge, Sir Richard (1855–1936), historian, was born on 20 June 1855 at Penkhull, Staffordshire, the fourth of the nine children born to Oliver Lodge (1826–1884), merchant, and his wife, Grace Heath (1826–1879). There was ability in the family; two of Lodge's siblings, Oliver *Lodge (1851–1940) and Eleanor *Lodge (1869–1936), also achieved academic eminence. After going from nine years at Christ's Hospital to Balliol College, Oxford, in 1874 as an exhibitioner, Lodge's scholarly abilities were rapidly declared in a succession of distinctions: a Brackenbury scholarship and the Stanhope essay prize in 1875, the Lothian essay prize in 1876, a first-class degree in modern history in 1877, and election to a fellowship of Brasenose College in 1878. Through the sixteen years that followed, Lodge made his mark as one of the group of young-ish college fellows, including A. L. Smith, A. H. Johnson, and C. R. L. Fletcher, whose tutorial zeal and scholarly professionalism were building firm foundations for Oxford's celebrated school of modern history. In 1885 he published *The Student's Modern Europe*, the first of the several textbooks that, in successive editions, were to spread his name far and wide. On 27 June 1882 he married Annie Gwendoline, daughter of Henry Morgan of Norwich.

Early in the 1890s, Lodge, like many other ambitious younger Oxford dons, sought one of the professorships of history that were beginning to become available elsewhere: in 1894 he was appointed to the chair of modern history newly established at Glasgow. When Glasgow's climate proved bad for his health, he applied for the equivalent chair at Edinburgh on its vacation by G. W. Prothero, and succeeded to it in 1899. At Edinburgh (which he would have preferred in the first place) he happily remained until his retirement in 1925.

By the time he left Edinburgh, Lodge had become one of the best-known names in the British historical profession; a status recognized in such distinctions as honorary degrees from the universities of Glasgow (1905), Manchester (1912), and Edinburgh (1926), and a knighthood in 1917. It was his generation of historians that first made British and European history a serious, respectable, and accessible subject of study at secondary and higher levels of education; and not the least of these men's services was to provide textbooks good enough to sustain it. The books they wrote, such as the volumes of the *Cambridge Modern History* to which Lodge contributed, came in course of time to seem overweighted on the political, institutional, and foreign relations sides; but being powerfully instructive and readily readable, they continued to perform yeoman service until the 1930s. Lodge wrote three of them. His *Modern Europe* went through many editions between 1885 and 1927, the last one co-authored with his most distinguished pupil and lieutenant at Edinburgh, D. B. Horn. His *Close of the Middle Ages* appeared in Rivington's series

Sir Richard Lodge (1855–1936), by Sir William Nicholson, 1925

Periods of European History in 1901; his *English Political History, 1660–1702* in Longman's Political History of England series was published in 1909. Beside these, his more research-based publications—learned articles and book reviews, and in 1923 the book of his Ford lectures, *Great Britain and Prussia in the Eighteenth Century*—may not have been his most important services to history.

Lodge and Scotland got on very well together. He climbed mountains and played golf. His Glasgow inaugural shows him well aware of the distinctive features of the society and culture into which he was moving, and ready to respect all the good in it—including, on its academic side, its approaching admission of women, on whose behalf he had consistently laboured at Oxford. One of the Glasgow heavyweights, the professor of humanity, George Ramsay, wrote on his behalf when he applied for the Edinburgh chair, 'He came to Glasgow with the resolve to enter into Scotch University life as heartily as before that he did into the Oxford life, and he has done so'. Other testimonials said he was 'active without being fussy', firm without being contentious, and possessing 'administrative ability, tact and common-sense' (*Application and Testimonials*). Above all he excelled in the art of lecturing, which mattered much more in Scotland than it did in England. His impressive presence no doubt was a help: he was over 6 feet tall, strong-looking, with piercing blue eyes, a rather ferocious Kitchener–Kipling moustache, and a good voice. But beyond that he won praise all through his life for the fine structure of his lectures, for his ability to convey quantities of information in measured and palatable style, and for the lively humanity which animated them. Students always respected and usually liked what they saw and heard of him.

The administrative ability that already showed at Glasgow blossomed to such an extent at Edinburgh that he soon became one of the weightiest figures in the university's governing assemblies. As dean of the faculty of arts from 1911 to 1924, in years when professors and *a fortiori* deans normally enjoyed powers much larger than today, he exercised near-regal authority, which inevitably excited resentment as well as respect. Whether his not being made principal in 1916 was in part due to his being thought too happy in the exercise of authority, or because he was, after all, not a Scot, remains debatable. In any case his daughter did not exaggerate when she said he became, in Edinburgh, 'a kind of institution'. She did not mean in the university alone: Lodge's principles regarding civic virtue and public service led him into the succession of good works and voluntary activities which formed part of the justification for his knighthood. Before the war he was, for example, one of the Industrial Council's team of arbitrators in industrial disputes, and the first chairman of the Edinburgh distress committee set up under the 1905 Unemployed Workmen's Act; from the first days of war until 1921 he was prominent in the administration of the prince of Wales's relief fund for the unemployed. The colour of his politics showed in his active support of the Navy League, the National Service League, and the Liberal League, the Rosebery-ite right-wing of the Liberal Party. It was not only the University of Edinburgh that felt the loss when he went back south in 1925.

Busy and productive for as long as his health permitted, Lodge finally settled in Harpenden, Hertfordshire. The years of his retirement saw him resume historical research, the fattest fruits of which were his *Studies in Eighteenth Century Diplomacy* (1930) and his edition of the copious *Correspondence of Sir Benjamin Keene* (1933). He continued through the Historical Association his lifelong support of the teaching of history in schools, helped to establish the Institute of Historical Research, and to manage the Royal Historical Society. He died after an operation in London at his home in Lane End, Harpenden, on 2 August 1936, mourned by his wife and his surviving children (one son and three daughters). A daughter and two sons had predeceased him. GEOFFREY BEST

Sources *DNB* · M. Lodge, *Sir Richard Lodge* (1946) · E. C. Lodge, *Terms and vacations*, ed. J. Spens (1938) · D. B. Horn, 'Sir Richard Lodge and historical studies at the University of Edinburgh, 1899–1925', *SHR*, 27 (1948), 77–85 · *Application and testimonials of Richard Lodge … candidate for the professorship of history in the University of Edinburgh* (privately printed, Oxford, 1894) · R. Lodge, 'History in Scottish universities: reminiscences of a professor', *University of Edinburgh Journal*, 4 (1930–31), 97–109 · m. cert. · *CGPLA Eng. & Wales* (1936)

Archives U. Edin. L., corresp., lecture notes, and papers

Likenesses W. Nicholson, oils, 1925, U. Edin. [*see illus.*] · W. Nicholson, oils, replica, 1925, U. Edin. · A. S. Watson, photograph, NPG

Wealth at death £17,930 6*s*. 3*d*.: probate, 30 Nov 1936, *CGPLA Eng. & Wales*

Lodge, Sir Thomas (1509/10–1585), merchant, the son of William Littleton, also known as Lodge, and his wife, Joan Burleton, was born at Cound in Shropshire; his father's use of the name Lodge was attributed to his living at Le Lodge, Cresset (Cressage?), in Shropshire, and to his claimed descent from Odard de Logis, Baron Wigton, of Cumberland, in the reign of Henry I. He was apprenticed in London to William Pratt, in the Grocers' Company, in 1528.

Lodge engaged in foreign trade in Antwerp and was an

enthusiastic supporter of schemes for opening new markets in distant countries. He was a member of the Grocers' Company, and served as warden in 1548 and as master in 1554–5 and again in 1559–60. In 1561 he was president of St Thomas's Hospital. He played a role in the government of the city of London, being sworn in as alderman of Cheap ward in 1553 and being chosen as sheriff in 1559. He was one of those who signed a document accepting Lady Jane Grey as queen in 1553.

Lodge married first Madwlyn (Magdalene) Vaughan (*d.* 1548), sister of Stephen *Vaughan, merchant. It was a brief marriage: begun about 1544, it ended with her death on 26 July 1548. In 1549 Lodge married Margaret Parker, who had 'well and truly served the said Sir Thomas Lodge in his house in the state of a mayden servant' (PRO, close rolls C54/463). She died on 26 April 1552, leaving him with daughters Sarah (*bap.* 1549) and Susan (*bap.* 1551), both of whom survived to a marriageable age.

Lodge was elected lord mayor in 1562, and became the first mayor to ignore the ancient custom of being clean-shaven. It was to be an eventful year for him; on 8 March 1563 he was knighted, and in April a son was baptized. The latter was one of five sons (among them the dramatist Thomas *Lodge (1558–1625)) and a daughter born of his marriage in 1552 to Anne Lane, *née* Loddington (1528–1579), the step-daughter of Sir William Laxton, a member of the Grocers' Company and a former lord mayor. However, the same year he had to contend with the effects of an outbreak of plague, and he also fell foul of Edward Skeggs, purveyor to the queen, who seized twelve capons provided for the lord mayor's table. Lodge compelled him to return six and threatened to lock him up in Newgate, which led both men to much public posturing and complaints to their patrons. Lodge was chastised and fined, but, because of the plague, not punished further.

The founding charter of the Merchants of Russia (the Russia Company) of 1555 names Lodge as among the first assistants to the governors, and by 1561 he was himself a governor. The Russia Company's interests were not limited to that region, and many members were keen to open trade with the Guinea coast of west Africa. Their first venture was in 1562; underwritten by Lodge, with Sir Lionell Duckett and others, three good ships sailed in October to Guinea to buy black Africans for shipment to the West Indies. 300 were sold there, and goods bought for sale in England when the ships landed in September 1563. This voyage is supposed to have inaugurated England's involvement in slave trading.

According to the antiquary Arthur Agarde (1540–1615), Lodge was responsible for bringing German metalworkers to England to refine the base coins which Queen Elizabeth had sent to the Tower. Lodge told Agarde that when these men fell sick (probably from inhaling the fumes of arsenic given off by the base metal) they found relief by drinking from human skulls, which Lodge obtained from those exhibited on London Bridge, under a warrant granted by the council.

Lodge seems to have been embroiled in later disputes; he was obliged to resign as alderman in 1566, and in 1576 was committed to Newgate for striking alderman John Braunche in the face. He suffered financial loss when one of his ships was seized by the French in a trade war, but the queen and the city tried later to help him. He died in February 1585 and was buried, with his first wife and her father, in St Mary Aldermary, in the vault of Henry Keble, 'whose bones were unkindly cast out, and his monument pulled down, in place whereof monuments are set up of the later buried' (Stow, 1.253). In his will, proved by his son-in-law Gamaliel Woodford, he describes himself as of West Ham, to whose poor he left £5, and he also possessed the manor of Malmeynes at Barking, Essex. He provided for a funeral sermon to be preached in the churches of St Peter, Cornhill, and St Mary Aldermary.

ANITA MCCONNELL

Sources *The diary of Henry Machyn, citizen and merchant-taylor of London, from AD 1550 to AD 1563*, ed. J. G. Nichols, CS, 42 (1848) · J. B. Heath, *Some account of the Worshipful Company of Grocers of the city of London*, 3rd edn (privately printed, London, 1869), 249–52 · A. B. Beaven, ed., *The aldermen of the City of London, temp. Henry III–[1912]*, 2 (1913), 172 · R. Thompson, *Chronicles of London Bridge* (1827), 586–8 · *CSP dom.*, *1547–80*, 105, 164, 183, 215 · R. Hakluyt, *The principal navigations, voyages, traffiques and discoveries of the English nation*, 3 vols. in 2 (1598–1600); repr. in Hakluyt Society, extra ser., 2 (1903), 307; Hakluyt Society, extra ser., 3 (1903), 14; Hakluyt Society, extra ser., 10 (1904), 7 · R. Tresswell and A. Vincent, *The visitation of Shropshire, taken in the year 1623*, ed. G. Grazebrook and J. P. Rylands, 2, Harleian Society, 29 (1889), 284 · 'Some account of Thomas Lodge', *GM*, 2nd ser., 2 (1834), 157 · J. Stow, *A survay of London*, rev. edn (1603); repr. with introduction by C. L. Kingsford as *A survey of London*, 2 vols. (1908); repr. with addns (1971) · 'Boyd's citizens of London', Society of Genealogists, London · C. J. Sisson, ed., *Thomas Lodge and other Elizabethans* (1933) · E. Cuvelier, *Thomas Lodge, témoin de son temps* (Paris, 1984) · will, PRO, PROB 11/68, sig. 29

Lodge, Thomas (1558–1625), author and physician, was born in London, the second surviving son and third of seven surviving children of Sir Thomas *Lodge (*d.* 1585), lord mayor of London, and his third wife, Anne (*née* Loddington; 1528–1579). The elder Thomas Lodge moved to London from Shropshire, was apprenticed to a grocer, and prospered. Anne was a stepdaughter of William *Laxton, a grocer and former mayor of London, and the widow of William Lane, also a grocer, who brought both money and land to the marriage. Like other men of his time and position, Sir Thomas invested in overseas trading ventures and real estate. In 1563, the final year of his mayoralty, Sir Thomas went bankrupt, a scandal Stow records. Both the land his wife brought to the marriage and the properties he purchased survived the bankruptcy, as attested by lawsuits that continued throughout the lives of his sons, many of which have been traced by Charles Sisson.

Education and early works Five years old at the time of his father's bankruptcy, Lodge spent some portion of his childhood in the household of Henry Stanley, earl of Derby, a circumstance Lodge acknowledges with gratitude in the dedication to *A Fig for Momus* (1595). The first definitive record of Lodge's education is his matriculation at the Merchant Taylors' School in 1571 as a 'poore scholar'. Three years later he went up to Trinity College, Oxford, where he received the BA in 1577. In the dedication to *Rosalynde* (1590), Lodge states that Edward Hoby was his tutor and names Edmund and Robert Carey, sons of the earl of Hunsdon, among his Oxford friends. In 1578 Lodge entered Lincoln's Inn. There is no evidence that he ever practised law, his perennial involvement in lawsuits notwithstanding. The provisions of his mother's will, drawn in 1579, suggest that Lodge's disinclination to the profession was evident early on: if he does not continue a good student at Lincoln's Inn, the will states, his portion is to be divided among his brothers. Evidence does suggest that Lodge continued a social and probably a residential relation to Lincoln's Inn for some years; *An Alarum Against Usurers* (1584) and *Scillaes Metamorphosis* (1589) both include dedications to the gentlemen of the inns of court and as late as *A Fig for Momus* (1595) the title-page advertises Lodge as 'of Lincolns Inne, Gentleman'.

Lodge first entered print in 1579. 'An Epitaph on Lady Anne Lodge' was entered on the Stationers' register in December by Edward White, who had married Lodge's half-sister, Sara Lodge. A reply to Stephen Gosson's *School of Abuse* (1579) survives in two copies, both lacking title-pages. Variously titled by others—*Honest Excuses*, *A Defense of Poetry*, *Reply to Gosson*—the importance of Lodge's pamphlet arises less from its intrinsic merits than from its position as the first defence of poetry in the long series of exchanges focused on drama and the theatre. Gosson replied to Lodge's pamphlet in *Plays Confuted* (1582) and Lodge to Gosson in the prefatory matter of *An Alarum Against Usurers* (1584). From these exchanges it appears that licence to publish Lodge's initial pamphlet was denied, and it was privately printed and circulated. One may read in the *Reply to Gosson* a sense of vocation when Lodge writes 'I affirme that poetry is a heavenly gift, then which I know not greater pleasure' (*Works*, 1.19).

Early Catholicism In 1581 Lodge's supplication for the MA at Oxford was initially accepted and then, later that year, denied. In the interim a Thomas Lodge, gentleman, was called before the privy council to answer 'certain matters' and a Thomas Lodge was imprisoned at the king's bench, according to the confession of an anti-Catholic informant. The coincidence between these records and the appearance of a Lodge (and a Loddington, potentially a cousin on Lady Lodge's side) on a list of recusants living in Paris in 1580, together with clear evidence of Lodge's Catholicism later in life, has led biographers to speculate that matters of faith underwrote the refusal of the MA, the privy council matter, and the imprisonment. It is also possible, as Charles Sisson argues, that the privy council interest in Lodge, if indeed he is the same Lodge, concerns his entry into the controversy about the stage. The stronger circumstantial argument, however, rests on the premise of Lodge's Catholicism, especially given that both Trinity College and Lincoln's Inn were sites resistant to the Reformation and hospitable to recusants. This circumstantial argument acquires greater force for biographers because it also helps to explain the omission of Thomas Lodge from his father's will in 1583.

Elaine Cuvelier's doctoral study of Lodge makes the strongest possible case for Lodge's early Catholicism and its determining impact on his life and writing. Arthur Kinney's discussion of Lodge's literary *œuvre* makes the contrasting case for a more general 'Christian humanism'. Lodge's Catholicism later in life is undisputed; after 1611 it also ceased to matter in significant practical ways, for 'Thomas Lodge, Dr. of Physike' was protected from prosecution for recusancy by order of the privy council. Assessment of the import of Lodge's Catholicism awaits both more extensive critical discussion of the work and a revisionist social history of the varieties of English Catholicism in the sixteenth and seventeenth centuries. The poets and writers among Lodge's contemporaries, whether of protestant or Catholic sympathy themselves, do not remark on Lodge's religion.

Sir Thomas Lodge died in 1585, the year after Thomas Lodge's *An Alarum Against Usurers* appeared. The exclusion of Lodge from his father's will may have been the obvious strategy of a man of Sir Thomas's diminished financial standing who had other children to consider, for Thomas had received land as well as money by his mother's will, albeit under the control of executors, or it may have been a silent expression of disapproval for his son's life, or both. In any case, Thomas Lodge never came into the lands his mother left him, having granted them to his brother William in 1583 for ready money and in acknowledgement of debts already paid on his behalf by William. Lawsuits involving Thomas Lodge reveal that he was repeatedly in need of ready money and of sufficient credit to get it, and that allegations of unpaid debt to various tradesmen pursued him for thirty years.

An Alarum Against Usurers offers an account of the practices by which a gentleman in need of ready money may be ruined and, in the event, forced into partnership with the usurer who ruined him. Although the correlation between Lodge's narrative and his life is obvious and tempting, the tone is reportorial rather than autobiographical even at those moments when the text approaches confession: 'truly gentlemen this that I write is true, I myselfe know the paymaster, naie more, I myselfe know certainly, that by name I can reckon among you some that have been bitten' (*Works*, 1.18). The volume in which *An Alarum Against Usurers* appeared also included a pastoral romance, 'The Delectable Historie of Forbonius and Prisceria', and a verse satire, 'Truth's Complaint over England'. The volume as a whole is dedicated to Philip Sidney and 'Forbonius and Prisceria' is obviously indebted to both Sidney's *Old Arcadia* and Lyly's *Euphues* in theme, style, and integration of verse into the narrative. Although most critics have treated the volume as a miscellany, Arthur Kinney argues that it forms a deliberate triadic structure, the circumstantial fiction of *Alarum* contrasted by the marvellous in 'Forbonius' and the contrast itself enclosed by the experientially focused satire of 'Truth's Complaint', written in the tradition of Chaucer, Skelton, Wyatt, and Gascoigne.

Between 1584 and 1589 Lodge wrote two plays, one in collaboration with Robert Greene, and made a sea voyage. In the dedication to *Rosalynde* Lodge refers to a voyage made 'with Captain Clarke … to the islands of Terceres and the Canaries'. Scholars have offered various possible voyages: a sailing in 1586 of the *Gold Noble*; a voyage in 1585 on the *Roebuck*; and a voyage in 1590 on the *Galleon Dudley*. Of these, the voyages made in 1585 or 1586 are most likely, but neither consensus nor any other evidence of Lodge's presence on any of the voyages has emerged. Lodge's play, *The Wounds of Civil War*, was, according to its title-page, performed by the Lord Admiral's Men. Both *Wounds* and the play Lodge wrote with Greene, *A Looking Glass for London and England*, were printed in 1594. *A Looking Glass* was first performed by either the Queen's Men or Lord Strange's Men; according to Henslowe's diary, it was revived by Lord Strange's Men and performed at the Rose in 1591 and 1592. Ferdinando Stanley, Lord Strange, was the son of Henry Stanley, the earl of Derby with whom Lodge spent some of his childhood. Charles Howard, the lord admiral, was uncle to Edward and Robert Carey, Lodge's Oxford friends.

Wounds tells the story of the Roman civil wars between Marius and Sulla. Drawn from the accounts of Appian and Plutarch, it is the earliest surviving example of a Roman history play from the Elizabethan repertory. Scholars have debated the question of Lodge's indebtedness to Marlowe or Marlowe's indebtedness to Lodge. Given the stiffness of the verse in *Wounds*, and the clumsiness of the plot, the current critical consensus is that Lodge's play predates *Tamberlaine* and *Edward II*, owing debts to *Gorboduc* by Thomas Norton and Thomas Sackville and to Gascoigne's plays, rather than to Marlowe's. *Looking Glass* seems to have been a greater success. Not only was it revived on stage, but the quarto was reprinted five times between 1594 and 1617. The plot is drawn from the biblical story of Ninevah and Jonah, but London is the clear allegorical referent and the scenes of the sub-plot feature satirical representations of contemporary urban life. In *Palladis tamia* (1598) Francis Meres named Lodge among 'the best for comedy' but no other plays survive.

Poetry and narrative fictions Lodge's position in the canon of English literature rests on the works published after 1589, particularly on his poetry and his narrative fictions. A volume called *Scillaes Metamorphosis* (1589) contains a long verse narrative, *Historie of Glaucus and Scilla*, a 100-line poem, 'The Discontented Satyre', and fifteen 'sonnets' or short poems. *Glaucus and Scilla* is an early and noteworthy example of the Ovidian minor epic poetry that was to become fashionable in the 1590s. Written in the six-line stanzas Shakespeare later used in *Venus and Adonis*, the story of Glaucus's unrequited love for Scilla and Scilla's belated response is told by a melancholy narrator whose presence in the poem lends it an ironic and arguably comic effect. The remaining poems in the volume are a mix of Horatian satires and 'sundrie sweet sonnets' that draw on French and Italian contemporaries and show Lodge experimenting with the possibilities of form, metre, and style. The volume seems to have sold slowly and was reissued with a new title, *A Pleasant Historie of Glaucus and Scilla*, in 1610.

Rosalynde: Euphues Golden Legacie, the best-known of Lodge's narrative fictions, was first published in 1590 and, by the time Shakespeare used it for *As You Like It*, had gone through four editions. Circumstantial evidence from the dedication to Lord Hunsdon suggests that it may have been written several years before and scholars have speculated that Robert Greene may have seen it through the press while Lodge was at sea. In any case, the pastoral romance with lyrics integrated into the narrative brings the formal work begun by 'Forbonius and Prisceria' to its full development. Arthur Kinney argues that the contrast achieved by the juxtaposition of the tract against usury and the romance of 'Forbonius' in the *Alarum* volume is fully integrated in the narrative of *Rosalynde* through its contrast between the cynical courtly world of Bordeaux and the pastoral forest of Arden. Lodge drew *Rosalynde*'s initial situation of the conflict between brothers upon their father's death and the wrestling match that eventually results in the exile of the second son from the fourteenth-century *Tale of Gamelyn*, but he developed the story away from bloody heroic revenge toward pastoral romance and euphuistic debate. The story is well-known from Shakespeare's use of it in *As You Like It*. Alan Brissenden provides an extensive discussion of that use in the Oxford edition of the play. Donald Beecher's introduction to the annotated text published by the Barnabe Riche Society discusses *Rosalynde*'s relation to contemporary texts in terms of genre, style, poetics, theme, and character. Of all Lodge's works, *Rosalynde* has attracted the most extensive critical attention, most of it focused through the lens of Shakespeare's play or through synthetic surveys of Elizabethan prose fiction. This critical attention shows how woven Lodge's work is into the literary culture of its time and how much work remains to be done tracing its affiliations (see, for example, *Modern Philology*, 95, 1998, 291–315).

Between 1590 and 1596 Lodge published four more prose fictions: *The Famous, True and Historical Life of Robert, Second Duke of Normandy* (1591), *Euphues Shadow* (1592), *The Life and Death of William Longbeard* (1593), and *A Margarite of America* (1596). *Euphues Shadow* clearly imitates Lyly's two *Euphues* volumes, some twelve years after their completed publication. *Robert, Duke of Normandy* (also known as *Robin the Devil*), *William Longbeard*, and *Margarite of America* all develop a sensational and often violent vision out of romance conventions, tempered, if at all, by an improbable spirituality or the presence of a hermit figure somewhat removed from violence. In *Robert, Duke of Normandy*, the title character spends his youth hurting, raping, and killing those he meets only to undergo a penitential conversion after receiving a mortal wound and being healed by a hermit. In *William Longbeard* William's vicious career ends with his hanging, and in *Margarite* the protagonist kills ten people, including himself. With the exception of *Margarite*, these fictions, if not dismissed altogether, have received little critical attention. One school of criticism suggests that in these late fictions Lodge is turning toward realism, either a psychological realism or a historiographical verisimilitude, an approach that positions the fictions in relation to the later development of the novel. A second line of argument sees an increasing preoccupation with problems of spirituality inflected by Lodge's Catholicism.

In 1591 Lodge sailed from England in one of five ships under the command of Sir Thomas Cavendish who had successfully circumnavigated the globe three years earlier. Although all five ships reached Brazil and stayed there for two months, Cavendish's second voyage was a disaster. Many men, including Cavendish, and at least two of the ships, were lost and those men and ships that returned gained no wealth from the voyage. In the prefatory material to *A Margarite of America* Lodge claims to have drawn the story from a Spanish manuscript found in a Jesuit library in Brazil and to have written it while 'at sea with M. Cavendish (whose memorie if I repent not, I lament not)' (*Works*, 3.3). However plausible either claim, the prefatory material is signed 'from my house the 4 Maie 1596', three years after Lodge's return. Arguably Lodge's most interesting fiction, *A Margarite of America*, is set in the New World and tells the story of a diplomatic marriage intended to avert war between Mosco and Cusco. Margarite is a chaste, innocent princess blindly trusting her father's arrangements and her intended husband, the Cuscan prince, Arsachadus, an unregenerately Machiavellian figure well versed in impeccable courtly appearances. The Petrarchan and pastoral conventions of Lodge's earlier romances are integrated into a story of unrelenting depravity and violence that anticipates the world of Jacobean tragedies. Claudette Pollack has drawn attention to the text's indebtedness to Castiglione's *Book of the Courtier* and Machiavelli's *The Prince* and *Discourses* ('Lodge's *A Margarite of America*: An Elizabethan medley', *Renaissance and Reformation*, 12, 1976, 1–11); Josephine Roberts argues that *A Margarite* presents a dystopian vision of the New World, ('Lodge's *A Margarite of America*: a dystopian vision of the New World', *Studies in Short Fiction*, 17, 1980, 407–15); and Joan Pong Linton locates the text in relation to the 'romance of empire' explored by Spenser and Ralegh, arguing that Margarite is figured in ironic relation to Spenser's Una and Elizabeth I's investments in the politics and rhetoric of empire (*The Romance of the New World*, 1998, 39–61).

Between 1590 and 1596 Lodge also published four other prose works and two volumes of poetry. *Catharos* (1591), *The Devil Conjured* (1596), and *Wits Miserie, or, The Worlds Madness* (1596) are all moral-philosophical writings: *Catharos* a dialogue featuring Diogenes and two interlocutors, *The Devil Conjured* a dialogue in which a Christian hermit counsels three young men, and *Wits Miserie* a satirical treatment of the seven deadly sins. The fourth prose piece, *Prosopopeia … the Teares … of Marie* (1596) explicitly declares its Catholic sympathies, using the figure of Mary to meditate on the sins of the world. *Phillis* (1593) is a volume of short lyrics, mostly sonnets, some of which also appeared in the Elizabethan verse miscellanies *Phoenix Nest* (1593), *Englands Helicon* (1600), *Belvedere* (1600), and *Englands Parnassus* (1600). The verse miscellanies also contained poems from Lodge's prose romances and poems Lodge had not printed elsewhere. *A Fig for Momus* (1596), Lodge's last volume of poetry, is a collection of epistles, satires, and eclogues modelled on the Roman satirists, especially Horace and Juvenal. Lodge's inclusion in the verse miscellanies attests to contemporary recognition of his accomplishments as a poet. Like the early Ovidian poem, *Glaucus and Scilla*, the late satiric collection, *A Fig for Momus*, has greater literary historical significance because it is an innovative exemplar. The poems of *A Fig for Momus* develop the heroic couplet and anticipate the satires of the late 1590s. Although Lodge's satires were imitated by John Marston and Edward Guilpin, the compression of his line and the detached quality of his persona bring his poems closer to those of his Augustan successors than those of his contemporaries.

Medical practice and translation In 1597 Lodge left England for France where he received a medical degree from the University of Avignon in 1598. In 1602 his medical degree was recognized by Oxford, though his application for a licence from the College of Physicians was denied. Between 1598 and 1610 Lodge practised medicine, at times in London and at times in the Low Countries and France. At some point within a few years of receiving his medical degree Lodge married Joan Aldred, *née* Ferneley (*b.* 1546, *d.* in or after 1625), widow of Simon Aldred. Simon Aldred had been an agent for both the pope and Francis Walsingham, but Joan Aldred evidently remained a constant Catholic, serving in the household of the countess of Arundel after separating from her husband. Lodge's shifting between the continent and England during this period, together with his marriage to a known Catholic, leads biographers to assume that his intermittent exile and the denial of a licence to practise from the College of Physicians resulted from his Catholicism and possible participation in Counter-Reformation activities. The intervention of Sir Thomas Edmondes, ambassador to France, made it possible for Lodge to resume permanent English residence. In 1610 Lodge was admitted to the College of Physicians and the next year he swore an oath of allegiance and the privy council issued the order effectively protecting him from prosecution for recusancy. Although his name appears on a list of recusants in 1618, there is no evidence that Lodge's Catholicism caused him trouble after 1611. Indeed, the biographical assumption is that he established a viable medical practice in London in part because he attracted Catholic patients.

Lodge continued to write and publish alongside his medical practice. His later literary reputation rests on two monumental translations, a folio volume of the works of the Jewish historian Josephus, and a folio volume of the prose works of Seneca. First published in 1602, *The Famous and Memorable Workes of Josephus* was reprinted at least nine times in the seventeenth century. Late sixteenth-century interest in Josephus's history of the Jews and its later redactions is well attested; a copy entry for a translation of Josephus was first made in the Stationers' register in 1591 and both Thomas Nashe's *Christs Teares Over Jerusalem* (1593) and Thomas Deloney's *Canaans Calamitie* (1598) use the fall of Jerusalem as a cautionary allegory for contemporary London. Lodge seeks, he says in his introduction to the reader, to make history available for study:

> it is the most exact and chiefest interest of historie to awaken mans idleness, and arme them against casualities, and the whole bent of example hath no other issue … For as life, so Historie (the image of life) is fraught with pleasure, and displeasure; and onely in the use of life, the wisdome of life consisteth. (*Works*, 4.25, 27)

Whether Lodge was the intended translator in 1591 or entered upon the task after the transfer of copy in 1598 is not known. The translation of Seneca also responded to an already established interest and occupied many years. An initial entry for the copy is dated 1600 and in a letter to Sir Thomas Edmondes in 1610 Lodge writes as though the translation were almost completed. The first edition of *The Workes both Morall and Naturall of Lucius Annaeus Seneca* appeared in 1614. Lodge prepared a revised edition, published in 1620, that was to become a standard translation until the twentieth century, and the basis of selection and redaction by others, beginning with Roger L'Estrange's *Seneca's 'Morals'* (1679).

While practising medicine and translating Josephus and Seneca, Lodge also published other smaller works. In 1601 he translated selections of Catholic devotional writings by Luis of Granada, *The Flowers of Lodowick of Granada*. Two years later a quarto volume, *A Treatise of the Plague*, reflects Lodge's vocational reading, his immediate practice as a physician, and his interest in making knowledge available to readers. Another text of popularized medical knowledge, 'The poore mans talentt', circulated in manuscript, the original dedicated to and evidently prepared for the countess of Arundel as an aid to her 'charitie' (*Works*, 4.3). Lodge's final published work, a translation of Simon Goulart's commentary on the poetry of Du Bartas, the French Huguenot poet, is contemporaneous with his revision of the Seneca translation. English poets had been interested in Du Bartas's poetry since the 1580s; Philip Sidney worked on a translation before his death in 1586 and Joshua Sylvester's translation of the complete works appeared in 1605. *A Learned Summary upon the Famous Poeme of … Du Bartas* was first published in 1621 and went through four editions before 1640.

Final years and reputation The last years of Lodge's life might have been lived in financial comfort. In 1612 the last of his brothers died and Lodge inherited an estate of enough value that a portion was leased for £200 a year. But as both Charles Sisson and Alice Walker have shown, Lodge continued to be embroiled in lawsuits over financial matters involving both debts and obligations that he owed and claims that he made upon the land of others. In any case, Lodge continued to practise medicine. In 1625 the London aldermen named Lodge as a physician who might be employed in relation to the plague. Early in the autumn of 1625 Lodge died, presumably of the plague. He died intestate; the administration of his estate was granted to his wife on 12 October 1625.

Although Lodge was occasionally recognized by his contemporaries, his name occurs less frequently than might be expected from the range of his work and the length of his life. Some of the mentions, moreover, are not easily understandable in relation to what is taken to be Lodge's *œuvre*. Francis Meres's naming Lodge as among 'the best for comedy' is one such example; Edmund Howe's listing him among the 'Latin poets' in his continuation of Stow's *Annales* is another. *The Returne from Parnassus* notes that Lodge has 'his oare in every paper boat' and 'turns over Galen every day' (*The Three Parnassus Plays*, ed. J. B. Leishman, 1949, 239). Lodge's dedications and direct or indirect autobiographical statements suggest personal friendships, some of long standing, but no permanent intellectual circle. The aristocratic Howard, Carey, and Strange families, the poets Spenser, Daniel, and Drayton, the professional writers Robert Greene and Barnabe Riche, the stationers Edward White and John Busbie, the professional secretaries and scribes Ralph Crane and Peter Bale may well have known each other, but they do not form any coherent social grouping.

Lodge's later reputation, the long life of *Rosalynde* and his translations of Josephus and Seneca notwithstanding, is eclipsed by that of his contemporaries, especially Shakespeare whose use of *Rosalynde* kept Lodge's name current even as critical comparisons inevitably slighted Lodge. In the *Dictionary of National Biography* Sidney Lee wrote that Lodge should be remembered primarily as a lyric poet. Edmund Gosse's edition, *The Complete Works of Thomas Lodge* (not including any of the translations), had been printed only ten years before Lee wrote. While Lodge's poetry still features in anthologies of Elizabethan verse, critical attention has turned toward the fictions in the century since Lee's comment and Gosse's edition. The convergence of literary and historical investigations at the end of the twentieth century suggests that Lodge merits continued and renewed attention for some of the very reasons that may have inhibited earlier recognition: the length of his active life as a writer, the range of his writing activity, his Catholic affinity or affiliation, as well as for the undisputed literary accomplishment of his best work. ALEXANDRA HALASZ

Sources E. Cuvelier, *Thomas Lodge, témoin de son temps* (Paris, 1984) · C. Sisson, 'Thomas Lodge and his family', *Thomas Lodge and other Elizabethans*, ed. C. Sisson (1933) · A. Walker, 'The life of Thomas Lodge', *Review of English Studies*, 9 (1933), 410–32 · A. Walker, 'The life of Thomas Lodge', *Review of English Studies*, 10 (1934), 46–54 · N. Burton Paradise, *Thomas Lodge: the history of an Elizabethan* (1931) · E. A. Tenney, *Thomas Lodge* (1935) · *The works of Thomas Lodge*, ed. E. Gosse, 4 vols. (1883) · A. Kinney, '"O vita! misero longa, foelici brevis": Thomas Lodge's struggle for felicity', *Humanist poetics: thought, rhetoric, and fiction in sixteenth-century England* (1986), 363–423 · T. Lodge, *Rosalind: Euphues golden legacy*, ed. D. Beecher (1997) · C. Whitworth, 'Thomas Lodge, Elizabethan pioneer', *Cahiers Elisabethains*, 3 (1973), 5–15 · R. Helgerson, *The Elizabethan prodigals* (1976), 105–23 · P. Salzman, *English prose fiction, 1558–1700* (1985) · J. Houppert, 'Thomas Lodge', *The predecessors of Shakespeare: a survey and bibliography of recent studies in English Renaissance drama*, ed. T. Logan and D. Smith (1973) · K. J. Donavan, 'Recent studies in Thomas Lodge (1969–1990)', *English Literary Renaissance*, 23 (1993), 201–11 · letters of administration granted to Joan Aldred, 12 Oct 1625, PRO, PROB 6/12, fol. 23v

Archives BL, medical handbook and papers, Add. MS 34212 | BL, letters to William Trumbull

Lodge, William (1649–1689), etcher and landscape draughtsman, born on 4 July 1649 at Leeds, the son of William Lodge and his wife, Elizabeth Sykes, came from families of merchants in the cloth trade; his mother's grandfather, Richard Sykes, was one of the first aldermen of Leeds when it was incorporated as a borough in 1629. He attended a school in Leeds before being admitted in 1666 to Jesus College, Cambridge, and in 1668 to Lincoln's Inn in London, but on inheriting an income of £300 a year had no further need to earn a living. He had taken up painting, drawing, and etching as an amateur at Cambridge.

In 1669–70 Lodge accompanied Thomas Belasyse, Lord Fauconberg, the new ambassador to Venice, and remained in Italy for two years, during which time he visited Rome and Provence. After his return he published in 1679 a translation of Giacomo Barri's *Viaggio pittoresco d'Italia* under the title *The Painter's Voyage of Italy*, which he illustrated with his own etchings of artists' portraits. In the mid-1670s he met members of the circle of 'virtuosi' in York, and one of these acquaintances, Mr Bolter of York, later gave George Vertue an account of his life. Vertue was given another account by Ralph Thoresby of Leeds, whose wife was a relation of Lodge's (Thoresby always referred to Lodge as 'cousin' in his diary, and Lodge's name frequently appears in his correspondence). These narratives remain the chief sources of information about Lodge's life.

Lodge was a close friend of the engraver Francis Place, with whom he made a sketching tour in Wales in 1678 at the height of the Popish Plot fever, when both men were arrested as Jesuit spies. He made copious drawings on many tours, some of which survive in Leeds Public Library, York City Art Gallery, and the British Museum. Most are made with a fine pen, and give the appearance of being studies for etchings. According to Vertue, Lodge also painted portraits in oils, but none is now traceable. Lodge's etchings have not been investigated since the list of fifteen that Thoresby gave Vertue. Among them are a pair of views of York, dated 1678; a *Book of Divers Prospects done after the Life*, containing small oblong Italian landscapes; and some miscellaneous views in London and near York. Some of these were published by his fellow Yorkshireman Pierce Tempest. Lodge also etched various plates of shells to illustrate papers by Martin Lister published in the Royal Society's *Philosophical Transactions*. Unlike Place and other members of the York circle, he seems never to have made a mezzotint. Lodge died, unmarried, on 27 August 1689, and Vertue records a curious anecdote that he was buried in Harewood church, against his expressed wishes, but as had been foretold in a dream he had had. ANTONY GRIFFITHS

Sources Vertue, *Note books*, 1.74–5, 119–21 • E. Croft-Murray and P. H. Hulton, eds., *Catalogue of British drawings*, 1 (1960), 426–8 • Venn, *Alum. Cant.*

Likenesses A. Comer, oils, *c*.1685, Patrick Allan-Fraser College of Art, Hospitalfield; on loan to York Art Gallery • G. Vertue, sketch, 1727 (after A. Comer), York Art Gallery • A. Bannerman, line engraving, BM, NPG; repro. in Walpole, *Catalogue of engravers* (1765) • F. Place, mezzotint, BM

Lodvill, Philip (*d.* 1767), religious writer, was born in Oxfordshire into an established family. He was the author of the first authoritative account in English of the doctrines and practices of the Orthodox church, which was published as *The Orthodox Confession of the Catholic and Apostolic Eastern Church* in 1762. It was a translation of a confession written in the seventeenth century by Pyotr Mogila, metropolitan of Kiev, and approved by a synod of Orthodox bishops. Lodvill was a regular attendant at the Russian Orthodox church at 32 Welbeck Street in London and received the prayer oil from the hands of Father Andrey Samborsky, who became confessor to Catherine the Great of Russia. Lodvill states in his brief preface that he intended his translation to spread understanding of his faith and to encourage others to join the Orthodox church.

Lodvill was married, probably to a Greek woman, and one of his daughters married the British consul at Salonika, Peter Paradise; their son was John *Paradise (1743–1795). Lodvill died on 14 March 1767 and was buried on 22 March in Bow church, London.

THOMAS SECCOMBE, *rev.* EMMA MAJOR

Sources *ESTC* • J. Boswell, *Life of Johnson*, ed. R. W. Chapman, rev. J. D. Fleeman, new edn (1970); repr. with introduction by P. Rogers (1980), 1349, n. 1 • P. Lodvill, *The Orthodox confession of the Catholic and Apostolic Eastern church* (1762), preface

Lodwick, Francis (*bap.* 1619, *d.* 1694), linguistic scholar, was baptized in the London Dutch church, his birth being registered on 8 August 1619 at St Nicholas Acons, London. His parents, Waldrave Lodwick and Judith Roussel, had been married in the French church, London, on 14 May 1616, the former being described as a native of 'Belle' (Bailleul), Flanders, and the latter as born in London. Waldrave, a protestant refugee, was a London merchant, Francis being his eldest surviving son.

In the introduction to his first published work, Lodwick described himself as not a scholar but a 'mechanick', but his surviving library catalogue demonstrates that, even if self-educated, he was extremely well read. He was engaged in trading abroad, in cloth and books, and by 1650 was an important member of the community associated with the London Dutch church; he was also a friend of Samuel Hartlib, who often described him as an 'informant'. By 1657 he owned a large house in rural Wandsworth; his London house, in Botolph Lane, was burned down in the fire of 1666, when he moved to Fenchurch Street. By 1672 he was a close friend of Robert Hooke, as the latter recorded in his diary; the two men met frequently to discuss linguistic matters. In 1681 Lodwick was elected to the Royal Society, and thereafter frequently acted as auditor to the society's council.

Lodwick published three works, leaving many others in manuscript. In 1647, in *A Common Writing*, he implemented a suggestion for a universal 'character' made by Francis Bacon (1605), and later by John Wilkins in *Mercury* (1641), by inventing a system of symbols which, like Arabic numerals, represented ideas or concepts which could be realized in any language. In 1652 he produced a more sophisticated system, in *The Ground-Work or Foundation Laid … for the Framing of a New Perfect Language*, in which he proposed the establishment of conceptual classes to which 'radical' symbols were assigned, with regular diacritics denoting subclasses. Although little more than a sketch, his work helped inspire John Wilkins's *An Essay towards a Real Character* (1668), in which Wilkins acknowledged his indebtedness to Lodwick. His third publication was a proposal for a phonetic alphabet in which related sounds were denoted by related symbols; this appeared in the Royal Society's *Philosophical Transactions* (1686). After Wilkins's death, Lodwick collaborated with John Aubrey and others in an unsuccessful attempt to improve the *Essay*. Lodwick's unpublished manuscripts, including an innovatory Dutch shorthand, are listed in V. Salmon, *The Works of Francis Lodwick* (1972); all display originality and intelligence, but failed to find practical implementation by his successors.

Lodwick seems to have been an attractive and popular person, to judge by the entries in Hooke's diary, and he was undoubtedly modest about his qualifications and achievements. However, he could display a hasty temper, as noted in an incident which took place in Wandsworth, and even on occasion came under suspicion of unethical behaviour. On 25 September 1645 Lodwick married, at the church of St Giles Cripplegate, Mary De le Bo. They had several children: a son Walraf was baptized in 1652, but only one son, Simon, and possibly a daughter, Mary, survived him. Simon too was a merchant, trading to New York, where his cousin, Charles Lodwick, formerly the master of Daniel Defoe, became mayor. Lodwick died in January 1694, and was buried on 5 January in St Mary Abchurch, London. VIVIAN SALMON, *rev.*

Sources V. Salmon, *The works of Francis Lodwick* (1972) · J. H. Hessels, ed., *Ecclesiae Londino-Batavae archivum*, 3: *Epistulae et tractatus cum Reformationis* (1897) · *The diary of Robert Hooke … 1672–1680*, ed. H. W. Robinson and W. Adams (1935) · D. Abercrombie, 'Forgotten phoneticians', *Studies in phonetics and linguistics* (1965), 45–75 · W. J. C. Moens, ed., *The marriage, baptismal, and burial registers, 1571 to 1874, and monumental inscriptions of the Dutch Reformed church, Austin Friars, London* (privately printed, Lymington, 1884) · *IGI*

Loe, Thomas (*d.* 1668), Quaker preacher, was probably born in Oxfordshire, the son of parents whose names are unknown. His father left him a house at Long Hanborough in that county upon his death, and his mother was still alive in September 1668. Loe certainly resided in Oxford, but nothing else is known of his background or early years. It is thought that he was an early Seeker and tradesman, and at an unknown date he married a woman named Mary (*d.* in or after 1669), whose surname was possibly Norton. Convinced by John Camm at Oxford in 1654, he afterwards travelled a great deal, despite his weak constitution. The Quaker Thomas Ellwood described him as 'a faithful and diligent labourer … in the work of the Lord' and as one who was possessed of 'an excellent ministerial gift' (Ellwood, 80).

In 1654 Loe and his wife, along with others, including the Quaker William Simpson, were imprisoned at Oxford 'for bearing the like Christian testimony, against vice and superstition, publicly in the assemblies and places of concourse at Oxford' (Besse, 1.563). At the Restoration he was again imprisoned at Oxford for several weeks for refusing the oath of allegiance.

Loe was one of the first generation of Quakers to visit Ireland. His initial sojourn seems to have been to Dublin in 1655, but he went there a second time in 1657, after travelling by foot from Munster. He spread the Quaker message and, according to John Tomkins, 'converted many to Truth, especially in Ireland, where he travell'd, thro' much Hardship' (Tomkins, 75). In 1660 he suffered incarceration, this time in Wexford, after he, his wife, and Sarah Holme visited a friend there. A letter to George Fox from Loe dated 17 August 1660 reveals that he was in the north of Ireland following travels in west Cork, Bandon, and Limerick, where he had attended meetings and where persecution had been rife. He appears to have returned to England later in the year.

It would seem that Loe regularly visited London, for John Tomkins recorded that he 'was divers times at London in the work of the ministry' (Tomkins, 75). He was one of a group of Quaker ministers who signed an important epistle in London in May 1666, which was a response to Quaker separatists such as John Perrot and John Pennyman and an attempt to strengthen authority within Quakerism.

Loe is most famous for his 'convincement' of the Quaker leader William Penn, who gradually inclined towards Quakerism after hearing Loe speak in Cork in 1667, though Penn had first heard and been impressed by him in Macroom, west of Cork, when he was a young boy of twelve. Penn was clearly very attached to Loe, and in a number of letters refers to his friend's sickness before his death. Loe had been at the duke of Buckingham's home along with Penn and George Whitehead 'in relation to Friends' liberty' when Loe was suddenly taken ill with fever and retching. Penn records that he died at nine in the morning on 6 October 1668 following a 'tedious sickness', and Quaker records reveal that this took place at the home of Thomas Mann, a hosier and prominent Friend of Bishopsgate Within, London.

Penn praised Loe and lamented his loss when he wrote that he had 'finisht his Testimony, & fought, like a Valiant souldier, the good Fight: Whose Works follow him, & have Eternis'd his Memorial amongst the Faithful. Whom my soul loved, whilst alive; & bemoanes, now dead' (Penn to Gulielma Springett, 7 Oct 1668, Dunn and Dunn, 1.68). Loe's dying message to Penn—'Dear heart, bear thy cross, stand faithfull for God, & bear thy testimony in thy Day & generation, & God will give thee an eternall crown of glory that none shall ever take from thee'—is thought to have provided the inspiration for Penn's famous work *No Cross, No Crown*, which he wrote a few months after Loe's death (Penn to Isaac Penington, 17 Oct 1668, ibid., 70). He was buried on 7 October 1668 at Chequer Alley.

CAROLINE L. LEACHMAN

Sources J. Besse, *A collection of the sufferings of the people called Quakers*, 1 (1753) · *The papers of William Penn*, ed. M. M. Dunn, R. S. Dunn, and others, 1 (1981) • A. R. Barclay, ed., *Letters, &c. of early Friends* (1841) • T. Ellwood, *The history of the life of Thomas Ellwood* (1714) • J. Tomkins and J. Field, *Piety promoted … in five parts* (1721) • W. C. Braithwaite, *The beginnings of Quakerism*, ed. H. J. Cadbury, 2nd edn (1955); repr. (1981) • W. C. Braithwaite, *The second period of Quakerism* (1919); 2nd edn, ed. H. J. Cadbury (1961); repr. (1979) • 'Dictionary of Quaker biography', RS Friends, Lond. [card index] • Quaker digest registers, RS Friends, Lond. • N. Penney, ed., *'The first publishers of truth': being early records, now first printed, of the introduction of Quakerism into the counties of England and Wales* (1907) • will, PRO, PROB 11/329, fol. 270r

Archives RS Friends, Lond., Swarthmore MSS, vol. 4, 238 (MS vol. 356); vol. 5, 28, 53 (MS vol. 357); vol. 6, 45, 46, 55 (MS vol. 358)

Loe, William (*d.* 1645), Church of England clergyman, may have been born in Kent. He graduated BA from St Alban Hall, Oxford, on 5 November 1597 and proceeded MA on 14 June 1600, at which time, Anthony Wood records, he 'was much in esteem for Latin, Greek and human learning'. On 8 June 1618 Loe graduated BD from Merton College, and he was awarded his DD on 8 July. In 1598 he was presented to the vicarage of Churcham, Gloucestershire, and in 1600 was appointed master of the college school in Gloucester. It may be that about this time Loe married, but nothing is known of his wife.

On 3 September 1602 Loe was presented by the queen to a prebend of Gloucester in succession to Samuel Proctor; he was installed on 30 September 1602. It was as the holder of this dignity that he preached *The Joy of Jerusalem*, a sermon at Paul's Cross on 18 June 1609. On 26 November 1611 he was presented to the rectory of Stoke Severn, Worcestershire, and in 1614 published four sermons preached in Gloucester Cathedral. However, this smooth progress did not continue for long. In 1617 William Laud, newly appointed dean of Gloucester, ordered the removal of the communion table in the cathedral to the high altar; there was strong opposition, and a protest or 'libel' was issued against Laud in which Loe appears to have been implicated. Perhaps it was this which helped earn the enmity of an unnamed powerful public man, later complained of. Yet Loe's reputation still stood high. Appointed chaplain to James I, he delivered a series of seven sermons at St Michael Cornhill and in the published version dedicated to the king was bold enough to suggest the need for moderate reform of 'the apparent errors and abuses crept into the church' (W. Loe, *The Mysterie of Mankind*, 1619, preface).

In 1618 Loe was appointed pastor of the English company of Merchant Adventurers at Hamburg, though his departure was delayed for almost a year. Yet the procedure was, on his own account, given in *The Merchant Reall*, a sermon published at Hamburg in 1620:

> both civil and honest. First by free election of your own fellowship. Secondly by approbation of the state whence I came. Thirdly by recommendation of his sacred majesty under his own hand, who pleased to grace me his unworthy servant with his royal letters, and of the most reverend archbishop of Canterbury … Fourthly with attestation from the famous university of Oxford, under their seal, and from the cathedral church.

Armed with such impressive credentials, Loe did not hesitate to give advice on matters of a political nature. He warned his audience to ensure the orthodoxy of their apprentices: 'Their hearts are alienated, so are their actions, their intendments, their purposes. Unite them once in religion, they are yours absolute, present or absent; sleeping or waking, by sea or land'; most unusually, he did not disown the label puritan but sought to distinguish between 'puritans in action … to whom all things are pure, altogether busy in honest action' and 'puritans in faction', that is, 'all papists, anabaptists, brownists, separatists, and all singularists whatsoever' (Loe, *Merchant Reall*, 1–2).

Loe remained in Hamburg almost a year, until at least 24 January 1620, when *Songs of Sion, Set for the Joy of God's Deere Ones* was signed 'from my study within the English house at Hamborough'. His eldest son **William Loe** (*d.* 1679) may have followed him in acting as a preacher to the Merchant Adventurers, issuing from Trinity College, Cambridge (from where he graduated in 1626 and of which he was a fellow), on 30 October 1627 *The Merchants Manuell* (1628), dedicated to the governor and members of the company. Loe records that the young William, having proceeded MA in 1629 and BD in 1636, was in Paris about 1638, where he was involved in discussions with leading Jesuits; he became vicar of Kirkby Masham, Yorkshire, in 1639.

Shortly after his own return to England, Loe senior issued his *Vox Clamantis: a Still Voice to the Three Thrice Honourable Estates of Parliament*, entered in the Stationers' register on 12 March 1621. In his epistle dedicated to George Villiers, duke of Buckingham, the author claimed that this work had 'lain suppressed some years, by means of a certain great one', recalling the 'aspersions of faction and sedition … which it pleased that great one mentioned to cast upon me at that time in an honourable assembly'. Loe also hinted darkly that this opponent would have had him put him to death:

> if some reverend fathers of the church, the blessed beaupeers of divinity, had not stayed that enraged fury against me: but not long after, the hand of almighty God surprised that greatness, clipped it, restrained it, that it might doe no more harm, and so it remains to this day.

Loe survived and prospered—he was again a chaplain to the king by 9 October 1622, when he preached at Theobalds *The Kings Shoe* (1623)—but he continued to take risks. In February 1623, in a sermon before James and Prince Charles, newly returned from his abortive expedition to Spain, Loe was careful to deny presuming to advise the king, but did actually urge him to the defence of the true religion by the sword, counselling military support for the Palatinate.

It was perhaps about this time that Loe was instituted to the vicarage of Putney, where he caused to have the entries from earlier registers of the parish copied into a new register, according to his statement on its flyleaf dated 17 January 1624 and signed 'William Leo, DD' (Bannerman, iii). He is also known to have been vicar of Wandsworth in 1631: a story is told of him that in a 'parish near London'—perhaps Wandsworth—at morning service, in the absence of a colleague named Adams, he preached on the text 'Adam, where art thou?' to which the missing cleric responded in the afternoon with an exposition of the words 'Lo, here am I!' (Chester, 140). In 1632 he published *The Incomparable Jewell*, a marriage sermon celebrating the virtuous wife. Loe is last heard of in connection with the death in April 1645 of the controversial figure Daniel Featley, whom he attended in his last sickness, and at whose funeral on 21 April he gave the oration, published later that year. Loe himself also died that year and was buried in Westminster Abbey on 21 September 1645.

STEPHEN WRIGHT

Sources Foster, *Alum. Oxon.* • Wood, *Ath. Oxon.*, new edn • *Fasti Angl., 1541–1857*, [Bristol] • W. Loe, *A sermon preached at Lambeth April 21 1645 at the funeral of … Daniel Featley* (1645) • J. L. Chester, ed., *The marriage, baptismal, and burial registers of the collegiate church or abbey of St Peter, Westminster*, Harleian Society, 10 (1876) • *CSP dom.*, 1611–18 • W. Loe, *The merchant reall, preached by William Loe, doctor of divinity chaplain to the king's sacred majesty, and pastor of the English church of Merchants Adventurers residing at Hamboroughe in Saxonie* (1620) • W. Loe, *Vox clamantis: a still voice to the three thrice honourable estates of parliament* (1621) • P. E. McCullough, *Sermons at court: politics and religion in Elizabethan and Jacobean preaching* (1998) [incl. CD-ROM] • *VCH Gloucestershire*, 10.26 • W. B. Bannerman, ed., *The parish register of Putney*, 1 (privately printed, Croydon, 1913) • *VCH Surrey*, 4.109 • Venn, *Alum. Cant.*

Loe, William (*d.* 1679). *See under* Loe, William (*d.* 1645).

Loebel, Hirsch. *See* Lyon, Hart (1721–1800).

Lóegaire Lorc (*supp. fl. c.*300 BC), legendary king of Leinster, was the son of Augaine Már and is said to have been also king of Ireland. He was described as *senathair Laigen*, 'the ancestor of the Leinstermen', and all kindreds who regarded themselves as true Laigin (Leinstermen) traced their descent back to Lóegaire Lorc. Lorcmag, 'the plain of Lorc', was used by medieval literati to describe the territory of the Leinstermen. The epithet *lorc* is variously explained as meaning 'fierce, dumb, tongue-tied'. The trait of dumbness, often associated with deities, links Lóegaire Lorc with his renowned grandson and other ancestor of the Laigin, Labraid Loingsech, whose original name was Móen, 'the dumb one'. They may ultimately be regarded as one character.

Lóegaire Lorc is one of the main protagonists in the original legend of the Laigin, *Orgain Denna Ríg*, 'The destruction of Dind Ríg', which in its earliest written form may date to the seventh century. Cobthach Cóel Breg, 'Cobthach the Thin of Brega', one of the reputed ancestors of the midland and northern dynasty, the Uí Néill, became jealous of Lóegaire and of his kingship of Leinster. The legend describes Cobthach and Lóegaire as brothers. Cobthach tricked Lóegaire into believing that he was dead and when Lóegaire came to grieve over his brother's body which was laid out in a chariot, Cobthach stabbed and mortally wounded him. An alternative version relates how Cobthach killed Lóegaire at the battle of Carman, the site where the kings of Leinster were inaugurated in the medieval period. This foul deed perpetrated by Cobthach is described as *fingal*, 'kin slaying', and is used to explain the continuous enmity between Cobthach's descendants, the Uí Néill, and Lóegaire's descendants, the Laigin. This act of kin slaying was avenged by Lóegaire's grandson, Labraid Loingsech, who returned from exile, seized the kingship of Leinster, and burned Cobthach in an iron house at Dind Ríg (claimed to be a site on the River Barrow near Leighlinbridge, co. Carlow).

EDEL BHREATHNACH

Sources M. A. O'Brien, ed., *Corpus genealogiarum Hiberniae* (Dublin, 1962) • D. Greene, ed., *Fingal Rónáin and other stories* (1955), 16–26 • T. F. O'Rahilly, *Early Irish history and mythology* (1946), 101–17 • H. Wagner, 'The archaic *Dind Ríg* poem and related problems', *Ériu*, 28 (1977), 1–16 • D. Ó Corráin, 'Irish origin legends and genealogy: recurrent aetiologies', *History and heroic tale: a symposium*, ed. T. Nyberg (1985), 51–96 • T. M. Charles-Edwards, *Early Irish and Welsh kinship* (1993), 119–21

Lóegaire mac Néill (*fl.* 5th cent.), high-king of Ireland, was a son of Níall Noígíallach, ancestor of the Uí Néill dynasties. He is associated with three elements of Irish mythology: the arrival of Patrick, the cattle tribute (or *bóroma*), and the Feast of Tara. His reign was dated by the seventh-century hagiographer Tírechán to about 427–63, but many or all of the dates associated with Lóegaire are based on the artificially constructed chronology surrounding St Patrick and it has been suggested that he died as late as the 480s.

According to the hagiographer Muirchú moccu Mactheni, who wrote *c.*700, Lóegaire, 'a great king, fierce and pagan, an emperor of barbarians' (Bieler, 74–7), dominated Ireland at the time of Patrick's arrival. One night he was celebrating a pagan festival at Tara, and it was forbidden for anyone to kindle a fire before the king's was alight. However, it was also Easter eve and Patrick lit a fire which was visible from Tara. Lóegaire's druids advised the king that the other fire should be put out that night, for it would otherwise never be extinguished. Patrick was summoned to Lóegaire and shamed the king's druids and advisers by a series of spectacular and violent miracles. A number of attempts were made by the king and others to kill Patrick, who warned Lóegaire that he must accept the faith or die. Having taken the counsel of his people, the king submitted, and was told by Patrick: 'Since you have resisted my teaching and been offensive to me, the days of your own reign shall run on, but none of your offspring shall ever be king' (ibid., 96–9). This curse served to explain the marginal status of Cenél Lóegairi, a Brega dynasty which traced itself to Lóegaire.

Muirchú's account differs from that of Tírechán, who said that Lóegaire remained a pagan in spite of Patrick's miracles. He had been bidden by his late father not to accept the faith but to be given a warrior's burial on the hill of Tara, bearing arms, his face towards Leinster. Lóegaire's hostility to Leinster is also seen in the chronicles, which indicate that his military activities were primarily against that province. The sons of Níall Noígíallach are said to have been bequeathed various attributes belonging to their father, and fittingly Lóegaire inherited 'warfare'.

Lóegaire's kingship is acknowledged by the chronicles, which say that he held the 'Feast of Tara'. This was probably originally a pagan ritual and it was celebrated only by the king of Tara, an office which later in the middle ages reflected a claim to the kingship of Ireland. Lóegaire is universally accepted as king of Ireland by the regnal lists, but at such an early date neither he nor any other king can have enjoyed such authority. However, he may have ruled Connacht, for, according to Tírechán, Patrick encountered Lóegaire's daughters at the royal site of Rathcroghan, in Roscommon.

Lóegaire is connected with legal matters in two notable ways: Tírechán shows him acting as a judge (along with Patrick) in a dispute about an inheritance; and the prologue to the law code *Senchas Már* says that Lóegaire summoned together the best of the men of Ireland, including Patrick, in order to discuss the arrangement of their laws. In the event, Lóegaire was only one of nine men entrusted by Patrick with the Christianizing of the laws, which became the *Senchas Már*.

The medieval *bóroma* saga tells of the heavy tribute which Leinster was expected to pay to the king of Ireland in reparation for an ancient treachery. Lóegaire invaded Leinster in order to exact the tribute and was captured following his defeat in the battle of Áth Dara. He was freed on a promise that he would remit the tribute and named the elements as his sureties. However, within three years he returned to Leinster and seized cattle. As a consequence of this he died by the elements: the sun burned him, the earth swallowed him, and the wind (that is, his breath) departed from him. However, there are alternative versions of his death. One account says that he died as a result of a curse by Patrick. Another says that there was a prophecy that he would die between Ireland and Britain. He tried to evade his fate by never going to sea, but the prophecy was fulfilled when he died between two hills called Ireland and Britain.

Tírechán names two of Lóegaire's daughters, and twelve sons are attributed to him, the mother of one of them being Muirecht ingen Echdach Muinremuir. He is also said to have been married to Angas ingen Ailella Tassaig of the Éoganachta dynasties of Munster. PHILIP IRWIN

Sources A. P. Smyth, 'The Húi Néill and the Leinstermen in the Annals of Ulster, 431–516', *Études Celtiques*, 14 (1974–5), 121–43 • G. S. Mac Eoin, 'The mysterious death of Loegaire mac Néill', *Studia Hibernica*, 8 (1968), 21–48 • L. De Paor, ed., *Saint Patrick's world: the Christian culture of Ireland's apostolic age* (1993), chaps. 27, 28 • J. Carey, 'An edition of the pseudo-historical prologue to the *Senchas Már*', *Ériu*, 45 (1994), 1–32 • *Ann. Ulster* • M. A. O'Brien, ed., *Corpus genealogiarum Hiberniae* (Dublin, 1962) • E. Mac Neill, 'The *Vita tripartita* of St Patrick', *Ériu*, 11 (1930–32), 1–41, esp. 25 • L. Bieler, ed. and trans., *The Patrician texts in the Book of Armagh*, Scriptores Latini Hiberniae, 10 (1979) [incl. Muirchú's *Life of Patrick*] • W. Stokes, ed. and trans., 'The Bóroma', *Revue Celtique*, 13 (1892), 32–124 • K. Mulchrone, ed. and trans., *Bethu Phátraic: the tripartite life of Patrick* (1939) • M. C. Dobbs, ed. and trans., 'The Banshenchus [pt 2]', *Revue Celtique*, 48 (1931), 163–234, esp. 179

Loehnis, Sir Clive (1902–1992), naval officer and civil servant, was born on 24 August 1902 at 21 Cadogan Gardens, London, the son of Herman William Loehnis, barrister, and his wife, Vera Geraldine, *née* Wood. He grew up as an only child, an elder brother having died as a baby. His father was brought up in England; earlier forebears had emigrated from Hamburg during the nineteenth century. His paternal grandfather was an entrepreneur in St Petersburg under the tsars. Loehnis went to Lockers Park preparatory school; he then joined the Royal Navy as a cadet in 1915 and went to the colleges at Osborne, Dartmouth, and Greenwich. As a midshipman he was in the battle cruiser *Renown* for the prince of Wales's Far Eastern tour, and he qualified as a signal officer in 1928. On 17 April 1929, as a lieutenant, he married Rosemary Beryl Ryder (*b.* 1909) at St Margaret's, Westminster. They had two children, Serena Jane (who in 1953 married James Wogan Remnant, later third Baron Remnant) and Anthony David, a diplomat and financier.

Loehnis retired from the navy in 1935 and went into film production with Anthony Kimmins (also ex-navy), but was recalled to the signal division in the Admiralty at the time of the Munich crisis in 1938. Soon after the outbreak of the Second World War he was posted to the operational intelligence centre in the Admiralty, and in 1942 he was appointed liaison officer between the centre and the Government Code and Cypher School at Bletchley Park. This led to close personal co-operation and friendship with Sir Edward Travis, the director at Bletchley Park, and Harry Hinsley, whose collaboration with the Admiralty had led to the regular breaking at Bletchley of the German naval and submarine 'Enigma' machine ciphers, which was of critical importance, especially in the battle of the Atlantic.

In March 1945 Loehnis (now a commander) accompanied Sir Edward Travis, Rear-Admiral Rushbrooke (the director of naval intelligence), and Harry Hinsley on a world tour through Egypt, India, Ceylon, Australia, New Zealand, and the USA, the objects of which were first to plan to transfer British signal intelligence resources from the German to the Japanese theatre of war; and second to discuss the possibility of post-war co-operation between the UK, the old Commonwealth countries, and the Americans. A direct result was that in September 1945 President Truman issued a secret order authorizing continued collaboration between US and British signal intelligence authorities, including in cryptanalysis. A top-secret Anglo-US conference followed in February–March 1946, under the chairmanship of Sir Stewart Menzies, chief of the secret service, with Loehnis and Hinsley as conference secretaries.

Loehnis, Joe to his friends, was demobilized in 1945 and joined the government communications headquarters in Cheltenham as a civilian. He was appointed a member of the directorate in 1951, deputy director in 1954, and director from 1960 to 1964. The period from 1951 to 1964 coincided with the growth of the cold war and requirements for greater intelligence effort against the Russians. Sociable and amusing, Loehnis also worked closely with the senior officials in Whitehall responsible for the provision of resources for intelligence, enabling requirements to be met.

Loehnis was an able administrator, insisting on some simple but sensible instructions; for example: 'a man's name is to him the most important thing. Letters from this office will always get the names right. If you don't, he won't believe the rest of the letter' (personal knowledge). He had something of a naval officer's manner of direction to his staff but got to know very many of them personally. To those whom he did get to know he was kind, and he would correct people by saying 'No, ducky, it's not like that' (personal knowledge). He smoked Turkish cigarettes and drank China tea from china cups, not mugs. He liked to drive fast. He did not move to Cheltenham but drove there from his London home in Eaton Place, Belgravia, his head only just showing over the steering wheel of his Jaguars. In 1959 he skidded on ice, was seriously injured in the resulting accident, and took six months to recover.

Like his predecessors as director, Sir Edward Travis and Sir Eric Jones, Loehnis believed that the UK should maintain the closest links in intelligence with the USA. He had excellent relations with his American opposite numbers—all the more important at a time when the enormous size of the Soviet armed forces and Soviet military investment, perhaps the greatest ever undertaken by a country in peacetime, was becoming clear.

After his retirement Loehnis was deputy chairman of the civil service selection board from 1967 to 1970. He was appointed CMG in 1950 and KCMG in 1962. He died at his home, 12 Eaton Place, on 23 May 1992 of pneumonia and a stroke, and was cremated at Putney Vale crematorium. He was survived by his wife and two children.

D. R. Nicoll

Sources *Daily Telegraph* (26 May 1992) • C. Andrew, *For the president's eyes only* (1995) • Government Communication Headquarters, Cheltenham • personal knowledge (2004) • *WWW*, 1991–5 • private information (2004) [Anthony Loehnis, Lady Remnant] • b. cert. • m. cert. • d. cert.

Archives Government Communication Headquarters, Cheltenham

Likenesses W. Bird, photograph, 1960–64, priv. coll.

Wealth at death £87,871: probate, 21 Aug 2000, *CGPLA Eng. & Wales*

Loewe, Louis (1809–1888), linguist, was born of Jewish parents at Zülz, Prussian Silesia. After attending successively Rosenburg Academy and the colleges of Lissa, Nicolsburg, and Presburg, studying theology, oriental languages, and the sciences, he matriculated at the University of Berlin, where he took the degree of PhD. His knowledge of languages and numismatics was already considerable, and on a visit to Hamburg he was entrusted with arranging the oriental coins in the Sprewitz collection. On arrival in London, he obtained introductions to the duke of Sussex and Admiral Sir Sydney Smith, through whom he became known to many leading scholars and patrons of learning in England. Pursuing his researches Loewe subsequently visited Oxford, Cambridge, and Paris. In 1836 he undertook, under the auspices of the duke of Sussex and Admiral Sir Sidney Smith, a three-year tour in the East for the purpose of extending his knowledge of such languages as Arabic, Coptic, Nubian, Turkish, and Circassian. Near Safed he was ill-treated and robbed by some Druses, and had to continue his journey through Palestine dressed as a Bedouin. In 1839 the duke of Sussex appointed him his lecturer on oriental languages.

On his return from his travels in 1839 Loewe went to study in the Vatican Library. At this time Sir Moses Montefiore passed through Rome on his second journey to the Holy Land, and Loewe, who had been Montefiore's guest at Ramsgate in 1835, readily accepted his invitation to accompany him to Palestine as his secretary. This close relationship with Sir Moses ceased only at the latter's death, and some regarded Loewe as 'the power behind the throne' (Morais, 208). In the memorable mission to Damascus and Constantinople in 1840, and on the thirteen succeeding journeys, extending from 1839 to 1874, Loewe accompanied Montefiore, to whom his linguistic acquirements and shrewd sense proved invaluable. In 1840 he addressed a large mixed congregation in the synagogue at Galata in four languages. His services to the missions and philanthropic schemes of Montefiore were frequently acknowledged by the Jewish board of deputies. On 25 March 1841 he was presented by Montefiore to Queen Victoria. He married in 1844.

In 1846 Loewe delivered two lectures on the Samaritans at Sussex Hall, Leadenhall Street, and in the same year he preached in the great synagogue at Vilna, on the occasion of Montefiore's mission to Russia. He was appointed first principal of Jews' College, Finsbury Square, in 1856, but soon resigned the office. He became examiner for oriental languages to the Royal College of Preceptors in 1858, and in the same year opened a Jewish boarding-school at Brighton. His advertisement in the *Jewish Chronicle* offered Hindustani and fencing, and the assurance that 'the pupils are permitted to write to their Parents or Guardians once a week, and their letters are NOT examined' (*The Jewish Chronicle, 1841–1941*, 39). He was naturalized on 12 July 1862. When in 1868 Montefiore founded the Judith Theological College at Ramsgate, he chose Loewe as principal and director, and Loewe filled that office for twenty years.

Sir Moses Montefiore by his will named Loewe one of his executors and entrusted him with all his diaries and other private papers to enable him to write a biography of Lady Montefiore. This became a biography of Sir Moses also, and an oblique record of Loewe's own work and travels. It was completed in June 1888, and published as *Diaries of Sir Moses and Lady Montefiore*, edited by Dr L. Loewe, 2 vols. (1890).

In 1841 Loewe prepared an English translation of J. B. Levinsohn's *Efês Dammîm* (1839), a series of conversations at Jerusalem between a Greek patriarch and a chief rabbi regarding the revival of the blood accusation in Soslow, Poland. In 1842 Loewe translated the first two conversations in *Matteh Dan* by Chacham David Nieto, as *The Rod of Judgment*. He also published *Observations on a unique Cufic gold coin, issued by Mustali, tenth caliph of the Fatimite dynasty* (1849) and *A Dictionary of the Circassian Language* (1854), originally printed in the *Transactions of the Philological Society*.

Loewe was a member of the Royal Asiatic and Numismatic societies, and of the Asiatic Society of Paris. He was a quiet, laborious scholar, with an aversion to public life and, except to those who knew him well, could seem cold and unsympathetic. Early in 1888 he moved to London where he died on 5 November 1888 at 53 Warwick Road, Maida Vale, leaving his wife, Emma, three sons and four daughters. He was buried at Willesden.

GORDON GOODWIN, *rev.* JOHN D. HAIGH

Sources L. Loewe, preface, in *Diaries of Sir Moses and Lady Montefiore*, ed. L. Loewe, 1 (1890), v–vi • H. S. Morais, *Eminent Israelites of the nineteenth century* (1880), 208–11 • *The Times* (6 Nov 1888) • *Jewish Chronicle* (9 Nov 1888) • *The Jewish Chronicle, 1841–1941: a century of newspaper history*, Jewish Chronicle (1949), 11 • *Men of the time* (1875) • Boase, *Mod. Eng. biog.* • d. cert.

Wealth at death £9356 12*s.* 11*d.*: administration, 14 Dec 1888, *CGPLA Eng. & Wales*

Loewenthal, Johann Jacob [*formerly* János Jakab Löwenthal] (**1810–1876**), chess player, son of a Hungarian merchant, was born at Budapest in July 1810. He was educated at the *Gymnasium* of his native town, and received his first chess lessons from Szen, the noted Hungarian player, then a clerk in the archives at Pest. In 1842–5 he helped Szen and Grimm win a correspondence match with the celebrated Cercle des Echecs of Paris. He also travelled to Vienna and Berlin to play von Heydebrandt and study under Lasa, Anderssen, and other masters. Though a non-combatant in the revolutions of 1849, Loewenthal was an ardent follower of Kossuth, and held a civil appointment under his administration; thus he was expelled from Austro-Hungary in 1849, and sought refuge in the United States of America. For some time he ran a club in Cincinnati; he also played the twelve-year-old Paul Morphy, who beat him twice, with one draw.

In 1851 Loewenthal visited Britain to take part in a chess tournament; being unsuccessful, he was reluctant to return to America. Howard Staunton procured him the secretaryship of the St George's chess club (1852–5). He also became chess editor of the *Illustrated News of the World* and of *The Era* (1854–67). He welcomed Morphy to London in 1858, accepted with a good grace defeat (by nine games to three with three draws) in a match with him, and published in 1860 *Morphy's Games of Chess, with Analytical and Critical Notes*.

Matches were never Loewenthal's forte: 'he was, indeed, the most uneven player of his time … Staunton complained most irascibly of his "glaring oversights" and "stupendous blunders"—and they were no less exasperating because he seemed to blunder against everyone except Staunton himself' (Cole and Diggle, 308); but 'it is not too much to say that his theoretical knowledge of the game was unrivalled' (*ILN*, 119). None the less, he won the tournament of 1857 at Manchester—beating Horwitz and Anderssen—and that of 1858 at Birmingham, beating Staunton. In 1853, unfortunately, being something of a protégé of Staunton, he was persuaded into a match, effectively as Staunton's representative, against the latter's rival Harrwitz. Sneered at by the *British Chess Review* as 'the wandering Jew' and harassed by Harrwitz's partisans with organ-grinders and cigar-smokers, the series' thirty-three games finally proved too much, and Loewenthal lost by ten games to eleven. Staunton was distinctly cooler to him thereafter.

Loewenthal was appointed manager of the great London chess congress of 1862, in which the first prize was taken by Anderssen, and in which he tied with Joseph Blackburne for eighth place after abandoning his last games. Thereafter, he concentrated on the administrative and literary side of chess. He edited the *Chess Player's Magazine* throughout its life from 1863 to 1867, and was, from 1865 to 1869, manager of the British Chess Association, of which Lord Lyttelton was president. After the secretaryship of the St George's (a post perhaps dependent on Staunton's continued patronage), he was from 1857 to 1864 president of the St James's chess club and from 1872 president of the City of London. Loewenthal became a naturalized British subject in 1866. The following year, a German speaker found: 'so anxious was he both in outward appearance and manner to be taken for an Englishman that he would rather converse in broken French … than have recourse to German, which of course he spoke fluently' (Hoffer, 754). Loewenthal was a friend and frequent opponent at chess of W. G. Ward, under whose influence he joined the Roman Catholic church. By 1874 he needed the support of a subscription fund of £500. He retired to the Sussex coast because of illness and died, unmarried, at Burlington House, St Leonards, Sussex, on 20 July 1876. The residue of the subscription funded a Loewenthal memorial cup for the county chess championship.

THOMAS SECCOMBE, *rev.* JULIAN LOCK

Sources R. N. Cole and G. H. Diggle, 'Johann Jakob Loewenthal', *British Chess Magazine*, 96 (1976), 308–14 • *British Chess Magazine*, 46 (1926), 345–8 • D. Hooper and K. Whyld, *The Oxford companion to chess*, 2nd edn (1992), 236–7 • *Westminster Papers*, 9 (1876–7), 69 • *The Field* (22 July 1876), 115 • *ILN* (29 July 1876), 119 • *The Times* (21 July 1876), 5 • Boase, *Mod. Eng. biog.* • L. Hoffer, 'The chess masters of today', *Fortnightly Review*, 46 (1886), 753–65 • F. M. Edge, *The exploits and triumphs in Europe of Paul Morphy, the chess champion* (1859); repr. with introduction by D. Lawson (1873) • H. Staunton, *The chess tournament* (1852); facs. edn (1986) • J. Loewenthal and G. W. Medley, *The chess congress of 1862: a collection of the games played, and a selection of the problems sent in for competition*, [another edn] (1889) • *CGPLA Eng. & Wales* (1876)

Likenesses group portrait, engraving, *c*.1858 (with Staunton and Boden.), repro. in Edge, *Exploits and triumphs in Europe*, facing p. 96 • A. Rosenbaum, group portrait, oils, 1880 (with Bird and Blackburne), repro. in K. Matthews, *British chess* (1948), 30 • photographs, repro. in Cole and Diggle, 'Johann Jakob Loewenthal', 309, 311 • portrait, repro. in *Illustrated News of the World*, 8 (1861), 164

Wealth at death under £450: probate, 6 Sept 1876, *CGPLA Eng. & Wales*

Lofft, Capel (1751–1824), radical editor and writer, was born on 14 November 1751 in London, the only son of Christopher Lofft, a former private secretary to Sarah, duchess of Marlborough, and his wife, Anne Capell, who was the sister of the Shakespearian scholar Edward Capell. He was educated at Eton College from 1759 to 1769, when he matriculated from Peterhouse, Cambridge. He did not take a degree and in 1770 was admitted to Lincoln's Inn, whence he was called to the bar in 1775. At Peterhouse, the college of John Jebb and John Disney, he

Capel Lofft (1751–1824), by William Ridley, pubd 1802 (after Thomas Holloway)

encountered a spirit of theological heterodoxy which influenced him for the rest of his life. He did not acquire a large legal practice, but in 1776 edited a compilation of reports of cases in king's bench, including several decisions of Lord Mansfield which were not recorded elsewhere. Lofft's report of Mansfield's crucial decision in the case of James Somerset—that the laws of England did not recognize slavery—allowed the nascent anti-slavery movement to derive a considerable political advantage. Thereafter Lofft was associated with movements for constitutional, legal, and religious reform. He was a strong critic of the British government's attempt to re-assert control over the North American colonies by force.

In 1778 Lofft married, as his first wife, Anne (*d.* 1801), daughter of the architect Henry *Emlyn; they had three children, of whom the second, Robert Emlyn Lofft (*d.* 1847), became an officer in the Bengal army. In 1781 Lofft inherited from his uncle Edward Capell substantial estates at Troston and Stanton in Suffolk, and for many years Troston Hall was his principal residence. He was now able to live independently of any profession; he became a prominent figure in Suffolk society, serving as a magistrate, and devoted his energy to writing and campaigns for reform. He was a founder member of the Society for Constitutional Information in 1780, organized a reform petition from Bury St Edmunds in 1783, and wrote many articles in favour of reform for the *Bury Journal*. James Boswell, who met Lofft in 1784 in company which included Dr Johnson, described him as 'a most zealous Whig', with 'a mind … full of learning and knowledge' (Boswell, *Life*, 4.258). Lofft indeed became something of a polymath, with a serious interest in English literature, history, classics, foreign languages, botany, and astronomy. He represented the best of the amateur tradition in learning, exemplified by the financially independent country gentleman.

Although brought up in the Church of England, by the 1780s Lofft had come to embrace Unitarian doctrines. In a letter to Joseph Parker in 1790 he described himself 'not as a Member of the Establishment but as a Dissenter so far removed from it as to be out of the Protection of the Act of Toleration' ('Letters and remains of Capel Lofft'). He gave strong support to the campaign for the repeal of the Test and Corporation Acts in 1787–90, contributing a *History of the Corporation and Test Acts* (1790), which included a valuable list of the minority of MPs who had voted for repeal on 8 May 1789. He remained convinced of the need for complete civil equality for protestant dissenters, but, as he told his fellow reformer Christopher Wyvill in 1809: 'I must acknowledge I scarcely can expect religious Freedom to come but as a consequence of a Reform in the Election & Duration of Parliament' (N. Yorks. CRO, Wyvill of Constable Burton MSS, ZFW 7/2/210/13).

During the 1790s Lofft vehemently opposed the ministry of the younger Pitt, especially in its war and taxation policies. He moved towards the more radical wing of the reform movement, arguing for the Society for Constitutional Information's programme of universal male suffrage and urging Wyvill himself to adopt a more radical approach. He used his influence in Suffolk in this cause, addressing several public meetings, and in 1800 his name was removed from the list of magistrates when he publicly opposed the imposition of the death penalty upon a young girl (*The New Suffolk Garland*, 52–4). A few years later he joined the Society for the Diffusion of Knowledge upon the Punishment of Death, which campaigned against capital punishment.

Anne Lofft died in 1801. The following year Lofft married, as his second wife, Sarah Watson, daughter of John Finch of Cambridge. She was an author and poet in her own right. They had a son and two daughters; the son, Capell *Lofft (1806–1873), became a miscellaneous writer of some note. Lofft himself maintained a high literary output, which included editions of Milton's *Paradise Lost* (1792) and of Virgil's *Georgics* (1803), together with a pamphlet entitled *On the Revival of the Cause of Reform in the Representation of the Commons in Parliament* (1809) and a collection of Shakespearian aphorisms (1812). He was the patron of the poet Robert Bloomfield, to whose *Farmer's Boy* he contributed a preface (1798). During the Regency period he maintained his radical political opinions; his closest associates were literary figures—S. T. Coleridge, W. Hazlitt, H. Crabb Robinson—who were also critics of the regime. Like Hazlitt, Lofft was a warm admirer of Napoleon Bonaparte. While remaining committed to strictly constitutional methods of proceeding, he refused to be deflected by a fear of popular pressure. As he told Wyvill in 1809: 'No violence, even of Mr Cobbett, shall make me other than a Friend to right Principles whencesoever they come' (N. Yorks. CRO, Wyvill of Constable Burton MSS, ZFW 7/2/208/48). In 1818 he embarked on a continental tour before settling at Turin four years later. Early in 1824 he moved to nearby Moncalieri, where he died on 26 May of the same year. He was buried in the protestant church of St Germain, Piedmont.

In its obituary the *Gentleman's Magazine* offered a description of Lofft's appearance: 'His figure was small, upright, and boyish; his dress—without fit, fashion or neatness; his speaking—small-voiced, long sentenced, and involved; his manner—persevering, but without command' (*GM*, 94/2, 1824, 184). His rather dishevelled person is captured, probably accurately, in S. Knight's cartoon *A View Near Bury-Suffolk*. He was a perfect example of a Cambridge-educated whig, brought up in a tradition of Anglican latitudinarianism and subsequently a Unitarian. He expressed a vigorously libertarian mentality, while not challenging the fundamental property relationships of the society within which he occupied an eminent position. According to Wyvill, he 'knew how to temper the ardour of his zeal with candour, moderation, and the most conciliatory prudence' (Wyvill, *Political Papers*, 5.88 n.). His energy was distributed over too many areas of interest for him to become an outstanding expert upon any particular subject, but he none the less established a secure niche within the second rank of literary and political figures of his age. G. M. Ditchfield

Sources *GM*, 1st ser., 94/2 (1824), 184 · R. A. Austen-Leigh, ed., *The Eton College register, 1753–1790* (1921), 339 · T. A. Walker, ed., *Admissions to Peterhouse or St Peter's College in the University of Cambridge* (1912), 331 · J. Glyde jun., *The new Suffolk garland* (1866), 52–4, 348–9 · *Monthly Repository*, 19 (1824), 481, 571–2 · Allibone, *Dict.* · Boswell, *Life*, 4.258 · J. A. Hone, *For the cause of truth: radicalism in London, 1796–1821* (1982), 147, 248 · I. R. Christie, *Wilkes, Wyvill and reform: the parliamentary reform movement in British politics, 1760–1785* (1962), 114–15, 189 · E. C. Black, *The Association* (1963), 99–100, 179–80, 201 · W. R. Cotter, 'The Somerset case and the abolition of slavery in England', *History*, new ser., 79 (1994), 35 · C. Wyvill, ed., *Political papers*, 6 vols. [1794–1804], vol. 1, pp. 297–323; vol. 5, pp. 180–83; 185–90 · 'Letters and remains of Capel Lofft, Esq.', DWL · will, PRO, PROB 11/1691, fols. 60–61 · N. Yorks. CRO, Wyvill of Constable Burton papers, ZFW 7/2/208/48, 7/2/210/13

Archives DWL | BL, Add. MSS 20,081, fol. 302; 28,721, fol. 36; 20,268, fols. 26, 30, 58–65, 128; 30,809, fols. 50, 52; 35,654, fol. 248 · N. Yorks. CRO, Wyvill of Constable Burton MSS · Suffolk RO, Ipswich, correspondence with James Boswell · Suffolk RO, Ipswich, correspondence with E. Cobbold

Likenesses W. Ridley, stipple, pubd 1802 (after T. Holloway), BM, NPG [*see illus.*] · S. Knight, cartoon, NPG · etching, BM, NPG

Wealth at death probably over £10,000; Troston Hall; also library and pictures to wife: will, 1802, PRO, PROB 11/1691, fols. 60–61; PRO, death duty registers, IR 26/1010, fols. 1100–02

Lofft, Capell (1806–1873), classical scholar, poet, and writer, fourth son of Capel *Lofft (1751–1824), and only son with his second wife, Sarah Watson, daughter of John Finch, was born on 9 March 1806 at Troston Hall, Suffolk. In 1814 he was placed on the foundation of Eton College, and from there proceeded in 1824 to King's College, Cambridge, where he became a fellow in 1827. Having obtained the Craven university scholarship—the highest classical distinction open in those days to King's men—in 1827, he graduated BA in 1829, MA in 1832. He was called to the bar of the Middle Temple in 1834, but never attained, if he sought, professional eminence. In October 1837 he vacated his fellowship by his marriage to Mary, daughter of William Anderson of Newnham House, Cambridge. They had two daughters, the elder of whom (wife of the Revd T. H. Irwin) was drowned, together with her only child, in a boating accident on Lake Geneva—a calamity to which Lofft alludes in his preface to the second edition of *Ernest* (xxv).

In 1837 Lofft published anonymously his first literary undertaking, a mental autobiography with a didactic purpose, entitled *Self-formation, or, The history of an individual mind, intended as a guide for the intellect through difficulties to success, by a fellow of a college*. Harriet Martineau said that every parent of boys ought to read the book. Lofft's object is 'to show, as the result of his own proper and personal experience, that self-instruction is the one great end of rational education', and 'to point out how habits of thoughtfulness are to be formed'. He extols religion as the very best way to foster intellectual and moral advancement, attributing the development of his own sense of religion to an excursion in Devon with the Bible as his only companion, and his subsequent perusal of William Law's *Serious Call to a Devout and Holy Life*. After his marriage Lofft resided for a short time in London, but a roving life was more to his taste, and he spent most of his time on the continent, where the strong liberal principles which he inherited from his father and visions of social perfectibility led him into the society of some of the chief radical figures of the time. His next publication, likewise anonymous, was an epic poem in twelve books, *Ernest*, dedicated to the memory of Milton, and printed for the author in 1839. It was soon withdrawn from circulation. The poem embodies a German tradition of Ernest, a parallel to the Welsh one of Arthur, both of whom are to return and reign and fulfil other patriot prophecies. It represents the growth, struggles, and triumph of Chartism. H. H. Milman, when noticing the poem in the *Quarterly Review* (December 1839), expressed the highest admiration of the genius of the unknown author, but condemned the work as wildly inconsistent and lawless in its style and object. A second edition was published in 1868 with the title *Ernest, the Rule of Right*. In the preface the author complained of the unreadiness of the English people to support the Chartist movement.

Lofft was in America during the civil war, and while living in Minnesota prepared an edition of the *Self-Communion* of Marcus Antoninus, with critical notes to the Greek text. The title ran *Markou … Ta es heauton Antōninou sive ad seipsum commentarii morales. Recensuit, denuo ordinavit, expurgavit, restituit, notis illustravit … C. L. Porcher, N. Eboraci U.S.,* A.D. *1861. A. liberatae reip. l.*. Despite its eccentricity, some of Lofft's emendations have been accepted by more recent editors. In 1868 Lofft published in London *New Testament: suggestions for reformation of Greek text from the self-conferred papal dictatorship and blind obstructiveness of mediaeval monkish copyists, on principles of logical criticism, by R. E. Storer* (that is, Restorer).

In his old age Lofft abandoned the radicalism of his youth and purchased two considerable estates, one in Sussex, and the other, called Millmead, in Amelia county, Virginia, USA. He died at Millmead on 1 October 1873.

H. A. HOLDEN, *rev.* RICHARD SMAIL

Sources Venn, *Alum. Cant.* • Boase, *Mod. Eng. biog.* • private information (1893) • *CGPLA Eng. & Wales* (1874)
Likenesses L. Lofft, oils, King's Cam.
Wealth at death under £600 and estates in USA: administration with will, 3 Sept 1874, *CGPLA Eng. & Wales*

Lofthouse, Mary. *See* Forster, (Emma Judith) Mary (1853–1885).

Loftie, William John (1839–1911), antiquary, was born at Tanderagee, co. Armagh, on 25 July 1839, the eldest son of John Henry Loftie of Tanderagee and his wife, Jane, daughter of William Crozier. After private education he entered Trinity College, Dublin, where he graduated BA in 1862. On 9 March 1865, at St George's, Hanover Square, London, he married Martha Jane (Jeannie), daughter of John Anderson and widow of John Joseph Burnett of Gadgirth, Ayrshire. They had one daughter. His wife was a writer on contemporary domestic life and the author of such books as *Forty-Six Social Twitters* (1878) and *Comfort in the Home* (1895). After taking holy orders in 1865, Loftie served curacies at Corsham, Wiltshire (1865–7), St Mary's, Peckham (1867–8), and St James's, Westmoreland Street, London (1869–71). He was assistant chaplain at the Chapel Royal, Savoy, from 1871 to 1895, when he retired from clerical work. He was elected fellow of the Society of Antiquaries of London in 1872, and of the Zoological Society of London in 1894.

Loftie devoted himself in London to literary and antiquarian study, and wrote voluminously in several periodicals. Initially, he contributed frequently to the SPCK's short-lived *People's Magazine* (1867–73), of which he became editor in 1872. He also wrote for the Church of England paper *The Guardian* from 1870 to 1876, and joined the staff of the *Saturday Review* in 1874, and of the *National Observer* in 1894. He also occasionally contributed to the *Quarterly Review* and other reviews. In 1868 he purchased the first drawings which Kate Greenaway sold publicly; he later published them in the *People's Magazine* and helped her to gain work as an illustrator.

Loftie's earliest field of interest was the history of printing. He compiled the *Catalogue of a Loan Collection of Books Printed before 1600* for an exhibition at the Royal Archaeological Institute in 1871, and his first book was *A Century of Bibles, or, The Authorized Version from 1611 to 1711* (1872). During many winter vacations in Egypt he visited out of the way parts of the country, and described one tour in *A ride in Egypt from Sioot to Luxor in 1879, with notes on the present state and ancient history of the Nile valley* (1879). Among his many contributions to the Royal Archaeological Institute's *Archaeological Journal* (1872–82) were several papers on Egyptology, published between 1878 and 1882. He described a fine collection which he formed of scarabs in an *Essay of Scarabs: with Illustrations by W. Flinders Petrie* (1884).

William John Loftie (1839–1911), by Lady Winchilsea, pubd 1907–9

Loftie described his chief recreation as 'searching for unrestored churches'. His article for *Macmillan's Magazine* ('Thorough restoration', June 1877) was praised by William Morris for encouraging support for the newly established Society for the Protection of Ancient Buildings, of which Loftie was an early committee member. His *Cathedral Churches of England and Wales* (1892) contains several attacks on the work of restoring architects and the Victorian Gothic revival.

From 1876 Loftie edited the Art at Home series in twelve volumes, including *The Dining Room* (1878), written by his wife. He contributed several articles on art and archaeology to *The Portfolio*, the *Magazine of Art*, and other journals. In the 1890s he wrote books on British art and architecture for the general reader, notably *Landseer and Animal Painting in England* (1891), *Reynolds and Children's Portraiture in England* (1891), and *Inigo Jones and Wren, or, Rise and Decline of Modern Architecture in England* (1893).

Loftie was a literary antiquary whose work may have lacked original scholarship but was usually well informed, written in an attractive style, and enlivened with strong personal opinions, especially on architecture. The history of London was his longest sustained interest and the subject that he researched the most thoroughly. He wrote several general works from *In and Out of London, or, The Half-Holidays of a Town Clerk* (1875) to *The Colour of London* (1907), and a number of guides to particular places in London and Windsor. *The Authorised Guide to the Tower of London* (1885) sold 10,000 copies in the first three weeks. Queen Victoria commissioned the brief *Memorials of the Savoy: the Palace, the Hospital, the Chapel* (1878). Loftie's most substantial work was the two-volume *A History of London*, published in 1883–4, whose chapters on the early history of central London provided a thorough review of research up to that time.

Loftie died on 16 June 1911 at his home, 3a Sheffield Terrace, Kensington, and was buried in Smeeth churchyard, Kent. His wife survived him.

W. B. OWEN, *rev.* BERNARD NURSE

Sources *Men and women of the time* (1899) • Allibone, *Dict.* • *WWW* • R. Engen, *Kate Greenaway: a biography* (1981) • Crockford • *Annual*

Report [Society for the Protection of Ancient Buildings], 1 (1878) · letter, 14 April 1894, S. Antiquaries, Lond., MS 451 [concerning *Memorials of the Savoy*] · *CGPLA Eng. & Wales* (1911)

Archives BL, corresp. with Macmillans, Add. MS 55075

Likenesses Lady Winchilsea, photograph, pubd 1907–9, NPG [*see illus.*]

Wealth at death £2228 8*s*. 9*d*.: resworn probate, 16 Aug 1911, *CGPLA Eng. & Wales*

Lofting, Hugh John (1886–1947), children's writer, was born on 14 January 1886 in Norfolk Road, Maidenhead, Berkshire, the fourth son in the family of five sons and one daughter of an Irishman, John Brien Lofting, clerk of works, and Elizabeth Agnes Cannon, his English wife. From the age of eight Lofting was a pupil at Mount St Mary's College, a Jesuit school in Chesterfield, Derbyshire. Despite an early passion for natural history (he had used his mother's linen cupboard as a combined zoo and museum) his first impulse was to train as a civil engineer, since he hoped thereby for opportunities to travel. In 1904 he began his studies in the USA at the Massachusetts Institute of Technology, but he returned to England a year later and completed the course at the London Polytechnic. He was in Canada in 1908–9 prospecting and surveying; he worked on the Lagos Railway in west Africa from 1910 to 1911, and in 1912 was employed as an engineer in Cuba by the United Railways of Havana. He gave up engineering that year and went to the United States, where, also in 1912, he married Flora Small of New York and settled to writing. He worked for the British Ministry of Information in New York during 1915, returning to England in 1916 to enlist with the Irish Guards, but was wounded and invalided out in 1917.

The family settled in Madison, Connecticut, in 1919, and Lofting began writing again. His first book appeared in New York in 1920, *The Story of Doctor Dolittle*, an account of the gently eccentric John Dolittle who gives up his medical practice in order to devote himself to treating animals, learning all their various languages with the help of Polynesia, his sage and authoritative parrot. The saga, which was illustrated with his own naïve pen-and-ink drawings, had its origins in the compassion he had felt for the sufferings of the animals in the past war—'If we made [them] take the same chances as we did ourselves, why did we not give them similar attention when wounded?' (Blishen, 12)—and in the letters about an imaginary horse surgery that he had written home from the front to his two children, Elizabeth and Colin (the latter of whom habitually called himself Dr Dolittle). It was an instant success and its sequel, *The Voyages of Doctor Dolittle*, received the American Library Association Newbery medal in 1923. The exploits of the doctor and his household of animals were to be recorded in twelve books, always set in England at some unspecified time in the middle of the nineteenth century. (None of his books indicated that he had spent so much of his life in America.)

At first Lofting took an exuberant delight in the books. The first book had been aimed at young children, and included much slapstick comedy (the tone of which was to become unacceptable to later readers) about the African court of the Jolliginki where the black Prince Bumpo yearns to be white. Its successors were increasingly sophisticated and inventive, embellished with fantastic quasi-scientific detail. But he became weary of his creation and with *Doctor Dolittle in the Moon* (1928) he hoped that he had seen the end of his hero. It was a time of great personal sadness; his first wife had died in 1927; he had married Katherine Harrower-Peters in the following year, but she too had died a few months later in an influenza epidemic. He was to marry in 1935 Josephine Fricker (*d.* 1966), of Toronto, with whom he had a son, Christopher.

Lofting brought the doctor back to earth in *Doctor Dolittle's Return* (1933), and there was to be one last book, *Doctor Dolittle and the Secret Lake*, built round the story of the flood with Dr Dolittle as a latter-day Noah and written when he was in poor health. It was published posthumously in 1948. Both these last books reflect his increasing pessimism about international affairs; as Edward Blishen says, 'the positive and determined John Dolittle has been replaced by an unhappy dreamer' (Blishen, 30). The two other posthumous Dolittle books are collections of short stories.

The unworldly, peace-loving doctor, oblivious of both material comfort and public opinion, is in some respects a self-portrait of the shy and gentle author. Lofting had expressed in articles in *The Nation* in 1923 and 1924 his strong feelings about the glorification of war and violence 'which seems as yet to be part of every child's metamorphosis' (Blishen, 30), and horror of war is the theme of the poem *Victory for the Slain* (1942), his only published work for adult readers. He wrote a handful of other books for children, which were mostly picture-books, but included a full-length fantasy, *The Twilight of Magic* (1930). Lofting died on 26 September 1947 at his home in Topanga, California, USA. GILLIAN AVERY

Sources *The Times* (30 Sept 1947) · E. Blishen, *Hugh Lofting* (1968) · *Wilton Bulletin* (6 Dec 1967) · b. cert.

Lofting, John (*c*.1659–1742), merchant and manufacturer of engines, was a native of the Netherlands, one of at least two brothers. He later recorded that he 'lived seven years at Amsterdam with one of the masters of the fire engines there, and is thoroughly acquainted with the methods practised in those parts in quenching of fires' (*DNB*). He came to England, obtaining grants of free denization in July 1686 and August 1688. At the time of his marriage, at St Nicholas Cole Abbey, London, on 3 May 1689, Lofting was described as a merchant, aged about thirty, and resident in the parish of St Thomas Apostle, London. His wife was Hester Bass of St Michael Queenhithe, London, aged nineteen, sister of Jeremiah Basse, future governor of New Jersey. In June 1689 Lofting enrolled in the Company of Free Shipwrights, paying quarterage until January 1699, thereby becoming a citizen of London.

In October 1689 Lofting and Nicholas de Wael petitioned for a patent for the sole making and selling of 'an engine for quenching fire, the like never seen before in this kingdom' (*CSP dom.*, *1689–90*, 283). A patent was granted to Lofting (no. 263) and a joint-stock company set up to exploit it. Lofting's fire engine was probably the first in England to use a wired suction hose to throw water as high as 400 feet, and could 'force the Water in a continued Stream into Alleys, Yards, Back houses, Stair-Cases; and other obscure places, where other Engines are useless' (Houghton, letter of 5 Jan 1694). The engines were employed at several royal palaces, and their use at a number of London fires was praised by Christopher Wren. In 1694 Lofting was involved in disputes with a rival, George Oldner, over advice to London aldermen on fire precautions. John Houghton advocated using Lofting's fire engines for drainage or the watering of agricultural land, and Lofting also marketed an engine for 'Starting of Beer and other Liquors' (*LondG*, 14–17 March 1691). After 1696 nothing is known of Lofting's engines, production may have ceased, but his advice on fire engines was sought at Marlow in 1730.

In April 1693 Lofting was granted a patent (no. 319) for making and selling an engine to replace hand punching in the manufacture of brass thimbles. He began producing thimbles and sewing rings shortly afterwards, the first important manufacturer in England. John Houghton's detailed description of the horse-powered thimble works at Islington shows that Lofting had imported skilled workmen from the continent as well as the technology. Shortly before July 1697, Lofting moved from Islington to a water mill at Marlow in Buckinghamshire in order to double production to over 2 million thimbles a year.

Throughout the 1690s Lofting continued as a merchant. He imported iron wire for his engines, dealt in wheat, exported upholstery ware and pewter to the Baltic and America, petitioned parliament about the import of French goods, traded with his brother in Amsterdam, and in 1696 was accused of setting up a lottery for illegal currency speculation. In 1698 Lofting and Jeremiah Basse shipped goods to Perth Amboy, East New Jersey, in the *Hester*, a sloop owned by Basse. It discharged without calling at or paying New York customs dues, and the governor of New York seized the ship and sold it. Lofting and Basse appealed to parliament and took legal action, eventually receiving damages and costs of £1890, but not before Lofting was declared bankrupt in March 1700.

About 1696 Lofting, in partnership with Gaspar Frederick Henning, a German immigrant, obtained a 31-year lease to Marlow corn mills. They continued grinding corn, but set up an oil mill and a thimble manufactory as well. Lofting took up residence at Marlow soon afterwards, and this business became the basis of his revived fortunes after the bankruptcy, receiving praise from Daniel Defoe in 1721. From 1714 Lofting had a new partner, a corn factor called Merrett, but from 1724 he operated alone. A London business address was maintained, at Broken Wharf in Thames Street. Making his will in 1733 Lofting described himself as a gentleman whose living now mainly arose from the good management of his mills, but a codicil in 1737 noted that 'my estate has been lessened by losses of Rent and other accidents' (PRO, PROB 11/719 sig. 193).

On 23 July 1709 Hester was buried at Marlow. On 16 December 1710 Lofting married Mary Carter of Eton at St Mary Magdalen, Old Fish Street, London. Mary died in October 1721 and Lofting never remarried. The first marriage produced at least one daughter and six sons, the second one daughter and two sons; but when Lofting died on 15 June 1742 only the six sons from the first marriage survived. The mills, the house he lived in, and the Three Tuns New inn in Marlow were left to his son Benjamin, who was to make payments to his brothers. Benjamin and his brother John continued the business, but do not seem to have renewed the lease to the mills in 1753. Samuel pursued a naval career until 1745, when he was dismissed, perhaps for suffering himself to be beaten by a marine, and William acquired wealth through a legal career and established a trust, Lofting's Charity, for the benefit of the poor of Marlow. K. R. Fairclough

Sources E. F. Holmes, 'A forgotten Buckinghamshire industry: thimble making at Marlow', *Records of Buckinghamshire*, 35 (1993), 1–10 · *DNB* · *CSP dom.*, 1689–90, 283 · W. A. Shaw, ed., *Denizations and naturalizations of aliens in England and Ireland, 1603–1700* (1911) · W. R. Scott, *The constitution and finance of English, Scottish and Irish joint-stock companies to 1720*, 3 vols. (1910–12) · R. Jenkins, 'Fire-extinguishing engines in England, 1625–1725', *Transactions* [Newcomen Society], 11 (1930–31), 15–25 · 'The answer of John Lofting of London, 1694', GL, Broadside 29.10 · PRO, PROB 11/179 sig. 193 · J. Houghton and R. Bradley, eds., *A collection for improvement of husbandry and trade*, 2nd edn, 4 vols. (1727–8) · *LondG* (14–17 March 1691) · *LondG* (21–5 March 1700)

Likenesses J. Kip, engraving, *c.*1690, repro. in Holmes, 'A forgotten Buckinghamshire industry' · Crowle, portrait, repro. in T. Pennant, *Some account of London*, 3rd edn (1793) [J. C. Crowle's expanded and illustrated copy, BL, print room, vol. 10, no. 76]

Wealth at death see will, PRO, PROB 11/719, sig. 193

Loftus, Adam (1533/4–1605), Church of Ireland archbishop of Dublin, was born at Swineside in the parish of Coverham, Yorkshire, the second son of Edward Loftus. His father was bailiff to the abbot of Coverham; Robert Loftus (*d.* 1606), father of Adam *Loftus, first Viscount Loftus of Ely (1568–1643), was his brother. His education at Cambridge University may have been at Trinity College, and he probably was appointed to the rectory of Outwell St Clement, Norfolk, in Edward VI's reign. He chose, however, to make his career in Ireland.

Loftus first went to Ireland as chaplain to Thomas Radcliffe, third earl of Sussex, who was reappointed lord lieutenant in May 1560. Sussex's instructions ordered him to establish the reformation by putting into effect the Acts of Supremacy and Uniformity of 1560. Loftus played a key role in formulating and implementing the policy of enforcement, an extremely complex task in a country where the power of the Irish privy council was politically and geographically limited. In this he had the backing of two influential patrons in England, both with special responsibility for Irish affairs, Sir William Cecil and Francis Walsingham. As a result, Loftus survived the dispatch and recall of all the Elizabethan governors, occasionally even deputizing for them, and successfully maintaining a working relationship with all but one, Sir John Perrot. He was nominated Church of Ireland archbishop of Armagh on 30 October 1562 and consecrated on 2 March 1563. He worked closely with Sussex during his lieutenancy (25 June 1560 to 25 May 1564) and with Sir Henry Sidney during his lord deputyship (20 January 1566 to 1 April 1571 and

Adam Loftus (1533/4–1605), by unknown artist

18 September 1575 to 14 September 1578), the latter hailing him as a great religious reformer on his translation to the archbishopric of Dublin on 9 August 1567. Later governors relied on Loftus's detailed knowledge of Irish affairs and his political judgement. He served as one of the lord justices on three occasions: from 31 August 1582 to 21 June 1584, with Sir Henry Wallop; from 27 November 1597 to 15 April 1599, with Robert Gardiner; and from 25 September 1599 to 26 February 1600, with Sir George Carey.

Ecclesiastical career Loftus was appointed chaplain to Alexander Craik, bishop of Kildare, by April 1561. Presented to the rectory of Painstown in co. Meath, he found that the distance from Dublin, where he was obliged to preach, made it impossible to fulfil reforming tasks in his living. Sussex's design to implement the reform programme envisaged a leading role for Loftus after his appointment as archbishop of Armagh. With the submission of Shane O'Neill (6 January 1562), the archbishop might act as a political watchdog there (like lord presidents of the queen's council in the north). To give the impression of continuity, Elizabeth I issued a *congé d'élire*, although this was unnecessary after the Acts of Supremacy and Uniformity. This stratagem to win over the Armagh chapter failed, as the dean, Terence Daniel, explained to the government on 2 September, because the chapter consisted mostly of Shane's horsemen. Loftus received permission to take the temporalities of the see from 30 October until his consecration. On 2 March 1563, in accordance with a royal mandate of 20 January, he was consecrated by Hugh Curwen, archbishop of Dublin. Dating his archiepiscopal title from 1562 insinuated a line of episcopal succession unbroken by the Reformation. The queen simultaneously appointed Loftus to the Irish privy council. He was in England for twelve months from August 1566 because of ill health due to the damp weather in Ireland, and was admitted DD at Cambridge University on 25 November.

Loftus could not act as a reformer in Armagh, because of the lack of control by the Dublin government over the area. Residing whenever possible in his official residence, Termonfeckin, near Drogheda, he complained that his temporalities were worth only £20 per annum. During a visit to England he was granted (on 6 January 1565) the deanery of St Patrick's *in commendam*, to improve his income until other suitable provision could be made. Loftus duly resigned the deanery to the new lord chancellor Robert Weston, and was then finally chosen to become archbishop of Dublin. The appointment had been hotly contested.

Throughout his career in Ireland, Loftus appears to have hankered after positions in England, in order either to cure his gout or to work more effectively. This was sometimes a device to remind the government of his indispensability. To abandon Ireland would have been impossible, considering his increasing commitments there.

Family networks Starting his work with no local connections, Loftus realized quickly that he needed his own supporters. The secret of his success as a political survivor lay in his wide circle of influential friends. He married Jane (*d.* 1595), eldest daughter of Adam Purdon of Lurgan Race, co. Louth, and they had twenty children, twelve surviving into adulthood. Through his own and his wife's families Loftus gained trustworthy associates among the gentry and Dublin patricians. His wife's relatives expected much from his episcopal patronage. In times of crisis, he cited his family commitments when asking the government for financial assistance. Irish clans periodically attacked Tallagh, his seat on the edge of the Wicklow mountains. A nephew and some of his men were killed at the gates of his castle in spring 1573. In 1580, during the rebellion of James Eustace, third Viscount Baltinglass, Loftus lived 'in a kind of imprisonment in his own house' (PRO, SP 63/84/1). In 1600 he reported that his daughters, married to the sons of servitors in King's county, now wasted by the O'Connors, had sought refuge in his house with their families and were utterly destitute. One of his sons, fighting in the queen's service, was still unpaid at the time. In 1589–90 times were better, however, and he had sufficient funds to build Rathfarnham Castle on the estate purchased from David Barry, third Viscount Barry.

Loftus's policy of promoting family interests made him vulnerable to accusations of covetousness, nepotism, and even neglect of his duties. Neither archdiocese yielded substantial or reliable financial rewards. He tried to make up for this by recovering church property alienated by his predecessor but apparently 'never gained a groat by any lease' (PRO, SP 63/72/52). He often asked for remission of debts and reminded the authorities that moneys were due to him. For example, as keeper of the great seal, he applied on 20 April 1580 for the 10s. a day to which he was entitled, because his 180 acres were not enough to make the necessary provision towards the education of his 'thirteen poor children' (ibid.). There is no doubt that most of his earnings came from his secular posts.

Puritan sympathies Loftus based his drive for reformation on his preaching, for which he was renowned. Reformation of religion meant 'extirpation of superstition' and ignorance, from which obedience and discipline were assumed to follow. He tried to recruit new preachers from England. Craik, after several unsuccessful attempts, warned the government that the livings were too small. Sussex too was aware that the problem lay in the inadequate remuneration of properly trained new clergy. In 1567 Sidney identified the government policy of giving the richest benefices to laymen as the greatest hindrance to the Reformation. The Reformation legislation of 1560 facilitated the more systematic use of church property to reward government officials in Ireland; bishoprics were treated as crown property. The benefices available to the preaching clergy were even worse than those in northern England. In addition, unsympathetic patrons hampered reform. These unfavourable conditions made the failure of the Reformation virtually inevitable.

As a religious reformer Loftus had obvious puritan leanings. During the vestiarian controversy (1565–6) he recorded his disapproval of the harsh treatment of London congregations and Cambridge men, arguing that the compromise promoted by the Church of England was the work of the devil. Loftus implored Cecil to ensure that the good and learned preachers who rejected 'the popish rags' should not be suspended. He was convinced that the restoration of 'the true and sincere ministry' required the removal of 'all the monuments, tokens and leavings of papistry; for as long as any of them remain, there remains also occasion of relapses unto the abolished superstition of Antichrist' (PRO, SP 63/14/22). That Loftus went unpunished for his stance seems to have been dictated by the government's political opportunism. Armagh was strategically important, especially in 1565, when Loftus acted as mediator between protestant Scottish nobles and the English government. His puritanism was ideally suited to gain credence with the Scottish nobility who justified their rebellion against Mary, queen of Scots, by the Calvinist theory of resistance. Loftus's attitude ensured that the rebellion was treated as religious and not political in origin. He relied on his family connections to gather information and apply pressure, using his brother-in-law John Douglas as his messenger.

Loftus's puritanism also prompted his recommendation of Thomas Cartwright and Christopher Goodman for preferment in Ireland. His advocacy of Cartwright in 1570 and again in 1577 shows that he valued the preacher. Goodman, like John Knox, elaborated the Calvinist theory of resistance in his *How superior powers oght to be obeyd of their subjects* (Geneva, 1558). Despite this radicalism, Sidney supported Loftus in his efforts to secure the service of Goodman. Loftus was consistent in his support for the established church, though, clearing himself of allegations of separatism in 1567 by arguing that its structure was sacrosanct. What was established by law must be followed, except when dealing with adiaphora such as vestments. Although corresponding with leading puritans, he declared himself ignorant of the term 'puritan'. An innovation such as moving the communion table out of the chancel and into the middle of St Patrick's Cathedral at Easter 1576 was not considered too radical, because the building was full of people and space was needed, and because this was done frequently in northern England. Loftus denounced his critics as papists and enemies of God in league with the pope. The articles of faith to be read by the Irish clergy were shorter and less precise than the ones used in England, allowing for a broader, more conciliatory interpretation of uniformity.

Reform by commission Ecclesiastical commissions were the preferred practical means of reform. When Loftus was nominated to the archbishopric of Armagh he was also commissioned (albeit to little effect) to hear ecclesiastical causes on 1 October 1565. Other local commissions followed. In the next few years he co-operated most effectively with Hugh Brady, bishop of Meath. Forming the central plank of the Reformation policy during these years, they dominated ecclesiastical commissions. Brady, an Irishman, urged caution. Relying on a network of traditionally loyal local families, he did not wish to 'correct their heresies' too vigorously. The instructions wisely allowed for personal judgement, and Loftus was content with outward conformity and consequent attendance at church services in which the new religion could be inculcated by sermons.

On 20 October 1563 the government appointed two Englishmen, Sir Nicholas Arnold and Sir Thomas Wroth, to assess progress, deal with irregularities in the payment of soldiers, and implement the religious legislation. Their devastating report associated 'blind ignorance' and 'superstition' with social disorder, but observed that people feared to offend. In autumn 1564 the more permanent high commission for ecclesiastical causes was established, recognizing Loftus's growing reputation. Against Brady's advice, in 1565 Loftus's main concern was the new commission's limited competence, since he wished to proceed against the refusal of nobility and gentry to attend divine service. When the commission was renewed in July 1568, the appointment of Robert Weston, the lord chancellor, was crucial to its success. That Weston provided the essential lay support and legal expertise emerged in November 1573, when Loftus complained that since the lord chancellor's death he was 'very slackly assisted' (PRO, SP 63/42/76).

In May 1577 the commission as a whole was renewed and the previous commissions revoked, but outstanding fines could be recovered. The instructions show a determination to assist the bishops with a very specific delineation of offences, revealing the failure of previous attempts to impose uniformity. They were concerned with heretical opinions, seditious books, conspiracies, scandalous words against the queen, absence from divine service, the correction of 'all heresies, schisms and ecclesiastical offences by censures, ecclesiastical deprivation, masterless men, quarrellers, vagrants and suspect persons, and all assaults and frays', measures to protect clerical marriage, adulteries, fornications, and other ecclesiastical crimes (*Irish Fiants*, Elizabeth, 3047). The commissioners had the power to summon witnesses and impose fines and imprisonment.

From 18 March 1577 to March 1579 Loftus devoted much energy to fighting an ecclesiastical device which the bishops resented as infringement of their rights: a commission of faculties, issued to the lawyers George Acworth and Robert Garvey to grant licences, dispensations, and faculties arising from a Henrician statute. The stated intention was to remove 'the inconvenience of having to apply to the archbishop of Canterbury' (*Irish Fiants*, Elizabeth, 2996). These commissioners had power to check titles, prove wills, and exercise ecclesiastical censure and coercion, and their activities proved lucrative. The real intention behind the commission, though, was the regulation of religious reform to the advantage of the queen and her secular officials. The consequent struggle between the bishops and the commission was acrimonious, but ultimately decided in favour of Loftus. In spring 1579 Garvey and he were appointed to a new commission for faculties; and since the ecclesiastical commission became active again, both commissions were firmly under Loftus's direction. Garvey was one of Loftus's trusted supporters and ran the commission of faculties until his death in April 1580, when he was replaced by Ambrose Forthe. Any plan to suspend the ecclesiastical commission was opposed, even by the lord deputy, Sir William Fitzwilliam, since this would cause Catholics 'to swell too high against his children' (PRO, SP 63/145/49). The ecclesiastical commission concentrated on urban reformation. The bishops began visitations too. Loftus hailed the advances made in Dublin as a true preaching reformation.

The ecclesiastical authorities were especially concerned with the new generation of Roman Catholic bishops sent to Ireland by the pope. Dublin officials took measures to prevent Roman Catholic bishops from establishing themselves in Ireland, especially in the light of fear that they were preparing the way for foreign invasions. In this activity they were largely successful. On 8 October 1583 Dermot O'Hurley, Roman Catholic archbishop of Cashel, was presented to the lord justices, not the ecclesiastical commission. His interrogation under torture and execution under martial law in 1584, while associated with the lord justices, Loftus and Wallop, proceeded from Walsingham's orders, sanctioned by the queen and privy council. In September 1590 Loftus admitted to Cecil (now Baron Burghley) that there was indeed a fairly recent 'general disposition to popery', leading to disloyalty 'under pretence of religion', but before Perrot's second year as lord deputy there were only twelve 'recusant gentlemen of account'. He added the revealing observation that, restrained by the ecclesiastical commission, they showed at least outward obedience and came to sermons and received communion (PRO, SP 63/154/37). Towards the end of Elizabeth's reign, there was much self-congratulation over the course of the Reformation in Ireland. On 3 February 1603 the Irish privy council assessed 'Reformation by commission' positively: impressive preaching, matched by a public lecture every week in the two cathedrals, made Dublin as good as any English city. Loftus was the driving force behind this.

Trinity College Since ignorance was seen as the origin of all disorder in Ireland, the government sought to support the Reformation by founding a university there. This issue had become more urgent because continental Roman Catholic seminaries sent able priests to Ireland. The privy council, however, had never before considered financing an Irish university to train protestant clergy. The far-reaching instructions to Perrot of 21 June 1584 included the authorization to consider a possible rededication of the revenues of St Patrick's to endow a university in Dublin. Curwen in the 1560s had vigorously opposed such a plan. In June 1565 Brady urged recalling Curwen to England and making provision for Loftus so that he could resign the deanery and then a university could be erected. He had stated the Tudor conviction about civility in its extended form: since ignorance bred murder, robbery, and adultery 'with vices infinite', a university was necessary to save the country (Shirley, 72). Loftus shared these sentiments, but as archbishop he needed no prompting to defend the integrity of St Patrick's. He agreed that a local university, the key to the reformation of religion, was long overdue, but the transformation of St Patrick's would mean that there would be no benefices for the preaching clergy. Loftus alleged that Perrot merely sought to gratify his ambition by creating 'Perrot's College'. The ensuing quarrel was resolved by the queen's order forbidding the dissolution, after Loftus had threatened to resign his archbishopric. It is unlikely that his threat tipped the balance, but his experience of Irish affairs could not be dispensed with.

Loftus's own university scheme mobilized private interest. He persuaded the corporation of Dublin to make a grant of the priory of All Hallows and its park as the first practical step to the foundation of Trinity College, Dublin. His speeches to this end are the only remaining evidence of his style of preaching. When the proposal was sanctioned by Elizabeth, Loftus himself also subscribed £100 towards the foundation. The charter of the college (3 March 1592) made him the first provost. On surrendering the office on 7 June 1594, to Walter Travers, a scholar of a strong puritan bias, he warned him to conform to 'the doctrine and discipline of this church … established by law … Both papists and schismatics are (tho' in different degrees of enmity) equally our implacable enemies' (BL, Lansdowne MS 846, fols. 205*r*–207*r*). His vision of the Reformation had shifted significantly from including puritanism within the parameters of uniformity to excluding puritans (schismatics) just as much as counter-reformation Catholics (papists) from the college.

Loftus's wife died in July 1595. He himself died at his palace of St Sepulchre in Dublin on 5 April 1605, at the age of seventy-one. He was buried in the choir of St Patrick's. His appearance and stature seem to be best captured in the anonymous portrait showing him as lord chancellor and first provost of Trinity College. He had stated his religious convictions in his last will, a rare account of faith unusual even among committed protestants at the time. He specifically renounced intercessions of saints and angels, and wished to rely only on the merits of Christ:

> which faith, since I was called to be Bishop and Minister of God's Holy Word, I have always both publicly preached and privately acknowledged, and I desire that this my Faith and Profession be made known to posterities hereafter as long as my memory be had of myself in this world.

Even today Loftus's intentions are much easier to assess than his actions and his impact. He made many enemies, and their vocal criticism has often dominated the verdicts of later historians. HELGA ROBINSON-HAMMERSTEIN

Sources State papers Ireland, Elizabeth, PRO, SP 63 • E. P. Shirley, ed., *Original letters and papers in illustration of the history of the church in Ireland* (1851) • *The Irish fiants of the Tudor sovereigns*, 4 vols. (1994), vols. 2–3 • J. Morrin, ed., *Calendar of the patent and close rolls of chancery in Ireland for the reigns of Henry VIII, Edward VI, Mary, and Elizabeth*, 2 vols. (1861–2) • J. Venn, ed., *Grace book Δ* (1910) • J. P. Mahaffy and others, *The book of Trinity College, Dublin, 1591–1891* (1892) • *Archbishop Adam Loftus and the foundation of Trinity College, Dublin: speeches by him* (Dublin, 1892) • H. Robinson-Hammerstein, *Erzbischof Adam Loftus und die elisabethische Reformationspolitik in Irland* (Marburg, 1976) • J. Murray, 'The Tudor diocese of Dublin: episcopal government, ecclesiastical politics and the enforcement of the reformation, c.1534–1590', PhD diss., TCD, 1997 • A. Ford, *The protestant Reformation in Ireland, 1590–1641* (Dublin, 1985) • S. G. Ellis, *Tudor Ireland: crown, community and the conflict of cultures, 1470–1603* (1985) • *DNB*
Archives TCD, MS 1065
Likenesses oils, 1619, NG Ire. • six portraits, TCD [*see illus.*] • stipple, BM
Wealth at death see will, *Journal of the Irish Memorials Association*, 11 (1921–5), 364–7

Loftus, Adam, first Viscount Loftus of Ely (1568–1643), lord chancellor of Ireland, was the second son of Robert Loftus (*d.* 1606) of Coverham in Yorkshire; his mother is unknown. His uncle, Archbishop Adam *Loftus of Dublin, also held the Irish chancellorship from 1578 until his death in 1605.

Early years and advancement Loftus matriculated from Jesus College, Cambridge, in 1586, graduating BA in the same year and proceeding MA in 1589. Three years later he appears as a member of Thavies Inn, subsequently entering Lincoln's Inn. Archbishop Loftus arranged preferments for his nephew in Ireland. In 1594 he appointed him archdeacon of Glendalough and Loftus retained the benefice until his death, despite never being *presbyteri canonici*, Archbishop Laud's disapproval, and an adverse judicial ruling in 1638. Three years later, in 1597, he married Sarah (*d.* 1650), widow of Richard Meredyth, bishop of Leighlin, and daughter of one Bathoe. They had four sons and two

Adam Loftus, first Viscount Loftus of Ely (1568–1643), by unknown artist, 1619

daughters. The same year he was made judge of the marshal court, in peaceful times a sinecure but not so when Loftus secured the post nor later, in 1608, during the repression of O'Doherty's rebellion. In 1598 he became a master in chancery. While his uncle was alive Loftus deputized on occasion for him in chancery and in the court of the prerogative as well as acting as his vicar-general. When he was created LLD, as has been claimed, is obscure.

Further advancement followed: a knighthood (1604), membership of the Irish privy council (1608), constable of Maryborough Castle (1611), and judge of the new Irish admiralty court (1612). This last appointment involved Loftus in questions of patronage and jurisdiction. He was thus soon to spend £200 in litigation to wrest the appointment of water bailiff back from the city of Dublin. Very much later, in 1637, he was to object to incursions into his admiralty jurisdiction by the common law courts, the corporate towns, and the manor courts. From 1613 to 1615 he sat in the Irish House of Commons as a member for King's county. The main prize, the lord chancellorship, fell into his hands in 1619. Early that year, the then chancellor, Archbishop Thomas Jones, Archbishop Loftus's successor, died. There were two contestants for the vacancy—Sir Francis Aungier, the master of the rolls, and Loftus. Offered £1000 by Loftus, the duke of Buckingham, then, as ever, in need of ready cash, made the self-evident choice: formal appointment by James I, on 13 May 1619, followed swiftly. More honours ensued. In May 1622 James raised Loftus to the peerage as Viscount Loftus of Ely: the viscountcy was intended, as the fulsome language of the accompanying patent had it, to 'descend upon his posteritie for his sake that thereby his vertues may be recorded for future ages, soe longe as there shall remaine an heire male of his howse' (*Ninth Report*, HMC, 2.303). The chancellor, meanwhile, at this point was associated with key investigations into the condition of church and state in Ireland—of which the king's directions for the courts of 1622 were one outcome—and into the Ulster plantation. In 1622, in the absence of a lord deputy, Loftus served alongside Viscount Powerscourt as lord justice. Further periods as lord justice followed—in 1629–33 alongside Richard Boyle, the earl of Cork, and in 1636 alongside Sir Christopher Wandesford.

Quarrels and the fall of Falkland Proud, overbearing, and jealous of his position—traits hardly in short supply in the king's servants of the period—Loftus was to prove a tiresome colleague for those with whom he was teamed in the administration. Quarrels were frequent and a source of annoyance in England to Buckingham, who had, after all, secured him the chancellorship, and, following the latter's assassination, even to Charles I. In 1625 Loftus complained to the privy council at the level of his remuneration, alleging that an undertaking given on his appointment as judge marshal that he would receive 6*s*. 8*d*. per diem had not been honoured:

> I have only £300 p.a. How farr short this poore some is of a competent maintenance for so great and chargible a place, and what disproportion there must needs be between my receipts and disbursments, and what contempt and other inconveniences the pooreness of this fee may bringe, I know your Lordshipps will in your greate wisdome redely apprehend. (*Ninth Report*, HMC, 2.294)

A king's letter wrought a modest amelioration, promising Loftus a moiety of all fines charged on writs issuing from the Irish chancery. How hard-pressed at this period Loftus actually was is impossible to determine. It may be significant that when, in October 1639, William Weston accused Loftus of having taken bribes, this was ascribed to the years 1620 to 1623 when Weston said he gave Lady Loftus, among other things, 'one suit of hangings of the value of £160, one dozen of silver plates with his lordship's arms thereupon [and] 32 ells [of] Polonie rich taffetie' (*CSP Ire.*, *1633–47*, 225).

Meanwhile, a major row was brewing with Henry Cary, Viscount Falkland, appointed lord deputy in 1622. Loftus had declined to sign fiants for grants of a tannery and a distillery; he had also refused to accept Falkland's nominations of judges to serve on the assize circuits and of JPs. In a letter to Falkland, Loftus stood his ground:

> If the sole command of the seal be in his Lordship's [Falkland's] power, vain and needless is the place of a Chancellor, and profane and impious were his oath taken at his entrance, if his conscience should be subject to the will and command of any other person. (*CSP Ire.*, *1615–25*, 533)

Falkland was not convinced, and replied dubbing Loftus's suggestion of a reference to the judges 'a specious subterfuge to color a disobedience' (ibid., 540). Falkland took steps to guard his position and, if possible, obtain the removal of the lord chancellor. Allegations reached London that Loftus had orchestrated opposition to Falkland over the financial negotiations of 1627 and, potentially more damning, allegations, too, of miscarriages of justice in the Irish chancery. A detailed list of such supposed miscarriages, meticulously, if anonymously, prepared, survives in the state papers. Loftus was called to London in June 1627 to justify his conduct. The result, announced before Loftus's return in August 1628, was his total vindication. The irony of this in light of Charles I's verdict on Loftus in not totally dissimilar circumstances a decade later cannot have been lost on contemporaries. A consequential instruction of the king's the following year must have been a particularly bitter pill for Falkland to swallow. It was, wrote Charles, 'just and fit that all those that have preferred any scandalous and false informations or charges against our Chancellor, for his carriage in the execution of his office, be proceeded against in our High Court of Castle Chamber' (Morrin, 3.464).

Loftus and the earl of Cork Between the recall of Falkland in the autumn of 1629 and the arrival of Viscount Thomas Wentworth, the future earl of Strafford, in the summer of 1633, the post of chief governor was shared by Loftus and Cork as lords justices. It was a strange alliance, stranger still that the king had endorsed it. Cork had earlier complained of the 'affronts and storms' he had encountered in legal proceedings before Loftus (Ball, 1.327), as a consequence of which Charles had rebuked his lord chancellor for failing to ensure that Cork received impartial justice; and a factor in Loftus's quarrel with Falkland had been the latter's nomination of a kinsman of Cork's to ride an assize circuit where lawsuits involving Cork were pending. So far as most items of official business were concerned the two preserved a united front. In the first months of office they thus both signed the decree ordering the suppression of religious houses throughout the kingdom, and in September 1632 they jointly ordered the destruction of buildings at St Patrick's Purgatory on Lough Derg in co. Donegal, in Queen Henrietta Maria's book an act of sacrilege over which she was later to protest to Wentworth. They were in unison, too, over the revival of recusancy fines. But the animosity between the two men—its precise origin is unclear—went deep, and could flare up on the least provocation. Gifts from Cork to Loftus of goshawks, falcons, and wine (not, so far as is known, reciprocated) and attempts by the king to secure the formal reconciliation of the two men—ordering handshakes before witnesses—achieved nothing. The capacity of both Loftus and Cork to use intemperate language to each other helped keep the relationship poisonous. Such an altercation occurred as the two accompanied Wentworth to Christ Church Cathedral on the day Wentworth was sworn in. And in 1635, at a meeting of the Irish council where the continuance of a lawsuit against Cork following a plaintiff's death was being debated, Cork attacked Loftus for expressing an opinion hostile to his own, whereupon Loftus, moved to anger, responded that he cared 'not a rush' for Boyle (Grosart, 1st ser., 4.109–10). At this uproar erupted.

Wentworth's installation as lord deputy signalled a complete change in the fortunes of the two erstwhile lords justices, and for the worse. Of the two Cork became the first casualty: in 1636 he was forced to purchase at a huge price immunity from a prospective castle chamber prosecution connected to his unscrupulous land dealings in Munster. If Loftus had already been targeted Wentworth for the moment at least played a waiting game. There were even conspicuous displays of friendship and support. In 1634 he wrote to the lords of the admiralty in London backing Loftus's claims to patronage in the Irish admiralty: 'I have a high opinion of his loyalty, and do not think the Chancellorship (not worth above £400 a year) is as well paid as it should be' (*CSP Ire.*, *1633–47*, 72).

Wentworth, downfall, and disgrace A brutal exchange of letters between Loftus and Wentworth over the choice of barrister to replace Serjeant Catlyn on the Leinster circuit after Catlyn's sudden death in April 1637 marked a deterioration of the relationship. But already there had been set in train a sequence of events that was to lead to Loftus's downfall and disgrace. Accused in February 1637 by Sir John Gifford, the half-brother of his daughter-in-law, Elinor, of failure to honour a promise to provide a settlement on the marriage of his eldest son, Sir Robert Loftus, and Elinor back in 1621, the lord chancellor was eventually, on 1 February 1638, found at fault by the council board presided over by Wentworth and ordered to make the necessary financial arrangements. Sir Robert and Elinor had lived with the lord chancellor in his house and at his expense until shortly before Gifford voiced his complaint. Elinor's sister's husband was none other than Sir George Wentworth, the lord deputy's younger brother. When Elinor died in May 1639 the lord deputy penned an extraordinary tribute. 'With her', he wrote, 'are gone the greatest part of my affections to the country, and all that is left of them shall be thankfully, and religiously paid to her excellent memory' (letter to Lord Conway, *Ninth Report*, HMC, 2.298). In such circumstances, but not least because there was found but a single witness to the promise Loftus was supposed to have given in 1621, suspicion necessarily attaches to Gifford's bona fides and, indeed, to Wentworth's role in the entire affair.

Yet for Loftus much worse was to come. Found contumacious in April 1638 for failing to comply with the decree of 1 February and for insults to Wentworth he was superseded from office and sent as a prisoner to Dublin Castle. And there he lingered until a bout of ill health secured a temporary respite in May 1639 and final release the ensuing July or August, having in the end complied with the decree of February 1638, apologized abjectly for his contempts, and in substantial measure beggared himself. The ferocity of the reported exchanges between Wentworth and Loftus during the latter's trial makes it hard to accept that they could ever have been on friendly terms. Loftus refused to kneel to receive his sentence on 20 April 1638. 'The Great Seal', he protested, 'ought not to creep on knees and elbows to any subordinate person in the world' (*Various Collections*, 3. 171). The next day, with Loftus still refusing to surrender the seal, Wentworth is reputed to have remarked that he 'did once believe he should never have been able truly to have said that he was sorry his Lordship was lodged so near him' (ibid.). Loftus appealed against his sentence to the king, but Charles dismissed this, and in December 1639 Sir Richard Bolton was named lord chancellor in his stead. Wentworth took no risks over the king's handling of the appeal. In the intervening months a great deal of new material was assembled touching on Loftus's conduct as a judge—material that included Weston's story of the acceptance of bribes—all of which helped to traduce the lord chancellor's character still further. Some items in the dossier, for example, Loftus's supposed violations of articles 18 and 21 of the king's directions for the courts of 1622 (which, ironically, Loftus as a lord justice that year had promulgated), however, do possess the ring of truth.

Last years Loftus lost considerable property, in excess of £10,000 in value, as a result of the Irish rising of October 1641. Soon afterwards he removed to Yorkshire, where he died at Middleham in the North Riding early in 1643. He was buried later that year at Coverham church. His widow died seven years later. Sir Robert Loftus, his eldest son, predeceased him. Alice, his younger daughter, married the second Viscount Moore of Drogheda. During her father's incarceration she had vainly petitioned the king on his behalf, earning from Wentworth the scarcely flattering description of Loftus's 'unclean mouth'd daughter' (letter to Sir John Wintour, 10 Dec 1638, *Ninth Report*, HMC, 2.297).

In the articles of impeachment drawn up against Wentworth in 1641, his conduct in *Gifford* v. *Loftus* received specific mention. The decree of February 1638 was itself set aside by the English House of Lords in May 1642: the decision ordered the conveyance back to the former chancellor of the lands taken from him. Reverberations from the great cause lasted down to 1678. The successor to the viscountcy in 1643, Loftus's second son, Sir Edward, faced an uphill struggle to obtain enforcement of the Lords' ruling of 1642. Pitted against him, in a series of fascinating, if tortuous, English and Irish lawsuits (easily followed through *Ninth Report*, HMC, and *Various Collections*, vol. 3) which happened to necessitate, on separate occasions, the interventions of Oliver Cromwell and Charles II—was Sir Robert and Elinor's daughter Anne, and, after the latter's death in 1659, Dacre Barrett, her son and heir.

W. N. OSBOROUGH

Sources F. E. Ball, *The judges in Ireland, 1221–1921*, 2 vols. (1926) • GEC, *Peerage* • R. Lascelles, ed., *Liber munerum publicorum Hiberniae … or, The establishments of Ireland*, later edn, 2 vols. in 7 pts (1852) • Venn, *Alum. Cant.* • *VCH Yorkshire North Riding*, vol. 1 • *CSP Ire.*, *1603–60* • J. S. Brewer and W. Bullen, eds., *Calendar of the Carew manuscripts*, *4: 1601–1603*, PRO (1870) • G. Radcliffe, *The earl of Strafforde's letters and dispatches, with an essay towards his life*, ed. W. Knowler, 2 vols. (1739) • A. B. Grosart, ed., *Lismore papers*, 2 series, 10 vols.

(1886–8) · H. Cotton, *Fasti ecclesiae Hibernicae*, 2 (1848) · G. J. Hand and V. W. Treadwell, 'His majesty's directions for ordering and settling the courts within his kingdom of Ireland, 1622', *Analecta Hibernica*, 26 (1970), 177–212 · V. Treadwell, *Buckingham and Ireland, 1616–1628: a study in Anglo-Irish politics* (1998) · A. Clarke, *The Old English in Ireland, 1625–1642* (1966) · H. F. Kearney, *Strafford in Ireland 1633–41* (1959) · *Ninth report*, 2, HMC, 8 (1884) · *Report on manuscripts in various collections*, 8 vols., HMC, 55 (1901–14), vol. 3 · J. Morrin, ed., *Calendar of the patent and close rolls of chancery in Ireland*, 3 vols. (1861–3), vol. 3 · J. R. O'Flanagan, *The lord chancellors and lord keepers of the great seal of Ireland*, 2 vols. (1870)

Archives Essex RO, Chelmsford, papers relating to case · TCD, corresp. and papers

Likenesses oils, 1619, NG Ire. [*see illus.*]

Wealth at death lost substantial property on Irish rising of 1641

Loftus, Lord **Augustus William Frederick Spencer (1817–1904)**, diplomatist, born in Clifton, Bristol, on 4 October 1817, was the fourth son of John Loftus, second marquess of Ely in the peerage of Ireland (1770–1845), and his wife, Anna Maria. She was the daughter of Sir Henry Watkin Dashwood, bt, of Kirtlington Hall, Oxfordshire, and his wife, Mary Helen. Loftus's mother was lady of the bedchamber to Queen Adelaide, and his sister-in-law, Jane (daughter of James Joseph Hope-Vere), wife of his brother, John Henry Loftus, third marquess, held the same post in the household of Queen Victoria from 1857 until 1889. Having been privately educated by Thomas Legh Claughton, later bishop of St Albans, Lord Augustus spent several months in 1836–7 abroad with his father, and saw King Louis-Philippe, Talleyrand, and other notables. He was soon introduced at the court of William IV, who undertook to 'look after him' in the diplomatic service. His first appointment, which he received from Lord Palmerston, was dated 20 June 1837, the day of the king's death, in the name of his successor, Queen Victoria.

Until 1844 he was unpaid attaché to the British legation in Berlin, at first under Lord William Russell, and from 1841 under John Fane, Lord Burghersh, later Lord Westmorland. This began an intimate relationship to the Prussian court lasting, with a few interruptions, until 1871. In 1844 he was appointed paid attaché in Stuttgart. Russia was represented there by Prince Gorchakov, with whom Loftus formed an enduring intimacy. Loftus married in Fulham, Middlesex, on 9 August 1845, Emma Maria (*d.* 1902), eldest daughter of Admiral Henry Francis Greville CB. They had three sons and two daughters. Their elder daughter, Evelyn Ann Frances, died in Berlin on 28 September 1861, and in her memory her parents began the building of the English church at Baden-Baden. Two of their sons, Henry John and Montagu Egerton Loftus, were also diplomatists.

Just before the outbreak of the revolutions of 1848, Loftus, at the request of Sir Stratford Canning (afterwards Viscount Stratford de Redcliffe), joined his special mission to several European courts, when on his way to Constantinople. He thus saw much of the various revolutions of 1848. He persuaded Canning not to attempt mediation in Venice between the insurgents and the government. During the Baden revolution of 1849 (the Stuttgart legation

Lord Augustus William Frederick Spencer Loftus (1817–1904), by Gustav Schauer

also being accredited to Baden) Loftus remained in Karlsruhe or Baden-Baden. In personal meetings with insurgents he showed himself cool and outspoken. He witnessed amid some personal danger the surrender of Rastatt to the prince of Prussia, which ended the rebellion.

An appointment in 1852 as secretary of legation in Stuttgart, to reside in Karlsruhe, was quickly followed in February 1853 by promotion to the equivalent post in Berlin. In September 1853 Loftus acted there as chargé d'affaires in the absence of the British minister, Lord Bloomfield. The moment was one of critical importance in European affairs. The Crimean War was threatening, and the direction of the foreign policy of Prussia was passing at the time into the hands of Bismarck, whom Loftus 'always considered to be hostile to England, however much he may have occasionally admired her' (Loftus, 1st ser., 1.207). Berlin was little involved with the diplomatic history of the Crimean War. Loftus warmly repudiated the charge brought against him in the memoirs of Count Vitzthum of having obtained by surreptitious means the Russian plan of proposed operations at Inkerman. The plan was supposed to have been communicated by the tsar to Count Münster, and by him to the king of Prussia. At the close of the war, Loftus reported on the British consulates on the German shores of the Baltic, several of which had been denounced for slackness in reporting intelligence, especially concerning the entrance into Russia of contraband of war. An appendix to his report descriptive of the state of local trade led to the subsequent Foreign Office regulation requiring all secretaries of embassies and legations to provide annual reports on the trade and finance of the countries in which they resided.

In March 1858 Lord Malmesbury appointed Loftus to be envoy-extraordinary to the emperor of Austria. He did all that he could to avert the coming war between Austria and France, but owing to a shy and reserved manner he did not exercise much influence in Vienna. He made clear to Count Buol, the head of the Austrian government, the sympathy felt in Britain for the cause of the national liberation of Italy. On the outbreak of the war with Italy in April 1859 Loftus continued to keep Austrian statesmen informed of the strength of British feeling against Austria.

Towards the end of 1860 the legation in Vienna was converted into an embassy, and Loftus was transferred to the legation in Berlin, where he was soon immersed in the Schleswig-Holstein crisis, in which at first he frankly expressed personal views which were favourable to Denmark. In September 1862 he met Lord John Russell, his chief, at Gotha during Queen Victoria's visit to Rosenau, and was informed of the intention of the government to raise the legation in Berlin to the rank of an embassy. He was naturally disappointed that he himself was not made the first ambassador; the office was conferred on Sir Andrew Buchanan. In January 1863 Loftus began three years' residence in Munich, where Lord Russell considerately made the mission first class. In Munich he formed the acquaintance of Baron Liebig, the chemist, of whose inventions he made useful notes.

In February 1866 Loftus returned to Berlin at last as ambassador. He at once perceived the determination of Prussia to solve her difficulties with Austria by 'blood and iron' (Loftus, 2nd ser., 1.43). The crisis soon declared itself. Loftus records a midnight talk with Bismarck on 15 June 1866, in the course of which the latter, drawing out his watch, observed that at the present hour 'our troops have entered' the territories of 'Hanover, Saxony and Hesse-Cassel', and announced his intention, if beaten, to 'fall in the last charge'. On the British declaration of neutrality, which immediately followed the outbreak of the Austro-Prussian War, Loftus commented: 'We are, I think, too apt to declare hastily our neutrality, without conditions for future contingencies' (ibid., 1.78). In July 1866 Loftus was created a GCB under a special statute of the order. During his residence in Berlin he was offered the order of the Black Eagle, but declined the honour. In March 1868 he was accredited to the North German Confederation. In November of the same year he was made a privy councillor. Loftus anxiously watched the complications which issued in the Franco-Prussian War of 1870–71 and when the conflict began he was faced by many difficulties. Bismarck took offence at the ready acceptance by the British government of the request that French subjects in Germany should be placed under its protection during the war. Loftus and his secretary, Henry Dering, managed the complicated system of *solde de captivité* for the 300,000 French prisoners of war in Germany to the satisfaction of those concerned.

After the creation of the German empire fresh credentials had to be presented to its sovereign ruler in Berlin. Loftus, who wanted a change, was at his own suggestion moved to St Petersburg in February 1871, where he remained eight years. The humane disposition of Alexander II, and the marriage of his daughter Marie to the duke of Edinburgh in January 1874 seemed to favour peace between Britain and Russia; but the period proved to be one of diplomatic difficulty. When the 'Eastern question' crisis of 1876–8 broke, Loftus was in a difficult position. He probably realized that his home government had little confidence in him—Disraeli thought him 'a mere Polonius' (Seton-Watson, 45)—but he was not recalled. He had little real knowledge of Russia and, despite his friendship with Gorchakov and Jomini, was not in the Russians' confidence. Not surprisingly, his attempt to arrange a conference in 1876 failed. During the Russo-Turkish War of 1877–8 he was often an object of suspicion to the Russian government. Before the Congress of Berlin met in July 1878, he wisely suggested a preliminary Anglo-Russian understanding. This was brought about by means of a discussion of the San Stefano treaty between Count Shuvalov, Russian ambassador in London, and Lord Salisbury, then British foreign secretary.

Early in 1879 Loftus expressed to Lord Salisbury his desire for a more attractive climate and less arduous duties. Accordingly Lord Dufferin succeeded him in St Petersburg, and he was appointed governor of New South Wales and Norfolk Island. He held office in Australia from 1879 to 1885. During his first year there he opened the first international exhibition held in Sydney. In 1881 he entertained princes Albert, Edward, and George (afterwards George V), while they were on their tour round the world in the *Bacchante*. The sending of a New South Wales contingent of troops to the Sudan expedition in 1884 was due to Loftus's suggestion.

After his return home Loftus wrote, at Linden House, Leatherhead, his *Diplomatic Reminiscences* (1st ser., 1837–62, 2 vols., 1892; 2nd ser., 1862–99, 2 vols., 1894). The personal element in these is small, and the chronological order is not always precise. Without literary pretensions, the reminiscences have few rivals among later English records as a continuous narrative of diplomatic life and letters extending over more than forty years. He died at Englemere Wood Lodge, near Ascot, the house of his sister-in-law, Lady Eden, on 7 March 1904. He was buried at Frimley.

Loftus was an adequate rather than an able diplomatist, promoted a little beyond his level. But he was not 'a mere Livadian parasite, afraid even of Gorchakov's shadow', nor was it true that he was 'not only absurd, he [was] mischievous' (Disraeli, cited in Seton-Watson, 45).

A. W. Ward, *rev.* H. C. G. Matthew

Sources *The Times* (10 March 1904) • A. Loftus, *The diplomatic reminiscences of Lord Augustus Loftus, 1837–1862*, 2 vols. (1892) • A. Loftus, *The diplomatic reminiscences of Lord Augustus Loftus, 1862–1879*, 2 vols. (1894) • R. W. Seton-Watson, *Disraeli, Gladstone and the eastern question: a study in diplomacy and party politics* (1935) • B. H. Sumner, *Russia and the Balkans, 1870–1880* (1937) • O. von Bismarck, *Gedanken und Erinnerungen*, ed. H. Kohl, 6 vols. (Stuttgart, 1898–1919) • Gladstone, *Diaries* • Count Vitzthum von Eckstädt, *Gastein und Sadowa*, 2nd ser., 2 vols. (1892–4) • *St Petersburg and London in the years 1852–1864:*

reminiscences of Count C. F. Vitzthum von Eckstädt, ed. H. Reeve, trans. E. F. Taylor, 2 vols. (1887)

Archives Duke U., Perkins L., corresp. · PRO, corresp. and papers, FO519 · U. Edin. L., travel journal | BL, letters to Sir Austen Layard, Add. MSS 39112–39135, *passim* · Bodl. Oxf., letters to fourth earl of Clarendon · Bodl. Oxf., letters to Lord Kimberley · Lpool RO, corresp. with fifteenth earl of Derby · NA Scot., letters to Sir H. B. Loch · NL Aus., dispatches to fifteenth earl of Derby [copies] · PRO, Ampthill MSS · PRO, corresp. with second Earl Granville, PRO 30/29 · PRO, corresp. with Lord John Russell, PRO 30/22 · PRO, corresp. with Odo Russell, FO 918 · Woburn Abbey, letters to Lord George William Russell

Likenesses Lock & Whitfield, woodburytype photograph, NPG; repro. in T. Cooper, *Men of mark: a gallery of contemporary portraits* (1880) · G. Schauer, photogravure?, NPG [*see illus.*] · chromolithograph (after photograph by C. Roesch), NPG · photogravure photograph (after Freeman & Co.), NPG

Wealth at death £298 11*s.* 5*d.*: administration, 23 March 1904, *CGPLA Eng. & Wales*

Loftus, Dudley (1618–1695), orientalist and jurist, was born at Rathfarnham Castle, co. Dublin, the third son of Sir Adam Loftus (*b.* 1590/91, *d.* in or after 1641), later lord justice and chancellor of Ireland, and his wife, Jane, daughter of Walter Vaughan of Golden Grove, King's county. He graduated BA from Trinity College, Dublin, in 1638 and then proceeded to Oxford, graduating MA from University College on 20 October 1640.

On his return to Ireland at the outbreak of the Irish rising of 1641 Loftus was entrusted with the defence of Rathfarnham Castle and ably protected both the castle and the city of Dublin. He then embarked on a political career and served in the Irish parliament as MP for Naas between 1642 and 1648, as MP for Kildare and Wicklow in the English parliament in 1659, and in the Irish parliament as MP for Bannow in 1661 and for Fethard, co. Wexford, from 1692 to 1695. Loftus prospered throughout the Cromwellian period, evidently presiding in Trinity College, Dublin, as professor of civil law, and no doubt through this position took part in a review of the University of Dublin in order to assess the need for a second college. He received a number of high-ranking legal appointments beginning in 1651 when he was made deputy judge advocate-general and commissioner of the revenue. Three years later he was appointed judge of the admiralty and in 1655 was made a master in chancery, ingrosser of the great roll of the clerk of the pipe, and chief ingrosser for life.

Edmund Borlase depicts Loftus as playing a key role in initiating the Convention of 1660 and although the issue remains in dispute, he certainly chaired a number of committees, among them the committee on religion. His innately conservative approach is evident in his support for 'ancients' rather then 'moderns', apparent in both his decision to produce an edition of an Aristotelian text and his later conflict with the Dublin Philosophical Society. No doubt it was this conservatism which allowed him to easily fit into the new Restoration regime, which not only renewed his position as master in chancery but also gave him new legal honours; in 1660 he was appointed vicar-general of Ireland and judge of the chancery. However, Loftus's impetuous nature led to his imprisonment in 1673, following his vocal denunciation of new rules concerning governmental control of the corporation, which he, as judge of the prerogative court, considered to be illegal. Yet by the time of the war of 1689–91 he was content to remain in his Exchange Street house in Dublin 'quietly at work upon his Syriac studies' (Stokes, 45).

Loftus's legal career is well reflected in both his manuscript collections and printed works (written not only under his own name but also that of Philo-Britannicus), such as *The Case of Ware and Shirley* (1669) and *Digamias adikia, or, The First Marriage of Katherine Fitzgerald* (1677). However, his fame is chiefly due to his linguistic ability and oriental studies, said to have been encouraged by James Ussher, archbishop of Armagh, who proved extremely influential in his intellectual development. By the age of twenty Loftus reputedly knew as many languages. A catalogue of 1697 which lists 128 manuscript works written by him demonstrates his interests in Arabic, Persian, Hebrew, Armenian, Syriac, and Ethiopian (several works were destroyed but the remainder are now scattered between the British Library, Bodleian Library, and Trinity College Dublin Library, and Marsh's Library, Dublin). His printed works continued these trends, his oriental studies being most evident in works such as his translation of the life of Abul Faraj from Arabic into Latin, and his famous translation of the Ethiopian version of the New Testament (1657) for Walton's influential polyglot Bible of the same year. Other works include his contribution to Edmund Castell's combined *Dictionary of Eastern Languages* (1667); *Anaphora* (1693); *An History of the Twofold Invention of the Cross* (1686); *Logica seu introductio* (1657); *Oratio funebris … Johannis Archepiscopi Armachani, … XVI die Julii 1663* (1663); *L'oratione del' eccellentissimo Signore Giacobo duca d'Ormondia* (1664); and *The Proceedings Observed in Order to, and in the Consecration of the Twelve Bishops* (1661).

Loftus was married twice. His first wife was Frances (*d.* 1691), the daughter and heir of Patrick Nangle, son of Thomas, styled baron of Navan. They had two sons, Dudley and Adam, and five daughters, Mary, Jane, Letitia, Frances, and Catherine, all of whom either died young or unmarried with the sole exception of Letitia, who married a Mr Bladen. Loftus's second marriage, to Lady Catherine Mervyn on 16 April 1693, caused some comment given his advanced age and in his brother-in-law Ware's view exemplified his improvident and foolish nature. Loftus died in Dublin two years later in June 1695 and was buried in St Patrick's Cathedral, Dublin, in the same month.

ELIZABETHANNE BORAN

Sources G. T. Stokes, *Some worthies of the Irish Church*, ed. H. J. Lawlor (1900), 35–62 · A. Clarke, *Prelude to Restoration in Ireland* (1999), 123, 167, 199, 211, 228, 235, 247, 252, 253, 310 · T. C. Barnard, *Cromwellian Ireland: English government and reform in Ireland, 1649–1660* (1975), 209, 259, 288 · K. T. Hoppen, *The common scientist in the seventeenth century: a study of the Dublin Philosophical Society, 1683–1708* (1970), 48, 159–166 · *The whole works of Sir James Ware concerning Ireland*, ed. and trans. W. Harris, 3/1 (1746), 254–6 · J. Lodge, *The peerage of Ireland*, rev. M. Archdall, rev. edn, 7 (1789), 258–61 · Wood, *Ath. Oxon.*, new edn, 4.428–30 · J. McGuire, 'The Dublin Convention, the protestant community and the emergence of an ecclesiastical settlement in 1660', *Parliament and community*, ed. A. Cosgrove and

J. McGuire (1983), 129, 142 · C. McNeill, ed., *The Tanner letters*, IMC (1943), 12, 425, 437, 441, 450, 454, 466, 470, 480 · R. L. Greaves, *God's other children: protestant nonconformists and the emergence of denominational churches in Ireland* (1997), 40–44, 60 · M. Mansoor, *The story of Irish orientalism* (1944), 24–5 · Foster, *Alum. Oxon.*, *1500–1714*, 3.934 · Burtchaell & Sadleir, *Alum. Dubl.*, 2nd edn

Archives King's Inns, Dublin, MS 33 · Marsh's Library, Dublin, MS Z.3.1.1; MS Z.3.2.17 (2); MS Z.4.2.11; MS Z.4.5.14; MS Z.4.2.7; MS Z.3.2.12 · TCD, MS 647, fols. 1*r*–2*r*; MS 844, fol. 136*r*; MUN/P/1/452; MUN/V/5/2, p. 47 · TCD, register book

Loftus [*née* Hope-Vere], **Jane, marchioness of Ely** (**1821–1890**), courtier, was born on 3 December 1821, fourth of the six daughters and two sons of James Joseph Hope-Vere (1785–1843), politician, of Blackwood House and Craigie Hall, Lanarkshire, and his wife, Lady Elizabeth Hay (*d.* 1868), fourth daughter of the seventh marquess of Tweeddale. Through her cousin and close friend Lady Douro, Jane Hope-Vere was befriended by the duke of Wellington; and under the chaperonage of Mrs Leicester Stanhope, she and her sister were regulars at the breakfasts given by the poet Samuel Rogers. She was married on 29 October 1844 at St George's, Hanover Square, London, to John Henry Loftus, Viscount Loftus (1814–1857), who succeeded the following year as third marquess of Ely. They had one son, who succeeded as fourth marquess of Ely, and one daughter. The Elys spent part of each year on their Irish estates, in Enniskillen and co. Wexford, and travelled regularly on the continent, enlarging their circle of acquaintances, notably Queen Sophie of Holland and the future Empress Eugenie of the French (whom Lady Ely chaperoned in London, and whom she attended on behalf of Queen Victoria during the birth of the prince imperial).

Lady Ely was an unlikely candidate for social, still less political, importance. She was exceedingly nervous, prone to ill health, and easily flustered and bullied. She was neither particularly discreet nor especially clever, and was excessively anxious about the opinions of those around her. But she was loyal, hard-working, and devoted. With the encouragement of Lord Ely she had solicited office at court, and on 15 July 1851 she was appointed lady of the bedchamber to the queen, and 'Dearest Jane' rapidly became indispensable. The queen was a domestic tyrant, requiring absolute devotion from her servants, and Jane Ely subjugated herself completely to her royal mistress's demands, to the detriment of her own peace of mind and sometimes her physical health. The queen used her constantly as a go-between and unofficial secretary, both within the royal household (where the use of indirect communication was brought to a fine art) and with politicians and the press, many of whom, like Clarendon, Disraeli, Salisbury, and J. T. Delane, the editor of *The Times*, took advantage of their social acquaintance with Lady Ely to gather information about the court or to pass information to the queen. When the queen fell out with her official private secretary Sir Henry Ponsonby, she circumvented him by using Lady Ely (and one or two of her other ladies) to correspond with Disraeli. However, there was never any question of Lady Ely's taking on the mantle of earlier women courtiers such as the duchess of Marlborough, who had manipulated Queen Anne to her own ends; Lady Ely had no ends separate from those of the queen. Her nervousness of the queen amounted sometimes to fear, and caused dismay among the more robust of her fellow courtiers: Mary Bulteel considered her 'utterly the reverse from what she ought to be', and wished the queen had a 'first lady with more natural dignity' (Ponsonby, 19). Lady Ely's anxieties encompassed the queen's reaction to several rumours of her impending remarriage (Lord Ely had died in 1857)—including one that had her married to the Piedmontese leader Count Cavour—and the queen's disapproval of the marital affairs of several members of Lady Ely's family. Her only daughter, Marion (described by Lord Clarendon as 'excessively nubile' (in Kennedy, 231), was a particular worry, and eventually married four times, her first marriage ending in divorce in 1875.

Following the marriage of Princess Louise in 1871, the queen invited Lady Ely to live with her as much as possible, and, despite several attempts to lessen her servitude, Lady Ely remained at court until April 1889, when the death of her only son and her own poor health finally released her (though she retained a nominal appointment, as extra lady of the bedchamber). She died at her home at 22 Wilton Place, Knightsbridge, London, on 11 June 1890, and was buried with her husband in Kensal Green cemetery. The formal notice of regret in the *Court Circular* of 14 June 1890 said she had been 'beloved and esteemed by the Queen's family and the whole Royal Household'; but the elderly queen was truly grieved at the loss of one she had depended on and considered a friend. She 'cried bitterly' on hearing the news, and for some days 'the talk has run continually on Kensal Green "worms and epitaphs" and most meals have been funereal', reported Marie Adeane (Mallet, 37–8). K. D. Reynolds

Sources W. A. Lindsay, *The royal household* (1898) · Burke, *Peerage* (1901) · Burke, *Gen. Ire.* (1937) · E. Longford, *Victoria RI* (1964) · K. D. Reynolds, *Aristocratic women and political society in Victorian Britain* (1998) · M. Ponsonby, ed., *Mary Ponsonby* [1927] · A. L. Kennedy, ed., *My dear duchess: social and political letters to the duchess of Manchester, 1858–1869* (1956) · Lady St Helier [S. M. E. Jeune], *Memories of fifty years* (1909) · *Life with Queen Victoria: Marie Mallet's letters from court, 1887–1901*, ed. V. Mallet (1968)

Archives BL, letters to Lady Holland, Add. MS 52134 · Bodl. Oxf., letters to Benjamin Disraeli · Bodl. RH, letters to Sir J. P. Hennessy · LPL, letters to T. J. Rowsell

Likenesses C. L. L. Muller, study, 1855, Royal Collection · F. X. Winterhalter, portrait, 1856, Royal Collection

Wealth at death £6602 5*s*. 8*d*.: probate, 7 Aug 1890, *CGPLA Eng. & Wales*

Loftus, William Kennett (*c.*1821–1858), archaeologist and traveller, was born at Rye, Sussex, the son of William Kennett Loftus (*d. c.*1860), a lieutenant in the Durham light infantry, and his first wife. He was the grandson of a well-known coach proprietor of the same name in Newcastle upon Tyne. He was educated successively at Newcastle grammar school, at a school at Twickenham, and at Gonville and Caius College, Cambridge, where, however, he took no degree. He acted for some time as secretary to the Newcastle Natural History Society, and his interest in geology attracted the attention of Professor Sedgwick and afterwards of Sir Henry De la Beche. Sedgwick proposed him as a fellow of the Geological Society, and De la Beche recommended him to Lord Palmerston for the post of geologist on the staff of Sir William Fenwick Williams on the Turco-Persian frontier commission. On this work Loftus was engaged from 1849 to 1852.

While the other members of the commission travelled to Muhammarah (the scene of the original border dispute) by boat, Loftus and his friend Henry Adrian Churchill (1828–1886), together with a detachment of troops, rode across the desert and marshes of Chaldaea from the Euphrates to the lower Tigris. On this journey Loftus observed the ruins of many sites which were later identified as biblical cities, including al-Muquayyar (Ur), Warka (Uruch or Erech), and Sankara (Ellasar). Williams was impressed by their reports and allowed Loftus to return to Warka to excavate for three weeks. He subsequently sent back finds, including some glazed 'slipper' coffins from the Parthian cemetery, and a report to the British Museum.

In 1853 Loftus returned to Warka to dig for three months under the auspices of the newly created Assyria Excavation Fund and gained an understanding of the size and complexity of the site. He discovered more coffins and important cuneiform tablets, and partly excavated some proto-Sumerian walls and the great Parthian temple. From Warka he moved to Sankara which Sir Henry Rawlinson, the learned political agent at Baghdad to whom Loftus sent any inscribed material which he discovered, identified as Larsa, the Ellasar of the Bible. Other important finds were made at Tell Sifr. In 1855 Loftus returned to England with material including over eighty tablets and a variety of vases and metal objects which were sent to the British Museum. He was then appointed to the geological survey of India, but his health broke down from sunstroke, following on repeated attacks of fever while in Assyria, and he was ordered to Rangoon to recuperate. Owing partly to the interruption of the survey by the mutiny, he embarked for England on the *Tyburnia* in November 1858, and died on board on 27 November within a week of starting, from the effects of an abscess of the liver, leaving a widow, Charlotte.

Loftus has been described by H. V. F. Winstone as 'the most underestimated of nineteenth century explorers and excavators. His work was thorough and his interpretation of finds scholarly'. In 1852 he issued a volume of lithographs of cuneiform inscriptions, without a title, and in 1857 he published *Travels and Researches in Chaldaea and Susiana*. This book caused a new burst of enthusiasm in America, France, and Britain for properly financed and organized excavations in the lower regions of Mesopotamia; it was reprinted in 1971. He also contributed papers to the *Quarterly Journal of the Geological Society* in 1851, 1854, and 1855, and to the *Journal of the Royal Geographical Society* in 1856 and 1857. Plants collected by him were sent to the herbaria at Kew and at the British Museum, and some antiquities were presented by him to the Newcastle Museum. RICHARD SMAIL

Sources *GM*, 3rd ser., 6 (1859), 435 · Venn, *Alum. Cant.* · R. Welford, *Men of mark 'twixt Tyne and Tweed*, 3 (1895), 66–72 · H. V. F. Winstone, *Uncovering the ancient world* (1985) · S. Lloyd, *Foundations in the dust*, new edn (1980), 131–40 · *Proceedings* [Royal Geographical Society], 3 (1858–9), 259 · A. H. Layard, *Nineveh and Babylon* (1853), 545 · *CGPLA Eng. & Wales* (1859)

Likenesses photograph, Newcastle Literary and Philosophical Society

Wealth at death under £5000: administration with will, 1 April 1859, *CGPLA Eng. & Wales*

Logan, Sir Douglas William (1910–1987), university administrator, was born in Liverpool on 27 March 1910, the younger son and youngest of three children of Robert Logan, cabinet-maker, of Newhaven, Edinburgh, and his wife, Euphemia Taylor Stevenson, of Kirkcaldy. He was educated at Liverpool collegiate school and at University College, Oxford, where he was a classical scholar and took firsts in classical honour moderations (1930), *literae humaniores* (1932), and jurisprudence (1933). In 1933 he was awarded an Oxford University senior studentship and the Harmsworth scholarship at the Middle Temple. During 1935–6 he held the Henry fellowship at Harvard, and in 1936–7 he was an assistant lecturer in law at the London School of Economics (LSE). In 1937 he was called to the bar (Middle Temple) and elected a fellow of Trinity College, Cambridge (until 1943).

During the Second World War, Logan worked as a temporary civil servant at the Ministry of Supply from 1940 until 1944, when he was appointed clerk of the court of London University. In 1948 he became principal, a post which he held until 1975. When he took office Logan faced some formidable problems. In 1948 Britain was still suffering from the hardships imposed by the war. Rationing of food and petrol was still in force, many necessities were in short supply, and the devastation caused to London by German bombs meant that a huge building programme would have to be undertaken. At the same time such developments as the planning of new comprehensive schools marked the increased demand for university education. Added to these difficulties was the inescapable dilemma that London University itself was a large and complex organization, made up of a number of colleges, medical schools, and other institutions covering a variety of specialities, powered by machinery which could work effectively only if controlled by somebody equipped with the capacity to take clear decisions and the determination and energy required to put such decisions into effect. Logan's character, education, and experience gave him the toughness to make this machinery work even when hampered by financial stringency, student militancy, and occasional academic obduracy.

From the outset Logan concentrated on the problems of reconstruction necessitated by the shortage of accommodation for students and the cost of building sites in central London. The outcome was the acquisition or construction of seven university halls of residence and the purchase of an extensive site in Bloomsbury on which important new university buildings could be erected.

At this time London, the largest university in Britain, also had responsibility for a number of colleges outside

London which took London degrees. Similarly, university colleges in Africa, the West Indies, and Malaya, together with the existing universities in Malta and Hong Kong, needed the assistance of London in maintaining their academic integrity through London degrees. Logan was actively involved in his membership of the Association of Commonwealth Universities, of which he was chairman in 1962–3.

Throughout Logan's term of office as principal and after his retirement he worked industriously to better the conditions of university staff and students. He fought a long campaign for the improvement of the pensions of university teachers and was virtually the author of the universities superannuation scheme, which came into force in 1974. He was its chairman in 1974–7, deputy chairman in 1977–80, and consultant from 1980 to 1986. In his youth he had been an enthusiastic player of rugby football, and, with the co-operation of his vice-chancellor, Sir David Hughes Parry, he took a leading part in the provision of social and athletic facilities for students on a university as opposed to a college basis. He was also particularly concerned with the problems of medical education, and the establishment of the National Health Service seemed to him to call for constant vigilance to safeguard the efficiency of the London hospital medical schools.

Logan also sat for many years on committees dealing with scholarships and grants for students from both Britain and overseas, including Athlone fellowships and Marshall scholarships. He was a member of the board of the National Theatre (1962–8), a governor of the Old Vic (1957–80), and a trustee of the City Parochial Foundation (1953–67). He was knighted in 1959 and received honorary fellowships from LSE (1962), University College, Oxford (1973), and University College, London (1975); honorary degrees were conferred upon him by universities from Melbourne to British Columbia. He was a chevalier of the Légion d'honneur, and an honorary bencher of the Middle Temple (1965).

In 1940 Logan married Vaire Olive, daughter of Sir Gerald Woods Wollaston, herald; they had two sons before they divorced in 1946. A year later he married Christine Peggy, daughter of William Arthur Walker, motor engineer inspector; they had one son and one daughter.

Jock Logan, as he was known to his colleagues, was well built, of medium height, and of somewhat shuffling gait. A prodigious worker, he had impressive organizing ability and was a consummate draftsman. He was impatient with inadequacy and with opposition based on ignorance or vested interest, and his brusque and forceful manner alienated many. He died in University College Hospital, London, on 19 October 1987, after suffering a stroke; his wife survived him. H. F. Oxbury, *rev.*

Sources *The Times* (20 Oct 1987) · N. B. Harte, *The University of London, 1836–1986: an illustrated history* (1986) · D. Logan, *The University of London: an introduction*, rev. edn (1956) · *CGPLA Eng. & Wales* (1988)
Archives LUL, papers
Wealth at death £60,737: probate, 25 March 1988, *CGPLA Eng. & Wales*

Logan, George (1678–1755), Church of Scotland minister and religious controversialist, was probably born in Glasgow, the son of George (or James) Logan, a merchant and burgess in the city, and his wife, Elizabeth, daughter of John Cunningham, minister of Old Cumnock. The family is thought to have originated in Ayrshire. Logan entered the Greek class at Glasgow University in 1693, and received the MA in 1696. Preparing for the ministry, he went on to study divinity and is listed as a student of that subject at Glasgow on 18 January 1697.

Logan was licensed to preach by the presbytery of Glasgow on 4 March 1703, and then became chaplain to John, earl of Lauderdale. On 6 February 1707 he was called to the parish of Lauder in Berwickshire, and was ordained on 8 May 1707. He married his first wife, Anne Home (*d.* before 1744), on 5 April 1711; the marriage produced a son and a daughter. On 16 October 1718 he was presented by the duke of Roxburghe to the parish of Sprouston in Roxburghshire, where he was admitted on 22 January 1719. He was transferred to the parish of Dunbar in Haddingtonshire on 24 January 1722, having again been presented by the duke of Roxburghe. While there he published his first work, the *Essay upon Gospel and Legal Preaching*, in 1723.

On 31 August 1732 Logan was called to Trinity parish in Edinburgh, and was admitted on 14 December. On 8 May 1740 he was elected moderator of the general assembly which deposed Ebenezer Erskine and other dissident ministers who had vehemently opposed the use of patronage in selecting parish ministers, thus officially confirming the first major secession of the eighteenth-century Church of Scotland. The hotly debated patronage issue provoked Logan's first controversial publications. In 1732 he published *A Modest and Humble Inquiry*, followed by *Continuation* in the following year. In 1733 he again wrote on church matters in *An Overture for a Right Constitution of the General Assembly* (1736). In the following year he supported the government's interpretation of events surrounding the Porteous riots in Edinburgh in *The lawfulness and necessity of ministers their reading the act of parliament for bringing to justice the murderers of Captain John Porteous*.

Some time after 1 January 1744 Logan married his second wife, Lilias Weir. As a confirmed whig and presbyterian Logan was naturally opposed to Jacobitism and strongly urged that Edinburgh be placed in a state of defence during the rising of 1745. When this was not done, and Edinburgh was occupied by Jacobite forces, Logan left the city, and his home on Castlehill was used by the Jacobite army as a guardhouse. After they left Logan inserted a satirical advertisement in the newspapers for the recovery of possessions which had been stolen by the recent occupants of his house.

Logan is best known for his contributions to the controversy between whigs and Jacobites over whether Scotland's monarchy was indefeasibly hereditary. Logan presented the whig presbyterian case for a limited monarchy that was not strictly hereditary, against the views of Thomas Ruddiman and other Jacobites. Already in 1717 Logan and other whigs, including the patriotic historian James Anderson, had formed a group of 'associated critics' to engage in whig / Jacobite controversy. Their object was to defend the reputation of the sixteenth-century Scottish historian George Buchanan, whose political and historical views were the cornerstone of Scottish whig-presbyterian ideology, and who had been attacked by Ruddiman in his edition of Buchanan's complete works. Their intention was to produce their own edition of Buchanan, refuting the slanders of Ruddiman. Although eighty pages of notes on Ruddiman's strictures were compiled the project was never completed. None the less, Logan spent the 1740s in lively literary combat with Ruddiman. In 1746 he argued in *A Treatise on Government* that the Scottish monarchy was not rigidly hereditary. Ruddiman's counter-arguments were answered by *A Second Treatise* (1747) and *The Finishing Stroke, or, Mr Ruddiman Self-Condemned* (1748). The battle continued in 1749 with Logan's *Second Letter … to Mr Thomas Ruddiman* and *The doctrine of the jure-divino-ship of hereditary indefeasible monarchy enquired into and exploded, in a letter to Mr Thomas Ruddiman*. The historical issues dealt with in these works were all central to the controversy, including the relative hereditary claims of Bruce and Balliol to the Scottish crown, and the legitimacy of Robert III and the contemporary Stuart pretender. Logan also defended the seventeenth-century presbyterian idol, Alexander Henderson, against slanders by the episcopalian Ruddiman, in a work published in 1749. He died in Edinburgh on 13 October 1755. His wife appears to have outlived him, but died before 17 December 1770.

ALEXANDER DU TOIT

Sources *DNB* · *Fasti Scot.*, new edn, 1.333, 407; 2.88, 153; 3.25 · Anderson, *Scot. nat.* · C. Kidd, *Subverting Scotland's past: Scottish whig historians and the creation of an Anglo-British identity, 1689–c.1830* (1993) · C. Innes, ed., *Munimenta alme Universitatis Glasguensis / Records of the University of Glasgow from its foundation till 1727*, 4 vols., Maitland Club, 72 (1854), vol. 1, pp.445–6; vol. 3, p.245 · Irving, *Scots.* · G. Chalmers, *The life of Thomas Ruddiman* (1794) · Chambers, *Scots.* (1855), 6.488–90

Archives BL, corresp. with duke of Newcastle, Add. MSS 32686–33078; 33157–33169; 33198–33201; 33325–33344; 33442, 64813, 69093 · NL Scot., Ruddiman collection · U. Edin. L., Laing collection

Logan, James (1674–1751), colonial official and scholar, was born on 20 October 1674 in Lurgan, co. Armagh, to Patrick Logan and Isabel Hume. Patrick Logan was a minister and an MA of Edinburgh University, who after becoming a Quaker had attempted to make a living as a schoolmaster. James knew Latin, Greek, and Hebrew when he was apprenticed at the age of thirteen to Edward Webb, a linen draper in Dublin, but he remained there only six months. During the conflicts in Ireland following the revolution of 1688 the Logan family fled to Scotland, and Patrick soon became master of the Friar Meeting-House Quaker school in Bristol. When the family returned to Ireland in 1693, James, aged nineteen, became a schoolmaster. While teaching he also perfected his Latin and Greek, learned French, Italian, and some Spanish, and, by studying William Leybourn's *Cursus mathematicus*, achieved knowledge of mathematics and astronomy, and built a library of more than 700 volumes. Discontented with being a schoolmaster, he sought to migrate to Jamaica and, when

James Logan (1674–1751), by Gustavus Hesselius, *c.*1716–45

his mother objected, sold his library and became a linen merchant in Bristol. In 1699 William Penn hired him as secretary to accompany him on his second trip to Pennsylvania.

Logan lived with Penn and his family at the Slate Roof House in Philadelphia until the proprietor moved to his estate at Pennsbury. Penn put Logan in charge of organizing land policy, a necessary task since proceeds from quit-rents and sales would help pay the proprietor's debts. With the aid of a new law regularizing land sales, Logan brought order to land policy but he found collecting money a frustrating task. Logan continued as the Penns' business agent for nearly thirty years, a role that was bound to bring conflicts with the settlers. Logan helped Penn negotiate the charter of privileges, though he later criticized that document for giving the assembly too much power and the council too little. Logan's ideal of government was of a balance of monarchy, aristocracy, and democracy, and he feared that Pennsylvania had too much democracy. He did not bother to hide his contempt for the 'mob', and his rather supercilious manner did not endear him to the people.

Before returning to England, Penn named Logan clerk of the council, secretary of the province, and one of three commissioners of property. Logan would serve on the council from 1702 to 1747. His new responsibilities brought him only £100 per year, so he began trading on his own account. Unable to make direct remittances from land sales to Penn in England, Logan began to invest such moneys in Pennsylvania commodities which could be sold elsewhere. By 1706 Logan had raised about £8000 in

Pennsylvania money for Penn, but the debts of the proprietor to the Ford family amounted to £30,000.

As Penn's primary agent in the colony, Logan became involved in political disputes with royal officials when Quaker lawyer David Lloyd questioned the Admiralty courts. Royal officials sought to make Pennsylvania a royal colony by proving the incompetence of proprietary government. Logan became the primary opponent of Lloyd, who emerged as a leader in the assembly's quest for power over land titles and fines at the expense of the proprietor. Logan also had to counter the politically disastrous policies of the new governor, John Evans, who issued a false alarm of a French attack in 1706 and sought to tax Philadelphia shipping to pay for a fort in Delaware. Other disputes centred on the rights of the assembly to set its own schedule for meeting and adjourning, and on whether the governor or assembly had the power to establish courts. The assembly attempted to impeach Logan, and thereby weaken Penn. The first trial failed when Governor Evans refused to preside as judge because the council was not equivalent to the House of Lords. When the new governor, Charles Gookin, argued that Logan's membership on the council made him immune, the impeachment ended, and in 1709 Logan sailed for England.

Logan's first two courtships failed because of his lack of property. In Philadelphia he had wooed Ann, the daughter of merchant Edward Shippen. Ann was also courted by Thomas Story, a wealthy Quaker minister and lawyer. Ann preferred Logan but her family preferred Story, and she married him. The disappointment was made public when the Philadelphia monthly meeting in 1703 arbitrated a resulting dispute between Logan and Story. In England Logan engaged the affections of Judith Crowley, but her family objected to his lack of wealth, and she, like Shippen, refused to disobey them. Determined now to gain wealth, Logan began buying at cheap prices the rights to unoccupied lands of Quakers who had not come to Pennsylvania. Logan ultimately married Sarah Read (*d.* 1754), a pious but not well-educated Quaker, on 9 December 1714. Their four children resembled their mother in piety, but did not share their father's intellectual acumen.

On his return to Pennsylvania in 1711 Logan engaged in the fur trade, using tactics described by Frederick Tolles as 'hard, venturesome, unscrupulous if necessary', as he got fur traders into debt and supplied them with rum for the Native Americans—even though the colony's laws and the Quaker meeting forbade selling alcohol to the American Indians (Tolles, 90). By 1715 he was sending £1000 in furs per year to England. He called the wagons for transporting the furs from his trading post on Conestoga Creek 'Conestoga wagons', and this continued to be the way Americans named the hooped, canvas-covered wagons used for westward migration.

Logan observed his first negotiations with the Native Americans at the gatherings at Pennsbury in 1701. When the War of the Spanish Succession broke out in America, Logan sought to create a common British Indian policy to wean American Indians away from the French, and saw keeping the loyalty of the Five Nations of the Iroquois as a key element in British imperial strategy. He also faced problems with settler encroachment on Indian lands. Anticipating changes that would not take place for three decades, in 1731 Logan composed a memorial to the British government asking for a unified command so that the colonists could effectively deal with the Indians and the French.

After Penn's stroke in 1711 and death in 1718, Logan continued to serve the Penn family loyally. He did extensive research on the disputed border between Pennsylvania, Delaware, and Maryland, finding maps to demonstrate what the crown thought was the border in 1681. When the Pennsylvania governor, William Keith (1717–26), ignored the council's advice before approving laws, and attempted to survey land and claim a copper mine for himself, Logan opposed him. Another issue was paper money, which Keith favoured but Isaac Norris opposed. Logan supported a modest circulation with sound backing, but feared depreciation if too much were issued. He approved of the assembly's issuing £15,000. In 1723 he returned to London to consult Hannah Penn, but before leaving he used his position as judge to lecture the people on the benefits of a mixed government. Logan returned with new instructions from Penn's widow, which Keith ignored. Instead Keith, aided by David Lloyd, commenced a pamphlet war with Logan and supporters of the proprietors. Keith and Lloyd won elections until Patrick Gordon arrived as new governor in 1726. When Keith tried to use the assembly as a new power base, an alliance of Logan, Norris, and even Lloyd defeated him. Keith's leaving Pennsylvania and David Lloyd's death in 1731 quieted political passions.

Logan, now tired of supporting the proprietors, tried to persuade the sons of William Penn to come to Pennsylvania to look after their own interests, and Thomas Penn came to the colony in 1732. In January 1728 a fall broke a bone that did not heal properly, leaving Logan disabled. He became chief justice of the Pennsylvania supreme court (1731–9) and, after Governor Gordon's death in 1736, became the executive of the colony by virtue of his position as president of the council.

Although Logan excelled at negotiating with American Indians, their confidence that he would treat them with the same care for justice as William Penn seems, in retrospect, misplaced. He co-operated with Thomas Penn in what was later known as the 'walking purchase', whereby the Lennai Lenape Indians lost a substantial amount of land by what many historians label a dubious interpretation of a previous purchase made by William Penn. Logan called upon the more powerful Five Nations, who claimed a kind of suzerainty over the region, to support his interpretation of the treaty and coerce the dwindling Lennai Lenape into accepting it. His last negotiation with the Indians, which occurred in 1742 when a delegation for the Five Nations visited Stenton, led in 1744 to a treaty at Lancaster, Pennsylvania, by which they pledged to support the British.

Logan, contrary to Quaker beliefs, was not a strict pacifist, at least not since his first journey to Pennsylvania. He believed there was little difference between a magistrate's use of force and a defensive war. Because he thought Quaker principles were incompatible with government, he had advised William Penn to sell the right to government. Seeing a coming imperial war with France, in 1741 at the Philadelphia yearly meeting (an annual gathering of Friends from Pennsylvania, Delaware, and West New Jersey) Logan sent a treatise justifying war and seeking to persuade Quakers to withdraw from government. Quakers' successful pursuit of wealth, he argued, made Pennsylvania a tempting target. The treatise had no immediate effect, but set a series of principles that would be considered in later wars.

Logan never lost his passion for learning and book collecting, being interested in astronomy, biology, optics, and numismatics as well as Greek and Latin classics. He collected a library of over 3000 volumes, which he bequeathed to the city of Philadelphia. He taught himself fluxions (calculus) by reading Newton's *Principia mathematica*. Logan conducted scientific experiments on the sexuality of plants, and his results were published by the Royal Society and praised by Linnaeus, who named the order Loganiaceae after him. He had discussions with and opened his library to young scientists, including John Bartram, Thomas Godfrey, and Benjamin Franklin. Logan defended Godfrey's claim to having invented the quadrant against John Hadley, and introduced Bartram's work to Linnaeus. Logan also carried on a learned correspondence on many subjects with such diverse scholars as Peter Collinson, Cadwallader Colden, and William Jones. Like many scientists of his time, Logan believed that reason could discover a cosmic order and that science helped religion by describing the works of God. Logan died on 31 October 1751 at his home, Stenton, Germantown, Pennsylvania, and was buried in the Friends' burial-ground, Arch Street, Philadelphia. J. WILLIAM FROST

Sources F. B. Tolles, *James Logan and the culture of provincial America* (1957) · J. Webb, 'Logan, James', *ANB* · R. N. Lokken, 'The social thought of James Logan', *William and Mary Quarterly*, 27 (1970), 68–89 · *The scientific papers of James Logan*, ed. R. N. Lokken (1972) · *The correspondence of James Logan and Thomas Story*, ed. N. Penney (1927) · 'A letter from James Logan to the Society of Friends, on the subject of their opposition in the legislature to all means for the defence of the colony, September 22, 1741', *Collections of the Historical Society of Pennsylvania* (1851), 36–42 · J. E. Johnson, 'A Quaker imperialist's view of the British colonies in America in 1732', *Pennsylvania Magazine of History and Biography*, 60 (1936), 97–130 · W. Armistead, *Memoirs of James Logan* (1851) · *The papers of William Penn*, ed. M. M. Dunn, R. S. Dunn, and others, 3–4 (1986–7) · E. Wolf, *The library of James Logan of Philadelphia, 1674–1751* (1974) · *Correspondence between William Penn and James Logan … and others, 1700–1750*, ed. D. Logan and E. Armstrong, 2 vols. (1870–72)

Archives Hist. Soc. Penn., corresp. and papers

Likenesses G. Hesselius, oils, *c.*1716–1745, Hist. Soc. Penn. [*see illus.*] · W. Cogswell, oils (after G. Hesselius), Hist. Soc. Penn.

Logan, James (1796/7–1872), writer on Scottish Gaelic culture, was born in Aberdeen, the son of a merchant there. He was educated at the local grammar school and afterwards at Marischal College. A fractured skull sustained while attending a highland games prevented him from following his intended career in law. From about 1821 it appears that he lived mainly in London, working as a writer and journalist, notably as a contributor to the *Gentleman's Magazine*. He served briefly as secretary of the Highland Society of London, and worked as a transcriber of the British Museum catalogue from 1838 to 1840. His failure to hold any formal post for long was owed apparently to his 'impatience of restraint' (*DNB*), and he returned to freelance work, being supported during his later years by highland friends in London. At different times he is supposed to have enjoyed the patronage of Prince Albert and the fourth earl of Aberdeen.

In the mid-1820s Logan made extensive walking tours of the highlands and islands, which led to his most significant work, *The Scottish Gael*, which first appeared in 1831 (2 vols.). The book, which was dedicated to William IV, encompassed a wide range of topics, from archaeology to early nineteenth-century Gaelic literature, and included chapters on war, arms, dress, hunting, food, poetry and music, and religion. Many of its archaeological and historical conclusions are no longer acceptable, and he relies overmuch on the Ossianica of James Macpherson, but the work contains a lot of valuable commentary on highland mores and traditional lore, and here he shows a fairly good knowledge of Gaelic. *The Scottish Gael* was reissued with a memoir of the author and notes by Alexander Stewart in 1876.

Following the enthusiastic reception of his 1831 book Logan was asked by John Mackenzie to write an introduction to his *Beauties of Gaelic Poetry* (1841), in which he summarized and occasionally expanded upon points made in his earlier work. He supplied the text for *The Clans of the Scottish Highlands* (2 vols., 1845–7), which consisted of original, if somewhat stereotyped, sketches of highland chiefs by R. R. McIan, and a 'Description and historical memoranda of character, mode of life, etc. etc.' by Logan. This work won contemporary praise for the verisimilitude of the tartans.

Logan died at 66 Whitfield Street, St Pancras, London, on 29 March 1872. Undoubtedly many of his conclusions need to be modified or challenged in the light of more modern Celtic scholarship, but his positive contribution to a more sympathetic and informed attitude to Gaelic history and culture deserves to be recognized.

DERICK S. THOMSON

Sources A. Stewart, 'Memoir', in J. Logan, *The Scottish Gael* (1876) · Allibone, *Dict.* · *DNB* · Boase, *Mod. Eng. biog.* · d. cert.

Logan, James Richardson (1819–1869), lawyer and newspaper proprietor, was born at Hutton Hall, Berrywell, Berwickshire, on 10 April 1819, the son of a gentleman farmer, Thomas Logan, and his wife, Elizabeth. A clever 'extra scholar' at Duns Academy, he trained with an Edinburgh barrister, and after a short spell planting indigo in Bengal moved to Penang in 1839, where he was admitted as an advocate in December 1841. His elder brother Abraham followed him to Penang and was admitted to the bar in April 1842, but soon moved to Singapore, where James joined him in partnership the following year. The brothers were to work closely together for nearly thirty years and were buried in the same grave. Abraham became editor-proprietor of Singapore's premier newspaper, the *Singapore Free Press*, secretary to the chamber of commerce, member of numerous public committees, and a champion of constitutional reform. In 1853 the more studious and reserved James returned to practise law in Penang, where he was made a justice of the peace and was much in demand as a lucid petition writer, an effective leader of deputations, and as a legal spokesman for the European and Chinese communities in opposing irksome official restrictions. In 1855 the brothers bought the *Pinang Gazette*, with James as editor, and their newspapers became particularly influential in the absence of representative institutions. In powerful editorials James argued Penang's case, criticizing dictatorial East India Company and government of India officials, championing free trade, and urging strong policies to protect commerce in the Malay states and Sumatra.

James Logan died in Penang at the home of his son Daniel, the solicitor-general, on 20 October 1869. His funeral that same day was attended by the entire European community and leading Asians; he was buried in the protestant cemetery, Penang, and a monument was erected in front of the supreme court by open subscription lamenting his untimely death as a public calamity: 'Unselfish to a degree he spared neither time nor money to promote Penang's welfare'.

But Logan's most lasting memorial was his *Journal of the Indian Archipelago and Eastern Asia*, always known popularly as Logan's journal. A fellow of the Geological Society of London, a member of the Asiatic Society of Bengal, and corresponding member of the Ethnological Society (of London) and the Batavian Society of Arts and Sciences, Logan contributed articles to prestigious journals of learned societies in London, Edinburgh, Calcutta, and Batavia. His own journal, the first attempt to promote a scientific periodical in the Straits Settlements at a time when most of the Malay peninsula was unexplored by Europeans, was unique in being conceived, edited, and financed single-handedly. Logan drew on the considerable expertise of officials, clergy, naval and military officers, lawyers, doctors, surveyors, businessmen, and planters of diverse nationalities, including one prominent Chinese merchant, while he himself contributed articles on a wealth of subjects: geology, exploration, piracy, Malay customs, aboriginal peoples, ethnology, and comparative philology. An indefatigable, ever inquisitive traveller, Logan braved hardship and often danger, which undermined his health. Sometimes he returned a living skeleton, fever-racked with malaria, which eventually killed him. Twelve volumes of Logan's journal were published between 1847 and 1859, until waning public enthusiasm and financial strain impelled Logan to abandon the journal and concentrate on public causes and the *Pinang Gazette*.

But Logan's enterprise inspired the formation in 1878 of the straits (later Malaysian) branch of the Royal Asiatic Society, with Daniel Logan as first vice-president, and the new society obtained a government grant to buy Logan's library. In his inaugural address, the president pledged to continue Logan's work, while avoiding the mistake of trying to carry the burden alone. While most of his geological and linguistic research was superseded or updated, Logan's journal remained of lasting interest to historians and anthropologists and the entire series was reprinted in 1970. C. M. TURNBULL

Sources J. T. Thomson, 'A sketch of the career of the late James Richardson Logan of Penang and Singapore', *Journal of the Straits Branch of the Royal Asiatic Society*, 7 (1881), 75–81 • *Penang Argus and Mercantile Advertiser* (21 Oct 1869) • *Penang Argus and Mercantile Advertiser* (28 Oct 1869) • *Pinang Gazette and Straits Chronicle* (25 Dec 1873) • G. F. Hose, 'Inaugural address of the president', *Journal of the Straits Branch of the Royal Asiatic Society*, 1 (1878), 1–12 • C. M. Turnbull, *The Straits Settlements, 1826–67* (1971) • W. Makepeace, G. E. Brooke, and R. St J. Braddell, *One hundred years of Singapore*, 2 vols. (1921); repr. (1991) • C. B. Buckley, *An anecdotal history of old times in Singapore*, 2 vols. (1902); repr. in 1 vol. (1965); new edn (1984) • *The Athenaeum* (18 Dec 1869), 820 • C. E. Buckland, *Dictionary of Indian biography* (1906) • GS Lond. • Royal Asiatic Society • J. Bastin and C. Bastin, 'Some old Penang tombstones', *Journal of the Malaysian Branch of the Royal Asiatic Society*, 37/1 (1964), 126–65, esp. 146 • b. cert.

Logan, John (1747/8–1788), Church of Scotland minister and writer, was born in late 1747 or early 1748 in Soutra, in the eastern Edinburghshire parish of Fala. The second son of George Logan, a farmer, and Janet Waterston of Stowe, he was sent to the grammar school in Musselburgh; it was probably there that he made the acquaintance of the local minister, Alexander Carlyle, who would remain a lifelong confidant. Some time during his youth the family moved to Gosford Mains, along the northern coast of Haddingtonshire. Although his parents frequented the congregation of the Revd John Brown of Haddington, the foremost minister of the Burgher branch of Presbyterian seceders, Logan gradually shifted his allegiance to the moderate party in the Church of Scotland. From November 1762 he was a student of arts, and subsequently divinity, at the University of Edinburgh, where his classmates included Thomas Robertson, later minister at Dalmeny and an intimate friend to the end, and Michael Bruce, whose *Poems on Several Occasions* Logan would publish in Edinburgh in 1770, three years after Bruce's untimely death. At the university Logan came under the influence of Adam Ferguson and Hugh Blair, both moderates in the Carlyle circle. On Blair's recommendation he travelled in the summer of 1768 to Caithness, in the far north of Scotland, to serve as tutor to fourteen-year-old John Sinclair, later Sir John *Sinclair of Ulbster, the famous agricultural improver, who remained a friend and patron for life. Logan received his licence to preach from the presbytery of Haddington on 27 September 1770, and the following year was called to the second charge at South Leith, near Edinburgh, although a dispute over a competing presentation provoked a heavy-handed satirical drama entitled *The Planters of the Vineyard* (1771) and delayed his ordination until 2 April 1773. He possessed a versatile intellect and in his early years at South Leith was supposedly an attentive pastor. Appointed in 1775 to a church committee charged with revising paraphrases and hymns for use in public worship, he was the largest contributor to the volume that the committee produced in 1781. Logan held strong whig views in politics, and in the general assembly of 1782 he broke with the moderates by delivering a powerful speech in support of an unsuccessful motion to congratulate the king on the recent change of ministries, from North to Rockingham.

During the 1779–80 college session, and again the following year, Logan delivered at St Mary's Chapel, Edinburgh, lectures on universal history which were, according to the recollection of Adam Smith, 'approved and even admired by some of the best and most impartial judges' (*Correspondence of Adam Smith*, 290). Logan hoped the lectures would establish his credentials for the chair of civil history at Edinburgh; when he heard that Principal William Robertson was supporting Alexander Fraser Tytler, who was appointed to the chair on 16 February 1780, he grew hostile to the principal, whom he subsequently called 'that impudent fellow Robertson' (letter to Carlyle, 12 April 1786, Logan MSS, Edinburgh University). On 10 November 1781, as he prepared to give his course of history lectures for a third time, Logan published, for the benefit of his hearers, *Elements of the Philosophy of History: Part First*, an extended outline of his views on the scientific nature of history and the progress of the ancient Greeks and Romans. He intended to add lectures on modern European history (the projected second part of his course), but the third lecture series was abruptly cancelled and the entire enterprise abandoned. In 1787, however, his brief *Dissertation on the Governments, Manners, and Spirit, of Asia* appeared in London, with a prefatory advertisement by William Creech (signed W. C.), a co-publisher of both works, identifying it as one of the lectures Logan delivered in Edinburgh in 1780, which Creech had taken down in shorthand on account of 'the high approbation which they met with, from a learned and respectable audience'. Like the *Elements*, the *Dissertation* is highly Eurocentric and dismissive of Asian culture, which it considers conducive only to despotism.

Meanwhile Logan's personal life was unravelling. Always prone to depression, he had also developed a serious drinking problem and had impregnated a servant girl, one Catharine Rogers, who gave birth to a son in 1781 (Donald Grant to Carlyle, 4 Dec 1788, Logan MSS). In March 1781 he went to London to escape the wrath of his parishioners and to arrange for the publication of a volume of poetry. Letters to Carlyle on 18 May and 22 June reveal him to be in a state of suicidal despair as he tries to explain away his alcoholism. Under these circumstances Logan must have received some satisfaction from the success of his *Poems*, published by Thomas Cadell in July 1781 and reissued in a second edition the following spring, but that work touched off an intense controversy centring on charges of plagiarism, particularly in regard to the celebrated 'Ode to the Cuckoo' which Logan placed at the head of his book. 'Cuckoo' had also appeared in the 1770 volume of *Poems on Several Occasions* by Michael Bruce, whose family and friends were adamant that it was his. In the course of an unsuccessful attempt to block the sale of a reprint edition of Bruce's *Poems* in 1782, Logan, or his lawyers, claimed that he was the real author of 'Cuckoo' and a number of other poems in the 1770 volume, and this point was later supported by Thomas Robertson and Henry Mackenzie, among others. Several pamphlets and articles supporting Logan's authorship of 'Cuckoo' also appeared during the 1870s, when the controversy was at its height, but since then the weight of scholarly evidence and opinion has favoured Bruce.

On 2 October 1781 Logan became a member of the Society of Antiquaries of Scotland, and on 12 June 1782 he donated to that society a copy of his *Poems*. The next year he completed a play, *Runnamede*, adapted from Voltaire's *Tancrède*, which Robert Anderson called 'the greatest effort of his genius' (Anderson, 1033), but which Henry Mackenzie considered flawed (though he penned an unused epilogue to it), and which Adam Smith did not admire 'in the least' (*Correspondence of Adam Smith*, 257, 290). It was banned from the stage at Covent Garden because the government considered its speeches on behalf of liberty too inflammatory. Although published in 1783 in London, and the next year performed in Edinburgh, the play proved to be another disappointment to Logan, who donated a copy of the London edition to the Society of Antiquaries of Scotland on 27 January 1784.

Authorship of a stage play added to Logan's list of offences in the eyes of pious parishioners, as did the news that he had impregnated a second woman in the parish. Logan found it prudent to leave Scotland in October 1785 for a short-lived career of hack journalism in London, where Old Slaughter's Coffee House was 'his common resort of an evening' (Thompson, 153). Using Hugh Blair as an intermediary he arranged to demit his parish on 27 December 1786 in exchange for an annuity of £40 (*Extracts*, 91). In London he worked with Gilbert Stuart on the *English Review* and wrote *A Review of the Principal Charges Against Mr. Hastings* (1788), a pamphlet so strident in its defence of Warren Hastings that the publisher, John Stockdale, was tried for libel (though acquitted). It is believed that Logan revised his Edinburgh lectures on ancient history from the Egyptians to the Greeks for publication in London in 1788 (second volume, 1791), by the Uxbridge schoolmaster William Rutherford, as *A View of Antient History*, which would be, Logan slyly assured Adam Smith on 20 August 1787, 'the very best [book] on the Subject' (*Correspondence of Adam Smith*, 307). In a letter to John Douglas, then bishop of Carlisle, on 9 November 1787, Carlyle recommended Logan for service in the Church of England, but the bishop, having heard stories of his conduct, made it clear in his reply of 25 November that this could not be. Meanwhile Logan's health was deteriorating. On 4 December 1788 the Revd Donald Grant, who would be one of the two executors of his estate, reported to Carlyle from London that Logan was in the last stage of a consumption, and on 6 January 1789 he wrote again to say that 'Your poor friend is now freed from all his trouble. He died on Sunday 28th Decr., & was decently & genteely buried under my direction on Friday 2d. Janry' (Logan MSS). He was just forty years old, and unmarried.

In his will Logan optimistically left £600 for his friends

and his two illegitimate children against the sale of his manuscripts, which are listed in a published letter from Thomas Robertson, the second of his executors (Anderson, 1029). In April 1790 a volume of his *Sermons*, including the programme for an entire Lord's supper celebration, was published in Edinburgh by Bell and Bradfute. A second edition was called for before the end of the year, and the following spring a second volume appeared, containing religious lectures as well as sermons; the two-volume set continued to be among the more popular works of its kind in early nineteenth-century Scotland. Both volumes of Logan's *Sermons* identify the author as a fellow of the Royal Society of Edinburgh on the title-page, and he appears as a non-resident fellow in the first volume of the society's *Transactions* (1788). On 14 May 1791 Donald Grant sent Logan's other manuscripts to Bell and Bradfute for evaluation, and on 26 November 1793 Thomas Robertson accepted an offer from that firm, giving the estate two-thirds of the profits in exchange for publication rights. The plan was for Blair (who had edited the *Sermons*) and Mackenzie to locate what Blair called 'sparks of the Loganic Genius' (Drescher, 1.166) and produce two large volumes of 'Miscellanies in Prose and Verse', followed by 'Lectures on Roman history'. In 1795 Robert Anderson announced that Robertson was planning to publish 'a full and candid representation of [Logan] and his writing' in an edition of his 'miscellaneous works' (Anderson, 1027). But none of these publications ever appeared, and it is not known what became of Logan's manuscripts after Mackenzie obtained them following Robertson's death in 1799. Mackenzie's final judgement of the unpublished poetry, plays, and periodical essays was that only the essays 'seem to possess enough general merit to entitle them to publication' (Drescher, 2.196). However, sales of Logan's *Sermons*, along with early nineteenth-century editions of his *Poems, and 'Runnamede'* (first published in 1805 with a biography that is believed to be by Logan's friend, the Revd Robert Douglas of Galashiels), brought the estate enough money to enable Grant to pay out all the legacies specified in Logan's will, including £200 to each of his children when they came of age. RICHARD B. SHER

Sources R. Anderson, 'The life of Logan', *A complete edition of the poets of Great Britain*, 13 vols. (1792–5), vol. 11, pp. 1027–34 · A. Chalmers, 'The life of John Logan', *The works of the English poets from Chaucer to Cowper*, ed. A. Chalmers, 18 (1810), 49–52 · Chambers, *Scots.* (1870), 2.541–3 · *The correspondence of the Right Honourable Sir John Sinclair, Bart.*, 2 vols. (1831) · R. Douglas, 'The life of the Rev. John Logan', in J. Logan, *Poems, and 'Runnamede, a tragedy'* (1812), v–xxxii · *Literature and literati: the literary correspondence and notebooks of Henry Mackenzie*, ed. H. W. Drescher, 2 vols. (1989–99) · J. Dwyer, *Virtuous discourse: sensibility and community in late eighteenth-century Scotland* (1987) · *Edinburgh Evening Courant* (3 Nov 1779) · *Edinburgh Evening Courant* (30 Oct 1780) · *Edinburgh Evening Courant* (20 Oct 1781) · *Edinburgh Evening Courant* (10 Nov 1781) · *Edinburgh Evening Courant* (27 May 1782) · W. Swan, ed., *Extracts from the registers of South Leith parish*, 2nd ser. (1925) · *Fasti Scot.*, new edn, 1.167–8 · J. C. Sharp, *'Ode to the cuckoo', 1770, with remarks on its authorship* (1873) · R. B. Sher, introduction, in J. Logan, *'Elements of the philosophy of history, part first' and 'Dissertation on the governments, manners and spirit of Asia'* (1995), v–xxi · R. B. Sher, *Church and university in the Scottish Enlightenment: the moderate literati of Edinburgh* (1985) · *The correspondence of Adam Smith*, ed. E. C. Mossner and I. S. Ross, 2nd edn (1987), vol. 6 of *The Glasgow edition of the works and correspondence of Adam Smith* · T. G. Snoddy, *Michael Bruce, shepherd poet of the Lomand Braes, 1746–1767* [1946] · *The anecdotes and egotisms of Henry Mackenzie, 1745–1831*, ed. H. W. Thompson (1927) · *DNB*

Archives BL, John Douglas, bishop of Salisbury, Egerton MS 2185, fols. 103–4, 151–2 · Edinburgh City Archives, Bell and Bradfute ledgers, SL 138/1/1 · NL Scot., Bell and Bradfute MSS, Acc 10,662 and Dep 317 · U. Edin. L., letters to Alexander Carlyle and others, Logan MS La.II.419

Likenesses J. Brown, pencil drawing, Scot. NPG · engravings (after J. Brown), BM, NPG

Logan, Robert, of Restalrig (1555–1606), landowner and conspirator, was the only son of Sir Robert Logan (*c*.1533–1561), sixth laird of Restalrig, and his wife, Agnes Gray (*c*.1540–1585), daughter of Patrick *Gray, fourth Lord Gray. He was descended from a family of Ayrshire origin which had acquired the barony of Restalrig, just outside Edinburgh, through marriage in the late fourteenth century. Logan's father died when he was only six years old, and after 1565 his mother married Alexander, fifth Lord Home. Logan and his mother and stepfather were among the Marian defenders of Edinburgh Castle when the fortress surrendered to the regent Morton in 1573, but the young laird and his mother were set free. Following the death of Lord Home in 1575 his mother was married a third time, to Thomas Lyon, master of Glamis. Logan himself married Elizabeth MacGill (*c*.1560–1622), daughter of David MacGill, later king's advocate, shortly before he was served heir to his Midlothian, Berwickshire, and Ayrshire estates in 1576. The marriage was short-lived, for by 1578 Elizabeth had returned to her father's household. The couple probably divorced some time in that year, for in spring 1579 she married Sir Thomas Kennedy of Culzean.

Logan supported the Ruthven raid in 1582 and after the new government had fallen in 1584 he was ordered to surrender his seaward seat, Fast Castle. In May 1586 he sat on the assize which acquitted Archibald Douglas of involvement in Darnley's murder. He was married again in October, to Marion Ker, of whom little is known except that she gave birth to his heir Robert as well as other children. In 1587 Logan accompanied the embassy of his cousin Patrick, master of Gray, to London to intercede for Queen Mary's life. When Gray fell from favour on their return, Logan was among those who stood surety that he would pass into exile. His taste for intrigue also drew Logan into association with Francis Stewart, first earl of Bothwell, and he was outlawed for conspiring with the earl in February 1593.

Fast Castle became a frequent point of arrival for foreign mail packets and persons illicitly entering Scotland. In December 1593 Logan stole gold and silver plate, valued at 3000 merks, from William Nesbit of Newton, and the following April two of his men assaulted and robbed James Gray, an Edinburgh burgess travelling on the road to Berwick, of £950. In July 1594 Logan contracted John Napier of Merchiston to use his arts to uncover treasure supposed to be secreted within Fast Castle. Napier was promised a third share and safe conduct back to Edinburgh. It is improbable that anything was found, but the episode evidently did not endear Napier to Logan, for when leasing property in 1596 he forbade his tenant to sublet to anyone of Logan's surname.

In the summer of 1600 Logan may have been drawn into the Gowrie conspiracy, though possible evidence of his culpability was not to emerge until after his death. Logan considered a venture with Peregrine Bertie, thirteenth Lord Willoughby of Eresby, to sail to the West Indies in 1601, but Willoughby's death in June arrested this scheme. Logan had meanwhile begun to dispose of his estates, for reasons which remain unclear, selling Fast Castle to Archibald Douglas of Pittendreich in November 1602, the barony of Restalrig to Lord Balmerino in 1604, and finally his Berwickshire lands to the earl of Dunbar. However, he had limited success in realizing the money from these sales and in 1605 travelled unsuccessfully to London to force the issue. Weakened by fever he died in Edinburgh's Canongate in July 1606. Two years after his death, his one time legal agent George Sprot, an Eyemouth notary, let slip while drinking that he had knowledge of the Gowrie conspiracy. Under arrest he confessed to possessing letters penned by Logan to the earl of Gowrie and others suggesting a plot to abduct the king to Fast Castle. Although Sprot admitted under torture that he had forged these letters, when the earl of Dunbar intervened in the interrogation he reverted to his original confession implicating Logan, while still maintaining the letters were themselves forgeries. Sprot was hanged for his part in the conspiracy in August, and the following June Logan's corpse was dug up and produced in court in the treason trial which forfeited his son. This outcome was of considerable benefit to Dunbar, who owed 15,000 merks to Logan's heir.

Willoughby perhaps best summarized Logan's character when he judged him 'a vain, loose man, a great favourer of thieves reputed, yet a man of good clan, as they here term it, and a good fellow' (Bain, 2.1034).

John Simmons

Sources M. Kennaway, *Fast Castle: the early years* (1992) • *Reg. PCS*, 1st ser., vols. 2–8 • *APS*, 1593–1625 • R. Pitcairn, ed., *Ancient criminal trials in Scotland*, 7 pts in 3, Bannatyne Club, 42 (1833) • J. Bain, ed., *The border papers: calendar of letters and papers relating to the affairs of the borders of England and Scotland*, 2 vols. (1894–6) • *CSP Scot.*, 1547–1603 • A. Lang, *James VI and the Gowrie mystery* (1902) • W. Fraser, *Memorials of the earls of Haddington*, 2 vols. (1889) • *Scots peerage*, vol. 4 • *Scots peerage*, vol. 6 • GEC, *Peerage*, 6.555

Logan, Sir William Edmond (1798–1875), geologist in Canada, was born on 20 April 1798 in Montreal, the second son in the family of nine children of William Logan (1759–1841), a baker and owner of real estate, and his wife, Janet, *née* Edmond (*d.* 1836). His grandfather was James Logan, a baker from Stirling who emigrated to Canada in 1784. Logan was educated at Alexander Skakel's school in Montreal and, from 1814 to 1816, at the Revd James Lippan's school in Edinburgh, where he was top of his class of 200. For one year he attended Edinburgh University, where he was registered in medicine, with classes in logic, mathematics, and chemistry; the last taught by Professor T. C. Hope, an opponent of James Hutton and Plutonism. In 1817 Logan moved to London, where he worked in

Sir William Edmond Logan (1798–1875), by Ernest Edwards, pubd 1865

accounting for his uncle. His evenings were spent studying geometry and languages, playing the flute, and painting, but he did not relish the evening social events which he attended with his uncle.

In 1831 Logan's uncle acquired an interest in the Forest Copper Works near Swansea and Logan was appointed to manage the accounts. However, he soon realized that a continuous supply of coal was essential to the works, and that reserves could only be determined from a precisely surveyed geological map. He set out to survey the area, plotting his findings on the available existing maps. At one point he wrote to his brother in London noting that 'if a pound or two would make the theodolite better, I should be disposed to give it.' Nevertheless, when his map was displayed in Liverpool at the 1837 meeting of the British Association for the Advancement of Science, Henry De la Beche, director of the geological survey, adopted it as the official map; Logan's name remains on the modern maps of the area. As a result of his work, in 1837 he was elected to the Geological Society of London.

Between February and April 1829 Logan travelled in Italy, possibly as a tourist. His diary contains notes about building stones, including granite, porphyry, travertine, and alabaster—indicating his knowledge, and possibly the nature of his uncle's business. In 1834 a business trip of several months was made to Spain, including Cadiz and Barcelona, possibly to visit copper mines. On this trip he was reading Charles Lyell's *Principles of Geology*, published in 1830, and probably made a number of watercolour paintings.

Although he continued map making in south Wales

until 1841, Logan had been without permanent employment since the death of his uncle in 1838. In late 1841 he applied for the position of founding director of the geological survey of Canada. William Buckland, Adam Sedgwick, Roderick Murchison, and Henry De la Beche all supported his application and he was offered the appointment, with headquarters in Montreal, and accepted on 14 April 1842. Within seven years, with four employees and field guides drawn from among the local people, he determined the general geology of the area which bordered the St Lawrence River and ran northwards from the Great Lakes shores. His first objective was to find coal. In May 1843 he measured a 14,570 foot section of sediments with coal at Joggins, Nova Scotia, but at that time Nova Scotia was not part of Canada. Further surveys, in 1843 and 1844, of the Gaspé coastline and a transect of the interior failed to reveal any coal deposits. Alexander Murray, Logan's able mapper in the field, confirmed the absence of coal in Upper Canada. As a result, in subsequent years Logan's objective was mineral deposits. He personally mapped along the Ottawa River, and the area east of Montreal where copper showings were found.

Using surveying instruments for field mapping proved impractical for Canada's vast area, much of it rugged wilderness. Logan perfected the 'pace and compass' method—counting paces along a line established by prismatic compass—which showed errors in the geographic maps made by earlier surveyors. While he was mapping the Gaspé coast local farmers and fishermen became concerned about this strange fellow walking in a seemingly erratic manner, mumbling to himself, cracking rocks with a large hammer, wrapping rock chips in paper, pencilling notes in a leather-bound book, and sleeping on the beach under a blanket hung over some sticks. On two occasions attempts were made to take him to an insane asylum, but his courteous manner, fluent French, and lucid explanations of the activity allayed fears.

Logan published thirteen annual reports, issued from 1845 to 1857; four copies had to be provided for the government, which he personally wrote with ink and paper. His workday in the office, and in the field, began two hours before breakfast. He seldom if ever had any lunch, and the lamp in his office was seen burning until midnight and beyond. Some wondered if he ever slept. In 1854 the government conducted an official inquiry on the value of the geological survey and Logan called prominent geologists from the United States and Britain to testify. As a result, the government doubled the survey budget. However, when government funds still proved inadequate, Logan used his own money to keep the survey going, spending C$10,000 by 1864. His major summary report, *Geology of Canada* (1863), contained 498 woodcuts, mostly of fossils and field sketches. A small atlas followed in 1865—it included a colour lithographed map covering parts of Newfoundland, Nova Scotia, northern United States, and Manitoba. In 1869 a 4 foot by 6 foot map was published, with individual copies hand coloured, possibly by Logan himself. It is not surprising that he suffered from eye strain.

In 1851 substantial collections of Canadian rocks and minerals were displayed at the Great Exhibition in London, and Logan was elected to the Royal Society; after a similar exhibition in Paris in 1855, Emperor Napoleon III of France appointed him to the Légion d'honneur. He was knighted on 29 January 1856, the first native-born Canadian to be so honoured. On his return to Canada, Toronto citizens organized a banquet; the Royal Canadian Institute commissioned his oil portrait by George Berthon; and Montreal citizens held a soirée and commissioned a 'silver fountain'. In a letter to his brother, Logan implied that if the price of fame was speaking in public, he would gladly forgo the fame. Among his many other awards were the Wollaston medal of the Geological Society of London (1856); royal medal of the Royal Society (1867); the degrees of doctor of civil laws of Bishop's University, Lennoxville, Quebec (1855), and doctor of laws of McGill University, Montreal (1856); and induction into the Canadian Mining Hall of Fame, in January 1992. Logan endowed the chair of geology at McGill.

Logan's chief contributions to geology included the first precise geological maps using surveying instruments, the realization that the underclay of coal beds with *Stigmaria* roots is evidence for the *in situ* origin of coal; and the establishment of the policies, philosophical objectives, and methodology of operation, of the geological survey of Canada, aims and methods which still prevailed in the late twentieth century.

About 5 feet 8 inches in height, with a muscular build, Logan had great stamina. In the spring of 1827 he and two brothers, together with a friend, travelled about 350 miles in ten days, from their father's estate, Clarkstone (now called Avondale), near Polmont, Scotland, by walking, carriage, rowing boat, farm wagon, and steam boat. In one day, they walked from Ballachulish to Fort William and to the top of Ben Nevis. Walking the Canadian wilderness was made more difficult by dense bush, clouds of biting insects, rain, and snow. B. J. Harrington, Logan's biographer (1883), described him as 'strong in body, of active mind, industrious and doggedly persevering, painstaking, a lover of truth, generous, possessed of the keenest knowledge of human nature, sound in judgment, but always cautious about expressing an opinion' (Harrington).

The Logan family were Presbyterians; William still attended church while living in London, but after his move to Wales in 1831 he worked seven days a week from before dawn to late evening, in office and field. In 1870 the Logan family donated a bell for the twin towered Presbyterian church in Polmont, in memory of their father. Logan retired as survey director on 30 November 1869 but continued fieldwork in the folded rocks east of Montreal where copper was being mined. He owned rental property in Montreal, probably inherited from his father and elder brother, James; some thought he might have been the richest man in Canada. He died on 22 June 1875 at his sister's home, Castle Malgwyn, near Llechryd in Cardiganshire, where he had spent the winters since 1869; he was buried on 29 June at St Llawddog's Church, Cilgerran,

Pembrokeshire. Logan was unmarried; mothers with daughters, perceiving Logan as an eligible bachelor, were told 'other rocks than "rock the cradle" claim my whole attention' (Bell, 23). Canada honoured a native son by giving the name Mount Logan to its highest mountain (elevation nearly 20,000 feet), located in the south-west corner of the Yukon, and in 1998 the Canadian news magazine *Macleans* named him among the most important figures in Canadian history. C. GORDON WINDER

Sources R. Bell, *Sir William E. Logan and the Geological Survey of Canada* [1907] • B. J. Harrington, *Life of Sir William Edmond Logan, kt.* (1883) • C. G. Winder, 'William Edmond Logan, 1798–1875', *Canadian Institute of Mining*, 954 (1991), 14–18; 956 (1992), 8–12; 957 (1992), 10–16; 958 (1992), 27–40; 959 (1992), 13–18; 960 (1992), 13–21 • C. G. Winder, 'Logan, Sir William Edmond', *DCB*, vol. 10

Archives BGS, notebooks and papers • McGill University, Montreal, McCord Museum, corresp. and papers • McGill University, Montreal, McLennan Library, corresp. and papers • Metropolitan Toronto Reference Library, journals and scrapbooks • NA Canada, papers relating to Great Lakes • NL Wales, journals on his work as provincial geologist in and around the Gaspé peninsula | McGill University, Montreal, McLennan Library, corresp. with Robert Bell • NMG Wales, letters to his patron, Sir H. T. de la Beche, relating to his appointment in Canada and progress of his work

Likenesses Berthon, oils, 1856, Royal Canadian Institute, Toronto • E. Edwards, photograph, NPG; repro. in *Portraits of men of eminence*, 3 (1865) [*see illus.*] • photographs, Geological Survey of Canada, Ottawa, Ontario

Wealth at death under £3000 in England and Wales: probate, 30 Nov 1875, *CGPLA Eng. & Wales*

Loggan, David (*bap.* **1634**, *d.* **1692**), artist and engraver, was born in Danzig, Poland, where he was baptized in the Calvinist church of St Peter and St Paul on 27 August 1634. He was the only son of John Loggan (*b.* 1608), a merchant, of a family of Scottish descent who had settled in Oxfordshire in the sixteenth century, and his wife, Margaret, the widow of John or Johann Klinge. Loggan is said to have learned engraving from Willem Hondius, who settled in Danzig in 1636, and, after Hondius's death in 1652, from the younger Crispijn de Passe (*c.*1597–1670) in Amsterdam. He apparently intended to continue his studies in France and Italy, but he settled in London between 1656, when some of his engravings were published in Amsterdam, and 1658, when he gained recognition through a pencil portrait of Oliver Cromwell, drawn shortly before the lord protector's death. He engraved a view of St Paul's Cathedral for Daniel King in 1658, and subsequently engraved a title-page to the Book of Common Prayer (1662) and some plates for William Dugdale's *Origines judiciales* (1666). In the early 1660s he became well known for his black lead (plumbago) portraits drawn on vellum from life, and he succeeded William Faithorne as the best-known exponent of this genre. The portraits, which include representations of Charles II and numerous Restoration courtiers and divines, are highly accomplished and full of character, and several of them were engraved. On 15 June 1663, when he was living in the parish of St Bride, Fleet Street, he married Anna (*c.*1644–1699), the daughter of John Jordan of the parish of St Andrew, Holborn, whose family owned property at Kencot, Oxfordshire. They had eight children, one of whom, John, became a fellow of Magdalen College, Oxford, and rector of Hanwell, Oxfordshire; another, Justinian, was a lieutenant in the Grenadier Guards.

In 1665 Loggan and his wife left London because of the plague and settled at Nuffield, Oxfordshire. An engraved portrait of an Oxford innkeeper, *Mother Louse*—supposedly the last woman in England to wear a ruff—brought him to the attention of the members of Oxford University, and he soon built up a flourishing local portrait practice. He is mentioned several times in the diaries of Anthony Wood, who appears to have introduced him to, among others, Elias Ashmole and John Aubrey, whose portraits he drew. By 1669 he had moved to Holywell Street, Oxford, where he had a 'rolling press' which he sold to Oxford University, and on 30 March 1669, probably through the influence of John Fell, he was appointed engraver to the university, with an annual salary of 20*s.*; his first official commission was for a pair of plates of the newly built Sheldonian Theatre, where the university press was housed. In 1672 he was made a member of the university, and he was naturalized in 1675. A book of plates of academic dress (*Reverendis … doctoribus academiae Oxoniensis haec omnium ordinium* [*sic*] *habituumque academicorum exemplaria*, 1674) has usually been ascribed to Loggan, though the plates are not signed; he and his assistants also engraved title-pages and plates for some of the university press's books. But the main legacy of his time in Oxford is his *Oxonia illustrata* (1675), a set of bird's-eye views of all the colleges, academic halls, and university buildings, together with a map. It was intended to accompany Wood's *The History and Antiquities of the University of Oxford* (1674), and was presented along with it by the university in the late seventeenth century to distinguished visitors to Oxford. Influenced by the work of Wenceslas Hollar, Loggan's meticulously detailed views were the first accurate representation of all the buildings and gardens of the university, and they have been an invaluable quarry for historians, antiquaries, and topographers ever since. In 1676 he engraved Christopher Wren's design for the new library at Trinity College, Cambridge, and in the same year he began work on *Cantabrigia illustrata*, a comparable volume of plates of all the Cambridge colleges and university buildings, for the production of which he was given a workshop and press at Trinity College; the book was published in 1690, when he was made engraver to the university. Some of his prints are preserved at Worcester College, Oxford.

Loggan moved from Oxford to London in 1675 and settled in a house in Leicester Fields (now Leicester Square) in a row on the St Martin's Lane side, next to the Golden Head. Here he continued to draw and engrave portraits; he also let rooms in his house to 'persons of Quality who desir to have Lodgings' (Loggan to Sir Thomas Isham, 21 Oct 1675, *Connoisseur*, 152, 1963, 85) and acted as an agent for portraits by Sir Peter Lely and members of his circle and for books and furniture. His clients included Sir Thomas Isham of Lamport (Northamptonshire) and his younger brother and heir, Sir Justinian Isham, to whom he wrote in 1682 that he was 'so plaged with besunes [business] more than ever I have bin' (Loggan to Sir Justinian Isham, 12 Sept 1682, *Connoisseur*, 154, 1963, 88). His portrait practice suffered from the rise of mezzotint engraving in the late 1670s, but he produced some mezzotints of his own about 1683 and two maps in 1687. Vertue recorded, but cast doubt upon, a story that 'he hurt his sight so in delineating of King's College Chappel [Cambridge] … that he engraved but little afterwards' (Vertue, *Note books*, 1.98).

In producing his plates of Oxford and Cambridge, Loggan was assisted by Robert White, who later became an accomplished portraitist in his own right, by Michael Burghers (1648–?1724), who succeeded him as engraver to Oxford University, and by another Dutchman, Everardus Kickius ('one Kickers'), who, according to Vertue, accompanied Loggan to Scotland, where they produced plates for *Theatrum Scotiae*. Among other pupils and assistants were Abraham Blooteling (1640–1690), Gerard Valck (1652–1726), and Edward (le) Davis, who departed for France after Loggan's wife 'woud have him follow her in a Livery & other servile offices, which he refus'd to do' (Vertue, *Note books*, 2.29).

Loggan died at his house in Leicester Fields in July 1692 and was buried on 1 August 1692 at St Martin-in-the-Fields. He left debts of £140, and, according to Vertue, 'little remaining substance … except for a few Copper graved plates' (Vertue, *Note books*, 6.182). They were sold to a printseller, Henry Overton, who republished the engravings of Oxford and Cambridge on which Loggan's later fame has largely rested. GEOFFREY TYACK

Sources C. F. Bell and R. L. Poole, 'English seventeenth-century portrait drawings in Oxford collections, pt 2', *Walpole Society*, 14 (1925–6), 49–80, esp. 55–64 • G. Isham, 'The correspondence of David Loggan with Sir Thomas Isham', *The Connoisseur*, 152 (1963), 231–6 • G. Isham, 'The correspondence of David Loggan with Sir Thomas Isham', *The Connoisseur*, 154 (1963), 84–91 • Vertue, *Note books*, vols. 1–2, 6 • E. Croft-Murray and P. H. Hulton, eds., *Catalogue of British drawings*, 1 (1960), 428–30 • A. Griffiths and R. A. Gerard, *The print in Stuart Britain, 1603–1689* (1998), 192–3, 198–202 [exhibition catalogue, BM, 8 May – 20 Sept 1998] • *The life and times of Anthony Wood*, ed. A. Clark, 2, OHS, 21 (1892); 3, OHS, 26 (1894), 394; 4, OHS, 30 (1895), 68; 5, OHS, 40 (1900), 184–90 • H. Walpole, *Anecdotes of painting in England: with some account of the principal artists*, ed. J. Dallaway, [rev. and enl. edn], 5 vols. (1826–8) • D. Loggan, introduction, *Cantabrigia illustrata*, ed. J. W. Clarke (1905) • H. Carter, *A history of the Oxford University Press*, 1: *To the year 1780* (1975) • N. Barker, *The Oxford University Press and the spread of learning, 1478–1978* (1978)

Wealth at death little remaining substance, except for copper plates; debts of at least £140: Vertue, *Note books*, vol. 6, p. 182; will, PRO, PROB 11/463, sig. 25 (7 June 1691, proved 23 Feb 1702)

Loggon, Samuel (*bap.* 1711, *d.* *c.*1778), Church of England clergyman and author, was baptized on 29 July 1711 at Cradley, Herefordshire, the son of William Loggon and his wife, Anna. He had at least four brothers and a sister. Loggon matriculated at Balliol College, Oxford, on 23 January 1730, graduated BA in 1733, and proceeded MA in 1736. He became curate of Eastrop and Sherborne St John, near Basingstoke. On 15 October 1740 he was elected usher of the free school of the Holy Ghost at Basingstoke by the corporation of Basingstoke, following a dispute over its patronage.

In 1743 he became curate of Stratfield Turgis in Hampshire, and on 18 July 1743, through the petition of Lord Portsmouth to the lord chancellor, he was appointed master of the free school of the Holy Ghost by letters patent. This ancient foundation was at the time in a ruinous condition, and in 1743 Loggon had the estate surveyed, and suggested that some of the income of the mastership be allocated for its improvement. In 1744 he presented a petition on the subject to Lord Hardwicke, and as he alleged that the corporation had wrongfully encroached on land owned by the foundation, he treated the town council with insolence. On 7 October 1745 the town clerk was authorized to take proceedings against him for neglecting his duties as schoolmaster, but as the inhabitants generally sided with Loggon nothing was done. In fact in 1747 the Sir John Deane lectureship was added to his preferment as master.

On 16 December 1746 Loggon was instituted to the rectory of Stratfield Turgis by George Pitt (afterwards Lord Rivers) of Stratfield Saye, a position he resigned in November 1748 on being presented, again by Mr Pitt, to the vicarage of Damerham in Wiltshire. He remained resident at Basingstoke and in periodic dispute with the corporation. He also appears to have undertaken duties as curate of the nearby parishes of Sherborne St John and Tunworth, providing both with 'double duty' each Sunday. He died unmarried at Basingstoke about 1778, and was buried, in accordance with his wishes, in a sawpit, in the churchyard of Stratfield Turgis.

Loggon was eccentric in his habits, wore two shirts, and drank stale beer. He collected a large number of manuscripts, which he offered to the corporation of Basingstoke in return for a piece of plate; the corporation would not accept this condition, and the manuscripts passed to his nephew. His selected translation *Colloquies of Corderius* (1759), which he had written for use at the school of the Holy Ghost, were extremely popular, running into twelve editions in his lifetime.

W. A. J. ARCHBOLD, *rev.* WILLIAM GIBSON

Sources Foster, *Alum. Oxon.* • F. J. Baigent and J. E. Millard, *A history of the ancient town and manor of Basingstoke …: with a brief account of the siege of Basing house,* AD *1643–1645*, 2 vols. (1889) • W. R. Ward, ed., *Parson and parish in eighteenth-century Hampshire*, Hampshire RS, 13 (1995) • *IGI*

Logie, John (*fl.* *c.*1365–*c.*1395). *See under* Margaret (*d.* in or after 1374).

Logier, Johann Bernhard (1777–1846), music teacher and composer, descended from a family of French refugees, was born on 9 February 1777 at Kassel in Hesse. His father and grandfather were musicians, and the former gave him his early musical education. About 1790 he travelled to England, and for two years played the flute and piano daily for an aristocratic patron. He then joined a regimental band conducted by John Willman, the father of the clarinettist Thomas Willman, with which he went to Ireland.

Johann Bernhard Logier (1777–1846), by Charles Turner, pubd 1819 (after James Lonsdale)

In 1796 he married Willman's daughter, and took to composing for and teaching military bands and the piano. On the disbanding of his regiment in 1807 he first became organist of Westport, co. Mayo, then moved to Dublin, where he conducted the orchestra at Johnson's theatre, ran a music shop, and was soon recognized as the city's leading music teacher. Among his piano pupils was his own daughter; and it was for her use that Logier initially designed the apparatus for guiding a pianist's hands that was to gain him celebrity. Known as the 'chiroplast', it was meant to ensure a correct wrist and hand position in the teacher's absence. (For a full description and illustration, see Rainbow, 193–4.)

Finding the device successful, Logier decided to use it for group teaching—making several pupils, twelve or more, play at the same time on as many pianos. The system led to much controversy. Musicians in general were opposed to it, but Spohr expressed himself in its favour (*Allgemeine Musikalische Zeitung*, 1820), and Samuel Webbe adopted it in London. Several hostile pamphlets and articles led to Logier inviting the Philharmonic Society and leading musicians to attend an examination of Webbe's pupils in London on 17 November 1817. The results of this examination are detailed in *An Authentic Account … by J. B. Logier* (1818), which was answered by *An Exposure of the New System … Published by a Committee of Professors in London* (1818). Many pamphlets followed.

In 1821 the Prussian government invited Logier to Berlin, where he established a chiroplast school with such good results that the king asked him to instruct twenty teachers to spread the system over the whole of Prussia. He remained for three years in Berlin, visiting England at intervals. By 1826 he had made enough money to retire. He settled near Dublin, where he died on 27 July 1846.

Logier arranged much music for the piano, and composed sonatas and other pieces, including an ode for the jubilee of George III, performed in Dublin. Several works were written especially for his peculiar system, and he was the author of sundry theoretical treatises and a *Complete Introduction to the Keyed Bugle*, an instrument he was said to have invented. He was not without a taint of charlatanism, establishing in Dublin a 'chiroplast club', with a special badge. He remarked to Mazzinghi that he 'considered himself an instrument in the hands of Providence for changing the whole system of musical instruction'. These pretensions were extravagant, but what he did undoubtedly had a beneficial influence on piano teaching long after his system and invention were abandoned.

J. C. Hadden, *rev.* Bernarr Rainbow

Sources F.-J. Fétis, *Biographie universelle des musiciens, et bibliographie générale de la musique*, 8 vols. (Brussels, 1835–44) • *New Grove* • J. B. Logier, *Companion to the royal patent chiroplast* (1817) • W. Gardiner, *Music and friends, or, Pleasant recollections of a dilettante*, 3 vols. (1838–53) • Franklin Taylor, 'The chiroplast', Grove, *Dict. mus.* (1904–10) • P. A. Scholes, *The mirror of music, 1844–1944: a century of musical life in Britain as reflected in the pages of the Musical Times*, 2 vols. (1947) • B. Rainbow, 'J. B. Logier and the chiroplast controversy', *MT*, 131 (1990), 193–6

Likenesses C. Turner, mezzotint, pubd 1819 (after J. Lonsdale), BM, NPG [*see illus.*] • Cruikshank, caricatures, BM, department of prints and drawings • H. Meyer, stipple (after J. R. Maguire), BM, NPG • portrait, repro. in Scholes, *The mirror of music*, facing p. 321

Login [*née* Campbell], **Lena, Lady Login (1820–1904)**, courtier, was born in Perth, the youngest of the eleven children of John Campbell and his wife, Ann. After the death of her parents she set out, in 1842, for India, where several members of her family were already established. In Lucknow she met Dr John Login (1809–1863), a fellow Scot, whom she married on 28 July 1842; they had six children.

John Login was residency surgeon at Lucknow; he was also physician at the court of Oudh, surveyor of roads, and postmaster. Lena Login, then as later, played an important part in his work. Learning the court language, she was readily accepted into the zenanas of the royal family and other nawabs, and greatly admired the intelligence and culture of their inmates. From within the zenana she was able to assist in the medical diagnoses of her husband, who was barred from a physical examination of his female patients, and in subsequent treatment. Dr Login also had political duties, and his wife, aware of the power exercised by the ladies of the zenana, was able to help him in an area otherwise closed to him.

On the conclusion of the Second Anglo-Sikh War in 1849 John Login was appointed guardian to Duleep *Singh, the deposed heir to the former ruler of the Punjab Ranjit Singh, who was then aged eleven. He moved with his entourage from Lahore to Fatehgarh Park, Fatehgarh, where John Login introduced an English type of education and environment. He attached considerable importance to his wife's role in establishing a suitable domestic life to inculcate 'respect for the character of an English lady' (Login, *Sir John Login*, 210). Her efforts were marked with success: 'From constant association with English ladies and gentlemen, he had rapidly acquired the usages of society, and his chivalrous courtesy to ladies became remarkable' (ibid., 275). Her influence was also used with the mother of a younger prince, Sheo Deo, who had accompanied Duleep Singh, to persuade her to allow her son an English education.

In 1854 the Logins went with Duleep Singh to England, where Dr Login was knighted by Queen Victoria in November. The Maharaja had converted to Christianity in 1853, and the search for a suitable wife became important. Princess Gouramma of Coorg had already been considered a candidate. Her father, the raja of Coorg, had brought her up in a European manner, and in 1852 had accompanied her to England for her education. She too became a Christian in an impressive ceremony at Windsor, when the queen stood as her godmother and named her Victoria. The queen took a keen interest in her Indian goddaughter, and in 1858 requested Lady Login to supervise her in preparation for her presentation in English society, and in expectation of her marriage to Duleep Singh. However, the projected marriage was thwarted by Duleep Singh. In Italy, where Lady Login had taken Princess Gouramma with two of her own children on the queen's instructions in 1859, he announced that he wished to marry an English wife, an ambition supported by the attention and flattery he had received from the English aristocracy. Lady Login then considered introductions to members of the European nobility, whom the queen also favoured as marriage partners for the princess. Unexpectedly, however, the princess married Lady Login's brother Colonel John Campbell, a widower some thirty years her senior, with whom she had a happy but brief union before her death in 1864 at the age of twenty-three.

Sir John died in 1863; during her long widowhood Lady Login devoted herself to their children, only three of whom survived her, and became the guardian of her niece, the daughter of her brother and Princess Victoria Gouramma. In 1890 she published *Sir John Login and Duleep Singh*, a record of their long and close relationship and of Duleep Singh's subsequent grievances against the British government, with which she sympathized. She died at her home, The Cedars, Aylesford, Kent, on 17 April 1904, and was buried beside her husband, in the parish churchyard at Felixstowe, Suffolk. ROSEMARY CARGILL RAZA

Sources E. D. Login, *Lady Login's recollections: court and camp life, 1820–1904* (1916) • Lady Login [L. C. Login], *Sir John Login and Duleep Singh* (1890) • E. D. Login, *The story of the Campbells of Kinloch* (1924) • d. cert. • M. Alexander and S. Anand, *Queen Victoria's maharajah: Duleep Singh, 1838–93* (1980)

Likenesses Fisher, miniature, 1850, repro. in Login, *Lady Login's recollections*

Wealth at death £4871 18*s*. 8*d*.: will, PRO

Logue, Lionel George (1880–1953), speech therapist, was born on 26 February 1880 in College Town, Adelaide, South Australia, the eldest of three children of George Edward Logue, clerk, and his wife, Lavinia, *née* Rankin. Logue was educated at Prince Alfred College, Adelaide, between 1889 and 1896, and studied elocution with Edward Reeves. As a Christian Scientist, Logue was dedicated to healing and had originally wanted to train as a doctor but soon realized that he did not like the sight of blood. Instead, in 1902, he became secretary and assistant teacher to Edward Reeves and also studied at the Elder Conservatorium of Music. For a while Logue's career changed direction and he moved to Western Australia to work with an electrical engineering firm at a goldmine in Kalgoorlie.

With the capital that he amassed from his engineering work Logue was able to return to his previous interest and he set up a school of elocution in Perth, where he taught elocution, public speaking, and acting. He enjoyed plays and reciting Shakespeare at concerts and founded a public speaking club. Logue also taught part time at the Young Men's Christian Association and later at Perth Technical School. It was during his residence in Perth that, on 20 March 1907 at St George's Anglican Cathedral, Logue married Myrtle Gruenert, a 21-year-old clerk, the eldest daughter of Francis Gruenert. They had three sons.

Logue came to speech therapy, like many other of his professional peers, during the First World War. He treated soldiers returned from fighting who were afflicted with a number of speech disorders as a result of shell-shock. Logue found that he had a special talent for the treatment of stammering and was said to have effected 'dramatic cures' (Judd, 97) on these soldiers. Logue's approach to the treatment of stammering was twofold, tackling both the psychological and physical aspects of the condition. He recognized the importance of building the patient's confidence and was always keen to stress that a cure could only be effected by the stammerers themselves. He used exercises to relax muscle tension, taught correct breathing, and also slowed the patient's rate of speech considerably.

In 1924 Logue and his family visited England for what was intended as a holiday. However, while staying in London he saw the possibilities of establishing a speech therapy practice in the capital and rented rooms at 146 Harley Street. Logue had no medical qualifications and, initially, little capital but he built up his practice steadily. The fees paid him by wealthier clients enabled him to treat poorer patients without charge.

Logue's association with his most famous client began in October 1925; he was present when the duke of York (later George VI) gave his closing speech as president of the British Empire Exhibition in which he stammered badly throughout. Logue is reported to have said to his son that he was sure that he could 'very nearly … manage a complete cure' (Bradford, 122). The duke was put in touch with Logue by Eileen Macleod, an eminent speech therapist, who when approached concerning treatment felt that a male therapist might be more effective. The first consultation took place on 19 October 1926 in Logue's rooms; despite an initial reluctance to attempt further therapy following several previous failures, the duke was deeply impressed by Logue's confidence and sincerity saying of him 'I wish I could have found him before, as now I know the right way to breathe my fear of talking will vanish' (Wheeler-Bennett, 214). He attended sessions almost daily for about two and a half months and strictly adhered to the exercises given to him by Logue which included intoning vowels by an open window and gargling with warm water. The treatment produced an almost instant improvement and while the duke still spoke slowly and deliberately his speech showed only occasional hesitations.

Logue was invaluable in preparing George VI for all his major speeches, using tongue twisters to aid practice and changing difficult words where necessary. He coached him in his responses for the coronation service on 12 May 1937, which he watched from a specially chosen seat in Westminster Abbey, and prepared the king for the live broadcast that evening and during which George VI did not stammer at all. During the Second World War, Logue frequently attended the king before most of his speech making engagements and broadcasts and it was often noted that his slow and measured pace while speaking added to the impact of his delivery. He continued to advise the king until the latter's death in February 1952. The only formal recognition of Logue's service to George VI was the ribbon of the Royal Victorian Order (elevated to CVO in 1944) presented to him by the king on the evening before his coronation. His friendship with George VI was said to be 'the greatest pleasure of Logue's life' (*AusDB*, 117).

Logue's contribution to the speech therapy profession was significant. He was a pioneer of work with shell-shocked soldiers, many of whom stammered as a result of their trauma. He was also active in the founding of the College of Speech Therapists, which was formed in 1945 when the British Society of Speech Therapists, of which Logue was a founder in 1935, and the Association of Speech Therapists were unified. Logue became a fellow enrolled on foundation and indeed it was he who, in 1948, wrote to George VI requesting his royal patronage, which was duly granted.

Logue was a freemason and was speech therapist to the Royal Masonic School in Bushey. His practice shrank during the Second World War and during the war he regularly acted as an air-raid warden. Logue's wife died in 1945 and he took up spiritualism. He retained his love of music and the theatre and also enjoyed gardening and walking.

Logue died of pneumonia on 12 April 1953 at his home, 68 Princes Court, Brompton Road, London, following a prolonged illness and was cremated. He was survived by his three sons. JANE H. SCHOFIELD

Sources *AusDB* • *Royal College of Speech and Language Therapists: a history of the college, 1945–1995* (1995) • S. Bradford, *George VI* (1989) • D. Judd, *King George VI* (1982) • J. W. Wheeler-Bennett, *King George VI: his life and reign* (1958) • *WWW* • d. cert. • *CGPLA Eng. & Wales* (1953)
Likenesses photograph, repro. in *Daily Telegraph* (13 April 1953), 7
Wealth at death £8605 12*s*. 10*d*.: probate, 17 Sept 1953, *CGPLA Eng. & Wales*

Logue, Michael (1840–1924), Roman Catholic archbishop of Armagh and cardinal, was born in Carrigart, near Millford, co. Donegal, on 1 October 1840, the second of six children of Michael Logue, innkeeper, and his wife, Catherine Durnan. He received his early education in a small school near Carrigart and continued his study of classical literature under a Mr Craig at the Robertson School of Kilmacrenan. He was to become perhaps the most spectacular failure of the late Colonel Robertson (who had endowed a school in each parish of the diocese of Raphoe) to achieve his hope that non-Anglican students would conform to the established church through 'the enlightenment of their understanding' (Carton, 4). Following further instruction by a Mr Campbell in Buncrana, Logue entered St Patrick's College, Maynooth, in 1857. At the national seminary he distinguished himself as an able and versatile student. In 1864 he was ordained a deacon, and in the following year he was admitted as a student in Maynooth's prestigious Dunboyne Establishment. Before he could complete the Dunboyne course, however, he was appointed professor of dogmatic theology in the Irish College, Paris. In December 1866 he was ordained a priest in the Vincentian Church, rue de Sèvres. It was during his residence in Paris that he made his only significant published contribution to theology, a series of articles in *Le Monde* on papal infallibility, which included a refutation of Bishop Dupanloup's views on the subject.

Having competed unsuccessfully for a theological professorship at Maynooth in 1874, Logue returned to Ireland and served at Glenswilly, near Letterkenny, as a curate of Bishop James MacDevitt's parish. In 1876 he was appointed dean and professor of the Irish language in Maynooth, and two years later he was also appointed to a professorship in dogmatic and moral theology. Following MacDevitt's death in 1879 he was placed highest (*dignissimus*) in the poll of parish priests in the diocese, a choice that was confirmed by the pope. On 20 July he was consecrated bishop of Raphoe in Letterkenny, his old protestant teacher, Mr Craig, insisting that, despite serious illness, he be brought on a stretcher to the ceremony. During the distress which prevailed in his diocese in 1879 and 1882 he was very active in raising and distributing relief funds, but he maintained an attitude of neutrality towards the Land League. Though he strongly opposed emigration as a solution to the economic problems of his flock, he launched a successful appeal to Donegal men throughout the world for funds to erect a new cathedral in Letterkenny.

The nearly unanimous choice of the parish priests of the archdiocese, Logue was named coadjutor with right of succession to the ailing Daniel McGettigan, archbishop of Armagh (and a native of the same parish as Logue) in 1887. He succeeded to the primacy before the end of the year, at a moment of crisis in the Irish Catholic church's relationships with the British state, the Holy See, and popular movements in Ireland. Over the preceding several years the Irish hierarchy had entered into a compact with Charles Stewart Parnell and his nationalist parliamentary party by which the bishops agreed to support the home-

Michael Logue (1840–1924), by London Stereoscopic Co.

rule cause on the condition that nationalist politicians would defend the church's vital interests, especially in education. At the time of Logue's succession this delicate relationship was under stress from the confrontation between the government and the renewed agrarian agitation known as the Plan of Campaign, as well as from the government's attempt to undermine the Irish hierarchy's position by playing upon Pope Leo XIII's wish for diplomatic relations with London. During McGettigan's illness, leadership of the hierarchy had devolved upon the very able young archbishop of Dublin, William Walsh, a fairly advanced nationalist.

The precedence of Armagh over Dublin in the hierarchy tended to compromise Walsh's ability to take bold initiatives after the succession of Logue, whom one bishop described as 'slow and indecisive' and 'not conscious of the importance of events because he does not understand them, or only partially understands them' (Larkin, *Roman Catholic Church … 1888–1891*, 191). Like nearly all Irish Catholic ecclesiastics, Logue was a nationalist who sympathized with popular discontent. He was genuinely outraged, for example, at the Conservative government's coercive measures against agrarian agitation in the late 1880s. What distinguished him from more politically creative prelates, such as Walsh, was a tendency to insist on explicit guarantees for the church's interests rather than to enhance and rely upon the church's identification with popular feeling to sustain its interests in an increasingly democratic age. Logue's cautious approach gained weight in the hierarchy's counsels after 1893, when Rome confirmed his precedence by conferring the cardinal's hat upon him rather than Walsh.

Although Logue happened to be in Rome at the time of the split in the parliamentary party in December 1890 over the divorce court revelations about Parnell, upon his return he was active in promoting the anti-Parnellite cause. More significantly, after the reunification of the party in 1900 Logue continued to act as the patron of T. M. Healy, who had led the clericalist faction of the anti-Parnellites in the 1890s and was the one important nationalist politician who remained outside the reunited party. Logue generally remained aloof from the party leaders (as indeed did Walsh after about 1905), and management of the hierarchy's relationship with the party devolved upon Logue's successor in Raphoe, Patrick O'Donnell.

The root of Logue's alienation was his suspicion that party leaders were becoming corrupted by secularist ideas concerning education by their alliance with the Liberals. He also shared with Walsh, however, an aversion to the tactics by which the party tried to maintain hegemony during the long years of waiting for another hung parliament, like that of 1886, in which the home-rule issue could be forced. Thus, for example, Logue condemned the Ancient Order of Hibernians while Joe Devlin, nationalist MP for West Belfast, was working to co-opt it to strengthen party organization in the north. A native speaker of Irish, Logue was a supporter of the Gaelic League, whose nominally non-political activities were mobilizing the generation of leaders who would supplant the party after 1916. If he perceived young cultural nationalists as anti-clerical, however, he could react quite sternly—for example, in his threat in 1906 to ban W. P. Ryan's paper, the *Irish Peasant*, in his diocese.

The 1910 elections, by returning no majority party, gave the Irish party leader John Redmond the whip hand over the Liberals and largely forestalled public attacks by his nationalist critics, even among the bishops. Privately, however, Logue was deeply troubled over safeguards for the protestant minority in the 1912 Home Rule Bill, for fear that they would lead to secularization of education. Though reluctantly willing in 1914 to go along with county plebiscites which party leaders were trying to negotiate as a solution to the Ulster problem, Logue was adamantly opposed to the six-county exclusion arrangement which was the best Redmond could obtain through negotiations in the wake of the 1916 Easter rising. 'It would be infinitely better to remain as we are for 50 years to come, under English rule', he declared 'than to accept these proposals' (Miller, 337).

Though the Irish party was clearly losing support, Logue was slower than other bishops to move towards an accommodation with the younger generation of nationalists associated with the Easter rising and loosely grouped under the label Sinn Féin. As late as November 1917 Logue probably retarded such an accommodation by issuing a pastoral against republicanism. The government's conscription proposals in the spring of 1918, however, galvanized him into action. The hierarchy, which he convened at

Maynooth on 18 April, conferred legitimacy upon Sinn Féin by receiving Eamon de Valera in a delegation of nationalist leaders with whom they developed a plan for nationwide resistance to conscription. The hopes of some bishops that this movement would lead to a *rapprochement* between the Irish party and Sinn Féin were to be disappointed, however, and on the eve of the 1918 general election Logue found himself allocating between the two parties eight Ulster constituencies with Catholic majorities in which a triangular contest might have allowed a Unionist victory.

During the Anglo-Irish war of 1919–21 Logue moved gradually towards open support for the revolutionary government. During the festivities in Rome connected with the beatification of Oliver Plunket in May 1920, Logue attended a reception held by the 'government of the Irish Republic'. In his public statements concerning violence he tended to compare the actions of the IRA with those of the crown forces. Nevertheless, in early 1921 he condemned guerrilla tactics and declined to take a specifically republican line when he was cast as an intermediary between the republican and British governments. He welcomed the Anglo-Irish treaty and was deeply suspicious of the anti-treaty faction. After the hierarchy condemned the anti-treaty side in the civil war, Logue, against the better judgement of other bishops, pressed the Vatican for what Walsh's successor, Edward Byrne, called a 'fulmination' against the anti-treaty camp. When Rome sent an envoy, Salvatore Luzio, Logue contemptuously dismissed his suggestion that the two of them undertake a peace mission to the irregulars.

During this period Logue was also quite concerned about the situation of Catholics under the new Northern Ireland government. He refused to nominate Catholic representatives to serve on a committee to recommend reforms in the educational system, and he remained deeply suspicious of the northern government's intentions. While he was travelling with Patrick O'Donnell, who became his coadjutor in 1922, his automobile was twice detained briefly at checkpoints by the special constabulary—actions which gave special offence to northern nationalists. Until he was succeeded by O'Donnell, however, his increasing infirmity meant that the task of day-to-day dealings with the northern government fell to Joseph MacRory, the bishop of Down and Connor, who resided in Belfast.

Logue's most ambitious ecclesiastical endeavour was the completion of the cathedral in Armagh. The National Cathedral Bazaar of 1900, which grew out of a pastoral which he issued, raised £30,000. He spent some months in Italy selecting furnishings for the edifice, which was consecrated in 1904. He also made several visits to America and attended the Eucharistic Congress in Montreal in August 1910. A very active advocate of temperance reform and supporter of the Irish Vigilance Society, which combated morally questionable literature and entertainment, he was a regular participant in the annual conferences of the Catholic Truth Society. In addition he was prominent in the meetings of the Maynooth Union, an association of the graduates of the national seminary which was sometimes referred to as the 'parliament' of the Irish Catholic church. In the Sacred College he served on the congregations of Propaganda, Indulgences, Ceremonial, and the Lauratana. Logue died of heart failure on 19 November 1924 at the archiepiscopal residence, Ara Coeli, Armagh. Following a pontifical requiem mass in his cathedral, he was buried on 25 November in St Patrick's cemetery, Armagh. David W. Miller

Sources *Irish News and Belfast Morning News* (20 Nov 1924) · D. W. Miller, *Church, state and nation in Ireland, 1898–1921* (1973) · E. Larkin, *The Roman Catholic church in Ireland and the fall of Parnell, 1888–1891* (1979) · E. Larkin, *The Roman Catholic church and the Plan of Campaign in Ireland, 1886–1888* (1978) · E. Larkin, *The Roman Catholic church and the creation of the modern Irish state, 1878–1886* (1975) · D. Keogh, *The Vatican, the bishops and Irish politics, 1919–1939* (1986) · M. Harris, *The Catholic church and the foundation of the Northern Irish state* (1993) · J. Healy, *Maynooth College: its centenary history* (1895) · *Irish Catholic* (22 Nov 1924) · M. Carton, *Kilmacrenan: guided trails* (1985) · *DNB* · S. Gwynn, *Saints and scholars* (1929) · *The Times* (26 Nov 1924)

Archives Armagh archdiocesan archive | Irish College, Rome, MSS of the rectors

Likenesses Lawrence, photograph, *c.*1895, NL Ire., Lawrence collection; repro. in Healy, *Maynooth College*, 564 · J. Lavery, oils, 1920, Ulster Museum, Belfast · London Stereoscopic Co., photograph, NPG [*see illus.*] · oils, probably St Patrick's College, Maynooth

Wealth at death £4287 1s.: probate, 24 April 1925, *CGPLA NIre.*

Lohmann, George Alfred (1865–1901), cricketer, was born at 3 Camden Hill Road, London, on 2 June 1865, the second son in the family of three sons and two daughters of George Stewart Cundell Lohmann, who worked in the City of London, and his wife, Frances Watling. When George was two the family moved to the less fashionable, yet booming, middle-class suburb of Clapham Common. He began playing cricket for the Church Institute Club on Clapham Common and between the ages of eleven and thirteen was the club's most successful batsman and bowler. After attending Louvain School, Wandsworth, he was employed in the London stock exchange, but his ability as a cricketer was spotted by the Surrey batsman W. W. Read and he joined the Oval ground staff as a professional in 1884.

Lohmann made his first-class début for Surrey on 30 May 1884 and in mid-June took his first wicket, that of England's premier batsman, W. G. Grace. He was selected for Surrey's first match in 1885 and was a regular member of the side until 1892. In those eight seasons Surrey won the county championship six times, with Lohmann taking 1415 wickets. Surrey's revival after a lean spell owed much to his right-hand, medium-paced bowling, in which he deployed a deceptive change of pace. A fine slip-catcher, he was also a hard-hitting lower-order batsman.

In July 1886 Lohmann made the first of his eighteen test appearances for England, at Manchester against the Australians. He toured Australia three times (1886–7, 1887–8, 1891–2); his best test performance was at Sydney in February 1887 when he took eight for 35 in Australia's first innings. In December 1892 he was diagnosed with tuberculosis and immediately left for Karoo in South Africa, hoping to benefit from the rain-free, dry air. He returned to England in 1895 to resume his cricketing career and toured South Africa in 1895–6 with Lord Hawke's England side. During the three test series, played in February and March 1896 at a time of political crisis following the Jameson raid, he took thirty-five wickets at an average of 5.80 on matting wickets. His nine for 28 in South Africa's first innings at Johannesburg made him the first bowler to take nine wickets in a test innings. His last test match was against the Australians at Lord's in June 1896. In his test career he took a total of 112 wickets at 10.75, placing him at the top of the all-time England bowling averages.

Aware of his talents, and prepared to market them, Lohmann was the first professional cricketer to negotiate a guaranteed season's income irrespective of performance. His contract of 1892 with Surrey ensured earnings of not less than £300. Before the third test against Australia at the Oval in August 1896 five established England players, led by Lohmann (the others were William Gunn, Tom Richardson, Bobby Abel, and Tom Hayward), demanded a £20 fee rather than the customary £10, citing the large sums which the Australians were making from the fixtures. The *Daily Mail* interviewed a player, thought to be Lohmann, who pointed out that the enormous crowds attracted to matches benefited the clubs but not the professionals who had helped to raise the popularity of the game. Three of the five backed down and apologized but Lohmann and Gunn refused and were left out of the test side. When told that he would not be selected for Surrey until the matter was settled, Lohmann made a public apology which was accepted by the Surrey committee. He never played for England again. In 1898 the fee for England appearances was increased to £20. He was keen to play for Surrey in 1897 but could not agree terms with the club, and returned to South Africa where he worked as a coach and tour manager, and was also employed by the Johannesburg Waterworks Company.

In 1899 Lohmann's tuberculosis worsened, though he was able to make a final trip to England in 1901 as assistant manager of the touring South African team. He died, unmarried, of tuberculosis at Worcester, Cape Colony, on 1 December 1901. He was buried in Matjiesfontein cemetery, where a white marble gravestone was paid for by his county colleagues at Surrey. Known affectionately as Our George, Lohmann was the greatest bowler of his time, a strong advocate of professional cricketers' being fairly rewarded, and a player who helped to make cricket a respectable profession. RIC SISSONS

Sources R. Sissons, *George Lohmann—the beau ideal* (1991) · Surrey county cricket club archives, London · R. Sissons, *The players: a social history of the professional cricketer* (1988) · *Cricket* (27 Aug 1885) · *Cricket* (30 July 1896) · *Cricket* (19 Dec 1901) · *The Clarion* (July 1892) · *Wisden* (1902) · *Wisden* (1889) · *The Times* (2 Dec 1901) · P. Bailey, P. Thorn, and P. Wynne-Thomas, *Who's who of cricketers* (1984) · Surrey county cricket club minute books, Surrey county cricket club, Kingston upon Thames · b. cert.

Archives Surrey county cricket club, Oval, Kennington, London, corresp.

Likenesses E. Hawkins, photograph, repro. in C. W. Alcock, ed., *Famous cricketers and cricket grounds* (1895), p. 1 · photograph, repro. in *Cricket* (27 Oct 1892) · stipple, NPG

Löhr, Marie Kaye Wouldes (1890–1975), actress, was born on 28 July 1890 in Sydney, New South Wales, Australia, the daughter of Lewis J. Löhr, treasurer of the opera house, Melbourne, and his English wife, Kate Bishop (1848–1923), who had acted on the London stage for twenty years and had been a member of the original cast of *Our Boys* at the Vaudeville Theatre in 1875: she was the sister of Alfred Bishop (1848–1928), the actor–manager. Marie Löhr first appeared on stage at the age of four in *The World Against her* in Sydney, and after moving to England made her London début in 1901 at the Garrick Theatre in *Shockheaded Peter*, a children's play by Philip Carr and Nigel Playfair, and *The Man who Stole the Castle*. She first went on tour with her god-parents, the actors William and Madge Kendal, in 1902, and continued to tour with the Kendals until 1907.

After the Kendals retired in 1908 Löhr embarked on a successful acting career, playing Mrs Reginald Bridgenorth in the original production of G. B. Shaw's *Getting Married* at the Haymarket Theatre in 1908. She was closely associated with Herbert Beerbohm Tree at His Majesty's Theatre, playing the part of Margaret in *Faust* in 1908, and Lydia in a revival of Shaw's *The Admirable Bashville* in 1909. Also in 1909 she was Lady Teazle to Tree's Sir Peter Teazle in R. B. Sheridan's *The School for Scandal* and Ophelia to his Hamlet. W. Somerset Maugham wrote the part of a country-bred parlourmaid for her in *Smith* (1909), and in 1911 she appeared with Sir John Hare (1844–1921) in *The Marionettes* by Gladys Unger, and *Better not Enquire*. She married Anthony Leyland Val (1888–1942), son of Val Prinsep RA, in 1911: they had one daughter. She continued to act leading roles for several West End managers, including Gerald Du Maurier and Charles Frohman, until January 1918, when in partnership with her husband she took on the management of the Globe Theatre in Shaftesbury Avenue (opened as the Hicks Theatre in 1906 and renamed the Globe in 1909). They opened in 1918 with Somerset Maugham's *Love in a Cottage*, and she went on to appear in several successful productions at the Globe, including *Nurse Benson* by R. C. Carton and J. H. McCarthy (1918), *The Voice from the Minaret* by R. S. Hichens (1919), and *A Marriage of Convenience* by Sydney Grundy (1920). After her New York début in 1922 as Lady Caryll in *The Voice from the Minaret* she returned to the Globe to appear in successful productions of *The Return* and Alfred Sutro's *The Laughing Lady* in the autumn of 1922. Her final role at the Globe was as the Hon. Margot Tatham in Frederick Lonsdales's *Aren't we All?* in 1923. After this she retired from active management of the theatre and was replaced as leading lady by Margaret Bannerman, who became Anthony Prinsep's second wife after he and Marie Löhr were divorced in 1928, when Prinsep also gave up the management of the Globe. Löhr continued to pursue a successful career as a light comedy actress. At Christmas 1927 she made the first of several appearances as Mrs Darling in J. M. Barrie's *Peter Pan*, and her successes in the 1930s included roles in Somerset Maugham's *The Breadwinner* (1930), Dodie Smith's *Call it a Day* (1935), Esther McCracken's *Quiet Wedding* (1938), and Lynne Dexter's *Other People's Houses* (1941). She played in several musicals, including *Casanova* (1932), and Ivor Novello's *Crest of the Wave* (1937).

Löhr was also a popular film actress, first appearing in the film version of *Aren't we All?* in 1932. Two of her best performances were in films of plays by G. B. Shaw, as Mrs Higgins in *Pygmalion* (1938), and as Lady Britomart in *Major Barbara* (1941), and in 1942 she was in the cast of the wartime thriller *Went the Day Well?* After several years' absence from the stage, she returned in 1947 in *Caste* by T. W. Robertson at the Duke of York's Theatre, and she continued to act in the West End for the next twenty years. She had parts in Terence Rattigan's *A Harlequinade* (1948), John Whiting's *A Penny for a Song* (1951), William Douglas-Home's *The Manor of Northstead* (1954), and Noël Coward's *Waiting in the Wings* (1960). She also continued to appear in musicals, including *Jubilee Girl*, which opened in Bristol in 1956, although it was so poorly received that she left the cast before its London opening. She took the part of Lady Bracknell in *Half in Earnest* (1958), a musical based on Oscar Wilde's *The Importance of being Earnest*, performed to inaugurate the new Belgrade Theatre in Coventry, and she was in John Osborne's *The World of Paul Slickey* (1959), which was booed on the opening night, and lasted only six weeks in the West End. She made her last stage appearance in 1966 as Mrs Whitefield in a revival of Shaw's *Man and Superman*. She died on 21 January 1975 at her home in Brighton, 24 Harrington Road, and was buried in the Brompton cemetery, West London, on 30 January.

ANNE PIMLOTT BAKER

Sources R. Mander and J. Mitchenson, *The theatres of London* (1979), 93–8 • P. Hartnoll, ed., *The Oxford companion to the theatre*, 4th edn (1983) • J. P. Wearing, *The London stage, 1890–1959* (1976–93) • K. Gänzl, *The British musical theatre*, 2 (1986) • *The Times* (24 Jan 1975) • *WW* • d. cert.

Likenesses photograph, repro. in *The Times*

Loingsech mac Óenguso (*d.* 704), high-king of Ireland, was also king of Cenél Conaill. He succeeded Fínśnechtae Fledach mac Dúnchada (*d.* 695) as high-king in 696 and reigned as such until his death. Loingsech was the first Cenél Conaill ruler to become king of Tara (high-king) in almost fifty years; the previous four kings to have attained to this position of overking of all the Uí Néill and their dependencies belonged to Síl nÁeda Sláine, a branch of the southern Uí Néill in whose territory the iconic site of Tara lay. The annalistic sources contain only two entries on Loingsech. The first is a bare notice of the year of his accession. The second is unusually precise: it states that he died in the battle of Corann (in south Sligo) and that this occurred on the fourth of the ides of July (12 July), at the sixth hour, on a Saturday.

Loingsech was fifth cousin to Adomnán, who had been abbot of Iona, and therefore head of the Columban *paruchia*, since 679. The fact that these Cenél Conaill cousins led the Uí Néill and the powerful Columban federation in the years 696–704 reinforced the prestige and power of both men. Throughout the seventh century, there was strong rivalry for ecclesiastical primacy between the various Irish *paruchiae*. From the middle of the century onwards the church of Armagh, situated in the Uí Néill vassal territory of Airthir, offered a series of challenges to the Columban *paruchia*, by promoting the cult of Patrick and by centring the cult on Armagh itself. The Uí Néill's traditional allegiance, however, was to the founder saint of the Columban churches; and his successor, Adomnán, had brought this *paruchia* to the peak of its power at the end of the seventh century. When the kingship of Tara returned to Cenél Conaill in the person of Loingsech, Adomnán was afforded his strongest chance of reasserting the primacy of the Columban federation. There is diplomatic evidence that Loingsech and Adomnán co-operated in at least one major enterprise: Loingsech's name appears first on the list of secular rulers who gave their support to the *Lex Innocentium*, a law promulgated by Adomnán in 697 *in Hibernia Britaniaque* ('in Ireland and Britain'), to which the church of Armagh gave its support.

Adomnán aspired to establish a Christian high-kingship but while he promoted the Uí Néill as the supreme federation, the high-kingship did not become a hegemony enforced by military power until after the mid-ninth century. Nevertheless, Loingsech, and his grandfather, *Domnall mac Áeda, are given the title *rex Hiberniae* ('king of Ireland') by the original hand of the annals of Ulster, the only two pre-ninth century kings so designated. As the annals before *c.*740 are based on a chronicle compiled at Iona, the designation can be taken to reflect Adomnán's concept of Christian *imperium*.

However, it is possible that Loingsech, as king of Tara, was attempting to assert a claim to the high-kingship at the time of his death at the battle of Corann. In leading an army southwards into Connacht, his first aim probably was territorial expansion: Cenél Conaill's opportunity for eastward expansion had diminished as a result of Cenél nÉogain aggrandizement. But Loingsech may also have hoped to deal a major blow to Connacht's ascendant dynasty, Uí Briúin Aí, and thereby gain the submission of the province: the accounts in the secondary hand of the annals of Ulster, in the interpolated annals, and in the narrative tale of the battle attribute the victory to Cellach mac Ragallaig, the Uí Briúin Aí king.

Cenél Conaill rulers occupied the kingship of Tara only twice more after Loingsech's death. The first of these was Loingsech's immediate successor and first cousin, Congal mac Ferguso (*r.* 704–10). The second was Loingsech's son, *Flaithbertach mac Loingsig, who began his rule in 728, was deposed in 734, and died in 765. It is therefore unlikely that Loingsech was over forty years of age at his own death.

MÁIRÍN NÍ DHONNCHADHA

Sources F. J. Byrne, *Irish kings and high-kings* (1973), 114, 256–8, 276, 283 • M. Ní Dhonnchadha, 'The guarantor list of Cáin Adomnáin, 697', *Peritia*, 1 (1982), 178–215, esp. 196–7 • M. Herbert, *Iona, Kells, and Derry: the history and hagiography of the monastic familia of Columba* (1988), 51, 55, 146

Lok, Henry (*d.* in or after **1608**), poet, was the third son of Henry Lok (*d.* 1571), a London mercer, and his wife, Anne *Locke, *née* Vaughan (*c.*1530–1590x1607). Sir William *Lok was his grandfather, the traveller Michael *Lok his uncle, and the versifier of the psalms Michael Cosworth his cousin. Nothing is known about his early life or education, other than Wood's unsubstantiated assertions that he was born early in Elizabeth's reign, spent some time at Oxford, and then gained the support of an unnamed nobleman at court—perhaps Henry Carey, Lord Hunsdon (Doelman, 5–6). Grosart was probably confused in stating that this Henry was the parent of one Zachary Lok who in 1598 described his father as a former Levant merchant of 'above 64 years of age' ('Poems by Henry Lok, gentleman', 2.20).

Lok married Ann Moyle of Cornwall, with whom he had two sons, Henry (*b.* 1592) and Charles. Perhaps motivated by these family responsibilities, Lok became one of the most productive writers of devotional poetry of the 1590s: his *Sundry Christian Passions* was published in 1593 and then reprinted in his volume entitled *Ecclesiastes* in 1597. The latter contained an unparalleled sequence of sixty dedicatory sonnets addressed to a veritable who's who of late-Elizabethan literary patrons. The survival at Lambeth Palace Library of a copy with the dedicatory sonnets cancelled, except for the one to Archbishop Whitgift printed alone on a leaf facing the title-page, suggests that Lok sometimes presented personalized copies to chosen individuals. Lok also contributed a commendatory poem to James VI of Scotland's *Poeticall Exercises at Vacant Houres* (1591), printed at Edinburgh but previously registered to Richard Field, the publisher of Lok's own two volumes.

The success of this literary frenzy of patronage hunting seems to have been limited. While Lok claimed in January 1597 that the countess of Warwick had encouraged him to seek a pension from Sir Robert Cecil until some suitable office became available, no employment seems to have come his way (Doelman, 8). By early 1598 he was petitioning unsuccessfully for the collectorship of Devon; and on 8 June 1598 he even put himself forward for the position of keeper of the queen's bears and mastiffs. 'It is better to be a bear herd', Lok bitterly mused, 'than to be baited daily with great exclamations for small debts' (*CSP dom.*, *1598–1601*, 60).

Eventually Cecil found some use for Lok in France and even acknowledged his service with the gift of a gelding. In 1599 Lok (who was skilled in cipher) was in Bayonne, assiduously collecting political information for Cecil. Unfortunately he also began to arouse the suspicions of the locals, who clearly did not believe his claim that he was merely an English traveller *en route* for Spain with the entourage of the French ambassador. Back home in England by April 1600 and living in the Strand, his services seem to have been dispensed with by Cecil. Despite his previous poetic commendation of King James's poetry, Lok fared no better during the new reign. By March 1606 he was imprisoned as an insolvent debtor in the Westminster gatehouse. In May 1608 he was again incarcerated for debt and pleaded with Cecil to be transferred to the Clink at Southwark. Desperate appeals in October 1608 to Cecil appear to have gone unanswered, after which time nothing else is known about Lok's fate. Doelman states that Lok died 'in Venice in 1611' (p. 11), but, in an otherwise densely noted article, he gives no citation for this assertion.

Lok is now best remembered for his two volumes of devotional verse, *Sundry Christian Passions* (containing 200 sonnets), and *Ecclesiastes*, which reprinted the first collection and added another 100 sonnets, along with a separate grouping of twenty sonnets or 'Peculiar Prayers'. Including introductory and concluding poems, this 1597 edition contained 328 sonnets which were memorably derided in *The Returne from Pernassus* (1606) as fit only 'to lie in some old nooks amongst old boots and shoes'.

More recently, however, it has been proposed that Lok's devotional poetry should be viewed as a historically important contribution to the emergence of an early seventeenth-century tradition of British devotional writing, culminating in William Drummond's *Urania* (1616) and John Donne's 'La corona' and 'Holy Sonnets' (Roche, 155). Lok presumably drew early inspiration from the pioneering devotional poetry of his mother, Anne Locke; and his own sonnets may have likewise influenced Barnabe Barnes's *A Divine Century of Spirituall Sonnets* (1595) and Nicholas Breton's *The Soules Harmony* (1602). Self-consciously learned and rich in biblical allegory, Lok's poems provide 'a kaleidoscopic sense of the Bible impinging on the repentant soul'. Despite their unevenness in quality, the best of Lok's work may still be usefully regarded as mediating 'between the assertiveness of Donne and the humility of Herbert' (Roche, 158). Lok also included 'Sundry psalmes of David' in his *Ecclesiastes* volume and contributed a commendatory verse to his cousin Michael Cosworth's own versification of the psalms (BL, Harley MS 6906). Lok was a showy metrical innovator and his *Ecclesiastes* was prefaced by a pair of dedicatory poems to Queen Elizabeth which are 'two of the most elaborately numerological poems' to be found in Elizabethan poetry (Roche, 164). Despite his literary effusions, Lok remains a poignant example of how the pursuit of court patronage through poetic dedications sometimes led only to destitution and despair. MICHAEL G. BRENNAN

Sources T. P. Roche, *Petrarch and the English sonnet sequence* (1989) · *DNB* · *CSP dom.*, *1595–7*, 348; *1598–1601*, 25, 60, 72, 74, 172, 201, 246, 262, 332, 361, 426, 495, 509; *1608–10*, 244, 307, 431, 463 · Wood, *Ath. Oxon.*, new edn · 'Poems by Henry Lok, gentleman', *Miscellanies of the Fuller Worthies' Library*, ed. A. B. Grosart, 4 vols. (1870–76), 2.1–389 · L. B. Campbell, *Divine poetry and drama in sixteenth-century England* (1959) · B. K. Lewalski, *Protestant poetics and the seventeenth-century religious lyric* (1979) · J. Doelman, 'Seeking "The fruit of favour": the dedicatory sonnets of Henry Lok's *Ecclesiastes*', *ELH: a Journal of English Literary History*, 60 (1993), 1–15

Lok, Michael (*c.*1532–1620x22), mercer, merchant adventurer, and traveller, was born in Cheapside, London, the youngest of five surviving sons of Sir William *Lok (1480–1550) and his second wife, Catherine, *née* Cooke (*d.* 1537), and the brother of Rose *Throckmorton. By his own account Lok was taught in 'scoles of grammar' until he was thirteen, and was then apprenticed to his family's mercery business in Flanders. He remained there until about 1552, when he and his brothers, moved by their father's death and the Antwerp trade crisis of 1550–51, began to seek more distant, innovative markets for their wares. The Loks were devout converts to protestantism, and during Mary Tudor's reign Michael remained abroad, travelling to France, Scotland, Spain, Portugal, Venice, the Greek islands, and the Levant, acting as his brothers' factor and trading on his own behalf. During this time the sight of the wares of the New World and Far East made a powerful impression on him; it was from this period that Lok himself dated his abiding obsession with the expansion of English commercial activities through the discovery and exploitation of new markets (Cotton MS, Otho E VIII, fols. 41–3). He collected a significant library of travel literature, charts, and other cosmographical data, to a value of some £500, which he later put at the disposal of Richard Hakluyt the younger during the preparation of his *Divers Voyages* (1582).

Lok returned to England at the accession of Elizabeth I. In 1562 he was admitted to the Mercers' Company, and about this time married Joan (*d.* 1571), daughter of Sir William Wilkinson, sheriff of London; they had eight surviving children. He continued to practise his mercery trade in London, and from 1571 to 1576 he was London agent of the Russia Company (Willan, 26–7). In 1574 he was approached by Martin Frobisher, with whom he may have had a prior acquaintance through his brothers' involvement in the Guinea voyage of 1554, in which Frobisher had sailed as a young man. Together they prepared a proposal to the privy council, to discover a sea route to 'Cathay' via the north-west. They secured a licence to attempt this from the Russia Company, whose charter privileges they were technically infringing, and secured investors from the city and court. For want of sufficient funds to dispatch a voyage during 1576, Lok was obliged to provide loans of over £800 from his own pocket. Two further voyages to Baffin Island followed, in which the queen herself invested, but the enterprise degenerated into a search for gold, incurring large losses (most spectacularly for Lok himself). Frobisher turned violently against Lok, whom he blamed for his own misfortunes, and led moves to impeach him for alleged financial irregularities. Effectively bankrupted, with his name on transactions entered into on behalf of his fellow adventurers, Lok was cynically abandoned to fight a series of creditors' suits. He went to debtors' prison upon at least eight occasions, and claimed to have seen the inside of every London gaol save the Fleet—to which he was also committed subsequently.

By this time Lok had fifteen children or stepchildren. He had married in 1576 or 1577 his second wife, Margery (*d. c.*1583), widow of Cesare Adelmare and mother of Julius Caesar Adelmare, later judge of the high court of admiralty. Lok emerged from prison for the final time in 1581 and spent most of the rest of his remarkably long life vainly attempting to recover some part of his former fortune and reputation.

In 1587 Lok was in Ireland on unspecified business, though so penurious that he was obliged to send his son Benjamin back to England to raise money to bring him home to fight a suit against one of his rare debtors. In 1591 he took up a four-year tenure as the Aleppan consul of the Barbary Company, where he immediately alienated all the company's merchants by enforcing the letter of its regulations scrupulously. On the initiative of the company's governor, Sir John Spencer (a distant relative), he was dismissed without compensation. Lok fled to Venice and initiated a suit in the courts there for compensation, which effectively paralysed the company's trade in the Levant. Finally, on the privy council's urging, Lok accepted a compromise settlement of £300 in 1601.

Lok retired from his business activities soon after returning to England on Christmas day 1602. He continued his studies, however. In 1612 he translated the last five decades of Peter Martyr's *De orbe novo* for a new edition published by Thomas Adams as *De Novo Orbe, or, The Historie of the West Indies*. For Samuel Purchas he made a translation from Spanish, the *Mexican History in Pictures*, and wrote a brief commentary, *Note on the Strait of Sea Commonly called Fretum Anian, in the South Sea*. As late as 1615 Lok was being sued for a debt of £200 incurred during the north-west enterprise. Little is known of his life subsequent to this, but the inquisition post mortem on his estate was conducted only in 1623, and he died in Cheapside, 'at the sign of the lock'—possibly his birthplace also—between 1620 and 1622. Lok's eldest sons, Zachary, Benjamin, and Matthew, predeceased him, and their wills (particularly the debts they forgive) offer ample evidence of their father's continuing penury. Lok's reputation remained poor; he is regarded as the role model for the merchant Shylock by those who regard the earl of Oxford as the author of the *Merchant of Venice* (Willan, 27). Hakluyt was more perceptive, regarding him as 'a man for his knowledge in divers languages & especially in Cosmographie, able to doe his country good, & worthie in my judgment for the manifold good partes in him, of good reputation & better fortune' (Hakluyt, 11).

JAMES MCDERMOTT

Sources BL, Cotton MS Otho E VIII, fols. 41–6 · PRO, SP/12/119, 29, SP/12/149, 42 · BL, Add. MS 43827 · J. Hunter, *Familiae minorum gentium*, ed. J. W. Clay, 4, Harleian Society, 40 (1896), 1306–8 · W. Newbold, ed., *Acts of court of the Mercers' Company* (1936) · inquisition post mortem, PRO, C 142/653, 25 · R. Collinson, *Three voyages of Martin Frobisher* (1867) · BL, Add. MS 12497, fols. 319–25 · BL, Lansdowne MSS 100/1, fols. 1–14v · BL, Lansdowne MS 82, fols. 190–91 · PRO, SP/99/1, 230–39 · J. Stow, *A survay of London*, rev. edn (1603); repr. with introduction by C. L. Kingsford as *A survey of London*, 2 vols. (1908), vol. 1, p. 269 · list of members of the Mercers' Company, Mercers' Hall, London · M. W. Douglas, *Lord Oxford and the Shakespeare group* (1948) · T. S. Willan, *The early history of the Russia Company, 1553–1603* (1956) · R. H. [R. Hakluyt], *Divers voyages touching the discoverie of America and the ilands adjacent unto the same* (1582) · PRO, PROB 11/33, sig. 20; PROB 11/101, sig. 27; PROB 11/105, sig. 34; PROB 11/118, sig. 72 [wills of William Lok and his eldest sons 1550, 1603, 1605, 1606]

Likenesses H. Watkins, albumen print, *c.*1885–1889, NPG

Wealth at death approx. £100 p.a. income from leasehold properties: PRO, C 142/653, 25

Lok, Sir William (1480–1550), mercer and merchant adventurer, was the second son of Thomas Lok and grandson of John Lok, sheriff of London in 1461, both of whom were also members of the Mercers' Company. Although formally admitted to the company only in 1507, Lok was already supplying clothes of gold and silver to the king in that year. His daughter Rose Hickman later claimed that he became the mercer and agent of Henry VIII 'beyond the seas'. Lok's strong Lutheran convictions—his first wife, Alice, was one of England's first converts to that doctrine—made him a willing servant of the early architects of the English Reformation. During annual visits to the Low Countries to trade at the marts of Antwerp and Bergen op Zoom, Lok provided intelligence to Cromwell or the king, reporting rumours concerning political and diplomatic developments in Europe. In a prophetic letter of February 1535 he commented upon the growing reaction against the Anabaptists: 'They be gon owte of every parte of this countre towards that town [Leeth: Liège], and that distrowyd, they schall go to the town of Mynster as they do say here…' (*LP Henry VIII*, 8.76). From further afield he passed on rumours that the Turks, fearful of Charles V's eastern ambitions, were attempting to form an alliance with any state who would join with them. In March 1527 Lok received official recognition in the form of an exclusive licence to import silks, jewels, and mercery wares for court revels. While in Dunkirk in December 1533 he tore down a papal bull excommunicating Henry VIII for his adulterous marriage to Anne Boleyn (who was herself supplied with French editions of the gospels, epistles, and Psalms by Lok), an incident which earned Lok a pension of £100 annually, the position of gentleman of the privy chamber, and, upon at least one occasion, the honour of entertaining the king at his home.

Lok's business activities were not confined solely to the importation of merceries; he was also involved in the export of beer, while in 1528 he sold 600 leather harnesses to the royal ordnance. In 1533 he was named in a letter to the king as someone known to have visited the island of Candia (Crete), which suggests that he was active in the wine or currant trade. In 1531 a ship jointly hired by Lok and John Gresham was detained at Lisbon *en route* for London from Chios, another indication of interests in foreign consumables. In 1535 Lok was rated—possibly for the king's subsidy—at £1000. On 20 October 1545 he was elected alderman of Vitry ward, and on 3 March 1549 created sheriff of London and knighted by Edward VI. On 10 October that year Lok was a member of the procession escorting the duke of Somerset to the Tower.

Lok was married four times: to Alice Spenser (*d.* 1522); Catherine Cooke (*d.* 14 Oct 1537); Eleanor Marsh (*d.* 1546); and Elizabeth Meredith (*d.* 1551). He fathered nineteen children, of whom twelve, five sons and seven daughters from his first two marriages, survived into adulthood. His children included Rose [*see* Throckmorton, Rose], Michael *Lok and Henry, father of the poet Henry Lok, all children of Catherine Cooke, and from his first marriage daughters Elizabeth (who married Nicholas Bullingham, later bishop of Lincoln and Worcester) and Jane, whose own three daughters all married members of the common council.

Lok died at his home in Cheapside, 'at the sign of the Padlock' on 24 August 1550, and was buried in the Mercers' Chapel, St Thomas Acres, with his parents and first and fourth wives, his coat of arms being set into a window there. Like many of his contemporaries, in later life Lok had converted much of his capital into property; in his will he bequeathed numerous houses and shops in Bow, Spitalfields, and Cheapside (including his retailing shop, the Lok), some twelve farms with land in Merton Holts and Tottenham, and at least one inn, the Dogges Head in the Potte, in White Leg Entry, Cheapside.

JAMES MCDERMOTT

Sources R. Hickman, BL, MS Add. 43827, fols. 1–18*v* • PRO, PROB 11/33, sig. 20 • G. S. Fry, ed., *Abstracts of inquisitiones post mortem relating to the City of London*, 1: 1485–1561, British RS, 15 (1896), 82 • *LP Henry VIII*, vols. 2, 7–8 • H. F. Y., 'Historical account of the Locke family', *GM*, 1st ser., 62 (1792), 798–801 • lists of members of the Mercers' Company, Mercers' Hall, London • L. Lyell and F. D. Watney, eds., *Acts of court of the Mercers' Company, 1453–1527* (1936) • J. Hunter, *Familiae minorum gentium*, ed. J. W. Clay, 4, Harleian Society, 40 (1896) • A. B. Beaven, ed., *The aldermen of the City of London, temp. Henry III–[1912]*, 1 (1908) • J. Stow, *A survay of London*, rev. edn (1603); repr. with introduction by C. L. Kingsford as *A survey of London*, 2 vols. (1908), vol. 1 • *The diary of Henry Machyn, citizen and merchant-taylor of London, from AD 1550 to AD 1563*, ed. J. G. Nichols, CS, 42 (1848) • Coll. Arms, MS I, 3, fol. 84*v* • BL, Cotton MS Galba B. x, fol. 58 • R. Hakluyt, *The principall navigations, voiages and discoveries of the English nation*, 3 vols. in 2 (1589) • BL, Cotton MS Cleopatra F. vi, fol. 344 • J. B. Heath, 'An account of materials furnished for the use of Queen Anne Boleyn, and the Princess Elizabeth, by William Loke, "The King's Mercer", between the 20 Jany, 1535 (27th of Henry VIII.) and the 27 April, 1536', *Miscellanies of the Philobiblon Society*, 7 (1862–3), 3–22

Wealth at death house and integral retailing shop in Cheapside; eight tenements; thirty-four messuages; several shops in Bow Lane, Spitalfields and Cheapside; farm properties; unspecified number of leasehold interests: will, PRO, PROB 11/33, sig. 20; C i, 82

Lokert [Lockhart], **George** (*c.*1485–1547), logician and theologian, was born in Ayr, to John Lokkert and Marion Multray (*d.* 1500). He entered the University of Paris, where he is first referred to in 1504 in the book of receipts of the German nation in the university, the 'nation' to which all Scottish students were assigned. Lokert studied arts, along with his half-brother John, under the Scot David Cranston at the Collège de Montaigu, and took his master's degree in 1505. In the same year he gave his inaugural lecture as regent in arts. With his theology studies underway he taught arts in the Collège de Rheims where he gave a full course of three and a half years, before returning to teach arts at Montaigu as a colleague of Noel Beda, John Mair, and David Cranston. In 1514, having taught a course on the *Sentences* of Peter Lombard, he became bachelor of theology, and in that same year he published his first book, on 'notions', concepts with which we represent the world to ourselves. The book, much the most popular he wrote, went into seven editions during his lifetime. In 1516 he published an important edition of fourteenth-century writings on physics by Buridan, Thimon, and Albert of Saxony, and three years later he prepared the alphabetic table of contents of the fourth edition of Mair's commentary on the *Sentences*, thereby providing evidence for the good relations between himself and Mair. Also in 1519 Lokert was elected prior of the Collège de Sorbonne, the headquarters of the faculty of theology in the University of Paris. About this time he moved from Montaigu to the Collège de La

Marche, where he lectured on logic; in 1520 he brought out a commentary on Aristotle's *Posterior Analytics*. In that same year he was awarded a doctorate in theology.

In 1521 Lokert returned to Scotland to take up a post as provost of the collegiate church of Crichton, in the village of Crichton, 6 miles south-east of Dalkeith. In December of the same year he was incorporated in the University of St Andrews, a move that seems to have been made as preparation for his election in February 1522 as rector of that university. In that post he deployed his skills to effect a grand revision of the examining procedures at the university, a revision that brought St Andrews quite closely into line with Paris practices. Lokert continued to publish works on logic during his three-year period as rector, bringing out in 1523 *De oppositionibus* (on the relations of contradiction, contrariety, and sub-contrariety), and around the same time publishing his *De terminis* (on the nature and variety of terms). The following year saw his *De sillogismis*, a very detailed investigation of syllogistic reasoning.

Near the start of 1525 Lokert returned to Paris to resume his fellowship of the Collège de Sorbonne and his membership of the faculty of theology. In addition he became head of the Scots College in Paris, a shadowy body founded in 1325 by David Moray, who as bishop of Moray had arranged for funds to be provided to enable scholars from his diocese to study in Paris. In January 1526 the then bishop of Moray, Robert Shaw, 'provydit Mr George Lokart, professor of theologie … then resident at Paris, ourseer of the studentis' of the Scots College (Durkan, 'George Lockhart'). Sadly none of the college papers of the period of Lokert's headship have survived. Other aspects of Lokert's work at this time are, however, well documented, especially his involvement in an attempt, masterminded by Noel Beda, administrative head of the faculty of theology, to have certain of Erasmus's works condemned as heretical. Lokert was one of the thirteen members of a commission established by Beda to investigate an attack by Erasmus on Beda. Lokert was in a difficult position, since Erasmus had the support of the king, François I, and Lokert no doubt felt his vulnerability as a foreign national criticizing a man whom the king was trying to attract to the newly founded Collège de France in Paris.

By this time Lokert had ceased to publish new works, and it may have been the increasingly stressful circumstances at Paris, with bitter in-fighting at the faculty of theology, including potentially lethal charges of heresy, that caused this cessation and led eventually to his return to the west coast of Scotland. For a brief period, from 1533 to 1534, he was archdeacon of Teviotdale, and in March 1534 he was appointed dean of Glasgow, a post he held until his death. As dean he was required to be in Glasgow for six months each year and to preside over chapter meetings. He died on 22 June 1547. In 1542 he had arranged for an anniversary mass for the souls of his parents to be said in the church of St John the Baptist in Ayr; he had also arranged that such a mass be said on his own death for himself and his half-brother John. Additionally, the register of decisions of the Sorbonne for 8 June 1549 records that 'with the consent of all' it was agreed that on the day after Quasimodo Sunday (the Sunday after Easter) an obit was thenceforward to be said for 'our master Loquart' (Durkan, 'George Lockhart').

George Lokert was a logician of formidable power, who wrote with great lucidity on highly technical and complex issues. In particular, his analysis of propositions which contain two quantifiers relates in interesting ways to modern problems in logic, and can be used to resolve difficulties which were thought insoluble before the work of Gottlob Frege (1848–1925). But he was also a devout man on the conservative wing of the church. The Reformation and the encroachment of Renaissance humanism must have been deeply distasteful to him. He dedicated himself to the maintenance of the old order, and died some thirteen years before the new order took a firm grip on his native country. ALEXANDER BROADIE

Sources A. Broadie, *George Lokert: late-scholastic logician* (1983) • A. Broadie, *The circle of John Mair* (1985) • J. K. Farge, *Biographical register of Paris doctors of theology, 1500–1536* (1980) • F. M. Higman, *Censorship and the Sorbonne* (1979) • H. Elié, 'Quelques maîtres de l'université de Paris vers l'an 1500', *Archives d'Histoire Doctrinale et Littéraire du Moyen Âge*, 18 (1950–51), 193–243 • J. Durkan, 'George Lockhart', *Innes Review*, 15 (1964), 191–2 • J. Durkan, 'Scots College, Paris', *Innes Review*, 2 (1951), 112–13 • J. Durkan, 'Grisy burses at Scots College, Paris', *Innes Review*, 22 (1971), 50–52 • G. Lokert, *Scriptum in materia noticiarum* (1514)

Lollard knights (*act. c.*1380–*c.*1414) is the name conventionally given to a close-knit group of influential courtiers, accused by contemporary chroniclers of promoting heretical Lollard doctrines during the reigns of Richard II and Henry IV. The Leicester chronicler Henry Knighton (writing during the 1380s) names **Sir Reynald Hilton** (*fl. c.*1380); **Sir John Pecche** (*c.*1360–1386); **Sir John Trussell** (1349–1424); **Sir Richard Stury** (*c.*1327–1395); Sir Lewis *Clifford (*c.*1330–1404), and Sir Thomas *Latimer (1341–1401) as 'the strongest promoters and most powerful protectors' of Lollard preachers (*Chronicon Henrici Knighton*, 295). The St Albans chronicler Walsingham also independently cites Stury, Clifford, and Latimer, along with Sir William *Neville (*c.*1341–1391); Sir John *Clanvow (*c.*1341–1391), and ('above all') Sir John *Montagu (*d.* 1400) as Lollard partisans in 1387: the same source names Stury ('the greatest supporter of perfidy'; Walsingham, *Annales*, 174), Clifford, Latimer, and Montagu as promulgators of the radical Lollard 'twelve conclusions' allegedly presented to parliament in 1395. Walsingham later added Sir John *Cheyne (*d.* 1414) to the list as a leading anti-clerical, and made further accusations against Montagu and Clifford.

The careers of these men were investigated by W. T. Waugh (1913), and far more thoroughly by K. B. McFarlane (1972). Of those named only by Knighton, Hilton cannot be satisfactorily identified—it is possible that the chronicler was mistaken in describing him as a knight, and that the Reynold Hilton whom he had in mind was a priest, a servant of Edward, the Black Prince, who was controller of the king's wardrobe (1377–81): but Pecche and Trussell (as well as Latimer) owned lands near the chronicler's Leicester, so that rumours of their activities may well have reached him. Pecche, who died young, was Sir Richard Stury's ward, while Trussell, a violent and lawless man, was associated with Lollard suspects much later, in 1418. The core of the group, however, were those accused either by both chroniclers (Stury, Clifford, and Latimer) or by Walsingham alone (Neville, Clanvow, Montagu, and Cheyne).

Though they were associated neither by area of origin nor blood relationship, these seven came to form a remarkably compact group: their careers were extraordinarily similar, and their public and private interrelationships very close. Again and again they appear together in documents as business partners, co-feoffees, and fellow executors, for each other or for mutual associates. All except Cheyne were career soldiers under Edward III; Clifford and Montagu were fellow knights of the Garter. Clifford, Stury, and perhaps Latimer were trusted retainers of the Black Prince, and by the 1380s all seven had achieved high status at the court of his son Richard II, five becoming knights of the king's chamber. In 1400 Montagu, now earl of Salisbury, was lynched for his share in a rising intended to restore the deposed King Richard. All except Latimer, moreover, served abroad as negotiators and diplomats. They were likewise a notably cultured group. Clifford, Stury, Neville, and Clanvow were all friends of Geoffrey Chaucer; Clifford also knew the French poet Eustace Deschamps, and Stury was an honoured associate of Froissart. Montagu was renowned in his own right for his French verse (now lost), while Clanvow wrote both an English love poem ('The Boke of Cupide') and a moralizing treatise (known as *The Two Ways*).

Whether this highly placed group also shared a real belief in heretical doctrines has been more controversial. Waugh concluded that they were the victims of chroniclers' prejudices, or at worst short-term and superficial supporters of heresy. McFarlane, basing his statements on much more wide-ranging investigation, conversely declared that their notoriety as protectors of Lollards was well founded. Their apparent immunity from persecution, he believed, was due partly to their influence at court and partly to the ambiguous attitude to heresy that prevailed among lay and ecclesiastical authorities before the passing of *De haeretico comburendo* under Henry IV in 1401. Subsequent research has confirmed McFarlane's view.

Latimer's support for Lollardy (which even Waugh admitted) is the best documented from non-chronicle sources. A forceful defender of heretical preachers from at least 1388, his Leicestershire and Northamptonshire properties remained important centres of Lollard activity long after his death. Neville clearly protected the leading Lollard Nicholas Hereford, and may even have procured his escape from prison: thereafter (according to Walsingham) Hereford took refuge with the 'arch-heretic' (as Walsingham saw him) and iconoclast Montagu. Neville's close friend Clanvow wrote an English pietistic treatise (itself a most unusual activity for a layman and courtier), which admits at least to accusations of heresy having been made against him and his friends. Clanvow's Herefordshire relations and associates, moreover, most probably lent powerful support to the Lollard evangelist William Swinderby. The evidence against Stury, admittedly, comes only from the repeated accusations of the chroniclers, but his association with the group is too close for these to be disregarded.

Clifford, Latimer, and Cheyne (as well as Latimer's widow, Cheyne's son, and Clanvow's heirs) moreover left wills remarkable for extravagant protestations of unworthiness, contempt for the body, and prohibition of funeral pomp—all sentiments compatible with the puritan strain in Lollardy. Among Clifford's executors, indeed, was the future Lollard rebel, Sir John Oldcastle.

By the time of Oldcastle's revolt in 1414 all the original Lollard knights (except the marginal Trussell) were dead. The support this influential group gave to Lollardy had been crucial to its growth, but it had been given in the milder climate of Richard II's reign, when such opinions in high places could be tolerated or tacitly disregarded, despite the chroniclers' fulminations. The new generation of Lollard knights, younger men who supported Oldcastle (five knights and more than twenty esquires and gentlemen, including three of Cheyne's cousins, were implicated in his rising), lived in a different world, where government attitudes to heresy had hardened. By resorting to rebellion, these later and far less influential Lollard knights inextricably entangled Lollardy with treason, and so destroyed it as anything more than a persecuted lost cause. CHARLES KIGHTLY

Sources K. B. McFarlane, *Lancastrian kings and Lollard knights* (1972) • W. T. Waugh, 'The Lollard knights', *SHR*, 11 (1913–14), 55–92 • K. B. McFarlane, *John Wycliffe* (1966) • C. Kightly, 'The early Lollards', DPhil diss., University of York, 1975 • P. McNiven, *Heresy and politics in the reign of Henry IV* (1987) • *Thomae Walsingham, quondam monachi S. Albani, historia Anglicana*, ed. H. T. Riley, 2 vols., pt 1 of *Chronica monasterii S. Albani*, Rolls Series, 28 (1863–4), vol. 2 • *Chronicon Henrici Knighton, vel Cnitthon, monachi Leycestrensis*, ed. J. R. Lumby, 2 vols., Rolls Series, 92 (1889–95) • 'Annales Ricardi secundi et Henrici quarti, regum Angliae', *Johannis de Trokelowe et Henrici de Blaneforde … chronica et annales*, ed. H. T. Riley, pt 3 of *Chronica monasterii S. Albani*, Rolls Series, 28 (1866), 155–420 • *Chancery records* • unpublished documents, esp. KB9 (king's bench, ancient indictments), PRO • 'The two ways … by Sir John Clanvowe', ed. V. J. Scattergood, *English Philological Review*, 10 (1967) • A. Hudson, *The premature reformation: Wycliffite texts and Lollard history* (1988)

Archives CUL, MS Ff.1.6 • University College, Oxford, MS (Coxe) 97

Lollard women (*act. c.*1390–*c.*1520) were a significant feature in nonconformist and heretical circles before the end of the fourteenth century, and remained so throughout the subsequent history of the Lollard movement. Most of the information about them, even more than for men, comes from the records of prosecuting authorities, and as a result is almost always tantalizingly brief—snapshots taken at the time of their appearance in court. Even so, a rich variety of characters and roles is revealed. It should be noted at the outset, however, that the appropriateness of the term 'Lollard' (which originated as a word of abuse) rather than 'Wycliffite', as well as the size of the movement and the extent of its dependence on John *Wyclif (whose earliest followers do not appear to have included women), are issues much debated by historians. There is also considerable discussion regarding the role of gender in Lollardy, and particularly whether the movement afforded women more, or fewer, opportunities than orthodox religion.

Early exemplars Looking at the best documented examples in chronological order, a formidable personality is presented by **Anna Palmer** (*fl.* 1393–1394). An anchoress living in a house next to St Peter's parish church in Northampton, in 1393 she was summoned before Bishop John Buckingham of Lincoln (*d.* 1399) on fifteen charges of heresy and the separate one of incontinence, as well as of being the principal hostess of Lollards (*receptrix lollardorum*) in the area. She was said to have received prominent Lollards in her house at night, while secret conventicles and illicit congregations were held. When she appeared before the bishop she denounced him as Antichrist and his clerks as Antichrist's disciples, and informed him proudly that she did not wish to answer the charges against her, except the charge of incontinence, which she denied. Her intransigence brought her detention in the episcopal prison at Banbury and a summons the next year to a further examination in London, at which point she disappears from record.

Christina More (*fl.* 1412–1414) and her husband, William (who was a member of the governing class of Bristol), formed a prominent Lollard household in that town in the early years of the fifteenth century. They kept a Lollard chaplain, William Blake. On her husband's death in 1412 Christina took over both the management of his estate and his patronage of Lollards, even to the extent of equipping Blake and a servant named James Merrshe, and perhaps other servants, for their part in Oldcastle's rising in 1414. On this account she was among eight Lollards from Bristol who were prosecuted by Bishop Nicholas Bubwith of Bath and Wells (*d.* 1424), and maybe her social position alone saved her from a worse penalty than trial and purgation.

Wives of Norfolk Between 1428 and 1431 Bishop William *Alnwick of Norwich (*d.* 1449) conducted a determined and unusually well-documented campaign against heretics in his diocese. Two women stand out in the records of the trials that resulted. The first of these, **Margery Baxter** (*fl.* 1428–1429), was described as the wife of William Baxter, wright, of Martham when she was brought to trial in October 1428. William had already been convicted as a heretic but his wife's greatest reverence was reserved for the former priest and Lollard evangelizer from Tenterden in Kent, William *White, whom she called 'a great saint in heaven and a most holy doctor ordained and sent by God' (Tanner, 47). She admitted having transported White's books from Yarmouth and hiding him in her house for five days, as well as having learned from him the six heretical articles charged against her. The articles are notable for their radical nature and social content: only the person who keeps God's commandments may be considered a Christian; the sacrament of confession is to be avoided because it implies a lack of hope in God's mercy; pilgrimages should be made only to poor people; capital punishment and all other killing of humans is wrong; every good person is a priest; oaths are permissible only in a law court. She abjured her errors and was sentenced to severe and exemplary penance: she was to receive four floggings at her parish church on successive Sundays, and two more in a market place—probably that of nearby Acle—and to present herself with other penitents to do 'solemn penance' in Norwich Cathedral on the next Ash Wednesday and Maundy Thursday.

Six months later, in April 1429, Margery was again brought before Bishop Alnwick charged with heresy. By this time she and her husband appear to have moved to Norwich. In these proceedings only the depositions against her survive, but they have a ring of truth about them, and once again suggest a formidable and intriguing personality, somewhat eccentric, an individualist remarkable for her strength of mind and irreverence, especially towards the clergy and orthodox religion. According to these depositions, she proselytized other people, sometimes alone and sometimes with her husband, both in their houses and in her own home, preferably, it seems, at night, or just as she met them. A vivid picture of her activities was given in evidence by Joan Clyfland of Norwich. Margery visited her home in midwinter and, 'sitting and sewing by the fire' (Tanner, 44), she instructed Joan and Joan's two teenage servants, Joan Grymle and Agnes Bethom, in a lengthy question-and-answer session. The situation provided perfect circumstances for an indoctrinating conversation—in all-female company, Joan Clyfland's husband being absent—and is very suggestive of how women might use their domestic roles to proselytize.

When a Carmelite friar threatened to denounce Margery as a heretic after she had tried unsuccessfully to convert him, she in turn threatened to denounce him for sexually harassing her, and warned that her husband wished to kill him, thus escaping detection. She denounced the whole ecclesiastical hierarchy of pope, cardinals, and bishops, 'for they falsely and cursedly deceive the people with their false mawmentries and laws to extort money from simple people in order to sustain their pride, luxury and idleness' (Tanner, 49). Her own bishop of Norwich she referred to as Caiaphas. Of her own invulnerability she was convinced: even if she was convicted of Lollardy she would not be burnt, since she had 'a charter of protection in her womb' (ibid.)—an interesting remark, suggesting the belief that women were exempt from being burnt if they were pregnant. In fact, however, she may have escaped death, the penalty of a relapsed heretic, by agreeing to witness against another person from Martham, John Pyry.

If Margery Baxter was something of a loner, the other prominent Lollard woman to appear in Alnwick's court, **Hawise Mone** (*fl.* 1428–1430), was a social Lollard *par excellence*. She was the wife of a prosperous shoemaker, Thomas Mone, of the town of Loddon. Their household was a hive of Lollard activity: those directly involved included, in addition to themselves, a daughter and three men who were, or had been, their servants or apprentices of Thomas. 'Schools of heresy' were held in 'privy chambers and places' of theirs (Tanner, 140)—presumably in their house in Loddon—which many people attended and in which William White and other leading Lollards taught. Hawise was also accused of organizing in her home what appears to have been a ritual breaking of the Lenten fast, in which she and several other people ate a meal of pork on the day before Easter Sunday. In the fast-breaking, moreover, she acted independently of her husband, who was absent from the proceedings. Indeed, she appears to have been at least as important as her husband for Lollardy in the area, perhaps more so, in both her organizational ability and her knowledge of the movement's teachings. Margery Baxter appreciated her highly. Hawise, she said, was the 'most distinguished and wisest woman' (ibid., 47) in her knowledge of the teaching of William White. She was tried and convicted in August 1430, a fortnight before her husband, and abjured her heresies. Nothing more is heard of her thereafter.

Early sixteenth-century Lollard women **Joan Washingby** [*née* Ward] (*d.* 1512) of Coventry was an enterprising Lollard of the late fifteenth and early sixteenth centuries. She had learned her heresy from Alice Rowley, a leading Coventry Lollard, about 1490. When still a young woman she had moved first to Northampton and then to London, perhaps going from one Lollard household to another. In London, where she stayed for three years and married, she lodged with a bedder called Blackbyre, whose wife, Joan, was already a Lollard. She and her husband, Thomas Washingby, a shoemaker who was also a heretic, then moved to Maidstone in Kent, possibly also a Lollard centre at this time, where in 1495 she had to abjure her heretical beliefs. Later she returned to Coventry and participated actively once more in the Lollard movement in the town. Finally the ecclesiastical authorities caught up with her again, and in March 1512 she was condemned as a relapsed heretic and handed over to the secular arm to be burnt. She is known to have owned at least one Lollard book, and there is some evidence to suggest that she used her travels to distribute such books among members of the movement.

Agnes Grebill (*d.* 1511) was a poignant case. Knowledge of her comes largely from the evidence given against her, mostly by members of her own family, at her trial in 1511. According to this information, her husband, John, was a weaver in Tenterden and later in neighbouring Benenden, Kent; she was first taught Lollard beliefs by him towards the end of the reign of Edward IV, when she was aged about thirty. She had two sons and a daughter, though whether John was the father of the sons is unclear, since at one point they are described as her 'natural sons'. Initially her husband appears to have continued to take the lead, but with her co-operation. They instructed the children in their beliefs and became central figures in a wide network of Lollards in Kent.

When in 1511 she was brought to trial before Archbishop William Warham of Canterbury (*d.* 1532), Agnes Grebill was at least sixty years old. Why members of her family betrayed her is unclear, especially since the family had sworn itself to secrecy at an earlier date; it may well be that those concerned were granted lenient treatment in their own trials in return for witnessing against her. She was accused of heretical beliefs and practices regarding the seven sacraments, especially the eucharist, images, pilgrimages, prayers to the saints, holy water, and blessed bread. Her husband provided the crucial depositions against her, supported by her two sons. Confronting them in person, she wholly rejected their allegations and wished her sons had never been born. Again, four days later, she protested her innocence. Rejecting her protestation, the archbishop pronounced her an obstinate heretic and handed her over to the secular arm to be put to death.

Functions and standing Other women provide some further glimpses. Many opponents of Lollardy, mainly clerics, criticized the movement for advancing women beyond their station in religious matters, notably as teachers and preachers; some thought that women priests existed among them. Of the last, no clear instances are known, and in any case, in view of the emphasis placed by Lollards on the priesthood of all believers and downgrading of the sacerdotal priesthood, the issue may have been not very important. Certainly there was a wide range of roles and activities within the Lollard movement that were open to women, as has already been seen.

Regarding the celebration of the eucharist by women, there was the case mentioned by Henry Knighton (*d.* *c.*1396), an opponent of Lollardy, under the year 1391:

> There was a certain matron in the city of London who had an only daughter whom she instructed to celebrate mass, and she set up an altar with its furnishings in her secret chamber, and got her daughter for many days to dress as a priest and go to the altar and to celebrate mass after her manner; but when she reached the sacramental words she prostrated herself before the altar and did not consecrate the sacrament; but rising completed all the rest of the mass to the end with her mother assisting and attending her devotion. (*Chronicon Henrici Knighton, vel Cnitthon, monachi Leycestrensis*, ed. J. R. Lumby, 2 vols., Rolls Series, 1889–95, 2.316–17; translation in Aston, 454–5)

A report eventually leaked out through a woman neighbour who attended the service, and the case came to the ears of the bishop of London. The daughter was discovered, her priestly tonsure was exposed to public view, and she herself was put to penance.

Recitation and rote learning were exercises in which women often seem to have played a leading role: Reginald Pecock, bishop of Chichester (*d.* in or after 1459), who was generally well informed about Lollardy, thought that quoting scripture was characteristic of women Lollards. In the early sixteenth century **Alice Colins** (*fl.* 1521), wife of the learned Richard Colins of Ginge in Berkshire, was reported as famous among Lollards for her good memory, so that 'when any conventicle … did meet at Burford, commonly she was sent for, to recite … the ten commandments and the epistles of Peter and James' (Hudson, 191);

her daughter, Joan, was able to recite the elements of religion and knew by heart the epistle of James, and the daughter of a fellow Lollard was sent into service in the Colins household, precisely so that 'she might be instructed there in God's law' (McSheffrey, *Gender and Heresy*, 98). Alice Rowley of Coventry, mentioned earlier, often read publicly before men. Alice Gardiner of Colchester, from the 1490s onward, was another woman who seems to have busied herself educating the next Lollard generation.

A broad spectrum of social backgrounds was represented among Lollard women, though the very highest ranks of society appear largely absent, as was the case among men. There is evidence of Lollard women among the urban élites of London, Coventry, and Bristol, at least in the late fifteenth and early sixteenth centuries. Lady Jane Yonge, who was suspected of heresy and may have died a Lollard martyr, was the widow of Sir John Yonge, lord mayor of London; her mother, Joan *Boughton, was burnt for Lollardy at Smithfield in 1494. There is some evidence of wives of *Lollard knights who sympathized with their husbands' views—for example, Dame Anne Latimer, widow of Sir Thomas *Latimer of Braybrooke (*d.* 1401)—but the majority seem to have come from the artisan classes, here too following the pattern among Lollard men. Of the several thousand Lollards who are identifiable between the 1370s and 1530s, women represented something like a quarter, though there seems to have been a marked increase, both proportionally and absolutely, in the years after about 1490. Most of them were married to Lollard men. That many women were Lollards must have feminized the movement in many ways. On the whole their roles were channelled within the accepted social norms, but some women, through favourable circumstances, were able to attain positions of prominence both within the movement and in society at large.

NORMAN P. TANNER

Sources *The acts and monuments of John Foxe*, ed. J. Pratt, [new edn], 8 vols. (1877) • A. Hudson, *The premature reformation: Wycliffite texts and Lollard history* (1988) • C. Cross, 'Great reasoners in scripture: the activities of women Lollards, 1380–1530', *Medieval women*, ed. D. Baker, SCH, Subsidia, 1 (1978), 359–80 • M. Aston, 'Women Lollard priests?', *Journal of Ecclesiastical History*, 31 (1980), 441–61 • N. P. Tanner, ed., *Heresy trials in the diocese of Norwich, 1428–31*, CS, 4th ser., 20 (1977) • S. McSheffrey and N. Tanner, eds., *Lollards of Coventry, 1486–1522*, CS, 5th ser., 23 [forthcoming] • A. Hope, 'Lollardy: the stone the builders rejected?', *Protestantism and the national church in sixteenth century England*, ed. P. Lake and M. Dowling (1987), 1–35 • S. McSheffrey, *Gender and heresy: women and men in Lollard communities, 1420–1530* (1995) • N. P. Tanner, ed., *Kent heresy proceedings, 1511–12*, Kent Records, 26 (1997)

Likenesses woodcut (*7 godly martyrs in Coventry, burned*), repro. in *Actes and monuments of John Foxe*, new edn (1583), 973

Lollius Urbicus, Quintus (*b.* after **100?**, *d.* after **150**), Roman governor of Britain, was born near Cirta in the province of Numidia (eastern Algeria), in north Africa, probably shortly after 100. He appears to have been the second of the three known sons of Marcus Lollius Senecio and Grania Honorata. His career can be calculated as starting soon after the accession of Hadrian in 118 and he served as: *quattuorvir viarum curandarum* (one of the officials in charge of the streets of Rome); *tribunus laticlavius* (senior tribune) in legion XXII Primigenia, stationed at Moguntiacum (Mainz) in Upper Germany; quaestor of the city of Rome; legate (adjutant) of the proconsul of Asia; tribune of the plebs and praetor, both as the emperor's candidate; legate (commanding officer) of the X Gemina at Vindobona (Vienna), in Upper Pannonia (Hungary); legate (staff officer) in the Jewish War of Hadrian (132–5), in which he was decorated; consul, probably in 135 or 136; *fetialis* (a member of one of the colleges of priests in Rome); governor of Lower Germany; governor of Britain from 139 to 142 or 143; and prefect of Rome, probably from 146 to at least 150.

Urbicus does not appear to have been the son of a senator; he was thus one of the new men who came into the aristocracy during the empire from the provinces. His early career is not distinguished, but it clearly acquired imperial support after his service as legate of the proconsul of Asia. Here he may have acquired a patron who helped further his career and this may have been Pompeius Falco, formerly governor of Britain. Urbicus held a staff post during the Jewish War of 132 to 135, serving under Sextus Julius Severus, also a former governor of Britain. At the end of the decade Urbicus was specially chosen by Antoninus Pius to reverse the frontier policy of his predecessor in Britain by conducting a new campaign to subdue the Britons north of Hadrian's Wall. It may be presumed that Urbicus had acquired some background knowledge of the province through his service with previous governors.

The emperor Hadrian died in July 138. The biography of his successor, Antoninus Pius, states that 'he conquered the Britons through the governor Lollius Urbicus and after driving back the barbarians built a new wall of turf' (Magie, v.4). An inscription from Corbridge demonstrates that Urbicus was governor of Britain by 139. In 142, following the end of the campaign, Pius was acclaimed *imperator* ('conqueror': the traditional acclamation by soldiers on the field of battle to their victorious commander was given under the empire to the emperor when his generals won victories in his name).

The reasons for the reconquest of southern Scotland are not known. The phrase 'drive back the barbarians' seems to imply that forcible action was necessary and this receives some support from an aside by Pausanias in his *Description of Greece*: 'Antoninus deprived the Brigantes in Britain of most of their territory because they too had taken up arms and invaded the Genunian district, the people of which are subject to Rome' (Pausanias, viii.43, 4). The passage as it stands makes little sense; nevertheless it presumably relates to the northward advance in the early 140s. Hence modern scholars have suggested that the reason for the reconquest of southern Scotland was that the northern tribes were causing trouble. A more subtle explanation is that Hadrian's Wall was a tactical success but a strategic failure, in that it was too distant from the main enemy in the north, the Caledonians, and that it was therefore necessary to move the frontier northwards.

More recently the necessity for the new emperor to gain a military triumph to secure his position on the throne has been emphasized, with Britain chosen as the location of this imperial triumph. Certainly the invasion of southern Scotland would have been the decision of the emperor, not of Urbicus, as the life of Antoninus Pius and a comment by Cornelius Fronto both imply.

Urbicus was clearly responsible for the preparations for the reconquest of southern Scotland, as the inscription from Corbridge indicates, and the preparations continued into the following season, as demonstrated by a second inscription from Corbridge. He is also recorded on two building inscriptions at the Roman fort at Balmuildy, one of the first forts to be constructed on the Antonine Wall. His name, however, does not appear on other inscriptions on that wall, which suggests that he left Britain during the building of the frontier, leaving completion of the task to his unknown successor. He is also recorded on a building stone at High Rochester on Dere Street to the south of the Antonine Wall. Clearly, Urbicus left his governorship only when work on securing its success through construction of the frontier and its attendant forts was well advanced. The close density of the forts and fortlets in southern Scotland was presumably ordered by Urbicus and may reflect his determination to ensure the enduring success of his military action. Nevertheless, the occupation of the Antonine Wall does not appear to have outlasted Antoninus Pius by many years. Modern opinion considers that it was abandoned within a decade of his death in 161.

Urbicus's career is further recorded on two inscriptions from Numidia. He left no known descendants and the author 'Lollius Urbicus' cited by the *Scriptores historiae Augustae* is now known to have been bogus.

David J. Breeze

Sources A. R. Birley, *The Fasti of Roman Britain* (1981), 112–15 • D. J. Breeze, *The northern frontiers of Roman Britain* (1982), 97–124 • D. Magie, ed. and trans., 'Antoninus Pius', *Scriptores historiae Augustae*, 1 (1921), v.4 • Pausanias, *Description of Greece*, ed. and trans. W. H. S. Jones and H. A. Ormerod, 5 vols. (1918–35), viii.43, 4 • R. G. Collingwood and R. P. Wright, eds., *The Roman inscriptions of Britain*, 2 vols. (1965), RIB 1147, 1276, 2191, 2192 • *Corpus inscriptionum Latinarum*, 6705

Lolme, John Louis de (1741–1806), political writer, was born in Geneva on 28 October 1741, the son of John de Lolme. He practised for a short time as an advocate in his home city. In 1768 he moved to England and began a lifetime's study of its government. His interest in this subject was stimulated, he later claimed, by the peculiarity of the system and by his experience of political troubles in his own country, which had given him 'insight into the first real principles of governments'. His views were heavily influenced by Montesquieu, whose writing he had encountered in Switzerland. In 1769 he began work on a major study of the English constitution that aimed to show the benefits of a balanced constitution, and claimed to have identified in English government the practical means by which freedom could be reconciled with political stability. He praised the jury system in particular, and admired the way in which monarchical authority had

John Louis de Lolme (1741–1806), by Heath, pubd 1784 (after Stoddart)

been effectively and beneficially limited by the settlement of 1688.

De Lolme's book was first written in French, and published in the Netherlands in 1771. The circumstances in which the work appeared in English are somewhat obscure. Parts of the study first appeared in English as an anonymous pamphlet, *A Parallel between the English Constitution and the Former Government of Sweden* (1772). Generally treated as de Lolme's work, though translated by another hand, the pamphlet attracted considerable attention in London political circles. An anonymous response attacked its factual inaccuracies while respecting its 'acuteness of comprehension'. At the same time, de Lolme was seeking subscriptions for the publication of a translation of his book, only to find that one had already been begun by two booksellers. He paid £10 for them to drop their undertaking, and the first full and credited English edition was published under the title *The Rise and Progress of the English Constitution* in 1775. It has been suggested that he was assisted in the translation by Baron Maseres, and the quality of the translation would appear to support this assertion. It is striking that a passage from the 1775 edition of *The English Constitution* appeared previously in the preface to the Junius letters written as early as November 1771 and published in 1772. This coincidence led to the conjecture that de Lolme and Junius were the same person. The theory was elaborately worked out by Thomas Busby in *Arguments and facts demonstrating that the letters of Junius were written by John Louis de Lolme* (1816). It is impossible to determine whether Junius saw the translation before publication or whether de Lolme adopted Junius's translation of the passage.

The English Constitution, which reached a fourth edition in 1784, proved a great success. For a time de Lolme was fêted by the London political establishment. Proceeds from the sale of the book should have given de Lolme a comfortable income, but through improvidence and, it was rumoured, dissipation, gambling, and speculation, he remained in almost constant poverty. Isaac Disraeli, who mentions that de Lolme received relief from the Literary Fund, and that 'the walls of the Fleet too often enclosed the English Montesquieu', considered his misfortunes a national reproach (D'Israeli, 2.262–3). Thomas Busby recalled that de Lolme was 'exalted and neglected, lauded with commendation and consigned to poverty' (Machelon, 30). Having great conversational powers—he 'has been compared to Burke', noted one of his editors, 'for the variety of his allusions, and the felicity of his illustrations' ('Preface' to *The English Constitution*, new edn, 1807)—he gained the acquaintance of most of the leading men of his time. On occasions he appeared in fashionable clothes and moved in the highest circles, but he was always in debt. He concealed his lodgings and changed them frequently; indeed he appears to have been homeless for long periods. A later admirer and editor of his works, the politician John MacGregor, described him as exhibiting 'the miserable and degraded appearance of a tattered and slovenly vagabond' (MacGregor, 3).

Beyond this, only the barest details are known of de Lolme's life. In 1775, according to Busby, he attempted to start a publication called the *News Examiner*, the object of which was to expose the party animosity and the inconsistency of the London journals by republishing their leading articles. However, he could not pay the stamp duty, and the project was abandoned. There followed a series of pamphlets, some more successful than others, which brought him his occasional bouts of prosperity. He wrote on a wide range of political issues. In 1788 he made a notable contribution to the debate on the window tax (the abolition of which he supported). He produced a tract on hawkers and peddlers and one which suggested the 'removal of Smithfield market to a more convenient location'. He wrote a history, the *British Empire in Europe* (1787), which was a rather impressionistic account of the English colonization of Ireland and the union of England and Scotland. In 1789 he used his authority as a constitutional expert to write a commentary on the regency question (*The Present National Embarrassment Considered*). This embroiled him in a bitter pamphlet war with the pseudonymous Neptune, who scorned de Lolme's contribution to the debate on the basis of his nationality and his disreputable private life. He appears to have remained in England until the beginning of the nineteenth century, when, having inherited property from a relative, he paid his debts and returned to Geneva. He was elected a member of the Council of Two Hundred, and shortly before his death is said to have been made a *sous-prefet* under Napoleon, although there is no evidence that he ever took up the post. He died in Seewen-sur-le-Ruffiberg in the canton of Schwitz on 16 July 1806. There is no evidence of a marriage or of any children.

De Lolme had an active and ingenious mind; Bentham went so far as to compare him with Blackstone. His work on the English constitution was for several decades the principal authority on the subject. It was influential in the United States, where, for example, it was cited by both supporters and opponents of the 1787 federal constitution. The book indeed contains many shrewd observations, but de Lolme had a cavalier attitude to research and the historical aspects of his analysis are full of errors. His principal legacy is to have helped disseminate the ideas of Montesquieu to the British reading public in a popular style. G. P. Macdonell, *rev.* Adam I. P. Smith

Sources J. P. Machelon, *Les idées politiques de J. L. de Lolme, 1741–1806* (1969) · E. Rutt, *Jean Louis de Lolme und sein Werk über die Verfassung Englands* (1934) · J. MacGregor, 'Introduction', in J. L. De Lolme, *The constitution of England*, ed. J. MacGregor (1853) · M. Moekli-Cellier, *La révolution française et les écrivains Suisses-romands, 1789–1815* (1931) · T. Busby, *Arguments and facts demonstrating that the letters of Junius were written by John Louis de Lolme, L.L.D.* (1816) · *Monthly Review*, 53 (1775), 281–92, 457–66 · [I. D'Israeli], *Calamities of authors*, 2 vols. (1812)

Likenesses Heath, line engraving, pubd 1784 (after Stoddart), NPG [*see illus.*]

Lombard, Adrian Albert (1915–1967), aeronautical engineer, was born in Coventry on 9 January 1915, the second son and third child of Arthur Henry Lombard, toolmaker, and his wife, Louisa Bartlett. Lombard was educated in Coventry at the John Gulson Central Advanced School and afterwards in evening classes at the Technical College. In 1930 he joined the Rover Company, beginning his training in the drawing office. He left in 1935 to join Morris Motors where, still only twenty years old, he was in charge of engine stress calculations.

In 1936 Lombard returned to the Rover Company and later became part of the design team under Maurice Wilks which in 1940 was given the task of making the Whittle W2B jet engine ready for production. In the same year the team moved from Coventry to Clitheroe, and at nearby Barnoldswick a factory was equipped to manufacture the engine. Thereafter, Lombard's main professional concern was the aircraft gas turbine, or jet engine.

Lombard's production design, known as B26, employed a different combustion system from Frank Whittle's W2B and was in fact the precursor of the highly successful Nene and Derwent engines which Lombard designed in 1944 and 1945. Early in 1943 Ernest Walter Hives, of Rolls-Royce, and Spencer Wilks, the chairman of Rover, completed a historic deal by which Rover exchanged its interest in the Whittle engine and the Clitheroe and Barnoldswick factories for the Rolls-Royce tank engine factory at Nottingham. The Rover engineers concerned were given the choice of staying with Rover and transferring to tank engine production or staying with the jet engine work and joining Rolls-Royce. Lombard was among the few who chose the latter.

Lombard had to create a fresh design organization and, with first-class recruits from Rolls-Royce, Derby, he quickly developed an efficient team. At Barnoldswick, he produced the W2B Whittle engine, of which 100 (at 1700 lb thrust) were built and used in the early Gloster Meteor twin-engined fighter aircraft. At the same time he supervised the design of the more powerful Derwent I engine (at 2000 lb thrust) which was interchangeable with the W2B in the Meteor. The Derwent I Meteors were in 1944 the first jet fighters to be used by the RAF.

Meanwhile Lombard had supervised the design of the Rolls-Royce Nene engine which first ran in 1944, achieving a world record thrust of 5000 lb. After the war the engine's design was sold to Pratt and Whitney in the USA and Hispano-Suiza in France. Twenty-five of the engines were sold to Russia, and a Russian version subsequently powered large numbers of MiG fighters.

In January 1945 Lombard began the design of the Derwent V engine, which was tested seven months later—an achievement which remains a testimony to Lombard's talent as a mechanical designer. Furthermore, in October 1945 a Meteor with Derwent V engines broke the world speed record at 603 m.p.h. In the same year his team designed the Avon engine, rated at 6500 lb thrust. During the design of this engine Hives decided to transfer the technical and design centre to Derby, where Lombard became chief designer (projects). The Avon proved to be a major success and provided the power plants of the Vickers Valiant, Hawker Hunter, English Electric Canberra, and English Electric Lightning. The Avon also powered the Fairey Delta experimental aircraft (the first to exceed 1000 m.p.h.), and was the first Rolls-Royce civil aircraft jet propulsion engine, being used in the De Havilland Comet and the Sud Aviation Caravelle.

In 1952 Lombard became chief designer (aero), and in 1954 chief engineer, of Rolls-Royce. In this period he was engaged on the Conway engine which became noted internationally in both military and civil roles. The Vickers VC10, with four Conway engines, was one of the finest civil jet aircraft of its time. He went on to develop other engines for military strike and vertical take-off aircraft.

Lombard served on the council of the Royal Aeronautical Society, on the Air Registration Board, and on the Aeronautical Research Council. Jointly with Stanley Hooker, he was awarded the James Clayton prize of the Institution of Mechanical Engineers. He was appointed CBE a month before his death.

Lombard, though lacking formal training in aerodynamics and thermodynamics, nevertheless had an intuitive grasp of the laws of nature. He was also an able leader of a team. Hooker, who knew Lombard well, aptly described him: 'He was dynamic in action, energetic in application, and determined in argument, but withal he had a strong sense of humour and a ready wit'. In stature he was a short, square person with an attractive smile, liked and respected by all who knew him. He married on 18 April 1940 Joan (*b.* 1918/19), daughter of George Chaffard Taylor, engineer. They had three sons, the second of whom died in infancy. When he died suddenly of a cerebral haemorrhage at Derbyshire Royal Infirmary, Derby, on 13 July 1967, Lombard was at the apex of his career, having been appointed director of aero-engineering in 1958 and a director of Rolls-Royce. His wife survived him. KINGS NORTON, *rev.*

Sources S. G. Hooker, *Journal of the Royal Aeronautical Society*, 71 (1967), 807–9 · personal knowledge (1981) · *The Times* (15 July 1967), 129 · d. cert. · m. cert.

Wealth at death £9663: probate, 9 Oct 1967, *CGPLA Eng. & Wales*

Lombard, Daniel (1678–1746), Church of England clergyman and author, was born at Angers, France, on 10 April 1678, the eldest son of the Revd John Lombard (*d.* 1721) and his wife, Francisca. Lombard's family travelled to London following the revocation of the edict of Nantes in 1685; his father, formerly a French protestant minister in Anjou, ministered in several French churches in London. Daniel Lombard was naturalized in England in January 1688. On 11 September of the following year he entered Merchant Taylors' School, London, and was then educated at St John's College, Oxford, where he matriculated on 7 July 1694; he was elected a scholar soon after. He graduated BA (17 May 1698); MA by diploma, being then abroad (16 March 1702); BD (26 April 1708); and DD (23 April 1714). Between 1697 and March 1718 Lombard was also a fellow at St John's College.

Lombard, ordained deacon by Henry Compton, bishop of London, on 26 May 1700, and priest on 9 January 1701, was appointed chaplain at Hanover to Princess Sophia and the embassy. His first published sermon, addressed to the recently deceased Sophia, appeared in 1714. After the accession of George I, Lombard was made chaplain to the princess of Wales, and on 24 February 1718 he was instituted to the rectory of Lanteglos with Advent, near Fowey, Cornwall. He retained this living for the rest of his life, but was absent for much of this period. His other published works include a comparison of the lines of François Eudes de Mézeray and his father, Daniel, printed in Amsterdam in 1723. The 1745 Jacobite rising prompted Lombard to write his own *Succinct History of Ancient and Modern Persecutions* (1747). He also contributed to his friend Francis Gregor's 1737 edition of Sir John Fortescue's *De laudibus legum Angliae*. Lombard was known to his parishioners for his learning, his simple lifestyle, and his attachment to French customs. He died at Camelford, near Fowey, Cornwall, on 30 December 1746 and was buried at Lanteglos on 2 January 1747. W. P. COURTNEY, *rev.* PHILIP CARTER

Sources Foster, *Alum. Oxon.* · *GM*, 1st ser., 17 (1747), 47 · D. C. A. Agnew, *Protestant exiles from France in the reign of Louis XIV, or, The Huguenot refugees and their descendants in Great Britain and Ireland*, 2nd edn, 3 vols. (1871–4) · C. J. Robinson, ed., *A register of the scholars admitted into Merchant Taylors' School, from AD 1562 to 1874*, 2 vols. (1882–3)

Archives Cornwall RO, Gregor MSS, correspondence with Francis Gregor

Lombard, Peter (*c.*1554–1625), Roman Catholic archbishop of Armagh, was born in Waterford town into an eminent and long-established merchant family. After receiving a good grounding in the classics at Peter White's school in Waterford, he went to the Spanish Netherlands and entered the University of Louvain to study philosophy. He graduated MA in 1572, coming first in his class, before studying theology, and eventually graduated DD in 1594. In the meantime, he was ordained a priest and began

Peter Lombard (*c.*1554–1625), by unknown artist, 1863 [original, 17th cent.]

lecturing at Louvain, earning a brilliant reputation as a professor first of philosophy and then of theology. In 1594 he was appointed provost of Cambrai Cathedral, and he was also made canon of the collegiate college at Siclin in Tournai.

By the late 1590s the Catholic church was increasingly divided over the issue of divine grace and the role of free will in salvation. The University of Louvain strongly opposed the new emphasis being placed by the Jesuits and their supporters on the importance of free will in securing salvation. In 1598 Lombard was chosen to participate on behalf of Louvain in the ongoing theological debates at Rome. He was also to defend the universities' privileges, which were being challenged by local Jesuits. On his arrival, Lombard quickly impressed Pope Clement VIII with his learning and ability; he spent the rest of his life at Rome, residing at the Palazzo Salviati and becoming theological counsellor to the Holy See.

In 1599 Lombard began acting as an agent at Rome for Hugh O'Neill, earl of Tyrone, who was then leading an uprising against English rule in Ireland. By 1600 he had written his most famous work, *De regno Hiberniae*, which is strongly supportive of Tyrone. It begins by defending the Gaelic Irish from charges of barbarity and stresses Ireland's glorious past as a civilized Christian nation, particularly during the early middle ages. Moving to the present, Lombard argued the legitimacy of Tyrone's uprising, declaring that the English had forfeited their right to rule Ireland, based as it was on a papal grant, through their actions against the church. However, many Old English Catholics in Ireland regarded the Gaelic Irish Tyrone as a very imperfect champion of the Catholic cause and remembered how he had failed to support James Fitzmaurice's papal-sponsored crusade to Ireland in 1579. To address these charges, Lombard stressed Tyrone's personal piety and claimed that the earl had long foreseen that the English were bent on the destruction of the Catholic church, but had prudently refrained from taking up arms until he was fully prepared. *De regno Hiberniae* was eventually published at Louvain in 1632.

At Rome, Lombard won many influential figures over to Tyrone's cause including Robert Parsons, rector of the English college there, and the duke of Sessa, Spain's papal ambassador. On 18 April 1600 Lombard's lobbying paid off when Pope Clement granted a bull of indulgence to Tyrone's supporters in Ireland and appointed Tyrone captain-general of the Catholic armies in Ireland. However, as Tyrone came under increased military pressure from the English in 1600–01, he badly needed more overt support from Rome. At Tyrone's behest Lombard pressed for Clement to excommunicate those Catholics who opposed Tyrone and to appoint a Spanish nuncio to Ireland. The ultimate goal was for the pope to grant Ireland to Philip II of Spain, who would send his forces to conquer it. However, Clement was strongly anti-Spanish and was not prepared to countenance a further expansion of Spanish power. Moreover, he was also aware that many Catholics in Ireland opposed Tyrone's uprising. As a result he appointed an Italian nuncio and refused to excommunicate pro-government Catholics. However, not wanting to disappoint Tyrone completely, he did make Lombard archbishop of Armagh on 9 July 1601. Lombard had not been Tyrone's first choice for the position, but the earl would be satisfied that a supporter was now head of the Irish church, while the Old English would also be reassured by the promotion of one of their own. As it happened, Lombard was consecrated in Rome, but never went to his archdiocese.

As events swung against Tyrone in Ireland, Lombard began to play a key role in the theological controversies raging at Rome. In 1602 he was appointed president of the special congregation, composed of cardinals and expert theologians, established to debate the issues of grace and salvation. As the congregation wound down its deliberations in 1607, he was authorized to draft the papal bull resolving the controversy. While the majority of the congregation wanted to condemn all forty-two of the propositions attributed to the Jesuit theologian Molina, Lombard's draft condemned only thirty. There is no doubting Lombard's opposition to the Molinists: throughout his career he was a vigorous critic of the Jesuits. His relative moderation on this matter simply reflected his anxiety to preserve the unity of the church. In the event, although Pope Paul V praised Lombard's draft highly, on 28 August 1607 the pontiff dissolved the congregation and ruled that each side should be allowed to follow its own teachings.

During this period Lombard remained deeply engaged in Irish affairs. Following Tyrone's submission to the English early in 1603, Lombard quickly changed his attitude toward the crown, taking the pragmatic view that the Catholic church in Ireland had no option but to accommodate itself to a protestant government. This shift was apparent from the contents of his *Episcopion doron*, written in 1604. Dedicated to King James I of England, the book argues that the Catholic church is the one true church and appeals for an end to the persecution of Catholics in Ireland. The deep roots of Catholicism in Ireland are stressed: Catholicism is an intrinsic part of being Irish. The work includes an oblique criticism of Tyrone for exploiting religion to further his own ends.

Thereafter, Lombard deviated from this conciliatory policy only in the immediate aftermath of the flight of Tyrone and Rory O'Donnell, earl of Tyrconnell, from Ireland in autumn 1607. Hoping that this development might precipitate a Spanish invasion of Ireland, Lombard wrote warmly to the earls and sought papal support for armed intervention in Ireland. However, by the time he received the two exiles outside Rome on 29 April 1608, it was clear that no military aid would be forthcoming from either Spain or the pope. Lombard reverted to his policy of appeasing the English in the hope of gaining better treatment for Catholics in Ireland, a decision which soon led to a rift with Tyrone. Indeed, prior to Tyrone's arrival in Rome, Lombard appears to have persuaded the pope not to appoint any of the earl's supporters to Irish bishoprics.

Denied military aid and even permission to travel to Spain, Tyrone cut an increasingly wretched figure at Rome. Despite Lombard's advice, the pope felt obliged to comply with Tyrone's repeated requests on behalf of Florence Conry, who became archbishop of Tuam in 1609, and Eugene McMahon, who was translated to the archbishopric of Dublin in 1611. Lombard was furious at these appointments, believing that the Catholic church should be trying to distance itself from Tyrone. In a memorandum of 1612 he argued that these promotions had precipitated a hardening of the Dublin administration's attitude towards Catholicism, culminating in the execution that year of Conor O'Devany, bishop of Down and Conor. He added that bishops who owed their appointment to Tyrone would achieve little, as they would be subject to constant government harassment. By contrast, Lombard pointed to the success enjoyed by his own deputy David Roth, who had been sent to Ireland about 1610. Roth had opened up informal communications with Sir Arthur Chichester, lord deputy of Ireland, informing him of Lombard's opposition to Tyrone. As a result, Roth was given considerable leeway by the government, being able to resolve a serious dispute between the secular and regular clergy and to hold a provincial synod at Drogheda in 1614.

The Vatican appears to have accepted Lombard's argument that future appointments to Irish bishoprics could not be associates of Tyrone. No further appointments were made until 1618, although ten were made between then and Lombard's death in 1625, and he appears to have had a major bearing on all or most of them. Indeed, in 1619, he was accused of trying to pack the Irish church with his own supporters. Although not averse to some self-aggrandizing, it must also be said that Lombard believed that the promotion of his own supporters was in the best interests of the church. When Tyrone attempted to canvass support for a Spanish invasion of Ireland in 1613–14, Lombard strongly opposed him, declaring that his religion commanded him to remain loyal to his rightful king. Lombard made sure through his nephew Robert that the English heard of this. However, if he was hoping for public appreciation of his efforts from King James, he was to be disappointed. On 21 April 1614, during the course of an address to a delegation of Catholic members of the Irish parliament at Whitehall, James roundly condemned Lombard as a traitor. However, the wily monarch's deeds did not match his words and, in practice, the Dublin government tacitly tolerated Roth's activities in Lombard's name.

An opportunity soon presented itself for Lombard to prove that Catholicism was compatible with loyalty to a protestant king. In England, a group of imprisoned Catholic priests was presented with twelve test questions concerning their attitude towards the king. As theological adviser to the pope, Lombard was charged with drafting the appropriate responses for Catholics in such a situation. The resulting 1052-page manuscript, which was completed in 1616, is Lombard's response to James's criticisms of him. He stresses that James is the rightful king of England, Scotland, and Ireland, and that all Catholics have a duty to acknowledge him as such. Although a heretic, James is a lawful king because he was raised from birth as a protestant and could not have known any better. Lombard does say, however, that Catholics are entitled to disobey laws passed by the king that adversely affect the Catholic religion and that the pope has the power to depose legitimate monarchs who behave like tyrants.

For the rest of his life Lombard was much in demand at Rome for his views on theological issues. On 24 February 1616 he gained an inauspicious place in history by heading the committee of eleven theologians which condemned Galileo's cosmology as heretical. The committee had debated the matter for only five days and showed little appreciation of the issues involved. A year later, Lombard advised the pope on how to approach proposals for a marriage alliance between England and Spain. He strongly endorsed the prospect of a marriage between a Catholic princess and a protestant prince, viewing it as a means of lessening the persecution of Catholics in England and Ireland. Recognizing that bargaining for formal toleration was unrealistic, he hoped that James could be persuaded to desist from enforcing the penal laws.

Apparently, Lombard planned to travel to Ireland in 1620 and again in 1622, but never went. This may have been because he became involved in the long-running controversy over the methods used to convert the natives in Madura. In 1621 he was appointed head of the papal commission to examine whether Jesuit missionaries were justified in adapting Christianity to Brahmin customs. The findings of the commission were substantially Lombard's work and had a major bearing on the papal bull issued on 31 January 1623 in favour of such methods. Lombard died shortly after September 1625 at Palombra, about 20 miles from Rome, and was buried in the parish church there. TERRY CLAVIN

Sources J. J. Silke, 'Later relations between Primate Peter Lombard and Hugh O'Neill', *Irish Theological Quarterly*, 22 (1955), 14–30 · J. J. Silke, 'Primate Lombard and James I', *Irish Theological Quarterly*, 22 (1955), 143–55 · P. Lombard, *De regno Hiberniae*, ed. P. F. Moran (1868) · J. J. Silke, *The Spanish intervention* (1970), 65–71, 80–81, 83 · J. J. Silke, 'Hugh O'Neill, the Catholic question and the papacy', *Irish Ecclesiastical Record*, 5th ser., 104 (1965), 65–79 · J. J. Silke, 'The Irish Peter Lombard', *Studies*, 64 (1975), 143–55 · L. Renehan, *Collections on Irish church history* (1801), vol. 1, pp. 20–24 · J. J. Silke, 'Bishop Conor O'Devany, OFM, *c*.1533–1612', *Seanchas Ardmhhacha*, 13/1 (1988), 9–32

Likenesses watercolour drawing, 1863 (over photograph of oils, University of Louvain), NG Ire. [*see illus.*] · oils, University of Louvain

Lombart, Pierre (**1612/13–1682**), engraver, was born and trained in France. At his death his age was given as sixty-nine, which places his birth in 1612 or 1613; Pierre-Jean Mariette, writing in the eighteenth century, says he was a Parisian. Nothing is known of his early career in France, though later writers variously thought that he was a pupil of Gérard Edelinck or François Poilly. A few signed plates may date from this period of his life. The first trace of him in London is in 1651, when he engraved the title-page to Jeremy Taylor's *The Rule and Exercises of Holy Dying*. Signed and dated plates, often with the words 'à Londres' added, continue through the 1650s, but Lombart was certainly back in Paris in 1663, when he engraved a dated portrait of Antoine Grammont after Wallerant Vaillant.

During the 1650s Lombart was the finest engraver working in England, and the principal competitor to William Faithorne. He made his name with two great portraits of Oliver Cromwell. The earlier, which can be dated between 1651 and 1653, shows him with a page and is after a painting by Robert Walker. The later, a full-length of Cromwell on horseback, followed in 1655. The portraits were dedicated by Lombart himself respectively to parliament and to the council of the Commonwealth. The 1655 print went through an unusual number of transformations through the years. G. S. Layard, who devoted a monograph to his researches into its history, identified seven states: the first shows Cromwell's head; in the second there is no head; in the third and fourth the head becomes that of Louis XIV; in the fifth it is Cromwell; in the sixth it is Charles I; and in the seventh it returns to Cromwell again. The plate survives in a private collection.

The principal achievement of Lombart's London years was a series of twelve portraits after paintings by Anthony Van Dyck, usually known as *The Countesses* because ten of them show ladies with the Latin title of comitissa. These bear a royal privilege, and so must have been made after the Restoration; however, they were published after Lombart's return to Paris, for each bears a French publication line as well. They are the prototype for the later series of full-length engravings after Van Dyck by Pieter Van Gunst and James McArdell, and perhaps inspired the set of *Beauties* by Kneller now at Hampton Court.

Lombart also worked extensively on the publications of John Ogilby, engraving most of the plates for his 1654 *Virgil* after Francis Clein. A few of the others were engraved by L. Richer, after whose designs Lombart engraved a set of *The Liberal Arts*. Richer is recorded in John Evelyn's *Diary* for 25 March 1653 as a 'rare graver in tallie douce … sent over by Card. Mazzarini to make collections of pictures' (Evelyn, *Diary*, 3.82), and it is possible that Lombart too travelled to London partly to profit from the dispersal of the royalist collections of paintings. After his return to Paris, Lombart was received into the Académie Royale de Peinture, but he never became a full member. He specialized in portraits, of which it seems that few, if any, can be dated later than the beginning of the 1670s. He died in Paris on 30 October 1682. His career still awaits a full study. ANTONY GRIFFITHS

Sources *Abécédario de P. J. Mariette, et autres notes inédites de cet amateur sur les arts et les artistes*, ed. P. de Chennevières and A. de Montaiglon, 6 vols. (Paris, 1851–60), vol. 3, pp. 214–19 · G. S. Layard, *The headless horseman* (1922) · A. Griffiths and R. A. Gerard, *The print in Stuart Britain, 1603–1689* (1998), 178–83 [exhibition catalogue, BM, 8 May – 20 Sept 1998]

Likenesses J. W. Cook, group portrait, medallion (with other engravers), BM; repro. in Walpole, *Anecdotes* (1828)

Lombe [*formerly* Beevor], **Edward** (*d.* **1852**), landowner and philanthropist, was the son of Edward Beevor, a barrister. He succeeded his father in 1847 as tenant for life to the Lombe estate of Melton Hall, Wymondham, Norfolk, both having taken, by act of parliament, the name of Lombe to comply with the conditions of the will of Sir John Lombe (*d.* 27 May 1817).

Lombe's father, on inheriting the life interest in the Lombe estate, proved to be a resolute, if contrary, individual. Sir John Lombe left a large sum held in trust specifically for the building of 'a mansion house' at Bylaugh in Norfolk as the seat of the Lombe estate; Edward Lombe senior resisted the trustees for thirty years. The building fund accumulated inexorably: by 1839 it stood at over £63,000. It was not until Edward Lombe the younger succeeded to the estate that the trustees were able to build Bylaugh Hall. It is ironic that the younger Lombe never saw the long-awaited mansion, for he lived abroad from the late 1820s until his death at Florence in 1852, and after 1830 never returned to England.

In 1826 Lombe was returned as MP for Arundel, a constituency in the gift of the duke of Norfolk. He received the duke's patronage on the understanding that he would vote for Catholic emancipation. Never in robust health, Lombe retired from politics in 1830. In the 1820s, when he had a leg amputated, he was nursed by a Mrs Lydia Emily Howis to whom he subsequently paid an allowance of £200 a year for over twenty years. She claimed that he had promised to provide for her after his death, and in support produced to Lombe's executors an 1828 will of Lombe's. She alleged also that he had driven one of her daughters to the grave through 'inconsistent waverings' and broken promises. To her anguish and grief, Lydia Howis was left nothing in Lombe's final will, executed in Florence in October 1851.

It was from Florence that Lombe ran his Norfolk estate on enlightened principles and also contributed to liberal causes in the United Kingdom. He described himself as 'ultra-liberal' in all matters of politics, philosophy, and religion. He gave financial support to W. E. Hickson, editor of the *Westminster Review*, by paying handsomely for articles commissioned on topics he himself suggested. Lombe's continuing support for the *Review* was a crucial factor in John Chapman's acquiring it from Hickson in 1851. George Eliot was Chapman's assistant editor and she attempted to incorporate Lombe's somewhat opaque notion of 'organic growth' into the prospectus for the *Review*. Lombe was a generous, but sometimes exacting, patron: it was Robert Browning, whom he knew in Florence, who identified the symptoms of 'Lombago'. But there were also unconditional offers of help, such as to Thomas Carlyle (via Browning) of £200 a year 'without strings'. On hearing that Harriet Martineau hoped to translate Auguste Comte's *Cours de philosophie positive*, he immediately arranged for £500 to be forwarded to her.

Lombe financed certain educational projects aimed at improving the economic prospects of the working classes. A firm believer in secular education, he gave financial support to George Combe (1788–1858) and others who were particularly active in promoting this cause. Lombe founded a college in Sheffield, and expended £1000 on the People's College in Norwich. A barque of 347 tons sailing out of London under the name *Edward Lombe* foundered on rocks during a storm on 25 August 1834 while entering Sydney harbour.

Lombe married a Frenchwoman, Maria Royer de St Julien. They had no children, and he died unexpectedly in Florence on 1 March 1852. His personal property was left to University College Hospital, London, with a life interest to his wife. It is poignant that he may never have met any of the individual beneficiaries of his gifts, nor witnessed the operation of the good causes he supported.

BRIAN CARTER

Sources UCL, Lombe Estate MSS • G. S. Haight, *George Eliot and John Chapman: with Chapman's diaries* (1940) • C. Gibbon, *The life of George Combe: author of 'The constitution of man'*, 2 vols. (1878) • G. S. Haight, *George Eliot: a biography* (1968) • 'Browning interest', *Baylor Bulletin*, 8th ser., 37 (1934) • *Index to local and personal acts … 1801–1947*, Statute law committee (1949), 1096 [Class XIII (3): Estates. Beevor, Edward to Lombe] • C. Mackie, *Norfolk annals: a chronological record of remarkable events in the nineteenth century … 1801–1900*, 2 vols. (1901) • G. A. Carthew, *The hundred of Launditch and deanery of Brisley, in the county of Norfolk*, 3 (1879) • *Lombe v. Stoughton* (1841), 59 ER 1148 • G. P. Judd IV, *Members of parliament, 1734–1832* (New Haven, 1955)

Archives UCL | Baylor University, Waco, Texas, Armstrong Browning Library, letters to Robert Browning • Duke U., special collections library, letters to John Chapman

Likenesses bust, *c*.1828; location unknown

Wealth at death approx. £28,000; left personal estate to University College Hospital: Lombe estate papers, UCL

Lombe, John (*c*.1693–1722). *See under* Lombe, Sir Thomas (1685–1739).

Lombe, Sir Thomas (1685–1739), merchant and inventor of silk-throwing machinery, eldest son of Henry Lombe, worsted weaver, of Norwich, was born at Norwich on 5 September 1685. The father died about 1695, leaving his sons Thomas and Henry under the care of his executors, while the surviving younger son John [*see below*] was to be brought up by his mother, Henry Lombe's second wife, formerly a Miss Wilmot. The family seems to have been long settled in Norfolk, and the name frequently occurs in local records.

In the early part of the eighteenth century Lombe found his way to London, where he was apprenticed to Samuel Totton, mercer, and was admitted to the freedom of the Mercers' Company in 1707. In the same year he became a freeman of the City of London, and he eventually established himself as a merchant. In 1718 he obtained a patent (no. 422) for:

> a new invention of three sorts of engines never before made or used in Great Britaine, one to winde the finest raw silk, another to spin, and the other to twist the finest Italian raw silk into organzine in great perfection, which was never before done in this country.

A specification was duly enrolled, as required by the letters patent, but was lost, and reappeared only in 1867, when it was printed for the first time. Lombe says:

> I declare that by constant application and endeavours for severall years past, and employing a great many agents and workmen both here and in foreigne parts, I have at very great expense and hazards found out, discovered, and brought into this country the art of making the three capital engines.

These are mentioned in the title of his patent. The description of the machinery is deliberately obfuscated and is interspersed with numerous Italian technical terms, the use of which Lombe justifies by alleging that there were no English terms applicable. In fact, it is clear that the real purpose of this obfuscation was to prevent the successful adoption of his process once the patent had expired.

Lombe employed his half-brother John, who, it is said, went to northern Italy, then the principal seat of the silk manufacture, and made himself thoroughly familiar with the various processes, sending back drawings made covertly on the spot, in bales of raw silk to be exported to England. These plans were realized on arrival, prototypes being erected in a room in Derby Moot Hall. Although long doubted, some evidence to support John's exploits has been found in archives at the University of Pisa. He probably worked for Glovere Urwin, silk exporters of Leghorn. This journey has been represented as a risky and daring enterprise, which may well constitute one of the first recorded instances of industrial espionage. The Piedmontese were said to have jealously guarded the secret of the manufacture, yet all the while a complete description of the Italian silk-throwing machinery, published as early as 1607 at Padua by V. Zonca in his *Novo teatro di machine*, was available in the collections of the Bodleian Library, Oxford. It contains engravings which show the construction of the machinery in great detail, and to an expert Zonca's book is to some extent more satisfactory than Lombe's specification. None the less, it is unlikely that anyone concerned with the possibility of throwing silk in Britain, least of all Lombe, was aware of its existence.

Moreover, a number of persons had unsuccessfully petitioned in 1692 for leave to be incorporated into a company for the purpose of introducing the Italian machinery and starting a manufactory in this country. The Lombes, therefore, can be credited with having introduced into this country a new and important trade, the main elements of which were the basic machinery and the factory method of working, long-established in Italy. Significantly, the machines could be adapted to other types of yarn and were to be of inestimable value to the silk and ultimately the textile industry as a whole.

In 1719 Thomas, John, and a cousin, William Lombe, in partnership began production at their mill, constructed from 1715, on an island in the River Derwent at Derby, adjacent to an unsuccessful silk mill built some fourteen years before by Thomas Cotchett, a local attorney. Eventually the mill became a prosperous concern, and Daniel Defoe records a visit to it in its first decade (Defoe, 3.38). The building, later known as the Old Silk Mill, was rebuilt after a fire in 1826. Subsequently the doubling shop collapsed in 1890 and the original building was extensively reconstructed after a fire which occurred on 5 December 1910, two years after silk throwing ceased. It was subsequently adapted to house the Derby Industrial Museum.

Lombe's patent was granted for fourteen years, and naturally expired in 1732, but on 28 January of that year he petitioned parliament for an extension, alleging that he had been put to great expense in training workmen, and that the Sardinian authorities had prohibited the importation of raw silk, so that a supply had to be obtained elsewhere. However, it would appear, from a letter written in 1739 by his successor as proprietor at Derby, William Wilson, to Samuel Lloyd, once Lombe's agent in Italy, that silk supplies were curtailed only from 1733 (letter of 2 October 1739, W. Yorks. AS, DB 32/44). This reinforces the claim by William Hutton that Lombe 'forgot to inform [parliament] that he had already accumulated more than £80,000' (Hutton, 203). The petition was referred to a committee, and evidence was produced showing that the machinery had rendered the manufacturers of England independent of Italy for the supply of organzine, thus reducing the price. There was considerable opposition to the petition on the part of the cotton and worsted spinners, who were keen to use a modified form of Lombe's machinery for making yarn, but who had been prevented by threats of legal action for infringement. The facts are set out in *The case of the manufacturers of woollen, linnen, mohair, and cotton yarn … with respect to … a bill for preserving and encouraging a new invention in England, by Sir Thomas Lombe* (n.d. [1732?]). The debate on the bill was thoroughly reported (*The Parliamentary History of England*, 1732, 924) and is of great interest, being the first instance of an application to parliament to prolong a patent beyond the limit fixed by the Statute of Monopolies. The bill was thrown out, but eventually an act was passed (5 Geo. II, c. 8) granting a reward of £14,000 to the inventor, one of the conditions being that Lombe should deposit models of his machinery in some public institution. Models were ultimately placed in the Tower (although this had clearly not happened as late as the 1750s). They later appear to have succumbed to the ravages of woodworm and the few surviving fragments later said to be in the Victoria and Albert Museum, London, were lost by 1974. Lombe's machinery was described and illustrated in Rees's *Cyclopaedia* (art. 'Silk') and a one-third scale model of the machinery was deposited in the Silk Museum, Macclesfield, Cheshire.

Lombe was an alderman of Bassishaw ward in the City of London, and was chosen sheriff in 1727. He was knighted on 8 July of the same year, when he attended at court to present a congratulatory address from the city to George II on his accession. He married Elizabeth Turner (*d.* 1753), and they had two daughters, Hannah and Mary Turner. Lombe died on 3 January 1739 at his house in Old Jewry, London, leaving a fortune estimated at £120,000 (*GM*, 9.47), which was bequeathed in equal portions to his widow and daughters. He desired his widow 'at the conclusion of the Darby concerns to reward the principal servants there as she shall think fit to the value of 500l. or 600l.' (will, PRO, PROB 11/694, sig. 14). His wife died on 18 November 1753, his daughters being married; Hannah in 1740 to Sir Robert Clifton, baronet, MP for East Retford, and Mary on 24 April 1749 to James Maitland, seventh earl of Lauderdale.

John Lombe (*c.*1693–1722), Sir Thomas's half-brother, born probably at Norwich, was probably apprenticed to Thomas, who subsequently encouraged him to visit Italy and make himself acquainted with the processes of silk throwing. He was referred to by Alderman Perry in his speech in the House of Commons when Sir Thomas Lombe's petition was being discussed as one 'whose head is extremely well turned for the mechanics'. He was further described in 1791 by William Hutton as 'a man of spirit, a good draughtsman and an excellent mechanic' (Hutton, 196). Hutton goes on to recount that John returned from Italy about 1717, bringing with him at least two Italians to assist him in starting the new factory. He adds that the silk throwers of Piedmont were so enraged at Lombe's success, and at the deception which had been practised upon them by the faithless Englishman, that they dispatched a woman to Derby to gain Lombe's confidence, and to administer a slow poison. In this she was successful, and her victim, after lingering for two or three years in great agony, died at his home, Silk Mill House, Derby, on 20 November 1722, and was according to Hutton buried with great pomp at All Saints' Church, Derby, on the 28th, when thousands of people attended the funeral. Hutton, who worked as a boy in the Old Silk Mill, related that Lombe's share of the mill passed 'into the hands of his brother, William' (actually his cousin), who, 'being of a melancholy turn, shot himself'. These events took place before Hutton was born (though he gleaned much from his grandfather) and his story must be received with some caution. It is likely that Lombe was actually buried in a mausoleum erected in a formal garden he had created on an island in the Derwent called the Little Bye-Flatt; the structure appears on Samuel Buck's *East Prospect of Derby* (1728) but later disappeared, probably destroyed in a flood. Sir Thomas Lombe makes no allusion to his brother's death in his petition to parliament for the renewal of his patent. John Lombe's will was proved in London in July 1724. He was unmarried.

R. B. PROSSER, *rev.* MAXWELL CRAVEN and SUSAN CHRISTIAN

Sources 'An old account of the … pedigree etc. of our family', 1782, Norfolk RO, MS MC 257/59/22 • T. Lombe, 'A short account of the character and pedigree of Mr William Lombe', *c.*1745, Norfolk RO, MS MC 257/59/22 • *GM*, 1st ser., 9 (1739), 47 • *GM*, 1st ser., 23 (1753), 541 • T. Lombe, patent no. 422, 1718 • V. Zonca, *Novo teatro di machine ed edificii per varie et sicure operationi con le loro figure* (1607) • G. Chicco, 'Il re e l'organzino: la filatura della seta in Piemonte nel sei-settecento', PhD diss., University of Pisa, 1988 • W. Wilson, letter to Samuel Lloyd, 2 Oct 1739, W. Yorks. AS, Bradford, MS DB 32/44 • W. Lombe, letter to B. Willis, 4 Jan 1723, Norfolk RO, MS MC 257/59/20 • [D. Defoe], *A tour thro' the whole island of Great Britain*, 3 vols. (1724–7) • J. Hunter, *Familiae minorum gentium*, ed. J. W. Clay, 4 vols., Harleian Society, 37–40 (1894–6), 134 • W. Hutton, *The history of Derby* (1791), 196–209 • *William Wolley's history of Derbyshire*, ed. C. Glover and P. Riden, Derbyshire RS, 6 (1981) • A. Calladine, 'Lombe's mill: an exercise in reconstruction', *Industrial Archaeology Review*, 16 (1993–4), 82–99 • W. Cunningham, *The growth of English industry and commerce*, 2 vols. (1890–92) • will, July 1724, Norfolk RO, MS MC 257/59/22 [John Lombe] • A. Rees, 'Silk', *Cyclopedia*, 39 vols. (1819–20) • will of Thomas Lombe, PRO, PROB 11/694, sig. 14

Archives Norfolk RO, MSS MC 257/59/22; MC 257/59/20 • W. Yorks. AS, Bradford, MS DB 32/44

Wealth at death approx. £120,000: *GM*, 9 (1739), 47

Lommán mac Dalláin (*fl.* **5th–early 6th cent.**). *See under* Meath, saints of (*act. c.*400–*c.*900).

Lonán mac Talmaig (*fl.* **5th–6th cent.**). *See under* Meath, saints of (*act. c.*400–*c.*900).

Londesborough. For this title name *see* Denison, Albert, first Baron Londesborough (1805–1860).

London, David of (*d.* **1189**), ecclesiastic and canon lawyer, was one of the many Englishmen who studied law at Bologna in the twelfth century; what sets him apart is the survival of his letter collection, 'The register of Master David', so that some details of his life, interests, and personality are unusually well documented. He was born in London, was a student in Clermont, where he acquired the title *magister*; he went on to Paris, and then to Bologna. He doubtless taught as well as studied at Bologna, and it is possible that he was 'D.', the glossator who appears in Bolognese glosses of the 1180s. While he was at Bologna, and at the latest by 1167, he was presented to the prebend of Brownswood in St Paul's, and he remained a canon of St Paul's until his death. In early days he enjoyed the patronage of Gilbert Foliot, bishop of London (*d.* 1187); Gilbert put him in charge of two of his own nephews who were also studying in Bologna—both dignitaries of St Paul's—and in 1169–70 sent Master David to Rome to plead his cause with the pope. The bishop had been excommunicated by Thomas Becket for his opposition to Becket's cause, and David's defence both of the bishop and of the king against Becket's attack impressed the pope and curia: the pope himself said that it was David who persuaded him to grant Gilbert absolution, and that he was worthy of a bishopric, not just of a canonry. With this and other testimonials David set off from the curia, and attempted to improve his endowments at home, winning a royal pension of £20 per annum, and one of £10 per annum from the bishop, pending further preferment which never came.

Late in 1170 Becket again excommunicated Gilbert Foliot, and David was once more at the curia. He gives a dramatic account of how he and his colleague Master Hugh were working hard in the cause when news came of Becket's murder on 29 December 1170. For a time the pope would not give audience to David and his colleagues; but he argued the case for king and bishop privately, and once again the pope bore witness to his fidelity and skill. Thus far he had worked wholly to Gilbert Foliot's satisfaction.

David's later years, however, seem to have brought disappointment: he held his pensions until his death, but remained only a canon of St Paul's. In 1179–80, it seems, he unsuccessfully intrigued to become dean of St Paul's; by then he had quarrelled with Gilbert Foliot and was working for Roger, bishop of Worcester (*d.* 1179). He continued to witness Gilbert's *acta*, especially those settling legal cases, throughout the 1170s, but not in the bishop's last years. Nevertheless David was resident at St Paul's for a part at least of his own later years. He probably died on 31 March 1189.

David's register survives in the Vatican Library, MS Lat. 6024, amid a remarkable group of letter collections. But it was evidently originally a separate double quire, fols. 140–154, and there can be little doubt that these quires were put together by David himself or under his eye. The register was edited by F. Liverani in 1863, very inaccurately, and became more widely known from the fundamental article by Z. N. Brooke of 1927; some of its contents have been re-edited since. Most, though not all, of the contents relate to David's own affairs: the chief exception is the dossier concerning the canonization of Edward the Confessor. But taken as a whole it is a fascinating revelation of the interests of an active and intelligent canonist involved in Anglo-papal relations and lawsuits in the late 1160s and 1170s.

C. N. L. BROOKE

Sources Z. N. Brooke, 'The register of Master David of London, and the part he played in the Becket crisis', *Essays in history presented to Reginald Lane Poole*, ed. H. W. C. Davis (1927), 227–45 • *Fasti Angl., 1066–1300*, [St Paul's, London], 30 • S. Kuttner and E. Rathbone, 'Anglo-Norman canonists of the twelfth century', *Traditio*, 7 (1949–51), 279–358, esp. 286 and n. 13 • A. Morey and C. N. L. Brooke, *Gilbert Foliot and his letters* (1965), 205–7, 277, etc. • *Letters and charters of Gilbert Foliot*, ed. A. Morey and others (1967), 17, 546 • F. Barlow, *Edward the Confessor* (1970), 309–24 [the dossier on Edward's canonization] • A. Duggan, *Thomas Becket: a textual history of his letters* (1980), 48–53 [on Vatican MS Lat. 6024] • F. Liverani, ed., *Spicilegium liberianum*, 1 vol. in 3 pts (Florence, 1863) [pt 1]

Archives Biblioteca Apostolica Vaticana, Vatican City, register, MS lat. 6024, fols. 140–54

London, George (*d.* **1714**), nurseryman and garden designer, was apprenticed to John Rose, gardener to Arthur Capel, earl of Essex, and Charles II. Rose recognized London's latent genius and sent him to study French gardens. It may be significant that Rose was working for Henry Compton, bishop of London, in 1675, for it was

Compton who, in the words of Stephen Switzer, was London's 'Great Encourager', employing him at Fulham Palace (Switzer, 70). Another catalyst in London's career may have been Lord Essex, who, with his gardener Moses Cook, laid out a forest garden at Cassiobury in 1677. With others, Cook and London were partners in 1681 in the founding of the Brompton Park nursery, where London secured control in 1687 in partnership with Henry Wise; thus began one of the great partnerships in garden history and the rise to European fame of the nursery. London and Wise were as one, not unlike Sir John Vanbrugh and Nicholas Hawksmoor; London was in the field and Wise administered the nursery.

An early reference to London's professional advice occurs jointly with mention of Cook, at Burghley House in 1683. In the same year the gardens at Longleat were begun, and also London's association with the court architect William Talman. Wherever Talman built, London gardened. Both Longleat and Burghley demonstrated London's virtuosity in the design of parterres, the creation of waterworks, and the planting of avenues, specialities which culminated in the huge works at Bretby House and Chatsworth in the 1680s and 1690s. If Longleat was the first of London's parterre designs, the scheme at Dawley (1695) perfected the style. However, nothing in England could match the stupendous parterre dug out of the hill at New Park, Richmond (1692), where London concurrently designed a forest garden, prophetic of the early liberated style at Wray Wood, Castle Howard. At Cholmondeley Hall (1693) London demonstrated his great skill in kitchen gardening, and he also showed an increasing interest in architectonic episodes. His best water gardens were at Bretby, and the art of fountain design seen here was never bettered in England. The contrast between Dyrham Park (1700) and Wanstead House (1706) tells of London's versatility. The former was empirical and *ad hoc* in composition, adumbrating the rococo garden, whereas the latter reflected the visit that London made in 1698 with William Bentinck, first earl of Portland, to study French gardens and to meet André Le Nôtre. For size and splendour Wanstead was excelled only by Versailles in the 1660s, and it earned London the sobriquet of the English Le Nôtre.

In 1688 Portland had become superintendent of the Royal Gardens, with London as his deputy. These two, with Talman (as comptroller of the works), formed a junta for architecture and gardening under the patronage of William III. London was involved in all the royal gardens, most notably at Hampton Court, and from 1694 he was assisted by Wise, who in 1702 succeeded Portland as superintendent. London's influence was thus widespread, and the gardens attributed to him may be numbered in their hundreds. Switzer noted that he could give 'directions once or twice a Year in most of the … Gardens in England' (Switzer, 81). L. Knyff's and J. Kip's *Britannia illustrata* (1707) is an engraved memorial of his achievement.

London died on 12 January 1714, leaving estates in Thames Ditton, purchased from Talman, who built there a small house for his lifelong friend. He was buried in Fulham, Middlesex. JOHN HARRIS, *rev.*

Sources S. Switzer, *Ichnographia rustica* (1718), vol. 1 · S. Morris, 'London and Wise, garden makers', essay, June 1988, Architectural Association · private information (1993)

London, Heinz (1907–1970), physicist, was born on 7 November 1907 at Bonn, the younger of the two sons of Franz London, mathematics professor at Bonn University, and his wife, Luise Hamburger (*d.* 1942). His father died when he was only nine and he was guided towards science by his brother, Fritz, seven years his senior, who became a leading figure in quantum chemistry. Following school in Bonn he studied at Bonn University and Berlin Technische Hochschule, and then from 1929 to 1931 at Munich University, where he was inspired by the lectures of Planck, von Laue, and Sommerfeld. He then started research in low-temperature physics at Breslau University under F. E. Simon, from whom he received a thorough grounding in thermodynamics, a discipline which London regarded with almost religious reverence. With Hitler's rise to power in 1933 Simon decided to leave Germany, and London joined his group in Oxford soon afterwards.

In Breslau, London looked for the appearance of resistance in a superconductor as the frequency of an alternating current was raised. Although he failed to find an effect because his frequency could not be raised sufficiently, his PhD thesis (Breslau, 1933) contained important new ideas about the nature of the superconducting state, which he then developed at Oxford in collaboration with his brother Fritz. Their 'phenomenonological' theory of superconductivity (1935) was an important step in the eventual development of the fundamental theory by John Bardeen, Leon N. Cooper, and John R. Schrieffer in 1956.

In 1936 London moved to Bristol, where he again took up the high-frequency resistance problem and at last found the effect in 1940. The effect was later more thoroughly studied by A. B. Pippard, and provided further vital clues to the fundamental theory. In parallel with his work on superconductivity, London also contributed to the understanding of superfluidity in liquid helium, most importantly by his thermodynamic interpretation of the fountain effect.

Early in the war, London was among the many German refugees who were interned, but he was soon released to work on problems of isotope separation for the atom bomb project (at Bristol and Birmingham universities, Imperial College, ICI Witton and Winnington, and the Ministry of Supply at Mold, Flintshire). In 1944 he was effectively leader of the Birmingham team. The anomaly of having a foreigner engaged on top secret work was eliminated by the simple expedient of naturalization in 1942.

After the war he joined the new Atomic Energy Research Establishment at Harwell as principal scientific officer and was later appointed senior principal scientific officer (1950) and deputy chief scientist (1958). There he continued for a while his isotope separation work, collaborated in various technical cryogenic projects, and worked on various ingenious ideas for the technical exploitation of superconductivity. His main contribution, however, was his invention of a new method of cooling to extremely low temperatures—the 'dilution refrigerator'. His first proposal of the basic idea in 1951 was very bold since it depended essentially on the use of the rare isotope helium-3, which was not then available in anything like sufficient quantities. However, helium-3 did soon become commercially available and after years of difficult development work (in collaboration with E. Mendoza and H. E. Hall) the dilution refrigerator eventually worked at Manchester in 1965. It went on to be manufactured commercially and in making readily accessible the millidegree range of temperatures it revolutionized low-temperature physics. London's fundamental contributions were recognized by the award of the first Simon memorial prize in 1959 and by his election as a fellow of the Royal Society in 1961.

Although London regarded himself as an experimentalist and most of his scientific life was spent in laboratories, he was appreciated more for his original ideas and inventions than for the experimental work he carried out himself. Indeed, he was rather ham-handed and things rarely went right until the actual manipulation was left to his assistants. He was much valued as an informal consultant and ideas man and could be relied on to get down to the fundamentals of a problem, especially if it involved classical disciplines such as electrodynamics or thermodynamics. In the familiar circle at the Harwell lunch table he would lose his customary shyness and hold forth in a lively way on many topics.

London's first marriage, to Gertrude Rosenthal in 1939, ended in divorce. He subsequently married Lucie Meissner, in 1945; they had two sons and two daughters. In spite of a somewhat withdrawn manner and a stooping stance, which made him look sad, London was very happy in his family life after his second marriage and much enjoyed simple recreations such as walking, climbing, and cycling. These recreations had to be much restricted after a mild coronary thrombosis in 1966, but he continued to be scientifically productive until the end of his life. Always a heavy smoker, he died of lung cancer at his home, 44 Cumnor Hill, Oxford, on 3 August 1970.

DAVID SHOENBERG, *rev.*

Sources D. Shoenberg, *Memoirs FRS*, 17 (1971), 441–61 · private information (1981) · personal knowledge (1981) · *CGPLA Eng. & Wales* (1970)

Archives University of Bristol, corresp., papers, notebooks | Bodl. Oxf., Society for Protection of Science and Learning and home office files

Likenesses D. Shoenberg, photograph, 1935, repro. in Shoenberg, *Memoirs FRS*, facing p. 441 · Ramsey & Muspratt, photograph, 1969, repro. in Schoenberg, *Memoirs FRS*, facing p. 441

Wealth at death £11,537: probate, 30 Dec 1970, *CGPLA Eng. & Wales*

London, Henry of [Henry de Loundres] (*d.* **1228**), archbishop of Dublin and justiciar of Ireland, was a member of the Blund family of London, one of five sons of Bartholomew Blund, alderman of that city (*d.* 1201). Although Henry is never called Blund in contemporary records, his presence in witness lists connected with the Blunds as well as his concern for and generosity to various members of the family make the link incontrovertible.

Loyal service to John Henry is occasionally referred to as *magister* but there is no indication as to where he earned this title. He first appears in the records *c.*1190 when Hugh de Nonant, bishop of Coventry, instituted him to the church of Mayfield in Staffordshire. He acquired the archdeaconry of Stafford *c.*1194, presumably again through Nonant's patronage. In 1195 he is found offering a fine of £200 to obtain the goodwill of the king, indicating that he had allied himself with the bishop of Coventry and Count John in the conspiracy against Richard I.

Once John became king, Henry of London's career in the royal administration commenced. He served the king in numerous capacities and has been described as 'typical of the *curiales* operating in a number of areas simultaneously who made Angevin government so effective' (Turner, 91). He served in the judiciary and acted as an officer of the chamber, supervising the transport of the king's treasure and regulating supplies for the court. He also took part in some important diplomatic missions, including a number of visits to Ireland. In 1204 he was among a party of three sent to Ireland to advise the justiciar Meiler fitz Henry and investigate his charges against William de Burgh. On this visit he also accompanied the justiciar to Connacht to negotiate with Cathal Ó Conchobhair.

Henry's service to the king was amply rewarded and he amassed a collection of benefices, prebends, and titles. Many of the rewards came during the years of the interdict when his continued loyalty to the king, and his efforts to delay public proclamation of John's excommunication, linked him firmly with the side of the state against the church. King John attempted on two occasions to have Henry appointed to an English bishopric but was foiled, first by the monks of Coventry and later by Archbishop Langton who refused to consecrate Henry as bishop of Exeter.

Archbishop of Dublin, justiciar, and papal legate In contrast, Henry's election to Dublin in 1212, although undocumented, appears to have provoked no hostility, either in Dublin or Rome. He was confirmed in his new position by Pope Innocent III at some date before March 1213. He was still in England in May 1213, when he was among those who witnessed the king's submission to the papal legate at Dover. However, he left for Ireland shortly afterwards. King John, meanwhile, lost no time in demonstrating that he expected the new archbishop to perform a dual role in Dublin, when in July 1213 he appointed him justiciar of Ireland.

Henry was in Ireland by August 1213 and he spent the next year and a half in his diocese. His first tenure of the office of justiciar spanned the period 1213–15 and it was marked by military and diplomatic successes. The archbishop enjoyed the support of the English barons in Ireland and ensured their loyalty to King John throughout the crisis in England. As justiciar, Henry was intimately concerned with the rebuilding of Dublin Castle as well as supervising the construction of several other castles in strategic parts of the colony. These included Roscrea

Castle from which a successful campaign against Muirchertach Ó Briain was mounted. The archbishop left Ireland in May 1215 and was present at Runnymede in June where he was named among the king's councillors and was one of the chief witnesses to Magna Carta.

Henry was relieved of the office of justiciar in July 1215, probably because he was about to set out for Rome. Accompanied by his suffragan bishops of Kildare and Ferns, he attended the Fourth Lateran Council, leaving the affairs of the province in the hands of the bishops of Ossory and Leighlin. There survives no information on the part played by Henry in the affairs of the council, although true to form he did use the occasion to further John's business at the papal court. He spent some of his time in Rome engaged in matters pertaining to the Dublin church, receiving four confirmations from Innocent III and a further three from his successor Honorius III. These included papal confirmations of the incorporation of the diocese of Glendalough into the metropolitan see of Dublin, confirmations of metropolitan rights and privileges, and confirmations of the possessions of the cathedrals of St Patrick's and Holy Trinity.

When Henry returned to Dublin in 1217 he held the post of papal legate to Ireland and he continued in this role for a period of three years. As papal legate he presided over a general synod of Irish clergy. The decrees of this synod have not survived, but according to the annals of Ireland in the chartularies of St Mary's, Dublin, 'he ordained many things useful for the condition of the Irish church' (Gilbert, 2.280). Henry's tenure of the office was controversial and was terminated abruptly in 1220 with the papacy all but asserting that the archbishop had accepted, if not actively supported, royal mandates relating to the exclusion of Irish clerks from ecclesiastical office. It is not clear how large a part Henry played in the formulation of the policy of 1217 which sought to prevent the election of Irishmen to cathedral churches in Ireland. However, he was closely involved with the administration that pursued this discriminatory policy and he did support the claims of the Anglo-Norman candidate in a number of disputed elections.

During this period Henry was justiciar of Ireland in all but name and very little was done by the administration without his counsel and consent. However, strains began to appear between the archbishop and other royal officials in Ireland and disputes flared up around the familiar topics of jurisdictional liberties. In 1218 the archbishop complained that the religious of his diocese were being unlawfully impleaded in lay courts. He also became involved in a dispute with Thomas fitz Adam, the royal forester in Ireland, over the temporal liberties of the Dublin church. His most serious dispute, again over jurisdictional liberties, was with the citizens of Dublin, who made a number of complaints to the king concerning Henry's attempts to obstruct secular justice.

The conflicts never erupted into an outright breach between the crown and the archbishop and in 1221 Henry III underlined his faith in Henry by appointing him justiciar of Ireland for a second time. This second term of office was, however, fraught with difficulty. It coincided with the rebellion of Hugh de Lacy (*d.* 1242), an event for which Henry appeared to be singularly unprepared. He was apparently forced to purchase a truce when Lacy threatened Dublin in 1224 and shortly after this, in June 1224, he was replaced in office by William (II) Marshal. Henry did not hold formal office in Ireland again and during his last years he was much occupied in attempts to obtain compensation for various expenses he had incurred during his years of service.

Soon after his replacement as justiciar Henry crossed over to England and in September 1225 he was present at the consecration ceremony of the new cathedral of Salisbury. He may also have visited the continent at this time as he had recently purchased an estate in the diocese of Autun in France for the use of the archbishops of Dublin. While his activities in the royal administration, coupled with the temporal responsibilities of his see, left Henry little time for more spiritual matters, he did complete the work of his predecessor John Cumin by raising St Patrick's to cathedral status and instituting the offices of dean, chancellor, treasurer, and precentor. He also continued the building work on the cathedral church of Holy Trinity. During his episcopate most of the nave was completed employing stone and sculptors brought over from England. In 1220 he granted rents to the prior and convent to enable them to construct a new entrance to their church. In return they agreed to celebrate his obit in perpetuity. The archbishop also made gifts to several religious houses in and around Dublin, including the hospital of St John the Baptist and the priory of Grâce Dieu. He also founded *c.*1216 the hospital of St James at the Steyne.

Death and assessment Henry of London died on 12 November 1228 in Dublin and was laid to rest the same month in the cathedral church of Holy Trinity. During his lifetime he held the highest offices of church and state in Ireland, as well as functioning as papal legate for three years. The events of his episcopate in Dublin clearly demonstrate the problems faced by a man with divided loyalties and responsibilities. His attempts to dispense simultaneously secular and spiritual justice involved him in frequent disputes which threatened to alienate the goodwill of the crown, while his identification with the discriminatory aims of the royal administration in Ireland caused him to lose the trust of the papacy. Although he demonstrated through his patronage and church-building a practical piety, his career as the second Anglo-Norman archbishop of Dublin, and one of the most active and controversial occupants of that see in the thirteenth century, was marked by his administrative expertise rather than by his spirituality. MARGARET MURPHY

Sources M. Murphy, 'Balancing the concerns of church and state: the archbishops of Dublin, 1181–1228', *Colony and frontier in medieval Ireland: essays presented to J. F. Lydon*, ed. T. B. Barry and others (1995), 41–56 • R. V. Turner, *Men raised from the dust: administrative service and upward mobility in Angevin England* (1988), 91–106 • M. Murphy, 'The archbishops and administration of the diocese and province of Dublin, 1181–1298', PhD diss., TCD, 1987 • J. A. Watt, *The church and the two nations in medieval Ireland* (1970) • M. Murphy, 'Ecclesiastical censures: an aspect of their use in thirteenth century Dublin',

Archivium Hibernicum, 44 (1989), 89–97 • M. P. Sheehy, ed., *Pontificia Hibernica: medieval papal chancery documents concerning Ireland, 640–1261*, 2 vols. (1962–5) • Giraldus Cambrensis, *Expugnatio Hibernica / The conquest of Ireland*, ed. and trans. A. B. Scott and F. X. Martin (1978) • J. T. Gilbert, ed., *Chartularies of St Mary's Abbey, Dublin: with the register of its house at Dunbrody and annals of Ireland*, 2 vols., Rolls Series, 80 (1884–6)

London, John of (*fl. c.*1260), mathematician, was praised by Roger Bacon (*d.* 1292/1294) in his *Opus tertium* as one of two 'perfect' mathematicians (the other being Peter of Maricourt, called Peregrinus, author of a noted tract on the magnet), and judged superior to two other 'good' mathematicians, namely, Campanus of Novara, the prolific editor and writer on geometry and astronomy, and Master Nicolas, tutor of Amaury de Montfort (*d. c.*1300), third son of Simon de Montfort, earl of Leicester (*d.* 1265). Thus ranked with Peter and Campanus, John must have been a mathematician of distinction, known to Bacon at Paris in the 1260s.

Further data are conjectural. John of London may perhaps be the John Bandoun whom Bacon cites at about the same time, in conjunction with Robert Grosseteste (*d.* 1253) and Adam Marsh (*d.* 1259), as having flourished in the mathematical sciences. He may also be the Paris master, John of London, author of a short letter on astronomical questions posed to him by his own master, 'R. de Guedingue', and the accompanying table of stellar co-ordinates, established by observation at Paris in 1246 (Paris, Bibliothèque Nationale, MS Lat. 7413/2, fols. 19*v*–21, 36). In an edition of the same star catalogue, dated four years later, its compiler, Roger of Lincoln, cites Master John of London as *astronomus famosus*, designer of a form of astrolabe used for verifying the star table (Erfurt, Stadtbibliothek MS Amplon. 4° 369, fol. 217). Kunitzsch, noting John's wide learning in astronomy and his unusual effort to establish the co-ordinates through observation, shows that John's table significantly influenced the tabulation and nomenclature of the stars in later catalogues. John may also be the Master John of London, owner and corrector of a copy of the *De aspectibus* of Alhazen (Ibn al-Haitham; *d.* 1038) that was consulted by Guido de Grana in his correction of another copy in 1269 (Edinburgh, Royal Observatory, MS Cr.3.3, fol. 189).

Other proposals made concerning Bacon's Master John of London doubtless are false. In particular, he cannot have been the gifted Franciscan friar John (not denominated 'of London', whose mathematical training was sponsored by Bacon; for the friar was barely twenty years old when Bacon wrote the *Opus tertium*.

Another **John London** (*fl. c.*1290–*c.*1325), astronomer, is recorded as the donor of a substantial collection of books to the library of the Benedictine abbey of St Augustine in Canterbury. From the extant inventory of the library, made late in the fifteenth century, it may be inferred that John London contributed over eighty books, including twenty-three in mathematics and astronomy, another twenty-three in medicine, and the balance in history, philosophy, and theology. Apart from works long standard, the astronomical titles display a concentration on research undertaken at Paris from the 1290s to the mid-1320s, for example, tracts by Peter of Denmark (Dacia) and Gillaume de St Cloud early in this period and by Jean de Lignières toward its end. No titles of later currency are discernible. Most of the thirteen surviving books from this donation have *ex libris* markings that identify the owner as either *magister* or *frater*. In one of them, Bodl. Oxf., MS Digby 174, fol. 99, a heading gives the owner's name as 'Johannes de Lond. cum monoculo', and affixes a rough sketch of a head, wearing a sort of master's cap, with a conspicuous left eye, but missing the right eye.

It can be inferred that John London was active as an astronomical master at Paris over three decades, before retiring to St Augustine's, where for a while he seems to have shared his astronomical interests with Michael Northgate. He appears not to be associable with anyone else attested under the same name. Against the suggestion that he may have been Bacon's protégé, the Franciscan friar John, is the later date of the book donor's activity, his Benedictine association, and the wealth implied by his substantial library. And against suggestions that he may have been the 'Dom. Joh. de London.' to whom the monk Reginald Lambourne wrote concerning the eclipse of 1363 (Bodl. Oxf., MS Digby 176, fols. 50–53*v*), is the implied gap of four decades between this date and the latest title in the book owner's astronomical collection; it has also been argued that this correspondent might be the Oxford scholar John Ashenden (*d.* in or before 1368).

WILBUR R. KNORR

Sources R. Bacon, 'Opus tertium', *Fr. Rogeri Bacon opera quaedam hactenus inedita*, ed. J. S. Brewer, Rolls Series, 15 (1859) • *Communia mathematica fratris Rogeri*, ed. R. Steele [1940], vol. 16 of *Opera hactenus inedita Rogeri Baconi*, ed. R. Steele and F. M. Delorme [1905–40] • P. Kunitzsch, *Typen von Sternverzeichnissen* (Wiesbaden, 1966) • N. R. Ker, ed., *Medieval manuscripts in British libraries*, 2 (1977) • Emden, *Oxf.*, 2.1157 • J. C. Russell, 'Dictionary of writers of thirteenth century England', *BIHR*, special suppl., 3 (1936) [whole issue] • M. R. James, *The ancient libraries of Canterbury and Dover* (1903) • A. B. Emden, *Donors of books to St Augustine's Abbey, Canterbury* (1968) • R. T. Gunther, *Early science in Oxford*, 2: *Astronomy*, OHS, 78 (1923) • L. Thorndike, *A history of magic and experimental science*, 8 vols. (1923–58), vol. 3

Archives Bibliothèque Nationale, Paris, MS Lat. 741 3/2, fols. 19*v*–21, 36

London, John of. *See* Bever, John (*d.* 1311?).

London, John (*fl. c.*1290–*c.*1325). *See under* London, John of (*fl. c.*1260).

London, John (*d.* 1428), Benedictine monk and recluse, entered Westminster Abbey in 1377–8 and said his first mass in 1379. The toponym may indicate his place of origin; his family is unknown. As keeper of the shrine of St Edward the Confessor, an office which he held as a junior monk, he was thrown into contact with pilgrims and sightseers. As the second of the two treasurers of Eleanor of Castile's manors in 1388–90 and 1391–3, he acquired experience of moneybags and the care of property, but without carrying the weight of responsibility falling on his senior colleague. A potentially useful, if not high-flying, career as an office-holder was terminated when he became a recluse. He probably took this step in or soon after 1393, when the monastery's *reclusorium*, formerly situated near the infirmary but now in the angle between the south transept and south ambulatory of the church, became vacant on the death of John Murymouth, its previous occupant. Murymouth was, it appears, the recluse to whom Richard II confessed on 14 June 1381, before his meeting with the rebels at Mile End, and whom Thomas Beauchamp, earl of Warwick (*d.* 1401), the former appellant, mentioned in his confession of treason in 1397.

In the later middle ages, the life of a recluse at Westminster was compatible with changes of scene, and London, accompanied by a servant, spent most of the year 1401–2, and possibly a longer period, at Little Malvern Priory, Worcestershire. Abbot William Colchester's willingness to pay the cost of his board there underlines the special status he now enjoyed in the community: an abbot would not normally do this for a monk. There appears to be no good reason to doubt that London, long since in residence again at Westminster, was the recluse to whom Henry V confessed on the night of his father's death. The claims of William Alnwick, later the first confessor-general of the Bridgettine order, to this distinction depend on the St Albans chronicler's reference to him as a monk and recluse of Westminster. But no one of this name occurs in either capacity in Westminster sources for the period. Like many other recluses, London was sought out by devout, if in some cases politically deviant, members of the aristocracy. The bequest to him by Henry, Lord Scrope of Masham, executed for treason in 1415, of a rosary and the sum of £5, a substantial legacy, points to more than a passing acquaintance between the two. A desire for greater solitude than could be enjoyed at Westminster may explain London's second absence, in 1416–19, but this time his whereabouts are unknown. The bequest to him of £10 by Thomas Beaufort, duke of Exeter (*d.* 1426), suggests that he again attracted an aristocratic clientele after his return to Westminster.

The St Albans chronicler believed that London died on or about the feast of St Scholastica (10 February), 1429. From Westminster sources, however, it appears that he died in 1428, in the late summer or autumn. He was probably buried in the monks' cemetery.

BARBARA F. HARVEY

Sources E. H. Pearce, *The monks of Westminster* (1916), 95, 115 • D. Knowles [M. C. Knowles], *The religious orders in England*, 2 (1955), 220–22, 367–8 • C. Peers and L. E. Tanner, 'On some recent discoveries in Westminster Abbey', *Archaeologia*, 93 (1949), 151–63 • *Annales monasterii S. Albani a Johanne Amundesham*, ed. H. T. Riley, 2 vols., pt 5 of *Chronica monasterii S. Albani*, Rolls Series, 28 (1870–71), vol. 1, pp. 27, 33 • A. K. Warren, *Anchorites and their patrons in medieval England* (1985), 200, 207 • V. H. Galbraith, ed., *The Anonimalle chronicle, 1333 to 1381* (1927), 146 • *The chronicle of Adam Usk, 1377–1421*, ed. and trans. C. Given-Wilson, OMT (1997), 35 • Westminster Abbey Muniments 24413

Archives Westminster Abbey Muniment Room

London, John (1485/6–1543), administrator, was a native of Hambleden, Buckinghamshire, the son of an Oxfordshire tenant farmer. In 1497, at the age of eleven, he was admitted a scholar of Winchester College, proceeding thence in 1503 as a scholar of New College, Oxford, where he was elected a full fellow in 1505. He graduated BCL in 1513, proceeded DCL in 1519, and was elected principal of Hinksey Hall in 1513. In 1526 he was elected warden of New College, a post he retained until 1542, while by 1533 he had been made a notary public by apostolic and imperial authority. Although he was not ordained priest until 1522, in April 1519 he became a canon of York Minster, holding the prebend of Bilton. He came to hold a number of other preferments, including a series of prebends in Lincoln Cathedral, and became a canon and prebendary at both Salisbury and Windsor in 1540. Appointed dean of Wallingford in 1536, and master of St John's Hospital there in 1541, on 1 September 1542 he was made dean of the new cathedral at Oxford, which was then in the former abbey of Osney.

Although London played an active role in the persecution of Lutherans in Oxford, both at his own college and at King Henry VIII College, his reputation as a bloodthirsty persecutor of heretics owes much to the highly coloured account of his actions provided by John Foxe in the *Acts and Monuments*. Certainly one member of New College, John Quinby, was in 1528 imprisoned in the steeple on London's orders, and died in captivity. When London's own nephew, Edward London, was heard to argue that papal supremacy had no legitimate foundation, his uncle summoned him and spent five hours trying to persuade him to disavow his opinions. Foxe claimed that London rejoiced in the arrest of Thomas Garrard (or Garrett) in 1540, and listed him among the 'pharisees troubled at Garrett's escape out of prison' (*Acts and Monuments*, 5.424). London's reputation as a defender of Catholic orthodoxy places him low in Foxe's estimation: the martyrologist describes London as 'puffing, blustering, and blowing, like a hungry and greedy lion seeking his prey'. However, it is clear from correspondence between London and John Longland, bishop of Lincoln, that London was following the instructions of Cardinal Wolsey in his actions against Garrard in 1528, and that he preferred that the case should receive 'gentle and discreet treatment' (ibid., 5, appx). Despite Foxe's interpretation of London's interview with his nephew, it was London who was to find himself forced to justify his conservative opinions after Edward had reported them to the council in 1536.

It is for his participation in the campaign for the dissolution of the monasteries in the 1530s that London is best remembered. He was responsible for the dissolution of houses in Oxford, Reading, Warwickshire, and Northamptonshire, and a number of letters between London, Cromwell, and Rich survive, many detailing the suppression of houses and the removal of images. David Knowles refers to him as a 'legendary figure' in the history of the period, while stopping short of Philip Hughes's description of London as 'one of the vilest men of all this vile time' (Hughes, 1.235). Although frequently regarded as a colleague of Layton, Legh, and ap Rice from the start of the process of visitation, London was not in fact active in the suppression of religious houses until 1538, and in many ways he was a strange choice as visitor: he had not been employed by the government prior to the dissolution, and played no role in the process of the official Henrician Reformation after this date. Earlier histories of the dissolution portray London as an enthusiastic destroyer and spoiler of the monasteries, removing everything of value and destroying what he could not remove. But more recently he has been viewed as a moderate and considerate agent of government, never making sweeping generalizations over the moral character of the monks, and making a deliberate effort to obtain financial security for those affected, for instance requesting favourable treatment for the abbess of Godstow. His own religious opinions were very much those of the conservative wing of the Henrician church; Knowles describes his motivation as an urge to reform rather than suppress, and there is little to suggest that he had any doctrinal interest in the obliteration of monasticism.

Despite London's role in the dissolution, his relations with Thomas Cromwell were not always amicable. He has been criticized for his 'oleagenous subservience to his political masters, especially to Thomas Cromwell' (Buxton and Williams, 45), but there were good reasons for his repeated protestations of loyalty to the Henrician cause. In 1532 it was suggested that his conservatism was standing in the way of his commitment to the crown: London responded by assuring Cromwell that all rumours of his opposition to royal policy were false, and claiming that he had publicly consented to Henry VIII's divorce before the whole university. London invoked the assistance of Cromwell in the government of his college, protesting against the demands of his fellows, but his defence of papal authority at this time made his position less secure. In 1533 his position was under threat again after one Richard Jones, arrested and imprisoned in the Tower of London after involvement in alchemy and prophecy, promised that he would reveal things about London 'that would make him smoke and others too of his affinity' (Elton, 56). In July 1536 London felt compelled to write to Cromwell once again with a declaration of his loyalty to the crown, and denying rumours that he had spoken openly in favour of purgatory, pilgrimages, and the papal supremacy.

London clearly feared that his position at New College was under threat: in a letter to Cromwell the latter's agent Thomas Bedyll outlined London's concerns and claimed that he was a dedicated servant of the crown. London enlisted the support of Bedyll again in 1537, protesting that Cromwell believed him to be a papist, and complaining again that he was troubled by the fellows of New College. The main causes of the clash with the fellows appear to have been his refusal to manumit bondsmen to college estates, and more particularly his hostility towards Lutheranism and the new learning. He had reported difficulties in maintaining discipline among the college membership, which included such conservatives as John and Nicholas Harpsfield alongside early evangelicals, John Man and John Philpot. His problems may indeed have been heightened by a clash between his obligation to enforce the will of the crown and his determination to suppress all heresy and innovation. London was clearly not the only conservative in New College, but his enemies were all too aware that any hint of opposition to the Henrician Reformation could be used against him.

With the fall of Cromwell in 1540 London aligned himself more firmly with Stephen Gardiner and the conservative members of the Henrician court and church. Having become a canon of Windsor he played an active role in the persecution of heterodoxy there. John Foxe lists him among the persecutors of the group of Windsor evangelicals in the spring of 1543, and at the same time he also played an important role in the conspiracy against Thomas Cranmer and the evangelicals at court, which culminated in the so-called prebendaries' plot. It was London who brought Stephen Gardiner into the orbit of the plotters, thereby forging a powerful alliance of conservative interests based in Kent, Oxford, and Winchester. In March 1543 London brought evidence of heresy in Windsor before the privy council, apparently with the prior knowledge of Gardiner. London and his ally William Symonds alleged that Anthony Peerson and his circle were acting in violation of the Act of Six Articles of 1539, which had set out official belief on a number of matters, most notably clerical marriage and the eucharist. Gardiner instructed London to return to Windsor to search for more concrete information, information that might be enough to tip the balance at court, and the mind of the king, in favour of the conservatives. London had an important part to play in the questioning of the suspects. The persecution of heresy in Windsor reached a peak in 1543, when it was believed that revealing the extent of heterodox belief there and in Kent would prove to be a decisive blow against the reformers, implicating Thomas Cranmer in the spread of evangelical beliefs in Kent and causing the king to turn against the archbishop.

Peerson and two of his followers were burnt on 28 July, but in November the king chose to stand by Cranmer, and John London was one of the first casualties. This may have been no accident: there are suggestions that London admitted full responsibility for the events, and particularly the questioning of members of the privy council, in an effort to preserve Gardiner's position. Accused of committing perjury in an attempt to exonerate himself after the Windsor trials, he was convicted and sentenced to ride through Windsor, Reading, and Newbury facing the tail of his horse with a paper on his head, before being committed to the Fleet. He had died in prison before the end of the year. News of his death was welcomed by contemporary evangelical writers, including John Bale, who recorded the event in the *Epistle Exhortatorye of an Englyshe Christiane* (1544; ESTC 1291; fol. 9*r*–*v*). The nature of London's involvement in the affairs of church and state has done much to shape his posthumous reputation—Catholic commentators and historians have condemned him for his involvement in the material destruction of the early Reformation, while protestant writers have criticized his continued conservatism and apparent allegiance to Rome.

H. L. PARISH

Sources D. Knowles [M. C. Knowles], *The religious orders in England*, 3 (1959) · D. MacCulloch, *Thomas Cranmer: a life* (1996) · T. Wright, ed., *Three chapters of letters relating to the suppression of monasteries*, CS, 26 (1843) · J. G. Nichols, ed., *Narratives of the days of the Reformation*, CS, old ser., 77 (1859) · *The acts and monuments of John Foxe*, ed. J. Pratt, [new edn], 8 vols. (1877) · Foster, *Alum. Oxon.* · *LP Henry VIII*, vols. 4–18 · G. W. O. Woodward, *The dissolution of the monasteries* (1966) · P. Hughes, *The Reformation in England*, 1 (1950) · Emden, *Oxf.*, 4.359–60 · G. R. Elton, *Policy and police* (1972) · J. Buxton and P. Williams, eds., *New College, Oxford, 1379–1979* (1979) · G. Redworth, *In defence of the church catholic: the life of Stephen Gardiner* (1990) · *State papers published under … Henry VIII*, 11 vols. (1830–52), vol. 11

London, William (*fl.* 1653–1660), bookseller, whose parentage, education, and private life are obscure, had a bookshop in Newcastle upon Tyne in the 1650s. His claim to fame derives mainly from *A Catalogue of the most Vendible Books in England*, which he published in 1657. In the preface London explained that he wanted to promote knowledge in the northern counties and had therefore compiled this catalogue which contained approximately 4500 titles and was arranged by subject category. The catalogue itself is preceded by 'An introduction to the use of books: in a short essay upon the value and benefits of learning and knowledge'. London claimed to be the first to list the books with their full titles, 'for a full title tels us the purport and intent of the books' contrary to the usual practice of listing short titles only which 'are great deluders and deceivers of mens expectations'. The title-page announces that besides the books in the catalogue maps, globes, paper, and wax may also be bought in his shop. The annual supplements promised are extant for 1658 (as part of the 1658 reissue of the catalogue) and for 1660 (also found as part of a 1660 reissue). The only other work known to be written by London is *The Civil Wars of France* (1655) where the author professes to be 'a true Protestant, and friend to the Common-wealth of England'. This claim seems to be contradicted by his association with the printer Stephen Bulkley (Buckley) who had to move several times rather hurriedly due to his support for the royalist cause and who printed several anti-Quaker tracts which, according to the imprint, were sold in London's shop. The first of these is J. Gilpin's *The Quakers Shaken* (1653). In the preface to his *Catalogue* London said that he 'will not stop the Currant of a generall knowledg of Books, by leaving out all that are accounted Heterodox'. The *Catalogue* was reissued twice with a cancel title-page and was possibly no great success, which may be the reason that the catalogue of Latin books London spoke of in his preface never materialized. MARJA SMOLENAARS

Sources H. R. Plomer and others, *A dictionary of the booksellers and printers who were at work in England, Scotland, and Ireland from 1641 to 1667* (1907) · W. K. Sessions, *Stephen Bulkley, peripatetic royalist printer* (1997)

London Corresponding Society (*act.* 1792–1799), radical society, was founded in January 1792 by Thomas *Hardy and owed its origins to his rereading, in late 1791, of the political writings first published by the Society for Constitutional Information during the American War of Independence as well as to the enthusiasm generated by the French Revolution and the publication of Thomas Paine's *Rights of Man*. The London Corresponding Society (LCS) had a somewhat tenuous beginning. Only nine men attended its first meeting at The Bell tavern in Exeter Street, London, but its popularity grew quite rapidly, and within two weeks a further fifteen had joined. By May 1792 the LCS comprised nine separate divisions, each with a minimum of thirty members. Unfortunately there are no records of the exact number who joined, and some estimates by contemporaries seem unrealistic—with figures varying from 28,000 to 80,000 members. It is known that at its lowest point in mid-1794 the LCS numbered only 241 paying members, while at its peak it probably counted some 5000 men among its ranks. Of the thousands who joined the society, occupational details of only 347 men are known; a significantly smaller number of personnel have left behind a traceable career, and it is, in these relative terms, that the LCS remains, by and large, an obscure and elusive group.

However, in addition to the thousands of LCS members who remain unknown or known only by name, there were also those who had significant careers and held professional positions. **Basil William Douglas**, Lord Daer (1763–1794) was born on 16 March 1763, the second but eldest surviving son of Dunbar Douglas, fourth earl of Selkirk (1722–1799), and Helen (1737/8–1802), daughter of John Hamilton of Blackadder, Berwickshire. A younger brother, Thomas *Douglas, fifth earl of Selkirk, achieved prominence as an advocate of colonization in North America. Daer was educated first at Anna and Rochemont Barbauld's school at Palgrave, Suffolk, and later at Edinburgh University under the moral philosopher Dugald Stewart. In 1789 he travelled to Paris, from where he returned with an enthusiasm for the French Revolution, becoming an active protagonist in the British reform movement. He was one of the earliest LCS activists and held concurrent membership of the Society for Constitutional Information and the Scottish Association of the Friends of the People. This provided the LCS with an important early link to other reform societies. Though a strong critic of the union (1707), Daer called for English and Scottish radical societies to work together 'to have mutually beneficial results: providing Scots with greater say in government while relieving you of that vermin from this country who infect your court, parliament and every establishment' (Daer to Charles Grey, 18 Jan 1793, quoted in Bewley, 54–5). Daer's radical career, however, was cut short when he died, unmarried, from tuberculosis on 5 November 1794 at Ivybridge, Devon; he was buried in Exeter Cathedral.

Over the years the LCS continued to attract men of prominent social and professional standing. Although the egalitarian nature and constitution of the society meant that these men were treated equally, there were distinct advantages in recruiting members from the higher social ranks. Many brought a certain image of respectability to the LCS, while others maintained important links with middle-class reform associations and provided, through their professions, a certain strategic advantage. Barristers and attorneys were particularly useful in providing advice during the society's continual legal engagements. Members among this group included James Agar, Peregrine Palmer, Felix Vaughan, and John Pierce, who served as assistant secretary to the LCS. Joseph *Gerrald was another attorney who played a particularly important role in the LCS during its formative years. In 1793, as delegate of the LCS, he travelled to the British Convention of the Friends of the People in Edinburgh, where he was arrested and subsequently transported to Botany Bay as one of the five 'Scottish martyrs'. Maurice *Margarot was another member of 'superior education, intellect, and information' (Thale, xxii) who accompanied Gerrald to the British Convention as an LCS delegate. Margarot was one of the first members, along with Hardy, to rise to a position of prominence within the society. He served as chairman, authored addresses, composed the society's correspondence, and contributed to the drafting of its constitution. His formal association with the LCS, however, ceased when he too was transported to Australia in 1794.

Physicians were also well represented, among them Richard Barrow, William *Hodgson, and Robert Thomas Crossfield, who served as president of the society in 1798. Undoubtedly the most significant physician active in the LCS was James *Parkinson, a prolific and powerful propagandist who was a regular contributor to the society's campaign. Another member, the surgeon John Gale *Jones, was an accomplished orator who displayed his skills at LCS mass meetings. In 1796 he was sent, along with John *Binns, on an important mission as a representative of the LCS to Birmingham, Maidstone, Portsmouth, Rochester, and other areas of southern England to gauge the state of reform activity and to enliven interest in the campaign for reform.

Apart from these well-placed members, the LCS also benefited considerably during the early stages from the contribution of educated men who were not formal members of the society but who were closely acquainted with Hardy and other early recruits. Veteran reformers such as Thomas Brand Hollis, John Cartwright, Daniel Stuart, and John Horne Tooke provided valuable advice which Hardy later acknowledged: 'Much political information I frequently received from gentlemen experienced in the cause of Reform which was communicated to the Society and received with great approbation, and which was of much use in regulating their conduct as a Society' (Thale, xxii).

Despite the influence of such individuals, the LCS was primarily conceived as a working-class organization—a forum for tradesmen, mechanics, and shopkeepers. As Hardy once asserted, the LCS was to represent those who were 'but few in number and humble in situation and circumstances' (Graham, 282). The low weekly subscription of 1*d.* reflected this aim, and the society's campaign for annual parliaments and universal manhood suffrage was designed to appeal to the disenfranchised citizens. Such inducements were indeed successful, with shoemakers, weavers, and tailors the three largest employment categories of the known members. To some contemporary detractors the LCS was nothing more than a group of illiterate rabble-rousers, 'the very lowest order of society … filthy & ragged … wretched looking blackguards' who were being unscrupulously led by a minority 'who possess strong but unimproved faculties' (Thale, xix). The general membership profile of the LCS was, however, quite unlike this characterization. The majority of members were recruited from a politically conscious and articulate artisan population, and those of higher social and professional standing were rarely placed in authoritative positions within the society for fear that, as Hardy stated, the ordinary members would be discouraged from 'exerting themselves in their own cause' (Goodwin, 197).

John Ashley (*c.*1762–1829), shoemaker and radical, served as secretary to the LCS after Hardy's resignation in 1794. On 12 November 1795 he addressed an outdoor LCS meeting near Copenhagen House, London, which attracted a crowd of some 300,000–400,000 people. He resigned as secretary in December 1796, and as a delegate of his division several months later, before leaving the society in June 1797. Ashley, described by one colleague as 'a serious thinking man' (Thale, xx), moved to Paris in June 1797, where he is thought to have prospered in business. There he maintained his radical activities, providing the French Directory with inflated estimates of the number of pro-French sympathizers in London who were 'active and decided men … ready to co-operate against the Government' (Goodwin, 437). He was also active in a militant circle of United Irish émigrés who worked for a rising in Ireland before his death in 1829.

It was Ashley who introduced Francis *Place to the LCS. Place quickly rose to prominence in 1795, serving as chairman of the general committee, which co-ordinated the activities of the different divisions, and of the executive committee, which dealt with the society's correspondence and the writing of addresses and resolutions. Like Place, John *Thelwall came from an artisan background to become a central character in London's reform movement, joining the LCS in 1793, where he proved a highly effective lecturer and propagandist. Not all working-class members were as gifted as Thelwall, nor did many have such enduring careers, yet the LCS provided ordinary and obscure men with the chance to acquire some standing within the society. Robert Oliphant, for instance, a tailor, and Anthony Beck, a saddler, served at various times as treasurer; John Philip Franklow, another tailor, James Savage, warehouseman, and Benjamin Pemberton Binns, a plumber and brother of John Binns, each served as assistant secretaries of the society.

John Baxter (*fl.* 1794–1816), silversmith and radical, also assumed some prominence within the LCS when he succeeded Margarot as chairman in 1794. He was arrested but not charged during the treason trials of the same year. Baxter was also a founder member, along with the bookseller Joseph Burks, of the Friends of Liberty, formerly division 16 of the LCS, which separated from the society in 1795. His *New and impartial history of England from the most* *early period of genuine historical evidence to the present important and alarming crisis* (1796) exhibited a politically articulate intellect. Details of his later career remain unclear: he was a known member of the United Irish movement, and in 1816 a satirical broadsheet, William Snow's *The Polemic Fleet*, listed him as a prominent member of the radical Spencean circle. Other sources suggest that the 'Impregnable' Baxter (*Polemics*) may by this date have been practising as a surgeon.

Like their middle-class counterparts, some of the working-class members of the LCS provided the group with strategic advantages through their occupations. With society meetings often held in taverns, publicans like John Barnes and Robert Boyd were particularly valuable associates. Of even greater use to the society's cause were the numerous booksellers and printers who joined the organization. In its campaign for parliamentary reform the LCS looked to use 'moral force' and to educate the people in their political rights through the publication of cheap democratic literature. The extensive publishing programme of the LCS consisted of about eighty separate pamphlets and broadsides between 1792 and 1798 as well as two periodicals, *The Politician* (1794–5) and the *Moral and Political Magazine* (1796–7). Booksellers and printers often subsidized and distributed these works for their society, and with the government's focus on the spread of seditious literature during the 1790s they were often faced with imprisonment. In the face of such adversity LCS members, such as Daniel Isaac *Eaton, who worked in the book trades, required amazing fortitude and endurance to remain loyal to the cause. Thomas *Spence, another bookseller who joined the LCS, showed similar tenacity and dexterity, and, like Eaton, composed radical propaganda of his own despite repeated intimidation. In 1794 he was one of the members imprisoned for six months without trial in the prelude to the infamous treason trials of that year.

Richard Lee (*c.*1774–1798?), publisher and radical, known as Citizen Lee, also joined the LCS and emerged from obscurity to play an intriguing and important role in London radicalism during the mid-1790s. Nothing is known of his background, but he appears to have grown up in poverty, and by 1794, aged about twenty, he lived in Orange Street, Leicester Fields. At that time he worked as a clerk in a merchant's office and became a frequent visitor to Eaton's bookshop. In this radical milieu Lee acquired an interest in political writing and poetry, and during the course of his career he published no fewer than fifty titles under his own imprint. Under the sign of the Tree of Liberty he moved premises frequently during 1795, trading at various times from his mother's shop in St Ann's Court, Soho, 47 Haymarket, 98 Berwick Street, Soho, and then 444 Strand. Lee's connection with the LCS proved brief and unstable. As a Methodist he disapproved of the society's growing tendencies to support deism and atheism in the mid-1790s and he was reputedly expelled for refusing to sell Paine's *Age of Reason* and Volney's *Ruins*. Despite distancing himself from the LCS, Lee was arrested in November 1795 for publishing the regicidal handbill *King Killing* (1795), Edward Iliff's *A summary of the duties of citizenship. Written expressly for the members of the London Corresponding Society* (1795), as well as two extracts from the radical pamphleteer Charles Pigott. On 19 December 1795 he escaped custody and within days was bound for Hamburg, ironically eloping with the wife of James Powell, one of the most diligent government spies to join the LCS. Within six months Lee had moved to Philadelphia, where he peddled copies of his publications and published the *American Magazine* until 1797. According to William Cobbett, Lee was in gaol during 1798, but nothing further is known of his career; it seems likely that he died, possibly from yellow fever, soon after his release from prison.

While booksellers and printers were important allies in the society's educative and 'moral force' programme, some also had close links with 'physical force' activists. The booksellers John Bone and Thomas *Evans, for example, both rose to prominence within the LCS and were members of the clandestine and revolutionary United Englishmen. Thomas Spence was also involved with a shadowy group known as the Loyal Lambeth Association (LLA), which drilled its members in the use of arms. There were significant overlaps in membership of the LLA and the LCS, with John Philip Franklow, one-time assistant secretary of the LCS, and John Shelmerdine, a hatter and member of division 12 of the Corresponding Society, the founders of the LLA in 1793. **Thomas Stiff** (*b. c.*1740, *d.* in or before 1808), hairdresser and radical, the son of a victualler Bartholomew Stiff of Lawrence Haltham, Berkshire, was another LCS member with an apparent interest in arming the society. On 2 April 1754 he was bound as an apprentice for seven years to Stephen Goodson, a barber, and on 2 June 1761 was admitted to the freedom of the Worshipful Company of Barbers. A year later he established a barber shop in Paternoster Row, London, and remained there for his entire career. By 1793 he was a member of the LCS and served as delegate to division 13. His premises were sometimes used as the meeting place for LCS committees and in 1794 he drew a print showing military and arming exercises. The print proved particularly useful, with one colleague commenting that, as a result of the drawing, 'many of the Members [of the LCS] already know their Exercise' and that Stiff was very capable at training those who were yet to learn (Thale, 149). Stiff disappears from LCS records after 1794 and is marked as dead in the records of the Worshipful Company of Barbers in 1808.

The subversive activities of the LCS were a great concern to the government, which employed an intricate network of spies to infiltrate the society. Often recruited from the working classes, men such as Henry Alexander, linen draper, Edward Gosling, hairdresser, George Lynam, ironmonger, and Frederick Polydore Nodder, botanic painter, blended with other members of the LCS and moved freely among their radical subjects. James Powell, a clerk, was something of a double agent, acting as assistant secretary to the LCS in 1797 and reporting frequently to the government. **William Metcalfe** (*fl.* 1778–1799), attorney and spy, was another informer who operated effectively within the society. His background remains obscure, but on 16 June 1778 he was elected clerk of the Tallow Chandlers Company, a position which he held by annual election until he was discharged on 5 September 1799 for financial irregularities. As an attorney he had been employed by the government in conducting criminal cases in the mid-1780s, and in 1793 he was again working in an official capacity on 'business of confidence and secrecy' in Shropshire, Worcestershire, and Liverpool (Thale, 126). Early in 1794 he began spying on the LCS and at Thelwall's lectures, for which he was to receive a sum of £300 per annum. His usefulness, however, came to an abrupt end in September 1794 when, at the request of the government, he was revealed as a spy during the capture of Paul Thomas Lemaitre and other LCS members accused of the so-called Popgun Plot to murder George III. Following this Metcalfe virtually disappears from public record apart from his involvement until 1799 with the Tallow Chandlers Company.

Reports of spies often provided the government with the bulk of evidence required to take legal action against those society members suspected of subversive intentions, and it was the treason trials of 1794 which marked a decisive point in the history of the LCS. In May thirteen men, all members of the LCS or the Society for Constitutional Information, were indicted for high treason. Hardy, Tooke, and Thelwall were the only men eventually brought to trial, and though each was acquitted many LCS members were subsequently discouraged, disillusioned, and frightened. While the society's membership showed signs of improving during the next twelve months, the government's Treason and Sedition Acts (1795) effectively sent the LCS into a downward spiral. Internal schisms had also fractured the group, with secessionist organizations such as the London Reforming Society, the Friends of Liberty, and the Friends of Religious and Civil Liberty (consisting of disgruntled Methodists) forming in 1795.

During 1796 the society fell into financial trouble through a combination of declining membership revenue and legal expenses, as well as costs associated with staging massive outdoor meetings and the unprofitable publication of the *Moral and Political Magazine*. By 1798 the government again adopted repressive measures to quell radical activity, and in April of that year mass arrests crippled the LCS. The Habeas Corpus Act was suspended, and some of the men captured were detained in prison without trial for up to three years. A few defiant LCS members continued to meet following these arrests, but the society, along with the United Englishmen, United Scotsmen, United Britons, and United Irishmen, was outlawed by name in legislation passed on 12 July 1799.

MICHAEL T. DAVIS

Sources J. Barrell, *Imagining the king's death: figurative treason, fantasies of regicide, 1793–1796* (2000) • M. T. Davis, ed., *The London Corresponding Society* (2002) • A. Goodwin, *The Friends of Liberty: the English democratic movement in the age of the French Revolution* (1979) • J. Graham, *The nation, the law and the king: reform politics in England, 1789–1799*, 2 vols. (2000) • M. Thale, ed., *Selections from the papers of the London Corresponding Society, 1792–1799* (1983) • G. A. Williams, *Artisans and sans-culottes: popular movements in France and Britain during the French Revolution* (1968) • H. Collins, 'The London Corresponding Society', *Democracy and the labour movement*, ed. J. Saville (1954) • C. Bewley, *Muir of Huntershill* (1981) • GEC, *Peerage*
Archives BL, minutes and letter-books, Add. MSS 27811–27813 | BL, Francis Place papers, Add. MSS 27811–27817 • PRO, corresp. with the British Convention, Edinburgh, TS 11/953/3497 • PRO, TS 11, HO 42, PC 1

Londonderry. For this title name *see* Ridgeway, Thomas, first earl of Londonderry (*c*.1565–1632); Pitt, Thomas, first earl of Londonderry (*c*.1688–1729); Stewart, Robert, first marquess of Londonderry (1739–1821); Stewart, Robert, Viscount Castlereagh and second marquess of Londonderry (1769–1822); Vane, Charles William, third marquess of Londonderry (1778–1854); Vane, Frances Anne, marchioness of Londonderry (1800–1865); Stewart, Charles Stewart Vane-Tempest-, sixth marquess of Londonderry (1852–1915); Stewart, Theresa Susey Helen Vane-Tempest-, marchioness of Londonderry (1856–1919) [*see under* Stewart, Charles Stewart Vane-Tempest-, sixth marquess of Londonderry (1852–1915)]; Stewart, Charles Stewart Henry Vane-Tempest-, seventh marquess of Londonderry (1878–1949); Stewart, Edith Helen Vane-Tempest-, marchioness of Londonderry (1878–1959).

Long [*née* Hume], **Amelia, Lady Farnborough** (1772–1837), watercolour painter, was born in Hill Street, Berkeley Square, London, on 29 January 1772, the elder daughter of the prominent art collector Sir Abraham *Hume (1749–1838) and his wife, Amelia Egerton (1751–1809). She was educated in the classics. On 28 May 1793 she married Charles *Long (1760–1838), a Treasury official who later became paymaster-general and in 1826 Baron Farnborough. He not only shared his wife's interests in the arts, but also took on the role of unofficial art adviser to the prince of Wales (later George IV). He drew and etched to a small extent and formed, no doubt with his wife's approval, a modest but significant art collection which included neo-classical sculpture, Dutch and Flemish paintings, and landscapes by Gainsborough, Claude, Rubens, Gaspard Dughet, and Sir George Beaumont.

Early in their marriage, the Longs acquired property and land in Bromley, Kent, where they finally settled in 1801. Situated on a hill and built in the Italian style, Bromley Hill Place was transformed into 130 acres of spacious lawn, wooded grounds, winding waterways and rock garden, with rustic bridges and seats 'for rest and contemplation', a summer house, farm buildings, carefully sited marble vases, and sun dial (Long to George Cumberland, Egerton, 384). The house subsequently became a meeting place for artists and royalty, as well as the arena for Amelia Long's works as a horticulturist and watercolourist.

In or shortly after 1796 Amelia Long took drawing lessons from the landscape painter Thomas Girtin, who reputedly 'told everything to his favourite pupil Lady Long' (Roget, 91). Early work shows her copying the masters of landscape painting, and employing the wide-angled topographical format and restricted tonal colour scheme characteristic of Girtin's work: a typical example is the *View of St Paul's from Thames* (National Galleries of Scotland,

Edinburgh). At the same time she was brought into contact with Dr Thomas Monro, the patron of aspiring watercolour painters and himself an amateur artist. Charles Long subscribed to the upkeep of J. R. Cozens, who was under Monro's care, and it may have been through the Monro Academy that Amelia Long was first introduced to Girtin.

Amelia Long's relationship with the portrait painter Henry Edridge (1769–1821) was even closer. Another member of the Monro circle, he was an important influence on her studies of natural foliage and vegetation, which were mainly executed in pencil or chalk, sometimes with charcoal. His style is also apparent in a series of picturesque continental townscapes in soft ground etching, the result of three visits to France and Holland between 1815 and 1819 (British Museum, London). During her earliest visit, at the height of the Napoleonic war, Amelia Long also painted the British troops at St Cloud (Fairhaven collection, Anglesey. Surviving sketchbooks—in the Victoria and Albert Museum in London and in Perth Museum and Art Gallery—show that Long otherwise confined her travels to the south of England. The limited number of oil paintings which she appears to have executed are serene, somewhat Italianate landscapes: contemporaries commented on their Corotesque and Wilsonic qualities. Watercolour, however, remained her favourite medium and Bromley Hill Place the subject depicted more than any other, as is evidenced by her *Views of Bromley Hill*, twelve soft ground etchings, now held in the British Museum, London. As a mark of the respect which she commanded among fellow artists, she was made an honorary exhibitor at the Royal Academy from 1807 to 1822 and at the British Institution in 1825. Lady Farnborough died at Bromley Hill Place on 15 January 1837, and was buried at St Lawrence's Church, Wormley, Hertfordshire. She is now recognized as one of the talented group of amateur women watercolourists who made a vital contribution to early English watercolour painting. TESSA SIDEY

Sources T. Sidey, *Amelia Long, Lady Farnborough, 1772–1837* [1980] [exhibition catalogue, Dundee Museums and Art Galleries] • J. L. Roget, *A history of the 'Old Water-Colour' Society*, 2 vols. (1891) • Graves, *RA exhibitors* • J. Egerton, *The British school* (1998) • G. Cumberland, *Bromley Hill, the seat of the Right Hon. Charles Long, MP*, 2nd edn (1816) • *The Farington diary*, ed. J. Greig, 8 vols. (1922–8) • S. R. Redgrave, *A history of water-colour painting in England* (1892) • M. Clarke, *The tempting prospect* (1981) • I. O. Williams, *Early English watercolours and some cognate drawings by artists born not later than 1785* (1952) • E. L. S. Horsburgh, *Bromley, Kent* (1929) • GEC, *Peerage* • monument, St Lawrence's Church, Wormley, Hertfordshire

Archives Bromley Central Library

Likenesses H. Edridge, engraving, *c.*1809, Bromley Public Library • H. Edridge, pencil with watercolour, *c.*1820, priv. coll. • S. W. Reynolds, mezzotint (after H. Edridge), BM

Long, Ann (1681?–1711), celebrated beauty, was born, probably in 1681, at Draycot Cerne, Wiltshire, the daughter of James Long (*d. c.*1690) and his wife, Susan, *née* Strangways. She was the granddaughter of Sir James Long, second baronet (1617–1692), the royalist soldier and politician, and of another leading civil war politician, Giles *Strangways (1615–1675). She was educated privately and never married. Most of what is known about her comes from Jonathan Swift, who admired her greatly, although their relationship never had the same intensity as those Swift had with Esther Johnson and Esther Vanhomrigh.

Ann Long may have first emerged as a famous figure in London society as early as 1703. She became a toast of the Kit-Cat Club and her name was engraved on the club's drinking glasses by Thomas Wharton, earl of Wharton:

> Fill the glass; let Hautboys sound
> Whilst bright Longy's health goes round
> With eternal beauty blest
> Ever blooming, still the best;
> Drink your glass, and think the rest.
> (*DNB*)

Her closest associate was Catherine Barton (*d.* 1739), niece of Sir Isaac Newton, who was rumoured to be the mistress of Charles Montagu, earl of Halifax, and later married the politician John Conduitt. She first met Swift in 1707 at the London home of her probable relatives the Vanhomrighs. In December 1707 or January 1708 Swift wrote 'A decree for concluding the treaty between Dr Swift and Mrs Long', published by Edmund Curll in *Letters, Poems and Tales: Amorous, Satyrical, and Gallant* in 1718. Her position in society was financially sustained by debts contracted against an inheritance expected from her grandmother Dorothy, *née* Leach, Lady Long, but Lady Long did not die until 1710. In September of that year Ann Long dissolved her London household and, to hold off her creditors, fled to King's Lynn, Norfolk, where she lived near St Nicholas's Chapel and passed herself off as 'being of George Smyth's family of Nitly' (*Correspondence of Jonathan Swift*, 1.274). Her grandmother's death did not improve her situation, as her brother Sir James Long, fifth baronet, withheld her legacy.

Ann Long's imprudence with money did not damage Swift's regard for her. He even used her as a confidante in his slowly and tortuously developing passion for Esther Vanhomrigh, his Vanessa. On one occasion, wishing to drop a gentle hint to Vanessa about her behaviour but not wishing to do it openly in case she might be offended, he hit on the device of addressing a letter about her to Ann but sending it via Vanessa, conveniently forgetting to seal the enclosure; thus Vanessa gets to know what he thinks about her but cannot protest or remonstrate, since to do so she would have to confess that she had read his private letter.

Ann Long's life must have become lonely after her exile to King's Lynn, although in her letters to Swift she enjoyed 'describing the rituals of provincial life and the mysterious figure that she cut there' (Nokes, 142). Only once did Swift turn against her, writing on 11 December 1710 that 'I had a letter from Mrs. Long, that has quite turned my stomach against her: no less than two nasty jests in it with dashes to suppose them. She is corrupted in that country town with vile conversation' (Swift, *Journal to Stella*, 1.118–19).

In late 1711, by careful management of her £100 annuity and £60 rental from 'Newburg-house' (Swift, *Journal to*

Stella, 2.446) in London, Ann Long had almost paid her debts and hoped to be able to leave King's Lynn. However, she was by this time suffering from asthma and from dropsy, and she died in King's Lynn on 22 December. The news reached Swift in London on 25 December, when he arrived at the Vanhomrighs' house for Christmas dinner: 'I never was more afflicted at any death … She had all sorts of amiable qualities, and no ill ones but the indiscretion of neglecting her own affairs' (ibid., 2.445–6). Swift suspected that Ann's brother intended to keep her death a secret to avoid the expense of a London funeral or public mourning. A notice of her death was placed by Swift in *The Post-Boy* of 27 December. Swift also wrote to the minister of St Nicholas's Chapel, Thomas Pyle, revealing Ann's true identity and asking that she be buried in the church and that a memorial stone be placed there at Swift's expense. Swift's private commemoration of Ann Long, entered in his account book, was perhaps his most eloquent appreciation of her: 'She was the most beautifull Person of the Age, she lived in, of great Honr and Virtue, infinite Sweetness and Generosity of Temper and true good Sense' (ibid., 1.277n.). ERIC SALMON

Sources I. Ehrenpreis, *Swift: the man, his works and the age*, 3 vols. (1962–83) · D. Nokes, *Jonathan Swift: a hypocrite reversed* (1985) · E. Hardy, *The conjured spirit* (1949) · J. Swift, *Journal to Stella*, ed. H. Williams, 2 vols. (1948) · *The correspondence of Jonathan Swift*, ed. H. Williams, 5 vols. (1963–5) · *DNB* · GEC, *Baronetage*

Long [*née* Walpole], **Lady Catharine** (**1797–1867**), religious writer, was the youngest child of the seven daughters and four sons of Horatio Walpole, second earl of Orford (1757–1822), and his wife, Sophia, *née* Churchill (*d.* 1797). Little is known of her early life, but on 25 July 1822 she married Henry Lawes Long of Hampton Lodge, Surrey. They had seven daughters and a son, and most of her writing appears to date from after her marriage.

Long's novels were religious in focus, although this did not insure her against adverse criticism. Her *Sir Roland Ashton: a Tale of the Times* (1844), a novel directed against the Tractarian movement, was described as 'feeble and second-rate' by an *Athenaeum* reviewer who felt that fiction was not 'a good medium for religious instruction' (*Athenaeum*, 24 Aug 1844, 771). She continued to work in this genre with some popularity, however, as she went on to write novels such as *The First Lieutenant's Story* (1853), favourably reviewed by the *London Daily News*. Both *Roland Ashton* and this later novel were reprinted in Routledge's cheap series in the mid 1850s.

Long also wrote pieces of music and poetry such as an Agnus Dei for four or five voices in 1848, and 'He is not dead, he cannot die', an elegy set to music upon the death of Prince Albert. Her collection of inspirational praise and verse, *The Midsummer Souvenir* (1846), contained original pieces, as well as selections from Felicia Hemans, Sarah Stickney Ellis, and other popular authors.

Lady Catharine Long died suddenly from heart failure after being alarmed by a thunderstorm at Landthorne Hatch, Farnham, Surrey, on 20 August 1867.

A. F. POLLARD, *rev.* MEGAN A. STEPHAN

Sources *The Athenaeum* (24 Aug 1844), 771 · Allibone, *Dict.* · Burke, *Peerage* (1907) · *GM*, 4th ser., 4 (1867), 408
Archives Cumbria AS, family corresp.
Likenesses J. Cochran, stipple (after A. E. Chalon), BM; repro. in *The Court Magazine*, 3 vols. (1832)

Long, Charles, **Baron Farnborough** (**1760–1838**), politician and connoisseur of the arts, was born in the City of London in January 1760, the fourth son of Beeston Long, the head of a well-known firm of West Indies merchants in the City. A senior branch of the family, established at Hurts Hall in Suffolk, had owned an estate in Jamaica since the conquest of the island in 1665. His mother, Sarah, was the daughter of Abraham Crop, another wealthy City merchant. Long was educated at a private school in Greenwich and at Emmanuel College, Cambridge, where he matriculated in 1779, but is not known to have taken a degree. Simultaneously he was entered at the Inner Temple, where he had chambers in Tanfield Court. From 1786 to 1788 he made the grand tour, exploring Rome under the tutelage of James Byres, and laying the foundation of his art collection.

Long's involvement in politics as a friend and ally of William Pitt, whom he had met at Cambridge, is attested as early as 1788, when he was canvassing for Lord Hood, the ministerial candidate in the Westminster election; and in January 1789 he himself entered parliament as member for Rye, a seat under Treasury control. He subsequently sat as member for Midhurst (1796–1802) and for Wendover (1802–6)—boroughs whose parliamentary representatives were nominated by Pitt's friend Lord Carrington—and for Haslemere (1806–26), where the Pittite earl of Lonsdale was sole patron. In 1791 he became junior secretary to the Treasury, in that capacity acting as parliamentary whip and teller and in 1796 undertaking much of the management of the general election on the government's behalf. In 1801 he insisted on following Pitt out of office, and was rewarded with a pension of £1500 per annum. At Pitt's behest he was prepared to advise Addington on Treasury matters and in 1802 was sworn of the privy council. In the following year he was the chief intermediary in negotiations between Pitt and Addington, which took place in his house at Bromley Hill in Kent. On Pitt's return to power in 1804 Long was made a lord of the Treasury (1804–6) and then chief secretary to the lord lieutenant of Ireland (1805–6). After Pitt's death in 1806 he took office in the Portland ministry as paymaster-general of the forces, a post which he retained until his retirement from politics in 1826. As a politician Long's ambitions were modest. 'Few persons', he told Lonsdale in 1809, 'have quitted an office with more reluctance than I retain mine.' He did not consider himself 'either disposed or fit for a cabinet office', and refused both the chancellorship of the exchequer and the secretaryship at war when they were offered to him by Perceval. He rarely spoke in the house except on matters arising from his ministerial responsibilities, and was a loyal and efficient political adjutant rather than an initiator of policy. He was the author of pamphlets on the French Revolution (1795) and the price of bread (1800), and in 1792 was instrumental, with Sir

Charles Long, Baron Farnborough (1760–1838), by Henry Edridge, 1805

James Bland Burges, in the foundation of the *Sun* newspaper as a tory organ. In 1820 Long was made a Knight of the Bath by George IV, and on his retirement from political life in 1826 he was created a peer with the title of Baron Farnborough (a village in Kent near his country residence). He was elected FRS in 1792, FSA in 1812, and was given an honorary LLD by his old university in 1833.

Long's real passion was for the arts. His resources were too small to allow him to be a major patron or collector in his own right, but as a minister and MP he used his influence to further artistic causes such as the purchase of the Elgin marbles and the establishment of the National Gallery. In 1792 it was he who acted as intermediary between Pitt and Humphry Repton over the improvement of the former's grounds at Holwood, and when the Altieri Claudes were brought to England in 1799 it was in Long's house in Grosvenor Place that they were first exhibited to English connoisseurs. In subsequent years his name appears repeatedly in connection with the public patronage of the arts. In 1802 he was the chairman of the committee of taste appointed to supervise the erection of monuments to the heroes of the Napoleonic wars, whose responsibilities were in 1809 extended to the repair (with money voted by parliament) of Henry VII's chapel at Westminster. Whether it was the appropriate order for the façade of the privy council offices in Whitehall (1824) or the need for a fig-leaf on the heroic statue honouring the duke of Wellington that had been subscribed for by the ladies of Great Britain (1821), Long was sure to be consulted. Such was his reputation as an arbiter of taste that in 1834, when steps were being taken to establish an Institution of British Architects, it was in the form of an open *Letter to Lord Farnborough* that the campaign was opened. He was an active trustee both of the British Museum and of the National Gallery (in whose establishment he played an important role) and as deputy director of the British Institution (or British Gallery) he was for many years a leading figure in its affairs.

Long's advice on artistic matters was valued at the highest level. Both as prince regent and as king, George IV frequently consulted him over the commissioning of architecture, painting, and sculpture. In Mrs Arbuthnot's opinion Long was 'a complete courtier, [who] always acquiesces in any thing the King says & never dares contest a point with him', but the prince's secretary told Farington that in matters of art, 'The Prince Regent saw through Mr. Long's spectacles'. It was Long who negotiated royal commissions with artists such as Canova, Westmacott, and Lawrence, and who (for instance) told the last of the prince's wishes that he should go to Rome to paint the portrait of Pope Pius VII for the Waterloo Chamber at Windsor. When the king determined to reconstruct Windsor Castle, Long drew up a detailed brief which envisaged every important feature of the castle as subsequently remodelled by Wyatville, from the heightening of the keep to the formation of the Grand Corridor, and he also suggested the sunken garden below the east terrace, for which he made a sketch-plan in 1823.

Long's own country villa at Bromley Hill in Kent, only a few miles from Pitt's at Holwood, was an elegant enlargement of an earlier house which he bought in 1801. Drawings made by Buckler at various dates between 1815 and 1835 (BL, Add. MS 36367, fols. 181–92) show a villa irregularly composed in the Italianate manner with neoclassical interiors. The extensive grounds were progressively improved to create a much-admired garden which by 1809 offered two picturesque walks, each a mile long, and a distant view of the dome of St Paul's Cathedral. Here Long entertained George IV, William IV, and Queen Adelaide, and here he died, childless, on 17 January 1838, leaving to the National Gallery paintings by Rubens, Vandyck, Canaletto, Teniers, Mola, Cuyp, and others.

As a young man Long had a mistress called Sophia Tarleton who died in Paris in 1789 or 1790, claiming that he had secretly married her. On 28 May 1793 he married Amelia [*see* Long, Amelia], daughter of Sir Abraham *Hume of Wormleybury, Hertfordshire; she died in January 1837. Lord and Lady Farnborough were both buried at Wormley church, where they are commemorated by a monument by Westmacott. HOWARD COLVIN

Sources J. F., 'Memoirs of the North and Long Families', *GM*, 1st ser., 99/1 (1829), 207–8, 417–18 • *GM*, 2nd ser., 9 (1838), 425–6 • HoP, *Commons, 1790–1820*, 4.448–52 • Farington, *Diary*, 6.182 • *The journal of Mrs Arbuthnot, 1820–1832*, ed. F. Bamford and the duke of Wellington [G. Wellesley], 1 (1950), 419 • W. T. Whitley, *Artists and their friends in England, 1700–1799*, 2 vols. (1928) • W. T. Whitley, *Art in England, 1800–1820* (1928); *Art in England, 1821–1837* (1930) • J. M. Crook and M. H. Port, eds., *The history of the king's works*, 6 (1973) • A. Aspinall, *Politics and the press, c.1780–1850* (1949), 78–9 • G. Cumberland, *Bromley-Hill* (1816) • E. L. S. Horsburgh, *History of Bromley* (1929), 240–46 • *IGI* • PRO, PROB 11/1893, fol. 238

Archives Birm. CA, letters to Boulton family • BL, corresp. with Lord Auckland, Add. MSS 34455–34456 • BL, corresp. with Jeremy Bentham, Add. MSS 33541–33543 • BL, letters to George Cumberland, Add. MSS 36492–36516, *passim* • BL, corresp. with Lord Harwicke, Add. MSS 35648–35768, *passim* • BL, corresp. with earls of Liverpool, loan 72 • BL, corresp. with Sir Robert Peel, Add. MSS 40222–40605, *passim* • Cumbria AS, Carlisle, letters to earls of Lonsdale • Glos. RO, letters to Lord Redesdale • NA Scot., letters to viscounts Melville • RA, corresp. with Thomas Lawrence

Likenesses H. Edridge, pencil drawing, 1805, NPG [*see illus.*] • J. Hoppner, oils, 1807, Tate collection • F. Chantrey, marble bust, 1820, NPG; copy, Powis Castle • F. Chantrey, marble bust, 1836, National Gallery, London • F. Chantrey, pencil drawing, NPG • G. Hayter, group portrait, oils (*The trial of Queen Caroline, 1820*), NPG • J. Heath, line engraving (after G. Chinnery), BM, NPG • P. C. Wonder, group portrait (*Patrons and lovers of art, 1826*), NPG

Wealth at death see will, PRO, PROB 11/1893, fol. 238

Long, Charles Edward (1796–1861), genealogist and antiquary, born on 28 July 1796 at Benham Park, Berkshire, was the elder and only surviving son of Charles Beckford Long (*d.* 1836) of Langley Hall in the same county and his wife, Frances Monro, daughter and heir of Lucius Tucker of Norfolk Street, Park Lane, London. Edward *Long (1734–1813), the historian of Jamaica, was his grandfather. Long was educated at Harrow School (1810–14) and at Trinity College, Cambridge (1815–19), where he gained a declamation prize. In July 1818 he won the chancellor's gold medal for English verse on the subject of imperial and papal Rome. He graduated BA in 1819 and MA in 1822. Possessed of an ample fortune, Long devoted himself to historical and genealogical studies, which were greatly facilitated by the access to the College of Heralds granted him by his uncle by marriage Lord Henry Molyneux Howard, deputy earl marshal.

Long always maintained a personal and scholarly interest in Harrow and materially assisted George Butler in his biographical notes to the lists of Harrow scholars (1849). In 1860 he wrote on the life of John Lyon (1514–1592), the founder of the school, for the *Harrow Gazette*. Long also took a considerable interest in the history of Wiltshire: he was an earnest promoter of the archaeological society for that county, and contributed to its magazine. During many years he was a frequent correspondent of the *Gentleman's Magazine*, and the leading antiquarian periodicals of his day.

In 1845 with the assistance of Sir Charles George Young, Garter king of arms, Long compiled a volume called *Royal descents: a genealogical list of the several persons entitled to quarter the arms of the royal houses of England*. In 1859 he edited for the Camden Society, from the original manuscript in the British Museum, the *Diary of the Marches of the Royal Army during the Great Civil War, Kept by Richard Symonds*. Long also made 'Genealogical collections of Jamaica families', which he presented to the British Museum (now Add. MS 27968). During 1857–9 he gave to the museum many valuable documents relating to Jamaica, and his letters to Joseph Hunter (1783–1861), extending from 1847 to 1859, are also preserved in the British Library.

Of Long's other publications, two may be mentioned. First, his pamphlet of 1832 in which he defends the conduct of his uncle Robert Ballard *Long (1771–1825) during the campaign of 1811; and, second, his volume *Considerations on the Game Laws* (1824; 2nd edn, 1825) in which he offered a robust and thoughtful argument for regarding game as property, thereby allowing the sale of game to become a legal transaction.

Long died unmarried on 25 September 1861 at the Lord Warden Hotel, Dover, on his return from a visit to Hamburg. He was buried at Seale churchyard in Surrey.

GORDON GOODWIN, *rev.* MICHAEL ERBEN

Sources Boase, *Mod. Eng. biog.* • *GM*, 3rd ser., 11 (1861), 568–9 • Burke, *Gen. GB* • Venn, *Alum. Cant.* • Allibone, *Dict.* • *CGPLA Eng. & Wales* (1861)

Archives Bath Central Library, papers • BL, collections relating to Jamaican families, Add. MSS 27968, 21931, 22639, 22676–22680, 24870 | Bodl. Oxf., corresp. with Sir Thomas Phillipps

Wealth at death £10,000: probate, 29 Oct 1861, *CGPLA Eng. & Wales*

Long, Edward (1734–1813), planter and commentator on Jamaican affairs, was born on 23 August 1734 at Rosilion, St Blazey, Cornwall, the fourth son of Samuel Long (1700–1757) of Longville, Jamaica, Tredudwell, Cornwall, and Bloomsbury, London, and Mary (*bap.* 1701, *d.* 1765), second daughter and coheir of Bartholomew Tate of Delapré, Northamptonshire. He was educated at Bury St Edmunds School, at Liskeard (*c.*1746–1752), and at home. He entered Gray's Inn, London, on 28 June 1753. On his father's death in early 1757, Long left his law studies and sailed to Jamaica, although he was called to the bar *ex gratia*, despite not having kept terms. The Longs had been connected with Jamaica since the 1660s. Long's great-grandfather Samuel had been speaker of the Jamaican assembly and was responsible for many of its procedures. His father, Samuel, born in Jamaica, was a member of the council and the owner of Lucky Valley sugar plantation, a rich property in Clarendon parish. Long took over the running of the plantation and became the private secretary of Lieutenant-Governor Sir Henry Moore, who had married his eldest sister, Catharina Maria. He was soon promoted to the position of judge of the vice-admiralty court in Jamaica. At St Catharine's Church, Jamaica, on 12 August 1758, he married Mary Ballard (1734/5–1797), second daughter and eventually heir of Thomas Beckford of Jamaica and widow of John Palmer. They had six children—three sons (including the army officer Robert Ballard *Long) and three daughters. Edward Long was elected a member of the Jamaican assembly for St Ann parish in 1761, 1765, and 1766. On 13 September 1768 he was elected speaker of the assembly, an office he held only until the house was dissolved on 22 September. In 1769 he left Jamaica because of ill health, and he lived the rest of his life in England. He retained his judicial office in Jamaica until about 1797 but never returned to the Caribbean.

In moving to Britain, Long detached himself from the day-to-day business of running an estate and participating in Jamaican government, and allowed himself the time in which he could take a longer view of Jamaican affairs. For many years he was a member of the West India merchants' and planters' committee, and from his properties in Berkshire, Surrey, Hampshire, and Sussex, and the London house he leased at 46 Wimpole Street, Marylebone, from 1781, he wrote numerous articles for London newspapers as well as pamphlets on the sugar trade and the game laws, and after 1783 wrote regularly about imperial politics as an ally of the Foxite whigs. His most influential work, which cemented his reputation as the leading contemporary commentator on the eighteenth-century British Caribbean, was the three-volume *History of Jamaica, or, General Survey of the Antient and Modern State of that Island*, published in 1774. Based on private papers, public records, and his own experience of living in Jamaica, this is an invaluable vade-mecum to the social, economic, and political life of Britain's largest and wealthiest West Indian colony. The book combines encyclopaedic detail with polemics and propaganda; some sections are plagiarized from other writers. The meteorology, botany, zoology, medicine, history, and laws of Jamaica are all covered, but *The History of Jamaica* is mainly consulted for its political arguments and its commentary on slavery. Long argued for better schools in Jamaica, for improved military defences, for a stronger militia, for more extensive white immigration, and for a solid church foundation. A staunch supporter of the elected Jamaican assembly, he criticized the governor's power to dismiss judges and suspend the assembly and council. He was a strong pro-slavery advocate who regarded enslaved Africans as subhuman, an inferior species. He thought that transporting enslaved Africans to the Caribbean instilled order and discipline into their lives. He associated slaves with apes in terms of lechery and feared the prospect of slave revolts. He considered the slave trade a profitable business for British interests and portrayed Jamaican slavery as a benevolent institution. He supported the rights of the plantocracy against the power of the imperial government and defended their cause when faced with humanitarian objections to slavery. He also argued, however, that plantation owners were inefficient managers. In his view this deficiency could be overcome when estate owners resided in Jamaica rather than returning as absentees to Britain. Long's work influenced Bryan Edwards's *History, Civil and Commercial, of the British Colonies in the West Indies* (1793), another important contemporary work on the Caribbean. Section 2 of Edwards's book, on the origin of the maroons, was in fact taken from Long's *History of Jamaica*. Long spent much time revising his *magnum opus* for a second edition, but this was never completed. His grandson Charles Edward Long gave the British Museum the manuscript sheets of the revision along with much other material on Jamaica gathered by Edward Long.

Long was a cultivated, studious man who wanted his family to be brought up in an intellectual atmosphere. He was an accomplished musician who played a Cremona violin and displayed an interest in science, corresponding with Dr Thomas Dancer, a botanist in Jamaica. Long's wife, Mary, died on 16 July 1797, aged sixty-two; Long himself survived until 13 March 1813, dying at Arundel Park, Sussex, the seat of his son-in-law, Henry Howard-Molyneux. He was buried on 20 March in the chancel of Slindon church, Sussex, where a memorial slab commemorates him. KENNETH MORGAN

Sources R. M. Howard, *Records and letters of the family of the Longs of Longville, Jamaica, and Hampton Lodge, Surrey*, 2 vols. (1925) • E. Long, *The history of Jamaica, or, General survey of the antient and modern state of that island*, 3 vols. (1774); new edn, with introduction by G. Metcalf (1970) • E. V. Foveia, *A study on the historiography of the British West Indies to the end of the nineteenth century* (Mexico City, 1956) • A. J. Barker, *The African link: British attitudes to the negro in the era of the Atlantic slave trade, 1550–1807* (1978) • *GM*, 1st ser., 83/1 (1813), 490, 659; 83/2 (1813), 215–16 • Boase & Courtney, *Bibl. Corn.*, 1.322–3; 3.1269 • *DNB* • D. Hall, *A brief history of the West India committee* (St Lawrence, Barbados, 1971)

Archives BL, collections and memoranda, corresp. and papers relating to Jamaica, Add. MSS 12402–12414; 12429–12432; 12435; 12438; 18270–18275; 18959–18963 • Suffolk RO, Ipswich, papers, incl. deeds, plans of land, and a ledger for Jamaican estate | BL, corresp. with Thomas Dancer upon scientific matters, Add. MS 22678 • Cumbria AS, Carlisle, letters to his children [copies]

Likenesses J. Scouler, pastels, 1774, priv. coll. • W. Sharp, line engraving, pubd 1796 (after J. Opie), BM; repro. in Howard, *Records and letters*, facing p. 122 • J. Opie, portrait, priv. coll. • miniature, priv. coll. • oils, priv. coll.

Long, Edwin Longsden (1829–1891), painter, was born at Bath on 16 July 1829, the son of James Long, of a family resident in Kelston in Somerset. He was educated at Dr Charles William Viner's academy at 15 Edward Street, Bath; he then moved to London in 1846 to pursue a career as a painter and enrolled as a student at James Matthew Leigh's School of Art, then at 18 Maddox Street. He began his professional life as a portrait painter in Bath, making his début at the Royal Academy in 1855 with three distinguished portraits. Other early portraits included likenesses of celebrated figures such as Lord Ellesmere (1856, National Portrait Gallery, London) and Charles Greville (exh. RA, 1856). On 19 March 1853 he married Margaret Jemima Aiton (1834–1907).

In 1857 Long returned to London, where he was to settle the following year, and came under the influence of John Phillip with whom he visited Spain and was introduced to the work of the great Spanish masters Velázquez and Murillo, as well as to the country which was to dominate his painting for the next seventeen years. In this period his output was prolific, and he produced a large number of Spanish genre scenes. His Spanish work also includes his first history paintings such as *The Suppliants* (1872, Royal Holloway and Bedford New College, University of London, Egham, Surrey) and *The Moorish Proselytes* (1873, Russell-Cotes Art Gallery and Museum, Bournemouth) which were significant markers in establishing him as a serious artist. The rise in his reputation was dramatic and came with *Babylonian Marriage Market* (1875, Royal Holloway and Bedford New College, Egham), which was exhibited at the Royal Academy exhibition of 1875. He had made an extensive visit to Egypt and Syria the year before, and the work had been some time in conception. The enthusiastic critical reception was unprecedented for Long and the work ensured his associateship to the Royal Academy in January 1876.

Subsequently Long's work was characterized by highly detailed and researched depictions of the ancient world. Works such as *An Egyptian Feast* (1877, Cartwright Hall Art Gallery, Bradford), *The Gods and their Makers* (1878, Towneley Hall Art Gallery and Museum, Burnley), and *Alethe* (1888, Russell-Cotes Art Gallery and Museum, Bournemouth)—all shown at the Royal Academy—illustrate his major achievement within this area. His works often contain a strong religious sentiment reflected in scenes which contrasted the early church with ancient religions, as well as more conventional biblical scenes. His successes, evident at the Royal Academy (he was elected a full academician on 13 July 1881), were also visible in the commercial galleries in Bond Street. Several were devoted exclusively to his work: Fairless and Beeforth set up a gallery of his work to follow up the success of their Doré Gallery and showed his ambitious *Anno Domini, or, The Flight into Egypt* (1883, Russell-Cotes Art Gallery and Museum, Bournemouth). Thomas Agnew & Sons, meanwhile, commissioned many works from him, including a series of twenty paintings entitled Daughters of Our Empire to coincide with Queen Victoria's golden jubilee year of 1887.

Long's commercial success was reflected in his lifestyle: he commissioned two grand studio houses from the fashionable architect Richard Norman Shaw, built next to one another in Hampstead. He did not have the personality of a natural celebrity, being a small and quiet man with a gentle disposition. M. H. Spielmann in his article in *The Graphic* of 1888 described him as 'reticent and retiring' (Spielmann, 612), while Julian Hawthorne in *Shapes that Pass* (1928) remembered him as a 'thin, unobtrusive man, with a brown beard, gentle of speech' (Hawthorne, 251). Long died of pneumonia caused by influenza on 15 May 1891 at his home, Kelston, 42 Netherhall Gardens, Hampstead, London, and was buried at Hampstead cemetery on 22 May. He left three sons, a daughter, and a bitterly contested fortune of about £120,000. His widow, Margaret Long, set up the Edwin Long Gallery at 25 Old Bond Street in 1893 to revitalize interest in his work. The principal public collection of his works is now in the Russell-Cotes Art Gallery and Museum in Bournemouth.

MARK BILLS

Sources M. Bills, *Edwin Longsden Long RA* (1998) • M. H. Spielmann, 'Painters in their studios, II—Mr Edwin Long', *The Graphic* (9 June 1888), 612–14 • R. Quick, *The life and works of Edwin Long R.A.* (1931) • A. Chester, 'The art of Edwin Long R.A.', *Windsor Magazine*, 27/158 (Feb 1908), 332–50 • *ILN* (6 May 1876) • *ILN* (23 May 1891), 667 • *The Times* (16 May 1891) • *Art Journal*, new ser., 11 (1891), 222 • *Magazine of Art*, 14 (1890–91), xl • *Daily Graphic* (16–18 May 1891) • *The Athenaeum* (23 May 1891), 676 • G. Walkley, *Artists' studio houses in London, 1764–1914* (1994) • G. A. Sala, *'Anno domini', painted by Edwin Long R.A., also 'Zeuxis at Crotona' etc.* (1885) [exhibition catalogue, Lawrence Gallery, London] • F. W. Farrar, *Descriptive catalogue of the pictures of the late Edwin Long RA* (1894) [exhibition catalogue, Edwin Long Gallery, London] • J. Hawthorne, *Shapes that pass* (1928) • m. cert.

Archives Courtauld Inst., Witt Library • National Gallery of Victoria, Melbourne, archive • RA • Royal Holloway College, Egham, Surrey • V&A, NAL

Likenesses C. B. Birch, pencil drawing, 1858, NPG • wood-engraving, 1876 (after photograph by C. Watkins), repro. in *ILN* (6 May 1876) • P. Renouard, drawing, 1888, repro. in *The Graphic* (9 June 1888) • R. W. Robinson, photograph, NPG; repro. in *Members and associates of the Royal Academy of Arts, 1891* (1892) • photograph, repro. in *Art Journal* • woodcut (after photograph by C. Watkins), NPG; repro. in *Year-book of Celebrities*

Wealth at death £74,411 8*s*.: probate, 24 June 1891, *CGPLA Eng. & Wales* [revoked by decree, Dec 1892] • estimated at £120,000—personal estate of £90,000; real estate of £20,000

Long, George (1780–1868), police magistrate, was the second son of Joseph Long of Shopwick, near Chichester, Sussex. He practised as an attorney in London and on 6 February 1806 he was admitted to Gray's Inn. He was called to the bar on 11 February 1811. He joined the home circuit and attended the Sussex sessions as a special pleader. In 1839 he was appointed a magistrate at Great Marlborough Street police court. From 1840 until 1842 he was recorder of Coventry. In 1841 he was transferred to Marylebone police court. He retired in 1859, by that time a bencher of his inn, and died on 26 June 1868 at his London home, 51 Queen Anne Street, Cavendish Square. He left a widow, Matilda Long.

Long wrote several legal works, including one relating to the sale of personal property, and another on poor relief. He also wrote texts on moral and religious matters.

GORDON GOODWIN, *rev.* ERIC METCALFE

Sources *Law List* • *The Times* (29 June 1868) • *CGPLA Eng. & Wales* (1868)

Wealth at death under £14,000: probate, 10 July 1868, *CGPLA Eng. & Wales*

Long, George (1800–1879), classical scholar, was born at Poulton, Lancashire, on 4 November 1800, the eldest of four children of James Long, a West Indies merchant, and his wife, Isabel Brodbelt. Educated at Macclesfield grammar school, he wanted to enter the army, but on the death of his father it was decided that he should seek his fortune at Cambridge, where he entered Trinity College as a sizar in 1818. In 1821 he was bracketed Craven scholar with T. B. Macaulay and Henry Malden. He graduated BA in 1822 as thirtieth wrangler and senior chancellor's medallist; in 1823 he was members' prizeman, and gained a fellowship at Trinity over the heads of Macaulay and Malden. In 1824 he was chosen professor of ancient languages in the new University of Virginia where Thomas Jefferson (third president of the United States) was rector. Long was a frequent guest of Jefferson who called him 'the boy professor'. He developed a deep love for America, marrying there in 1827 Harriet *née* Gray (*d.* 1841), widow of Lieutenant-Colonel Joseph Selden, judge of the supreme court of Arkansas. They had four sons and a daughter who died in infancy.

In 1828, at the invitation of Lord Brougham, Long returned to England as professor of Greek in the newly founded University of London (afterwards University College, London). His 1830 lectures, published as *Observations on the Study of the Latin and Greek Languages*, are of interest as an early instance of the use of the comparative method in classical philology. Long held the Greek chair until August 1831 when he resigned in protest at the dismissal of Professor G. S. Pattison and became editor of the radical *Quarterly Journal of Education* (10 vols., 1831–5), published by the

George Long (1800–1879), by unknown photographer, 1871

Society for the Diffusion of Useful Knowledge (SDUK), of whose committee Long was an active member. He made the *Quarterly Journal* a champion for the reform of secondary education, attacking the public schools and calling for new schools to meet the needs of the middle classes. He was later a supporter of the Central Society of Education. Long had a special interest in geography. In 1830 he was one of the founders of the Royal Geographical Society and was for many years a member of the council, serving as honorary secretary from 1846 to 1848. He wrote a paper on its teaching to *The Schoolmaster* (1836), and contributed to volumes 3 and 12 of the Royal Geographical Society's *Journal*, and to William Smith's *Dictionary of Greek and Roman Geography*. He edited for the SDUK *The Geography of America and the West Indies* (1841) and wrote with G. R. Porter *The Geography of Great Britain* (1850). His *Atlas of Classical Geography* (1854) and smaller *Grammar School Atlas of Classical Geography* became standard works.

From 1833 to 1846 Long was engaged on the laborious task of editing for the SDUK the twenty-nine volumes of the *Penny Cyclopaedia*. He was himself an extensive contributor and an unwearied editor, the regular issue of the monthly parts being never interrupted. He simultaneously contributed to the SDUK's *Biographical Dictionary* (7 vols., 1842–4; the letter 'A' only). In 1842 Long became professor of Latin in University College, in succession to his great friend and former colleague at Virginia, Thomas Hewitt Key. He resigned the chair in 1846, and for a short time was lecturer on jurisprudence and civil law in the Middle Temple, having been called to the bar at the Inner Temple in 1837. He wrote all the articles on Roman law in William Smith's *Dictionary of Greek and Roman Antiquities* (1842) and published in 1847 *Two Discourses on Roman Law*. In his knowledge of Roman law he stood alone among English scholars of his time, and he contributed greatly to the revival of its study in England. But that lay in the future.

Exasperated by the indifference of his students, who were not then obliged to attend law lectures, and by the lack of encouragement which the Middle Temple authorities gave to his teaching, Long became a schoolmaster. From 1849 until midsummer 1871 he held the position of classical lecturer at Brighton College, a new school founded on progressive lines. There he found his métier, applying the principles he had advocated in the *Quarterly Journal*. He used visual aids and insisted that a classical author be read as a modern one. An inspiring teacher, he was revered and held in affection by his pupils. He established for the infant school a formidable reputation in classical scholarship. Those years also produced his most important books. He edited various Latin texts, notably for the Grammar School Classics series. In conjunction with Brighton's principal, Revd Arthur J. Macleane (*d.* 1858), he established and edited the Bibliotheca Classica, contributing himself an edition of Cicero's *Orations* (4 vols., 1851–8). He also published an admirable translation of Marcus Aurelius with the title *Thoughts on the Emperor M. Aurelius Antonius* (1862) and began the publication of his reflective but vigorous *Decline of the Roman Republic* (5 vols., 1864–74). In his *Essays in Criticism* Matthew Arnold praised Long for treating Roman history 'not as a dead and dry matter of learning', but as having 'a side of modern applicability and living interest'. During the American Civil War Long staunchly supported the South and the 1869 edition of his *Marcus Aurelius* commended Robert E. Lee. Later Long urged Lee 'to write his "Commentaries" to stand beside those of Caesar'.

In 1871 Long retired to Portfield, near Chichester, 'to tend my little garden and rose trees'. He lived a frugal life with his parrot George, his dog Caesar, and his housekeeper, Esther Lawrence, who was an executor of his will and is buried in his grave. In 1873 he was granted a civil-list pension of £100 a year for his services to learning. He once confessed that 'I live for my pen', but in old age complained ruefully that it 'never made me a living'; at one time his Cambridge medal was in pawn. Although he was said to have married three times, it is probable that he was only married twice; his second wife, of German extraction, ran off with one of his Brighton College pupils. Long died on 10 August 1879 at 2 Rhine Villas, Portfield, near Chichester, after six months' illness. He was buried at Portfield cemetery. A memorial tablet was erected at Brighton College, and a scholarship established there in his memory.

As a teacher and writer Long exercised much influence on classical scholarship in England, which he wanted to save from 'dusty pedantry'. He was a man of extensive learning, gifted with a powerful memory and 'a clear judicial intellect'. He was even more remarkable for a rare simplicity, elevation, and integrity of life. 'No one', an obituarist remarked, 'ever lived the life recommended by Marcus Aurelius more completely' (*Spectator*, 23 Aug 1879). W. W. WROTH, *rev.* MARTIN D. W. JONES

Sources H. J. Mathews, 'In Memoriam. George Long', *Brighton College Magazine*, 3 (1879–80), 154–76 • *Letters of George Long*, ed. T. Fitz-Hugh (1917) • G. Long, *An old man's thoughts about many things* (1862) • J. S. Cotton, *The Academy* (23 Aug 1879), 140 • *The Athenaeum* (23 Aug 1879), 239–40 • C. Knight, ed., *The English cyclopaedia: biography*, 6 vols. (1856–8) [suppl. (1872)] • *Encyclopaedia Britannica*, 9th edn (1875–89) • *Alumni Bulletin of the University of Virginia*, 17 (July 1924), 355–9 [bibliography] • *Recollections of Thomas Graham Jackson*, ed. B. H. Jackson (1950) • H. H. Bellot, *University College, London, 1826–1926* (1929) • P. A. Bruce, *The history of the University of Virginia, 1819–1919*, 5 vols. (*c.*1920–1922) • B. Simon, *Studies in the history of education* (1960)

Archives Brighton Reference Library • University of Virginia, Alderman Library | Cumbria AS, Carlisle, letters to John Burton • Duke U., Perkins L., letters to Henry Tutwiler • DWL, letters to Henry Crabb Robinson • UCL, letters to Society for the Diffusion of Useful Knowledge

Likenesses two photographs, *c.*1860–1871, priv. coll. [*see illus.*]

Wealth at death under £200: resworn probate, June 1881, *CGPLA Eng. & Wales* (1880)

Long, Sir James, second baronet (*bap.* **1617**, *d.* **1692**), politician, was the only son of Sir Walter Long (*b.* in or before 1594, *d.* 1637) of Draycot Cerne, Wiltshire, and his first wife, Lady Anne Ley (*d.* 1627), second daughter of James *Ley, first earl of Marlborough, and nephew of Sir Robert Long, later chancellor of the exchequer to Charles II. He was born at South Wraxall, Wiltshire, and baptized at Bradford-on-Avon on 12 January 1617. He may have travelled in France before being admitted to Lincoln's Inn in 1634. In the following year he was settled with jointure lands at his marriage to a daughter of Sir William Dodington, and at his father's death in 1637 he inherited the bulk of the Wiltshire estate, including Draycot House. His first wife had died by 1640, when he married Dorothy Leach (*d.* 1710), a daughter of Sir Edward Leach of Shipley, Derbyshire, a master in chancery.

In 1642 Long became a captain in Sir Thomas Glemham's royalist regiment of horse. By 1644 he had risen to the rank of colonel in Sir Francis Dodington's brigade, and in the same year was appointed sheriff of Wiltshire in the king's interest. Early in 1645 he escorted the prince of Wales to Bristol, and was leisurely returning eastwards when, on 12 March 1645, he was overtaken by a superior force of parliamentarians under Waller and Cromwell at Devizes. Retreating to Bath while hotly pursued by Waller, he was intercepted near Potterne by Cromwell, who suddenly appeared before him with an advance guard, and the high thickset hedges prevented his escape. Long was captured and of his 400 horse only some thirty succeeded in getting away. Clarendon ascribed the disaster to Long's 'great defect of courage and conduct' (Clarendon, *Hist. rebellion*, 4.12). He was soon exchanged, and in August 1645 captured Chippenham. On 4 May 1649 he was allowed to compound for his estates at the Goldsmiths' Hall, the assessment being fixed at £300. He thereupon paid his fine of £714 and sued out his pardon. Shortly afterwards, or so Aubrey relates, 'Oliver, Protector, hawking at Hounslow Heath, discoursing with him, fell in love with his company, and commanded him to weare his sword, and to meet him a hawkeeing, which made the strict cavaliers look on him with an evill eye' (*Brief Lives*, 2.37).

In 1673, by the death of his uncle Sir Robert Long, James succeeded to the baronetcy and estates in Yorkshire. He was admirably adapted for a country gentleman's life, if Aubrey is to be believed; he states that, in addition to his intellectual attainments—recognized by his election as a fellow of the Royal Society in 1663—Long was a 'good swordsman, great memorie, great falconer and for horsemanship. For insects exceedingly curious and searching long since in naturall things'. He was also something of an antiquary: in a letter to Aubrey in 1688, preserved in the Bodleian Library, Long describes a number of Roman coins found at Heddington, Wiltshire. In the same year he wrote a short account of his family history, which is preserved in Wotton's *Baronetage* (1771). Long often went hawking near Avebury, occasionally in the company of Aubrey, who once noted that 'our sport was very good … but the flight of the falcons was but a parenthesis to the colonell's facetious discourse, who was "tam Marti, tam Mercurio", and the Muses did accompany him with his hawkes and spaniells' (*Wiltshire: the Topographical Collections*, 315–16). Aubrey avers that Long wrote a great work, the 'History and causes of the civill war', as well as a tract entitled 'Examinations of witches at Malmesbury', but neither work appears to survive. His letters to Aubrey 'mention astrology, witchcraft and natural magic; he hoped to combine an account of these with conjectures concerning unicorns and a natural history of animals in a demonstration of God's wisdom in the creation' (Hunter, 135). In 1690 Edward Wells dedicated to Long his geographical table.

Long represented Malmesbury in the three exclusion parliaments, 1679–81, and again from 1690 until his death. Considered 'moderately active' in the 1679 parliaments, he was, by 1681, 'clearly an opponent of exclusion' (Henning, 2.758). By 1688 he gave his opinion in favour of repeal of penal laws and James II's agents reported, and supported, his proposed election for Wiltshire in that year. After his election in 1690 he 'was regarded as "doubtful" by the Government' (Henning, 2.758). He died in London, reportedly of an apoplexy, on the night of 22–23 January 1692. His body was carried to Draycot, where it was buried in the family vault on 3 February.

By his second marriage Long had four daughters and one son, James, who died in his father's lifetime, leaving, by his first marriage to Susan, daughter of Colonel Giles Strangways of Melbury, Dorset, three sons—Robert, Giles, and James—who were successively baronets. James, Long's grandson, became fifth baronet in 1697, and was admitted to Balliol College, Oxford, on 1 February 1699. From 1705 he was MP successively for Chippenham, Wootton Bassett, and Wiltshire, until his death on 16 March 1729. His elder sister was Ann *Long, friend of Jonathan Swift. THOMAS SECCOMBE, *rev.* HENRY LANCASTER

Sources G. D. Squibb, ed., *Wiltshire visitation pedigrees, 1623*, Harleian Society, 105–6 (1954) • *Wiltshire: the topographical collections of John Aubrey*, ed. J. E. Jackson, Wiltshire Archaeological and Natural

History Society, 1 (1862) · N. Luttrell, *A brief historical relation of state affairs from September 1678 to April 1714*, 6 vols. (1857) · J. Burke and J. B. Burke, *A genealogical and heraldic history of the extinct and dormant baronetcies of England, Ireland and Scotland*, 2nd edn (1841); repr. (1844) · E. Peacock, ed., *The army lists of the roundheads and cavaliers* (1863) · M. A. E. Green, ed., *Calendar of the proceedings of the committee for advance of money, 1642–1656*, 1–2, PRO (1888), 624, 983 · *Brief lives, chiefly of contemporaries, set down by John Aubrey, between the years 1669 and 1696*, ed. A. Clark, 2 vols. (1898) · M. Hunter, *The Royal Society and its fellows, 1660–1700: the morphology of an early scientific institution*, 2nd edn (1994) · *The memoirs of Edmund Ludlow*, ed. C. H. Firth, 2 vols. (1894) · W. P. Baildon, ed., *The records of the Honorable Society of Lincoln's Inn: admissions*, 2 vols. (1896) · Clarendon, *Hist. rebellion* · C. H. Firth and G. Davies, *The regimental history of Cromwell's army*, 2 vols. (1940) · T. Wotton, *The baronetage of England*, ed. E. Kimber and R. Johnson, 3 vols. (1771) · B. D. Henning, 'Long, Sir James', HoP, *Commons, 1660–90*, 2.757–8 · M. Hunter, *John Aubrey and the realm of learning* (1975) · parish register, Bradford-on-Avon [baptism], 12/1/1617 · BL, Add. MS 37047, fol. 242

Archives BL, letters to John Aubrey, MS Aubrey 12

Likenesses oils, NPG

Wealth at death at least five Wiltshire manors; £3500 portions for two granddaughters: will, PRO, PROB 11/409, fol. 326

Long, James (1814–1887), missionary and Indian scholar, was born in Bandon, co. Cork, the eldest son of John Long, clerk and Methodist local preacher. While a pupil at Bandon grammar school he excelled in classics and developed an interest in languages. He also came under the influence of the evangelical revival of the time, and was converted at a Wesleyan Methodist meeting at the age of fourteen—an experience which determined the direction of his future career. After volunteering for service with the Church Missionary Society (CMS) in 1838, he was sent to its training institution at Islington, London, where he impressed the principal, the Revd C. F. Childe, with his extensive knowledge of languages. He was ordained deacon in the Church of England in 1839 and priest in the following year, shortly before his departure for India in July 1840. He acted as superintendent of the CMS Anglo-vernacular school at Mizapore, Calcutta, for most of the period between 1840 and 1849. He married Emily Orme (*d.* 1867) on 10 June 1848; they had no children.

Although a friend and admirer of the Scottish missionary Dr Alexander Duff, Long became increasingly disillusioned with education through English as an instrument of evangelism and as a means of creating a class who would spread knowledge and enlightenment among the masses. While acting as pastor at Thakurpukur, a small village a few miles south of Calcutta, he experimented with methods of improving elementary vernacular education, illustrating his teaching by referring to familiar objects of everyday life and to local proverbs, metaphors, and similes. His innovative methods, emphasis on practical subjects, and introduction of a broad academic syllabus, including geography, history, and science, showed what might be done through the utilization and improvement of the traditional village system. Long's schools, acclaimed as model institutions, combined with his own arguments and lobbying of government officials, influenced the Bengal government's educational policy in the 1850s and 1860s, especially its attempts to develop the 'circle school system'. Increasingly convinced of the importance of conveying Christian 'truths' and Western scientific ideas and learning through the idiomatic language of ordinary people, Long was active on a large number of influential committees which were attempting to develop and disseminate a 'sound' vernacular literature. He was a member of the Calcutta School Book Society, the Vernacular Translation Committee, the Calcutta Auxiliary Bible Society, and the Calcutta Christian Tract and Book Society, for which he wrote an unusually sympathetic life of Muhammad founded exclusively on Arabic sources. In addition he greatly extended the work of collecting and publishing collections of Bengali proverbs and soon became the best-known authority on the subject.

Long wrote on both historical and social issues. He believed that knowledge was the basis of real sympathy and that the study of society provided essential insights into the condition of the people and a meaningful basis for both Christian mission and social improvement. He was one of the founders of sociology in India. When Duff reorganized the Bethune Society in 1860 Long pioneered the branch dealing with sociology, and when Mary Carpenter visited Bengal in 1866 Long was largely instrumental in persuading her to found a branch of the Social Science Association in Calcutta—an organization he continued to support until his retirement.

Long, whose attacks in 1859 on European racism and claims to cultural superiority infuriated some of the Europeans in Calcutta, was further involved in controversy in the 1860s. In evidence before the indigo commission of 1860 he claimed, on the basis of vernacular publications, that few words could describe the state of feeling against the European planters in the indigo districts. In 1861 he received a copy of a vernacular play, *Nil darpan, or, Mirror of Indigo*, and brought it to the attention of government officials as, in his view, it reflected feelings which he feared would lead to further violence and bloodshed. The play attacked all involved in the indigo business and was extremely popular in indigo districts; it was written by Dinabhandu Mitra and purported to show the devastating effect of the indigo system on the life and livelihood of a peasant family. Seton-Karr, secretary to the Bengal government, asked Long to prepare a translation. When this was completed by Michael Datta (under Long's instructions) and after Long himself added a preface in which he declared that the effects of the indigo system were pointed out in language 'plain but true', Seton-Karr had the play and preface circulated under government frank. The planters, already shaken by the findings of the commission, were furious. Having failed to obtain the names of the government officials responsible for 'a foul and malicious libel' on the planters of Lower Bengal, they sought to discredit the government by indicting Long for libel in the supreme court of Calcutta in July 1861. After a trial which was characterized by the ineffectiveness of the counsel for the defence and the extreme partiality of Sir Mordaunt Wells, the presiding judge, whose violent language shocked even some of the planters, Long was found guilty and sentenced to a fine of 1000 rupees and a month's imprisonment.

Kaliprosanna Sinha, a well-known Bengali writer and millionaire stepped forward immediately and paid the fine. Government officials, missionaries, and Bengalis of all religious persuasions visited Long in prison. Before the imprisonment and even outside Bengal he was regarded as 'one of the best friends of the peasantry', and addresses of sympathy and support came from associations and meetings in cities as far away as Allahabad, Madras, and Bombay. These events, which made Long a popular, India-wide hero, coincided with the beginnings of nationalist sentiment and gave him a degree of access into all levels of Indian society probably unprecedented for a European in the 1860s.

Owing to ill health Long was forced to return to England in 1872. However, while in retirement he continued to campaign on Indian issues and was able to consolidate his links with Russia. His first visit to Russia had been in 1863 when, after the publicity surrounding his imprisonment, he was invited by liberal reformers within the administration to visit the country and report on the progress of serf emancipation. The report of his findings was published in a series of articles in the *Anti-Slavery Reporter* in 1864. On later visits to Russia in 1872 and 1876 he made further enquiries into the condition of the peasantry, including the progress of education and spread of the Christian literature among them. While his writings on the similarities between India's and Russia's social systems reflect his interest in comparative sociology, his basic concern was, as hitherto, with the social and religious improvement of the masses. He dwelt on the improvement of collaboration between the Anglican and Orthodox churches and on the need for a greater understanding in England of Russia's civilizing and Christianizing mission in central Asia, a process which he argued was a major factor in the containment of Islam.

In England, Long was a member of the Royal Asiatic Society and a fellow of the Royal Geographical Society. A short time before his death he assigned to the Church Missionary Society £2000 to provide popular lectures on the religions of the East. He died at his residence, 3 Adam Street, Adelphi, London, on 23 March 1887.

GEOFFREY A. ODDIE

Sources *Register of missionaries … from 1804 to 1904*, Church Missionary Society (privately printed, *c*.1905) • G. A. Oddie, *Social protest in India: British protestant missionaries and social reformers, 1850–1900* (1979) • E. Stock, *The history of the Church Missionary Society: its environment, its men and its work*, 4 vols. (1899–1916) • Church Missionary Society, *Intelligencer* (1887) • G. A. Oddie, *James Long of Bengal, 1814–1887: missionary scholar and people's hero* [forthcoming] • J. Long, *Russia, central Asia and British India* (1865) • J. Long, *A visit to Russia* (1876) • *CGPLA Eng. & Wales* (1887) • d. cert. • G. A. Oddie, *Missionaries, rebellion and proto-nationalism: James Long of Bengal, 1814–87* (1999)

Archives BL OIOC • U. Birm. L., Church Missionary Society archive, corresp. and papers

Wealth at death £691 10s. 5d.: administration, 3 Sept 1887, *CGPLA Eng. & Wales*

Long, John (1547/8–1589), Church of Ireland archbishop of Armagh, was born in London in 1547 or 1548. He was educated at Eton and contributed four Latin epigrams to the verses presented by Eton scholars to Queen Elizabeth at Windsor Castle in 1563. He was admitted as a scholar to King's College, Cambridge, on 13 August 1564. While there is no record of his having taken a degree when he left Cambridge three years later, Ware identified him as a doctor of divinity. He became the vicar of Stanwell, Middlesex.

Elizabeth appointed Long archbishop of Armagh and primate of the Church of Ireland on the recommendation of her viceroy, Sir John Perrot, and the council of Ireland; he was consecrated on 13 July 1584. He became a member of the Irish privy council in the following year, also on Perrot's recommendation. Long was a rigorous protestant who reckoned that there were not forty Irish born Christians in all of Ireland. At first he advocated a sturdy policy of enforcing the Reformation in Ireland, prosecuting recusants and preventing Catholic priests from exercising their ministries, but was obliged to accept that that did not accord with the wishes of the crown. Thereafter he concentrated his energies on advancing the Reformation by teaching and persuasion, not with very significant success. In 1589 Barnaby Rich remarked that in Drogheda, the chief town in Armagh diocese and in close proximity to Long's residence, 'the Word of God has been for many years most plentifully preached but to such a froward and obstinate people that willfully resist the truth … [and] do as their [Catholic] fathers have done before them' ('Rich', fol. 10).

Long died at Drogheda in January 1589 and was buried in the vault of Primate Octavian del Palatio in St Peter's Church, Drogheda. A month after his death, Lord Deputy Fitzwilliam commented in a letter to William Lyon, bishop of Cork, that the late archbishop 'loved good cheer but too well' (*DNB*). His widow, Anne, petitioned Perrot's successor for relief on account of the small estate left to her and her children, and the fact that many of her goods had been confiscated to pay some of the arrears of the tax of a twentieth owed by her late husband as archbishop of Armagh. Her petition was granted on 15 May 1589.

HENRY A. JEFFERIES

Sources Venn, *Alum. Cant.* • *CSP Ire.*, 1589 • Cooper, *Ath. Cantab.*, vol. 2 • *The whole works of Sir James Ware concerning Ireland*, ed. and trans. W. Harris, rev. edn, 1 (1764) • W. Sterry, ed., *The Eton College register, 1441–1698* (1943) • W. M. Brady, ed., *State papers concerning the Irish church* (1868) • R. Rawlinson, ed., *Sir John Perrot* (1728) • B. Bradshaw, 'Sword, word and strategy in the Reformation in Ireland', *HJ*, 21 (1978), 475–502 • 'Book of Barnaby Rich on the Reformation of Ireland', 1589, PRO, SP Ireland, MS 63/144/35, fol. 10

Long, John St John (1798–1834), quack and painter, was born at Newcastle West, co. Limerick, the second of three children of John Long and Anne St John. His father was a basket maker and handyman, and both parents were protestant. After demonstrating an ability in sketching, Long was sponsored in 1816 for two years by local residents in Doneraile, co. Cork, to undertake art classes at Dublin Academy, where he became a pupil of the still-life painter Daniel Richardson (*fl.* 1783–1830). After his return to Limerick, Long painted still lifes, landscapes, and portraits, and supported himself by giving drawing and painting

John St John Long (1798–1834), by James Fahey, 1831

lessons. He added St John to his name some time before 1822, the year he moved to London, where he assisted in the studios of Sir Thomas Lawrence, John Martin, and William Young Ottley. Long's own paintings, which were chiefly of biblical, allegorical, and historical subjects, were exhibited at the Society of British Artists, and at the British Institution in 1824–5.

However, Long could not support himself by painting alone, and he turned instead to medicine. Although unqualified, he had gained some knowledge of anatomy from his art training. Initially he began practice in chiropody, but soon he effected his first 'cure' for consumption, in 1826. Long claimed that bodily impurities could be removed by his unique lotion, which was rubbed onto the back, shoulders, and chest, or, alternatively, inhaled. After his death, this lotion was found to consist of turpentine, acetic acid, and egg yolk. This counter-irritation cauterized the skin, and was designed to draw inflammations and lung ulcers to the surface. Once the impurities had been removed, the resulting blister was soothed with cabbage leaves. The corrosive liniment was claimed to cure consumption, rheumatism, gout, measles, smallpox, and even insanity. Long began this treatment in Howland Street, Fitzroy Square, in 1827, but soon after moved to 41 Harley Street. A tall, dark-complexioned, and handsome man, with a slender figure and impeccable manners, Long was particularly successful in gaining a large female clientele. Indeed between 1827 and 1834 he undoubtedly enjoyed the most lucrative and fashionable quack medical practice in London.

In 1830, Long was indicted in two court cases involving consumptive female patients who had died after being 'rubbed' with Long's lotion. While Long was acquitted in one case, he was found guilty of the manslaughter of Miss Catherine Cashin at the Old Bailey on 23 October 1830 despite the favourable testimony of sixty-three of his patients. Long was discharged on payment of a fine of £250, which he flamboyantly paid on the spot. His practice did not suffer adversely from the publicity. The coroner in the second case was Thomas Wakley, editor of *The Lancet*. Wakley described Long as the 'king of humbugs' (Wakley, 'John St John Long', 506) and his patients as the 'willing dupes and fools of a dishonest and tricking knave' (Wakley, 'Second trial', 726). The cases brought against Long provoked him to write two books setting forth his methods: *Discoveries in the Science and Art of Healing* (1830) and *A critical exposure of the ignorance and malpractice of certain medical practitioners, in their theory and treatment of diseases* (1831).

Long, who did not marry, died on 2 July 1834, at Elm Grove, near Roehampton. His death was allegedly due to consumption, which he had steadfastly refused to treat by his own methods. This story is almost certainly apocryphal. Long had fallen from his horse in May 1834, and a later bad cough caused a ruptured blood vessel. His tomb was erected in Kensal Green cemetery, Middlesex, and was built in the style of a Greek temple, decorated with Aesculapian emblems. His epitaph noted that he had 'many enemies and few friends'. The secret of his lotion was later purchased from his executors, allegedly for £10,000, by Lewis C. Kinchela, an Irish medical practitioner—to unknown success. Although a minor talent as a painter, Long exemplified how swiftly fame and fortune could be achieved by unqualified medical practitioners in early nineteenth-century London. MARTEN HUTT

Sources R. Herbert, *Worthies of Thomond* (1944) · *A defence of St. John Long* (1831) · *Annual Biography and Obituary*, 20 (1836), 436–8 · C. Pelham, *The chronicles of crime*, [another edn], 2 vols. (1886) · W. G. Strickland, *A dictionary of Irish artists*, 2 vols. (1913) · 'Composition of the notorious quack liniment of St. John Long', *The Lancet* (30 June 1838), 485–6 · *DNB* · [T. Wakley], 'John St John Long', *The Lancet* (9 Jan 1830), 506 · [T. Wakley], 'Second trial of Long the quack', *The Lancet* (26 Feb 1831), 724–6 · *London Medical and Surgical Journal*, 5 (1834), 760–61 · *The Lancet* (6 Nov 1830), 210–14 [editorial] · 'Dr Kinchela on the practice of Mr St John Long', *Dublin Journal of Medical Science*, 9 (1836), 139–44 [review] · H. Boylan, *A dictionary of Irish biography* (1978) · 'Dr Ramadge and the quack Long', *The Lancet* (16 April 1831), 90–93 · 'Completion of Dr Ramadge's letter to Long the quack', *The Lancet* (30 April 1831), 154–6 · J. McCabe, 'Remarks on the late trials of Long the quack for manslaughter', *The Lancet* (11 June 1831), 333–5 · *Fraser's Magazine*, 3 (1831), 365–8 · *GM*, 1st ser., 100/2 (1830), 461 · *GM*, 2nd ser., 2 (1834), 656 · J. S. Crone, *A concise dictionary of Irish biography*, rev. edn (1937) · S. Maunder, *The biographical treasury*, new edn, rev. W. L. R. Cates (1870) · Redgrave, *Artists* · Bryan, *Painters*

Likenesses J. Fahey, lithograph, 1831, NPG [*see illus.*] · engraving, repro. in Herbert, *Worthies of Thomond*, facing p. 26 · lithograph, BM, NPG

Wealth at death 'secret' lotion allegedly sold by brother for £10,000 after death; also alleged that Long left £1000 in will for tomb

Long, Lislebone [created Sir Lislebone Long under the protectorate] (*bap.* **1613**, *d.* **1659**), politician, was the eldest son of William Long (*d.* 1645) of Stratton on the Fosse in Somerset, and his wife, Mary (*d.* 1660), daughter of Thomas Loviband of Shorwell, Isle of Wight. Related to the Longs of Devizes and Trowbridge in Wiltshire, he was baptized at Beckington in Somerset in 1613 as Loveban, although he later changed his name to Lislebone. Educated at Magdalen Hall, Oxford, where he matriculated on 4 December 1629 and graduated BA on 1 February 1631, he was subsequently called to the bar at Lincoln's Inn in February 1640. Held by contemporaries in the highest esteem as 'a person of great integrity in the profession of law' (Manning, 377) he was described by Whitelocke as 'a very sober, discrete gentleman and a good lawyer' (Whitelocke, 4.341). He and his wife, Frances (*d.* 1691), daughter of John Mynne of Epsom, had several children, including his heir, George (1644–1705).

In local affairs Long identified both before and during the civil wars with his Wiltshire relatives, who were outspoken critics of the king. Apparently a presbyterian in religion, he became an elder in parliament's presbyterian national church and a member of the committee established to administer the solemn league and covenant in Somerset (1644), and was later appointed to the parliamentary committee charged with settling the form of church government in England (1648). He eventually became a member of parliament's county committee in Somerset after its revival in 1645, following the ending of royalist occupation. However, although the committee was increasingly dominated by Colonel John Pyne's radical war party faction, Long himself had by then emerged as a moderate in politics.

Long's moderate stance was also demonstrated in parliament, following his election to the Long Parliament as a recruiter MP for Wells (1645–53). He strongly opposed Pride's Purge (6 December 1648), though he was not secluded, as shown when he acted as a teller on a critical vote on the day following the purge. After a period of hesitation, during which he made occasional appearances, he eventually absented himself from the Commons in protest (25 December). However, although he played no part in the trial and execution of the king he became a conformist by taking his dissent (22 February 1649) and resuming his seat in the Rump Parliament. Thereafter, like many other conformists, he played an active role in the work of committees, exercising a moderating influence on government policies. He allied closely with a group of conservative lawyers (including Bulstrode Whitelocke, Roger Hill, and Edmund Prideaux) most of whom opposed proposals for reform of the legal system. Together they were entrusted with drafting much of the Rump's legislation and organizing the work of its committees.

Long also participated regularly in parliamentary debates. He served as MP for Wells in the first protectorate parliament (1654–5); for Somerset in the second protectorate parliament (1656–8); and again for Wells in Richard Cromwell's parliament (1659). He made intelligent contributions during sessions of the Cromwellian parliaments on points of law, precedent, and procedure, and spoke convincingly in the debates on James Nayler (5 December 1656), the Excise Bill (8 January 1657) and the powers of the 'other house' (22 February 1658). He also submitted, as chairman of the committee charged with defining the powers of the lord protector, a paragraph to be inserted in 'The humble petition and advice' (22 May 1657). After being elected recorder of London (1 June 1655) he was knighted by Oliver Cromwell (15 December 1656) and appointed treasurer of Lincoln's Inn, a master of requests, and a commissioner of treasons (all in 1656). Much respected within his local community, he was appointed JP for Somerset 1654–9.

On 9 March 1659 Challoner Chute, the speaker of Richard Cromwell's parliament, suddenly became indisposed as a result of being 'tired out with the long debates and late sitting' (*Diary of Thomas Burton*, 4.92). Whereupon, after Sir Arthur Hesilrige had proposed that Long should take the chair during the speaker's illness, Sir Lislebone was duly elected 'by general consent of the House' (*JHC*, 7.612). Although this was a tribute to the high regard in which he was held, his fame was sadly short-lived. One week later (16 March) Burton recorded in his diary that Long 'being very sick, could not attend' (*Diary of Thomas Burton*, 4.419). He died later the same day and was buried at Stratton on the Fosse, leaving an estate which included a number of ecclesiastical and royalist lands purchased after confiscation by parliament.

John Wroughton

Sources R. L. Woods, 'Long, Sir Lislebone', Greaves & Zaller, *BDBR*, 20 • S. W. Bates-Harbin, *Members of parliament for the county of Somerset* (1939) • B. Worden, *The Rump Parliament, 1648–1653* (1974) • *Pedigrees of the family of Long: Wiltshire, Somerset and Hampshire* (1878) • Foster, *Alum. Oxon.*, 1500–1714 [Sir Leileboune Long] • D. Underdown, *Somerset in the civil war and interregnum* (1973) • D. Underdown, *Pride's Purge: politics in the puritan revolution* (1971) • J. A. Manning, *The lives of the speakers of the House of Commons* (1850) • *Diary of Thomas Burton*, ed. J. T. Rutt, 4 vols. (1828), vol. 4 • B. Whitelocke, *Memorials of English affairs*, new edn, 4 vols. (1853), vol. 4 • A. I. Dasent, *The speakers of the House of Commons* (1911) • *JHC*, 7 (1651–9) • *DNB*

Wealth at death see administration, PRO, PROB 6/35, fol. 149

Long [*née* Campbell], **Margaret Gabrielle Vere** [*pseuds.* Marjorie Bowen, Joseph Shearing, George Preedy] (**1885–1952**), writer, was born Margaret Gabrielle Vere Campbell on 1 November 1885 at Hayling Island, Hampshire, the second of three daughters (the first died very young) of Vere Douglas Campbell and Josephine Elisabeth Bowen Ellis, writer and daughter of a Moravian clergyman. The poverty, deprivation, verbal denigration, and emotional abuse she experienced in youth are detailed in her autobiographical *The Debate Continues* (1939). Her parents separated when she was four. Her mother's compromised status as a woman living apart from her husband, her temperament, and her connections to the theatre resulted in a bohemian lifestyle which Margaret despised. Food was often scarce and frequent moves occurred to avoid paying bills. Moreover, the disparaging comparison of Margaret to her attractive and frivolous younger sister undermined her confidence, causing her to withdraw to a life of the mind.

Margaret was not sent to school but was taught to read and write at home. She voraciously accumulated knowledge, developed her artistic abilities, and by early adolescence had taught herself to read French, Italian, and a bit of Latin. Her mother wanted to send her to the Royal College of Art in South Kensington, but she failed the entrance examination. A second try at formal education was an equally dismal experience. At the Slade School of Fine Art she was isolated from other students by her poverty, often went the entire day without food, and failed the first exam. She worked for a time as a research assistant at the British Museum. Her mother then sent her to Paris to study art but did not send money for board or school fees. Isolated from others because of her poverty, she turned to writing for consolation. After rejection by eleven publishers, the eventual success of *The Viper of Milan* (1906), a historical fantasy, created further bitterness on the part of her mother, who had long and vainly sought literary fame herself. The book launched a writing career that helped support Margaret's family, and a new identity as Marjorie Bowen.

On 11 October 1912 Bowen married Zeffirino Emilio Costanzo (1882/3–1916), an employee in an engineering and mining company. Although the marriage offered a socially acceptable escape from the turmoil of life with her mother and sister, it was fraught with difficulty. Bowen continued to send money to her mother and sister, leaving herself and her husband poorly off. They settled for a time in Tuscany before returning to England at the outbreak of the First World War. In Kent her husband embarked on a disastrous venture as a poultry farmer, and their first child, a daughter, died of meningitis at five months. Costanzo, who was suffering from tuberculosis, returned to Italy leaving Bowen pregnant with their second child. She was forced to leave her infant son in England while she nursed her ailing husband in Italy. Bowen fictionalized this episode of her life in *Stinging Nettles* (1923). After Costanzo's death in 1916 she had a doomed affair with her husband's physician and returned to England. On 4 December 1917 she married Arthur Leonard Long (*b.* 1885/6), an army officer. They had two sons, and in this relationship she seems finally to have achieved the domestic stability she longed for.

During the decade since *The Viper of Milan* Marjorie Bowen had been remarkably prolific, publishing about twenty books, including the supernatural gothic novel *Black Magic: a Tale of the Rise and Fall of the Antichrist* (1909), and numerous historical romances such as *A Knight of Spain* (1913). Later she turned her hand to novels and short stories with modern situations such as *Stinging Nettles* and *The Pagoda* (1927), coinciding with the general shift away from the swashbuckling romance. She began a Renaissance trilogy in the 1920s which comprised *The Golden Roof* (1928), *The Triumphant Beast* (1934), and *Trumpets at Rome* (1936), and a further trilogy in the 1930s of the spiritual life of seventeenth-century England, *God and the Wedding Dress* (1938) *Mr. Tyler's Saints* (1939), and *The Circle in the Water* (1939). In 1920 she adopted the pseudonym George Preedy to write more historical novels, including the best-seller *General Crack* (1928), made into a film starring John Barrymore in 1929; several biographies, such as *This Shining Woman* (1937); a life of Mary Wollstonecraft Godwin; and drama. She used pseudonyms throughout her life, she said, in order to demarcate her separate creative personalities. In 1932 she began to use the name Joseph Shearing for reconstructions of nineteenth-century crimes starting with *Forget-me-Not* (1932), based on the murder of the duchesse de Praslin, and followed by treatment of the Maybrick poisoning in *Airing in a Closed Carriage* (1943). As Joseph Shearing she was similarly prolific and successful; her identity was not revealed until 1942. As John Winch and Robert Paye she wrote children's literature, and as Margaret Campbell her candid autobiography *The Debate Continues: being the Autobiography of Marjorie Bowen* (1939). In *Ethics in Modern Art* (1939) she reflected on the social function of art and the place of women in the literary arena.

Bowen died in St Charles Hospital, Kensington, London, on 23 December 1952 of haemorrhage due to a fractured skull, the result of a fall at her home at 34 Holland Park, Kensington; her husband survived her. She was cremated on 31 December at Putney Vale, London.

While Bowen believed she necessarily sacrificed her art to write so prolifically in order to earn a living, she has had her share of supporters who believe she should be taken seriously as a literary writer. Edward Wagenknecht has noted that she was a superb storyteller, presenting rich, accurate, and well-researched background for her historical works he ranked her with Wilkie Collins for her skill in the creation of atmosphere. While Wagenknecht believed she was one of the best writers of stories of the supernatural, Hugh Walpole proclaimed her the most important historical novelist of her generation. Befriended by Mark Twain, she dedicated one of her novels to him. Graham Greene, in *The Lost Childhood* (1951), credited a reading of *The Viper of Milan* when he was fourteen with the awakening of his writing career.

FRANCES M. MALPEZZI

Sources M. Campbell, *The debate continues, being the autobiography of Marjorie Bowen* (1939) · E. Wagenknecht, 'Bowen, Preedy, Shearing & Co.: a note in memory and a check list', *Boston University Studies in English*, 3 (1957), 181–9 · M. A. S. Ferreira, 'Marjorie Bowen', *Late-Victorian and Edwardian British novelists: first series*, ed. G. M. Johnson, DLitB, 153 (1995), 39–50 · E. Wagenknecht, *Seven masters of supernatural fiction* (1991) · M. J. DeMarr, 'Joseph Shearing', *British mystery writers, 1860–1919*, ed. B. Benstock and T. F. Staley, DLitB, 70 (1988), 269–76 · F. M. Malpezzi, 'A woman of many names', *Cimarron Review*, 83 (April 1988), 83–9 · J. W. Stedman, 'Joseph Shearing', in J. M. Reilly, *Twentieth-century crime and mystery writers* (1980), 1311–17 · S. J. Kunitz and H. Haycraft, eds., *Twentieth century authors: a biographical dictionary of modern literature* (1942) · *The Times* (27 Dec 1952) · *New York Times* (27 Dec 1952) · *Time* (5 Jan 1953) · *Wilson Library Bulletin* (Feb 1953) · 'Miss Marjorie Bowen: verdict of accidental death', *The Times* (30 Dec 1952) · M. Ashley, *Who's who in horror and fantasy fiction* (1977) · E. Martell, L. G. Pine, and A. Lawrence, eds., *Who was who among English and European authors, 1931–1949*, 3 vols. (1978) · D. C. Browning, ed., *Everyman's dictionary of literary biography: English and American*, rev. edn (1962) · S. J. Kunitz, 'The Roving Eye', *Wilson Library Bulletin* (Nov 1942), 242 · N. O. Ireland, *Index to women of the world: from ancient to modern times* (1970) · b. cert. · m. cert. · d. cert.

Likenesses H. Coster, photographs, *c.*1930–1939, NPG · photograph, 1932, Hult. Arch.

Wealth at death £2118 4*s.* 4*d.*: probate, 22 April 1953, *CGPLA Eng. & Wales*

Long, Sir Richard (*c.*1494–1546). *See under* Henry VIII, privy chamber of (*act.* 1509–1547).

Long, Sir Robert, first baronet (*c.*1602–1673), politician and exchequer official, came from an old Wiltshire family. His father, Sir Walter Long (1560–1610), married twice and left his principal estate to the son of his first marriage; but he was still able to settle property at Draycot Cerne on Long's eldest brother of the whole blood. Long was the eighth (but fourth surviving) son, being the youngest son of Sir Walter and his second wife, Katherine (*d.* 1613), daughter of Sir John Thynne of Longleat. As a widow she married into a Shropshire family called Fox, and her eldest son and two of her six daughters settled in that county without much éclat. Long was admitted to Lincoln's Inn in 1619 and called to the bar eight years later. By then he was acting as secretary to his brother's father-in-law, the decrepit lord treasurer, the first earl of Marlborough, on whose interest he was elected for Devizes to the parliaments of 1626 and 1628–9. A totally inactive member and none too reliable an administrator, he devoted his energies to ingratiating himself with the newly arrived queen, Henrietta Maria, whose creature he became. After Marlborough's long-overdue resignation, Long entered the royal service, though for many years under the personal government of Charles I he had to be content with minor commissions and reversions. He was chiefly engaged as undertaker in a Lincolnshire drainage project, a work sufficiently important to excuse him from military service against the Scots in 1639. One of his reversions as receiver of recusant revenue south of the Trent fell in at this juncture, and the queen made him her surveyor-general. From her jointure he acquired an interest in the forest of Galtres, between York and Boroughbridge, and he became a gentleman of the chamber. He sat for Midhurst in the Short Parliament on the interest of the Roman Catholic Viscount Montagu, but he stood down at the autumn election.

During the civil war Long joined the king at Oxford, where, as reversioner to the parliamentarian Sir Robert Pye, he was appointed writer of tallies in the exchequer. More significant to his career was his appointment as secretary to the young prince of Wales, whom he attended in the west country. Long was accused of precipitating the final royalist collapse here by providing parliament with intelligence about divisions among the commanders. He himself made his way to London, and thence to Paris, where he was welcomed by the queen and sent to rejoin the prince in Jersey, primarily to manage correspondence with royalist conspirators. Nevertheless on 19 November 1646 the parliamentary authorities received a petition from Long, offering to compound for his estates; but all the papers are missing from their records. When a part of the parliamentary fleet placed itself at the prince's disposal in 1648, Long went aboard to replenish the royalist coffers from a blockade of the Thames. Prizes were taken, but the results were disappointing, and Long, who was 'thought to love money too well' (Clarendon, *Hist. rebellion*, 4.415), was accused of lining his own pockets.

The execution of Charles I left the Louvre faction, controlled by Henrietta Maria and her favourite Henry Jermyn, dominant in royalist counsels. They relied on Long to keep the prince steady and fast to the presbyterian alliance, and accordingly he warmly supported the move to Scotland. But Long was himself unacceptable to the Scots and had to return to the continent, while his property in England was included in the Act of Sale of 16 July 1651. On the surrender of Jersey at the end of the year, the Commonwealth government came into possession of a trunkful of compromising letters. Long 'had not the good fortune to be generally well thought of' (Clarendon, *Hist. rebellion*, 4.323). His duties as secretary of state were transferred to Sir Edward Hyde, and Long left the court, though he still tried to make trouble for his supplanter by supporting an absurd allegation of a secret interview with Cromwell in London.

At the Restoration, Long wrote from Rouen to beg Hyde's forgiveness, urging compassion on his 'destitute condition' (*Clarendon State Papers*, 4.676), from which he was to emerge, after thirteen years of office, as owner of 'a very vast estate' (Christie, *Letters to Williamson*, 118). Giving his triumphant rival no further trouble, he regained his post as the queen's surveyor-general, acquiring from her Worcester Park in Surrey and Higham Ferrars Park in Northamptonshire, and ultimately became receiver-general of her revenues. It was on her interest that Long was elected for Boroughbridge in 1661, but in the first ten sessions of the Cavalier Parliament he was named to only forty-three committees, none of them of much political significance. When in 1662 he at last succeeded Pye as auditor of the lower exchequer, he was made a baronet. Much matured from the incompetent young secretary of 1626, Long now showed himself 'exceptional among 17th century Exchequer officials in having a conscientious devotion to the personal performance of his duties' (Roseveare, 30). Perhaps the mistrustful nature shown in his will left him incapable of delegating responsibility. Even more unexpectedly, while eschewing politics, he became a vocal supporter of the reforms introduced by the niggardly Sir George Downing, on whose behalf he had regularly to entertain officials from other departments, such as Samuel Pepys. This modest expense he was well able to afford while purchasing three Yorkshire manors and Athelhampton in Dorset, and spending £2500 on repairs to Worcester Park. With the collapse of Downing's 'payment in course' on the stop of the exchequer in 1672, Long could no longer avoid involvement in politics. He was restored to the privy council in July, and on 21 December attended a small meeting in Lord Arlington's lodgings to prepare for a stormy session in parliament. But he was not to face it after the recess of 29 March 1673. Weak of body with a long and lingering disease, Long was under the care of the Shropshire-born Dr Walter Needham. A lifelong bachelor, Long had secured a special remainder to his baronetcy for his nephew Sir James *Long of Draycot Cerne. The other executor was Sir Richard Mason, a household official from a minor Shropshire family who had married James Long's daughter. But the bulk of the estate was entailed on his great-nephew James Long junior, who had made a much grander match with a daughter of a prominent Dorset churchman, Giles Strangways. A codicil added two months later, however, might be interpreted as evidence of a different spiritual allegiance, for he left £600, half of which consisted of a debt due from an English merchant in Rouen, 'for the good and benefitt of my Soule' (PRO, PROB 11/341/236), as privately communicated to Mason. Long died on 13 July 1673, and was buried on 28 July in Westminster Abbey according to the Anglican rite.

JOHN FERRIS

Sources HoP, *Commons, 1660–90* • H. Roseveare, *The treasury, 1660–1870: the foundations of control* (1973) • G. E. Aylmer, *The king's servants: the civil service of Charles I, 1625–1642*, rev. edn (1974), 139, 368 • D. Underdown, *Royalist conspiracy in England, 1649–1660* (1960), 10, 32, 63 • *Miscellanea genealogica at heraldica*, ser. 2, vol. 3 (1880), 46 • C. Holmes, *Seventeenth-century Lincolnshire*, History of Lincolnshire, 7 (1980) • Clarendon, *Hist. rebellion*, 4.341, 373, 415; 5.2, 134, 323 • W. D. Christie, ed., *Letters addressed from London to Sir Joseph Williamson*, 1, CS, new ser., 8 (1874), 104, 106, 118 • *Calendar of the Clarendon state papers preserved in the Bodleian Library*, 2: *1649–1654*, ed. W. D. Macray (1869); 4: *1657–1660*, ed. F. J. Routledge (1932), 676 • *CSP dom., 1629–43; 1660–72* • R. P. Cust, *The forced loan and English politics, 1626–1628* (1987), 148 • will, PRO, PROB 11/341, fols. 234–7 • HoP, *Commons, 1558–1603*

Archives BL, official corresp., Add. MS 37047 • BL, proceedings in House of Lords, Add. MSS 27232–27237 • Bodl. Oxf., corresp. and papers • Magd. Cam., corresp.

Likenesses P. Lely, portrait; formerly in possession of Earl Brownlow, 1891 • oils (after P. Lely), NPG

Wealth at death will, PRO, PROB 11/341, fols. 234–7 • 'a very vast estate': Christie, ed., *Letters to Williamson*, 118

Long, Robert Ballard (1771–1825), army officer, one of the six children of Edward *Long (1734–1813), judge and historian of Jamaica, and his wife, Mary Ballard (*d.* 16 July 1797, aged sixty-two), widow of John Palmer, and daughter and heir of Thomas Beckford of Jamaica, was born in Chichester on 4 April 1771, the elder of twin sons. He was educated at Dr Thomson's school, Kensington, Harrow School (1780–89) under Dr Drury, and at the University of Göttingen, in Hanover, where he took a course of military instruction. On 4 May 1791 he was appointed cornet in the 1st King's dragoon guards, in which he became lieutenant in April and captain in November 1793. He served with the regiment in Flanders under the duke of York in 1793–4, and was deputy adjutant-general to General Sir George Don in the winter retreat to Germany in 1794–5. He returned home from Cuxhaven in January 1796, and after serving at Portsmouth as brigade-major and aide-de-camp to General Sir William Pitt, whose friendship subsequently helped his career, he became a major in the York rangers (though he probably did not serve with them). He bought the lieutenant-colonelcy of the Hompesch mounted riflemen from the regiment's proprietor, Baron Hompesch, Long's father paying £2000 for this. Long became lieutenant-colonel of the regiment on 3 March 1798, and commanded it in Ireland against the 1798 uprising when it was employed under General John Moore in Wexford. In 1800 he was transferred to the York hussars, a fine foreign unit, which he commanded, chiefly at Weymouth, until it was disbanded in 1802 at the peace of Amiens. After studying at the senior department, Royal Military College, High Wycombe, Long was appointed lieutenant-colonel in the 16th light dragoons, and was transferred in December 1805 to the 15th light dragoons, of which Ernest, duke of Cumberland (later Ernest I of Hanover) was colonel. Cumberland repeatedly interfered, and relations between him and Long were hostile. Nevertheless Long remained lieutenant-colonel of the 15th for the rest of his life. Under Long's command the regiment was converted in 1806 to hussars, and its distinctive headdress was copied from the York hussars. Long was appointed brevet-colonel on the staff in Spain in 1808. He landed on 15 January 1809 at Corunna, the night before the battle, at which he was present, but held no command. He was adjutant-general to Lord Chatham on the disastrous 1809 Walcheren expedition. In 1810 he joined Wellington's army in Portugal, with the rank of brigadier-general, and commanded a brigade of cavalry under General William Carr Beresford in the actions of Campo Maior and Los Santos, and under Sir Rowland Hill in the operations of 1811–12. At Campo Maior, on 25 March 1811, he initially fought well; then he 'lost his head completely' (Fortescue, *Brit. army*, 8.133). Near Santa Marta on 15 May 1811 Long retreated, in the judgement of Beresford and his staff, with unjustified haste and showing insufficient resistance. Near Elvas on 23 June 1811, partly through Long's faulty dispositions, the British lost relatively heavily in casualties and captives; Wellington reprimanded Long. He commanded a brigade, composed of the 19th and 13th light dragoons, at the battle of Vitoria, 21 June 1813 (gold medal), and in Hill's operations in the Pyrenees and the investment of Pamplona. Wellington privately considered Long incompetent and, at Wellington's request, the commander-in-chief (Frederick, duke of York) in December 1812 recalled Long, against his wishes. Long returned, indignant, and declined an offer of a command in Scotland.

After his return home Long, who had become major-general in 1811, and was made lieutenant-general in 1821, resided in various places before finally settling at Barnes Terrace, Surrey. He died at Berkeley Square, London, on 2 March 1825, and was interred in the family vault in the church at Seale, Surrey.

Long had disagreements with Marshal Beresford when under his command in the Peninsula. After Long's death his nephew, Charles Edward Long, published in 1832 and 1833 two pamphlets, attempting to vindicate his uncle's conduct, especially at Campo Maior, from criticism in W. F. P. Napier's *History of the Peninsular War* (6 vols., 1828–40), and in some letters of Lord Beresford (see *Naval and Military Gazette*, April and 31 Aug 1833). Long's Peninsular War correspondence, edited by T. H. McGuffie, was published in *Peninsular Cavalry General (1811–13)* (1951).

H. M. CHICHESTER, *rev.* ROGER T. STEARN

Sources *Army List* • *Peninsular cavalry general, 1811–13: the correspondence of Lieutenant-General Robert Ballard Long*, ed. T. H. McGuffie (1951) • *The dispatches of … the duke of Wellington … from 1799 to 1818*, ed. J. Gurwood, new edn, 4–6 (1837–8) • *Supplementary despatches* *(correspondence) and memoranda of Field Marshal Arthur, duke of Wellington*, ed. A. R. Wellesley, second duke of Wellington, 15 vols. (1858–72), vols. 7–8, 13, 15 · R. Cannon, ed., *Historical record of the fifteenth, or king's regiment of light dragoons, hussars* (1841) · R. Cannon, ed., *Historical record of the thirteenth regiment of light dragoons* (1842) · *GM*, 1st ser., 83/1 (1813) · Fortescue, *Brit. army*, vols. 8–9 · E. Longford [E. H. Pakenham, countess of Longford], *Wellington*, 1: *The years of the sword* (1969) · R. Muir, *Britain and the defeat of Napoleon, 1807–1815* (1996)

Archives NAM, papers | Royal Military Academy Library, Sandhurst, corresp. with General Le Marchant on military affairs

Likenesses C. Turner, mezzotint, pubd 1827 (after W. Fowler), BM, NPG

Wealth at death over £6000: McGuffie, ed., *Peninsular cavalry general*

Long, Roger (1680–1770), astronomer, was born on 2 February 1680 at Croxton Park, Norfolk, the son of Thomas Long, a gentleman. Following an early education at Norwich grammar school he was admitted as a sizar at Pembroke College, Cambridge, on 4 March 1697. He graduated BA in 1701, was elected fellow in 1703, and graduated MA in 1704.

At the commencement of 1714 Long delivered a 'music speech' in Latin prose and English verse as a petition on behalf of Cambridge women who had previously been able to sit in that part of the university church known as the throne, but who had recently been forced to sit in the chancel, out of sight and unable to view the proceedings. The speech was well received and continued to be reprinted well into the nineteenth century, because in addressing the vice-chancellor, whom university wags usually styled 'Miss Greene', he assumed his native Norfolk dialect and, instead of saying 'Domine Procancellarie', 'did very archly pronounce the words thus, *Domina Procancellaria*, which occasioned a general smile in that grave Auditory' (Nichols, liv).

Long was ordained deacon at Lincoln on 25 September 1716 and priest at Norwich on 23 December 1716. He was rector of Overton Waterville, Huntingdonshire, from 1716 to 1751, then of Bradwell-on-Sea, Essex. He had become DD in 1728, and was appointed vicar of Cherry Hinton, Cambridgeshire, in 1729, the same year he was elected a fellow of the Royal Society. On commencement Sunday June 1728 Long preached a sermon entitled 'The Blessedness of Believing'. He declared that

> vain therefore are all our attempts to conceive or explain, further than the Scripture will bear us out, the mysteries of faith: as well may we hope to measure the Heavens with a span, as with the short line of human reason to fathom the depths of them. (Long, *Blessedness*, 18)

His faith did not preclude his later astronomical work, some of which did involve measurement; at the beginning of his *Astronomy in Five Books* he quoted an ancient source, noting that 'it is an observation of a philosopher that mathematical sciences have a tendency to purify the soul' (Long, *Astronomy*, 1.vii).

Long was master of Pembroke College from 1733 to 1770 and vice-chancellor of the University of Cambridge in 1733–4. He was elected the first Lowndean professor of astronomy and geometry in 1750. A broadside was published, apparently in the 1760s and presumably written by Long, protesting the encumbrance of Lowndes's estate by the Admiralty, which prevented the university from benefiting fully from his bequest.

Long's *Astronomy, in Five Books* took some time to be completed: the first volume was published in 1742, part of the second in 1764, the remainder, posthumously, in 1784, having been prepared for publication by Richard Dunthorne (who served as butler and astronomer at Pembroke under Long) and the astronomer and mathematician William Wales. The astronomer royal, Nevil Maskelyne, offered his help as well.

Long was very interested in teaching devices. In the first volume of his *Astronomy* he described what he referred to as 'an astronomical apparatus', a hoop about 20 feet in diameter and 3 feet in breadth, which he had installed at Pembroke, 'whereon are delineated the constellations of the zodiac, with the ecliptic and such other circles as I thought proper' (Long, *Astronomy*, 1.x). He went on to describe in some detail his ideas for a similarly sized celestial sphere, which would rotate around a stage and which could be used to demonstrate astronomical phenomena to younger members of the university. Noting that he had little reason to expect encouragement in such an undertaking, he did eventually build such a sphere at Pembroke. Called the 'Uranium', the sphere was 18 feet in diameter and capable of seating thirty people; it was entered by climbing steps situated at the south pole. The inner surface was painted to represent the stars and constellations, there was a planetarium in the middle, and the entire sphere could be turned by a winch. The sum of £6 was set aside annually to pay for someone, generally an undergraduate, to look after the sphere, which stood until it was torn down some time after 1871. Photographs (in Pembroke College archives), as well as a sketch by William Stukeley (Bodl. Oxf., Gough maps 230, fol. 12), survive. Long's enthusiasm for teaching apparently extended to the very young; his commonplace book (in Pembroke College Library) contains 'An essay concerning teaching children to know their letters by a pack of cards', with various games described.

Long was a member of the Gentlemen's Society at Spalding, Lincolnshire. Several amusing anecdotes were published, including the following, in the *Gentleman's Magazine*:

> That [Mr Bonfoy] and Dr Long walking together in Cambridge, in a dusky evening, and coming to a short post fixed in the pavement, which Mr B. in the midst of chat and inattention took to be a boy standing in his way, he said in a hurry, 'Get out of my way, boy.' That boy, Sir (said the Doctor very calmly and slily), is a post-boy, who turns out of his way for nobody. (*GM*, 924)

Long died on 16 December 1770. His portrait, conveying a pleasant visage, hangs in Pembroke College, and suggests the sense of humour for which he was known.

LIBA TAUB

Sources R. Long, *Astronomy, in five books*, 1 (1742), ii, x; 2 (1764), 241–9, esp. paragraphs 729–31 · 'Memoir of Roger Long', *Two music speeches at Cambridge, spoken at public commencements in the years 1714 and 1730, by Roger Long … and John Taylor*, ed. J. Nichols (1819), liv–lviii · W. Cole, notes for the *Athenae Cantabrigienses*, BL, Add. MS

5875, fols. 65–6 [renumbered in pencil, 72–73] • R. T. Gunter, *Early science in Cambridge* (1937), 97, 163–7, 189, 409 • R. Long, *The blessedness of believing* (1728), 18 • [R. Long], 'The case of Mr Lowndes's salt', CUL, broadsides, b.76.1 • R. Long, 'An essay concerning teaching children to know their letters by a pack of cards', Commonplace book, Pembroke College Library, 2.71 • 'Original anecdotes of Dr Long', *GM*, 1st ser., 53 (1783), 923–4 • Venn, *Alum. Cant.* • J. H. Le Keux, *Memorials of Cambridge* (1847), 1.219–20 • W. H. Smyth, *Bedford cycle of celestial objects*, 2 (1844), 179 • A. L. Attwater, *Pembroke College, Cambridge: a short history*, ed. S. C. Roberts (1936), 91–3

Archives Pembroke Cam., notebooks and photographs

Likenesses E. Fisher, mezzotint, pubd 1769 (after B. Wilson), BM, NPG • B. Wilson, oils, 1769, Pembroke Cam.

Long, Samuel (1638–1683), planter and politician in the West Indies, was born in Wiltshire, the second son of Timothy Long (1610–1691) and his wife, Jane, the only daughter of Oliver Brunsell, the vicar of Wroughton. Nothing of his early life is known, except that on 20 October 1661 he married Elizabeth Streete.

Long participated in the conquest of Jamaica, as a lieutenant in Colonel Edward D'Oyley's regiment, led by Admiral William Penn and General Robert Venables in 1655. He acted as secretary to the commissioners, which placed him at the centre of political affairs in the new colony and which may explain the considerable land grants he received after the war. As one of the largest landowners in the island, he subsequently played an instrumental role in limiting the prerogative powers of the royal governors and in championing the corporate rights of the elected assembly. He was elected as a member for Port Royal in the first meeting of an assembly, in which he served as clerk in 1664. He was later chosen speaker in four successive assemblies from 1672 to 1675. On the last occasion he was nominated by the members, not the governor, which henceforth became the established practice. He was sworn a member of the council and was appointed chief justice in 1674. He played a crucial role in ensuring the support of the council for the constitutional claims of the assembly against the governors. He said of his political stance that 'he asked nor desired nothing but his rights and privileges as an Englishman' (*CSP col.*, 10, no. 1512) which included the right of the assembly to enjoy the same privileges in Jamaica as the House of Commons. He believed that the assembly alone should have the right to tax the colony, and he anticipated many claims later contended by the North Americans during the American War of Independence, saying 'that His Majesty's commission was no law to them, and that there might be that which was unlawful in such commissions' (ibid., *1677–80*, no. 270). After the meeting of the first assembly in 1664 he was charged with treason primarily because of his success, with his ally and fellow planter William Beeston, in the passage of three acts which gave the legislature, not the governor, control of the revenue even before these powers were assumed by the House of Commons. The charges against him were dropped in recognition of the popularity of his stance. He was the first speaker to request the privileges of the house, possibly as early as 1672. He consolidated his earlier success with the alteration of the Revenue Act, in which the king's name was removed and the assembly won more control over the revenue, in 1675. He similarly orchestrated the reduction of the military powers of the governor in the Militia Act of 1677. He foiled the 'new frame' of government in 1678 in which the imperial authorities attempted to recover the powers lost to the assembly and to undo his work. His opposition to the proposed changes caused his suspension from the council and his dismissal as chief justice. He was arrested with William Beeston and sent to England in 1680. He used the opportunity not only to gain his acquittal but to contrive a deal with the lords of trade in which the assembly passed a permanent Revenue Act in return for the guarantee of existing laws giving control of the revenue to the assembly. He acted informally as the colony's agent in London and obtained permission for a permanent agent to represent Jamaica in Britain. He died in Jamaica on 28 June 1683 and was buried in the parish of St Katherine's. He had accumulated seven plantations, 11,183 acres in six parishes, and 288 slaves. He kept a particularly splendid residence in the capital at Spanish Town, far more elaborate than his plantation houses, which had a hall large enough for sixty chairs and seven tables. His career was synonymous with the rise of the sugar planters who dominated island politics. He and Beeston had created an assembly in Jamaica which surpassed the claims of peer institutions in North America even though the island did not rebel in 1776.

Andrew J. O'Shaughnessy

Sources Jamaica Inventories, Spanish Town RO, Jamaica • *CSP col.*, vols. 1, 5, 7, 9–45 • A. M. Whitson, *The constitutional development of Jamaica, 1660 to 1729* (1929) • R. S. Dunn, *Sugar and slaves: the rise of the planter class in the English West Indies, 1624–1713* (1972); repr. (1973) • A. P. Thornton, *West India policy under the Restoration* (1956) • W. A. Fuertado, *Official and other personages of Jamaica from 1655 to 1790* (1896) • S. A. G. Taylor, *The western design: an account of Cromwell's expedition to the Caribbean* (1965)

Archives Spanish Town Archives, Jamaica | PRO, Colonial Office papers, 139–42

Wealth at death £12,000 in local currency (excl. value of land, buildings, and two mansions): Jamaica Inventories, Spanish Town RO, Jamaica

Long, Sidney Selden (1863–1940), army officer and transport entrepreneur, was born on 31 March 1863, the fifth son of James Long, commissary-general, and his wife, Anna, daughter of Andrew Kirkwood, of Clongoonah, Ireland. Educated privately, Long followed his father into a military career, eventually in what would now be termed logistics, entering via the militia, from which he moved to the Durham light infantry in 1884. Five years later he transferred to the Army Service Corps (ASC, later the Royal Army Service Corps, RASC), a move possibly influenced by his father's example. His career was now set in the path it would follow through military into civilian life. Service in south China as deputy assistant adjutant-general (DAAG), 1896–9, was followed by distinguished service in the Second South African War (1899–1902). He became DAAG (later assistant adjutant-general) for transport, commandant of the ASC training establishment, Aldershot (1908–9), assistant director of supplies (1909–12), and director of supplies and quartering (1913–14). For the first half of the First World War (1914–16) he was director of supplies and transport at the War Office. He was made a companion in the Order of the Bath in 1914.

Long's background and career experience thus led him to, and fitted him for, a key post in the first major war mechanized on any scale; and this, in turn, opened the way for a pioneering role in commercial road transport and distribution. The official history of the RASC describes Long's role as director of supplies and transport as 'to initiate upon the right lines the gigantic task of expanding a force of 500 officers and 6000 men (the pre-war RASC) into one which ultimately reached … 12,000 officers and 320,000 men'. To achieve this, Long had to organize 'the training of all ranks in all descriptions of the work of transport and supply', and 'the provision of motor vehicles and … all that was needful for vast armies scattered all over the world' (Reader, 15–16). Long's origins in the protestant ascendancy and his military experience and success helped to create a personality described as 'direct, impetuous, even irascible' (Reader, 16). His military career effectively came to an end in May 1915, when he stood out against Lloyd George's plan, implemented through Sir Eric Geddes, to take over motor vehicle production and the supply of motors for the army. Long resisted the loss of the army's independence in procurement for some time, but resigned in March 1916, with the rank of major-general.

Long had apparently served on an official committee with Sir William Lever (later first Baron Leverhulme) in the early part of 1916. At this time Lever, who, years before, had shown an appreciation of the motor vehicle in its infancy, was concerned with improving the efficiency of group transport operations. In consequence, Long joined Lever Brothers in late 1916; by the summer of 1917 he was advocating the establishment of a separate transport company within the group, replacing the independent operations of the individual manufacturing companies. It took more than six months for Long's views to prevail, and then he was successful only in part—achieving the centralized distribution of finished products, crucial for both soap and margarine, but not the collection of raw materials. SPD Ltd (the initials derived from 'speedy prompt delivery') was incorporated in July 1918, and Long was its first chairman (as well as a director of Lever Brothers, which changed its name to Unilever in 1929), serving with SPD until the end of 1931. He spent his first years as a Lever director at Port Sunlight, where he and his wife 'took an active interest in the life of the village and its institutions' (Leverhulme, 14). He was given an appreciative profile in the Unilever house journal on his retirement, yet he did not record his civilian career in *Who's Who*. His service with SPD was not without controversy, probably attributable not only to his strong personality, but also to intra-group rivalries and genuine, if unfounded, fears about the common transport of foodstuffs and cleaning materials.

In addition to his work for SPD, Long was a member of the Commercial Motor Users' Association, and also served as its president. Between the wars Long played an important role in national transport bodies. During the 1920s he was an assiduous chairman of the transport committee of the Federation of British Industries, retiring at the end of 1931. Little is known about his private life, but it is known that he married Augusta Elizabeth, daughter of Colonel T. G. Glover, and they had one son. Long's wife predeceased him in 1938, and he died on 31 January 1940 at 16 Fitzroy Square, London. RICHARD A. STOREY

Sources W. J. Reader, *Hard roads and highways: SPD Ltd, 1918–68, a study in distribution* (1969) · Lord Leverhulme [W. Lever], 'Major-General S. S. Long, C. B.', *Progress* (Jan 1932), 14–15 · *WWW* · J. Fortescue and R. H. Beadon, *The royal army service corps: a history of transport and supply in the British army*, 2 vols. (1930–31) · Federation of British Industries minute books, U. Warwick Mod. RC, MSS 200/F/1/1 · d. cert. · *CGPLA Eng. & Wales* (1940)

Archives Unilever Archives, Leverhulme corresp.

Wealth at death £15,141 4s: administration with will, 9 April 1940, *CGPLA Eng. & Wales*

Long, Thomas (*bap.* **1621**, *d.* **1707**), Church of England clergyman, was the son of Richard Long of Exeter and was baptized at St Lawrence's Church there on 14 December 1621. Thomas matriculated servitor at Exeter College, Oxford, on 5 April 1639. He graduated BA in 1642, but left soon afterwards because of the turmoil in Oxford due to the civil war. He must have married by 1648 or 1649, when his eldest son Thomas was born, but we do not know the name of his wife (or wives).

Long became vicar of Clyst St Lawrence, near Exeter, in 1652. In April 1684 Bishop Lamplugh of Exeter claimed in a letter to Archbishop Sancroft that Long was sequestered during the interregnum because of his loyalties and churchmanship: Long 'lay under a long Sequestration & yet held up against all interests, but the kings & the churchs, which he constantly asserted both by preaching & printing against the ringleaders of the Rebellion' (*Walker rev.*, 118). However, whether Long actually was sequestered is questionable; John Walker, who knew Long well, and Long was indeed the 'ancient clergyman' who inspired him to write his account of the sufferings of the loyalist and Anglican clergy, fails to mention any such sequestration (ibid., v). A book published by Long in 1658 does not answer the question directly, but clearly shows his sense of persecution and alienation. He implied that the puritan authorities—'those who are named by the name of Christ'—were committing 'iniquities' just as were the 'enemies of Jerusalem'. That these 'veterane Souldiers, and houshold-servants, who yet remain in his Tents, should conspire with his enemies to betray his fortresses, cast away their armes, and desert his cause, is of very sad consideration' (T. Long, *An excercitation Concerning the Frequent Use of our Lords Prayer in the Publick Worship of God. And a View of what hath been Said by Dr. Owen Concerning that Subject*, London, 1658, preface). In a letter of 1703 Long claimed that the number of ejected Anglican priests during the interregnum was much higher than Edmund Calamy's estimate—perhaps as high as 10,000. All this, plus Long's later vitriolic attacks on dissent, suggest that, even if he was not sequestered, he certainly carried a grudge because of his treatment during the interregnum.

Long was created BD by royal mandate at the Restoration and was created prebendary of Exeter Cathedral on 18 January 1661. He was a prolific writer, and in this period was best known for his bitter pamphlet wars against dissenters, particularly against the presbyterians. In *Calvinus redivivus* (London, 1673) he argued that Calvin 'sets himself in the breach that is made, to prevent any farther separation, and to recall those that are departed to their former Communion' (Long, *Calvinus*, epistle). He went on to quote the reformer on his views of 'Anabaptists' and 'Libertines', and applied these comments to dissenters. This did not mean that Calvin would agree with Anglicans on all things: 'I know he differs in some things from us; but in many more from our Adversaries' (Long, *Calvinus*, 14). The interregnum—and very likely his own experience during the interregnum—was always in his mind when he wrote these tracts. In *No Protestant but the Dissenters Plot* (London, 1682) he maintained that dissenters had persecuted Anglicans far more in the 1650s than vice versa during the Restoration. Dissenters, moreover, would go to any length to destroy the Church of England: 'By which we see, that the help of any Party, Anabaptists or Papists, are acceptable to the Dissenters, when there is any probability of afflicting or destroying the established Church' (Long, *No Protestant*, 11). He often lumped dissenting and papist plots together, and made an attempt at cataloguing their long, nefarious business in *History of all the popish and fanatical plots and conspiracies against the established government … from the first year of Queen Elizabeth's reign to this present year 1684* (London, 1684). Long's greatest target among the presbyterians was Richard Baxter, against whom he wrote a great deal. Wood observed that he had 'undergone that very toilsome drudgrey of reading many or most of Mr. Richard Baxter's Books, and hath published Reflections and Animadversions on several of them' (Wood, *Ath. Oxon.*, 2.951). Baxter took umbrage at Long's 1678 book, *Mr. Hales's Treatise of Schism Examined and Censured* (London, 1678), in which he accused nonconformists of being 'schismaticks'. Baxter replied to Long in a letter in which, with biting sarcasm, he said that he understood 'by your Book that you think that you are in the Right; which is the most that I have yet learned out of it, unless it be also that you think the Nonconformists be not yet hated and afflicted enough' (Keeble and Nuttall, 2.197–8). The attacks and recriminations between Long and Baxter continued until Baxter's death. In fact, Long was determined to have the last say, so after Baxter died he penned a *Review of Mr. Richard Baxter's life, wherein many mistakes are rectified, some false relations detected, [and] some omissions supplyed* (London, 1697). When Edmund Calamy took over Baxter's *Reliquiae* project, he inherited the battle with Long as well. Long sparred with him as he did with Baxter (*A Rebuke to Mr. Edmund Calamy, Author of the Abridgment of Mr. Baxter's Life*, Exeter, 1704).

Archbishop Sancroft offered Long the bishopric of Bristol in 1684, but he declined that poor diocese because of his age and the size of his family. Long also served as proctor for convocation in 1689, 1693, and 1694. Numerous sources report that he refused the oaths in 1689, but this is clearly not the case and seems to have arisen from confusion with his son, Thomas [*see below*], who also had a prebend at Exeter. Long was, it is true, a staunch advocate of passive obedience, but in *Reflections upon a Late Book, Entituled 'The Case of Allegiance Consider'd'* (London, 1689), he argued that it was lawful to take the oaths of allegiance to William and Mary, who 'had a right Title to the Succession of the Crown of England'. James had clearly abdicated, since he

> deserted first the Government, and then the Land, and fled to an inveterate Enemy of our Religion and Nation, … and leaving us under a standing Army, wherein was a considerable party of Irish Papists, who … were likely to be very injurious to the English subjects. (Long, *Reflections*, 5–6)

Long maintained, however, that the best security that English subjects could give to the present government was to hold fast to the doctrines of non-resistance and passive obedience.

Long had a reputation for erudition. He published sermons, works critical of heterodoxy (*Answer to a Socinian Treatise called 'The Naked Gospel'*, London, 1691) and Lockean toleration (*The Letter for Toleration Decyphered*, London, 1689), books against alteration of the liturgy of the Church of England (*Vox cleri, or, The sense of the clergy, concerning the making of alterations in the established liturgy*, London, 1690), and a defence of Charles I's authorship of *Eikon basilike*.

Though he resigned his prebend in 1701, Long apparently remained at Clyst St Lawrence, though by the time he made his will, on 4 June 1706, he appears to have given up the living, as he merely described himself as a clerk of Exeter. The will, proved on 8 October 1708, lists eight children as survivors: Joseph, Nicholas, Thomas (who died not long after the will was made), John, Richard, Elizabeth, Dorothy, and Susanna. Long died on 7 December 1707 and was buried four days later in the parish where he had been baptized, St Lawrence, Exeter.

Long's son, also **Thomas Long** (1648/9–1707), Church of England clergyman, also attended Exeter College, Oxford, where he matriculated, aged fifteen, on 1 April 1664, but graduated from Corpus Christi College, Oxford, in February 1668 and proceeded MA in 1671. He was rector of Whimple, Devon, from 1676. After 1679 he served as chaplain to Anthony Sparrow, bishop of Norwich (and previously bishop of Exeter) whose daughter Bridget Sparrow (*d.* 1712) he had married on 15 August 1676. He became a prebendary of Exeter in 1681. Long lost living and prebend in 1689 when he became a nonjuror. He died in Exeter in 1707, and was buried in St Lawrence's on 28 July, less than five months before his father, and five years before his widow.

J. S. Chamberlain

Sources T. Long, *Calvinus redivivus* (1673) • T. Long, *No protestant but the dissenters plot* (1682) • [T. Long], *Reflections upon a late book, entituled 'The case of allegiance consider'd'* (1689) • Wood, *Ath. Oxon.*, 2nd edn • Foster, *Alum. Oxon.* • will, Devon RO, Moger transcripts [Thomas Long the elder] • *Calendar of the correspondence of Richard Baxter*, ed. N. H. Keeble and G. F. Nuttall, 2 (1991), 197–8 • N. H. Keeble, *N&Q*, 230 (1985), 190–91 • *Walker rev.* • G. B. Tatham, *Dr. John Walker and the 'Sufferings of the clergy'* (1911) • Watt, *Bibl. Brit.* • Allibone, *Dict.* •

T. Lamplugh, bishop of Exeter, letter to Sancroft, 16 April 1684, Bodl. Oxf., MSS Tanner, fol. 30 • Bodl. Oxf., MS Rawl. C. 739 • *The registers of baptisms, marriages, and burials of the city of Exeter*, 1, ed. W. U. Reynell-Upham and H. Tapley-Soper, Devon and Cornwall RS (1910) • *DNB*

Archives Bodl. Oxf., letters, MSS Rawl.

Wealth at death £33 in cash, lands in Exeter and Devon: will, Moger transcripts, Devon RO

Long, Thomas (1648/9–1707). *See under* Long, Thomas (*bap.* 1621, *d.* 1707).

Long, Sir Walter, first baronet (*c.*1591–1672), politician, was the second son of Henry Long (*d.* 1612), a wealthy clothier and landowner from Whaddon, Wiltshire, and Rebecca Bailey (*d.* 1655). Educated at Lincoln's Inn, he spent the latter half of the 1610s at Salisbury with his mother and her second husband, Henry Sherfield, a prominent lawyer who became the town's recorder. He had inherited no land at his father's death and in 1620, having completed his legal training, joined Sir Robert Mansell's fleet at Tilbury as it prepared for an expedition against Algerian corsairs. Long's return to England soon afterwards was hastened by his elder brother's death, and thereafter he struggled with the family's extensive but encumbered estate. On 26 December 1621 he married Mary Coxe (*d.* 1631). By 1623 his debts had grown alarmingly. With his father-in-law's assistance he obtained a seat for Salisbury in the 1625 parliament, perhaps as a means to evade creditors. He was elected knight of the shire in 1626, and on this occasion probably had the backing of William Herbert, third earl of Pembroke.

A vocal supporter of the remonstrance defending the Commons against the charge of unparliamentary proceedings, Long played an active part in supporting Pembroke's attack on the duke of Buckingham, making several speeches questioning the duke's protestantism and implying that the duke had a hand in precipitating the death of James I. The crown endeavoured to prevent Long's return to parliament in 1628 by pricking him as sheriff for Wiltshire, but he managed to secure a seat for Bath in Somerset nevertheless, arguing on tentative legal grounds that he was not breaking the law since the constituency lay outside his county. Again he was one of the principal voices in attacking Buckingham, and he played a significant part in promoting the petition of right. His continuing opposition to Buckingham was not tolerated, however, and in October 1628 he was silenced by the solicitor-general, Sir Robert Heath, who in a star chamber suit argued that Long had not only acted unlawfully in securing his election but also neglected his shrieval duties. Long quickly withdrew to Wiltshire in an attempt to avoid censure, but he returned to parliament for the 1629 session. He took a leading part in the tumultuous scenes on 2 March, when the speaker was forcibly prevented from adjourning the house. He was arrested and appeared before king's bench for offences committed within the house while simultaneously facing ongoing star chamber proceedings concerning his shrievalty. His appeals for clemency, and attempts by his counsel and sympathetic friends to secure his release, were unsuccessful. He agreed to be bound over but, fearing that he should be considered weak in his resolution, he retracted on learning that the other prisoners had refused to be bailed. He was fined 2000 marks and sent to the Tower until his release in 1633, by which time both his first wife and his political confidant and fellow prisoner Sir John Eliot had died.

Forced to sell much of his Wiltshire property to pay his fine, Long spent most of the 1630s on the Shropshire estates of his second wife, Anne Foxe (*née* Cage; *d.* 1665). His subsequent opposition to ship money was consistent with his earlier hostility towards arbitrary government taxes. He was elected to the Long Parliament as member for Ludgershall, Wiltshire, in December 1641, and a sympathetic house soon afterwards granted him compensation for his former ill usage. His continuing opposition to the court led to his exemption from the royal pardon in November the following year, and during the civil war he took an active part in parliament's cause. Severely wounded at Edgehill, he subsequently raised a troop of horse and helped to organize parliamentary forces in Wiltshire and Shropshire, but it is uncertain whether he saw further action. He gained the position of chief register in chancery but was to acquire a degree of notoriety as a prominent member of the presbyterian faction in the Commons. He twice assaulted members who disputed his views and by 1647 was acting as 'a recognizable party Whip' for the presbyterians (Underdown, 69). It was this latter role that saw Long included among the eleven presbyterian members the army sought to remove from parliament in 1647. After escaping to France he fell in with royalists and disaffected parliamentarians. The role he played, if any, in promoting the royalist cause while abroad is uncertain. However, sensing the changing political tide, he returned to England in late 1659, and after the restoration of the monarchy he was given a baronetcy in 1661, either as a reward for his endeavours on behalf of the exiled king or to placate an influential former foe. He died on 15 November 1672 at Whaddon, where he was later buried. A portrait of Long, now lost, was referred to in the will of his third wife, Anne Cotes (*d.* 1688), whom he married on 2 January 1666. HENRY LANCASTER

Sources Wilts. & Swindon RO, 947; 1676 • Hants. RO, 44M69L34 • *JHC*, 1–5 (1547–1648) • J. Eliot, *'De jure maiestatis, or, Political treatise of government' (1628–30) and the letter-book* (1625–1632), ed. A. B. Grosart, 2 vols. (1882) • G. E. Aylmer, *The state's servants: the civil service of the English republic, 1649–1660* (1973) • B. Whitelocke, *Memorials of the English affairs*, new edn (1732) • will, PRO, PROB 11/393, fol. 176v [Anne Long, Lady Long, third wife] • Keeler, *Long Parliament* • *VCH Wiltshire* • GEC, *Baronetage* • PRO, C 142/331/11 • BL, Add. MS 11757, fol. 147 • C. Russell, *Parliaments and English politics, 1621–1629* (1979) • *IGI* • D. Underdown, *Pride's Purge: politics in the puritan revolution* (1971) • W. P. Baildon, ed., *The records of the Honorable Society of Lincoln's Inn: admissions*, 2 vols. (1896)

Archives Wilts. & Swindon RO, family MSS | Hants. RO, Sherfield MSS

Wealth at death substantial: owed £37,036 at death: Wilts. & Swindon RO, 947/1132; 1676/1, 2

Long, Walter Hume, first Viscount Long (1854–1924), politician, was born at Bath on 13 July 1854, the eldest son

Walter Hume Long, first Viscount Long (1854–1924), by Elliott & Fry

of Richard Penruddocke Long (1825–1875), a country gentleman and MP, and his wife, Charlotte Anna (*d.* 1899), daughter of William Wentworth Fitzwilliam Hume (later Dick). He was educated privately and at Harrow School, where he distinguished himself as a sportsman (he played for his school at the Eton and Harrow cricket match of 1873). In 1873 he went up to Christ Church, Oxford, where fox-hunting and driving his coach-and-four proved to be more absorbing pursuits than the formal academic curriculum. The death of his father in 1875 brought the burdens of property, and heralded the end of his playful undergraduate career: Long left Oxford without a degree, and took on the management of his patrimony—an estate of some 15,400 acres with an income of £23,200. Like his father, Long found a bride among the southern Irish landed élite: on 1 August 1878 he married Lady Dorothy Blanche (1858–1938), the fourth daughter of Richard Edmund St Lawrence Boyle, ninth earl of Cork and Orrery. The couple had five children, two sons and three daughters.

Parliamentary career The Long family had owned land in Wiltshire since the fourteenth century, and had an extended tradition of parliamentary representation: 'our parliamentary record', Long boasted, 'is, I believe, unique' (Long, 2). In addition Long's maternal family, the Humes, had sat in the Commons for co. Wicklow over several generations. There was, however, little distinction in the families' recent parliamentary offerings: Long's two grandfathers, who represented Wiltshire and Wicklow, maintained the tradition of silent county members, and contributed one speech between them to the Commons debates. Long upheld his family's claims to one of the Wiltshire seats; but he swiftly demonstrated both a rather greater political energy than his predecessors and an appeal which transcended the county boundaries. He was elected for North Wiltshire in 1880, and held the seat until 1885, when he moved to the eastern division of the county: here he remained until the election of 1892.

Long was a casualty of the Liberal victory of that year, but in 1893 found a seat in the West Derby division of Liverpool, which he occupied until 1900. He was MP for South Bristol from 1900 until 1906, when he was again defeated. But he had taken the precaution of accepting nomination for South County Dublin, a constituency with a comparatively strong Irish unionist presence: he won this contest, and represented the division until 1910. In January 1910 his electoral peregrination took him back to England, and to the Strand division of Middlesex, where he was MP until 1918. In that year he made his final move, to the St George's division of Westminster. In 1921 he left the Commons on being raised to the dignity of a viscountcy (4 June).

Long represented seven constituencies in a parliamentary career of some forty years. Some of his moves had been forced upon him through defeat or through boundary changes; but there may also have been an element of political calculation. By the time of his retirement Long had served the electors of his home county, and—as befitted a squire—had represented the needs of different agrarian interests. But he had also represented constituencies in other, far-flung strongholds of late Victorian and Edwardian toryism: he had established or consolidated connections with the tory working men of Liverpool, the Irish unionists of south Dublin, the suburban tories of South Bristol, the metropolitan tories of the Strand and of St George's. Long's parliamentary *cursus honorum* reveals something of his carefully won national significance: it also suggests the ambition and calculation of a man often (wrongly) dismissed as a booby squire.

Early ministerial career, 1886–1905 Long's ministerial career confirms this image of shrewd, strategically alert, political intelligence. In 1886 he was appointed as parliamentary secretary to the Local Government Board, with C. T. Ritchie as president of the board. The two men had complementary skills and experience: Ritchie represented urban and metropolitan toryism, while Long at this stage had an exclusively agrarian base. Long had responsibility for the administration of the poor law. In addition he was one of the architects of the Local Government Act of 1888, through which were established elected county councils. Ritchie, who generally handled the urban aspects of the board's activities, championed the creation of the London county council. Ritchie's absence from the House of Commons between 1892 and 1895 gave Long an opportunity to act as the senior opposition spokesman on local government matters; and this in turn reinforced his claims on further ministerial advancement.

With the tories back in power in 1895, Long was offered the presidency of the Board of Agriculture and a seat in the cabinet. Here he consolidated his reputation as a politically courageous and pragmatic reformer who was informed, but not unduly constrained by his rural constituency. He was keen to preserve the quality of British livestock, and moved quickly—despite opposition from the colonies—against imported animals of inferior quality. But rabies was the issue which dominated his time at the board, and here he fell foul of rural opinion. He fought to conquer the disease in Britain—through quarantine and other import restrictions, by muzzling animals in areas where an outbreak had occurred, and by the seizure and destruction of animals suspected of contamination: he took on the pet-loving British middle classes as well as farmers and huntsmen. He was bombarded with more hate-mail and with more threats than at any other period of his political career (including his service in Ireland); but he stood his ground, and the new regulations were successfully enforced. The episode, important in itself, also illustrated that Long was not wholly tied to agrarian prejudices, and that he was by no means an uncomplicated spokesman for rural opinion. It illustrated that he had the capacity to defy key elements of his support, a capacity which would also be clear in his handling of the Government of Ireland Bill in 1919–20.

In 1900 Long was translated to the presidency of the Local Government Board. The two measures which chiefly distinguished his tenure of this office were the Metropolitan Water Act (1902) and the Unemployed Workmen's Act (1905). Through the first of these the property of the eight water companies which supplied London was bought up, and their functions delegated to a new elective authority. The Unemployed Workmen's Act was an initiative designed to address the needs of the rising numbers of the jobless: the measure created an unemployment board which was intended to give work and training through centrally supported funding mechanisms. Long's enthusiasm for this measure was not widely shared among his colleagues, who felt that he had extended the bounds of paternalist toryism towards the heresies of socialism. He was deemed to be 'a radical at heart' by the tory whip Lord Balcarres (Vincent, 43): other senior party figures felt that he had sold out to the challenge of Labour. The accusations read somewhat strangely in the light of Long's reputation as an immoveable hardliner.

Ireland, 1906–1914 In what might have been an effort to terminate his socialist education, Arthur Balfour offered Long the first lordship of the Admiralty early in 1905. But the proposal was spurned, and in March 1905 Long took the opportunity instead to succeed George Wyndham as chief secretary for Ireland. Here Balfour's intention was unmistakable: he wanted a minister who would bring the increasingly wayward Irish Unionist Party back into line with British Conservatism and Unionism (indeed the position had earlier been offered successively to two Irish Unionist MPs, Edward Carson and John Atkinson). Long was well qualified for this task, having connections with southern Irish Unionism through both his mother's family and that of his wife. In addition he had a long-standing friendship with Edward Saunderson, the leader of the Irish Unionist parliamentary party, and effective commander of the broader Irish unionist movement. There was no absolute collapse to Irish unionist demands, just as there had been no slavish following of rural opinion at the Board of Agriculture: Long resisted pressure to remove Sir Antony MacDonnell, the under-secretary for Ireland, and a Catholic, who was thought by Irish loyalists to have been the malevolent grey eminence behind the Wyndham regime. On the other hand, Long satisfied the concerns of loyalists and others with regard to policing: he launched a programme to consolidate the strength of the Royal Irish Constabulary, a force which had been somewhat neglected by Wyndham. In addition Long was attentive to the patronage demands of Irish unionists (again, in contradistinction to the record of his predecessor): in a significant gesture, Long moved to offer the post of solicitor-general for Ireland to William Moore, one of Wyndham's most ferocious loyalist critics. In the event the appointment was never made, for the Unionist government fell in December 1905, before the negotiations had been concluded. Long was out of office, but—unlike many of his former ministerial colleagues—he remained in the Commons. For, thanks in no small part to his record as chief secretary, the unionists of South County Dublin had nominated him as their candidate; and on 26 January 1906 he had gone on to take the seat, defeating his nationalist opponent.

Ireland was a significant—though by no means an exclusive—preoccupation until the outbreak of the First World War. Long was keen to emphasize his claims to be a major arbiter of Conservative policy on Ireland, and he jealously monitored Wyndham's efforts to claw back an influence over Irish matters. But there were limits to Long's concern for Ireland, and—more obviously—limits to the interest of the wider Conservative Party. In 1907 Long helped to found the Union Defence League, a body designed to re-energize unionist opinion in Great Britain: its evangelizing activities were complemented by an Irish sister body, the joint committee of the Unionist associations of Ireland. The efforts of these two organizations were tardily rewarded, however: Long found it very difficult to rouse enthusiasm even among his front-bench colleagues when he was seeking patronage for the Union Defence League. He was a leading opponent of the third Home Rule Bill, and there are good grounds for believing that he had connections with the most hawkish of the Ulster unionists. It is certainly the case that Long's parliamentary lieutenant, Sir William Bull, actively facilitated the arms-smuggling schemes of the Ulstermen. The protagonist of the Larne gun-running episode of April 1914, F. H. Crawford, claimed that Long had not only been aware of the plans for the coup, but had been closely involved with its finances.

On the other hand, there is a suggestive ambiguity (or at least hesitation) in Long's actions. As early as 1908, despite his protestations of empathy with Irish Unionism, he was preparing to move out of his South Dublin constituency to the safer tory environment of the Strand division. Moreover, he did not identify himself quite as closely with Carson as some other British Conservative MPs (F. E. Smith, for example): he emphatically did not 'play the Orange card' with any abandon. It seems that he was willing to aid even the most extreme expressions of Ulster unionist militancy; but it also seems to be the case that he was happiest doing so discreetly, and through intermediaries. The explanations for this comparative restraint are not hard to find. His health, for example, was beginning to break down: he was compelled in 1909 to take a four month break from politics, and recuperate on a cruise to South Africa. But it was also probably the case that Long did not want to become too narrowly identified with the Irish unionist cause, and too publicly identified with militant Ulster Unionism. For, unlike Carson, he had much wider political concerns and ambitions; and, unlike James Craig, he was temperamentally unsuited to playing a supporting role in someone else's drama.

The leadership contest, 1911 Long played across a wide political repertoire. His early observations of rural poverty, and of the unpopularity of the 'fair trade' proposals of the early 1880s made him cautious about tariff reform. However, just as with Ireland, he was careful not to position himself too far from the median of party opinion on this question. He declared himself from the start to be 'more or less' a follower of Joseph Chamberlain's policy; but coyness remained the hallmark of his approach (Fitzroy, 1.138). He was a moderate tariff-reformer; but at the same time he acted as an intermediary between free-trade unionists and the party leadership. During the constitutional crisis of 1909–11 he displayed the same mixture of strategic self-interest and political pragmatism. He was anxious not to be upstaged by any of his front-bench rivals in opposing Lloyd George's budget of 1909; but he emerged as a comparative moderate in responding to the challenge of the Parliament Bill of 1911 (Long favoured acquiescence in the measure, without forcing the issue). As always, his choleric defence of his position distracted from its essential moderation: Lord Balcarres recalled some menacing observations (Vincent, 214) offered by a 'vermilion' Long to a bemused Carson on the issue of the bill (Carson favoured last-ditch resistance to the government).

Long's careful manoeuvrings and ministerial experience placed him in a commanding position in November 1911, when Balfour chose to resign from the party leadership. Indeed, he was widely regarded—certainly in the Carlton Club—as the likely winner of any contest for the succession. Long had thirty-five years' ministerial experience. He had moved with party opinion on the tariff-reform question; he had promoted the cause of the Irish unionists without becoming ensnared in the minutiae of loyalist politics; he had fought the budget tenaciously without becoming identified with any extremist position. He had been seen to remain loyal to Balfour, while contributing fully to the resentful murmurings which had helped to precipitate his chief's resignation.

However, Austen Chamberlain, representing the Liberal Unionist and advanced tariff-reform interests, also had a wide following: in addition Chamberlain, a former chancellor of the exchequer, had occasionally deputized for Balfour. Divided by principle, there were also personal tensions separating the two men. A highly divisive contest was only avoided when—on 10 November—Chamberlain offered to withdraw his candidature, if Long did likewise. The two men united in endorsing the claims of a *tertium quid*, Andrew Bonar Law, who was duly elected on 13 November. Long later claimed that he, and not Chamberlain, was the architect of the great compromise (Long, 191): the surviving evidence does not support his claim. However, a remark made by Chamberlain on 22 October suggests the faint but pleasing possibility that Long may have had deeply laid plans: 'Walter Long has abandoned claims for the leadership, and has settled to put forward Bonar Law as his nominee when a vacancy occurs' (Vincent, 234). In addition, it was widely noticed that Long, in proposing Bonar Law for the leadership, had been on top form: 'his speech was one of the best things I ever heard', observed Robert Sanders, '[it was] manly and rather touching. The country gentleman at his very best' (Ramsden, *Real Old Tory Politics*, 35). Long's 'masterpiece of plain speaking and noble devotion to the interests of the Party and Country' (Williamson, 54) helped to silence the resentful murmurings prevalent in some quarters of the party against the leadership deal.

Wartime ministerial service With the formation of the first coalition government in 1915 (the prospect of which had originally raised his suspicions), Long returned to office as president of the Local Government Board. Here he was responsible for the welfare of the many thousands of Belgian refugees who had fled their homeland under the threat of the German advance. In addition he was charged with the task of framing the conscription measures which were enacted in 1916. He was closely involved with the lengthy debates on the franchise which were eventually formalized within the speaker's conference (August 1916): he may be regarded as one of the architects of the Representation of the People Bill (1917). He shifted ground on the issue of women's suffrage, moving from outright opposition in the pre-war period to a grudging and pragmatic acquiescence by 1916. But for the moment he remained a critic of home rule: he was an influential opponent of the proposed Irish settlement formulated by Lloyd George in the aftermath of the 1916 rising.

On the formation of the second coalition, in December 1916, Long was moved to the Colonial Office, where he remained for the rest of the war. He sought to bind the empire ever more closely to the British war effort: he chaired the imperial conferences of 1917 and 1918, and developed better communication links between London and the various colonial administrations. He had additional responsibilities. He was the cabinet member responsible for liaison with Dublin Castle. Lloyd George delegated to him the further task of improving the supply of oil to the British forces. This charge, of pressing significance in terms of the war effort, was a major preoccupation in 1917–18.

The Admiralty and Ireland, 1918–1921 Long's last ministerial posting came in 1918, when he was appointed first lord of the Admiralty. Here he oversaw the downsizing of the Royal Navy, as well as improvements in the pay and conditions of those officers and men who survived the cuts. He fought inter-departmental battles to preserve the navy from the crusading ambitions of the new Air Ministry and of its secretary of state, Winston Churchill. He was responsible for the navy's contribution to the campaigns in support of the White Russian cause. But he was also ailing (observers began to comment on his frailty); he was burdened by extra-departmental administrative challenges. That he survived unscathed (at least in political terms) for three years at the Admiralty reflects on his own powers of delegation, and on the quality of his parliamentary support: his parliamentary secretary in 1920–21 was James Craig, tipped as a rising ministerial star, but soon to be diverted into Ulster politics.

In October 1919 Long was asked to chair the cabinet committee on Ireland, a body which was charged with the task of preparing a measure of home rule for Ireland. Like other tories, Long had become reconciled to the idea of home rule for Ireland by 1918—a change of heart which 'gives the lie to the oft repeated allegation that he was a diehard reactionary' (Murphy, 'Walter Long and the making of the Government of Ireland Act', 95). Still, his legislative assignment raised some eyebrows: Almeric Fitzroy quoted the wry observation (made perhaps by Carson) that 'to set Walter Long drafting a Home Rule Bill is like asking the Bishop of London to draft the regulations of a maison tolérée' (Fitzroy, 2.674). The resultant Government of Ireland Act (1920) made provision for the creation of two home-rule parliaments and governments, one in Belfast for the new Northern Ireland, and one in Dublin for a proposed southern Ireland. The relevance of the measure to the south of Ireland was rapidly overturned by the Anglo-Irish treaty of 1921, and by the Irish Free State Constitution Act of 1922. But Long's Government of Ireland Act survived as the founding charter for Northern Ireland, and for the constitutional arrangements which operated there until 1972.

Summation Walter Long retired and was created a viscount in 1921. He died at his home, Rood Ashton, Trowbridge, Wiltshire, on 26 September 1924. In some ways he had been an archetypal tory gentleman, and it was in this light that he was viewed by many contemporaries and by posterity. But with Long appearances were often deceptive. He looked and sounded like a squire from the pages of Fielding: he was stout, rubicund, and was armed with an explosive temper. Surviving photographs suggest a casual, tweedy, dress sense. Yet behind the apparent carelessness there ran a streak of vanity. It is quite clear from the surviving images that he liked to be photographed in profile: it is clear, too, that he was cussedly prepared to spoil the symmetry of group portraits in order to display what he presumed was his best side.

Long was a firm unionist, and yet was one of the architects of the Government of Ireland Act, the fourth home-rule measure. He was strongly interested in the armed forces (his eldest son, Brigadier-General Walter Long, was killed in action in France in 1917, and his grandson, the second Viscount Long, fell in 1944, during the Second World War). Yet as first lord of the Admiralty he presided over a massive demobilization and retrenchment within the Royal Navy. He was a squire, deeply interested in the problems of rural Britain: he strongly believed that the creation of a bulwark of small landowners in the British countryside would be an insuperable barrier to socialism. But he was not excessively rigid or romantic in his convictions: here was no representative of 'the stupid party'. It has been rightly said that 'when it came to landed society and rural property he approached the diehards, but he had a receptivity to opportunism when it was applied to the urban sector' (Fforde, 79). He was thought by his colleagues to have dangerously radical leanings: Lord Balcarres complained that

> he is the most paradoxical and ill-balanced person I know. One day he delivers a speech of sturdy and uncompromising Toryism, and the next day he larks off … to deliver … an address in which he tries to go one better than the Socialists. (Vincent, 182)

The complexities of Long's politics reflected to some extent the complexities of his personality. He could be generous and chivalrous in his personal relations. He valued personal and political loyalty (he knew well the value of his patronage, and few of those who served him went unrewarded). His political intelligence was acute, though sometimes underestimated; his unsophisticated tastes, hectoring manner, and meandering style were unhelpful to his reputation—Balfour remarked in September 1911 that Long was 'too discursive, too quick-tempered, and above all too complimentary' (Vincent, 225). An accusation of discursiveness from Balfour may be thought a little hard to credit; and yet others also complained of Long's occasionally unfocused and emotive modes of disquisition. There is, however, a case for seeing his uncertainty as pragmatism, and for judging his volatility in the light of his political ambitions.

Long was intensely jealous of rivals. He was easily driven to anger, and especially by perceived slights to his position within the party. He was a complainer: Austen Chamberlain observed in November 1911 that 'Long had been at the centre of every coterie of grumblers for the last five years' (Chamberlain, 387). He may also have been an intriguer (though here the evidence is a little less certain). He was unquestionably highly ambitious; and it is likely that, had his health been better, he would have pushed his claims on the party leadership much more vigorously than in fact was the case. As it was, he survived for twenty-six years in tory cabinets or shadow cabinets: he had twenty-five years of ministerial experience and achievement in five different departments of state.

Some thought that Long's anger and uncertainty

betrayed an intellectual and emotional weakness; Balcarres remarked that his 'nervous and protean excitability must arise from some latent affectation of the nerves' (Vincent, 186). And yet his careful cultivation of a wide base within the party, combined with his rich ministerial experience, had brought him, in 1911, to within reach of the succession to Balfour. Some, who thought that his elevation was likely, feared for the consequences. Was he, then, the worst leader the Conservatives never had?

ALVIN JACKSON

Sources W. Long, *Memories* (1923) • R. Murphy, 'Walter Long and the conservative party, 1905–1921', PhD diss., University of Bristol, 1984 • C. Petrie, *Walter Long and his times* (1936) • E. H. H. Green, *The crisis of conservatism: the politics, economics and ideology of the Conservative Party, 1880–1914* (1995) • A. Jackson, *The Ulster party: Irish unionists in the House of Commons, 1884–1911* (1989) • R. Murphy, 'Walter Long and the making of the Government of Ireland Act, 1919–20', *Irish Historical Studies*, 25 (1986–7), 82–96 • M. Fforde, *Conservatism and collectivism, 1886–1914* (1990) • *The Crawford papers: the journals of David Lindsay, twenty-seventh earl of Crawford … 1892–1940*, ed. J. Vincent (1984) • A. Chamberlain, *Politics from inside: an epistolary chronicle, 1906–1914* (1936) • A. Fitzroy, *Memoirs*, 2 vols. [1925] • F. H. Crawford, *Guns for Ulster* (1947) • *Real old tory politics: the political diaries of Robert Sanders, Lord Bayford, 1910–35*, ed. J. Ramsden (1984) • *The modernisation of conservative politics: the diaries and letters of William Bridgeman, 1904–1935*, ed. P. Williamson (1988) • M. Pugh, *Electoral reform in war and peace, 1906–18* (1978) • J. Ramsden, *The age of Balfour and Baldwin, 1902–1940* (1978) • R. Shannon, *The age of Salisbury, 1881–1902: unionism and empire* (1996) • Burke, *Peerage* (1939)

Archives BL, corresp. and papers, Add. MSS 62403–62443 • IWM, letters from his son • PRO, papers, ADM 116/3623 • Wilts. & Swindon RO, corresp. and papers | BL, corresp. with H. H. Asquith and wife, Margot, Add. MS 62404 • BL, corresp. with Arthur James Balfour, Add. MS 62403 • BL, corresp. with Arthur James Balfour, Add. MSS 49776–49777, *passim* • BL, corresp. with Admiral Lord Charles de la Poer Beresford, Add. MS 62407 • BL, corresp. with Arthur John Bigge, Baron Stamfordham, Add. MS 62405 • BL, corresp. with Lord Cecil, Add. MS 51072 • BL, corresp. with Austen Chamberlain, Add. MS 62405 • BL, corresp. with Henry Chaplin, Add. MS 62406 • BL, corresp. with Albert Venn Dicey, Add. MS 62406 • BL, corresp. with Lord Gladstone, Add. MS 46082 • BL, corresp. with Andrew Bonar Law, Add. MS 62404 • BL, corresp. with Henry Charles Keith Petty-Fitzmaurice, fifth marquess of Lansdowne, Add. MS 62403 • BL, corresp. with Edward George Villiers Stonely, seventeenth earl of Derby, Add. MS 62405 • Bodl. Oxf., corresp. with Herbert Asquith • Bodl. Oxf., corresp. with H. A. Gwynne • Bodl. Oxf., letters to Lord Hanworth • Bodl. Oxf., corresp. with Sir William Harcourt and Lewis Harcourt • Bodl. Oxf., corresp. with John Sandars, etc. • Bodl. Oxf., corresp. with Lord Selborne • Bodl. RH, corresp. with Lord Lugard • CAC Cam., corresp. with Sir William Bull • CKS, letters to Aretas Akers-Douglas • Durham RO, letters to Lady Londonderry • Glos. RO, letters to Sir Michael Hicks Beach • HLRO, letters to R. D. Blumenfeld • HLRO, corresp. with J. C. C. Davidson and Andrew Bonar Law • HLRO, corresp. with Andrew Bonar Law • HLRO, corresp. with David Lloyd George • HLRO, corresp. with Herbert Samuel • Lpool RO, corresp. with Lord Derby • NA Scot., corresp. with A. J. Balfour and G. W. Balfour • NA Scot., corresp. with Philip Kerr • National Archives of Zimbabwe, Harare, corresp. with Francis Chaplin • NL Aus., corresp. with Lord Novar • NMM, letters to David Beatty • NRA, priv. coll., corresp. with Lord Balfour of Burleigh • PRO, corresp. with Lord Kitchener, PRO 30/57; WO 159 • PRO, corresp. with Lord Midleton, PRO 30/67 • PRO NIre., corresp. with Edward Carson, D1507 • PRO NIre., letters to Lady Londonderry, D2846 • U. Birm. L., corresp. with Austen Chamberlain • U. Newcastle, Robinson L., corresp. with Walter Runciman • University of Sheffield, corresp. with W. A. S. Hewins | FILM BFI NFTVA, film footage (speech) • IWM FVA, current affairs footage

Likenesses J. Brown, stipple, pubd 1882 (after photograph by Downey), NPG • B. Stone, photograph, 1897, NPG • A. H. Collins, oils, 1918, Steeple Ashton, Wiltshire; copy, Harrow School, Middlesex • Elliott & Fry, photograph, NPG [*see illus.*] • Spy [L. Ward], chromolithograph caricature, NPG; repro. in *VF* (16 Oct 1886)

Wealth at death £103,990 2*s*. 11*d*.: probate, 17 Dec 1924, *CGPLA Eng. & Wales*

Long, William (1817–1886), antiquary, born on 15 August 1817, was the second son of Walter Long (1788–1871) of Corhampton, Hampshire, and his wife, Lady Mary (*d.* 1875), eldest daughter of William *Carnegie, seventh earl of Northesk. He matriculated from Balliol College, Oxford, on 5 June 1835; he graduated BA in 1839 and proceeded MA in 1844. Long was a justice of the peace for Somerset and an FSA (from 1871) and he passed his life as a country gentleman and a local antiquary. His exhaustive articles on Avebury and Stonehenge, which appeared in the *Wiltshire Archaeological and Natural History Magazine*, were later expanded for publication in 1858 and 1876 respectively.

Long married, on 13 April 1841, Elizabeth Hare (*d.* 1874), only child of James Hare Joliffe; they had two sons and one daughter. He died at 2 Onslow Gardens, South Kensington, on 14 April 1886.

W. A. J. ARCHBOLD, *rev.* PENELOPE RUNDLE

Sources Foster, *Alum. Oxon.* • *The Times* (20 April 1886) • *The Athenaeum* (24 April 1886), 562 • *Wiltshire Archaeological and Natural History Magazine*, 23 (1887), 98 • Burke, *Gen. GB* • *Proceedings of the Society of Antiquaries of London*, 2nd ser., 11 (1885–7), 375 • *CGPLA Eng. & Wales* (1886)

Wealth at death £46,482 7*s*. 2*d*.: resworn probate, Jan 1887, *CGPLA Eng. & Wales* (1886)

Longchamp, William de (*d.* 1197), administrator and bishop of Ely, probably born near Argenton, Normandy, was a son of Hugh de Longchamp, who was a servant of Henry II, farmer of the revenues of the honour of Conches, Normandy, at the time of his death (probably in 1187). Hugh held land in Herefordshire, including a knight's fee of Hugh de Lacy's honour, the marriage portion of his wife. Apparently, her father was a tenant of the Lacys. Although William de Longchamp's modest knightly background was typical of the 'new men' whom the Angevins were recruiting into their service, chroniclers' complaints against his low birth are unusually harsh, repeating the charge levelled by Hugh de Nonant, bishop of Coventry and Lichfield, that Longchamp was the grandson of a peasant, 'who being of servile condition in the district of Beauvais, had for his occupation to guide the plough and whip up the oxen; and who at length to gain his liberty fled to the Norman territory' (*Chronica … Hovedene*, 3.142; *Gir. Camb. opera*, 4.418). He began his career as a clerk of Geoffrey Plantagenet (*d.* 1186) then became chancellor of Richard, count of Poitou. When Richard acceded to the English throne in 1189 he named Longchamp royal chancellor, a title that he held until his death. He paid £3000 for the office, and an increase in fees charged for sealing chancery documents may have been intended to provide funds for paying this fine. At the Council of Pipewell (15 September 1189) Richard I elevated four long-time royal servants to bishoprics; among them was Longchamp, who became bishop of Ely, being consecrated on 31 December 1189.

The king's first scheme for government of England during his absence on crusade broke down almost at once with the death in December 1189 of one of the two co-justiciars he had named, William de Mandeville, earl of Essex. Richard I then substituted William de Longchamp to serve alongside Hugh du Puiset, bishop of Durham. A second regency scheme was adopted at a council held at Nonancourt, Normandy, in mid-March 1190. The king named Longchamp chief justiciar of England, with Hugh du Puiset's authority confined to the lands north of the Humber. This, plus the fact of Longchamp's custody of the king's seal as chancellor, made his paramount authority clear.

By late spring 1190 Longchamp had left the king's entourage on the continent and returned to England to take control of the government. His custody of important castles reinforced his authority, and on 5 June Pope Clement III named him papal legate for England, adding to his power and prestige. As legate he presided over ecclesiastical councils at Gloucester on 1 August and at Westminster on 13 October 1190. Richard's new commission to Longchamp, dated 6 June 1190, failed to define the role of Hugh du Puiset, justiciar for the north; and Longchamp chose to bar him from any role in the central government, excluding him from the exchequer and requiring him to surrender castles in his custody. Longchamp acted vigorously as justiciar and chancellor in 1190. He took firm steps to restore order and do justice at York, following the massacre of the Jewish community there. He also organized a general eyre in the summer of 1190; and himself headed the panel of justices sitting at Westminster from Easter term 1190 to Easter term 1191. Again in 1190 Longchamp launched an expedition against Rhys ap Gruffudd, the most powerful prince in south Wales. And he made a concerted effort to raise as much money as possible for the king—for example, setting up a special exchequer to collect the enormous debts owed to Aaron, the Jewish moneylender of Lincoln. Longchamp left his mark on the English chancery. He is probably responsible for the precise dating clauses of Richard I's charters, and for substitution of the 'plural of majesty' for the first person singular—innovations doubtless reflecting the chancellor's familiarity with the papal chancery's practice.

Despite Longchamp's ability as an administrator, as a low-born foreigner he lacked the respect of the English baronage. He caused resentment by his financial exactions and the extravagance of his entourage as he moved about the country. His imperious manner and his ignorance of English customs soon aroused their incipient xenophobia, and brought mocking descriptions of his personal appearance and scurrilous attacks on his private life, including accusations of homosexuality. An accusation about his public activity, probably unjust, was that he ignored his associate justiciars; they were actually playing an important part in the administration, as barons of the exchequer, royal justices, and sheriffs. Yet he did seek to insinuate his own men into the government; by autumn 1191 a dozen counties had new sheriffs selected by the chancellor, and among them were two of his brothers. But Longchamp's chief problem in governing the kingdom was the powerful position of the king's brother, John, count of Mortain, whose position, not only as a great magnate but as a likely inheritor of the English crown, presented insurmountable difficulties for the chancellor. John knew how to exploit baronial opposition to Longchamp's authoritarian rule. One source of friction was the succession to the archbishopric of Canterbury, vacant in November 1190. Longchamp had some ambition of securing election for himself, but John wanted a say in the election. A more significant source of conflict was custody of royal castles. Longchamp was determined to keep royal control over key castles within John's domains, and in 1191 he began preparing for combat, importing mercenary soldiers from overseas. Richard I did not deal with complaints against his justiciar until the late spring of 1191, when he sent Walter de Countances, archbishop of Rouen, to England with two letters that directed the chancellor and others to take counsel with him, and implied that the archbishop should have an authority equal to the chancellor's own. Such orders were certain to undermine Longchamp's position, which was likely to be weakened further by the prospect of losing his position as papal legate; for Clement III died on 20 March 1191, and his commissions died with him. By midsummer, however, the new pope, Celestine III, had confirmed him in that office.

Meanwhile Gerard de Camville, who had purchased the shrievalty of Lincolnshire and custody of Lincoln Castle from Richard I, had renounced the chancellor's authority and done homage to John. Longchamp then laid siege to Lincoln Castle, whereupon John occupied Tickhill and Nottingham castles, and commanded Longchamp to lift his siege of Lincoln, saying, 'It is not fitting to take their custodies away from law-worthy men of the realm … and hand them over to foreigners and unknown men' (*Chronicon Richardi Divisensis*, 30–31). Walter de Coutances stepped forward at the end of April to act as mediator, and although both John and the chancellor appeared at the council at the head of large armed forces, the two opponents agreed to name arbitrators to settle the issue. Agreement was reached at a council at Winchester on 28 July 1191. There it was agreed that Gerard de Camville could keep his custody of Lincoln Castle and that John would surrender the castles he had taken. Also John obtained Longchamp's promise of support for his succession if the king died.

Another crisis soon followed, and led to Longchamp's fall from power and his exile from England. Fearful of the implications for his own authority if the king's half-brother, the bastard Geoffrey Plantagenet, archbishop of York, should return to England to take up possession of his see, Longchamp ordered the sheriff of Sussex to prevent Geoffrey from landing at any port under his jurisdiction. The resulting scandal, when Geoffrey's goods were seized by the constable of Dover Castle, and the archbishop himself was forcibly dragged from the church of St Martin's Priory in Dover, where he had taken refuge, gave John an opportunity to discredit Longchamp, and he convened a great council at Marlborough, accusing him of breaking the peace sworn at Winchester. The council summoned Longchamp to come before it at Loddon Bridge, between Reading and Windsor, on 5 October; and after some hesitation the chancellor duly appeared. Walter de Coutances finally revealed the contents of the two royal letters that he had brought from Sicily, and complained that Longchamp had never sought his counsel. The chancellor left the council to return to London, having heard a rumour that Count John was preparing to seize the city by force. He asked the citizens to bar the gates to the count, but they refused to obey and denounced him as a traitor. He then took refuge in the Tower of London, but surrendered after three days. John and the magnates followed him to London, where they reconvened, hearing accusations from Geoffrey of York and from Hugh de Nonant. On 10 October Longchamp came before the council, maintaining that Archbishop Geoffrey had been seized without his knowledge or consent and declaring his readiness to account to the last farthing for his spending of the king's money. When he refused to lay down the duties assigned him by the monarch, the council stripped him of his offices, and required him to hand over hostages for the return of all castles held by his dependants. The great council declared John supreme governor of the kingdom, and granted him custody of all royal castles.

Longchamp surrendered the Tower and Windsor Castle, and went to Dover in preparation for sailing to the continent. He was forbidden to leave England, however, and his efforts to escape in disguise made him a laughing-stock. He was variously described as having been caught fleeing in a monk's habit and in women's clothing, while a letter of Hugh de Nonant vividly depicts the fallen chancellor on Dover beach, dressed as a whore, being assaulted by a fisherman who had understandably assumed that he was encountering a prostitute. Eventually Longchamp sailed to Flanders on 29 October; he continued to Paris and then to Normandy. When he placed his diocese of Ely under an interdict and excommunicated his former colleagues at the exchequer, the archbishop of Rouen responded by seizing his episcopal estates and denouncing him throughout Normandy as an excommunicate. In 1192 Eleanor of Aquitaine persuaded the chancellor to withdraw the excommunication of his associate justiciars, and the archbishop to revoke his excommunication of Longchamp and restore his Ely estates to him. Having sent an agent to Palestine to inform Richard I of his fate, Longchamp returned to England in the spring of 1192, in an attempt to resume his duties as papal legate and to bribe John into supporting his restoration to his offices. John informed the bishops and barons meeting in a great council that the chancellor had promised him £700; they then offered him a larger sum of 2000 marks, and Longchamp had to leave the kingdom. In February 1194 a council at Westminster wrote to the pope protesting against Longchamp's continued legation, and some time after that he lost his commission.

Richard I's capture on the journey from the Holy Land took Longchamp to England once more in the spring of 1193 on the king's order, to attend a council at St Albans where the raising of Richard's ransom was to be discussed. He brought with him a copy of the treaty between the king and the German emperor, and royal commands for a number of the king's English subjects to return with him to Germany as hostages to the emperor. The barons received him badly, and were unwilling to entrust their sons to him. The king's captivity led to other diplomatic missions by Longchamp. He was with Richard at Worms in late June 1193, when the emperor reopened the question of the amount of ransom to be paid. He left for an embassy to Mantes on 9 July to conclude a peace settlement between the English and French kings. Richard's release led to Longchamp's resumption of duties as chancellor, and also to royal favours. He received custody of the honour of Eye, and after a modest gift of 10 marks, was appointed sheriff of Essex and Hertfordshire, a post he held until 1196. Longchamp continued to serve on diplomatic missions; he negotiated the truce of Tillières with Philip Augustus (23 July 1194) and returned to the emperor's court in July and November 1195. He died at Poitiers at the end of January 1197 (probably on the 28th, but perhaps on the 31st), on his way to Rome for negotiations about Richard's quarrel with the archbishop of Rouen over the king's construction of Château Gaillard on land of his see, and was buried at the abbey of Le Pin.

William de Longchamp had a number of brothers who followed him to England to seek their fortunes. Stephen, who became a steward in the royal household and accompanied Richard I on crusade, and Osbert and Henry, both of whom acted as sheriffs in the 1190s, followed William into the service of the crown. Robert, a monk, became successively prior of Ely and of St Mary's, York. A nephew and niece made profitable marriages, while his sister Richeut married Matthew de Clere, whom Longchamp appointed constable of Dover Castle. Another sister, Melisend, is also known to have come to England. A man of considerable education and culture, Longchamp was one of a number of Anglo-Norman canonists active in the late twelfth century, composing a treatise *Practica legum et decretorum*. His friends included such prominent writers as Nigel of Canterbury, who addressed to him a work warning against the courtier's life, *Contra curiales et officiales clericos*, and Peter of Blois, who wrote to Hugh de Nonant to complain of his treatment of the fallen chancellor. Richard Barre, a member of his household, dedicated to him a compendium of passages from the Old and New testaments arranged by topics. Described at the height of his power as 'Caesar and more than Caesar' (*Gir. Camb. opera*, 4.399), Longchamp suffered resentment and humiliation as a result of the very ability that raised him to greatness. He was probably also the first Norman to be regarded as a 'foreigner' by members of the aristocracy in post-conquest England.

RALPH V. TURNER

Sources *Chronicon Richardi Divisensis / The Chronicle of Richard of Devizes*, ed. J. T. Appleby (1963) • *Chronica magistri Rogeri de Hovedene*, ed. W. Stubbs, 4 vols., Rolls Series, 51 (1868–71) • W. Stubbs, ed., *Gesta regis Henrici secundi Benedicti abbatis: the chronicle of the reigns of Henry II and Richard I, AD 1169–1192*, 2 vols., Rolls Series, 49 (1867) • *Gir. Camb. opera* • *Pipe rolls* • L. Landon, *The itinerary of King Richard I*, PRSoc., new ser., 13 (1935) • W. Stubbs, *Historical introductions to the Rolls Series* (1902); repr. (New York, 1968) • L. Boivin-Champaux, *Notice sur Guillaume de Longchamps, évêque d'Ely, vice-roi d'Angleterre* (1885) • *DNB* • *Fasti Angl., 1066–1300*, [Monastic cathedrals] • D. Balfour, 'The origins of the Longchamp family', *Medieval Prosopography*, 18 (1997), 90
Likenesses seal, BL; Birch, *Seals*, 1493

Longden, Sir Henry Errington (1819–1890), army officer, son of Thomas Hayter Longden, was born in January 1819. He was educated at Eton College and at the Royal Military College, Sandhurst. He was appointed to an ensigncy without purchase in the 10th regiment on 16 September 1836. His subsequent commissions—all the regimental ones in the 10th regiment—were lieutenant (1840), captain (1843), brevet major (1849), major (1850), brevet lieutenant-colonel (1856), lieutenant-colonel (1858), and colonel (1859).

After taking a certificate of proficiency in higher mathematics and military drawing at the senior department, Royal Military College, in May 1842, Longden served with his regiment in India, and was present in the First Anglo-Sikh War of 1845–6, including the battle of Sobraon, and in the Second Anglo-Sikh War of 1848–9, including the two sieges of Multan, where he commanded the regiment at the attack on the heights on 27 December 1848, and was acting field engineer at the fall of the city. He was also at the capture of Chiniot and the victory at Gujrat, and was promoted brevet major. He served in the Indian mutiny and in September 1857, before Sir Colin Campbell advanced from Allahabad, he dispatched Longden from Benares with a small field force, to assist the Nepali troops in driving the rebels from the Azamgarh and Jaunpur districts. Longden commanded a party of picked marksmen, covering Brigadier Franks's force in the advance to Lucknow, and was attached to the Gurkhas during the siege and capture of the city; he was mentioned in dispatches. He was with Lord Mark Kerr at the first relief of Azamgarh on 6 April 1858, and was chief of the staff of Brigadier Edward Lugard's force at the second relief of Azamgarh, and the operations in the Jagdispur jungles. Longden afterwards retired on half pay, and was adjutant-general in India in 1866–9. He was promoted major-general in 1872 and lieutenant-general in 1877, and retired with the honorary rank of general in 1880.

Longden was a KCB and CSI, and colonel in succession of the Hampshire regiment and the Lincolnshire regiment (late 10th regiment). He died in Bournemouth on 29 January 1890, from a chill caught at the funeral of his old friend Lord Napier of Magdala.

H. M. Chichester, *rev.* James Falkner

Sources *Army List* • *Hart's Army List* • A. Lee, *The history of the tenth foot, the Lincolnshire regiment* (1911) • *CGPLA Eng. & Wales* (1890)
Likenesses engraving, *c*.1880, repro. in Lee, *History of the tenth foot*
Wealth at death £20,147 13*s*. 3*d*.: probate, 10 March 1890, *CGPLA Eng. & Wales*

Longden, Sir James Robert (1827–1891), colonial governor, was the youngest son of John R. Longden, a proctor, of Doctors' Commons, London. In 1844, two years after the establishment of a civil government, he was appointed government clerk in the Falkland Islands, and became acting colonial secretary the year after. In 1861 he was appointed president of the Virgin Islands, in 1865 governor of Dominica, in 1867 governor of British Honduras, in 1870 governor of Trinidad, and in December 1876 governor of Ceylon, which post he held until his retirement in 1883. In 1864 he married Alice Emily, the daughter of James Berridge of the island of St Kitts, West Indies.

Longden was made CMG in 1871, KCMG in 1876, and GCMG in 1883. After his retirement he resided at Longhope, near Watford, Hertfordshire, and took a very active part in county affairs. He was a JP and alderman for the county under the Local Government Act. He died at Longhope on 4 October 1891 and his funeral took place at Woking crematorium on 9 October. His wife survived him.

H. M. Chichester, *rev.* Lynn Milne

Sources *The Times* (6 Oct 1891) • *The Times* (10 Oct 1891) • *Colonial Office List* (1891) • Burke, *Peerage*
Archives Bodl. Oxf., corresp. with Lord Kimberley
Wealth at death £24,937 3*s*. 4*d*.: probate, 11 Nov 1891, *CGPLA Eng. & Wales*

Longe, Francis Davy (1831–1910), civil servant, was born at Coombs, Suffolk, on 25 September 1831, the second son in the family of three sons and one daughter of Robert Longe (1800–1890) of Spixworth Park, Norfolk, vicar of Coddenham-cum-Crowfield, and his wife, Margaret Douglas (*d*. 1873), daughter of Charles Davy, rector of Barking, Suffolk. Educated from 1845 to 1850 at Harrow School, where he was captain of the cricket eleven, he matriculated as a commoner at Oriel College, Oxford, in 1850, and went on to take third-class honours in classics in 1854, and to represent Oxford against Cambridge at cricket. George Goschen was a college contemporary and lifelong friend. After graduating BA in 1854, Longe was admitted to the Inner Temple in April 1855 and called to the bar in April 1858. On 27 September 1864 he married Sara Rose (*d*. 1905), daughter of the Revd Thomas Patteson, rector of Hambledon, Hampshire; they had no children.

Longe was a member of the Social Science Association committee which produced the important report on trade unionism *Trades' Societies and Strikes* (1860). His own contribution to the contemporary debate on unionism was a pamphlet, *An Inquiry into the Law of 'Strikes'* (1860), which advanced the novel, and subsequently influential, contention that the common-law doctrines against trade combinations rested on extremely shaky foundations. He also observed the historic tendency of the statute law to favour the interests of the consumer and employer over those of the labourer. From 1862 to 1867 he was an assistant commissioner on the children's employment commission, and prepared reports on the employment conditions of women and children ranging across several industries and regions, including the Staffordshire potteries (1863), the Yorkshire textile trades (1863), the midlands iron trades (1864), copperworks in south Wales (1865), and the agricultural gangs of the East Anglian fens (1866).

Longe's observation of the damaging moral and social effects of low wages, and a practical interest in social reform, informed his most significant work, *A refutation of the wage-fund theory of modern political economy as enunciated by Mr Mill, M.P. and Mr Fawcett, M.P.* (1866). The first systematic critique of the theory that wages were paid from a predetermined sum of capital, Longe's pamphlet contended that the existing orthodoxy obstructed attempts to improve the position of the most depressed groups of workers by popularizing the idea that the aggregate rate of wages could not be raised. His arguments were not immediately noticed by political economists, and it was another writer, W. T. Thornton, who drew a recantation from Mill in 1869, but the significance of Longe's pioneering work was later more widely recognized. It was reprinted in 1903 in the series of economic tracts edited by the American labour economist Jacob Harry Hollander, to whom Longe supplied details of its publishing history (Vint, 179–80 n.). His work was, moreover, acknowledged in contemporary official circles, as were the implications of his comparative researches into the law of trade unions and strikes in France, published in the *Fortnightly Review* (1867).

In 1868 Goschen appointed Longe to be his private secretary at the poor-law board. He was made a general inspector at the successor department, the Local Government Board, in 1871, and had responsibility for supervising the administration of poor relief in the Gloucestershire district. His last annual report was dated 1 May 1896. His official career in a department whose routine work was described by his colleague Herbert Preston-Thomas in *The Work and Play of a Government Inspector* (1909) seems to have been unremarkable. In retirement he was a prominent member of the Norfolk Naturalists' Society, and published the results of some antiquarian researches, *Lowestoft in Olden Times* (1898; 2nd edn, 1905). Longe died at his home in Ipswich, Suffolk, on 20 February 1910.

M. C. CURTHOYS

Sources Burke, *Gen. GB* • *Oriel Record*, 1 (March 1910), 80 • J. Foster, *Men-at-the-bar: a biographical hand-list of the members of the various inns of court*, 2nd edn (1885) • M. G. Dauglish, ed., *The Harrow School register, 1801–1900*, 2nd edn (1901) • J. Vint, *Capital and wages: a Lakatosian history of the wages fund doctrine* (1994) • *CGPLA Eng. & Wales* (1910)

Wealth at death £2471 2s. 5d.: probate, 18 March 1910, *CGPLA Eng. & Wales*

Longespée [Lungespée], **William (I), third earl of Salisbury** (*b.* in or before **1167**, *d.* **1226**), magnate, was the natural son of *Henry II and an unknown mother. His contemporary epithet Longespée, or Lungespée, may be a conscious invocation of his namesake, William Longsword, the second duke of Normandy (*c.*928–942), or the second King William, called Longespée as well as Rufus. He used it himself in several charter attestations, and a sword appears as a rebus on his seal and on those of his sons. More certainly, Longespée's adoption of the coat of arms of his paternal grandfather, Geoffrey Plantagenet, namely azure, six lioncels rampant or, emphasized his descent from the counts of Anjou. Nothing is known of the date or circumstances of his birth, and the sixteenth-century legend that he was the son of Rosamund Clifford (Fair Rosamund; *d.* 1175/6) is without foundation. Although Longespée later laid claim to the lands of one Roger d'Acquigny, it is equally unlikely that he was son of Ykenai or Hikenai, who according to Walter Map was the mother of another of Henry's bastards, the considerably older Geoffrey Plantagenet (*b.* 1151?).

Early career Little is known of Longespée's upbringing or early career, although in a letter of 1220 to Hubert de Burgh he reminded the justiciar that they had been brought up together. He received Appleby, Lincolnshire, from Henry II in 1188, which suggests that by then he had attained his majority. In 1196 his half-brother Richard I gave him in marriage *Ela (or Isabel), countess of Salisbury (*b.* in or after 1190, *d.* 1261), the infant daughter and heir of William Fitzpatrick, earl of Salisbury. William and Ela had four sons: William (II) *Longespée, Richard, a canon of Salisbury, Stephen (*d.* 1260), a soldier and administrator made seneschal of Gascony in 1253 and lord justice of Ireland in 1259, and Nicholas (*d.* 1297), bishop of Salisbury from 1291 to 1297. Of four daughters, Isabel married William de Vescy, Petronilla died unmarried, Ela married first Thomas, earl of Warwick (*d.* 1242), then Philip Basset, and Ida married first Walter Fitzrobert and second William de *Beauchamp [*see under* Beauchamp, de, family].

Salisbury was in close attendance on Richard in Normandy from 1196 to 1198, when he attested charters at Château Gaillard and doubtless gained military experience in the campaigns against Philip Augustus. He was with the king shortly before Richard routed Philip outside Gisors on 28 September 1198, although his presence in the engagement is not recorded. He took part in John's coronation on 27 May 1199, and thereafter was frequently with the king, with whom he seems to have enjoyed most cordial relations. The rolls reveal the two gaming together, and Salisbury received a steady stream of royal favours, from gifts of wine to an annual pension, against which he was frequently lent money by the king. His earldom, however, conferred more status than wealth, for although the barony commanded fifty-six fees and he was custodian of Salisbury Castle, an important royal fortress on which the Angevins expended large sums, he held no castle of his own. Although the king resisted his claim as earl to hold the shrievalty of Wiltshire by hereditary right, he was appointed to this office three times: 1199–1202, 1203–1207, and 1213–1226. In his capacity as sheriff, it was Salisbury's men who besieged the outlaw knight Fulk Fitzwarine in Stanley Abbey in 1202, but Salisbury himself was among those who procured John's pardon for Fitzwarine and his men the following year. Salisbury held a variety of other offices, being custodian of the castle and honour of Eye in February 1205, keeper of Dover Castle, most notably in 1212–13, when French invasion threatened, and sheriff of Cambridgeshire and Huntingdonshire from May 1212 to

1216. In 1208, when John moved to anticipate the interdict, Salisbury took custody of the lands of clergy in the diocese of Ely who refused to celebrate mass, and in August 1212 became supervisor of the keeper of the archbishopric of Canterbury. The same year, possibly in order to secure Salisbury's support in a time of increasing political disaffection, John supported his claim to the barony of Trowbridge, which he received in 1213 when the king disseized Henry de Bohun.

Diplomacy and soldiering Salisbury's diplomatic abilities are reflected in a series of important missions entrusted to him. Early in 1202 he negotiated a treaty between John and Sancho VII, king of Navarre. In 1204, together with the earl marshal, he escorted Llywelyn to the king at Worcester, was among those sent to treat with the king of Scots in November 1205, and accompanied William the Lion to meet John at York in November 1206. In March 1209 he headed an embassy to the princes of Germany on behalf of John's nephew Otto, who was subsequently crowned emperor, and in May 1212 he went on a mission to Ferrand, count of Flanders.

Salisbury's most prominent role, however, was as a military commander of considerable ability on both land and sea. In August 1202, together with William (I) Marshal and the earl of Surrey, he shadowed Philip Augustus's army as it withdrew in close order from the siege of Arques on learning of John's victory at Mirebeau. The lightly armed earls, however, only narrowly escaped capture by a counter-attack led by William des Barres. In 1203, he received back the important castle of Pontorson on the Breton border, which he had earlier exchanged for lands in England, and this, together with his being keeper of the castle of Avranches, suggests a marcher command against Breton attack. With the fall of Normandy he was given command of Gascony in May 1204, and in September made constable of Dover and warden of the Cinque Ports, which offices he retained until May 1206. In June 1205 he sailed to reinforce the garrison of La Rochelle, with the only part of the great force collected by John to see active service. In 1208 he was appointed keeper of the March of Wales, and he accompanied John on the Irish expedition of 1210. In May 1213, together with the counts of Holland and Boulogne, Salisbury led a powerful expeditionary force to aid Count Ferrand against Philip Augustus, the earl himself having been given a magnificent ship by King John. On 30 May the allied force attacked a large French fleet moored off Damme, a little north-east of Bruges, burning many ships but sending a great number back to England laden with arms and provisions. Although Salisbury and the forces which disembarked to raid inland were driven off on 1 June by the arrival of Philip's larger army, the naval victory was significant, and forced the French king to abandon his planned invasion of England. According to the *Histoire de Guillaume le Maréchal* Salisbury, with William Marshal and the count of Boulogne, had been instrumental in advising this pre-emptive strike. Earlier that May he was one of the earls who swore that John would observe the papal terms concerning satisfaction to the bishops, and witnessed his declaration of homage to the papal see.

Later in 1213 Salisbury returned to Flanders with troops and a credit of over 20,000 marks. In 1214, as marshal of the king of England, he led the allied forces that recovered almost all of Flanders for Ferrand. At the fateful battle of Bouvines on 27 July 1214 he commanded the right wing of the allied army with Renaud de Dammartin, count of Boulogne. He fought bravely, but was clubbed from his horse by Philippe, the militant bishop of Beauvais, and taken captive. The *Histoire de Guillaume le Maréchal* explicitly absolves him from blame for the failure at Bouvines, stating indeed that the battle was fought against his advice, and that the emperor Otto would have been taken or slain without Salisbury's aid. His release was still being negotiated in February 1215, but he was eventually exchanged for Robert, son of the count of Dreux. Back in England by May he was among those appointed to examine the state of royal castles, but his attempt to prevent London falling to the barons was unsuccessful. Dispatched with a force of Flemish mercenaries against insurgents in Devon, Salisbury succeeded in forcing the rebels to abandon Exeter.

Magna Carta and its aftermath It is uncertain whether Salisbury was present at Runnymede for the initial negotiations on 15 June, but he was named among those on

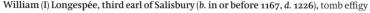

William (I) Longespée, third earl of Salisbury (*b.* **in or before 1167**, *d.* **1226**), tomb effigy

whose advice Magna Carta had been granted, which suggests he was with John by 19 June. Salisbury received extensive grants from the royal demesne in August in compensation for the honour of Trowbridge, restored to Henry de Bohun by the baronial committee of twenty-five as one of the king's unjust disseisins.

In October 1215 John ordered Salisbury to relieve Oxford and Northampton with a small field force drawn from the garrisons of ten royal castles, but it seems that Falkes de Bréauté led the expedition. Following the fall of Rochester Castle in December Salisbury was one of the commanders left to contain the rebels in London while John led his forces north. With Falkes de Bréauté and Savaric de Mauléon he conducted a punitive *chevauchée* through the predominantly rebel counties of Essex, Hertfordshire, Middlesex, Cambridgeshire, and Huntingdonshire. During the ravaging of the Isle of Ely in the early weeks of 1216, however, it was Salisbury who protected the womenfolk from the worst excesses of Walter Buc's Brabançon mercenaries. He rejoined the king and aided him in the siege of Colchester, pledging on John's behalf to observe the surrender terms agreed with the French and baronial garrison, terms which the king subsequently violated.

After Louis's landing on 21 May 1216 Salisbury adhered to John until rapid French gains in the southern counties led the earl to submit to Louis at Winchester in late June. Little credence, however, need be given to the rumour recorded by William the Breton that Salisbury's defection was caused by John's seduction of Countess Ela while Salisbury had been a prisoner in France. Rather, he was prompted by the widely held belief that John's cause was now lost; nevertheless the king was still able to order his lands to be seized by 30 August. Following the death of John (19 October), Salisbury remained in Louis's camp and, according to Wendover, he attempted to persuade Hubert de Burgh to surrender Dover to the French. On 5 March 1217, however, during Louis's absence in France, Salisbury re-entered the king's faith and was absolved from excommunication. He brought with him William Marshal the younger, who was a close friend and ally, and around one hundred lesser men from Wiltshire and the south-west. A considerable blow to Louis, his return had been influenced by the worsening military position of the French, the fact that Henry de Bohun, his rival for the castle and honour of Trowbridge, was one of Louis's leading English supporters, and the regent's promise to him of Sherborne Castle and the counties of Somerset and Devon, simply in return for his 'homage and service'.

Having witnessed the surrender of Knepp Castle near Shoreham, Salisbury and the younger Marshal laid siege to Winchester, taking the fortified episcopal palace of Wolvesey. On the arrival of the regent they were sent to Southampton, which they took, installing a constable before returning to share in the rich booty which had accrued from the surrender of Winchester (before 14 March). At the battle of Lincoln (20 May 1217) Salisbury commanded the third squadron of the royalist forces, and with the younger William Marshal led the charge through the west gate of the city against the French and English besieging the castle from the south and east. According to the *Histoire de Guillaume le Maréchal* the Marshal saved Salisbury from the lance of Robert of Ropsley by felling this assailant, and together they proceeded to engage the count of Perche in front of the cathedral. After the royalist victory Salisbury was rewarded with custody of the city and county of Lincoln 'by common council' of the king's supporters, although Ranulf (III) of Chester received the earldom. Later, in 1218, he and the regent partitioned the English manors of the count of Perche who had been killed in the battle; Salisbury gained those of Aldbourne and Wanborough in Wiltshire and adopted the latter as his chief seat in the shire. Salisbury took part with Hubert de Burgh in the naval victory off Sandwich on 24 August, in which the English intercepted a French fleet bringing vital reinforcements to Louis. He was closely involved in the resulting peace negotiations which culminated in the treaty of Lambeth, 12 September, and Louis's departure from the kingdom.

A man of power From 1217 until his death in 1226 Salisbury enjoyed a position of considerable power, his career epitomizing both the centrifugal and the centripetal forces which so characterized the minority of Henry III. Within his areas of influence he sought to exercise effective local autonomy without the interferences of central government. Between March 1217 and 1219 he tried to make effective the grants of the lordship of Somerset and Dorset and, later, of Alnwick, extorted from the regency, but failed against the power of John's sheriffs. He made repeated efforts to secure Lincoln Castle from the redoubtable Nicola de la Haie, the hereditary castellan, claiming both custody of the castle and wardship of the rich Haie barony in Lincolnshire, since his eldest son, still a minor, was betrothed to Idonea, daughter and heir of Richard de Camville (*d.* 1217). In May 1220, on the death of Robert of Berkeley, Salisbury seized Berkeley Castle and Robert's lands and chattels in a pre-emptive bid for wardship of his heir, 'against justice, the custom of the kingdom and the law of the land', as the earl of Pembroke complained to the justiciar, Hubert de Burgh (Shirley, no. clv, p. 179).

Salisbury nevertheless professed himself strongly committed to government by the king's council, stating forcefully in 1220 that the only legitimate orders were those sanctioned by 'the magnates of England who are held to be and are of the chief council of the king, with other chief men' (Carpenter, 204). He supported the king and the justiciar Hubert de Burgh at crucial moments in the restoration of royal authority. In 1221 he opposed both the count of Aumale and Peter de Mauley. At Christmas 1221, and again at Northampton in December 1223, when the country came to the verge of civil war, he stood with the justiciar against the powerful dissident faction of the earl of Chester, Falkes de Bréauté, Engelard de Cigogné, Brian de Lisle, and other castellans reluctant to yield up their shrievalties and castles. In this Salisbury represented, in his own words, 'we native-born men of England' against those 'aliens' who were felt to be fomenting war within the kingdom (Shirley, no. cxcvi, p. 221). In June 1222, on

Henry's second act of resumption of royal demesnes, he yielded a number of royal manors, and in February 1223 he surrendered Salisbury Castle, only to receive it back directly, with the custody of the castles of Shrewsbury and Bridgnorth, and the shrievalties of Shropshire and Staffordshire.

Last years, death and reputation Salisbury retained his role as a leading military commander until his death. In mid-1223 Salisbury was joint leader with William Marshal of a force of 140 knights, sent by Hubert de Burgh against Llywelyn, which established control over Kidwelly and Ceredigion. In 1225 he accompanied Richard of Cornwall, then only sixteen, as the effective leader of the successful expedition to Gascony, which reasserted English control in the province and secured it from the invasion of Louis VIII. Before La Réole fell on 13 November, however, Salisbury had fallen sick and embarked on a difficult three-months voyage home. Driven ashore on the Île de Ré, held for Louis by Savaric de Mauléon, he took shelter in the abbey of Notre Dame de Ré. He was warned to escape, according to Matthew Paris, by two of Savaric's men, to whom he gave £20, and set sail again. He landed in Cornwall at Christmas, and in January was received with great rejoicing in Salisbury Cathedral. Paris relates an implausible tale of an attempted poisoning of the earl by Hubert de Burgh. The story is undoubtedly false, for the two men were close and the earl's death at Salisbury Castle on 7 March 1226 was almost certainly the result of the illness contracted in Gascony. He was buried in the lady chapel of Salisbury Cathedral, whose foundation stones he and his countess had laid on 28 April 1220, with the assistance of the legate Pandulf. Later moved to the easternmost bay of the south arcade of the nave, his tomb, carved *c.*1240 by craftsmen of the Wells school, was one of the finest military effigies of its period. On an arcaded oak tomb chest enriched with mosaic inlay on gesso, the originally richly coloured effigy of local Doulting stone depicted Salisbury in gilded mail armour with armorial surcoat and shield.

Despite his prominence Salisbury's character remains enigmatic. His support for John during his excommunication led Wendover to number him among the king's evil counsellors, while the annals of Dunstable believed it was Salisbury who, on John's orders, arrested Geoffrey of Norwich who later died in captivity as a result of his harsh treatment. The opprobrium of monastic chroniclers, however, was short-lived. Wendover approvingly noted his especial veneration of the Virgin, before whose altar he had kept a light burning since the day of his knighthood, and who it was claimed had appeared to Salisbury during his shipwreck in 1225. The same chronicler accords him a pious end, when, stripped and with a halter round his neck, he knelt before Richard Poor, bishop of Salisbury, declaring himself a traitor to God and refusing to rise until he had confessed and received the sacrament. His salvation was betokened by the fact that the candles in his funeral procession from the castle to the cathedral remained alight despite a raging storm. 'When William, the flower of earls resigned his princely breath', ran the epitaph added by Matthew Paris, 'his long sword was content to find a shorter sheath' (Paris, 3.105).

Certainly Salisbury and his wife seem to have been more than conventionally devout. His will largely comprises benefactions to religious houses. He endowed the Augustinian house of Bradenstoke, Wiltshire, founded by Ela's great-grandfather, Walter of Salisbury, and was commemorated at the hospital of St Nicholas, Salisbury. In 1222 he gave the manor of Hatherop, Gloucestershire, for a Carthusian foundation, adding further endowments in his will, although at the monks' request his widow afterwards moved them to her manor of Henton (or Hinton), Somerset, where the monastery of Locus Dei was dedicated in 1232. The same year Ela began an Augustinian nunnery at Lacock, where she herself took the veil in 1238 and became abbess in 1239.

Longespée was a political figure of the first rank, symbolizing not only the important role played by royal bastards, but the multifaceted competence in administration, diplomacy, and war which characterized leading figures in the Angevin regime. He has been labelled among the 'conspicuous trimmers' (Carpenter, xviii) during the period of crisis in 1216–17, but the *Histoire de Guillaume le Maréchal*, written in the 1220s, and possibly after Salisbury's death, passes over his temporary defection to Louis in silence. Rather he is portrayed with no little justification as a loyal, courageous, and skilful commander, 'whose mother was largesse and whose banner was prowess' (Meyer, ll. 12125–8), the former compliment perhaps being a tactful inversion of his illegitimacy.

MATTHEW STRICKLAND

Sources Paris, *Chron.*, vols. 2–3 • P. Meyer, ed., *L'histoire de Guillaume le Maréchal*, 3 vols. (Paris, 1891–1901) • F. Michel, ed., *Histoire des ducs de Normandie et des rois d'Angleterre* (Paris, 1840) • T. D. Hardy, ed., *Rotuli litterarum clausarum*, 2 vols., RC (1833–4), vol. 1; vol. 2, p. 71 • T. D. Hardy, ed., *Rotuli litterarum patentium*, RC (1835) • *Radulphi de Coggeshall chronicon Anglicanum*, ed. J. Stevenson, Rolls Series, 66 (1875) • GEC, *Peerage* • D. A. Carpenter, *The minority of Henry III* (1990) • S. Painter, *The reign of King John* (1949) • J. C. Holt, 'The making of Magna Carta', *EngHR*, 72 (1957), 401–22 • G. Drury, *William Longespée, earl of Salisbury* (1954) [incl. repro. of family seals and of effigy] • W. W. Shirley, ed., *Royal and other historical letters illustrative of the reign of Henry III*, 1, Rolls Series, 27 (1862) • W. H. Rich Jones, ed., *Vetus registrum sarisberiense alias dictum registrum S. Osmundi episcopi: the register of St Osmund*, 2 vols., Rolls Series, 78 (1883–4)
Likenesses tomb effigy, Salisbury Cathedral [*see illus.*]

Longespée, Sir William (II) (*c.*1209–1250), magnate, was the eldest son and heir of *Ela, countess of Salisbury (*b.* in or after 1190, *d.* 1261), in whom the earldom was vested, and William (I) *Longespée (*b.* in or before 1167, *d.* 1226). He had three brothers and four sisters. His marriage to Idonea, heir of Richard de Camville and Eustacia, daughter of Gilbert *Basset, was arranged in April 1216; they married between 1226 and 1230.

Military service and royal favour A minor at his father's death, Longespée was knighted by his cousin Henry III at Gloucester at Whitsuntide 1233, but he must have attained his majority before that since Henry had intended to knight him at Easter 1230. Moreover, in March 1230 Countess Ela was instructed to surrender to William all the lands she held of inheritance as the wife of William (I) Longespée, along with other properties granted to her son by Henry in 1228–9; and in November 1230 William paid homage for the lands claimed by his wife, Idonea, as of hereditary right. Earlier that year, he had accompanied Henry III on his ill-fated expedition to Brittany. This was his first taste of military action, and for the rest of his short life he was to be closely associated with his royal cousin, largely in a military capacity. In the autumn of 1233, during the rebellion of Richard Marshal, earl of Pembroke, he was at Henry's side in the operations against the Welsh and other supporters of the earl. In 1234 he was engaged in the pursuit and arrest of Peter des Rivaux. After returning from his first crusade (discussed below), he played a leading role in Henry III's expedition to Gascony in 1242–3. The number of royal charters he attested there, and the fact that he generally heads the list of lay witnesses, indicates his high standing in the king's regard and counsels. He fought at the battle of Saintes (July 1242), and was appointed captain of a number of subsequent operations, including the raid into Périgord in late 1242 and the siege of Garro in 1243. Back in England, Longespée went in royal service to Wales in June 1245, in response to the Welsh rising of 1244–5 under Dafydd ap Llywelyn.

Longespée did well from his career in royal service, as the favours showered upon him in these years indicate, but the earldom of Salisbury was denied him. He clearly expected to receive the comital title, for a number of his *acta* (1231–7) contain explicit statements of his hopes. In 1237–8 he claimed by hereditary right custody of Salisbury Castle and the *comitatus* of Wiltshire, of which Patrick, earl of Salisbury, had been seised in Henry II's reign. Judgment against Longespée may have been given before his departure on crusade in 1240; if so, he did not give up, for he was pestering the king during 1242 when both were in Gascony. On 16 October 1242 Henry promised that on his return to England he would judge concerning the county of Wiltshire and Salisbury Castle. If judgment went against Longespée he and his heirs would receive 40 marks per annum from the revenues of the county; if he were successful, the king would be quit of that sum and of the 60 marks per annum granted to Longespée until judgment were made. Since judgment indeed went against him, for reasons that remain somewhat puzzling, it is not surprising that Longespée does not appear so high in Henry's counsels after their return to England in 1243; he was much less frequently at court in the following years. Relations were certainly not embittered, however, for Henry continued to dispense patronage and favours to him, and, according to Matthew Paris, he was not unduly aggrieved. He apparently accepted, however reluctantly, the crown's arguments regarding the comital title, and he possessed, of course, the lands attached to the earldom, concentrated largely in Wiltshire and Dorset. Lesser holdings, including those brought to him through acquisition and marriage, were located in Berkshire, Oxfordshire, Buckinghamshire, Surrey, Hampshire, Gloucestershire, Northamptonshire, and, more importantly, Lincolnshire and Somerset.

Religion and the crusades Longespée was a man of some piety. He patronized the Franciscans of Salisbury and Oxford, and the Dominicans of Wilton, besides making notable grants to monastic houses of his family's connection, especially Lacock Abbey and Bradenstoke Priory. He also twice went on pilgrimage overseas: in 1232 to an unknown shrine, and in 1245 to Santiago de Compostela. This behaviour, combined with his active military career, helps to explain his particular association with crusading. He went on crusade twice, something that marks him out from most of his contemporaries and suggests a genuine crusading enthusiast. He first took the cross in June 1236 at Winchester, along with Richard, earl of Cornwall, and other associates. They left Dover in June 1240, travelled across France for embarkation at Marseilles, and landed at Acre in October. This crusade was marked by its lack of action in the field, and it can be assumed that Longespée performed no memorable deeds, especially since no later source in his praise makes anything of his first crusading venture. After witnessing a charter drawn up at Acre on 2 May 1241 he almost certainly sailed home on 3 May, when Earl Richard left the Holy Land. He arrived back in England in early March 1242. Within weeks he was off again, to attend Henry III in Gascony.

Sir William (II) Longespée (*c.*1209–1250), tomb effigy [identification uncertain]

Longespée took the cross once more in May 1247, encouraged, apparently, by the example of Louis IX and the French. Much is known of his preparations for this crusade. One of his first acts against his crusade passage was a journey to Lyons to petition the pope for financial subsidy. After an audience with Innocent IV he was duly promised moneys from the redemption of English crusading vows on 6 June, but he experienced difficulties in securing the cash and further papal mandates were required in 1248 and 1249 to ensure payment of the 2000 marks eventually assigned to him. Money was raised in other ways, including the lease of four of his manors for four years from Michaelmas 1248 and the grant of a charter to his burgesses of Poole in return for 70 marks. His royal patron and cousin came to his assistance with further grants of money. He also took measures to settle disputes over property and to ensure the security of his interests and family during his absence. These included the drawing up of a will, duly confirmed by the king, the securing of a royal judicial protection, the appointment of executors and attorneys, and the concluding of a number of quitclaims and final concords. In 1249, for the good of his soul, he secured a grant from his mother, now abbess of Lacock, that he would be received into all spiritual benefits and prayers of the house in perpetuity, and it was probably around this time that he requested his body be buried at Lacock. With his mother's blessing he left England in 1249, an essoin on his behalf, taken at Wilton on 18 April, indicating that he had already left, though other evidence makes a date in late June or early July more likely. He joined the army of Louis IX at Damietta in Egypt, with around 200 English knights under his command, at some point in late 1249, certainly before the general advance up the Nile that began on 20 November. If Matthew Paris (uncorroborated) is to be believed, he had previously attended Louis. But following an ugly clash with certain French nobles, Robert, count of Artois, at their head, over the spoils from successful raids he had mounted out of Damietta, Longespée withdrew to Acre, having failed to secure justice from Louis in the matter. He returned to Damietta, according to Paris, only on Louis's prompting.

A famous death It is upon the circumstances and manner of his death on crusade that Longespée's later, posthumous, fame rested. Following further reinforcement from France in October 1249, which may well have included Longespée and his knights, the strategic decision was taken to advance on Cairo. The army travelled slowly up the right bank of the Damietta branch of the Nile, until it was halted, unable to cross, on the north bank of the al-Bahr al-Saghir, opposite Mansourah where the bulk of the Egyptian forces were located. Eventually a local revealed the existence of an unguarded ford downstream, and on 8 February 1250 the vanguard, comprising the best cavalry and including the English under Longespée, crossed the ford at dawn led by Robert of Artois. Louis had instructed Robert to secure a bridgehead and advance no further, so that the main body of the army could cross safely. But Robert, rashly disobeying orders, insisted upon further attack, first into the Egyptian camp at Jadila and then into the town of Mansourah itself, though the vanguard was now isolated with no prospect of support. In the narrow streets of Mansourah, unable to manoeuvre, they were largely destroyed. As contemporaries, Muslim and Christian, appreciated, this proved to be the turning point of the entire crusade, so it is not surprising that the incident attracted much comment in Western sources, especially English and French ones, and that the attempt should be made to find a scapegoat for the crusade's failure.

Longespée was but one of those who died at Mansourah, but within twenty-five years he was emerging in English sources as a heroic figure, an ideal, exemplary crusader who fought to the death while the cowardly French, led by Robert of Artois, sought to flee the field, his arrogance and greed having doomed all of them. A legend rapidly developed: Longespée was transformed into an English 'national' crusading hero, and his fame continued for a century and more. That the nature of his supposed last stand, and the deaths of his loyal English crusading companions, met with favour in English chivalric circles is amply proved by the Anglo-Norman poem in his and their honour, composed *c.*1275–1300, and then copied. Matthew Paris, plainly, was exposed to earlier, oral analogues in the 1250s, and the diffusion of his works contributed to the making of Longespée's legend in other social circles as well.

Despite his wishes it seems that Longespée's bodily remains came to be buried in the cathedral at Acre, not at Lacock, and that his family and descendants made no attempt to translate them. The fine knightly effigy in the nave of Salisbury Cathedral is said, traditionally, to be of him, and produced on his mother's order, but the grounds for this are no more than romantic. He and his wife, Idonea, left one son, William (III) Longespée, and one daughter, Ela, who married James *Audley.

SIMON LLOYD

Sources *Chancery records* (RC) · F. Michel, C. Bémont, and Y. Renouard, eds., *Rôles Gascons*, 4 vols. (1885–1962), vol. 1 · K. H. Rogers, ed., *Lacock Abbey charters*, Wilts RS, 34 (1979) · V. C. M. London, ed., *The cartulary of Bradenstoke Priory*, Wilts RS, 35 (1979) · Paris, *Chron.*, vol. 5 · *Ann. mon.*, vols. 1–4 · Lacock Abbey MSS · S. Lloyd, 'William Longespée II: the making of an English crusading hero', *Nottingham Medieval Studies*, 35 (1991), 41–69; 36 (1992), 79–125

Archives Lacock Abbey, Wiltshire, papers

Likenesses tomb effigy (possibly William (II) Longespée), Salisbury Cathedral [*see illus.*]

Longfield, Mountifort (1802–1884), jurist and economist, was born at Church Hill, Desertserges, near Bandon, co. Cork, the second son of the Revd Mountifort Longfield, vicar of Desertserges, and his wife, Grace, daughter of William Lysaght of Fort William and Mount North, near Mallow in co. Cork. He had two brothers and three sisters. After first being educated by Thomas Dix Hincks, probably at Fermoy Academy, Longfield entered Trinity College, Dublin, in 1818 and graduated as moderator and gold medallist in natural science in 1823. He was elected a fellow of the college in 1825, but as jurist, for at that time the college regulations required all fellows to be in holy orders, except five, of whom one was elected as 'medicus', the other four as jurists. Called to the Irish bar in 1828, Longfield proceeded to the degree of MA in the same year and to LLD in 1831. In that year he lectured in the law school of Trinity College as deputy for the professor of feudal and English law, Philip Crampton. In 1832 a new professorship of political economy was established in Trinity College; Longfield applied for it and was appointed, on the results of an examination set by Richard Whately, archbishop of Dublin, who funded the chair. This appointment was tenable for five years only, and in 1834 Longfield, who had drawn attention to himself by his zeal and ability as a teacher of law when serving as deputy for Crampton, was appointed to succeed him in the regius professorship of feudal and English law, resigning his fellowship in order to do so. He held this office for the rest of his life, although from 1871 he employed a deputy to carry out its duties.

Longfield had already earned a high reputation as a real property lawyer when he became a QC in 1842. When the Incumbered Estates Act became law in 1849 he was selected to be one of the three commissioners by whom it was administered. With the extension of the act to unincumbered estates in 1858, the commission was replaced by the landed estates court, of which Longfield then became a judge. He continued to sit in this court until 1867, when he retired and was sworn of the Irish privy council.

In his later years Longfield maintained an interest in economic and social questions. In 1847 he became one of the founder members of the Dublin Statistical Society (later renamed the Statistical and Social Inquiry Society of Ireland) and in 1863 succeeded Whately as its second president. He was also active in the National Association for the Promotion of Social Science and gave the opening address as president of its social economy section at its Dublin meeting in 1861. Longfield was appointed a commissioner of Irish national education in 1853, and also gave much voluntary service to the Church of Ireland, acting as an assessor to its general synod on several occasions after its disestablishment in 1869; at that period he was also instrumental in developing new methods for financing the church. His experience in the landed estates court led Longfield to recognize the need to strengthen the legal rights of tenants to compensation for improvements. In an essay published by the Cobden Club in 1870 he outlined what came to be known as the 'Longfield scheme of parliamentary tenant-right', which attracted wide interest and support, but which Gladstone felt unable to incorporate into his first Irish Land Bill.

In 1845 Longfield married Elizabeth Penelope, daughter of Andrew Armstrong, of Kilsharvan, co. Meath; there were no children of the marriage, and she died in 1882. Longfield died at his home, 47 Fitzwilliam Square, Dublin, on 21 November 1884, and was probably buried in the city's Mount Jerome cemetery. Although he had virtually retired from public life a decade earlier, at his death he was still known and highly regarded as a learned and impartial judge, a man of vigorous and independent mind, with more liberal views on social and economic issues than might have been expected in his day from a long-established expert in real property law.

Longfield's former position as the first incumbent of the first chair of political economy to be founded in Ireland received little or no mention in his obituaries—not surprisingly, for he had left the chair almost half a century earlier; it was a forgotten interlude in a long and distinguished legal career. Almost twenty years later, in 1903, the American economist E. R. A. Seligman published two articles in the *Economic Journal*, 'On some neglected British economists', which drew attention, among others, to the work of Longfield as evidenced in the three volumes which he published during his tenure of the Whately chair: *Lectures on Political Economy*, *Four Lectures on Poor Laws*, and *Three Lectures on Commerce and one on Absenteeism* (1834–5). Since then it has come to be recognized by economists throughout the world that in these lectures Longfield produced work of outstanding originality, and his posthumous reputation in economics eclipsed that which he had in his own lifetime as a jurist. In 1833 when Longfield gave his first lectures on political economy, which (as his appointment required) he afterwards published, the theories of value and distribution developed by David Ricardo and propagated by James Mill dominated the subject. Having shown that he understood these theories better than many contemporary interpreters, Longfield rejected them and presented his own analysis in five lectures. His explanation of value emphasized market prices rather than natural values, stressing utility as of at least equal importance with labour costs in determining value. His theory of distribution was perhaps his most original contribution: in it he put forward a theory of profits as determined by the marginal productivity of physical capital and of wages as determined, not by subsistence, but by the specific productivity of each labourer.

Unlike Ricardo, Longfield took an optimistic view of the long-term prospects for economic development, and predicted that the effects of increased population would be offset by technical progress in agriculture and that increased capital accumulation, while lowering profits, would improve the productivity of labour and allow real wages to rise, with consequent economic and social benefits. While his two other published courses of lectures dealt primarily with current Irish economic problems, in his *Lectures on Commerce* he again showed his originality as an economic theorist, specifically treating the case of trade in more than two commodities and explaining the causes of international specialization in terms of variations in factor endowments. He thus foreshadowed developments in this field which were not generally known and accepted until almost a century later. Longfield's ideas in political economy had considerable influence on his successors in the Whately chair—indeed he really founded a distinctive 'Trinity College Dublin school of value theory'—but until Seligman wrote they remained completely unknown to economists outside Ireland, and this state of affairs Longfield himself appears never to have sought to alter. R. D. Collison Black

Sources E. R. A. Seligman, 'On some neglected British economists', *Economic Journal*, 13 (1903), 335–63, 511–35 [rev. version in Seligman's *Essays in economics* (1925)] • *The economic writings of Mountifort Longfield*, ed. R. D. C. Black (1971) • R. D. C. Black, 'Trinity College, Dublin, and the theory of value, 1832–1863', *Economica*, new ser., 12 (1945), 140–48 • L. S. Moss, *Mountifort Longfield, Ireland's first professor of political economy* (1976) • A. E. Murphy, 'Mountifort Longfield's appointment to the chair of political economy in Trinity College, Dublin, 1832', *Hermathena*, 135 (1983), 13–24 • 'Law School of Dublin University', *Dublin University Magazine*, 1 (1833), 93–7 • Burke, *Gen. Ire.* (1976), 735–6 • *The Times* (24 Nov 1884) • *Irish Law Times and Solicitors' Journal* (29 Nov 1884), 606 • *Annual Register* (1884)

Archives BL, corresp. with Sir Robert Peel, Add. MS 40218 • TCD, MUN/DEED (1845) 2885 • TCD, MUN/LIB/12/21 1843

Wealth at death £68,942 9*s*. 6*d*.: probate, 15 Dec 1884, *CGPLA Ire.*

Longford. For this title name *see* Aungier, Francis, first earl of Longford (*c*.1632–1700).

Longhurst, Henry Carpenter (1909–1978), golf journalist and television broadcaster, was born on 18 March 1909 at Bromham, Bedfordshire, the only child of (William) Henry Longhurst, the owner of a large furnishing business in Bedford, and his wife, Constance Smith. From St Cyprian's, Eastbourne, he won a classical scholarship to Charterhouse, whence he proceeded to Clare College, Cambridge. He obtained third classes in both parts (1929 and 1930) of the economics tripos. He won a golf blue as a freshman, and played four years in the university match; in his last year he was captain and led his side to victory. He was a very good golfer, if a little short of the top rank; he won the German amateur title (1936), and was runner-up for the French (1937) and the Swiss (1938) titles, and he was an essential part of the Old Carthusian team which used so regularly to win the Halford-Hewitt cup at Deal.

When therefore Longhurst soon settled into golf journalism, he did so with the advantage of knowing not only the personalities involved but also, from firsthand experience, the difficulties as well as the delights, the troughs as well as the peaks, of this most subtle of games. It was Bernard Darwin who, in *The Times* and *Country Life*, had made the writing of golf a literary exercise with a following among many who never handled a club. Where Darwin led the way, Longhurst followed. Neither made the mistake of treating the game too seriously, nor of confusing ordinary mortals by the excessive use of technicalities.

When Longhurst first took up his pen in the early 1930s, Darwin was the uncrowned king of responsible games writers, the model towards which others vainly aspired. Longhurst wisely took his own line, quickly becoming adept at the shorter essay. He acknowledged in later life his debt to P. G. Wodehouse, who taught him, he said, that 'to write well you did not have to write on a serious subject', and also that 'good writing flows'. It was important not only to have the right words but to put them in the right order. Though most of Longhurst's work was done

Henry Carpenter Longhurst (1909–1978), by unknown photographer, 1972

on the spot and against time—he left his untopical pieces to the last minute—he never wrote an ugly sentence.

Success in his chosen profession came to Longhurst very quickly. His first (unpaid) efforts in a small periodical, *Tee Topics*, in 1931 led to an offer in 1932 from the *Sunday Times*, which had not previously employed a golf correspondent. Neither had *The Tatler*, the next to sign him on. Then the *Evening Standard* reporting job became vacant. These last appointments ended with the war in 1939, but his association with the *Sunday Times* extended over forty-five years. Longhurst's five-minute pieces, on the back page, always on a given point and usually containing a quotable anecdote, were required early morning reading in the golf world and beyond, and he was proud of having written more than a thousand of them without missing a Sunday. He had a keen ear for an amusing story, and in his travels round all the continents, taking in more than four hundred clubhouses, picked up an unending store of them. At Turnberry over breakfast he discovered Lord Brabazon of Tara poring over what turned out to be a chess match, played with a friend by correspondence. It was midsummer and his lordship said he had lost a bishop in February and had been in difficulties ever since. When next they met Brabazon confided, said Longhurst, '"I was mated last week". We agreed that he might add to his many other distinctions that of being the only peer to have been mated by post.'

Longhurst began the war with the Home Guard (as they became), spent the bulk of it as an anti-aircraft gunnery officer, and the last two years (1943–5), having fought a by-election, as the Conservative member of parliament for Acton. He emerged with an undying devotion to Winston Churchill, duly lost his seat at the 1945 general election, and was soon adding to his writing activities the pioneering of golf presentation on BBC television. It is scarcely too much to say that Longhurst 'made' golf on television. He conveyed with an enviable economy of words, to handicap players and non-golfers, the emotions of the player in the eye of the camera. So often a word or a phrase conveyed everything, his dry laconic comments interspersed by brilliant flashes of silence. His technique caught on in the United States, where the viewers had been fed on far too much talk and too many superlatives.

Indispensable to the BBC, Longhurst also became an institution in America, and was specially proud in 1973 of winning the Walter Hagen award 'for furtherance of golfing ties between Great Britain and America'. He had been appointed CBE a year earlier. At the autumn meeting of the Royal and Ancient Golf Club in 1977 came the honour which he prized most of all. Amid the warmest possible acclaim (and, like his hero Bobby Jones before him) he was made an honorary life member. Not a few who were then present at St Andrews will have contrasted the master of his crafts, serene and benevolent, with the somewhat prickly, outspoken undergraduate who had made his first mark on the golfing scene all but fifty years before. He also wrote twelve light-hearted books, including an autobiography.

Longhurst married in 1938 Claudine Marie Berthé, daughter of Horace Evelyn Sier, senior partner of the accountants Viney, Price, and Goodyear and chairman of Burroughs Wellcome, pharmacists. They had two children: Oliver William Henry, killed in a motor accident aged thirty-one, and Susan Jane, widowed when thirty. There were six grandchildren. Longhurst died on 21 July 1978 at his home, Clayton Windmills, Hassocks, Sussex.

E. W. SWANTON, *rev.*

Sources H. Longhurst, *My life and soft times* (1971) · *The best of Henry Longhurst*, ed. M. Wilson and K. Bowden (1979) · personal knowledge (1986) · *CGPLA Eng. & Wales* (1979)
Archives SOUND BL NSA, 'Conversation', 10 Jan 1961, T6914WTR1C1 · BL NSA, 'Bitten by golf', 1LP0058658 S2BD 7 BBC
Likenesses photograph, 1972, Hult. Arch. [*see illus.*] · portraits, repro. in Longhurst, *My life*
Wealth at death £41,003: probate, 1979, *CGPLA Eng. & Wales*

Longhurst, Margaret Helen (1882–1958), museum curator, was born on 5 August 1882 at Windsor Street, Chertsey, Surrey; she is believed to be the youngest of the five children of Henry Longhurst (1824–1895), draper, and his second wife, Caroline Louisa, daughter of William Taylor. Margaret Longhurst was an innately private person who remained unmarried, and little is known about her life before she joined the Victoria and Albert Museum, London. In her *Who's Who* entries she is simply noted as being educated privately; there is no reference to either her parents or her siblings. Her father, Henry Longhurst, was a well-respected businessman in Chertsey, entering his stepfather's drapery business at the age of thirteen and taking over the business from 1864 until his retirement in 1888. In an obituary in *Rawlings's Year Book and Trade Guide for 1896* he was described as 'a quiet, benevolent man, whose acts of charity and goodness were none the less frequent for being unostentatious'. His effects amounted to a substantial sum of £41,955 13*s*. 9*d*. The 'modest income', noted in her obituary in *The Times*, which enabled Margaret Longhurst to travel 'early in the century', was almost certainly the result of a bequest to her in her father's will. These travels furthered her interest in European art, which was to form the foundation of her career.

Margaret Longhurst's distinguished career was entirely devoted to the department of architecture and sculpture at the Victoria and Albert Museum, which she joined as a temporary cataloguer in September 1924, having previously worked as a volunteer shortly after the end of the First World War. A known authority on medieval sculpture prior to her appointment, she took her first permanent position at the museum as an assistant, commencing employment in August 1926. In December 1930 she became assistant keeper (second class), and in August 1934 she was promoted to assistant keeper (first class). Only four years later, in June 1938, she was made keeper (second class) of the department of architecture and sculpture, becoming—though she was too modest to have recognized this herself—the first woman in Britain to attain the post of keeper in a national museum. She held this post until her retirement on 27 August 1942, during which she keenly pursued hobbies of gardening and travel. During her career she published on ivories and Italian sculpture, her primary areas of interest: *English Ivories* (1926) and *Catalogue of Carvings in Ivory* (V&A, part 1, 1927, part 2, 1929), which were pioneering works in the field; and, with Eric Maclagan, *Catalogue of Italian Sculpture* (V&A, 2 vols., 1932). She also wrote numerous articles for the *Burlington Magazine*. Margaret Longhurst was elected fellow of the Society of Antiquaries on 2 May 1929, and was on the council in 1941. As a fellow she gave a paper on the museum's newly acquired Easby cross, which was published in *Archaeologia* in 1931.

Margaret Longhurst died on 26 January 1958 at her home, Wayside, Castle Street, Aldbourne, near Marlborough, Wiltshire. Her obituary in *The Times* was written by her former colleague Hender Delves Molesworth, who also acted as her executor and was a beneficiary in her will, where she entrusted to him her 'manuscripts, books, photographs and other written printed or pictorial material relating to the Italian Monuments Tombs and Sculptures', and a portion of her estate which she hoped might enable him to 'arrange for the collation, editing and if possible publication'. Edited transcripts of Longhurst's unfinished manuscripts were prepared about 1963; copies are held at the Victoria and Albert Museum and at the University of London, Warburg Institute, although they remain unpublished.

DIANE BILBEY

Sources H. D. Molesworth, *The Times* (28 Jan 1958) · P. Williamson, 'Longhurst, Margaret Helen', *The dictionary of art*, ed. J. Turner (1996) · *WW* (1947), 1838 · *Rawlings's year book and trade guide for*

1896, 115–16 • *Surrey Advertiser & County Times* (24 Aug 1895), 3 • *Museums Journal*, 38 (1938/9), 32 • nominal file on Margaret Helen Longhurst, V&A • history of employment for Margaret Helen Longhurst, V&A • will, Probate Department of the Principal Registry of the Family Division, London • records, Surrey HC [baptism, marriage, burial] • census returns, 1881, 1901 • b. cert. • d. cert. • *CGPLA Eng. & Wales* (1958) • *CGPLA Eng. & Wales* (1895) [Henry Longhurst, father] • will, Probate Department of the Principal Registry of the Family Division, London [Henry Longhurst, father]

Archives V&A, notes on Italian monuments • Warburg Institute, notes on Italian monuments

Likenesses photograph, *c.*1938, V&A

Wealth at death £6442 1*s.* 11*d.*: probate, 14 April 1958, *CGPLA Eng. & Wales*

Longhurst, William Henry (1819–1904), organist and composer, the son of the organ builder James Longhurst and the brother of the composer John Alexander Longhurst (1809–1855), was born at Lambeth, London, on 6 October 1819. In 1821 his father started business in Canterbury. Longhurst began his seventy years' service for the cathedral there when he was admitted a chorister in January 1828. He had lessons from the cathedral organist, Highmore Skeats, and afterwards from Skeats's successor, Thomas Evance Jones, and in 1836 he was appointed under-master of the choristers, assistant organist, and lay clerk. In 1845 he edited *A Collection of Anthems as Performed at Canterbury Cathedral*. In 1865 he became the thirteenth successful candidate for the fellowship diploma of the College of Organists, founded in 1864. He succeeded Jones as organist of Canterbury Cathedral in 1873, and held the post until 1898. He was also a lecturer in music at St Augustine's College in Canterbury. On his retirement the dean and chapter granted him a full stipend, together with the use of his house in the precincts. The degree of MusD was conferred on him by the archbishop of Canterbury in 1875. He died at 5 Summerhill, Harbledown, Canterbury, on 17 June 1904. A brass tablet was placed upon the organ console in Canterbury Cathedral to commemorate the length of his service.

As a composer Longhurst devoted himself chiefly to church music. His published works include twenty-eight short anthems in three books, and many separate anthems; a morning and evening service in E; a cantata for female voices, *The Village Fair*; an *Andante and Tarantella* for violin and piano; and many hymn tunes, chants, songs, and short services. An oratorio, *David and Absalom*, and other works remained unpublished.

J. C. Hadden, *rev.* Nilanjana Banerji

Sources Grove, *Dict. mus.* • Brown & Stratton, *Brit. mus.* • J. D. Brown, *Biographical dictionary of musicians: with a bibliography of English writings on music* (1886) • D. Baptie, *A handbook of musical biography* (1883) • Dotted Crotchet, 'Canterbury Cathedral', *MT*, 47 (1906), 373–83, esp. 382 • H. H. Nelson, 'William H. Longhurst, Mus. D.', *Musical Age* (Aug 1904), 151–2

Likenesses portrait, repro. in Nelson, 'William H. Longhurst'

Wealth at death £813 8*s.* 5*d.*: probate, 17 Aug 1904, *CGPLA Eng. & Wales*

Longland, Charles (*d.* 1688), merchant, was born at Tingewick, Buckinghamshire, probably a descendant of John Longland (*d.* 1589), archdeacon of Buckingham from 1544 to 1554 and 1559 to 1589. After apprenticeship to a merchant he set up business as a factor at Leghorn and by 1651 was one of the wealthiest English residents. He generously assisted the parliamentarian fleet with £1000 and was chosen by the council of state on 30 October that year as the local agent to fund and supply shipping.

The Dutch conflict led to privateer attacks and Longland appealed for naval assistance, but the arrival of Richard Badiley's squadron produced tension with Grand Duke Ferdinand of Tuscany. When in November 1652 the expedition cut out a Dutch prize, the *Phoenix*, inside Leghorn harbour and shot a Tuscan sentry, Ferdinand arrested Captain Henry Appleton, whom Longland had to rescue. Relationships with Appleton deteriorated as the Dutch blockaded his ships in Leghorn in 1653. It was arranged that when Badiley arrived Appleton would sail out to link up, but on 14 March Appleton engaged the Dutch alone and was captured, losing five of his six ships. Longland paid for the officers' parole, aided their sailors, and tried to form a force of merchant ships including his own *Mary Rose*. Back in England, Appleton denounced Longland's conduct in a pamphlet, and in his reply to the council on 14 November Longland denied causing Appleton's arrest or enjoying his sufferings and insisted that he had warned him not to engage the Dutch alone. He blamed Appleton's 'own ignorance and rashness' for the disaster, said that one of his captains had assaulted him after it, and accused Appleton of depriving him 'most maliciously of the only jewel and riches that I had in the world, my credit and good name' (*CSP dom.*, 1652–3, 243–8), thus ruining his livelihood. The investigating parliamentary committee chose to believe Longland and his supporter Badiley; Appleton was not re-employed.

Thereafter Longland served a vital role in England's Mediterranean policy in assisting Oliver Cromwell's squadrons and collating intelligence. A strong supporter of the war against Spain, he wrote to John Thurloe, who replaced the Admiralty commissioners as the main recipient of his reports, that it would ruin 'the Beast'—the Papal Antichrist—and help Charles X of Sweden to clip the wings of the Habsburg eagle (Thurloe, *State papers*, 4.295). He warned of the new Pope Alexander VII's machinations for Franco-Spanish peace, and assisted Cromwell's dispatch of a spy to Rome. Anglo-Tuscan relations were threatened by the uneasy visits of the English navy, particularly that of Captain John Stokes in the spring of 1658, and by episodes such as the capture of English vessels. Longland's own *Tripoline* was seized by a Tuscan privateer off Salonika in 1658, and Cromwell wrote to Ferdinand on his behalf on 12 June. Longland also helped to repatriate captives from north Africa, on which matter he had dispatched his envoy Edward Goodwin to Tripoli in December 1653.

Making his own suggestions to Thurloe for commercial advantage, Longland proposed to import 200 tons of Zante currants in foreign ships despite the Navigation Act, pleading that no English ships were available. During the Spanish war he urged Thurloe to allow local Englishmen to import goods that Tuscany needed from Spain's

American dominions in neutral Dutch ships. He pressed for a permanent English base in the Strait of Gibraltar, and when Cromwell conquered Dunkirk from Spain proposed that it be exchanged for Oran in a peace treaty. In December 1657 he requested a patent to trade with the Mozambique coast, declaring that it was surely against Cromwell's intentions that the East India Company 'keep in their power such large territories without making the least use of them' (Thurloe, *State papers*, 6.671).

Longland continued to help government shipping in the western Mediterranean after the Restoration, operating at both Leghorn and Lisbon. By 1670 he was trading as Charles Longland & Co., and in February 1671 was criticized by the local navy agent, Thomas Clutterbuck, for his 'very violent', 'clamorous and malicious persecutions' over overdue bills drawn on the Admiralty (*CSP dom.*, *1671*, 100). In 1672 he was deputy consul at Leghorn to Ephraim Skinner, but seems to have played less part in supplying English ships thereafter. He died at Florence in 1688, described as resident in Leghorn and unmarried, and was buried there. In his will he did not forget his home village of Tingewick, to which he bequeathed money to purchase a 'yardland' of 4½ acres, the rent of which was to support poor widows. He was a talented trader who acquired substantial wealth from humble provincial beginnings and a capable organizer on whose efficiency and financial generosity the English naval presence in the Mediterranean relied for logistical support in several crucial years in the 1650s. His correspondence with Thurloe shows a vigorously anti-papist protestantism and a shrewd nose for financial and strategic advantage. He played a crucial role in minimizing the effect of English naval commanders' arrogance and blunders on relations with a neutral Catholic power, not helped by men such as Appleton.

TIMOTHY VENNING

Sources Thurloe, *State papers* · PRO, SP 98/4 [Tuscany, 1653–63] · Longland letters, BL, Add. MS 19770 · Longland letters, BL, Add. MS 18986, fol. 717 · *CSP dom.*, *1651–72* · *CSP Venice*, *1647–56*; *1675–9* · C. H. Ridge, ed., *Index to wills proved in the prerogative court of Canterbury*, 11: *1686–1693*, Index Library, British RS, 77 (1958) · J. R. Powell, *Robert Blake: general-at-sea* (1972) · T. A. Spalding, *A life of Richard Badiley* (1899) · *VCH Buckinghamshire*, vol. 4 · Foster, *Alum. Oxon.* · [C. B. Heberden], ed., *Brasenose College register, 1509–1909*, 2 vols., OHS, 55 (1909) · *Fasti Angl.*, *1541–1857*, [Lincoln]

Archives BL, letters, Add. MS 18986 | BL, letters to admiralty, Add. MS 19770 · PRO, state papers, domestic, interregnum, letters to admiralty · PRO, state papers, Tuscany papers, 98/4

Wealth at death legacy to Tingewick, Buckinghamshire; house and mercantile business at Leghorn, Italy: implied in will, PRO, PROB 11/392, sig. 96: Ridge, ed., *Index to wills*; *CSP dom.*

Longland, John (1473–1547), bishop of Lincoln, was born at Henley-on-Thames, Oxfordshire, the son of Thomas Longland (*d.* 1529) and Isabel Staveley, who had a shop in Henley. By the time of his mother's death in 1530, the family was clearly a prosperous one.

Education and early preferments John Longland went to school in Henley, and his parents were said to have promoted his education: 'I was entrusted by my parents to a school of good and sound learning' (Longland, *Quinque sermones*, 4, fol. 88*v*). He may have gone from Henley to Eton College, a foundation of which he was very fond, and in which he was eventually to be buried. From Eton he went by 1491 to Oxford, where he became a scholar and fellow (and bursar) of Magdalen College, and was for a year (1506/7) principal of Magdalen Hall. By 1509 he was BTh, and DTh by 1511.

Longland was from the first a scholar, and by the time of his death had accumulated a very large library. He received his first preferments in 1505, but they were not of a particularly significant kind until he became dean of Salisbury in December 1514 and a canon and prebendary of St Stephen's Chapel, Westminster, in 1517 and of St George's Chapel, Windsor, in 1519. He was singled out for advancement by the quality of his preaching, which was admired by such serious churchmen as Thomas More, Richard Kidderminster, and William Warham. Warham wrote to Longland commending a published volume of his sermons, for his 'fervent zeal for reformation to be made as well of heretical doctrines as of misbehaviours in manners', and he assured him that his sermons would give Longland a 'perpetual memory' (Lincoln Archives Office, register 26, fols. 206–206*v*). Longland was also in correspondence with Juan Luis Vives and with Erasmus on matters of church reform. So influential a preacher gained the notice of Henry VIII, perhaps partially because Thomas Wolsey had been at Magdalen with Longland. He was, therefore, a strong candidate for preferment, and on 20 March 1521 Longland was provided to the see of Lincoln; he was consecrated on 5 May and the temporalities were restored on 26 June. Almost immediately afterwards he became the king's almoner, and by 1524 the royal confessor.

Wolsey's hand may be seen in these marks of favour. Wolsey often used Longland to help him with his most cherished projects. It was Longland who in 1525 preached at the laying of the foundation stone of Cardinal College, who was Wolsey's agent in acquiring 'singing men' for the college, and on whom Wolsey relied for his projected reformation of the statutes of the University of Oxford; and it was to Wolsey that Longland wrote some of his most personal letters. For Longland, unlike Wolsey, the combination of these posts meant that, like other bishops before him, he was always torn between his obligations to his diocese and those of the court. He had been present at the Field of Cloth of Gold in June 1520 and he was required to preach at court for most major festivals and in Lent. In 1525 he told Wolsey that he was at court for Trinity Sunday (11 June) and for Corpus Christi eve and day (14 and 15 June). On the eve 'the king his grace was shriven and on the morrow was shriven and houselled' (Ellis, 3/1, 251–4). As though this were not enough, plague was raging and the bishop could not even find safe refuge at his favourite manor of Buckden, in Huntingdonshire.

Bishop of Lincoln His duties to his diocese Longland saw mainly in terms of dealing with the larger institutions within it, the monasteries and the cathedral church. He was installed in this latter in September 1522, and two years later began a personal visitation of it. He wrote new rules for the poor clerks, whose truancy had become legendary. In his requirements for them, some written in his own hand, he ordered them not to keep hawks, dogs, and ferrets, but a single dog for them all, and not to play cards or dice, or to hunt, or 'use any other unlawful or unhonest games or play'. Fines were imposed for slander, drawing a knife, and for assault which 'God forbid … draw blood of any of his fellows' (Lincoln Archives Office, dean and chapter MSS, A.2.10[8]). There were other penalties for leaving gates open or using doors as privies. All to no avail, since a mere two years later the fines levied were finding their way back to the clerks themselves, whose games now included playing with loaded dice.

Longland also found that the religious houses of his diocese fell short of his exacting standards. Before he came to the see of Lincoln, he had preached to the monks of Westminster and had roundly condemned the laxity of the religious:

> Woe unto them who do not devote themselves to prayer and reading … but they give themselves over to gourmandising and self-indulgence. When they have filled their bellies, they belch, they sit idle, they laugh and pass most of the time in relaxation and idle vanities. The pure will see God and rejoice in the sight; the impure will neither rejoice nor see … Our true predecessors, both monks and secular clergy, led a holy and hard life, we a much easier and softer one, we who have stained her pristine beauty and devotion with worldly desires. (Longland, *Tres conciones*, 1, fols. 7v, 9–10)

In visiting some of the most severely disordered monasteries of his diocese, Longland showed that his view of them was not merely idealistic. He was apt to embellish his injunctions with quotations in his own hand from the rule of St Benedict. He confined his visitations to the most intransigent of the monastic orders in his diocese, and the houses he visited clearly shocked him. At the Augustinian priory of Dorchester he took the unusual step, in June 1529, of appointing a new prior. A year later, he found that his nominee did not read his injunctions to the community, and that he was dallying with a local lady. At Great Missenden, to which he made injunctions in 1531, he was forced to admit that the monks were uneducated, and he told them that 'ye be ignorant and have small understanding of Latin [so] we have drawn our said injunctions in our vulgar English tongue' (Lincoln Archives Office, register 26, fol. 212). Where monks and nuns could not feign ignorance of his wishes, they went behind his back to court, pretending that he was the cause of the undoing of a place. No amount of energy expended either by him or by his deputies appeared to make any difference. It is hardly surprising that when the monasteries were dissolved, Longland made no move to defend them.

Counteracting heresy Longland could not evade the enormous challenges that heresy posed to a diocese which certainly had a Lollard community in Buckinghamshire. Moreover, the diocese included the University of Oxford, where Luther's views, in whole or in part, were much debated. In Luther, Longland recognized a formidable adversary:

> You, Luther, already turn everything upside down and confound everything … You revile the holy sacraments from which we derive every remedy and help against all the diseases of the soul. You want everything to be in common, you want the human race to be a wanderer on the earth as it was in the beginning, without a leader, without a ruler … without authority … without virtue, without grace. (Bodl. Oxf., MS Arch.A.d.11, fol. 44)

Within a week of his consecration, Longland was present at Paul's Cross for the condemnation of Luther, the public burning of his books, and a penetrating sermon against Luther preached by John Fisher in 1521. He followed this by ordering a search for Luther's books in Oxford and by a further examination of those Buckinghamshire Lollards, drawn mainly from Amersham, who came under suspicion of heresy as a result of having been required to abjure their opinions before his predecessors. Four of them were condemned to the stake and many more were imprisoned in monasteries as a form of penance. But by 1526 Longland's activities in Oxford went well beyond that. Booksellers were to be searched and scholars' rooms scoured for the works of Luther. But vigilant as he might be, the bishop's commissary in Oxford realized that Lutherans like Thomas Garrett had made contact with scholars who were 'given to Greek, Hebrew and the polite Latin tongue' (*Acts and Monuments*, 5, appendix 1). He could not stop the distribution of books. Like Bishop Nicholas West of Ely, between 1527 and 1532 Longland took the unusual measure of asking any priest suspected of heretical views for an oath of orthodoxy before he was admitted to a benefice. He also alerted the archdeacon of Lincoln to the danger that the Lincolnshire coast presented for the import of heretical books.

The king's divorce and the royal supremacy At the height of Longland's campaign against Lutheranism came another threat: it was that of the king's marriage. Wolsey's biographer, George Cavendish, thought that the king first raised doubts about the validity of his marriage with Longland, but others were of the opinion that the cardinal prompted Longland to raise the question. Certainly Longland was at the centre of the affair and at all times seems to have taken the king's side. He was the obvious person to solicit the views of the University of Oxford on the marriage, and though he encountered much hostility, he was selected by the king to be chancellor of the university in 1532. He accompanied Henry and Anne Boleyn to France in 1532 and was a strong candidate for the archbishopric of Canterbury on the death of William Warham in August 1532. Longland's favoured position was, however, weakened by the disgrace of his friend Thomas Wolsey, and still more by Wolsey's replacement at court, Thomas Cromwell. Longland's correspondence with Cromwell reveals the bishop's meticulous attention to detail, but clearly no love was lost between the two, and there are no references to the personal problems that he shared so readily with Wolsey.

If Longland had no doubts about the Boleyn marriage, he had some problems with its sequel. He was not, like John Fisher and Thomas More, in total opposition to the royal supremacy over the church, nor was he against the succession passing to the issue of Anne Boleyn. The challenge, however, to ecclesiastical jurisdiction posed by the threat to the clergy of *praemunire* and eventually of the delegation of the supremacy to Thomas Cromwell as vicegerent, was a different matter. In 1534 the Spanish ambassador reported 'the Bishop of Lincoln … has said several times since Christmas that he would rather be the poorest man in the world than ever have been the King's councillor and confessor' (*LP Henry VIII*, 7, no. 14). That was but the beginning. Longland could and did argue with Cromwell about the extent of the invasion of his jurisdiction by archbishop or vicegerent or anyone else. He sent carefully worded letters and a well-chosen gift in order to safeguard the rights of future bishops of Lincoln, but it was not until 1538 that he actually made public his views on the supremacy of the bishop of Rome.

Preaching before the king at Greenwich on Good Friday 1538, Longland said that there is only one great bishop and:

> he did penetrate the heavens whose name is Jesus the Son of God … The bishop of Rome therefore ought … to be abashed, ashamed and to abhor his own pride. For … he outrageously doth offend God and blasphemeth him in that he presumeth to take this high name [*summus maximus* and *universalis pontifex*] from our bishop Christ … He is the mighty Bishop. We are not so. (*A Sermonde Made before King* [*Henry VIII*])

It was, however, one thing to accept a royal supremacy under Christ, but Longland was discriminating in his attitude to the various reforms of the church that resulted from it. Not surprisingly, he does not appear to have objected to the dissolution of the monasteries, and he seems to have remained consistently in favour of a vernacular scripture. In a sermon reminiscent of Erasmus, he said:

> We rejoice much that we have it in our own vulgar speech, that we hear it, that we read it, that we have it in our bosoms, and hanging at our girdles, and it is daily preached among us. But what shall this profit if we live not thereafter? If we live not well and Christianly? (ibid.)

A conservative prelate For Longland, to live as a Christian was not necessarily to adopt the views of Cromwell, Cranmer, or Martin Luther, and he took very good care to control preaching in his diocese and to limit it to the uncontentious exposition of scripture. A printed copy of the agreed declaration about the royal supremacy was sent to all his clergy in 1535, and in the following year preaching on opinions which had no authority from king or bishop was forbidden. By 1540 he was keeping records of preachers and having an eye to what they preached. He was equally careful to control any spread of heresy, either through books smuggled into the University of Oxford, or through the network of Lollard communities. He wrote to his archdeacons to make sure that anybody transgressing his orders about preaching was to be reported to him at once.

But there were some changes that Longland disliked but could not stop. He clearly objected to the plunder of church treasure and the attempt by the crown to extend its control of the church by influencing bishops and deans and chapters of cathedrals in their grants of lands and advowsons. As early as 1534 he insisted that his dean and chapter should not allow any such grants to be made unless his explicit approval had been obtained. In his leasing of episcopal lands, he attempted after 1540 to concentrate them in a few hands, and these were mainly those of his family and most trusted servants. The charge of nepotism can obviously be made against him, but it was not nepotism in its usual derogatory sense, simply to benefit the family: he was attempting to keep the wealth of the church in conservative hands—a purpose that is very marked in his will. In his later years he invested his money in building a chantry in Lincoln Cathedral, thereby placing his faith in the idea of intercession for the dead and its institutionalization which disappeared from England even as he lay dying. His last years were spent mainly at Wooburn, Buckinghamshire, and he began to visit some of his archdeaconries, notably that of Buckingham, in person. He recognized that the defence of the church in the 1540s lay in the hands of the secular clergy, whose welfare he had delegated to others in the early part of his episcopate.

Legacies Longland died at Wooburn on 7 May 1547. He asked that his body be buried at Eton College, and that his heart be taken to his cathedral church and buried before 'the most blessed sacrament at the high altar' (PRO, PROB 11/31, fol. 305*v*). All parishes through which his body passed between his house at Wooburn and Eton were to receive 6*s*. 8*d*. for the maintenance of their churches. His will reveals the scholar and theologian that he had been. To a Dr Roydon, he left his smaller astrolabe and a clock, with a small book about making dials. To many different people, he left a large quantity of books. From his library at Buckden '[books of] the greatest and best sort' were to go to Lincoln Cathedral, but the smaller ones were to be distributed among the rectors and vicars of the county. Additionally he left books to be chained in the libraries of Eton College and, at Oxford, in those of the colleges of Magdalen, Lincoln, Oriel, and Brasenose. He left to his nephew Edward Longland a commentary on the Bible and three of his best books of sermons from his study at Buckden. He was a wealthy man, and his servants and relatives received from him horses and harnesses, large quantities of bedding, and a considerable amount of silver. He pardoned the debts of those who owed him less than 40 shillings, and was extremely generous to another nephew, Thomas Longland, who was apparently setting up house and needed his linen and household utensils. To the dean and chapter of Lincoln he left a considerable number of copes and for his successors to the bishopric, his red silk gloves and episcopal sandals, together with books needed for giving orders and consecrating bishops. He also left to them a book of blessings for the use of future bishops of Lincoln, but with the prudent condition that it might not be taken away from the cathedral. The furnishings for his own chantry chapel were provided for, and a psalter was to be chained there.

Longland seemed at his death to be aware of his own humble origins as well as of his evangelical duty to care for the old and poor. He provided for an almshouse at Henley for five men and five women, and his own devotional rigour was in part demanded of them. They had, among other devotions, to be able, twice daily, to say (five times, in honour of the five wounds of Christ) the Our Father and the Ave, together with the creed. Most importantly of all, they were not to hold 'any erroneous opinions' under pain of dismissal (PRO, PROB 11/31, fol. 306*v*).

Longland may seem to have been a time-server who had the power to influence Henry VIII and did not use it. But as the royal confessor he had access to information which perforce is now lost. Henry VIII trusted his integrity, and that is most evident in his protection of Longland against another royal servant, Thomas Cromwell. Cromwell might bully Longland but did not oust him. Longland could not avoid the diminution of his diocese with the formation of the dioceses of Oxford and Peterborough, with all the loss of status and wealth that this implied. The Lincolnshire rebels in 1536 derided him and murdered his vicar-general, even though they were as doctrinally conservative as he was. His sermons reveal a rigorous attitude to his faith and a stern and somewhat joyless attitude to the gospel. His own death saved him from changes in royal policy of which he would not have approved. He remained throughout his life aware, almost too aware, that he would account for all his actions 'at that great day of examination' ('A Sermonde Made be for the Kynges Hyghenes'). MARGARET BOWKER

Sources M. Bowker, *The Henrician Reformation: the diocese of Lincoln under John Longland, 1521–47* (1981) • Lincs. Arch., Episcopal MSS, registers 26 and 27 • R. E. G. Cole, ed., *Chapter acts of the cathedral church of St Mary of Lincoln*, 1–2, Lincoln RS, 12–13 (1915–17) • *The acts and monuments of John Foxe*, new edn, ed. G. Townsend, 8 vols. (1843–9) • *LP Henry VIII* • will, PRO, PROB 11/31, sig. 39 • *A sermonde made before King [Henry VIII] an. MDXXXVIII by John Longlande*, BL, MS C.53.14 • [J. Longland], *Tres conciones* and *Quinque sermones*, Bodl. Oxf., MS Arch. A. d.11 • J. Longland, 'A sermonde made be for the kynges hyghenes at Rychemunte upon good fryday the yere of our lord MCCCCCXXXVI by Johan' Longlond bysshope of Lincoln', Trinity Cam., MS C.7, 79[2] • Lincs. Arch., dean and chapter papers, A.2.10[8] • H. Ellis, ed., *Original letters illustrative of English history*, 3rd ser., 4 vols. (1846) • Emden, *Oxf.*, 2.1160–62 • G. E. Wharhirst, 'The Reformation in the diocese of Lincoln, illustrated by the life and work of Bishop Longland, 1521–47', *Associated Architectural Societies Reports*, 1 (1939) • Lincs. Arch., registers 26, 27 • Trinity Cam. • BL, MS C. 53. 14

Archives Brasenose College, Oxford, books • Lincoln College, Oxford, books • Magd. Oxf., books • Oriel College, Oxford, books

Likenesses portrait, BL, missal, Add. MS 21974

Longley family (*per. c.*1860–1994), builders and contractors, came to prominence with **James Longley** (1836–1915), who was born on 6 June 1836 and baptized at Lindfield, Sussex, the eldest son of fourteen children of James Longley (1810–1874), a timber merchant of Turners Hill, Sussex, and his wife, Jane, *née* Beard, of Lindfield. His Sussex ancestry stretched back many generations. He was educated privately. On 13 September 1858 he married Louisa (1833–1902), the daughter of Thomas Fuller of St Mary Newington, Surrey, and Turners Hill. They had seven sons and one daughter.

James Longley was originally apprenticed as a carpenter to a Mr Anscombe, a builder in Lindfield. At the age of twenty-five he entered into partnership as a builder with his father-in-law, whom he bought out quite soon. In 1882 James moved to Crawley, where he established a steam joinery works, and in 1888 he took his own sons Charles [*see below*] and George into partnership. The business flourished as a result of the late railway boom, the development of Brighton, and church building. A peak of activity came at the turn of the century with contracts for the West Sussex Asylum, Chichester (1895), Christ's Hospital, Horsham (1896), and the King Edward VII Sanatorium, Midhurst (1903). About 1890 the firm invented and patented an interlocking wood-block flooring which was later used throughout the country. In 1897 James and Charles established the Crawley and District Water Company to provide the first public supply in the area.

During this pre-First World War period the partnership carried out many works in Brighton, especially on the seafront, including swimming baths, a refuse destructor, groynes, sewers, schools, churches, roads, and bridges. The London, Brighton, and South Coast Railway Company commissioned dozens of stations including the whole of the Cuckoo line, Newhaven harbour (twice as a result of fire), East Croydon, Lewes, and Eastbourne. Church work, not necessarily complete churches, ranged from Bideford and Beaulieu to Harrow chapel and Eastbourne. A man of great energy, enthusiasm and ambition, James served on the local board of guardians and rural district council. He died on 23 June 1915, at his home, The Beeches, Crawley, Sussex, and was buried at St John's Church, Crawley.

A key role in the firm was played by James Longley's second child. **Charles John Longley** (1862–1931) was born on 1 February 1862 at Turners Hill and educated locally. He began work in his father's building business at the age of fourteen and was taken into partnership in 1888. On 6 December of that year he married Alice Amelia (1863–1897), the daughter of John Howell of Newick. They had one son and two daughters, as well as three other children who died in infancy. Following his wife's death in 1897 Charles married, on 12 April 1899, Anna Gibson (1871–1938), the daughter of Henry Marchant of Eastbourne. They had two sons, Norman and Basil [*see below*]. Charles's younger brother, George Thomas Longley (1863–1926), also entered the firm, but he is a shadowy figure, and appears to have played a supporting role to his father and elder brother.

The business was incorporated in 1924 as James Longley & Co. Ltd, with Charles, George, and Charles's sons Norman and Basil as directors. The next year the company's joinery works was destroyed by fire but was soon rebuilt in spite of being underinsured. Charles inherited his father's energy and took a major part in the running of the firm but he became confined to a wheelchair by 1925 and died on 17 December 1931 at The Beeches, Crawley. He was buried at St John's, Crawley. He had served as overseer of the parish of Ifield.

Following their father's death the two sons of Charles Longley became joint managing directors of the firm. The elder, **Sir Norman Longley** (1900–1994), was born on 14 October 1900 at Rathcote, Goffs Park Road, Crawley, and was educated at Clifton College. On 6 June 1925 he married Dorothy Lilian (*b.* 1903), the daughter of George Baker of Horley. They had two sons and one daughter. The company just managed to survive the depression, in which it carried out every type of building work. During the Second World War, however, it played a major role in the war effort, concentrating on invasion defences and radar stations, followed by airfield construction and repair. The joinery works made pontoons for Bailey bridges and balsa wood life-rafts. After the war the company was fortunate to be on the site of one of the first new towns, Crawley, and it also took advantage of the development of Gatwick airport, which started in 1953. In parallel with the local activities, the company specialized in department store building, first at Plymouth, and then eight stores for Debenhams. In the 1960s extensive work was carried out at Oxford, Sussex, and Surrey universities, and, following work at Eton College, other work at public schools.

In 1968 the company changed its name to James Longley (Holdings) Ltd. Norman Longley was successively president locally, regionally, and nationally of the National Federation of Building Trades Employers, of which he also served as treasurer, and he was president of the International Federation of Building and Public Works Contractors from 1955 to 1957. Chairman of the Federated Employers Press, he was trustee of the industry pension scheme, a director of the industry's holiday-pay scheme, and a member of the joint contracts tribunal. His service to the industry culminated in his appointment as first chairman of the Construction Industry Training Board from 1964 to 1970. He retired as a director of the family firm in 1970.

In local government Norman Longley served on Crawley parish council, Horsham rural district council, and West Sussex county council, retiring as an alderman in 1960. He served on the board of Crawley College, Chichester, and on Graylingwell Hospital committee and the Industrial Disputes Tribunal. He gave forty-three years' service to the special constabulary, retiring as commandant of West Sussex. Other appointments included secretary of Crawley and District community association for twenty years, chairman of Crawley disablement advisory committee, director of Redland Holdings Ltd, member of the Wilson committee on noise, and the building regulations advisory committee. He was appointed CBE in 1954, knighted in 1966, and made a deputy lieutenant of West Sussex in 1975. He died on 24 January 1994 at The Beeches, Crawley; he was cremated and his ashes were placed on his parents' grave at St John's Church.

His younger brother, **Basil Longley** (1904–1979), was born on 19 January 1904 at Rathcote, Goffs Park Road, Crawley, and educated at Clifton College. On 3 June 1931 he married Sylvia Hannah (1908–1990), the daughter of F. H. Garnett of Skipton, Yorkshire. They had two sons, Oliver, born in 1933, and Richard Paul, born in 1939, and one daughter, Gillian, born in 1936. The marriage was dissolved in 1940 and on 5 December 1942 he married Phyllis Lattey, *née* Henderson (*b.* 1905). They had a daughter, Charis, born in 1944. Basil Longley qualified as a chartered surveyor, but devoted his whole life to running the company. This enabled his brother Norman to participate in industry-wide organizations and public affairs. Basil was above all a technical man and involved himself closely in estimating and surveying. He was identified with the success of the company in carrying out a series of department store and university contracts in the 1950s and 1960s. He died on 13 September 1979 at West Chiltington, Sussex, and was buried at the parish church there.

The Longley family thus ran one of the most important building firms in Sussex from the second half of the nineteenth century. Their business flourished during the railway boom, and they constructed many stations as well as churches. During the twentieth century they benefited from the inauguration of new towns, and in later years specialized in the construction of new department stores, as well as undertaking a number of university buildings. In the late twentieth century, under the direction of the fourth and fifth generations of the Longley family, the firm continued to undertake all types of building construction. PETER LONGLEY

Sources personal knowledge (2004) · private information (2004) · C. J. Longley, *Recollections* (1923) · C. J. Longley, *A short history of Crawley and District Water Company* (1926) · R. Smith, *Longleys of Crawley* (1983) · W. T. Pike, ed., *Sussex in the twentieth century* (1910) · J. Hime, ed., *People of Sussex* (1991) · N. Longley, 'James Longley & Co., 1939–45', 1946, James Longley (Holdings) Ltd, Crawley, Sussex, James Longley & Co. MSS · N. Longley, 'Appreciation of Basil Longley', 1946, James Longley (Holdings) Ltd, Crawley, Sussex · parish register, St John's, Crawley, Sussex, 26 June 1915 [burial, James Longley] · parish register, St John's, Crawley, Sussex, 21 Dec 1931 [burial, Charles John Longley] · parish register, Linfield, Sussex, 10 July 1836 [baptism, James Longley] · parish register, Crawley Down, Sussex, 7 March 1862 [baptism, Charles John Longley] · parish register, Crawley, Sussex, 16 Nov 1900 [baptism, Sir Norman Longley] · parish register, Crawley, Sussex, 17 April 1904 [baptism, Basil Longley] · *CGPLA Eng. & Wales* (1915) [James Longley] · *CGPLA Eng. & Wales* (1932) [Charles John Longley] · *CGPLA Eng. & Wales* (1979) [Basil Longley] · *CGPLA Eng. & Wales* (1994) [Sir Norman Longley]

Archives James Longley (Holdings) Ltd, Crawley, Sussex, family MSS · W. Sussex RO, records

Likenesses bust (James Longley), James Longley (Holdings) Ltd, Crawley, Sussex · bust (Sir Norman Longley), James Longley (Holdings) Ltd, Crawley, Sussex · photograph (James Longley), James Longley (Holdings) Ltd, Crawley, Sussex · photograph (Charles John Longley), James Longley (Holdings) Ltd, Crawley, Sussex · photograph (Sir Norman Longley), James Longley (Holdings) Ltd, Crawley, Sussex · photograph (Basil Longley), James Longley (Holdings) Ltd, Crawley, Sussex

Wealth at death £55,887 11*s.* 7*d.*—James Longley: probate, 1915, *CGPLA Eng. & Wales* (1915) · £56,916 13*s.* 7*d.*—Charles John Longley: probate, 1932, *CGPLA Eng. & Wales* (1932) · £105,040—Basil Longley: probate, 1979, *CGPLA Eng. & Wales* (1979) · £413,237—Sir Norman Longley: probate, 1994, *CGPLA Eng. & Wales* (1994)

Longley, Basil (1904–1979). *See under* Longley family (*per.* *c.*1860–1994).

Longley, Charles John (1862–1931). *See under* Longley family (*per. c.*1860–1994).

Longley, Charles Thomas (1794–1868), archbishop of Canterbury, was born at Boley Hill, Rochester, Kent, on 28 July 1794. He was the fifth son of John Longley, recorder of Rochester and a magistrate of the Thames police court,

Charles Thomas Longley (1794–1868), by Mayall, *c.*1863

and his wife, Elizabeth, daughter of Thomas Bond, a London timber merchant. He was the last but one of seventeen children born to the couple, several of whom died in infancy. He was educated at Cheam School before his election as a king's scholar at Westminster School in 1808 and as a Westminster student of Christ Church, Oxford, in 1812. He graduated BA in 1815 with a first in classics; he proceeded MA in 1818, and BD and DD in 1829. He held several offices at Christ Church, where he was tutor and censor between 1825 and 1828, and was a university proctor in 1827, leaving the first proctor's handbook for his successors. He was genuinely popular throughout the university. He was ordained deacon in 1818 and priest in 1819, and served as curate to Thomas Vowler Short, incumbent of Cowley (and later bishop of St Asaph). He became vicar of the parish in November 1823, and in August 1827 rector of West Tytherley in Hampshire, which involved resigning his Christ Church studentship. He was much in demand as a tutor for the sons of the aristocracy and gentry. Bishop C. R. Sumner appointed him rural dean. In March 1829, after Vowler Short had canvassed his name among the governors, Longley was invited to become headmaster of Harrow. The roll increased and Longley enlarged the syllabus, but his regime's lack of discipline was notorious. He was also believed to have become very wealthy through capitation fees.

On 15 December 1831 Longley married Caroline Sophia, eldest child of Henry Brooke *Parnell, first Baron Congleton. Parnell was paymaster-general in Melbourne's administration and he suggested Longley's name for a bishopric to the prime minister. Longley was appointed bishop of the newly created see of Ripon in October 1836. Despite the method of recommendation for appointment, Melbourne agreed that Longley need not be constrained to vote with the government on matters of Irish church policy. Longley actually voted against the government on other issues besides the Irish church, to Melbourne's pain and displeasure.

Longley threw great energy into engendering diocesan spirit in what was the first new diocese in England since the Reformation. Initially he had the practical problem of finding a suitable episcopal residence. He was given permission by the ecclesiastical commissioners to look for a suitable site for a new palace. Eventually land at Bramley Grange Farm, close to Ripon, was purchased from the lessee, and the archbishop of York, its ultimate landlord, passed the property to the see of Ripon. The minster in Ripon became the new diocese's cathedral church. The diocese included the countryside of the North Riding as well as the growing industrial towns of Barnsley, Bradford, Dewsbury, Halifax, Huddersfield, Leeds, and Wakefield. There was a glut of school and church building during his twenty-year episcopate, W. F. Hook's legendary efforts in Leeds being merely the most prominent. Stephenson (*Victorian Archbishops*, 23) calculates an increase in churches from 307 to 432, in vicarages from 170 to 301, and in curates from 76 to 146.

The controversy over the church of St Saviour's, Leeds, remains the most famous issue of his episcopate. In 1839 Hook, vicar of Leeds, had tried to persuade both J. H. Newman and E. B. Pusey of the need for more churches in Leeds and of the opportunity that this would give to the Oxford men for widening their influence. Pusey's wife had recently died and he conceived the church as both a memorial to her and a testimony to his church principles. Pusey's church would serve a very deprived part of the city, where brothels were numerous and which was later to suffer appallingly from cholera. Pusey was an anonymous donor. Both Longley and Hook soon became concerned about Pusey's ideas. In particular Pusey insisted on an inscription exhorting prayer for the builder of the church—himself. Longley and Hook both protested that when he died such an inscription would encourage prayers for the dead, which they found unacceptable.

The foundation-stone of the church was laid in 1842 and the next three years until its consecration were filled with disagreements. Longley refused to dedicate the church to the holy cross, as Pusey wished; he objected to a stone altar and there were many other minor disputes. It was agreed to dedicate the new church to St Saviour. Although Longley did consecrate the church in October 1845, unhappiness about its practices and its clergy continued throughout Longley's time at Ripon. Naturally these altercations gave Longley a poor reputation among advanced Tractarians and even led to him being wrongly described as low-church by the intemperate W. H. B. Proby. Longley, like Hook and many fellow bishops, was a staunch high-churchman, whose support for the Tractarians diminished as they became ever more 'Romish'.

Longley opposed the Oxford University Bill of 1854 which, among other things, reduced the proportion of clerical fellows in each college and reconstituted the central government of the university. In 1854 Longley was named as one of two churchmen who would join the executive commissioners empowered to revise the statutes of the university and colleges of Oxford. He was later one of the five referees who produced a new constitution for Christ Church, Oxford, in 1867.

On Palmerston's nomination Longley was translated to the see of Durham on 13 October 1856. He had previously declined a move to Lincoln. Here he began again the work of church building. His wife died in October 1858 at Auckland Castle. After four years he succeeded Thomas Musgrave as archbishop of York on 1 June 1860. In the brief time that he was at York the Northern convocation was revived (1861). Archbishop Musgrave had refused to let the convocation transact active business. One of its first acts was to condemn *Essays and Reviews*, to Longley's satisfaction.

Longley stayed only two years at York before Palmerston nominated him to his fourth see. He succeeded J. B. Sumner at Canterbury on 20 October 1862. Doctrinal disputes figured large. Longley and William Thomson, the archbishop of York, were dissenting members of the judicial committee of the privy council which overturned the verdict of heresy in the court of arches against the authors of *Essays and Reviews*. The law lords on the committee and Bishop A. C. Tait of London had exonerated them. The two archbishops issued pastoral letters which explained that the committee had only judged extracts of the book. Longley was also firmly convinced of the unsoundness of Bishop J. W. Colenso's writings, and thought him properly deposed from his Natal bishopric by Bishop Gray of Cape Town, his metropolitan. At the same time Longley dissuaded W. J. Butler, vicar of Wantage, from agreeing to election in Colenso's place.

By far the most important event of Longley's primacy was the first Lambeth conference, which met in London on 24–27 September 1867. The furore over Colenso was but one of the pressures that necessitated a meeting of Anglican bishops. J. B. Sumner had resisted calls for a meeting of bishops as he had resisted the revival of the Canterbury convocation. Longley, by contrast, had welcomed visits by American and Scottish bishops while still at Ripon. On 24 September seventy-eight British, colonial, and foreign bishops inaugurated the Lambeth or Pan-Anglican synod. Longley insisted that the meeting was a conference not a synod: no declaration of faith was to be made nor were canons to be enacted.

Even the description of the faith held by Anglicans was a subject of haggling. Reference to the first four ecumenical councils was finally included. Initially the case of Colenso was not scheduled for discussion, but pressure from the colonial bishops overturned this. A large majority of the bishops were united in condemnation of Colenso, although Longley forestalled a proposition to do so formally by appointing a committee to consider the matter. Nevertheless Samuel Wilberforce had a statement of support for Colenso's deposition signed by fifty-six bishops. The whole issue of appeal from the colonies to a spiritual tribunal in England was discussed. There were many who were suspicious of the whole proceeding, including William Thomson, the archbishop of York, who stayed away along with most bishops from the northern province, fearing that the Thirty-Nine Articles would be compromised. Dean A. P. Stanley refused the use of Westminster Abbey for the closing service because he was afraid that the bishops would censure Colenso.

Longley had to contend with the constant pressure of Lord Ebury, who wished to amend the form of clerical subscription. Ebury believed that many were deterred from ordination because they could not assent to every word in the prayer book and the articles. Eventually a royal commission on subscription (1864–5), of which Longley was inevitably a member, was conceded and minor changes were enacted. Henceforth clergy gave assent that the prayer book and articles were 'agreeable' to the word of God. Ebury's attempts to change the burial service were quashed.

Longley was also faced with the increase of ritualism during his primacy. Ebury's continuing attempts to reform the liturgy were included in the remit of the commission on ritual which was set up in 1867 and of which he was part. The first report, in August, condemned eucharistic vestments.

Although the bishops still had great influence over internal church affairs, the state got its own way more and more. In 1868 compulsory church rates were abolished and disestablishment of the Irish part of the United Church of England and Ireland, which Longley had opposed in parliament and at public meetings, became imminent. A fatigued Longley developed bronchitis after a holiday intended for recuperation and died at Addington Park, Croydon, on 27 October 1868. He was buried in the churchyard there. Longley had three sons and four daughters; his eldest son, Sir Henry Longley (1833–1899), became chief charity commissioner. Longley's personal charm and striking good looks (he was C. L. Dodgson's most photographed male subject), and his intellect and energy, served him very well throughout his life. His fame, though inflated by virtue of being primate when the Lambeth conference was first called together under his chairmanship, is not undeserved. J. R. Garrard

Sources A. M. G. Stephenson, *The Victorian archbishops of Canterbury* (1991) · A. M. G. Stephenson, *The first Lambeth conference, 1867* (1967) · A. M. G. Stephenson, *Anglicanism and the Lambeth conferences* (1978) · D. A. Jennings, *The revival of the Convocation of York, 1837–1861*, Borthwick Papers, 47 (1975) · N. Yates, *The Oxford Movement and parish life: St Saviour's, Leeds, 1839–1929*, Borthwick Papers, 48 (1975) · M. A. Crowther, *Church embattled: religious controversy in mid-Victorian England* (1970) · W. H. B. Proby, *Annals of the 'Low Church' party*, 2 vols. (1888) · Boase, *Mod. Eng. biog.* · *The Guardian* (28 Oct 1868) · *The Guardian* (4 Nov 1868) · *The Times* (29 Oct 1868) · *The Times* (30 Oct 1868) · *The Times* (3 Nov 1868) · *The Times* (4 Nov 1868) ·

E. G. W. Bill and J. F. A. Mason, *Christ Church and reform, 1850–1867* (1970) · *CGPLA Eng. & Wales* (1868) · *DNB*

Archives Bodl. Oxf., corresp. · Harrow School, corresp. and papers as headmaster of Harrow School · LPL, corresp. and papers · U. Leeds, Brotherton L., notebooks relating to Ripon diocese | BL, corresp. with W. E. Gladstone, Add. MSS 44361–44412, *passim* · BL, corresp. with Sir Robert Peel, Add. MSS 40399–40607 · Bodl. Oxf., corresp. with Samuel Wilberforce · Durham RO, letters to Lady Londonderry · LPL, corresp. with Angela Burdett-Coutts · LPL, corresp. with A. C. Tait · LPL, corresp. with Christopher Wordsworth · NRA, priv. coll., letters to S. H. Walpole · Pusey Oxf., corresp., mainly relating to St Saviour's, Leeds · U. Durham L., letters to third Earl Grey

Likenesses H. P. Briggs, oils, exh. RA 1838, Christ Church Oxf. · E. Davis, marble bust, exh. RA 1844, LPL · F. Grant, oils, *c.*1849, Bishop Mount, Ripon, North Yorkshire · portrait, 1859, repro. in *Church of England photographic portrait gallery* (1859) · G. Richmond, chalk drawing, *c.*1862, NPG · Mayall, carte-de-visite, *c.*1863, NPG [*see illus.*] · G. Richmond, oils, LPL · carte-de-visite, NPG · portrait, repro. in *ILN*, 41 (1862), 381 · portrait, repro. in *Illustrated News of the World*, 8 (1861) · portrait, repro. in *Illustrated Times* (25 Oct 1862), 417

Wealth at death under £45,000: resworn probate, July 1869, *CGPLA Eng. & Wales* (1868)

Longley, James (1836–1915). *See under* Longley family (*per. c.*1860–1994).

Longley, Sir Norman (1900–1994). *See under* Longley family (*per. c.*1860–1994).

Longman family (*per.* **1724–1972**), publishers, had their origins at Winford near Bristol. The family tree has been traced back to Thomas Longman, a Somerset yeoman, whose third son, also named Thomas, born *c.*1612, was apprenticed to a Bristol 'sopemaker' in 1626, being made free in 1633. He married Ann, the daughter of Ezekiel Wallis, an alderman and one-time mayor of Bristol. There were three generations of Longman soapmakers before the advent of seven generations of Longman publishers. The local soap trade was in decline, however, after 1738. When Ezekiel Longman, sheriff, died in 1708, the London book trade, through which the Longmans made their way into history, was already flourishing, offering, if never without risk, expanding markets and rising profits.

Thomas Longman (1699–1755), the first in the line of publishers, was born at Bristol in 1699, the son of Ezekiel Longman's second marriage, and he was nine years old when his father died. No evidence survives about why in 1716 his guardians sent him to London to be apprenticed to a Lombard Street bookseller, John Osborn (*d.* 1734), at the sign of the Oxford Arms. In 1724, one year after his articles expired, Thomas (remembered in the firm as Thomas I), using an inheritance from his Bristol relatives, acquired for £2282 9*s.* 6*d.* a publishing house at the sign of The Ship. It had been in existence since 1640, owned by different families, the last of them that of William Taylor, remembered as publisher of Daniel Defoe's *Robinson Crusoe* (1719). John Osborn was an executor. Taylor had moved premises to Paternoster Row, occupying a property later numbered 39, in 1711 and had also acquired the Black Swan, an adjacent property, at the corner of Paternoster Row and Ave Maria Lane.

The sense of a dynasty Thomas, who did not immediately acquire all the Taylor copyrights—*Robinson Crusoe* was not one of them—always called himself a bookseller and not a publisher (the term was not then used in its current sense), and he never printed any of the books that bore his imprint, usually an imprint shared with others. From 1725, moreover, he was joined as a partner by John Osborn's son, also called John, who died without issue in 1733 six months before his father. There was one even closer family connection with the Osborns. Thomas married the elder Osborn's daughter, Mary (*d.* 1762), on 27 January 1731, in St Paul's Cathedral. They too had no children.

Almost at once Thomas had added to the shares in the titles of books he acquired from Taylor at a time when such shares were bought and sold at convivial but exclusive sales. He paid particular attention to science titles, beginning with an edition of the works of the chemist Robert Boyle, prepared by Peter Shaw, his doctor, who helped Mary through a serious illness in 1735. Seven years earlier he had been one of a consortium which published the influential *Cyclopaedia of Arts and Sciences* compiled by Ephraim Chambers, whom he is said to have treated with 'the liberality of a prince and the tenderness of a father' (H. Curwen, *A History of Booksellers*, 1873, 82). His best-remembered enterprise, however, is that of being one of a later consortium which produced Samuel Johnson's *Dictionary of the English Language* in 1755. Thomas died on 18 June that year, nine years to the day from when the agreement with Johnson was signed.

It was Mary who on Thomas's death became the senior partner in what was by then a thriving business, alongside Thomas's nephew **Thomas Longman** (1730–1797), who was keenly interested in the theatre and married Elizabeth Harris, the sister of a proprietor and manager of Covent Garden. Without him the Longman business, thriving though it was, might have come to an end very near its beginning; and it was fortunate for its survival and further growth that he had no fewer than twelve children. His eldest son, **Thomas Norton Longman** (1771–1842), was an outstanding figure in the Longman line of publishers. The second son, George (1776–1822), provided further dynastic connection, highly valuable in trading terms. With the fortune bequeathed to him by his father, he went into business with the enterprising paper maker John Dickinson, and was the first Longman to become a member of parliament.

The connections continued and became more intricate. In 1843 **William Longman** (1813–1877) married Emma Pratt-Barlow, daughter of a rich railway director, whose brother had married John Dickinson's daughter, and in 1874 **Thomas Norton Longman** (1849–1930), eldest son of **Thomas Longman** (1804–1879), married Florence Pratt-Barlow, Emma's niece. Six years later **Charles James Longman** (1852–1934) married Harriet Ann, the daughter of Sir John Evans, who was a treasurer of the Royal Society and president of the Society of Antiquaries as well as a paper maker.

There was another connection, this time with printing.

Mary (1801–1870), one of the daughters of Thomas Norton Longman (1771–1842), married Andrew Spottiswoode, later printer to Queen Victoria, a member of the famous printing house founded by his grandfather William Strahan, main printer for the early Longmans.

The name Norton had come into the Longman family in 1736 following the purchase by Thomas Longman (1699–1755) and Samuel Buckley from the Norton family, its patentees, of the royal grant and privilege of printing William Lily's *Latin Grammar* dating back to the sixteenth century. The last Thomas Norton Longman was always known in the business as Mr Norton.

Such family connections and convergences have often been noted, as they were in 1854 by a publisher very different from the Longmans, Charles Knight; and in 1924, the *Publishers' Circular*, a valuable periodical launched in 1837 by a group of publishers including William Longman, numbered Longman names, as Knight had done, like sovereigns. Five were called Thomas, and it was only because there were by then too many Longmans in the business that the last Thomas Norton Longman dropped the numbering.

Yet there remained a strong sense of family hierarchy. In 1924, at the time of the much celebrated bicentenary of the house, Harold Cox—the last editor of the *Edinburgh Review*, the quarterly which Longmans had owned throughout most of its history—suggested as a firm believer in the 'principle of heredity' that 'the example of the firm of Longmans' was of more than family interest. Through six generations (and there was to be a seventh) a single family had 'successfully administered an important and constantly expanding business', preserving 'the traditions on which the original success of the firm was based', but developing them 'to meet new needs or to seize new opportunities' (Cox and Chandler, 48).

Even more eloquently, Sir George Otto Trevelyan, the nephew of Macaulay, paid tribute at the time of the bicentenary to the house with which his own family had been and remained in such close dynastic connection. It was not, he said, 'a creature of the State, nor of the Church, nor of the Universities, nor of any corporate body'. Nor was it 'the creation of the money-making impulse'. The house stood both for 'self-help and the effort of the individual' and for 'family tradition, for ideals of public usefulness and assistance to the cause of literature and science, handed on from generation to generation' (Cox and Chandler, 56). In the Trevelyan family that cause was perpetuated by Sir George's son G. M. Trevelyan, who had already written several books for Longman by 1924, including his *British History in the Nineteenth Century*, published two years before. His *English Social History* (1944) was as much of a Longman bestseller as Macaulay's five-volume *History of England* (1849–61). The cheque for £20,000 paid to Macaulay by Longman on account in 1855 has been carefully preserved.

Dynastic links were present inside the Longman business at almost every level as well as between the Longmans and other families. Thus the Greens, father and son, Bevis (1793–1869) and William Ellerby (1836–1918), spanned almost a century of the business, and from 1889 to 1926 the imprint used by the Longmans was 'Longmans Green'. Not until 1959 did it become 'Longmans'. The success of the family, as the Longmans themselves appreciated, always depended on the taking in of 'outsiders', the first of them Owen Rees (1770–1837), a Welsh dissenter from a very different background from the Longmans, who was made a partner in 1797 before the death of Thomas Longman on 5 February 1797. There were many non-Longman partners in the nineteenth century, their names recorded in the successive imprints of the house. The longest list of names, six of them—Longman, Hurst, Rees, Orme, Brown, and Green—was on the imprint between 1823 and 1825.

In briefly describing the house of Longman & Co. in 1859, the year of the retirement of Thomas Brown and the death of Cosmo Orme, *The Times* (6 September) claimed that 'perhaps nothing more has tended to raise the House to its present position than the plan adopted by the principals of introducing fresh blood from time to time'. It noted also, however, that 'like some of our other well-known institutions, its origin is lost in obscurity'. The family itself made every effort to find out, and this remark could not have been made ten years later.

Leviathan, 1842–1877 In 1842, before the mid-Victorian boom years in the history of publishing, an obituary notice of Thomas Norton Longman in the *Annual Register*, in which the Longmans had had a share since 1805, described him as the head of a house 'which has for more than a century been distinguished as the Leviathan of publishing and bookselling'. The description was to become more familiar between 1851 and 1870, when the mid-Victorian publishing business was dominated by a few great leviathans, as they were called at the time, with the house of Longman heading or near the head of them.

The basis of the house's strength was capital. Thomas Norton Longman had left nearly £200,000 in 1842, when he died accidentally after falling from his horse on his way back from Paternoster Row to his house in Hampstead; and Bevis Green, who died in 1869, left about the same sum. Nevertheless, success depended not only on capital but on the display of publishing skills. A new phase in the history of the family began in 1842, when for the first time two sons, Thomas and William, succeeded to the control of the firm. They were given good advice by the aged Sydney Smith, then a canon of St Paul's living not far from Paternoster Row. 'You and your brother', he told them, 'are arrived at years of great maturity and are quite capable of conducting your own business … I expect you [both] to live together upon the strictest terms of friendship and to be ready to make mutual concessions' (Wallis, 19–20). They followed his advice, whether they needed it or not, and from the start divided their responsibilities in a sensible manner. By virtue of his age Thomas Longman (1804–1879) was chairman, but William, who was born on 9 February 1813, was a more dynamic businessman, although, like earlier Longmans, he was singled out by contemporaries less for his dynamism than for his 'courtesy, geniality, kindliness and ready hospitality'. The latter quality had always been stressed by his father, who generously entertained his authors as well as published them.

In 1873 it was said of William by Henry Curwen, author of an early history of the book trade, that he succeeded through a combination of enterprise and discretion, and the former quality was evident in 1863 when he arranged the acquisition of the business of J. W. Parker, not the first or last of Longman acquisitions, which greatly strengthened the Longman list of authors. John Stuart Mill was one of them, and his *Subjection of Women* (1869) and his revealing *Autobiography* (1873) were major Longman publications in a completely different genre from John Henry Newman's *Apologia pro vita sua* (1854), a book published by Longman at Newman's own request.

In the Parker list there were three historians very different from Macaulay and from each other—J. A. Froude, who became a close friend of the Longman family, H. T. Buckle, and W. E. H. Lecky. Two other of Longman's highly successful mid-Victorian publications were P. M. Roget's *Thesaurus* (1852), frequently re-edited, first in dynastic fashion by his son and grandson, and *Gray's Anatomy* (1863), a far less original work, but one which was also to go through many new and distinctly different editions, including a lavish centenary edition in 1958. In this and other books the Longmans paid particular attention to illustrations.

The mid-Victorian theological list was extremely varied, and while it included Newman, with very different religious views from those of the family, it also included the highly controversial works of J. W. Colenso, deposed for heresy—and reinstated—bishop of Natal: Colenso had written many successful mathematical textbooks at various levels for Longman, to whom he sold the copyright for £10,000. Education was already a Longman speciality, but the width of their publishing list is demonstrated by the presence in it of the novelist Anthony Trollope (*The Warden*); the traveller Richard Burton (Longmans did not publish his erotica); the sociologist, would-be psychologist, Herbert Spencer; the philologist Max Müller; the soldier Evelyn Baring, later Lord Cromer, whose *Staff College Essays* appeared in 1870 when he was a lieutenant; the man of many parts Sir John Lubbock, later Lord Avebury, *qua* anthropologist; and the widely read writer on cookery Eliza Acton.

Longman was the second of the publishing leviathans to be described at length in a series of three anonymous articles in *The Critic* in 1860, written by a well-known Victorian journalist, Francis Espinasse. (Murray was the first, Blackwood the third.) He traced the story of the dynasty back to Bristol and described its association under Thomas Norton Longman and Rees with an at least equally remarkable list of pre-Victorian authors, some of whom had already become leading names in English literature—Samuel Taylor Coleridge, William Wordsworth, Robert Southey, and Sir Walter Scott. The second edition of the *Lyrical Ballads* (1800), with its famous preface, had already joined Johnson's *Dictionary* in a Longman hall of fame. And before Macaulay there had already been one other long-remembered record payment, that of £5000 presented to Tom Moore for his now largely forgotten Romantic poem *Lalla Rookh* (1817), which went through six impressions in its first year. Espinasse ended his article with a reference to a new edition of Johnson's *Dictionary*. Only the house of Longman had survived from the original consortium.

A regular Longman publication that survived all rival publications was the *Edinburgh Review*, the whig quarterly through which Macaulay came to fame. Launched in 1802 in association with the Scottish firm of Archibald Constable, it remained in joint Constable-Longman hands after only a short break until it became Longmans' exclusive property in 1826 after the collapse of the Constable business. Edited by Francis Jeffrey, it had established substantial political importance before the advent of its Victorian editor Henry Reeve, a personal friend of the Longman family, who stayed in his chair for forty years from 1855. In unpublished memoirs the last Thomas Norton Longman could write in 1921, eight years before the review ceased to appear, that the family had been fortunate in all 'our editors, and all has been such smooth running that there is little or nothing to report'.

Into the twentieth century: 1877–1906 This last Thomas Norton Longman, son of Thomas Longman (1804–1879), was one of a new generation of Longmans who took over at Paternoster Row following the death of the first William Longman on 13 August 1877. He had joined the business as a young man of twenty and had become a partner in 1873. Four years later William's son, Charles James Longman, with impeccable whig first names, became a partner too. A third Longman, George Henry (1852–1938), also entered the business and became a partner in 1879. He took little part in the literary side of the house, but had responsibility for foreign trade and, loosely, for financial affairs before the advent of professional accounting. A fourth Longman, Hubert Harry Longman (1856–1940), was not much involved in the business at Paternoster Row, but for a time was given charge of the Ship Binding Works at Great Saffron Hill, conveniently not far away. This was a subsidiary company, formed in 1887. Hubert Harry's main interest was in Liberal politics in Surrey, and he was the only Longman to be made a baronet—in 1909.

Effectively publishing control of the house of Longman was now in the hands of Thomas Norton Longman and Charles James Longman (1852–1934), the latter the junior but the more powerful of the two. Known as CJ, he was educated at Harrow School and at University College, Oxford; he was also known in the book trade as Black Longman on account of his square-cut black beard. He could be autocratic in his treatment of employees and even of authors. It was reputed that he lost the young Winston Churchill, whose first books were published by Longman, because Churchill lit a cigar in his presence. It was CJ, however, who was largely responsible for the negotiations leading up to the acquisition in 1890 of the house of

Rivington (founded in 1711), which involved more complex issues than the acquisition of J. W. Parker in 1863. CJ was surprised to be approached by Francis Hansard Rivington about a take-over since Rivington had been in charge of the business for thirty-nine years.

The Rivington deal strengthened the Longman theological list even more than the Parker deal had done, and Longmans were now the publishers of Newman the Anglo-Catholic as well as of Newman the Roman Catholic. They were placed in direct contact too with the high-church party in Oxford. Yet this was not the only new link forged during the period. CJ was a close friend of the novelist Rider Haggard, and it was through this and similar links that Longmans published Robert Louis Stevenson's *Dr Jekyll and Mr Hyde* (1886). On very different fronts CJ fostered the increase in the number of school textbooks and the expansion of the overseas side of the business, two developments which converged with the development of English language teaching. A key appointment was that of J. W. Allen in 1884, who arrived at Paternoster Row with teaching experience with the Liverpool school board. His experience and acumen added to Longman family profits, but he did not become a partner until 1918 on the death of W. E. Green, who left him his shares.

The head of the house of Longman, the last Thomas Norton Longman, claimed in typewritten memoirs that as 'Longman the 5th' he had the right to have the casting vote on all details relating to the form and price of any book: 'my very blood is printer's ink and my very bones are made of a mixture of type and paper'. In one of his very first business transactions, however, that with Disraeli, then Lord Beaconsfield, he yielded to the author in 1880 on many points in relation to the publishing of Disraeli's *Endymion*. He confessed that he was surprised too by the immediate great success of *The Voyage of the Sunbeam* (1877) written by Lady Brassey, widow of the great contractor: it sold a quarter of a million copies in a popular edition and was translated into every European language.

Like his cousin, Thomas Norton Longman later put much of his trust in the unremitting literary advice given to the house by Andrew Lang: Lang had been at Oxford with Frederick William Longman (1846–1908), who because of an accident became a lifelong invalid and could not take part in the business. Lang also wrote a regular column, 'At the sign of The Ship', for *Longman's Magazine*, founded in 1882, priced 6*d*., and edited by CJ, which lasted until 1905 without ever acquiring the reputation and prestige of the *Cornhill* or *Macmillan* magazines.

Scientific and medical books fell within Thomas Norton's range of responsibilities, with CJ cultivating the history side of the business. In 1881 the *English Historical Review* was launched, edited by a Longman author, Mandell Creighton, later bishop of London, to be followed in 1905 by a new twelve-volume series on the political history of England, the first of many later Longman series. One of these was to be the responsibility of Cyprian Blagden, formerly a public schoolmaster, an inspector of schools, who came to know more about the history of the Longman business than any member of the family. In his penetrating booklet *Fire More than Water* (1959) he claimed that those Longmans who had controlled the business during the 107 years since 1842 had provided no new 'publishing answers'. They had provided the old answers 'over and over again under new conditions and with changing problems' (Blagden, 29). There was limited truth in the remark as far as the first seventy years were concerned, for by 1964 the house of Longman was making more of its longevity than of its enterprise, and at the end of the First World War Thomas Norton and CJ were still in charge at the top. Thomas Norton retired a year later; CJ, increasingly conservative, not until 1928: in his last years he refused to keep a telephone in his room. He died in 1934.

It made very little difference to the daily business routines of the family when in 1889 Longmans Green became a family company, or, indeed, when in 1926 a limited liability company transformed the partners into directors. Each lunchtime they held a meeting to discuss business after a boy employee had taken round the relevant papers to each director's room, using the words 'Mr Green desires your presence' long after the last Green had died. No formal votes were taken at the meetings.

Nevertheless, emphases were changing, with an increased concentration on education and on overseas expansion. School textbooks became increasingly profitable after the Education Acts of 1870 and 1902, and so did textbooks in English and vernacular languages for overseas, some of them produced abroad. There had been an early Longman connection with America when Thomas Longman (1730–1797) was chairman, and in 1889 a branch of Longmans Green was opened in New York. By 1918 it had built up a substantial independent business, not only in textbooks. A branch in Toronto followed in 1922. In India branches had been opened in Bombay in 1895 and in Calcutta in 1906. Blagden headed the Indian operations from 1941 to 1948.

The sixth generation: 1906–1946 Two new Longmans arrived in Paternoster Row in 1906—**Robert Guy Longman** (1882–1971), the younger son of George Henry Longman, and his cousin **William Longman** (1882–1967), the son of C. J. Longman, the first of them educated at Eton College and Trinity College, Cambridge, and the second at Harrow School and University College, Oxford. They both became partners three years later, once again specializing in their interests. Robert Guy was a highly intelligent and sensitive publisher with a lively interest in music and literary tastes of his own. It was he who encouraged novelists as different as Elizabeth Bowen, Stella Gibbons, and Mary Renault and the American author and playwright Thornton Wilder. He did not retire until 1948. William, always known in Paternoster Row as Mr Willie, concentrated on finance and accounts, inheriting a traditional and ritualized system, but, following the Companies Act of 1914, one required to follow standard procedures of accounting.

William was a shy man, who by the time when he retired in 1964 after thirty years as chairman was something of a recluse. Yet, like his father, he was involved in the higher politics of publishing. C. J. Longman had been first president of the newly formed Publishers' Association in 1896 and again from 1902 to 1914, and had given his full support to the net book agreement, regulating the retail prices of books, which had been initiated by Frederick Macmillan. William, who was president from 1929 to 1931, was described by a fellow publisher, Stanley Unwin, as the best president the association ever had.

In their own publishing Robert Guy Longman and William Longman had to help steer their ship, still the Longman publishing logo, through the troubled seas of two wars and unprecedented depression. There was one family tragedy too. Eight weeks after the beginning of the First World War William's younger brother Frederick (1890–1914) was killed in action. During the depression the house of Longman had to turn for financial assistance to an outsider, Kenneth Boyd Potter, a member of a shipping family with its own rich and varied dynastic history, who became a director, bringing in necessary capital in 1926 and playing a bigger part than any of the Longmans when it became a public company in 1948. He was one of three directors who then disposed of some of their shares as part of a capital reorganization, William receiving £57,252 for his and Robert Guy £72,996.

It would have been impossible to foresee this outcome on 29 December 1940 when at the height of the German air assault on Britain 39 Paternoster Row was totally destroyed along with neighbouring buildings. The fires that burnt there, started by incendiary bombs, were far more devastating than those of an earlier fire in 1861 which led the Longmans to have built on the site an imposing new building in Portland stone 'in the Renaissance style'. Literature, supported by the Arts and Science, was represented in the keystone of the main arch. It was with these two fires in mind—and the great fire of London of 1666—that Blagden wrote *Fire More than Water*, noting that fires had their phoenixes, a lesson of 1940 as much as of 1861.

In 1939 part of the Longman business had already been transferred to Wimbledon, and it was to suburban houses there that Robert Guy and William Longman now moved out, carrying on their business as far as possible as usual after a back list of nearly 6000 titles had been reduced to twelve. And there was further fire to come, for in April 1941 the old Ship Binding Works was put out of action. Even then the trials were not over, but in 1947 it was possible for the Longmans and their employees to return to London, this time to the West End not the City—first to 6 and 7 Clifford Street, and next, in 1961, to 48 Grosvenor Street, not far away. These had been eighteenth-century domestic houses, built about the time when Thomas Longman started his business in 1724.

Residences There was no one single domestic residence passed on from one generation to another. The first Thomas Longman had lived and worked in Paternoster Row. So, too, had several of the later members of his family. Thomas Norton Longman (1771–1842) was the first to move out from the City to Mount Grove, Hampstead, in 1798: all his children were married in Hampstead parish church, and a bust in memory of him was placed there, donated by J. R. McCulloch, the political economist, and other friends.

After his marriage in 1838 Thomas Longman (1804–1879) moved to a Nash house in Hanover Terrace, Regent's Park, moving again further out of London ten years later, but keeping a London house in Sussex Gardens, where the youngest of his five daughters was born. It was the daughters whom he commemorated in a stained glass window in the Grosvenor Chapel, South Audley Street, complete with ships and black swans. Thomas moved later to Hampshire, where in 1860 he built an imposing new house at Farnborough Hill, designed in deep rose brick by Henry Edward Kendall, and set in a substantial estate. It too incorporated a frieze of stone terracotta panels depicting in high relief ships in full sail and swans swimming on water surrounded by palm trees. It was not bequeathed to any of his children, however, and two years after his death in 1879 it was acquired by the exiled French Empress Eugénie, who lived there until her own death in 1920.

Thomas Longman's brother, William, who produced an even larger family consisting of seven daughters and three sons, lived in Hyde Park Square in London before acquiring houses first in Chorleywood and later in Berkhamsted, so that the Longman family, while mostly retaining London houses, was now scattered geographically. It was not until 1908 that the last Thomas Norton Longman, Thomas Longman's eldest son, acquired a substantial country house, Shendish, near Apsley, Hertfordshire, which had been built by Charles Longman, the Dickinson partner, in 1853 and which was occupied after his death in 1873 by his son Arthur (1843–1908), also a partner in the Dickinson paper business. Thomas Norton Longman retired to Shendish in 1919 exactly fifty years after his first arrival at Paternoster Row. He was buried there in a churchyard which was built at the expense of the Longman, Dickinson, Pratt-Barlow, and Evans families.

Charles James Longman, Thomas Norton Longman's nephew, had a country house in Hertfordshire, Upp Hall, Braughing, near Ware, coincidentally not far from Harlow, where the Longman business was to move in 1968. His elder son, William, recorded that CJ was the last member of the family to live in style. He had four children, three of whom were given public-school and university educations, and possessed a town house, complete with mews and a coachman, as well as his country estate, where he employed seven domestic servants, two gardeners, two labourers, and two gamekeepers.

The gamekeepers were more than status symbols, for most of the Victorian Longmans, beginning with Thomas Longman (1804–1879), were keenly interested in sports, a few of them more than they were in the business. The first William, deeply involved as he was in business affairs and in his own historical researches, which led him to write several books mainly on medieval English history and the architecture of St Paul's, was a founder member of the Alpine Club and its president from 1871 to 1874. C. J. Longman was an association football blue at Oxford and champion of England at archery in 1883, and along with his partner, the last Thomas Norton Longman, produced many books on different sports in their Badminton Library, begun in 1885 with the duke of Beaufort as its editor. CJ himself contributed the volume on archery. The series was supplemented later by a monthly *Badminton Magazine*. George Henry Longman captained the Eton cricket eleven and Cambridge University, played regularly for the Gentlemen against the Players, and sponsored a Longman cricket club for employees of the business. Arthur Longman (1843–1908), like his father a partner in Dickinson & Co., was master of the Old Berkeley hunt.

The last of the Longmans, Mark Frederick Kerr Longman (1916–1972), was more interested in the arts than in sports, but he had a country house at Bishopstone, on the top of a hill near Salisbury, an eighteenth-century rectory with Victorian connections. It is reputed to have been the model for Anthony Trollope's Plumstead Episcopi in *The Warden*, which was published by Mark's great-grandfather in 1855.

The last of the Longmans Mark was the son of Henry Kerr Longman, who never entered the Longman business, but who came to its rescue as a stockbroker when for the only time in its history it faced banking problems in 1932. Mark's three forenames all came from the female side of his inheritance. In 1874 George Henry Longman had married Mary Frances Kerr, the daughter of Lord Frederic Kerr, whose brother was called Mark, and since the last Thomas Norton Longman had no male heir—he had four daughters—and William Longman had no children, it was through Henry Kerr Longman that the two of the last generation of Longmans entered the publishing business. Of his five sons, John Cecil Longman (1912–1965), who never intended to become a publisher, was made a director on the same day as his younger brother Mark, and their cousin, Thomas Michael Longman (1917–1978), only son of Robert Guy Longman. Thomas Michael was the only member of the family to leave the house of Longman. In 1959, unhappy about the decision of his fellow directors not to allow him to extend the theological side of their business, he set up a publishing business of his own, taking with him as partners two of his house colleagues, G. C. Darton and John Todd.

Mark Longman had joined the house straight from Cambridge in 1938, returning after war service in 1946. Described in the headline of his *Times* obituary (6 December 1972) as an 'outstanding publisher', he had become head of what was now simply called Longmans in 1964. An effective chairman and a brilliant speaker, he was president of the Publishers' Association from 1969 to 1971, following in the footsteps of an earlier generation of Longmans. He was also an energetic president of the National Book League, believing strongly in the future of the book in an age of new electronic media.

There were great hopes for the future of the Longman business when it moved out in 1967 to a new building in Harlow New Town. It was designed by Sir Frederick Gibberd and proudly named Longman House. The warehouses had moved out earlier in 1959. The business was still expanding on the educational side with non-Longmans, like John Chapple and John Newsom, who inspired the move to Harlow, playing a major part. The expansion overseas, particularly in Commonwealth countries, had been so substantial that in 1966 a Longman Group of companies was constituted, their locations ranging from Nigeria to Australia, the Caribbean to the Pacific, with Mark as its first chairman. Exports and overseas sales then accounted for three-quarters of the Longman total. They depended on enterprise on the periphery rather than at the centre, where there was a shortage of family capital. In 1968, therefore, Mark initiated and carried through friendly negotiations that resulted in the take-over of the Longman Group by the Financial and Provincial Publishing Company, owned by S. Pearson & Son, and two years later Pearson Longman Ltd was formed. The pedigrees of the Longman and Pearson families, the latter with its origins in Bradford in 1856, sharply contrasted, but the first chairman of Pearson Longman, Patrick Gibson, had been at Eton with Mark and was proud to link the two family names in the company's new title.

In the same year Mark became vice-chairman of Penguin, and after the death of Sir Allen Lane, founder in 1936 of the famous paperback business, he played a major part in arranging a merger between Pearson Longman Ltd and Penguin. It was not to last, but both companies continued to operate within the Pearson Group, a large conglomerate, dealing in many other products besides books, including porcelain and wine, until Pearson Longman, which flourished in the 1980s under the leadership of Tim Rix, a non-Longman and a non-Pearson, ceased to exist in 1994. That decision was taken not at Harlow but by the Pearson Group in London.

Mark's widow, Lady Elizabeth Lambart, daughter of the tenth earl of Cavan, who had seen Mark through a long and crippling illness, survived this last landmark event in the Longman story. She had worked briefly inside Longmans as a secretary, and she was proud of the part that Mark, her second cousin, had played not only within the business, but within publishing as a whole. He was also chairman of the Fine Art Society, and his portrait by Graham Sutherland is a worthy memorial. ASA BRIGGS

Sources H. Cox and J. E. Chandler, *The house of Longman: a record of their bicentenary celebrations* (1925) • C. J. Longman, *The house of Longman, 1724–1800: a bibliographical history with a list of signs used by the booksellers of this period* (1936) • C. Blagden, *Fire more than water* (1959) • P. Wallis, *At the sign of The Ship, 1924–1974* (1974) • A. Briggs, ed., *Essays in the history of publishing* (1974) • *IGI*

Archives U. Reading, business archive | BL, letters to Harvey Napier, Add. MSS 34619–34626, *passim* [Thomas Longman] • CUL, letters to Sir George Stokes [William Longman] • Herts. ALS, letters to Lord Lytton [Thomas Longman] • U. St Andr. L., corresp. with James David Forbes [Thomas Longman]

Likenesses C. Moore, bust, *c.*1845 (Thomas Norton Longman), parish church St John, Hampstead

Wealth at death approx. £200,000—Thomas Norton Longman: 1842 • £200,000—William Longman: probate, 12 Sept 1877, *CGPLA Eng. & Wales* • under £100,000—Thomas Longman: probate, 28 Oct 1879, *CGPLA Eng. & Wales*

Longman, Charles James (1852–1934). *See under* Longman family (*per.* 1724–1972).

Longman, Robert Guy (1882–1971). *See under* Longman family (*per.* 1724–1972).

Longman, Thomas (1699–1755). *See under* Longman family (*per.* 1724–1972).

Longman, Thomas (1730–1797). *See under* Longman family (*per.* 1724–1972).

Longman, Thomas (1804–1879). *See under* Longman family (*per.* 1724–1972).

Longman, Thomas Norton (1771–1842). *See under* Longman family (*per.* 1724–1972).

Longman, Thomas Norton (1849–1930). *See under* Longman family (*per.* 1724–1972).

Longman, William (1813–1877). *See under* Longman family (*per.* 1724–1972).

Longman, William (1882–1967). *See under* Longman family (*per.* 1724–1972).

Longmate, Barak (1737/8–1793), genealogical editor and heraldic engraver, was the only son of Barak Longmate (*d.* 1763/4), of the parish of St James's, Piccadilly, who was descended from a Lincolnshire family, and his first wife, Elizabeth Weston. His mother seems to have died soon after his birth, and certainly before 29 October 1741, when his father married Mary Yeomans. In 1752 he was bound apprentice to James Wigley, citizen and clothworker of London, for £10. On 2 July 1764, at Greenwich, he married Elizabeth Thompson (*d.* 1781).

Longmate seems to have begun heraldic engraving in private practice as early as 1760. By the 1770s he was contributing work to heraldic and genealogical publications, and by the end of the decade was also working on the editorial side. He was responsible for the fifth edition of Collins's *Peerage*, which came out in eight volumes in 1779, as well as for a supplementary volume in 1784; in the preface to the latter he announced a plan to publish an 'Extinct Peerage of England', but this was not accomplished. In 1788 he produced a small, two-volume work, *The Pocket Peerage*; popularly known as 'Longmate's Peerage' this achieved some success, and he produced two further editions before his death. The small compass of these books did not allow much elaborate engraving but he continued to execute more distinguished work in other contexts, and regarded a large, separately produced plate, 'A genealogical history of the family of O'Sullivan More from Duach Donn, monarch of Ireland. Anno Mundi 3912', as his masterpiece. Hugh Clark, later editor of the successful *Introduction to Heraldry*, considered himself Longmate's pupil in heraldic engraving; how formal the relationship was is not clear.

To assist his editorial work and his private engraving commissions Longmate collected genealogical and heraldic manuscripts, and also compiled many of his own. Among the latter was a great 'alphabet', or dictionary of arms, such as engravers relied on when selecting arms for clients who did not know, or claim to know, what their arms were. Though of dubious function this dictionary (later owned by Thomas Willement; BL, Add. MS 30373) is important because it cites its sources. Compiled between 1760 and 1793 it illuminates how the published armories of this and later periods—such as those by Joseph Edmondson, William Berry, and John Burke—came into being. Longmate also made detailed extracts from William Segar's 'Baronagium' (probably in connection with the projected 'Extinct Peerage'), noted church monuments in the counties around London, and copied and updated many of the heralds' visitations, several contemporary manuscripts of which he possessed.

Longmate died at his house at 11 Noel Street, Soho, on 23 July 1793, leaving three sons and two daughters, and was buried four days later in the churchyard of St Marylebone. Part of his library was sold by Leigh and Sotheby, raising £235 9*s.* 9*d.* His eldest son, **Barak Longmate** (1768–1836), succeeded him both in his business and as editor of *The Pocket Peerage*, of which he produced four further editions. By the time of the seventh, in 1813, the success of John Debrett's rival work was hampering sales, and no further editions followed. The younger Longmate was a friend and assistant of John Nichols and other antiquaries in his circle. His obituary in the *Gentleman's Magazine* states that about 1801 he made church notes in many parishes of Gloucestershire with a view to continuing the work of Ralph Bigland on that county, but that the project was abandoned after the disastrous fire at Nichols's printing house in 1808. On 12 August 1793, at St Paul's, Covent Garden, he married Elizabeth, daughter of Jeremiah Locke, of the parish of St Martin-in-the-Fields; they had no children. Having lived for many years in Margaret Street, off Cavendish Square, Longmate retired in his sixties first to Camden Town and then to Edward Street, Hampstead Road, east of Regent's Park. There he died, after a long paralysis, on 25 February 1836, and was buried on 3 March at St Marylebone. He was survived by his wife.

C. E. A. Cheesman

Sources *GM*, 1st ser., 63 (1793), 679; 2nd ser., 6 (1836), 441 · Nichols, *Lit. anecdotes*, 9.4, 51 · GL, MS 11936/261, no. 389643 [Sun Fire Office policy list, 1777] · typescript index of London apprenticeship records, Society of Genealogists · T. Moule, *Bibliotheca heraldica* (1822), 447, 464 · will of Barak Longmate (*d.* 1763/1764), PRO, PROB 11/896, sig. 56 · will, PRO, PROB 11/1236, sig. 425 · will, PRO, PROB 11/1859, sig. 174 [Barak Longmate (1768–1836)] · H. W. Fincham, *Artists and engravers of British and American bookplates* (1897), 59 · B. N. Lee, *British royal bookplates* (1992), 95 · parish register, Greenwich, 2 July 1764 [marriage: E. Thompson] · parish register, St James's, Piccadilly, 29 Oct 1741 [marriage: M. Yeomans] · parish register, St Paul's, Covent Garden, 3 Sept 1793 [marriage: E. Locke] · H. Clark and T. Wormull, *A short and easy introduction to heraldry*, 7th edn (1794) · death duty entry, PRO, IR 26/1423 [Barak Longmate (1768–1836)] · *DNB* · parish register, St Marylebone, 3 March 1836, LMA, vol. 21 [burial]

Archives BL, alphabet of arms of English families and other heraldic papers, Add. MSS 12478, 30373; Ro King's MS 423 · Bodl. Oxf., pedigrees mostly of Berkshire families copied by him from various visitations, MSS Rylands b 1, c 10 · S. Antiquaries, Lond., heraldic notes, collection of monumental inscriptions, and other papers | BL, Add. MSS 26758, 38728 fol. 180; 39991 fols. 83, 85 [Barak Longmate] · BL, Add. MSS 8848, 26704, 26781 · Bodl. Oxf., letters to Mark Noble · Bodl. Oxf., Top. Gen. C. 74 · Coll. Arms, four MSS in presses RR/42/A, RR/25/A, RR/19D/A, RR/35/E

Wealth at death £1500; business insured at £400 by Sun Fire Office in 1777; library sold for £235 9*s*. 9*d*. on death; Barak Longmate: death duty registers, PRO, IR 26/1423

Longmate, Barak (1768–1836). *See under* Longmate, Barak (1737/8–1793).

Longmore, Sir Arthur Murray (1885–1970), air force officer, was born on 8 October 1885 at St Leonards, New South Wales, Australia, the youngest son of Charles Croker Longmore (1855–1930), stationmaster at Yarrara, and his wife, Janet Murray (*d*. 1942). He was brought to England by his mother when he was seven, and educated at Benges School, Hertford, and Foster's Academy, Stubbington. The sea held a great attraction for him as a boy and, after showing considerable aptitude at school, he joined the Royal Naval College, Dartmouth, as a naval cadet in May 1900. After he received his commission into the Royal Navy in 1904, his early career followed the normal pattern of a junior officer. During this period he took a great interest in, and followed the exploits of, the early pioneers in aviation.

It was a coincidence that in 1910, when Longmore was commanding a torpedo boat based at Sheerness, one of the early flying schools was being established near by at Eastchurch on the Isle of Sheppey. Such was his enthusiasm for aviation that he was one of the first four naval officers selected to attend a course of flying instruction there. In less than two months he was awarded Royal Aero Club certificate no. 72, which put him high among the ranks of the pioneers of naval aviation.

Longmore then had a brief period as a flying instructor at the newly opened Central Flying School, where John Salmond was also an instructor. After this he took command of Cromarty air station and subsequently of the experimental seaplane station at Calshot, where he was able to pursue his great interest in the development of float-planes. Before aircraft-carriers were introduced, these were regarded as the most suitable aircraft to provide support for the Royal Navy. On 23 April 1913 he married Marjorie (*d*. 1959), the only child of William James Maitland, of Witley Manor, Godalming, Surrey, formerly deputy governing director of Indian Guaranteed Railways. They had three sons and a daughter.

When war broke out in 1914 Longmore was sent to Dunkirk to carry out some of the first bombing missions, during which the small bombs were literally thrown over the sides of the cockpit. After a few weeks of these haphazard and largely ineffectual operations, he was given the task of forming and commanding 1 squadron, Royal Naval Air Service, which had considerable success in the Dunkirk area against Zeppelins, then beginning to attack England with increasing frequency.

It came as a disappointment to Longmore to be transferred back to naval duties in January 1916, when he was appointed to HMS *Tiger* of the first battle-cruiser squadron as a lieutenant-commander, relinquishing the rank of wing commander, Royal Naval Air Service. This was his last seagoing appointment and it gave him a unique opportunity to be present at the battle of Jutland during which the experience he had acquired as an airman made him an admirable adviser on air matters to the commander of the battle-cruiser force. In this capacity he was highly critical of the failure to make adequate use of aircraft during the battle, and considered that they could have made an invaluable contribution in a reconnaissance role.

After a brief spell in London on the Air Board, where he was responsible for aircraft and equipment development, Longmore, now a wing captain, Royal Naval Air Service, went to Malta. There he joined the staff of the commander-in-chief, Mediterranean, and was responsible for air operations. On 1 April 1918 the Royal Air Force was formed; Longmore became a lieutenant-colonel, RAF, and was given his first RAF command, the Adriatic group at Taranto, a post he held until after the armistice in November 1918. He waged a vigorous and successful campaign against U-boat bases in the Mediterranean, for which he was appointed to the DSO in 1919.

The post-war years were unstable and frustrating for the new service, and Longmore filled several posts for short periods before being posted to Iraq in 1923 as a group captain on the staff of air headquarters. This was a period of great interest for him since Iraq had been placed under 'air control' by the Cairo conference of 1921; this gave the RAF its first opportunity to demonstrate how it could control large, sparsely populated areas of difficult terrain. Longmore deserves much of the credit for the success of the experiment, later extended to Aden and other theatres. He was appointed CB on his return home in 1925 for a tour of duty in the Air Ministry as director of equipment.

Longmore then became commandant of the RAF College, Cranwell, and shortly afterwards was promoted to air vice-marshal at the early age of forty-five. His great experience and somewhat gregarious nature qualified him admirably for this appointment. He passed two of the happiest years of his career in the Lincolnshire countryside, where he was able to indulge his enthusiasm for hunting and shooting. Under his guidance the permanent college building was completed at Cranwell and opened in 1933.

After leaving Cranwell, Longmore commanded in succession Inland Area and Coastal Area, which later became Fighter Command and Coastal Command respectively. These years involved him in constant struggles to preserve his forces against the wholesale reductions and economies which were prevalent, and it was not until 1933, when he was promoted to air marshal, and in the following year, when he became commandant of the Imperial Defence College, that the RAF began to expand to meet the growing threat from Germany. At the Imperial Defence College he devoted much time and effort, with little response, to fostering closer relations between the three services. He was appointed KCB in 1935.

For a brief period in 1939–40 Longmore was commander-in-chief, Training Command; as such, he played a notable part in initiating the highly successful empire air training scheme under which thousands of wartime aircrews were trained in Canada, Rhodesia, Australia, and New Zealand. Shortly after the outbreak of war, however, he was transferred to the important post of air officer commanding-in-chief, Middle East, which turned out to be his most challenging appointment. When he assumed command in May 1940, the pressing demands of the European theatre had resulted in a serious dearth of modern aircraft and equipment in the Middle East. In the following month, Italy declared war and Longmore's small force was soon heavily engaged against the Italian air force in north Africa, Greece, and Abyssinia. As he slowly built up and modernized his squadrons, their commitments, notably in Greece, became increasingly heavy.

On 9 December 1940 the offensive in the western desert opened, with all the air support that Longmore could assemble. It turned out to be the first British success of the war on land, and the Italian air force in north Africa was virtually put out of action. Unhappily the triumph was short-lived. Germany came to the assistance of her Italian ally both in Africa and in Greece, and within four months the Germans had recaptured all the army's earlier gains and overrun Greece. Longmore's constant demands for reinforcements resulted in some unwelcome attention from Churchill, who hated pessimists and senior commanders who complained about their lack of resources. After some acerbic correspondence, in which Churchill accused Longmore of failing to make proper use of the manpower and aircraft he had, Longmore was recalled to London in May 1941. He was succeeded in the Middle East by Air Chief Marshal Sir Arthur Tedder, and was made inspector-general of the RAF, a post which he held until the following year, when he retired officially from the service, having been appointed GCB.

After his retirement Longmore returned to his home in Lincolnshire. He contested the March 1942 by-election in Grantham as a Conservative candidate, and was narrowly defeated. His RAF career was not finished, however. In August 1943 he was recalled to serve on the post-hostilities planning committee, which considered problems concerned with the reshaping of combatant countries in peacetime. This valuable work took him to his final retirement in May 1944, but he continued to help the war effort by joining a voluntary organization, the 'yachtsmen's emergency service'. As a lifelong sailing enthusiast he was of immense value to this organization, which provided water-borne transport for the invasion fleet forming in the channel ports. From the end of the war until his death he led an active life and gave a great deal of his time to the Imperial War Graves Commission, of which he was vice-chairman. He also continued to indulge his love of sailing as a member of the Royal Yacht Squadron.

Two of Longmore's sons joined the RAF, one being killed in action in 1943 while serving with a Coastal Command anti-submarine squadron, and another joined the Royal Artillery. His wife, Marjorie, died in 1959 and he married, secondly, on 20 May 1960, Enid, the widow of Lieutenant-Colonel Geoffrey Bolster, and daughter of Colonel M. R. de B. James. During his long and distinguished career Longmore received many foreign decorations—from Belgium, France, Italy, and Greece—and he wrote his autobiography, *From Sea to Sky*, which was published in 1946. He also wrote a chapter on air forces in *The Era of Violence, 1898–1945* (1964), volume 12 of the *New Cambridge Modern History*.

Longmore died on 10 December 1970 at his home, Little Trees, Broomfield Park, Sunningdale, Berkshire. Before his death, Longmore expressed a wish for his ashes to be scattered over the Solent, and this was duly done in January 1971 by four Nimrod maritime patrol aircraft. He was described in official records as having been 'exceedingly popular with officers but also with the rank and file'.

DAVID LEE, *rev.* CHRISTINA J. M. GOULTER

Sources *The Times* (12 Dec 1970) · A. Longmore, *From sea to sky, 1910–1945* (1946) · air historical branch (RAF) records · Burke, *Peerage* (1967) · Burke, *Gen. GB* (1952) · J. Terraine, *The right of the line* (1985)

Archives Commonwealth War Graves Commission, Maidenhead, notebooks relating to Imperial War Graves Commission | FILM IWM FVA, documentary footage · IWM FVA, news footage | SOUND IWM SA, oral history interview

Likenesses W. Stoneman, two photographs, 1931–53, NPG · W. Rothenstein, portrait, 1939, Royal Air Force College, Cranwell · J. Hughes-Hallett, oils, Royal Air Force Museum, Hendon

Wealth at death £5089: probate, 30 March 1971, *CGPLA Eng. & Wales*

Longmuir, John (1803–1883), poet and lexicographer, was born on 13 November 1803 near Stonehaven, Kincardineshire, the son of John Longmuir and his wife, Christian Paterson. In 1814 his parents moved to Aberdeen, where he was educated at the grammar school, and at Marischal College. After graduating MA he completed divinity studies. In 1825 he published *The College and other Poems*, the title poem of which criticizes the academic system of the time.

After leaving university Longmuir taught for some years in schools at Stonehaven and Forres. In July 1833 he was licensed to preach by the presbytery of Forres. On 2 January 1835 he married Lillias, daughter of Alexander Milne, a bookseller in Forres. He was appointed evening lecturer at Trinity Chapel, Aberdeen, in 1837, and in September 1840 was ordained minister to the city's Mariner's Church. At the Disruption of 1843 he went over with most of his congregation to the Free Church of Scotland. For some years he was lecturer on geology at King's College, Aberdeen. His first wife having died, he married, second, Dorothy Hawthorn Dixon in 1857. On retiring from lecturing in 1859 he was granted the degree of LLD.

Longmuir published three further collections of verse, *Bible Lays* (1838), *Ocean Lays* (1854), and *Lays for the Lambs* (1860). He produced a popular guidebook to Dunnottar Castle in 1835, and one to Speyside in 1860. He also published a volume on a local monolith, *The Maiden Stone of Bennachie* (1869), *A Run through the Land of Burns and the Covenanters* (1872), and an edition of Alexander Ross's *Helenore* (1866).

In addition to his other accomplishments Longmuir was a noted lexicographer. He edited a dictionary combining the work of Walker and Webster in 1864, and revised

Walker's *Rhyming Dictionary* in 1865. His revision of Jamieson's *Scottish Dictionary* appeared in an abridged edition in 1867 and in four volumes between 1879 and 1912, and is probably his most important work. As a preacher Longmuir was noted for his conversational style, and several of his sermons were published. He was popular as a platform speaker, particularly in the cause of temperance. He died at 5 Dee Place, Aberdeen, on 7 May 1883, survived by his wife and at least one son, A. D. Longmuir.

J. C. Hadden, *rev.* Douglas Brown

Sources Irving, *Scots.* • Boase, *Mod. Eng. biog.* • W. Walker, *The bards of Bon-Accord, 1375–1860* (1887) • D. H. Edwards, *Modern Scottish poets, with biographical and critical notices*, 2 (1881) • private information (1893) [A. D. Longmuir] • personal knowledge (1893) • d. cert. • m. cert.

Wealth at death £620 10s. 3d.: confirmation, 30 May 1883, *CCI*

Longridge, Thomas (*bap.* 1751, *d.* 1803). *See under* Hawks family (*per. c.*1750–1863).

Longrigg, Stephen Hemsley (1893–1979), military governor and petroleum company executive, was born on 7 August 1893 at Sevenoaks, Kent, the younger son of William George Hemsley Longrigg (1859–1941), a banking official and businessman, and his wife, Kate Thorp (*d.* 1937).

Longrigg attended Highgate School in north London and subsequently went up to Oriel College, Oxford, in 1911. He read classics and obtained a first-class degree. Because of army service in the Royal Warwickshire regiment in 1914–21 (major in 1918) he received his MA degree in 1921 when on home leave from Iraq. Early during his subsequent service in the Iraq government, from 1918 to 1931, he married, in 1922, Florence (1890–1976), daughter of Henry Aitken Anderson. They had two sons (John and Roger) and a daughter. In the Iraq administration Longrigg rose rapidly and at an early age became inspector-general of revenue, from 1927 to 1931. In addition to his official duties he developed his authorial talents by writing a highly competent history of Iraq entitled *Four Centuries of Modern Iraq* (1925), which has not been superseded. This work established his reputation as a serious historian and orientalist. His familiarity with Iraq extended beyond its borders to the whole of the Fertile Crescent and the Arabian peninsula.

The success of Longrigg's first work was followed by several other books, many articles, and a steady stream of lectures throughout his life. His firsthand knowledge of the scene and personalities of the area enlivened both his felicitous pen (put to paper in a fine hand) and his remarkable fluency as a speaker. When on one occasion, during a lecture to a university audience, the lights failed, he discarded his script and continued without hesitation or pause.

His long service in Iraq enabled Longrigg to acquire an admirable command of Arabic. This facility served him in good stead when, from 1931 to 1951, he became a senior executive of the Iraq Petroleum Company and in this capacity negotiated oil contracts with some of the rulers of the Arabian peninsula. King Ibn Saʿud was one of the principal partners of his negotiating skills.

The Second World War ushered in a third career as proconsul. Longrigg became a brigadier for the duration of the war and served on the general staff of general headquarters Cairo, mainly concerned with the preparations for the military administration of the expected occupation of the Italian colonial possessions in Africa. When he was appointed chief administrator (military governor) of Eritrea, he was fully ready for the task, which he always considered the high point of his career. For the best part of three years, from 1942 to 1944, he presided over a military (yet quasi-colonial) government which reflected Longrigg's own efficiency and humaneness.

Longrigg was fortunate in having on his staff a number of officers of high calibre who were skilled in colonial administration, anthropology, and some of the languages of the area. Longrigg himself was initially no expert in Ethiopian history or languages, but he acquired a knowledge of the former by remarkably skilful and eclectic reading, while for the latter he made use of his extremely serviceable Italian and his command of Arabic. Although the lowlands of Eritrea were predominantly inhabited by Muslims who knew little or no Arabic, he would insist on talking to them in that language—suggesting that it was sheer quirkiness on their part to claim that they could not understand him.

Longrigg's governorship was undoubtedly the most prosperous as well as the most quiescent time during the eleven years of British military administration in Eritrea. In his official capacity Longrigg could be aloof and gubernatorial, with the natural air of authority which he so amply possessed, but as host at the Villa Vicereale he was relaxed and attentive to the comfort of his guests. The less cerebral among his officers might have been slightly restive during his weekly lectures, but the majority enjoyed his intellectual vigour as much as the lecturer himself did.

Towards the end of his governorship Longrigg wrote *A Short History of Eritrea* (1945) which, though not primarily based on independent research (as he himself stressed repeatedly), gave an excellent and succinct picture of country and people, their past and prospects for the future. His views on that future (the Christian highland provinces to go to Ethiopia, the Muslim lowlands to be annexed to Sudan) bore fruit only with regard to the former proposal.

On Longrigg's return to England he rejoined the Iraq Petroleum Company until his retirement in 1951. As well as accepting a number of honorary positions, he continued his literary activities at an astonishing pace. His earlier book on Iraq was now brought up to date in *Iraq, 1900 to 1950* (3rd impression, 1968) and was followed by works on oil, on the Middle East, and on Syria and Lebanon. He was much in demand as a lecturer, particularly in the USA.

Longrigg was appointed OBE in 1927, and in 1955 he supplicated successfully for an Oxford DLitt. He received the

Lawrence of Arabia medal in 1962 and the Richard Burton medal in 1969. His wife predeceased him in 1976 and he himself died on 11 September 1979 at the Otara Nursing Home, Kingsley Green, Sussex.

EDWARD ULLENDORFF

Sources personal knowledge (2004) · private information (2004) [J. S. Longrigg and R. Longrigg] · *WWW* · *Daily Telegraph* (13 Sept 1979) · *CGPLA Eng. & Wales* (1979)
Archives St Ant. Oxf., Middle East Centre, reports on Cyrenaica and notes on Occupied Enemy Territory Administration | St Ant. Oxf., Middle East Centre, corresp. with C. J. Edmonds · University of Warwick, BP archive
Wealth at death £80,888: probate, 10 Dec 1979, *CGPLA Eng. & Wales*

Longstaff [*née* Donald], **(Mary) Jane** (1855–1935), biologist, was born on 27 August 1855 at 16 Cavendish Place, Carlisle, Cumberland, the eldest of four children of Matthewman Hodgson Donald, manufacturer, and his wife, Henrietta Maria Roper, daughter of the Hon. J. H. Roper Curzon. She was educated at a private school in London before entering Carlisle School of Art. Interested in all aspects of natural history from an early age, Jane Donald became an authority on land and freshwater mollusca, her first paper on the mollusca of Cumberland being read to the Cumberland Association for the Advancement of Science in 1881. J. G. Goodchild of the Geological Survey, himself active in the Cumberland Association, encouraged her to study fossil shells, and her notes on Carboniferous gastropods from Penton and elsewhere, published in the *Transactions of the Cumberland Association* (1885), constituted the first of twenty papers on the neglected subject of Palaeozoic gastropods; these she expanded into a systematic revision of fossil genera and families, which she published in the *Quarterly Journal of the Geological Society* in the years up to 1933. She joined the Geologists' Association in 1883 and received its Murchison Fund award in 1889. Though never formally connected with any museum or institute, by visiting various museums, and with the help of private means, she produced some remarkable papers, with her own illustrations, most of which were published by the Geologists' Association. She was also a good botanist and was elected fellow of the Linnean Society in 1906.

On 29 August 1906 Jane married a widower, George Blundell Longstaff (1848/9–1921), himself an entomologist; they travelled abroad together, visiting north Africa and South Africa, Australia, the West Indies, and South America. George Longstaff's interest lay in butterflies; Jane always brought back recent (not fossil) shells from these regions. Her most important paper was on the non-marine mollusca of southern Sudan, in 1914. For several years she undertook breeding experiments with the large South African land snail *cochlitoma*, the results of which she published in 1921. She also provided appendices to her husband's works, notably his *Butterfly Hunting in many Lands* (1912). Jane Longstaff died at the Spa Hotel, Bath, on 19 January 1935. Her nephew inherited her collections, which he presented to the Natural History Museum.

ANITA MCCONNELL

Sources *Proceedings of the Geological Association*, 47 (1936), 97 · *Nature*, 135 (1935), 297 · L. R. Cox, 'Mrs Mary Jane Longstaff (*née* Donald)', *Proceedings of the Linnean Society of London*, 147th session (1934–5), 183–4 · b. cert. · m. cert. · d. cert. · *CGPLA Eng. & Wales* (1935)
Wealth at death £24,110 8*s*. 2*d*.: resworn probate, 22 Feb 1935, *CGPLA Eng. & Wales*

Longstaff, Tom George (1875–1964), mountaineer, was born on 15 January 1875 at Summergangs Hall, Hull, the eldest son of Llewellyn Wood Longstaff (1841–1918), merchant, and his wife, Mary Lydia, daughter of Thomas William Sawyer, of Southampton. It was his father who made possible the first Antarctic expedition under Captain Scott by an early contribution of £25,000. Longstaff was educated at Eton College and Christ Church, Oxford, where he obtained a third class in physiology in 1897. He proceeded BM, BCh in 1903, and DM in 1906 (Oxford and St Thomas's), but he never took up regular practice thereafter.

Although he often visited the Alps during his childhood and adolescence, it was not until he was twenty-two that Longstaff began serious mountaineering; then, during several alpine seasons, he learned the art under the tuition of some of the leading alpine guides of the period. In 1903 he undertook a climbing expedition in the Caucasus, where, with his single companion, L. W. Rolleston, he made the first ascent of five peaks. In 1905 Longstaff went to the Himalayas with two Italian guides, Alexis and Henri Brocherel, with the intention of exploring the vicinity of Nanda Devi. His plans were curtailed when he accepted an invitation to join C. A. Sherring, deputy commissioner of Almora, on a journey to Tibet. Before setting off, however, Longstaff and his guides spent a month exploring the eastern approaches to Nanda Devi, and reached a 19,000 feet col on the rim of the basin which gave them the first view of its interior. The Tibetan journey took them through little-known country to Lake Manasarowar, the source of the Sutlej River. On the way, Longstaff and the Brocherels made a bold attempt to climb Gurla Mandhata (25,350 feet). Swept away by a snow avalanche which carried them 3000 feet down the mountainside, they renewed their ascent next day but abandoned the attempt 1000 feet below the summit after they had spent the night in the open at an altitude of 23,000 feet.

Two years later Longstaff returned to the Himalayas with the same guides, this time accompanied by Charles Bruce and Arnold Mumm. They approached Nanda Devi from the west and, by discovering and crossing the Bagini Pass (20,000 feet), they reached the middle gorge of the Ganges, the only outlet from the basin. From there Longstaff and the guides made the ascent of Trisul (23,360 feet), climbing the final 6000 feet in a single day. This was to remain for twenty-three years the highest summit reached. They then attempted to penetrate the upper gorge of the Ganges into the Nanda Devi basin. Although they failed, the first party to accomplish this project twenty-seven years later owed its success largely to this

Tom George Longstaff (1875–1964), by unknown photographer

reconnaissance. They spent the rest of the summer exploring the glaciers of the Kamet group.

In 1909 Longstaff turned his attention to the Karakoram. It was there that he made his most notable contribution to geography when, accompanied by A. Morris Slingsby, he crossed the legendary Saltoro Pass to discover the upper portion of the Siachen glacier, one of the greatest ice-streams outside polar regions, and the lofty massif of Terim Kangri beyond. Then, with D. G. Oliver he followed the Nubra River to its source in the glacier; and continuing up the glacier was able to confirm his identification. These discoveries established the position of an important section of the continental watershed between the Indus and the Tarim basin of Chinese Turkestan. All these expeditions he conducted with Spartan simplicity, unencumbered by elaborate equipment and living largely upon local produce. This was from choice, not necessity; for he was a keen exponent of light travel which not only gave him freedom of movement but enabled him more easily to establish contact with the local people and to achieve close harmony with his chosen environment. Following the tradition of the nineteenth-century travellers, he recorded detailed observations of the natural history of the regions he visited; but his special interest was ornithology. His affection for mountain people and his understanding of their way of life are revealed in his autobiography, *This my Voyage* (1950).

In 1910 and 1911 Longstaff climbed in the Canadian Rockies. During the First World War he served in India and, as assistant commandant of the Gilgit scouts (1916–17), in the course of his duties travelled widely in the Hindu Kush. In 1922 he joined the second expedition to Mount Everest, where his experience of high-altitude climbing and his medical knowledge were of great value to the party. Apart from this, his pioneer travels during this period were in the Arctic. He took part in two expeditions to Spitsbergen (1921 and 1923) and three to west Greenland (1928, 1931, and 1934).

Longstaff's short, spare frame belied his exceptional powers of endurance; but his dynamic character was revealed by a high-bridged, patrician nose and lively eyes, and emphasized by a jutting red beard. For more than half a century he was a leading figure in geographical and mountaineering circles. He served for many years on the council of the Royal Geographical Society, as vice-president in 1934–7, and as honorary secretary in 1930–34. In 1908 he was awarded the Gill memorial and in 1928 the Founder's medal. He was elected president of the Alpine Club in 1947 and was made an honorary member in 1956. It was, however, through his personal contacts that Longstaff's influence was most widely felt. His great experience was at the disposal of all who sought it and successive generations of young mountaineers and explorers owed much to his encouragement and sage advice. He would discuss their plans with as much enthusiasm as though he himself were taking part in their projects, and he was equally generous in his praise of their success. He never hesitated to say what he thought and he was fiercely critical of humbug and ostentation. Typical was his remark to a member of one of the many abortive attempts to climb Everest which in his opinion received excessive publicity: 'For Heaven's sake climb the wretched thing and let's get back to real mountaineering.'

In 1911 Longstaff married Dora Mary Hamilton, daughter of Bernard Scott MRCS, of Bournemouth; they had seven daughters. The marriage was dissolved in 1937 and in 1938 he married Charmian Dorothy Isabel, daughter of Duncan James Reid MB CM, of Ealing, London, with whom he settled in Wester Ross. In this wild setting, so well suited to his tastes, he spent the main part of his last twenty-five years, keeping open house to his wide circle of friends, including many of the foremost naturalists of the day, and visited, as always, by young men seeking his advice. He died at his home, Badentarbet Lodge, Achiltibuie, Ross-shire, on 27 June 1964. His second wife survived him.

ERIC SHIPTON, *rev.*

Sources personal knowledge (1981) • private information (1981) • *The Times* (29 June 1964) • T. G. Longstaff, *This my voyage* (1950) • P. Lloyd, *Alpine Journal*, 69 (1964), 322–5 • Burke, *Gen. GB* (1937) • b. cert. • d. cert.

Archives Alpine Club, London, diaries • U. Oxf., Edward Grey Institute of Field Ornithology, notes | Bodl. Oxf., corresp. with T. R. E. Southwood • Rice University, Houston, Texas, Woodson Research Center, letters to Sir Julian Huxley | FILM BFI NFTVA, record footage

Likenesses photograph, repro. in Lloyd, *Alpine Journal*, facing p. 323 • photograph, Alpine Club, London [*see illus.*]

Wealth at death £17,238: probate, 13 Jan 1965, *CGPLA Eng. & Wales*

Longstrother, John. *See* Langstrother, Sir John (*d.* 1471).

Longueville, William (1639–1721), lawyer, was the only son of Sir Thomas Longueville, knight, of Bradwell Abbey, Buckinghamshire, and his wife, Anne Ashcombe, second daughter and coheir of Sir William Ashcombe of Alvescot, Oxfordshire. He was entered as a student at the Inner Temple in November 1654; he then matriculated at Christ Church, Oxford, on 25 July 1655 and was created MA in special congregation on 28 September 1663. He was called to the bar at the Inner Temple in 1660, was called to the bench in 1677, and he became an autumn reader in 1682, a Lent reader in 1685, and treasurer in 1695. He was one of the six clerks in chancery from 1660 to 1678. These were six officers who received and filed bills, answers, replications, and other documents on the equity side of the court. He was a successful conveyancer, and by his practice was able to restore the fortunes of his family, which his father had ruined. He married Elizabeth (1647–1716), third daughter and coheir of Sir Thomas Peyton, second baronet, of Knowlton, Kent, and his second wife, Cecilia. They had two sons, Charles and William, who died in the East Indies, and two daughters, Catherine and Elizabeth.

Longueville was a close friend of Sir Francis North, the lord keeper, and his brother Roger. The best account of him is given by Roger North in the *Life* of his brother; there he is described as one of the lord keeper's most intimate friends, valued for his 'fluent, witty, litterate, copious and instructive' conversation and for his knowledge and love of the classics and poetry (North, *Life of the Lord Keeper*, 458). For a time Roger North, who had leased Sir Peter Lely's house in Covent Garden, London, lived near to Longueville, who occupied a house in Bow Street, Covent Garden, but the connection and friendship between the Norths and Longueville may have been closer. The Peytons of Knowlton, the family of Longueville's wife, Elizabeth, were a branch of the Peytons of Isleham; Thomas Peyton of Isleham married Elizabeth, daughter of Sir William Yelverton, of Rougham, Norfolk, the property that Roger North bought in 1690–91. As early as 1672 Francis North was given a mortgage over this property by Yelverton Peyton, and in the mid-1680s his sister Elizabeth Wiseman also held a mortgage over Rougham.

Longueville was also a close friend of the poet Samuel Butler. Roger North describes him as 'the last patron and friend poor old Butler, the author of Hudibras had, and in his effete old age he supported him, otherwise he might have bin literally starved'. Butler repaid him by making him his heir: 'that is gave him his remaines, but in loos papers, and indegested'. Longueville 'reduced them to method and order, where they lye out of reach of the tapstering printers' (ibid.). They are now in the British Library (Add. MS 32625). An edition with notes was published by Robert Thyer in 1759.

William Longueville has been identified as the Mr Longueville who is referred to by George Farquhar in his preface to *The Twin Rivals* (1703), of whom Farquhar says he 'must own [him]self obliged … for some lines in the part of Teague, and something of the lawyer; but above all, for his hint of the twins, upon which I formed my plot'. That this refers to the William Longueville discussed here was questioned by Charles Stonehill in a note to his edition of Farquhar's *Works*, who refers to

> a marginal note in the *Biographia Britannica* (ed. 1793, vol. 5) [which] says that Longueville was 'as we are told, our author's countryman, and a fencing master, as was also his son, James …' It does seems unlikely that anyone but an Irishman could have given help in composing the lines of Teague. (1.398)

Letters from Longueville are preserved in the Hatton papers in the British Library (Add. MSS 29550–29586), some of which are printed in the Camden Society edition of the *Correspondence of the Family of Hatton*.

Longueville died on 21 March 1721 in London and was buried on 30 March in Edward the Confessor's chapel, Westminster Abbey. Apart from his property, which passed to his son, and mourning for his two daughters, he left £50 each to the school of St Clement Danes and 'to the poor of the said parish as my executor shall finde to be objects of pitty'. MARY CHAN

Sources J. Burke and J. B. Burke, *A genealogical and heraldic history of the extinct and dormant baronetcies of England, Ireland, and Scotland*, 2nd edn (1841) • Foster, *Alum. Oxon.* • F. A. Inderwick and R. A. Roberts, eds., *A calendar of the Inner Temple records*, 2 (1898); 3 (1901) • G. Lipscomb, *The history and antiquities of the county of Buckingham*, 4 vols. (1831–47), vol. 1 • R. North, *The life of the Lord Keeper North*, ed. M. Chan (1995), 39, 458–9 • E. M. Thompson, ed., *Correspondence of the family of Hatton*, 2 vols., CS, new ser., 22–3 (1878) • G. Farquhar, *'The recruiting officer' and other plays*, ed. W. Myers (1995), 84, 345 n. • R. North, *The autobiography of the Hon. Roger North*, ed. A. Jessopp (1887), 237–9 • *The complete works of George Farquhar*, ed. C. Stonehill, 2 vols. (1930) • *The genuine remains in verse and prose of Mr. Samuel Butler*, ed. R. Thyer, 2 vols. (1759) • *DNB*

Archives Harvard U., law school, legal notes, memoranda, and cases | BL, letters to Lord Hatton, Add. MSS 29550–29586 • priv. coll., MSS of Thomas North, Box 23.D.4

Longworth, Maria Theresa (1833–1881), plaintiff in a case of disputed marriage and author, was born at Cheetwood, near Manchester, the youngest of six children of Thomas Longworth, silk manufacturer, and his wife, Ann, *née* Fox. Thomas Longworth's business, and at one time his residence also, was in a large house at the corner of Quay Street and Longworth Street, Manchester. Maria's mother died when she was very young, and she was educated at an Ursuline convent school in Boulogne, France, where she became a Roman Catholic. She spent two years in Italy completing her education. On her return to her father's house at Smedley near Manchester, disagreements with him on religious subjects arose, and she spent much of her time with a married sister in Boulogne, or on visits to friends.

In the summer of 1852, while crossing the channel with some friends, Maria Longworth was introduced to William Charles *Yelverton, afterwards fourth Viscount Avonmore, and a correspondence between them began. In 1855 she served as a nurse with the French Sisters of Charity during the Crimean War, and met Yelverton again at the Galata Hospital, when she accepted his proposal of

Maria Theresa Longworth (1833–1881), by unknown engraver

marriage. Yelverton's relatives disapproved of the engagement and it was broken off for a time; but on 12 April 1857 the couple went through a private ceremony of marriage in Scotland, when Yelverton read aloud the Church of England marriage service at Maria Longworth's lodgings at 1 Vincent Street, Edinburgh. They were afterwards married by a priest at the Roman Catholic chapel at Rostrevor in Ireland, and then lived together in Ireland and Scotland.

On 26 June 1858, while Maria was in Edinburgh, Yelverton formally married Emily Marianne Forbes, widow of Professor Edward *Forbes. On 31 October 1859 Maria Longworth, claiming to be Yelverton's wife, sued him for restitution of conjugal rights in the London probate court, but the court decided that it had no jurisdiction over the marriage. In 1861 an action was brought in Dublin by Mr Thelwall, in whose house Maria Longworth had been living, to recover from Yelverton money Thelwall had supplied to her. This action lasted from 21 February to 4 March 1861, and the validity of both the Scottish and the Irish marriage was established in the Irish court. In July 1862 on appeal the Scottish court of session annulled the marriage, and the judgement was affirmed by a majority of the House of Lords on 28 July 1864, although Lord Brougham declared in Maria Longworth's favour. Her attempt to reopen the case at Edinburgh in March 1865 failed, and the House of Lords on 30 July 1867 supported the Scottish court. Finally her appeal to the court of session, on 29 October 1868, to set aside the judgment of the House of Lords was rejected. Much sympathy was shown to her in this long and unsuccessful struggle, and a subscription was raised on her behalf in Manchester. A novel based on the affair, *Gentle Blood*, was published by J. R. O'Flanagan in 1861. In 1867 *A Wife and not a Wife* by Cyrus Redding appeared, similarly inspired by Maria Longworth's case.

Maria Longworth spent her later years in travel, and died of dropsy at Pietermaritzburg, Natal, on 13 September 1881. She was buried the next day in the Church of England cemetery in Pietermaritzburg.

What money Maria Longworth had was spent in the litigation, and she largely supported herself by writing. Her chief works were *Martyrs to Circumstance* (1861), *The Yelverton Correspondence, with Introduction and Connecting Narrative* (1863), *Zanita: a Tale of the Yo-Semite* (1872), and two books about travel.

ALBERT NICHOLSON, *rev.* CATHERINE PEASE-WATKIN

Sources D. Crow, *Theresa: the story of the Yelverton case* (1966) • J. Thelwall, ed., *The Yelverton marriage case, Thelwall v. Yelverton, an account of the trial* (1861) • *BL cat.* • Boase, *Mod. Eng. biog.* • Ward, *Men of the reign*

Likenesses drawing, repro. in Crow, *Theresa* • engraving, NPG [*see illus.*]

Lonsdale. For this title name *see* Lowther, Katherine, Viscountess Lonsdale (1653–1713); Lowther, John, first Viscount Lonsdale (1655–1700); Lowther, Henry, third Viscount Lonsdale (1694–1751) [*see under* Lowther, John, first Viscount Lonsdale (1655–1700)]; Lowther, James, earl of Lonsdale (1736–1802); Lowther, William, first earl of Lonsdale (1757–1844); Lowther, William, second earl of Lonsdale (1787–1872); Lowther, Hugh Cecil, fifth earl of Lonsdale (1857–1944).

Lonsdale [*formerly* Leonard], **(Lionel) Frederick** [Freddy] (**1881–1954**), playwright, was born in St Helier, Jersey, on 5 February 1881, the third and youngest son of Frederick Leonard, a tobacconist, and his wife, Susan, daughter of James Belford, also a tobacconist. He was educated locally and on leaving school at seventeen immediately joined the South Lancashire regiment as a private. Within three months he found the discipline of army life uncongenial, and, his parents lacking the money to buy him out, he managed to persuade a sympathetic doctor to provide him with a medical discharge. On returning to Jersey he found work as a railway clerk in the London and South Western Railway office. However, clerkship did not appeal for long. In 1901 he formed an attachment with a Canadian girl holidaying in St Helier with her family, and on her return to Canada he pursued her, working his way across the Atlantic as a steward on a liner. Once in Canada, he was rebuffed both by the girl and by her shotgun-wielding father and, crestfallen, he returned to England, where he worked for a time on Southampton docks.

During this picaresque youth Leonard had begun to write plays, encouraged by the favourable reception of the barracks entertainments he had produced while briefly in the army. In 1903 his comedy *Who's Hamilton?*

(**Lionel**) **Frederick Lonsdale** (**1881–1954**), by Simon Elwes, 1940s?

was performed in Jersey to a packed and appreciative house. It was the only play he acted in himself (he took the role of leading man) and the only one written under his real name. The following year he eloped with Leslie Brooke Hoggan (*b.* *c.*1886), the daughter of Lieutenant-Colonel William Brooke Hoggan RA of St Helier. The couple were married in Scotland on 4 August; they had three daughters.

In 1908 Leonard changed his name to Lonsdale by deed poll (apocryphally to evade his creditors), and he sold the libretto for *The King of Cadonia*, a musical comedy with lyrics by Adrian Ross and music by Sidney Jones, to the producer Frank Curzon. It was a success, and later that year Curzon produced Lonsdale's farce, *The Early Worm*, at Wyndham's. With Curzon's production of *The Best People* at Wyndham's the following year, and *The Balkan Princess*, a musical play, in 1910 at the Prince of Wales's, Lonsdale's reputation was established. These early comedies set the tone for later pieces. He specialized in producing 'adroit and witty trifles' (*The Times* 11b): frothy comedies of manners centring on the unlikely exploits of the rich and titled. His plays were known for their cynical, epigrammatic wit, sparkling dialogue, and deft manipulation of farcically unlikely situations. Contemporaries compared him with the older W. Somerset Maugham or the younger Noël Coward. Lonsdale 'aped his betters' in parodying the manners, behaviour, and jargon of a class from which he did not spring, but his success, self-confidence, and reputation as an entertaining talker and bon viveur won him many friends among that class.

The skill which enabled Lonsdale to produce a new play almost every year seemed to come in cycles. Thus it was not until 1915 that he produced his next batch of successes, namely the musicals *Betty* (Daly's, 1915), *High Jinks* (Adelphi, 1916), and *The Maid of the Mountains* (Daly's, 1917). This last was a tremendous success and ran for 1352 performances. It was produced by Oscar Asche, with José Collins as Teresa. *Monsieur Beaucaire*, a romantic opera (Prince's Theatre), came in 1919 and *The Lady of the Rose*, another musical at Daly's, in 1922.

The comedy *Aren't we All?*, produced at the Globe Theatre in 1923, was a particular success, and Lonsdale considered it his best play. It was followed by five plays in two years—*Madame Pompadour* (Daly's, 1923), *The Fake* (Apollo, 1924), *The Street Singer* (Lyric, 1924), *Spring Cleaning* (Eltinge Theatre, New York, 1923; St Martin's Theatre, London, 1925), and *Katja the Dancer* (Gaiety, 1925). On several occasions in the 1920s, three of his comedies ran simultaneously in the West End.

In 1925 *The Last of Mrs Cheyney* was produced at the St James's Theatre, with the leading roles played by Gladys Cooper, Ellis Jeffreys, Ronald Squire, and Sir Gerald Du Maurier. This, Lonsdale's most famous play, ran for 514 performances in London, and enjoyed comparable popularity in New York, Berlin, and Paris. *The Last of Mrs Cheyney* complicates Lonsdale's more usual exposure of upper-class insincerities with a thriller theme—Mrs Cheyney, masquerading as one of the smart set, conceals her shop-girl past in order to conspire with an aristocrat disguised as her butler to defraud her wealthy friends. In 1930 the play was adapted into a popular novel by Denys Herriot, and it was twice made into a film by MGM, first in 1937 and again as *The Law and the Lady* in 1951. Tom Walls produced *On Approval* at the Fortune Theatre in 1927 and also *The High Road* at the Shaftesbury Theatre in the same year. Other successes included *Lady Mary* (Daly's, 1928), *Canaries Sometimes Sing* (Globe, 1929), and *Once is Enough* (Henry Miller Theatre, New York, 1938). *Foreigners* was one of his few failures; it ran for only a week at the Belasco Theatre, New York, in 1939.

Lonsdale's later plays, such as *Another Love Story* (Fulton Theatre, New York, 1943; Phoenix Theatre, London, 1944) and *The Way Things Go* (Phoenix, 1950), were not as popular. Since his work always dealt with the activities of the worldly and well-bred, his plays became dated. His audience's taste was modified by the depression and the Second World War, and playgoers were no longer as willing to be entertained by the drawing-room comedy and the problems of the rich. Lonsdale's heyday was the 1920s, and towards the end of his life he became acutely aware of and much distressed by his decline in popularity, which carried none of the variety and colour of the life which he had enjoyed. He turned to writing for the cinema, producing two scripts for MGM, *The Devil to Pay* (1930) and *Lovers Courageous* (1932); and for Alexander Korda he wrote the screenplay for *The Private Life of Don Juan* (1934).

In 1938 Lonsdale decided to settle in the United States and he remained there throughout the war. After the war he returned, occasionally, and rather sadly, to England, and after 1950 lived mostly in France. On his last visit to

London in 1954 he died, on 4 April, at 40A Hill Street, Piccadilly, as he was walking home after dining with friends. He was survived by his wife. KATHERINE MULLIN

Sources *DNB* • *The Times* (6 April 1954), 11b • A. G. S. Enser, *Filmed books and plays* (1987) • D. L. Kirkpatrick, ed., *Reference guide to English literature*, 2 (1991), 884–5 • F. Donaldson, *Freddy Lonsdale* (1957) • *CGPLA Eng. & Wales* (1954)

Likenesses S. Elwes, oils, 1940–49, NPG [*see illus.*] • photographs, repro. in Donaldson, *Freddy Lonsdale*

Wealth at death £2234 11*s*. 6*d*.—in England: probate, 14 July 1954, *CGPLA Eng. & Wales*

Lonsdale, Henry (1816–1876), physician and biographer, was born in St Mary, Carlisle, on 25 February 1816, the son of Henry Lonsdale, a tradesman there, and his wife, Hannah. After attending a local school he was apprenticed in 1831 to Messrs Anderson and Hodgson, at that time the leading medical practitioners in Carlisle. In 1834 he went on to study medicine at Edinburgh, and after a very successful course was in his third year appointed assistant to Robert Knox (1791–1862), the anatomist, whose biographer he later became, and also to John Reid, the physiologist. Lonsdale studied during the summer of 1838 in Paris; he also went to London, and became a member of the Royal College of Surgeons and licentiate of the Society of Apothecaries. On his return to Edinburgh in 1838 he graduated MD; his thesis, 'An experimental inquiry into the nature of hydrocyanic acid', was printed in the *Edinburgh Medical and Surgical Journal* in 1839.

In the autumn of 1838 Lonsdale, who was suffering from overwork, took temporary charge of a country practice at Raughton Head, Cumberland, where he helped to found the Inglewood Agricultural Society, a monthly club and the first of its kind in the county. He also gave a course of popular lectures on science, and he became interested in the work of Susanna Blamire, 'the muse of Cumberland', whose poems he subsequently collected. In 1840 he returned to Edinburgh, and from May of that year he was a partner with his former principal, Robert Knox, giving a daily demonstration in anatomy in the classroom and managing the dissecting rooms. In 1841 he was appointed physician to the Royal Public Dispensary, where for the first time in Edinburgh he introduced the use of cod-liver oil. During an epidemic of relapsing fever in Edinburgh in 1843, he took charge of the largest district, and when the health of his three assistants broke down he did the work single-handed.

Lonsdale was admitted fellow of the Royal College of Physicians of Edinburgh, in 1851, and at one of their monthly meetings he read the paper 'On the terminal loops of the nerves in the brain and spinal cord of man'. These loops, which he had discovered when examining an infant suffering from deformities, he exhibited under a powerful microscope. The history of the case was recorded in the *Edinburgh Medical and Surgical Journal* in 1843 and attracted some attention. Lonsdale was soon afterwards appointed a senior president of the Royal Medical Society, to which he made a notable contribution on diphtheria, based chiefly on observations of the disease at Raughton Head. He was also for two sessions the senior president of the Hunterian Medical Society, and was at the same time senior president of the Anatomical and Physiological Society, which had been resuscitated by Knox and himself.

In 1845 Lonsdale's increasing susceptibility to bronchitis induced him to relinquish his growing practice in Edinburgh and to return to Carlisle, where he settled in the autumn of 1845. In 1846 he was appointed physician to the Cumberland Infirmary, an office which he held for twenty-two years. Lonsdale attributed an epidemic of scurvy occurring in a district north of Carlisle to the lack of vegetables following the potato blight of 1846. His observations enabled him to dismiss the theories of Robert Christison, who had assigned the disease to a defective supply of milk, and to reassert the traditional explanation for scurvy. When in the winter of 1847–8 cholera seemed to be threatening western Europe, Lonsdale established a sanitary association in Carlisle. He contributed many articles promoting the Health of Towns Act to the *Journal of Public Health*, a London periodical supported by the early sanitary reformers. His report on the health of Carlisle was quoted with commendation in the House of Commons by Lord Morpeth. A careful essay which Lonsdale wrote on the health of bakers also attracted notice and was reprinted in *Chambers's London Journal*.

In 1851 Lonsdale married Eliza Indiana, only daughter of John Smith Bond, of Rose Hill, near Carlisle, whose residence subsequently became his own. After his marriage Lonsdale occupied himself in reading, travelling in southern and eastern Europe, interesting himself in Italian art and archaeology, and collecting materials for the biographical studies that he undertook. The writing of biographies of a number of local notables and medical practitioners became his main work during the 1860s. After producing several individual works, he published in 1867 the first volume of his *Worthies of Cumberland*, a six-volume series of short biographies. In them he attempted to avoid political bias and aimed to pursue the 'brevity, conciseness of arrangement, and the use of terse and simple language' which he felt suited to the region's character (Lonsdale, *Worthies*, vol. 1, preface). The collection was well received by contemporaries.

Lonsdale died at Rose Hill on 23 July 1876, and was buried on 27 July in Stanwix churchyard. He left three sons and three daughters. A man of genial and kindly temperament, Lonsdale was in politics a philosophical radical, and took a special interest in the cause of Italian unity. He helped to collect subscriptions for Garibaldi's expedition to Sicily in 1860, and was the friend of Mazzini and Kossuth, as well as of Garibaldi.

GORDON GOODWIN, *rev.* PATRICK WALLIS

Sources Ward, *Men of the reign* • *London and Provincial Medical Directory* (1868) • H. Lonsdale, *The worthies of Cumberland*, 6 vols. (1867–75) • *BMJ* (5 Aug 1876), 195 • *Carlisle Journal* (28 July 1876) • *Carlisle Express* (29 July 1876) • *IGI* • *CGPLA Eng. & Wales* (1876)

Wealth at death £10,000: probate, 17 Aug 1876, *CGPLA Eng. & Wales*

Lonsdale, James (1777–1839), portrait painter, was born at Lancaster on 16 May 1777 and baptized on 15 June at St

John's, Lancaster, the son of Francis Lonsdale and his wife, Anne. It is believed that he attended a charity school in Lancaster. He worked as a pattern designer at Margerison and Glover's printworks, Catterall, near Garstang, Lancashire. About 1799 Lonsdale moved to London, where he briefly became a pupil of George Romney, who retired to Kendal late in 1799, and in October 1801 he entered the Royal Academy Schools. In that year he painted a copy of Van Dyck's Ghent masterpiece *The Crucifixion*, as the altarpiece for the Roman Catholic chapel of St Mary and St Michael, Garstang, where it still hangs. In 1806 he presented to Lancaster his *Admiral Lord Nelson* (Lancaster town hall), for which he received the freedom of the city. With encouragement from Richard Threlfall, a local Lancaster architect, whose portrait by Lonsdale was exhibited at the Royal Academy in 1809, he soon received commissions from Archibald, ninth duke of Hamilton of Ashton Hall near Lancaster, of whom he exhibited one portrait in 1804 and another in 1819. Between 1802 and 1838 Lonsdale exhibited 138 paintings at the Royal Academy, eighty-seven with the Society of British Artists (which he had helped to found) in Suffolk Street, and seven with the British Institution. He was painter to the Sublime Society of Beefsteaks, a dining club limited to twenty-four members, more familiarly known as the Beefsteak Club, founded in 1735 by the theatre manager John Rich, which included Hogarth among its founding members.

On 7 April 1807 Lonsdale married Jane Thornton (1776/7–1827), who came from Lancaster, in Edmonton, Middlesex. On the death of John Opie in 1807 Lonsdale bought that painter's house in Berners Street, Marylebone, where the couple lived thereafter. They had three sons, all baptized at St Marylebone, Middlesex: Richard Threlfall Lonsdale, who became a painter; James John Lonsdale, who became a circuit judge in the West Riding of Yorkshire (1855–67) and recorder of Folkestone (from 1847 to his death, *c.*1886); and Edward Francis Lonsdale, who became a surgeon. It is thought that a descendant, Henry Lonsdale, wrote a life of James Lonsdale which was published in 1870, although no copy of this work appears to be extant. Jane Lonsdale died on 28 April 1827.

Lonsdale's commissions included one in 1820 from the lord mayor of London for a portrait of Queen Caroline; on Henry Meyer's stipple engraving of that portrait Lonsdale is described as 'Principal Painter in Ordinary to the Queen', a description that Cross questions in his biography of Romney (Cross, 241). Another portrait of Queen Caroline painted by Lonsdale *c.*1821 is in the National Portrait Gallery, London. Further aristocratic and royal commissions included *HIH Archduke Maximilian* (exh. RA, 1819); the king of the Belgians; the tsar of Russia; *Lord Hamilton* (exh. RA, 1822; Royal Collection), and portraits of the duke of Wellington (1815; Gov. Art Coll., HM embassy, Vienna) and the duke of Sussex (exh. RA, 1817; Trinity College, Cambridge). Famous sitters included the *Right Honourable William Pitt* (1807; Lancaster town hall); the French tragic actor François-Joseph Talma as Hamlet (exh. RA, 1818); the sculptor Joseph Nollekens (*c.*1818; NPG); Henry Brougham, first Baron Brougham and Vaux (1821; NPG), and the scientists Sir William Congreve (exh. RA, 1812; NPG); John Dalton (exh. Society of British Artists, 1825; Manchester University), and Sir Humphry Davy (exh. RA, 1822). Also of interest are his *King John Signing Magna Charta* painted for the duke of Norfolk and later executed in stained glass, and *A Game at Chess* (exh. British Institution, 1837; Castle Museum and Art Gallery, Nottingham) which includes a self-portrait of Lonsdale and portraits of his three sons.

Commentators note Lonsdale's bold, accurate portrayal of faces with 'little attempt at flattery' (Redgrave, *Artists*, 75). This may explain why his clientele was 'chiefly confined to male sitters' (Bryan, *Painters*, 3.244). Lonsdale died at his home in Berners Street on 17 January 1839. A memorial to him and his wife was placed in St Mary's Priory church, Lancaster. L. H. Cust, *rev.* Dennis Child

Sources *Art Union*, 1 (1839), 22 · *James Lonsdale exhibition* (1993) [exhibition catalogue, Lancaster City Museums] · Graves, *RA exhibitors* · Graves, *Artists* · R. Walker, *National Portrait Gallery: Regency portraits*, 2 vols. (1985) · Bryan, *Painters* (1903–5) · Redgrave, *Artists* · B. Stewart and M. Cutten, *The dictionary of portrait painters in Britain up to 1920* (1997) · J. Johnson, ed., *Works exhibited at the Royal Society of British Artists, 1824–1893, and the New English Art Club, 1888–1917*, 2 vols. (1975) · D. A. Cross, *A striking likeness: the life of Geoge Romney* (2000) · C. Brown and others, *Van Dyck, 1599–1641* (1999) [exhibition catalogue, Koninklijk Museum voor Schone Kunsten, Antwerp, 15 May – 15 Aug 1999, and RA, 11 Sept – 10 Dec 1999] · *IGI* · will, PRO, PROB 11/1905, sig. 42 · S. C. Hutchison, 'The Royal Academy Schools, 1768–1830', *Walpole Society*, 38 (1960–62), 123–91, esp. 160 · Lancs. RO · memorial, St Mary's Priory church, Lancaster

Likenesses J. Lonsdale, self-portrait, miniature, oils, *c.*1810, NPG · J. Lonsdale, self-portrait, oils, *c.*1826–1829, Lancaster City Museums · C. Turner, mezzotint, pubd 1830 (after self-portrait by J. Lonsdale), BM, NPG · J. Lonsdale, oils, 1837 (*A game at chess*, including self-portrait and his three sons), Castle Museum and Art Gallery, Nottingham · E. H. Baily, bust, NPG

Wealth at death £330—in bequests: will, PRO, PROB 11/1905, sig. 42

Lonsdale, James Gylby (1816–1892). *See under* Lonsdale, John (1788–1867).

Lonsdale, John (1788–1867), bishop of Lichfield, born on 17 January 1788 at Newmillerdam, near Wakefield, Yorkshire, was the eldest son of John Lonsdale (1737–1807), vicar of Darfield and perpetual curate of Chapelthorpe, and his wife, Elizabeth, *née* Steer (1750–1827). His education commenced under the Revd Robert Wilkinson at the grammar school in Heath, near Halifax, and continued at Eton College from 1799, where Joseph Goodall pronounced him the best Latin scholar he had ever had. In 1806 he went up to King's College, Cambridge, where he twice won the Browne medal for a Latin ode, and was said to have penned the best Latin since the Augustan age in winning a university scholarship in 1809. In the same year he became a fellow of King's, taking his BA in 1811. Lonsdale commenced at Lincoln's Inn in 1811, but returned to King's in 1814 as a tutor. In 1815 he was ordained deacon and then priest within a month, relinquishing his fellowship on his marriage (25 November 1815) to Sophia (*d.* 16 Oct 1852), daughter of John Bolland MP, a London hop merchant. They had five children.

Shortly after his ordination Lonsdale was appointed

John Lonsdale (1788–1867), by Ernest Edwards, pubd 1865

chaplain to Archbishop Manners-Sutton (remaining in post when Howley succeeded), and the master of the Temple, Dean Rennell, advanced him to an assistant preachership. In 1822 Lonsdale became Christian advocate at Cambridge, succeeding Rennell's son, Thomas, of whom Lonsdale published a memoir in 1824. He soon resigned, however, when the archbishop appointed him rector of Mersham, Kent. From 1827 the same patron advanced him in succession to a prebendal stall at Lincoln, the precentorship at Lichfield (1828), and a prebend at St Paul's (1831). In 1828 Lord Lyndhurst made him rector of St George's, Bloomsbury, where he remained until he removed to Regent's Park in 1834, holding no cure before becoming preacher of Lincoln's Inn (1836–43) and rector of Southfleet, near Gravesend (1836–42). Throughout these years Lonsdale was a prominent figure in London religious life, being an active member of the National Society, the Society for the Propagation of the Gospel, the Society for Promoting Christian Knowledge, and the Incorporated Church Building Society. He served on the provisional committee and then on the council of King's College, London; in 1830 he declined to become the first principal. In January 1839, however, he took the post, having assumed its responsibilities during the illness of Hugh James Rose the previous year. As principal he secured the position of the medical school, and after resigning in 1843 he remained a council member until his death. Lonsdale also maintained a lifelong interest in Eton. In 1840 he was elected provost, only to decline in favour of Francis Hodgson, the crown nominee, whom the fellows had refused since he did not possess a BD (which Lonsdale, himself a fellow in 1827–8, acquired in 1824). In January 1843 Blomfield appointed Lonsdale archdeacon of Middlesex, and in October Peel made him bishop of Lichfield, Howley having recommended him as possessing 'perfection of temper, and extraordinary fairness of mind'.

Lonsdale was widely acknowledged as an outstanding bishop, distinguished by his unswerving attention to diocesan duty and his lack of partisanship. He rarely ventured onto the national stage in print or in person—Howley judged him 'too thin-skinned'—and the only major publication of his later career was *The Four Gospels with Annotations* (1849) (prepared with W. H. Hale), which like his sermons concentrated on a clear exposition of fundamental doctrines. In 1847 he chaired the royal commission on Lord Lyndhurst's act prohibiting marriage with a deceased wife's sister, but despite condemning the act was not present to vote for its repeal. He was briefly chair of the Cambridge University commission in 1857. When he did speak out, Lonsdale was a voice of moderation, warning convocation against extreme resolutions against Bishop Colenso, and protesting against the decision of the council of King's College to ask F. D. Maurice to resign his professorship in 1853.

Lonsdale consecrated 156 new churches in his diocese; he himself contributed £3,700 to this work. His personal wealth, drawn partly from profits obtained through improvements to an estate leased on Sunk Island at the mouth of the Humber, enabled him to become a net contributor to his see. Lonsdale also fostered the corporate life of the diocese, encouraging the meeting of ruridecanal chapters, lodging ordinands at the episcopal palace, and reserving his patronage exclusively for its clergy. At the time of his death he was contemplating summoning a diocesan conference. His most controversial innovation came when, despite considerable evangelical opposition, he supported the establishment of a diocesan theological college, opened in 1857. Lonsdale died suddenly from the rupture of a blood vessel on the brain on 19 October 1867 at Eccleshall Castle. He was buried at Eccleshall.

Tall and thin but broad shouldered, Lonsdale was fond of shooting, fishing, and the theatre, regretting that public opinion frowned on this last enthusiasm in a clergyman. His theology was that of 'the *old* high church school … but broadened by experience' (Denison, 240). He had little sympathy with ritualism, but in private preferred Tractarians to evangelicals, since they more generally conformed with his vision of a gentleman clergy.

James Gylby Lonsdale (1816–1892), classical scholar and Church of England clergyman, the bishop's eldest son, was born at the Clapham home of his grandfather, John Bolland, on 14 October 1816. He was educated at a Kensington school, then at Laleham School under the Revd J. Buckland (brother-in-law of Thomas Arnold), and from 1828 at Eton College, where in March 1834 he won the Newcastle scholarship. In 1833 he was elected open scholar of Balliol College, Oxford, graduating BA in 1837 with a first in classics and a second in mathematics, and proceeding MA in 1840. He became fellow of Balliol in

1838, counting among his friends Benjamin Jowett and A. P. Stanley, and was a tutor from 1841 to 1842.

In June 1842 Lonsdale took holy orders. It was about this time that he developed a liver complaint which forced him to leave Oxford (though he retained his fellowship until his marriage in 1864), and which afflicted him throughout the remainder of his life. Lonsdale accepted the post of chaplain to Bishop Tomkinson of Gibraltar, returning in 1843. He undertook cures at Malvern and Bowness, where he remained from 1844 to 1849. He then taught at the Royal Institution School in Liverpool, and in 1851 became a tutor at the University of Durham, serving as censor of University College and junior proctor (1852–3). In 1853 he was appointed principal of Hatfield Hall, but resigned the following year as illness again took its toll. In 1854 he was encouraged to offer himself for election to the mastership at Balliol, but instead turned to parochial work as a curate at Duddon, Cheshire, and then at Holt, Worcestershire. After brief spells at Whitchurch grammar school and as assistant preacher at Lincoln's Inn, in 1863 Lonsdale was appointed professor of classical literature at King's College, London. In the following year he married Amelia Mary Peake. In 1870 he retired to the Balliol living of South Luffenham, Rutland, and in 1873 became rector of Huntspill, Somerset, where he remained until 1878. During these years, with his friend Samuel Lee, he produced his major publications—prose translations of Virgil (1871) and of Horace (1873), the former going through twelve editions. After leaving Huntspill he moved to Mayfield, Sussex, and finally to Weybridge in 1885. He died of a chill at 6 Queen's Parade, Bath, on 25 April 1892, and was buried in Bath.

The testimonials Lonsdale received for King's College in 1862 bear witness to the high regard in which he was held, both as a scholar and as a teacher whose 'presence and manner act like a spell in enlivening dullness' (H. Montagu Butler). In person he was melancholic and retiring, but with a winning, boyish sense of humour. Conservative in his politics, he was a high-churchman with little time for ritualism (although he fraternized with nuns at Mayfield), favouring a practical piety: as he observed in one of his sermons, 'Of theology we can have too much; of true religion we cannot' (*Sermons*, 188). ARTHUR BURNS

Sources E. B. Denison, *The life of John Lonsdale, bishop of Lichfield* (1868), 51, 240 • *Recollections of Sophia Lonsdale*, ed. V. Martineau (1936) • F. J. C. Hearnshaw, *The centenary history of King's College, London, 1828–1928* (1929) • P. Virgin, *The church in an age of negligence: ecclesiastical structure and problems of church reform, 1700–1840* (1989), 84–5 • *The life of Frederick Denison Maurice*, ed. F. Maurice, 2 (1884), 196–7 • *The Times* (23 Oct 1867) • *The Times* (25 Oct 1867) • *GM*, 4th ser., 4 (1867), 815–19 • M. S. Watts, *George Frederic Watts*, 1 (1912), 241–4 • Venn, *Alum. Cant.* • R. Duckworth, *A memoir of the Rev. James Lonsdale* (1893) • J. T. Fowler, *Durham University: earlier foundations and present colleges* (1904) • T. A. Whitworth, *Yellow sandstone and mellow brick: an account of Hatfield College, Durham, 1846–1971* (1972) • J. G. Lonsdale, *Sermons*, ed. E. L. Bryans (1893)

Archives BL, letters to Sir Robert Peel and corresp. concerning his elevation, Add. MSS 40534–40593 • King's Lond. • King's Lond., testimonials supporting application for professorship, 1862 [James Lonsdale]

Likenesses G. F. Watts, alabaster effigy, *c*.1869, Lichfield Cathedral • E. Edwards, photograph, NPG; repro. in *Portraits of men of eminence*, 3 (1865), 88 [*see illus.*] • Maull & Co., photograph, repro. in Denison, *Life of John Lonsdale*, frontispiece • Maull & Co., photograph, LPL, MS 2155 • D. J. Pound, engraving, LPL, MS 2547 fol. 81 • D. J. Pound, stipple and line engraving (after photograph by Maull & Polyblank), NPG • photograph (James Lonsdale), repro. in Duckworth, *Memoir of Rev. James Lonsdale*, frontispiece • portrait (James Lonsdale), probably Eton

Wealth at death under £90,000: probate, 14 Nov 1867, *CGPLA Eng. & Wales* • £21,747 19*s*. 11*d*.—James Lonsdale: probate, 30 May 1892, *CGPLA Eng. & Wales*

Lonsdale [*née* Yardley], **Dame Kathleen** (**1903–1971**), crystallographer and pacifist, was born Kathleen Yardley in Newbridge, Ireland, on 28 January 1903, the youngest child of Harry Frederick Yardley (*d.* 1923), the local postmaster, and his wife, Jessie Cameron. In 1908 Kathleen's mother, who had been brought up in north London, decided that the family should leave Ireland on account of increasing political uncertainty, and the family moved to Seven Kings, Essex. Kathleen attended Downshall elementary school from 1908 to 1914, and then won a scholarship to the Ilford County High School for Girls which she attended from 1914 to 1919. At the age of sixteen she won a place at Bedford College for Women in London. At college she changed her subject from mathematics to physics because she enjoyed the experimental aspects of physics and saw her future in experimental work rather than teaching. Having achieved the top place in the university BSc list in 1922 she was offered a research position at University College, London, by W. H. Bragg who had been one of the examiners on her course. In 1923 she, along with Astbury, Bernal, and others, accompanied Bragg when he moved to the Royal Institution, London. She began publishing in 1924, including a joint paper with Astbury, 'Tabulated data for the examination of the 230 space-groups by homogenous X-rays' in the Royal Society's *Philosophical Transactions*.

In 1927 Kathleen married Thomas Jackson Lonsdale, whom she had met during her postgraduate study at University College. They then moved to Leeds, where he had a post in the Silk Research Association based in the textile department at Leeds University. They returned to London in 1929, after the birth of their first child, and in 1931 Kathleen Lonsdale took a position at the Royal Institution, where she remained until after the war. She returned to University College, London, in 1946, as reader in crystallography; in 1949 she was appointed professor of chemistry and head of the department of crystallography. According to Dorothy Hodgkin, herself a distinguished X-ray crystallographer, there was a sense in which Kathleen 'appeared to own the whole of crystallography in her time' (Hodgkin, 467). She greatly enjoyed day-to-day laboratory work, carrying out experiments and calculations herself when time permitted and noting technicians' contributions by sharing with them authorship of many published papers.

In Leeds Kathleen had worked on the structure of crystals of hexamethylbenzene, proving that carbon atoms in the benzene nucleus are coplanar and hexagonally

Dame Kathleen Lonsdale (1903–1971), by Charles Hewitt, 1948

arranged. At the Royal Institution during the 1930s she worked on magnetic anisotropy of crystals, particularly of aromatic compounds, for which she was in 1957 awarded the Davy medal of the Royal Institution. In the early 1940s she developed an interest in the thermal movement of atoms in crystals and her work on thermal vibrations strengthened her case for nomination for fellowship of the Royal Society which she achieved in 1945. She organized undergraduate and postgraduate lecture and practical courses at University College and built up a research school of her own. She became editor of the *International Tables for X-Ray Crystallography* in 1946 and despite this heavy workload continued her own research which included work on synthetic diamonds and on endemic bladder stones. The latter was a new departure for Kathleen in the 1960s, since it moved her research into the field of medical science and she continued the work after she retired in 1968.

Kathleen had been brought up as a strict fundamentalist Baptist, but this had always seemed at odds with her questioning, sceptical frame of mind. The Lonsdales became Quakers by convincement in 1935 and Kathleen saw her life as scientist, Quaker, and mother as inextricably linked. She gave the Eddington lecture in 1964 and described how the practice of science, of religion, and of child rearing should be founded on common themes of scepticism and of knowledge gained at first hand. She agreed with Eddington that Quakerism 'holds out a hand' to the scientist because it avoids the dogma of specific creeds, and relies on Friends' own experience. Kathleen felt that religion and science had much in common. For her, religious faith came from personal experience not from religious texts, and scientific knowledge was generated through experience and experiment. She stated that she believed that current scientific knowledge was probably true but kept an open mind with regard to new and better theories. However, she acknowledged that most scientists were in agreement, at least in part, because of similar training and education. For Kathleen, the upbringing of children should also mirror the questioning concepts of Quakerism: children should not be told what to believe but should be encouraged to find their own faith through personal experience. Likewise, Kathleen adhered to prevailing educational concepts which held that children should have the opportunity of learning by experience rather than learning by rote.

As a Quaker Kathleen believed in absolute pacifism and believed all war to be morally wrong. In the Swarthmore lecture of 1953 she talked at length regarding the causes of war and of her opinion of international affairs. She considered that no permanently armed nation could be free and that complete world disarmament was the only solution to international problems. Again, her inclusiveness of the personal and political, and association of family life with public life was clear. She considered that the same principles should apply in the home as in national and international affairs: as violence does not further peace in the home, neither would it in world politics. She was a firm believer in Gandhian non-violent resistance and in civic disobedience. During the Second World War she refused to register for civil defence and when she refused to pay the fine for this, was committed to Holloway prison for one month. Although she would have been exempt from civil defence duties, it seemed important to her that she should make the point as a conscientious objector. According to her husband the time spent in prison was the most formative experience of her life and she retained an interest in penal reform and became a member of the board of visitors at Aylesbury prison and Borstal institution in 1949.

Kathleen was always concerned about the ethical dimensions of science, especially with regard to the use of science in war. After the war she became vice-president of the Atomic Scientists Association and she was also president of the British section of the Women's International League for Peace and Freedom, originally formed during the First World War at The Hague. She attended meetings of the Pugwash movement, the scientists' anti-nuclear group, and was also a member of the east–west committee of the Society of Friends. Her peace and prison work were of great importance to Lonsdale and this emphasis was shared by her husband; in fact when he retired he took on some of the correspondence regarding this work.

Kathleen was one of the first two women to be elected to the Royal Society as fellows (the other being Marjorie Stephenson). In 'Women in science: reminiscences and reflections' in *Impact of Science on Society* (1970) she attributed the scarcity of women in the top ranks of science to the lack of role models. She considered that both schools and parents had a role to play in encouraging more girls to take up the study of science and technology. In Kathleen's obituary in *Biographical Memoirs of Fellows of the Royal Society* Dorothy Hodgkin stated that when Kathleen wrote regarding women in science, she was, in fact, writing of her own life and her prescription for scientific success. Kathleen assumed that women wanted to marry and have a family life in addition to a fulfilling career. She considered that a woman should choose a husband with care; he should have the ability to share her problems, and domesticity would be a bonus. With regard to the woman herself, in order to be a first-class scientist one must be a good organizer, work twice the usual hours, and learn to concentrate in any available moment of time.

Kathleen worked extremely hard all her life; she travelled widely in association with her science, prison, and peace work, including trips to Europe, the United States, India, the Soviet Union, and the People's Republic of China. She was vice-president of the International Union of Crystallography from 1960 to 1966 and became the first woman president of the British Association in 1968. She was appointed DBE in 1956 and received honorary degrees from the universities of Wales, Leicester, Manchester, Lancaster, Oxford, Bath, Leeds, and Dundee.

In 1961, when Thomas Lonsdale retired, he and Kathleen moved to Bexhill, Sussex; she continued working in London, commuting five hours a day. Despite Kathleen's busy public life, there was always time for her three children and ten grandchildren, who were a source of great pride to her. She died in University College Hospital, London, on 1 April 1971. GILL HUDSON

Sources *The Times* (2 April 1971) · D. M. C. Hodgkin, *Memoirs FRS*, 21 (1975), 447–84 · H. J. Milledge, *Acta Crystallographica*, 31A (1975) · K. Lonsdale, 'Women in science: reminiscences and reflections', *Impact of Science on Society*, 20/1 (1970) · K. Lonsdale, *I believe…* (1964) · K. Lonsdale, *Removing the causes of war* (1953) · K. Lonsdale, 'Women in science', *Proceedings of the Royal Institution of Great Britain*, 43 (1970) · K. Lonsdale, 'The structure of the benzene ring', *PRS*, 123A (1929), 494–515 · J. P. Glusker, ed., *Structural crystallography in chemistry and biology* (1981) · d. cert. · *DNB*

Archives NRA, priv. coll. | Bodl. Oxf., correspondence with C. A. Coulson · Bodl. Oxf., letters to Dorothy Hodgkin · Bodl. Oxf., correspondence relating to Society for Protection of Science and Learning · CAC Cam., correspondence with A. V. Hill · ICL, correspondence with Herbert Dingle · U. Leeds, Brotherton L., correspondence with W. T. Astbury

Likenesses C. Hewitt, photograph, 1948, Hult. Arch. [*see illus.*] · photographs, 1948, Hult. Arch. · J. Pannett, pastels, UCL

Wealth at death £16,575: probate, 5 Nov 1971, *CGPLA Eng. & Wales*

Lonsdale, Margaret (*fl.* 1317). *See under* Women in trade and industry in York (*act. c.*1300–*c.*1500).

Lonsdale, William (1794–1871), geologist, youngest son of William Lonsdale (1742–1813), a silk mercer from Skipton, Yorkshire, and his wife, Mary Wagstaffe (1745?–1832) of Higham Ferrers, Northamptonshire, was born on 8 September 1794, probably in Bath, where he spent his early years. In February 1810 he was commissioned, without purchase, as ensign in the 4th (King's Own) regiment of foot. He served at Salamanca in 1812 and Waterloo in 1815, but soon afterwards, as a retired lieutenant on half pay, he returned to Bath.

By chance, Lonsdale became interested in Bath's geology, which William Smith (1769–1839) had there made so popular. He began by working out the sequence of the strata and collecting, examining, and identifying their associated minerals and fossils. His appointment as the first honorary curator of the Bath Literary and Philosophical Institution in 1825, and his personal donation of over 1000 geological specimens to its museum collections, testify to his growing reputation for preparing, labelling, and cataloguing accessions. Described by his early acquaintance Roderick Impey Murchison, as a 'tall, grave man with a huge hammer on his shoulder' (A. Geikie, *Life of Sir Roderick I. Murchison*, 1875, 1.128), Lonsdale the fossil-hunter daily advanced his geological studies during the 6 mile return walk from his mother's Batheaston home to his work in Bath.

Lonsdale's 1827 report 'On the occurrence of galena in the Inferior Oolite' [near Frome] (*Philosophical Magazine*, 2, 1827, 234–5) resulted from his enquiries into the forces governing deposition of ore in Carboniferous Limestone as compared with other strata. He believed that the age formerly assigned to these metallic veins was 'too remote' and with better knowledge of the unconformable superposition of rocks, similar finds could be expected in more recent secondary formations. He next earned high praise for his definitive geological colouring of areas of the midland counties on Ordnance Survey maps, and greater recognition, in February 1829, for his paper 'On the oolitic district of Bath' (*Transactions of the Geological Society of London*, 3, 1835, 241–75). This was the first comprehensive analysis of the classic Bath area, within a 70 mile radius of the city. Lonsdale described the sequence of the strata from the Lias to the Lower Chalk and their associated fossils, and complemented six geologically coloured sections with descriptive tables of organic remains featuring only those specimens which he had personally collected and identified.

Lonsdale was elected fellow of the Geological Society of London in June 1829 and, later that year, appointed as its curator, librarian, and indexer; in this capacity he found himself carrying out nearly all the work which had previously fallen on the honorary secretaries. In 1832 he was first awarded the society's Wollaston fund, to extend his investigation of the oolites to the southern boundaries of Warwickshire and Oxfordshire. He determined the Stonesfield Slate's position as in the lower part of the Great Oolite and defined the 'Cotteswold' hills escarpment as a prolongation and much expanded layer of the Inferior Oolite. In March 1840, Lonsdale's 'Notes on the age of the limestones of south Devonshire' (*Transactions of the Geological Society of London*, 2nd ser., 5, 1840, 721–38) showed they had often been assigned to the transition series but that their similarity in character with the Old Red Sandstone had been noticed by various field workers. In

December 1837, Lonsdale had proved that 'shells resembling or identical with mountain-limestone species … Silurian corals, the *Calceola sandalina*, and various distinct Testacea' were all present in these beds. This showed that the south Devonshire limestones were 'of an intermediate age between the Carboniferous and Silurian systems, and consequently of the age of the Old Red Sandstone' (*Transactions of the Geological Society of London*, 2nd ser., 5, 1840, 727). Lonsdale thereby played a significant role in the introduction of the new Devonian system.

Lonsdale's advice was constantly sought both for identifying fossils and editing manuscripts and his role as mentor is exemplified by his relationship with Charles Darwin, whom he greatly assisted in the study of corals. Six species from the Palaeozoic formation of Van Diemen's Land were described by Lonsdale in an appendix to Darwin's book on volcanic islands, published in 1844. Problems caused by persistent ill health, however, forced Lonsdale into early retirement from the geological society in 1842, but the gift of more than £600 from his friends at the society allowed him to continue his studies in the west country while looking for a healthy place to live. In 1844 he again received the Wollaston fund to aid his research, and in 1846 he was awarded the fund, and now the Wollaston medal, for his contributions to geological science in describing Silurian and Devonian corals and for his papers, 'Corals from the Tertiary formation of North America' and 'Corals from the Palaeozoic formations of Russia'. Finally rewarded with a fourth Wollaston fund in 1849, Lonsdale produced a memorandum respecting *Choristopetalum impar* and *Cyathophora? elegans* (*Quarterly Journal of the Geological Society of London*, 7, 1851, 113–17), and a note on the genus *Lithostrotion* (*Annals of Natural History*, 8, 1851, 451–77), both papers reflecting his concentration on physical and taxonomic differentiation between genera and species. Lonsdale's unpublished *magnum opus* featuring the Palaeozoic tabulate corals, '*Alveolites*, *Favosites*, and *Heliolites*', reveals the facility with which he had interpreted the languages of science in conjunction with his own work, either to endorse or to challenge orthodox opinion. As an evolutionist and pioneer of microscopy, every aspect of geological determination was important to him. He was aware of the effects which 'permanent alteration in the inhabiting medium' (Lonsdale MSS, Bath RO) might have on the form and size of a shell or coral, and he knew that every factor which might affect the development of animal life had to be taken into account before the distribution of species could be properly judged. Stratigraphy, Lonsdale believed, should be based on evidence derived not only from fossils, but also from order of superposition, mineral composition, and lithological structure. His own work on stratigraphy, taxonomy, and corals constituted an outstanding and invaluable gift to geological science. Lonsdale, who never married, died of tuberculosis on 10 November 1871, at his home, 12 City Road, Bristol, and was buried four days later at Arnos Vale cemetery. STELLA WHYBERD PIERCE

Sources W. S. Mitchell, 'Notes on early geologists connected with the neighbourhood of Bath', *Proceedings of the Bath Natural History and Antiquarian Field Club*, 2 (1872), 332–42 • H. S. Torrens, 'The Bath geological collections', *Geological Curators Group Newsletter*, 1/3 (1975), 88–108 • H. B. Woodward, *The history of the Geological Society of London* (1907) • J. Murch, *Biographical sketches of Bath celebrities, ancient and modern* (1893) • M. J. S. Rudwick, *The great Devonian controversy: the shaping of scientific knowledge among gentlemanly specialists* (1985) • P. Tasch, 'Darwin and the forgotten Mr. Lonsdale', *Geological Magazine*, 87 (1950), 292–6 • *The correspondence of Charles Darwin*, ed. F. Burkhardt and S. Smith, 1–3 (1985–7); 8 (1993) • parish register (baptism), 23 March 1800, Bath, St James's • Bath RO, Lonsdale MSS • d. cert. • *IGI* • Arnos Vale cemetery records

Archives Bath and North East Somerset RO, papers • Bath Central Library, catalogues • Bath RO • Bath Royal Literary and Scientific Institution, Bath, MSS catalogues, geological specimens, etc. • Devon RO, papers • GS Lond., letters and maps • NHM, report • U. Lpool L., papers • University of Bristol, department of geology • University of Bristol Library | GS Lond., letters to Roderick Impey Murchison • NHM, letters to members of Sowerby family

Wealth at death under £1000: probate, 16 Jan 1872, *CGPLA Eng. & Wales*

Looker [Lucre, Lukar], **Roger** (*d.* **1685**), gardener and nurseryman, was in charge of the garden of William Cecil, second earl of Salisbury, at Hatfield in 1661, when Samuel Pepys met him there on 22 July. By 1671 he had a nursery near St Martin-in-the-Fields, for from there he sold fruit trees for the gardens at Woburn Abbey. In 1681 he described himself as 'gardener to her Majestie'; this was probably Henrietta Maria, the dowager queen, at Somerset House, before she left England in 1665, rather than Catherine of Braganza, Charles II's consort, who is not recorded as sharing her mother-in-law's interest in gardening.

Also in 1681 Looker was the senior member of the group of four gardeners who joined forces in London to establish the Brompton Park nursery, a large concern covering 100 acres on the site later covered by the Victoria and Albert Museum and its neighbours in South Kensington. The other three were John Field (*d.* 1687), the head gardener at Woburn; Moses Cook (*d.* 1715), the gardener from Cassiobury, who had published a book on trees and their culture; and George London. The nursery was the first to offer garden designs and the workmen to carry them out. It also stocked all the necessary plants, from forest trees to flowering bulbs and evergreens—especially citrus trees, myrtles, jasmines, and other tender shrubs for the greenhouse—and fruit trees, vegetables, and everything needed in the kitchen garden. A large collection of fruit trees in the nursery was used in an attempt to settle standard names for the varieties available, which were often known by different labels in different regions, or even in different gardens.

Several other gardens were supervised by Looker, among them those of Henry Hyde, second earl of Clarendon, at Cornbury in Oxfordshire and Swallowfield in Berkshire; of Richard Boyle, first earl of Burlington, in London and at Londesborough in Yorkshire; and of Elizabeth Murray, duchess of Lauderdale, at Ham House, Surrey. Looker died on 3 March 1685, leaving a widow, Bridgett, and a son, William, who inherited his father's share of the Brompton Park nursery, but who died before 1687.

SANDRA RAPHAEL, *rev.*

Sources J. Harvey, *Early nurserymen* (1974)

Lookup, John (*fl.* **1739–1740**), theologian, the details of whose upbringing and parentage are unknown, was a disciple of the philosopher John Hutchinson (1674–1737). In 1739 Lookup published *The erroneous translations in the vulgar versions of the scriptures detected in several instances taken from the original, with a previous essay upon the doctrine of the Trinity*, the 'Essay' having been written in deprecation of Edward Merchant Johnson's pamphlet, *A Plain Account of the Trinity from Scripture and Reason* (1739). In the following year Lookup produced his translation, *Berashith, or, The First Book of Moses, Call'd Genesis*, which is inscribed to John Potter, archbishop of Canterbury. Lookup had previously shocked the archbishop by his 'incorrect sentiments' on the doctrine of the Trinity. His translation shows him to have possessed a creditable knowledge of Hebrew.

GORDON GOODWIN, *rev.* PHILIP CARTER

Sources Allibone, *Dict.*

Loop, George [*name in religion* Edmund of St Joseph] (**1648–1716**), Discalced Carmelite friar, was born in Herefordshire, the son of George Loop, of a long-established Catholic family from Garway in Herefordshire, and his wife, Winifred. He was sent to Flanders for his education and found his vocation in the order of Discalced Carmelites who maintained a priory at Louvain. He was professed on 22 October 1667 aged nineteen, taking the name Edmund of St Joseph. He continued his studies at Louvain and at the Missionary College of St Pancras in Rome.

In September 1677, shortly after his ordination as a priest, Loop returned to England to minister in Hereford. He had hardly begun his apostolate when he became a victim of the Popish Plot. His presence in the county became known to John Scudamore of Kentchurch, a justice of the peace, who instigated a search for him. He was forced to take flight, finding refuge in woods and outhouses. He was once hiding in a haystack which the searchers investigated with their swords, but managed to escape detection and injury. He fled disguised as a farmer's wife and reached London where his pursuers soon caught up with him. He had several more remarkable escapes. On one occasion his was the only room in the house where he was lodging which was not searched and another close call came when pursuivants crawled from the roof of an adjoining house and reached his window but were unable to break in.

In 1680 Loop moved to Worcester where there had been no priest for over a year because of the furore resulting from the plot. He ministered to the scattered Catholic community and was renowned for his poverty of life and generosity to the poor, giving away the alms which richer people gave him for his own subsistence. He travelled on foot and dressed in the rags of a beggar. His austere lifestyle not surprisingly led to a breakdown in health. The Worcester Catholics pleaded that he should not be taken from them and he was given an assistant, Francis of the Child Jesus, who was able to share the labours of the mission.

The accession of James II in 1685 permitted the provision of a public Catholic chapel in Worcester which was opened with solemn mass on Christmas eve 1686 in a house in Foregate Street. When James II fled in 1688 the priests also had to leave as the mob prepared to attack and wreck the chapel. They were able to return to Worcester about 1690 and the mission remained in their care until about 1720. The English vicar provincial, Lucian of St Teresa, died in 1691 and Loop succeeded him, holding the office for at least twelve years. He moved to London where he also ministered as chaplain to a Catholic family.

During his early years as provincial Loop wrote *The Queen of Heaven's Livery*, subtitled 'A short treatise of the institution, excellency, priviledges, and indulgencies of the most famous confraternity of our Blessed Lady of Mount Carmel, commonly called the Scapular: together with a brief relation of the antiquity and never-interrupted succession of the religious order of the Carmelites, to whom the B. Virgin Mary gave this her sacred livery', printed in Antwerp in 1709, although a first edition appeared in 1706. A proposal to publish a new edition in 1725 was suppressed by Bonaventure Giffard, vicar apostolic of the London district, in the light of virulent attacks on the work by Richard Jameson, an eccentric secular priest in Lancashire. Jameson published his criticisms in 1726 in a pamphlet entitled *The Queen of Heaven's Livery is Quite Worn Out with Ould Age, and Past Mending*. Loop died in London on 6 February 1716.

BRIAN DOOLAN

Sources B. Zimmerman, 'Father Edmund of St Joseph', *Carmel in England: a history of the English mission of the Discalced Carmelites, 1615 to 1849* (1899), 330–37 • Gillow, *Lit. biog. hist.*, vol. 4 • D. A. Bellenger, ed., *English and Welsh priests, 1558–1800* (1984) • H. A. Leicester, *Notes on Catholic Worcester* (1929)
Archives Herefs. RO, papists' oaths

Loor, Pieter van. *See* Vanlore, Sir Peter (*c.*1547–1627).

Loosemore, George (*bap.* **1619**, *d.* in or before **1682**). *See under* Loosemore, Henry (1605x9–1670).

Loosemore, Henry (**1605x9–1670**), composer and organist, was born probably at Barnstaple, Devon, son of Samuel Loosemore (*bap.* 1577, *d.* 1642) and his wife, Gillian Maney (*bap.* 1584), and brother of John *Loosemore (1613/14–1681), the Exeter organ builder, and George Loosemore [*see below*]. Although his ancestors had lived at Bishop's Nympton since the early sixteenth century, Henry may have been a chorister in one of the Cambridge colleges and spent most of his adult life in the service of King's College. At Michaelmas 1627 he was listed for the first time as lay clerk and organist, and he continued to receive regular payments in respect of both posts for the rest of his life.

In his long career at King's, Loosemore apparently served the college well. At Christmas 1627 he was paid for copying a new organ book (probably New York Public Library, MS Drexel 5469), and during the next three years he received further payments for augmenting the college's choral partbooks and for binding his organ book. Most of Loosemore's extant compositions are choral and were composed for liturgical use at King's, though six keyboard dances and two consort pieces by him also survive. Loosemore's sacred music includes two services, full anthems (one of which, 'O Lord, increase my / our faith', was long attributed to Orlando Gibbons), and verse anthems. Although the quality of his music is variable, his best work is very well crafted and bears comparison with that of his more famous contemporaries.

On 17 February 1634 Loosemore married Elizabeth Brooke (*bap.* 1595, *d.* 1660) at St Botolph's, Cambridge. In 1640 he took the Cambridge MusB degree. Between 1640 and 1652 Loosemore was paid for teaching the choristers at King's, though with the cessation of choral services by 1643 all his college posts probably became sinecures. Between 1652 and 1660 he is said to have acted as organist and music teacher to the family of Dudley, third Baron North, at Kirtling, Cambridgeshire, but he evidently resumed his full college duties at the Restoration. On 7 July 1670, having 'died suddenly in a privy house' (Shaw, 357), he was buried at St Botolph's, Cambridge.

Loosemore's brother **George Loosemore** (*bap.* 1619, *d.* in or before 1682), composer and organist, was baptized on 12 September 1619 at Barnstaple. Having been a chorister at King's College, Cambridge, he was from 13 June 1635 organist at Jesus College.

Most of Loosemore's music, which is both sacred and incomplete, survives in two autograph manuscripts at the British Library, London, and at Trinity College, Cambridge, where he became organist in 1660. He is known also to have composed fancies for viols, now lost, which were admired by Baron North, of Kirtling, whose family Loosemore served as organist and music teacher between 1660 and 1666, following in his brother Henry's footsteps. Loosemore possessed neither the technical fluency nor the creative talent of his brother, to whose best music his own is inferior. In October 1665 he was paid by Jesus College for copying choral music, and in the same year he obtained the Cambridge MusD degree. He was dead by 11 September 1682, and his widow, Honorah, died on 3 February 1692. IAN PAYNE

Sources I. Payne, *The provision and practice of sacred music at Cambridge colleges and selected cathedrals, c.1547–c.1646* (1993) • I. Payne, 'George Loosemore at Trinity College, Cambridge, 1660–1682', *Proceedings of the Cambridge Antiquarian Society*, 77 (1988), 145–50 • J. Morehen, 'Loosemore, Henry', *New Grove* • J. Morehen, 'Loosemore, George', *New Grove* • private information (2004) • H. W. Shaw, *The succession of organists of the Chapel Royal and the cathedrals of England and Wales from c.1538* (1991) • V. Brookes, *British keyboard music to c.1660: sources and thematic index* (1996) • Venn, *Alum. Cant.* • *DNB*

Archives CUL, Peterhouse 'Caroline' part-books • NYPL, New York, Drexel MS 5469

Loosemore, John (1613/14–1681), organ builder, was born probably at Bishop's Nympton, Devon, the son of Samuel Loosemore (*bap.* 1577, *d.* 1642), organ builder, and his wife, Gillian Maney (*bap.* 1584). He was the brother of George *Loosemore [*see under* Loosemore, Henry] and Henry *Loosemore, who were both organists and composers. He was baptized at Barnstaple on 25 August 1616. Nothing is known of his life until the period 1635–8, when he looked after the organ at Hartland church, Devon. At the Restoration he was at Exeter Cathedral, where for the rest of his life he was clerk of works and lived in the cathedral close. In November 1660 he was paid £5 by the chapter towards 'the making of a sett of pipes to' a temporary organ used in the cathedral until a new one was built. Another instrument, a small chamber organ for the choir school, survived until the twentieth century.

In January 1663 Loosemore was sent at the expense of the chapter to Cornwall, where he selected tin for a new organ that he was to build in the cathedral. Later that year he went to examine Thomas Harris's organ in Salisbury Cathedral, 'the better to inform himself to make the new organ' at Exeter, and in 1664 he visited London 'about the church's business'. His new cathedral organ, completed about 1665, was one of the largest built in the years after the Restoration, and was Loosemore's most important work. Its specification was unadventurous and representative of several new cathedral instruments of the time in its continuation of the English organ building style before the civil war. In these organs there were few if any signs of the continental devices—such as reed, mixture, and mutation ranks—adopted by the Dallams, who had recently returned to Britain from Brittany. Despite the essential conservatism of the Exeter organ, its great double diapason with large pipes was a notable feature, though perhaps more for its ostentatiousness than for its musical value. Indeed, a contemporary visitor thought the organ's visual qualities outweighed its aural ones. Loosemore's organ case survives. His autograph note of 'what the organ cost' gives £847 7*s.* 10*d.* as the total sum, owing to 'not bying tinne in seson'.

Among other organs built by Loosemore was one for Sir George Trevelyan of Nettlecombe Court, Somerset (*c.*1665); its reed stop suggests that Loosemore was not entirely immune to French influence, though he remained at heart a member of the old English school. He was also a maker of virginals, and, like other makers of his time, used boxwood for naturals in the keyboards. One of his virginals (1655) is in the Victoria and Albert Museum. Loosemore was married, and in 1674 his daughter, Joane, married John Shearme, who was also an organ builder and probably Loosemore's assistant. Loosemore died in Exeter on 18 April 1681, in his sixty-eighth year, and was buried in Exeter Cathedral on 20 April. His epitaph on a gravestone in the transept records that he was 'easily the chief among craftsmen of his kind' (translation from the Latin; Edmonds, 31). L. M. MIDDLETON, *rev.* PETER LYNAN

Sources B. B. Edmonds, 'John Loosemore', *Journal of the British Institute of Organ Studies*, 5 (1981), 23–32 • *New Grove* • S. Bicknell, *The history of the English organ* (1996)

Looten, Jan (*c.*1618–*c.*1680), landscape painter, was born in Amsterdam. He appears in a group portrait of a company of militia dated 1642, and was married in Amsterdam in September 1643, when he was about twenty-five years old. He moved to London early in the reign of Charles II. The Ogdens, writing about the English taste in landscape in the seventeenth century, rate him the 'most important landscape painter of the Northern tradition active in England' during the 1660s, and one of the few to use 'English scenery consciously in composing their ideal landscapes' (Ogden and Ogden, 116). He painted landscapes 'of a sublime or romantic description' (*DNB*), with dark woods and waterfalls, in the style of Roelant Roghman, Allart van Everdingen, Jacob van Ruisdael, or Meindert Hobbema. Looten also painted some views of the Alps in Switzerland, where he is said to have lived for several years. He generally used larger than average canvases, and the figures in his paintings were often the work of Jan Lingelbach. Jan Griffier was his pupil and, according to George Vertue, 'became a more pleasant Painter than his Master' (Vertue, *Note books*, 1.50). In 1669 Looten was living in St James's Market, where he was visited on 11 April by Samuel Pepys, who 'there saw no good pictures' but was introduced to another painter, Simon Verelst (*Diary*, 514). Vertue states he 'died poor in Yorkshire' (Vertue, *Note books*, 1.77). That he was in Yorkshire and in straitened circumstances is suggested by a letter of 1678 from William Lodge in London to Henry Gyles in York saying 'as for those things of Mr Loton they are out of my way … tell honest Cowell as a secret that I would not have him putt so much confidence in his Landskip painter, by what I have heard of him here being in debt to severall he delt withall and so left em' (Hake, 64). He died in London or York about 1680. Administration of the effects of Johanes Looton was granted to one of his creditors in London in February 1691.

Four landscapes attributed to Looten are in the Royal Collection; of the three originally in the collection of James II, *Landscape with an Estuary* and *A Wooded Landscape* were probably painted for him about 1675. Looten landscapes in national collections include those at Cheltenham Art Gallery, falsely signed and dated 'Hobbema pinx 1686'; Temple Newsam House, Leeds; and Beecroft Art Gallery, Southend-on-Sea. The *River Landscape* in the National Gallery, thought to be by Looten, is now attributed to Joris van der Haagen. There are also earlier landscapes in Amsterdam (figures by Lingelbach), Nancy (1655), Copenhagen (two, 1656; figures by Lingelbach), Rotterdam (1658), Hamburg, Berlin (two), and elsewhere. Numerous Looten landscapes have passed through the auction houses over the years.

L. H. Cust, *rev.* Arianne Burnette

Sources [B. Buckeridge], 'An essay towards an English school of painting', in R. de Piles, *The art of painting, with the lives and characters of above 300 of the most eminent painters*, 3rd edn (1754), 354–439 · Vertue, *Note books*, 1 · H. V. S. Ogden and M. S. Ogden, *English taste in landscape in the seventeenth century* (1955) · *The diary of Samuel Pepys, a new and complete transcription, 1668–1669*, ed. R. Latham and W. Matthews, 9 (1976) · N. MacLaren, *National Gallery catalogue: the Dutch school* (1960) · H. M. Hake, 'Some contemporary records relating to Francis Place, engraver and draughtsman, with a catalogue of his engraved work', *Walpole Society*, 10 (1921–2), 39–69 · Thieme & Becker, *Allgemeines Lexikon* · C. Wright, *Paintings in Dutch museums: an index of oil paintings in public collections in the Netherlands by artists born before 1870* (1980) · C. Wright, *Dutch painting in the seventeenth century: images of a golden age in British collections* (1989) · C. Wright, *Old master paintings in Britain* (1976) · administration, London, GL, MS 9168/27, fol. 5r · O. Millar, *The Tudor, Stuart and early Georgian pictures in the collection of her majesty the queen*, 2 vols. (1963) · N. MacLaren, *The Dutch school, 1600–1900*, rev. C. Brown, 2 vols. (1991) · Bénézit, *Dict.*, 4th edn · W. Bernt, *The Netherlandish painters of the seventeenth century*, 2 (1970) · H. Walpole, *Anecdotes of painting in England: with some account of the principal artists*, ed. R. N. Wornum, new edn, 2 (1849); repr. (1862) · E. K. Waterhouse, *The dictionary of British 16th and 17th century painters* (1988) · *DNB*

Likenesses N. E. Pickenoy, group portrait (*The company of Captain Jan Claesz Vlooswijck and Lieutenant Gerrit Hudde, Amsterdam, 1642*), Rijksmuseum, Amsterdam

Wealth at death died poor: Vertue, *Note books*

Lopes, Henry Charles, first Baron Ludlow (1828–1899), judge, was born at Devonport on 3 October 1828, the third son of Sir Ralph Lopes, second baronet (*d.* 1854), of Maristow, Devon, and his wife, Susan Gibbs, the eldest daughter of Abraham Ludlow of Heywood House, Wiltshire. He was the great-nephew of Sir Manasseh Masseh *Lopes, first baronet, who was imprisoned for political corruption and bribery. Sir Lopes Massey *Lopes, third baronet (1818–1908), was his brother. He was educated first at Winchester College and then at Balliol College, Oxford, where he matriculated on 12 December 1845 and graduated BA in 1850. He joined Lincoln's Inn on 5 June 1849, but moved on 26 May 1852 to the Inner Temple, where he was called to the bar on 7 June 1852, and elected bencher on 31 May 1870 and treasurer in 1890. On 20 September 1854 he married Cordelia Lucy, daughter of E. Clarke, of Efford Manor, Devon; they had at least one son.

Lopes practised first as a conveyancer and equity draftsman, later as a pleader on the western circuit and at Westminster. He was appointed recorder of Exeter in 1867 and became QC on 22 June 1869. He was returned unopposed as Conservative member for the rotten borough of Launceston on 9 April 1868 and in the general election of 1874 wrested Frome from the Liberals. In 1876 he was appointed justice of the High Court and knighted (28 November). He then sat in the Common Pleas and Queen's Bench divisions until advanced in 1885 to the Court of Appeal (1 December), when he became member of the privy council (12 December). He was made a peer on the queen's jubilee in 1897 (26 July), as Baron Ludlow of Heywood, Wiltshire, retiring shortly afterwards for health reasons.

Ludlow died of influenza at his London house, 8 Cromwell Place, Kensington, on 25 December 1899, his wife having died before him, in 1891. His son, Henry Ludlow, succeeded as the second Baron Ludlow. Although not a great lawyer, Lopes was an able judge in *nisi prius* and divorce cases, and an admirable chairman of quarter sessions.

J. M. Rigg, *rev.* Hugh Mooney

Sources *The Times* (26 Dec 1899) · *Annual Register* (1899) · *Law Magazine*, 5th ser., 25 (1899–1900), 311–36 · Burke, *Peerage* · J. Foster, *Men-at-the-bar: a biographical hand-list of the members of the various inns of court*, 2nd edn (1885)

Likenesses Lock & Whitfield, woodburytype photograph, repro. in T. Cooper, *Men of mark: a gallery of contemporary portraits* (1881), vol. 5, pl. 9 · Quiz, chromolithograph caricature, NPG; repro. in *VF* (25 March 1893), pl. 40 · portrait, repro. in *Green Bag*, 7 (1895), 381 · portrait, repro. in *ILN*, 111 (1897), 601 · portrait, repro. in *ILN*, 116 (1900), 7

Wealth at death £161,563 6*s*. 1*d*.: resworn probate, March 1901, *CGPLA Eng. & Wales* (1900)

Lopes, Sir Lopes Massey, third baronet (1818–1908), politician and agriculturist, born at Maristow, Devon, on 14 June 1818, was the eldest son of Sir Ralph Lopes, second baronet (*d*. 1854), and his wife, Susan Gibbs, eldest daughter of Abraham Ludlow of Heywood House, Wiltshire. His brother was Henry Charles *Lopes, first Baron Ludlow (1828–1899). The family having forsworn Judaism, he was educated at Winchester College and at Oriel College, Oxford, where he graduated BA with a fourth class in *literae humaniores* in 1842 and proceeded MA in 1845. His initial attempt to follow his father into tory politics failed, for in 1852 he was defeated standing for Westbury, the seat held by his father until 1847. Elected for Westbury in 1857, he held it unopposed until 1868, when he defeated Lord Amberley in South Devon and represented it until ill health forced his retirement in 1885.

In the Commons, Lopes joined a group of members, including Henry Chaplin, Albert Pell, and Clare Sewell Read, who supported farming interests, and was chairman of the agricultural business committee. He effectively harassed the Gladstone government of 1868–74 on the question of local taxation; on 16 April 1872 he carried a resolution against the government declaring that it was unjust to impose taxation for national objectives on real property only, and demanding the transfer to the exchequer in whole or in part of the cost of administering justice, police, and lunatics. Lopes's speech showed mastery of his subject. Relief came to landowners and farmers in the Agricultural Ratings Act, passed by the Conservative government in 1879. Lopes was also the author of an amendment to the Public Health Bill of 1873, transferring to the national exchequer the payment of half the salaries of medical officers and inspectors of nuisances. He advocated, but without success, the division of local rates between owner and occupier.

From 1874 to 1880 Lopes was Disraeli's civil lord of the Admiralty. He chaired a committee which reorganized the Admiralty office, and added to the efficiency of the Naval College, Greenwich, by causing the property of the foundation to give a better return. Ill health compelled him in 1877 to refuse the secretaryship to the Treasury in succession to W. H. Smith. On his retirement from parliamentary life in 1885 he was sworn of the privy council, but declined a peerage.

Lopes, who had succeeded to the baronetcy in 1854 and had been high sheriff of Devon in 1857, continued to make his influence felt in local politics, though his public appearances were infrequent. From 1888 to 1904 he was an alderman of the Devon county council, and in the latter year he resigned the directorship of the Great Western Railway, which he had held for forty years. A generous supporter of the charitable institutions of Plymouth, he endowed the South Devon and East Cornwall Hospital with £14,000. He was also a large subscriber to Church of England extension and endowment. A scientific farmer of much sagacity, he greatly increased the value of his estates at Maristow. On his accession to the property he

Sir Lopes Massey Lopes, third baronet (1818–1908), by Maull & Polyblank, 1860s

had to rebuild throughout because, owing to the system of long leases, tenants had had control over leasehold property and it had been neglected; he calculated that in forty years he spent £150,000. He gave prizes to encourage cattle breeding and started a pension scheme for the elderly poor.

Lopes was twice married: first, to Bertha (*d*. 1872), daughter of John Yarde-Buller, first Lord Churston; and, second, to Louisa (*d*. 27 April 1908), daughter of Sir Robert W. Newman, first baronet, of Mamhead, Devon. With his first wife he had three children, Henry Yarde Buller Lopes, fourth baronet, and two daughters. He died at Maristow on 20 January 1908 after a few days' illness.

L. C. Sanders, *rev*. H. C. G. Matthew

Sources *The Times* (21 Jan 1908) · *Western Morning News* (21 Jan 1908) · H. C. G. Matthew, *Gladstone*, 2 vols. (1986–95); repr. in 1 vol. as *Gladstone, 1809–1898* (1997) · C. S. Read, 'Large and small holdings', *Journal of the Royal Agricultural Society of England*, 2nd ser., 23 (1887), 1–28

Archives Devon RO, corresp. relating to Plymouth water supply

Likenesses Maull & Polyblank, carte-de-visite, 1860–69, NPG [*see illus.*] · A. S. Cope, oils, 1900; in South Devon and East Cornwall Hospital, 1912 · Ape [C. Pellegrini], chromolithograph caricature, NPG; repro. in *VF* (15 May 1875), 270

Wealth at death £655,988 9*s*. 6*d*.: probate, 24 March 1908, *CGPLA Eng. & Wales*

Lopes, Sir Manasseh Masseh, first baronet (1755–1831), landowner and politician, was born Manasseh Lopes in Jamaica on 27 January 1755, only son of Mordecai Rodriguez Lopes (*d.* 1796), plantation owner, and Rebecca, daughter of Manasseh Pereira of Jamaica. He came from a family of Sephardic Jews who had become very wealthy as sugar planters in Jamaica and he inherited a substantial fortune on the death of his father in 1796, who had settled in Clapham, Surrey. Lopes was believed to have spent £100,000 buying the Heywood estates at Maristow, Devon, in 1798 and he continued to buy land around Plymouth, so that by 1820 he was one of the largest landowners in Devon. He also invested heavily in the East India Company and gave £5000 to the loyalty loan of 1797. On 19 October 1795 he married Charlotte Yeates, daughter of John Yeates of Monmouthshire; they had one child, Esther, who died on 1 July 1819. In 1802 Lopes was baptized in the Church of England and the same year was returned to parliament for New Romney, Kent. He became a firm supporter of Pitt and for his loyalty received a baronetcy on 1 November 1805; he also obtained a royal licence to add Masseh to his name. He was not a candidate at the 1806 general election and his election as MP for Evesham, Worcester, in 1807 was declared void on the grounds that some of his votes had been illegal. In 1810 he purchased the borough of Westbury from Montagu Bertie, fifth earl of Abingdon, at a cost of some £75,000 with the intention of ensuring his electoral success, although he decided to contest Barnstaple in Devon at a by-election in January 1812. Defeated by the opposition candidate, William Busk, he succeeded at the general election later that year, as did the two government candidates at Westbury, but he found himself considerably out of pocket as a result. After failing to receive compensatory patronage from Lord Melbourne, he voiced his dismay to Lord Liverpool and claimed that he had been treated with 'total neglect and disregard' by those he had so faithfully supported (Fisher, 456).

It is possible that Lopes's discontent, coupled with his political ambition, tempted him into using corrupt practices to win votes. With the assistance of a contingent of electors, his agent secured Lopes's return for Grampound in Cornwall by bribing forty voters with £35 apiece. This bribery became known only after a petition was lodged against Lopes following his 1818 election in Barnstaple, in which he was accused of making payments to voters. For his first offence he was brought to trial at Exeter assizes before Mr Justice Holroyd and a special jury on 18 March 1819 and he was convicted. He then stood trial for the allegations made at Barnstaple where it was found he had spent £3000 in bribes, and had bribed 63 of the 300 resident electors at £5 each. Although the house saw fit to unseat him, he was acquitted 'from defect of proof' at Devon assizes in August 1819 (Fisher, 457). On 13 November he was sentenced to two years' imprisonment and a fine of £10,000 by the court of king's bench. In the eyes of a number of MPs, such as Lord John Russell and even Lopes's counsel, James Scarlett, his sentence was seen as a necessary measure against electoral corruption. Brougham and the Holland House set, however, thought that he had been unfairly singled out for a crime of which many MPs were guilty. On his release from prison Lopes continued in public life and was returned in 1823 for his pocket borough of Westbury. Despite his unpopularity he successfully stood again in 1826, but later resigned his seat to provide for Peel on his rejection by Oxford University in 1829. Lopes, who served as a magistrate for Devon and Wiltshire, and from 1810 was recorder of Westbury, died at his seat, Maristow House, on 26 March 1831 and was buried at Bickleigh, Devon. He left a fortune of £800,000, principally in government and East India stock, but also in land. His nephew and heir, Ralph Franco, assumed the surname Lopes on succeeding to the baronetcy.

J. A. HAMILTON, *rev.* HALLIE RUBENHOLD

Sources D. R. Fisher, 'Lopes, Manasseh', HoP, *Commons* • *GM*, 1st ser., 101/1 (1831), 465–6 • C. Redding, *Fifty years' recollections, literary and personal*, 2nd edn, 3 vols. (1858) • Farington, *Diary*, vol. 5
Archives Devon RO, corresp. relating to Plymouth water supply
Wealth at death £800,000 chiefly in East India and government stock: *GM*, 465

Lopez, Aaron [*formerly* Duarte] **(1731–1782)**, merchant in America, was born Duarte Lopez in Lisbon, Portugal, the son of Diego Jose Lopez and his second wife (name unknown). Nothing is known of his early life. In 1752 Lopez left Lisbon, taking his wife, Anna (*d.* 1762), to Newport, Rhode Island, where his brother, Moses, had already settled. Abandoning their Christian names, Duarte and Anna, for Aaron and Abigail, they soon dropped the outward appearances of practising Christianity and publicly displayed the Jewish faith they had hidden in Lisbon.

Lopez was quickly accepted in the Jewish community in Newport and began to develop his position as a merchant. He worked primarily in the trade of spermaceti candles, so named because of their construction from the head matter of sperm whales, which he and Jacob Rodrieguez Rivera pioneered in America. In 1761 he joined the United Company of Spermaceti, a consortium of nine firms designed to regulate the trade and arrange price agreements. For a short period in 1762 Aaron resided in Swansea, Massachusetts. His wife, with whom he had seven children, died on 14 May 1762. Five months later he received his naturalization papers, which did not give him political rights but guaranteed him all the commercial rights of his fellow colonists. The following summer he married the daughter of his spermaceti candle commercial associate, Jacob Rodrieguez Rivera, Sarah (*b.* 1747), with whom he had ten further children.

Lopez struggled initially, enduring the disruption of trade in the Seven Years' War and the post-war depression. Towards the end of the 1760s, however, his business prospects soared. In the 1770s he experienced a tremendous increase in shipping, having complete or part ownership in over thirty vessels by 1775. His vessels traded in Jamaica, Hispaniola, Surinam, Honduras, Newfoundland, England, the Netherlands, Spain, Portugal, Africa, the Azores, and the Canary Islands. He also extended his commercial ventures into new and varied avenues, including real estate, manufacturing, and trading other goods. During Newport's 'golden age', he was one of its most prosperous citizens.

The outbreak of the American War of Independence was disastrous for Lopez's business. British troops occupied Newport from 1776 to 1779, forcing him to move to Leicester, Massachusetts, where he tried to continue some of his mercantile activities despite a general British naval blockade. Towards the end of the war, in 1782 he returned to Newport with his family and readied himself to re-establish his former business activities. However, on a family outing on 27 May 1782 he tried to drive his carriage through a shallow pond, Scott's Pond, Smithfield, Rhode Island. The carriage tipped over, and Lopez, unable to swim, drowned before his onlooking family. He was buried in the Jewish cemetery in Newport.

MURNEY GERLACH

Sources S. F. Chyet, *Lopez of Newport: colonial merchant prince* (1970) • M. A. Gutstein, *Aaron Lopez and Judah Touro: a refugee and a son of a refugee* (1939) • D. S. Lovejoy, *Rhode Island politics and the American revolution, 1760–1776* (1958) • M. J. Kohler, 'The Lopez and Rivera families of Newport', *American Jewish History Society Publications*, 2 (1894) • B. M. Bigelow, 'Lopez, Aaron', *DAB* • S. L. Skemp, 'Lopez, Aaron', *ANB* • B. M. Bigelow, 'Aaron Lopez: colonial merchant of Newport', *New England Quarterly*, 4 (1931), 757–76 • L. M. Friedman, 'Some further sidelights on Aaron Lopez', *Jewish Quarterly Review*, new ser., 45 (1954–5), 562–7 • J. R. Rosenbloom, *A biographical dictionary of early American Jews: colonial times through 1800* (1960) • L. Huhnet, 'A merchant prince of colonial New England', *Jewish Comment* (26 May 1905); (2 June 1905) • *Collections of the Massachusetts Historical Society*, 7th ser., 9–10 (1914–15) [*Commerce of Rhode Island, 1726–1800*]

Archives American Jewish Archives, Cincinnati, Ohio, papers • American Jewish Historical Society, Waltham, Massachusetts, papers • Newport Historical Society, Providence, papers • Rhode Island Historical Society Library, Rhode Island, papers

Likenesses miniature, American Jewish Historical Society, Waltham, Massachusetts

Lopez [Lopes], **Roderigo** [Ruy, Roger] (*c.*1517–1594), physician and alleged conspirator, was born in Portugal, where his father, António Lopes, was physician to João III. A New Christian, or son of a Jew baptized by force in 1497, he studied at the University of Coimbra, graduating BA on 7 February 1540 as Ruy Lopes, MA on 4 December 1541, and going on to enrol for the medical course on 23 December 1541. The university's degree registers for the period from 1537 to 1550 have not survived, but it is likely that he received his degree in medicine in 1544. Lopez settled in London in 1559, soon after Elizabeth I's accession. He was admitted as a fellow of the College of Physicians (the date is not recorded) and was the first appointee as physician to St Bartholomew's Hospital following its refoundation in 1547. He received £2 a year with a house and garden nearby in Little Britain. One of his colleagues at the hospital, William Clowes, noted in his work on gunshot wounds (1591) that Lopez showed himself to be both careful and very skilful, not only in his counsel in dieting, purging and bleeding, but also for the direction of Arceus's apozema. About 1563 he married Sarah (*b.* 1550), daughter of Dunstan *Anes, citizen and grocer of London. She was English born of Portuguese Jewish parents. They conformed to the established church but secretly adhered to Judaism. Their eldest daughter, Ellyn or Elinor, was baptized on 9 January 1564 at St Bartholomew-the-Less, as were other children: Ambrose on 6 May 1565, Douglas on 13 May 1573, William on 24 October 1577, and Ann on 1 March 1579. Their son Anthony was sent to Winchester College. In the 1571 census of aliens in the parish of St Andrew's, Holborn, Lopez is described as 'Doctor Lopus, Portingale, howsholder, denizen came into this realm about xij yeares past to get his lyvinge by physycke; and Lewis Lopez, his brother, is a soiourner in his howse and a joyner' (Huguenot Society). Another brother, Diego Lopes Aleman, was a merchant in Antwerp and Venice.

Lopez became physician to the earl of Leicester and after the death of Giulio Borgarucci he was appointed physician to the queen and her household in 1581. As such he received a life pension of £50 a year. In June 1584, by way of reward, he was granted a monopoly of the importation of sumach and aniseed for ten years. This was renewed again in January 1593. In 1588 he was granted land and tithes in Worcestershire belonging to the bishop of Worcester. Lopez lived at one time in Wood Street and later in Mountjoy's Inn, Fenchurch Street.

In 1580 King Henrique of Portugal died and Philip II of Spain invaded and seized the country. The other claimant to the Portuguese throne, Dom António, prior of Crato, took refuge in France and then in England with his followers. Lopez, who was among his keen supporters, helped to persuade the queen to recognize him as king of Portugal. However, Dom António's cause did not prosper and after the failure of his counter armada attack on Lisbon, in 1589, his followers gradually defected and made their peace with Philip.

In 1584 *Leicester's Commonwealth*, an anonymous Roman Catholic tract attacking the earl of Leicester, mentioned Lopez among his instruments: 'Iulio the Italian and Lopes the Iewe, for Poysoning & for the arte of destroying children in women's bellies' (*Leicester's Commonwealth*, 116). This was the first suggestion made that Lopez was a poisoner. A second such suggestion was made in 1586 by António da Veiga, one of Dom António's turncoat followers. In a letter to Don Bernardino de Mendoza, the Spanish ambassador to France, he claimed that in 1572 Don Gerau de Espes, the Spanish ambassador in London, had persuaded Lopez to sabotage Bartolomeo Bayon's voyage to the Spanish Indies by giving him a purge, which, however, Lopez did not do. Veiga claimed that he could persuade Lopez to poison Dom António. The Spaniards did nothing about it.

In 1590 Lopez himself approached Mendoza, through the intermediacy of Manuel de Andrada, who was a double agent, possibly on the initiative of the secretary of state, Sir Francis Walsingham, who had used Hector Nunes in 1586 to open negotiations with Spain. Lopez, who was Walsingham's physician, was an obvious alternative intermediary. Mendoza sent Andrada on to Spain, where he was interviewed by the Portuguese secretary of state, Dom Cristovão de Moura. Andrada proposed two things: first the opening of peace negotiations through

Lopez, and second the immobilization of Dom António by getting the English to agree either to his house arrest or else to his expulsion. The Spaniards were also interested in persuading Dom António's son Manuel to defect. The correspondence between Dom Cristovão de Moura and Philip II in the Spanish state papers makes it quite clear that these were then their sole aims in opening negotiations with Lopez. They gave Andrada a jewelled ring worth £100 as a gift for Lopez's daughter. Walsingham died in 1591 and Lopez continued his correspondence with the Spanish officials without the knowledge or authority of the English government.

Lopez also incurred the enmity of his former patient, the earl of Essex. In a conversation with Dom António and with Philip II's former secretary, António Perez, who lived at Essex House, Lopez told them of what diseases he had treated Essex, 'which did disparage his honour' (Goodman, 1.152–3). Perez reported this back to Essex, who was understandably furious.

After Walsingham's death in 1591 Essex took the latter's principal cryptologist, Thomas Phelipes of the Customs House, into his service and he discovered a secret correspondence between Estevão Ferreira da Gama, one of Dom António's erstwhile supporters, and the count of Fuentes, in the Spanish Netherlands. This was followed by the arrest of Lopez's courier, Gomez d'Avila, a Portuguese New Christian living in London, and of one Manuel Luis Tinoco, who was carrying letters from Spanish officials in the Netherlands to Ferreira da Gama. When they were interrogated they implicated Lopez. On 28 January 1594 Essex wrote to Anthony Bacon,

> I have discovered a most dangerous and desperate treason. The point of conspiracy was Her Ma[ties] death. The executioner should have been Dr Lopus. The manner by poison. This I have so followed that I will make it appeare as cleere as the noone day. (LPL, MS 653 fol. 312, vol. 7, no. 17)

Once Essex had committed his reputation to this thesis Lopez's fate was sealed. Matters were also made worse by a letter which Manuel Andrada had sent to Lord Burleigh in 1591, in which he wrote, 'The King of Spain had gotten three Portuguese to kill her Majesty and three more to kill the King of France' (*CSP for.*, 1591–2). Once a clandestine correspondence with Spain had been discovered this naturally left William Waad and Sir Robert Cecil keen to unmask Andrada's three unnamed Portuguese assassins. Tinoco was tortured and Ferreira da Gama threatened with torture until their confessions confirmed Essex's preconceptions. Ferreira da Gama was asked if Lopez would have been willing to poison the queen and confirmed that he would have been. Philip's main concern was to neutralize Dom António and to eliminate António Perez. Lopez had acted stupidly and dishonestly. Once his intrigues came to light, and these included passing information about the English court to Spain and a cryptic letter concerning his donation to a secret synagogue in Antwerp, the privy council, including William Waad and Robert Cecil, were ready to believe the worst. Lopez's claim that the sole purpose of his intrigue was 'to deceive the Spaniard and wipe him of his money' (Camden, 484) was not believed. Lopez, Manuel Luis Tinoco, and Estevão Ferreira da Gama were tried at Guildhall. The attorney-general, Sir Edward Coke, made great play with Lopez's secret Judaism. All three were convicted of high treason and hanged, drawn, and quartered at Tyburn on 7 June 1594. The government published an official account of the plot, stressing the criminal conduct of Philip of Spain in trying to murder the queen of England, whereas she never had and never would attempt to murder him.

Many people, influenced by the flow of polemics after the event, were shocked at Lopez's alleged venality and ingratitude to the queen, who had been his benefactress. Christopher Marlowe's play *The Tragedy of the Rich Jew of Malta* with its villainous Jewish character, Barabbas, was revived. William Shakespeare responded by writing and

Roderigo Lopez (*c.*1517–1594), by Frederik van Hulsen, 1627 [right, with a Spanish gentleman]

staging *The Merchant of Venice* with its murderous Jewish character, Shylock, who hates all Christians. Their audiences would have been well aware of the story of Lopez's alleged plot.

Some ten years later Count Gondomar wrote to Philip III about the affair, alleging that Lopez and Ferreira da Gama had been innocent and unjustly convicted. He wrote,

> the King our master had never conceived nor approved such measures … the Count of Fuentes neither received nor gave such an order, moreover it is understood that Dr Lopez never passed through his thoughts, because he was a friend of the Queen and a bad Christian. (Documentos ineditos, 196–8)

Sarah Lopez petitioned the queen to be allowed her late husband's estate. The queen kept King Philip's ring and most generously gave her back the rest, which was little enough. EDGAR SAMUEL

Sources autos e provas de curso, University of Coimbra Archives, A. U. C. IV-1ªD-1-1-3, V. 3° cad. 98v.; 158v, V. 2° cad., 191 • *CSP dom.*, 1591–4; 1593–4, 800 • *Report on the manuscripts of the family of Gawdy, formerly of Norfolk*, HMC, 11 (1885) • *Calendar of the manuscripts of the most hon. the marquis of Salisbury*, 4, HMC, 9 (1892) • LPL, Bacon MSS, MS 653, fol. 312, vol. 7, no. 17 • BL, Sloane MS 4112 • BL, Harleian MS 871 • R. E. G. Kirk and E. F. Kirk, eds., *Returns of aliens dwelling in the city and suburbs of London, from the reign of Henry VIII to that of James I*, Huguenot Society of London, 10/1 (1900) • 'A true report of the detestable treason intended by Dr Roderigo Lopez, a physician attending upon the person of the Queen's majesty', *The works of Francis Bacon*, ed. R. L. Ellis, J. Spedding, and D. D. Heath, 8 (1861), 274–87 • M. A. S. Hume, 'The so-called conspiracy of Dr Ruy Lopez', *Transactions of the Jewish Historical Society of England*, 6 (1908–10), 32–55 • *CPR*, 1580–82, 103, no. 647 • *CSP for.* • *Documentos ineditos para la história de España*, 1 (1936), 196–8 [dispatches of Count Gondomar] • G. Goodman, *The court of King James the First*, ed. J. S. Brewer, 1 (1839), vol. 1 • D. C. Peck, ed., *Leicester's commonwealth: the copy of a letter written by a master of art of Cambridge (1584) and related documents* (1985), 116 • *CSP Spain* • *A true report of sundry horrible conspiracies* (1594) • J. Gwyer, 'The case of Dr Lopez', *Transactions of the Jewish Historical Society of England*, 16 (1945–51), 163–84 • L. Wolf, 'Jews in Elizabethan England', *Transactions of the Jewish Historical Society of England*, 11 (1924–7), 1–91, esp. 32–55 • A. Dimock, 'The conspiracy of Dr Lopez', *EngHR*, 9 (1894), 440–72 • H. A. Harben, *A dictionary of London* (1918) • C. Hilton, 'St Bartholomew's Hospital, London, and its Jewish connections', *Jewish Historical Studies*, 30 (1987–8), 21–50 • M. A. S. Hume, *Treason and plot: the struggle for Catholic supremacy in the last years of Queen Elizabeth* (1901) • C. Read, *Lord Burghley and Queen Elizabeth* (1960) • E. R. Samuel, 'Dr Rodrigo Lopes' last speech from the scaffold at Tyburn', *Jewish Historical Studies*, 30 (1987–8), 51–3 • private information (2004) [David Harley] • W. Camden, *Annales rerum Anglicarum et Hibernicarum regnante Elizabetha* (1727), 484 • R. Cooke, *Visitation of London, 1568*, ed. H. Stanford London and S. W. Rawlins, [new edn], 2 vols. in one, Harleian Society, 109–10 (1963), 74–5 • J. J. Howard and G. J. Armytage, eds., *The visitation of London in the year 1568*, Harleian Society, 1 (1869), 65 • private information (2004) [D. N. Harley]

Archives BL, Add. MS 871 • BL, Add. MS 4122 • PRO • University of Coimbra archive, Portugal, autos e provas de curso, A. U. C. IV-1ª D-1-1-3, V. 3° cad. 98v; 158v; V. 2° cad., 191 | HMC, Gawdy MSS • HMC, Hatfield MSS • LPL, Bacon MSS

Likenesses F. van Hulsen, engraving, 1627, BL [*see illus.*]

Wealth at death 'little enough'; Elizabeth I kept King Philip's ring but returned the rest of Lopez's estate to his wife

Lopokova, Lydia Vasilievna [Lidiya Vasilyevna Lopukhova; *married name* Lydia Vasilievna Keynes, Lady Keynes] (**1892–1981**), ballet dancer, was born on 21 October 1892 at St Petersburg, Russia, the third of five children

Lydia Vasilievna Lopokova (1892–1981), by Duncan Grant, early 1940s

(three sons and two daughters) and second daughter of Vasily Lopukhov, an impassioned theatre lover and an usher at the Imperial Aleksandrinsky Theatre, and his wife, Rosalia Constanza Karlovna Douglas, daughter of the clerk to the municipality of Riga, of Scottish ancestry. Lopokova was educated at the Imperial Ballet School, St Petersburg, which she entered shortly before her ninth birthday in 1901. She graduated into the Imperial Ballet at the Maryinsky Theatre, St Petersburg, in 1909. Although a *demi-caractère* dancer, she could also shine in the purely classical roles because of her strong technique, extreme lightness in jumping, and stylistic sensitivity.

In 1910 Serge Diaghilev included Lopokova in the company he had formed for the second summer running to tour European capitals. Although only seventeen when thrust among Diaghilev's exalted group of artists, Lopokova quickly established herself and successfully danced Tamara Karsavina's roles, including those in *Firebird* and *Carnaval* (with Nijinsky) when Karsavina was away fulfilling other contracts.

Following the tour Lopokova, with her sister and elder brother, both dancers, sailed for America on eight-month contracts. She never returned to the Imperial Ballet nor danced again in Russia. When her brother and sister went home, she chose to stay on to dance in assorted ballet groups, shows, and musicals, making a name for herself. She also ventured into straight acting.

In 1916 Diaghilev sent his Ballets Russes to America and Lopokova rejoined the company as the leading ballerina. During the tour she married in 1916 Randolfo Barocchi,

Diaghilev's business manager and an older man of great charm. Thus Lopokova returned to Russian ballet and with it to Europe for the first time in six years. There followed seasons in Europe and North and South America but it was not until 1918 that Lopokova first danced in London. Her triumphs were now crowned by the roles created for her by Léonide Massine in *The Good-Humoured Ladies* (1917–18) and *La boutique fantasque* (1919). Such was her fame that when she abruptly left her husband and the ballet company simultaneously in July 1919 her mysterious disappearance caused banner headlines in the London press. Once again Lopokova had abandoned the Russian ballet as though it meant nothing to her. Yet two years later she returned to Diaghilev's company in Paris and then starred among five important ballerinas in Diaghilev's 1921 London production of *Sleeping Beauty*.

At this time the economist (John) Maynard *Keynes (1883–1946) became her ardent admirer. He was the brother of the scholar and surgeon Geoffrey Langdon Keynes (1887–1982), and the son of (John) Neville Keynes, registrary of Cambridge University. Belonging to the Bloomsbury group, he brought Lopokova into the circle—which was difficult at times for her, and for its members. When Keynes began to think of marriage, some of his friends were filled with foreboding. They tended to find Lopokova bird-brained. In reality she was intelligent, wise, and witty, but not intellectual. E. M. Forster, T. S. Eliot, and Picasso were among her close friends. She artfully used, and intentionally misused, English to unexpectedly comic and often outrageous effect. Keynes was constantly amused and enchanted. Lopokova idolized him and they married on 4 August 1925 (the year of her divorce from Barocchi) at St Pancras Central register office, visiting Russia on their honeymoon. The marriage inspired the couplet:

> What a marriage of beauty and brains
> The fair Lopokova and John Maynard Keynes.

They had no children. When they were apart they wrote daily, if only between King's College, Cambridge, of which Keynes was the bursar, and Bloomsbury.

Lopokova continued to dance and act intermittently, playing Ibsen, Molière, and Shakespeare, albeit with her charming Russian accent; and she helped the burgeoning British ballet tremendously. But from when Keynes suffered his first serious illness in 1937 until his death in 1946 the total dedication she had never quite mustered for her career came to flower. She was a devoted wife, forsaking all interests save her husband's health and work while entertaining him and their friends with her unpredictable remarks. They now lived mostly at Tilton in Sussex, sharing their love of poetry, literature, and the countryside. Lopokova accompanied her husband on his economic missions abroad. Keynes was raised to the peerage as Baron Keynes of Tilton in 1942.

Lopokova was a diminutive figure with the natural air of an eager, enquiring child which caused her to hold her head tilted up towards anyone with whom she was conversing. This could give the impression that her nose, too, was up-tilted whereas, unusually, just the tip turned down, as a Picasso drawing of 1919 clearly shows. Her face was round with alert eyes under perfectly curved eyebrows; her mouth was a well-defined feature. Both her face and hands were remarkably expressive. On or off the stage her vitality, originality, humour, and youthful enthusiasm were irresistible. Gaiety and good humour prevailed. In addition she was devoid of jealousy, malice, vanity, meanness, or pretension. After her husband's death she adopted a retired way of life but lost none of her originality and charm. She died at Threeways Nursing Home, Seaford, near Tilton on 8 June 1981.

MARGOT FONTEYN, *rev.*

Sources M. Keynes, ed., *Lydia Lopokova* (1983) · P. Hill and R. Keynes, eds., *Lydia and Maynard: letters between Lydia Lopokova and John Maynard Keynes* (1989) · personal knowledge (1986) · *The Times* (9 June 1981) · H. Koegler, *The concise Oxford dictionary of ballet* (1977) · R. Shone, *Bloomsbury portraits: Vanessa Bell, Duncan Grant and their circle*, 2nd edn (1993) · *CGPLA Eng. & Wales* (1981) · R. F. Harrod, *The life of John Maynard Keynes* (1951) · R. J. A. Skidelsky, *John Maynard Keynes*, 3 vols. (1983–2000), vols. 1–2

Archives King's AC Cam., corresp. and papers · King's AC Cam., letters and postcards to G. H. W. Rylands

Likenesses P. Picasso, drawing, 1919 · D. Grant, oils, 1940–44, NPG [*see illus.*]

Wealth at death £109,163: probate, 13 Aug 1981, *CGPLA Eng. & Wales*

Loraine, Sir Percy Lyham, twelfth baronet (1880–1961), diplomatist, was born in London on 5 November 1880, the second son and second child in the family of two sons and two daughters of Rear-Admiral Sir Lambton Loraine, eleventh baronet (1838–1917), and his wife, Frederica Mary Horatia (*d.* 1933), daughter of Captain Charles Acton Broke, of the Royal Engineers, who brought him the Suffolk property of Bramford Hall, near Ipswich. Loraine was educated at Eton College and entered New College, Oxford, in 1899, but left to serve in the Second South African War as a lieutenant with the East Kent imperial yeomanry. He entered the diplomatic service in March 1904, and served in Constantinople from 1904 to 1907 and in Tehran from 1907 to 1909. He learned both Turkish and Persian. In 1909 he was posted to Rome with the rank of second secretary, and in 1911 temporarily to Peking (Beijing). He next served in Paris, from 1912 to 1916, and in Madrid (with the rank of first secretary) from 1916 to 1918. He succeeded his father as twelfth baronet on 13 May 1917, his elder brother, Eustace Broke, a captain in the Grenadier Guards, having died in a flying accident in 1912.

In 1918–19 Loraine was attached to the peace conference delegation in Paris, but found that working for tired and overburdened men was disheartening; more congenial was battling with the Bolsheviks in eastern Europe. In October 1919 he was appointed Sir George Clerk's assistant on the mission which thwarted Bela Kun in Hungary, and from there went immediately to Poland where he witnessed the Polish success in repelling the Bolshevik armies from Warsaw; he helped to moderate extravagant Polish frontier demands.

The foreign secretary, Lord Curzon, had spotted Loraine's zeal, and in 1920 offered him the counsellorship in Tehran to help win ratification for 'his' treaty; but Loraine, who had just inherited Northumbrian estates, pleaded for a home posting, and joined Curzon's personal staff. The two north-country landowners, with their shared feudal outlook, found that they had much in common; nevertheless Loraine was astounded when in July 1921 Curzon begged him to become minister to Persia and salvage what he could from a treaty which the Persians had rejected. Loraine early recognized Reza Khan (later Reza Shah Pahlavi) as the likely winner of the local struggle for power; he appreciated Reza's directness. But his assignment was dogged by conflicting British obligations—to the sheikh of Muhammarah in the oil province of Khuzestan, and to Reza, who was bent on controlling all Persia. In bad faith, Reza seized the sheikh and removed him to Tehran, where he later died. Loraine spent much effort trying to correct this injustice, and to combat Soviet influence in Persia. He was advanced to KCMG in June 1925, having been made a CMG in June 1921.

An interesting pen portrait of Loraine in middle age was provided by Lord Gladwyn, who served under him in Tehran. Gladwyn found Loraine to be a 'brooding presence' but 'fine-looking … highly industrious and pretty shrewd'. Loraine was rather remote in his relations with Foreign Office subordinates and acquired the nickname Ponderous Percy, but Gladwyn judged ultimately that 'within his limits he was a model diplomat' (Gladwyn, 23). Superiors at the Foreign Office, however, like Sir Orme Sargent, found his dispatches wordy, and occasionally vapid.

Loraine's posting to Tehran coincided with his marriage, on 23 October 1924, to Louise Violet Beatrice (*b.* 1893), elder daughter of Major-General Edward James Montagu-Stuart-Wortley, of Highcliffe Castle, Hampshire. His wife was a noted beauty and a considerable support for him in his diplomatic career. They had no children, and Lady Loraine suffered severely from arthritis in later life, which made her a semi-invalid.

Loraine next served for three years as minister in Greece, from December 1926 until August 1929, when he was appointed high commissioner for Egypt and Sudan, succeeding the imperious Lord Lloyd. Here his technique of establishing personal relations with a leader failed him. Leaving King Fuad to sort out differences with his ministers yielded neither a treaty with Britain nor mitigation of the tussle between king, parties, and residency. To Loraine's disappointment he was replaced and in December 1933 transferred to Ankara. Even appointment to the privy council in the same month did not reconcile him to that 'godforsaken hole'.

But Loraine was mistaken. His Turkish service was a success. He established with Mustafa Kemal Atatürk relations even closer than those with Reza Shah. They played bridge and poker together, talked far into the night, and agreed on Anglo-Turkish friendship. Loraine's biographer, Gordon Waterfield, pointed out, however, that embassy staff in Ankara thought that Loraine overdid his hero worship of Atatürk, and his attempt to pretend that Atatürk was not a dictator because he was deliberately trying to create a system of government that would survive him did not convince. Loraine left Turkey shortly after Kemal's death, confident that Anglo-Turkish friendship was firm. He had been advanced to GCMG in May 1937.

Loraine was a strong candidate for the vacant post in Berlin in 1937 when Sir Eric Phipps was recalled, but Anthony Eden wanted him to remain in post in Ankara. Later Eden was to write of his deep regret that he did not choose Loraine or Miles Lampson, rather than the more controversial Nevile Henderson. Loraine had been 'stunned and disheartened', according to his biographer (Waterfield, 224), when Eden told him that he was not to get the Berlin post, but he was promised an important one within a year or two. He was a convinced supporter of appeasement and approved of the 1938 Munich agreement which, he told Lord Halifax, had avoided 'another gruesome and futile slaughter' (Loraine to Halifax, 25 Nov 1938, PRO, FO 424/282).

The new posting to Rome duly came in May 1939, and Loraine earned the respect of the Italian foreign minister Count Galeazzo Ciano for standing up to Mussolini. Crucially, however, Churchill was critical of Loraine's diplomacy in Rome when he joined Chamberlain's government in September 1939. Nevertheless, there was little Loraine could have done to prevent Mussolini's madcap slide into war in June 1940. On his return to England Loraine much resented official failure to use his talent; Churchill would not see him; he thought his Middle East experience wasted; and he spent the war in frustration.

Tall, discreet, immaculately dressed, Loraine nevertheless looked forbidding; he would have liked to unbend, but found this difficult, being essentially shy. He never discussed ideas, and preferred cards or backgammon to chat. His memory was excellent and his judgement good, but he delegated too little. Gladwyn was not the only diplomat to find him intimidating. But he mellowed in old age, became a keen racehorse owner and was described by the *Times* racing correspondent on his death as a 'charming and enthusiastic owner' (*The Times*, 24 May 1961). One of his horses won the One Thousand Guineas in 1948, and another came third in the Derby. His most enduring contribution to racing was his role as chairman of the Race Finish Recording Company from 1946 until 1959, from which position he oversaw the introduction in Britain and elsewhere of the photo finish. He died at his home, 19 Wilton Crescent, London, on 23 May 1961, and was buried at Kirkharle, Northumberland. The baronetcy became extinct on his death.

ELIZABETH MONROE, *rev.* PETER NEVILLE

Sources PRO, Loraine MSS • G. Waterfield, *Professional diplomat: Sir Percy Loraine of Kirkharle, bt, 1880–1961* (1973) • Lord Gladwyn [H. Jebb], *Memoirs* (1972) • D. C. Watt, *How war came* (1989) • N. Henderson, *Water under the bridges* (1945) • *Ciano's diplomatic papers*, ed. M. Muggeridge (1948) • *The Times* (24 May 1961) • *The Times* (26 May 1961) • *The Times* (30 May 1961) • *The Times* (13 June 1961) • R. Lamb, *The drift to war, 1922–1939* (1989) • *CGPLA Eng. & Wales* (1961)

Archives Bodl. Oxf., corresp. relating to Egypt • Bodl. Oxf., diary as high commissioner to Egypt and the Sudan, MS Eng. hist. d 308 • PRO, corresp. and papers, FO 1011 • St Ant. Oxf., Middle East Centre, press cuttings | BL OIOC, letters to Lord Reading, MSS Eur. E

238, F118 • CAC Cam., corresp. with Sir Edward Spears, SPRS • PRO, Halifax MSS • U. Newcastle, letters to Gertrude Bell • University of York, Halifax MSS | FILM BFI NFTVA, news footage • IWM FVA, actuality footage

Likenesses T. Geraldy, 1913, NPG; repro. in Waterfield, *Professional diplomat* • Histed, photograph, NPG

Wealth at death £505,430: probate, 13 June 1961, *CGPLA Eng. & Wales*

Loraine, Robert (1876–1935), actor, was born on 14 January 1876 at New Brighton, Cheshire, the son of Henry Loraine (1819–1899), actor, and his wife, Edith Kingsley (*d*. 1895). Robert Loraine, who was educated privately, made his first appearance on the stage at the age of thirteen and was first seen in London in 1894 at the age of eighteen. He quickly became a leading player in both London and New York, appearing constantly in both cities: *Who's Who in the Theatre* lists his roles in fifty-six London productions and twenty-seven New York productions between 1894 and 1932.

A man of action, between 1899 and 1901 Robert Loraine served as a volunteer in the Second South African War. During the First World War he distinguished himself in the Royal Flying Corps (RFC), winning the MC and the DSO in 1917 and twice being seriously wounded. He retired from the army at the end of the war with the rank of lieutenant-general and immediately returned to the stage.

In 1901 Loraine married Winifred Lydia, daughter of Sir Robert Strangman; they had three daughters. Loraine's range as an actor was very wide and throughout his career he was just as ready to play in light, popular box-office successes as in plays of more substance. The remarkable fact was that he was equally adept in either. While he was still in his early twenties he established himself as a leading 'romantic' actor (a 'matinée idol', in fact) in such popular melodramas as *The Prisoner of Zenda* by Anthony Hope and *The Three Musketeers*, in which he played D'Artagnan in 1899. Lightweight comedies were also Loraine's forte, and he starred in *Frocks and Frills* (by S. Grundy), *Pretty Peggy* (a musical play by A. Rose and C. Austin), and *Dolly Reforming herself* (by H. A. Jones), as well as a number of others.

In addition Loraine appeared in a number of major Shakespearian roles between 1896 and 1927. His Prince Hal impressed H. M. Walbrook, the critic of the *Pall Mall Gazette* in 1909, who commented that his association with Falstaff 'was at least as much a matter of intellectual curiosity as of any particular partiality towards riot and dishonour' (Walbrook, 96). Loraine's other 'classical' parts included Young Marlow in Oliver Goldsmith's *She Stoops to Conquer* (1909), Charles Surface in R. B. Sheridan's *The School for Scandal* (1909), Bob Acres in Sheridan's *The Rivals* (1910), and Mirabell in W. Congreve's *The Way of the World* (1924). He played the eponymous hero in two different productions of Rostand's *Cyrano de Bergerac*, one in 1919 in Edinburgh and the other in 1927 in London.

Loraine was especially associated with Bernard Shaw: they once went for a balloon flight together, along with Harley Granville Barker, over London and almost drowned together on a seaside holiday in Wales. Loraine played Jack Tanner in *Man and Superman* in 1907 (taking over the part from Granville Barker) and again under his own management in 1911 and on subsequent occasions in London and New York. His other Shavian parts included Bluntschli in *Arms and the Man* in 1907 and again in 1919 and 1926, St John Hotchkiss in *Getting Married* in 1908, and O'Flaherty in *O'Flaherty VC* at an army camp in Belgium in February 1917 while he was a serving RFC officer. This being the first production of the play, Shaw himself attended the dress rehearsal, in spite of the curious location and the dangers of war. Shaw, in fact, was very fond of Loraine, whom he saw as a good example of the man of action who is also an artist, a type he greatly admired. On his army enlistment papers Loraine listed Shaw and Mrs Shaw as next of kin. In some ways Loraine stood in the same relationship to Shaw that Granville Barker had stood before him and T. E. Lawrence was to stand after him—the ardent young man who became a surrogate son.

Robert Loraine (1876–1935), by Bassano, 1919

Throughout his long career Loraine was an actor who was very popular with the general public. Yet a number of leading theatre critics commented favourably on the quality and depth of his work in serious drama. In 1907 Max Beerbohm considered he was excellent as Jack Tanner at the Court Theatre in the first production of Shaw's *Don Juan in Hell* (derived from act III of *Man and Superman*). Beerbohm wrote that 'He seems to be really thinking, really evolving the ideas he has to express, and really rejoicing, too, in his mastery of debate' (*Saturday Review*, 8 June 1907). Shaw directed the play and, ten days before it opened, wrote to Granville Barker that Loraine 'who always starts a company by sacking at least three members of it after the first rehearsal to intimidate the rest' had 'got all the comedy side of the part capitally and does it quite in my old-fashioned way, with a relish and not under protest, like you' (Purdom, 85). Desmond MacCarthy, reviewing Loraine's performance of the title part in *Deburau* (by Sacha Guitry, translated by Granville Barker) in May 1921 agreed that Loraine was 'a most accomplished elocutionist; indeed, about the best on the stage' (MacCarthy, 69). James Agate, the leading British theatre critic of his day, noted the excellent pairing of Loraine's Mirabell with the Millament of Edith Evans in *The Way of the World* in 1924: 'The part was beautifully spoken and the actor used only the suavest and most gentle notes in his voice. He listened exquisitely' (Agate, *Red Letter Nights*, 35).

Loraine's stature as an actor was perhaps shown to best effect in his Strindberg performances in the late 1920s: he got excellent notices for his major roles in *The Father* (1927) and *The Dance of Death* (1928). Agate, reporting in 1928 on Loraine's performance as Edgar in the latter play, considered that Loraine's acting was

> magnificent throughout, and as masterly in its implications as in its detailed craftsmanship. While fully satisfying the eye in the matter of the paralytic stroke and so forth, he kept our minds occupied not with the tricks of the crumbling body but with the cancerous sweep of evil imagination. (Agate, *Red Letter Nights*, 123)

Writing in 1951, J. C. Trewin got the measure of Robert Loraine when he described him as 'an actor never afraid of mountaineering' (Trewin, 194). Daring in his choice of roles, he refused to follow, unthinkingly, earlier and traditional interpretations.

Loraine died in the Golden Square Hospital, Westminster, London, on 23 December 1935. In 1938 his widow published a popular biography of him.

Eric Salmon

Sources I. Herbert, ed., *Who's who in the theatre*, 17th edn, 2 vols. (1981) • W. Loraine, *Robert Loraine, actor* (1938) • D. MacCarthy, *Drama* (1940) • J. Agate, *Red letter nights* (1944) • H. M. Walbrook, *Nights at the play* (1911) • J. Agate, *The contemporary theatre, 1924* (New York, 1969) • *Collected letters: Bernard Shaw*, ed. D. H. Laurence, 2 (1972) • W. Archer, *The theatrical 'World' of 1897* (1898); repr. [1969] • J. C. Trewin, *The theatre since 1900* (1951) • *CGPLA Eng. & Wales* (1936) • C. B. Purdom, *The Shaw–Barker letters* (1956)

Likenesses Bassano, photograph, 1919, NPG [*see illus.*] • photographs, Mander and Mitchenson Theatre Collection; repro. in Shaw, *Letters*, vol. 2

Wealth at death £2689 4*s*. 8*d*.: probate, 1936, *CGPLA Eng. & Wales*

Loraine, Violet [*real name* Violet Mary Tipton; *married name* Violet Mary Joicey] (**1886–1956**), actress, was born in Kentish Town, London, on 26 July 1886, the daughter of Henry Edmund Tipton, commercial clerk, and his wife, Mary Ann Eliza Garrod. She was educated at Trevelyan House, Brighton, and went on the stage at the age of sixteen as a chorus girl. Although her status was humble her surroundings were not, for her first job was in the Drury Lane pantomime of 1902, *Mother Goose*. Small parts in musical plays followed at once and carried her through to 1905, in which year she had her first taste of straight acting, in a revival of the old farce *Our Flat* by Mrs Musgrave at the Comedy Theatre, and of the variety stage when she appeared in revue at the Palace. By now well launched, she toured for George Edwardes in the George Grossmith musical comedies *The Spring Chicken* and *The Girls of Gottenburg*; made her first venture on to the 'halls' as a single turn at the old Oxford Theatre; became a popular principal boy in provincial pantomimes; and in 1911 returned with glory to her starting point, playing lead in the Drury Lane pantomime *Hop o' my Thumb*. When war broke out in 1914 she was already a well-known performer. In 1914 and 1915 she found a place in a series of revues at the London Hippodrome: *Hullo, Tango!*, *Business as Usual*, and *Push and Go*. Her big chance came in April 1916 when *The Bing Boys are Here* was put on at the Alhambra in Leicester Square and she was given the leading female part, Emma, with George Robey playing Lucius Bing. This entertainment caught the special taste of the troops on leave and, with its two sequels—the not altogether successful *The Bing Girls are There* (1917) and the immensely popular *The Bing Boys on Broadway* (1918)—it made the Alhambra a rallying place for men in uniform until long after the fighting was over.

Violet Loraine became a considerable star. With her warm, friendly personality, her gaiety, her rich humour, and the sincerity she could bring to such basically sentimental songs as 'If you were the only girl in the world' or 'Let the great big world keep turning', she was a symbol of delight; the public—armed forces and civilians alike—took her to its heart. As often happens when a stage artist makes a popular hit, the magnitude of Violet Loraine's success was due to the chance that she was on a particular spot with particular talents at a particular time. There was a public need, and she was there to supply it. The success itself, however, she had earned for herself by hard work. After the war she appeared in *Eastwood Ho!* by Oscar Ascho and Dornford Yates at the Alhambra (1919), and in the revues *The Whirligig* at the Palace (1920), and *London, Paris and New York* at the London Pavilion (1921). In September 1921 she announced her retirement from the stage and married, on 22 September, Edward Raylton Joicey MC (1890–1955), eldest son of Colonel Edward Joicey, of Blenkinsopp Hall, Haltwhistle, Northumberland. They had two sons.

In May 1928 Violet Loraine took part in a charity performance of *The Scarlet Pimpernel* by Baroness Orczy and Montague Barstow at the Palace and later that year she made a return to the professional stage, playing the name part in *Clara Gibbings*. This was not the kind of venture to appeal to her old public and it seemed—like other returns that she made in 1932 and 1934—to be evidence of a passing desire for a glimpse of her old world of the theatre rather than a serious intention to win back her former place in it. She died at the Royal Victoria Infirmary, Newcastle upon Tyne, on 18 July 1956.

W. A. Darlington, *rev.* K. D. Reynolds

Sources J. Parker, ed., *Who's who in the theatre*, 6th edn (1930) • Burke, *Gen. GB* (1937) • *The Times* (20 July 1956) • private information (1971)

Archives sound BL NSA, performance recordings

Likenesses four photographs, 1915–34, Hult. Arch. • C. Buchel and Hassall, lithograph, NPG

Wealth at death £52,846 19*s*. 2*d*.: probate, 1956, *CGPLA Eng. & Wales*

Lorant, Stefan [*formerly* István Reich] (**1901–1997**), magazine editor and historian, was born on 22 February 1901 at Dohány utca 10, Budapest, the first son and eldest of three children of Izsó Reich (1868–1917), a portrait photographer and manager of a photographic studio, and his wife, Irén (1878–1934), daughter of Mihály Guttmann-né, and his wife, Cenci. Both his parents were Hungarian Jews. Born István Reich, he changed his name to Lóránt in 1917, a few months after the death of his father. He was educated at a number of schools in Budapest, at the Academy of Economics, Budapest, and at Harvard University.

Between 1920 and 1925, first in Austria and then in Germany, Stefan Lorant (as he thereafter called himself) worked on fourteen films for the emerging silent film industry. Initially he made still photographs, before becoming a cameraman, a scriptwriter, and finally a director, all within a single year. His first film, on Mozart's life, loves, and suffering, *Mozart, Leben, Lieben und Leiden* (1920), established him as a much sought-after cameraman. Then, in 1925, after having mastered the German language, he began writing articles for Berlin magazines based primarily on his knowledge of the film industry and its film stars.

Lorant observed life visually and laterally. For him there was no difference between telling stories with pictures on a screen and telling stories with pictures on a page. The narrative was the same, though the concept of using pictures rather than words proved a major leap in the public's understanding. Technical innovations allowed the promotion to and rapid expansion of a visually receptive audience. Within a few years Lorant had become the editor of four new picture magazines: *Das Magazin* (1925), *UFA Magazin* (1926), *Bilder Courier* (1927–8), and in 1928 Berlin editor of the *Münchner Illustrierte Presse*, for which he eventually rose to be editor-in-chief (1932–3). After being released from six and a half months' 'protective custody' in Munich following the Nazis' seizure of power in Bavaria in 1933, he returned to Budapest, where he wrote *I was Hitler's Prisoner*, published in London in 1935, and later as one of the first Penguin paperbacks. During this period in Budapest he edited *Pesti Napló Magazin* (1933–4), an early example of a weekly illustrated newspaper supplement. Shortly after his arrival in England in April 1934, he created the influential *Weekly Illustrated*, and in 1937 founded *Lilliput*, the pocket-sized publication that included visually surrealistic photographic 'juxtapositions', followed in 1938 by his *tour de force*, the influential weekly picture magazine *Picture Post* which he edited along with *Lilliput* until 1940. Within a year he brought *Picture Post* to a circulation of 1.7 million, and statistics from the time indicate that it was read by half the adult population of England. *Picture Post* provided a logical progression in and arguably the pinnacle of his creative achievement.

Lorant emigrated to America in 1940, like many of his creative and talented peers. He lived there primarily as an author and biographer, and is acknowledged as the creator of the pictorial biography. Only a year after his arrival in America, Lorant's first pictorial biography, *Lincoln, his Life in Photographs* (1941), was published. Later editions provide the most complete collection of Lincoln portraits. Politically astute, Lorant visually analysed and illustrated the development of American democracy through its people and its cities. *The New World* (1946) brought together the earliest authentic representations of aboriginal life in North America (1564–90). Then came a biography of Franklin D. Roosevelt (1950), followed by *The Presidency* (1951), and a biography of Theodore Roosevelt nine years later. *The Glorious Burden* (1968) depicted a history of each of the American presidential elections from Washington to Carter and is essential to an understanding of the American experience. *Pittsburgh, the Story of an American City* was published in 1964; and *Sieg Heil!*, an illustrated history of Germany from Bismarck to Hitler, in 1974. In all, Lorant was the author of about twenty books, including major revisions.

On 21 August 1930 Lorant married the dancer Niura Fainleib (*b*. 1911) in Berlin, later divorcing her in Budapest on 30 March 1932. The only child from their marriage was Andrew (*b*. 1930). Lorant's second child, Virginia (*b*. 1938), was born as the result of a long liaison with the journalist Alison Blair Hooper (1906–1995). On 17 September 1957 Lorant married Louise Ottinger in City Hall, New York, divorcing her on 31 March 1960 at Reno. His final marriage was on 1 November 1963, to the writer and teacher Laurie Robertson (*b*. 1940), from whom he was divorced on 18 September 1978. There were two children from this marriage: Christopher Stefan (*b*. 1964) and Mark Imre (1965–1984). From 1946 he enjoyed living in the heart of the Berkshires in Lenox, Massachusetts, until his death on 14 November 1997 at the Mayo Clinic, Rochester, Minnesota, from pancreatic cancer. He was cremated the same day. He sold his remarkable collection of photographs, and some boxes of correspondence, to the Getty Research Institute for the History of Art and the Humanities in Los Angeles in 1991; catalogued, the collection occupies about 45 feet of shelving.

Lorant's work as a visual and literary editor allowed him to pioneer and develop the genre of picture-based journalism at a period that saw the emergence of modern mass communication. Internationally he became a guiding force, disseminating his ideas and political knowledge throughout Europe in the late 1920s and 1930s by working in Germany, Hungary, and England, eventually spreading his sphere of influence to America. He stretched the concept of what people needed, admired, and regarded as good taste. His innovative layouts, his 'exclusive' interviews and thirst for knowledge became a familiar part of millions of everyday lives, largely through the pages of his own creations, and in particular through the legendary media icon *Picture Post*. His vision of photography as a documentary medium inspired *Life* and *Look* magazines in America, and paved the way for the eventual emergence of the television documentary. MICHAEL HALLETT

Sources M. Hallett, *Stefan Lorant: messages and myths* [forthcoming] [working title] • M. Hallett, *The real story of Picture Post* (1994) • J. Cardwell, 'At 82, Stefan Lorant remembers his six lives', *Boston Globe* (26 Feb 1983) • B. Dobler, 'An afternoon with Stefan Lorant', *Pittsburgh Magazine* (Feb 1989) • *The Independent* (17 Nov 1997) • *Daily Telegraph* (18 Nov 1997) • *The Guardian* (17 Nov 1997) • *The Times* (18 Nov 1997)

Archives International Center of Photography, New York, collection • J. Paul Getty Museum, California, collection | FILM Stiftung Deutsche Kinemathek, Berlin, Germany | SOUND BL NSA, 'Oral history of British photography', Feb 1994

Likenesses R. Mahrenholz, photograph, 1933, Berlin • K. Hutton, double portrait, photograph, 1938 (with Tom Hopkinson), Hult. Arch. • K. Hutton, double portrait, photograph, 1939 (with Winston Churchill), Hult. Arch.; repro. in *The Independent* • double portrait, photograph, 1957 (with John F. Kennedy) • A. Frejndlich, portrait, 1987

Lord, Cyril (1911–1984), carpet manufacturer, was born on 12 July 1911 at 129 Moorside Street, Droylsden, Manchester, the son of Richard Lund Lord and his wife, Kate, *née* Hackney. His family had impeccable textile connections linking Macclesfield and Saddleworth hand-loom weavers, and his was a Wesleyan Methodist upbringing within a close mill community. In later life he rebelled against many of his early associations, was educated at the central school in Manchester, and defied his father, a worker in the co-operative movement, by taking an apprenticeship with a local textile firm. Working in the expanding rayon industry, he studied at the Manchester College of Technology and in 1935 moved to a London firm of wholesalers and merchant converters. During the Second World War he was an adviser to the Cotton Board and an instructor in the weaving of 'cotton' from utility fibres in Northern Ireland.

By 1945 the basis of Lord's remarkable post-war rise had been laid. A specialist in man-made fibres and their applications, he had connections with both producers and those in merchandising, and was a remarkable salesman. A short but strong man, intolerant of bureaucracy and compromise, he showed bravery verging on recklessness in business. With the support of the Irish banks, and in association with William McMillan, the assemblage of his company began with the purchase of two mills in Chorley. Its partial flotation in 1954 was oversubscribed twelvefold. Following a world tour in 1953, Lord was to the forefront of the campaign for trade protection, culminating in the Cotton Industry Act (1959). He gained much publicity when he sent 1200 members of the political and economic establishment spindles of cotton and wallets stuffed with Japanese money. Specializing in 'from the factory' sales, and the Taiho fabric, his mills made good profits, making him a millionaire by the early 1960s.

Lord responded to the further contraction of the cotton industry with an ill-fated enterprise in South Africa, and by diversifying into carpet production. Backed by government funds, he established a large factory at Donaghadee, co. Down, Northern Ireland, in 1956. His greatest venture, this plant could produce 5 yards of carpet per minute, and employed 800 people in a town of only 3700. Relentless sales campaigns, in which Lord, with his jingle 'This is luxury you can afford by Cyril Lord', was much to the fore, fed

Cyril Lord (1911–1984), by Ida Kar, 1950s

the consumer boom of the 1960s. The pace of expansion could not be maintained, new product lines failed, and, amid increasing difficulties, Lord's health broke down in September 1967, and he retired to the West Indies. The collapse of his firm in October 1968 was one of the spectacular failures of the period. The firm's prospects, trumpeted in a second share issue in 1965, were revealed to have been unfounded, and directors had much reduced their holdings. The collapse was the subject of a libel action in 1974, and a final payment to creditors was made only in 1987.

Lord was a colourful personality who played the part of the millionaire to the full: a character based on him appeared in a 1967 episode of the American television series *Batman* in the shape of 'Mat Man, the Karpet King of Europe'. Though principally remembered for the spectacular demise of his company, Lord was a genuine innovator, whose career, up to a point, represented a logical, if individualistic, business response in a declining industry.

Lord was married three times: on 26 December 1936 to Bessie Greenwood (*b.* 1913/14), whom he divorced in 1959 and with whom he had two sons and two daughters; on 17 January 1960 to the journalist and novelist Shirley Florence Hussey, *née* Stringer (*b.* 1932/3), whom he divorced in 1973; and in 1974 to Aileen Parnell, widow of impresario Val Parnell. Lord died after a long illness at his home in Barbados on 29 May 1984. DAVID HUNT

Sources *The Times* (4 June 1984) • K. Ullyett, ed., *My key to life by fifteen famous men and women today* (1958) • 'Rolling up the mat man saga', *Financial Times* (29 Aug 1987) • 'The Times diary', *The Times* (4 Feb 1983) [Shirley Lord] • *Supplement to Tattersall's Weekly Survey*, no. 1403 (Nov 1968) • share prospectus, *The Times* (14 May 1954) • press cuttings, 1954–68, Lancs. RO, Barber Lomax Collection • 'High court libel action', *The Times* (19 Nov 1974) • *Cyril Lord Journal* (April 1958) • b. cert. • m. certs.

Likenesses I. Kar, photograph, 1950–59, NPG [*see illus.*]

Lord, Henry (*b.* 1563), clergyman and ethnographer, was born in Oxfordshire; his parents' names are unknown. He matriculated from Magdalen Hall, Oxford, on 15 April 1580, but seems to have left without a degree. In January 1624 the East India Company appointed him chaplain to the company factory at Surat in Gujarat for five years at a salary of £60 per annum, and advanced him two months' pay and £20 to buy books. Lord arrived with the rest of the English fleet in October 1624; by December 1625 he was threatening to return to England, but the president of the factory, Thomas Kerridge, forbade him to go.

At Kerridge's urging Lord studied the religion of the Hindu Banias, 'out of their Manuscripts, and by renewed accesse, with the helpe of Interpreters, made my collections out of a booke of theirs called the SHASTER' (H. Lord, *Display of Two Forraigne Sects*, pt 1, sig. B2r), as well as the Zend-Avesta of the Parsis. He gave accounts of these in his two-part work, *A display of two forraigne sects in the East Indies vizt: the sect of the Banians the ancient natives of India and the sect of the Persees the ancient inhabitants of Persia* (1630), which he dedicated to Archbishop Laud and to the East India Company. The book offered an invaluable account of Hindu and Parsi cosmography for European readers, albeit framed by a condemnation of their 'vaine Superstitions, and composed Forgery' (Lord, *Display*, pt 1, 93) deployed 'to beget in good Christians, the greater detestation of these Heresies' (ibid., pt 2, 53). Pierre Briot translated the work into French in 1667, and it was reprinted repeatedly, for example in Awnsham Churchill and John Churchill's *Collection of Voyages and Travels* (1732, 1744, 1752), in Bernard Picart's *Cérémonies et coutumes religieuses de tous les peuples du monde* (1723–42), and in John Pinkerton's *General Collection of the Best and most Interesting Voyages* (1808–14). The date and place of Lord's death are not known. DAVID ARMITAGE

Sources *CSP col.*, vols. 4, 6 • W. Foster, ed., *The English factories in India*, 3 (1909) • Foster, *Alum. Oxon.* • S. J. McNally, 'The chaplains of the East India Company', 1976, BL OIOC, OIR 283.54 • B. G. Gokhale, *Surat in the seventeenth century: a study in the urban history of pre-modern India* (1979) • P. Briot, trans., *Histoire de la religion des Banians* (1667) • B. Picart and others, eds., *Cérémonies et coutumes religieuses de tous les peuples du monde* (1723–42) • A. Churchill and J. Churchill, eds., *A collection of voyages and travels*, [another edn], 6 vols. (1732) • A. Churchill and J. Churchill, eds., *A collection of voyages and travels*, 3rd edn, 6 vols. (1744) • A. Churchill and J. Churchill, eds., *A collection of voyages and travels*, [another edn], 8 vols. (1752) • J. Pinkerton, ed., *A general collection of the best and most interesting voyages and travels in all parts of the world*, 17 vols. (1808–14)

Lord, John Keast [*pseud.* the Wanderer] **(1818–1872)**, naturalist and traveller, was probably born in Cornwall, the son of Edward Lord. He was taken to Tavistock, Devon, with his brother, William Barry Lord, and educated by an uncle named Luscombe, a man of some local position. About 1840 Lord was apprenticed to Edgecombe and Stannes, chemists, in Tavistock, and afterwards entered the Royal Veterinary College, London, on 4 November 1842. He received his diploma (MRCVS) on 29 May 1844 and established himself as a veterinary surgeon at Tavistock, but his convivial tastes led him astray, and he suddenly disappeared. He is said to have made a whaling voyage and been shipwrecked, and to have been for some years a trapper in Minnesota and the Hudson's Bay fur countries. On 19 June 1855 he was appointed to the British army in the East as a veterinary surgeon with local rank, and attached to the artillery of the Turkish contingent, with which he served in the Crimea. He received the rank of lieutenant on 4 January 1856. In August of that year he was acting as veterinary surgeon with local rank and senior lieutenant of the Osmanli horse artillery.

When British Columbia was formed into a colony after the gold discoveries on the Fraser River in 1858, Lord was appointed (1 February 1858) naturalist to the British North American boundary commission sent out to run a boundary line along the forty-ninth parallel of north latitude, separating the new colony from United States territory. He was detached to San Francisco to buy mules, and to his skill and energy the success of the transport arrangements of the expedition was largely due. He lived for some time at Vancouver Island, but returned to England on 14 July 1862. The valuable collections he made of mammals, birds, fishes, insects, and other specimens are now in the Natural History Museum, London. Two new mammals, a muskrat which he called *Fiber osoyooensis* and another animal, related to the hare and the rabbit, which he called *Lagomys minimus*, were described by him in the *Proceedings of the Zoological Society* (1863, 95–8), where he argued that these should be classified as new species rather than simply varieties. In the same year, dressed in the garb of a trapper, he delivered lectures entitled 'The canoe, the rifle, and the axe' at the Egyptian Hall, Piccadilly, London, and there he became acquainted with the naturalist Francis Trevelyan Buckland. At Buckland's suggestion Lord became a contributor to *The Field*, and joined the staff of Buckland's journal, *Land and Water*, on its establishment on 1 January 1866.

Subsequently Lord was employed by the viceroy in archaeological and scientific researches in Egypt. While there he made many observations on snakes and exposed the tricks of the snake charmers, who, seeing his dexterity in handling venomous snakes made him a 'sheikh' of their craft. He brought to London collections of remains from ancient mines and sent them back to Egypt after arranging them. Catalogues of collections of Lepidoptera and Hymenoptera formed by him in Egypt were published in London in 1871. Lord was appointed the first manager of the Brighton aquarium, which was opened on 10 August 1872, but four months later, on 9 December, he died aged fifty-four at his home, 17 Dorset Gardens, Brighton. His friend Buckland described him as a big, unostentatious, large-hearted man, a delightful companion, and a first-rate practical naturalist.

Lord's most enduring work was perhaps *The Naturalist in Vancouver Island and British Columbia* (2 vols., 1866), at the end of which are lists of his collections in north-west America. He also wrote, under the pseudonym of the Wanderer, *At Home in the Wilderness* (1867, 2nd edn, 1876), and helped in an enlarged edition of Francis Galton's *Art of Travel* (new edn, 1867). In addition he was a contributor to the *Leisure Hour*, *Temple Bar*, the *Intellectual Observer*, and other journals, and as the Wanderer contributed many papers on sea fisheries and other topics to *Land and Water*, which for a short time he edited as Buckland's substitute.

H. M. Chichester, *rev.* Andrew Grout

Sources F. T. Buckland, *Land and Water* (14 Dec 1872), 387, 395 · Boase, *Mod. Eng. biog.* · D. B. Baker, 'Two little-known nineteenth century collectors: Dr Thomas Dowler and John Keast Lord, Esq., FZS', *Archives of Natural History*, 23 (1996), 385–98 · J. Ewan and N. D. Ewan, *Biographical dictionary of Rocky mountain naturalists … 1682–1932* (1981) · private information (1893) · *Army List* (1856) · D. B. Baker, *John Keast Lord: material for a life* (Leiden, 2002)
Archives NHM, specimens
Likenesses etching (after J. Kirkwood), NPG · portrait, repro. in *Leisure Hour*, 22 (1873), 696–9 · portrait, repro. in *The Graphic*, 7 (1873), 3, 12

Lord, Percival Barton (1808–1840), diplomatic agent and surgeon, was born at Cork. He was the son of John Lord, chaplain to an institution founded by the Kingston family at Mitchelstown, co. Cork, for the relief of decayed gentlewomen. After being taught by his father he went to Trinity College, Dublin, where he graduated BA in 1829 and MB in 1832. From Dublin he went to Edinburgh, where he zealously studied anatomy and physiology and acted as resident superintendent of a hospital during an epidemic of cholera. Following completion of his course in Edinburgh he went to London, and there contributed some valuable medical reviews to the *Athenaeum*, notably two on consumption in the numbers for 15 and 22 March 1834, which were reprinted by medical journals on the continent and in America.

On 23 November 1834 Lord was appointed assistant surgeon in the service of the East India Company, and proceeded to Bombay. On the voyage he studied Persian. He was appointed to the native cavalry in Gujarat, and afterwards accompanied, as surgeon, the embassy (the 'commercial mission') which was sent under Sir Alexander Burnes to Kabul. At Kabul he won the friendship of Dost Muhammad Khan and other Afghan chiefs, and his fame reached the ears of Murad Beg, the dreaded emir of Kunduz, who sent a mission to request his attendance on his brother, then threatened with blindness. Accordingly, late in November 1837, Lord penetrated into Tartary through the mountains of the Hindu Kush. He found the case of Murad Beg's brother hopeless, but he embodied valuable observations in a report to the government, which met with the highest approval.

Lord was consequently, on 1 October 1838, named political assistant to William Hay Macnaghten, the envoy dispatched to Kabul, and was sent to Peshawar to collect and arm all the natives who were ready to fight on behalf of Shah Shuja, whom the English government had determined to place on the throne of Afghanistan instead of Dost Muhammad. At Peshawar he wrote to his mother that he was 'busied in casting cannon, forging muskets, raising troops, horse and foot, talking, persuading, threatening, bullying, and bribing'. Lord determined on a vigorous forward policy to extend the authority of Shah Shuja even beyond the Hindu Kush. Initially he had a series of successes, and a mixture of bluff and modest force gained

Percival Barton Lord (1808–1840), by John Kirkwood, pubd 1843 (after Charles Grey)

step-by-step advances towards Turkestan. But Macnaghten and the Indian government were always ambivalent and, in a confused situation, drew back. The first phase of the forward movement ended, Lord being killed in a minor engagement at Purwan on 2 November 1840. One of the early players of 'the great game', Lord was 'an unfortunate choice, for while he did not lack intelligence, there was an errant impulsiveness about his judgement which … cost Britain dear' (Yapp, 353).

Gordon Goodwin, *rev.* H. C. G. Matthew

Sources *Athenaeum* (1841), 36, 287, 428 · *GM*, 2nd ser., 15 (1841), 320–21 · M. E. Yapp, *Strategies of British India: Britain, Iran and Afghanistan, 1798–1850* (1980) · J. W. Kaye, *History of the war in Afghanistan*, 2 vols. (1851)
Likenesses J. Kirkwood, etching (after C. Grey), NG Ire.; repro. in *Dublin University Magazine*, 21 (1843) [*see illus.*] · etching (after J. Kirkwood), NPG

Lord, Thomas (1755–1832), founder of Lord's cricket ground and businessman, was born on 23 November 1755 at Thirsk, Yorkshire, the son of William Lord, a labourer from a Roman Catholic family. Lord's ancestors had suffered for their allegiance to the Jacobite cause and had had their lands sequestered, forcing his father to work as a labourer. The family moved to Diss, Norfolk, where Lord was educated. He then moved to London, and at the age of twenty-one was employed as attendant and bowler at the *White Conduit Cricket Club in Islington.

In 1786 Lord was approached by several members of the club, most notably George Finch-Hatton, later ninth earl of Winchilsea, and Charles Lennox, later fourth duke of Richmond, who suggested that he should find a new

Thomas Lord (1755–1832), by unknown artist

ground for them, because they wanted the privacy of an enclosed ground near the centre of London. They guaranteed to indemnify him against any financial loss. Lord acted on this suggestion, and took out a lease on a 7 acre field on the Portman estate in Marylebone, later Dorset Square. The venture was immediately successful. On 31 May and 1 June 1787 Middlesex beat Essex on Lord's new ground in Dorset Fields. By the end of the 1787 season the White Conduit Club had merged with the new Marylebone Cricket Club. As early as 1788 the Marylebone Cricket Club revised the laws of the game, thus taking on a role it retains to this day.

When the lease ended in 1810, Lord transferred his ground to North Bank, Regent's Park, in order to avoid a greatly increased rent bill, and the MCC moved there in 1811. This venture was short-lived, as the Regent's Canal was cut right through the middle of the pitch. In 1814 Lord moved again, to another site in St John's Wood. The first function to take place in the new headquarters of cricket was a reception for the bishop of London, who had just consecrated the adjacent St John's Wood church. Lord's connection with his ground ceased rather abruptly in 1825. He informed the MCC that he was going to build several houses on the ground, leaving only 150 square yards for cricket. A member of the MCC, William Ward MP, bought the ground for £5000 and saved Lord's from such a fate.

Lord himself was a capable but not an outstanding player. He generally fielded at point and his underhand bowling was formidable. Possibly his best batting performance was scoring 56 for Middlesex against the MCC at Lord's in 1790. Lord did not confine his ventures to cricket. He ran a successful wine business in Marylebone, supplying wine to the royal family, and was a property speculator, buying and selling leases and properties. In 1807 he was made a member of the Marylebone vestry. He was a handsome man, standing 5 feet 9 inches and weighing 12 stone. He possessed a charming personality which enabled him to deal easily with all members of the club.

In 1793 Lord married Amelia Smith, *née* Angell. She came from a well-known north London family, and was the widow of a proctor. They had one son. Lord died at West Meon in Hampshire on 13 January 1832 and was buried there. STEPHEN GREEN, *rev.*

Sources archives, Marylebone Cricket Club, Lord's, London · G. R. C. Harris and F. S. Ashley-Cooper, *Lord's and the M.C.C.* (1914) · P. Warner, *Lord's, 1787–1945* (1946) · T. Lewis, *Double century: the story of MCC and cricket* (1987) · private information (1993) · [A. Haygarth], *Frederick Lillywhite's cricket scores and biographies*, 1 (1862) · J. Pycroft, *The cricket field* (1851)

Archives Marylebone Cricket Club, Lord's, London

Likenesses Morland, portrait, Marylebone Cricket Club, Lord's, London · G. Shepheard, two watercolour sketches, Marylebone Cricket Club, Lord's, London · portrait, Marylebone Cricket Club, Lord's, London [*see illus.*] · silhouette, Marylebone Cricket Club, Lord's, London

Lord, Thomas (*fl.* 1791–1796), ornithologist, was a protégé of the painter the Revd Matthew William Peters RA (1742–1814), and under his 'inspection and patronage' published at London, in folio numbers, from 1791 until 1796, a work entitled *Lord's Entire New System of Ornithology, or, Oecumenical History of British Birds*. This consisted of 114 plates painted and engraved by Lord himself, with a brief descriptive text revised by Dr Dupree, master of Berkhamsted grammar school. The figures were mostly life size, and the book is now very rare. In October 1796 Lord was living at 6 Lambeth Road, near the Obelisk in London.

GORDON GOODWIN, *rev.* YOLANDA FOOTE

Sources T. Lord, *Lord's entire new system of ornithology, or, Oecumenical history of British birds* (1791–6) · *BL cat.* · Royal Society archives

Lord, Thomas (1808–1908), Congregational minister, was born of poor parents at Olney, Buckinghamshire, on 22 April 1808. His father was John Lord and his mother Hannah, *née* Austin. Mainly self-taught, he was apprenticed to a shoemaker. His family moved to Northampton in 1816 where they joined Doddridge Chapel and Thomas began to preach and distribute tracts. He was ordained into the Congregational ministry on 14 October 1834 and was successively pastor at Wollaston, Northamptonshire (1834–45); Brigstock (1845–63); Horncastle, Lincolnshire (1863–6); Deddington, Oxfordshire (1866–73); and Salem, Great Bridge, Staffordshire (1873–9). His resignation from this last post was prompted not by old age but by the economic decline which had hit his congregation hard. From 1879 to 1899 he preached frequently in the West Bromwich area. Lord published a memorial sermon on Sir Arthur de Capel Broke (1859), *Heavenly Light the Christian's Desire* (1861), and *Precept and Practice* (1864). He was one of the founders of the Congregational Total Abstinence Association and the United Kingdom Alliance, and was an active member of the Peace and Liberation societies. He was three times married, his first wife, Elizabeth, *née* Whimple, dying in 1889, and his third wife in 1899. In that year he returned to Horncastle to live with his only daughter, Mrs Hodgett. In his 101st year he was still preaching in Lincolnshire. He died in Horncastle on 21 August 1908.

CHARLOTTE FELL-SMITH, *rev.* IAN SELLERS

Sources *Congregational Year Book* (1909) • *Transactions of the Congregational Historical Society*, 3 (1907–8) • *The Times* (22 Aug 1908)
Likenesses portrait, repro. in *Congregational Year Book*
Wealth at death £151 10*s.* 5*d.*: probate, 7 Sept 1908, *CGPLA Eng. & Wales*

Lorde, Elizabeth (*d.* **1551**), prioress of Wilberfoss, was the daughter of Robert Lorde of Kendal. Her brother, Brian Lorde, migrated to York and established himself as a merchant in the parish of St Michael, Ousebridge, and her sister, Mary Lorde, married George Gale, goldsmith, lord mayor of York in 1534 and 1539. Elizabeth Lorde probably became a nun in the Benedictine priory of Wilberfoss, a few miles east of York, while still very young; in October 1512, following the death of Margaret Easingwold, she became prioress. About this time the convent gained a favourable reputation for educating well-born girls, in 1537 counting Thomas Cromwell's granddaughter among its pupils. The Lorde family forged very close connections with the nunnery; the prioress's niece, Alice Mabel, had joined the community before 1526 and in that year Brian Lorde made his sister one of the supervisors of his will and entrusted her with his daughter, Isabel, together with her portion. Others besides her relatives valued her administrative skills; the chaplain of Wilberfoss, John Watte, in 1537 appointed her the joint executor of his will.

Cromwell's commissioners uncovered no scandals at their visitation early in 1536, and even though with an annual income of a little under £22 it clearly came within the provisions of the first Dissolution Act, the priory was allowed to continue for a further three years. Then on 20 August 1539 Elizabeth Lorde together with her convent of nine nuns surrendered the house to the crown. The prioress herself received a rather generous pension of £8, her nuns pittances of between 33*s.* 4*d.* and £1.

After the dissolution Elizabeth Lorde moved to Goodramgate in York to take up residence in the affluent household of her sister and brother-in-law, Mary and George Gale, mixing on terms of equality with the civic élite. By the time she came to draw up her will on 18 January 1551 she had amassed a sizeable fortune of well over £65 in ready money in addition to a considerable amount of plate which she conferred almost exclusively upon members of her extensive family. She asked to be buried in the lady choir of Holy Trinity, Goodramgate, requesting her executor to distribute £4 for the welfare of her soul. The largest legacy, a silver pot and £20 in money towards her marriage, went to Ursula Gale, with a further £10 to Thomas Gale. She bestowed three gilt standing pieces with covers, three goblets parcel gilt, her silver salt, half a dozen silver spoons and sums of money ranging from £10 to 4 gold angels upon seven sets of cousins, Francis Gale, Robert Peacock and his wife, Ralph Hall, Brian Lorde, John Rokeby and his wife, Christopher Clapham and his wife, and Robert Garbray and his wife, remembering her geographically more distant relative Mabel, the wife of Henry Wilson of Kendal, with a pair of coral beads and a gold sapphire ring.

Despite her concern for her family Elizabeth Lorde had not completely forgotten her previous existence, for she provided 6*s.* 8*d.* apiece to Agnes Barton, Alice Thornton, Joan Andrew, and Margery Browne 'which was sisters with me in the house of Wilberfoss'. She gave the residue of her estate to her executor, her 'loving and kind brother', Alderman George Gale, and was dead before 20 February 1551 when a grant of probate was made (Borth. Inst., prob. reg. 13, pt 2, fol. 705*r–v*). In April 1553 George Gale and his wife bought the site of Wilberfoss Priory for just over £615.

CLAIRE CROSS

Sources confirmation of Elizabeth Lorde's election, Borth. Inst., Abp. reg. 26, fols. 42*v*–43*r* • will, Borth. Inst., prob. reg. 9 [Elizabeth Lorde's brother, Brian Lorde], fol. 368*v* • will, Borth. Inst., prob. reg. 11 [Sir John Watte, chaplain of Wilberfoss], pt 1, fol. 229*r–v* • will, Borth. Inst., prob. reg. 13 [Dame Elizabeth Lorde], pt 2, fol. 705*r–v* • J. W. Clay, ed., *Yorkshire monasteries: suppression papers*, Yorkshire Archaeological Society, 48 (1912), 166–7 • *LP Henry VIII*, 12/2, no. 549; 15, nos. 431, 553 • C. Cross and N. Vickers, eds., *Monks, friars and nuns in sixteenth century Yorkshire*, Yorkshire Archaeological Society, 150 (1995), 543–7 • G. W. O. Woodward, *The dissolution of the monasteries* (1966), 156 • *VCH Yorkshire*, 3.125–6
Wealth at death bequests of a considerable amount of plate; cash in excess of £65: will, Borth. Inst., probate register 13, pt 2, fol. 705*r–v*

Lords appellant (*act.* **1387–1388**), bringers of trial proceedings against royal favourites, numbered five nobles who came together in the autumn of 1387. Their aim was to compel *Richard II to agree to the trial of five of his favourites in the parliament that assembled in February 1388, and which is known as the Merciless Parliament. They were *Thomas of Woodstock, duke of Gloucester (1355–1397), Richard (III) *Fitzalan, fourth earl of Arundel and ninth earl of Surrey (1346–1397), Thomas *Beauchamp, twelfth earl of Warwick (1337x9–1401), Henry, earl of Derby, son of John of Gaunt, duke of Lancaster [*see* Henry IV (1366–1413)], and Thomas (I) *Mowbray, first earl of Nottingham (1366–1399). The accusations that they made against the king's favourites were contained in a document called an appeal of treason, a device borrowed from civil law, and the five lords were thus known as the lords appellant.

The origins of the appellants' coalition probably go back no further than the so-called Wonderful Parliament of October 1386. The three lords who were then prominent in opposition to the crown—Gloucester, Arundel, and Warwick—were not close blood relatives, and although they had all taken part in Richard II's expedition to Scotland in the previous year, they had not served together on military campaigns earlier in the reign. Arundel and Warwick had been members of the commission to reform the royal household in 1381, but otherwise the lords had not worked together in government. Each had his own reasons for hostility to the king and his favourites, but in 1386 they were united by a common wish to call some of his favourites to account. Both Gloucester and Arundel were forceful, not to say overbearing, personalities; Warwick was perhaps a milder man, though not as pathetic and malleable as he tried to portray himself when on trial for his life in 1397. All three, however, had the wealth to command substantial retinues, and extensive influence in those parts of the country where their main estates lay.

Although Gloucester had acquired by marriage the Bohun lands in Essex and elsewhere, he depended for part of his income on exchequer annuities, and he watched with concern as Robert de *Vere, earl of Oxford, and Michael de la *Pole, first earl of Suffolk, used royal favour to enhance their standing in East Anglia. Arundel's criticism of the king had earlier taken the form of a generalized attack on 'evil counsellors', but both he and Gloucester had misgivings about the king's pacific policy towards France. Warwick is more of an enigma: he had not expressed open hostility to those round the king, or criticized policy towards France, but presumably he had silently sympathized with Gloucester and Arundel. He was also, perhaps, unhappy about the rise in influence at court of a member of a cadet branch of his family, John Beauchamp of Holt, who used his favour with the king to aggrandize himself in the west midlands.

When parliament met in October 1386, John of Gaunt was absent in Castile, and the Commons were in hostile mood. The three lords now saw their opportunity to make their will prevail. They argued, according to the author of the continuation of the *Eulogium*, that parliament should deal first with enemies within the realm rather than the threat of invasion from France. By enemies within the realm they probably meant the chancellor, Michael de la Pole, and Robert de Vere, now duke of Ireland: it is possible that the three lords initially had de Vere rather than de la Pole in their sights, but turned their attention to de la Pole when the Commons made it clear that their priority was his dismissal. Gloucester and Arundel's brother, the bishop of Ely, took the lead in pressing the king to agree to the removal and impeachment of de la Pole, while at this stage Warwick was perhaps less forthright in his views. After de la Pole's removal from office Gloucester and Arundel (though not Warwick) were appointed to the commission that was to control the government of the country for one year from 19 November 1386.

Richard II's response to the imposition upon him of the commission was to ask his judges whether it had been lawful, and they replied that those who had coerced him into agreeing to the commission should be punished 'as traitors'. The judges' answers were a threat to the lives and inheritances of Gloucester and Arundel, and they, together with Warwick, determined on a pre-emptive strike against the king and his favourites. Gloucester and Warwick were probably the first of the five lords to take up arms. They assembled their retinues at Harringay, north of London, in mid-November; on 13 November Arundel joined them, and on the following day the three marched to Waltham Cross, where they formally submitted their appeal of treason against de la Pole, de Vere, Alexander *Neville, archbishop of York, Nicholas *Brembre, mayor of London, and Robert *Tresilian, chief justice of the king's bench. Three days later they came into the presence of the king at Westminster and repeated their appeal. The king took both sides under his protection and agreed that the appeal should be heard in the parliament that was due to open on 3 February.

De Vere, however, raised an army in Cheshire to resist the appellants by force. The three original appellants were now joined by the earls of Derby and Nottingham. Both were younger men, who had played no part in the events of the Wonderful Parliament, but who were probably motivated mainly by hostility to de Vere. Nottingham in particular may have thought that de Vere had usurped his own place in Richard II's favour. The five lords marched from London to Huntingdon, and on 12 December moved westwards to intercept de Vere on his march southwards from Cheshire. At Radcot Bridge on 20 December the appellants routed de Vere's army. De Vere himself fled overseas, and the five appellants marched to London, where they confronted Richard in the Tower on 27 December.

Tensions between the appellant lords now revealed themselves. Most sources suggest that the appellants criticized Richard's misgovernment, and insisted on the imprisonment of those appellees who had not fled overseas. Richard, these sources say, eventually agreed under threat of deposition. The Whalley Abbey chronicle, however, suggests that Richard was actually deposed for a few days, and then reinstated: a story that is given further credence by a statement in Gloucester's confession in 1397 that the king had been deposed for two or three days. The story may well be true, and the Whalley chronicler maintains that Richard was reinstated because the appellants could not agree among themselves about who should reign in Richard's place. The earl of Derby (who would eventually become king as Henry IV) seems to have resisted Gloucester's designs on the crown, not least because he and his father had a superior claim as Richard's nearest male heirs.

If the first crack in the appellant coalition appeared during these last days of December 1387, the five put on a ceremonial show of unity at the opening of parliament on 3 February 1388, when the five lords entered the White Hall at Westminster arm in arm and dressed in cloth of gold. The appeal of treason was then read. In essence, the charges against the five favourites alleged that they had accroached royal power and used their influence over the king to persuade him to adhere to their unwise counsel and to procure favours for themselves. The appeal itself was a device fraught with procedural difficulties. It had not been used hitherto as a means of initiating prosecutions in parliament, and in any case it was doubtful whether the charges against the favourites amounted to treason under the statute of 1352. That statute, however, allowed the king in parliament to decide whether acts that were not specifically defined as treasonable under the statute were in fact treason, and the appellants argued that 'in so high a crime as is claimed in this appeal, which touches the person of our … lord the king and the estate of the whole realm, perpetrated by persons who are peers of the realm, with others', the trial should take place in parliament and according to the law and course of parliament (*RotP*, 3.236). The lords agreed, and parliament proceeded to hear the appeal.

De la Pole, de Vere, and Neville had fled overseas; they were found guilty in their absence, and de la Pole and de Vere were sentenced to death and forfeiture of their lands and possessions; Neville was sentenced to loss of his temporalities. Tresilian, who had sought sanctuary in Westminster Abbey, was also sentenced to death and forfeiture: he was later dragged out of sanctuary and executed. Brembre was the only appellee who could be tried in person, and the appellants found difficulty in procuring his conviction. He sought, but was denied, trial by battle, and in the end the appellants resorted to the device of asking the mayor and aldermen of London whether he was guilty. They replied that he probably was, and this was sufficient for the appellants to have him executed. Thus far the appellants had met little resistance; but when they turned to the impeachment of other royal officials and chamber knights, the strains within the group began to show once again. There was little disagreement over the fate of the judges and three chamber knights, Sir John Beauchamp of Holt, Sir James Berners, and Sir John Salisbury. All were sentenced to death, though the death sentence on the judges was later commuted to exile in Ireland. A bitter argument broke out, however, over the fate of the third chamber knight to be impeached, Sir Simon *Burley. He was found guilty of offences which amounted to exercising undue influence over the king and was sentenced to death; but Derby and Nottingham, together with the duke of York, tried to win a reprieve for him, perhaps out of respect for his age and his status as a member of the Order of the Garter, and perhaps also because he was apparently in poor health. York and Gloucester publicly called each other a liar, and both Richard and the queen interceded on Burley's behalf, but to no avail and he was executed on 5 May.

At the end of the parliament all five appellant lords renewed their oath of homage to the king in another show of unity. They had tried to give the impression that they were acting for the benefit of king and kingdom in bringing the king's evil counsellors to justice; but in reality they were united by little more than hostility to de la Pole, de Vere, and to a lesser extent Neville, Tresilian, and the other judges, Brembre, and some of the chamber knights. The dispute over Burley's fate was the defining moment for the appellants: it exposed even more than Derby's resistance to Gloucester's ambitions in December the fragility of the coalition, and Richard II never forgave Gloucester and Arundel for their insistence that Burley should die.

Gloucester and Arundel, together perhaps with Warwick, retained some responsibility for the supervision of government and for initiatives in foreign policy after the end of the Merciless Parliament, but with the destruction of the favourites their real work was done. Derby and Nottingham appear to have gone their own way after the end of the parliament, and although the period of appellant rule formally came to an end on 3 May 1389, when Richard resumed personal control of government and dismissed Gloucester and Arundel from the council, the five lords did not again act as a group after parliament was dissolved on 4 June 1388. Even when Richard brought those who had opposed him in 1387 and 1388 to justice in parliament in 1397, only Gloucester, Arundel, and Warwick were tried and convicted. Burley's fate still rankled with Richard in 1397, and the part that Gloucester and Arundel had played in it was held against them at the time of their arrest and trial. Derby and Nottingham, however, escaped punishment for their lesser part in the appellant coalition.

ANTHONY TUCK

Sources *RotP*, vol. 3 • L. C. Hector and B. F. Harvey, eds. and trans., *The Westminster chronicle, 1381–1394*, OMT (1982) • *Knighton's chronicle, 1337–1396*, ed. and trans. G. H. Martin, OMT (1995) [Lat. orig., *Chronica de eventibus Angliae a tempore regis Edgari usque mortem regis Ricardi Secundi*, with parallel Eng. text] • M. McKisack, ed., 'Historia, sive, Narracio de modo et forma Mirabilis Parliamenti apud Westmonasterium', *Camden miscellany, XIV*, CS, 3rd ser., 37 (1926) • *Thomae Walsingham, quondam monachi S. Albani, historia Anglicana*, ed. H. T. Riley, 2 vols., pt 1 of *Chronica monasterii S. Albani*, Rolls Series, 28 (1863–4), vol. 2 • F. S. Haydon, ed., *Eulogium historiarum sive temporis*, 3 vols., Rolls Series, 9 (1858–63) • M. V. Clarke, *Fourteenth century studies*, ed. L. S. Sutherland and M. McKisack (1937) • N. Saul, *Richard II* (1997) • A. Goodman, *The loyal conspiracy: the lords appellant under Richard II* (1971) • A. Tuck, *Richard II and the English nobility* (1973) • A. Rogers, 'Parliamentary appeals of treason in the reign of Richard II', *American Journal of Legal History*, 8 (1964), 95–124 • C. Given-Wilson, *The royal household and the king's affinity: service, politics and finance in England, 1360–1413* (1986) • J. G. Bellamy, *The law of treason in England in the later middle ages* (1970)

Lords ordainer (*act.* 1310–1313), group of administrators commissioned in 1310 to reform the realm, numbered twenty-one prelates, earls, and barons. They were elected following the concession by *Edward II on 16 March 1310 that such a body should be created to 'ordain and establish the estate of the king's household and realm' (Rymer, *Foedera*, 2/1, 105). They were: Robert *Winchelsey, archbishop of Canterbury; John *Langton, bishop of Chichester; John of *Monmouth, bishop of Llandaff; Ralph *Baldock, bishop of London; John *Salmon, bishop of Norwich; David Martin (*d.* 1328), bishop of St David's; Simon *Ghent, bishop of Salisbury; Edmund *Fitzalan, earl of Arundel; Gilbert de *Clare, seventh earl of Hertford and eighth earl of Gloucester; Humphrey (VII) de *Bohun, fourth earl of Hereford and ninth earl of Essex; *Thomas, earl of Lancaster; Henry de *Lacy, fifth earl of Lincoln; Aymer de *Valence, earl of Pembroke; John of *Brittany, earl of Richmond; Guy de *Beauchamp, tenth earl of Warwick; Hugh Courtney; Robert Fitzroger; John *Grey, second Lord Grey of Wilton; William le Mareschal; William Martin; and Hugh de Vere.

The making of the ordinances Although it has been suggested that there were 'probably as many "baronial policies" as there were barons', and 'probably as many points of view as there were Ordainers', nevertheless the baronial opposition to Edward II was as united at this point as it ever would be (Prestwich, 'Ordinances', *Politics and Crisis*, 1; Phillips, 31). Indeed, just three days after the king authorized the election of the ordainers, on 19 March 1310, a set of six preliminary ordinances was issued. These were drafted even before the ordainers technically had been elected, and they are generally illustrative of the magnates' long-standing concerns, particularly with the king's favouritism and his irregular financial policies. Along with general calls to protect the franchises of the church and to maintain Magna Carta, these preliminary ordinances are directed at specifics: the king is prohibited from making gifts without the counsel and assent of the ordainers; customs are to be paid into the exchequer to Englishmen so that the king will not need to resort to prises; foreign merchants are to be arrested and their accounts examined. Provision is also made to support the work of the ordainers, in London, throughout the duration of their commission. These six preliminary ordinances reflect the concerns voiced repeatedly since the crisis of 1297, and indeed their language, and it is noteworthy that they would remain essentially intact in the first eight articles of the final ordinances in 1311.

The lords ordainer set about their work at once, and on 29 May 1310 the mayor and aldermen of London were ordered to keep the city safely guarded and to prevent any evil or damage being done to the ordainers. It is difficult to say who took the lead in drafting the ordinances in 1310–11. The earl of Lincoln and the archbishop of Canterbury were both elder statesmen who had been active in the difficult last years of Edward I, and both men were considered influential by contemporary chroniclers. Nevertheless, the well informed author of the *Vita Edwardi secundi* divided the ordainers into two groups: a group of genuine reformers led by the earl of Warwick; and another group that comprised the earls of Hereford, Lancaster, and Pembroke, who were said to be motivated by their hatred for Piers Gaveston, earl of Cornwall, Edward's notorious favourite. These four earls were consistently present together in London on occasions when the ordinances were apparently drafted and seem to have been the core element in framing the document. In August 1310 the earls of Arundel, Hereford, Lancaster, and Pembroke refused to leave their business in London to attend the king's council at Northampton. Similarly, the determination of the ordainers to keep to their task is well illustrated by the fact that the only earls to serve in Scotland with Edward II in 1310–11 were Gaveston, Gloucester, and Warenne. Lincoln, it is true, was serving as keeper of the realm in London, but he threatened to resign this position when on 28 October the king ordered the removal of the exchequer and the benches to York by the following Easter. The ordainers, who would thus have been deprived of expert advice, in contravention of the preliminary ordinances, were said to have dispersed to their own districts following the king's order, but in February 1311 Hereford, Lancaster, Pembroke, and Warwick were all once again together in London—as they still were in July—and it may have been during this period that revisions were made to an earlier draft of the ordinances now preserved in the Durham archives. Although it has been suggested that Archbishop Winchelsey also played an important role in the drafting process, both the earlier and final version of the ordinances are decidedly 'baronial' in character, and what little sign there is of clerical involvement in the authorship of the ordinances may better be attributed to earlier attempts to limit royal authority in the *confirmatio cartarum* of 1297, the *articuli super cartas* of 1300, and the Statute of Stamford of 1309, than to a decisive clerical presence in 1310–11.

The content of the ordinances On 3 August 1311 a draft copy of the ordinances was sent to the king, and on 16 August parliament met, the mayor of London having taken steps to safeguard the ordainers in the city. The ordinances, composed of forty-one clauses, were finally published on 27 September 1311 by the bishop of Salisbury in Archbishop Winchelsey's stead, in the presence of the earls of Arundel, Hereford, Lancaster, Oxford, Pembroke, and Warwick. This was just two days before the commission of the lords ordainer was set to expire. On 11 October the ordinances, sealed with the king's great seal, were sent to the sheriffs for publication. Their primary thrust was aimed at the king and his household, but there was also an important emphasis upon the role of parliament. Parliament was to be regularly summoned (ordinance 29), to give consent for military expeditions (ordinance 9), to consent to any change in coinage (ordinance 30), and to appoint numerous officials including the chancellor, the chief justices of the king's bench and the common pleas, the treasurer, the chancellor and chief baron of the exchequer, the steward of the household, the controller of the wardrobe, the keeper of the privy seal, the keepers of the forests, and the escheators (ordinance 14). There were also articles that called for the abolition of prises (ordinance 10), and new customs (ordinance 11), and for restrictions on royal pardons (ordinance 28), privy seal writs (ordinance 32), and the jurisdiction of the household steward and marshal (ordinance 26). Most noteworthy to contemporary chroniclers and presumably the general populace, however, were the personal clauses of the ordinances, which called for the removal of evil counsellors such as the Frescobaldi, the Beaumonts, and of course Gaveston (ordinance 13, 20–23). The *Vita Edwardi secundi* claims that 'there was one of those Ordinances that more than the rest distressed the king, to wit the expulsion of Piers Gaveston and his exile' (Denholm-Young, 17). In this context it may be significant that in late November 1311 a supplementary set of ordinances, sometimes referred to as the household ordinances, was issued, which specifically names twenty-seven persons to be excluded from the king's household, the majority of whom had connections to Gaveston. This supplement is generally thought to have been the work of the earls of Lancaster and Warwick alone, hereafter the most stalwart supporters of the ordinances.

The implementation of the ordinances The implementation of the ordinances was vigorously resisted by Edward II, although they dominated political thought and activity throughout the next decade. As early as 12 January 1312 the king issued a proclamation that the ordinances should be observed only in so far as they were not prejudicial to him. Later in the year Edward sent a delegation to the pope at the Council of Vienne requesting that the ordinances be annulled if they should prove prejudicial to the crown, and similar embassies were sent to the king of France as well later in 1312. By this time, of course, Gaveston had been captured and executed by the barons, and England was poised on the edge of civil war. In the protracted negotiations between the king and his magnates that stretched through to November 1313, Edward II determinedly avoided confirmation of the ordinances. This policy, however, proved impracticable after the disaster at Bannockburn (24 June 1314) and with both his Scottish and domestic policy in disarray, the king was forced to allow the baronial reforms to be implemented.

The earl of Lancaster now emerged fully as the leader of the baronial opposition, and in the York parliament of September 1314 and the Westminster parliament of January 1315 he insisted on the enforcement of the ordinances, to which the king now conceded. Most dramatically, the resumption of all royal grants made since March 1310 was ordered. Other ordinances were also observed with greater rigidity: the wool custom of London was surrendered by a French merchant; commissions for perambulation of the forests were issued; the king's wardrobe drew its revenues from the exchequer. This pattern was further accelerated following the Lincoln parliament of January 1316, in which Lancaster was made the king's chief councillor, but by late in that year tensions between the king and earl had again arisen, ostensibly over the king's unwillingness to enforce the ordinances. Indeed, in December 1316 the king sent a delegation including the earl of Pembroke to the pope, apparently once again seeking the annulment of the ordinances. Tensions were relieved somewhat by the treaty of Leake in August 1318, by which a standing council was formed to provide or deny assent to all actions taken outside parliament, and which again reaffirmed the ordinances.

Repeal of the ordinances and their legacy A Scottish failure, this time the siege of Berwick, along with the rise of another unpalatable royal favourite, this time the younger Despenser, led to another crisis and a further showdown between the king and the earl of Lancaster, who continued to demand strict adherence to the ordinances at every point. This crisis would lead to civil war and to the execution of Lancaster following his defeat at Boroughbridge (16 March 1322). Edward II followed up his greatest victory by having the ordinances repealed in parliament by the Statute of York in 1322. Indeed, not only were they repealed, it was decreed that never again was the royal power to be so constrained. The Statute of York has been the source of considerable debate, particularly with regard to its language concerning the role of parliament. In the context of the ordinances of 1311, however, the Statute of York was clearly an effort to reset the political clock to the *status quo* before 1310. Interestingly, several 'good points' of the ordinances were preserved, taken either directly or indirectly from the legislation of 1311. As a programme, however, the ordinances ceased to exist. Nevertheless, the ordinances and the lords ordainer would be remembered and invoked by subsequent opponents of royal authority, as in the crisis of 1340. Thomas of Lancaster, the individual most closely associated with the ordinances, was to become the focus of a popular cult and an attempt at canonization. The work of the lords ordainer was the watershed of the reign of Edward II.

J. S. HAMILTON

Sources A. Luders and others, eds., *Statutes of the realm*, 11 vols. in 12, RC (1810–28), vol. 1, pp. 157–67 • N. Denholm-Young, ed. and trans., *Vita Edwardi secundi* (1957) • Rymer, *Foedera*, new edn • J. C. Davies, *The baronial opposition to Edward II* (1918) • M. Prestwich, 'A new version of the ordinances of 1311', *BIHR*, 57 (1984), 189–203 • M. Prestwich, 'The ordinances of 1311 and the politics of the early fourteenth century', *Politics and crisis in fourteenth-century England*, ed. J. Taylor and W. Childs (1990) • J. R. Maddicott, *Thomas of Lancaster, 1307–1322: a study in the reign of Edward II* (1970) • J. R. S. Phillips, *Aymer de Valence, earl of Pembroke, 1307–1324: baronial politics in the reign of Edward II* (1972) • J. H. Trueman, 'The personnel of medieval reform, the English lords ordainers', *Mediaeval Studies*, 21 (1959) • J. H. Trueman, 'The privy seal and the English ordinances of 1311', *Speculum*, 31 (1956), 611–25 • J. S. Hamilton, *Piers Gaveston, earl of Cornwall, 1307–1312: politics and patronage in the reign of Edward II* (1988) • T. F. Tout, *The place of the reign of Edward II in English history: based upon the Ford lectures delivered in the University of Oxford in 1913*, rev. H. Johnstone, 2nd edn (1936)
Archives BL, Cotton Charter 43 D 18 • Canterbury Cathedral, MS K 11 • Ordinances of 1311

Loreburn. For this title name *see* Reid, Robert Threshie, Earl Loreburn (1846–1923).

Lorimer, David Lockhart Robertson (1876–1962), diplomatist and linguist, was born in the Free Church manse, Strathmartine, near Dundee, on 24 December 1876, the son of Robert Lorimer, a minister of the Free Church of Scotland, and his wife, Isabella Lockhart Cornish Robertson. His elder brother was John Gordon *Lorimer (1870–1914), who became an administrator in India. Educated at Dundee high school, David Lorimer entered the Indian army in 1896. After seven years attached to different regiments he was seconded to the political department of the government of India, and spent most of the rest of his professional life as a vice-consul, consul, or political agent in various parts of the Persian Gulf and (after 1920) on the north-west frontier of British India. In the course of his time as vice-consul for Khuzestan (at Ahvaz between 1903 and 1909) he developed a close friendship with the semi-independent ruler of the region, the wali of Posht-e-Kuh, which proved politically useful at the time of the British occupation of Iraq in the First World War.

After marrying Emily Overend [*see below*] in 1910, Lorimer served in Bahrain, Kerman, and ʿAmara in lower Iraq between 1911 and 1920; he was created CIE in 1917. After the war the Lorimers returned to India, where David Lorimer spent four years as political agent in Gilgit. He retired from the service in 1927, and the Lorimers spent most of the rest of their lives in Welwyn Garden City. They had an adopted daughter.

David Lorimer is best known for a number of descriptive grammars of some of the languages spoken in or around the north-west frontier of India, the area that is now northern Kashmir and northern Pakistan. As one of his obituarists remarked, 'From the very beginning of his career the study of the life and languages of the various peoples among whom chance led him to work provided him with a "spare time" interest which was to last throughout his life' (Mackenzie, 181–2). Either by himself or with his wife, he published a dozen books of descriptive grammar and dialectology on Pashtu (1915), Badakshani and Bakhtiari (1919), Dumaki (1939), Werchikwar (1962), and Burushaski (3 vols., 1935 and 1938), a 'philologically unconnected language' (ibid.). He was awarded one of the first Leverhulme research fellowships to visit Hunza to work on Burushaski from 1933 to 1935.

Lorimer was a member of the Norwegian Academy of Science and Letters and, jointly with his wife, was awarded the Burton medal of the Royal Asiatic Society in 1948. During the Second World War he assisted with postal censorship, and also became associated with the School of Oriental and African Studies of the University of London, which appointed him an honorary fellow in 1953. Lorimer died in Queen Victoria Memorial Hospital, Welwyn Garden City, on 26 February 1962. He bequeathed his large collection of linguistic materials, slides, photographs, cine films, and other materials to the library of the School of Oriental and African Studies (PP MS 60), where it remains. The University of Copenhagen published a three-volume study on Bahktiari ethnography, poetry, and linguistics based on this collection: *West Iranian Dialect Materials: from the Collection of D. L. Lorimer*, edited by F. Vahman and G. S. Asatrian (1987–95).

Lorimer had been predeceased by his wife, **Emily Martha Lorimer** [*née* Overend] (1881–1949), who was born in Dublin on 10 August 1881, the daughter of Thomas George Overend (1846–1915), county court judge and recorder of Londonderry. Educated at Alexandra School and Alexandra College, Dublin, she graduated from the Royal University of Ireland in 1904 with first-class honours in French and German. After studying in Paris and Göttingen she entered Somerville College, Oxford, and took first-class honours in German in 1906, remaining there as tutor in Germanic philology until her marriage to David Lorimer. She collaborated in his work on Persian dialects and the languages of the north-west frontier of India.

During the First World War, Emily Lorimer was director of the Red Cross missing and wounded enquiry department in Egypt. In 1916 Emily and David Lorimer were posted to Mesopotamia: while her husband was political officer at ʿAmara, Emily edited the *Basra Times* (1916–17). In 1917 she was mentioned in dispatches from Mesopotamia and was appointed OBE in the same year. On their return to England from India in 1927, she became a deputy commissioner of the Girl Guides (1927–30) and spent a year (1930–31) as acting warden of Bedford College House, University of London. She was correspondent for *The Times* on the expedition with her husband to Hunza (1933–5), of which she wrote a vivid account for the general reader entitled *Language Hunting in the Karakoram* (1939). She translated numerous German works (publishing under the name Emily Overend Lorimer), including Hitler's *Mein Kampf* which appeared as a Penguin Special, *What Hitler Wants* (1939). Like her husband she worked during the Second World War on postal censorship. She died in the Cottage Hospital, Welwyn Garden City, on 10 June 1949.

PETER SLUGLETT

Sources D. N. Mackenzie, *Journal of the Royal Asiatic Society* (1962), 181–2 • *The Times* (27 Feb 1962) • A. Wilson, *Loyalties: Mesopotamia, 1914 to 1917: a personal and historical record* (1930) • *WWW* • D. N. Mackenzie, note accompanying PP MS 60, SOAS • *Somerville College register, 1879–1971* (1976) • matriculation records, Oxf. UA

Archives BL OIOC, corresp. and papers, MS Eur. D 1168 • BL OIOC, family corresp., MS Eur. F 177 • SOAS, notebooks and papers relating to his linguistic studies

Wealth at death £27,398 2*s*. 8*d*.: probate, 3 July 1962, *CGPLA Eng. & Wales* • £1184 10*s*.—Emily Overend Lorimer: probate, 22 Oct 1949, *CGPLA Eng. & Wales*

Lorimer, Emily Martha (1881–1949). *See under* Lorimer, David Lockhart Robertson (1876–1962).

Lorimer, (Elizabeth) Hilda Lockhart (1873–1954), classical scholar, was born at 38 India Street, Edinburgh, on 30 May 1873, the eldest daughter of the Revd Robert Lorimer (1840–1925), minister of the Free Church of Scotland at Mains and Strathmartine, Forfarshire, and his wife, Isabella Lockhart Cornish Robertson (1849–1931). She was the second of eight children; her two eldest brothers became distinguished oriental scholars and a third, William, became professor of Greek at St Andrews and translated the New Testament into Scots. She was educated at Dundee high school and, 1889–93, at University College, Dundee, earning a first-class BA (London). In 1893 she won an open scholarship to Girton College, Cambridge, and three years later was placed in the first class of the (old) classical tripos. From the Michaelmas term 1896 she was appointed fellow and classical tutor at Somerville College, Oxford, where she remained for the rest of her career. On resigning in 1934 as classical tutor she was instead appointed tutor in classical archaeology and, for five years, Lady Carlisle research fellow. After her retirement in 1939 the college made her an honorary fellow. From 1920 she shared with Professor John Myres in the teaching of Homeric archaeology, in which she was from 1929 to 1937 university lecturer. She occupied a distinguished place in the Oxford classical establishment, illustrating in her own person the distance travelled since her appointment in 1896 when, advised by the college to consult Professor Pelham (the Roman historian) about her research, he told her it was not necessary (or, he indicated, desirable) for her to take up any, since all advanced teaching would be provided by friends from the men's colleges. After her retirement she moved to 26b Norham Gardens, Oxford, but was a frequent and always welcome visitor at Somerville.

Hilda Lorimer took an Oxford MA at the first opportunity, in 1920, and went specially to Girton to take her Cambridge MA in 1948, when degrees were at last open to women. She valued highly her ties with Girton and often stayed there in the long vacation. She was made honorary fellow in 1951, and left her library to the college.

Hilda Lorimer was no armchair scholar. In 1901–2 she travelled widely in Greece, as (Somerville) Pfeiffer student at the British School at Athens; it was at this time that she studied under W. Dörpfeld, for whom her admiration never wavered. Later she assisted W. A. Heurtley in his excavations in northern Greece, in 1927 at Boubousti and in 1930 at Servia, and again in 1931–2 at Aetos in Ithaca, where she undertook much of the publication (see *Annual of the British School at Athens*, 33, 1932–3, 22–36). In 1934 she spent part of a term's leave of absence excavating with S. Benton in Zakynthos. In spite of the copious and important results of the series of Ithaca excavations she never wavered from her belief in Dörpfeld's identification of Homeric Ithaca with Levkas.

Hilda Lorimer's interests were not confined to Greece, and her travels included Turkey, Albania, and the Slav lands which became Yugoslavia. In 1917 she went to Salonica to work as nursing orderly in the Scottish Women's Hospital. In 1918 her services were requisitioned by the Foreign Office historical department; with R. D. G. Laffan she produced *The Slovenes* (1920) and *The Yugoslav Movement*, and later contributed to volumes on *Yugoslavia* (1923) and *The History of Serbia up to 1914* in the Nations of Today series.

Scholarship was Hilda Lorimer's life; the acquisition of knowledge was her passion, her use of it meticulous. Articles published from 1912 ('Dress in Homer') to 1947 ('The hoplite phalanx') show how Homeric studies came to preoccupy her, and the breadth of her knowledge is fully displayed in *Homer and the Monuments*, published, after wartime delays, in 1950. This majestic work demonstrates both her mastery of all the evidence bearing upon the *Realien* of the Homeric poems and its dispassionate discussion. Its results and conclusions were described by Myres in *Homer and his Critics* (1958) as 'perhaps as near to historical truth as it is possible to go'.

Hilda Lorimer seems never to have used her first name. The family knew her as Hiddo; in Oxford she was affectionately termed Highland Hilda. She was slight but wiry, and her Scottishness was never in doubt. She is remembered as 'sitting very erect, on a bicycle with high handlebars, still (at 76) attracting the attention of the casual passer-by'. The beauties of landscape and the study of birds meant much to her. Colleagues delighted in her witty and learned conversation; her pupils found her rigorous standards tempered by kindness and understanding. She died in hospital in Oxford on 1 March 1954.

HELEN WATERHOUSE

Sources K. T. Butler and H. I. McMorran, eds., *Girton College register, 1869–1946* (1948) · M. Hartley and S. Benton, *Girton Review* (1954), 26–9 · M. Hartley, *Somerville College Report* (1954), 24–7 · correspondence, Somerville College Archive, Oxford · private information (2004) · P. Adams, *Somerville for women: an Oxford college, 1879–1993* (1996)

Archives Somerville College, Oxford | Bodl. Oxf., corresp. with Sir J. L. Myres

Likenesses J. A. Grant, portrait, after 1954 (posthumous; after photograph), Somerville College, Oxford

Wealth at death £7581 16*s*. 9*d*.: confirmation, 17 April 1954, *CCI*

Lorimer, James (1818–1890), jurist, was born at Aberdalgie, Perthshire, on 4 November 1818, the son of James Lorimer (1779–1868), factor of the earl of Kinnoul, and Janet Webster (1776–1866). Initially educated at home, he

James Lorimer (1818–1890), by John Henry Lorimer, 1890

briefly entered Perth grammar school, before matriculating with his only brother, Thomas W. Lorimer, in the University of Edinburgh in 1834. After a year of study, he was apprenticed to a merchant in Glasgow with the ultimate intention that he should pursue a career in India. Thomas was apprenticed to a writer in Perth. A breakdown in James's health in Glasgow resulted in his return to Aberdalgie to recuperate. In 1837 he resumed study in Edinburgh, completing the regular curriculum in 1840. The greatest influence on him was the class in moral philosophy of Sir William Hamilton, who combined a critical reading of Kantianism with the Scottish philosophy of common sense.

Recurrence of the asthma that was to plague Lorimer all his life led to his going abroad to study in September 1840. He travelled first to Geneva where he remained until September 1841, attending classes in natural sciences at the Academy, before embarking on a tour of Italy and Germany. He next intended to study law in Berlin. After an interview with the great scholar F. C. von Savigny which left Lorimer embarrassed as he had not appreciated the importance of the professor to whom he had been given a letter of introduction, he spent the winter of 1841–2 learning German, and started classes in the spring, studying Roman law with G. F. Puchta, chemistry with E. Mitscherlich, and legal philosophy with Adolf Trendlenburg. Of the three Lorimer considered that the most influential on him were the lectures in chemistry. He spent the summer session of 1843 at the University of Bonn, attending F. C. Dahlmann's lectures on politics and history, and G. Kinkel's on art history. He returned home to Scotland in the autumn to matriculate as a law student in the University of Edinburgh. After two sessions, on 8 March 1845, he was admitted to the faculty of advocates. He intended his membership of the faculty to help him pursue an essentially literary career. He was active in the Speculative Society. The patronage of Lord Kinnoul secured him the sinecure post of lyon clerk in 1848: a deputy carried out the duties.

With a weak voice and continuing poor health, Lorimer had only a slight practice at the bar, and, although he sometimes acted as sheriff substitute of Midlothian, he devoted his energies to a variety of other interests such as *Chambers's Encyclopaedia*. From the late 1840s and early 1850s he started to write in the *Quarterly Journal of Agriculture*, the *North British Review*, and the *Edinburgh Review*. Putting his legal knowledge to use he wrote a *Handbook of the Law of Scotland*. Aimed at the general public, and first published in 1859, this reached a sixth edition in 1894. Lorimer's interest in constitutional reform led to *Political Progress not Necessarily Democratic* in 1857 and *Constitutionalism of the Future* in 1865. He favoured complex voting systems in which individuals would have votes linked to various qualifications. He corresponded on these issues with a number of individuals including J. S. Mill, whose work on representative government he discussed in the *North British Review* (November 1861). By 1851 he felt sufficiently secure in his literary career to marry and on 22 December that year he married Hannah (1835–1916), daughter of John Riddel Stodart, writer to the signet, and Jemima Henrietta Brown. The couple had three sons and three daughters, the most noted of whom were the artist, J. H. Lorimer RSA, and the architect R. S. *Lorimer ARSA (1864–1929). One important fruit of Lorimer's literary labours was his election as a fellow of the Royal Society of Edinburgh in 1861.

In the 1850s the agitation for reform of the Scottish universities that had existed since the royal commission in the 1820s culminated in the Universities (Scotland) Act of 1858. Having first written on the need for reform in the *North British Review* in 1850, Lorimer played a notable part as secretary of the Association for the Extension of the Scottish Universities which he founded in 1853. He also served on the committee of the faculty of advocates that proposed radical new requirements for admission in 1854. Lorimer was critical of the existing Scottish universities as being merely an extension of high school. He considered they should be centres of teaching and original research that promoted the creation of an educated professional élite which could lead the country. The influence of what R. D. Anderson has called 'the neo-humanist ideal of the German universities' (Anderson, 60) is evident in this. Lorimer most clearly expounded these views in *The Universities of Scotland, Past, Present, and Possible* in 1854, and in the *Edinburgh Review* in 1858.

Owing much to Lorimer, reform of the faculties of law favoured a broad liberal approach to legal education. The regius chair of public law and the law of nature and nations in the University of Edinburgh was accordingly revived in 1862 with Lorimer appointed to it through the influence of Sir George Cornewall Lewis. Here Lorimer found his métier and exerted a profound influence, even if he was perhaps not the best of teachers. His class started with an account of the law of nature, and then moved on to public international law and next to private international law. His account of the last was much influenced by F. C. von Savigny. It was Lorimer's practice to begin each year with a special lecture on some topic of current interest, and many of these lectures, which were often separately published at the time as pamphlets or in periodicals and sometimes reported in the Edinburgh newspapers, were collected and published posthumously in 1890 as *Studies National and International*.

The first part of Lorimer's course resulted in his *Institutes of Natural Law* in 1872. This reached a second edition in 1880 and was reprinted in Germany in 1987. Rejecting the historical school and the legal positivism and utilitarianism of Jeremy Bentham and John Austin no less than he rejected the Kantian categorical imperative, Lorimer, following the German Karl C. F. Krause, founded law scientifically in certain universal facts of human nature. He emphasized the autonomy of the individual, by which he meant that one was able to find within oneself the rules of nature that had to be obeyed. In this he showed the influence, as well as of Krause, of his old teacher Adolf Trendlenburg, who also had emphasized that one should view one's ethical life as the result of one's nature as a whole. This led Lorimer to reject any distinction between ethics and law. Moreover, this view of Trendlenburg, reinforced by a reading of Spinoza, led Lorimer to the view that every natural thing had as much right by nature as it had power to enforce. This *de facto* principle led him to the view that there was a natural right to aggression. While to some extent undoubtedly influenced through Hamilton by the Scottish school of common sense, Lorimer in reality developed a complex system of natural law derived from contemporary German *Naturrecht*, but rejecting a foundation of natural law in mind or reason. Natural law realized in time or place was 'positive law', by which Lorimer meant (rather than the common meaning) the idealized law best suited to the society. It was the duty of legislators and judges to turn this positive law into enacted law.

Lorimer's account of public international law was founded on these views of natural law, and thus differed radically from that of many of his contemporaries in Britain. He was therefore roundly criticized by the English positivists. Sir Frederick Pollock in particular made a notable attack on his mode of theorizing. For Lorimer, international law was the branch of positive law (in his special sense) by which the freedom of different nations was realized through the reciprocal recognition and enforcement of their real powers. Lorimer thus applied to states his views of the autonomy of individuals, with a similar justification of aggression. Though criticized for cloudy abstractions, Lorimer in fact put considerable intellectual effort into thinking out the institutions necessary for a system of international law. He proposed their creation through an international treaty under which there would be a proportional reduction of national armed forces which would preserve the balance of power but leave money in states' hands to fund an international government with legislative, judicial, executive, and financial powers. Authority to make decisions was to be weighted in favour of the great powers, since they would have to implement them. This aspect of his teaching was published in two volumes in 1883–4 as *Institutes of the law of nations: a treatise of the jural relations of separate political communities*.

Lorimer continued to campaign energetically for the further improvement of the Scottish universities and legal education. His active public presence alone achieved much in this respect, especially for his own university and faculty. This ultimately has proved to be of more lasting importance than his scholarly contributions. While his attempt to work out an institutional structure for international law still arouses interest, his theories of natural law and his approach to national and international law are superseded. His *de facto* principle would now be rejected, as would his right of aggression and his often explicitly racist opinions that some societies are progressive and others degenerative.

Though Lorimer was awarded the honorary degree of LLD by the University of Glasgow (where, before the institution of a public law lectureship, he had lectured for several summers) in 1882, he generally achieved a greater reputation in continental Europe than in the United Kingdom. He was awarded another honorary doctorate by the University of Bologna in its anniversary year of 1888, while an abridged version of his work on international law—translated into French by Lorimer's close associate the Belgian professor E. Nys—was published in Brussels in 1885. This French version was translated into Spanish by A. L. Lopez Coterilla and published in Madrid in 1888. In 1890 Nys published a translation in abridgement of Lorimer's work on natural law. With Nys, Lorimer was one of the founders of the Institute of International Law in 1873, devoting considerable time to its activities, and through it he became acquainted with many scholars of similar interests in other European countries. He was also honoured by appointments as corresponding member of the Academy of Jurisprudence of Madrid, honorary member of the imperial universities of St Petersburg and Moscow, and member of the Royal Academy of Belgium.

For the sake of his always precarious health, Lorimer preferred to spend his summers outside Edinburgh. On his father's death in 1868 he inherited the small estate of Kellyfield near Dundee. This was too far for him to use regularly in the summers and in 1878 he leased Kellie Castle in Fife, devoting many years to its restoration. He died at his home, 1 Bruntsfield Crescent, Edinburgh, of pleurisy and pneumonia on 13 February 1890.

JOHN W. CAIRNS

Sources R. Flint, 'Professor Lorimer', *Juridical Review*, 2 (1890), 113–21 • 'The late Professor Lorimer', *Journal of Jurisprudence*, 34 (1890), 132–9 • 'The late Professor Lorimer's services to jurisprudence and legal education', *Journal of Jurisprudence*, 34 (1890), 118–24 • P. J. Hamilton Grierson, 'The *de facto* principle in jurisprudence', *Juridical Review*, 2 (1890), 245–55 • U. Edin. L., MS Gen 103 • [W. M. Watson], ed., *The history of the Speculative Society, 1764–1904* (1905) • R. D. Anderson, *Education and opportunity in Victorian Scotland: schools and universities*, [new edn] (1989)

Archives Kellie Castle, Fife, artefacts • U. Edin. L., papers | NL Scot., letters to Alexander Campbell Fraser

Likenesses J. H. Lorimer, oils, 1878, U. Edin. • drawing, 1878, U. Edin. • J. H. Lorimer, oils, 1890, Scot. NPG [*see illus.*] • T. & R. Annan, engraving (after oil painting? by J. H. Lorimer), repro. in J. Lorimer, *Studies national and international* (1890) • W. Hole, etching, NPG; repro. in *Quasi cursores portraits of … professors of the University of Edinburgh* (1884), 171 • photograph, repro. in Flint, 'Professor Lorimer', facing p. 113

Wealth at death £19,123 8*s*. 3*d*.: confirmation, 24 March 1890, *CCI* • £2460 12*s*. 6*d*.: additional estate, 19 May 1917, *CCI*

Lorimer, John Gordon (1870–1914), administrator in India, was born at 6 Woodside Place, Glasgow, on 14 June 1870, the son of Robert Lorimer, a minister of the Free Church of Scotland, and his wife, Isabella Lockhart Cornish Robertson. David Lockhart Robertson *Lorimer was his younger brother. While an undergraduate at Edinburgh University, Lorimer was selected for the Indian Civil Service, and subsequently spent a year at Christ Church, Oxford (1889–90), following the course for Indian Civil Service probationers. He served as assistant commissioner in various parts of the Punjab between 1891 and 1897, and held a number of other administrative positions, mostly on the north-west frontier until his appointment to the foreign department of the government of India in Simla, where he served briefly from 1899 to 1900 and then between 1904 and 1908. On 8 October 1903, while on leave in Edinburgh, he married Marian Agnes Maclean (*b*. 1875/6), daughter of George Campbell Maclean, secretary of the Scottish Amicable Assurance Society; they had two daughters.

Lorimer is known principally for his massive compilation in six volumes entitled *Gazetteer of the Persian Gulf, Oman and Central Arabia*, published by the government of India in 1908 and 1915, based on 'personal enquiries carried out between 1902 and 1906' (Wilson, 79). The *Gazetteer*, republished in 1970, is part geographical and navigational handbook, part historical survey, and part detailed account of Britain's relations with the Ottomans and the other political authorities in Arabia and the Gulf. It is the fullest account of the state of knowledge of the region in the late nineteenth and early twentieth centuries, and as such is still an important tool for researchers. Its principal drawback, noted by a leading Russian scholar, is that Lorimer does not always quote his sources, so that it is not clear whether he is relying on the published work of travellers or on less publicly accessible reports from British consular and other agents (Vassiliev, 18). In that sense the *Gazetteer* needs to be supplemented by the various works by his contemporary, J. A. Saldanha, such as *Précis of Koweit Affairs, 1896–1904* (Simla, 1904) and *Précis of Nejd Affairs, 1804–1904* (Simla, 1904). The *Gazetteer* remained 'on the "secret" list until 1930 when it was declassified, but marked "for official use only"' (Winstone, 58).

In 1909 the foreign department of the government of India appointed Lorimer political resident in Turkish Arabia, stationed at Baghdad; in April 1911 he became consul-general. Like his friend and contemporary Captain Shakespear, Lorimer felt that Britain should take due note of the weakening Ottoman position in northern Arabia and commit itself more firmly to the rising star of Ibn Saʿud.

On 9 February 1914 Lorimer died at Bushehr while cleaning a loaded gun: his colleague and contemporary Arnold Wilson noted that his death 'deprived the Government of India of one of its most brilliant servants' (Wilson, 79). In addition to the *Gazetteer*, Lorimer published *Customary Law of the Main Tribes in the Peshawar District* (Lahore, 1899) and *Grammar and Vocabulary of Waziri Pashto* (Calcutta, 1902).

PETER SLUGLETT

Sources *WWW* • A. T. Wilson, *Loyalties: Mesopotamia, 1914–1917* (1930) • A. Vassiliev, *The history of Saudi Arabia* (2002) • H. F. V. Winstone, *The illicit adventure: the story of political and military intelligence in the Middle East from 1898 to 1926* (1982) • b. cert. • m. cert. • J. Foster, *Oxford men, 1880–1892: with a record of their schools, honours, and degrees* (1893)

Lorimer, Peter (1812–1879), minister of the Presbyterian Church of England, born in Edinburgh, was the eldest son of John Lorimer, builder. He was educated at the Royal High School and George Heriot's Hospital in that city, and thereafter proceeded, with a bursary, to the University of Edinburgh in 1827. In 1836 he was ordained minister of the Presbyterian church, River Terrace, London, which was then connected with the Church of Scotland. After the Disruption of 1843 he and his congregation joined the synod at Berwick in 1844. On the establishment of the English Presbyterian College, London, in 1844, he was appointed professor of theology; he became its first principal in 1878. In June 1857 the college of New Jersey conferred on him the degree of DD. From his marriage in 1840 to Hannah Fox (1817–1884) of Whitehaven he had a son, John Archibald, surgeon, of Farnham, Surrey, and a daughter, Annie, the wife of James Austin, barrister. He died on 29 July 1879 at Whitehaven, Cumberland, and was buried in the Grange cemetery at Edinburgh.

Lorimer's Scottish presbyterian background helped shape his approach to church history and to the topics which attracted his attention. His main interest focused on the Scottish Reformation and its leading exponents. As a contribution to tercentenary celebrations of the Reformation in Scotland he published in 1860 *The Scottish Reformation: a Historical Sketch*, exploring the subject through the careers of such early reformers as Patrick Hamilton, Sir David Lindsay, Alexander Alesius, Alexander Seton, Henry Forret, George Wishart, and John Knox. He drew attention, too, to the numerous early protestant exiles who settled in England, Germany, and Denmark, and to their contribution to the Reformation on the continent. Earlier, in 1857, his study *Precursors of Knox*, covering similar ground, attached priority to the careers of Hamilton, 'first martyr', Alesius, 'first academic theologian', and Lindsay, 'first poet' of the Scottish Reformation. In that volume Lorimer utilized fresh material by Alesius on Hamilton preserved in the library at Wolfenbüttel, and he dedicated the volume to Thomas M'Crie (1797–1875), professor of church history and systematic theology in the London college of the English Presbyterian church and son of the Scottish presbyterian church historian of the same name. Lorimer's *John Knox and the Church of England* (1875), his most significant historical work, incorporated fresh source material on Knox's relations with his congregation at Berwick, his 'Memorial' to the privy council on Edward VI's second prayer book, and contacts with English puritans uncovered among the Morrice manuscripts in Dr Williams's Library in London. Appended to that work is 'The life and death of Mr William Whittingham, deane of Durham', printed from Anthony Wood's manuscripts in the Bodleian Library. His encouragement of record scholarship is apparent, too, in his support, as a founding member, for the Wodrow Society, named after the Scottish historian and antiquary Robert Wodrow, and established in Edinburgh in 1841 'for the publication of the works of the fathers and early writers of the Reformed Church of Scotland'.

Lorimer's other works included *Healthy Religion Exemplified in the Life of … Andrew Jack of Edinburgh* (1852), *The Function of the Four Gospels Viewed in Connection with Recent Criticism* (1869), and *A Good and Faithful Servant: Memoir of the Rev Archibald Jack of South Shields* (1871). He also translated from German, with additional notes, G. V. Lechler's *John Wiclif and his English Precursors* (2 vols., 1878) and edited, with notes, M. Stuart's *Critical History of the Old Testament Canon* (1849). He wrote an introduction to the reprint of Thomas Cartwright's *Book of Discipline, or, Directory of Church Government* (1872).

GORDON GOODWIN, *rev.* JAMES KIRK

Sources *The Times* (31 July 1879), 5f • *Edinburgh Courant* (1 Aug 1879), 5 • *BL cat.* • private information (1893) • *CGPLA Eng. & Wales* (1879)

Archives Westminster College, Cambridge | U. Edin. L., letters to David Laing

Wealth at death under £5000: probate, 18 Oct 1879, *CGPLA Eng. & Wales*

Lorimer, Sir Robert Stodart (1864–1929), architect, was born at 21 Hill Street, Edinburgh, on 4 November 1864, the third and youngest son of James *Lorimer (1818–1890), regius professor of public law at Edinburgh University, and his wife, Hannah (1835–1916), daughter of James Riddell Stodart, writer to the signet. J. R. Stodart's father, Robert, was a piano maker, who in 1777 patented the first British grand action, and it was from his maternal side that Lorimer inherited his lifelong passion for music. He first showed enthusiasm for architecture, and for the company of craftsmen, when his father leased and repaired the castle of Kellie, Fife, as a weekend residence in 1878. Educated at Edinburgh Academy and Edinburgh University, he left the latter in 1884 without graduating to enter the office of Robert Rowand Anderson and Hew Montgomerie Wardrop (1856–1887). He stayed there four and a half years. In 1889 he left for London, where he made the acquaintance of John James Stevenson, James Marjoribanks MacLaren, and, slightly later, Richard Norman Shaw. He obtained a place in the office of George Frederick Bodley, who encouraged his love of fine craftsmanship. After a year he moved to the office of MacLaren's successors, William Dunn and Robert Watson, working on the tactful remodelling and extension of the ancient

Sir Robert Stodart Lorimer (1864–1929), by John Henry Lorimer, 1886

house of Glenlyon and on the associated hotel and village of Fortingal, Perthshire. The subtle synthesis of Scottish and English vernacular traditions created by MacLaren, Dunn, and Watson had a profound influence on Lorimer, who developed the theme from 1893 onwards in a remarkable series of roughcast medium-sized houses and cottages built in Colinton, in Midlothian, North Berwick and Gullane, both East Lothian, and elsewhere; the finest example was built at Wayside, St Andrews, Fife, in 1901. These buildings paralleled the work of William Richard Lethaby and Charles Voysey, with whom Lorimer had become more closely associated through election to the Art Workers' Guild in 1897.

Lorimer's return to Edinburgh in 1892 had, however, been primarily to restore the dilapidated sixteenth-century house and garden of Earlshall, Fife (1892–1900), for a friend of his father's, R. W. Mackenzie. In it he applied the same principles as his father had done at Kellie, respecting what existed and avoiding additions as far as practicable. He also designed for Earlshall some very fine marquetry furniture. In 1894 he reconstructed St Marnock's, Dublin, as a handsome house in a symmetrical seventeenth-century style. These led to many commissions for tactful restoration and sympathetic extension later, most notably at Pitkerro, Forfarshire, Craigmyle, Aberdeenshire, and Barton Hartshorn, Buckinghamshire (all 1902), Lympne Castle, Kent (1907), Dunderave, Argyll (1911), and Balmanno, Perthshire (1921); the two last were the finest of the series.

Lorimer's earliest commissions for large houses built completely anew were commuter-belt country houses in England. They included Whinfold, Hascombe, Surrey (1899), the early Lutyens-like High Barn, Godalming, Surrey (1901), and the arts and crafts brick-and-tile Weaponess House, Scarborough, Yorkshire (1902). The largest house he ever built, the rambling neo-Jacobean Brackenburgh, Penrith, Cumberland, a true country house, followed in 1901, and challenged comparison with the very best work of his English contemporaries. Lorimer's first comparable commission in Scotland came in 1903 with Rowallan, Ayrshire, a large house in Scottish sixteenth-century style for Cameron Corbett (Lord Rowallan), which drew themes from the ruined Auchans House near by. The project was curtailed after the death of Corbett's wife, Alice, which resulted in problems with the building which were perhaps never fully resolved. The commission for Ardkinglas, Argyll, for Sir Andrew Noble, followed in 1906, and in it the picturesque but compact style of Lorimer's best medium-sized houses was applied to a really large one. Both these houses were built of carefully crafted rubble, rather self-consciously arts and crafts, but at Briglands, Kinross-shire, where his large addition of 1898 was extended to the scale of a great house for Lord Clyde in 1908, a roughcast treatment was adopted. By far the most successful example of his great houses was the stone-slated Formakin, Renfrewshire (1912–14), 'the purest Scotch I've ever done' (letter to R. S. Dods, Savage, *Edinburgh Craft Designers*, 115), for the collector John A. Holms, in which the ideas behind his unbuilt house for the shipowner Sir William Burrell were more than realized. With its gate lodges, great garden, tower-house-like bothy, farm court, and mill, it is a place of extraordinary magic in which the visitor is left wondering what is old and what is new, when only the farmhouse is ancient. Similar qualities on a much smaller scale were achieved at Laverockdale, Colinton, in 1912.

Although not by temperament a classicist, Lorimer was a successful designer in a late Stuart, early Georgian manner. In 1907–9 he built the Carnegie Library at the University of St Andrews, the only major public commission of his earlier years, and Hill of Tarvit, Fife (1907), a symmetrically fronted house for the collector F. B. Sharp. The Scottish dormered mid-seventeenth-century form originally proposed for that house was subsequently adopted, with asymmetrical elements in the composition, at Woodhill, Forfarshire, and the granite Rhu-na-Haven, Aberdeenshire (both 1908). In the internal remodelling of the great mid-Georgian pile of Galloway House, Wigtownshire (1909), Lorimer achieved a confident early Georgian style not easily distinguished from original work. Similar qualities are to be found in his more extensive remodelling of Midfield, Midlothian, and his finest work in that idiom, the reconstruction of the mid-eighteenth-century Marchmont, Berwickshire, for R. F. McEwan (both 1914–15). Another major remodelling, though in a neo-Jacobean idiom, was the restoration after a fire of the interior of Sir Charles Barry's Dunrobin Castle, Sutherland, for the duke of Sutherland (from 1915).

All Lorimer's larger houses were remarkable for the craftsmanship of their interiors, with rich plasterwork modelled by Thomas Beattie and Sam Wilson, stonecarving by Joseph Hayes, and wrought-iron work by Thomas Hadden. For several he designed superb furniture, often to complement the collections of his clients. His gardens, which were designed with just as much care, were influenced by his friendship with Gertrude Jekyll from 1901 onwards, although only at Whinfold, Surrey, and Barton Hartshorne, Buckinghamshire, was she directly involved. His work attracted a great deal of contemporary attention, notably from Hermann Muthesius (in

Das englische Haus, translated as *The English House*, ed. D. Sharp, 1979) and in *Country Life*.

Lorimer's career as an ecclesiastical architect was at first slow to develop, despite his early success with the church of the Good Shepherd, Edinburgh (1897), which owed more to J. D. Sedding and Harry Wilson than to Bodley. Subsequent commissions were mainly for high-quality woodwork within existing churches, but in 1909 he replaced Thomas Ross as architect of the Thistle Chapel at St Giles's Cathedral, Edinburgh. The chapel is very much in Bodley's manner—tall, slim, and apsed externally with boldly stepped basecourses, and vaulted within. The rich stallwork was executed by Nathaniel Grieve and the brothers W. Clow and A. Clow, working from maquettes by Louis Deuchars. The chapel was a most remarkable revival of medieval crafts. It brought Lorimer a knighthood in 1911 and established his reputation for restoring and refurnishing medieval churches. In 1912 he furnished the choir at Dunblane Cathedral, Perthshire, disregarding the surviving medieval stalls in favour of a richer scheme; in 1915 he was entrusted with the restoration of the burnt-out Whitekirk, East Lothian, and in 1923 with the reinstatement of the divided St John's Church in Perth, and the completion of the choir and tower at Paisley Abbey, Renfrewshire. In his new-build churches he tended to adopt a simpler idiom, most notably at the large red tile-roofed Italianate St Peter's, Edinburgh, for André Raffalovich and Canon John Gray (1906), and at the brick St Andrew's, Aldershot, Hampshire (1926), with a 'pencil' tower of early Scots-Irish type.

Lorimer's absorbing occupation between 1918 and 1927 was the Scottish national war memorial, for whose construction his whole development had prepared him. His first scheme (1919) was for a gothic memorial cloister attached by a low passage to a lofty octagonal shrine crowning the highest point of Edinburgh Castle Rock. This cloister was subsequently (1922) redesigned as a 'hall of the regiments'. But J. S. Richardson, the principal inspector of ancient monuments and a disaffected former assistant of Lorimer's, had a canvas montage built to demonstrate the effect of the shrine on the profile of the castle; and, although Lorimer's scheme was robustly defended by Sir John Burnet, public protest at alteration of the familiar skyline resulted in a complete redesign. The barrack block on the site was recast as the hall, and the shrine reduced to a lower apse. The details are in a very personal, rugged late Scottish gothic with some early Renaissance elements within, and draw inspiration from James V's palace block at Stirling. It was a commission which suffered from having to take account of too much advice, but the craftsmanship was superb, and the concept of the shrine with its suspended figure of St Michael fulfilled the emotional requirements of a national war memorial. The response was popular and immediate. In 1928 Lorimer was made KBE. In parallel with the national war memorial, Lorimer designed a great many local memorials, notably those at Paisley and Galashiels, Selkirkshire, and the naval war memorials at Chatham, Portsmouth, and Plymouth. He also carried out a great deal of good work for the Imperial War Graves Commission in Italy, Germany, Egypt, and Macedonia, although at none of these was he asked to design on a truly monumental scale.

Until 1913 Lorimer had tended to avoid public and commercial buildings, as he disliked being rushed and the fluctuating demand on staff resources. But in that year he was asked to prepare sketch designs for the proposed Scottish Office buildings on Calton Hill, Edinburgh. To his bitter disappointment he was not recommissioned when the project was revived in 1928. But with his first apprentice—by then his partner, John Fraser Matthew (1875–1955)—he designed the University of Edinburgh zoology and animal genetics blocks at King's Buildings, the former austere classical modern, the latter in a more characteristic style (1927–30). The best works of his later years were the classical chapel at Stowe School, Buckinghamshire (1927–8), for the interior of which the Temple of Concord was robbed of its columns, and the Scandinavian gothic St Margaret's Knightswood, Glasgow (1929–30).

On 2 October 1903 Lorimer married Alicia Violet (1875–1940), daughter of Edward Wyld of Denham, Buckinghamshire, with whom he had three sons and a daughter. In the same year he was elected ARSA. Election to ARA followed in 1920, and RSA in 1921. In appearance he was handsome and alert, with large keen eyes of grey-blue. His strength as an architect lay in an obstinate idealism, an instinctive perception of the elements on which the character and psychological effect of a design depended, and his love of fine craftsmanship. Nearly all his work has a lyrical quality, but a very few of his designs are overworked, sometimes from a reluctance to discard designs with which he was dissatisfied and start afresh, sometimes from being called upon to alter and extend what was already as good as it could be. When his plans for his own country house at Auchentrail, Fife, proved unrealizable, he bought and adapted a good late Georgian one nearby at Gibliston.

Lorimer died suddenly following an operation for appendicitis on 13 September 1929 in Edinburgh. His body was cremated and the ashes buried in the family burial-ground at Newburn, Fife. Of Lorimer's sons, Hew became a pupil of Eric Gill and was a distinguished sculptor. An almost complete archive of Lorimer's drawings is held by the Royal Commission on the Ancient and Historical Monuments of Scotland, Edinburgh.

DAVID M. WALKER

Sources P. D. Savage, 'Sir Robert Lorimer', PhD diss., U. Edin., 1973 • P. D. Savage, *Lorimer and the Edinburgh craft designers* (1980) • C. Hussey, *The work of Sir Robert Lorimer* (1931) • F. Deas, 'The work of Sir Robert Lorimer', *RIBA Journal*, 38 (1931–2), 239–49 • L. G. Thomson, 'The late Sir Robert Lorimer and his work', *Quarterly Journal of the Royal Incorporation of Architects in Scotland*, 31 (1929), 63–76 • *The Times* (14 Sept 1929) • m. cert. • E. M. Ripin and others, 'Pianoforte', *New Grove* • private information (2004) [Alfred George Lochhead]

Archives NL Scot., corresp. and papers relating to Scottish national war memorial • NRA, priv. coll., letters and plans for Charleton House • RIBA BAL, office papers • Royal Commission on the Ancient and Historical Monuments of Scotland, Edinburgh, National Monuments Record of Scotland, prints, drawings, and plans • U. Edin. L., corresp. and papers incl. letter-book | PRO

NIre., corresp. with Sir K. MacDonnel • U. Edin. L., letters to R. S. Dods

Likenesses J. H. Lorimer, oils, 1875, Tate collection • J. H. Lorimer, oils, 1876, repro. in Savage, *Lorimer* • J. H. Lorimer, oils, *c*.1883, repro. in Savage, *Lorimer* (1980) • J. H. Lorimer, oils, 1886, Scot. NPG [*see illus.*] • photograph, repro. in Hussey, *Work* • photographs, repro. in Savage, *Lorimer*

Wealth at death £82,134 4*s*. 11*d*.: Scottish confirmation sealed in London, 9 Jan 1930, *CGPLA Eng. & Wales*

Lorimer, Sir William (1844–1922), locomotive engineer and industrialist, was born on 4 November 1844 in Sanquhar, Dumfriesshire, son of William Lorimer, house factor, and Margaret Whigham. Little is known about his family origins and early life in Sanquhar. He attended the local parish school and at the age of fifteen joined the Edinburgh and Glasgow Railway Company, probably as an apprentice or clerk. In 1864 he moved into locomotive engineering as a cashier in the newly founded business of Dübs & Co. This firm became one of the principal locomotive engineering companies in Glasgow, and was founded by Henry Dübs at the Glasgow locomotive works, later known as the Queen's Park works, Polmadie, on the south side of Glasgow. Lorimer made an impression on Dübs and was made his principal assistant in 1867. By 1875 Lorimer was made a partner in the firm and only one year later Dübs died, leaving the business in the hands of his two sons, Henry and Charles, and William Lorimer. As managing partner Lorimer held a key role in the firm with the Dübs sons assuming a lower profile.

In 1874 Lorimer began a long association with the Steel Company of Scotland Ltd. He acted as its general manager, in a caretaker role between 1874 and 1878. He then joined the board, following in the footsteps of Henry Dübs, who had also been a director. From 1878, under the chairmanship of Sir Charles *Tennant, the company went through a period of technical innovation and expansion. However, it was also a period of over-expansion which brought the company close to bankruptcy. When Tennant resigned in 1895 it was Lorimer who took over as chairman and restored business confidence and a measure of stability, in an industry where economic fluctuations and market forces caused uncertainty. He resigned in 1918, but was then given the position of honorary president.

Such qualities of leadership also led to Lorimer's appointment as chairman of the North British Locomotive Company in 1903. This firm was an amalgamation of Sharp Stewart & Co. Ltd, Neilson, Reid & Co., and Dübs & Co., all leading Glasgow companies. Unity in the face of competition, increasing overheads, and declining markets created a company which dominated locomotive engineering in Britain and Europe with a combined workforce of nearly 8000 and a capacity to produce some 600 engines per annum at the Hydepark and Atlas works, Springburn, and at the Queen's Park works, Polmadie. It was typical of Lorimer and his interest in the welfare of his workers that, in order to mark the amalgamation in 1903, he conveyed to trustees a large number of shares in the North British Locomotive Company to provide pensions for aged and infirm workmen.

Despite the dual role which Lorimer fulfilled at the head of two leading Scottish companies, he also devoted much of his time to a wide range of public duties and activities. His interests were wide-ranging over education, politics, and local issues. As an extension of his business interests he was a director of the Glasgow and South Western Railway Company. He was elected a member of the Institution of Engineers and Shipbuilders in Scotland in 1896 and also was a member of the West of Scotland Iron and Steel Institute. From 1900 he was chairman of the Locomotive Manufacturers' Association of Great Britain. As a resident of the south side of Glasgow he took an interest in local issues and was one of the main campaigners in the 1880s to establish a third voluntary hospital on the south side of Glasgow, which resulted in the opening of the Victoria Infirmary in 1890. He was appointed vice-chairman of the board of governors.

Education was also close to his heart and Lorimer served on various bodies. He was appointed a governor of the Royal Technical College of Glasgow, serving on its university advisory joint committee for a while. As a governor of Hutcheson's Education Trust he served as a representative on the burgh committee of secondary education. He was also a member of the juvenile delinquency board. However, his greatest involvement was in university education. In 1905 he was appointed lord rector's assessor to H. H. Asquith, who had become lord rector of Glasgow University. Three years later under Lord Rosebery he became chancellor's assessor until 1913. The university conferred on Lorimer the honorary degree of LLD in 1910.

Lorimer's university service was closely linked to his political stance as a Liberal Unionist and free trader. He had been an active member of the Glasgow parliamentary debating society and was a fluent speaker. While his political activities were confined to promoting local campaigns they were none the less important; and when Rosebery arrived in Glasgow on 10 September 1909 to deliver his famous budget speech it was Lorimer who welcomed him to the city and chaired the meeting. Indeed, Lorimer had been the chairman of the committee promoting the Glasgow meeting. On the same day Lorimer also organized the formal opening by Lord Rosebery of the new administrative building of the North British Locomotive Company.

In 1911 Lorimer was appointed to the dominions commission, a body set up to survey the natural resources of the overseas dominions and to assess the possible trade links. Despite increasing deafness, Lorimer took on this task with the same dedication and application so characteristic of his business career, travelling extensively overseas between 1911 and 1917.

Lorimer was a man of simple tastes and outlook. In his younger years he developed an interest in literature and through his membership of several literary societies and clubs became a keen collector of books. On 4 February 1869 he married Jane Gray Smith (*d*. 1902); they had four sons and four daughters. Two sons followed their father into locomotive engineering; and in 1903 Lorimer passed the day-to-day running of the Queen's Park works to his son William, one of the joint managing directors. His daughter Janie was one of the early women medical graduates from Glasgow University. He married for a second time on 18 September 1913; his new wife was Mary Elizabeth Muir Simpson, a widow, the daughter of John Sieber, a calico printer. Although not a pioneer or an innovator, Lorimer displayed great leadership skills and business acumen. After an outstanding career in Scottish industry, recognized by a knighthood in 1917, he died on 9 April 1922 at home at 27 Mansionhouse Road, Glasgow; his second wife survived him. He was buried at Cathcart cemetery on 12 April. SHEILA HAMILTON

Sources *Glasgow Herald* (10 April 1922) • *Glasgow Herald* (11 April 1922) • *Transactions of the Institution of Engineers and Shipbuilders in Scotland*, 65 (1921–2), 718–19 • *WWW* • G. E. Todd, *Who's who in Glasgow in 1909* (1909) • 'Men you know series', *The Bailie*, 1639 (16 March 1904); 1978 (14 Sept 1910); 2485 (2 June 1920) • North British Locomotive Company Ltd, *A history of the North British Locomotive Co. Ltd* (1955) • *An account of the manufactures of the North British Locomotive Co. Ltd during the period of the war, 1914–1919: with a short history of the firms which constituted the company when formed in 1903*, North British Locomotive Company Ltd (*c*.1920) • M. Nicolson and M. O'Neill, *Glasgow: locomotive builder to the world* (1987) • *The Times* (31 May 1922) • *Glasgow Herald* (25 Nov 1914) • *Glasgow Herald* (13 April 1922) • *Glasgow Herald* (31 May 1922) • *Glasgow Herald* (1 June 1922) • P. L. Payne, *Colvilles and the Scottish steel industry* (1979) • d. cert. • *DSBB*

Likenesses G. F. Watt, portrait, 1914 • photograph, Mitchell L., Glas., North British Locomotive Co. collection

Wealth at death £445,339 18*s*. 2*d*.: confirmation, 1922, Scotland • £477,170 7*s*. 4*d*.: inventory of estate, NA Scot. SC 36/48/331

Lorimer, William Laughton (1885–1967), classical scholar and translator, was born in Strathmartine, near Dundee, on 27 June 1885, the son of the Revd Robert Lorimer (1840–1925), a minister in the United Free Church of Scotland, and his wife, Isabella Lockhart Robertson (1849–1931). Lorimer was educated at Dundee high school, at Fettes College, Edinburgh, and at Trinity College, Oxford. After graduating from Oxford in 1910 he lived permanently in St Andrews, except for a period of military service in the First World War. A fondness for Italy, developed during a few months' residence there in 1904–5, later prompted him to active efforts in support of Italian prisoners of war. Lorimer held teaching posts in Latin and Greek at St Andrews University and University College, Dundee. In 1915 he married Marion Rose Gordon (*d*. 1922). They had one son, Robert Lewis Campbell (Robin) Lorimer (1918–1996). A second marriage, made in 1929 during a period of extreme distress and despondency, was annulled within a year. From his boyhood Lorimer had shown a consuming interest in Scots vernacular speech, beginning by collecting words from the dialect of Strathmartine in Angus (his father's parish): the knowledge so obtained enabled him to become a valuable informant and consultant for the *Scottish National Dictionary* and latterly also its chairman.

Despite valuable publications on Greek and Latin texts and on the demographic history of Gaelic, Lorimer's most important achievement was the work of his retirement from the chair of Greek at St Andrews. This was his Scots translation of the New Testament, made directly from the Greek originals and prepared for by a long and distinguished life of scholarship in classical literature and lexicography, the written and spoken forms of Scots, and the tradition of Bible translation in many European languages and dialects. Lorimer's aim was to revitalize the declining Scots vernacular tongue by producing a monumental prose work exploiting the full resources of the language. In this he succeeded triumphantly. As a literary and linguistic achievement, the only parallel in Scots letters to his testament is the sixteenth-century translation of the *Aeneid* by Gavin Douglas. Lorimer's translation contains many rare words of local currency but almost none of the literary archaisms frequent in modern Scots writing, and conveys the rhythms, cadences, and idiomatic phrasing of spoken Scots with unerring skill. Perhaps uniquely among Bible translations, his style is deliberately varied to reflect the characteristics of the original books. The complete work, edited by his son Robin Lorimer, was not published until 1983, sixteen years after William Laughton Lorimer's death of cancer at 18 Eglinton Crescent, Edinburgh, on 25 May 1967. His body was cremated and the ashes interred in the cemetery at Sanquhar, Dumfriesshire, where a memorial to him was erected in the church. Lorimer's Scots New Testament has been widely read and appreciated, sometimes being used in services of worship, and is recognized as the most complete demonstration in recent literature of the expressive power of Scots. J. DERRICK MCCLURE

Sources R. L. C. Lorimer, 'Introduction', *The New Testament in Scots*, trans. W. L. Lorimer (1983), vii–xxv • K. Dover, 'William Laughton Lorimer, 1885–1967', *PBA*, 53 (1967), 437–48 • private information (2004) [Mrs Priscilla Lorimer] • NA Scot., SC 20/50/261/1534–9

Archives NL Scot., MSS • U. St Andr. L., papers | NL Scot., corresp. with *Scottish National Dictionary*

Likenesses G. Borrowman, drawing, priv. coll. • photograph, repro. in Dover, 'William Laughton Lorimer' • photographs, priv. coll.

Wealth at death £21,652 4*s*. 4*d*.: confirmation, 10 July 1967, NA Scot., SC 20/50/261/1534-9

Loring, Frederick George (1869–1951), naval officer and wireless expert, was born on 11 March 1869 at Stonelands, Ryde, Isle of Wight, the eldest son of Admiral Sir William Loring (*d*. 1895), and his wife, Frances Louisa Adams. From a naval family—his grandfather Sir John Wentworth *Loring (1775–1852) was lieutenant-governor of the Royal Naval College, Portsmouth, 1819–37—Loring was destined for the Royal Navy. He entered *Britannia* in July 1882 as a naval cadet, going out to Australia as a midshipman. As a sub-lieutenant he served in the royal yacht, *Victoria and Albert*, in 1891 and was promoted lieutenant on 1 September 1891. He was a lieutenant in HMS *Victoria* when she was rammed and sunk by *Camperdown* off Tripoli on 22 June 1893 with terrible loss of life. Loring was awarded a bronze medal by the Royal Humane Society for saving two lives.

Loring undertook the long torpedo course at HMS *Vernon* in 1894, qualifying as a torpedo lieutenant in 1896. The same year he married Charlotte Elizabeth Arbuthnot (1862–1933), daughter of the Hon. James Edward Arbuthnot of Mauritius; they had two daughters, Evelyn Frances and Iris. Loring joined the staff of *Defiance*, the torpedo school at Devonport, where Captain Henry Jackson was experimenting with wireless telegraphy for naval purposes. Loring was one of the first to specialize in wireless telegraphy, becoming one of the navy's leading wireless experts. He served in the fleet during 1900–02 and from 1902 was in charge of the Admiralty shore wireless stations. Loring was selected to accompany Guglielmo Marconi to America in 1904 for wireless experiments, and in 1906 he was the Admiralty representative at the second International Wireless Telegraphy Conference at Berlin. In the same year he was elected as a member of the Institution of Electrical Engineers.

Although specially recommended for promotion, Loring was found to be unfit for further sea service, but permission was given for him to accept the appointment as inspector of wireless telegraphy under the Post Office from 1 July 1908. He received an expression of the Admiralty's appreciation of his services in charge of war signal and wireless telegraphy stations and finally retired from the Royal Navy at his own request with the rank of commander in December 1909. In 1914 Loring was released from liability for naval service, but refused further promotion.

Loring remained as inspector of wireless telegraphy at the Post Office, responsible for the operating staff, until 1930, and represented the Post Office at the international radio-telegraphy conferences at London in 1912 and Washington in 1927. He also acted as an assessor for wireless telegraphy for the Board of Trade, attending the safety at sea conferences in London in 1914 and 1929. Appointed a civil OBE in 1926 for his services to the development of radio, Loring retired from the Post Office in January 1930. He joined the International Marine Radio Company, of which he later became a director, and represented that company at the conferences in Copenhagen in 1931, Madrid in 1932, Lisbon in 1934, Bucharest in 1937, Cairo in 1938, and Stockholm in 1948. He finally retired from the company in 1950, having devoted over fifty years of his life to the interests of maritime radio. In 1949 he married Margaret Mackenzie, daughter of Montague S. Napier.

Apart from his many naval and technical interests Loring had a distinct literary bent. In his early days at sea he wrote for a naval technical journal, and was the naval correspondent for the *Western Morning News*. He also wrote poems and short stories, one of which, 'The Tomb of Sarah', achieved considerable success. He was co-author of a paper, 'A survey of marine radio progress, with special reference to RMS *Queen Mary*', published in the Institution of Electrical Engineers' *Journal* in 1937. Loring died of cardiac failure at his home, the Old House, Footscray, Sidcup, Kent, on 7 September 1951, aged eighty-two.

A. J. L. BLOND

Sources PRO, naval service record, ADM 196/43, 55 · *Journal of the Institution of Electrical Engineers* (1952), 92 · Post Office Archive, London, minute 1802 (1916), pensions 512 (1930) · *WWW*, *1951–60* · 'Loring, Sir John Wentworth', *DNB* · A. J. L. Blond, 'Technology and tradition: wireless telegraphy and the Royal Navy, 1895–1920', PhD diss., University of Lancaster, 1993 · *CGPLA Eng. & Wales* (1951) · b. cert. · m. cert.

Wealth at death £5734 5*s*. 0*d*.: probate, 8 Nov 1951, *CGPLA Eng. & Wales*

Loring, Sir John Wentworth (1775–1852), naval officer, born in America on 13 October 1775, was the grandson of Commodore Joshua Loring (*d*. 1781), who commanded the flotilla employed on the North American lakes in the Seven Years' War. His father, Joshua Loring, was high sheriff of Massachusetts before the American War of Independence; he moved to England and settled in Berkshire.

John Loring entered the navy in June 1789 on the *Salisbury*, flagship of Vice-Admiral Milbanke on the Newfoundland station. He returned to England in 1791, continued on the home station and in the Mediterranean, and as midshipman of the *Victory* was severely wounded at the evacuation of Toulon on 17 December 1793. He commanded a gunboat at the siege of Bastia. On 24 May 1794 he was promoted lieutenant of the sloop *Flêche* and was shortly afterwards moved to the *St George*, flagship of Sir Hyde Parker. In her he was present in the two actions off Toulon on 13–14 March and 13 July 1795. At the beginning of 1796 he followed Parker to the *Britannia*, in which he returned to England, and towards the end of the year went out to the West Indies in the fireship *Comet* to rejoin Parker, then commander-in-chief at Jamaica.

In June 1798 Loring was appointed acting commander of the sloop *Rattler* (16 guns), and in September of the *Lark* (18 guns), to which he was confirmed on 3 January 1799. In the *Lark* he cruised successfully against enemy privateers and merchant ships, for which he was publicly thanked by Sir Hugh Seymour, and appointed acting captain of the *Abergavenny* (54 guns) in April 1801. In October 1801 he was moved to the frigate *Syren* (32 guns), and in March 1802, while cruising off Cape François, suppressed a dangerous mutiny with a coolness that drew the praise of Sir John Duckworth. On Duckworth's recommendation the Admiralty confirmed Loring's post rank to 28 April 1802, the day before the general promotion in honour of the peace. Loring married on 18 July 1804 Anna, daughter of Vice-Admiral Patton, then a lord of the Admiralty. They had three daughters and three sons, the second of whom was Admiral Sir William Loring KCB (*d*. 1895).

In 1803–4 Loring commanded the *Utrecht* (64 guns), flagship of successive admirals in the Downs, and in 1805 the *Aurora*, in a voyage to Bermuda and back; but his war service was chiefly identified with the *Niobe*, a 38-gun frigate, which he commanded on the coast of France from November 1805 until 1813. On the dark night of 28 March 1806 he pursued and took silent possession of the brig *Néarque* (16 guns) out of a squadron of three frigates of equal or superior force. On 13 November 1810 he took part with Captain Grant of the *Diana* (38 guns) in driving under the batteries of La Hougue two 40-gun French frigates, one of which got on the rocks and was burnt by her own people, while the other escaped, only to be driven on shore and burnt at Cape Barfleur on 24 March 1811, by a British squadron, of which the *Niobe* was one. Thirteen days previously the *Niobe*, while watching the port of Le Havre, had captured the privateer *Loup Marin* (16 guns).

In 1813–14 Loring commanded the *Impregnable* as flag captain to Admiral William Young in the North Sea. On 4

June 1815 he was made CB. From 1816 to 1819 he was superintendent of the ordinary at Sheerness, and from 4 November 1819 lieutenant-governor of the Royal Naval College, Portsmouth, until his promotion to flag rank on 10 January 1837. He was made KCH on 30 April 1837, KCB on 4 July 1840, became vice-admiral on 9 November 1846, and admiral on 8 July 1851. He settled in 1837 at Ryde in the Isle of Wight, where he died on 29 July 1852.

J. K. LAUGHTON, *rev.* ANDREW LAMBERT

Sources D. Syrett and R. L. DiNardo, *The commissioned sea officers of the Royal Navy, 1660–1815*, rev. edn, Occasional Publications of the Navy RS, 1 (1994) • C. Lloyd, 'The Royal Naval College at Portsmouth and Greenwich', *Mariner's Mirror*, 52 (1966), 145–56 • O'Byrne, *Naval biog. dict.*, [2nd edn] • *GM*, 2nd ser., 38 (1852), 312–13 • W. James, *The naval history of Great Britain, from the declaration of war by France in 1793, to the accession of George IV*, [5th edn], 6 vols. (1859–60) • J. Marshall, *Royal naval biography*, 2/2 (1825), 544–9

Archives BL, letters to the second Earl Spencer

Loring, Sir Neil [Nigel] (*c*.**1315–1386**), soldier and administrator, was the son of Roger Loring of Chalgrave, Bedfordshire, and Cassandra, daughter of Reginald Perot. The family seems to have been established there since the twelfth century, and Sir Piers Loring served in Edward I's Scottish wars. His mother's family were also from Bedfordshire. Loring apparently entered the royal service at an early age. On 6 October 1335 he was granted a pension of 100*s*., and had further grants from the king on 24 September 1338 and in 1339. He married Margaret, daughter and heir of Ralph Beauple of Cnubeston, Devon, with whom he had two daughters. Isabel, the elder, married first William Coggan, and second Robert *Harrington, third Baron Harrington [*see under* Harrington family]; her tomb is in Porlock church, Somerset. Margaret, Loring's younger daughter, married Thomas Peyvre of Toddington, Bedfordshire.

Loring fought with distinction at the battle of Sluys on 24 June 1340, and was rewarded with the honour of knighthood and a pension of £20 yearly. In 1342 he served in Brittany under Sir Walter Mauny. On 23 February 1345 he went with Michael Northburgh on a mission to the pope to obtain a dispensation for the marriage of the prince of Wales with a daughter of the duke of Brabant. Later in this and in the following year he served under Henry, earl of Derby, in Aquitaine; a grant of 12 November 1346 implies that he was still with the earl following the latter's raid into Poitou and Saintonge during the autumn. Unlike most founder knights of the Garter he almost certainly did not fight at Crécy, but he was in the king's retinue at Calais in 1347, with three esquires and a hobelar. When the Order of the Garter was instituted in 1348–9 Loring was one of the original knights, occupying the tenth stall on the prince's side. On 16 December 1350 he was one of the commissioners appointed to treat concerning the payments due to the king for the government of the Low Countries. By 1351 he had become chamberlain to the prince of Wales and a member of his council. He accompanied the prince to Aquitaine in 1353, and served in the campaign of Poitiers in 1356, distinguishing himself in the skirmish before Romorantin on 29 August.

Sir Neil Loring (*c*.**1315–1386**), manuscript painting

After the battle on 19 September, during which he was 'appointed to be in attendance on the prince's person', he was sent home to England with the news of the victory. Like many other members of the prince's retinue he was handsomely rewarded for his service, being given a pension of £83 6*s*. 8*d*. for life, as well as lands in Wales. In November 1359 Loring accompanied the king on his expedition into France, which was followed by the treaty of Brétigny on 25 May 1360. He was one of the guardians of the truce on 7 May, and was one of the commissioners appointed to supervise the transfer of lands and redress any violations.

In July 1362 Loring went out to Aquitaine to prepare for the arrival of the prince of Wales later that summer. He was one of the four knights whom the prince sent to England in 1366 to obtain the king's opinion on the Spanish expedition, but returned to France in time to join the army at the beginning of the following year. At the battle of Nájera on 3 April he fought in the prince's division. Loring was one of the knights whom the prince dispatched at the end of June from Valladolid to Seville in order to urge Pedro the Cruel of Castile to send the assistance he had promised. In 1369 he served under Sir Robert Knolles on his expedition into the Agenais, at the siege of Domme, and in the following year, under John Hastings, earl of Pembroke, in Poitou.

Loring returned to England and took up residence on his

ancestral estate at Chalgrave, where, in 1365, he had obtained leave to enclose a park. He died on 18 March 1386, and was buried in Dunstable Priory church, of which he was a benefactor. Loring also founded a chantry in Chalgrave church, and contributed to building the cloister at St Albans. He made a large number of legacies to religious foundations, including the friars at Truro, Bodmin, and Plymouth, reflecting the places where he had worked in the prince's service. He left his daughters a gold circlet valued at £40 and 2367 'great marguerite pearls' to be divided between them. There is a miniature representing him in his robes as a knight of the Garter in BL, Cotton MS Nero D.vii, fol. 105*v*.

C. L. KINGSFORD, *rev.* RICHARD BARBER

Sources G. F. Beltz, *Memorials of the most noble order of the Garter* (1841) • H. Jenkinson and G. H. Fowler, 'Some Bedfordshire wills at Lambeth and Lincoln', *Bedfordshire Historical Record Society*, 14 (1931), 97–103 • M. C. B. Dawes, ed., *Register of Edward, the Black Prince*, 4 vols., PRO (1930–33) • *Chroniques de J. Froissart*, ed. S. Luce and others, 15 vols. (Paris, 1869–1975) • Rymer, *Foedera*, new edn, 2.2, 3.1, 3.2 • *CClR*, *1339–74* • *CPR*, *1335–9* • *CIPM*, 16, nos. 7–15, 96–7
Likenesses manuscript painting, BL, Cotton MS Nero D.vii, fol. 105*v* [*see illus.*]
Wealth at death lands in Cornwall and Devon: *CIPM*, 16, nos. 7–15

Lorkin, Thomas (*c.*1528–1591), physician, was born at Frindsbury in Kent, to Thomas Lorkin and Joan Huxley. He matriculated at Pembroke College, Cambridge, on 12 November 1549, graduated BA in 1552, proceeding MA in 1555, and was created MD in 1560. Lorkin married Catherine (*d.* 1582), daughter of John Hatcher, regius professor of physic, in November 1560. They had a son and six daughters, one of whom married Edward Lively, regius professor of Hebrew at Cambridge.

Lorkin was at first, from 1551 to 1553, a fellow of Queens' College, but from 1553 until 1560 was a fellow of Peterhouse. On 21 April 1564 he was created regius professor of physic; he was respondent in the Physic Act kept before the queen in the same year, and in 1590 he obtained a grant of arms for the five regius professors. From 1572 until 1585 he was rector of Little Waltham in Essex. He had become a Catholic in his youth, and in later years opposed puritan preaching in the university.

Lorkin published one work: *Recta regula et victus ratio pro studiosis et literatis* (1562). His 'Carmen Latinum decastichon' is prefixed to the manuscript *Historia Anglicana* by John Herd (Cotton. MS Julius, C., ii.136).

Lorkin died on 1 May 1591, and was buried in Great St Mary's Church, Cambridge. In his will he left certain estates to Pembroke College, Queens' College, and Peterhouse. His medical books he bequeathed to the university library. About 140 volumes reached the library in December 1594; many of them contain annotations by Lorkin, and have his monogram on the title page.

Thomas Lorkyn (*d.* 1625), diplomat, graduated BA from Emmanuel College, Cambridge, in 1601, proceeded MA in 1604, and was incorporated at Oxford on 30 August 1605. He accompanied Thomas Puckering on his travels between 1611 and 1613, and in 1619–20 he journeyed with the second son of Robert Cary, earl of Monmouth. In 1623 he was secretary to the embassy at Paris which negotiated the marriage of Prince Charles and Henrietta Maria. He continued to correspond with Puckering after they had parted, and many of his letters appear in Birch's *Court and Times of James I* (1848). Two addressed to the earl of Carlisle are in the British Library (MS Egerton 2596, fols. 57, 112). Lorkyn was drowned in a channel storm about November 1625.

W. A. J. ARCHBOLD, *rev.* SARAH BAKEWELL

Sources Venn, *Alum. Cant.* • C. Sayle, 'The library of Sir Thomas Lorkyn', *Annals of Medical History*, 3 (1921), 310–13 • P. M. Jones, 'Thomas Lorkyn's dissections, 1564/5 and 1566/7', *Transactions of the Cambridge Bibliographical Society*, 9 (1986–90), 209–29 • Cooper, *Ath. Cantab.*, 2.102, 545 • Foster, *Alum. Oxon.*
Archives CUL

Lorkyn, Thomas (*d.* 1625). *See under* Lorkin, Thomas (*c.*1528–1591).

Lorne. For this title name *see* MacDougall, John, lord of Lorne (*d.* in or after 1371) [*see under* MacDougall, John, lord of Argyll (*d.* 1316)]; Campbell, John George Edward Henry Douglas Sutherland, marquess of Lorne and ninth duke of Argyll (1845–1914).

Lorrain, Paul (*d.* 1719), Church of England clergyman and criminal biographer, was a Huguenot immigrant to England. Neither the names of his parents nor the details of his education are known, but in 1681 his employer, Samuel Pepys, recorded that, 'his whole family, both by father and mother, are known protestants in France, and sufferers for being so,—and himself by them bred up as such from the cradle' (*Life, Journals*, 1.262). Some of Lorrain's kin found refuge in the Netherlands, while one Pierre Lorrain was admitted a member of the French church at Threadneedle Street, London, on 25 April 1671, bearing a certificate from his old congregation in Paris, where Paul is known to have had family. Paul had arrived in England by the late 1670s. There were those later who certainly thought that Lorrain had come as a religious refugee, but when in 1685 he praised Charles II for the safe haven he had provided for Huguenots, he wrote not of a personal debt he owed the king, but rather in third-person terms of:

> my deep Resentment [sense] of the Favours that many of my owne Country and Religion have so plentifully and seasonably receiv'd from His Bounty Basilick (which has been so graciously pleas'd so as to afford them a sanctuary in His Dominions, whilst it appear'd the whole World besides had no Place of Refuge for them). (BL, Stowe MS 987, fol. 8*r*)

Secretary to Samuel Pepys By the beginning of 1678 Lorrain was employed by Samuel Pepys as secretary, translator, and copyist, a position he held until 1700. He came recommended by 'a protestant minister, a man very eminent both at home and abroad' (*Life, Journals*, 1.262). On 1 January 1678 Lorrain presented Pepys with 'Mulieres non Homines, ou, La Femme Deshumanisée' ('Women not Men, or, The Female Dehumanized') as a new year's gift, a beautifully copied translation into French that he had made of a notorious spoof polemic originally published in Latin in 1595. He had, he explained, often heard Pepys in conversation with the fair sex tell them that they were not of the human race, nor capable of salvation, a paradox that he had put down to his master's good humour, but now, coming across this eighty-year-old text, found the argument neither as new nor as extravagant as he had thought. He rounded off the translation with a gallant apology 'Aux Dames'. Lorrain was drawn into the problems of his master as Pepys, who came under suspicion in the wake of the Popish Plot, was falsely accused of treason and for a time imprisoned in the Tower of London. On 4 November 1678 Lorrain was required, as a member of Pepys's household, to display his protestant conformity by receiving the Anglican sacrament. In the following years Lorrain actively helped his master in his attempts to clear his name. In October 1679 he provided letters to two of his kinsmen in Paris as contacts for Pepys's brother-in-law. In January 1680 he witnessed a written statement against the sacked butler who had testified against Pepys in parliament. Most notably, in the summer of 1680 Lorrain helped his master in compiling—and copied in his own hand—the two volumes of evidences against Pepys's main accuser, John Scott, known as the Book of Mornamont. Lorrain himself came under suspicion of popery, and in January 1681 dared not leave Pepys's house until he had put together the evidence to prove his protestantism. There was thus something more than the conventional when Lorrain, who had witnessed Pepys's dangers at first hand, alluded to 'YOUR KNOWN INTEGRITY and FORTITUDE', in the dedication of a book to him in 1683 (P. Lorrain, *Rites of Funeral*, 1683, sig. A3*r*). His inscription of the copy he presented to Pepys underlined the debt he owed to his master:

> SAMUELL PEPYS
> Anagram
> ALMES-SUPPLIE
> Whilst Godlike Charity's so much neglected,
> And by the most as fruitless quite rejected
> You do regard the Poor with Piteous Eye,
> And are to them an Heav'n-sent Alms-Supply.
> (Lorrain, *Rites of Funeral*, BL copy)

Lorrain elaborated his taste for anagrams with his new year's gift to Pepys on 1 January 1685, a small handwritten book which echoed his master's toryism by disclosing the secret meaning contained within the letters of Charles II's formal title:

> He's God on Earth,
> an Angelic Blessing of the Land,
> Releef of the Church,
> (that can defend it),
> and Dear Frend of God.
> (BL, Stowe MS 987, fol. 2*v*)

Lorrain's thoughts carried on in similarly extravagant loyalist vein, in the course of the book condemning those 'moderne Writers, such as pen Romances, Novels, Pamphlets, and the like', who tailored their style:

> to please the gust [taste] of the Sick, than to give them good and wholesome Food, and choosing rather to set forth a bad piece that will take (as they call it) than a good one that will not relish the distemper'd palate of the squeamish Multitude. (ibid., fol. 6*v*)

Lorrain was granted letters of denization on 31 January 1690. In the years following he helped his master in organizing his great library. During his years with Pepys, Lorrain also published a number of translations of protestant polemic and devotion. The first was *Marcus Minucius Felix Octavus, or, A Vindication of Christianity Against Paganism* (1682), using a French translation collated with the original Latin. Dedicating the book to John Tillotson, dean of Canterbury, Lorrain made clear the contemporary relevance of this third-century apologetic when he praised him as 'a Zealous Defender of our Christian religion against Atheism; of our Reformed Religion against the Romish Superstition, which is the old Paganism reviv'd and varnish'd over' (sigs. A2*v*–A3*r*). *Rites of Funeral, Ancient and Modern*, a translation of a work by the French priest Pierre Muret, followed in 1683, excising a chapter on 'The funerals of hereticks' which Lorrain regarded as 'little less or more, than an Invective against Protestants, in reference to their Rites of Burial' ('The translator to the reader'). There followed three translations of works of Huguenot piety. In 1688 Lorrain published as *A Preparation of the Lord's Supper, to which are Added, Maxims of True Christianity*, a compilation of two works by Pierre Allix. *A discourse of Christianity: laying open the abuses thereof in the Anti-Christian lives and worship of many of its professors; especially the Romanists; and shewing the way to a holy life in the character of a true Christian* (1693) was the translation of a work by Jean Ogier de Gombauld. *A way to salvation, or, The way to eternal bliss; being a collection of meditations and prayers suited to the exercise of a true Christian*, published in the same year, included pieces by Pierre Du Moulin, Pierre Drelincourt, and others, 'with some Additions of my own' (sig. A3*r*)—an interesting authorial intervention given that Lorrain was at this point himself still a layman.

By the late 1690s Lorrain's piety was drawing him to a career in the Church of England. He also had practical matters to consider: a future livelihood without his ageing patron and, probably, family responsibilities. The first surviving mention of a wife is in a letter dated 25 March 1700. He does not name her there, and—especially given evidence of his (also unnamed) wife's bouts of serious illness in the summer of 1700 and in May 1709—it not certain that Sarah, his widow, was his first and only wife. In January 1699 Pepys wrote supporting Lorrain's intention of 'consecrating the remainder of his life to His service in the Church, by entring into Holy Orders' and praised his 'sobriety, diligence and integrity' (*Private Correspondence*, 1.168). By October Pepys was complaining, in terms which convey both how dependent Pepys had become upon Lorrain and the latter's increasing absorption into his clerical role, of:

> the little time I have Lorraine with mee, and the restraint his praesent character putts upon me as to the uses I should have to make of him relateing to my books, papers and clerkelike services, other than bare sitting at his deske upon solemne works only; the generality of my studys, businesse, and domesticks subjecting mee to many lesser uses for an assistant-pen, more than hee is either in the way for, or I doubt would readily apply himselfe to if hee were … Nor is this a small difficulty with mee, as knowing too well my having no choice towards the solving it, there being noe

> body but hee that knows my businesse and manner of workeing, and at the same time qualifyed in every respect for doeing it. (ibid., 1.200–01)

Lorrain nevertheless continued to act as Pepys's copyist when the latter was unable to write letters himself, and continued to show concern for his master: in March 1700 he disobeyed Pepys's wishes and wrote a letter to his nephew John Jackson warning him of his uncle's ill health. At Pepys's funeral in 1703 he received a mourning ring worth 15*s*.

The ordinary of Newgate his account Well before that date Lorrain had left Pepys's service. On 7 November 1700 he was appointed ordinary (prison chaplain) of Newgate by the court of aldermen. 'I (who all along have endeavoured to live blameless and suitable to my Holy Profession) was by order of that Court committed to New-gate', he wrote to Jackson, begging his prayers that 'God will enable me to go through that great and important work, and to discharge the office incumbent on me to the Glory of God and the good of those poor wretched souls that shall come under my care' (*Private Correspondence*, 2.120). Lorrain's application had been supported by, among others, bishops Edward Fowler of Gloucester and Richard Kidder of Bath and Wells. As ordinary, his responsibility was not only to preach in the chapel and provide spiritual counsel to the prisoners and especially to the condemned. He also was to produce the semi-official broadsheet which followed each execution day, *The ordinary of Newgate his account of the behaviour, confessions, and last speeches of those that were executed at Tyburn*, a publication which had emerged in the 1670s and taken firmer shape under Samuel Smith, ordinary from 1676 to 1698. Lorrain's predecessor but one, John Allen, had been dismissed five months earlier for corrupt practices, which included 'his frequent prevarications in the printing and Publishing the pretended Confessions of the respective Criminalls That are executed at Tybourne' (Corporation of London RO, REP 104, fol. 340).

An important duty of Lorrain's was, therefore, to guarantee the integrity of the ordinary's *Account*, as it recounted the crimes and fate of the condemned, its record of their confessions to him in Newgate, and behaviour at the gallows dramatizing tales of sin and hard-won redemption. The *Account* was at once true-crime story and religious tract, and at once moral and commercial in its functions. Lorrain took both functions very seriously.

In 1712 Lorrain claimed in the case he addressed to the Commons that the *Account* should be exempt from stamp duty because it was a religious work, but he nevertheless implied the mingling of religious and secular considerations in its intentions. The *Account* contained 'nothing but DIVINITY, DEVOTION, and what may be most Useful to the World', appearing 'for the general satisfaction of the Publick' and of value both to 'Good Men, in informing them in what they desire and have an Interest to Know' and

> to the Wicked, in reforming them in what they are so very defective, and making them sensible of the Dangers and Miseries which attend a vicious and ill Course of Life, and plainly shewing them how to avoid an Untimely and Shameful Death in this World, and an Eternal one in the next. (Lorrain, *Case*)

As the way to personal salvation lay through the atonement of public confession and execution for sins committed against society and against God, the *Account* (at its fullest) included details of the early life of the condemned and of how their sins had led them into crime. Lorrain could provide details of receivers and accomplices. Moreover, the *Account* sought to demonstrate that the condemned criminal was different in degree, not in kind, from the ordinary sinner, who faced the same crisis of salvation, a message underlined by placing criminals not as a breed apart but as ordinary members of the working population of London. Thus Lorrain became the sole biographer of many humble criminals: women such as Elizabeth Tethrington, aged twenty-nine, condemned for housebreaking, who had come to London from Ormskirk in Lancashire six years before to become an oyster-seller at Billingsgate before falling into bad company; or men such as Thomas Hunter, aged twenty-three, another housebreaker, born in St Botolph without Bishopsgate, who after serving a hard master for seven years fled, worked in victualling, and joined the navy before deserting and falling into a life of thieving.

In the *Account* Lorrain presented his energetic attempts to win such criminals to salvation: in private and public meetings in the chapel, and in the condemned hold, and in the sermons of repentance he preached on the Sundays between trial and execution. How his message was received has been a matter of debate at the time and among modern scholars, the latter disturbed by the shaping of the experience of the condemned criminal to stereotyped models of the descent into sin and the obvious element of gaining the criminals' consent to the righteousness of the political and social order which was about to hang them. Were the condemned indifferent to Lorrain's message, or angry at the spiritual harrying that it entailed, or did they genuinely find solace in his words? His own accounts provide evidence for all three positions, and in the same person at different times in their last days. At the time observers disagreed on the effectiveness of his ministry. *The History of the Press-Yard* (1717) condescendingly noted that Lorrain:

> indeed did according to his Sufficiency, read Prayers tolerably well, and gave such Exhortations as might have been of benefit to the poor Souls they were directed to, but they had conceived such an indifferent Opinion of him from common Report, that all he said—*was made to go in at one Ear and out at the other.* (p. 49)

The 'tradesman' The profits of the *Account* in the early eighteenth century have been estimated as £200 per annum, easily exceeding Lorrain's formal emoluments: each year he received a salary of £35, supplemented by a charitable bequest of £6 for preaching to the condemned and the grant to sell each year (usually) one City freedom, worth perhaps £25. Its profitability evidently owed much to Lorrain's own energies. The most thorough study of the *Account* has argued that 'It would seem that much of the credit for firmly establishing the *Account* as not only a "semi-official" publication, but as a lucrative commercial enterprise in its own right rests with Paul Lorrain' (McKenzie, 239). He standardized the title and format (always writing in the first person). He carefully distinguished the authority of his text from the advertisements which appeared at the bottom of the *Account*, informing any readers who objected to their content that 'I have nothing to do with whatever comes in after my Name' (Harris, 18). Indeed, while the advertisements were often for works of piety—very often Lorrain's own—they could also include less obviously improving items such as a face-wash which 'plumps and softens the Skin, making it as smooth and tender as a sucking Child's' and *The court of Venus, or, Cupid restor'd to right, being a history of Cuckolds and Cuckold-makers* (Lorrain, *Account*, 7 Dec 1715). On several occasions he warned readers of the *Account* to accept no unreliable substitutes. Readers should spurn the 'sham-papers' purporting to be the *Account* which often got the names and crimes wrong and misrepresented the spiritual state of the condemned. The only true account was the one which came out about eight o'clock the morning after the day of the execution under his name with its standard title and format.

Above all Lorrain maintained editorial and commercial control of the *Account*, frequently changing publishers and printers—he employed at least seven over the years. One, Dryden Leach, bitterly complained in 1707 of Lorrain's hard-headed dealings, alleging that, although he had always 'very honestly' paid Lorrain for every copy of the *Account*, when offered with better terms by another printer, Lorrain told Leach:

> in plain Terms, *That truly he must take him that would pay him best*, by this he excluded me: And now whether this is a Practice becoming a Clergyman or a Tradesman, I leave to the judicious part of Mankind, to make their own just Reflections. (McKenzie, 69)

Leach further claimed that he had often received copies of the *Account* two days before the execution day it was alleged to report. This was not the only charge made against Lorrain to suggest that his greed got the better of his clerical duties. He was accused of having accepted bribes to work to obtain reprieves, and of having administered the sacrament to unworthy recipients for money. He was also charged with accepting cash to soften his account of some criminals.

Many of these accusations arose from the ambiguity of Lorrain's position as somebody who, through the *Account*, was profiting from his spiritual functions, and as somebody who turned tales of crime into tales of redemption. Daniel Defoe suggested that his high-flown tales of low criminals reaching salvation rather discredited the authority of the church, in *A Hymn to the Pillory* (1703):

> Where lies the Secret, let us know,
> To make a *Sheep-stealer* a *Saint*? …
>
> If this *Wise Precedent* the World receives,
> *Newgate* shall ne're be call'd a *Den of Thieves*:
> What Rev'rence ought to such a Place be given,
> That Ships so many Loads of *Saints to Heaven*?
> (pp. 1–2)

The riposte by or on Lorrain's behalf, *Remarks on the author of the hymn to the pillory, with an answer to the hymn to the funeral sermon* (1703), not unreasonably cited in his defence the example of the thief on the cross beside Christ. Defoe's attack was sparked by the funeral sermon that Lorrain had delivered at St James, Clerkenwell, for Thomas Cook. Lorrain did indeed speak strongly of Cook's pious death, but the desire to preach a powerful sermon on repentance and salvation to a congregation whom he would not normally have reached was evidently Lorrain's motivation, rather than the fee as Defoe alleged. This is confirmed by reading the published text, *Walking with God*, with its insistent warning that its hearers might not be as lucky as Cook in being able to avoid damnation by timely repentance, and by who Cook actually was. Cook, a booth performer at the May fair, had been hanged a few days earlier for murdering a constable associated with the Reformation of Manners societies who had been trying to implement the queen's proclamation against vice at the fair. Cook, by profession and by his particular crime, was the embodiment of the sin that Lorrain was struggling against. His sincere repentance at the end was a pure example of what God's mercy and a willing soul could achieve.

Lorrain continued to publish other works. In 1702 he published *The dying man's assistant, or, Short instructions how to prepare sick persons for death: which are no less worthy the consideration of all good Christians in time of health, as shewing the importance of an early preparation for their latter end*. In 1707 he published the sermon he had preached for the fast day to commemorate the great fire of London, with alternative endings to its message of atonement adapted to the two congregations who heard it: to the worthy parishioners of St Dunstan's-in-the-West he exhorted charity to the poor; to the prisoners of Newgate he preached prayer and sincere repentance. In 1712, in *Popery Near a-kin to Paganism and Atheism*, he returned to his anti-popish strain, on the occasion of the abjuration of a Catholic priest accused of blasphemy.

Pirates and Jacobites Lorrain's struggle to save the souls of the condemned appeared at its most dramatic at the execution of William Kidd for piracy at Execution Dock, Wapping, on 23 May 1701. Kidd had proved fairly resistant to Lorrain's exhortations in Newgate, believing (not without reason) that he was paying for the faults of his crew and his political patrons. Only when it was clear that there would be no reprieve did he at last make the briefest and most general of confessions. While he eventually promised to make a full confession at the gallows, he turned up at Wapping drunk, and 'was unwilling to own the Justice of his Condemnation, or so much as the Providence of God, who for his Sins, had deservedly brought him to this untimely End'. While Lorrain sang psalms with the other pirates who were to die, their captain loudly warned all masters of ships to have a care of themselves and take warning by him. When the condemned were turned off,

Kidd's rope split; he was again tied from the gallows. 'Now I found him in much better temper than before', Lorrain recorded, and with Kidd at the top of the ladder and himself perched half-way up, Lorrain redoubled his efforts, urging him to 'embrace (before it was too late) the Mercy of God, now again offer'd him, upon the easy Conditions of stedfast Faith, true Repentance, and perfect Charity. Which now indeed he did so fully and freely express, that I hope he was hearty and sincere in it' (Lorrain, *Kidd*).

The Jacobite prisoners in 1715 and 1716 faced Lorrain with another set of challenges. His role as the voice of the state condemning the sin of rebellion earned him an abusive and threatening letter in the autumn of 1715, attacking him as a sycophant to the usurper. It demanded:

> Is there one syllable in all the Doctrine of the Church of England (of which you now declare yourself to be a Member) that can Justifie Deposing King James or abjuring his Son, on acco[un]t of Religion? I know not what you think now, but turn the tables, & I dare say you'l be of my opinion, & soe let me ask you, whether you did not think it a hardship to be driven out of France for your principles? & shall not King James & his Son have the same regard? (BL, Add. MS 38507, fol. 172*r*)

This was evidently only one of several Jacobite 'Vile and unseemly Elegies' directed against Lorrain (*Weekly Journal, or, British Gazetteer*, 10 Oct 1719, 1419). Other Jacobite prisoners showed the same refusal to accept that their rebellion was a crime. He urged the men awaiting execution in December 1715 that they make 'some publick Token of their Repentance for the publick Crime that had deservedly brought them to this open Shame'. They replied that 'They would not hear me if I harp'd any longer upon this string: and what they only desired of me was, my reading to them the Prayers and Lessons appointed for the Day and no more' (Lorrain, *Account*, 7 Dec 1715). The nonjuror John Hall was even more shocking in his resolution and breach of the basic tenets of civility. At the gallows he refused to join Lorrain in prayer, 'but all the while turn'd his back upon me; a Thing which no Protestant ever did before on such an Occasion'. 'Mr Hall, methinks you might have been more serious, and more civil; what harm have I now done to you, in imploring God's Mercy to your Soul?' (Lorrain, *Account*, 13 July 1716).

Bolstered by their refusal to accept the validity of Lorrain's claims, these prisoners offered perhaps the most extreme form of resistance to his authority. It was reinforced by suspicions of him as an informer, exploiting his position to 'Expose some things which fell in his way, to the Service of the Government' (*Weekly Journal, or, British Gazetteer*, 10 Oct 1719, 1419).

In the *Account* of May 1719 Lorrain offered a reward for discovering the author and publisher of a libel which had accused him of getting drunk on gin in a brandy-shop in Newgate Street; going the day after to condemned prisoners in the chapel, 'he shamefully spue'd upon his Cushion and then dy'd'. It went on to accuse him of having been before he took holy orders a French dancing-master who had himself been tried at the Old Bailey (McKenzie, 202). Lorrain showed his accustomed sensitivity to attacks on his position. The kernel of truth may be that he was already ill. He died five months later about 6 p.m. on 7 October 1719, in his house in Town Ditch (now Houndsditch), near Christ's Hospital, where he had moved from the house near St Bartholomew's Close, West Smithfield, in which he had been living in 1715. His will, made on 14 March 1712 and proved by his widow, Sarah, nine days after his death, inevitably paid a more than formulaic attention to the state of his soul: 'I nothing doubting but firmly beleiving that by the power & mercy of Almighty God I shall receive the same [my body] again Glorious and Immortall at the Generall Resurrection in the last day Amen'. To his immediate (unnamed) heir at law he left a mere twelve pence should he demand it; otherwise he left everything to 'my loving and most dearly beloved Wife' (GL, MS 9051/11, fol. 245). The *Weekly Journal, or, Saturday Post* reported that he left an estate of £5000, but no inventory survives to substantiate this claim. TIM WALES

Sources A. McKenzie, 'Lives of the most notorious criminals: popular literature of crime in England, 1670–1770', PhD diss., University of Toronto, 1999 • L. B. Faller, 'In contrast to Defoe: the Rev. Paul Lorrain, historian of crime', *Huntington Library Quarterly*, 60 (1976), 59–78 • P. Linebaugh, 'The ordinary of Newgate and his account', *Crime in England, 1550–1800*, ed. J. S. Cockburn (1977), 246–69 • M. Harris, 'Trials and criminal biographies: a case study in distribution', *Sale and distribution of books from 1700*, ed. M. Harris and R. Myers (1982) • *Private correspondence and miscellaneous papers of Samuel Pepys*, ed. J. R. Tanner, 2 vols. (1926) • *The life, journals and correspondence of Samuel Pepys*, ed. J. Smith, 2 vols. (1841), 1.261–2 • P. Lorrain, 'The royal anagram of Charles the second', BL, Stowe MS 987 • P. Lorrain, *The case of Paul Lorrain, ordinary of Newgate, most humbly offer'd to the honourable House of Commons* (1712) • P. Lorrain, *The ordinary of Newgate his account of the behaviour, confessions, and dying-words of Captain William Kidd, and other pirates … May 23, 1701* (1701) • P. Lorrain, *The ordinary of Newgate his account* (21 July 1703), (21 June 1704), (25 Oct 1704), (5 Dec 1715), (7 Dec 1715), (13 July 1716) • P. Lorrain, *Walking with God* (1703) • P. Lorrain, *A sermon preached … on the … fast-day for the fire of London* (1707) • repertories of the court of aldermen, 1698–1720, CLRO, REP 104–REP 124 • *The letters of Samuel Pepys and his family circle*, ed. H. T. Heath (1955) • R. L. Ollard, *Samuel Pepys: a life* (1984) • D. Defoe, *A hymn to the pillory* (1703) • A. Bryant, *Samuel Pepys: the years of peril* (1948) • will, GL, MS 9051/11, fols. 244–6 • *Weekly Journal, or, British Gazetteer* (10 Oct 1719), 1419 • *Weekly Journal, or, Saturday Post* (10–17 Oct 1719), pp. 268, 274 • *The Original Weekly Journal* (10 Oct 1719), 1556 • *The history of the press-yard* (1717), 50–52 • letter from Paul Lorrain to Dr Hans Sloane, BL, Sloane MS 40976, fol. 38*r* • threatening letter, 1715, BL, Add. MS 38507, fols. 172*r* and *v* • W. A. Shaw, ed., *Letters of denization and acts of naturalization for aliens in England and Ireland, 1701–1800*, 2, Huguenot Society of London, 27 (1923), 221 • W. Minet and S. Minet, eds., *Livre des tesmoinages de l'église de Threadneedle Street, 1669–1789*, Huguenot Society of London, 21 (1909), 181 • 'Mulieres non homines, ou, La femme deshumanisée', Bodl. Oxf., Rawl. MS D421

Wealth at death £5000: *Weekly Journal, or, Saturday Post*, 10 Oct 1719, 268

Lort, Michael (1724/5–1790), antiquary, a descendant of a Pembrokeshire family, was the eldest child of Roger Lort (1693/4–1745) of Tenby, a major in the Royal Welch Fusiliers who died of wounds after the battle of Fontenoy, and his wife, Anne (1697/8–1767), only child of Edward Jenkins, vicar of Fareham in Hampshire. His brothers and sisters all died before him; his sister Anne was the mother of William Lort Mansel, bishop of Bristol. Lort was educated at Evans's school, Tenby, and William Cole claimed that

Michael Lort (1724/5–1790), by John Downman, 1777

he went on to Westminster School, but there is no evidence of that in the school registers (Brydges, 1.469). He entered Trinity College, Cambridge, in June 1743 as a pensioner aged eighteen and proceeded BA (1747), MA (1750), BD (1761), and DD (1780). He was incorporated at Oxford on 7 July 1759. Trinity elected him to a fellowship in 1749 and he vacated it in March 1781.

After graduation Lort became librarian to one of the great collectors of the age, Dr Richard Mead, until Mead's death in 1754. He was ordained priest in March 1754 and for the rest of his life he held numerous appointments both clerical and lay. Elected to the regius professorship of Greek at Cambridge in 1759 he enjoyed it virtually as a sinecure for twelve years, and left not even so much as a faded reputation as a classicist. Even the Greek verses above his name in several university collections were not his own but those of Thomas Zouch. He was debarred by the terms of this professorship from holding other offices in Cambridge and from proceeding to his doctor's degree so that by 1764 he was considering whether to apply for the university librarianship if it fell vacant. This came to nothing, and in 1768 he also failed to secure the regius professorship of modern history which went to his friend Thomas Gray.

In 1761 Lort had become chaplain to the bishop of Peterborough, and was vicar of Bottisham, Cambridgeshire, from 1763 to 1770; from 1771 until his death he was rector of St Matthew's, Friday Street, London. During 1776 he accompanied Levett Hanson on a continental tour. He served as domestic chaplain to Archbishop Frederick Cornwallis, a great friend of the dean of Ely whose wife was a kinswoman of Lort, between September 1779 and 1783 when a visiting American, Thomas Hutchinson, heard him race 'through the litany as fast as a clerk would have gone through an instrument which was mere matter of form' (*Diary and Letters of … Thomas Hutchinson*, 2.318). He was given a prebend at St Paul's Cathedral in 1780 which he held until his death. Lort married on 19 May 1783 Susannah (*bap.* 1741, *d.* 1792), the daughter of William Norfolk, a Cambridge alderman, and his wife, Susannah. They had no children. In 1785 he became librarian to the archbishop at Lambeth, and he also had a position in the duke of Devonshire's household as keeper of his coins and medals; he was described in the *Public Advertiser* as 'the Duke's Antiquary' (15 Sept 1788). To these preferments Lort added the living of St Michael, Mile End, near Colchester, to which he was collated in 1789, and the sinecure rectory of Fulham, Middlesex, for six months before his death.

Lort was in touch with many scholars whose tastes and interests he shared, and he was a fellow of both the Society of Antiquaries from 1755 (he resigned after some time as its vice-president in 1788) and of the Royal Society from 1766. A great deal of his correspondence survives and parts of it, such as those with Walpole and Bishop Percy, have been printed. He was a friend and executor of the numismatist George North and inherited (with Anthony Askew) his books and other collections, and gave John Nichols a memoir of him. He was generous in supplying information to others, and especially obliging to Horace Walpole who had a high regard for him, and was indebted to him for many researches and for acting as an intermediary with Richard Gough. He made careful investigations into Chatterton and the Rowley forgeries, even travelling to Bristol to interview those who knew the poet; he resolutely defended Walpole's conduct in the affair. He helped James Granger with his book on portraiture and was an early patron of John Carter, the architectural draughtsman. His manuscripts are the basis of certain biographies in Alexander Chalmers's biographical dictionary, and of 'The whole duty of man', an account that Nichols later printed in *Literary Anecdotes*. He also gave Nichols assistance with his history of Lambeth.

Lort published only a few short pieces on his own account: an obsequious sermon given to the university on the anniversary of the accession of George II (1760), and another preached at Lambeth on the consecration of the bishop of Peterborough (1770); a Tudor document given him by Thomas Astle concerning the constitution and officers of the university whose publication in 1769 coincided with the installation of the duke of Grafton as chancellor; a short commentary on the Lord's prayer (1790); a letter to the *Public Advertiser* (5 September 1771) to complain of scurrilous attacks on the king in the press; a few notes for the *Gentleman's Magazine*; and papers for *Archaeologia*. Like many of his kind he projected works that never appeared; there are, for example, fragmentary notes for a history of Trinity College (Bodl. Oxf., MS Gough Camb. 54), and a life of Bentley was hardly started. He wrote to Walpole in 1760 to say he lived among books and loved to 'tumble them over' (Walpole, *Corr.*, 16.141), and he was an inveterate annotator of his library, which was sold after his death in April and May 1791. Fanny Burney met Lort often and found that—when not inadvertently embarrassing her with talk of *Evelina*—he could be 'comical and diverting', in manner 'somewhat blunt and odd', and 'curious in every species of antiquity, and difficult in none', while Susannah Lort was 'a most light and merry-hearted dame' (*Diary and Letters of Madame D'Arblay*, 1.91, 476, 4.408–9).

In August 1790 Lort was thrown from his carriage on a hill at Colchester; he died from his injuries on 5 November at his London home, 6 Savile Row. He was buried in St Matthew's, Friday Street, where Susannah Lort erected a memorial tablet; she died on 5 February 1792 and was also buried there. When the church was demolished in 1883 their remains were removed to the City of London cemetery at Ilford. JOHN D. PICKLES

Sources Nichols, *Lit. anecdotes*, 2.594–605 • Walpole, *Corr.*, 16.137–228; 46.1578–9 • Nichols, *Illustrations*, 7.438–565 • D. A. Winstanley, *Unreformed Cambridge: a study of certain aspects of the university in the eighteenth century* (1935), 114, 117, 120, 265 • *Diary and letters of Madame D'Arblay (1778–1840)*, ed. C. Barrett and A. Dobson, 6 vols. (1904–5), vol. 1, pp. 91, 476; vol. 4, pp. 408–9; vol. 6, p. 477 • 'Observations on Celts', *Archaeologia*, 5 (1779), 106–18 • 'Account of an ancient inscription in North America', *Archaeologia*, 8 (1787), 290–301 • 'Extract of a letter from Col. Sydenham to Lord Macartney dated St. Thomas Mount, near Madras, Oct 14 1786', *Archaeologia*, 9 (1789), 81–3 • *GM*, 1st ser., 53 (1783), 451 • *GM*, 1st ser., 60 (1790), 1055, 1199 • *GM*, 1st ser., 61 (1791), 577 • *GM*, 1st ser., 74 (1804), 511 • *GM*, 1st ser., 81/1 (1811), 526 • W. M. Palmer, *William Cole of Milton* (1935), 172 • E. Brydges, *Restituta, or, Titles, extracts, and characters of old books in English literature*, 4 vols. (1814–16), vol. 1, p. 469; vol. 3, pp. 59, 226–7; vol. 4, p. 370 • *The diary and letters of His Excellency Thomas Hutchinson*, ed. P. O. Hutchinson, 2 (1886), 318 • *DNB* • *IGI* • Bodl. Oxf., MS Gough Camb. 54

Archives BL, copy of Pope's *Essay on man* with MS notes and additions • Bodl. Oxf., collections for Trinity College, Cambridge • Boston PL, letters • NL Wales • Yale U. | BL, corresp. with William Cole, etc., Add. MSS 5811-6401, *passim* • BL, letters to Lord Hardwicke, Add. MSS 35350–35658 • BL, letters to Horace Walpole, Add. MS 12527 • Bodl. Oxf., corresp. with John Charles Brooke • JRL, letters to Hester Lynch Thrale • S. Antiquaries, Lond., letters to Richard Gough

Likenesses J. Downman, chalk drawing, 1777, FM Cam. [*see illus.*] • J. Hawksworth, engraving, 1777 (after J. Downman), repro. in Nichols, *Illustrations*, facing p. 438 • F. Grose, etching (*The antiquarian mastiff*), BM, NPG • S. Harding, watercolour, BM • etching, BM

Lort [Lorte], **Sir Roger, first baronet (1607/8–1664)**, Latin poet, was the eldest son of Henry Lort of Stackpole, Pembrokeshire. He was admitted as a gentleman commoner to Wadham College, Oxford, in 1624, aged sixteen, sharing a chamber there in 1625 with his brother Sampson. He matriculated on 3 November 1626, graduated BA on 11 June 1627, and proceeded to the Middle Temple. In 1632 he married Hester, daughter of Francis *Annesley, second Viscount Valentia (*bap.* 1586, *d.* 1660). The 'ambidextrous' Lorts played a leading role in Pembrokeshire. In 1643 Lort was an active royalist, commissioned by Lord Carbery to raise a regiment, and on 19 April of that year Lort and Robert Rudd, archdeacon of Carmarthen, were sent for as delinquents by parliament. In August 1643 Lort secured possession of Tenby for the king, by threats and lavish financial guarantees. Carbery's royalists then dissipated their forces and Lort's fortified house at Stackpole, a few miles south of Pembroke, was the first garrison attacked, falling on 30 January 1644. He rapidly submitted to parliament, agreed to serve on parliamentary committees (like many other former royalists), and was freed from delinquency and restored to his estates on 26 July 1644, though a fine of £1000 was imposed on 8 September 1645.

While in London securing his future Lort published his 'first book' of Latin epigrams, *Epigrammatum Rogeri Lort, armigeri, Cambro-Britanni, Oxoniensis … liber primus* (1646), comprising fourteen pages of reasonably accomplished elegiacs—evidence of the value of Latin for furthering personal ambition. The book was rare by Wood's time, though Nicholas Lloyd 'commended the poems therein to be very good' (Wood, *Ath. Oxon.*, 3.232). Lort reveals a genuine interest in poetry (including Christopher Ocland's *Anglorum praelia*), and close friendship for Archdeacon Rudd and former Middle Temple colleagues. He presents himself as a loyal parliamentarian, moderate in religion, lamenting the cruelties of civil war (worse than the conduct of wild bears or boars; Lort, *Epigrammatum*, 1), the proliferation of newspapers, and the unsightly brawls of Independents and presbyterians. Driven from home and family by Sir Charles Gerard, leader of a royalist counter-offensive, he describes how he undertook a perilous sea voyage to London. Fairfax receives extravagant praise, as equal to Gustavus Adolphus. The fiercest scorn is reserved for 'J. P. Pembrochiensem rapacissimum' (John Poyer, parliamentary governor of Pembroke Castle), who resented the Lorts' successful trimming. The feud with Poyer continued and Poyer imprisoned the Lorts in 1647, refusing Fairfax's order for their release. Soon afterwards Poyer was in revolt against parliament, with the Lorts now acting as loyal parliamentary commissioners and suppliers. One contemporary thought Roger Lort 'of any principle or religion to acquire wealth', and Sampson no better (Leach, 221); another that Roger fought 'in preservation of no cause but his own' (Jenkins, 26). By the Restoration, Lort was a royalist again, and in 1662 he was created a baronet. He died in 1664, survived by his second wife, Ann Wyndham (who later married Sir Edward Mansel); Lort was buried at St Petrox Church, Stackpole. The baronetcy passed to his son John; it died out in 1698 with Lort's grandson Gilbert. Lort's final epigram of 1646 promises further compositions, if they please the reader (if not, he says, that is more than enough); for whatever reason, there was no second book. D. K. MONEY

Sources A. L. Leach, *The history of the civil war (1642–1649) in Pembrokeshire and on its borders* (1937) • R. B. Gardiner, ed., *The registers of Wadham College, Oxford*, 2 vols. (1889–95) • Wood, *Ath. Oxon.*, new edn • G. H. Jenkins, *The foundations of modern Wales, 1642–1780* (1987) • W. S. K. Thomas, *Stuart Wales, 1603–1714* (1988) • J. R. Phillips, *Memoirs of the civil war in Wales and the marches, 1642–1649*, 2nd edn (1878) • J. Burke and J. B. Burke, *A genealogical and heraldic history of the extinct and dormant baronetcies of England, Ireland and Scotland*, 2nd edn (1841); repr. (1844) • *DNB* • R. Lort, *Epigrammatum liber primus* (1646)

Wealth at death property in Pembrokeshire to be used to provide money for daughters: will

Loryng, Sir Nigel. *See* Loring, Sir Neil (*c*.1315–1386).

Losey, Joseph Walton (1909–1984), film director, was born on 14 January 1909 in La Crosse, Wisconsin, USA, the first of two children of Joseph Walton Losey (1879–1925) and his wife, Ina Higbee (*c*.1879–1959). An unhealthy, asthmatic child, his upbringing was middle-class and Episcopalian, though as a young man he abandoned religious belief for Marxism. His first four decades were lived in the USA, and, though he left in 1951, never to return to live or to make films, he remained an American citizen. 'British' only by prolonged residence (from 1953 to 1975, and then again at the end of his life from 1983 to 1984), despite much operating in the world of international film production, he directed enough films of British subject matter, from a British base, with British actors and other collaborators, to be considered a British director. Indeed in the three major works he directed from scripts by the English dramatist Harold Pinter—*The Servant* (1963), *Accident* (1967), and *The Go-Between* (1971)—he made films which must be accounted in the top echelon of British productions of the second half of the twentieth century.

Aged forty-four when he settled in Britain in 1953, Losey had already had two careers, the first in New York theatre (1933–8) and radio (1937–43), the second as a Hollywood director with films released between 1948 and 1951. Educated at La Crosse High School, then Dartmouth and Harvard universities (at the first of which he switched from medicine to arts), he developed theatrical interests which he followed up on the New York theatre scene, as a critic, then as a director. Though less sensationally successful, his progress paralleled that of his contemporary Orson Welles. Both established reputations in the febrile off-Broadway theatre, both worked in radio, and both showed little initial interest in film. However, where Welles's work was fundamentally apolitical, Losey's was allied to left-wing projects, most famously *The Living Newspaper* documentary theatre. In 1936 he got to know Bertolt Brecht, who was visiting the USA, an association that was to reverberate throughout his life, politically and aesthetically.

Losey's introduction to film came through two ideologically clashing routes—first, the animated cartoon *Pete Roleum and his Friends* (1939), propaganda for American oil interests, and second, work for various progressive educational foundations on documentaries (1940). In 1943 he was invited to Hollywood by MGM, where his career, slow to start, was interrupted by brief wartime military service (ended with an honourable discharge for health reasons). Though initially frustratingly inactive in Hollywood, he directed, under Brecht's supervision, the now legendary stage production, starring Charles Laughton, of Brecht's *Life of Galileo* in Hollywood and New York (August, then December, 1947). On returning to film, he worked across a number of studios. Losey's first feature film was *The Boy with Green Hair* (1948), an inventive socially conscious allegory. Four films followed, of which *The Prowler* and *M* (both 1951), both thrillers, the second an Americanization of Fritz Lang's famous film, are best-known, and already mature and highly disturbing works. However, Losey's communist activities, including his friendship with Brecht and Hanns Eisler, which had led to his being under FBI surveillance from 1943, and the growing House Un-American Activities Committee (HUAC) pressure on Hollywood culminated in Losey's being subpoenaed to testify at the hearings, and led him to abandon his American career. Though he later painfully revoked his Stalinism, and indeed dropped all formal political commitment, the HUAC were not misled about his beliefs at this point.

Joseph Walton Losey (1909–1984), by Norman Hargood, 1963

As a blacklisted film-maker, Losey's earliest work in Britain had to be done under pseudonyms. After minor television work his British film career began, dogged by financial and residency problems, with a string of mainly low-budget films: *The Sleeping Tiger* (1954), *The Intimate Stranger* (1956), and *Time without Pity* (1957; the first made under his own name). These won him a three-film contract and a near £1 million budget from Rank for *The Gypsy and the Gentleman* (1958), but its lack of success resulted in Rank settling the contract. Then followed *Blind Date* (1960), and two films, *The Criminal* (1960) and *The Damned* (1963), which enhanced his reputation in Britain and, particularly, in France.

Eve (released in Europe as *Eva*, 1962–3) was a watershed in Losey's career. It marked his beginnings as an international director, using major international stars (here Jeanne Moreau; later Monica Vitti, Richard Burton, and Elizabeth Taylor), and moving into the hazardous world of internationally financed big-budget films. *Eve*, disputed over by director and producers, displays some of these hazards, finally cut without directorial approval, and not available for viewing in its original form until a sole surviving (Swedish and Finnish subtitled) copy was released on American DVD (2002). Back in Britain, Losey made *The Servant* (1963), then the trenchant *King and Country* (1964), where he found in British class relations a complex and psychically violent reality to match the entrapments of the American psyche in a film such as *The Prowler*. He then made that wittily playful product of the 'swinging 60s' *Modesty Blaise* (1966), and between *Accident* (1967) and *The Go-Between* (1971) pursued two expensive star-laden projects, *Boom!* (1968; with Burton and Taylor and a Tennessee Williams script) and *Secret Ceremony* (1968; with Mia Farrow, Taylor, and Robert Mitchum), films both admired and heavily criticized for their mannerism, adding to the debate about the meaningfulness of the 'baroque' elements in Losey's visual style.

The pre-eminent films of Losey's British period, *The Servant*, *Accident*, and *The Go-Between*, were wholly individual in tone but linked together by their intense reworking of preoccupations evident in the earlier British films—thematics of power relations mediated by class and sexuality, and formal inventiveness with regard to *mise-en-scène*, sound, and various distancing devices. These expanded under the acknowledged influence of Resnais's film *Muriel* (1963) into an appropriation of avant-garde elements, in particular the temporal dislocations of the two later works, ingenious but muted enough to avoid too much narrative disturbance. In this Losey successfully negotiated between the worlds of high popular and art cinema. Of the trio of Losey–Pinter collaborations, *The Servant* was distinctive in its evocation of early 1960s London decadence, an enigmatic parable of decline suffused with class hostilities in which an indolent upper-class James Fox is subverted by his butler Dirk Bogarde, and the sexuality of Sarah Miles. *Accident*, shot in colour, like *The Go-Between*, enacted its more subterranean violences in Oxford settings, as Bogarde and Stanley Baker, playing academics, jostle for personal predominance with an enigmatic foreign student. While both films explored the atmospherics and mores of very different areas of contemporary England, their successor, *The Go-Between*, adapted from L. P. Hartley's novel of childhood trauma and its adult consequences, recreated a pre-First World War Edwardian past. If its eye for nostalgic beauty suggests aspects of what has been later identified as 'heritage cinema', those typical ever-present Losey elements of mordant class relations, sexual struggle, and violence—both covert and overt—and the discreet glimpses of the ruined protagonist in the present, refuse the viewer easy luxuries. All three films, in the performances of Dirk Bogarde, Stanley Baker, James and Edward Fox, Sarah Miles, Julie Christie, Margaret Leighton, and others, confirmed Losey's reputation as a great director of actors.

In the last phase of his career Losey worked predominantly outside Britain, first on *The Assassination of Trotsky* (1972; with Burton), *A Doll's House* (1973; with Jane Fonda), *Galileo* (1975; reworking the 1947 stage production), and *The Romantic Englishwoman* (1975). Losey's late residence in Paris (1975–82) led to a number of French-language films—*Mr Klein* (1976), *Les routes du sud* (1978), and *La truite* (1982). Of these *Mr Klein*, set amid the antisemitism of Nazi-occupied Paris, gained wide critical acceptance as a late masterpiece, alongside *Don Giovanni* (1979), a version of Mozart's opera, which has claims to be the greatest opera film of all. Now gravely ill, Losey directed only one more film after returning to Britain in 1983, *Steaming* (released in 1985).

Joe Losey was a large, physically imposing man, described more than once as looking like a Red Indian. He suffered continually from asthma, and in later life heavy drinking contributed to failing health and difficult professional and personal behaviour. Such characteristics were no doubt exacerbated by the strain of dealing with collapsing projects. Accounts of him by his contemporaries—in their statements, often contradictory, of admiration and dislike—vary more than with more serene personalities.

Like his professional life, Losey's personal life was less than serene. He married four times. On 23 July 1937 he married Elizabeth Jester, *née* Hawes (1904–1971), a fashion designer, journalist, and author. They were divorced in 1944. The marriage produced one son, Gavrik (*b.* July 1938). Losey's second marriage, to Louisa Stuart (Louise Moss), an actress, on 19 October 1944, was dissolved in 1953. He then married Dorothy Bromiley, also an actress, in Britain on 16 June 1956; they were divorced in 1963. Losey's second son, and last child, Joshua (*b.* 1957), was the product of this marriage. Losey's last marriage, to Patricia Mohan, *née* Tolusso (*b.* 1930), on 29 September 1970—like his previous two wives, she was considerably younger than Losey—lasted until his death. She has a credit as screenwriter on *Steaming*.

Losey's career was symptomatic of the pressures operating on the independent high commercial film director with artistic aims but working in the market place on large projects demanding expensive stars. The list of abandoned Losey projects (usually when finance fell through) is very large, several for every film made. The best-known of these was the collaboration with Pinter on a version of Proust's *Remembrance of Things Past*.

Losey's films are distinguished by the psychic violence of his characters; by the pessimism, including a marked sexual pessimism, of his narratives; by an ambivalent attraction–repulsion to the high bourgeoisie who were often his subjects; by his brilliant work with actors such as Stanley Baker, Jeanne Moreau, Dirk Bogarde, and Alain Delon; by creative use of sound and fastidious attention to details of photographic reproduction; and by inventive and meticulous *mise-en-scène* (there are many stories of his extreme attention to details others felt would not be noticed). Though Losey wrote no autobiography, his intellectuality and articulateness made him a suitable subject for extended interviews by critics. In these he gave much biographical and artistic information about himself. A well-researched biography by David Caute (1994) adds much further information, though its hostility to its subject makes it a complicated source. Before he died the film-maker lodged his archive of materials related to his films at the British Film Institute.

Losey remains a controversial figure, for most critics one of very uneven production, but certainly one who made major films in each of his main periods, and a dominating presence on the British and international film scene from the 1960s to the 1980s. He died of cancer at his home, 29 Royal Avenue, Chelsea, London, on 22 June 1984, and was cremated at Putney Vale crematorium.

BRUCE BABINGTON

Sources D. Caute, *Joseph Losey: a revenge on life* (1994) • T. Milne, ed., *Losey on Losey* (1967) • M. Ciment, ed., *Conversations with Losey* (1985) • BFI, Joseph Losey collection • D. Bogarde, *Snakes and ladders* (1978) • V. Navasky, *Naming names* (New York, 1980) • M. Riley and J. Palmer, *The films of Joseph Losey* (New York, 1993) • H. Pinter, *Five screenplays* (1971) • F. Hirsch, *Joseph Losey* (Boston, 1980) • R. Durgnat, *A mirror for England: British movies from austerity to affluence* (1970) • d. cert. • *CGPLA Eng. & Wales* (1984)

Archives BFI, corresp., papers, scripts | FILM BFI NFTVA, *Cinema*, 2 Sept 1971 • BFI NFTVA, 'il cinema di Joseph Losey', 1981 | SOUND BL NSA, recorded talks

Likenesses N. Hargood, photograph, 1963, NPG [*see illus.*] • photograph, 1968, Hult. Arch. • double portrait, photograph, 1969 (with his wife), Hult. Arch. • A. Springs, bromide print, 1979, NPG

Wealth at death £2844: probate, 24 Sept 1984, *CGPLA Eng. & Wales*

Losh, James (**1763–1833**), barrister, was born on 10 June 1763 in Woodside, Wreay, near Carlisle, the fourth child and fourth of the eight sons (one of whom died shortly after birth) and one daughter of John Losh, gentleman, of Woodside, and his wife, Catherine, daughter of John Liddell of Moorhouse, Burgh by Sands, Cumberland. Educated privately, he went to Trinity College, Cambridge, in 1782, and graduated BA in 1786. He then entered himself at Lincoln's Inn, and, after being called to the bar in 1789, began to practise on the northern circuit.

On a visit to Paris in 1792, Losh narrowly escaped from the city during the September massacres, possibly owing his escape to the influence of Jean-Paul Marat, who had practised as a veterinary surgeon in Newcastle. Ill health later led him to spend some time in the Bristol area, where he cemented his friendship with William Wordsworth, whom he had met in 1795 at a gathering of radical friends (including George Dyer, William Frend, William Godwin, and John Horne Tooke). He also became a friend of Samuel Taylor Coleridge and Robert Southey.

In 1799 he settled as a barrister in Newcastle upon Tyne, rapidly acquiring an enviable reputation as a man of strict integrity and sound judgement, whether in the courts or as an arbitrator in industrial disputes. As a Unitarian he was debarred from holding civic appointments or public office, but, following the repeal of the Test and Corporation Acts in 1828, for the annulment of which he had campaigned, the corporation of Newcastle in 1832 invested him with the highest judicial function in their gift, the recordership, and shortly afterwards with the honorary freedom of the city.

Losh was an active reformer and philanthropist. Among the causes which he espoused with fervour were the abolition of the slave trade, Catholic emancipation together with total religious freedom, and, above all, parliamentary reform. A friend of both Charles (later second Earl) Grey and Henry Brougham, he used his influence in the northern counties to speed the passing of the Reform Bill. In the smaller world of Newcastle, Losh did valuable work towards the relief of indigence and the betterment of social conditions and educational standards; he was a leading figure in the improvement of services in the infirmary and the fever hospital, and the establishment of Sunday schools, infant and secondary schools, and mechanics' institutes. Always forward-looking, and abreast of industrial developments, he was a prime mover, as chairman of the directors, in the construction of the Newcastle and Carlisle Railway.

Very widely read and a lover of drama and music, Losh was for some thirty years one of the most influential members of the famous Literary and Philosophical Society of Newcastle upon Tyne. In 1791 he published an edition of *Areopagitica* by John Milton, and in 1831 a translation of Benjamin Constant's *Collection complète des ouvrages publiés sur le gouvernement représentatif et la constitution actuelle de la France* (1818–20), as *Observations on the Strength of the Government in France*, and some of his reforming speeches were printed. He had a fine presence and was a forceful speaker. He was a devoted family man, and a friend to men of all religious creeds and political persuasions.

In 1798 Losh married Cecilia, daughter of the Revd Roger Baldwin of Aldingham, Lancashire. They had five sons and three daughters. Losh died in Greta Bridge, Yorkshire, on 23 September 1833.

T. S. DORSCH, *rev.*

Sources *The diaries and correspondence of James Losh*, ed. E. Hughes, 2 vols., SurtS, 171, 174 (1962–3) • H. Lonsdale, *The worthies of Cumberland*, 4 (1873) • R. Welford, *Men of mark 'twixt Tyne and Tweed*, 3 (1895)

Archives Carlisle Library, diaries • NRA, priv. coll., letters and papers | Herts. ALS, letters to James Thain • U. Durham L., letters to Charles, second Earl Grey • UCL, letters to Henry Brougham

Losh, Sara (*bap.* **1786**, *d.* **1853**), architect, was born at Woodside, Wreay, near Carlisle, and was baptized on 6 January 1786, the oldest of the four children of John Losh (1756–1814), landowner and industrial entrepreneur of Woodside, and his wife, Isabella (1765–1799), daughter of Thomas Bonner of Callerton Hall, Northumberland. Of their four children, John (*b.* 1787) died in infancy and Joseph (1790–1848) was mentally handicapped. The Loshes had lived at Woodside since the sixteenth century, progressing from yeomanry to squirearchy, and John extended his interests into the chemical industry on Tyneside. Sara and her sister, Katherine (1788–1835), inherited their father's estate equally, and on Katherine's death Sara succeeded to the whole substantial estate, including the Walker alkali works managed by her uncle William. The sisters were very close, and Sara—who was quieter and more studious than Katherine—was deeply affected by her sister's death. Neither ever married, though one of them may have been romantically attached to a schoolfellow, Major Thain, killed in the Khyber Pass by a poisoned arrow in 1842, and commemorated by Sara in a pine cone

Sara Losh (*bap.* 1786, *d.* 1853), by unknown engraver (after Thomas Heathfield Carrick)

vigorously carved on a large irregular shaped slab in the churchyard.

None of Sara's journals or drawings has survived, and our information about her life comes chiefly from a memoir by Henry Lonsdale in his *The Worthies of Cumberland* (1867; new edn, 1873). He says she was educated at school in Wreay, London, and Bath, and travelled in France, Italy, and Germany in 1814 and 1817. She read widely and deeply, mixed with the intellectual élite of the north, spoke French and Italian fluently, and could translate Latin extempore. Lonsdale says, 'Her intellect … almost approached in power that of my friend "George Eliot"' (Lonsdale, 215).

Losh would not have described herself as an architect. Apart from restoring the south front of Woodside (mostly dem.) she did not start building until 1828, and most of her eighteen architectural projects, from simple wells to village schools, were built in Wreay at her own expense. All her early designs were copies of what she had seen in her travels or studied in Britain; for example, during the 1830s she adapted the Bewcastle cross in Wreay churchyard to commemorate her parents, and copied a Pompeian villa for her schoolmaster's cottage. But her masterpiece, St Mary's Church, Wreay, was astoundingly original.

In 1840 Losh offered to donate a site and pay for replacing the dilapidated Wreay chapel 'on condition that I should be left unrestricted as to the mode of building it' (Drew, 29). A faculty was granted in May 1841 and the completed church was dedicated in December 1842 at a cost of £1200. She herself described it as 'early Saxon or modified Lombardic' (ibid., 34), and similarities have been found with foreign churches she may have seen, and such English curiosities as the contemporary Christ Church, Streatham, which she almost certainly had not. But whatever her sources, the finished building has a total coherence and affecting simplicity. Losh aimed to reproduce an early Christian basilica. The aisleless nave opens into a semicircular colonnaded apse forming thirteen seats, with the altar (Italian marble supported by brass eagles) on the chord. She designed the prolific, vigorously expressive decoration, inside and out; the local builder's son William Hindson jun. executed the stone carving, and the woodcarving was by her gardener. Sara and her cousin William themselves carved the alabaster font. The profusion of naturalistic ornament (including a snake and crocodile as gargoyles) is best explained as an attempt to express a pantheistic celebration of creation. Pevsner likened it to arts and crafts work of 1900 (*Cumberland and Westmorland*, 212) and D. G. Rossetti described it, in a letter to Janey Morris in 1869, as 'very original and beautiful … very much more so than the things done by the young architects now' (Kemp, 125). There is no distinctive Christian symbolism, not even a cross, but the vitality of the carvings and the use of natural forms reflects the cycle of death, rebirth, and eternity. In addition Losh deploys her own symbolism and draws on fossil forms studied in the new science of geology. Hill states that

> If there is any explanation for her anticipation of Ruskin it is surely that her imagination, like his, had been fired by Romanticism, by a desire to express in architecture the sympathy of humanity and the natural world … How important is Sara Losh's work? … If artistic value is to be measured by an ability to seize the currents of thought and feeling that flow through the age and give them fresh and vital expression, Sara Losh and her church are very important indeed. (Hill, 39)

Wreay church was Sara's last building. Subject to bronchitis in her later years, she died at Woodside on 29 March 1853 after catching a chill, and was buried on 4 April in her sister's grave in the Losh enclosure which she had designed in Wreay churchyard. CHARLES PLOUVIEZ

Sources H. Lonsdale, *The worthies of Cumberland*, 4 (1873), 197–238 · K. Drew, 'Sara Losh and "the Chapel of Ease"', BArch diss., U. Newcastle, 1987 · L. Kemp, *Woodside* (1997) · *Cumberland and Westmorland*, Pevsner (1967) · *The diaries and correspondence of James Losh*, ed. E. Hughes, 2 vols., SurtS, 171, 174 (1962–3) · N. Pevsner, 'Sara Losh's church', *ArchR*, 142 (1967), 65–7 · Cumbria AS, Wreay parish archive, PR118 · parish registers, St Cuthbert's, Carlisle, Cumbria AS, Carlisle · Mannix and W. Whellan, *History, gazetteer and directory of Cumberland* (1847), 169, 173–4 · S. Jenkins, *England's thousand best churches* (1999), 103 · R. Hill, 'Romantic affinities: Sarah Losh's Cumbria church anticipates Ruskin and the arts and crafts movement', *Crafts*, 166 (Sept–Oct 2000), 35–9

Likenesses T. H. Carrick, miniature, 1836, repro. in Lonsdale, *Worthies of Cumberland* · D. Dunbar the younger, bust · engraving (after T. H. Carrick), repro. in Lonsdale, *Worthies of Cumberland* [*see illus.*] · oils, Wreay church, Cumbria

Wealth at death probably wealthy: Lonsdale, *Worthies of Cumberland*; Losh, *Diaries*

Losinga, Herbert de (*d.* 1119), abbot of Ramsey and bishop of Norwich, was one of the most prominent English ecclesiastical leaders of his time.

Origins Herbert was born at Exmes, in the old *vicomté* of the Oximin in southern Normandy, the son of Robert de Losinga. Various explanations of his name have been advanced. That it is of Suffolk origins (from Lothingland hundred, Lowestoft) is patently mistaken; and the chronicler John of Worcester's remark that he was called Losinga because of his skill in flattery (*lozenga* is first recorded as meaning flatterer in 1384) is extremely unlikely, since his father bore the same name. The most likely explanation is that, as in the case of another Robert de Losinga, bishop of Hereford, it is a corruption of Lotharingia, and that Herbert's ancestors had come from that region to Normandy.

Herbert's career Herbert entered the abbey of Fécamp, where he rose to the office of prior. William Rufus (*d.* 1100), soon after his accession, summoned Herbert to England, and in 1087 or 1088 he was appointed abbot of Ramsey. Three years later, on the death of William de Beaufou, he was elevated to the bishopric of East Anglia, recently moved to Thetford, and was consecrated before 27 January 1091, probably on 5 January. There is no doubt that he paid money to the king for his appointment, and for that of his father as abbot of the New Minster at Winchester (subsequently Hyde Abbey)—one source specifies £1000—and thus committed simony, one of the sins most abhorred by reformers who took their lead from Rome. The episode is the subject of an early thirteenth-century wall painting in Norwich Cathedral.

In the next three years there is little information concerning Herbert; he attested three royal charters and was present on 4 December 1093 at the consecration of Archbishop Anselm, who may have had considerable influence on his subsequent decision and actions. On 2 February 1094 the king deprived Herbert of office. The reason for this was the bishop's repentance of his simony and his intention to resign his see into the hands of Pope Urban II who, in a time of schism, was not yet recognized by Rufus. The chronology of events is not absolutely clear, but it seems almost certain that the royal action preceded rather than followed Herbert's visit to the pope, who absolved him and restored him to his bishopric. It is remarkable how quickly he was forgiven and reinstated by the king, but Herbert repaid Rufus by joining all the bishops except Rochester in supporting him against Archbishop Anselm at the Council of Rockingham in February 1095. There is, indeed, no evidence of any further conflict between Herbert and the king or his successor. In 1101 he was dispatched by Henry I as one of the envoys to the papal curia to discuss Anselm's refusal of homage; an embassy disrupted by Herbert's capture for ransom in 1102 by Guy of Lyons, and one which was ultimately hardly a success, since not only did Pope Paschal II fully support Anselm, but the envoys misunderstood his message, and a second delegation had to be sent. When Herbert, with other bishops, wrote to the archbishop urging him to return from exile, this was certainly not done against the king's wishes. Although, again with other bishops, Herbert deplored Henry I's depredations of the church during Anselm's exile, he mentioned his affection for the king in a letter to a close friend, and he corresponded with Queen Matilda, for whom he composed a prayer.

That Anselm did not bear any resentment is suggested by his choice of Herbert in 1108 as his envoy to York to negotiate in the primacy dispute between the two archiepiscopal sees. Herbert attended councils of the English church in 1102, 1108, and 1109, and appears to have supported the archbishop's reforming measures, although after the council of 1102 he told Anselm that pastoral ministry in his diocese would almost come to a stop if all married clergy were to be suspended. On at least five occasions between 1096 and 1115 he was present at the consecration of bishops. He was a prominent figure within the English church, and the abbot of Ely at least hoped that he might emerge as successor to Anselm at Canterbury; it is interesting, however, that Herbert sharply refused the abbot's invitation to become involved in the simmering conflict between regulars and seculars as the champion of the monastic order.

Establishment of his see at Norwich In the history of his own diocese, Herbert's most obvious contribution is the removal of the see from Thetford to Norwich and his establishment there of a magnificent new cathedral staffed by a chapter of Benedictine monks. The tradition that the bishop embarked on its construction largely at his own expense as atonement for his simony need not be entirely discarded, as his foundation charter stresses the value of penitence; but it is not in fact necessary to explain the move, which was entirely in accord with the programme adopted by the Norman episcopate as a whole to move their sees to thriving urban centres. Although the removal from North Elmham to Thetford was recent, the church of St Mary there was small and was, moreover, held by the sons of Bishop Herfast, while the great magnate houses of Bigod and Warenne had a strong hold on the two halves of the town. The later tradition is that the establishment of the cathedral at Norwich took place on 9 April 1094, but this is too soon after Herbert's deprivation and probably during his journey to Rome. It is likely, in fact, that the king's permission was obtained in 1095, when a royal commission determined the bounds of the land to be handed over to the bishop in addition to the site of Holy Trinity Church, given to the bishopric by the Conqueror, and now to be demolished. Building probably began in 1096. There was inevitably a period of transition; the church of Thetford was not handed over to Roger (I) Bigod for the establishment of a Cluniac priory until 1103, and for some years Herbert was described as bishop of either place.

By early September 1101 Herbert made reference to the church of Holy Trinity, which he had built and consecrated. This obviously refers to the eastern end of the church, and possibly only the choir. By Herbert's death in 1119 building had progressed probably as far as the fourth or fifth bay of the nave. The building, which substantially survives, was completed under his successor, Everard, and is remarkable both for its scale (a nave of fourteen bays) and for its cosmopolitan sophistication. In essence an ancient Roman basilica, its elaborate decoration broke with the stark simplicity of the first generation of Anglo-Norman Romanesque. Much of the episcopal palace, akin to a miniature keep, was also built by 1119, although the monastic complex was not completed until the late twelfth century. The construction of the cathedral, following on that of the royal castle, totally transformed both the topography and the social structure of medieval Norwich. The liturgy introduced in the cathedral was that of Fécamp, the house of Herbert's profession, and, as the customs of Fécamp were themselves derived from Cluny, Norwich was drawn into one of the great reforming movements of the eleventh and early twelfth centuries.

Bishop Herbert in the initial years made substantial donations to the new community out of the revenues of the bishopric, both on the outskirts of Norwich and further afield in East Anglia. He imposed an aid on the whole diocese, collected in parishes, to finance the programme. He was also careful to obtain the support of both king and pope. Rufus almost certainly charged heavily for land around Holy Trinity Church, but Henry I gave the manor of Thorpe specifically to fund the building, and also granted valuable privileges. The earliest papal document in the Norwich archives is a bull of Pope Paschal II, issued in April 1102, when Herbert was in Rome. This confirmed the founder's own intentions, that a community of monks should for ever be established in the church of Norwich, and that no future bishop should expel them or in any way infringe the rights granted to them by the king and others of the faithful.

Development of religious life in his diocese In fact, lay investment in the new cathedral was not lavish. This did not denote lack of enthusiasm for the monastic order, but was rather the consequence of the foundation by the Norman aristocracy of East Anglia of numerous religious houses, which had first claim on the generosity of the tenants of the honours and which were encouraged by the bishop himself. In 1087 the only Benedictine communities in the region were Bury St Edmunds, St Benet of Hulme and the small cell at Rumburgh, and the earliest Norman foundation by William Malet at Eye. Thereafter, before Herbert's death in 1119, communities of French monks were established at Castle Acre (by the Warenne family, 1089), Clare (1090), Binham (Valognes, *c.*1093), Thetford (Bigod, 1103), Horsham St Faith (Robert fitz Walter and Sybil, his wife, 1103), and Wymondham (d'Aubigny, 1107). The ecclesiastical geography and religious practice of East Anglia was totally transformed and, as the buildings gradually rose, the influence of Herbert's architectural model at Norwich became apparent. His personal influence in this revolution is more difficult to document, as few episcopal charters survive from the period, which still relied largely on oral testimony. There are, in fact, only twenty episcopal *acta* for an episcopate of twenty-eight years. Hints are given, however, by Herbert's notification that a monastery was being built at Castle Acre in accordance with his wishes, by a reference to his confirmation for Clare, and by the indulgence which he granted to visitors to Horsham St Faith. His awareness of new trends in religion is indicated by his support for the foundation, towards the end of his life, of a house of Augustinian canons at Great Bricett.

Herbert's policy as diocesan bishop was assertive. He continued his predecessors' attempts to undermine the exempt status of the great Suffolk monastery of Bury St Edmunds, albeit ultimately unsuccessfully. He was alarmed by the exemption claimed by Thetford as a daughter house of Cluny, and waged a successful battle to ensure that the body of the founder, Roger Bigod, was buried in the cathedral rather than in his own monastery. The cathedral was intended to be a liturgical model for the diocese, and its influence was extended by the foundation of dependent cells at St Leonard's in Norwich and at Aldeby, Lynn, and Yarmouth; at the last of these, episcopal rights were staunchly defended against the claims of the local citizens. The best evidence for Herbert's aspirations is architectural. He built on a grand scale, modelled on the style of the cathedral, at the new town of Bishop's (now King's) Lynn, at Yarmouth, and at North and South Elmham, to the extent that his architectural programme has been described as a manifestation of 'episcopal imperialism' (Batcock, 188).

His sermons and letters It is possible to obtain some appreciation of Herbert's character and intellect because of the rare survival of collections of fourteen sermons and fifty-nine letters. The sermons, which were probably delivered to a monastic audience, reveal an encyclopaedic knowledge of scripture and a determination always to extract a moral from the text; Herbert was an expert in allegory. His knowledge of patristic writers may well have been derived from florilegia rather than from profound study of the texts themselves. His theology was generally conservative, and there is little hint of the application of reason to faith, which was the path of the future. His emphasis on the Real Presence in the eucharist is probably the legacy of Lanfranc. In only one instance does his preaching reflect a theological development of his own time; his Marian theology has been described as more advanced than that of any contemporary except Eadmer, and Herbert described himself as 'pious client of the Mother of God' (Alexander, 204). His effectiveness as a preacher, which of course cannot be fully appreciated from the written word, is suggested by an account of how his sermon at Ely at the translation of St Æthelthryth (Etheldreda) in 1107 reduced the congregation to tears.

Many of the letters are addressed to monastic students. They indicate that there was a school of liberal arts at Norwich and that the bishop took a keen interest in the education of oblates. The letters reveal a very traditional Benedictine attitude, compassionate and sensible, rigid in essentials and especially on obedience to the rule, flexible on peripheral matters. Herbert appreciated the dangers and temptations of the celibate life, especially for the young, and understood the difficulties caused by the simultaneous study of both Christian and pagan literature. Most especially, in letters and sermons, he stressed continually the obligation of charity: 'the church's poor people are the Body of Christ' (Alexander, 216), and 'alms extinguish sin as water does fire' (*Life, letters and sermons*, 2.27).

Death and reputation Late in 1116 Herbert set out again for Rome, this time with Archbishop Ralph of Canterbury, who was intent on resolving the dispute with York. He fell ill at Piacenza and returned to Normandy. Thereafter he attracted no notice from chroniclers until his death on 22 July 1119. He was buried before the high altar of his cathedral. It is no longer believed that the episcopal figure set in the north wall of the north transept is Herbert's image from his tomb (probably it rather represents St Felix) but the vestments are of the early twelfth century and its presence here is strangely appropriate. At Norwich the memory of the founder was, naturally, still cherished in the early fourteenth century. More significantly, both Orderic Vitalis and William of Malmesbury, who had fiercely condemned Herbert's simony, believed that by his record as bishop he had atoned for his sin.

CHRISTOPHER HARPER-BILL

Sources *The life, letters and sermons of Bishop Herbert de Losinga*, trans. E. M. Goulbern and H. Symonds, 2 vols. (1878) • *Herberti de Losinga primi episcopi Norwicensis epistolae*, ed. R. Anstruther (1846) • C. Harper-Bill, ed., *Norwich, 1070–1214*, English Episcopal Acta, 6 (1990) • B. Dodwell, ed., *The charters of Norwich Cathedral priory*, 1, PRSoc., 40, new ser., 78 (1974) • H. W. Saunders, ed., *The first register of Norwich Cathedral priory*, Norfolk RS, 11 (1939) • *Reg. RAN*, vols. 1–2 • J. W. Alexander, 'Herbert of Norwich 1091–1119: studies in the history of Norman England', *Studies in Medieval and Renaissance History*, 6 (1969), 115–232 • B. Dodwell, 'The foundation of Norwich Cathedral', *TRHS*, 5th ser., 7 (1957), 1–18 • I. Atherton and others, eds., *Norwich Cathedral: church, city and diocese, 1096–1996* (1996) • Ordericus Vitalis, *Eccl. hist.* • William of Malmesbury, *Gesta regum Anglorum / The history of the English kings*, ed. and trans. R. A. B. Mynors, R. M. Thomson, and M. Winterbottom, 2 vols., OMT (1998–9) • *Willelmi Malmesbiriensis monachi de gestis pontificum Anglorum libri quinque*, ed. N. E. S. A. Hamilton, Rolls Series, 52 (1870) • N. Batcock, 'The parish church in Norfolk in the eleventh and twelfth centuries', *Minsters and parish churches: the local church in transition, 950–1200*, ed. J. Blair (1988), 188

Archives CUL, MS Ii.2.19 • Royal Library of Belgium, Brussels, MS 3723 • Acta

Losinga, Robert de. *See* Robert the Lotharingian (*d.* 1095).

Loss, Joshua Alexander [Joe] **(1909–1990)**, bandleader, was born on 22 June 1909 in Spitalfields, London, the youngest of the family of two sons and two daughters of Israel Loss, of Russian origin, a cabinet-maker who had an office furnishing business, and his wife, Ada Loss. His mother and father were first cousins. Israel Loss recognized his son's musical talents and started him with violin lessons at the age of seven. It was hoped that he might become a concert violinist, and, after education at the Jewish Free School, Spitalfields, he studied at the Trinity College of Music and the London College of Music.

Loss's interests lay in lighter fields and, after playing in cinemas during silent films and in various bands, at the end of 1930 he formed his own first band to play at the Astoria Ballroom (then known as the Astoria Danse Salon) in Charing Cross Road, becoming, at the age of twenty-one, the youngest bandleader in the West End of London. Under the name of Joe Loss and his Harlem Band, his musicians first played as the number two unit, Joe Loss leading on violin, with three saxophones, trumpet, piano, and drums. Later they added a special tango section, which

Joshua Alexander [Joe] **Loss (1909–1990)**, by unknown photographer, 1950

featured two accordions and two violins. Occasionally they deputized for the Percival Mackey band at the Kit-Kat Club, and, when Mackey left to go into vaudeville at the beginning of 1932, Joe Loss took over to initiate a new 'popular price' policy, playing for daily tea, dinner, and supper dances, supported by and often combining with Fred Spedbury's Coney Islanders. He returned to the Astoria in 1934 to become the number one band and remained there until the outbreak of the Second World War in 1939.

During this period Loss began to record for the Regal-Zonophone label and his first really big hit came with a recording made in July 1939 of 'Begin the Beguine', with Chick Henderson (who was killed by shrapnel in 1944) as vocalist. During the war years Joe Loss toured the country and after D-day (6 June 1944) played to the forces at various venues in Europe. His was to become the most prestigious society dance orchestra in the country, its qualities based on his love of a strong rhythm. From 1939 it played a regular engagement at Buckingham Palace and later at the weddings of Princess Margaret, Princess Anne, and Princess Alexandra. After the war there were residencies at the Hammersmith Palais, the Villa Marina in the Isle of Man, and Green's Playhouse, Glasgow, and there were frequent trips on the liner *Queen Elizabeth II*. The band was now always at least eighteen strong, usually with three vocalists—his singers, at various times, including Monte Rey, Howard Jones, Ross McManus, and Rose Brennan. Vera Lynn was among those given encouragement in the early stages of an illustrious career. In 1970, when Loss left Hammersmith, the band, in the face of economic demands, became smaller.

Loss's recording career was a busy one. In 1940 he had a second big hit with 'In the Mood', which became his signature tune, and many others followed. Despite the emergence of pop, he continued to record his swinging strict-tempo music, and in the 1970s had two albums which sold a million copies—*Joe Loss Plays Glenn Miller* and *Joe Loss Plays the Big Band Greats*. He continued to record with EMI until the end of his career, and became a well-known name on radio and television, notably with the long-running *Come Dancing* series.

Loss was a great supporter of such charities as the Variety Artists' Federation Sunshine Coach Fund. He was appointed OBE in 1978 and LVO in 1984. He was awarded the queen's silver jubilee medal in 1978 and became a freeman of the City of London in 1979. Posthumously, he was made a fellow of the City University when his wife, who continued to run the Joe Loss Agency, started in the 1930s, presented the library with his collection of big-band scores.

Loss's generosity, kindness, and courtesy, and his dislike of star treatment, made him one of the best-liked figures in the world of popular music. He was 5 feet 8 inches in height, with a trim figure, and sleek black hair, which tumbled over his face when he was conducting in his typically energetic way. He was always well dressed, in later years in a white silk suit, and usually had a broad, friendly smile. Away from the relentless hard work of sixty years as a bandleader, celebrated by a Variety Club luncheon in 1989, he was a devoted family man. In 1938 he married Mildred Blanch Rose, daughter of a Latvian from Riga, Barnet Rosenberg (who later changed his name to Rose), master tailor. They had a son and a daughter and were delighted to have grandchildren who followed in Loss's musical footsteps. Loss, who lived latterly at 89 North Gate, Prince Albert Road, London, died in a London hospital on 6 June 1990. PETER GAMMOND, *rev.*

Sources *The Times* (7 June 1990) · *The Independent* (7 June 1990) · personal knowledge (1996) · private information (1996) · *CGPLA Eng. & Wales* (1991)
Likenesses photograph, 1950, Hult. Arch. [*see illus.*]
Wealth at death under £115,000: probate, 17 July 1991, *CGPLA Eng. & Wales*

Lote, Stephen (*d.* 1417/18). *See under* Yevele, Henry (*d.* 1400).

Lothian. For this title name *see* Gospatric, first earl of Lothian (*d.* 1138); Gospatric, second earl of Lothian (*d.* 1166); Waltheof, third earl of Lothian (*d.* 1182); Ker, Mark, first earl of Lothian (*b.* in or before 1559, *d.* 1609); Kerr, William, third earl of Lothian (*c.*1605–1675); Kerr, Robert, first marquess of Lothian (1636–1703); Kerr, William, second marquess of Lothian (*bap.* 1661, *d.* 1722); Kerr, William Henry, fourth marquess of Lothian (*c.*1712–1775); Kerr, Cecil Chetwynd, marchioness of Lothian (1808–1877); Kerr, Schomberg Henry, ninth marquess of Lothian (1833–1900); Kerr, Philip Henry, eleventh marquess of Lothian (1882–1940).

Lothian, William (1740–1783), Church of Scotland minister and historian, was born in Edinburgh on 5 November 1740, the son of George Lothian, an Edinburgh surgeon, and Elizabeth Hutchison. His mother having died when he was an infant, and his father when he was five years old, he was raised by relatives. After attending Edinburgh high school, he proceeded to the arts and divinity courses at the University of Edinburgh, where he took an active part in the Belles Lettres Society and the Theological Society. Licensed to preach by the presbytery of Edinburgh in October 1762, he was presented to the first charge at the Canongate church on 12 April 1764 and was ordained there on 16 August. A supporter of the moderate party on the controversial subject of church patronage, he represented the presbytery of Edinburgh at the annual general assembly of the church in regular rotation, in 1768, 1773, 1778, and 1783, and earned the respect of his brethren for his 'sound understanding' and 'firmness of mind' in the assembly and other ecclesiastical courts (Dalzel, 50).

On 1 October 1776 Lothian married the daughter of an Edinburgh jeweller, his cousin Elizabeth Lothian (*d.* 1815), with whom he had six children, five of whom survived him. In the same year two of his sermons were published in *The Scotch Preacher* (vol. 2). His major work was a large quarto, *The history of the united provinces of the Netherlands, from the death of Philip II, king of Spain, to the truce made with Albert and Isabella* (1780), published by James Dodsley and Thomas Longman of London and James Dickson of Edinburgh. John Murray had originally planned to publish it but, in a letter of 29 June 1779, declined to do so, citing unfavourable economic circumstances caused by the Spanish war and the closing of the American trade as factors in his decision. Lothian then approached the Edinburgh bookseller William Creech, who raised the matter with his primary publishing partner in London, William Strahan. Lothian viewed his book as a continuation of Robert Watson's successful *History of the Reign of Philip the Second, King of Spain*, which Strahan, Creech, and other partners had published in 1777, and he was apparently unaware that Watson himself was engaged in continuing that work. On 6 August 1779 Strahan informed Creech that they 'can have nothing to do' with Lothian's manuscript because the subject infringed on Watson's. While Lothian continued to negotiate with booksellers, he was granted an honorary DD by the University of Edinburgh on 15 October 1779. His work is for the most part a dry narrative of the Dutch struggle for independence that concludes with praise for the 'firm and determined spirit' of the Dutch, in opposition to the 'oppression' and 'tyranny' of Spanish rule (W. Lothian, *The History of the United Provinces*, Dublin edn, 1780, 455).

Elected fellow of the Royal Society of Edinburgh on 17 November 1783, Lothian died one month later on 17 December, after a long and painful illness, and was buried in the Canongate churchyard. A memorial by John Logan was inscribed in the wall behind the church's gallery. On

15 March 1784 Andrew Dalzel read a brief biography of Lothian to the Royal Society of Edinburgh, the first eulogy in the history of the society, which was published four years later in its *Transactions*. RICHARD B. SHER

Sources P. Bator, 'The University of Edinburgh Belles Lettres Society (1759–64) and the rhetoric of the novel', *Rhetoric Review*, 14 (1996), 280–98 • Chambers, *Scots.* (1835) • A. Dalzel, 'Account of William Lothian, DD', *Transactions of the Royal Society of Edinburgh*, 1/1 (1788), 47–50 • D. D. McElroy, *Scotland's age of improvement* (1969) • *Fasti Scot.*, new edn, 1.25 • [W. Mure], ed., *Selections from the family papers preserved at Caldwell*, 2 vols. in 3 (1883–5) • R. B. Sher, *Church and university in the Scottish Enlightenment: the moderate literati of Edinburgh* (1985) • T. Somerville, *My own life and times, 1741–1814*, ed. W. Lee (1861) • W. Zachs, *The first John Murray and the late eighteenth-century book trade* (1998) • NA Scot., RH 4126

Archives NL Scot., Advocates' Library, notes and attributed speeches, MS 22.3.8 | NA Scot., William Robertson corresp. in the letter-books of Robert Dundas, RH 4/15/5

Lothropp, John (*bap.* 1584, *d.* 1653), minister in America, was baptized on 20 December 1584 at Etton in the East Riding of Yorkshire, the son of Thomas Lothropp (*d.* 1606) and his second wife, Mary (*d.* 1588/9), of Cherry Burton and Etton. He had two brothers, Thomas (*d.* 1629), later rector of Dengie, Essex, and William, and two sisters, Mary and another who later married William Akett of Leconfield, Yorkshire. After matriculating on 15 October 1602 at Christ Church, Oxford, where he was a sizar to Dr John King, he moved to Queens' College, Cambridge, where he graduated BA in 1606 and proceeded MA in 1609. He was ordained a deacon at Lincoln on 20 December 1607, and served as curate of Bennington, Hertfordshire, before becoming perpetual curate of Egerton, Kent, in 1609. On 10 October 1610 he obtained a licence to marry Hannah, daughter of John Howse, minister of Eastwell, Kent. Their children included five sons, Thomas (21 Feb 1613–29 Sept 1675), Samuel, Joseph (*b.* 1624), Benjamin, and Fuller (married 8 April 1635), and three daughters, Jane (1614–1634/5), Barbarah (*bap.* 31 October 1619; married 19 July 1638), and Elizabeth.

About 1624 Lothropp, perhaps influenced by discussions with a group of separatists at Egerton led by John Fenner, resigned his curacy, renounced his ordination, and moved to Southwark. There he joined the Independent congregation founded by Henry Jacob, was elected its pastor in 1625, and was reordained. The congregation split in 1630 after one of the members had a child baptized in the Church of England, an act that sparked calls by some to renounce the established church and become fully fledged separatists, a course recommended by John Canne. When Lothropp and his supporters refused to do so, 'not knowing what in time to come God might further manifest to them' (Burrage, 2.301–2), John Dupper and his followers seceded. In 1632 Lothropp, having obtained notes of John Davenport's sermon against Independency, sent him a substantive critique that changed his mind. On 29 April 1632 Bishop William Laud's pursuivant, one Tomlinson, arrested Lothropp and approximately forty-one of his adherents as they worshipped in the house of a brewer's clerk in Blackfriars. Eighteen members of the church were either absent or escaped. When Lothropp appeared before the court of high commission on 3 May, he claimed that 'the Lord hath qualified me' to be a minister and refused to take the oath *ex officio*, a position he reiterated before the commission on 8 May (Gardiner, 281). While he was incarcerated, some of his church members left in September 1633 to establish a separatist congregation, the first pastor of which was Samuel Eaton. Lothropp's wife also died while he was in prison.

On 12 June 1634 the high commission ordered Lothropp's release on bond, with the stipulation that he return in Trinity term and not attend conventicles. When he failed to appear, the commission ordered his arrest on 19 June and again on 9 October, and on 19 February 1635 it cited him for contempt and repeated the call for his apprehension. By this time he had sailed for Massachusetts with his church's approval, taking approximately thirty members with him. Nine days after arriving in Boston on 18 September 1634, he went to Scituate at the invitation of its settlers to organize a church. He had the support of the Plymouth congregation, which dismissed its members in the Scituate area on 23 November so they could join Lothropp's group. Following the church's foundation on 8 January 1635, Lothropp was ordained on 19 January. Some time after 8 January Lothropp remarried, for his new wife, Ann, joined the congregation on 14 June 1635. They had six children, Barnabas (*bap.* 6 June 1636, *d.* 1715), Abigail (*bap.* 2 Nov 1639), Bathsua (*bap.* 27 Feb 1642, *d.* 1724), John (1645–1727), and two who died at or near birth (1638, 1650). On 7 June 1637 Lothropp was admitted as a freeman of the colony of New Plymouth.

On 1 January 1638 Lothropp and other freemen of Scituate complained to the colony's court of assistants about a shortage of suitable land, and the following month he reported to the governor that he was experiencing numerous problems, including suspicions (which proved unfounded) of plotting between local residents and people in England. He sought new land on which to settle his flock, but not until October 1639 could he and some of his members relocate to Barnstable, in the same colony. He sold his farm at Scituate to Christopher Blackwood, who subsequently returned to England and became a prominent Particular Baptist. A new church was formally organized at Barnstable on 31 October 1639, and John Mayo became Lothropp's assistant the following year. Lothropp served as minister until his death on 8 November 1653. His will bequeathed two houses and several lots at Barnstable to his wife and eldest son, and he left goods valued at £72 16*s.* 5*d.* Nathaniel Morton described him as a humble man, a 'lively' preacher, and 'studious of peace, furnished with godly contentment' (Morton, 141).

RICHARD L. GREAVES

Sources C. Burrage, *The early English dissenters in the light of recent research (1550–1641)*, 2 vols. (1912) • S. R. Gardiner, *Reports of cases in the courts of star chamber and high commission*, CS, 39 (1886) • *CSP dom.*, *1633–4*, 583; *1634–5*, 112, 118, 261, 550; *1641–3*, 529 • 'Scituate and Barnstable church records', *New England Historical and Genealogical Register*, 9 (July 1855), 279–87; 10 (Jan 1856), 37–43 • Venn, *Alum. Cant.*, 1/3.104 • Foster, *Alum. Oxon.*, *1500–1714*, 3.945 • J. Winthrop, *The history of New England from 1630 to 1649*, ed. J. Savage, 2 vols. (1825–6); repr. (1972) • *DAB* • N. Morton, *New-Englands memoriall*

(1669) • J. Lathrop, 'Biographical memoir of Rev. John Lothropp', *Collections of the Massachusetts Historical Society*, 2nd ser., 1 (1838), 163–78 • W. Bradford, *History of Plymouth plantation, 1620–1647*, ed. W. C. Ford, 2 vols. (1912); repr. (1968) • G. A. Moriarty, 'Lothrop', *New England Historical and Genealogical Register*, 84 (Oct 1930), 438–9 • E. B. Huntington, *A genealogical memoir of the Lo-Lathrop family* (1884) • J. G. Bartlett, 'House', *New England Historical and Genealogical Register*, 66 (Oct 1912), 357

Archives Bodl. Oxf., MS Rawl. A128 • Regent's Park College, Oxford, Gould MSS

Wealth at death two houses; lots at Barnstable; £72 16*s*. 5*d*. in goods: Lathrop, 'Biographical memoir'

Loudin, Frederick J. (1840–1904), choirmaster, was born in Portage county, Ohio, in 1840, the son of a farmer. His colour severely restricted his opportunities although Ohio was not a slave state. His father had contributed funds to a nearby college, but Loudin was refused a place because of his colour. Educated in Ravenna, Ohio, then as a printer's apprentice, he was refused entry into the choir of the local Methodist church. White printers would not work with him.

With the expansion of opportunities for blacks after the American Civil War, Loudin migrated to Nashville, Tennessee, and its all-black Fisk University. Fisk's need for financial support had encouraged eleven students to form a choir which presented negro spirituals to white audiences. The tour of 1871 netted $20,000 for the college; in 1873 the choir crossed the Atlantic and performed before Queen Victoria, Gladstone, Lord Shaftesbury, and Charles Spurgeon, and returned with $50,000. In 1875, now with Loudin, a Fisk choir returned to Britain. All-black choirs were so popular in Britain that charlatans organized groups. But the Fisks retained prestige and fame, returning to Nashville in triumph in mid-1878.

The Fisk Jubilee Singers now became a commercial venture, under the leadership of Loudin, although other groups, some with Fisk veterans, also used the Fisk name. Loudin's choir came back to England in 1884 on the first leg of a global tour that also took them around Australia. They received numerous notices and reviews in British, Australian, and other newspapers. Fisk veterans reached South Africa, where Will P. Thompson influenced music-making in Kimberley and the McAdoo brothers entertained before relocating to Australia; Thompson and Eugene McAdoo worked together in England in the 1900s, where Loudin's choir had spread negro spirituals across the nation, having returned in August 1897.

Every year Hodder and Stoughton reprinted *The Story of the Jubilee Singers with their Songs*, with a fresh photograph of the latest group, Loudin's tall, bearded figure usually at the centre. The books were sold at their recitals, and parlour pianists and domestic singers added 'Oh! Sinner man', 'Swing low, sweet chariot', and 'Nobody knows the trouble I see, Lord' to their repertory. The choir paid homage at the home of anti-slavery campaigner William Wilberforce in Hull in 1898. On this and many other occasions these men and women, who had experienced the time of slavery in America, by their presence testified to the humanity of African people.

Loudin became a friend of the London-born composer Samuel Coleridge-Taylor, whose music was duly influenced by that of Loudin and his choir. The two men with their wives participated in the Pan-African Congress in London in July 1900, and both men were on the Pan-African Association's committee, for Loudin was now a London resident.

Over the years Loudin's choir members changed, taking up opportunities elsewhere or retiring from the gruelling routine of touring. He insisted on 'none but ladies and gentlemen' (A. C. Hill and M. Kilson, eds., *Apropos of Africa*, 1969, p. 125), for his choir deliberately took a stance distant from the fun and foolishness of minstrelsy and black-face entertainers. Neatly dressed and with polished manners, Christian, and refined, Loudin and his choir were welcome in churches and chapels, palaces and castles, and their renditions of spirituals had a huge impact. In Bournemouth in October 1900, recalled ex-slave Thomas L. Johnson, 'Wealthy ladies and gentlemen were making appointments with Mr. Louden [*sic*] to come and sing before them, for which they [the choir members] were remunerated, but it did just seem to me that God sent them to sing' (T. L. Johnson, *Twenty-Eight Years a Slave*, 1908, 240–41). Loudin died at Ravenna, Ohio, on 3 November 1904.

The spread of negro spirituals around Britain was largely due to Frederick Loudin's choirs. The manner in which they were presented, and the explanations and introductions provided by Loudin at each recital, provided their audiences with a music that showed a distinct and developed art form. These religious folk-songs of African America continued in concert performance in Britain into the 1950s, being performed before royalty and ordinary people. Fisk University again became formally involved with the Jubilee Singers around 1950.

JEFFREY GREEN

Sources J. B. T. Marsh, *The story of the Jubilee Singers with their songs* (1876) [further editions until 1902] • D. Seroff, 'The Fisk Jubilee Singers in Britain', *Under the imperial carpet: essays in black history, 1780–1950*, ed. R. E. Lotz and I. Pegg (1986) • M. Pickering, '"A jet ornament to society": black music in nineteenth-century Britain', *Black music in Britain*, ed. P. Oliver (1990) • I. Geiss, *The Pan-African movement* (1974) • R. Tames, 'Americans in London', *The peopling of London*, ed. N. Merriman (1993)

Archives Detroit Public Library, Fisk Singers scrapbooks

Likenesses photograph, *c*.1876, repro. in Marsh, *Story of the Jubilee Singers* • photograph, *c*.1884, repro. in Merriman, *The peopling of London*, 66

Loudon, Charles (1801–1844), medical writer, was born in Barony, Lanarkshire, and baptized there on 11 October 1801. He matriculated at the University of Glasgow in 1818. By 1826 he had become a member of the Royal College of Surgeons in London; in that year he published his first work, *A short inquiry into the principal causes of the unsuccessful termination of extraction by the cornea*. In 1827 he graduated MD at Glasgow.

Loudon established himself in 1828 as a physician at Leamington Spa, Warwickshire, where he published his second work, *A Practical Dissertation on the Waters of Leamington Spa*, which went through three editions between 1828 and 1831. He described the forms of treatment and the amenities that were available in this new spa resort that was already attracting an aristocratic and royal clientele. Contrary to the more 'quack' medical writers of the day he described the waters as 'inapplicable to every ailment'. In Leamington, Loudon first practised at Bedford House before moving to the newly built 3 Clarendon Place, Clarendon Square—both in the fashionable new town being built north of the River Leam. On 12 July 1830, at Leamington Priors, he married Margracia Ryves of Castle Ryves, co. Limerick. They had no children.

In 1833 Loudon was appointed one of the royal commissioners for inquiring into the employment of children in factories. One of three medical commissioners, he investigated conditions in the north-eastern district of Yorkshire, in Leicestershire, and in Nottinghamshire. He contributed articles to medical journals, including a paper in 1832 on the use of leeches on the breasts to cure amenorrhoea and a contribution on the medicinal use of laurel leaves for *The Lancet*. In 1836 he published the first of two works on population and subsistence, *The equilibrium of population and sustenance demonstrated, showing on physiological and statistical grounds the means of obviating the fears of the late Mr Malthus*. One of many publications of the time that sought to contradict the notion of the 'positive check' to population advanced by Thomas Malthus, this was followed in 1842 by a volume published in Paris, *Solution du problème de la population et de la subsistance*. In a series of thirteen epistles, Loudon concluded that an extended physical, moral, and religious education would make for a contented population. Loudon had retired to Paris in 1841, and he died there at 9 rue neuve du Luxembourg, on 2 February 1844. GORDON GOODWIN, *rev.* DAVID SOUDEN

Sources *GM*, 2nd ser., 21 (1844), 657 • members' lists, RCS Eng. • F. Cave, *Royal Leamington Spa* (1988) • 'Report … inquiring into the employment of children in factories', *Parl. papers* (1833), vol. 20, no. 450; vol. 21, no. 519 [royal commission] • J. M. Collinge, *Officials of royal commissions of enquiry, 1815–70* (1984), 19 • W. I. Addison, *A roll of graduates of the University of Glasgow from 31st December 1727 to 31st December 1897* (1898) • W. I. Addison, ed., *The matriculation albums of the University of Glasgow from 1728 to 1858* (1913), 302 • bap. reg. Scot. • parish register, Leamington Priors, Warwickshire, Warks. CRO [marriage]

Loudon [*née* Webb], **Jane** (1807–1858), writer on botany and magazine editor, was born on 19 August 1807 at Ritwell House, near Birmingham. Her mother died when she was twelve, and her father, Thomas Webb, a businessman, suffered financial reverses a few years later. Little is known of Jane Webb's early education, but, following the death of her father in 1824, she set out to earn money by writing. In addition to *Prose and Verse* (1824) she published anonymously *The Mummy! A Tale of the Twenty-Second Century* (1827), a pioneering work of science fiction that brought together political commentary, Egyptomania, and interest in technology. References to a steam mowing device, telegraph, and other innovations led John Claudius *Loudon (1783–1843) to review the book favourably and to seek out the acquaintance of the writer, whom he believed to be male. They met in February 1830, and on 14 September of that year Jane Webb married Loudon, then forty-six, who was an indefatigable landscape designer.

Jane Loudon (1807–1858), by unknown photographer

They lived with their daughter, Agnes (*b.* 1832), at 3 Porchester Terrace, Bayswater, London, in a suburban villa with an attached circular conservatory and a garden, all designed by Loudon.

Jane Loudon worked closely with her husband on his *Gardener's Magazine*. Embarrassed about how little she knew about plants when they married, she attended lectures in London given by the botanist John Lindley, and wrote up her notes as articles. During the 1830s and early 1840s she accompanied her husband on tours through England and into Scotland. She served as his amanuensis, recording his observations about kitchen gardens, conservatories, and great houses and their grounds, as he recommended improvements and endeavoured to promote a taste for gardening as art.

When production of her husband's *Arboretum* (1838) saddled the family with debts of £10,000, Jane Loudon turned again to authorship, and tapped the ready Victorian market for books popularizing horticulture, botany, and natural history. *Instructions in Gardening for Ladies* (1840) was hugely successful; 1350 copies were sold on the day of publication alone. *The Ladies' Flower-Garden of Ornamental Annuals* (1840), the first in a much-reprinted series of informative illustrated books, was followed by others about bulbs, greenhouse plants, and perennials.

Jane Loudon also brought information about the natural system of plant classification to popular audiences, in *The First Book of Botany … for Schools and Young Persons* (1841) and *Botany for Ladies* (1842). Identifying with readers who had little or no science education, she wrote:

> It is so difficult for men whose knowledge has grown with their growth, and strengthened with their strength, to imagine the state of profound ignorance in which a beginner is, that even their elementary books are like the old Eton Grammar when it was written in Latin. (*Botany for Ladies*, vi)

To make scientific knowledge more accessible and interesting, Loudon used familiar narrative forms; *The Young Naturalist's Journey* (1840) features rail travel by 'Agnes Merton and her Mamma' across the British Isles.

Jane Loudon was widowed in 1843, and debts from her husband's publications put her into financial hardship for the rest of her life. She received an award from the Royal Literary Fund in 1844, and a civil-list pension of £100 in 1846, and continued to produce many illustrated botanical books and popular natural history titles. She edited the *Ladies' Companion at Home and Abroad* (1849–51), a weekly magazine that promoted mental cultivation along with 'separate spheres', 'Not to make women usurp the place of men, but to render them as rational and intelligent beings' (29 Dec 1849). Although she did not support feminist initiatives in her day, she wrote sympathetically about women in distress. She died at 3 Porchester Terrace on 13 July 1858, aged fifty, survived by her daughter who later applied to the Royal Literary Fund for money to erect a monument to her mother in Kensal Green cemetery.

ANN B. SHTEIR

Sources Royal Literary Fund Archives, file nos. 648, 1101 · J. Loudon, *The mummy! A tale of the twenty-second century*, ed. A. Rauch (1994) · P. Boniface, ed., *In search of English gardens: the travels of John Claudius Loudon and his wife Jane* (1987) · J. Loudon, 'A short account of the life and writings of John Claudius Loudon', in J. Gloag, *Mr Loudon's England* (1970) · *DNB* · B. Howe, *Lady with green fingers: the life of Jane Loudon* (1961) · *CGPLA Eng. & Wales* (1858)

Archives NL Scot., corresp. | Royal Literary Fund · U. Newcastle, Robinson L., letters to Sir Walter Trevelyan

Likenesses miniature, repro. in Howe, *Lady with green fingers* · photograph, NPG [*see illus.*]

Wealth at death under £800: probate, 25 Aug 1858, *CGPLA Eng. & Wales*

John Claudius Loudon (1783–1843), by John Linnell, 1840–41

Loudon, John Claudius (1783–1843), landscape gardener and horticultural writer, was born on 8 April 1783 at Cambuslang, Lanarkshire, the eldest son of William Loudon (*d.* 1809), farmer, of Kerse Hall, Lothian, and his wife, Agnes, *née* Somers (*d.* 1831).

Early years In 1794 Loudon began working part-time as an assistant to John Mawer, a nurseryman and landscape gardener at Dalry; on Mawer's death in 1798 he became a part-time apprentice to Dickson and Shade, nurserymen at Leith Walk, Edinburgh. At the same time he entered the University of Edinburgh, where he studied until 1802, attending Andrew Coventry's lectures on agriculture, as well as classes in botany and chemistry. While at university, according to his wife's account, he developed the habit of staying up two nights a week to study. His first publication, a translation of the life of Abelard for an encyclopaedia, took place in 1802.

In 1803 Loudon visited London with letters of introduction from Coventry, and met James Sowerby, Sir Joseph Banks, and Jeremy Bentham, the last of whom became a major influence on his social and political thinking. His first horticultural publication, 'Hints respecting the manner of laying out the grounds of the public squares in London', was published in the *Literary Journal* for 31 December of that year; it revealed him as a follower of Sir Uvedale Price and a critic of Humphry Repton. His first book appeared in 1804: *Observations on the Formation and Management of Useful and Ornamental Plantations*, which was followed in 1805 by *A Short Treatise on Several Improvements Recently Made in Hot-Houses* and in 1806 by a two-volume *Treatise on Forming, Improving, and Managing Country Residences.*

In 1804, meanwhile, Loudon had exhibited three landscapes at the Royal Academy. On 13 March 1805 he was elected to the Society of Arts, and the following year he was made a fellow of the Linnean Society. He had already begun a career as a landscape gardener in 1803, with proposals for improvements to the grounds of Scone Palace, Perthshire, the seat of Lord Mansfield; 1804 saw commissions from the duchess of Brunswick and others, for properties in the London vicinity and in Scotland (some of these early commissions he was to describe in his book on Scottish farms in 1811).

In 1806 Loudon moved to 90 Newman Street, London, and exhibited the first symptoms of the ill health that affected him for the rest of his life: following an attack of rheumatic fever, his knee became ankylosed and his right arm permanently contracted. In 1807 he retired to Wood Hall Farm in Pinner, Middlesex, and with his father took out a lease on the nearby Kenton Farm. The following year he published a pamphlet, *An Immediate and Effectual Mode of Raising the Rental of the Landed Property of England*, as a result of which he was invited by General George F. Stratton to appraise his property at Great Tew, Oxfordshire; Loudon took over the tenancy of Tew Lodge Farm on an undertaking to double its rental value. In 1809 he established a small agricultural college at Tew, and in 1811 he published *Designs for Laying out Farms and Farm-Buildings, in the Scotch Style* (reprinted the next year as *Observations on Laying out Farms …*), celebrating his accomplishments there. General Stratton bought back the lease in February 1811, but the agricultural reversals of the Napoleonic wars meant that his expected profits did not materialize. Loudon moved to 42 Pall Mall. His father had died on 29 December 1809, and was buried in the churchyard of St John the Baptist, Pinner; Loudon designed a unique monument for the grave, in the form of a pyramid from whose sides projected the ends of a sarcophagus carrying inscriptions on their end-panels.

Continental visits Loudon had amassed £15,000 by the time he left Tew. In 1812 he published *Hints on the Formation of Gardens and Pleasure Grounds*, which included designs for formal gardens as well as informal landscapes. He journeyed though the south of England, and in 1813 and 1814 travelled on the continent, visiting Germany, Latvia, St Petersburg, Moscow, and central Europe. According to his wife's account, 'he proceeded by Grodno to Wilna, through a country covered with the remains of the French army, horses and men lying dead by the road-side, and bands of wild-looking Cossacks scouring the country' (J. Loudon, xxii). He arrived in Moscow in time for the celebrations on learning of the allied armies' entry into Paris. When he returned to England he found that his banker had mishandled his finances and largely dissolved the fortune he had built up. During the following year he 'made several fruitless journeys [including one to Paris] in the hope of recovering some part of the property', but ultimately had to resign himself to its loss (ibid., xxv). In 1816 he moved to Bayswater.

In 1817 Loudon published *Remarks on the Construction of Hot-Houses* and the next year *A Comparative View of the Common and Curvilinear Mode of Roofing Hot-Houses* and *Sketches of Curvilinear Hot-Houses*. Following a suggestion by Sir George Mackenzie, that the ideal design for a greenhouse was spherical, so that light would be admitted equally at all times of day, Loudon invented a glazing bar in wrought iron that could be made in curvilinear sections. He later recorded that he sold his design to Messrs W. and D. Bailey of Holborn, and the patent (no. 4277, granted 11 July 1818) was taken out by them; Loudon's name does not appear on it. Loudon collaborated with Baileys on an unascertained number of glasshouses in the following years. Grandiose plans for glasshouses characterized his plans in 1831 for the Birmingham Botanic Garden, but on these he was overruled by the town council.

In 1819, carrying letters of introduction from Sir Joseph Banks, Loudon visited France, Italy, Switzerland, and the Low Countries to gather material for a proposed *Encyclopaedia of Gardening*. The book was published in 1822 as an octavo of nearly 1500 pages, covering plant culture, botany, garden design, and an international survey and history of gardening. It went through six editions, with varying degrees of revision and expansion, during Loudon's lifetime, and posthumous editions continued to appear into the 1870s. The period of writing of this work was one of great physical pain for Loudon: in 1820, an attempted operation fractured his right arm, which in 1825 was amputated. During the intervening years he had become addicted to laudanum as a painkiller, but after the amputation he broke his addiction by progressively diluting the dose he took. Other works of these years include *The Different Modes of Cultivating the Pine-Apple* (published anonymously, 1823), *The Green-House Companion* (1824, with further editions in 1825 and 1832), and *An Encyclopaedia of Agriculture* (1825). In 1823–4 Loudon designed and supervised the building of a villa at 3 Porchester Terrace, Bayswater, which incorporated an entrance conservatory with a wrought-iron dome; he lived there until his death. (The house now bears an LCC plaque, installed in 1953.)

The Gardener's Magazine In 1826 Loudon began publishing the *Gardener's Magazine*, first as a quarterly, priced 5*s.*; according to Jane Loudon, 4000 copies of the first issue were sold. From 1827 it appeared bi-monthly, and from 1831 as a monthly, the price per issue declining until in 1834 it reached 1*s.* 2*d.* Loudon's magazine, which reached nineteen volumes before it ceased on his death at the end of 1843, was soon imitated by magazines edited by Joseph Paxton, George Glenny, and others, and accusations of plagiarism passed between rival editors; but, in its early years in particular, Loudon himself had republished much material from the more expensive *Transactions* of the Horticultural Society. The *Gardener's Magazine* became a forum for the exchange of ideas on gardening on a national scale; it also served as Loudon's main forum for promoting his ideas on a variety of subjects. He recounted in it his various journeys around Great Britain, describing the gardens he visited and commenting freely on how they could be improved. In 1829 he published in it articles recommending a national system of education, workers' dwellings, and a plan for the controlled expansion of London through concentric circles of alternating open space and residential and commercial development.

The *Gardener's Magazine* was not Loudon's only venture in periodical publication. Between 1828 and 1836 he edited the *Magazine of Natural History*, and between 1834 and 1839 the *Architectural Magazine*, which provided the young John Ruskin's first opportunity at publication. In 1830 Loudon also launched a folio publication, *Illustrations of Landscape-Gardening and Garden Architecture*, but this was poorly subscribed to and was discontinued after its third number in 1833.

In March 1828 Loudon had reviewed an anonymous novel called *The Mummy*, published the year before, which favourably impressed him by its account of the scientific and technological advances made in its imagined future. In February 1830 he met the author, who proved, to his surprise, to be a young woman, Jane Webb (1807–1858) [*see* Loudon, Jane], and he married her on 14 September. They had one child, Agnes (married name Spofforth), who was born in 1832.

Botanical publications 1828 saw Loudon's third continental tour, in France and Germany. In 1829 came the first of his important botanical publications: *An Encyclopaedia of Plants*, with the botanical text contributed by John Lindley. This was followed in 1830 by *Hortus Britannicus* and an anonymous *Manual of Cottage Gardening*, and in 1832–3 by *An Encyclopaedia of Cottage, Farm, and Villa Architecture and Furniture*.

In 1835 Loudon designed a small public garden at an unnamed location, which has been identified as Gravesend, Kent; the site, although built over in the 1870s, marked his practical involvement with the movement in favour of creating public walks and gardens for the country's congested towns. In 1839 he was commissioned by Joseph Strutt to design a public garden for Derby; the 11 acre Derby Arboretum was opened in 1840, and Loudon published a book about its design in the same year.

Two publishing projects occupied Loudon between the years 1836 and 1838. The first of these was *The Suburban Gardener and Villa Companion* (1838). Much of the material had been published in the *Gardener's Magazine*; additional material from that source was included in the second, posthumous, edition of 1850 (retitled *The Villa Gardener*). A sequel devoted to practical gardening, mostly dealing with the kitchen garden, was published in 1842 as *The Suburban Horticulturist*.

The second project was the *Arboretum et fruticetum Britannicum* (1838), a survey on a scale never before attempted of all the trees grown in the British Isles, whether native or exotic. Again, John Lindley provided botanical assistance. The illustrations for the *Arboretum* required the employment of seven artists, including James De Carle Sowerby and G. R. Lewis and H. W. Jukes, both of whom were employed by the owners of the estates where the trees were drawn. Even with Jane acting as amanuensis, the expenses of its production left Loudon £10,000 in debt. He placed his other publications in Longmans' hands as a pledge for the debt, and, by the end of 1841, when financial depression hit the book trade, the debt was reduced to £2600. Loudon compiled two smaller publications from the text of the *Arboretum*: the *Hortus lignosus Londinensis* (1838) and the *Encyclopaedia of Trees and Shrubs* (1842).

In 1840, besides another continental tour, Loudon undertook the editing, in a handy, inexpensive, and pocket-sized volume, of *The Landscape Gardening and Landscape Architecture of the Late Humphry Repton*. He also, for several months in 1840–41, conducted the horticultural department of the weekly newspaper the *Gardener's Gazette*, founded in 1837 by his rival George Glenny, who had been ousted from editorship by the publishers. In 1841 he laid out the grounds of Castle Kennedy, Stranraer.

Cemeteries The last direction which Loudon found for his talents was the creation of cemeteries. In 1842, with Edward Buckton Lamb as his architect, he designed the Histon Road cemetery in Cambridge, which was laid out on a strict grid plan to facilitate the location of graves, and was planted with specimen trees, mostly evergreen, arranged geometrically. A series of articles on cemetery design, criticizing various aspects of the layout and management of the new cemeteries which had been opened in the preceding twenty years, and advocating grid layout and evergreen planting, was published in the *Gardener's Magazine* in 1843, to be published towards the end of the year as *On the Planting, Managing, and Laying out of Cemeteries*. Loudon's financial difficulties led him to accept two commissions for cemeteries in 1843, one for a private company (Bath Abbey cemetery) and one for a local authority (Southampton cemetery). He saw neither project to completion, and his plans for Southampton were the subject of much controversy with the council.

Loudon had suffered inflammation of the lungs in 1842, which left him in declining condition throughout 1843. Despite his poor health, he was overworking frantically in an attempt to work off his debt resulting from the *Arboretum*, for one of the creditors, the engraver (whose name does not appear in the work), became bankrupt, and his assignees threatened to arrest Loudon for the required sum of £1500. The other creditors refused their consent to the threat, and on 1 December Longmans issued a plea for the sale of additional copies of the *Arboretum* to help clear the debt (copies to the value of £300 were sold in the next two weeks). Loudon was working simultaneously on plans for Coleshill House, Berkshire, and his two cemeteries, when he was taken ill on a visit to the Isle of Wight. Not long after returning to London he died at his home, 3 Porchester Terrace, on 14 December 1843; his death certificate attributed his death to chronic bronchitis. He was buried in Kensal Green cemetery on 21 December. A public meeting was held in February 1844 to raise funds to clear the remaining debt, and Sir Robert Peel provided Mrs Loudon with an annuity. Loudon's last work, *Self-Instruction for Young Gardeners*, was published in 1845, with a biographical notice by his widow. BRENT ELLIOTT

Sources J. Loudon, memoir, in J. C. Loudon, *Self-instruction for young gardeners* (1845), ix–li • Desmond, *Botanists*, rev. edn, 438 • M. Simo, *Loudon and the landscape* (1988) • J. C. Loudon, *Observations on laying out farms … in the Scotch style* (1812) • J. C. Loudon, *Gardener's Magazine* (1826–43), *passim* [articles describing his travels] • B. Howe, *Lady with green fingers* (1961) • *DNB* • P. Ballard, *An oasis of delight: the history of the Birmingham Botanical Gardens* (1983), 17–24 • R. Desmond, 'Loudon and 19th-century horticultural journalism', *John Claudius Loudon and the early nineteenth century in Great Britain*, ed. E. B. Macdougall (1980), 77–97 • W. Roberts, 'The centenary of Loudon's *Arboretum*', *Journal of the Royal Horticultural Society*, 61 (1936), 277–84

Archives Linn. Soc., papers | Glos. RO, letters to Dan Ellis • Linn. Soc., letters to William Swainson • NHM, letters to the Sowerby family • Oxf. U. Mus. NH, letters to J. O. Westwood • W. Sussex RO, letters to duke of Richmond

Likenesses J. Linnell, oils, 1840–41, Linn. Soc. [*see illus.*] • stipple, repro. in Loudon, *Self-instruction*, frontispiece

Wealth at death died in debt; approx. £1000 of debt paid off by February 1844; widow continued to carry burden of debt

Loudoun. For this title name *see* Campbell, John, first earl of Loudoun (1598–1662); Campbell, Hugh, third earl of Loudoun (*c*.1673–1731); Campbell, John, fourth earl of Loudoun (1705–1782).

Lough, Ernest Arthur (1911–2000), singer, was born at 56 Glenparke Road, Forest Gate, London, on 17 November 1911, the son of Arthur Henry Lough, cashier to a lace merchant, and his wife, Caroline Ellen Frisby. He sang as a treble in the choir of his local church, St Peter's, but failed an audition for Southwark Cathedral. He was, however, accepted in 1924 by the Temple Church choir, whose organist and choirmaster, Dr George Thalben-Ball, had a reputation as a superb trainer of boys' voices. At the same time, Lough became a pupil at the City of London School, where all the Temple choristers were educated.

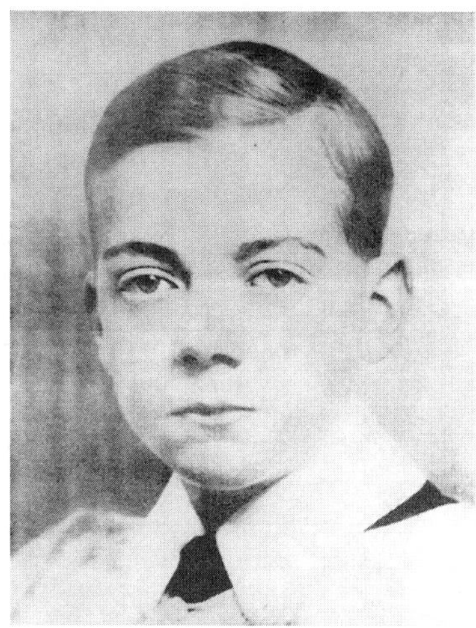

Ernest Arthur Lough (1911–2000), by Foulsham & Banfield, 1927

The idea that one of the treble soloists in the choir should make a recording came, apparently, from Lord Justice Eldon Bankes, and was enthusiastically taken up by 'Doctor', as the boys all called Thalben-Ball. HMV had very recently introduced a special mobile van, which made recordings outside a studio possible. In addition, the Temple Church had a particularly fine acoustic, perfect for recording. The piece chosen was Mendelssohn's 'Hear my prayer', better known as 'O for the wings of a dove', from the oratorio *St Paul*. Ernest Lough, then aged fifteen, was chosen because his voice was, at that moment, in the most perfect condition.

'We did four or five takes', recalled Lough some sixty years later (*Daily Telegraph*):

> One was discarded because a child was whistling outside; another because the Temple clock chimed. I wasn't aware that I was making history. I was so small I had to stand on a couple of Bibles so the single microphone would pick up my voice.

Lough was indeed making history. Record C1329 was issued by HMV in June 1927. So many copies were sold during the first six months that the matrix wore out, and another version had to be made. Later there was a third recording. People came from all over the UK, North America, and Australia to hear Ernest Lough at the Temple Church, and tickets had to be issued for all services until his voice broke two years later.

In *The Record Guide*, published in 1951, Edward Sackville-West and Desmond Shawe-Taylor wrote that:

> the famous record [of 'Hear my prayer'] made in 1927 by Master Ernest Lough still survives … This was one of the outstanding best-sellers of gramophone history. The touching purity of the singer's tone can still be appreciated in spite of the age of the record.

The 78 r.p.m. version stayed in the catalogue until the late 1950s. The recording was reissued as an extended-play record in 1961, and in the following year Lough received a golden disc, though the sales of the recording had exceeded 1 million some years before. By 2000 worldwide sales exceeded 5 million. 'O for the wings of a dove' and a dozen other solos recorded by Lough as a treble were made available on CD.

Lough's own favourite among his recordings was 'Hear ye, Israel' from Mendelssohn's *Elijah*, recorded on the spur of the moment at the end of another recording session when two 10 inch waxes were left unused. Lough did not previously know the piece, but learned it in half an hour. After his voice broke, or 'slid down' as he himself said, Lough remained with the Temple Church choir as a baritone until 1971. During the Second World War he worked in the fire service, and in 1942 had to look on helplessly when the Temple Church was destroyed by fire bombs. Services were held in the ruins until 1958, when the church was rededicated by the archbishop of Canterbury, Dr Geoffrey Fisher.

Ernest Lough made very little money from the phenomenal sales of his recording. Royalties of 5 per cent were paid to the Inner Temple, and half the sum was shared by Dr Thalben-Ball and the twenty-four members of the choir. When he reached the age of twenty-one, Lough received £200. By then he had become tea-boy and general dogsbody in the advertising department of HMV. One of his superiors was Ethel Winnifred Charlton (*b.* 1912/13), known as Charlie. On 25 June 1938 he and Charlie were married. They had three sons—Peter, Robin, and Graham—all of whom became choristers. Peter, who sang at the Chapel Royal, took part, together with his father, in the coronation of Queen Elizabeth II in 1953. Robin and Graham sang with the Temple Church choir.

After the war Lough joined the advertising agency Mather and Crowther, which later became Ogilvy and Mather. He was not tempted to become a professional singer, as his serviceable baritone was nothing remarkable. He always attributed the phenomenal success of 'O for the wings of a dove' to the training of Thalben-Ball, and no doubt there is some truth in that, but the angelic sound of the young voice and its wonderful musicality were his alone. After he left the Temple Church choir at the age of sixty, he sang for a further ten years with the Bach Choir, conducted by Sir David Willcocks. A Radio 4 programme celebrated the recording's sixtieth anniversary in 1987, and Robin Lough made a television documentary about his father for Channel 4 in 1994. Ernest Lough died at Watford General Hospital in Hertfordshire on 22 February 2000, survived by his wife and three sons.

ELIZABETH FORBES

Sources *The Times* (24 Feb 2000) • *Daily Telegraph* (24 Feb 2000) • *The Guardian* (24 Feb 2000) • *The Independent* (24 Feb 2000) • K. J. Kutsch and L. Riemans, *Grosses Sänger-Lexicon* (1987) • E. Sackville-West and D. Shawe-Taylor, *The record guide* (1951) • b. cert. • m. cert. • d. cert.

Likenesses Foulsham & Banfield, photograph, 1927, repro. in *The Times* [*see illus.*] • D. Mansell, photograph, repro. in *The Guardian*

Lough, John (1913–2000), French scholar, was born on 19 February 1913 at 2 Hollywood Avenue West, Jesmond, Newcastle upon Tyne, the second son and third of the five children of Wilfrid Gordon Lough (1880–1962), proprietor of a family firm of butchers in Jesmond, and his wife, Mary Turnbull Millican (1885–1979). He was educated at the Royal Grammar School, Newcastle, won a scholarship to St John's College, Cambridge, in 1931, and graduated in 1934 with a first-class degree in modern and medieval languages. He was awarded the PhD by Cambridge University in 1937, after a period of research that included an Esmond scholarship at the British Institute in Paris for study at the Sorbonne and a Jebb studentship at Cambridge. His first academic appointment, in 1937, was as assistant lecturer, later lecturer, in French at the University of Aberdeen, whence he returned to Cambridge as lecturer in French in 1946.

On 3 July 1939 Lough married Muriel Alice Barker (1913–1998), daughter of Ernest and Annie Barker. Their daughter, Judith, was born in 1952. His wife was also a scholar of French language and literature, and held a doctorate obtained at Nottingham, then under the aegis of the University of London. She collaborated with Lough on some of his publications. With his sister E. Merson he published a biography of their ancestor *John Graham Lough, [1798–1876]: a Northumbrian Sculptor* (1987). In 1952 Lough was appointed professor of French at the Durham Colleges, soon to be Durham University, and remained in that position until his retirement in 1978. Honours awarded during the course of his career included honorary doctorates from the universities of Clermont-Ferrand (1967) and Newcastle (1972); he was made an officier de l'ordre national du mérite in 1973 and a fellow of the British Academy in 1975.

Lough's research expertise and his flair for narrative history, on which he built his very considerable reputation as a scholar, both in Great Britain and France, were concentrated in three main areas: French theatre history; the history of Enlightenment thought; and, in a more relaxed mode perhaps, the memoirs of travellers between Britain and France in the seventeenth and eighteenth centuries. (He himself disliked travel, even to France.) He was essentially a historian rather than a literary critic, but the enormously detailed information he assembled with admirable clarity constituted a crucial point of reference for critical inquiry in both fields for many years. Of particular importance was his bibliographical and archival research into the material history of the Paris theatre, from which he vividly reconstructed the experiences of actors and audiences, notably in *Paris Theatre Audiences in the Seventeenth and Eighteenth Centuries* (1957). He wrote authoritatively and extensively on that vast compendium of Enlightenment thought the *Encyclopédie*, engaging with zest in the academic detective work of tracking down the authors of its many anonymous articles (*The Contributors to the 'Encyclopédie'*, 1973), and tracing its reception in eighteenth-century England (*The 'Encyclopédie' in Eighteenth-Century England and other Studies*, 1970). His first book had been *Locke's Travels in France* (1953), and in retirement he returned to that theme with *France Observed in the Seventeenth Century by British Travellers* (1985) and *France on the Eve of Revolution: Observations by British Travellers, 1763–1788* (1987).

Lough did not publish solely for the scholarly community. He was concerned with education at all levels, not least with facilitating the access of pre-university students to the historical periods and topics on which he was an expert. His *An Introduction to Seventeenth-Century France* (1954) and *An Introduction to Eighteenth-Century France* (1960), in particular, were standard sixth-form reading for many years, and for many students they were their first experience of works of scholarship bearing on the historical and social context of literary production.

Lough also promoted the study of the French language at schools as well as universities. The compilations of passages for translation between French and English that he published in collaboration with his wife were familiar textbooks. As a teacher, Lough used lectures to impart information, and in tutorials he encouraged the sceptical questioning of received ideas, unobtrusively pushing his students to attend to evidence and think for themselves. Lough was very much a man of the Enlightenment. He was rational, humane, tolerant, and very shrewd, and observed the follies and foibles of his fellows with more than a touch of Voltairean irony. He regarded all irrational and ill-founded convictions with a confident and benign suspicion. He died in Dryburn Hospital, Durham, on 21 June 2000, and was cremated in Durham on 5 July.

Ann Moss

Sources *WW* (2000) • private information (2004) [Judith Lough, daughter] • personal knowledge (2004) • *The Times* (11 July 2000) • *The Independent* (5 July 2000) • b. cert. • m. cert. • d. cert.

Wealth at death £372,981—gross; £367,715—net: probate, 30 Aug 2000, *CGPLA Eng. & Wales*

Lough, John Graham (1798–1876), sculptor, was born on 8 January 1798 in Black Hedley Port, Greenhead, Shotley, Northumberland, the third son of William Lough (1764–1850), a blacksmith and small-holder, and his wife, Barbara Clemitson (1767–1852). John Lough (who later added the middle name Graham, his grandmother's maiden name) is said to have followed the plough in his youth and was apprenticed (*c*.1815–*c*.1823) to a stonemason, Jonathan Marshall of Shotley Field. He afterwards gained employment in Newcastle upon Tyne as an ornamental sculptor, and carved decorations on the building of the Literary and Philosophical Society in Westgate Road. In early 1825 Lough went to London—he made the journey on a collier, the captain of which, on their arrival, took him to see the Elgin marbles in the British Museum—and on 15 December 1826 he was admitted to the Royal Academy Schools.

Lough gained unusual early success as a sculptor in London. He became the protégé of the painter Benjamin Robert Haydon, who organized an exhibition of two of Lough's early works in June 1827 at rooms in Maddox Street. These sculptures, a colossal statue entitled *Milo* and *Samson Slaying the Philistines*, were hailed by contemporaries as works of remarkable power and originality, based on a study of Phidian sculpture and Michelangelo rather than the standard Graeco-Roman models. Lough received several commissions for these works at this time, and in March 1828 he held a second private exhibition in Regent Street.

In 1832 Lough married Mary North (1791/2–1888), the daughter of a domestic chaplain of the duke of Kent; they had two daughters, Mary Rebecca (*b.* 1832) and Georgina (*b.* 1834). In 1834 the family travelled to Italy, where they remained for three years. Little is known of this period, though Lough seems to have kept himself apart from the English community of sculptors in Rome and was beset by financial problems and health worries caused by outbreaks of cholera.

After his return, Lough led a productive career as a sculptor in London, though he perhaps never regained the reputation he had enjoyed in his early years. He was not elected a Royal Academician nor even an associate, though he exhibited some fifty works at the Royal Academy between 1826 and 1863, and he was unsuccessful in major public competitions such as that for the Nelson monument in Trafalgar Square. He did, however, produce some notable public memorials, including those to Thomas Fanshaw Middleton, bishop of Calcutta (1832), for St Paul's Cathedral, and the inventor George Stephenson (1862) for Newcastle upon Tyne. His church monuments included those to the poet Robert Southey (1845) in Crosthwaite, Westmorland, and Bishop William Grant Broughton (1855) in Canterbury Cathedral. He also made a large number of portrait busts.

Lough designed many 'ideal' works in marble, an area in which he was fortunate to gain the patronage of certain wealthy noblemen. In particular, Sir Matthew White Ridley, fourth baronet, commissioned a large series of Shakespearian statues (*c.*1840–*c.*1871) from the sculptor, as well as a bronze version of the *Milo* (1863) and other imaginative pieces. Lough also made ideal works for Charles Hanbury-Tracy of Toddington, Gloucestershire. His work reflected an impulse towards novelty in form and subject matter, and an eclectic mixture of sources—from Roman to high Renaissance, Gothic revival (in his church monuments), and modern pictorialism—which mark him as a 'transitional' sculptor, seeking to break the mould of neoclassicism. The results were sometimes boldly original, at other times unconvincing, overambitious, and strangely mannered.

The writer Cecilia Toulmin described Lough as 'A handsome man … with magnificent eyes that lighted up the whole countenance' (Toulmin, 142), and a painting by an unknown artist portrays the sculptor in his youth as a Romantic, Byronic figure standing before his statue of *Satan* (Lough and Merson, pl. 4). In old age he was, according to his nephew, the biographer and surgeon Stephen Paget, a 'dear, simple, philosophical old boy, with a tremendous broad accent', the son of a Greenhead blacksmith who had married well (Paget MSS, 10). John Graham Lough died of bronchitis on 8 April 1876 at his home, 42 Harewood Square, London. Soon afterwards his widow presented a large number of the sculptor's models and casts to Elswick Hall, Newcastle upon Tyne, where unfortunately, together with other works given by the Ridley family, they were later destroyed.

MARTIN GREENWOOD

Sources J. Lough and E. Merson, *John Graham Lough, 1798–1876: a Northumbrian sculptor* (1987) [incl. bibliography] · R. Gunnis, *Dictionary of British sculptors, 1660–1851*, new edn (1964), 242–4 · T. S. R. Boase, 'John Graham Lough: a transitional sculptor', *Journal of the Warburg and Courtauld Institutes*, 23 (1960), 277–90 · J. Robinson, *Descriptive catalogue of the Lough and Noble models of statues, bas-reliefs and busts in Elswick Hall, Newcastle upon Tyne*, 6th edn (1914) · Graves, *RA exhibitors* · *The diary of Benjamin Robert Haydon*, ed. W. B. Pope, 5 vols. (1960–63) · *DNB* · B. Read, *Victorian sculpture* (1982) · M. Greenwood, 'Lough, John Graham', *The dictionary of art*, ed. J. Turner (1996) · *Art Journal*, 38 (1876), 202–3 · C. A. Allen, 'John Graham Lough and the neo-classical tradition', BA diss., U. Newcastle, 1958 · S. C. Hall, *Retrospect of a long life, from 1815 to 1883*, 2 vols. (1883), 2.241–2 · Mrs N. Crosland [C. Toulmin], *Landmarks of a literary life, 1820–1892* (1893) · Paget MSS, Bodl. Oxf., MS Eng. misc. d. 1175 · *CGPLA Eng. & Wales* (1876)

Archives V&A, Forster MSS

Likenesses B. R. Haydon, pen-and-ink sketch, 1828, Harvard U., Houghton L.; repro. in Lough and Merson, *John Graham Lough*, pl. 3 · portrait, oils?, *c.*1832, repro. in Lough and Merson, *John Graham Lough*, pl. 4; priv. coll. · J. G. Lough, self-portrait, plaster bust, 1843–7, Laing Art Gallery, Newcastle upon Tyne; repro. in Lough and Merson, *John Graham Lough*, pl. 32 · photograph, 1860–69, repro. in Lough and Merson, *John Graham Lough*, pl. 6 · R. Hedley, oils, 1881 (*An incident in the life of Lough*), Laing Art Gallery, Newcastle upon Tyne

Wealth at death under £7000: probate, 20 May 1876, *CGPLA Eng. & Wales*

Loughborough. For this title name *see* Hastings, Henry, Baron Loughborough (1610–1667).

Lougher, Robert (*d.* 1585), ecclesiastical lawyer, was born at Tenby, Pembrokeshire, the younger son of Thomas Lougher, alderman and former mayor of the town, and Maud, daughter of Rhys ap Gwilim of Betws, Carmarthen. Elected a fellow of All Souls College, Oxford, as of founder's kin in 1553, he graduated BCL (9 July 1558) and proceeded DCL (19 February 1565), having in the meantime been collated to the archdeaconry of Totnes (21 February 1562). Holding a number of Devon rectories in plurality, he was on the commission of the peace for this county from 1561 and of the quorum from 1564. As proctor for the clergy of the diocese of Exeter in the convocation of 1563, he subscribed the Thirty-Nine Articles, but disapproved even of the watered down version of puritan demands embodied in the six articles.

In 1564 Lougher was elected principal of New Inn Hall, Oxford. On 25 February 1565 he was admitted a member of Doctors' Commons, and about this time became chancellor of Exeter diocese. Appointed regius professor of civil law at Oxford on 10 January 1566, he was among the disputants before Queen Elizabeth on her visit to the university in the following September; and he was one of the original fellows of Jesus College on its foundation in 1571, having resigned the headship of New Inn Hall the previous year. In 1572 he was returned to parliament for Pembroke, being named on 13 March 1576 to a committee to consider a Bill for Relief of Vicars and Curates. In 1574 he became a master in chancery, and on 10 May 1575 was re-elected to the headship of New Inn Hall, which he held for the ensuing five years. In 1576 Archbishop Grindal appointed him as one of the visitors of the diocese of Gloucester. From 1577 he was a justice of the peace for Pembrokeshire (of the quorum from *c.*1583) and was eventually appointed deputy lieutenant. But these positions were probably chiefly honorary, since in May 1577, resigning his professorship, he was appointed official of the consistory and vicar-general in spirituals to Edwin Sandys, archbishop of York, who described him in a letter to Burghley as 'an honest, learned and wise man' (BL, Lansdowne MS 27, art. 12). As vicar-general he was a leading member of the northern high commission and among the most regular attenders. However, on account of his frequent absences from York, he relied heavily on an unqualified surrogate to preside over cases in the consistory court. Perhaps as a result, testamentary cases were shifted to another of the York diocesan courts, the exchequer, despite Lougher's attempts to prevent the change.

Lougher married Elizabeth, granddaughter of John Rastell, the printer. They had three sons, John (the heir), Thomas, and Robert, and three daughters, Elizabeth, Jane, and Lettice. Lougher's nuncupative will was made at Tenby (where he was afterwards buried) on 3 June 1585, and proved six days later. Unfortunately his fortune attracted the predatory attention of a certain Rice Morgan, who claimed to have been betrothed to Elizabeth before Lougher married her; his attempts to force the widow into a union with him were foiled only with the assistance of Star Chamber. It was not until 1593 that the terms of Lougher's will were finally confirmed.

Martin Ingram

Sources HoP, *Commons, 1558–1603*, 2.490 • R. A. Marchant, *The church under the law: justice, administration and discipline in the diocese of York, 1560–1640* (1969), 42–4, 63, 79, 96–9 • P. Tyler, 'The ecclesiastical commission for the province of York, 1561–1641', DPhil diss., U. Oxf., 1965, 174–5, appxs, xviii • *Reg. Oxf.*, 1.237 • C. Plummer, ed., *Elizabethan Oxford: reprints of rare tracts*, OHS, 8 (1887), 173, 184, 201 • J. Strype, *Annals of the Reformation and establishment of religion … during Queen Elizabeth's happy reign*, new edn, 1/1 (1824), 489, 505 • *Fasti Angl.* (Hardy), 1.403, 3.511, 589 • G. D. Squibb, *Doctors' Commons: a history of the College of Advocates and Doctors of Law* (1977), 156 • PRO, PROB 11/68, fol. 232v • PRO, PROB 11/81, fols. 342v–343 • PRO, PROB 11/85, fols. 13v, 202v–203 • PRO, STAC 5/L10/6, 40; L40/21; M17/6 • *Hansard 1* • *JHC*, 1 (1547–1628), 115 • BL, Lansdowne MS 27, art. 12

Loughlin, Dame Anne (1894–1979), trade unionist, was born on 28 June 1894 in Leeds, the daughter of Thomas Loughlin, an Irish boot and shoe maker. Her mother died when Anne was twelve, and she subsequently took over the responsibility of looking after her younger brothers and sisters. Four years later, on the death of her father, she began working in a Leeds clothing factory to support the family. She soon became an active trade unionist and by 1915 was a full-time organizer, leading the Hebden Bridge strike of 6000 clothing workers in 1916. In 1920 she became national organizer of what became the National Union of Tailors and Garment Workers, charged with rebuilding the union after the First World War when membership was declining drastically.

Anne Loughlin's post involved travel throughout the country, and her task was made difficult by falling wages, rising unemployment, and the hostility of the union men to women members. Union tactics were to hold limited strikes in order to establish union rates and conditions, town by town. It was alleged that when Anne Loughlin appeared in any town, employers immediately called a

Dame Anne Loughlin (1894–1979), by Bassano

meeting to plan defensive action. They would be faced by all 5 feet of a severely but stylishly dressed woman with fair hair, innocent blue eyes, and a schoolgirl complexion, who would tell them in an incisive way exactly what she intended to do. She had the knack of inspiring loyalty and confidence among women; her explanations were lucid and she spoke their language. She was elected to the TUC general council in 1929 from the organization's women's group, and was one of those who pressed successfully for the establishment of the national women's advisory committee within the TUC.

During the 1930s Anne Loughlin served on royal commissions and government committees on health and safety, industrial insurance, equal pay, and holidays with pay. She was a member of the Joint Committee of Working Women's Organizations and was also active in the International Labour Organisation and International Federation of Trade Unions. She was appointed OBE in 1935.

During the Second World War, Anne Loughlin was frequently consulted by the government. Ernest Bevin, while still minister of labour, appointed her to a board advising on the working conditions and social problems encountered by thousands of women who switched from civilian to munitions industries. She was involved in the organization of clothing prices, utility production, austerity restrictions, and the output of 409 million uniforms and other garments for the armed forces. In recognition of her wartime work she was made a dame of the British empire in 1943.

In 1942, as the longest serving TUC general council

member, Anne Loughlin became its chairman and president of the 1943 congress. She was the first woman and first titled person to hold the post. She urged the TUC to plan for a future of social, economic, and industrial change in accordance with its socialist aims. She believed equal pay was the just reward for women's war effort. The post-war concern with exports and the shortage of both cloth and textile workers evoked her scathing criticism of the Dior 'new look' in 1947, with its long, full skirts.

Dame Anne Loughlin became general secretary of the Garment Workers' Union in 1948, and the first woman to become a trade group member of the TUC general council. Early in 1950 she served on a wages council (formerly trade boards) for her industry and a development council looking at ways to increase efficiency, productivity, and working conditions in the clothing industry. The final report, presented with recommendations in 1952, was scrapped by the Conservative government of the day.

In 1953 Anne Loughlin retired from her union post on grounds of ill health, probably caused by years of hard work. By then, she was seen as part of the union establishment in contrast to her youthful reputation as a radical firebrand. Nevertheless, her concern throughout her career that women should be treated in the same way as men in the workplace and union, and her service to the clothing industry as a whole, made her fully deserving of the accolade given by the National Union of Tailors and Garment Workers when the Anne Loughlin Room was opened at union headquarters in 1975: 'An International Women's Year tribute to an outstanding pioneer woman, member and leader' ('Appreciation', 1975). Anne Loughlin never married; she died at her home, 147 Trinity Road, Tooting, London, on 14 July 1979. JANET E. GRENIER

Sources H. Chevins, *Garment Worker* (Aug 1979), 4–5 [repr. of 'Appreciation' on occasion of naming ceremony of Anne Loughlin Room, March 1975, National Union of Tailors and Garment Workers] · M. Stewart and L. Hunter, *The needle is threaded* (1964) · *The General Council's Report to the Annual Congress* [Trades Union Congress], 111 (1979), 359–60 · *The Guardian* (17 July 1979) · *DLB*, 6.246; 9.125 · *The Times* (6 Sept 1943) · *The Times* (7 Sept 1943) · *Daily Telegraph* (19 July 1979) · S. Lewenhak, *Women and trade unions: an outline history of women in the British trade union movement* (1977) · N. C. Solden, *Women in British trade unions, 1874–1976* (1978) · *WWW* · d. cert.

Archives London Metropolitan University, TUC library

Likenesses Bassano, photograph, NPG [*see illus.*] · photograph, repro. in Stewart and Hunter, *The needle is threaded*, 165 · photograph, repro. in *Labour Woman*, 19 (Jan 1931), 7

Wealth at death £34,159: administration, 25 Oct 1979, *CGPLA Eng. & Wales*

Louis, Alfred Hyman (1829–1915), scholar and visionary vagrant, was born in 1829 in Birmingham, the eldest son of Hyman Tobias (or Tobar) Louis, a well-to-do merchant. At fifteen he entered King Edward's School, Birmingham, where he began long friendships with Edward White Benson, later archbishop of Canterbury, and Joseph Lightfoot, later bishop of Durham. Although born a Jew, Louis was strongly attracted to Anglicanism, and his schooldays were full of precocious religious and literary projects. He matriculated at Trinity College, Cambridge, in 1847, and showed exceptional brilliance and learning, but he left Cambridge two years later without a degree.

Alfred Hyman Louis (1829–1915), by Histed

In 1851 Louis was admitted to Lincoln's Inn, and during the next decade associated with leading London intellectuals and reformers. He was deeply influenced by Frederick Denison Maurice and other Christian socialists. It was Maurice who baptized him into the Church of England. At the Working Men's College he was on close terms with Charles Kingsley, J. M. Ludlow, and Frederick Furnivall, and knew Ruskin, Burne-Jones, and Rossetti. His prodigious legal learning was also acquired during these years, and he was called to the bar in 1855. Nothing is known of his legal practice, or indeed if he had one, though he always styled himself 'barrister of Lincoln's Inn'. In 1861 he published a knowledgeable and opinionated volume, *England and Europe*, calling for vigorous British moral leadership in continental affairs. During the electoral reform crisis of 1867 his pamphlet *The Ministry, Reform, and the Constitution* affirmed that he was 'a reformer to the very core', but urged restraint on both political parties.

In 1869 Louis voyaged to America with letters of introduction but no funds or friends. In Chicago he carried on a romance by letter with Cornelia Lunt, an heiress, but her parents persuaded her to ignore him. In Boston he visited Henry Wadsworth Longfellow with annoying frequency in 1872, and tried unsuccessfully to get William Dean Howells to publish his poetry. Longfellow claimed that Louis was twice married, and that his first wife, a Miss Anthony, had died leaving two children, but no evidence to support these assertions has been found. The claim of his *Times* obituary that he married one Eliza Telfer in 1869 is disputed by his biographer. In New York, Louis was befriended for a time by Rabbi Gustav Gottheil, for whom he translated from German a small book published in 1875 as *Hebrew Characteristics*. His wanderings thereafter may have taken him to India, or Australia, or New Zealand, but there is no record of his activities. He was in London again in 1876–7, writing *The Conference and the Crisis*, a condemnation of British interference in Turkish affairs at the Constantinople peace conference—a book somewhat at odds with his earlier *England and Europe*.

Louis sometimes appeared among the distinguished Sunday afternoon guests of George Eliot and George Henry Lewes at The Priory, and later claimed that he was the prototype of Mordecai, the consumptive mystic of *Daniel Deronda*. In The Priory circle he was befriended by the Catholic writers Wilfrid and Alice Meynell, and dined with their protégé Francis Thompson. Through them he met Cardinal Manning, who received him into the Roman Catholic church.

In New York again by 1890, Louis lived in a garret as a virtual pauper, occasionally selling poems to newspapers and magazines. Algernon Blackwood, then a struggling journalist, came upon him in a waterfront warehouse in 1894 and marvelled at the contrast between his miserable condition and the eloquence of his utterance. He similarly fascinated the young Edwin Arlington Robinson, who transformed him into the subject of his poem *Captain Craig*, the 'hoboscholiast'. His New York friends were too poor to support him, but one helped him to return to London in 1903. Living in rooms opposite the British Museum, and later in Hampstead, he occasionally saw the Meynells. By now he had apparently returned to Judaism. Conversing with anyone willing to listen, he drifted increasingly into reverie and delusion, resembling a picturesque aged Hebrew of Rembrandt. He died on 10 October 1915 at St Marylebone Infirmary and was buried in Plashet Jewish cemetery in Manor Park.

Louis's personality, rather than his attainments, made him memorable. In his earlier years he was noted for his wit, vehemence, and advanced social views. In his later years it was his pathetic shabbiness, rhapsodic recitations, and pontific manner that first fascinated, and usually later alienated, his acquaintances. He often wore out his welcome. Diminutive, with a prophet's beard and sharp eyes, he had a resonant voice and dignified demeanour. He was a pianist, a poet, an encyclopaedia of European literature. A man of mystery and contradictions, unrevealing about his history, he hinted at his past eminence and implied that some tragedy had denied him his destiny. He was gentle and unworldly, but actively despised Gladstone and Spencer. His successive religious conversions were unexplained, as were his transatlantic travels. Differing accounts circulated of a marriage, or marriages, and children. One third of his adult life was spent in America, but how and where he lived are hardly known; and of his years in Britain there are desultory allusions but little documentation. ALBERT R. VOGELER

Sources W. D. Sutcliffe, 'The original of Robinson's Captain Craig', *New England Quarterly*, 15 (1943), 407–31 · A. Blackwood, *Episodes before thirty* (1923) · *The Times* (20 Oct 1915) · E. Neff, *Edwin Arlington Robinson* (1948) · H. Hagedorn, *Edwin Arlington Robinson* (1938) · M. Ffoulkes, *My own past* (1915) · R. B. Martin, *The dust of combat: a life of Charles Kingsley* (1959) · N. C. Masterman, *John Malcolm Ludlow: the builder of Christian socialism* (1963) · R. Gottheil, *The life of Gustav Gottheil* (1936) · W. D. Howells, *Literary friends and acquaintance* (1901) · *The letters of Henry Wadsworth Longfellow*, ed. A. Hilen, 5 (1982)

Likenesses Histed, photograph, repro. in Ffoulkes, *My own past* [*see illus.*]

Louis, Sir Thomas, first baronet (*bap.* **1758**, *d.* **1807**), naval officer, was baptized at Holy Trinity Church, Exeter, on 11 May 1758, the son of John Louis (1720–1815), a schoolmaster, and Elizabeth, *née* Atkinson (*c.*1724–1798). His grandfather, according to family tradition, was an illegitimate son of Louis XIV. In November 1769, aged eleven, Louis joined his first ship, the sloop *Fly* (Captain Mitchell Graham); he served on the home station until September 1771 when he transferred to the frigate *Southampton* (Captain John Macbride). With Macbride he moved to the frigate *Orpheus* in April 1773 and thence to the *Kent* (74 guns). In June 1775 he joined the sloop *Martin* (Captain William Parker) and saw his first foreign service, off Newfoundland.

On his return home in January 1776 Louis rejoined Graham in the frigate *Thetis* in which he remained—visiting Ascension Island and St Helena—until November when he transferred to the *Bienfaisant* (64 guns), again with Macbride. On 18 July 1777 he was promoted lieutenant and in 1780 he became the ship's first lieutenant. He was present at Augustus Keppel's action off Ushant on 27 July 1778 and, on 16 January 1780, at Admiral Sir George Rodney's 'Moonlight Battle' off Cape St Vincent which led to the relief of Gibraltar. The Spanish flagship *Phoenix* (80 guns) struck to the *Bienfaisant*, and Louis was appointed her prize-master. With great skill he took her, in her shattered condition and in stormy weather, to Gibraltar. Macbride wrote to Rodney on 20 January 1780: 'I beg leave to recommend to your attention Mr Thomas Louis to whose diligent and active behaviour the safety of the prize is in a great measure owing. This is the second line of battle ship he has had the charge of within these eight days' (*Private Papers of … Sandwich*, 3.197). The first had been the *Guipuzcoana* (64 guns) taken on 8 January 1780.

Louis took the much-damaged *Phoenix* to England, before rejoining the *Bienfaisant* in time to partake in the skilful capture of the unusually large privateer *Comte d'Artois* (60 guns) off southern Ireland in August. Louis was again the prize-master. In January 1781 he followed Macbride to the frigate *Artois*, a recently taken French prize, and on 9 April he was promoted commander with command of the armed vessel *Mackworth*, convoying the Milford–Plymouth trade. Fifteen months later Louis was appointed to the impress service at Sligo and Cork (again under Macbride) where he raised 5000 men, and on 20 January 1783 he was promoted captain. During the ten years of peace he was on half pay, living near Torquay. On 15 July 1784 he married Jacquetta (1752–1824), daughter of Samuel Belfield of Stoke Gabriel. They had three daughters and four sons, of whom the eldest, Sir John Louis, second baronet, died an admiral in 1863 having gone to sea with his father in 1793, and the third fought in the Royal Horse Artillery at Waterloo.

On the resumption of war in March 1793 Louis commissioned the *Cumberland* (74 guns); a year later he transferred to *Minotaur* (74 guns) as flag-captain to Macbride, now a vice-admiral and commander-in-chief in the Downs. In 1796 he escorted a convoy to the West Indies and back, and late the next year he joined the Mediterranean Fleet. His was one of the ships under Captain Thomas Troubridge which, in June 1798, reinforced Nelson's small squadron and won the battle of the Nile on 1–2 August.

On that night the *Minotaur* anchored next ahead of Nelson's flagship and received the surrender of the *Aquilon* (74 guns) after a two-hour duel. Nelson, who had been badly wounded, summoned Louis to his flagship at about 9 p.m. as 'he could not have a moment's peace until he had thanked him. "Farewell dear Louis, I shall never forget the obligation I am under to you for your brave and generous conduct; and now, whatever may become of me, my mind is at peace"' (*Naval Chronicle*, 1, 1799, 287; 3, 1800, 183). The *Naval Chronicle* emphasizes that the incident is 'perfectly correct' (ibid.), though it is doubted in Nicolas's *Dispatches and Letters … of Nelson* (3.56). With the other captains, Louis received the gold medal for the victory.

In September 1799 the *Culloden* (Commodore Troubridge) and the *Minotaur* liberated Civita Vecchia from the French with their marines and seamen, while Louis himself 'went to Rome and arranged the evacuation and taking possession of that place … with great ability and exertion', hoisting British colours over the Capitol (T. Troubridge to the Admiralty, 6 Oct 1799, PRO, ADM 1/2599/211B). For this he received the Neapolitan order of St Ferdinand and of merit.

In May 1800 Lord Keith flew his flag in the *Minotaur* during the siege of Genoa, and as a private ship the *Minotaur* took part in the Egyptian operations of 1801. She returned home the following year.

On the resumption of war in 1803 Louis commanded the *Conqueror* (74 guns) off Brest and in the channel until he was promoted rear-admiral of the blue on 23 April 1804. He immediately hoisted his flag in *Leopard* (50 guns), with Francis Austen (Jane Austen's brother) as his flag-captain, and commanded some forty vessels off Boulogne where Napoleon was preparing his invasion force.

In January 1805 Louis (with Austen) sailed to the Mediterranean, joining *Canopus* (80 guns) just in time to join Nelson, as his second-in-command, in the chase of the Franco-Spanish fleet to the West Indies and back. Off Cadiz on 11 October he was sent by Nelson with six ships to Gibraltar to water, provision, and store, then to escort an east-bound troop convoy past Cartagena, and to return with fresh provisions for the fleet. 'You are sending us away', Louis is said to have reproached Nelson; 'the enemy will come out, and we shall have no share in the battle', at which Nelson explained that he had no choice but to send his ships to water and provision in detachments. 'I look upon *Canopus* as my right hand, and I send you first to insure your being here to help to beat them' (*Dispatches and Letters*, 7.63).

In November, having missed Trafalgar, *Canopus* sailed from Cadiz under Vice-Admiral Sir John Duckworth to the West Indies and fought in the battle of St Domingo on 6 February 1806, a brilliant piece of service in which all five French ships-of-the-line were either captured or destroyed, and for which Louis, the second-in-command, was created a baronet (March 1806) and received a second gold medal.

In November 1806 he was dispatched by Lord Collingwood with a small squadron to reconnoitre the defences of the Dardanelles as a preliminary to the impending expedition to Constantinople to be led by Duckworth. Three months later Louis in the *Canopus* led Duckworth's squadron up the straits 'with the gallantry and cool judgement which mark his character' (Duckworth to his squadron, 4 March, H. B. Louis, 117); on the return (3 March) through the straits the *Canopus* was struck by huge stone shots fired by the Turks which carried away her wheel and caused much damage to her hull. The squadron then sailed to the coast of Egypt where Louis was left in command. On 17 May 1807 he died on board the *Canopus* in Alexandria harbour, aged forty-nine, of a 'sort of complaint' picked up in the West Indies the previous year. His body was taken to Malta where he was buried on Manoel Island on 8 June. To his sailors he was 'our most noble Admiral … all that was good and just' (petition, May 1806, PRO, ADM 1/5127/34). C. H. H. OWEN

Sources *DNB* · admiralty documents, PRO, ADM 1; ADM 36; ADM 51; ADM 52; ADM 107/6 [captain's letters for Louis and Troubridge; ships' muster books; captain's logs; master's logs; lieutenants' passing certificates] · 'Biographical memoir of Sir Thomas Louis', *Naval Chronicle*, 16 (1806), 176–93 · H. B. Louis, *One of Nelson's band of brothers, Admiral Sir Thomas Louis, bt.* (1951) · *The dispatches and letters of Vice-Admiral Lord Viscount Nelson*, ed. N. H. Nicolas, 7 vols. (1844–6) · NMM, Louis MSS · NMM, Keith MSS · *The private papers of John, earl of Sandwich*, ed. G. R. Barnes and J. H. Owen, 3, Navy RS, 75 (1936) · parish register, Exeter, Holy Trinity Church, 11 May 1758 [baptism] · *IGI*

Archives NMM, corresp. and papers | BL, letters to Lord Nelson, Add. MSS 34908–34930 · NMM, letters to Lord Keith · NMM, letters to Lord Nelson

Likenesses R. Smirke, group portrait, print, *c*.1799 (with Nelson's captains at the Nile), NMM · W. Bromley, J. Landseer, and Leney, group portrait, line engraving, pubd 1803 (*Naval victories, Victor of the Nile*), BM, NPG · N. Freese, engraving, *c*.1805 (after unknown portrait), repro. in *Naval Chronicle* · J. Downham, portrait, *c*.1806, repro. in Louis, *One of Nelson's band of brothers* · Ridley and Holl, stipple, pubd 1806 (after Freese), NPG · J. Daniell, mezzotint, pubd 1807 (after R. Livesay), BM · J. Daniell, engraving (after R. Livesay, 1807), NMM

Wealth at death under £15,000: PRO, death duty registers, IR 26/133, no. 231

Louisa, Princess (1724–1751). *See under* Anne, princess royal (1709–1759).

Louisa [Louisa Stuart], **styled countess of Albany** (1752–1824), consort of Charles Edward, Jacobite claimant to the English, Scottish, and Irish thrones, was born Louisa Maximiliana Carolina Emmanuel in Mons, Hainault, in the Austrian Netherlands. She was the first child of Prince Gustav Adolf of Stolberg-Gedern (*d.* 1757); her mother was a daughter of the earl of Elgin. Following Prince Gustav's death at the battle of Leuthen (1757) his widow and daughter came under the protection of the Austrian empress, Maria Theresa. Louisa, who was raised a Roman Catholic, became at seventeen a canoness of the prestigious chapter at Mons. She was promoted as a suitable bride for *Charles Edward (1720–1788) by the duke of Berwick, one of whose family was married to another Stolberg sister. The purpose of the marriage was to secure a dowry and an heir as quickly as possible—the marriage contract stipulated consummation on the night of the marriage. Additionally, France had offered Charles a pension of 40,000 crowns upon his marriage. For these reasons, and to prevent the interference of the empress, then an ally of Hanoverian Britain, a quick proxy marriage was performed in Paris on 22 March 1772 (with Berwick as proxy for Charles) and the real wedding took place in Italy on 17 April. The news soon reached Britain: Horace Walpole described her erroneously as sixteen and a Lutheran; others noted that via the earls of Elgin she was a direct descendant of Robert the Bruce. Bishop James Gordon dubbed her the Queen of Hearts, and pictures of her were much in demand.

Politically and connubially the marriage was a failure. France did not pay the promised pension, and Pope Clement XIV continued to refuse to recognize the royal title, referring to 'Baron and Baroness Renfrew'. Charles, against familial custom, employed the Albany title, first used by him as an incognito in 1737 and which he would pass to his natural daughter Charlotte as a duchy in 1783. No heir was forthcoming, although the later Sobieski Stuart pretenders would base their claim upon contemporary rumour concerning a boy who had been spirited overseas soon after birth. The 52-year-old Charles was a political refugee who took took refuge in heavy drinking. Within four years Louisa had begun a series of affairs, first with the grand tourist Thomas *Coke of Holkham, and in 1776, on the royal couple's removal to Florence, an enduring liaison with the Piedmontese poet Count Vittorio Alfieri (*d.* 1803). Following an alleged drunken attack by Charles in November 1780, Louisa fled to the convent of the little white nuns and thence to the protection of Charles's brother Henry, Cardinal York. The breach was recognized by observers such as Horace Mann as a more or less final blow to the dynastic hopes of the exiled line. York's protection ceased in 1783 when he was enlightened as to the (continuing) Alfieri affair. An official separation was negotiated by Gustav III of Sweden in 1784.

Louisa and Alfieri moved to Paris; there they heard of Charles's death in 1788, but did not move to regularize

Louisa [Louisa Stuart], **styled countess of Albany** (1752–1824), by François-Xavier Fabre, 1793

their liaison. In 1791 Louisa visited England and was presented at court, Horace Walpole commenting upon her unregal demeanour. After fleeing Paris in 1792, the couple formed part of an émigré minor intellectual salon in Florence. Alfieri died in April 1803 and appears to have been succeeded in the countess's affections by the painter François-Xavier Fabre. On the death of Cardinal York in 1807 Louisa became a pensioner of the British government and died in Florence on 29 January 1824. Her bequests are the foundation of the Musée Fabre, Montpellier, and she is buried in the church of Santa Croce, Florence.

Changing perceptions of the last Stuarts and the coincidence of her own lifetime with revolutionary Romanticism to some extent coloured the contemporary image of Louisa. Disparity in age and expectations prejudiced the marriage from the outset. Her deception of Cardinal York and her exploitation of his estrangement from his brother are discreditable. She may yet be reclaimed as the emancipated survivor of domestic abuse, but a recent verdict is of a calculating 'little vixen who richly deserved what she got in the way of marital deserts' (Douglas).

Eirwen E. C. Nicholson

Sources M. Crosland, *Louise of Stolberg, countess of Albany* (1962) • H. Douglas, *Bonnie Prince Charlie in love: the private passions of Prince Charles Edward Stuart* (1995) • F. P. Lole, 'The title of Albany', *The Jacobite*, 98 (1998), 2–3

Likenesses O. Humphrey, miniature, *c.*1772, Burghley House, Northamptonshire • C. Marsigli, oils, *c.*1772, Scot. NPG • oils, *c.*1772, Stonyhurst College, Lancashire • A. Giardoni, line engraving, pubd 1773 (after C. Marsigli), BM • O. Humphrey, pencil and chalk, *c.*1776 • attrib. H. D. Hamilton, portrait, *c.*1785, NPG •

F.-X. Fabre, oils, 1793, Uffizi Gallery, Florence [*see illus.*] • attrib. H. D. Hamilton, pastel drawing, Musée Fabre, Montpellier • miniature, U. Edin. • oils, Scot. NPG

Louise, Princess, duchess of Argyll (1848–1939), was born Louise Caroline Alberta at Buckingham Palace, London, on 18 March 1848, the sixth of Queen *Victoria's nine children. Although she was the queen's most beautiful daughter, Louise suffered from occupying a middle position in a large family. Queen Victoria underrated Louise's intelligence and her artistic talents were only belatedly recognized. After being taught modelling by Mary Thornycroft, the princess enrolled at the National Art Training School, Kensington, in 1868 but her duties as the queen's social secretary prevented regular attendance. Much of her subsequent artistic progress came through her association with the portrait sculptor Joseph Edgar Boehm.

Princess Louise's reaction against Queen Victoria's morbid widowhood took the form of moodiness, alternating with sporadic artistic and political enthusiasm. Alone of royalty she supported the women's movement, writing to Josephine Butler to praise her *International Women's Review* and privately visiting the woman doctor, Elizabeth Garrett. Her position within the royal family meant that such activities were severely circumscribed. However, Louise served as foundation president of the Women's Educational Union in 1871 and the following year she helped launch the Girls' Public School Day Company. Her support for non-denominational education as a means of advancing women's individuality as well as lessening class distinctions contrasted with the court's conservatism.

Queen Victoria reacted with some annoyance and alarm towards her daughter's feminism and liberalism. When these sympathies were coupled with rumours of romantic liaisons, she resolved upon an appropriate marriage for her daughter. Princess Louise married John (Ian) Douglas Sutherland *Campbell, marquess of Lorne, later ninth duke of Argyll (1845–1914), on 21 March 1871. The queen claimed that the marriage was 'the most popular act of my reign' (Fulford, 305) and the press generally hailed it for striking a 'democratic' note, Louise being the first daughter of a sovereign since 1515 to marry a commoner. Although the marriage was initially happy, the couple's childlessness, the constraints on their activities imposed by the queen, and Lorne's failure to fulfil his early promise all affected Louise. Of Lorne's alleged, unprovable homosexuality, Elizabeth Longford concludes that he was 'indeed mildly ambivalent' (54).

From 1878 to 1883 Princess Louise was Lorne's consort as governor-general of Canada but after sustaining injuries in a sleigh accident in February 1880 she spent protracted spells in Britain. Homesickness, marital tensions, and her dislike of Ottawa society explained the situation, which resulted in her loss of popularity in Canada. Her main, enduring contribution to Canadian culture was her support for the foundation of the Royal Canadian Academy in 1880. Her decorative paintings at Rideau Hall, Ottawa, have affinities with the aesthetic movement and her portrait of Henrietta Montalba (1880; National Gallery of Canada, Montreal) is a convincing essay in realism.

Princess Louise, duchess of Argyll (1848–1939), by unknown photographer

The later 1870s and 1880s witnessed the princess's extensive involvement with the art world. She exhibited at the Royal Academy, the Society of Painters in Watercolour, and the Grosvenor Gallery. Her avant-garde tastes were evident in her admiration of James Whistler and her commission of Edward Godwin to design her studio at Kensington Palace. Louise's presence in Boehm's studio at the time of his sudden death in December 1890 provoked press gossip and subsequent, unsubstantiated speculation upon their possible sexual relationship. Boehm and Alfred Gilbert had assisted Louise with her best-known sculpture, the seated marble statue of Queen Victoria (1890–93; Kensington Gardens, London), a conscientious if vapid work. Another portrait statue of Queen Victoria is at McGill University, Montreal (1890). More innovative are two near-identical memorials reflecting Louise's admiration of Gilbert: Prince Henry of Battenberg (1897; Whippingham church, Isle of Wight) and the Second South African War 'colonial soldiers' memorial (1904; St Paul's Cathedral, London).

Politically, Princess Louise was similarly progressive: she disagreed with Lorne's opposition to Irish home rule; she supported the creation of life peers; she advocated conciliation in India; and she urged Queen Victoria to co-operate with the Liberal ministry of 1892–5. In later years, however, she apparently shared the reactionary opinions of her brother Prince *Arthur, duke of Connaught. By the 1890s, her relations with Queen Victoria had improved, although Louise's beauty, flirtatiousness, unconventionality, and wit aroused sisterly jealousy and court gossip. Her marriage survived thanks to long periods of separation; however, Argyll's deteriorating health from 1911 brought them closer together. His death in May 1914 led to Louise's nervous breakdown and 'terrible' loneliness. The outbreak of the First World War provided an outlet for her grief and the opportunity to perform 'good works'.

Among Princess Louise's presidencies were the Soldiers' and Sailors' Family Association, the Ladies' Work Society, and the National Trust. Never a figurehead, she was appointed DBE in 1918 for her war work, which included visits to hospitals, canteens, and servicemen's clubs. She housed wounded officers at Kensington Palace and at her Scottish residence, Rosneath Castle. The president of twenty-five hospitals, Louise's closest links were with the Princess Louise Hospital for Children, Kensington, founded in 1924. After taking an energetic interest in its building, the elderly princess often paid unscheduled visits to patients and staff. Such activities typified her resolve to be considered a private individual, detached from the stereotypical role of a member of the court, yet never compromising her dignity or style. Princess Louise, duchess of Argyll, died on 3 December 1939 at Kensington Palace, London. Her obituary in *The Times* considered her 'the least bound by convention and etiquette of any of the Royal Family'. MARK STOCKER

Sources J. Wake, *Princess Louise: Queen Victoria's unconventional daughter* (1988) • D. Duff, *The life story of H. R. H. Princess Louise, duchess of Argyll* (1940); repr. (1971) • S. Gwyn, *The private capital: ambition and love in the age of Macdonald and Laurier* (1984) • J. Roberts, *Royal artists: from Mary queen of Scots to the present day* (1987) • R. M. Stamp, *Royal rebels: Princess Louise & the Marquis of Lorne* (1988) • E. Longford, ed., *Darling Loosy: letters to Princess Louise, 1856–1939* (1991) • *Your dear letter: private correspondence of Queen Victoria and the crown princess of Prussia, 1865–1871*, ed. R. Fulford (1971), 303–10 • *The Times* (4 Dec 1939) • *The Times* (8 Dec 1939)

Archives Royal Arch. | BL, Flower MSS • BL, Holland MSS • BL, Knightley MSS • BL, Paget MSS • Hove Central Library, Sussex, Wolseley MSS • NA Canada, Lorne MSS • NL Scot., Campbell MSS • priv. coll., Inveraray MSS • priv. coll., Bevills MSS • priv. coll., Probert MSS • PRO NIre., Dufferin MSS

Likenesses F. X. Winterhalter, portrait, 1865, Royal Collection • M. Thornycroft, bust, 1870, Royal Collection • P. F. Connelly, bust, 1874, Inveraray Castle, Argyll • P. F. Connelly, bust, 1879, Royal Collection • H. von Angeli, portrait, 1892, Royal Collection • P. A. de Laszlo, portrait, after 1914, HRH Prince and Princess Michael of Kent Collection • L. Béroud, pencil drawing, Scot. NPG • attrib. C. Louise, self-portrait, bust, NPG • M. Thornycroft, statuette, Royal Collection • photograph, NPG [*see illus.*]

Wealth at death £239,260 18*s*. 6*d*.—save and except settled land: probate, 7 Feb 1940, *CGPLA Eng. & Wales*

Louise, princess royal and duchess of Fife (1867–1931), was born Louise Victoria Alexandra Dagmar on 20 February 1867 at Marlborough House, London. She was the third child and eldest daughter of the prince and princess of Wales—the future *Edward VII (1841–1910) and Queen *Alexandra (1844–1925). Her mother went down with rheumatic fever five days before her birth, and took many months to recover. Princess Louise, with her two sisters, Victoria and Maud, received a conventional, restricted education from governesses; their mother ('Darling Motherdear') was the greatest—and not entirely benign—influence on their lives. None of them inherited their mother's beauty, and, although all were boisterous and high-spirited children, as they grew up they became shy, even listless, and were referred to as 'the whispering Wales girls'. The princess of Wales saw no reason for her daughters to marry, but in July 1889 Louise became engaged to the wealthy Alexander William George Duff, sixth Earl Fife (1849–1912), and married him within the month, on 27 July. On their marriage, Fife (a descendant of one of the illegitimate children of William IV) was created a duke, despite the initial objections of Queen Victoria. The Fifes had two daughters, among them Princess *Alexandra (1891–1959), and a stillborn son; by a special remainder of 1900, the dukedom of Fife passed to the princess's daughters and their male issue. This marriage, although welcomed by Queen Victoria, added to her anxieties about the future succession to the throne after the death of the duke of Clarence in 1892: should the prince of Wales's only other son die, or leave no children, the throne would go to the withdrawn princess, whose children would (without royal intervention) be commoners. The engagement of Prince George to Princess May of Teck, which took place in Princess Louise's garden at Sheen Lodge in Richmond Park, effectively removed her from the succession.

Marriage enabled the princess to live in entire privacy, at Mar Lodge, near Braemar, and at Duff House, near Banff, where she became a skilled salmon-fisher. In 1905 she was declared princess royal, and her two daughters were created princesses with the title of highness. In 1911 the family travelled to Egypt, and their ship, the *Delhi*, ran aground off the coast of Morocco; their lifeboat also sank. They went on to Khartoum and Cairo, and the duke of Fife developed pneumonia and died at Aswan on 29 January 1912. After the duke's death, the princess became still more reclusive, and died at her London house in Portman Square on 4 January 1931. K. D. REYNOLDS

Sources *DNB* • J. Pope-Hennessy, *Queen Mary* (1959) • C. Hibbert, *Edward VII* (1976) • T. Aronson, *Grandmama of Europe* (1973) • *The Times* (5 Jan 1931) • K. Rose, *King George V* (1983)

Archives FILM BFI NFTVA, news footage

Likenesses K. W. F. Bauerle, double portrait, oils, 1871 (with sister Victoria), Royal Collection • K. W. F. Bauerle, group portrait, oils, 1872 (with brothers Albert Victor and George), Royal Collection • J. Sant, group portrait, oils, *c*.1872 (*Victoria with three of her grandchildren*), Royal Collection • M. Thornycroft, marble statuette, 1877, Royal Collection • H. von Angeli, oils, 1878, Royal Collection • S. P. Hall, group portrait, oils, 1883 (with sisters Victoria and Maud), NPG • L. Tuxen, group portrait, oils, 1887 (*The Royal Family at the Time of the Jubilee*), Royal Collection • W. & D. Downey, double portrait, photograph, 1889 (with Duke of Fife), NPG • W. & D. Downey, group portrait, photograph, *c*.1891 (with Duke and daughter Alexandra), NPG • L. Tuxen, group portrait, oils, 1893 (*Marriage of King George and Queen Mary*), Royal Collection • L. Tuxen, group portrait, oils, 1896 (*Marriage of Princess Maud and Prince Charles of Denmark*), Royal Collection · A. Corbett, double portrait, photograph, *c*.1910 (with Duke), NPG · A. Corbett, group portrait, photograph, *c*.1910 (with daughters Alexandra and Maud Duff), NPG · L. Charles, group portraits, photographs, *c*.1911 (with daughters), NPG · Graphic Photo Union, double portrait, photograph, 1923 (with daughter Maud), NPG · R. Faulkner, photograph, NPG; repro. in *ILN* (16 Feb 1884) · J. Sant, oils (study for *Victoria and grandchildren*), Royal Collection · photographs (as infant), NPG · photographs, Royal Collection

Lound, Thomas (**1802–1861**), landscape painter, worked in the family brewery in Norwich and spent his spare time painting landscapes in oils and watercolours. He is said to have had lessons from John Sell Cotman, whose influence is greater in his oil paintings, and his works show the influence of watercolours by John Crome, David Cox, and Joseph Stannard. He collected paintings by other Norfolk artists, including Henry Bright, and at his death he owned seventy-five paintings by John Thirtle. Many of his best pictures are of scenery near Cromer, on Norfolk's north coast; during summer holidays he also painted in Wales and Yorkshire.

Although not a member of the Norwich Society of Artists, Lound exhibited there regularly from 1820 to 1833 and later at the Norfolk and Norwich Fine Arts Association. Between 1845 and 1857 he showed eighteen watercolours at the Royal Academy, all of which were Norfolk scenes. He was one of the most prolific watercolourists of the Norwich school. *Framlingham Castle, Suffolk*, *View Looking up the Wensum at Norwich* (1832), and *View from Rusthall Common, Near Tunbridge Wells, Kent* (1845) are in the Victoria and Albert Museum, London, and *Yarmouth Beach*, *Richmond Castle*, and *Ely Cathedral* are in the British Museum in London. Two of his etchings are in the National Maritime Museum, Greenwich.

He was married, though nothing is known of his wife. They had two daughters. Thomas Lound died following a stroke at his home in King Street, Norwich, on 18 January 1861. ANNE PIMLOTT BAKER

Sources H. A. E. Day, *East Anglian painters*, 2–3: *The Norwich school of painters* (1979), 246–59 · Mallalieu, *Watercolour artists*, vols. 1–2 · Wood, *Vic. painters*, 3rd edn · L. Lambourne and J. Hamilton, eds., *British watercolours in the Victoria and Albert Museum* (1980) · Graves, *RA exhibitors* · *GM*, 3rd ser., 10 (1861), 468 · *Norwich Mercury* (23 Jan 1861) · Redgrave, *Artists* · 'Catalogue of prints and drawings', www.nmm.ac.uk, 3 Jan 1999

Likenesses photograph, repro. in Day, *Norwich School of painters*, 347

Wealth at death £3000: probate, 25 Feb 1861, *CGPLA Eng. & Wales*

Loundres, Henry de. *See* London, Henry of (*d*. 1228).

Louth. For this title name *see* Bermingham, John, earl of Louth (*c*.1290–1329).

Louth, Gilbert of (*fl*. *c*.**1148**–*c*.**1180**). *See under* Saltrey, H. of (*fl*. *c*.1184).

Louth, William of (*c*.**1240–1298**), administrator and bishop of Ely, was presumably born at Louth in Lincolnshire, probably *c*.1240, judging by the chronology of his career. His parentage is unknown, but besides his early benefices in the diocese, which are not significant in themselves, there are some slight indications of a connection with the county. His appellation of master in the chancery rolls implies that he completed a course of study at a university before he entered the royal service, as one of an increasing number of graduates there.

Louth probably became a royal clerk in the last years of Henry III's reign. He went to Rome in the spring of 1272, and, although there is no record of his journey, his companion Hugh Warwick, who appointed an attorney, seems to have been subordinate to him. As Louth's earliest known preferment came in 1277, it is likely that he was sent on a mission rather than travelling to seek his own fortune. He was described as clerk of the royal household in 1275, but was cofferer of the wardrobe during the keepership of Thomas (I) Bek from 1274 to 1280. Bek, a doctor of civil law and chancellor of the University of Oxford in 1270, was the son of the lord of Eresby in Lincolnshire. Louth, who had some private transactions in the county during the same decade, may have owed something to local patronage.

The wardrobe was in origin the storehouse and safe deposit of the royal household in the same sense as the chamber was the king's bedroom. It became the household's accounting office, just as the exchequer became the accounting office of the treasury. Louth joined it at a significant time, when the wardrobe was emerging as a compact and efficient office, staffed by men of wide and varied experience who were closely in touch with the king. Under Edward I it was made to function both as a second chancery and a second treasury, and had to deal with an endless variety of administrative demands. In the course of any year Louth had to collect and dispense cash, negotiate and record credits of all kinds, and discharge commissions at home and abroad of widely varying delicacy. In the spring of 1283 he held a commission to raise loans for the Welsh expedition from foreign merchants, at his own discretion, and was equipped with sealed letters of credit for the lenders. All those matters were more or less urgent, and maintaining royal credit was not made easier by repeated application. None of the additional duties facilitated the day-to-day routines of the office, and many were deleterious to them. Diplomatic and other extraneous business, such as the negotiation of loans, or exercise of patronage upon some particular instruction, complicated the accounts as well as consuming time, in a period when the wardrobe's annual turnover was £44,000 as against £24,000 under Bek, and the exchequer was providing rather less than half the wardrobe's income.

The most significant episode in Louth's career was probably the work that fell to him in 1278–80 when Edward built a castle and a new town at Rhuddlan in the county of Flint, which served as a major base in the second Welsh war in 1282–3. The project involved extensive surveying and civil engineering, the co-ordination of labour and supplies on a large scale, and eventually the settlement of the town. Louth was involved at every level with its organization and finance. He was rewarded with prebends at Beverley and Lincoln in 1279, and succeeded Bek as keeper of the wardrobe on 20 November 1280. In the spring of that year he was appointed with the chief justice of Chester to oversee the settlement of the remaining plots at Rhuddlan.

In the 1280s Louth spent some time abroad, chiefly in Gascony, both with and without the king. Early in 1283 he became dean of the collegiate church of St Martin's-le-Grand, London, a preferment more imposing in style than in substance, which was reinforced within a year by the archdeaconry of Durham. On that occasion he received a papal licence to hold his benefices for up to five years without taking holy orders. He then spent the autumn abroad, and in 1286 went to Gascony with the king, after which he had letters of protection and attorney, renewed on various occasions until the autumn of 1289.

Louth was elected bishop of Ely on 12 May 1290 and was finally constrained to take orders. He was consecrated and enthroned on 1 October following. Walter Langton, later treasurer, succeeded him at the wardrobe, but Louth continued to render accounts for several years. In 1291 he was appointed to a commission to determine the dispute in the Welsh march which led to the imprisonment of the earls of Gloucester and Hereford, Gilbert de Clare and Humphrey (VI) de Bohun. In the remaining years of his life he probably gave as much attention to public affairs in London and abroad as to those of his diocese. The chapel of St Etheldreda, Ely Place, the last remnant of Ely House, is probably his work.

Louth died on either 25 or 27 March 1298, and was buried in the south choir aisle at Ely. Only the canopy of his tomb survives, but its design and sculpture has a close affinity with the monument to Edmund (Crouchback), first earl of Lancaster, in Westminster Abbey. It is almost certainly a product of the royal workshops: a last recognition by the king of Louth's faithful service. The executors of Louth's will included Richard of Gravesend (*d.* 1303), bishop of London, and Walter Langton. All that is known of his next of kin is that his heir was a nephew, William Tuchet.

G. H. MARTIN

Sources *Chancery records* · Tout, *Admin. hist.* · *CEPR letters*, 1.505 · *Cambridgeshire*, Pevsner (1954) · W. D. Sweeting, *Ely*, Bell's Cathedral Guides (1901) · M. W. Beresford, *New towns of the middle ages* (1967) · E. B. Fryde, ed., *Book of prests of the king's wardrobe for 1294–5* (1962) · *Fasti Angl., 1066–1300*, [Monastic cathedrals], 47 · Emden, *Oxf.*, 3.2191

Archives PRO, chancery records · PRO, exchequer records

Loutherbourg, Philippe Jacques [Philip James] **de** (**1740–1812**), landscape painter and scene designer, was born on 31 October 1740 according to the baptismal register of the Neue Kirche in Strasbourg, Alsace. However, his monument in the cemetery of St Nicholas in Chiswick, London, notes his birth as taking place on 1 November in Fulda, some 60 miles north of Darmstadt, Germany. His mother was Catherine Barbe Heitz and his father Philippe Jacques (or Jacob) Loutherbourg (1698–1768), who worked as a miniaturist and engraver to the court of Darmstadt. The painter Johann Rudolf Loutherbourg (1652–1727), noted by Bénézit as working in Basel, is likely to have been the artist's grandfather. His father planned an engineering career for his son, while his mother held hopes for his future in the ministry of the Lutheran church. He studied mathematics, theology, and languages at the University of Strasbourg, but a talent for drawing led him to seek instruction from his father. On the family's move to Paris in 1755, he began his formal artistic training with Carle Van Loo, rector of the Académie Royale. He studied engraving with Jean-Georges Wille and began his lifelong concern for the chemistry and technology of pictorial reproduction. While still a pupil of Wille, Loutherbourg worked in the studio of François Joseph Casanova, and exhibited his first paintings at the salon, in 1763. Critical acclaim was swift, and Diderot identified the abilities to depict space and atmosphere that were to become distinctive features of de Loutherbourg's work, both in the theatre and for the easel (D. Diderot, *Salons*, ed. J. Seznec and J. Adhémar, 2nd edn; 1975, 1.225).

Loutherbourg regularly exhibited in subsequent salons and, in 1766, he was nominated as a 'peintre du roy' of the Académie Royale. In the following year he was elected a full member—a mark of his celebrity in that he was three years away from the qualifying age of thirty. He was now unhappily living with Barbe Burlat, whom he had married in 1764. But rumours of criminal activity on her part sufficiently tainted the painter's name to prevent the final bestowal of the Académie award. His father died in 1768, and it was perhaps a combination of personal reasons (as well as artistic imperatives) that caused Loutherbourg to leave Paris that year. Significantly, he chose to make his grand tour to southern France, Switzerland, and the Rhineland, and not to Venice, Naples, and Rome. By 1771 he was the most prolific painter exhibiting at the salon. He adopted the 'de' and used this almost exclusively with his name thereafter.

It is possible that de Loutherbourg considered his journey to England in the autumn of 1771 as a continuation of his tour of Europe, and not with a view to permanent residence. Although there is no direct evidence of theatrical activity in Paris, de Loutherbourg's letter of introduction was from Jean Monnet (1703–1785), the retired manager of the Opéra Comique, and a friend of David Garrick, who was patron to a number of easel artists, including Zoffany, Gainsborough, and Richard Wilson. On arrival in London, de Loutherbourg stayed with Domenico Angelo, a fencing-master, stage machinist, and good friend of both Monnet and Garrick. It was here, according to Henry, Domenico's son, that de Loutherbourg met Garrick.

The result of this meeting was de Loutherbourg's letter to Garrick that proposed radical change to the scenic arrangements at Drury Lane Theatre (Harvard Theatre Collection). Garrick was sufficiently impressed to engage de Loutherbourg and to give him control over all aspects of the scenic department at Drury Lane. He was paid an unprecedented salary of £300, which was increased to £500 during his second season for Garrick.

De Loutherbourg's most significant designs were for Garrick's pantomime *A Christmas Tale* (1773); Alexander Dow's tragedy *Sethona* (1774); John Burgoyne's comedy *The Maid of Oaks* (1774); Henry Woodward's pantomime *Queen*

Mab (1775); and Charles Dibdin's ballad opera *The Waterman* (1776). Contemporary comment valued his work for the unification of all scenic elements; for his skill in creating lighting effects of considerable sophistication; and for his ability to create scenes of great topographic power and association.

Sheridan continued to employ de Loutherbourg when he took over the management of Drury Lane in 1776. New work included Sheridan's afterpiece *The Camp* (1778), which was noted for its representation of the military camp at Cox-Heath and in which reference is made to de Loutherbourg as 'Mr Leatherbag the great painter'. Sheridan's comedy *The Critic* (1779) presented de Loutherbourg's recreation of Tilbury Fort and battle against the Armada for which 'The deception of the sea was very strong, and the perspective of the ships, together with the mode of their sailing truly picturesque' (*General Advertiser*, 1 Nov 1779). The harlequinade-travelogue written by Sheridan and de Loutherbourg, *The Wonders of Derbyshire* (1779), for which a model survives in the Theatre Museum, London, may well have been his finest work in this period. The scenographic coherence of this is probably rare, and Sheridan increasingly economized by extracting scenic effects from earlier work, or requiring de Loutherbourg to design a spectacular scene to rejuvenate revived pieces—for example the revival in 1780 of Isaac Bickerstaff's *Love in a Village*, concluded with 'a Grand View of Greenwich Hospital'.

Sheridan's financial mismanagement may well have prompted de Loutherbourg to leave Drury Lane after completing *Robinson Crusoe* in 1781. Additionally, de Loutherbourg was elected a member of the Royal Academy early in 1781 and the next decade saw him committed to pursuing his easel career. He undertook extensive tours of the Peak District of Derbyshire, the Lake District, and north Wales, and exhibited some twenty-one paintings between 1784 and 1787. Some of his most powerful and typical landscapes include: *Dovedale in Derbyshire* (exh. RA, 1784; York City Art Gallery), *View of Snowdon from Llan Berris Lake* (exh. RA, 1787; Musée des Beaux-arts, Strasbourg), and *Smugglers Landing in a Storm* (1791, Victoria Art Gallery, Bath).

De Loutherbourg made two important interventions in matters theatrical during the 1780s. In 1782, at his home in Lisle Street, London, he presented his actor-less miniature theatre, the Eidophusikon, which presented scenes from Milton; topographical scenes that prefigured the great panoramas and dioramas of the nineteenth century; and scenes of immediate interest such as the loss at sea in January 1786 of the Indiaman *Halsewell*. De Loutherbourg perhaps achieved the visual unity and compositional control in miniature that current theatre technology was unable, or unwilling, to allow.

With John O'Keefe, de Loutherbourg prepared the pantomime *Omai, or, A Trip Round the World* (1785) at Covent Garden Theatre. This built upon the excitement created by Captain Cook's voyages in the south seas. John Webber, the artist who accompanied Cook, assisted and added authority to the scenic spectacle. Two models survive in the Theatre Museum, London, and seventeen costume designs exist in the Commonwealth National Library, Canberra, Australia.

In 1781 de Loutherbourg transformed rooms at Fonthill Abbey, Wiltshire, into an environment of Arabian fantasy for William Beckford, and concerns with alchemy, mysticism, and the occult underlie his later career. In 1787 he left England with the notorious theologian and freemason Count Cagliostro. Their partnership ended acrimoniously and de Loutherbourg and his wife, Lucy, returned to London to offer faith-healing services through 'heavenly and divine Influx'. He abandoned this in late 1789 and returned to his easel. During the 1790s he celebrated Britain's growing naval eminence in *The Battle of Camperdown* (1797) and *The Battle of the Nile* (1800; both Tate collection). Robert Bowyer published William Pickett's engravings of de Loutherbourg's *The Picturesque Scenery of Great Britain* (1801) and *The Romantic and Picturesque Scenery of England and Wales* (1805). He contributed many of the plates in Thomas Macklin's Bible (1800) and to Robert Bowyer's *History of England* (1812). In 1807 he was made 'Historical painter to HRH the Duke of Gloucester', but no paintings have been identified from this appointment. He died peacefully at his home in Hammersmith, Middlesex, on 11 March 1812, and was buried at St Nicholas's Church, Chiswick, where his second wife, Lucy, who died in 1828, and his son, William Philip James Lodder (1779–1867), were also interred.

CHRISTOPHER BAUGH

Sources C. L. Baugh, *Garrick and Loutherbourg* (1990) · R. Joppien, *Philippe Jacques de Loutherbourg RA, 1740–1812* (1973) [exhibition catalogue, Kenwood, the Iveagh Bequest, London, 2 June – 13 Aug 1970] · Highfill, Burnim & Langhans, *BDA* · S. Rosenfeld, *Georgian scene painters and scene painting* (1981) · C. L. Baugh, 'Philip James de Loutherbourg and the early pictorial theatre: some aspects of its cultural context', *The theatrical space*, ed. J. Redmond (1987), 99–128 · C. L. Baugh, 'Three Loutherbourg "designs"', *Theatre Notebook*, 47 (1993), 96–103 · S. Rosenfeld and E. Croft-Murray, 'A checklist of scene painters working in Great Britain and Ireland in the 18th century [pt 3]', *Theatre Notebook*, 19 (1964–5), 102–13 · R. G. Allen, 'Topical scenes for pantomime', *Educational Theatre Journal*, 17/4 (1965), 289–300 · R. Allen, 'The Eidophusikon', *Theatre Design and Technology*, 7 (1966), 12–16 · J. Gage, 'Loutherbourg: mystagogue of the sublime', *History Today*, 13 (1963), 332–9 · R. Joppien, 'Die Szenenbilder Philippe Jacques de Loutherbourgs, eine Untersuchung zu ihrer Stellung zwischen Malerei und Theater', PhD diss., University of Cologne, 1972 · R. Joppien, 'Philippe Jacques de Loutherbourg's pantomime Omai, or, A trip round the world and the artists of Captain Cook's Voyages', *British Museum Yearbook* (1979), 81–136 · F. Nunnez [P. Coxe], *A catalogue of all the valuable drawings, sketches, sea-views and studies of that celebrated artist, Philip James de Loutherbourg* (1812) · G. Ashton, *Pictures in the Garrick Club*, ed. K. A. Burnim and A. Wilton (1997) · Bénézit, *Dict.*

Archives Commonwealth National Library, Canberra, Australia, costume designs · Theatre Museum, London, designs and models · V&A

Likenesses T. Gainsborough, oils, 1772, Dulwich Art Gallery, London · stipple, pubd 1798 (after S. Singleton), BM, NPG · P. J. de Loutherbourg, self-portrait, oils, 1805–10, NPG · Page, stipple, pubd 1814, BM, NPG · H. Meyer, stipple, BM, NPG; repro. in *Contemporary portraits* (1813) · H. Singleton, group portrait, oils (*Royal Academicians, 1793*), RA

Loutit, John Freeman (1910–1992), radiobiologist and haematologist, was born on 19 February 1910 at 16

Almondbury Road, Mount Lawley, Perth, Western Australia, the only child of John Freeman Loutit (1868–1950), a mechanical and locomotive engineer, and his wife, Margaret Gould, *née* Broadfoot (1878–1971), whose family were also engineers. His antecedents had emigrated from the Orkneys to Australia in the 1850s. He was educated at the local Church of England grammar school and the universities of Western Australia and Melbourne (Trinity College). In Hilary term 1931 he took up a Rhodes scholarship at St John's College, Oxford, where he read physiology and graduated with a second-class degree in natural sciences in 1933. He later completed his medical training at the London Hospital medical college, winning prizes there. On 14 June 1941 he married Thelma Salusbury (1913–1992); they had a son and two daughters. Also in 1941 Loutit was appointed to take charge of the south-west London blood supply depot, where his research career began. He made contributions to knowledge of the preservation of blood for transfusion, and also of types of haemolytic anaemia. At the end of the Second World War he took part in work on the treatment of starvation in Holland and was made an officer of the order of Orange Nassau.

After the end of the Second World War the government felt the need for a research unit to investigate the biological hazards of radiation, in view of the use of atomic weapons and also of nuclear power. Loutit was invited to be the director of the Medical Research Council (MRC) radiobiology unit located initially at the Atomic Energy Research Establishment at Harwell, but independent of it. He set out to collect a nucleus of talented physicists and biologists to investigate various fundamental aspects of the hazards of ionizing radiation. The unit's programme encompassed the effects of radiation on cellular function, induction of chromosome aberrations, the pathogenesis of injury in various organs, the absorption and retention of radioisotopes by the body, and the genetic effects of radiation.

Loutit was a hands-on scientist (personally ingesting small quantities of radioactive material in order to assess their biological effects) and made many contributions to knowledge of the uptake and retention of radioactive isotopes from the air and the food chain, particularly isotopes of strontium and iodine. However, his most important contribution was the demonstration of the immunosuppressive effect of radiation. Using a strain of mouse with a chromosome translocation resulting in a recognizable cell marker, Loutit and his colleagues showed that mice treated with high doses of X-rays would accept bone marrow grafts from genetically incompatible donors, and could thus be rescued from the lethal effects of irradiation. This discovery led to major advances in knowledge of the effects of radiation, and also to advances in the treatment of leukaemia and other malignancies, and was relevant to organ transplantation. For it, Loutit, jointly with his colleagues David Barnes, Charles Ford, and John Hamerton, was awarded the Robert Roesler de Villiers award of the Leukemia Society of the USA. He was also elected a fellow of the Royal Society in 1963 and was awarded honorary degrees by the universities of St Andrews and Stockholm. He served on many national and international committees concerned with radiation, often as chairman. He was appointed CBE in 1957 for his services to radiation protection.

Throughout the roughly twenty years that Loutit was director the MRC radiobiology unit grew and came to be of major international status, being particularly strong in genetics and cell biology, Loutit having appreciated early on the importance of the genetic effects of radiation. However, in 1969 the MRC recommended that the unit should be reduced to half its size. Loutit was unhappy with this decision and resigned. He returned to work full time at the bench for another nineteen years. During this time he worked on haematopoietic stem cells and their function. He argued that there was a variety of stem cells in the bone marrow giving rise to all the different types of blood cells, and also bone forming cells, osteoblasts, and bone destroying cells, osteoclasts. He also studied the induction of myeloid leukaemia and of bone tumours by bone seeking radioactive isotopes. In his last field of work he continued his lifetime interest in using gene mutations to answer biological problems, and studied various mouse mutants of haematological importance. During his career he published two books and more than 200 scientific papers.

Loutit was a kind-hearted, reserved, somewhat taciturn man, who never spoke ill of others, and was always modest. He was devoted to his family, with whom he lived in the village of Steventon, Oxfordshire, from the 1940s until the end of his life. He was a convinced Christian and attended Steventon church regularly. He brought to his hobbies the same enthusiasm and attention to detail that he brought to his work, and was a keen gardener and cricketer. His skill in cooking was legendary, and he regularly cooked for dinner parties at his home. He died of pneumonia and dementia at the Grange Nursing Home, Stanford in the Vale, Oxfordshire, on 11 June 1992. He was buried on 21 June 1992 in the graveyard of St Michael's Church, Steventon, Oxfordshire. He was survived by his wife and their three children. MARY F. LYON

Sources M. F. Lyon and P. L. Mollison, *Memoirs FRS*, 40 (1994), 239–52 • private information (2004) [A. Loutit] • *The Times* (19 June 1992) • *The Independent* (17 June 1992) • *WWW* • A. Sillery and V. Sillery, *St John's College biographical register, 1919–1975* (1978)

Likenesses photograph, RS; copy, Medical Research Council, Harwell, Didcot, Oxon. • photograph, repro. in *The Times* • photograph, repro. in *The Independent*

Wealth at death £478,106: probate, 13 Nov 1992, *CGPLA Eng. & Wales*

Louvain, Joscelin de (*d.* 1180), magnate, was the youngest son of Godefroi, duke of Lotharingia (or Brabant; *d.* 1140) and count of Louvain. He first appears at Reading, with his elder sister, the widowed queen, *Adeliza of Louvain, when on 1 December 1136 she made a grant to the abbey on the anniversary of Henry I's death. It seems likely that he had only recently come to England so that his sister might make his fortune for him. On his father's death in 1140 Louvain had no portion of the paternal estate, which his elder brothers Duke Godfrey (*d.* 1144) and Count Henry (retired 1149) divided between them.

The queen made use of Louvain as her deputy in her lands. His usual title was 'the castellan' or 'the castellan of Arundel', which implies that the queen had adopted the Brabazon method of local government at Arundel, confiding power to castellans (such as those at Brussels and Louvain). To maintain his status he had a grant of a large estate at Petworth in Sussex to which were attached twenty-two knights' fees. Louvain seems to have worked well with his sister's second husband, William d'*Aubigny, called earl of Arundel, Chichester, or Sussex after 1140. He frequently attested his brother-in-law's charters, and continued to do so long after his sister's death in 1151.

Despite the queen's death, Louvain's career in England continued to prosper. He was among those favoured magnates whose future support was solicited by Duke Henry in his 1153 progress around England. Following Henry's accession he became a frequent witness to royal acts. It may have been this connection which provided him with his marriage (before 1166) to Agnes, coheir of William de Percy, a leading Yorkshire baron. Louvain was involved with the Becket affair, being one of three royal knights who were sent to warn Becket, just before his death in 1170, not to go to meet Prince Henry, the Young King, at Woodstock. He was loyal to Henry II during the rebellion of 1173–4. In April 1175 he led a party of Sussex and Hampshire knights to join the count of Flanders on his pilgrimage to the Holy Land. While in Palestine, one of his party, Henry Hose, died, and Louvain himself sealed Henry's testament and sent it back to England with Hugh Hose, brother of the deceased. On his return Louvain succeeded to his portion of the Percy honour. The inquest before royal justices establishing this share survives, and demonstrates that his interest at court obtained for him the lion's share: the lowland estates in Yorkshire, the centres of Topcliffe and Seamer, and the Percy lands in Lincolnshire and Hampshire.

Louvain died early in 1180, probably in his early sixties. His wife survived him for over twenty years and did not remarry. They had three legitimate sons, Henry de Percy (*d. c.*1198), Richard de *Percy (*d.* 1244), and Joscelin, as well as four daughters. Ralph 'the castellan's son' who appeared as holder of lands in the honour of Petworth in 1190 was probably an illegitimate son.

David Crouch

Sources E. de Dynk, ed., *Chroniques des ducs de Brabant*, 2 vols. (1854) · C. T. Clay, ed., *The Percy fee* (1963), vol. 11 of *Early Yorkshire charters*, ed. W. Farrer (1914–65) · H. Hall, ed., *The Red Book of the Exchequer*, 3 vols., Rolls Series, 99 (1896) · W. Farrer, *Honors and knights' fees … from the eleventh to the fourteenth century*, 3 vols. (1923–5) · B. R. Kemp, ed., *Reading Abbey cartularies*, 2 vols., CS, 4th ser., 31, 33 (1986–7) · C. J. Holdsworth, ed., *Rufford charters*, 4 vols., Thoroton Society Record Series, 29, 30, 32, 34 (1972–81) · J. C. Robertson and J. B. Sheppard, eds., *Materials for the history of Thomas Becket, archbishop of Canterbury*, 7 vols., Rolls Series, 67 (1875–85) · *Pipe rolls*

Lovat. For this title name *see under* Fraser family (*per. c.*1300–*c.*1500) [Fraser, Hugh, lord of Lovat (*d.* in or before 1440); Fraser, Hugh, first Lord Lovat (*d.* 1501)]. *See also* Fraser, Simon, eleventh Lord Lovat (1667/8–1747); Fraser, Simon, master of Lovat (1726–1782); Fraser, Simon Joseph, fourteenth Lord Lovat and third Baron Lovat (1871–1933); Fraser, Simon Christopher Joseph, fifteenth Lord Lovat and fourth Baron Lovat (1911–1995); Fraser, Simon Augustine, master of Lovat (1939–1994) [*see under* Fraser, Simon Christopher Joseph, fifteenth Lord Lovat and fourth Baron Lovat (1911–1995)].

Love, Augustus Edward Hough (1863–1940), mathematician and geophysicist, was born on 17 April 1863 at Weston-super-Mare, the second son of John Henry Love, surgeon, and his wife, Emily Serle. He grew up in Wolverhampton, where his father was police surgeon. He had two sisters, to the younger of whom, Blanche, he was especially close; after their father's death she kept house for him for the rest of his life. He was unmarried.

Love entered Wolverhampton grammar school in 1874. In 1881 he was awarded a sizarship at St John's College, Cambridge, to which he went up in 1882. He was at first doubtful whether to read classics or mathematics, but chose the latter and gradually came to the top of his year. He was elected scholar of the college in 1884 and was second wrangler in the mathematical tripos of 1885; he was awarded the first Smith's prize in 1887 after being elected the previous year to a fellowship at St John's which he retained until 1899, occupying the post of college lecturer in mathematics most of that time. He was elected FRS in 1894. During his Cambridge days he began his long association with the London Mathematical Society, which he served as secretary (1895–1910) and as president (1912–19). In 1926 he was awarded the society's De Morgan medal. In 1911 he won the Adams prize of the University of Cambridge for an essay on geodynamics.

In 1898 Love was elected to the Sedleian chair of natural philosophy at Oxford, a position which he held until his death. He was elected a fellow of Queen's College, Oxford, in 1927, when he was also elected an honorary fellow of St John's College, Cambridge. He was awarded a Royal medal of the Royal Society in 1909, and its Sylvester medal in 1937. He became an associate of the Italian Accademia dei Lincei, and a corresponding member of the Institut de France.

Love's chosen field of research was the mathematical theory of elasticity, and its application to geophysics. On this subject, and on problems of hydrodynamics and electromagnetism involving similar differential equations, he contributed to various journals some fifty memoirs. He is now known mainly for his important contributions to theoretical geophysics, published chiefly in his Adams prize essay, *Some Problems of Geodynamics* (1911). Several of his concepts are still in use. His model for the propagation of (purely distortional) surface waves, known as 'Love waves', brought the mathematical theory of surface waves into concordance with the observational data of the seismologist. Moreover, his work made possible the detection of differences of thickness in the crust of the earth, and he also made significant contributions to the dynamical theory of tides and to tidal measurement. During his lifetime, however, Love was mainly known as the author of what was a standard work, *A Treatise on the Mathematical Theory of Elasticity* (1892–3). This is a scholarly work, written with a historical sense; it is comprehensive, elegantly written, and became a classic in the field. Though Love was none too familiar with the practical application of the field the book remains a permanent monument to the academic aspect of elasticity. The treatment is rigidly analytical throughout, but it took form too early to incorporate tensor calculus.

Love had a certain whimsicality of manner and appearance which endeared him to his many friends. Although no experimenter, in his emphasis on clear exposition, logical tidiness, and foundational knowledge, he continued the conservative tradition of applied mathematics earlier exemplified by Sir George Stokes. His 'architectural' style, described as 'savouring of a more leisurely age' (Milne, 475), and equally his emphasis on theory rather than application, fitted well the educational priorities of Oxford science. Love died at 25 Banbury Road, Oxford, on 5 June 1940, and was buried at Wolvercote, Oxford. E. A. MILNE, *rev.* JULIA TOMPSON

Sources E. A. Milne, *Obits. FRS*, 3 (1939–41), 467–82 · *The Times* (6 June 1940) · *Nature*, 146 (1940), 393–4 · *Journal of the London Mathematical Society*, 16 (1941), 68–80 · *DSB* · Venn, *Alum. Cant.* · *CGPLA Eng. & Wales* (1941)

Archives Air Force Research Laboratories, Cambridge, Massachusetts, letters to Lord Rayleigh · St John Cam., letters to Sir J. Larmor

Likenesses Elliott & Fry, photograph, RS

Wealth at death £5248 8s. 10*d*.: administration with will, 6 May 1941, *CGPLA Eng. & Wales*

Love, Christopher (1618–1651), clergyman, born in Cardiff, Glamorgan, was the youngest son of parents 'of the middle sized people, who had neither poverty nor riches' (DWL, MS 38.34, pp. 278–9). In his youth Love was brought up to play cards in the houses of local gentlemen, but he was converted to evangelical Christianity in 1633 when he heard William Erbury preach.

A 'young Puritaine' Under Erbury's ministry Love became depressed for the 'fifteen years of his life past which he had spent in vanity' (Sloane MS 3945, fol. 81*r–v*). His father, Christopher Love, a merchant, suggested that he play cards with local gentlemen to take his mind off his anxieties, but Love declared that he could no longer 'endure to see cards or dice in any hand or house' (ibid.). This newfound faith caused a rift between Christopher and his father, who complained that his son had changed from having 'the name of a young Gaimester' to being known as 'a young Puritaine' (ibid.). In an attempt to stop this new faith Love's father confined his son in the top room of the family house. Yet Christopher, who had an 'impatient longing desire to heare the Word' (ibid.), escaped to church by sliding down a rope attached to the window of the room.

At seventeen Love's father arranged for his son to be apprenticed in London. However, Erbury had coached Love for the ministry and, with the support of his mother,

Christopher Love (1618–1651), by Abraham J. Conradus, 1651

Love convinced his father to let him go up to Oxford. Although poor, Love arrived in Oxford desiring to attend a college where he could share the fellowship of the godly. Love decided to go to New Inn Hall when he heard some students complain that Christopher Rogers, the college's principal, was 'an Arch Puritaine' (Sloane MS 3945, fol. 81*v*). He matriculated as a servitor in July 1635. Love's poverty at New Inn Hall meant that he worked hard to finish his degree early in order to enter the ministry. While at Oxford he practised the skills that would allow him to follow this calling. Wood relates that he preached in St Peter's Church, 'prating for more than an hour before academical as well as lay auditors' (Wood, *Ath. Oxon.*, 3.228).

At New Inn, Love was 'looked upon by the generallity as a melancholy [and] sad dejected man' (Sloane MS 3945, fol. 82), but this was perhaps due as much to dire poverty as to worries about his salvation. Love could not afford to complete his degree and so resolved to go to London to join the godly as a schoolteacher. But Love fortunately benefited from the estate of a gentleman who left money for poor scholars in his will, and he was able to proceed BA on 2 May 1639. However, he refused episcopal ordination, considering it corrupt.

In June 1639 Love became chaplain to the household of John Warner, the newly elected sheriff of London. His role followed a rigorous pattern of puritan spiritual exercise. Every morning he examined the family's knowledge of scripture, and he marked Mondays as a day for catechizing. Saturday afternoon and evening would be spent preparing the family for the sabbath with tests on the catechism and on the previous week's sermon. While in Warner's household Love met his wife, Mary Stone [*see* Love,

Mary (*fl.* 1639–1660)], an orphaned daughter of Matthew Stone, a wealthy London merchant: they married some six years after they first met. As Warner's chaplain Love was well protected in his nonconformity. In 1640 he was the first clergyman to refuse subscription to the Laudian canons. His notoriety brought him to the notice of William Juxon, the Laudian bishop of London, who used Love's refusal of episcopal ordination as a pretext to suspend him. Prior to his suspension Love received the call of the parish of St Anne and St Agnes within Aldersgate, London. In order to preach again Love needed ordination and so sought to receive holy orders from a presbytery in Scotland. However, the Scots refused Love on the basis that he had no call to a cure of souls in their national church.

On his return from Scotland, Love was invited to preach in Newcastle; he took this opportunity to attack the Book of Common Prayer and the Laudian ceremonies, an act that earned him a spell in prison. He was removed to London on a writ of habeas corpus but was acquitted after trial at king's bench. Despite his suspension, Love appears to have been something of a wandering firebrand: on 26 March 1642 he proceeded MA but was also expelled from the University of Oxford for his nonconformity. Later that year he preached a sermon at Tenterden in Kent on the lawfulness of a defensive war against the king. This brought a charge of treason, but Love was again acquitted. In Autumn 1642 Love and George Lawrence, a fellow New Inn Hall student, published *The Debauched Cavaleer, or, The English Midianite*. This tract compared royalists to the biblical enemies of Israel and advised parliament to prepare for a bloody war.

Civil war preacher Love's talents as a parliamentarian preacher did not go unrecognized and in late 1642 he was appointed chaplain to the regiment of the parliamentarian MP John Venn, later governor of Windsor Castle. While at Windsor, Love excelled as a chaplain, catechizing soldiers and, when plague broke out, caring for the sick and dying. He also earned the respect of Sir Thomas Fairfax by preaching a sermon on the sixtieth psalm, comparing the parliamentarian forces to the army of biblical Israel. On 23 January 1645 Love finally received presbyterian ordination when the House of Lords empowered the Westminster assembly to form an *ad hoc* presbytery to ordain clergymen. Love's ordination took place at St Mary Aldermanbury, London, under a presbytery presided over by Thomas Horton.

During the peace talks between parliament and the royalists at Uxbridge, Love was invited to preach the market day sermon in that town. His sermon, *England's Distemper Having Division and Error as its Cause*, preached on 30 January 1645, was a warning to parliament not to appease the crimes of the cavaliers in order to obtain peace. Love counselled the parliament not to 'doate … too much on this Treaty of Peace' because the royalists 'lye under the guilt of much innocent blood, and are not meet persons to be at peace with, till all the guilt of blood be expiated and avenged, either by the sword of Law, or law of the Sword' (C. Love, *England's Distemper*, 1645, 42, 37). Love's sermon caused immediate scandal and the royalist newspaper *Mercurius Aulicus* falsely reported that he preached that the king himself was to be punished as a man of blood. This led the royalist commissioners at Uxbridge to lodge a complaint; on 3 February the House of Commons ordered that Love be put into safe custody pending investigation. Love's arrest, however, seems to have been merely to appease royalists; he was confined to his garrison at Windsor and on 5 March, after the Uxbridge negotiations collapsed, the Commons ordered that his confinement be lifted.

On 25 November 1646 Love was chosen to preach the afternoon fast sermon to the House of Commons. He used his sermon to advise Fairfax and parliament to purge the army of heretics, preaching that 'the requittal of men for their good service, must not extend so farre as to tolerate them in their evils' (C. Love, *Short and Plaine Animadversions*, 1646, sig. A2*v*.). Love also caused some scandal when he broke both ministerial and parliamentary protocols by disputing with William Dell on the floor of the Commons. Dell, an antiformalist who opposed all fixed church structures, had used the morning fast sermon to preach against a presbyterian reformation of the Church of England. When Dell published his sermon without the consent of the Commons, he added criticisms of Love's principles as an appendix. Love was forced to reply with some *Short and Plaine Animadversions*, arguing that a presbyterian national church was the divinely warranted prescription for 'peace, union, and brotherly love' in a Christian commonwealth (ibid., 25). Love argued that the purpose of formal church government was to win souls to Jesus Christ, to nurture them in their growth, and to protect them from soul-damning errors. In defence of church discipline Love cited Jude 23: 'others save with fear, pulling them out of the fire; hating even the garment spotted by the flesh' (ibid., 12).

Presbyterian minister Although Love had been nominated by parliament to become the preacher at Newcastle, in May 1645 he was re-elected to the parish of St Anne and St Agnes within Aldersgate and so left the service of Venn's regiment to take up the cure of souls. In London, Love joined with the other ministers who were constructing a presbyterian church government in the City. From 1646 the London ministers increasingly believed that heretics in the army were the greatest threat to presbyterianism and so became vocal critics of the army's activities. Love appears to have been a central figure in this attack. In May 1647 Colonel John Lambert's regiment petitioned the council of officers at Saffron Walden, complaining that 'the ministers in their public labour … do make us odious to the kingdom … [and] have printed many scandalous books against us, as Mr Edwards's *Gangraena* and Mr. Love's *Sermons*' (Woodhouse, 399).

The fruit of Love's sermons appeared in his pamphlet *Works of Darkness Brought to Light*. In this tract, published in July 1647 under the pseudonym Tom Tell-Troth, Love accused the army of rigging elections, of desiring to abolish the House of Lords, and of having designs on the life of the king. He declared:

> O Ye Inhabitants of ENGLAND ... Wil ye suffer the Army under pretence of justice to bring you under oppression, and under the notion of Liberty to bring you into bondage, and under the name of the Saints of Light to act the part of Angels of darkness? (Love, *Works of Darkness*, 7)

Like many presbyterian ministers, Love opposed the call for religious toleration on the grounds that it would encourage religious libertinism and lead to social turbulence. Instead of tolerating error, Love counselled his flock not to get lost in trivial doctrinal speculation but to 'let it be your endeavour to get Christ's kingdom to be erected in your hearts' (Love, *Heaven's Glory*, 76). The volumes of posthumously published sermons show that Love was an able preacher whose method was to apply Calvinist doctrine to both comfort and humble his flock before God.

In March 1649 the vestry of St Lawrence Jewry, London, offered to make Love its minister. In return for his stipend Love was asked to preach twice on the sabbath and once on fast days. Love followed the policy of his fellow presbyterian ministers by insisting that parishioners were conversant with the fundamentals of Reformed Christianity before they attended holy communion. This policy resulted from the presbyterians' insistence that communicants should be able to examine their consciences in line with St Paul's instructions in 1 Corinthians 11: 26–34. Upon election to St Lawrence Jewry, Love was asked 'To admit all of his parish to that table that desire it, and are not knowne to be either grosly scandalous, or notoriously ... of ill and scandalous life'. Despite this request, the figures for the purchase of communion wine in the churchwardens' accounts suggest that Love admitted no more communicants to the Lord's supper than his presbyterian predecessor Anthony Burges.

With the army's purge of parliament on 6 December 1648 and the trial of Charles I, Love joined his fellow presbyterian ministers in condemning the army's political *coup d'état*. Between 28 December 1648 and 20 February 1649 Love joined the London presbyterians in holding private prayer meetings designed to 'find out some way to disappoint ... [the regicides'] bloody intentions' (DWL, MS PP.12.50*.4 (21), fol. 85). Love was also a signatory to the printed letters published by the London presbyterian ministers in January 1649 protesting against the regicide and revolution.

After the regicide Love declared that he was 'a friend to a regulated Monarchy, a free Parliament, an obedient Army, and a Godly ministry; but an enemy to Tyranny, Malignity, Anarchy and Heresie' (Love, *A Modest and Clear Vindication*, frontispiece). He accused the army of political cynicism and selfish factionalism. At the same time he attempted to counter allegations that the presbyterians had converted to royalist principles. Love declared that although the presbyterians were 'zealous Anti-Cavalierists' they were not 'Anti-Carolists'. Likewise, the presbyterians were 'for the Army while they used the sword to subdue malignants in arms; but against them when they use the sword to cut off the King and force the Parliament'.

Love was at the forefront of the presbyterians who attacked the republic. He opposed the engagement of loyalty and preached against the millenarian fantasies of the republican 'saints'. On 29 July 1649 he told his flock: 'This is not the way to usher in Jesus Christ; to cut off Protestant kings, destroy lawes, government and rule, this is not the fruit of saintshipp' (DWL, MS PP.12.50*.4 (21), fol. 88). Because of his opposition to the republic, Love was soon in trouble with the new regime. On 6 September 1649 he appeared before the parliamentary committee for plundered ministers charged with seditious preaching but was acquitted when witnesses failed to show. A newspaper reported that 'a great company of people' gathered to meet him after his acquittal, crying out 'Not a persecutor durst appear against him' (*Perfect Weekly Account*, 5–13 Sept 1649, 596).

Conspiracy and execution In summer 1649 Love became involved in a plot to assist the Scottish covenanters to bring the exiled Charles II to the throne of England. The ringleader of the plot was William Drake, a mercer, who was in contact with presbyterian leaders at the exiled royal court. Drake convinced Love to convene meetings at his house, and some of the most committed presbyterian ministers and laity were invited to attend. The purpose of these meetings, which continued until April 1651, was to hear letters detailing the efforts of the Scottish covenanters and their allies to restore the Stuart monarchy. The exiled royalists hoped that the presbyterian ministers would use their influence with London's merchants to fund a Scottish invasion of England. Despite these plans, Love and his fellows continually refused to send money; Love wrote to Major-General Edward Massey, telling him that 'it was neither safe, nor fit for us to ingage in a business of that nature' (*State trials*, 5.118; *Mr. Love's Case*, 12).

The plot was discovered by the republican regime when Thomas Coke, a royalist agent, was arrested in March 1651. His long depositions led the government to Love and the presbyterian conspirators and on 2 May 1651 Love was arrested on suspicion of treason. Love's trial for treason took place in late June and early July 1651; unsurprisingly, he was found guilty and condemned on 5 July. Although Love was technically guilty, it is clear that the trial was little more than a demonstration of the republic's brute power dressed up as legal sovereignty. This point is graphically exemplified by Sir Henry Vane, who told Cromwell that Love should be executed because the presbyterians 'do not judge us a lawful magistracy, nor esteem anything treason that is acted by them to destroy us, in order to bring in the king of Scots as the head of the Covenant' (B. Worden, *The Rump Parliament*, 1974, 244).

Love himself admitted to the high court that he desired an 'agreement between the king and Scots' and was unrepentant for his actions. After sentence he told his wife:

> I bless my God that, notwithstanding all that is come upon me, I have not forsaken Him, nor dealt falsely in his Covenant, and therefore ... never had I more joy in my spirit ... than when the sentence of death was this day read against me. (DWL, MS PP.12.50*.4 (21), fols. 115–16)

A campaign was organized by Love's wife and friends to get his condemnation overturned. Many petitions were submitted to parliament for Love's release. However, the pleas for Love's life were to no avail. Although on 15 July Love earned a month's reprieve, it appears that ardent republican Independents were set on Love's destruction. In a last, desperate attempt to save her husband's life, Mary Love sent a petition to Cromwell in Scotland. It arrived on 29 July, and the council of war debated whether to intervene in the affair. Colonels Goffe and Okey were 'tooth and nayle' for Love, but colonels Pride and Lambert spoke 'high against' a pardon. In the end the council advised Cromwell that he 'should not at all ingage or write in the businesse for him' (F. M. S. Henderson, 'New material from the Clarke manuscripts: political and official correspondence and news sent and received by the army headquarters in Scotland, 1651–1660', DPhil diss., University of Oxford, 1998, 80).

The last petition for Love's pardon was rejected on 18 August and he learned that on 22 August 1651 he would die by beheading on Tower Hill. With his death imminent, the London presbyterian ministers spent the days preparing Love for martyrdom. On the morning of his execution Love told his friend James Lever that he 'blessed God [that] his heart did not soe much as leape or pant in his breast, but hee was as cheerfull as hee were to live till the Day of Judgement' (A. Wallis, 'The diary of a London citizen in the seventeenth century', *The Reliquary*, new ser., vol. 3, 1889, 89). His wife relates that the grim procession to the scaffold 'made the hill ring with [the] bitter-weeping and lamentations' of the crowd gathered to witness his death (DWL, MS PP.12.50*.4 (21), fol. 137).

In a long execution speech Love declared himself to be 'a Spectacle unto God, Angels and men, … a Grief to the Godly; a Laughing stock to the wicked and a Gazing stock to all'. He declared that 'I desire this day to magnifie God … that such a one as I, born in an obscure Country in Wales … that God should look upon me, and … single me out to be an Object of his everlasting Love'. However, he warned the republic that 'my blood will be bad food for this Infant Commonwealth … Mine is not malignant blood, though here I am brought a grievous and notorious Offender' (*Mr. Love's Case*, 25–6).

Love's body was privately buried at his parish church, St Lawrence Jewry, three days later. After his death his executors, including the London presbyterian ministers Edmund Calamy, Simeon Ashe, William Taylor, and Matthew Poole, published fifteen volumes of Love's sermons. The thought behind this endeavour, they claimed, was not 'to make old sores bleed' but to mourn the 'great loss the Church of God had in the death of so useful and hopeful a minister'. Thirteen days after Love's execution his widow, Mary, gave birth prematurely to the fifth of their children. Mary Love later wrote a manuscript biography of her husband.

By the late eighteenth and early nineteenth centuries Love had gained a further reputation. In a host of cheap pamphlets in both Britain and America, sometimes laced with versions of last letters to his wife or his scaffold speech to lend verisimilitude and the authority of a martyr, Love was reinvented as a prophet of the last days. He had foretold the Restoration, the plague of 1665, and the great fire of London. From his studies of Daniel and Revelation he had predicted the American War of Independence and the French Revolution, the last 'the destruction of popery, or Babylon's fall', 'the revolution in France, which is properly Babylon's fall, as it hath broken off the tenth horn of the beast, so that the Pope hath become as weak as another man' (*The Strange and Wonderful Predictions of Mr Christopher Love*, n. d., 8; *Prophecies of the Reverend Christopher Love: and his Last Words*, 1794, 7). E. C. Vernon

Sources biography of Love by his widow, Mary, DWL, MS PP.12.50*.4 (21) · BL, Sloane MS 3945 · DWL, MS 38.34, vol. 1 · E. C. Vernon, 'The Sion College conclave and London presbyterianism during the English revolution', PhD diss., U. Cam., 1999 · GL, MS 259011 · [C. Love], *Works of darkness brought to light* (1647) [Under pseudonym Tom Tell-Troth: how he appears in BL catalogue] · *Mr. Love's case* (1651) · C. Love, *A cleare and necessary vindication of the principles and practices of me Christopher Love* (1651) · C. Love, *Heaven's glory, hell's terror* (1653) · [C. Love], *A modest and clear vindication of the serious representation* (1649) · A. S. P. Woodhouse, ed., *Puritanism and liberty: being the army debates (1647–9) from the Clarke manuscripts, with supplementary documents*, 2nd edn (1974) · Wood, *Ath. Oxon.*, new edn, 3.228 · *DNB*

Archives BL, biography, Sloane MS 3945 · DWL, biography [copy]

Likenesses A. J. Conradus, line engraving, 1651, BM, NPG [*see illus.*] · T. Cross, print, BM, NPG; repro. in C. Love, *Grace* (1652) · woodcut, repro. in C. Love, *The souls cordiall* (1653) · woodcut, BM; repro. in C. L. [C. Love], *The Christian's combat* (1664)

Love, David (1750–1827), pedlar and poet, was born at Torriburn (Torryburn) on the north shore of the Firth of Forth in Fife, Scotland, on 17 November 1750 and baptized in nearby Culross on 2 January 1751. His parents were Anne, *née* Robertson (*d. c.*1773), and her husband, William Love (1696–1788), a work-shy, hard-drinking coalminer, who had two sons and three daughters by a previous marriage. Another son, John, was baptized at Culross on 22 June 1752, soon after which William abandoned his family and Anne lost her sight and became a wandering beggar.

David had a year's schooling to the age of nine, probably in Culross, then worked as an errand boy and farmer's boy, and spent a year driving ponies underground in the earl of Dundonald's coalmines at Culross, where his arm was broken; he kept a village school for five months, but from an early age his chief occupation was selling tracts and small books as a pedlar.

About 1775, having accumulated £3, Love married Mary Thomson (*c.*1755–1806), with whom he had five sons and a daughter in eight years. They kept a shop in a village near Falkirk, but when they ran into debt Love resumed his itinerant bookselling as a 'flying-stationer' (*Life, Adventures*, 31) and began to print, sing, and sell satirical ballads, 'godly poems for Christians of all denominations', and other verse of his own composition. He advertised himself as 'a lame man, who makes verse on any subject, if employed' (Love, *A Few Remarks*, title-page). Sadly, the verse is also lame.

Love served for about four years (probably 1778–82) in the duke of Buccleuch's regiment of fencibles before resuming his pedlar's and balladeer's trade, which he now extended into England. If his wife was as shrewish as he claimed (*Life, Adventures*, 36–7) this may have been because she was obliged to leave their children with her sister in Scotland and unwillingly take to the road with her husband. They travelled over much of England, with settled spells in London and Bristol, where Love met his aged father, now a reformed pedlar of religious books, and they spent nearly a year in Gosport, Hampshire, where there was good trade among sailors just returned from Earl Howe's victory on 1 June 1794. Love experienced religious conversion at Newbury, Berkshire, on 17 April 1796, and thereafter celebrated that date as a new birth, but he had been writing and publishing religious verse from the 1770s.

Mary Love died in November 1806. On 20 July 1807, at Duffield, Derbyshire, Love married Mary Falconer, *née* Thomson, aged about forty-nine and widow of an artilleryman. She died in March 1809. Both wives were buried at Rugby, Warwickshire: the first on 26 November 1806, the second on 17 March 1809.

Love married his third wife, Elizabeth Laming (*c.*1775–1853), a silk spinner, on 21 May 1810 at Nottingham and they had five children together, the last when David was nearly seventy. Nottingham now became their chief home, though they still sometimes tramped as pedlars and were persuaded by the poor-law overseers to travel to Edinburgh in 1812 and later to London: Love published his prose account of the second trip in *David Love's Journey to London and his Return to Nottingham* (*c.*1814). A stay in Nottingham workhouse as well as occasional imprisonment in other towns for vagrancy and a spell on the treadmill in Hull at the age of seventy-five provided further material for Love's rough, comic, topical ballads. Nicknamed Old Glory, singing his own hymns and ballads, composing acrostics on demand, selling haberdashery as well as books, and proclaiming his evangelical faith, Love became a familiar figure in Nottingham, and very popular 'considering his extreme lack of talent' (Sutton, 18).

Love undertook to publish his autobiography by penny numbers at least three times. Incomplete sets of a chapbook version in stanzaic verse (n.d.) and of a different broadside version in octosyllabic couplets (*c.*1818) survive, as do complete sets of *The Life, Adventures, and Experiences of David Love, Written by himself* in twenty-four numbers (1814–23). This largely prose autobiography thriftily incorporated his stanzaic *Life* as well as many other poems, and ran to a fifth edition (1825). Some copies contain an engraved portrait of the author, aged seventy-four.

Love remained active to within a few weeks of death. He died in Nottingham on 12 June 1827 and was buried on 14 June in St Mary's churchyard.

> In person David was below the middle stature; his features were not unhandsome for an old man; his walk was exceedingly slow, deliberately placing one foot before the other, in order perhaps to give his customers time to hear what he had got; his voice was clear, and strongly marked with the Scotch accent. He possessed a readiness of wit and repartee. (Hone, 3, col. 179)

JAMES SAMBROOK

Sources *The life, adventures, and experiences of David Love, written by himself* (1814–23) • *The life of David Love: part 1* [n.d.] • *The life of David Love in verse* (*c.*1818) [broadside] • *The life of David Love, part the third* (*c.*1818) [broadside] • W. Hone, *The Every-day Book and Table Book*, 3 vols. (1830), vol. 2, cols. 225–30, 1575; vol. 3, cols. 177–81 • *N&Q*, 7th ser., 8 (1889), 234, 333, 411–12, 474 • *Transcript of registers: Rugby, Warwickshire*, Society of Genealogists • *Derbyshire parish registers: marriages*, ed. W. P. W. Phillimore and others (1907), 74 • *Nottingham parish registers: marriages*, ed. W. P. W. Phillimore and J. Ward (1900), 286 • J. F. Sutton, *The date-book of remarkable and memorable events connected with Nottingham* (1852), 18–19 • D. Love, *A few remarks on the present time with a serious advice to the redeeming our time here, so that we may be blessed and happy, when TIME shall be no more* (1777?) • D. Love, *A new and correct set of godly poems, for the benefit of all Christians of all denominations* (1782) • 'Scott, Henry, third duke of Buccleuch', *DNB* • C. Bonnell, 'David Love (Prince of Ballad Mongers)', *Nottingham Daily Express* (8–15 March 1904)

Likenesses coloured engraving, repro. in Love, *Life, adventures* (1823–4) [BL copy] • engraving, repro. in Love, *Life, adventures* (1823–4), frontispiece

Love, Geoffrey [Geoff] (**1917–1991**), popular composer, bandleader, and trombonist, was born on 4 September 1917 in Todmorden, Yorkshire, the only son and younger of the two surviving children of Thomas Edward (Kidd) Love (*c.*1886–1923/4), a dancer and guitarist, and his wife, Frances Helen Maycock (1892–1975), an actress and singer from a touring theatrical family. His father was African American, his mother was English.

Love travelled on the road with his family until the age of six, when his father died and the family returned to their grandmother's house. In Todmorden, where Frances Love worked winding cotton in a factory, Love's elder sister Cornelia played violin in the junior section of the amateur symphony orchestra. He also attempted to learn the instrument but abandoned it shortly in favour of the trombone. He took lessons from his doctor who was a music student, and from the local brass band, but found their music too loud. He left school to work in a garage, and at the age of fifteen began to play trombone for local dances. He abandoned manual labour at seventeen in favour of a professional career in music and joined the band of Freddie Platt.

In 1936 Love joined Jan Ralfini's band and travelled to London with them to work in cine-variety, singing and tap-dancing as part of his act. He learned to play jazz at after-hours West End 'bottle-parties' such as the Bag O'Nails and the Nest, where he got to know and was influenced by trombonists George Chisholm and Ellis Jackson. He worked with Alan Green on Hastings pier, then with Syd Millward's Nitwits until his wartime call-up in February 1940. He joined the King's Royal Rifle Corps and, after initial training, helped re-form the Green Jackets' regimental dance band. During six years' military service he taught himself orchestration through the expedient of asking individual musicians the best way to write for their instrument.

On demob Love worked as a freelance trombonist and arranger, and, while with Stanley Black's BBC orchestra, he absorbed further ideas about orchestration from the harpist Marie Goossens. He played film music sessions, then joined saxophonist Harry Gold in whose Pieces of Eight he played Dixieland jazz for the first time, eventually becoming a business partner in the band with Gold,

Geoffrey Love (1917–1991), by Derek Allen, 1955

his brother Laurie Gold, and pianist Norrie Paramor. He worked as an arranger for the Paramor/Gold Orchestral Service, then as a staff writer at Kassner's music publishers (1950–55).

As a trombonist Love worked with the bandleader Lew Stone and continued to do session work, but increasingly he was in demand for his arrangements. He wrote for the Ambrose and Ken Mackintosh dance bands, for television and radio orchestras and the Cliff Adams Singers, then formed an eight-piece band to play dances and concerts for American servicemen. He broadcast with his own group and as guest soloist on BBC *Jazz Club* with trumpeter Kenny Baker and other important jazz musicians. He continued to do cabaret and make guest appearances, then, with the launch of commercial television, wrote the music and organized a new band for the fifty-week series *On the Town*.

In the mid-1950s Love was contracted by several record labels to write for their artists. From Philips he moved to Polydor and Polygram before settling with EMI, where he arranged for Alma Cogan, Frankie Vaughan, Anne Shelton, and others on the HMV label and also recorded orchestral singles under his own name, notably a 1958 'cover version' of Perez Prado's 'Patricia'. As staff arranger–conductor at Columbia, he was responsible for the huge success of Laurie London's gospel song 'He's Got the Whole World in His Hands', which topped the American music charts in 1957. The same year he wrote the score for *6.5 Special*, the film version of television's hit rock and roll show, but this type of music was not really his métier.

Love was an unashamed populist who enjoyed creating melodic and uncontroversial arrangements of tunes that would sell. For forty years he had a working relationship with recording manager Norman Newell, whom he described as the man who 'hears what Mrs Smith in Wigan will hear', and who would bring him suitable material (interview with Val Wilmer, BL NSA). Wally Stott's arrangement of Mikis Theodorakis's 'The Honeymoon Song' was such a tune and, to Love, 'it suggested harps, guitars and voices' (ibid.). He combined these elements for what he called 'Theme from Honeymoon' (1959), and created the ethereal, guitar-heavy sound that became known internationally as Manuel and his Music of the Mountains. His intention was to keep Manuel's identity secret but an American album success in 1959 and that of 'Never on Sunday' (1960) made this impossible.

In a spectacular career that garnered one platinum, fifteen gold, and thirteen silver discs, and a special trophy for the sale of 2.5 million records, Love (as Manuel) spent several weeks in the British popular music charts. 'Somewhere my Love' (1966) was another major success although the number one position eluded him (his recording of the theme from the second movement of Rodrigo's guitar concerto 'De Aranjuez' (1976) was acknowledged to have reached that position but is omitted from the *Guinness Book of Hit Singles*, exact computation being impossible during the week in question).

As musical director and arranger, Love's list of recording credits encompassed Judy Garland, Paul Robeson, Mel Tormé, Marlene Dietrich, Gracie Fields, Randy Crawford, Hinge and Bracket, and Danny La Rue, but he first became known to the public in this role through television appearances with the pianist Russ Conway and the comedian–singer Max Bygraves. His comedy speaking parts in the latter's live shows and spectaculars made his friendly, open face and Todmorden accent familiar in every British home.

Love was a popular figure with other show business professionals. He was kind, generous, and witty, but he was also a stickler for discipline, professionalism, and timing, attributes that ensured he remained at the top of his profession. On 4 April 1942 he married Cicely Joyce (Joy) Peters (1923/4–1993). She played a notable part in his success, relieving the pressures of an extraordinarily hectic life by organizing his business, booking his session musicians, and doing accounts. They had two sons, Adrian (1944–1999), who became a well-known radio presenter, and Nigel (*b.* 1947).

In 1981 Love co-founded (with Bill Starling) the Young Person's Concert Foundation. A charitable body aimed at introducing orchestral music to youngsters, its patrons and benefactors came from the world of commerce—Sir Charles Forte and Ford's—and music—Ron Goodwin, Vera Lynn, Harry Secombe, and Sir Georg Solti. Love travelled the country with an orchestra of student musicians, giving schools a concert of accessible musical pieces with linking commentary on the various instruments provided by his son Adrian or by the entertainer Rolf Harris.

Despite his early antipathy towards brass bands, Love

returned to his Yorkshire roots in the late 1980s. He became involved with various brass band traditions, participated in the Saddleworth Whit Friday contest and played with the local band in annual concerts at Todmorden town hall. While he kept a house in Bush Hill Park, Enfield, he did most of his writing in Spain. His successes continued. As he explained: 'I'm not playing for musicians or people who listen to jazz, I'm just playing for Joe Public' (interview with Val Wilmer, BL NSA). He died at University College Hospital, Camden, London, on 8 July 1991.

VAL WILMER

Sources C. Ellis, *The Independent* (10 July 1991) • V. Wilmer, *The Independent* (17 July 1991) • M. Martingale, 'Love story in black and white', *News of the World* (17 June 1990) • D. Wicks, *The ballad years: from the bombs to the Beatles* (1997) • private information (2004) • personal knowledge (2004) • *The Times* (12 July 1991) • *The Guardian* (10 July 1991) • *Daily Telegraph* (9 July 1991) • d. cert.
Archives SOUND BL NSA, oral history interview
Likenesses D. Allen, photograph, 1955, NPG [*see illus.*] • photographs, priv. coll.
Wealth at death £222,906: probate, 16 Oct 1991, *CGPLA Eng. & Wales*

Love, James. *See* Dance, James (1721–1774).

Love, Sir James Frederick (1789–1866), army officer, son of John Love and his wife, Mary (*née* Wyse), was born in London. Commissioned ensign in the 52nd foot (26 October 1804), he advanced to lieutenant (5 June 1805), and served with the regiment during 1808 in Sweden and in Portugal, where after the convention of Cintra (30 August 1808) he was one of 107 officers and men to escort repatriated French troops to their point of embarkation. The following year he took part in the retreat of Lieutenant-General Sir John Moore's force to Corunna, but returned to Portugal with the 1st battalion of the 52nd later in 1809, fighting with it in various engagements until 1812 and securing a captaincy (11 July 1811). On the night of 11 March 1810, with courage and initiative, Love discovered that the enemy had abandoned Pombal, and at Busaco on 27 September 1810 he took prisoner the French general Simon. On 3 April 1811 at Sabugal, with his company he recaptured a howitzer lost by the 43rd earlier in the day, and three weeks later repulsed a dangerous French attack on the Marialva Bridge. With good sense and knowledge of his men, at Aruda in October 1810 he refused to declare one soldier a deserter, and shortly afterwards was vindicated when Tobin reappeared, having escaped from captivity. At Fuentes de Oñoro, on 5 May 1811, compassionately he released an enemy sergeant who had strayed across the line, after addressing him in fluent French.

Having returned to England in December 1813 with the 52nd's 2nd battalion, Love joined Lieutenant-General Sir Thomas Graham's expedition to the Netherlands, and three months later was engaged in the attack on Merxem and bombardment of Antwerp, after which he commanded the rear-guard as British troops withdrew. In January 1815 he acted as Major-General Sir John Lambert's aide-de-camp during the assault on New Orleans, where he was wounded in the arm and had two horses killed under him. Promoted brevet major (16 March 1815), he rejoined the 52nd in time to fight at Waterloo, where he was wounded four times during the regiment's decisive advance against the imperial guard on the evening of 18 June. Subsequently, he served with the 52nd in North America, and was made inspecting field officer of the New Brunswick as a brevet lieutenant-colonel on half pay (5 May 1825). In 1825, also, he married Mary Heaviside of Halifax, Nova Scotia; they had no children, and she survived her husband. He resumed regular service after obtaining a majority in the 11th foot on 9 November 1830. Learning of anti-reform riots in Bristol on 31 October 1831, while commanding troops in Cardiff, he swiftly gathered 170 men, commandeered a steamer at Newport, and that evening restored order to the relief of worried citizens: 'Thanks, thanks, brave fellows, you are come to save us from pillage and death' (Aggett, 44). He became lieutenant-colonel of the 76th (6 September 1834), then of the 73rd foot (6 March 1835), for three years commanding it in the Mediterranean, while also acting as British resident at Zante. He took the 73rd to Canada in May 1838, where it successfully quelled unrest, and returned with the regiment to England in June 1841. Meanwhile, he had been promoted colonel (28 June 1838) and appointed CB (30 March 1839), the same year that he became KH. Back in south Wales, he deployed troops effectively during the Chartist and Rebecca riots in 1842–3.

Love went on half pay on 23 September 1845, having surrendered nominal command of the 73rd the previous day. Promoted major-general (11 November 1851), he was appointed lieutenant-governor of Jersey (1 April 1852), becoming KCB (4 February 1856) after leaving that post. He then briefly commanded the training camp at Shorncliffe, and became colonel of the 57th foot (24 September 1856) and temporary lieutenant-general (6 January 1857). He served as inspector-general of infantry for four years from April 1857, being promoted substantive lieutenant-general on 26 September 1857. Having advanced to general (10 August 1864), he was appointed colonel of the 43rd foot (5 September 1865) and GCB that same year. He died at 17 Ovington Square, Brompton, London, on 13 January 1866.

JOHN SWEETMAN

Sources *Army List* • W. S. Moorsom, ed., *Historical record of the fifty-second regiment (Oxfordshire light infantry), from the year 1755 to the year 1858* (1860) • W. J. P. Aggett, *The bloody eleventh*, 2 (1994) • H. H. Woollright, *History of the 57th regiment of foot* (1893) • C. Dalton, *The Waterloo roll call*, 2nd edn (1904); repr. (1971) • Fortescue, *Brit. army*, vol. 9 • R. Cannon, ed., *Historical record of the seventy-third regiment* (1851) • L. C. Cornford and F. W. Walker, *The great deeds of the black watch* (1915) • *A short history of the black watch, 1725–1907* (1908) • W. Siborne, *The Waterloo campaign, 1815* (1895) • W. Leeke, *The history of Lord Seaton's regiment (the 52nd light infantry) at the battle of Waterloo*, 1 (1866) • Boase, *Mod. Eng. biog.* • *CGPLA Eng. & Wales* (1866)
Archives NL Scot., Sir George Brown MSS • W. Sussex RO, Gordon-Lennox MSS
Likenesses A. Baccari, portrait; formerly at United Service Club, London
Wealth at death under £1500: probate, 12 Feb 1866, *CGPLA Eng. & Wales*

Love, John (1695–1750), literary scholar, was born at Dumbarton in July 1695, the son of John Love, bookseller and stationer; he was probably the John Love presented for baptism there on 11 July 1695 by John Love and Elizabeth Thomsone. From about 1700 he was educated at Dumbarton grammar school and then at Glasgow University; later he became assistant, and in 1721 successor, to his old schoolteacher. The school was inspected in 1729 by a presbytery committee which found it to be in a flourishing condition and expressed full satisfaction with the master. Smollett was among his pupils and later showed his regard by seeking help for one of Love's sons. Love married Elizabeth, daughter of Archibald Campbell, a Glasgow surgeon, in 1722, and they had thirteen children. He also had two children from his second marriage, to Gelis Elphinston, a minister's daughter. At Dumbarton, Love was also clerk to the presbytery from 1717 to 1735; his minister, Archibald Sydserf, was forced to apologize following an accusation of brewing on a Sunday. In 1735 Love was appointed a master of the high school in Edinburgh and in 1739, at the request of the duke of Buccleuch, he moved to his final post as rector of Dalkeith grammar school.

Love's publications centred on three controversies. First, he produced in 1733 two treatises on Latin grammar, criticizing a grammar by Robert Trotter, schoolmaster at Dumfries, and defending Thomas Ruddiman's *Grammar* respectively. The second controversy concerned the Latin paraphrase of the Psalms by George Buchanan. With Robert Hunter, later professor of Greek at Edinburgh University, Love prepared an edition of this work in 1737 that made considerable use of Nathan Chytraeus's commentary to earlier editions and emphasized the work's educational as well as religious value. In 1740, writing as 'Philo-Buchananus', Love defended Buchanan against William Lauder and William Benson who had asserted the superiority of the version of the Psalms by Arthur Johnston. Thus far Love had the support of Thomas Ruddiman. Third, in his *Vindication of Mr. George Buchanan* published in 1749, Love discussed other aspects of the author's life, refuting the accusation of ingratitude to Mary, queen of Scots, and William Camden's suggestion that at the end of his life Buchanan had repented of his treatment of her. By this time, however, Ruddiman's estimation of Buchanan had fallen for political reasons and he wrote a critical reply to Love.

Love also corresponded with Sir John Clerk on literary matters and he appointed John Traill, bookseller in Edinburgh, as factor and curator to his children. He died at Dalkeith on 20 September 1750, survived by his second wife.

GORDON GOODWIN, *rev.* D. M. ABBOTT

Sources D. Duncan, *Thomas Ruddiman* (1965) · W. Steven, *The history of the high school of Edinburgh* (1849) · *The new statistical account of Scotland*, 1 (1845) · Dumbarton presbytery records, NA Scot., CH2/546/7–9 · *IGI* · commissary court records, NA Scot., CC/8/8/14, 9 July 1752

Archives NA Scot., letter to Sir John Clerk, GD 18/5065

Wealth at death £674 5*s.* 8*d.* Scots [£56 3*s.* 9*d.* sterling]: 9 July 1752, commissary court records, NA Scot., CC 8/8/14

Love, John (1757–1825), Church of Scotland minister, was born at Paisley on 15 June 1757, the son of James Love of Paisley and his wife, Margaret Lang. He was educated at Paisley grammar school and, aged ten, entered the University of Glasgow, where he received a bursary for his excellent performance in Latin, Greek, and mathematics. On 24 December 1778 he was licensed by the presbytery of Paisley and was assistant in the parishes of Rutherglen and Greenock before being ordained to the Hoxton Presbyterian congregation at Artillery Street, Bishopsgate, London, on 22 August 1788.

During his residence in London, Love was active in moves to promote the foreign missions movement and, in January 1795, published on this subject in the *Evangelical Magazine*. Along with Alexander Waugh and David Bogue he was a co-founder of the London Missionary Society (LMS) at Aldersgate Street in September of that year. Thereafter he served as the society's secretary for five years and, on his return to Glasgow in 1800, he performed the same role for the Glasgow Missionary Society. Love was especially interested in missions to the south Pacific and in 1796 published his *Addresses to the People of Otaheite* which provided the Tahitians with a highly personal 'system of Christian theology' (Morison, 261). The Church of Scotland's first important missionary station in Africa, at Kaffaria (established in 1830), was named Lovedale in his honour.

Despite the success of the LMS and his reputation as a dignified and well-respected preacher, Love felt increasingly dissatisfied with his London ministry. He returned to Scotland after twelve years to become minister of the Anderston chapel of ease in Barony parish, Glasgow, where he was inducted on 11 July 1800. In 1815 he was a candidate for the chair of divinity at Aberdeen University and, though unsuccessful, he was awarded the degree of DD at Marischal College in the following year. Love remained at Anderston until his death at his manse in Clyde Street, Glasgow, on 17 December 1825. He was survived for several years by his wife, further details of whom are unknown.

In addition to his *Addresses*, during his lifetime Love published a collection of *Nine Occasional Sermons* (1788) and several additional sermons, including *Benevolence Inspired and Exalted in the Presence of Jesus Christ* (1794). After his death there appeared his *Discourses on Select Passages of Scripture* (1838), *Letters of the Late John Love, DD* (1838 and 1840), and, best-known, his *Memorials* (1857–8) which were praised as models of forthright evangelical devotion. According to the ecclesiastical historian John Macleod it was once said in criticism that his written works were only skeletons, to which came the reply that, if so, they were the bones of a mammoth.

JOHN R. MCINTOSH

Sources *DNB* · *Fasti Scot.*, new edn, vol. 3 · *Some notices of the character of … John Love* (1827) · J. Macleod, *Scottish theology in relation to church history since the Reformation* (1943) · J. M. Calder, *Scotland's march past: the share of Scottish churches in the London Missionary Society* (1945) · 'Memoir of the Revd John Love', J. Morison, *The fathers and founders of the London Missionary Society* [1844]

Likenesses W. Ridley, stipple, 1797, NPG; repro. in *Evangelical Magazine* (1797)

Love, Joseph (1796–1875), colliery owner, was born in co. Durham, but little else is known about his early life. Born into a poor family, he started work as a pit boy at the age of eight, and at fourteen he was supporting his parents. He subsequently moved from the pit to become an itinerant packman, selling soft goods around the colliery villages, and at the age of twenty-five he used his savings to open a shop. In 1825 he married Sarah, the daughter of Isaac Pearson, a prosperous timber merchant of North Shields. Love then became a speculative builder, winning profitable contracts for colliery housing before being ruined by a bank failure. He continued in the timber trade, selling pit props, and in 1840 he purchased Brancepeth colliery, his first pit. At that time the iron and steel industry, shipbuilding, and the railways were beginning a period of expansion in the north-east of England which created an immense demand for coal and the means to export it to London and beyond. Because of his entry into the coal industry in this period of highly profitable expansion, Love came to own or part-own six pits in mid-west Durham.

Love was prominent in the Methodist New Connexion. In 1819 he was on the plan as a preacher, and throughout his life he lived with discipline and frugality. Love funded chapels and chapel-related activities throughout the country, but especially in Durham. The neo-classical Bethel Chapel in Durham North Road was the most architecturally distinguished monument to his generosity. He also supported overseas missions in Canada and Australia. Towards the end of his life Love was plagued by frequent requests to clear the debts of New Connexion chapels that he considered ill managed, notably the Chelsea Chapel. In 1873 he wrote that he felt like advertising that 'I have washed my hands of the New Connexion, being fairly pressed out' (William Cooke Collection, John Rylands Library). By this time he was suffering from the wasting disease that was to lead to his death. He does not seem to have acted on his threat by the time of his death, though the relative absence of published obituaries and eulogies, especially in the Methodist press, suggests some distancing of Love from his previous commitments. None the less, Dr Cooke, the president of the Methodist New Connexion, preached at Love's memorial service and a chapel was dedicated to his memory shortly afterwards.

Methodist accounts of Love record a life of piety and good works. But a different Love appears in the records of the labour and trade union movement, leading one historian to conclude that 'Mr Love's business actions were in sharp contrast to the piety of his private life … He belonged to a school which had learned well the lesson, to hide from the right hand what its left hand did' (Welbourne, 121). Love gave key managerial posts in his enterprises to his relatives, and it was a cause of complaint that others could not gain promotion. He victimized men who supported trade unionism and was instrumental in breaking the third union of the Durham and Northumberland miners in 1863 through the 'rocking' strike in his pits (1863–4). The men working in low seams were unable to fill their tubs sufficiently to prevent the coal settling below the rim during the journey to the surface. The men claimed they were paid nothing for each such tub. When they went on strike Love evicted the miners and their families from their homes, in severe winter weather, and he cut their credit through his role as the shopkeepers' landlord. His actions earned the hostility of both the Durham newspapers and *The Times*, in whose letter columns Love sought to defend his actions.

Joseph Love was important in the history of British entrepreneurialism. Like many other businessmen he was able to reconcile his Methodism with running a business empire in harshly competitive conditions. He also represented a phase of British capitalism in which labour and capital met face to face. Later employers were able to acquire anonymity, protecting their interests behind the names of joint-stock companies, while their private lives became increasingly remote from those of their employees. Unlike these corporate owners of modern firms Love was in close contact with his enterprises and the daily life of his workforce. He was unable, therefore, to avoid facing the conflict between his own economic interests and the welfare of his workers. Nevertheless, Love was very successful: he was one of a small group of nineteenth-century figures to rise from a working-class background to riches through hard work, frugality, and enterprise—an exemplar of Samuel Smiles's 'self-help'. He died on 21 February 1875 at his house, Mount Beulah, Durham, and left an estate worth about £1 million to his wife, making her one of the richest women in Britain. Their one child, Isaac Pearson Love, predeceased Joseph. ROBERT MOORE

Sources E. Welbourne, *The Miners' Union of Northumberland and Durham* (1993) · G. E. Milburn, 'Piety, profit and paternalism', *Proceedings of the Wesley Historical Society*, 49 (1993–4) · *Durham County Advertizer* (23 Oct 1863–3 Feb 1864) · *Durham County Advertizer* (5 March 1875) · *Durham Chronicle* (23 Oct 1863–3 Feb 1864) · *Durham Chronicle* (5 March 1875)

Archives JRL, corresp.

Wealth at death under £1,000,000: probate, 23 March 1875, *CGPLA Eng. & Wales*

Love [*née* Stone], **Mary** (*fl.* **1639–1660**), religious writer and biographer, was the daughter of Matthew Stone, a London merchant. Following the deaths of both her parents she lived in the household of the London alderman, John Warner, where in 1639 she met and was spiritually inspired by Warner's chaplain Christopher *Love (1618–1651), whom she married about 1645. Before Love's death they had four children, of whom two, Kit and Mall, lived past infancy.

Mary Love was pregnant with her fifth child when Christopher was convicted of treason in 1651. She worked tirelessly to save his life and, more importantly, his reputation. At the cost of £100 she sent messages to Cromwell and his officers in Scotland begging for her husband's life, and 'stood dailie with her petition at [parliament's] doors' (DWL, MS PP.12.50*.4 (21), 118). Shortly after his death her petitions were published, as were copies of letters written by the couple as Christopher awaited execution. The letters, in which Mary and Christopher prepare one another for his impending death, were included in a manuscript collection of exemplary Christian letters by Nehemiah Wallington and reprinted frequently in the latter part of the eighteenth century, appended to numerous editions of *The Strange and Wonderful Predictions of Mr Christopher Love* (alternatively titled *The Remarkable Predictions of Mr C. Love*). Their more immediate political purpose, however, was as part of the propaganda campaign by London presbyterians to cast Christopher Love as a martyred saint. Mary Love must be seen as an important contributor to that project.

Mary Love's most elaborate effort on Christopher's behalf was her 'Life of Mr Christopher Love', a biographical narrative based in part upon first-hand knowledge and in part on what was told to her by her husband and others about his life. The manuscript was never printed. It exists now in two versions, an apparently complete text in an eighteenth-century hand in Dr Williams's Library and an incomplete copy in an apparently earlier hand in the British Library. Its date of composition and the extent of its circulation are unknown. Two prefatory letters attached to both copies of the manuscript (the first apparently by Mary Love herself and the second by an unidentified 'T. H.') suggest that the work was intended to be printed or perhaps widely circulated in manuscript after the Restoration; T. H.'s letter, which wonders 'how the intention was frustrated of sending forth this narrative about the time of his majesties restoration', suggests that it may have been completed in the interregnum. Whether the manuscript was ever intended for print, why it wasn't printed, why it exists in so few copies, why the British Library copy is incomplete, and how the eighteenth-century copyist of the Dr Williams's version had access to the portion missing from the former, all remain intriguing questions.

The 'Life of Mr Christopher Love' provides many colourful details absent from other accounts, such as John Quick's biography of Christopher, 'Icones sacrae', in Dr William's Library. It opens a window into the practices of the godly in the 1630s and 1640s, detailing Christopher's early conversion by William Erbury and rebellion against his father, his methods of catechizing the members of the Warner household, his physical asceticism, his relations with the individuals and communities to whom he ministered, his gradual assurance of his own election, and his elaborate preparations for death. It also reveals considerable anxiety about his reputation, responding to slanders that were published or circulated at the time of his trial and execution. Mary Love responded in detail to charges that her husband lacked 'natural affection', that he was an extortioner, that he was arrested with a prostitute, and that he slandered Charles I in his Uxbridge sermon of January 1645. The latter part of the work (intriguingly, the part missing from the British Library copy) attacks the council of state for its spying on and harassment of Love, and its manipulation of the law and subornation of witnesses to achieve his conviction. By weaving biblical prototypes into the story Mary Love casts her husband as a prophet who has been murdered for speaking the truth (specifically, for condemning the regicide and the engagement oath), and whose murderers will shortly suffer divine vengeance. This last aspect of the text may explain why it was not more widely disseminated. The author's joyous expectation, for example, that 'he who is cloathed with a vesture dipped in blood will make his arrows drunk with the blood of those who have dyed their garments in the blood of his servants the prophets' (BL, Sloane MS 3945, fol. 101) would have sat awkwardly with some post-Restoration dissenters' desire to portray themselves as politically quiescent.

Mary Love's texts, taken collectively, provide a complex case of female authorial self-presentation. Her petitions portray her as a vulnerable, pregnant wife and mother, repeatedly threatening that the shock of her husband's death will cause her to have a miscarriage. In her letters, by contrast, she eschews her wifely status, admonishing Christopher, 'think not that it is your wife but a friend that now writeth to thee' (*Loves Letters*, 1) and celebrating instead the new marriage of Christopher and his 'bridegroom', Jesus Christ. Her preface to the 'Life of Mr Christopher Love' takes yet another tack, elaborately comparing the manuscript to a birth. The human being behind the female author, alas, remains mostly hidden, for in her manuscript she speaks of herself only in passing. She can be glimpsed, for example, as a competent manager of her family's practical affairs, her husband being:

> careful not to intangle himself with the business of the world, … committed the whole care and ordering of his family occasions and outward estate which he had by her unto his wife, with whom he lived as a man of knowledge. (BL, Sloane MS 3945, fol. 105)

Evident, too, is her commitment to a learned ministry, and distress at 'our abuse of light' (ibid., fol. 96). She never said, though, what she knew or thought of her husband's involvement in plots to restore the king, although the fact that she obtained a pass to travel to Amsterdam on 18 December 1650 suggests that she may have participated in attempts to send money to royalists abroad.

Mary Love did not, as she feared, miscarry at Christopher's death, but the child died within six months of his birth. She later married Edward Bradshaw (1604?–1671), who was mayor of Chester in 1647 and 1653. In June 1660 she and her brother (or brother-in-law) James Winstanley petitioned the House of Commons, unsuccessfully, for reparations from the judges who had condemned Christopher. Nothing more is heard of her, and the date of her death is unknown. RACHEL WEIL

Sources *Loves letters* (1651) · *Love's name lives* (1651); (1663) · G. Cuitt, *History of the city of Chester* (1815) · *CSP dom., 1650* · E. C. Vernon, 'The Sion College conclave and London presbyterianism during the English revolution', PhD diss., U. Cam., 1999 · M. Love, 'Life of Mr Christopher Love', DWL, MS PP.12.50.4 (21) · M. Love, 'Life of Mr Christopher Love', BL, Sloane MS 3945 · Wood, *Ath. Oxon.*, new edn · *IGI* · *DNB*

Archives BL, Sloane MS 3945 · DWL, MS PP.12.50.4 (21)

Love, Nicholas (*d.* 1423/4), prior of Mount Grace and religious writer, may have been born in the area of Coventry, or somewhere in the south-eastern or east midland counties. He may have been the Augustinian friar, Nicholas Love, referred to in 1389 and, or alternatively, the Augustinian prior of York, Nicholas, referred to in 1400; but all aspects of his background are obscure. He was appointed fourth rector of the Charterhouse of Mount Grace in Yorkshire *c*.1409 and its first prior in 1410, when the house was formally recognized by the Carthusian general chapter. He left office possibly *c*.1417 but more probably *c*.1421, and died in 1423 or 1424.

Love's only known work is his *Myrrour of the Blessed Lyf of Jesu Christ* (also entitled the *Speculum vitae Christi* or *Vita Christi* in early printed editions), an English translation of the best-known Latin life of Christ, the *Meditationes vitae Christi*, attributed in the middle ages to St Bonaventure (*d.* 1274) but now to Johannes de Caulibus, a fourteenth-century Franciscan. According to his own preface he produced his work 'at þe instance & þe prayer of some deuoute soules' for 'symple creatures' (Love, 10). He envisaged an audience of men and women, literate and illiterate, religious and lay.

Love may have begun, and may even have finished, a version of the *Myrrour* before Archbishop Arundel's constitutions of 1407–9 restricted the translation of scriptural and theological works; and he certainly completed a form of it by about 1411, when Arundel approved its publication 'for the edification of the faithful and the confutation of heretics' (Love, 7). Although the *Myrrour* had almost certainly been designed to counter the challenges of the Lollards, and had circulated previously, this official sanction contributed to the quantity, quality, and uniformity of the subsequent manuscripts. His determination to address contemporary devotional and ecclesiastical needs also explains many of the additions and omissions which Love made to the source text and which heightened the affective, didactic, and meditative sides of the translation. He adapted and expanded the constructions and expressions of the Latin to bring them closer to the English speech idiom and rhythm of his own writing, and his ability to blend what was best in both traditions was his most original and valuable contribution to the development of English prose style.

The quality and suitability of the *Myrrour*, as well as the circumstances of its production and publication, explain not only its popularity but also the comparative lack of popularity in England of other lives of Christ. Among the most popular devotional works in England in the fifteenth and early sixteenth centuries, it survives in fifty-six originally complete manuscripts, was printed by Caxton in 1484 and 1490, and reprinted by Pynson and de Worde seven times between 1494 and 1530 (*STC*, nos. 3259–67). It is the best-known Carthusian English translation, the first complete English translation of the *Meditationes vitae Christi*, and among the most important of the many vernacular versions. W. N. M. Beckett

Sources J. Hogg and others, eds., *The chartae of the Carthusian general chapter*, Analecta Cartusiana, 100/1–24 (1982–94) • N. Love, *Mirror of the blessed life of Jesus Christ: a critical edition based on Cambridge University library additional MSS 6578 and 6686*, ed. M. G. Sargent (1992) • M. G. Sargent, 'Versions of the life of Christ: Nicholas Love's *Mirror* and related works', *Poetica*, 42 (1995), 39–70 • A. I. Doyle, 'A survey of the origins and circulation of theological writings in English in the 14th, 15th and early 16th centuries, with special consideration of the part of the clergy therein', PhD diss., U. Cam., 1953 • A. I. Doyle, 'Reflections on some manuscripts of Nicholas Love's *Myrrour of the blessed lyf of Jesu Christ*', *Essays in memory of Elizabeth Salter*, ed. D. Pearsall, Leeds Studies in English, new ser., 14 (1983), 82–93 • E. Zeeman, 'Nicholas Love: a 15th-century translator', *Review of English Studies*, new ser., 6 (1955), 113–27 • E. Salter, *Nicholas Love's 'Myrrour of the blessed lyf of Jesu Christ'* (1974) • I. R. Johnson, 'The Latin source of Nicholas Love's *Mirrour of the blessed lyf of Jesu Christ*: a reconsideration', *N&Q*, 231 (1986), 157–60 • B. Nolan, 'Nicholas Love', *Middle English prose: a critical guide to major authors and genres*, ed. A. S. G. Edwards (1984), 83–95 • J. M. Mueller, *The native tongue and the word: developments in English prose style, 1380–1580* (1984) • J. Hogg, ed., *Mount Grace Charterhouse and late medieval English spirituality*, [1] (Salzburg, 1980), 1–43 • S. Furnish, 'The *ordinatio* of Huntington Library, MS HM 149: an East Anglian manuscript of Nicholas Love's *Mirrour*', *Manuscripta*, 34 (1990), 50–65

Archives CUL, Add. MSS 6578, 6686

Love, Nicholas (*bap.* **1608**, *d.* **1682**), politician and regicide, was baptized on 26 October 1608 in St Swithun's, Winchester, the son of Dr Nicholas Love (*d.* 1630), headmaster of Winchester College, and his wife, Dousabell Colnett. He matriculated at Wadham College, Oxford, on 3 November 1626. On 12 November the next year he was admitted to Lincoln's Inn, whence he was called to the bar on 4 February 1636. He was created MA at Oxford on 31 August 1636. At Lincoln's Inn he appears to have formed some kind of connection with the Lenthall family of Oxfordshire, which helps explain his appointment in 1644 to one of the six clerkships, a lucrative office in the court of chancery under the master of the rolls, a post then held by the speaker of the House of Commons, William Lenthall. He was made an associate to the bench at Lincoln's Inn on 26 November 1644 and a bencher on 18 November 1648.

Love was active on behalf of parliament in his native Hampshire by the end of 1643 and was recruited to the House of Commons, winning election to one of the vacant seats at Winchester in November 1645. Having strongly opposed the conclusion of talks with the king at Newport in 1648, he was appointed to the high court of justice in January 1649, serving on four of its committees, including those for drawing up the charge against the king and for drafting the sentence. He was present at the sentencing of the king, though he did not sign the royal death warrant, and has been called as good a king-killer as any of the signatories [*see also* Regicides]. Certainly he became a forward revolutionary but his express confidence, before the trial began, that the charge would be 'nothing, but what he knew the K[ing] could cleerely acquit himselfe of' (Bodl. Oxf., MS Clarendon 34, fol. 17*v*) suggests a more moderate spirit. It also lends some credibility to the otherwise standard self-exculpatory rhetoric of Love's plea for mercy in 1660.

Love was closely involved in the constitutional revolution which ran parallel with developments in the great hall at Westminster, and served energetically the kingless Commonwealth set up in the wake of the regicide and the abolition of the monarchy. In parliament he chaired the debates of the committee of the whole house which issued in the passage of the Navigation Act in November 1651. In the following year he shared special responsibility for the legislation annexing Scotland with his fellow Winchester MP, Lord Commissioner John Lisle. He also sat on the last three councils of state down to the interruption in

1653. In the year of Worcester he had assumed some of the conciliar responsibility for placing urgent matters of home defence and militia organization before the house. At the council board he also had a hand in Scottish and Irish affairs, foreign policy, trade, and government finance, as well as press regulation. Finally he was influential in the transformation of English political iconography witnessed under the Commonwealth.

It has been claimed that Love joined the angry chorus of dissent which greeted Cromwell's abrupt termination of the council of state on 20 April 1653, but an unfortunate gap in the state papers precludes confirmation of Love's presence in council on that occasion. Certainly by 1655 Major-General William Goffe, keeping a watchful eye on Hampshire, appears to have had his suspicions about Love's intentions towards the Cromwellian regime. But if he had gone into overt opposition, his hostility to the protectorate was doubtless connected with the controversial ordinance of 1654 for the reform of chancery, which abolished Love's office as one of the six clerks in chancery. At least one of his colleagues protested mightily against this arbitrary destruction of patentees' property rights.

The six clerks' low fortunes revived in 1659, when the Rumpers, Love included, returned to government. Yet within months the Commonwealthsmen were once again assailed by their military protectors and by December Love was at Portsmouth, where the corporation had raised the standard of opposition to the military junto. There he joined the co-ordinators of the resistance to Fleetwood and Lambert, Sir Arthur Hesilrige MP and Valentine Walton MP. All three were made burgesses of the town. In January 1660 the Rump, returned to power, elevated Love to the council of state (where he was appointed president), and gave order for repayment of his substantial expenditure for the Commonwealth cause during the stand-off at Portsmouth.

By 1660 Love had become too big a fish, and his appetite for church and royalist lands too rapacious, for his plea for leniency to receive special treatment from the restored Stuart regime. In the spring he arranged to embark for the continent together with Hesilrige and Robert Wallop, but when the other two changed their minds Love was left to make the voyage alone, 'he being resolved not to trust the mercey of enraged beastes of prey' (Ludlow, 281). He survived pirates and tempests in his passage to Hamburg via Norway before joining his friend Edmund Ludlow and other *regicides in Vevey, Switzerland, where he died on 5 November 1682; he was buried in St Martin's Church there. The fate of his wife, Elizabeth (*née* Buggs), of Lambeth, whom Love had married on 6 October 1655, is unknown. SEAN KELSEY

Sources W. Berry, *County genealogies: pedigrees of the families of the county of Hants* (1833), 266–7 · W. P. Baildon, ed., *The records of the Honorable Society of Lincoln's Inn: admissions*, 1 (1896), 204 · W. P. Baildon, ed., *The records of the Honorable Society of Lincoln's Inn: the black books*, 2 (1898), 326, 331, 338, 365, 379 · *JHC*, 6 (1648–51), 93, 110, 138, 143, 185, 524, 532–3, 593, 600 · *JHC*, 7 (1651–9), 4, 7, 11, 14–15, 19, 42, 220, 654–5, 800, 823 · *JHL*, 9 (1646–7), 32, 52, 101 · C. H. Firth and R. S. Rait, eds., *Acts and ordinances of the interregnum, 1642–1660*, 1 (1911), 91, 113, 230, 335, 450, 1255 · *CSP dom.*, *1649–53*; *1659–60* · Thurloe, *State papers*, 4.408; 5.215 · D. Dymond, *Portsmouth and the fall of the puritan republic* (1971) · E. Ludlow, *A voyce from the watch tower*, ed. A. B. Worden, CS, 4th ser., 21 (1978), 61, 89, 103, 274, 281–2 · *Seventh report*, HMC, 6 (1879), 119 · G. E. Aylmer, *The state's servants: the civil service of the English republic, 1649–1660* (1973), 90–93 · J. L. Chester, ed., *The marriage, baptismal, and burial registers of the collegiate church or abbey of St Peter, Westminster*, Harleian Society, 10 (1876), 2 · *N&Q*, 5th ser., 6 (1876), 13 · parish register, Winchester, St Swithun, 26 Oct 1608, Hants. RO, 74M81/PR1 [baptism], fol. 6 · PRO, LR2/266, fol. 1v

Archives Winchester College, letters and MSS

Likenesses oils, Winchester College

Wealth at death entire English estate forfeit in 1660 (valued at £846 12*s*. p.a.); much of the estate forfeit in 1660 was encumbered with debts; valuation may or may not include investments in episcopal estate totalling £4605 18*s*. 18½*d*.: PRO, LR2/266, fol. 1v, 4

Love, Richard (**1596–1661**), college head, was born on 26 December 1596 in Great St Mary's parish, Cambridge, the second of three children and the only son of Richard Love (*d.* 1605), an apothecary, and Margaret, daughter of William Bosome. Margaret remarried in 1607, her new husband being Henry Mowtlowe (*d.* 1634), Gresham professor of law and public orator, one of the friends the apothecary entrusted with his son's education in the advent of Margaret's death. Love matriculated from King's College, Cambridge, in 1611, gaining his BA in 1615 from Clare College and proceeding MA in 1618. He was ordained deacon and priest in 1624, was a university taxor in 1625–6, and became a fellow before 1628, the year in which he was senior proctor. He was in La Rochelle when that stronghold of Calvinism was besieged in the summer of 1628, and about the same time was made chaplain in ordinary to Charles I, who on 27 October 1629 presented him to the living of Eckington, Derbyshire. In January 1631 he proceeded DD on the king's recommendation. The following October he received the prebend of Tachbrook in Lichfield Cathedral.

By mandate from Charles I, Love was made master of Corpus Christi College on 4 April 1632, immediately after Dr Butts's suicide. A quarrel followed between Love and the earl of Warwick that demonstrates Love's tactfulness and powers of persuasion. Warwick, supported by Charles, tried to press his nominee for a vacant fellowship, but the master and fellows resisted. The king eventually withdrew his candidate, after receiving a letter of apology and explanation from Love. His most notable act as vice-chancellor in 1633/4 was to cause the arrest of Peter Hausted in the pulpit of St Mary's while preaching a sermon against the neglect of religious duties in the university. Love also contributed on occasions when the university presented congratulatory verses.

Love married, about 1632, Grace, his stepfather's daughter, and settled in St Benedict's parish, Cambridge. Their daughter Anne (*b.* 1633) later married Thomas Tenison, archbishop of Canterbury, who bequeathed Love's portrait to Corpus Christi College. Grace (*b.* 1635) married John Lawson, an eminent physician. Sons Richard (*b.* 1637) and Thomas (*b.* 1638) followed; Henry (*b.* 1640) died soon after birth; John arrived in 1648.

Despite the difficulties of the times Love retained his

headship during the civil war. He preached a sermon at Whitehall to parliament at the monthly fast on 30 March 1642, 'The watchman's watchword', in which he criticized the threats both from Laudianism and from radical protestants' attacks on church hierarchy, and appealed for the promotion of preaching. It was subsequently published by royal command at Cambridge with the aim of attracting religious moderates to Charles's side. This did not make Love's position in parliamentarian-controlled Cambridge untenable. He probably took the solemn league and covenant as, when in July 1643 a general leave of absence was granted to the fellows, he was one of the four heads of college at Cambridge who, 'by the special favour of the friends and their own wary compliance, continued in their places' (Fuller, *History of Cambridge*, 169). When in December 1643 William Dowsing cleansed the colleges' chapels he found Love's conservatism had prevented the installation of Laudian furnishings at Corpus Christi. Love survived the rash of ejections prompted by the earl of Manchester's visitation of the university, and was included in February 1646 with those heads directed by parliament to preach at St Mary's. In 1647 he was appointed to a syndicate to maintain the university muniments.

Love also remained in place throughout the interregnum. Oliver Cromwell addressed him as 'my worthy friend' in 1649. In the same year he was made Lady Margaret professor of divinity, and despite staunchly defending Anglican doctrines and disciplines appears to have retained his prebend. Love's friend Colonel Valentine Walton, the regicide, was said, at an unspecified time, to have protected him. When faced with the engagement in 1650, Love joined other heads of colleges in petitioning, requesting that a promise not to disturb the present government might be accepted as their subscription. Grace informed a relative that they anticipated ruin if he was compelled to resign the professorship and claimed the stress of the situation prompted the return of 'His Olde Disease of the Spleen' (*Masters' History*, appx, 73). By November he was suspended, but rumours that a way would be found for him to appear to have satisfied the engagement proved correct, and he retained his preferments. Love's retrospective explanation was that, having demonstrated his disapproval of the trial and execution of Charles I, inviting an expulsion would be abandoning what power he retained to do good. His sermons about this time questioned the Calvinist emphasis on faith rather than works. He was appointed a member of the assembly of divines, but took no part in the proceedings. Although he survived the purge of college masters, he was omitted from the 1654 commission to regulate the university. In 1656, however, he and Anthony Tuckney were praised in the *Publick Intelligencer* for the international eminence they brought to the university and the nation. Love undertook a limited smartening up of the college chapel in 1659–60. J. B. Mullinger states he was the only head to retain his position until the Restoration.

Love composed two Latin congratulatory pieces. The first, delivered at Cambridge, discusses the calamities of the rebellion and excuses his temporary acquiescence. The second (published by the king's command) was presented by Love in person, acting as deputy vice-chancellor at Whitehall on 5 June 1660. He also contributed to the Cambridge collection of verses which were published at the Restoration. He made such a good impression that Charles II, besides allowing him to retain his posts, made him dean of Ely by patent dated 14 August; he was installed on 28 September.

Love died at the beginning of February 1661, and was buried in his college chapel. In his will, which was proved on 26 May 1661, his wife was the executor and main beneficiary and was entrusted with the education of their son John. Love's Latin books were bequeathed to John if he fulfilled his father's hopes that he would join the ministry. His daughters were provided with dowries, but his sons Richard and Thomas were intentionally omitted from his will. Among the larger bequests he laid out £100 on the college, gave a window to the master's lodge, and left £10 and a polyglot Bible. To his old college, Clare, whose master, Dr Paske, was his friend, he left £50. Love's moderation and remarkable levels of tact and discretion, which allowed him to retain the good opinion of so many enemies in such turbulent times, no less than his eminent reputation, suggest he was an extraordinary man.

E. T. Bradley, *rev.* S. L. Sadler

Sources will, PRO, PROB 11/303, sig. 26 • will, 1605, CUL, department of manuscripts and university archives, trans 111/46; inv 1605; adm 1607, 1611 [R. Love, father] • parish register, Cambridge, St Benedict's, Cambs. AS [baptism] • parish register, Cambridge, Great St Mary's, Cambs. AS [birth] • *CSP dom.*, 1640, 518–19, 531–2, 550–51 • *Masters' History of the college of Corpus Christi and the Blessed Virgin Mary in the University of Cambridge*, ed. J. Lamb (1831), 152, 170–71, appx 72–3, 149–50, 178–9 • C. H. Cooper, *Annals of Cambridge*, 3 (1845), 263, 264, 365, 440, 491 • E. Carter, *The history of the University of Cambridge* (1753), 92, 95, 96 • J. Twigg, *The University of Cambridge and the English Revolution, 1625–1688* (1990), 25, 27, 31–2, 34, 53, 105, 112, 114, 116–17, 129, 154, 156, 159, 171, 178–9, 196, 199, 238–9, 247, 250, 272, 290 • Venn, *Alum. Cant.*, 1/2.107; 1/3.55, 225; 1/4.214 • J. B. Mullinger, *The University of Cambridge*, 3 (1911), pp. 114n., 117, 147n., 220n., 247, 270–71, 295, 338, 378, 535, 557, 562–4 • W. Kennet, *A register and chronicle* (1728), 188, 215–16, 393 • *Walker rev.*, 36 • T. Cooper, ed., *The journal of William Dowsing: iconoclasm in East Anglia during the English civil war* (2001), 167–8, 276, 467 • J. Bentham, *The history and antiquities of the conventual and cathedral church of Ely* (1771); repr. in 2 vols. in 1 (1771), 232–3, 236 • R. Parr, ed., *The life of the most reverend father in God, James Usher … with a collection of three hundred letters* (1686), 470–71 • H. Cary, ed., *Memorials of the great civil war in England from 1646 to 1652*, 2 (1842), 234–9, 244–9 • G. D'Oyly, ed., *The life of William Sancroft, archbishop of Canterbury* (1821), 1.55–7 • *VCH Cambridgeshire and the Isle of Ely*, 3.201 • F. J. Varley, *Cambridge during the civil war, 1642–1646*, 60–67 • J. Walker, *The sufferings of the clergy during the Great Rebellion*, ed. [W. E. Flaherty] (1862), pt 2, pp. 41, 133 • Wing, *STC*

Archives Bodl. Oxf., Tanner CLVIII.20; CLVIII, 116; LII 98

Likenesses M. Tyson, etching (after oil painting), BM, NPG • oils, CCC Cam.

Wealth at death left dowries of £700 and £1000 to daughters: will, PRO, PROB 11/303, sig. 26, fols. 208–9

Love, William (*c*.1620–1689), merchant and politician, was the eldest son of William Love of Aynho, Northamptonshire, and his wife, Mary, daughter of John Uvedale. His family were members of the minor gentry, armigerous since Elizabeth I's reign. As an adolescent he was apprenticed to Roger Vivian, an assistant of the Levant Company, and during the 1640s served as a factor to him in Smyrna. In 1650 he returned to London with 'a great estate', and in July of that year took his freedom of the Drapers' Company and the Levant Company. On 1 February 1651 he married Elizabeth (*d.* 1694), daughter of Sir John Burgoyne of Sutton, Bedfordshire.

Love quickly became an important figure in the business world. His commercial activities centred on the Levant trade, in which he invested heavily until his retirement some time in the late 1670s. He exported large amounts of cloth and tin and imported diverse goods, chiefly Persian silk, but also including galls, cordevants (articles made of leather), worm-seeds, and gum ammoniac. In recognition of his eminence within the trade, the Levant Company elected him assistant in 1653, a post which he held until 1670, except for a brief stint as deputy governor in 1661. He also invested in a number of trading voyages to the East Indies, and between 1657 and 1662 the East India Company elected him to their court of directors. These commercial ventures led to many disputes, and Love was extremely litigious, appearing often as a plaintiff in chancery.

From his base in the business world Love became active in first City and then national politics, concerning himself mainly with issues of trade and religion. He was an alderman between 1659 and 1662, sheriff in 1659, and master of the Drapers' Company in 1660. Before the Restoration he was councillor of state in January and February of 1660, and he was subsequently elected to the Cavalier Parliament of 1661 as one of four MPs for London. On election, however, his refusal as a Congregationalist to take the sacraments debarred him from the House of Commons and caused his removal from the aldermanic bench under the Corporation Act. Upon reinstatement in the Commons after the impeachment of Edward Hyde, earl of Clarendon, in 1667 he was prominent in advocating toleration for nonconformists. Engaged in the reform of the Board of Trade in 1668, he then served as a commissioner for trade between 1668 and 1672. His most active period in the Commons came during the three Exclusion Parliaments: he served on no fewer than fifty-two committees, involving a wide range of issues. Love voted for exclusion and concerned himself with related topics. His dissenting and mercantile interests came together most poignantly when he attacked the East India Company under the leadership of the court-connected Sir Josiah Child. He did not seek re-election to the parliament of 1685 and supported the revolution of 1688, subscribing money to the new regime. Returned to the convention of 1689, he attended only briefly before his death in April. He was buried on 1 May 1689 at St Andrew Undershaft in London.

Love lived most of his life in London, in the parishes of St Andrew Undershaft, St Martin Orgar, and in Lime Street, St Mary Axe. His will indicates that he also acquired property in Clapham, Surrey. Although three sons and a daughter survived infancy, only his daughter, Sarah, and second son, John, survived him, the latter to pursue a successful career in the City, centred on the Levant trade. Love left £50 to the poor and, except for small legacies to his daughter and next of kin, he divided his estate between his wife, Elizabeth, and son John.

TREVOR DICKIE, *rev.*

Sources J. R. Woodhead, *The rulers of London, 1660–1689* (1965) · J. B. Whitmore and A. W. Hughes Clarke, eds., *London visitation pedigrees, 1664*, Harleian Society, 92 (1940) · HoP, *Commons, 1660–90* · D. R. Lacey, *Dissent and parliamentary politics in England, 1661–1689* (1969) · will, PRO, PROB 11/395, sig. 67 · PRO, SP 105/151/39 · PRO, SP 105/152/20 · PRO, SP 105/166

Wealth at death left £50 to the poor, all else to family: will, PRO, PROB 11/395, sig. 67

Love, William Edward (1806–1867), impressionist, the son of a merchant in the city of London, was born in London on 6 February 1806, and was educated at Harlow in Essex and at Nelson House Academy, Wimbledon, Surrey. At the age of twelve, while still at school, he began to imitate the noises of machinery and other objects, and soon went on to mimic the sounds made by musical instruments, beasts, birds, and insects. From about 1820 to 1826 he was connected with London journalism, but he then turned his attention to the theatre, and in 1827 performed throughout England and France. One year later he appeared for a benefit in a solo entertainment at the Olympic Theatre entitled *The False Alarm*, a performance whose success, it was said, led to his professional career in the theatre. Thereafter he became renowned as the best ventriloquist in England; he assumed various characters, making rapid changes in dress while talking, singing, and displaying remarkable powers of mimicry and ventriloquism.

In June 1829, at the start of his theatrical career, Love produced and appeared solo in *The Peregrinations of a Polyphonist*, with which he toured major English towns. He then went to Scotland, where in 1830 he brought out *Love in a Labyrinth, or, The Adventures of a Day*, and in 1833 he opened at Oxford with a piece called *Ignes fatui*. In 1834 he made his first appearance in London, and acted at the City of London assembly rooms, Bishopsgate Street, for several months. Over the following years he divided his time between touring in France, America, and the West Indies, and performing in London in such theatres as the Strand, Almack's, and the Hanover Square Rooms. On 26 December 1854 he took possession of the Upper Hall, 69 Quadrant, Regent Street, London, where he produced *The London Season*. On 8 February 1856 Love played at the Regent Gallery for the 300th consecutive night, which was reputed to be his 2406th performance in London. In 1858 he became paralysed and, in keeping with the professional benevolence of the time, his colleagues at Sadler's Wells organized a benefit for him. He died at his home, 33 Arundel Street, Strand, on 16 March 1867.

G. C. BOASE, *rev.* BRENDA ASSAEL

Sources Boase, *Mod. Eng. biog.* · 'Death of Mr Love, polyphonist', *The Era* (24 March 1867), 11 · Hall, *Dramatic ports.*

Likenesses C. Baugniet, lithograph, 1844, Harvard TC · C. Baugniet, two woodcuts, Harvard TC · T. B., woodcut, Harvard

TC · four lithographs, Harvard TC · two woodcuts, Harvard TC · woodcut (as Mr Tranquillus Calm in *The London season*), BM

Loveday, John (1711–1789), antiquary and traveller, was born on 5 February 1711 at Cateaton Street, London, the elder child of Thomas Loveday (1680–1720) of Caversham and Feens and his wife, Sarah Lethieullier (1682–1761), daughter of William Lethieullier of Clapham, a Turkey merchant, and his wife, Mary. His paternal grandfather, a successful London goldsmith who had bought the lease of the old rectory at Caversham in 1666, had left the family well off financially. In 1739 Loveday married Anna Maria Goodwin (1717–1743), daughter of William Goodwin of Arlescote, near Edgehill. They had a son, John [*see below*], and a daughter, Mary (1741–1749). He married, secondly, in 1745, Dorothy Bagshaw (1709–1755), daughter of Revd Harington Bagshaw of Bromley, Kent. His third marriage was in 1756 to Penelope Forrest (1723–1801), daughter of Thomas Forrest of Jamaica. They had a son, Arthur (*d.* 1827), and three daughters: Penelope (1759–1846), who married Revd William Benwell (1765–1796) in 1796 and Revd John Hind (1759–1882) in 1808; Sarah (1766–1832); and Mary (1768–1840), who remained single.

Loveday had been educated at Reading School, under the sympathetic supervision of H. J. Hiley. He matriculated at Oxford as a gentleman commoner of Magdalen College in 1728, graduated BA in 1731, and proceeded MA in 1734. On arrival at Oxford he called on the antiquary Thomas Hearne, with whom he had corresponded, volunteering information about St Anne's Chapel on Caversham Bridge. A lasting friendship was struck up, and Hearne described Loveday in his diary as 'an ingenious Gentleman [who] takes great delight in antiquities' (*Remarks*, 9.402). Loveday became a youthful member of Hearne's antiquarian circle in Oxford. Until his death in 1735 the older man was supplied by the younger with information from churches and graveyards, both near and far. Loveday made many friends and enjoyed Oxford life so much that he kept rooms there for ten years. In the vacations he returned to Caversham but from 1730 began to travel further afield and, undeterred by the poor roads, made a number of extensive tours on horseback throughout the British Isles, often with one or two companions. He described in great detail the architecture and monuments of many cathedrals and churches and also visited numerous country houses. He noted the progress of new buildings and gardens and was especially interested in the paintings and sculpture. He recorded on loose papers over 100 tours and short visits between 1729 and 1765, to which he added references throughout his life. His only visit to Europe was in 1737, when he travelled through the Low Countries to Aachen. His 'Diary of a tour in 1732 through parts of England, Wales, Ireland and Scotland' was published in 1890 by his great-grandson J. E. T. Loveday as a contribution to the Roxburghe Club.

Loveday was brought up and remained a deeply committed member of the Church of England, regularly attending Magdalen College chapel or St Mary the Virgin at Oxford, and St Peter's in Caversham. He adhered to high-church principles and was always a tory, but not an Oxford high-church tory in the political sense, as was Hearne. He bought and read books extensively, being particularly interested in church history. He assembled a fine library and a good collection of coins. His only publications were occasional articles for the *Gentleman's Magazine* under pseudonyms. He corresponded with many scholars, to whom he was always ready to give assistance. Thanking him for 'many useful corrections and excellent hints', Thomas Warton begged in vain for permission to disclose his name, arguing that 'the public have a right to know by whom they have been obliged' (Loveday MSS). In 1802 Charles Coates used his notes on Reading (*The History and Antiquities of Reading*, preface and text) and those on the margins of his copy of Wood's *Athenae Oxonienses* were used by Arthur Bliss in his edition (preface, 14). Loveday always kept open house at Caversham. The 'old Tory country gentleman' was described in a visit by Mary Berry in 1774 as 'an elegant and accomplished scholar' (*Extracts*, 1.9), and John Byng referred to the 'well-known hospitality … where learning and virtue grace the mansion' (*Torrington Diaries*, 1.195).

Loveday was short and slight in stature, but blessed with physical courage and stamina. He died at the old rectory, Caversham, on 16 May 1789 of an internal disorder, leaving between £5000 and £6000 in bank stock. He was buried at St Peter's Church, Caversham, on 22 May. His directions for his diaries, excluding the tours, to be burnt were eventually carried out by his grandson Thomas, after he had copied the major part.

John Loveday (1742–1809), antiquary, born at the old rectory, Caversham, on 11 November 1742, was also educated at Reading School and Magdalen College. He graduated BCL in 1766, was made DCL in 1771, and was admitted an advocate in Doctors' Commons in 1771. He retired in 1777 on his marriage to his ward Anne Taylor Loder (1756–1837), daughter and heir of William Taylor Loder (*d.* 1772) of Williamscote, near Banbury, where they continued to live. They had four sons and a daughter. He assisted his friend Richard Chandler, and compiled the index for the *Marmora Oxonienses*. He contributed papers on antiquarian and orthographic subjects to the *Gentleman's Magazine* and continued to correspond with many other British and foreign scholars. In 1788 he inherited Arlescote from his grandmother Abigail Goodwin. He succeeded to the Caversham property in 1789 and retained it until his sons left Reading School. He sold the lease in 1799 and transported the books and their presses to a new library wing he had built for them and his own at Williamscote. He died there of pneumonia on 4 March 1809 and on 11 March was buried at the church of St Mary the Virgin at Cropredy. Over 2000 volumes from his library were acquired by Pennsylvania State University in 1969.

SARAH MARKHAM

Sources priv. coll., Loveday family MSS · S. Markham, *John Loveday of Caversham, 1711–1789* (1984) · S. Markham, *A testimony of her times* (1990) · letters of Thomas Hearne, Bodl. Oxf. · *Remarks and collections of Thomas Hearne*, ed. C. E. Doble and others, 9, OHS, 65 (1914) · *The Torrington diaries: containing the tours through England and Wales of the Hon. John Byng (later Viscount Torrington) between the years*

1781 and 1794, ed. C. B. Andrews, 1 (1934) • C. Coates, *The history and antiquities of Reading* (1802); suppl. (1810) • *Extracts of the journals and correspondence of Miss Berry*, ed. M. T. Lewis, 2nd edn, 3 vols. (1865–6), vol. 1 • R. Churton, *GM*, 1st ser., 79 (1809) • *DNB*

Archives BL, corresp. and papers • Bodl. Oxf., corresp. and papers • Bodl. Oxf., notes on Shenington church • NRA, priv. coll., family MSS • Pennsylvania State University | BL, corresp. with John Ward, Add. MSS 4284, 4312, 6265 • Bodl. Oxf., Ashmole MS 1822 • Bodl. Oxf., Ballard MSS, 10, 37 • Bodl. Oxf., corresp. with A. C. Ducarel • Bodl. Oxf., corresp. with Thomas Hearne

Likenesses B. Schwartz, oils, 1721, priv. coll. • miniature, *c.*1780, priv. coll. • T. Gibson, oils; last known at Williamscote, 1966

Wealth at death £5000–£6000 bank stock: priv. coll., Loveday family MSS

Loveday, John (1742–1809). *See under* Loveday, John (1711–1789).

Loveday, Robert (1620/21–1656), translator, was a scion of the Loveday family seated at Chediston, Suffolk, but his exact parentage is unclear. He went to school at Metfield, Suffolk, was admitted as a pensioner at Peterhouse, Cambridge, on 20 December 1636, aged fifteen, and matriculated in the following year. Loveday did not complete his studies because of the civil war, and became a secretary in the Clinton family; in this capacity he travelled extensively throughout England, spending time at the Clintons' seat, Tattershall Castle, Lincolnshire, and at the Clares' residence, Thurland House, Nottinghamshire (a county Loveday disliked).

Having become proficient in French and Italian under the instruction of another member of the Clinton household, Loveday translated into English the first three parts of La Calprenède's *Cléopâtre* under the title *Hymen's præludia, or, Love's master-piece*; these appeared respectively in 1652, 1654, and 1655, and were reprinted many times. Despite the erroneous attribution of other parts of the romance to Loveday's hand in some later editions, it was only with the collaboration of John Coles that part 4 was completed and published in 1656. Loveday was an agreeable writer, and his translation is accurate and idiomatic. After Robert Loveday's death his brother Anthony edited a selection from his correspondence under the title *Loveday's Letters, Domestick and Forrein* (published 1659, reprinted several times), at the beginning of which is a portrait of the author by Faithorne. The work includes some verses by Loveday that intimate a facility in metre. A hard-working and kind man, Loveday was also sickly and died, probably of a consumptive disease, in 1656. As he has been plausibly but contentiously identified with the patient in Sir Thomas Browne's *A Letter to a Friend* (published 1690), his death may have taken placed in mid-May 1656.

Ross Kennedy

Sources Venn, *Alum. Cant.*, 1/3.107 • W. C. Metcalfe, *The visitations of Suffolk* (1882), 150 • T. A. Walker, ed., *Admissions to Peterhouse or St Peter's College in the University of Cambridge* (1912), 58 • F. L. Huntley, *Sir Thomas Browne: a biographical and critical study* (1962), 188–97 • N. J. Endicott, 'Browne's *Letter to a friend*', *TLS* (15 Sept 1966), 868 • K. J. Höltgen, 'Browne's *Letter to a friend*', *TLS* (20 Oct 1966), 966

Likenesses W. Faithorne, line engraving, BM, NPG; repro. in R. Loveday, *Letters* (1659), frontispiece

Loveday, Samuel (1619?–1677), General Baptist preacher, was the son of William Loveday, scissorer (tailor) of Helions Bumpstead, Essex. On 5 October 1638 he was bound apprentice in London to John Hanson, a member of the Company of Merchant Taylors. At an unknown date he married his wife, Jane; they brought up several children, of whom at least five survived him.

In 1642 Loveday published in defence of recent damage caused to Cheapside Cross (or Jasper), a 'monument of idolatry':

> Old Charing Cross has lost its head
> and so't may be your feare
> that Jasper's noddle would be gone
> but for the watchman's care
> His case is bad, but to conclude
> If Jasper for me send
> when he assaulted is againe
> No help to him I'll lend
> (Loveday, *Cheap-side Crosse*, 4)

Loveday was made free of the Company of Merchant Taylors on 12 November 1645. About this time, and until at least 1651, he seems to have been living and perhaps working with another Baptist merchant tailor, Edward Barber, in Threadneedle Street, London. In late 1645, it was reported, Barber, assisted by another unnamed, instituted the ceremony of the laying on of hands in his congregation, and in 1654 a church now led by Loveday was reported to be one of those which followed the custom of 'the supper', a church meal, usually preceding communion, which was accepted only by churches which baptized by the laying on of hands. All this may suggest that Loveday acted at first as Barber's assistant.

In November 1650 Loveday published his *Hatred of Esau* as a 'Servant of the Church of Christ', which suggests he was an elder or pastor. By that time, he had come to the view that saints might fall away, the first General Baptist known publicly to embrace that doctrine, and eagerly anticipated the imminent conversion of the Jews: 'none of us shall enter into glory until the Jews come up too; therefore let us use all means possible to publish that light, and put forth that power we have to bring them up' (Loveday, *Hatred of Esau*, 15).

In September 1654 there were plans to divide Loveday's congregation, apparently because of internal dissension, though the source of this is unknown. Loveday's name does not appear as an elder or messenger in the reports of the intercongregational assemblies of the General Baptists in 1654 and 1656. In October 1655, however, members of his congregation subscribed a petition in support of the Socinian John Biddle, though apparently not unanimously, and perhaps against the opposition of the pastor himself.

Reports of December 1657 indicate that there were close and continuing links between Loveday's congregation and the influential church of Fenstanton, Huntingdonshire, whose members sometimes lodged with Loveday's on visits to London. By this time the church was meeting at Tower Hill. In March 1660 Loveday and several followers subscribed *A Brief Confession … of Faith*, and in January 1661 they joined in the denunciations of Thomas Venner's uprising. Most of the Baptist churches were anxious to dissociate themselves from Venner, and were generally drawn towards quietism after the Restoration. The government was not always convinced by this. In 1670 Loveday's meeting-place, now at Looking Glass Alley in East Smithfield, was raided, and many of the congregation, who had come to hear a sermon by John Jennings, were arrested.

But Loveday himself had never been a very militant or populist leader in the style of Samuel Oates or Jeremiah Ives. Crosby tells us he was 'noted for his great moderation, and very seldom concerned himself with controverted points' (Crosby, 4.250). His interpretation of the twenty-fifth chapter of Matthew was expounded over 'the space of one year' in 'that small congregation over which I am concerned by the providence and grace of God as a pastor or feeder' (Loveday, *Alarm*, 'Letter to the reader').

Loveday seems to have prospered in business: on 3 October 1673 he was admitted to the livery of the Company of Merchant Taylors, and at his death was able to leave two houses to his wife, Jane. There were bequests of £50 to his two sons, John and Samuel, but £150 to Elizabeth, evidently his favourite; Mary and Hester, on the other hand, got 'twenty shillings apiece', in satisfaction of 'all claims they may have or pretend to have on my estate' (PROB 11/355, sig. 128, fol. 262*r*). We may suspect their mode of life and belief, or their marriages, did not meet with his approval.

Loveday retained firm Baptist convictions until his death. *An elegy on the much lamented death of Mr. Samuel Loveday … on the 15th of December 1677 in the 59th year of his age* stresses the many years of his service to the congregation in east London—'bless the Lord that lent us him so long'—and warmly recalls his 'pious, rare and vertuous life'.

STEPHEN WRIGHT

Sources T. Edwards, *Gangraena, or, A catalogue and discovery of many of the errours, heresies, blasphemies and pernicious practices of the sectaries of this time*, 3 vols. in 1 (1646) • S. Loveday, *An answer to the lamentation of Cheap-side Crosse* [1642] • S. Loveday, *The hatred of Esau and the love of Jacob* (1850), E1380(3) • T. Crosby, *The history of the English Baptists, from the Reformation to the beginning of the reign of King George I*, 4 vols. (1738–40), vols. 3–4 • *A brief confession or declaration of faith: set forth by many of us whoare, falsely, called Ana-Baptists* (1660); another edn (1854) [repr. in E. B. Underhill, ed., *Confessions of faith and other public documents, illustrative of the history of the Baptist churches of England in the 17th century*, Hanserd Knollys Society, 9 (1854), 107–20] • 'To the king of these nations', *Confessions of faith and other public documents, illustrative of the history of the Baptist churches of England in the 17th century*, ed. E. B. Underhill, Hanserd Knollys Society (1854), 357 • *The petition of divers churches*, Td 23 Oct 1655 E856(3) [supported Biddle] • *To the officers and soldiers*, Td 2 Feb 1656/7 E902(4) [listed congregations supporting Biddle, and place of meeting, p. 3] • S. Loveday, *An alarm to slumbering Christians* (1675) • *An elegy on the much lamented death of Mr. Samuel Loveday* (1677) • PRO, PROB 11/355, sig. 128 • M. Tolmie, *The triumph of the saints: the separate churches of London, 1616–1649* (1977), 80 • Merchant Taylors' Company apprentice bindings, vol. 11; court minutes, vols. 9, 11, GL • St Benet Fink churchwardens' accounts, GL, MS 1303/1 • E. B. Underhill, ed., *Records of the Churches of Christ, gathered at Fenstanton, Warboys, and Hexham, 1644–1720*, Hanserd Knollys Society (1854), 238

Wealth at death four houses; specified bequests of £262 15*s*.: will, PRO, PROB 11/355, sig. 128

Lovegrove, William (1778–1816), actor, the son of a plumber, was born at Shoreham, Sussex, on 13 January 1778, and was apprenticed to his father. After playing Hamlet as an amateur at a private theatre in Tottenham Court Road, London, he made his first professional appearance at the Richmond theatre in June 1799. From there he went to Dublin, where he appeared as Anhalt in *Lovers' Vows*, an adaptation from the German by Elizabeth Inchbald. In a stagecoach on his way to Manchester he was shot in the leg when a passenger's pistol was accidentally discharged. This delayed his arrival, and hampered his eventual performance in the city. After playing in Guernsey and Plymouth he made his first appearance at Bath in November 1802 in the part of Lazarillo in Robert Jephson's farce *Two Strings to your Bow*. During the season he played other roles, including Edgar in *King Lear*, and gained some popularity. When John Edwin left Bath for Dublin, a large range of comic characters fell to Lovegrove, whose name appeared in Bath and Bristol in roles from Dr Pangloss in George Colman's *The Heir-at-Law*, Sir Anthony Absolute in *The Rivals*, and Isaac in *The Duenna*, to Autolycus, Dogberry, Sir Martin Marall, and Alphonse in Beaumont and Fletcher's *The Pilgrim*. During the summer season he played at Margate and Worthing. Bath proved, as it often did, the portal to London, and Lovegrove appeared on 3 October 1810 at the Lyceum, the temporary home of the Drury Lane company, as Lord Ogleby in Colman and Garrick's *The Clandestine Marriage*. Job Thornberry in Colman's *John Bull* and many favourite characters followed, and he played original parts in dramas by Dimond, Masters, Millingen, Arnold, and other writers. His Lopez in *Kiss*, an alteration of Beaumont and Fletcher's *The Spanish Curate*, won him much applause.

Lovegrove remained with the company in the new Drury Lane Theatre until his retirement, and rose to be one of the principal supports of the house. He married a Miss Weippert, the daughter of a harp player; she died shortly after giving birth to a daughter, who did not long survive her. These two shocks produced a visible effect on Lovegrove's health. He took a benefit in June 1814, when he appeared as Wilford in Colman's tragedy *The Iron Chest* and played in a piece entitled *Cheating*, by a friend named Parry. In October that year he was the original Old Fathom in *Policy, or, Thus Runs the World Away*, attributed to Henry Siddons. Soon afterwards he broke a blood vessel and was ill for many months. He did not reappear until June 1815, when for the first time, for his benefit, he played Sir Peter Teazle; his reception was enthusiastic. He acted during the next season and was allowed a full salary until a relapse occurred and his recovery was seen to be hopeless. He was granted a half salary until his death, on 25 June 1816, near Bath, where he had been taken by his sister.

Lovegrove was an excellent actor, and his premature death was a misfortune. A prudent and a reserved man, he mixed little with his colleagues and though much respected had few close friends. He was the victim either of a singular outrage or of an extraordinary delusion. George Raymond, the biographer of R. W. Elliston, records how Lovegrove once rushed to the Lyceum at midnight, covered with brickdust and mortar, and in a state of frenzy, stating that at the end of Dyott Street, Bloomsbury, he had been seized and pinioned by two stalwart women, forced into a house, and thrust into a room, where a third woman was dying from the result of violence. By supreme efforts he escaped. After his recovery he took refuge in customary taciturnity, and no elucidation was afforded of the story. Raymond says that Lovegrove was strong, natural, and free from caricature.

JOSEPH KNIGHT, *rev.* NILANJANA BANERJI

Sources *Monthly Mirror*, new ser., 8 (Nov 1810), 110 · 'Biographical memoir of Mr Lovegrove', *Theatrical Inquisitor, and Monthly Mirror*, 9 (1816), 83–8 · Genest, *Eng. stage* · Hall, *Dramatic ports.* · G. Raymond, *Memoirs of Robert William Elliston* (1844–5)

Likenesses S. De Wilde, two watercolour drawings, 1810–15, Garr. Club · five prints, Harvard TC · portrait, repro. in *Monthly Mirror* · portrait, repro. in 'Biographical memoir of Mr Lovegrove' · prints, BM, NPG

Lovekyn, John (*d.* 1368), merchant and lord mayor of London, was descended from an ancient Surrey family. The sources variously describe him as the son of Edward Lovekyn, citizen of London, and a native of Kingston, who built a chapel in that parish in 1309, and of Edward's brother, Robert, who left lands and rents for the endowment there of various family obits. John is described in letters patent of 26 Edward III as the son of Edward, but in the register of Bishop Stratford as the son and heir of Robert. The former seems more likely to have been his father. He re-endowed the family chapel in 1352 with two messuages in the parish of St Michael, Crooked Lane, of the annual value of £4.

A wealthy man, recorded at different times as a stockfishmonger, pepperer, and draper, John Lovekyn carried on an extensive merchandise in salted or stockfish, corn, wheat, oats, beans, herrings, and sea coal, and traded much abroad. In 1358 he claimed as a citizen of London the right to bring a freight of sea coal from Newcastle to London free of custom. In 1360 he supplied provisions to the royal army in Normandy, and in 1365 he successfully protested through the mayor and aldermen to the authorities of Nieuport in Flanders against the seizure of a cargo of red herrings which he and his agents at Great Yarmouth were importing to London. Lovekyn first lived in the parish of St Mary-at-Hill, in a house afterwards occupied by his 'servant' and apprentice, Sir William Walworth. Early in Edward III's reign he moved to the parish of St Michael, Crooked Lane, where his large mansion in Thames Street overlooked the river between Oystergate and Ebbegate by the bridge foot. He brought with him his fellow tradesmen, and the locality became known as Stockfishmongers' Row. His mansion descended to Walworth, and afterwards to Henry Preston, citizen and stockfishmonger, who left it in 1434 to the Fishmongers' Company for their hall.

Lovekyn was alderman of Bridge ward, became sheriff in 1342, and was one of the representatives of the city in parliament in 1344, 1346, 1348, and 1365. He was four times lord mayor, in 1348, 1358, 1365, and 1366. He owed his third tenure of office to the direct appointment of the king on 21 January 1365, in place of Adam Bury, who was discharged by a royal order, although he had been re-elected after serving as mayor in the previous year. He also held numerous other civic offices, including city attorney at Boston fair, in Lincolnshire (1333), warden of London Bridge (1342–50), auditor of the bridge accounts (1351), and supervisor of the city's supply of ships to the royal fleet (1359). Leader of the Fishmongers in 1351, he had contributed to a gift by the city to the king in 1337, and to London's loans to the crown in 1340 and 1346. He lent sums ranging from £100 to £200 to the king between 1356 and 1365.

In 1338 Lovekyn went overseas in the king's service, and later held royal appointments in Surrey. He stood surety for Adam Fraunceys, mercer and citizen of London, as guardian of Simon, son of Thomas Leggy, skinner, and he benefited his ancestral home at Kingston by repairing his father's chapel and making further endowments. He was also the second founder of the church of St Michael, Crooked Lane, which he entirely rebuilt at his own cost. According to Leland, he founded St Michael's College, in connection with the church. John Stow says that Walworth was the founder, 'peradventure for John Lofkin his master' (Herbert, *History and Antiquities*, 125).

Lovekyn was married twice: first to Mabel, who brought him a stepdaughter, Leticia, and then to Margaret. He died on 4 August 1368 and was buried in the choir of St Michael, Crooked Lane, under a handsome tomb, with images of himself and his first wife in alabaster. Stow relates that Lovekyn's monument was removed, and a flat stone of grey marble, garnished with plates of copper, substituted. The brass plate containing his epitaph in three Latin verses found its way to Walkern church, Hertfordshire, where it served as a palimpsest brass inside the church for Richard Humberstone, who died in 1581. Both Lovekyn's and Walworth's monuments were restored by the Fishmongers' Company in 1562, with the addition of an English inscription in doggerel verse. In the original Latin inscription Lovekyn is erroneously said to have died in 1370. His will, dated 25 July 1368, was enrolled in the court of husting on 11 November 1368. Walworth acted as his executor and later married his widow. He appears to have possessed, besides his house in Thames Street, other houses further east towards Billingsgate, and property in St Martin Vintry, Crooked Lane, Candlewick Street, Oyster Hill, and Tower Street. Lovekyn left no issue, but he bequeathed some London property to a nephew, John.

CHARLES WELCH, *rev.* ROGER L. AXWORTHY

Sources R. R. Sharpe, ed., *Calendar of wills proved and enrolled in the court of husting, London, AD 1258 – AD 1688*, 2 vols. (1889–90) · R. R. Sharpe, ed., *Calendar of letter-books preserved in the archives of the corporation of the City of London*, [12 vols.] (1899–1912), vols. F–G · R. Newcourt, *Repertorium ecclesiasticum parochiale Londinense*, 2 vols. (1708–10) · *Registrum Henrici Woodlock, diocesis wintoniensis, AD 1305–1316*, ed. A. W. Goodman, 2 vols., CYS, 43–4 (1940–41) · J. Weever, *Antient funeral monuments*, ed. W. Tooke (1767) · W. Herbert, *The history of the twelve great livery companies of London*, 2 vols. (1834–7) · P. Metcalf, *The halls of the Fishmongers' Company* (1977) · J. Gough Nichols, 'Notices of John Lovekyn', *Transactions of the London and Middlesex Archaeological Society*, 3 (1865–9), 133–7 · J. Gough Nichols and A. Heales, 'Notices of John Lovekyn', *Transactions of the London and Middlesex Archaeological Society*, 6 (1890) • Exchequer documents, PRO • *Chancery records* • *VCH Surrey* • W. Herbert, *History and antiquities of the parish church of St Michael, Crooked Lane* (1833) • S. L. Thrupp, *The merchant class of medieval London, 1300–1500* (1948)

Lovel, Mary [*née* Jane Roper], **Lady Lovel** (*c.*1564–1628), founder of the English Carmelite convent at Antwerp, was the third of the three children of John Roper, Baron Teynham (*c.*1534–1618), of the Lodge, Linsted, Kent, chief clerk of the common pleas, and his first wife, Elizabeth (1544–1567), daughter of Richard Parke of Pluckley in Kent. Probably named Jane at birth she was later known as Mary. Little is known of her early education, although presumably she received a thorough grounding in Catholic teachings at her home in Kent. She and her older sister, Elizabeth Vaux, were some of the best-known and most fervent recusants of their era. She married Sir Robert Lovel, soldier, of Martin Abbey, Surrey, some time before the birth of her eldest child, Christina (1597–1639), who became a Benedictine nun at Brussels. They had another child in 1601. Her husband predeceased her although the exact date of his death is unknown; Anstruther believed he was dead by 1606.

Lady Lovel devoted a great deal of energy and financial resources to recusant causes. In 1606 she petitioned the earl of Salisbury for permission to go to Spa in the Spanish Netherlands to cure her breast cancer. After this favour was granted she again wrote to the earl. This time she raised his ire by indiscreetly stating that she would not take an anti-Catholic oath even if it were a precondition for her travel pass. She wrote, 'I am resolved to undergo any misery that may be imposed upon me rather than do that thing which a religious and Catholic conscience cannot justify' (*Salisbury MSS*, 18.419).

In 1608, the English agent at Brussels, Thomas Edmondes, reported that Lovel was considering joining the English Benedictine convent at Brussels. This was the first stage in her lifelong spiritual quest to ascertain her vocation. Lovel's passionate temperament and her changeable commitments to various religious orders resulted in a peripatetic and tumultuous life. Her contemporaries criticized her plan to join the cloister in 1608 because of the 'great neglect' that she would demonstrate in 'abandoning the care of her children' (Guilday, 360). In 1609 Lovel left the cloister when her lifelong devotion to Jesuit confessors put her at odds with Abbess Mary Percy. She then proceeded to Louvain and planned to establish a Benedictine convent. Acting on instructions that she received in a Marian vision she attempted to found a Carmelite convent at Liège and at Malines in 1616. In 1619 Lovel settled on Antwerp, where she founded the English Carmelite convent with a cash donation of £1600 and a gift of ornate church ornaments worth £600.

Tensions soon arose, however, on several fronts. Lady Lovel was committed to the principle of freedom of choice in confessors. The question arose as to whether Carmelite or Jesuit influence should predominate at the Antwerp convent. Furthermore, Lovel believed that as the cloister's founder she deserved a significant voice in the institution's internal governance. She disapproved of how the nuns were using her money. By 1620 Lovel went so far as to spread rumours against the cloister to those outside its walls. In 1622 she went to England to raise more funds for the establishment. When she returned to Antwerp in 1623 she was angered to learn that the sisters had accepted several Flemish women as novices in her absence. She threatened to withdraw her financial support were the Flemish members allowed to remain. They departed and began a new convent in 1624. By 1625 Lovel's relations with the Antwerp convent had ceased as she began a new quest—to found a Bernardine cloister at Bruges, which she considered joining. She died at Bruges on 12 November 1628 before her plan reached fruition. Lady Lovel was interred on the gospel side of the high altar of the church of Notre Dame at Bruges.

Colleen M. Seguin

Sources P. Guilday, *The English Catholic refugees on the continent, 1558–1795* (1914) • A. Hardman, *English Carmelites in penal times* (1936) • *Calendar of the manuscripts of the most hon. the marquis of Salisbury*, 24 vols., HMC, 9 (1883–1976), vols. 17–18 • H. Foley, ed., *Records of the English province of the Society of Jesus*, 7 vols. in 8 (1875–83) • *John Gerard: the autobiography of an Elizabethan*, trans. P. Caraman (1951) • C. S. Durrant, *A link between Flemish mystics and English martyrs* (1925) • G. Anstruther, *Vaux of Harrowden: a recusant family* (1953) • Burke, *Peerage* • *Miscellanea, IX*, Catholic RS, 14 (1914) • L. C. Sheppard, *The English Carmelites* (1943) • T. Hunter, *An English Carmelite: the life of Catharine Burton, Mother Mary Xaviera of the angels, of the English Teresian convent at Antwerp*, ed. H. J. Coleridge and others (1876)

Lovel, Philip (*d.* 1258), administrator and royal counsellor, was a kinsman of the Lovels of Minster Lovell in Oxfordshire, perhaps a younger son of William Lovel (*d.* 1213); the kinship is proved by the fact that the manor of Snorscomb, Northamptonshire, in Philip's possession in 1257, passed after his death to John Lovel the justice, an illegitimate son of John Lovel of Minster Lovell (*d.* 1287). Before entering the church Philip Lovel had married and fathered at least three children. He first appears in 1223, as witness to a grant of property in Blewbury, Berkshire, involving Richard Poore, bishop of Salisbury (*d.* 1237), and had been ordained subdeacon by 1231/2, when he was presented to the living of Lutterworth in Leicestershire by Nicholas de Verdun. The Verduns were subtenants of the earls of Winchester, and it may have been through his Verdun connection that Lovel entered the service of Roger de Quincy, earl of Winchester, lord of Galloway, and constable of Scotland (*d.* 1264). He witnessed Earl Roger's charters from before 1240, and rose to become the earl's steward for his English estates, earning the favour of the Scottish royal family. In 1246/7 he obtained promotion to the church of Hanslope at the presentation of William Mauduit, chamberlain of the English royal exchequer, which suggests that he was already active on the fringes of the court. By the time of his death, he was also rector of Stanground in Huntingdonshire, and of Rock in Worcestershire, and was a canon of London, with the prebends of Weldland (from *c.*1255) and (later) Islington.

By 1249 Lovel had entered court service and in November of that year, through the influence of John Mansel (*d.* 1265), was appointed a justice of the Jews. In 1250, styled clerk and counsellor of the king, he took the cross but did not go on crusade. At Michaelmas next year he was accused of taking bribes from various wealthy Jews of the north of England, in return for a reduction in their liability for tallage, allegations which the chroniclers suggest were inspired by the personal rivalry of Robert de la Ho, another of the justices of the Jews. Lovel was briefly disgraced, but on offering a fine of 10 marks of gold, and through the mediation of John Mansel and Alexander III of Scotland, he recovered the king's favour. On 27 August 1252 he was appointed treasurer of the royal exchequer, again through Mansel's advice, and in 1255 he was appointed to an inquiry into the king's revenues and rights in eight midland counties, an inquiry he is said to have conducted with great harshness. In 1257 Henry III unsuccessfully petitioned the monks of Coventry to elect Lovel as their bishop. His years as treasurer coincided with a crisis in royal finance, resulting in the levying of forced loans, harsh exploitation of Jewish debt, and a great increase in the sums demanded from the king's sheriffs. In the early stages of the baronial reform movement Lovel was allowed to retain his offices, but in October 1258 he was arraigned on a series of trumped-up charges relating to his infringement of forest law, and on 2 November 1258 he was replaced as treasurer by a candidate more acceptable to the baronial council. He was handed over to the keeping of the earl marshal, but released on the payment of large sums of money. He retired to his rectory of Hanslope, where he died on 29 December 1258, through vexation at the king's refusal of reconciliation, according to Matthew Paris. His estates at Little Brickhill in Buckinghamshire, Littlebury in Essex, Dunton in Warwickshire, and Snorscomb in Northamptonshire, for the most part acquired by purchase after 1252, were seized by the crown, but were eventually divided between his kinsman John and his own three children, Philip the younger, Amicia, the wife of Richard de Curzon of Derbyshire, and Master Henry Lovel, a clerk who served as his father's executor.

NICHOLAS VINCENT

Sources *Chancery records* (RC) • *Pipe rolls* • Paris, *Chron.* • W. P. W. Phillimore and others, eds., *Rotuli Hugonis de Welles, episcopi Lincolniensis*, CYS, 1, 3 (1907–9) • F. N. Davis, ed., *Rotuli Roberti Grosseteste, episcopi Lincolniensis*, CYS, 10 (1913) • F. N. Davis and others, eds., *Rotuli Ricardi Gravesend, diocesis Lincolniensis*, CYS, 31 (1925) • *Ann. mon.* • *CEPR letters*, vol. 1 • G. Wrottesley, 'Plea rolls, *temp.* Henry III', *Collections for a history of Staffordshire*, William Salt Archaeological Society, 4/1 (1883), 1–215 • GEC, *Peerage* • W. H. Rich Jones, ed., *Vetus registrum sarisberiense alias dictum registrum S. Osmundi episcopi: the register of St Osmund*, 2 vols., Rolls Series, 78 (1883–4) • W. H. Rich Jones and W. Dunn Macray, eds., *Charters and documents illustrating the history of the cathedral, city, and diocese of Salisbury, in the twelfth and thirteenth centuries*, Rolls Series, 97 (1891) • A. M. S. Leys, ed., *The Sandford cartulary*, 2 vols., Oxfordshire RS, 19, 22 (1938–41) • J. M. Rigg, ed., *Calendar of the plea rolls of the exchequer of the Jews*, Jewish Historical Society, 1 (1905) • E. Stokes and F. C. Wellstood, eds., *Warwickshire feet of fines*, 1, Dugdale Society, 11 (1932) • M. W. Hughes, ed., *A calendar of the feet of fines for the county of Buckinghamshire*, Buckinghamshire RS, 4 (1940, [1942]) • G. G. Simpson, 'The "familia" of Roger de Quincy, earl of Winchester and constable of Scotland', *Essays on the nobility of medieval Scotland*, ed. K. J. Stringer (1985)

Lovelace. For this title name *see* individual entries under Lovelace; *see also* Byron, (Augusta) Ada [(Augusta) Ada King, countess of Lovelace] (1815–1852); Milbanke, Ralph Gordon Noel King, second earl of Lovelace (1839–1906).

Lovelace, Francis (*c.*1621–1675), colonial governor, was the fourth of eight children of Sir William Lovelace (*bap.* 1584, *d.* 1627), politician and army officer, of Bethersden and Woolwich, Kent, and Anne (*d.* 1633), daughter of Sir William Barne and his wife, Anne Sandys. Lovelace was a zealous supporter of Charles I in the English civil war, serving as a colonel in the royalist forces. In June 1644 he was appointed governor of Carmarthen Castle in Wales. He lost the castle to parliamentary forces in October 1645, after a sharp fight in which his brother William was killed. Another brother, Richard *Lovelace, the cavalier poet, memorialized these events in *Lucasta*. For a time he served on the continent with his brothers Richard and Dudley in the forces of Louis XIV, then in 1650 joined his sister Anne Gorsuch in Virginia. When the colony was seized by parliamentary commissioners in 1652, Governor Sir William Berkeley dispatched him to France to inform Charles II. In 1658 he returned to England to aid the royalist cause. About a year later he secretly married Blanche Talbot. They had two children. On 5 August 1659 he was arrested and thrown into the Tower of London, but was freed in 1660 when Charles II ascended the throne.

In the years following the Restoration, Lovelace apparently lived in London and worked for the Admiralty. He appears to have been appointed deputy governor of Long Island in 1665 but it is unclear if he took up the post. In 1667 he succeeded Richard Nicolls as governor of New York. Samuel Maverick, a New Englander in high standing with the royalists, had recommended Lovelace to the earl of Clarendon, lord high chancellor, as a person eminently qualified for the office. A contemporary newsletter announcing the appointment mistakenly identified him as the brother of Lord Lovelace, which has led to him being confused with his near contemporary Francis Lovelace, son of Richard, first Baron Lovelace of Hurley, who died in 1673. On 13 June 1667 Lovelace was commissioned lieutenant-colonel in Sir Walter Vane's regiment. He arrived in New York in March 1668, and spent the summer receiving instruction from Nicolls in his new duties. In August he assumed full powers, attempting to maintain English authority over the diverse Dutch, Swedish, and English populations while keeping frictions to a minimum. Unlike Nicolls, he held regular council meetings, but usually did not follow the councillors' advice. Recognizing the religious diversity among New Yorkers, he guaranteed them liberty of conscience, 'provided they raise not fundamentalls'. He expressed his concern for the American Indians by sending missionaries among them and by paying them for Staten Island. He stimulated prosperity by developing land and water transportation, founding new townships, establishing a merchants' exchange, and regularizing postal service between New York and Boston. Looking to the colony's defences, he organized infantry and militia companies and enlarged New York's fortifications.

Over the years Lovelace's conduct in office was generally prudent and cautious, but difficulties mounted. He had altercations with neighbouring colonies over borders, and in 1672 had to contend with a political uprising in New Jersey. Frontier Indians were a continual concern; on one occasion he rushed troops to Esopus to defend settlers. His colony was rent by religious and cultural squabbles between fractious nationalities, and he lived in constant dread of Dutch invasion. He sometimes acted unilaterally, without taking into account the wishes of the Dutch residents. In 1672 he refused to entertain citizens' demands for a representative assembly, and, when they in turn communicated their refusal to pay taxes, 'he was so wroth he ordered the papers publicly burned'. A year later, while he was visiting Connecticut, a Dutch fleet seized New York with little opposition, and he was arrested and shipped off to England.

Lovelace was not responsible for this loss, but he was undone by it. Dutch creditors seized his New York property, and the duke of York confiscated his English estates for a debt of £7000. Other creditors enmeshed him for years in litigation. In January 1675 he was imprisoned in the Tower, and on 2 and 9 March 1675 crown officials questioned him about the loss of New York. His answers were deemed unacceptable, but the matter was not pursued and he was released in April because of his health. He retreated to Woodstock, Oxfordshire, where he had died by 22 December 1675, when administration of his estate was granted to his brother Dudley, a further administration being granted on 10 May 1686 to his sister Joan Caesar. PAUL DAVID NELSON

Sources E. B. O'Callaghan, ed., *Documentary history of the state of New York*, vol. 1 (1849) • E. B. O'Callaghan and B. Fernow, eds., *Documents relative to the colonial history of the state of New York*, vol. 2 (1858); vols. 3–4, 9 (1854–5) • 'The Golden letters on Smith's history', *Collections of the New-York Historical Society for the year 1868* (1868), 177–235 • 'The Clarendon papers', *Collections of the New York Historical Society* (1869) [whole issue] • B. Fernow, ed., *Records of New Amsterdam*, vols. 6–7 (1897) • V. H. Palsits, ed., *Minutes of the executive council of the province of New York: administration of Francis Lovelace, 1668–1673*, 2 vols. (1910) • E. Doremus, *Lovelace chart* (1900?) • *The manuscripts of S. H. Le Fleming*, HMC, 25 (1890) • E. C. Delavan, *Colonel Francis Lovelace and his plantation on Staten Island* (1902) • J. H. Pleasants, 'Francis Lovelace, governor of New York, 1668–1673', *New York Genealogical and Biographical Record*, 51 (1920), 175–94 • J. Brodhead, *History of the state of New York*, 2 (1871) • B. Lossing, *History of New York City*, vol. 1 (1884) • P. D. Nelson, 'Lovelace, Francis', *ANB* • E. H. Roberts, *New York: the planting and the growth of the empire state*, vol. 1 (1892) • J. Overton, *Long Island's story* (1929) • R. Gilder, *The battery* (1936) • V. H. Palsits, 'Lovelace, Francis', *DAB* • administration, PRO, PROB 6/50, fol. 151v; 6/62, fol. 76v • J. W. Raimo, *Biographical directory of American colonial and revolutionary governors, 1607–1789* (1980), 240

Archives PRO, Colonial Office MSS

Wealth at death see Palsits, 'Lovelace, Francis'

Lovelace, John, third Baron Lovelace (*c*.1640–1693), politician, was the only son of John Lovelace, second Baron Lovelace (1615/16–1670), and his wife, Anne (*bap*. 1623, *d*. 1697), third daughter and ultimately coheir of Thomas *Wentworth, earl of Cleveland. His father supported the

John Lovelace, third Baron Lovelace (*c*.1640–1693), by Marcellus Laroon the elder, 1689

royalist cause during the English civil wars, much to his financial detriment, and subsequently served as lord lieutenant of Berkshire from the Restoration until 1668. His mother was the Lady Anne to whom Richard Lovelace dedicated his poem *Lucasta*.

Lovelace matriculated from Wadham College, Oxford, on 25 July 1655 (the same year that his father was briefly incarcerated in the Tower of London on suspicion of plotting against the government) and was created MA on 9 September 1661. He married Martha Pye (*c*.1642–1704?), the eldest daughter and coheir of Sir Edmund Pye, baronet, of Bradenham, Buckinghamshire, on 28 August 1662. Their only son died an infant; of three daughters—Anne, Martha, and Catherine—only Martha survived her father. She subsequently succeeded to the title of Baroness Wentworth upon the death of Lovelace's mother, while the Lovelace title passed to a collateral male heir, John Lovelace [*see below*], at the time of her father's death.

Country and whig politician Returned to the House of Commons in 1661 as one of the members for Berkshire, Lovelace's opposition to the hearth tax (which extended outside the house as far as beating up a collector) attracted a reference by Andrew Marvell in his 'Last instructions to a painter' (1667). In 1667 Lovelace was a teller against the bill imposing double taxation on nonconformists. Otherwise he seems not to have distinguished himself in the Commons and, notwithstanding these policy stands, both in

1664 and later in 1669–71 he was noted as a court dependent and supporter. After the death of his father in 1670, however, Lovelace took his seat in the House of Lords and by the end of the 1670s he had emerged as a leading whig partisan. In 1675 he was one of the country peers who voted against the government's attempt to impose an oath on all peers, MPs, and office-holders to forswear any attempt to alter the government of church or state. Two years later he was one of the two country peers who, like the duke of York (the future James II) and his supporters, dissented from the government's bill to impose limitations on a Catholic successor, but for very different reasons to theirs: to Lovelace, the bill provided too weak a bulwark against what a Catholic monarch could do.

Lovelace was an active participant in the upper chamber's continuing investigation of the Popish Plot in 1678 and 1679. At the local level, Anthony Wood reported sourly his success at influencing the election of whig burgesses at Oxford (and elsewhere) to the exclusion parliaments. Made a freeman of Oxford in the summer of 1680, Lovelace further scandalized Wood by drinking a health to the king at the entertainment that followed, and then, in a deliberate insult to the duke of York, a second health to the confusion of all popish princes. In September of the same year he arranged for the duke of Monmouth to visit Oxford, an occasion studiously ignored by the university community and the bishop of Oxford but one which prompted a considerable popular response. 'My Lord Lovelace', according to one report, 'rode all about the town shouting … he was for a Protestant Duke, no Papist, and God damn him, he was for the Protestant religion' (*Ormonde MSS*, new ser., 5.449). Lovelace was also a member of the Green Ribbon Club. Not surprisingly, tokens of royal displeasure multiplied over these years. In 1679 he lost his place as steward of Woodstock manor and park, to which he responded by inviting Titus Oates to preach there twice while attending the horse races as his guest. In 1680 he was removed from the commissions of the peace for both Berkshire and Oxfordshire and then two years later he was dropped from the deputy lieutenancy of Berkshire.

It has been suggested that Lovelace's political views, and perhaps also his outlook on religion, were shaped in his early youth by John Owen, the prominent Independent minister who had served as his father's chaplain. If so this would have depended on continuing links between Owen and the Lovelaces, as the clergyman had moved on from his chaplaincy when Lovelace was only a small child. The most that can be proved is that Lovelace had connections with the nonconformist leadership in Berkshire and Oxfordshire during the exclusion crisis, and that he continued to meet with Owen and others even after the dissolution of the third Exclusion Parliament in March 1681, with a view to preparing a suitable slate of candidates in case new elections were held. Such planning came to nothing after the revelations of the Rye House plot rapidly transformed the political landscape, and in early July 1683 Lovelace found himself briefly incarcerated in the Tower of London at the same time that William, Lord Russell, and a number of other whig extremists were arrested on charges of having participated in the plan to assassinate Charles II and his brother. Certainly Lovelace's penchant for political provocation was sufficient to have raised suspicions, but even in the charged atmosphere of the moment no solid evidence against him could be found. Released on bail after an appearance before the council, Lovelace was hardly intimidated by this brush with royal authority and was again in the newsletters in 1684 having tried, albeit unsuccessfully, to persuade both Oxford and Reading not to surrender their charters.

The revolution of 1688 His earlier support for Monmouth notwithstanding, Lovelace steered clear of any involvement in that duke's futile rebellion. However, his name subsequently appears on almost every list of those opposed to the policies of James II and, later, of those peers of the realm who might be expected to countenance a movement against the king. In February 1688 he again found himself hauled before the council, this time accused of telling some constables that they need not obey Roman Catholic justices of the peace. According to Lord Macaulay's version of the incident, Lovelace was closely examined but managed to extricate himself from trouble, although not before James personally taxed him severely for playing political tricks. Lovelace's record of rash behaviour and his reputation as a whig extremist probably account for the fact that he was not included in the early network of contacts established by the prince of Orange, but he was finally drawn into the conspiracy against James shortly after the die was cast by the dispatch of the invitation to William in late June. Tradition has it that, in a series of meetings held in the cellars of his house at Hurley, Lovelace plotted his part in the uprisings to occur when William landed. More certain is the fact that his high tolerance for risk was put to good use when he served as courier for a final round of messages from the prince to his associates in England. To this end, Lovelace left for the continent early in September, travelling on an official pass permitting him to go abroad to take the waters. Although a warrant for his arrest as an abetter of the prince was issued just after he returned at the end of the month, he successfully managed to drop out of sight.

Within a week after William landed at Torbay—well before most of the other principal conspirators were in motion—Lovelace gathered a party of some fifty horse made up of tenants and neighbours. From a staging point at Woodstock the group moved on to Cirencester to spend the night of 12 November, but there it encountered a detachment of militia horse sent out by the duke of Beaufort, perhaps the only lord lieutenant actually to make some effort to block supporters from reaching the prince. In one of the few violent encounters in England of the 'bloodless' revolution, a confused skirmish ensued during which the commander of the militia unit and his son were killed and Lovelace and several of his followers arrested; a few days later they were taken under close guard to Gloucester Castle. News of the affair circulated quickly and widely, with Lovelace's fate becoming a matter of some concern to both James and William at a point in time when many had yet to decide whether to take an active role in the events unfolding or, in some cases, which way to jump. According to the earl of Clarendon, James was anxious to have Lovelace sent to Salisbury, presumably so that an example could then be made of what would happen to anyone taking up arms against the king. William is also supposed to have made vigorous efforts to secure his release or at least to guarantee his personal safety, including a threat to burn Badminton as a way to put pressure on the duke of Beaufort. In the end Lovelace was freed by an advance party of troops accompanying Lord Delamer and the earl of Stamford on their march south to join the prince. James having long since withdrawn to London, it was apparently decided that Lovelace should take a party of men and occupy Oxford in anticipation of the arrival of Princess Anne and the sizeable force escorting her south from Nottingham. On 5 December Lovelace entered the city at the head of some 200 horse and was welcomed by the mayor and council and, with the writing on the wall, by the university community as well.

Last years In the Convention Parliament, Lovelace was a strong proponent of declaring the throne vacant and William and Mary king and queen, and he was suspected by Clarendon of having incited popular protests to accelerate the political process. Once the new regime was settled in, Lovelace was rewarded for his efforts almost immediately by appointment as captain of the band of gentlemen pensioners, a position that carried an annual stipend of £1000 and, more to the point, was sufficiently important to please Lovelace but also keep him well removed from the front lines of administration. He was also named chief justice in eyre of royal parks and forests south of Trent, a post largely without function but one with a variety of perquisites to supplement the annual salary of £165. That same spring a regiment of foot was raised in his name to be sent to Ireland, but it was poorly officered and organized from the first and was disbanded within less than a year. Both in 1689 and 1690 Lovelace was active in the House of Lords, taking an interest in legislation intended to improve the lot of dissenters, to protect the rights of peers, and generally to set right the wrongs of the past decade. As the record of his protests reveal, he not infrequently ended up voting with a small minority of the more radical whigs when it came to matters such as the attempt to pass a bill reversing the 1685 conviction of Titus Oates for perjury or abolishing the strictures of the Test Act for the benefit of the protestant nonconformists.

Although he cut a dashing figure during his time, Lovelace's political extravagance and flaws of character were such that neither contemporary chroniclers nor more recent commentators have always treated him kindly. Elias Ashmole used the phrase 'vitae virtutis degener heres' ('a moral degenerate, you cling to a life of virtue') to signal his conflicted view of this intemperate whig partisan who almost certainly was an alcoholic as well as a compulsive gambler and given to sexual excess (Ashmole, 2.478). Thomas Hearne weighs in with the opinion that he was 'a Man of good natural parts, but of very ill and very loose principle' (T. Hearne, *Remarks*, ed. C. E. Doble, 3, 1889, 349). Hearne then goes on to report hearsay to the effect that Lovelace was rarely sober, a point echoed on more than one occasion by Narcissus Luttrell and other observers of the period. Certainly Lovelace wasted whatever remained of his patrimony, and after his death the estate at Hurley was sold for £41,000 by order of the court of chancery to help pay off accumulated debts. In spite of his personal failings, however, it would be a mistake to dismiss Lovelace as no more than a Restoration rake. He contributed significantly to one extreme in the political dialogue of the period, used his personal popularity and public flair effectively to rally support for the whig cause before and during the revolution of 1688, and played a role of some substance in the overthrow of James II. Only in the year or two before he died in London on 27 September 1693 did his personal habits and declining health overwhelm all capacity for effective action. He died at Lincoln's Inn Fields and he was buried at Hurley on 6 October 1693.

John Lovelace, fourth Baron Lovelace Lovelace was succeeded in the peerage by a second cousin, another **John Lovelace**, fourth Baron Lovelace (*d.* 1709), army officer and colonial administrator. He was the son and heir of William Lovelace (*d.* 1676) of Hurst, Berkshire, and grandson of Francis Lovelace, the second son of the first baron. His mother, Mary, was the sister and co-heir of Sir Edward Nevill, baronet, of Grove, Nottinghamshire. A chance contemporary reference suggests a birth date sometime during the decade before his father's death in 1676. About 20 October 1702 Lovelace married Charlotte Clayton (*d.* 1749), daughter of Sir John Clayton of Richmond, Surrey. The couple had four children: three sons—John, Nevill, and Charles—and a daughter, Martha.

Lovelace inherited little but a title from his cousin and was reputed to be of relatively modest means himself. He took his seat in the House of Lords on 11 November 1693 but was not very active politically. None the less, the family's whig connection was sufficiently strong to secure him a series of appointments in the military, starting in the Life Guards in 1699 and then as colonel of his own regiment of foot in 1706. Two years later Lovelace was appointed governor of New York and New Jersey as replacement for Lord Cornbury, an administrator singularly deficient in talent and much disliked. (Lovelace was, incidentally, no relation of the Francis Lovelace who had served as governor of New York some forty years earlier.) He first arrived in the New World in the late autumn of 1708 after a difficult transatlantic crossing. He adopted a conciliatory stance with his constituents, even allowing the assemblies in both colonies for the first time to make specific appropriations of tax revenues rather than simply delivering up a lump sum to the governor. However, his death from a stroke on 6 May 1709 cut short Lovelace's administrative career at too early a stage for there to be a record of significant accomplishment or any challenge to his initial popularity. Six days later, after a funeral at Trinity Church, New York, Lovelace was buried in the churchyard there. DAVID HOSFORD

Sources N. Luttrell, *A brief historical relation of state affairs from September 1678 to April 1714*, 6 vols. (1857), vols. 1–2 · *The life and times of Anthony Wood*, ed. A. Clark, 2, OHS, 21 (1892), 250, 308; 3, OHS, 26 (1894) · *The manuscripts of S. H. Le Fleming*, HMC, 25 (1890) · *CSP dom.*, 1682–4; 1689–93 · *The manuscripts of the House of Lords*, 4 vols., HMC, 17 (1887–94), vol. 1 · *Calendar of the manuscripts of the marquess of Ormonde*, new ser., 8 vols., HMC, 36 (1902–20) · J. E. Thorold Rogers, ed., *Complete collection of the protests of the Lords*, 3 vols. (1875), vol. 1 · E. Ashmole, *The antiquities of Berkshire*, 2 (1719) · D. Lacey, *Dissent and parliamentary politics in England, 1660–1689* (1969) · E. Chamberlayne, *Angliae Notitia* (1692) · C. Dalton, ed., *English army lists and commission registers, 1661–1714*, 6 vols. (1892–1904) · W. Smith, *The history of the province of New-York* (1757); repr. M. Kammen, ed., 2 (New York, 1972) · E. P. Tawney, *Province of New Jersey* (1908) · letter re Lovelace's appearance before privy council, BL, Add. MS 34515, fol. 57r · GEC, *Peerage* · HoP, *Commons, 1660–90* · A. Swatland, *The House of Lords in the reign of Charles II* (1996) · D. L. Kemmerer, *Path to freedom: the struggle for self-government in colonial New Jersey, 1703–1776* (1940)

Archives Berks. RO, marriage settlement papers · BL, corresp. and papers, Add. MS 63465 · Bodl. Oxf., letters to the officers of the ordnance and Sir Henry Goodricke

Likenesses M. Laroon the elder, oils, 1689, Wadham College, Oxford [*see illus.*]

Wealth at death see Ashmole, *Antiquities of Berkshire*, vol. 2; GEC, *Peerage*

Lovelace, John, fourth Baron Lovelace (*d.* 1709). *See under* Lovelace, John, third Baron Lovelace (*c.*1640–1693).

Lovelace, Richard (1618–1657), poet and army officer, was the eldest of five sons and three daughters of Sir William Lovelace (*bap.* 1584, *d.* 1627) of Woolwich, Kent, and his wife, Anne Barne (*d.* 1633). No record of the birth exists among the parish registers of Kent, where the Lovelaces had been an established Bethersden family since the reign of Edward III, and possibly Richard was born in the Netherlands during his father's military service. Before Captain Lovelace lost his life at the August 1627 siege of Grol, the man whom James I knighted in 1609 had, as his widow notes, 'served about thirty yeares in the warres', part of which time she was with him 'in the Low Countries' (*Poems*, xvi). Later their son Richard would also live in the Netherlands; he too would follow the family tradition of military service. His grandfather Sir William Lovelace (1561–1629) had been knighted by the lord lieutenant of Ireland during Essex's 1599 Irish campaign; other forebears further justified the contemporary reputation of the Lovelaces as 'a Race of Gentlemen … who have in Military Affairs atcheived Reputation and Honour, with a prodigal Losse and Expence' (T. Philipot, *Villare Cantianum*, 1659, 72). Though Richard Lovelace's military exploits are largely unrecorded, chivalric honour has long been associated with his life and poetry.

Study at Oxford and Cambridge The essential source of his biography, Anthony Wood's account in *Athenae Oxonienses* (1691), states that Lovelace studied at Charterhouse School, though other than a 1629 petition of the widowed mother on behalf of 'one of hir Sonnes' no records have survived. A warrant in the Public Record Office dated 5 May 1631 does, however, document the appointment of

Richard Lovelace (1618–1657), attrib. William Dobson

Richard Lovelace to the honorary position of 'A Gent Wayter extraordinary' to the king (Berry and Timings, 396). He matriculated as a gentleman commoner at Gloucester Hall, Oxford, on 27 June 1634, 'being then accounted the most amiable and beautiful person that ever eye beheld, a person also of innate modesty, virtue and courtly deportment'; two years later he received a master of arts degree, not merely because he had won the favour of a 'great lady belonging to the queen' as Wood suggests (Wood, *Ath. Oxon.*, 3.460). Among the 'persons of quality' honoured with this degree on 31 August 1636 at the conclusion of Charles and Henrietta Maria's visit to Oxford, the strikingly handsome, remarkably prepossessing young man had by then shown a precocious literary promise by writing a comedy entitled *The Scholars*. The only parts of the play that remain, the prologue and epilogue, indicate that Henrietta Maria's company performed the comedy at Whitefriars, probably after late 1637, when the theatres closed by the plague reopened. Meanwhile, if Wood is correct, Lovelace 'retired in great splendor to the court'. But he did not abandon the scholarly world: at Cambridge his name was entered in the book of subscriptions on 4 October 1637.

During an indeterminate stay at Cambridge, Lovelace probably met Andrew Marvell and some of the other writers who later commended the publication of his first volume of poetry; his relationship with Oxford and the court, however, occasioned his first datable poems. An elegiac piece by 'Rich. Lovelace. Mag. Art. A. Glouc.' was added to the Oxford University collection of verse, *Musarum Oxoniensium Charisteria* (1639), commemorating the 20 January 1639 death of the infant Princess Catherine. Among the contributors was Anthony Hodges, whose translation of a Greek romance Lovelace had praised the year before in verses prefaced to its Oxford publication, and George Ashwell, perhaps the 'learned Friend' G. A. similarly honoured in another prefatory poem. Court connections may then have brought Lovelace and the earl of Norwich's son George, Lord Goring, together, for with the outbreak of the bishops' wars the former Oxford poet and playwright served in Goring's regiment as an ensign and later a captain. The royalist poem to General Goring written after the first Scottish expedition ended badly at Berwick in June 1639 softens the defeat of a peace achieved 'at the Foes rate' with rounds of drink celebrating the general and his wife Lettice. During the second unsuccessful campaign the next year Lovelace apparently expressed a more sombre note in *The Soldier*, an unpublished tragedy that was not staged before the theatres were closed in 1642 and was later lost.

'Confin'd to peace' during the civil war With the cessation of armed hostility Lovelace withdrew to Kent and his recently inherited family estate at Bethersden, where he became embroiled in the growing national conflict. On 29 April 1642 he and other young Kent royalists disrupted the Maidstone quarter sessions at which parliament supporters were discussing a response to the moderate Kentish petition advocating, among other local concerns, 'just and regal authority' (Everitt, 97). The intruders 'in a furious manner cried, "No, No, No", and then with great contempt of court clapped on their hats'; raising a copy of the parliamentarian counter petition above his head, Captain Richard Lovelace tore it to pieces (Steele Young and Snow, 2.249). At the head of between 280 and 500 Kent supporters, Lovelace then marched from Blackheath to London. The next day, 30 April, he and Sir William Boteler delivered to the House of Commons a petition similar to the one already burnt by the hangman. For their defiance Lovelace was sent to the Gatehouse at Westminster and Boteler committed to the Fleet. During the seven weeks spent in prison Lovelace possibly, though not probably, 'made that celebrated song called Stone Walls do not a Prison make, &c' (Wood, *Ath. Oxon.*, 3.461). A petition from prison written in his own hand does survive, however, requesting 'conditionall freedome' and the opportunity to serve 'his Kinge and Countrie' in Ireland (*Poems*, xxxviii–xxxix). After he was released on bail on 21 June his whereabouts are less certain.

Lovelace seems to have taken no active role in the military conflicts that threatened the monarchy; instead he appears to have been, in the words of his close friend and distant cousin Thomas Stanley,

> During our Civill Wars confin'd to peace,
> Expos'd to Forrein Wars, when ours did cease.
> (T. Stanley, 'Register of Friends', in *Poems and Translations*, ed. G. M. Crump, 1962, 360)

Part of that confinement was passed in London; there, Wood reports, Lovelace lived beyond his means 'by furnishing men with horse and arms, or by relieving ingenious men in want, whether scholars, musicians, soldiers, &c' (Wood, *Ath. Oxon.*, 3.462). His presence, if not his patronage, is apparent in the 1643 dedication to him of poems written by Henry Glapthorne, who the year before had named his daughter Lovelis. William Lawes also set three of Lovelace's lyrics to music during this period, and the first of the manuscript versions of 'To Althea, from Prison' began to circulate. But Lovelace did not remain solely in London. A poem, 'Upon my Noble Friend, *Richard Lovelace*', written no later than 1645 by John Tatham stresses the absence of the author's friend, 'his being in Holland' (J. Tatham, *Ostella*, 1650, 82–3). Another by Samuel Holland published in broadside recalls that France and Holland had found Lovelace 'excellent in Arms, and Art' ('On the Death of my much Honoured Friend, Colonel *Richard Lovelace*', 1660?). Although no record of military service in Holland has been found, he may have accompanied Goring on the mission in late 1642 to recruit volunteers from the English soldiers there. Lovelace's poem on the exiled queen of Bohemia's daughter Louise Hollandine does confirm his presence in The Hague, where his 'Art' might have been both developed and known. Unlike his brothers, one of whom was mortally wounded during a royalist campaign in Wales, he may well have taken up arms only in France. He was in the service of the French at Dunkirk, and Wood reports that he was wounded before the siege ended in October 1646.

Back in England by 1647, Lovelace seems to have been among the authors gathered at Stanley's Middle Temple chambers. By then the reputation of his 'Art' was not limited to poetry. Along with Peter Lely he and two others were given the freedom of the Painter–Stainers Company on 26 October 1647, the same year he contributed one of the poems prefaced to the folio edition of the plays of Beaumont and Fletcher. A year later, however, he was once again imprisoned and his lands sequestered. Some time in October, following a search of his lodging in connection with the 1648 uprising in Kent, he was committed to Peterhouse 'upon pretence of answering some matters contained in papers of his' (D. Gardiner, ed., *The Oxinden and Peyton Letters*, 1937, 145). While in prison, Wood believes, 'he fram'd … for the press' the collection dedicated to his relative Anne Lovelace entitled *Lucasta*.

The 1648 *Lucasta* The volume of poems licensed on 4 February 1648 and entered for publication on 14 May 1649, a month after Lovelace's release from Peterhouse, was not written during his incarceration; nor has the Lucasta said to have inspired them been identified with any certainty. The licensing implies the completion of a collection whose publication was delayed, Marvell speculates in one of the dedicatory poems, because Lovelace had supported the Kentish petition, 'wrong'd' the 'Houses Priviledge', and was now 'under sequestration'. The 'gentlewoman of great beauty and fortune named Lucy Sacheverel', who in Wood's account married soon after she heard falsely that Lovelace was fatally wounded at Dunkirk, appears at the very least to have been someone the poet knew, though the suggestions that she was the daughter of Ferdinando Sacheverel or a member of the Lucas family remain unsubstantiated. She is in the poetry 'Lucasta that Bright

Northerne Star', literally perhaps from the north but figuratively *lux casta* or pure light. As such she recalls William Habington's Castara and to a lesser extent Edmund Waller's Sacharissa or Thomas Carew's Caelia. Among the other verses in the volume to Althea, Amarantha, Ellinda, and Gratiana, those to Lucasta are not limited to deft variations of Petrarchan conventions or graceful formulations of Caroline compliment. Her symbolic light illuminates a darkening world of civil conflict.

The love and honour commonly associated with Lovelace's cavalier loyalties and unmistakable in the initial poems addressed to Lucasta 'Going beyond the Seas' and 'Going to the Warres' are distinctly Caroline and chivalric. Lucasta resembles the transcendence and inspiration celebrated in the court masques; the lovers' world of Mars and Venus recalls on a lesser scale the valour of Rubens's *Landscape with St. George and the Dragon*. The royal dimensions of her radiance and his own devotion are explicit in a poem written about the time of the Kentish petitions, 'To Lucasta: from Prison'. England itself metaphorically becomes the prison, and the king both displaces and merges with Lucasta as the light that might dispel the enveloping world of darkness. By the end of the volume in 'Calling Lucasta from her Retirement' a triumphant Lucasta assumes the mythic proportions accorded the royal couple in the Whitehall masques; the hope that she too can reorder the world is, however, now limited to the realm of the lovers. Ultimately the long pastoral 'Amarantha' added to the completed collection abandons the world of Mars and its honour for the love the poems have come to value more.

Though Lovelace recognizes the destruction and futility of civil war, the poems in *Lucasta* never forsake a loyalist commitment, embracing neutralism or succumbing to disillusionment. The poem he allegedly wrote in the Gatehouse, 'To Althea, from Prison', stoically sings the goodness and greatness of the king. 'Stone Walls' and 'Iron bars' cannot confine 'Mindes innocent and quiet'. It is a belief affirmed in his complex royalist tribute to the image of Charles and his son James captured by Peter Lely in the portrait painted at Hampton Court by late 1647. The tacit recognition of the king's separation from his wife adds a poignant note to the heroic resolve Lovelace sees in 'griefe triumphant' despite 'clouded Majesty'. Earlier he encouraged Francis Lovelace to accept the battlefield death of their brother William with a similar 'firme selfe' and 'thorough-made Resolve'. Caught now in the bleak winter realities of 'The Grasse-hopper', a poem fraught with royalist overtones, Lovelace assures Charles Cotton that together they can recreate 'A Genuine Summer in each others breast'. The friendship, abundant wine, and good poetry celebrated in this justly famous poem are meant to sustain the spirits of loyalists forced to turn inward.

The posthumous poems The volume of poetry entered in the Stationers' register on 14 November 1659 and published posthumously the next year by Lovelace's brother Dudley Posthumus and Eldred Revett reflects the suffering brought about by the civil war. Lovelace had sold the Bethersden property, Lovelace Place, to Richard Hulse in 1649, and his diminished fortunes and whereabouts after his release from prison remain largely unresolved. He may have been in Holland during part of this time; later in London he might have been subjected to the searches in 1656 for royalists in the city who had not posted required securities. *Lucasta: Posthume Poems* and its appended *Elegies Sacred to the Memory of the Author* question, at the very least, the image Wood creates of an increasingly melancholic author reduced to dependence upon the charity of his friends before he died of consumption in 1657 amid the squalor of Gunpowder Alley and was buried in nearby St Bride's. None of the elegies mentions the dire straits, which Wood elsewhere says are the curse of poets; the various poems Lovelace addressed to his peers in the last years of his life suggest, moreover, that he was neither isolated nor disconsolate, though his tribute to Charles Cotton and especially the long final poem on Sanazar may convey personal dismay about the lot of the writer. An allusion to William Davenant in the Sanazar satire and the dating of Revett's elegy on Lovelace, in any event, indicate that the poet died in 1657 (Duncan-Jones, 408–9; *Poems*, liv). Whether his final days were spent in Gunpowder Alley, Long Acre, or the Strand, as other contemporaries report, his life after the king's execution and his release from prison altered but did not entirely transform his spirited convictions.

Though the much less familiar poems in Lovelace's posthumous collection were long ignored as decidedly inferior, their increasing sense of detachment and even alienation provides a valuable complement to the first volume. Lucasta's light belongs to the initial poems, her radiance now dimmer and more limited. Opposing her invitation to sportful play in the last of the Lucasta poems is the austere ant, an obvious counterpart to the grasshopper. In a significant series of poems the fates of the ant, the fly, the spider, the falcon, and the toad bleakly underscore the realization that all are caught up in consuming forces, destroyed as they themselves destroy. Without the conviviality celebrated in the earlier poems, libertine abandonment is attractive; the graceful saraband of the previous volume becomes a drunken dance suited to a reeling world scornful of honour. An alternative, however, is the composure of the self-contained snail and the brave struggle of the dying falcon to rise triumphant. In a benighted and treacherous world Lovelace can still counsel his brother Francis once again to defy fate; he also sees in Charles Cotton a semblance of the enclosed life celebrated in the earlier grasshopper poem addressed to Cotton's father. While the optimism is tempered, the final poem, 'On Sanazar's being Honoured', nevertheless invokes a spirit of stoic integrity despite isolation and rejection.

Together the two volumes of *Lucasta* modify the long-established impression that Lovelace is an uneven, careless poet who wrote several memorable verses. The handsome features in the Dulwich portrait, a painting that re-enforces a common comparison to Sir Philip Sidney, only adds to the romantic biography of a dashing poet driven by his lofty ideals to imprisonment, poverty, and early death. The poems themselves, especially those in the posthumous publication, challenge the stereotype of chivalric love and cavalier honour. Sensitive to the earlier writing of John Donne as well as Ben Jonson and an influence on the verse of Andrew Marvell, Richard Lovelace embodied in his life and poetry the loyalties, conflicts, and violent loss of the Caroline world.

The two volumes of *Lucasta* are the only legacy of the poet who never married; contemporary paintings, engravings, and songs, however, further confirm the spirit of his life and poetry. Besides the portrait of 'Colonel Lovelace' in the Dulwich Picture Gallery, an oil painting at Worcester College, Oxford, attributed to John de Critz is said to be the young Lovelace richly robed in the academic regalia of the Oxford MA. A Wenceslaus Hollar engraving depicts Lovelace in his early twenties; another Hollar engraving of the poet drawn by his brother Francis appears in *Lucasta: Posthume Poems*. Lovelace is also seen as Orpheus in an engraving attributed to Richard Gaywood, and engraved variations of the Dulwich portrait exist. Musicians Lovelace knew at court or in private circles set sixteen of the poems in *Lucasta* to music; many of the songs in the settings of Henry Lawes, Thomas Charles, John Gamble, John Cave, and John Wilson are reprinted in Wilkinson's 1925 Oxford edition and in a series of articles by Willa McClung Evans. Numerous twentieth-century musical transcriptions and recordings attest to the enduring attraction of Richard Lovelace's lyric poetry.

RAYMOND A. ANSELMENT

Sources Wood, *Ath. Oxon.*, new edn • *Brief lives, chiefly of contemporaries, set down by John Aubrey, between the years 1669 and 1696*, ed. A. Clark, 2 vols. (1898) • *The poems of Richard Lovelace*, ed. C. H. Wilkinson (1953) • A. E. Waite, 'Richard Lovelace', *GM*, 257 (1884), 459–77 • A. J. Pearman, 'The Kentish family of Lovelace', *Archaeologia Cantiana*, 10 (1876), 184–220 • A. J. Pearman, 'The Kentish family of Lovelace', *Archaeologia Cantiana*, 20 (1893), 54–63 • R. A. Anselment, 'Richard Lovelace and the "gallant thorough-made resolve"', in R. A. Anselment, *Loyalist resolve: patient fortitude in the English civil war* (1988) • T. N. Corns, *Uncloistered virtue: English political literature, 1640–1660* (1992) • G. Hammond, 'Richard Lovelace and the uses of obscurity', *PBA*, 71 (1985), 203–34 • M. Weidhorn, *Richard Lovelace* (1970) • H. M. Margoliouth, review of *The poems of Richard Lovelace*, ed. C. H. Wilkinson, *Review of English Studies*, 3 (1927), 89–95 • W. C. Hazlitt, ed., *Lucasta* (1864) • A. Everitt, *The community of Kent and the great rebellion, 1640–60* (1966) • A. Steele Young and V. F. Snow, eds., *The private journals of the Long Parliament*, 2: *7 March to 1 June 1642* (1987) • H. Berry and E. K. Timings, 'Lovelace at court and a version of his "The scrutinie"', *Modern Language Notes*, 69 (1954), 396–8 • E. E. Duncan-Jones, 'Two allusions in Lovelace's poems', *Modern Language Review*, 51 (1956), 407–9 • W. A. Shaw, *The knights of England*, 2 vols. (1906) • Foster, *Alum. Oxon.* • Venn, *Alum. Cant.* • G. E. Bentley, *The Jacobean and Caroline stage*, 7 vols. (1941–68), vol. 4, p. 724

Archives Worcester College, Oxford, letters to Matthew Parker

Likenesses attrib. J. de Critz, oils, Worcester College, Oxford • attrib. W. Dobson, oils, Dulwich Picture Gallery, London [*see illus.*] • attrib. R. Gaywood, etching (as Orpheus), BM • W. Hollar, engraving, BM • W. Hollar, engraving (after bust by F. Lovelace) • W. Hollar, etching, BM • F. Lovelace, pen-and-ink drawing (after unknown artist), NPG • portraits, repro. in C. H. Wilkinson, ed., *The poems of Richard Lovelace* (1925)

Wealth at death died in abject poverty: Wood, *Ath. Oxon*

Loveless, George (1797–1874), leader of the 'Tolpuddle martyrs', was born in Tolpuddle, Dorset, the seventh of the ten surviving children of Thomas Loveless, a labourer, and his wife, Dinah. From boyhood he worked on local farms and became an itinerant Methodist preacher. During the suppression of the agrarian unrest of 1830 he attempted, unsuccessfully, to improve the wages of labourers around Dorchester. Concluding that 'it would be vain to seek redress either of employers, magistrates or parsons' (Selley, 14), he formed a Friendly Society of Agricultural Labourers in Tolpuddle in October 1833. Its modest objectives were to be pursued peacefully, and the society would 'not countenance any violation of the laws' (15).

The repeal of the Combination Acts in 1824–5 had given trade unions a precarious legality, and Loveless's initiative was apparently protected. However, a resurgence of working-class agitation during 1833–4 alarmed the whig government and the propertied classes in general. The home secretary, William Lamb, second Viscount Melbourne, and many other landowners were anxious to stifle any revival of agrarian disorder, and the men of Tolpuddle became their first victims [*see also* Tolpuddle Martyrs].

On 21 February 1834 the Dorchester magistrates, having consulted Melbourne, declared that membership of the tiny society was a crime, and Loveless was arrested and accused of administering oaths illegal under largely forgotten statutes of 1797 and 1819. This charge, designed to circumvent the repeal of the Combination Acts, was technically defensible in that most trade unions, oblivious of the possible consequences, still imposed such oaths. The subsequent trial was a travesty, and, as a deterrent, an inexperienced judge sentenced Loveless and his five associates to seven years' transportation. Within weeks they were sent to Australia, where they suffered many privations.

What Sidney and Beatrice Webb saw as 'a scandalous perversion of the law' (Webb, Webb, and Peddie, 130) led to an outcry that coincided with the dramatic emergence of the short-lived Grand National Consolidated Trades Union founded by Robert Owen, which organized a massive protest in London on 21 April 1834. Loveless's cause was also taken up by defenders ranging from William Cobbett and Edward Bulwer Lytton (later first Baron Lytton) to Joseph Hume and Daniel O'Connell. With their support, the London Dorchester Committee, under the future Chartist William Lovett, persuaded the home secretary, Lord John Russell, to pardon the 'martyrs' in March 1836.

Loveless returned to England in June 1837 and the committee, financed by working-class subscriptions, leased an Essex farm for his family. He then wrote two dignified pamphlets, *The Victims of Whiggery* (1837) and *The Church Shown up* (1838), which revealed his commitment to a moderate, anti-Anglican radicalism.

In 1824 Loveless married Elizabeth Snook Sprachlen (*d.* 1868) of Dewlish, Dorset. They had five children. In 1846 they emigrated to Canada, settling near London, Ontario, where Loveless died on 6 May 1874, in very prosperous circumstances. He was buried in Siloam cemetery. For a generation he and his fellow 'martyrs' were forgotten men, but by the end of the century their brief celebrity had become a hallowed memory. Loveless, imposing and eloquent, critical of landlords and farmers, lay and ecclesiastical, was enshrined as a working-class hero, his *cause célèbre* revered as an emotive moment in the development of trade unionism. A. F. THOMPSON, *rev.*

Sources S. J. Webb, B. P. Webb, and R. A. Peddie, *The history of trade unionism* (1894) • E. Selley, *Village trade unions in two centuries* (1919) • J. Marlow, *The Tolpuddle Martyrs* (1971)
Likenesses engraving, pubd 1838, Mitchell L., NSW; *see illus. in* Tolpuddle Martyrs (*act.* 1834–*c.*1845)

Loveless, James (**1808–1873**). *See under* Tolpuddle Martyrs (*act.* 1834–*c.*1845).

Loveling, Benjamin (*b.* **1711**), poet, was baptized on 17 July 1711 at Banbury, Oxfordshire, where his father, Benjamin Loveling (*fl.* 1690–1727), was incumbent. He was educated at Winchester College (1722?–1727) and at Trinity College, Oxford, where he matriculated as a commoner on 13 July 1728; he left without taking a degree. After this little is known about his life. Nichols claims Loveling 'was ordained deacon, lived gaily and died young' (p. 30), while Dr Johnson possibly had Loveling in mind when describing 'a wit about town, who wrote Latin bawdy verse' (J. Boswell, *Life*, 16 Oct 1769).

Clues to Loveling's later life must be gleaned from his collection of Latin and English verse, *Poems by a Gentleman of Trinity College, Oxford* (1738 and 1741), which hints at an uproarious existence in London. His chief occupations appear to have been boozing and whoring, and his poetry catalogues in salacious detail the pleasures available in Drury Lane brothels. However, it seems Loveling was forced to leave London for a lengthy exile in the country, perhaps in Northamptonshire. His reasons for fleeing the city are unclear; if he was not avoiding imprisonment for debt, he might have been trying to escape his wearing lifestyle. Indeed, his friend Thomas Gilbert cites:

> This strange apostasy from wine
> Which makes the dullest genius shine

worrying lest it should 'lessen your poetic merit' (*Poems on Several Occasions*, 1747, 254). In addition to a poetic correspondence with Gilbert, Loveling penned verse epistles to other friends, in which the exile's melancholy in 'loca deliciis invidiosa meis' ('places hostile to my pleasures') mellows to Arcadian delight:

> Pars nulla immensi ridet mihi gratior orbis,
> Non habet angellum terra Britanna parem
> ('I love nowhere as much in the whole wide world,
> no corner of Britain is its equal.')

Some of the pieces are by other poets (for example, Anthony Alsop), and the longest one in the book, 'Baptizatio rustica' ('A country baptism'), was probably the same as 'Festum lustrale, sive, Baptizatio rustica', published ten years earlier at the end of William Pattison's posthumous *Poetical Works* (1728). Loveling's *Imitation of Persius' First Satire* (1741) is a short, derivative tract expressing hackneyed oppositional ideas, which nevertheless shows some skill in creative translation.

Loveling's licentiousness is mitigated by the genuine depth of feeling he exhibits for the Hogarthian *demimonde* of his urban poetry. His admirable command of Latin versification owes its greatest debt to Horace, which is visible in an occasional overreliance on direct borrowings. This notwithstanding, picturesque passages from his rural poetry prove that it did not need the impetus of alcohol. ROSS KENNEDY

Sources Foster, *Alum. Oxon.* • J. Nichols, *Biographical anecdotes of William Hogarth, and a catalogue of his works chronologically arranged with occasional remarks*, 3rd edn (1785), 30 • T. F. Kirby, *Winchester scholars: a list of the wardens, fellows, and scholars of … Winchester College* (1888) • C. W. Holgate and H. Chitty, eds., *Winchester long rolls, 1723–1821* (1904) • *IGI* • A. Beesley, *The history of Banbury* (1841), 150 • C. S. Dessen, 'An eighteenth-century imitation of Persius, *Satire I*', *Texas Studies in Language and Literature*, 20 (1978), 433–56 • *N&Q*, 7th ser., 7 (1889), 49 • *N&Q*, 12th ser., 11 (1922), 269, 414

Lovell, Daniel (*d.* **1818**), journalist, was for many years proprietor and editor of *The Statesman* (1806–24), a radical daily newspaper projected in 1806 by John Hunt. His outspoken criticism of the tories subjected him to much government persecution. In 1811 he was sentenced to twelve months' imprisonment for copying the remarks of the Manchester papers on the conduct of the troops at Sir Francis Burdett's arrest, while the originators of the libel were only called upon to express regret at their carelessness.

In August 1812 Lovell was tried and found guilty of a libel on the commissioners of the transport service. He pleaded that it was published without his knowledge or sanction while he was in prison, but was sentenced to pay a fine of £500, to be imprisoned in Newgate for eighteen months, and to find securities for three years, £1000 on his own account and two sureties of £500 each. Unable to pay the fine or find sureties, he remained in gaol.

At last on 23 November 1814, Samuel Whitbread MP presented a petition from Lovell asking for a remission or reduction of his fine, and after some time the government remitted the fine and reduced the amount of security; but he was still unable to obtain this, and on 17 March 1815 Whitbread again presented a petition from him, stating his complete inability to obtain the required security, and seeking the merciful consideration of the house of his sorry condition, having been confined nearly four years in Newgate. He was finally released, broken in health and financially ruined.

In 1817 Lovell was again heavily fined for speaking of the ministerial evening journal as 'the prostituted *Courier*, the venerable apostate of tyranny and oppression, whose full-blown baseness and infamy held him fast to his present connections and prevented him from forming new ones', while he further accused the editor, Daniel Stuart, of pocketing £600 or £700 of the Society of the Friends of the People. Lovell died in Salisbury Court, Fleet Street, London—probably his business address—on 27 December

1818, shortly after selling *The Statesman* to Sampson Perry, formerly editor of *The Argus*.

In his will, Lovell bequeathed an annuity of £50 yearly to Ann Field, formerly Ann Hill, of whom he speaks as 'now residing with me'. This wording indicates that it was unlikely that they were married, although Lovell goes on to speak of their son and daughter, born in 1810 and 1814 respectively. GORDON GOODWIN, *rev.* JOHN D. HAIGH

Sources *GM*, 1st ser., 88/2 (1818), 647 • K. Gilmartin, *Print politics: the press and radical opposition in early nineteenth-century England* (1996) • H. R. Fox Bourne, *English newspapers: chapters in the history of journalism*, 1 (1887), 368 • A. Andrew, *The history of British journalism*, 2 vols. (1859), 2.71, 91, 98 • will, PRO, PROB 11/1613, sig. 77
Archives Beds. & Luton ARS, letters to Samuel Whitbread
Wealth at death financially ruined: will, PRO, PROB 11/1613, sig. 77, fols. 223–4

Lovell, Francis, Viscount Lovell (*b. c.*1457, *d.* in or after 1488), administrator and rebel, was the only son of John, Lord Lovell, and Joan, daughter of John, first Viscount Beaumont. Francis Lovell is variously described as aged seven and nine at his father's death in January 1465; given the date at which he received livery of his lands the former is more likely. The wardship and custody of Lovell and his lands were granted on 13 November 1467 to Richard Neville, earl of Warwick. Lovell had already married (by 17 February 1466) the earl's niece, Anne Fitzhugh, the daughter of Henry, Lord Fitzhugh, and Alice, daughter of Richard Neville, earl of Salisbury. Henry Fitzhugh followed Warwick into rebellion in 1469–70, and Lovell and his wife were among those pardoned by Edward IV in September 1470. After Warwick's death at Barnet, Lovell's wardship was granted, on 11 July 1471, to the king's brother-in-law John de la Pole, duke of Suffolk, although the grant specifically excluded lands which Lovell had yet to inherit—notably those of his grandmother Alice Deincourt, which passed to the crown rather than to Suffolk at her death in February 1474. Lovell was still regarded as a minor on 19 February 1477, but on 28 February he was given livery of his Cheshire lands, and was licensed to enter his land elsewhere, including substantial estates in Yorkshire, on 6 November.

In 1480 Lovell was named to commissions of array in the North Riding as a preliminary to the planned Scottish campaign, in which he served under Richard, duke of Gloucester, and was knighted by him beside Berwick on 22 August 1481. On 4 January 1483 Lovell was elevated to the rank of viscount. His rise to power accelerated a few months later with the accession of Richard III. While still protector of the young Edward V, Gloucester made Lovell chief butler of England and granted him effective control of the castle and manor of Thorpe Waterville, Northamptonshire, part of the Holland inheritance which Lovell had previously been disputing with Edward IV's stepson Richard Grey. Two days after Richard's assumption of the throne, Lovell replaced Grey as constable of Wallingford and was made the king's chamberlain. The latter post, which set him at the head of that part of the household closest to the king, is the clearest evidence for Lovell's intimacy with the new king. He was also a councillor and was elected knight of the Garter early in the reign. Lovell and his wife attended Richard's coronation, where Lovell bore the third sword of state.

When the duke of Buckingham rebelled in October 1483 Lovell deputed William Stonor to raise his men in Oxfordshire and bring them to the king. Stonor, however, joined the rebels, and the episode suggests that Lovell was out of touch with his family interests in the south. Certainly most of the men who can be closely associated with him after his coming of age were northerners. Richard III may have hoped that Lovell would strengthen his links with Oxfordshire and Berkshire, where, as the rebellion had showed, he was in need of reliable allies. Lovell was given extensive grants of forfeited land in the region, including several Stonor manors, but there is little evidence of his involvement there, although in 1484 he joined with the duke of Suffolk in refounding a fraternity in St Helen's Church, Abingdon. His power seems to have been primarily exercised at the centre, within the royal court, where his influence is suggested by the gifts of those anxious for the king's favour, including Selby Abbey and the city of Salisbury, and by his inclusion in William Collingbourne's famous couplet:

> The Cat, the Rat and Lovell our Dog
> Rule all England under the Hog.
> (Horrox, 222)

Lovell continued to receive royal patronage throughout the reign, including (with William Catesby) the constableship of Rockingham (Northamptonshire).

As the threat of invasion intensified in the summer of 1485, Lovell was sent to guard the south coast. Henry Tudor landed instead near Milford Haven, and Lovell had probably rejoined Richard in time to fight at Bosworth on 22 August. Although he is not mentioned in any of the chronicle accounts of the battle, his presence is suggested by early reports that he was among the dead. In fact he escaped and took sanctuary at Colchester. He was attainted in Henry's first parliament. In spring 1486 Lovell and his companion in sanctuary, Humphrey Stafford of Grafton (Worcestershire), sought to stir up rebellion against the new regime: Stafford in the west midlands and Lovell in Yorkshire. But the leading northern families failed to support the rising, and by the time Henry VII entered York on 20 April Lovell's forces had dispersed. By 19 May Lovell was believed to be in the Isle of Ely, seeking to escape abroad or take sanctuary once again. He subsequently made his way to the court of Margaret of York, dowager duchess of Burgundy, where he was joined in the following spring by John, earl of Lincoln, the son of Lovell's former guardian, Suffolk.

In 1486 Lovell and Lincoln, with military backing supplied by Margaret, launched an invasion of England. They went via Ireland, where, on 24 May, a boy claiming to be Clarence's son, Edward, earl of Warwick, was crowned 'King Edward VI' in Dublin Cathedral. The rebels landed on the Furness peninsula, near the lands of one of their allies, Sir Thomas Broughton, on 4 June, and moved rapidly south. As in the previous year, few former Ricardians of any standing joined them. On 16 June the rebels met the king's army at Stoke, near Newark (Nottinghamshire), and were routed. Lincoln was killed. Lovell, according to the reports which reached York, 'was discomfited and fled' (Attreed, 2.573). His fate thereafter is obscure, but there seems no reason except coincidence to identify him with the body of a man said to have been found in a hidden room in Minster Lovell in the early years of the eighteenth century. After the battle he probably headed northwards. It was to the north that his wife sent his associate Edward Franke in search of him, although by the following February Franke had reported failure. Lovell ultimately arrived in Scotland, where on 19 June 1488 James IV granted a safe conduct to him, Sir Thomas Broughton, Sir Roger Hartlington, Oliver Frank, and their associates. Hartlington, reduced to his former status of gentleman (which perhaps implies that his knighthood had been conferred by 'Edward VI'), was pardoned in July 1489, but there is no further official reference to Lovell or Broughton. In July 1491 a 'simple and poor person' of the city of York was said to have spoken to Lovell and Broughton in Scotland, although he subsequently denied it and no date is given for the meeting.

Lovell's wife was granted an annuity of £20 p.a. from the exchequer in December 1489. She was still alive in 1495, when her interests were protected in her husband's attainder. The 1487 act had omitted him—negligently, it was claimed, although it is more likely to have been because he was then already under attainder. Lovell had no children, and his heirs were his sisters Joan Lovell, who married Sir Brian Stapilton, and Frideswide Lovell, who married Edward Norreys. Henry VIII later granted their heirs some of the Beaumont lands, but Lovell's attainder was never reversed. ROSEMARY HORROX

Sources *Chancery records* • GEC, *Peerage* • *RotP* • R. Horrox and P. W. Hammond, eds., *British Library Harleian manuscript 433*, 4 vols. (1979–83) • J. Williams, 'The political career of Francis Viscount Lovell', *The Ricardian*, 8 (1988–90), 382–402 • N. Davis, ed., *Paston letters and papers of the fifteenth century*, 2 vols. (1971–6) • L. C. Attreed, ed., *The York House books, 1461–1490*, 2 vols. (1991) • R. Horrox, *Richard III, a study of service*, Cambridge Studies in Medieval Life and Thought, 4th ser., 11 (1989) • M. Bennett, *Lambert Simnel and the battle of Stoke* (1987)

Lovell, George William (1804–1878), playwright and novelist, was for many years secretary of the Phoenix Insurance Company. Little is known of his early life, but in 1830 he married Maria Ann Lacy, an actress, who, after her marriage, became a playwright under her married name, Maria Ann *Lovell (1803–1877). Lovell himself wrote six plays starting with *The Avenger*, staged at the Surrey Theatre in 1835. This was followed by the tragedy *The Provost of Bruges* in 1836, produced at Drury Lane with W. C. Macready and Ellen Tree in the leading roles. Lovell based the work on a story called 'The Serf' found in Leitch Ritchie's *Romance of History*. According to *The Times*, the opening night 'audience applauded loudly and unanimously, and the public may be congratulated on the appearance of a play which presents such unquestionable claims to their favour as this' (*The Times*, 11 Feb 1836). In 1841 Lovell's literary career was further enhanced with the publication of

George William Lovell (1804–1878), by unknown engraver, pubd 1878

his novel *The Trustee*. On 12 September 1842 his play *Love's Sacrifice, or, The Rival Merchants* was staged by Charles Kemble at Covent Garden and had George Vandenhoff in the lead role. The *Theatrical Journal* praised the author's wit in the humorous sections of the play and *The Times* noted that Lovell had written 'a *very* clever piece' (*The Times*, 13 Sept 1842). A comedy, dealing with the romantic lives of two Oxford students of differing temperaments, entitled *Look before you Leap*, was then produced at the Haymarket on 29 October 1846. *The Times* stated that:

> The merit of the piece lies in the freshness and cheerfulness with which the subject is treated. There is little or no repartee properly so called, but the language flows on smoothly and naturally, and the characters speak out for themselves with much force. (*The Times*, 30 Oct 1846)

The first production of Lovell's most famous play, *The Wife's Secret*, took place at the Park Theatre, New York, on 12 October 1846, and proved to be a success with American audiences. The work was staged at the Haymarket, London, on 17 January 1848, and ran thirty-six nights with Mr and Mrs Charles Kean in the lead roles. According to Wilbur Dunkel, Charles Kean paid Lovell £300 for the piece and then gave the author an extra £100 when the play was performed in London. The work became popular and there were notable revivals staged in October 1850, at the Princess's Theatre, and in February 1861, at Drury Lane with the Keans again taking the lead roles. Later productions took place at the Surrey in November 1868, the Olympic in March 1877, and at the St James's in April 1888. This final revival was produced by John Hare with Lewis Waller and Mr and Mrs W. H. Kendal taking the leads. Regarding the original London production, *The Times* said:

> the *Wife's Secret* is a plain story effectively told, with the advantage that the ruling sentiment, though often treated before, is one that is sure to appeal to a large portion of an audience. And it may be laid down as a fixed maxim, that he who can tell a story well upon the stage has accomplished nine-tenths of his work as a practical dramatist. (*The Times*, 18 Jan 1848)

The noted theatre historian Allardyce Nicoll stated that *The Wife's Secret* was 'certainly one of the best plays I have read in this period' (Dunkel, 52). Lovell's last play, *The Trial of Love*, was written for Charles Kean and staged at the Princess's Theatre on 7 June 1852. It ran for twenty-three nights, but was not critically acclaimed. Lovell's playwrighting career is best summed up by Wilbur Dunkel: 'His was not a distinguished talent. Yet he wrote highly actable plays which kept alive original playwrighting at the nadir of the English theatre' (ibid., 58). Lovell died on 13 May 1878 at his home, 18 Lyndhurst Road, Hampstead, leaving at least one daughter and one son, William Henry Lovell. BARRY YZEREEF

Sources *Era Almanack and Annual* (1869), 19 • *Theatrical Journal* (17 Sept 1842) • *Theatrical Journal* (15 Aug 1846) • *Theatrical Observer*, 4415 (10 Feb 1836) • *Theatrical Observer*, 4416 (11 Feb 1836) • *Theatrical Observer*, 6464 (12 Sept 1842) • *Theatrical Observer*, 6465 (13 Sept 1842) • *The Times* (11 Feb 1836) • *The Times* (13 Sept 1842) • *The Times* (30 Oct 1846) • *The Times* (18 Jan 1848) • W. D. Dunkel, 'The career of George W. Lovell', *Theatre Notebook*, 5 (1950–51), 52–9 • *ILN* (8 June 1878), 533 • V. Francisco, 'Charles Kean's acting career, 1827–1867, and the development of his style', PhD diss., Indiana University, 1974 • D. Mullin, ed., *Victorian plays: a record of significant productions on the London stage, 1837–1901* (1987) • d. cert.

Archives BL, letters to Royal Literary Fund | CUL, Phoenix archive, legal, financial, and family MSS

Likenesses engraving, NPG; repro. in *ILN* (8 June 1878) [*see illus.*]

Wealth at death under £16,000: probate, 29 June 1878, *CGPLA Eng. & Wales*

Lovell, James (*d.* 1778), sculptor and interior decorator, was active from the mid-1740s. Nothing is known of his birth, parentage, or childhood. His work shows stylistic affinities with that of Peter Scheemakers—who like Lovell worked at Stowe in Buckinghamshire—and it seems likely that he trained in the studio of Scheemakers and Laurent Delvaux. Although the account books at Stowe refer to two sons, John and James Lovell, nothing is known either of Lovell's marriage. He apparently went bankrupt in 1768. Given the slight biographical knowledge of Lovell, an account of his life therefore must focus almost entirely on the evidence of his works.

Lovell worked mainly on houses and estates in Warwickshire: Radway Grange and the neighbouring Hagley Hall, Arbury Hall, Warwick Shire Hall, and Newnham Paddox. Many sources suggest that—despite his large practice in this county—he lived in London for most of his life. In 1756 Bishop Richard Pococke noted in the garden at Radway Grange a statue of Caractacus in chains, 'modeled … by a countryman of genius now established in London' (L. Dickens and M. Stanton, eds., *An Eighteenth-Century Correspondence*, 1910, 270); Horace Walpole supplies a more precise address when he refers to him as a 'statuary in Mortimer Street, near Oxford Road' (Walpole, *Corr.*, 35.644). An account presented by Lovell to Lord Temple's steward in 1775 provides a different, later address, revealing that the sculptor had rented a house in Wall Street, London, for the previous three years from his patron; this rental is again mentioned in a final settlement of his account for work at Stowe, dated 10 October 1777, and it may be presumed to be the place of his death the following year.

Lovell's works may be divided into three categories: plasterwork and fittings for interiors of the early Gothic revival; funerary monuments for church interiors; and neo-classical monumental statuary in relief and in the round, mostly to be found at Stowe. He was a stylistic chameleon throughout his career, and early neo-Gothic and rococo elements persist until the final decade, when he executed the architectural and figurative sculpture of the south front of Stowe in the most advanced neo-classical taste. Stylistic variations may be attributed to the tastes of his patrons rather than to personal convictions. First and chief among these seems to have been Sanderson Miller of Radway: at the centre of the early Gothic revival, he was designer of plasterwork at his own Radway Grange, at Sir Roger Newdigate's Arbury Hall, at Lord Dacre's Belhus in Essex, and at Lord North's Wroxton Abbey in Oxfordshire, as well as at the house and church at Hagley in Worcestershire belonging to Lord Lyttleton. Through Lord Lyttleton, Miller was also involved in continuing restorations to the house and garden buildings at Stowe in Buckinghamshire. James Lovell was employed at all of these estates.

Lovell's principal funerary monuments are to Earl Fitzwalter in Chelmsford Cathedral and to the Montagu family at Horton church, Northamptonshire (both 1756). Horace Walpole admired the latter particularly, writing to Richard Montagu that 'There is a helmet that would tempt one to enlist' (Walpole, *Corr.*, 9.200). It was probably therefore through Walpole's intervention that Lovell sculpted the monument to Galfridus Mann in the church at Linton in Kent (1756), to the designs of Richard Bentley. Although a small monument, it was important as one of the earliest funerary monuments in the early Gothic revival style. Also in Kent is Lovell's monument to General Wolfe in his birthplace, Westerham (1760). Finally, there is the monument to Thomas Trotman in the church at Bucknell, Oxfordshire (1777).

Such occasional commissions for fireplaces, plasterwork, and funerary monuments would have made James Lovell an exemplary jobbing sculptor and stuccoist of the period but nothing more. What distinguishes him is the ensemble of relief and free-standing sculpture of the south front of Stowe, monumental in scale and marking a new departure in style. Executed in the final decade of his life, it was the culmination of a series of involvements by Lovell in the interior of the house and in the ornamentation of the garden buildings. The most conspicuous of these was the architectural ornament of the Corinthian arch framing the new south front and designed—as the south front was—by Lord Temple's nephew, Thomas Pitt, later Lord Camelford. The architectural ornamentation and the sculpture and stucco-work of the south front of Stowe made pioneering use of newly published sources: Robert Wood's *The Ruins of Palmyra* (1753) and *The Ruins of Baalbek* (1757), and the first volume of James Stuart and Nicholas Revett's *The Antiquities of Athens* (1762). This is the earliest and most comprehensive programme of sculpture of the age of neo-classicism.

There is clearly no argument to be made for originality in design on behalf of James Lovell: he was a master craftsman and not an artist. His most impressive early sculpture was the chimney-piece in the saloon of Hagley Hall in

Worcestershire for Lord Lyttleton in 1759, and it is decidedly rococo in style. But his major work is the most public manifestation of the transition from the rococo to the neo-classical style in sculpture, and his own career marks the end of the predominance of foreign sculptors in England and the coming-of-age of native sculptors.

MICHAEL MCCARTHY

Sources R. Gunnis, *Dictionary of British sculptors, 1660–1851* (1953); new edn (1968) • M. McCarthy, 'James Lovell and his sculptures at Stowe', *Burlington Magazine*, 115 (1973), 221–32 • Walpole, *Corr.* • G. Beard, *Georgian craftsmen and their work* (1966) • M. D. Whinney, *English sculpture, 1720–1830*, 17 (1971)

Archives Essex RO, Belhus MSS • Hunt. L., Stowe building and repair accounts • Warks. CRO, Sanderson Miller MSS

Lovell [Lovel], **John, fifth Baron Lovell** (*c.*1342–1408), courtier and royal councillor, was the second son of John, third Lord Lovell (1314–1347), and Isabel (*d.* 1349), who may have been a Zouche. He succeeded his elder brother, John, fourth Lord Lovell (*d.* 1361). He played an influential part in the political life of late fourteenth-century England and, by his abilities, conclusively established his family in the ranks of the parliamentary peerage. Lovell's early career was a varied one. After serving in Brittany with Sir Walter Hewet in 1364, he was one of the party accompanying Lionel, duke of Clarence, to Milan in 1368. He received letters of protection before journeying overseas again in 1371 and it may be on this occasion that he fought, as eye witnesses later testified, in Prussia and the eastern Mediterranean. These exploits, together with the considerable increase in his landed resources his marriage, before May 1373, to Matilda (*c.*1356–1423), daughter and heir of Sir Robert Holland, had brought him, earned Sir John a personal summons to parliament from December 1375 and brought him to the attention of Edmund Mortimer, earl of March. Lovell went in Mortimer's company to Brittany in 1374–5 and to Ireland in 1380 and he was granted the manor of Great Hambleton, Rutland, for life by the earl in recognition of his services.

Edmund (III) Mortimer's death in December 1381 closed this lucrative avenue of advancement but, by this time, Lovell was already well established at the court of Richard II: he is described as a 'knight of the king's house' when assisting Henry Percy, first earl of Northumberland, at the recapture of Berwick Castle in November 1378. Appointed master of the king's hounds in December 1377, Lovell was a king's knight by 1383 and served as one of a group of ten bannerets attached to the royal household between 1385 and 1387. It was in this capacity that he had joint command of a force of 300 men within the king's 'battle' during the Scottish campaign in 1385. Although the appellant lords used Sir John as an intermediary between themselves and the king in the early stages of the political crisis of 1387–8, his close links with Richard's household rendered him suspect and he was among a group of courtiers whom the appellants banished from the king's presence. Lovell's rehabilitation was swift once Richard resumed power, however, for he was certainly present at meetings of the royal council by September 1389, and for the next decade he acted as one of the king's regular advisers: present at most of the more important council meetings; a consistent witness of royal charters; and frequently chosen as a trier of parliamentary petitions. Lovell was formally retained by Richard in February 1395, during the king's first Irish expedition, at a fee of 200 marks p.a., and he returned to Ireland with Richard in May 1399.

Lovell managed the revision of loyalties required by the Lancastrian usurpation as adroitly as he had negotiated the appellancy crisis. Neither the first nor the last to abandon the Ricardian cause, he submitted to Henry Bolingbroke at Chester and participated fully in the formal acts of deposition. He had soon won Henry's trust, for he sat on the judicial commissions investigating the 'Epiphany rising' and was granted the office of constable of Corfe Castle, Dorset, forfeited by one of the rebel earls, in January 1400 because 'the king wishes to remove all suspicion of the safety of the castle' (*CPR, 1399–1401*, 182). Lovell played his part in defending the new Lancastrian regime: he served on the king's Scottish expedition in 1400, undertook to meet the costs of fitting out a warship in 1401, and accompanied the king towards Wales in 1405. It was as an experienced voice in the new king's counsels that Lovell made his principal contribution to Henry IV's rule, however. He continued to attend council meetings—in 1405–6 he was the most frequent attender among the lay peers—and was earlier (in 1401) one of the four names considered by the council as suitable to act as governor to the prince of Wales. He was a member of the Lords' committee chosen to intercommune with the Commons in November 1402 and was named as a royal councillor in full parliament in both January 1404 and May 1406. On this second occasion, however, Lovell expressed his reluctance to accept the responsibility and seems thereafter to have retired from public life.

Underpinning Lovell's public prominence were considerable private resources and a growing regional dominance. His marriage to Matilda Holland had brought him an inheritance that both complemented and consolidated his own estates and enabled him to style himself Lord Lovell and Holland. Taken together with his royal annuities, his lands can hardly have yielded an income less than £1000 p.a.—enough to place him among the richest of the baronage. Though spread through thirteen counties, these lands were most thickly concentrated in Oxfordshire and Wiltshire and it was there that Lovell was most frequently called upon to exercise his local influence. He was a justice of the peace in Oxfordshire from 1381 to 1389 and again from 1397 to 1407, and in Wiltshire from 1386 to 1389 and 1391 to 1407, intermittently heading the commission in both counties. It was in Wiltshire, however, that Lovell's local ambitions were most clearly evident. He had been keeper of the castle of Devizes since 1381 and also held the manors of Rowde and Corsham, together with the forests of Melksham, Chippenham, and Pewsham, by royal grant; added to the several further manors he acquired in the county by purchase and inheritance, Lovell's control of these estates made him the dominant local figure. His aspirations in this regard were announced by the castle he built at Wardour, Wiltshire: a striking hexagonal courtyard house, begun in 1393, that proclaimed both his wealth and his familiarity with court fashion. Persistent allegations of maintenance and threats of violence against Lovell suggest, however, that his local ascendancy was ruthlessly enforced; one opponent complained that most of the Wiltshire justices were retained by him, while Lovell is certainly known to have made substantial payments to ensure favourable juries. Constant and usually acrimonious litigation is, indeed, a feature of his later years; pressure of business in the courts was the explanation that Lovell gave for his reluctance to continue to act as a councillor in 1406. The most prominent legal action Lovell was involved in was, however, the court of chivalry case he brought against Thomas, Lord Morley, in 1386 for the right to bear the arms of Burnell—a case in which Lovell seems, characteristically, to have been less concerned with vindicating his chivalric honour than with establishing an indirect claim to the barony of Burnell.

John, Lord Lovell, and his wife, Matilda, had at least five children: John (*d.* 1414), who married Eleanor, daughter of William, Lord Zouche [*see under* Zouche family]; Robert, who married Elizabeth, daughter and coheir of Sir Guy Brian; Ralph; Thomas; and Philippa, who married Sir John *Dinham (*d.* 1428) [*see under* Dinham family]. Lovell died at his castle of Wardour on 10 September 1408. In his will he left vestments and a lectionary (BL, Harleian MS 7026), illustrated by the Dominican artist John Sifrewast, to Salisbury Cathedral and desired to be buried in the church of St John's Hospital, Brackley. It was presumably in fulfilment of his intentions that his widow, to whom Lovell had entrusted absolute discretion in the disposal of his goods for pious purposes, proposed to convert the Brackley hospital into a Dominican house of thirteen friars.

SIMON WALKER

Sources PRO · *Chancery records* · estate papers, Magd. Oxf., 36/9; MS Misc 315 · *RotP* · N. H. Nicolas, ed., *Proceedings and ordinances of the privy council of England*, 7 vols., RC, 26 (1834–7), vol. 1 · Rymer, *Foedera*, 2nd edn · register of Archbishop Arundel, LPL · A. L. Brown, 'The Commons and the council in the reign of Henry IV', *EngHR*, 79 (1964), 1–30 · R. B. Pugh and A. D. Saunders, *Old Wardour Castle, Wiltshire* (1968) · *Knighton's chronicle, 1337–1396*, ed. and trans. G. H. Martin, OMT (1995) [Lat. orig., *Chronica de eventibus Angliae a tempore regis Edgari usque mortem regis Ricardi Secundi*, with parallel Eng. text] · G. B. Stow, ed., *Historia vitae et regni Ricardi Secundi* (1977) · *CIPM*, 19, no. 29, [C 137/66] no. 12 [E 149/90] · *CClR, 1361–8* · *CPR, 1377–81; 1399–1401* · GEC, *Peerage* · H. L. Gray, 'Incomes from land in England in 1436', *EngHR*, 49 (1934), 607–39

Archives BL, lectionary, Harley MS 7026 · Magd. Oxf., MS 36/9; MS misc. 315

Likenesses J. Sifrewast, portrait, *c.*1400, BL, Harley MS 7026 f. 4v

Wealth at death £426 p.a.: *CIPM*, 19, nos. 404–17 · properties yielded £460 in 1400–01: Magd. Oxf. MS misc. 315 · estates assessed at £1000 p.a.: Gray, 'Incomes'

Lovell, Sir Lovell Benjamin Badcock (**1786–1861**), army officer, a descendant of Sir Salathiel *Lovell, was the eldest son of Stanhope Badcock of Little Missenden Hall and Maplethorpe Hall, Buckinghamshire, who served in the American War of Independence as a subaltern in the 6th regiment, and with the Royal Buckinghamshire militia in Ireland in the 1798 rebellion. His mother was the daughter of William Buckle of Mythe Hall and Chasely, Gloucestershire. Educated at Eton College, he was appointed cornet on 18 December 1805 in the 4th light dragoons, in which he became lieutenant on 19 May 1808 and captain on 12 December 1811. He served in the expedition to Montevideo in 1807, on the staff of Sir Samuel Auchmuty. After landing with his regiment in Portugal in December 1808, he served with it throughout the Peninsular campaign of 1809–14, much of the time with the light division. He was present in all at ten general actions, seven sieges, and forty other engagements. In 1811 he was much employed on the left of the army as an unofficial intelligence officer, and was strongly recommended by Wellington for promotion. After the war Badcock was given a brevet majority (21 January 1819) for his Peninsular services.

On 28 October 1824 Badcock was brought into the 8th light dragoons, after the return of that regiment from India, and on 21 November 1826 obtained a lieutenant-colonelcy, half pay unattached. He was one of the military reporters under Lord William Russell at the siege of Oporto during the Miguelite War in Portugal. He published *Rough Leaves from a Journal in Spain and Portugal in 1832, '33, and '34* (1835). On 21 March 1834 he exchanged to the command of the 15th light dragoons (later hussars) with Lord Brudenell, later earl of Cardigan. In 1835 he was made KH. In 1839 he took his regiment out to Madras. In 1840, together with his brother, Captain William Stanhope Badcock KH, Royal Navy, he assumed the surname of Lovell under royal sign manual. He became brevet colonel on 23 November 1841. On 8 March 1850 he exchanged from the 15th hussars to half pay with the 11th hussars. He became major-general on 20 June 1854, and in 1856 was made KCB and appointed colonel of the 12th (Prince of Wales's) Royal lancers. He died at his residence, Brunswick Terrace, Brighton, on 11 March 1861, aged seventy-five.

H. M. CHICHESTER, *rev.* JAMES FALKNER

Sources *Army List* · *Hart's Army List* · *GM*, 3rd ser., 10 (1861), 473 · *Dod's Peerage* (1858)

Archives Derbys. RO, corresp. · W. Sussex RO, corresp. and papers | Woburn Abbey, Bedfordshire, letters to Lord George William Russell and Oporto journal

Likenesses T. W. Mackay, oils, *c.*1850 · G. T. Payne, mezzotint (after T. W. Mackay), BM · photograph (after oil painting by T. W. Mackay, *c.*1850), priv. coll.

Wealth at death £800: probate, 16 April 1861, *CGPLA Eng. & Wales*

Lovell [*née* Lacy], **Maria Ann** [*performing name* Mrs Haller] (**1803–1877**), actress and playwright, was born in London on 15 July 1803, the daughter of Willoughby Lacy (*d.* 1831), patentee of Drury Lane. She first appeared on the Belfast stage in 1818 as Mrs Haller, and achieved a certain degree of fame as an actress while in Ireland. In 1820 she performed at Glasgow and Edinburgh in conjunction with Edmund Kean and Charles Young. She was later engaged at Covent Garden where, on 9 October 1822, she performed the role of Belvidera, which she followed with the representation of Isabella. Henry Harris, who was the lessee of the theatre, then engaged her for three years. In *Our Actresses* Mrs C. Baron states that Maria excelled in pathetic parts. According to the *Theatrical Journal*, Maria was 'a good actress of secondary standing' (*Theatrical Journal*, 16, 31 Oct 1855), and the *Era Almanack* described her as 'an esteemed tragic actress' (*Era Almanack*, 1869, 19).

On her marriage in 1830 to George William *Lovell (1804–1878), playwright, Maria retired from the stage and employed herself in writing plays. Her five-act drama *Ingomar the Barbarian, or, The Son of the Wilderness* was adapted from the German and was produced at Drury Lane in June 1851. According to the *Theatrical Journal*, the play 'was very successful', owing mostly to the performance of Miss Charlotte Vandenhoff in the character of Parthenia, who 'was truly the Greek heroine, nothing more truly Greek in look, and generally in spirit it is possible to conceive'. It was also noted that 'At the fall of the curtain the lady authoress curtsied to the audience from a private box' (*Theatrical Journal*, 12, 12 June 1851). In contrast, *The Times* complained that the 'idea might have been fairly worked out in a couple of acts, with plenty of room for all the graduations in Ingomar's character' (*The Times*, 10 June 1851). The play was staged again in October of the same year at Sadler's Wells with Samuel Phelps taking the title role and Fanny Elizabeth Vining playing Parthenia. According to the *Theatrical Journal* the production 'attracted a large audience … although its novelty was forestalled at Drury Lane a few months ago' (*Theatrical Journal*, 12, 29 Oct 1851). The play was also revived in June 1854, December 1867, and at the Victoria Theatre in June 1857. An 1883 staging by the American actress Mary Anderson at the Lyceum in London met with mixed critical response.

Another of Maria's plays, *The Beginning and the End*, was a four-act drama first staged at the Haymarket in 1855, but, despite the talents of Charlotte Cushman, William Henry Chippendale, and Henry Howe, the play was a failure. The *Theatrical Journal* noted, 'It is a drama of the Victorian stamp, the plot hinging on a forged will; and contains neither exciting interest nor well developed character' (*Theatrical Journal*, 16, 31 Oct 1855). *The Times* mockingly cited the moral of the play as: 'When you burn a will in the kitchen, take care that no one is in the pantry' (*The Times*, 30 Oct 1855). Maria Lovell died on 2 April 1877 at her home, Grove Lodge, 18 Lyndhurst Road, Hampstead.

BARRY YZEREEF

Sources *Theatrical Journal* (12 June 1851) · *Theatrical Journal* (29 Oct 1851) · *Theatrical Journal* (31 Oct 1855) · *The Times* (10 June 1851) · *The Times* (30 Oct 1855) · *The Times* (5 April 1877) · *The Times* (6 April 1877) · D. Mullin, ed., *Victorian actors and actresses in review: a dictionary of contemporary views of representative British and American actors and actresses, 1837–1901* (1983) · *Era Almanack and Annual* (1869), 19
Likenesses theatrical prints, BM · theatrical prints, Harvard TC

Lovell, Patience. *See* Wright, Patience Lovell (1725–1786).

Lovell, Robert (1630?–1690), naturalist, was born at Lapworth, Warwickshire, the son of Benjamin Lovell (*b.* 1607/8), rector of Lapworth, and his first wife, Mary Godwin (*d.* 1658). Sir Salathiel *Lovell was his brother. In 1648 he became a student of Christ Church, Oxford 'by favour of the visitors appointed by Parliament' (Wood, 296), studying botany with the benefit of the recently established Physic Garden, zoology, and mineralogy. He graduated BA in 1650 and MA in 1653.

Lovell was apparently still in Oxford when his two books were published. The first, *Pambotanologia* (1659), was a pharmacopœia rather than the 'compleat herball' that its sub-title proclaimed. Dedicated to Charles II, it demonstrated Lovell's industry in ransacking libraries to list nearly two hundred and fifty authors, rather than any understanding of botany. There was nothing original in its content or arrangement, which followed the antique Galenic principles of the four elements, temperaments, and qualities. Remarkably, the work reached a second edition in 1665, Lovell having meanwhile issued a companion volume, *Panzōoryktologia*, claiming to be a complete history of animals and minerals.

'Afterwards he retired to Coventry, professed physic, and had some practice therein, lived a conformist, and died [there] in the communion of the church' (Wood, 296). Lovell died in November 1690 and was buried in Holy Trinity Church, Coventry.

G. S. BOULGER, *rev.* ANITA MCCONNELL

Sources C. E. Raven, *English naturalists from Neckam to Ray: a study of the making of the modern world* (1947), 46–7 · R. Pulteney, *Historical and biographical sketches of the progress of botany in England*, 1 (1790), 181–3 · Wood, *Ath. Oxon.* · F. L. Colvile, *The worthies of Warwickshire who lived between 1500 and 1800* [1870], 516

Lovell, Robert (1771–1796), poet, was born at his parents' home in Thomas Street in Bristol on 25 October 1771, the son of a wealthy Quaker, initially a cabinet-maker and later a pin manufacturer, Robert Lovell (*d.* 1804), and his first wife, Edith, *née* Bourne (1741–1781), a Quaker minister. He probably followed some business (he was described on his death as a pin manufacturer), but the vehemence of his *Bristoliad*, a satire in Churchill's style and not deficient in vigour, shows that he was ill at ease in the commercial atmosphere of Bristol. He estranged himself still further from his original circle when on 20 January 1794 he married Mary (1771–1861/2), daughter of Stephen Fricker, a girl of much beauty and some talent, with whom he had one child, Robert Lovell the younger (*b.* 1795). Lovell's family disapproved of the match because she was not only a non-Quaker, but had become an actress after her father's bankruptcy. It is not precisely clear when Lovell first made Southey's acquaintance, but it was early enough for Southey to have become engaged to his sister-in-law, Edith, before Coleridge's visit to Bristol in August 1794. Lovell introduced the two poets to Joseph Cottle and before long Coleridge was betrothed to a third Fricker sister, Sara, whom he married on 14 November 1795. In the same month of August 1794 the three friends co-operated in the production of a wellnigh improvised three-act tragedy on the fall of Robespierre. Each wrote an act, but Lovell's was rejected as out of keeping with the others, and Southey filled the void. The tragedy was published as Coleridge's at Cambridge in September 1794. Southey and Lovell nevertheless combined to publish a joint volume of poetry under the title of *Poems by Bion and Moschus* (1794); this was mistaken for a translation, and so was reissued in 1795 in an edition bearing the authors' names. Southey's mature opinion of his own pieces may be inferred from the fact that he reprinted none of them. This notwithstanding, they were reprinted in Park's *British Poets* with the addition of the *Bristoliad*, which does not seem to have been published before.

Next to their poetry, the young men were chiefly occupied with the project for their Pantisocratic colony. This was an idealized democratic community of self-governing equals with no private ownership of land and an emphasis on living in harmony with nature. It was to be based in Kentucky, and Lovell was to have brought to it not only his wife but his brother and two sisters. The design had practically collapsed before Lovell's death from a fever contracted at Salisbury and aggravated by his travelling home without taking medical advice. Edith Southey, in Southey's absence, nursed him for three nights at the risk of her life. After his death in Bristol on 3 May 1796, Lovell's father refused all aid to his daughter-in-law on the ground of her having been an actress and she and her infant son were provided for by Southey. Mary Lovell lived in his family during his life, and afterwards with his daughter Kate until her death at the age of ninety. Robert Lovell the younger settled in London as a printer in 1824. Some years afterwards he went on a tour of Europe and mysteriously disappeared, last being heard of at Marseilles. Enquiries were made by the Foreign Office, and Henry Nelson Coleridge journeyed in quest of him, but no trace was ever discovered. RICHARD GARNETT, *rev.* REBECCA MILLS

Sources *Letters of Samuel Taylor Coleridge*, ed. E. H. Coleridge, 2 vols. (1895) · J. Cottle, *Early recollections; chiefly relating to the late Samuel Taylor Coleridge, during his long residence in Bristol*, 2 vols. (1837) · *IGI* · [D. Rivers], *Literary memoirs of living authors of Great Britain*, 1 (1798), 381 · *The life and correspondence of Robert Southey*, ed. C. C. Southey, 6 vols. (1849–50), vol. 1, pp. 262–7 · K. Jones, *A passionate sisterhood: the sisters, wives and daughters of the lake poets* (1997) · 'Dictionary of Quaker biography', RS Friends, Lond. [card index]

Lovell, Sir Salathiel (1631/2–1713), judge, was the son of Benjamin Lovell (*b.* 1607/8) and his first wife, Mary Godwin (*d.* 1658). The naturalist Robert *Lovell was his brother. Benjamin Lovell was rector of Preston Bagot, Warwickshire, from 1636. During the civil war Benjamin exchanged the word for the sword; he served briefly as a captain in the cavalry regiment raised in the county by Colonel William Purefoy and was present at the siege of Gloucester in 1643. He became rector of Lapworth, Warwickshire, where he resisted paying the sequestered minister's wife her due out of the revenues of the parish. In 1646 he was threatened with the loss of the living unless he did so, and by May 1649 owed her two years' arrears. Benjamin Lovell conformed at the Restoration, and was still alive in 1677.

Northampton and the law In June 1648 Lovell was admitted to Gray's Inn. In 1652 he was created one of the trustees for the parish lands in Lapworth (and twenty-five years later he helped defeat an attempt to convey the lands into the trusteeship of local gentry rather than of parishioners). For a time he worked as an attorney's clerk in Buckingham, and was called to the bar in November 1656. By 1661 he had moved to Northampton, where on 2 June he and his wife, Mary (1641/2–1719), baptized their son Salathiel in the parish church of All Saints. They may already have had a daughter, Maria. Nine sons and three daughters followed between September 1662 and June 1681.

Lovell established himself as a significant figure in the politics of Northampton. In 1663 he acted as the local agent for Christopher Hatton when the latter stood in a parliamentary by-election in the town with the backing of the town's dissenting interest and the council members recently secluded under the Corporation Act. On 31 January Lovell headed the list of signatories—'your vestalls'—appealing to Hatton to stand as 'our Publicola & most noble Consull, to see restored our faythfull Senators of late most violently irregulated' (BL, Add. MS 29551, fol. 9*r*). On the day of the election, while the corporation proceeded to choose Sir William Dudley on a restricted franchise in the town hall, Hatton's supporters elected him at the market cross on an open franchise, and Lovell importuned the sheriff for four hours to issue a double return (unsuccessfully, though Hatton won on appeal to the Commons). Lovell's local position was doubtless advanced by the triumph by 1672 of the 'fanatic party'—the secluded councillors and their supporters on the corporation—and by their demand for his legal expertise as Northampton's partisan politics were fought out in king's bench. He became deputy recorder (the town's chief legal officer, as the recordership itself was always held by an influential local peer), a testimony both to his local importance and to the success of his legal career in London. Following the devastation of Northampton by fire in 1675 Lovell was one of the named commissioners appointed to adjudicate in disputes arising from the rebuilding of the town. He also picked up the post of deputy to the earl of Arlington as steward of the royal manor of Higham Ferrers, Northamptonshire. At some point he acquired an estate at Harleston, 4 miles to the west of Northampton.

Lovell also became a significant figure in Gray's Inn. Although in November 1669 he had to apologize to the pension (the meeting of the governing bench) for 'his error in his Behaviour and carriage and for words spoken at a former Pencon' (Fletcher, 2.4), he was called to be an ancient of the inn in November 1671 and became a bencher in November 1677; thereafter he was a frequent attender at the pensions until 1688.

Early in 1684 Lovell's politics brought him under suspicion with the government, when he was accused of involvement with the fugitive radical whig Thomas Hunt. On 18 January Sir Roger L'Estrange wrote to Secretary of State Jenkins that a prominent Northampton tory had informed him that Hunt had 'sent his libels to Northampton as by direction from Mr Lovell of Gray's Inn, and that the thing is proved upon Lovell, it appears under Hunt's own hand that he corresponds with Lovell, who knows where he is' (*CSP dom.*, *1683–4*, 219). L'Estrange recommended that Lovell's chambers be searched. However, Lovell had already written to Arlington to forestall the charge a few days earlier. About midsummer 1682, he explained, Hunt, a fellow member of Gray's Inn whom he hardly knew, had asked him what booksellers there were in Northampton; he had given him a couple of names and thought nothing more of it. However, on 9 January, while attending the sessions on behalf of a client, Lovell heard Hunt's *Postscript* (an attack on the clergy who preached up passive obedience and the divine right of kings from their pulpits) presented as a seditious book, and saw a letter produced in court from Hunt to one of the booksellers which had been sent with a consignment of 150 copies of the book, asking him to send the money for them by Lovell. Lovell protested that he had known nothing of this: 'I never read that book and am far from promoting that or any book touching the government and have never concerned myself in public affairs' (ibid., 206). Lovell's protests appear somewhat disingenuous (Hunt was already a notorious figure when he spoke to Lovell), and later in 1684 he acted as counsel for the whig William Sacheverell and others charged with riot in the disputes in defence of the borough charter of Nottingham.

Superficially, Lovell accommodated to the regime of James II. He was one of a group of lawyers installed as serjeant on 26 June 1688. The rings which they presented by custom at Westminster Hall acknowledged the recent birth of the king's son and the declaration of indulgence with the inscription 'Rex princeps et Christiana libertas' ('King, prince, and Christian liberty'; Baker, *Serjeants*, 418). However, Lovell's name also appeared on a list drawn up by an unknown but evidently informed hand of those who might act in opposition to James.

Recorder of London On 10 June 1692 Lovell was elected as recorder of London by the court of aldermen; the defeated candidates were the whig MP and lawyer Sir John Tremayne and James Selby, and, in a tied vote with Selby, Lovell was elected on the casting vote of the lord mayor. On 22 October 1692 he was knighted when the City dignitaries attended the king at Kensington Palace to congratulate him on his safe return from the Netherlands. In 1695 Lovell was made a king's serjeant and appointed second justice of Chester and of Denbighshire, Flintshire, and Montgomeryshire, a position he held in tandem with the recordership.

Lovell showed himself a loyal agent of William III's regime. In September 1695 at the Old Bailey he heard the case of the Jacobite Captain Waugh, charged with procuring an escape from a government messenger: where the judges in king's bench had worried away at the legal technicalities in a similar case, Lovell 'cut asunder the Gordian knots of law he could not untie, and the fact being proved refused a special verdict, and directed the jury to bring him in guilty, which they did' (*Downshire MSS*, 1.691). Later that year Lovell helped prepare the evidence for the bill of attainder against Sir John Fenwick.

Lovell became recorder at a time of rising concern with crime in the metropolis, fed by economic disruption and by political and religious anxieties. The 1690s saw high levels of prosecution of thieves, and of the coiners and clippers who endangered a currency in a state of crisis; it also witnessed the drive against vice offences by the societies for the reformation of manners (of which Lovell was a supporter). Lovell was a very active magistrate, and, when in 1702 he sought the grant of the forfeited estate of a convicted coiner, he presented himself very much as the committed crime fighter, declaring that over the past nine years he had had more 'trouble & fateague in the discovery and Conviccon of such Offenders [coiners] and other Criminalls than any person in the Kingdome' (PRO, T1/78, fol. 130).

Others took a less positive view of Lovell's activities. Daniel Defoe was savage in his denunciation in *The Reformation of Manners* (1702), portraying him as the archetype of the bad judge who shamelessly played to the gallery in his public pronouncements

> The *City-Mouth*, with eloquence endu'd,
> To Mountebank the list'ning Multitude

glorying in his power of life and death, and sadistically hectoring the condemned from the bench:

> L—l, the Pandor of thy Judgment-Seat,
> Has neither Manners, Honesty, nor Wit;
> Instead of which, he's plenteously supply'd
> With Nonsense, Noise, Impertinence, and Pride...
> With awkward scornful Phiz, and vile Grimace
> The genuine Talents of an ugly Face;
> With haughty Tone insults the Wretch that dies
> And sports with his approaching Miseries
> God-like he nods upon the Bench of State;
> His Smiles are Life, and if he Frown 'Tis Fate:
> Boldly invading Heaven's Prerogative;
> For with his Breath he kills, or saves alive.
> (Defoe, 70–71)

This much is arguably no more than condemning Lovell as the hard face of the war against crime and vice: at each sessions at the Old Bailey, Lovell not only sat in judgment on many of the cases, but at the end delivered the sentences on all of them. But most troubling of all to his critics was precisely how Lovell pursued the 'discovery and Conviccon' of offenders: the linked questions of his relationship with thief-takers and his role in the granting of royal pardons.

Even the rulers of the City had serious reservations about the report that Lovell presented to the king and (increasingly) the cabinet after each sessions recommending who should be pardoned, apparently appropriating to himself the role of sole intermediary between the Old Bailey bench and the City on the one hand, and Whitehall on the other. Seven months after his appointment, on 15 January 1693, the court of aldermen complained that a pardon of Newgate convicts was passing the great seal without their prior notification. Three days later they ordered that after every sessions, 'Mr Recorder doe before he attend his Matie with his Report Come unto this Court and take the sense and Judgment of the same in what Character and Circumstance he shall Represent to his Majesty the severall Condemned Persons' (CLRO, REP 97, 100). The issue rumbled on until September, when Lovell himself admitted that 'the present Method of reporting to their Majesties' had led to 'great and intollerable troubles and many unjust Jealousies and Reflections'. The court accepted his proposal that the justices present should together decide before the end of each sessions who should be recommended for pardon (ibid., 454–5). Nevertheless, in spring 1700 the court of aldermen again attacked Lovell for making his report to the cabinet without due consultation, and unanimously voted to deny him the recorder's customary annual gratuity of 100 guineas 'for his disrespects to the Chayre and his not Obeying the Orders of this Court' (CLRO, REP 104, 296). The aldermen relented a few months later upon Lovell giving them 'full Satisfaccon' (CLRO, REP 105, 4).

The court's objections were in part a matter of defending jurisdictional territory, and it is uncertain how far the aldermen were responding to a real rather than a formal change in the recorder's role in the pardoning process; the impetus for the change probably came more from the cabinet than the recorder, and their objections did little to halt it. In 1693 the aldermen were also responding to complaints that far too many criminals were being reprieved. Some may have opposed Lovell for his whig politics. But the court was evidently concerned about his lack of accountability and about *who* was being pardoned. What the court thought of Lovell's motives is unknowable, but they were addressing an issue which in the bitter satire of Defoe and Tom Brown was taken as evidence of corruption. To them Lovell was a man who misused the power of life and death, which he exercised through his influence in court and his voice in the granting of royal pardons; to Defoe, Lovell was a man who could be bought, who actively shielded and took a share of the spoils of criminals:

> Definitive in Law, without Appeal,
> But always serves the Hand who pays him well:
> He trades in Justice, and the Souls of Men,
> And prostitutes them equally to Gain:
> He has his Publick Book of Rates to show,
> Where every Rogue the Price of Life may know
> Fraternities of Villains he maintains,
> Protects their Robberies, and shares the Gains;
> Who thieve with Toleration as a Trade,
> And then restore according as they paid.
> (Defoe, 70–71)

This was an accusation about Lovell's relationship with thief-takers, the ambiguous figures who inhabited the borderland between the law and crime, mediating between the authorities and victims of theft on the one hand and criminals on the other. They detected and brought to trial some offenders for private or official reward, while often simply helping people get their stolen goods back for a fee. These were men who in some cases were as much organizers as detectors of crime.

The charges of corrupt dealings with thief-takers dogged Lovell's memory. In 1725, at the time of the downfall of Jonathan Wild and twelve years after Lovell's death, a correspondent of the *British Journal* related how Lovell had colluded with the thief-taker John Connell in his attempt to get one of the latter's clients, Rogers, acquitted of theft. Connell brought into court one of his henchmen, Joseph Hatfield, who swore that he and Morris Evans (who was then a prisoner in Newgate, and whom Connell tried to bribe to confess to the crime) were the actual thieves. Lovell spoke in Hatfield's favour and attempted to have the case dismissed, then and at the next sessions. In the hope of getting a judge other than Lovell, the prosecutors then had the case held over to a further sessions, when Lovell defended Hatfield to the presiding judge, the lord chief justice, Sir John Holt, as:

> a poor young unhappy Man, that had been drawn in to be an assistant in conveying away a Truck with some Clothes in it … who was now dead in Prison; and that Hatfield's Conscience having prick'd him, he came voluntarily, and made a Confession in Court of his Crime, to prevent another Man's being wrongfully hang'd for what he had done; and that we [the accusers] had been maliciously and cruelly prosecuting several Sessions for it, when he appeared to be a true Penitent, that it was hoped he would never attempt a dishonest Act again. (*British Journal*, 24 April 1725, 2)

According to Morris Evans, 'Hatfield had always a Purse of five or six hundred Pounds to bribe the R—r, and Court Officers, or their Servants, and had, by that Means, many Times escap'd hanging'. And if Evans was doing no more than retail street gossip or tell the writer what he thought he wanted to hear, the latter noted that at the trial,

> it look'd as if the Lord Chief Justice thought H. had then brib'd the R—r for his Speeches in his Favour: For he reproached him for it with such a Shew of Contempt, as one would scarcely use to a Slave. (*British Journal*, 1 May 1725, 1)

This account, made many years later, receives some support from the bare record of the case in the Middlesex sessions rolls, while Hatfield is elsewhere identified as helping Connell in an attempted extortion by helping him frame someone with a theft. And Hatfield was at the least remarkably lucky: a frequent defendant at the Old Bailey in the years around 1700, he survived to die in Newgate in 1725, while other men and women no more guilty than he had been hanged long before.

Ultimately, it can never be known whether Lovell took bribes from the thief-takers. He undoubtedly looked to them for many prosecutions. He inevitably knew these men: they came to him with accusations seeking arrest warrants (though he was certainly not the only magistrate they resorted to), and his signature appears on the depositions they made and on the bonds to prosecute that they took out. In May 1693 he threw his weight behind the petition for reward of Anthony Dunn and Anthony St Leger as men 'Eminently Serviceable to the Government' in the prosecution of clippers and coiners, who had 'Apprehended prosecuted and Convicted near Forty such notorious Offenders' (PRO, T1/22, fol. 152*v*). He failed to mention that they were also convicts who had been pardoned only the previous January in the pardon which had so concerned the court of aldermen. They went on to be leading thief-takers, frequently bringing their accusations to Lovell. In 1698 the forger William Chaloner alleged that he was being pursued by Lovell and his thief-catchers.

Lovell's relationship with thief-takers provided grounds for his own claim to be a vigorous crime fighter as much as it did for his critics' charge of corruption. The combination of policing, judicial, and pardoning functions offered an active recorder both a powerful weapon against crime and the opportunity for favour and corruption. Doubts about his partiality in pardoning evidently stemmed from how he exercised this range of powers in his dealings with thief-takers and (at the least) high-profile examples of its deployment on behalf of particular offenders such as Dunn, St Leger, and Hatfield. The institution of statutory rewards (against highwaymen in 1693 and especially against coiners in 1695) encouraged reservations about the motives of prosecutors, especially when the offence was the apparently 'victimless' one of coining, where thief-takers were particularly prominent in obtaining convictions. The relationship between Lovell and the thief-takers was mutually beneficial. They could provide him with names, information, and prisoners at the bar, using their influence within, and knowledge of, the capital's criminal networks. In turn, Lovell could protect them and their clients, in practice upholding their authority by allowing them to demonstrate their powerful connections. Lovell was neither the first nor last recorder to work with thief-takers, and some degree of horse-trading with criminal contacts is no doubt an essential part of policing in any period. Nevertheless, Lovell and the thief-takers exploited the particular opportunities provided by the anxieties and reforms of the 1690s. The evidence of his relationship with the thief-takers is consistent with either outright bribery or with favour derived from sacrificing the stricter tenets of justice to the demands of policing the city, which mainly required that the authorities inflict exemplary punishment on some individuals, while at the same time acquiring a sense of the criminal networks of the capital. These readings of Lovell's behaviour—outright corruption or a ruthlessly pragmatic partiality—need not be mutually exclusive.

Baron of the exchequer Lovell himself claimed in 1702 that the recordership was 'a place of great trouble & little profitt' and that he had 'long served the public at his own charge, to the damage of his fortune' (*Calendar of Treasury Papers, 1697–1702*, 561, 89), although in declaring his salary to be only £80 per annum he omitted both the City's annual 100 guinea gratuity and the £100 a year he received for the Chester and Welsh judgeships. The king accepted that Lovell 'hath been a great loser by that servis', noting that recorders were usually quickly promoted to a judgeship in the great common-law courts of Westminster Hall (ibid., 562). Lovell's career had stalled. In June 1700 he was expected to succeed Sir Nicholas Lechmere as baron of the exchequer, but the king opposed his appointment because he had impeded his attempts to woo the tories by refusing to make way for Sir Bartholomew Shower as recorder. Five years later it was noted that Lovell 'is pushing hard for the Judge's place and is like to have it', but that the plan to appoint his intended replacement, upon which his promotion depended, was unlikely to pass the court of aldermen (*Downshire MSS*, 1.842).

By now Lovell was in his seventies. As early as 1693 Jacobites gleefully retailed his unfortunate choice of words at the trial of highwayman James Whitney, condemning him for his cruelty in shedding Christian blood by shooting his pursuers' horses from under them. As he grew older, other stories accrued around his alleged senility: that he should be called Obliviscor ('forgetter') rather than recorder. His great-grandson Richard Lovell *Edgeworth told a story of Salathiel inadvertently condemning his failing memory out of his own mouth. When a young lawyer protested that Lovell had forgotten the law on a certain point, he replied, 'Young man, I have forgotten more law than you will ever remember' (a story which, however, has been told about several judges). In 1707 Lovell resigned the Chester and Welsh judgeships. However, in June 1708 he was finally promoted and sworn in as an additional baron of the exchequer when John Smith was appointed to serve in the newly created Scottish court of exchequer. Lovell's new position carried a salary of £1000 per annum. He resigned the recordership and was succeeded by Peter King. He continued to advise on matters of crime, writing to the Treasury in October 1709 about rewards for the conviction of burglars.

While on the western circuit in April 1710 Lovell's charge to the grand jury at the Devon assizes was in large part a rant against the high Anglican toryism of Henry Sacheverell and the riots which had accompanied the latter's trial. Intemperate and intellectually somewhat incoherent, it is interesting for what it says about Lovell's lifelong politics. He drew on the classic seventeenth-century smear of identifying the political threat of popery—'A Wild Fire is running about, to the great Disturbance of the Peace. And whence comes it? From Priests and Jesuits' (Lamoine, 77). In his contempt for the high Anglican doctrine of passive obedience to the monarch, Sir Salathiel was very much the son of the martial Benjamin Lovell, very much the man who had advised Thomas Hunt on booksellers:

> I would ask you of all those, that cry up the Doctrine of Passive Obedience what they mean; or what Necessity there is for trumping up that damnable Doctrine? Many may say I am hot; I am fervent as the Subject on which I am requires. I doubt not, but some may still remember the dismal Consequences of it some 60 Years ago and upwards. Or at least most of you have heard the deplorable Calamities it drew upon this Nation. (ibid., 78)

Lovell died on 3 May 1713, aged eighty-one, and was buried at Harleston ten days later. His widow, Mary, survived him by six years, dying on 9 December 1719, aged seventy-seven. Their son Samuel had become a Welsh judge, but like all but one of the Lovells' sons did not outlive his parents, although at least two of their daughters shared their longevity. TIM WALES

Sources Baker, *Serjeants* • Foss, *Judges*, 7.395–7 • G. Baker, *The history and antiquities of the county of Northampton*, 1 (1822–30), 166–76 • J. Bridges, *The history and antiquities of Northamptonshire*, ed. P. Whalley, 1 (1791), 515 • M. A. Kishlansky, *Parliamentary selection: social and political choice in early modern England* (1986) • C. A. Markham and J. C. Cox, eds., *The records of the borough of Northampton*, 2 vols. (1898), 2.244–7 • R. J. Fletcher, ed., *The pension book of Gray's Inn*, 2 (1910) • J. M. Beattie, 'The cabinet and the management of death at Tyburn after the revolution of 1688–1689', *The revolution of 1688–1689: changing perspectives*, ed. L. G. Schwoerer (1992), 218–33 • J. M. Beattie, *Policing and punishment in London, 1660–1750* (2001) • T. Wales, 'Thief-takers and their clients in later Stuart London', *Londinopolis: essays in the social and cultural history of early modern London*, ed. P. Griffiths and M. S. R. Jenner (2000), 67–84 • G. Howson, *Thief-taker general: the rise and fall of Jonathan Wild* (1970), 34–43 • D. Defoe, 'Reformation of manners: a satyr', in D. Defoe, *A true collection of the writings of the author of the true born English-man* (1705), 66–109 [first pubd as an individual vol. in 1702] • *British Journal* (24 April 1725) • *British Journal*

(1 May 1725) · J. Redington, ed., *Calendar of Treasury papers*, 1–3, PRO (1868–74) · W. A. Shaw, ed., *Calendar of treasury books*, [33 vols. in 64], PRO (1904–69) · *CSP dom.*, *1682*, 303; *1683–4*, 205–6, 219; *1692–1704* · *Report on the manuscripts of the marquis of Downshire*, 6 vols. in 7, HMC, 75 (1924–95), vol. 1 · repertories of the court of aldermen, 1691–1708, CLRO, REP 96–112 · J. Foster, *The register of admissions to Gray's Inn, 1521–1889, together with the register of marriages in Gray's Inn chapel, 1695–1754* (privately printed, London, 1889) · A. Browning, *Thomas Osborne, earl of Danby and duke of Leeds, 1632–1712*, 3 (1951), 157–61 · G. Lamoine, ed., *Charges to the Grand Jury, 1689–1803*, CS, 4th ser., 43 (1992), 77–9 · N. Luttrell, *A brief historical relation of state affairs from September 1678 to April 1714*, 6 vols. (1857), 1.446; 2.476, 478, 598; 3.477; 4.642; 6.166, 316–17 · *Letters illustrative of the reign of William III from 1696 to 1708 addressed to the duke of Shrewsbury by James Verno*, ed. C. P. R. James, 3 vols., 3 (1841), 74 · Lovell's petition for grant of an estate, 1702, PRO, T1/78, fol. 130 · BL, Add. MS 35107, fol. 28*v* · R. Hudson, *Memorials of a Warwickshire parish: being papers mainly descriptive of the records and registers of the parish of Lapworth* (1904) · *Walker rev.*, 363 · *VCH Northamptonshire*, vol. 3 · J. P. Ferris, 'Northampton', HoP, *Commons*, *1660–90*, 1.338–41 · P. Halliday, *Dismembering the body politic: partisan politics in England's towns, 1650–1730* (1998), 106–8 · private information (2004) [Dr Paul Hopkins] · Foster, *Alum. Oxon.* · Hatton corresp., BL, Add. MS 29551, fols. 9–78 · will, PRO, PROB 11/534, fols. 201*r*–202*r*

Archives BL, corresp. with Christopher Hatton, Add. MS 29551, fols. 9–78

Sir Thomas Lovell (*c*.1449–1524), by Pietro Torrigiano, *c*.1518

Lovell, Sir Thomas (*c*.1449–1524), administrator, was the son of Ralph Lovell of Beachamwell, a cadet of the Lovells of Barton Bendish, a minor family of Norfolk gentry. Like many men of his station, he sought his fortune through study of the law. He was admitted to Lincoln's Inn in 1464, when he was perhaps about fifteen, was treasurer there from 1472 to 1475, and rose to be reader in autumn 1475 and Lent 1482, meanwhile developing a practice among East Anglian clients and finding a seat on the Norfolk commission of the peace. He joined the revolt of 1483 against Richard III, probably as a follower of Thomas Grey, marquess of Dorset, and was attainted in the following year's parliament. His resultant attachment to the cause of Henry Tudor, though it cannot be shown to have led to his fighting for Tudor at Bosworth, was the key to his subsequent career. In 1485 he served as speaker of the Commons in Henry's first parliament. In the years that followed he became an established member of the inner ring of less than a dozen councillors most influential with the king.

Lovell's primary responsibilities were financial. He was treasurer of the king's chamber from 1485, an increasingly important office as Henry gradually restored the chamber to the supremacy it had enjoyed in Yorkist financial administration but lost for some years after Bosworth. From 12 October 1485 he was also chancellor of the exchequer, smoothing relations between the older financial institutions and the new. By 1503, when much of his work in the chamber seems to have been taken over by his former clerk John Heron, he became treasurer of the king's household. These offices were combined with more flexible but no less important roles. He regularly travelled to Calais to collect the king's French pension, audited accounts with the king and other councillors, and took bonds for payment from many victims of the king's exactions.

Lovell also worked to ensure Henry's security on the throne. As deputy lieutenant and later, from Michaelmas 1512, lieutenant of the Tower of London, he took custody of many state prisoners. By the end of his life he was keeping Lambert Simnel, pretender to the throne in 1487, as a falconer in his household. In a task of similarly sensitive implications, he and Sir Reynold Bray arranged for the construction of Richard III's tomb. He fought at Stoke in 1487, where he was knighted, in France in 1492, and at Blackheath in 1497, where he was made banneret. In 1500 his loyalty was rewarded with election to the Order of the Garter. His relationships with other leading councillors were close, in particular, it would seem, those with Richard Fox, bishop successively of Exeter, Durham, and Winchester, with Giles, Lord Daubeney, and with John de Vere, thirteenth earl of Oxford. Their co-operation was an important key to the stability of Henry's regime.

Henry's councillors took their judicial function very seriously, and Lovell was no exception. Statistics based on the thin surviving records make him the second most regular attender of the reign in the Star Chamber, and one of the most regular in the judicial sessions of the council attendant. He was frequently involved in the arbitration of suits and attended occasional sessions of the commission of the peace in half a dozen counties. As steward of the universities of Oxford from 1507 and Cambridge from 1509 he oversaw the exercise of their privileged jurisdictions. As steward of the manorial courts of many crown and church estates, he administered through his deputies justice at the most local level.

Such stewardships were also the foundation of Lovell's considerable military power. In 1492 he raised 143 men for the king; in 1497 it was 493. By 1508, when he listed the followers he had been allowed to retain under royal licence, they numbered 1365, more than half drawn from estates on which he was steward, including significant boroughs such as Derby, Lichfield, and Nottingham. These retainers were often the leading men in their communities: seven past and future mayors of Walsall, seven churchwardens of Thame, seven of the nine richest men in Hitchin. Lovell acted as their patron at the centre of power and reaped his reward not only in service but also in gratitude. In 1507, after he had helped secure a new borough charter, the town council of Wallingford ordered that he be prayed for in each of the town's parish churches every Sunday for the rest of his life. Thus he helped to tie the élites of towns and villages to the developing Tudor regime.

Lovell made considerable profits in Henry's service. His fees for offices and the pensions paid to him by those who valued his influence with the king enabled him to spend freely on the land market, until by 1522–3 he enjoyed a clear landed income of over £450 a year, from estates spread across twelve counties from Yorkshire to Kent and from Wiltshire to Norfolk. Between 1486 and 1513 perhaps double this sum accrued to him annually from the estates of his brother-in-law, Edmund, Lord Ros. In 1485 or 1486, doubtless with the king's backing, he had married Isabel (1451–1508/9), daughter of Thomas, Lord *Ros, and widow of Sir Thomas Everingham (*d.* 1484/5). She brought him not only a share in the Tiptoft inheritance derived from her mother, but also, under the terms of a deal struck with the king in 1486, the keeping of her brother's lands, he being adjudged mentally incapable of managing them. Lovell extended the lands under his control yet further by leases from the crown, religious houses, university colleges, and noblemen. Some of his profits he put into building: a brick house with battlemented gatehouse and polygonal turrets at East Harling, Norfolk, a London house next to Holywell Nunnery in Shoreditch, and a brick palace sufficient to receive the court on progress at Elsings in Enfield. He also made generous contributions to other building projects: the clerestory and glazing of Enfield parish church, the windows of Malvern Priory (where the remains of his likeness survive), the gatehouse of Lincoln's Inn, the walls of Gonville Hall, Cambridge, and the repair of Dover harbour. He made large donations to Holywell Nunnery, where he built himself a burial chapel inscribed:

> All the nunnes in Holywel
> Pray for the soul of Sir Thomas Lovel.

Enough remained to sustain a splendid style of life, with eighty-five liveried servants, expensive tapestries on the wall, and scores of printed books. For the subsidy of 1524 he was taxed on goods worth £2000. Little of this grandeur survives except for his portrait, executed in a bronze medallion attributed to Pietro Torrigiano, now at Westminster Abbey. His interests seem to have been wide: he often made use of his ecclesiastical patronage to support clerics who were continuing their education, and at the end of his life he made efforts to meet the explorer Sebastian Cabot.

At the accession of Henry VIII, Lovell remained a leading member of the king's council. He continued to sit regularly in Star Chamber, helped untangle the complex financial legacy of the previous reign, and became involved in new ventures such as the campaigns against enclosure in 1517 and vagrancy in 1519. On 6 February 1510 he became chief justice of the royal forests south of Trent and from 14 June 1513 he served as master of the wards, improving the local administration of what would later become the court of wards. In the wars of 1511–14 he supervised the procurement of artillery and the fortification of Calais. Advancing age reduced his activity and he gave up some of his offices: the treasurership of the household in 1519, the mastership of the wards in 1520. Yet he remained a trusted councillor, taking part in the interrogation of Edward Stafford, third duke of Buckingham, in 1520. At length, after a year or more of illness, he died on 25 May 1524 at his house at Elsings in Enfield. After a sumptuous funeral he was buried in his chapel at Holywell Nunnery on 8 June. Having no children, he had made arrangements for the advancement of the children of his brother Sir Robert and of his cousin Sir Gregory. His niece Ursula he had married to William Hussey, son of his colleague Sir John, at a cost of £666 13*s.* 4*d.*; her sister Elizabeth he had matched with his great-nephew Thomas Manners, heir to the Ros estates and later first earl of Rutland. The bulk of his estates he left to Francis, second son of Sir Gregory, who founded the Norfolk gentry family of Lovell of East Harling.

S. J. GUNN

Sources G. L. Harrison, 'A few notes on the Lovells of East Harling', *Norfolk Archaeology*, 18 (1912), 46–77 • S. J. Gunn, 'Sir Thomas Lovell (*c.*1449–1524): a new man in a new monarchy?', *The end of the middle ages? England in the fifteenth and sixteenth centuries*, ed. J. L. Watts (1998), 117–53 • *Chancery records* • *LP Henry VIII*, vols. 1–4 • [C. H. Hunter Blair], ed., *Visitations of the north*, 3, SurtS, 144 (1930), 163

Archives Belvoir Castle, Leicestershire, household accounts, MS account, no. 4 • Belvoir Castle, Leicestershire, retinue list, Add. MS 97 • BL, estate accounts, Add. MS 12463

Likenesses P. Torrigiano, bronze relief medallion, *c.*1518, Westminster Abbey [*see illus.*] • P. Torrigiano, bronze relief medallion, plaster cast, NPG • portrait, Malvern Priory

Wealth at death assessed on £2000 goods in 1524 subsidy; goods worth £840 14*s.* 0*d.* listed in probate inventory: PRO, PROB 2/199

Lovell, Thomas (*d.* in or after **1615**), engineer and soldier, was probably from a family that farmed lands in Huntingdonshire and Norfolk (though he should not be confused with the prominent Norfolk gentleman Sir Thomas Lovell). In 1596 he recalled that he had served for thirty years in the wars of foreign countries, so he may have first fought for the Huguenots in the French wars of religion. In 1572 the Netherlands revolted against Catholic Spain and among the many Englishmen who crossed to Flushing to aid the Dutch was Lovell, who was reported to 'have served very valiantly' (Longleat, Devereux MS 2, fol. 9*r*). Many volunteers returned home in 1573, downcast by defeats, but Lovell's 'desire heartily to bear arms here against the enemey' resulted from a belief that the Spanish were 'enemies of God's gospel' (*CSP for.*, *August 1584–August 1585*, 440) and he stayed on. He evidently distinguished himself, for by the early 1580s he was a sergeant-major, an administrative command of considerable responsibility. Probably in this period he learned and developed the skills of an engineer—by 1585 he had responsibility for inspecting fortifications in southern Holland.

Lovell was one of the informants of Sir Francis Walsingham, the principal secretary, and was keen to return to the service of his 'own prince and natural country' (*CSP for., August 1584–August 1585*, 440); the intervention of England in the Dutch revolt provided an opportunity. Like many Englishmen, Lovell saw the conflict in apocalyptic terms, writing early in 1585 of a Dutch offer of sovereignty to Elizabeth I:

> No doubt but through God's help it will turn to good effect and establish His Word through Christendom within few years and the putting down of Antichrist, for this is the way by land to Rome and her Majesty being master here, will make all her enemies to quake. (ibid., 402)

Commissioned into the English army, he was wounded and sought a place as sergeant-major. Eventually, after temporary (unpaid) service in the cautionary town of Brill, he was appointed sergeant-major of Bergen-op-Zoom in February 1587. Lovell won plaudits from the Dutch for his part in the heroic defence against the Spanish siege in 1588 that resulted in a famous (and decisive) victory for the Anglo-Dutch forces.

In 1596 Lovell returned to England. The reasons are unknown, but he was probably about fifty and may have had enough of active service. He now put his 'great knowledge in fortifications, inundations of flooeds, water courses, and work of rivers and streams' (*Salisbury MSS*, 6.237) to good use. He promoted land reclamation schemes in fens around Peterborough and Ely and in parts of Lincolnshire, under the patronage of the Cecil family. These were not very successful and ruined Lovell's finances, but he and other veterans of the Dutch wars played an important developmental role in fen drainage that culminated in the great works of Sir Cornelius Vermuyden, while Lovell is notable as one of the first English engineers to master Dutch techniques. It is not known when he died but he was still alive in 1615.

D. J. B. TRIM

Sources *CSP for., 1584–5* · Longleat House, Wiltshire, Devereux MS 2 · *Calendar of the manuscripts of the most hon. the marquis of Salisbury*, 6, HMC, 9 (1895) · *Calendar of the manuscripts of the marquis of Bath preserved at Longleat, Wiltshire*, 5 vols., HMC, 58 (1904–80), vol. 5 · BL, Cotton MS Titus B vii · Nationaal Archief, The Hague, Archief van de Raad can State 1524 · T. Churchyard and R. Ro[binson], *A true discourse historicall of the succeeding governors in the Netherlands and the civil wars there begun in the yeere 1565* (1602) · *Draft calendar of patent rolls, 1585–7*, Lists and Index Society, 243 (1991), pt 2 · D. W. Davies, *Dutch influences on English culture, 1558–1625* (1964) · A. Hassell Smith, *County and court: government and politics in Norfolk, 1558–1603* (1974) · M. F. Kennedy, 'Fen drainage, the central government and local interest: Carleton and the gentlemen of South Holland', *HJ*, 26 (1983), 15–37

Archives BL, Cotton MS Titus B vii · Hatfield House, Hertfordshire, Cecil Papers, Salisbury MSS, 41, fol. 109; 43, fol. 15 · PRO, state papers, Holland, i.46, i.62, i.96, i.114, ii.23

Lovelock [*née* Northover Smith], **Irene May** (1896–1974), founder of the British Housewives' League, was born on 26 May 1896 at Wood Green, London, the elder daughter of William Northover Smith (1864–1953), ironmonger, and his wife, Florence Minnie Heath (1869–1943). She was educated at schools in Margate and Finchley, and at Birmingham School for Young Ladies. She married the Revd John Herbert Lovelock (1903–1986), a Church of England clergyman; they had three children. Irene Lovelock undertook a busy round of parish work in support of her husband. She became involved with the local Mothers' Union and helped with the Sunday school. It was a labour of love. She was a devout believer; her family joked that if St Peter would not let her enter through the gates of heaven she would have said 'Well, really!'

During the Second World War, Irene Lovelock's husband held the parish at Selhurst, London. In addition to her parish duties, Mrs Lovelock became an air raid warden and a firewatcher; she was subsequently awarded a civil defence medal for this work. During this time, too, both she and her husband's parishioners struggled with the difficulties of housekeeping in an era of rationing and shortages, experiences which undoubtedly provided the backdrop to her decision to establish the British Housewives' League (BHL).

The BHL was the best-known of a number of predominantly middle-class housewives' organizations which sprang up around Britain at the end of the war. According to an unpublished memoir written by Irene Lovelock later in her life, the idea for the BHL originated with her anger at the sight of women and children queuing for food one cold and rainy morning in June 1945. She called a meeting in her husband's parish hall in protest at the hardships of queuing. The meeting generated great local interest, and the league was officially constituted the following month. A BHL committee was formed, with Mrs Lovelock as chairman. In April 1946 she resigned from that post to become president of the league.

The league's interests quickly widened to embrace a range of issues affecting housewives and their families. Its main activities centred around the quality, quantity, and cost of food and other household commodities, concerns which, although rooted in an era of rationing and shortages, in many ways foreshadowed those of a later generation of consumer activists. In the immediate post-war period the BHL attracted national attention with a series of high-profile activities. It launched a 'bacon and egg campaign', to demonstrate dissatisfaction with aspects of the government's food policy; a 'vegetable boycott', to highlight what the league considered to be unacceptably high vegetable prices; a 'campaign for cleaner food', which focused on improving hygiene conditions in shops; and a protest against the use of agene in flour for bread. From the early 1950s the league waged a long battle against proposals to fluoridate drinking water.

The BHL also campaigned against what it termed 'over-control by the state'. Mrs Lovelock warned of the dangers of socialism in language which echoed much contemporary Conservative Party propaganda aimed at women: 'The sturdy independent character of the British Home is being lost in a welter of Control which the State does so badly and which the Mother, given the tools and opportunity, does so well' (British Housewives' League newsletter, July 1946). The league was often accused of being an offshoot of the Conservative Party, a charge it always vigorously rebutted. Like a number of other contemporary women's organizations, the league insisted that it was independent of party political allegiances, regarding this as a source of moral strength. Certainly, it sought initially to maintain a political balance of sorts. Both the Labour MP Edith Summerskill and the former Conservative MP Mavis Tate were involved with the league in its early days (although, significantly, Summerskill's relations with the league rapidly soured). However, the league's criticisms of the Attlee governments became increasingly vehement; in the second half of the 1940s it was supported by a number of prominent Conservatives. For their part, the Conservatives came to regard the BHL as something of a mixed blessing. The party was anxious that the BHL was drawing women away from its own women's organizations. It was also reluctant to be associated with the league's increasingly libertarian stance at a time when it was trying to emphasize its commitment to social reform.

The BHL did not view itself as a feminist organization. Its members none the less drew inspiration from the suffrage movement, and its methods—parades, deputations, demonstrations—recalled suffragette tactics. The league's advocacy of an expanded, public role for the housewife, albeit one grounded in a traditional view of women's domestic role, may also have issued an inadvertent challenge to contemporary conceptions of 'a woman's place'.

In terms of membership, the league enjoyed its greatest success in the first few years of its existence. In 1948 it claimed to have in excess of 70,000 members, although it would appear that its newsletter, *Housewives Today*, had a circulation of about 3000 at the time. The membership dwindled from the late 1940s, partly as a result of a number of bitter (and public) disagreements among the committee over the finances and direction of the league.

Irene Lovelock's direct involvement with the league gradually declined, although she remained as president for many years. She maintained that the league's major achievement had been 'to make the nation "housewife conscious"'. Irene Lovelock died at George's Hospital, Tooting, on 9 August 1974. After cremation her ashes were deposited at South London crematorium, Streatham Vale. ELIZABETH A. MCCARTY

Sources I. Lovelock, 'British housewife', unpub. MS, not dated, priv. coll. • *Housewives Today* (1948) • circular to branches, British Housewives' League, not dated, priv. coll. [occasional pubn] • newsletter, British Housewives' League, July 1946, priv. coll. [occasional pubn] • Bodl. Oxf., conservative party archive [various] • d. cert. • private information (2004) [Keith Lovelock] • Crockford

Lovelock, John Edward [Jack] (**1910–1949**), athlete and physician, was born on 5 January 1910 at Crushington, near Reefton, New Zealand, the son of John Edward Jones Lovelock (1869–1923), a goldmine battery superintendent, and his wife, Ivy Evelyn, *née* Harper (1883–1959). He had a sister and younger brother. His father, never in good health, died in 1923 while manager of the Mount Cook Motor Company at Fairlie in South Canterbury. Having attended Temuka primary school and Fairlie district high school, Lovelock in 1924 became a boarder at Timaru Boys' High School, where the oak he won as a seedling at the Berlin Olympics now flourishes. He became head prefect, a university scholar, and an outstanding boxer and runner. From the University of Otago medical school (1929–30) he gained a Rhodes scholarship to Exeter College, Oxford, in October 1931.

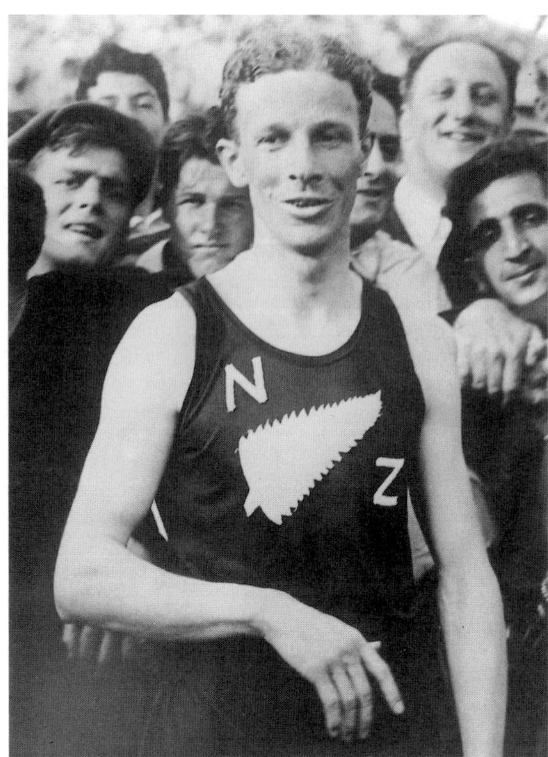

John Edward Lovelock (1910–1949), by unknown photographer, 1935 [after his victory in the Mile of the Century at the Princeton invitational meeting, New York, 15 June 1935]

At this time Lovelock began to keep diaries (still unpublished) which articulate the medical, intellectual, and psychological aspects of top-class racing and training. He improved dramatically as a runner in 1932, setting a British and empire mile record (4 min. 12.0 sec.), breaking the 37-year-old world record for the three-quarter mile (3 min. 2.2 sec.), and representing New Zealand at the Los Angeles Olympics. After finishing seventh, as Luigi Beccali of Italy and his Oxford team-mate Jerry Cornes took the top places, he promised in his diary 'to square my account with Beccali and Co.'.

A perfectly judged training programme produced, on 15 July 1933, 'the greatest mile of all time' (*Morning Post*, 16 July 1933), when Lovelock defeated the powerful American Bill Bonthron at Princeton University, breaking the world record by almost 2 seconds (4 min. 7.6 sec.). At the World University Games in Turin he was photographed with black-shirted Fascist students and placed second to Beccali in a fast 1500 metres. Following knee surgery, and a successful season as president of Oxford University Athletic Club, he moved to St Mary's Hospital medical school in Paddington. During 1934, which was a busy year for Lovelock, he also won the mile at the English championships and the British empire games in London, in a style described by the *Daily Telegraph* as 'melodious prose … with perfect serenity' (*DNZB*). Meanwhile the world records for 1500 metres and 1 mile had fallen to the Americans Bonthron and Glenn Cunningham. With Beccali, Cornes, and the rising Gene Venzke (USA) and Sydney Wooderson (England), this remarkable vintage attracted unprecedented attention from radio and film newsreels and the golden age of print journalism. In June 1935 Lovelock won a race at Princeton promoted as the Mile of the Century, which aroused what his diary calls 'terrific enthusiasm' from 'the great American public'.

Lovelock's finest moment was the 1500 metres final at the Berlin Olympic games on 6 August 1936. His diary calls it 'an artistic creation'. While Beccali shadowed Cunningham, Lovelock's unexpected acceleration 300 metres from the finish gave him a decisive victory by 4 metres in 3 min. 37.8 sec., a world record by a second, with Cunningham also under the previous best and Beccali third. The race's legendary quality comes not only from its being, as he put it, 'perfectly executed', but from the highly charged context of Nazi Germany's imperial arrogance and the new myth-making power of the media. It is now almost inseparable from the BBC radio commentary by Harold Abrahams, with its boyishly biased ecstasy and famous cry of 'Come on, Jack!'

After an unhappy official tour of New Zealand (30 October to 8 December 1936) Lovelock returned to England, graduated MB ChB, and practised in London, specializing in rheumatic diseases. He also worked as a freelance in sports journalism and broadcasting. His self-published booklet *Athletics* (1937) ends with the elegiac advice that 'athletic fame is fleeting'. In the Second World War he served as major in the Royal Army Medical Corps, rehabilitating the wounded. A fall from a horse in 1940 left him with severely damaged vision. On 26 March 1945 in London he married Cynthia Wells James (*b.* 1915), an American from Brooklyn employed in the office of strategic services and secretary of the American Hospital in England. They had two daughters, Janet and Mary. In 1947 they moved to Flatbush in Brooklyn and Lovelock worked as assistant director of physical medicine and director of rehabilitation at the New York Hospital for Special Surgery. In 1948 he received a Winfield Baird fellowship for research in rehabilitation. On 28 December 1949, suffering from influenza, having phoned his wife to say he was dizzy and too ill to stay at work, Lovelock fell beneath a subway train at Church Avenue Station, Brooklyn, and was killed. His strong pebbled spectacles were found in his pocket. He was cremated at Fresh Pond crematorium, Maspeth, New York, on 30 December.

Numerous accounts, which besides sports writings include two biographies, a novel, and stage and television plays, have sought to define the fey, elusive personality behind Lovelock's public achievements. He continues to exert the charisma that aroused 'terrific enthusiasm' in America, perplexed Hitler, and reduced the urbane voice of the BBC to a schoolboy babble. ROGER ROBINSON

Sources N. Harris, *The legend of Lovelock* (1964) • C. Tobin, *Lovelock: New Zealand's Olympic gold miler* (1984) • R. Robinson, 'Lovelock, John Edward (Jack)', *DNZB*, vol. 4 • J. Lovelock, *Athletics* (1937) • J. McNeish, *Lovelock* (1986) • *New York Times* (29 Dec 1949) • *Brooklyn Eagle* (30 Dec 1949) • N. Harris, *Lap of honour: the great moments of New Zealand athletics* (1963) • N. Harris and R. Clarke, *The lonely breed* (1967) • D. Hart-Davis, *Hitler's games: the 1936 Olympics* (1986) • R. Quercetani and C. Nelson, *The 1500 metres and mile*, 2nd edn (1994) • P. Heidenstrom, *Athletes of the century: 100 years of New Zealand track and field* (1992) • 'Lovelock, Jack', *Oxford companion to New Zealand literature*, ed. R. Robinson and others (1998), 312 • S. Fordyce, 'Lovelock's labour lost', *New Zealand Runner*, 60 (1989), 31–4 • S. Fordyce, 'Lovelock's labour lost', *New Zealand Runner*, 61 (1989), 37–9 • b. cert. • m. cert. • private information (2004)

Archives NL NZ, Turnbull L., MS-Group-0012 WTU • Timaru Boys' High School War Memorial Library, Wellington, New Zealand | FILM BFI NFTVA, documentary footage

Likenesses photograph, 1935, NL NZ, Turnbull L. [*see illus.*] • Associated Press, photographs • Sport and General, photographs • World Wide Photos, photographs • photograph, Hult. Arch. • portraits, Timaru Boys' High School, New Zealand

Lover, Samuel (1797–1868), miniature painter and author, was born in Dublin on 24 February 1797, the eldest son of William Frederick Lover (*d.* 1833) and his wife, Abigail Maher (*d.* *c.*1810). His father was a stockbroker and had various other commercial interests. His mother was an accomplished singer and musician, who encouraged the young Samuel's artistic and musical interests, in particular an appreciation of Irish poetry and songs. As a child Lover suffered from poor health and at the age of twelve he was sent for a rest-cure to a farm in co. Wicklow. There he was introduced to the customs and traditions of country people. Despite his artistic interests and against his will, Lover was sent to work in his father's office and in 1814 he went to London to work in another business house. Lover thrived on the artistic atmosphere of London and on his return to Dublin there was a family disagreement and Lover left home to pursue a career as an artist.

It was probably at this time that Lover attended the Dublin Society's drawing schools: his presence there is recorded by James Dowling Herbert (1762/3–1837) in his memoirs. Lover supported himself by painting marine views and landscapes, copying music, and teaching drawing. He became a pupil of the prolific miniaturist John Comerford, and as a result of his influence Lover turned to miniature painting and adopted his master's meticulous technique. Lover had learned to draw at the Dublin Society schools and he combined this skill with painting in watercolour on ivory to produce extremely accomplished portraits. His work gradually became larger and he relished the details of theatrical props and fancy dress which he included in much of his work. His portraits are posed and he often painted his sitters singing or reading, as may be seen in the many examples of his work in the National Gallery of Ireland. Lover passed on his skill as a miniaturist to his pupil Frederic William Burton.

However, it was as a songwriter that Lover was first celebrated. In 1818 he composed a musical tribute to Thomas Moore which he performed at a banquet held in Dublin for the poet. In the song, entitled 'Election of a Poet Laureate for Olympus', Venus and the Graces vote for their favourite, Moore, who of course wins the award. Lover's connection with Moore and Moore's family proved useful: he drew on Moore's work for inspiration for his pictures, such as *Flow on thou Shining River* (National Gallery of Ireland, Dublin) from Moore's *Irish Melodies* (1807), and many of his early commissions were from people in the musical, literary, and theatrical world. His artistic and social accomplishments obtained for him an entrée into Dublin society. His friend and patroness Lady Morgan, the art historian and novelist, was the doyenne of literary and musical society. She encouraged him to paint and to write musical comedy; he produced several portraits of her (National Gallery of Ireland and the Royal Irish Academy, Dublin). Lover was also introduced to the LeFanu family and their intellectual circle.

Lover began publishing and illustrating stories about Ireland in the leading literary journals of the 1820s and 1830s such as the *Dublin Penny Journal*, the *Dublin Literary Gazette*, the *Irish Penny Magazine*, and the *Dublin University Magazine*; with Charles Lever, George Petrie, and William Carleton he was joint founder of the last of these publications, an anti-nationalist journal which was something of an innovation in its commitment to serialized fiction. He was a member of a number of convivial clubs in Dublin, and the official portrait painter of the Burschenschaft Club, founded by Lever; Lover was also a prominent member of the Dublin Glee Club. In 1826 Lover wrote his most famous ballad, 'Rory O'More', and in 1827 he composed his first musical drama, *Grana Uile*, based on the story of Grace O'Malley, the pirate queen. In that year he married Lucy (*d.* 1847), the daughter of a Dublin architect, John Berrel.

In 1817, 1819, and 1823 Lover exhibited drawings at the Artists of Ireland exhibitions. He began to exhibit at the Royal Hibernian Academy at its first exhibition in 1826. In 1828 he was elected an associate of the academy, becoming a full academician in 1829; he was appointed trustee and secretary in 1831. Between that first exhibition and 1863 he exhibited 115 pictures at the Royal Hibernian Academy. In 1831 Lover was commissioned to paint a portrait of the violinist Paganini when he came to Dublin. The portrait was exhibited at the Royal Academy in 1832 and at the Royal Hibernian Academy in 1833. This important commission led to requests from other well-known sitters. He was offered a commission to paint Princess Victoria, but this never materialized because family circumstances prevented him from travelling to England.

In the early 1830s Lover developed a new talent for humorous political caricature, a medium that had become very popular due to the skill of John Doyle, the principal exponent of the genre at the time. The *Parson's Horn Book*, a satire on religion, was published in 1830: Lover contributed the illustrations and much of its literary content. The book gained notoriety as a result of a crown prosecution. In 1832 Lover published a less contentious work, *Legends and Stories of Ireland*, which he also illustrated. This drew on his knowledge of rural Ireland, its customs, and characters.

Through his writings and the success of his portrait painting—such as the Paganini portrait—Lover had become known in London. In 1835 he went to live there permanently and he quickly established himself as a miniaturist. He became a member of the Garrick Club and part of London-Irish literary, musical, and artistic society. Among his friends were Father Mahony, who wrote under the pseudonym Father Prout; Michael Banim; John Banim; and Anna Jameson, the art historian and daughter of the miniaturist Denis Brownell Murphy. Through the literary patroness Lady Blessington, Lover became a friend of Charles Dickens, with whom he was associated in founding *Bentley's Miscellany*; he made an important contribution to the design of the journal, which was characterized by an effective combination of text and image.

In 1837 Lover published his first novel, *Rory O'More: a National Romance*, set at the time of the 1798 rebellion. This he successfully dramatized, but it was just one of a series of plays: *The Beau Ideal* (1835), *The White Horse of the Peppards* (1838), and *The Happy Man* (1839). He subsequently composed a musical drama, *The Greek Boy* (1840), and a burlesque opera, *Il Paddy Whack in Italia* (1841), which was produced by Michael William Balfe in the Lyceum Theatre. In 1842 he published *Handy Andy*, his most significant novel and the vehicle for a hero who has been described as 'the great, amiable, awkward, moronic lout of Irish literature' (Hogan, 725); in 1844 he published *Treasure Trove*.

In 1844 Lover abandoned miniature painting as a result of failing eyesight but continued to paint and exhibit landscapes. He invented a new form of entertainment which he called Irish Evenings, a monologue of songs, recitations, and stories, all of his own composition. These he performed at the Princess's Concert Rooms, London. Lover spent the years 1846–8 touring North America with a theatrical company, performing his Irish Evenings with great success, and painting landscapes and views such as *The Cabildo, New Orleans* (British Museum, London). He composed his best-known song 'The Alabama' there. Back in London, he continued to perform his Irish Evenings, which he renamed Paddy's Portfolio, and wrote the drama *The Sentinel of Alva* (1854) for the Haymarket Theatre; he also composed two librettos for Balfe.

While Lover was in the United States his wife died and on his return in 1848 his daughter, Meta, died. On 1 January 1852 he married Mary Jane Wandby from Cambridgeshire, and in 1856 was granted a civil-list pension of £300 p.a. in recognition of his services to art and literature. In 1858 he published *The Lyrics of Ireland* with biographical and musical notes. In 1860 the London Irish rifle volunteers was formed and Lover took an active part, writing songs which were published in *Original Songs for the Rifle Volunteers*. He fell ill in February 1864 and in 1865 he went to live in the Isle of Wight and then in St Helier, Jersey. He died at Clear View, St Lawrence Valley, Jersey, on 6 July 1868 and was survived by his second wife, Mary. Lover was buried in Kensal Green cemetery, London, on 15 July. His memory is commemorated on a tablet in St Patrick's Cathedral, Dublin.

Lover's career as artist, writer, and composer reflects his versatile talent; as a painter he produced not only miniatures but also landscapes and literary and historical genre paintings. His wide-ranging productivity has attracted the criticism that he spread his talents too thinly: his biographer in the *Dictionary of National Biography* comments that he 'never reached a great height in any department of his many-sided efforts' and describes his literary works rather harshly as 'only those of a second-rate Lever and a third-rate Moore'. His novels made an important contribution to the development of Anglo-Irish literature, and recently his artworks have deservedly attracted more attention (although his miniatures can vary in quality). He belonged to an important generation of Irish literary and artistic figures who achieved success in England and America in the early nineteenth century.

PAUL CAFFREY

Sources B. Bernard, *The life of Samuel Lover*, 2 vols. (1874) · A. J. Symington, *Life sketch of Samuel Lover* (1880) · W. G. Strickland, *A dictionary of Irish artists*, 2 (1913), 25–9 · P. Caffrey, 'Samuel Lover's achievement as a painter', *Irish Arts Review*, 3/1 (1986), 51–4 · P. Caffrey, 'Samuel Lover: his life and work', 2 vols., BA diss., University of Dublin, 1985 · P. Caffrey, 'Irish portrait miniatures, *c*.1700–1830', 3 vols., PhD diss., Southampton Institute, 1995 · P. Caffrey, *Portrait of Master John Russel Moore* (1989) [exhibition catalogue, Gorry Gallery, Dublin] · J. D. Herbert, *Irish varieties for the last fifty years* (1836), 55 · A. Crookshank and the Knight of Glin [D. Fitzgerald], *The painters of Ireland, c.1660–1920* (1978), 242 · A. Le Harivel, ed., *National Gallery of Ireland: illustrated summary catalogue of drawings, watercolours and miniatures* (1983), 475–80 · A. M. Stewart, ed., *Royal Hibernian Academy of Arts: index of exhibitors and their works, 1826–1979*, 2 (1986), 2.203–5 · A. M. Stewart, ed., *Irish art loan exhibitions, 1765–1927*, 1 (1990), 422–3 · NG Ire., Bartlett MSS · *DNB* · B. Sloan, *The pioneers of Anglo-Irish fiction, 1800–1850* (1986) · R. Hogan, ed., *Dictionary of Irish literature*, rev. edn, 1 (1996) · *CGPLA Eng. & Wales* (1868) · J. Sutherland, *The Longman companion to Victorian fiction* (1988)

Archives BL, letters and plays · NG Ire. | NG Ire., Barton MSS · NL Ire., Larcom MSS · NL Ire., LeFanu MSS

Likenesses S. Lover, self-portrait, watercolour on ivory, *c*.1825, NG Ire. · S. Lover, self-portrait, chalk, 1828, NG Ire. · E. A. Foley, marble bust, 1839, NPG; repro. in Caffrey, 'Samuel Lover's achievement', 51 · S. Lover, self-portrait, chalk on paper, *c*.1840, priv. coll. · C. Baugniet, lithograph, 1844, BM, NPG, NG Ire. · H. Watkins, print, *c*.1855, NPG · J. Harwood, oils, 1856, NG Ire. · S. Lover, self-portrait, pencil, NPG · Maull & Co., photograph, NPG · ceramic bust, NG Ire. · engraving (after drawing by D. Maclise), repro. in *Fraser's Magazine* (1836), 211 · stipple, NG Ire. · wood-engraving (after photograph by Maull & Co.), NPG; repro. in *ILN* (1868)

Wealth at death under £800: probate, 25 Nov 1868, *CGPLA Eng. & Wales*

Lovetot, Sir John de (*b*. in or before **1236**, *d*. **1294**), administrator and justice, was a younger son of the Richard de Lovetot (*d*. 1235), who was lord of one-third of the Huntingdonshire barony of Southoe, and his wife, Christine, who survived him. John cannot therefore have been born later than 1236. He was probably the John de Lovetot who acted as bailiff of the escheated honour of Peverel of Nottingham from 1258 to 1260 or 1261, while in 1263–4 he was one of four men who administered the county of Yorkshire in opposition to its royalist sheriff. In the late 1260s he was an under-sheriff in Norfolk, and in the early 1270s successively steward of Norwich Cathedral priory and in the service of Robert de Vere, earl of Oxford, again possibly as his steward. By 1269 he had been knighted.

Lovetot may have owed his entry into royal service to Robert Tiptoft or Tibetot (*d*. 1298), whom he represented when Tiptoft went on crusade with the future Edward I in 1270. He had certainly entered Edward's service by 1274, when he was appointed joint custodian of the vacant see of Durham. Lovetot was appointed a justice of the common bench in Easter term 1275, and the formal records of the court show him serving as a justice continuously until the end of 1289. He is, however, known to have been sent abroad by the king on at least eight different occasions during these years, both on diplomatic missions and on commissions concerning the administration of Ponthieu, in northern France, and these overseas journeys caused him to miss part or all of several law terms. Lovetot was also active during the same period as an assize and gaol delivery justice, and managed to find time to fulfil duties as one of the trusted servants of Edward's wife, Queen Eleanor.

Lovetot was disgraced early in 1290 with his judicial colleagues, for failing to prevent the chief justice of the court, Thomas Weyland (*d*. 1298), from altering the record of a case heard in the court. Between June 1290 and October 1293 he paid the fine of £1000 that had secured his release from the Tower of London. In 1293 he was committed to the Tower for a second time, perhaps for misconduct in the service of Queen Eleanor, and only released for a second fine of 1000 marks.

John de Lovetot's first wife, Margaret, was the daughter of Robert d'Eyville and his wife, Denise. They were certainly married by 1268 and she died in the late 1280s. His second wife, Joan, daughter of William of Standon, had previously been married to Bartholomew de Briaunzon. This marriage probably took place in 1290 or 1291. Lovetot had at least four sons and three daughters, probably all with his first wife. He died shortly before 5 November 1294. In 1301 his son and heir, also John, alleged that Lovetot had been murdered at the instigation of Walter Langton, bishop of Coventry (*d*. 1321). The younger John claimed that Langton had been conducting an adulterous relationship with his stepmother, Joan, who died about August 1302, but although proceedings continued until 1303, he was unable to prove his allegations.

PAUL BRAND, *rev.*

Sources court of common pleas, feet of fines, PRO, CP 25/1 · exchequer, king's remembrancer, memoranda rolls, PRO, E 159 · court of common pleas, plea rolls, PRO, CP 40 · *Chancery records* · Rymer, *Foedera*, new edn, 1/2.956–7 · T. F. Tout and H. Johnstone, eds., *State trials of the reign of Edward the First, 1289–1293*, CS, 3rd ser., 9 (1906) · P. Brand, *The making of the common law* (1992)

Lovett, Richard (*bap*. **1692**, *d*. **1780**), writer on electricity, was baptized on 31 July 1692 at Chalfont St Giles, Buckinghamshire, the son of Richard Lovet, member of a landed family long established in the district. On 25 November 1722 he was admitted to a lay clerkship in Worcester Cathedral, and retained this position until his death. The name of his wife is not known; a son, Timothy, a pupil at Worcester Infirmary, predeceased him. Lovett witnessed the lectures given by J. T. Desaguliers in 1739, which included simple demonstrations of electrical phenomena. From about 1750, when he was able to obtain a friction machine, electricity became Lovett's main interest. He read widely, in particular the works of Benjamin Franklin, and wrote a number of books and pamphlets for the benefit of his provincial neighbours.

Lovett's interest soon concentrated on the medical effects of electricity and his books included lists of those afflicted by a wide variety of ailments and disabilities; he claimed to have cured many of these or at least to have alleviated their suffering. In 1758 he advertised himself as able to effect cures, especially of a sore throat, by electricity. His first book was *The subtil medium prov'd, or, That … power … call'd sometimes aether, but oftener elementary fire, verify'd* (1756): it was savaged in the *Monthly Review* of December 1756, and Lovett was condemned as ill-educated, ignorant of his subject, and adding nothing beyond the lengthy title, a view echoed by Augustus De Morgan in *The Athenaeum* of 1863.

While this criticism was justified, Lovett, with his 'electrical fluid', was only one of many would-be natural philosophers seeking to explain effects for which adequate concepts and vocabulary did not yet exist. Lovett responded in 1759 with *Sir Isaac Newton's aether realised, or, The second part of the subtil medium proved and electricity rendered useful*, in which he admitted a lack of polite education and contested at length the arguments made against him. His *Philosophical essays … containing an enquiry into the nature and properties of the electrical fluid etc.* (1766) contained lengthy extracts from the *Philosophical Transactions* of the Royal Society and from the works of Franklin, and drew praise from the editor of *Critical Review* in October 1766, who considered it 'evidently a work of genius' (Chambers, 364). In 1774 Lovett published *The electrical philosopher: containing a new system of physics, founded upon the principle of an universal plenum of elementary fire*. This was cast as a dialogue, which Lovett considered the easiest form to convey his unfamiliar material to local uneducated readers, whom he sought to impress with copious extracts ranging from Newton and Franklin to minor writers on electrical science. In the latter part of the book Lovett dealt with what he considered to be related effects: lightning, magnetism, earthquakes, gravity, and motion. In reaction to the criticism voiced against his *Philosophical Essays*, he appended 'a postscript containing strictures upon the uncandid animadversions of the monthly reviewers on those essays'. He died on 8 June 1780 and was buried on 11 June at St Swithin's Church, Worcester.

T. B. SAUNDERS, *rev.* ANITA MCCONNELL

Sources J. Chambers, *Biographical illustrations of Worcestershire* (1820), 363–4 · A. De Morgan, 'A budget of paradoxes', *The Athenaeum* (12 Dec 1863), 800–01 · parish register (baptism), Chalfont St Giles, Buckinghamshire, 31 July 1692 · parish register, St Swithin, Worcester · R. Lovett, *The subtil medium prov'd* (1756) · R. Lovett, *Philosophical essays* (1766) · *Monthly Review*, 15 (1756), 561–4

Likenesses R. Hancock, mezzotint (after oil painting; after J. Wright), BM, NPG · oils (after J. Wright), NMM · portrait, MHS Oxf.

Lovett, Richard (1851–1904), author, son of Richard Deacon Lovett and Annie Godart, his wife, was born at Croydon on 5 January 1851. Nine years of boyhood (1858–67) were spent with his parents at Brooklyn in the United States. Leaving school there at an early age, he was employed by a New York publisher. In 1867 he returned to England, and in 1869 entered Cheshunt College, whose president, Dr Henry Robert Reynolds, powerfully influenced him. He graduated BA with honours in philosophy at London University in 1873, and proceeded MA in 1874, when he left Cheshunt and was ordained into the ministry of the Countess of Huntingdon's Connexion. He began ministerial work at Bishop's Stortford, also acting as assistant master at the school there.

In 1876 Lovett accepted an independent charge as minister of the Countess of Huntingdon church at Rochdale. On 29 April 1879 he married Ann Hancock, daughter of William Reynolds of Torquay. Lovett was a thoughtful, able preacher, and he made many friends in Lancashire. But his leaning was towards writing rather than pastoral work, and in 1882 he was appointed book editor of the Religious Tract Society in London. In his new office Lovett's interest in foreign missions grew. He became a director of the London Missionary Society, and wrote the society's history for its centenary (1899). Interest in missionary work brought him into close touch with James Chalmers of New Guinea and James Gilmour of Mongolia, both of whose lives he wrote. He revisited the United States as a delegate to the ecumenical missionary conference of 1900.

Lovett was a close student of all that concerned the English printed Bible, and especially the works of William Tyndale; when the John Rylands Library at Manchester was founded, he gave advice on the biblical section, and compiled its bibliographical catalogue of Bibles. He also had his own collection of early English Bibles and kindred works, which was dispersed after his death. In 1899, on the retirement of Samuel Gosnell Green, Lovett became one of the secretaries of the Religious Tract Society, with responsibility for the society's continental interests, while retaining much of his former work as book editor. Towards the end of his life the affairs of Cheshunt College, of which he acted as honorary secretary, gave him anxiety, and he was among the early workers for the reconstitution of the Congregational Union. Overwork impaired his health, and he died suddenly of heart failure at his house, 74 Victoria Road, Clapham, London, on 29 December 1904. His wife, one son, and two daughters survived him.

Lovett was a prolific author, contributing frequently to periodical literature. He also published a series entitled Pictures (of Norway, Holland, Ireland, London, and the USA), *The English Bible in the John Rylands Library* (1899), and other works.

A. R. BUCKLAND, *rev.* H. C. G. MATTHEW

Sources *Christian World* (5 Jan 1905) · A. Peel, *These hundred years: a history of the Congregational Union of England and Wales, 1831–1931* (1931) · personal knowledge (1912) · *CGPLA Eng. & Wales* (1905)

Wealth at death £5724 9s. 11½d.: probate, 3 Feb 1905, *CGPLA Eng. & Wales*

Lovett, William (1800–1877), Chartist and radical, was born in Newlyn, Cornwall, on 8 May 1800, the son of William Lovett, captain of a small trading vessel and a native of Hull, who was drowned before Lovett's birth. His mother, Kezia (*née* Green) (*c.*1778–1852), proceeded to raise Lovett and his four siblings with the help of her family and by her own efforts, which included selling fish in Penzance market. He was sent to the local dame-schools, but he was always to regret the limitations of this education and of the reading materials available during his youth, inadequacies accentuated by his strict Methodist upbringing. After serving seven years' apprenticeship to a rope maker, he was unable to secure employment at the trade and turned instead to his natural skills as a woodworker. So it was that when, in June 1821, he left Cornwall for London he was to learn a second trade of cabinet-making by working for 'a trade-working master' in Somers Town (*Life and Struggles*, 28). Within a few years he was able to serve a qualifying period at a respectable shop and eventually gain admittance to the élite West End Cabinet-makers' Society, of which, remarkably, he was later elected president.

It was as a young man in London that Lovett was able to indulge his passion for the pursuit of knowledge, by joining several mutual improvement societies and attending lectures, as he recalled, at the recently opened mechanics' institute, as well as frequenting the radical coffee houses, where he was influenced by such speakers as John Gale Jones, Richard Carlile, and the Revd Robert Taylor. On 3 June 1826 at All Souls, Langham Place, he married Mary Solly, a lady's maid from Pegwell, Kent, who was to be his unobtrusive, uncomplaining support. Of their two daughters, Kezia died from an accident in infancy, and the other, also Mary, was at the end of Lovett's life attempting to make a living in the theatre. The Lovetts proceeded to open a confectioner's shop off St Martin's Lane, but this was the first of several failed business ventures.

By now an advocate of Owenism, Lovett had joined the First London Co-operative Trading Association and, having given up the shop, he took over from James Watson as storekeeper at the close of 1829. This position too did not provide a livelihood and he was for much of 1831 secretary of the nationally important British Association for Promoting Co-operative Knowledge, launched after the First London Association had hived off its propagandist functions. By the late 1820s, in addition to Watson, Lovett had also got to know his other principal lifelong radical associates Henry Hetherington and John Cleave. This key grouping, which was to provide a highly visible leadership within metropolitan working-class radicalism for most of the 1830s, differed from Owen himself in considering political reform to be as important as the transforming powers of co-operation, and they engaged in both activities concurrently.

The first political society to which Lovett belonged was Henry Hunt's Friends of Civil and Religious Liberty of 1827. Two years later this was renamed the Radical Reform Association, with a programme of universal male suffrage, annual parliaments, and the ballot, and held weekly meetings at the Rotunda amid the excitement occasioned by the French revolution of July 1830 and Wellington's cancellation in November of the king's annual visit to the City for fear of insurrection. Lovett's traditional reputation as an uncompromised proponent of moral force, while entirely valid for the Chartist period, is out of kilter with his outspoken militancy during the years of the reform agitation. An experienced police spy described him as 'a dangerous man' for advocating arming and declaring 'he for one would fight' against the aristocracy (Large, *Pressure from Without*, 116); and Lovett vehemently opposed Hunt's efforts to prohibit the display of the tricolour at meetings and to purge Gale Jones, Carlile's supporters, and other revolutionaries when the Radical Reform Association disintegrated in December 1830.

William Lovett (1800–1877), by unknown photographer

Although Lovett was also a member of the councils of both the Metropolitan Political Union and the National Political Union, these were organizations created by the middle-class reformers—at the inaugural mass meeting of the latter, after Cleave was howled down for seconding his amendment in favour of universal suffrage, he denounced the middle class for wanting to make the working class 'tools of their purposes' (Large, *DLB*, 167)—and it was the National Union of the Working Classes, founded in April 1831, that was the ultra-radical successor to the Radical Reform Association. Despite joining the union belatedly, in September 1831, he rapidly became a member of its committee and one of the twenty-four class leaders, as well as drafting with Watson the rules, including the widely circulated 'Declaration of the National Union of the Working Classes'. The union's most successful demonstration was against the national fast day of 21 March 1832, proclaimed by the whig government in expiation of the outbreak of cholera, when tens of thousands attempted to march from Finsbury Square to Westminster. Lovett, Watson, and William Benbow were arrested but acquitted, amid acclamation, of the charge of causing a riot. The previous year, on refusing as a non-voter either to serve in the militia or to find a substitute, Lovett had had, to great publicity, his household goods distrained and auctioned; balloting for the militia was thereafter discontinued. His intensive activity of these years also included a significant contribution to the campaign for an unstamped press, for whose victim fund, in operation from July 1831, he acted as sub-treasurer and secretary.

Lovett was 'a tall, gentlemanly-looking man with a high and ample forehead, a pale, contemplative cast of countenance, dark-brown hair, and … a very prepossessing exterior, in manner quiet, modest and unassuming, speaking seldom, but when he does so always with the best effect', although for Place 'his is a spirit misplaced', being 'in ill-health', and 'somewhat hypochondriacal'; 'a man of melancholy temperament, soured with the perplexities of the world' (Hovell, 55–6).

From 1832 the Lovetts took over the former Hatton Garden premises of the First London Co-operative Trading Association and ran them as a coffee house and discussion centre, with a reading-room and library. While financially unsuccessful, these two years served as a key transitional phase for Lovett, in the aftermath of the failure of both co-operative trading and radical parliamentary reform. He began to allot education a major role in the attainment of political and social change, and to move towards his ultimate repudiation of Owenism. He was shortly to enter into collaboration with the middle-class reformers Dr James Roberts Black and Francis Place.

The outcome of these developments was the foundation on 16 June 1836 of the (London) Working Men's Association (LWMA), with Lovett as secretary, whose membership, costing 1s. monthly, was further restricted to 'persons of a good moral character among the industrious classes' (Goodway, 22)—over three years only 318 were admitted—although honorary members could be elected from the middle class. During its first year the working men listened receptively to lectures on, and discussed, orthodox political economy. In February 1837 a public meeting was held at the Crown and Anchor tavern in the Strand to petition parliament for what were to become known as the 'six points' of the People's Charter. Meetings in May and June between the working men and radical members of parliament led to a committee of six from each group, and then (probably in December) to Lovett and J. A. Roebuck alone being appointed to draw up a parliamentary bill incorporating the Crown and Anchor petition. When Roebuck withdrew from the task it was Place who provided the drafting expertise. The writing of the Charter was therefore the combined work of Lovett and Place, although suggestions of the committee of twelve and of the LWMA did result in revisions to the original document.

The People's Charter was published on 8 May 1838 and adopted by the Birmingham Political Union, but was also taken up by the very different movement which was mobilizing in the north and the midlands and increasingly under the influence of Feargus O'Connor and his *Northern Star*. Already the LWMA had been wrong-footed when in the winter of 1837–8, during the trial—ending in the transportation—of the five Glasgow cotton spinners, Daniel O'Connell, one of its parliamentary coadjutors, made his extreme hostility to trade unions explicit and was successful in instituting a select committee to investigate them. In February O'Connor's attack on the LWMA was answered by Lovett's denunciation of him as 'the great "I AM" of politics, the great personification of Radicalism' (*Life and Struggles*, 161). Open conflict between its two opposing wings had broken out even before the new movement of Chartism had emerged. The LWMA was still able to control events in the capital sufficiently to fix the election of its eight candidates, including Lovett, at the New Palace Yard meeting of September as London's delegates to the first Chartist convention, which when it met in February 1839 unanimously appointed him as its secretary; but both the LWMA and its leading member, Lovett, were now relegated to the sidelines, never to recover their former influence.

After the convention had moved to Birmingham, Lovett, as the signatory of its resolutions condemning the Metropolitan Police's dispersal of the Bull Ring meetings, was arrested on 6 July and sentenced four weeks later at Warwick assizes to twelve months' imprisonment for seditious libel. On his release from Warwick gaol in July 1840, he declined to join the newly established National Charter Association, which he condemned as an illegal organization; and, after publishing the short book *Chartism: a New Organization of the People* (1840), which he had written in prison with John Collins, he proceeded to launch in 1841 in London only the National Association for Promoting the Political and Social Improvement of the People, which it had proposed. This ambitious vision of a network of halls, schools, and libraries was denounced as 'knowledge chartism' and a 'new move' by the National Charter Association and the *Northern Star*, and all who wished to participate were compelled to isolate themselves from mainstream Chartism. Financial support was barely enough for a national hall to be opened in High Holborn in 1842; W. J. Linton, himself a member, provided a damning assessment: 'Lovett was impracticable; and his new association, after obtaining a few hundred members, dwindled into a debating club, and their hall became a dancing academy, let occasionally for unobjectionable public meetings' (Goodway, 41). Lovett's espousal of class collaboration made him a natural supporter of the Complete Suffrage Union, of which he became a council member; yet at its second conference, in December 1842, he rejected a proposed 'bill of rights' in place of the Charter and, seconded by O'Connor, his resolution was carried overwhelmingly. This caused the exodus of the middle-class delegates but, equally, Lovett spurned the detested O'Connor's offer of reconciliation.

For the remainder of his career Lovett scraped a living as a teacher in various schools and published two textbooks, one on *Elementary Anatomy and Physiology* (1851); but in old age he was reduced to poverty, dependent on the charity of friends: 'Perhaps few persons have worked harder, or laboured more earnestly, than I have; but somehow I was never destined to make money' (*Life and Struggles*, 400). Although he had begun his memoirs as early as 1840, not until the year before his death at his home, 137 Euston Road, London (long since a deist inclining to Christianity), on 8 August 1877, did he publish *The Life and Struggles of William Lovett, in his Pursuit of Bread, Knowledge, and Freedom*. It is one of the outstanding working-class autobiographies, but in it Lovett underplays the importance of his early political activities and excises their extremism, distortions that have been followed until recently by most historians. He was buried in Highgate cemetery.

Lovett was a creative leader of metropolitan artisan radicalism in the late 1820s and early 1830s, he was joint author of the Charter, and he was the perfect political secretary. He also became a respectable Victorian Liberal and thereby estranged himself from the great and turbulent movement of Chartism which he had helped to create.

DAVID GOODWAY

Sources *The life and struggles of William Lovett, in his pursuit of bread, knowledge, and freedom* (1876) • 'William Lovett', *Howitt's Journal* (8 May 1847) • J. Wiener, *William Lovett* (1989) • D. Large, 'Lovett, William', *DLB*, vol. 6 • D. Large, 'William Lovett', *Pressure from without in early Victorian England*, ed. P. Hollis (1974), 105–30 • I. J. Prothero, *Artisans and politics in early nineteenth-century London: John Gast and his times* (1979) • D. Goodway, *London Chartism, 1838–1848* (1982) • M. Hovell, *The chartist movement*, 2nd edn (1925) • B. Harrison, '"Kindness and reason": William Lovett and education', *Victorian values*, ed. G. Marsden (1990), 13–28 • E. J. Yeo, 'Will the real Mary Lovett please stand up?', *Living and learning*, ed. M. Chase and I. Dyck (1996), 163–81 • G. D. H. Cole, *Chartist portraits* (1941) • minutes of the Working Men's Association, BL, Add. MS 37773 • *CGPLA Eng. & Wales* (1877)

Archives Birm. CA, corresp. and papers • BL, corresp. and papers as Chartist National Convention secretary, Add. MS 34245 • BL, papers, Add. MSS 78161–78164 • NRA, priv. coll., MS autobiography | BL, corresp. with Francis Place, Add. MSS 35149–35151, *passim* • BL, minutes, mainly in his hand, of Working Men's Association, Add. MSS 37773–37776

Likenesses A. Harral, woodcut (after drawing by H. Anelay), repro. in 'William Lovett', 253 • engraving, repro. in *Reynolds's Political Instructor* (12 Jan 1850) • photographs, NPG [*see illus.*]

Wealth at death under £450: probate, 17 Oct 1877, *CGPLA Eng. & Wales*

Lovibond, Edward (*bap.* 1723, *d.* 1775), poet, was the son of Edward Lovibond (*d.* 1737), a director of the East India Company, and his wife, Mary, and was baptized at St James's, Clerkenwell, London, on 6 July 1723. He was educated at Kingston upon Thames under Richard Wooddeson and at Magdalen College, Oxford, where he matriculated as gentleman commoner on 15 May 1739. Having inherited a competence from his father, Lovibond spent the greater part of his life in the neighbourhood of Hampton, Middlesex, 'where he seems to have divided his time between the occupations of rural economy, the amusements of literature and poetry, and the gaieties of elegant society' (Anderson, 577). On 26 December 1744 he married Catherine Hamilton, third daughter of Gustavus Hamilton of King's county, Ireland. The marriage was reputed to have been unhappy. Lovibond died on 27 September 1775 at his home in Hampton, which had formerly belonged to Charles Jervas. In 1776 Horace Walpole bought some pictures, including one by Cowley, 'at Mr. Lovibond's sale', which he had admired previously on a visit to Lovibond's estate in the early 1770s (Walpole, letter to Lady Ossory, 20 June 1776; 'Walpole's journals', 69).

Through his involvement with Edward Moore's weekly newspaper *The World*—to which he contributed five papers (Chalmers, 283–4)—Lovibond may have been acquainted with Walpole, who was one of the paper's original contributors. His best-known piece, 'Tears of Old May Day', occasioned by 'the reforming our style or calendar to the general usage of the rest of Europe', first appeared in *The World* on 25 July 1754 and was praised for its 'plaintive melody which has only been surpassed by the inimitable Churchyard Elegy' (Anderson, 577, 579). This poem, along with another entitled 'Mulberry Tree', on the contrasting characters of David Garrick and Johnson, was later noted with approval by Boswell (Boswell, 1.70–71).

Although it circulated privately in his lifetime, the majority of Lovibond's poetry was published posthumously as *Poems on Several Occasions* (1785) under the superintendence of his brother, Anthony Lovibond Collins. Lovibond's poetical voice chiefly draws its inspiration from Gray, though in the case of 'Julia's Printed Letter' Pope's 'Eloisa to Abelard' is evidently his model. His 'demi-platonic' love verses directed to Miss K— P—, identified by Chalmers as Miss Kitty Philips, also suggest the influence of his subject's namesake, Katherine Philips, the matchless Orinda. Lovibond's poems were reprinted in Anderson's *British Poets* (1794), together with a panegyric sneeringly described by Croker as 'hyperbolic' (Boswell, 1.71). His life was subsequently revised by Alexander Chalmers for the *General Biographical Dictionary* (1816) and his edition of the *British Poets* (1820). Selections of his poetry reappeared in two early nineteenth-century collections.

JEFFREY HERRLE

Sources A. Chalmers, 'The life of Edward Lovibond', *The works of the English poets from Chaucer to Cowper*, ed. A. Chalmers, 16 (1810), 283–4 • R. Anderson, 'Life of Lovibond', *A complete edition of the poets of Great Britain*, 13 vols. (1792–5), vol. 11, pp. 577–9 • Foster, *Alum. Oxon.* • J. Boswell, *The life of Johnson*, new edn, ed. J. W. Croker, 5 vols. (1831) • Walpole, *Corr.*, vol. 32 • H. Walpole, 'Horace Walpole's journals of visits to country seats', *Walpole Society*, 16 (1927–8), 9–80 • *IGI* • *DNB* • *GM*, 1st ser., 7 (1737), 514

Wealth at death see will, Surrey HC, 258/2/19

Loving, Henry (1790–1850), newspaper proprietor in the West Indies, was born a slave on Antigua and manumitted at the age of nine. He was probably the son of a white slave owner and a black slave. The rest of his early life is obscure, and he first came to prominence in 1814 when he founded the *Weekly Register* newspaper. The *Register* was one of the first newspapers in the British West Indies run by free coloureds, but as Loving later admitted it was for many years reluctant to discuss political matters in any real depth. This seems to have been due to the influence of Loving's partner, William Hill, a trained printer, who when asked to join the paper in 1815 evidently assumed responsibility for editorial decisions. He proceeded cautiously, probably anxious to avoid alienating the white oligarchy which controlled the colony.

After Hill's death in July 1827 the way was open for Loving to change the whole tenor of the paper. The time and circumstances were certainly propitious for such a move; the slave question was preoccupying the British government and by 1830 Antigua's other newspaper, the *Free Press*, was starting to argue for immediate abolition. Loving perhaps directed more energy to securing his political and civil rights as a free coloured, but he never neglected the plight of the slaves, and he seems to have possessed considerable influence over them. Although he had no direct connection with the plantation economy, he owned at least one domestic slave himself. He was married, with at least eight children, but the name of his wife is unknown.

In tightly controlled and racially stratified societies like Antigua, radicalism of this kind was fraught with danger. Dubbed a 'compound of mustard and malevolence' by the pro-planter journalist James MacQueen, Loving suffered attacks which went beyond mere verbal abuse. In October 1828 the *Register*'s contract to print government notices was cancelled and a year later its editor was charged with libelling the whole community of Antigua. Loving conducted his own defence and eloquently exposed the absurdity of the charge, but his acquittal did not mark the end of his troubles. In May 1831 he was attacked and horsewhipped by a white man claiming that Loving had traduced the memory of his recently deceased brother in the *Register*. Loving pressed charges against his assailant, and the affair resulted in several serious disturbances which highlighted the island's acute racial divisions.

Shortly after this incident Loving travelled to England as the official representative of the Antigua free coloured corresponding committee, a group lobbying to gain full political and civil rights. While in England he addressed anti-slavery meetings and entered into a correspondence on the slave question with the under-secretary of state for the colonies, Lord Howick. Loving published this correspondence as a pamphlet, somewhat disingenuously claiming that he had been in direct contact with the secretary of state, Viscount Goderich. He also gave impressive testimony before the government select committee on the extinction of slavery throughout the British empire.

Loving returned to Antigua in June 1832, having been instrumental in obtaining the concession of civil rights to Antiguan free coloureds. He resumed the editorship of the *Register* but for less than a year; in May 1833 he announced his retirement from both the newspaper and from journalism. The battles he had been involved in may have taken a personal toll and comments he made later indicated a deep disillusionment with politics. He briefly ran a general store in St John's but in July 1834 the governor of the Leewards, Sir Evan Murray-MacGregor, appointed him superintendent of the Antigua police. Again controversy dogged him as the decision provoked an outcry from white people who were appalled at the prospect of a coloured man occupying such an important position. By March 1836 he was acting private secretary to Murray-MacGregor and in July of the following year was appointed as a stipendiary magistrate in Barbados, charged with ensuring the smooth working of the apprenticeship system. In March 1838 he took up the post of secretary and clerk to the crown on Montserrat, despite Murray-MacGregor's caution about accepting the post. The move proved a mistake; not only was his salary cut drastically but at one point he went for two years without receiving any pay at all. He attempted to solicit promotion from the Colonial Office but failed and eventually returned to Antigua. For two years before this he had suffered a debilitating illness, which robbed him of his mental powers. He probably died at St John's, Antigua, in 1850.

A. P. Lewis

Sources A. P. Lewis, 'The British West Indian press in the age of abolition', PhD diss., U. Lond., 1994 • PRO, Colonial Office records, CO7, 10, 33/4, 300/2, 393, 714 • 'Select committee on the extinction of slavery in the British dominions', *Parl. papers* (1831–2), vol. 20, no. 721 • W. Green, *British slave emancipation: the sugar colonies and the great experiment, 1830–65* (1976) • D. Hall, *Five of the Leewards, 1834–70* (1971) • [Mrs Flannigan], *Antigua and the Antiguans: a full account of the colony and its inhabitants*, 1 (1844) • V. L. Oliver, *The history of the island of Antigua*, 3 (1899) • C. Wesley, 'The emancipation of the free coloured population in the British empire', *Journal of Negro History*, 19 (1934) • *Port of Spain Gazette* (11 Jan 1833) • R. Lowe, *The Codrington correspondence, 1743–1851: being a study of a recently discovered dossier of letters* (1951)
Archives PRO, CO records

Low, Alexander, Lord Low (**1845–1910**), judge, the son of James Low of The Laws, Berwickshire, and his wife, Jessy, daughter of George Turnbull of Abbey St Bathans, Berwickshire, was born at The Laws on 23 October 1845. After education at Cheltenham College and from 1862 to 1864 at St Andrews University, he went up to St John's College, Cambridge, where he matriculated in Michaelmas term 1864 and graduated BA in 1867, taking a first in the moral science tripos.

Low was originally intended for the army, but he failed the medical test. He therefore decided to take law classes at Edinburgh University, and was called to the Scottish bar on 22 December 1870. He joined the Juridical Society on 18 January 1871. For some time he edited the *Scottish Law Reporter*, while establishing himself at the bar. He was able to build up a good practice in spite of a weak constitution, which at times prevented him from undertaking all the work sent to him. Low's hard work and conscientiousness, so apparent whenever his health allowed, coupled with his clear and persuasive advocacy, ensured his success at the bar. Low was a conservative, but was never active in politics. He married, on 23 December 1875, Annie Adèle (*d.* 1925), daughter of the Hon. Lord Mackenzie (a judge of the

Court of Session). They had one son, James, and two daughters.

In 1889 Low was appointed sheriff of Ross, Cromarty, and Sutherland, and on 25 November 1890 he was raised to the bench of the Court of Session, taking the courtesy title of Lord Low. His success at the bar was repeated in his judicial career. Again, his hard work and natural abilities enabled him to carry out his functions in the outer house (where he sat for some considerable time before being transferred to the inner house) with great efficiency and success.

Causes célèbres were not unknown to Lord Low who, as a judge of first instance, heard *The General Assembly of the Free Church of Scotland* v. *Lord Overtoun* (1904), in which the property of the Free Church—worth some £2 million—was claimed by members of that body who objected to its union with the United Presbyterians. Low decided against the claim, and his judgment was adhered to by the inner house. On appeal to the House of Lords, the lord chancellor Lord Halsbury engineered a reversal of the previous decisions (1904). However, this decision of the majority of their lordships met with a hostile public reaction, and the government had to appoint a commission and effectively overrule it.

On the bench Lord Low was renowned for his courtesy and consideration to counsel. His written judgments were invariably pellucid and logical, but he also had a gift for delivering very sound extempore judgments. He never succumbed to the temptation to include extraneous matters when giving judgment. Lord Low resigned, owing to bad health, in the autumn of 1910. He died only two days later at his home, The Laws, on 14 October. His wife survived him. He was buried at Whitsome, Berwickshire.

NATHAN WELLS

Sources *The Times* (15 Oct 1910) • F. J. Grant, ed., *The Faculty of Advocates in Scotland, 1532–1943*, Scottish RS, 145 (1944) • *Scots Law Times* (20 May 1893) • R. Stevens, *Law and politics: the House of Lords as a judicial body, 1800–1976* (1979) • *Juridical Review*, 22 (1910–11) • *Scottish Law Review*, 26 (1910), 262–3 • Venn, *Alum. Cant.*
Likenesses G. F. Watt, oils, exh. 1908?, Faculty of Advocates, Edinburgh • photograph, repro. in *Scots Law Times* (20 May 1893)
Wealth at death £36,297 17s. 9d.: confirmation, 18 Nov 1910, *CCI*

Low, Austin Richard William [Toby], **first Baron Aldington (1914–2000)**, soldier and politician, was born on 25 May 1914 at 16 Launceston Place, Kensington, London. He was the elder son and eldest of the three children of Lieutenant-Colonel Stuart Low (1888–1942), financier and army officer, and his first wife, the Hon. Lucy Gwen, *née* Atkin (*d.* 1957), eldest daughter of James Richard *Atkin, Baron Atkin of Aberdovey, judge. Low's family had connections with Grindlays Bank dating back to 1845 and his father was chairman of the bank before the Second World War, in which he was killed at sea by enemy action.

Toby Low, as he was invariably known, was educated at Winchester College, where he was head of the commoners and rowed for the college. He went on to New College, Oxford, where he read jurisprudence and graduated with a second-class degree in 1936 before being called to the bar at the Middle Temple in 1939. Although Oxford undergraduates had earlier voted in the union against fighting for king and country, Low reacted to the rise of fascism by joining the Territorial Army (King's Royal Rifle Corps), and had risen to the rank of captain by the outbreak of war.

Low had a most active and distinguished war. He served in Greece, where he was awarded the DSO during the allied retreat, and went on to serve in Crete, the western desert, and Tunisia. In 1943 he was attached to the Eighth Army staff for the Sicilian campaign, where he was made MBE, and then served as a lieutenant-colonel on the staff of 13 corps in Italy. In 1944 he was promoted brigadier (one of the youngest in the army) and was attached to general staff of 5 corps for the advance from Italy into Austria. It was in this role that he became involved in the return of Cossack and Yugoslav prisoners of war to their countries of origin, an involvement which led to a notorious and harrowing libel case that (despite his winning the case) blighted the later years of his life. In the course of his front-line service he was on one occasion briefly captured but took advantage of the chaos following an artillery attack to seize an enemy vehicle and escape to the allied lines. His war service received much recognition: he was appointed CBE in 1945 as well as receiving the French Croix de Guerre (with palms) and being appointed to the American Legion of Merit (commander).

On return to civilian life, Low stood for parliament as a Conservative and won the Blackpool North seat in the general election of July 1945. He married on 10 April 1947 (Felicité Anne) Araminta Bowman, daughter of Sir Harold Alfred *MacMichael, colonial governor, and formerly wife of Captain Paul Humphrey Armytage Bowman, officer in the Coldstream Guards, from whom she had obtained a divorce. The marriage was an enduring and happy one, and resulted in one son, Charles (*b.* 1948), and two daughters, (Priscilla) Jane (*b.* 1949) and (Lucy) Ann (*b.* 1956).

With the return of a Conservative government in October 1951, Low was appointed parliamentary under-secretary to the Ministry of Supply, and in July 1954 was promoted by Churchill to be minister of state at the Board of Trade. He was an energetic minister who travelled widely and established a reputation as an able negotiator, and was sworn of the privy council in 1954. But in January 1957 he left office at his own request to seek better-paid work in the City, and he was appointed KCMG the same year for his services to exports. It was not, however, the end of his active participation in politics: he remained MP for Blackpool North until 1962 and in 1959 he was appointed deputy chairman of the Conservative Party with special responsibility for its organization, a post he held until 1963. During this period he established a particularly close rapport with Edward Heath, and was created a hereditary peer (one of the last) in 1962, when he took the title Baron Aldington of Bispham.

Having entered the City, Aldington embarked on a career even more successful than his former military and political ones. In 1964 he became chairman of GEC, where he worked closely with Arnold Weinstock. It also gave him particular satisfaction to take on the chairmanship of

Grindlays Bank and to mastermind the acquisition of Brandts bank and the establishment of close links with First National City Bank of New York and Lloyds Bank, both of whose boards he joined. He did much to modernize banking methods and to encourage overseas expansion. He also took on the chairmanship of the Port of London Authority in 1971 and (together with Jack Jones, leader of the Transport and General Workers' Union) produced a report which went some way towards restoring order to London's dockland. He was appointed chairman of the Sun Alliance insurance group in 1971, and of Westland aircraft in 1977. But not everything went without a hitch: in 1975 Brandts had to write off £14 million as a result of property losses and Aldington felt it necessary to resign the chair of Grindlays.

The Sun Alliance connection was also in part responsible for the subsequent attack on Aldington's reputation. A relative of a disgruntled policy holder of Sun Alliance, Nigel Watts, held Aldington responsible for the company's refusal to pay out on an accident policy after the death of his brother-in-law in 1975, the grounds for non-payment being that relevant information had been withheld by the insured. With the encouragement of Count Nikolay Tolstoy (who had earlier associated Aldington with the sending back, to their death at the hands of Stalin and Tito, of those Cossacks and Yugoslavs who had fought with the Germans and surrendered to the British in 1945) he circulated a pamphlet accusing Aldington of war crimes. The attack was both vivid in its charges and designed to cause maximum embarrassment by its circulation. Aldington was accused of 'a combination of duplicity and brutality without parallel in British history since the massacre of Glencoe', and his behaviour was compared to 'the worst of the butchers of Nazi Germany' (*Daily Telegraph*, 8 Dec 2000). The pamphlet was sent to politicians, the press, Aldington's neighbours, and the parents and old boys of Winchester, where Aldington was at the time warden (or chairman of the governors). Not unnaturally, although contrary to some of the advice he was given which recommended a simple denial, Aldington felt he had no honourable alternative other than to sue for libel.

Aldington, then in his mid-seventies, was given access to the official records to prepare his case, and the trial lasted nine weeks. Watts maintained that Aldington 'had issued every order and arranged every detail of the lying and brutality' (*Daily Telegraph*, 8 Dec 2000) and Tolstoy argued that Aldington had laid down definitions of Soviet nationals which included Cossacks who had never fought for the Germans but were fleeing from Stalin. Aldington for his part maintained that the definitions had been approved by higher authority; that no Cossacks had been handed over before the date of his own return to the UK; that he had never imagined they would be massacred without trial; that if he had known what was to happen he would 'have taken steps to ensure it did not' (ibid.); and that, above all, in the military and political climate of the time, the first priority was perceived as fulfilling the Yalta agreement on return of prisoners so that the British prisoners of war held by the Russians should be promptly repatriated.

The court found in favour of Aldington, who, far from being a war criminal, was generally felt to have been caught up in a tragic and violent situation for which he was in no way responsible. He was granted unprecedentedly high damages of £1.5 million, and £500,000 costs. Tolstoy declared himself bankrupt and paid nothing, while Watts paid only a sum which left Aldington with massive costs to be repaid to Sun Alliance, who had largely financed him in view of their connection with the reasons for the libel. Tolstoy launched various appeals against the findings and award, and in 1994 the European Court of Human Rights pronounced the extent of the damages as constituting a violation of the right of freedom of expression. The whole affair cast a shadow over Aldington's declining years.

As he became less involved in City affairs, Aldington took on a number of voluntary and public activities. He chaired the management committee of the Institute of Neurology, of Leeds Castle Foundation, and of the BBC General Advisory Council. He was a keen and expert golfer. In retirement he continued to live at Aldington in Kent; he had become a deputy lieutenant of the county in 1973. Latterly he became increasingly blind and he died of cancer on 7 December 2000. He was survived by his wife and children and was succeeded in his peerage by his son, Charles Harold Stuart Low. His old friend Sir Edward Heath gave a moving address at his memorial service.

Aldington was a quintessentially 'establishment' figure: a Wykehamist who rose through his courage, ability, and industry to hold high positions in the wartime army, in the Conservative Party, and in the City of London. He could be relied on to deal fairly and sensibly with complex issues, and it was ironic that he should have been unjustly pilloried for involvement in one of the vicious tragedies of war which he regretted as deeply as anyone. His former friend Nigel Nicolson, who had been present at the handover of the Cossacks, was among those who felt that Aldington had been haunted by the thought that, though in no way responsible, he might have done more to avoid the tragedy.

John Ure

Sources *Daily Telegraph* (8 Dec 2000) · *The Times* (9 Dec 2000) · *The Guardian* (9 Dec 2000) · *The Independent* (8 Dec 2000) · *Financial Times* (11 Dec 2000) · Burke, *Peerage* · *WWW* · personal knowledge (2004) · personal information (2004) · b. cert. · m. cert.

Archives King's Lond., Liddell Hart C., corresp. with Sir B. H. Liddell Hart · U. Birm. L., corresp. with Lord Avon

Likenesses R. Baker, photograph, *c.*1989, repro. in *The Guardian* · photograph, 1989, repro. in *Daily Telegraph* · photograph, *c.*1989, repro. in *Financial Times* · photograph, repro. in *The Times*

Wealth at death £525,786—gross; £416,919—net: probate, 18 April 2001, *CGPLA Eng. & Wales*

Low, David (1768–1854), Scottish Episcopal bishop of Ross and Argyll and the Isles, was born in November 1768 in Brechin, Forfarshire, one of four children. He came from a traditional Episcopalian family which was staunchly Jacobite, and his father, a tradesman, was particularly solicitous of his education. Educated in the local school, he later attended Marischal College, Aberdeen, in preparation for his ordination in the Scottish Episcopal church. Episcopalian necessity dictated that he receive his theological education in the home of one of the more learned clergy, in Low's case with Bishop George Gleig at Stirling. He was then tutor to the family of a Mr Patullo of Balhouffie, Fife, for a year and a half. Appointed to the tiny nonjuring congregation at Perth, he was ordained deacon on 5 December 1787 and priest on 4 February 1789. In September 1789 he was elected priest of the nonjuring congregation at Pittenweem, an appointment he retained until his death. Much of his local influence was due to his alliance with influential local gentry, particularly Archibald, earl of Kellie. Low's ministry was hampered by shyness and a disposition to solitude, which could become irritability under pressure. This did not prevent him from also ministering to nearby congregations in Craill and Cupar. Low's personal appearance was described by a contemporary as 'most striking—thin, attenuated, but active—his eye sparkling with intelligence' (*GM*, 2nd ser., 43, 1855, 423).

In 1819 Low was elected bishop of the united dioceses of Ross and Argyll and the Isles; he was consecrated bishop at Stirling on 14 November 1819. Marischal College consequently awarded him a DD in 1820. Two of his charges to his diocesan clergy, in 1823 and 1826, were his only publications, although he retained a particular interest in genealogy. He was a constant, though necessarily intermittent, visitor throughout his huge dioceses with their small Episcopalian populations. To support them, he was instrumental in 1831 in founding the Episcopalian Gaelic Society to provide Gaelic religious literature and financial support. Low was also active in the wider support of his church, lobbying influential peers and MPs during the 1820s for the resuscitation of the *regium donum* grant to the Episcopal church, which became regular again in 1830. He also pressed for the removal of the legal disabilities on Episcopalian clergy ministering in England, a restriction resulting from the legal toleration granted to the Episcopal church in 1792. This concern made Low hostile to Episcopalian traditions at odds with the Church of England; he desired the suppression of the Scottish communion office traditional to nonjuring episcopalianism. He was elected bishop of Moray in 1838.

Low was a central figure in the legal mitigation of Episcopalian disabilities in 1840, but his most enduring legacy to his own church was a consequence of his unmarried state and frugal nature. As incumbent of one of the few wealthy Episcopalian incumbencies, he was able to become a generous benefactor to various Episcopal causes, such as the Episcopalian Church Society for the development of church infrastructure and Trinity College, Glenalmond, as a public school and seminary. When Argyll and the Isles became a separate diocese in 1847, he was able to endow it with £8000. Low kept up a regular correspondence with American Episcopalians, which resulted in the award in 1848 of an honorary DD from Hartford College, Connecticut, and another from Geneva College, New York. He was also an early connection between the Episcopal church and the Oxford Movement in the Church of England through his practice of inviting English priests to tour his dioceses with him during the summer months. In 1838 John Henry Newman's curate, William Copeland, was his chaplain.

In his last years Low was able to overcome his lack of self-confidence to an extent and became in Episcopalian circles a figure venerated for his personal connections with the penal days of their church. He died at his home in the restored Pittenweem priory on 26 January 1854. His funeral at the Pittenweem Episcopal Church was on 1 February 1854; he was buried at a specially consecrated site adjacent to the chancel of the priory's chapel.

ROWAN STRONG

Sources W. Blatch, *A memoir of the Right Rev David Low* (1854) · J. Archibald, *The historic episcopate in the Columban church and in the diocese of Moray* (1893) · *The letters and diaries of John Henry Newman*, ed. C. S. Dessain and others, [31 vols.] (1961–), vol. 6
Archives NRA Scotland, MSS of diocese of Moray and Ross
Likenesses C. Lees, portrait · Quilley, engraving (after C. Lees) · C. Warren, stipple and line engraving (after C. Lees), BM, NPG

Low, David (1786–1859), university professor, was born on 25 November 1786, probably at Woodend, Berwickshire, the eldest son of Alexander Low, land agent, of Laws, Berwickshire, and his wife, Susan Anderson. He was educated at Perth Academy and the University of Edinburgh. He assisted his father on his farms, and soon showed special aptitude as a land agent and valuer. In 1817 he published *Observations on the present state of landed property, and on the prospects of the landholder and the farmer*, dealing with the slump which followed the battle of Waterloo (1815). In 1825 he settled in Edinburgh, and in the following year the *Quarterly Journal of Agriculture* was established at his suggestion; he edited it from 1828 to 1832.

On the death of Professor Andrew Coventry in 1831 Low was appointed professor of agriculture in the University of Edinburgh. His first step was to urge on the government the necessity of forming an agricultural museum, for which the chancellor of the exchequer, Thomas Spring-Rice, consented in 1833 to allow £300 a year. Low also contributed collections of his own, and employed the artist William Shiels to travel, taking portraits of the best specimens of different breeds of animals. Altogether £3000 was expended on the museum—£1500 from the government, £300 from the Reid fund, and the rest from the professor's private resources. The museum led to increased attendance in the class of agriculture.

In 1834 Low published *Elements of Practical Agriculture* (4th edn, 1843); it was translated into French and German. In 1842 he brought out a splendid work in two volumes, *The Breeds of the Domestic Animals of the British Islands*, with coloured plates. This was translated for the French government immediately on its appearance. Two years later he published *On Landed Property and the Economy of Estates*, and in 1850 an *Appeal to the Common Sense of the Country Regarding the Condition of the Working Classes*. He was also much devoted to chemistry and had a private laboratory. His controversial work *An Inquiry into the Nature of the Simple Bodies of Chemistry* (1844) suggested that carbon and hydrogen were the only fundamental chemical elements, and opposed the atomic theory of John Dalton. It provoked a reply from J. J. Berzelius.

Low resigned his chair in 1854, and died, unmarried, at Mayfield, Edinburgh on 7 January 1859. He was buried at the Edinburgh cemetery, Warriston.

G. C. BOASE, *rev.* DAVID KNIGHT

Sources A. Grant, *The story of the University of Edinburgh during its first three hundred years*, 2 (1884), 456–7 • Irving, *Scots.*, 290–91 • D. M. Knight, *The transcendental part of chemistry* (1978), 204–9 • Anderson, *Scot. nat.* • b. cert. • d. cert.

Low, Sir David Alexander Cecil (1891–1963), cartoonist and caricaturist, was born on 7 April 1891 in Dunedin, New Zealand, the third son among the four children of David Brown Low, a businessman, and his wife, Jane Caroline Flanagan. His father's family emigrated from Fife, Scotland, in the 1860s and his mother's from Dublin, Ireland, in 1850.

Early years Low's father's uneven commercial fortunes took the family to Christchurch. After a few months at Christchurch Boys' High School, Low was removed at the age of eleven, following the death of his eldest brother from peritonitis. His parents believed the boy had been weakened by too much study and they wished to protect David from the same risk. Thereafter Low was educated at home. He read widely, and his lively curiosity was fed by a disputatious father. From the age of eight he devoured—and studiously copied—British comics. He also relished the *Punch* cartoons of Charles Keene, Linley Sambourne, and especially Phil May. 'Once having discovered May', he recalled, 'I never let him go' (Low, 27).

Borrowing from the stock of joke ideas which, as he saw, cropped up repeatedly, Low posted his own efforts to London and Australia. His first success, when eleven, was in a British comic, the *Big Budget*. Next a Christchurch political weekly, *The Spectator*, accepted a cartoon. Other successes soon followed, including commercial work and police court sketches for the sensational *New Zealand Truth*. *The Spectator* paid him to illustrate two jokes a week. Perhaps because of these encouragements, he failed a two-year course at a local business college. Formal instruction at Canterbury Art College proved no more inspiring. He learned more from watching a local caricaturist, Fred Raynor, who hired him in 1907 to draw for a new magazine. Next year he went full time to *The Spectator* and thence, after falling out over its politics, to the *Canterbury Times*. Here he had twice the salary and more space.

Low routinely mailed copies of his *Spectator* work to editors in Australia, and the Sydney weekly *Bulletin* began publishing his drawings. Out of the blue, in 1911, *The Bulletin* offered a six-month contract as its Melbourne cartoonist. This was to be the making of Low. Known across Australia as 'the bushman's bible', the irreverent *Bulletin* had a reputation for spotting talent. The contract was followed by another, to travel the country and caricature local notables (a selection being republished as *Caricatures*, Sydney, 1915); and then, after a spell as a general cartoonist, by appointment as *The Bulletin*'s regular Melbourne political cartoonist in 1914.

Low found an ideal foil in William M. (Billy) Hughes, prime minister of the Labor government and its wartime coalition successor. Short, with a large nose and a volatile, dominating personality, Hughes—more than his policies—provoked *The Bulletin*. As a gift to the caricaturist, he in turn was provoked by Low. The resulting rows were grist to *The Bulletin's* mill. Low became news. He was exempted from conscription because of his 'national importance'. His anthology, *The Billy Book* (Sydney, 1918), quickly sold 60,000 copies—remarkable in a population of five million.

Sir David Alexander Cecil Low (1891–1963), by Yousuf Karsh, 1943

The *Evening Standard* To some colleagues Low seemed rather obviously on the make. He continued the habit of sending copies of his work overseas, and some of his Hughes cartoons were reprinted in the *Manchester Guardian*. This policy paid off, when the owner of the Liberal *Daily News*, Henry Cadbury, offered him a job in 1919. When he arrived in November, with his mother, sister, and brother in tow, the job turned out to be on the less prestigious London *Evening Star*. Worse still, Low had to fight for space and for scope to develop his own style, rather than compete with the celebrated Poy (Percy Fearon) of the rival *Evening News*. But he won his way, making a butt of Lloyd George, prime minister of the post-war rump coalition, as he did of Hughes. To represent the Liberal and Conservative halves of the coalition, Low invented a two-headed ass. Such symbols became a memorable feature of his work, the most famous being the choleric and befuddled Colonel Blimp and the benign but lumbering TUC carthorse. Others, more ephemeral, included Joan *Bull, a 'flapper' version of John, and

Blimp's left-wing counterpart, standing on his head, called Pmilb. In 1920 Low married Madeline Grieve Kenning, of New Zealand. He proposed by cablegram, prepaying for a one-word reply. They had two daughters.

The freshness of Low's ideas and the quality of his drawing gave his work 'pep', to use the idiom of a critic in 1921. In 1927, after repeated attempts, Lord Beaverbrook succeeded in wooing him to the *Evening Standard*. The two men had sharply differing political attitudes. But each was a showman and a colonial boy made good, with an element of detachment about Britain, and they thrived on mutual flattery. Beaverbrook paid extremely well, and the *Evening Standard* had a more sophisticated, if less numerous, readership. Above all, cartoonist and proprietor played up to the claim that Low was entirely free to express his own opinions. Low enjoyed a reputation for outspoken independence, Beaverbrook for proprietorial tolerance. The arrangement was set out in a letter of agreement and lasted until Low left in 1949. The key paragraph read: '*Policy*: It is agreed that you are to have complete freedom in the selection and treatment of subject-matter for your cartoons and in the expression therein of the policies in which you believe' (Beaverbrook MSS). Yet in context this paragraph was not everything it seemed. Low could not be required to draw to order: but nor was Beaverbrook required to publish everything he drew. Over the years, at least forty cartoons were omitted and others were modified.

The great international issue that gives the letter of agreement its interest was the appeasement of the fascist dictators in the 1930s. Beaverbrook—with probably the majority of readers—was in favour, Low against. More than anyone, Low defined the image of Hitler which the history books perpetuate: a strutting figure, with toothbrush moustache and diagonal forelock. His cartoons got the *Evening Standard* banned from Nazi Germany (not alone, among British papers), and later from Italy. Low was added to a Gestapo priority list of persons to be arrested after invasion.

Low's principal weapon was ridicule, not the arousal of hate or horror. He believed people were vulnerable to 'the criticism of the grin', and also that there was 'more stupidity than wickedness in the world' (Seymour-Ure and Schoff, 143, 153). Since 'the person is merely the symbol of an idea', he attacked stupidity through drawing persons (Low, 'Adventures with my pencil', *Strand Magazine*, September 1926, 266). In style, he saw himself as heir to Gillray and Rowlandson more than to Tenniel and the Victorian *Punch* tradition. The latter, in Max Beerbohm's phrase, dealt in 'comic ideas seriously illustrated', while Low, like the former, preferred serious ideas comically illustrated (Seymour-Ure and Schoff, 148). Part of his humour came from the cartoonist's traditional armoury of exaggeration, distortion, neat and expressive metaphors. Part, too, came from caricature. Low could capture a likeness in a few lines. He was master of 'the tab of identity', those few strokes making a figure instantly identifiable. While some were facial, such as Hitler's moustache, others were like stage props. Neville Chamberlain was identified so much with his umbrella that at length he was identifiable as it—an umbrella with a handle in the shape of his features. Similarly the Labour politician J. H. Thomas, who adopted the dress code of the upper classes, was drawn as 'The Rt. Hon. Dress Suit, Wearing his Jimmy Thomas'.

Low could draw with palpable menace, when depicting Nazi blackshirts or serried ranks of goose-stepping stormtroopers. But his line was intrinsically gentle. His lions and tigers might spit, but it would have been fun to own a toy one. He worked with a brush and ink, over a painstaking pencil sketch. The impression of fluency, or what Ronald Searle called 'an almost oriental facility', was contrived (*The Guardian*, 21 Sept 1963). There was too much talk about 'the gift for drawing', Low complained. 'It is a capacity for work that gets you there' (Seymour-Ure and Schoff, 124). He habitually drew from models. His technique developed little after his arrival in England, the main change being a reduction of shading and cross-hatching. He was adept at handling large blocks of contrasting black and white, and in the grouping of figures within the frame—a full half-page at the tabloid *Evening Standard*. The eye would be drawn from group to group, and also, perhaps, to panels of text: a Low drawing might incorporate fifty words, in addition to the caption beneath. Low often included a tentative version of himself, too, as an internal commentator. By these means he engaged the reader in the cartoon's argument.

At home Low's victims were more inclined than the dictators to see the funny side. In domestic as in foreign politics Low was at odds with Lord Beaverbrook. He was too much of an individualist to be a good party man, and too practical to be a keen theoretician. At most he was left-liberal, with reformist instincts rooted in 'common sense' and predictable in an antipodean autodidact. He had the cartoonist's capacity to distil an idea to its essence. This made him the envy of journalists—and a crisp essayist and broadcaster himself. From 1941 to 1944 he broadcast monthly to North America and the Far East. He also started writing for the Sunday *New York Times*.

The force, consistency, and eventual vindication of Low's anti-appeasement drawings helped make him internationally celebrated—eventually the most famous newspaper cartoonist of his time. Already before the war, his cartoons were widely syndicated in Europe and the anglophone world. His style was closely imitated. He produced several drawings during the war, such as *Very Well, Alone!*, after the fall of Dunkirk, which were deeply affecting at the time and still illustrate the quintessence of the Dunkirk spirit. Some of his wartime work was inevitably propagandistic, but he did not get much involved with official propaganda.

Low was in sympathy with the Attlee government after 1945. With the enemy abroad defeated too, he grew restless, and in 1949, after his space was cut, he decided to leave the *Evening Standard*. Beaverbrook was saddened, but his editors were not altogether sorry: they felt Low was losing his touch, and they wanted the space. Joining the *Daily Herald* in 1950 proved a mistake. This was a mass circulation working-class paper, whose owners, Odhams, left editorial policy to the TUC and the Labour Party. Low soon chafed both at people who thought he had become a Labour cartoonist and at readers who complained he had not. In June 1952 he put out feelers to the *Manchester Guardian*, the paper which by now was surely his spiritual home. He was welcomed with delight, was paid more than the editor, and stayed until April 1963, shortly before his death.

Low worked from a studio at 13A Heath Street, Hampstead, within walking distance from home. His cartoon was collected by courier. At the *Evening Standard* in the 1930s he was doing four cartoons a week. Between 1934 and 1940 he also drew a full-page Saturday *Topical Budget* of comments on the week's news. Here Colonel Blimp made his appearance in 1934, as did, from 1937, an occasional strip about 'Hit and Muss' (Hitler and Mussolini). After discreet official German complaints, Low substituted a composite dictator, Muzzler.

Later work Low's contracts always allowed for freelance work, including up to twelve cartoons a year for *Punch* during his *Star* years. In 1932 he travelled in the Soviet Union and published *Low's Russian Sketchbook* (1932) with Kingsley Martin, editor of the *New Statesman*. He occasionally illustrated the *New Statesman*'s annual anthologies of ludicrous remarks, published under the title *This England*, and he became a director of the magazine in 1933. When he visited the United States in 1936, he was fêted. While still on the *Star*, he collaborated with F. W. Thomas in a series of features about London landmarks, such as Billingsgate fish market and the zoo, published together in *Low and I: a Cooked Tour in London* (1923). The series continued with a new collaborator when Low moved to the *Evening Standard*. More ambitious was *The Modern 'Rake's Progress'* (1934), a handsome Hogarthian pastiche with twelve double-page watercolours and a text by Rebecca West. Conceived as a parody of the prince of Wales and his set, it was toned down and broadened, with recognizable characters from the arts and public life. Low also illustrated a minor political novel by H. G. Wells (*The Autocracy of Mr Parham*, 1930), and a prescient novella by Peter Fleming, *The Flying Visit* (1940), which fancied Hitler parachuting into Britain, a year before his deputy, Rudolf Hess, in fact did so. Other ventures tantalizingly came to nothing. These included a book of historical caricatures, with text by the historian Philip Guedalla; and a satirically illustrated version of Hitler's *Mein Kampf*. He briefly tried 'animated editorial cartoons' for the cinema, with which he had a lifelong fascination. He wrote many essays on cartoon and caricature and a short book, published in 1935 as *Ye Madde Designer*. He contributed *British Cartoonists, Caricaturists and Comic Artists* (1942) to the popular Britain in Pictures series published by Collins.

Low made considerable claims for caricature, which he described as the art of 'all-in portraiture' (*Ye Madde Designer*, 1935, 10). His own caricatures, in the tradition of the *portrait chargé*, were admired by many, including Max Beerbohm. His practice of seeking a sitting was a shrewd way of meeting well-known people when he went to London. Two series were published as supplements in the *New Statesman* and separately as *Lions and Lambs* (1928) and *Caricatures by Low* (1933). Drawings for an earlier Australian series, clearly a model, were not published because of a libellous text; they are in the Mitchell Library, Sydney. After 1945 Low produced a further series, less finely observed (*Low's Company*, 1952).

Low's newspaper cartoons were anthologized as early as 1908 (*Low's Annual*). The first British collection was *Lloyd George & Co* (1921). Later came *The Best of Low* (1930), *Low's Political Parade* (1936), *Low Again* (1938), and three wartime Penguin paperbacks—*Europe since Versailles* (1940), *Europe at War* (1941), and *The World at War* (1941). *Europe since Versailles* quickly sold a quarter of a million copies. Many of these volumes were repackaged by American publishers. Three post-war anthologies appeared, the last in 1960.

In 1958 Low was made an honorary LLD of the University of New Brunswick, which had strong associations with Lord Beaverbrook. In 1962 he accepted a knighthood, first offered in the 1930s. He had bouts of poor health in the last three years of his life and died of pneumonia with complications in hospital in London on 19 September 1963. He was cremated at Golders Green and was survived by his wife.

Low was of medium height. He had strong features, heavy eyebrows, alert eyes, a moustache, and in middle life a pointed beard (which he shaved in 1940). When famous, and although clubbable, he could leave an impression of self-importance. A self-portrait in oils is in the National Portrait Gallery, London, which also possesses some 400 studies for caricatures. Several thousand original cartoons are in the possession of the Beaverbrook Foundation. A small collection formerly at New Zealand House, London, is in the Centre for the Study of Cartoons and Caricature at the University of Kent at Canterbury, which also has copies of cuttings books and correspondence, microfilms, and a computer database of his cartoons. A comprehensive collection of cuttings books is at the London School of Economics. Low's papers are in the Beinecke Library, Yale University.

COLIN SEYMOUR-URE

Sources C. Seymour-Ure and J. Schoff, *David Low* (1985) • D. Low, *Low's autobiography* (1956) • Yale U., Beinecke L., Low papers • House of Lords, Beaverbrook MSS • T. Benson, 'Low and Lord Beaverbrook', PhD diss., University of Kent at Canterbury, 1999 • *DNB* • private information (2004) [R. Whear] • *CGPLA Eng. & Wales* (1963) • H. R. Westwood, *Modern caricaturists* (1932), ix–xiv, 3–22 • *The Times* (21 Sept 1963) • M. Bryant, ed., *The complete Colonel Blimp* (1991)

Archives Mitchell L., NSW • University of Kent, Canterbury, Centre for the Study of Cartoons and Caricature, family MSS (copies) • Yale U., Beinecke L., collection | Bodl. Oxf., letters to E. J. Thompson • HLRO, corresp. with Lord Beaverbrook • King's Lond., Liddell Hart C., corresp. with Sir B. H. Liddell Hart, with other printed ephemera | FILM BBC-TV film documentary, c.1985

Likenesses D. Low, self-portrait, oils, *c.*1924–1925, NPG • W. Lewis, pencil drawing, 1932, Wakefield education committee, West Yorkshire • H. Coster, photographs, 1935, NPG • Y. Karsh, photograph, 1943, NPG [*see illus.*] • A. Gray, bust, repro. in *The Times* (30 Nov 1963) • W. Rothenstein, drawing, repro. in W. Rothenstein, *Contemporaries* (1937)

Wealth at death £100,311: probate, 2 Dec 1963, *CGPLA Eng. & Wales*

Low, George (1747–1795), naturalist, born at the farm of Meikle Tullo, near Edzell, Forfarshire, and baptized at Edzell on 29 March 1747, was the third of five children of John Low (*d.* 1760), tenant farmer and church officer, and his wife, Isobel Coupar (or possibly Cooper; *fl.* 1730–1760). He was educated at the parish school, and then for one year at Brechin grammar school. In 1762 he enrolled in the faculty of arts at Marischal College, Aberdeen, but left the following year for the University of St Andrews, where he studied first under Robert Watson, professor of philosophy, at St Salvator's College (1763–6), and then took up divinity at St Mary's College (1766–7). A remarkable commonplace book written by him while at St Andrews, entitled 'A cabinet of curiosities' and dated 1766, is still extant in manuscript and indicates his early eclectic interests.

Low went to Orkney in late 1767 or early in 1768 as tutor to the sons of Baillie Robert Graham, merchant of Stromness, where he devoted most of the remainder of his life to the study of the natural history and antiquities of the Orkney and Shetland archipelagos. He commenced by careful observations of the birds, fishes, and flora of Orkney, and became enthralled with the study of microscopy, constructing a 'water microscope', and in 1769 beginning a series of 'Microscopical observations', a work illustrated with attractive Indian-ink sketches.

Isolated as he was from other scientific workers, with much of his time occupied as a tutor (an occupation which he disliked), and possessing hardly any books, the zeal with which he conducted these pioneer studies can hardly be overestimated. He also set to work about 1770 upon what became perhaps his major work, a 'History of Orkney', in which he contemplated embodying accounts of the history and antiquities, as well as of the natural history and topography of the islands, and for this purpose translated into English Torfaeus's *Orcades* (1697), a history of Orkney. Low was licensed as minister by the presbytery of Cairston in 1771, but remained for three years longer at Stromness.

In 1772 Sir Joseph Banks visited Orkney on his return from Iceland, in company with Daniel Solander and James Lind. Low acted as their guide and assisted them in the excavation of Bronze age burials at Skaill, an event which probably first aroused his interest in antiquities. Low was introduced by them to the antiquary and bibliophile George Paton of Edinburgh, who lent him books and became his friend, and to Thomas Pennant, with whom he began corresponding, and from whom his antiquarian studies derived further important stimulus. In the summer of 1774 Low made, at Pennant's expense, an extended tour of the south islands of Orkney and the whole of the Shetland group, and sent Pennant some materials for his *Tour in Scotland* (1776). Low began writing, with a view to publication, an exhaustive account of his tour, which dealt with the commerce, the population, and language, as well as with the archaeological and other records of the islands. On 14 December 1774 he was appointed minister to the remote parish of Birsay and Harray, on the mainland of Orkney, through the patronage of Sir Laurence Dundas. On 25 August the following year he married Helen, only daughter of James Tyrie, minister of Stromness and Sandwick; she died on 2 December 1776, after giving birth to a stillborn child.

In the seclusion of Birsay, Low completed his 'History' together with his accounts of 'Fauna' and 'Flora' respectively of the islands of Orkney. In 1778 to complete his survey of the islands he made a tour through the north isles of Orkney, the manuscript of which was published eventually in 1915. In 1781 he became a corresponding member of the Society of Antiquaries of Scotland. From this date until 1790 he was engaged in a succession of futile endeavours to get his manuscripts published. Though not published during his lifetime, his writings were extensively circulated and employed by others. Richard Gough introduced quotations from him into his *British Topography* (1780), and Pennant inserted, besides descriptions, several engravings from Low's drawings into his *Arctic Zoology* (1784–7). The manuscript of Low's 'History' was extensively plagiarized by George Barry in his *History of the Orkney Islands* (1805), which includes important samples of the Norn language of Shetland (a dialect of West Norse) collected by Low in 1774. Such was the extent of use of Low's information by others that Samuel Hibbert, writing in 1822, managed only with some difficulty to cull information respecting the earlier customs of Shetland that had not already been used. The *Fauna Orcadensis* was eventually published in 1813 by William Elford Leach. Pennant's attempts to find a publisher for Low's 1774 tour proved futile, and it remained unpublished until edited by Joseph Anderson, with an introduction containing extracts from Low's correspondence, in 1879.

The fate of Low's manuscripts became the subject of an increasingly acrimonious correspondence between Pennant, Gough, and Paton. Disappointed at the scant recognition of his labours, and embittered and disillusioned by the increasing coldness of Pennant and other friends, Low's health began a steady decline from about 1781, with recurrent episodes of cough, pleurisy, and latterly of rheumatism and weight loss. In particular, his eyesight began to fail, and from 1793 he became almost completely blind. Nevertheless, he did manage to provide a description of Birsay parish for Sir John Sinclair's *Statistical Account* (1791–94). Low died on 13 March 1795 at Birsay, and was buried on the 16th beneath the pulpit in Birsay church. He was clearly a good naturalist and was remembered as an eloquent preacher. His hobbies included fishing and shooting, and, particularly after his eyesight failed, music.

Many of the unfortunate naturalist's manuscripts fell into the hands of his friend Paton, at whose death they were distributed; their subsequent history is complex. Important collections were made during the nineteenth century by Dr Omand, Professor Thomas Stewart Traill, and David Laing. These manuscripts, including those of the important 'Tours', the 'Flora Orcadensis', and the 'History of Orkney', are now located mainly in Edinburgh University Library, the National Museums of Scotland, and the National Library of Scotland.

THOMAS SECCOMBE, *rev.* ANDREW GROUT

Sources O. D. Cuthbert, *The life and letters of an Orkney naturalist: Rev. George Low, 1747–1795* (1995) • G. Low, *A tour through the islands of Orkney and Schetland ... with an introduction by Joseph Anderson* (1879) • A. Jervise, *Epitaphs and inscriptions from burial grounds and old buildings in the north-east of Scotland*, 2 vols. (1875), 310; 2 (1879), 88 • *Fasti Scot.*, new edn, 7.241 • A. Goodfellow, *Birsay church history, including Harray, with sketches of the ministers and people from the earliest times* (1903) • L. Rendboe, *Det gamle shetlandske sprog: George Low's ordliste fra 1774* (1987) [incl. Eng. summary] • *Fasti academiae Mariscallanae Aberdonensis: selections from the records of the Marischal College and University, MDXCIII–MDCCCLX*, 2, ed. P. J. Anderson, New Spalding Club, 18 (1898), 334 • M. Spence, *Flora Orcadensis* (1914), xxxi, xxxvii–xxxviii • J. M. Anderson, ed., *The matriculation roll of the University of St Andrews, 1747–1897* (1905), 14 • parish register (baptism), 29 March 1747, Edzell, Forfarshire

Archives Museum of Scotland, Edinburgh, papers • NL Scot., notes, papers relating to Orkney • U. Edin. L., papers relating to Orkney | NL Scot., letters to George Paton • Warks. CRO, letters to Thomas Pennant

Low, George Carmichael (1872–1952), physician and specialist in tropical diseases, was born on 14 October 1872, the third son of Samuel Millar Low, an engineer, at Monifieth in Forfarshire. He was educated at Madras College, St Andrews, St Andrews University, and Edinburgh University, where he graduated with a first-class MB degree in 1897. His first post was at Edinburgh Royal Infirmary, though he was soon lured by the exciting opportunities opening up in tropical medicine to work with Patrick Manson in London. After fieldwork in the early 1900s Low demonstrated that it was possible to have a successful and prosperous career in tropical medicine in the metropolis, based on teaching, research, consultancy, and a clinical practice serving travellers and returning colonial personnel. However, like most of his contemporaries he spent the early part of his career overseas on a variety of short-term contracts and projects.

Low's first overseas venture at Manson's prompting was to visit Heidelberg and Vienna, where he learned new methods of taking cross-sections of insects for microscopical observation. With this technique Low disproved Manson's notion that filarial parasites were carried in the water supply, finding instead that they were transmitted in mosquito saliva during biting. In 1900 he achieved some public fame when, again at Manson's behest, he was a human guinea-pig, with Louis Sambon and Signor Terzi, in an experiment in the marshes around Rome to show the effectiveness of anti-mosquito measures in preventing malaria. The three men spent the daylight hours in ordinary work, but at nightfall, when the mosquitoes emerged, they retired to huts that were screened with mosquito-proof netting. They maintained their strict regimen throughout the late summer and none caught the disease. This not only confirmed the malaria-mosquito theory but also showed the effectiveness of individual precautions. Low was next sent to the West Indies, as a Cragg's scholar, to investigate filarial parasites. In 1903 he was appointed to the Royal Society's commission sent to Uganda to investigate the epidemic of sleeping sickness. Manson wanted his colleague in the team as he suspected a filarial worm was the cause. The commission was dogged with problems and it was left to a second commission, led by David Bruce, to show that the specific cause was a trypanosome parasite borne by the tsetse fly.

On his return from Uganda, Low accepted the position of superintendent of the London School of Tropical Medicine; he continued to serve there until 1937, apart from a period of four years as pathologist to the West London Hospital. Having begun as pathologist and lecturer he eventually concentrated on clinical work, becoming director of the department of clinical tropical medicine. He also served as physician to the Albert Dock Hospital and as senior physician at the new Hospital for Tropical Diseases that opened after the First World War. During the war Low was an officer in the Indian Medical Service (IMS), treating troops returning home from tropical theatres. He was a founding member of the Royal Society of Tropical Medicine and Hygiene in 1907 and played a leading role in its affairs throughout his life, especially in securing its long-term solvency. On Manson's death Low assumed a leading role in tropical medicine in London. His main contributions to the literature were in textbooks, most notably his collaboration with Sir Neil Hamilton Fairley on the tropical section of F. W. Price's *Textbook of the Practice of Medicine* (1941). Low was awarded the Straits Settlements gold medal by the University of Edinburgh in 1912 and the Mary Kingsley medal in 1929. He was renowned as a methodical observer and recorder, with an encyclopaedic knowledge of tropical diseases.

Low was admired by his colleagues, being noted for his kindliness, dry Scottish humour, and clear teaching style. He was prone to use Spooneresque aphorisms and always greeted people with a friendly 'How's yoursel?'. However, he often presented a gruff exterior, being known as a disciplinarian, and was circumspect about taking up new ideas. On 1 December 1906 in Bexhill, Sussex, he married Edith, daughter of Joseph Nash; there were no children. When not at work Low was an enthusiastic ornithologist and showed his organizational skills as secretary and treasurer of the British Ornithological Club. He pioneered bird-watching at the new reservoirs in Staines, Middlesex, and in London became official bird-watcher in Kensington Gardens and published on birds with the Zoological Society. He died at his home at 7 Kent House, Kensington Court, London, on 31 July 1952, and was survived by his wife.

MICHAEL WORBOYS

Sources N. H. Fairley, *Transactions of the Royal Society of Tropical Medicine and Hygiene*, 46 (1952), 571–3 • *The Lancet* (9 Aug 1952), 296–7 • *BMJ* (9 Aug 1952), 341–2 • *WWW* • *CGPLA Eng. & Wales* (1952) • m. cert. • d. cert.

Archives Wellcome L., corresp. and obituaries | Wellcome L., Manson MSS

Likenesses R. Haines, photograph, repro. in Fairley, *Transactions* • R. Haines, photograph, Wellcome L. • Navana Ltd, photograph, Wellcome L. • photograph, Wellcome L. • photograph (after drawing), Wellcome L.

Wealth at death £81,674 14*s.* 10*d.*: probate, 14 Oct 1952, *CGPLA Eng. & Wales*

Low, James (*d.* 1852), army officer in the East India Company and Siamese scholar, received a Madras army cadetship in 1811, and on 11 June 1812 was appointed ensign 25th Madras native infantry. He became lieutenant in 1817, and captain 46th native infantry in 1826. He retired as lieutenant-colonel 16th native infantry in 1845. He was for many years in civil charge of Wellesley Province, Penang, in the Straits Settlements, Malaya. He published *A Dissertation on the Soil and Agriculture of … Penang* (1828), *A Grammar of the T,Hai, or Siamese Language* (1828), *On Buddha and the Phrabat* (1831), and treatises on the literature and laws of Siam. Low died on 2 May 1852. Copies of his Siamese drawings were deposited in the British Museum.

H. M. Chichester, *rev.* Roger T. Stearn

Sources *East-India Register and Army List* • E. Balfour, *The cyclopaedia of India and of eastern and southern Asia*, 3rd edn, 2 (1885) • Boase, *Mod. Eng. biog.* • F. Swettenham, *British Malaya: an account of the origin and progress of British influence in Malaya* (1907) • T. A. Heathcote, *The military in British India: the development of British land forces in south Asia, 1600–1947* (1995)

Low, Sir John (1788–1880), army officer in the East India Company and political officer in India, born at Clatto, near Cupar, Fife, on 13 December 1788, was the eldest son of Captain Robert Low of Clatto, and his wife, the daughter of Dr Robert Malcolm. He was educated at St Andrews University, attending the sessions of 1802–3, and in 1804 obtained a Madras cadetship on the nomination of J. Hudleston. On 17 July 1805 he was appointed lieutenant in the 1st Madras native infantry. For the part taken by six of its companies in the uprising at Vellore the regiment was disbanded in January 1807, the loyal men and the officers (Low included) being re-formed into the 24th Madras infantry; in 1816 it was renumbered the 1st Madras infantry, for its conduct at the battle of Sitabaldi. Low became captain in the regiment in 1820, major 17th Madras infantry (late 2nd battalion 24th Madras infantry) in 1828, and lieutenant-colonel 19th Madras infantry in 1834. In 1839 he obtained the colonelcy of the 1st Madras infantry, which he held up to his death.

Low saw in his early years varied military service. He was attached to the office of the quartermaster-general from 11 May 1810, rejoined his regiment in February 1811, was attached to the 59th regiment in the Java expedition of 1811, and was wounded at the storming of Fort Cornelis. He was afterwards brigade major in the Ceded Districts, and was Persian interpreter and head of the intelligence staff to Colonel Dowse in the southern Marattha country in 1812–13; he was in commissariat charge of Brigadier William Tuyl's force sent against the Guntur rebels in 1816, and was present at the final defeat of the Maratthas at Mehidpur in Malwa, on 21 December 1817, as extra aide-de-camp to Sir John Malcolm. In March 1818, as first political assistant to Malcolm, he was employed with a force of over 3000 men and ten guns in pacifying the Chindwara district, and his services were afterwards publicly acknowledged. He efficiently performed the delicate task of inducing the peshwa, Baji Rao, to place himself under British protection; and when Baji Rao retired to Bithur, near Cawnpore, Low was appointed resident there. He filled that post for six years to the entire satisfaction of governors-general the marquess of Hastings and Lord Amherst. From that time onwards Low's services were chiefly political, although later at Lucknow and afterwards at Hyderabad his functions included the control of large local contingents of Indian troops. In 1825 he became political agent at Jaipur. In 1830 he was appointed by Lord William Henry Cavendish-Bentinck political agent at Gwalior, where he displayed much determination and wisdom in defeating the intrigues of the regent Baï. In 1831 he was sent as resident to Lucknow. Low married in 1829 Augusta Ludlow, second daughter of John Talbot Shakespear of the Bengal civil service, and sister of Sir Richmond Shakespear, one of Low's assistants at Lucknow; they had four sons and two daughters. The eldest son, William Malcolm Low (1835–1923), Bengal civil service, was Conservative MP for Grantham from 1886 to 1892. Another son was General Sir Robert Cunliffe *Low.

In 1837 the long misrule in Oudh caused the court of directors to agree to a proposal of Lord William Bentinck for the temporary assumption by the East India Company of the government of that state. Low was certain that this effective annexation would be misunderstood by the inhabitants, and suggested instead deposing the king and placing the heir-apparent on the throne. The new governor-general, Lord Auckland, left the decision to Low. Meanwhile the king died suddenly—from poison, or possibly from strong drink. A pretender, the favourite of the late king's chief widow, had been placed on the throne, the palace and city swarmed with turbulent soldiers, and the rightful heir was a prisoner. Summoning a Bengal regiment to his aid, Low, after unsuccessful negotiation, had the gates of the palace blown open and the pretender seized. The rightful heir was then installed by the British resident. In recognition of his services Low received the special thanks of the court of directors, and was made CB (20 July 1838). Low was not the author of the Oudh treaty which was subsequently quashed. Ill health compelled him to return to Britain in 1842, after thirty-eight years of almost uninterrupted service in India.

Low returned to India in 1847, and in 1848 was appointed governor-general's agent in Rajputana and commissioner at Ajmer and Mewar, where he remained until 1852, when he was sent by Lord Dalhousie to Hyderabad, in succession to James Stuart Fraser, as resident with the nizam. There he negotiated the treaty by which Berar was assigned to the British government in return for the organization and maintenance of the Hyderabad subsidiary force. For his services on this occasion he again received the special thanks of the court of directors. On 22 September 1853 Low was appointed a member of council.

In 1854 he was promoted major-general. Low's experience of Indian princes was by then unrivalled. In two able minutes (both dated in February 1854) he protested against the impolicy and injustice of the Nagpur annexation; but on this, as on other occasions, his views were largely ignored by Dalhousie. In the deliberations that ended with the annexation of Oudh, Low strongly advocated interference, showing in a minute drawn up in March 1855 that the paramount government was bound, by considerations of justice as well as by treaty obligations, to interfere. The king, he showed, would never become an efficient ruler, and the non-enforcement of Lord Hardinge's threats of seven years previously had had a widespread influence for dissatisfaction and uncertainty. When, early in May 1857, news arrived of the mutinous refusal of the 7th Oudh irregulars to use the greased cartridges, Low advocated leniency. He refused to credit the troops with disloyalty or disaffection, but only with fear that biting the cartridges would injure their caste. The news of the outbreaks at Meerut and Delhi was received a day or two later, and Low—in opposition, it is said, to his civilian colleagues—advised a determined and immediate effort for the recovery of Delhi, an enterprise which might have cut short the uprising. In April 1858, when the rising was practically suppressed, Low returned to Britain, receiving, as on many previous occasions, the thanks of the government of India. Lord Canning described his services as 'invaluable', and acknowledged that he had exceptional knowledge of the people of India. Low was promoted lieutenant-general in 1859 and general in 1867, and was placed on the retired list in 1874. He was made KCB in 1862, and GCSI in 1873. He died at Strathallan, Upper Norwood, Surrey, on 10 January 1880, in his ninety-second year, and was buried at Kemback, Fife. His wife survived him.

H. M. CHICHESTER, *rev.* JAMES FALKNER

Sources *East-India Register* · *Indian Army List* · *The Times* (12 Jan 1880) · *Army List* · *Hart's Army List* · *Journal of the Royal Asiatic Society of Great Britain and Ireland*, new ser., 12 (1880), xv–xvi · J. W. Kaye and G. B. Malleson, *Kaye's and Malleson's History of the Indian mutiny of 1857–8*, 6 vols. (1888–9) · *CGPLA Eng. & Wales* (1880)

Archives NA Scot., 1848–56 letters to Lord Dalhousie, GD45 · U. Nott. L., 1831–5 letters to Lord William Bentinck, MSS Dept., PW JF 1250–93

Likenesses engraving, repro. in *ILN* (*c*.1875)

Wealth at death £17,889 8*s*. 6*d*.: confirmation, 2 Feb 1880, *CCI*

Low, (Helen) Nora Wilson [*pseud.* Lorna Moon] (**1886–1930**), novelist and screenwriter, was born on 16 June 1886 in North Street, in the village of Strichen, Aberdeenshire, the second of the four daughters and a son of Charles Low (1860/61–1952) and Margaret Benzies (1863–1945). Charles was registered at birth as the illegitimate son of Mary-Ann Low and Charles May, the butler of a family for whom Mary-Ann had worked in Deeside. Family rumour, however, speculated that his father may have been a more aristocratic member of the household. Brought up by his grandmother, Charles Low followed his grandfather into the family trade of stone-dressing and plastering. While Nora (as she wanted to be known) was growing up, her father worked abroad. After returning to Strichen he became landlord of the Temperance Hotel. An atheist and socialist who enjoyed discussing politics, her father was a powerful figure, who has been described as widely experienced, extremely intelligent, and well read. Local anecdote also paints him as rejecting the success of his daughter, who dedicated her first book, *Doorways in Drumorty*, to him: 'To My Dad This, His Wee Nottie's First Book.' His granddaughter Evelyn and eldest daughter, Annie, are both quoted as disputing this account and claim that he was proud of her writing (de Mille, 124). Margaret Benzies, her mother, suffered considerable hardship bringing up the family. Anecdotal evidence also describes her character: 'She wis a woman like this; she'd a likit to be upper class' (William Center, quoted in *Leopard Magazine*, February 1981). Nora Low grew up in the small community she depicts with such detail in her fiction. She received an elementary education at the local Episcopal school, but according to various sources had a passion for reading and attended evening classes in an attempt to further her education. The few surviving photographs show that Nora possessed a dark red-haired and intense beauty. In 1907 a commercial traveller staying at the Temperance Hotel, 29-year-old William Hebditch (1878–1960) from Yorkshire, fell in love with Nora and they secretly arranged to be married on Christmas eve of that year in Aberdeen. They left for Selby in Yorkshire, where Nora had a child, Bill, but soon emigrated to Entwistle in Alberta, Canada.

Information on the intervening years was for some time sketchy and contradictory. Research by her son has, however, established that Nora left Hebditch in 1913 for another Yorkshireman, Walter Moon (1890–1971), moving first to Winnipeg then Minneapolis in 1917, where she worked as a journalist. She also bore Moon a child, Mary, in 1914, but the child was sent back to Moon's family in England. Accounts of her transition to Hollywood are again contradictory; her son concedes there is a problem in that she 'told so many false stories' and liked to create a mythical background for herself (de Mille, 259). She appears, however, to have left Walter Moon and found herself employment, working for Cecil B. DeMille on *The Affairs of Anatol* (1921). Hollywood at the time was keen to attract new and marketable writers into the developing field of screenwriting, and Lorna Moon, as she was now known, achieved success very quickly. She also appears to have became the mistress of William de Mille (1878–1955) and to have borne another son, Richard de Mille, the 'foundling' child who was adopted by William's brother, Cecil, in 1922. While pregnant she was also diagnosed as having tuberculosis, and spent a considerable amount of time in a sanatorium, while working on her fiction.

In Hollywood, Nora worked on a number of screenplays. Her greatest success was *Mr. Wu* (1927), produced by MGM and starring Lon Chaney, but she also worked in screenwriting teams on a variety of silent films, including the romantic comedy *Don't Tell Everything* (1921) starring Gloria Swanson, and *Her Husband's Trademark* (1922), again with Gloria Swanson, the latter directed by Cecil B. DeMille, *Love* (1927), a version of *Anna Karenina* with Greta Garbo, *After Midnight* (1927), and *Women Love Diamonds* (1927). She was also involved with the storylines of *Too much Wife* (1922) and *Upstage* (1926). The last film with which she is accredited, a comedy, *Min and Bill*, brought out in 1930, appears to have been a much changed, Americanized, version of her novel, *Dark Star*, which she had sold to MGM at the suggestion of her friend and fellow screenwriter, Frances Marion, as a means of raising funds. Marion, one of the best-known of Hollywood screenwriters, describes how, 'all of us loved this girl, who had blithesome flights of fancy and a rare sense of humour' (Marion, 204). In her obituary the *Los Angeles Times* acknowledged Moon as one of the three best scenario writers in Hollywood. While the exotic quality of her Hollywood career may appear surprising given her origins in rural Aberdeenshire, her fiction demonstrates the writing talent which won her acclaim.

Both the collection of short stories, *Doorways in Drumorty* (published in America in 1925, in Britain in 1926), and Nora's novel, *Dark Star* (1929), draw on her experiences of growing up in a small and inward-looking community, presenting this world with a vividness and harshness which distinguishes her writing from other fiction of the Scottish kailyard school, and aligns it more closely with the work of Lewis Grassic Gibbon (Leslie Mitchell), another novelist from north-east Scotland. Drawing upon local characters and tales for her inspiration, she also parallels Gibbon in having offended the local community. Various accounts suggest that her father was particularly upset by a story 'The Funeral', in *Doorways in Drumorty*, which depicts the pride and suffering of a mother whose child is dying, and whose husband, working abroad, leaves her in poverty. Some commentators suggest this story, which does seem to draw upon her own memories of her father working away, shows the guilty man as living 'in elegance' while his wife suffers. The story, however, suggests he is unable to get work, and that the community is at fault for creating a code of pride whereby the mother cannot confess her poverty. It is therefore more focused on the tensions experienced by the woman, and less directly critical of the father, than some readings suggest. All the stories in *Doorways in Drumorty* explore similar themes: the particular codes and conventions created by such a closed community, patterns of surveillance, strictures of public morality, evidence of private despair. They engage with the margins of this world, presenting itinerants, outcasts, and misfits with a distinct lack of sentimentality. Low's work is also striking in its awareness of the position of women in the community: her stories deal with minutiae, with networks of power which operate in apparently insignificant areas.

Nora's novel, *Dark Star*, which was well received in both America and Britain, presents a similarly uncompromising picture of rural life, and again has a local setting, drawing on Strichen, but also nearby fishing villages such as Broadsea, Pennan, or Gardenstown. The plot may, in fact, have been based on stories Nora Low heard as a child when visiting relatives in Broadsea. The novel dissects, with an odd mixture of realism and melodrama, the plight of Nancy, illegitimate and an outsider in her narrow world. While delineating her attempts to escape its confines through romance, the text explores the precarious social structures, the sexual instabilities, and the surface hypocrisies which define it. This book too appears to have been unpopular in Strichen and was, according to some reports, banned from the local library because its depiction of a legless librarian was rather too close to the actuality.

Nora's books (published under the name Lorna Moon) remained unknown to the mainstream of Scottish literature for a considerable time although, through the advocacy of David Toulmin, both were republished in 1980 and 1981 by Gourdas House publishers. After that her work was given growing attention, in particular through feminist interest in its depiction of women's lives, although her name is still not widely known, even in Scotland. Nora was ill with tuberculosis in the last few years of her life and, the subject of much media interest in America, died from a fatal haemorrhage in Albuquerque, New Mexico, on 1 May 1930. On 3 June that year her ashes were brought home by a young American man she had met in a sanatorium, Everett Marcy (1902–1948?), and, according to her wishes, were scattered 'to the four winds' on Mormond Hill, behind Strichen. GLENDA NORQUAY

Sources R. de Mille, *My secret mother Lorna Moon* (1998) · D. Toulmin, 'Moondust on Mormond hill', *Leopard Magazine* (Nov 1980), 23–4 · 'Lorna Moon', *Leopard Magazine* (Feb 1981), 15 · A. Edwards, *The DeMilles: an American family* (1988) · L. Riddoch, 'Lost-lost Moon', *Leopard Magazine* (May 1992), 12 · S. Hamilton, 'The missing years of the exile of Drumorty', *Aberdeen Evening Express* (5 Oct 1981) · *Aberdeen Press and Journal* (5 May 1930) · *Los Angeles Times* (3 May 1930) · L. Moon, *Doorways in Drumorty* (1981) [with an introduction by D. Toulmin] · L. Moon, *Dark star* (1980) [with an introduction by D. Toulmin] · G. Norquay, 'Dark star over Drumorty: the writing of Lorna Moon', *Studies in Scottish fiction: twentieth century*, ed. J. Schwend and H. Drescher (1990), 117–31 · J. Webster, *Grains of truth* (1994) · F. Marion, *Off with their heads!* (1972) · C. Higham, *Cecil B. DeMille* (1974) · d. cert. [Charles Low] · G. Norquay, ed., *The collected works of Lorna Moon with a foreword by Richard de Mille* (2002)

Archives Indiana University, Bloomington, Lilly Library, Bobbs-Merrill Manuscript Collection, Lorna Moon author file · Strichen Public Library | priv. coll., corresp.

Likenesses photograph, repro. in Edwards, *The DeMilles* · photograph, repro. in Webster, *Grains of truth* · photographs, repro. in *Aberdeen Evening Express* (5 Oct 1981) · photographs, repro. in *Leopard Magazine* (Feb 1981) · photographs, Strichen Public Library, Aberdeenshire · photographs, repro. in de Mille, *My secret mother*

Low, Sir Robert Cunliffe (1838–1911), army officer, born at Kemback, Fife, on 28 January 1838, was second in a family of four sons and two daughters of Sir John *Low (1788–1880), general in the Indian army, and his wife, Augusta, second daughter of John Talbot Shakespear of the East India Company's civil service. His eldest brother was William Malcolm Low (1835–1923), Bengal civil service, who was MP for Grantham from 1886 to 1892.

After education at a private school Low received a commission as cornet in the Bengal army on 26 August 1854, and was posted to the 9th Bengal light cavalry. His first service was in the expedition against the rebellious Santals, and won him promotion to lieutenant on 29 September 1855. On the outbreak of the Indian mutiny his regiment joined the rebels, and Low was subsequently attached to the Delhi field force. He took part in the action at Badli-ki-sarai on 8 June 1857 and in the victory of John Nicholson at Najafgarh (25 August). During the siege and fall of Delhi (20 September) he served as aide-de-camp to General Archdale Wilson, and was mentioned in dispatches. After accompanying Sir Colin Campbell on his march to the second relief of Lucknow (19 March 1858), Low was appointed brigade major to the Agra field force, and was engaged in the pursuit and capture of rebels in central India. At the end of the campaign he received the thanks of the governor-general. In 1862 Low married Mary Constance (*d.* 1900), daughter of Captain Taylor of the East India Company's service; they had two sons and three daughters.

Promoted captain on 1 January 1862, Low commanded a company in the second Yusufzai expedition in 1863 under Sir Neville Chamberlain. He was promoted brevet major on 15 February 1872 and lieutenant-colonel on 8 February 1878. The following year he commanded the 13th Bengal lancers in the Second Anglo-Afghan War campaign against the Zakha Khel Afridis of the Bazar valley, took part in the punitive expedition against the Zaimukhts in December 1879, and was at the assault of the Zava heights. In June 1880 Sir Frederick (afterwards Lord) Roberts secured his appointment as director of the transport service. Under Low's energetic and intelligent management the transport organization worked smoothly and efficiently; his invaluable services on the march from Kabul to Kandahar were generously acknowledged by the commander-in-chief, and he was made a CB.

Low became colonel on 8 February 1882, and was nominated brigadier-general in May 1886 to command the second-class district of Bareilly. In the following July he was detached for service in Upper Burma, where a desultory armed resistance continued for two years after its annexation. He commanded a brigade at Minbu, and during the period of pacification was engaged in arduous guerrilla warfare. He was mentioned in dispatches, received the thanks of the viceroy of India, and was made KCB. In 1888 he resumed charge of the Bareilly district, and held the command of the first-class district of Lucknow from 1892 to 1895. He was promoted major-general on 5 October 1893.

Low's well-known capacity for organization led to his appointment as commander-in-chief of the Chitral relief expedition. Advancing from Nowshera in the spring of 1895 he concentrated his whole force on the Malakand Pass, and on 3 April stormed the heights. The enemy were again defeated at the Panjkora River, and a flying column, dispatched by Low under Sir William Gatacre, reached Chitral on 15 May after a most difficult journey through the Lowari Pass. But meanwhile the garrison had already been relieved by Colonel Kelly's force from Gilgit. It was generally recognized that the success of the campaign was mainly due to Low's dispositions and the rapidity of his movements, and he received the thanks of the viceroy of India. Next year he was promoted lieutenant-general and advanced to GCB. From 1898 to 1903 he commanded the Bombay army and, after attaining the rank of general in 1900, retired in 1905. In 1909 he became keeper of the crown jewels at the Tower of London. He died at his home, 20 Cornwall Road, Dorchester, Dorset, on 4 August 1911, and was buried at Dorchester.

G. S. Woods, *rev.* James Falkner

Sources *Army List* • *The Times* (7 Aug 1911) • *Indian Army List* • H. B. Hanna, *The Second Afghan War*, 3 vols. (1899–1910) • *Hart's Army List* • *LondG* (15 Dec 1857) • *LondG* (7 Nov 1879) • *LondG* (3 Dec 1880) • *LondG* (2 Sept 1887) • *LondG* (15 Nov 1895) • Lord Roberts [F. S. Roberts], *Forty-one years in India*, 30th edn (1898)

Likenesses E. Taylor, portrait, 1907; in possession of Robert Balmain Low, 1912 • engravings, repro. in *Navy and Army Illustrated* (3 April 1896)

Wealth at death £15,702 15*s.*: resworn probate, 3 Oct 1911, *CGPLA Eng. & Wales*

Low, Sampson (1797–1886), publisher, was born in London in November 1797, the son of Sampson Low (*d.* 1800), printer and publisher, of Berwick Street, Soho. He served an apprenticeship with Lionel Booth, the proprietor of a circulating library, and, after a few years spent in the house of Longman & Co., began business in 1819 at 42 Lamb's Conduit Street, London, as a bookseller and stationer, with a circulating library attached. His reading-room was frequented by many literary men, lawyers, and politicians. In 1821 Sampson married; his wife's name was Mary (1796/7–1881), and they went on to have several children, among whom his eldest son, Sampson Low jun. (1822–1871), and his second son, William Henry Low (*d.* 1881), were to assist with the family business.

Until 1837 *Bent's Literary Advertiser* was the only trade journal connected with bookselling; at this period the publishers became dissatisfied with the manner in which it was conducted, and established a periodical of their own called the *Publishers' Circular*, appointing Low as editor. The first number appeared on 2 October 1837. Low gradually introduced many changes and improvements, and in 1867 the *Circular* became his sole property. The periodical, which was published fortnightly, supplied a list of new books, and from these lists an annual catalogue was made up, the first appearing in 1839. Upon these annual catalogues Low based his *British Catalogue*, the first volume of which, containing titles under authors' names of all books issued between 1837 and 1852, was published in 1853; it was continued as the *English Catalogue*, with four further volumes appearing between 1864 and 1882. Subject indexes were issued in 1858 and in 1876, the first being reprinted in 1976 and the second in 1979, as important sources for literary historians. Low was also manager of a society for the protection of retail booksellers against undersellers until the dissolution of the society in 1852. In 1841 Low compiled and published *Low's Comparative Register of the House of Commons, 1827–1841*, six years later producing an updated version covering the years 1841 to 1847. About 1844 he met Fletcher Harper of New York, and became his literary agent and correspondent, and one of the chief American booksellers in London. In 1848, in conjunction with his eldest son, Low opened a publishing office at the corner of Red Lion Court, Fleet Street. In 1852 they moved to 47 (and later to 14) Ludgate Hill, where, with the aid of David Bogue, an American department was opened. In 1856 Edward Marston became a partner, and Bogue retired. The firm moved in 1867 to 188 Fleet Street, and, two years after publishing *Low's Literary Almanack and Illustrated Souvenir for 1873*, Low retired in 1875. In 1887 the firm moved again, to St Dunstan's House, Fetter Lane, and subsequently to Paternoster Row.

In addition to his business commitments, Low found time for many philanthropic projects. With his son he was mainly instrumental in establishing in 1843 the Royal Society for the Protection of Life from Fire, and supervised it until 1867, when it was taken over by the Metropolitan Board of Works. From its foundation in 1837 he took the deepest interest in the Booksellers' Provident Institution, serving on the committee and acting as a vice-president, and bequeathing it a handsome legacy in his will.

The death of Low's eldest son on 5 March 1871 was a great blow. Sampson Low jun. had been an invalid, but had taken a considerable share in the business, compiling *The Charities of London* in 1850, a popular and useful reference work which formed the basis for four further editions between 1854 and 1870. Low's wife died on 26 May 1881, in her eighty-fourth year, within a month of their anticipated diamond wedding anniversary, and a few months later, on 25 September 1881, Low lost his second son. Low himself died at home on 16 April 1886, at 41 Mecklenburgh Square, London, and was buried in Highgate cemetery. He was survived by his daughter, Mary Ann. G. C. Boase, *rev.* M. Clare Loughlin-Chow

Sources *Publishers' Circular* (16 May 1879) · *Publishers' Circular* (1 June 1881), 435 · *Publishers' Circular* (1 Oct 1881), 763 · *Publishers' Circular* (1 May 1886), 431–3 · *The Bookseller* (3 May 1886), 418–20 · *The Times* (21 April 1886), 9 · *Harper's Weekly*, 30 (1886), 268 · *CGPLA Eng. & Wales* (1886)
Likenesses portrait, repro. in *Publishers' Circular* (1 May 1886)
Wealth at death £24,248 14*s.* 9*d.*: probate, 25 May 1886, *CGPLA Eng. & Wales*

Low, Sir Sidney James Mark (1857–1932), journalist, historian, and essayist, was born at Blackheath, London, on 22 January 1857. His father, Maximilian Loewe (*b. c.*1830), a Hungarian Jew, had fled to England in 1848, established himself successfully in business in the City of London, and married Therese Schacherl (*d.* 1886), daughter of a Viennese rabbi. Sidney was the eldest child in their family of six sons and five daughters. He was educated at King's College School, Strand, from 1870, and won a scholarship to Pembroke College, Oxford, in 1876. The following year he migrated to Balliol, where he later became a Brackenbury scholar. Tutored by the respected Revd James Bright (1832–1930), Low achieved a first class in modern history in 1879, and then worked for four years as a private tutor. Between 1883 and 1885 he lectured on constitutional history at King's College, London; and in 1884 he published his first book, *The Dictionary of English History*, jointly edited with Professor Frederic Pulling.

Low's journalistic career began in 1883 when he started writing for the *St James's Gazette*, a periodical he looked upon as 'the organ of the governing classes'. Low edited the *St James's* between 1888 and 1897, eventually resigning after a series of disagreements with its proprietor, Edward Steinkopff. The two distinguishing features of his editorship were the unfailing support of the journal for empire builders such as Rhodes, Curzon, Cromer, and Milner, and its very high literary standards. Notable and regular contributors recruited by Low included Rudyard Kipling, Gilbert Parker, J. M. Barrie, Andrew Lang, and Edmund Gosse. After leaving the *St James's* Low was appointed a leader writer on *The Standard* in 1898. But when Arthur Pearson purchased the paper in November 1904, appointing the passionate tariff reformer H. A. Gwynne (1865–1950) as its editor, Low's free trade sympathies prohibited him from writing on home politics. He was made literary editor instead, and in the autumn of 1905 dispatched to India to act as the special correspondent of *The Standard* during the visit of the prince and princess of Wales. This journey led to the publication of *Vision of India* (1906), by far Low's most popular work, and less a record of the royal tour than a subtle and sensitive portrayal of Indian life and society. In particular, his account of the *swadeshi* movement and the growth of a nationalist consciousness was remarkably perceptive and prescient. In 1908 Low's position on *The Standard* was terminated by Pearson; thereafter, he contributed articles to the paper on a freelance basis. He was bitterly disappointed not to succeed Fabian Ware as editor of the *Morning Post* in 1911, passed over because his views on the fiscal question proved unacceptable to its owner, Lady Bathurst. During the First World War Low's talents eventually received proper recognition when, in 1918, he was asked to take charge of the wireless service of the Ministry of Information.

Of Low's publications, the *Governance of England* (1904) stands out as the most important, reflecting his longstanding interest in the working of the English constitution since 1867. Other books included a volume in Longman's *Political History of England* (with L. C. Sanders, 1907); a literary study, *De Quincey* (1911); *Egypt in Transition* (1914); and *Samuel Henry Jeyes* (1915). Low was also a regular contributor to monthly journals. His brief biographical sketch of Cecil Rhodes in the *Nineteenth Century and After* (May 1902) remains one of the most insightful and illuminating pieces on the beliefs and personality of that figure.

Low's political ambitions were mainly confined to the London county council, of which he was a Conservative member from 1901 to 1906, active on the highways committee and displaying a particular interest in London's growing traffic problems. He fought shy of Westminster, declining an offer to become a Conservative parliamentary candidate for Bethnal Green in 1895. He did, however, firmly believe that a newspaper had an essential function to play in party politics, both in expounding policy and maintaining morale. Low's enthusiasm for the empire found a very practical expression in the active role which he played in the founding of the faculty of imperial studies at King's College, London. He was especially eager that the school should cover the history of the British in India under the company and the crown, and addressed the British Academy on this matter in 1912.

Low was called to the bar in 1892, and knighted in 1918. He was twice married: first, on 16 June 1887, to Eliza (1854/5–1921), daughter of John Davison, a cabinet-maker; second, on 23 October 1924, to Ebba Cecilia, daughter of

Captain Gustaf Byström of Stockholm. Low had no children. He died at his home, 45 Campden Hill Court, in Kensington, on 13 January 1932. ANDREW S. THOMPSON

Sources D. Chapman-Huston, *The lost historian: a memoir of S. Low* (1936) • S. E. Koss, *The rise and fall of the political press in Britain*, 2 (1984) • D. Griffiths, *Plant here The Standard* (1996) • *The Times* (14 Jan 1932), 14 • A. T. C. Pratt, ed., *People of the period: being a collection of the biographies of upwards of six thousand living celebrities*, 2 vols. (1897)
Archives Bodl. Oxf., Milner MSS • Richmond Local Studies Library, London, corresp. with Douglas Sladen • U. Leeds, Brotherton L., letters to Edmund Gosse
Likenesses two photographs, *c.*1887–1932, repro. in Chapman-Huston, *Lost historian*, 132, 180
Wealth at death £2092 0s. 4d.: probate, 12 March 1932, *CGPLA Eng. & Wales*

Low, William (1814–1886), civil engineer, was born on 11 December 1814 at Rothesay, Bute, Scotland, the eldest son of John Low, a leather currier, and Mary McKinzie, a labourer's daughter. In 1815 the family moved to Glasgow where William was raised. He was apprenticed to Peter MacQuisten, a Glasgow engineer and surveyor.

In the late 1830s Low was at Bristol working on the construction of the Box Tunnel near Bath for the Great Western Railway, and while there married Elizabeth Cameron (*d.* 1896) in October 1838. By 1841 Low was an assistant engineer to Isambard Kingdom Brunel, moving to Chester to work on the Chester to Holyhead line. He was also consulted on the Shrewsbury to Hereford, and the Shrewsbury to Chester lines, especially about tunnelling. He probably returned to Glasgow to work in partnership with MacQuisten until the latter's death about 1847. In 1850 Low submitted plans for a loan fund to finance the construction of railways in Ireland.

In 1852 Low became joint owner with Mortimer Maurice of the Vron colliery, near Wrexham, and Low set up home at Adwy'r-clawdd near Coed-poeth, moving in 1864 to Roseneath, a house he built himself, in Wrexham. He pursued a career locally, as the managing partner of Vron colliery with about 400 employees, and as a consulting colliery engineer. He advocated the Vale of Llangollen Railway, which opened in 1858; subscribed to Wrexham Infirmary; served as a Denbighshire JP; and was an active supporter of the local Liberal Party. In 1875 Low built the Westminster Buildings in Wrexham for the Great Exhibition of Industry and Art in 1876.

Low maintained professional interests at the national level, and was especially known for his advocacy of the channel tunnel. In the 1860s he worked with Sir John Hawkshaw on plans for a tunnel, but disagreed with Hawkshaw's proposals for a single-bore tunnel with a double-track railway, arguing that a twin-bore tunnel with a single track in each would be cheaper to construct and could be better ventilated. His suggestions are considered to be the first practical proposals for a channel tunnel, and the present tunnel was constructed on similar principles. He and a colleague, George Thomas, submitted plans to Napoleon III in 1867, and Low played an important role in subsequent Anglo-French investigations and reports in favour of the scheme.

The Franco-Prussian War interrupted these discussions, but afterwards interest arose once more, and in England two competing private companies emerged, one backing Hawkshaw's proposals, while that of the railway entrepreneur Sir Edward Watkin backed those of Low. Both companies obtained enabling legislation, both sank trial shafts, and drove short stretches of tunnel, but the idea aroused opposition, and in 1883 British military authorities vetoed construction on the grounds of national security. All work on both sides of the channel came to a halt. Such was Low's enthusiasm that his study at Roseneath became known as the Channel Tunnel Office, and it may have been a reason for his move to London in 1882.

In 1867 Low was elected a member of the Institution of Civil Engineers. In 1871 he and Thomas submitted plans for a railway from England to India, Low having surveyed part of the route in 1870, and in 1876 he advocated a line from Constantinople to Karachi. In the mid-1870s Low advocated a tunnel under the Mersey, and a bridge over the Severn, both of which were authorized but remained unbuilt. Some years before his death an attack of paralysis compelled him to cease active work, and his colliery may have closed down during the 1878–9 trade depression. In 1882 Low moved from Wrexham to 88 West Cromwell Road, London. He died there on 10 July 1886 and was buried at Brompton cemetery on 13 July. His widow lived in Oswestry until her death in 1896. The 1861 census records ten children. K. R. FAIRCLOUGH

Sources *DNB* • 'William Low and the Channel Tunnel', Wrexham Maelor Heritage Centre information sheet 2, Wrexham • M. Hughes, 'William Low (1814–86) and the channel tunnel idea', *Transactions of the Denbighshire Historical Society*, 22 (1973), 331–4 • P. Haining, *Eurotunnel: an illustrated history of the channel tunnel scheme* (1973) • R. Ryves, *The channel tunnel project* (1929) • M. Bonavia, *The channel tunnel story* (1987) • *Wrexham Advertiser* (17 July 1886) • W. Low and G. Thomas, *The proposed England and India railway* (1871) • E. Rogers, 'The history of trade unionism in the coal mining industry of north Wales … Twelve years of sectional movements (1848–1860)', *Transactions of the Denbighshire Historical Society*, 16 (1967), 100–27 • E. Rogers, 'The history of trade unionism in the coal mining industry of north Wales … force and arbitration (1870–1875)', *Transactions of the Denbighshire Historical Society*, 19 (1970), 188–216 • G. C. Lerry, *The collieries of Denbighshire past and present* (1968) • *The Times* (16 July 1886) • index, Katherine House marriage registers
Archives Clwyd RO, reports on Westminster colliery
Likenesses photograph, Wrexham Maelor Hospital, Wrexham, Denbighshire; repro. in 'William Low and the Channel Tunnel' • photograph negative, priv. coll. • portrait, repro. in Haining, *Eurotunnel*, 25
Wealth at death £5182 10s.: probate, 26 July 1886, *CGPLA Eng. & Wales*

Lowder, Charles Fuge (1820–1880), Church of England clergyman, the eldest of the two sons and four daughters of Charles Lowder (1789–1876), banker, and his wife, Susan Fuge (1788–1871), was born at 2 West Wing, Lansdown Crescent, Bath, on 22 June 1820. After early schooling in Bath (1827–34) and at Bruton grammar school (1835), he attended King's College School, London, from 1835 to 1839 and in February 1840 went up to Exeter College, Oxford, from which he received his BA, a second in classics, in 1843, and an MA in 1845. Ordained deacon at Michaelmas 1843, he went as curate to Walton, near Glastonbury, and following his priesting in December 1844 began work as chaplain to the Axbridge workhouse. In 1846 he became curate of Tetbury, and in September 1851 moved to London as assistant curate to James Skinner, senior curate of St Barnabas's, Pimlico, then a chapel of ease to St Paul's, Knightsbridge, and in the vanguard of the Anglo-Catholic revival.

In 1854 Lowder was briefly suspended for encouraging choirboys to throw eggs at the placard-bearer of an anti-ritualist churchwarden. During the suspension he read Louis Abelly's *Vie de S. Vincent de Paul* (1664) and conceived the idea of a secular order of priests to upgrade the clergy's spiritual life and to establish home missions among the poor. In February 1855, with five other priests, he founded the Society of the Holy Cross, which in the following February, at Lowder's suggestion, both revived retreats in the Church of England and began a home mission in Bryan King's parish of St George-in-the-East. As the Society of the Holy Cross grew and came to include most of the notable figures in the Anglo-Catholic movement, it exercised an increasing influence on its members and the church through its rules of life, its publications and monthly chapters, and its support for Anglo-Catholic parishes and beleaguered ritualist priests.

On 20 August 1856 Lowder left St Barnabas's to take charge of St George's mission, living in the recently bought mission house in Calvert Street, Wapping. In November 1856 the mission opened the iron chapel of the Good Shepherd in Wapping, and in the following March began services in the rented Danish chapel of St Saviour at Wellclose Square. Elizabeth Neale, sister of John Mason Neale, came in May 1857 to found under Lowder's aegis the Community of the Holy Cross, which enabled the mission to expand its work in the provision of schools, a refuge for prostitutes, a hostel for homeless girls, night classes and parish clubs, visiting, and general poor relief. From the opening of the iron chapel Lowder wore eucharistic vestments, almost certainly the first priest in London to do so. Bishop Tait complained of this and other ritual, but from May 1859 attention focused on the parish church, which with brief interludes was the scene of riots, ostensibly about ritual, until the summer of 1860. The mission clergy, especially Lowder and A. H. Mackonochie (Lowder's assistant from November 1857 to Easter 1862), bore the brunt of the disturbances, but the mission chapels themselves were relatively free of trouble. Despite accusations of Romanism Lowder was resolutely loyal to the Church of England. The secession to Rome of some of his assistants and curates in 1857–8 and 1868 deeply distressed him, and on his deathbed he instructed that it should be witnessed he died an Anglican.

In 1860 Lowder acquired a site for a church and began to raise funds to build St Peter's, London Docks, which was consecrated on 30 June 1866. Lowder was first licensed as perpetual curate and then, on the resignation of the rector of St George's in 1873, became vicar. From July until September 1866 cholera attacked the East End, with Wapping one of the worst hit districts. The work of the clergy and sisters during the epidemic ensured their acceptance among the people, and from then on Lowder was known simply as 'the Father'. The love of his parishioners and the esteem in which he was held in the wider church, even by those who disagreed with him, foiled efforts to prosecute him for allegedly illegal ritual. A complaint by the Church Association in 1869 under the Church Discipline Act was quashed by Bishop Jackson, and an attempt in 1877–8 under the Public Worship Regulation Act was vetoed by Archbishop Tait on the advice of Jackson, who in November 1878 wrote privately to Tait that, if the prosecution of Lowder proceeded, he doubted whether the unamended Public Worship Act 'could ever be put in force again'. The failure of the prosecution and the unabated ritual at St Peter's was a moral victory for the Anglo-Catholic movement, and undoubtedly contributed to the eventual acceptance of high-church ritual within the Church of England.

Throughout the 1870s Lowder struggled to raise the funds needed for parish work. In 1877 he published *Twenty-one Years in St George's Mission*, an update of his earlier *Ten Years in St George's Mission* (1867), in the hope of re-exciting interest and encouraging contributions. At the same time, the combination of overwork and what was probably a peptic ulcer told on his health, and he was increasingly forced to spend time out of the parish. During the 1870s his self-imposed reserve and sternness mellowed, and he allowed a natural warmth and sense of humour to show itself to colleagues and parishioners. Tall for his generation, slimly but strongly built, he impressed those who knew him with his physical courage and self-discipline, and as he grew older he won those who knew him by his gentleness and love.

Lowder died at Hotel Krone, in all likelihood from a perforated ulcer, while on a climbing holiday at Zell-am-See, Austria, on 9 September 1880. After a requiem at St Peter's on 17 September, several hundred clergy and a few thousand parishioners and friends made their way to St Nicholas's churchyard, Chislehurst, for his burial.

LIDA ELLSWORTH

Sources L. E. Ellsworth, *Charles Lowder and the ritualist movement* (1982) • [M. Trench], *Charles Lowder: a biography*, 3rd edn (1882) • *The Guardian* (15 Sept 1880) • *The Guardian* (22 Sept 1880) • *Church Times* (17 Sept 1880) • *Church Times* (24 Sept 1880) • *Tower Hamlets Independent* (18 Sept 1880)

Archives NRA, corresp. and papers • St Peter's parish archives, London Docks, London | CKS, Society of the Holy Cross MSS • GL, London diocese MSS • LPL, corresp. with Archbishop Tait

Likenesses photograph, 1850–59, Pusey Oxf. • two photographs, 1860–79, St Peter's, London docks • stained-glass window, after 1945, St Peter's, London docks • G. Cook, stipple, NPG

Wealth at death under £600: resworn administration, May 1881, *CGPLA Eng. & Wales* (1880)

Lowe, Arthur (1915–1982), actor, was born on 22 September 1915 at Hayfield, Derbyshire, the only child of Arthur Lowe (*fl.* 1900–1950), railwayman, and his wife, Mary Ford (*fl.* 1900–1960). Between the wars the family lived in Manchester, where Mr Lowe worked as a bookings manager for excursion trains. After grammar school, where he was a promising boxer, young Arthur started work at sixteen pushing a barrow for a cotton mill. He had a spell with Fairey Aviation, then joined another local firm, Brown

Arthur Lowe (1915–1982), by unknown photographer, *c.*1974

Brothers, selling motor parts. His skill at mimicking the foremen showed where his real talent lay, and the Second World War gave him the chance to exploit it. Fellow recruits had been amused at his characterization of a Nazi officer with the catchphrase 'Velcome to my vahr' and when Lowe was posted to a REME (Royal Electrical and Mechanical Engineers) depot in Egypt he formed a theatre group. After producing *The Monkey's Paw* he joined a field entertainment unit and helped to run fortnightly repertory in Alexandria.

Home again in 1945, Lowe decided on a stage career. His father, whose customers included touring theatre companies, persuaded the impresario Frank H. Fortescue to give him an audition, and he was soon in demand for character parts at the Hulme Hippodrome, Manchester. There he met a married actress, Joan Cooper (1923–1987?), later to be his wife and stage partner. She was instantly struck by his ability to claim an audience's attention in the most minor role. They spent 1947 with a company in Hereford, where Lowe appeared in forty-two plays; a lasting tendency not to know his lines properly was already evident. Joan Cooper divorced and on 10 January 1948, while playing in repertory around London's southern fringe, they married. A year later Lowe made the most of the part of a reporter in the film *Kind Hearts and Coronets*. The notebook in which he recorded a lifetime's work lists nearly fifty plays in Bromley during 1950 and 1951. He escaped briefly for a first West End appearance in the Guy Bolton comedy *Larger than Life*, but in 1952 began an eighteen-month run as Senator Brockbank in the musical *Call me Madam*. His talent for singing and dancing brought him parts in *Pal Joey* and *The Pajama Game* (1954 and 1955), but in a later career résumé he maintained he first 'really came to notice' in *A Dead Secret* by Rodney Ackland at the Piccadilly Theatre in 1957. Philip Hope-Wallace in the *Manchester Guardian* noted 'the mean, respectable cousin (beautifully played by Arthur Lowe)' (Lowe, 58). By this time a son, Stephen, had been born, and, together with Joan's son David, the family lived in a succession of Knightsbridge flats. Acting then as his own agent, Lowe was never slow to remind producers of his availability, and worked regularly in films, broadcasting, and commercials. 'I took everything that was going,' he said. 'How can you say you're an actor if you're not acting?' (Morley).

During the early 1960s Lowe reached a wider audience as the self-important Leonard Swindley in the television series *Coronation Street*, but was contracted for only half the year and made notable appearances in Lindsay Anderson's film *This Sporting Life* (1963) and in the John Osborne play *Inadmissible Evidence* at the Royal Court. Reviewing Henry Livings's play *Stop it Whoever You Are*, one critic wrote that Arthur Lowe seemed less like an actor than a Manchester alderman who had strayed by accident onto the stage of the Arts Theatre (Lowe, 64). It was one of many tributes to the naturalness of his performances. His portrayal of Mr Swindley, the draper fussily upholding the standards of forty years before, became so popular that in 1965 he left *Coronation Street* to play the same part in a new series, *Pardon the Expression*. The following year he earned high praise as the cuckold Sir Davy Dunce in *The Soldier's Fortune* by Thomas Otway at the Royal Court. 'Mr Lowe can speak the most insignificant line with such a point that it gets a laugh … His pathos is all the deeper for being expressed in comic terms', said the *Financial Times* (ibid., 91). In 1968 he played an ineffectual housemaster in Lindsay Anderson's film *If* … but it was another part during the same year which transformed him from a well-regarded actor into an enduring national favourite.

When Jimmy Perry suggested Arthur Lowe for the role of Captain Mainwaring in a television comedy series he had devised about the Home Guard, the BBC were doubtful. The response—'We don't know him, do we?'—indicated a sniffy view of Lowe's starring roles for ITV (Lowe, 102). Perry persisted and he and his co-writer and producer David Croft invited Lowe to lunch. The meeting got off to a bad start, with Lowe expressing reservations about the sitcom genre, and unguardedly citing *Hugh and I*, which Croft had produced, as particularly dreadful. Croft let it pass and the three went on to establish a classic of British sitcom. There were eighty-three episodes of *Dad's Army* between 1968 and 1977, and the repeats later became part of the staple of television, attracting large audiences long after most of the participants were dead. As Mainwaring, the bank manager-cum-Home Guard officer, Lowe defended his dignity against a world unwilling to acknowledge it, and led a memorable supporting cast through action and cross-talk of high inventiveness. His genius was to put his physical limitations—short sight and stature, baldness, and *embonpoint*—at the service of his art—timing and mastery of vocal and facial expression. The alchemy turned standard scriptwriter's fare into gold, so that when he declared (of a Lewis gun position), 'This'll cover the High Street from Timothy Whites to the Novelty Rock Emporium', he made millions laugh at the incongruity. Mainwaring's determination to excel was doomed to failure—fate and the rest of the platoon saw to that. He was guaranteed to come off worse in his exchanges with the effortlessly superior Wilson (John *Le Mesurier)—his junior in the bank *and* the Home Guard, but several rungs higher on the social ladder.

Lowe's triumph was to make Mainwaring likeable despite the testiness and vainglory. That he was able to do so without always being confident of his lines only adds to the achievement. Many stories were told of his delaying tactics as he put off the moment for proper study of the script. Once when David Croft suggested he take a copy home he replied: 'I don't want a thing like that in my house' (Lowe, 106). Colleagues suspected the hesitations that became Mainwaring's stock-in-trade ('I say, Jo … Jo … Jo … Jones …') gave Lowe the chance to think of the next line. In one episode Mainwaring's social pretensions were threatened by a visit from his brother, a bibulous traveller in novelties. The two characters were poles apart, but Lowe played both with a virtuosity which made Perry rate him among the best comic actors of the century. Away from work he was a private man who shrank from the demands of celebrity, yet everything he did had the air of a performance. Choosing from a menu took on the solemnity of a board meeting, with earnest enquiries into whether the ham was off the bone, or the kippers still had their heads. There was something of Mainwaring in him, which he played up for effect, muttering 'That'll have to change' to one of the production staff when a junior member of the cast hailed him as 'Arthur' on the location bus. It was very much in the mould of his withering 'Stupid boy!', directed at Private Pike, which soon went into the language.

In latter years the Lowes moved to Little Venice in London, and bought a boat, *Amazon*, which they moored at Teddington and occasionally took to France or the Isle of Wight. He remained hectically busy, with much-praised performances in films—playing a boozy and rebellious butler in *The Ruling Class* (1972), and three different parts in *O Lucky Man* (1973), which won him a British Film Academy award for best supporting actor. On stage he appeared as Ben Jonson in *Bingo* with Sir John Gielgud, and took the *Dad's Army Stage Show* into the West End and on tour. There were further television series, radio adaptations of *Dad's Army*, and many voice-overs for commercials. But behind the success, Lowe's last years were difficult. He began to suffer from narcolepsy and would fall asleep without warning, even on stage. Life was further complicated by his wife's alcoholism. Only the discipline of the theatre kept her sober, and when offered a play he would stipulate that she must appear with him. The scheme worked on tour, but West End managements doubted her competence and Lowe turned down a number of opportunities because there was no part for her. He found solace in entertaining old friends on the boat, and in food, of which he consumed large quantities. He was touring in R. C. Sheriff's play *Home at Seven* when he died on 15 April 1982 in the General Hospital, Birmingham, having had a stroke in his dressing-room at the Alexandra Theatre, Birmingham. He was sixty-six, and was survived by his wife.

James Hogg

Sources S. Lowe, *Arthur Lowe: Dad's memory* (1996) • private information (2004) • B. Pertwee, *'Dad's army': the making of a television legend* (1989); repr. (1994) • R. Webber, *'Dad's army': a celebration* (1997) • R. Fawkes, *Fighting for a laugh* (1978) • J. Le Mesurier, *A jobbing actor* (1985) • S. Morley, *The Times* (10 Aug 1974) • B. Pertwee, *A funny way to make a living* (1996) • d. cert.

Archives FILM BFI NFTVA, 'A life on the box', BBC 1, 21 Feb 1999 • BFI NFTVA, 'The unforgettable Arthur Lowe', ITV 1, 18 Sept 2000 • BFI NFTVA, news footage | SOUND BBC WAC • BL NSA, *With great pleasure*, 1976, T1291R • BL NSA, performance recordings

Likenesses photograph, *c*.1974, Hult. Arch. [*see illus.*] • photographs, Hult. Arch.

Wealth at death £240,273: probate, 11 Aug 1982, *CGPLA Eng. & Wales*

Lowe, Douglas Gordon Arthur (1902–1981), athlete, was born on 7 August 1902 at 314 Lower Broughton Road, Broughton, Salford, the son of Arthur John Lowe, a wool merchant, and his wife, Emily Mary, *née* Read. After attending Manchester grammar school and Highgate School he went up to Pembroke College, Cambridge, in 1921 where he read for the medieval and modern languages tripos; he gained a second in French in 1923 and a lower second in German in 1925. Lowe was a superb all-rounder who demonstrated his athleticism both at Highgate, where he won the public schools' half mile in 1920, and at Cambridge, where he won blues for athletics and football. He was honorary secretary and then president (1924–5) of Cambridge University athletic club. In appearance he was 'trim and dark, with sleek hair parted in the centre'. He had 'clean-cut features and a glittering smile that might have made him a matinée idol' (Lovesey, 68).

Though he won the 880 yards for Cambridge against Oxford three years in succession (1922–4), Lowe failed to finish in the first three at the Amateur Athletic Association (AAA) championships in either 1922 or 1923. In 1924 he came a close second to Henry Stallard, and both men were selected to represent Britain in the Olympic games in Paris. But it was Stallard rather than Lowe who was considered the first-string runner, and in the final of the 800 metres he set a fast pace in an attempt to break the field. Stallard's tactic, however, played to Lowe's advantage, for as the former faded in the final straight, Lowe came through to take the Olympic gold medal in a British record time of 1 min. 52.4 sec. Stallard came fourth. Two days later Lowe narrowly missed out on a medal in the 1500 metres final, when Stallard won the bronze.

Lowe was Olympic champion at the age of twenty-one and yet still had a point to prove. Press accounts of the Paris race praised him but were also 'heavy in sympathy for the luckless Stallard' (Lovesey, 71). And the Olympic champion, it was noted, had yet to win an AAA title. Lowe, a 'dignified, self-possessed man', waited for his moment to reply (ibid.). In 1925 he raced in America with the Oxford and Cambridge team and his next AAA championships came in 1926. A week before the championships he set a new world record of 1 min. 10.4 sec. for the 600 yards, an indication of his superb form. But barring his way to a title was the impressive Otto Peltzer, German champion at 400 and 1500 metres. It was the first time since the war that Germans had been invited to compete at the championships and in the 880 yards final the 27,000 spectators at

Stamford Bridge saw a duel worthy of the occasion. Lowe was determined to make his mark and led at the halfway mark, which he reached in world record pace, 54.6 sec. Peltzer, though, proved the stronger and came from behind to win in 1 min. 51.6 sec. The German had broken Ted Meredith's world record of 1 min. 52.2 sec., as indeed had Lowe, who was unofficially credited with 1 min. 52.0 sec.

Peltzer also ran in the 440 yards, where he showed impressive speed in coming second, and this persuaded Lowe to race at the shorter distance himself. At the AAA championships in 1927 he won both the 440 and 880 yards, and was in the Achilles club team that won the 440 yard relay. In 1928, an Olympic year, he repeated his 440 and 880 yard double. In two years he had won five AAA titles and he approached the defence of his Olympic 800 metres title in Amsterdam with justifiable confidence. In the weeks before the games, though, the world record was twice lowered, by Lloyd Hahn of the United States and Séra Martin of France respectively. Both men were in the world-class field for the final. Lowe drew the last of the cards for the start positions and got pole, his favourite. He led to the first bend and then took up second place, behind Hahn, ready to respond to any move from the field. Off the final bend he produced a devastating burst of speed to win in 1 min. 51.8 sec., a new Olympic record. It was a perfectly run tactical race and Lowe became the first man successfully to defend the Olympic 800 metres title.

In August 1928 Lowe accepted an invitation to run in Berlin against Peltzer, who at the Olympics had been below par through injury. Lowe won a close contest in a British record time of 1 min. 51.2 sec. It was his last race before retirement and a fitting end to a magnificent career. Lowe had contributed to a golden age of British middle-distance running, when Britons won the Olympic 800 metres title four times in succession. 'He was the perfect Olympic champion, and the perfect artist on the track' (Killanin and Rodda, 52).

After his running career was over Lowe made a significant contribution to the administration of athletics. He was honorary secretary of the AAA (1931–8), and in this capacity drafted, with Harold Abrahams, the constitution of the body that became, in 1937, the British Amateur Athletic Board. He thus helped to resolve the crisis over British representation on the International Amateur Athletic Federation, clarifying the distinction between teams representing Great Britain and Northern Ireland, and the home nations. He also wrote on athletics, and with Arthur Porritt published *Athletics* (1929), a training manual for track and field which included a history of the Olympic movement. In 1936 he published *Track and Field Athletics* (reissued in 1961), an illustrated guide for the aspiring beginner.

Lowe also pursued a distinguished career as a barrister and judge. In 1928 he was called to the bar at Inner Temple, of which he became a bencher in 1957, and in 1964 was made queen's counsel. He was chairman of Warwickshire quarter sessions (1965–71), recorder of Lincoln (1964–71), and a recorder of the crown court (1972–7). He was a chairman of the governors of Highgate School. In 1930 he married Karen, daughter of Surgeon Einar Thamsen; they had one son. Lowe died of heart disease on 29 March 1981 at his home, 26 Great Maytham Hall, Rolvenden, Cranbrook, Kent.

MARK POTTLE

Sources *The Times* (11–12 Nov 1927) · *The Times* (2 April 1981) · *The Times* (7 April 1981) · I. Buchanan, *British Olympians: a hundred years of gold medallists* (1991) · P. Lovesey, *The official centenary history of the Amateur Athletics Association* (1979) · F. A. M. Webster, *Great moments in athletics* (1947) · J. Huntington-Whiteley, ed., *The book of British sporting heroes* (1998) [exhibition catalogue, NPG, 16 Oct 1998 – 24 Jan 1999] · M. Watman, *History of British athletics* (1968) · J. Arlott, ed., *The Oxford companion to sports and games* (1975) · R. L. Quercetani, *A world history of track and field athletics, 1864–1964* (1964) · Lord Killanin and J. Rodda, eds., *The Olympic games* (1976) · D. G. A. Lowe, *Track and field athletics* (1961) · D. Lowe and A. E. Porritt, *Athletics* (1929) · private information (2004) [the honorary archivist, Pembroke Cam.] · b. cert. · *WWW* · d. cert.

Archives FILM BFI NFTVA, news footage · BFI NFTVA, sports footage

Likenesses Topical Press, photograph, 1923, repro. in Huntington-Whiteley, ed., *Book of British sporting heroes*

Wealth at death £31,075: probate, 8 Oct 1981, *CGPLA Eng. & Wales*

Lowe, Sir Drury Curzon Drury- (1830–1908), army officer, born at Locko Park, Denby, Derbyshire, on 3 January 1830, was second of the five sons (in a family of eight children) of William Drury-Lowe (1802–1877) of Locko Park and his wife, the Hon. Caroline Esther (*d.* 1886), third daughter of Nathaniel Curzon, second Baron Scarsdale. William, the son of Robert Holden of Darley Abbey, Derbyshire, and his wife, Mary Anne, only daughter and heir of William Drury-Lowe (*d.* 1827), assumed the surname of Drury-Lowe in 1849 on the death of his wife's mother. Educated privately and at Corpus Christi College, Oxford, Drury-Lowe graduated BA in 1853. Resolving on a military career at a comparatively late age, he obtained a commission in the 17th lancers on 28 July 1854, and was promoted lieutenant on 7 November 1854 and captain on 19 November 1856. He was associated with the 17th lancers throughout his active service.

Drury-Lowe joined the regiment in the Crimea (18 June 1855), and took part in the battle of the Chernaya, and the siege and fall of Sevastopol. He also served in the concluding episodes of the Indian mutiny, including the pursuit of the force under Tantia Topi during 1858 and the action of Zerpur, when Evelyn Wood, who had just exchanged into the 17th lancers, was for the first time in action with him: both won distinction, and Drury-Lowe was mentioned in dispatches. He became major on 10 June 1862, lieutenant-colonel on 15 June 1866, and colonel on 15 June 1871. In 1876 he married Elizabeth, daughter of Thomas Smith; they had no children.

In the Anglo-Zulu War Drury-Lowe commanded the 17th lancers and the cavalry of the 2nd division, and was at the battle of Ulundi, where he was slightly wounded. He was made CB on 27 November 1879. On his return to South Africa to serve under Sir Evelyn Wood in the Transvaal campaign of 1881, he commanded the cavalry brigade, and was promoted major-general in December 1881.

Sir Drury Curzon Drury-Lowe (1830–1908), by Bassano

It was in the Egyptian campaign (1882) that Drury-Lowe made his reputation; he commanded a cavalry brigade, and afterwards the cavalry division. After taking part in the action at Tell al-Mahuta and the capture of Mahsama (25 August 1882), he made a cavalry charge by moonlight at the first action of Qassasin (28 August), which effectually assured the British forces their victory under Sir Gerald Graham. He was at the battle of Tell al-Kebir, pursuing the enemy and occupying Cairo, where he received the surrender of Arabi Pasha. He was mentioned in dispatches, thanked by both houses of parliament, and received the Osmanieh (second class). On 18 November 1882 he was made KCB.

In 1884 Drury-Lowe was put in command of a cavalry brigade at Aldershot, and from 1885 to 1890 was inspector-general of cavalry, but made no innovations at Aldershot. Promoted lieutenant-general on 1 April 1890, he was during 1890–91 inspector-general of cavalry at the Horse Guards. On 24 January 1892 he was appointed colonel of the 17th lancers, and on 25 May 1895 was made GCB. On his retirement he lived at Key Dell, Horndean, Hampshire. He died at 7 Gay Street, Bath, on 6 April 1908 and was buried at Denby, Derbyshire. His wife survived him.

H. M. Vibart, *rev.* James Falkner

Sources *The Times* (7 April 1908) • *Army List* • *Hart's Army List* • Burke, *Gen. GB* • C. N. Robinson, *Celebrities of the army*, 18 pts (1900) • *LondG* (17 July 1860) • *LondG* (21 Aug 1879) • *LondG* (8 Sept 1882) • *LondG* (19 Sept 1882) • *LondG* (6 Oct 1882) • *LondG* (2 Nov 1882) • F. E. Colenso, *History of the Zulu War* (1880) • R. H. Vetch, *Life of Sir Gerald Graham* (1901) • J. F. Maurice, *Military history of the campaign of 1882 in Egypt*, rev. edn (1908)

Archives U. Nott. L., papers relating to the Egyptian campaign

Likenesses A. Bassano, photograph, 1892 (after portrait), repro. in J. W. Fortescue, *17th Lancers* (1895), 179 • H. T. Wells, portrait, 1892 • Bassano, photographs, NPG [*see illus.*] • photograph, repro. in *ILN* (1 May 1896)

Wealth at death £26,655 1*s*. 2*d*.: probate, 25 May 1908, *CGPLA Eng. & Wales*

Lowe, Edward (*c*.1610–1682), organist and composer, was born in the parish of St Thomas's, Salisbury, probably into the family of John Lowe (*d*. 1632), lawyer, of Salisbury, and his second wife, Elizabeth (*d*. 1639?), daughter of Thomas Hyde, chancellor of Salisbury Cathedral from 1588 to 1618. Although there is no direct evidence that Edward Lowe was their son, he called a Humphrey Hyde 'cousin' (BL, Add. MS 29396). According to Anthony Wood, Lowe was 'bred a chorister' (Bodl. Oxf., MS Wood D.19 (4), fol. 87*v*) at Salisbury Cathedral under John Holmes, master of the choristers from about 1621 to 1629.

After Michaelmas 1631, but before 1641, Lowe succeeded William Stonard as organist and master of the choristers at Christ Church Cathedral, Oxford. On 14 December 1633 he married Alice (1607/8–1649), daughter of Sir John Peyton of Doddington, Isle of Ely, at St James's, Clerkenwell, in London; they had nine children. Since Alice's coat of arms was depicted with Lowe's in a pane of painted glass in the house at Hampton Gay, near Shipton-on-Cherwell, Oxfordshire, which he occupied fifty years later, he may already have been living there during this period. Alice died on 17 March 1649, and Lowe probably married his second wife, Mary, about 1654.

During the interregnum Lowe gave private lessons and took part in weekly music meetings at the house of William Ellis, formerly organist of St John's College, Oxford. The vice-chancellor's accounts for 1657–8 name him as university organist, and he acted as deputy to the professor of music appointed in 1656, John Wilson, whom he succeeded in 1661.

Soon after the Restoration Lowe became one of the three organists of the Chapel Royal (with William Child and Christopher Gibbons), a post he retained along with his Oxford appointments until his death, and he compiled *A short direction for the performance of cathedrall service, published for the information of such persons as are ignorant of it, and shall be call'd to officiate in cathedrall, or collegiate churches where it hath formerly been in use* (1661; rev. 1664), containing simple settings of the liturgy for newly reconstituted choirs. Lowe's enduring achievement, however, was in administration. As professor of music he fostered performance at the Thursday afternoon meetings of the music school and continued the development of the school's music collection (Bodl. Oxf., MSS mus. sch.), an outstanding source of English music of the early and mid-seventeenth century. Despite his long service in Oxford, however, Lowe was not granted university privileges until 19 August 1667.

The music school's holdings at Lowe's death are outlined in a catalogue made in 1682 by his successor Richard Goodson (Bodl. Oxf., MS mus. sch. C.204* [R]), which also lists 'The Gift of Mr Lowe late Professour'. Manuscripts purchased for the music school during Lowe's professorship included the North family's collection of works by John Jenkins and other composers, bought for £22 from 'Mr Wood' (possibly but not certainly Anthony Wood) in 1667 (MSS mus. sch. C.81–91, C.98–101, and E.406–9). Lowe's regular contact with court musicians was a great advantage: John Hingeston, formerly Cromwell's household musician, presented music of his own, encouraged by 'what I have heard & seen of the care, dilligence and industry, of the present Professor of that faculty in the University, my Honored frind and fellow servant Mr Edward Lowe' (MSS mus. sch. D.205–11), and four books in William Lawes's autograph (MSS mus. sch. D.229 and 238–40), together with mus. sch. B.2 and 3 in Lowe's private collection, were probably given by Henry Lawes, whose will Lowe witnessed in 1662. Other material was donated by Oxford musicians, commissioned from copyists or copied by Lowe himself, many manuscripts being annotated by Lowe with informative practical or historical details.

The professor's duties included the organization of music for the degree ceremony or 'act' and for other official occasions. Lowe copied performing parts for several of the odes, known as act songs, performed at these events, among them two works of his own; one of these, *Nunc est canendum*, might have been composed for the opening of the Sheldonian Theatre on 9 July 1669; the other, *Eia eruditam*, was performed on 7 July 1671 and may have given rise to the unfounded assertion that he was not formally installed as music professor until that year. For Christ Church Lowe copied twenty-seven anthems, including several composed by himself, into the cathedral partbooks (Mus. 1220–24): a competent but minor composer, he also wrote a few songs and partsongs, and one keyboard piece is ascribed to him (Christ Church, Mus. 1177). Further sources in Lowe's handwriting include a Christ Church organ accompaniment book (Mus. 1002), a collection of voluntaries in Christ Church (Mus. 1176), and a song anthology at Edinburgh University Library (MS Dc.I.69) and its companion volume (Bodl. Oxf., MS Mus.d.38).

Lowe was described by Anthony Wood as 'a proud man' who 'could not endure any common Musitian to come to [Ellis's] Meeting, much less to play amongst them' (Clark, 1.205), but this observation may reflect Lowe's concern for the status and standards of his profession rather than personal vanity. In his will he described Richard Goodson, an Oxford innkeeper's son who succeeded him in his university appointments, as his friend, and his manuscripts suggest that he actively encouraged local composers, including at least one, Henry Bowman, with no official connection with the university.

Lowe died on 11 July 1682 and was buried near his first wife in the divinity chapel of the cathedral. Two children were living from that marriage: Edward (1635–1711), who had become vicar of Brighton in 1674 and rector of Slinfold, Sussex, in 1681, and Elizabeth, who had married Thomas Burtchall of London, a comb maker and dissenter, at St James's, Duke's Place, in 1667. There were also at least two surviving children from his second marriage: Susanna, who married John Strype, the church historian, at Christ Church on 7 February 1682, and, almost certainly, Charles Lowe (*b.* 1654/5), of St Katharine Cree, London, who was aged twenty-three when on 28 August 1678 he obtained a faculty office licence to marry Mary Downes. Lowe's place in the Chapel Royal was granted to Henry Purcell; at Christ Church the next organist was probably William Husbands, then too young to collect his payment in person. ROBERT THOMPSON

Sources Edward Lowe's will, PRO, PROB 11/370, fols. 245v–246v • E. Lowe, autograph songbook, BL, Add. MS 29396, fol. 62v • A. Wood, *The history and antiquities of the colleges and halls in the University of Oxford*, ed. J. Gutch (1786) • *The life and times of Anthony Wood*, ed. A. Clark, 5 vols., OHS, 19, 21, 26, 30, 40 (1891–1900) • J. Hawkins, *A general history of the science and practice of music*, new edn, 3 vols. (1853); repr. in 2 vols. (1963) • H. W. Shaw, *The succession of organists of the Chapel Royal and the cathedrals of England and Wales from c.1538* (1991) • M. Crum, 'Early lists of the Oxford music school collection', *Music and Letters*, 48 (1967), 23–34 • Foster, *Alum. Oxon.* • R. E. C. Waters, *Genealogical memoirs of the extinct family of Chester of Chicheley*, 2 vols. (1878) • A. Ashbee, ed., *Records of English court music*, 1 (1986) • A. Ashbee, ed., *Records of English court music*, 5 (1991) • J. R. Magrath, ed., *The Flemings in Oxford*, 1, OHS, 44 (1904), xvi, 541, 552; 2, OHS, 62 (1913), xix • I. Spink, *Restoration cathedral music, 1660–1714* (1995) • G. S. Fry and E. A. Fry, eds., *Abstracts of Wiltshire inquisitions post mortem … in the reign of King Charles the First*, British RS, 23 (1901) • G. D. Squibb, ed., *Wiltshire visitation pedigrees, 1623*, Harleian Society, 105–6 (1954)

Archives BL, Add. MS 29396 • Bodl. Oxf., Anthony Wood's MS notes, MS Wood D.19 (4) • Bodl. Oxf., MS Mus.d.38; Music School MSS • Christ Church Oxf., disbursement books • Christ Church Oxf., music MSS • U. Edin. L., MS Dc.I.69

Wealth at death comfortably off; pictures, furnishings: will, PRO, PROB 11/370, fols. 245v–246v

Lowe, Edward William Howe de Lancy (1820–1880), army officer, youngest son of Sir Hudson *Lowe (1769–1844), colonial governor, and his wife, Susan (*d.* 1832), daughter of Stephen de Lancey and widow of Colonel William Johnson, was born in St Helena on 8 February 1820. He was educated at the Royal Military College, Sandhurst, and on 20 May 1837 was appointed ensign in the 32nd regiment. He became lieutenant in 1841, captain in 1845, major in 1857, lieutenant-colonel in 1858, and colonel in 1863. He served with the regiment in the Second Anglo-Sikh War of 1848–9, including the two sieges and capture of Multan and the battle of Gujrat. He was with the regiment at Lucknow at the outbreak of the Indian mutiny, and on 18 May 1857 was sent with his company to Cawnpore. General Wheeler, on hearing the state of affairs at Lucknow, sent the reinforcement back some days later, which thus escaped the massacres. When Inglis took command at Lucknow, on Sir Henry Lawrence's death, Lowe took command of the 32nd, which he held throughout the defence of the residency. On 26 September 1857 he commanded a sortie which captured seven guns, and he also commanded the party sent out to bring in the guns and stores with the rear-guard of Havelock's relieving force, which had arrived the day before. In these operations he was severely wounded. After the second relief by Colin Campbell, in October, Lowe commanded the 32nd at the defeat of the Gwalior rebels at Cawnpore on 6 December

1857 and during the ensuing campaign in Oudh from July 1858 to January 1859. He was mentioned in dispatches, given brevet promotion, and made a CB. Some letters sent by Lowe to his sister during the defence of the residency formed the basis of an article in the *Quarterly Review* (vol. 103, 1858). Lowe afterwards commanded in succession the 2nd battalion 21st regiment (Royal North British Fusiliers) and the 86th Royal County Down regiment. He retired on half pay in 1872 and became a major-general in 1877. He married Anne Louisa Russell, daughter of Maurice Peter Moore (1809–1866) of Sleaford, Lincolnshire, solicitor and clerk of the peace for Kesteven; she survived her husband. Lowe died at his home, 11 Upper Berkeley Street, London, on 21 October 1880.

H. M. Chichester, *rev.* James Falkner

Sources *Army List* • *Hart's Army List* • J. W. Kaye and G. B. Malleson, *Kaye's and Malleson's History of the Indian mutiny of 1857–8*, 6 vols. (1888–9)

Wealth at death under £6000: probate, 17 Nov 1880, *CGPLA Eng. & Wales*

Lowe, Elias Avery (1879–1969), palaeographer, was born on 15 October 1879 in Moscow, Russia, the son of Charles Loew, a silk and embroidery merchant, and his wife, Sarah Ragoler. In 1892 he emigrated with his parents to New York city, where he became a United States citizen in 1900. He was educated at the College of the City of New York (1894–7), Cornell University (1899–1902, BA), the University of Halle (1902–3), and the University of Munich (1903–7, PhD). On 10 February 1911 he married Helen Tracy Porter (a writer and later a translator of Thomas Mann under the name H. T. Lowe-Porter). They had three daughters: Prudence Holcombe (1912–1967), Frances Beatrice (Lady Fawcett; *b.* 1913), and Patricia Tracy (*b.* 1917). He changed the spelling of his name to Lowe in 1918.

Lowe's formal teaching of palaeography was all done, with negligible exceptions, at Oxford, where he first lectured in 1913 and was given a regular appointment as lecturer in 1914 and as reader in 1927. As an American and a Jew he represented a rare, if not unique, species at the time of his original appointment. After 1936, when he became one of the first professors at the Institute for Advanced Study in Princeton, to which he would be attached for the rest of his life and where no teaching was required, he continued to lecture at Oxford during Trinity terms, except for the war years, until 1948.

Preceding or concurrently with his Oxford and Princeton careers Lowe was a fellow of the American School of Classical Studies in Rome (1907–8, 1909–11), a research associate in palaeography of the Carnegie Institution of Washington (1911–53), and a consultant in palaeography for the Library of Congress. Corpus Christi College, Oxford, made him an honorary fellow in 1954. The Medieval Academy of America, of which he was a fellow, awarded him its Haskins medal (1957) and the Bibliographical Society gave him its gold medal (1959). He was a corresponding fellow of the British Academy and received similar recognition from academies or institutes in Boston, Dublin, Madrid, Munich, Paris, and Rome. Honorary doctoral degrees were conferred on him by Oxford (1936),

Elias Avery Lowe (1879–1969), by Sir Jacob Epstein, 1953

North Carolina (1946), and the National University of Ireland (1964).

Lowe always maintained that he became a palaeographer—with the motto he devised, 'He is concerned with trifles'—by a series of accidents, the most crucial being his encounter in 1903 with Ludwig Traube, a charismatic professor of medieval Latin philology in Munich who made the study of manuscripts somehow come alive. But he would not have met Traube if he had not gone to study classical philology with Georg Wissowa in Halle in 1902, and he would not have gone to Halle if Charles Bennett, his Latin professor at Cornell, had not incidentally mentioned to him that Halle abounded in 'fresh running water', which to Lowe meant the promise of trout fishing, his favourite form of recreation. Traube's suggested dissertation topic—Monte Cassino as a centre for the transmission of the Latin classics—deflected Lowe from Latin philology to palaeography, since he decided, in order to deal with this topic adequately, that he first needed to study the script used at Monte Cassino, the mother house of Benedictine monasticism. Ironically, he undoubtedly made more contributions to philology indirectly through palaeography than he would have made directly as a philologist.

Lowe's dissertation, *Die ältesten Kalendarien aus Monte Cassino* (1908), and his next major work, *Studia palaeographica: a contribution to the history of early Latin minuscule and to the dating of Visigothic manuscripts* (1910), did not deal formally with the script of Monte Cassino. His long investigations into this subject came to fruition only in 1914 with the publication of *The Beneventan Script*. This rigorously systematic study of the main script used for the copying of books not only at Monte Cassino but in much of southern Italy from the eighth to the fourteenth century became a landmark in Latin palaeography. It set new standards for treating the history of a script and so overwhelmed the palaeographical world that it had the unintended effect of discouraging further serious research on the Beneventan script for more than a generation. Meant to be published with *The Beneventan Script* but delayed until 1929 by the First World War and then by other projects were two folio-size volumes entitled *Scriptura Beneventana* and containing facsimiles with transcriptions and descriptions of the main monuments in this script.

Lowe next turned his attention to uncial, a script that had originated probably in the third century, if not the second, and became the most popular medium for the copying of books until well into the eighth century. What particularly excited his interest in this script was the discovery in 1915 of a fragment of the *Letters* of Pliny the younger in uncial that was clearly at least several centuries older than any previously known copy of this text. Lowe's attempt to date and localize this fragment more precisely, published as part of *A Sixth-Century Fragment of the 'Letters' of Pliny the Younger* (1922), forced him to enucleate objective criteria by which uncial manuscripts can be dated and placed. This work of enucleating criteria for dating and placing and of further clarifying the methodological assumptions underlying the interpretation of palaeographical evidence continued in his *Codices Lugdunenses antiquissimi* (1924), dealing with the oldest manuscripts in Lyons, and in his *Regula S. Benedicti* (1929), a study of the oldest extant manuscript of St Benedict's rule, now preserved in Oxford. During this period he also made his lone attempt at a comprehensive overview of Latin scripts in a chapter on handwriting in *The Legacy of the Middle Ages* (1926; an expanded edition, *Handwriting: our Medieval Legacy*, was published separately in 1969). This essay forced him to deal with Caroline minuscule, the medieval script to which modern printing is most indebted.

Unquestionably the greatest of Lowe's contributions to palaeography and perhaps unequalled in value by any other palaeographical publication of the twentieth century is his *Codices Latini antiquiores* (*CLA*). This work is a palaeographical guide in eleven folio-size volumes plus a supplement (1934–71; 2nd edn of vol. 2, 1972) to all the Latin literary manuscripts that survive in scripts antedating the ninth century. It contains detailed descriptions of 1811 manuscripts now preserved in libraries in twenty-one different countries and it provides one or more facsimiles of each manuscript. On the basis of the information in these descriptions Lowe was able to supply each manuscript with an exact or approximate place and date of origin, thus enabling the history of early Latin scripts to be put on a much sounder footing, and he himself began the needed work of synthesis in extensive introductions to several of the volumes. The project, which officially began in 1929 with a substantial grant from the Rockefeller Foundation and the promise of further financial or moral support from numerous other organizations including the Clarendon Press, occupied the remaining forty years of Lowe's life, with the Institute for Advanced Study in Princeton eventually becoming its main source of funding. In the first volumes he was greatly aided by William J. Anderson and from volume 2 onwards especially by Bernhard Bischoff of the University of Munich. While working on *CLA* Lowe managed to publish many other important contributions to palaeography well into his eighties.

Lowe was wide-ranging in both his personal and his literary interests and they added a humanizing dimension to his scholarship. He was a persuasive speaker, a gifted conversationalist, and a genial host, capable of great friendships. Although physically small in stature, there was nothing small about his spirit, which could resolutely both face and overcome adversity. His eyesight so deteriorated from cataracts in his late sixties that he needed others to read for him; after successful surgery he wore glasses with thick lenses. From his mid-sixties onwards he was afflicted with angina pectoris and frequently had to resort to nitroglycerin. With his health so precarious, only an indomitable will to live enabled him to bring *CLA* to a successful conclusion. Here he was strengthened by a religious disposition, which convinced him that Providence, and perhaps more particularly the intercessory power of St Benedict, whom he had done his best to honour, would see the project through. He never abandoned his solidarity with the Jewish people, but he did not practise Judaism and in later life told a daughter that if he were to adhere to any religion it would be the Roman Catholic. He died in Bad Nauheim, Germany, on 8 August 1969, shortly after seeing the proof sheets of the last volume of *CLA*. His ashes were interred at Corpus Christi College, Oxford.

JAMES J. JOHN

Sources E. A. Lowe, *Palaeographical papers, 1907–1965*, ed. L. Bieler, 2 vols. (1972), 2.591–3, 575–82, 595–611 [incl. work list] · B. Bischoff, 'Elias Avery Lowe', *Bayerische Akademie der Wissenschaften, Jahrbuch* (1970), 199–203 · J. Brown, 'E. A. Lowe and *Codices Latini antiquiores*', *Scrittura e Civiltà*, 1 (1977), 177–97 · J. J. John, 'E. A. Lowe and *Codices Latini antiquiores*', *American Council of Learned Societies Newsletter*, 20/5 (Oct 1969), 1–5 · J. J. John, 'A palaeographer among Benedictines: a tribute to E. A. Lowe', *American Benedictine Review*, 21 (1970), 139–47 · H. Mayo and S. Sharma, 'The E. A. Lowe papers at the Pierpont Morgan Library', *Scriptorium*, 46 (1992), 90–107 · R. W. Hunt, 'E. A. Lowe and the University of Oxford', Lowe lecture delivered at Corpus Christi College in 1978 · books, photographs, notes, diaries, correspondence, and other papers, Morgan L. · E. A. Lowe file, Cornell University Library, Dept of Manuscripts and University Archives · Institute for Advanced Study, Princeton, records of the School of Historical Studies · personal knowledge (2004) · private information (2004)

Archives BL, lectures on palaeography, Add. MS 39174 · Morgan L., MSS | BL, letters to J. P. Gilson, Add. MSS 47686–47687

Likenesses J. Epstein, bronze scultpure, 1953, Metropolitan Museum of Art, New York [*see illus.*] · J. Epstein, bust, Institute for

Advanced Study, Princeton · portrait, Morgan L. · portrait, priv. coll.

Lowe, Elizabeth (1828/9–1897), journalist and newspaper editor, was the daughter of James Lowe, a successful Liverpool solicitor, and his wife, Elizabeth. The second of three children, Elizabeth Lowe and her younger sister, Anne, were fortunate that their parents considered it important for the girls to share an education at home with their brother, James. They had tutors in classics, mathematics, and modern languages. However, the premature death of their father, when the children were still young, left the family in straitened circumstances. James took up journalism while Elizabeth spent three years travelling in France, Germany, and Italy before returning to England to find work.

By this time her brother was editor of *The Critic*. For Elizabeth Lowe, like many women journalists of her day, the encouragement, position, and contacts of a brother were to prove invaluable in starting out. James Lowe trained his sister in journalism and then commissioned her to supply book reviews and articles about art to *The Critic* and later *The Queen*. This journal, originally founded by Samuel Beeton, was bought in 1862 by Serjeant Cox, owner of *The Critic*. The following year Cox bought its rival, the *Ladies' Paper*, and the two then merged. Elizabeth Lowe was thus associated from the start with the new, enlarged magazine, called *The Queen: the Lady's Newspaper*, and in 1864 was offered the editorship of the combined journals while Horace Cox, nephew of Serjeant Cox, retained overall responsibility as manager and head of the enterprise.

When Lowe first took over, the magazine contained sixteen pages and was a rather prim society journal. By the time of her death it numbered 144 pages, including some ten pages of advertisements, and had become one of the most important magazines primarily for rich and leisured women, steering their sphere of interest towards politics and social matters without in any way neglecting the practical and domestic. Key elements in its success were the high-quality coloured fashion plates included in every issue as well as paper patterns as supplements, with designs for a variety of handwork such as decorative fretwork, lace, and Berlin woolwork. However, the success was not immediate. It was not until Lowe introduced the idea of dividing the paper into departments—dress, home decorations, fashion, gardening, cooking, charities, women's employment—and answered readers' queries on all these, that the circulation picked up. It then increased dramatically, although no figures have been kept. The response was enormous and a lively correspondence began between Lowe and her readers on almost all issues.

One of Lowe's most important editorial skills was an ability to attract very high profile contributors. She managed, for example, to secure original sketches by Queen Victoria for publication in the magazine, as well as articles and short stories by Mrs Lynn Linton, Walter Besant, and several princesses. At the same time she acquired a reputation as a generous supporter of struggling writers and artists and an editor who inspired her staff with her composure, strong personality, and powers of leadership. However sympathetic an ear she proffered to female journalists, she did not put aside her sound editorial judgement merely because a woman needed work. 'They make me feel like a brute because I must cut down or return their articles', she once said in a rare interview (*The Queen*, 12 June 1897).

Elizabeth Lowe must have moved effortlessly in the top echelons of British society to produce the journal which *The Queen* became, and yet she steadfastly avoided making herself well known to a wider public. She refused nearly every request for an interview or for her portrait to be published. Her own magazine admitted in an obituary notice that a picture of its former editor would be of great interest to its readers, yet refused to publish one, adding that 'she retained her good looks and fine presence to the last'.

Elizabeth Lowe lived for her work and had little recoverable private life beyond it. However, she had regular Sunday afternoon At Homes where a large circle of friends would gather. She would never discuss politics on these occasions, but was a born raconteur with a shrewd and racy humour. In *The Queen* too, she retained an objectivity on political matters and refused to give a platform to any one view. The last issue she produced carried an article on the subject of women's suffrage in New Zealand, which commented:

> That the influence of women in politics and their voting will not be different from that of their husbands and brothers may be regarded as foregone conclusion, and should this much debated reform come into actual operation in the UK it is probable that it will not produce the effects that are hoped for by its promoters and apprehended by its adversaries. (1 May 1897)

Elizabeth Lowe died at Victoria House, 46 Gillingham Street, London, on 1 June 1897, from a skin and ear complaint after an illness lasting some five months. She was sixty-eight. She was buried on 4 June at Brookwood cemetery, Woking, in Surrey, in the same grave as her brother, James, who had died, aged thirty-seven, in November 1865. Her sister's husband, Richard Scott Deane, was with her when she died, and the editorship of *The Queen* passed to his daughter, Lowe's niece, Ethel Deane. From the poverty of her young womanhood, Lowe acquired a considerable fortune, leaving more than £20,000 in her will.

Anne M. Sebba

Sources National Magazine House, London, *The Queen* archives · *Englishwoman's Review*, 28 (1897), 202–3 · *Daily News* (4 June 1897), 5 · *The Queen* (12 June 1897), 1176 · d. cert. · *CGPLA Eng. & Wales* (1897)

Archives National Magazine Company, London, *The Queen* archives

Wealth at death £20,048 1*s*. 1*d*.: probate, 2 July 1897, *CGPLA Eng. & Wales*

Lowe [*née* Farren], **Eveline Mary** (1869–1956), local politician, was born in Rotherhithe on 29 November 1869, the daughter of the Revd John Farren, a Congregational minister, and his wife, Sarah Saint Giles. She was educated at

Eveline Mary Lowe (1869–1956), by Alfred Kingsley Lawrence, 1940

Milton Mount College, Gravesend, where all the pupils were daughters of Congregational ministers, and trained as a teacher at Homerton College. In 1893 she became a lecturer at the college and then vice-principal in the following year, when the college moved from London to Cambridge. She retired in 1903 on her marriage to George Carter Lowe (*d.* 1919), a veterinary surgeon who qualified as a doctor in 1911; he subsequently became a partner in the Bermondsey medical practice of Alfred Salter.

Eveline Lowe's relationship with Alfred Salter and his wife, Ada, was central to her subsequent political career. The Bermondsey practice, staffed by socially progressive doctors, was a critical ingredient in the development of a local socialist movement. The Bermondsey Independent Labour Party (ILP) was formed in May 1908; an unsuccessful parliamentary contest in the following year led to the adoption of a patient strategy of propaganda backed by an alliance with the strengthening local trade unions. The objective was to win majorities in all municipal institutions; Eveline Lowe, who was elected to the Bermondsey board of guardians, played a thorough part, collecting subscriptions, attending meetings, and selling the local party magazine. The ILP activists endured the difficult war years; the strategy quickly reaped post-war dividends. In November 1919 Labour swept the Bermondsey borough council capturing all the seats. In the following month George Lowe died. Eveline Lowe, childless, became more committed than ever to her public activities. In 1919, on the nomination of Charles George Ammon, she was co-opted a member of the London county council (LCC) education committee, and she was subsequently appointed a JP. In 1922 she and Ada Salter gained the two West Bermondsey seats on the LCC. She retained her position for twenty-four years. In working-class London the Liberals (Progressives on the LCC) were in retreat, and Labour frequently reaped the benefits.

It would be easy to depict Lowe's career as a classical demonstration of Labour's advance to power in urban Britain. Yet her politics had its complexities. Throughout the 1920s she combined office in Bermondsey Labour Party and the local ILP. Stylistically she found the ILP culture highly congenial, and that party remained significant in Bermondsey. Yet Labour strength in Bermondsey was founded not just on ILP high-mindedness but also on trade unionism and its appeal to solidarity. As the ILP moved further to the left, Eveline Lowe and the Bermondsey ILP became a minority unhappy about this development and thoroughly opposed to any break with the Labour Party. With the ILP's disaffiliation in 1932, she and her Bermondsey colleagues ended their tie with the party that had founded the local socialist movement.

The development from 1918 of women's organization within the Labour Party also brought Eveline Lowe into controversy. She represented the London Labour Party executive on the London women's advisory committee and became involved in the debate over the character of women's representation within the party. In April 1921 the party's National Women's Conference debated a proposal that they should nominate and elect the four women's section representatives on the party's national executive. This would replace a situation in which the women were chosen by the delegates to the party conference, who were almost entirely male. Eveline Lowe opposed the change: 'it would mean preferential treatment for women … they wanted to be in the Labour Party, not as representatives of a sex but as representatives of the people' (*Labour Woman*, June 1921). Her appeal failed at the women's conference, but it was the view of the party leadership and of many within the wider party.

Lowe's increasing prominence on the LCC and the advent of a Labour government in 1929 facilitated her selection as a member of the royal commission on the civil service chaired by Lord Tomlin. This dealt essentially with staff questions, and among them were issues of sexual equality. With five women members, including three Labour Party supporters, some division over the recommendations was predictable. The commissioners agreed that on appointments there should be 'a fair field and no favour' (*Parl. papers*, 1930–31, 10.115, Cmd 3909) but certain posts remained reserved for men. There was also agreement on an end to segregation in the organization of work, but there was division over equal pay and the abolition of the marriage bar.

Above all, however, Eveline Lowe's principal activities were within the LCC. She specialized in education and established herself as Labour's expert in this field. When Labour won its first LCC majority in 1934 she became chair of the education committee. She held the post for three years and helped to establish Labour's credibility as an effective party for London. Her approach conformed with Herbert Morrison's vision of Labour municipal strategy and style—a clear, reforming, and attractive agenda, and a courteous response to the criticisms of opponents.

From 1937 Lowe chaired the establishment committee and then in March 1939 became the first woman to chair the LCC. The terms of her office acknowledged the established characterization of women within Labour Party culture. She was addressed as 'Mr Chairman' and 'Sir' (*Manchester Guardian*, 15 March 1939). She insisted that gender was irrelevant to service in local government. 'She did not want them as women but as thoroughly efficient people' (*The Times*, 18 April 1939). Her year in office was marked by the LCC's golden jubilee and by the outbreak of war. She retired from the LCC in 1946; in that year she became a freeman of Bermondsey. In 1950 London University conferred on her the honorary degree LLD.

Eveline Lowe's career reflects one route by which progressives formed in religious nonconformity came through ethical socialism into Labour politics. In style she could seem not really a partisan politician, but she was thoroughly loyal to the Labour Party and its dominant sentiments. Her appearance could be rather austere; above all she was a solver of problems. Yet children of her Bermondsey comrades of the early years recalled another Eveline Lowe 'who after tea would sit at the piano playing and singing old airs and folk songs' (*The Times*, 5 June 1956). She died in Dulwich, London, on 30 May 1956.

David Howell

Sources *DNB* • A. Fenner Brockway, *Bermondsey story* (1946) • press cuttings, People's History Museum, Manchester [incl. profile in *Labour Woman* (March 1939) with photograph, obits. in *The Times* (31 May 1956, 5 June 1956)] • P. M. Graves, *Labour women: women in British working class politics, 1918–1939* (1994) • *Labour Woman* (June 1921) • BLPES, Francis Johnson MSS, Independent Labour Party Archive • *CGPLA Eng. & Wales* (1956)

Archives Women's Library, London, papers | BLPES, Francis Johnson collection | FILM BFI NFTVA, news footage

Likenesses A. K. Lawrence, oils, 1940, Guildhall Art Gallery, London [*see illus.*]

Wealth at death £17,061 8*s*. 2*d*.: administration with will, 21 Aug 1956, *CGPLA Eng. & Wales*

Lowe, Sir Hudson (1769–1844), army officer and colonial governor, born in Galway, Ireland, on 28 July 1769, was the son of Hudson Lowe (*d*. 1801) and his wife, the daughter of J. Morgan of Galway.

Family and early army career The elder Hudson Lowe, from a Lincolnshire family long settled near Grantham, was for over thirty years surgeon of the 50th foot, and afterwards, as staff surgeon-major and assistant inspector of hospitals, head of the medical department at Gibraltar, where he died. The younger Hudson was born while his father was with his regiment in Galway, and he went with it to Jamaica in late 1772. After nearly four years the 50th moved to North America, where most of the men were dispersed to other regiments. However, in November 1776 Lowe's father returned to England with a recruiting party to Salisbury, and the younger Hudson attended school there. In the autumn of 1778 the regiment, now up to

Sir Hudson Lowe (1769–1844), by unknown engraver, pubd 1853 (after Wyville?, 1832)

strength, settled at Plymouth. Hudson Lowe apparently became an ensign in the East Devon militia, passing review with it before the age of twelve, which does not necessarily prove that he joined his father at Plymouth. The 50th moved to Gibraltar in 1784, where Lowe served as a volunteer in 1785–6, and was gazetted ensign on 25 September 1787, advancing to lieutenant in the regiment on 16 November 1791, and captain-lieutenant and captain on 6 September 1795. Meanwhile, he had travelled on leave through Italy, picking up an intimate knowledge of Italian and French. On the outbreak of war he rejoined his regiment at Gibraltar and served with it at Toulon (1793) and at the capture of Corsica (1794), taking part in the attack on the great Martello tower, the storming of the Convention redoubt, and the sieges of Bastia and Calvi. He remained two years in garrison at Ajaccio, then went with the 50th to Elba, where he was deputy judge-advocate. Subsequently he was stationed in Portugal for two years and became proficient in Portuguese, having already obtained a good knowledge of Spanish. From Lisbon he moved in 1799 to Minorca, where he was made one of the inspectors of foreign corps and put at the head of 200 anti-republican Corsicans—styled the Corsican rangers—with the rank of major-commandant from 5 July 1800. He commanded the corps in Egypt in 1801 at the landing and in the operations before Alexandria and the advance on Cairo, winning the approval of Brigadier-General John Moore, who remarked on one occasion: 'When Lowe's at the outposts I'm sure of a good night'. For his services in Egypt he received the Turkish gold medal. The Corsican rangers were disbanded at Malta after the peace of Amiens, and Lowe was put on half pay.

War in the Mediterranean In 1803, on the recommendation of Moore, Lowe was appointed one of the new permanent assistants in the quartermaster-general's department and was stationed at Plymouth, from where, in July, he was dispatched to Portugal to inspect the troops and defences on the north and north-eastern frontiers; and he reported the feasibility of defending the country with a mixed British and Portuguese force. He was then sent to Malta to raise a new and larger corps of foreign men, to be called the Royal Corsican rangers, as major-commandant from 15 October 1803 and lieutenant-colonel-commandant from 25 June 1804. Following a mission to Sardinia, where his report on the state of the island saved a proposed subsidy, in 1805 Lowe went with his corps to Naples, under Lieutenant-General Sir James Henry Craig, and commanded the advance from Castellamare towards the Abruzzi. When the British retired to Sicily he was detached with part of his corps, the rest joining him, after the battle of Maida in July 1806, at Capri, where he was reinforced later by the Malta regiment. On his own responsibility he humanely appealed to Marshal Louis-Alexandre Berthier, chief of the staff of the army of Naples, against the frequent French military executions of Calabrese fugitives. Lowe occupied Capri from 11 June 1806 until 20 October 1808, when, after thirteen days' siege—the Malta regiment having been made prisoners and the defences of Capri breached—he surrendered to a French force under General Count Jean-Maximin Lamarque. He blamed the disaster on the absence of naval aid and the conduct of the Malta regiment. Deeply upset by the omission from the *London Gazette* of his detailed dispatch, he thought of leaving the service.

Lowe commanded the Royal Corsican rangers in the expedition to the Bay of Naples in 1809 and distinguished himself at the capture of Ischia. He then acted as second in command of the expedition to the Ionian Islands (1809–10), led the attacking force at Zante (Zákynthos), was present at the capture of Cephalonia and Ithaca, and the capture of Santa Maura (Leukas). Lowe was put in command of the left division of the troops in the Ionian Islands and entrusted with the provisional government of Cephalonia, Ithaca, and Santa Maura, which he administered without remuneration for two years. He also addressed a general report about the Ionian Islands to the Colonial Office. On leaving, the inhabitants presented him with a sword of honour. He was promoted colonel-commandant of the Royal Corsican rangers on 1 January 1812 and retained that post until the corps was disbanded at the beginning of 1817. He returned home on leave in February 1812, reputedly having been on active service continuously since 1793, with only six months in England during the peace of Amiens.

In northern Europe In January 1813 Lowe was sent to inspect the Russian German Legion—a force composed of German fugitives from the Moscow retreat—which was to be paid by Britain. He travelled to Stockholm, then crossed the Gulf of Bothnia on the ice to inspect the legion, which was scattered along the Baltic coasts. Afterwards, he went on to Kalisch (Kalisz) in Poland, where an anti-French treaty had been signed by Russia and Prussia. He remained with the Russian army for the ensuing campaign, being present at the battles of Bautzen (where he first saw Napoleon) and Würschen. During the short-lived armistice (June–July 1813) he inspected some 20,000 levies in British pay in north Germany, and joined Major-General Sir Charles Stewart at the headquarters of Crown Prince Bernadotte of Sweden. Stewart sent Lowe to the headquarters of the Prussian army of Silesia under Marshal Blücher, with whom he was present at Möckern, at the great battles around Leipzig, and at the pursuit of the French to the Rhine. He then resumed his inspections in north Germany and at the end of the year was ordered to organize a new body of Dutch levies in the Netherlands. This plan was abandoned, apparently at his own request, and on 24 January 1814 he rejoined Blücher at Vaucouleurs, being subsequently present with the Prussians at thirteen general engagements. As the only British officer of rank with Blücher's army, Lowe was privy to many important deliberations, especially during the conferences at Châtillon, where he strongly advocated the advance on Paris. He was the first officer to bring to England the news of Napoleon's abdication, arriving in London on 9 April 1814, after having ridden from Paris to Calais through potentially hostile country attended by a single cossack.

Lowe was knighted on 26 April 1814 and promoted major-general on 4 June. He also received the Russian cross of St George and the Prussian order of military merit. When the allies withdrew from France, he became quartermaster-general of the army in the Low Countries under the command of William Frederick, prince of Orange. Upon the news of Napoleon's return from Elba, which reached Brussels early in March 1815, Lowe, with permission of the prince of Orange, dispatched a British staff officer to the Prussian commanders between the Rhine and Meuse, urging a concentration on the Meuse, to co-operate in the defence of the Southern Netherlands. After the Prussians had begun to move, the prince of Orange changed his mind; but Lowe refused to issue counter-orders. Six years later, on 18 March 1821, in a letter to Earl Bathurst from St Helena, Lowe asserted that Napoleon had made a firm proposal for the king of the Netherlands to give up his claims to the Southern Netherlands, offering to procure for him indemnities in the north of Germany. The duke of Wellington assumed command in the Netherlands early in April 1815, and Lowe remained for a few weeks under him as his quartermaster-general, but he was condemned by the duke as a 'damned old fool' (Longford, 482) for hesitant map-reading and was replaced in May by Colonel Sir William Howe de Lancey. The day after the battle of Waterloo, Lowe took command at Genoa of troops gathered to co-operate with Austro-Sardinian forces. In July, in conjunction with a naval squadron under Admiral Sir Edward Pellew, he occupied Marseilles, and then marched against Toulon, where, in concert with the royalists, he drove out the Napoleonic garrison.

Guarding Napoleon, 1815–1821 At Marseilles, on 1 August 1815, Lowe received intimation that he would have the custody of Napoleon, who had taken refuge on the *Bellerophon*, in Aix Roads, a fortnight previously. On Lowe's departure from Marseilles, the citizens of the town presented him with a silver urn bearing an inscription alluding to his having saved the city from being pillaged. The island of St Helena in the south Atlantic was a possession of the East India Company, and on 23 August the court of directors notified him that they had appointed him governor with a salary of £12,000 a year. No stipulation was made as to pension, which explains why his critics could later claim that he was not considered eligible for pension. On 12 September he received from Bathurst, secretary of state for war and the colonies, preliminary instructions about dealing with Napoleon. He obtained the local rank of lieutenant-general on 9 November, and on 4 January 1816 he was made KCB.

In London, on 16 December 1815, Lowe married Susan Johnson (1779/80–1832), daughter of Stephen de Lancey, sister of Colonel Sir William Howe de Lancey, and widow of Colonel William Johnson. From her first marriage she had two daughters surviving, one marrying Count Balmain, the Russian commissioner at St Helena during Napoleon's captivity. With Lowe she had two sons and a daughter, all of whom were born on St Helena. The younger son was Edward William Howe de Lancy *Lowe. Lady Lowe died in Hertford Street, Mayfair, Westminster, on 22 August 1832.

In mid-January 1816 Lowe left Portsmouth for St Helena, accompanied by his wife and her two daughters; they reached the island on 14 April. Two days earlier, a warrant had been issued, addressed to Lowe as 'lieutenant-general of his Majesty's army in St Helena and governor of that island', requiring him to detain and keep Napoleon as a prisoner of war, under such directions as should be issued from time to time by one of the principal secretaries of state. Indeed, frequent dispatches from Bathurst would reiterate Napoleon's status as a prisoner and the government's persistent fear that he might again escape captivity, as he had from Elba. Lowe, therefore, felt compelled to restrict Napoleon's freedom of movement. Nevertheless, he was not inhumane: shortly after his arrival, he raised the annual allowance for running Longwood, where Napoleon and his entourage lived, from £8000 to £12,000.

Lowe was unable, however, to establish a satisfactory relationship with Napoleon. Supposedly at their first meeting, when the governor addressed him as 'General Buonaparte', Napoleon observed: 'His eye is that of a hyena caught in a trap' (Rosebery, 66); and his dislike intensified, as Lowe insisted on still-tighter security. Lowe and Napoleon met six times in four months, then no more. The last two encounters were particularly acrimonious; though, by all accounts, Lowe maintained self-control in the face of considerable verbal abuse. After 18 August 1816 he refused to make further visits to Longwood, though a contrary version holds that Napoleon declined to see Lowe again because 'he makes me too angry and I lose my dignity' (Markham, 235). He also told a nephew of the prime minister, Lord Liverpool, that Lowe 'was one of the few men that your uncle should never have sent here', due to his association with 'the Corsican battalion', which Napoleon considered a collection of renegades and deserters (ibid., 233). Indeed, views similar to Napoleon's were independently expressed. Wellington thought Lowe 'a very bad choice … wanting in education and judgement … a stupid man … [who] was suspicious and jealous' (Rosebery, 69). Count Balmain (who later married Lowe's stepdaughter) declared him 'not a tyrant, but he is troublesome and unreasonable beyond endurance' (ibid.). Officers who were on the spot all the time, and were personal friends of various members of Napoleon's staff, pointed to the real origin of many calumnies that have found general acceptance. Walter Henry, assistant surgeon in the 66th foot, which formed part of the St Helena garrison from 1816 to 1821, became convinced that Lowe's vigilance and his firmness in suppressing plots at Longwood were the cause of the hostility towards him, rather than any want of temper or courtesy. Lieutenant Basil Jackson, a Royal Staff Corps officer at St Helena, after noting reliance placed by the exiles on party sympathy in England, concluded:

> The policy of Longwood—heartily and assiduously carried out by Napoleon's adherents, who liked banishment as little as the great man himself—was to pour into England pamphlets and letters complaining of unnecessary restrictions, insults from the governor, scarcity of provisions, miserable accommodation, insalubrity of climate, and a host of other grievances, but chiefly levelled at the governor as the head and front of all that was amiss. (Jackson, 104)

Napoleon died on 5 May 1821. At the end of July Lowe handed over the governorship to Brigadier-General John Pine Coffin and left St Helena. Peace was made, at the dying wish of Napoleon, between the exiles and the governor before the general exodus. At his departure, the people of the island presented Lowe with an address praising his rule. The confidence felt in him was evinced by the unanimous acceptance of his measures for the abolition of slavery (without compensation), which took effect from Christmas day 1818. The abolition of slavery was also warmly acknowledged by Sir Thomas Fowell Buxton in the House of Commons in May 1823.

Controversy and last years, 1821–1844 Back in England, Lowe was cordially received by George IV; and on 4 June 1822, he was appointed colonel of the 93rd foot (Sutherland Highlanders).

In August 1822 Barry Edward O'Meara, who had been Napoleon's doctor at St Helena, and who had resigned complaining of restraints placed on him by the governor, had been ordered off the island in July 1818, and on 2 November 1818 had seen his name removed from the navy list for defamatory allegations about Lowe, published in London his highly critical *Napoleon in Exile: a Voice from St. Helena*. The glaring inconsistencies between some of its statements and others previously made by O'Meara were exposed in the October 1822 issue of the *Quarterly Review*;

nevertheless, the book went through five editions in a few months. Lowe sought legal redress, and a rule *nisi* for a criminal information against O'Meara was obtained in Hilary term 1823 but was afterwards discharged on a technical objection in respect of time. Lowe was then advised that he had done everything necessary by denying the various charges on affidavit, as O'Meara, if he challenged the truth of the denials, could proceed against him for perjury. He was, therefore, dissuaded from further proceedings against O'Meara, though he was strongly advised by Lord Bathurst to publish a full and complete vindication of his governorship of St Helena from the materials in his possession. He appears, however, to have thought that the government was bound to defend his character as a public servant, whose conduct it had approved.

In 1823 Lowe was appointed governor of Antigua but quickly resigned for domestic reasons. He was then appointed to the staff in Ceylon as second in command under Lieutenant-General Sir Edward Barnes. He left his family in Paris and late in 1825 set out for Ceylon, where he remained until 1828, at which time implied criticisms in the last volume of Sir Walter Scott's *Life of Napoleon* brought him home on leave. He met with a hearty welcome at St Helena on the way, but his return was not well received in official quarters because the reasons for it were deemed inadequate. Appeals to Bathurst and also to Wellington, who advised him to go back to Ceylon and look forward to succeed to the chief command, proved fruitless. His promotion to lieutenant-general on 22 July 1830 virtually coincided with the opposition party coming to power. Ceylon received a new governor, and Lowe's hopes of further preferment or pension were never fulfilled. He returned to England in 1831 and from that time until his death in 1844 incessantly pressed the government in respect of his claims. Letter after fastidious letter went to the Colonial Office, year by year, without result. He became colonel of the 56th foot on 22 July 1832, and then, on 17 November 1842, of his old regiment, the 50th. In 1842 also, he advanced to the highest class of the Prussian order of the Red Eagle, which was notified in a highly flattering letter from Baron von Bülow recalling his 'signal services to the common cause in the glorious campaigns of 1813–14'. Previously, in 1838, he had been made a GCMG.

Lowe was a slightly built man of below average height. He had reddish hair, bushy eyebrows, a ruddy freckled face, an aquiline nose, and a tight mouth. His manner was quick and restless, though he was never a fluent speaker.

On leaving St Helena, Lowe possessed £20,000 and much valuable property, including a fine and extensive library. However, before his death the heavy expenses in which he had been involved made him a much poorer man. He died at Charlotte Cottage, near Sloane Street, Chelsea, London, of paralysis on 10 January 1844, aged seventy-four.

Lowe's papers were entrusted to Sir Harris Nicolas to prepare for publication, but the arrangement was abandoned after many delays. Subsequently, they were placed by the publisher of the *Quarterly Review* in the hands of William Forsyth, who compiled the *Captivity of Napoleon at St Helena, from the Letters and Journals of Sir Hudson Lowe* (3 vols., 1853). H. M. CHICHESTER, *rev.* JOHN SWEETMAN

Sources *Army List* • Colonel Fyler [A. E. Fyler], *The history of the 50th or (the queen's own) regiment, from the earliest date to the year 1881* (1895) • R. Holloway, *The queen's own royal west Kent regiment* (1973) • Earl of Rosebery [A. P. Primrose], *Napoleon: the last phase* (1900) • F. Markham, *Napoleon* (1963) • J. Kemble, *Napoleon immortal* (1959) • E. Longford [E. H. Pakenham, countess of Longford], *Wellington*, 1: *The years of the sword* (1969) • B. Jackson, *Notes and reminiscences of a staff officer* (privately printed, London, 1877)

Archives Bibliothèque Nationale, Paris, corresp. and papers • BL, corresp. and papers, Add. MSS 15729, 20107–20140, 29543, 36297, 41192, 45517, 49528, 56088–56091 • BL OIOC, corresp. and papers, MS Eur. E 398 • Suffolk RO, Bury St Edmunds, memoranda relating to Napoleon | BL, corresp. with Earl Bathurst, loan 57 • BL, corresp. with Lord Goderich, Add. MS 40879 • NL Scot., corresp. with Hugh Elliot • NL Scot., corresp. with Sir A. Walker

Likenesses engraving, pubd 1853 (after Wyville?, 1832) [*see illus.*] • J. M. Fontaine, line engraving (after J. N. Frémy), BM • Wyville, oils, NAM

Lowe, James (1796–1866), inventor of a screw propeller, whose early life is unknown, was initially apprenticed on 2 November 1813 to Edward Shorter, a London master mechanic and a freeman of the City, who had in 1800 taken out a patent for propelling vessels, which he had named 'the perpetual sculling machine'. In 1816 Lowe joined a whaling ship, but after three voyages returned to his master. Later on he commenced business as a mechanic and a manufacturer of smoke jacks for roasting spits. On 30 May 1825 he married Mary, the eldest daughter of a Mr Barnes of Ewell, Surrey.

Lowe's spare time was subsequently taken up with experimenting on screw propellers for ships. On 24 March 1838 he took out a patent, no. 7599, for 'improvements in propelling vessels' by means of a screw of one or more curved blades, set or fixed on a revolving shaft below the waterline of the vessel. His propeller was first practically used in the *Wizard* in 1838, and then in the navy's steamships the *Rattler* and the *Phoenix*. On 16 December 1844 he brought an action in the court of queen's bench against Penn & Co., engineers at Greenwich, for infringement of the patent. The evidence was contradictory, but it was shown that Lowe, although not the original inventor of propellers, was the inventor of a combination of them never before applied to the propulsion of vessels. This combination consisted of three parts: a segment of a screw; a segment of a screw applied below the waterline, so as to be totally immersed; a segment of a screw applied on an axis below the water. The jury gave a verdict in his favour.

However, it was a popular field for inventors: at least forty other people proposed screw propellers before 1836. The main advantage of a submerged propeller was to reduce its risk of damage from naval bombardment; side and centre paddle wheel propulsion was developed earlier, but found to be too exposed. F. P. Smith (1808–1874) and John Ericsson (1803–1889) in the USA are generally accorded recognition for the innovation of practical marine screw propulsion (see *Introduction of the Ironclad Warship*, 1933, by J. P. Baxter).

On 19 August 1852 Lowe took out another patent, no. 14263, for his propeller. He apparently spent his wife's fortune of £3000 in his experiments, reduced himself to poverty, and never succeeded in obtaining any compensation for the use of his invention. On 12 October 1866 Lowe was run over by a wagon in London and killed. His wife died in 1872. Their daughter, Henrietta [*see* Vansittart, Henrietta], who in July 1855 married Frederick Vansittart, continued her father's experiments, and on 18 September 1868 took out a patent, no. 2877, for a further improvement, which she called 'the Lowe–Vansittart propeller'. This useful device was subsequently fitted to many government ships. G. C. Boase, *rev.* W. Johnson

Sources J. P. Baxter, *The introduction of the ironclad warship* (1933) · *The Times* (17 Dec 1844) · *The Times* (24 Dec 1869) · *Mechanics Magazine*, 37 (1842), 462 · *GM*, 4th ser., 2 (1866), 705 · H. Vansittart, *History of the Lowe–Vansittart propeller* (1882) · R. Armstrong, *Powered ships* (1975), 106 · *CGPLA Eng. & Wales* (1866)
Wealth at death under £50: administration, 31 Oct 1866, *CGPLA Eng. & Wales*

Lowe, James (*d.* **1865**), journalist and translator, was the only son of James Lowe of Liverpool. In his early career he was editor of a newspaper at Preston, and from 1843 to 1863 edited *The Critic of Literature, Science, and the Drama*. He was also a contributor to *The Field* and *The Queen*, and was one of the secretaries of the Acclimatisation Society.

Lowe projected a *Selected Series of French Literature*, to consist of translations from memoirs and letters, of which the first volume, containing part of Madame de Sévigné's correspondence, appeared at London in 1853; no more seems to have been published. In 1857 he published a translation of Victor Schoelcher's *Life of Handel*. He died of erysipelas on 29 October 1865 in London, at 10 Lancaster Place, the Strand. J. M. Rigg, *rev.* Zoë Lawson

Sources *London Review* (4 Nov 1865) · catalogue [BM] · *Annual Report* [Society for the Acclimatisation of Animals … within the United Kingdom], 3 (1863) · *The Times* (31 Oct 1865), 1

Lowe, John (*c.*1385–1467), bishop of Rochester, is said by the Worcestershire antiquarian T. R. Nash (*d.* 1811) to have been a member of the Lowe family of Lindridge parish in that county. His namesake John Lowe (archdeacon of Rochester from 1452 until at least 1467), who was probably a relation, was described as of noble birth. Born near Droitwich about 1385, Lowe entered the Augustinian friary in that town, but in 1400 moved to the Lincoln house where, aged at least fourteen, he was ordained acolyte (18 September 1400) and deacon (22 December 1403). He studied theology in Oxford; by 1420 he was a master of arts, and received his doctorate in theology by 1426. In 1420 he obtained conventuality in the London house of Augustinian friars, and was its prior by 1423. He was prior provincial of the order in England from December 1427 to December 1433. He was provided to the bishopric of St Asaph on 17 August 1433, and consecrated on 1 November 1433. On 22 April 1444 he was translated to the bishopric of Rochester, which he held until his death.

Lowe was a learned man and a strongly orthodox theologian, who before and after he became a bishop was a noted prosecutor of heretics. He was involved in the examination of William Taylor, burnt in 1423, of Ralph Mungyn and others in 1428, and above all in the condemnation of Reginald Pecock, bishop of Chichester, in 1457. He was also involved with the production of the detailed refutation of Pecock's errors written by Master John Bury of Clare, the *Gladius Salomonis*, and Lowe's learning and orthodoxy were praised by Bury in his dedicatory letter to the archbishop of Canterbury. On 23 July 1441 Lowe preached at the public recantation of the necromancer Roger Bolingbroke. John Capgrave (*d.* 1464), a fellow Augustinian friar, dedicated his *Corona super libros regum* to Lowe. John Bale credits Lowe with a number of sermon collections and theological writings. He also left many manuscripts to the library of the Augustinian friars in London which Bale and Leland credit him with having built up. Little is known of his period as bishop in St Asaph, but his register shows him to have been a conscientious bishop of Rochester. He attended parliaments and convocations regularly, but spent most of his time in his diocese, in particular at his episcopal manor of Halling, Kent. He was responsible for some rebuilding and remodelling of the episcopal palace in Rochester before 1459.

Lowe probably owed his introduction to court circles to Humphrey, duke of Gloucester (*d.* 1447). On 25 February 1432 he became confessor to the king, delegating his duties as provincial, and was dispensed from the liturgical rules of his order while at court. Although Gloucester may have been behind his promotion to the episcopate in the following year, it is also true that Lowe ceased to be the king's confessor, so his provision to St Asaph may have represented a discreet dismissal when Duke Humphrey's brief period of dominance ended. But he retained his connection with the court, where he was a noted preacher, and he has been suggested (by R. A. Griffiths) as a possible author of the treatise *On the Rule of Princes* written for Henry VI between about 1436 and 1442. In 1440 he was one of the twelve feoffees in whom all alien priory lands in royal hands were vested so as to provide an endowment for Eton College, and in the decade following was among the men responsible for overseeing various aspects of the development of Eton and of King's College, Cambridge. He was paid £100 for his services on a diplomatic mission to the emperor Friedrich III (*r.* 1440–93) at Frankfurt, Germany, between 15 March and 14 August 1442. Late in 1443 he became a member of the king's council, attending its meetings with moderate regularity. Late in 1455 he was a member of the committee appointed to define the powers of the duke of York as protector, and like many Augustinian friars, he adopted a political stance increasingly favourable to York. In June 1460 he joined the earls of Warwick and March at Rochester, and in the following month was sent as an emissary to Henry VI at Northampton. In the Yorkist administration established at the end of July, Lowe was appointed master of the mints. In February 1461, after the second battle of St Albans, Lowe formed part of a deputation from the citizens of London to ask Edward of York his intentions, and in the first months of

Edward IV's reign he was one of the bishops who lent money to the new king.

According to Hardy's edition of Le Neve's *Fasti*, in 1465 Edward IV wrote to the pope seeking his permission for the aged and infirm Lowe to resign. However, Lowe died in 1467, probably in September and certainly by 21 November, at Halling, before permission could be obtained. His will, dated 15 August 1467, includes bequests to his cathedral of vestments and a 'beautiful chalice' depicting Christ and his apostles. He was buried in an inscribed tomb (later moved), sited before the 'golden image of St Andrew' opposite the bishop's chair in Rochester Cathedral. VIRGINIA DAVIS

Sources F. X. Roth, *The English Austin friars, 1249–1538*, 2 vols. (1961–6) • Emden, *Oxf.*, 2.1168–9 • R. Pecock, *The repressor of over much blaming of the clergy*, ed. C. Babington, 2 vols., Rolls Series, 19 (1860) • *CEPR letters*, vols. 8–11 • *Chancery records* • J. Thorpe, ed., *Registrum Roffense, or, A collection of antient records, charters and instruments … illustrating the ecclesiastical history and antiquities of the diocese and cathedral church of Rochester* (1769) • [T. Netter], *Fasciculi zizaniorum magistri Johannis Wyclif cum tritico*, ed. W. W. Shirley, Rolls Series, 5 (1858) • *Recueil des croniques … par Jehan de Waurin*, ed. W. Hardy and E. L. C. P. Hardy, 5 vols., Rolls Series, 39 (1864–91), vol. 5 • R. A. Griffiths, *The reign of King Henry VI: the exercise of royal authority, 1422–1461* (1981) • T. Nash, *Collections for the history of Worcestershire*, 2 vols. (1781–2) • *Fasti Angl.* (Hardy), vol. 2 • R. A. Griffiths, 'The trial of Eleanor Cobham: an episode in the fall of Duke Humphrey of Gloucester', *Bulletin of the John Rylands University Library*, 51 (1968–9), 381–99; repr. in R. A. Griffiths, *King and country: England and Wales in the fifteenth century* (1991), 232–52, esp. 240 • P. A. Johnson, *Duke Richard of York, 1411–1460* (1988) • J. Watts, *Henry VI and the politics of kingship* (1996) • will, PRO, PROB 11/5, sig. 32

Archives CKS, register

Wealth at death see will, PRO, PROB 11/5, sig. 32

Lowe, John (1750–1798), poet, was born in Kenmure, parish of Kells, East Galloway, the son of a gardener at Kenmure Castle. Having left the parish school he was apprenticed in New Galloway with John Heron, hand-loom weaver, father of Robert Heron (1764–1807). He improved his education at Carsphairn parish school, and with the help of friends (he was handsome, talented, and always popular) entered Edinburgh University in 1771 to prepare for the church. He studied for two sessions, being tutor in the interval in the family of Mr M'Ghie of Airds on the Dee, East Galloway. He became engaged to Jessie M'Ghie and found the subject for 'Mary's Dream', his chief lyric, in the grief of her sister, whose lover, a ship surgeon, had been recently drowned. Near the house he had constructed an arbour in which he studied and which, known as 'Lowe's seat', Burns piously visited when he was in the neighbourhood in 1793.

Doubtful of success in the Scottish church Lowe went to the United States in 1773 as tutor to the family of a brother of George Washington, leaving Jessie behind to follow at an unspecified date. Later he ran a private school at Fredericksburgh, Virginia, which failed in 1784. There he shortly afterwards took orders and obtained a living as a clergyman of the Church of England. For a time he was, at least poetically, faithful to Jessie but he was at length fascinated by a beautiful Virginian, whose indifference impelled him to marry her more accommodating sister 'from a sentiment of gratitude'. Burns reproved this treatment of Jessie, and the marriage proved unhappy. When Lowe discovered that his wife was unfaithful he began to drink, and a downward spiral ensued. He died in poverty in December 1798 of an overdose of laudanum, at Windsor Lodge, Culpepper county, Virginia, and was buried in the cemetery of Little Fork church, in the same county.

The remaining fragments of Lowe's poems (quoted from manuscript by Gillespie and Murray in their notices of him) show a vein of deep genuine feeling. His command of pathos is fully displayed in 'Mary's Dream', his only complete lyric, which seems to have circulated in Galloway in a printed form before appearing in any collection. When Robert Hartley Cromek was preparing his *Remains of Nithsdale and Galloway Song* (1810) Allan Cunningham foisted upon him as an antique an ingenious Scottish paraphrase of 'Mary's Dream'. Cromek was fooled and gives both versions. T. W. BAYNE, *rev.* JAMES HOW

Sources A. Trotter, *East Galloway sketches, or, Biographical, historical and descriptive notices of Kirkcudbrightshire, chiefly in the nineteenth century* (1901) • W. Gillespie, 'Brief memoir of the life of John Lowe', in R. H. Cromek, *The remains of Nithsdale and Galloway song* (1810), 342–60 • J. G. Wilson, ed., *The poets and poetry of Scotland*, 2 vols. in 4 (1876–7) • Chambers, *Scots.*, rev. T. Thomson (1875) • Allibone, *Dict.* • Anderson, *Scot. nat.* • P. Ross, *The Scot in America* (1896) • Irving, *Scots.* • T. Murray, *The literary history of Galloway* (1822)

Lowe, Mauritius (1746–1793), painter, was the illegitimate son of Thomas, second Baron Southwell (1698–1766), from whom he had a small annuity, but he claimed connection with the family of John Lowe, bishop of Rochester in 1444. He studied with G. B. Cipriani RA at the duke of Richmond's gallery, and was one of the first students to enter the Royal Academy Schools on 9 August 1769, in which year through the interest of Giuseppe Baretti he was the first to obtain the gold medal awarded by the Royal Academy for a historical painting, *Time Discovering Truth*. In 1771 he was the first student selected to receive the travelling scholarship for study at Rome, but was 'indolent and spent his time in dissipation' and, as he failed to comply with the regulations of the academy, the scholarship was withdrawn in 1772 (Redgrave, *Artists*, 276).

Lowe exhibited at the Society of Artists in 1776 and 1779, sending miniatures and his picture *Venus*. Lowe enjoyed the friendship and protection of Dr Samuel Johnson, who left him a small legacy. In 1783 he sent a huge picture to the Royal Academy, entitled *The Deluge—there were Giants on the Earth in those Days*. This was justly rejected, but at the earnest solicitation of Dr Johnson it was ultimately admitted, though it was hung in an empty room by itself, and universally condemned. In 1777 he exhibited his drawing *Homer Singing the Iliad to the Greeks*. He was reputed to be the author of the *Ear-Wig* 'an abusive art periodical published in 1787' (Redgrave, 277). Lowe married Sarah, a servant, and had a large family, to one of whom Johnson was godfather. In her diary (2.41) Madame d'Arblay described Johnson's efforts to obtain work as a portrait painter for Lowe, and the state of filth and misery to which Lowe and his family were reduced. Lowe resided for some time in Hedge

Lane, London, and later in a miserable lodging in Westminster, where he died on 1 September 1793, leaving one son and two daughters. (For Johnson's god-daughter see *The Examiner*, 28 May 1873.) In the print room at the British Museum there are three drawings by Lowe, two being for a large painting, *Royal Power, assisted by Wisdom and Virtue, defending the constitution of Great Britain against the attacks of Sedition and Licentiousness*, which was engraved by George Graham and published in 1793. Other drawings, in the style of Fuseli, are *Abraham Offering up Isaac*, *Adam and Eve*, and *Daedalus and Icarus*. L. H. CUST, *rev.* J. DESMARAIS

Sources Redgrave, *Artists* · *GM*, 1st ser., 63 (1793), 867 · Bryan, *Painters* (1866); (1886–9) · W. Sandby, *The history of the Royal Academy of Arts*, 2 vols. (1862) · J. Northcote, *The life of Sir Joshua Reynolds*, 2nd edn, 2 vols. (1818) · J. Boswell, *The life of Samuel Johnson*, 2 vols. (1791) · E. Edwards, *Anecdotes of painters* (1808); facs. edn (1970) · M. Pilkington, *A general dictionary of painters: containing memoirs of the lives and works*, ed. A. Cunningham and R. A. Davenport, new edn (1857) · Waterhouse, *18c painters* · H. Hammelmann, *Book illustrators in eighteenth-century England*, ed. T. S. R. Boase (1975) · M. Brownell, *Samuel Johnson's attitude to the arts* (1989) · N. L. Pressly, *The Fuseli circle in Rome: early Romantic art of the 1770s* (New Haven, CT, 1979) [exhibition catalogue, Yale U. CBA, 12 Sept – 11 Nov 1979] · S. C. Hutchison, 'The Royal Academy Schools, 1768–1830', *Walpole Society*, 38 (1960–62), 123–91, esp. 134
Likenesses M. Lowe, self-portrait, oils, 1770, probably RA

Lowe, Peter (*c.*1550–1610), surgeon and founder of the Faculty of Physicians and Surgeons of Glasgow, may have been born in the west of Scotland. The exact date and location of his birth are unknown and have been the subject of debate. Lowe described himself variously as 'Arellian' (perhaps relating to Errol, or to the University of Orléans) and 'Scottishman'. He left Scotland about 1566 and travelled to France, where he remained for some thirty years, serving the Spanish army, the French army, and the French royal household, and experiencing the traumas of events such as the St Bartholomew's day massacre, when he is reputed to have been hidden in the king's wardrobe to avoid capture and probable execution (Finlayson, *Life*, 23). The nature of his medical and surgical training is unclear, although the available evidence suggests that he may have received some medical training at the University of Orléans and also become a master surgeon (academic, or 'gown-surgeon') of the College of St Côme, the historic fraternity of surgeons in Paris, the latter being the stronger possibility. Travel, study, and service abroad were entirely typical pursuits for the physicians and surgeons of the time, and the natural destination for Scots was Europe. Whatever his real qualifications, Lowe was clearly an educated man and highly regarded within the upper ranks of French society. He left France around 1596 after serving as surgeon to Henri IV for some six years, and was in London at the time of the publication of his treatise *An Easie, Certain and Perfect Method to Cure and Prevent the Spanish Sickness*, dedicated to Robert Devereux, earl of Essex.

Lowe returned to Scotland and was in residence in Glasgow by early 1598. In August of that year he fell foul of the Glasgow presbytery, being ordered to 'mak as yet two Sondayes his repentance on the pillar', no doubt for some minor moral misdemeanour (Finlayson, *Life*, 26). In March 1599 he was contracted by the town council to treat the poor of the town, at a salary of 80 merks a year. Later that year, after petitioning James VI about the unorganized and primitive state of medicine and surgery in Glasgow, Lowe, together with physician Robert Hamilton and apothecary William Spang, was granted a charter (dated 29 November 1599) allowing them to supervise and examine all surgical practitioners in the west of Scotland. Thus came into being a unique organization, encompassing both physicians and surgeons, which continues as the Royal College of Physicians and Surgeons of Glasgow.

In addition to his historical significance in terms of the Glasgow institution, Lowe's publications were equally important. His major work, *The Whole Course of Chirurgerie* (1597), was written in the vernacular, a move which could have attracted much criticism from contemporaries, who favoured Latin as the legitimate medium for academic discourse. It was constructed partly in the form of a catechism, or conversation between the author and a student, and partly a description of surgical techniques, medical treatments, and examples from his practice in France. The second edition of the book implies that his son John was the second party in the catechism, although at the time he was still a child. Lowe's translation, probably from the French, of the *Presages of Hippocrates* is included in the work, which was republished on a number of occasions, being retitled *A Discourse of the Whole Art of Chirurgerie* from the second edition, published in 1612. Interestingly, though perhaps typically, many of the illustrations in the book are copied directly—in some cases with the French titles reproduced—from the works of Ambroise Paré. He refers frequently in his published works to several other books in preparation, notably a 'poor man's guide', a treatise on parturition and the diseases of women, sometimes referred to as the 'Book of the infantment', and a book on the plague, but there is no evidence that any of these was published formally.

It is evident from his testament that Lowe had married twice, as it is stated that 'Helen Wemyss now his spous should have nane of his guidis nor geir quhill his first wyffis bairnes were payit of sevin thousand and fyve hundreth merkis' (Finlayson, *Testament*, 2). Helen Wemyss was the daughter of David Wemyss, the first protestant minister in Glasgow after the Reformation, who was rector of Glasgow University on several occasions between 1593 and 1602. Lowe's son John was apparently the son of his first wife, while Helen Wemyss was the mother of his daughter Christian, who was also provided for under the terms of the testament. Lowe died in Glasgow on 15 August 1610 (Finlayson, *Testament*, 2, from Commissariot Records). The preface to the second edition of *Chyrurgerie* is dated 1612, but this is likely to be a publisher's error. He was buried in the grounds of Glasgow Cathedral. He had been active in practice until a few months previously, as he was paid £40 by the Glasgow town council on 15 May 1610 as his fee for 'bowelling' (embalming) the laird of Houston. Lowe's memorial stone bears an appealing inscription:

Stay, passenger and view this stone, for under it lyis such a
one who cuired many whill he lieved, soe gracious he noe
man grieved. Yea when his phisicks force oft failed, his
pleasant purpose then prevailed. For of his God he got the
grace to live in mirth and die in peace. Heavin hes his soul,
his corps this stone, sigh, passenger, and soe be gone.

HELEN M. DINGWALL

Sources J. Finlayson, *Account of the life and works of Maister Peter Lowe, the founder of the Faculty of Physicians and Surgeons of Glasgow* (1889) • J. Finlayson, *The last will and testament with the inventory of the estate of Maister Peter Lowe, founder of the Faculty of Physicians and Surgeons of Glasgow* (1898) • P. Lowe, *A discourse of the whole art of chirurgerie* (1612) • D. Hamilton, *The healers: a history of medicine in Scotland* (1981) • A. Duncan, *Memorials of the Faculty of Physicians and Surgeons of Glasgow* (1896) • J. D. Comrie, *History of Scottish medicine*, 2 vols. (1932) • J. Geyer-Kordesch and F. Macdonald, *Physicians and surgeons in Glasgow: the history of the Royal College of Physicians and Surgeons of Glasgow, 1599–1858* (1999)

Likenesses oils, Royal College of Physicians and Surgeons of Glasgow

Wealth at death £5562, Scots (£463 sterling); plus property valued at £2666 Scots (£221 sterling): Finlayson, *Last will and testament*

Lowe, Richard Thomas (1802–1874), naturalist, was born on 4 December 1802 in Derbyshire, the only child of Thomas Lowe (*d.* 1803/4), a naval officer, and his wife, Susanna Dorothy (1778/9–1841). He was educated at Brewood School, Staffordshire, and in 1821 entered Christ's College, Cambridge. In 1825 he graduated BA as senior optime, and in the same year took holy orders. In 1831 he graduated MA, and in 1843 was admitted *ad eundem* at Oxford. At university he acquired a fondness for natural history from his friend, the botanist Miles Joseph Berkeley (1803–1889), who introduced him to the professor of mineralogy at Cambridge, John Stevens Henslow (1796–1861). Henslow, a founder of the Cambridge Philosophical Society, was responsible for organizing botanizing tours of the local countryside for a number of students, including Charles Darwin (a devoted beetle hunter) and Lowe's lifelong friend, the entomologist Thomas Vernon *Wollaston (1822–1878).

In 1827 Lowe was awarded a travelling bachelorship for a year. It enabled him to visit Madeira with his mother in May 1828—a visit partly intended to improve his health. On arriving at Funchal Lowe took up rooms at the Quinta da Lavada, and soon began attending the English church there. His botanical field trips and collecting of specimens began almost immediately. He sent copies of his work, along with specimens, to the professor of botany at Glasgow, William Jackson Hooker (1785–1865).

In 1830 Lowe returned to England owing to his mother's ill health, and in November that year the Cambridge Philosophical Society agreed to publish his work, 'Primitiae faunae et florae Maderae et Portus Sancti', in its *Transactions*. In January the following year he returned to Madeira, again accompanied by his mother. Soon after arriving he was offered the chance to stand in for the Anglican chaplain, and about 1832/3 he took up the post on a permanent basis. On reading *Tract Number One*, a pamphlet of the Oxford Movement, Lowe became the cause's first and most 'notorious' combatant abroad. His support for the movement and Tractarianism led him into a prolonged conflict both at home and with a number of his fellow islanders on Madeira.

In the spring of 1835 Lowe once again visited England. He published papers on the flora of Madeira in several periodicals; his 'Novitiae florae Maderensis' (1838), also published in the *Cambridge Philosophical Transactions*, was perhaps his most valuable contribution. Lowe's mother died in 1841. In 1843 he again returned to England, to organize the publication of his work *A History of the Fishes of Madeira* (1843). While in England, on 5 July 1843, he married Catherine Maria (*bap.* 1802, *d.* 1874), eldest of seven children of the Revd Joseph Guerin (*d.* 1863), rector of Norton Fitzwarren, Somerset. The couple had no children.

In January 1844 Lowe and his wife travelled to Madeira. In the winter of 1847 Wollaston visited the island, and accompanied Lowe on one of his explorations of its flora and fauna. While Lowe worked on describing new species, Wollaston concentrated on examining species variation and distribution. Lowe was still embroiled in conflict with some of his parishioners, and with the church in England—a situation which Queen Adelaide attempted to resolve during her 1847 visit to the island. However, on 22 December Lord Palmerston removed Lowe from his position as chaplain, to be replaced by Thomas Kenworthy Brown within a couple of months. On 28 March 1852 Lowe and his wife sailed back to England.

On his return to England Lowe accepted the living at Lea, near Gainsborough, Lincolnshire, given to him by Sir Charles Anderson, a cousin of his wife. Wollaston was a frequent visitor to Lea, and Lowe also paid visits to his botanist friend Berkeley, who lived nearby at King's Cliffe. Lowe made a further journey to Madeira in January 1855, returning to England in August the same year. At Lea he set to work on *A Manual Flora of Madeira and the Adjacent Islands of Porto Santo and the Desertas*, of which the first part of volume one appeared in 1857; the fifth (and concluding) part of the volume appeared in 1868. In August 1857 Lowe returned to Madeira to collect more botanical specimens. He made further journeys to his beloved island and its neighbours in 1860, 1863, 1865, and 1871. He also made trips to the Cape Verde and Canary Islands. He continued work on his *Manual Flora of Madeira*, but did not publish more than the first part of the second volume, which was issued in 1872.

On 10 April 1874 Lowe and his wife sailed from Liverpool for Madeira on the steamship *Liberia*. However, the ship never reached its destination. In the following month the *Volta* arrived in Liverpool with news of *Liberia* wreckage observed 200 miles off the Isles of Scilly; it was assumed that the *Liberia* sank with all hands at some time between 11 April and mid-May 1874. Wollaston, as executor of Lowe's will, carried out his friend's wishes to destroy all his notes (scientific and religious), but Lowe's botanical collection was presented to the herbarium at Kew, and the British Museum. The botanist John Lindley (1799–1865) dedicated the rosaceous genus *Lowea* (which has subsequently been absorbed in *Hulthemia*) to him, and a memorial was erected in the English cemetery at Funchal, in honour of both Lowe and his wife. YOLANDA FOOTE

Sources *Journal of Botany, British and Foreign*, 12 (1874), 192, 287–8 · *Men of the time* (1875) · R. Nash, *Scandal in Madeira: the story of Richard Thomas Lowe* (1990) · Venn, *Alum. Cant.* · *DNB*
Archives NHM · RBG Kew · U. Cam., Botany School Library
Wealth at death under £3000: probate, 18 Dec 1874, *CGPLA Eng. & Wales*

Lowe, Robert, Viscount Sherbrooke (**1811–1892**), politician, born at Bingham, Nottinghamshire, on 4 December 1811, was the second son of Robert Lowe (1780–1845), rector of that parish and prebendary of Southwell, and Ellen (*d.* 1852), second daughter and coheir of the Revd Reginald Pyndar, rector of Madresfield in Worcestershire. He was an albino, and his eyes were extremely sensitive to light; moreover, he had imperfect vision in both eyes, and one was useless for reading. At Winchester College, which he entered as a commoner in 1825, he was much bullied, and unable to identify his tormentors; later in life, too, he suffered from his inability to recognize people, especially in large groups. Lowe was, however, very intelligent and very determined. Conscious that his logical mind and taste for scholarship would be his best assets in life, he responded to his affliction by developing great powers of memory and labour. He also became very self-reliant. Confident in his superior intellectual ability and the correctness of his views, he quickly developed a talent for blunt, fearless assertions, and never lost the clever schoolboy's pleasure in undermining established orthodoxies and pricking complacency. He matriculated at University College, Oxford, on 16 June 1829. At Oxford he spoke often at the union, adopting unpopularly radical opinions and relishing the controversy and notoriety that this brought him. He retained his intellectual ambitions too; but though he took a first class in classics in 1833, he achieved only a second in mathematics, which he later claimed was unsuited to his questioning mind and imperfect eyesight.

Seeking a career The church was among the institutions against which the young Lowe rebelled, and so that career was closed to him (in 1841 he was to conduct a pamphlet war with the Tractarians about the interpretation of the Thirty-Nine Articles). He decided to read for the bar, and so remained in Oxford as a private tutor until a lay fellowship at Magdalen College, for which he was eligible, became vacant in 1835. But he resigned this after his impetuous marriage to Georgiana (*d.* 1884), second daughter of George Orred of Tranmere, Cheshire, on 29 March 1836. In order to make a living, he had to return to private tutoring. He quickly developed a reputation as the most efficient coach in the university, but the work was hard. His experience of it intensified his contempt for the low general standard of university education and his animosity to the complacency of college fellows, which he thought was caused by the protection given to them by lavish college endowments. It also convinced him that teaching was drudgery. Having failed to be appointed professor of Greek at Glasgow University in 1838 he gave up

Robert Lowe, Viscount Sherbrooke (1811–1892), by George Frederic Watts, *c*.1874

hope of an academic career, and in 1840 went to London to resume his law studies. He was called to the bar at Lincoln's Inn on 28 January 1842. Shortly afterwards he decided to emigrate to Australia in the hope of making a quick fortune at the Sydney bar, a decision which he later claimed was the consequence of mistaken medical advice that he must expect to be blind in seven years.

In Australia Lowe spent eight years in Australia. He was quickly drawn into New South Wales politics, at first in the hope of benefiting his legal practice. He was a member of the legislative council from November 1843, nominated by the governor, Sir George Gipps. Lowe justified this allegiance on the grounds that Gipps's opponents were supporters of tariffs and the manipulation of interest rates in order to benefit vested interests; but he soon came to quarrel with Gipps, and in August 1844 resigned his nominated seat, claiming that Gipps was abusing his powers by taxing graziers in order to pay immigrants to come to the colony. In the following year he returned to the council as an elected representative, but quickly became a vigorous opponent of his former allies, the graziers, who used their influence to acquire quasi-permanent tenure of many thousands of acres under an act of 1846. Lowe's opposition to this assertion of vested influence in turn made him a hero of the populace, and he was elected for Sydney as their candidate in 1848. However, he then refused to support many of their demands. Though abused for lack of principle throughout his Australian political career, Lowe was in fact consistent in his stand against the potential domination of powerful interests, wherever he encountered them. He opposed the Australian constitutional reforms brought in by the British government in 1850, partly on the ground that they failed to provide guarantees against such domination. His major legislative achievement was the abolition of imprisonment for debt; he battled with less success to establish a system of non-denominational schools. He also acquired substantial sums from his law practice, which he judiciously invested in the purchase of real property at Sydney. In 1850 he returned to England with enough money to be able to afford a small country house at Warlingham in Surrey as well as a town residence.

Early career in British politics Lowe aimed at a political career in Britain, and was elected to the Reform Club soon after his return. From April 1851 he was a regular leader writer in *The Times*, and moved in the circle of its editor, John Delane. Like most of that group Lowe was a Liberal but not an admirer of the government of Lord John Russell, which seemed too socially exclusive, dominated by 'the family system' and other manifestations of patronage, and insufficiently attuned to the sentiments of middle-class administrative reformers. Through his contacts with this group, Lowe was returned MP for Kidderminster at the general election of 1852, presenting himself to Lord Ward, whose influence carried the seat, as an independent Liberal beholden to neither Russell nor Lord Palmerston. *The Times* was then at the height of its influence, and the need to conciliate it probably explains his appointment as joint secretary to the Board of Control in the Liberal–Peelite coalition government formed by Lord Aberdeen in December 1852. In this post Lowe was largely responsible for the India Act of 1853, which threw open all writerships to public competition. But he quickly became bored by the routine of subordinate office, and when, on the break-up of the Aberdeen ministry in early 1855, he was offered the same post by the new premier, Lord Palmerston, he declined it.

This decision may not have been unconnected with the fragility of Palmerston's position and the vociferous public criticism of the military and political conduct of the war. Lowe joined in this criticism, blaming the patronage system for the appointment of so many incompetents. However, he did not work against Palmerston, believing that the war must be won and that he was by far the best man to do this. (Lowe's attitude to foreign policy in the 1850s was that Britain had a major role to play in Europe; that a strong, reformed, professional army was needed in order to assert her place; and that Russia was the enemy of civilization and progress.) In August 1855, after the clamour had died down, and with Palmerston still in place but needing to strengthen his position, Lowe was offered and accepted the vice-presidency of the Board of Trade, and was sworn of the privy council. His most significant achievement in this post, which he held until the fall of Palmerston in early 1858, came in 1856, when he had charge of the act allowing associations of seven or more shareholders to become limited liability companies. Previously the Board of Trade had had discretion over the award of limited liability status. Lowe hoped that the reform would liberate capital for investment and allow poorer men access to the benefits of free enterprise. In the same session he demonstrated his shortcomings as a parliamentarian by an ill-fated attempt to reform the structure of shipping dues, offending many representatives of shipping interests by casting aspersions on their motives and causing Palmerston to abandon the reform. None the less, his combination of Palmerstonianism in foreign policy and advocacy of administrative reform at home gave him a high profile among commercial men and led to a request to be the Palmerstonian candidate for Manchester at the 1857 general election. Lowe declined this request on account of the difficulty he faced in seeing large audiences and deputations. He was elected for Kidderminster in 1857 and in 1859 for Calne (by most of its 174 electors), which he held until 1868.

Education and the revised code When Palmerston returned to power in June 1859 Lowe was again—to his resentment—given a difficult but non-cabinet post, this time at the privy council. His major responsibilities were to the committee of council on education and to the medical department, which had taken over the bulk of the state's duties in the sphere of public health on the demise of the General Board of Health in 1858. Health and education were difficult areas for central government, since social conditions supplied weighty reasons for an assertive approach but this generated a great deal of local jealousy. As he was not in cabinet, Lowe could not change broad policy in either area, but he was determined to use his powers to the utmost to improve efficiency and attack complacency. In dealing with health, this meant strengthening the hand of the civil servant who was secretary to the medical department, John Simon. Simon's position was subject to annual review by parliament, which greatly reduced his scope for innovation. In 1859 Lowe persuaded the Commons to give him permanent tenure. Thereafter he gave Simon substantial independence, which he used in a number of ways, such as by building up a powerful vaccination inspectorate. By these means government influence over sanitation could be improved without enduring risky divisions in parliament. Lowe and Simon also raised public consciousness about sanitary matters through the publication of official reports and through Lowe's leading articles in *The Times*.

Lowe's task in education was harder. There was great opposition in parliament to the idea of a national system of elementary education imposed by central government, yet there was also strong feeling against the ever expanding annual grant given to assist existing voluntary schools, while it was believed that the only alternative, local rating, would create too many tensions between sects about the kind of religious teaching which the locality should offer. Lowe and the civil servant in charge of education, Ralph Lingen, did not wish to increase substantially the power of the central educational bureaucracy, but were anxious to raise the committee's profile, to improve standards, and to prevent public money being wasted on inefficient teaching, mostly in church schools protected by over-sympathetic inspectors. In 1861 they responded to parliamentary pressure for cost cutting by issuing a revised code. This laid down that the grant would in future be allocated on the basis of the number of children in each school passing an examination by inspectors in reading, writing, and arithmetic, a system notoriously known as 'payment by results'. The code was greeted with great hostility by schoolteachers, inspectors, and Anglican and dissenting opponents of state activity, a hostility all the more intense because it had, provocatively, been published just as the parliamentary session ended.

Palmerston ordered a delay in the introduction of the code until 1862, when it was amended so that some money would be paid no matter how badly children performed. Between 1862 and 1866 the grant fell by 16 per cent, while average attendance increased by 18 per cent. But the opponents of the code depicted Lowe in an unfairly philistine and anti-clerical light. Its object was not to save money at the expense of standards, since the cost to government was potentially open-ended. The 'three Rs' were chosen not because these were deemed to be the only proper components of an elementary education but because they could be examined most easily and provided a good basic test—a test which many schools failed. The grant continued to depend on schools satisfying inspectors about the general quality of their education, including religious instruction.

Opposition to the code was motivated primarily by clerical hostility to the assertiveness of the committee of council on education, exacerbated by anger from inspectors and schoolteachers at the extra workload imposed on them. Relations between the government and the voluntary schools did not improve, and in April 1864 Lord Robert Cecil persuaded the Commons to censure the committee of council for heavily editing inspectors' reports before publishing them. The charge was not quite justified, and a select committee subsequently acquitted the committee of impropriety; but Lingen frequently returned offending reports to inspectors for amendment as part of a mission to infuse professionalism into a self-indulgent corps of amateur, strongly Anglican gentlemen. Lowe resigned his post immediately on the censure.

Lowe was out of office until 1868, and free to speak his mind. During these years he came to acquire an extraordinary reputation as a parliamentary debater; Gladstone later said that in 1866 Lowe was 'at the very top of the tree'. He had believed since 1859 that he deserved cabinet office but was being sacrificed to the 'domination of cliques and coteries' in the Liberal–Peelite coalition government and forced to tackle the dangerous and thankless tasks which aristocrats would not touch. His resentment partly explains his vehemence in the mid-1860s, especially after the advent of Earl Russell to the premiership on Palmerston's death in October 1865. But the basic cause of his behaviour was his increasing determination to make a controversial name for himself by opposing what he saw as the illogical and dangerous fad of parliamentary reform.

Electoral reform, 1866–1867 Why did Lowe's views on government lead him to oppose the reform bills of 1866 and 1867? His aim for politics can be deduced from a definition he later gave (1877) of the 'ideal of the Liberal party': 'a view of things undisturbed and undistorted by the promptings of interest or prejudice, … a complete independence of all class interests, and [a reliance] for its success on the better feelings and higher intelligence of mankind' ('A new reform bill', *Fortnightly Review*, Oct 1877, 441). Lowe was an admirer of Bentham and Adam Smith (he was elected a member of the Political Economy Club in 1852). He believed that men tended to be selfish and pleasure seeking, and that while their search for pleasure was in general to be encouraged, because it was the motor of human progress, there was a constant temptation for powerful men to advance their own interests, sometimes in ways contrary to the general good. Government should provide security and justice, and restrain these anti-social tendencies by opposing monopolies, oligarchies, and other vested interests. Lowe disapproved of government interference where it distorted the workings of the natural laws which determined human progress, but not if it worked to uphold them. Government had to be conducted by someone; ideally, it should be entrusted to those committed to empirical, unprejudiced analysis of data and human behaviour in order to identify those natural laws. 'The cause of true progress' could be promoted only 'by pure and clear intelligence' (Martin, 2.263). Lowe was a meritocrat.

In the 1850s Lowe's meritocratic image had driven him to team up with radicals in criticizing the social exclusiveness and legislative timidity of official Liberalism. He remained an opponent of the patronage network all his life. But Lowe was never a fully-fledged radical. He preferred to promote his ideas anonymously through the columns of *The Times* (and later in periodicals) rather than through mass meetings. When he became a minister and mixed with men like Palmerston, he quickly saw that the greatest threat to good government was not the selfishness of propertied Liberals but the unpredictability and narrow-mindedness of parliament, much of which was caused by ignorant and obstructive pressure from popular representatives. Appreciating the merits and sharing the prejudices of his leading civil servants at the Board of Trade, such as Thomas Farrer and Henry Thring, he wrote an article in 1857 criticizing parliament as venal and superficial, and advocating giving more power to central regulatory agencies staffed by disinterested officials—'true votaries'. His experience at the privy council intensified these views, as did the furore over the cattle plague of 1865–6, when he criticized, on the one hand, the delay in response caused by the selfish behaviour of railways and farming interests in parliament and, on the other, the narrow-minded commercial Liberals who resisted compensation to farmers who had served the public interests by killing their cattle.

In the mid-1860s, then, Lowe was impatient at the obstacles to good government thrown up by parliament even under the existing franchise. He feared that the evils would multiply if the electorate was expanded. Lowe argued that working-class voters would be bound to follow their interests as they perceived them—that is, as trade union leaders and other demagogues portrayed them. A reformed parliament would press for sectional legislation to benefit trade unions against employers at law, to reduce the stringency of the poor law, and to redistribute taxation. The changes would strike at the principles of political economy which Lowe believed that educated men should uphold. And some working-class voters would act in the way that Lowe had witnessed as a candidate at Kidderminster in 1857, when he had stood out against the beer and other wealthy lobbies and had been viciously stoned by the mob, who fractured his skull. In other words, they would respond to bribes and influence, to the benefit of a plutocracy of elderly commercial men who would uphold their own interests in parliament and be useless for administrative work.

Lowe's opposition to the 1866 Reform Bill threw him into alliance with aristocratic Palmerstonian Liberals such as Earl Grosvenor—an alliance which, to some of his critics, appeared inconsistent with his earlier radical politics. Lowe in fact believed that property and intellect stood or fell together. He was a staunch defender of property rights and freedom of contract. For example, he regarded the cry for land reform as outdated, suited to a period when peasants sought land for subsistence but not to a modern economy in which capital investment was as badly needed in land as it was in manufacturing industry.

Lowe was the intellectual leader of the so-called 'Adullamites', who irritated the Russell ministry throughout the 1866 session and finally defeated its Reform Bill in June, causing its resignation. Lowe may have hoped that this would lead to a coalition of talented politicians from both parties who were lukewarm about reform, supplanting the patronage-driven party system. But this did not materialize, and Lowe and other Adullamites declined office in the minority Conservative government formed by Lord Derby. In 1867 this government passed a much more radical Reform Bill than the one defeated in 1866. Lowe, impotent to resist it, felt 'deceived and betrayed' by Disraeli, the Commons leader. On its third reading, Lowe told the Commons: 'I believe it will be absolutely necessary that you should prevail on our future masters to learn their letters' (*Hansard* 3, 188, 15 July 1867, col. 1549); this was soon attributed to him as 'We must educate our masters.' Other such trenchant phrases on the political capacity of working-class voters were widely publicized in exaggerated form by radical reformers, and his political future looked uncertain.

Politics, 1867–1868 In 1868 Lowe was elected for the new London University seat, owing to the support of doctors who admired his work for public health reform, and other intellectuals with whom Lowe's élitist but meritocratic views struck a chord (he was made LLD by Edinburgh University in 1867 and DCL at Oxford in 1870). He further appealed to such men because of his urgent advocacy of education reform in the winter of 1867–8 in speeches at Edinburgh and Liverpool.

Despite his warning to the Commons in 1867, his interest in the next twelve months was not in elementary education so much as in its higher branches, with a view to improving the quality of the political leadership given by the élite and the political judgement exercised by the middle classes. In particular he urged an overhaul of the syllabuses in universities and middle-class schools so as to embrace more science, history, and language work, and to develop the power of dispassionate and discriminating reasoning and criticism. He also advocated the separation of teaching from examining (as in London University) and the rational reorganization and regulation of school endowments by the state.

Lowe's liberalizing educational agenda extended to Ireland; he mounted a fierce opposition to the Conservative government's Irish university policy of 1868, which he thought retrograde in its encouragement of a separate Catholic university. He used this episode to justify his adhesion to Gladstone's alternative policy of Irish church disestablishment. Though Lowe did not believe that disestablishment was a panacea for Ireland, or indeed that any concession compatible with Liberal ideals could conciliate Irish Catholic activists, this return to the party fold made him a strong candidate for a post in the new Liberal cabinet which Gladstone formed after the 1868 election. In order to facilitate this eventuality, Lowe finally broke his connection with *The Times* in April 1868. Gladstone, impressed with Lowe's expenditure reductions as education minister and his capacity for resisting pressure, made him chancellor of the exchequer in December, supplying him with a detailed list of 'remnants' left from his own chancellorship and needing attention (Gladstone, *Diaries*, 10 Jan 1869).

Cabinet minister, 1868–1874 Lowe's outstanding achievement at the Treasury was the introduction of competitive examinations almost across the civil service by an order in council of 1870. He was single-handedly responsible for the change, for which there had been little public pressure; it developed naturally from his views about the importance of trained administrators and his dislike of the patronage system, which had been only slightly damaged by the introduction of limited competition in 1855. Lowe was responsible for the division of appointees into two rigid classes—policy makers and clerks. The qualifications for the higher grade were set so as to complement university syllabuses, in the hope that the new administrative class would enter a 'freemasonry' of educated gentlemen, able to hold their own in parliamentary company. He also devised the machinery for the scheme, which was controlled by the Treasury and greatly increased its dominance of the service. Departments were given incentives to participate, and after Lowe himself ended the Home Office's resistance when he became home secretary in 1873, the Foreign Office was the only significant department to opt out.

Lowe also had considerable influence on government policy in other areas. For example, he approved the mixture of central and local powers created by the 1870 Elementary Education Act. In particular he was responsible for the dual system by which voluntary schools were funded from central taxation while the new board schools were to be supported from local rates. This pragmatic and successful solution to the religious difficulty which had obstructed the development of a national system was the result of Lowe's long-held awareness of ratepayers' unwillingness to pay for sectarian teaching. He influenced the separation of teaching and examining in Gladstone's failed Irish university scheme of 1873 (though he disliked the arrangement whereby subjects like history and philosophy might not be examined in deference to Catholic scruples). But he was dissatisfied with the handling of the reform of middle-class education (1869) and the failure to take English university reform beyond the abolition of tests (1871).

Despite his early successes, Lowe's time at the exchequer became unhappy and unsuccessful because of the controversy surrounding his budget policy. Taxes were cut, but his supervision of departmental expenditure was not rigorous enough to satisfy Gladstone, while his parsimony on small points lowered his reputation among the electorate.

During Lowe's tenure, £12.5 million was cut from taxes and over £26 million from the national debt; income tax was reduced from 6*d.* to 3*d.*; the 1*s.* duty on a quarter of corn was abolished (1869); the sugar duty was halved in 1870 and again in 1873, and that on coffee halved in 1872. But the uncommon economic prosperity of these years played the major part in this success: in 1873 the government's surplus reached £6 million. Lowe was overcautious about cutting taxes and Gladstone complained that he was 'wretchedly deficient' in reducing expenditure. One of the reasons for Lowe's caution was his favouritism for particular civil servants and spending projects, which he probably thought needed defending against popular pressure for economy. Lowe was generous, for example, to both education and health: the number of assistant secretaries in the education department was doubled and many more inspectors were appointed as a result of the 1870 act, while Simon persuaded him to sanction the appointment of five permanent general health inspectors between 1869 and 1871, despite opposition elsewhere in the Treasury. On several occasions he overruled the parsimonious policy of the first commissioner of works, A. S. Ayrton. More important was Lowe's ambivalence about cuts in defence expenditure. Though the prosperity and reforming atmosphere of 1869–70 provided fertile ground for reductions in the army and navy, this mood ended with the outbreak of the Franco-Prussian War, which forced government to budget for a temporary increase in the army. Lowe, who before taking office had hoped for a large trained professional militia and a 'very strong Navy', now indicated his anxieties about Britain's international position; thenceforth he became less aggressive in demanding defence cuts and less confident about the wisdom of tax cuts.

Paradoxically, Lowe's indifference to giving offence and tendency to preach sermons on the merits of self-reliance and political economy encouraged in the public mind the view that he was a brutal cost-cutter of the Ayrton breed; in 1873 they were the subject, with Gladstone, of a memorable burlesque at the Court Theatre, *The Happy Land*, co-written by W. S. Gilbert. In particular, some of Lowe's policies damaged his reputation among working men already suspicious of his attitude towards them because of the reform debates. This was the effect, for example, of his attempt in 1871 to sell crown land in Epping Forest, depriving working-class voters of access to it; he gave way after an embarrassing defeat in the Commons. His worst mistake also came in 1871, when he needed to raise taxes in order to fund the extra defence spending. He planned to distribute the burden between the classes by increasing the succession duties and the income tax, and by putting a small stamp tax on each box of matches sold. This created fears of unemployment among match girls, many of whom marched on the Commons in protest; Lowe had to be conducted into the Palace of Westminster through the passage from the underground station. He had introduced the tax with a Latin tag, *Ex luce lucellum* ('Out of light, a little gain'); a *Punch* writer retorted with the couplet,

> Ex luce lucellum, we all of us know,
> But if Lucy can't sell 'em, what then, Mr. Lowe?

Characteristically Lowe thought this very funny; but the furore did him great damage. He was forced to withdraw his budget (largely, in fact, because of propertied objections to the increased succession duties, which the match tax drama allowed them to disguise), and never recovered his standing.

In 1873 Lowe's reputation was also worsened by financial irregularities at the Treasury involving the Post Office and the Zanzibar mail contract—a legacy of his excessive trust of his officials (this was partly explained by his appalling eyesight). These scandals made it possible and probably necessary for Gladstone to move him. He became home secretary in August 1873, and produced an important plan to revise legislation of trade unions, but the government was defeated at the general election in February 1874.

Final years, death, and reputation Lowe never held office again. For some time he played an active part on the opposition front bench, where his most important achievement was to amend the Conservative government's trade union legislation of 1875 so as to clarify the legality of peaceful picketing. This solved a major union grievance; Lowe justified it on the ground that the existing law discriminated against union members. He was also a fierce critic of the imperial policy and posturing of Disraeli—whom he disliked intensely. Disraeli's behaviour entrenched his view that democracies could not be trusted to conduct an aggressive foreign policy responsibly, and this led him to cause a pleasurable stir by asserting, in the *Fortnightly Review* in November 1877, that Britain's colonies brought her fewer benefits than costs. Eighteen months earlier he had unwisely implied in public that Queen Victoria had previously urged her prime ministers to make her empress of India, but that only Disraeli had been craven enough to agree; he was forced to retract.

Lowe expected to be offered a cabinet post on the formation of the Liberal government in 1880, but was not. Despite the queen's reluctance, Gladstone obtained a viscountcy for him; Lowe chose the title Sherbrooke, the name taken by his elder brother on inheriting their great-grandmother's estate. He refused a government pension in 1882 and was made GCB in 1885. His lack of sympathy for Irish grievances about religion and land, his defence of political economy, his distrust of politicians who gave way to populist sectional pressures, and his belief in the crucial significance of the Union for the international standing of Britain all made him a convinced Liberal Unionist in 1886. But he now took little part in politics. His plain-spoken, garrulous, eccentric wife, Georgiana, from whom he had unsuccessfully tried to separate in the late 1860s, suffered a stroke in 1882 which left her partially paralysed; he tended her until she died on 3 October 1884 after another seizure. On 3 February 1885 he married Caroline Anne Sneyd, daughter of Thomas Sneyd of Ashcombe Park, Staffordshire. His sight declined further and in the late 1880s failed completely, a condition which he tolerated with equanimity. After sustained weakness he died on 27 July 1892 at his home, Sherbrooke Lodge, Warlingham, Surrey, and was buried at Brookwood cemetery, Woking. He left no children.

Lowe saw himself as an outsider who had overcome inherited adversity by dint of hard work and intelligence. He accepted his lot without bitterness. Indeed, he had an enormous capacity for enjoying life. He was placid, cheerful, and blessed with great energy, a strong muscular body, and a lack of fear. He relished athletic sports—rowing, horse-riding, skating, and, as he aged, fast rides in carriages and tricycles down Surrey lanes. He was a bright, charming, and stimulating conversationalist with a clear, penetrating voice and a fine head and face, and a great taste for witty epigrams, dexterous repartee, and apt quotations. He was a popular and invigorating member of London intellectual society—an enthusiastic debater at the Political Economy Club, the Metaphysical Society, and the X-Club. He was a trustee of the British Museum and a fellow of the Royal Society. He sat on many royal commissions, especially in the 1860s. Though blunt and sceptical about human nature and incapable of suffering fools gladly, he was neither malicious nor pompous and was always true to himself; in that respect, he was a real Victorian gentleman. He did not disguise his principles in order to curry political favour; but nor was he as dogmatic as he sometimes appeared. In fact he delighted—too much for his own good—in questioning orthodoxies and fashions of the day. His real dislikes were bigotry, injustice, complacency, and inefficiency, especially in the upper classes and in religion (he had no time for London club life and preferred the company of ladies such as the countess of Derby, the countess of Airlie, and the duchess of St Albans, who also provided sympathy and relief from his trying wife). He was, as his niece remarked, a firm protestant. His motivating beliefs were in the need to strive for disinterested government and in the capacity of energetic, ambitious, and open-minded men like himself to offer it.

Jonathan Parry

Sources J. Winter, *Robert Lowe* (1976) · A. Patchett Martin, *Life and letters of the Right Honourable Robert Lowe, Viscount Sherbrooke*, 2 vols. (1893) · D. W. Sylvester, *Robert Lowe and education* (1974) · R. Lowe, *Speeches and letters on reform*, 2nd edn (1867) · R. Lowe, *Middle class and primary education: two speeches* (1868) · R. Knight, *Illiberal liberal: Robert Lowe in New South Wales, 1842–50* (1966) · R. Lambert, *Sir John Simon, 1816–1904, and English social administration* (1963) · M. Wright, *Treasury control of the civil service, 1854–74* (1969) · Gladstone, *Diaries* · *CGPLA Eng. & Wales* (1892)

Archives HLRO, corresp. and papers · News Int. RO, papers relating to *The Times* · priv. coll. | BL, corresp. with W. E. Gladstone, Lord Ripon, and others · Bodl. Oxf., letters to Lord Clarendon · Bodl. Oxf., letters to Lord Kimberley · Bodl. Oxf., letters to A. C. Tupp · CKS, corresp. with duke of Cleveland and duchess of Cleveland · Hunt. L., letters to Lord Aberdare · NRA, priv. coll., corresp. with duke of Argyll · PRO, corresp. with Lord Cardwell, PRO 30/48 · PRO, corresp. with Lord Granville, PRO 30/29

Likenesses Ape [C. Pellegrini], terracotta statuette, 1873, NPG · R. Lehmann, drawing, 1874, BM · G. F. Watts, oils, *c.*1874, NPG [*see illus.*] · E. Mortlock, oils, *c.*1878, Castle Museum, Nottingham · Ape [C. Pellegrini], chromolithograph caricature, NPG; repro. in *VF* (27 Feb 1869) · C. Baugniet, lithograph, BM · L. C. Dickinson, group portrait, oils (*Gladstone's cabinet of 1868*), NPG · Elliott & Fry, cartes-de-visite, NPG · H. Furniss, caricatures, pen-and-ink drawings, NPG · F. Holl, stipple (after G. Richmond), BM · John & Charles Watkins, photographs, NPG · Lock & Whitfield, woodburytype photograph, NPG; repro. in T. Cooper, *Men of mark: a gallery of contemporary portraits* (1878) · A. J. Melhuish, photographs, NPG · H. S. Mendelssohn, photograph, NPG · photogravure photograph, NPG · prints, NPG

Wealth at death £15,768 8*s.* 9*d.*: probate, 30 Sept 1892, *CGPLA Eng. & Wales*

Lowe, Roger (*d.* 1679), diarist and shopkeeper, was born in Leigh, Lancashire. His parents, of whom almost nothing is known, were both dead by 1663, leaving four children. He attended the grammar school in Leigh and then between 1657 and 1658 was in service with the vicar of Great Budworth, Cheshire. Subsequently apprenticed to Hammond, a Leigh mercer, he kept a general shop for his master at Ashton in Makerfield, near Wigan, from 1660, and from 1 January 1663 until 1669 (with occasional later entries) he also kept a diary. Since its first publication in the 1870s this rare survival has been a primary document in the history of social attitudes and popular presbyterianism in seventeenth-century England. Its wealth of incidental detail records a great variety of social interaction, centred on the alehouse as much as upon the religious meeting.

Roger Lowe was a busy member of Ashton's local society. He acted as a scribe and notary, being paid in ale as often as in cash. He dealt in a wide variety of commodities, from cloth and ribbon to scythes, candles, and currants, with only occasional visitations from his master and an annual reckoning that usually showed a decent profit. The credit he offered was an important lubricant in the local economy. The diary was a vehicle for his personal piety, and recorded devotional works read, sermons heard, religious meetings attended, and occasional encounters with local ministers, notably Adam Martindale. Lowe's presbyterianism did not prevent him from appreciating music, especially organs that had only recently been reinstated in churches after the interregnum.

Lowe remained as apprentice in sole charge of the Ashton shop until November 1665. He had been keen to gain his freedom, and was given it along with continued charge of the shop. He found trading on his own account difficult and by the spring of 1667 considered re-entering service. At the end of that September he left Ashton to serve Thomas Peake of Warrington, Lancashire, for three years; unhappy in this service and then ill, he returned to Ashton now a married man. The diary had recorded Lowe's somewhat erratic love life: he remarked on a succession of sweethearts and broken hearts. Finally, on 23 March 1668, Lowe was married to Emma, daughter of John Potter of Ashton, by Joseph Ward, the rector of Warrington, at a cousin's house. After that the diary entries are spasmodic, mainly consisting of obituary lists and funerals attended.

Lowe's own funeral occurred in the early months of 1679; he died intestate. A post-mortem inventory was taken on 22 April 1679. Half of its value (£29 3*s.* out of £60 6*s.* 4*d.*) was accounted for by goods in the shop, another £6 in debts he was owed. The diary, in private hands locally when first published in 1877, was his gift to posterity.

David Souden

Sources *The diary of Roger Lowe*, ed. W. L. Sachse (1938) • diary, Wigan Archives Service, Leigh, MS D/DZA58 • *The diary of Roger Lowe* (1877) • *The diary of Roger Lowe*, ed. [I. Winstanley] (1994) • R. Houlbrooke, ed., *English family life, 1576–1716: an anthology from diaries* (1988) • R. C. Latham, 'Roger Lowe, shopkeeper and nonconformist', *History*, new ser., 26 (1941–2), 19–35 • T. S. Willan, *The inland trade: studies in English internal trade in the sixteenth and seventeenth centuries* (1976)

Archives Wigan Archives Service, Leigh, diary

Wealth at death £60 6*s.* 4*d.*: post-mortem inventory (diocese of Chester), 5 May 1679 (administration), dated 22 April 1679, in *Diary*, ed. Sachse

Lowe, Thomas (*c.*1719–1783), singer and actor, was probably born in London. His singing career began when he was a child; a benefit was held for him on 27 March 1732, and on 2 May that year he sang in Handel's oratorio *Esther* at the King's Theatre.

Lowe was singing professionally as a tenor by 1740, when in August he took part in the performance of the masque *Alfred* at Cliveden, the Buckinghamshire residence of Frederick, prince of Wales. *Alfred*, written by James Thomson and David Mallet, with music by Thomas Arne, saw the first performance of 'Rule, Britannia'. Lowe's début at Drury Lane was on 11 September, when he appeared as Sir John Loverule in Charles Coffey's *The Devil to Pay* and introduced the popular song with which he was identified throughout his career, 'The Early Horn' by John Ernest Galliard. In the course of his first two seasons he played or sang a wide variety of roles, including Macheath (John Gay's *The Beggar's Opera*, 17 October 1740), songs in Arne's *Oedipus* (19 November), Bacchanal (Arne's *Comus*, 10 December), Amiens (with Arne's music, in *As You Like It*, 20 December), Arne's songs in *Twelfth Night* (15 January 1741), Welford (*The Blind Beggar of Bethnal Green*, by John Day, adapted by Robert Dodsley, 3 April), Lorenzo (*The Merchant of Venice*, 11 January 1742), and Marcus (in Joseph Addison's *Cato*, 4 March).

While Lowe passed the winters at Drury Lane, he spent summer 1741 in Bristol and summer 1742 in Dublin. In protest at Charles Fleetwood's management of Drury Lane he remained in Dublin during the 1742–3 season, not returning until December 1743. In summer 1744 he joined the Arnes at Smock Alley in Dublin. His greatest achievement there was to sing the lead in the first performance of Arne's *The Death of Abel*. He was again at Drury Lane for the 1744–5 season and, after a winter at Aungier Street Theatre in Dublin, he returned to Drury Lane for 1747–8.

The great tenor John Beard returned after five years' absence to supersede Lowe at Drury Lane, and Lowe migrated to Covent Garden, where he appeared on 26 September 1748 as Macheath. His Arviragus in *Cymbeline* (15 February 1749) and Colonel Bully in John Vanbrugh's *The Provoked Wife* (4 October 1752), appear to have been, with some small singing parts, the most notable impersonations which he added to his Drury Lane repertory. It was probably at some point during his Covent Garden period that he married his wife, Mary (*d.* 1770).

Beard moved to Covent Garden in 1759, and the two tenors shared roles for a season. When Beard moved to Covent Garden Lowe returned to Drury Lane, taking part, among other performances, in John Stanley's *The Tears and Triumphs of Parnassus* (first performed 17 November 1760), in Shakespeare's *Much Ado about Nothing* (as Balthazar), and in *The Tempest* (as Hymen). After summer 1763 his connection with the great theatres ceased.

During his career in the patent houses Lowe was associated with several roles, but most particularly with musical comedy and with 'speciality' songs introduced to vary otherwise non-musical pieces. He was also a member of Handel's oratorio company between 1742 and 1760, most often taking secondary roles. Prominent among his performances were Zadok in *Solomon* (1749) and Septimus in *Theodora* (1760). Lowe was a member of the Madrigal Society between 1741 and 1751, and he sang at a number of public gardens. By 1750 he was regularly to be seen at Vauxhall, and in August of that year he made his first appearance at Marylebone, with which he remained associated for twenty-five years.

For five years, beginning in 1763, Lowe was lessee and manager of Marylebone Gardens, succeeding John Trusler. 'The orchestra', wrote J. T. Smith:

> before which I have listened with my grandmother to hear Tommy Lowe sing, stood upon the site of the house now (1828) No. 17 Devonshire Place, and … nearly opposite to the old church still standing in High Street. (J. T. Smith, *Nollekens and his Times*, 2 vols., 1829, 1.33)

The elder Stephen Storace and Dr Arnold supported the enterprise, and the first season was prosperous; but in spite of Miss Catley's singing, Miss Trusler's plum puddings, and the rousing choruses (by the audience) to Lowe's 'Fellowcraft' and other songs, Lowe was ruined in 1767, following an exceptionally wet summer. He assigned all receipts to his creditors in 1768, and sold the gardens in

1769. Thenceforward his efforts to gain a livelihood met with scanty success. After holding an engagement at Finch's Grotto Gardens and managing the wells at Ottersley Pool, near Watford (1770), where his wife died, he was engaged by Tom King, on his purchase of Sadler's Wells, to sing there from 20 April 1772. He retained this engagement until his death, on 1 March 1783, in his lodgings in Aldersgate Street.

Lowe's voice was said by Dibdin to be more even and mellow than that of Beard, 'and in love songs, when little more than mere utterance was necessary, he might be said to have exceeded him. … Lowe lost himself beyond the namby-pamby poetry of Vauxhall; Beard was at home everywhere' (C. Dibdin, *A Complete History of the English Stage*, 5 vols., 1800, 5.364).

Burney concurred that Lowe's talents suffered from his lack of education: 'he could never be safely trusted with any thing better than a ballad, which he constantly learned by ear' (Highfill, Burnim & Langhans, *BDA*, 9.374). However, he was popular with audiences, particularly as 'huntsmen, naval officers, rustics both realistic and classically pastoral' (ibid.). Portraits of Lowe were published with many songs, several engraved by George Bickham, and often showing him with his 'early horn' of the song.

Lowe's son Halifax Lowe, who was said to resemble his father in voice and manner, made his first appearance as a singer at Sadler's Wells on 15 April 1784. He died in 1790.

L. M. MIDDLETON, *rev.* MATTHEW KILBURN

Sources Highfill, Burnim & Langhans, *BDA* • W. Dean, 'Lowe, Thomas', *New Grove* • M. Sands, *The eighteenth-century pleasure gardens of Marylebone, 1737–1777* (1987) • *London Daily Post and General Advertiser* (1740–63) • M. Kelly, *Reminiscences*, 1 (1826), 96 • *GM*, 1st ser., 53 (1783), 272 • *GM*, 1st ser., 60 (1790), 980 • *European Magazine and London Review* (1790), 319 • *London Magazine*, 52 (1783), 146 • Burney, *Hist. mus.*, 4.447, 663, 667 • T. Oliphant, *A brief account of the Madrigal Society* (1835) • R. Percival's collection relating to Sadler's Wells Theatre, BL, Crach. 1.4.b & 5.b

Likenesses J. Macardell, mezzotint, pubd 1752 (after R. E. Pine), BM • J. Bew, engraving, 1778 (after unknown artist), Harvard U.; repro. in *Vocal Magazine* • R. E. Pine, line engraving, pubd 1778 (after engraving by unknown artist), BM • line engraving, pubd 1778, BM • R. E. Pine, painting, Folger • portrait, Harvard U.

Lowenfeld, Margaret Frances Jane (1890–1973), child psychiatrist and child psychotherapist, was born on 4 February 1890 in Lowndes Square, London, the younger of the two daughters of Henry (born Heinz) Lowenfeld (1859–1931), a businessman and property owner of Polish Jewish origin, and Alice Evens (*c.*1863–1930), daughter of a Welsh naval captain from a nonconformist background. Margaret's elder sister, Helena, became well known as Helena *Wright (1887–1982), gynaecologist and a pioneer of birth control. Both daughters were brought up in the Church of England and as British citizens. However, Poland exerted a strong influence. Their father was the third son in a landowning and mining family from Chrzanow, near Cracow, in what was then the Austrian part of Poland. He came to Britain in the early 1880s and was rapidly successful financially, eventually owning several hotels and theatres. This allowed him to take over the ownership of the Polish estate. His daughters regularly accompanied him on trips to Poland.

Lowenfeld's education was, in many respects, liberal. She attended kindergarten at the Froebel Educational Institution in Talgarth Road, London, the first Froebel school in England. From eight years old she was a pupil at the Church of England High School for Girls, Graham Street, London, before joining her sister, in 1902, at Cheltenham Ladies' College. However, despite cultural and educational opportunity Lowenfeld's childhood was not entirely happy. Her mother enjoyed the lifestyle provided by her husband's success and was well known as a society hostess. But differences in the parents' temperaments and background finally led to a particularly complex divorce in 1902. Margaret was deeply affected by the divorce. As a child she had often been ill. In her teens she was under great emotional strain. She was sustained particularly by her active involvement in the Student Christian Movement and by her growing interest in science.

In 1912 Lowenfeld entered the London School of Medicine for Women, following her sister, Helena. She passed her intermediate MB examination shortly before the outbreak of the First World War. By 1918 she had obtained the minimum qualifications entitling her to practise. However, before taking the examination for the MB BS a request from the family village in Poland led her to join a League of Friends typhus mission. The Polish-Russian War was still continuing and epidemics of influenza, cholera, and typhus ravaged much of Europe. Entering Poland in 1919 Lowenfeld witnessed extreme examples of distress and survival in children and adults which made her particularly interested in what promoted resilience in mental health and on relations between psyche and soma. Later, difficulties in conveying the horror of what she observed convinced her of limitations in the capacity of verbal language for conveying emotional experience.

On returning to London in 1921 Lowenfeld spent a period as an in-patient at Bowden House Nursing Home, London, under the care of Wilfred Trotter, a well-known advocate of psychodynamic psychology, gaining public recognition for its success in treating shell-shock victims. Lowenfeld continued her career by becoming a research student at the Mothercraft Training Centre dedicated to promoting infant health according to methods advocated by Truby King, before contributing to two major research projects, on infant feeding and on rheumatism in childhood. In 1928 she established the Clinic for Nervous and Difficult Children, a community based drop-in centre at 12 Telford Road, London. In the same year, on rather different lines, the Child Guidance Council was established in Britain. The Paediatric Association was also started, with Lowenfeld as a founder member.

The success of the clinic led to several changes of premises. Moving to Warwick Avenue in 1931 it acquired the name Institute of Child Psychology (ICP). By 1935 annual attendance had risen to over thirteen hundred. Lowenfeld's historical survey and observational research had led to the publication of *Play in Childhood* (1935), and the first child psychotherapy training was established. In

1937 she gave her paper ‘A thesis concerning the fundamental structure of the mento-emotional processes in children’ to the general section of the British Psychological Society. This outlined her views on the primacy of an integrative mental function, simultaneously cognitive and affective, which functioned in infancy, and which required non-verbal means for its expression. She later called this the proto system. The work was partly influenced by her close friendship with the philosopher R. G. Collingwood, whose *Essay on Philosophical Method* (1933) had recently been published. The work was well received. But within the year Lowenfeld was strongly criticized by psychoanalysts present at her reading of ‘The world pictures of children’ given to the general section of the British Psychological Society. Though personally devastated by the criticism, her enthusiasm was encouraged by a further move of the institute to new premises at 6 Pembridge Villas, on 23 June 1938.

Unfortunately, the Second World War broke out within fifteen months. The clinic was evacuated to Berkhamsted, Hertfordshire, under the name of the Children's Clinic. During the war, though suffering mentally and physically, Lowenfeld continued to generate new ideas. After the war the formation of the National Health Service in 1948 introduced further complications. The clinic changed its status from a friendly society to a non-profit making limited company taking children from poorer families via a special arrangement with the North West Regional Health Authority. The ICP functioned side by side with the child guidance clinics which increased numerically immediately after the war. Along with other child psychotherapy trainings recently established, regulation of the ICP training came under the auspices of the new professional body, the Association of Child Psychotherapists. Unfortunately, in 1978 with the recession the health authority withdrew its financial support, affecting a large proportion of clients. The ICP was forced to close. The training was discontinued more or less simultaneously five years after Margaret Lowenfeld's death.

After the war Lowenfeld's friendship with the anthropologist Margaret Mead, whom she met in London at the World Federation of Mental Health Conference in 1948, was particularly important in fuelling a growing interest in using Lowenfeld's mosaics in cross-cultural work. Mead also encouraged Lowenfeld's interest in educational research, culminating in the kaleidoblocs and poleidoblocs tests used in psychological assessment and to enable children to discover mathematical concepts. The latter, in particular, continued to be used for many years.

In the late 1960s Lowenfeld spent less time at the ICP, focusing on writing on private work with adults. She lived alternately at her Harley Street flat and at East Wing, a house in Cholesbury, Buckinghamshire, which she had bought on the death of her mother. She was supported by her close friend and living companion, Ville Andersen, a Danish citizen who had trained at the ICP in the 1950s.

Lowenfeld published some nine medical research papers, about twenty-three papers on psychological work, many popular papers, and three books: in addition to *Play in Childhood* there was *The Lowenfeld Mosaic Test* (1955), and *The World Technique* (1979), published posthumously. She is particularly well known for the world technique in which in the course of non-directive psychotherapy the patient uses a sand tray and model figures to create an imaginary world.

Always a person of firm ideas, in her last years Lowenfeld suffered increasingly from confusion and alteration of mood. After going into a coma she died in the Hospital of St John and St Elizabeth, near her sister's flat in St John's Wood, London, on 2 February 1973. She was buried at the church of St Lawrence, Cholesbury, Buckinghamshire. After a brief career in medical research Lowenfeld became a crucial figure in establishing child psychotherapy in Britain as the importance of mental health reached public awareness after the First World War.

CATHY URWIN

Sources C. Urwin and J. Hood-Williams, eds., *Child psychotherapy, war and the normal child* (1988) • B. Evans, *Freedom to choose: the life and work of Helena Wright, pioneer of contraception* (1984) • H. V. Dicks, *Fifty years of the Tavistock Clinic* (1970) • M. Davis, ‘Play and symbolism in Lowenfeld and Winnicott’, *Free Associations*, 2, 3/23 (1991), 395–421 • U. Cam., Centre for Family Research, M. Lowenfeld archive • d. cert. • *CGPLA Eng. & Wales* (1973)

Archives U. Cam., Centre for Family Research, papers

Wealth at death £27,097: probate, 9 May 1973, *CGPLA Eng. & Wales*

Lower, Mark Antony (1813–1876), antiquary, was born on 14 July 1813 at Chiddingly, Sussex, the fourth of seven surviving children of Richard *Lower (1782–1865), schoolmaster, and his wife, Mary Oxley (*b.* 1780), daughter of William Oxley of Heathfield, Sussex. He was educated by his father. In 1830 he briefly assisted his sister at her school at East Hoathly, before establishing a school for himself at Cade Street, Heathfield, and then a larger one at Alfriston, Sussex, in 1832. There, in conjunction with John Dudeney, he also founded a mechanics' institution. He moved to Lewes about 1835, and conducted his school there initially in an old chapel. On 8 January 1838 he married, at Bromley, Kent, his first wife, Mercy Holman (1813–1867), daughter of William Holman of Bentley in Framfield, Sussex; they had four sons and five daughters. After several moves within Lewes, the school settled at St Anne's House in the High Street about 1853 and was restricted to boarders. He served as one of the headboroughs of Lewes in 1860–61, but held no other significant public office.

As early as 1831 Lower had printed *Sussex*, a guidebook, parish by parish, for which he found 250 subscribers. His next publication, *English Surnames* (1842), went through four editions and, with *Patronymica Britannica, a Dictionary of the Family Names of the United Kingdom* (1860), was the work by which he was most widely known. But the majority of his writing was related to Sussex. He was one of the prime movers in the foundation of the Sussex Archaeological Society in 1846 and conducted much of its routine business in the early years under the supervision of W. H. Blaauw (1793–1870), the first secretary. At an annual salary of £50 he served as the society's editor and corresponding secretary in 1865–70, but his overspending brought him into conflict with the committee. All but one of the first twenty-six volumes of the society's *Collections* (1848–75) contain at least one article by him, and some as many as five, as well as short notes. His translation called *The Chronicle of Battel Abbey* appeared in 1851. Two encyclopaedic works were *The Worthies of Sussex* (1865), giving biographical sketches, and *A Compendious History of Sussex* (2 vols., 1870), greatly enlarging his 1831 book. His evangelical, low-church beliefs and radical political opinions were reflected in his historical writings, for instance *The Sussex Martyrs* (1851)—which inaugurated a cult that survived well into the next century—and his lectures to the mechanics' institute on the Bayeux tapestry.

Lower was active in the British Archaeological Association from 1844. In 1852 he was elected a fellow of the Society of Antiquaries, for which he acted as local secretary. His honorary MA degree was awarded by a college in Connecticut, USA, about 1846.

The large amount of time which Lower devoted to archaeology and literature interfered with his profession, and the loss of his wife on 31 May 1867, as well as his own failing health, precipitated his giving up the school in that year and moving to nearby Seaford, where he continued to take only a few French boys. A local subscription raised about £400 as a mark of appreciation for his services to the history of Sussex. On 4 May 1870 he married his second wife, Sarah (*bap.* 1813, *d.* 1875), daughter of Henry Scrase and his wife, Sarah, and from 1871 he lived in Peckham, London. A trip to Denmark and Sweden in search of health in 1873 brought no benefit. After his wife's death in 1875, he lived with his youngest daughter at 4 Percival Villas, Sydney Road, Enfield, Middlesex, where he died on 22 March 1876. He was buried in St Anne's churchyard, Lewes.

Lower was a large man with, in middle age, a full beard. In a small county town he cut a flamboyant figure, and his enthusiasms may have outrun his judgement.

JOHN H. FARRANT

Sources H. Campkin, 'The late William Durrant Cooper … and the late Mark Antony Lower', *Sussex Archaeological Collections*, 27 (1877), 117–51 [incl. list of pubns] • L. F. Salzman, 'The history of the Sussex Archaeological Society', *Sussex Archaeological Collections*, 85 (1946), 1–76 • m. cert. • *DNB* • M. A. Lower, 'An historical sketch of the family of Lower', 1835 • Sussex Archaeological Society Library, Lower papers, MSS • MS pedigree by W. S. Ellis, *c.*1840, Sussex Archaeological Society Library • register transcript, Heathfield Independent Chapel, E. Sussex RO; parish register, Lewes, St Anne's, E. Sussex RO • A. S. Gratwick and C. Whittick, 'The Losely list of "Sussex martyrs"', *Sussex Archaeological Collections*, 133 (1995), 225–6 • J. H. Farrant, 'John Collingwood Bruce and the Bayeux tapestry', *Archaeologia Aeliana*, 5th ser., 25 (1997), 110–12

Archives S. Antiquaries, Lond., drawings and papers relating to excavations at Pevensey • Sussex Archaeological Society, Lewes, notebooks, sketchbooks, and letters on genealogy and heraldry | Bodl. Oxf., letters to Sir Thomas Phillipps

Likenesses Dalziel, woodcut (after H. Weir), BM • portrait, oils, Sussex Archaeological Society, Lewes; repro. in Salzman, 'History of the Sussex Archaeological Society'

Wealth at death under £600: probate, 21 April 1876, *CGPLA Eng. & Wales*

Lower, Richard (1631–1691), physician and physiologist, was born at Tremeer House, near Bodmin, Cornwall, the son of Humphry or Humfry Lower (*bap.* 1597, *d.* 1683) and Margery Billing (*d.* 1686). He was baptized at St Tudy's, Cornwall, on 29 January 1632. A prominent and affluent Cornish family, the Lower clan included Sir William Lower, a poet and dramatist. Richard's younger brother, Thomas *Lower, was also a physician, whose religious beliefs led to his imprisonment with George Fox, the Quaker leader.

Lower's early education was at Westminster School under the tutelage of Richard Busby. In 1649 he received a studentship to Christ Church, Oxford, and matriculated on 27 February 1651. He graduated BA on 17 February 1653, proceeding MA in June 1655, and BM and MD on 28 June 1665. While at Oxford, Lower was praelector in Greek (1656–7) and censor in natural philosophy (1657–60), and by 1659 he had established an active medical practice there. During his Oxford years he secured his reputation as a skilled medical scientist, particularly through his work with Thomas Willis, Sedleian professor of natural philosophy. For much of his period at Oxford, Lower worked as research assistant to Willis, a collaboration that yielded numerous important neuroanatomical and physiological advances. Lower also studied chemistry under Peter Stahl. Following in the experimental traditions of William Harvey, Lower and Willis were part of an extraordinary scientific circle at Oxford that, during the 1650s and 1660s, included Robert Boyle, Christopher Wren, and John Mayow. From this background Lower emerged as one of the most talented and important medical researchers in the history of physiology and anatomy, a position derived from his insistence on careful experimentation and direct observation. Lower relied heavily on vivisection of animals to study physiological questions, and his publications were characterized by a terse, clear writing style. Lower continued his association with Oxford until 1666, when, following Willis, he relocated to London to establish a medical practice. On 17 November 1666 Richard married Elizabeth (*d.* 1704), daughter of John Billing of Hengar, and widow of Samuel Trelawny.

Lower maintained his research activities for several years after arriving in London, primarily through his involvement with the Royal Society, whose meetings he attended as early as 1666. In May 1667 Boyle formally introduced Lower to the society, and on 17 October of that year Lower was elected a fellow. In November 1667 the society offered him the position of curator, but he declined the appointment. Many of Lower's most important medical contributions were presented at the Royal Society, but in less than two years after becoming a member, his participation in the society declined notably. He ceased regular attendance by March 1669 and resigned his fellowship in 1678. As his research activities waned, Lower devoted himself increasingly to clinical medicine, where he soon established a prominent and lucrative practice in London. Lower lived initially at Hatton Garden, but as his practice thrived, he relocated to increasingly fashionable addresses, including Salisbury Court near Fleet Street,

Bow Street, and finally to King Street near Covent Garden. On 22 December 1671 he was a candidate for the College of Physicians, where he became a fellow on 29 July 1675. His practice eventually involved royal appointments, and he became increasingly active in the political intrigues of the times. Following the death of Thomas Willis in 1675, Lower was appointed royal physician. At that time Anthony Wood noted that Lower was 'esteemed the most noted physician in Westminster and London, and no man's name was more cried up at court than his' (Wood, *Ath. Oxon.*, new edn, 1813–20, 4.297). Eventually, however, Lower's strongly held political opinions adversely affected his medical career, as his protestant religious beliefs and close affiliation with the whig party led to his loss of court appointments and a considerable decline in his reputation and practice. Lower actively opposed the policies of James II, who once remarked that he 'did him more mischief than a troop of horse' (Gunther, p. xxv), although Lower seems to have spent much of his time in Cornwall while James was in power. Following the revolution of 1688, Lower was again involved with the court, providing advice to the crown regarding medical services for the navy.

Lower's reputation in neuroanatomy derives principally from his collaborative research with Thomas Willis, whose *Cerebri anatome* (1664) was a major landmark in descriptive anatomy of the central and the autonomic nervous systems. Willis and Lower had begun their research as early as 1658 and by January 1661 were actively involved in dissection studies with the intent of publishing a book summarizing their studies. Their research continued until summer 1663, with Christopher Wren providing the illustrations for the text. The *Cerebri anatome* contained the first functional account of the cerebral blood circulation and provided a detailed description of the basal ganglia, medulla, cerebellum, and ten of the twelve cranial nerves, as well as an account of the vagus nerve and sympathetic nervous system. Although several of Lower's contemporaries claimed that he deserved more credit than Willis for the book, it appears that Willis was responsible for the organization and interpretation of their studies, while Lower performed most of the exacting dissections. In the preface to *Cerebri anatome*, Willis praised Lower as 'an anatomist of supreme skill' whose 'most skillful dissecting hand' and 'indefatigable Industry, and unwearied Labour' had provided Willis with the data needed to describe the 'structure and function of bodies, whose secrets were previously concealed'. The following year Lower published his first book, *Diatribae Thomae Willissi de febribus vindicatio* (1665), which aggressively defended concepts earlier proposed by Willis in *Diatribae duae medico-philosophicae* (1658–9). Although Lower subsequently changed the views he expressed in the *Diatribae* concerning pulmonary circulation, the book indicates his interest in questions of cardiorespiratory function that would later be addressed in his *Tractatus de corde*. The *Tractatus* contained the results of Lower's extensive physiological research and a summary of his pioneering work in blood transfusion.

Lower is generally credited with being the first to perform successful blood transfusions, despite some lingering uncertainty over priority. Lower's transfusion studies were a logical continuation of work at Oxford by Christopher Wren and Robert Boyle, who, as early as 1656, were using quills and special bladders to inject medications and other fluids into the bloodstream of dogs. By January 1661 Lower mentioned to Boyle an interest in trying to infuse broth into the veins of dogs; and by June 1664, Lower wrote to Boyle concerning plans to experiment on blood transfusion between dogs. Because blood coagulates rapidly after removal from the circulation, prior attempts to transfuse had met with questionable or no success. Lower decided to try direct transfusion from arterial to venous circulation in hopes that clotting could be avoided by minimizing the time that the blood was outside the vascular system. In late February 1665 at Oxford, Lower successfully performed the first direct blood transfusion, involving the transfer of blood from the carotid artery of one live dog into the jugular vein of another. The experiment demonstrated that blood transfusion was possible and that the technique was effective in reviving an animal that would otherwise have died from severe blood loss. A report of the event was conveyed to the Royal Society by September 1666, and Lower's work quickly became the subject of widespread interest and discussion. In November 1666 the dog transfusion experiments were repeated before the Royal Society at Gresham College, London. Accounts of Lower's transfusions were published in November and December of that year in the *Philosophical Transactions* (vol. 1, pp. 252, 353–8). Meanwhile, Jean-Baptiste Denis, professor of philosophy and mathematics in Paris, had learned of Lower's work as early as 1665, transfused blood between calves and dogs, and published the results in the *Journal des Scavans* in March and April 1667 (pp. 69–72, 96). Subsequently, in June 1667, Denis performed the first adequately documented blood transfusions involving human subjects, using sheep blood infused into two volunteers. Denis sent a letter to the Royal Society describing the experiments, which was printed in the *Philosophical Transactions* (no. 27, 22 July 1667, pp. 489–504). Denis did not provide any details of the technical methods, and his claim of French priority for the concept of transfusion provoked Henry Oldenburg, secretary of the Royal Society, to suppress the volume and to replace it with his own version of number 27. In response to the experiments that Denis had reported from France, Lower and an associate, Dr Edmund King, successfully transfused sheep blood into a volunteer, Arthur Coga of Cambridge, on 23 November 1667. By the late 1670s, ensuing events in both countries resulted in a ban on transfusions, which effectively prevented clinical research on the subject until the early 1800s.

Lower's investigations in cardiopulmonary physiology and blood transfusion were summarized in his major work, the *Tractatus de corde*, containing in its five chapters a succinct exposition of his most important discoveries. The first three chapters reviewed his work on the comparative anatomy and functional physiology of the heart, blood vessels, and lungs. Chapter four contained the results of his experiments in blood transfusion, and chapter five described his concepts on chyle and its transformation into blood. Lower intended to extend the work of William Harvey by addressing questions raised by Harvey that had not yet been resolved. While at Oxford in 1658, Lower and Willis attempted to discover the cause for the commonly recognized difference in colour between venous and arterial blood. Willis in his *Diatribae duae medico-philosophicae* proposed that the vivid colour of arterial blood was due to its having become lighter as it 'effervesced' out of the left ventricle. At the time it was generally believed that movement of blood in the circulation was due to this spontaneous effervescence rather than to any mechanical pumping by the heart. Although Lower initially accepted this concept, his extensive comparative anatomy studies of the heart and a series of elegant experiments led him to conclusions that differed quite dramatically from traditional notions. In October 1667 Lower began collaborative work with Robert Hooke using vivisection studies on dogs, which demonstrated that the colour change in blood occurred during its passage through the lungs and that 'penetration of particles of air into the blood' were responsible for this alteration. Lower further concluded that the heart was a muscle, whose structure and function were designed to propel blood through the circulation by contractile and expulsive movements. His investigations in comparative anatomy delineated the muscular nature of the heart and its nerve supply in man and other vertebrates. Lower also measured the velocity of blood movements through the circulation and attempted to calculate cardiac output.

The *Tractatus* gained rapid acceptance as an important work in cardiopulmonary physiology. In his *De sanguinis accensione* (1670) Willis subsequently abandoned his earlier concepts about the roles of the heart and lungs and embraced Lower's findings and conclusions, and John Mayow revealed his debt to the book in his own *Tractatus quinque* (1674). The *Tractatus de corde* was translated into English and French, and sixteen editions were published, continuing its recognition well into the mid-eighteenth century as an important scientific study.

Subsequent works by Lower included *Dissertatio de origine catarrhi* (1670), which summarized experiments he had conducted with Willis to demonstrate that nasal secretions were not due to the discharge of fluid from cerebral ventricles through the palate, a concept that had been widely held at the time. Other publications attributed to Lower include *Bromographia* (1669) and *Receipts, or Dr Lower's and Several other Eminent Physicians Receipts* (1700).

Lower contracted a fever after attempting to extinguish a chimney fire at his home in King Street, and died, probably from pneumonia, on 17 January 1691. His body was returned to Cornwall and interred at the church of St Tudy on 3 February. He was survived by his wife and two daughters, Loveday and Philippa, neither of whom married. Lower remains best known for his seminal contributions to neuroanatomy, cardiopulmonary physiology, and blood transfusion. MARCUS B. SIMPSON JUN.

Sources R. G. Frank, *Harvey and the Oxford physiologists* (1980) • R. Lower, *Tractatus de corde* (1669) • E. C. Hoff and P. M. Hoff, 'The life and times of Richard Lower', *Bulletin of the Institute of the History of Medicine*, 4 (1936), 517–35 • A. D. Farr, 'The first human blood transfusion', *Medical History*, 24 (1980), 143–62 • R. Lower, *De corde: London, 1669*, ed. R. T. Gunther, trans. K. J. Franklin (1932) • J. F. Fulton, *A bibliography of two Oxford physiologists: Richard Lower, John Mayow* (1936) • Wood, *Ath. Oxon.*, new edn • Foster, *Alum. Oxon.* • H. E. Hoff and R. Guillemin, 'The first experiments on transfusion in France', *Journal of the History of Medicine and Allied Sciences*, 18 (1963), 103–24 • T. Willis, *Cerebri anatome* (1664) • H. Isler, *Thomas Willis, 1621–1675: doctor and scientist* (1968) • H. Brown, 'Jean Denis and transfusion of blood, Paris, 1667–1668', *Isis*, 39 (1948), 15–29 • *IGI*

Likenesses portrait, AM Oxf., Sutherland collection; repro. in W. Feindel, ed., *Thomas Willis: the anatomy of the brain and the nerves* (1978), 8 • portrait, AM Oxf., Hope collection; repro. in J. T. Hughes, *Thomas Willis, 1621–1675* (1991), 43

Lower, Richard (1782–1865), poet, was born at Alfriston, Sussex, on 19 September 1782, the son of John Lower, bargeman, and his wife, Sarah. His father owned the barge the *Good Intent*, and was the first person to navigate the little River Cuckmere from the sea to Longbridge. Richard Lower was physically too weak to adopt his father's calling; having received a fair education, he opened a school about 1803 in the parish of Chiddingly, where he resided until within a few months of his death. He also carried on the business of land surveyor.

From the time of his childhood Lower was addicted to rhyming, much to his mother's displeasure. His best-known production is *Tom Cladpole's jurney to Lunnon, told by himself, and written in pure Sussex doggerel by his Uncle Tim*, printed in 1830 as a sixpenny pamphlet and reprinted at least twice. Of this upwards of twenty thousand copies were sold, chiefly among the cottagers in east Sussex, who, however, resented Lower's sarcasms at their expense. It was followed in 1844 by *Jan Cladpole's trip to Merricur, written all in rhyme by his father, Tim Cladpole*, which expressed the author's anti-slavery sentiments.

Lower married Mary Oxley (*b.* 1780) on 9 April 1803, and he died at the residence of their third son, Joseph Richard Lower, surveyor, at Swan Lane, Tonbridge, Kent, on 30 September 1865. His second son, Mark Antony *Lower FSA (1813–1876), wrote several antiquarian works. His eldest daughter, Mrs Quaife, was well known as a nurse in America in the Federal army.

G. C. BOASE, *rev.* MEGAN A. STEPHAN

Sources *GM*, 3rd ser., 19 (1865), 792 • *IGI* • Boase, *Mod. Eng. biog.* • d. cert. • M. A. Lower, *An historical sketch of the family of Lower* (1835)

Archives Sussex Archaeological Society library, Lower papers

Lower, Thomas (*bap.* 1633, *d.* 1720), Quaker activist and physician, was baptized at St Tudy, Cornwall, on 11 August 1633. He was the son of Humfry Lower of Tremeer, St Tudy (*bap.* 1597, *d.* 1683), and his wife, Margery Billing (*d.* 1686). Thomas received a good education and was elected scholar of Winchester College in 1646.

Lower was living with his aunt Loveday Hambly at Tregangreeves, St Austell, Cornwall, in 1656, at the time that George Fox was thrown in Launceston gaol. Lower visited him there and offered him money. This was declined, but when he was released on 13 September 1656 Fox held a meeting at Tregangreeves and Lower became a convert to

Quakerism around this time. Although Lower qualified as a physician (like his elder brother the physiologist Richard *Lower) and apparently practised in London, he seems to have spent most of his time in promoting the movement's growth.

Lower's first wife was Elizabeth Trelawny (*bap.* 1617, *d. c.*1662), who died childless. On 26 October 1668 he married at Swarthmoor Hall, near Ulverston, Mary Fell (1643/4–1719), fifth daughter of Judge Thomas *Fell and his wife, Margaret *Fell, and stepdaughter of George Fox. They had ten children, nine daughters and one son, Richard (1682–1705), but it would appear that five of them died in infancy. Lower's wife and children lived at Swarthmoor Hall until 1676, when Lower purchased the estate of Marsh Grange in Furness from the Fells. There Fox sometimes came to stay with the family and dictated letters to his son-in-law.

In 1673 Fox and Lower were arrested for holding meetings at Armscott, Worcestershire, and taken to Worcester gaol, where they remained for more than a year. A letter which would have secured Lower's release was obtained through the interest of his brother Richard, but as it did not mention Fox, Lower chose to stay in prison with Fox. In 1675, or perhaps earlier in 1674, Fox began dictating his autobiography to Lower. In 1683 Lower went into Cornwall to transact some private business, and after holding a religious meeting at Tregangreeves was arrested and sentenced to imprisonment. His name is first on a petition of Quakers from Launceston gaol dated 1 August 1683 which was presented to Sir Job Charlton, the assize judge, but despite occasional periods of liberty he remained a prisoner until released by royal proclamation in 1686. In 1687 he received Fox's instructions respecting the disposal disposition of his property. Under Fox's will Lower received legacies of books, dials, and other property, and it was added that he could assist in compiling an account of the travels and sufferings of the Friends.

About 1693 Lower moved to London, probably living in Hammersmith, practised as a physician, and became involved in the activities of the Friends in the capital. In 1695, for example, he was a signatory to a petition of Quakers to parliament, the aim of which was to try and ease Friends' sufferings for refusing to swear oaths. He was also chosen, along with George Whitehead and Daniel Quare, to present an account of Quaker sufferings to William III on behalf of imprisoned Friends. Not a prolific writer, he wrote a few tracts around this time which were largely defences of Quakerism, for example, *An Answer to Francis Bugg's Presumptious Impeachment … Against the Quakers' Yearly Meeting* (1695) and *A Modest Vindication of the People called Quakers* [n.d., 1701?]. In 1696, perhaps in recognition of his work as a doctor, Lower was among those to whom Daniel Phillips dedicated his treatise on smallpox upon commencing as doctor of physic at Leiden.

At an unknown date Lower provided the Quaker burial-ground at Tregangreeves, Cornwall, and in 1715 he purchased some of the American property which had belonged to Fox. In 1719 Mary Lower died, aged seventy-five. Thomas died on 5 May the following year, aged eighty-eight, and was buried at Bunhill Fields on 9 May 1720.

CAROLINE L. LEACHMAN

Sources M. Webb, *The Fells of Swarthmoor Hall*, 2nd edn (1884) • A. C. Bickley, *George Fox and the early Quakers* (1884) • L. V. Hodgkin, *A Quaker saint of Cornwall: Loveday Hambly and her guests* (1927) • I. Ross, *Margaret Fell: mother of Quakerism*, 2nd edn (1984) • J. Besse, *A collection of the sufferings of the people called Quakers*, 2 vols. (1753) • Boase & Courtney, *Bibl. Corn.*, vol. 1 • J. Morgan, *Phoenix Britannicus* (1732) • H. L. Ingle, *First among Friends: George Fox and the creation of Quakerism* (1994) • W. Sewel, *The history of the rise, increase and progress of the Christian people called Quakers*, 6th edn, 1 (1834) • digest registers of births, marriages, and burials, RS Friends, Lond.

Archives RS Friends, Lond., Abraham MSS, 17 (MS vol. 364) • RS Friends, Lond., Spence MSS vol. III (MS vol. 378)

Lower, Sir William (*c.*1570–1615), politician and natural philosopher, was the eldest of the six sons of Thomas Lower and his wife, Jane, *née* Reskimer, minor Cornish gentry of St Winnow, near Lostwithiel. His father 'thrust forth his sonnes to be trayned in martiall knowledge and exercise for the publike service of the country' (MacLean, 3.378). In 1586 Lower matriculated at Exeter College, Oxford, where he maintained a connection at least until 1593. In 1589 he entered the Middle Temple, where he was penalized on several occasions for riotous behaviour. He became member of parliament in 1601 for Bodmin, and in 1604 was returned—for seven years—as member for Lostwithiel. The same year he and his brothers Nicholas and Francis were knighted by James I. Lower married Penelope, the daughter of Sir Thomas Perrott and stepdaughter of Henry Percy, ninth earl of Northumberland, at some unknown date, most likely following his move to London in 1601 since Penelope, apparently, was only twenty-five when Lower died in 1615. His marriage brought him about 3000 acres in Carmarthenshire, with a home farm in Tra'venti, near Laugharne. Percy and Walter Ralegh—who was a friend of Thomas Perrott's—were both patrons of the mathematician and natural philosopher Thomas Harriot. It was most likely through these connections that Lower and Harriot became acquainted and that Lower began to study astronomy, mathematics, and alchemy under Harriot's tutelage.

Nine letters survive from Lower to Harriot, spanning the period 1607–11. They reveal that Lower studied advanced algebra, geometry, and trigonometry, read Kepler in Latin and repeated many of Kepler's calculations, used a telescope in 1610 to observe the heavens, made a celestial sphere from 'the desolution of a hogshead' and discussed these matters with Harriot as well as with other 'Traventane philosophers' (*Miscellaneous Works*, 25–6, 28, 42–5). In a letter to Harriot, Lower has left a record of the cross-staff observations which he made of the comet of 1607, later known as Halley's comet. His suggestion in 1610 to Harriot that Kepler's elliptical orbits for the planets might also apply to comets may be the earliest surviving record of what is now the accepted theory of comet orbits.

Lower's presence with Northumberland at a dinner on 4 November 1605, the eve of the Gunpowder Plot, led to his interrogation concerning the conversation at dinner. His association with the disgraced Ralegh and Percy, and with Harriot, who was under suspicion of atheism, must have made his position difficult. He had other problems: in a letter of 1611 to Harriot, following a discussion of trigonometry and Kepler, Lower concluded, 'I have lost my second boy also, and wel neere eighty catle of the murraine, and they die still; now you know all my discomforts and losses' (Halliwell, 40). He died at Tra'venti on 12 April 1615, on the same day as his mother, Jane, leaving his wife, a daughter, Dorothy, and a posthumous son, Thomas. Although he has no scientific achievement or publication to his credit Lower was a competent astronomer and mathematician and a stimulus to Harriot. His letters capture the excitement generated among natural philosophers by Kepler's discovery of elliptic orbits, the invention of the telescope, Galileo's telescopic discoveries, and the new symbolic algebra. J. J. ROCHE

Sources BL, Add. MS 6789, fols. 425–38, 444 · Petworth House, HMC 214/vii, fols. 1–7 · J. O. Halliwell, ed., *A collection of letters illustrative of the progress of science in England from the reign of Queen Elizabeth to that of Charles the second* (1841), 38–42 · J. Maclean, *The parochial and family history of the deanery of Trigg Minor in the county of Cornwall*, 3 (1879) · *Reg. Oxf.*, vol. 2/2 · C. H. Hopwood, ed., *Middle Temple records*, 4 vols. (1904–5) · Bodl. Oxf., MS Rigaud 35, fols. 108–28 · *Miscellaneous works and correspondence of the Rev. James Bradley*, ed. [S. P. Rigaud] (1832), account of Harriot's astronomical papers, 68–70 [separate pagination] · W. J. Jones, 'Lower, William', HoP, *Commons, 1558–1603* · F. Maddison, 'The earliest users of the refracting telescope in Britain: Thomas Harriot, Christopher Tooke, Sir William Lower and John Protheroe', MHS Oxf. · J. W. Shirley, *Thomas Harriot: a biography* (1983), 388–411 · J. D. North and J. J. Roche, eds., *The light of nature* (1985)

Archives BL, letters to Harriot, Add. MS 6789, fols. 425–38, 444 · Petworth House, West Sussex, letters to Harriot

Wealth at death 3000 acres in Tra'venti in Carmarthenshire; manors of St Winnow, Bridge-End, and Trelaske in Cornwall: Maclean, *Parochial and family history*, vol. 3, p. 379

Lower, Sir William (*c.*1610–1662), playwright and translator, was born in Cornwall, the only son of John Lower of Tremere (*c.*1584–1645, the second of six sons of Thomas Lower of St Winnow) and his first wife, Jane (*d.* before 1640). He was probably born about 1610; he may be the William Lower, son of John, baptized on 7 March 1609 at Constantine, Cornwall (about 20 miles south-west of St Winnow), but proof is lacking. There is no record of Lower at either Oxford or Cambridge, but his kinsman Dr Richard Lower told Anthony Wood that William 'spent some time in Oxon, in the condition of an Hospes for the sake of the public Library and Scholastic Company … but his Fancy being gay, he troubled himself not with the crabbed studies of Logic and Philosophy' (Wood, *Ath. Oxon.*, 2.272).

The documentary silence is broken by the publication in 1639 of Lower's first play, *The Phoenix in her Flames*, dedicated to the author's cousin, Thomas Lower. This play is a competent but conventional tragic romance set in Arabia, involving a kidnapped princess who falls in love with a hero reduced from his rightful station, a battle in which the hero rebuffs an enemy army, and a tragic ending in which all the main characters die. It has no major source, but shows the influence of Greek romances and Marlowe's *Tamburlaine*. The play displays considerable military knowledge, and in the dedication Lower implies that he had seen military service. In 1640 he was a lieutenant in the regiment of Sir Jacob Ashley in the army of the earl of Northumberland, and later that year, now a captain, he gave an account of his company's mutiny near Brackley.

For the next four years there is no record of Lower's activities; the outbreak of the civil war presumably put his literary endeavours on hold. In June 1644, now a lieutenant-colonel in the king's army and lieutenant-governor of Wallingford, he was ordered by the crown to levy a weekly tax of £50 on the town of Reading for the garrison at Wallingford. When the town refused to pay, Lower kidnapped the mayor of Reading as a hostage. A series of letters ensued, in which the town's aldermen reiterated their inability to pay and Lower attempted without success to reach a compromise. Eventually the council of war at Oxford remitted part of the levy. On 27 March 1645 Lower was rewarded for his service by being knighted. Less than a year later, on 19 January 1646, he was captured by the parliamentary garrison of Abingdon and sent to London as a prisoner. He apparently remained there until 11 January 1647, when he was discharged and permitted to go overseas, as long as he promised not to act against the parliament.

Lower's whereabouts over the next seven years are unclear. At some point after 1647 he married and had a daughter, Elizabeth, but it is impossible to say exactly when or where this daughter was born, and nothing is known of his wife, except that she died before 1661. Lower probably spent some time in the Low Countries, since his uncle Sir Nicholas Lower owned lands in Holland and Zeeland. Sir Nicholas died in 1653, leaving most of his estate to Sir William and his cousin Thomas, but they encountered difficulties gaining title to their inheritance because of the wars. Lower was in England in July 1654 petitioning for permission to go to the Low Countries to settle his uncle's estate, but he had to wait more than a year before receiving it. He was in The Hague in October 1655, bringing news of Cromwell's weakness back in England, and he apparently stayed there for the next six years, finally resolving the estate difficulties in 1660.

During this time Lower began to publish translations of various French works. He translated three non-dramatic works of René de Ceriziers concerning religious martyrs: *The Innocent Lady* (1654), *The Innocent Lord* (1655), and *The Triumphant Lady* (1656). He also translated two plays by Corneille (*Polyeuctes* in 1655 and *Horatius* in 1656), two by Paul Scarron (*Don Japhet of Armenia*, preserved as British Library Add. MS 28723, and *The Three Dorothies*, now lost), and two by Quinault (*The Noble Ingratitude* in 1659 and *The Amorous Fantasme* in 1660). The latter two were dedicated, respectively, to the princess royal of Orange (for whom Lower published a funeral elegy in 1661) and to Elizabeth, queen of Bohemia, indicating Lower's close connection with the exiled royal family. In 1660 he translated a French description of Charles II's residence in Holland, publishing it in an elaborate engraved folio. In addition to his translations, Lower wrote a second original play, *The Enchanted Lovers* (1658). This is a pastoral set on the island of Erithrea, with lovers disguised as shepherds, enchantments, and the goddess Diana appearing as a *deus ex machina* at the end. The Folger copy of *The Noble Ingratitude* and *The Enchanted Lovers* (bound together, Folger L3314/Q218) is inscribed 'For Mris. Elizabeth Lower 1659' and 'Corrected by the Author's own hand', with about fifteen manuscript corrections, all in Lower's hand. Lower also wrote a manuscript set of paraphrases on the apostolic epistles, preserved as Harleian MS 4611.

In 1661 Thomas Lower died and left most of his estate to his cousin Sir William, prompting the latter's return to England. Early the following year, however, Sir William himself died, and his will was proved on 7 May 1662. He left most of his estate to his daughter, Elizabeth, with trustees holding it until she turned twenty-one. Wood supposed that he was buried in St Clement Danes, Westminster (Wood, *Ath. Oxon.*, 2.273), but there is no record of his burial there, nor in St Winnow, Cornwall.

DAVID KATHMAN

Sources *The dramatic works and translations of Sir William Lower, with a reprint of 'The enchanted lovers'*, ed. W. B. Gates (1932) · Wood, *Ath. Oxon.*, 2nd edn, 2.272–3 · J. Maclean, *The parochial and family history of the deanery of Trigg Minor in the county of Cornwall*, 3 (1879), 386–7 · J. L. Vivian, ed., *The visitations of Cornwall, comprising the herald's visitations of 1530, 1573, and 1620* (1887), 300 · *IGI*

Likenesses print, BM; repro. in W. Lower, *The noble ingratitude* (1659)

Wealth at death estates in Cornwall, Holland, and Zeeland; plus £1300 in cash bequests: will, repr. in *Dramatic works of William Lower*, ed. Gates, 19

Lowerison, Bellerby [Harry] **(1863–1935)**, socialist and schoolmaster, was born on 13 July 1863 in Great Lumley, co. Durham, son of George Lowerson, a coalminer, and his wife, Dorothy Richardson. Very little is known about his early life and some basic facts are unclear. The family's name on his birth certificate is Lowerson but he always kept the 'i' in his surname. He called himself Harry until 6 May 1910, when, in an article in the socialist newspaper *The Clarion*, he adopted the forename given on his birth certificate, which was Bellerby. He left his family after disagreements with them over their strict religious views and later attended St Bede's College, Durham, where he trained as a teacher. Any record of his life has to begin in earnest in 1889, when he became a socialist as a result of meeting participants in the London dock strike.

Lowerison joined the east London branch of the Fabian Society and by 1891 was joint secretary of what was the biggest branch of the society in London; it met at his home in Homerton. In April 1891 he was elected to the national executive committee of the society, on which he served for a year. He was widely recognized as a very hard-working socialist propagandist (see *Justice*, the paper of the Social Democratic Federation, 18 April 1891). He wrote numerous articles for *The Clarion*, his most productive year being 1911, and he addressed socialist meetings throughout the country. On 23 July 1892 he married Alice Mabel Dutton, a Post Office clerk; they had two children, Gordon and Elaine.

Despite Lowerison's staunch secularism, a central component of his socialism was the idea that

> there is lot of miserable cant talked about religion necessarily making a milksop of a man, when the truth is that unless a man has a religion of some sort or other he is either a brute or a madman. (H. Lowerison, *Mother Earth*, 1902, 136)

The co-operative commonwealth based on fellowship could not be brought about by means inimical to its ends. Though economic reform was vital, so too was change in the people's moral outlook. This change could be accomplished by bringing people into closer contact with each other, with learning, and with nature. To achieve the closer harmony of man and nature Lowerison helped to set up and organize the Clarion field clubs, the subject of his *Fields and Folklore* (1899). He envisaged the clubs as the collective stewards of the people's heritage. His essays in the collections *Sweet Briar Sprays* (1899), *Mother Earth* (1902), and *In England now* (1906) merged his political and naturalist interests; much of his later journalism blended politics and astronomy.

From 1894 to 1899 Lowerison taught at Wenlock Road School in the London school board division of Hackney. He was repelled by the physical surroundings for, like many schools of the time, the school was overcrowded and filthy. But most of all he loathed the character of the education that he was employed to deliver, particularly the religious elements of the curriculum. While he was a teacher he tried to improve the education of his pupils and struggled to open the eyes of his colleagues to more progressive teaching methods. It was to these ends that he helped to establish the London School Swimming Association and attempted to set up a London schools rambling club.

However, by the end of the 1890s Lowerison was running up against the system, and in particular against the headmaster, at Wenlock Road. In July 1898 letters he had written to *The Clarion* brought him to the attention of the school board and in November 1899 his lack of respect for the headmaster led to his dismissal without a reference. The offending letters were entitled 'My ideal school', in which he set out the principles on which he would found Ruskin School (*The Clarion*, 15 July, 7 Oct, and 18 Nov 1899). He planned, first, to teach the laws of health and exercise, second, to teach, by example, habits of justice and gentleness, and, third, to discover, draw out, and develop the natural capabilities of each child.

After Lowerison's dismissal from Wenlock Road School his scheme was realized with funds donated by readers of *The Clarion*. Ruskin School was opened in Hunstanton, Norfolk. In February 1902 the school moved to new premises a few miles away at Heacham. Lowerison's preferred method of teaching was to link subjects such as astronomy, literature, and art and then to arouse children's interest in this unified body of knowledge. He did this by allowing them to find one aspect that excited their imaginations, and using this as a gateway to the whole.

These methods were detailed in his book *Star Lore for Teachers* (1911) and exemplified in *From Palaeolith to Motor Car* (1906). Given that Lowerison, in common with most socialists of his day, viewed the ends of struggle and the means of getting there as being of necessity the same, he structured the school so that it was as deinstitutionalized as possible. He therefore allowed children considerable freedom to roam the countryside and to pursue and develop their own interests. A. S. Neill visited Ruskin School and may well have been influenced by what he saw there.

Ruskin School Home was busiest in 1909–10, when it had fifty pupils, but it declined after the war and closed in 1926. The school's decline was matched, if not caused, by Lowerison's political drift. By 1914 his socialism had changed into a form of paternalism and with the outbreak of war he became a rampant nationalist baying for German blood (*The Clarion*, 13 Nov 1914). When the school closed he retired to Green Garth, Houghton, near Huntingdon, where he died on 6 June 1935; he was buried later that month in Houghton on Whit Monday.

KEVIN MANTON

Sources K. Manton, 'Establishing the fellowship: Harry Lowerison and Ruskin School Home, a turn-of-the-century socialist and his educational experiment', *History of Education*, 26 (1997), 53–70 • P. Pugh, *Educate, agitate, organize: 100 years of Fabian socialism* (1984) • W. McCann, 'Trade unionist, co-operative and socialist organisation in relation to popular education, 1870–1902', PhD diss., University of Manchester, 1960 • *Peterborough Herald* (14 June 1935) • *Lynn Advertiser* (14 June 1935) • b. cert. • d. cert. • private information (2004)

Archives BLPES, Fabian Society Archive • Durham RO, MSS of the College of St Hilda and St Bede, University of Durham • LMA, London School Board archives, Wenlock Road School entries, SBL 650–662 • Lynn Museum, King's Lynn, Norfolk, notes on Ruskin School

Likenesses photograph, repro. in *Peterborough Advertiser* (21 June 1935)

Wealth at death £1367 10*s.* 4*d.*: administration with will, 20 Sept 1935, *CGPLA Eng. & Wales*

Lowery, Robert (1809–1863), Chartist, born on 14 October 1809 at North Shields, was the eldest of a sailor's four sons; his mother was the daughter of a local master shoemaker. Educated at North Shields, Banff, and Peterhead until aged nine, he took a pithead job when illness threw his father out of work. His mother, who opened a school for girls, encouraged ambition in a son who was mischievous as a child but alert and inquisitive as a teenager. Thirteen when his father died, Lowery got himself apprenticed as a sailor, but within two years a rheumatic illness had lamed him for life.

Long convalescence brought wide reading, which was carried further with the encouragement of his wife, a cousin whom Lowery married at eighteen. With two daughters before he was twenty-one, he was apprenticed to a Newcastle tailor, trained himself in public speaking, and became secretary to the North Shields Political Union. An active trade unionist, he was secretary to the tailors' branch of the Consolidated Trades' Union, lost his job, and was at times very poor, but published his pamphlet *State Churches Destructive of Christianity and Subversive to the Liberties of Man* in 1837.

After being elected Newcastle delegate to the Chartists' Palace Yard meeting of 17 September 1838, he became a Chartist lecturer. Over-optimistic and somewhat stagy in style, he displayed the provincial Chartist's jaunty irreverence and delight in taunting authority. Fascinated by history and admiring the seventeenth-century puritans, he was proud of his class. As Newcastle delegate to the Chartist convention at Christmas 1838, his actions were more moderate than his speeches. His autobiography (penetrating on the art of oratory and alert to regional contrasts) vividly describes a Chartist missionary's experience in Cornwall and Dublin. In 1839 his published address recommended exclusive dealing, and he opposed physical force during the Frost rising and at the Chartist convention's second session in 1839–40. He relished Scottish intelligence and religiosity and lectured there, managing to evade arrest.

Serious illness in 1839–40 launched Lowery on religious conversion, political quietism, and commitment to moral reform. Urquhartites—influential in Newcastle, with a programme that required class harmony—helped him through this personal crisis, and sent him on a Russophobe mission to Paris in autumn 1840. Defeated as radical candidate at Edinburgh and Aberdeen in the general election of 1841, he was persuaded by Aberdeen teetotallers to take the pledge, and temperance lecturing became his new route to respectability. He supported the Complete Suffrage Union in 1842 and drifted away from Chartism via Lovett's moralistic and gradualist 'new move'. In 1848 he was first secretary to Lovett's People's League, which aimed to head off revolution through a wider franchise and lower taxes. Less prominent as a temperance reformer than as a Chartist, Lowery was a respected lecturer for several temperance organizations until rheumatism and a failing voice compelled him to retire in 1862. With a public subscription raised for his support, he emigrated in September to his daughter Sarah Edwards in Canada, and died at Woodstock, Ontario, on 4 August 1863. He was buried in the Baptist cemetery there, together with his daughter, son-in-law William Edwards, and some of his grandchildren.

In his public life Lowery was neither as distinctive nor as prominent as some, but no Chartist published an autobiography of such quality so soon after the event. Vivid, evocative, and reflective, the thirty-three anonymous instalments of his 'Passages in the life of a temperance lecturer … by one of their order' in the *Weekly Record of the Temperance Movement* for 1856–7 recount his life up to 1841. Somewhat wistful in tone, his autobiography shows zest for dramatic scenery, historic events, and the Romantic poets, and displays shrewd insight into personality. Lowery's taste for anecdotes, his ear for dialect, and his fine visual memory reveal an attractive personality who consistently pursued the Chartist aim of justifying his own class to society at large, fair-mindedly and without apology. Chartism, he insisted, was a respectable movement, and its supporters' actions should be judged in contemporary context. But his career fitted awkwardly into the pedigree that led from Chartism to socialism and the Labour Party, so he sank from public view until he was rediscovered in the 1960s. BRIAN HARRISON

Sources B. Harrison and P. Hollis, eds., *Robert Lowery, radical and chartist* (1979) • B. Harrison and P. Hollis, 'Chartism, liberalism and the life of Robert Lowery', *EngHR*, 82 (1967), 503–35 • B. Harrison and P. Hollis, 'Lowery, Robert', *DLB*, vol. 4
Archives Balliol Oxf., Urquhart MSS • National Temperance League, Sheffield, archives
Likenesses portrait, repro. in *The Charter* (28 April 1839), 215

Lowick, Robert (1655–1696), army officer and Jacobite conspirator, was a Yorkshireman, born at Stokesley in the North Riding, into its small Catholic community, on 12 March 1655, son of Robert Lowick (*b*. 1624, *d*. after 1690) and, almost certainly, Mary Lowick (*d*. 1693?). His family were perhaps related to the extinct petty-gentry recusant Lowickes of nearby Osmotherley, and his 1696 indictment ranked him 'gentleman'; but his father's house had only two hearths. The Benedictine monk Henry Benedict Lowick (*d*. 1720), who became prior of St Leonard's, Dieulouard, Lorraine, was probably Robert's brother; he had at least two other brothers and one sister—perhaps four.

Under James II Lowick became ensign in the Catholic Sir Thomas Haggerston's independent company, commissioned on 26 June 1685 to garrison Berwick, afterwards incorporated into Sir William Clifton's regiment and by 1687 into the Royal Fusiliers. He was among the officers pardoned for Catholicism in November 1685. When the rich Catholic George Holman's new cavalry regiment was commissioned on 10 October 1688, Lowick was his cornet; but the regiment disbanded that December.

In Ireland in 1689 Lowick became a lieutenant in the cavalry regiment freshly raised for King James by Colonel John Parker. Lowick displayed, besides professional abilities, his characteristic humanity, particularly in saving captured Williamite officers' lives after a skirmish in June 1690. Parker's regiment was largely destroyed fighting at the Boyne. Lowick, having afterwards risen to major, returned to England in 1691.

From 1692 to 1694 Parker was organizing the Lancashire and northern Catholic gentry for a rising. He appointed Lowick major—the professional officer's post—in his own theoretical cavalry regiment. Since half its troops were scattered between Northumberland and southern Lancashire, and half in London, the post was burdensome, especially after Parker fled to France. Lowick lodged mainly in London.

In the 1696 assassination plot, Lowick, who was closely involved with Robert Charnock and Father Henry Joseph Johnston over regimental matters, bought a periwig to disguise Sir George Barclay. Lowick was to join the force attacking William and his guards, bringing two other horsemen—unsubsidized by Barclay, he remarked. Like Ambrose Rookwood, he expressed disgust at the plot among comrades, but resolved to obey Barclay's orders, assuming that he acted on James's. Afterwards, two proclamations offered £1000 for him among others, and he was arrested on 23 March in Golden Lane, London. Refusing inducements to confess, then or after condemnation, he was arraigned, with Rookwood and Charles Cranburne, in the court of king's bench on 14 April, and tried and convicted on 22 April. The main witnesses, the turncoat George Harris and Thomas Bertram, a relative from Stokesley whom he had often charitably assisted, showed uneasy consciences; but the government had reliable evidence of his complicity from an undercover spy. Lowick prepared a last paper in which, like earlier executed whigs and Jacobites, he used legal shortcomings in prosecution testimony to imply his moral innocence. However, when he, Rookwood, and Cranburne were executed at Tyburn on 29 April 1696, the sheriff's appeal to his piety, and guilt at having drawn others in, made him admit his knowledge and involvement.

A proclamation's description of Lowick—tall, lean, of sanguine complexion, with high cheekbones and hollow cheeks—calls into question the etching of the conspirators. Unmarried, he used his limited means charitably and was generally loved. PAUL HOPKINS

Sources *State trials*, vols. 12–13 • J. Hawell, ed., *The registers of the parish church of Stokesley, co. York, 1571–1750*, Yorkshire Parish Register Society (1901) • *An account of the execution of Brigadier Rookwood, Major Lowick, and Mr Cranburn at Tyburn, April 29th 1696* (1696) • *Report on the manuscripts of the marquis of Downshire*, 6 vols. in 7, HMC, 75 (1924–95), vol. 1 • Trumbull's cabinet minutes, 5 March, 14 March, 24 March, 27 April, 1696, BL, Add. MSS 72566–72567 • H. Aveling, *Northern Catholics: the Catholic recusants of the North Riding of Yorkshire, 1558–1790* (1966) • P. A. Hopkins, 'Aspects of Jacobite conspiracy in England in the reign of William III', PhD diss., U. Cam., 1981, chaps. 4, 9 • *The Hearth Tax list for the North Riding of Yorkshire, Michaelmas 1673*, 5: *Langbarugh West, Langburgh East and Whitby Strand Wapentakes* (1991) • *CSP dom.*, 1685–9; 1696 • *True copies of the papers which Brigadier Rookwood, and Major Lowick, delivered to the sheriffs* (1696) • *Observations upon the papers which Mr Rookwood and Mr Lowick deliver'd to the sheriffs* (1696) • J. D'Alton, *Illustrations historical and genealogical of King James's Irish army list (1689)*, 2 vols. (1861), 1.246–70 • T. B. Snow, *Obit book of the English Benedictines from 1600 to 1912*, rev. H. N. Birt (privately printed, Edinburgh, 1913) • J. C. Atkinson, ed., *Quarter sessions records*, 6, North Riding RS, 6 (1888) • Lowick's examination, 24 March 1696, U. Nott. L., Portland MSS, PWA 2484 • N. Luttrell, *A brief historical relation of state affairs from September 1678 to April 1714*, 4 (1857)
Likenesses etching, 1696, NPG • etching, 1697, repro. in R. Sharp, *The engraved record of the Jacobite movement* (1996), no. 688

Lowin, John (*bap*. 1576, *d*. 1653), actor, the son of Richard Lowin of London, was baptized on 9 December 1576 at St Giles Cripplegate. His father was a currier, or tanner of leather (not a carpenter, as early authorities state), and must have been a fairly well-to-do craftsman, for he apprenticed his son to a goldsmith: this was a desirable trade that could be entered only by boys whose fathers owned property. Lowin was bound to Nicholas Rudyard for eight years from Christmas 1593, and although he is not recorded achieving freedom of the trade, he probably completed his apprenticeship since notices of him as an actor begin only in 1602. Additional testimony comes from the City pageant by Anthony Munday (or Mundy) entitled *Chrusothriambos, or, The Triumphs of Gold* (October 1611), in which

John Lowin (*bap.* 1576, *d.* 1653), by unknown artist, 1640

Lowin played the goldsmith Leofstane, supposedly the first mayor of London. This spectacular parade was mounted by the Goldsmiths' Company to celebrate the election of a goldsmith, Sir James Pemberton, as lord mayor, and a company document recording Lowin's agreement to perform calls him 'one of his Majesty's players and brother of this company' (Gordon and Robertson, 81). We can only speculate how he had migrated from Cheapside to the Bankside, but he was not the only goldsmith's apprentice to follow this route: the comedian Robert Armin, Lowin's colleague in the King's Men, was another prominent example.

Lowin first appears as a player in the records of the Earl of Worcester's Men, during their time at the Rose playhouse in Southwark. Until recently a provincial company, Worcester's became established in London in 1601 after the appointment of their patron as Elizabeth's master of horse; in the next reign they acquired Queen Anne's patronage. Lowin appears in the books of the Rose's impresario, Philip Henslowe, during the winter of 1602–3, usually through business concerning the purchase of new plays. In March 1603 Henslowe lent him 5*s*. 'when he went into the country with the company to play' (*Henslowe's Diary*, 212). But later that year he moved into London's premier troupe, the King's Men. The playhouses were closed for twelve months from March 1603 because of Elizabeth's death and the plague, during which period the companies were reallocated to new royal patrons. Lowin does not appear in the official company lists of May 1603 or March 1604, but in Ben Jonson's *Works* (1616) he is listed seventh among the performers of *Sejanus*, which play, it is believed, the King's Men premièred at court late in 1603. He remained with the King's Men until the end of his career, by which time he was their longest-serving player.

Lowin had a high company profile from the first, since he was one of five actors featured in the induction added in 1604 by John Webster to John Marston's *The Malcontent* for its performances at the Globe. Webster's amusing scene stages a 'real-life' conversation between audience and performers before the play begins. Two troublesome spectators (played by actors) try to sit on the stage as was the practice at the Blackfriars Theatre, and have to be persuaded to enter the boxes by three cast members, Richard Burbage, Henry Condell, and Lowin. As the most junior, Lowin's part is small, but it testifies to his standing with the company that he was singled out. Over the next forty years he played important roles in some of the best-known dramas of the time, including the Shakespeare, Jonson, Fletcher, and Massinger plays that formed the core of the King's Men's repertoire. He stands eleventh among the actors listed in the Shakespeare first folio (1623), and heads the signatories of the dedication to the 1647 Beaumont and Fletcher folio.

Lowin was an imposing individual. His portrait in the Ashmolean Museum, painted when he was sixty-four, depicts him as bulky but dignified, possessed of both power and grace. These qualities are reflected in his roles. In the 1690s James Wright recollected seeing him as Falstaff ('with mighty applause'), as the bluff soldier Melantius in Beaumont and Fletcher's *Maid's Tragedy*, and in several Jonsonian parts: the title role in *Volpone*, the misanthrope Morose in *Epicene*, and the sensualist Epicure Mammon in *The Alchemist* (Bentley, 2.505). Wright would have witnessed Lowin in the 1630s, so these were not all parts he had created; Volpone was one of Burbage's roles, and *Epicene* was originally a boys' play. Lowin also took over Belleur, a gentleman 'of a stout blunt humour', in revivals of Fletcher's spirited comedy *The Wild Goose Chase*. Of the roles he himself created, he had leading parts in some two dozen plays by Fletcher, but his greatest was the self-doubting criminal Bosola in Webster's *Duchess of Malfi* (1613). He also played Massinger's despotic Romans Domitian in *The Roman Actor* (1626) and Flaminius in *Believe as you List* (1631), the wealthy citizen Undermine in John Clavell's *The Soddered Citizen* (1630), and the title character, 'of great beard and bulk', in Arthur Wilson's *The Swisser* (1631). A late tradition recorded by John Downes has him as Shakespeare's original Henry VIII (1611): Downes says he passed his interpretation to Sir William Davenant, having 'had his instructions from Mr Shakespeare himself' (Bentley, 2.502, 506). Evidently Lowin excelled in commanding and authoritative roles, but had considerable range in both tragedy and comedy. In the Caroline period he and Joseph Taylor, Burbage's successor as principal tragedian, were the King's Men's most senior actors and typically appeared in tandem, Taylor playing Mosca to Lowin's Volpone, Arbaces to his Melantius, Paris to his Domitian, and Ferdinand to his Bosola.

In the prologue to Davenant's *The Platonic Lovers* (1635), Lowin reminded his audience that he had:

laboured here
In buskins and in socks this thirty year
(Bentley, 2.503)

His labours, though, were increasingly consumed by company administration. He became a company shareholder in the reorganization of 1627, with two out of seventeen shares, making him one of the six people with a controlling financial stake in the troupe. Then in 1630, after the death of John Heminges, Lowin and Taylor became the company's business representatives. For the next twelve years they acted as its day-to-day agents, and took over the responsibility for liaison between the King's Men and the authorities at court, an onerous and important job. Lowin's status with the company had already helped him to achieve a small court office, since at some point before the end of James's reign he acquired the post of porter, for which he paid £200. He also acquired a family. It is unclear whether he was the John Lowin who married Joan Hall, a widow, at St Botolph without Bishopgate in 1607, but in 1620 he certainly married Katherine Wooden at St Saviour's, Southwark, the parish he resided in for most of his working life. A son, John, was baptized there in 1639. By this time Lowin was sixty-two; the 1640 portrait depicts a man conscious of his prosperity and achievements.

Lowin's career was abruptly interrupted in September 1642, when the theatres were closed by order of parliament, not to reopen officially in his lifetime. The activities of his final decade can only be tentatively reconstructed. The next five years are a blank, though he had capital to fall back on, since the King's Men sharers liquidated their stock when the theatres closed. Although the company was effectively dissolved, its network held together, for the 1647 Beaumont and Fletcher folio was published with a dedicatory letter from the actors, and in 1652 Fletcher's *Wild Goose Chase* was separately published with a preface by Lowin and Taylor. And even though playing was banned, some surreptitious performances by unlicensed troupes continued, the peak period coming in 1648. In January of that year seven former King's Men, headed by Lowin, contracted to pay a debt due to the widow of an eighth, and it was possibly this group that illegally staged the King's Men's play *Wit without Money* at the Red Bull in February. James Wright claimed that a troupe led by Lowin and Taylor were covertly performing at the Drury Lane Cockpit late in 1648, and that one afternoon, while playing Fletcher and Massinger's *The Bloody Brother*, they were arrested by soldiers, briefly imprisoned, and lost their costumes. Wright's notes date from 1699, so their details may not be reliable, but other sources show that at least three unlicensed companies had resurfaced, and were suppressed in similar circumstances as security measures before the king's execution. This arrest seems to have ended Lowin's acting career, and subsequent financial problems are signalled by the 1652 edition of Fletcher's *Wild Goose Chase*, which was printed to raise money for Lowin and Taylor. Wright says Lowin ended his days as innkeeper of the Three Pigeons at Brentford, 'and his poverty was as great as his age' (Bentley, 2.505). He was buried at St Clement Danes on 24 August 1653.

The only serious puzzle around Lowin relates to the tract *Conclusions upon Dances* (1607). This decidedly pious treatise, that censures most kinds of dancing on the grounds of profanity, was published with an epistle signed 'I. L., Roscio'—that is 'player', after the Roman actor Roscius. Lowin is the only Jacobean player whose initials fit, and the attribution, originally made by John Payne Collier, has been generally accepted. It is not impossible to reconcile the pamphlet's opinions with the outlook of an actor who came from citizen stock, and who achieved such heights of social respectability. Yet if Lowin really was the author, his theology was so much in tension with his calling that it must have made his professional life a never-ending source of scruple.

MARTIN BUTLER

Sources G. E. Bentley, *The Jacobean and Caroline stage*, 7 vols. (1941–68) • R. Bowers, 'John Lowin, actor-manager of the King's Company, 1630–1642', *Theatre Survey*, 28 (1987), 15–35 • R. Bowers, 'John Lowin's *Conclusions upon dances*: puritan conclusions of a godly player', *Renaissance and Reformation*, 23 (1987), 163–73 • I. L., *Conclusions upon dances, both of this age and of the old* (1607) • J. Robertson and D. J. Gordon, eds., 'A calendar of dramatic records in the books of the livery companies of London, 1485–1640', *Malone Society Collections*, 3 (1954) • *Henslowe's diary*, ed. R. A. Foakes and R. T. Rickert (1961) • J. Milhous and R. D. Hume, 'New light on English acting companies in 1646, 1648, and 1660', *Review of English Studies*, new ser., 42 (1991), 487–509 • L. Hotson, *The Commonwealth and Restoration stage* (1928) • S. Kawai, 'John Lowin as Iago', *Shakespeare Studies*, 30 (1992), 17–34 • A. Gurr, *The Shakespearian playing companies* (1996) • A. Mundy, *Chruso-thriambos: the triumphs of gold*, ed. J. H. P. Pafford (1962)

Likenesses oils, 1640, AM Oxf. [*see illus.*]

Wealth at death died in poverty: Bentley, *Jacobean and Caroline stage*, vol. 2, p. 505

Lowke, Wenman Joseph Bassett- (1877–1953), model-maker and businessman, was born Joseph Wenman Bassett Lowke at 13 Kingswell Street, Northampton, on 27 December 1877, the elder son of Joseph Tom Lowke, agricultural engineer, and Eliza Goodman. He was educated at Kingswell Street College and All Saints' Commercial School until the age of thirteen. He worked for his father in the firm of J. T. Lowke & Sons, engineers and boiler-makers, of Northampton, founded as Bassett & Sons by his step-grandfather in 1859. He soon left to work for an architect but, after eighteen months, returned to his father's firm.

There, with Harry Franklin, the company's bookkeeper, Lowke took up model engineering, making small engines and boilers. He spent two years, 1898–1900, as a student apprentice with Crompton & Co. Ltd of Chelmsford; during that time, in 1899, he founded the firm of Bassett-Lowke & Co., so named to distinguish it from his father's firm. At the same time he adopted this as his own surname. Franklin helped to run the nascent company, a small, mail-order business selling component parts for model engines. In 1898 Bassett-Lowke had forged a relationship with Percival Marshall, editor of the new magazine *Model Engineer and Amateur Electrician*. He was thus soon able to advertise regularly and reach a wide public. His first catalogue appeared in 1900, the year in which he made, at the Paris Exhibition, important contacts with

Bing Brothers and Carette & Cie, both of Nuremberg, who were able to manufacture and supply steam engines of British railway design to a standard of precision not yet achieved in Britain.

With works established in Northampton and with the supply of parts from abroad and from such home suppliers as Cornish and Claret, business flourished. Always a prolific writer, Bassett-Lowke, known to his friends as Whynne and to his employees as Mr Whynne, contributed articles to numerous magazines and produced many brochures. The first edition of *Model Railway Handbook* which he edited appeared in 1906, and it passed through countless editions until 1953. Bassett-Lowke's first retail shop was opened in High Holborn in London in 1908, and others were subsequently opened in Edinburgh and Manchester. The business became a limited liability company in 1910 as it branched out from model railways and stationary engines into flying machines, electrical equipment, and, especially, ships. A miniature railway run at Blackpool from 1905 to 1910 was highly successful. From 1911 there were regular contracts with the Admiralty. Bassett-Lowke was able to anticipate trends and so to diversify and establish subsidiary companies to supply and market a vast range of products. He 'was like a magnet, drawing to him all the best craftsmen, engineers, draughtsmen and designers' (Fuller, 330).

After the First World War the field of exhibition and industrial models was greatly expanded. Railway and shipping companies asked Bassett-Lowke to supply training models, and electricity in models was developed. His company, Narrow Gauge Railways Ltd, re-created and ran the Ravenglass and Eskdale Railway from 1915 to 1925. He lectured and broadcast, and the name Bassett-Lowke became renowned to museums, institutions, companies, and collectors across the world. In the Second World War Bassett-Lowke was called upon by the services to provide countless training models of vessels and models of Mulberry harbours, Bailey bridges, and landing equipment for vital operational planning purposes.

In 1912 Bassett-Lowke, earlier a member of the Fabian Society, joined the Labour Party. George Bernard Shaw was a close friend who sometimes stayed with him in Northampton. Bassett-Lowke was a town councillor in Northampton from 1930 and an alderman from 1945. In 1948 he declined an invitation to be mayor, not wishing to sit on the bench and pass judgment on others. He served a number of committees and was successful in having the council build a modern public baths. He was a founder member of the town's Rotary Club, of which he was president in 1934, and founder director of its repertory theatre; he enjoyed taking part in amateur dramatics. Northampton Central Museum and Art Gallery has a three-view oil painting of him by John A. A. Berrie.

On 21 March 1917 Bassett-Lowke married Florence Jane, daughter of shoe manufacturer Charles Jones. There were no children. Bassett-Lowke was a founder member of the Design Industries Association and was always interested in architecture: he had Charles Rennie Mackintosh carry out alterations to his first marital home, and in 1926 his second was designed by Peter Behrens. As a young man he was interested in swimming and cycling. He had a lifelong interest in photography, both still and cine, becoming vice-president of the Institute of Amateur Cinematographers. Throughout his life he was a great traveller, both on business and for pleasure. In 1904 he became a member of the Junior Institution of Engineers and, in 1911, of the Institution of Locomotive Engineers. He was the first president of the Model Engineers' Trade Association. He became a fellow of the Royal Society of Arts in 1946. In the last two years of his life Bassett-Lowke showed marked signs of senility. He died at St Andrew's Hospital, Northampton, on 21 October 1953 of broncho-pneumonia. He was buried at Billing Road cemetery, Northampton, on the 23rd. His wife survived him. ROBERT SHARP

Sources R. Fuller, *The Bassett-Lowke story* (1984) · G. Holland, *Fifty years of model-making* [1949] · *Northampton Independent* (23 Oct 1953) · J. Bassett-Lowke, *Wenman Joseph Bassett-Lowke: a memoir of his life and achievements, 1877–1953* (1999) · m. cert. · b. cert. · d. cert. · burial records, Billing Road cemetery, Northampton, Oct 1953 · *CGPLA Eng. & Wales* (1954)

Archives Northants. RO | Northampton Central Museum and Art Gallery, exhibition about Bassett-Lowke

Likenesses J. A. A. Berrie, oils, Northampton Central Museum and Art Gallery

Wealth at death £22,992 8*s*. 1*d*.: probate, 22 April 1954, *CGPLA Eng. & Wales*

Lowman, Moses (*bap.* **1679**, *d.* **1752**), nonconformist minister and writer, was baptized on 25 January 1679 at St Gabriel Fenchurch, London, the son of Moses and Anne Lowman. His father, who was educated at Merton and Magdalen colleges, Oxford, and proceeded MA on 21 June 1660, was ordained in the Church of England but left it for 'employment in the public revenues' (*Protestant Dissenter's Magazine*, Dec 1794, 465). Nothing is known of Moses's early schooling, but it is unlikely to have taken place among the dissenters. Destined for a career in the law, he entered the Middle Temple in March 1698, but left a year later to study divinity at the universities of Leiden and Utrecht. It is also unclear how he became a dissenter or trained for the ministry, but in 1710 he became assistant minister at the Presbyterian chapel in Grafton Square, Clapham. From 1714 until his death he was chief minister to the congregation.

Lowman's reputation rests on his scholarship, in particular his published works on the Bible, the various defences he made of protestant dissent, and theological controversy with members of the established church. His two works on Jewish history and worship 'contain many things in them not only curious but entirely new … He determined to follow and embrace the truth wherever he should find it' (Chandler, 41–2). His commentaries and paraphrases on books of the Bible were widely read and appreciated by both churchmen and dissenters. His *Paraphrase and Notes on the Revelation of St John* (1737), praised by Philip Doddridge, went to four editions, the last being as late as 1807. He was an active and public-spirited pastor, serving not only his own congregation but assisting other chapels in a poor financial position. However, more than one source states that he was a poor preacher.

> His discourses were obscure, the respect and esteem of his congregation must be due not on evidence for the acceptableness of his sermons [but] to the excellence and weight of his character, and of the candour of his hearers, who, possessed of high sentiments of the latter passed over the unpleasing defects of the former. (*Protestant Dissenter's Magazine*, 1794, 465–7)

Lowman sat lightly in the denominational setting. He was recognized at various times as a Presbyterian and an Independent. Voting with the Presbyterian majority for non-subscription at Salters' Hall in 1719, he was also a founder member of the London Congregational board in 1727. His style appeared to match the religious sentiments of the time. 'His piety was rational, not superstitious; the effect of principle not enthusiasm; grave but not morose; and serious without being disfigured by sourness' (*Protestant Dissenter's Magazine*, 1794, 469).

Lowman was married to Martha (*d.* 1771), daughter of John Travers, a wealthy London merchant; they had two sons and a daughter. He died at Clapham on 3 May 1752; according to Samuel Chandler, who preached his funeral sermon, 'he continued in his ministerial labours till accident and disorder put an end to his services' (Chandler, 39–40). ALAN RUSTON

Sources S. Chandler, *The character and reward of a Christian bishop: a sermon occasioned by the death of Mr Moses Lowman … preached at Clapham* (1752), 38–46 • *Protestant Dissenter's Magazine*, 1 (1794), 465–70 • *Protestant Dissenter's Magazine*, 2 (1795), 46–7 • *IGI* • Foster, *Alum. Oxon.* • J. Waddington, *Surrey Congregational history* (1866), 185 • W. D. Jeremy, *The Presbyterian Fund and Dr Daniel Williams's Trust* (1885), 134 • D. Bogue and J. Bennett, *History of dissenters, from the revolution in 1688, to … 1808*, 3 (1810), 384–6 • T. G. Crippen, 'London Congregational Board', *Transactions of the Congregational Historical Society*, 2 (1905–6), 50–60, esp. 50–57 • will, 1752, PRO, PROB 11/795, sig. 241 • will, Martha Lowman, 1772, PRO, PROB 11/974, sig. 18 • R. Thomas, 'Presbyterians, Congregationals, and the Test and Corporation Acts', *Transactions of the Unitarian Historical Society*, 11/4 (1955–8), 117–27, esp. 117 • H. A. C. Sturgess, ed., *Register of admissions to the Honourable Society of the Middle Temple, from the fifteenth century to the year 1944*, 1 (1949)
Archives DWL
Wealth at death see will, 1752, PRO, PROB 11/795, sig. 241

Lowndes, Alan Bailey (1921–1978), landscape painter, was born on 23 February 1921 in Stockport, Cheshire, the fourth child of Samuel Lowndes (*d. c.*1955), railway clerk, and his wife, Helen Morrey (*d.* 1924), daughter of a blacksmith from Kilmarnock, Scotland. Lowndes grew up in impoverished circumstances in a working-class neighbourhood, Heaton Norris, in Stockport. He began attending Christ Church School, Heaton Norris, in 1926. He received little formal art training. After leaving school in 1935 an apprenticeship as painter, decorator, and signwriter proved useful, equipping the emerging painter with a suitably robust feeling for paint's expressive qualities.

Having joined the Territorial Army in September 1939, Lowndes received call-up papers shortly after the outbreak of the Second World War. He was shipped out to the Middle East, where he served in the north African desert. He later became a draughtsman for the Royal Army Service Corps in Italy. Also in Italy, Lowndes produced landscapes in watercolour, which were shown after the war to Emmanuel Levy, the Manchester portrait painter, who gave Lowndes instruction in evening classes at Stockport School of Art. He was otherwise self-taught.

Lowndes's earliest pictures depict the streets, mills, factories, and prominent viaduct of post-war Stockport. They are richer in colour than Lowry's equivalent subjects. They also focus, in an anecdotal and affectionate way, on working-class rituals such as queuing for fish and chips, gossiping on street corners, or walking to football matches. Lowry's vision, in contrast, was more detached and impersonal, the overlap between their shared industrial subject matter notwithstanding. Living in poverty in his studio at St Petersgate, Stockport, Lowndes was discovered by the ambitious Hungarian émigré Andras Kalman, founder of the Crane Gallery, which opened in 1950 in South King Street, Manchester. From 1950 onwards Lowndes exhibited regularly with Kalman, who sold Lowndes's paintings to emerging playwrights, actors, and local businessmen. After Kalman's relocation to Knightsbridge, London, in 1958, Lowndes's paintings sold to many well-known actors, whose northern backgrounds were echoed in pictures with an obvious documentary value and nostalgic appeal. One typical street scene, *Coronation Street* (1950), was an influence on the conception of the long-running television soap opera.

Encouraged by Kalman, Lowndes began visiting St Ives, Cornwall, during the early 1950s. The vibrant Cornish art colony galvanized Lowndes, who started to introduce local harbour and fishing subject matter in his work. He alternated this with northern industrial landscapes, both of which proved popular in solo and group exhibitions at the Crane Kalman Gallery. In 1958 he worked as a scene painter for the Belle Vue circus in Manchester, an experience that led to several paintings of clowns and other circus performers.

During a trip to the south of France in the summer of 1959 Lowndes met Valerie Holmes (*b.* 1928), a secretary at the Karolyi Foundation, Vence. They married on 12 October 1959 and settled in St Ives during the late autumn of that year. The couple had three children, Amanda (*b.* 1960), Martin (*b.* 1962), and Rosalind (*b.* 1964). While living in Cornwall, Lowndes enjoyed three solo shows at the Crane Kalman Gallery, in 1961, 1965, and 1968, and held a one-man exhibition at the Osborn Gallery, New York, in 1964. Among the pictures exhibited were *Sunset Fishing* (1963), *The Lone Fisherman* (1966), and *A Rough Day* (1967), all in private collections, which reflect an empathy with the sea and emulate the intense visual poetry of Christopher Wood.

Lowndes's figurative paintings ran counter to the orthodox abstraction of the modern St Ives movement. The directness of his work reflected an idiosyncratic and gregarious character. A searching, original thinker, he sought a fresh challenge. In 1970 the Lowndes family left Cornwall to live near Dursley, Gloucestershire. From then onwards Lowndes's pictures embraced rural subjects and local landscapes. Paintings of Slimbridge, Tetbury market, and the railway at Cam were complemented by a series based on Cardiff docks. In 1972 the municipal art gallery of his home town, Stockport, gave him a major retrospective exhibition. Lowndes died in Gloucester Royal Hospital on 22 September 1978, and was buried on 1 October in St George's Church, Upper Cam, Dursley. Several posthumous shows, including two at the Crane Kalman Gallery in 1984 and 1995, proved the enduring popularity of this colourful painter of everyday life. His work is held by Manchester City Galleries, Stockport Art Gallery, and the Mappin Art Gallery, Sheffield. PETER DAVIES

Sources P. Davies, *A northern school* (1989) • P. Davies, *St Ives revisited* (1994) • J. Willett, introduction, *Alan Lowndes: paintings, 1948–1972*, ed. L. Klepac (1972) [exhibition catalogue, Crane Kalman Gallery, London] • MS notes by Alan Lowndes, priv. coll. • artist's file, archive material, Courtauld Inst., Witt Library • b. cert. • m. cert. • d. cert. • *CGPLA Eng. & Wales* (1978)

Archives Courtauld Inst., Witt Library, photographic archive of paintings and catalogues • priv. coll., corresp. and notes

Likenesses photographs, 1940–60, priv. coll. • photographs, Crane Kalman Gallery, London

Wealth at death £4316: administration, 3 Nov 1978, *CGPLA Eng. & Wales*

Lowndes, Marie Adelaide Elizabeth Renée Julia Belloc (1868–1947), author, was born on 5 August 1868 at 11 George Street, Marylebone, London, the first of two children of Louis Marie Belloc (1830–1872), French barrister, and his wife, Elizabeth (Bessie) Rayner *Parkes (1829–1925), great-granddaughter of Joseph Priestley, formerly editor of the *English Woman's Journal* and an active British feminist, who had converted to Catholicism. Marie Belloc and her younger brother, Hilaire *Belloc, were brought up as Catholics, spending most of their time at La Celle St Cloud, then a rural suburb of Paris. During the Franco-Prussian War of 1870 and the Paris commune of 1871 the family lived in London at 11 Great College Street, Westminster. Although their house in France had suffered badly from the war, they returned, and continued to spend much of the year there even after the death of Louis Belloc in August 1872. Both Marie and Hilaire considered themselves at least half French, and Marie always seemed to speak English with a slight French accent (although she was known as Mary to her brother and most of her friends). When not in France they lived with Mrs Eliza Parkes, Bessie's mother, at 17 Wimpole Street. However, in 1877 Mrs Parkes died, and shortly afterwards Bessie Belloc lost much of her money through an unfortunate investment, which forced the family to move to a cottage at Slindon in Sussex.

Marie Belloc's life was thus subject to disruption; her formal education seems to have consisted of two years in a convent at Mayfield in Sussex, and even in old age she regretted her poor spelling of both French and English. Despite this, in her teens she decided to become a writer, and in 1888 Cardinal Manning, a family friend, introduced her to W. T. Stead, who accepted her as a contributor to the *Pall Mall Gazette* under the tutelage of Edmund Garrett. Her first major assignment was collaborating on a guide to the 1889 Paris Exhibition. From then on she continued to write for the *Pall Mall Gazette*, among other periodicals, mainly on French matters, making numerous trips to France, and meeting many prominent French writers of the day, including Edmond de Goncourt, Paul Verlaine, and Jules Verne. In this way she contributed to the family income, helping among other things to subsidize Hilaire Belloc's education. On 9 January 1896 she married Frederick Sawney Archibald Lowndes (1867–1940), a staff writer on *The Times*; they had one son and two daughters.

Although she had a reasonably successful career as a journalist, Marie Belloc Lowndes's main ambition was to write books, especially fiction. Shortly after their marriage Frederick Lowndes was left a legacy of £2000 and suggested that they live on this while Marie tried her hand at writing. Her first two books had little success, but she soon began to make a name for herself. In the course of the next fifty years she published at least seventy books of various kinds, mainly under her own name, but for two works using the pseudonyms Philip Curtin and Elizabeth Rayner. Her books included biographies of royal persons, but more usually they were romances or crime novels. It was the last genre with which she came to be most associated, especially through her novels *The Chink in the Armour* (1912) and most of all *The Lodger*, published in 1913, a story of a London couple in the 1880s who suspect that their lodger is Jack the Ripper; this has undergone various adaptations, as a stage play, several films (including an early Alfred Hitchcock), and an opera by Phyllis Tate. *The Lodger* was a best-seller in its day, yet Marie Belloc Lowndes found herself constrained in the summer of 1914 to borrow £350 from her brother, Hilaire Belloc, to pay off an overdraft, a debt which seemed to rankle over the years, although in general brother and sister remained friends.

In 1909 Marie Belloc Lowndes and her husband had set up house at 9 Barton Street, just round the corner from her childhood home at Great College Street. Even before her marriage she had enjoyed an active social life, among other things attending the Sunday 'at homes' of Constance and Oscar Wilde, and after her marriage her husband's unsocial working hours allowed her to lead, as she put it, 'the life of a happy widow'. During the day she wrote (with a quill pen), but from late afternoon she regularly went visiting or entertained. She made friends with (among many others) Henry James, Rhoda Broughton, and George Meredith, as well as Margot Asquith; during Herbert Asquith's premiership she was a frequent guest at 10 Downing Street. She also helped younger writers, encouraging among others Graham Greene, Hugh Walpole, Margaret Kennedy, E. M. Delafield, and L. P. Hartley. Like her mother, but unlike her brother, she was a strong supporter of women's rights, being president of the Women Writers' Suffrage League in 1913. Also, like many suffragists at this time, she was always a smart dresser, asserting that every woman ought to dress as far as she could afford to do so in the fashion. She was a frequent traveller, especially to the USA, to which she made annual visits in the 1930s, and where she had many admirers—some unexpected, such as Ernest Hemingway, to whom her books had been recommended by Gertrude Stein.

On the outbreak of war in 1939 Marie Belloc Lowndes and her husband (now retired) moved to 28 Crooked Billet, near Wimbledon Common, where her husband died in 1940, to her great grief. Henceforward she embarked on autobiography, producing four highly successful volumes: *I, too, have Lived in Arcadia* (1941), *Where Love and Friendship Dwelt* (1943), *The Merry Wives of Westminster* (1946), and *A Passing World* (1948). In 1942 she had moved back to Barton Street, this time to no. 1, and she spent the rest of her life between there and Parfetts House, Eversley Cross, Hampshire, where her daughter Lady Iddesleigh lived. She died at Parfetts House of stomach cancer on 14 November 1947. DAVID DOUGHAN

Sources *Diaries and letters of Marie Belloc Lowndes, 1911–1947*, ed. S. Lowndes (1971) • M. Belloc Lowndes, *I, too, have lived in Arcadia: a record of love and of childhood* (1941) • M. Belloc Lowndes, *Where love and friendship dwelt* (1943) • M. Belloc Lowndes, *The merry wives of Westminster* (1946) • M. Belloc Lowndes, *A passing world* (1948) • *WWW, 1941–50* • P. Schlueter and J. Schlueter, eds., *An encyclopedia of British women writers* (1988) • J. Todd, ed., *Dictionary of British women writers* (1989) • A. N. Wilson, *Hilaire Belloc* (1984) • b. cert. • d. cert. • m. cert.

Archives Boston College, Massachusetts, Belloc papers • Girton Cam., corresp. and papers for biography of Bessie Rayner Parkes • Ransom HRC, corresp. and literary papers • Richmond Local Studies Library, London, corresp. and literary papers | BL, corresp. with the League of Dramatists, Add. MS 63359 • BL, corresp. with the Society of Authors, Add. MSS 56739–56740 • Col. U., Melony papers • Georgetown University, Washington, DC, Iddesleigh and Marques papers • Indiana University, Bloomington, Pearson MSS • U. Cam., Templewood papers • University of Arkansas, Fayetteville, Swinnerton papers • University of Waterloo, Ontario, women writers' letters

Likenesses photograph, repro. in Lowndes, ed., *Diaries and letters* (1971) • photograph, repro. in Belloc Lowndes, *Where love and friendship dwelt* • photograph, repro. in Belloc Lowndes, *A passing world* • photograph?, repro. in *Sunday Telegraph* (28 May 2000)

Wealth at death £2126 15*s*. 3*d*.: probate, 16 March 1948, *CGPLA Eng. & Wales*

Lowndes, Mary (1856–1929), stained-glass artist, was born on 30 December 1856 at the rectory, Poole Keynes, near Cirencester, the eldest in the family of four sons and four daughters of Richard Lowndes (1821–1898) and Annie Harriet Kaye (1827–1907), eldest daughter of William Kaye of the Inner Temple and Ampney Park, Gloucestershire. Her father was vicar of St Mary's Church, Sturminster Newton, Dorset, which was dedicated to her paternal grandfather, William Loftus Lowndes (1793–1865), barrister and QC; he was also a canon of Salisbury. When she was nine a large east window produced in the factory of John Hardman of Birmingham, depicting *Christ in Majesty* and surrounded by the *Acts of Mercy*, was erected in the church, and appears to have inspired Mary's future vocation.

At twenty-seven, and after an education described by her sister Rebe as by a long line of mostly very inefficient governesses, Mary Lowndes left for London, where in 1883 she entered the Slade School of Fine Art. She also studied privately with the stained-glass artist Henry Holiday (1839–1927), with whom she learned to make cartoons. In the 1890s she taught herself the techniques of glass painting as well as designing; her first commissions were made in collaboration with the firm of Britten and Gilson, in whose premises in Southwark Street she took a glass painting studio. Her work was much influenced by the designs and craftsmanship of another studio holder, Christopher Whall, who became the leading stained-glass artist of the arts and crafts movement. The firm had developed a new type of glass initiated by the architect Edward Prior and known as 'Prior glass' or 'slab glass', which was characterized by uneven thickness and great brilliancy of colour. Though she made extensive use of slab glass (for example, in the centre east lancet of Lamarsh church, Essex, in 1896), it was expensive to buy and time-consuming to lead. In 1897 she formed a business partnership with Alfred J. Drury, head glazier at Britten and Gilson, and set up the firm of Lowndes and Drury to provide facilities and permanent staff including cutters, glaziers, and kiln-men, to enable stained-glass artists to participate in the whole process of carrying out a design. Materials and services were to be paid for by artists out of commission fees. The firm was a success and moved from its small premises at 35 Park Walk, Chelsea, to purpose-built studios and workshops, known as the Glass House in Lettice Street, Fulham. These attracted artists, many of them women, from all over the country who went to work or to study there. Drury oversaw the practical side of the business, and Lowndes continued to design and collaborate on stained-glass projects with other artists, including the illustrator Isobel Gloag (1865–1917) and the painter Emily Ford (1851–1930). She designed and made over 100 windows from the 1890s to the 1920s, including figurative and decorative designs for churches, commercial premises, and houses. Two of her earliest works were of a personal nature and comprise two windows: a *Nativity* (1895) dedicated to her grandmother Ella Lowndes, and a *Resurrection* (1898), of an elegant arts and crafts design, dedicated to her father in the church at Sturminster Newton.

From 1907 Mary Lowndes was active for about nine years, as a non-militant, in the last phase of the women's suffrage movement. She was chairman of the Artists' Suffrage League, and a committee member of the London Society for Women's Suffrage and of the National Union of Women's Suffrage Societies. She designed many of the banners executed for the latter, including those for the demonstration of 21 June 1908, and for the Women's Pageant of Trades and Professions held the following year at the Albert Hall as part of the International Woman Suffrage Alliance Congress. Many of her banner designs are in an album, together with her treatise *On Banners and Banner-Making*, in the Fawcett Library, London Guildhall University. From 1910 to 1920 she was a prolific contributor to *The Englishwoman*, and was active in the organization of the Women Welders' Union during the First World War. After the war Lowndes and Drury produced many war memorial windows. Though she sometimes grumbled about her committee work, Lowndes was an inspiring leader, and very generous. She worked hard (in spite of suffering from asthma) and to high standards. She never married. Following her death on 28 February 1929 at her home, 27 Trafalgar Square, London, she left most of her estate to her friend and companion Barbara Forbes.

NANCY ARMSTRONG

Sources P. Cormack, *Women stained glass artists of the arts and crafts movement* (1985) [exhibition catalogue, William Morris Gallery,

London, 7 Dec 1985 – 2 March 1986] · L. Tickner, *The spectacle of women: imagery of the suffrage campaign, 1907–14* (1987) · L. Lee, G. Seddon, and F. Stephens, *Stained glass* (1982) · M. Harrison, *Victorian stained glass* (1980) · F. Miller, 'Women workers in the art crafts', *Art Journal*, new ser., 18 (1898), 116–18 · E. Crawford, *The women's suffrage movement: a reference guide, 1866–1928* (1999) · N. Armstrong, 'The stained glass windows in St Mary's Church, Sturminster Newton, Dorset', Dorchester Museum, Dorset · M. Lowndes, 'Genius and women painters', *Women's Suffrage* (17 April 1914), 31 · M. Lowndes, 'On banners and banner-making', *The Englishwoman*, 7 (Sept 1910), 172–8 [subsequently published as a pamphlet by the Artists' Suffrage League] · M. Lowndes, 'The little new trade union', *The Englishwoman*, 34 (1917), 20–32 · private information (2004) · b. cert. · *The Guardian* (26 Oct 1898) [obit. of Richard Lowndes] · photocopy of Mary Lowndes's will, dated 14 June 1929 · *CGPLA Eng. & Wales* (1929) · d. cert.

Archives priv. coll., notebooks · Women's Library, London, 'Mary Lowndes album' | London Metropolitan University, papers of Artists' Suffrage League

Wealth at death £15,837 2*s*. 8*d*.: probate, 14 June 1929, *CGPLA Eng. & Wales*

Lowndes, Noble Frank (1896–1972), underwriter and insurance company manager, was born on 28 August 1896 at Gisborne, New Zealand, the eldest of the six sons of Frank Forbes Lowndes, wool shipper, and his wife, Laura Louisa. After primary school, Lowndes worked in Gisborne in his father's firm, and later was employed by a large export firm in Auckland. At the outbreak of the First World War, Lowndes volunteered for the army and was sent to German Samoa, where he landed on his eighteenth birthday and raised the flag as a member of the 1st New Zealand expeditionary force. After six months he was invalided with tropical fever, and later, with the Anzacs, he was also wounded on the Western Front.

After the war Lowndes returned to New Zealand to work for his father's transport business, but this became bankrupt in the post-war depression, and Lowndes found employment selling life assurance in Auckland. Promoted to head the firm's pension unit, he attempted to promote more sophisticated employee benefit schemes such as combined pension, life, sickness, and accident insurance, but his employers objected. He resigned to join an Australian company, Mutual Life and Citizens, and moved to Sydney, where he became the youngest ever life manager for New South Wales. In 1928 he married Maisie Hennessy of Gisborne; but they were later divorced.

In 1932 Lowndes became manager of a newly opened branch of Mutual Life in London, but was again frustrated by opposition towards his underwriting ideas. In 1934 he therefore left Mutual Life to set up his own broking firm in London. His partners included his brothers Roy and Colin, and in 1938 the firm moved to 38 Lowndes Street in Belgravia, a street named after one of Lowndes's ancestors, a secretary to the Treasury under Queen Anne.

Over the next thirty-five years, Noble Lowndes & Partners expanded to become an international business, specializing in the design of company pension schemes, insurance broking, and life assurance. By 1939 Lowndes was already regarded as one of the leading life insurance agents in the City of London. From the outbreak of the Second World War he enthusiastically promoted innovative endowment assurance schemes, under which premium contributions could be offset against the rising burden of taxation. He also persuaded insurance companies to issue full war-risk cover on all schemes arranged by his firm. After the war further innovations included the notorious 'top hat scheme' of 1946, criticized as a form of tax evasion. Under this scheme the nominal salary of a senior executive was reduced, and the difference paid by the employer as a premium on an endowment assurance. The object was to maximize the amount of premiums paid towards the pension, at no extra cost to the employer, while reducing the amount of income lost to taxation.

By 1960 the success of this and other schemes had made Noble Lowndes the largest firm of pension consultants in the world. One in four British companies had a pension scheme devised by Noble Lowndes. The firm, which became a limited company in 1949, also expanded overseas, and business was extended to offer personal financial services to senior executives, most of whom came to Noble Lowndes through their pension schemes.

Although intensely proud of British traditions, Lowndes saw himself as a wild colonial boy who had come back to the mother country to make good. A staunch New Zealander, during the Second World War he had kept open house at his Warlingham home in Surrey for New Zealand and Australian fighter pilots based at Biggin Hill. He retired to Jersey in 1960, a few years before the firm of Noble Lowndes was taken over by the merchant bank Hill Samuel. In 1964 he declined the offer of a life peerage to join the new Labour government in a finance portfolio, because 'it would have been the icing on the cake for my Establishment foes in the City'. He did, however, continue to act as an adviser to the government on national pensions. After his divorce from his first wife Lowndes remarried, and he and his second wife, Jane Hose, had a son and a daughter. He spent his leisure time sedately, gardening and playing bridge. He died in Jersey on 9 May 1972.

ROBIN PEARSON

Sources H. Woolhouse, 'Lowndes, Noble Frank', *DBB* · *The Times* (10 May 1972) · N. Lowndes & Partners, 'The story of Noble Lowndes', Sedgwick Noble Lowndes Ltd, Norfolk House, Croydon · *The Times* (27 June 1972) · private information (2004)

Likenesses photograph (after portrait), repro. in Woolhouse, 'Lowndes, Frank Noble' · portrait, priv. coll.

Lowndes, Rawlins (*c*.1721–1800), lawyer and revolutionary politician in America, was born on the island of St Kitts in the British West Indies, the youngest of three sons of Charles Lowndes (*d*. 1736) and his wife, Ruth, *née* Rawlins (*d*. 1763). The family migrated to South Carolina in 1730 but after the death of Charles, Ruth and her eldest son, William, returned to St Kitts. Young Lowndes and his brother Charles were placed in the care of Robert Hall, provost marshal of the colony, under whom they studied law. From 1742 to 1752 Rawlins was deputy provost marshal. On 15 August 1748 he married Amarinthia (1729–1750), daughter of John Elliott and his wife, Mary. A second marriage, following the death of Amarinthia, was to Mary (*d*. 1770), daughter of Daniel Cartwright and his wife,

Sarah, *née* Butler, on 23 December 1751. They had seven children. By the 1760s Rawlins had a home on West Tradd Street, Charles Town, 3800 acres in the low country, a warrant for 7300 acres in Georgia, and at least three houses and other property in the city. His third marriage, in January 1773, was to Sarah (1757–1800), daughter of Charles Jones of Georgia, with whom he had a further three children. Crowfield plantation was added to his Goose Creek and Horseshoe estates in 1775.

Lowndes's political career spanned nearly fifty years and included service in the South Carolina Commons house of assembly (1749–54, 1757–75), where he served as speaker of the house (1763–5, 1772–5). He was also a member of the first and second South Carolina extra-legal provincial congresses (1775, 1776) and of the state's revolutionary general assemblies (1776–8, 1787–90). During this time he was also an associate judge of the South Carolina court of common pleas (1766–73). A hallmark of his service was resistance to arbitrary authority whether exercised by British ministers, royal governors, placemen, or an arrogant governor's council. His opposition to Governor Thomas Boone (1761–4) in a case involving a disputed assembly election was successful. From the bench on 13 May 1766 he ruled that the Stamp Act of 1765, by which parliament taxed internal colonial trade, was against the common rights of the people. The motion to advance £7000 to erect a statue of William Pitt, earl of Chatham, in Charles Town to honour Pitt's effort to repeal the Stamp Act was made by Lowndes. In 1772, when Governor Charles Greville Montagu tried to deny Lowndes the speakership, the Commons house gave Lowndes its unanimous support, forcing the governor to back down. A ruling by Lowndes in 1773 stating that the governor's council could not act as a house of peers, thus limiting their power and increasing that of the Commons house, was sustained by the British House of Lords on 11 May 1775.

In the period of transition from royal to revolutionary government, Lowndes was a leading advocate of moderation. He hoped for reconciliation with Great Britain, respected British law, and initially opposed the Declaration of Independence, but when it was adopted he supported it. A member of the committee of eleven who wrote the South Carolina state constitution, he became president of South Carolina on 10 March 1778. He did not seek re-election the following year, choosing to retire to his plantation, Crowfield, rather than face continuing political turmoil and invading British forces. When Charles Town surrendered to the British on 10 May 1780, Lowndes was present. Soon afterwards he petitioned the town's new government for a return of his rights as a British subject, having suffered substantial losses of property when his plantation was pillaged. Although he was acting in conjunction with other prominent patriot South Carolinians, the former president was heavily criticized. When the conflict ended in 1783, he successfully petitioned the new state government for the return of his citizenship and re-entered the political arena. In the debate over the adoption of the federal constitution of 1787 Lowndes was an ardent critic, arguing that the document lacked sufficient safeguards to protect minority and southern interests. An anti-federalist, he was convinced that government responded more to sectional forces than to idealistic arguments. His memorable comment was: 'Here lies the man who opposed the Constitution because it was ruinous to the liberty of America' (Ravenel, 30). The inauguration of the new federal government coincided with the close of his public career.

Rawlins Lowndes rose to become a prominent figure in South Carolina, demonstrating a strong sense of duty, personal merit, character, and industry. Concurrent with his notable political career was his service in local offices as a commissioner of revenue, vestryman of St Michael and St Philip parishes, justice of the peace, commissioner of a free school, warden of ward six and intendant of Charles Town (in 1783 renamed Charleston), a member of the South Carolina Society, and the St Cecilia Society. Earnest and paternal in manner, he left a numerous family well positioned. He died in Charleston on 24 August 1800 and was buried there in St Philip's Church. Sarah, Lowndes's third wife, was killed in an accident only a few months later. FREDERICK V. MILLS, SR.

Sources W. B. Edgar and N. L. Bailey, eds., *Biographical directory of the South Carolina house of representatives*, 2 (1977) • C. J. Vipperman, *The rise of Rawlins Lowndes, 1721–1800* (1978) • G. B. Chase, *Lowndes of South Carolina: an historical and genealogical memoir* (1876) • St J. Ravenel, *Life and times of William Lowndes of South Carolina, 1782–1822* (1901) • E. McCrady, *The history of South Carolina under the royal government, 1719–1776* (1899); repr. (New York, 1969) • M. E. Sirmans, *Colonial South Carolina: a political history, 1663–1763* (Chapel Hill, NC, 1966) • J. P. Greene, *The quest for power: the lower houses of assembly in the southern royal colonies, 1689–1776* (1963) • S. W. Crompton, 'Lowndes, Rawlins', *ANB*

Archives L. Cong. | University of North Carolina Library, Chapel Hill, Southern Historical collection

Wealth at death at least $70,000; plus city properties, lands, and plantations: will, Charleston county wills, 28.26–36, South Carolina Archives and History Center, Columbia

Lowndes, Thomas (*bap.* **1692**, *d.* **1748**), colonial official and benefactor, was baptized at Astbury, Cheshire, on 7 December 1692. He was the second son of William Lowndes of Overton, an estate at Astbury, and his wife and cousin Elizabeth, daughter of Ralph Lowndes of Lea Hall. Thomas spent his childhood at Lea Hall, and through family influence became a clerk to the Treasury.

On 27 September 1725 Lowndes received from the lords proprietors of South Carolina the patent of provost marshal. He never visited the colony, entrusting his duties to a deputy, but he profited substantially from financial dues paid to him as holder of the position. In this capacity he urged the crown's purchase of the colony, arguing for the colony's fertile soil, ease of defence, disunion among its proprietors, and its potential to restrain French and Spanish expansion. He also advanced schemes promoting foreign emigration to the colony, the manufacture of potash, and the incorporation of North Carolina with Virginia.

On 30 November 1730 George II renewed Lowndes's patent of provost marshal, which he had surrendered at the transference of the colony to the crown in 1727. However, its value was greatly reduced by an act declaring all process null and void unless served by the provost marshal or his deputy in person. Lowndes did his utmost to have the Summons Act, which in the days of the lords proprietors had screened the abuses of the provost marshals, restored. When the assembly rejected this proposal he accused—possibly upon false information—Governor Robert Johnson of purposely withholding the motion. Johnson, writing from Charles Town on 28 September 1732, warned the Board of Trade against listening to the insinuations of a man who 'by the neglect of the late lords proprietors had made the province his property to the extent of £4,000 or £5,000, by no other merit than a consummate assurance'. In 1733 Lowndes resigned his patent of provost marshal, and it was not again renewed.

In the following decade Lowndes turned his attention to questions of domestic trade. In 1745 he published *A Method to Prevent, without a Register, the Running of Wool from Ireland to France*, in which he blamed the decay of the British woollen manufacture on the restrictions placed on Irish trade. Appealing to the example of the Netherlands, Lowndes proposed to allow Ireland to manufacture in the Isle of Man home-grown wool into cloth and from there import it into England duty-free. The proposal met with no success and his attempt to introduce the measure in parliament came to nothing. He had better fortune with a project to supply the navy with salt, much of which then took the form of poor-quality imports. He developed his own method of producing salt which he advocated in a pamphlet in 1746. His specimens were highly praised by the Royal College of Physicians (their report, dated 27 August 1745, was printed with the pamphlet), but the Admiralty refused his terms. Lowndes carried the scheme to the House of Commons, and in June 1746 the house petitioned the king to instruct the Admiralty to accept the terms. Additional statements on the merits of his proposal included *A Seasonable Hint for our Pilchard and Coast Fishery* and a letter from Lowndes 'to the salt proprietors of Great Britain' (both 1748). However, he did not see his plan fully tested: he died, unmarried, on 12 May 1748, at Overton Manor. By his will he left the estate at Overton, bought from his elder brother's daughter, and all his other property in Cheshire to found a chair of astronomy in Cambridge University, the Lowndean professorship of astronomy and geometry. The first professor, Roger Long, was appointed in 1750. J. A. CRAMB, *rev.* TROY O. BICKHAM

Sources W. Lowndes, *A Cheshire family: Lowndes of Overton* (1972)
Archives PRO, Colonial Office MSS for South Carolina
Wealth at death left a house and land to University of Cambridge: Lowndes, *A Cheshire family*, 20–21

Lowndes, William (1652–1724), Treasury official, was born at Winslow, Buckinghamshire, on 1 November 1652, the younger son of Robert Lowndes (*bap.* 1619, *d.* 1683) and his wife, Elizabeth, the daughter of Peter Fitzwilliams. Lowndes was descended from an old Cheshire gentry family, a cadet branch of which had established itself at Winslow early in the sixteenth century. His father had avoided participation in the civil war by emigrating to the American colonies, but returned to Winslow after the execution of Charles I. The family were impoverished minor

William Lowndes (1652–1724), by or after Sir Godfrey Kneller

gentry, and young William's formal education advanced no further than his attendance at the free school at nearby Buckingham. In 1667 he went to live in London. Precisely when his lifelong connection with the Treasury began has not been ascertained, but the records reveal that he was established there as a clerk by 1675, which may suggest that his government career had begun in a minor capacity some years before.

Lowndes quickly excelled as a versatile and promising government servant. At first under the tutelage of the lord treasurer, Danby, he impressed Charles II in 1676 with the thoroughness of an investigation he conducted into racketeering by the sub-farmers of the coffee duties, and was afterwards regularly on duty at Treasury board meetings at Windsor and Newmarket, depending on where the royal court was based. His varied responsibilities in these early years also brought him closely in touch with the House of Commons. Here, he acted as an essential channel of communication to Lord Danby, advising him in relation to the detail and progress of money bills through the house, and providing drafts of proposed clauses requiring the consideration of the various revenue departments. In March 1679 Danby procured for him a customs sinecure (surrendered in 1680) and the reversion to an office in the duchy of Cornwall, though Lowndes subsequently regarded these as inconsiderable rewards.

Late in 1679 Henry Guy, a financier with strong connections at court, was appointed secretary to the Treasury and soon came to regard Lowndes as a rare talent in the running of the Treasury office. He chose Lowndes as his chief or senior clerk, though it is not known when this appointment was actually made. Initially, it may not have been a formal arrangement, but it is clear that Lowndes began deputizing for Guy in Treasury affairs as early as 1680. Their association endured with mutual benefit for many years. Lowndes operated alongside the small number of other senior clerks, including such long-serving men as Robert Squibb, William Shaw, and Samuel Langford. The 1680s saw a significant expansionist phase in the development of the Treasury, during which Guy was ably assisted by Lowndes's financial expertise and command of administrative detail. Lowndes became an expert on the complex and arcane workings of the exchequer, upon which he produced a handbook in 1684–5, and was highly skilled in drafting complex documentation. By the mid-1680s he was suggesting important improvements in procedure, and in 1685 Guy procured for him the additional post of agent for taxes, responsible for co-ordinating the work of the provincial receivers-general, with a salary of £200.

Lowndes was less fortunate in his personal life. He married four times between 1679 and 1691, each of his first three wives dying young. His first wife was Elizabeth (*d.* 1680), the daughter of Sir Roger Harsnett of Dulwich, Kent, whom he married on 26 October 1679, and with whom he had one son, Robert (*d.* 1727). His second wife, whom he married on 25 November 1683, was Jane (*d.* 1685), the daughter of Simon Hopper of Richmond, Surrey, with whom he had a daughter. On 12 July 1686 he married, third, Elizabeth (*d.* 1689), the daughter of the Revd Dr Richard Martin, and added another son and daughter to his family. He married, fourth, on 29 November 1691, Rebecca (*d.* 1742), the daughter of John Shales, a colleague of Lowndes in the exchequer, a relationship which endured fruitfully until Lowndes's death. Between 1692 and 1710 their marriage produced seven sons and seven daughters, though Lowndes was survived by only two of the sons and four of the daughters.

Although for political reasons Guy was removed from the Treasury following the revolution of 1688 until being reinstated in 1691, Lowndes remained in his post unscathed. The turning point in his career came suddenly in February 1695 when Guy was sent to the Tower on charges of corruption. The Treasury lords immediately nominated Lowndes as acting secretary, a role he had briefly performed in 1691, but left open the question of Guy's successor. Guy's destruction at the hands of the junto Whigs had in fact been only partial since his patron, Lord Sunderland, retained the goodwill of William III who allowed Guy the liberty of naming his successor. Lowndes was a natural choice, not only on account of his mastery of Treasury business, but also because he lacked political experience and was without political connection. With Lowndes in charge of the Treasury secretariat, Guy could expect to exercise a continuing influence in Treasury business, which would serve both his own and Sunderland's purposes. In facilitating this arrangement, Lowndes agreed that Guy should continue to receive the profits of the secretary's office while restricting himself to a salary of £1000 (later increased to £1200), which in the mid-1690s was less than half the net value of the secretary's office. Even after Guy's career had faded by the end of the decade, the payments to him continued, possibly until his death in 1710, and were justified by Lowndes to the Treasury board in 1702 as 'an acknowledgement to a person he had been so beholden to' (PRO, T64/126, fols. 247–8, quoted in Baxter, 201).

Lowndes kissed the king's hand for his new office on 24 April 1695. He had already become involved in the government's efforts to resolve the worsening coinage crisis. The practice of 'clipping' hammered silver coin had reached the point where it was seriously affecting the Treasury's ability to pay its way in the war with France, and in late 1694 confidence in the silver coinage weakened dramatically. A complete reminting of the coinage was now imperative, but the problem facing a House of Commons committee early in 1695 was whether there should be a temporary devaluation in order to stabilize the currency while the old money was reminted, a primary concern being to offset the inevitable loss in the value of tax receipts. Earlier generations of historians, focusing upon the publication of opposing views on the subject by Lowndes and the philosopher John Locke, have portrayed Lowndes as the main exponent of devaluation and refer to the public difference of opinion between the two men as 'the Locke–Lowndes controversy'. More recent investigation, however, casts doubt on whether the views published under Lowndes's name on the Treasury's behalf represented his personal views. In a written report to the Treasury board in January 1695 Lowndes actually ruled out any suggestion of devaluation. While modestly conceding a limited grasp of the complexities behind the issue, he envisaged an immediate loss of some £150,000 in revenue, which would have to be met by a 'public tax', and a worrying increase in the cost of England's military payments abroad.

The recoinage proposals put forward by the House of Commons in April 1695 embodied a nominal rate of 9 per cent devaluation, but received little notice, largely because Locke had earlier published a pamphlet against devaluation. But as the situation grew more urgent, Lowndes was instructed by the Treasury board in August to prepare a detailed scheme for recoinage, and since majority opinion on the board favoured devaluation it would appear that Lowndes was instructed to follow the scheme already proposed by the Commons. By mid-September his 'book', *A Report Containing an Essay for the Amendment of the Silver Coins*, was in Treasury hands. It embodied the Commons committee's resolutions and was fleshed out with much historical detail, but owing to the rapid increase in the market price of silver a devaluation rate of 20 per cent would now be necessary. William III and his ministers acknowledged Lowndes's ingenuity and scholarship but, disagreeing with the Treasury board, saw greater virtue in Locke's arguments for a recoinage at the old standard. Thus it was largely to assist the ministry's own scheme for recoinage in parliament that Lowndes's *Report* was subsequently published in November 1695, followed by Locke's *Further Considerations Concerning Raising the Value of Money*. While paying tribute to Lowndes's erudition, Locke was quick to point out that some of his arguments tended in fact to condemn devaluation of any kind. Moreover, the encouragement which Lowndes gave to Locke and other critics to publish their rebuttals of his *Report* would likewise suggest that Lowndes had never personally favoured devaluation. In January 1696 an act was passed for a recoinage at the existing standard.

At the general election in November 1695 Lowndes entered parliament for the Cinque Port town of Seaford in Sussex, a seat procured for him by the Pelham family, one of whom was a former member of the Treasury board. Lowndes's work as Treasury secretary settled in to a complex routine that would dominate the rest of his life. His controlling hand in all major aspects of Treasury administration was soon apparent in his deep involvement in the 'recoinage' of 1696–7, and in his initiation in 1697 of a major overhaul of exchequer procedure. His house, situated in the Broad Sanctuary near the west door of Westminster Abbey, proved a convenient meeting place for the Treasury commissioners after fire destroyed most of Whitehall, including the Treasury chambers, on the night of 4–5 January 1698. He played an important part each year in planning the government's financial measures to be laid before the House of Commons. To this end he maintained close liaison with the various spending departments and revenue boards, and oversaw the collation of data for compiling the annual accounts of overall government income and expenditure. He was also involved in the finalization of borrowing arrangements with the monied companies and with individual financiers and bankers. In the Commons, Lowndes's special sphere of responsibility was the committee of ways and means; there he proposed and explained each year the agendas of financial measures which had originated under his scrutiny at the Treasury. Not infrequently, during the financial stress of war, the angry criticism of MPs placed heavy demands on his ingenuity, forcing him to find ways of modifying proposals, and on occasion he was forced to abandon them altogether. The task of managing major pieces of fiscal legislation through the house usually fell to others, but it was Lowndes who ensured that bills contained the correct level of detail needed to regulate the levy and collection of new duties.

Lowndes's mastery in Treasury matters was unchallenged for nearly thirty years, and he is recognized as one of the key figures in the 'financial revolution'. During his early years as secretary, the Treasury began to consolidate its control over parliamentary finance, a process which saw much refinement under Lowndes's continued lead. The Treasury machinery itself underwent much rapid change during Queen Anne's reign under the pressure of an increasing wartime workload, and the expanded Treasury 'establishment' which had emerged by 1714 bore characteristics which were to endure well into the nineteenth century. When faced with administrative failure or neglect, however, as often tended to occur among exchequer officials in their auditing of departmental accounts, Lowndes's improving hand entailed no more than an insistence on the observation of 'ancient' rules. He was loyal to successive Treasury ministers regardless of their politics, and he became, in effect, a permanent secretary. His longest and closest working association, however, was with Lord Godolphin, who was lord treasurer during 1700–01 and from 1702 until 1710. His scrupulous avoidance of party intrigue, and the fixed support which he gave to each ministry, was an important factor in the unstinting professionalism with which Lowndes approached his duties. He defied attempts by political analysts to classify him in terms of whig or tory, and at various times either party label was attached to him.

Portraits of Lowndes depict a man of stern countenance although he was said to be 'a sociable, good companion' and a devoted Anglican (*Portland MSS*, 5.99). All too often, however, his colleagues saw a man whose almost constant engrossment in work was difficult to penetrate. His piety and rectitude were deeply ingrained features of his personality, and his long involvement in organizing the nation's finances was entirely without taint of peculation. Like most men in the higher echelons of government, Lowndes was nevertheless able to profit greatly from the perquisites of office. A shrewd manager of his own money, he bought up land in and around his native Winslow during the 1690s, purchasing the manor of Winslow itself in 1697 and rebuilding Winslow Hall over the next five years. He acquired other property: at Chesham, also in Buckinghamshire, at Berkhamsted in Hertfordshire, and in the fashionable metropolitan districts of St James's and Chelsea. It was appropriate, too, that he should use his position to secure salaried places at the Treasury and other government offices for several of his sons and sons-in-law, thus establishing a dynastic involvement in government administration which would continue for several generations.

Lord Treasurer Oxford's appointment of a joint secretary to the Treasury in June 1711 was primarily for political purposes, and Lowndes's hold over financial administration remained largely untouched. There was likewise never any doubt of his being retained at the Treasury after the Hanoverian succession. At the general election of 1715 he lost control of the seat he had held for many years at Seaford, but transferred to the Cornish pocket borough of St Mawes. A major Treasury priority during the early years of whig rule was to find ways of controlling the escalating national debt. In May 1717 he thus gave full support to the scheme for a 'sinking fund', designed ostensibly to reorganize the debt in such a way as would ensure its liquidation in the foreseeable future. The scheme had been devised by Robert Walpole but, amid the opening stages of the 'whig schism', was unveiled in the Commons by Walpole's opponent, the Treasury's new first lord, James Stanhope. In 1720 Lowndes had a large share in drafting the South Sea Act which gave authorization to the company's disastrous scheme for dealing with unfunded national debt, and which resulted in the South Sea Bubble and its bursting later in the year. He subsequently assisted Walpole, following the latter's return to the Treasury in April 1721, with the task of framing the Act to Restore the Public Credit which restructured the company's finances and its government obligations. It was duly introduced to the house by Lowndes on 2 August.

Renouncing his Cornish seat at the election of 1722, Lowndes stood for the populous London constituency of Westminster, but was defeated after a fierce contest. An alternative seat was found for him in October that year when he was brought in at a by-election for another Cornish borough, East Looe. Lowndes's death occurred on 20 January 1724, just four days after a routine appearance at the house; he was buried on 3 February in the family vault at Winslow constructed in 1700 when the church was handsomely refurbished at his expense. Walpole told MPs that they 'had lost a very useful Member, and the public as able and honest a servant as ever the crown had' (*JHC*, 20.242). According to Lord Chesterfield, writing in 1747, Lowndes was the originator of the maxim, 'take care of the pence for the pounds will take care of themselves' (Chesterfield, *Letters to his Son*, 6 Nov 1747).

A. A. Hanham

Sources 'Lowndes', HoP, *Commons, 1690–1715* [draft] • HoP, *Commons, 1715–54*, 2.225–6 • S. B. Baxter, *The development of the treasury, 1660–1702* (1957), 20, 87, 117, 198–202, 230, 236–9, 258 • D. W. Jones, *War and economy in the age of William III and Marlborough* (1988), 244–5 • H. Roseveare, *The treasury, 1660–1870: the foundations of control* (1973), 51, 57, 77–81, 138–41 • J. C. Sainty, ed., *Treasury officials, 1660–1870* (1972), 137–8 • *Locke on money*, ed. P. H. Kelly (1991), 20–32, 106–9, 140, 405, 407 • P. G. M. Dickson, *The financial revolution in England* (1991), 58–9, 103, 175 • J. Carswell, *The South Sea Bubble* (1960), 248, 252, 259 • BL, Add. MS 5840, fols. 177–80 • Lowndes pedigree, Lowndes's family notes, Bucks. RLSS, Lowndes MSS D/LO/5/12, D/LO/6/18/1 • W. A. Shaw, ed., *Calendar of treasury books*, 6, PRO (1913), 619, 630, 753; 8 (1923), 78–9; 10 (1935), 70, 480; 13 (1933), 52 • *IGI* • *DNB* • G. Lipscomb, *The history and antiquities of the county of Buckingham*, 3 (1847), 543–4 • A. Boyer, *The political state of Great Britain*, 27 (1724), 103 • *The manuscripts of his grace the duke of Portland*, 10 vols., HMC, 29 (1891–1931), vol. 5

Archives Bucks. RLSS, notebooks • PRO, electoral corresp., papers and accounts of revenue of various government departments, T48 • U. Edin. L., army and navy accounts | Hunt. L., letters to W. Blathwayt • Yale U., Beinecke L., letters to W. Blathwayt

Likenesses by or after G. Kneller, oils, Gov. Art Coll. [*see illus.*] • R. Philips, oils, Bank of England, London; repro. in Dickson, *Financial revolution*

Lowndes, William Thomas (*bap.* 1793, *d.* 1843), bibliographer, was baptized at St Luke's, Chelsea, on 8 December 1793, the son of William Lowndes (1753?–1823), bookseller at 77 Fleet Street and Bedford Street, Covent Garden, and his wife, Mary Ann. He came from a well-known bookselling family, originally from Cheshire, of which several members were liverymen of the Stationers' Company. His grandfather Thomas Lowndes and his father were noted dramatic publishers; his cousin Henry Lowndes recovered from bankruptcy to become a prosperous bookseller and Stationers' Company court assistant. W. T. Lowndes was apprenticed to his father at Stationers' Hall on 7 July 1807 and freed on 8 September 1814, but not admitted to the livery. On 11 October 1828 he married Susan Cooper at St Paul's, Covent Garden. They had two children, one of whom, a daughter, was born in 1830. Lowndes may well have scratched a living as a freelance cataloguer but little is known of his life up to its last few years. In January 1841 he wrote applying for relief to the Royal Literary Fund. It was a charity that at that time insisted on its pensioners possessing moral probity as well as literary merit, and Lowndes hoped to conceal from its committee his 'one great offence committed many years ago' which had been 'within the knowledge of everybody connected with literary affairs in the metropolis' (P. Hall, letter of apology, Royal Literary Fund). In 1833 Lowndes had 'sold £300 worth of books from the collection of Richard Heber, which had been placed in his hands to be catalogued' (*N&Q*, 10th ser., 12, 1909, 228). He apparently asked his three sponsors, who included the well-known booksellers Thomas Rodd and Henry Stevens, to speak only of his penury and the worth of *The Bibliographers' Manual* but the book theft came to the ears of the committee and the appeal was rejected as 'unworthy of consideration' (Royal Literary Fund). Lowndes removed his letter of application and the biographical information it would have contained. There is no other evidence of shiftiness, yet it is strange that a young man of twenty-seven, in 1820, should have had the leisure to embark on a bibliography designed to supplement 'in relation to *British* literature' (Lowndes, 1834, i) Brunet's *Manuel du libraire*. He was known within the trade for his 'bibliographical drudgery', encouraged by booksellers and collectors alike, and was, perhaps, accounted so brilliant a cataloguer that booksellers would be prepared to risk losing a few books by employing him. Bibliophiles such as Richard Heber and Thomas Grenville offered him the use of their libraries. Thomas Rodd 'especially gave constant advice and useful suggestions' (Lowndes, 1834, xii) and put the first and no longer extant edition of *The Bibliographer's Manual* in fifteen parts (1828–32) on his 1832 catalogue. After publication of the *Manual* Lowndes 'designed to supplement' his 'defective treatment of theology' by compiling *The British Librarian* (1839–42). He was 'confident', he told the Royal Literary Fund, 'that when completed its sale would sufficiently remunerate' (Royal Literary Fund) him, but he was by then 'so dogged by ill health, mental instability and failing eyesight' (ibid.) that the work was published in an incomplete form. At the end of his life Lowndes lodged at 4 Calthorpe Place, Gray's Inn Road. He spent his last years working for Bohn as a cataloguer, but in his employer's words:

> his long course of bibliographical drudgery had reduced him, both in body and mind, to a mere wreck of his former self … and in his own history he realised a fact, of which he was always conscious, that Bibliography has no recognised status in England. (Bohn, appx V)

He died in London on 31 July 1843.

Lowndes's posthumous fame rests on *The Bibliographer's Manual* (1834), the first systematic work of its kind. At the close of the twentieth century this was still a standard bibliographical reference tool, particularly useful to librarians and bibliophiles for its details of provenance. It was an attempt to produce a bibliographical manual for the whole of English literature on the pattern of Watt's *Bibliotheca Britannica*. After Lowndes's death Bohn expanded it to 6 volumes (1858–68). In an eminently respectable book trade family, he appears to have been the black sheep.

ROBIN MYERS

Sources W. T. Lowndes, *The bibliographer's manual of English literature*, 4 vols. (1834) [address and preface] · H. G. Bohn, preface and appx V, in W. T. Lowndes, *The bibliographer's manual of English literature*, ed. H. G. Bohn, [new edn], 6 vols. (1864) · Stationers' Company apprentice memorandum books, 1794–1807 · Stationers' Company freedom register, 1796–1830 · Royal Literary Fund, Case 1019 [application, committee minutes, correspondence from sponsors] · *IGI* · census returns, 1841 · Nichols, *Lit. anecdotes*, 3.646–7 · *GM*, 2nd ser., 20 (1843), 326 · *DNB* · D. F. McKenzie, ed., *Stationers' Company apprentices*, [3]: 1701–1800 (1978) · I. Maxted, *The London book trades, 1775–1800: a preliminary checklist of members* (1977) · *N&Q*, 10th ser., 12 (1909), 228

Lowry, Henry Dawson (1869–1906), journalist and novelist, only son of Winifred Dawson, of Redhill, Surrey, and Thomas Shaw Lowry, was born at Truro, Cornwall, on 22 February 1869. His father was a bank clerk and afterwards bank manager at Camborne; both parents were staunch Wesleyans who intended Lowry for the ministry. He was educated at a Wesleyan school at Taunton called Queen's College, and then attended Oxford University (unattached), where he graduated in the honour school of chemistry in 1891. Described by his friends as a 'little, delicate, nervous, romantic, high-strung, wilful and affectionate boy', Lowry was never entirely comfortable with the career in journalism he thereafter pursued, preferring to spend his time writing verse, playing the piano, and collecting antique china. None the less, he began to write for the *National Observer* under W. E. Henley in 1891, arriving in London two years later. He also wrote for the *Pall Mall Gazette*, joining the staff in 1895, as well as *Black and White*, *The Speaker*, *English Illustrated*, and the *Daily Express*; he also edited the *Ludgate Magazine*, before joining the staff of the *Morning Post* in 1897.

During this time Lowry published several delicate volumes, mostly on religious themes, in the style of the decadent poet Ernest Dowson; the best of these are *A Man of Moods* and *Make-Believe* (1896), illustrated by Charles Robinson of *The Yellow Book*; *Strange Happenings* (1901); and *The Hundred Windows* (1904). In addition to his journalism, he also wrote fiction, often focusing on Cornish life; examples include *Wreckers and Methodists* (1893) and *Women's Tragedies* (1895). His final novel, *The Happy Exile* (1898), is semi-autobiographical, about a Cornish poet living in London yet longing 'for the Idyll of the Daffodils' he knew with his mother. Always sickly, Lowry died at his home, 49 Dulwich Road, Herne Hill, London, of pneumonia and 'a wasting disease' in the early hours of 22 October 1906. He never married. He was buried in a suburban London churchyard at Norwood. As Edgar Preston wrote in his 1912 memoir, 'his whole story was composed of a few small volumes of verse, some earnest friendships, one passion, and a premature death'.

T. F. HENDERSON, *rev.* KATHARINE CHUBBUCK

Sources *Morning Post* (23 Oct 1906) · E. A. Preston, 'Memoir', in H. D. Lowry, *A dream of daffodils: last poems*, ed. G. E. Matheson and C. A. Dawson Scott (1912) · C. A. D. Scott, introduction, in H. D. Lowry and C. A. D. Scott, *Wheal darkness* (1927) · *WWW* · *Men and women of the time* (1899)
Archives Redruth Public Library
Likenesses photograph, repro. in Preston, 'Memoir'

Lowry, John (1769–1850), mathematician, was born in Cumberland, and was for some time an excise officer at Solihull, near Birmingham. Little is known of his background and personal life. In 1804 he was appointed teacher of arithmetic in the new military college at Marlow. He held this post until 30 June 1840, when failing sight compelled him to resign on a pension. About 1846 he became totally blind. He died at Pimlico, London, on 3 January 1850. Lowry was one of the earliest and most frequent contributors to Thomas Leybourn's *Mathematical Repository* (1799 to 1819). He was the author of a section on spherical trigonometry included in the second volume of Dalby's *Course of Mathematics*, the textbook in use at Sandhurst during the early nineteenth century. The writer of Lowry's obituary in the *Gentleman's Magazine* claims that he wrote the sections on arithmetic and algebra also .

CHARLES PLATTS, *rev.* JULIA TOMPSON

Sources *GM*, 2nd ser., 33 (1850), 330 · records of Royal Military College, Marlow

Lowry, Joseph Wilson (1803–1879). *See under* Lowry, Wilson (*bap.* 1760, *d.* 1824).

Lowry, Laurence Stephen (1887–1976), painter, was born on 1 November 1887 at 8 Barrett Street, Stretford, in Manchester, the home of the industrial revolution. He was the only child of Robert Stephen McAll Lowry (1857–1932), an estate agent's clerk, and his wife, Elizabeth (1858–1939), daughter of William Hobson, a member of a Manchester firm of hatters. His mother regarded herself as socially superior to her husband, and his failure to earn enough money to keep her in the style which she felt she deserved may have been at the root of her increasing self-imposed isolation, and her growing disappointment with her son, who, nevertheless, remained devoted to her. Lowry later refused a knighthood, proposed in 1967 by the prime minister, Harold Wilson, on the grounds that he did not see the point of it now that his mother was dead. She was an accomplished pianist and Lowry, who shared her love of classical music, kept her piano in his sitting-room, though he could not play it himself.

Lowry began his education in 1895 at Victoria Park School in Rusholme, Manchester. When he was fifteen there were heated family arguments about what career he should follow. Since childhood he had been interested only in drawing, and wanted to continue. This distressed his mother, who considered it a useless pursuit and beneath his station in life. The outcome was a compromise. In 1904 he began work with a Manchester firm of accountants, and in 1905 he started to attend evening classes at the Manchester Municipal School of Art. His teacher, Adolphe Valette, a Frenchman, was an exponent of the post-impressionist style. He exerted a profound influence upon the young artist, by teaching him the importance of drawing and observing atmospheric effects. He also demonstrated to him that being an artist was not just a job but a highly professional calling.

In 1910 Lowry became a rent collector and clerk with the Pall Mall Property Company in Manchester, in whose employ he was to remain until his retirement on full pension in 1952, by which time he had risen to the rank of chief cashier. The fact that for almost fifty years he was in a 'nine-to-five' job was the most closely guarded secret of his life, for the good reason that he had a horror of being thought of as a Sunday painter. He lied to Sir John Rothenstein, then director of the Tate Gallery, London, claiming that he had never had to work for his living because his mother had left him an ample inheritance. Not until after his death in 1976 was the truth made public.

After ten years as a student at Manchester, Lowry began attending evening classes at the Salford School of Art at the Royal Technical College, where he remained for a further five years. It was about this time (*c.*1915) that he 'discovered' the industrial scene. 'One day he missed a train from Pendlebury, and as he left the station he saw the Acme Spinning Company's mill … he experienced an earthly equivalent of some transcendental revelation', was how Sir John Rothenstein described it in *Modern English Painters* (2, 1976), based on his discussions with the artist. This was almost certainly a lie too, or rather a dramatic over-simplification. Lowry tended to let his interviewers believe what they wanted to believe and Rothenstein was interested particularly in the spiritual inspiration of art. The evidence of Lowry's work suggests that he did not have a single 'visionary' experience. Instead his subject matter grew naturally and methodically out of his observations of life around him. Nevertheless, there was an aspect of his work which could be called 'spiritual'. He confided to close friends that he often found himself looking at a scene as if he were an outsider, cut off from it. The high viewpoints from which his pictures are seen reflect these 'out-of-body' experiences.

Lowry occasionally made thumbnail sketches of scenes he had witnessed on his rounds as a rent collector, but these were rarely if ever used literally. His paintings are, rather, an imaginative re-creation of the industrial scene, made at night, after supper. He often worked until 2 a.m., always by artificial light. It is remarkable that he produced such a huge body of work.

It is often thought that Lowry tended to repeat himself. However, familiarity with his work reveals that each painting is different and about something new. Over the years his style changed considerably, becoming increasingly expressive of his personal feelings. In 1939 he painted an anguished portrait of himself (Salford Art Gallery) with red eyes and a violent stare, which expressed his suffering at his mother's death and his troubled experiences working as a fire-watcher during the war. In the late 1940s and 1950s he produced a sequence of seascapes in which each has nothing in it but an empty white sky, a horizon, and a few low, rippling waves. Few artists have ever managed to capture such a complete feeling of emptiness. Lowry once had a dream that one day the tide would not turn, but just go on rising. These sea paintings were an evocation of that. Like so many of his pictures they are about death as a background to life.

During the 1960s and 1970s Lowry peopled his white canvases increasingly with single figures often drawn from his macabre imagination, such as tramps, drunks, bearded ladies, and people with deformities. However freakish they may appear, there is always a liveliness

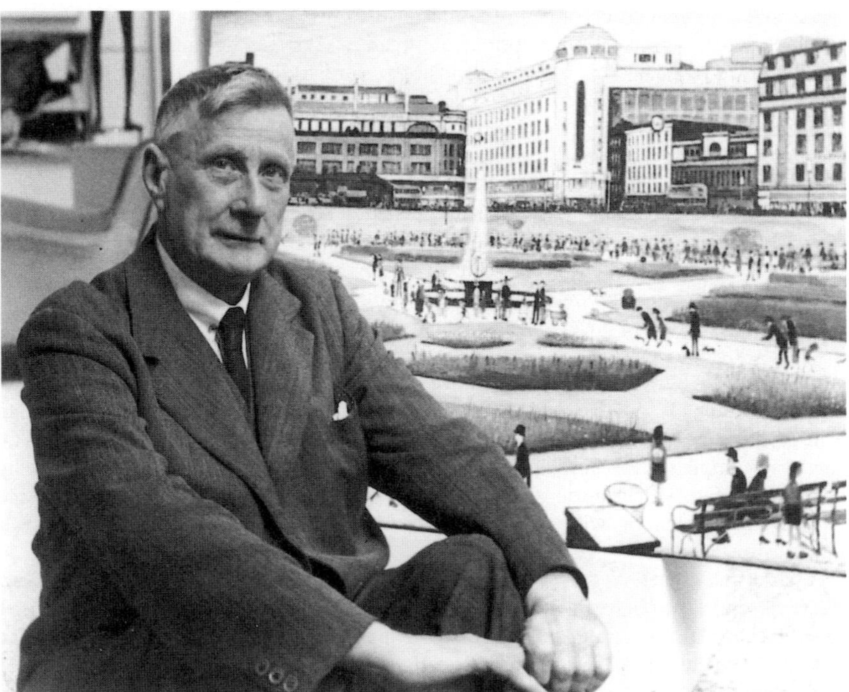

Laurence Stephen Lowry (1887–1976), by Ida Kar, 1954 [with his painting *Piccadilly Gardens*]

about them—a sense that they are kicking back. After his death a small group of rather beautiful but essentially private drawings were discovered, showing buxom young girls wearing men's clothes and being tortured with whips or knives. He never married, but had a sequence of obsessional friendships with young women, many of whom appear to have been called Anne. Shelley Rohde, who wrote a biography of the artist, unearthed quite a lot of information about these shadowy figures.

Lowry's public reputation as an artist began in 1930, when the Manchester City Art Gallery purchased *An Accident* (1926). In 1934 he was elected to the Royal Society of British Artists. But the major event of his life was the chance discovery of his work by the art dealer A. J. McNeil Reid of the Lefevre Gallery, London, who in 1938 noticed some of the artist's paintings on the premises of James Bourlet & Sons, picture framers. Reid instantly recognized the importance of this work and in 1939 gave Lowry his first one-man exhibition. In 1948 he moved to The Elms, the bleak house at Mottram in Longdendale, Cheshire, where he lived until his death. He was awarded an honorary MA (1945) and LLD (1961) by Manchester University. He was elected an ARA in 1955 and an RA in 1962. In 1965 he received the freedom of the city of Salford, and in 1967 the General Post Office issued a stamp reproducing one of his industrial scenes. In 1975 the universities of Salford and Liverpool conferred upon him the honorary degree of DLitt.

As a man Lowry was an eccentric in the grand tradition. Tall in build, he cared nothing for appearances, and in the 1970s frequently wore the mackintosh and cap in which he had painted his celebrated *Self-Portrait* of 1925 (Salford Art Gallery). He collected Pre-Raphaelite drawings and paintings and at his death possessed a notable group of female portraits by Dante Gabriel Rossetti. His recreation was listening to music, especially Donizetti and Bellini.

The main collection of Lowry's work—over 150 drawings and paintings—is owned by the Salford Art Gallery. A selection is regularly exhibited at the Lowry, the major new concert hall and gallery in Salford named after the city's most famous artist. There are portraits of him by Mervyn Levy (pencil, 1961, Herbert Art Gallery and Museum, Coventry) and Olwyn Bowey (oil, 1963–4, Tate collection). There is a bronze bust (1967) by Leo Solomon in the Royal Academy of Arts, London. Lowry died on 23 February 1976 at Woods Hospital, Glossop, Derbyshire, following an attack of pneumonia, and was buried on the 27th in the southern cemetery, Manchester.

Lowry is a unique figure in British and, possibly, in world art. No other artist caught so completely the new townscape the industrial revolution created, with its horizons of smoking chimneys and streets teeming with people. He lived long enough to see the factories he loved bulldozed to make way for car-parks and offices. As this happened they faded from his art, leaving only solitary figures isolated on a field of white. He realized that the industrial landscape is not dark, but light. The light from overcast skies not only banishes all shadows but also reflects back from the often wet pavements, with the result that the figures and buildings stand out against a misty haze. Lowry used this to express both his sense of loneliness and his love of life. MERVYN LEVY, *rev.* JULIAN SPALDING

Sources S. Rohde, *A private view of L. S. Lowry* (1979) · A. Andrews, *The life of L. S. Lowry* (1977) · M. Levy, *The paintings of L. S. Lowry* (1978) · M. Levy, *The drawings of L. S. Lowry* (1978) · T. Marshall, *Life with Lowry* (1981) · J. Spalding, *Lowry* (1979) · J. Spalding, *Lowry* (1987) [exhibition catalogue, Cleveland Art Gallery, Middlesbrough] · M. Leber and J. Sandling, *L. S. Lowry* (1987)

Archives V&A NAL, miscellanea | Salford Museum and Art Gallery, letters to Mr Timperley and Mrs Timperley · V&A NAL, corresp. with Bernhard Baer · V&A NAL, corresp. with Geoffrey Bennett · V&A NAL, letters to D. Carr

Likenesses L. S. Lowry, self-portrait, pencil, *c.*1920, NPG · L. S. Lowry, self-portrait, oils, 1925, Salford Art Gallery · I. Kar, photograph, 1954, NPG [*see illus.*] · M. Levy, pencil drawing, 1961, Herbert Art Gallery and Museum, Coventry · O. Bowey, oils, 1963–4, Tate collection · J. S. Lewinski, photograph, 1965, NPG · L. Solomon, bronze bust, 1967, RA · S. Samuels, photographs, 1968, NPG · S. Tonkiss, bronze head, 1971, NPG · P. Thompson, photograph, 1973, NPG · R. Birch, photograph, 1975, NPG · S. Samuels, photograph, 1975, NPG

Wealth at death £298,459: probate, 29 June 1976, *CGPLA Eng. & Wales.*

Lowry, (Clarence) Malcolm (1909–1957), author, was born on 28 July 1909 at Warren Crest, North Drive, New Brighton, Cheshire, the youngest of the four sons of Arthur Osborne Lowry (1870–1945), cotton broker, and Evelyn (1873–1950), daughter of John Lyon Boden, master mariner, of Toxteth, Liverpool, and his wife, Betsy, *née* Potter. Both of his parents were born in Toxteth but, after marrying in 1894, moved to the Wirral, settling finally in Caldy. His early education was at Braeside School, West Kirby, Cheshire, and Caldicott preparatory school, Hitchin, Hertfordshire. While at the Leys School in Cambridge, at fifteen Lowry began writing for his school magazine and at the same time discovered alcohol; at sixteen he was composing popular songs. A short, muscular, blue-eyed, copper-haired youth, gifted with a photographic memory, he loved jazz and the ukulele, swam, played hockey, and won golf competitions at Hoylake. However, he feared his autocratic father and despised his socially pretentious mother.

In May 1927 Lowry shipped as a deckboy on a Liverpool freighter trading to Yokohama in Japan, a searing experience which provided him with the persona of 'drunken sailor-poet', a phobia about syphilis, and material for his first novel, *Ultramarine*. In 1929 he was tutored for three months by the American poet Conrad Aiken in Cambridge, Massachusetts, before going to St Catharine's College, Cambridge, to read English. In his first term, when drunk, he helped a friend, Paul Fitte, to gas himself. His feelings of guilt over this only served to intensify his drinking.

Ultramarine (1933), greatly influenced by Aiken's *Blue Voyage* and Nordahl Grieg's *The Ship Sails on* (Lowry visited Grieg in Oslo in 1931), grew into a highly wrought, stream-of-consciousness novel laden with literary allusions. His third-class degree at Cambridge (1932) owed much to extracts from it being submitted for examination. Thereafter, he received a stipend from his father, who was determined to keep his violently drunken son away from home. In London, his manuscript of *Ultramarine*, the result of four years' painful work, was stolen, and he considered suicide. Luckily, a carbon was found and Jonathan Cape agreed to publish it.

While in Spain with Aiken in 1933, Lowry met a young American, Janine Vanderheim (1911–2001), who acted and wrote under the name Jan Gabrial; he married her in Paris on 6 January 1934. Their stormy relationship was sustained mostly by Jan's enduring faith in Lowry's genius. The muted reception of *Ultramarine* helped persuade him to follow his wife to the United States in 1934. In New York he began *In Ballast to the White Sea*, a novel inspired by his fascination with Grieg. But heavy drinking following a charge of plagiarism brought him close to collapse, and he spent a brief time in the psychiatric ward of Bellevue Hospital in May 1936, an ordeal he portrayed in *Lunar Caustic* (1963), a brilliant surrealistic story of the modern lunatic city.

The Lowrys left New York and settled in Cuernavaca, Mexico, in a villa with views of the volcano Popocatépetl. The Mexican atmosphere—the cult of death, the clash of cultures, the dramatic landscape—mesmerized Lowry. A dying Indian by the roadside, encountered during a bus journey, sparked 'Under the Volcano', a story he soon expanded into a novel. But visits from Aiken and the author Arthur Calder-Marshall led to alcoholic fugues, prompting Jan to leave for Los Angeles—experiences he religiously incorporated into his narrative. Seeking more Mexican background, he visited Oaxaca, where he was jailed on suspicion of spying, and Acapulco, where he almost drowned. In July 1938 his father's lawyers barely saved him from deportation, and he joined Jan in Los Angeles, where, because of his drinking, they lived apart and eventually divorced in 1940.

After a year struggling against alcohol and working on his novel, Lowry met the former silent film actress Margerie Bonner (1904–1988), who had previously been married to Jerome Chaffee. When Lowry's father moved him to Canada she followed, marrying him in Vancouver, British Columbia, on 2 December 1940. In that year *Under the Volcano* was rejected by thirteen American publishers. Meanwhile, the couple moved into a squatter's shack at Dollarton on Burrard inlet, near Vancouver, a magnificent lakeside setting where he began to rewrite his novel. Alcohol made Lowry accident-prone. In 1944 the shack burnt down and the manuscript of *In Ballast* was destroyed. He and Margerie rebuilt the shack, and he revised *Under the Volcano*—now a brilliant, multifaceted novel about the last day of Geoffrey Firmin, an alcoholic former British consul in Mexico. The setting—the Day of the Dead beneath Popocatépetl, with the Spanish Civil War approaching its tragic end—provided a rich mix of images and allusions which could be interpreted variously as a religious or political parable, a Faustian story, or an elaborate film scenario. (The novel was filmed by John Huston in 1984 with Albert Finney hypnotic as the consul.)

In 1946 Lowry returned to Mexico where news of a friend, murdered while drunk on *mescal* like his consul, and the experience of being deported at gunpoint, led to two further novels—*Dark as the Grave wherein my Friend is Laid* (1969) and *La mordida* (1996). In Cuernavaca he wrote a remarkable 15,000-word letter defending *Under the Volcano* against cuts proposed by Jonathan Cape, and then heard of the book's acceptance in both London and New York. It was published in 1947, was poorly received in Britain and soon remaindered, but was hailed as a work of genius in North America, becoming a best-seller.

A disastrous European trip gave Lowry material for some subtly allusive short stories, published posthumously in *Hear Us O Lord from Heaven thy Dwelling Place* (1961). He returned to Canada and produced a grandiose plan, *The*

(Clarence) Malcolm Lowry (1909–1957), by unknown photographer, 1946 [in Tlaxcala, Mexico]

Voyage that Never Ends, which embraced all his completed and projected works; it was commissioned by Random House. But he was soon diverted, first into writing a screenplay for F. Scott Fitzgerald's *Tender is the Night*, and then *October Ferry to Gabriola* (1979), a novel of remorse based on the suicide of his old friend Paul Fitte, and his threatened expulsion from Dollarton. Random House rejected *October Ferry*. Lowry returned devastated to Europe and suffered a mental collapse. Back in England, he received aversion therapy for his alcoholism. He was found dead on 27 June 1957 at the White Cottage, Ripe, near Lewes, Sussex, that he and Margerie had rented. The inquest recorded death by misadventure. He had swallowed half a bottle of gin, twenty of Margerie's sodium amytal tablets, and had inhaled his own vomit. He was buried on 3 July in the churchyard of Ripe parish church.

Lowry produced one great novel, acknowledged as influential by writers such as Anthony Burgess, Thomas Pynchon, and Gabriel García Márquez. His other Mexican novels, involving constant reflections on *Under the Volcano*, are powerful works of metafiction. He wrote brilliant short stories and some fine poems—hymns to nature and the sea. His 'confessional' letters are fascinating insights into the workings of a highly complex and disturbed creative mind. At his death none of his work was in print in English. GORDON BOWKER

Sources b. cert. • d. cert. • G. Bowker, ed., *Malcolm Lowry remembered* (1985) • G. Bowker, *Pursued by furies: a life of Malcolm Lowry* (1993) • *Sursum corda: the collected letters of Malcolm Lowry*, ed. S. Grace, 2 vols. (1995–6) • D. Day, *Malcolm Lowry: a biography* (1972) • private information (2004) • personal knowledge (2004) • G. Bowker, ed., *Malcolm Lowry, 'Under the volcano': a casebook* (1987)
Archives Hunt. L., Conrad Aitken collection | FILM BBC Film Archives • CBA, Toronto • National Film Board of Canada • University of British Columbia | SOUND BBC Sound Library • BL NSA • National Film Board of Canada • University of British Columbia
Likenesses photograph, 1946, priv. coll. [*see illus.*] • photographs, University of British Columbia • photographs, priv. coll.
Wealth at death £11,018 17*s*. 6*d*.: probate, 11 Nov 1957, *CGPLA Eng. & Wales*

Lowry, Robert Lynd Erskine, **Baron Lowry of Crossgar** (**1919–1999**), judge, was born on 30 January 1919 in Belfast, the only son of William Lowry (*d*. 1949), lawyer, politician, and judge, and his wife, Catherine Hughes Lynd, daughter of the Revd Dr Robert John Lynd, Presbyterian minister. His father was a founding member of the bar of Northern Ireland, Stormont MP for Londonderry City from 1939 to 1947, attorney-general for Northern Ireland from 1944 to 1947, and a Northern Ireland High Court judge from then until shortly before his death. Robert Wilson *Lynd, journalist and essayist, was Lowry's maternal uncle.

Lowry was educated at the Royal Belfast Academical Institution and was awarded an exhibition in classics at Jesus College, Cambridge, where he gained first-class honours in part one of the classical tripos in 1939. On the outbreak of the Second World War he volunteered for military service but was instructed to complete his degree at Cambridge, which he did in 1940, being awarded another first in part two of the classical tripos. He then enlisted in the Royal Inniskilling Fusiliers and was commissioned

Robert Lynd Erskine Lowry, Baron Lowry of Crossgar (1919–1999), by unknown photographer

into the Royal Irish Fusiliers in 1941. He served through the Tunisian and Italian campaigns and became brigade intelligence officer of the 38th Irish infantry brigade. He was demobilized with the rank of major and subsequently became honorary colonel of successively the 5th and 7th battalions of the Royal Irish Fusiliers (1967–8 and 1969–71) and the 5th battalion of the Royal Irish Rangers (1971–6).

Lowry was called to the bar of Northern Ireland in 1947. His ability was such that he quickly established himself as a leading junior in civil work. In 1948 he was appointed junior counsel to the attorney-general for Northern Ireland, which was a part-time post so he was still able to carry on a large private practice. He took silk in 1956 and soon became one of the leading members of the senior bar. His father, whom he greatly admired and for whom he had a deep affection, had been a flamboyant advocate, but although Lowry was a powerful advocate his style was quiet and restrained and his success flowed, particularly in appellate work, from his powers of acute analysis and the clarity of his submissions. It was clear that he was destined for high judicial office and he was appointed a judge of the High Court in 1964 at the early age of forty-five. As a High Court judge he sat in the chancery court. His judgments were models of cogency and lucidity, and he tried the cases before him with quiet courtesy and care which brought out the best in the counsel who appeared before him.

Lowry was appointed lord chief justice of Northern Ireland on the retirement of Lord MacDermott in 1971, at a time of growing violence and turbulence in the province and just a week before the introduction of internment without trial. During the next seventeen years he presided in the Court of Appeal through a period of grave terrorist violence, and he also took his turn as a trial judge in the non-jury Diplock courts trying those accused of terrorist crimes. Many of the cases which came before him in the Court of Appeal were appeals in criminal cases, and although his work, both at the bar and as a chancery judge, had related to civil cases, he displayed a mastery of the criminal law and delivered judgments of the highest quality. In the case of *R.* v. *Maxwell* he delivered a judgment upholding the conviction of the defendant which clarified the law as to the degree of knowledge required for liability to attach to an accomplice who assisted the principal offender. The defendant appealed to the House of Lords, which dismissed the appeal, and in his judgment Lord Edmund-Davies (himself a master of the criminal law) said that Lowry's judgment was so clear in its review of the facts and so comprehensive in its consideration of the relevant statutory and case law that he had concluded that it would be 'a sleeveless errand' were he to proceed himself to deliver a judgment.

Throughout the years of terrorist violence and communal strife in Northern Ireland, Lowry was unswerving in his determination to uphold the rule of law, to administer justice with complete impartiality, and to protect the rights of individual citizens against unlawful actions by the state. He also sought to ensure, when emergency legislation was enacted for Northern Ireland, that the rights given by the common law and the well-established principles of fairness enshrined in it were preserved to the greatest possible extent permitted by the terms of the legislation. He voiced this determination in his judgment in *R.* v. *Gibney* in 1983, when he said:

> 'Amid the clash of arms the laws are silent' so Cicero exclaimed over 2000 years ago. During the greatest conflict in our history Lord Atkin bravely ventured to contradict this assertion. Now, too, peace, order and society itself are under fierce and constant attack and that is why we must remember Lord Atkin's famous dictum: 'In this country, amid the clash of arms the laws are not silent. They may be changed, but they speak the same language in war as in peace.' This war is being waged by organisations which style themselves armies and observe military procedures, but it has not invaded, and will not be allowed to invade, the courts. The rule of law has prevailed and will continue to prevail there.

His determination to uphold the rule of law was exemplified in numerous cases. In 1972, before the emergency provisions legislation was enacted, the army set up a detention centre in an army barracks near Belfast, where IRA suspects were interrogated. Lowry excluded confessions made by suspects in the centre on the ground that they were not voluntary because the interrogation set-up, organized and operated to obtain information from persons who would otherwise have been less willing to give it, would have constituted oppressive conduct in the investigation of ordinary crime. In 1973, when emergency provisions legislation provided that a confession was admissible in evidence in a criminal trial unless it had been obtained by violence, torture, or inhuman treatment, Lowry held that the trial judge still retained a discretion under common law to exclude the confession if its admission would not be in the interests of justice. In 1977, in a case where John Hume, the well-known nationalist politician, challenged the validity of a regulation made under the Special Powers Act of the Northern Ireland parliament empowering a soldier to order an assembly of three or more persons to disperse, Lowry held that the regulation was *ultra vires* as being in contravention of section 4 of the Government of Ireland Act 1920, which provided that the parliament of Northern Ireland should not have power to make laws in respect of (*inter alia*) the army.

Throughout his years as lord chief justice, Lowry continued to administer justice with the same courtesy and patience which he had displayed as a chancery judge. His fairness and impartiality were widely recognized and respected throughout both sections of the community in Northern Ireland and he was held in great respect and affection by his judicial colleagues and by the members of the bar and the solicitors' profession. The years during which he was lord chief justice were dangerous years for him and his fellow judges and they lived under the threat of terrorist attack. Five of them were murdered by the IRA, one was severely wounded, and other attacks were carried out on their homes. Lowry himself survived an assassination attempt by gunmen who fired at him from a nearby house when he arrived at Queen's University in Belfast to give a lecture. The bullets aimed at him missed and wounded a member of the academic staff close to him, but Lowry was unperturbed and went ahead and delivered his lecture as planned. On another occasion a bomb exploded outside his house in co. Down and blew in the windows, and once a motor cyclist blew himself up on a border road shortly before Lowry's car was due to pass. Lowry gave admirable leadership to his colleagues by the calm and unruffled manner in which he carried out his work and his example and encouragement were an important factor in ensuring that Northern Ireland's judges came through this period with their morale strong and unimpaired.

Lowry was one of the British members of the joint law enforcement commission established by the British and Irish governments in 1974 to consider how to deal with the problem of terrorists who committed crimes in Northern Ireland and then fled across the border into the Republic of Ireland, where they successfully resisted extradition on the ground that the crimes they carried out were political offences. The British members recommended a change in the law to permit extradition in such cases. However this recommendation was not accepted by the Irish members of the commission, who considered that such a change would be contrary to the principles of international law and in contravention of the Irish constitution. Therefore the British members recommended, as their second choice, the course proposed by the Irish members, which was that extra-territorial jurisdiction should be conferred on the courts in each part of Ireland to try terrorist offences committed in the other part.

After the collapse of the Sunningdale agreement in 1974 Lowry was appointed a year later to be chairman of the Northern Ireland constitutional convention, which was established to decide on the most acceptable form of democratic government for the province. It was at a time of deep political divisions, and the convention collapsed in 1976, but Lowry's chairmanship of the convention and his handling of the political personalities taking part in it were widely admired.

Lowry was knighted in 1971, sworn of the privy council in 1974, and became a life peer as Baron Lowry of Crossgar in 1979. Thereafter he frequently sat in appeals to the House of Lords while continuing his work as lord chief justice in Northern Ireland. He was appointed a lord of appeal in ordinary in 1988 and sat full time in the House of Lords where he delivered lucid and elegantly written judgments until his retirement in 1994. He was awarded honorary degrees by Queen's University, Belfast (1980) and the University of Ulster (1981) and he became the visitor of the latter university in 1989.

Lowry had two very happy marriages. In 1945 he married Mary Audrey, only daughter of John Martin, of 12 Deramore Park, Belfast; they had three daughters. Following her death in 1987 he married, in 1994, Barbara Adamson Calvert QC (*b*. 1926), barrister and recorder of the crown court, the daughter of Albert Parker, chemical engineer, and widow of John Thornton Calvert; through her Lowry acquired a stepson and a stepdaughter.

Lowry was a fine games player in his younger days and was selected for the Irish schools cricket team. He was an excellent golfer until late in life (at one time playing to a three handicap) and he played in the former Oxbridge Blues' president's putter at Rye at the age of seventy-two. He was president of the Royal Portrush golf club from 1974 until 1997. Through his first wife and his daughters, who were devoted to showjumping, he became keenly interested in that sport and became a skilled judge at showjumping competitions, travelling to judge international events in different parts of the world.

Lowry was an unselfish and compassionate man. Amid a busy life in dangerous and stressful times he found happiness in his family and pleasure and relaxation in his friends and in sporting activities. At gatherings of sporting friends or fellow lawyers, which he greatly enjoyed, he was the best of company. He died at Beaumont House, Beaumont Street, Westminster, on 15 January 1999, following a stroke, and was survived by his second wife, the three daughters of his first marriage, and the two stepchildren from his second marriage. BRIAN HUTTON

Sources *The Guardian* (16 Jan 1999) • *The Times* (17 Jan 1999) • *The Independent* (18 Jan 1999) • *WWW* • private information (2004) • personal knowledge (2004)

Likenesses photograph, repro. in *The Guardian* • photograph, repro. in *The Times* [*see illus.*] • photograph, repro. in *The Independent*

Lowry, Thomas Martin (1874–1936), physical chemist, was born on 26 October 1874 at Low Moor, Bradford, the second son of Edward Pearce Lowry, Methodist minister, and his wife, Jemima Hofland. He was educated at Kingswood School, Bath, and then, from 1893, at the Central Technical College at South Kensington. His outstanding chemical ability was recognized, and in 1896 he was invited to assist the professor of chemistry at the Central Technical College, H. E. Armstrong; he retained that responsibility for the next seventeen years. From 1904 he also held a lectureship at Westminster Training College. In 1913 he was appointed head of the chemistry department at Guy's Hospital, London, becoming the first academic at a medical school to hold a chemical professorship at London University. Seven years later he became the first professor of physical chemistry at the University of Cambridge, retaining that position until his death.

Under Armstrong, Lowry's earliest researches were in organic chemistry, relating to α-derivatives of camphor, which on dissolving were discovered to change their optical activity to that of a mixture of the original substance and an isomer of it. The two isomers were shown to be in equilibrium with each other, and the optical phenomenon, hitherto noted only in sugars, was given the name 'mutarotation'. Lowry further declared that the interconversion of isomers was a case of 'dynamic isomerism'. This appeared to take place by removal of a hydrogen ion (proton) and its reattachment elsewhere in the molecule. Lowry called this 'prototropy'.

The variation of optical activity with wavelength, or optical rotatory dispersion, had been little studied since its discovery by A. Cotton in 1896. It now became Lowry's most important research topic. He confirmed the essential correctness of an equation advanced by P. Drude in 1900 connecting wavelength and angle of rotation, and showed that one of the characteristic frequencies of the rotatory dispersion of camphor coincides with that known for the carbonyl group. From this he was led to his concept of 'induced dissymmetry'. This was fundamental work in physical chemistry; it was to be many years before such studies could be used to gain structural information about a molecule.

Lowry's examination of isomeric change led him to a generalized theory of catalysis by acids and bases and to a recognition of the special ability of water to act as both. Inspired by the electronic theory of valency advanced by G. N. Lewis and others early in the century, Lowry applied it to both structures and reactions, stressing that polar activation is often a prerequisite to reaction. He organized a conference at Cambridge in 1923 on such matters, one of the attendees being N. V. Sidgwick, who was shortly to take the subject much further.

Other scientific work included studies of the chlorides of sulphur and the oxides of nitrogen. During the war Lowry investigated the troublesome interconversions of the various forms of ammonium nitrate, an important constituent of several major explosives. He became director of shell filling (1917–19) and served on several other military committees. He was elected FRS in 1914, and appointed OBE in 1918 and CBE in 1920. He also received honorary doctorates from the universities of Brussels and Dublin. He was president of the Faraday Society (1928–30), and vice-president of the Chemical Society (1922–4) and of the Oil and Colour Chemists' Association (1925–8). Lowry was an excellent teacher and wrote several books, including *Historical Introduction to Chemistry* (1915), *Inorganic Chemistry* (1922), and *Optical Rotatory Power* (1935).

In 1904 Lowry married Eliza, eldest daughter of a Methodist minister, Cornelius Wood. They had two sons and one daughter. He enjoyed the companionship of his dogs and, especially, summer camping with his family in Cornwall. He acknowledged the supreme importance to him of Methodist Christianity and loved to preach at village chapels, which he did with great power and simplicity. He died at his home, 54 Bateman Street, Cambridge, on 2 November 1936, and was buried in Cambridge four days later. COLIN A. RUSSELL

Sources A. Findlay and W. H. Mills, eds., *British chemists* (1947) · W. J. Pope, *Obits. FRS*, 2 (1936–8), 287–93 · *Chemistry and Industry* (1 Dec 1936), 282 · *Methodist Recorder* (12 Nov 1936), 4 · *Methodist Recorder* (19 Nov 1936), 28 · *The Times* (4 Nov 1936) · *DNB* · *CGPLA Eng. & Wales* (1936)

Archives CUL, corresp. | RS, corresp. with Sir Robert Robinson on electronic theory

Likenesses W. Stoneman, photograph, 1931, NPG · photograph, repro. in Pope, *Obits. FRS*, 38 · photograph, repro. in Findlay and Mills, eds., *British chemists* (1947) · photographs, Royal Society of Chemistry, London

Wealth at death £8,298 1s. 7d.: probate, 23 Dec 1936, *CGPLA Eng. & Wales*

Lowry, Wilson (*bap.* 1760, *d.* 1824), engraver, was baptized at St James's, Whitehaven, Cumberland, on 30 April 1760, the son of Strickland Lowry (1737–1780x85), portrait and landscape painter, and his wife, Sarah, *née* Watson. It is thought that he was named after the Belfast-born painter Joseph Wilson, with whom his father worked in Ireland. Lowry's childhood saw the family living for a time in Staffordshire, Shropshire, and Ireland. His first job was as a house-painter on the exterior of Warwick Castle. This was followed by a period in London and Arundel, Sussex. At about seventeen he was working for an engraver named Mr Ross in Worcester, where his family had finally settled.

Lowry's first plate was a trade card for a local fishmonger, for which he received as payment a large quantity of red herrings. In 1779 he produced illustrations for *The History and Antiquities of Shrewsbury* by Thomas Phillips, a resident of the town. At about eighteen he returned to London, took lodgings in Vauxhall, and began working for the prominent printer John Boydell. His works for Boydell included engravings after landscapes by Gaspar Poussin, Salvator Rosa, and George Robertson. Boydell introduced Lowry to William Blizard, surgeon at the London Hospital, for whom he made a drawing of the hot-air balloon flown by the pioneering aviator Vincenzo Lunardi in 1784. Blizard encouraged Lowry to practise surgery, but after four years spent training he abandoned this plan and instead returned to engraving. Though he never formally enrolled as a student, it is said he took drawing lessons in the Royal Academy Schools and was taught perspective by Thomas Malton the elder.

Lowry found work with John Browne, James Heath, and William Sharp, preparing the plates for works such as Sharp's version of Sir Joshua Reynolds's portrait of John Hunter, physician to George III. He also assisted William Byrne in etching the *Antiquities of Great Britain* drawn by Thomas Hearne, and published several portrait prints under his own name. But it was as an engraver of architecture and mechanism that Lowry earned distinction. Early examples include his illustrations for James Murphy's *Description of the Church of Batalha in Portugal* and *Travels in Portugal* of 1795; architectural prints for the 1796 edition of Lord Macartney's *Embassy to China*; and illustrations to Alexander Tilloch's *Philosophical Magazine*, first published in 1798, and the *Journal of the Society of Arts*. In 1800 Lowry began work on plates for Dr Abraham Rees's *Cyclopaedia*, which was to become the most successful reference book of its day. This was a mammoth task not only because the publication ran for the next twenty years, but also because each design had to be engraved twice over in order to print the 6000 copies required. Where no artist is given, the original drawing was made by Lowry or one of his daughters. The volumes contain some of Lowry's finest representations of machinery.

While working on the *Cyclopaedia* Lowry also contributed many of the illustrations to *The Antiquities of Magna Graecia*, written in 1807 by William Wilkins, future professor of architecture at the Royal Academy, and also the same author's translation of Vitruvius (1812). In 1809 he engraved twelve plates for Jane Marcet's *Conversations on Chemistry* and also several for Jeremiah Joyce's *Scientific Dialogues*. He contributed the plates to works by the builder and mathematician Peter Nicholson, including *The Principles of Architecture* (1795–8); *A Treatise on Practical Perspective* (1815); an *Architectural Dictionary* (1819); and *The Rudiments of Practical Perspective* (1822). In 1820 his engravings were used in Thomas Squire's *A Popular Grammar of the Elements of Astronomy* and Frederick Nash's *Picturesque Views of the City of Paris*. Lowry's last works appear to be illustrations for George Crabb's *Universal Technological Dictionary* (1823) and Samuel Taylor Coleridge's *Encyclopaedia metropolitana*, published from 1817 onwards.

To ensure his engravings achieved an accuracy worthy of their scientific subjects, in 1798 Lowry became the first engraver to use diamond points for ruling. About 1790 he designed a ruling machine, which he first employed upon a plate in James Stuart's *Antiquities of Athens*; in 1801 he invented an instrument for striking elliptical curves, and in 1806 another for making perspective drawings. These were described and highly praised by John Landseer in his lectures on engraving at the Royal Institution. Though none of the above were patented, Lowry sold the formula of his prized etching fluid to Jacob Perkins, the American inventor, and Charles Heath, the engraver.

Lowry was a founder member of the Geological Society and in 1812 he was elected a fellow of the Royal Society. He kept his own collection of geological specimens and, in a letter published in the *Imperial Magazine* in January 1820, contended that the formation of the earth had taken at least a million years with only the alluvial soils deposited by the biblical flood. He wrote many of the minor articles in Rees's *Cyclopaedia*. Undoubtedly it was Lowry's genuine interest in science and mechanics that enabled him to design and engrave his plates with such clarity.

Lowry was married twice, first to Miss Porter of Birmingham, with whom he had two daughters, Anne and Matilda. After she died he married Rebekah Eliza Delvalle (1761–1848), a mineralogist of Spanish descent. The wedding took place on 16 June 1796 in the parish of St Marylebone, Middlesex. They had a daughter, Delvalle, and a son, **Joseph Wilson Lowry** (1803–1879), who was born on 7 October 1803 and baptized in March 1804 at St Marylebone, Middlesex. Lowry died at his home, 57 Great Titchfield Street, London, on 23 June 1824 after a two-year illness. He had by this time lost his wealth and was reliant on the Artists' Annuity Fund. His daughter Anne married the Greek scholar Hugh Stuart Boyd. His daughter Matilda married Mr Heming, an Oxford astronomer, and became a successful portrait painter, exhibiting four works at the Royal Academy in 1808 and 1809. In 1822 his daughter Delvalle wrote and illustrated *Conversations on Mineralogy* and in 1825 she married as his second wife John Varley, the painter, with whom the family had been friends since 1802. In 1846 she wrote the *Engineer's Manual of Mineralogy and Geology*, followed by *Rudimentary Geology* in 1848. Lowry's son, Joseph Wilson Lowry, also worked as an engraver. He collaborated with his father on the *Encyclopaedia metropolitana*, and later specialized in topographical and geological subjects, exhibiting two works at the Royal Academy in 1829 and 1830. He died, unmarried, on 15 June 1879 at Robert Street, Hampstead Road, London.

A portrait of Wilson Lowry, drawn by John Linnell and engraved by Linnell and William Blake, was published soon after his death. There are also two known portraits of Lowry drawn by his daughter Matilda. One is a watercolour dating from about 1810 which is now in the collection of the National Portrait Gallery. The second was engraved by James Thomson for the *European Magazine* (August 1824), and by Henry Meyer for the *Imperial Magazine* (February 1825). Examples of Lowry's work can be found in the British Museum, the National Portrait Gallery, and the Victoria and Albert Museum. MARY GUYATT

Sources 'Memoir of Wilson Lowry', *Imperial Magazine*, 7 (1825), 113–28 • B. Hunnisett, *A dictionary of British steel engravers* (1980), 87–8 • Redgrave, *Artists* • Bryan, *Painters* (1903–5), 3.253 • A. Crookshank and the Knight of Glin [D. Fitzgerald], eds., *Irish portraits, 1660–1860* (1969), 61 [exhibition catalogue, Dublin, London, and Belfast, 14 Aug 1969 – 9 March 1970] • Graves, *RA exhibitors* • *IGI* • will, PRO, PROB 11/1168, sig. 424

Likenesses attrib. M. Heming, watercolour, *c.*1810, NPG • J. Thomson, engraving, 1824 (after M. Heming), repro. in *European Magazine* (Aug 1824) • J. Linnell and W. Blake, engraving, 1825 (after drawing by J. Linnell) • H. Meyer, engraving (after M. Heming), repro. in *Imperial Magazine*

Wealth at death none: 'Memoirs', *Imperial Magazine*; will, PRO, PROB 11/1168, sig. 424

Lowson, Sir Denys Colquhoun Flowerdew, first baronet (1906–1975), financier, was born on 22 January 1906, at Snitterfield House, Wootton Wawen, near Stratford upon Avon, Warwickshire, youngest of three children of James Gray Flowerdew Lowson (1860–1942) and his wife, Adelaide Louisa (1867/8–1948), daughter of Courtenay Harvey Saltren Scott, colonel in the Bengal staff corps. Registered at birth as Denis, he always spelt his name Denys. His father had studied physics at the Sorbonne and at Heidelberg University before making a fortune from paper manufacture and buying the estates of Snitterfield Park, and later Quarwood, Stow on the Wold, Gloucestershire. The latter was a major house of the Gothic revival designed by John Pearson in 1857; as Denys Lowson's elder brother was killed in action in 1917, he inherited the property, which he owned until 1958. The Lowsons improved the grounds at Quarwood, but destroyed most of Pearson's work. Denys Lowson was first cousin of Sir William Lowson Mitchell-Thomson, created Baron Selsdon in 1932.

Lowson was educated at Winchester College (1919–24) and at Christ Church, Oxford, where he obtained a third class in modern history (1927) and a fourth class in jurisprudence (1928). He shot for Oxford against Cambridge, Harvard, and Yale, and was called to the bar at the Inner Temple (1930). He spent one year working for a bank in London and Berlin, and another year with the Investment Trust Corporation (founded 1888), before joining the London stockbroking firm of Quilter. He visited South Africa, Madagascar, Mauritius, and Zanzibar during the 1930s, and made several trips to North America. In 1936 he married Anna Patricia (1919–2003), daughter of James Ian Macpherson, first Baron Strathcarron. They had one son and two daughters.

Following the crash of pyramided investment trusts in New York in 1929, George Macaulay Booth had experimented in London with alternatives for the investor: he issued the first fixed unit trust in 1931 and the first unit trust with a flexible portfolio in 1934. Building on this innovation, the merchant bank of Dawnay, Day, led by Guy Dawnay, in 1935 formed the Security First Trust, managed by Security Trust Managers Ltd, with Lowson as managing director. In the next few years Lowson founded the Fifteen Moorgate group of unit trusts (which bought out Dawnay, Day's unit trust management interests in 1941), and became managing director of the British Isles and General Investment Trust and vice-chairman of Domestic Trust Managers. During the war he gained control of the National group of unit funds. When his father James Lowson was granted arms by the lord Lyon's office in 1906, he took as his motto *Deus dat incrementum*, a sentiment which Denys Lowson took rather too earnestly. From the outset he worked for his own advantage rather than to fulfil his fiduciary duty to the companies he directed. His reputation in this respect was established early, and his methods never represented best City practice. Typically he bought shares through brokers for undesignated accounts: bad performers were later allotted to unit trust accounts, while the winners went to Lowson or his entourage. He gained control of several investment companies through the funds he managed in unit trusts, and secured that control by interlocking shareholdings: each of ten trusts would hold five per cent of the eleventh. Shares in these investment companies were rarely available for trading on the stock exchange; he was thus able to manipulate share prices and inflate his companies' balance sheets. As a result of Lowson's identification with unit trusts, they were considered shady by the City establishment, and their development was retarded for years. Although he sat on the London City board of General Accident Fire and Life Assurance Corporation in his mid-thirties, he was not offered major City directorships.

Lowson shared with his father a somewhat bombastic tendency. Loving pomp and ceremony, he sought distinction in the liveries and hierarchies of the City of London. At the early age of thirty-three he was sheriff of the City of London (1939–40) and at forty-four he served as lord mayor of London during Festival of Britain year (1950–51). He received a baronetcy in June 1951. He was master of the Glaziers' Company (1947–8), the Loriners' Company (1950–51), and the Gold and Silver Wyre Drawers (1951–2), and prime warden of the Shipwrights' Company (1955–6). As a freemason, he was grand warden of the United Grand Lodge of England. He was a church commissioner for England (1948–62) and a member of the Royal Company of Archers (HM bodyguard for Scotland) from 1948. He was honorary treasurer of the Princess Louise Hospital for Children in Kensington (1938–48) and, until the institution of the National Health Service in 1948, was life governor and almoner of St Bartholomew's Hospital (chairing its finance committee), vice-president of St Mary's Hospital, Paddington, and governor of Bridewell, Bethlem, and the royal hospitals. He served on the board of St Bartholomew's Hospital under the National Health Service Act (1948–67) and was active in the St John Ambulance Brigade. He rejoiced in a string of minor foreign decorations, acquired Brantridge Park, Balcombe, in Sussex (1948) and a sporting estate at Bandirran, Balbeggie, in Perthshire (1956/7). Although he was very rich, he siphoned money from his companies to subsidize the expenses of these properties and to provide such luxuries as shoots and fishing rights.

The Prevention of Fraud and Investment Act of 1958 finally imposed tighter standards of procedure for fund managers, and Lowson's ethical deficiencies were increasingly resented in the City. He had a phenomenal memory for financial intricacies and controlled his interests autocratically. By 1972 his financial empire was worth about £200 million. Its investments included Canadian and South American railways, oriental merchant trading, Australian cattle and sheep ranching, as well as goldmines, rubber plantations, and restaurants. Fourteen interrelated investment trusts controlled a tangle of cross-shareholdings involving some hundred trading and industrial companies. In June–July 1972 Lowson bought shares from his National group of unit trusts for about 62 pence each, selling them in January 1973 for £8.67 each. This transaction personally gained him about £5 million. After exposures in the *Investors' Chronicle* (supplied by a disaffected employee), the secretary of state for trade and industry in June 1973 appointed inspectors to investigate (following precedents established with Robert Maxwell in 1969). Their report published in July 1974 was damning. Although Lowson's lawyers attributed his conduct to illness, obstinacy, and secretiveness rather than dishonesty, he was obliged to resign from the companies which he had so long controlled. The merchant bankers Hill, Samuel were enlisted to unravel the cross-holdings; civil proceedings were launched against him by several litigants; and the affairs of Australian Estates, of which he had been chairman and managing director, were also investigated by the inspectors, copies of whose documentary evidence were sent to the directorate of public prosecutions. Lowson was served with an indictment summons, but before his case could come to court he died from 'diabetes and cirrhosis of the liver (certified as non-alcoholic)' on 10 September 1975, in the London Clinic, 20 Devonshire Place, Marylebone. He was buried in Scotland, possibly at Kinfauns, Perthshire, where other members of his family were buried. He was survived by his wife.

RICHARD DAVENPORT-HINES

Sources *The Times* (11 Sept 1975) • *The Times* (13 Sept 1975) • *The Times* (18 Sept 1975) • *The Spectator* (3 Aug 1974) • *The Spectator* (10 Aug 1974) • *The Spectator* (24 Aug 1974) • D. Kynaston, *The City of London*, 3 (1999) • *CGPLA Eng. & Wales* (1975) • b. cert. • d. cert. • *DNB*

Likenesses oils, *c*.1948, Glaziers' Company, London • oils, *c*.1951, Loriners' Company, London • oils, *c*.1952, Gold and Silver Wyre Drawers' Company, London • oils, *c*.1956, Shipwrights' Company, London

Wealth at death £154,216: probate, 29 Oct 1975, *CGPLA Eng. & Wales*

Lowth, Robert (1710–1787), biblical critic and bishop of London, was born in his father's house in the cathedral close at Winchester on 27 November 1710. He was the second son of William *Lowth (1661–1732), prebendary of Winchester, and his wife, Margaret (*fl.* 1675–1735), daughter of Robert Pitt of Blandford, Dorset. He attended Winchester College, as a scholar, from November 1721 until September 1729. He matriculated as a commoner at St John's College, Oxford, on 26 March 1729 but was admitted as a scholar at New College in January 1730. He graduated BA in October 1733 and MA in June 1737, and became a fellow of New College.

Lowth made a name for himself as a very young man through his composition of verses in both English and Latin. To the pious stanzas that he wrote in his bed at the age of fourteen, 'On a Thunder Storm by Night', he soon added a poem (printed in 1729) on the genealogy of Christ as displayed in the east window of Winchester College chapel, and another, written as a school exercise, 'Katherine-Hill, Near Winchester', in which he turned a consideration of the place where he played as a schoolboy into an elegy on the fate of Charles I and of Winchester during the civil war. Lowth's career as a poet developed at Oxford, where he published Latin verses in several collections of poetry from the university, as well as in the *Gentleman's Magazine*. His poem *The Judgment of Hercules* was printed in 1743. Conservative in tone and essentially predictable in style, Lowth's poetry nevertheless commanded the attention of Christopher Pitt and Joseph Spence; it was frequently anthologized later in his life. Yet it was Lowth's skill as a critic, not a writer, of verse that would win him genuine and widespread fame.

In June 1741 Lowth was elected professor of poetry at Oxford, a chair that Spence had held. Re-elected in 1746, he served for a total of ten years, in the course of which he

Robert Lowth (1710–1787), by John Keyse Sherwin, pubd 1777 (after Robert Edge Pine)

delivered the thirty-four *Praelectiones de sacra poesi Hebraeorum* that were to make his name. Published in 1753, together with a short confutation of Bishop Francis Hare's system of metre, Lowth's lectures established a new method for reading and understanding those passages of the Hebrew Bible, such as the Psalms and many of the writings of the prophets, that were traditionally considered as verse, as well as a means to expand and define the canon of biblical poetry. Building on the work of contemporary Oxford scholars, notably Thomas Hunt, Lowth urged the importance of setting biblical poetry in the context of oriental rather than classical style and the impossibility of ever determining the ancient vocalization of the Hebrew Bible with sufficient accuracy to identify its true metrical structure. In place of metre Lowth argued that the structure of Hebrew verse could be identified by its often parabolic or figurative mode of expression, and in particular by the parallelisms, or repetitions of similar words or phrases, sometimes in a regular order, sometimes not, that gave rhythm to Hebrew poetry and song, and served almost as an alternative to metre. Using these critical tools Lowth also tried to identify a sublime, and divinely inspired, quality in Hebrew verse.

In December 1741, shortly after his election as professor of poetry, Lowth was ordained deacon by Bishop Thomas Secker; he became a priest in December 1742. In July 1744 Bishop Benjamin Hoadly collated him to the rectory of Ovington, Hampshire, and in August 1750 promoted him archdeacon of Winchester, adding the rectory of East Woodhay to his preferments in June 1753. The University of Oxford created him DD by diploma on 18 July 1754. In March 1748 Lowth travelled with the embassy of Henry Bilson-Legge to Berlin, where he took the opportunity to instruct Frederick the Great, king of Prussia, about the principal English poets. He returned in February 1749 but was soon travelling again with lords George and Frederick Cavendish, sons of William Cavendish, third duke of Devonshire. They journeyed together through France and Italy, visiting Herculaneum in the spring of 1750. Lowth thus established firm connections with prominent whig noblemen and with influential figures in the ministry. He also cemented his own place in the life of his native county. On 26 December 1752 he married Mary (*d.* 1803), daughter and heir of Laurence Jackson of Christchurch, Hampshire, in the process securing substantial property and a considerable fortune. Despite the careful financial arrangements that preceded it this seems also to have been a loving marriage, and Lowth evidently took pleasure in the family that resulted. Two sons and five daughters were born between December 1753 and June 1765, but Lowth's later life was increasingly tinged by sadness as a result of the premature deaths of some of his children, of whom only Martha (1760–1812) and Robert (1762–1822), later vicar of Halstead, in Essex, and prebendary of St Paul's, survived their father. In 1768 Lowth composed a moving epitaph on the death of his eldest daughter, Mary, whom he had celebrated as 'a little brown Beauty' after her birth in 1755 (Bodl. Oxf., MS Eng. lett. c. 572, fols. 66–7).

In spite of his personal success Lowth complained in March 1755 that 'my affairs seem to be at a dead stand' (Bodl. Oxf., MS Eng. lett. c. 572, fol. 9*r*). As a result he felt bound to accept appointment as chaplain to William Cavendish, then marquess of Hartington, who was appointed lord lieutenant of Ireland in 1755. He extracted a promise that Hartington would intercede with Thomas Pelham-Holles, duke of Newcastle, then prime minister, to exchange any Irish preferment that Lowth might obtain for a suitable position at home. Lowth sailed for Dublin in May 1755, by which time Hartington was pursuing another scheme that would allow Lowth to change places with someone who would have liked an Irish bishopric '& had the wherewithal to pay well for it' (ibid., fols. 15–16). Lowth was granted the freedom of Limerick in June 1755 and soon afterwards Hartington's plans began to bear fruit. Protracted negotiations involving Joseph Butler, bishop of Durham, and Benjamin Hoadly, bishop of Winchester, as well as the duke of Newcastle eventually resulted in the appointment of James Leslie as bishop of Limerick, an office that Lowth had declined, and the transfer to Lowth of a prebendal stall at Durham. In place of Leslie's other preferments Lowth was granted the valuable living of Sedgefield. He took up his new positions and moved to co. Durham in October 1755, purchasing a post-chaise to facilitate communication with his family in Hampshire. Through Hartington, who had become duke of Devonshire, he was appointed a royal chaplain on 18 August 1757. Lowth was now free to pursue literary and theological controversy, and although further preferment took some time he was also set on a significant career within the Church of England. He was considered a candidate to be warden of Winchester College in 1764. In 1765 he became a fellow of both the Royal Society of London and that of Göttingen. On 15 June 1766, as one of the final beneficiaries of Newcastle's ecclesiastical patronage, he was consecrated bishop of St David's. On 16 October, however, he was translated to the see of Oxford, and on 12 April 1777 he was nominated bishop of London. He was made dean of the Chapel Royal, was sworn of the privy council, and from 1786 was a member of the committee for trade and plantations. He was also a governor of the Charterhouse and a trustee of the British Museum. On the death of Frederick Cornwallis, archbishop of Canterbury, in 1783, he declined the offer of the primacy.

Although Lowth had been astute in the pursuit of worldly success, and of the patronage necessary to achieve it, he was nevertheless a dedicated and effective churchman and administrator. He preached regularly, and although his conclusions were often predictable the subjects that he tackled were sometimes controversial ones, such as the importance of instructing African slaves in Christian religion or the need to overcome the weakening of the constitution by 'a general national depravity' (*Sermons, and other Remains, of Robert Lowth*, 194). Richard Price attacked Lowth's Ash Wednesday sermon in 1779, arguing that he had abandoned the concern with freedom and the constitution that had been expressed in some of his earlier sermons, but others praised his love of liberty. More significant than Lowth's preaching, however, was his concern for the godly administration of the church. He was an efficient archdeacon, and as bishop of London conducted a campaign in the early 1780s against the practice of some lay patrons in forcing clergymen to accept bonds of resignation before instituting them to their livings. After legal battles lasting two and a half years the House of Lords finally ruled in Lowth's favour, upholding the principle that the beneficed clergy should be able to act as freeholders, without obligation to their patrons. Like Secker he was amenable to the revision of the Thirty-Nine Articles and showed some sympathy for those who felt unable to subscribe to their current form. More significantly Secker drew on Lowth's learning for support in his efforts to promote a revision of the Authorized Version of the Bible, a project that Lowth continued to encourage after his own consecration as bishop. His reputation for scholarship and good sense ensured that individuals as different from one another as John Wesley and Alexander Geddes could enjoy his company and regard him as sympathetic and encouraging to some of their ideas. He was a prominent supporter of Benjamin Kennicott's collation of Hebrew manuscripts of the Bible and, later, of Robert Holmes's work on the text of the Septuagint.

To other eyes, however, Lowth's career was marred by his tenacity in controversy. *The Life of William of Wykeham*, which first appeared in 1758 and was based on considerable research in the Winchester archives, contained a dedication to Lowth's patron, Bishop Hoadly, that reignited debate over Hoadly's role in the election of Christopher Golding as warden of Winchester College and led to a sharp exchange of pamphlets. Lowth's care in revising subsequent editions of this biography, in 1759 and 1777, did not extend to any softening of his support for Hoadly. His Hebrew scholarship won him many admirers, especially among his contemporaries at Oxford and at the University of Göttingen, where J. D. Michaelis in particular championed his interpretation. Michaelis added his own notes to an edition of Lowth's *Praelectiones* (1758–61), which were included in the translation by George Gregory, published in 1787. But the regard for Lowth's work in Germany and, following its translation in 1812, in France did not lessen the offence that it gave to some English critics. His attack on Bishop Hare generated a hostile reception, notably from Thomas Edwards, to which he characteristically responded by amplifying his criticisms in *A Larger Confutation of Bishop Hare's System of Hebrew Metre* (1766).

More heat and less light were produced by the quarrel that ensued with William Warburton and his followers as a result of Lowth's remarks in the *Praelectiones* about the punishment of idolatry by the civil power among the ancient Hebrews. Lowth's arguments called into question some of the conclusions of Warburton's *Divine Legation of Moses*. A long correspondence developed in 1756, into which Warburton's criticisms of the work of Lowth's father were drawn. The dispute eventually appeared to have been settled but it was reignited by Warburton's comments on Job in the appendix to the sixth book of the *Divine Legation*. As part of his reply Lowth printed the correspondence from 1756, angering Warburton, who objected to the publication of private letters, and generating a torrent of pamphlets from his friends. By the summer of 1766 Secker was concerned about the open and petty quarrel between two of his most prominent churchmen and struggled to bring about a rapprochement that recognized 'the Relation, in which you are soon to stand, as Bishops in the same Church, obliged frequently to meet & act together' (BL, Add. MS 42560, fols. 147–8). Nevertheless Warburton's followers continued to worry at the sore that had been created, and as late as 1796 were still trying to retaliate for the injury inflicted on their champion.

In 1762 Lowth published *A Short Introduction to English Grammar*, in which he extolled the simplicity of the form and construction of the English language while remarking that it could still not rival the most ancient of languages, Hebrew, in this respect. Lowth intended his work to provide a succinct guide to grammar and to overcome imperfect or imprecise usage, even when found in the Authorized Version of the English Bible. It proved immensely popular in both Britain and America and was republished dozens of times during the eighteenth century alone; more than 34,000 copies had been printed by 1781. A German translation with critical notes by Christian Heinrich Reichel appeared in 1790. The most substantial of Lowth's publications was his new translation, with notes, of the book of Isaiah. This came out in 1778, with a second edition in the following year. It enabled Lowth to work out his interpretations of the form and structure of

Hebrew poetry, as well as to set out his conjectures about the original text and his opinions about its translation. It was the first and most successful example of a short-lived genre of biblical criticism and commentary that was emulated by several Oxford scholars and that owed much to Secker's desire that there should be progress towards a new English translation of the Bible. A German translation by Johann Benjamin Koppe, a professor of theology at Göttingen, appeared between 1779 and 1781. As usual, however, Lowth's work proved controversial; David Kocher in particular attacked Lowth's doubts about the value of vowel points for an understanding of the Hebrew text. When selections from Lowth's *Isaiah* were published in parts by the Society for Promoting the Knowledge of the Scriptures in the mid-1780s they were criticized by Michael Dodson.

In his old age Lowth was hampered by fits of bladder and gall stones, and he became incapable of travel. He died at Fulham Palace, London, between 2 p.m. and 3 p.m. on 3 November 1787, probably following a stroke, and was buried at Fulham church on 12 November. He had already given the copyright in his lectures on Hebrew poetry to the University of Oxford, and that in his life of William of Wykeham to New College, Oxford. His will honoured the terms of the trust set up when he married.

SCOTT MANDELBROTE

Sources Bodl. Oxf., MSS Eng. lett. c. 572–574 · Bodl. Oxf., MSS Eng. misc. c. 816–817 · Bodl. Oxf., MS Rawl. J, 4, fols. 53–5 · Bodl. Oxf., MS Eng. misc. d. 1236 · BL, Add. MSS 42560, fols. 145–54; 4297; 32976, fols. 287–8; 33070; 35339 · *Sermons, and other remains, of Robert Lowth*, ed. P. Hall (1834) · *GM*, 1st ser., 57 (1787), 1028–30 · J. L. Kugel, *The idea of biblical poetry* (1981)

Archives BL, letters · Bodl. Oxf., corresp. and papers · Bodl. Oxf., letters · LPL, diocesan corresp. · New College, Oxford, letters · St David's College, Lampeter, Founder's Library, letters | BL, letters to Robert Dodsley and James Dodsley, Add. MS 35339 · BL, corresp. with W. Warburton, Add. MS 4297 · NL Scot., letters to Lord Hailes · Yale U., Beinecke L., letters to Gloster Ridley

Likenesses R. E. Pine, oils, *c.*1777, New College, Oxford · J. K. Sherwin, line engraving, pubd 1777 (after R. E. Pine), BM, NPG [*see illus.*] · J. Cook, line engraving (after R. E. Pine), repro. in *Memoirs of the life and writings of the late Right Reverend Robert Lowth* (1787) · Dean, line engraving (after R. E. Pine), repro. in Hall, ed., *Sermons, and other remains*

Wealth at death over £14,000: PRO, PROB 11/1160, sig. 561

Lowth, Simon (*bap.* **1636**, *d.* **1720**), nonjuring Church of England clergyman and writer, was baptized at Dingley, Northamptonshire, on 30 October 1636, where his father, Simon Lowth (1600–1679) was the rector. His mother was Elinor Paddon, of whom little is known. Lowth was the third son of four sons and two daughters baptized at Dingley between 1633 and 1641: the eldest, William, was the father of the theologian William *Lowth and grandfather of Robert *Lowth, bishop of London. Lowth's father suffered sequestration in 1655 for reading the Book of Common Prayer, bowing at the name of Jesus, preaching only once on Sundays, and general insufficiency, but in 1658 became rector of Tilehurst, Berkshire. Lowth senior may have been the author of *Catechetical questions* (1673), and he was buried at Tilehurst on 21 June 1679.

Lowth was admitted to Clare College, Cambridge, on 29 June 1653; he graduated BA in 1657 and proceeded MA in 1660. He served as vicar of St Dunstan's, Canterbury (1665–89), rector of St Michael's, Harbledown, Kent (1670–90), and vicar of St Cosmus, Blean, Kent (1679–89). On 8 November 1679 he was licensed to marry Jane Austin (*b.* 1654/5, *d.* in or after 1720) of Canterbury.

Lowth appears to have found a patron in Samuel Parker, archdeacon of Canterbury, and in 1685 he published *Of the Subject of Church Power*, which upheld the role of the bishops in the governance of the church, and was an attack on the Erastian leanings of Edward Stillingfleet, John Tillotson, and Gilbert Burnet. He published several other pamphlets on this theme before the revolution of 1688, mainly contesting the claims of Burnet. He was probably the Mr Lowth who preached the sermon at the consecration of bishops Samuel Parker (his old patron), Thomas Cartwright, and William Lloyd on 17 October 1686. He seems to have been in royal favour because James II presented him to the deanery of Rochester on 6 November 1688, and Bishop Thomas Sprat instituted him on 12 November. However, Sprat then discovered that Lowth's degree of MA was insufficient for the post and he wrote to the chapter on the 14th advising them not to install Lowth. The chapter duly refused installation on 27 November. By the time Lowth proceeded BD and DD at Cambridge (delayed because there was no vice-chancellor) on 18 January 1689, and again claimed installation on 19 March 1689, William III had presented Henry Ullock in his place, and installation was again refused. This disappointment may have coloured Lowth's subsequent reaction to the new regime, because the register of St Cosmus, Blean, indicates that Lowth prayed in public for the new regime until the deanery was disposed of elsewhere.

Lowth's refusal to take the oaths of allegiance led to his suspension from his Kentish parishes in August 1689, and to his deprivation in February 1690. Lowth was an important contributor to the controversy following the deprivation of the nonjuring bishops in 1691; in particular in his *Historical Collections Concerning Church Affairs* (1696), he refuted the arguments of Humphrey Hody, who used medieval documents to provide precedents of the practice from the early church. Hody in response referred to Lowth as a 'foul mouthed collector', whose work was a 'long wild rage of impertinences' (Champion, 49). Other historically based tracts followed, such as *Ekalogai, or, Excerpts from the Ecclesiastical History* (1704), and *Historical Collections Concerning District Successions and Deprivations* (1713), both of which upheld the power of episcopacy against that of the state in spiritual matters.

Lowth was living in London in the parish of St Andrew's, Holborn, when he made his will on 27 April 1713. The amounts he bequeathed were small, and most of his estate was left to his wife. He republished his will in a memorandum of 22 June 1717. He died on 3 July 1720, and was buried in the new cemetery of the parish of St George the Martyr, Queen Square. He was survived by his wife, whose date of death is unknown, and by at least two children, Simon and Anne.

STUART HANDLEY

Sources Venn, *Alum. Cant.* • W. B. Bannerman and A. W. H. Clarke, eds., *Miscellanea genealogica et heraldica*, ser. 5, 1 (1916), 201–2 • *Fasti Angl., 1541–1857*, [Canterbury], 56 • G. J. Armytage, ed., *Allegations for marriage licences issued by the vicar-general of the archbishop of Canterbury, July 1679 to June 1687*, Harleian Society, 30 (1890), 11 • J. A. I. Champion, *The pillars of priestcraft shaken: the Church of England and its enemies, 1660–1730* (1992), 47–9, 88–9 • J. Spurr, *The Restoration Church of England, 1646–1689* (1991), 130–31, 156 • J. Gregory, *Restoration, reformation and reform, 1660–1828* (2000), 93 • *The diary of Thomas Cartwright, bishop of Chester*, ed. J. Hunter, CS, 22 (1843), 6 • J. Thorpe, *Custumale Roffense* (1788), 224, 238–9 • will, PRO, PROB 11/575, sig. 158, fols. 85v–86r • J. H. Overton, *The nonjurors: their lives, principles, and writings* (1902), 485 • T. Birch, *The life of Dr. John Tillotson* (1752), 64–5 • *Walker rev.*

Lowth, William (1661–1732), theologian, was born in the parish of St Martin Ludgate, London, at 4 p.m. on 11 September 1661 and baptized there at 5 p.m. on 1 October, the son of William Lowth, apothecary, and his wife, Mary Short. His father, who was the brother of Simon *Lowth (*bap.* 1636, *d.* 1720), was 'burnt out with great loss at the fire of London' (*GM*, 1st ser., 57/2, 1787, 1028). At the time of the great fire, Lowth was receiving a preparatory education under his grandfather Simon Lowth (1600–1679), rector of Tilehurst, Berkshire. He was admitted to Merchant Taylors' School on 11 September 1672 and was elected scholar of St John's College, Oxford, on 11 June 1675. He became a fellow and graduated BA in 1679, proceeding MA (1683) and BD (1688). On 25 May 1684 he was ordained deacon at Christ Church, Oxford; he was made a priest on 20 September 1685, subsequently becoming vicar of St Nicholas, Rochester, and rector of Overton, Hampshire.

In 1692 Lowth published *A vindication of the divine authority and inspiration of the writings of the Old and New Testament*, in which he attacked Hobbes, Spinoza, and other critics of the integrity and inspiration of scripture and answered many of the points raised by Jean Le Clerc's *Five Letters* (1690). Lowth defended the Oratorian Richard Simon from some of Le Clerc's remarks and from the misrepresentation of his ideas given in the poem *Religio laici* by John Dryden. This work found favour with Peter Mew, bishop of Winchester, who made him his chaplain, gave him a prebendal stall at Winchester on 8 October 1696, and presented him to the benefice of Buriton with Petersfield, Hampshire, in May 1699, which he held until his death. In 1697 he was an unsuccessful candidate for the presidency of St John's College, Oxford. A second edition of the *Vindication*, with a new preface in which Lowth defended the authority of the Pauline epistles against some remarks of John Locke, appeared in 1699. On 15 November 1700 he married, at St Bride's, Fleet Street, London, Margaret, daughter of Robert Pitt of Blandford Forum, Dorset.

In 1708 Lowth printed *Directions for the Profitable Reading of the Holy Scriptures*; six editions of this book had been published by 1799. It aimed to serve as a practical guide for lay readers to safe and profitable texts in the Bible. His skill as an expositor, whose work appealed to lay people as well as divines, was confirmed by the success of a series of commentaries on the prophetic books of the Old Testament that he published between 1714 and 1726. These were frequently reprinted later in the century as a companion to the commentaries of Simon Patrick on the historical books of the Old Testament. Lowth effectively summarized the most advanced orthodox ideas of post-Restoration churchmen in his commentaries, which treated Israelite prophecy as foreshadowing the teaching of Christ and the history of the church. A dedicated advocate of the established church, Lowth preached against separation in June 1722 following the opening of a dissenting meeting-house at Petersfield. In his sermon, and in the ensuing pamphlet controversy with John Norman, Lowth defended the apostolical institution of episcopacy and the record of the Church of England in promoting knowledge of the Bible. He was, however, a somewhat reluctant controversialist and he withdrew from lengthy engagement with Norman, sending his adversary manuscript responses that he refused to allow to be printed. He was highly regarded as a critic by his contemporaries and assisted John Potter in an edition of Clement of Alexandria and John Hudson with his work on Josephus. He also contributed to William Reading's edition of early ecclesiastical historians and advised Edward Chandler in his controversy with Anthony Collins. Lowth died at Buriton on 17 May 1732 and was buried in the churchyard there. He was survived by his wife, two sons, and three daughters.

SCOTT MANDELBROTE

Sources GL, MS 10213 • [R. Lowth], 'Lowth, William', *Biographia Britannica, or, The lives of the most eminent persons who have flourished in Great Britain and Ireland*, 5 (1760), 3010–13 • M. J. Simmonds, *Merchant Taylor fellows of St John's College Oxford* (1930), 40 • Bodl. Oxf., MS Rawl. J, fol. 4, fols. 57–60 • *GM*, 1st ser., 57 (1787), 1028 • *DNB*

Wealth at death £3500; goods and chattels: will, PRO, PROB 11/652, sig. 169

Lowther family (*per.* c.**1270**–c.**1450**), gentry, took their name from Lowther in north Westmorland, a few miles south of Penrith. They traced their ancestry back to a certain Dolfin in the late twelfth century, but the first member of the family to achieve more than local eminence was **Sir Hugh** [i] **Lowther** (*d.* 1317), a lawyer recorded as engaged in pleas relating to north-west England from 1274. In the early 1280s he was employed as a serjeant by Isabella de Forz, lady of Cockermouth, and became increasingly active in the bench. Between 1290 and 1292 he was a king's serjeant, and in that capacity prosecuted *quo warranto* actions in the eyres of the west midlands. By September 1293 he had been knighted. Professional success enabled Lowther to build up an estate in the north-west; he purchased lands in and around Lowther itself, and bought the manor of Newton Reigny in south Cumberland from the chancellor, Robert Burnell, for 400 marks.

On 19 July 1294 Lowther was appointed steward of the lands of the archbishop of York, with an annual salary of £40, a move that signalled a change of professional course, from law to administration, which lasted for several years. By 1296 he was in Scotland, serving as sheriff of Edinburgh, Linlithgow, and Haddington, and attending parliament at Berwick, where he was assaulted by the earl of Angus's son. But by 21 July 1297 Lowther had left the king's service for that of Sir Robert Clifford, whose tenant he was at Lowther. He acted as Clifford's attorney, but also as his knight, in the garrison at Carlisle and on campaign in Scotland. By 1300, however, Lowther was again principally employed as a lawyer; in November that year he acted as a justice for Bishop Antony (I) Bek of Durham, who subsequently granted him the manor of Thorpe Thewles, near Stockton. He was also employed by the king, acting regularly as a justice of assize and gaol delivery and on commissions in the north of England. A knight of the shire for Westmorland in 1305, he was summoned to parliament among the justices in 1307 and 1313. Lowther's last commission was issued on 1 March 1317, but he was dead by 21 April following. With his wife, named Ivetta or Jenet, to whom he was married by 1286, he had two sons, Hugh and John.

The heads of the Lowther family in the three generations following Hugh [i] all bore the forename Hugh, and this unadventurous baptismal policy, combined with an absence of secure evidence for their dates of death, often makes the fortunes of these Lowthers hard to differentiate. Even before 1317 it can be difficult to distinguish commissions directed to Hugh [i] from those intended for his heir, **Sir Hugh** [ii] **Lowther** (*d.* 1338?). Given livery of his father's lands on 1 June 1317, when northern England was coming under acute pressure from Scottish raids, Hugh [ii] was principally active as a soldier, not always successfully—he was captured by the Scots, and ransomed for at least £300. In 1319 he served at the siege of Berwick, and was knighted at about that time. The fact that he was deputy sheriff of Westmorland (1320–22) shows that he had maintained his family's links with the Cliffords, hereditary sheriffs of the county; following Roger Clifford's execution for treason after the battle of Boroughbridge in 1322, Lowther found it advisable to obtain a royal pardon. He subsequently proved his loyalty as one of the small group of knights who on 25 February 1323 surprised and arrested Andrew Harclay, earl of Carlisle, before he could implement a treasonable alliance with the Scots.

As a reward Lowther received a life grant of Harclay's manor of Hartley. He also consolidated his inherited estates at Lowther, while by his marriage (before 1317) to Margaret, daughter of John Lucy of Cockermouth, he acquired the manor of Wythop, south-east of Cockermouth, which became one of his family's principal residences. On 12 July 1318 he was granted licence to crenellate there. Knight of the shire for Westmorland in 1320, and for Cumberland in 1324, he acted as a commissioner of array in both counties, and in 1331 served briefly in Ireland. Hugh [ii] was believed to be still alive on 28 June 1338, when he was reportedly engaged in a collusive action with John Harclay over the manor of Hartley, but had apparently died by 10 July following, when a Hugh Lowther who was probably his son made an enfeoffment to uses of the manor of Newton Reigny, in terms implying that his father was now dead. Hugh [ii] left two other sons, Robert and Thomas.

Sir Hugh [iii] **Lowther** (*d.* in or before 1367) was already a father and a knight when his own father died; with his wife, Margaret, daughter of William Whale, whom he probably married about 1333, he had five sons and two daughters. MP for Westmorland in 1339, and for Cumberland in 1341 and 1344, he was active on the Anglo-Scottish march in the 1340s, as a soldier and commissioner of array, and was sheriff of Cumberland almost continuously between November 1351 and January 1355. His marriage brought him the manor of Whale, and he also acquired property in Knipe, but in 1359 his purchase of lands and rights in Askham was challenged in the bench, and he may have allowed himself to be bought out again. Hugh [iii] seems to have been dead by 20 April 1367, when a dispute was settled between his wife and eldest son, probably over the former's dower rights; the fact that Margaret Lowther died in 1370 meant that these constituted no lasting drag upon the fortunes of her descendants.

Like his predecessors, **Sir Hugh** [iv] **Lowther** (1326–1382?) succeeded his father in full adulthood. Said to be aged forty-four in 1370, when he was already a knight, he had married Matilda, daughter of Sir Peter Tilliol of Scaleby, in 1338; they had six sons, three of whom were said in 1376 to have abetted their father in a series of assaults at Penrith. Such charges were seldom an impediment to office and employment. Sir Hugh had been knight of the shire for Westmorland in 1371 and 1372. A commissioner of the peace there in 1373, 1377, and 1380, and of array in 1377 and 1380, he was an assessor of Westmorland's poll tax in 1379. His eldest son, **Sir John Lowther** (*d.* 1382?), one of the alleged abettors of 1376, represented Westmorland in parliament every year between 1377 and 1380. But although Sir Hugh was reappointed to the Westmorland bench on 20 December 1382, a revised commission, issued on the same day, replaced him not with his son but with his grandson, **Sir Robert Lowther** (*d.* 1430), the elder of the two sons of John Lowther's marriage to Margaret Preston. The likelihood is that the substitution followed hard upon Sir Hugh's death, and that Sir John had lately predeceased his father.

Robert Lowther was influential in the affairs of north-west England for nearly fifty years. For much of that time he had the support of his brother **William Lowther** (*d.* 1421?), and together the two men substantially raised the standing of their family. Both acted as sheriff and escheator, and both sat in parliament. Robert, as befitted the elder, was the first into parliament, representing Cumberland in 1391, and being returned on a further six occasions between 1394 and 1417. William was MP in 1393, and in 1404 was returned alongside his brother. Sir Robert (knighted by 1404) was sheriff of Cumberland in 1407–8 (in succession to William, who held the shrievalty in 1406–7, and also in 1400–01) and 1418–19, and was three times appointed escheator of either Cumberland or Cumberland and Westmorland together. William was twice escheator. Their shrievalties and parliamentary associations, taken together with the fact that Robert was appointed only at intervals to the Westmorland bench, but sat continuously as a Cumberland JP from 1397 until his death, point to a shift in interest from the former to the latter county.

This development probably stemmed largely from political developments in the region, from the advance of the Nevilles, who became dominant in Cumberland, at the expense of the Cliffords, lords of Westmorland. In 1379 John Lowther had indented to accompany the young Thomas Clifford to war should the need arise. But in the 1390s his sons attached themselves to the Nevilles. By January 1397 Robert was lieutenant to Ralph Neville, earl of Westmorland, in Inglewood Forest. With Neville he transferred his allegiance from Richard II to Henry of Lancaster two years later, and in May 1402 was commissioned to act against trouble-makers and Ricardian propagandists in Cumberland, while in 1405 Robert and William were together appointed to take custody of the Percy castle at Cockermouth. On 28 June 1406 Sir Robert was simultaneously a commissioner to investigate concealed royal revenues, and to raise a loan for the king, again in Cumberland, and he was ultimately to be an executor of Ralph Neville's will. In the meantime William Lowther, to whom Neville made a grant for life of lands in his Yorkshire manor of Eastburne, was in 1407 appointed master forester of Inglewood for life. Apparently unmarried, he was less prominent in public affairs than his brother, but the fact that until he died, probably in 1421, he often acted as a surety or trustee suggests that he was widely respected.

Sir Robert did not advance his career by political means only. By 1398 he had married Margaret, widow of Sir John Derwentwater and daughter of William *Strickland, who in 1400 became bishop of Carlisle. They had six sons and three daughters. Born before her father took major orders, Margaret was probably the only legitimate child of a medieval English bishop. The marriage brought her husband the Cumberland manors of Castlerigg and Tallentire, as well as estates in southern Westmorland. It also brought a useful connection with the see of Carlisle, enabling Lowther to secure the constableship of Rose Castle, the bishop's residence, for his second son, William. When Bishop Strickland died in 1419, leaving 100 marks for prayers for his soul, Sir Robert, as his principal executor, used the money to buy land for himself, arranging for the chantrist's stipend to be paid out of the issues. Lowther was making provision for his children well before his death, which had occurred by 20 April 1430, a few weeks after he dictated his will. His body was to be buried in Lowther church, but he endowed prayers for his own and his father-in-law's souls in Carlisle Cathedral. As well as making bequests of cash, he disposed of a number of cows and of four flocks of sheep, one of which was left to his widow. Margaret Lowther lived until 1449; in her will, dated 3 February, she instructed that she be buried in Carlisle Cathedral, next to Bishop Strickland's grave, and left money to celebrate masses for her own soul, her father's, and the souls of both her husbands. To her eldest son, Hugh Lowther, she left a silver cup engraved with his father's arms, presumably with the intention that it should serve as an heirloom. Such commemoration would have been appropriate. Sir Robert and his forebears had raised their family to a high place among the gentry of north-west England; able, energetic, and fertile, their descendants continued to flourish there, until raised to the peerage with the titles of successively viscount (1696) and earl (1784) of Lonsdale.

The arms of the Lowther family were or, six annulets, three, two and one, sable. HENRY SUMMERSON

Sources deeds, Cumbria AS, Carlisle, Lonsdale papers, D/Lons • *Chancery records* • F. W. Ragg, 'Early Lowther and de Louther', *Transactions of the Cumberland and Westmorland Antiquarian and Archaeological Society*, 2nd ser., 16 (1916), 108–68 • C. M. L. Bouch, 'The origins and early pedigree of the Lowther family', *Transactions of the Cumberland and Westmorland Antiquarian and Archaeological Society*, 2nd ser., 48 (1949), 114–24 • F. W. Ragg, 'Medieval Knipe: Gnype, Cundal and Gnype Patrick', *Transactions of the Cumberland and Westmorland Antiquarian and Archaeological Society*, 2nd ser., 19 (1919), 118–39 • F. W. Ragg, 'Helton Flechan, Askham and Sandford of Askham', *Transactions of the Cumberland and Westmorland Antiquarian and Archaeological Society*, 2nd ser., 21 (1921), 174–233 • F. W. Ragg, 'De Cundal, Bampton Cundal and Butterwick', *Transactions of the Cumberland and Westmorland Antiquarian and Archaeological Society*, 2nd ser., 22 (1922), 281–328 • F. W. Ragg, 'Early Barton', *Transactions of the Cumberland and Westmorland Antiquarian and Archaeological Society*, 2nd ser., 24 (1924), 295–350 • F. W. Ragg, 'Cliburn Hervy and Cliburn Tailbois, pt 2', *Transactions of the Cumberland and Westmorland Antiquarian and Archaeological Society*, new ser., 28 (1927–8), 179–272 • inquisitions post mortem: chancery, PRO, C139/44 no.4; C139/133 no.2 • P. A. Brand, ed., *The earliest English law reports*, 2, SeldS, 112 (1996) • HoP, *Commons, 1386–1421*, 2.639–42 • *CIPM*, 6, 12, 13 • R. L. Storey, 'The chantries of Cumberland and Westmorland, part 1', *Transactions of the Cumberland and Westmorland Antiquarian and Archaeological Society*, 2nd ser., 60 (1960), 66–96 • *RotP*, vols. 1–2, 4 • F. Palgrave, ed., *The parliamentary writs and writs of military summons*, 2 vols. in 4 (1827–34), vols. 1/2, 2/3 • *CDS*, vols. 2–3, 5 • *RotS*, vol. 1 • *The registers of John le Romeyn, lord archbishop of York*, ed. [W. Brown], 2, SurtS, 128 (1917) • *'Registrum palatinum Dunelmense': the register of Richard de Kellawe, lord palatine and bishop of Durham*, ed. T. D. Hardy, 4 vols., Rolls Series, 62 (1873–8) • A. Hughes, *List of sheriffs for England and Wales: from the earliest times to AD 1831*, PRO (1898); repr. (New York, 1963), 26–27 • J. Nicolson and R. Burn, *The history and antiquities of the counties of Westmorland and Cumberland*, 2 vols. (1777), 1.429–31 • *Returns of members of parliament: England, 1213–1702* (1878) • H. Summerson, *Medieval Carlisle: the city and the borders from the late eleventh to the mid-sixteenth century*, 2 vols., Cumberland and Westmorland Antiquarian and Archaeological Society, extra ser., 25 (1993)

Lowther, Sir Christopher, first baronet (1611–1644), merchant and landowner, born in early 1611 at Skirwith Hall, Kirkland parish, Skirwith, Cumberland, and baptized on 4 May 1611, was the second son of Sir John *Lowther (1582–1637), lawyer and landowner, of Lowther Hall, Westmorland, and Ellinor Fleming of Skirwith (*c*.1583–1659). He was admitted to the Inner Temple in 1627, and matriculated a pensioner at St John's College, Cambridge, in the Easter term of 1628, but he also spent a period learning mercantile skills from his uncle Robert Lowther, a London merchant, although apparently not as an indentured apprentice. This was probably because his father, in dividing responsibility among his sons for the Lowther enterprises, intended Christopher to run the Irish branch from the small haven of Whitehaven, part of the manor of St Bees in Cumberland which Sir John had purchased from the head of the Ingleton branch of the family in 1630. Set in a district rich in out-cropping coal and promising to be profitable for salt-boiling, Whitehaven had the potential to grow in wealth and population as Dublin grew in importance as a port and a market. Lowther visited Dublin twice in 1632. In June he sold West Riding cloth and visited Clonmel, Kinsail, Wicklow, Wexford, Bandon, Mallow, Carlow, and Cork, investigating the pilchard and herring fisheries, the trade in pipe and barrel staves from Wexford, and shipbuilding. In the autumn he organized a venture in wheat to the Canary Islands on a ship sent from London by his uncle Robert and investigated the possibilities of other Irish exports.

Lowther's correspondence shows him resourceful, confident, and committed to a merchant's life. From 1633 until his father's death in 1637 he was occupied in a multiplicity of ventures in textiles, beef, salt, coal, herring, and iron (iron ore to Ireland, pig iron home). He developed salt manufacturing in Whitehaven in association with Sir George Radcliffe, friend and chief adviser of Sir Thomas Wentworth, the lord deputy of Ireland, and Richard Marris, Wentworth's chief steward. One fruit of that collaboration was the construction of the first Whitehaven pier, which transformed a poor haven into a port. His textile trading took him as far as Hamburg, where he spent most of 1637.

After their father's death, on which Christopher Lowther inherited the manor of St Bees, Whitehaven, and much against Sir John's wishes, Christopher and his brothers appear to have separated their concerns. On 6 September 1638 Christopher married Frances Lancaster (*c*.1624–1647), to whom his father had betrothed him five years earlier when she was aged only eight. She brought as her dowry the Westmorland manors of Sockbridge and Hartsop.

Public affairs increasingly absorbed Lowther's energies. While serving as sheriff of Cumberland in 1641 the outbreak of the Irish rising destroyed his Irish iron-forging enterprise and disrupted his other commercial activities. In May 1642, in return for raising a troop of horse for Ireland, the king gave him a baronetcy, although the estate was then scarcely large enough to sustain such a status. In the civil war, at least nominally he commanded a regiment of foot in the marquess of Newcastle's army, and he was appointed governor of Whitehaven and of Cockermouth Castle. However, he played little part in the campaigning, probably because of worsening health.

In February 1644, foreseeing his imminent death, Lowther made a settlement of his estate into the hands of trustees (his mother Dame Ellinor Lowther, his brother William *Lowther (*bap.* 1612, *d.* 1688), and his neighbour and nephew John Lamplugh of Lamplugh) for the benefit of his infant son, John *Lowther (*bap.* 1642, *d.* 1706), and his still unborn daughter, Frances. He died shortly after, at Whitehaven, at the age of thirty-three, and was buried on 24 April 1644 in St Bees parish church.

D. R. HAINSWORTH

Sources Cumbria AS, Carlisle, Lonsdale papers, D/Lons/W, Sir Christopher Lowther • *Commercial papers of Sir Christopher Lowther, 1611–1644*, ed. D. R. Hainsworth, SurtS, 189 (1977) • D. R. Hainsworth, 'Christopher Lowther's Canary adventure', *Irish Economic and Social History*, 2 (1975) • J. V. Beckett, *Coal and tobacco: the Lowthers and the economic development of west Cumberland, 1660–1760* (1981) • H. Owen, *The Lowther family: eight hundred years of 'A family of ancient gentry and worship'* (1990) • Venn, *Alum. Cant.* • W. H. Cooke, ed., *Students admitted to the Inner Temple, 1547–1660* [1878]

Archives Cumbria AS, Carlisle, corresp. and papers, mainly relating to his business affairs

Lowther, Claude William Henry (1870–1929), politician and art connoisseur, was born at Binstead on the Isle of Wight on 26 June 1870, the third child and only son of Francis William Lowther (1841–1908), an officer in the Royal Navy, and his wife, Louise Beatrice de Fonblanque. His father was an illegitimate son of William *Lowther, the second earl of Lonsdale, and received a legacy of £125,000 on the latter's death in 1872. Educated at Rugby School, Lowther entered the diplomatic service and was honorary attaché at Madrid in 1894. Early in 1900 he joined the eighth battalion, imperial yeomanry, an irregular force of mounted infantrymen who embodied the national resolve to defeat the Boers. On 30 March 1900 he was a member of a composite force, commanded by Sir Charles Warren, defending Faber's Put farmhouse. During the Boer attack Lowther, assisted by two troopers, rescued two severely wounded men under heavy fire, an action which led Warren to recommend him, unsuccessfully, for the Victoria Cross.

In the 'khaki' election of October 1900 Lowther was elected the Unionist MP for North Cumberland, a constituency which included part of the family's estate. He was defeated in the general election in 1906 and, dismayed by his rejection by the voters, spoke out against the threat which socialism posed, in his view, to the survival of the crown, Lords, and empire. He was an enthusiastic tariff reformer and asserted the cause of 'national efficiency', including provision for infant welfare and pensions. Defence of empire and functional privilege, interest in selective social reform, and indictment of collectivism were sustained themes of his political life. As chairman of the Anti-Socialist Union, in 1908–11, he made bitter, forthright, and often personalized attacks on the leaders of parliamentary Labour. After a further defeat in January 1910, he regained the North Cumberland seat in December 1910, and from 1918 to 1922 he was MP for the Lonsdale division of Lancashire as a coalition Unionist.

Although Lowther made politics his profession, he cultivated wider interests in the theatre and connoisseurship. Out of friendship Herbert Beerbohm Tree presented his play *The Gordian Knot* at His Majesty's Theatre in 1903. The text does not survive. It was heartily booed on its first performance and, courageously, Tree came before the curtain at the end of the performance to mollify the audience. Their friendship survived. Max Beerbohm, brother of Tree, drew two caricatures of Lowther.

In 1910 Lowther bought Herstmonceux Castle, near Hailsham, Sussex, which was the picturesque ruin of one of the finest domestic buildings of the fifteenth century. He rebuilt the great gateway tower, south front, and large parts of the banqueting hall. The inhabitable parts of the castle were refurnished. Lowther collected Flemish tapestries, Jacobean oak furniture, and old English glass to recreate an enchanted twilight castle where he met his guests 'dressed in black knee breeches, black silk stockings and buckled shoes as though for a Court Ball' (Carter, 462–3).

Lowther owned only 183 acres and was barely capable of obtaining squirearchical influence over the fiercely independent trug makers of Herstmonceux. However, this 'Sussex man' (*Sussex Daily News*, 13 Nov 1914) received official sanction to raise new battalions of the Royal Sussex regiment in September 1914 which quickly overtook, in efficiency and popularity, the efforts of traditional raisers of manpower in the county. His three Southdown battalions acquired a distinctive character as 'Lowther's own'. Among the small villages and seaside resorts of Sussex he successfully applied the 'pals' principle which ensured that men who enlisted together, trained, fought (and died) alongside each other. It echoed the imperial yeomanry of 1900 as an expression of active citizenship in time of national crisis. The raisers of service battalions rarely, however, commanded their own formations in France and Lieutenant-Colonel Lowther was no exception. He returned to Herstmonceux Castle a disappointed man.

In 1916 Lowther clamoured for conscription for both military and industrial purposes. He identified with the powerful sacrificial impulse in wartime Britain. Early in 1918 he urged the creation of an army of veterans above military age because it was 'the tragedy of their lives' for fit older men not to be able to fight for their country (*Hansard 5C*, 101, 24 Jan 1918, 1242). He had a Milnerite regard for the uniformed patriotic working man.

At the end of the war Lowther's preoccupations were those of an anti-modernist. He expressed dissatisfaction with the design of the victory medal and hoped that Kipling would become poet laureate. His voice was among those which demanded massive financial compensation from Germany. At home his attachment to national efficiency was not translated into a vision of social reconstruction but ended in the mire of the 'anti-waste' movement. His support for Horatio Bottomley's 'Economy with Efficiency' campaign confirmed his hostility to Lloyd George. He was among the majority of Unionist MPs who voted to end the coalition with Lloyd George at the celebrated meeting held at the Carlton Club on 19 October 1922. In declining health, he withdrew from politics at the general election held in November 1922.

Lowther's letters to political allies reveal a pungent and witty observer of high politics. His intellectual arrogance, poetic instinct, mild eccentricities, and hostility to coalition unionism damaged his parliamentary career but conveyed his insistence on remaining an independent-minded country gentleman. His capacity for friendship was demonstrated in his correspondence with Winston Churchill, who in August 1916, at a low point in his political career, was lent a cottage in the grounds of the castle. Lowther died, unmarried, at his London home, 43 Catherine Street, Westminster, on 16 June 1929. No parliamentary colleagues were present at his memorial service. His two sisters erected a plaque in his memory in All Saints' Church, Herstmonceaux. In his restoration of Herstmonceux Castle, Lowther created a monument of beauty but the contents were auctioned at his death and this great pleasure ground of Sussex slid once more from public view.

KEITH GRIEVES

Sources *The Times* (18 June 1929) · b. cert. · H. Owen, *The Lowther family: eight hundred years of 'A family of ancient gentry and worship'* (1990) · K. Grieves, '"Lowther's lambs": rural paternalism and voluntary recruitment in the First World War', *Rural History*, 4 (1993), 55–75 · W. W. Williams, *The life of General Sir Charles Warren* (1941) · H. Pearson, *Beerbohm Tree: his life and laughter* (1956) · M. Beerbohm, *A book of caricatures* (1907) · K. D. Brown, 'The anti-socialist union, 1908–49', *Essays in anti-labour history*, ed. K. D. Brown (1974) · G. D. Martineau, *A history of the royal Sussex regiment* [1955] · *Sussex Daily News* (Aug 1914–April 1915) · Sussex marching song, 'Lowther's own', W. Sussex RO, 11/60 · V. B. Carter, *Winston Churchill as I knew him* (1965) · Viscountess Wolseley, 'Herstmonceux Castle', *Sussex County Magazine*, 2 (1928), 180–84 · sale catalogues (1929) [Christie, Manson & Woods] · *The valuable contents of Herstmonceux Castle, Sussex* [sale catalogue, 5–6 Nov 1929] · inscription to the memory of Lt. Col Claude Lowther, All Saints' Church, Herstmonceux · sale particulars, Herstmonceux Castle Estate, Chichester, E. Sussex RO, MSS 21/4

Likenesses M. Beerbohm, caricature, exh. Carfax Gallery 1907, repro. in Beerbohm, *A book of caricatures* · M. Beerbohm, caricature, repro. in *The Sketch* (20 May 1903)

Wealth at death £100,554 2*s*. 1*d*.: probate, 17 Aug 1929, *CGPLA Eng. & Wales*

Lowther, Sir Gerard (*d.* 1624). *See under* Lowther, Sir Gerard (*c.*1590–1660).

Lowther, Sir Gerard (*c.*1590–1660), judge, was according to Sir William Betham the illegitimate son of Sir Christopher Lowther (*d.* 1617) of Penrith, Cumberland. Raised within the family circle, he is probably the Gerard Lowther who entered Queen's College, Oxford, in 1605. After call to the bar by Gray's Inn in 1614, he elected to pursue his fortunes in Ireland where two of his uncles, one of whom was also called Gerard, were to attain judicial office in the 1610s. The elder **Sir Gerard Lowther** (*d.* 1624) was a younger son of Sir Richard *Lowther (1532–1608) of Lowther, Westmorland, and his wife, Frances, daughter of John Middleton of Middleton, Westmorland. He entered the Inner Temple in 1580 and was called to the bar in 1590. Appointed a justice of common pleas in Ireland by patent dated 12 October 1610, he was recorded the following year as 'like to do good service' in a court whose judges were characterized by age and infirmity (Bewley, 3). A friend of Richard Boyle, earl of Cork, he was returned MP for Tallow, a borough in the earl's sway, in 1613. In 1616 he served as treasurer of King's Inns and in 1618 was knighted by the lord deputy. By then he had acquired land in co. Fermanagh and co. Tyrone under the Ulster plantation and he was granted market and fair privileges for Lowtherstown in co. Fermanagh. He married, first, Grace (1557/8–1594), daughter of Alan Bellingham of Levens, Westmorland, and widow of Edmund Cliburn, and second, Anne Welbury (*née* Bulmer), daughter and coheir of Sir Ralph Bulmer of Wilton, Durham. There were no children by either marriage and at his death, on 14 October 1624, he bequeathed the bulk of his property to his nephew Richard Lowther and his godson the younger Gerard Lowther. He was buried on 16 October in Christ Church, Dublin.

Admitted to King's Inns, Dublin, in 1619, the younger Gerard Lowther was named attorney-general of Munster three years later at the salary of 20 marks a year. Through the influence of Richard Boyle, earl of Cork, he was made a baron of the Irish exchequer in 1628, where, for some years, he served on the same bench with his other uncle, Lancelot Lowther. With the removal from office of Dominick Sarsfield, the chief justice of the Irish common pleas, in 1633, the younger man, who had been knighted two years earlier, was destined to secure an even higher prize. Boyle pressed for the promotion of the new Sir Gerard to fill the vacancy, greasing the palm of Sir Thomas Wentworth, recently installed as Irish lord deputy, with the promise of £1000 if he carried out his side of the bargain. The new chief justice, not for the last time, then altered his allegiance, attaching himself to Wentworth and helping to oversee the legal and administrative reforms that the latter was to implement. The fall from favour of Wentworth (now earl of Strafford) in late 1640 threatened Lowther's career with an abrupt termination. In February 1641 impeachment proceedings were commenced in the Irish parliament against four of Wentworth's most prominent Irish associates, including Lowther. The proceedings dragged on, but those directed against Lowther and Lord Chancellor Bolton were eventually dropped in June 1642.

Prominent in the business of the Irish privy council in the mid-1640s, Lowther emerged as a member of the faction opposed to accommodation with the Catholics of the confederation of Kilkenny. The impending collapse of the royalist cause in Ireland led to his changing sides yet again, surviving the change of regime after the trial and execution of the king to be confirmed in judicial office in 1651. He is best glimpsed in this final phase of his career as the author of the harangue delivered by him at the inauguration the following year of the special non-jury high court of justice set up to try assorted rebels, traitors, and malefactors, later printed in Edmund Borlase's *History of the Execrable Irish Rebellion* (1680). Though one of the commissioners of the great seal of Ireland in 1655–6, Lowther's chameleon past earned him no special favours, and he was a conspicuous absentee from the Irish council on which he had previously served under Wentworth and Ormond. Throughout his career, as the Dublin statute staple records make clear, Lowther loaned substantial sums of money: £ 15,000 between 1628 and 1659. He married, first, in 1621, Ann (*d.* *c.*1634), the daughter of Sir Laurence Parsons, whom he succeeded on the exchequer in 1628, and, second, Margaret (*d.* 1658), daughter of Sir John King, the muster-master general of Ireland. Lowther died in Dublin on 3 April 1660 on the eve of the Restoration, and was buried at St Michan's Church, Dublin. He left no children. W. N. Osborough

Sources F. E. Ball, *The judges in Ireland, 1221–1921*, 1 (1926) · E. T. Bewley, 'Some notes on the Lowthers who held judicial office in Ireland in the 17th century', *Transactions of the Cumberland and Westmorland Antiquarian and Archaeological Society*, new ser., 2 (1901–2), 1–28 · [E. Borlase], *The history of the execrable Irish rebellion* (1680), esp. 376ff. · *CSP Ire.*, *1633–60* · *The Lismore papers, first series: autobiographical notes, remembrances and diaries of Sir Richard Boyle, first and 'great' earl of Cork*, ed. A. B. Grosart, 5 vols. (privately printed, London, 1886), vols. 3, 4 · R. Lascelles, ed., *Liber munerum publicorum Hiberniae … or, The establishments of Ireland*, 2 vols. [1824–30], vol. 1, pt 2, pp. 36, 51 · *The journals of the House of Commons of the kingdom of Ireland*, 1.166ff. and passim [1641 impeachment proceedings] · *Lords' Journals, Ireland*, 1, 170ff [1641 impeachment proceedings] · R. Steele, ed., *A bibliography of proclamations of the Tudor and Stuart sovereigns*, 2 vols. (1910), vol. 2 · T. C. Barnard, *Cromwellian Ireland: English government and reform in Ireland, 1649–1660* (1975), 282–3 · V. Treadwell, *Buckingham and Ireland, 1616–28: a study in Anglo-Irish politics* (1998) · G. Watson, 'Gerard Lowther's house, Penrith', *Transactions of the Cumberland and Westmorland Antiquarian and Archaeological Society*, new ser., 1 (1900–01), 94–103 · J. Ohlmeyer and E. O. Ciardha, eds., *The Irish statute staple books* (1998)

Wealth at death substantial land holdings: will, 14 Nov 1659, inquisition, 2 Sept 1662, in Bewley, 'Some notes on the Lowthers', 21–4

Lowther, Henry, third Viscount Lonsdale (1694–1751). *See under* Lowther, John, first Viscount Lonsdale (1655–1700).

Lowther, Sir Hugh (*d.* **1317**). *See under* Lowther family (*per.* *c.*1270–*c.*1450).

Lowther, Sir Hugh (*d.* **1338**?). *See under* Lowther family (*per.* *c.*1270–*c.*1450).

Lowther, Sir Hugh (*d.* in or before **1367**). *See under* Lowther family (*per.* *c.*1270–*c.*1450).

Lowther, Sir Hugh (**1326–1382**?). *See under* Lowther family (*per.* *c.*1270–*c.*1450).

Lowther, Hugh Cecil, fifth earl of Lonsdale (**1857–1944**), sportsman, was born at 21 Wilton Crescent, London, on 25 January 1857, the second surviving child of Henry Lowther (1818–1876), MP for West Cumberland and later third earl of Lonsdale, and his wife, Emily Susan (Pussy) Caulfeild (1832–1917), daughter of Francis St George Caulfeild. Hugh was at Eton College for only two years, before leaving at the age of twelve to pass his time learning outdoor sports (and particularly fox-hunting) in his father's stables at Ashfordby, near Melton Mowbray. Horses remained his lifelong passion. He entered London society under the shadow of his elder brother, St George, who himself inherited the earldom in 1876.

Hugh Lowther was not rich, handsome, or sophisticated but he had energy and a taste for self-advertisement. He fell in love with Lady Grace Cecilie Gordon (1854–1941), third daughter of Charles Gordon, tenth marquess of Huntly. She was one of a slightly impoverished family of twelve, kind if strait-laced, but she shared Hugh's passion for hunting. In spite of her family's opposition they married (quietly) on 27 June 1878, ten days after Hugh had attracted public attention by winning a walking match over a 100 mile length of the Great North Road. He completed the course in 17 hours 21 minutes, stopping for a change of shoes and socks every 5 miles and for three rests of one hour each, so averaging nearly 6 miles an hour.

The following year took the Lowthers to the American

Hugh Cecil Lowther, fifth earl of Lonsdale (**1857–1944**), by Sir John Lavery, 1930

Middle West. Hugh returned with trophies and a conviction that he might make a fortune out of cattle ranching with his fox-hunting friend Moreton Frewen. Because he was heir presumptive of the family estates (if his brother St George, who had now married, died without an heir) he possessed a contingent reversionary interest which he sold for £40,000. (The family trustees soon repurchased it.) He invested the money in cattle in Wyoming but by spring the herds had starved, and the venture collapsed.

The Lowthers took a cottage near Oakham and tried to live on Hugh's allowance from his brother of £1000 a year. Grace found herself pregnant. It did not stop her from hunting. After a bad fall she lost the baby and was declared incapable of bearing children. She remained a partial invalid for the rest of her life. But on 8 February 1882 St George died and Hugh found himself at twenty-five the fifth earl of Lonsdale, one of the richest men in England. He acquired an income of over £70,000 from land, as well as the huge royalties from the Whitehaven collieries which ran miles out under the sea on the west Cumberland coast. His houses were Lowther Castle, Whitehaven Castle, the large hunting-box at Barleythorpe in Rutland, and two houses in Carlton House Terrace knocked into one.

At once Lonsdale indulged his taste for immaculate appearances. His own dress, his long cigars and a fresh gardenia in his buttonhole, his beautifully matched chestnuts, his yellow carriages and yellow-liveried footmen were soon famous in London and at the meets of the Woodland Pytchley, of which he was master. He gave himself a groom of the bedchamber, a chamberlain, and a master of music to supervise the twenty-four musicians who travelled with him from house to house. His household travelled in a special train, and stationmasters would be rewarded with £5 notes given by his valet.

But Lonsdale's income was not his own. It was controlled by the 1876 estate resettlement trustees, the chief of whom was his uncle William Lowther and (after 1904) the latter's son James William Lowther, speaker of the House of Commons. They had a duty to preserve and maintain the castles and estates. They failed in this, but still nettled Hugh, who declared that because of his childlessness he was the last of the Lowthers. This ignored his younger brother Lancelot, who was to inherit the peerages and the remains of the estate after his death.

An attempt by Lonsdale to ride in Hyde Park with Lillie Langtry led to a scuffle with Sir George Chetwynd, who was trying to do the same. But boxing was an art which both men knew. Lonsdale indeed claimed that he had beaten the American John L. Sullivan, heavyweight champion of the world. On this reputation he became chairman of the boxing committee of the Pelican Club, an aristocratic sports club in Gerrard Street. There he worked to reform the abuses of boxing and to seek its recognition as a sport. Another member of the club, John Sholto Douglas, the ninth marquess of Queensberry, gave his name to the laws of boxing, the 'Queensberry rules', but credit for their devising must be given to Lonsdale.

In 1885 Lonsdale was in love with the stage beauty Violet *Cameron and financed an opera company for her. When cited by her husband in the divorce petition, he took Violet and the whole company to New York. But the scandal followed, and they all returned to London, where Violet bore a daughter. In Whitehaven the radical *Northern Counties Gazette* called it all 'Lowtherism'. In February 1888 he departed for a long stay abroad, reportedly to shoot bear in Arctic Canada.

Lonsdale told the *New York Herald* that he was to collect specimens for a body called the Scotch Naturalist Society. He took a train to Fort Qu'Appelle, beyond Winnipeg, and told Bishop Bompas that he had been commanded by Queen Victoria to report on the state of the Indians. Then his party set off in bad weather by horse sleigh, dog sleigh, and boat and reached the Arctic circle by July 1888. In conditions of great hardship he then travelled 6000 km up the Mackenzie River and across northern Alaska, reporting his impressions in some lurid letters home. Sled dogs died of cold or ate his snow-shoes. He shot the quarrelsome ones and knocked out hired Indians who were insubordinate. 'Indians can stand half the cold white men can', he recorded in his diary on 14 February 1889 (Beckett, 87). He reappeared in San Francisco in April 1889, to the applause of the world's press. He fed them an exaggerated account of his travels. But his achievement had been remarkable. His knowledge of dogs, wildlife, and hunting had enabled him to understand and obtain artefacts from Indians and Inuit, whose way of life was now being destroyed. He presented most of his huge collection to the British Museum on his return, and 100 years later it formed an exhibition about him.

Back in London 'the yellow earl' was now a press hero,

and as 'Lordy' in the north Lonsdale was popular even with his west Cumberland miners, whose living conditions he did nothing to improve. He was reconciled to his wife, and resumed his love of display and the encouragement of boxing. He hired Sir Charles Russell and Edward Marshall Hall to defend boxers charged with breach of the peace and manslaughter. He became the first president of the National Sporting Club, which in due course introduced a new boxing championship trophy, named the Lonsdale belt after he donated the first belt in 1909.

In August 1895 the Kaiser visited Lowther Castle for some grouse-shooting. The road from Penrith Station was lined with police and yeomanry and a cheering crowd. The nine carriages drawn by matching chestnuts were escorted by the hunt servants of the Quorn (of which Hugh was now master) in dark red coats with Lonsdale coronets on the buttons. The imperial flag flew over the castle. On the last evening, while Lonsdale's orchestra was playing 'Heil dir in Siegerkranz', the Kaiser called for silence and presented a marble bust of himself. The kings of Italy and Portugal later came to stay, and the Kaiser a second time in 1902: he gave Lonsdale the order of the Prussian crown (first class) and a Mercedes with a driver called Kieser. Lonsdale returned the car to Berlin to have its chrome fitting replaced with silver.

Lonsdale's enthusiasm for cars made him the first president of the Automobile Association, which adopted his livery colour as its own. But horses remained his passion. In 1907 he was the first president of the International Horse Show at Olympia. As master of the Quorn for six years he was a disciplinarian with the field. When the First World War came he helped to found the Blue Cross (Grace was appointed CBE for her Red Cross work). His chief role was as a recruiter both of horses and men. 'Are you a man or a mouse?' asked his posters, distributed among the northern towns. The enlisted men, officially named the 'Lonsdale battalion', were reduced to scarcely a quarter of their number at the Somme. Meanwhile he resumed his mastership of the Cottesmore, which he justified as entertainment for officers on leave.

After the First World War Lonsdale gave up hunting and became more involved with racing. This was partly because the wartime government had surprisingly set up a national stud and allowed him to run its horses under his own colours. He became a senior steward of the Jockey Club, and gained his only classic win, the St Leger, in 1922. Rarely seen in the House of Lords, he had few friends of his own class. One was George V, who would ride with him before breakfast when they stayed at Goodwood each year and who appointed him a GCVO in 1925 and awarded him the Garter in 1928. Lonsdale continued ostentatious and generous, but money was running short. In 1921 Whitehaven Castle was sold, and in 1926 Barleythorpe. The same year the west Cumberland coalmines closed. But his popular esteem was such that in 1928 the *Sporting Chronicle* launched a fund in his name for incapacitated sportsmen and entrusted to him the whole proceeds, said to be £250,000, together with a gold box presented by the prince of Wales. No one afterwards enquired where the *Sporting Chronicle* funds had gone. Financial pressure closed down Lowther Castle itself in 1936. On 12 May 1941 Grace died, and was followed by Lonsdale himself, at his home, Stud House, Barleythorpe, Oakham, Rutland, on 13 April 1944. Both were buried at Lowther.

MARK BLACKETT-ORD

Sources J. V. Beckett, *A Victorian earl in the Arctic: the travels and collections of the fifth earl of Lonsdale, 1888–9* (1990) [biographical introduction by S. Krech] • H. Owen, *The Lowther family: eight hundred years of 'A family of ancient gentry and worship'* (1990) • D. Sutherland, *The yellow earl: the life of Hugh Lowther, fifth earl of Lonsdale* (1965) • G. MacDonogh, *The last Kaiser: William the impetuous* (2000) • J. Gore, *King George V: a personal memoir* (1941) • *The Field* (April 1894) • GEC, *Peerage* • L. Dawson, *Lonsdale: the authorized life of Hugh Lowther, fifth earl of Lonsdale* (1946) • J. Harding, *Lonsdale's belt: the story of boxing's greatest prize* (1994) • *DNB*

Archives Cumbria AS, Carlisle, personal, estate, and official records | BLPES, letters to E. D. Morel | FILM BFI NFTVA, news footage • BFI NFTVA, sports footage

Likenesses M. Beerbohm, caricature, *c.*1894, U. Texas • J. Lavery, oils, 1930, NPG [*see illus.*] • J. Lavery, oils, 1930, Mansion House, Dublin • Bede, mechanically reproduced caricature, repro. in *VF* (7 Dec 1905) • Beerbohm, caricature; Sothebys 22 April 1979, lot 201 • J. Brown, stipple (after photograph by J. Mayall), NPG; repro. in *Baily's Magazine* (1884) • H. Coster, photographs, NPG • D. Low, portrait, NPG • B. Partridge, caricature, pen-and-ink sketch, NPG; repro. in *Punch* (21 May 1928) • A. P. F. Ritchie, cigarette card, NPG • J. Simpson, chalk caricature, BM • Spy [L. Ward], chromolithograph caricature, NPG; repro. in *VF* (10 July 1896) • Spy [L. Ward], chromolithograph caricature, repro. in *VF* (6 Dec 1894) • Spy [L. Ward], chromolithograph caricature, repro. in *VF* (28 Nov 1895) • WH, chromolithograph caricature, NPG; repro. in *VF* (19 June 1912) • A. Wysard, watercolour drawing, NPG

Wealth at death £28,798 5*s*.—save and except settled land: probate, 30 June 1945, *CGPLA Eng. & Wales* • £91,312 10*s*.—limited to settled land: probate, 17 Oct 1945, *CGPLA Eng. & Wales* • £10,728 15*s*.—limited to settled land: probate, 18 Oct 1945, *CGPLA Eng. & Wales*

Lowther, Sir James, fourth baronet (*bap.* **1673**, *d.* **1755**), politician and coal owner, was baptized on 5 August 1673 at St Giles-in-the-Fields, London, the second son and the youngest of the three children of Sir John *Lowther, second baronet (*bap.* 1642, *d.* 1706), MP, and landowner of Whitehaven, and his wife, Jane (*d.* 1678), daughter of Woolley Leigh of Addington, Surrey. He was educated privately in London, then at Queen's College, Oxford, and finally at the Middle Temple. He succeeded as fourth baronet in 1731.

In 1694 Lowther was returned to parliament, beginning a career in the Commons which lasted for more than sixty years: he was MP for Carlisle (1694–1702), Cumberland (1708–22 and 1727–55), and Appleby (1723–7). He held various positions at the Ordnance office between 1696 and 1708. A whig in parliament, but of an independent disposition, he spoke only occasionally during debates on national affairs, but he actively promoted local causes on behalf of his Cumbrian constituents.

Lowther's lifelong interest was in the development of his estates in Cumberland. Although a younger son, he inherited the property on the death of his father in 1706 after his elder brother, Christopher (a notorious spendthrift), was disinherited. In the years which followed Lowther increased the family estates through land purchase

Sir James Lowther, fourth baronet (*bap.* **1673**, *d.* **1755**), by Jonathan Richardson the elder, 1734

and invested heavily in developing collieries in west Cumberland. He sought a monopoly of the coal trade, with its lucrative market in Dublin, and to this end he played a vital role in developing the harbour facilities in Whitehaven. Partly as a result, Whitehaven came to prominence in the Virginia tobacco trade during the 1740s, though Lowther had only indirect links with the merchant community. Lowther also sought to promote the local iron industry, and to continue the development of Whitehaven as a planned town along lines laid down by his father in the 1680s. All this, together with a parsimonious outlook on life, brought him great wealth. By the 1730s he was considered by many to be the richest commoner in England, and at his death his income from landed property, coalmining, investments in government funds, and mortgage holdings was around £25,000 annually.

Lowther was interested not merely in profits but also in ways of solving some of the immense technological difficulties confronting coalmining in the eighteenth century. He was an early investor in Newcomen steam engines, which were used for mine drainage, and in 1736 he conducted an experiment before the Royal Society (as a result of which he was elected FRS) relating to the problems caused in coalmines by inflammable gases.

Lowther was a man of immense stamina. Almost every year he undertook the arduous journey from London to Whitehaven, where he spent the summer months discussing business with his stewards. He continued to travel north, despite frequent attacks of gout from the age of fifty, even after surviving the amputation of his right leg at the age of seventy-seven in 1750. Such was his energy that in 1753 he steered through parliament no fewer than six separate bills on turnpike trusts, all of which related to Whitehaven.

Lowther was unmarried. He died in London on 2 January 1755. J. V. BECKETT, *rev.*

Sources J. V. Beckett, *Coal and tobacco: the Lowthers and the economic development of west Cumberland, 1660–1760* (1981) • H. Owen, *The Lowther family: eight hundred years of 'A family of ancient gentry and worship'* (1990)

Archives Cumbria AS, Carlisle, papers, incl. corresp. relating to elections and as principal storekeeper of the ordnance

Likenesses J. Richardson the elder, oils, 1734, Holker Hall, Lancashire [*see illus.*] • J. Richardson the elder, portrait, Whitehaven Museum, Cumbria

Wealth at death richest commoner in England: 1730s

Lowther, James, earl of Lonsdale (1736–1802), politician and landowner, was born on 5 August 1736 at Maulds Meaburn, Westmorland, the fourth child and eldest surviving son of Robert Lowther (1681–1745), landowner, of Maulds Meaburn and Katherine Pennington (1712–1764), only daughter of Sir Joseph Pennington, second baronet, of Muncaster, Cumberland. His father, sometime governor of Barbados, came from a junior branch of the Lowthers of Lowther, who were the most powerful aristocratic proprietors in Cumberland. The Maulds Meaburn family properties lay in a compact area south of Appleby. In addition to the manor of Maulds Meaburn they included property in Crosby Ravensworth and Asby Grange. Part of the property was already encumbered when Robert Lowther succeeded his father in 1703, and financial considerations seem to have dictated his marriage the following year to an elderly widow whose inheritance included an estate in Barbados. As a result of this windfall Lowther was gradually able to turn his fortunes around. His wife died in 1722 and in 1731 he married Katherine Pennington; they had five children. James Lowther was just nine when his father died in 1745.

The creation of the Lowther interest Lowther was educated at schools in London and Hertfordshire, and in 1752 at Peterhouse, Cambridge. By 1757, when he came of age, he was one of the wealthiest men in northern England, largely because several senior branches of his family were childless. On 6 March 1751 he inherited estates worth more than £6000 annually from the third Viscount Lonsdale of Lowther Hall. The title lapsed, but he succeeded to Lonsdale's baronetcy. Four years later, on the death of Sir James Lowther of Whitehaven, he inherited estates in Westmorland and Middlesex with an annual rental value of £1200. On 15 April 1756 Sir William Lowther of Holker Hall died aged only twenty-nine, and Lowther inherited by the terms of Sir James Lowther's will extensive land and colliery interests in west Cumberland. As a result of these various inheritances the young man now had an income of about £45,000 per annum. Horace Walpole claimed that 'though not of age [he] becomes master of one or two and forty thousand pounds a year' (Walpole, *Corr.*, 9.185). The duke of Newcastle told George II that he was 'perhaps the richest subject that His Majesty has' (Owen, 283).

Lowther was not frightened of spending this fortune,

James Lowther, earl of Lonsdale (1736–1802), by Thomas Hudson, *c.*1755

notably in the pursuit of electoral success. While still a teenager, in 1754 he contested with the earl of Thanet the right to control the parliamentary borough of Appleby. When subsequently his candidates were defeated in the borough, he challenged the result in the Commons and backed down only after the king had suggested a compromise with Thanet. As a result, the original election was declared void and at the by-election in 1756 Thanet and Lowther duly returned one member each. In 1756 Lowther spent £58,000 buying up the burgage borough of Cockermouth, and in April 1757, still a few months short of his twenty-first birthday, he was returned on the whig interest for Cumberland at a by-election. These activities did not make him popular. Joseph Waugh, dean of Worcester, wrote of him in 1759:

> I should think from what I hear in the country this young gentleman carries matters so imperiously, without any pretence but having money, that at the general election he will meet with some stand against the career he at present runs. (HoP, *Commons, 1754–90*, 3.56)

Waugh predicted correctly, because, although in 1761 Lowther secured the return of eight MPs—two each for Cumberland, Westmorland, and Cockermouth, and one each for Appleby and Carlisle—he was unsuccessful in the second seat at Carlisle. One of his nominees was forced to withdraw when it was clear that there was to be a revolt against 'the all-grasping and monopolizing spirit of the baronet' (ibid.).

Marriage and ministerial ambitions In 1755 Henry Fox had tried unsuccessfully to negotiate for Lowther a marriage with the duke of Marlborough's daughter—she turned him down—but potentially Lowther made an even better match when on 7 September 1761 he married Lady Mary Stuart (1740–1824), daughter of George III's prime minister John *Stuart, third earl of Bute, and Mary Wortley Montagu. Bute subsequently agreed that Lowther should nominate to all Treasury appointments in Cumberland and Westmorland, and Sir James was annoyed when this arrangement was not automatically continued on George Grenville's appointment as prime minister in 1763. By then Lowther had extended his demands to include military and ecclesiastical appointments in Cumberland, and when he fell out with Grenville over the deanery of Carlisle, Bute refused to intervene on the grounds that he by now expected his son-in-law to make unreasonable claims. With the death of Lord Egremont in August 1763 Lowther recommended himself unsuccessfully for a position at the Board of Trade, despite both his lack of empathy with Grenville and his apparent lack of interest in the business of parliament. Subsequently, in 1765, on hearing that George III had offered the Treasury to Rockingham, Lowther threatened to break his political connection with Bute on the grounds that he had been neglected by the ministry, and to align himself with the opposition.

In 1765 the third duke of Portland, partly out of enmity towards Bute, and partly because of his political rivalry with Lowther in Cumberland, filed bills in chancery against Lowther and Carlisle corporation alleging that he was the owner of a fishery in the River Eden which had been rendered valueless by the mode of fishing adopted by the defendants. Lowther had been elected mayor of Carlisle, where he instituted a rigorous examination of the corporation's accounts, and subsequently endeavoured to swamp the constituency by creating honorary freemen. In response to Portland, Lowther's legal advisers subsequently found that in William III's original grant to the first earl of Portland of the honour of Penrith, the forest of Inglewood, and the socage manor of Carlisle had been expressly omitted. This put Portland's case in a new light since it was under the general wording of the grant that he claimed the socage manor of Carlisle, but since these places had been in the undisturbed possession of the Portland family for sixty years their title could be impeached only by the crown. On 9 July 1767 Lowther petitioned the Treasury for a grant of the crown interest in these two properties 'for three lives, on such terms as to their lordships should seem meet'. Portland protested, but the grant was made to Lowther on 18 December 1767.

The decision in this case was used by Portland and his friends to claim that no possessions were safe if the legal maxim *nullum tempus occurrit regi* was to be enforced. On 17 February 1768 Sir George Savile sought leave to introduce into the Commons a Nullum Tempus Bill, designed to abrogate the legal maxim and thereby deprive Lowther of his rights under the crown leases, but his motion was defeated by 134 votes to 114. The following year a compromise was found and Savile's bill passed with a provision excluding grants of the crown made prior to 1 January 1769 from the operation of the legislation as long as grantees prosecuted their claims within the year. Lowther immediately filed a bill against Portland, and served around 300 ejectments on his tenants. In February 1771 Sir William Meredith attempted to carry a bill in the Commons to repeal the clause. Subsequently the court of exchequer found against Lowther on the technical grounds that the original grant was unacceptable under the Civil List Act of 1702 because the rent reserved to the crown was insufficient. As a result, the question of Portland's title to the forest of Inglewood and the socage manor of Carlisle was never tested in the courts, and he sold the property in 1787 to the duke of Devonshire.

At the 1768 general election Lowther encountered unexpectedly firm opposition. He nominated two Scots at Carlisle, neither of whom had any connection with the borough and both of whom were defeated. In Cumberland the duke of Portland won one seat, and although Lowther was returned for the other he was unseated on petition and Portland's second nominee was declared duly elected. He did not stand in Westmorland where he lost one seat to a weak candidate who declared only a few days before the poll. Thus in Cumberland, Westmorland, and Carlisle, where he had secured five seats in 1761, he returned only one in 1768 and that was in Westmorland where his candidate, John Robinson, had a considerable interest of his own.

For three months Lowther was out of the house, and Grafton turned down his application for a peerage. He was returned as MP for Cockermouth in March 1769, but his position at Westminster was temporarily damaged and Grafton refused him the exclusive right to nominate to government places in Cumberland. Such was his annoyance that he briefly contemplated joining the opposition.

In 1773 Lowther reluctantly agreed with Thanet to continue the Appleby arrangement and divide the borough for their joint lives. The following year he negotiated a compromise with Portland whereby they were to divide Cumberland and Carlisle to avoid an expensive repetition of the events of 1768. At the 1774 general election Lowther won back the second Westmorland seat and returned a total of seven members. He himself was elected for both Cumberland and Westmorland and opted to sit for Cumberland. By the later 1770s he had joined the opposition to North's ministry, and in 1781–2 he opposed further prosecution of the war in America. After the change of administration Shelburne refused to promote with the king his claim to a peerage. During 1783 he was courted by both government and opposition, but he did not stand at the 1784 general election because he had by then been promised a peerage. On 24 May 1784 he was created Baron Lowther of Lowther, baron of the baronies of Kendal and Burgh, viscount of Lonsdale and of Lowther, and earl of Lonsdale. This was little short of a thank-offering by William Pitt the younger to a boroughmonger who had provided him with his first parliamentary seat at Appleby in 1781 and who had subsequently placed at the disposal of the prime minister the seats under his control. Lowther took his seat in the Lords on 2 June 1784, and normally thereafter supported Pitt's administration, although in 1792 he was said to be considering transferring his support to the opposition because the prime minister had refused him a dukedom.

Electoral dominance of the Lowther interest Although the 1774 compromise had apparently blunted his strength in Cumberland and Westmorland, Lowther set out to restore his position by buying the estates of the duke of Portland and the earl of Egremont. He acquired neither, even though he offered Egremont £5000 above the price to be fixed by an independent referee, and the borough of Haslemere (which he had bought in 1780). Even so, at the 1784 election Lowther was at the height of his boroughmongering powers, returning both members for Cockermouth, Westmorland, and Haslemere, and single MPs for Cumberland, Carlisle, and Appleby—Sir James's Ninepins, as they were colloquially known. At a by-election in Carlisle in 1784 he sought to dominate the second seat through the creation of honorary freemen, a move which led to post-election petitioning. In both 1786 and 1790 he also tried expensively and unsuccessfully to return a member for Lancaster. Throughout his life Lowther lavished money on elections, including £15,000 at Appleby in 1754, at least £20,000 for Cumberland and Carlisle in 1768, and over £25,000 at Lancaster in 1786. In all he must have spent well in excess of £100,000 on contests.

Lowther chose the candidates himself, sometimes following the recommendations of friends, and once elected he expected them to follow his own political line. He even forced his brother in 1763 to resign his seat for Westmorland when he voted against Grenville's administration. In 1781 he told his cousin William Lowther, MP for Carlisle, that:

> it will affect me very much that a person so nearly connected with me should not be present the first day of the meeting of Parliament. It has not happened to me before, and if you cannot give your attendance *constantly* in Parliament, which I must expect, you had better resign your seat that a person who will attend the duty may be chose to succeed to you. (HoP, *Commons, 1754–90*, 3.59)

In January 1782 he wrote that his members were 'not accountable to any person but myself' (ibid.). However, many of the MPs returned on his influence by the 1780s were men of no political standing, entirely dependent on him for patronage, and they seldom if ever spoke in the house. In 1788 he ordered all his 'people' in the Commons to oppose Pitt's regency resolutions, but his political voice was never as loud as his electoral control might have implied.

Lowther inherited a vast estate, but he extended it through land purchases, notably in coal-bearing west Cumberland where he spent £55,000 acquiring the Workington estate of Charles Pelham in 1758 as well as substantial sums on the manors of Millom, Whicham, Greysouthen, and Clifton. He was active in promoting his colliery interests, and annual profits were about £10,000 in the 1770s, doubling by the time of his death. Despite his wealth Lowther often failed to pay bills. As a landlord he had a reputation for meanness and ruthlessness, extracting every penny he could from tenants while maltreating his Whitehaven steward John Wordsworth whose fees he refused to pay. At the same time he built a 'planned village' at Lowther in Westmorland for his estate employees, and for a number of years provided additional employment in a carpet factory in the village. He spent little on his main seat, Lowther Hall, which had been rebuilt in 1718 following a fire, but he turned his Whitehaven residence, Flatt Hall, into Whitehaven Castle. By repute the plans, by Robert Adam, were never paid for.

Lowther held many other positions including *custos rotulorum* (3 August 1758) and lord lieutenant (14 August 1758) of Westmorland; lord lieutenant (13 December 1759) and *custos rotulorum* (18 October 1759) of Cumberland; brigadier-general of the Cumberland and Westmorland militia (25 June 1761), vice-admiral of Cumberland and Westmorland (15 April 1765), steward and bailiff of Inglewood forest (18 December 1767), steward of Lonsdale (23 November 1793), and colonel in the army during service (14 March 1794).

Reputation and death Lowther was a man of mixed reputation, acquiring epithets such as the Bad Earl and 'Jimmy, Grasp-all, earl of Toadstool' (GEC, *Peerage*). According to Nathaniel Wraxall he was 'tyrannical, overbearing, violent, and frequently under no restraint of temper or of reason' (Wraxall, 378). Horace Walpole considered him to be 'equally unamiable in public and private' (Walpole, *Memoirs*, 3.195). Edward Knubley told James Boswell that Lowther 'had a most tyrannical temper and not a spark of gratitude' (HoP, *Commons, 1754–90*, 3.60). Boswell, who hoped Lowther would bring him into parliament, was grossly insulted by 'this brutal fellow' during 'a most shocking conversation' in June 1790 (*Letters of James Boswell Addressed to the Rev. W. J. Temple*, ed. P. Francis, 1857, 323–5). Richard Penn complained of Lowther's 'shocking ferocity and undignified manner of living', and according to Sir Edward Blackett he was 'one of the most worthless men in his Majesty's dominions … you never hear him spoken of but with the greatest abhorrence' (HoP, *Commons, 1754–90*, 3.60). To the Revd Alexander Carlyle he was 'more detested than any man alive as a shameless political sharper, a domestic bashaw, and an intolerant tyrant over his tenants and dependents'. In Carlyle's view he was 'truly a madman, though too rich to be confined' (*Autobiography of the Rev Dr Alexander Carlyle*, ed. J. H. Burton, 3rd edn, 1861, 418–19). Occasionally, Lowther's sense of humour made a better impression. When staying at Whitehaven, Boswell was pleased to discover that 'when he choses to pay a compliment nobody can do it more gracefully', and Walter Spencer-Stanhope believed him to possess the ability and mind 'that would have enabled him to have played a distinguished part on the theatre of the World' (Owen, 297, 301).

Lowther's marriage was not particularly happy. There were no children, and after about fifteen years he and his wife lived apart. He is known subsequently to have had a number of mistresses. With no son to whom he could pass the property, he obtained on 26 October 1797 the barony and viscountcy of Lowther of Whitehaven, with special remainder to the male heirs of his cousin the Revd Sir William Lowther, second baronet, of Swillington, Yorkshire. Lowther died at Lowther Hall on 24 May 1802 and was buried at Lowther on 9 June. He had been ill for some time and the cause of death was a 'mortification of the bowels'. His widow died at Broom House, Fulham, on 5 April 1824, aged eighty-four.

J. V. BECKETT

Sources H. Owen, *The Lowther family: eight hundred years of 'A family of ancient gentry and worship'* (1990) · O. Wood, *West Cumberland coal, 1660–1982/3* (1988) · B. Bonsall, *Sir James Lowther and Cumberland and Westmorland elections, 1754–75* (1960) · J. V. Beckett, 'Inheritance and fortune in the eighteenth century: the rise of Sir James Lowther, earl of Lonsdale', *Transactions of the Cumberland and Westmorland Antiquarian and Archaeological Society*, [new ser.,] 87 (1987), 171–8 · J. V. Beckett, 'The making of a pocket borough: Cockermouth, 1722–56', *Journal of British Studies*, 20/1 (1980–81), 140–57 · GEC, *Peerage* · N. W. Wraxall, *Historical memoirs of my own time*, ed. R. Askham (1904), 378 · Walpole, *Corr.*, 9.185 · H. Walpole, *Memoirs of the reign of King George the Third*, ed. G. F. R. Barker, 4 vols. (1894) · *GM*, 1st ser., 72 (1802), 586–8 · HoP, *Commons, 1754–90*

Archives Cumbria AS, Carlisle, corresp. and papers | BL, corresp. with first earl of Liverpool, Add. MSS 38198–38310, 38458, 38469, 38570 · Carlisle Public Library, corresp. with Henry Dundas · Cumbria AS, Whitehaven, letters to Humphry Senhouse · Yale U., Beinecke L., corresp. with James Boswell

Likenesses T. Hudson, oils, *c*.1755, priv. coll. [*see illus.*]

Lowther, James (1840–1904), politician and sportsman, born at Swillington House, Leeds, on 1 December 1840, was the younger son in the family of two sons and a daughter of Sir Charles Lowther, third baronet (1803–1894), of Swillington House, Leeds, and Wilton Castle, Redcar, and his wife, Isabella (*d.* 1887), daughter of Robert Morehead, rector of Easington. James's grandfather, Sir John (created a baronet in 1824), was the second son of Sir William Lowther, who succeeded his cousin as Baron and Viscount Lowther in 1802 and was created earl of Lonsdale in 1807. James Lowther was educated at Westminster School and at Trinity College, Cambridge, graduating BA in 1863 and proceeding MA in 1866. He entered the Inner Temple on 1 November 1861, and was called to the bar on 17 October 1864, but never practised.

Lowther's interests were divided between public affairs and sport. Throughout his life he championed the uncompromising principles of Conservatism in which he was brought up. In 1865 he stood for York City in the Conservative interest, and was returned at the head of the poll. His maiden speech was delivered in opposition to the abortive Reform Bill brought in by Lord Russell's government in 1866. He also opposed the Derby–Disraeli bill of 1867, denouncing it as an extremely bad measure and speaking disrespectfully of Disraeli. But his independent action did not prevent him from being offered, nor from accepting, the post of parliamentary secretary to the Poor Law Board for the last three months of Disraeli's first administration (1867–8).

At the general election of 1868 Lowther was again returned at the head of the poll at York, and in the following years he took a vigorous part in opposition to Gladstone's government in parliament. He was never afraid of controversy with the prime minister, and was one of the

James Lowther (1840–1904), by Maull & Fox

minority of 11 out of 442 who voted against on the second reading of the Irish Land Bill (1870).

At the general election of 1874 Lowther was for a third time returned for York, but on this occasion second at the poll. Disraeli then appointed him under-secretary for the colonies. In 1878 Disraeli, now Lord Beaconsfield, gave further proof of his confidence in Lowther by nominating him chief secretary to the lord lieutenant of Ireland (though he remained outside the cabinet) in succession to Sir Michael Hicks Beach. He was sworn of the privy council at the same time.

The post of chief secretary was Lowther's highest official appointment, and his last. It caused surprise at the time as his character and temperament always appeared to greater advantage in the freedom of opposition than under the restraint of office, and it was remembered to his detriment in Ireland that he had voted against the Land Bill of 1870. He was unable to prevent the surge of Irish support for home rule in the late 1870s and the early stages of the Land League; his position outside the cabinet but responsible for Irish affairs in the Commons was not easy. During his secretaryship the Royal University, Ireland, was founded, in 1879. He left office with the tory government in 1880, leaving it to his successor to renew expiring measures of coercion, and lost his seat at York after a fifteen-year tenure.

For eight years his efforts to re-enter the House of Commons proved unsuccessful. In February 1881 he stood and was beaten in East Cumberland, and in September in North Lincolnshire. At the general elections of 1885 and 1886 he was defeated in the Louth division of Lincolnshire and the Eskdale division of Cumberland. In 1888 he was returned at a by-election for the Isle of Thanet, and he represented that constituency until his death. On his return to the Commons he developed a reputation for himself as a rare survival of old toryism. He deplored Ritchie's bill for the establishment of county councils (1888), which he was unable to resist as it was debated before he took his seat. He was always an unwavering advocate of protection, and welcomed the acceptance of tariff reform as a principle of a section of his party during his last year in parliament. He had great knowledge of parliamentary procedure and paid constant attention to forms and precedent. He was popular among all parties in the house. It was his annual habit during his last years in parliament to oppose the sessional order of the house prohibiting lords lieutenant and peers from taking part in elections, on the ground that it was an anomaly and was not rigidly enforced. It continued to be passed until 1910, when it was finally dropped.

Outside politics Lowther had many public interests. He served as alderman of the county council for the North Riding of Yorkshire and on the Tees fishery board, and he was one of the founders and sometime president of the Darlington chamber of agriculture. In 1873 he began to breed horses at Wilton Castle, and registered his colours—blue and yellow hoops, red cap. He trained until 1902 at Newmarket with Joseph Enoch, Lord Zetland's private trainer, and then with John Watts and with Golding. His first success was in 1877, when he won the Gimcrack Stakes with King Olaf, ridden by Fred Archer. His most successful horse was King Monmouth, which began by winning the Great Yorkshire Handicap in 1885, and ended in 1889 with a career record of twenty-three races and upwards of £11,000 in stakes. Lowther's best year was 1889, when he won fourteen races and over £7000 in stakes. He ran his horses regularly in the north of England, and was a constant attendant at meetings at York, Stockton, and Redcar.

Lowther's sporting reputation did not, however, depend on his achievements as an owner. He did not bet, was a good judge of racing, and demanded high standards of honesty in its conduct. He became a member of the Jockey Club in 1877 and first served as a steward in 1880. When senior steward in 1889 he was appointed a member of a special commission with Prince Soltykoff and Lord March to inquire into the charge of slander brought by Sir George Chetwynd against Lord Durham in consequence of words uttered in a speech at the Gimcrack Club dinner. Sir George claimed £20,000 damages; on 29 June 1889 Lowther and his colleagues awarded him a farthing.

Lowther was senior trustee of the Lonsdale estates and as such responsible for trying to contain his extravagant cousin, Hugh Cecil Lowther, fifth earl of Lonsdale (the 'Yellow Earl'). On his father's death in 1894 he inherited Wilton Castle, Redcar, and took a personal interest in his estate. One of the best-known Yorkshiremen of his time, Lowther had an exceptional knowledge of slang, but his public speaking was cumbrous. When in London he dressed for the country, and vice versa. The Lowther Inn in York is named after him and his uncle, J. H. Lowther.

In 1903 Lowther's health was obviously failing. He sold

his horses and was obliged to forgo active work in parliament. On 12 September 1904 he died, unmarried, at Wilton Castle, which passed to his nephew, John George Lowther. His body was cremated at Darlington and his ashes were deposited in Wilton churchyard, Yorkshire.

REGINALD LUCAS, *rev.* H. C. G. MATTHEW

Sources *The Times* (13 Sept 1904) · *Yorkshire Post* (13 Sept 1904) · *The Sportsman* (13 Sept 1904) · *The Field* (17 Sept 1904) · H. Owen, *The Lowther family: eight hundred years of 'A family of ancient gentry and worship'* (1990) · R. Mortimer, *The Jockey Club* (1958) · D. Thornley, *Isaac Butt and home rule* (1964) · *CGPLA Eng. & Wales* (1904)

Archives CUL, letters to duke of Marlborough · Glos. RO, letters to Sir Michael Hicks Beach

Likenesses H. Furniss, pen-and-ink caricature, NPG · London Stereoscopic Co., photograph, NPG; repro. in *Our conservative and unionist statesmen*, 2 [1898] · Maull & Fox, cabinet photograph, NPG [*see illus.*] · E. Miller, oils?; last known at Wilton Castle, Yorkshire, in 1912 · W. Roffe, stipple and line engraving (after photograph by W. T. & R. Cowland), NPG · Spy [L. Ward], chromolithograph caricature, NPG; repro. in *VF* (8 Dec 1877), 358 · Spy [L. Ward], chromolithograph caricature, NPG; repro. in *VF* (1 March 1900) · photograph, repro. in Owen, *The Lowther family* · stipple, NPG · wood-engraving, NPG; repro. in *ILN* (18 May 1878)

Wealth at death £91,698 1*s.* 11*d.*: probate, 24 Nov 1904, *CGPLA Eng. & Wales*

Lowther, James William, first Viscount Ullswater (1855–1949), speaker of the House of Commons, was born at 56 Park Street, Oxford Street, London, on 1 April 1855, the son of William Lowther, a diplomatist, and his wife, Charlotte Alice, daughter of Sir James *Parke (later Lord Wensleydale), the judge, and his wife.

Lowther was educated at Eton College (1868–70), King's College, London, and Trinity College, Cambridge (1874–8), where he gained a third in law. At Cambridge he acted with the Amateur Dramatic Club and retained a lifelong interest in its affairs. He was called to the bar at the Inner Temple in 1879, taking the degree of LLM at Cambridge in 1882. He practised in the early 1880s on the north-western circuit, but, like several in his family, was drawn into tory politics. In September 1883 he was elected as a tory for Rutland at a by-election; in the redistribution of 1885 Rutland was reduced to a single member constituency and Lowther, as the junior member, was squeezed out. He stood unsuccessfully in 1885 for Cumberland (Penrith) in family territory and next door to his father's seat, but won this in 1886, holding the seat for the rest of his time in the Commons.

On 1 March 1886 Lowther confirmed his position at the centre of tory politics by his marriage to Mary Frances, daughter of Alexander James Beresford-*Hope and his wife, Mildred, who was daughter of J. B. W. Gascoyne-Cecil and niece of Robert, third marquess of Salisbury, the tory prime minister. He thus moved on the outskirts of the 'Hotel Cecil', as Salisbury's coterie of relatives was known. Lowther was soon in office, first in 1887 as fourth charity commissioner (unpaid), and in 1891–2 as under-secretary for foreign affairs, speaking for them in the Commons as the foreign secretary was Lord Salisbury.

Lowther's career was not, however, to be that of ministerial office. In 1890 he briefly served as a deputy chairman of the house, having been spotted by A. W. Peel, the

James William Lowther, first Viscount Ullswater (1855–1949), by Philip A. de Laszlo, 1908

speaker, as a person suitable for such duties. Peel may have enjoyed Lowther's temerity in rebuking G. J. Goschen, a senior Liberal, for irrelevance. In 1895 W. C. Gully, a Liberal, succeeded Peel as speaker and later that year Lowther became chairman of ways and means, in effect deputy speaker. He carried out his duties competently, especially when A. J. Balfour rather controversially carried the reform of the procedures for supply in 1896, which included an automatic guillotine. Lowther was sworn of the privy council in 1898. He kept clear of Unionist in-fighting over tariff reform in the early 1900s and when Gully retired as speaker he succeeded him to general acclaim on 8 June 1905. Lowther had been unopposed at the election of 1900 and as speaker he was unopposed by custom (despite the Unionists' flouting of it in 1895 when Gully had been opposed) in 1906 and at subsequent general elections.

Lowther became speaker six months before the election to the Commons of a large majority of Liberals, who enacted a series of major legislative reforms, opposed with increasing stridency by the Conservatives, with whom he had a natural sympathy. Lowther managed the difficult task of maintaining good relations with both sides. Asquith, who was prime minister during the political crisis which began with the rejection of Lloyd George's budget in 1909 by the House of Lords and who did not flatter Unionists, said of him that he 'combined deep and accurate knowledge, quick judgment, dignity, urbanity, and tact with a keen insight into human nature, and an unfailing dexterity in the employment of the lighter as well of the heavier weapons in the dialectical armoury' (Asquith, 1.186). Indeed, Lowther's presence in the chair probably assisted the government as he was in a good position to curb some of the excesses of his own party. In 1911 he was thought of as a possible Unionist leader when A. J. Balfour resigned. Though usually cautious, Lowther was prepared on occasion to give bold rulings, notably in 1905 when his procedural ruling ruined A. J. Balfour's plan of redistribution, and on 27 January 1913 when he ruled unexpectedly, and in the view of one historian in a 'dubious and political slanted ruling' (Pugh, 42), that an amendment on women's suffrage would so change the bill it amended as to require the measure to be reintroduced. This was, Asquith told the king, 'in flat contradiction of the assumption upon which all parties in the House hitherto treated the bill … the Speaker's judgment is entirely wrong' (Jenkins, 278). Despite the prime minister's view, the bill was lost. On 21 May 1914, when suspending the house, which was in uproar over Ireland, Lowther criticized Bonar Law, the Unionist leader, and received a fulsome apology.

During the First World War, Lowther was in 1916 offered, a little improbably, the post of controller of food, which he declined. Earlier that year, Asquith (encouraged by Walter Long) persuaded Lowther to chair the novel device of a speaker's conference on electoral reform, which reported in January 1917. The appointment of the conference was a means of escape for a government caught in the confusion of wartime franchise registration expedients; it was not anticipated that the conference would generate a sweeping measure of electoral reform. However, it proposed what was in effect adult male suffrage, extensive redistribution, a reduction of plural voting, proportional representation in some seats, new registration procedures to increase the size of the electorate, and votes for many women over thirty. Many of these proposals were enacted in 1918. 'It is entirely thanks to you that the Conference has come through so triumphantly', Walter Long told Lowther (Pugh, 85). The conference formed the precedent for subsequent speaker's conferences. Lowther also chaired a conference on federal devolution in 1919.

In his later years Lowther seemed rather austere as speaker—his clerk, G. F. M. Campion, recalled him as 'a little formidable' (*DNB*)—but he never lost his good humour. He had played an important part in the modernization of his office. In 1921 he retired as speaker, being created Viscount Ullswater and appointed GCB. In 1907 he had received honorary degrees from Oxford and Cambridge, and in 1910 from Leeds. He recorded his experiences in *A Speaker's Commentaries* (2 vols., 1925). He remained active in local and national affairs, as a county alderman for East Suffolk, and on other bodies and royal commissions (including those on London government 1921–2, political honours 1923–4, Cambridge University 1923, electoral reform 1929–30, agricultural wages 1930–40, and the BBC 1935). He was a trustee of the National Gallery from 1924 and of the British Museum from 1922 to 1931.

Ullswater's wife died on 1 May 1944 and his son and heir, Christopher, in 1935; his grandson and heir, John Arthur, secretary to the duke of Kent, was killed in a flying accident with the duke in 1942. Ullswater was vigorous into his nineties, riding his sturdy white cob, shooting, and tending his large estates. He retired as alderman in 1946. He died at his home, High House, Campsey Ashe, near Woodbridge, Suffolk, on 27 March 1949, and was succeeded by his great-grandson, Nicholas James Christopher Lowther. H. C. G. MATTHEW

Sources GEC, *Peerage* · *DNB* · H. H. Asquith, *Memories and reflections, 1852–1927*, ed. A. Mackintosh, 2 vols. (1928) · R. Jenkins, *Asquith* (1964) · M. Pugh, *Electoral reform in war and peace, 1906–18* (1978) · P. Laundy, *The office of speaker in the parliaments of the Commonwealth* (1984) · Burke, *Peerage* · H. Owen, *The Lowther family: eight hundred years of 'A family of ancient gentry and worship'* (1990) · J. Hart, *Proportional representation* (1992) · *The Crawford papers: the journals of David Lindsay, twenty-seventh earl of Crawford … 1892–1940*, ed. J. Vincent (1984)

Archives PRO, corresp. and papers, FO 800/28, 34 | BL, corresp. with Lord Gladstone, Add. MSS 46050, 46068, 46083–46084, *passim* · HLRO, letters to David Lloyd George · HLRO, letters to Andrew Bonar Law · HLRO, corresp. with Samuel Herbert · NRA, priv. coll., letters to Sir Thomas Wrightson · Surrey HC, corresp. with Lord Onslow

Likenesses P. de Laszlo, oils, 1907, Inner Temple, London · P. de Laszlo, portrait, 1908, priv. coll. [*see illus.*] · G. F. Watt, oils, 1922, Palace of Westminster, London · G. F. Watt, oils, exh. RA 1922, Ipswich county hall · P. de Laszlo, oils, 1959, Carlisle law courts · H. Furniss, caricature, pen-and-ink sketch, NPG · R. T. & Co., wood-engraving, NPG; repro. in *ILN* (10 Oct 1891) · Spy [L. Ward], caricature, mechanical reproduction, NPG; repro. in *VF* (24 Oct 1906) · Spy [L. Ward], caricature, watercolour study, NPG; repro. in *VF* (19 Dec 1891)

Wealth at death £229,073 18*s*. 7*d*.: probate, 25 July 1949, *CGPLA Eng. & Wales*

Lowther, Sir John (*d*. 1382?). *See under* Lowther family (*per*. *c*.1270–*c*.1450).

Lowther, Sir John (1582–1637), landowner and barrister, was born at Lowther, Westmorland, on 4 February 1582 and baptized in Lowther church on 24 February, the second (but first surviving) son in the family of eight sons and one daughter of Sir Christopher Lowther (1557–1617) of Lowther and his first wife, Eleanor (*d*. 1597), daughter of William Musgrave esquire of Hayton, Cumberland. He was educated at Appleby grammar school and in 1599 was admitted to the Inner Temple. He was called to the bar in 1609.

Lowther was active as a barrister and, according to his autobiography, the circuit judges nominated him in 1616 as a JP for Westmorland; he joined his father on a bench which welcomed his legal knowledge. The nomination helped him avoid the feuds between Francis Clifford, fourth earl of Cumberland, and Lord William Howard (1563–1640), and signalled that he was 'tied to none in dependancie'. Westmorland elected him MP in 1623, twice in 1625, and, with his son John, in 1627; and he kept diaries of proceedings in the Commons. In parliament he seems to have been happiest with the common-law politics of Sir Edward Coke but disapproving of faction. Nevertheless, in June 1626 he was introduced to George Villiers, first duke of Buckingham, who had him knighted and appointed KC on the council of the north. If Buckingham's policies fitted Lowther's perception of good government, his reputation as an unaligned member survived his links with the duke. He was active in Westmorland over the forced loan. In October 1626 he had been drafted onto the loan commission for Yorkshire, and was also a commissioner in June 1627 to finance shipbuilding using recusancy fines, which commissions were headed by Sir John Savile (later first Baron Savile of Pontefract). Lowther's service under Savile probably explains why Sir Thomas Wentworth (later first earl of Strafford) removed him from the commission to compound with recusants in July 1630. Notwithstanding, Lowther remained active in the council of the north until his death.

Until he inherited in 1617, Lowther's professional income and a jointure estate of £72 per annum supported him. Thereafter his landed income always exceeded that from the law, and was wisely diversified by moneylending, often on mortgage, and by investment in trade, coalmining, and salt manufacture. In 1617 in Westmorland £710 gross was the income of a substantial landed family. Lowther purchased additional land worth over £1200 per annum at a cost of £28,085, mostly in Cumberland, though some was in Yorkshire. He kept a demesne farm, and improved both land and rents, so that his landed income was over £2000 at his death. Land was the basis of Lowther's county and parliamentary position; the law gave him added influence and opportunity.

Sir John had married in 1602, at his father's prompting, Ellinor (*c*.1583–1659), daughter of William Fleming esquire of Rydal, Westmorland. They had two daughters and three sons, John *Lowther (1606–1675), of Lowther, Christopher *Lowther (1611–1644), of Whitehaven, and William *Lowther (*bap.* 1612, *d.* 1688), of Swillington. Sir John died at Lowther on 15 September 1637 and was buried there on the following day. C. B. Phillips, *rev.*

Sources Cumbria AS, Carlisle, Lonsdale papers · C. B. Phillips, ed., *Lowther family estate books, 1617–1675*, SurtS, 191 (1979) · H. Owen, *The Lowther family: eight hundred years of 'A family of ancient gentry and worship'* (1990)

Archives Cumbria AS, Carlisle, parliamentary diaries

Likenesses portrait, 1630, repro. in Owen, *The Lowther family*, 153

Wealth at death £2024 p.a.; inventory £1000; debts £4823; also land: Phillips, ed., *Lowther family*, xv

Lowther, Sir John, of Lowther, first baronet (1606–1675), landowner and local politician, was born on 20 February 1606, probably at Rydal Hall, Westmorland, and baptized on 27 February, the eldest of five children of Sir John *Lowther (1582–1637) of Lowther, and of his wife, Ellinor (*c*.1583–1659), daughter of William Fleming esquire of Rydal. Like his father, he was educated first at Appleby grammar school and then at the Inner Temple, where he was admitted in 1621. On 1 February 1626 he married Mary (*d.* 1648), daughter of Sir Richard Fletcher of Hutton, Cumberland, who came from a Cockermouth merchant gentry family; they had five sons and six daughters.

Lowther and his father sat as knights of the shire for Westmorland in the 1628 parliament. Called to the bar in 1630, he then practised in York and accumulated influential local stewardships and recorderships, including that

Sir John Lowther of Lowther, first baronet (1606–1675), by unknown artist

of Kendal. Both he and his father purchased estates in Yorkshire, and in 1637, on the latter's death, Lowther's lands were worth some £1800 a year. In 1638 he was made a baronet of Nova Scotia.

Although he twice unsuccessfully contested the county seat against Sir Philip Musgrave of Edenhall in the elections of 1640, by 1641 Sir John, as head of a long-established landowning family, was at the forefront of county society. He stayed in Westmorland in the early years of the civil war, and tried at the end of 1642 to negotiate a county defence alliance with Yorkshire, from where, by this date, 42 per cent of his landed income came. He was a royalist commissioner of array and nominally a colonel, but quarrelled with Musgrave over the latter's desire to use the Westmorland militia as a royalist force, and later claimed never to have taken up arms against parliament. However, despite the fact that he took the covenant, when the Scots invaded the north in 1644, parliament classed Lowther as a delinquent and he was fined £1500: if he had done little for the king, he had done nothing for parliament. None the less, acting for Lady Anne Clifford in Westmorland from 1644, he maintained informal contacts with parliamentarian officials, and may have been reappointed as a JP.

Through the 1640s, 1650s, and early 1660s Sir John continued as an active land purchaser in present-day Cumbria, but increasingly spent in Yorkshire, as well as investing in the London money market, laying him open to the charge that he was exporting wealth from his native Westmorland. Connections with Yorkshire were enhanced by the marriages of four of his daughters and by investments with his brother Sir William *Lowther (*bap.* 1612, *d.* 1688) of Swillington. However, his attachment to Lowther is evident in the care he expended on maintenance and innovation on his Westmorland estates, for instance in his modest building works and by tree planting for 'shelter and ornament' (Phillips, *Lowther Family Estate Books*, 253). He noted the 'difference of the condicion of Cuntryes and manor of liveinge betwixt north and south' (ibid., 68) when, following the death of his wife, Mary, on 9 February 1648, he married on 9 April 1652 a southerner, Elizabeth (1621–1699), daughter of Sir John Hare of Stow Bardolph, Norfolk, and widow of Woolley Leigh of Addington, Surrey. The couple had three sons and three daughters.

In 1660 such was Lowther's position in Westmorland society that he topped the poll for the Convention Parliament. That autumn his crown stewardship was renewed, with reversion to his royalist son John. He saw his appointment as sheriff of Cumberland in 1661 as recognition of his political loyalty to the new regime. A frequent attender at quarter sessions for north Westmorland in the 1660s, Sir John headed special sessions against conventicles in 1664. Although a justice, he does not appear to have acted in Cumberland or Yorkshire (North Riding).

A demanding, if fair, landlord of his customary tenants throughout Westmorland and Cumberland, Lowther shrewdly set rents on his Yorkshire estates at levels which would be paid. None the less, declining returns from land in all three counties frustrated him, and he made no major purchases after 1667. Instead, he continued to lend money across the north (some £4000 in 1670) and invested in a Yorkshire alum mining project and more extensively in the London money market. At the time of his death two London scriveners were managing £47,000 of his wealth and generating £2200 a year. He died at Lowther on 30 November 1675, and was buried there on 4 December. His chief heir was his eldest grandson, John *Lowther, later Viscount Lonsdale (1655–1700). C. B. PHILLIPS

Sources C. B. Phillips, ed., *Lowther family estate books, 1617–1675*, SurtS, 191 (1979) • H. Owen, *The Lowther family: eight hundred years of 'A family of ancient gentry and worship'* (1990) • C. B. Phillips, 'The gentry of Cumberland and Westmorland, 1600–1665', PhD diss., University of Lancaster, 1973 • C. B. Phillips, 'The royalist north: the Cumberland and Westmorland gentry, 1642–1660', *Northern History*, 14 (1978), 169–92 • Cumberland quarter sessions register, 1667–95, Cumbria AS, Carlisle, CQ1/1 • Kendal sessions indictment book, 1655–67, Cumbria AS, Kendal, WQ/I 1 • Appleby sessions indictment book, 1661–85, Cumbria AS, Kendal • J. C. Atkinson, ed., *Quarter sessions records*, 4–6, North Riding RS, 4–6 (1886–8) • R. T. Spence, *Lady Anne Clifford: countess of Pembroke, Dorset and Montgomery, 1590–1676* (1997) • *CSP dom.*, 1660–61, 284 • W. A. Shaw, ed., *Calendar of treasury books*, 1, PRO (1904), 98, 145 • M. W. Helms and L. Naylor, 'Lowther, Sir John I', HoP, *Commons, 1660–90*, 2.768–9 • J. Heelis, 'Appleby grammar school', *Transactions of the Cumberland and Westmorland Antiquarian and Archaeological Society*, 8 (1885–6), 404–12 • GEC, *Baronetage*, 2.440 • W. H. Cooke, ed., *Students admitted to the Inner Temple, 1547–1660* [1878]

Archives Cumbria AS, Carlisle, corresp. and papers | Cumbria AS, Kendal, corresp. with Daniel Fleming

Likenesses portrait, priv. coll. [*see illus.*]

Wealth at death over £7600—land in possession incl. some land not of inheritance, and some belonging to grandson, in 1675; over £50,000 personal estate; est. £5000 p.a.: lands of inheritance: Phillips, ed., *Lowther family estate books*, xv, 149–151

Lowther, Sir John, second baronet (*bap.* **1642**, *d.* **1706**), politician and industrialist, was born in Whitehaven in the parish of St Bees and baptized on 20 November 1642, the son (there was also a daughter) of Sir Christopher *Lowther, first baronet (1611–1644), and his wife, Frances (*c.*1624–1647), heir of the Lancasters of Sockbridge, Westmorland. His grandfather was Sir John *Lowther of Lowther. Orphaned in infancy, Lowther, together with his sister, Frances, was in the guardianship of trustees, two of whom—his grandmother, Dame Ellinor Lowther, and his uncle, Sir William Lowther—were probably responsible for his upbringing. He was educated at a school in Ilkley and at Balliol College, Oxford. In March 1660 he married Jane (*d.* 1678), daughter of Woolley and Elizabeth Leigh, the stepdaughter of his uncle, the younger Sir John Lowther of Lowther, who had married Jane's widowed mother in 1652. Having first established himself at Sockbridge Hall, Lowther moved to London permanently in 1663. In 1665 a contested by-election began a long parliamentary career, Lowther representing Cumberland thereafter in every parliament until illness compelled his retirement in 1699.

Lowther was a confirmed Londoner and an absentee landlord who nevertheless took a keen interest in the detailed affairs of his estate. Making all decisions and directing all developments through his estate and colliery stewards, Lowther vigorously expanded his collieries, selling their produce to ships freighting to Dublin; he also planned and developed the port town of Whitehaven, the first planned town built in England after the middle ages. Lowther encouraged the building of a church and a nonconformist chapel, built a mathematical school to encourage navigation, enlarged the pier, and invested in trading voyages to Virginia and the Baltic. However, his relations with his tenants were never happy, because while Lowther believed his town and harbour should be developed largely at the expense of the inhabitants, with modest financial encouragement from himself, he could never bring himself to make those concessions of self-government which might have persuaded his tenants to co-operate. His long struggle to prevent the development of a rival port in neighbouring Parton was finally lost in the last months of his life.

Lowther was an active parliamentarian, serving on 141 committees in his first decade in politics, during which he was a reliable supporter of the government; he also received a grant of lands between the tides at Whitehaven–St Bees from Charles II, which proved of considerable importance in his local battles. However, by 1675 Lowther was turning against the government, though he voted against the first Exclusion Bill, in 1679. He welcomed the revolution of 1688 and William III appointed him a commissioner of the Admiralty, a responsibility Lowther took very seriously, effectively using Whitehaven for gathering intelligence during the Irish war of

Sir John Lowther, second baronet (*bap.* **1642**, *d.* **1706**), by unknown engraver, *c.*1684 (after Sir Peter Lely)

1689–90. However, during the 1680s and 1690s it is difficult to distinguish his parliamentary activities from those of his younger but politically more significant cousin, John *Lowther of Lowther, first Viscount Lonsdale, William III's first lord of the Treasury and leader of the Commons. In 1696 Lowther of Lowther, tired of contesting elections, employed his cousin to seek a viscountcy for him from the king.

A man of broad cultural interests, as his library and collection of pictures attest, Lowther was an active member of the Royal Society, serving on committees with Samuel Pepys, Sir Christopher Wren, and Sir Isaac Newton. Illness permanently trapped him in Whitehaven on a rare visit in 1698. (For most of his adult life he had suffered in his wrists and legs a condition diagnosed as 'gout'.) He died there in January 1706 (and was buried there on 17 January), having disinherited his heir, Christopher, third baronet, who was a compulsive drinker and gambler, in favour of his younger son, Sir James *Lowther, fourth baronet (*bap.* 1673, *d.* 1755), who, building on his father's industrial foundations, came to be reputed the richest commoner in England. James never married, and as neither Christopher nor Lowther's only daughter, Jane, left any offspring the Whitehaven dynasty died with James in 1755.

D. R. HAINSWORTH, *rev.*

Sources Cumbria AS, Carlisle, Lowther of Whitehaven papers • *Commercial papers of Sir Christopher Lowther, 1611–1644*, ed. D. R. Hainsworth, SurtS, 189 (1977) • *The correspondence of Sir John Lowther of Whitehaven, 1693–1698*, ed. D. R. Hainsworth (1983) • J. V. Beckett, *Coal and tobacco: the Lowthers and the economic development of west Cumberland, 1660–1760* (1981) • H. Owen, *The Lowther family: eight hundred years of 'A family of ancient gentry and worship'* (1990) • HoP, *Commons, 1660–90*

Archives Cumbria AS, Carlisle, Lowther of Whitehaven archives | BL, letters to Sir Charles Hedges, Add. MS 25098 • Cumbria AS, Kendal, corresp. with Sir Daniel Fleming

Likenesses engraving, *c.*1684 (after P. Lely), NPG [*see illus.*]

Lowther, John, first Viscount Lonsdale (1655–1700), landowner and politician, was born on 25 April 1655 at Hackthorpe Hall, Westmorland, the third of the four children of Colonel John Lowther of Hackthorpe (1628–1668), politician, and his first wife, Elizabeth (*d.* 1662), daughter and coheir of Sir Henry Bellingham.

The dominant influence on John Lowther's early life was his grandfather. His mother died when he was six. His father then remarried against the will of his own father, Sir John *Lowther of Lowther, first baronet (1606–1675), who promptly disinherited him. Sir John sent his grandson to Kendal grammar school, but withdrew him after a year. Subsequently he was educated at Lowther Hall, Westmorland, under the supervision of Sir John's butler 'whose cruelty and blows did no good to my tender years', as he later recalled in his memoirs (Lonsdale papers). He went next to Sedbergh School, and then on 12 July 1670 entered Queen's College, Oxford. He left after eighteen months without taking a degree, and subsequently spent a year at an academy in Paris. Returning to England after a further six months in France, he attended lectures at the Inner Temple, from whence he was subsequently called to the bar in 1677.

As early as 1671, when Lowther was just sixteen, his grandfather was anxious to see him settled. He resisted until 1674 when, on 3 December, he married Katherine Thynne [*see* Lowther, Katherine (1653–1713)], daughter of Sir Henry Frederick Thynne, in Henry VII's chapel in Westminster Abbey. John Lowther was nineteen and his bride twenty-one. When his grandfather died on 30 November 1675 Lowther inherited both the family estate and—his own father having died in 1668—the baronetcy. Having reached the age of twenty-one, in March 1677 he was returned to parliament for Westmorland. Apart from the brief session of October 1680–January 1681 he was re-elected to every parliament until his elevation to the House of Lords in 1696.

Lowther made his maiden speech in the Commons on 19 December 1678 during a debate on the Popish Plot, but undertook little further political involvement until 1685, when he opposed James II in parliament. He came to political prominence in 1688 when he took the lead in securing Cumberland and Westmorland for William of Orange, in the face of opposition from Sir Christopher Musgrave and Sir George Fletcher. On 9 December he and his tenants secured a ship at Workington harbour bound for Ireland with arms, and several days later they were largely responsible for the fall of the Carlisle garrison. Lowther was hailed as a hero for securing the border region for William. He was made vice-chamberlain in the new king's household, a privy councillor, and lord lieutenant of Cumberland and Westmorland. On 18 March 1690 he was appointed first lord of the Treasury and leader of the

John Lowther, first Viscount Lonsdale (1655–1700), attrib. Mary Beale, 1677?

House of Commons. He was subsequently one of the nine members of the council appointed in June 1690 to advise Queen Mary during her husband's campaign in Ireland. She later described Lowther as 'a very honest but weak man' (Owen, 205).

Lowther was not considered a success as first lord of the Treasury, and he was replaced by Sidney, Lord Godolphin, on 15 November 1690. A contemporary squib derided 'the dull, insipid stream of his set speeches, made up of whipt cream', and dismissed him as 'an empty piece of misplaced eloquence' (*Poems on Affairs of State: Augustan Satirical Verse, 1660–1714*, ed. G. de F. Lord and others, 7 vols., 1963–75, 2.211). The king refused to allow him to retire altogether, and Lowther remained on the Treasury board as second commissioner. He also stayed on Queen Mary's council, suggesting that he retained the king's confidence, and he continued as leader of the Commons. As one of only two commoners on the council, he had to defend the government's policies in the Commons, often against accusations levelled from the leader of the opposition, his fellow Cumbrian and arch political rival, the tory Sir Christopher Musgrave. He was frequently criticized in the house as a former country politician who now held two lucrative places, in the Treasury and (as vice-chamberlain) the royal household, and the situation did not improve when he received a gift from the king of 2000 guineas. With some relief Lowther left the Treasury board in March 1692. Among recommendations in a later letter to his son Lowther warned him to avoid government office and the Treasury in particular.

Lowther continued as vice-chamberlain until January 1693 and government spokesman in the Commons until February 1694. He resigned the lord lieutenancy to the earl of Carlisle in June 1694, but despite claiming he wished to live quietly in the country he took his wife and family to Bath and London and he was re-elected for Westmorland in October 1695. The election was 'a great expense', and he decided to 'begg an honour of the King' because 'securitie and eas are to be had no other way' (*Correspondence*, 241). On 28 May 1696 he was created Baron Lowther of Lowther and Viscount Lonsdale in the county of Westmorland. He was introduced in the House of Lords on 13 January 1697. Shortly after taking his seat, Lonsdale suffered a serious illness. On recovery he told Sir Daniel Fleming of Rydal that 'it hath not pleased God so to dispose off me yett' (Owen, 211). For a while Lonsdale stayed out of politics, but in March 1699 he was summoned by the king to London and made lord privy seal. Subsequently he was appointed one of the nine lords justices to govern the country as regents in the king's absence on the continent. In December 1699 he was elected a fellow of the Royal Society.

Lowther inherited from his grandfather the family estates in Westmorland, which included the chief seat at Lowther and a second family home at Hackthorpe Hall, and lands in Cumberland, Yorkshire, and co. Durham. He made no fewer than eighty-one separate purchases of property in Cumberland and Westmorland, at a cost of £33,731, and he spent a further £10,000 on property in Yorkshire, again designed to consolidate the existing estates. His landed income was £6387 in 1694–5, and in 1696 he wrote to his son that 'I would not if I might wish have the estate of my family swell above £10,000 a year, and even now when it is but little more than six, in my opinion it is great enough' ('Letter to his son', Lonsdale papers). He maintained a garden at Lowther to help supply the family with food, and a flourishing stud. In 1696 an Irish correspondent claimed to have heard 'so much of your lordship's breed of horses that I am ambitious to have one of them' (Lonsdale papers). He advised his son to adopt improved methods of husbandry, although he did not necessarily take his own advice.

Lonsdale built a new house at Lowther. Between 1681 and 1684 he bought various properties and rehoused those displaced in what is now called Lowther Newtown. This cost him £1300. Lonsdale then built his new hall at cost of £6460, new stables (£1500), and new offices (£1200). He employed William Talman of the king's office of works, and deputy to Wren, to prepare a design based 'principally on my own thought' ('Letter to his son', Lonsdale papers). The building costs included £195 for marble from London, and £430 paid to the Italian artist Antonio Verrio (1639–1707), who spent nine months painting the hallway. Celia Fiennes described how it 'looks very nobly, with severall rows of trees which leads to large iron gates' (*The Journey of Celia Fiennes*, ed. C. Morris, 1947, 199). It is known today only from the painting by Matthias Read. At the same time, Lonsdale laid out gardens and a park. He also almost completely rebuilt the Norman church at a cost of £300. The building was described by the bishop in 1703 as 'in the fairest condition of any parish church in the diocese' (Owen, 209). He had 'hoped to establish some manufacture for the benefit of the poor, to which purpose I had built a house convenient for it' ('Letter to his son', Lonsdale papers). This cost £600 but the attempt to promote textile manufacturing failed, and the building was converted into a school 'for none but gentlemen's sons' (ibid.). Two masters were appointed, the boys were boarded in the village, and Lonsdale endowed the school in his will.

By early 1700 Lonsdale's health was giving cause for concern. During April he was visibly ill while leading the opposition to the resumption bill sent from the Commons, which the king wanted to see defeated but which the earl of Marlborough was supporting. The king eventually gave way, but Lonsdale was by now in the hands of Dr John Ratcliffe, the king's own doctor. On 23 May William agreed that he should return to Westmorland. He went via Bath, where the waters apparently brought him no relief. Although on 30 June he was again appointed a lord justice on the council of regency, he died on 10 July at Lowther. James Brydges, later duke of Chandos, wrote that Lonsdale was 'a man very eminent for many great qualities which, joined with the opinion the world had of his integrity, could not fail to add very great strength to the side he was of' (Owen, 215). Lonsdale was buried at Lowther church on 15 July 1700. A magnificent memorial by William Stanton was erected above his tomb. Katherine, his widow, died aged fifty-nine in January 1713 and was buried at Lowther on the 28th; her name was added to her husband's memorial in the church. The couple had had five sons and nine daughters, and at Lonsdale's death the three surviving sons were all under age: Richard, the eldest, inherited the title, but died only months after he came of age, on 1 December 1713; the title and estate passed to his brother Henry.

Henry Lowther, third Viscount Lonsdale (1694–1751), court official and gambler, distinguished himself in the defence of Cumberland and Westmorland during the 1715 Jacobite rising. In 1717 he was appointed a lord of the bedchamber, accepting the position without enthusiasm because he was 'afraid that a Court employment will require more attendance than I (who am at present very fond of the country) can have inclination to give' (Lonsdale to Lowther, 21 July 1717, Lonsdale papers). He nevertheless retained the position for ten years. In 1726 he was appointed a governor of the Tower of London, but resigned in 1731 according to Sir James Lowther of Whitehaven, because 'he is desirous to live more in the country than he thinks is fit for one of that place' (Lowther to Spedding, 6 May 1731, Lonsdale papers). He was briefly lord privy seal (1733–5). On the death of Lord Carlisle in 1738 he was appointed lord lieutenant of Cumberland and Westmorland, and was responsible for the defence of the two counties during the 1745 Jacobite rising. He remained at his sister Elizabeth's home at Byram, near Pontefract in Yorkshire, passing much of his responsibility to Sir George Fleming, the octogenarian bishop of Carlisle.

Lonsdale spent little time at Lowther Hall. In March 1718 it was badly damaged by fire. The main central building and most of the inner east, or chapel, wing were gutted. Pictures, furniture, and Verrio's great hall paintings were all lost. Subsequently Lonsdale lived in a converted office wing on his infrequent visits, and he attributed his absence in 1745 to 'some alterations in my house which are now in hand … [and] make it impossible for me to be there' (*The Jacobite Risings of 1715 and 1745*, ed. R. C. Jarvis, 1954, 94). He closed the school at Lowther in 1739 and converted the building for textile manufacture. He was a compulsive gambler, both on horses and in the City. He lost heavily during the South Sea Bubble crisis and as a result had to sell estates valued at more than £26,000. He may have lost more than £30,000. Although he left a depleted estate, his acquisition of burgages in Appleby helped to secure the borough for the Lowthers. Horace Walpole thought him 'no great genius' (H. Walpole, *Memoirs of King George II*, ed. J. Brooke, 3 vols., 1985).

Lonsdale died unmarried at Byram on 7 March 1751 and was buried at Lowther on 18 March. The peerage became extinct, although the baronetcy and estates passed to James *Lowther, later earl of Lonsdale. J. V. BECKETT

Sources H. Owen, *The Lowther family: eight hundred years of 'A family of ancient gentry and worship'* (1990) • J. V. Beckett, 'Landownership in Cumbria, 1680–1750', PhD diss., University of Lancaster, 1975 • J. V. Beckett, 'The eighteenth-century origins of the factory system: a case study from the 1740s', *Business History*, 19 (1977), 55–67 • J. V. Beckett, 'Lowther College, 1697–1740: "for none but gentlemen's sons"', *Transactions of the Cumberland and Westmorland Antiquarian and Archaeological Society*, [new ser.], 79 (1979), 103–7 • J. V. Beckett, 'Cumbrians and the South Sea Bubble, 1720', *Transactions of the Cumberland and Westmorland Antiquarian and Archaeological Society*, [new ser.], 82 (1982), 141–50 • D. R. Hainsworth, 'The Lowther younger sons: a seventeenth century case study', *Transactions of the Cumberland and Westmorland Antiquarian and Archaeological Society*, [new ser.], 88 (1988), 149–60 • *The correspondence of Sir John Lowther of Whitehaven, 1693–8*, ed. D. R. Hainsworth (1983) • GEC, *Peerage*, new edn, vol. 8 • *Cumberland and Westmorland*, Pevsner (1967) • Cumbria AS, Carlisle, Lonsdale papers, fols. 370–7 • J. F. Haswell and C. S. Jackson, eds., *The registers of Lowther, 1540–1812*, Cumberland and Westmorland Antiquarian and Archaeological Society, parish register section, 21 (1933), 156

Archives Cumbria AS, Carlisle, corresp. • Cumbria AS, Carlisle, corresp. and papers • Cumbria AS, Carlisle, MSS | BL, letters to second marquess of Halifax • Cumbria AS, Kendal, corresp. with Sir Daniel Fleming • U. Nott. L., letters to first earl of Portland

Likenesses attrib. M. Beale, oils, 1677?, Longleat, Wiltshire [*see illus.*] • H. Rigaud, oils, Gov. Art Coll.; repro. in Owen, *Lowther family*

Lowther [*née* Thynne], **Katherine**, **Viscountess Lonsdale (1653–1713)**, electoral patron, was born on 21 September 1653 at Caus Castle, Shropshire, the daughter of Sir Henry Frederick Thynne, first baronet (1614–1680), landowner, of Kempsford, Gloucestershire, and his wife, the Hon. Mary (*b.* 1618), daughter of Thomas *Coventry, first Baron Coventry of Aylesborough.

On 3 December 1674 Katherine married John *Lowther (1655–1700), of Lowther, Westmorland. They had five sons (two of whom died young), and nine daughters (four of whom survived her). Their first child, Mary, was born at Drayton, Staffordshire, a residence of Katherine's brother, Thomas *Thynne, created Viscount Weymouth in 1682. On 30 November 1675 John Lowther succeeded his grandfather as second baronet. There followed several years of living in London, where several more children were born. However, after 1680, all but two of her children were born at Lowther.

The Lowthers had much political influence in the north-west: Lady Lowther's husband served as MP for Westmorland, with a break of only one short parliament, from 1677 until his elevation to the peerage as Viscount Lonsdale on 28 May 1696. He also served in high office from 1689 to 1694. His retirement in 1694 was interrupted by the illness of his wife following the birth of his son, Henry, and the death of a daughter, Dorothy, which necessitated a trip to Bath and an extended stay in London to aid her recovery. Lonsdale returned to high office in 1699 and was still in office when he died on 10 July 1700.

Lady Lonsdale's most immediate problem was her husband's will, Lord Weymouth fearing 'a good deal of trouble in the execution' of it (Weymouth to Lady Lonsdale, 21 July 1700, Lonsdale MSS, D/Lons/L1/1/44). She certainly sought advice from Weymouth and her husband's cousin Sir John *Lowther, second baronet (*bap.* 1642, *d.* 1706), of Whitehaven, on estate matters, and on the education of her son Henry. Lady Lonsdale, however, made it a guiding rule of her conduct to act as her late husband would have done, which included scrupulously following the instructions left in his will. She also became the head of the Lonsdale political interest during her eldest son's minority. By late August 1700 she was living in Chelsea, seeing no-one but her 'brothers and sisters and some particular relations' (James Lowther to Sir John Lowther, 29 Aug 1700, Lonsdale MSS, D/Lons/W2/2/3). Initially she was advised by her brother Weymouth to stand neutral in the impending by-election for Westmorland, but she seems to have realized that this would weaken her interest. She then seems to have taken advice from Sir John Lowther, who was keen for the Lowther/Howard (earl of Carlisle) interest to thwart the Musgraves, even though Musgrave was a political ally of her brother Weymouth. In the general election of January 1701 she was 'resolute to do as my Lord would have done had he been alive' (James Lowther to Sir John Lowther, 5 April 1701, Lonsdale MSS, D/Lons/W2/2/4). In December 1702 James *Lowther reported to his father Sir John that 'my Lady Lonsd[ale] calls herself a Whig' (James Lowther to Sir John Lowther, 1 Dec 1702, Lonsdale MSS, D/Lons/W2/2/5).

In June 1705 a family crisis erupted when Lady Lonsdale's daughter Barbara was 'clandestinely married' to the Catholic Thomas Howard of Corby, Cumberland. This necessitated a series of delicate negotiations covering the security of the bride's portion and the children, not completed until September 1706. The viscountess's political sympathies were shown again in November 1705 when, according to Bishop Nicolson of Carlisle, the young Viscount Lonsdale was 'brought into' the house of Lords by the whig Lord Wharton without the tory Lord Weymouth's being given notice, even though Lady Lonsdale had dined with her brother the evening before.

Lady Lonsdale was vital in establishing James Lowther as knight of the shire for Cumberland in the 1708 election, now that his father had died. He was confident in expecting that the interest of Lonsdale and Carlisle would carry the election for him, but he was careful to approach her before taking any action. Again, in 1710, she promised to send orders to her bailiffs to campaign for James Lowther once anybody stirred in the county.

Katherine Lonsdale died in London on 7 January 1713, and was buried in Lowther on the 28th, 'none invited formally … yet great crowds' ('Nicolson's diaries', pt 5, 61). Her will left tokens to her three sons, to three of her daughters, and to her sons-in-law, including Sir John Wentworth, whose wife (Lady Lonsdale's daughter Mary), had died in 1706. Her daughter Barbara was not mentioned. STUART HANDLEY

Sources GEC, *Peerage*, new edn • Lowther correspondence, Cumbria AS, Carlisle, Lonsdale papers, D/Lons, L1/1/44; L1/1/46; W1/20; W1/27; W2/1/40–46; W2/2/3–5 • H. Owen, *The Lowther family: eight hundred years of 'A family of ancient gentry and worship'* (1990), 64–5, 198–223 • J. F. Haswell and C. S. Jackson, eds., *The registers of Lowther, 1540–1812*, Cumberland and Westmorland Antiquarian and Archaeological Society, parish register section, 21 (1933), 46–50, 154–6 • will, PRO, PROB 11/534, sig. 139 • Bishop of Barrow-in-Furness, 'Bishop Nicolson's diaries, pt 2', *Transactions of the Cumberland and Westmorland Antiquarian and Archaeological Society*, new ser., 2 (1901–2), 155–230 • L. Naylor, 'Lowther, Sir John III, 2nd bt', HoP, *Commons, 1660–90* • S. Rudder, *A new history of Gloucestershire* (1779), 511 • *IGI*

Archives Cumbria AS, Carlisle, Lonsdale MSS • Longleat House, Wiltshire, Thynne MSS

Likenesses P. Lely, oils, repro. in Owen, *Lowther family*, 199

Wealth at death see will, PRO, PROB 11/534, sig. 139

Lowther, Sir Richard (1532–1608), landowner and soldier, was born on 14 February 1532 in Hartsop Hall, Westmorland, the eldest of the six children of Hugh Lowther (*c.*1510–1555) and Dorothy Clifford (*d.* 1562). She was the daughter of Henry *Clifford, tenth Baron Clifford (*d.* 1523), the Shepherd Lord, and his second wife, Florence. Lowther's ancestors had lived in Lowther, Westmorland, certainly since the twelfth century, and since 1305 at least eight of his direct ancestors had represented Westmorland or Cumberland in parliament, three Lowthers fought at Agincourt, and his grandfather Sir John led his tenantry into battle at Solway Moss and was captain of Carlisle Castle from 1544 until his death in 1553. Lowther was also legitimately descended from William *Strickland (*d.* 1419), bishop of Carlisle, whose wife died giving birth to a daughter before he took orders.

Nothing is known of Lowther's early years or education; he may have studied law at Lincoln's Inn, but he is not recorded as entering the inn until 1560. When aged twenty he took over the family estates on his grandfather's death, his ne'er-do-well father having been disinherited for his 'great unthriftiness' (Cumbria AS, Carlisle, D/Lons/L3/1/7). In 1553 he married Frances Middleton (*d.* 1597) of Middleton Hall in south Westmorland; they had eight sons and seven daughters, of whom three sons and five daughters died young. All but the first were born in Lowther Hall.

In 1566 Lowther was pricked sheriff of Cumberland and in the same year Lord Scrope, lord warden of the west march and captain of Carlisle Castle, appointed him his deputy in both posts. On 16 May 1568, Mary, queen of

Scots, landed on the Cumberland coast on her escape from Scotland, and she was greeted at Cockermouth the next day by Lowther with a force of 400 horsemen to conduct her to Carlisle. Here she was lodged in the castle 'with such entertainment as I well can or am able upon such sudden' (PRO, SP 53/1/2). Four days later the Catholic earl of Northumberland tried to take custody of Mary which, despite the earl's anger, Lowther refused to allow without orders from London. On 27 May Sir Francis Knollys (to whom Queen Elizabeth entrusted Mary's security) and Lord Warden Scrope arrived from London. When Northumberland complained of the treatment he received from Lowther, regarding him as 'too mean a man to have such a charge', he was told that Lowther 'did dutifully and wisely and he [Northumberland] had overshot himself very much to the discontentation of Queen Elizabeth' (PRO, SP 59/15; Sharp, 341). Mary for her part thanked Elizabeth 'for the good reception I have had in your country, and principally from Mister Lowther who received me with all courtesy' (BL, Cotton MS Caligula C. i, fol. 106*v*, 28 May). The story in the *Dictionary of National Biography* and elsewhere that Lowther injudiciously permitted the duke of Norfolk to meet Mary and was heavily fined in Star Chamber has no truth in it. Norfolk was in London throughout.

On 13 July 1568 Mary was removed from Carlisle, which was considered too dangerously close to the Scottish border, and taken to Bolton Castle. Knollys chose Lowther Hall for her first night as it 'standeth farther from the rescue of the Scots than any other house we could have chosen' (BL, Cotton MS Caligula C. i, fol. 163, 14 July). Lowther family tradition recalled that Mary was deeply touched by the affectionate reverence she received from Lowther and his family and, as Sir William Lowther wrote in 1765, she 'knelt down upon the floor and prayed earnestly a blessing on him and his family' (Cumbria AS, Carlisle, D/Lons/L3/5/155).

In 1569 Lowther, by now receiver of the duke of Norfolk's rents in Cumberland and Westmorland and therefore beholden to him, together with his younger brother Gerard, became involved in the plot (led by the earls of Northumberland and Westmorland and not discouraged by the duke) to depose Elizabeth and supplant her by Mary. Gerard Lowther escaped to Scotland, as did the earls, but Richard was incarcerated in the Tower of London from January to August 1570 with Norfolk and twenty-three other prisoners. In October 1571 he was again in the Tower following the Ridolfi plot, which had the same aims. Norfolk was executed in June 1572 and Lowther was not released until the following January. Apart from the mental anxiety that it induced, his imprisonment appears from his own account to have been relatively comfortable. On both occasions his release from the Tower was suitably celebrated by the arrival of a son about ten months later.

Lowther next came to prominence in 1588 when he was pricked sheriff of Cumberland on the recommendation of the agent of Sir Francis Walsingham—he:

> had disgrace by the cause of the late Duke of Norfolk, which is a thing common when the master gets a fall … Yet quit himself very worshipfully of that action … There is no man in the West Marches so sufficient for Border causes. (BL, Cotton MS Caligula D.i, fol. 315)

In 1590 Scrope again appointed him deputy warden of the march. On 4 June 1592, only four days after Scrope's death, Lowther was appointed by the queen to succeed him as lord warden and to assume responsibility for keeping 'the country in good order and the laws of the borders towards Scotland duly observed' (PRO, SP 15/32/34). He was known to be well respected by the Scots and had experience of conducting difficult business with them. He was the first commoner lord warden since 1327; nevertheless he was a stopgap until the new Lord Scrope was appointed the following year. From 1597 to 1601 he was again deputy warden.

In September 1597 Lowther's wife died. He subsequently married Margaret Eden, widow of John Threlkeld, who outlived him. On 17 April 1603 he was knighted at York by James I on his journey south to his new capital, the ninth member of his family to receive the honour, and in the following year he served for the third time as a commissioner for border affairs to negotiate a treaty with the Scots. Of the gentry who played a part in the government of the west march and the counties of Cumberland and Westmorland in Elizabeth's reign, Lowther was probably the most active.

Sir Richard died at Lowther Hall a great-grandfather aged seventy-five on 21 January 1608, and was buried four days later in Lowther church, where there is a monument to him with a full-length effigy. To his grandson, Sir John *Lowther (1582–1637), he was 'my memorable grandfather—I have ever given great regard to his sayings' (Cumbria AS, Carlisle, D/Lons/L3/1/1). Of Sir Richard's five surviving sons, Christopher (1557–1617) commanded Scrope's escort when he greeted King James at Newcastle in 1603 and was knighted by the king; Sir Gerard *Lowther (*d.* 1624) [*see under* Lowther, Sir Gerard (*c.*1590–1660)] was a judge of the common pleas in Ireland; and Sir Lancelot (1571–1638) was solicitor-general to James I's queen, Anne of Denmark, and later a baron of the court of exchequer in Ireland. Sir Richard's descendants are still seated at Lowther. C. H. H. Owen

Sources Cumbria AS, Carlisle, Lonsdale papers · PRO, C142/321/92 (inquisition post mortem); SP 53/1/2; SP 59/15; SP 15/32/34 · H. Owen, *The Lowther family: eight hundred years of 'A family of ancient gentry and worship'* (1990) · BL, Cotton MSS, Caligula C.i, fol. 106*v*, 163: D.i, fol. 315 · J. Bain, ed., *The border papers: calendar of letters and papers relating to the affairs of the borders of England and Scotland*, 2 vols. (1894–6) · J. Nichols, *The progresses, processions, and magnificent festivities of King James I, his royal consort, family and court*, 1 (1828), 82 · C. Sharp, ed., *Memorials of the rebellion of 1569* (1840) · W. P. Baildon, ed., *The records of the Honorable Society of Lincoln's Inn* [incl. *Admissions*, 2 vols. (1896), and *Black books*, 6 vols. (1897–2001)] · Lowther parish register · W. Jackson, 'Threlkeld of Melmerby', *Transactions of the Cumberland and Westmorland Antiquarian and Archaeological Society*, 10 (1889), 1–47

Archives BL · PRO

Likenesses alabaster effigy, *c.*1611, Lowther parish church, Cumbria

Wealth at death manors of Lowther, Hackthorpe, Newton Reigny, and part of Holton; twenty messuages and 160 acres in Penrith; advowson of Lowther church: inquisition post mortem, PRO, C 142/321/92 (1611)

Lowther, Sir Robert (*d.* **1430**). *See under* Lowther family (*per.* *c.*1270–*c.*1450).

Lowther, William (*d.* **1421**?). *See under* Lowther family (*per.* *c.*1270–*c.*1450).

Lowther, Sir William (*bap.* **1612**, *d.* **1688**), merchant and landowner, of Swillington, Yorkshire, baptized at Holy Trinity Church, Kendal, Westmorland, on 28 September 1612, was the third son of Sir John *Lowther (1582–1637), of Lowther Hall, Westmorland, and Ellinor Fleming (*c.*1583–1659), of Skirwith, Cumberland. Destined, like his elder brother Christopher *Lowther (1611–1644), for commerce, he was apprenticed to his uncle Robert Lowther of the Drapers' Company. He did not serve out his time, but even his unbending father was inclined to blame the master more than the man.

Throughout the 1630s Lowther and his brother Christopher collaborated in trading ventures, and he resided variously in Leeds, London, and Hamburg. In March 1635 he was admitted free of the Merchant Adventurers of London. In 1636 he married Jane (1615–1686), second daughter of William Busfield, merchant, of Leeds, and his wife, Elizabeth Metcalfe. He thereby knowingly frustrated deep-laid plans of his father's, and forfeited the landed settlement Sir John had intended for him, receiving only a grudging £1000 under his will.

Lowther was at Leeds at the outbreak of the civil war but withdrew to Rotterdam in 1643. Though he had not taken up arms in the royal cause, in 1646 he was fined £200 for helping to raise a loan to the king and contributing to his northern forces; another transaction to furnish £1000 to Lord Goring in the Netherlands was adjudged to have been merely commercial.

After ten years of trading at Rotterdam Lowther returned to England in 1653 to invest the profits in land around Leeds. He bought Roundhay for his own residence, but later sold it to his nephew, Sir John Lowther of Whitehaven. He joined with his eldest brother, John *Lowther of Lowther, in lending money to distressed royalists on the security of their estates. In 1656 they purchased Great Preston for £6100, and two years later William bought his brother's half and rebuilt the house to live in. He laid out a further £9000 for neighbouring Swillington. The coal deposits beneath these two estates sustained successive generations of his descendants.

Lowther first served as a JP for the West Riding of Yorkshire in 1632 and was a deputy lieutenant from 1667 to 1676. He was knighted on 30 December 1661. Meanwhile election for the nearby borough of Pontefract in May 1660 had launched him into nineteen years of parliamentary service, in which his industry is witnessed by membership of 617 committees. He was chairman of the Commons committee which examined the naval accounts for the Second Anglo-Dutch War. Often named to committees for enforcing uniformity in religion, in the debate on the 1671 bill for suppressing conventicles he argued the need for churchmen to gather in dissenters by good example rather than compulsion. He was one of the six commissioners of the customs appointed in 1671, but his own surviving papers exhibit hardly a trace of his work, and fire has destroyed the official record at the London Custom House.

In surviving personal letters Lowther exercises a calming but hardly inhibiting influence on his wife and their nine surviving children. 'I know your eagerness for long journeys,' he wrote to Jane on 23 September 1673 after thirty-seven years of marriage, 'when we came down if you had overruled me the horses had been spoilt'. 'Her humour and yours suits well,' he protested on the same day to their eldest son, William, 'to be all upon the spur' (W. Yorks. AS, NCB Swillington, box 14). William, left in charge of his two youngest sisters, was advised to take a walk in the garden if his sisters provoked him. Indulgent, Lowther quickly forgave the daughter who married against his wishes. For his daughters and younger sons, he explained to his son Richard on 16 October that year, he had early undertaken to provide portions of £1500, 'much above any of my degree in those parts that had as good as I have now from their forefathers and not got it themselves' (ibid.).

His wife having died in March 1686, Lowther himself died on 20 February 1688 at Great Preston, and was buried in his parish church at Kippax, near Leeds. His eldest surviving son, William Lowther (1639–1705) was a whig MP for Pontefract between 1695 and 1698.

Christine Churches

Sources W. Yorks. AS, Leeds, Lowther of Swillington papers, NCB Swillingham, 14 • Denbighshire RO, Ruthin, Sir William Lowther of Swillington MSS, DD/L • C. B. Phillips, ed., *Lowther family estate books, 1617–1675*, SurtS, 191 (1979) • Cumbria AS, Carlisle, Lonsdale MSS, D/Lons/A1/1 [for material not printed in Phillips] • H. Owen, *The Lowther family: eight hundred years of 'A family of ancient gentry and worship'* (1990) • HoP, *Commons, 1660–90* • A. Grey, ed., *Debates of the House of Commons, from the year 1667 to the year 1694*, new edn, 1 (1769), 23, 116, 280–81, 307, 408, 420; 5 (1769), 200, 381 • *JHC*, 8 (1660–67), 311, 368, 373–4, 537, 550, 580, 584, 655, 661, 669, 674 • *The diary of John Milward*, ed. C. Robbins (1938), 26–7 • C. M. L. Bouch, 'Lowther of Swillington from its origins till 1788', *Transactions of the Cumberland and Westmorland Antiquarian and Archaeological Society*, new ser., 42 (1941–2), 67–102, esp. 67–76 • *Commercial papers of Sir Christopher Lowther, 1611–1644*, ed. D. R. Hainsworth, SurtS, 189 (1977) • Burke, *Gen. GB*

Archives Denbighshire RO, Ruthin, letter-book relating to cloth trade, in-letters, and papers • W. Yorks. AS, Leeds, papers and memorandum book | Cumbria AS, Carlisle, Lonsdale papers

Likenesses double portrait, oils, *c.*1640–1649 (with Jane Busfield), repro. in Owen, *Lowther family*, p. 312

Lowther, William, **first earl of Lonsdale** (**1757–1844**), landowner and literary patron, was born on 29 December 1757 at Little Preston Hall, near Leeds, the elder son of the Revd Sir William Lowther, baronet (1707–1788), rector of Swillington, and Anne Zouch (1723–1759), daughter of the Revd Charles Zouch, vicar of Sandal near Wakefield. He was educated at Felsted School, Essex (1769–71), Westminster School (1771–2), by private tutor (1773–5), and at Trinity College, Cambridge (1776–8) where he became a friend of Pitt.

In 1780 Lowther was elected MP for Carlisle under the

patronage of his godfather and third cousin once removed, the tyrannical Sir James Lowther (later earl of Lonsdale), and a year later, on 12 July 1781, married Lady Augusta Fane (1761–1838), daughter of John *Fane, ninth earl of Westmorland [*see under* Fane, John, seventh earl of Westmorland]. They had two sons, including William *Lowther, and five daughters. In the 1784 election Lowther was returned for Cumberland but in 1790 was dropped by Lonsdale 'without any reason … and without Lonsdale even signifying any offence' (*Journal of Boswell*, 80). In 1788 he had succeeded his father as second baronet, of Swillington, and inherited the family's large Yorkshire estate with its collieries. In 1796 he re-entered parliament as member for Rutland, where he now lived, and was free from the tight political reins of his godfather; but he was a reluctant speaker in the house.

In 1797 the childless earl of Lonsdale received the additional titles of Viscount and Baron Lowther of Whitehaven with special remainder to Sir William, his nearest male Lowther relative. The distant cousins were back on speaking terms. On Lonsdale's death on 24 May 1802 Sir William became Viscount Lowther and inherited the family's vast estates in Cumberland and Westmorland including the lucrative collieries and flourishing harbour of Whitehaven. By a previous arrangement the family's Yorkshire estates then passed to Sir William's brother.

William Lowther became overnight one of the wealthiest men in the kingdom (his annual income was estimated to be nearly £100,000), the controller of eight (later nine) seats in parliament, the patron of thirty-two parishes, and lord lieutenant of Cumberland and Westmorland (appointed 16 June 1802). His newly acquired wealth brought him great influence which, in contrast to his predecessor, he used generously and with sympathy. Immediately on inheriting, he arranged a compromise with the duke of Norfolk over the filling of the two seats for Carlisle to avoid an expensive and unseemly campaign at the forthcoming election. Soon afterwards he repaid, with full interest, the earl's twenty-year-old debt of £5000 to William and Dorothy Wordsworth, a debt which arose from legal and political fees owing to the poet's father, who had been Lonsdale's law agent and land steward in Cockermouth for twenty-three years until his death in 1783. Throughout the succeeding years Lonsdale had resisted a series of lawsuits brought by the guardians of the Wordsworth children for payment of the debt. Repayment of £8500 was made by William Lowther within eighteen months of his inheritance.

In 1806 Lowther was selected by the earl of Chatham to be one of the six assistant mourners at Pitt's funeral 'as one of the nearest of his friends' (Chatham to Lowther, 17 Feb 1806, *Lonsdale MSS*, 166). In the following year he was created earl of Lonsdale and received the Order of the Garter for his part in negotiating the duke of Portland's new administration after the resignation of Grenville, but he declined a seat in the cabinet.

On inheriting Lowther Hall, the family seat in Westmorland, Lowther found it in a deplorable state and commissioned Robert Smirke, the future architect of the British Museum, to build Lowther Castle. It was the young architect's first major commission, described by Wordsworth as 'a baronial castle' of 'majestic pile' (*Poetical Works*, 477). The artist Jacob Thompson was another whom Lonsdale set on the road to fame.

William Wordsworth and Lonsdale became firm friends and mutual admirers, and in 1818 Lonsdale was able again to ease the poet's financial position by arranging his appointment as distributor of stamps for Westmorland. For their part Wordsworth and his sister worked tirelessly in the Lowther interest during the general election campaigns of 1818 and 1820. In 1828 Lonsdale presented Wordsworth's clergyman son to the first of three livings in his gift.

For many years Wordsworth paid an annual visit of a week or more to Lowther Castle and sometimes stayed also at Whitehaven Castle. Occasionally he even sent his verse to Lonsdale for comment and accepted the earl's suggestions for changes. 'He was to myself and my children the best benefactor', Wordsworth wrote to Lady Frederick Bentinck on 31 March 1844 (De Selincourt, 7.539).

Lonsdale died on 19 March 1844 at York House, Twickenham, aged eighty-six, and was buried on 1 April in Lowther church beside his wife (*d.* 1838). 'How much is there to be thankful for in every part of Lord Lonsdale's life to its close', wrote Wordsworth (De Selincourt, 7.539).

C. H. H. Owen

Sources H. Owen, *The Lowther family: eight hundred years of 'A family of ancient gentry and worship'* (1990) • Cumbria AS, Carlisle, Lonsdale papers • Clwyd RO, Ruthin, Lowther MSS • *The letters of William and Dorothy Wordsworth*, ed. E. De Selincourt, 2nd edn, rev. C. L. Shaver, M. Moorman, and A. G. Hill, 8 vols. (1967–93) • *The manuscripts of the earl of Lonsdale*, HMC, 33 (1893) • *The journal of James Boswell, 1789–1794*, ed. G. Scott and F. A. Pottle (New York, 1934), vol. 18 of *Private papers of James Boswell from Malahide Castle* (1928–34) • HoP, *Commons* • PRO, Pitt MSS • M. H. Port, 'Lowther Hall and Castle', *Transactions of the Cumberland and Westmorland Antiquarian and Archaeological Society*, [new ser.,] 81 (1981), 122–36 • *The poetical works of William Wordsworth*, ed. T. Hutchinson, new edn (1904); repr. (1908) • parish register, Swillington, Yorkshire, 29 Dec 1757 [birth] • parish register, Swillington, Yorkshire, 2 Feb 1758 [baptism]

Archives Clwyd RO, Ruthin, Lowther MSS • Cumbria AS, Carlisle, Lonsdale MSS | BL, letters, Add. MSS 58989, 38242–38328, 38450, 40410–40532 • CKS, correspondence • Harrowby Manuscript Trust, Stafford, correspondence (priv. coll.) • NRA Scot, Edinburgh, correspondence • PRO, Richmond, letters, PRO 30/8/104, 153

Likenesses J. Downman, chalk, 1778, FM Cam. • J. Opie, oils, 1806, repro. in Owen, *Lowther family*, 383; priv. coll. • T. Lawrence, oils, 1812, priv. coll.; photograph, NPG • Hayter, oils, *c.*1820; photograph NPG • T. Campbell, marble bust, 1830, Apsley House, London • J. Thompson, chalk, *c.*1839, BM; repro. in Owen, *Lowther family*, 387 • J. Thompson, oils, *c.*1839; photograph, NPG • M. L. Watson, statue, 1845, Carlisle • E. B. Stephens, statue, 1863, Lowther mausoleum, Westmorland • prints, BM, NPG

Wealth at death approx. £200,000: PRO, death duty registers, IR26/1681, fol. 2/393

Lowther, William, second earl of Lonsdale (1787–1872), politician, was the eldest son of Sir William *Lowther (1757–1844), subsequently Viscount Lowther and first earl of Lonsdale, and Lady Augusta (1761–1838), daughter of John *Fane, ninth earl of Westmorland [*see under* Fane, John, seventh earl of Westmorland]. He was born at Uffington, near Stamford, Lincolnshire, on 30 July 1787, and educated at Harrow School and Trinity College, Cambridge, whence he graduated MA in 1808. Thanks to the strength of the Lowther interest in Westmorland, he was returned as MP for Cockermouth in 1808–13, and for Westmorland in 1813–31 and 1832–41. The crumbling of the Lowther interest in 1831 over their resolute stance against reform forced him to seek a seat elsewhere, and he represented the pocket borough of Dunwich for the 1832 sessions.

Lowther first took office under Perceval, succeeding Palmerston as junior lord of the Admiralty in 1809; from 1813 to 1826, with a short interval, he was on the Treasury board, and was made first commissioner of woods and forests by the duke of Wellington in 1828. He was president of the Board of Trade in 1834–5, and postmaster-general with a seat in the cabinet in 1841. He was summoned to the House of Lords in his father's barony on 6 September 1841 and succeeded to the earldom in 1844. He was president of council in 1852 in Derby's administration. Although a good business man, Lonsdale was no orator, and took no real initiative in politics. His great wealth, however, and the influence of his family gave him importance in his party, and extra-parliamentary meetings of the tories were frequently held at his house in Carlton House Terrace.

Lonsdale invested greatly in his estates, especially in drainage; he had been in his earlier days a patron of Macadam, the road-maker, and was at his death chairman of the metropolitan roads commission. He was something of a sportsman (his horse Spaniel won the Derby in 1831), paid large subsidies for the maintenance of Italian opera in London, and was an enthusiastic collector of porcelain. He was the distant original of Lord Eskdale in Disraeli's *Tancred*, 'a man with every ability, except the ability to make his powers useful to mankind'. Unmarried, he acknowledged three children, whose mothers were believed to be opera singers. Marie Caroline was born in Paris in 1818, the daughter of Caroline Saintfal; nothing further is known of her. Frances (*d.* 1890) married Henry Broadwood MP, in 1840, and was left a substantial sum in her father's will, as was Francis William (1841–1908), the son of Emilia Creosotti.

Lonsdale died at his London house, 14 Carlton House Terrace, on 4 March 1872, and was buried in the mausoleum which he had built at Lowther Castle. He was succeeded by his nephew, Henry Lowther (1818–1876).

THOMAS SECCOMBE, *rev.* K. D. REYNOLDS

Sources GEC, *Peerage* • HoP, *Commons* • H. Owen, *The Lowther family: eight hundred years of 'A family of ancient gentry and worship'* (1990) • M. Brock, *The Great Reform Act* (1973) • N. Gash, *Politics in the age of Peel* (1953) • T. Rankes, *Journal*, 4 (1857), 198–9

Archives Cumbria AS, Carlisle, corresp., diaries, and papers, incl. Walcheven diary, 1809 | BL, corresp. with Lord Aberdeen, Add. MSS 43234–43239 • BL, corresp. with Sir Robert Peel, Add. MSS 40391–40578, *passim* • BL, corresp. with Lord Ranelagh, Add. MS 62522 • Bodl. Oxf., corresp. with Benjamin Disraeli • Northumbd RO, family corresp. • PRO, corresp. with Lord John Russell, PRO 30/22

Likenesses R. and E. Taylor, wood-engraving, NPG; repro. in *ILN* (1872) • J. Ward, portrait, possibly BM; repro. in Owen, *The Lowther family* • marble bust, Hughenden Manor, Buckinghamshire

Wealth at death under £700,000: probate, 26 March 1872, *CGPLA Eng. & Wales*

Löwy, Albert [*formerly* Abraham] (**1816–1908**), Hebrew scholar, born on 8 December 1816 at Aussee in Moravia, was the eldest son of thirteen children (seven sons and six daughters) of Leopold Löwy and his wife, Katty. Löwy was called after Rabbi Abraham Leipnik, an ancestor who wrote an account in Hebrew of the destruction of the synagogue in Aussee in 1720. In 1822 his father left Aussee for Friedland, on the border of Silesia, where he owned a brewery, and in 1829 the child was sent to school in Leipzig. After his schooling at Leipzig, Jägendorf, and Olmütz, he matriculated at the University of Vienna, where fellow students included Moritz Steinschneider, the German Hebraist, and Abraham Benisch, with whom Löwy founded Die Einheit, an association for the promotion of the welfare of the Jews. The ultimate aim of the society was to colonize Palestine.

Löwy intended, on the completion of his studies, to move to Italy, where Jews were much freer than in Austria, but the foundation in 1838 of Die Einheit, a society of some two hundred students, involved his efforts and so required his continued presence in Vienna. The society operated under the guise of a literary society in order to escape discovery by and the censure of the government. In 1840 Löwy visited England to seek support for the scheme; the result was that he settled there for life. A section of the Jewish community in London was at the time seeking to reform both ritual and practice. The reformers seceded from the main body of their co-religionists, opening on 27 January 1842 the West London Synagogue of British Jews, in Burton Street. Löwy became one of the first two ministers (and remained in that post until 1892), David Woolf Marks being the other. Together they edited the prayer book of the new congregation. In 1851 Löwy had married Gertrude Levy Lindenthal; they had nine children before her death in January 1879.

In 1870 Löwy founded the Society of Hebrew Literature, editing its publications until its dissolution in 1877. With the help of Benisch, in 1870 he also helped to found the Anglo-Jewish Association, whose aims were to champion the cause of persecuted Jews and to maintain Jewish schools in the Orient. After attending a Jewish conference at Königsberg on the Russo-Jewish question, Löwy was sent by the Anglo-Jewish Association on a secret mission to Russia, in 1874. His report on the position of the Russian Jews was published as an appendix to the *Annual Statement of the Anglo-Jewish Association* in 1874. Löwy was secretary of the Anglo-Jewish Association from 1875 until his resignation in 1889. On 31 October 1892 he also resigned his ministry at the West London Synagogue, but he continued to take part in public affairs. He was made honorary LLD of St Andrews University in 1893. Löwy died in St John's Wood, London on 21 May 1908. He was buried on 24 May at the cemetery of the West London Synagogue of British Jews, in Upper Berkeley Street, where a tablet was erected to commemorate his fifty years' ministry.

Löwy was an accurate and erudite Hebrew scholar. In 1872 Lord Crawford entrusted him with the preparation of a catalogue of his unique collection of Samaritan literature, and the *Catalogue of Hebraica and Judaica in the Library of the Corporation of the City of London* was published in 1891. Löwy also became involved in the controversy over the Moabite stone at the Louvre, whose authenticity he disputed. In 1903 he printed for private circulation *A Critical Examination of the So-called Moabite Inscription in the Louvre*. Löwy's reputation as an excellent teacher made him a fashionable tutor in high society, and his pupils included Archibald Tait, archbishop of Canterbury, the marquess of Bute, and the editor of *The Times*, Thomas Chenery. Löwy was a member of the council of the Society of Biblical Archæology. One of his daughters, Bella Löwy, edited the English translation (5 vols., 1891) of Heinrich Graetz's *Geschichte der Juden*. M. EPSTEIN, *rev.* SINÉAD AGNEW

Sources *The Times* (22 May 1908), 12 · *Jewish Chronicle* (15 Feb 1907), 16–17 · *Jewish Chronicle* (27 May 1908), 1, 7–8 · private information (1912)

Likenesses J. Solomon, double portrait (with his son Ernest), RA · photograph, repro. in *Jewish Chronicle* (27 May 1908) · tablet, West London Synagogue, Upper Berkeley Street, London

Wealth at death £1224 1s. 8d.: probate, 6 June 1908, *CGPLA Eng. & Wales*

Loy [*formerly* Lowy; *married names* Haweis, Lloyd], **Mina Gertrude** (1882–1966), poet and painter, was born on 27 December 1882 in Hampstead, London, the first of the three daughters of Sigmund Felix Lowy (1848–1917), a Hungarian Jewish tailor, and Julia Bryan (1860–1942), daughter of George Bryan, carpenter and cabinet-maker, and his wife, Ann. Mina adapted Lowy to Loy in 1904, for her submission to the Salon d'Automne in Paris.

Loy spent her childhood in London; she was educated first at home in Hampstead, and then at a progressive school nearby. Her parents wanted nothing more for her than a good marriage, but she was able to escape her repressive upbringing and domineering mother by attending art school: in 1897 she went to St John's Wood School and in 1900–01 spent a year at the Munich Künstlerinnenverein, the Society of Female Artists' school. She completed her art training at the Académie Colarossi in Paris (1902–3). It was Loy's fellow students, however, who provided her with a more lasting influence than any artistic instruction she received, initiating her in the bohemian ways of life as artistic creation.

Loy's first marriage on 31 December 1903 to the painter and photographer Stephen Haweis (Hugh Oscar William Haweis; *b.* 1878) was not happy and after the death from meningitis of their one-year-old daughter they separated in 1906. Loy's subsequent affair with Henry Joël le Savoureux, a French doctor, resulted in a daughter, Joella, but Loy and Haweis were later reconciled (Loy's income from her father was dependent on the success of her marriage). In 1907 they settled in Florence where they had a son, Giles.

During her years in Florence, Loy came into contact with futurism: she showed some of her paintings at the first Free Futurist International Exhibition in Rome, and had a brief affair with F. T. Marinetti. Loy was impressed by Marinetti's *parole-in-libertà* and his bold assault on language inspired her to try writing herself. Her 'Aphorisms in Futurism', a cross between a prose poem and a futurist-style manifesto, was published in *Camera Work* in 1914, introducing Loy to an American audience.

In 1916 Loy left her children in Florence and moved to New York. There she met the boxer and poet Arthur Cravan (Fabian Avenarius Lloyd; 1887–1918). She fell deeply in love and, when Cravan left America to evade military service, Loy went with him. After her divorce from Haweis in 1917, they married in Mexico on 25 January 1918; they lived for a year in squalid poverty before Cravan disappeared while testing a boat he planned to escape in. He was presumed drowned, but reported sightings continued to haunt Loy for the rest of her life.

After Cravan's disappearance Loy, who was four months pregnant, travelled via South America to England where she gave birth to a daughter, Fabienne. Loy then returned briefly to Florence to see her other children, before leaving them behind to settle once more in New York. This was a particularly productive period for Loy and her poetry began to appear in some of the many small magazines, such as *Little Review* and *Dial*. However, provoked by the news that Haweis had moved with Giles to the Caribbean, Loy returned to Florence. Loy found that in her absence her daughters had become staid and middle-class and so she took them with her to Berlin where Joella was enrolled in a dance school. Yet the reunion did not last long: this time Loy was drawn to Paris and her daughters were once again left in the charge of their nurse. Giles wrote to her in Paris but, with perhaps characteristic obduracy, Loy refused to reply and only a few years later he died of cancer.

Celebrated for her beauty and vivacity, Loy moved within the large circle of artists and intellectuals living in Paris, which included Joyce, Brancusi, Pound, and Duchamp, as well as Gertrude Stein, whose vital approach to language influenced Loy's work. It was also during this time that her first book was published, a collection of thirty-one poems entitled *Lunar Baedeker*. It included in abbreviated form her best-known work, 'Love Songs', a thirty-four poem sequence, which is at once passionate and analytical. The first four poems had been published in *Others* in 1915, but their sexual explicitness had provoked a violent reaction, which made it difficult to publish the rest.

Loy returned to New York in 1940 and in 1946 she became a naturalized American citizen. Fabienne looked after her mother until 1948 when she moved into a rooming house. There, inspired by the people living on the streets, Loy began making three-dimensional collages using rubbish she had picked up. In 1958 she had a second volume of poems published, *Lunar Baedeker & Time-Tables* and in 1959 there was an exhibition of her 'constructions' at the Bodley Gallery in New York. However, over the last decades of her life, Loy became increasingly eccentric and withdrawn, unable to come to terms with her age and fading beauty. Her final move, to be nearer her two daughters, was in 1953 to Aspen, Colorado, where she died of pneumonia on 25 September 1966; she was buried there.

In her time, Loy was considered a representative 'modern woman' and she is perhaps remembered more for her charm, wit, and beauty than for her work. Her painting has almost completely disappeared from view and, until recently, her writing had similarly been neglected and forgotten. As well as poetry, Loy wrote a novel, *Insel*, essays, plays (two of which, following futurist rules for the reinvention of drama, take about one minute to perform and contain no dialogue), memoirs, and a utopian tract, *Psycho-Democracy: a Movement to Focus Human Reason on the Conscious Direction of Evolution* (1921). The advent of feminist criticism led to republication of Loy's poetry, and a reappraisal of its place in the modernist enterprise. The structural law breaking of her poetry was influenced by her ideas about sexual difference, and the subject matter of her writing also frequently returns to women's experience. The poem 'Parturition' (1914), for example, attempts to speak directly from the female body and capture the rhythms of labour. While Loy's writing is certainly of historical interest, as an expression of a particular time and milieu, her poetic achievement was uneven and it is perhaps for this reason that the question of her reputation remains unsettled. RACHEL COTTAM

Sources C. Burke, *Becoming modern: the life of Mina Loy* (1996) • C. Burke, 'Mina Loy', *The gender of modernism: a critical anthology*, ed. B. K. Scott (1990) • Y. Winters, *The Dial*, 80 (1926), 496–9 • J. E. Miller, 'Pig Cupid's rosy snout', *The London Review of Books* (19 June 1996) • S. Benstock, *Women of the left bank: Paris, 1900–1940* (1987) • J. Rothenberg, ed., *Revolution of the word: a new gathering of American avant garde poetry, 1914–1945* (1974) • V. M. Kouidis, *Mina Loy: American modernist poet* (1980) • R. L. Conover, 'Introduction', *The last lunar Baedeker*, ed. R. L. Conover (1982) • M. Shreiber and K. Tuma, eds., *Mina Loy: woman and poet* (1996) [incl. annotated bibliography of pubd work and references to her by others]

Archives Yale U., MSS | Col. U., Stephen Haweis MSS

Likenesses M. Loy, self-portrait, *c*.1905, Joella Bayer collection; repro. in Conover, ed., *Last lunar Baedeker* • S. Haweis, photographs, Haweis family collection • S. Haweis, portrait, University of Columbia, Rare Book and Manuscript Library

Loyd, Samuel Jones, Baron Overstone (1796–1883), banker, was born on 25 September 1796 at 43 Lothbury, in the City of London, the only child of the Revd Lewis Loyd (*d*. 1858), a nonconformist clergyman and banker, and his wife, Sarah (*d*. 1821), the daughter of John Jones, a Manchester banker and manufacturer. Lewis Loyd came from a Carmarthenshire family and it was probably he who was responsible for the change in the family name from Lloyd to Loyd. Having given up his ministry, Lewis Loyd was employed at the Manchester bank owned by Jones, and in 1793 married his daughter.

Lewis Loyd proved to be a brilliant banker and, together with his brothers-in-law, Samuel and William Jones, was one of the founders of Jones, Loyd & Co. Loyd moved to London to establish a branch office there, and went on to transform a small country bank into one of the leading

Samuel Jones Loyd, Baron Overstone (1796–1883), by Frank Holl, 1881

private banks in the country. After the death of Sarah, he married again, and increased his already large fortune considerably. He retired from business and bought Overstone Park, and an estate of 15,000 acres, near Northampton; in 1854 he also acquired the manor of East Lockinge in Berkshire. Lewis Loyd died in 1858 at the age of ninety-one, leaving an estate of several million pounds.

Samuel Jones Loyd was born over the bank's premises in the heart of London. His birth was registered with the Unitarians at Dr Williams's Library, but he was brought up a member of the Church of England. He was educated privately before going to Eton College (*c*.1808–*c*.1813). He then spent some time as a private pupil with C. J. Blomfield, later bishop of London, before going on to Trinity College, Cambridge. He graduated in 1818, but had already become a partner in his father's bank, being admitted on 26 December 1816. His father retired in 1844 and the Manchester and London businesses were formally divided in 1848. In 1819 Loyd was elected liberal member of parliament for Hythe, by a majority of sixty-seven, remaining member until 1826, when he did not offer himself for re-election. In December 1832 he stood for Manchester, but was defeated, coming third in the poll. He never again stood for parliament.

In 1829 Loyd married Harriet (*d*. 1864), daughter of Ichabod Wright, a Nottingham banker. They had two children, a son who died aged only three months, and a daughter, Harriet Sarah (*b*. 1837), who married Robert Lindsay in 1858 [*see* Lindsay, Harriet Sarah Loyd-]; at their marriage the Lockinge estate was settled on the couple. Samuel Loyd's wife died in November 1864, and it is clear from his surviving correspondence that he was overwhelmed with grief.

Samuel Loyd exhibited great skill as a banker, and the continued profitability and development of the bank's business was largely due to him. It has been estimated that between 1817 and 1848 the bank returned profits of £2.2 million, 'of which Overstone collected £563,000 or an average of £18,161 per annum as his share' (Michie, 60). Nevertheless, as a practising banker he was always very cautious, carefully weighing risk, especially on loans, with the result that during the years of his association with his bank it never made a loss. At the same time, however, it slowly stagnated, as he refused to countenance the changes in banking practice which were taking place in the 1840s, his real interests lying in currency theory. Thus he always remained opposed to the joint-stock principle, believing it would reduce the personal element in banking and that joint-stock banks did not keep stable reserve ratios. He also remained committed to unlimited liability, thinking this would induce a proper caution in a banker's activities.

In 1831 Loyd was elected a member of the Political Economy Club, remaining a member until 1872, when he was chosen as an honorary member. Also in 1831 he was appointed an exchequer bill commissioner and in 1832 he appeared before the select committee on the renewal of the charter of the Bank of England. In 1837 he published his first pamphlet, *Reflections suggested by a perusal of Mr. J. Horsley Palmer's pamphlet on the causes and consequences of the pressure on the money markets*, which recognized the importance of psychological factors on the trade cycle. The pamphlet was very well received and marked Loyd's début as an influential figure in banking and financial circles. Between 1837 and 1840 he was a member of the commission on hand-loom weavers, and in 1838 he appeared before the select committee on postage. Further pamphlets on currency matters appeared in 1840, including *Remarks on the Management of the Currency*, in which he strongly defended convertibility.

In 1844 Loyd's *Thoughts on the Separation of the Departments of the Bank of England* appeared. This work had been privately printed in 1840, and was particularly influential. It made Loyd the chief spokesman of the currency school of monetary theorists. In it he advocated a single bank of issue of paper money, as well as the separation of the banking and issue departments of the Bank of England. The proper function of the Bank of England was, in his opinion, to regulate the amount and secure the solidity of the paper issues, and to afford a safe place of deposit for government and public money. Loyd undoubtedly influenced the content of Sir Robert Peel's Bank Charter Act of 1844, for his views were closely reflected in the terms of the act. He had appeared before the select committee on banks of issue in 1840, and was able to put his views before Sir Robert Peel, who attended meetings regularly. The act provided for the division of the Bank of England into an issue department and a banking department, as Loyd had proposed, and prohibited the issue of bank notes by anyone who was not already an issuer. Loyd came to feel an almost personal responsibility for the act and its workings, so that the suspension of the act during the financial crisis of 1857 disturbed him greatly.

Loyd now commanded wide public respect, but consistently refused all invitations to stand again for parliament. His advice was widely sought, for example by Lord John Russell, and by Sir Charles Wood, later first Viscount Halifax, who consulted him for thirty years and, on becoming chancellor of the exchequer in 1846, openly acknowledged his debt to him. In 1846 he became chairman of the British Association for the Relief of the Extreme Distress in Ireland and Scotland, making his own considerable personal contributions to the funds of the association.

In October 1849 he was offered a peerage by Lord John Russell, for whom he had considerable respect. He was both surprised and dismayed at this offer, and took a fortnight to decide to accept; it was March 1850 before he took his seat in the House of Lords. He rarely spoke in the house, but served on a number of select committees, including that on the Turner and Vernon bequests. In 1850 he became a trustee of the National Gallery, and he was one of the commissioners for the Great Exhibition of 1851. His interest in art was genuine, and he formed his own collection of paintings, which included works by Ruysdael, Hobbema, Rembrandt, Lorrain, Murillo, Cuyp, Crome, and Stanfield.

A member of the British Association for the Advancement of Science, in June of 1864 Loyd was created honorary DCL by the University of Oxford. He was a member of the commission appointed to consider decimal coinage, to which he was always strongly opposed. He became a member of the council of the University of London in 1828, serving until 1844. He was a member of the senate of the university from 1850 until 1877, when he resigned in opposition to proposals to award degrees to women.

Loyd gave up direct involvement in banking upon his elevation to the peerage. When the other partners wished to retire the two branches of his bank were taken over by joint-stock companies, the Manchester branch in 1863 by the Manchester and Liverpool District Bank and the London branch by the London and Westminster Bank in 1864. As his interests in banking and currency matters receded, so he became increasingly interested in the management of his estates. Loyd bought 5000 acres at Wing, in north Buckinghamshire, and rebuilt the house at Overstone, employing the architect William Milford Teulon. He also spent much money on improving the dwellings of the agricultural labourers on his estates.

In his last years Loyd became increasingly conservative and withdrew more and more from public life. His eyesight began to fail, and for at least the last two years of his life he seems to have been confined to a wheelchair. His religious beliefs became steadily more austere, and he became more and more lonely and dependent upon his daughter, spending much of his time with her at Lockinge. Nevertheless, he retained a strong sense of humour. He died peacefully on 17 November 1883 at his London home, 2 Carlton Gardens, a house which he had bought from the widow of William Huskisson, shortly after that MP's death. He was buried at Lockinge beside his wife. The prince of Wales sent a letter of condolence to his daughter, and Queen Victoria was represented at his funeral. He left securities valued at £2,118,084 and landed property worth £3,114,262, making him one of the wealthiest men in the country at that time.

The important role that Loyd played in banking reform was well described in a *Times* obituary, which also mentioned that he was

> one of those men who in a measure outlive their reputation as they survive their contemporaries. He did his country most valuable service in his time but the time was long ago … and it is nearly a quarter of a century since his name has come prominently before the public.

The obituary continued, however:

> in the fulness of his practical knowledge he submitted the whole of our banking system with its subsidiary monetary questions to a severely scientific analysis, bringing theories and ideas to the test of experience, drawing logical deductions from closely sifted premisses, and marshalling deliberate conclusions in his mind with a wonderful lucidity of method. (*The Times*, 19 Nov 1883)

MICHAEL REED

Sources *The correspondence of Lord Overstone*, ed. D. P. O'Brien, 3 vols. (1971) • R. C. Michie, 'Loyd, Samuel Jones', *DBB* • *The Times* (19 Nov 1883) • *The Times* (20 Nov 1883) • *The Times* (29 Nov 1883) • M. A. Havinden, D. S. Thornton, and P. D. Wood, *Estate villages: a study of the Berkshire villages of Ardington and Lockinge* (1966) • B. Hilton, *The age of atonement: the influence of evangelicalism on social and economic thought, 1795–1865* (1988) • S. J. L. Overstone, rev., *Catalogue of the library, Overstone Park* (privately printed, 1867), 355 [This library consisted mostly of the collection of Jonathan Ramsay McCulloch, which was purchased by Lord Overstone. This catalogue is one of a few copies printed for the owner's private use.] • R. C. Michie, 'Income, expenditure and investment of a Victorian millionaire: Lord Overstone, 1823–83', *BIHR*, 58 (1985), 59–77

Archives LUL, corresp. and papers • Northants. RO, account books | Borth. Inst., letters to Lord Halifax • PRO, letters to Lord Granville, PRO 30/29

Likenesses photograph, *c*.1866, repro. in O'Brien, ed., *Correspondence of Lord Overstone*, vol. 1, frontispiece • F. Holl, oils, 1880, U. Reading; repro. in O'Brien, ed., *Correspondence of Lord Overstone*, vol. 3, frontispiece • F. Holl, oils, 1881, priv. coll. [*see illus.*] • Count Gleichen, statue, 1883, U. Reading L.

Wealth at death £2,118,803 17*s*. 3*d*.: probate, 31 Dec 1883, *CGPLA Eng. & Wales* • £2,118,084 securities • £3,114,262 landed property: O'Brien, *Correspondence*

Lozikeyi (*c*.**1845–1919**), Ndebele queen of Bulawayo, was one of Cecil Rhodes's most effective opponents. Her father was Ngogo Dlodlo, and her mother was MaTshabalala, whose mother was Nxongo. Ngogo Dlodlo's family are said to have been kings in Zululand. A Dlodlo called Mpangazitha was inyanga (healer) to Matshobane, King Lobengula's grandfather. Lozikeyi was brought up in what is now Matabeleland South and, at her marriage (date unknown) to King *Lobengula (*c*.1835–1893/4?), moved to his court at (Old) Bulawayo.

Lozikeyi was the king's senior wife, and after 1880 was given control of the Ndebele (Matabele) war medicines. Marie Lippert describes her as controlling immigration at Bulawayo in October to November 1891. Surgeon-general Melladew describes her leading the nation at the *inxwala*, the most important Ndebele ceremony, in 1890. Lozikeyi had no children born to her, perhaps because barrenness was associated with the ceremonial role. Her surrogate, Mamfimfi, had a daughter Sidambe.

In 1893, as Dr L. S. Jameson and the British South Africa Company troops approached Bulawayo, King Lobengula had his capital destroyed. Queen Lozikeyi accompanied the king north to the last battle at Pupu near the Shangani River. After the king disappeared Queen Lozikeyi led Lobengula's other queens and the royal herds back towards the Ndebele heartland, settling at what is now Inkosikazi communal land (or Queen's Kraal) in Matabeleland North. In 1894 the land commission recommended, and the British South Africa Company subsequently granted, this area as a 'reserve' for Lobengula's widows. Queen Lozikeyi's court became a centre of resistance to the white regime: the local native commissioner Val Gielgud called her 'a most dangerous and intriguing woman' (Gielgud to chief native commissioner, 9 April 1897, Bulawayo, National Archives of Zimbabwe, LO 5/6/8, vol. 2).

In 1896 the Ndebele rose in revolt. Lozikeyi seems to have worked with her brother Umuntuwani Dlodlo, one of Rhodes's most implacable enemies, to organize resistance. Native commissioner Gielgud believed she distributed to Ndebele soldiers the Martini-Henry rifles given to King Lobengula under the Rudd concession. However, the uprising failed and the white invaders occupied most of the useful land in Matabeleland. By 1910 Queen Lozikeyi's people could nowhere freely grow crops or herd their cattle. She saw a vacuum of ideology: someone in authority had to interpret the terrible new reality and weave together the different religious traditions practised in northern Matabeleland. She therefore helped to make Christianity—according to the London Missionary Society—the hegemonic ideology of Matabeleland North.

Lozikeyi asked the Welsh London Missionary Society missionary Bowen Rees to send Matambo Ndlovu, an outstanding convert whom she considered to be of good clan, to preach at her court, where traditional Nguni practices from Zululand continued. Rees also collaborated with priests of the indigenous Mwali religion. London Missionary Society Christianity in Matabeleland North was therefore an inclusive religion and it fully involved women. The society brought reading and writing to fuel resistance to the invaders and it later provided inspiration to the nationalist Zimbabwe African People's Union which grew up around the mission stations.

Queen Lozikeyi died at Queen's Kraal, Matabeleland, on 23 February 1919, of febric cellulitis and sepsis following influenza. She left 901 cattle, a considerable herd. Native commissioner C. L. Carbutt described her as 'a woman of outstanding intelligence and personality, who maintained great influence over the Matabele' ('A brief account of the rise and fall of the Matebele', *Native Affairs Department Annual of Rhodesia*, 25, 1948, 43).

Queen Lozikeyi resisted the white invaders so effectively that Ndebele people still ask for help at her grave at Queen's Kraal. During the 1970s war of liberation, soldiers from the Zimbabwe people's revolutionary army put bullets on her grave to request her guidance. To Lozikeyi's other titles may be added 'Foremother of the Zimbabwe People's Revolutionary Army' and 'Foremother of Zimbabwe's Freedom'. MARIEKE FABER CLARKE

Sources National Archives of Zimbabwe [*passim*] · interview with Queen Lozikeyi's maid, MaTshuma [Mrs Sasiya Ndlovu] · T. O. Ranger, *Revolt in Southern Rhodesia, 1896–1897: a study in African resistance* (1967) · private information (2004) [governor of Matabeleland North Welshman Mabhena, and Mrs Mabhena; Mrs Elizabeth Mzilethi; ZIPRA soldiers; Pathisa Nyathi] · unpublished MSS of Bowen Rees translated by his grandson · *Native Affairs Department Annual of Rhodesia* (1948) · R. Palmer, *Land and racial discrimination in Rhodesia* (1977) · M. Lippert, *Matabele travel letters of Marie Lippert, 1891* (1960) · E. P. Mathers, *Surgeon-General Melladew in 'Zambesia'* (1891) · letter from V. Gielgud to chief native commissioner, 9 April 1897, National Archives of Zimbabwe, Bulawayo, MS LO 5/6/8, vol. 2

Archives SOAS, Council for World Mission (formerly LMS)

Likenesses J. Colenbrander, photograph, Bodl. RH · B. Rees, photographs, priv. coll.; copies, Bodl. RH, SOAS

Wealth at death 901 cattle: National Archives of Zimbabwe, Harare, native commissioner of Imyathi reports, 6 Dec 1919

Luard, (David) Evan Trant (**1926–1991**), politician and writer on international affairs, was born on 31 October 1926 at Park Cottage, Addington, Kent. He was the third child and second son of Colonel Trant Bramston Luard (1873–1976) of the Royal Marines, and his wife, Helen Anne Frances (1893–1981), *née* Evans. His father served in many countries and was awarded the DSO for service in the Middle East in the First World War; after his retirement he published a number of philosophical articles, in the *Hibbert Journal* and elsewhere. Luard grew up in Kent, and from 1934 in Cambridgeshire. In 1934–40 he attended (not as a chorister) King's College choir school, Cambridge, and in 1940–45 Felsted School, which had been evacuated from Essex to near Ross-on-Wye, Herefordshire. Towards the end of the Second World War, while still at school, he volunteered for the Fleet Air Arm, serving in it for a few days before the war ended, when his services were no longer needed. He arranged to take up, in 1946, a scholarship he had been awarded at King's College, Cambridge. In the meantime he worked at Miller's music shop in Cambridge, and learned to play the piano, remaining an enthusiastic pianist thereafter. In 1947 he achieved a first in part one in modern languages (doing French and German). He then switched to music, doing another part one examination in 1949, in which he got a disappointing third. Passing two part one examinations allowed the candidate to graduate with an ordinary BA, that is a pass degree, without honours. An active sportsman, he was president of the King's College Athletics Club in 1948–9.

When he left Cambridge in 1949, Luard expected to do national service—only to be told that his three days' service in 1945 sufficed. He applied to the Foreign Office, but had to wait a year before he could take an entry examination. In the meantime, to broaden his outlook, he worked in a factory in Shepherd's Bush, London. In October 1950 he entered the foreign service, learned Chinese in London and Hong Kong, and was then posted to Beijing (Peking), from September 1952 to August 1954. During the Suez crisis he was serving in London. On 5 November 1956, when the Anglo-French military action against Egypt was running into heavy criticism inside the Foreign Office as well as at the United Nations and elsewhere, he submitted a letter of resignation, stating

(David) Evan Trant Luard (1926–1991), by Godfrey Argent, 1970

> I belong to a generation which was brought up in the belief that for one nation to undertake the use of armed force against another in order to promote its own interests is morally wrong. I grew up during a war which, I understood, was fought for the establishment of that principle. When I joined the Foreign Service I was conscious that this country was a member of the United Nations and had entered into a solemn undertaking to act in accordance with the Charter of that Organisation. … Here it is a question of an action of the Government that I serve which in my eyes seems to have betrayed everything for which I had believed that this country stood … (Luard to Henniker-Major, 5 Nov 1956)

Luard was one of a very few members of the diplomatic service who resigned over Suez. Others were persuaded not to do so by, among others, Anthony Nutting, the junior minister at the Foreign Office whose own resignation was announced on 3 November.

Having left the foreign service at the age of thirty, Luard turned to research and writing on international relations. In 1957 he was appointed to a research fellowship at St Antony's College, Oxford. He was to retain an association with the college, and to live in Oxford, for the rest of his life. His research on China was funded for two years by the Eastern Metals and Mining Company, and then by a grant from the Leverhulme Trust for a book, *Britain and China* (1962). St Antony's was not always able to find funding for him thereafter, but it provided accommodation for him until 1980, when he bought his own small terraced house nearby in Observatory Street. He did occasional teaching at Oxford, mainly in the earlier years, but never held a university post. It was at Oxford that he wrote his books, embarked on a political career first on the city council (1958–61) and then in parliament, and performed many services for Oxfam (for which he worked from 1980 to 1983).

In 1966–70 and 1974–9 Luard served as the first (and, as it transpired, only) Labour MP for the Oxford constituency, subsequently dissolved in boundary revisions. Characteristically active and conscientious as an MP, at the same time he continued writing and took on other responsibilities. He was a member of the UK delegation to the UN general assembly in 1967 and 1968; and in 1975 he was appointed by the UN secretary-general to the ad hoc committee on the restructuring of the economic and social sectors of the UN system. In violation of the unwritten rule that ministers should be lay figures unburdened by professional expertise, he had two spells (from October 1969 to June 1970 and from April 1976 to May 1979) as under-secretary of state at the Foreign Office. In this situation, where irritation or offence might easily have been caused—both on account of his knowledge, and on account of his earlier resignation—he earned the affection and respect of both the diplomats and the ministers with whom he worked. David Owen, foreign secretary from February 1977 to May 1979, later wrote:

> He was an unassuming, quiet person but of firm determination and tenacious will … I found Evan's specialised knowledge immensely valuable when we both served together in the FCO. He brought to United Nations matters and all aspects of international law an attractive mix of enthusiasm and calculation. (*Daily Telegraph*)

Luard's political position, reflected in all his work, can be crudely summarized as right-wing Labour, but with an exceptionally strong admixture of belief in the centrality of moral principle, international organization, and overseas aid. In the early 1980s he joined the newly formed Social Democratic Party, which was at that time the party that most closely reflected his political philosophy. His last parliamentary campaign was fought unsuccessfully in June 1983 under its colours for the new Oxford West and Abingdon constituency.

Between 1959 and his death Luard wrote no fewer than eighteen books, co-authored one, and edited seven. Of these twenty-six books, five were reissued in revised editions. All these works, as well as numerous articles and pamphlets, were in the field of international relations broadly conceived. Following the concentration on China in the first two works, his *Peace and Opinion* (1962) staked out a number of themes which were to remain central to his world vision: man is more adaptable than other species, though not perhaps enough for the dangers he now faces; it is of limited use to set up systems of authority called states, if between them there is still murderous anarchy; nuclear weapons, horrific as they are, may have reduced the likelihood of war; general and complete disarmament is not going to be achieved; a more peaceful world must be sought by reforming the behaviour of states; and international society is slowly becoming more law-abiding. Of his subsequent works, *The Control of the Sea-Bed* (1974; rev. 1977) was a notably well-timed call for international regulation of under-sea resources, appearing as it did early in the negotiations (1973–82) which led to the adoption of the UN convention on the law of the sea. One book sold particularly well: the comparatively short *The United Nations: How it Works and What it Does* (1979). Luard also embarked on a multi-volume *History of the United Nations*, and by the time of his death had published the first two volumes (1982, 1989), covering the years 1945–65.

In his substantial writings Luard did not claim to be an academic historian working on original documents. He was not a discoverer of new facts, or an inventor of new theories. He covered a vast canvas, the world; and a huge time span, centuries past, present, and future. He often wrote prescriptively, especially in calling for redistribution between richer and poorer countries. In the age of the specialist it was impossible to do these things without risking criticism. Yet his works had solid merits. He was knowledgeable on all the subjects he tackled. Eschewing rhetoric, he wrote elegantly and clearly. He was less interested in addressing topical issues of the day, whether Vietnam or nuclear weapons deployments, than deeper and longer-term questions. His books tackled subjects—including human rights and the internationalization of civil wars—which were often neglected during the cold war, but which later proved to be of enduring importance. The fact that certain themes were repeated was a reflection of his moral concern about them. Above all, he sought to make sense of the times through which he lived. Towards the end of his life the crumbling of communist regimes and the growing role of the UN suggested that his cautious belief in progress was not misplaced.

A slim, wiry figure of medium height, Luard's manner was unassuming. His performance at public meetings, including political ones, was judicious, reasonable, and understated. Generous with his time in helping others, he combined friendliness, charm, and clarity of mind. He lived unostentatiously in Oxford, often on a modest income. The disciplined austerity of his life was tempered by a love of gardening as well as of the piano. He never married, but had many friends. Although he cut down on public speaking when (about five years before his death) he lost his larynx, he worked hard to recover a natural articulation, and was proud that he could still give the occasional talk. He died of lung cancer on 8 February 1991 at his sister's home, 1 St Mary's Grove, Putney, London, and was cremated at Mortlake crematorium. A memorial meeting was held at St Antony's College, Oxford, on 1 June 1991.

ADAM ROBERTS

Sources E. Luard, letter of resignation to J. P. E. C. Henniker-Major, 5 Nov 1956, priv. coll. • C. S. Nicholls, *The history of St Antony's College, Oxford, 1950–2000* (2000), esp. pp. 23, 77, 81–3, 250, 257 • A. Roberts, 'Evan Luard as a writer on international affairs', *Review of International Studies*, 18/1 (Jan 1992) • private information (2004) [Pauline Williamson (sister); J. Bennett; A. Shlaim] • *Daily Telegraph* (11 Feb 1991) • *The Guardian* (11 Feb 1991) • *The Independent* (11 Feb 1991) • *The Times* (11 Feb 1991) • *WWW*, 1991–5 • *Annual Report of the*

Council [King's College Cambridge] (1992), 63–4 • *Historical register of the University of Cambridge*, 11 vols. (1917–91) • A. E. Campbell, P. A. Cornthwaite, and H. B. F. Dixon, *Register of admissions to King's College, Cambridge, 1919–1990* (1998) • *Yearbook—United Nations* (1967), 1019 • *Yearbook—United Nations* (1968), 1123 • A. Nutting, *No end of a lesson: the story of Suez* (1967)

Archives priv. coll., MSS • priv. coll., letters and papers

Likenesses G. Argent, photograph, 1970, NPG [*see illus.*] • photograph, repro. in *Daily Telegraph* • photograph, repro. in *The Guardian* • photograph, repro. in *The Independent* • photograph, repro. in *The Times* • photographs, priv. coll.

Wealth at death £242,667: probate, 4 Sept 1991, *CGPLA Eng. & Wales*

Luard, Henry (1792–1860), banker, was born on 4 December 1792, the fifth son of Captain Peter John Luard (*d.* 1830) of Blyborough Hall, Lincolnshire, and his wife Louisa, daughter of Charles Dalbiac, of Hungerford Park, Wiltshire. Luard was one of eight brothers; he had no sisters. His eldest brother inherited the Lincolnshire property on the death of their father in 1830. Of the remaining six, three entered the army, two the church, and one took up a medical career.

By contrast, Henry Luard, the only son not educated for a profession, was taken on at an early age by a mercantile trading house, probably in the City of London. His intuitive grasp of figures was recognized at once and he was quickly promoted to the responsible position of ledger keeper. This provided him with a sound commercial education, laying the groundwork for a long career in banking and commerce. A man of stout physical appearance, Luard, with widespread family connections and a number of distinguished musical attainments, moved easily between the business world of the City and the pleasant diversions of polite metropolitan society. On 13 November 1824 he married Jane, daughter of William Richards of Clatford, Hampshire. Together they had four sons, the eldest being Henry Richards *Luard, university registrary.

By the 1830s Luard's career was firmly in the ascendant, with appointments as director of the London Life Association and deputy chairman of the Southampton Dock Company. Luard was chiefly known, however, for his role as general manager of the London and County Bank between 1841 and 1856. Established in 1836, the London and County Bank was one of the new wave of joint-stock banks formed in the metropolis following the liberalization afforded by the Bank Charter Act of 1833. Despite considerable business success, the bank quickly gained a reputation as a somewhat unlucky institution, and its first two decades were marred by ill-judged and, on occasion, fraudulent activities on the part of its most senior managers. Luard's appointment in 1841 was, in fact, occasioned by the unexplained disappearance of the previous general manager Thomas Dighton in connection with serious errors of commercial judgement.

Showing strong determination of character, allied to his long-standing financial experience and an iron constitution, Luard worked unceasingly to remedy the bank's affairs, instituting a series of structural reforms in the operation and management of the bank. That he did so with the full co-operation, even admiration, of his colleagues is clearly evident in the report of a testimonial organized in 1853 by his branch managers:

> to record their high and grateful sense of the valuable and effective management of Henry Luard, Esq., the company's general manager. To his urbanity and gentlemanly deportment, combined with those rare talents which so eminently qualify him for the responsible post he fills, may be attributed, they feel, in a very great degree, the well-regulated and gratifying harmony which has characterised the conduct of their business for the several past years. (*Bankers' Magazine*, 13, 1853, 752)

Within three years such sentiments must have carried a distinctly hollow ring: on 25 March 1856 Henry Luard resigned as general manager of the London and County Bank, on the grounds of irregular conduct of the bank's affairs which had left him deeply indebted both to the bank and to several other parties connected with it. An internal investigation following the suicide of the bank's chairman, John Sadler MP, who had been forging shares, revealed a number of dubious transactions, including unsecured loans (likely to produce a loss of £10,000 for the bank) in favour of parties to whom Luard was personally indebted. It appeared also that his personal finances bordered on insolvency.

Despite this fall from grace, which brought such a sudden end to Luard's banking career, recognition is due for the many sound advances in the treatment of bank employees that he helped to promote, of which the establishment of a provident fund for their long-term protection was of especial note. Within a few short years Luard was dead. His body was found in a field at Thornbury, Devon, on 20 May 1860. An inquest held on the 21st revealed that he died suddenly, of unknown causes.

IAIN S. BLACK

Sources 'Biographical sketch of Henry Luard', *Bankers' Magazine*, 14 (1854), 1–11 • T. E. Gregory and A. Henderson, *The Westminster Bank through a century*, 1 (privately printed, London, 1936), 353–66 • 'London and County Joint-Stock Bank: testimonial to Mr Henry Luard, the chief manager', *Bankers' Magazine*, 13 (1853), 752–4 • I. S. Black, 'Money, information and space: banking in early nineteenth-century England and Wales', *Journal of Historical Geography*, 21 (1995), 398–412 • Burke, *Gen. GB* • *IGI* • *Bankers' Magazine*, 20 (1860), 525 • d. cert.

Likenesses Denison, daguerreotype, in or before 1854, repro. in 'Biographical sketch of Henry Luard, Esq.'

Wealth at death bordered on insolvency at death; deeply indebted both to London and County Bank and to others connected with it; owed the bank £5500 for loans

Luard, Henry Richards (1825–1891), university administrator, eldest son of Henry *Luard (1792–1860), London banker, and his wife, Jane Richards, was born in London on 17 August 1825. His uncle was John *Luard. He was educated at Cheam School under Charles Mayo, and between 1841 and 1843 at King's College, London. He took up residence at Trinity College, Cambridge, in October 1843. In 1846 he obtained a college scholarship, and in 1847 graduated BA. He was fourteenth in the first class of the mathematical tripos, lower than expected, but he was later said to have been in bad health at the time of the examination. In 1849 he was elected to a fellowship at Trinity College.

Henry Richards Luard (1825–1891), by unknown photographer

He proceeded MA in 1850, BD in 1875, and DD in 1878. He was for a short time mathematical lecturer in Trinity College, and was junior bursar from 1853 to 1862. In 1855 he was ordained deacon and priest, and from 1860 to 1887 he was vicar of Great St Mary's, Cambridge. In January 1862 he was elected registrary of the university, in succession to Joseph Romilly, and on 19 June in the same year he married Louisa Calthorpe, youngest daughter of George Hodson, archdeacon of Stafford and canon of Lichfield; they had one son, who died in June 1891. In 1875 he was elected honorary fellow of King's College, London.

Luard was a pre-Tractarian high-churchman opposed to ritualism, but tolerant of those who differed from him. He was an energetic parish clergyman, an active parish visitor and an eloquent preacher. During his incumbency much of Great St Mary's was restored. He found the church still encumbered by the eastern gallery, nicknamed Golgotha, in which the vice-chancellor and heads of colleges sat; but he persuaded the senate to accept a plan which included the removal of both eastern and western galleries, and the reseating of the nave and chancel. These works were carried out in 1863, and the church was reopened for services on 2 February 1864.

Although he took his degree in mathematics, Luard was a good classical scholar, with a particular interest in the English critics of the eighteenth and early nineteenth centuries. Among these his hero was Richard Porson, whose work he began to collect and edit even as an undergraduate. He contributed a 'Life of Porson' to the *Cambridge Essays* (1857), and to the ninth edition of the *Encyclopaedia Britannica*, and he bequeathed his extensive collection of Porsoniana to the library of Trinity College. It had been anticipated that he would collaborate with W. G. Clark in editing the Cambridge Shakespeare (1863–6), but his appointment as university registrary prevented more than a preliminary edition of Act I of *Richard II* (1860). As registrary of the university he was accurate and industrious. With the help of his clerk he rearranged the documents under his charge, binding each group in a volume, with a separate index. These indices were afterwards united so as to form a comprehensive guide to the whole body of records. In 1870 he published *A chronological list of the graces, documents, and other papers in the university registry which concern the university library.* He took a close interest in the university library, sharing in the printed catalogues of manuscripts (1856–67) and of adversaria (1864). Luard was by temperament and conviction a conservative, and he was opposed to most of the changes during his lifetime in the university and in Trinity College: he wrote several fly-sheets and short pamphlets on the subject.

In addition to his university duties and influenced by S. R. Maitland, Luard edited for the Master of the Rolls series a long list of works, upon which his reputation as a historian chiefly rests. He approached his task with scrupulous care, and compiled the indices with precision, but at the same time the introductions are distinguished by wide historical knowledge. The first of these, *Lives of Edward the Confessor*, was published in 1858, when Luard, still a novice, was much helped by J. E. B. Mayor. The principal piece in the volume is a metrical life of the saint in old French (Cambridge UL, MS Ee.3.59), to which Luard appended a translation and glossary. Sixteen years afterwards Robert Atkinson of Dublin published 'Strictures on Mr. Luard's edition of a French poem on the life of Edward the Confessor' in *Hermathena* (1, 1–81). Undoubtedly Luard had made mistakes but the attack was ill-tempered and tardy, especially in view of Luard's fine record as a Rolls Series editor: his *Annales monastici* (1864–9) is still the standard and unchallenged edition of this text. Luard made no reply to Atkinson but it was well known that the attack affected him greatly, and probably contributed to the illness which he suffered between 1877 and 1880. During those years he was obliged to go abroad and to ask the university to appoint a deputy registrary. Returning in better health, he continued to work for the Rolls Series on Matthew Paris's *Chronica majora* (1872–83), one of the best editions in the series. He also contributed articles to the *Dictionary of National Biography.* His recovery was, however, followed in 1889 by the death of his wife, to whom he was much attached; other symptoms appeared, and he died, after a long period of weakness and suffering, on 1 May 1891 at his home, 4 St Peter's Terrace, Cambridge. He is buried with his wife in St Giles's cemetery, Cambridge.

J. W. Clark, *rev.* David McKitterick

Sources J. W. Clark, *Old friends at Cambridge and elsewhere* (1900) • admission book, Trinity Cam. • Boase, *Mod. Eng. biog.* • S. Sandars,

Historical and architectural notes on Great Saint Mary's Church, Cambridge (1869) • Venn, *Alum. Cant.* • Burke, *Gen. GB* (1965–72)
Archives CUL • Trinity Cam. | U. Nott. L., letters to C. B. Marley
Likenesses L. Dickinson, oils, 1897, Trinity Cam. • photographs, Trinity Cam. [*see illus.*] • photographs, CUL • photographs, CUL, Cambridge Antiquarian Society collection
Wealth at death £31,618 4*s*. 6*d*.: resworn probate, Dec 1891, *CGPLA Eng. & Wales*

Luard, John (1790–1875), army officer, author, and artist, was the fourth son of Captain Peter John Luard (*d*. 23 May 1830) of the 4th light dragoons and of Blyborough, Kirton in Lindsey, Lincolnshire, and his wife, Louisa, daughter of Charles Dalbiac of Hungerford Park, Berkshire. He was born on 5 May 1790, served in the Royal Navy 1802–7, and on 25 May 1809 obtained a cornetcy without purchase in his father's former regiment, with which he served through the Peninsular campaigns of 1810–14. Afterwards he served with the 16th light dragoons (later lancers) as lieutenant at Waterloo and as captain at Bharatpur in 1825. In India he instructed his regiment in the use of the lance and was reportedly the first to use it in the British army, at Bharatpur. He exchanged to the 30th regiment in 1832, retired as major in 1834, and obtained a brevet lieutenant-colonelcy in 1838. In retirement he was a director of the London and South-Western railway. He had married in 1826 Elizabeth, daughter of Colonel William Scott HEICS; they had two daughters and four sons including Lieutenant-General Richard Luard and Major-General Frederick Luard.

Like others of his family, Luard had much artistic talent. He published *Views in India, St Helena, and Car Nicobar* (1835), illustrated by himself, and *History of the Dress of the British Soldier* (1852), which includes original sketches of military characters and costume from the Peninsular War. Luard died on 24 October 1875 at his home, The Cedars, Farnham, Surrey.

His second son, **John Dalbiac Luard** (1830–1860), army officer and artist, born at Blyborough on 31 October 1830, was educated at the Royal Military College, Sandhurst. He was appointed ensign without purchase in the 63rd in 1848, and transferred to the 82nd regiment. After obtaining his lieutenancy in 1853, he left the service to devote himself to art, and studied for a time under John Phillip RA. He exhibited his first picture at the Royal Academy in 1855, *A Church Door*. He spent the winter of 1855–6 in the Crimea with his brother, Major Luard, then on the headquarters staff at Sevastopol. In 1857 he exhibited a Crimean subject, *The Welcome Arrival* (National Army Museum), which, engraved, had some popularity, and two others in 1858. He was a friend of Millais, with whom he shared lodgings for a time. His health failed, and he died at Winterslow, near Salisbury, on 9 August 1860.

H. M. CHICHESTER, *rev.* JAMES FALKNER

Sources *Army List* • Burke, *Gen. GB* • *Hart's Army List* • Boase, *Mod. Eng. biog.* • Wood, *Vic. painters*, 2nd edn • J. Lunt, *Scarlet lancer* (1964) • Bryan, *Painters*
Likenesses portrait, repro. in Lunt, *Scarlet lancer* • woodcut, NPG; repro. in *The Graphic*, 12 (1875)
Wealth at death under £9000: probate, 2 Dec 1875, *CGPLA Eng. & Wales*

Luard, John Dalbiac (1830–1860). *See under* Luard, John (1790–1875).

Luard, Sir William Garnham (1820–1910), naval officer, born on 7 April 1820 at Witham, Essex, was eldest son in a family of five sons and six daughters of William Wright Luard (1786–1857) of Witham, and his wife, Charlotte (*d*. 1875), daughter of Thomas Garnham. The family was of Huguenot origin and had migrated to England on the revocation of the edict of Nantes, the chief branch settling at Blyborough, Lincolnshire, in 1747. To the elder line belonged Henry Richards Luard, John Luard, John Dalbiac Luard, and Charles Edward Luard (1839–1908) of Ightham, Kent, who served in the Royal Engineers, becoming colonel in 1886 and major-general in 1887.

William was educated at the Royal Naval College, Portsmouth, and in 1835 was rated midshipman and appointed to the frigate *Actaeon*. By his service as mate of the *Samarang* during the First Opium War he earned his commission as lieutenant, dated 4 May 1841. He was present in the squadron under Sir Gordon Bremer at the storming of Fort Taecockow on 7 January 1841, and at the capture of the Bogue (Humen) forts on 25 February, when the ships silenced the batteries at Anunghoy (Yaniangxie) and on North Wantong, which the Chinese believed to be impregnable. As a lieutenant he served in the *Isis* (44 guns), on the Cape of Good Hope station, and in the sloop *Grecian* (16 guns) on the south-east coast of the USA, and in April 1848 was appointed first lieutenant of the *Hastings* (72 guns), flagship of Sir Francis Collier in the East Indies. On 29 September 1850 he was promoted commander, and on the same day was appointed to command the *Serpent* (12 guns), in which he continued during the Second Anglo-Burmese War, taking part in the capture of Rangoon in April 1852, of Pegu in the following June, and other operations, and was mentioned in dispatches. He commanded the sloop *Star* on the south-east coast of the USA and from her was in August 1855 moved into the flagship as executive officer. On 11 March 1857 he was promoted captain. In 1858 he married Charlotte, third daughter of the Revd Henry du Cane of Witham, Essex. They had eight daughters and three sons, one of whom was Commander Herbert du Cane Luard RN.

In July 1860 Luard was appointed flag captain to the commander-in-chief at the Nore, and in November to the screw battleship *Conqueror* for the China station. In her he took part in the operations in Japan, superintending the landing of storming parties at the destruction of the Nagato batteries in the Strait of Shimonoseki in September 1864, for which he received the CB and was made a member of the Légion d'honneur (fourth class). In January 1869 he became flag captain to the admiral-superintendent of naval reserves, and was captain-superintendent of Sheerness Dockyard from May 1870 until he was promoted to flag rank on 1 January 1875.

Luard had no employment afloat as a flag officer, but was superintendent of Malta Dockyard from March 1878 until promoted vice-admiral on 15 June 1879. He afterwards served as chairman of several departmental committees, including that which inquired into the bursting of the *Thunderer*'s gun in January 1879, and in November 1882 he succeeded Sir Geoffrey Hornby as president of the Royal Naval College, Greenwich. He reached the rank of admiral on 31 March 1885, and a week later was placed on the retired list under the age clause. However, he held his appointment at Greenwich for six months after retirement. He was a deputy lieutenant and JP for Essex, and in 1897 was created KCB. He died at his home, The Lodge, Witham, Essex, on 19 May 1910, as the result of a carriage accident, and was buried at All Saints', Witham. He was survived by his wife.

L. G. C. Laughton, *rev.* Roger Morriss

Sources *The Times* (20–25 May 1910) • Burke, *Gen. GB* • G. S. Graham, *The China station: war and diplomacy, 1830–1860* (1978) • B. English, *John Company's last war* (1971) • E. Holt, *The opium wars in China* (1964) • Kelly, *Handbk* • O'Byrne, *Naval biog. dict.* • *CGPLA Eng. & Wales* (1910)

Likenesses S. Luard, portrait, 1905; last known at Ivy Chimneys, Witham, Essex, 1912

Wealth at death £18,421 3*s.* 3*d.*: resworn probate, 8 July 1910, *CGPLA Eng. & Wales*

Lubbock, John, first Baron Avebury (1834–1913), banker, politician, and scientific writer, was born on 30 April 1834 at 29 Eaton Place, London, the eldest of eleven children of Sir John William *Lubbock, third baronet (1803–1865), and his wife, Harriet Hotham (*d.* 1873). His father and grandfather were both partners in the London banking firm of Lubbock, Foster & Co. (called Robarts, Lubbock & Co. between 1860 and its merger with Coutts & Co. in 1914). Lubbock moved to High Elms, near Downe, in Kent, in 1840, when his father succeeded to the baronetcy. Sir John William Lubbock was a successful amateur mathematician and astronomer and a good friend of Charles Darwin, who moved to Down in 1841 and acted as the younger Lubbock's informal tutor in natural history. Between 1845 and 1849 Lubbock attended Eton College, the last formal education he would receive. In 1849 his father assumed active duty at the family bank following the death of both his partners, and called on the younger Lubbock to assist as a clerk.

In 1856 John Lubbock married Ellen Frances (Nelly) Hordern, the daughter of a Lancashire Anglican minister, and they had three sons and three daughters. Until her death in 1879, the Lubbocks split their residence between London and High Elms, with the exception of 1861–5 when Chislehurst was their country home. In 1884 Lubbock married Alice A. L. L. Fox Pitt, daughter of the archaeologist, Augustus Pitt-*Rivers, and with her he had three more sons and two more daughters. After he was named to the peerage in 1900, Lubbock and his family increasingly spent their time refurbishing Kingsgate Castle on the Kent coast.

Upon his father's death in 1865, Lubbock took over as head of the family bank, a position he continued to fill until his death. From the 1850s onwards he divided his

John Lubbock, first Baron Avebury (1834–1913), by Barraud, pubd 1889

time evenly between banking, politics, and scientific and popular writing. As a banker, Lubbock was instrumental in the formation in 1860 of a separate clearing facility for provincial banks, which prevented the need to post cheques to London. In 1863 he took over his father's long-held job as secretary of the London Bankers' Clearing House, breaking with tradition in 1867 by commencing annual publication of the average volume of business transacted by the clearing banks. Lubbock also served as the first president of the London Institute of Bankers upon its establishment in 1879, and was an important representative of the banking interest in the House of Commons, where he defended the gold standard and helped to revise various niceties in commercial law.

Lubbock's lifelong interest in natural history started with his early introduction into Darwin's 'inner circle' and membership of such groups as the Royal Institution, the Geological Society, the Royal Society (FRS 1858), and the X Club, and persisted through his enduring idea that natural selection provided a 'true cause' that could be applied to such disparate fields as archaeology and entomology. His first major scientific contribution was *Pre-Historic Times as Illustrated by Ancient Remains* (1865), in which he coined the distinction between palaeolithic and neolithic man, summed up existing evidence in favour of human antiquity, and made much of the similarity between prehistoric tools and those in use by 'modern savages'. In *The Origin of Civilisation and the Primitive Condition of Man* (1870), Lubbock provided a more explicitly evolutionary account connecting 'savage' with 'civilised' societies.

All his anthropological work exuded a relentless optimism, emphasizing the potential for all cultures to progress through stages. His work on insects, which he pursued most actively in the 1870s, carried this evolutionary model back from the human to the animal world. He professed to observe hunting, pastoral, and agricultural societies in different species of ants, and was intrigued by the possibility that they exhibited rational behaviour. Most of his published research concerned the social behaviour of insects, based in part on an ants' nest he and his daughters kept under constant observation in his room between 1874 and 1882; but he also published an account of a three-month experiment in teaching his pet poodle how to read.

After 1880 Lubbock's banking and political duties increasingly took time away from his original scientific work. After failing in his attempts to win a seat in the Commons in 1865 and 1868, Lubbock successfully stood for Maidstone in 1870; upon losing that seat in 1880, he stood for the safe borough of London University (which he had served as vice-chancellor since 1872), and represented it for the next twenty years. He was a Liberal until 1886, when he broke with Gladstone over home rule, and he continued to support the Unionist case on Ireland, at times marshalling ethnological evidence on his side of the debate. He was also outspoken on labour issues, championing early-closing bills in the 1870s (which he saw mainly as a question of occupational health among clerks); he also drafted the Bank Holiday Bill of 1871, which, when it was passed, created the first secular holiday in British history, popularly called 'St Lubbock's day' in his honour. A self-professed 'scientific' MP, Lubbock pushed through a bill to preserve ancient monuments in 1873, and upon being named to the peerage in 1900 chose the title Avebury after an ancient druidical site which he had long fought to save from being 'destroyed for the profit of a few pounds' (*Scientific Lectures*, 2nd edn, 1890, 170). He was also an advocate of voting reform, founding, with his brother Beaumont and with Leonard Courtney, the Proportional Representation Society in 1884. On economic issues he remained a strong advocate of free trade, despite his break with the Liberals. He was a member of the royal commission on trade depression of 1885. In 1905 he opposed both Joseph Chamberlain's imperial preference scheme and Arthur Balfour's compromise plan for retaliatory duties.

Like many economic liberals, Lubbock assumed Britain could maintain its economic position by improving its system of education, especially in the sciences and modern languages. To that end he published a number of extremely popular didactic books late in his life, including *The Pleasures of Life* (1887), *The Use of Life* (1894), and *The Beauties of Nature* (1896). Lubbock also pursued his economic and social interests through local London politics. As president of the London chamber of commerce between 1888 and 1893, and chairman of the London county council from 1890 to 1892, he took a strong line against municipal socialism and in favour of technical education. A few years after being created Baron Avebury he retired from public life. He died from anaemia on 28 May 1913, at Kingsgate Castle, and was buried three days later in Farnborough churchyard, High Elms. He was survived by his wife.

TIMOTHY L. ALBORN

Sources H. G. Hutchinson, *Life of Sir John Lubbock, Lord Avebury*, 2 vols. (1914) • G. W. Stocking, *Victorian anthropology* [1987] • Y. Cassis, *City bankers, 1890–1914*, trans. M. Rocque (1994) [Fr. orig., *Banquiers de la City à l'époque édouardienne, 1890–1914* (1984)] • *DNB*

Archives BL, corresp., diaries, and papers, Add. MSS 49638–49681; Add. Ch 76145–76147 • CKS, corresp. and business papers • Committee of the London Clearing Bankers, minute books • Electoral Reform Society of Great Britain and Ireland, papers • LUL, corresp. and papers relating to elections • RS, notebooks • U. Warwick Mod. RC, papers relating to shop hours | BL, letters to W. E. Gladstone, Add. MSS 44434–44789 • BL, corresp. with Macmillans, Add. MSS 55213–55214 • BL OIOC, letters to Grant Duff family, MS Eur. F 234 • CUL, letters to Sir George Stokes • Elgin Library, Moray, letters to George Gordon • ICL, letters to Thomas Huxley • Oxf. U. Mus. NH, letters to Robert McLachlan • Oxf. U. Mus. NH, corresp., mainly letters to E. B. Poulton • Salisbury and South Wiltshire Museum, letters to A. H. L. F. Pitt-Rivers • Surrey HC, letters to Lord Farmer • U. Edin. L., corresp. with Sir Charles Lyell • UCL, corresp. with Sir Edwin Chadwick

Likenesses G. Richmond, drawing, 1867, repro. in Hutchinson, *Life*, vol. 1 [frontispiece] • G. Richmond, chalk drawing, 1869, NPG • G. B. Black, lithograph, 1871, NPG • lithograph, 1871 (after G. B. Black), NPG • H. von Herkomer, painting, 1911, repro. in Hutchinson, *Life*, vol. 2 [frontispiece] • Barraud, photograph, NPG; repro. in *Men and Women of the Day*, 2 (1889) [*see illus.*] • M. Klinkicht, wood-engraving (after photograph), BM; repro. in *ILN* (1890), supplement • Maclure & Macdonald, lithograph, NPG • Pet, chromolithograph caricature, NPG; repro. in *Monetary Gazette* (10 Jan 1877) • Spy [L. Ward], chromolithograph caricature, NPG; repro. in *VF* (23 Feb 1878) • lithograph (after photograph by London Stereoscopic Co.), NPG • print (after H. T. Wells), NPG

Wealth at death £362,877 9s. 11d.: probate, 17 July 1913, *CGPLA Eng. & Wales*

Lubbock, Sir John William, third baronet (1803–1865), astronomer and banker, was born on 26 March 1803 in Duke Street, Westminster, London. He was the only child of Sir John William Lubbock, second baronet (1773–1840) and Mary Entwistle (*d.* 1845) of Manchester. The elder Lubbock, the eldest of six children of William Lubbock (1746–1823), inherited his baronetcy from his childless uncle Sir John Lubbock (1744–1816) who helped establish the banking firm of Sir William Lemon, Buller, Edward Forster, John Lubbock & Co. in 1772. This partnership, which Sir John Lubbock and Forster mainly ran after 1800, would later pass down to the younger J. W. Lubbock through his father.

Education and banking career Lubbock received his early education at Eton College and privately from William Maltby, and in 1821 convinced his father, who had intended to send him to Oxford, to enrol him instead at Trinity College, Cambridge. He spent more time studying astronomy and algebra with William Whewell and other younger Trinity fellows than he did cramming for the mathematics tripos, and graduated first senior optime in 1825. While an undergraduate he vacationed in Milan and Paris, where he steeped himself in the scientific and mathematical work of Laplace and Lagrange.

In 1827 Lubbock entered his father's banking firm at 15 Lombard Street, London, then known as Sir John William

Sir John William Lubbock, third baronet (1803–1865), by Thomas Phillips, 1843

Lubbock, Forster & Co. In 1833 he married Harriet Hotham (1810–1873), daughter of a York military officer. This marriage produced eight sons (all of whom attended Eton) and three daughters, between 1834 and 1849. From 1827 to 1834 Lubbock's London address was 23 St James's Place, across from the Royal Society; between 1834 and 1840 he lived at 29 Eaton Place, London, and Mitcham Grove, Surrey. Upon succeeding to the baronetcy at his father's death on 22 October 1840, he moved his country home to High Elms, Farnborough, Kent. For the next twenty years he divided his weeks between working as senior partner of his bank in London and presiding over his estate in High Elms. Besides supervising the primary education of his own sons and establishing three village schools he spent his leisure time in Kent breeding sheep and cattle, planting conifers, and conversing with his neighbour Charles Darwin.

Scientific interests Most of Lubbock's published work in science and mathematics appeared in the 1830s when he was still only a junior partner at the bank. In addition to original research on planetary motion, lunar theory, and tide tables, he played an important role in introducing British men of science to the work of Europeans, including the Frenchmen Augustin-Louis Cauchy, Phillippe de Pontécoulant, and François Pambour; the Italian astronomer Giovanni Plana; and the Norwegian mathematician Niels Abel. In his original scientific work Lubbock was consistently drawn to topics which allowed him to relate mathematical theories with observations that had been collected by practical men with little formal scientific training.

Lubbock contributed to a uniquely eclectic array of scientific societies. On the one hand he put in long hours at the Society for the Diffusion of Useful Knowledge (SDUK), Henry Brougham's project for making science intelligible to mechanics. On the other he was elected to the Royal Society in 1829, regularly read papers there in the 1830s, and served as its treasurer and vice-president from 1830 to 1835 and from 1838 to 1847—a time when the society's aristocratic bent was under constant fire from reformers like Charles Babbage. He also regularly contributed to the Royal Astronomical Society (RAS), which he joined in 1829, and belonged to the Geological Society of London (to which he contributed only one paper, on the climatic effects of the earth's rotation). And, while he was much less active in the British Association for the Advancement of Science (BAAS) than most of his friends, Lubbock did serve occasionally as vice-president of section A (astronomy), and he gladly accepted a BAAS grant in 1834 for his tidal research, although he published the findings in the Royal Society's *Philosophical Transactions* rather than the annual BAAS *Report*. Less formally Lubbock maintained a lengthy correspondence with several important men of science including Babbage, Whewell, John Herschel, and Augustus De Morgan, some of whom failed to agree about very much apart from their friendship with Lubbock.

One of the founders of the SDUK's *British Almanac* in 1827, Lubbock contributed an article on tides to its *Companion* in 1830, which he continued to update for the rest of the decade and revised as *An Elementary Treatise on the Tides* in 1839. In 1830 he also published for the SDUK with J. E. Drinkwater (later Lord Bethune) the essay entitled *On Probability*, which expounded Laplace's probability theory with examples from horse-racing, juries, and life assurance; this was a popular version of a highly abstract pair of papers on probability theory which Lubbock had delivered to the Cambridge Philosophical Society in 1828–9. A final SDUK project which Lubbock supervised in 1830 was the publication of a set of six star maps on the 'gnomonic projection', which displayed the constellations, in Lubbock's words, 'as they would be … by a Camera Lucida' (Lubbock, *The Stars*, preface). He also published articles in the *Philosophical Magazine* during the 1830s on cask-gauging and achromatic lenses, which combined esoteric forays into pure mathematics with respectful nods to the 'experience' of barrel makers and lens grinders.

In most of his work on the practical applications of science Lubbock urged scientists to band together with artisans in order to dethrone what were, in his view, the inept and corrupt practices of untrained placemen who held official scientific jobs. In the 1830s he joined with John Herschel and Francis Baily to try to reform the Admiralty office and its nautical almanac, after failing in his attempt to win the post of superintendent of the almanac in 1831. And he sided with commercial actuaries against the census official John Rickman, whose overly optimistic population figures had failed to square with life assurance companies' tables of mortality. Lubbock also served, alongside Herschel and George Biddell Airy, on two royal commissions on weights and measures (1838–41 and 1843–54), which among other things recommended in 1853 that Britain switch to a decimal coinage. At the heart of his lifelong interest in the practical side of science was a sincere belief that skilled labourers, with suitable direction from their social superiors, could turn their practical knowledge into social and political progress. This belief also motivated him to stand, unsuccessfully, as a radical MP for Cambridge in 1832, to serve as the first vice-chancellor of London University (1837–42), and to act as a treasurer of the Great Exhibition in 1851.

Royal Society administration Yet, at the same time that he was working so diligently on behalf of populist causes in the 1830s, Lubbock was displaying similar levels of administrative and intellectual toil at the openly élitist Royal Society of London. Between 1831 and 1837 he published six papers in the society's *Philosophical Transactions* (including the Bakerian lecture of 1836) that extended the work on tides he had commenced at the *British Almanac*. Together with William Whewell's concurrent work at the Royal Society and the BAAS, these papers did much to refine the methods of Daniel Bernoulli and Laplace for relating the moon's transit with observed tidal fluctuations. Lubbock's share of the labour consisted in tabulating large data series which had been privately collected by dock employees in London and Liverpool, then comparing their regularities with each other and with Bernoulli's predictions. He left to Whewell the more ambitious (and, for the time being, fruitless) task of co-ordinating a standardized set of tidal observations around the world in order to produce an accurate map of co-tidal lines for use in navigation. In addition to his tidal research, for which the Royal Society awarded him a medal in 1834, Lubbock published an important set of papers in *Philosophical Transactions* on physical astronomy. These investigations, which were also published in serial form by Charles Knight, supplemented Laplace's theories of planetary and lunar motion with a series of constants which made better allowance for disturbing forces.

As Royal Society treasurer, Lubbock worked closely with its librarian, James Hudson, at building up its collection of books and journals; besides charging Hudson with keeping the shelves full, he supervised as the librarian took round-the-clock meteorological measurements from the society's rooms in 1832. Lubbock's library work also led him to publish a short work *On the Classification of Different Branches of Human Knowledge* (1838), which originated in part from a dispute with the British Museum librarian Antonio Panizzi over the proper method of classifying books. Although his last published memoir in *Philosophical Transactions* appeared in 1840, he continued to provide the society with referee reports (typically of a forbidding nature) into the 1850s.

Astronomy The Royal Astronomical Society was the only group to which Lubbock continued to send papers into the 1860s. Most of his efforts followed on from his earliest interests in tightening the fit between existing physical laws and available observations. In a set of papers delivered to the RAS between 1829 and 1833 Lubbock derived cometary orbits from his new laws of planetary motion in order to predict more precisely where to look for Halley's comet upon its predicted return in 1835. His RAS paper on 'The theory of astronomical refractions' (1855) summed up earlier findings he had published in the *Philosophical Magazine* in 1840, in which he applied to astronomical observations Gay Lussac's law concerning the expansion of gases. Starting with this law and a set of observed pressures at different altitudes, he interpolated constants that could be used to correct for the distorting effect of atmospheric pressure, and thereby provide astronomers with more accurate angles of refraction. (In 1840, challenged by Sir James Ivory about the accuracy of these constants, Lubbock tried unsuccessfully to raise £1500 for a ballooning expedition in order to confirm them.)

Lubbock's final RAS paper, 'On the lunar theory', restated the conclusions of his earlier Royal Society papers on the moon in order to claim priority for his own theoretical innovations, along with the empirical contributions of Plana and Pontécoulant, against recent claims made by the American astronomers M. F. Longstreth and Benjamin Peirce. In this paper he credited himself and his two European colleagues with 'bringing to perfection the solution of the problem of finding the longitude at sea by means of lunar observations' (Lubbock, 'Lunar theory', 12). For his work on lunar and planetary astronomy Lubbock was one of twelve astronomers who received a testimonial from the RAS in 1849 as part of a compromise stemming from the society's inability to decide which of the co-discoverers of Neptune (J. C. Adams or U. J. J. le Verrier) should receive its annual medal.

Banking and City life Lubbock's scientific avocations, both in outlook and in their successful results, owed much to his equally successful vocation as a private banker in the City of London. He was one of London's leading financiers, both at the family bank and as a director of the Royal Exchange Assurance company. Lubbock's bank was a relatively small but very influential concern, which provided him with a prominent seat in the London Bankers' Clearing House and with easy access to polite society. He inherited his position on the court of directors at the Royal Exchange, like his senior partnership at the bank, upon the death of his father, who had been the insurance company's governor from 1838 to 1840. Lubbock became close friends with the firm's actuary, J. A. Higham, who abetted his lifelong interest in probability theory, and with the economist Thomas Tooke, its governor from 1840 to 1852.

Lubbock's day-to-day experience in the City served him well in his interactions with men of science. He frequently passed along to Babbage and Whewell information on commercial matters like prices and exchange rates, which were readily accessible in his capacity as a private banker but which were next to impossible for a gentleman of science to discover on his own. Lubbock also periodically sought jobs for relatives of his scientific friends, as when he lobbied the Royal Exchange in 1861 to hire John Herschel's son as a successor to Higham. Men of science were often quick to return the favour: Whewell, Babbage, and David Ricardo all offered their support when Lubbock stood for parliament in 1832. More generally he used his social connections in the City to gain access to much of the practical information (typically held in private hands) which he was forever squaring with scientific theory. Among other contacts Lubbock relied heavily in his scientific work on such men as Sir John Hall, secretary of the St Katherine's Dock Company, who relayed to Lubbock the practical wisdom of his dock master and harbour master; Isaac Solly, chairman of the London Dock Company, who handed over twenty-six years of private tidal data to Lubbock; Captain Eastfield of the East India Company, who superintended a year's worth of careful observations at Lubbock's behest; and M. J. F. Dessiou of the Admiralty office, who constructed many of the tables that Lubbock analysed.

Lubbock's scientific pursuits, however, did not always serve him so well at his desk in the City. He frequently complained that fellow financiers thought the less of him for his achievements in astronomy, and on the few occasions when he tried to apply scientific methods to financial questions the results were mixed at best. In his pamphlet entitled *On Currency* (1840), he used the latest algebraic techniques to determine that no firm predictions about the effects of competing monetary schemes could be reached without far more evidence—a conclusion few financiers were interested in hearing in the midst of a heated currency debate. And in 1860 he presented a paper to the Institute of Actuaries which appealed to probability theory as a means of convincing London's leading banks to move their cash reserves from the Bank of England to a collectively held mutual fund—a suggestion which none of his fellow bankers, who revered the bank as a symbol of financial stability, would take seriously for decades to come.

Lubbock's scientific and financial activities alike came to an abrupt end in 1860 when he was stricken by gout. That year Lubbock arranged for a merger between his bank and the London firm of Robarts, Curtis & Co., a comparably influential Lombard Street concern which had been founded in 1791. Shortly after closing the deal, which created the new firm of Robarts, Lubbock & Co., Lubbock passed along his senior partnership in the bank to his eldest son, John *Lubbock, who was already well on the way to inheriting his father's scientific laurels as well: the younger Lubbock, later Lord Avebury, would go on to a brilliant career as a banker, anthropologist, politician, and popularizer of science. In 1861 J. W. Lubbock resigned his directorship of the Royal Exchange, a post which was later taken up in 1865 by his third son, Neville Lubbock, who remained on the court until his death in 1914. Sir John William Lubbock spent the last five years of his life mainly at High Elms, where he died of heart disease on 20 June 1865. TIMOTHY L. ALBORN

Sources J. W. Lubbock, 'On the tides at the Port of London', *PTRS*, 126 (1836), 217–66 • J. W. Lubbock, *On currency* (1840) • J. W. Lubbock, 'On the lunar theory', *Memoirs of the Royal Astronomical Society*, 30 (1860–61) • J. W. Lubbock and J. E. Drinkwater, *On probability* (1830) • J. W. Lubbock, *The stars, in six maps, on the gnomonic projection* (1830) • J. W. Lubbock, 'The tides', in *Companion to the almanac, or, Year-book of general information for 1830*, Society for the Diffusion of Useful Knowledge [1830], 49–64 • J. W. Lubbock, 'On the census', *Philosophical Magazine*, new ser., 7 (1830), 416–21 • J. W. Lubbock, *Remarks on the classification of different branches of human knowledge* (1838) • J. W. Lubbock, *On the heat of vapours and on astronomical refractions* (1840) • J. W. Lubbock, 'On change of climate resulting from a change in the earth's axis of rotation', *Quarterly Journal of the Geological Society*, 5 (1849), 4–7 • J. W. Lubbock, 'On the clearing of the London bankers', *Assurance Magazine and Journal of the Institute of Actuaries*, 9 (1860) • M. Deacon, *Scientists and the sea, 1650–1900: a study of marine science* (1971) • J. P. Henderson, 'Sir John William Lubbock's *On currency*: "an interesting book by a still more interesting man"', *History of Political Economy*, 18 (1986), 383–404 • J. Morrell and A. Thackray, *Gentlemen of science: early years of the British Association for the Advancement of Science* (1981) • election certificate, RS • *DNB*

Archives RS, correspondence • UCL, letters to RAS • UCL, letters to SDUK | BL, correspondence with Charles Babbage, Add. MSS 37185–37200 • Bodl. Oxf., letters to Mary and William Somerville • RS, correspondence with Sir John Herschel • TCD, correspondence with Sir William Hamilton • Trinity Cam., correspondence with William Whewell

Likenesses T. Phillips, oils, 1843, U. Lond. [*see illus.*]

Wealth at death under £120,000: probate, 10 Oct 1865, *CGPLA Eng. & Wales*

Lubbock, Percy (1879–1965), writer, was born on 4 June 1879 in London, the fourth child of Frederic Lubbock, merchant banker, and his wife, Catherine, daughter of John Gurney of Earlham Hall, Norfolk. Both lines of Lubbock's family produced distinguished citizens. On his mother's side was Elizabeth Gurney Fry, famed prison reformer and Quaker activist; on his father's, the writer and scientist John Lubbock, first Baron Avebury. Percy Lubbock was raised in splendour and educated at Eton College, then at King's College, Cambridge, where he was placed in the first class for the classical tripos in 1901.

After university Lubbock worked for the Board of Education in a post he found 'uncongenial' (*DNB*). In 1906 he was elected Pepys librarian at Magdalene College, Cambridge. In that year his first book, *Elizabeth Barrett Browning and her Letters*, was published, establishing his penchant for biography. In 1908 he gave up his post in order to devote himself to writing, and in 1909 he published *Samuel Pepys* as a homage to the Magdalene College graduate while providing ingenious commentary on Pepys's *Diary*.

Lubbock contributed regularly to the *Times Literary Supplement* between 1908 and 1914 and during the First World War worked on behalf of the Red Cross. His most concerted biographical and critical work emerged through his association with Henry James—his idol and friend. After James's death in 1916 Lubbock orchestrated the publication of the unfinished works (*The Ivory Tower*, *The Sense of the Past*, and *The Middle Years*), a two-volume collection of letters, and a memoir. He also wrote the entry on James for the *Dictionary of National Biography*.

Yet it was *The Craft of Fiction* (1921) that established Lubbock as a thoroughly modern scholar. There he set out to show readers that the novel is a series of mechanical, even musical, progressions and that within these one discovers true art. Lubbock's work inaugurated the modernist revaluation of the novel, as exemplified by Virginia Woolf's *Mr Bennett and Mrs Brown* (1924) and E. M. Forster's *Aspects of the Novel* (1927). What distinguishes *The Craft of Fiction* as crucial to modern understanding of the novel is its reverence for technique. Lubbock was the first to associate art and form so completely, describing the work of innovators and stylists—Tolstoy, Flaubert, Thackeray, James, Dickens, Balzac—as both revolutionary and absolutely intelligent. *The Craft of Fiction* also presaged formalism, which may be one reason for the popularity of the text throughout the 1960s.

Two of Lubbock's most important books may be read together as examples of his fancy and intelligence. *Roman Pictures* (1923) involves related characters who usher the narrator from naïvety into urbanity. It is, however, demanding in a way that most social comedies are not. The narrator, while guileless, is philosophical about human nature, in particular about the nature of Britons abroad. In the end his idealism trumps British snobbery and Italian indifference; Lubbock's narrator records the splendours of Rome and the Italian countryside that both groups outwardly (and foolishly) disdain. Critically acclaimed, *Roman Pictures* won the Prix Fémina-Vie Heureuse in 1924.

Roman Pictures is non-fiction for only half the time. The biographical portraits are embellished and the narrator is more sagacious than he lets on. *The Region Cloud* (1925), in contrast, represents Lubbock's only published fiction. The novel is built around a chance encounter between the protagonist, Austin, and John Cannon, who is reminiscent of Sir Herbert von Herkomer, a famous Victorian painter whom Lubbock met while visiting Toledo in 1906. The novel may well be read as a dubious homage to Henry James, as it presents the figure of a great artist whose throng of young admirers makes him feel powerful. While its rambling narrative may have alienated some readers, its series of fleeting impressions that combine to signal a life-changing experience confer on *The Region Cloud* the stamp of the modern.

Although dramatic impressionism is one hallmark of modernity, it was countered in British fiction of the 1920s by post-war nostalgia. One recognizes deep appreciation for a childhood world lost to time in Lubbock's *Earlham* (1922), for which he received the prestigious James Tait prize. The book describes the Gurney family home where Lubbock spent much of his youth. The portraits of family, the splendiferous descriptions of Earlham (worth reading for Lubbock's passion alone), and appreciation for neighbouring landscapes are conveyed with elegance. Above all, *Earlham* spoke to a generation that had been brought up Victorian but had been transfigured by war and social change. Its appeal was reinforced by the appearance of the equally sentimental *Shades of Eton* (1929), which punctuated Lubbock's and his peers' aggrandizement of the past.

Lubbock also published a number of 'sketches from memory' of his friends: *George Calderon* appeared in 1921 and *Mary Cholmondeley* in 1928. In 1925 he published an edition of A. C. Benson's *Diary*, commemorating the Eton schoolmaster whose recommendation had secured Lubbock the post of Pepys librarian.

In 1926 Lubbock married Lady Sybil Marjorie Scott (1879–1943), *née* Cuffe, daughter of the fifth earl of Desart and widow of W. C. Cutting of New York and of Geoffrey Scott. They lived at Villa Medici in Fiesole, Italy, for the next fourteen years. In his personal life Lubbock was by all accounts ensconced in love and admiration, beloved as much for his devotion to literature as for his own contributions to British letters. He was tall and pale (described as 'the colour of putty' by Virginia Woolf) and suffered blindness in his old age (*Letters*, 2.494). In the late 1940s Lubbock moved to Lerici on the Gulf of La Spezia and into his much prized Gli Scafari. This second home presents a striking vision on the cliffs of the Mediterranean—white, ethereal, yet imposing. Lubbock spent his remaining days at this idyllic retreat. His last published work, *Portrait of Edith Wharton*, was published in 1947. He was appointed CBE in 1952.

In 1957 a revised edition of *The Craft of Fiction* appeared, complete with a new preface by Lubbock in which he explained that all literary criticism is engineered for 'the detection of the writer at work, for catching him in the act, always supposing that he has watched his own practice as narrowly as any other'. The quotation is prophetic, for it is through Lubbock's own craft that one discerns glimpses of the man working on behalf of a subject he loved: the development of the artist's mind.

Percy Lubbock died at Gli Scafari on 2 August 1965 and was buried at Lerici. Although he attracted only moderate public attention, it would be a mistake to class him with the lesser lights of early twentieth-century literary scholarship. Intellectual vivacity, nostalgia for England's past, many and diverse writings, as well as a profound influence on major novelists of his day comprise Percy Lubbock's legacy. ELIZABETH MACLEOD WALLS

Sources P. Lubbock, *Earlham: reminiscences of the author's early life at Earlham Hall, Norfolk* (1922) · M. G. Harkness, ed., *The Percy Lubbock reader* (1957) · *The Times* (3 Aug 1965) · A. O. Bell, ed., *The letters of Virginia Woolf*, 5 vols. (1977) · *DNB*

Archives BL, corresp. with Macmillans, Add. MS 55033 · Bodl. Oxf., corresp. with Sibyl Colefax · Harvard University, near Florence, Italy, Center for Italian Renaissance Studies, letters to Bernard Berenson and Mary Berenson · U. Birm. L., letters to Francis Brett Young and Jessica Brett Young · U. Hull, Brynmor Jones L., letters to Irene Forbes Adam · U. Leeds, Brotherton L., letters to Sir Edmund Gosse

Likenesses photograph, Lerici, Italy; repro. in Harkness, ed., *Percy Lubbock reader*, jacket

Wealth at death £681: probate, 26 April 1966, *CGPLA Eng. & Wales*

Lubetkin, Berthold Romanovich (1901–1990), architect, is believed to have been born on 14 December 1901 in Tiflis, Georgia, son of Roman (Rubin) Aronovich Lubetkin (*d.* *c.*1941), engineer, and his wife, Fenya (Hassya) Menin (*d.* 1941?). A different place and year of birth—Warsaw, 1903—are noted in several student certificates and in Lubetkin's British passport: these were explained by Lubetkin himself as false information to eliminate an early period of cadet service with the Red Army about

Berthold Romanovich Lubetkin (1901–1990), by Baron, 1948

1919–20. An authenticated birth certificate has not been traced. He was educated at Tenishev Gymnasium in St Petersburg and the Medvednikov Gymnasium in Moscow. His family was of Jewish origin, moderately prosperous, and well-travelled; Lubetkin had visited France, Germany, England, and Scandinavia by 1914.

Lubetkin's artistic education is believed to have begun with his early enrolment at the Stroganov Art School in Moscow about 1916. After the Russian Revolution he attended the SVOMAS (free art) studios in St Petersburg and Moscow, and the VkhUTEMAS (advanced state workshops of art and industrial art) in Moscow. He participated in several revolutionary groups, including Proletkult and ASNOVA, and came into contact with leading figures of the constructivist period, including Rodchenko, Tatlin, Malevich, Mayakovsky, Vesnin, Popova, and Gabo. This breadth of acquaintance was to be widened still further in Europe, where he would meet Klee, Grosz, Picasso, Braque, Léger, Gris, Soutine, Cocteau, Ernst May, Bruno Taut, and many others.

Lubetkin accompanied the first Exhibition of Russian Art to Berlin in 1922, and thereafter attended the Bauschule at the Technische Hochschule, Charlottenburg, and the Höhere Fachschule für Textil und Bekleidungsindustrie (1922–3). After a short study scholarship in Vienna, he moved to Poland and took his diploma in architecture at the Warsaw Polytechnic (1923–5). In 1925 he moved to Paris to continue his professional education and assisted in the construction of the Soviet pavilion at the Exposition des Arts Décoratifs, where he first met Le Corbusier. He attended the École Spéciale d'Architecture, the Institut d'Urbanisme, the École Supérieure de Béton Armé, and the École des Beaux-Arts; he also participated in the independent atelier of Auguste Perret, to whom Lubetkin later acknowledged an enduring debt of design skill.

Lubetkin maintained contact with the Russian avant-garde and entered several architectural competitions of the 1920s, including the Urals Polytechnic at Sverdlovsk and the Tsentrosoyus in Moscow. In the most important of these, for the Palace of Soviets in Moscow, Lubetkin and his team gained an award. He also worked for the USSR trades delegation in France curating a travelling exhibition of Russian goods in a demountable timber pavilion designed with the architect J. Volodko.

Lubetkin's first significant building was a nine-storey apartment block in avenue de Versailles, Paris, undertaken with Jean Ginsberg and completed in 1931. Though both designers were still under thirty, it exhibited a mature grasp of the aesthetic and technical concepts of contemporary modernism. With little prospect of further work in Paris, Lubetkin made several exploratory trips to London, where, in 1931, he was offered a commission to design a private house in Hampstead for Ralph and Manya Harari. Although this was not realized, Lubetkin was attracted by English traditions of tolerance and scientific progress, and by the possibility of making his mark in a country where continental modern architecture had yet to arrive. In 1932—with six graduates of the Architectural Association—he formed the Tecton partnership and set up a practice in London. This relocation to England, seemingly an unlikely choice for someone of Lubetkin's radical disposition, was not initially intended as permanent, but was consolidated with the rapid establishment of Tecton's reputation, and his growing misgivings over developments in the Soviet Union.

Although nominally a group of equals, Tecton was dominated by Lubetkin with his rich European experience, charismatic personality, and clear sense of artistic direction—attributes that also made him a figure of interest in contemporary English intellectual and society circles. His belief in building design as an instrument of social progress was underlaid by a profound appreciation of architecture's rational disciplines and emotive power. His Marxist convictions and his experience of the Russian Revolution implanted high expectations of architecture's role in transforming society, both through the provision of new and relevant building types—'social condensers'—and through its aesthetic capacity to project the image of an oncoming better world.

Lubetkin's buildings were characterized by clear geometric figures, technical ingenuity, and intensive functional resolution. He dissociated himself, however, from the contemporary doctrine of functionalism, and sought a deeper synthesis of human, architectural, and philosophical values. Formal composition and a lyrical playfulness differentiate his designs from much of the work associated with the international style; also unusual was Tecton's method of presentation whereby the rationale of a scheme was depicted in didactic analyses, witty cartoons, and slogans.

Tecton's output included several private houses, a series

of zoological pavilions and structures at London Zoo, Whipsnade, and Dudley, a pair of apartment blocks, Highpoint in Highgate, Middlesex, and a health centre and housing for Finsbury borough council. Many of these projects made innovative and expressive use of structural reinforced concrete through collaboration with the Danish engineer Ove Arup. The penguin pool at London Zoo (1934), with its interlocking spiral ramps, and Highpoint I (1935), an elegantly planned eight-storey apartment building, brought Lubetkin and his firm international recognition, including praise from Le Corbusier, who described Highpoint as 'an achievement of the first rank' ('The vertical garden city', *Architectural Review*, 79/470, January 1936, 10). The second Highpoint block (1938) employed a richer array of materials and controversially incorporated facsimile Greek caryatid figures to support the entrance canopy. The penthouse flat, designed by Lubetkin for his own occupation, achieved an interior sophistication unequalled in England at the time. Finsbury health centre—the first commission by a metropolitan authority of a firm of modern architects—was opened in 1938 and, in both its architectural and social programme, anticipated the National Health Service reforms of the post-war period. Tecton's works were well received when first built and have remained highly regarded; many are now protected by statutory listing, three at grade I. The zoo buildings were especially popular, with Dudley Zoo attracting crowds of 250,000 at its opening in 1937.

Lubetkin was active in several radical professional associations of the 1930s, notably the Modern Architecture Research (MARS) Group and the Architects' and Technicians' Organisation. In both cases Lubetkin contributed to exhibition projects, but the Architects' and Technicians' Organisation was more politically engaged and involved him in campaigns against government housing policy. (In 1935 Tecton had won a competition for the design of an ideal scheme of working-class flats.) Tecton's work with Finsbury was due to continue with several housing projects but was halted in 1939. Meanwhile, following the Munich crisis, Lubetkin and his team, together with Ove Arup, were commissioned to plan a scheme of air-raid protection for the entire borough population. Their proposals, involving a series of deep bomb-proof shelters, were politically controversial and eventually rejected. Lubetkin's architectural activity ceased with the onset of the war, although in 1942, following the entry of the USSR on the allies' side, he designed a memorial to mark Lenin's association with Finsbury.

In 1939 Lubetkin was naturalized and on 1 April of that year he married Margaret Louise Church (1917–1978), an assistant architect in Tecton and the youngest of three daughters of the barrister Harold Church. In the same year they moved from London to acquire and manage a farm in Upper Kilcott, Gloucestershire. This relocation is commonly misinterpreted as Lubetkin's retirement from architectural practice, but he resumed work on Finsbury's housing projects in 1943, when the council began to plan for reconstruction. Three large-flatted estates for Finsbury were completed by the 1950s, with a fourth being undertaken for Paddington borough council and completed by Denys Lasdun, a post-war partner in Tecton until the firm's dissolution in 1948.

Peterlee New Town, to which Lubetkin was appointed architect–planner in 1947, should have been the crowning achievement of his career. Designated on a spectacular site near Durham, this project to build an urban centre for the local mining community presented Lubetkin with the ideal opportunity to apply the full range of his mature skills to a commensurate social programme. But the project was flawed by prior development restrictions and the considerable technical difficulties of building over the active coalfield. Although Lubetkin argued for co-ordinated over- and underground planning, thereby permitting the coherent civic development he desired, the necessary departmental support was lacking. He left Peterlee in 1950, having built nothing. In the same year he was interviewed for the master planning of Chandigarh, the new capital of Punjab, though the commission was subsequently awarded to Le Corbusier.

These disappointments are often cited as marking the end of his career, but Lubetkin resumed private practice in partnership with Francis Skinner (formerly of Tecton) and Douglas Bailey, his deputy at Peterlee. The firm produced several housing schemes in Bethnal Green, London, details of which—notably the public staircases—display the sculptural vigour of Lubetkin in his prime. However, from the mid-1950s Lubetkin increasingly withdrew from professional attention and in 1957 considered emigrating to China. Margaret Lubetkin's deteriorating health caused them to give up the farm and move to Clifton, Bristol, in 1969. Following her death in 1978 Lubetkin began writing a personal memoir, which is still unpublished. He emerged from seclusion in 1982 to receive the award of the royal gold medal for architecture. This marked a renewal of interest in the man and his work and, in the following years, he re-entered the architectural arena and travelled extensively, giving lectures and interviews. He died at his home, 113 Princess Victoria Street, Clifton, Bristol on 23 October 1990, survived by two daughters and a son; a second son had died in childhood following a tonsillectomy. He was cremated on 27 October.

Berthold Lubetkin (Tolek to his friends) was a man of complex character, a maverick who none the less inspired devotion in his collaborators. He was a captivating conversationalist but described himself as a 'rootless journeyman' and could be elusive in personal relations. Many details of his early life and family background remain uncertain or uncorroborated by documentary record. He had strong left-wing political allegiances and a distinguished analytical mind that ranged widely over many subjects. His intermittent writings, invariably directed from a rationalist philosophical viewpoint, combined architectural critique, social polemic, and a sardonic humour enlivened by idiomatic polyglot wordplay. His tastes—whether in art, literature, or food—were discerning, cosmopolitan, and idiosyncratic. He was of short but powerful physique with handsome features and a pronounced 'foreign' accent, despite his long English domicile. He is widely regarded as the outstanding architect of his generation to have practised in England, his work encapsulating the early optimistic vision of modernism at its most poetic and poignant. JOHN ALLAN

Sources J. Allan, *Berthold Lubetkin: architecture and the tradition of progress* (1992) • P. Coe and M. Reading, *Lubetkin and Tecton: architecture and social commitment* (1981) • J. Allan, 'The passing of a modern master', *Architects' Journal* (31 Oct 1990), 5 • J. Allan, *RIBA Journal*, 97 (Dec 1990), 30–32 • P. Moro and J. Allan, *ArchR*, 188 (1990), 4 • J. Allan and M. von Sternberg, *Berthold Lubetkin* (2002) • *The Times* (24 Oct 1990) • *Daily Telegraph* (25 Oct 1990) • *The Guardian* (24 Oct 1990) • *The Independent* (25 Oct 1990) • L. Kehoe, *In this dark house* (1995) • personal knowledge (2004) • private information (2004) • G. Nelson, 'Architects of Europe: Tecton, England', *Pencil Points*, 16 (Oct 1936) • R. F. Jordan, 'Lubetkin', *ArchR*, 118 (1955), 36–44

Archives RIBA, archive | FILM BBC TV, Arena (transmitted 31 March 1989), 'Lubetkin: thoughts of a twentieth century architect' | SOUND BBC Radio 4, 1975: Open University arts course: History of architecture and design, 1890–1939; A305/14 Lubetkin 'Art, ideology and revolution'; A305/27 Lubetkin 'A commentary on Western Architecture'

Likenesses Baron, photograph, 1948, NPG [*see illus.*] • Lord Snowdon, photograph, 1985, repro. in Allan, *Berthold Lubetkin*

Wealth at death under £115,000: probate, 17 Dec 1990, *CGPLA Eng. & Wales*

Luby, Thomas (1800–1870), mathematician, was born at Clonmel, co. Tipperary, the son of John Luby and Eleanor Fogarty. His father was descended from a Huguenot family that had settled in Canterbury, and his mother came from the old Irish family of Castle Fogarty. Luby entered Trinity College, Dublin, as a sizar in 1817, obtained a scholarship in 1819, graduated BA in 1821, and was awarded an MA in 1825 and DD in 1840. He was elected to a junior fellowship in 1831 and was co-opted as senior fellow in 1847. Among the various college offices filled by him were those of university preacher, censor, junior dean, bursar, and senior dean; he was also senior lecturer, Donegal lecturer, and mathematical examiner in the school of civil engineering. He married, first Mary Anne Wetherall, niece of General Sir Frederick Wetherall, and second Jane Rathborne of Dunsina; he was the father of six sons and four daughters. His popularity as a college tutor was unrivalled. He was a member of the Royal Irish Academy and he wrote two textbooks for college use: *An Introductory Treatise on Physical Astronomy* (1828), and *The Elements of Plane Trigonometry* (1825; 3rd edn, 1852). He also edited John Brinkley's *Elements of Astronomy* (1836).

Luby was a friend and colleague of Sir William Rowan Hamilton, with whom he discussed difficult mathematical questions. In his capacity as a university administrator he helped ensure that Hamilton was given the research time and financial support needed for the publication of his seminal works. Luby died at his home, 43 Lower Leeson Street, Dublin, on 12 June 1870.

A. M. CLERKE, *rev.* JULIA TOMPSON

Sources W. B. S. Taylor, *History of the University of Dublin* (1845), 524 • *Irish Times* (13 June 1870) • *The Athenaeum* (18 June 1870), 811 • R. P. Graves, *Life of Sir William Rowan Hamilton*, 3 vols. (1882–9) • *CGPLA Ire.* (1870) • private information (1893)

Wealth at death under £70,000: probate, 1 Aug 1870, *CGPLA Ire.* • under £20,000: Irish probate sealed in London, 15 Aug 1870, *CGPLA Eng. & Wales*

Luby, Thomas Clarke (1822–1901), revolutionary, was born on 15 January 1822 in Dublin, the only son of James Luby (*c.*1800–*c.*1853), a Church of Ireland priest, and Catherine Mary Meynell (*c.*1796–1870), a Catholic. After attending several boarding-schools he began his studies at Trinity College, Dublin, in July 1839, and graduated BA in the spring of 1845. He studied law at the King's Inns, Dublin, and Gray's Inn, London, from 1845 to 1848, completing the required number of terms; he abandoned his plans for a career at the bar as a result of his growing interest in nationalist politics. In July 1848 Luby participated in an abortive attempt by Meath and Dublin Irish Confederation members to seize Dunshaughlin constabulary barracks and Navan town. In 1849 Luby was one of the five-man directory headed by James Fintan Lalor which planned a rebellion in various parts of Munster. In September 1849, after unsuccessfully inciting a gathering of peasants in Cashel to rebel, he was arrested and lodged in Cashel bridewell for a few days. In 1850 he wrote numerous articles in *The Irishman* newspaper, advocating independence from Britain and the establishment of a peasant proprietary in Ireland.

On 23 September 1852 Luby married Letitia Ffraser (*d.* 1903), the daughter of one of the *Nation* poets, Jean de Jean Ffraser. Shortly afterwards he emigrated to Melbourne, but he returned to Ireland in October 1854. From 3 November 1854 to 9 February 1855 Luby edited *The Tribune* newspaper, and in 1856 he accompanied James Stephens on a tour of Ireland to ascertain the prospects of establishing a conspiratorial republican organization. On 17 March 1858 Stephens founded the Irish Republican Brotherhood (IRB): Luby formulated the society's oath and administered it to Stephens. Luby became the second sworn member of the IRB and for the next seven years he played a central role in it. He made numerous organizational trips in Leinster and Munster from 1858 to 1860. In 1859, when Stephens travelled to America to consult with the leaders of the IRB's sister organization, the Fenian Brotherhood, Luby was left in charge of the Irish society. He spent five months in Paris consulting with Stephens on the latter's arrival from America, and returned to Ireland in July 1859. He was mainly responsible for foiling an attempt made in the autumn of 1860 to remove Stephens and John O'Mahony from the Irish and American branches, respectively, of the republican movement. Also in the autumn of 1860 Luby recruited into the IRB in Dublin a number of members, including Edward Duffy, who were to have a very important impact on the future growth of the organization, not only in Dublin but also in Ulster and Connaught. In November 1861 he thwarted an attempt by Father John Kenyon and a number of other ex-Young Irelanders to use the funeral of Terence Bellew McManus for their own political purposes; the subsequent IRB-dominated funeral gave a very significant boost to the society's recruitment efforts.

In February 1863 Luby went to America on a fund-raising

and organizing trip. He returned to Ireland in July of the same year, and in November 1863 he became one of the editors of the *Irish People* newspaper, the organ of the IRB. He made a few further organizing trips in Britain and Ulster in 1865. On 16 September 1865 he was arrested by the Dublin Metropolitan Police, the morning after they raided the *Irish People* offices. He was tried for treason felony, found guilty, and sentenced to twenty years' penal servitude. In January 1871 he received an amnesty on condition that he remain outside the United Kingdom for the unexpired portion of his sentence. He went at first to Antwerp, and emigrated to New York in May 1871. His wife and three children, James, John, and Catherine, joined him in the United States in September 1871. In May 1871 Luby was elected to the directory of the newly established Irish Confederation, and on 4 October 1871 he replaced John Devoy on the joint council of the Irish Confederation and the Fenian Brotherhood. In April 1873 Luby was largely responsible for the dissolution of the Irish Confederation and shortly afterwards he joined the Fenian Brotherhood. He was a prominent member of the brotherhood's central council until his resignation from the organization shortly after the death of its 'head centre', John O'Mahony, in February 1877. Luby remained active in Irish-American political affairs as a member of Clan na Gael. In April 1877 he was appointed a trustee of the Skirmishing Fund, and was a participant in the meeting of trustees which decided to fund John Holland's submarine scheme. Luby tentatively and briefly supported the 'new departure' in which Irish-American extremists agreed to co-operate with constitutional nationalists in a campaign to achieve agrarian reform and Irish independence. Luby resigned from the Skirmishing Fund (renamed the Irish National Fund) late in 1879. Shortly afterwards he resigned from Clan na Gael. He played no further part in Irish nationalist politics, although he remained convinced of the necessity of a violent revolution to achieve Irish independence.

Luby contributed a number of articles to the *Irish Nation* newspaper from 1881 to 1884 in which he described his activities in the 1849 revolutionary movement. His earlier writings included *The Life, Opinions, Conversations and Eloquence of Daniel O'Connell* (1872) and *The Lives and Times of Illustrious Irishmen* (1878). In 1893 he wrote, with Robert F. Walsh and Jeremiah C. Curtin, *The Story of Ireland's Struggles for Self-Government*. John O'Leary incorporated large sections of Luby's manuscript memoirs in his *Recollections of Fenians and Fenianism* (1896). Thomas Clarke Luby died at his residence in Jersey City on 29 November 1901.

BRIAN GRIFFIN

Sources S. Pender, 'Luby, Kenyon and the MacManus funeral', *Journal of the Cork History and Archaeological Society*, 56 (1951), 52–65 · D. Ryan, 'James Stephens and Thomas Clarke Luby', *The Fenian movement*, ed. T. W. Moody (1967), 49–62 · J. O'Leary, *Recollections of Fenians and Fenianism* (1896) · T. C. Luby, letters to J. O'Leary (28 Jan 1885, 10 Dec 1901), NL Ire., MS 5926

Archives NL Ire. | NL Ire., John O'Leary MSS

Likenesses photograph, repro. in *Gaelic American* [NY] (24 June 1911) · photograph, NL Ire. · photographs, repro. in Moody, ed., *The Fenian movement* · photographs, repro. in M. Kenny, *The Fenians: photographs and memorabilia* (1994), 9, 12

Lucan. For this title name *see* Sarsfield, Patrick, Jacobite first earl of Lucan (*d.* 1693); Bingham, Margaret, countess of Lucan (*c.*1740–1814); Bingham, George Charles, third earl of Lucan (1800–1888); Bingham, (Richard) John, seventh earl of Lucan (*b.* 1934, *d.* in or after 1974).

Lucan, Arthur [*real name* Arthur Towle] (**1885–1954**), comedian, was born in Sibsey, Boston, Lincolnshire, on 16 September 1885, the second of five children of Thomas Towle, a groom, and his wife, Lucy Ann Mawer. Educated at a local national school, from an early age he became interested in theatre and frequented Shodfriars Hall, a civic centre in nearby Boston, which included a small auditorium. He saw his first pantomime there in 1892 and was inspired to build a model theatre, staging productions for his own amusement. His first stage role was one of the wise men in a nativity play at the national school. Eventually the young Arthur, then aged eight, was offered a job by the manager of Shodfriars, sweeping the stage in the mornings and selling programmes at night. This gave him the opportunity to watch the weekly shows free, and in 1895, when a measles epidemic decimated the cast of *Robinson Crusoe*, he was asked to play the part of a native.

In 1899 Towle took a job, still selling programmes, at Boston Corn Exchange. He auditioned for the proprietor and began to be used regularly in shows there. His next engagement was in a pierrot troupe, after he had decided to run away from home when his family disapproved of his theatrical activities. Towle began busking on the sands in Skegness and Blackpool. He signed a contract for a seven-year apprenticeship with the Musical Cliftons, at the age of fourteen, and appeared at Colwyn Bay and Llandudno. Danny Clifton and his wife, Vera, 'adopted' the young performer and taught him all they could about comedy. In 1909 they toured Ireland with their barnstorming fit-up show (travelling with a portable stage and scenery by horse and cart).

On hearing that the manager of the Queens Theatre, Dublin, wished to book an English pantomime in 1910, Towle (by then using the surname Clifton professionally) wrote his own script for *Little Red Riding Hood*, which was accepted for the seasonal attraction; he was allowed to play the part of Granny and produce it himself. The title-role was given to a local thirteen-year-old girl singer Towle had discovered at the penny arcade song booth in Henry Street, where potential buyers of sheet music could hear new compositions before they bought them. This was **Kathleen** [Kitty] **McShane** (1897–1964), actress, who was born Catherine McShane in Dublin on 19 May 1897, the fourth child of Daniel McShane, a fireman, and his wife, Kate Hudson, a midwife. During rehearsals for *Little Red Riding Hood* Kitty was prevented from appearing as she was under age, but the show was still a success, with Towle creating his first part as a dame. On a visit to the village of Lucan, outside Dublin (named after Lord Lucan who owned the estate), he noticed the sign 'Lucan's Dairies' on a milk float and decided it would be ideal for his stage

Arthur Lucan (1885–1954), by unknown photographer [as Old Mother Riley, with Kitty McShane as Kitty]

name. His next professional engagement was with the White Coons concert party in Carnoustie, Scotland, where he was to develop his talents as a sketch writer.

Lucan and Kitty McShane were married in Dublin on 25 November 1913 and formed an act that combined their talents. The first sketch Lucan created—based on characters he had observed in the Dublin backstreets—featured him playing a bibulous, aged Irish washerwoman of the period, with hair in a bun, bonnet and shawl, flowing black dress worn with many underskirts, apron, red flannelette bloomers, and elastic-sided boots. Lucan's dexterous gift for visual humour was given full scope as his washerwoman whirled her arms and legs in a startlingly non-geriatric way. Her homely dialogue was full of puns and non sequiturs. This was to be the basis of the Old Mother Riley persona that would make Lucan famous for the rest of his career. McShane played the harridan's glamorous daughter, Bridget, allowing her to show off her singing voice. With sketches including 'Come Over' and 'The Match Seller', Lucan and McShane, as they were now billed, toured the variety circuits in such revues as *Irish Follies*. They journeyed as far afield as South Africa, New Zealand, and Australia. Their 'Bridget's Night Out' sketch was selected for the royal variety performance at the London Palladium in 1934 and its finale, with a hail of flying crockery, was said to have amused George V and Queen Mary greatly. In the following year the *Liverpool Echo* wrote:

> His acting was something quite outside the range of the ordinary 'dame' comedian. Mr Lucan does not, of course, play the part straight, but he never gets completely out of character … in effect realistic acting with excursions into slapstick comedy. (Fisher, 78)

By that time Lucan and McShane were referred to as 'The hottest property in the business today' (King, 63) and, inevitably, films followed—they appeared in fifteen low-budget productions between 1936 and 1951. Lucan's screen and stage character became known as Old Mother Riley after he starred in the film of that title in 1937 with his wife as his daughter Kitty. He appeared solo in his last film with imported Hollywood horror star Bela Lugosi. None of his films received critical acclaim but all made profits at the box office. The Old Mother Riley duo were also a popular cartoon feature in *Film Fun* comic for many years. The BBC gave them their own radio series, *Old Mother Riley Takes the Air*, in 1941. They appeared in many radio variety shows and featured in a post-war series, *Old Mother Riley and her Daughter Kitty* (1948) as well as making four 78 r.p.m. records for Columbia.

The stormy off-stage relationship between Lucan and McShane was an open secret within the variety profession. It reached such a pitch that when filming they had their scenes shot separately and edited together later. Max Wall recalled that it was his impression that Lucan in reality suffered as a battered husband. McShane assumed the position of business manager and hired and fired supporting acts when they took their own shows on tour. According to Jack Le White, whose family speciality act often toured on bills hired by McShane, when the Lucan and McShane stage partnership split up in the 1950s and Kitty started her own Mayfair beauty salon:

> Arthur did his best to carry on with the show, but Kitty took to following after him and creating scenes until it became necessary to ban her from going backstage. So many times we had heard her telling Arthur to drop dead in her reverberating stage whisper. In the end, that is what he did. (Le White and Ford, 218)

Lucan died on 17 May 1954. The *Daily Telegraph* reported next day:

> Old Mother Riley—Arthur Lucan, the comedian—is dead. Lucan, whose crotchety feather-bonneted character brought him stage and film fame and fortune, collapsed in the wings of the Tivoli Theatre, Hull, last night … the curtain was about to go up on his latest revue *Old Mother Riley In Paris*. He was carried to his dressing room and died ten minutes later. (*Daily Telegraph*, 18 May 1954)

Lucan had suffered a heart attack, perhaps exacerbated by the fact that he was in the middle of a long dispute with the Inland Revenue over a matter of £10,000 surtax. His understudy, Frank Seton, made up as Lucan's character, donned his costume and went on in his place. Lucan was buried in Hull's eastern cemetery on 21 May 1954. Kitty McShane died, an alcoholic, in London on 24 March 1964, aged sixty-six. MICHAEL POINTON

Sources S. King, *As long as I know, it'll be quite alright!* (1999) • b. cert. • d. cert. • m. cert. • b. cert. [K. McShane] • G. B. Bryan, ed., *Stage deaths: a biographical guide to international theatrical obituaries, 1850–1990*, 2 vols. (1991) • *Daily Telegraph* (18 May 1954) • *Daily Telegraph* (25 March 1964) [K. McShane] • private information (2004) • press cuttings file, Theatre Museum, Covent Garden, London [obituaries of Lucan and McShane confirming dates] • British Music Hall Society, press cuttings [article in *Call Boy*, 3 (March 1966)] • J. Le White and P. Ford, *Rings and curtains* (1992) • *CGPLA Eng. & Wales* (1964) [Kathleen McShane] • *The Times* (25 March 1964) [Kathleen [Kitty] McShane] • J. Fisher, *Funny way to be a hero* (1973)

Archives FILM BFI NFTVA, advertising film footage • BFI NFTVA, performance footage • BFI NFTVA, propaganda film footage (ministry of information) | SOUND BBC WAC • BL NSA, performance recordings

Likenesses double portrait, photograph (with K. McShane), Old Mother Riley, Arthur Lucan Appreciation Society, Market Rasen, Lincolnshire [*see illus.*]

Wealth at death £3400—Kitty McShane: administration with will, 1 June 1964, *CGPLA Eng. & Wales*

Lucar, Cyprian (1544–1611?), author, was born in London, the eldest of several sons and a daughter of Emanuel Lucar (1494–1574) and his second wife, Joan, daughter of Thomas Turnbull. Emanuel Lucar's forebears had their roots in the west country but he and his family lived in the parish of St Botolph, Billingsgate, in the city of London. He was an active and generous member of the Merchant Taylors' Company and its master in 1560–61, the year in which Merchant Taylors' School was founded. He was one of the merchants who by Protector Somerset's order accompanied the lord mayor to Greenwich in support of a plot to place Lady Jane Grey on the throne, but suffered no punishment under Queen Mary for this act. He was a juryman at the trial of Sir Nicholas Throckmorton for complicity in the insurrection led by Sir Thomas Wyatt the younger in 1554, which sought to prevent the marriage of Mary with Philip of Spain. Throckmorton was found not guilty and in consequence the jurymen were summoned to the Star Chamber and committed to prison, Emanuel Lucar to the Tower of London, to be released on payment of £1000 fine, his fellow jurymen to the Fleet.

Cyprian Lucar was admitted scholar of Winchester College in 1555 and was at New College, Oxford, in 1561–3. In 1568 he entered Lincoln's Inn. He was still living with his widowed mother, brothers, and sisters in St Botolph's Lane at the time when he and Richard Madox paid a visit to Robert Norman, about 1581, to see his new magnetic dipping needle. The date of his marriage to Joan is unknown. She survived him, as did their son Anthony, who entered the Middle Temple, and his brother Mark, who succeeded to family property in Somerset.

In 1588 Lucar published *Three Bookes of Colloquies concerning the Arte of Shooting in Great and Small Peeces of Artillerie*, a translation of the first systematic treatise on ballistics written by Niccolò Tartaglia in 1537. Lucar himself contributed an appendix, somewhat longer than the original Italian text, containing allied material from some twenty continental and five English authors. In fact Lucar had been anticipated by William Bourne, whose *Arte of Shooting in Great Ordnaunce* (1587) was based on Tartaglia. Lucar also produced *A Treatise Named Lucarsolace*, a small volume on current surveying practice, illustrating the instruments and methods used, and including aspects of estate management. It was dedicated to William Roe, alderman of London, who had married Lucar's sister.

Lucar's death probably occurred in 1611; his will, proved that year, described him as 'of Isleworth in Middlesex' (PRO, PROB 11/118). In it he requested that he be buried in St Botolph, Billingsgate, alongside his parents.

Anita McConnell

Sources T. F. Kirby, *Winchester scholars: a list of the wardens, fellows, and scholars of … Winchester College* (1888), 133 • *Reg. Oxf.*, 2/2.21 • will, PRO, PROB 11/118 • W. P. Baildon, ed., *The records of the Honorable Society of Lincoln's Inn: admissions*, 1 (1896), 75 • E. G. R. Taylor, *The mathematical practitioners of Tudor and Stuart England* (1954), 175–6, 328, 330 • C. M. Clode, *The early history of the Guild of Merchant Taylors of the fraternity of St John the Baptist, London*, 2 vols. (1888) • *N&Q*, 176 (1939), 37 • *DNB* • Foster, *Alum. Oxon.*

Lucas. For this title name *see* individual entries under Lucas; *see also* Herbert, Auberon Thomas, eighth Baron Lucas of Crudwell and fifth Lord Dingwall (1876–1916).

Lucas, Anthony (1633–1693), university professor and experimental philosopher, was born on 18 October 1633 in co. Durham. From about 1650 he studied at the Jesuit school at St Omer in Flanders, and he entered the Society of Jesus in May 1662. The next year he joined the English Jesuit college at Liège, and in 1672 became professor of theology there. Liège professors boasted expertise in mathematical and experimental subjects they judged fashionable in England, especially at the Royal Society. In the 1670s Lucas maintained contacts with the society's secretary, Henry Oldenburg, via the ex-Jesuit controversialist and St Omer graduate Robert Pugh, and through the virtuoso John Aubrey, who also proposed to his friend Lucas the making of French translations of English scholarly texts.

Lucas became involved with the Royal Society after Isaac Newton's doctrine of colours was attacked in September 1674 by the elderly Francis Line, mathematics professor at Liège. Newton passed sunlight from a small window-hole into a darkened room then transversely and symmetrically through a prism near the hole, making an oblong spectrum on a distant wall. He claimed that the spectrum's shape showed that rays had intrinsically different refrangibilities. Line reckoned such a shape could only be obtained were the sky cloudy and the prism far from the hole and parallel to the light. After Line's death in November 1675 his student John Gascoines insisted Line had successfully performed many trials before witnesses at the college. In January 1676 Oldenburg sent to Liège Newton's instructions on orienting the prism and darkening the room, and in April organized a Royal Society demonstration of the prism trial.

In May 1676 Lucas joined the fight, interpreting the Royal Society's demonstration as a confirmation of Line's reports. He reproduced a slightly less lengthy oblong spectrum, but his views of spectral colours, coloured silks, and paper discs through lenses and prisms suggested coloured rays did not intrinsically experience different refractions. Lucas's letter on the subject was published in the society's *Transactions* in September 1676. Newton worried about the difference in spectral length but ignored Lucas's other trials, which concerned phenomena Newton had treated in writings of the early 1670s. He wanted Lucas to check prism angles and concave sides, measure spectral lengths, and attend to Newton's crucial experiment, in which well-separated rays were subjected to a second refraction to show each ray's constant refrangibility. In October, Lucas made further trials to challenge intrinsic differences in refrangibility, denied the logical force of the crucial experiment, and appealed to the precedent of Robert Boyle, preferring accumulation of relevant experiments to a single decisive trial. Newton reacted with fury, again demanding that Lucas report on prism size and quality. In early 1677 Lucas conceded that the difference in spectral length, a matter he judged trivial, was perhaps due to his prism's concave sides, glass quality, and the time of day, but repeated that extrinsic factors could explain colours' different refractions.

At the end of 1677 Newton, Aubrey, and Robert Hooke, the Royal Society's new secretary, discussed publication of the optical debate, as Lucas also wanted. In early 1678 Lucas sent copies of his previous letters via Pugh and Hooke, adding that his prism angles were slightly smaller than Newton used and that he had difficulty getting good glass. In Newton's final response to Lucas, sent via Aubrey and Pugh in March 1678, he explained away all Lucas's trials of 1676. Lucas's prism had too small an angle, he had confused mixed with simple colours, and he believed that microscope glasses behaved like fine lenses, ignored differences in angles of incidence, and assumed the crucial experiment was supposed to show that different colours had different refrangibilities, whereas, Newton now claimed, the experiment had nothing to do with colour. Lucas sent Aubrey further letters in the summer of 1678, but Newton withdrew from debate and publication, charging Lucas with conspiracy to embroil him and save Jesuit honour. Lucas, responsible for redirecting Newton's optical project and for some of Newton's anguish about public controversies, has occasionally been treated sympathetically, notably in Johann von Goethe's late eighteenth-century history of optics.

After the end of the debate with Newton, Lucas's English connections were disrupted. In the winter of 1678–9 Jesuits at St Omer were implicated in the Popish Plot, and Pugh, Lucas's contact, died in a London gaol. In 1684 Lucas took part in debates at Ghent about a Jesuit history of the plot. Between 1680 and 1685 he was rector of the Jesuit school for novices at Watten, near St Omer. In 1686 Liège seminarians established a pilgrimage chapel in honour of the Virgin Mary, and it has been suggested that Lucas composed a manuscript account of her life and death. He achieved promotion as James II's regime began encouraging English Jesuits during 1687 and Flemish colleges grew. In March 1687 Lucas became rector of the Liège College, and in October rector of the English College at Rome. In August 1693 he was made provincial superior of the English Jesuits, but he died of fever at the age of fifty-nine, at Watten, on 3 October 1693. SIMON SCHAFFER

Sources G. Holt, *The English Jesuits, 1650–1829: a biographical dictionary*, Catholic RS, 70 (1984) • G. Oliver, *Collections towards illustrating the biographies of the Scotch, English and Irish members of the Society of Jesus*, 2nd edn (1845) • H. Foley, ed., *Records of the English province of the Society of Jesus*, 7/1 (1882) • *The correspondence of Isaac Newton*, ed. H. W. Turnbull and others, 1–2 (1959–60) • *The correspondence of Henry Oldenburg*, ed. and trans. A. R. Hall and M. B. Hall, 12–13 (1986) • H. Chadwick, *St Omers to Stonyhurst* (1962) • [J. Keynes and T. Stapleton], *Florus Anglo-Bavaricus* (Liège, 1685) • *John Aubrey: 'Brief lives' and other selected writings*, ed. A. Powell (1949) • R. S. Westfall, 'Newton defends his first publication: the Newton–Lucas correspondence', *Isis*, 57 (1966), 299–314 • S. M. Gruner, 'Defending Father Lucas: a consideration of the Newton–Lucas dispute on the nature of the spectrum', *Centaurus*, 17 (1973), 315–29

Archives Archives of Society of Jesus, Rome, Epistolae Generalium [Anglia] • RS, correspondence with Oldenburg • Stonyhurst College Archives, Anglia V

Lucas, Bryan Keith- (1912–1996). *See under* Lucas, Keith (1879–1916).

Lucas, Sir Charles (1612/13–1648), royalist army officer, was the youngest of three sons of Thomas Lucas (*d.* 1625), a barrister of St John's, Colchester, and his wife, Elizabeth Leighton (*d.* 1647), a London heiress. His eldest brother, Sir Thomas *Lucas, like Charles a professional soldier, was to serve the king in Ireland, while the royalism of the middle brother, Sir John *Lucas, was to make him the prime target of Colchester rioters in the uneasy weeks which preceded the outbreak of war in 1642. Charles Lucas's youngest sister was Margaret *Cavendish, duchess of Newcastle upon Tyne. The Lucas family had been prominent in Colchester and Essex affairs since the fourteenth century, and these strong local connections played a part in Lucas's later career. Sir Charles Lucas was a brave and capable cavalry commander, but he owes his measure of fame to the manner of his death. He was executed after the surrender of Colchester in 1648 and became, after Charles I, the pre-eminent royalist martyr of the civil wars. The justice of his fate was hotly debated at the time and continued to divide latterday 'royalists' and 'parliamentarians'.

Lucas was educated by a private tutor in Colchester before entering Christ's College, Cambridge, on 7 June 1628 as a fellow commoner, aged fifteen. In May 1637 he went as a cornet in his brother Sir Thomas's troop of horse to serve in the Netherlands, but though he gained useful experience his stay was brief. With the advent of the Scottish wars the Lucas brothers were high on the list of officers with experience abroad who were now 'elected' to serve the king (NL Wales, MS Chirk F 7042). Charles was knighted by the king at Berwick on 27 July 1639. In July 1640 he commanded a troop of horse in Sir Thomas's regiment in Yorkshire, and by September he was in command of the garrison at Richmond. By 1641 he had established himself as an able and responsible officer.

The first civil war Lucas was active in the king's service from the beginning of the civil wars. Between September 1642 and 1644 his actions at Powick Bridge, Edgehill, Cirencester, Nottingham, Doncaster, and elsewhere earned him a reputation for acting '*resolutely and bravely*' (*Mercurius Aulicus*, 1642 [1644], 342). On Prince Rupert's recommendation he became the earl of Newcastle's lieutenant-general of horse. At Marston Moor on 2 July 1644 his brigade, on the royalist left wing, routed Sir Thomas Fairfax's horse, but in a later charge Lucas's horse was killed and he was taken prisoner. After the battle he was taken around the field to identify the eminent royalist dead so that they might be reserved for honourable burial. He is said to have wept at their numbers.

Lucas was finally freed by exchange in the winter of 1644–1645 and soon afterwards was appointed governor of Berkeley Castle. Consequently he was not present at Naseby in June 1645. At Berkeley, Lucas's position was

Sir Charles Lucas (1612/13–1648), by William Dobson, 1645

weakened by disaffected troops, local hostility, and unreliable officers. His subsequent surrender, after parliamentarian troops under Colonel Rainsborough stormed the outer works and undertook a heavy bombardment, did not tarnish his character as 'a souldier of reputation and valour' (I. Sprigge, *Anglia rediviva: Englands Recovery*, 1647, 125), for Berkeley had been 'well defended' (E. Walker, *Historical Discourses*, 1705, 142).

Lucas next joined Prince Maurice and Prince Rupert but he cannot have accompanied them into exile, for late in 1645 he was appointed lieutenant-general of horse to Sir Jacob Astley's force. On 21 March 1646 they were defeated at Stow on the Wold in the last major engagement of the first civil war and Lucas was captured. This appears to have been the occasion on which Fairfax released him on parole.

Lucas's property had been sequestered, but by April 1646 he was petitioning for relief. On 28 February 1648 he compounded for his delinquency in arms and took the requisite oaths, and on 16 March his fine was set at £508 10*s*. 0*d*. He paid half, but on 28 July the suspension of penalties against him was revoked on the ground of failure to pay the remainder. By this time, however, non-payment was the least of his sins.

The siege of Colchester Lucas claimed that he was forced to fly from London when the Derby House committee put a price on his head (probably in fact a reward for information against royalists illegally remaining in London). Commissioned by the prince of Wales to command in Essex, he joined the earl of Norwich and his royalist forces at Chelmsford after they crossed the Thames from Kent early in June 1648. Closely pursued by Fairfax, they marched to Colchester, reaching it on 10 June. In both towns Lucas's exploitation of his local connections was crucial in winning support. On 13 June he was one of a small band of gentlemen who, by a heroic stand at one of the town gates, thwarted Fairfax's attempt to take Colchester by storm. In the long siege of attrition that followed, Lucas, Lord Capel, and Lord Loughborough managed royalist military organization and logistics, and Lucas led several daring raids outside the walls. In negotiations between besiegers and besieged Fairfax refused to deal directly with him:

> for that he, … being his prisoner upon his Parole of Honour, and having appear'd in Arms contrary to the Rules of War, had forfeited his Honour and faith, and was not capable of command or trust in Martial affairs.

Lucas, stung by this attack on his honour and his professionalism, sent back what even a royalist reporter significantly described as 'his excuse for his breech of his Parole' (*Buckinghamshire MSS*, 284).

The bitter siege was marked by hunger, fire, and sickness. Lucas shared the blame for conducting a defence that had no care for civilian suffering, and he was accused of individual acts that breached the rules of war and humanity. At last on 17 August, hunger, mutiny, desertion, civilian protests, and the impossibility of relief drove the royalist leaders to seek a treaty, but their demands were unrealistic and Fairfax was in no mood to be generous. Finally on 27 August they agreed to his terms. On 28 August, at about two in the afternoon, Fairfax entered Colchester.

Execution The provisions were harsh. Junior officers and lower ranks were granted quarter, but senior officers were forced to accept a surrender to mercy. Both terms had specific and well-known military meanings. Quarter preserved the prisoner's life; mercy left it at the discretion of the victorious commander. Surrender to mercy came, in Fairfax's words, 'without certain Assurance of Quarter; so as the Lord General may be free to put some immediately to the Sword, if he see cause' (Rushworth, 7.1247).

Those selected for 'cause' were the most active royalist leaders in Colchester, with the addition of a turncoat, Colonel Farr, who eluded capture. Capel and Norwich were reserved for the judgment of parliament. The immediate victims were Lucas, Sir George Lisle, and Sir Bernard Gascoigne, speedily condemned in absentia by a council of war. They were taken to the castle, and Colonel Henry Ireton, the commissary-general, told them to prepare to die. An extraordinary debate between Lucas and Ireton followed, which ranged over questions of the authority by which they were condemned; the proper jurisdiction, whether civil or military, that covered their case; and ultimately the site of sovereignty and whether it lay in king or parliament (Firth, *Clarke Papers*, 2.35–8). Ireton insisted that the army acted by authority of parliament; Lucas argued that their case should fall under civilian law while denying the charge of treason that this would entail, for service to the king could not be treason. At the same time, however, he appealed to military precedent. At last he desisted. He prayed again with his two friends, asked God to forgive his executioners, and to be laid down decently when he fell and buried with his ancestors. He was shot by six dragoons. Lisle kissed him, and was shot in his turn. Gascoigne, an Italian, was reprieved.

Lucas and Lisle became instant royalist martyrs. A flood of extravagant panegyrics followed. They were noble, heroic, and loyal, and Fairfax and his colleagues were excoriated as unsoldierly murderers and barbarians who had killed in cold blood. Fairfax felt himself on the defensive, though he had acted with perfect legality according to the laws of war that, though unwritten, governed the conduct of the armies of both sides. He was correct in arguing that 'by delivering upon mercy is to be understood, that some are to suffer, and the rest to go free' (Fairfax, Bodl. Oxf., MS Fairfax, 36, fol. 6). Furthermore military law in practice was both discretionary and exemplary; though rules were clear, the rigour with which they were enforced varied according to circumstances. At Colchester, Lucas and Lisle were the 'Persons pitched upon for this Example' (Rushworth, 7.1243). Yet if Fairfax was legally correct he had none the less moved into new territory. Soldiers had surrendered to mercy before in the civil war but their lives had not been forfeited. If he had not breached the laws of war he had breached conventions of practice. The executions were 'new, and without Example', said Clarendon (Clarendon, 3.138).

The reasons offered for the new severity were varied. Royalists attributed it to Fairfax's spleen and pique and his desire for revenge for Lucas's routing of his horse at Marston Moor, and to Ireton's 'unmerciful and bloody Nature' (Clarendon, 3.138). Fairfax's own justification for the selection of Lucas and Lisle was patently disingenuous: they were 'mere soldiers of fortune' and, unlike Capel and Norwich, not 'considerable for estates and family' (Fairfax, Bodl. Oxf., MS Fairfax, 36, fol. 6). Lucas's breach of parole and of the oaths at his composition not to take arms against parliament, both potentially capital charges, and accusations of himself killing in cold blood, were also adduced. In fact Lucas and Lisle, as leading officers, were selected as exemplary victims and by the rules of surrender to mercy no specific charges were needed. More broadly, the need to engage in draconian justice can be explained by the shock and fear the second civil war produced among the victors of the first, by anger at extensive breach of royalist oaths not to take arms again, and by the frustration of a long, bitter, and increasingly pointless siege.

Soldier and martyr Lucas's character remains elusive. Clarendon found him rough, proud, uncultivated, 'morose', and, off the battlefield, intolerable (Clarendon, 3.138). Yet though Lucas professed himself no 'rhetorician' and others granted that 'persuasion was not his talent' (Firth, *Clarke Papers*, 2.32; *Beaufort MSS*, 21), he successfully swayed the unruly crowds at Chelmsford in 1648, and in debate with Ireton he was agile and resourceful. His lost 'Treatise of the arts in war', largely in cipher, suggests an intellectual as well as a practical approach to war, while a letter to Prince Rupert in 1644 reveals a talent for the conventional arts of clientage and flattery (Warburton, 2.370–71). At Colchester he took some steps to mitigate the sufferings of the inhabitants of his home town, but he allowed them no weight in military calculations. The evidence suggests a tough soldier in the mould of the professionals of his age, whose severities were thrown into harsher relief by the 'softness' and 'kindness' of his fellow victim Lisle. Even Clarendon granted that his ability and courage inspired men to follow him (Clarendon, 3.138).

Ultimately the victims triumphed. After their execution Lucas and Lisle were privately buried in St Giles's Church with Lucas's family, but on 7 June 1661, the anniversary of their entry into the king's service, a great funeral was magnificently solemnized in Colchester after a procession through the town of soldiers, gentlemen, and civic dignitaries. The black marble stone placed over their vault recorded that they were 'by the command of Sir Thomas Fairfax, the General of the Parliament army, in cold blood barbarously murdered' (Morant, 1.68). Tradition held that grass would not grow on the spot where they fell.

BARBARA DONAGAN

Sources Margaret, duchess of Newcastle [M. Cavendish], *The life of William Cavendish, duke of Newcastle*, ed. C. H. Firth (1886) • *The Clarke papers*, ed. C. H. Firth, 4 vols., CS, new ser., 49, 54, 61–2 (1891–1901) • M. C. [M. Carter], *A … true … relation of that as honourable as unfortunate expedition of Kent, Essex, and Colchester* (1650) • J. Rushworth, *Historical collections*, 5 pts in 8 vols. (1659–1701) • Thomas, Lord Fairfax, 'Short memorialls', Bodl. Oxf., MS Fairfax 36 [also exists in other MS collections: BL, Harleian MS 2315 and 6390; BL, Add. MS 25, 708. Differences from printed version, *Short Memorials of Thomas Lord Fairfax* (1699), are few but significant] • E. Hyde, earl of Clarendon, *The history of the rebellion and civil wars in England*, 3 vols. (1702–4) • *A great and bloudy fight at Colchester* (1648) • *The manuscripts of the duke of Beaufort … the earl of Donoughmore*, HMC, 27 (1891) [Beaufort MSS] • *The manuscripts of the earl of Buckinghamshire, the earl of Lindsey … and James Round*, HMC, 38 (1895) [Round MSS] • M. A. E. Green, ed., *Calendar of the proceedings of the committee for compounding … 1643–1660*, 5 vols., PRO (1889–92) • P. Morant, *The history and antiquities of the county of Essex*, 2 vols. (1768) • Venn, *Alum. Cant.* • D. J. Appleby, *Our fall our fame: the life and times of Sir Charles Lucas, 1613–1648* (1996) • *The letter books of Sir Samuel Luke, 1644–45*, ed. H. G. Tibbutt, Bedfordshire Historical RS, 42 (1963) • A. H. Woolrych, *Battles of the English civil war* (1961) • C. H. Firth, 'The battle of Marston Moor', *TRHS*, new ser., 12 (1898), 17–79 • *Memoirs of Prince Rupert and the cavaliers including their private correspondence*, ed. E. Warburton, 3 vols. (1849) • J. Vicars, *The burning-bush not consumed* (1646), 399 [bound in *Magnalia Dei Anglicana* (1646)] • R. Bell, ed., *Memorials of the civil war … forming the concluding volumes of the Fairfax correspondence*, 2 vols. (1849) • *CSP dom.*, 1645–6, 215 • *Ninth report*, 2, HMC, 8 (1884), 437 [Morrison MSS]

Likenesses W. Dobson, oils, 1645, priv. coll. [*see illus.*] • W. Dobson, oils, copy, Moot Hall, Colchester • engraving (after M. A. Wagemans?), repro. in *Memoirs of Prince Rupert*, ed. Warburton, vol. 3, facing p. 406 • woodcut, repro. in *The Loyall Sacrifice* (1648)

Wealth at death estate in Horsey, Essex, and apparently property in Suffolk; £2000 in debts at death: *CCC*, 3.1821–2; *CAM*, 1.59

Lucas, Charles (1713–1771), politician and physician, was born on 16 September 1713 in co. Clare, a younger son of Benjamin Lucas (*d. c.*1727), a gentleman farmer of Ballingaddy, and Mary Blood. His great-grandfather, Lieutenant-Colonel Benjamin Lucas, was a Cromwellian officer who had been granted lands in co. Clare after service in the wars of the 1640s. Little is known about Lucas's early

Charles Lucas (1713–1771), by James Macardell (after Sir Joshua Reynolds, 1755)

years, but the assertion that his father had squandered his estate (*DNB*) is belied by the fact that he left effects worth in excess of £900 to his wife and their large family, the sum of £80 being apportioned to Charles.

Early career After his father's death about 1727, Lucas was apprenticed as an apothecary in Dublin city and set up shop there in the 1730s. He married his first wife, Anne Blundell, in 1734. Undeterred by the fact that he was a newcomer to the apothecary's trade, he wrote against frauds and abuses in the preparation and sale of drugs. His campaign was instrumental in securing legislation in 1736 which authorized the Royal College of Physicians of Ireland to inspect apothecaries' shops. His stance also provoked the enduring enmity of many of his colleagues, and may have contributed to an initial failure in business which necessitated a temporary retreat to London about 1737.

Lucas's political involvement began with his appointment in 1741 as a representative of the Barber–Surgeons' Guild on the common council of Dublin corporation, where he soon demonstrated that attachment to radicalism which would mark his later career. The council of Dublin corporation was bicameral, the upper house consisting of the lord mayor and 24 aldermen, the lower house of a maximum 48 sheriff's peers, 96 representatives of the city's guilds, and 2 sheriffs who presided jointly. The corporation's constitution was based partly on royal charters and established usage, but principally on 'New Rules' passed in 1672 during the viceroyalty of the earl of Essex. These rules were designed to strengthen the role of the lord mayor and aldermen by vesting in them power to appoint higher city officers and to vet guild representatives on the council. Though regarded by whigs and radicals on the council as a product of Stuart despotism, the New Rules survived into the Hanoverian period. An attempt was made by William Howard to have the rules repealed following his election as MP for Dublin in 1727, and a corporation committee considered municipal reforms in the 1730s.

In alliance with James Digges La Touche, a Merchants' Guild representative and a member of the wealthy Huguenot merchant and banking family, Lucas commenced a new campaign for municipal reform in 1742. They sought to limit the oligarchic powers of the upper house and to increase the influence of the lower house. The reformers represented the protestant freemen or enfranchised citizens of Dublin only, whose entitlement to participate in municipal and parliamentary elections depended on their membership of the city's exclusive trade guilds. Under the penal laws Catholics were denied participation in politics even at the municipal and guild level. Lucas issued a series of pamphlets in support of the campaign for municipal reform, the most notable being *A Remonstrance Against Certain Infringements* (1743) and *Divelina libera* (1744). The campaign culminated in a lawsuit in the court of king's bench in 1744, when Lucas and La Touche unsuccessfully challenged the aldermen's power of self-election, and shortly thereafter the two lost their seats on the city council.

In January 1747 an outbreak of rioting occurred in Smock Alley Theatre as a result of attempts by the manager, Thomas Sheridan, to curb rowdy excesses by 'gentlemen' members of the audience. Lucas entered the fray as a champion of Sheridan and produced several pamphlets in letter form in February and March 1747, in which, untypically, he concealed his identity behind a pseudonym, 'A Freeman, Barber and Citizen'. Noting that the most prominent rioter, one Kelly, was a Catholic from the province of Connaught, Lucas warned of a relapse into the slavery and barbarism that had characterized the ancient Irish. He claimed that there was more to the riots than a mere theatrical dispute, and that they were the work of a group of 'professed Papists' and 'mercenary converts' preparing for 'a foreign invasion, a western insurrection or an universal massacre' (C. Lucas, *A [First] Letter*, 1747, 2; C. Lucas, *A Second Letter*, 1747, 10). Taken by themselves, these letters are undoubtedly unpleasant and seem to confirm that Lucas was a bigot, and the memory of them would live on to become the principal basis for Lucas's reputation as an ultra-protestant zealot. Yet the obsessive anti-Catholicism of his 'Barber' persona was in fact uncharacteristic of Lucas, and in later years he would become less preoccupied with the dangers of popery and more favourably disposed towards Catholics and ancient Ireland.

The political constitutions Lucas's next opportunity for political action came during the Dublin by-election of 1748–9, when the city's two parliamentary seats fell vacant due to the deaths of the aldermanic incumbents. He declared himself a candidate and, in uneasy alliance with La Touche, sought to end the virtual monopoly of Dublin city's parliamentary representation by aldermen of Dublin corporation. As well as making fiery speeches in the guild halls, Lucas bombarded the voters with pamphlet addresses and letters designed as much to educate them in correct political principles as to advance his own candidacy. He reprinted these tracts in a collected edition in 1751, under the title *The Political Constitutions of Great Britain and Ireland*. This publication may be one of the more important but neglected Irish political texts of the eighteenth century, as well as being Lucas's most coherent work. Though Lucas was a somewhat quixotic personality, and his style not infrequently emotive and pedantic, the *Political Constitutions* is quite readable, as well as being fairly systematically laid out and containing much matter of interest.

The *Political Constitutions* is composed of lengthy prefatory material, twenty election addresses, and six letters to the citizens of Dublin, all written by Lucas, together with selected reprints from Lucas's election newspaper, *The Censor*, many of the latter articles being written by other authors. Lucas's election campaign was not confined merely to municipal matters, as has sometimes been implied, but encompassed much larger political issues. It was in his attempt to demonstrate that the British constitution was also the birthright of the Irish that Lucas was to be most controversial, and indeed original, making a distinct but still not adequately recognized contribution to the development of Irish nationalist thought. In his tenth address, of 13 January 1749, Lucas paraphrased the ideas of the constitutionalist William Molyneux, to the effect that Ireland was not a conquered colony dependent on Great Britain. He then went on to make a radical statement which eventually would land him in serious trouble with the authorities: 'It must now be confessed that there was no general rebellion in Ireland, since the first British invasion, that was not raised or fomented by the oppression, instigation, evil influence or connivance of the English' (C. Lucas, *Political Constitutions*, 1751, 123). In his eleventh address, of 31 January 1749, Lucas went even further in his critique of English misgovernment, claiming that although the native Irish in medieval times had shown their willingness to submit to English law, they had been treated as badly 'as the Spaniards used the Mexicans, or as inhumanly as the English now treat their slaves in America' (ibid., 134). He concluded with an attack on the Declaratory Act of 1720, which he saw as evidence of the increase of the 'destructive excrescence of English power' (ibid., 143), thereby signalling clearly that his words had a contemporary as well as a historical import.

Lucas did not pursue his ideas concerning the treatment of the native Irish, and indeed it is remarkable that he advanced them at all given his protestant prejudices. Yet he more than hinted at the existence of an inclusive Irish nation that transcended the anglican and dissenter sections of the population and had a common interest in resisting English domination, even if he was not prepared to concede that all sections of society should possess a complete equality of civil rights.

A tract dated 18 August 1749, reprinted in the *Political Constitutions*, in the form of a letter to the citizens of Dublin, is evidence that Lucas's views on the Catholic question had also softened. Lucas claimed that he pitied rather than condemned the religious errors of the 'Papists or Romanists', and had the popes not claimed temporal power, he would 'know no difference between the civil rights of a Papist and a Protestant' (Lucas, *Political Constitutions*, 443). Hence he believed that Catholics should be free to worship according to their consciences, and should be compelled only to pay 'due allegiance to the established civil constitution' (ibid., 443). Lucas concluded his religious reflections by stating that all subjects, 'whether Papist or Protestant, Jew or Gentile', should have 'the full protection and benefit of the law' and the liberty to dispose of their persons and property as they chose, subject to the just laws of God and man (ibid., 443–4). Lucas's comments in this letter show that he had undoubtedly modified his position since 1747, and while not committing himself to a call for their repeal, he displayed none of the enthusiastic support for the penal laws which might be expected from a bigot.

It is also significant that Charles O'Conor of Belanagare, the leading Catholic spokesman and writer against the penal laws, was sufficiently interested in the Dublin election controversy to issue a pamphlet in Lucas's defence in 1749, entitled *A Counter-Appeal to the People of Ireland*. Unfortunately this has tended to be overshadowed or negated by a letter hostile to Lucas which was fabricated by O'Conor's grandson and biographer, the Revd Dr Charles O'Conor. This forgery coloured the hostile attitude towards Lucas shown by nineteenth-century historians such as Plowden and Lecky, and remains to influence the unwary today due to its inclusion in the 1988 edition of O'Conor's correspondence. A further indication that those with pro-Catholic sympathies were inclined to support Lucas in 1749 exists in the form of five articles in *The Censor*, which may have been the work of the young Edmund Burke. The articles, some of which were signed with the letter 'B', a signature used by Burke in his own journal, *The Reformer*, exhibit a lofty tone and support Lucas in a relatively cautious and moderate way, but include a specific recommendation that 'penal laws' should now be relaxed.

Parliamentary investigation and exile As the election paper war raged in the summer and autumn of 1749, the controversy surrounding Lucas's candidacy came to a head. Following pointed comments by the lord lieutenant, the earl of Harrington, in his opening speech to the Irish parliament on 10 October 1749, the House of Commons mounted an investigation into Lucas's election writings and summoned him for questioning. Even as the house deliberated on his case, in *The Censor* of 14 October a defiant Lucas courageously but unwisely quoted from a work by James Anderson DD, which claimed that Ireland was a distinct kingdom, that Catholics had believed they were taking arms in their own defence during the rising of 1641, and that both sides in the conflict had been guilty of atrocities. Belief in Catholic guilt in 1641 was almost an article of faith among moderate as well as extreme protestants, and Lucas's stance on 1641 and Irish risings must surely call into question his reputation as an extreme anti-Catholic bigot.

On 16 October 1749 the House of Commons voted that certain of Lucas's election publications were seditious and promoted insurrection, that he had justified past rebellions and reflected scandalously on the lord lieutenant and parliament, and that he was an enemy to his country and should be imprisoned in Newgate. Fearing that his angry followers would attempt a violent uprising and that his health would not withstand imprisonment, Lucas yielded to the pleas of friends and fled by boat to the Isle of Man. He was by this stage a widower, and was obliged to leave his children behind him.

The removal of Lucas from the scene was probably a satisfactory outcome so far as the government and his enemies were concerned, and polling commenced in his absence on 24 October. Although Lucas's running mate La Touche won one of the two parliamentary seats, he was later to be unseated by the House of Commons on the grounds of alleged electoral irregularities, and the representation of Dublin city therefore remained safely in the hands of the aldermanic party for the time being.

Lucas made his way from the Isle of Man to London, where he issued some pseudonymous pamphlets and endeavoured to interest the corporation of London in his case. He then 'threw aside the political pen' and travelled to the continent to study medicine (Lucas, *An Appeal to the Commons and Citizens of London*, 1756, p. 1). Having studied at the University of Paris, he graduated MD at the University of Rheims in 1751, and secured a further MD from the University of Leiden in 1752. The title of his Leiden thesis was *De gangrena et spacelo*.

Lucas returned to England in 1753, and while he maintained an interest in matters political, most of his energies in the years following seem to have been devoted to building up his medical practice, and publishing the results of his research on European spas, his principal work in this area being *An Essay on Waters* (1756). Samuel Johnson reviewed this work, and while expressing scepticism concerning the curative effects of cold bathing, he took a surprisingly sympathetic view of Lucas's political misfortunes, observing that he had been 'driven into exile for having been the friend of his country' (Boswell, *Life*, 1.311). Lucas brought his genius for controversy to his medical activities also, becoming involved in acrimonious debate with the medical faculty at Bath in the late 1750s, on the subject of the professional methods of its members.

Parliamentary success The more relaxed political conditions immediately following the accession of George III in 1760 encouraged Lucas to return to Ireland in order to contest the subsequent general election. In May 1761 he won one of Dublin's two parliamentary seats by a narrow margin, having established in a court action that the legal proceedings initiated against him in 1749 were no longer pending. Lucas threw himself with enthusiasm into his new role as a parliamentarian, his most important legislative achievement being the Octennial Act of 1768, which provided for regular general elections; he also secured additional legislation controlling the sale of drugs. Having been derided earlier for being a mere tradesman, Lucas was now subject to the charge that he was a corporation politician out of his depth in parliament, but his legislative record shows that his transition from municipal to parliamentary politics was perhaps not quite so unsuccessful as claimed.

While there is no evidence that Lucas exerted himself in support of the developing Catholic campaign for relief from the penal laws in the 1760s, neither is there any evidence that he wrote systematically in a bigoted fashion against Catholics, as was alleged by Madden for example. Lucas was closely associated with the radical newspaper, the *Freeman's Journal*, which although it published letters hostile to Catholics, also gave space to some pro-Catholic correspondence, indicating an attitude of growing tolerance if not sympathy among protestant radicals. Yet Lucas did support 'quarterage', an unjust exaction which Catholics had to pay to the protestant-controlled trade guilds, despite not being allowed to become full members.

Lucas had remarried on 27 March 1760 at St James's, Westminster, his bride being Penelope (*d. c.*1765), daughter of Colonel Robert Catherwood. Following Penelope's death Lucas married again in 1768, his third wife being Elizabeth Hely, who survived him. All three of Lucas's wives bore children; of these only the eldest son, Henry *Lucas (*c.*1740–1802), rose to prominence, achieving some minor fame as a court poet.

Final years Lucas's final years were marked by even more intense conflict with the administration, particularly over the issue of augmenting the army in Ireland, and he continued to assert the Irish right to autonomy, never moderating his criticisms of English misgovernment. His relations with the lord lieutenant, Viscount Townshend, were particularly poor, and the latter wrote of him in 1768: 'Here is a Dr Lucas, the Wilkes of Ireland, who has been playing the devil here and poisoning all the soldiery with his harangues and writings' (*Rutland MSS*, 2.303). In the wake of Townshend's prorogation of parliament in December 1769 in response to its refusal to pass a money bill, Lucas issued a strongly worded denunciation entitled *The Rights and Privileges of Parliament Asserted* (1770). The parallels between events in Ireland and those in the increasingly restive American colonies were clear to Irish patriots, and following the Boston massacre in 1770 the townsmen sent Lucas an account of the incident.

So disabled by gout that he frequently had to be carried to and from the House of Commons, Lucas died aged fifty-eight on 4 November 1771 at his home in Henry Street, Dublin. He was buried on 7 November in Dublin's St Michan's churchyard (where his gravestone may still be seen). As well as his son Henry and other relatives, the large funeral procession included members of Dublin corporation and the city guilds, over 200 scholars of Trinity College, and friends and colleagues such as the earl of Charlemont and Henry Flood.

Lacking independent means, Lucas's participation in unremunerative politics meant that he was not infrequently financially embarrassed, and his widow Elizabeth was obliged to apply for a municipal pension after his death. There are several portraits of Lucas, by Reynolds and Hickey among others, but the physical frailty and nervous energy of the man are perhaps best captured in the statue by Edward Smyth in Dublin's City Hall in Dame Street. This remarkably realistic piece of work shows Lucas in full oratorical flight, and also portrays an injured eye which he had sustained in a laboratory accident in his younger days.

Townshend's 'the Wilkes of Ireland' is the best remembered description of Lucas, although it obscures the fact that his campaigns antedated those of the English radical. The relative obscurity into which Lucas fell after his death may be due first to the fact that his period has been overshadowed by the more dramatic events of the late eighteenth century, and second to the absence of a substantial body of surviving personal papers or a near-contemporary published memoir or biography. The lack of personal papers is compensated for significantly by Lucas's copious published writings, and it may be that the unfounded belief that they are uniformly tedious and unimportant has discouraged historians from paying them due attention. Lucas's medical career was also significant, and his efforts to control the manufacture and sale of drugs are actually somewhat better remembered today than his political campaigns. Lucas's personality could be difficult and his habits were certainly independent, yet his reputation for anti-Catholicism has been greatly exaggerated, and his significant contribution to the evolution of Irish nationalism has not received the recognition it deserves.

SEAN J. MURPHY

Sources S. Murphy, 'Charles Lucas, Catholicism and nationalism', *Eighteenth-Century Ireland*, 8 (1993), 83–102 • S. Murphy, 'The Lucas affair: a study of municipal and electoral politics in Dublin, 1742–9', MA diss., University College Dublin, 1981 • S. Murphy, 'Charles Lucas and the Dublin election of 1748–9', *Parliamentary History*, 2 (1983), 93–111 • S. Murphy, 'Burke and Lucas: an authorship problem re-examined', *Eighteenth-Century Ireland*, 1 (1986), 143–56 • *DNB* • E. K. Sheldon, *Thomas Sheridan of Smock-Alley: recording his life as actor and theater manager in both Dublin and London* (1967), 81–95 • *Letters of Charles O'Conor of Belanagare*, ed. R. E. Ward and others (1988), 3.11 • A. P. I. Samuels, *The early life, correspondence and writings of the Rt. Hon. Edmund Burke, LL. D.* (1923), 389–95 • R. R. Madden, *The history of Irish periodical literature*, 2 vols. (1867), 1.43; 2.373–4, 388 • J. Hill, *From patriots to Unionists* (1997) • *The manuscripts of his grace the duke of Rutland*, 4 vols., HMC, 24 (1888–1905) • Genealogical Office, Dublin, MS 142

Archives Royal Irish Acad., Charlemont MSS, personal papers

Likenesses T. Hickey, chalk drawing, 1758, NG Ire. • W. Jones, print (after unknown artist, 1747), NL Ire. • J. Macardell, mezzotint (after J. Reynolds, 1755), BM, NPG [*see illus.*] • E. Smyth, statue, Dublin city hall • print (after J. Reynolds, 1755), NG Ire., NL Ire.

Wealth at death house in Henry Street, Dublin; interest in house at Ballybough Bridge; debts: *Freeman's Journal* (31 Dec 1771)

Lucas, Charles (1769–1854), writer and Church of England clergyman, was the son of William Lucas of Daventry. He was educated first at the school in the close of Salisbury, then at Harrow School. He was admitted a student of Oriel College, Oxford, on 15 July 1786, and he styled himself 'A. M.' on the title-pages of his books, but the university register does not recognize him as a graduate. In 1791 he became curate of Avebury, Wiltshire, where he devoted himself to writing novels and religious poems. Among these are: *A Descriptive Account in Blank Verse of the Old Serpentine Temple of the Druids at Avebury* (1795; 2nd edn with notes, 1801), *The Castle of St Donat's, or, The History of Jack Smith* (1798), and *The Infernal Quixote: a Tale of the Day* (1801). On 5 January 1803 he married Sarah Ann Williams, sister of the Revd H. Williams; they had a large family. Lucas continued to write, producing a novel entitled *The Abissinian Reformer, or, The Bible and the Sabre* (1808) and *Joseph* (1810), a religious poem in two volumes. Lucas left Avebury in 1816 and settled at Devizes, where he died in 1854.

A. F. POLLARD, *rev.* M. CLARE LOUGHLIN-CHOW

Sources [J. Watkins and F. Shoberl], *A biographical dictionary of the living authors of Great Britain and Ireland* (1816) • Boase, *Mod. Eng. biog.* • Watt, *Bibl. Brit.* • *IGI* • Foster, *Alum. Oxon.*

Lucas, Charles (1808–1869), composer, cellist, and conductor, was born at Salisbury, Wiltshire, on 28 July 1808, the son of a music-seller. He was a chorister at Salisbury Cathedral for eight years under Arthur Thomas Corfe. In 1823 he was admitted to the Royal Academy of Music, where he studied the cello with Robert Lindley and composition with William Crotch. He was made a sub-professor of composition in 1824, and won several prizes. In 1830 he joined Queen Adelaide's private band, and about the same time became music tutor to Prince George (later duke) of Cambridge and the princes of Saxe-Weimar. In 1832 he succeeded Cipriani Potter as conductor at the Royal Academy, and in 1839 became organist of Hanover Chapel, Regent Street. He was for some time conductor of the Choral Harmonists' Society, and from 1840 to 1843 occasionally conducted at the Ancient Concerts. From 1859 to 1866 he was principal of the Royal Academy, and from 1856 to 1865 a member of the music-publishing house of Addison, Hollier and Lucas. He was in much demand as a cellist and succeeded Robert Lindley as principal cellist of the Italian Opera and the Philharmonic Society. His compositions included an opera, *The Regicide*, three symphonies, string quartets, anthems, songs, and a cello concertino, and he edited *Esther* (1851) for the Handel Society. Several of his works were performed at concerts of the Philharmonic Society.

Lucas married Helen Taylor (*d.* 1866), a soprano. A Charles Lucas married Frances Short at St Thomas, Salisbury, on 15 March 1832, and may be our subject; Zoë Wilson (*b.* 1840), who married Walter Hawken *Tregellas, was described as the third daughter of Lucas and his wife Frances. He died on 23 March 1869 at his home, 9 Louvaine Road, Wandsworth, London, and was buried at Woking. The Royal Academy of Music set up a gold medal for composition in his memory. His executors were his two sons, Stanley and Radnor.

J. C. HADDEN, *rev.* ANNE PIMLOTT BAKER

Sources F. Corder, *A history of the Royal Academy of Music from 1822 to 1922* (1922) • *Magazine of Music* (Oct 1890) • *New Grove* • W. W. Cazalet, *The history of the Royal Academy of Music* (1854) • J. F. Waller, ed., *The*

imperial dictionary of universal biography, 3 vols. (1857–63) • *CGPLA Eng. & Wales* (1869)
Likenesses portrait, repro. in Corder, *History of the Royal Academy of Music*, 71 • portrait, repro. in *Magazine of Music*, 183
Wealth at death under £3000: probate, 11 May 1869, *CGPLA Eng. & Wales*

Lucas, Sir Charles Prestwood (1853–1931), civil servant and historical geographer, was born at Glanyrafon, Crickhowell, Brecknockshire, on 7 August 1853. He was the fourth and youngest son of Henry John Lucas MD, of Glanyrafon and his wife, Elisabeth, daughter of George Bevan, vicar of Crickhowell. He was educated at Winchester College, and won an open exhibition to Balliol College, Oxford, where he was a contemporary of Alfred Milner. He gained first classes in classical moderations (1873) and *literae humaniores* (1876), and was awarded the chancellor's Latin essay prize (1877).

Lucas was placed first on the civil service examination list of 1877, and was appointed to the Colonial Office, serving *inter alia* in the West Indian department and the dominions department (the latter created in 1907 from the department dealing with the 'self-governing colonies') as joint head (he had become an assistant under-secretary in 1897). He had been appointed in 1886 to serve on the managing council of the emigrants' information office. Lucas was much in sympathy with the imperial ideologies of Joseph Chamberlain (appointed colonial secretary in 1895), but with the coming to power of a Liberal government in 1905 the prospects of Lucas's promotion as head of the Colonial Office receded. In 1911, at the age of fifty-eight, he retired. He had been appointed CB in 1901, and was made KCMG in 1907 and KCB in 1912. He was called to the bar by Lincoln's Inn in 1885.

Lucas spent the rest of his life, supported by a fellowship at All Souls College, Oxford, 1920–27 (in acknowledgement of his services to colonial history), writing and lecturing on the British empire, and was a major advocate of the study of imperial history and geography in schools and universities. He continued the work that he had begun in 1881 of teaching and assisting at the Working Men's College in Great Ormond Street, London. He became a member of the council of that college in 1892 at the age of thirty-nine, and was vice-principal 1896–1903 and principal 1912–22. The college, founded in 1854, linked intellectuals, administrators, writers and artists, and working people in London who wished to advance their knowledge and education. Among the college's early impressive array of voluntary lecturers was J. R. Seeley, whose imperial ideas had an important influence on Lucas's own work.

From 1887 to 1925 Lucas edited a book series entitled A Historical Geography of the British Colonies. An introduction to the series, written by Lucas himself, was published in 1887; he was also responsible for volumes 1–4 and part 1 of volume 5 (1888–1901). The volumes of the series were frequently revised up to about 1925. His other works included *Greater Rome and Greater Britain* (1912), which compared attitudes to race in the classical Roman and contemporary British empires, *The British Empire* (1915),

Sir Charles Prestwood Lucas (1853–1931), by Walter Stoneman, 1917

The Beginnings of English Overseas Enterprise (1917), *The Partition and Colonization of Africa* (1922), *The Story of the Empire* (British Empire series, vol. 2, 1924), and *Religion, Colonising and Trade* (1930). He edited and wrote much of *The Empire at War* (5 vols., 1921–6).

The institutions through which Lucas purveyed his views on empire included the Royal Colonial Institute, to which in 1894 the Geographical Association had sent copies of replies to a questionnaire about the teaching of geography in schools, and the Geographical Association, of which he was president in 1920 and subsequently vice-president. His writings accorded respect to the factual and historic details of individual colonies, but while emphasizing the need for a sensitive and sympathetic view of their potential also expressed concern at the developing critiques of British imperialism. They reflect some of the contemporary views on acclimatization, exhibit awareness of the speed of change within the empire, and provide a liberal and enlightened perspective on the need for racial equality. Lucas died, unmarried, at his London home, 65 St George's Square, Westminster, on 7 May 1931. ROBIN A. BUTLIN

Sources *The Times* (8 May 1931) • *Geography*, 16 (1931), 153 • R. A. Butlin, 'Historical geographies of the British empire', *Geography and imperialism, 1820–1940*, ed. M. Bell, R. Butlin, and M. Heffernan (1995), 151–88 • B. L. Blakely, *The colonial office, 1862–92* (1971) • J. F. C. Harrison, *A history of the Working Men's College, 1854–1954* (1954) • T. R. Reese, *The history of the Royal Commonwealth Society* (1968) • R. Symonds, *Oxford and empire: the last lost cause?* (1991) • *DNB*
Archives NL Aus., corresp. with Alfred Deakin • NL Scot., letters • Working Men's College, Camden, London
Likenesses W. Stoneman, photograph, 1917, NPG [*see illus.*] • A. G. Wyon, marble bust, *c.*1933, Gov. Art Coll.
Wealth at death £8490 16*s.* 7*d.*: probate, 21 Aug 1931, *CGPLA Eng. & Wales*

Lucas, Charles Thomas (1820–1895), public works contractor, was born on 26 October 1820 in Greenland Place, Cromer Street, St Pancras, London, the second son and fourth child of James Jonathan Hughes Lucas, a plasterer, said to be of Norfolk and Quaker descent, but born and baptized in the City of London, and his wife, Elizabeth Pearman. After serving articles with Stokes, a London builder, Lucas joined his father; he was soon employed by Samuel Morton Peto (1809–1889) to superintend construction of the Norwich and Brandon Railway. In 1842 he set up his own contracting business in Norwich, where he was joined by his younger brother Thomas [*see below*] in founding Lucas Brothers at Lowestoft; they were extensively involved in the development of the town, the construction of waterworks, and the rebuilding of nearby country houses, including Somerleyton for Peto from 1844, Henham, and Rendlesham. The brothers moved in 1850 to London, where they secured riverside premises at Belvedere Road in Lambeth, aiming from the outset 'to become one of the first firms in London' (*The Builder*, 17 Nov 1860, 757). In 1849 they had leased Peto's Somerleyton brickworks; the railway made off-site production profitable, and these became the focus of works that produced the vast quantities of building materials required for their undertakings. In the later 1850s they appeared frequently in *The Builder*'s lists of competitive tenders, but as unsuccessful, suggesting both that they had become one of the 'inevitable' major contractors, and that their amount of work in hand made it generally unnecessary to quote very low prices.

This picture is confirmed by Lucas's statement, at a dinner to his workmen in the volunteer corps (of which he was a lieutenant-colonel) given in 1860, that they had had the same number of men in their employ 'upwards of ten years, and who had never yet had to work an hour's short time'. They had 'felt it their duty at times to take works at a loss in order to keep their old hands on', but none the less their overall profit had been beyond anything they could have anticipated (*The Builder*, 17 Nov 1860, 757). Indeed, the firm obtained a commanding position in the construction of railway termini and vast hotels. Major works included Covent Garden Opera House and Floral Hall (1858, 1860), stations and hotels at Charing Cross, Cannon Street, Liverpool Street (1863–4, 1867, and 1874), and York (1877–8), and other leading hotels in London including the Palace (1860–61), London Bridge (1861, at a cost of £110,000), the Langham (1864, at a cost of £300,000), and De Keyser's (1874). They also built King's College Hospital (1862), the Junior Carlton Club, Pall Mall (1866), the Royal Albert Hall (1867), and Charterhouse School (1872). The country houses they built included Cliveden for Lord Westminster and Normanhurst for Lord Brassey. They undertook in partnership with Kelk the huge building (largely intended to be temporary) at South Kensington to house the 1862 International Exhibition, a £300,000 job. The South Kensington exhibitions of 1867 and 1871 were also their construction. Works for the war department included the reconstruction of Woolwich arsenal and Colchester camp, and contracts at Aldershot and Shorncliffe. In 1861, when they were building the new Blackfriars Bridge, Lucas Brothers were employing about 3000 men.

In the 1860s the brothers turned to railway contracting on their own account, though often in collaboration with other firms. Kelk and Lucas were contractors for the Metropolitan District Railway, and Lucas joined Brassey and Wythes in the East London Railway, tunnelled under the Thames. Their main railway work for the Great Eastern Railway was in 1865–75. They also worked on the London, Chatham, and Dover Railway, and the West Highland. In 1870 they took John Aird into partnership, forming two new companies, Lucas and Aird, 'one of the largest employers of labour in the country', and John Aird & Sons, to specialize in railway and commercial contracting. 'Heavily engaged in all directions on railways, dock and harbour construction, and gas- and water-works, … besides work for most of the principal railway companies' (*PICE*, 149, 1902) they built the Royal Albert and the rival Tilbury docks (1880, 1882–6), and undertook the Suakin–Berber Railway in the Sudan in 1885.

Lucas married Charlotte Emma, daughter of Charles Tiffin, on 27 April 1842; they had five sons and two daughters. In London he lived at 9 Belgrave Square. Of kindly manner and homely appearance, he nevertheless had a reputation for strength of will and the exercise of great authority, and for utter integrity in his business life. He acquired a country seat at Warnham Court near Horsham, Sussex, and became the complete squire, making large additions to the estate, restoring the church, laying out gardens, and rearing horses, sheep, and cattle, 'his various herds being well known in the agricultural world' (*PICE*, 144, 1896, 438). 'A generous landlord and a popular county man' (ibid.), he was a JP, and high sheriff, and also a deputy lieutenant for Sussex. He was a Conservative and was consulted by ministers on labour questions, but declined offers of an unopposed return to parliament because of his business commitments. His wife predeceased him; he provided for three of his younger sons in brewery businesses and left his Sussex estates to his eldest son, with the bulk of his personal property, for the upkeep of Warnham Court, expressing the wish that the estate should descend in the male line. He retired from business about 1891 and died of old age at Warnham Court on 4 December 1895.

His brother **Sir Thomas Lucas**, first baronet (1822–1902), public works contractor, was born on 18 July 1822, also in Greenland Place, Cromer Street, St Pancras, London, the third son and fifth child of James and Elizabeth Lucas. About 1844 he joined Charles in establishing Lucas Brothers. Active like his brother in the volunteers, Thomas gave evidence to a War Office committee on the question of reserves and terms of service. In a trifling railway accident he received a blow on the knee that affected him for forty years and ultimately made him a confirmed invalid, leading a retired life. He was keenly interested in politics and a member of the Carlton Club, and was closely concerned with Viscount Cross's schemes for artisans' dwellings. He received a baronetcy from Salisbury's government in 1887, possibly inspired by his building Princess Alexandra's house for female students, South Kensington, at cost.

Thomas Lucas was twice married, first, in 1845, to Jane Rolfe (*d.* 1849), daughter of Charles Golder, with whom he had one daughter; and second, on 2 June 1852, to Mary Amelia, daughter of Robert Chamberlain of Catton

House, Norfolk, with whom he had six sons and four daughters. His principal recreation was the opera. He collected paintings and *objets d'art* in his mansion at 12A Kensington Palace Gardens, where in 1871 his family was supported by a large resident staff of governess, eight female, and five male servants. He was socially aspirant and was described in the 1871 census as a magistrate and deputy lieutenant for Middlesex. He purchased Ashtead House, Surrey, in 1880 but sold it in 1888, although retaining the advowson; instead, Heatherwood, Ascot, Berkshire, became his summer residence. He commonly wintered at Cannes, and was closely involved in establishing St George's Anglican Church there.

Much richer (and better-looking) than his brother, Sir Thomas Lucas at his death left an estate valued at £775,984; he possessed, in addition to shares in Lloyds Bank, mines and mining companies and the Hull, Barnsley, and West Riding Junction Railway and Dock Company, real estate in Norfolk, Suffolk, Middlesex, Surrey, Berkshire, and elsewhere, which he instructed in his will should be sold. He died on 6 March 1902 at 12A Kensington Palace Gardens, London. He was survived by his wife.

M. H. PORT

Sources *PICE*, 124 (1895–6), 438–41 • *PICE*, 149 (1901–2), 366–8 [obit. of Thomas Lucas] • 'Messrs Lucas and the volunteers', *The Builder*, 18 (1860), 756 • parish register, Holborn, St Andrew's, 19 Nov 1820 [birth; baptism] • parish register, Holborn, St Andrew's, 6 Aug 1822 [Sir Thomas Lucas: birth, baptism] • census returns, 1871, PRO, RG 10/131/75; 1881, RG 11/121/48 • *The Times* (8 March 1902) • *London Directory* • Burke, *Peerage* • d. cert. [Sir Thomas Lucas]

Likenesses group portrait, engraving, 1862 (with T. Lucas and J. Kelk; after photograph), repro. in *ILN*; copy, NPG • H. O'Neil, painting, exh. RA 1871 • L. Dickinson, painting, 1880 (Sir Thomas Lucas); Christies, 9 Dec 1981, no. 192

Wealth at death £312,078 13*s*. 1*d*.: probate, 17 Jan 1896, *CGPLA Eng. & Wales* • £775,984 5*s*. 9*d*.—Sir Thomas Lucas: probate, 17 April 1902, *CGPLA Eng. & Wales*

Lucas, David (1802–1881), mezzotint engraver, was born on 18 August 1802 in Geddington Chase, between Rushton and Brigstock, Northamptonshire, the eldest of seven children of Charles Lucas (1765/6–1852), farmer and grazier, and his wife, Sarah (1775/6–1849). He was baptized in Brigstock's Independent church on 28 January 1808. In April 1820, while working on his father's farm in Brigstock, he had a chance encounter with the mezzotint engraver S. W. Reynolds, who was travelling in the district and, having stopped for a drink of water, serendipitously discovered that Lucas was a talented (presumably self-taught) landscape draughtsman. Having seen a few drawings scattered about the farmhouse, but knowing nothing else about Lucas's suitability for the profession, Reynolds none the less offered him an engraving apprenticeship, which his father managed to secure for a token sum of 10*s*. Lucas immediately moved to London, where he lived with Reynolds at Ivy Cottage, Bayswater, until his apprenticeship (renegotiated when he came of age in 1823) ended in 1827. By that year he had moved to 18 Wyndham Street, Bryanston Square, from where he published his first independent mezzotints. Several more plates appeared in 1828, including a portrait of the duke of Wellington, after

David Lucas (**1802–1881**), attrib. Robert William Satchwell, *c*.1820

Sir T. Lawrence, and *The Bride*, after J. Masquerier, which was praised by *The Athenaeum* (21 May 1828, 470) for its 'fine disposition of the lights and shadows'.

By May 1829 Lucas had come to the attention of John Constable and began what was to be the most important artistic alliance of his career. As a former agricultural labourer and able landscape draughtsman, well trained by an accomplished painter and engraver of landscapes, Lucas was especially suited to a collaboration with Constable. Although he did continue to produce competent reproductive engravings of portraits and genre subjects after various artists, evidence of his remarkable interpretative powers and technical mastery can only fully be seen in his landscape mezzotints, particularly those created under Constable's obsessively close supervision. Between June 1830 and July 1832 Constable's *Various Subjects of Landscape, Characteristic of English Scenery* (generally known as *English Landscape*) was published in five parts, containing twenty-two plates. Hundreds of progress proofs chronicle their complex development during, and even after, their publication as Lucas constantly reworked the plates in an effort to incorporate Constable's numerous instructions, typically conveyed by scribbled notes, touched impressions, and marginal drawings. While preparing these plates Lucas worked on additional ones intended for the series but temporarily laid aside as Constable dithered about the final scope of his publication. He continued to work on at least six of them under Constable's supervision but plans for their publication were halted by the artist's death in 1837. Impressions issued by F. G. Moon and dated 1838 suggest that Lucas further prepared them for publication, presumably with the co-operation of Constable's children, with whom he maintained friendly relations for many years. Two of these plates, plus others prepared with the guidance of C. R. Leslie, were published by Lucas in his 'new series' of *English Landscape* in 1846. Although he no longer had the volatile and demanding Constable to cajole and inspire him Lucas was still able in several of these mezzotints to convey the depth and power of the artist's expressive chiaroscuro and unorthodox handling. In addition to these plates Lucas engraved six large ones after Constable, all begun in the artist's lifetime but only two of which were published before his death. *The Lock* and *The Cornfield*, issued by Moon in 1834, were praised as 'powerful and noble' by the *Literary Gazette* (27 Dec 1834), whose reviewer thought Lucas 'eminently successful in exhibiting the peculiar and characteristic manner of their execution' (p. 869).

Lucas, perhaps because he was known as Constable's engraver, remained peripheral to the vast commercial print publishing industry. Information about his work for other artists is fragmentary but prints after R. Smirke, R. P. Bonington, E. Isabey, D. Roberts, T. Girtin, J. D. Harding, and several others are known, including *A Devonshire Water Mill*, after F. R. Lee, published for the Art Union in 1839. Scientific publications by George Field and J. H. Kyan include small, but most unusual, Lucas engravings. His last known employment was to rework Constable's *English Landscape* plates for their republication by H. G. Bohn in 1855. Despite evidence that alcoholism plagued the final decades of his life and prevented any further work Lucas inexplicably took on an apprentice, J. B. Pratt, from 1868 to 1873.

Lucas was a knowledgeable printer, sensitive to selective inking and wiping. He relied primarily on mezzotint but would use other techniques to achieve his effects. Occasionally his signature or monogram appears in the mezzotint ground or inscription space. The most complete collections of Lucas prints are in the Fitzwilliam Museum, Cambridge (together with his engraving tools and extensive correspondence from Constable), the British Museum, the Metropolitan Museum of Art, New York, the Tate collection (including ten steel plates), and private collections.

On 9 October 1830 Lucas married a widow, Jane Smith, *née* Prece (*b. c.*1802, *d.* in or before 1881), a nurse, with whom he had three daughters and five sons, one of whom was born before the marriage. They lived in Paddington until 1833, when they moved to Pimlico. Suffering from paraplegia and senile decay Lucas died in Fulham union workhouse on 22 August 1881, unaware that his mezzotints were featured that year in an exhibition at the Burlington Fine Arts Club. He was buried in a pauper's grave in Fulham cemetery on 26 August 1881.

JUDY CROSBY IVY

Sources A. Shirley, *The published mezzotints of David Lucas after John Constable, RA* (1930) • FM Cam., Charrington collection • *John Constable's correspondence*, ed. R. B. Beckett, 4, Suffolk RS, 10 (1966), 314–463 • F. Wedmore, *Constable: Lucas: with a descriptive catalogue of the prints they did between them* (1904) • private information (2004) [including C. Lennox-Boyd] • L. Parris, *John Constable and David Lucas* (New York, 1993) [exhibition catalogue, Salander–O'Reilly Galleries, New York, 6 May – 5 June 1993] • L. Parris and I. Fleming-Williams, 'The English landscape mezzotints', in L. Parris and I. Fleming-Williams, *Constable* (1991), 318–57 [exhibition catalogue, Tate Gallery, London, 13 June – 15 Sept 1991] • J. Gage, *George Field and his circle* (1989) [exhibition catalogue, Fitzwilliam Museum, Cambridge, 27 June – 3 Sept 1989] • *Catalogue of engravings in mezzotinto, illustrating the history of that art down to the time of David Lucas*, Burlington Fine Arts Club (1881) • E. E. Leggatt, *Catalogue of the complete works of David Lucas* (1903) • private information (2004) • d. cert. [Charles Lucas] • d. cert. [Sarah Lucas] • marriage register, St Marylebone, 9 Oct 1830 • *IGI* • parish register, Fulham, 26 Aug 1881 [burial] • d. cert. • indenture papers

Archives Museum of Fine Arts, Boston, MSS • Tate collection, MSS • U. Cam., MSS

Likenesses attrib. R. W. Satchwell, watercolour miniature, *c.*1820, NPG [*see illus.*] • G. Lucas, pen-and-ink and wash drawing, 1876, priv. coll. • J. B. Pratt, pencil drawing, 1898, priv. coll. • T. H. Hunn, chalk drawing, 1902 (after J. Lucas), NPG

Wealth at death died a pauper: parish register, Fulham, 26 Aug 1881; d. cert.

Lucas, David Keith- (1911–1997). *See under* Lucas, Keith (1879–1916).

Lucas, Edward Verrall (1868–1938), essayist and biographer, was born at the Villa Stresa in Wellington Road, Eltham, Kent, on 12 June 1868, the second son of the four sons and three daughters of Alfred Lucas (1841–1895) of Sussex, agent for insurance companies and building societies and formerly a woollen merchant, and his wife, Jane Drewett (*b.* 1844), daughter of William Drewett of Luton, Bedfordshire, baker and later a corn dealer. Both parents were Quakers, and members of families whose interests had been banking and brewing, but on his mother's side he was related to Joseph Lister and Arthur Woollgar Verrall. Lucas's parents moved to Brighton not long after he was born, so that he was able to call himself a Sussex man. Always devoted to his mother, who encouraged his taste in literature, he had less affection for his father, whose laxity in financial matters led to Lucas's being placed in nine different schools before being apprenticed, aged sixteen, to a bookseller in Brighton. He deeply regretted the loss of a classical education, and frequented poetry readings to make up for it. In 1886 he wrote to Andrew Lang and journeyed to Oxford to hear Walter Pater lecture on the history of the Renaissance.

In 1889 Lucas joined the staff of the *Sussex Daily News*, and his first volume of poetry, *Sparks from a Flint*, was published the following year. His literary skill convinced an uncle to donate £200 for him to go to London to attend the lectures of W. P. Ker at University College, where Lucas read assiduously, founded two university magazines, and in 1893 was recruited to the staff of *The Globe*, a leading evening paper. *The Globe's* loose schedule allowed him to spend most of his time in the reading room of the British Library, which he later called his 'alma mater'. He spent many of his evenings translating Maupassant, not for publication but as practice in style.

When Lucas was twenty-four the Society of Friends asked him to write a book on Charles Lamb, as well as *Bernard Barton and his Friends: a Record of Quiet Lives* (1893), and to edit a Quaker magazine, *The Essayist*. His success in these endeavours led to a commission from Smith, Elder & Co. for *Charles Lamb and the Lloyds* (1898), and from Methuen for a new edition of Lamb, which ran to seven volumes, and a biography. These works established him as a critic, and his *Life of Charles Lamb* (1905) is considered seminal.

In 1897 Lucas married (Florence) Elizabeth Gertrude, daughter of James Theodore Griffin, a colonel in the

Edward Verrall Lucas (1868–1938), by Howard Coster, 1931

United States army; the couple had one daughter, Audrey. Elizabeth was a talented literary woman, writing under the name Mr C. Greene, and was a close friend of J. M. Barrie. Lucas collaborated with her on several children's books. Among his other publications—there were 180 before he died—were many anthologies and about thirty collections of light essays. Some of the titles he gave them—*Fireside and Sunshine* (1906), *A Swan and her Friends* (1907), *Cloud and Silver* (1916), and *The Vermillion Box* (1916)—indicate sufficiently the lightness and gaiety of their contents. He published parodies of well-known literary works and his growing reputation as a humorist gained him a position at *Punch* in 1904, where he remained for thirty years.

Lucas also became notable as a travel writer, publishing *Highways and Byways in Sussex* (1904), *A Wanderer in Holland* (1905), *A Wanderer in Florence* (1912), and *Zigzags in France* (1925). He wrote articles on India, Japan, and Jamaica, and published short books on painters, notably *Vermeer of Delft* (1922), *John Constable the Painter* (1924), and *Vermeer the Magical* (1929). He attempted to turn playwright, collaborating with Barrie on *The Visit of the King*, performed at the Palace Theatre in London in 1912, and independently writing several comedies including *The same Star* (1924), but all were failures. He wrote romances, including *Rose and Rose* (1921) and *Genevra's Money* (1922), which were slight, sentimental, and charming. And he established himself as an expert essayist on cricket, Pekinese dogs, Japanese scrolls, and Chinese rice-paper, books which were by far his most popular. In 1924 he became chairman of Methuens publishing company, with which he had long been connected.

Lucas once remarked of the painters he praised: 'I know very little about pictures, but I like to write about them for the benefit of those who know less'. This same statement might be applied to much of his work, for he undoubtedly broadened the horizon of culture for a great number of readers by the easy introduction he gave them to books which they would not otherwise have read, and pictures they would not have seen. At the same time, he helped liberate the language of the critic from undue pedantry and affectation. Often preferring the quaint to the profound, and claiming neither deep study nor creative imagination, he established himself by dint of good taste. In later years a member of many social clubs, he added to the reputation of a writer that of a connoisseur who was both bon vivant and lavish host. He received the honorary degree of LLD from the University of St Andrews and DLitt from the University of Oxford and was appointed CH in 1932. After he died, aged seventy, on 26 June 1938 in a nursing home at 20 Devonshire Place, London, he was warmly eulogized by his daughter, Audrey, and by A. A. Milne. Nor did Lucas ever forget the start of his success. Throughout his life he paid for the upkeep of Charles Lamb's grave, and when he died he left a sum for that purpose in perpetuity. E. V. KNOX, *rev.* KATHARINE CHUBBUCK

Sources A. Lucas, *E. V. Lucas: a portrait* (1939) · C. A. Prance, *E. V. Lucas and his books* (1988) · E. V. Lucas, *Reading, writing and remembering: a literary record* (1932) · E. V. Lucas, *The old contemporaries* (1935) · C. Asquith, *Portrait of Barrie* (1954) · D. Mackail, *The story of J. M. B.: a biography* (1941) · A. St John Adcock, *The glory that was Grub Street* [1928] · A. P. Hudson, ed., *Collins encyclopaedia* (1968), vol. 15 · *The Times* (27 June 1938) · 'Dictionary of Quaker biography', RS Friends, Lond. [card index] · b. cert. · *WWW, 1941–50* · *The Friend* (1 July 1938) · *CGPLA Eng. & Wales* (1938)

Archives Dartmouth College, Hanover, New Hampshire, corresp., literary MSS, and papers · Ransom HRC, corresp. and papers | BL, letters to William Archer, Add. MS 45293 · BL, corresp. with G. K. Chesterton and others, Add. MS 73195, fols. 168–212 · BL, corresp. with Macmillans, Add. MS 55034 · BL, corresp. with Society of Authors, Add. MS 63282 · Bodl. Oxf., corresp. with Sibyl Colefax · Bodl. Oxf., letters to Bertram Dobell · Bodl. Oxf., letters to Sidney Lee · Cheltenham College, letters to Charles Turley · Col. U., Rare Book and Manuscript Library, corresp. with Arnold Bennett · Elgar Birthplace Museum, Worcester, letters to Edward Elgar · Forbes Magazine, New York, letters to John Galsworthy · Keele University Library, letters to Marguerite Bennett · LUL, letters to Austin Dobson · NRA, priv. coll., letters to Sir Norman Moore · Richmond Local Studies Library, London, Sladen MSS · U. Edin. L., corresp. with Charles Sarolea · U. Leeds, Brotherton L., letters to Clement Shorter

Likenesses photographs, 1904–31, repro. in Lucas, *E. V. Lucas* · H. Leslie, silhouette, 1925, NPG · H. Coster, photographs, *c*.1931, NPG [*see illus.*] · R. Guthrie, pen-and-ink drawing, 1937, NPG · R. Peacock, portrait, *Punch* offices, London · J. Tweed, plaster bust, priv. coll.

Wealth at death £24,670 2*s*. 2*d*.: probate, 21 July 1938, *CGPLA Eng. & Wales*

Lucas, Frank Laurence (1894–1967), author and classical scholar, was born on 28 December 1894 at Hipperholme in Yorkshire, the elder son of Frank William Lucas, headmaster of the grammar school there, and his wife, Ada Ruth

Blackmur. Educated at Colfe's Grammar School, Lewisham, where his father was then headmaster, and at Rugby School, he went up to Trinity College, Cambridge, in 1913 with a classical scholarship and in 1914 won the Pitt University scholarship and the Porson prize for Greek iambics. The war interrupted Lucas's university career and in November 1914 Peter, as he was always called, was commissioned in the Royal West Kent regiment. He served throughout the war on the western front and the *Official History* mentions his 'daring and resourceful reconnaissance ... conducted whilst British shrapnel was bursting behind him', which brought the first indication of the German retreat to the Hindenburg line. After being dangerously wounded in 1916 and gassed in 1917, he was transferred to the intelligence corps. The war left him partially deaf.

Back in Cambridge in 1920, where he was numbered among the Apostles, he won the Chancellor's medal for classics and a Browne medal for Latin ode, was placed in the first class in part one of the classical tripos, and was elected to a fellowship in classics at King's. His first two published works were in this field, *Seneca and Elizabethan Tragedy* (1922) and *Euripides and his Influence* (1924), but he was then attracted to the newly established English faculty. Meanwhile on 17 February 1921 he had married the novelist Emily Beatrix Coursolles (Topsy) *Jones (1893–1966), and had become associated with the Bloomsbury group of writers and artists. Virginia Woolf knew him well and described him to Ottoline Morrell as 'an academic poet; pure Cambridge: clean as a breadknife and as sharp' (*Letters of Virginia Woolf*, 5.357).

His career as a writer now entered its most productive and versatile period. His edition in four volumes of the plays of John Webster (completed 1927) was hailed as a supreme work of scholarship. A first book of poems, *Time and Memory* (1929), was admired by T. E. Lawrence among others and was followed by *Marionettes* (1930) and *Poems 1935* (1935). His early semi-autobiographical novel, *The River Flows* (1926), was followed by two historical novels, *Cécile* (1930) and *Dr. Dido* (1938). Also in the thirties two of his plays reached the London stage, though neither had a long run. In criticism, where many will think his special talents lay, *Authors Dead and Living* (1926), *Tragedy in Relation to Aristotle's 'Poetics'* (1927)—still a standard work after fifty years—and *Eight Victorian Poets* (1930) were followed by *Studies French and English* (1934), the fruit of a lifelong love of French literature and civilization, and *The Decline and Fall of the Romantic Ideal* (1936), perhaps his best work of historical criticism. In it he defended classical and romantic poetry against the 'moderns' praising the vitality of Rupert Brooke's poems while tilting at Ezra Pound and T. S. Eliot. When he had been under fire in No Mans's Land, Lucas recalled, it was Homer, Morris, and Housman who sustained him: 'I doubt if there is much modern literature that would stand that test' (Lucas, *Decline and Fall*, 236).

In 1932 Lucas married his second wife, Prudence Dalzell Wilkinson, a graduate of Girton College: their passion for wild scenery and arduous walking is vividly displayed in their companion-guide to Greece, *From Olympus to the Styx* (1934).

Lucas had now an international reputation as a writer. In the later thirties he earned a second reputation, as an outspoken opponent of totalitarianism. His *Delights of Dictatorship* (1938) and *Journal under the Terror, 1938* (1939) reflect those times, the latter recording his growing anger at appeasement, culminating in the Munich agreement of September: '"It is peace for our time". My God! The man must be intoxicated' (Lucas, *Journal*, 276). During the Second World War he was employed in the highly secret Ultra project at Bletchley Park in Buckinghamshire, and was a central figure in hut 3, which produced intelligence reports from the Enigma decodes of German army and Luftwaffe high-grade ciphers. The value of his work there was recognized in 1946 by his appointment as OBE. In 1940 he married his third wife, the Swedish psychologist Elna Julie Dagmar Constance Kallenberg, with whom he had a daughter and a son. From his first two marriages, both of which were dissolved, he had no children.

In Cambridge after the war Lucas resumed lecturing and writing with all his old energy and was university reader in English from 1947 to 1962. The influence of F. R. Leavis and his school was then in the ascendant in the English faculty, however, and to Lucas this approach to literature was an aberration. His own settled outlook had been shown in the brilliant chapter on English literature which he contributed to Harold Wright's *Cambridge University Studies* (1933). It was that of an uncompromising traditionalist in the line deriving from Sainte-Beuve and exemplified by his own friend and mentor Sir Desmond MacCarthy, who remained for him always the 'wisest of readers to-day' (Lucas, *Journal*, dedication). As a tutor Lucas was always solicitous for the interests of his students, but he was less concerned to hear their views than to impart his own, and if his supervisions were entertaining they were also somewhat pedagogic in style.

In two large volumes of verse translation, *Greek Poetry for Everyman* (1951) and *Greek Drama for Everyman* (1954), Lucas met a popular need. *Style* (1955) was illuminated by a wealth of examples drawn from a lifetime of voracious reading in half a dozen literatures. In *The Search for Good Sense* (1958) and *The Art of Living* (1959) he returned to his old love of the eighteenth century; and another earlier interest was revived in *The Drama of Ibsen and Strindberg* (1962) and *The Drama of Chekhov, Synge, Yeats and Pirandello* (1963).

Lucas was an immensely clever man, yet in some moods he himself valued most highly the life of action, and thought the most useful years of his life had been those of the two world wars. The dominant impression he made was of an exhilarating and masterful vitality. Gay and charming in congenial company, he could also be formidable and, once he had decided on a course of action, was apt to pursue it with a single-mindedness which, despite a native considerateness towards others, could sometimes be disconcerting. In appearance he retained in later life 'the sensitive face of a poet' which, after half a century, the writer Henry Williamson, a contemporary at Colfe's

Grammar School, remembered in him as a schoolboy. He died at his home, The Pavilion, 20 West Road, Cambridge, on 1 June 1967, his wife surviving him.

R. H. L. Cohen, *rev.* Mark Pottle

Sources J. E. Edmonds, ed., *Military operations, France and Belgium, 1917*, 1, History of the Great War (1940) · C. Bell, *Old friends* (1956) · *Selected letters of T. E. Lawrence*, ed. D. Garnett (1938) · personal knowledge (1981) · private information (1981) · G. Welchman, *The Hut Six story: breaking the Enigma codes* (1982) · F. H. Hinsley and A. Stripp, eds., *Codebreakers: the inside story of Bletchley Park* (1993) · *The letters of Virginia Woolf*, ed. N. Nicolson, 4 (1978) · *The letters of Virginia Woolf*, ed. N. Nicolson, 5 (1979) · R. V. Jones, *Most secret war: British scientific intelligence, 1939–1945* (1978) · *The diary of Virginia Woolf*, ed. A. O. Bell and A. McNeillie, 5 vols. (1977–84), vol. 2, p. 156; vols. 3–5 · F. L. Lucas, *The decline and fall of the Romantic ideal* (1936); 2nd edn (1948) · F. L. Lucas, *Journal under the terror, 1938* (1939) · *The Times* (24 Oct 1935) · *The Times* (2 June 1967) · *CGPLA Eng. & Wales* (1967)

Archives State University of New York, MSS and letters | JRL, letters to the *Manchester Guardian* · King's Cam., letters to Clive Bell · King's Cam., letters to John Maynard Keynes

Wealth at death £51,620: probate, 25 Aug 1967, *CGPLA Eng. & Wales*

Lucas, Frederick (1812–1855), journalist and politician, born in Westminster, London, on 30 March 1812, was the son of Samuel Hayhurst Lucas (*d.* in or after 1840), a corn merchant in the City of London, and a member of the Religious Society of Friends. Samuel *Lucas (1811–1865) was his elder brother. After spending eight years in a Quaker school at Darlington, he became, in his seventeenth year, a student at the London University, then recently established. He took a leading part in almost every discussion in the college debating club, or Literary and Philosophical Society. At this period the Roman Catholic claims were the principal topic of discussion, and he eagerly espoused the cause of emancipation, and devoted much attention to Irish politics. When he left the university, which had not then the power to confer degrees, he took up the study of the law, first in the chambers of Revell Phillips, and afterwards in those of Duval. He was called to the bar at the Middle Temple in 1835.

In 1838 Lucas delivered two lectures on education in the Literary and Scientific Institution at Staines. In these lectures, which excited some attention at the time, and were afterwards published, he bestowed his warmest sympathies on the feudal and Catholic spirit of medieval Christendom. Early in 1839, in the course of some conversations with Thomas Chisholm Anstey, he was led seriously to examine the doctrines of Roman Catholicism, and in less than a week he was reconciled to the Roman church by Father Lythgoe SJ. He forthwith published a pamphlet entitled *Reasons for Becoming a Roman Catholic, Addressed to the Society of Friends* (1839). This offended many of his former acquaintances, but later his wife and two of his brothers followed him into the Roman communion, and he maintained an intimacy with many persons of opposite and irreconcilable views and principles. The most conspicuous of these, outside the Catholic body, were John Stuart Mill and Thomas Carlyle. On 5 August 1840 he married Elizabeth Skidmore, daughter of William Ashby of Staines, Middlesex; they had two sons.

About this time Lucas wrote for the *Dublin Review*, and acquired a literary reputation which made his co-religionists desirous that he should be permanently engaged in the support of their cause. With the aid of some wealthy Catholics he was enabled to start *The Tablet*, a weekly London newspaper, the first number of which appeared on 16 May 1840. In conducting this journal he advocated the most advanced ultramontane and pro-Irish opinions with such zeal and occasional asperity of language that he soon found himself in opposition to powerful sections of his own religious community. An attempt to force his removal as editor in 1842 led him to start a rival journal, the *True Tablet*, which won the support of other English Catholics and of Daniel O'Connell and triumphed over its opponent, resuming the name of *The Tablet* in 1843. He identified himself with the Irish national movement and supported O'Connell in his demand for repeal of the Union. Towards the end of 1849 he moved the publishing offices of *The Tablet* to Dublin.

Lucas became an Irish political figure, leading in the foundation of the tenant-right agitation in 1850 and of the Independent Irish Party in 1851. In 1852 he was returned to parliament as one of the members for the county of Meath. He soon became a prominent debater in the House of Commons, and by his ability and evident sincerity, even when urging unpopular opinions, he gained the respect of many of his opponents. In 1853, when dissensions arose among the tenant-right party, Dr Cullen, archbishop of Dublin, and some other bishops prohibited the priests in their dioceses from interfering in political affairs. Lucas denounced in *The Tablet* this action of the archbishop, and determined to appeal from the episcopal decision to the Holy See. In the autumn of 1854 he started on a mission to Rome. He had two interviews with Pope Pius IX, at whose suggestion he began to write a full 'Statement' of the condition of affairs in Ireland and of the questions at issue between himself and Dr Cullen.

In May 1855, his health having broken down, Lucas returned to England, so altered in appearance that when he presented himself at the House of Commons the door-keepers did not know him. He stayed with friends and relatives, and finally moved to the house of his brother-in-law at Staines, where he died of heart disease on 22 October 1855. He was buried in Brompton cemetery on 27 October.

Lucas's 'Statement' was not quite completed at the time of his death. This document occupies more than 300 pages in the second volume of Lucas's *Life* by his brother Edward. About six months after his death the 'Statement' was presented to the pope. It failed to achieve its object.

Thompson Cooper, *rev.* Josef L. Altholz

Sources E. Lucas, *The life of Frederick Lucas, MP*, 2 vols. (1886) · C. J. Riethmüller, *Frederick Lucas: a biography* (1862) · J. H. Whyte, *The independent Irish party, 1850–9* (1958) · E. Larkin, *The making of the Roman Catholic church in Ireland, 1850–1860* (1980) · M. Walsh, *The Tablet, 1840–1990: a commemorative history* (1990) · J. L. Altholz, 'The Tablet, the *True Tablet*, and nothing but the *Tablet*', *Victorian Periodicals Newsletter*, 9 (1976) · S. Gilley, 'Frederick Lucas, "The Tablet" and Ireland: a Victorian forerunner of liberation theology', *Modern religious rebels: presented to John Kent*, ed. S. Mews (1993), 56–87 · m.

cert. • d. cert. • *The Tablet* (27 Oct 1855) • *The Tablet* (3 Nov 1855) • *The Tablet* (10 Nov 1855) • *Weekly Register and Catholic Standard* (27 Oct 1855)
Archives NL Ire., papers
Likenesses photograph, repro. in Walsh, *The Tablet, 1840–1990*, 2

Lucas [*née* Goldsmid], **Helen** (**1835–1918**), philanthropist and social worker, was born on 10 August 1835, the first of the nine children of Frederick D. Goldsmid (1812–1866), a financier and MP for Honiton, and his wife, Caroline Samuel (1814–1885) of Somerhill, Kent. She married Lionel Lucas (1822–1862), a merchant, on 25 July 1855 and had two children, F. L. Lucas and Ethel R. Mozley. After her husband's death in 1862, Helen Lucas devoted her life and considerable family wealth to philanthropy. She served as president (from 1880) of the ladies' conjoint visiting committee of the Jewish Board of Guardians (JBG), and assisted with its adult workroom. From 1896 she was president of the JBG's workrooms, where girls learned embroidery and needlework, skills that directed them away from crowded trades. She provided religious instruction during weekly visits. Lucas also promoted the virtues of cleanliness, tidiness, and punctuality; she expected women to arrive at the workrooms wearing bonnets.

Lucas was known for her passionate interest in the poorest, and for her generosity to Jews and Christians alike. She was patron of the City of London Widows' Benevolent Society, treasurer of the Jewish Ladies' West End Charity, honorary secretary of the Jewish Ladies' Benevolent Society, contributed generously to the JBG's building fund and the Jewish Religious Education Board, and visited Jews in the workhouse infirmary. Lucas was also involved in the National Union of Women Workers and the Union of Jewish Women.

Lucas, who had very definite views and a strong character, regularly commented on communal affairs in the Jewish press, and was especially opposed to girls' clubs. Unlike most workers, she encouraged girls to spend evenings at home helping their mothers. She believed that clubs destroyed home and family life, once a source of pride for Jews. Concerned that human nature loved change, Lucas contended that girls would lose interest in clubs. They would resort to questionable activities, increasing the need for rescue organizations. She also opposed day nurseries, convinced that they encouraged mothers to shirk their duties to their infants.

In 1885 Lucas and Lady Louisa de Rothschild paid for a nurse to work among the Jewish poor, and in 1891 Lucas supplied a second and, a year later, a third nurse. Some critics viewed her as a traditionalist, implying that her nurses did not employ the most modern methods available. While supportive of efficient charitable methods, she cautioned that the contemporary emphasis on science added layers of bureaucracy. At the first study circle of the Union of Jewish Women, held in May 1906, Lucas noted that her half-century of experience in relief work led her to conclude that unnecessary hardship often resulted when there were delays in providing assistance. At the meeting, covered by the *Jewish World* (18 May 1906), Lucas argued that relief workers needed 'common sense and sympathy' and ought to 'give less attention to statistics and clerical duties'.

As a member of the ladies' committee of the Jews' Free School, Lucas was especially involved in girls' education. She presided over numerous prize distributions at Jewish voluntary and board schools. At awards day at Westminster Jews' Free School in 1900, Lucas admonished the girls to dress more simply, not to wear white shoes, nor lace on their dresses. She thought that cookery was as important as history and geography and that girls who kept tidy homes would be able to keep their husbands at home. She supported physical education, because drill kept children strong and healthy. She was particularly dedicated to Hebrew, the language of divine law and religious instruction.

Lucas was an active member of the West London (Reform) Synagogue, which her family helped to found. She was present at the opening of their original house of worship. Religiously conservative, she opposed innovation, and sought to prevent change in the congregation's liturgy. She felt great loyalty to the synagogue, and preferred to retain her membership, but made clear to the leadership that she would leave if they introduced English. Lucas's own religious education started at the age of six, when her father began teaching her Hebrew, and she recalled crying if denied the opportunity to attend worship services. Helen Lucas died, aged eighty-three, on 3 January 1918 at her home, Harewood Lodge, Sunninghill, Berkshire, and was buried at the West Ham cemetery on 8 January. SUSAN L. TANANBAUM

Sources *Jewish Chronicle* (1880–1918) • E. C. Black, *The social politics of Anglo-Jewry, 1880–1920* (1988) • L. Marks, *Model mothers: Jewish mothers and maternity provision in east London, 1870–1939* (1994) • *The Times* (21 Jan 1918) • *The Times* (11 March 1918) • m. cert. • *Annual Report* [Board of Guardians for the Relief of the Jewish Poor] (1880–1918) • *Jewish Chronicle* (11 Jan 1918) • d. cert.
Likenesses portrait, repro. in *Jewish Chronicle* (3 Aug 1906), 12
Wealth at death £154,953 11*s*. 9*d*.: probate, 26 April 1918, *CGPLA Eng. & Wales* • £122,585 15*s*. 8*d*.: further grant, 18 July 1918, *CGPLA Eng. & Wales*

Lucas, Henry (*bap.* **1587**, *d.* **1663**), founder of the Lucasian professorship of mathematics at Cambridge University, the son of Edward Lucas (*bap.* 1566, *d.* 1601) of Thriplow, Cambridgeshire, and his wife, Mary Covert, daughter of Sir Nicholas Heron, was baptized at St Giles Cripplegate, London, on 11 November 1587. Lucas was educated at the village school at Thriplow, and according to his will 'receaved … part of my education' at St John's College, Cambridge, although there is no evidence that he matriculated (Clark, 165). Lucas also states in his will that his patrimony 'was snatched from him by unhappy suits in law during his childhood'. Following the death in 1595 of Poynings Heron, Mary Lucas's brother, Edward Lucas acquired a trusteeship or executorship in respect of the interests of his children. This led to a series of lawsuits which after Edward's death were pursued against his widow and the young Henry; these depleted their wealth and compelled Henry to seek his own fortune.

Lucas was admitted to the Middle Temple on 6 February 1606 but was never called to the bar. His first recorded employment was in 1618 when as one of four agents of Lucy, countess of Bedford, he was responsible for the collection of tolls on coal shipped from the Tyne. In May 1629 Lucas was appointed secretary to Dudley Carleton, Viscount Dorchester and secretary of state. This post resulted in Lucas's meeting Henry Butts, vice-chancellor of Cambridge University. Following the death of Dorchester in 1632, Lucas became secretary to Henry Rich, first earl of Holland, chancellor of Cambridge University. As Holland's secretary Lucas was placed in the profitable position of being able to benefit from receiving favours granted from above and petitions presented from below. In his inaugural lecture as the first holder of the Lucasian professorship, Isaac Barrow claimed that 'while he [Lucas] managed the affairs of his patron so well, … he did not look badly to his own; but stored up some fruit into his own barn, from so plentiful a harvest'.

Lucas was admitted MA of St John's College on 4 February 1636. It was also as a result of being Holland's nominee that he was elected one of the university's representatives in parliament on 24 October 1640. As an MP, Lucas was an influential protector of the university's interests. Holland's support wavered between the Commons and the king until 1648 when he rose in arms for Charles I. Holland was defeated at Nonsuch on 7 July and taken prisoner three days later. In the aftermath of the fiasco, twenty-nine of the earl's attendants including Lucas surrendered to the Hertfordshire militia and were sent to Peterhouse prison. Lucas and two others were released on 16 November 1649. It is probable that his links with Holland had inadvertently embroiled him in an event which he did not personally support.

Following Holland's trial and execution Lucas retired. According to his will, he concentrated on developing a library of 'Bookes of diverse subjects'. Lucas frequently inscribed the books with his name, the year of purchase, and the cost, and in some of the more expensive texts he provided elevated comment in Latin.

Lucas died at his residence in Chancery Lane, London, in July 1663 and was buried in the Temple Church on the 21st of that month.

Lucas's most significant legacy was the establishment of the Lucasian professorship of mathematics at Cambridge University. He instructed his executors to 'purchase lands to the value of one hundred pounds by the yeare to be imployed and setted as a yearely stipend and sallerie for a professor and reader of the mathematicall sciences' (Clark, 165). The professorship was founded in 1663 and was endowed with an estate in Bedfordshire; Isaac Barrow was elected the first professor on 20 February 1664.

Lucas also bequeathed to the university library his collection of '812 bookes in folio, 326 books in Quarto, Octavo, and other small volumes and 29 bundles of several pamphletters' (draft in CUL archives, graced 12 Sept 1664, Grace book H, 335). His gift of books is comparable with the benefactions provided by the better-documented donations of Richard Holdsworth and John Hacket, bishop of Lichfield. The remainder of Lucas's estate, amounting to about £7000, he bequeathed for the establishment of a hospital in Berkshire or Surrey. The foundation, consisting of a chaplain or master, was intended to assist as many poor people as could be looked after; they were to be selected from the poorest inhabitants of the forest division in Berkshire and the bailiwick of Surrey. The hospital was built in 1665 on Luckley Green, Wokingham, Berkshire, with lands in Bedfordshire being purchased for its endowment. In 1666 Lucas's executors established 15 July as the commemoration day of the Lucas Hospital. JOHN MARTIN

Sources J. C. T. Oates, *Cambridge University Library: a history from the beginnings to the Copyright Act of Queen Anne* (1986) • will, PROB 11/311, fols. 354v–356r • Venn, *Alum. Cant.* • Burke, *Peerage* • I. Barrow, 'Oratio praefatoria', *Lectiones mathematicae*, 23 (1685) • F. Peck, ed., *Desiderata curiosa*, new edn, 2 vols. in 1 (1779) • *N&Q*, 10th ser., 4 (1905), 166 • D. Lysons and S. Lysons, *Magna Britannia* (1813) • J. W. Clark, ed., *Endowments of the University of Cambridge* (1904) • J. R. Tanner, *The historical register of the University of Cambridge … to the year 1910* (1917) • private information (2004) [R. J. Griffiths]

Wealth at death see will, PRO, PROB 11/311, fols. 354v–356r

Lucas, Henry (*c.*1740–1802), writer and lawyer, was born in Dublin, the son of Charles *Lucas (1713–1771), the radical Irish politician, and his first wife, Anne, *née* Blundell. His father had to flee Ireland in 1749 after his election campaign for the Dublin city seat in the Irish House of Commons resulted in a charge of seditious libel. It is not clear if Henry remained with his mother and family in Dublin while his father subsequently studied medicine in Europe. However, the family was with Charles while he practised medicine in London and Bath in the 1750s. Henry returned to a scholarship at Trinity College, Dublin, in 1757. There he was taught by Thomas Leland, a supporter of his father's. He tactfully subscribed to Leland's *The History of the Life and Reign of Philip, King of Macedon* in 1758. He graduated BA in 1759, the year his father returned from exile, and obtained his MA in 1762. He was admitted to the Middle Temple the following year (as had been his father during a brief spell in London after his flight from Ireland and before taking up his medical studies). He seems to have made the law his occupation and was called to the bar in 1790.

In his later twenties Henry rode on the coat-tails of his father in Dublin. Indeed, his father may have been grooming him for a political career, for Dr Lucas's stalwart supporters the Dublin Guild of Barber Surgeons admitted Henry as a freeman in 1767. In 1770, the year before his father's death, Lucas was involved in a fracas at a meeting of the Constitutional Free Debating Society. After drawing with Richard Brinsley Sheridan for a medal, with a group of 'ignorant, giddy, young men' he attacked the chair and attempted to take it (*Freeman's Journal*, 30 May–1 June 1770, 471). His expulsion from the society is the last record of his Irish involvements, and after his father's death in 1771 he appears to have transferred his attentions to London and to writing.

Lucas shared his father's interest in the theatre, and his first attributed work was an opera in 1776. He attempted to obtain patronage from the duke of Northumberland with a 'pastoral elegy' on the death of the duchess in 1777.

Northumberland had been Irish viceroy from 1763 to 1765, and Lucas was possibly acquainted with him thus. Samuel Johnson was a connection of Lucas's father from the time of his exile, and Lucas asked him for advice on his historical play *The Earl of Somerset* in 1777. The subject of the play was the fall of Robert Cauvs the earl of Somerset following his unjust treatment of Sir Thomas Overbury. Johnson said that it was 'but a poor performance', but which given it might 'put money into his [Lucas's] pockets [and] contains nothing immoral or indecent … we may very well wish success' (*Letters of Samuel Johnson*, 3.21). (The remark of Johnson, 'I never did the man an injury', has been wrongly attributed to this episode and actually refers to Joseph Reed.) However, Johnson was annoyed two years later when Lucas used his name in association with attempts to get the work staged. The play received mixed notices the best of which, in the *London Review*, said it contained 'more beauties than defects' (*London Review*, 11 Feb 1780, 143). When Lucas published the play by subscription in 1779, describing himself on the title-page as a 'student of the Middle Temple', he complained about the difficulties of getting work staged, and was still making similar complaints twenty years later with the publication of his last work, shortly before his death in 1802.

Lucas's other published works are either poetical or dramatic, and in subject and tone highlight Lucas's pressing need to attract remunerative patronage. Examples include: *A Visit from the Shades, or, Earl Chatham's Adieu to his Friend Lord Cambden* (1778); *Poems to her Majesty* (beginning with the unfortunately titled 'Ejaculation Occasioned by Seeing the Royal Children', published together with *The Earl of Somerset* in 1779); and *The cypress-wreath, or, Meed of honour: an elegio-heroic poem, to the memory of Lord Robert Manners* (1782).

Neither Lucas's legal nor his literary career seem to have been much of a success, and in 1818, sixteen years after his death, his stepmother and sister were in such financial straits that a public subscription had to be launched in Dublin for their support. Like his father's political pamphlets, his poetry and dramatic works stress the theme of personal virtue. MIHAIL DAFYDD EVANS

Sources M. D. Evans, '"A very devil of a fellow", Charles Lucas MD, MP (1713–1771): a reappraisal', BA diss., U. Wales, 1995 • D. J. O'Donoghue, *The poets of Ireland: a biographical dictionary with bibliographical particulars*, 1 vol. in 3 pts (1892–3) • J. Hutchinson, ed., *A catalogue of notable Middle Templars: with brief biographical notices* (1902) • H. W. Liebert, 'An addition to the bibliography of Samuel Johnson', *Papers of the Bibliographical Society of America*, 41 (1947), 231–8 • *The letters of Samuel Johnson*, ed. B. Redford, 3 (1992)

Lucas, Horatio Joseph (1839–1873), etcher, was born in London on 27 May 1839, the fourth son of William Jeremiah Lucas, a West India merchant, and his wife, Esther Louis. He belonged to an old Jewish family. He was educated at Brighton and at University College, London, and studied painting under Francis Stephen Cary. He married Isabel Olga, the daughter of Count d'Avigdor and the niece of Sir Francis Goldsmid, bt, with whom he had four children. He was a member of the Langham Sketching Club, and between 1870 and 1873 he exhibited architectural views, landscapes, and an interior at the Royal Academy and at the Salon in Paris. Lucas was a proficient etcher and contributed to the various black and white exhibitions; a selection from his etchings is in the print room at the British Museum. One drawing, *The Sangreal*, was published in *Good Words* in 1863. In 1862 Lucas joined his father's business, so that he was able to devote only his leisure time to art. He was an accomplished musician and an active and useful member of the Jewish community in London. He died at his home, 5 Westbourne Terrace, Hyde Park, on 18 December 1873.

L. H. CUST, *rev.* JOANNA DESMOND

Sources R. K. Engen, *Dictionary of Victorian wood engravers* (1985), 166 • *The classified dictionary of artists' signatures, symbols and monograms*, rev. H. H. Caplan, 2nd edn (1982), 279 • G. White, *English illustration, 'the sixties': 1855–70* (1897); repr. (1970), 454 • S. Houfe, *The dictionary of 19th century British book illustrators and caricaturists*, rev. edn (1996), 214 • K. M. Guichard, *British etchers, 1850–1940* (1977), 73 • I. Mackenzie, *British prints: dictionary and price guide* (1987) • Graves, *RA exhibitors* • *CGPLA Eng. & Wales* (1874) • *IGI*

Archives BM, prints

Wealth at death under £70,000: probate, 17 Feb 1874, *CGPLA Eng. & Wales*

Lucas, James (1813–1874), eccentric, was born on 21 December 1813 in Hackney, Middlesex, the second (but first surviving) son and fourth child of James Lucas, a wealthy West India merchant and partner in the Liverpool-based firm of Chauncey, Lucas, and Lang, and his wife, whose maiden name was Beesly. He was educated at a private school in Clapham, from which he ran away at the age of fourteen, and then at a school in Richmond for a short time. Proving to be an awkward youth, he was sent to a medical man at Whitwell, a Mr Hicks, with a view to moral restraint and discipline, but quickly ran away back to his home, Elm Wood House, at Redcoat's Green, Great Wymondley, near Hitchin, which his father had purchased. An attempt to place him with a clergyman for his moral education met with no greater success. When thwarted he would shut himself in his bedroom for days on end. 'His meals were taken to him and left at his door, which he did not object to eat, but resolutely refused to return the plates. At length the plates and dishes became scarce in other parts of the household, as his bedroom contained nearly the whole supply in the way of crockery' (Tuke, 363). His father's death in 1830 gave encouragement to this promising start on a life of eccentricity, for his mother humoured all his many whims and saw nothing odd about his going hunting in a nankeen suit or with his shirt outside his breeches, his riding in a carriage with his hair in curl papers, or his unsuccessful courting of a local lady with a pair of doves in a cage, although medical opinion was later to regard these as undoubted symptoms of incipient madness. But it was his mother's death in 1849 which removed all restraints on oddity and launched him on the life of a hermit.

Mrs Lucas died on 24 October 1849, but Lucas refused to part with her corpse until the following January, when his younger brother (who was their mother's executor) intervened and enforced her interment. This caused James to barricade himself into the kitchen of Elm Wood House, which was to be his abode for the next twenty-five years. He rarely left the one room, let alone the house. Window panes were broken by stones thrown at the time of the 'papal aggression' in 1850, as he was thought to have Catholic tendencies, and were replaced by iron bars through which he could be viewed, if permitted by the guards he employed to protect him from harassment. Particularly after Charles Dickens visited him and wrote him up in the Christmas 1861 number of *All the Year Round*, thinly disguised as Mr Mopes, he became an object of fashionable curiosity; he was visited by Lord Lytton, Sir Arthur Helps, John Forster, and others, and became known as the Hertfordshire Hermit. Dickens thought he was a fraud, 'an abominably dirty thing', an intolerably conceited sluggard, 'a slothful, unsavoury, nasty reversal of the laws of human nature' who ought to be put on a treadmill (Tuke, 370). Others, although inarticulate, probably took a more generous view. He was fond of children and tramps. On Good Fridays he doled out sweets, coppers, and gin and water to upwards of 200 children; he was visited by swarms of tramps, giving them gin and pennies, always more to Catholics than protestants. A rich man—he left some £120,000 at his death—he lived on a simple but ample diet of bread, cheese, red herrings, eggs, milk, and gin. Always suspicious that people were trying to poison him, he rejected many of his supplies; after his death a whole cartload of hard, untouched loaves, suspected of being poisoned, was taken away by a farmer, and after soaking in water they were fed to his chickens. He was also infested with rats, and kept his victuals in baskets hanging from the ceiling as a precaution. Once thought to be a good-looking man, 5 feet 6 inches tall, rather muscular, and with dark hair and eyes, he lived in filth and squalor, unwashed, clothed only in an old blanket, and sleeping simply on the ashes that built up to a depth of several feet (fourteen cartloads were removed after his death). But his conversation remained lucid and well informed, his memory was good, his conviction of the illegitimacy of the queen and his refusal therefore to execute any document requiring a stamp was consistently maintained, and he managed his bank account and his cheque book competently.

Lucas's manner of life being so bizarre and irrational, medical opinion puzzled over how to classify him, and in the end the best view was that this was 'a case of moral insanity, madness of action rather than language' (Tuke, 371). He died of apoplexy on 19 April 1874, at Titmore Cottage, near Elm Wood House, and was buried beside his mother in Hackney churchyard on 21 April. Moral insanity or no, the sensational and curio trades had no doubt of his value, and within weeks of his death 10,000 copies of a biographical sketch had been sold, and a brisk trade was going on in a range of mugs and tea services carrying pictures of the hermit and his strange dwelling.

F. M. L. THOMPSON

Sources *DNB* • D. H. Tuke, 'The hermit of Redcoat's Green', *Journal of Mental Science*, 20 (1875), 361–72

Wealth at death under £120,000: administration with will, 18 Dec 1874

Lucas, John, first Baron Lucas of Shenfield (1606–1671), royalist landowner, was born on 23 October 1606, the eldest legitimate heir of Thomas Lucas (*c.*1573–1625), of St John's, near Colchester in Essex, and his wife, Elizabeth (*d.* 1647), daughter of John Leighton, gentleman, of London. Lucas was a prominent supporter in Essex of Charles I, which helps to explain the episode in 1642 in which crowds, numbered in their thousands, attacked and plundered his house. This has featured prominently in accounts of popular politics in the English revolution since its inclusion in Clarendon's *History of the Rebellion*. Lucas succeeded to a prosperous landed estate in Essex in 1625. His earlier education is unknown, and although he appears not to have attended either Oxford or Cambridge his sister Margaret, later Margaret *Cavendish, duchess of Newcastle upon Tyne (1623?–1673), described him as 'a great scholar'. As he was in France at his father's death he may have been sent abroad for part of his education. On 17 December 1628 he married Anne Nevill (*d.* 1660), daughter of Sir Christopher Nevill.

While the Lucas family traced their descent to the younger son of a fifteenth-century Suffolk gentry family, their fortune had been made by John's great-grandfather who as town clerk of Colchester married into the town's élite and later purchased the estates of the dissolved abbey of St John's. This purchase simultaneously removed the family to the 'country' seat of St John's—in reality little more than a stone's throw from the walls of Colchester—and bequeathed to them a series of conflicts between the abbey and Colchester that ran back to the peasants' revolt of 1381. Margaret Lucas's detailed, if eulogistic, account of the family's upbringing—emphasizing the care their mother took to instil in her children the values of a culture of honour appropriate to their gentle status—provides a key to Lucas's later history: the family conflicts gained an added edge from his readiness to detect a slight to his and his family's honour, and his religion provided another source of conflict with a town noted for the strength of its puritanism. The anti-Calvinist Samuel Harsnett, then bishop of Norwich, a Colcestrian and friend of the family (who had been his early patrons), had acted as his informal guardian. That Lucas was later suspected, wrongly, of popery probably reflected his patronage of ceremonialist ministers; among them was his chaplain Thomas Newcomen, who may have been Lucas's agent in ensnaring Dr John Bastwick, one of the famous puritan martyrs of the 1630s.

Lucas was a member of a protoroyalist group within Essex and probably played a key role in the group's attempt to win the county for the king in preparation for civil war. Although he never served as a JP, he became sheriff in 1636 and succeeded, where his predecessor had failed, in collecting the unpopular ship money tax. Success won him the public thanks of the king and doubtless helped to win him a knighthood in 1638, but it also gained him enemies in a county dominated by the parliamentarian and puritan earl of Warwick and his allies. Lucas's attempt in August 1642 to steal away from Colchester with horse and supporters to join Charles I led to the attack on his house. Although this has been represented, then and later, as an example of class hostility, the reality was more complex: Lucas had angered both the godly rulers of Colchester and the parliamentarian élite within the county, and there is reason to suspect the involvement of the former, and at least the acceptance of the latter, in the attack.

After his imprisonment by the House of Commons, Lucas fled to Oxford and served as colonel of horse in the royalist army. In 1645 he secured the title of Baron Lucas of Shenfield as compensation for his sufferings, though Clarendon implied that a gift from Lucas was also involved. Despite his support for the royalist cause he was not involved in the 1648 siege of Colchester, in the aftermath of which his brother Sir Charles *Lucas (1612/13–1648) was executed; indeed, when the royalist army came into the county he fled to London to avoid any suspicion of involvement. Nevertheless, he was again imprisoned briefly in 1655. The Restoration brought him revenge over his enemies at Colchester, who were forced to participate in the reburial of his martyred brother in the family church of St Giles. Lucas was made a fellow of the Royal Society on 20 May 1663 but was inactive and was expelled in 1666. In 1671 the printed copy of a speech he had made in the Lords against the subsidy was ordered to be burnt by the public hangman. Lucas, it was reported, died of chagrin at this public disgrace—a strange end for a man whose life had been marked by loyalty to the royal cause. He died on 2 July and was buried at St Giles, Colchester.

JOHN WALTER

Sources J. Walter, *Understanding popular violence in the English revolution: the Colchester plunderers* (1999) • B. Ryves, *Mercurius rusticus, or, The counties complaints of the murthers, robberies, plundrings, and other outrages, committed by the rebels on his majesties faithfull subjects* (1643) • E. Hyde, earl of Clarendon, *The history of the rebellion and civil wars in England*, 3 vols. (1702–4) • Margaret, duchess of Newcastle [M. Cavendish], 'A true relation of my birth, breeding and life', *The life of William Cavendish, duke of Newcastle*, ed. C. H. Firth (1886), 275–318 • *My Lord Lucas his speech on the house of peers, Feb. the 22. 1670/1, upon the reading of the Subsidy Bill the second time, in the presence of his majesty* • *CSP Venice*, 1671–2 • *CSP dom.*, 1625–49 • C. H. Firth, 'Verses on the cavaliers', *N&Q*, 7th ser., 10 (1890), 41–2 • *JHC*, 2 (1640–42) • will, PRO, PROB 11/338, fol. 37 • W. A. Shaw, *The knights of England*, 2 vols. (1906) • *The life of Edward, earl of Clarendon … written by himself*, new edn, 3 vols. (1827), vol. 1 • W. C. Metcalfe, ed., *The visitations of Essex*, 2 vols., Harleian Society, 13–14 (1878–9) • Essex RO, Colchester, MSS D/Y 2/10; D/DRg 1/226

Wealth at death see will, PRO, PROB 11/338, fol. 37; administration, 21 Jan 1672

Lucas, John (1807–1874), portrait painter, was born in London on 4 July 1807, the son of William Lucas (*bap.* 1775, *d.* 1819), whose family came from King's Lynn in Norfolk, and a Miss Calcott. His father began his career in the Royal Navy, but later styled himself a literary man, publishing poems such as *The Fate of Bertha* (1800) and acting as editor of *The Sun* newspaper. Lucas was apprenticed to Samuel William Reynolds, the mezzotint engraver, at the same time as Samuel Cousins. During this time he also studied and practised oil painting. When his tenure with Reynolds ended in the late 1820s, Lucas established his practice as a painter while continuing as a member of the Clipstone Street Academy, working with William Etty and other artists.

John Lucas (1807–1874), by Lucas

Lucas exhibited his first portrait at the Royal Academy in 1828 and thereafter gained fame as a fashionable society portraitist. He painted the likeness of Queen Adelaide, the prince consort (four times), the princess royal, the duke of Wellington (eight times), Lord and Lady Palmerston, and William Ewart Gladstone, among others. His portrait of Mary Russell Mitford was purchased by the National Portrait Gallery after his death. The National Portrait Gallery also has Lucas's *Conference of Engineers, Britannia Bridge*, which features portraits of Robert Stevenson and Isambard Kingdom Brunel. This work was later engraved by J. Scott, as were other portraits by Lucas. Lucas himself employed his training as an engraver, producing engravings after Sir Thomas Lawrence.

In 1836 Lucas married Milborough Morgan, a woman of Welsh descent, with whom he had three sons and two daughters. He often exhibited his works publicly, showing ninety-six portraits at the Royal Academy from 1828 to the time of his death on 30 April 1874 at his home, 22 St John's Wood Road, London. He was buried on 5 May 1874 at

Kensal Green cemetery, London. Christies auctioned the contents of his studio on 25 February 1875. Lucas's artistic legacy lived on in the work of his sons: William Lucas became a watercolour painter and Arthur Lucas became an art publisher. His nephew John Seymour Lucas RA was his pupil. His eldest son, **John Templeton Lucas** (1836–1880), perhaps achieved the most renown. Born in London, he concentrated on landscape painting, exhibiting seven landscapes at the Royal Academy between 1859 and 1876. Like his grandfather, he turned to literature, publishing a farce entitled *Browne the Martyr* and a book of fairy tales, *Prince Ubbely Bubble's New Story Book*, in 1871. He died at Bagdale, Whitby, in Yorkshire, on 13 September 1880. MORNA O'NEILL

Sources Bryan, *Painters* • Graves, *Brit. Inst.*, 354 • J. Johnson, ed., *Works exhibited at the Royal Society of British Artists, 1824–1893, and the New English Art Club, 1888–1917*, 2 vols. (1975), 309 • *The Times* (6 May 1874), 5 • *The Times* (17 Sept 1874), 6 • *Art Journal*, 36 (1874), 212 • Redgrave, *Artists* • Wood, *Vic. painters*, 3rd edn • A. Lucas, *John Lucas: portrait painter* (1910) • *The Academy* (25 Sept 1880), 221 • d. cert. • *CGPLA Eng. & Wales* (1881) [John Templeton Lucas]

Archives V&A NAL, personal papers | City Westm. AC, letters to Mr and Mrs Acton Tindal

Likenesses Lucas, photograph, carte-de-visite, NPG [*see illus.*] • wood-engraving, NPG; repro. in *ILN* (16 May 1874)

Wealth at death under £300: 10 June 1874, *CGPLA Eng. & Wales* • under £400—John Templeton Lucas: probate, 1881, *CGPLA Eng. & Wales*

Lucas, John Templeton (1836–1880). *See under* Lucas, John (1807–1874).

Lucas, Joseph (1834–1902), lamp manufacturer, was born on 12 April 1834 at Carver Street, Birmingham, the eldest son of Benjamin Lucas, a plater, and his wife, Catharine, *née* Ball. He received his basic education, probably only on Sundays, at a school attached to the church of the Saviour in Edward Street, Birmingham, run by the non-denominational Unitarian minister George Dawson, who was the first to articulate the notion of civic enterprise and to find in Joseph Chamberlain its greatest disciple. At the age of about thirteen, Joseph Lucas followed his father and was apprenticed to H. and G. R. Elkington, a firm of Birmingham silversmiths; he served seven years before qualifying as an electro-plater journeyman by the time of his first marriage, to Emily Stevens (*d*. 1885), on 20 July 1854. Over the next eleven years they had six children, his eldest son, Harry, becoming his lifelong business partner.

In 1860 Lucas began in business, selling buckets, shovels, and other items of hollow ware door-to-door, which led in 1869 to his first entry in White's *Birmingham Directory* as a dealer in lamps and oils. As business prospered, Lucas took on a small three-storey terraced house, 209 Great King Street, and in 1872 seventeen-year-old Harry Lucas joined his father. Within three years they had set up the Tom Bowling lamp works in Little King Street, Birmingham, producing a lamp of the same name for the fishing industry. Both were agreed on the need to find a more profitable adjunct to lamp oil, which had been selling well after fish oil had been replaced by paraffin and petroleum in the late 1850s. Their decision to concentrate on lamps which would burn the new fuel turned out to be an astute move. The growing popularity of the bicycle created an unprecedented demand for lamps, and Lucas was quick to realize that if he was to make any impression on this new market he would have to make the move from trader to manufacturer. In 1878, when laws were being passed requiring bicycles to carry lamps after dusk, Lucas decided on his first cycle lamp, the 'King of the Road'. It was certainly a gamble, since the bicycle was still expensive, difficult to handle, and many years from becoming universally popular. Even though Lucas was running his business very much on a hand-to-mouth basis, he had enough confidence to take advantage of the growing number of cycling clubs springing up all over the country. In 1880 he was granted a patent for his new lamp, nicknamed 'His Majesty', and in the same year the first signs of interest were shown from across the Atlantic. In the spring of 1881, the first consignment of King of the Road lamps was shipped to the States.

In 1882, after ten years in the business, Harry was brought into formal partnership, creating the firm of Joseph Lucas & Son. It was a difficult period for both men. Joseph's wife died, aged fifty-two, in February 1885, and he married, with some haste, his 51-year-old widowed cousin, Maria Tyzack, *née* Lucas (*d*. 1900), in November of the same year. The new business partnership also had to deal with stresses relating to cash flow and the potentially more serious threat from infringement of patent rights. Joseph Lucas was never slow to invoke the law if his designs were being pirated, but being litigious only served to detract from harnessing trade in a still fickle market. With this in mind, Lucas typically ensured that his lamp designs kept in fine tune with bicycling trends.

The development of the first pneumatic tyre for bicycles, patented in 1888 by a Belfast veterinary surgeon, John Boyd Dunlop, put paid to the 'boneshaker', and transformed the bicycle industry. Cycling now became a popular pastime for countless people and, in 1891, Lucas launched the Tom Bowling Lamp Works Cycling Club for the benefit of staff members. However, it was becoming increasingly obvious that if he was to take full advantage of the expanding business, Lucas would need to build new premises. Funds being in as short supply as floor space, Lucas decided to form a public limited company to raise the necessary capital to finance the building of a five-storey factory close to the original site in Little King Street. In 1892 the firm of Joseph Lucas & Son Ltd was incorporated, with Joseph as chairman, and himself and his son Harry as joint managing directors. The new company, with 700 personnel on the payroll, appointed Walter Chamberlain, youngest son of Joseph Chamberlain, to the board. Walter, who was then working for Nettlefolds, was to be part of the team that ran the company throughout the Edwardian years and into the age of the motor car. In 1895, Lucas patented perhaps his most profitable accessory, the legendary Silver King of the Road, which remained the company's best-selling line over the next decades. After 1898, the influence of the company having spread beyond the midlands, he opened an office in Holborn, London.

Lucas showed a great deal of kindness towards members of staff, and certain people who had displayed great loyalty over the years were remembered in his will. He was a great exponent of the views of George Dawson, who held that public service was a religious duty. But, as a devout teetotaller, abstinence was the order of the day. Lucas would have no truck with an inebriated worker and had no compunction in dismissing without notice anyone found smelling of alcohol. He had been a member of the Birmingham Temperance Society since 1877, and in 1888 was elected to the board of directors of the Temperance Hall Company. Through his munificence the hall was rebuilt and in October 1901 Joseph Chamberlain, the secretary of state for the colonies, performed the opening ceremony. Ironically, Lucas died of typhoid fever at the Hotel Bristol, Naples, on 27 December 1902, after the ship he was sailing in called at the port. Had he drunk the wine and kept off the local water he might not have fallen ill.

Lucas was survived by his third wife, Mary Anne (*b.* 1850/51), daughter of Samuel Owen, whom he had married on 30 July 1901, just one year after the death of his second wife. He left the bulk of his estate to his wife, children, and grandchildren, but he set aside £4000 to enable a special trust to be set up for 'the diffusion and promotion of the principles and practice of total abstinence from alcoholic liquors among the inhabitants of the city of Birmingham and its neighbourhood'. Lucas was buried at Moseley parish church, Worcestershire, on 14 January 1903. BARBARA TROMPETER

Sources H. Nockolds, *Lucas: the first hundred years*, 1 (1976) • m. certs. • d. cert.
Archives Lucas Varity, Lucas Industries archives
Likenesses daguerreotypes, *c.*1854, repro. in Nockolds, *Lucas*, 48 • photograph, 1902, repro. in Nockolds, *Lucas*, 1, 48 • painting, repro. in H. Nockolds, *Lucas: the first hundred years*, 2 (1978), 72
Wealth at death £94,552 6*s.* 0*d.*: probate, 16 Feb 1903, *CGPLA Eng. & Wales*

Lucas, Keith (1879–1916), physiologist and instrument designer, was born at Greenwich on 8 March 1879, the second son of Francis Robert Lucas (*d.* 1931), managing director of the Telegraph Construction and Maintenance Company of Greenwich, and inventor of improvements in submarine cables and cable laying, and his wife, Katharine Mary; she was the daughter of John Riddle, headmaster of Greenwich Hospital schools, and the granddaughter of Edward Riddle, both of whom were fellows of the Royal Astronomical Society and well known in nautical astronomy. Educated at the Revd T. Oldham's preparatory school, Blackheath, London, and at Rugby, where he was head of School House, Lucas proceeded, with a scholarship in classics, to Trinity College, Cambridge, in 1898. Abandoning classics, he gained a first class in the first part of the natural science tripos in 1901, but deferred the second part of the tripos until 1904, to make an extended visit to New Zealand. He was elected a fellow of Trinity College in 1904, and became college lecturer in natural science in 1906. Lucas married Alys, daughter of the Revd Cyril Egerton Hubbard, in 1909, living initially on the Huntingdon Road, Cambridge, before moving to Fen Ditton. They had three sons, Alan (*b.* 1910), David [*see below*], and Bryan [*see below*].

Between the years 1904 and 1914 Lucas undertook a series of studies, publishing some twenty-five papers in the *Journal of Physiology*, several in conjunction with students including A. V. Hill and E. Adrian; the results of these studies gave a fresh impetus to the study of muscle and nerve. His physiological research work was almost entirely on the physico-chemical properties of nerves and muscles. Among other discoveries, he showed that the 'all-or-none' law, that a given stimulus evokes either the maximum contraction or no contraction at all, applied to skeletal muscle. This was a fundamental principle, which his pupil Adrian later proved to be applicable to motor nerve fibres. Lucas also determined the temperature coefficient of nerve conduction, and examined in detail the nature of the nervous impulse and its propagation, work summarized in his posthumous *Conduction of the Nervous Impulse* (1917), prepared for publication by Adrian. In the course of this work, besides formulating fundamental questions and answering them, Lucas devised instruments of remarkable ingenuity, elegance, and precision. By 1914 he was recognized as a leader in this field of science. He took his DSc in 1911, and was elected FRS in 1913, having given the Croonian lectures the preceding year.

Lucas had a significant advantage in his physiological researches: he had the ability to design and build very sensitive instrumentation. His designs were so remarkable that they were manufactured and marketed by the Cambridge Scientific Instrument Company, and Horace Darwin, chairman of the company, made Lucas a director in 1906. Both Lucas and Darwin followed Clerk-Maxwell's principles of geometric design in all instrument design—for example, that accuracy should not deteriorate with wear.

In 1914, following the outbreak of war, Lucas was encouraged by Darwin, as a member of the Aeronautical Research Committee, to join the growing group of scientists being mobilized by Mervyn O'Gorman at the Royal Aircraft Factory, Farnborough. Puzzled on his first day by a Royal Flying Corps report from the western front that their aircraft compasses were useless, he started a series of ground and flight tests to examine the problems for himself. His experiments showed that severe compass error could be caused by engine vibration irrespective of the heading of the aircraft, and a more subtle heading error caused by the vertical component of the earth's magnetic field when the aircraft turned off a northerly course. This second error, of which even the Admiralty was unaware and which Lucas termed 'northerly turning error', explained why pilots were finding it impossible to navigate through cloud using their compass, the only aid they had at that time.

Lucas established new design features, which were incorporated into future aircraft compasses, including Darwin's suggestion to reverse the cup and pivot to eliminate vibration error. Turning next to bomb aiming, it was quickly obvious to him that the accuracy of any simple aiming device was affected by the aircraft's natural oscillations. He designed a photo-kymograph, using the sun as both reference and light source to measure accurately aircraft oscillations, conducting all his own flight experiments, usually piloted by R. H. Mayo; and he built the first gyroscopic aiming device. Convinced that his experimental work would benefit if he became a pilot, he attended a flying course at Upavon, where he was tragically killed in a mid-air collision on 5 October 1916.

Lucas was buried in the Aldershot military cemetery. After his death his wife Alys changed the family name, and, as Alys Keith-Lucas, edited a short book describing his life and work and listing his published papers (*Keith Lucas*, 1934). Following his death, Lucas's pioneering work on cloud flying and bomb aiming was continued and advanced over the next two years by F. A. Lindemann, while his photo-kymograph continued in use at Farnborough for many years.

Lucas's second son, **David Keith-Lucas** (1911–1997), aeronautical engineer, was born on 25 March 1911 at Cambridge; he and his brothers adopted the surname Keith-Lucas as a memorial to their dead father. Educated at Gresham's School, Holt, from 1924 to 1929, he read engineering at Gonville and Caius College, Cambridge, overlapping in his final year with an apprenticeship at Metropolitan-Vickers, which he continued at C. A. Parsons & Co. In 1940 he joined Short Bros. at Rochester, where he soon rose to be chief aerodynamicist. He married in 1942 Dorothy De Bauduy Robertson (*d.* 1979); they had two sons and a daughter. After the war he accompanied Shorts to Belfast, holding successively the posts of chief designer, technical director, and research director, contributing to the design of various swept-wing and vertical take-off planes. In 1965 he was appointed professor of aircraft design in the College of Aeronautics, Cranfield (later the Cranfield Institute of Technology); in 1972 he became professor of aeronautics. He served on numerous boards and committees, notably the Roskill commission for the third London airport; he was president of the Royal Aeronautical Society in 1968 and was awarded its gold medal in 1975. In 1979, visiting the site of the world's first powered flight at Kitty Hawk, North Carolina, the Keith-Lucases were involved in a serious motor accident, which resulted in his wife's death. In 1981 he married Phyllis Marion Everard, *née* Whurr, whom he had known earlier at Short Bros. He died on 6 April 1997, survived by his second wife and the three children of his first marriage.

Lucas's third son, **Bryan Keith-Lucas** (1912–1996), political scientist, was born on 1 August 1912 at Fen Ditton, Cambridgeshire, and was educated at Gresham's School from 1924 to 1930. He read history and economics at Pembroke College, Cambridge, then joined the town clerk's department at Kensington, west London, qualifying as a solicitor in 1937. During the Second World War he served in north Africa, Italy, and Cyprus with the Buffs and Sherwood Foresters, ending the war as a major. He then returned to local government in Nottingham. His marriage in 1946 to Mary Hardwicke brought a son and two daughters. In 1948 he moved into academic life, being appointed senior lecturer in local government at Oxford University. He was elected a fellow of Nuffield College in 1950 and domestic bursar in 1957. He served as an Oxford city councillor for the Liberal Party, sat on several governmental committees, and advised on aspects of local government for Britain's former colonies, including Sierra Leone (1954), Mauritius (1955–6), Nigeria (1963), and Fiji (1975). In 1965 he was appointed professor of government in the new University of Kent, and from 1970 to 1974 he was master of Darwin College, where he and his wife played host to numerous undergraduates and visiting academics. After retirement in 1977 he taught politics part-time at King's School, Cambridge. In 1983 he was appointed CBE. Among his publications were *The English local government franchise* (1952), *The mayor, aldermen and councillors* (1961), which anticipated the much later introduction of democratically elected mayors, and (with P. G. Richards) *A history of local government in the 20th century* (1978). In 1970 he produced a second edition of Josef Redlich's and Francis Wrigley Hirst's *History of local government in England*. His wife was also a Liberal Party supporter; she served as a Canterbury councillor and as sheriff. He died at Canterbury on 7 November 1996, survived by his wife and their three children.

JOHN K. BRADLEY

Sources A. Keith-Lucas, ed., *Keith Lucas* (1934) • H. Darwin and W. M. Bayliss, *PRS*, 90B (1917–19), xxxi–xlii • J. K. Bradley, The history and development of early aircraft instruments, 1909–1919, PhD diss., U. Lond., 1994 • B. Melvill Jones, 'Cloud flying in the First World War', *Journal of the Royal Aeronautical Society*, 70 (1966), 207 • M. J. G. Cattermole and A. F. Wolfe, *Horace Darwin's shop: a history of the Cambridge Scientific Instrument Company, 1878–1968* (1987) • personal knowledge (1927) [*DNB*] • *CGPLA Eng. & Wales* (1917) • *The Guardian* (21 April 1997) • *Daily Telegraph* (23 April 1997) • *The Times* (15 April 1997) • *The Independent* (29 May 1997) • *Daily Telegraph* (23 Nov 1996) • *The Guardian* (2 Dec 1996) • *The Times* (20 Nov 1996) • *The Independent* (20 Nov 1996)

Archives RS

Likenesses photograph, repro. in Darwin and Bayliss, *PRS*, xxxi

Wealth at death £6782 12*s.* 6*d.*: administration, 16 March 1917, *CGPLA Eng. & Wales* • £649,528—David Keith-Lucas: probate, 3 Sept 1997, *CGPLA Eng. & Wales* (1997) • £239,503—Bryan Keith-Lucas: probate, 9 Jan 1997, *CGPLA Eng. & Wales* (1997)

Lucas, Louis Arthur (1851–1876), merchant and traveller in Africa, was born on 22 September 1851 at Temple House, Cheetham, Manchester, the only surviving son of Philip Lucas and his wife, Juliana. **Philip Lucas** (*b.* 1797, *d.* before 1876), cotton merchant, was born in 1797 in Kingston, Jamaica, the son of Sampson Lucas, a cotton trader who made his fortune in the West Indies before settling in London where he died in 1820. Philip was connected to wealthy Jewish merchant circles in London, through his elder brother Louis, and in Manchester, through his sister Anne, who was the wife of S. L. Behrens, one of the earliest and most successful Jewish immigrants in Manchester. Philip was the senior partner in Lucas and Micholls: Henry Micholls was Lucas's nephew and married Frederica, Behrens's daughter, strengthening family and business ties. In 1834 the firm set up in Brown Street, Manchester, as merchants and cotton spinners at a time when many merchants from London and continental Europe were establishing agencies in the town to gain a stake in the lucrative cotton trade. Lucas and Micholls was one of several Jewish firms to join this trend, but was unusual in setting out to control all stages in the cotton business, from the manufacturing and finishing of cottons and calicoes to their distribution in the overseas market. In Manchester, Lucas rapidly assumed a high place in middle-class Jewish and gentile circles. He supported Jewish institutions, such as the Jewish school in the foundation of which he was instrumental, and followed Moses Montefiore in standing against antisemitism. None the less, he sent his own son to a non-Jewish school and hoped for a national secular school system into which Jewish children could be integrated. He was a moderating influence and mediator between the groups into which Manchester Jews were split. He was an active anti-cornlaw campaigner, was elected a city councillor in 1851 (to the approval of Jew and gentile), and in 1858 was elected to the board of the very influential Manchester chamber of commerce. He maintained a fine residence at Temple House, Cheetham Hill Road, where he lived with his wife, Juliana, *née* Gomperty, his one surviving son, Louis, and seven domestic servants. His wife undertook philanthropic work among Jews. Lucas is known to have died before his son. After his death he lapsed into an obscurity from which he has only recently been rescued, while his son, an unremarkable explorer, able to travel because of his father's wealth, had his exploits and death widely noticed.

Louis Lucas was educated at University College School, London, and at University College, where he showed a preference for scientific subjects. After a trip to Switzerland in 1870, he visited the United States in 1872, reaching as far west as Nebraska. At the end of 1873 he set out for Egypt hoping to improve his health, but contracted typhoid fever and spent some months convalescing. In July 1875 he announced his intention of exploring Africa, beginning in the Congo, despite his poor health. He organized an expedition independent of the Royal Geographical Society, of which he was an associate. He left London on 2 September 1875 and spent some weeks in Cairo learning Arabic and engaging servants. He travelled via Suez, Suakin, and Berber to arrive in Khartoum in January 1876. After making preparations there for an absence of several years, he left in April and sailed up the White Nile in a steamboat lent by Colonel Charles George Gordon to Lado, where he met Gordon. Together they travelled to the Albert Nyanza (Lake Albert) and Lucas was the first to sail on its northern waters in a steamship. Gordon persuaded Lucas to return to Suez, go thence to Zanzibar, reorganize his expedition, and make a fresh start for the interior; but at Khartoum, Lucas was delayed two months by fever and dysentery. He reached Suakin on 18 November and embarked for Suez but died on board the steamship *Massowah* in the Red Sea on 20 November 1876. He was buried at Jiddah. He compiled a Bishareen vocabulary which was published in the Anthropological Institute's *Journal*. Lucas's fortune was valued for probate record at under £60,000: he was described in his probate record as a merchant. ELIZABETH BAIGENT

Sources R. Alcock, *Proceedings* [Royal Geographical Society], 21 (1876–7), 418–21, 465 • *The Athenaeum* (9 Dec 1876), 766 • *The Athenaeum* (23 Dec 1876), 838 • *The Times* (26 Dec 1876), 4 • *Jewish Chronicle* (15 Dec 1876), 588 • B. Williams, *The making of Manchester Jewry, 1740–1875* (1976); repr. (1985) • b. cert. • *DNB* • Boase, *Mod. Eng. biog.*

Wealth at death under £60,000: probate, 29 Dec 1876, *CGPLA Eng. & Wales*

Lucas, Margaret Bright (1818–1890), temperance activist and suffragist, was born on 14 July 1818 at Rochdale, Lancashire, the youngest daughter of Jacob Bright (1775–1851), cotton mill proprietor, and his second wife, Martha, *née* Wood (*d.* 1830). Several of her ten siblings, notably John *Bright and Jacob *Bright, became prominent in politics and reform. Educated 'in the institutions of the Society of Friends', she recalled: 'I developed slowly for we were strictly brought up and told that "children should be seen and not heard"' (M. Parker). On 6 September 1839 Margaret married Samuel *Lucas (1811–1865), a London corn exchange merchant and a fellow Quaker. The pair moved to Manchester in 1845, when Samuel took up a cotton mill partnership, but the family settled permanently in London in 1850. Margaret became politicized during the anti-cornlaw agitation, when, in 1845, she aided her husband in organizing meetings and raising money. Until her husband's death in 1865, however, her main burdens remained within the family, including the rearing of her two children, Samuel Bright Lucas, a deaf mute, and Katharine. By 1870 both children had married, Katharine to John Pennington Thomasson (later MP for Bolton).

Relieved from the cares of immediate family, Lucas now sought a clear plan to fit her Quaker moral purpose. Suffering from bronchial trouble, and seeking a change of climate, she went to North America to stay with a cousin, Esther Blakey, in Halifax in 1870. Lucas easily mixed in the trans-Atlantic reform network that included strong Quaker participation. Woman suffragists and temperance reformers in the north-eastern United States warmly welcomed her as 'John Bright's sister'. She would reciprocate the hospitality when American reformers came to Britain.

The American visit was a turning point in Lucas's public temperance career. There she witnessed 'the advanced views and institutions of a less trammelled social system', influences she found 'congenial' (*Memoir*, 14–28). She had signed the temperance pledge at the age of sixteen, but joined the American-devised Independent Order of Good Templars in 1872, and became a grand worthy vice-templar in 1874. The Good Templars organized the British tour of 'Mother' (Eliza) Stewart, whose social protest against saloons in the Woman's Crusade had stimulated the creation of the Woman's Christian Temperance Union (WCTU) in 1874. Lucas and Stewart spoke at a Newcastle upon Tyne meeting in 1876 which led to the founding of the British Women's Temperance Association (BWTA). Elected BWTA president in 1878, Lucas also supported peace and anti-prostitution work, and served on the executives of the National Society for Women's Suffrage and the Ladies' National Association. Yet temperance took her chief labours, and she remained BWTA president until her death. In 1885 American WCTU leader Frances Willard selected Lucas as first World's WCTU president, in order to emphasize the organization's global commitment. As a consequence, Lucas crossed the ocean again in 1886 to attend an American WCTU convention in Minneapolis, at which she was fêted.

Lucas represented the phase of women's temperance that located the movement's power primarily in the home and in the superiority of women's moral virtues. In her fourth annual report she stated: 'I believe in the household women have a greater power over men, than men have over women, in inducing abstinence from intoxicating drinks' (*Memoir*, 32). She also made, in the 1870s, more conservative assessments of the possibility of social protest than Americans did. British women would not, Lucas believed, emulate the American crusade marches. 'It is hardly likely we can go through the streets and kneel at the doors of the gin palaces' (*Crusader*, 51), she argued, but temperance women could in Britain hold processions and assemblies. They could also petition, and in 1879 she took the first women's petition in favour of Sunday closing to the House of Commons.

By 1883–4 the general failure to convert men to temperance led to a more radical conclusion: 'The conviction grows upon me that while Petitions educate the workers and the people something more is needed to make them effectual'. Had not 'the time come', she asked, 'when it becomes a duty to claim the right to vote on the side of Temperance?' (*Memoir*, 32). Nevertheless the BWTA remained only one of several women's temperance organizations, and it did not embark on its major period of expansion until after her death from tuberculosis on 4 February 1890 at her London home, 7 Charlotte Street, Bloomsbury. She was buried in Highgate cemetery.

Colleagues described Lucas variously as a 'homely British matron' (C. E. Parker, 36), and yet 'well-preserved, erect and vigorous' (Willard, 120), an earnest speaker, 'tall and stately' (M. Parker) with an impressive shock of silvery hair when in her sixties. The BWTA achieved greater heights under her successor, Lady Henry Somerset, but Lucas was an important link in the Anglo-American women's reform networks and a pioneer in British women's temperance. IAN TYRRELL

Sources *Memoir of Margaret Bright Lucas: president of the British Women's Temperance Association* (1890) · M. Parker, *Union Signal* (13 Jan 1887) · *Union Signal* (26 Aug 1886) · *Union Signal* (11 Nov 1886) · F. Willard, *Woman and temperance, or, The work and workers of the Woman's Christian Temperance Union* (1883) · E. H. Cherrington and others, eds., *Standard encyclopedia of the alcohol problem*, 6 vols. (1924–30), vol. 4, p. 1612 · *DNB* · *The crusader in Great Britain, or, The history of the origin and organisation of the British Women's Temperance Association* (1893) · C. E. Parker, *Margaret Eleanor Parker: a memoir* (1906) · d. cert. · m. cert. · I. Tyrrell, *Woman's world, woman's empire: the Woman's Christian Temperance Union in international perspective* (1991) · *CGPLA Eng. & Wales* (1890)

Likenesses portrait, repro. in Willard, *Woman and temperance*, 118 · portrait, repro. in Cherrington, ed., *Standard encyclopedia of the alcohol problem*

Wealth at death £5891 17s. 4d.: probate, 14 March 1890, *CGPLA Eng. & Wales*

Lucas, Norman Bernard Charles (1901–1980), headmaster, was born on 2 January 1901 at 3 Salisbury Terrace, Craven Road, Newbury, Berkshire, the son of Allan Lucas, solicitor, and his wife, Norah Eveline Brooks. Lucas's troubled experiences as a child had a significant influence on his work as a teacher. At the age of three he was boarded out, but rejoined his parents aged six, when his father's business difficulties led to the removal of the family to Winnipeg, Canada. Here his parents' marriage broke up and he was eventually sent back to an aunt in England. By his ninth birthday he had been transferred to his tenth home, that of his maternal grandparents in a village near Newbury. In 1912 he gained a scholarship to Newbury grammar school but had to leave at fifteen to work for his grandfather as a baker's roundsman. A year or so later in Newbury he happened to meet his headmaster, who asked him home and offered him a place at his own expense in the sixth form as a boarder from September 1917. Four terms later Lucas won an open scholarship in history at Cambridge. One significant consequence of this was that as headmaster of Midhurst grammar school many years later he took on as boarders at his personal expense some able boys who needed the support of a boarding education to achieve their potential, including, at one stage, some from Germany and Austria threatened with persecution by the Nazi regime.

In 1919 Lucas went up to Emmanuel College, Cambridge; he graduated in 1922 with a first-class degree. He taught in France and Egypt for three years. On returning to Britain he taught from 1925 at Rendcombe College in Cirencester, an experimental boarding-school, whose headmaster, J. H. Simpson, had been greatly influenced by the ideas of Homer Lane. Simpson's main aim was to enable pupils to combine acceptance of authority with much freedom and a considerable degree of self-government, and within this framework to achieve a high academic standard. Lucas believed that it was here that he learned much of the art of headmastership which he later put into practice at Midhurst. In 1927 he moved to London and taught at Highgate School for three years before undertaking research in France, with financial support from the Rockefeller Foundation, on the thought of Georges Sorel. He returned to England in 1933 to teach history at the Royal Grammar School, Newcastle upon Tyne, and on 2 August 1934 he married Vera Agnes Douglas (1908–1971), whom he had met when both were engaged on research in the Bibliothèque Nationale in Paris. She had read modern languages at Somerville College, Oxford, taken a first-class degree, and then held successively the Zaharoff travelling fellowship and the Esmond senior scholarship, before becoming a schoolteacher.

Lucas was appointed headmaster of Midhurst grammar school in 1938. No new staff had been appointed there since 1927 and the number of pupils had declined to about 150. The boarders and most day boys were fee payers; a fifth held free places. The current level of achievement was such that the county education authority would give no guarantee that it would continue to support the school. Sixth-form work was virtually non-existent. The most urgent task facing Lucas was to see that far more attention was given to study and achievement. The first group of sixth formers under the new arrangements consisted of seven boys, six of whom got open awards at Oxford and Cambridge. During a period of twenty-five years the sixth form increased from 7 to over 130. The outbreak of war in 1939 led to the evacuation to Midhurst of a London girls' grammar school, which meant that the main school buildings had to be shared. This facilitated radical change in that for half of each day pupils had to use the large boarding-house, where less formal group teaching, clubs, and discussion groups were organized, and fuller use was made of the extensive playing fields. Weekly meetings of boys to deal with school matters in the boarding-house were used to accustom pupils to a considerable degree of self-government.

Within a few years the school became a community based on mutual respect in which pupils, including those with emotional or social disabilities, were enabled to develop independent personalities so that they could accept with assurance and sensitivity their place in the community, be it school, place of employment, or society generally. Under Lucas's guidance Midhurst grammar school became co-educational in 1956 to help overcome the shortage of places for girls in the area. A girls' boarding-house was built to balance the boys' house while preserving the value that Lucas saw in a part boarding, part day school. Ten years later there was further change when the school became comprehensive. Lucas was asked to stay for a further year beyond retirement age to see through the fusion of the county secondary school with the grammar school voluntary-controlled foundation. Throughout the three decades of Lucas's headmastership his wife, through both her ideas and her teaching (she was head of the modern languages department from 1939 and senior mistress when the school went co-educational), made a vital contribution to the school.

In 1967 Lucas retired to Haslemere, Surrey. In 1972, the year after Vera Lucas's death, he married on 25 July Doreen Mary Bassett (1913–1995), who had worked at the school as secretary and later caterer for a quarter of a century. In retirement he wrote *An Experience of Teaching* (1975), in which he set out many of his ideas and described his work in a unique and outstandingly successful school community. Lucas died at his home, Coombe Cottage, Grayswood Road, Haslemere, Surrey, on 12 July 1980, of coronary thrombosis. PETER GOSDEN

Sources N. B. C. Lucas, *An experience of teaching* (1975) • C. Hannam, 'The right kind of authority', *Times Educational Supplement* (12 Sept 1975) • K. C. Leslie, *Midhurst grammar school tercentenary, 1672–1972* (1972) • T. Aston, 'Vera Lucas, 1908–1971', address given at the memorial service for Vera Lucas (30 April 1971), 17 • personal knowledge (2004) • private information (2004) • *Midhurst Petworth and District Observer* (18 July 1980), 1 • b. cert. • m. cert. • d. cert.
Archives Midhurst grammar school, Sussex
Likenesses photograph, repro. in Lucas, *An experience of teaching*, jacket
Wealth at death £6829: probate, 28 Sept 1980, *CGPLA Eng. & Wales*

Lucas, Percy Belgrave [*called* Laddie Lucas] (**1915–1998**), air force officer, politician, and golfer, was born on 2 September 1915 at The Lodge, Sandwich Bay, Worth, Kent, the son of Percy Montagu Lucas, the secretary of Prince's Golf Club, Sandwich, and his wife, Charlotte Gertrude, *née* Bone. Lucas acquired his nickname from enquiries by Highland light infantry soldiers billeted in Sandwich as to 'How's the wee laddie?' and learned his golfing skills from his father. It was said that, had he fallen out of bed at the clubhouse, he would have dropped on to the first tee. In 1944 he force-landed his damaged Spitfire on the Sandwich links.

Lucas was educated at Stowe School, where he excelled at rugby, cricket, and golf (winning the English boys' championship in 1933), and at Pembroke College, Cambridge, where he read economics and represented the university at golf. In 1936 he was a member of the Walker cup team which toured the USA. The following year he entered journalism as a sports writer for the *Sunday Express*, and in 1939 he volunteered for the RAF, being posted to 1 initial training wing at Cambridge on 16 January 1940. He was then sent to Canada in the first group of novice pilots to be taught to fly under the empire air training scheme, gaining his wings at 2 service flying training school, Ottawa, in February 1941 as a newly commissioned pilot officer.

Posted back to the UK, Lucas was sent in May 1941 to 52 operational training unit, Debden, and from there to 66 squadron, based at Perranporth in Cornwall with Spitfire Is on convoy patrols. Wanting more action, he volunteered to serve in Burma; instead he was sent to Malta, as one of fifteen Spitfire pilots flown out there by Sunderland flying boat, where he arrived in February 1942.

Malta was then at the nadir of its wartime misfortunes, short of supplies and constantly under air attack: its defending Hurricanes were outclassed and outnumbered. Only when Spitfires arrived, flown off the aircraft-carriers *Eagle* and *Wasp* by RAF pilots (including Lucas), did the tide turn; and it was in the counter-offensive which saved Malta from invasion that Lucas first showed his genius as a fighter leader. For a brief period in February 1942 he flew with a Hurricane squadron (185), then from the 27th with 249 squadron, which from March was re-equipped with Spitfire VCs. As a flight commander, then as commanding officer, he led the Takali wing (nos. 249 and 603 squadrons) in Malta's successful repulse of axis air attacks. In July he was awarded the DFC, then flown back to the UK.

By now a squadron leader, Lucas was first posted to Fighter Command headquarters, then to the school of tactics, and on 18 April 1943 he took command of a Spitfire VI squadron, 616, at Ibsley. After three months he was appointed wing commander flying at Coltishall, where he led two Spitfire VB Squadrons, nos. 64 and 611. In January 1944 he was awarded the DSO and posted to air defence of Great Britain headquarters, where he was involved in planning tactical air support for operation Overlord, the allied invasion of Europe.

But in September Lucas began a further tour of operations, on Mosquitos in the intruder role, commanding

613 squadron—following a conversion course at 13 operational training unit and two months at 2 group support unit—from December to the end of hostilities. For his leadership he was awarded a bar to his DSO and the Croix de Guerre with palm.

In the wake of his brilliant wartime career Lucas decided to take on a new challenge—politics—and in June 1945 he was granted special leave to fight the West Fulham parliamentary seat. Though defeated in Labour's landslide victory, he became MP for Brentford and Chiswick five years later.

After his leave for the general election Lucas was posted to 11 group, Fighter Command, then from 3 September to his release from service in January 1946 he commanded RAF Bentwaters. One of his frequent visitors there was the legless fighter ace Group Captain Douglas Bader; and on 18 May 1946 they became brothers-in-law when Lucas married Jill Addison (*b*. 1921), the sister of Bader's wife, Thelma. They had three sons: Christopher (*b*. 1947), who died before his fourth birthday, Jeremy (*b*. 1952), and David (*b*. 1955).

In 1946 Lucas joined the Greyhound Racing Association (GRA) through his friendship with one of its founders, Brigadier-General A. C. Critchley, who had told him in 1942 that there would be a job for him after the war. He had worked at the GRA, unpaid, in his university vacations, and his post-war career there prospered: initially assistant to the administrative director, he became assistant managing director in the mid-1950s, then was appointed managing director in 1957 and elected chairman in 1965. After the war Lucas maintained his golfing prowess, captaining the Walker cup team in 1949, and he combined his GRA work with his parliamentary duties. In 1957 the prime minister, Harold Macmillan, offered him the post of under-secretary of state at the Air Ministry, but he declined, feeling that he could not maintain his family and educate two sons on a junior minister's salary. He decided not to stand for parliament again.

In eight years as managing director of the GRA, followed by eleven as chairman until his retirement in 1976, Lucas was involved in many hard-fought boardroom battles. These he vividly described in his crisply written autobiography, *Five up* (1978), the first of eight books he produced in his retirement. These comprised a biography of his famous brother-in-law (*Flying Colours: the Epic Story of Douglas Bader*), two golfing books, an account of the siege of Malta, and three titles in co-operation with the leading fighter pilot Air Vice-Marshal 'Johnnie' Johnson.

Lucas was made CBE in 1981, a civil honour crowning his awards for bravery in the air. Of exceptional charm and charisma, he succeeded in all the roles he played: as golfer, journalist, fighter pilot, business executive, MP, and author. Lucas died at his home, Flat 2, 11 Onslow Square, Chelsea, on 21 March 1998. His widow, Jill, received more than 400 letters of condolence—indicating the wide and affectionate esteem in which he was held. He was buried at St Clement's Church, Sandwich, on 27 March.

Humphrey Wynn

Sources b. cert. • m. cert. • d. cert. • RAF record of service and gazetted details, RAF Innsworth, Gloucester, RAF Personnel Management Agency • P. B. Lucas, *Five up* (1978) • P. B. Lucas, 'The Royal Air Force and the battle of Malta', lecture to the RAF Historical Society, 11 March 1991 • private information (2004) [Mrs Jill Lucas, widow] • *The Times* (23 March 1998) • *The Guardian* (23 March 1998) • *The Scotsman* (25 March 1998) • *The Independent* (3 April 1998) • personal knowledge (2004) • *WWW*

Archives FILM 'The air battle for Malta', 1982, TV documentary

Likenesses photograph, repro. in *The Times*

Wealth at death £569,124: probate, 8 July 1998, *CGPLA Eng. & Wales*

Lucas, Philip (*b*. **1797**, *d*. before **1876**). *See under* Lucas, Louis Arthur (1851–1876).

Lucas, Richard (**1648/9–1715**), Church of England clergyman, was born at Presteigne, Radnorshire, the son of Richard Lucas. He matriculated at Jesus College, Oxford, on 3 March 1665, aged sixteen, graduating BA in 1668 and proceeding MA in 1672 (incorporated at Cambridge in 1677). He appears to have travelled around France for a while with his friend William Powell, later rector of Llanwenarth, Monmouthshire. For some time Lucas worked as the master of the free school at Abergavenny, Monmouthshire. In 1677 Lucas published his *Practical Christianity*, which offered discourses and accompanying prayers on Christian living. In this work Lucas stressed the importance of shared beliefs in the fundamentals of the Christian faith as overriding doubts and scruples over liturgy and ceremonies. He also emphasized that the active life was more Christian than the contemplative life as it presented greater challenges to faith and more opportunities for the exercise of Christian charity.

It was probably the popularity of this work and his reputation as a preacher that gained Lucas the rectory of St Stephen, Coleman Street, London, in 1678. In October 1683 he was made lecturer of St Olave, Southwark. Some time around 1683 his eyesight, which had always been weak, completely failed him. Rather than impair his work as a preacher and devotional writer his disability spurred him on to write the most famous of his works, his *Enquiry after Happiness*. First published in 1685 the work was divided into three parts, the first showing the possibility of obtaining happiness, the second the true notion of life, and the third treating religious perfection. These works are dominated by the notion that happiness is attainable on earth via the exercise of right reason and, as in his *Practical Christianity*, there is an emphasis on the importance of an active life. Lucas stated that the whole work was inspired by his friend Dr Thomas Lamb's dictum that 'the life of man is to be estimated by its usefulness in the World'. The work was very popular and went through a number of editions. John Wesley, who had had the book recommended to him by his mother, remained an unshakeable admirer of Lucas's writing.

Aside from the *Enquiry*, Lucas published many other devotional works, including *The Duty of Servants* (1685), which contained guidance and prayers for those entering domestic service. He was also a regular preacher before the mayor and court of aldermen and he preached before the queen on 31 July 1692. These sermons, like his other works, are dominated by the theme of Christian charity. Lucas also revised and corrected a translation of de Castiniza's *The Spiritual Combat* (1698). He conformed at the revolution and in his sermons urged that the oaths of allegiance to William and Mary should not be interpreted to 'weaken and subvert' but only 'strengthen and preserve' the constitution (R. Lucas, *A Sermon Preached at the Assizes*, 1691, 18). He insisted that it was necessary to pay higher taxes to defend England against French tyranny. He was created BD and DD in 1691. In 1697 he was appointed to a prebend at Westminster and in 1701 became president of Sion College. (His election as president was, however, completely unconstitutional as he had never served in any office on the court of governors.) Lucas had a high reputation for piety and was one of the clerics who visited the godly household of Lady Elizabeth Hastings at Ledsham in Yorkshire.

Lucas died at Westminster on 29 June 1715 and was buried in Westminster Abbey on 5 July. He was survived by his widow, Anne (1658/9–1727), and three sons, of whom the two younger also went on to become clergymen. Richard Lucas (1692/3–1747) was ordained deacon at Ely in 1717 and later became rector of Foots Cray, Kent, a living he held until his death. William (1702/3–1753) was a fellow of Corpus Christi College, Cambridge, from 1723 to 1733 and rector of Benington, Hertfordshire, from 1736 to 1753.

EDWARD VALLANCE

Sources *DNB* • Venn, *Alum. Cant.* • R. Lucas, *Practical Christianity* (1677) • E. H. Pearce, *Sion College and library* (1913), 345 • I. Green, *Print and protestantism in early modern England* (2000), 251, 358–9, 638 • J. L. Chester, ed., *The marriage, baptismal, and burial registers of the collegiate church or abbey of St Peter, Westminster*, Harleian Society, 10 (1876), 283, 320–21 • Foster, *Alum. Oxon.*

Likenesses G. Vandergucht, line engraving, BM, NPG

Lucas, Richard Cockle (1800–1883), sculptor, was born on 24 October 1800 in Salisbury, the son of Richard Lucas and his wife, Martha Sutton. At the age of twelve he was apprenticed to an uncle, a cutler at Winchester. Becoming proficient at carving knife-handles, he decided to become a sculptor. In 1828 he entered the Royal Academy Schools, when his age was incorrectly given in the register as twenty-five, and from that year he was a regular contributor to the Royal Academy, receiving a silver medal for an architectural drawing in 1828 and 1829. Over the next thirty years he exhibited over a hundred works at the academy, the British Institution, and the Suffolk Street Gallery of the Society of British Artists, including busts, medallions, and classical subjects, such as those of Dr Johnson at Lichfield, Dr Watts at Southampton, and Richard Colt Hoare at Salisbury Cathedral. His marble, wax, and ivory medallion portraits, many of which were displayed at the Great Exhibition, were more successful, however, and have subsequently been purchased by the Bethnal Green Museum and the National Portrait Gallery, London, which holds his wax medallion of Sir Anthony Panizzi (1850). Two self-portraits, an etching dated on the plate 1858, and a plaster cast of a bust, incised and dated 1868, are also in the National Portrait Gallery collection. Lucas's popular wax relief *Leda and the Swan* was subsequently purchased by the Victoria and Albert Museum. Lucas made a study of the Parthenon marbles, of which he made two large wax models, the first showing the Parthenon as it appeared after bombardment by the Venetians in 1687; the second was made according to a plan of reconstruction according to his own theories as to the original arrangement of the sculptures. The latter was the subject of much public interest when exhibited at the British Museum, where it stood in the Elgin room. In 1845 he published his *Remarks on the Parthenon*, illustrated with fifteen etchings. A decade later he designed and built himself a house which he called Tower of the Winds at Chilworth, near Romsey, Hampshire, an account of which he entitled 'The artist's dream realised, being a residence designed and built by R. C. Lucas, sculptor, 1854; etched and described 1856 with seventeen plates'. Lucas produced many popular etchings depicting his own sculptural works, biblical stories, and scenes from eighteenth-century poetry, including that of Thomas Gray, Oliver Goldsmith, and Robert Burns. A nearly complete series of these, mounted in an album bound by Lucas himself, and including a frontispiece portrait of the artist, is in the print room of the British Museum. Lucas also frequently contributed to the periodical presses where there was some debate as to whether his *Flora*, purchased by the Kaiser Friedrich Museum, Berlin, was by Leonardo da Vinci.

Towards the end of his life, Lucas's conversational prowess ensured that he was a frequent guest at Broadlands, the seat of Lord Palmerston, who obtained for him a civil-list pension in June 1865. Lucas made three wax portraits of Palmerston, and a statuette which formed his last exhibit at the Royal Academy in 1859. In 1870 he published *An Essay on Art*. Lucas died of paralysis at Tower of the Winds, Chilworth, on 18 May 1883, leaving a son, Albert Durer Lucas (1828–1918), a flower painter who exhibited at the British Institution and with the Society of Artists between 1859 and 1874. Grant noted that although Lucas was 'somewhat forgotten today', he was 'one of the leading sculptors of his time', whose sculptural portraits of women were particularly sensitive (Grant, 153). Gunnis described Lucas as an artist of 'great originality' whose works were characterized by their use of contrasting perspective (Gunnis, 245).

F. M. O'DONOGHUE, *rev.* JASON EDWARDS

Sources *Hampshire Independent* (20 Jan 1883) • *The Athenaeum* (27 Jan 1883), 127–8 • *The exhibition of the Royal Academy* (1828–59) [exhibition catalogues] • *Great Exhibition* (1851) [exhibition catalogue, London] • R. Gunnis, *Dictionary of British sculptors, 1660–1851* (1953); new edn (1968) • M. H. Grant, *A dictionary of British sculptors from the XIIIth century to the XXth century* (1953) • *CGPLA Eng. & Wales* (1883) • S. C. Hutchison, 'The Royal Academy Schools, 1768–1830', *Walpole Society*, 38 (1960–62), 123–91, esp. 180 • K. K. Yung, *National Portrait Gallery: complete illustrated catalogue, 1856–1979*, ed. M. Pettman (1981) • *IGI* • Wood, *Vic. painters*, 3rd edn

Archives Bethnal Green Museum, London, works • BM, works • NPG, works

Likenesses R. C. Lucas, self-portrait, pen and wash etching, 1858, NPG • R. C. Lucas, self-portrait, plaster bust, 1868, NPG • etching, BM • photograph, BM

Wealth at death £573 6s. 6d.: resworn probate, Aug 1883, *CGPLA Eng. & Wales*

Lucas, Robert (1747/8–1812), Church of England clergyman and poet, was born in Northampton and was educated at the free grammar school there. He was admitted to Trinity College, Cambridge, in December 1776 and graduated BD as a ten-year man in 1787. In 1793 he graduated DD. In 1772 he may have been acting as curate of Brixworth, and in 1778 he was curate of Hardingstone, Northamptonshire, but on 8 March 1782 he was instituted to the vicarage of Pattishall in the same county. Lucas married a daughter of Thomas Hurd, the younger brother of Bishop Richard Hurd. They had a son, Richard Hurd Lucas (*b.* 1789), and a daughter, Harriet Charlotte. The marriage probably took place before 1787, in which year, on 20 March, Lucas was collated by Bishop Hurd to the rectory of Ripple, Worcestershire, which he held with his vicarage.

Lucas produced two volumes of poetry: *Hymn to Ceres* (1781), a translation into English heroic verse of the Homeric hymn, and *Poems* (1810), which included a reprint of his translation. His relationship to Hurd prompted a further publication, *A Letter to the Reverend Doctor Parr* (1789), defending the reputation of his patron, and he may also have written the memoir of Hurd in the *Ecclesiastical and University Annual Register* for 1809. As a clergyman Lucas was an enthusiastic proponent of the Sunday school movement and published a number of sermons in its support. These were reprinted with other predominantly charity sermons in *Occasional Sermons* (2 vols., 1809). He died at Ripple on 1 March 1812.

GORDON GOODWIN, *rev.* SARAH BREWER

Sources Venn, *Alum. Cant.* • H. I. Longden, *Northamptonshire and Rutland clergy from 1500*, ed. P. I. King and others, 16 vols. in 6, Northamptonshire RS (1938–52) • E. H. Pearce, *Hartlebury Castle* (1926), 278, 308, 311 • F. Kilvert, *Memoirs of the life and writings of the Right Rev. Richard Hurd* (1860), 171, 371 • G. Baker, *The history and antiquities of the county of Northampton*, 2 vols. (1822–41) • *GM*, 1st ser., 82/1 (1812), 497 • *N&Q*, 2nd ser., 8 (1859), 416

Lucas, Samuel (1805–1870), painter, was born at Hitchin in Hertfordshire, the son of William Lucas, a brewer. He was educated at Hitchin and at a Quaker school in Bristol, and wanted to be an artist, but his Quaker religion at that time forbade an artistic education. He was apprenticed to a shipowner at Shoreham in Sussex, but managed to practise painting as an amateur. After his marriage in Norfolk to Matilda, daughter of John Holmes, a farmer, on 7 September 1837 he settled at Hitchin, where he resided for the remainder of his life. Though he carried on his father's business, Lucas continued to devote himself to his favourite art; his wife, son, daughters, and granddaughters also painted.

In 1830 Lucas sent to the Royal Academy *The Ship 'Broxbournbury' off the Islands of Amsterdam*. He also exhibited at the British Institution and Society of British Artists in Suffolk Street, but such public displays were rare. His subjects were mainly landscapes, carefully studied from nature, and he painted both in oil and in watercolours. He was an excellent ornithologist, and also painted birds, animals, and flowers. Some of his drawings of flowers were engraved in *The Florist*. His pictures were much admired, and he enjoyed the friendship of many leading artists. Good examples of his drawings are in the British Museum, and there is a picture by him, *The Old Hitchin Market*, in the Corn Exchange at Hitchin. Lucas was struck with paralysis in 1865 and died in Tilehouse Street, Hitchin, on 29 March 1870. His wife survived him.

L. H. CUST, *rev.* EMILY M. WEEKS

Sources Wood, *Vic. painters*, 3rd edn • Thieme & Becker, *Allgemeines Lexikon* • M. H. Grant, *A dictionary of British landscape painters, from the 16th century to the early 20th century* (1952) • H. M. Cundall, *A history of British water colour painting* (1908); 2nd edn (1929) • L. Binyon, *Catalogue of drawings by British artists and artists of foreign origin working in Great Britain*, 3 (1902) • Mallalieu, *Watercolour artists* • private information (1893) • m. cert. • d. cert.

Wealth at death under £16,000: resworn probate, April 1871, *CGPLA Eng. & Wales* (1870)

Lucas, Samuel (1811–1865), journalist and educational reformer, was the eldest son of Samuel Hayhurst Lucas, a Quaker corn merchant of Wandsworth, Surrey. His younger brother was Frederick *Lucas, who converted to Roman Catholicism and founded *The Tablet*; Samuel, by contrast, remained a Quaker all his life, and opposition to the established church was a steady theme throughout his career. His childhood and early adult years were spent in Surrey and in London. On 6 September 1839 he married Margaret Bright (1818–1890) [*see* Lucas, Margaret Bright], daughter of Jacob Bright and sister of John Bright, of the Anti-Corn Law League. In 1845 they moved to Manchester, where Lucas became a partner in a cotton mill. He was involved in the later campaigns of the Anti-Corn Law League, having been active from 1844 in the Anti-State Church Association (from 1853 the Society for the Liberation of Religion from State Patronage and Control).

In August 1847 Lucas became one of the six veterans of the anti-cornlaw campaign who founded the Lancashire Public Schools Association (LPSA), which was organized along similar lines to the league, and used petitioning and pamphleteering as its chief campaign tools. Lucas chaired the LPSA committee, in which capacity, according to his colleague J. Alfred Steinthal, he demonstrated his 'sweet temper' and 'rare tact and judgement', most notably in smoothing differences arising from divergences in religious outlook (Jones, 38). Lucas's *Plan for the Establishment of a General System of Secular Education in the County of Lancaster* (1847), written on behalf of the LPSA, advocated a decentralized scheme of public schools' administration similar to that which operated in Massachusetts. From June 1849 he edited a journal, the *Education Register*, which ran until early the following year. In August 1849 he returned to London, where he set up in business as a corn merchant.

Late in 1849 the LPSA changed its name to the National Public Schools Association (NPSA), having recruited Richard Cobden as a powerful advocate. Lucas continued to be active in the cause: in 1850 he edited a collection of essays entitled *National Education not Necessarily Governmental, Sectarian or Irreligious*. His anxiety to keep the NPSA firmly to a secularist path led him to oppose compromise with religious bodies and occasionally placed him at odds with

Cobden. He was frustrated by the indifference or hostility that met NPSA proposals in the House of Commons, and, dissatisfied at coverage in the mainstream press, in August 1853 he started the *Advocate for National Instruction*, which ran for four issues. More significantly, from the summer of 1857 until his death Lucas served as editor of the *Morning Star*, the radical newspaper started by Cobden and Bright in March 1856. As an 'active managing partner', with a financial stake in the paper (Koss, 126), he was successful at bringing in Justin McCarthy and Edmund Yates as contributors, and was involved in the takeover of the *People's Charter* and *The Dial*. Lucas was active in the Association for the Repeal of Taxes on Knowledge, particularly at the time of the House of Lords' rejection of Gladstone's attempt to repeal the paper duty in 1860. During the American Civil War he was a prominent supporter of the North, helping to found the Emancipation Society, which opposed slavery, in 1862.

Lucas died from a bronchial illness at 4 Gordon Street, Gordon Square, London, on 16 April 1865, and was buried in Highgate cemetery in north London. Many of the proposals contained in his 1847 *Plan* subsequently found their way onto the statute book in the Education Act of 1870.

MILES TAYLOR and H. J. SPENCER

Sources *DNB* • J. T. Mills, *John Bright and the Quakers*, 2 vols. (1935) • S. E. Koss, *The rise and fall of the political press in Britain*, 2 vols. (1981–4); repr. (1990) • D. K. Jones, 'Samuel Lucas, 1811–1865, journalist, politician and educational reformer', *Biography and education: some eighteenth and ninteenth century studies*, ed. R. Lowe (1980)
Archives Man. CL, National Public Schools Association archives • NL Scot., corresp. with George Combe • U. Birm., Harriet Martineau MSS • W. Sussex RO, corresp. with Richard Cobden
Wealth at death under £3000: probate, 3 June 1865, *CGPLA Eng. & Wales*

Lucas, Samuel (1818–1868), journalist and author, eldest son of Thomas Lucas, a Bristol merchant, initially trained to enter his father's business. When his literary tastes became apparent, he was sent to Queen's College, Oxford, as preparation for a legal career. He matriculated in 1838, graduating BA in 1842 and MA in 1846. At Oxford he won the Newdigate prize for English verse in 1841 and the chancellor's prize for the English essay in 1845.

In 1846 Lucas was called to the bar at the Inner Temple, and became a barrister on the western circuit. He abandoned his legal practice after seven years to become a journalist. On 8 May 1853, with the backing of Disraeli and other leading Conservatives, he founded *The Press*, a tory weekly, which he edited until May 1854. It was to some extent a baptism of fire for the inexperienced editor, as the contributors were mainly public men with little grasp of journalistic practices. Lucas was replaced by David Coulton (1810–1857) and in 1855 began reviewing for *The Times*.

Lucas worked for *The Times* for ten years, despite differences with the editor, J. T. Delane, which seem to have led him to offer his resignation on one occasion. As a man of wide reading and urbane manner, Lucas was a successful, witty, and largely generous reviewer. He seems to have dealt mainly with non-fiction, reviewing Thomas Carlyle's *Frederick the Great*, Macaulay's *History of England*, Sir Robert Peel's *Memoirs*, and (with much expository clarity) Buckle's *History of Civilization*. He was an early appreciator of George Eliot, praising her *Scenes of Clerical Life* for their combination of pathos and humour, and he wrote a strikingly perceptive and unusually favourable review of George Meredith's *Richard Feverel* (1859).

Lucas published several volumes of his collected journalism and other minor works, including *History as a Condition of National Progress* (1853) and *Illustrations of the History of Bristol and its Neighbourhood* (1853). He also edited the poems of Thomas Hood (2 vols., 1867). In 1858 Lucas was appointed stamp distributor for Derby. He edited *Once a Week* from 1859 until 1865; his final journalistic venture was to launch the *Shilling Magazine*, which lasted only a few months. In 1866 his health began to fail, and he left London. He died at Molesey House, Eastbourne, Sussex, on 27 November 1868, leaving a widow, Jane.

JOSEPH COOHILL

Sources *The Times* (2 Dec 1868) • [S. Morison and others], *The history of The Times*, 2 (1939), 467–92 • S. E. Koss, *The rise and fall of the political press in Britain*, 1 (1981), 90–91 • D. Griffiths, ed., *The encyclopedia of the British press, 1422–1992* (1992) • Allibone, *Dict.* • C. Knight, ed., *The English cyclopaedia: biography*, 3 (1856) • Foster, *Alum. Oxon.* • *CGPLA Eng. & Wales* (1868) • d. cert.
Archives Bodl. Oxf., letters to Benjamin Disraeli • NL Scot., corresp. with Blackwoods • U. Birm. L., letters to Harriet Martineau
Wealth at death under £5000: probate, 19 Dec 1868, *CGPLA Eng. & Wales*

Lucas, Simon (*fl. c.*1766–1799), explorer and diplomat, was the son of a London wine merchant. He was wrongly identified in the *Dictionary of National Biography* as William Lucas. While still a boy he was sent to Cadiz to be trained as a merchant, but was captured on his return voyage by a Salé rover and pressed into slavery in the imperial court of Morocco. After three years' captivity he was freed and went to Gibraltar and was thence sent back to Morocco as vice-consul and *chargé d'affaires* by General Edward Cornwallis, governor of Gibraltar from 1762 to 1773. He remained in Morocco for sixteen years.

In 1785 Lucas returned to England and was appointed oriental interpreter to the British court. Soon afterwards he volunteered to undertake a journey in Africa in the service of the newly formed Association for Promoting the Discovery of the Interior Parts of Africa, commonly known as the African Association. This was founded in 1788 to undertake geographical exploration, not least with the aim of opening the continent to British trade and influence. Lucas volunteered his services to the society, suggesting that his knowledge of Arabic and of north African lands would be useful. He stipulated that he must receive his salary of £80 per annum in his absence from his post as interpreter. The African Association accepted his offer, secured his paid leave from his position, and furnished him with presents and other equipment to the value of £250, subscribed personally by the association's committee members.

Lucas left England in August 1788 with instructions to

cross the desert from Tripoli to Fezzan collecting information from the local people and traders about the interior of Africa and returning home via the Gambia or the Guinea coast. He landed at Tripoli on 25 October and was well received by the pasha, whom he told that his mission was to investigate antiquities and medicinal plants. He secured leave to travel to Fezzan, but his departure was delayed by the revolt of the Arab peoples who occupied the territory through which he was intending to pass. This made it impossible for him to proceed alone as planned, but the arrival in Tripoli of two sherifs, both claiming descent from Muhammad and one, Imhammed, being the son-in-law of the king of Fezzan, offered a way out. Their positions allowed them to take responsibility for his safe conduct, and Lucas set out in their company on 1 February 1789. They had, however, travelled only a short distance when it became obvious that the disturbed conditions would make it impossible for the party to reach Fezzan before the winter, and the caravan determined to break up. But before the party dispersed, Lucas used his time to gain from Sherif Imhammed much geographical information about Fezzan, Bornou, and Nigritia. Lucas left Memoon on 20 March 1789 and reached Tripoli on 6 April and England on 26 July of that year.

Lucas's account of his voyage in Africa was published in the *Proceedings* of the African Association (vol. 1, 1790) but it was clear that the association felt it had got little for its money. Joseph Banks, its president, commented: 'Mr Lucas and Major Houghton [Daniel Houghton, the next explorer sent out by the association] do not appear to have been well chosen; the inexperience of Your Committee in the selection of proper persons must plead their excuse' (Hallett, 168). Frederick Hornemann, also sent out by the association to Africa, met Lucas in Tripoli in 1799 and commented: 'I don't know if the Committee believes his excuses for his returning to England, or if they give them so little credit as I do myself' (ibid., 189). Indeed the consul for Morocco remarked of Lucas in a letter to Banks that he 'has got such a determined habit of lying that he is quite a proverb not only over all Barbary but at this place [Gibraltar]' (ibid., 155n.).

If the information which Lucas brought back was not wrong, neither was it particularly original, and memories of his journey for the association were rapidly eclipsed by those of other explorers sent out by the association. In 1793 he was appointed consul at Tripoli, a result perhaps due in part to his attempts to discredit Mr Tully, the previous consul. He was last heard of in October 1799 by the report of Hornemann. ELIZABETH BAIGENT

Sources R. Hallett, *Records of the African Association, 1788–1831* (1964) • *Proceedings of the Association for Promoting the Discovery of the Interior Parts of Africa*, 1 (1790), esp. 47–74

Lucas, Theophilus (*fl.* 1714), writer on gambling, inherited, according to his own assertion, an estate of £2000 a year, which he lost at the gaming tables. To deter his son, who was the 'very next heir to £1,500 per annum by the death of an uncle' (Lucas, vi), from following his example, or, at best, to put him on his guard against the tricks of card-sharpers, he wrote an entertaining and, in places, scandalous, book, *Memoirs of the lives, intrigues and comical adventures of the most famous gamesters and celebrated sharpers in the reigns of Charles II, James II, William III and Queen Anne* (1714). In addition to the biographical information, Lucas provided a history of gaming which exposed the method of cheating in various card games. A third edition, with additions, was published without the author's name in 1744. The accuracy of this book, which does not draw on earlier studies such as Charles Cotton's *Compleat Gamester* (1674), remains questionable. Indeed with so few known details it is also debatable whether Lucas was a real-life author, a pseudonym for a similarly reformed gamester, or a fictitious character—the story of financial loss being intended to give validity to the work.

GORDON GOODWIN, *rev.* PHILIP CARTER

Sources T. Lucas, *Memoirs of the lives, intrigues, and comical adventures of the most famous gamesters and celebrated sharpers in the reigns of Charles II, James II, William III and Queen Anne* (1714)

Lucas, Sir Thomas (1597/8–1648/9), royalist army officer, was the eldest and illegitimate son of Thomas Lucas (*d.* 1625) of Colchester and Elizabeth Leighton (*d.* 1647). His parents' failure to marry before his birth may be explained by his father's exile from England in Queen Elizabeth's later years for participation in a fatal duel. Despite his illegitimacy Thomas was fully integrated into his family and his father provided carefully for him, buying him the manor and estate of Lexden, close to Colchester, about 1612, and on his death in 1625 dividing his own estate between his wife, Elizabeth, and his sons Thomas Lucas, John *Lucas, and Charles *Lucas. Thomas's brother John secured the reversion of his barony (1645) first to his legitimate brother Charles but after him to Thomas and his heirs. The career of the younger Thomas exemplifies the way in which many pre-civil war Englishmen pursued military careers on the continent and later formed a professional nucleus in the armies of both sides in the civil war.

Lucas matriculated at Pembroke College, Cambridge, at Easter 1615. He was probably in the Low Countries as early as 1625; in 1637 he commanded a troop of horse there. He was knighted on 14 April 1628 at Whitehall and on 27 January 1629 married Anne Byron (*b.* 1612/13, *d.* in or after July 1653), the daughter of Sir John Byron; he was thirty-one and she was sixteen. In the 1630s he was involved in a dispute with the undertakers engaged in piping water to Colchester, claiming that the disorderly patrons of the alehouse at the waterworks damaged his warren. In 1639 the privy council decided in his favour, but relations between the Lucases and the town corporation remained uneasy, and the dispute may partly account for the plundering of Sir Thomas's records in the popular violence that erupted in Colchester in August 1642. With the approach of the Scottish war he was, with his brother Charles, among those 'elected' to serve the king (NL Wales, MS Chirk, fol. 7442). In December 1638 Lord Deputy Wentworth recommended that he be given command of a troop to march in

Ireland, with the intention of gaining him to the king's service, an indication that his support was held to be worth winning.

Early in 1640 Lucas was trying to extricate himself from his command of a troop in the Low Countries and was also, in London and the Netherlands, engaged in inspecting and procuring equipment for war in Scotland. In February he was appointed commissary-general of horse in Ireland at a fee of 20*s*. per day, with an additional 10*s*. per day if employed in the king's wars. He commanded a regiment in Yorkshire in July 1640, but the main theatre of his service to the king was in Ireland. He was present at the battle of Kilrush on 15 April 1642 and was badly wounded at Ross on 18 March 1643. He was a member of the Irish privy council, and participated in negotiations for the cessation of 1643 and the treaty of 1646. He had returned to England by October 1646 with members of the committee of both kingdoms, to whom he had personally applied for consideration. In February 1647 he compounded for delinquency. In March his fine was set, at one-tenth, at £1194; in May 1648, after he demonstrated that he had only a life interest in his estate, he was assessed at £800, and finally in September 1648 his fine was set at £637. The date of the last reduction suggests that he was not implicated in the second civil war. However, the sequestration of his estate imposed in May 1647 was not discharged until 19 October 1649, after Sir Thomas's death. His sister, Margaret, duchess of Newcastle, believed that his life had been shortened by a severe head wound which he had suffered in Ireland.

BARBARA DONAGAN

Sources *CSP dom., 1625–49* • M. A. E. Green, ed., *Calendar of the proceedings of the committee for compounding … 1643–1660*, 5 vols., PRO (1889–92) • M. A. E. Green, ed., *Calendar of the proceedings of the committee for advance of money, 1642–1656*, 3 vols., PRO (1888) • Margaret, duchess of Newcastle [M. Cavendish], *The life of William Cavendish, duke of Newcastle*, ed. C. H. Firth (1886) • *DNB* • Venn, *Alum. Cant.* • GEC, *Peerage* • J. Walter, *Understanding popular violence in the English revolution: the Colchester plunderers* (1999) • D. J. Appleby, *Our fall, our fame: the life and times of Sir Charles Lucas, 1613–1648* (1996) • G. Radcliffe, *The earl of Strafforde's letters and dispatches, with an essay towards his life*, ed. W. Knowler, 2 vols. (1739), vol. 2, pp. 254, 262 • NL Wales, MS Chirk, fol. 7442

Wealth at death unknown, but fined; also wife had lands in Lancashire; several years of army pay (30*s*. per day if actually paid): Green, ed., *Calendar of the proceedings of the committee for compounding*, 3.1675, 2338; 4.2880–81; Green, ed., *Calendar of the committee for advance of money*, 2.821; Margaret, duchess of Newcastle, *Life*

Lucas, Sir Thomas, first baronet (1822–1902). *See under* Lucas, Charles Thomas (1820–1895).

Luce, Sir (John) David (1906–1971), naval officer, was born on 23 January 1906 at Halcombe St Mary, Malmesbury, Wiltshire, the son of Admiral John David Luce (1870–1932), and his wife, Mary Dorothea Tucker. Luce senior had commanded the cruiser *Glasgow* at the battles of the Coronel and the Falklands. One of four brothers, David Luce, as he was generally known, entered the Royal Naval College, Dartmouth, in 1919. He decided to enter the Submarine Service in 1927. In 1935 he married Mary Adelaide Norah

Sir (John) David Luce (1906–1971), by Walter Bird, 1960

Whitman; they had two sons. Luce received his first command, the boat *H44*, in 1936. This was followed by two more submarine commands in the early years of the Second World War, *Rainbow* (1939–40) and *Cachalot* (1940–41). His achievements in a number of hazardous patrols were rewarded by appointment to the Distinguished Service Order in November 1940. Both submarines were sunk shortly after Luce relinquished command of them.

Promoted commander, Luce served in the plans division at the Admiralty before joining Mountbatten's combined operations organization in 1942. He was made OBE for skill and resources displayed in the attack on Dieppe and remained as an acting captain on the books of HMS *Vectis*, the combined operations base in the Isle of Wight. This period of Luce's career culminated in duty as chief staff officer to the forces engaged in operation Neptune, the amphibious attack on Normandy in June 1944. He received a bar to his DSO. Two months later and in his substantive rank once more Luce went east as executive officer of the cruiser *Swiftsure* allocated to the British Pacific Fleet. Promoted captain in June 1945 he joined Admiral Fraser's Pacific Fleet staff as assistant chief of staff, plans, in the battleship *Duke of York*. With the war's end the staff moved ashore at Hong Kong and by the end of the year Luce had become chief of staff, operations.

Luce broadened his experience further by commanding the royal naval air station Ford from late 1946 to 1948. He then moved back to the plans division at the Admiralty as deputy director, a key appointment as his department evolved definitive post-war plans. He also had to respond to the demands of planning the effects of the sudden and massive Korean rearmament. Sea command then followed in two successive cruisers, *Liverpool* in the Mediterranean in 1951–2 and *Birmingham* in the Far East in 1952–3. Under Luce's command the latter ship took part in bombardment operations against the North Korean coastline. Luce next became director of the Royal Naval Staff College at Greenwich, a position he held until the following year. This saw his move to the Admiralty as naval secretary to the first lord, an influential post in charge of officer appointments. He was promoted rear-admiral in 1955.

Luce went back to sea as flag officer (flotillas) Home Fleet, being promoted vice-admiral in 1958. His appointment in his new rank was flag officer, Scotland, a post he carried out with the expected success. Promotion to full admiral came in 1960 together with the main operational command of the contemporary Royal Navy, commander-in-chief, Far East Fleet. When under Mountbatten's influence joint theatre commands were set up, Admiral Sir David Luce was appointed the first commander-in-chief, British forces, Far East, in 1962. As such Luce commanded the rapid and successful response to the Brunei uprising in December 1962. Luce's qualities of diplomacy and tact were much at a premium in setting up this tri-service enterprise.

Luce succeeded Sir Caspar John as first sea lord in 1963. He was the first sea lord to be a submariner and the last to sit on the old Board of Admiralty that was absorbed into the new Ministry of Defence in 1964. When Luce took over, the Admiralty had just succeeded in obtaining authorization for a new large carrier, CVA01, HMS *Queen Elizabeth*. The new carrier became a major item of dispute when the newly elected Labour government of 1964 began a major defence review. Luce led the naval staff's defence against a direct attack from the Royal Air Force, which argued that its land-based aircraft could carry out the power projection task 'East of Suez' more cost-effectively than could CVA01. Luce, a kindly man with much joint experience, would not countenance a direct naval counter-attack against the sister service. Some felt that his submarine background meant that he lacked the instinctive passion to support carriers that John as an airman had possessed, but the reasons were probably more a reflection of Luce's gentle and statesmanlike character. He would not allow the naval staff to expose what the latter regarded as sharp practice by the junior service. The carrier case as developed by Luce and his colleagues was to argue for increased expenditure beyond the government's plans in order to sustain operations east of Suez. This was unacceptable to the government. Within the new ministry Luce lacked the support both of the Admiralty secretariat and the political position of the first lord of the Admiralty, both of which had been of inestimable value to his predecessors in the shark infested waters of Whitehall. When the decision was taken in February 1966 to cancel *Queen Elizabeth* in favour of the RAF's F-111 aircraft Sir David Luce felt that there was no alternative but to resign. A popular officer, he became president of the Royal Naval Association. Luce was made CB in 1947 and KCB in 1960. He was promoted GCB in 1963. He died on 6 January 1971 at the Lansdown Nursing Home, Bath.

Eric J. Grove

Sources E. J. Grove, *Vanguard to Trident: British naval policy since World War II* (1987) · *WWW*, 1971–80 · *CGPLA Eng. & Wales* (1971)
Archives PRO, Admiralty MSS, ADM · U. Southampton, Mountbatten MSS | FILM IWM FVA, actuality footage
Likenesses W. Bird, photograph, 1960, NPG [*see illus.*]
Wealth at death £41,644: probate, 21 April 1971, *CGPLA Eng. & Wales*

Lucius (*supp. fl.* 185), supposed king in Britain, was the fruit of simple unpremeditated error, which then gave rise to a story of considerable historical importance. The *Liber pontificalis*, in its biography of Pope Eleuther (*fl. c.*180), has the following brief sentence: 'He received a letter from Lucius, a British king, who wanted to become a Christian on his authority' (*The Book of Pontiffs*, 6). The names of the consuls imply a date of 185. It is very probable, as shown by Harnack, that this is the outcome of a confusion between Birtha (the castle of Edessa) and Britain; the ruler of Edessa, Abgar IX (Lucius Aelius Septimius Megas Abgarus), was thus transformed into a British king. It is highly unlikely that there was any propagandist intent behind the error, since the sixth-century author of the early part of the *Liber pontificalis* showed no interest in papal sponsorship of missions: the role of Celestine in authorizing the sending, as his representative, of Palladius as first bishop of the Irish is passed over.

The *Liber pontificalis*, however, was one of the most important historical texts of the early middle ages. The story thus passed to Bede, where it was repeated in his *Historia ecclesiastica*: for Bede, this papal mission to the Britons was rapidly successful and Christianity then remained 'unharmed and undiminished in serene peace up to the time of the emperor Diocletian' (Bede, *Hist. eccl.*, 1.4). Bede associated the end of this golden age of the British church—a happy period before heresy, first Arianism and then Pelagianism, poisoned the island—with the persecution of Diocletian; the persecution then accounted for the martyrdom of St Alban. The unstated implication, for Bede, appears to be that the Britons, many of whom currently refused to accept the Roman Easter and tonsure, should remember their papal origins and conform.

The *Historia Brittonum* (829–30) also included the story: the embassy, however, was no longer from Lucius to the pope, but from the Roman emperors and the pope (named 'Eucharistus') to the Britons. The role of Lucius is also significantly glossed: he is still 'the British king' but his baptism is followed by those of 'all the under-kings of the British people' (*Historia Brittonum*, chap. 22). The author has made Lucius part of a Britain ruled by British kings, but subject to Roman emperors; the role of the papacy has become secondary. The conversion, however, was seen to be just as complete as it was by Bede.

By the ninth century, therefore, the early papal origins of British Christianity were authoritatively established both among the Britons themselves and among the English. Although the story might later be overshadowed by mistier and more exciting tales of Joseph of Arimathea, it remained standard until, in modern times, ancient historians observed that there could hardly have been a second-century British king at all south of Hadrian's Wall, let alone one in a position to send an embassy to the pope.

T. M. Charles-Edwards

Sources Bede, *Hist. eccl.*, 1.4 • T. Mommsen, ed., 'Historia Brittonum', *Chronica minora saec. IV. V. VI. VII.*, 3, MGH Auctores Antiquissimi, 13 (Berlin, 1898), 111–222 • J. G. Evans and J. Rhys, eds., *The text of the Book of Llan Dâv reproduced from the Gwysaney manuscript* (1893) • R. Davis, ed. and trans., *The Book of Pontiffs ('Liber pontificalis'): the ancient biographies of the first ninety Roman bishops to* AD *715* (1989) • A. Harnack, 'Der Brief des britischen Königs Lucius an dem Papst Eleutherus', *Sitzungsberichte der Königlich-Preussischen Akademie der Wissenschaften* (1904), 900–16 • H. Williams, *Christianity in early Britain* (1912), 60–66

Luckock, Herbert Mortimer (1833–1909), dean of Lichfield, born on 11 July 1833, at Great Barr, Staffordshire, was the second son of the Revd Thomas George Mortimer Luckock and his wife, Harriet, daughter of George Chune of Madeley, Shropshire. Educated at Marlborough College (1848–50) and Shrewsbury School (1850–53), he was elected to a scholarship at Jesus College, Cambridge, and graduated BA with a second class in the classical tripos in 1858, proceeding MA in 1862 and DD in 1879. In 1859, 1861, and 1862 he won the members' prize for an essay. In 1860 he was placed in the first class of the theological examination (middle bachelors), and won the Carus and Scholefield prizes for proficiency in the Greek Testament and the Septuagint. In 1861 he was awarded the Crosse scholarship and in 1862 the Tyrwhitt Hebrew scholarship. Ordained deacon in 1860 by the bishop of Oxford, he worked for a time at Clewer with T. T. Carter and as a private tutor at Eton. He was elected to a fellowship at Jesus College, took priest's orders in 1862, and was appointed to the college living of All Saints, Cambridge. From 1863 to 1865 he was rector of Gayhurst with Stoke-Goldington, Buckinghamshire, but returned to the vicarage of All Saints in 1865, held it for ten years, and completed a new church for the parish. He was select preacher at Cambridge in 1865, 1874, 1875, 1883, 1884, 1892, and 1901. He married in 1866 Margaret Emma (*d.* 1890), second daughter of Samuel Henry Thompson of Thingwall, Liverpool; they had eight children.

In 1873 Bishop J. R. Woodford of Ely (three volumes of whose sermons he afterwards edited) appointed Luckock one of his examining chaplains, made him honorary canon of Ely in 1874, and entrusted him with the organization of Ely Theological College. He was principal of the college from 1876 to 1887, exercising a marked influence on the men under his care. He was residentiary canon of Ely from 1875 to 1892 and warden of the society of mission preachers in the diocese. In 1892 he was appointed dean of Lichfield, where he advanced the character of the cathedral services and promoted the restoration of the fabric, rebuilding at his own cost St Chad's Chapel. He died at the deanery, Lichfield, on 24 March 1909 and was buried there in the cathedral close. Six of his children survived him.

A decided high-churchman, though standing aloof from party organizations, a born teacher, unemotional and precise, Luckock exercised a wide influence, largely through his many publications, of which the most notable are *After Death* (1879; 5th edn, 1886) and its sequel, *The Intermediate State* (1890), a history of Jewish and Christian marriage (1894), and several devotional expositions.

A. R. Buckland, *rev.* H. C. G. Matthew

Sources *The Guardian* (31 March 1909) • *Church Times* (26 March 1909) • Venn, *Alum. Cant.* • *CGPLA Eng. & Wales* (1909) • Crockford (1908)
Archives BL, letters to W. E. Gladstone, Add. MSS 44492–44525
Likenesses wood-engraving, NPG; repro. in *ILN* (22 Oct 1892)
Wealth at death £24,563 15s.: resworn probate, 14 May 1909, *CGPLA Eng. & Wales*

Luckombe, Philip (*bap.* 1730, *d.* 1803), printer and writer, was born in Exeter and baptized in the church of St Lawrence, Exeter, on 8 November 1730, son of John Luckombe, tailor. His brother John was baptized on 17 November 1728 in the same church. Philip, a printer by trade, was made a freeman of Exeter by succession in 1776, probably in order to vote in the general election of 1776. A report that he entered one of the Oxford colleges (Nichols, *Illustrations*) seems highly doubtful and is not corroborated by any university register. Luckombe did leave Exeter but settled in London, from where he did much miscellaneous literary work; in 1803 he was resident in the parish of St Dunstan-in-the-West in the City. Besides editing several dictionaries and encyclopaedias, he wrote books on printing and made a special study of conchology. His collection of shells was large, and his learning brought him into contact with Thomas Percy, bishop of Dromore and author of the famous collection of ballads *Reliques of Ancient English Poetry*.

Of Luckombe's several works, perhaps the liveliest was *A Tour through Ireland in Several Entertaining Letters* (1748), which he co-wrote with William Rufus Chetwood. Chetwood knew Ireland well through his links with the Smock Alley Theatre in Dublin. The letters are addressed to 'Ned', that is 'E. H. esq', in his chambers in the Middle Temple. There are several lively incidents, from the party's being surrounded by straw plaiters and having to buy a woman's hat to make their escape, to stories of grizzly murders, and hanged men brought back to life, all recalled with relish and showing Chetwood's sense of the dramatic. This *Tour* seems to have relied at least in part on firsthand information, though antiquarian details are culled from elsewhere. Luckombe's *Tour through Ireland* of 1780 is more extensively plagiarized from others, including Richard Twiss, though Luckombe was in Ireland in 1779. Luckombe also wrote guides to England and Wales.

Luckombe published anonymously in 1770 *A Concise History of the Origin and Progress of Printing* and the following year published a second edition under the title *The History and Art of Printing* (2 parts) which went out over his name. The work was based on his own firsthand experience of the printing trade, and the technical information it provides led to its being reprinted in 1965.

Luckombe died in September 1803. He seems to have

been unmarried, as his will (January 1803) mentions only male friends and his brother, John Luckombe of Exeter, his executor and the main beneficiary of his will.

ELIZABETH BAIGENT

Sources will, PRO, PROB 11/1400, fol. 1r–v • *IGI* • Watt, *Bibl. Brit.* • 'The Devon book trades: a biographical dictionary', www.devon.gov.uk/library/locstudy/bookhist/devexei.html, 8 Aug 2002 • Foster, *Alum. Oxon., 1715–1886* • Nichols, *Illustrations*, vol. 8

Likenesses T. Kearsley, mezzotint • R. H. Laurie, mezzotint (after T. Kearsley), BM, NPG • H. Mutlow, line engraving, NPG

Wealth at death see will, PRO, PROB 11/1400, fols. 1r–1v

Lucy [*née* Spencer], **Alice, Lady Lucy** (*c.*1594–1648), puritan gentlewoman, was the only surviving child and heir of Thomas Spencer esquire of Claverdon, Warwickshire, and his wife, Mary, daughter of John Cheke. About 1605, at the age of eleven, she was introduced to her future husband, Sir Thomas *Lucy (*d.* 1640) of Charlecote, Warwickshire, at the London house of Thomas Egerton, Lord Ellesmere, the lord keeper, whose third wife Alice, countess of Derby, was Alice's aunt. They married about 1610.

Alice Lucy's main claim to fame was as the archetype of a godly gentlewoman. Little is known of her life while Sir Thomas was alive, but she did succeed in establishing a reputation as a model of feminine piety. John Ley, puritan minister of Great Budworth in Cheshire, dedicated his life of Jane Ratcliffe, published in 1640, to Alice Lucy and Brilliana, Lady Harley. He described them both as 'Elect ladies' whose 'names are registered together in the booke of life' and whose virtuous and religious example was an inspiration to the 'communion of saints here on earth'. He also thanked them for their support and encouragement of godly ministers, including himself (Ley, A3–A5).

After her husband's death Alice took over the running of the household at Charlecote and established a godly regime, described later in her funeral sermon by Thomas Dugard, who had served as household preacher for three years. She was an invalid for much of this period and, unable to attend the parish church, 'she made a church of her house'. Much of her time was spent working her way through the large library of devotional literature which she and her husband had collected at Charlecote. She led the household in regular psalm singing and each Sunday arranged for a minister to visit and preach an evening sermon which the whole family was required to attend. She also took charge of the religious upbringing of her younger children, requiring them to read the Bible and godly sermons out loud each day and 'frequently instilling into them sweet instruction and exhorting them to a religious walking'. Dugard hailed her as the most 'virtuous woman' in a county well furnished with such paragons (Dugard, 46–52).

Dugard also made much of Lady Lucy's exemplary marriage and generosity to the poor. She was devoted to Sir Thomas during his lifetime and after his death erected a lavish marble monument to the two of them at Charlecote in which she rehearsed his virtues at length while modestly forbearing to mention her own. In her charitable work she followed the example he had set. Every Christmas she toured the local townships doling out bread and meat, and during the dearth which struck Warwickshire in 1647–8 she took particular care to ensure that the poor were relieved at her gate and that corn was sold in small enough quantities for them to purchase.

Alice Lucy stood alongside such other contemporaries as Lady Harley and Joan, Lady Barrington, as a role model for the godly gentlewoman. Her greatest impact was on her immediate family and household, which she regarded as her principal sphere of responsibility, but beyond this she made a considerable contribution to the growth of support for puritanism, through her encouragement of godly ministers and the example of her piety and charity described by Dugard and others. Since most of the evidence relating to her takes the form of hagiography, it is hard to form a clear picture of her personality. However, her will, which provided generously for her children and grandchildren, confirms the impression of a godly and loving mother. She died in August 1648 leaving six sons and four daughters, and was buried alongside her husband in Charlecote parish church.

RICHARD CUST

Sources A. Fairfax-Lucy, *Charlecote and the Lucys: the chronicle of an English family* (1958) • A. Hughes, *Politics, society and civil war in Warwickshire, 1620–1660* (1987) • J. Ley, *A patterne of pietie* (1640) • T. Dugard, *Death and the grave* (1649) • PRO, PROB 11/205/125 • H. Summerson, 'The Lucys of Charlecote and their library', *National Trust Studies* (1979) • *Charlecote Park, Warwickshire*, National Trust, [new edn] (1979) • J. T. Cliffe, *The puritan gentry: the great puritan families of early Stuart England* (1984)

Archives Warks. CRO, collection, LC

Likenesses C. Johnson, group portrait, oils, *c.*1628, Charlecote Park, Warwickshire • attrib. N. Stone, marble sculpture on funeral monument, *c.*1645, St Leonard's Church, Charlecote, Warwickshire

Lucy, Anthony, first Lord Lucy (*c.*1283–1343), soldier and administrator, was the second son of Sir Thomas de Lucy (*d.* 1305) and his wife, Isabella (*fl.* 1282–1319), the eldest daughter of Adam of Boltby. His father was a considerable landowner in Cumberland, by virtue of his descent from Amabilla, the second daughter of William fitz Duncan, lord of Allerdale, Cumberland, and Skipton, Yorkshire, and his wife, Alice de Rumilly; he also had claims on the inheritance of Amabilla's two sisters. His mother brought the Lucys the manor of Langley and other lands in Northumberland. Anthony is first recorded in 1301, when his father made provision for him, appropriate to a second son, with lands in Cumberland and Ireland. When Thomas de Lucy died in 1305 he was succeeded by his eldest son, another Thomas, whose death without a direct heir in 1308 brought their father's estates to Anthony.

By this time Cumberland was increasingly exposed to Scottish attack. Anthony Lucy served on the English west march in 1309 and 1311. He had been knighted by 1314, when he fought at Bannockburn under the leadership of Humphrey (VII) de Bohun, fourth earl of Hereford. In the aftermath of defeat he was among fugitives who were captured in Bothwell Castle, and was not released until early in 1315. At the end of the year he was appointed to the custody of Hexham, and was encouraged to raid into Scotland by Edward II. Following the capture of Sir Andrew Harclay by Scots at about this time Lucy became increasingly prominent in the defence of north-west England. With Ranulf Dacre he had custody of the west march between November 1316 and November 1317; their deployment of a force of hobelers (light cavalry) was doubtless intended to counteract the mobility of similarly mounted Scottish raiders. On 20 July 1318 he was appointed sheriff of Cumberland.

By now Harclay had been released, and he and Lucy competed for pre-eminence in Cumberland and Westmorland. In April 1319 Harclay replaced Lucy as sheriff. Both men took contingents to the siege of Berwick later in 1319, and in the years that followed often served together on border commissions. But although each received a personal summons to parliament on 15 May 1321, Lucy being thereby deemed to have become Lord Lucy, Harclay had the edge, and his supremacy was confirmed by his victory over Thomas, earl of Lancaster, at Boroughbridge on 16 March 1322, and by his being created earl of Carlisle on 25 March. Claiming (baselessly) that Lucy had shown rebel sympathies, he promptly took his rival's lands into the king's hand, and though compelled to restore them, subsequently sued Lucy in king's bench, alleging trespass and contempt. But Lucy made a decisive riposte when Harclay concluded an unauthorized peace treaty with the Scots at the beginning of 1323. Remaining close to the earl, who showed no signs of suspecting his loyalty, with a few followers he arrested him on 25 February in Carlisle Castle, and on 3 March carried out the sentence of execution ordered by royal justices.

Lucy was rewarded for his services with a grant of 100 marks per annum, and also with the honour of Cockermouth and manor of Papcastle which he had claimed as the descendant of Alice de Rumilly. He was constable of Carlisle Castle from 1323 to 1328, and carried out extensive repairs to its fabric. But the years between 1323 and 1332 saw the Anglo-Scottish borders relatively at peace, which made it possible for Edward III to appoint Lucy justiciar of Ireland on 27 February 1331, with £500 per annum towards his expenses. He arrived in Ireland on 3 June, accompanied by a staff on which fellow Cumbrians featured prominently, and also by his wife and children, and proceeded to administer his charge with a strong hand. As well as revoking grants made during the king's minority, he took energetic action against the turbulent earl of Desmond, whom he imprisoned in Dublin Castle, while in July 1332 he had the hardly less influential Sir William Bermingham hanged. His energy and rigour provoked opposition, but it was not this that led to Lucy's recall, but the reopening of hostilities in the Anglo-Scottish borders in August 1332. A successor as justiciar was appointed on 30 September, and Lucy left Ireland on 3 December.

Lucy was at once in action on the borders, on 24 or 25 March 1333 leading a plundering force into Scotland, and heavily defeating the garrison of Lochmaben when it tried to cut off his retreat. For the rest of his life he was continually engaged in the marches, both east and west. Between June and September 1334 he had the custody of Berwick, before being transferred to the west march. In 1335 he took part in the invasion of Scotland led by Edward III and Edward Balliol, and in May 1336 was appointed keeper of Berwick and justiciar of English-controlled Scotland, offices he retained until the end of 1337. He himself received grants of land in Scotland, including the manor of Earlston (Berwickshire). In 1336 he campaigned in south-west Scotland with a force from Cumberland and Westmorland, and in 1337 raided into Galloway and attacked a Scottish force invading Cumberland, before helping to raise the siege of Edinburgh in November with troops from Berwick. Appointed sheriff of Cumberland again in May 1338, he took part in the relief of Perth in the following year; shortly afterwards, the men of Cumberland asked that he be excused attendance at parliament, so that he could defend the west march. In August 1340 he was reported to be preparing to lead a force to the relief of Stirling, and, though replaced as sheriff in November 1341, he was still active in June 1342, when he undertook to stay on the march with thirty men-at-arms and thirty archers. He received his last appointment, as a commissioner to maintain a truce, on 20 May 1343, and was dead by 10 June 1343, when the escheators were ordered to take his lands into the king's hand. His heir, the son of his marriage to Elizabeth—her surname is unknown, though she may have been a daughter of Robert Tilliol of Scaleby—was another Thomas Lucy, who succeeded to estates worth at least £300 per annum, and also to the title of Lord Lucy. Lands and title eventually passed, with Thomas's daughter Matilda, to her second husband, Henry *Percy, first earl of Northumberland. HENRY SUMMERSON

Sources *Chancery records* • GEC, *Peerage*, new edn, 8.247–53 • Lucy cartulary, Cockermouth, Cumbria AS, Carlisle, D/Lec/301 • *CDS*, vol. 3 • *RotS*, vol. 1 • *RotP*, vols 1–2 • F. Palgrave, ed., *The parliamentary writs and writs of military summons*, 2/2 (1830) • *CIPM*, 4, no. 322; 5, no. 146 • H. Maxwell, ed. and trans., *The chronicle of Lanercost, 1272–1346* (1913) • J. T. Gilbert, ed., *Chartularies of St Mary's Abbey, Dublin: with the register of its house at Dunbrody and annals of Ireland*, 2, Rolls Series, 80 (1884), 375–7 • C. M. Fraser, ed., *Northern petitions*, SurtS, 194 (1981), 144–5 • H. Summerson, *Medieval Carlisle: the city and the borders from the late eleventh to the mid-sixteenth century*, 2 vols., Cumberland and Westmorland Antiquarian and Archaeological Society, extra ser., 25 (1993) • *CClR, 1343–6*, 257–60 • A. Hughes, *List of sheriffs for England and Wales: from the earliest times to AD 1831*, PRO (1898); repr. (New York, 1963) • G. Neilson, 'The battle of Dornock', *Transactions of the Dumfriesshire and Galloway Natural History and Antiquarian Society*, new ser., 12 (1897), 154–8 • R. Frame, *English lordship in Ireland, 1318–1361* (1982) • H. G. Richardson and G. O. Sayles, *The administration of Ireland, 1172–1377* (1963), 85 • G. O. Sayles, 'The rebellious first earl of Desmond', *Medieval studies presented to Aubrey Gwynn*, ed. J. A. Watt, J. B. Maxwell, and F. X. Martin (1961), 203–29

Archives Cumbria AS, Carlisle, D/Lec/301

Wealth at death over £300 p.a.: *CClR*

Lucy, Charles (1814–1873), history painter, was born at Hereford. His parentage is unknown; and the information concerning his first thirty years is, at times, puzzling. He reputedly was apprenticed to his uncle, a chemist in Hereford; he preferred to embark on a career in art, left Hereford for Paris, and studied at the École des Beaux-Arts under Paul Delaroche. After returning to England, he entered the Royal Academy Schools in London. Subsequently, according to the *Art Journal* (July 1873), he executed commissions as a copyist in Paris and The Hague,

Charles Lucy (1814–1873), by Rolfe's Portrait Studio

returned briefly to London, and then took up residence in France at Barbizon, near Fontainebleau, for 'nearly sixteen years'; dates are not given. Samuel Redgrave's *Dictionary of Artists of the English School* (1874) mentions no protracted sojourn in France. In 1838, 'then living at Hereford', according to Redgrave, Lucy exhibited a portrait at the Royal Academy. In 1840 he exhibited *The Interview between Milton and Galileo*; in 1844, *The Good Samaritan* and *Burns and his Mary*.

By 1844 or 1845 Lucy was probably married (he had at least one child, a son, Charles Hampden Lucy) and certainly in London, where he shared a studio with Ford Madox Brown. For the Fine Arts Commission's second competition (1844) he painted *The Roman empress Agrippina interceding with the emperor Claudius on behalf of the family of Caractacus*; he won a premium of £100, but not appointment to prepare a design for one of six arched compartments in the House of Lords. When the commission reopened the competition in 1845, he submitted an unsuccessful cartoon of *Religion Supported by Faith, Hope, and Charity*. For the final competition (1847) he made a sketch, *The Burial of Charles I*, which was rejected, and a painting, *The departure of the 'primitive puritans', or 'Pilgrim Fathers', to the coast of America, AD 1620*, for which he received a premium of £200. These subjects, two of the eight planned for the Peers' Corridor, were entrusted in 1853 to the history painter Charles West Cope; but seventeenth-century history continued to hold Lucy's interest.

Many of Lucy's paintings were engraved; few gained lasting notice. *Nelson Meditating in the Cabin of the 'Victory' Previously to the Battle of Trafalgar* (exhibited in the Royal Academy in 1854), bought at auction in 1855 by Sir Robert Peel, reappeared in the sale of Peel heirlooms in 1900. *Cromwell and his Family Listening to Milton Playing the Organ at Hampton Court*, signed 1863, was presented in 1870 by William Graham, the Liberal MP, to the Glasgow Art Gallery and Museum. Eight portraits commissioned by the Liberal politician Sir Joshua Walmsley, completed in 1869, are now in the Victoria and Albert Museum, London. The subjects are Oliver Cromwell, Horatio Nelson, Joseph Hume, Richard Cobden, John Bright, Gladstone, Disraeli, and Giuseppe Garibaldi.

For some years, with health failing, Lucy taught at a drawing-school in Camden Town, London. He died on 19 May 1873 at 13 Ladbroke Crescent, Notting Hill, where he lived with his son. William Michael Rossetti (*Some Reminiscences*, 1906) remembered him as a friend of Madox Brown: 'He was a short man, of very ordinary appearance and address, more like a country estate-agent than an artist. He was married, friendly and accommodating in disposition'. DAVID ROBERTSON

Sources Redgrave, *Artists* · *DNB* · D. Robertson, *Sir Charles Eastlake and the Victorian art world* (1978) · W. M. Rossetti, *Some reminiscences*, 1 (1906), 139 · F. M. Hueffer [F. M. Ford], *Ford Madox Brown: a record of his life and work* (1896), 37–8, 62, 75, 90 · A. Graves, *Art sales from early in the eighteenth century to early in the twentieth century*, 2 (1921); repr. (1973) · F. T. Roberts and F. Hicklin, eds., *Summary catalogue of British paintings: Victoria & Albert Museum* (1973) [catalogue, V&A] · *Summary catalogue of British oil paintings*, Glasgow Art Gallery and Museum (1971) · *Art Journal*, 35 (1873), 208 · *CGPLA Eng. & Wales* (1873)

Archives NPG

Likenesses Rolfe's Portrait Studio, photograph, NPG [*see illus.*] · R. & E. Taylor, wood-engraving (after J. Watkins), NPG; repro. in *ILN* (7 June 1873)

Wealth at death under £450: probate, 10 Oct 1873, *CGPLA Eng. & Wales*

Lucy, Godfrey de (*d*. 1204), bishop of Winchester, was the second son of Richard de *Lucy (the Loyal) (*d*. 1179), chief justiciar of England. Attached to the court from youth, he became a favoured member of the royal household, and between the early 1170s and Henry II's death in 1189 witnessed thirty royal charters, nine of them in France. He attended schools in London, studying under Master Henry of Northampton; and he also studied abroad, earning the title *magister*. Then, having taken holy orders, he became a royal clerk, and received a long series of ecclesiastical preferments, being appointed dean of St Martin's-le-Grand in 1171, canon of Lincoln, St Paul's, London, and Exeter, and of the collegiate church of Bampton, Oxfordshire; he was archdeacon of Derby *c*.1174, and he was also archdeacon of Richmond (1181–4) and parson of the church of Wye. While his elder brother, Geoffrey de Lucy (*d*. 1170x73), was heir to their father's holdings, Godfrey inherited a portion of them; and he was custodian of his two nephews' honour of Ongar, Essex, from *c*.1181 until their deaths some time before 1194, when they left two sisters as their heirs.

Godfrey de Lucy (*d.* 1204), seal [obverse]

This set off a series of lawsuits over the Lucy inheritance lasting into Henry III's reign.

On the resignation of the justiciarship by his father and the subsequent division of England into four circuits at the Council of Windsor in 1179, Godfrey de Lucy was appointed leader of the itinerant justices for the northern eyre. He participated in the remaining judicial eyres of Henry II's reign, also serving as a justice at Westminster, where he continued to sit throughout Richard I's reign as well as acting as a justice on eyre. In 1184 he was dispatched by Henry II to Normandy, together with the bishops of Lincoln (Walter de Coutances) and Norwich (John of Oxford), to arrange terms between Philip Augustus and the count of Flanders. In 1186 he was elected by the chapter of Lincoln to fill the vacant see, but was rejected by Henry, who was resolved on the appointment of Hugh of Avalon (*d.* 1200). From 1184 to 1186 he was royal custodian of the abbey of St Mary's, York.

Godfrey de Lucy was in 1186 elected to the see of Exeter, which he declined on the ground of the insufficiency of the income to meet the expenses of the office. On the accession of Richard I in 1189 he took a prominent part in the coronation ceremony, and bore the king's linen cap. When Geoffrey Plantagenet (*d.* 1212) was elected to the archbishopric of York in August 1189, Lucy was absent, but as canon and archdeacon he signified his consent by letter. That same year he reached the episcopate, being one of the five bishops—'all, with one exception, faithful servants of his father, as lawyers or ministers' (*Works of Gervase of Canterbury*, 1.458)—nominated by Richard I at the great Council of Pipewell on 15 September. His see was Winchester, to which he was consecrated by Archbishop Baldwin in St Katherine's Chapel, Westminster Abbey on 22 October 1189. One of the earliest acts of his episcopate was to reclaim the manors of Meon and Wargrave, of which the see had been deprived. He proceeded *ordine judiciario*, but according to the chronicler Richard of Devizes took care to secure a favourable verdict by a secret gift to Richard of £3000 in silver, obtaining at the same time the post of sheriff of Hampshire, the confirmation of his own paternal inheritance, together with indemnity for the treasure of his church, and the constableship of the castles of Portchester and Winchester, for which he had to pay another 1000 marks. Not having the means to pay so large a sum, he was unwillingly compelled to borrow it from the treasury of his cathedral, binding himself and his successors to its repayment; the larger part was restored by himself on 28 January 1192.

In November 1189 Lucy was one of the arbitrators appointed by the king to compromise the long-standing dispute between Archbishop Baldwin and the monks of Canterbury over the proposed collegiate church of Hackington. When Richard left early in 1190 for the crusade, Lucy accompanied him as far as Tours (25 June). But he opposed the domination of the government in 1190–91 by William de Longchamp (*d.* 1197), chancellor and bishop of Ely, as chief justiciar, for he had close ties to the co-justiciar in the north, Hugh du Puiset (*d.* 1195), bishop of Durham. One of the earliest of Longchamp's high-handed acts was to deprive Lucy, who was detained by sickness in Normandy, of his post as sheriff of Hampshire, custody of his castles, and his paternal inheritance. On his return to England, Lucy lost no time in confronting Longchamp, whom he found at Gloucester besieging the castle. Longchamp received him warmly, followed his advice in giving up the siege, and restored his patrimony, retaining, however, the shrievalty and the castles. At the council held by Longchamp as papal legate at Westminster in October 1190 Lucy sat at his left hand, the bishop of London to his right. The management of the arbitration between Longchamp and Count John, the king's brother, at Winchester on 25 April 1191 was entrusted to him, in conjunction with the bishops of London and Bath.

Further trouble arose in the following September, when Geoffrey Plantagenet, the new archbishop of York, on his landing at Dover was dragged from the church in which he had taken refuge and thrown into prison by the orders of Longchamp. The chancellor's attempt to explain and justify his conduct called forth from Lucy a letter addressed to the prior and convent of Canterbury expressing his grief and indignation, but declining to give them any advice until he had taken counsel with his brother prelates. In the struggle that then ensued between Longchamp and Count John, Lucy took a leading part against the justiciar, attending the meetings of the barons and ecclesiastics summoned at Marlborough, Loddon Bridge, and finally on 8 October 1191, at St Paul's. He was one of the four bishops deputed by the assembly to communicate to Longchamp, who had taken refuge in the Tower of London, their resolution that he must resign; and on Longchamp's deposition, Lucy was reinstated in the custody of the castles of which Longchamp had deprived him. In the crossfire of anathemas that followed he was excommunicated by the pope, in company with John and the chief enemies of Longchamp. One of those commissioned by Richard I on 8 June 1193 to assist the queen mother in securing Hubert Walter's election as archbishop of Canterbury, Lucy joined with the new primate, Hugh of Lincoln, and other prelates in February 1194 in pronouncing excommunication on Count John.

Immediately after Richard's arrival at Winchester on his return from captivity on 15 April 1194, Lucy was once more deprived of the custody of the castles, the shrievalty, and the manors that he had bought of the king five years before, although the bishop repurchased them in 1199, offering a fine of £1000. When Richard I solemnly wore his crown in Winchester Cathedral, Lucy's name is absent from the long list of prelates who took part in the ceremony. But the bishop was in Normandy for several months in 1198, probably summoned by the king in the vain hope that his mediation could effect a reconciliation between Archbishop Geoffrey and the York chapter.

Lucy took part in John's coronation on 27 May 1199, and witnessed a number of royal charters in 1200. Sickness prevented his presence at the great council held by Archbishop Hubert Walter at Westminster on 19 September 1200, but he took part in the obsequies of Bishop Hugh in Lincoln Cathedral on 23 November. The close of Lucy's episcopate was signalled by large additions to the fabric of his cathedral. In 1199 a tower, not now identifiable, had been begun and finished. In 1202 he instituted a confraternity for the repair of the church, to last for five years, by which a spacious retrochoir was created for St Swithun's shrine and a lady chapel was erected with two flanking chapels. The lady chapel is among the earliest examples of the Gothic style in England.

Lucy died at Winchester on 11 or 12 September 1204, and was buried outside the lady chapel he had caused to be built. He had apparently had a long-lasting relationship, possibly a clandestine marriage, with Agatha, a wet-nurse employed by Eleanor of Aquitaine who later married William of Gaddesden, a royal falconer. Evidence exists for three illegitimate sons of Godfrey de Lucy: Geoffrey (*d.* 1241), archdeacon of London, dean of St Paul's, and chancellor of Oxford University; John, to whom his father gave houses in the Strand, London; and Philip, a clerk of the chamber until 1207.

That Lucy's character for practical wisdom stood high with his sovereigns is shown by the various delicate missions with which he was entrusted. Henry II, a good judge of character, formed a high opinion of him. Lucy was the first English bishop systematically to date his letters, inspired by his experience in royal government. The editor of *Glanvill* suggests his authorship of the pioneer law book as 'an intriguing possibility'. Described by Bishop William Stubbs, the great nineteenth-century scholar, as 'a good average bishop' (Stubbs, xxxi), Lucy conferred a great benefit on his episcopal city by restoring the navigation of the River Itchen from Southampton by means of an artificial channel he caused to be dug, extending up to Alresford, where he constructed a large reservoir, Alresford pond, for its supply; he reserved to himself the revenues from the river and the customs on goods entering the city by the canal, obtaining a charter from John. In 1199 he established a market at Alresford and in 1202 a three-day fair; he also reconstructed the town centre to create a large market square. He augmented the revenues of Lessness Abbey (or Westwood), founded by his father the justiciar on his retirement from public life, and where he had died a canon in 1179. Apparently the bishop planned that Lessness should be the Lucy family mausoleum.

EDMUND VENABLES, *rev.* RALPH V. TURNER

Sources M. J. Franklin, ed., *Winchester, 1070–1204*, English Episcopal Acta, 8 (1993) · *Ann. mon.*, vol. 2 · *The historical works of Gervase of Canterbury*, ed. W. Stubbs, 2 vols., Rolls Series, 73 (1879–80) · *Chronica magistri Rogeri de Hovedene*, ed. W. Stubbs, 4 vols., Rolls Series, 51 (1868–71) · *Chronicon Richardi Divisensis / The Chronicle of Richard of Devizes*, ed. J. T. Appleby (1963) · D. M. Stenton, 'Development of the judiciary, 1100–1216', *Pleas before the king or his justices, 1198–1212*, ed. D. M. Stenton, 3, SeldS, 83 (1967), xlvii–ccxliv · *Pipe rolls* · R. W. Eyton, *Court, household, and itinerary of King Henry II* (1878) · R. V. Turner, 'Who was the author of *Glanvill*?', *Law and History Review*, 8 (1990), 97–127 · GEC, *Peerage* · *VCH Wiltshire* · *Fasti Angl., 1066–1300*, [Monastic cathedrals] · W. Stubbs, ed., *Chronicles and memorials of the reign of Richard I*, 2: *Epistolae Cantuarienses*, Rolls Series, 38 (1865)

Likenesses seal, BL; Birch, *Seals*, 2245 [*see illus.*]

Lucy, Sir Henry William (1843–1924), journalist, was born at Crosby, Lancashire, the son of Robert Lucy, a rose-engine turner in the watch trade, and his wife, Margaret Ellen Kemp. He was probably born towards the end of March 1843 for he was baptized (as William Henry) on 23 April of that year. While he was still an infant the family removed to Everton, Liverpool, where he attended the private Crescent School until August 1856; thereafter until 1864 he was junior clerk to Robert Smith, hide merchant, of Redcross Street, Liverpool.

Lucy began to write at an early age. During his clerkship he contributed verse to the *Liverpool Mercury*, and, having taught himself shorthand, he sought a post as reporter on one of the Liverpool papers. Eventually, without experience but with a testimonial from Edward Russell, then assistant editor of the *Liverpool Post*, he became chief reporter to the *Shrewsbury Chronicle* in July 1864. He soon began to contribute leader notes to the local *Observer* and the *Shropshire News*; for a short time in 1865 he was editor and part proprietor of the former. Then he became secretary to Richard Samuel France, railway contractor, and at the same time greatly enlarged his experience as a freelance journalist.

From May to December 1869 Lucy lived in Paris, learning French; thereafter he was for a short time (January to June 1870) in London as a sub-editor on the newly founded morning edition of the *Pall Mall Gazette*, and for eighteen months (June 1870 to January 1872) in Exeter as assistant editor of the *Exeter Gazette*. Returning to London he was a freelance for some months, until he secured a regular engagement on the *Daily News* in October 1872. He was soon in the full tide of success: John Richard Robinson made him manager of the *Daily News* parliamentary staff and writer of its parliamentary summary; in addition he contributed London letters to several provincial papers. A journalistic venture of his own, *Mayfair*, started in December 1877, never paid its way, and after two years collapsed.

Sir Henry William Lucy (1843–1924), by John Singer Sargent, 1905

In 1880 he began a connection with *The Observer* which lasted for twenty-nine years (he wrote the 'Cross bench' column), and in 1881 he succeeded Shirley Brooks as the writer of 'Essence of parliament' for *Punch*, continuing to write as 'Toby, MP' until February 1916.

Lucy's industry, fertility, humour, and remarkable flair for politics and parliamentary affairs soon brought him to the front rank of his profession. Two further promotions were in store. In July 1885 Henry Labouchere offered him the editorship of the *Daily News*; he refused, out of loyalty to Frank Harrison Hill, who was then editor, but in December, Hill having had his *congé*, Lucy took the post. He was a poor editor—Labouchere thought his style 'that of a washer-woman' (Koss, 269); P. W. Clayden was brought in to write the leaders, and Lucy returned to the press gallery. Ten years later (April 1897) he again showed his loyalty, this time to F. C. Burnand, by refusing the editorship of *Punch*, offered to him by William Agnew. Notwithstanding his copious output as a journalist, Lucy found time to write two novels and a collection of short stories, two studies of W. E. Gladstone (the first with an edition of his speeches, 1885, the second published in 1895; 2nd edn, 1898), and two popular political handbooks—*Parliamentary Procedure* (1880) and the *Law and Practice of General Elections* (1900). He also produced several volumes of personal reminiscences, including *The Diary of a Journalist* (3 vols., 1920–23), which also contain correspondence. He made huge sums out of his writing, leaving over £250,000 when he died. He was probably the wealthiest Victorian journalist who was not a proprietor.

Lucy's lasting memorial is in the volumes he compiled from his *Punch* parliamentary sketches: *A Diary of Two Parliaments* (2 vols., 1885–6); *A Diary of the Salisbury Parliament, 1886–1892* (1892); *A Diary of the Home Rule Parliament, 1892–1895* (1896); *A Diary of the Unionist Parliament, 1895–1900* (1901); and *The Balfourian Parliament, 1900–1905* (1906). These amount to a history of the Commons in its heyday, and have been over-extensively quarried by historians. Lucy was, on the whole, an accurate chronicler, but it is often forgotten that he was originally writing for a supposedly humorous magazine. His portrait gallery of the Commons is thus too whimsical. Lucy was a committed Gladstonian Liberal, but, like F. Carruthers Gould (his cartoonist equivalent), was affectionate about Unionist perversity. He was the first lobby correspondent to be seen as the social equal of the politicians in the Commons whom he reported, a fact reflected in his knighthood (1909).

Lucy married on 29 October 1873 Emily Anne, daughter of his old schoolmaster at Liverpool, John White. There were no children of the marriage. The Lucys built Whitehorn, a country house at Hillside Street, Hythe, Kent, in 1883 for weekending; 42 Ashley Gardens was their London house. Lucy died intestate, from bronchitis, at Whitehorn on 20 February 1924.

H. B. Grimsditch, *rev.* H. C. G. Matthew

Sources *The Times* (22 Feb 1924) · H. W. Lucy, *Sixty years in the wilderness*, 1 (1909) · *Fifty years of Fleet Street: being the life and recollections of Sir John R. Robinson*, ed. F. M. Thomas (1904) · S. E. Koss, *The rise and fall of the political press in Britain*, 2 vols. (1981–4); repr. (1990) · Gladstone, *Diaries* · *WWW*

Archives Bodl. Oxf., letters · CAC Cam. | CAC Cam., corresp. with Lord Randolph Churchill · NL Scot., corresp., mainly with Lord Rosebery · Richmond Local Studies Library, London, Sladen MSS

Likenesses J. S. Sargent, oils, 1905, NPG [*see illus.*] · S. P. Hall, pencil drawing, NPG · John Russell & Sons, photographs, NPG · Spy [L. Ward], chromolithograph caricature, NPG; repro. in *VF* (31 Aug 1905) · photograph, repro. in H. Lucy, *The diary of a journalist* (1922) · photograph, repro. in H. Lucy, *Memories of eight parliaments* (1908)

Wealth at death £263,672 1s. 5d.: probate, 14 April 1925, *CGPLA Eng. & Wales*

Lucy, Richard de (*d.* 1179), soldier and administrator, was born early in the twelfth century, of a family with lands in both Normandy and England. His mother, Aveline, is mentioned in association with the young Richard in several records; his father's name is unknown. The family originated in Normandy, at Lucé, near Domfront; Richard's brother Walter, later abbot of Battle in Sussex, was at first a monk at Lonlay-l'Abbaye, near Lucé. Other brothers were Robert and possibly Herbert. Richard married a woman named Roysia, whose origins are unknown, and they had sons named Geoffrey and Godfrey, and daughters Matilda, Aveline, and Alice who married Odinel de *Umfraville (*d.* 1182) [*see under* Umfraville family (*per. c.*1100–1245)].

Lucy may have begun his career of royal service under Henry I, from whom he was later said to have received a grant of royal land in Suffolk. By 1136 he was in the service of King Stephen, for whom he daringly and successfully defended the castle of Falaise against Geoffrey of Anjou in October 1138. After this he returned to England, where he remained in almost constant attendance upon the embattled king. Although his only official title in Stephen's reign was apparently that of local justice in Middlesex, London, and Essex from *c.*1143 onwards, he gradually became one of Stephen's closest associates and right-hand men, steadfast in his service to the king even in the most troubled periods of the anarchy. He served as an intermediary between the king and Archbishop Theobald of Canterbury in 1148, while in the summer of 1153, when support for Stephen was waning among the barons, Richard de Lucy helped lead a raid up the Thames valley into the territory held by Henry of Anjou, who would soon force Stephen into negotiations over the throne. The treaty of Westminster, later the same year, demonstrated the esteem in which both sides held Richard de Lucy, naming him guardian of the Tower of London and Windsor Castle, which he was to hand over to Henry upon Stephen's death; Richard's son was to be a hostage for his father's good faith.

During Stephen's reign Lucy had begun to collect the estates that would eventually form his barony of Ongar. His English inheritance, worth some seven knights' fees, included lands at Diss and Stowe in East Anglia and Newington in Kent; in the latter county he was a tenant of the archbishop of Canterbury. From Stephen he received generous grants from the king's honour of Boulogne, including Chipping Ongar in Essex; here Lucy built a castle and promoted the growth of the town. Concentrated in eastern England, his territorial interests coincided with those of the royal family, and royal grants strengthened the connection.

When Stephen died in 1154 and was succeeded by Henry II, Richard de Lucy moved easily into the new royal administration, and was almost immediately named co-justiciar with Robert, earl of Leicester. Both his familiarity with English government and his unblemished record of loyalty, albeit to Henry's rival, doubtless commended him to the new king, as did his continuing competent service. For the first few years of this reign he served as sheriff of Essex and Hertfordshire and was in charge of several royal manors as well. Then he turned more exclusively to the concerns of central government. In 1166 he was one of those sent on the first of the revived judicial eyres. He also continued to carry out occasional military tasks, in 1167 repelling an attempted landing by Matthew, count of Boulogne, claimant to the English honour of Boulogne. As justiciar Lucy often filled a viceregal role while the king was overseas, and he himself was sent on frequent foreign missions.

On the king's orders Lucy played an important role in securing the election of his colleague Thomas Becket as archbishop of Canterbury in 1162; he also helped to draw up the constitutions of Clarendon, which led in 1164 to Becket's quarrel with Henry II. Later that year, when overseas on royal business and possibly returning from a pilgrimage to Santiago de Compostela, he met with the exiled archbishop to urge a reconciliation between him and the king. Instead the two argued bitterly, and Lucy renounced his homage. In 1166 Becket excommunicated him at Vézelay for his role in drafting the constitutions and for his support of the king. Soon after this Lucy was said to have taken a crusader's vow, but if he did he never fulfilled it. Instead he was absolved by the bishop of St Asaph in 1167, and excommunicated by Becket once again in 1169.

As a servant of Henry II, Lucy continued to increase his lands and wealth. From the king himself he received large 'gifts' from the royal revenues, confirmation of Stephen's grants, and (*c.*1174) a new grant of Ongar hundred. In addition Richard de Lucy became the ally and tenant of various intimates of the new king. Already in 1155 he and his brother Walter enjoyed a 'treaty of friendship' with the king's uncle, Reginald, earl of Cornwall, and the royal constable Richard du Hommet, as well as less formal alliances with other *familiares* of the king. By 1166 he was holding ten knights' fees from Reginald; nine fees from Reginald's tenant Adam Malherbe; and one fee from the honour of Clare in Suffolk. A few years later he was enfeoffed by the king's cousin William, earl of Gloucester, with ten knights' fees at Greenstead in Essex.

Richard de Lucy was left sole justiciar upon the earl of Leicester's death in 1168. It was in the next decade that he reached the pinnacle of his career, being called the king's *familiarissimus* and 'the most powerful man in the kingdom' (*Gesta … Benedicti*, 1.124; *Works of Gervase of Canterbury*, 1.241). During the rebellion of 1173–4 he was the leader of the king's forces in England. With Reginald of Cornwall he besieged and captured the town of Leicester, then he and Humphrey (III) de Bohun led a force into northern England and Scotland against the Scottish king, William, who had invaded Northumberland. But, hearing of the landing of the rebellious earl of Leicester in the south, Lucy arranged a truce with William and returned to the midlands, where he laid siege to Huntingdon Castle, which belonged to the Scottish king's brother David. Lucy's prudence, energy, and success during this lengthy crisis permanently increased not only his own reputation but also the power and prestige of the justiciarship itself. Henry was said to call him 'de Lucy the loyal' (*Gesta … Benedicti*, 1.124), and it was a surprise to contemporaries when Ongar Castle was among those confiscated by the king in the post-rebellion repossessions of 1176. Lucy was sure enough of his standing with the king to reprimand him for later ignoring the forest privileges he had granted to his servants during the rebellion.

Lucy's eldest son, Geoffrey, predeceased his father, leaving his young son Richard as the justiciar's heir. For his second son, Godfrey de *Lucy, the elder Richard arranged a church career, which culminated in his election to the see of Winchester in 1189. For his daughters Lucy achieved marriages into some of the leading families of Essex: Matilda married Walter fitz Robert de Clare, and Aveline married Gilbert de Montfichet. Alice married Odinel de Umfraville. Richard de Lucy was a benefactor of Holy Trinity Priory in London, where his wife was buried, and a champion of Battle Abbey, where his brother was abbot. His interest in religion increased in the later years of his life. In 1178 he founded a house of Augustinian canons on his land at Lessness, or Westwood, in Kent, not far from Ongar. The foundation was dedicated to the Virgin and St Thomas of Canterbury—the latter an unexpected dedication, in the light of Lucy's difficult relations with the archbishop. He retired from the justiciarship in 1178 or 1179, and entered this house as a canon. He died at Lessness on 14 July 1179, and was buried in the abbey there. He was succeeded by two young grandsons in turn, and eventually by his daughters and granddaughters. EMILIE AMT

Sources *Reg. RAN*, vols. 2–3 • *Pipe rolls* • H. Hall, ed., *The Red Book of the Exchequer*, 3 vols., Rolls Series, 99 (1896) • E. Searle, ed., *The chronicle of Battle Abbey*, OMT (1980) • R. W. Eyton, *Court, household, and itinerary of King Henry II* (1878) • J. C. Robertson and J. B. Sheppard, eds., *Materials for the history of Thomas Becket, archbishop of Canterbury*, 7 vols., Rolls Series, 67 (1875–85) • E. Amt, 'Richard de Lucy, Henry II's justiciar', *Medieval Prosopography*, 9 (1988) • J. H. Round, 'The honour of Ongar', *Transactions of the Essex Archaeological Society*, new ser., 7 (1898–9), 142–52 • A. Saltman, *Theobald, archbishop of Canterbury* (1956) • *The historical works of Gervase of Canterbury*, ed. W. Stubbs, 2 vols., Rolls Series, 73 (1879–80) • R. Howlett, ed., *Chronicles of the reigns of Stephen, Henry II, and Richard I*, 4 vols., Rolls Series, 82 (1884–9) • St Aelred [abbot of Rievaulx], 'Relatio de standardo', *Chronicles of the reigns of Stephen, Henry II, and Richard I*, ed. R. Howlett, 3, Rolls Series, 82 (1886) • *Chronica magistri Rogeri de Hovedene*, ed. W. Stubbs, 4 vols., Rolls Series, 51 (1868–71) • W. Stubbs, ed., *Gesta regis Henrici secundi Benedicti abbatis: the chronicle of the reigns of Henry II and Richard I, AD 1169–1192*, 2 vols., Rolls Series, 49 (1867)

Lucy, Sir Richard, first baronet (1592–1667), politician, was the second of six sons of Sir Thomas Lucy (1551–1605) of Charlecote, Warwickshire, and his second wife, Constance Kingsmill. He matriculated at Magdalen College, Oxford, in 1607, and graduated BA from Exeter College in 1611; he was a student of Lincoln's Inn in 1608. Sir Thomas *Lucy (1583x6–1640) and William *Lucy, bishop of St David's, were among his brothers. About 1617 Lucy married the twice-widowed Elizabeth, Lady Oxenbridge (*b.* before 1600, *d.* 1645), daughter and coheir of the chairman of the Hertfordshire bench, Sir Henry Cocke, thus becoming life owner of the Broxbournebury estate. At the time of his first marriage he was described as having 'tossed back red hair & a long pointed chin', 'all ease and confidence' and 'as if he took his puritanism lightly' (Fairfax-Lucy, 127–8). Between 1645 and 1647 he married Jane, daughter and coheir of Thomas Chapman of Wormley, Hertfordshire, a draper of London. She predeceased him. Their only son, Kingsmill, failed to become MP for Brecon in 1661, but was returned for Andover in 1673.

Lucy inherited land in Hampshire, leased the parsonage of Broxbourne from the bishop of London, and accumulated property in four Hertfordshire parishes. He gained a knighthood and a baronetcy in 1618 and between 1630 and 1658 was chairman of the Hertfordshire bench on fifty-three occasions. He was noted for his temperate nature and ability to find compromises, as in a confrontation at Ware in 1639 over Lord Carr's seizure of post horses when Lucy prevented a duel; Lucy, 'a more temperate man, would rather use his authority than his courage' (*CSP dom.*, 1638, 137–9). He was instrumental in implementing Charles I's Book of Orders in the 1630s and in encouraging parishes to subsidize bread for the poor. He was particularly concerned about young children falling idle and finding 'such small work as is most meet for them according to the tenderness of their age, that idleness may not fasten in them' (Lucy to the council, PRO SP 16/189/79). He established the referral of business to divisional monthly meetings of JPs, a practice revived by him in the 1650s, but led the local opposition to purveyance, suggesting that the court of the verge should be abolished and defending county against court interests. He established the principle of no double rating for ship money and as deputy lieutenant opposed increased exactions over the militia, the payment of the muster master, and coat and conduct money. In 1642 he was placed on both the parliamentary assessment commission and the king's commission of array, and signed the county accommodation petition. He was in France from March 1643 to mid-1644 and on his return was placed on most of parliament's local assessment and other military committees, having given up his neutrality.

In 1647 Lucy was returned to the Long Parliament for the earl of Salisbury's seat of Old Sarum, one of the recruiter MPs elected to fill vacancies in the Commons. He dealt largely with financial and religious matters and acted as a teller against both the 'presbyterian' Holles and the 'Independent' Hesilrige. He was not secluded at Pride's Purge in December 1648 but protested at the army's action and withdrew from the house. He returned to take his seat in the Rump in the following July and served on committees to consider the maintenance of the ministry, seditious writings, plundered ministers, and the corporation of the poor in London. He specialized in financial, religious, and poor-law legislation, notably that for reducing the price of corn and setting the poor on work. He opposed Hesilrige over raising militia horses for the Scottish expedition, Thomas Scott over the sale of traitors' lands, and Sir Henry Vane over the discharge of the sheriff of Nottingham. More conservative than most, he protected Salisbury's interests in the Commons and was part of his Hertfordshire syndicate in the protectorate parliaments, representing the county. In the 1656–7 session he was teller against the motion for including the title lord protector in 'The humble petition and advice', for amendments to the catechism allowing non-compulsion, and against high assessments for the army. With the return of the Rump in 1659 he again took his seat for Old Sarum. He died on 6 April 1667, probably at Broxbourne, and left a bequest to establish a free school there, to teach the poor to read and write, as well as extensive legacies and pensions to his own servants. He was buried at Broxbourne on 12 April. ALAN THOMSON

Sources A. Fairfax-Lucy, *Charlecote and the Lucys: the chronicle of an English family* (1958) • M. E. Lucy, *Biography of the Lucy family* (1862) • *DNB* • GEC, *Baronetage*, 1.113–14, 220 • *N&Q*, 2nd ser., 7 (1859), 86–7 • K. W. Murray, 'Chapman of Hertfordshire and London', *The Genealogist*, new ser., 34 (1917–18), 1–5 • *CSP dom.*, *1623–65* • Foster, *Alum. Oxon.* • J. Burke and J. B. Burke, *A genealogical and heraldic history of the extinct and dormant baronetcies of England, Ireland, and Scotland*, 2nd edn (1841), 329 • *JHC*, 2–8 (1640–67) • *VCH Hertfordshire*, 3.432, 4.13 •

Calendar of the manuscripts of the most hon. the marquis of Salisbury, 24 vols., HMC, 9 (1883–1976), vol. 22, pp. 127, 136, 152, 300–01, 311; vol. 24, pp. 266–74 · will, PRO, PROB 11/323, sig. 47 · B. Worden, *The Rump Parliament, 1648–1653* (1974) · D. Underdown, *Pride's Purge: politics in the puritan revolution* (1971) · A. M. Mimardière, 'Lucy, Sir Kingsmill', HoP, *Commons, 1660–90*

Archives Herts. ALS, Broxbournebury MSS · Herts. ALS, quarter sessions books · Herts. ALS, Wittewrong MSS, papers relating to 1656 parliamentary election · PRO, state papers relating to Charles I, returns from magistrates under the Book of Orders, 1631–9, SP 16

Likenesses portrait, repro. in Fairfax-Lucy, *Charlecote and the Lucys*

Wealth at death over £6460 in landed wealth, incl. £124 p.a. from Weld and Gosfield manors, from which half annual wage to be paid to household servants for life; £685 in individual bequests: will, 1667, PRO, PROB 11/323, sig. 47

Lucy, Sir Thomas (*b*. in or before **1532**, *d*. **1600**), gentleman, of Charlecote, in Warwickshire, was the eldest son of William Lucy (*d*. 1551) and his wife, Ann (*d*. 1550), daughter of Richard Fermor of Easton Neston in Northamptonshire. The family could trace its tenure of Charlecote back at least to the end of the twelfth century, when the village was recorded in the possession of Walter, son of Thurstan of Charlecote. Walter's son and heir, William, assumed the surname Lucy, possibly that of the family of his mother, Cecilia. Over the next three hundred years the family estate descended from father to son, augmented from time to time by advantageous marriages, particularly that of Thomas Lucy (*d*. 1415) to Alice Hugford, heir to extensive estates in Bedfordshire and Shropshire.

Thomas Lucy was educated at home, at one time by John Fawkener, an Oxford graduate, and then, for a year or so between the summer of 1545 and early in 1547, by John Foxe, the martyrologist. During this period Thomas, still only fourteen or so, was betrothed to Joyce (1532–1595), the twelve-year-old only child and heir of Thomas Acton of Sutton Park, in Worcestershire. Their marriage settlement is dated 1 August 1546, the marriage itself presumably taking place shortly afterwards. Five months later, in January 1547, Acton died, and his extensive estates, subject only to his wife's dowry, were thus inherited by his daughter. In 1551 Thomas Lucy inherited Charlecote itself on the death of his father, William, and, in 1553, having reached the age of twenty-one, was granted admission to his estates. Within a few years he began rebuilding the family home at Charlecote, which was completed, according to William Dugdale's *Antiquities of Warwickshire*, in 1559/60. It was an imposing brick building, half-H in plan, with a detached gatehouse. Despite major renovation and improvement during the first half of the nineteenth century, the building still retains these original features. At the same time Lucy was building up his Warwickshire estates. In 1553 he acquired from the crown the nearby manor of Sherbourne by exchanging for it land in Bedfordshire, and four years later was granted by Queen Mary the reversion of the adjacent manor of Hampton Lucy. For the next ten years or so there is further evidence of his selling off his more distant estates, especially those in Bedfordshire that had formed part of his wife's inheritance. This policy was facilitated by the death, in 1564, of his mother-in-law, which had freed the estates from dower.

From 1559 Lucy entered on the life of public service to be expected of a man in his position. He sat as a member of parliament for Warwickshire in 1559, 1571, and 1584, was sheriff of Warwickshire and Leicestershire in 1559/60, of Warwickshire in 1578/9, and of Worcestershire in 1585/6, and served as a justice of the peace in Warwickshire from *c*.1559 and in Worcestershire from *c*.1582. He was knighted in 1565, and entertained Elizabeth I at his house at Charlecote during her visit to nearby Kenilworth in August 1572. In 1590 he was appointed a member of the council of Wales and the marches.

In his religious views Lucy was clearly a vigorous protestant. This is best illustrated in the contributions he made to parliamentary business, particularly in the parliaments of 1571 and 1584. In the former he was appointed to a committee concerned with defects in the prayer book, and was involved in legislation against the practice of Catholic priests' disguising themselves in serving-men's apparel, and to enforce church attendance and the taking of communion. In the 1584 parliament he introduced one of the petitions concerning godly preachers, and took a leading role in pressing for more stringent punishment for the Welsh lawyer William Parry, who had spoken out against anti-Catholic legislation. Locally he was concerned with the prosecution of recusants, and in 1583 was closely involved in the arrest of Edward Arden and other Catholic families after the uncovering of the so-called Somerville conspiracy. However, it would be unwise to argue from this that Lucy was a representative of the puritan interest. His record differed little from that of other local gentry entrusted with the implementation of government policy in their areas of influence.

Thomas Lucy might not now be so well known had his name not come to be associated with one of the earliest examples of Shakespeare folklore. Nicholas Rowe was the first to publish this, in 1709 and in some detail, but similar stories can be found in three other autonomous sources of late seventeenth-century date, all ultimately derived, no doubt, from local Stratford gossip. Rowe's account records that the young William Shakespeare, having got into bad company, had more than once stolen deer from Thomas Lucy's park at Charlecote, that he had been caught and rather too severely punished, and that in revenge had composed a ballad satirizing Lucy, which got him into such trouble that he had to leave Stratford for London. Another version of the story introduces the concept that Shakespeare's revenge included a caricature of Lucy in the person of Justice Shallow. Further embellished, this has proved to be one of the most popular and enduring Shakespeare legends, and has provoked much debate as to its authenticity. Some writers have drawn attention to inconsistencies (there was, for example, no formal park at Charlecote at this date), and few claim that the story can be true throughout. Nevertheless, during Shakespeare's youth Thomas Lucy was certainly well known in Stratford.

He was regularly entertained by the corporation when visiting the town on official business, is recorded as an arbitrator in a Stratford dispute in 1571, and attended a wedding in the town in 1575. A case can also be made that the account in the opening scene of *The Merry Wives of Windsor* of Justice Shallow's coat of arms, with its twelve white luces, or pikes, may be an oblique reference to that of the Lucy family itself, with its three silver luces. That the dialogue caricatures Shallow as an ignorant country justice, and includes a disrespectful pun ('louses' for 'luces') and a reference to deer-killing has then been used to argue that Shakespeare, in this scene, was paying off old scores arising out of his youthful crimes recorded in the later stories. If Shakespeare did have Thomas Lucy in mind when, about 1598, he wrote these lines, then clearly he must have had scant regard for this local Stratford figure. However, it need have meant nothing more than that. Furthermore, whether or not deliberate caricature was intended, it is not difficult to see how this passage, when it later became more generally known in Stratford circles, could have been interpreted as hostile to the Lucy interest, and, with its reference to deer-stealing, then turned into the folk-tale which surfaces in the written record at the end of the seventeenth century. We may also note that a payment in 1584 by Coventry corporation to 'Sir Thomas Lucies players' does not make Lucy an obvious target for a playwright's satire, and that Shakespeare in *1 Henry VI* introduces in a far more flattering light another member of the Lucy family, William, thought to be William Lucy of Charlecote, who died in 1466.

Sir Thomas's wife, Joyce, died on 10 February 1595, and was buried in the parish church at Charlecote on 10 March. She is commemorated in a fine alabaster tomb, with a full-length effigy and a charming inscription composed and 'set down by him that best did know what hath been written to be true: Thomas Lucy'. He continued in the execution of his local duties: as late as February 1600 he received a letter from the privy council acknowledging that it had 'good cause to note your diligence and endeavour'. He died on 7 July of that year, and was buried alongside his wife on 7 August. Her tomb appears to have been modified to accommodate his full-length effigy. Three heralds attended the funeral, William Camden, as Clarenceux, superintending the ceremonies.

Sir Thomas and Joyce had only two children, Anne and Thomas. Anne married Edward Aston of Tixhall, in Staffordshire, in 1580. The marriage was not a happy one, and led to bitter family feuding. In a letter to his cousin Richard Bagot, Aston paints a dramatic picture of these disagreements, and casts his mother-in-law, in particular, in a light very different from the epitaph on her tomb. Anne died in 1596 and four of her children came to live at Charlecote. This led to a scandalous liaison between one of the daughters, Elizabeth, and a manservant, John Sambach, which clouded Sir Thomas's final days. The couple were married two weeks after his death.

Thomas's son, also Thomas (1551–1605), who survived him by only five years, married twice. His first wife, whom he married on 27 January 1574, was Dorothea, only daughter of Roland Arnold of Highnam in Gloucestershire. She died in 1580, a month after giving birth to a son who did not survive her long. His second wife was Constance, daughter of Sir Richard Kingsmill of Highclere in Hampshire; they had fourteen children. Their eldest son, Thomas (1585–1640), succeeded to the family estates on his father's death in July 1605. ROBERT BEARMAN

Sources A. Fairfax-Lucy, *Charlecote and the Lucys: the chronicle of an English family*, rev. edn (1990) • HoP, *Commons*, *1558–1603* • S. Schoenbaum, *Shakespeare's lives*, new edn (1991) • E. L. Fripp and R. Savage, eds., *Minutes and accounts of the corporation of Stratford-upon-Avon, … 1553–1620*, 5 vols., Dugdale Society, 1, 3, 5, 10, 35 (1921–90) • R. W. Ingram, ed., *Records of early English drama: Coventry* (1981) • W. Dugdale, *The antiquities of Warwickshire illustrated*, rev. W. Thomas, 2nd edn, 2 vols. (1730) • C. C. Stopes, *Shakespeare's Warwickshire contemporaries* (1907) • *CPR*, esp. 1548–9; 1553; 1555–7; 1563–9 • T. Kemp, ed., *The Black Book of Warwick* [1898] • parish register, Charlecote, Warwickshire, 7 Aug 1600 [burial] • parish register, Charlecote, Warwickshire, 1595 [burial: Joyce Lucy, wife] • parish register, Charlecote, Warwickshire, June 1551 [burial: William Lucy, father] • parish register, Charlecote, Warwickshire, July 1550 [burial: Ann Lucy, mother] • 'Foxe, John', *DNB*

Archives Warks. CRO, Charlecote House MSS, Charlecote MSS

Likenesses alabaster effigy, *c.*1600, St Leonard's Church, Charlecote, Warwickshire

Lucy, Sir Thomas (1583x6–1640), magistrate and politician, was the eldest surviving son of Sir Thomas Lucy (1551–1605), of Charlecote, Warwickshire, and his second wife, Constance, daughter and heir of Richard Kingsmill of Highclere, Hampshire. He matriculated at Magdalen College, Oxford, on 8 May 1601, was admitted as a student at Lincoln's Inn on 13 May 1602, and was knighted in 1603.

As a young man Lucy was drawn into the intellectual and literary life of London. He made the acquaintance of John Donne at the London house of his fellow Warwickshire landowner, Sir Henry Goodere, who was also patron to Ben Jonson, he was eulogized by a minor poet, John Davis, as a 'Bright spark of wit and courage' (Fairfax-Lucy, 114n.), and he developed a close friendship with the unconventional polymath Lord Herbert of Cherbury. Lucy spent much of his time in the household maintained by Herbert's mother and the two men had their portraits painted in classical attire by William Larkin. In 1608 Lucy joined Herbert in Paris, where he shared his study of music and also became involved in two abortive duels. On their return to Dover in February 1609 the two men nearly perished in a shipwreck.

With his wife, Alice *Lucy (*d.* 1648), daughter of Thomas Spencer of Claverdon, Warwickshire, whom he married about 1610, Sir Thomas appears to have settled down to living at his ancestral home at Charlecote Park, where they had six sons and four daughters. He did not abandon his literary interests but continued to correspond with Donne and Herbert, maintained his acquaintance with Goodere and built up a large library at Charlecote which was later illustrated on his funeral monument. He also developed an interest in antiquarianism which brought him into contact with William Dugdale. He was said to be 'so rare and proficient' in either 'sacred or secular learning' that 'he was accounted a living library' (Dugard, postscript).

Sir Thomas, however, made his principal mark in local affairs. His family had been a significant presence in Warwickshire since at least the thirteenth century and the marriages of his father and grandfather brought extensive additional estates which made him one of the wealthiest landowners in the shire, with an annual income of over £3500. From the 1610s through to the end of the 1630s he served in the principal county offices of justice of the peace and deputy lieutenant and established a reputation as a conscientious and diligent administrator. He regularly attended quarter sessions, took responsibility for the military affairs of the shire, acted as the arbiter of disputes involving his neighbours and became a principal benefactor of the boroughs of Stratford upon Avon and Warwick. For much of this period he was the most influential landowner in the southern half of the shire and his status was acknowledged in his apparently uncontested election to parliament as knight of the shire in 1614, 1621, 1624, 1625, 1626, 1628, and the Short Parliament of 1640. He was also returned as MP for Warwick borough to the Long Parliament, but it is doubtful that he ever took his seat as he was already ill in the spring of 1640.

In national politics Lucy was a much less significant figure. He is not recorded as having made any major speech in parliament, and his most significant contribution was, perhaps, to present Warwickshire's complaints against patentees in 1621. However, he does provide a good example of the growing disillusionment among county gentry with the political and religious policies of the Caroline regime. He kept himself informed about national politics as part of a network of local gentry corresponding with the London newsletter writer John Pory and he was on good terms with lord keeper Coventry and secretary of state Sir John Coke who shared his moderate views. While in most respects he served the regime loyally, he was also involved in opposition to some of its more contentious policies. There were rumours that he was opposed to the forced loan and when the levy was being collected in Warwickshire in 1627 he was conspicuous by his absence, preferring to pay in London. During the 1630s he was closely associated with the opposition peer Lord Brooke and at dinner parties at Warwick Castle he met with other leading critics of the crown, such as John Pym, Lord Saye and Sele, and his brother-in-law, Richard Knightley. Finally in February 1640, a few months before his death, he was removed from the commission of the peace, probably because he was seen as obstructing the collection of ship money in south Warwickshire.

Lucy's service in local office and his readiness to challenge the crown on sensitive issues helped to establish a reputation as the archetypal 'patriot' or 'public man', devoted to the service of the common weal. He was also a moderate puritan and patron of godly ministers, such as Robert Harris of Hanwell, and he was acclaimed for his hospitality towards the poor and for generosity to his tenants. Lucy died at Charlecote Park on 8 December 1640 following a fall from a horse, and was buried, as he requested, among his ancestors in the chancel of the parish church at Charlecote. The tribute paid to him by Harris at his funeral was a classic description of the role to which he had aspired:

> A noble lady hath lost not an husband (as she saith) but a father.
> Many children have lost not a father, but a counsellor.
> An houseful of servants have lost not a master but a physician who made (as I am informed) their sickness his, and his physic and cost theirs.
> Townes full of tenants have lost a landlord that could both protect and direct them in their own way.
> The whole neighbourhood have lost a light.
> The countie a leader.
> The countrey a patriot, to whom he was not wanting till he was wanting to himself in his former vigour and health.
> (Harris, 25–6)

Richard Cust

Sources A. Fairfax-Lucy, *Charlecote and the Lucys: the chronicle of an English family* (1958) • A. Hughes, *Politics, society and civil war in Warwickshire, 1620–1660* (1987) • Keeler, *Long Parliament* • R. Harris, *Abners Funerall* (1641) • T. Dugard, *Death and the grave* (1649) • PRO, PROB 11/185, sig. 20 [Sir Thomas Lucy's will] • *The life of Edward, first Lord Herbert of Cherbury written by himself*, ed. J. M. Shuttleworth (1976) • H. Summerson, 'The Lucys of Charlecote and their library', *National Trust Studies* (1979) • *Charlecote Park, Warwickshire*, National Trust, [new edn] (1979)

Archives Warks. CRO, Lucy Collection L6

Likenesses W. Larkin, oils, *c*.1608, Charlecote Park, Warwickshire • C. Johnson, group portrait, oils, *c*.1628, Charlecote Park, Warwickshire • attrib. N. Stone, marble sculpture on funeral monument, *c*.1645, St Leonard's Church, Charlecote, Warwickshire

Wealth at death approx. £3500 p.a.: Hughes, *Politics*, 34n.

Lucy, William (1594–1677), bishop of St David's, was born at Hurstbourne, Hampshire, the fourth son of Sir Thomas Lucy (1551–1605) of Charlecote, Warwickshire, and his second wife, Constance, daughter and heir of Richard *Kingsmill (*c*.1528–1600) of Highclere, Hampshire; Sir Thomas *Lucy (1583x6–1640) and Sir Richard *Lucy (1592–1667) were his elder brothers. In 1610 he was admitted to Trinity College, Oxford, where he graduated BA on 18 November 1613. He was admitted to Lincoln's Inn on 25 May 1614 but 'upon second thoughts, and perhaps a desire of a sedate and academical life' (Wood, *Ath. Oxon.*, 3.1127) he entered Gonville and Caius College, Cambridge, as a fellow-commoner on 12 June 1615. He proceeded MA the following year and was ordained deacon at London on 21 December 1617. In 1619 Lucy became rector of Burghclere, Hampshire. In 1621 he also obtained the living of Highclere and about the same time was appointed chaplain to the duke of Buckingham, on the recommendation of James I. Appointed as a university preacher at Cambridge in 1620 Lucy gained notoriety for delivering on commencement Sunday 1622, before the largely Calvinist university, an anti-Calvinist sermon which Joseph Meade described as being 'totally for Arminanisme, wonderfully bold and peremptorily, styling some passages to the contrary by names of blasphemie etc.' (BL, Harley MS 389, fol. 213). The scandal over the sermon led to calls for Lucy to be denied higher degrees, but he escaped censure and in 1623 proceeded BD and DD with the support of the king against what appears to have been heavy opposition. On 12 February 1629 at St Bride's, Fleet Street, London, Lucy married Martha (1608–1674), daughter of William Angel. They had two daughters and five sons, including Spencer Lucy (1643/4–1691).

Lucy lived at Burghclere until the outbreak of the civil war, when, as a staunch royalist, he was 'both active and passive to his ability in the great cause' (Bodl. Oxf., MS Tanner 146, fol. 133). His house was searched and his extensive library seized. An informer suggested that he was raising money for the duke of York. In April 1651 the committee for compounding ordered his estates in Hampshire to be seized. After being sent a copy of Thomas Hobbes's *Leviathan* (1651), and noting its popularity with local gentlemen, Lucy composed *Examinations, Censures and Confutations of Divers Errours in the Two First Chapters of Mr Hobbes his Leviathan* (1657), published under the pseudonym William Pike (a play on his name). He followed this with *Observations, Censures and Confutations of Divers Errors in the 12, 13 and 14 Chap. Of Mr Hobs his Leviathan* (1658), dedicated to William Seymour, marquess of Hertford. These two works were extended and republished as *Notorious Errours in Mr Hobbes his Leviathan* (1663), dedicated to the earl of Clarendon. Lucy completed his critique of *Leviathan* with his *Second Part of Observations, Censures and Confutations* (1673); this work included a postscript censuring Hobbes's Latin edition of *Leviathan* (1668). Lucy's often obtuse animadversions of Hobbes's ideas rarely achieve great originality and largely rely upon the restatement of traditional scholastic ideas which were fast moving out of fashion. For this reason his critique did not find much favour among contemporaries. Henry Stubbe commented that many of the things that Lucy objected to in Hobbes were 'admitted generally, by those who had learned to search into nature, & not to acquiesce in ye traditions of others' (*Correspondence of Thomas Hobbes*, 1.440). In addition to his work against Hobbes, Lucy also composed in the 1650s *A Treatise of the Nature of a Minister*, a defence of episcopal authority in the apostolic church against the New England congregationalist Thomas Hooker's *A Survey of the Summe of Church-Discipline* (1648). Lucy eventually published his book in 1670.

At the Restoration, Lucy's loyalty was rewarded when, on 11 October 1660, he was elected bishop of St David's, his confirmation and consecration taking place on 17 and 18 November 1660. He is recorded as being present at the Savoy conference, but he took no part in the debates. Lucy faced a difficult task at St David's. Episcopal administration of the diocese, one of the largest and poorest in Britain, had effectively ceased in 1640. The cathedral at St David's, the collegiate church at Brecon, and the bishop's houses at Brecon and Abergwili were practically in ruins, the decay exacerbated by plundering during the interregnum. Lucy's effectiveness as an administrator is a subject of some debate. He was posthumously charged with having 'lived in a woeful and culpable omission of many of the direct and important as well sacred as other duties of his office' (Ferguson, 21–2). He is said to have neglected to hold confirmations in his diocese and to have connived at the exaction of exorbitant fees, as well as filling the cathedral with non-residents and preferring royalists and his own family exclusively to benefices in the diocese. Some of these charges were justified: his son Spencer, for instance, became in 1669 vicar of Penbryn, Cardiganshire, and canon and treasurer of St David's. However, Lucy's transgressions went hand in hand with his attempts to combat religious dissent and revive the fortunes of the church in his diocese. He does appear to have made considerable efforts to improve the condition of the diocese. Large sums were spent in the restoration of the collegiate church and the bishop's and prebendary's houses at Brecon as well as sums in augmentation of poor vicarages. Bishop Thomas Burgess, Lucy's nineteenth-century successor and champion, considered that Lucy could be considered 'the second founder of the College at Brecknock' (Burgess, 25–6).

Lucy also fought tenaciously to preserve his authority as bishop in the see. William Nicholson, bishop of Gloucester, had been allowed to retain his archdeaconry of Brecon *in commendam*. In 1663 he claimed the right of holding visitations and correcting faults in the clergy of Lucy's diocese. Lucy denied Nicholson's claims, although the extent of the archdeacon's jurisdiction was far from clear. The controversy led to the suspension of archidiaconal visitations and the controversy had to be referred to the bishops of London and St Asaph who in 1665 finally ruled in favour of Lucy. One result of the quarrel was that the right of holding visitations in the diocese of St David's remained in abeyance until the nineteenth century. However, *Articles of Visitation and Enquiry* were published not only in 1662 but also in 1671, revealing Lucy to be an early exponent, among Restoration bishops, of railing in the altar at the east end of the chancel.

Lucy's final years at St David's were marked by his progressive physical deterioration, which prevented him from travelling. In a letter to Archbishop Gilbert Sheldon in 1675 he describes himself as a 'poor old man, who hath not beene 2 miles from his house this 3 last yeares' (Bodl. Oxf., MS Tanner 42, fol. 142). However, when he drew up his will, on 3 September 1677, he pronounced himself in perfect health, apart from a little lameness, stemming from gout. This scourge of sectaries and dissenters declared himself convinced of the validity of the Church of England as by law established, but conceded 'some things may be amended in it as whatsoever is ordered by humane Reason will have deficiency in it (although such reason doth take scripture for its guidance)'. However, 'I feare he who shall undertake to amend it may probably doe harme then good by that adventure' (PRO, PROB 11/355, sig. 99). He died on 4 October 1677 and was buried in the collegiate church of Brecon. JON PARKIN

Sources Venn, *Alum. Cant.* • Foster, *Alum. Oxon.* • Wood, *Ath. Oxon.*, new edn, vol. 3 • Bodl. Oxf., MSS Tanner 42, fol. 142; 146, fol. 133 • *The correspondence of Thomas Hobbes*, ed. N. Malcolm, 1 (1994) • R. Ferguson, *A large review of the summary view of the articles exhibited against the bishop of St David's* (1702) • T. Burgess, *Bishops and benefactors of St David's vindicated from the misrepresentations of a recent publication, in a charge delivered to the chapter of St David's at his primary visitation of the cathedral church on the 30th July 1811* (1812) • will, PRO, PROB 11/355, sig. 99 • B. Willis, *A survey of the cathedral church of St David's* (1717) • W. B. Jones and E. A. Freeman, *The history and antiquities of St David's* (1856) • W. L. Bevan, *St David's* (1888) • *Walker rev.* • *The nonconformist's memorial … originally written by … Edmund Calamy*, ed. S. Palmer, 2nd edn, 1 (1777) • F. L. Colvile, *The worthies of Warwickshire who lived between 1500 and 1800* [1870] • *Fasti Angl.*, *1541–1857*, [St Paul's, London] • *CSP dom.*, *1623–5* • M. A. E. Green, ed., *Calendar of the proceedings of the committee for compounding … 1643–1660*, 4, PRO (1892) • C. H. Cooper, *Annals of Cambridge*, 3 (1845) • J. B. Mullinger, *The University of Cambridge*, 2 (1884) • N. Tyacke, *Anti-Calvinists: the rise of English Arminianism*, *c.1590–1640* (1987) • P. White, *Predestination, policy and polemic* (1992) • [T. Birch and R. F. Williams], eds., *The court and times of Charles the First*, 2 (1848) • J. Spurr, *The Restoration Church of England, 1646–1689* (1991) • S. Mintz, *The hunting of Leviathan* (1962) • J. Bowle, *Hobbes and his critics* (1951) • G. H. Jenkins, *The foundations of modern Wales* (1993)

Archives Bodl. Oxf., Tanner MS 42, fols. 43, 84, 142; MS 43, fol. 74; MS 47, fol. 51; MS 146, fols. 113, 126, 133, 139; MS 314, fol. 40

Ludd, Ned (*fl.* 1811–1816), mythical machine-breaker, was the name signed by the authors of letters threatening the destruction of knitting frames. Luddism emerged initially in the small villages of Nottinghamshire and Leicestershire (the address affixed to some of the letters was Sherwood Forest) and later spread to Lancashire and the West Riding of Yorkshire (where the *nom de guerre* used was often Enoch). The first incidence of Luddism, according to the *Nottingham Review*, occurred in December 1811 when a boy apprentice named Ludlam from the village of Anstey, near Leicester, attacked his frame after his master complained of poor work. Framework knitters appealed to a charter granted by Charles II which authorized them to destroy frames that fabricated articles in a deceitful manner, but in a short space of time Luddism became a catch-all term applied to food riots, incendiarism, and political militancy. The assassination of the prime minister, Spencer Perceval, on 11 May 1812 was initially thought to be the work of the Luddites. Many Luddite leaders were executed, but the identity of Ludd remained a mystery. Although local figureheads such as Gravenor Hensen and James (Jem) Towle (in Nottinghamshire) and George Mellor (in Yorkshire) were strongly suspected, no one individual was ever identified as Ludd (or General Ludd), and the letters and threats were issued by divers hands.

MILES TAYLOR

Sources R. A. Church and S. D. Chapman, 'Gravener Henson and the making of the English working class', *Land, labour and population in the industrial revolution: essays presented to J. D. Chamber*, ed. E. L. Jones and G. E. Mingay (1967), 131–61 • F. O. Darvall, *Popular disturbances in Regency England* (1934) • J. L. Hammond and B. Hammond, *The skilled labourer*, 2nd edn (1927); repr. (1979) • F. Peel, *The rising of the Luddites* (1895) • M. I. Thomis, *The Luddites: machine-breaking in Regency England* (1970)

Luders, Alexander (*d.* 1819), legal writer, was the second son of Theodore Luders of Lyncombe and Widcombe, Somerset. He was probably of German extraction, and when admitted a member of the Inner Temple on 10 July 1770 was described in the books of the inn as 'Sacri Romani Imperii nobilis Eques'. He was called to the bar on 6 February 1778, and became a bencher of his inn on 10 May 1811. He was probably the father of Alexander Luders, who matriculated at Brasenose College, Oxford, in 1806, aged seventeen, and died in 1851 as rector of Woolstone, Gloucestershire.

Luders wrote widely on legal and constitutional history. He edited three volumes of a Commons committee dealing with 'controverted elections' (1785–90); and in 1807 his essay on the use of French in ancient laws and acts of state appeared. A clutch of other writings dealt with aspects of the law of treason, on the right of succession to the crown in the reign of Elizabeth I, and also on the constitution of parliament in the reign of Henry VIII. His final works included an essay on Henry V (1813), a study of the monarch's title of 'defender of the faith', and a monograph on the constitution of parliament in the reign of Edward I (1818).

These writings made a valuable contribution to legal history and were cited by Henry Hallam in his constitutional histories. Luders died on 25 November 1819. Some of his books were bequeathed to the Inner Temple Library.

C. L. KINGSFORD, *rev.* ROBERT BROWN

Sources private information (1893) [H. W. Lawrence, of the Inner Temple] • Watt, *Bibl. Brit.* • Foster, *Alum. Oxon.* • H. Hallam, *The constitutional history of England from the accession of Henry VII to the death of George II*, 4 vols. (1827) • H. Hallam, *View of the state of Europe during the middle ages*, 2 vols. (1818)

Archives Inner Temple, London, legal papers

Ludford, Nicholas (*c.*1490–1557), composer, whose early musical training is unknown, may have originated from London. In 1495 the composer John Ludforde, perhaps his father, joined the fraternity of St Nicholas, the London Guild of Parish Clerks; Nicholas Ludford himself joined in 1521. The composer occupied the majority of his adult working life employed at the royal collegiate chapel of St Mary and St Stephen in the palace of Westminster. From its foundation in 1348 by Edward III the college comprised a dean, twelve secular canons, thirteen vicars-choral, four clerks or singing men, six choristers (a seventh chorister being added some time in the late fifteenth century), a verger, and a sacristan. St Stephen's was one of the highest-ranking collegiate churches in late medieval England, being a sister foundation of St George's, Windsor. It was a customary venue for royal baptisms and memorials, and stood within the old palace of Westminster, adjacent to the south-east end of Westminster Hall. The post of verger seems to have incorporated the post of organist by the middle of the fifteenth century, and thereafter was occupied by the chief musician of the chapel. The instructor of the choristers at St Stephen's was normally appointed from among the vicars-choral and clerks; there is no evidence that Ludford ever held the post.

The earliest reference to Ludford in Westminster is in January 1517 when he rented lodgings from the abbey. It is likely that he had found employment in one of Westminster's musical establishments; certainly he was employed at St Stephen's by the early 1520s, perhaps as a lay clerk of the choir, and probably he had acquired a probationary appointment as chief musician (nominally occupying the office of verger) by 1525. 30 September 1527 marked his formal appointment as verger with an annual income of £9 2*s.* 6*d.*, and 13*s.* 4*d.* each year at Christmas towards his chapel livery; as organist he received an additional stipend of 40s. Ludford's duties included singing in the chapel services and playing the organ. It is also possible that he would have been responsible for leading the processions and, perhaps, for chapel maintenance.

Upon the dissolution of St Stephen's in March 1548, Ludford received a substantial annual pension for the rest of his life, and remained active in the administration of the church of St Margaret in Westminster, in the parish of which he was resident. By 1541 he resided in Longwolstable Street, which was located immediately outside the north wall and gate of New Palace Yard; he is also known in 1549 to have held property in King Street. He regularly maintained his pew at St Margaret's from 1525, and was present (along with a number of other parishioners) at the drawing of the churchwardens' accounts at various times between 1537 and 1556. He probably did not participate much in the music-making there, though in 1534 the churchwardens paid him 20s. for 'a pryke songe boke'. Between 1552 and 1554 Ludford was himself elected a churchwarden of St Margaret's, where his first wife, Anne, was buried on 9 December 1552; on 21 May 1554 he married Helen Thomas, who survived him.

Ludford was a local composer, and seems not to have travelled much outside the orbit of London and Westminster. His musical style owes much to his earlier contemporary Robert Fayrfax (1464–1521), who was instrumental in refining cyclic mass composition in England. Indeed Ludford and Fayrfax's works sit side by side in a number of contemporary sources, and there are certain similarities between the beginning of Fayrfax's mass *O bone Jesu* and that of Ludford's mass *Christi virgo dilectissima*. Ludford's musical style may be considered to represent a trend away from the more melismatic and embellished style of composition found in the Eton choirbook (compiled *c.*1505). The Eton technique was further developed and championed by his more direct contemporaries Hugh Aston (*d.* 1558) and John Taverner (*d.* 1545), but in contrast Ludford (like Fayrfax) preferred a more homogeneous soundscape, in which overall texture and sonority took precedence over the floridity and individuality of each vocal line. Nevertheless, Ludford was also capable of drawing out important melodic ideas from the richness of his texture. This latter point certainly seems to have been his hallmark, though he also dabbled in the melismatic style of the old school, as is evident in his six-part mass *Videte miraculum* on a plainsong for the feast of the Purification (arguably one of his earliest and most brilliant surviving works), which is unusually scored for two equal treble parts throughout.

Ludford's festal masses are preserved in three sources: the so-called Caius and Lambeth choirbooks of *c.*1521–7 (the only English manuscripts of their type to have survived from the reign of Henry VIII), and the Peterhouse partbooks of *c.*1539–40. Caius and Lambeth are enormous productions, in the same hand, and, at least in the case of Caius, commissioned by Edward Higgons, a prominent royal lawyer who held a canonry of St Stephen's from 1517, and who held the mastership of Arundel College in Sussex from 1520. A manuscript roll in Arundel Castle archives containing the bass part of Ludford's antiphon *Gaude flore virginali* is also in the same hand as the choirbooks, and it has been argued that the Caius book was prepared in Arundel as a presentation manuscript from Higgons to St Stephen's (possibly to mark Ludford's formal appointment as verger of the chapel in 1527).

None of Ludford's compositions can be confidently assigned to a particular event, but it would appear that most if not all of his works were Westminster productions. The patronal mass *Lapidaverunt Stephanum* was almost certainly written for St Stephen's, and he may have received commissions from elsewhere in the city or indeed from one of the various guilds connected with St Margaret's Church. The most prominent and influential of these guilds was that of the Assumption of the Virgin Mary, which controlled a number of properties in the parish and maintained its own chapel in St Margaret's. While there is no evidence that Ludford himself was a member of this guild, he can be associated with a number of known members; it may be that his great six-part mass and Magnificat cycle *Benedicta et venerabilis* (based on the Assumption chant *Beata es virgo*) was commissioned by the guild at some point after 1521 (after which time the guild account books are no longer extant). It is difficult to imagine that this cycle was composed with the choir of St Stephen's in mind, as it is scored with two low bass parts throughout (utilizing the opposite end of the vocal spectrum as *Videte miraculum*); only four singing men were employed in the chapel. But it is also possible that extra singers might have been brought in for large occasions, as was certainly the case with a number of similar institutions.

Ludford's festal masses are all based on a cantus firmus assigned to a particular liturgical festival, although it is likely that they were not restricted to 'seasonal' performance. *Lapidaverunt Stephanum* (St Stephen's day, 26 December) may have been a show-piece that was employed at grand chapel occasions; *Christe virgo dilectissima* is constructed around chant for the feast of the Annunciation; *Regnum mundi* is based on the ninth respond at matins for the feast of Virgins not Martyrs; and *Inclina cor meum* draws its chant from a terce responsory for the feast of Epiphany (the latter mass is paired with Ludford's antiphon *Ave Maria, ancilla trinitatis*). The cantus firmus of each mass is usually confined to the tenor part of the 'full' choral sections. *Videte miraculum* is slightly unusual in that its cantus firmus migrates to other voices during some sections for reduced scoring, but the construction of *Inclina cor meum* is indeed rare among the entire repertory of the period. Here, the melody is stated several times in each movement, and by all voices in turn in both full and reduced passages. Lost masses include a *Requiem eternam* and a *Sermone blando*.

Ludford's seven settings of the Lady mass, one for each day of the week, are the sole contents of a set of four partbooks which can be dated from between *c.*1515 and *c.*1525 (the fourth book contains the cantus firmus or 'squares', which are thought to have been used as the basis of organ improvisation *alternatim* with the choir). This collection is a unique survival among the repertory, and the decoration on their leather covers suggests they were a gift to Henry VIII and Katherine of Aragon (the books are recorded in an inventory made in 1542 of Henry VIII's books in Westminster). It may be that the Lady masses were commissioned by the royal couple for performance in the lady chapel at St Stephen's (the under-chapel, St Mary in the Vaults), or even for Katherine's private devotions, although there is no direct proof to support either suggestion. The fragmentary four-part 'Le roy' Kyrie is evidence of another Lady mass cycle by Ludford; here the same square is used as in Taverner's 'Le roy' Kyrie.

Four of Ludford's six surviving antiphons can be reconstructed. While the majority are set to general Marian texts (*Ave cuius conceptio*, *Ave Maria, ancilla trinitatis*, *Gaude flore virginali*, and *Salve regina, mater misericordie*), others like *Salve regina, pudica mater* and *Domine Jesu Christe* may have been composed in response to a particular event or circumstance. The former (of which only the *medius* part survives) contains a verse which invokes the Virgin Mary as 'protectress and patroness to the English', while another begs her to 'protect the king and also the queen with their children and subjects'. The text of *Domine Jesu Christe* appears in a number of fifteenth- and sixteenth-century prayer books of various uses, where it is prescribed for recitation 'in the agonie and laste ende of man and woman labourynge agaynst the dethe'. By 1530 a Jesus chapel was completed in Westminster Abbey where weekly memorials were performed for Abbot John Islip, who died in 1532. (Ludford witnessed the will of John Ellys, one of the workmen on the chapel, who painted an image of the five wounds on the entrance stairs.) It is known that the choirs of St Stephen's and the abbey occasionally joined forces at St Margaret's for certain festivals, and it is not beyond the bounds of possibility that Ludford's *Domine Jesu Christe* was written as a musical 'suffrage' for the late abbot.

There is no evidence that Ludford composed in the new pithy and condensed style of writing that became fashionable in the 1530s and 1540s (Taverner certainly began to compose in this style towards the end of his life), and it is unlikely that he wrote music for the reformed church after his time at St Stephen's. His music is nowhere to be found in the Elizabethan collections of John Baldwin and John Sadler, where many of his contemporaries are well represented, although Thomas Morley lists him as one of the composers consulted for his *Introduction to Practicall Musicke* (1597).

Ludford died in 1557 and was buried in the vaults of St Margaret's Church on 9 August next to his first wife. His will, dated 5 August 1557, mentions no surviving child, though the registers of St Margaret's record the marriage of a Thomas Ludford on 27 January 1566 as well as the marriage of an Anne Ludford on 7 November 1574 (the latter was buried in St Margaret's churchyard on 2 April 1597).

DAVID SKINNER

Sources H. Baillie, 'Nicholas Ludford (*c*.1485–*c*.1557)', *Musical Quarterly*, 44 (1958), 196–208 • H. Baillie, 'Squares', *Acta Musicologica*, 32 (1960), 178–93 • J. Bergsagel, 'An introduction to Ludford', *Musica Disciplina*, 14 (1960), 105–30 • J. Bergsagel, 'On the performance of Ludford's *Alternatim* masses', *Musica Disciplina*, 16 (1962), 35–55 • R. Bowers, 'The music and musical establishment of St George's in the 15th century', *St George's Chapel, Windsor Castle, in the late middle ages*, ed. C. Richmond and E. Scarff (2001) • F. L. Harrison, *Music in medieval Britain*, 4th edn (Büren, 1980) • F. Kisby, 'Music and musicians of early Tudor Westminster', *Early Music*, 23 (1995), 223–40 • N. Sandon, 'The manuscript British Library Harley 1709', *Music in the medieval English liturgy*, ed. S. Rankin and D. Hiley (1993), 355–79 • D. Skinner, 'At the mynde of Nycholas Ludford: new light on Ludford from the churchwardens' accounts of St Margaret's, Westminster', *Early Music*, 22 (1994), 393–413 • D. Skinner, 'Nicholas Ludford (*c*.1490–1557): a biography and critical edition of the antiphons, with a study of the collegiate chapel of the Holy Trinity, Arundel, under the mastership of Edward Higgons, and a history of the Caius and Lambeth choirbooks', DPhil diss., U. Oxf., 1995, esp. 2–68 • D. Skinner, 'Discovering the provenance and date of the Caius and Lambeth choirbooks', *Early Music*, 25 (1997), 245–66 • D. Skinner, 'Ludford's lady masses, *XX songes* and a Westminster inventory of 1542' [forthcoming] • private information (2004) [J. Smart]

Archives City Westm. AC, MSS • Westminster Abbey, MSS

Ludford, Simon (*d.* 1575), physician, was a native of Bedfordshire, and entered the Franciscan order. After the dissolution of the monasteries he became an apothecary in London. He supplicated for the degree of BM from the University of Oxford on 6 November 1553, and despite claims that he was 'a man utterley unlearned' (Lewis, 232), he was admitted to the degree and to practice on 27 November 1554. However, the College of Physicians objected. On hearing of Ludford's admission as a bachelor, John Caius, president of the college, sent a letter reprimanding the university, and stating that Ludford had been examined by the College of Physicians on 12 February 1553, and had been found ignorant, not only of medicine but of philosophy and letters, and that he was completely uneducated. In January 1556 an angry letter from Caius and the college was read out in convocation two months after John Lawton, another candidate rejected by the college, had been admitted bachelor of physic. The matter ended inconclusively. Ludford then studied at Cambridge, but was eventually admitted DM at Oxford on 26 June 1560. He was elected a fellow of the College of Physicians on 7 April 1563, and was chosen a censor in 1564, 1569, and 1572.

Ludford's only extant composition is a manuscript copy of verses written on a blank space at the end of the preface of Charles Estienne's *De dissectione partium corporis humani libri tres* (1545). Ludford had paid 8*s*. for the book, and he states that he was in want of money at the time. Ludford, who was married to Jane (*d.* 1597), with whom he had a son, William (*d.* 1578), died in 1575 and was buried at St Stephen Walbrook on 21 August. He left some books to the library of the College of Physicians, including his copy of the works of Avicena and Estienne's *De dissectione*.

NORMAN MOORE, *rev.* SARAH BAKEWELL

Sources Munk, *Roll* • Foster, *Alum. Oxon.* • G. Lewis, 'The faculty of medicine', *Hist. U. Oxf.* 3: *Colleg. univ.*, 213–56, esp. 232, 234 • will, PRO, PROB 11/57, sig. 38 • W. B. Bannerman and W. B. Bannerman, jun., eds., *The registers of St Stephen's, Walbrook, and of St Benet Sherehog, London*, 1, Harleian Society, register section, 49 (1919)

Ludlam, Henry (1824–1880), mineralogist, was born on 14 October 1824, probably in London. He was the youngest of the fifteen children of James Ludlam, a tradesman, and his wife, Sarah Barton. He studied architecture, but became instead a land surveyor, and subsequently a hosier. However, his passion was mineralogy and he amassed one of the finest private collections of minerals in the country. It incorporated those made by Charles Hampden Turner (which in turn included earlier collections by Jacob Forster and Henry Heuland) and William Nevill (which included the collection of the diplomat William Garrow Lettsom). A wealthy man, Ludlam bought extravagantly at mineral auctions and was one of the best customers of Cornish dealer Richard Talling (1820–1883). In 1876 Talling discovered a new iron phosphate mineral; it was named ludlamite in Ludlam's honour by Frederick Field in 1877.

Ludlam died, unmarried, on 23 June 1880 at his home, 174 Piccadilly, London, leaving his collection to the Museum of Practical Geology, London. His own descriptive catalogue of the 18,000 specimens was unfinished at his death. At the museum the collection formed the backbone of what was described by F. W. Rudler in 1905 as the finest topographical display of British minerals ever seen in this country. Ludlam was a fellow of the Geological Society of London and a member of the Mineralogical Society. MICHAEL P. COOPER

Sources T. Davies, *Mineralogical Magazine*, 4 (1880–81), 132 · F. W. Rudler, *A handbook to a collection of the minerals of the British Islands mostly selected from the Ludlam collection* (1905) · *DNB* · A. Lévy, *Description d'une collection de minéraux formée par M. Henri Heuland et appartenant a M. Ch. Hampden Turner* (1837) · W. Nevill, *Descriptive catalogue of minerals, being the collection of William Nevill* (1872) · E. G. Allingham, *A romance of the rostrum* (1924) · F. Field, 'On ludlamite, a new Cornish mineral', *Proceedings of the Crystallographical Society*, part 1 (1877), 23–31 · *CGPLA Eng. & Wales* (1880) · d. cert. · census return for 174 Piccadilly, London, 1871 · *IGI* · parish register (baptism), 8 Nov 1824, London, St Marylebone

Archives NHM, corresp. and collection of minerals

Wealth at death under £45,000: probate, 14 Aug 1880, *CGPLA Eng. & Wales*

Ludlam, Isaac (*d.* 1817), rebel, is of unknown origins and upbringing. He earned his living as a quarryman and owned 'considerable property' at South Wingfield, Derbyshire (Thompson, 667). He was a Methodist who actively engaged in preaching.

In June 1817 Ludlam took a prominent part in the 'Derbyshire insurrection' or 'Pentrich rising' promoted by Jeremiah Brandreth, which saw an assembly of stockingers, quarrymen, and ironworkers march to Nottingham from a handful of villages in the Derby Peak. Before the outbreak Ludlam occupied himself in the manufacture of pikes, which were stored in a quarry near his house. On 8 June he went with another of the rebels, William Turner, to the White Horse inn at Pentrich. Here a meeting presided over by Brandreth took place, at which Ludlam read out a list of those persons in the neighbourhood from whom it was proposed to rob firearms. On the night of Monday, 9 June, Ludlam, accompanied by his three sons, joined the rebels under Brandreth at Topham Close, and the party of 200–300 men set out towards Nottingham. Ludlam, who acted as a rear-guard, was active in demanding arms from houses on the road, and compelled several persons to join in the movement against their will. When the party went into an inn at Codnor, Ludlam was stationed outside as sentinel to prevent waverers from escaping. In the course of the march Ludlam frequently stated that the object of the party was to join another body of men in Nottingham Forest, and then proceed to the town itself to guard an insurrectionary parliament which had been assembled there.

Ludlam escaped capture by the dragoons, who dispersed the rebel band on 10 June, but was subsequently arrested, and tried for high treason by the special commission at Derby. His counsel attempted to show that he was only Brandreth's dupe, which seems to have been true, and that his offence amounted to riot only. But he was found guilty, and executed with Brandreth and William Turner in front of the county gaol at Derby on 7 November. His corpse was then beheaded in line with the punishment for high treason. Ludlam's body was later that day buried, without a service, at St Werburgh's Church, Derby. His sons, despite pleading guilty at the trial, were discharged. G. P. MORIARTY, *rev.* PHILIP CARTER

Sources *GM*, 1st ser., 87/2 (1817), 358–9, 461–2 · *A full and particular account of the execution of Jeremiah Brandreth, Isaac Ludlam and William Turner* (1817) · E. P. Thompson, *The making of the English working class* (1963); repr. (1964) · J. L. Hammond and B. Hammond, *The skilled labourer, 1760–1832* (1919) · *State trials*, vol. 32

Ludlam, Thomas (1727–1811), theologian and essayist, born in Leicester and baptized at St Mary's on 3 March 1727, was the youngest son of Richard Ludlam (1680–1728), physician, and brother of William *Ludlam (*bap.* 1717, *d.* 1788), mathematician and writer on theology. After being educated at Mr Andrew's school in Leicester he was admitted to St John's College, Cambridge, as a pensioner on 9 May 1745; he graduated BA in 1749 and proceeded MA in 1752. Following his ordination as deacon by the bishop of Ely in 1750 he spent some time as chaplain in the navy, and on 31 May 1750 he was appointed chaplain to the *Prince Henry*. He was ordained priest by the bishop of Lincoln in 1753 and, with the help of John Jackson, was appointed confrater of Wigston's Hospital, Leicester, in 1760 and rector of Foston, Leicestershire, in 1791.

At a time when the importance of religious experience was being urged by those influenced by the evangelical revival Ludlam remained committed to the widespread eighteenth-century belief in the basic consonance between Christianity and reason, and suspicion of 'enthusiasm'. In particular, as a devoted disciple of Locke, he argued that religious experience, like all forms of experience, should be subject to the tests of demonstration and analysis, a view he argued at length in his tellingly entitled *Four essays, on the ordinary and extraordinary operations of the Holy Spirit; on the application of experience to religion; and on enthusiasm and fanaticism* (1797). He conceded that infallible knowledge might be received from God but claims to such knowledge had to be closely scrutinized since 'the knowledge men receive by the use of their various faculties is very imperfect' (*Four Essays*, 67). As he made plain, such a critique was directed particularly at those like the Methodists who mistake 'the confidence of expectation for the certainty of experience, the positiveness of opinion for the convictions of reason' (ibid., 44). His writings in the same vein in the *Orthodox Churchman's Review* earned him a reputation as 'one of the most formidable opponents of the Calvinistic writers' (*GM*, 81/2, 492). Predictably such views led to tension with such prominent evangelicals as his former friend, Isaac Milner, who, in his edition of the sermons of his brother, Joseph Milner, characterized Ludlam's work as being written 'with an unexampled self-sufficiency, arrogance, and contempt of others' (Milner, 1.102). A more charitable view of his forthright style was that of his obituarist in the *Gentleman's Magazine* who claimed that 'he was in temper, independent, frank, and friendly, not unobservant of human follies, nor unwilling to expose them' (*GM*, 81/2, 492). Ludlam died on 13 November 1811 in Leicester.

JOHN GASCOIGNE

Sources *GM*, 1st ser., 81/2 (1811), 492 · *GM*, 1st ser., 77 (1807), 1144 · Nichols, *Illustrations*, 5.349–52 · M. Milner, *Life of Isaac Milner* (1842), 54 · F. Kilvert, *Memoirs of the life and writings of the Right Rev. Richard Hurd* (1860), 156 · I. Milner, preface, in J. Milner, *Practical Sermons* (1804), i.102 · *DNB* · Venn, *Alum. Cant.* · *IGI* · *Annual Register* (1811), 166

Ludlam, Thomas (*c.*1775–1810). *See under* Ludlam, William (*bap.* 1717, *d.* 1788).

Ludlam, William (*bap.* **1717**, *d.* **1788**), mathematician and writer on theology, was baptized at St Mary's, Leicester, on 8 April 1717, the son of Richard Ludlam (1680–1728), physician, and his wife, Anne, daughter of William Drury of Nottingham. His father graduated MB at St John's College, Cambridge, in 1702, and practised medicine at Leicester. His uncle Sir George Ludlam (*d.* 1726) was chamberlain of the City of London. Thomas *Ludlam, the theologian, was his younger brother, and one of his sisters became the stepmother of the writer, Joseph Cradock, and another the mother of Gerrard *Andrewes (1750–1825), dean of Canterbury.

After attending Leicester grammar school Ludlam became a scholar at St John's College, Cambridge, where he matriculated in 1734. There he graduated BA in 1738, MA in 1742, and was elected to a fellowship in 1744. He was rector of Peckleton, Leicestershire, 1743–9, having been ordained deacon in Lincoln in 1741 and priest in the following year. In 1749 he gained his BD and in the same year became vicar of Norton by Galby in Leicestershire, on the nomination of Bernard Whalley. From 1754 to 1757 he was junior dean of his college, and from 1767 to 1769 he was Linacre lecturer in physic. He was, however, unsuccessful in his bid for the Lucasian chair of mathematics in 1760, losing the contest to Edward Waring despite powerful support from William Samuel Powell, then principal tutor of St John's.

Ludlam enjoyed a considerable reputation at the time for his skill in practical mechanics and astronomy, as well as for his mathematical lectures. In 1765 he was a member of the committee of outside experts appointed by the board of longitude to examine John Harrison's fourth chronometer. His report, published in the *Gentleman's Magazine* (1st ser., 35, 1765, 412), was cautiously favourable. In 1768 he accepted from his college the rectory of Cockfield in Suffolk, thereby vacating his fellowship, and moved to Leicester where he spent the remaining twenty years of his life, at first living with his brother Thomas in Wigston's Hospital. In 1772 he married: his wife's name is not known. Two of their children survived him.

While Ludlam appears to have contributed in early life to the *Monthly Review*, most of his writings were produced during his Leicester years. His *Rudiments of Mathematics* (1785) became a standard Cambridge textbook, passed through several editions, and was still being used in 1815. His 'Essay on Newton's second law of motion' was, however, rejected by the Royal Society. He wrote extensively on issues relating to astronomy, mechanics, and mathematical instruments, his main publications in these fields appearing between 1761 and 1771. Later works included *An Introduction to and Notes on Mr Bird's Method of Dividing Astronomical Instruments* (1786) and some mathematical essays. He also contributed to the *Gentleman's Magazine* 'A short account of church organs' (1st ser. 42, 1772, 562), and various papers relating to mechanical inventions and to astronomical observations which appeared in *Philosophical Transactions of the Royal Society*.

In 1788 Ludlam published *Two Essays on the Justification and Influence of the Holy Spirit*; this followed some earlier theological essays published in 1785. Together with some others, written by himself and by his brother Thomas Ludlam, these essays were republished posthumously under the title *Essays, Scriptural, Moral, and Logical* (1807). The essays on the Holy Spirit which came out in 1788 brought a sharp response from the evangelical academic Isaac Milner (1750–1820), whose brother, the historian and Christian apologist Joseph Milner (1744–1797), Ludlam had forcefully criticized. Such plain speaking was typical of Ludlam's life and writings and was one of the traits for which he was best remembered. Thomas Vaughan, a Leicester contemporary, presented him as a man of independent character, sound judgement, and pungent wit.

Ludlam died at Leicester on 16 March 1788; he is commemorated in a tablet on the south wall of St Mary's, Leicester, where he was buried. His instruments and models (said to have been very valuable) were sold by auction on 6 May 1788.

Thomas Ludlam (*c.*1775–1810), colonial governor, was the elder of William Ludlam's two surviving children. In early life he was apprenticed to a printer, and later joined the Sierra Leone Company. After going out to Africa he became a member of the colony's council and later served as its governor. He retired his governorship when the company's rights were ceded to the British government, and was commissioned to explore the neighbouring coast of Africa. He died on the frigate *Crocodile* at Sierra Leone on 25 July 1810.

CHARLES PLATTS, *rev.* H. K. HIGTON

Sources Venn, *Alum. Cant.* · J. Nichols, *The history and antiquities of the county of Leicester*, 2/2 (1798); repr. (1971), 733–4, 738; 4/2 (1811);

repr. (1971), 873 • E. T. Vaughan, *Some account of the Rev. Thomas Robinson* (1815) • J. Cradock, *Literary and miscellaneous memoirs*, ed. J. B. Nichols, 4 vols. (1828) • *GM*, 1st ser., 58 (1788) • *GM*, 1st ser., 80 (1810), 386–7 [Thomas Ludlam] • Nichols, *Lit. anecdotes*, 2.525; 3.639–40 [Thomas Ludlam]

Archives MHS Oxf., letters

Likenesses L. Vaslet, pastel drawing, 1785, Queen's College, Oxford

Ludlington, William [William of Littlington] (*d. c.*1310x12), Carmelite friar, probably joined the order in Stamford; his name may have derived from nearby Lyddington. He had completed his studies at Oxford and incepted as a doctor of theology when, in 1301, he was elected provincial. A few years before, the general chapter of the order had ordered the separation of the Irish and Scottish houses into a separate province; however, Ludlington, supported by many other senior Carmelites, led so fierce a resistance to this move that the prior-general, Gerardo da Bologna, was forced to appoint two commissaries, William Newenham and William Pagany, to resolve matters. Ludlington and his supporters refused to accept their commission, in spite of a chancery warrant issued on 21 January 1303 by Edward I at Gerardo's request. Finally the prior-general appealed to Pope Benedict XI (*r.* 1303–4), whose delegate, Cardinal Gentilis Montefiore, sent two German Carmelite provincials to preside over the English provincial chapter in London on 28 August 1305. At this chapter Ludlington was deposed and he and his supporters punished, Ludlington himself being sent to Paris to 'fast and study the holy scriptures' (Bale, BL, Harley MS 3838, fol. 27*v*). After completing this penance he was appointed provincial of the Holy Land and Cyprus, an honorary position by this time, and retired to Stamford. He died at the Carmelite house, Stamford, *c.*1310–12 and was buried there. Bale notes five works by him, of which only one, on St Matthew's gospel, survives in Oxford, New College, MS 47. The other four, which lack incipits, consist of a book of *determinationes*, a collection of sermons, lectures on theology, and a defence against the decision of the general chapter. RICHARD COPSEY

Sources J. Bale, BL, Harley MS 3838, fols. 26*v*–28, 58*v*–59, 162*v* • Emden, *Oxf.*, 2.1146 • Bale, *Cat.*, 1.360–61 • A. Staring, 'Guillaume Ludlington', *Dictionnaire d'histoire et de géographie ecclésiastiques*, ed. A. Baudrillart and others, 22 (Paris, 1988), 945 • J. Bale, Bodl. Oxf., MS Bodley 73 (SC 27635), fols. iv, 79*v*, 118*v*, 133 • J. Bale, Bodl. Oxf., MS Selden supra 41, fol. 162 • J. Bale, *Illustrium Maioris Britannie scriptorum … summarium* (1548), fol. 122*v* • *Commentarii de scriptoribus Britannicis, auctore Joanne Lelando*, ed. A. Hall, 2 (1709), 341 • J. Pits, *Relationum historicarum de rebus Anglicis*, ed. [W. Bishop] (Paris, 1619), 394 • Tanner, *Bibl. Brit.-Hib.*, 357–8 • C. de S. E. de Villiers, *Bibliotheca Carmelitana*, 2 vols. (Orléans, 1752); facs. edn, ed. P. G. Wessels (Rome, 1927), vol. 1, p. 603 • B. Zimmerman, ed., *Monumenta historica Carmelitana* (1907), i, 104 n., 225–7, 433

Archives New College, Oxford, MS 47

Ludlow. For this title name *see* individual entries under Ludlow; *see also* Lopes, Henry Charles, first Baron Ludlow (1828–1899).

Ludlow [Ludlowe], **Edmund** (**1616/17–1692**), army officer and regicide, was born in Maiden Bradley, Wiltshire, the son of Sir Henry Ludlow (1592?–1643) of Maiden Bradley and his wife, Elizabeth (*d.* 1660), daughter of Richard Phelips of Montacute, Somerset.

Edmund Ludlow (1616/17–1692), by Robert White, 1689

Early career Ludlow (who used the spelling Ludlowe) matriculated at Trinity College, Oxford, on 10 September 1634, aged seventeen. He graduated BA on 14 November 1636, and in 1638 was admitted to the Inner Temple. Sir Henry Ludlow represented Wiltshire in the Long Parliament, and was one of the most extreme critics of the crown. On 7 May 1642 he was rebuked by the speaker for saying that the king was not worthy to be king of England. Edmund Ludlow, moved by his father's persuasion, enlisted at the beginning of the civil war among the hundred gentlemen who formed the bodyguard of the earl of Essex. He was present at the skirmish at Worcester (23 September 1642), where the guard ran away, and at Edgehill (23 October 1642), where it distinguished itself in a more honourable manner. At the close of the first campaign he returned to his native county and became captain of a troop of horse for Sir Edward Hungerford's regiment (10 April 1643). When Hungerford took Wardour Castle, Wiltshire (8 May 1643), he appointed Ludlow its governor. Ludlow made himself famous by the tenacity with which he endured a three months' siege. His answer to the summons sent him by Sir Francis Dodington was published by the newspapers of both parties—by *Mercurius Aulicus* to show his obstinacy, by *Mercurius Britannicus* to show his fidelity.

After a short imprisonment at Oxford, Ludlow was exchanged early in the summer of 1644 and became major of Sir Arthur Hesilrige's regiment of horse in the army under Sir William Waller (10 May 1644). On 30 July 1644, however, Waller gave him a colonel's commission and sent him into Wiltshire to raise a regiment of horse. Parliament about the same time made Ludlow sheriff of his native county, and for the rest of the war he was engaged in endeavouring to reduce it to obedience. He took part, however, in the second battle of Newbury (27 October 1644), in the siege of Basing House (November 1644), and in an expedition for the relief of Taunton (December 1644). At the beginning of January 1645 his regiment was surprised by Sir Marmaduke Langdale at Salisbury, and Ludlow himself escaped with great difficulty. On the formation of the New Model the committee for the selection of officers, ardently backed by Sir Arthur Hesilrige, recommended Ludlow for the command of a regiment, but the Wiltshire committee professed that they could not spare him. Ludlow was elected as member for Wiltshire on 12 May 1646. To him the parliamentary cause was God's cause, to be understood in providentialist and apocalyptic terms. He believed in the almost total separation of church and state. He was a Baptist and worked closely with other Baptists. In theology he was a firm Calvinist predestinarian. His religious intensity did not impede his co-operation with men of other priorities. In parliament he allied with Henry Marten and the most radical critics of the monarchy. He sympathized with the Levellers and was trusted by them.

As a parliamentary speaker Ludlow did not distinguish himself, and his later political importance was due to his influence outside the Commons rather than within it. He took the part of the army in their quarrel with parliament in the summer of 1647, and signed the engagement of 4 August. But the negotiations of the army leaders with the king, and their suppression of the army Levellers, roused his suspicions. He opposed the vote of thanks given to Cromwell for his conduct at the Ware rendezvous, and was still further alienated from him by his avowed preference for monarchy. Nevertheless in the summer of 1648, when Major Huntington accused Cromwell, Ludlow wrote to encourage the latter and to promise him support. Convinced of the danger of a treaty with the king he urged Ireton and Fairfax to put an end to the proposed negotiation by force, and was one of the chief promoters of Pride's Purge in December 1648. He was appointed one of the king's judges, was present at eleven meetings of the court, and his name is the fortieth in the list of those who signed the king's death warrant [*see also* Regicides]. Charles's execution was to Ludlow a righteous use of the sword, demanded by biblical injunction, to punish tyranny and bloodguilt.

The interregnum On 7 February 1649 Ludlow was ordered to draw up instructions for the proposed council of state. He was himself elected a member of that body on 14 February, and was also a member of the second council elected in February 1650. He married, about 1649, Elizabeth (1629/30–1702), daughter of William Thomas of Wenvoe, Glamorgan, and his wife, Jane, daughter of Sir John Stradling of St Donatus in the same county.

When Cromwell returned from Ireland in June 1650 he thought it necessary to appoint a second in command to Ireton who would replace him in case of death or illness. For this post he selected Ludlow, to whom he privately vindicated his former conduct, and professed his desire to effect that reformation of the clergy and the law on which Ludlow had set his heart. Ludlow hesitated to accept, pleading the condition of his estate, but was nominated by the council of state on 27 June and approved by parliament on 2 July following. He received a commission from Cromwell as lieutenant-general of the horse in Ireland, and from parliament as one of the commissioners for the civil government of that country. In the latter capacity he was paid a salary of £1000 a year. Ludlow, however, complained that during the four years he served in Ireland he expended £4500 out of his own estate over and above his pay. He landed in Ireland in January 1651, passed the Shannon with Ireton in June, and took part in the siege of Limerick. On the death of Ireton (26 November 1651) the commissioners of the parliament issued a circular letter ordering the army to give obedience to Ludlow, but on 9 July 1652 parliament voted Fleetwood commander-in-chief.

Fleetwood did not land until October 1652, so that Ludlow held the chief command for nearly a year. Galway, the only important place in the possession of the Irish at Ireton's death, surrendered in April 1652, and the rest of the war consisted of skirmishes and capitulations. Ludlow narrated at length the hardships of campaigning in Ireland, and the severe measures which he used to force the Irish to submit. The royalist lord deputy, the earl of Clanricarde, proposed to Ludlow (March 1652) a treaty for the settlement of the country, which the latter refused, saying that the settlement of the nation belonged to the English parliament. On 22 June 1652 Ludlow concluded an agreement with Lord Muskerry for the surrender of his forces, and on 28 June the earl of Clanricarde also capitulated. Ireland was practically conquered before Fleetwood landed.

In the settlement of Ireland the confiscated estate of Walter Cheevers of Monkstown, near Dublin, was granted to Ludlow as satisfaction for his pay. Of the policy of the transplantation, and of the principles on which the settlement was based, he thoroughly approved, and he took part in the preliminary measures. The news that Cromwell had expelled the Long Parliament (20 April 1653) did not prevent Ludlow continuing to act both in his civil and military capacity. He broke with Cromwell in December, when Barebone's Parliament was dissolved and Cromwell became protector. Detestation of that 'usurpation', which Ludlow regarded as a fatal sacrifice of God's cause to the 'lust' of Cromwell's 'carnal' ambition, would stay with Ludlow all his days. On hearing of the coup he rallied opposition among the Baptists in Ireland. He obstructed for several weeks the proclamation of Cromwell as protector, and refused to sign it himself (30 January 1654).

After it took place he refused to act further as civil commissioner, lest he should seem to acknowledge Cromwell's authority as lawful, but he resolved to keep his commission as lieutenant-general until it should be forced from him. Cromwell's son Henry, who had been sent to Ireland to assess the state of feeling among the officers, attributed Ludlow's stance to the fact that the military office was the more profitable. After failing to convince Ludlow of the lawfulness of the government, Henry recommended his removal. But the protector was reluctant to proceed to extremities, and Ludlow was allowed to continue in his anomalous position until January 1655, when it was found that he was circulating pamphlets hostile to the government. Fleetwood then demanded the surrender of his commission. To avoid this Ludlow engaged to appear before Cromwell within a couple of months in order to answer the charge, and meantime to act nothing against his government (30 January 1655). But Cromwell's council preferred to keep Ludlow in Ireland, and forbade him to come to England. On receiving a second and still more definite engagement (29 August), Fleetwood gave him leave to go, but the Irish council was against it and had him arrested as soon as he landed in England (October 1655).

After remaining six weeks a prisoner at Beaumaris, Ludlow was allowed to proceed. He had an interview with Cromwell at Whitehall on 12 December 1655. Throughout he persistently refused to engage not to act against the government. He asserted that the present government was unlawful and, while denying that he was privy to any plot against it, refused to pledge loyalty lest providence should lead him into opposition. On 1 August 1656 Ludlow was again summoned before the council and ordered to give security to the amount of £5000 for his peaceable behaviour. Though threatened with imprisonment for his refusal to give security he was allowed to retire with his relations to Essex, where he spent the rest of the summer. His whereabouts in the remainder of Cromwell's lifetime are uncertain. The government was anxious to keep him out of his own county for fear he should obstruct the election of its partisans to the ensuing parliament. Both in 1654 and in 1656 a numerous party in Wiltshire wished to elect Ludlow as one of their members, but in each case the opposition of the presbyterian clergy and the influence of the government prevented it. After Cromwell's death, however, Ludlow was returned to the parliament of January 1659 to represent Hindon. At first he would not take his seat, as he objected to the oath by which members were required to oblige themselves not to act or contrive anything against the protector. Then he slipped in quietly, and, though attention was called to the fact that he had not taken the oath, was allowed to continue sitting.

Before the parliament met, Ludlow and the other leaders of the opposition had arranged their plan of campaign. He spoke often, though apparently not at length. He opposed the bill for the recognition of Richard Cromwell as protector, and sought to set limits to the protector's power over the military forces. 'I honour his highness', he declared, 'as much as any man that sits here. I would have things settled for his honour and safety, but if we take the people's liberties from them, they will scratch them back again'. He denied also the right of the members for Ireland and Scotland to sit in the house, and attacked the new upper house with special vehemence. 'The men who sat there', he protested, 'had been guilty of all the breaches upon the liberty of the people' (*Diary of Thomas Burton*, 3.145, 282; 4.173). Before and after the dissolution of the parliament he negotiated with the army leaders for the overthrow of Richard Cromwell and the recall of the Long Parliament.

The recall of the Long Parliament (7 May 1659) and the re-establishment of the Commonwealth made Ludlow a man of great importance. The parliament at once appointed him a member of the committee of safety (7 May), one of the council of state (14 May), and one of the seven commissioners for the nomination of the officers of the army (4 June). He obtained the command of a regiment in the English army (9 June), but was next month chosen commander-in-chief of the Irish army with the rank of lieutenant-general and the command of a regiment of horse and another of foot (4 July). At the end of July he landed in Ireland. There he reorganized the army, changed many of the officers, and put in their places men of his own principles. He also dispatched a brigade to England to aid in the suppression of Sir George Booth's rising. When his work was finished he appointed Colonel John Jones to command in his absence, and returned to England.

Ludlow landed at Beaumaris in October 1659 and was met by the news that Lambert and the army had again expelled the Long Parliament. After hastening to London he used all his efforts to reconcile the army and the parliament, and in conferences with the leaders of the two parties strove to moderate their animosities and make them sensible of the danger of their quarrels to the republic. The army endeavoured to win him by appointing him one of their committee of safety (26 October) and one of the committee for the consideration of the form of government (1 November). He refused to act with them, but complied so far that his parliamentary friends suspected him. He opposed the calling of a new parliament which the army announced, and objected to their scheme for the establishment of a select senate. His own plan was to summon a representative army council and to recall the expelled parliament. The essentials or fundamentals of the republican cause were to be clearly stated and declared inviolable, and twenty-one 'conservators of liberty' were to be appointed to watch over them and decide any difference between parliament and army (*Memoirs*, 2.749, 756, 759, 766).

During these discussions Ludlow learned first that Jones and the Irish army had declared for the army, and next that Sir Hardress Waller and other dissentient officers had seized Dublin Castle (13 December), arrested Jones and the other commissioners, and declared for the restoration of the Long Parliament. Accordingly he set out to restore order, and arrived off Dublin on 31 December 1659. Waller and the officers at Dublin not only refused obedience but prepared to arrest him if he landed. A few officers, however, still adhered to Ludlow, and the governor of Duncannon received him into the fort there (5 January). The Dublin officers openly charged him with neglecting his duty in Ireland and in parliament and with encouraging the usurpation of the army, accusations which he indignantly refuted in a correspondence with Waller.

Sir Charles Coote drew up articles of treason against Ludlow and the three commissioners for the civil government of Ireland, which were presented to the now restored parliament on 19 January 1660 by Colonel Bridges. The news of this impeachment met Ludlow on his return to England, and he hastened to demand a hearing. But before he could be heard Monck arrived in London. Both in his speech to the parliament on 6 February and in his letter of 11 February Monck supported Ludlow's accusers. Privately, however, he told Ludlow that he had nothing to object against him but his favour to the sectaries in Ireland, and protested his own faithfulness to the republic. Ludlow nevertheless urged his friends, in vain, to adjourn parliament to the Tower and collect their scattered forces for armed resistance. Nor was he more successful in getting parliament to set a day to justify his own conduct.

The readmission of the secluded members (21 February) put an end to all hope of maintaining the Commonwealth by parliamentary means, and Ludlow plotted a rising of the republican regiments. Obliged to leave London for fear of arrest he succeeded in getting the electors of Hindon to return him to the Convention (4 April 1660), though he dared not appear personally at the election. He was preparing to join Lambert in his abortive insurrection when he received the news of Lambert's recapture. Thereupon he went to London. He took his seat in parliament on 5 May, and distinguished himself at once by refusing to take any part in nominating the commissioners sent to Charles II at Breda. On 14 May the House of Commons ordered that all persons who had sat in judgment on the late king should be forthwith secured, and on the 18th Ludlow's election was voted void. As he lay concealed in a house near Holborn, he saw the crowds returning from welcoming Charles II to London.

Exile Ludlow did not long remain in hiding. Though he was not one of the seven regicides capitally excepted by the Commons from the Act of Indemnity, he was included among the fifty-two persons excepted for penalties less than death. At the request of the Commons the king issued a proclamation (6 June) summoning all the judges of Charles I to surrender on pain of entire exemption from pardon. Relying on the implied promise contained in this proclamation Ludlow surrendered himself to the speaker on 20 June, hoping to escape with a fine and to gain time to settle his estate. The speaker committed him to the custody of the serjeant-at-arms, who allowed him his liberty, accepting sureties for his appearance when wanted. Ludlow provided four men of straw, and waited to see what the king and the lords would do. Before long he discovered that his life was in imminent danger, and at the end of August 1660 made his way to Lewes, and escaped to Dieppe.

The government, ignorant of Ludlow's movements, thought he was still in England and offered a reward of £300 for his arrest (1 September 1660). Twice during the autumn his capture was actually announced. In October 1661 he was said to be lurking in Cripplegate. Spies reported that 40,000 old soldiers were pledged to rise in arms, and sectaries asserted that a few days would see Ludlow the greatest man in England. In reality, although Ludlow remained closely in touch with the nonconformists in England, he advised them against precipitate action, warning them that 'the Lord's tyme is not yet come' (Ludlow, *Voyce*, 1978, 11). No rumour about him was too absurd to find credit. In July 1662 he was to head a rising in the west of England. In November he had been seen at Canterbury, disguised as a sailor, and soldiers scoured Kent and Sussex to find him. It was believed that Ludlow had bound himself by an oath never to make his peace with the king, to refuse pardon and favour if they were offered to him, and to wage perpetual war with all tyrants.

Meanwhile Ludlow quietly travelled through France and established himself at Geneva. On arrival he learned of the executions of ten of his fellow regicides in England. He interpreted that measure, and the executions of four more roundheads in 1662, as barbarous acts of revenge which were certain to provoke divine vengeance. Not finding himself sufficiently assured of safety in Geneva, he moved in April 1662 to Lausanne, and in the following autumn to Vevey. On 16 April 1662 the government of Bern granted to Ludlow and his fellow fugitives, Lisle and Cawley, an act of protection by which they were permitted to reside in any of the territories of that canton. Ludlow paid a personal visit to Bern to thank the magistrates, who received him with great kindness and honour.

As soon as the English court discovered that Ludlow had found refuge at Vevey plots against his life began. Irishmen, Savoyards, and Frenchmen were successively engaged in these designs. John Lisle was assassinated at Lausanne on 11 August 1664, but the vigilance of the authorities of Vevey and his own caution frustrated all attempts against Ludlow.

The war between England and the Netherlands (1664–7) seemed to many of the exiled republicans an opportunity for re-establishing by Dutch aid the English republic. Ludlow was urged to come to the Netherlands, and was promised high command in the Dutch service and armed support in this enterprise. D'Estrades, the French ambassador there, sent him a passport to guarantee his safe passage through France. Ludlow resisted these offers. He distrusted the sincerity of the Dutch. He also regarded their decision to hand over to the English government, in 1661, three fugitive regicides, John Barkstead, Miles Corbet, and John Okey, who were executed the following year, as an act of treachery and bloodguilt, of which the Dutch must repent before God's servants could join with them. His friends were disgusted by his caution, and Colonel Blood, who was sent over to persuade Ludlow to head a rising in

England, described him as very unsuited to such an employment.

In exile Ludlow watched with great keenness the course of events in England. For more security he adopted a variant of his mother's name, and signed the letters Edmund Phillips. His wife had joined him in 1663, and remained with him for the rest of his exile. One by one he lost the companionship of his fellow regicides. Cawley died in 1666, Nicholas Love in 1682, and Andrew Broughton in 1687. In April 1684 some of the exiled whigs endeavoured to persuade Ludlow to head a rising in the west of England. Their agent found him 'no ways disposed to the thing, saying he had done his work, he thought, in the world, and was resolved to leave it to others' (*Confession of Nathaniel Wade*, BL, Harley MS 6845, fol. 269). The revolution of 1688 seemed to open to him the prospect of a return to England. The preface to the first edition of his memoirs states that he was sent for as a fit person to be employed in the reconquest of Ireland. On 25 July 1689 he took a solemn farewell of the magistrates of Vevey, telling them that the Lord had called him home to strengthen the hands of the English Gideon. He went to London, where his house became the rendezvous of the survivors of the godly and republican party. On 6 November 1689 Sir Joseph Tredenham called the attention of the House of Commons to his presence in England, and they resolved to ask the king to issue a proclamation for apprehending Ludlow, who still stood attainted of high treason. An address to this purpose was presented to the king by Sir Edward Seymour on 7 November. William III answered that the desire of the Commons was reasonable and just, and published a proclamation offering £200 reward for Ludlow's arrest. Ludlow escaped to the Netherlands, according to tories with the connivance of the king, and returned in safety to Switzerland. His death, probably in Vevey, is mentioned in Narcissus Luttrell's diary under 26 November 1692.

Ludlow was buried in St Martin's Church, Vevey, and the monument erected there by his widow in 1693 states that he died in the seventy-third year of his age. The epitaph is printed in Joseph Addison's *Travels through Italy and Swisserland* (1745, 264) and in the preface to the 1751 edition of Ludlow's *Memoirs*. Over the door of his house at Vevey Ludlow placed a board with the inscription 'Omne solum forti patria quia patris', a Christianized version of a line of Ovid ('to the brave man every land is a fatherland because God his father made it'). The authorities of Vevey set up during the nineteenth century an inscription marking the site of the house in which Ludlow lived. But in one view the inscription is wrongly placed, and should be on the house at 49 rue du Lac.

Ludlow left no children. His widow married, in 1694, Sir John Thomas, bt, and died on 8 February 1702, aged seventy-two. The best portrait of Ludlow is that prefixed to the *Memoirs*. According to a note by Thomas Holles in the copy of the 1751 edition which he gave to the public library at Bern, it is 'a bad print from a very good drawing on vellum by R. White, taken from the life when the general was in England in the reign of King William' (A. Stern, *Briefe Englischer Flüchtlinge in der Schweiz*, 1874, xi).

Ludlow's memoirs In exile Ludlow composed a huge autobiographical work, 'A voyce from the watch tower'. By the later 1660s his narrative had reached recent times, and thereafter the story, which he took up to 1685, was a record of more or less contemporary events. After Ludlow's death his manuscript came into the hands of Slingsby Bethel, who had earlier visited him in Switzerland. Although most of it is lost a substantial portion of it, covering the years 1660–77, was recovered in 1970 and is in the Bodleian Library in Oxford. A heavily rewritten and heavily abbreviated version of 'A voyce' appeared as the *Memoirs of Edmund Ludlow* in 1698–9 in three volumes, nominally published at Vevey but in reality printed by John Darby of Bartholomew Close, London. The editor was probably the deist and republican John Toland. The *Memoirs* belonged to a cluster of late seventeenth-century publications printed by Darby which included the *Discourses* of Algernon Sidney and the works of John Milton and James Harrington. They took advantage of the standing army controversy that followed the peace of Ryswick in 1697 to promote the cause of the radical and country whigs. Ludlow's puritanism was eliminated, and his views overhauled so as to make him a republican of secular outlook and country party sympathies. Although most of the autobiographical material in the *Memoirs* has a basis in Ludlow's own words, his style is transformed and there are passages of pure invention. Some doubts were expressed at the time, and again at various moments in the eighteenth century, about the authenticity of the *Memoirs* but until the 1970s they were generally accepted as authentic.

Ludlow was a prominent figure of the puritan revolution, but it is the *Memoirs* that have constituted his principal claim on posterity's attention. They have generally been at their most influential at those points where his manuscript was most extensively revised, but Ludlow's editor treated his facts less unfaithfully than his character and views, and the work, which supplies vivid accounts of Ludlow's military and political career, can still be profitably consulted. Ludlow and the *Memoirs* were admired by eighteenth-century Commonwealthsmen and radical whigs, though by the nineteenth century judgements of both the man and the work had become more critical. There were editions in 1720–22, 1751, and 1771, but that by C. H. Firth (2 vols., Oxford, 1894) supersedes earlier versions. It has extensive supplementary material. The portion of 'A voyce from the watch tower' that covers the years 1660–62 was published in the Camden series of the Royal Historical Society in 1978.

In 1691–3 four pamphlets were published, ostensibly at Amsterdam, in Ludlow's name, but really by another person or persons. Attacking the tyranny of Charles I and praising the Long Parliament they, like the *Memoirs* after them, were contributions to the radical whig cause. Comtemporaries variously attributed them to Slingsby

Bethel, John Phillips (Milton's nephew), Thomas Percival, and John Toland. An ode to Ludlow is in Thomas Manley's *Veni, vidi, vici*, 1652. C. H. FIRTH, *rev.* BLAIR WORDEN

Sources *The memoirs of Edmund Ludlow*, ed. C. H. Firth, 2 vols. (1894) • E. Ludlow, *A voyce from the watch tower*, ed. A. B. Worden, CS, 4th ser., 21 (1978) • B. Worden, 'Whig history and puritan politics: *The memoirs of Edmund Ludlow* revisited', *Historical Research* [forthcoming] • *Diary of Thomas Burton*, ed. J. T. Rutt, 4 vols. (1828) • E. S. de Beer, 'Edmund Ludlow in exile', *N&Q*, 207 (1962), 223 • E. Ludlow, 'A voyce from the watch tower', Bodl. Oxf., MS Eng. hist. c. 487 • A. Fletcher, *The outbreak of the English civil war* (1981) • R. L. Greaves, *Deliver us from evil: the radical underground in Britain, 1660–1663* (1996) • R. L. Greaves, *Enemies under his feet: radicals and nonconformists in Britain, 1664–1667* (1990) • A. Clarke, *Prelude to Restoration in Ireland* (1999) • B. Worden, *Roundhead reputations: the English civil wars and the passions of posterity* (2000) • Foster, *Alum. Oxon.* • *JHC* • *CSP dom.* • Thurloe, *State papers*

Archives Bodl. Oxf., 'A voyce from the watch tower', MS Eng. hist. c. 487

Likenesses R. White, drawing, 1689, Yale U. CBA, Paul Mellon collection [*see illus.*] • I. B. Cipriani, drawing and etching, 1760, repro. in F. Blackburne, ed., *Memoirs of Thomas Hollis*, 2 vols. (1780), 67 • Ravenet, engraving (after R. White), repro. in *Memoirs of Edmund Ludlow*, 3rd edn, 3 vols. (1751) • M. Vandergucht, line engraving, BM, NPG; repro. in E. Ward, *The history of the grand rebellion*, 3 vols. (1713) • R. White, line engraving (after drawing by R. White), BM, NPG; repro. in *Memoirs of Edmund Ludlow*, 3 vols. (1698–9)

Ludlow, George (*bap.* **1596**, *d.* **1655**). *See under* Ludlow, Roger (*bap.* 1590, *d.* after 1664?).

Ludlow, George James, third Earl Ludlow (**1758–1842**), army officer, was born on 12 December 1758, the second son of Peter, first Earl Ludlow (1730–1803), comptroller of the household to George III, and his wife, Lady Frances Lumley-Saunderson (*d.* 1796), the eldest daughter of Thomas, third earl of Scarbrough. On 17 May 1778 he was appointed ensign in the 1st foot guards, in which he rose to the rank of regimental major on 9 May 1800. He was appointed brevet colonel (1795), major-general (1798), lieutenant-general (1805), and general (1814).

Ludlow embarked for America in the spring of 1781, and was with Lord Cornwallis at the surrender of Yorktown on 17 October 1781 when he was taken prisoner and narrowly escaped execution. George Washington sent him to New York with dispatches relating to Captain Charles Asgill, who was then being held captive by revolutionary forces. After his return from America Ludlow served in Flanders in 1793–4 and lost his left arm in the affair near Roubaix on 17 May 1794. In 1800 he went to Ireland with the 2nd brigade of guards (consisting of the 1st battalions of Coldstream and 3rd foot guards), which he commanded in the Vigo expedition and in the Egyptian campaign of 1801, including the battles before Alexandria and the city's blockade. Following the breakup of the army in Egypt he held major-general's commands in the eastern counties and in Kent during the invasion alarms of 1803–4, and commanded a division in the Hanover expedition of 1805 and in the Copenhagen expedition of 1807.

Ludlow was made KB on 26 September 1804 and GCB on the reconstitution of the order in 1815. He succeeded his brother Augustus, second Earl Ludlow, as third Earl Ludlow, Viscount Preston, and Baron Ludlow, all in the peerage of Ireland, in 1811. He was created Baron Ludlow in the United Kingdom peerage on 10 September 1831. He was equerry to the prince of Wales (1784–95), a deputy governor of Berwick upon Tweed, a member of the consolidated board of general officers, a colonel in succession of the old 96th, of the 38th foot (from 1808 to 1836), and of the Scots Fusilier Guards, to which he was appointed on 30 May 1836. He died, unmarried, at his residence, Cople Hall, near Bedford, on 16 April 1842, when the titles became extinct and the Irish estates passed to the duke of Bedford. H. M. CHICHESTER, *rev.* PHILIP CARTER

Sources GEC, *Peerage* • *Army List* • *GM*, 2nd ser., 18 (1842), 92 • F. W. Hamilton, *The origin and history of the first or grenadier guards*, 3 vols. (1874)

Ludlow, John Malcolm Forbes (**1821–1911**), lawyer and social activist, was born in Neemuch, India, on 8 March 1821, the youngest in the family of two sons and three daughters of Lieutenant-Colonel John Ludlow of the East India Company, and his wife, Maria Jane, eldest daughter of Murdoch Brown, a merchant and traveller of Edinburgh. His father died very shortly after the birth, and his mother took the family back to England, and then to France in 1826. From 1829 to 1838 he was educated at the fashionable Collège Bourbon in Paris. He visited Martinique, learned a hatred of slavery, and considered becoming a French subject. He returned to Britain and was called to the bar at Lincoln's Inn on 21 November 1843, having been influenced by Bellenden Ker, the head of his chambers and a noted whig radical. Until 1874 he practised as a conveyancer.

It was for his contribution to social reform that Ludlow is most remembered. While still at Lincoln's Inn he had joined the British India Society and the Anti-Corn Law League, both of which confirmed his radical political leanings. In 1839 he also underwent a religious conversion experience which was associated, in a direct echo of his French background, with the humanitarian ideals of socialism. In 1841 he again visited the West Indies, suffering an attack of haemoptysis. His humanitarianism drew him into the company of Frederick Denison Maurice and the band of young men who surrounded him, and the combination of their enthusiasm and insights produced the Christian socialist movement of 1848 to 1854. Ludlow may reasonably be taken as the actual founder of the movement: it was his experience from 1847 of social visiting among the London poor, and his knowledge of the French co-operatives, which gave content to Maurice's theological groundwork. Whereas Maurice was always reluctant to involve himself in practical agitation and action, Ludlow was a concrete thinker who was never satisfied until ideals received some sort of institutional expression. Despite adopting the political label of socialism, however, he was always insistent that social reform rather than political organization was the appropriate priority for nineteenth-century England. He was a convinced domocrat and, unlike the other Christian socialists, he had a genuine vision of social transformation.

During the revolution of 1848 in Paris, Ludlow went there to help his sisters, and made speeches in the streets.

John Malcolm Forbes Ludlow (1821–1911), by E. Braconnier

In Britain, he went with Charles Kingsley to the Chartist demonstration. In May 1848 *Politics for the People* began publication; it lasted only until July, but the founders continued to meet, usually in Ludlow's chambers, and a night school for working men was begun. Thomas Hughes, the novelist and politician, became a helper and friend. In December 1849 Ludlow and his friends drew up the first code of rules in Britain for a working people's co-operative society. In 1850 Ludlow founded and edited a penny weekly, the *Christian Socialist*. Lectures and classes for working people were held in Castle Street East from 1853, Ludlow often teaching French. From these developed the Working Men's College, founded in Great Ormond Street in November 1854, with Ludlow as its chief lecturer, lecturing on law, English, and Indian history (the latter published in two volumes in 1858).

Ludlow was also an invaluable representative in the legislative attempts to protect working-class enterprise; in 1850 he gave evidence to the House of Commons select committee on middle-class and working-class savings, and he appeared before the royal commission on limited liability set up in 1853. In 1870 he was appointed secretary to the royal commission on friendly and benefit building societies, and from 1874 until 1891 he was chief registrar of friendly societies—years he described as 'the happiest of my life'. To the very end of his long life he continued to be consulted about these types of issues, and lived to be present at the Pan Anglican Congress of 1908, at which so many of his ideals were acclaimed. He was appointed CB in 1887.

A small, slightly built man of mild manners, a finely shaped head, and very bright, brown eyes, Ludlow was always energetic, and in addition to his legal and lecturing work maintained a steady flow of publications on a variety of subjects, and published many articles in the *Edinburgh Review*, *Fraser's*, *Macmillan's*, and the *Contemporary* and *Fortnightly* reviews. *Progress of the Working Classes, 1832–1867* (1867), written with Lloyd Jones, reflects his general position.

Though remaining attached to French protestantism—he attended the French church in London—Ludlow's contribution to Anglican social thought was important. Through his advocacy of a heightened place for deaconesses in the church, made in 1865, he may indeed be categorized as an early champion of the modern women's ministry, writing *Woman's Work in the Church: Historical Notes on Deaconesses and Sisterhoods* (1865).

In 1869 Ludlow married his cousin, Maria Sarah (*d.* 1910), daughter of Gordon Forbes of Ham Common. They had no children. Ludlow died at his home, 35 Upper Addison Gardens, London, on 17 October 1911.

E. R. NORMAN, *rev.* H. C. G. MATTHEW

Sources N. C. Masterman, *John Malcolm Ludlow* (1963) • A. D. Murray, ed., *John Ludlow: the autobiography of a Christian socialist* (1981) • E. R. Norman, *The Victorian Christian socialists* (1987) • *The Times* (19 Oct 1911) • *Working Men's College Journal* (Nov 1911) • *Co-operative News* (21 Oct 1911) • *Co-operative News* (28 Oct 1911) • *The Working Men's College, 1854–1904* (1904)

Archives CUL, corresp. and papers | Bodl. Oxf., Kingsley MSS • UCL, letters to Society for the Diffusion of Useful Knowledge

Likenesses E. Braconnier, photograph, repro. in Davies, ed., *The Working Men's College, 1854–1904* [*see illus.*]

Wealth at death £5488 17*s.* 1*d.*: probate, 22 Dec 1911, *CGPLA Eng. & Wales*

Ludlow [Lodelowe], **Lawrence of** (*d.* **1294**), merchant, was the son of **Nicholas of Ludlow** (*d.* in or before 1279), also a merchant, and his first wife, Margery, to whom he was married by 1267. Although his family took its name from Ludlow in Shropshire, the centre for Nicholas's operations was Shrewsbury, where the fine wools of the Welsh borderlands provided the basis for his fortunes. Active in the wool trade by the mid-1260s, Nicholas had important court connections; he was described as merchant to Edward I, as both prince and king, and bought cloths and skins for Edward's cousin, Henry of Almain. In the 1270s Nicholas was exporting wool (often through London) on a considerable scale, and inevitably suffered from the disruption of trade caused by English disputes with successive rulers of Flanders between 1270 and 1276, even though he was several times licensed to export wool at times of embargo—in 1274 his losses were estimated at £1928. His personal involvement made him an appropriate person to be sent to Flanders in 1276 to demand reimbursement for English losses. But in spite of his difficulties his profits remained such as to enable him to sell silver to the mint worth £900 per annum. Nicholas was dead by 20 August 1279; Margery had predeceased him, and he left a widow named Idonia. His children, at least four sons and two daughters, all appear to have been born of his first marriage.

Lawrence of Ludlow was probably the eldest of Nicholas's sons. Active as a merchant by 1272, he seems sometimes to have traded in partnership with his father and brothers, two of whom (John and Thomas) also dealt in wool. Indeed, it may not be an exaggeration to describe him as the head of a family business. His sister Cecilia's first husband, John Adrian, was a London draper who traded in wool, while her second, John Banquell, was a lawyer who might act as Lawrence's attorney. Like his father, Lawrence exported wool to the Low Countries in the 1270s (200 sacks in 1277, for instance) and afterwards; in 1285 he complained that 60 sacks destined for sale abroad had been arrested at Boston fair at the suit of a merchant of Arras. And he continued to trade in his native Shropshire—at the 1292 Shropshire eyre his name headed the list of those infringing the assize of cloth at Ludlow. His wealth enabled Lawrence to lend money to the king, who in 1291 made arrangements to repay a loan of 1000 marks, and also to lay and ecclesiastical magnates in and around Shropshire, including the earl of Arundel, Edmund Mortimer of Wigmore, Roger Mortimer of Chirk, John (V) Lestrange of Knockin (who acknowledged owing £4000), the abbot of Buildwas, and Worcester Cathedral priory. Another outlet for his capital was real estate. Lawrence bought several properties in Ludlow itself, and at the time of his death was in process of acquiring the Shropshire manors of Rowton and Ellerdine. But his most notable purchase was the manor of Stokesay, some 7 miles north-west of Ludlow, which he bought in 1281. Since he obtained rights of common for his livestock in the neighbouring manor of Sibdon, Lawrence probably did not intend Stokesay to be only a country retreat. Even so, the grant of free warren which he obtained in the year of purchase, and still more the fortified manor house which he constructed there, obtaining a licence to crenellate in 1291, may still point to social ambitions for himself and his family. The structure surviving in the late twentieth century incorporated earlier work, but the three-storied south tower, the impressive hall, with the fine timberwork of its cruck roof and staircase, and the handsome stone fireplace and decorated floor tiles in the north tower, all of the late thirteenth century, proclaimed their owner and creator as a man of wealth, taste, and standing.

Lawrence of Ludlow was clearly a capable man of affairs, with talents extending beyond commerce. In June 1294 Ralph de Tosny, lord of Painscastle in Shropshire, who was about to go overseas, made Lawrence his principal agent for the administration of his estates during his absence. The king, too, made use of Lawrence's organizational skills. 1294 saw the outbreak of war with France, and Edward I, badly in need of funds, devised ways of raising money with Lawrence's assistance. The annals of Dunstable specifically attributed a new tax on exports of wool, the so-called 'maltôte' of 40s. per sack, to Lawrence of Ludlow, describing him as *nominatissimus mercatorum* ('most renowned of merchants'; *Ann. mon.*, 3.389). And he was also involved in an accompanying scheme for raising money from wool, which was to be shipped under royal supervision to the Low Countries, and customs duties paid to the king's officers on its arrival, while its owners would also make loans to the king from the proceeds of subsequent sales. The money thus raised would go towards the substantial sums which Edward I undertook to pay to his allies, the archbishop of Cologne and the count of Bar. The latter had earlier visited England, and Lawrence was apparently involved in negotiations with the count, who was later said to have received £200 from him in London.

The fleet carrying the wool left from London under the command of Lawrence of Ludlow, whose own contribution to the king's finances was later calculated at just over £1000 in customs payments and loans, and the royal clerk Roger of Lincoln, but ran into a storm. Most of the fleet escaped destruction, but the ship carrying Lawrence and Roger was driven onto the Suffolk coast at Aldeburgh on the night of 26 November 1294, and both men were drowned. Lawrence's body was recovered from the sea and buried at Ludlow on 20 December following. With his wife, Agnes, he had at least five sons, and some of his purchases of land may have been intended to provide for them—a fragment of his will records a bequest of two messuages and seven shops in Ludlow to his youngest son, Richard. After his death his widow herself traded in wool, and in company with her eldest son, William, devoted much energy to the recovery of her husband's debts. She later married Simon Leyburn. The descendants of Lawrence of Ludlow deserted trade for a country life in Shropshire, remaining lords of Stokesay until 1497.

HENRY SUMMERSON

Sources justices itinerant assize rolls, PRO, JUST/1 · court of king's bench plea rolls, PRO, KB 27 · exchequer, king's remembrancer's memoranda rolls, PRO, E 159 · court of common pleas, plea rolls, PRO, CP 40 · court of common pleas, feet of fines, PRO, CP 25/1 · *Chancery records* · Shropshire deeds, Bodl. Oxf., MS Craven 63 · T. H. Lloyd, *The English wool trade in the middle ages* (1977) · E. Power, *The wool trade in medieval English history* (1941) · *Ann. mon.*, vols. 3–4 · M. Faraday, *Ludlow, 1085–1660* (1991) · G. A. Williams, *Medieval London: from commune to capital* (1963) · J. Munby, *Stokesay Castle, Shropshire* (1993) · J. de Sturler, 'Deux comptes enrôlés de Robert de Segre, receveur et agent payeur d'Edouard 1er, roi d'Angleterre, aux Pays-Bas (1294–1296)', *Bulletin de la Commission Royale d'Histoire*, 125 (1959), 561–612 · R. R. Sharpe, ed., *Calendar of letter-books preserved in the archives of the corporation of the City of London*, [12 vols.] (1899–1912), vol. A

Wealth at death very wealthy; properties in Ludlow: PRO, JUST/1/1413, m. 420 · loaned moneys; debts owed to him

Ludlow, Nicholas of (*d.* in or before **1279**). *See under* Ludlow, Lawrence of (*d.* 1294).

Ludlow, Roger (*bap.* **1590**, *d.* after **1664**?), colonial governor and jurist, was baptized on 7 March 1590 at Dinton, Wiltshire, the second son of Thomas Ludlow (1550–1607), landowner, and his wife, Jane (1561–1648), the daughter of Thomas Pyle of Bapton, Wiltshire. He was admitted to Balliol College, Oxford, on 16 June 1610, then entered the Inner Temple in November 1612, but was not called to the bar. He married Mary Endecott, whose parentage is unknown but who was the sister of John *Endecott, later governor of Massachusetts Bay. His first wife having died, he is said to have married Mary (1604–1664?), daughter of Philobert Cogan, in 1624. Ludlow's legal training, in combination with his devout commitment to Congregationalism, probably influenced his election as an assistant by the Massachusetts Bay Company in February 1630, during the company's final meeting in England. As an assistant and a lay leader, Ludlow, accompanied by his younger brother George [*see below*] and approximately 140 others, sailed to New England on the *Mary and John*, one of the ships that made up John Winthrop's fleet, and arrived in Massachusetts Bay in May 1630. There, they created a settlement which they named Dorchester.

Ludlow held a position of prominence in the fledgeling Massachusetts Bay Colony, becoming one of its leading citizens and a major landowner. He served for four years as an assistant to the company in Boston, and in 1634 he became deputy governor of the colony, but he was not elected to office in 1635, either because of his opposition to increasing democracy in the election of magistrates, or because he may already have had plans to leave the colony. In the same year he led a migration of Dorchester residents to Connecticut, where they settled at Windsor. In Connecticut Ludlow served as the chief officer of the commission set up by the Massachusetts government to govern the new colony, as well as holding the office of deputy governor in alternate years. His responsibilities included signing a treaty with the Pequot nation after the brief but bloody war between the settlers and the Indians in 1637–8, and serving as a delegate to the Cambridge synod of 1637, which met in order to formulate a response to the challenge presented by Anne Hutchinson and the Antinomians. By 1639 he had moved to the south-west of the colony and helped to found Fairfield.

Although Ludlow was 'stern, passionate, and demanding' and possessed a 'quick temper and a sharp tongue' (Jones, 74), he was greatly respected for his commitment to the young colony and especially for his extensive knowledge of the law. In 1639 he was involved in putting together the 'fundamental orders' which provided the basis for Connecticut's constitutional arrangements; setting out the authority of the government and methods of election. In 1646 the general court of Connecticut commissioned him to codify the laws of the colony. The resulting Code of 1650 contained some twenty original provisions, the other fifty-eight being derived substantially from Massachusetts laws, particularly the Massachusetts Bay laws and liberties of 1648. It was 'a sweeping corpus of law that described the duties and powers of every colony and town official' (Daniels, 66), and it gave Ludlow a posthumous reputation as the 'Father of Connecticut Jurisprudence'.

Ludlow had helped to set up the united colonies of New England in 1643, the first federation of the American colonies, and in 1648, 1651, and 1653 was Connecticut's commissioner to the federation. In 1653 the colonies were bitterly divided on the issue of whether to go to war with the Dutch, and Connecticut, frustrated at the delays, appointed Ludlow as their commander in preparation for an attack on the Dutch. Events went no further before the First Anglo-Dutch War ceased in 1654, by which time Ludlow had sold his Connecticut lands and sailed for Dublin, where on 3 November 1654 he was appointed commissioner for forfeited lands (perhaps on the recommendation of his relation Edmund *Ludlow, lieutenant-general of Ireland), and later the same year JP for Dublin and Cork. In February 1660 he filed a suit in chancery in England against his nephew Thomas, in which he described himself as of Dublin, and he may have been still alive in 1664 when a Mary Ludlow, wife of Roger Ludlow, was buried on 3 June at St Michan's parish church, Dublin.

Ludlow's younger brother **George Ludlow** (*bap.* 1596, *d.* 1655) was baptized at Dinton on 15 September 1596. He accompanied his brother to the Massachusetts Bay Colony on the *Mary and John* in 1630, and became a freeman of Massachusetts later that year. In 1631 he returned to England, but by 1638 had established himself in Virginia, where the land registry records that he was granted 17,000 acres of land. He served for many years as the lieutenant of York County, bearing the title of colonel, and served as a member of Virginia's council from 1642 to 1655. He died about 23 October 1655, having had no children with his wife, Elizabeth. NATALIE ZACEK

Sources *DNB* • *IGI* • B. C. Daniels, *The Connecticut town* (Middletown, CT, 1979) • A. Johnston, *Connecticut: a study of a commonwealth-democracy* (Boston, 1887) • M. J. A. Jones, *Congregational commonwealth: Connecticut, 1636–1662* (Middletown, Conn., 1968) • R. J. Taylor, *Colonial Connecticut: a history* (Millwood, NY, 1979) • A. E. Van Dusen, *Connecticut* (New York, 1961) • J. M. Taylor, *Robert Ludlow: the colonial lawmaker* (1900) • R. V. Coleman, *Roger Ludlow in chancery* (1934) • R. V. Coleman, *Mr Ludlow goes for England* (1935) • T. W. Jodziewiez, 'Ludlow, Roger', *ANB*

Ludmer, Maurice Julian (1926–1981), journalist and political activist, was born at 42 Hilton Street, Salford, on 7 August 1926, the son of Ben Ludmer, a self-employed hairdresser, and his wife, Becky, *née* Lazarus, a teacher of Hebrew. The family moved to Birmingham in 1939 where Maurice Ludmer attended Handsworth Technical College and fostered his lifelong passion for sport. He began to read avidly, joining the Left Book Club and starting to build his impressive collection of radical literature. He started an apprenticeship at the Austin Motor Works and joined the Young Communist League.

Called up for military service, Ludmer was seconded to the War Graves Commission in Europe. He visited the concentration camp at Belsen, an experience that set the tone for the rest of the twenty-year-old's life; standing at the site of atrocities which had taken place in the heart of Europe, he pledged himself to work to ensure it would never happen again. After returning to England, he did several jobs before becoming quality controller in a Birmingham knitwear factory. He met Elizabeth (Liz) Nancy Miller (1929/30–2001), a fellow political activist, in 1954, and they married at Birmingham register office on 25 June 1956. She was the daughter of Harry May, a market trader; her previous marriage had been dissolved. They had four daughters and a son, who died young, and they brought up Liz's son from a previous marriage.

Ludmer was an active Communist in the 1950s, campaigning in several local elections in Balsall Heath and working with local tenants' associations. In the late 1950s, following the Notting Hill and Nottingham race riots, he became involved with activists from racial minorities who were concerned at the development of organized racism. Ludmer, Jagmohan Joshi of the Indian Workers' Association, and others set up the first broadly based anti-racist campaign, the Co-ordinating Committee Against Racial Discrimination, which demonstrated against the first immigration control bill, passed in 1961, and in favour of legislation against racial discrimination. The need for active intervention on race issues was particularly evident in Birmingham, where immigration control committees were set up in Handsworth, West Bromwich, and Smethwick. The last became a byword for racism when the Conservative candidate won in the general election of 1964 after a blatantly racist (though unofficial) campaign which he refused to condemn. In looking back on that period Ludmer wrote, 'When people ask "How did Hitler do it?" the answer is to look at Smethwick and the way people were swept up in a tide of carefully manipulated racial hatred' (*Searchlight*).

The formation of the National Socialist Movement in 1962 was a harbinger of fascism's new role as a mass movement; this was taken a step further with the founding of the National Front, in 1967. Ludmer became involved with Searchlight Associates, a body of individuals set up to provide journalists with research material on the extreme right. In the late 1960s he resigned from the Communist Party for its failure to respond sufficiently to working-class racism, and devoted increasing time to anti-racist activity. He became a hero of the Asian community in the midlands when he played a leading role in strikes at Mansfield Hosiery in Loughborough and Imperial Typewriters in Leicester, where National Front activists were promoting racial disunity among the workforce.

From 1973 Ludmer worked full time as a freelance journalist. He collaborated with Gerry Gable in 1974 to produce *A Well Oiled Nazi Machine*, a booklet exposing the nature of the National Front, the title taken from the words of one of the party's leaders. He played a leading role in launching *Searchlight* magazine in 1975, and served first as managing editor then as full-time editor. The magazine became the culmination of his life's work, crude early issues developing into an authoritative international monthly journal exposing the British far right and their links with terror networks abroad. *Searchlight* exposed the illegal and anti-social activities of leading fascists and, most importantly, the direct ideological links between the Nazis of the 1930s and the National Front who presented themselves as an anti-immigration pressure group. For years no fascist candidate could stand for election without Ludmer providing the media with material exposing their extremism or criminality.

Anti-fascist work, while never comfortable, became more dangerous as organized skinhead gangs were recruited to the ranks of the neo-Nazis. Ludmer often suffered attack and abuse but was never intimidated. In the late 1970s he helped to found the Anti-Nazi League, which introduced a generation of young people to anti-fascist activity. He masterminded the translation of a Jewish experience into a common British one. As the obituary in his own magazine stated, his commitment was not only that of a young Jew horrified by what had been done to his people, 'for him racism was indivisible, and what had happened to the Jews in Nazi Germany could equally well happen to West Indians and Asians in post-war Britain' (*Searchlight*). The fact that such a belief became the mainstream accepted wisdom with regard to Britain's post-war fascist groups was due in no small measure to Ludmer. He suffered a stroke in February 1980 and returned to work after what was thought to be a full recovery, but had a heart attack and died at his home in Birmingham on 14 May 1981. He was buried in a Birmingham Jewish cemetery.

JAD ADAMS

Sources *Searchlight* (July 1981), 3–7 • M. Walker, *The national front* (1977) • personal knowledge (2004) • b. cert. • m. cert. • d. cert.
Wealth at death £36,878: administration, 16 July 1981, *CGPLA Eng. & Wales*

Ludovici, Anthony Mario (1882–1971), author, was born on 8 January 1882 at 88 St Augustine's Road, London, the third of the six children of Albert Ludovici (1852–1932), an artist, and his wife, Marie Cals (1850–1914). He was educated at a small private school in London and started his career as a book illustrator, then in 1906 became private secretary to the sculptor Auguste Rodin. The following year he spent in Germany, studying Nietzsche, to whose ideas he subsequently devoted himself; he was among the translators of the first English edition of Nietzsche's works and a close friend of its editor, Oscar Levy. Other readers at the British Library nicknamed the two men 'the lion and the jackal' (Levy, 126), and Ludovici portrayed Levy as Doctor Melhado in his first novel, *Mansel Fellowes* (1918). After lecturing on Nietzsche at University College, London (1909–10), he published three books about him, in which he developed the theory that 'the strong will and *must* discharge their strength, and in doing so, the havoc they may make of other beings in their environment is purely incidental' (*Who is to be Master of the World?*, 1909, 43), a belief he never abandoned. Ludovici was wounded and made a captain in the First World War in 1916, when he returned to London and worked for MI6. He was demobilized in 1919, and on 20 March 1920 he married Elsie Buckley (*d.* 1959), the daughter of Justice Buckley.

In his biweekly art column in the *New Age* (1912–14) Ludovici attacked abstraction as 'anarchy in art', leading to a fierce dispute with T. E. Hulme. He was much influenced by Nietzsche, and wrote eight novels (the best being *What Woman Wishes*, 1921) and thirty books and numerous articles on topics including aristocratic revivalism, Conservatism, social Darwinism, anti-feminism, sexology, anti-liberalism, anti-democracy, anti-alienism, race, anti-semitism, health, birth control, eugenics, and religion. Among them are *A Defence of Aristocracy* (1915), *Man: an Indictment* (1927), *The Future of Woman* (1936), and *The Specious Origins of Liberalism* (1967). Notably, he published only one of these under the pseudonym Cobbett: the antisemitic *Jews, and the Jews of England* (1938).

With Lord Willoughby de Broke, the leader of the 'diehard' peers between 1911 and 1914, Ludovici developed theories of tory revivalism, and later with Viscount Lymington and William Sanderson he established the English Mistery, a proto-fascist group devoted to creating an organic, monarchical, racially homogeneous society. In 1933 the English Mistery published Ludovici's most striking piece, *Violence, Sacrifice and War*, in which he argued that 'sacrifice' was necessary for society to function, given that excess energy had to be expended, and that the time had come consciously to select those who were to be the victims. In 1936 the group split, and Ludovici formed with Lymington the more politically oriented English Array. In the years before the war, which he called 'the war for Polish independence' (*The Child*, 1948, 20), he wrote for the English Array's *Quarterly Gazette* and for Lymington's journal, the *New Pioneer*. He wrote favourable reports on the Third Reich in 1936 for the *English Review*, travelled to Nuremberg to attend a Nazi rally, and, although not interned during the war, he was associated with the British pro-Nazis William Joyce and Francis Beckett. His claim to be a patriotic Englishman rather than a Nazi sympathizer is reminiscent of Oswald Mosley's claims.

Blaming Socrates and Christianity for society's physical and mental degeneration, under the Nietzschean slogan 'transvaluation of all values' Ludovici advocated a 'masculine renaissance', the subordination of women, the Alexander technique and correct body control, the need to apply the stock-breeder's perspective to human mating, post-natal selection, racial segregation, and a corporate community under the leadership of an aristocracy. Though involved with the Eugenics Society, he refused to join because he disagreed with its support for birth control, which he believed would be practised only by the 'better' classes.

Ludovici was noted for his striking good looks, his sartorial elegance, and his charm. He opposed the use of all bodily stimulants (though he opposed prohibition), banned his housekeeper from keeping sugar in his house in Ipswich (where he moved to escape the decadence of London), and attacked what he conceived as all forms of ugliness, bad taste, prudery, and hypocrisy in social and sexual relations. His writings on sexology, in particular, are characterized by striking frankness about sexual matters combined with an attitude towards women which sees them solely as breeding machines, physically incapable of a fulfilling sexual life which is not oriented towards child bearing. He scorned female emancipation ('no reform can come of teaching women anything'; *Man's Descent from the Gods*, 1921, 222), and at the end of his life he despaired that British society had entered into irreversible decline. Nevertheless, despite their marriage being childless, Ludovici spoke of his wife as 'one of the greatest blessings of my life' (*Confessions of an Anti-Feminist*, MS, 172).

By the end of his life Ludovici was a curious 'relic of a bygone age' (Stone, 211). A Luddite-like attack on the motor car could be combined with a call for the 'revivification of the English race through … mass murder' (ibid.). Although a key figure in the early reception of Nietzsche's ideas in Britain, he deserves to be remembered not for any direct influence he exerted, even on extreme right structures: he played no role in organized anti-feminism and held aloof from the British Union of Fascists, and it is a testimony to the strength of liberal opinion in twentieth-century Britain that his numerous writings had little influence on public discussion. His significance lies rather in the evidence his career provides that there were indigenous strains of fascism, however weak, within British thought, which in very different circumstances might have been nourished into more vigorous growth. Perhaps, too, he should be remembered for a personality which enabled him unashamedly to propagate with remarkable tenacity throughout his long life views which were politically impracticable.

Ludovici died in his London home, 78 Cadogan Place, Chelsea, on 3 April 1971 from bronchopneumonia and was buried near Diss, Norfolk. DAN STONE

Sources D. Stone, 'The extremes of Englishness: the "exceptional" ideology of Anthony Mario Ludovici', *Journal of Political Ideologies*, 4/2 (1999), 191–218 · O. Levy, 'Autobiography', MS, priv. coll. · *WW* (1970) · *Contemporary Authors: Permanent Series*, 1 (1975) · A. Ludovici, *An artist's life in London and Paris, 1870–1925* (1926) · *CGPLA Eng. & Wales* (1971) · d. cert.

Archives Bodl. Oxf., letters · Bodl. Oxf., letters, MS AUTOGR.c.26, fols. 41–67 · U. Edin., MSS, MS 3121 · University of North Carolina, Greensboro, books | JRL, letters to Francis Neilson · Wellcome L., corresp. in Eugenics Society papers, SA/EUG/C.212

Likenesses photograph, priv. coll.

Wealth at death £79,112: probate, 23 July 1971, *CGPLA Eng. & Wales*

Ludwell, Philip (*b. c.*1637, *d.* after 1710), colonial official, was the youngest child of Thomas Ludwell (*d.* 1637), a churchwarden of the parish of Bruton in Somerset, and his wife, Jane, the only daughter of James Cottington (brother to Philip, Lord Cottington) of Discoe in Bruton parish. Neither his birth nor his death is well documented. He was born shortly before, or even after, his father's death in July 1637, and he lived well beyond 1710, and perhaps 1720. His remains are in the family vault in Stratford-le-Bow churchyard, London.

The Cottingtons were royalists, and relatives of Sir William Berkeley, who was named royal governor of the Virginia colony in 1642. As a young man, therefore, Ludwell ventured to America, joining his elder brother Thomas, who was serving on the Virginia council under the autocratic Berkeley. (Since all three men were Anglicans from Bruton parish, in 1674 they bestowed that name on a newly formed Virginia parish that became the seat of the capital, Williamsburg, twenty-five years later.) In 1675 Berkeley appointed Philip Ludwell to the council and made him deputy secretary of state under his brother. (He served briefly as secretary after 1677 when his brother was absent from Virginia.) During Bacon's rebellion in 1676 he remained loyal to Berkeley's Green Spring faction, taking a key role in battles and in the trials that followed.

In or before 1667 Ludwell married Lucy (*d.* 1675), the daughter of Captain Robert Higginson and Joanne Tokesay, and the widow of Major Lewis Burwell and of Colonel William Bernard. They lived at Fairfield plantation in Gloucester county, where she bore two children who lived to maturity (Philip and Jane). But she died in 1675, so when Governor Berkeley (who also held a proprietorship in Carolina) died in England two years later, Ludwell lost little time in marrying his widow, which happened in October 1680. The powerful Frances, Lady Berkeley (1634–90), had migrated to Virginia in 1650 with her parents, Thomas and Katherine Culpeper of Feckenham parish, Worcestershire, and she was the cousin of Lord Thomas Culpeper, the grasping courtier who succeeded Berkeley as governor. Ludwell moved into his wife's estate at Green Spring, and he broadened his political base by siding with Virginia's assembly, the house of burgesses, against the governor and council.

For such bold behaviour Ludwell was twice briefly removed from Virginia's council, but he impressed the disgruntled burgesses with his opposition to the governor, Francis Howard. So in 1689 they sent him to England as their agent, where he petitioned successfully against excessive fees before the new government of King William. In London he sold off to friendly Carolina proprietors the proprietorship his wife had inherited from Sir William. In turn the proprietors of Carolina made Ludwell governor of North Carolina (5 December 1689), then of South Carolina too (2 November 1691), hoping he would improve on his corrupt predecessor, Seth Sothel. But he proved an absentee leader, looking after Culpeper land interests in Virginia and serving on the first board of visitors for William and Mary College. When he did spend a year in Charles Town he found himself caught between fierce factions on key issues—American Indian relations, illicit trade with pirates, and unfair land policies.

The proprietors replaced Ludwell as governor of South Carolina in November 1693 and of North Carolina in mid-1695, but not before he had improved land policies in that region. In 1695 he was speaker of the Virginia burgesses, continuing in that house for three years and then retiring to relative obscurity in England several years later. His son became prominent in Virginia politics, and his son-in-law Daniel Parke served as governor of the Leeward Islands. PETER H. WOOD

Sources L. S. Butler, 'Ludwell, Philip', *ANB* • M. E. E. Parker, 'Ludwell, Philip', *Dictionary of North Carolina biography*, ed. W. S. Powell (1979–96) • W. M. Billings, *Virginia's viceroy: their majesties' governor general Francis Howard, Baron Howard of Effingham* (1991) • R. L. Morton, *Struggle against tyranny, and the beginning of a new era: Virginia, 1677–1699* (1957) • C. Dowdey, *The Virginia dynasties: the emergence of 'King' Carter and the golden age* (1969) • K. M. Brown, *Good wives, nasty wenches, and anxious patriarchs: gender, race, and power in colonial Virginia* (1996) • S. S. Webb, *1676: the end of American independence* (1984) • M. E. Sirmans, *Colonial South Carolina: a political history, 1663–1763* (Chapel Hill, NC, 1966) • W. E. Washburn, *The governor and the rebel: a history of Bacon's rebellion in Virginia* (1957)

Lugaid [Lughaidh] **mac Lóegairi** (*d.* 507), high-king of Ireland, was one of twelve sons attributed to Lóegaire mac Néill; his mother was said to have been Angas ingen Ailella Tassaig. He became high-king of Ireland at some point after 482, when Ailill Molt, his predecessor, was killed. Some chronicle accounts say that Lugaid was part of an alliance which defeated Ailill Molt, but the main hand of the annals of Ulster—in general the most reliable of the chronicles—ignores him utterly, save in a brief notice of his death (in 507, repeated in 508). During his reign battles were regularly undertaken by other descendants of Niall Noígiallach, such as Coirpre and Muirchertach Mac Erccae, but Lugaid himself appears wholly inactive, which is somewhat unusual for a high-king of Ireland. It has even been suggested that he was never high-king at all, but was inserted into the regnal scheme in order to fill a gap caused by a backdating of the mission of St Patrick. However, his reign is attested in the earliest king-list, *Baile Chuinn*, and indeed in all subsequent lists.

Lugaid had at least two sons, one called Guaire, and is said to have been married to Niam, daughter of the king of the Ulstermen. His progeny, Clann Lugdach, was a lowly Uí Néill dynasty and no high-kings of Ireland came from it. The tripartite life of Patrick, with the benefit of hindsight, tells how Lugaid's father, Lóegaire, was converted by the saint while Lugaid was in his mother's womb. Patrick cursed Lóegaire on account of earlier disobedience, saying that only one king, Lugaid, would come of his offspring (that concession was granted on account of the mother's petition). Patrick said of the unborn child, 'Till he opposes me, I will not curse him' (Stokes, 1.61). However, after Lugaid became king he uttered a mocking remark about the curse on his father's descendants and in consequence was struck dead by a thunderbolt in 507, at 'Achad Forcha'. He was one of at least three fifth-century high-kings of Ireland to die by the elements and so it is possible that the story of Patrick's malediction has overlain an earlier legend of Lugaid's death by lightning. PHILIP IRWIN

Sources A. P. Smyth, 'The Húi Néill and the Leinstermen in the Annals of Ulster, 431–516', *Études Celtiques*, 14 (1974–5), 121–43 • W. Stokes, ed. and trans., *The tripartite life of Patrick, with other documents relating to that saint*, 1, Rolls Series, 89 (1887), 61 • *Ann. Ulster* • G. Murphy, 'On the dates of two sources used in Thurneysen's *Heldensage*: 1. *Baile Chuind* and the date of *Cin Dromma Snechtai*', *Ériu*, 16 (1952), 145–56 • G. Keating, *The history of Ireland*, ed. and trans. P. S. Dineen, Irish Texts Society, 9 (1908), 47–9 • M. C. Dobbs, ed. and trans., 'The Ban-shenchus [pt 2]', *Revue Celtique*, 48 (1931), 163–234, esp. 180 • M. A. O'Brien, ed., *Corpus genealogiarum Hiberniae* (Dublin, 1962)

Lugar, Robert (1772/3–1855), architect, was the son of Edward Lugar, a carpenter of Colchester. He established himself in London *c.*1799, and exhibited at the Royal Academy from that date on; in due course he developed a very widespread practice as a country-house architect, which extended to Scotland and Wales as well as throughout much of England. He also published a number of books of his designs, which doubtless served to publicize his name. The first two—*Architectural Sketches for Cottages, Rural Dwellings, and Villas* (1805; repr. 1815 and 1823) and *The Country Gentleman's Architect … Designs for Farm Houses and Farm Yards* (1807)—were purely pattern books, but the subsequent volumes were records of executed projects: *Plans and Views of Buildings Executed in England and Scotland, in the*

Castellated and other styles (1811; 2nd edn, 1823) and *Villa Architecture: A Collection of Views, with Plans, of Buildings Executed in England, Scotland* (1828). The last of these was dedicated to the south Wales ironmaster William Crawshay, for whom Lugar designed his largest work, Cyfartha Castle, Glamorgan (1825).

Lugar was a practitioner of the Picturesque after the manner of John Nash and Humphry Repton, working in a wide variety of architectural styles including the 'Grecian', the Tudor Gothic, and that of the *cottage ornée* as well as the castellated. At Gold Hill (later Dunstall Priory), Shoreham, Kent (1806), he produced a notably early example of a villa in the Italianate vernacular style of Nash's Cronkhill, Shropshire, and at Balloch Castle, Dunbartonshire (1809), he was among the first to introduce the picturesquely asymmetrical castle form into Scotland; but he was a designer of only limited ability, who frequently reduced the process of picturesque composition to a meagrely detailed routine formula of only marginal asymmetry.

Lugar also served as county surveyor for Essex from 1812 to 1816, and became a freeman of Colchester in 1812. The architect Archibald Simpson of Aberdeen was his pupil. He died in Pembroke Square, Kensington, where he lived in retirement, on 23 June 1855, aged eighty-two.

PETER LEACH, *rev.*

Sources Colvin, *Archs.* • [W. Papworth], ed., *The dictionary of architecture*, 11 vols. (1853–92)

Dame Flora Louise Lugard, Lady Lugard (1852–1929), by George Charles Beresford, 1908

Lugard [*née* Shaw], **Dame Flora Louise**, **Lady Lugard** (**1852–1929**), journalist and author, was born on 19 December 1852 at 2 Dundas Terrace, Woolwich, the fourth of fourteen children of Captain George Shaw (1822–1892) of the Royal Artillery and Marie Adrienne Josephine, *née* Desfontaines (1826–1871), of Mauritius. She had nine sisters, the first and last dying in infancy, and four brothers. Her paternal grandfather was Sir Frederick *Shaw, third baronet (1799–1876), of Bushy Park, Dublin, and a member of parliament from 1830 to 1848, regarded as the leader of the Irish Conservatives. Her paternal grandmother, Thomasine Emily, was the sixth daughter of the Hon. George Jocelyn, and granddaughter of Robert, first earl of Roden. Although the children of George and Marie Shaw were baptized in their mother's Roman Catholic faith, they were brought up in the Anglo-Irish protestant tradition of their father. As a young woman Flora Shaw had a crisis of faith during her mother's fatal illness; later she explored different religious traditions and found spiritual renewal in the beauty of nature. Identifying her heritage as Irish and French, she became fluent in French on visits to relatives in France. She closely followed the politics of Ireland, initially approving Gladstone's moves for home rule, but soon opposing; in 1914 she actively supported Ulster resistance to home rule.

Flora Shaw, who became the first woman on the permanent staff of *The Times* and its colonial editor from 1893 to 1900, had no formal schooling, but read widely in the library of the Royal Military Academy in Woolwich. When she was seventeen John Ruskin, then Slade professor at Oxford, became her mentor and introduced her to the ageing Thomas Carlyle. She left home at the age of twenty, after the remarriage of her father, to visit relatives in France and Ireland, and, in the role of housekeeper-governess, to stay with the family of Colonel Brackenbury (a cousin by marriage) at Aldershot and then at Waltham Abbey. Encouraged by Ruskin, she wrote her first children's book, *Castle Blair* (1877), set in contemporary Ireland, which gained wide acclaim and was reprinted in numerous editions. This was followed by two novels serialized in *Aunt Judy's Magazine*, *Hector* (1880–81) and *Phyllis Browne* (1882–3), the former published as a book in 1881, and then by *A Sea Change* (1885). All four books were published in the United States as well, but she never again attained her initial success. After the failure of her novel for adults, *Colonel Cheswick's Campaign* (1886), she gave up writing fiction.

In 1883 a rented room in Little Parkhurst, a cottage in the Surrey woods near Abinger, became Flora Shaw's retreat from London and eventually—remodelled with an adjoining cottage—her lifetime home. Like many unmarried women of her social class, she undertook charity work in the slums of London's East End, where she became convinced that Britain's poverty could be solved only by emigration to its colonies. Required to earn her living, she took up journalism at the suggestion of her Surrey neighbour George Meredith. He introduced her to the editor of the *Pall Mall Gazette*, W. T. Stead. On Gibraltar, accompanying elderly family friends in the winter of 1886–7, Shaw interviewed the political prisoner Zobehr

Pasha, who claimed he could have saved General Gordon's life had the British government granted Gordon's request for Zobehr to join him in Khartoum. In her article, featured on the front page of the *Pall Mall Gazette* on 28 June 1887, she pointedly questioned British justice. Within six weeks Zobehr was released and on his way back to Cairo. Shaw's apprenticeship under Stead, who conducted numerous newspaper campaigns to rouse public opinion, led her to view journalism as a form of politics.

In Egypt during the winter of 1888–9 Shaw became correspondent for both the *Pall Mall Gazette* and the *Manchester Guardian*. With frequent briefings from Sir Evelyn Baring, consul-general advising the khedive, she reported on progress under the British occupation. Back in London she continued freelance journalism. She began her long association with Cecil Rhodes, whose visionary ideas on the expansion of self-governing colonies within the empire she found compelling. Her opportunity to write for *The Times* came in the spring of 1890 when C. F. Moberly Bell, its correspondent in Egypt, who had been impressed with her abilities, was recalled to London as assistant manager. He told her, 'If you were a man you would be Colonial Editor of *The Times* tomorrow' (Bell, 92). She began writing articles and, in November, initiated a fortnightly column, 'The colonies', which was to continue throughout the decade. Charles Mills, the London agent for Cape Colony, described her as 'an exceedingly clever, fascinating lady who has thoroughly studied and mastered South African politics' and recalled how Joubert, whom she interviewed, 'was delighted with her, and could not believe that a Lady could know so much, and ask such searching and pertinent questions' (letter to J. X. Merriman, 14 Aug 1890; *Selections*, 2.8).

In order to recover from severe influenza in early 1892, Shaw sailed to South Africa. Here she went down diamond and goldmines, investigated labour conditions, and assessed prospects for agriculture. Her 'Letters' so impressed the management of *The Times* that she was asked to report from Australia and New Zealand. After circling the globe, she returned to London in July 1893 to gain a permanent position as colonial editor at an annual salary of £800, higher than other women journalists of her day. Macmillan published her *Letters from South Africa* and *Letters from Queensland* in 1893. With an assured income, she set up a household with three younger unmarried sisters at 130 Cambridge Street, London. She was generous in helping her family, particularly with funds for her nephews' schooling.

During the 1890s, when imperial rivalry among European powers reached its highest pitch, Flora Shaw wrote over 500 articles, leaders, and columns for *The Times* promoting British imperial interests. Later she assessed her achievements:

> To have helped to rouse the British public to a sense of Imperial responsibility and an ideal of Imperial greatness, to have had a good share in saving Australia from bankruptcy, to have prevented the Dutch from taking South Africa, to have kept the French within bounds in West Africa, to have directed a flow of capital and immigration to Canada, to have got the Pacific cable joining Canada and Australia made, are all matters that I am proud and glad to have had my part in. (Shaw to Sir Frederick Lugard, 13 Nov 1904, Lugard MSS)

She coined the name Nigeria on 8 January 1897 in an article in *The Times* about the west African territories under the jurisdiction of the Royal Niger Company. The first woman to speak at the Royal Colonial Institute, she talked on 'the Australian outlook' and colonial expansion in 1894, and on the Klondike in 1899. She also spoke at the Scottish Geographical Society and the Royal Society of Arts. Her younger contemporary Mary Kingsley described her as

> a fine, handsome, bright, upstanding young woman, as clever as they make them, capable of any immense amount of work, as hard as nails and talking like a *Times* leader all the time. She is imbued with the modern form of public imperialism. It is her religion. (Kingsley to John Holt, 20 Feb 1899, Holt MSS)

The extent of Shaw's involvement in imperial politics became dramatically exposed in 1897 when on 25 May and 2 July she was called before a select committee of the House of Commons inquiring into Jameson's military raid into the Transvaal. She had to explain incriminating telegrams discovered between her and Rhodes, which raised suspicions that she had been the link in a collusion between Rhodes and the colonial secretary, Joseph Chamberlain. She deftly parried questions, protecting the reputation of *The Times* and the colonial secretary. When gold was discovered in the Klondike she travelled for five months in 1898 to the Canadian far north and roused political controversy by exposing official corruption in the Yukon. During the dark days of the Second South African War in February 1900 she wrote four patriotic articles asserting Britain's sovereignty over the Dutch republics in South Africa, which were republished in several European languages as a propaganda pamphlet subsidized by the government. Exhausted by a decade of intense work, she resigned from *The Times* on 1 September 1900.

Flora Shaw had deep romantic attachments—with Colonel Charles Brackenbury during the years before his death in 1890 and, in the late 1890s, with Sir George Goldie, founder of the Royal Niger Company; but there is no evidence that these relationships went beyond Victorian propriety. On 11 June 1902, in Madeira, at the age of forty-nine, she married Sir Frederick John Dealtry *Lugard (later Baron Lugard) (1858–1945), then high commissioner of Northern Nigeria, and later governor of Hong Kong (1907–12) and governor-general of Nigeria (1912–19). Ill health in Nigeria caused Lady Lugard to return to England, where she wholeheartedly supported her husband's career through her political and social networks and by praising his administration in Northern Nigeria in her book *A Tropical Dependency* (1905). She accompanied him to Hong Kong and, despite illness, helped gain financial support for founding the University of Hong Kong, and travelled extensively in Japan and China. Her work for Belgian refugees during the First World War led to her creation as a DBE in 1916. A full partner in her marriage, she regarded both to be serving the imperial cause. She died after chronic illness at her home,

Little Parkhurst, on 25 January 1929 and was cremated at Woking on 30 January. She was considered 'a crusader and an intriguer' by historians of *The Times*, who stated, 'By her powerful mind and compelling personality she directly influenced policies and statesmen and did much to restore the somewhat battered image of *The Times* bequeathed by the episode of the Pigott forgeries' (Woods and Bishop, 158).

DOROTHY O. HELLY and HELEN CALLAWAY

Sources E. M. Bell, *Flora Shaw (Lady Lugard D.B.E.)* (1947) • *Selections from the correspondence of J. X. Merriman*, ed. P. Lewsen, 4 vols. (1960–69), vol. 2 • M. Perham, *Lugard*, 2 vols. (1956–60) • O. Woods and J. Bishop, *The story of The Times: bicentenary edition, 1785–1985* (1985) • F. Shaw, *The work of the War Refugees Committee: an address by Lady Lugard to the Royal Society of Arts, March 24, 1915, and reports of the Lady Lugard Hospitality Committee* (1915) • [S. Morison and others], *The history of The Times*, 3 (1947) • birth record, St Catherine's House • *The Times* (28 Jan 1929) • Bodl. RH, Lugard MSS • Bodl. RH, Holt MSS

Archives Bodl. RH | BL, corresp. Lord Gladstone, Add. MSS 46078–46081 • CAC Cam., Stead MSS • Harvard U., Houghton L., Norton MSS • News Int. RO, *The Times* archive

Likenesses photograph, *c*.1866–1869 (portrait in pearls, white dress), priv. coll. • photograph, *c*.1880–1889 (portrait with high ruffled collar), Harvard U., Houghton L., Charles E. Norton MSS • photograph, *c*.1880–1889, repro. in [Morison and others], *History of the Times*, 162 • photograph, *c*.1902 (in white dress at time of marriage), repro. in Bodl. RH, MSS Lugard 160/4, no. 1 • photograph, 1902 (in professional black silk gown), repro. in *Lady's Pictorial* (March 1902), Bodl. Oxf., N. 2288, b.21, 316 • two photographs, *c*.1902–1916, repro. in Bell, *Flora Shaw*, 34, 274 • photograph, *c*.1904 (in front of new door to home, Little Parkhurst, Abinger, Surrey), repro. in Bodl. RH, MSS Lugard 160/4, no. 2 • photograph, *c*.1907, Bodl. Oxf. • photograph, *c*.1907, repro. in A. Wright, ed., *Twentieth century impressions of Hong Kong* (1907), frontispiece • G. C. Beresford, photograph, 1908, NPG [*see illus.*] • J.-E. Blanche, portrait, 1909, priv. coll. • photograph, *c*.1910 (formal pose, sitting in draped chair), Yale U., Howell Wright Papers • photograph, *c*.1912 (on balcony at 51 Rutland Gate, London), priv. coll. • A. Cluysenaar, portrait, 1919?, repro. in Bell, *Flora Shaw*, frontispiece • caricature, repro. in *Punch* (20 Jan 1894) • caricature, repro. in *Punch* (29 May 1897)

Lugard, Frederick John Dealtry, Baron Lugard (1858–1945), governor-general of Nigeria, was born at Fort St George, Madras, on 22 January 1858, the eldest son of Frederick Grueber Lugard (1808–1900), a senior chaplain on the Madras presidency establishment, and his third wife, a missionary, Mary Jane (*d*. 1865), daughter of John Garton Howard, vicar of Stanton by Dale, Derbyshire. The family returned to England in 1863 and soon settled in Worcester, where Lugard's father had obtained a living. Two years later his mother died. In 1871 he was admitted to Rossall School, from where he passed into the Royal Military College, Sandhurst, chosen over a possible career in the Indian Civil Service under the influence of the fact that his uncle General Sir Edward Lugard, who had earned distinction in the Anglo-Sikh wars and the Indian mutiny, was permanent under-secretary at the War Office from 1861 to 1871.

Soldier, 1878–1886 Lugard was commissioned into the 9th (East Norfolk) regiment in 1878, after only eight weeks at Sandhurst, and in the same year joined the 2nd battalion in India. He served in Afghanistan in 1879–80 but because of illness saw little action and was soon invalided home.

Frederick John Dealtry Lugard, Baron Lugard (1858–1945), by Elliott & Fry, 1893

Slight but wiry in build, he was endowed with great powers of endurance, and on his return to India in 1881 he developed a reputation for big game hunting and pig-sticking. He applied this stamina equally to his soldiering, managing to pass the higher standard examinations in Hindustani and in Urdu at the same time as his promotion exam. His lifelong habit of working far into the night dates from this double undertaking. His private means, however, were scant, and it was this that led him to put in for leave in 1884 and secure secondment to the better paid military transport service under Captain (later General Sir James) Willcocks. Lugard's first contact with the civil side of imperial administration came when he joined his half-brother Henry, now in the Indian Civil Service, on a tiger hunt. His first encounter with Africa came in the following year when his unit was ordered to the Sudan to support the expedition for the relief of Khartoum. He saw action in the severe fighting round Suakin. In 1886 he went as transport officer with the field force dispatched to Burma following the overthrow of King Thibaw. For these services he earned four mentions in dispatches and was made DSO in 1887. Lugard was well on the way to becoming a successful soldier.

Adventurer Six months later Lugard's military career had ended and he found himself without employment, penniless, and contemplating suicide as he headed for an uncertain job in an unknown land. Towards the end of his

Burma posting, and ill with fever, he had received a telegram from India which prompted him to apply for immediate leave. While in command of transport at Lucknow in 1886 he had met an attractive and high-flying divorcée. She felt challenged by his image as a man's man, he found an outlet for his deeply affectionate nature, and a brief but intense relationship ensued. Known only as Celia, she is today identified as Frances Catherine Gambier. Injured in a coach and four accident in Lucknow and apparently on her deathbed, she called for him. He hastened to India, only to find she had already recovered enough to sail for England. He followed at once, to be shattered at catching up with a different kind of woman from the one he had known, and already re-engaged in her philandering ways. Disillusioned and distraught, his reaction was to throw himself into danger, seeking destruction as a volunteer in London's new fire brigade. His resignation of his commission was not accepted, and even a posting to the 1st battalion of his regiment in Gibraltar was still too near to Celia, though she continued to write until at least 1903 (in 1899 she sent him a poem she had written for him entitled 'Adieu') about her daughter, Kitty Maunsell, who twice stayed with the Lugards at Abinger after her mother's death. Placed on medical leave, and knowing something of Sir John Kirk's work against the slave trade in Zanzibar as well as coming across a copy of Rider Haggard's novel *The Witch's Head* (1884) in which the hero, crossed in love, flees to Africa, Lugard too now headed for oblivion. Nothing came of his hope for anti-slavery work in Zanzibar, so he altered course for Abyssinia (Ethiopia), to join the Italian army in Massawa. Discouraged by the lack of action there ('active hard work' was his prescription for recovery), he crossed to Aden; he toyed with the idea of being a white hunter in Somaliland, thought about making his way to the beleaguered Emin Pasha on the upper Nile, contemplated applying for a job with the new East Africa Company, and ended up in Mozambique, hired to hunt elephants and sell their tusks to the African Lakes Company in Nyasaland. Lugard's initiation into Africa was under way.

Company employee: (i) Central Africa, 1888–1889 Lugard's first assignment was to lead the company's expedition against Arab slave traders. He had already seen enough of the effects of slaving by Arabs along the east African coast to be convinced that the only solution was to take action against the raiders in the hinterland. Nyasaland was then one of the principal centres of slave-taking. Thus satisfied of the morality of the company's occupation, Captain Lugard assumed its command and reached the station at Karonga in May 1898. His force was ill equipped but Karonga was saved, though he himself was severely wounded and temporarily lost the use of his left arm.

(ii) East Africa, 1889–1890 Following a disagreement with Gerald Portal, consul-general in Zanzibar, on what should be done in Nyasaland, Lugard reached England in 1889. His exploits had brought his name to the attention of Cecil Rhodes and also of William Mackinnon, founder of the Imperial British East Africa Company. When Rhodes backed out of a proposal that Lugard should administer the interests of his British South Africa Company in Nyasaland, and after bitterly watching the official appointment there, which he felt he deserved himself, go to Harry H. Johnston, Lugard, still on the army list, accepted Mackinnon's offer of opening up a new route from Mombasa into the interior. No sooner had he pushed through as far as Machakos than the Imperial British East Africa Company ordered him to proceed to Uganda. After a forced march, much of it through Maasai country, his caravan crossed the Nile in December 1890. The second phase of his African career had opened. For the next four years Uganda was to dominate Lugard's attention.

(iii) Uganda, 1890–1892 Affairs in Uganda were in chaos. Anglican missions had established themselves in 1877 and French Catholic ones in 1879, but in 1882 Muslim propaganda gained ascendancy among the Ganda. Mwanga, *kabaka* of Buganda, was deposed and in 1888 the Muslims temporarily occupied his capital, Mengo. They were driven out a year later and Mwanga, now under the patronage of the French White Fathers, was restored. Finally, in 1890 Karl Peters secured a treaty from Mwanga which favoured German intervention. Lugard set up camp in nearby Kampala, running up the company flag on 18 December 1890. He obtained a treaty from Mwanga granting him, as the company's agent, the right to intervene in the affairs of Buganda. With his escort of Sudanese soldiers reinforced by a small detachment serving the company, he now set about imposing some kind of order on Buganda and the other chiefdoms, crushing opposition when he encountered it. Penetrating to the south, he enlisted a further 600 Sudanese soldiers left behind by Emin Pasha and Stanley.

On returning to Kampala, Lugard found that fighting had broken out between the two Christian factions. His headquarters were attacked by the French Catholics. Lugard received orders to evacuate Uganda because the company could no longer afford to maintain its presence there. Although temporary respite was secured through the raising of funds from the missionary societies in England, Lugard decided to go to London and appeal against the withdrawal, which he considered a tragedy for the fractured Uganda. The British government's decision not to intervene over the company's evacuation led him publicly to participate in the campaign by the missionary and anti-slavery societies to force Gladstone to assume responsibility for the administration of Uganda. The affair took on an international as well as a political dimension, during which Lugard's own conduct in Uganda was attacked by French missionaries and by the French government on the ground of alleged atrocities.

Most disturbing of all, a secret report had been written by Captain R. L. Macdonald, who had arrived in Kampala as head of the railway survey party on the eve of Lugard's departure in 1892. Junior to Lugard in every respect, Macdonald had nevertheless been commissioned to draw up a report for the British government to 'explain the causes of the outbreak and the action of British officials'. It was eighteen months beyond the events it described before the cabinet took the report; by then its faith in Portal's endorsement was shaken by reservations about Macdonald's own conduct. A cabinet committee was set up and Lugard was invited to defend himself against the charges. His reputation and future were on the line. In the end Lugard's character was vindicated as much by the course of events in Uganda as by the government's shelving of the report (it was never published) as inconclusive and by the Foreign Office's readiness to drop the whole affair. By this conclusion Lugard's actions were explained and excused, if not justified. Anxious to clear his name as well as to persuade the government to accept responsibility for Uganda, he now publicly presented his case in a somewhat hastily written book, *The Rise of our East African Empire* (1893). Overall, his vigorous involvement in the campaign to retain Uganda can be said to have influenced the government to dispatch a commissioner to Uganda, resulting in the country's being declared a British protectorate in 1894. Yet once again, as with Nyasaland and the appointment of Johnston, it was a moment of chagrin for Lugard: the commissioner was not to be himself but Portal.

(iv) West Africa, 1894–1895 Despite any disenchantment over his experience of two companies and his longed for but dwindling hope of returning to east Africa in senior government service, Lugard now embarked, however hesitatingly, on another roving company expedition. An offer of service came from Sir George Goldie, who had obtained a charter for his Royal Niger Company and in 1894 was busily concluding treaties with local chiefs so as to strengthen the company's capacity to repel the encroachments of the French in the Niger region. Aware that they were preparing an expedition to Borgu, Goldie wanted Lugard to proceed to Nikki, its chief town, and to forestall the French and Germans by securing a treaty from the ruler. In a rapid and remarkable march through unexplored country, Lugard won the so-called 'steeplechase to Nikki', to the dismay of the French, who had no doubt about the motives of one whom they stigmatized as 'the conqueror of Uganda'.

(v) Southern Africa, 1896–1897 A brief interlude in southern Africa followed. Lugard left the Niger in April 1895, still hoping that the government would ask for his services in Africa. Agonizingly, his appointment as CB brought nothing more with it, so he accepted an offer from yet another African company, the new British West Charterland Company, and set off to explore a mineral commission near Lake Ngami in Bechuanaland. Here the main problem was not fighting but transport. The journey involved 700 miles across the Kalahari Desert, and a rinderpest epidemic had emptied the country of trek cattle. Nevertheless, the journey was accomplished by September 1896. In the following August, Lugard received an urgent and surprise message from the new colonial secretary, Joseph Chamberlain, inviting him to take up work in west Africa. It was an imperial appointment at last. What Lugard called his 'destiny to Africa' entered its third phase: after central and east Africa, henceforth it was to be west Africa. It turned out to be the longest connection of them all.

Imperial appointments: (i) Nigeria, 1897–1906 The cause of this turnabout in Lugard's fortunes was basically that which had previously taken him to Borgu. In the interval, continuing French expansion had built up such a perilous state of tension in the region that Chamberlain—whom Lugard knew and who had earlier shown sympathy with Lugard's assessment of the French presence there—determined to check France on the Niger by creating a military force of 2000 African soldiers. The fact that his chosen man of action was hated by the French was, in Chamberlain's eyes, a bonus. Lugard was appointed in 1897, with the dual title of her majesty's commissioner for the Nigerian hinterland and, in the temporary rank of colonel, commandant of the West African frontier force which he was to raise. As his second in command he asked for his old transport chief from India, Colonel Willcocks. The force was soon committed to implementing the Chamberlain–Lugard policy on the Niger, though Lugard's strategy was a far more forward one than Chamberlain's chessboard policy. Lugard's promotion to substantive major came in 1896 and to lieutenant-colonel in 1899.

In 1900 the government terminated the Niger Company's charter and declared a protectorate over Northern and Southern Nigeria. Lugard's African record made him a prime candidate for the first charge of the north. Although the company had entered into treaties with a number of chiefs, it had taken no effective steps to bring the area above the Niger–Benue confluence under administration. Some of the Fulani states in Hausaland enjoyed an established military history and could be expected to fight for their independence. Lugard's time in Africa had taught him how a combination of military force and firm diplomacy could ensure control. It had also given him a realistic and statesmanlike conception of the relationship which could most effectively exist between an administrator and chiefs. A long-suffering War Office gazetted him in the temporary rank of brigadier-general and in 1900 Lugard assumed office as high commissioner of Northern Nigeria, and was appointed KCMG a year later. Thus reinstated in official esteem, Lugard's transformation from seconded soldier to imperial administrator was complete.

It was not in public life alone that Lugard now entered the establishment. He came to know well Flora Louise Shaw [*see* Lugard, Dame Flora Louise (1852–1929)], the brilliant colonial editor of *The Times*, whom he had first encountered, in reproof, when he had gone to seek a sympathetic review of his forthcoming book on east Africa. Her admiration of Chamberlain and Goldie brought her and Lugard closer. Their friendship deepened, and during his first tour in Nigeria they married, in Madeira, on 11 June 1902, he sailing from Lagos and she, a month before the wedding, from England. Together they returned to Nigeria, sailing up the Niger to Government House at Lokoja.

Lugard's administrative staff was small and his finances restricted, but the speed with which he brought the protectorate under control was remarkable. A measure of force was inevitable, but by 1902 the kingdoms of Nupe,

Kontagora, Yola, and Bauchi had submitted, and Bornu too, despite the confusion generated in the north-east by Rabeh, the French, and the Germans. A greater trial of strength, however, would clearly be called for in such traditional strongholds of Fulani supremacy as the emirates of Sokoto, Kano, and Katsina. Lugard, well aware that the Colonial Office was opposed to armed intervention, did not hesitate: the office could be told later that the expeditionary force had already been ordered to advance. He marched against Kano, which surrendered in early 1903, and Sokoto fell in March after a brief battle. Lugard, gaunt and dust-covered, and looking anything but a high commissioner, rode into the sultan's capital, and on 21 March delivered a subsequently famous address in which he elaborated the principles of British rule outlined in Kano a fortnight earlier. The chiefs were to be recognized and supported, yet firmly guided by British officials in their rule and unambiguously controlled in the abolition of slave trading and the administration of taxation and justice. Under this system of indirect rule, which Lugard codified and with which both his name and his major writings are indissolubly linked, the traditional rulers were not to be treated as semi-sovereign princes in the Indian and Malayan fashion but as an integral part of a single administration. By 1905 the protectorate was functioning well, though in the first months of 1906 the thunderclap news of a grave setback at Satiri, where British officials were murdered, and of an armed revolt in Hadeija—both resulting in military reprisals and heavy casualties—clouded his achievement.

Lugard resigned his post in September 1906. If he felt dissatisfied with the restraints put on him, the Colonial Office was equally disturbed by the frequent friction that coloured relations and by his military tendency to act first and request permission after. On both sides, too, there was the irritation of the idea he urged on Whitehall of allowing him, quite exceptionally, to carry on the administration of Northern Nigeria while he was on leave in England. The scheme had been devised by both the Lugards, combining his continuous distrust of the Colonial Office and its senior officials, his reluctance ever to take a holiday, and his inability to delegate with his desire to spend as much time as possible in England with his wife, whose health had broken down after five months in Nigeria and who could not return there. Together they conjured up a new dimension of tropical administration at the Colonial Office, with Lugard spending half the year in his territory and the other half administering it from Downing Street. The office was less than enthusiastic, especially when Lady Lugard published an article in *The Times* praising the merits of the scheme. Colonial Office staff felt alienated and sidetracked. In March 1906 the much lobbied scheme was ruled out and Lugard was recalled for consultation. Disappointed by what he interpreted as Lord Elgin's reneging on a promise given by his predecessor, Alfred Lyttelton, disillusioned by his reception at the Colonial Office, and determined never again to let Africa come between him and Flora, Lugard sent in his resignation.

(ii) Hong Kong, 1907–1912 But private leisure and unemployment were to the taste of neither Lugard: both were essentially public figures. So, somewhat surprisingly, within the year the Colonial Office offered, and Lugard accepted, the governorship of Hong Kong. Although the routine duties of a long-established governorship and the ceremonial functions it involved had little appeal for him, he found some outlet for his energy in educational enterprise and he was largely responsible for the creation of the University of Hong Kong, which he opened a few days before he left in March 1912. At the same time Hong Kong offered a better likelihood of Flora's coming out to join him, though in the event her poor health quickly militated against a shared life in Government House. Lugard was advanced to GCMG in 1911.

(iii) Nigeria, 1912–1918 Hong Kong turned out to be only an interlude in Lugard's fifteen years' service in Nigeria. In 1911 the Colonial Office had privately sounded him out on whether he would consider the post of governor of the single unit of Nigeria which it intended to create out of the current two protectorates and colony. 'We are agreed that you are the right man', Sir Reginald Antrobus added. Lugard weighed grave considerations of his wife's health against his belief that here was 'the biggest job in the whole empire' and one which would set the seal on his work in Nigeria. He accepted, taking his Chinese servant, A. You, with him. From September 1912, as governor of both territories, he drew up a plan of amalgamation (not of unification), and from December 1913 he was given the personal title of governor-general against the inauguration of the single Nigeria on new year's day 1914. It was a rank not revived until 1954.

Despite the extra burden resulting from establishing a new government during a war which brought severe fighting to its eastern border, Lugard did not shirk the labour involved. His industry was indomitable and his abnormal hours of work were legendary; so too was his will to retain everything possible in his own hands. Yet a grim crisis occurred in his confident extension of the principles of indirect rule from the emirates, where the system had worked well, to the very different kingdoms of Yoruba. It took place in Abeokuta, the capital city of Egbakoo, initially in 1914 with disorders centred on his interpretation and definition of sovereignty, and again in 1918, when a grave breakdown of law and order occurred. Troops were ordered in, over 500 people were killed, and a commission of inquiry was set up. The report, which was critical of the local administration, was not submitted until after Lugard had left Nigeria. It criticized him for pushing through a major reorganization during wartime and with insufficient staff. The report was not made public, but the tragedy cast a shadow over his last year in Lagos. A quarter of a century later he confided to his biographer, 'You will blame me about Abeokuta.'

Indeed, however justifiably his name is linked with Nigeria, much of Lugard's term of office there was scarred. There was, as always, frustration and friction with the Colonial Office, Lugard describing the new permanent under-secretary, Sir George Fiddes, as the rudest man he had ever met. If Lugard refused to admit he was tired by 1914, half-way through the war he acknowledged that he was becoming tired. When it ended he wrote to Walter Long, the secretary of state, to express his grievance over the fate of his scheme for continuous administration, adding that his task in Nigeria was concluded. Perversely or ironically, this was taken in the office to be his resignation. Long accepted it, thanked him for his work, and offered to recommend him as GBE. Lugard replied that it was not his intention to resign from the colonial service, but the answer made it clear that he was unlikely to be offered any further crown appointment. He retired in November 1918.

Retirement, 1919–1945 Lugard's retiring was bitter-sweet, the resentment at the Colonial Office for having virtually dismissed him balanced against the joy that he and Flora could at last live, unseparated, at Little Parkhurst, the Abinger home which on their marriage she had created out of the two cottages she owned on Leith Hill. It was to become the base for Lugard's activities for the rest of his life.

First came the period of the peak of Lugard's third career, that of writer, when he finished two books of lasting importance and, during it, wrote hundreds of articles, letters to the press, forewords, lectures, speeches, and broadcasts. Immediately, however, he completed his version of the instructions he had issued to his staff in the founding years of Northern Nigeria, now titled *Political Memoranda* (1919), though the book did not come into the public domain until 1970. Next he saw through the press his detailed report on the amalgamation of Nigeria and of his administration since 1912, which appeared as a command paper in 1919. Then, the record of his Nigerian years completed, he turned to organizing his long accumulated ideas about colonial government. *The Dual Mandate in British Tropical Africa*, which appeared in 1922, won him instant recognition as the outstanding authority, in Europe as well as in Britain, on how colonial powers ought, morally and materially, to administer their possessions. In the wake of post-war concern and sensitivity over the colonial question and the dominance of superpowers in Africa and Asia, Lugard set up a broadly acceptable standard by which their stewardship could be judged. Maintaining that empire was no monolithic layer of mastery, he argued that its justification lay in its capacity to evolve a reciprocal benefit, to the colonized peoples as well as to the colonial power, and that the aim of every colonial administration should be to fulfil that dual mandate.

Books apart, there was no let-up in practical work. Lugard interrupted his writing to make a quick visit to Ethiopia for the Abyssinian Corporation in 1920. In the same year he was sworn of the privy council. In 1922 he became Britain's member on the permanent mandates commission of the League of Nations. Once more, he was separated from Flora for weeks at a time. If he was periodically irked by the commission's absorption in legalistic issues, he won respect by his deep courtesy and by his conscientious analysis of the record of the mandatory administrations. But he remained inflexible in his rejection of any form of international control.

Geneva was but one of Lugard's numerous public duties. He was a member of the league's permanent slavery committee (from which he was brusquely removed in 1933) and of the International Labour Office's committee of experts on native labour in 1925–41; he served on the colonial advisory committee on education from 1923 to 1936, working closely with his friend Dr J. H. Oldham; he was involved with the International Colonial Institute in Brussels; he was a member of the governing body at the School of Oriental Studies, where he successfully added 'and African' to the name; and in 1926 he became chairman of the International Institute of African Languages and Cultures (today's International African Institute), in the promotion of which he played a leading part. Additionally he went on the boards of four companies of whose work in Africa he approved, among them the Colonial Bank (Barclays), the Empire Cotton Growing Board, and the Lever Brothers subsidiary Huileries du Congo. His club was the Athenaeum. Raised to the peerage in 1928 as Baron Lugard of Abinger in the county of Surrey, he took a vigorous part in the joint select committee on closer union in east Africa and from 1923 to 1936, again with Oldham, in the wider arena of conflict which led to the campaign against the incorporation of the three high commission territories into the Union of South Africa. Age brought no decline in the attention he devoted to colonial affairs, including robust contributions to the press on Germany's claim for the return of her colonies.

Final years and death Flora died in 1929. Inconsolable, Lugard kept her room unused, exactly as she had left it; her spirit lived on in his life, of which she had been such a major part. He sought distraction in even more public engagements; 'life is still interesting even though all the sunshine and pleasure have gone out of it', he observed. A procession of visitors called on him at Little Parkhurst, among them old Nigerian officials who came to greet their 'Chief', successive groups of Nigerian emirs and obas, notably between 1933 and 1937, and, in 1943, the west African press delegation, one of whose members, Abubakar Imam, initiated a significant series of letters, the last of which was written by Lugard a few days before the onset of his fatal illness. Even the Colonial Office now consulted him. Growing deafness made him give up his Geneva assignment in 1936, when he found the procedures in rapid French harder to follow. Typically, he continued to prepare a revised edition of his *Dual Mandate*, which had seen four reprints in its first seven years (albeit with fewer than 2500 copies sold). In the end the accumulated material was too much to marshal and the need perhaps reduced by the publication of Lord Hailey's *An African Survey* in 1938—'my one failure' he conceded. His pension was the meagre income of one who had joined the colonial service late, supplemented by a small allowance from the War Office. In his own affairs he was the most economical of men and did not own a car. It was the fees from his directorships which enabled him to spend so much time on unpaid public service.

Lugard was taken ill on 2 April 1945. He died at Little Parkhurst on 11 April without regaining consciousness and was cremated on 16 April at St John's, Woking. The memorial plaque in the church at Abinger concludes: 'All I did was to try and lay my bricks straight.' A memorial service was held in Westminster Abbey on 26 April. The Lugards had no children. In his affections, next to Flora stood his *alter ego*, his brother Ned (*b.* 1865): 'you who know me better than any other living soul.' It was on Ned he relied and to him he confided throughout his life. He chose Ned, then Major Lugard DSO, as his second-in-command on his Bechuanaland mission and arranged to have him seconded as political assistant when he was high commissioner of Northern Nigeria, and again as his political secretary when governor-general of Nigeria. It was a bond of intimacy that Flora freely entered into.

Lugard was made commander of the Légion d'honneur (1917) and held the grand cross of the order of Leopold II of Belgium (1936). He received the honorary degree of DCL from the universities of Oxford (1912) and Durham (1913), and was made LLD at Hong Kong (1916), Cambridge (1928), and Glasgow (1929). He was a gold medallist of the Royal Geographical Society (1902), the Royal African Society (1925), and the Royal Empire Society (1926), and a silver medallist of the Royal Scottish Geographical Society (1892). An annual Lugard lecture was established by the International African Institute in 1950 and a Lugard scholarship at Rossall School in 1951.

Retrospect Lugard's life and work spanned all but the final stage of the whole history of British rule in tropical Africa. Three periods were of special importance: his vigorous action in Uganda in 1890–92, his influential administration of Northern Nigeria in 1900–06, and his amalgamation of the two Nigerias into one administrative entity in 1912–18. The consequences of both Nigerian exercises were identifiable long after his death and into the country's independence. His ultimate objective, running through *The Dual Mandate*, was progressively to prepare colonial peoples for some form of self-rule, yet to be defined in detail, under a tutelage which would give prominence to their own cultural institutions without the deracinating impact of premature modernization through European influences. The key lay in gradualism—his own precept of *festina lente*—and in his confidence that this could best be achieved under British rule. At the same time, his experience left him in no doubt that the best results could be gained only through the maximum measure of responsibility being devolved by Whitehall to its man on the spot—the interesting reversal of his own practice of delegation to his subordinates.

Emphatically a product of his time and age, Lugard was an imperial soldier before he became a colonial administrator. As a man of action and outspoken principles, and a latecomer to the still evolving colonial service, he found it hard to conceal his impatience with his superiors at the Colonial Office. Confident of his own judgement and driven by a monumental capacity for hard work reinforced by an ability to work far into the night, delegation was an administrative art he never learned. Short of stature, gaunt, and angular, he was described in 1902, with a little licence, as having 'the hollowed cheeks [and] sunken eyes … of a man who has struggled for life … square-jawed, ferocious moustache and keen black eyes … a relentless disciplinarian [who] can unbend and be as gentle as a woman' (Perham, 1.70). A man of personal gentleness and deep feelings, he did not suffer fools gladly, above all if they were his seniors in office. While in the pantheon of Britain's African pro-consuls Lugard's name continues to lead all the rest, he twice resigned a governorship, and with his record of friction between him and the Colonial Office he would have been the last to claim the status of the beau idéal colonial governor—or to have wanted to. His genuinely unassuming simplicity of manner in public was matched by the ever present modesty of his private means, together revealed in his disinclination to pay heed to his own comfort and convenience. The respect in which his pro-consular achievements were held and the influence on colonial thinking he exercised after his retirement, particularly from *The Dual Mandate* and in the mandates commission, placed him in a unique position of authority.

In the immediate post-imperial age, Lugard's reputation, enhanced but not irredeemably sanctified by his biographer Margery Perham, was assailed along with that of the whole imperial establishment. In particular, charges were now levelled against him for his obstinate refusal to halt the Kano–Sokoto expedition (Muffett), for his disastrous handling of the Abeokuta uprising (Gailey), and for an anti-Southern bias in his passionate preference for the Northern administrative system (Nicolson). For all the fickle fashions of post-imperial deconstruction and hindsight denigration, fifty years beyond his death Lugard's record and reputation as Britain's most famous African colonial governor in the age of empire and as a pre-eminent colonial thinker in the inter-war years look set to survive and to enable historians to widen their perspective on the exemplars of Britain's imperial moment.

A. H. M. Kirk-Greene

Sources Bodl. RH, Lugard MSS • M. Perham, *Lugard*, 2 vols. (1956–60) • *DNB* • *The Times* (12 April 1945) • 'Lugard: a book of remembrance' [obits. and tributes compiled for priv. circulation by E. J. Lugard, 1946] • *The diaries of Lord Lugard*, ed. M. Perham and M. Bull, 4 vols. (1959–63) • E. Moberly Bell, *Flora Shaw* (1947) • J. Willcocks, *The romance of soldiering and sport* (1925) • I. F. Nicolson, *The administration of Nigeria, 1900–1960* (1969) • D. J. M. Muffett, *Concerning brave captains* (1964) • H. A. Gailey, *The road to Aba* (1971) • [F. J. D. Lugard], *Lugard and the amalgamation of Nigeria*, ed. A. H. M. Kirk-Greene (1968) • B. Mellor, *Lugard in Hong Kong* (1992) • d. cert. • m. cert. • *The Times* (17 April 1945)

Archives Bodl. RH, corresp., diaries, and papers • RGS, corresp. with Royal Geographical Society | Bodl. Oxf., corresp. with Lewis Harcourt • Bodl. Oxf., corresp. with Gilbert Murray • Bodl. RH, Anti-Slavery and Aborigines Protection Society • Bodl. RH, corresp. with Granville Orde Browne • Bodl. RH, letters to Ernest Gedge • Bodl. RH, corresp. with Joseph Oldham • Bodl. RH, corresp. with Margery Perham and related papers • Bodl. RH, corresp. with Lord Scarbrough • Duke U., Perkins L., letters to J. W. Robertson-Scott • HLRO, corresp. with Lord Samuel • HLRO, letters to John St Loe

Strachey • NA Scot., corresp. with Lord Lothian • NL Scot., corresp. with Blackwoods • Stanton Harcourt, Oxfordshire, Harcourt MSS • U. Birm., Chamberlain MSS | SOUND BL NSA

Likenesses Elliott & Fry, photograph, 1893 [*see illus.*] • C. E. Howard [Mrs E. J. Lugard], miniature, 1893, NPG • W. & D. Downey, woodburytype, pubd 1894, NPG • ivory and oils miniature, *c.*1910, priv. coll. • A. Cluysenaar, oils, 1915, University of Hong Kong • W. Stoneman, photographs, 1924–36, NPG • W. J. Carrow, oils, 1936 (after photograph), NPG • C. d'O. P. Jackson, plaster bust, 1960, NPG; bronze bust, University of Hong Kong • H. H. Cawood, bronze statuette • Spy [L. Ward], chromolithograph caricature, NPG; repro. in *VF* (19 Dec 1895) • photographs, Bodl. RH

Wealth at death £23,548 10*s.* 5*d.*: probate, 28 July 1945, *CGPLA Eng. & Wales*

Lugge, John (*bap.* 1580, *d.* 1647x55?), organist and composer, was baptized at Barnstaple on 24 October 1580, the second son of Thomas Lugge, a prominent citizen and shoemaker there, and his wife, Joan Downe, and not, as has often been stated, of Thomas Lugge, a vicar-choral at Exeter Cathedral from 1570. Nothing is known of his early musical education; he may have served as a cathedral chorister at Exeter, though there is no evidence for this. By 1602, when his first child was born, he had married.

Lugge spent his adult life in the service of Exeter Cathedral. The date of his arrival is not recorded; but he was certainly organist there during the quarter ending on 25 March 1603, when he signed in receipt of the salary for this post. On 24 June 1605 Lugge was admitted a lay vicar-choral, having enjoyed the profits of the vicar's stall of one Upcott (whom he had presumably replaced) for half of the previous quarter. Up until June 1608 Lugge received the £10 annual salary attached to the joint office of organist and master of the choristers, but by Michaelmas of that year he was sharing the salary (and therefore probably also some of the duties) with Edward Gibbons. This division of salary persisted up until the mid-1640s.

On 10 December 1617 Lugge's brother, Peter, 'a Spanish sympathizer' (Shaw, 109), wrote Lugge a letter, which was intercepted by Bishop William Cotton of Exeter. Cotton duly examined John Lugge but found that he had no popish sympathies, though his religion was 'as the market goes' (ibid.). According to Cotton's report, dated 14 January 1618, Lugge had had nothing to do with his brother for seven years and had never promised to become a Catholic. Cotton continued: 'though I fear, and by conference do suspect that he hath eaten a little bit, or mumbled a piece of this forbidden fruit, yet I verily believe he hath spit it all out again' (Steele, 310). His vicar-choral colleagues certified his innocence, and a search of his house three years later turned up no evidence against him. None the less, the fact that John's youngest son, Robert (organist of St John's College, Oxford, since 1635), some time prior to April 1639 'went beyond the seas and changed his religion for that of Rome' (*John Lugge*, iv) must raise the distinct probability that John may also have harboured Catholic views.

Lugge apparently served Exeter Cathedral well. The dean and chapter granted to him and his family permission to live in his house in Kallendarhay (as the vicars' close was called) until their deaths and, on 18 October 1617, the profits of a vacant clerkship of the second form to supplement his income. There is also evidence that he was allowed a deputy organist, for on 21 March 1618 it was decreed that Hugh Facy, one of the lay clerks, 'should sometimes play on the organs at service tyme' (Payne, 234). On 12 August 1644 Lugge's wife, Rebecca, died, having borne six children between 1606 and 1622. By the summer of 1646 choral services had been abandoned: Lugge is mentioned for the last time in a vicars-choral account book for 1647, and in the same year he transferred the lease of his house to his daughter, Mary. He may have died before 1655.

Lugge was one of the most talented English provincial composers of the period and is remembered for his outstanding organ music, especially the three voluntaries for double organ, which is well written, imaginative, and technically demanding. He also left three short keyboard dances, and a small quantity of church music comprising three service-settings (one of which was praised by the eighteenth-century music historian Charles Burney) and four anthems. IAN PAYNE

Sources *John Lugge: the complete keyboard works*, ed. S. Jeans and J. Steele (1990) • I. Payne, *The provision and practice of sacred music at Cambridge colleges and selected cathedrals, c.1547–c.1646* (1993), 234 • J. Steele, 'Lugge, John', *New Grove* • H. W. Shaw, *The succession of organists of the Chapel Royal and the cathedrals of England and Wales from c.1538* (1991), 108–9

Archives Devon RO, Exeter dean and chapter MSS

Lughaidh. *See* Lugaid mac Lóegairi (*d.* 507).

Lugidus. *See* Mo Lua moccu Óche (554–609) *under* Munster, saints of (*act. c.*450–*c.*700).

Luke. For this title name *see* Johnston, George Lawson, first Baron Luke (1873–1943); Johnston, Ian St John Lawson, second Baron Luke (1905–1996) [*see under* Johnston, George Lawson, first Baron Luke (1873–1943)].

Luke de Tany. *See* Tany, Sir Luke de (*d.* 1282).

Luke, Sir Harry Charles (1884–1969), colonial governor, was born on 4 December 1884 at 6 Emperor's Gate, London, the eldest child of Joseph Harry Lukàch (*d.* 1930), an international businessman of Hungarian descent, and his wife, Eugénie Caroline Zamarksa (*d.* 1940), of Vienna. On both sides Luke inherited cosmopolitanism, culture, and sensitivity. His features were always to be slight. In 1919 he changed his surname by deed poll from Lukàch to Luke.

From preparatory school Luke went to Eton College in 1898, where the lively teaching of the classics instilled a strong urge to Mediterranean travel. He went up to Trinity College, Oxford, in 1903. After obtaining a second class in modern history in 1906, Luke carried out an extensive tour in Greece, Turkey, Cyprus, Palestine, Syria, and northern Mesopotamia. This perambulation through the Ottoman empire during the last months of the regime of Sultan Hamid II provided Luke with a lasting feel for Near Eastern affairs. He returned home in May 1908, and in September took up the position of private secretary to the governor of Sierra Leone, Sir Leslie Probyn. So began an association of thirty-five years with the colonial service.

When Probyn went to Barbados as governor in early 1911, Luke accompanied him, but soon left with the intention of obtaining a position in Cyprus, whose Levantine atmosphere had already gripped his imagination. After attachment to the Colonial Office in London on coronation duties, Luke went to Cyprus in November 1911 as private secretary to the new governor, Sir Hamilton Goold-Adams. At the end of 1912 Luke moved to a junior administrative position in the secretariat. Particularly absorbing to him were researches with the chief cadi into the manuscripts in the main Muslim seminary in Nicosia. It was Luke's rapport with Muslim notables which on 5 November made him an excellent choice, following Turkey's entry into war against Britain, to draw up in appropriate language the necessary proclamation concerning the annexation of the island, and to inform the local *mufti* and his colleagues that they were no longer Ottoman citizens.

At the end of 1914 the Cyprus government agreed to loan Luke as interpreter on HM cruiser *Doris*, which inaugurated a peripatetic war career in the eastern Mediterranean and Aegean. His involvement in conferences with army intelligence in Cairo broadened his experience and afforded him useful contacts with such figures as W. H. Deedes, Aubrey Herbert, T. E. Lawrence, and Ronald Storrs. During several extensions of his period on loan as a political officer with the eastern Mediterranean Fleet, Luke was involved in the administration of the islands of Mudros and Lemnos during the Gallipoli campaign. In June 1916 he returned to Cyprus, where in the autumn of 1917 he was appointed commissioner of Paphos. He recalled this as the most congenial job he ever held, permitting ample scope for contact with a largely village population (Luke, 2.33). In 1918 Luke became commissioner for Famagusta. The same year he married Joyce Evelyn Fremlyn in the Anglican church of St Helena in Larnaca. They had two children, the elder of whom, Peter, gained renown for his play *Hadrian the Seventh*. The marriage was dissolved in 1949.

In the autumn of 1919 Luke was recruited by Admiral De Robeck as a political officer on his staff as high commissioner in Constantinople. It was Luke's aptitude for gently placating Muslims which led to his drafting the proclamation for the allied military occupation of the city in March 1920. Some hectic and insecure months followed as British chief commissioner in the disturbed countries of Georgia, Armenia, and Azerbaijan; Luke later remembered the Armenian capital, Erivan, as 'the saddest town' he ever saw (Luke, 2.170). He was at heart more interested in the ethnography of the Caucasus than in its contemporary politics, and although De Robeck valued his services, in the Foreign Office Luke's abilities were sometimes regarded more sceptically. When his secondment as chief commissioner ended, Luke sought the vacancy as chief secretary of Cyprus, and when he was not successful, accepted a post in the Palestine administration of assistant governor of Jerusalem under Sir Ronald Storrs.

Luke did much to protect the beauty of the Holy City. Jerusalem suited his fascination with eastern Christianity, and he enjoyed acting as a special commissioner respecting the affairs of the patriarchate of Jerusalem, *The Times* duly noting the anomaly whereby a Jewish high commissioner, Lord Samuel, empowered two Anglicans to give a ruling on orthodox canon law. Less consonant with Luke's natural preferences was his participation in the commission of inquiry into the bloody Arab-Jewish disturbances of May 1921.

The Jerusalem job was not pensionable in the colonial service, and in February 1924 Luke was appointed colonial secretary in Sierra Leone. While there he resumed a previous interest in local bibliography; it also fell to him, as acting governor in September 1927, to sign the ordinance ending slavery in the protectorate. In May 1928 Luke was transferred to Palestine as chief secretary. Immediately on his arrival in that territory, the high commissioner, Lord Plumer, departed on completion of his tenure, leaving Luke as acting head of government to contain the riots which broke out by the Wailing Wall on 23 August. Luke described the decision to disarm the special Jewish constables in the Palestine police as the most difficult he had ever taken, and during the subsequent commission of inquiry he was stringently criticized by Jewish representatives. Although the report refuted these complaints, it was slightly lukewarm in concluding that there was no serious criticism to be made of Luke for the delay in mobilizing troops to restore order. In mid-1930 Luke was promoted to the post of lieutenant-governor of Malta.

Luke had a penchant for taking jobs just when they were becoming awkward and he arrived in Malta as it was gripped by controversy involving the rights of the Roman Catholic establishment, resulting in the suspension of the constitution for two years. He was attacked by nationalist newspapers in the island and expansionist organs in Italy. As lieutenant-governor, Luke took a close interest in the problems of the Maltese diaspora in the Mediterranean, visiting Tripoli, Tunis, and Corfu. He also furthered study into the antiquities of the island, and provided regular hospitality in his summer palace at Verdala during a time when Malta was a magnet for the peacetime Royal Navy. As acting governor, it pleased Luke in January 1936 to proclaim king Edward VIII in the throne room of the palace in Valletta. The following year Luke was offered the governorship of Mauritius, but refused on the understanding that he would be considered for the impending vacancy in Cyprus. This position subsequently went elsewhere, and in 1938 he became governor of Fiji and high commissioner in the Western Pacific.

Regretful at leaving the Mediterranean, Luke was none the less 'thankful to be done' with its embittered politics (Luke, 3.112). The Western Pacific had its own political problems, not least those posed by relations with the French. Tensions on this front eased when the administration in New Caledonia adhered to the Gaullist cause after June 1940, and Luke's own Francophilia and *savoir-faire* assisted matters thereafter. Supervision of the local war effort did not stop Luke visiting every part of his hugely dispersed domain, except for remote Pitcairn Island. In June 1942 Luke resigned from his position. In thanking him for his services, the secretary of state for colonies highlighted the contribution he had played in preparing Malta for the present ordeal of war.

After his retirement in April 1943 Luke became chief representative of the British Council in the Caribbean. He chose Trinidad as his base, but never spent more than one week in any territory—his wanderings took him also to such 'non-British' places as Cuba, Haiti, the Central American republics, and Yucatan. After leaving British Council employment in 1947, he was able to extend his itinerary in South America with interludes elsewhere. He was very active as an office-holder of the order of St John of Jerusalem, being made a grand officer of merit of the sovereign military order in Rome in 1966. Yet no honour pleased him more in his closing years than his honorary fellowship at Trinity College, Oxford.

Luke's literary output was prolific, extending even to a witty cookery compendium, *The Tenth Muse* (1954). Perhaps most enduring were his books on Malta (1949) and Cyprus (1957). His three-volume autobiography, *Cities and Men* (1953–6) was one of the most engaging, if not most revealing, of his generation. Ronald Storrs, whose experience was scarcely confined, said that Luke had lived 'the most unwasted life of any man I have known' (*DNB*). Luke was appointed CMG in 1926, knighted in 1933, and promoted KCMG in 1939. He was a DLitt of Oxford (1938) and an honorary LLD of the Royal University of Malta. Luke died in Cyprus on 11 May 1969; his ashes were interred in the crypt of the conventual church of the order of St John of Jerusalem in Clerkenwell, London. ROBERT HOLLAND

Sources H. Luke, *Cities and men*, 3 vols. [1953–6] • R. Storrs, *Orientations* (1937) • N. Bentwich and H. Bentwich, *Mandate memories, 1918–1948* (1965) • G. S. Georghallides, *A political and administrative history of Cyprus, 1918–26* (1979) • PRO, FO 371 • 'Report of the commission on the Palestine disturbances of August, 1929', *Parl. papers* (1929–30), 16.675, Cmd 3530 • *DNB* • *WWW* • *CGPLA Eng. & Wales* (1969)
Archives Bodl. RH, papers relating to Malta • Leventis Museum, Nicosia • Order of St John Library and Museum, London, papers • St Ant. Oxf., Middle East Centre, diaries and papers | BL, corresp. with Society of Authors, Add. MS 63283 • Bodl. RH, corresp. with Sir Harry Batterbee
Likenesses E. Caruana-Dingli, oils, 1933, priv. coll. • W. Stoneman, photograph, 1934, NPG
Wealth at death £6883: probate, 16 Sept 1969, *CGPLA Eng. & Wales*

Luke [*née* Thompson], **Jemima** (1813–1906), hymn writer, daughter of Thomas Thompson (1785–1865) and Elizabeth Pinckney (*d.* 1837), was born at Islington, London, on 19 August 1813. Her father was one of the pioneers of the Bible Society, assisted in the formation of the Sunday School Union, and helped to support the first floating chapel for sailors. In 1819 he founded the Home Missionary Society; he was also a prominent member of the London Missionary Society (LMS) from 1827. Jemima and her sisters were educated at home by a governess. She imbibed her parents' missionary enthusiasm, and strongly supported 'female agency' in church life and missions. After her mother's death, and her father's remarriage in 1839, she planned to go to India as a missionary for the LMS, but was prevented by ill health. She taught at the normal infant school in Gray's Inn Road, and became honorary secretary to the Female Missionary Society in the East. In 1843 she married Samuel Luke, a Congregationalist minister; they had one child, a son.

Jemima Luke's literary career had begun when she published some verses in the *Juvenile Friend* at the age of thirteen. Shortly before her marriage she became the editor of the *Missionary Repository*. The hymn on which her reputation rests, 'I think when I read that sweet story of old', was largely written on the back of an envelope while she was travelling in a stagecoach between Wellington and Taunton. It was first published in the *Sunday School Teacher's Magazine* in 1841; in 1853 it appeared anonymously in *The Leeds Hymn Book*, and subsequently it was included in other collections. She also published *The Female Jesuit* (1851), a curious account of a deception passed off on her own family by 'Marie', an apparent convert from Roman Catholicism; *A Brief Memoir of Eliza Ann Harris* (1859); and *The Early Years of my Life* (1900), an autobiographical record of her life before her marriage.

After her husband's death in 1868 Jemima Luke lived at Newport, Isle of Wight. An ardent nonconformist, she was an active opponent of the Education Act of 1902, which she feared would expose large numbers of children to ritualist teaching. She was summoned among the Isle of Wight 'passive resisters' in September 1904—the oldest passive resister in the country. She died at Newport on 2 February 1906.

J. C. HADDEN, *rev.* ROSEMARY MITCHELL

Sources J. Luke, *The early years of my life* (1900) • *British Weekly* (8 Feb 1906), 523 • *MT*, 46 (1905), 124 • J. Julian, ed., *A dictionary of hymnology*, rev. edn (1907) • J. Luke, *Sketches of the life and character of Thomas Thompson* (1868) • private information (1912)
Likenesses photograph, *c.*1900, repro. in Luke, *Early years*, frontispiece
Wealth at death £2738 19*s.* 10*d.*: probate, 16 March 1906, *CGPLA Eng. & Wales*

Luke, Sir Samuel (*bap.* 1603, *d.* 1670), parliamentarian army officer, was baptized at Southill, Bedfordshire, on 27 March 1603, the eldest son of Sir Oliver Luke (*b.* 1574, *d.* in or after 1650) of Woodend in Cople, Bedfordshire, and his first wife, Elizabeth (*d.* 1607), daughter of Sir Valentine Knightley of Fawsley, Northamptonshire. Samuel was born into one of the great political networks of the early seventeenth century, which encompassed not only his mother's immediate family but also the Fleetwoods, Lyttons, and Barringtons.

Luke attended Eton College between 1617 and 1619. He and a younger brother travelled in Europe in 1623. On 2 February 1624 he married Elizabeth, daughter of William Freeman, a London merchant and member of the Haberdashers' Company. Together they had six sons and four daughters. Luke was knighted later that year, on 20 July. His name appears in 1625 listed in the burgess rolls of Bedford, which lay 3 miles from the family seat; by 1636 he was a member of the Bedfordshire commission of sewers and by 1640 a JP for the borough of Bedford.

In both the Short Parliament of April 1640 and the Long Parliament Luke was elected for Bedford, evidently on an anti-court ticket, while his father was one of the members for the county. Sir Samuel's election to both parliaments was a matter of dispute: four days before the Short Parliament ended he still had not been allowed to sit, and he did not begin his work in the Long Parliament until August 1641. When war broke out in England both father and son took the side of parliament. In July 1642 Samuel was wounded in endeavouring to arrest Sir Lewis Dyve. He was present at the battle of Edgehill as captain of a troop of horse, and on 4 January 1643 was commissioned by the earl of Essex to raise a regiment of dragoons in Bedfordshire. His newly raised regiment was surprised by Prince Rupert at Chinnor, Oxfordshire, on 18 June 1643; 50 were killed and 120 taken prisoner. Luke himself was absent, but fought by John Hampden's side in the defeat at Chalgrove Field, Oxfordshire, on the same day, where he greatly distinguished himself by his courage. 'Great-spirited little Sir Samuel Luke', says a parliamentarian paper, 'so guarded himself with his short sword, that he escaped without hurt, though thrice taken prisoner, yet rescued, and those to whom he was prisoner slain' (J. Forster, *John Pym, 1584–1643—John Hampden, 1594–1643*, 1837, 371). On 5 July 1643 and again on 28 September Luke was thanked by parliament for his services. He became scoutmaster-general of Essex's army, assisted in the recovery of Newport Pagnell, Bedfordshire, on 29 October 1643, and became its governor when it was made a permanent garrison.

Luke co-operated with Oliver Cromwell in the capture of Hillesdon House, Buckinghamshire, of which he sent a detailed account to the speaker. On 26 May 1644 Luke surprised Fortescue's regiment of royalist horse at Islip, Oxfordshire. As both governor and scoutmaster Luke was extremely energetic and efficient. 'This noble commander', *Mercurius Britanicus* declared, 'watches the enemy so industriously that they eat, sleep, drink not, whisper not, but he can give us an account of their darkest proceedings' (*Mercurius Britanicus*, 218; quoted in *GM*): a claim confirmed by the journal that he maintained of his scouts' reports, covering the period 9 February 1643 to 29 March 1644. The fall of Leicester to the royalists seemed to endanger Newport, and Luke complained that he had only 600 men at his disposal to defend works requiring 2000 men to man them. 'We want all provisions,' he wrote, 'and if we escape storm we cannot hold out long' (Rushworth, 6.38). But the victory of Naseby saved Newport from attack, and on 26 June 1645 the operation of the self-denying ordinance put a term to Luke's command. On 11 January 1647 parliament ordered him to be paid £4482 13*s.* 6*d.* for arrears of pay.

Luke was a strong presbyterian, and his time at Newport Pagnell was marked not only by his problems with an ill-paid and discontented garrison, but by his anxiety over the social and religious threat posed by sectaries. He suppressed conventicles and dismissed an officer 'for disaffection to the service and perverseness to all religious exercises' (Hill, 49). He complained that it was 'far easier to breed people up to wickedness than to godliness, especially when under profession of the latter they may with allowance practice the former', and edgily reported tales of sexual disorder. Unless he could rid the town of sectaries Luke feared that Newport Pagnell would go the way of Sodom and Gomorrah. He attempted to counter the threat with a roster of divines, regular sermons three times a week, and prayers and Bible reading every morning at the changing of the guard. Matters came to a head on 15 June 1645, the day after Naseby, when Luke ordered a service of thanksgiving for the victory. Passing through the town were two New Model Army captains, the Particular Baptist preacher Paul Hobson and Richard Beaumont—'tailor Hobson' and 'druggist Beaumont', as Luke, who firmly believed that officers should be gentlemen, dismissed them: 'Anabaptists, who cannot consent with magistracy or government' (Hill, 50). When Hobson chose to ignore the official church parade and instead himself preached openly Luke had the two men arrested for transgressing the orders of parliament against unlicensed preaching. He thus became involved in a quarrel with their commanders, Charles Fleetwood and Sir Thomas Fairfax, and continued to pursue the matter even after he had ceded the governorship, having Hobson rearrested and sent before a parliamentary committee; his efforts succeeded only in incurring the hatred of the Independent party in the army.

On 1 August 1647 Luke was seized by a party of soldiers on suspicion that he was raising the forces of Bedfordshire to assist the city against the army, but he was speedily released by Fairfax. On the occasion of Pride's Purge (6 December 1648) Luke was again arrested, having been readily identified as a keen supporter of the treaty of Newport, but he was set at liberty on 20 December, and no charge was brought against him. Luke took no part in public affairs during the Commonwealth and protectorate. He literally cultivated his own garden, swapping plants and cuttings with his neighbour Dorothy Osborne who described him as 'a nice florist' (*Letters of Dorothy Osborne*, 46). As the Restoration approached in early 1660 he received a militia command. He was returned to the Convention parliament as MP for Bedford, but was defeated in the election the following year. In his later years he was perhaps in some financial difficulty, alienating one of his main estates, at Hawnes, Bedfordshire, to Sir George Carteret. Luke died in 1670, and was buried at Cople on 30 August.

Luke was a very little man, and his size made him a butt for royalist satire. His reputation has suffered from the supposition that he was the original of Samuel *Butler's Sir Hudibras. The key to *Hudibras* attributed to Sir Roger L'Estrange explained that Sir Hudibras was 'Sir Samuel Luke of Bedfordshire, a self-conceited commander under Oliver Cromwell' (Butler, vol. 1). However, Butler himself said that his model was a west-country knight, and a more plausible candidate is Sir Henry Rosewell of Ford Abbey, Devon. Claims that Butler had been Luke's servant seem to rest on the original misattribution. The estimate which Luke's own party formed of his character is shown by the posts with which parliament entrusted him, and by the panegyrics of parliamentarian writers such as Josiah

Ricraft, to whom 'the valiant victorious Sir Samuel Luke' was 'a true-hearted publike ingaged Covenant keeping and vertuous true-hearted English Knight' (J. Ricraft, *A Survey of Englands Champions and Truths Faithfull Patriots*, 1647, 78). Both Luke's journal and his letter-books have been published (as has his diary of the siege of Reading in 1643) and prove him a vigilant and energetic officer, and a man of sense and courage. His correspondence offers clues as to his personality: a mainstream puritan gentleman concerned with the maintenance of the social order, but also fond of fine clothes, good cheer, and good claret, who showed 'fatherly concern for the education of his son in Italy and in the Netherlands armies, and an interest in falconry which he shared with his powerful kinsman, Lord Saye and Sele' (Keeler, *Long Parliament*, 262).

SEAN KELSEY

Sources M. W. Helms, L. Naylor, and G. Jagger, 'Luke, Sir Samuel', HoP, *Commons, 1660–90* • Keeler, *Long Parliament*, 261–2 • D. Underdown, *Pride's Purge: politics in the puritan revolution* (1971) • *Journal of Sir Samuel Luke*, ed. I. G. Philip, 1–3, Oxfordshire RS, 29, 31, 33 (1950–53) • *The letter books of Sir Samuel Luke, 1644–45*, ed. H. G. Tibbutt, Bedfordshire Historical RS, 42 (1963) • C. Hill, *A turbulent, seditious, and factious people: John Bunyan and his church* (1988), 47–52 • *JHL*, 5 (1642–3), 246 • *JHC*, 3–5 (1642–8) • *His highness Prince Rupert's late beating up of the rebels' quarters at Portcomb and Chinner* (1643) • *A letter from Robert, earl of Essex, relating the true state of the late skirmish at Chinner* (1643) • F. A. Blaydes, ed., *The visitations of Bedfordshire, annis Domini 1566, 1582, and 1634*, Harleian Society, 19 (1884) • *The manuscripts of his grace the duke of Portland*, 10 vols., HMC, 29 (1891–1931), vol. 1 • *CSP dom.*, 1644 • J. L. Sanford, *Studies and illustrations of the great rebellion* (1858), appx B • H. Ellis, ed., *Original letters illustrative of English history*, 3rd ser., 4 (1846), 217–67 • J. Rushworth, *Historical collections*, new edn, 8 vols. (1721–2), 6.38; 7.740, 1355, 1369 • H. Cary, ed., *Memorials of the great civil war in England from 1646 to 1652*, 1 (1842), 325 • S. Butler, *Posthumous works in prose and verse*, 3 vols. (1715), vol. 1 • *The letters of Dorothy Osborne to William Temple*, ed. G. C. Hoare Smith (1828), 46 • C. Coates, *The history and antiquities of Reading* (1802), 31–9 • *GM*, 1st ser., 93/2 (1823), 124

Archives BL, letter-books, Egerton MSS 785–787, 3514; Stowe MS 190 • Bodl. Oxf., book of reports from scouts and messengers • Bodl. Oxf., journal, MS Eng. hist. c. 53 | Beds. & Luton ARS, letters to Sir William Boteler • Bodl. Oxf., Tanner MSS

Likenesses C. Jansen, oils, repro. in Philip, ed., *Journal of Sir Samuel Luke* • G. Soest, oils, repro. in Tibbott, ed., *The letter-books of Sir Samuel Luke* • oils, Woburn Abbey, Bedfordshire • oils, Bedford town hall

Luke, Stephen (*bap.* **1763**, *d.* **1829**), physician, was born at Penzance, Cornwall, and baptized at Madron on 4 June 1763, the second son of Stephen Luke (*b.* 1727/8), of Madron, and his wife, Margaret Trewarvas. He was educated at the school of the Revd James Parker, before being apprenticed to Richard Moyle, apothecary, of Marazion, near Penzance, and he subsequently studied medicine in London and Paris for three years and became a member of the Company of Surgeons in London. While in Paris he became the pupil of the celebrated surgeon Pierre-Joseph Desault, whom he never ceased to hold in the highest esteem.

After a short period of practice in London, Luke returned to Cornwall. He practised at Helston, where he entered into partnership with Zachary John, a surgeon apothecary, and afterwards with Isaac Heard. He married Harriet Vyvyan (*bap.* 1758?), daughter of Philip Puron Vyvyan of South Petherwin, Cornwall, probably in 1792, and in the same year he obtained the degree of MD from the University of Aberdeen. He then settled as a physician at Falmouth, where he was elected mayor in 1797. Luke was captain of the Pendennis volunteer cavalry in the same year and he was the original promoter of the Pendennis artillery volunteers.

Luke remained at Falmouth for seventeen years, and was said to have attained a large practice and the highest reputation in the county of Cornwall. According to Munk his health had never been very robust and in 1808 he decided to leave Falmouth to enter Jesus College, Cambridge; he then moved to Edinburgh for the session 1808–9. He practised at Exeter from 1811, and about 1815 returned to Cambridge where it was said that he was instrumental in saving the life of Dr Pearce, the master of his college, who had suffered from an apoplectic attack. Having been an extra-licentiate of the Royal College of Physicians since 23 July 1806, he was admitted a licentiate of the college on 26 June 1815, and took a house in Cavendish Square, London. He graduated MB at Cambridge later in 1815 and MD in 1821. In 1828 he was made physician-extraordinary to George IV.

Luke was said to be remarkable for his prompt and accurate perception of the seat and cause of disease, imparting a boldness and decisiveness of action that was generally successful. He was well known for his gentlemanly manners and his tenderness and solicitude in the sick room. He also contributed an essay on nitrous acid in dropsy to Thomas Beddoes's *Contributions to Physical and Medical Knowledge* (1799), detailing a single case of cirrhosis of the liver in which, after tapping, nitrous acid was of use as a diuretic; and he added 'Observations on the diseases of Cornwall' to Richard Polwhele's *History of Cornwall* (1806).

Luke died at his house in Cavendish Square, London, on 30 March 1829.

NORMAN MOORE, *rev.* ALICK CAMERON

Sources Munk, *Roll* • *GM*, 1st ser., 99/1 (1829), 641 • R. Polwhele, *Biographical sketches in Cornwall*, 1 (1831), 50–52 • Venn, *Alum. Cant.* • register, Madron, 4 June 1763, Cornwall RO [baptism]

Lukin, Henry (1628–1719), clergyman and ejected minister, was born on 1 January 1628 in Great Baddow, Essex. He was the younger son of Henry Lukin and his second wife, Hannah. After studying at Mansfield School (under Halliwell) he went to Christ's College, Cambridge (8 July 1645), where he joined his elder brother William (admitted 1641). He was ordained and adopted puritanism, then became rector of Chipping Ongar, Essex, on 23 March 1659. Soon afterwards he resigned and perhaps was associated with Lindsell, a parish 3 miles from Great Dunmow, but without benefice or cure. At the Restoration he was in France, probably as tutor for about three years with Sir William Masham, second baronet, of High Laver, Essex. He was still abroad at the passing of the Act of Uniformity (1662) and, according to Calamy, was 'silenced … tho' not ejected'. In 1663, after Masham died, Lukin returned to England and lived for many years with Mrs Masham (apparently Sir William's mother, Elizabeth) of Matching Hall, near which he preached regularly. Under Charles II's declaration of indulgence Lukin was licensed a Congregationalist on 11 April 1672. Calamy described him as a 'man of great note and eminence … a judicious and learned divine' (*Nonconformist's Memorial*, 1.529–30).

Most of Lukin's written works were learned but practical devotional guides or instructional manuals for his friends and hearers. *The Practice of Godliness* (1658; 3rd edn, 1690), dedicated to Mrs Masham, gave brief rules directing Christians how to keep their hearts holy and how to order their behaviour. *An Introduction to the Holy Scripture* (1669) exhaustively catalogued the types of figurative language in the Bible, showed readers how to interpret and apply their meanings to salvation and obedience, and encouraged them to claim God's promises revealed in the text. *The Interest of the Spirit in Prayer* (1674) was a classically puritan work with its emphases on: the role of the Holy Spirit, practical moral application, 'experimental' knowledge of the Christian graces, genuine piety instead of formalism, God's grace and providence, and man's impotence and total dependence on God. In *The Chief Interest of Man* (1665; 3rd edn, 1718), Lukin reflected on his cosmopolitan experiences, and used biblical citations, historical examples, and practical insights to argue the benefits of religion for building strong societies. Identifying Christianity as the religion best fitted to do this because it possessed the greatest truth he called for unity among Christians in moral living: 'let us pray like Calvinists, endeavour like Arminians, act like Legalists, hope like Antinomians; be Papists in our works, Protestants in our Faith' (pp. 188–9). This was an uncommonly latitudinarian perspective for a Congregationalist of his day. In 1705 Simon Priest produced a Latin translation of this entitled *Lucrum hominis praecipuum, sive, De religione tractatus*. Lukin's *A Remedy Against Spiritual Troubles* (1694) was a practical theological discourse derived from sermons and transcribed for a friend to guide him from faith to assurance and holiness. Lukin's other major works were *The Life of Faith* and *A Discourse of Right Judgment*, both published in 1660.

Lukin was also a key source of information about the ejected dissenting ministers of Essex, which Edmund Calamy was gathering for inclusion in his *Abridgment of Mr. Baxter's 'History'* (1702). Through the Masham family Lukin became a close friend of the philosopher John Locke, who lived with Sir Francis Masham, the third baronet, and his wife, Damaris, at Otes, Essex, from 1691 until his death in 1704, and supposedly was with him when he died. Lukin died on 13 September 1719 at Matching Green, Essex. Afterwards Lauchlan Ross of Abbots Roothing and George Wiggett of Hatfield Heath supplied the ministry at Matching Green every Sunday morning. Their successors continued this until 1743, when George Ross became the minister there. Shortly after this Ross left the neighbourhood, the congregation dispersed, and the chapel was closed.

JIM SPIVEY

Sources *The nonconformist's memorial … originally written by … Edmund Calamy*, ed. S. Palmer, 1 (1775) • Venn, *Alum. Cant.* • *DNB* • H. Lukin, *The chief interest of man* (1665), preface • *Calamy rev.* • R. E. McFarland, 'Lukin, Henry', Greaves & Zaller, *BDBR*, 208 • T. W. Davids, *Annals of evangelical nonconformity in Essex* (1863) • W. C. Metcalfe, ed., *The visitations of Essex*, 2 vols., Harleian Society, 13–14 (1878–9), vol. 1, p. 438

Lukin, Sir Henry Timson (1860–1925), army officer, was born at Fulham on 24 May 1860, the only son of Robert Henry Lukin, barrister-at-law, of St Peter's-in-Thanet, and his wife, Ellen, daughter of Richard Watson of Northampton. He was educated at Merchant Taylors' School, London, from 1869 to 1875. The family had distinguished military associations, and the boy ardently wanted to become a soldier; but he failed to pass into the Royal Military College, Sandhurst. It was typical of him that, on the prospect of war with the Zulu, he sailed for Durban in January 1879 and worked as a road foreman in Natal until he obtained a commission in Bengough's horse, a native cavalry contingent. Severely wounded at the battle of Ulundi (4 July), Lukin saw no more of that campaign, but on 23 March 1881 he was promoted lieutenant in the Cape mounted riflemen. He served with that regiment in the protectorate of Basutoland in 1881 and as field adjutant in the Bechuanaland field force through the Langeberg operations, 1896–7, which completely crushed the Bechuana rebellion. In the course of these services he was several times decorated and mentioned in dispatches. On 1 July 1891 he married Lily, daughter of Michael Herbert Quinn, landowner, of Fort Hare, Victoria East, Cape Colony; they had no children.

In the Second South African War (1899–1902) Lukin particularly distinguished himself in command of the Cape mounted rifles' artillery in the defence of Wepener, Orange Free State, in April 1900, and was awarded the DSO. Subsequently he commanded a mounted column in Cape Colony. When, in December 1901, the Cape government formed a colonial division Lukin was given command of it. After the war he was created CMG (1902). In 1904 he was appointed commandant-general of the Cape colonial forces. In 1912 he was made inspector-general of the permanent force, Union of South Africa.

In the First World War Lukin was first given command of a mixed force in the operations in South-West Africa (March to July 1915). On the conclusion of that campaign he organized and commanded the 1st South African infantry brigade. In January 1916, after a few months in England, this brigade was dispatched to Egypt, where the commander-in-chief, Lieutenant-General Sir John Maxwell, had been obliged to evacuate the coast between Matruh and Sollum in November 1915 on the threat of an invasion of Egypt by the Senussi. With the South African brigade available, he adopted a forward policy. At Agagia on 26 February 1916 Lukin fought a minor tactical masterpiece, capturing the able Turkish commander, Ja'far Pasha. On 14 March he reoccupied Sollum.

The South African brigade proceeded to France in April 1916, and became part of the 9th (Scottish) division. In the battle of the Somme the brigade distinguished itself in the capture of Delville Wood on 15 July, though at great cost. In December Lukin took command of the 9th division, thus keeping under his orders the brigade which he had raised and trained. He commanded the division in the battle of Arras in April 1917, achieving all his objectives, and in the third battle of Ypres (Passchendaele) in the following September and October. In January 1918 he was created KCB. He returned to England in February, and was in command of the 64th division at home until the end of the war.

Lukin retired in 1919 and returned to South Africa where he played a leading part in defence and ex-servicemen's affairs. Tim Lukin was a popular commander, tough and brave. The welfare of his men was paramount with him and he was often seen in the front line. His health never really recovered from his being gassed and he died at Muizenberg, Cape Province, on 16 December 1925. He was buried in Plumstead cemetery, Cape Town.

CYRIL FALLS, *rev.* J. M. BOURNE

Sources R. E. Johnston, *Ulundi to Delville wood: the life story of Major-General Sir Henry Timson Lukin* (1931) • J. Ewing, *The history of the 9th (Scottish) division* (1921) • *DSAB* • *The Times* (17 Dec 1925) • F. Uys, *Roll call: the Delville wood story* (1991) • W. Nasson, 'South Africans in Flanders: le Zulu Blanc', *Passchendaele in perspective*, ed. P. Liddle (1997), 292–304 • *CGPLA Eng. & Wales* (1926)

Archives FILM IWM FVA, actuality footage • IWM FVA, news footage

Likenesses W. Stoneman, photograph, 1918, NPG • J. S. Sargent, group portrait, oils, 1922 (*General officers of World War I*), NPG • portrait, Cape Town City Hall, South Africa • portrait, Durham Town Hall • statue, Military Museum of Cape Town Castle, South Africa

Wealth at death £1505 14*s*. 6*d*.: probate, 25 June 1926, *CGPLA Eng. & Wales*

Lukin, Lionel (1742–1834), lifeboat designer, was born at Dunmow, Essex, on 18 May 1742, the youngest son of William Lukin, of Blatches, Little Dunmow, and Anne, daughter of James Stokes. His father belonged to an old Essex family, one of his ancestors being Henry Lukyn (1586–1630), who is described by Anthony Wood as a mathematician, and who is mentioned by Thoroton in his *History of Nottinghamshire* as having 'dwelt before the wars at South Holme' (369). On his mother's side he was descended from a Lionel Lane, one of Blake's admirals.

Lukin was for many years a fashionable London coachbuilder in Long Acre. He became a member of the Coachmakers' Company in 1767, and did not finally retire from business until 1824. He was twice married, and with his first wife, born Walker, and widow of Henry Gilder of Dunmow, had a daughter, and a son of the same name, who patented several inventions, and died in 1839. Lukin appears to have been a man with a taste for science and possessed of a fertile mechanical mind.

Being a personal favourite of the prince regent and connected with William Windham, secretary of state for war and the colonies, Lukin had many opportunities to bring some of his inventions to public attention. Among these was an 'unsubmergible' boat. He began by making certain alterations to a Norway yawl which he purchased in 1784, the efficacy of which he tested as far as was practicable in the River Thames. He obtained a patent in 1785 for his invention, by which 'boats and small vessels … will neither overset in violent gales or sudden bursts of wind, nor sink if by any accident filled with water' (patent no. 1502, 1785). The patent specification explained that this was to be accomplished by fitting

> to the outsides of vessels … projecting gunnells sloping from the top of the common gunnell in a faint curve towards the water … and from the extreme projection … returning to the side in a faint curve at a suitable height above the water-line. The projections are very small at the stem and stern, and increase gradually to the dimensions required. (ibid.)

The specification further provided that ports of the inside of the boat should be filled up with airtight and watertight compartments or with cork or other light material that would repel water, whereby 'the boat or vessel will be much lighter than any body of water it must displace' (ibid.) Lukin submitted his invention to the prince of Wales, the dukes of Portland and Northumberland, Admiral Sir Robert King, Admiral Schank, and Admiral Lord Howe, who gave him strong encouragement but no official support.

Lukin's first boat, the *Experiment*, was tested by a Ramsgate pilot but, after crossing the channel several times in rough weather, the boat disappeared—it may have been confiscated in a continental port. His second boat, the *Witch*, was tested by Sir Sydney Smith and other naval officers, and its qualities were publicly displayed at Margate. But Lukin had to contend with seafaring prejudices, and his 'unsubmergible boats', though they attracted attention, were in little demand. Apart from one built for the Bamborough Charity, only four were ordered, one of which proved very useful at Lowestoft.

In 1790 Lukin published a description of his lifeboat, with scale-drawings. Some time after the date of Lukin's patent a lifeboat was built (not patented) by Henry Greathead, who was rewarded with a parliamentary grant. Lukin declared that Greathead's boat was in general built according to the principles set out in his patent, and had no additional safety features. In 1806 a Mr Hailes put forward the claims of Wouldham of Newcastle as an inventor of lifeboats, and Lukin wrote three letters in 1806 in the *Gentleman's Magazine*, in which he set out his claims to priority. These he afterwards published as a pamphlet dedicated to the prince of Wales, entitled *The Invention, Principles of Construction, and Uses of Unimmergible Boats* (1806).

Lukin also invented a raft for rescuing persons from under ice, which he presented to the Royal Humane Society, and an adjustable reclining bed for patients, which he presented to various infirmaries. He invented a rain gauge, and kept a daily record of meteorological observations for many years until his sight failed in 1824. He died on 16 February 1834 at Hythe, Kent. A headstone, marking his grave in the parish churchyard, described him as the 'inventor of the lifeboat principle.' A memorial window in the local parish church was unveiled on 3 October 1892.

H. M. CHICHESTER, *rev.* R. C. COX

Sources *GM*, 2nd ser., 2 (1834), 653 • *The Times* (8 Nov 1890), 6 • private information (1893)

Lukis, Frederick Corbin (1788–1871), antiquary and natural historian, was born on 24 February 1788 at La Grange, St Peter Port, Guernsey, the last of the four children of John Lukis (1753–1832), captain in the Royal Guernsey militia, and Sarah Collings (1749–1816). His father having made a substantial income from privateering and from the lucrative wine trade, the family had a fine house built in the elegant Grange Road, leading out of St Peter Port. As a young man Lukis became interested in a wide variety of disciplines, including natural history, botany, geology, conchology, and science. He was elected a fellow of the Society of Antiquaries on 28 April 1853 but never published in their journal, *Archaeologia*, although he wrote many letters to the secretary and other members. He served in the local Guernsey militia, which later became the Royal Guernsey militia; he became a colonel and served as aide-de-camp to the governor of Guernsey in 1820. In 17 February 1813 he married his first cousin Elizabeth Collings (1791–1865), with whom he had six sons and three daughters. In the same year he became a constable of St Peter Port.

In 1811, while still a young man, Lukis was taken by Joshua Gosselin (1739–1813), an elderly cousin and a noted local botanist, to examine a chambered tomb on L'Ancresse Common. The tomb had been uncovered by soldiers working on the common to make a redoubt; they thought they had discovered an artificial cavern, and were digging through pottery and bones when Gosselin and Lukis arrived. It is said that the young Lukis went away with a human skull under his arm. This brush with the past at the age of twenty-three was the start of Lukis's lifelong fascination with archaeology and the natural sciences. Self-taught, he went on to discover, record, and protect as best he could the remains of Guernsey's heritage. Although to present-day archaeologists his methods may seem crude, he made meticulous notes and etchings, and left superb watercolour sketches, many of which were painted by his youngest daughter, Mary-Anne (1822–1906), who lived with her father and devoted much of her time to this exercise. Lukis also collected artefacts from these investigations, and in addition to the papers he published nationally on Guernsey his greatest endeavour was an archive called the Collectanea Antiqua, in which he recorded his excavations and fieldwork. This unpublished opus, in six volumes, is housed at Guernsey Museum together with a number of his letters, notebooks, and diaries; this body of work, amassed without the scientific basis of modern studies, still forms the basis for any serious study of Guernsey's prehistoric past.

Lukis was also intensely involved in the study of local natural history and was the local secretary of the Botanical Society of the British Isles. From his studies in geology he left a collection of over 900 entries; the material collected by him, and later by his family, forms the nucleus of the collections of the Guernsey Museum and Galleries. He died on 15 November 1871 at his home, La Grange, St Peter Port. A local obituarist recorded:

> Like all true sons of science he combined the humility and simplicity of a child with the depth and wisdom of a philosopher. Never was he so happy as when unfolding to the youngest the interesting marvels of natural history, and many who are besides his own more favoured children, have received their earliest impulses and most abiding inspirations from him. (*Gazette de Guernesey*, 18 Nov 1871)

Several of Lukis's children did indeed follow in his footsteps. His second son, John Walter Lukis (1816–1894), who moved to northern France, was a mining engineer and collected many geological samples; he also carried out a number of excavations in Brittany. His eldest daughter, Louisa (1818–1887), married her cousin William Collings, who was seigneur of Sark. She collected lichens, and over 1000 of her specimens are in the Guernsey museum collections. William Collings Lukis (1817–1894), the third son, was born and educated in Guernsey and is best remembered in England for his work on the megaliths of Great Britain and France; with his university friend Sir Henry Dryden he surveyed the megalithic monuments of Brittany. He was ordained in Salisbury in 1845, and after holding several livings in Wiltshire he moved to Wath in Yorkshire, where he carried out a number of excavations. He published a treatise on ancient church plate in 1845 and was a regular contributor to the journals of the British Archaeological Association and other learned societies. His collection of artefacts was bought by the British Museum after his death. Lukis's fifth son, François du Bois Lukis (1826–1907), a lieutenant in the 64th regiment and an archaeologist, was also born and educated in Guernsey. On his retirement from the army in 1870 he dedicated his time to archaeology, mainly excavating in Alderney. He inherited his father's collections and archive, and in accordance with his wishes bequeathed them to the states of Guernsey. The Lukis collection formed part of the nucleus of the present Guernsey Museum.

H. R. Sebire

Sources E. F. Lukis, 'The Lukis family of Guernsey', *Quarterly Review of the Guernsey Society*, 30 (1974), 79–83 · W. de Guérin, *Our kin* (1890) · parish register, 1788, St Peter Port, Guernsey [birth] · parish register, 1871, St Peter Port, Guernsey [death] · parish register, 1813, St Peter Port, Guernsey [marriage] · T. D. Kendrick, *The bailiwick of Guernsey* (1928), vol. 1 of *The archaeology of the Channel Islands* · Guernsey Museum, Collectanea Antiqua MSS · *Gazette de Guernesey* (18 Nov 1871)

Archives Guernsey Museum, Lukis collection, archaeological, geological, and natural history objects · Guernsey Museum and Galleries, Candie Gardens, Guernsey, Collectanea Antiqua, letters, MSS

Likenesses photograph, Guernsey Museum

Lul [St Lul, Lullus] (*c*.**710–786**), archbishop of Mainz, was born in Wessex, probably about 710, and entered the abbey of Malmesbury, apparently at a young age. In 738, while in Rome on a pilgrimage, Lul encountered his fellow countryman Boniface, who was then, on his third visit to the city, appointed papal legate in Germany. Lul was one of those whom Boniface persuaded to accompany him back to his mission field east of the Rhine. The prominence which he quickly achieved in the mission, and his closeness to Boniface, are evident from his correspondence, some of which survives among that of his master in three ninth-century, and a number of later medieval, copies. These letters show Lul near the centre of a network of English clerics that covered both those who accompanied Boniface on his continental mission, including Burchard, later bishop of Würzburg, and their acquaintances and supporters in England. Prominent among the latter, at least during the earlier part of Lul's career, were a number of abbesses: Lul asked that they support him through their prayers. This notion of confraternity through prayer was one of the English mission's significant contributions to continental religious life. The surviving correspondence reveals that Lul had become a deacon by 745–6, an archdeacon by 746–7, and was employed by Boniface to take letters to Rome. In 752 Boniface made Lul one of two *chorepiscopi* (assistant bishops) to help him in his efforts to mould a diocesan organization in Germany. Shortly afterwards he wrote to Fulrad, the abbot of St Denis and one of the most influential figures at the court of the new Frankish king, Pippin III, asking that Lul be his successor.

On Boniface's death in 754, Lul duly succeeded to the bishopric of Mainz. He did not, however, also acquire the metropolitan status that Pope Gregory III (*r.* 731–41) had granted to Boniface. Nevertheless, there are signs that Lul was considered pre-eminent among the bishops of the Anglo-Saxon mission. From the time of his accession onwards, he was in correspondence with the leading members of the English church, including two archbishops of Canterbury and one of York, in a network of mutual support animated by prayer and the exchange of gifts. Furthermore, it was to Lul that King Alchred of Northumbria wrote in 773, asking that he lend his aid to the legates that the king had sent to Charlemagne and confirming his spiritual confraternity with Lul. Other English correspondents of Lul included King Eardwulf of Kent and King Cynewulf of Wessex; the extent of his influence in his native land is also amply demonstrated by his excommunication of the English abbess Switha. On the continent, Lul's advice on the administration of family monasteries and on questions of marriage law was sought by the Frankish bishop Megingoz, who had succeeded Burchard at Würzburg. The limit to Lul's episcopal power is evident from his failure to end the privilege of direct jurisdiction from Rome that Boniface's foundation of Fulda had enjoyed since 751. Between 769 and 775, however, Lul established his own foundations at Hersfeld in Hesse and Bleidenstadt in Nassau. He was also able to incorporate into his diocese the short-lived missionary bishoprics of Buraburg and Erfurt.

His correspondence reveals Lul as a pivotal figure in the dissemination of Anglo-Saxon learning on the continent. He wrote requesting the works of Aldhelm, and sent presents to the tomb of Bede at Jarrow, in return for which Abbot Cuthbert dispatched copies of Bede's prose and verse lives of St Cuthbert: he would, he said, have provided more had not the cold of winter hampered the hand of the scribe. Lul had, in any case, also acquired a copy of Bede's *Historia ecclesiastica gentis Anglorum*. The list of that author's other works which it contains prompted Lul to send further requests to Abbot Cuthbert and to Archbishop Ælberht of York: a copy of Bede's *De templo*, at least, was forthcoming. Lul had himself been taught metrics by Boniface in Rome and before he became bishop he sent a specimen of his efforts to an abbess and a nun in England. Later he wrote to Milred, bishop of Worcester, asking for a book of the egregiously florid picture poems of Optatianus Porfyrius (*fl.* 325–333), which, however, Milred could not send, because it had not been returned by Cuthbert, archbishop of Canterbury.

Apart from his letters, with their included snatches of poetry, the only other work of Lul to survive is his profession of faith. This he made *c.*780, when Pope Hadrian I (*r.* 772–95), prompted by Charlemagne's desire to complete Boniface's work of diocesan organization, ordered an examination by the bishops of Rheims, Trier, and (perhaps) Tarentaise of Lul's consecration. On the basis of the resulting profession, Hadrian granted Lul the pallium, indicating metropolitan status, probably in the following year.

Lul died on 16 October 786 and was buried at Hersfeld. His epitaph survives in the same manuscript as his profession of faith. Lampert of Hersfeld wrote a life of Lul *c.*1070 which adds nothing to historical knowledge of him. His cult never took hold in his native England, but there are many dedications to him in Germany.

MARIOS COSTAMBEYS

Sources M. Tangl, ed., *Die Briefe des heiligen Bonifatius und Lullus*, MGH Epistolae Selectae, 1 (Berlin, 1916) • W. Levison, *England and the continent in the eighth century* (1946) • Lampert von Hersfeld, 'Vita Lulli', *Lamperti monachi Hersfeldensis opera*, ed. O. Holder-Egger, MGH Scriptores Rerum Germanicarum, [38] (Hannover, 1894)

Lulach [Lulach mac Gille Comgáin] (*d.* **1058**). *See under* Macbeth (*d.* 1057).

Lulls, Arnold [*formerly* Arnout] (*fl.* **1584–1642**), merchant and jeweller, was born in Antwerp, Spanish Netherlands. Members of the Lulls family had lived in England since the 1550s, but Arnold himself arrived some time between 1580 and 1584, when he became a member of the Dutch church, Austin Friars. On 12 June 1593 he married another member of the church, English born Susanna de Beste (*bap.* 1574, *d.* 1597), daughter of Geleyn de Beste and Locoyse zen Moenen; their son Arnold was baptized there on 26 October 1595 and their daughter Susanna on 2 January 1597. His wife died later that year and was buried on 16 November at St Magnus the Martyr, London. On 11 December 1599 Lulls married Margriete Raket, widow of Abraham van Hawijck, and had three further daughters, Maria (*bap.* 1601), Margriet (*bap.* 1603), and Sara (*bap.* 1605); his second wife died early in 1615. Returns of aliens describe the family as living in a succession of different properties, mostly in Billingsgate and Bridge wards.

Although never recorded as a member of the Goldsmiths' Company, Lulls became rich through supplying jewellery to the royal court and to foreign ambassadors. By 1597 he was sufficiently well placed to petition the privy council on behalf of Peter and Hans Lulls (probably his brothers), the owners of a Dutch flyboat whose cargo had been seized by the earl of Cumberland. Four years later he survived apparently unscathed the suspicions of Matthew Greenesmith, secretary of state Robert Cecil's agent in Middleburg, that he had been engaged in illegal pearl trading through Emden. In the first decade of James's reign Lulls was paid thousands of pounds for pearls, diamonds, emeralds, gold buttons, and small jewels, provided in partnership with Sir John Spelman and Sir William Herricke, the king's jewellers. In June 1604 he received £260 for 'a jewel AR set with diamonds', presumably destined for the queen, and in February 1605 £700 for 'A jewel R with thistles & a jewel like a lance' (PRO, SP 14/24, fol. 21). A letter preserved in Lulls's design book (V&A, department of prints, MS 91, A.83), datable to 1612 and signed by George Calvert, then temporarily secretary of state, lists £3000 worth of jewels supplied by Herricke and Lulls for gifts at the new year last past, including a rope of pearls (£740) and 'a great round pearle' (£900) for the queen, and a chain of stones and a George (£800) for Prince Henry. The designs themselves are mostly of pendants, earrings, and brooches; notes in Dutch point to a partnership between Lulls and his brother Peter and to continuing links with Antwerp.

Lulls was naturalized on 7 May 1618, being variously described in returns of aliens that year as having lived in England for thirty and for thirty-eight years. The same year his son died. In his will dated 4 April 1618 and proved on 7 September, Arnold the younger revealed kinship and friendship connections spanning native, stranger, and foreign mercantile communities. Legatees included the son of his uncle Peter (a Hamburg merchant), his cousin Jane Vanlore (granddaughter of merchant stranger and Berkshire landowner Sir Peter Vanlore), a London draper, cooper, and mercer, and the poor of both the Dutch church and St Mary-at-Hill, Billingsgate. He left £500 to his sister Susanna, and £600 and a property in Lime Street between his stepsisters.

Late that year Sir Peter Vanlore and other members of the Dutch born mercantile community who had previously advanced significant loans to the king were accused of the illegal export of bullion. By 1619 his kinsmen Arnold and Jehan Lulls and Jacques de Beste had also been implicated and called before Star Chamber. Henry Rowland of London, goldsmith, testified on 3 March that between about 1598 and 1606 he had delivered a total of £65,000 in gold to Arnold Lulls and £50,000 to de Beste; these and sums delivered to others had, it was alleged, unaccountably disappeared. On 11 December 1619 Lulls was fined £8000; together with de Beste's fine of £7000 this was granted to Sir James Erskine the following month. It is not clear when, or to what extent, it was ever paid. After widespread protest, and in particular the intervention of the Dutch ambassador, Sir Noel de Caron, in 1620 the overall level of the merchant strangers' fines was reduced.

The episode bred considerable insecurity among the immigrants. It was thus perhaps in a bid to gain advantageous patronage that on 23 June 1621 Lulls promised a handsome dowry worth over £5350 in settlements attendant on the marriage of his daughter Susanna on 27 June to John *Newdigate (1600–1642), a Warwickshire gentleman of very modest wealth but with valuable kinship connections. Guarantors of the settlements included Jehan Lulls and Jacques de Beste, but none of them proved able to honour in full their respective commitments, and Newdigate was unable to take possession of a house and shops at the corner of Thames Street and St Michael's Lane, London, supposedly conveyed to him. Financially disastrous as this was for the Newdigates, Lulls remained on good terms with his son-in-law throughout the 1620s. Integrated in a circle which included Newdigate's friend Gilbert Sheldon, in correspondence he supplied European and metropolitan news until at least 1629.

Thereafter little is known of Lulls. His second daughter married Andrew Blackwell, minister of Tilehurst, Berkshire, a living in the gift of Sir Peter Vanlore. As a 'gentleman' Lulls was party to a settlement made in December 1642 following Newdigate's death, but may have died before his daughter Susanna remarried in May 1646. At that time she reached an agreement with her future husband over the disposal of what seems to have been a significant inheritance, devolving on her as the only daughter of Lulls's first marriage. He was not mentioned at all in her will, drawn up in 1653, but jewels similar to those depicted in his design book were prominent among Susanna's bequests. The design book itself passed to the Blackwell family. VIVIENNE LARMINIE

Sources records of the Dutch church, Austin Friars, GL, MSS 7402/7, 7403, 7404 · W. J. C. Moens, ed., *The marriage, baptismal, and burial registers, 1571 to 1874, and monumental inscriptions of the Dutch Reformed church, Austin Friars, London* (privately printed, Lymington, 1884) · R. E. G. Kirk and E. F. Kirk, eds., *Returns of aliens dwelling in the city and suburbs of London, from the reign of Henry VIII to that of James I*, 4 vols., Huguenot Society of London, 10 (1900–08) · W. A. Shaw, ed., *Letters of denization and acts of naturalization for aliens in England and Ireland, 1603–1700*, Huguenot Society of London, 18 (1911), 6, 25 · W. D. Cooper, ed., *Lists of foreign protestants and aliens resident in England, 1618–1688*, CS, 82 (1862), 63 · PRO, STAC 8, 25/19, part 1 · PRO, E 159/457 · PRO, SP 14/24, fol. 21; SP 14/26, fol. 94 · will, PRO, PROB 11/132, fol. 83 [Arnold Lulls, son] · *CSP dom.*, *1603–10*, 217, 338, 352; *1619–23*, 119, 474 · A. Lulls, letters to J. Newdigate, Warks. CRO, CR 136, B 265–8 · private information (1978) [Beric Lloyd] · *Calendar of the manuscripts of the most hon. the marquis of Salisbury*, 24 vols., HMC, 9 (1883–1976), vol. 14, p. 11; vol. 18, p. 105 · *Report of the Laing manuscripts*, 1, HMC, 72 (1914), 122 · A. Heal, ed., *The London goldsmiths, 1200–1800: a record of the names and addresses of the craftsmen, their shop-signs and trade-cards* (1935), 197 · V. M. Larminie, *Wealth, kinship and culture: the seventeenth-century Newdigates of Arbury and their world*, Royal Historical Society Studies in History, 72 (1995) · J. Hayward, 'The Arnold Lulls book of jewels and the court jewellers of Queen Anne of Denmark', *Archaeologia*, 108 (1986), 227–37
Archives V&A, department of prints and drawings, MS 91 A.83 · Warks. CRO, letters to John Newdigate, CR 136, B 265–8

Lumby, Joseph Rawson (1831–1895), author and Church of England clergyman, the only son of John Lumby (1799/1800–1864), a joiner, and his first wife, Sarah (*d.* 1844), was born at Stanningley, near Leeds, on 18 July 1831. On 2 August 1841 he was admitted to Leeds grammar school and in March 1848 he left to become master of a school at Meanwood, a village soon to be absorbed in Leeds, where his ability attracted attention. He was encouraged to attend university, and in October 1854 he entered Magdalene College, Cambridge; in the following year he was elected to a Milner close scholarship. In 1858 he graduated BA, being bracketed ninth in the first class of the classical tripos, and was ordained in the following year. He was awarded an MA in 1861, a BD in 1873, and a DD in 1879.

Within a few months of graduation Lumby was made Dennis fellow of his college, and began to take pupils. He forfeited his fellowship on his marriage on 11 April 1859 to Susanna Mary Parsons (*d.* 1873) of Darlington. In 1860 he gained the Crosse theological scholarship, the chaplaincy of Magdalene, and the curacy of Girton. In the following year he won the Tyrwhitt Hebrew scholarship, and was appointed classical lecturer at Queens' College. In 1873 his name was added to the list of the Old Testament Revision Company; when the Old Testament was completed, he worked with equal enthusiasm on the revision of the Apocrypha, just living to see the publication of the latter work. In 1874, then a widower after the death of his first wife in May 1873, he was chosen fellow and dean of St Catharine's College, Cambridge; having resigned his curacy at Girton he became curate of St Mark's, Newnham. In the following year he was appointed, on the nomination of Trinity Hall, to the non-stipendiary cure of St Edward's, Cambridge, where his sermons were much appreciated by undergraduates. In 1879 he was elected to the Norrisian professorship of divinity; he was also Lady Margaret preacher for that year. Having vacated his fellowship at St Catharine's because of his second marriage—on 16 June 1880 to Luise Theodore Ernestine Albertine Dahlmann (1856/7–1915), second daughter of a German lawyer—he was appointed to a professorial fellowship in that college in 1886. In 1887 he was made prebendary of Wetwang in the cathedral church of York, and acted as examining chaplain to the archbishop of York and the bishop of Carlisle. On the death of F. J. A. Hort in 1892 he was unanimously chosen to succeed him as Lady Margaret professor of divinity. After an illness of several months he died at Merton House, Grantchester, near Cambridge, on 21 November 1895, leaving a large family. He was buried on 25 November in Grantchester parish church.

Lumby habitually rose early and worked diligently. H. J. Roby, who taught him, remembered him as 'of all my pupils the one who made the most evident progress from day to day', who winced at criticism but did not repeat mistakes (*Cambridge Review*, 23 Jan 1896, 144). Anecdotes about him later entered the folklore of the university, where his omnivorous reading and capacious memory for recondite and often trivial information were a source of wonder and amusement. A large and powerful man, he was reputedly able to twist pokers. He was kindly but, some thought, deficient in humour. The famous observation (attached to more than one scholar, before and since) 'Lumby is omniscient and omnipotent but (thank Heaven!) not omnipresent' and the verses 'I heard the voice of Lumby say' (repeated in full in Venn's *Alumni Cantabrigienses*) are attributed to A. W. Spratt of St Catharine's.

Lumby's literary career, especially as editor and annotator, was unflagging and wide-ranging. He often had several works, large and small, in preparation and others at press, chiefly in the fields of biblical scholarship and medieval English literature and history. He was co-editor of the Cambridge Bible for Schools series and a contributor to the Speaker's Commentary, the Expositor's Bible, the *Cambridge Companion to the Bible*, and the ninth edition of the *Encyclopaedia Britannica*. Among his other works were editions of More's *Utopia* (1879) and *History of Richard III* (1883), Cowley's *Essays* (1887), a *History of the Creeds* (1873), *A Popular Introduction to the New Testament* (1883), sermons, and contributions to learned journals. A fairly full list of his publications is included in the *Dictionary of National Biography*.

But Lumby attempted too much: although he was active in the Early English Text Society from its beginning, his editions of Old and Middle English texts such as *Be domes daege* (1876) and *Ratis Raving* (1867) were indifferent and soon superseded. He stood unsuccessfully against Walter Skeat for the new professorship of Anglo-Saxon in 1878. Above all, the poor reputation of what could have been a worthy memorial, nine large (and to him lucrative) volumes for the Rolls Series, has most damaged his memory. He edited seven volumes of Ranulf Higden's *Polychronicon* (1871–86), in which some errors and omissions misled scholars badly, and his edition of the *Chronicon* of Henry Knighton (1889–95) was one of the worst of the whole enterprise, causing James Tait to remark that he 'lacked much of the elementary equipment of an editor of a medieval chronicle' (Tait, 569). JOHN D. PICKLES

Sources *Armley and Wortley News* (29 Nov 1895), 3 · *Biograph and Review*, 5 (1881), 419–21 · *Cambridge Review* (28 Nov 1895), 115–16 · *Cambridge Review* (23 Jan 1896), 144 · G. G. Coulton, *Fourscore years: an autobiography* (1943), 118–20 · Venn, *Alum. Cant.* · *Cambridge Chronicle* (17 May 1873) · *Cambridge Chronicle* (19 June 1880) · *Cambridge Chronicle* (22 Nov 1895) · *Cambridge Chronicle* (29 Nov 1895) · R. L. Poole, review, *EngHR*, 6 (1891), 172–3 · J. Tait, review, *EngHR*, 11 (1896), 568–9 · J. A. Robinson, 'An unrecognized Westminster chronicler, 1381–1394', *PBA*, [2] (1907–8), 61–92 · L. C. Hector, 'An alleged hysterical outburst of Richard II', *EngHR*, 68 (1953), 62–5 · *Cambridge Chronicle* (4 Dec 1895), 4 [account of sermon at Great St Mary's, Cambridge, by G. F. Browne] · G. F. Browne, *St Catharine's College* (1902), 226–7

Likenesses G. G. Coulton, cartoon, repro. in G. G. Coulton, *Fourscore years*, 119 · photograph (in middle age), repro. in E. Wilson, *Leeds grammar school admission books* (1906) · wood-engraving (after photograph by Russell, 1880–1889?), NPG; repro. in *ILN* (30 Nov 1895), 662

Wealth at death £4669 8*s*. 5*d*.: resworn probate, 4 Feb 1896, *CGPLA Eng. & Wales*

Lumisden, Andrew (1720–1801), Jacobite politician and antiquary, was the only son of William Lumisden (1688–1756), an Edinburgh law agent and burgess, and Mary (*d.* 1755), daughter of Robert Bruce, a merchant of the same city; and the grandson of another Andrew Lumisden, the nonjuring bishop of Edinburgh (1654–1733). Born into a family with marked Jacobite sympathies, he was educated for a career in the law, following both the precedent of his father and the traditional path for a Scottish gentleman into the respectable professions. However, the arrival in September 1745 of the highland army into Edinburgh prompted a dramatic break with his former existence. Having been deprived of the services of his original secretary, Prince Charles Edward, the Young Pretender, had asked Alexander Cunningham to fill the vacancy. Though

Andrew Lumisden (1720–1801), by James Tassie, 1784

refusing the offer himself, Cunningham warmly recommended Lumisden—his second cousin—as an individual who would ideally suit the post. Thereafter Lumisden served as the under-secretary and the first clerk of the treasury to the Young Pretender throughout the campaign of 1745–6. He accompanied the army into England, supplied money for its current expenses, and left detailed and graphic manuscript accounts of the battles of Prestonpans, Falkirk, and Culloden, at which he was present (now in NL Scot., MS 279). On the eve of the battle of Culloden (15 April 1746) special orders were given to ensure his safety, as he carried with him 'the sinews of war' (Dennistoun, 1.85), and following the defeat he fled the field, having first been entrusted with the safe keeping of the prince's seal. He obeyed the order to rendezvous with the other remnants of the Jacobite army at Ruthven on 17 April, only to hear that the Young Pretender had advised his followers to disband and to 'Let every man seek his own safety the best way he can' (Youngson, 261).

As a consequence of this Lumisden spent the next four months wandering the highlands as a hunted fugitive, his importance to the authorities underlined by his inclusion in the act of attainder issued by the Hanoverian government. He returned to Edinburgh heavily disguised as a lady's servant: his yellow hair hidden beneath a black wig and his eyebrows corked to match. Taking refuge at his father's house, he remained hidden in Edinburgh until October 1746, when, having assumed the dress and manner of a poor schoolteacher, he made the acquaintance of a king's messenger and with 'happy audacity' journeyed to London under his protection (H. W. Lumsden, 106). In contrast to his later pursuit of a quiet scholarly life, at this point he seems to have delighted in his various disguises—passing his old schoolmates by unnoticed in the streets of Edinburgh and slipping into Newgate gaol so that he might visit his friends who had been captured after the failure of the rising. For this latter escapade his father remarked that he truly deserved to be hanged for jeopardizing himself in such a rash and foolish manner. Taking a boat at Tower stairs, he finally made his escape to the continent and journeyed to Paris via Rouen.

From his place of exile Lumisden maintained a lively correspondence with his family, written in various sorts of sympathetic ink, including milk and water, in order to preserve its secrecy. However, both the novelty of life in a foreign land and his early optimism about his prospects soon evaporated under the grim realities of poverty and unemployment. His application for a commission in Lochiel's regiment was submitted late, and his fluent command of the French language did not, as he had hoped, ensure him a place in a prominent mercantile company. His father's unwillingness to provide credit for his private trading schemes spelt the end of his dreams of financial independence, and he turned instead to the exiled Jacobite court as his primary means of subsistence. Unable to afford the rent in Paris he returned to Rouen, but on the strength of favourable references provided by the officials of the Scots College he secured an annual pension of 600 livres in June 1749. Before the end of that year he had travelled to Rome in the hope of securing employment in the service of the Old Pretender, but had to wait another year to acquire the post of his assistant secretary, working under the direction of James Edgar. On assuming his duties he began to keep scrupulous notes of his correspondence, and his letter-books for the period 1751–73 provide a vital source for reconstructing the diplomatic and social life of the exiled court during those years.

Lumisden distinguished himself as a competent and dutiful servant, concerned above all with the promotion of a noble and seemly image for the leadership of the Jacobite movement. In the winter of 1758–9 he was dispatched on a secret mission through France and the Italian states to drum up support for a projected French raid upon the coast of England. In Paris he attempted to heal the rift between the Old Pretender and his son, and to urge Charles Edward to reconcile himself to the French crown. After the death of Edgar in September 1764 he became the secretary of state to the Jacobite court. In this capacity he served the Old Pretender faithfully until the latter's death in January 1766 and officiated at his funeral, discharging his last duty to his master by placing three seals in his coffin and seeing that it was closed up.

Though Lumisden was there to greet Charles Edward upon his entry into Rome on 23 January 1766, and had been quick to congratulate him on his accession to the 'throne', he enjoyed none of the rapport that he had had with his late father. The hero worship which had characterized his accounts of the prince's role in the battles of the 'Forty-Five had rapidly dissipated during his years of exile, and his letters of the 1750s and 1760s speak all too often of a thinly veiled contempt for his new royal master. In particular he strongly disapproved of the prince's drinking and womanizing, and he joined forces with Cardinal Henry Stuart and John Waters, the Parisian banker and factor for the exiled court, to exert pressure on Clementine Walkinshaw to sign a declaration, dated 9 March 1767, that she had never been married to the Young Pretender. It seems likely that Lumisden had threatened her with the severance of her pension if she did not comply with their demands.

In this light, Lumisden's dismissal by the Young Pretender on 8 December 1768 did not come as a surprise, but formed part of a dramatic incident none the less. After an evening witnessing the prince's heavy drinking at the dining table, a quarrel arose as Lumisden and his friends refused to accompany their master to an oratorio on the grounds that he was too hopelessly drunk to appear in public. Undaunted, Charles Edward staggered out to his coach commanding that they follow him, but when they refused he dismissed them all on the spot. Within two days the prince had thought better of his rash decision and commanded Lumisden to return to his duties. However, on the advice of Cardinal Henry Stuart, Lumisden had resolved to quit his service as secretary of state. He had long complained of Rome's hot climate and mosquitoes, and been shunned by many of the local élites on the grounds of his staunch protestantism.

From 1769 to 1773 Lumisden resided in Paris and was visited by many British tourists and gentlemen on the grand tour. From 1772 he discontinued his practice of writing an annual letter to the Stuart princes and increasingly distanced himself from their cause. This did much to hasten the raising and acceptance of a petition to allow him to revisit his native land (dated 15 February 1773), which was signed by forty-five of the most distinguished men in Edinburgh society, including David Hume and eight members of the judiciary. Lumisden arrived back in Edinburgh in June and chose to divide his time between Scotland, Paris, and Bath. While in Paris he put himself at great pains to buy up a collection of rare books for George, prince of Wales, which greatly helped to secure him a full pardon from the British government in 1778.

A member of the royal and antiquaries' societies of Edinburgh, Lumisden corresponded with Joseph Banks, James Boswell, Adam Smith, and David Hume. In 1797 he published his *Remarks on the Antiquities of Rome and its Environs*, the product of almost forty years of intermittent research, which contained a thorough description of those classical remains still extant in the city, as well as copious engraved illustrations. The book was well received and ran to a second edition in 1812. His last years were spent in Edinburgh, sharing apartments with another elderly bachelor, John McGowan, first in Luckenbooths—which had gained a reputation for its literary salons—and then in the more fashionable new developments of Princes Street. Lumisden was renowned as a popular and sociable figure in Edinburgh society, much in demand as a dinner guest. On Christmas night 1801 he went to bed in good health, but was seized by a sudden fit of apoplexy at some point in the early hours of the morning and was found dead upon the floor the following day. Writing in 1855, James Dennistoun mentioned that his copious anecdotes and stories were still fondly remembered by those that knew him (Dennistoun, 2.274). Distinguished for his contemporaries by his singularly old-fashioned, *ancien régime* manners and 'natural mildness of disposition' (*Scots Magazine*, 182), Lumisden, it should not be forgotten, was also committed to the absolute necessity of divine-right monarchy, with an almost total distrust of democratic institutions, and manifested a fierce and brutal antisemitism in many of his writings (Dennistoun, 1.174; A. Lumisden, *Remarks on the Antiquities of Rome*, 299).

John Callow

Sources *DNB* • J. Dennistoun, *Memoirs of Sir Robert Strange … and of his brother-in-law Andrew Lumisden*, 2 vols. (1855) • N. K. Strange [Mrs. Gower Stanley], *Jacobean tapestry* (1947) • J. Maidment, ed., *Analecta Scotica: collections illustrative of the civil, ecclesiastical and literary history of Scotland*, 2 vols. (1834–7), vol. 2 • *Scots Magazine*, 64 (1802), 182 • H. W. Lumsden, *Memorials of the families of Lumsdaine, Lumisden or Lumsden* (1889) [repr. 1994] • A. Lumsden-Bedingfeld, *Genealogical records of the family of Lumsden* (1928) [repr. 1994] • A. Cameron, *Two accounts of the escape of Prince Charles Edward by Dr. Archibald Cameron and another, with twelve letters from Lord George Murray to Andrew Lumisden*, Luttrell Society Reprints (1951) • A. J. Youngson, *The prince and the pretender* (1985)

Archives NL Scot., account of battles of Prestonpans, Falkirk, and Culloden • NL Scot., letter-book, ACC 11328 • NL Scot., letter-books and corresp., MSS 14260–14265; Ch 10674–10683 | Yale U., corresp. with James Boswell and others

Likenesses J. Tassie, paste medallion, 1784, Scot. NPG [*see illus.*] • W. Dickinson, engraving (after J. Tassie), repro. in A. Lumisden, *Remarks on the antiquities of Rome and its environs* (1797), frontispiece • W. Ridley, stipple, BM, NPG; repro. in *European Magazine* (1798)

Wealth at death Stuart pensions presumably given up some time between 1768 and 1773; able to claim upon father's estate after 1756; took possession of it after 1773

Lumley, Benjamin (1811/12–1875), opera manager and author, was the son of Louis Levy, a Jewish merchant of Canada, who died in London about 1831. Benjamin Levy assumed the name Lumley early in life. After being educated at King Edward's School at Birmingham, he was admitted a solicitor in London in 1832. Within a few years he was solicitor to the Herne Bay Steam Packet Company and had separate chambers as a parliamentary agent. He was studying for the bar when, in 1835–6, Pierre-François Laporte, manager of Her Majesty's Theatre, employed him first on legal and then on financial business. For five years he worked as Laporte's assistant, and after the latter's death (on 25 September 1841) he took over as manager from 1842. Her Majesty's Theatre had practically been the sole home of Italian opera since its establishment in England. When Lumley took over, the repertory was all Italian as to language and largely Italian in provenance. Even more than in Italy the genre was dominated by virtuoso singers, in particular by the '*Puritani* quartet' of Giulia Grisi, G. B. Rubini (G. M. Mario soon stepping into his place), Antonio Tamburini, and Luigi Lablache, who together with Fanny Tacchinardi-Persiani were widely known as 'la vieille garde'. Lumley was later blamed by J. E. Cox for having alienated these remarkable artists by choosing to show himself 'sole master … ostensibly and positively'; he himself gloried in his 'policy of silence and reserve' and enjoyed being known as 'l'homme mystérieux'. There is no sign that he was opposing the star system in general in the name of ensemble. He began by dropping Tamburini, with whom the management was already in

Benjamin Lumley (1811/12–1875), by Alfred, Count D'Orsay, 1847

dispute. In 1844 he made no effort to retain Persiani; a year later he seemed to show greater interest in ballet by setting up the famous *Pas de quatre* with Marie Taglioni, Carlotta Grisi, Fanny Cerrito, and Lucille Grahn. In 1846 he refused the demand of Michael Costa, the conductor, to be allowed to accept the conductorship of the Philharmonic Society's orchestra. Costa may have had other reasons for discontent—his own music was not being performed often enough. He seceded, with Grisi, Mario, and the greater part of his fine orchestra, to the new Royal Italian Opera House at Covent Garden in 1847. Lablache alone remained faithful to Lumley.

Up to 1847 Lumley's management met with brilliant success. Among contemporary critics, often partisan, some credited him with 'revolutionizing' a shabby system, but H. F. Chorley—always hostile—thought Costa's discipline had educated the audience to expect 'the entire performance … to be the real object of interest', and, once Costa left, Lumley's reliance on singers brought 'systematic deterioration'. Lumley's cult of ballet was similarly controversial. Besides the four ballerinas already named, he engaged Fanny Elssler and the male dancers Perrot and St Leon, altogether an epitome of Romantic ballet. His success enabled him in 1845 to acquire the lease of Her Majesty's.

The opening of the rival opera house in 1847 imperilled Lumley's position. He replaced Costa with Michael Balfe and, for the 1847 season, engaged Jenny Lind, paying for her to break a previous contract and gradually overcoming her scruples. He also secured a new opera from the young Verdi (*I masnadieri*, a relative failure); an attempt to procure one from the more prestigious Mendelssohn foundered. From Lind's opening performance on 4 May, as Alice in Meyerbeer's *Robert le diable*, she exerted an extraordinary spell over the English public and temporarily saved Lumley from disaster. At the end of her third season at Her Majesty's, in 1849, she retired from the stage, and Lumley's financial embarrassment thenceforth grew rapidly. Far from relying on her alone, he engaged some of the leading Italian singers of the day, as well as the Germans Henriette Sontag and Sophie Cruvelli, who made a considerable impression; but, Marietta Alboni apart, his Italians failed to counter the prestige of Grisi and Mario, and Chorley may have been right in denouncing these seasons as undisciplined 'sham'. Lumley attempted to keep up their social prestige by throwing lavish parties at his riverside house in Fulham, at which artists mingled with 'society'. He also took the classic gambler's step of throwing good money after bad by taking on, from 1850, the winter season at the Théâtre Italien in Paris; theoretically this fitted in with the London spring season, but in practice it was difficult to supervise both. Though subsidized, the Paris seasons suffered from political disturbances, cripplingly so after the December 1851 *coup d'état*. Lumley lost at least £14,400. In 1852 it is clear even from his disingenuous memoirs (*Reminiscences of the Opera*, 1864) that he was failing to pay his artists both in London and in Paris; they were leaving or, like Johanna Wagner, turning to the rival Covent Garden management (Lumley won the resulting lawsuit, but no damages). Various devices—a subscribers' committee, formed to safeguard the wages of permanent staff, and an attempt at limited liability through an act of parliament—failed. Lumley fled to Paris. Her Majesty's remained closed from 1853 to 1856. In the latter year the burning of Covent Garden led Lord Ward (later earl of Dudley) to reopen Her Majesty's. He bought up Lumley's debts and his lease and reinstalled him as manager and sub-lessee. Until 1858 Lumley secured some good singers, among them Alboni, Giuglini, and the young Therese Titjens; his greatest draw was Marietta Piccolomini, less a singer than a personality for whom there was a craze. The commercial panic of 1857, however, influenced the receipts; it is again clear, between the lines of Lumley's account, that he owed Lord Ward rent, as well as earlier debts, and on 10 August 1858 he had to give up his sublease. In 1863, three benefit performances were given at Her Majesty's on his behalf.

The few new works put on under Lumley's management included, besides Verdi's, Halévy's *La tempesta*, loosely based on Shakespeare and notable chiefly for Lablache's Caliban. Operas by Costa and Sigismond Thalberg failed. The usual repertory of Bellini, Donizetti, and early Verdi (eight of whose works Lumley introduced to London) was supplemented with a little French grand opera by Meyerbeer and Auber.

Lumley perhaps did not deserve the description (by the singer Gilbert-Louis Duprez, *Souvenirs d'un chanteur*, 1880, 202) 'faiseur [crook or charlatan] habile et audacieux', but he seems to have left an ambiguous impression which his memoirs do not dispel.

After resigning Her Majesty's Theatre, he returned to the practice of law, and wrote several books. In 1838 he had published a standard book on *Parliamentary Practice on Passing Private Bills*. In 1862 appeared, published anonymously, a work of fiction, *Sirenia*, followed in 1873 by *Another World, or, Fragments from the Star City of Montallayah by Hermes*; both were experiments in what would later be called science fiction. *Another World* reached a third edition within a year. Lumley also published a pamphlet (1863) about his legal and financial disputes with Lord Dudley. He died, aged sixty-three and unmarried, at his home, 8 Kensington Crescent, London, on 17 March 1875, and was buried at West Ham.

L. M. MIDDLETON, *rev.* JOHN ROSSELLI

Sources B. Lumley, *Reminiscences of the opera* (1864) • A. Soubies, *Le Théâtre-Italien de 1801 à 1913* (1913), 141–9 • *The Times* (19 March 1875) • D. Nalbach, *The King's Theatre, 1704–1867* (1972) • J. E. Cox, *Musical recollections of the last half-century*, 2 (1872), 130, 145, 153–4, 165 • H. F. Chorley, *Thirty years' musical recollections*, 2 (1862), 179, 196 • J. Budden, *The operas of Verdi*, 3 vols. (1973–81), 1.315–19 • d. cert. • Boase, *Mod. Eng. biog.*

Archives BL, corresp. with Charles Babbage, Add. MS 37193

Likenesses J. Brown, lithograph, 1847 (after sketch by Count D'Orsay), NPG; repro. in Lumley, *Reminiscences*, frontispiece • Count D'Orsay, lithograph, 1847 (after his portrait), NPG [*see illus.*] • portrait, repro. in *ILN*, 3 (1843), 124 • portrait, repro. in *ILN*, 4 (1844), 237 • prints, Harvard TC

Wealth at death under £1000: probate, 27 April 1875, *CGPLA Eng. & Wales*

Lumley [*née* Cornwallis], **Elizabeth**, **Viscountess Lumley of Waterford** (*c*.**1578–1658**), benefactor, was the second daughter of Sir William Cornwallis of Brome, Suffolk (*c*.1549–1611), and his first wife, Lucy (*c*.1549–1608), daughter and coheir of John Neville, fourth Baron Latimer, and his wife, Lucy. Her father's profligacy at court lost £20,000; he left debts amounting to £4000, to settle which five manors had to be sold. He even allegedly remarked: 'So that I may be about her Majesty, I care not to be groom of the scullery' (HoP, *Commons, 1558–1603*, 1.659). On 22 November 1596 at her father's house in St Botolph without Bishopsgate, London, she married Sir William Sandys (*d*. 1629) of Mottisfont, Hampshire, son and heir of Sir Walter Sandys and a grandson of Thomas, Lord Sandys of the Vyne. On 11 May 1630 at St Bride's, London, she married Richard Lumley, Viscount Lumley of Waterford [*see below*].

Elizabeth Lumley's second marriage was unhappy as conflict grew over her husband's aid in clearing her debts to the earl of Danby. He petitioned the king on 30 March 1640, complaining of his great costs, and that owing to the differences between him and his wife just satisfaction was denied him. On 18 May 1640 a day was appointed for the House of Lords to hear their differences. Elizabeth's breach with her husband appears to have been unresolved as their wills failed to address each other as husband and wife. Elizabeth's will lamented 'these long miseries of scarcity' and that her personal effects were 'soe poor through my long continued sufferings as I may well shame to have anie eyes upon them' (will, PROB 11/293, sig. 356). She left £2000 towards a marriage portion for her niece, Henrietta Maria Cornwallis. She was 'strong minded, independent and thoughtful' (Jordan, *Charities of Rural England*, 279), and warned the viscount to 'interrupt not nor meddle with anie thing in my possession' (will, PROB 11/293, sig. 356).

Elizabeth Lumley's greatest significance rests in her foundation of almshouses and schools in the North Riding of Yorkshire and London, which reached the substantial total of £5750. They included almshouses in St Botolph Aldgate, London, and Thornton-le-Dale, the Yorkshire parish in which she usually resided. Her concern for education was such that she also founded grammar schools in Thornton-le-Dale and Pickering, and left an endowment of £40 per annum to support scholarships at Oxford and Cambridge for inhabitants of her three local Yorkshire parishes. She died childless and was buried on 2 February 1658 in Westminster Abbey.

Her second husband, **Richard Lumley**, first Viscount Lumley of Waterford (*bap*. 1589, *d*. 1661x3) was baptized at Chester-le-Street, co. Durham, on 7 April 1589, the son and heir of Roger Lumley and his wife, Anne Kurtwich. Educated at Cambridge, he was awarded the degree of MA in 1609, in which year he also succeeded to the estates of his cousin, John, Baron Lumley. On 17 August 1614 he married his first wife, Frances (1592–1627), widow of William Holland of Chichester, Sussex, and daughter of Henry Shelley of Warminghurst, Sussex.

Lumley was admitted to Gray's Inn on 2 March 1615, knighted at Theobald's on 19 July 1616, and created Viscount Lumley of Waterford in the peerage of Ireland on 12 July 1628. He had been living on his Sussex estates, but was ordered to return to Lumley Castle, co. Durham, on 27 January 1638. He was a commissioner for the duchy of Cornwall in 1641. He garrisoned Lumley Castle for the royalists during the civil war and was president of Prince Rupert's council of war at the surrender of Bristol in 1645. He petitioned that he left Stansted in January 1644 to join the king, but never bore arms nor contributed to the royalist service. He took the national covenant and the negative oath, and his composition fine was later reduced to £1925 15*s*. In 1646 he petitioned against local people felling wood on his Stansted estate. In 1654 he was granted a pass to travel abroad. Before the meeting of the Convention Parliament in 1660 he signed a declaration of moderate royalists pledging not to take revenge upon old enemies. His will, dated 13 April 1661, was proved on 12 March 1663. He was buried in the vault at Cheam parish church, Surrey. His son John had died in 1658, and he was succeeded as second viscount by his grandson, Richard Lumley, later first earl of Scarbrough.

ANDREW J. HOPPER

Sources GEC, *Peerage*, new edn, vols. 7–8 • E. Milner, *Records of the Lumleys of Lumley Castle*, ed. E. Benham (1904) • HoP, *Commons, 1558–1603*, vol. 1 • J. L. Chester, ed., *The marriage, baptismal, and burial registers of the collegiate church or abbey of St Peter, Westminster*, Harleian Society, 10 (1876) • M. A. E. Green, ed., *Calendar of the proceedings of the committee for compounding … 1643–1660*, 5 vols., PRO (1889–92) • M. A. E. Green, ed., *Calendar of the proceedings of the committee for advance of money, 1642–1656*, 3 vols., PRO (1888) • *CSP dom.*, *1640*, with *addenda, March 1625 – Jan 1649* • J. Foster, *The register of admissions to Gray's Inn, 1521–1889, together with the register of marriages in Gray's Inn chapel, 1695–1754* (privately printed, London, 1889) • Venn, *Alum. Cant.*, 1/3 • will, PRO, PROB 11/293, sig. 356 • will, PRO, PROB 11/310, sig. 37 [Richard Lumley] · T. W. Beastall, *A north country estate: the Lumleys and Saundersons as landowners, 1600–1900* (1975) · L. G. H. Horton-Smith, *The ancient northern family of Lumley and its Northamptonshire branch records of the past 680 years* (1948) · W. K. Jordan, *The charities of rural England, 1480–1660* (1961) · W. K. Jordan, *The charities of London, 1480–1660: the aspirations and achievements of the urban society* (1960) · *VCH Yorkshire North Riding*, vol. 2

Archives Sandbeck Park, Rotherham, Yorkshire, MSS · Suffolk RO, Ipswich, Cornwallis of Brome MSS

Wealth at death £1570 bequeathed gifts, incl. many charitable gifts; £2000 portion to niece; £391 annuities; estates in Hampshire, Yorkshire, London: will, PRO, PROB 11/293, sig. 356

Lumley, George, third Baron Lumley (*d.* 1507), nobleman, was the eldest son and heir of Thomas, second Baron Lumley, and Margaret, daughter of Sir James Harrington. Forty years old and more at his father's death in 1485, he received licence for entry into his inheritance on 12 May 1486. Following an early visit to Newcastle upon Tyne, in the wake of his victory at Towton in March 1461, Edward IV entrusted the defence of Tynemouth Castle to Lumley and a garrison of forty men; even with a reduced force of twenty-four from September he managed to hold this northern fortress until 11 January 1462. On 13 November 1461 he was named a commissioner to array men in the county of Northumberland for defence against Henry VI, Margaret of Anjou, and their adherents, and the king's enemies in Scotland. Lumley also held office as sheriff of the county from November 1461 to November 1463. Significantly, in June 1464, he was excused payment of arrears arising out of his shrievalty, partly because the devastation wrought by the king's rebels and traitors had been so great that he had not been able to collect what was due, and partly because he had resisted them at great expense to himself. In the North Riding of Yorkshire he was justice of the peace from May 1461 to June 1464, a commissioner to arrest and imprison rebels there in May 1461, and, jointly with his father, became constable of Scarborough Castle on 14 December 1461.

Elected member of parliament for Northumberland on 23 April 1467 Lumley also served as deputy sheriff of Northumberland under John Neville, earl of Northumberland, in the later 1460s and became sheriff of Durham and Sedbergh in 1471. During the 1470s, following Edward IV's decision to entrust the rule of the north to his brother, Lumley entered the service of Richard, duke of Gloucester. In 1480–81, at a time when the threat from Scotland was once more manifesting itself strongly, he became lord lieutenant of the county of Northumberland; in 1482 he took part in a major expedition into Scotland led by Richard of Gloucester; and, for his services against the Scots, he was created a knight-banneret. Although probably among the northerners who supported Richard III at the battle of Bosworth he rapidly entered the service of Henry VII, appearing on a commission as early as 25 September 1485 to array men in the northern counties in readiness for a Scottish invasion. In April 1486 he attended on the new king during his first northern progress; in 1497 he took part in an expedition against the Scots led by Thomas Howard, earl of Surrey; and when, in 1503, Henry VII's daughter Margaret married James IV of Scotland, he and his son were among those who escorted her from Darlington to the Scottish border.

Lumley married Elizabeth, daughter and heir of Roger Thornton, a wealthy merchant of Newcastle upon Tyne, and granddaughter of John, Lord Greystoke: as a result he seems to have obtained possession of estates including Ludworth and the Isle, co. Durham, and Witton, in Northumberland. Traditionally he is said to have married Elizabeth, bastard daughter of Edward IV, but there is no reliable evidence for this. Lumley died on 13 November 1507 and was buried at Chester-le-Street. Thomas Lumley, his son and heir, had predeceased him and, consequently, in his will George Lumley left his estates in trust for his grandson Richard. KEITH DOCKRAY

Sources GEC, *Peerage* · W. E. Hampton, *Memorials of the Wars of the Roses: a biographical guide* (1979), 245 · *CPR, 1461–94* · C. L. Scofield, *The life and reign of Edward the Fourth*, 1 (1923)

Lumley, George (*d.* 1537). *See under* Lumley, John, fifth Baron Lumley (*b.* in or before 1492, *d.* 1545).

Lumley, Henry (*c.*1658–1722), army officer, was the second son of John Lumley, whose burial is recorded for 10 October 1658. Henry Lumley, however, was described as in his sixty-third year at the time of his death, on 18 October 1722. His mother was Mary, daughter of Sir Henry Compton, and his elder brother Richard *Lumley, first earl of Scarbrough. He was probably raised a Roman Catholic, and may have converted to protestantism in 1687. On 13 June 1685 he had attained the rank of captain in the Queen's regiment of horse (later 1st dragoon guards), and served with it throughout the wars of William III and Anne, gaining a high reputation for courage. When Sir John Lanier, the colonel of the Queen's Horse, was killed at Steenkerke in 1692, Lumley was made colonel (10 August) in his stead, and in February 1693 he was promoted brigadier-general. He was at Neerwinden and Landen in 1693, covering the retreat on 19 July, and saving William III from capture by the enemy. In 1695 he was at the siege of Namur. On 1 January 1696 he became major-general. After the peace of Ryswick (1697) he returned to England, and his regiment, though reduced, was one of those which were not disbanded in February 1699. Lumley married, first, Elizabeth Thimbleby of Lincolnshire, and, second, Anne, daughter of Sir William Wiseman of Great Canfield Hall, Essex. A daughter, Frances, by his second marriage, died in 1719.

Lumley was elected MP for Sussex in 1701 and 1702, and for Arundel in 1715 in his brother's interest. On 27 February 1702 he embarked at Woolwich for the campaign in Flanders, and was promoted lieutenant-general on 11 February 1703. He became governor of Jersey in 1703, and in 1710 he was given the office for life, on the recommendation of Marlborough; he never visited the island, although he was very attentive to the interests of the inhabitants in London. In July 1704 he took part in the bloody assault on the Schellenberg and with the horse prevented some of the young recruits from running away. At Blenheim he was on the left wing, and he afterwards fought at Ramillies, Oudenarde, and Malplaquet. On 30 January 1711 he was promoted full general. In 1717 he resigned the command of his regiment, and died on 18 October 1722. He was buried in the church at Sawbridgeworth in Hertfordshire, where there is an inscription to his memory.

W. A. J. ARCHBOLD, *rev.* TIMOTHY HARRISON PLACE

Sources R. R. Sedgwick, 'Lumley, Henry', HoP, *Commons, 1715–54* • GEC, *Peerage*, new edn, vol. 11 • *The letters and dispatches of John Churchill, first duke of Marlborough, from 1702 to 1712*, ed. G. Murray, 5 vols. (1845) • N. Luttrell, *A brief historical relation of state affairs from September 1678 to April 1714*, 6 vols. (1857) • N. B. Leslie, *The succession of colonels of the British army from 1660 to the present day* (1974) • R. Beatson, *A political index to the histories of Great Britain and Ireland*, 2nd edn, 1 (1788) • P. Falle, *Caesarea, or, An account of Jersey, the greatest of the islands remaining to the crown of England of the ancient Dutchy of Normandy*, 2nd edn (1734)

Likenesses portrait, Lumley Castle, co. Durham

Lumley [*née* Fitzalan], **Jane**, **Lady Lumley** (**1537–1578**), translator, was the eldest child of Henry *Fitzalan, twelfth earl of Arundel (1512–1580), and his first wife, Katherine (*d.* 1542), daughter of Thomas Grey, second marquess of Dorset, and his second wife, Margaret. She had two siblings: Henry, Lord Maltravers (1538–1556), and Mary *Howard, duchess of Norfolk (1539/40–1557); and one stepbrother, John, son of her father's second wife, Mary, and her first husband, Robert Radcliffe, earl of Sussex. She married, as his first wife, John *Lumley, first Baron Lumley (*c.*1533–1609), a university friend of her brother, probably by 1550 and certainly before 1553, when she attended Queen Mary's coronation as his wife. The couple then spent some time at Lumley's ancestral home, Lumley Castle in co. Durham, before joining Arundel's household at Nonsuch Palace in Surrey, where Jane nursed her father through considerable illness following the deaths of her brother in 1556, and both her sister and stepmother in 1557. Jane died at Arundel Place in London, predeceasing her father on 27 July 1578. Her funeral took place at St Clement Danes, the Strand, on 19 August. Her body was presumably re-interred by Lumley when he erected her tomb at Cheam in Surrey in 1596. Jane had two sons and one daughter, who all died in childhood.

Jane Lumley's considerable learning was made possible by her father's particular care to educate all of his children, allowing his daughters to continue their studies at home when, unlike their brother, they could not pursue them at university. Partly to this end, the twelfth earl of Arundel built up an impressive library and offered patronage to scholars and practitioners of the arts. His library, which passed to Jane's husband on Arundel's death and is therefore known as the Lumley Library, was the means by which Jane's work was preserved. As well as housing the books that she collected, it was the repository for her manuscript translations. When the library passed into royal ownership in 1609, Jane's work became part of what is now the British Library. BL, Royal MS 15 A. i and ii are Latin translations selected from the orations of Isocrates, as are folios 2–62 of Royal MS 15 A. ix, with the exception of two Latin dedications to her father on folios 4 and 23. Most significant, however, are folios 63–97, which contain *Iphigenia at Aulis*, her English translation from Euripides. This work has the distinction of being both the first translation of one of Euripides' plays into English, and also the earliest piece of extant English drama by a woman.

STEPHANIE HODGSON-WRIGHT

Sources *DNB* • 'The life of Henry Fitzallen', BL, Royal MS 17 A.ix • S. Jayne and F. R. Johnson, eds., *The Lumley library: the catalogue of 1609* (1956) • GEC, *Peerage* • BL, Royal MS 15 A.i, ii, ix • M. F. S. Hervey, 'A Lumley inventory of 1609', *Walpole Society*, 6 (1917–18), 36–50 • E. McCutcheon, *Sir Nicholas Bacon's Great House Sententiae*, English Literary Renaissance Supplements, 3 (1977) • Euripides, *Iphigenia at Aulis*, ed. H. H. Child, trans. Lady Lumley [J. Lumley] (1909) • L. Cust, 'The Lumley inventories', *Walpole Society*, 6 (1917–18), 15–35

Likenesses Steven, oils

Lumley, John, **fifth Baron Lumley** (*b.* in or before **1492**, *d.* **1545**), landowner and rebel, of Lumley, co. Durham, was born in or before 1492, being at least eighteen in 1510. He was the son and heir of Richard Lumley, fourth Baron Lumley (*b.* in or before 1477, *d.* 1510), landowner, of Lumley, co. Durham, and his wife, Anne (*d.* 1530), daughter of Sir John Conyers, of Hornby, North Riding of Yorkshire, and his wife, Alice. He succeeded his father, as fifth Baron Lumley, in May 1510 and received his first summons to parliament on 23 November 1514. Surprisingly, he did not take livery of his lands until 18 July 1515.

From his youth, Lumley followed the traditional chivalric ideals of the nobility. Indeed, members of his family aspired to the crusading values associated with the cult of St George. As such, Lumley participated in several military campaigns during the early years of Henry VIII's reign. He distinguished himself at the battle of Flodden on 9 September 1513 and was knighted on the field by Thomas Howard, earl of Surrey. In 1519 he participated in a raid to destroy fortresses in Scotland and was later involved in the Scottish campaign of 1522–3, where he was mentioned in reports from the commander. More spectacularly, in June 1520 he accompanied Henry to France and was present at the Field of Cloth of Gold. In addition to his military exploits, Lumley participated in the administration of co. Durham, serving as JP. However, his relations with the early Tudor bishops of Durham were strained. In 1508 his father and he had been appointed, jointly, to the office of chief forester of Weardale, a position which had been held, in hereditary succession, by members of the Lumley family since 1436. Lumley's period of tenure was, however, punctuated by disputes with the episcopal administration, and his involvement in the Pilgrimage of Grace in 1536–7 signalled the end of the family's longstanding connection with the office. The office of coroner of Chester Ward, which had likewise been in the family for several generations, was also granted to others. Dissatisfaction at the erosion of his traditional position within Durham society may well have been a factor in his later decision to rebel against the crown.

On 13 July 1530 Lumley signed the petition from the House of Lords calling on Clement VII to consent to the king's request for a divorce. He felt sufficiently at odds with royal policy in the north by the autumn of 1536 to take a rebel stance in the Pilgrimage of Grace. His Catholicism was probably a strong motivating factor too. As with many of the aristocratic pilgrims, Lumley claimed that he had been coerced into joining the revolt. He had been ordered by the king to raise 100 men to suppress the revolt. Instead, he played a leading role in it, adopting, in the process, an uncompromisingly hard-line approach in terms of rebel demands. Despite this, he came, subsequently, to accept the terms of the peace agreement, as one of their chief negotiators, drawn up at Doncaster in early December. While Lord Lumley avoided further involvement in the revolt, his eldest son and heir, George Lumley [*see below*] of Thwing in the East Riding of Yorkshire, was not so fortunate.

During the closing years of his life Lord Lumley suffered poor health, although he continued to play some part in public life, being appointed JP for the North Riding in 1539 and 1540. He was also summoned to sit in the parliament which met in January 1541. He concerned himself with local affairs and his estates during the last years. He died between 23 November and 16 December 1545 and was buried at Guisborough Priory, not far from his North Riding manor of Kilton. He had married Joan (*d*. in or after 1545), daughter of Henry Le Scrope, seventh Baron Scrope of Bolton, and his second wife, Mabel or Margaret. They had two sons, George and Percival Lumley. The few details about Percival are contained in the family papers; he married Elizabeth Hussey in 1543. Upon Lord Lumley's death his peerage was forfeited as a result of his heir's attainder. The Lumley estates, however, were settled upon his grandson, John *Lumley, first Baron Lumley (*c*.1533–1609), the son and heir of George Lumley. In 1547 John Lumley successfully petitioned for the restoration of the barony.

George Lumley (*d*. 1537), rebel, had his marriage settled with Jane (*d*. in or after 1537), second daughter and coheir of Sir Richard Knightley of Upton and Fawsley, Northamptonshire, and his wife, Joan, on 20 May 1524. The couple were married before 1533 and had one son, John Lumley, and two daughters, Jane and Barbara. George Lumley became involved in the second phase of the Pilgrimage of Grace, led by Sir Francis Bigod in January 1537. He participated, with 400 men, in the capture of Scarborough, North Riding of Yorkshire, which the rebels held for several days. He gave himself up on 20 January. As a result of this activity he was attainted and found guilty of high treason on 27 May. He wrote to his wife before his execution, 'good mother and natural to my three children, to whom I give God's blessing and mine', asking her to teach his heir to be a faithful servant to the king and a good Christian (Milner, 30). He was hanged, drawn, and quartered at Tyburn on 2 June and buried in the Crutched Friars, London. CHRISTINE M. NEWMAN

Sources GEC, *Peerage* • M. James, *Family lineage and civil society: a study of society, politics and mentality in the Durham region, 1500–1640* (1974) • M. H. Dodds and R. Dodds, *The Pilgrimage of Grace, 1536–1537, and the Exeter conspiracy, 1538*, 2 vols. (1915) • *LP Henry VIII* • M. Bush, *The Pilgrimage of Grace: a study of the rebel armies of October 1536* (1996) • M. Bush and D. Bownes, *The defeat of the Pilgrimage of Grace* (1999) • M. Bush, *Durham and the Pilgrimage of Grace*, Durham County Local History Society (2000) • E. Milner, ed., *Records of the Lumleys of Lumley Castle* (1904) • J. L. Drury, 'More stout than wise: tenant right in Weardale in the Tudor period', *The last principality: politics, religion and society in the bishopric of Durham, 1494–1660*, ed. D. Marcombe (1987)

Archives priv. coll., family deeds, estate papers, etc.

Lumley, John, first Baron Lumley (*c*.1533–1609), collector and conspirator, was the only son of George *Lumley (*d*. 1537) [*see under* Lumley, John, fifth Baron Lumley (*b*. in or before 1492, *d*. 1545)], conspirator, of Thwing, East Riding of Yorkshire, and his wife, Jane (*d*. in or after 1537), second daughter and coheir of Sir Richard Knightley of Upton, Northamptonshire. His father was executed for high treason on 2 June 1537 for his part in the Pilgrimage of Grace. Lumley inherited the family estates around Durham on the death of his grandfather John *Lumley, fifth Baron Lumley (*b*. in or before 1492, *d*. 1545), by virtue of a settlement made after his father's attainder. He inherited extensive estates and was the greatest coal owner among the English aristocracy, obtaining a charter of incorporation for Hartlepool, co. Durham, on 3 February 1593 in order to erect a pier for shipping coal to the south. More important, he was also a committed Catholic. On his petition to parliament in 1547 he was restored in blood and created Baron Lumley.

Life and political career Lumley's destiny was determined by his marriage, in or before 1550, to Jane (1537–1577) [*see* Lumley, Jane], translator, eldest child of Henry *Fitzalan, twelfth earl of Arundel (1512–1580), and his first wife, Katherine (*d*. 1542), daughter of Thomas Grey, second marquess of Dorset. Lumley met her brother, Henry Fitzalan, Baron Maltravers (1538–1556), at Cambridge, where they matriculated as fellow-commoners at Queens' College in May 1549. Lumley's manuscript translation of Erasmus, *Institution of a Christian Prince* (BL, Royal MS 17 A.xlix) is inscribed to Arundel at the end, 'your lordshippes obedient sone, J. Lumley 1550', suggesting that he was married by that date. The couple had two sons and a daughter, none of whom survived to adulthood. Lumley was created KB on 29 September 1553 and attended Mary I's coronation on 1 October.

The death of Arundel's second wife, Mary, in October 1557 and the deaths of Lady Lumley's siblings during these years increased Lumley's importance; Arundel began to look on him as a son. The Lumleys may have spent the first years of their married life at Lumley's London house in Hart Street near Tower Hill (a house built for the poet Sir Thomas Wyatt) and at Lumley Castle, near Chester-le-Street, co. Durham. However, Arundel's various bereavements led them to move to his new residence, Nonsuch Palace, Surrey. Lumley was keeper of the great park of Nonsuch from 20 August 1559 until his death, a position which carried an annual fee of £4 8*s*. 4*d*. Both Arundel and he made various alterations to Nonsuch, the most important of which was the creation of extensive gardens.

Lumley became high steward of the University of Oxford on 24 February 1559 on the elevation of Arundel to chancellor. He maintained a relationship with the university throughout his life, donating forty books to the Bodleian Library in 1599. He also gave eighty-seven duplicate books from his own library to the University of Cambridge Library in 1598.

John Lumley, first Baron Lumley (*c*.1533–1609), attrib. Steven van der Meulen, *c*.1560–63

A steady adherent of Arundel's, Lumley was deeply implicated in the Ridolfi Plot of 1571 for the re-establishment of Roman Catholicism and in the marriage negotiations of his brother-in-law, Thomas *Howard, fourth duke of Norfolk (1538–1572), to Mary, queen of Scots. His involvement in these intrigues, which went on for a number of years and included telling Guerau de Spes, the Spanish ambassador, in August 1569 that he could raise men, led to incarceration in the Tower of London after September 1571. He was then held at several other locations until released in April 1573. These activities ended any political ambitions he had. It seems likely that Lumley erected the grove of Diana, England's first allegorical garden (an area of inscriptions, sculptures, and tableaux away from the formal privy garden) at Nonsuch as an apology for his involvement in the Ridolfi Plot.

Despite his long imprisonment on Mary's account, Lumley avoided association with the subsequent plots for her escape and accepted nomination as one of the commissioners for her trial. He was present at Fotheringhay Castle, Northamptonshire, and in the court of Star Chamber in October 1586. He sat in judgment on a number of important trials, including those of Henry Grey, duke of Suffolk, in 1554, Dr Rowland Taylor in 1557, and William Davison in 1587. He was also appointed commissioner for settling claims for the coronations of both Elizabeth I (whom he attended on her journey from Hatfield to London at her accession in November 1558) and James I, and for the creation of the knights of the Bath in 1603.

Arundel died at Arundel House, Westminster, on 24 February 1580 and Nonsuch passed to Lumley, along with his father-in-law's huge arrears in debt. The greatest single amount owed was the so-called 'Florentine debt'. This was a loan of £11,000 owed to Henry VIII by a group of Florentine merchants. Arundel and Lumley were given responsibility in 1564 for repaying the money, now owed to Elizabeth; they hoped to make money on the deal but were unable to fulfil their promise. Lumley began to negotiate terms for the payment of the debt in 1590 and in 1592 it was agreed that he would give Nonsuch to the queen but remain resident as keeper. He was allowed a lease on the great park and was excused from paying after a few years. Lumley was also the owner of a number of properties in and around Chichester (because of its proximity to his wife's family base at Arundel) and exercised patronage over its parliamentary seat. He sponsored Anthony Watson, rector of Cheam, Surrey, who became bishop of Chichester in 1596, and wrote the most important description of Nonsuch and its gardens. Lumley also had a house at Stanstead, Sussex (which had been the property of his first wife), where it is said that Henry, prince of Wales, visited him in September 1603.

By the time of Lumley's second marriage, in 1582, to Elizabeth (*d*. 1617), daughter of John Darcy, second Baron Darcy of Chiche, and his wife, Frances, he was no longer a significant figure at court; he seems to have spent more time at Lumley Castle, where he gradually expressed his interest in ancestry and genealogy through a series of decorative embellishments. There were no children of his second marriage. It is said that James I visited Lumley Castle on his journey south to London in 1603 but, Lumley being absent, he was shown around by Tobras Matthew, bishop of Durham, who lectured him on the baron's long and noble pedigree. The king is supposed to have become bored by this lengthy diatribe and stopped the bishop, saying 'oh, mon, gang na futher. I maun digest the knowledge I ha' this day gained, for I didna' ken Adam's ither nam was Lumley' (Milner, 92).

Collections and patronage Lumley was one of the great Elizabethan collector-patrons. His collections, which included books, paintings, and marbles, were catalogued during his lifetime and transcriptions of the manuscripts published during the twentieth century. The significance of these inventories cannot be underestimated—they provide a unique illustration of his particular interests and intellectual pursuits as well as a more general picture of aristocratic taste in Elizabethan England. Unfortunately there is no trace of the gardens at Nonsuch, but this complex project was Lumley's other significant contribution to Elizabethan culture.

Lumley's library was one of the largest in Elizabethan England. It was housed at Nonsuch and contained nearly 3000 books. Remarkably, the majority of the books listed in the catalogue survive in the British Library as they passed from Lumley to Henry, prince of Wales (exactly how this happened is not known), and thence into the

Royal Library. The books are inscribed with the original purchaser's name. Thomas Cranmer, archbishop of Canterbury, Arundel, and Lumley's brother-in-law, the Welsh antiquary Humphrey Lloyd (*c*.1527–1568), all contributed significant numbers of books. However, the vast majority were collected by Lumley himself.

The catalogue is divided by subject and size and is remarkable for the wide range of titles it contains, but the predominance of scientific, medical, and geographical titles should be noted. Lumley's interest in medicine led to his sponsorship of a regular surgery lecture at the Royal College of Physicians between 1582 and 1583. The other significant group of titles, although small in number, is listed at the end under the heading *Musici*. These include religious works by the Catholic composer William Byrd, one of which is dedicated to Lumley, as well as one of the earliest sets of madrigals to be seen in England. This was commissioned by Arundel while in Italy in 1566 and 1567 and sent to him by the composer Innocenzo Alberti.

Lumley's collection of paintings, furniture, and stone sculptures is included in the famous illustrated inventory, known as the Red Velvet Book (because of a later binding), which remains in the possession of Lumley's descendant the earl of Scarbrough. The inventory includes the contents of all of Lumley's residences and was drawn up in 1590 during his financial negotiations with Elizabeth (presumably in order to establish exactly which of the contents were Lumley's). Unfortunately this inventory does not list the continu by location, but another, of Lumley Castle, dated 1609, helps to establish the locations of at least some of the items in 1590.

The Red Velvet Book starts with a written account of Lumley Castle, followed by transcripts of various historic deeds and detailed heraldic descriptions. The inventory proper begins with a series of hand-coloured illustrations of sculptures, fountains, and furniture. Notable among the statuary are the free-standing fountains and obelisks, which were situated in the privy garden at Nonsuch. These are remarkable for their classical form and can be related to continental examples. It is possible that Lumley may have known of them through engravings or drawings or perhaps the accounts of Arundel and Lloyd after their journey to Italy. Many of the other objects illustrated were to be found at Lumley Castle, as they can be identified through the description of the castle at the start of the Red Velvet Book, including marble busts of Henry VIII and his children (presently at Leeds Castle, Kent). Sadly, none of the furniture illustrated in the inventory survives.

The inventory continues with a list of paintings. These are described in more detail than almost any other contemporary inventory, often including the artist's name, and it has been possible to identify the hand of at least one artist using evidence from this inventory. As with Lumley's books, it is still possible to identify some of his paintings as each was painted with the so-called 'Lumley cartellino'—a fictive scrap of paper with the sitter's name written on it. The predominance of portraits in the collection has often been noted, and it has been assumed that Lumley's interests lay more with the sitters than the artists. However, the list includes a number of other genres, such as still lifes and religious works.

The grove of Diana at Nonsuch is known only through written accounts, the most detailed (and most florid) being the Latin description written by Watson before 1592. The grove was constructed in order to lead the visitor past a series of sculptures, fountains, and buildings which conveyed a complex allegorical message. This type of garden, using all of the senses and many media, was developed in northern Italy during the late first half of the sixteenth century, particularly at the Medici villas outside Florence. Lumley's inspiration must have come through written and verbal descriptions of these gardens, as the grove of Diana was unlike anything else built in England at the time. It portrayed Elizabeth as Diana, while Lumley is both characterized as Acteon and as the apologetic 'smitten fisher'.

Lumley's concern with family ancestry and genealogy was remarkable and it is not surprising that he is often incorrectly described as being a member of the Society of Antiquaries. It is still possible to appreciate this aspect of his personality through an examination of the various tombs (all surviving) that he erected, as well as through his books and building projects. These interests may also reflect his concern to portray himself as a member of the ancient nobility. The first group of tombs, for himself, his wives, and children, is to be found in the Lumley chapel at St Dunstan's, Cheam. They are all illustrated in the Red Velvet Book. Lumley's own tomb concentrates on genealogy, while that for Jane Lumley is remarkably classical in its decoration and detail. Between 1594 and 1597 he also arranged for the installation of a group of tombs at the church of St Mary and St Cuthbert in Chester-le-Street. These fourteen tombs to his ancestors included real monuments removed from Durham Cathedral, as well as fictive examples that Lumley had made in an appropriately medieval style. In 1596 he erected a tomb to the tenth, eleventh, and twelfth earls of Arundel in the Fitzalan chapel at Arundel Castle. This was deliberately evocative of a medieval chantry chapel, such as that to William Fitzalan, ninth earl of Arundel, opposite, and is yet another example of Lumley's historicizing attitude.

Certain of Lumley's building projects were intentionally historicizing, particularly his alterations to Lumley Castle of the 1580s, which included the addition of rows of heraldic shields in the main courtyard and the erection of the 'Lumley horseman' (now at Leeds Castle) in the hall. This polychrome wooden equestrian monument (illustrated in the Red Velvet Book) represents Edward III in whose time the castle was founded. It relates to the similar monuments and paintings commissioned by various Italian city states (particularly Venice) in honour of foreign warriors, especially the *condottieri*, like Sir John Hawkwood, and it is possible that Lumley was told of these statues by Arundel and Lloyd on their return from Italy. It was the first statue of its kind to be made in England.

The greatest myth about Lumley is that he travelled to Italy and that this provided him with the inspiration for his collecting and building projects, especially the grove of Diana. Although it is absolutely clear from the documentation that Lumley did not go to Italy, it is easy to understand why historians have made this assumption. Modern research into patterns of patronage and manufacture in Elizabethan England (especially the availability of printed sources and the activities of northern artists and craftsmen) helps to explain how Lumley could have built and collected as he did without leaving England.

Death and burial Lumley died on 11 April 1609 at his residence in London and was buried at night (presumably with Catholic ritual) in the Lumley chapel at St Dunstan's, Cheam. In 1607 he had entailed the lands and castle of Lumley on Richard *Lumley, first Viscount Lumley of Waterford (*bap.* 1589, *d.* 1661x3) [*see under* Lumley, Elizabeth, Viscountess Lumley of Waterford (*c.*1578–1658)]. From him descended the earls of Scarbrough.

KATHRYN BARRON

Sources A. Wells-Cole, *Art and decoration in Elizabethan and Jacobean England* (1997) • K. Barron, 'Classicism and antiquarianism in Elizabethan patronage: the case of John, Lord Lumley', MLitt diss., U. Oxf., 1996 • E. Milner, ed., *Records of the Lumleys of Lumley Castle* (1904) • L. Cust, 'The Lumley inventories', *Walpole Society*, 6 (1918), 15–35 • S. Jayne and F. Johnson, eds., *The Lumley Library: the catalogue of 1609* (1956) • A. Watson, 'Description of the Palace of Nonsuch', trans. C. F. Ball and A. W. Carr, MSS, Bourne Hall Library, Ewell, Surrey • J. G. Nichols, 'Life of the last Fitz-Alan, earl of Arundel', *GM*, 1st ser., 103/2 (1833) • M. Biddle, 'The vanished gardens of Nonsuch', *Country Life* (26 Oct 1961), 1008–10 • GEC, *Peerage* • *DNB* • J. Dent, *The quest for Nonsuch* (1962) • F. Edwards, *The marvellous chance: Thomas Howard and the Ridolphi Plot* (1968) • J. Pollen, ed., 'Unpublished documents relating to the English martyrs, 1584–1603', *Catholic Record Society*, 5 (1908), 30 • F. W. Steer, 'Lord Lumley's benefaction to the College of Physicians', *Medical History*, 2 (1958), 298–305 • Trinity Cam., MS R.7.22

Archives Surrey HC, rentals, memoranda book, and accounts | BL, MS and printed book collection, Royal MSS

Likenesses attrib. S. van der Meulen, portrait, *c.*1560–1563, NPG [*see illus.*] • J. Fittler, line engraving, pubd 1789, BM • line engraving, pubd 1791, BM • attrib. W. Segar, portrait, Sandbeck Park, Yorkshire • lithograph (after picture at Lumley Castle), BM, NPG

Lumley, Lawrence Roger, **eleventh earl of Scarbrough** (**1896–1969**), civil servant, was born at York on 27 July 1896, the second son of Brigadier-General Osbert Victor George Atheling Lumley (1862–1923) and his wife, Constance Eleanor (*d.* 1933), eldest daughter of the late Captain Eustace John Wilson Patten, and a grandson of the ninth earl of Scarbrough. He was first educated at Eton College (1909–15) and at the Royal Military College, Sandhurst. His elder brother, Richard, fighting with their father's regiment, the 11th hussars, was killed in action in 1914. From 1916 Lumley himself fought with the 11th hussars and was wounded on the western front in March 1918.

After the war Lumley went up to Magdalen College, Oxford, graduating BA in 1921. On 12 July 1922 he married Katharine Isobel (*d.* 1979), daughter of Robert Finnie McEwen of Marchmont, Berwickshire, and Bardrochat, Ayrshire. Four months later he was elected as Conservative member for Hull East, a seat which he held until the Labour victory of 1929. From 1931 until 1937 he was the member for York. Neither strikingly handsome nor an outstanding personality, Lumley did not make a splash in the Commons. But he was efficient, decisive, and imperturbable, ideal qualities for administrative and advisory work, and he served a range of Conservative ministers as parliamentary private secretary, including Anthony Eden at the Foreign Office, who became a close friend. Throughout his parliamentary years he kept up his military connections as an officer of the Yorkshire dragoons (1921–36) and author of *The History of the 11th Hussars* (1936).

Lawrence Roger Lumley, eleventh earl of Scarbrough (1896–1969), by Walter Stoneman, 1937

In 1937 Lumley was appointed governor of Bombay, just as the Indian National Congress was taking provincial power under the new 1935 constitution. He was a realistic and clear-sighted governor who gave full and public backing to the new order, a stance which enabled him to maintain cordial, workmanlike relations with a government whose members were bound by party policy to reject his hospitality. Congress resigned office at the outbreak of war in 1939, and in August 1942, with the launch of the militant Quit India movement, Lumley was forced to find penal accommodation for the Congress leaders, including his own former ministers. In February 1943 the most famous of the prisoners, M. K. Gandhi, embarked upon a 'fast unto the capacity', a nightmare scenario for which Lumley had been preparing for months. He repeatedly warned that the frail and ageing Gandhi could not be allowed to die in detention, but was overruled by the viceroy, Lord Linlithgow, and the cabinet. Gandhi confounded everyone by surviving his three-week ordeal, but the fast cost Lumley the viceroyalty. Leo Amery had marked him out as the most capable successor to Linlithgow, but Churchill flatly refused to consider him in the light of what he interpreted as Lumley's 'weakness'. Had Gandhi died in detention, history would almost certainly have proved Lumley right in predicting a catastrophic breakdown in British-Indian and Anglo-American relations. Churchill's scorn aside, Lumley's governorship was regarded as a success, especially by Linlithgow who thought him the most competent of his governors. He held the civil service firm when many Indian officers were suffering conflicts of loyalty, and with his energetic wife presided over a massive local contribution to the war effort. He himself did not want the viceroyalty and gratefully returned to military service in Britain in mid-1943 as acting major-general of the Yorkshire dragoons.

In 1945 Lumley briefly served in Churchill's caretaker government as parliamentary under-secretary of state for India and Burma before accepting the chairmanship of the 1945–6 commission on oriental, Slavonic, east European, and African studies. His final report laid the foundations for a new, purposeful era of British scholarship on non-Western cultures and languages. His interest in Asia never diminished: chairman of the School of Oriental and African Studies in 1951–9 and of the Commonwealth Scholarship Commission in 1960–63, he also presided over the Royal Asiatic Society (1946–9), the East Indian Association (1946–51), and the Royal Central Asian Society (1954–60).

In 1945 Lumley succeeded his uncle as eleventh earl of Scarbrough, after which his duties in Yorkshire increased markedly. He was lord lieutenant of the West Riding of Yorkshire and the city of York from 1948 and chancellor of the University of Durham from 1958. In May 1967, as high steward of York Minster, he launched and shepherded the minster's restoration appeal for £2 million, half of which was collected within four months. Always an active freemason, in 1951 he was installed as grand master of the United Grand Lodge of England at a huge ceremony in the Royal Albert Hall. In 1967 he became pro-grand master. He was many times honoured by his country, a tribute to his unflagging observance of the obligations of aristocratic duty and service. He was made GCIE in 1937 and GCSI in 1943, KG in 1948, GCVO in 1953, a privy councillor in 1952, lord chamberlain of the royal household in 1952–63, and a permanent lord-in-waiting from 1963, in which year he also received the Royal Victorian Chain. Durham, Sheffield, Leeds, and London universities all recognized him with honorary degrees. His wife, too, was honoured with the DCVO (1962) and, for her war work in Bombay, the kaisar-i-Hind gold medal (1941).

Of all these honours, Scarbrough's appointment as lord chamberlain was perhaps the most fitting. His aristocratic pedigree amply equipped him for the 'pomp and splendour' duties of the job, but in the shifting world of post-war Britain he had to muster all of his administrative experience to carry out the lord chamberlain's archaic role of stage censor. In 1957, before the tabling of the Wolfenden report and after five years of wielding the blue pencil against perversion and indecency, he lifted the ban on plays dealing with homosexuality, providing they were 'sincere and serious' (*The Times*, 30 June 1969, 10). He also eased the restrictions on swearing and provocative statements. He was by no means a radical reformer, but he brought to the role of censor a new readiness to listen to the arguments of playwrights and producers.

Scarbrough died at home, Sandbeck Park, Rotherham, Yorkshire, on 29 June 1969, aged seventy-two, and was buried privately. He was survived by his wife and their four daughters and one son, Richard Aldred (*b.* 1932), who succeeded his father as twelfth earl of Scarbrough.

KATHERINE PRIOR

Sources *The Times* (30 June 1969) · *The Times* (3 July 1969) · *The Times* (12 July 1969) · N. Mansergh and E. W. R. Lumby, eds., *The transfer of power, 1942–7*, 2 (1971) · N. Mansergh and E. W. R. Lumby, eds., *The transfer of power, 1942–7*, 3 (1971) · BL OIOC, Lumley MSS, esp. MS Eur. F 253 (19–20) · A. Aldgate, *Censorship and the permissive society, British cinema and theatre, 1955–65* (1995) · Burke, *Peerage* (1959) · *The Eton register*, 8 (privately printed, Eton, 1932) · *WWW*, *1961–70* · *WWBMP*, vol. 3 · *DNB* · *The Times* (15 July 1969)

Archives BL OIOC, papers relating to India, MS Eur. F 253 · priv. coll., family MSS | BL OIOC, corresp. with Lord Brabourne, MS Eur. F 97 · BL OIOC, Linlithgow collection · Freemasons' Hall, London, grand masters' MSS · U. Birm. L., corresp. with Lord Avon and Lady Avon | FILM IWM FVA, actuality footage

Likenesses W. Stoneman, three photographs, 1937–58, NPG [*see illus.*] · W. Langhammer, portrait, before 1944, Bombay Freemasons · J. Gunn, portrait, Freemasons' Hall, London · D. Hill, portrait, Sandbeck Park, Rotherham

Wealth at death £422,922: probate, 18 Aug 1969, *CGPLA Eng. & Wales*

Lumley, Marmaduke (*c.*1390–1450), administrator and bishop of Carlisle, was the fourth son of Ralph, first Baron Lumley, a major landowner in co. Durham and other northern shires, and Eleanor, sister of Ralph Neville, earl of Westmorland. Ordained in 1414, he was a bachelor of civil law by 1422, probably of Cambridge, where he was later chancellor of the university for at least two years (1425–7) and master of Trinity Hall (1429–43). Before his elevation he was a regular 'chopchurch', being presented to numerous livings, including prebends in Chichester Cathedral and in the Yorkshire secular colleges of Hemingbrough, Harden, and Osmotherley, and the archdeaconry of Northumberland, many of which he later exchanged. His powerful Neville relations and the patronage of Queen Catherine and Henry Beaufort, bishop of Winchester (*d.* 1447), his uncle by marriage, must have assisted him to so much preferment. The latter probably secured the bishopric of Carlisle for Lumley in December 1429, in spite of opposition from the duke of Gloucester. He was consecrated on 16 April 1430. The promotion proved a mixed blessing as it confirmed Lumley's commitment to the interests of Beaufort in return for an impoverished and often war-ravaged diocese.

In 1431 Lumley's partisanship for Beaufort appears to have led to his eclipse, for his name disappears from among the personnel attending the king's council. He was nominated to attend the councils of Basel (1433) and Ferrara (1438) but, since the exchequer made no payments to him, he probably did not go; his activities from the mid-1430s to the 1440s seem to have been largely confined to his bishopric. His episcopal register has not survived so these have been reconstructed from other sources. He was a commissioner to regulate the keeping of the truce with the Scots in 1433 and 1434. On the latter occasion it proved impossible to secure a permanent peace and, following the expiry of the truce, the Scots besieged Roxburgh in August 1436. Lumley's role in organizing the raising of the siege may have persuaded the government that, unusually, a bishop would be a suitable warden for Carlisle and the west march. It may also have been attracted by his willingness to receive a reduced salary of £1050 p.a. Perhaps too the royal council thought he would be easier to control from London than a lay magnate. Lumley took up office as warden on 12 December 1436. The earl of Salisbury and Lord Dacre certainly seem to have resented his appointment: the former was soon suing for the restoration of the post, and Dacre had to give a bond for 1000 marks in 1443 in the course of a dispute between himself and the bishop. Lumley's rivalry with Dacre also spilled over into the political life of Carlisle, as mayors favourable to one or other magnate alternated in office. Lumley's poverty led to great difficulties in the administration of his bishopric, and his estates were devalued by Scottish raids. He seems only to have been able to afford the services of one lawyer, Alexander Cok, and he relied principally on his relatives and servants to defend the march. In part his problems were due to the fact that his salary was neither fully nor regularly paid. Nevertheless, he completed his seven-year term.

As the power of Gloucester waned and that of the earl of Suffolk waxed, Lumley's political career at last revived. Late in 1446 he reappeared as a member of the king's council and was appointed treasurer of England on 18 December. He took effective steps to address the financial crisis he inherited. The increasing household expenses of the king and his educational foundations, along with the costs of the French war, coincided with a sharp fall in the yield from customs, the most important source of royal income. In 1447 he effectively put a stop on the exchequer by dismissing a number of customs collectors, so that the tallies they had issued to authorize payments from their revenues could be cancelled. He then controlled an orderly provision for the expenses of the royal households and partial repayment of the most pressing debts to holders of invalidated tallies. By 1448 his policies had been moderately successful and he also initiated a survey of outstanding debts and the effectiveness of revenue collection. However, the deteriorating military situation and plummeting customs receipts combined to provoke a financial catastrophe. Lumley continued to follow the model established by his predecessors, repaying long-outstanding debts instead of satisfying the urgent demands of the commanders and garrisons in France, as they came under increasing pressure in 1448 and 1449. When the military crisis was eventually recognized, royal credit was so bad that revenue could only be raised by loans, and in seriously inadequate amounts. In September 1449 he resigned the treasurership.

In the previous year Henry VI and Suffolk, who clearly wanted both to reward Lumley and to keep him close at hand, had proposed him for the see of London, contradicting their own earlier recommendation of Thomas Kemp. The pope refused to accept the change, and rebuked king and duke for their ineptitude. On 28 January 1450, however, Lumley was provided to the even more desirable see of Lincoln; the temporalities were restored on 14 March. His failure to defend Suffolk in that year, like his resignation as treasurer, may have been due less to timidity than to bodily infirmity—his age (about sixty) was one of the reasons given by the pope for allowing him to appoint a deputy for a visitation of his diocese. He did, however, spend some time there between April and October 1450, but he returned to London early in November, perhaps for that month's session of parliament, and died in London on a day variously reported as 20 November and 5 December. No will survives, but he had made gifts of books to the London Charterhouse and Queens' College, Cambridge.

MARGARET LUCILLE KEKEWICH

Sources R. L. Storey, 'Marmaduke Lumley, bishop of Carlisle, 1430–51', *Transactions of the Cumberland and Westmorland Antiquarian and Archaeological Society*, new ser., 55 (1956), 112–31 • G. L. Harriss, 'Marmaduke Lumley and the exchequer crisis of 1446–9', *Essays presented to J. R. Lander*, ed. J. G. Rowe (1986), 143–78 • H. Summerson, *Medieval Carlisle: the city and the borders from the late eleventh to the mid-sixteenth century*, 2, Cumberland and Westmorland Antiquarian and Archaeological Society, extra ser., 25 (1993) • R. A. Griffiths, *The reign of King Henry VI: the exercise of royal authority, 1422–1461* (1981) • G. L. Harriss, *Cardinal Beaufort: a study of Lancastrian ascendancy and decline* (1988) • C. M. L. Bouch, *Prelates and people of the lake counties: a history of the diocese of Carlisle, 1133–1933* (1948) • Emden, *Cam.* • *Francisci Godwini primo Landavensis dein Herefordensis Episcopi De praesulibus Angliae commentarius*, ed. G. Richardson (1743) • R. Virgoe, 'The composition of the king's council, 1437–61', *BIHR*, 43 (1970), 134–60 • *VCH Cumberland*, 2.46 • J. M. George, 'The English episcopate and the crown, 1437–50', PhD diss., University of Columbia, 1976 • *CPR*, 1422–52 • *Calendar of the fine rolls*, PRO, 15–18 (1935–9) • *CClR*, 1422–52

Likenesses episcopal seal, repro. in *VCH Cumberland*

Wealth at death estates and income of bishopric of Lincoln; personal wealth probably small

Lumley, Richard, first Viscount Lumley of Waterford (*bap.* **1589**, *d.* **1661x3**). *See under* Lumley, Elizabeth, Viscountess Lumley of Waterford (*c.*1578–1658).

Lumley, Richard, first earl of Scarbrough (**1650–1721**), politician, was the eldest son of John Lumley (*d.* 1658) and his wife, Mary Compton (*d.* after 1667), daughter of Sir Henry Compton. Richard *Lumley, first Viscount Lumley of Waterford [*see under* Lumley, Elizabeth] was his grandfather, and the army officer Henry *Lumley his younger brother. He was educated as a Roman Catholic and in October 1667 went overseas on the grand tour accompanied by his mother and the Roman Catholic divine Richard Lassels (Lascelles). A favourite of Charles II, he accompanied the duke of York to Scotland in 1679 before serving as a volunteer with the reinforcements sent to Tangier in 1680. From 11 September 1681 to 23 February 1682 he served as the earl of Feversham's replacement as master of the horse to Queen Catherine and may have held simultaneously a commission in the 1st troop of Life Guards. Having already succeeded to his grandfather's Irish title, on 31 May 1681 he was created Baron Lumley of Lumley Castle in the English peerage. On 25 October 1684 he replaced the earl of Clarendon as treasurer to Queen Catherine. He married Frances Jones (*c*.1665–1722), daughter of Sir Henry Jones of Aston, Oxfordshire, on 17 March 1685 at St Giles-in-the-Fields.

Following the outbreak of Monmouth's rebellion Lumley was commissioned to raise an independent troop of horse in Hampshire on 18 June 1685. Accompanied by cavalry from the Sussex militia, his men concentrated at Ringwood in Hampshire, whence patrols captured Lord Grey of Wark on 7 July and Monmouth himself on the following day. Lumley was appointed colonel of a new regiment of cavalry, the queen dowager's, on 31 July 1685, but was sacked in 1686 because of his opposition to the projected repeal of the Test Acts and the penal laws. Converting to protestantism in 1687—thereafter his politics were whig—and piqued at his dismissal, he joined the conspiracy against James II in 1688, helped to organize the petition in support of the seven bishops, and signed the 30 June invitation to William of Orange to intervene militarily in England. Despite repeated orders for his arrest he secured Durham for the prince of Orange on 5 December before claiming Newcastle upon Tyne. During the Convention Parliament he strongly supported the contention that the throne was vacant. His rewards were considerable: he was made a privy councillor on 14 February 1689; a gentleman of the bedchamber on 23 February; colonel of the 1st troop of Life Guards on 2 April; and lord lieutenant of co. Durham and of Northumberland. He was created Viscount Lumley of Lumley Castle on 10 April 1689 and earl of Scarbrough five days later.

Scarbrough, a conscientious officer, crossed to Ireland with William III in 1690 and fought at the Boyne. Transferred to the Netherlands in 1691, he was promoted to major-general on 1 April 1692 and lieutenant-general on 4 October 1694. He left the army in 1699, selling his colonelcy of the Life Guards to the earl of Albemarle on 9 March. Queen Anne continued him in his appointments, including his membership of the privy council, and he was appointed a commissioner for the union with Scotland on 10 May 1708. Unlike most of his co-commissioners he took his responsibilities in this regard seriously. Although he lost his offices during the tory purge of 1712, he was reinstated by George I and readmitted to the privy council. On 21 November 1714 he was appointed to the court martial that adjudicated on the seniority of regiments and on 9 March 1716 became chancellor of the duchy of Lancaster. Resigning the latter position in May 1717, he received in compensation the vice-treasurership of Ireland jointly with Matthew Ducie, later first Lord Ducie. He died at his home, Lumley Castle, of apoplexy on 17 December 1721 and was buried in Chester-le-Street. His widow, with whom he had seven sons and four daughters, and who had been a lady of the bedchamber to Queen Mary and to Queen Anne, died on 7 August 1722. His second but eldest surviving son and heir, Richard, was summoned to the House of Lords on 10 March 1714, installed as a knight of the Garter on 28 July 1724, appointed a privy councillor in 1727, and commissioned as a lieutenant-general in the army on 2 July 1739. He died by suicide, unmarried, on 29 January 1740. John Childs

Sources C. Dalton, ed., *English army lists and commission registers, 1661–1714*, 6 vols. (1892–1904) · GEC, *Peerage*, new edn · M. S. Child, *Prelude to revolution: the structure of politics in county Durham* (1972) · *Memoirs of Sir John Reresby*, ed. A. Browning (1936) · D. H. Hosford, *Nottingham, nobles and the north: aspects of the revolution of 1688* (1976) · N. Luttrell, *A brief historical relation of state affairs from September 1678 to April 1714*, 6 vols. (1857) · *The autobiography of Sir John Bramston*, ed. [Lord Braybrooke], CS, 32 (1845) · R. Surtees, *The history and antiquities of the county palatine of Durham*, 4 vols. (1816–40)

Lumley, Sir William (1769–1850), army officer, seventh and youngest son of Richard Lumley, fourth earl of Scarbrough (*c*.1725–1782), and his wife, Barbara (*d*. 22 July 1797), sister and heir of Sir George Savile, seventh baronet, of Rufford, Nottinghamshire, was born on 28 August 1769. He was educated at Eton College and in 1787 was appointed cornet in the 10th light dragoons (later hussars), in which he obtained his lieutenancy in 1791, and his troop in 1793. In 1794 he was made major in Ward's corps of foot, and on 24 May 1795 lieutenant-colonel of the 22nd light dragoons (the third of four regiments that successively bore that number). He commanded the 22nd dragoons during the Irish uprising, and on 7 June 1798 was severely wounded at Antrim, where he prevented the sack of the town by the rebels, and saved the lives of the magistrates, except Lord O'Neil. He also commanded the regiment in Egypt, where it served during the latter part of the campaign of 1801. He superintended the embarkation at Alexandria of the French garrison of Cairo. The 22nd dragoons regiment was disbanded in 1802.

In 1803 Lumley was appointed colonel of the 3rd battalion of the army of reserve, and thereafter he took much interest in its organization. When the army of reserve was ordered to be broken up, Lumley induced all the men of the battalion who passed the required test (400 in all) to re-engage for life service, but the authorities then changed their plans, and ordered the men to be disbanded. Lumley, who became a major-general in 1805, commanded a brigade in the London district that year; with his brigade he was afterwards at the recapture of the Cape of Good Hope in 1806, and in the operations in South America in 1806–7, where he commanded the advance of the army in the landing at Maldonado and the attack on Montevideo. He also served with General Whitelocke in the disastrous attempt on Buenos Aires. He held a like position in Sicily, and commanded the light brigade, which formed the advance of Sir John Stuart's expedition to the coast of Italy in 1809, and captured Ischia. An account of the expedition, and of the situation in Sicily, is given by Sir H. E. Bunbury (see *Narratives of some Passages in the Great War with France*, 1854).

Lumley joined Wellington's army in the Peninsula in 1810. He commanded the attack on the Fort Christoval side during the first siege of Badajoz, and commanded the allied cavalry with Beresford at the battle of Albuera (gold medal), and in the cavalry action at Usagre. He was invalided home in August 1811, and did not serve in the

Peninsula again. He became lieutenant-general in 1814. He was governor and commander-in-chief at Bermuda from 1819 to 1825, during which time, in his *ex officio* position as 'ordinary', or person possessing episcopal authority in ecclesiastical matters, he had disputes with the church-wardens of the colonial parish of St George. A case arising ultimately went before Lord Chief Justice Tenterden, who expressed an opinion that if Lumley possessed the powers claimed, he had used them illegally, and a verdict, with £1000 damages, was given against him.

Lumley was made KCB in 1815, GCB in 1831, and general in 1837. He was colonel in succession of the 3rd battalion of reserve, the Royal West Indian rangers (disbanded in 1818), the 6th Inniskilling dragoons, and the 1st King's dragoons guards, to which he was appointed in 1840. He was a groom of the bedchamber from 1812 to 1841, and in 1842 was made an extra groom-in-waiting. He married, first, on 3 October 1804, Mary, daughter of Thomas Sutherland of Ulverstone; she died in July 1807. His second marriage, on 3 March 1817, was to Louisa Margaret (*d.* 11 Sept 1859), widow of Colonel Lynch Cotton (*d.* 1799 in India) and daughter of John Robbins. Lumley had no children from either marriage. He died at his residence in Green Street, Grosvenor Square, London, on 15 December 1850.

H. M. CHICHESTER, *rev.* ROGER T. STEARN

Sources J. Philippart, ed., *The royal military calendar*, 3rd edn, 3 (1820) • *The dispatches of … the duke of Wellington … from 1799 to 1818*, ed. J. Gurwood, new edn, 3–5 (1837–8) • *Supplementary despatches (correspondence) and memoranda of Field Marshal Arthur, duke of Wellington*, ed. A. R. Wellesley, second duke of Wellington, 15 vols. (1858–72), vols. 6–7, 13, 15 • *Annual Register* (1829) • GEC, *Peerage* • Burke, *Peerage* • A. J. Guy, ed., *The road to Waterloo: the British army and the struggle against revolutionary and Napoleonic France, 1793–1815* (1990) • R. Muir, *Britain and the defeat of Napoleon, 1807–1815* (1996) • *GM*, 2nd ser., 35 (1851)

Archives Notts. Arch., personal corresp. | Derbys. RO, letters to Sir R. J. Wilmot-Horton

Lumsden, Frederick William (1871–1918), Royal Marines officer, was born on 14 December 1871, at Benaris, Bengal, India, the son of J. J. F. Lumsden of the Bengal civil service. He was commissioned in the Royal Marine Artillery in 1890. As an officer he acquired appropriate qualifications expected of him, in gunnery, torpedo, musketry, signalling, equitation, and military law. These he gained at the Royal Naval College, Greenwich, in HMS *Excellent*, and in army schools. On 16 December 1894 he married Mary Ellen Agusta Harward, the second daughter of Lieutenant-General Thomas N. Harward of the Royal Artillery; they had one daughter.

In 1908 Lumsden graduated from the Army Staff College, Camberley. Ironically, in retrospect, the final report of the commandant in December 1908 stated, 'He will be better in an office than in the field and would do well as a Staff Officer in a fortress' (PRO, ADM 196/62). He obtained six months' leave in 1909 in Germany to study German—and in 1910 was certified an interpreter. Between 1910 and 1914 Lumsden was seconded to the straits settlements as GSO2, and received exceptional reports from his commanding general. He was judged thoughtful, capable, reliable, and hard-working; his commander in 1912 wrote of him that he had 'the greatest respect for his tact and judgment', and in 1913 that 'I have recommended him for accelerated promotion on account of his excellent work on the Staff and because, being 42 years of age, he is liable to be retired compulsory as promotion in the R. M. A. is slow' (ibid.). Before 1914 his career generally had been normal for a marine officer, with rotations between the Royal Marine Artillery division, Eastney, and sea duty plus an assignment at Ascension Island between 1896 and 1899. Promotions came in due course, including that to brevet major in 1911, the substantive rank following in 1913.

The First World War changed both Lumsden's life and his career. After short service at sea in 1914 he joined the Royal Marine howitzer brigade in France in February 1915, and was seconded to the army in July of that year. Lumsden served as GSO3 at First Army, as a staff officer at the headquarters of the Canadian corps, and as GSO2 at 5th corps and then the 32nd division. He also had temporary command of the 17th battalion of the Highland light infantry in 1917 before being promoted temporary brigadier-general in command of the 14th infantry brigade on 12 April 1917; for distinguished service he was promoted to the substantive rank of lieutenant-colonel.

Lumsden's DSO was gazetted in January 1917 for distinguished service in the field. In May 1917 the first bar was awarded after he made a reconnaissance of the enemy's position, moving over open ground under heavy fire and bringing back valuable information. A second was given for his personally leading a reconnaissance party with conspicuous success, the citation noting that his conduct, rapid decision, and good judgement saved many casualties. Then came the Victoria Cross, awarded on 8 June 1917: after six enemy guns had been captured he personally led the operation in bringing them back into British lines over a distance of 300 yards, under enemy rifle, machine gun, and shrapnel fire, while making several trips between the lines and in close contact with the Germans. In May 1918 he was awarded a third bar to his DSO for personally leading a raid against the enemy and successfully returning his force to friendly lines. 'Such coolness, determination to succeed, and absolute disregard of danger, not only ensured the success of the operation' stated the citation, 'but afforded a magnificent example to all ranks, the value of which can hardly be exaggerated' (*London Gazette*, supplement, 22 April 1918). Lumsden was mentioned in dispatches four times and wounded in action twice. He was awarded the Belgian Croix de Guerre and, on the day before his death the CB. His death occurred on the western front on 4 June 1918 from a rifle wound to the head; he was buried at the new military cemetery, Berles-au-Bois, near Arras, France.

Lumsden was a distinguished military officer, a combat leader, and a legitimate war hero. In a corps with a tradition of service and sacrifice, but limited recognition in awards, he was its most highly decorated officer (although he received all his awards while seconded for duty with the army). As a fellow officer wrote on 4 June 1918 after describing his death, 'All the honours he gained … in every case were won over and over again, as there was hardly a day when he did not expose himself to danger in a way which was an example to all' (Lumsden papers; *The Times*, 11 June 1918). His medals were put on display at the Royal Marines Museum, Eastney, where a large stone memorial to him was erected on the parade deck in front of the former officers' mess and marines' barracks.

DONALD F. BITTNER

Sources PRO, ADM 196/62, pp. 231, 418, with attachments • Lumsden papers, Royal Marines Museum, Eastney barracks, Southsea, Hampshire [collection of personal papers, mostly pertaining to the First World War; accessioned 17 July 2000; with rough inventory] • *Globe and Laurel*, 24/255 (Jan 1917), 25/260 (June 1917), 113; 25/261 (July 1917), 128, 132; 25/6 (June 1918), 93; 25/7 (July 1918), 125, 127 • *The Times* (1 Jan 1917); (23 July 1917); (27 Sept 1917); (7 Nov 1917); (23 April 1918); (3 June 1918); (10 June 1918); (11 June 1918) • E. Fraser and L. G. Carr-Laughton, *The royal marine artillery, 1804–1923*, 2 (1930) • H. E. Blumberg, *Britain's sea soldiers: a record of the royal marines during the war, 1914–1919* (1927) • J. Thompson, *The royal marines: from sea soldiers to a special force* (2000) • S. D. Jarvis and D. B. Jarvis, *Cross of sacrifice: officers who died in the service of the Royal Navy, royal naval reserve, royal naval volunteer reserve, royal marines, royal naval air service, and Royal Air Force, 1914–19* (1993) • P. C. Smith, *Per mare per terram: a history of the royal marines* (1974) • F. Smith, *A history of the royal army veterinary corps, 1796–1919* (1927) • *The Royal Navy list, or, Who's who in the navy* (1917); repr. as *The naval who's who, 1917* (1981) • *Hart's Army List* (1913)

Archives Royal Marines Museum, Eastney barracks, Southsea, Hampshire, personal papers, medals | FILM IWM FVA, actuality footage | SOUND IWM SA, oral history interview

Likenesses A. Durrant Smyth, portrait, Royal Marines Museum, Eastney barracks, Southsea, Hampshire • photograph, repro. in Fraser and Carr-Laughton, *The Royal Marine Artillery*, facing p. 964 • stone obelisk memorial, bust in relief bronze, Royal Marines Museum, Eastney barrackes, Southsea, Hampshire

Wealth at death £1290 8*s*. 6*d*.: probate, 18 Oct 1918, *CGPLA Eng. & Wales*

Lumsden, Sir Henry Burnett [Harry] (**1821–1896**), army officer, born on 12 November 1821 on the East India Company's ship *Rose*, in the Bay of Bengal, was the eldest son of Colonel Thomas Lumsden (1789–1874), Bengal artillery, of Belhelvie Lodge, Aberdeenshire, and his wife, Hay (*d.* 11 Oct 1873), youngest daughter of John Burnett of Elrick, Aberdeenshire. Lumsden was sent home from India in 1827 and educated at Bellevue Academy, Aberdeen, and at Mr Dawes's school, Bromley, Kent. He returned to India as a cadet at the age of sixteen, and on 1 March 1838 was commissioned ensign in the 59th Bengal native infantry.

Lumsden displayed a marked aptitude for languages and in the spring of 1843 was attached as interpreter and quartermaster to the 33rd Bengal infantry, which formed part of the army, under the command of Sir George Pollock, that during the First Anglo-Afghan War forced the Khyber Pass. He first saw action on 5 April 1842. While at Kabul, Lumsden struck up a close friendship with John Nicholson. On 16 July 1842 he was promoted lieutenant, and early in 1843 returned to join the 59th native infantry at Ludhiana. Lumsden fought with his regiment during the Sutlej campaign and in February 1846 was severely wounded at the battle of Sobraon.

When Sir Henry Lawrence was made resident at Lahore, he appointed Lumsden on 15 April 1846 as one of his assistants. Lumsden accompanied Lawrence to Kashmir in October, and in December was sent with 3000 Sikh troops and six guns through Hazara. Lumsden's force encountered resistance from 7000 hostile tribesmen, but he successfully forced the passage of the two tributaries of the Jhelum, near Muzaffarabad, and following two sharp engagements eventually forced them to submit. He received the thanks of government and was given responsibility by Lawrence for raising the corps of guides for frontier service. Lumsden enjoyed complete freedom regarding the recruitment, training, and equipment of this force, which initially consisted of 100 horsemen and 200 infantrymen. Its recruits were chosen from the warlike frontier tribes who knew the terrain of the border hills—in his own words, men 'accustomed to look after themselves, and not easily taken aback by any sudden emergency'. Lumsden directed that the new unit wear a serviceable khaki uniform, later adopted by the rest of the Indian army, ideally suited to military operations on the north-west frontier. The guide cavalry distinguished itself under Lumsden's command during the siege of Multan in 1848, and again on 3 January 1849, when it surprised and destroyed a Sikh raiding force near the border with Kashmir. For these actions Lumsden again received the thanks of government.

On 21 February 1849 Lumsden fought at the battle of Gujrat, for which he was mentioned in dispatches and received the Punjab medal with two clasps. On 19 June the strength of the corps of guides was increased to 400 horsemen and 600 infantrymen, in recognition of its success. Following the occupation of the Punjab, Lumsden was appointed assistant commissioner in Yusufzai, in addition to his military duties, and for a short time was placed in charge of Peshawar district, where he had to deal closely with the frequently hostile border tribes over whom he exercised considerable personal influence. He developed an intimate knowledge of the language and of the inhabitants of the tribal territory, demonstrating his ability both as an administrator and as a skilled frontier soldier during repeated skirmishes and punitive campaigns. As Lord Dalhousie wrote: 'A braver or better soldier never drew a sword. The governor-general places unbounded confidence in him and in the gallant body of men he commands.'

Lumsden went home on leave in November 1852 after fifteen years of continuous service in India. He was promoted captain on 1 March 1853, and on 6 February 1854 he was given a brevet majority for his services during the Second Anglo-Sikh War. He returned to India at the end of 1855 and assumed command of the guides, now permanently deployed in the trans-Indus areas of the Punjab. In 1857 he was sent on a mission to Kandahar, accompanied by his brother Lieutenant Peter Lumsden and by Dr Henry Walter Bellew, to ensure that subsidies paid by the government of India to the amir were used for the payment of troops employed to defend Afghanistan against Persia following the recent capture of Herat. The mission was also responsible for advising and assisting the amir as far as possible without arousing the hostility of the Afghan population. On 25 April they reached Kandahar, but news of the outbreak of the Indian mutiny made their position extremely hazardous. Despite a constant fear of attack by the local population Lumsden remained at Kabul throughout the uprising, in order to maintain British prestige and influence over the amir. He finally returned to India on 15 May 1858 when he was promoted lieutenant-colonel. For his services, and for the sound judgement he displayed at Kabul, Lumsden was made a civil CB on 5 December 1859. However, this proved little reward for the opportunities he had missed for command on active service during the Indian mutiny. On 5 September 1866 he married Fanny, daughter of Charles Myers of Dunningwell, Cumberland, vicar of Flintham, Nottinghamshire; she survived her husband.

Lumsden was promoted major-general on 6 March 1868, and was made a KCSI on 24 May 1873. He became lieutenant-general on 1 December 1873, and general on 1 January 1880. His later career suffered, however, from his absence from India during the mutiny, when many other senior officers came to prominence. Lumsden was not offered further employment in the army, and he refused civil posts, for which he was qualified, as he intensely disliked official routine. He retired from the army on 15 September 1875, and spent the remainder of his life at Belhelvie Lodge, Aberdeenshire, which he had inherited on his father's death in 1874. He occupied his time with sport, photography, and wood-carving. Lumsden died at Belhelvie Lodge on 12 August 1896. T. R. MOREMAN

Sources P. S. Lumsden and G. R. Elsmie, *Lumsden of the guides: a sketch of the life of Sir Henry Burnett Lumsden* (1899) • *The Times* (13 Aug 1896) • *General report on the administration of the Punjab, for the years 1849–50 and 1850–51* (1854) • H. Daly, 'The Punjab frontier force', *Journal of the Royal United Service Institution*, 28 (1885), 907–24 • H. W. Bellew, *Journal of a political mission to Afghanistan in 1857, under Major (now Colonel) Lumsden with an account of the country and people* (1862) • V. C. P. Hodson, *List of officers of the Bengal army, 1758–1834*, 3 (1946) • *DNB*

Archives NAM, letters to W. S. R. Hodson

Likenesses photograph, 1860–70, BL OIOC • R. J. Lane, lithograph, 1865, NPG • lithograph, BM • portraits, repro. in Lumsden and Elsmie, *Lumsden of the guides*

Wealth at death £27,038 0s. 7d.: confirmation, 23 Nov 1896, *CCI*

Lumsden, Sir James, of Innergellie (*fl.* 1629–1651), army officer, was a son of Robert Lumsden of Airdrie, Fife; his mother's name is unknown. Two of his brothers, Robert Lumsden and William Lumsden [*see below*], are known to have become soldiers.

James Lumsden first appears in Swedish service as an ensign in Colonel James Spens's regiment in 1629. He must have proved a skilful soldier; by February 1631 he was a colonel and Field Marshal Gustav Horn specifically requested the use of his 600 infantry for his campaign in northern Germany. Colonel Robert Monro recorded his exploits with Lumsden as they led their pikemen into Frankfurt an der Oder and claimed the town for the Swedes. Lumsden also distinguished himself at the battle of Leipzig in September 1631. The following year the Scottish privy council granted permission for Colonel

Sir James Lumsden of Innergellie (*fl.* 1629–1651), by unknown artist

Lumsden to raise a further 1200 troops for Swedish service. He became the commandant in 1635 of Osnabrück, where eight companies of his regiment were still serving in March 1637.

Lieutenant-General James King called in at Osnabrück in February 1639 and probably passed on the news from Scotland that hostilities were afoot with King Charles I. At this point Lumsden made his first request to be released from Swedish service, with the intention of returning home in order to safeguard not only his property but also his honour. The field marshal, Johan Banér, was, however, not keen to lose his service. Lumsden suggested that his brother Robert could replace him as governor of Osnabrück, but Banér did not consider Robert either capable or qualified for that position. Lumsden continued to seek his release until September 1639, when it was noted that he had been provided with an annual pension, along with Field Marshal Alexander Leslie (later earl of Leven) and Patrick Ruthven (later earl of Forth and of Brentford). The Scottish cleric John Dury informed Sir Thomas Roe, the Stuart agent in Hamburg, that Colonel Lumsden and Colonel David Leslie were travelling to Stockholm to petition the Riksråd (Swedish state council) for permission to leave Swedish service, and in August 1640 this was finally granted to them. They left Sweden to serve in the covenanting army during the bishops' wars in Scotland. Lumsden and Leslie received not only a pension of 1000 daler for life and a gold chain with Queen Kristina's image on it from the Swedes, but also 200 muskets and 200 suits of armour. Days later another Scot, Lieutenant-Colonel George Monro, received permission to leave, and they decided to depart for Scotland by 1 November from Hamburg. Sir Thomas Roe suggested that the men could be intercepted upon arrival, but most of them got through.

On his return to Scotland, Lumsden bought land at Innergellie in Fife and married Catherine (or Christianne) Rutherford, although it is unknown exactly when this occurred. Of his children, all that is known is that a daughter, Magdalen, later married her first cousin William Erskine. From 1644 until 1649 Lumsden served on various shire committees for the Scottish parliament, representing Fife. He was also an officer in the army of the solemn league and covenant. From 1643 to 1644 he was lieutenant-colonel of Lord Gordon's foot, which became known as Lumsden's foot when he took over from Gordon in 1644. He was at the siege of York in June, when he served alongside Lord Fairfax's troops. Lumsden's plan for the battle of Marston Moor still exists. He was in charge of the reserve Scottish foot, with which he successfully supported the first line of infantry.

Lumsden became the governor of Newcastle upon Tyne on 23 November 1644, although his appointment was ratified by the English only in March 1645. Six companies of Colonel Sinclair's regiment of foot, the Galloway foot, the Mearns and Aberdeen foot, the Merse foot, the Nithsdale and Annandale foot, the Perthshire foot, and Strathearn foot, all came under Lumsden's command at Newcastle. An undated letter signed by William Weems survives in the Swedish archives, referring to Lumsden as the governor at Newcastle and seeking to obtain the remaining balance of Lumsden's pension from Sweden. The Swedish chancellor, Axel Oxenstierna, had released 4000 riksdaler for Lumsden in Hamburg, but there were still 2000 riksdaler lacking.

On 30 January 1647 the earl of Leven permitted Lumsden to see Charles I, making him the only noble serving in the army of the solemn league and covenant to do so. Lumsden and his forces left Newcastle later that afternoon, and in February the regiment was disbanded. At some point after this Lumsden must have been knighted, as he is subsequently referred to as 'Sir'.

In 1649 Lumsden was colonel of a regiment of foot raised in the presbytery of St Andrews for the army of the covenant. In August 1650 the earl of Loudoun wrote to King Charles II describing Lumsden's loyalty to his cause. David Leslie appointed him lieutenant-general of horse in 1650, and he served as the brigade commander at Dunbar. The regiment was destroyed and both Lumsden and his brother William were taken prisoner. A ship belonging to Sir James Lumsden had been impounded, along with all its contents, at Whitby in January 1651. A month later the English council of state ordered the commissioners of customs to release the ship and make restitution for all the goods as Lumsden had both Cromwell's protection and a pass for the ship. On 10 June 1651 the committee of estates provided Lumsden with maintenance of £240 collected through voluntary contributions for prisoners of war. From the end of February 1652 the English council discussed the release of a Scotsman, Lieutenant-Colonel James Lunden, from captivity. He was to pay £1000 sterling, report to the commander-in-chief, and offer a further £1000 as security for his good behaviour. He was eventually released from English captivity in September 1652. It has not been determined whether this man was the same as James Lumsden. Some sources imply that Lumsden died in 1660, but this has not been verified.

James's brother **Robert Lumsden of Montquhanie** (*d.* 1651), army officer, appears to have entered Danish service as a lieutenant-colonel in the regiment of Colonel Donald Mackay (Lord Reay) in 1628. He later served as a colonel in the Green regiment in Swedish service from 1630 to 1632. It is uncertain when he returned to Scotland, but by 1644 Robert was a major-general in the army of the solemn league and covenant under Lord Callander. He also sat on parliamentary war committees in 1647 as Major-General Robert Lumsden of Montquhanie. He was acting as governor of Dundee when General Monck stormed the town, and was killed in the fighting on 1 September 1651.

Another brother, **William Lumsden** (*fl.* 1645–1650), army officer, is believed to have entered Swedish service during the Thirty Years' War, but no proof has yet been found of this. He was probably the Major Lumsdale of the Merse foot in 1643–4, although that officer is listed without a forename. From 1645 to 1647 he served as lieutenant-colonel of the Strathearn foot in the army of the solemn league and covenant. William led the regiment during its campaigns in 1646. He was captured along with his brother James at the battle of Dunbar in 1650. In December of that year he appealed for the payment of his arrears, but nothing further is known of him after this.

A. N. L. Grosjean

Sources military muster rolls, Krigsarkivet, Stockholm, 1629/22 · riksregistratur, 1639, Riksarkivet, Stockholm, vol. 197, fols. 192–4 · bref till Axel Oxenstierna, Riksarkivet, Stockholm, E655 · biographica, Riksarkivet, Stockholm, vol. 44 · N. A. Kullberg, S. Bergh, and P. Sondén, eds., *Svenska riksrådets protokoll*, 18 vols. (Stockholm, 1878–1959), vol. 8 · *Rikskansleren Axel Oxenstiernas skrifter och brefvexling*, 2/7–9 (Stockholm, 1895–8) · *APS*, 1643–60 · *Reg. PCS*, 2nd ser., vol. 4 · J. M. Thomson and others, eds., *Registrum magni sigilli regum Scotorum / The register of the great seal of Scotland*, 11 vols. (1882–1914), vol. 9 · *CSP dom.*, 1640–41; 1644; 1651 · *The Swedish discipline* (1632) · R. Monro, *Monro his expedition with the worthy Scots regiment (called Mac-Keyes regiment) levied in August 1626* (1637); new edn, with introduction by W. S. Brockington (1999) · J. Grant, *Memoirs and adventures of Sir John Hepburn* (1851) · S. R. Gardiner, ed., *Letters and papers illustrating the relations between Charles the Second and Scotland in 1650*, Scottish History Society, 17 (1894) · T. Fischer, *The Scots in Germany* (1902) · T. A. Fischer [E. L. Fischer], *The Scots in Sweden* (1907) · E. M. Furgol, *A regimental history of the covenanting armies, 1639–1651* (1990) · *Scots peerage* · G. Ridsdill-Smith and M. Toynbee, *Leaders of the civil wars, 1642–1648* (1977) · P. Young, *Marston Moor, 1644* (1970) · *DNB*

Archives Riksarkivet, Stockholm, letters and MSS

Likenesses double portraits (with wife, Catherine Rutherford), priv. coll. · portrait, priv. coll.; on loan to Scot. NPG [*see illus.*]

Wealth at death house at Innergellie, 1000 daler p.a. pension from Sweden: Bergh, ed., *Svenska riksrådets protokoll*; *CSP dom.*

Lumsden, James (1778–1856), banker, was born at Glasgow on 13 November 1778, the eldest son of James Lumsden, a printer and engraver in the city, and his wife, Janet Craig. His education was obtained in the grammar school (later Glasgow high school), where he was a contemporary of the poet Thomas Campbell, and immediately after leaving school he entered his father's business as an apprentice. He succeeded to control of the business upon his father's death (*c.*1820). In Lumsden's hands it grew rapidly and diversified into manufacturing stationery and printing diaries, almanacs, and guidebooks.

Lumsden was a man with an enormous range of interests. An eager innovator, he was on board Henry Bell's famous experimental trip across the River Clyde in his steamship *Comet* in 1812. He was keen on the arts and encouraged painters such as Horatio McCulloch and Sir Daniel Macnee. He gave over fifty years of public service to the city of Glasgow. During the 1820s he spent a few years on the unreformed town council, but his reforming ideas made him unpopular with the tories and he was not re-elected until 1833, in the first open election to the new council. He became a magistrate at that time and served until 1853, save for the period 1838–41 when the tories regained control. From 1843 until 1846 he was lord provost. He belonged to a group of reforming whigs, known locally as 'the clique'. This group were free-traders, and strongly opposed to the corn laws, but it was in local politics that they made their mark.

During his time as provost Lumsden was largely responsible for extending the boundaries of the city into the burghs of Anderston, Gorbals, and Calton. As a member of the Clyde Trust he took a major role in improving the navigability of the river. He was also a justice of the peace and deputy lieutenant for Lanarkshire. Lumsden's great energies were also devoted to social and philanthropic matters. He was treasurer of the Royal Infirmary for nineteen years, and used his many networks to raise funds. One of the promoters of the first model lodging houses, he took an interest in providing homes and night refuges for the homeless. He helped to found the City of Glasgow Native Benevolent Society and the Glasgow Athenaeum, and was three times president of the Incorporated Company of Stationers. The formation of what became the Glasgow Savings Bank in 1836 owed much to his energy and enterprise.

Lumsden's first real involvement with banking came in 1830, when he was one of the original promoters of the Glasgow Union Bank, but a dispute over the powers of the chairman occasioned his withdrawal. In 1838 he was involved, with a group of Glasgow businessmen 'of the middling order, liberal-radicals' (Checkland, 335), in the formation of one of the strongest joint-stock banks, the Clydesdale Bank. Although aged sixty, Lumsden was the moving spirit in the enterprise. There were 776 shareholders, and within a year the paid-up capital was £375,000; by 1841 it was £500,000. The bank had strong Edinburgh support, and Lumsden organized the purchase of the fine offices of Ramsay-Bonars as the Clydesdale's Edinburgh branch.

The bank had nine branches by the end of 1840, and in 1844 it took over the Greenock Union Bank. The founders of the bank have been aptly portrayed as 'thoroughly middle-class' and, in spite of their mildly radical politics, as 'hard-headed and cautious' (Checkland, 336). Lumsden served as chairman in 1838–41, and again in 1847. He retired from the bank in 1848. The records of the bank bear witness to his energy, imagination, and humour. The Clydesdale was one of only two of the Glasgow banks to maintain an independent existence into the twentieth century.

In the business world Lumsden also helped found the City of Glasgow Life Assurance Company, the City and Suburban Gas Company, and the Caledonian Railway Company. His involvement with railway companies seems to have been relatively modest, and he did not get heavily involved in the speculations of the late 1840s. For a time he was involved in running river steamers, but withdrew in 1841.

In 1802 Lumsden married Margaret (*d.* 1819), the daughter of William Mirrlees, a saddler in Glasgow; they had two sons and a daughter. His wife's brother William was closely involved with Lumsden in many of his business pursuits, as was his son-in-law, Peter White, an accountant in Glasgow. Sir James Lumsden, one of his sons, was closely involved with the Clydesdale Bank; he served as a director and was chairman for a number of years. Throughout his life Lumsden was a faithful member of the Church of Scotland, and in 1850 he endowed a bursary for students of theology at Glasgow University.

A man of many talents and connections, Lumsden died on 16 May 1856 from an inflammation of the stomach and bowels at 208 St Vincent Street, Glasgow. An obituarist recalled that 'It is scarcely possible to mention a single local cause or event of a public nature with which he was not intimately associated' (Munn, 308).

CHARLES W. MUNN

Sources M. M. Ramsay, 'Biographical sketches of the directors of the Clydesdale Bank', Clydesdale Bank archives, Glasgow • C. W. Munn, *Clydesdale Bank: the first one hundred and fifty years* (1988) • J. M. Reid, *The history of the Clydesdale Bank* (1938) • S. G. Checkland, *Scottish banking: a history, 1695–1973* (1975) • d. cert.

Archives U. Glas., Archives and Business Records Centre, corresp. and papers | Clydesdale Bank, Glasgow, archives

Likenesses J. Mossman, statue, Glasgow Royal Infirmary

Lumsden, Dame Louisa Innes (1840–1935), promoter of women's education, headmistress, and suffragist, was born on 31 December 1840 in Aberdeen. She was the seventh and youngest child of Clements Lumsden (*d.* 1853), advocate and writer to the signet, and his wife, Jane (*d.* 1883), daughter of James Forbes of Echt, Aberdeenshire.

Early life A gentle, happy family, the Lumsdens were devout Anglicans, attending St Paul's Church of England Chapel twice on Sundays; by her own admission they spoilt their youngest daughter and left her early education largely to chance. Taught to read by her nurse, Louisa could read fluently by the age of six; she briefly shared an English governess with her sisters—'a silly woman', with whom Louisa would argue the merits of 'the old quarrel between Scotland and England' until both were in tears (Lumsden, *Yellow Leaves*, 7). Unsurprisingly, after the governess left no further attempt was made to educate Louisa, apart from some lessons from her sister. From this

Dame Louisa Innes Lumsden (1840–1935), by Olive Edis, *c.*1925

period of freedom developed two of Louisa's lifelong passions: her love of the highlands and her fondness for animals.

In 1853 Clements Lumsden died, and his wife moved the family to Cheltenham. There Louisa attended school for the first time, before being sent to the Château de Koekelberg, a boarding-school near Brussels. At this progressive establishment, whose regime included gymnastics, fresh air, and plenty of homemade entertainments, Louisa spent two happy years before she was sent to a London finishing school which, by contrast, she found excruciatingly dull. In her memoirs she likened the waste of women's abilities to 'that rather puzzling parable of the Talents', in which more talents 'awaken a stimulus and incentive to work, while the receiver of only one talent loses all hope and hides it away unused. So with girls and many women in the past' (Lumsden, *Yellow Leaves*, 24).

In 1857 Louisa returned home to Scotland, where she continued to enjoy great freedom, riding or walking in the countryside, dancing until dawn, and returning home full of energy. Although she read widely and mastered Latin, it quickly became obvious that her intellectual energy was going to need some other outlet. Of this period, her sister said that living with Louisa was like living beside a suppressed volcano (Lumsden, *Yellow Leaves*, 41). Travel abroad and the family's purchase of an old Lumsden property at Glenbogie in Aberdeenshire, which was to be her home for much of her life, made these years happy, but could not make them satisfying. When she heard of a course of lectures for women by professors of Edinburgh University she enrolled at once. Throughout the winter of 1868–9 she worked tirelessly and made many friends.

A Girton pioneer Upon hearing that Emily Davies was recruiting for a new women's college at Hitchin, near Cambridge, Louisa applied immediately. Although she met opposition from members of her family, she was supported by her mother, who also accepted the decision of two of her sisters to become nurses. Emily Davies wrote of her: 'she is 28, manifestly a lady, as well as an eager student, and I should think eminently desirable for us to have in our first group' (Stephen, 216). In the autumn of 1869 Louisa joined the group that came to be known as the Girton Five or the Girton Pioneers. Hard intellectual work, companionship, and the pioneering fervour of Davies and her recruits gave Louisa the aim in life she had been looking for. Asked what were her feelings in that first term she replied, 'Gladness' (ibid., 223). What tensions there were in the first year arose from the pioneering nature of the enterprise and from Davies's tendency to treat her five strong-minded charges as if they were schoolgirls. Davies was eager to demonstrate that her students were ladies, so recreations had to be carefully selected: gymnastics and even wrestling (at which Louisa excelled), walking, and rambling were acceptable, while rough team games were not. Theatricals with women dressed in men's clothing were forbidden, although Louisa protested that they had often performed these at home. These, however, were minor disagreements compared with the problems posed by the curriculum.

In Cambridge there were two competing visions of how higher education for women should be pursued. The Sidgwicks at Newnham were prepared to adapt the course to women's needs: to allow them to study for short periods, for instance, and to dispense with the previous examination in classics and mathematics, for which many of the first women students were poorly prepared. Davies, on the other hand, believed that in order to be accepted at a men's university, women must complete the course on precisely the same terms as men. Girton students found the necessity of cramming for the previous and then returning to work for their tripos in the short time remaining unbearably stressful, and on occasion voiced their envy of the Newnham system. While Louisa agreed with Davies in theory (she once set Benjamin Jowett severely to rights when he advocated separate courses of study for the sexes) she reacted to the distress which the Girton course caused her friends, and, in her role as their leader and spokeswoman, began to clash with Davies.

Louisa Lumsden passed the classical tripos in the third class in 1873, a result which she considered disappointing and ascribed to nervousness. In her memoirs she recalled the tension of not knowing until the hour of the examination whether they would be allowed to sit it and, as background, the clicking of Emily Davies's knitting needles as she waited to supervise the candidates. The following autumn Louisa was appointed classical tutor to the college, now moving to its new site in Girton, but the newly confident graduate clashed with the autocratic Davies, and Lumsden resigned in 1875. The students had wanted her to represent their interests on the college committee, an innovation displeasing to Davies and to some members of the committee. As the youngest member of the college staff, Louisa had felt lonely and isolated, neither staff nor student.

Headmistress of St Leonards During her student days Louisa had embarked on a stormy and passionate affair with fellow student Constance Maynard. Whether or not this constituted a fully fledged sexual liaison, the two women kept their own counsel, but it did provide an absorbing emotional focus for nearly ten years. In 1876 Louisa was appointed to teach classics at Cheltenham Ladies' College and persuaded Constance to accompany her. In 1877 the two were recruited to head a new school for girls in St Andrews, Louisa as headmistress and Constance as head teacher. The school (which later took the name St Leonards) has been called a project of St Andrews academics for the education of their daughters (Anderson, 256). Certainly it was the first girls' school to be modelled on the English public schools, incorporating a house system and a sixth form collectively responsible for the duties of prefect. Louisa was enthusiastic about its location, as she had been sorry to see Scottish girls having to travel to England to attend a first-rate school. At St Leonards she put into practice Davies's idea of an identical curriculum for boys and girls, with classics and mathematics forming the staples of the curriculum, with 'accomplishments' such as music firmly relegated to leisure time. Science was taught by Jane Frances Dove, one of the first women to sit the Cambridge natural sciences tripos, and, in keeping with a characteristic interest of Louisa's, the school placed a strong emphasis on games and exercise. A rare glimpse of a radiant and supremely happy Louisa dates from this period, as described by Constance, being fêted by St Andrews society, 'a stately queen in thick white ribbed silk edged with swan's down', charming all who met her (Firth, 153).

It has been said that Louisa was 'a starter, not a stayer', and this was certainly true of her five years at St Leonards (Walker, *Celebrating a Centenary*, 7). Once the initial impetus of the new venture was over, her undiplomatic nature led to conflicts with her staff; her temper could flare abruptly, responsibility for the daily life of the girls bored her, and, perhaps most disastrously, her relationship with Constance Maynard was coming to an end. The two women had been inseparable for four years, their lives marked by a series of quarrels, tears, and tender reconciliations, but Constance grew restless under the rule of Louisa's dominant personality and they disagreed about religion. While Constance channelled all her energy into fervent emotional religious belief, Louisa remained a cool, cerebral believer, who frowned on the emotional excesses of her friend's Christianity and disapproved of her proselytizing among the girls. Constance left St Andrews in 1880, and in 1882 became the first mistress of Westfield College.

In 1882 Louisa, ill and deeply concerned for her mother's health, resigned as headmistress, despite pleas from the council for her to stay. After Jane Lumsden's death in late 1883 she stayed alone in the highlands, then travelled to Canada and the United States in the summer of 1884, where she spoke on the education of women at a meeting of the British Association. On her return she stood for the post of mistress of Girton, but was not entirely sorry when she lost by one vote. In her memoirs she wrote: 'I had already suffered so much at Girton' (Lumsden, *Yellow Leaves*, 104). She toyed with the idea of moving to London, but in the end kept the family home at Glenbogie in order to be near her sisters. Friends gave her her first dog, whose companionship she treasured, as she was often alone in those years. She became chair of Rhynie school board and served on another; she and her dog would walk 2 miles to meetings along icy roads. Characteristically she counted as her greatest achievement in this role the introduction of physical education in Aberdeenshire rural schools. She was well liked locally and a member of her parish church.

In 1895 Louisa Lumsden was at work on one of her rare books, a German grammar, when she was asked to return to St Andrews as warden of a new hall of residence for women at the university. The scheme, conceived by Professor William Knight, was intended to evolve into a 'Scottish Girton', and Louisa fought for that ideal with her usual determination, but she met formidable opposition to the plan (Lumsden, *Yellow Leaves*, 118). Residence in hall formed no part of the Scottish tradition, women students often preferred the freedom of lodgings, while the principal of St Andrews University himself was publicly scornful of those who chose 'conventual rule under Miss Lumsden!' (ibid., 119). For five years she struggled to make the hall a success, winning the devotion of her residents and the respect of some non-residents, to whom she did her best to extend the benefits of residential social life, but she never succeeded in establishing her authority with the hall committee or obtaining a free hand in running the hall. Conflicts with the committee over the extent of the warden's powers, and with certain of the non-resident women who resented her tendency to treat them as schoolgirls, led to an untenable situation. Depressed and physically ill, Louisa resigned as warden in 1900. She would have been the last to admit how much she had learned about the exercise of authority from Emily Davies.

Retirement: writings, war work, and her legacy In retirement Louisa Lumsden travelled in Scotland and on the continent with her sister Rachel. They bought a house in Midlothian and travelled there with Louisa's dog in a horse-drawn caravan. Their last trip aboard was in 1906; Rachel died in 1908, and Louisa at last sold Glenbogie and moved to The Chanonry in Aberdeen. 'And though life and work seemed to have come to an end', she wrote, 'new interests came and new work' (Lumsden, *Yellow Leaves*, 170). She was asked to be president of the Aberdeen Suffrage Association and she agreed, on condition that it would not take up much time. This hope soon proved unfounded, and Louisa, now in her seventies, became absorbed in the politics of the non-militant suffragists. She was a popular and energetic speaker, and became one of ten vice-presidents of the non-partisan Scottish Churches' League for Woman Suffrage. In 1913, after she had delivered a speech on behalf of the Scottish Federation in Hyde Park, she recalled, 'when I stepped from the platform a gentleman on one side and a policeman on the other handed me carefully down and people came up to congratulate me' (ibid., 180). She believed passionately in the cause, scorning what she called the 'irresponsible backstairs influence' of women in the past and calling for 'responsibility, equal laws and an equal place in the national life' (ibid., 170–71). She contributed an essay on the position of women in history to a collection entitled *The Position of Woman: Actual and Ideal* (1911), in which she cited the protestant reformation as the root of contemporary women's servile status. As always in her writing, education and useful work were the keys to emancipation.

In 1911 Louisa Lumsden was awarded an honorary LLD degree by St Andrews University; her robes were a gift to her from her former pupils at St Leonards. She chose to interpret the honour as amends for the university's treatment of her in the past.

Louisa Lumsden spent the First World War recruiting—using her formidable powers of oratory on behalf of the war effort, speaking to highland audiences who understood little of the reasons for going to war; fund-raising; and doing what she mysteriously referred to as 'humble work' in the chemical laboratory at St Andrews (Lumsden, *Yellow Leaves*, 182). After the war she continued to work on behalf of the Unionist Party and women's rural industries, in addition to her lifelong interest in the welfare of animals. She was for many years editor of an anti-cruelty periodical, *Our Fellow Mortals*.

In 1919 Louisa Lumsden spoke at the Girton College jubilee as the last survivor of the Girton Pioneers, where she was given a triumphant reception. In 1925 she was created DBE in recognition of her services to education. She wrote her memoirs at the age of ninety-two; one visitor recalled seeing the chapters 'laid out on the sofa like so many eras of womankind awaiting the synthesis of memory from a very old lady' (Cowan, 8). As a historical document, the autobiography is disappointing, explaining little about her relations with Emily Davies or the trouble at St Andrews; indeed, even contemporaries felt it conveyed little sense of her tremendous energy (Trail, 52–3). It is a very old woman's memoir, an attempt to make peace with old adversaries and to live again in happier times. Visitors now found her sadly aged, although possessing all her old mental acuity and fire. Her devoted family of servants, the Wilsons, said serving her was like serving a queen, and her friends called themselves the 'Ladies in Waiting' (Cowan, 9).

Louisa Lumsden died at her Edinburgh home, 1 Doune Terrace, on 2 January 1935 at the age of ninety-four. In her old age somebody asked her if, when St Leonards School began, she had imagined the great future it would have. She said no, she had never thought about it: 'I was far too hard at work laying foundations to have time to dream' (Grant, 149). Throughout her long and active life, Louisa Lumsden remained largely unreflective, thrusting forward almost as if eager to leave the past behind. She liked endeavours that attracted controversy, from the college at Hitchin to the suffrage movement, but it is likely that her own quick temper and inability to conciliate led her into more personal disputes than the novelty of the enterprises merited. She possessed great personal charm and magnetism, but outside her own family she was often alone. Despite her many friendships she appears to have had no further romantic attachments after the relationship with Constance Maynard ended in grief. She was a large woman, tall, dark-haired, with a lovely speaking voice, and capable of a certain statuesque elegance, even beauty, when at her ease. A more characteristic impression comes from a group photograph of the women at Hitchin; Louisa faces the camera defiantly, her chin set hard, one hand involuntarily clenched into a fist (Stephen, facing 219).

Louisa Lumsden is claimed by both St Leonards School and University Hall, St Andrews, as their founder and inspiration; she is remembered justly as an eloquent advocate of women's right to education and careers, as a suffragist, and as an early champion of animal rights. Her greatest fame, however, lies in her earliest achievement, as the leader of the Girton Pioneers.

ELIZABETH J. MORSE

Sources L. I. Lumsden, *Yellow leaves: memories of a long life* (1933) · B. Stephen, *Emily Davies and Girton College* (1927) · J. Grant and others, *St Leonards School, 1877–1927* (1927) · O. Banks, *The biographical dictionary of British feminists*, 2 vols. (1985–90) · M. Vicinus, *Independent women: work and community for single women, 1850–1920* (1985) · C. B. Firth, *Constance Louisa Maynard* (1949) · A. M. Adam, *Girton Review*, Lent term (1935), 3–7 · M. G. Cowan, *Girton Review*, Lent term (1935), 8–9 · K. Trail, *S. L. S. Gazette* [St Leonards School] (Feb 1935), 52–3 · *Annual Register* (1935), 103–4 · L. I. Lumsden, 'The position of woman in history', in L. I. Lumsden, *The position of woman: actual and ideal* (1911) · L. Walker, ed., *Celebrating a centenary* (1996) · L. Walker, ed., *Dame Louisa Innes Lumsden: a pioneer* (1996) · *WWW* · R. McWilliams-Tullberg, *Women at Cambridge: a men's university—though of a mixed type* (1975) · C. Dyhouse, *No distinction of sex? Women in British universities, 1870–1939* (1995) · R. D. Anderson, *Education and opportunity in Victorian Scotland: schools and universities* (1983) · A. J. R., ed., *The suffrage annual and women's who's who* (1913)

Archives Westfield College, Constance Maynard's unpublished diary and autobiography

Likenesses Mrs Donders (later Grandmont), portrait, 1892, St Leonards School, St Andrews · O. Edis, photograph, *c*.1925, NPG [*see illus.*] · group photograph (with other students at Hitchin), repro. in Stephen, *Emily Davies and Girton College*, facing p. 219 · photographs, repro. in Grant, *St Leonards School*, facing pp. 1, 10, 149

Wealth at death £22,031 2*s*. 9*d*.: confirmation, 23 Feb 1935, *CCI*

Lumsden, Matthew (1777–1835), orientalist, was fifth son of John Lumsden of Cushnie, Aberdeenshire, and a cousin of Sir Harry Burnett Lumsden (1821–1896), army general. After education at King's College, Aberdeen, he went to India as assistant professor of Persian and Arabic in the College of Fort William, and in 1808 succeeded to the professorship. In 1812 he was appointed secretary to the Calcutta Madrasa, and superintended various translations of English works into Persian then in progress. From 1814 until 1817 he had charge of the East India Company's press at Calcutta, and in 1818 he became secretary to the stationery committee.

Owing to ill health Lumsden left India on leave in March 1820, and travelled with his cousin, Thomas Lumsden, through Persia, Georgia, and Russia to England. An account of this journey was published by Thomas Lumsden in 1822. Lumsden returned to India in 1821. In 1808 he received the degree of LLD from King's College, Aberdeen. He died at Tooting Common, Surrey, on 31 March 1835.

Lumsden published books on the grammars of Persian and Arabic, as well as editing Firdausi's *Shah Namu*, to which he added an English preface.

GORDON GOODWIN, *rev.* PARVIN LOLOI

Sources Anderson, *Scot. nat.* • catalogue, Library of the Faculty of Advocates, Edinburgh • private information (1893) • Irving, *Scots.* • Allibone, *Dict.* • C. E. Buckland, *Dictionary of Indian biography* (1906) • [J. Watkins and F. Shoberl], *A biographical dictionary of the living authors of Great Britain and Ireland* (1816) • J. Haydn, *A dictionary of biography, past and present*, ed. B. Vincent (1877)

Lumsden, Robert, of Montquhanie (*d.* 1651). *See under* Lumsden, Sir James, of Innergellie (*fl.* 1629–1651).

Lumsden, William (*fl.* 1645–1650). *See under* Lumsden, Sir James, of Innergellie (*fl.* 1629–1651).

Lunardi, Vincenzo (1759–1806), balloonist, was born at Lucca, Tuscany, on 11 January 1759, and passed his early years in the East Indies before becoming, through the patronage of his guardian, Chevalier Gherado Compangi, secretary to the Neapolitan ambassador to the Court of St James, Prince Caramanico. In July 1784 he obtained permission from Sir George Howard, governor of Chelsea Hospital, to make a balloon ascent from the hospital grounds. This permission was subsequently revoked after onlookers turned violent when the balloon of a French rival, the Chevalier de Moret, failed to inflate at the demonstration on 4 August planned to pre-empt Lunardi's. John Sheldon also attempted an ascent before Lunardi's but on 16 August his balloon managed only a modest captive ascent before it caught fire. Lunardi finally secured permission from the Honourable Artillery Company to use their ground at Moorfields and on 15 September, in the presence of spectators estimated variously to number between 30,000 and 300,000, he made a successful ascent. His balloon was about 32 feet in diameter, and was filled with hydrogen under the direction of the physician and chemist George Fordyce. The balloon, known as a Charlière after Jacques Alexandre César Charles who made the first hydrogen-filled balloon, contrasted with that of the Montgolfier brothers and most other contemporaries whose Montgolfière balloons rose after the common atmospheric air that they contained had been heated. The only new features of the balloon were the oars by which Lunardi hoped to steer the balloon downwards without needing to lose hydrogen, and the wings with whose flapping he hoped to move the balloon horizontally. These additions had no scientific rationale. He claimed that the use of the oars helped his descent but it seems more probable that loss of gas was responsible for this. The balloon lacked a valve at the top to control the

Vincenzo Lunardi (1759–1806), by Francesco Bartolozzi, pubd 1784 (after Richard Cosway)

escape of gas. It is not known how far Lunardi was responsible for the design; his partner George Biggin is spoken of warmly in Lunardi's account of the voyages, and may have been responsible for the design, being something of an inventor. Lunardi flew over London before making a brief landing at what is now known as Balloon Corner, Welham Green, where a stone marks his landing and the ejection from the balloon of a cat. He finally descended about 24 miles from his starting point in Stanton Green End, Thundridge, north of Ware, Hertfordshire, where a monument was later erected to mark the event, and shortly afterwards waited on the prince of Wales and other patrons, who had been present at the ascent, with an account of his journey. A *March for the Flight of an Air Balloon* was composed for the occasion by Samuel Wesley. Lunardi became the hero of the moment. A balloon-shaped bonnet was named after the aeronaut (see Robert Burns, 'To a Louse', 1789, where it is used to signify the social pretensions of a country girl), and Lunardi skirts, decorated with balloon motifs, and Lunardi garters were also fashionable. Several descriptions were printed, the best by Lunardi himself in *An Account of the First Aerial Voyage in England* (1784). Numerous prints depicting the event were published and a drawing by Paul Sandby (Patent Office) survives. A medal was struck to mark the event and Lunardi exhibited himself and his balloon to enthusiastic crowds at the Pantheon.

Lunardi subsequently made numerous other more or less successful ascents, including one from St George's Fields, Newington Butts, on 29 June 1785, when Mrs L. A. Sage, a London beauty, ascended and thus became 'the first English female aerial traveller', according to the title-page of her *Letter Describing … her Expedition with Lunardi's*

Balloon (1785). (She flew without Lunardi who gallantly left the balloon when her ample bulk put a strain on its lifting power.) Moving north he made successful ascents from Liverpool, Edinburgh, Glasgow, Kelso, and York, each time to acclaim. A memorial stone marks the place at North Callange Farm, Pitscothe, where he landed after leaving Edinburgh on 5 October 1784. Lunardi took pains to describe himself as 'the first aerial traveller in the English atmosphere' as James Tytler had already ascended in Scotland on 27 August 1784, a fact which is graciously mentioned in Lunardi's *Account of Five Aerial Voyages in Scotland* (1786). But his string of successes came to an end after a planned ascent on 23 August 1786 from Newcastle upon Tyne at which a young man, Ralph Heron, became entangled in one of the balloon's ropes, rose with it, fell, and died from his injuries, the country's first victim of air travel. The press turned against Lunardi as quickly as they had fêted him, thus ending his career, which depended on his being able to raise money by subscription to pay for his balloons. In 1787 he was in London experimenting with a device for saving life at sea, but he was evidently pressed for money, and had turned his hand to other ventures including hotel keeping.

Having left Britain in August 1787, Lunardi continued his ballooning exploits across Italy, Spain, and Portugal, his last recorded ascent being from Lisbon on 24 August 1794. He died in the convent of Barbadinas, Lisbon, on 31 July 1806 'of a decline'.

Lunardi added nothing to the technical or scientific development of ballooning (his only innovations being his wings and oars which seemed to be of little use, and a 'double balloon' which he advertised that he would use but never did), but he was a likeable and courageous opportunist who brought the spectacle of ballooning to a wide British public and deserved his description in his death notice in the *Gentleman's Magazine*: 'Mr Vincent Lunardi, the celebrated aeronaut'.

ELIZABETH BAIGENT

Sources Vincent Lunardi, *An account of the first aerial voyage in England* (1784) • Vincent Lunardi, *An account of five aerial voyages in Scotland* (1786) • J. E. Hodgson, *The history of aeronautics in Great Britain* (1924) • *Morning Post* (16 Sept 1784) • L. T. C. Rolt, *The aeronauts: a history of ballooning, 1783–1903* (1966) • R. Newsome, *Doctor Denis: the life and times of Dr Denis Wright* (1995) • *GM*, 1st ser., 76 (1806)

Likenesses F. Bartolozzi, stipple (after miniature by R. Cosway), BM, NPG; repro. in Lunardi, *An account … in England*, frontispiece [*see illus.*] • J. Kay, caricature, etching, BM • portrait (after etching by Duché de Vaney, pubd 1784), BM

Lund, John (*fl.* 1785), humorous poet, of Pontefract, is said to have been a barber in that town. Little else is known of his life, although a contemporary declared that his satires 'would not disgrace the pen of a Churchill' (Boothroyd, 495). In 1771 Lund published *The mirrour: a poem, in imitation of C. Churchill, to which are added three tales, in the manner of Prior*. In 1777 he published *A collection of original tales in verse, in the manner of Prior; to which is added a second edition of 'Ducks and pease, or, The Newcastle rider'*. The story is rudimentary, being that of a rider (that is, bagman) who, when airing himself as a person of quality, is suddenly confronted by his master; but it proved extremely popular, passing through numerous editions down to 1838 and was reprinted in Richardson's *Table Book* . In 1779 there followed *A collection of oddities in prose and verse, serious and comical, by a very odd author*. Also often attributed to Lund is a piece entitled *The Bath Comedians*, but its publication date of 1753 casts doubt on the matter. The British Library refers to this piece's author simply as 'L., J. M.'.

THOMAS SECCOMBE, *rev.* GRANT P. CERNY

Sources B. Boothroyd, *The history of the ancient borough of Pontefract* (1807) • W. T. Lowndes, *The bibliographer's manual of English literature*, ed. H. G. Bohn, [new edn], 3 (1864), 1413 • *N&Q*, 3rd ser., 5 (1864), 282–3 • D. E. Baker, *Biographia dramatica, or, A companion to the playhouse*, rev. I. Reed, new edn, rev. S. Jones, 1 (1812), 464 • M. A. Richardson, ed., *The local historian's table book … legendary division*, 3 vols. (1843–6), vol. 1, p. 169

Lund, Sir Thomas George (1906–1981), lawyer, was born at 8 Collingham Road, Kensington, London, on 6 January 1906, the younger son of Kenneth Fraser Lund, physician and surgeon, and his wife, Elsie Lisette Silley. He was educated at Westminster School (1919–24). After articles in private practice he was admitted a solicitor in December 1929. Like most solicitors until the 1960s he was not a university graduate. On 25 July 1931 he married Catherine Stirling, the daughter of Arthur John Audsley, company manager, with whom he had a daughter, who subsequently qualified as a solicitor.

In 1930 Lund joined the Law Society as an assistant solicitor. He became an assistant secretary in 1937, and in 1939 was promoted to the most senior post of secretary-general, which he held for thirty years. During the Second World War his capacity for creating new roles for solicitors and the Law Society first emerged. For more than 100 years there had been various scandals about solicitors who had stolen their clients' money. One of these delinquents had been president of the Law Society, but still the professional body showed a distinct reluctance to take practical steps to reduce this possibility as well as to compensate members of the public who were victims. Lund was one of the driving forces behind the compensation fund set up in 1941. From this he turned his attention to the wartime problem of a huge increase in the number of marriage breakdowns. In 1942, with the support of the government, the Law Society set up its own divorce department employing solicitors and supporting staff to act as practitioners on behalf of a divorcing spouse. This was against a background of consistent opposition within the profession to state-employed lawyers providing services for private clients. The divorce service however was deemed a great success.

Reputedly developing this next big idea in his bath, Lund proposed to the Rushcliffe committee, appointed by the lord chancellor in 1944, that there should be a national legal aid scheme extending legal services to people of moderate means, with the whole system being run by the Law Society. This idea was embodied in the 1949 Legal Aid and Advice Act. No private body before or since has been given responsibility for spending so much taxpayers' money. Lund's advocacy, and subsequently his administrative skills, produced a model, which was the legal equivalent of the National Health Service. The fact that these arrangements remained until 1989, when a government body assumed control, was a tribute to the structure which Lund devised. He received a knighthood in 1958.

This visionary zeal also assumed an international dimension. Lund simply loved travelling. Throughout the common-law world he was treated as something of a deity. National and local bar associations often modelled themselves on the Law Society and incorporated the principles of professional etiquette and conduct which Lund had prepared for domestic consumption. He was behind the foundation of an organization of English-Speaking Secretaries of European Bar Associations. They included most European countries apart from France and southern Europe. His attendance at this body was demanded long after his retirement, because of his wisdom but also his outstanding sociability.

Lund saw an opportunity to enhance the quality of education for solicitors by arranging the merger of the private tutors Gibson and Wheldon with the Law Society's own school of law to become a new chartered entity, the College of Law, in 1962. Despite the existence of more than twenty licensed competitors by the 1990s, the College of Law still commanded over 75 per cent of the market. Unlike many of his generation Lund was strongly in favour of the rise of women in the profession and appointed many to work with him in the Law Society. Among his publications was *A Guide to the Professional Conduct and Etiquette of Solicitors* (1967).

Without its ever occurring to him that this might seem to be a boast, Lund indicated that he saw one of the most important parts of his role as that of 'thinking for the profession'. It was much needed because most of his members were myopic about the opportunities for more business, or the qualities required to meet the needs of modern clients. A famous lecture he gave at the third Commonwealth and Empire Law Conference at Sydney in 1965 ('The future pattern of the profession', *Law Society's Gazette*, 63, 1966, 127–31) foreshadowed the emergence of multi-disciplinary practices in which members of many different professions would practice under the same business and professional umbrella. This was just one of the bold steps that he proposed that worried his professional masters in the council of the Law Society. Many of them in the past had admired him hugely, but some had come to resent his influence.

Such wranglings did not affect Tommy Lund's popularity in the ranks of the provincial profession, whose dinners he graced with superb after-dinner speaking skills. A tall imposing man, with a twinkle in his eye, for them he was the best of the Law Society. When he was told by the council that his time at the Law Society was over, in 1969, he moved on to be director-general of the International Bar Association. This was both a recognition of his international reputation and also a means of providing this body with a professional structure less reliant on its volunteers. Lund died at the Middlesex Hospital, Westminster, on 20 April 1981. JOHN HAYES

Sources *WWW, 1981–90* · *The Times* (25 April 1981) · H. Horsfall Turner, *Law Society's Gazette* (29 April 1981), 445 · *Old Westminsters*, vol. 3 · H. Kirk, *Portrait of a profession: a history of the solicitor's profession, 1100 to the present day* (1976) · b. cert. · m. cert. · d. cert. · private information (2004)

Wealth at death £77,558: probate, 7 Sept 1981, *CGPLA Eng. & Wales*

Lundgren, Egron Sellif (1815–1875), watercolour painter, was born in Brunkerberg, Stockholm, Sweden, on 18 December 1815, the sixth child of Erik Lundgren (*d.* 1840x49?) and his wife, Maria Elisabeth Fåhreus (*d.* 1846). He trained at the Tekniska Högskola (College of Technology) in Stockholm and, from 1832, at the gun foundry at Finspång, but he decided to change careers and in 1835 began to study at the Kungliga Akademien för de Fria Konsterna (Royal Academy of Fine Arts) in Stockholm under A. J. Fägerplan. In 1839 he went to Paris, where he trained for two years under Léon Cogniet. With a scholarship from the Kungliga Akademien in Stockholm he then travelled to Switzerland and Italy, settling in Rome with a group of Scandinavian artists led by Bertel Thorvaldsen. In 1848 he was conscripted into Garibaldi's Guardia civica but escaped to Spain in March 1849, leaving behind an illegitimate son, Luigi, and the boy's mother, Eleonora Gonzales. When his travel grant expired he decided to develop his watercolour technique abroad rather than to return to Sweden to take up a professorship.

In 1852 Lundgren met the English artists John Phillip and Francis William Topham in Seville; on their advice he went to England in 1853 and was introduced to Thomas Oldham Barlow, who later engraved many of his works. Lundgren concentrated on watercolour painting in England, thereafter producing few pictures in oil. His work was shown to Queen Victoria, for whom he completed over thirty theatrical scenes in watercolour illustrating many of Charles Kean's Shakespearian and other productions. He also painted private royal events, including *The Marriage of the Princess Royal* (which took place on 25 January 1858), and two military occasions (Royal Collection) for the queen. This royal patronage assisted his career and he established himself in a large studio in London. After a visit to the portrait painter Francis Grant at Melton, he was invited to paint for the earl of Wilton at Egerton Lodge, for the Coventry family, and for the Exeter family at Burghley; at Badminton he drew four large oval pastels of the sons of the eighth duke of Beaufort.

On 4 February 1858, with a letter of recommendation from Queen Victoria, Lundgren was sent to India by Thomas Agnew & Sons; he reached Calcutta on 20 March. He accompanied the commander-in-chief, Lord Clyde, on his journey of reoccupation after the Indian mutiny, making numerous studies of camp scenes, Sepoy prisoners, and soldiers after the fall of Oudh. His portraits included those of Lord Clyde, Sir William Mansfield, the king of Oudh, and the captured Chinese former governor-general, Ye. He made studies to illustrate a book on the mutiny (which was never published), and his sketches were sent back to England for use by Thomas Jones Barker in his oil painting *The Relief of Lucknow, November 1857*. The majority of Lundgren's Indian sketches were acquired from Agnews by Sam Mendel of Manley Hall, Manchester. (They were sold after Mendel's death at Christies on 16 April 1875.) Barker's completed oil painting and Lundgren's sketches were exhibited in London from 1 May 1860: the oil was damaged and destroyed in the Art Gallery and Museum, Glasgow, during the Second World War; a smaller version is now in the National Portrait Gallery, London. Lady Canning, wife of the governor-general of India, described the sketches to Queen Victoria as 'very rough but full of cleverness' (Royal Archives, Z 502/55), and on Lundgren's return from India in April 1859 the queen acquired over thirty of them. In September 1859 she invited the artist to Balmoral Castle, where he spent over three weeks painting Scottish scenes and making studies at a highland gathering (Royal Collection; Nationalmuseum, Stockholm).

Lundgren visited Stockholm and Oslo in 1860 before travelling to Cairo in November 1861, where he shared a studio with Frank Dillon and George Price Boyce. In 1862 he was made a knight of the order of Vasa by Karl XV, king of Sweden, and in the same year exhibited two works at the Royal Academy. He was elected an associate of the Society of Painters in Water Colours in 1864 and became a full member in 1865; between 1865 and 1875 he sent fifty-eight watercolours to the society's winter exhibitions and thirty-five to the summer exhibitions at the Pall Mall East Gallery in London. He visited Italy in 1865 and returned to Seville for the winter of 1867–8, and to England in the spring of 1868. He settled in Stockholm with his brother, Mildhog, in the autumn of that year and there received commissions from the Swedish royal family. A talented letter-writer, Lundgren was described by J. L. Roget as 'a gifted artist with keen perceptive and poetic eyes' and a style 'easy, pure, elegant, charming, pleasing, humorous' (Roget, 2.409). He wrote *En målares anteckningar* ('A painter's notes'), published in 1873–9, which included extracts from his journals and letters.

Lundgren died of apoplexy on 16 December 1875 at 4 Oxtorget, Stockholm; he was buried in Stockholm. He bequeathed many of his works to his brother, Mildhog, who presented them to the Nationalmuseum in Stockholm and the Göteborgs Konstmuseum; the manuscripts of his books are in the Kungliga Biblioteket (royal library) in Stockholm. A retrospective exhibition was held at the Kungliga Akademien (Royal Academy of Sweden) from March to July of 1876. DELIA MILLAR

Sources K. Montgomery, S. A. Nilsson, and D. Millar, *Egron Lundgren: en målares anteckningar* (1995) [exhibition catalogue, Nationalmuseum, Stockholm, 23 Sept – 3 Dec 1995] • D. Millar, *The Victorian watercolours and drawings in the collection of her majesty the queen*, 1 (1995) • J. L. Roget, *A history of the 'Old Water-Colour' Society*, 2 (1891), 402–11 • K. Asplund, *Egron Lundgren*, 2 vols. (1914–15) • S. Nilsson, 'Egron Lundgren: reporter of the Indian mutiny', *Apollo*, 92 (1970), 138–43 • S. Nilsson and N. Gupta, *The painter's eye: Egron Lundgren and India* (1992) • Royal Arch., royal archives, Z 502/55/23 February 1859

Archives Kungliga Biblioteket, Stockholm • Uppsala University Library

Likenesses E. S. Lundgren, three self-portraits, 1841–55, repro. in Montgomery, Nilsson, and Millar, *Egron Lundgren*, nos. 18, 24, 134 • photograph, 1860, repro. in Montgomery, Nilsson, and Millar, *Egron Lundgren*, 55 • wood-engraving (after photograph, 1874), NPG; repro. in *ILN* (8 Jan 1876) • woodcuts, BM

Lundie, John (*b. c.*1600), poet, is of unknown parentage. He was admitted to King's College, Aberdeen, in 1618, proceeded AM in 1622, and was elected a regent in 1626. Having become humanist in 1629, he was advanced in 1631 to the title of 'professor of humanity in the university of Aberdeen', though, says Gordon, he was 'raither maister of the grammar scoole' (Gordon, 1.154). On 16 November 1640 he was chosen dean of the faculty of philosophy. On 12 July 1647, at Gordon's Mill, he married Margaret Gordon.

In contrast to the general opposition to the national covenant in Aberdeen, Lundie secretly subscribed it in July 1638 and refused the king's covenant in October. He was chosen to represent his university at the general assembly at Glasgow in November of that year: his commission extended to little more than reporting news to his superiors in Aberdeen, but the moderator, Alexander Henderson, got wind that he was a covenanter and granted him a voice. On 15 December Lundie asked the assembly to send a committee of visitors to Aberdeen on the grounds that the bishop was unlawfully taking up rents. Lundie returned to Aberdeen and subscribed the king's covenant on 14 January 1639. In the following month he was accused of having exceeded his powers by the Aberdeen authorities, to whom he pleaded guilty. There is, however, a suggestion that Lundie's petition had been engineered by the covenanters to furnish them with a pretext for sending arms against the marquess of Huntly (Gordon, 3.224–5).

Besides his 'Oratio eucharistica et encomiastica', which was delivered on 27 July 1631 (Marischal College Library, Aberdeen), on the occasion of a gift to the university from Dr Alexander Read, Lundie wrote the dedicatory poem prefixed to Bishop Patrick Forbes's *Funerals*. The other verses from his pen contained within this volume (pp. 370, 414) are reproduced in the largest collection of his work, which is appended to the Abbotsford Club's edition of *A Garden of Grave and Godlie Flowers* (1845) by Alexander *Garden, who was probably Lundie's brother-in-law. Lundie's miscellaneous verses rarely sparkle and, while they have potential for grace and light-heartedness, they are too often weighed down by an overpowering use of classical allusion. Some show feeling, such as his Latin elegiacs on the death of his son (p. 29), but even these are marred by the admission of a false quantity. Several of the poems are addressed to Garden and to David Leech. Lundie is also supposed to have written in Latin the 'Comedy of the twelve patriarchs' (preface to Garden's *Garden*, xvi).

Lundie was a baillie for the town of Aberdeen and is recorded in council minutes until 1655. He was predeceased by his son, John, but survived by his wife.

THOMAS SECCOMBE, *rev.* ROSS KENNEDY

Sources C. Innes, ed., *Fasti Aberdonenses … 1494–1854*, Spalding Club, 26 (1854) • A. M. Munro, ed., *Records of Old Aberdeen: MCLVII–MDCCXCI*, 2 vols. (1899–1909) • J. Gordon, *History of Scots affairs from 1637–1641*, ed. J. Robertson and G. Grub, 3 vols., Spalding Club, 1, 3,

5 (1841) · P. Forbes, *Funerals of a right reverend father in God, Patrick Forbes* (1635)

Lundy, Robert (*d.* before 1717), army officer, was a Scot, probably from Fife. He was commissioned in Lord Dumbarton's regiment (later the Royal Scots), which served on the continent in the French service until 1678, by which time he was a captain. He served in England and Ireland until 1680, when the regiment was sent to Tangier. He was seriously wounded while leading an attack on the trenches in the victory over the Moors on 27 October 1680. He received £80 bounty in compensation for his wounds in 1683.

Lundy married Martha, a daughter of Rowland *Davies, later dean of Cork, and with her had at least one son and one daughter who survived him. Through his wife's connections he was able to get the duke of Ormond to secure him a commission as lieutenant-colonel in the regiment of William Stewart, Viscount Mountjoy, in Ireland in 1685. Under Lundy's command the regiment formed the garrison of Londonderry until November 1688, when it was recalled to Dublin so as to make way for a newly raised Catholic regiment. Mountjoy's regiment was sent straight back to Londonderry after the citizens rebelled and shut the gates on the replacement garrison. Mountjoy signed articles promising that he would seek a pardon for this act of rebellion and left Lundy as the governor of Londonderry and the commander of the troops in the north-west.

In March 1689, when civil war was inevitable, Lundy ordered Lord Kingston to evacuate Sligo, and advised Gustavus Hamilton to abandon Coleraine. On 21 March he swore, albeit in private, an oath of allegiance to William and Mary and received his new commission as governor of Londonderry. When the Irish army crossed the River Bann in early April 1689, Lundy consolidated his position by ordering his outlying garrisons back to the city. He burnt the Waterside to deny the enemy shelter, and in a hurried council of war on 13 April he ordered all his troops to assemble at the fords on the rivers Finn and Foyle, which he hoped to be able to hold against King James's army. The plan resulted in a precipitate flight back to Londonderry on 15 April. Lundy was criticized for his handling of the affair and for failing to get those troops commanded by Lord Kingston to join him. This criticism grew after he held a council of war on 16 April with the officers from two English regiments who had been sent by sea to join the garrison. It was concluded that, as there were not enough provisions in Londonderry and as the city was untenable in any event, the reinforcements should not disembark. As soon as it was realized that Lundy had sent the reinforcements away, it was rumoured that he was planning to surrender. He was forced to take refuge in his house from a violent mob led by Adam Murray who had let in to the city all those fugitives whom Lundy had locked out. He called a further council in which he was asked to resume his governorship. Having no control over the mob, he refused, and on 19 April Henry Baker and George Walker were elected joint governors in his place. On the evening of 20 April Lundy disguised himself as a common soldier and with Walker's connivance he slipped out of the city with four others and managed to cross in an open boat to Islay where he was arrested. He was released by the governor of Dumbarton, a relation of his, and made his way to London where he was placed in the Tower. He was in the meantime attainted by King James's Dublin parliament.

There has over the centuries been an unresolved debate as to whether Lundy was a Jacobite agent intent on preventing resistance or a Williamite who honestly thought that Londonderry would not be able to withstand the Irish army. The fact that Lundy chose to make a hazardous escape to avoid falling into Jacobite hands makes his being a traitor unlikely. In August 1689 he was brought before a House of Commons committee appointed 'to inquire into the miscarriages relating to Ireland and Londonderry'. It was initially recommended that he be sent back to Londonderry to face trial for treason, but this never happened since George Walker let it be known that Lundy still had his supporters there. Lundy remained in the Tower until February 1690, when he was produced on a writ of habeas corpus and bailed in the sum of £12,000, £2000 of which was put up by the earl of Clarendon, the erstwhile lord lieutenant of Ireland. He was never brought to trial but left military life until after the death of King William in 1702. In 1704 he travelled to Lisbon with Queen Anne's letter of recommendation for employment and was appointed the adjutant-general of the king of Portugal's forces in the queen of England's pay, a post he held until 1712. He brought reinforcements to Gibraltar in December 1704 and served there until the siege was raised in the following March. He was later captured by the French at sea in April 1707 and taken to France. He was exchanged for twenty men in June 1709. He died some time before 1717. Since 1788 he has been remembered in Londonderry by the annual burning of his effigy bearing the sign 'Lundy the traitor'. PIERS WAUCHOPE

Sources J. Hempton, ed., *The siege and history of Londonderry* (1861) · C. D. Milligan, *History of the siege of Londonderry, 1689* (1951) · J. Michelburne, *Ireland preserv'd, or, The siege of London-Derry*, 2 pts (privately printed, London, 1705) · C. Dalton, ed., *Irish army lists, 1661–1685* (privately printed, London, 1907) · 'Tangier 1680: the diary of Sir James Halkett', ed. H. M. McCance, *Journal of the Society for Army Historical Research*, 1 (Dec 1922) [whole issue] · *The correspondence of Henry Hyde, earl of Clarendon, and of his brother Laurence Hyde, earl of Rochester*, ed. S. W. Singer, 2 vols. (1828) · N. Luttrell, *A brief historical relation of state affairs from September 1678 to April 1714*, 6 vols. (1857) · *Report on the manuscripts of Allan George Finch*, 5 vols., HMC, 71 (1913–2003), vol. 3, pp. 434–6 · W. A. Shaw, ed., *Calendar of treasury books*, 24, PRO (1950–52) · Lundy's account of events, NA Scot., GD 26
Archives NA Scot., Lundy's account of events, GD 26

Lunn, Sir Arnold Henry Moore (1888–1974), skier and religious controversialist, was born in Madras on 18 April 1888, the eldest in the family of three sons (the second of whom was Hugh Kingsmill [*see* Lunn, Hugh Kingsmill]) and one daughter of Sir Henry Simpson *Lunn (1859–1939), medical missionary and travel agent, and his wife, Ethel, eldest daughter of Canon Thomas Moore, rector of Midleton, co. Cork, and headmaster of Midleton College.

He was educated at Harrow School and Balliol College, Oxford. He failed to take a degree but founded two clubs: the Oxford University mountaineering club and the Alpine Ski Club. He also became secretary of the Oxford Union and edited *The Isis*. In 1915 he went to France with a Quaker ambulance unit, and, having returned home and been medically rejected for military service, went to work at Mürren on behalf of British and French internees.

In 1910 Sir Henry Lunn had opened up Mürren for winter sports and the Swiss hamlet was transformed into one of the most favoured resorts in Europe. It was here that Arnold Lunn invented the modern slalom in 1922 and gained, against great opposition, the international and Olympic recognition of both downhill and slalom racing. In 1931 he organized in Mürren the first world championships in these events; he arranged another in 1935. He introduced these races into the 1936 Olympic games. When barely twenty, he was exploring the high Alps and crossed the Bernese Oberland on skis from end to end. He also made the first ski ascent of the Dom, the highest mountain entirely in Switzerland. In 1909 he suffered a serious fall when making a solo descent from the east ridge of Cyfrwy in Wales. His right leg was shattered and shortened permanently by 3 inches. He suffered constant pain from this accident for the rest of his life but never complained. His disability did not prevent him from making the first ski ascent of the Eiger in 1924. Actively engaged in skiing and mountaineering as he was from his early years, Lunn marked these also with a succession of books on various aspects of the subject, twenty-three in all, as well as editing the *British Ski Year Book* from 1919 to 1971.

The physical and mental effort involved in so many alpine activities would exhaust the capabilities of most men, who would also be content with the wide recognition accorded for such achievements. Lunn, however, also made a reputation in quite a different field, that of religious controversy. Of his sixty-three published books sixteen were in the field of Christian apologetics, or what he preferred to call advocacy. They began with *Roman Converts* (1924) before he himself became one in 1933 (he had been brought up a Methodist) and continued with epistolary arguments with Ronald Knox (*Difficulties*, 1932), with C. E. M. Joad (*Is Christianity True?*, 1933), with J. B. S. Haldane (*Science and the Supernatural*, 1935), and with G. G. Coulton (*Is the Catholic Church Anti-Social?*, 1946). Six books of somewhat repetitive memoirs published in this period and later also dwelt largely on his religious views.

During the Second World War Lunn was a press correspondent in the Balkans, Chile, and Peru. In June 1941 he was attached to the Ministry of Information. The liberalism which he inherited from his father had inspired in him a passionate opposition to Hitlerism and he went on many government-sponsored lecture tours to the USA and elsewhere during the war. He also denounced communism, which he saw as the ultimate enemy of his faith. The Spanish Civil War was to him a communist rehearsal of a worldwide attack on Christian civilization, a threat both to the arts which he loved and the spiritual way of life which he followed with dogged devotion and exemplary moral courage.

Lunn's achievements in the two totally different areas of skiing and Christian apologetics may suggest a dual or split personality, but he was very much himself and the same person on the ski slopes and on the uplands of religious speculation and argument. Although he liked to think of himself as a rationalist in matters of religion, he had an almost mystical apprehension of eternal beauty as he contemplated his beloved mountains. Conversely, the zest and dexterity of his endless religious discussions had their counterpart in the expertise of all his alpine enterprises. He kept these disparate interests together with the help of a multitude of friends in both camps. High-spirited and gregarious, he was also unworldly and absent-minded to a degree. Those who would accuse him of egotism and even arrogance in his writings might also recognize a certain selflessness and humility in his way of life.

Lunn was very happy and well cared for in his two marriages. He married first in 1913 Lady Mabel (*d.* 1959), daughter of Revd the Hon. John Stafford Northcote and sister of the third earl of Iddesleigh; they had two sons and one daughter. The elder son, Peter, was captain of the British ski team at the 1936 Olympics. In 1961 he married Phyllis, elder daughter of Oliver Needham Holt-Needham, who farmed his own land in Gloucestershire.

Lunn was knighted in 1952 for his services to British skiing and Anglo-Swiss relations and was a recipient of many civic and academic awards in Switzerland, France, and Spain. He is commemorated by the annual Arnold Lunn memorial lecture held under the auspices of the Ski Club of Great Britain and the Alpine Ski Club. He died in London on 2 June 1974. T. F. BURNS, *rev.*

Sources *The Times* (3 June 1974) • personal knowledge (1986) • private information (1986) • I. Elliott, ed., *The Balliol College register, 1900–1950*, 3rd edn (privately printed, Oxford, 1953) • *CGPLA Eng. & Wales* (1974)

Archives Georgetown University, Washington, DC, corresp. and papers

Wealth at death £5740: probate, 9 Sept 1974, *CGPLA Eng. & Wales*

Lunn, Sir George (1861–1939), local politician and educational administrator, was born at 121 Percy Street, Newcastle upon Tyne, on 26 November 1861, the son of John Ramsay Lunn, bricklayer, and later contractor, and his wife, Jane, *née* Hindmarch. He was educated at the Wesleyan Orphan House School, Newcastle, and the city's fee paying Royal Grammar School. He began working in the shipping business in 1887 and, by the turn of the century, had joined John MacCoy to form the firm of Lunn and MacCoy. When this partnership dissolved he became an arbitrator and spoke with pride on a number of occasions of having spent the whole of his working life on the quayside. On 1 March 1887 he married Charlotte Reeves (*b.* 1863/4), daughter of James Reeves of Newcastle, a clerk at the county court.

Lunn's interest in education was lifelong and his achievements came to be known 'throughout the world' (Newcastle council reports, 1929/30, 762). After being elected to the city council in 1901 he also served on the Newcastle school board. Following the educational changes of 1902 he became vice-chairman of the newly formed council education committee. In 1905 he was elected chairman, a post he held for the rest of his life. At the national level he served on, and at one point chaired, the National Association of Education Committees of England and Wales, and was a member of the Burnham committee on teachers' salaries. He was also an active member of the governing body of the Royal Grammar School for many years.

Lunn was a Liberal and a member of the Newcastle Liberal Club and of the National Liberal Club. He also attended meetings of the National Liberal Federation and was duly appointed president. His efforts to move into national politics proved a failure when he failed to win the North Newcastle seat in 1918. He was more successful as a local politician. For many years he chaired the parliamentary committee of the city council. He served three times as mayor between 1915 and 1918 and was later described by a fellow councillor as 'the Lloyd George of Newcastle' (Arthur Lambert, in Newcastle council reports, 1929/30, 821). He was knighted in 1918 for his services to the state. He was also a justice of the peace, honorary doctor of civil law of the University of Durham, deputy lieutenant of Northumberland, and member of the Tyne improvement commission. In 1919 he became an alderman and in 1930 was made a freeman of Newcastle. His Liberalism fitted neatly with his Methodism. After his early Methodist education he became a lay preacher at the age of twenty-one and retained links with the Newcastle Brunswick Chapel until his death. He served on the Wesleyan national conference and carried a Bible daily.

All records point to Lunn's being an uncomplicated character. He was firm but fair, with a good sense of humour and a strong sense of social justice, and, by all accounts, a dominating personality. Aspects of his work as governor of the Royal Grammar School fill out the picture. He fought for the school to remain open during the First World War yet was first in line to open the doors to those who could not afford to attend. When national teaching salaries were cut by 10 per cent in the 1930s the governors voted for 5 per cent for their staff. Lunn left the meeting 'breathing fire and slaughter and vowing that he would take steps to bring the governors into line' (Mains and Tuck, 195). Using his national clout he won the day and promptly resigned from the governors.

Lunn died at his home, Moorfield, Kenton Road, Gosforth, just north of Newcastle, on 21 July 1939. He was seventy-seven and had been in ill health despite an operation earlier in the year. He was cremated after a service held at the Brunswick Chapel on 24 July. He was survived by his wife, three sons, and five daughters. At his golden wedding presentation ceremony he had said he would like his epitaph to be 'he lived a useful life' (Newcastle council reports, 1936/7, pt 1, 427). It was an apt choice.

KEITH GREGSON

Sources *Newcastle Journal* (22 July 1939) • *North Mail* (22 July 1939) • *WWW*, 1929–40 • annual reports of Newcastle upon Tyne council 1900–39, council report, 1929/30, 762, 821, 1043–58 • annual reports of Newcastle upon Tyne council 1900–39, council report, 1936/7, pt 1, 423–9 • annual reports of Newcastle upon Tyne council 1900–39, council report 1938/9, pt 1, 892 • B. Mains and A. Tuck, eds., *Royal Grammar School, Newcastle upon Tyne: a history of the school in the community* (1985) • b. cert. • m. cert. • *IGI*

Wealth at death £8744 5*s*. 7*d*.: probate, 1939, *CGPLA Eng. & Wales*

Lunn, Sir Henry Simpson (1859–1939), worker for ecclesiastical reunion and travel agent, was born on 30 July 1859 at Bridge Street, Horncastle, Lincolnshire, the eldest son of Henry Lunn, greengrocer and lay preacher, and Susanna, daughter of Simpson Green, of Horncastle. His parents were both Wesleyan Methodists. He was educated at Horncastle grammar school and, following two conversion experiences at the ages of nine and seventeen, became convinced of a call to the Wesleyan Methodist ministry and in particular to missionary work in India. He studied simultaneously for the Methodist ministry and a degree in medicine, enrolling at the Methodist Training College in Headingley, Leeds, and at Trinity College, Dublin. He was ordained in 1886 and graduated with degrees in theology and medicine in 1887.

Following his marriage in 1887 to Ethel, daughter of Canon Thomas Moore, which brought them three sons and a daughter, Lunn took a six month placement as assistant to Hugh Price Hughes at the West London Mission, then sailed for India to work as a missionary. His expectations of mission work were disappointed by a placement in a wealthy and medically overstaffed area of India and his own ill health. He returned to England in 1888 and resumed his work with Hughes who was a great influence on his own thinking. In April 1890 his frustration with the organization of missionary work led him to write four articles for the *Methodist Times* under the pseudonym 'A Friend of Missions'. The articles raised a storm of controversy; following further comments on the opium trade and on the question of the Contagious Diseases Act, Lunn was forced to resign as a Methodist minister. Having seriously considered entry into the Anglican ministry, he chose instead to enter the ministry of the American Methodist Episcopalian church, with the right to live in England. His isolation from the main body of that church caused him to resign his position in 1895 and he reluctantly returned to the status of a Methodist layman. He was confirmed into the Anglican church in 1910 and again considered ordination into its ranks in 1931. He held that his position reflected that of John Wesley, a Methodist within the Anglican church.

Lunn's lifelong interest in the cause of church reunion began in 1891 when he founded an interdenominational periodical, the *Review of the Churches*. Its success inspired him to organize a series of conferences at Grindelwald in Switzerland to which he invited leaders from the Anglican and major nonconformist churches. The conferences, spanning the years 1892–6, attracted hundreds of delegates concerned to promote reunion, including influential Anglican, Methodist, Congregationalist, Baptist, Presbyterian, and Old Catholic delegates. Lunn terminated the

Sir Henry Simpson Lunn (1859–1939), by Sir Benjamin Stone, 1894

Review of the Churches in 1895 as a result of falling subscriptions, but revived it in 1924 to accompany a second series of reunion conferences, held at Mürren in Switzerland. In the intervening period Lunn was British treasurer at the Universal Conference of Life and Work at Stockholm in 1925 and one of the six international chairmen of the World Conference of Faith and Order at Lausanne in 1927. He worked closely with ecumenical leaders of the time including Bishop George Bell of Chichester, Archbishop Söderblom of Uppsala, and Archbishop Germanos of Thyateira. He travelled widely in his promotion of ecclesiastical reunion and international co-operation. In 1924 he embarked upon a world tour to promote church unity and the League of Nations with the support of the archbishop of Canterbury. He made a further tour in 1926.

The termination of Lunn's ministerial career in 1895 and the logistical organization of the Grindelwald conferences for reunion caused him to enter the sphere of travel agency and hotel work in Europe. The arrangement of tours, particularly to Switzerland but also to Italy and Israel, proved highly successful. He pioneered the promotion of winter sports and was responsible for opening up large areas of Switzerland to the English public, forming the Hellenic Travellers' Club, Alpine Sports Limited, the Church Travellers' Club, and the Free Church Touring Guild. His cultural cruises, combining travel with lectures by well-known speakers, were also highly successful. His firm survived into the twenty-first century as Lunn-Poly.

In politics Lunn was a staunch Liberal. He believed in free trade and the need for education, progress, and freedom. He retained his faith in Liberalism after the First World War, believing fervently in providence and in the inevitability of progress. He stood for parliament in 1910 and 1923, but without expecting success, and was committed to the work of the Liberal Council. Throughout his life he upheld the cause of minorities, in particular chairing the Assyrian and Iraq Committee in 1925 which raised £22,000 for those suffering persecution. He was knighted in 1910.

In character Lunn was determined and forceful. His optimism and desire for progress were infectious but were accompanied by an impatience and oversensitivity which sometimes made him difficult to work with.

Lunn's publications included two autobiographies, *Chapters from my Life* (1918) and *Nearing Harbour* (1934). In addition he published several devotional works, *Retreats for the Soul* (1913) and *The Secret of the Saints* (1923), which reveal the catholicity of his spirituality. He died at the Hospital of St John and St Elizabeth, Marylebone, London, on 18 March 1939. He was survived by his sons, Arnold Henry Moore *Lunn, Hugh Kingsmill *Lunn, and Brian, his daughter, Eileen, having died in 1921. STELLA WOOD

Sources H. S. Lunn, *Chapters from my life* (1918) · H. S. Lunn, *Nearing harbour* (1934) · H. S. Lunn, *Round the world with a dictaphone* (1927) · H. S. Lunn, *The secret of the saints: studies in prayer, meditation and self-discipline* (1933) · S. M. Wood, 'Nonconformity, theology, and reunion', DPhil diss., U. Oxf., 1995 · d. cert.

Archives Georgetown University, Washington, DC, papers · priv. coll., personal diaries | Bodl. Oxf., letters to Lewis Harcourt · King's AC Cam., letters from subject and his brother to Oscar Browning · LPL, Benson MSS · LPL, Bell MSS · LPL, Lang MSS

Likenesses B. Stone, photograph, 1894, NPG [*see illus.*] · Elf, caricature, Henschel-colourtype, NPG; repro. in *VF* (6 Oct 1909) · photographs, priv. coll.

Lunn, Hugh Kingsmill [*pseud.* Hugh Kingsmill] (**1889–1949**), writer, was born at 46 Torrington Square, London, on 21 November 1889, the second son and second child of the three sons and one daughter of Sir Henry Simpson *Lunn (1859–1939), founder of a travel agency and a pioneer of skiing holidays, and his wife, Ethel, daughter of Canon Thomas Moore, rector of Midleton, co. Cork, and headmaster of Midleton College. Lunn was educated at Harrow School (1903–8), won an exhibition to New College, Oxford, where he studied from 1908 to 1911 but failed to take a degree, and finally went to Trinity College, Dublin (1911–12), graduating BA and MA (1919). In 1912–13 he worked for his early literary hero, James Thomas (Frank) Harris, on the journal *Hearth and Home*. On 10 March 1915 he married Eileen FitzGerald, daughter of Horace Turpin, a solicitor from Maryborough (Port Laoise), Queen's county, Ireland. They had one daughter.

At the outbreak of the First World War Lunn enlisted in a regiment of cyclists and in 1916, having received a commission in the Royal Naval Volunteer Reserve, was sent to France, where he was soon captured. His twenty-one months as a prisoner of war at Karlsruhe in Germany would have been satisfactory, he later calculated, 'had I been able to bank them and draw them two or three weeks at a time whenever I wanted a respite from ordinary experience'. From 1921 to 1927 his ordinary experience was comfortably divided between employment in his father's travel business in Lucerne and the writing of fiction. His first novel, *The Will to Love* (1919), appeared under the name Hugh Lunn. For the rest of his career he used his two Christian names, Hugh Kingsmill, as a *nom de plume*. This was partly to distinguish himself from his elder brother, Sir Arnold *Lunn (1888–1974), and partly to disengage himself from his father, with whom his relationship was fractured by the breakup of his marriage to Eileen in 1927. His biography of Matthew Arnold (1928), written somewhat under the influence of G. Lytton Strachey, was disordered by the working out of personal grievances. In 1930 he settled with Dorothy, the daughter of Thomas Vernon, a servant, and they married on 21 January 1934. She had one son of her own, and she and Kingsmill themselves had two daughters and a son.

Over the next twenty years Kingsmill earned most of his income from writing. *The Dawn's Delay* (1924) and *The Fall* (1940) were his best volumes of fiction, but he became chiefly known for his essays and biographies. One maverick publication, *The Return of William Shakespeare* (1929), featured an inspired chapter of Shakespearian criticism framed by an unconvincing science-fictional device which consigned it to shelves not visited by scholars. Of the four biographies he published in the 1930s, *Frank Harris* (1932) was a witty and ironic exercise in demythology, identifying his one-time literary hero as an inverted puritan 'with a heart of borrowed gold'; and *Samuel Johnson* (1933) was a succinct and humane study of 'an intensely loving and compassionate soul handicapped in its expression by lifelong disabilities of mind and body'. His other biographies, being cases for the prosecution, provoked hostile reviews. Yet George Orwell judged *The Sentimental Journey* (1934), his life of Charles Dickens, 'a brilliant book' and still the best study of Dickens fifteen years after its publication; and William Empson described his *D. H. Lawrence* (1938) as 'the best book about him', being 'funny with the human breadth that the subject requires'.

Kingsmill's biographies tended to start brilliantly and end hurriedly, owing to his pressing financial difficulties. His volumes of essays, *After Puritanism* (1929), *The Poisoned Crown* (1944), and *The Progress of a Biographer* (1949), were more satisfactory as finished books. He supplemented his income with a number of anthologies, of which the most celebrated is *Invective and Abuse* (1929), and by working as literary editor of *Punch* (1942–4) and the *New English Review* (1945–9).

The main impulse in Kingsmill's writings was the theme of will versus imagination. In his biographical criticism this took the form of showing how popular sentiment acting on suggestible minds simplified people into myths. His ideal was 'the complete sympathy of complete detachment', but in practice he distanced himself from his subjects and stressed his severity over the underlying sympathy. His fate was that he was to be valued as a conversationalist rather than as a writer, and to have a profound effect on those who were to become better known than himself. Kingsmill died of cancer in the Royal Sussex County Hospital, Brighton, on 15 May 1949.

MICHAEL HOLROYD

Sources H. Pearson and M. Muggeridge, *About Kingsmill* (1951) • M. Holroyd, *Hugh Kingsmill: a critical biography* (1964) • R. Ingrams, *God's apology: a chronicle of three friends* (1977) • *DNB* • *CGPLA Eng. & Wales* (1949) • b. cert. • private information (2004) [friends]

Archives priv. coll., corresp. with Hesketh Pearson | CUL, corresp. with W. A. Gerhardie • Georgetown University, Washington DC, corresp. with Sir Arnold Lunn

Likenesses Illingworth, pencil drawing, repro. in Holroyd, *Hugh Kingsmill*, jacket • photographs, repro. in Pearson and Muggeridge, *About Kingsmill* • photographs, repro. in Holroyd, *Hugh Kingsmill* • photographs, repro. in Ingrams, *God's apology*

Wealth at death £555 16*s*. 9*d*.: probate, 11 Oct 1949, *CGPLA Eng. & Wales*

Lunn, Joseph (1784–1863), playwright, of whose early life nothing is known, had his earliest work, *The Sorrows of Werther*, a burlesque, with music by Henry Rowley Bishop, produced at Covent Garden on 6 May 1818 with John Liston and his wife in the chief parts. Liston was successful in four pieces by Lunn produced at the Haymarket between 1822 and 1825. These were: *Family Jars*, a farce in one act produced on 26 August 1822 (acted nineteen times and printed both at New York and in London, in Lacy's Acting Edition of Plays, 14, 1850); *Fish out of Water*, another one-act farce, produced on 26 August 1823 (acted twenty-eight times and printed in Lacy, vol. 16); *Hide and Seek, Petit opéra*, adapted from the French, in two acts, produced on 22 October 1824 (revived at Covent Garden, 11 November 1830, and printed in Cumberland's *British Theatre*, 12, 1829); and *Roses and Thorns, or, Two Houses under one Roof*, a comedy in three acts produced on 24 August 1825 (printed in Cumberland, vol. 12). Henry Compton also appeared with great success in *Family Jars* and *Fish out of Water*, and the latter when revived at the Lyceum in the autumn of 1874 ran for over one hundred nights.

Several of Lunn's plays were translations or adaptations of French originals. These included *Management, or, The Prompter Puzzled*, a comic interlude in one act, a free translation from *Le bénéficiaire* by Théaulon de Lambert and Étienne, which was produced at the Haymarket Theatre on 29 September 1828 and published separately in 1830 and again in Richardson's *British Drama* and in Cumberland. *The Shepherd of Derwent Vale, or, The Innocent Culprit*, a drama in two acts given at Drury Lane on 12 February 1825, was issued in London in 1825 and reprinted in Lacy.

Lunn also wrote *Horae jocosae, or, The Doggerel Decameron*, ten facetious tales in verse (1823). He lived some time in Craven Street, Strand, London, and was an original member of the Dramatic Authors' Society. Lunn died at Grand Parade, Brighton, on 12 December 1863, aged seventy-nine, leaving at least two sons, William Arthur Brown Lunn and Henry Charles Lunn.

G. LE G. NORGATE, *rev.* JOHN D. HAIGH

Sources Genest, *Eng. stage*, 8.659; 9.167, 210, 268, 316 • *GM*, 3rd ser., 16 (1864), 134 • *Theatrical Journal* (16 Dec 1863) • C. Mackenzie,

Memoir of Henry Compton, ed. C. Compton and E. Compton (1879) [Henry Compton pseud. of Charles Mackenzie]
Archives Theatre Museum, London, corresp.
Wealth at death under £1500: probate, 4 Feb 1864, *CGPLA Eng. & Wales*

Lunn, Sally (*supp. fl.* 1680x1800), supposed baker, first appears as a historical figure in the *Gentleman's Magazine* for 1798, where a correspondent stated that 'a certain sort of hot rolls, now, or not long ago, in vogue at Bath, were gratefully and emphatically styled "Sally Lunns"' after their inventor (*GM*). By 1831 a more elaborate version of the story was being told:

> The bun so fashionable, called the *Sally Lunn*, originated with a young woman of that name in Bath, about thirty years ago. She first cried them, in a basket with a white cloth over it, morning and evening. Dalmer, a respectable baker and musician, noticed her, bought her business, and made a song, and set it to music in behalf of 'Sally Lunn'. This composition became the street favourite, barrows were made to distribute the nice cakes, Dalmer profited thereby, and retired; and to this day, the *Sally Lunn* cake, not unlike the hotcross bun in flavour, claims preeminence in all the cities in England. (Hone, 2.1561–2)

These two items appear to be the only evidence available for Sally Lunn's existence. Her bun is first mentioned in 1780 in a fashion that suggests it was already an established part of Bath life. The author of *The Valetudinarian's Bath Guide* wrote that his brother died suddenly 'after drinking a large quantity of Bath Waters, and eating a hearty breakfast of spungy hot rolls, or *Sally Luns*' (Thicknesse, 12). The waters, not the buns, were at fault. The bun remained part of the English tea throughout the nineteenth century and was mentioned alongside muffins and crumpets by Charles Dickens in *The Chimes* (1845). A recipe for the bun appeared in Eliza Acton's *Modern Cookery for Private Families* (1845), which gave the alternative spellings 'solemena' or 'soel leme'. By the early twentieth century the term Sally Lunn was also being applied to different kinds of bread in North America. In 1954 the British food historian Dorothy Hartley, commenting on the 1831 story, wrote: 'we do not dispute the existence of the cook, nor the baker, but the "cry" she yelled in good west-country French was "Solet Lune! Soleilune!"' (Hartley, 512), representing the gold top and white base of the bun.

Whether a person or an accident of popular etymology, in the twentieth century Sally Lunn became an integral part of the folklore of Bath. By 1917 *The Original Bath Guide* was stating that at 4 North Parade Passage 'Sally Lunn sold the tea cakes still known by her name' (Lewis, 79), and that same house, 'an ancient shop in Lilliput Alley' (Sturge Cotterell, 14), was by the early 1930s marked on Bath corporation's *Historic Map of Bath* as Sally Lunn's house. A plaque was fixed to the wall of the house, asserting that Sally Lunn had arrived there in 1680, much earlier than might previously have been inferred, as a Huguenot refugee from France. The house, itself probably built in the mid-sixteenth century, was claimed to have been a coffee house where 'Beau Nash, Ralph Allen and their friends came to their morning coffee and [where], no doubt, they would have had a *Sally Lunn* as well' (Borsay, 141). At the end of the twentieth century the house was the home of a successful restaurant, serving a Sally Lunn bun with a variety of savoury and sweet toppings; its authenticity rested on the reported discovery of a secret recipe 'in a panel above the fireplace' in 1966 (Simmonds and Carter, 27). In this way Sally Lunn was used 'to provide a tangible link, of place and taste, between the eighteenth century and the present' (Borsay, 141) and demonstrated the power of the legend-making process in the twentieth-century British tourist economy. MATTHEW KILBURN

Sources P. Borsay, *The image of Georgian Bath, 1700–2000: towns, heritage and history* (2000) • 'Sally Lunn', *Oxford English dictionary*, online edn (2000) • W. Hone, *The Every-day Book and Table Book*, 2 (1831), 1561–2 • D. Hartley, *Food in England* (1954) • *GM*, 1st ser., 68 (1798), 931 • P. Thicknesse, *The valetudinarian's Bath guide, or, The means of obtaining long life and health*, 2nd edn (1780), 12 • W. Lowndes, *They came to Bath* (1982) • T. Simmonds and M. Carter, *This is Bath* (1991) • H. Lewis, *The original Bath guide* (1917) • T. Sturge Cotterell, *Historic map of Bath* (1931) • 'Sally Lunn's, 1680', www.sallylunns.co.uk • 'Gadsby's tavern Sally Lunn bread recipe', www.whitington.com/wash99/gadbread.html

Lunn, William (1872–1942), trade unionist and politician, was born in the pit village of Rothwell, 4 miles south-east of Leeds, on 1 November 1872, the son of Thomas Lunn, a coalminer, and his wife, Mary Emma Jackson. After attending Rothwell board school he followed his father into the pits and union politics, starting work at Rothwell Haigh colliery aged twelve and being victimized at the age of sixteen for organizing a strike. Aged nineteen he succeeded his father as president of the Yorkshire Miners' Association (YMA) branch at Rothwell. His high standing among the miners was reflected in his election at the early age of twenty-seven to the responsible and sensitive post of checkweighman at Middleton colliery, a post which he held until entering parliament in 1918. When he was twenty-nine Lunn, by then a leading local union and political activist, married Louise Harrison, daughter of Henry Hill, a warehouseman, at Rothwell on 16 August 1902. Louise was a twenty-eight-year-old widow with two children, who supported herself by taking in washing.

After the 1893 lock-out and strike Lunn helped found in 1895 one of the first Independent Labour Party (ILP) branches in the Yorkshire coalfield at Rothwell, inspired by hearing Keir Hardie. Until the affiliation of the YMA and Mineworkers' Federation of Great Britain to the Labour Party in 1909 Lunn was one of the leading members of the ILP in west Yorkshire; he later became secretary of the Normanton Labour Party. Lunn's vocal support for Pete Curran in the 1897 Barnsley by-election did little to endear him or the ILP to the then devoutly Lib-Lab leadership of the YMA, who endorsed the Liberal candidate, James Walton, a Durham coal owner. Lunn's union and political activity was local and practical, dedicated to improving the lot of the miners and their families. He served on the Rothwell school board and management committee, Hunslet board of guardians, and was a member of Rothwell urban district council for fifteen years. He belonged to the Rothwell Primitive Methodist congregation and was a temperance supporter. His local political reputation and activism secured his election to the YMA's panel of parliamentary candidates, from where he was selected to fight the Holmfirth by-election in June 1912. In a three-cornered fight against a Liberal and a Conservative, Lunn came third, partly because many local miners were still not committed to voting Labour; his manifesto shows him to have favoured *inter alia* the eight-hour day, mines nationalization, and votes for women.

Lunn was elected MP for Rothwell in 1918, retaining the seat until his death. The 1918 Parliamentary Labour Party, largely because of the number of miners it contained, has been dubbed 'a party of checkweighmen', and to a large degree Lunn fitted the stereotype. In other ways, he departed from it. He was, for example, an effective speaker (a product of his ILP membership and Methodism) and, despite his blunt personality and imposing presence, was easy to get on with. He had also experienced the hardships of working-class life and politics at first hand and saw political activity in pragmatic terms, although he seems never to have lost his radical sympathies. His experience of industrial unrest and the general strike, however, convinced him of the need for caution, and that a majority Labour government offered the best hope of progress for the working class. Lunn served on Arthur Henderson's 1921 inquiry into British policy in Ireland; he was very interested in overseas issues (he visited Egypt in 1922), was an active member of the Empire Parliamentary Association, was keenly interested in emigration to Canada, and visited coalfields in Europe. He served as whip and as parliamentary secretary for overseas trade under Sidney Webb at the Board of Trade in the 1924 Labour government, and as under-secretary of state for the colonies, and then dominions, between 1929 and 1931, again under Webb (by then Lord Passfield). He was also chairman of the overseas settlement committee and vice-chairman of the Empire Marketing Board. Although Lunn did not reach the highest levels of government, he was, unlike most of the miners' MPs, thought capable of holding office. He was regarded by those worked with him, including Sidney Webb, as an effective minister.

Lunn died on 17 May 1942 in Leeds General Infirmary; he was survived by his wife and three children. His marriage had been a political partnership, as Louise was a community politician in her own right, becoming a West Riding justice of the peace in 1922 (Lunn himself joined the bench in 1929) and the first woman to sit on the West Riding bench at Leeds. Lunn is fairly typical of those who began Labour's forward march at the turn of the nineteenth century. Although influenced by Methodism and temperance, influences which a few years earlier might have drawn Lunn to Liberalism, his personal experiences of labour relations in the pits, especially in 1893, and the perceived failure of Lib-Labism to deliver benefits to the miners, drew him to the ILP. From this amalgam of a Lib-Lab political culture with the ILP emerged a radical labourism which influenced Labour and trade union politics for the next fifty or so years. The result was a deep commitment to, and involvement in, grass-roots labour movement politics, with an emphasis on the improvement of everyday life in the mining communities.

ANDREW TAYLOR

Sources R. Gregory, *The miners and British politics, 1906–1914* (1968) • *Rothwell Advertiser* (23 May 1942) • *The Times* (18 May 1942) • *Wakefield Express* (23 May 1942) • A. J. Taylor, 'Trailed on the tail of a comet: the Yorkshire miners and the ILP, 1885–1908', *The centennial history of the independent labour party*, ed. D. James and others (1992), 229–58 • *DLB* • D. Rubinstein, 'The independent labour party and the Yorkshire miners: the Barnsley by-election of 1897', *International Review of Social History*, 23 (1978), 102–34 • D. Butler and G. Butler, *British political facts, 1900–1994*, 7th edn (1994) • Yorkshire Miners' Association, minutes and proceedings • D. Howell, *British workers and the independent labour party, 1888–1906* (1983) • b. cert. • m. cert.

Wealth at death £2756 4s. 11d.: probate, 11 July 1942, *CGPLA Eng. & Wales*

Lunsford, Henry (*bap.* **1611**, *d.* **1643**). *See under* Lunsford, Sir Thomas (*b. c.*1610, *d.* in or before 1656).

Lunsford, Sir Herbert (*b. c.***1610**, *d.* in or after **1667**). *See under* Lunsford, Sir Thomas (*b. c.*1610, *d.* in or before 1656).

Lunsford, Sir Thomas (*b. c.***1610**, *d.* in or before **1656**), royalist army officer, was possibly the third of four sons (there were also four daughters) of Thomas Lunsford (*d.* 1637), of East Hoathly, Sussex, and his wife, Katherine (*d.* 1642), daughter of Thomas Fludd, treasurer of war in France and the Low Countries under Elizabeth I, and sister of Robert *Fludd, the celebrated Rosicrucian.

The Lunsford family was established in Sussex before the Norman Conquest, but its fortunes seem to have decayed in the early seventeenth century, and by the 1630s its insecurity had helped provoke a feud with a relative, Sir Thomas Pelham, of Halland, whose parkland abutted the Lunsford property. The Lunsfords seem to have poached Pelham's deer, and on 27 June 1632 a Lunsford servant killed one of Pelham's hounds; the family were fined £1750. In August 1633 Lunsford foolishly fired his pistol at Pelham's coach outside East Hoathly church after Sunday morning service; the bullet passed through the coach, lodging in the church door, where it remained for many years. Although no one was seriously hurt the incident was generally regarded as attempted murder, and Lunsford was ostracized by Sussex society and imprisoned in Newgate by privy council warrant on 16 August 1633. Allowed to lodge outside the prison, he contrived in October 1634 to escape, despite a game left leg.

Lunsford entered French service, and in April 1636 he was in Picardy, raising a foot regiment, of which he became colonel. In the mid-1630s Lunsford married Anne Hudson (*d.* 1638), of Peckham, Surrey; their only child, a son, died in infancy. The Pelham case finally reached Star Chamber in June 1637: Lunsford was fined £8000 and was outlawed for failing to appear to receive judgment. Two years later he returned to England, was pardoned, and had his fine remitted (24 April 1639). He joined the royal army against the Scots, and in 1640 commanded a regiment of trained bands raised in Somerset. Although he complained that 'all are forward to disband' (*CSP dom.*, *1640*,

Sir Thomas Lunsford (*b. c.*1610, *d.* in or before 1656), by unknown artist

327) and boasted of having shot a couple of mutineers out of hand, he managed to conduct it from Warwick to Newcastle (June–3 August 1640) and fought bravely at the rout of Newburn (28 August), so retaining a special hold on the king's affections. In 1640 Lunsford married his second wife, Katherine (*d.* 1649), daughter of Sir Henry Neville, of Billingbear, Berkshire; they had three daughters.

On 22 December 1641 the king, apparently on the recommendation of George Digby, issued an ill-timed warrant appointing Lunsford lieutenant of the Tower of London. Many saw this as a calculated affront to parliament, signalling an impending coup, since the Tower was the key to military control of the capital. The following day the common council of London petitioned the House of Commons against the appointment, depicting Lunsford as an indebted, quarrelsome desperado and a non-attender at church (a charge they later withdrew). On 24 December the Commons voted him unfit to be lieutenant; the same day Lunsford's superior, the earl of Newport, who enjoyed the complete confidence of the anti-court party, was dismissed as constable of the Tower. John Pym declared that Lunsford's appointment was proof that the popish conspiracy was nearing maturity; Londoners feared that Lunsford might use the cannon in the Tower to pound the city to rubble; reports circulated that the City merchants were withdrawing their bullion from the mint within the Tower, to the potential damage of trade; and libels soon appeared that Lunsford was a cannibal, with a penchant for eating children.

Although the king, on the advice of the lord mayor (who suggested that Lunsford's appointment would lead to an apprentice assault on the Tower), replaced Lunsford with Sir John Byron on 26 December, this was clearly a response to popular protest. The following three days saw a wave of demonstrations by the citizenry, who feared the testy, braggart professional soldiers who hung about London, waiting for their pay arrears and pressing for new commands in Ireland. Lunsford led a party of these officers who were prepared to confront the populace and were not averse to shedding blood. On 27 December, after Lunsford had been examined by the Lords, they drove the citizens out of Westminster Hall (though Lunsford had to escape by wading out to a boat in the Thames); clashes at Westminster Abbey on 28 December were followed by the fiercest fighting the following day round Whitehall. Lunsford received compensation for his dismissal in a knighthood on 28 December and, apparently, a pension of £500 per annum.

Lunsford accompanied the king in his attempted arrest of the five members on 4 January 1642, and he was with him when he finally left Whitehall six days later. On 12 January, with a large force, he was reported to be at the noted but ill-defined hurly-burly at Kingston-on-Thames, Surrey, site of the county magazine, which it was widely believed the king aimed to seize *en route* to capturing Portsmouth. An alarmed House of Commons ordered Lunsford's arrest, and on 13 January he was captured at Billingbear, Berkshire, the home of his father-in-law. Bailed on 2 February, he was at liberty before June. On 1 July he was at York with the king, and on 14 July he had an hour-long private interview with him at Beverley. He was present at the armed demonstration against Hull on 29 July and by 3 August was based at Wells, Somerset.

At Banbury on 8 August Lunsford helped capture parliamentarian ordnance destined for Warwick Castle, and on 14 August he rescued Colonel Hastings near Loughborough from impending imprisonment in Leicester. On 19 August Lunsford received a commission to raise 1000 foot in Yorkshire, and the following day he was appointed governor of Sherborne Castle, Dorset, by the marquess of Hertford, with whom he retired into Glamorgan on 23 September.

After the battle of Edgehill on 23 October 1642 Lunsford was taken prisoner at Kineton, Warwickshire, and incarcerated in Warwick Castle until early May 1644. Arriving on 6 May at Oxford, where he was given command of a regiment, he was one of those chosen to assist Sir Arthur Aston in his government of the city. After relieving Greenland House (8 June) he entered the service of Prince Rupert, and was at Bristol, possibly as lieutenant-governor, in March 1645. By April he had become governor of Monmouth, a post he resigned to his brother Herbert [*see below*] before 7 July. After suffering defeat at Stoke

Castle, Shropshire, on 9 June 1645 he received a royal commission to consolidate royalist forces in Wales; he escaped an assassination attempt, but on 8 December was captured at the taking of Hereford. Imprisoned in the Tower of London on a charge of treason, he remained there, with his wife, until 1 October 1647, when he was removed to Lord Petre's house in Aldersgate Street.

By 29 June 1648 he had secured his liberty, and in December Lunsford was in Amsterdam, ready to cross to England. He seems to have given up the Stuart cause as hopeless, and on 7 August 1649, having compounded for his delinquency at a sixth (£300), and described as having no personal estate and much indebted, he secured a pass for himself and his family to Virginia. Early in 1650 he was depicted feasting and carousing at Ralph Wormeley's plantation on the York River, and on 24 October he was granted 3423 acres on the south side of the Rappahannock River, known as Portobacco. He was made lieutenant-general of the Virginia militia and a member of the council by the governor, Sir William Berkeley. At some point he married his third wife, Elizabeth, daughter of Henry Wormeley, of Riccall, Yorkshire, and widow of Richard Kempe, secretary of Virginia; they had a daughter. Lunsford probably lived at Richneck, his wife's home; after his death she married Major-General Robert Smith of Middlesex county. Lunsford died in or before 1656 and was buried near Greenspring, Berkeley's residence, where he shared a monument with Richard Kempe and Thomas Ludwell, Kempe's successor as secretary; this was moved to the churchyard at Bruton parish church, Williamsburg, where it remains at the beginning of the twenty-first century.

Red-haired, and of a markedly turbulent temperament, Lunsford clearly had an unsavoury reputation for sadism, brutality, and violence in the early 1640s, and he was depicted by his cousin, Lord Dorset, as 'a young outlaw who neither fears God nor man, and who, having given himself over to all lewdness and dissoluteness, only studies to affront justice, [taking] a glory to be esteemed … a swaggering ruffian' (Newman, *Royalist Officers*, 242). He was typical of the hard men upon whom Charles I increasingly relied, to the annoyance of moderate royalist opinion. His reputation for cannibalism arose because a libeller had written he was fierce enough to eat children; Sir Walter Scott, in *Woodstock*, mentions drawings in which he was depicted about to cut an infant into steaks. Yet Clarendon, by no means a sympathetic source, merely characterized Lunsford as a man 'of a very small and decayed fortune, and of no good education … who had been forced to fly the kingdom to avoid the hand of justice for some riotous misdemeanours'. If by 1641 he had acquired 'an ill character', he had also earned himself 'the reputation of a man of courage and a good officer of foot' (Clarendon, *Hist. rebellion*, 1.478). Indeed, Lunsford's characterization has been largely couched in parliament's terms, based on hearsay, insinuation, and the vestiges of an unbridled youth. 'Nothing in his wartime career suggests excesses' (Newman, *Old Service*, 145), and Sir John Coke, suffering depredations from royal troops in June 1640, and soliciting Lunsford's help, found him 'a brave gentleman and discreet' (ibid., 144).

Sir Herbert Lunsford (*b. c.*1610, *d.* in or after 1667), royalist army officer, brother (and possibly twin) of Sir Thomas, like him seems to have experienced the wars in the Netherlands and Germany. In 1630 he was fined £10 for failing to take up the honour of knighthood. It was he who ordered one of his servants to kill Pelham's hound in June 1632. In 1640 he was a captain in his brother's regiment, and he was present at Edgehill. He distinguished himself at Rupert's capture of Cirencester, and, having been made governor of Malmesbury, was taken prisoner when it was captured by Sir William Waller (23–5 March 1643). He commanded Patrick Ruthven, earl of Forth's, foot, at the siege of Bristol (July 1643). By March 1644 he was in command of a regiment, and he fought at Cropredy Bridge, Oxfordshire, on 29 June. He was knighted on 6 July 1645, by when he had succeeded his brother Thomas as governor of Monmouth; he surrendered the town to Colonel Morgan in October and went over to France.

On 29 February 1648 Sir Herbert was licensed to transport soldiers into Europe from Erith, Kent, and in 1652 he petitioned the council of state for permission to transfer 3000 Irishmen into the king of Spain's service. In 1658 he was temporarily in command of three regiments, and the following year he was Charles II's emissary to Marshal Turenne. He returned to England some time after the Restoration and in 1667 was in command of a company of foot. He married (probably in the early 1640s) Margaret, daughter of Sir Thomas Engham, of Goodnestone, Kent; they had a son and two daughters. His captain's commission in March 1667 is the last certain reference to him.

Henry Lunsford (*bap.* 1611, *d.* 1643), royalist army officer, another brother of Sir Thomas, was baptized at Framfield, Sussex, on 29 September 1611. After serving in Europe he was lieutenant-colonel in Thomas's regiment at York in 1640. He raised 240 foot for the regiment in Somerset, and was active in one of the first confrontations in the civil war, when on 4 August 1642 he led a successful ambuscade at Marshall's Elm, Somerset, before the king's formal declaration of hostilities. He fought at the action near Sherborne Castle on 26 August, retired into Wales, and, after being present at Edgehill, succeeded to the colonelcy of his brother's regiment, fighting at Brentford (12 November) and the defence of Reading (April 1643). After commanding Prince Rupert's foot at Chalgrove Field (18 June), he was wounded at the siege of Bristol (26 July) and, carrying on in command, was shot through the heart the following day on Christmas Steps, long afterwards known as Lunsford's stairs. Clarendon refers to him as an officer of 'extraordinary sobriety, industry, and courage' (Clarendon, *Hist. rebellion*, 3.114). Basil Morgan

Sources *DNB* • *GM*, 2nd ser., 5 (1836), 350–57, 602–4; 6 (1836), 32–5, 148–53 • 'Sir Thomas Lunsford', *William and Mary Quarterly*, ser. 1, vol. 8 (1899–1900), 183–6 • P. R. Newman, *The old service: royalist regimental colonels and the civil war, 1642–1646* (1993) • *CSP dom.*, *1633–7*; *1640–43*, with *addenda 1625–49*; *1651–2*; *1666–7*, 554 • *Collectanea topographica et genealogica* (1837), vol. 4, p. 142 • A. Fletcher, *The outbreak of the English civil war* (1981) • A. Fletcher, *A county community in* *peace and war: Sussex, 1600–1660* (1975) · P. R. Newman, *Royalist officers in England and Wales, 1642–1660: a biographical dictionary* (1981) · C. Russell, *The fall of the British monarchies, 1637–1642* (1991) · B. Manning, *The English people and the English revolution*, 2nd edn (1978) · D. Underdown, *Somerset in the civil war and interregnum* (1973) · R. L. Morton, *Colonial Virginia*, 2 vols. (1960) · J. Horn, 'Tobacco colonies: the shaping of English society in the seventeenth century Chesapeake', *The origins of empire: British overseas enterprise to the close of the seventeenth century*, ed. N. Canny (1998), 170–92 · Clarendon, *Hist. rebellion*

Likenesses J. W. Cook, engraving, pubd 1641? (after print by unknown artist), BM, Bodl. Oxf.; repro. in E. Warburton, *Memoir of Prince Rupert*, 3 vols. (1849), vol. 1, p. 428 · W. N. Gardiner, portrait, BM, NPG; repro. in F. G. Waldron, *The biographical mirrour*, 1 (1795) · oils, Audley End House, Essex [*see illus.*]

Luny, Thomas (*bap.* **1759**, *d.* **1837**), marine painter, son of Thomas Luny and his wife, Elizabeth Wallace, was probably born in Cornwall, being baptized at St Ewe near Mevagissey on 20 May 1759. His mother had a son from a previous marriage, James Wallace (1754–1832), a Royal Navy captain who fought at Copenhagen with Nelson in 1801. By 1773 Luny was apprenticed to the marine painter Francis Holman from whose address, Johnson Street, St George's, London, he first exhibited at the Society of Artists in 1777 and 1778. He first exhibited at the Royal Academy in 1780 from nearby Anchor and Hope Street, with Ratcliffe Highway being his academy exhibiting address from 1782 to 1790. In 1783 his picture *Battle of the Dogger Bank* (1781) was his only appearance at the Free Society of Artists, submitted from the address of Mr Merle, a frame maker in Leadenhall Street, near East India House, who appears to have been an outlet for many of Luny's ship portraits of East Indiamen and similar compositions. Luny exhibited annually at the Royal Academy until 1793, then again in 1802, when he showed *Battle of the Nile* (1798).

A belief that Luny joined the navy as a purser in 1793 and retired on a pension when incapacitated is now discounted, despite the absence of exhibited works between then and 1802. Many of his subjects suggest that he travelled, but there is no direct evidence of this save for a visit to Paris in 1777. In 1791 he bought a property at 16 Mark Lane, between Leadenhall Street and the Thames, and by January 1795 was earning enough to begin regular investment in interest-bearing government stocks. In mid-1807 he moved to Teignmouth, a fashionable watering place on the Devon coast, probably for health reasons. In 1808–9 he built a home there in Teign Street, later called Luny House. From February 1807 to December 1835 he kept a list of paintings, purchasers, and prices: it includes over 2200 works, but there must have been many more. The earliest paintings listed include views of London and Blackfriars bridges, but Teignmouth features from June 1807. Thereafter picturesque local coastal views, shipping scenes, and naval events were his stock-in-trade, most selling for under £5, some at £10, and a few up to £25. Again he did well: his link with Merle lasted to 1817 and he established others with frame-maker–dealers in Bristol and Plymouth as well as finding many local clients. These included Admiral George Tobin, an amateur artist who retired to Teignmouth in 1814 and with whom his supposed naval career was previously linked.

Luny was able to paint occasional large pictures (up to 5 ft x 8 ft) as late as about 1821 but by the mid-1820s he was confined to a wheelchair by some form of arthritis, which deprived him of the use of his hands and forced him to work with his brush held between both fists or strapped to his wrist. At their best Luny's naval battles, shipping, and wreck scenes are dramatic, strongly drawn, and colourful, with many of the small coastal scenes he did around Teignmouth having a picturesque, atmospheric charm. Unsurprisingly, given his disability, the drawing of some later work is weak and his original bright colour also became increasingly muted. He exhibited a pair, of the battles of the Nile and Trafalgar, at the British Institution in 1825. His last pictures were shown at the Royal Academy in 1837, just before 130 were exhibited for sale in Old Bond Street, when a report states he had given up painting about two years before (*Literary Gazette*, 24 June 1837), no doubt because of the arthritis which had then crippled him. The last known date on a painting is in fact 1836. He also painted in watercolour and a number of his pictures, both naval and topographical, were engraved.

Luny was described by a friend of the late 1820s as probably of medium height, had he been able to stand, and 'as a man of broad and well-nurtured frame, of fair and somewhat florid complexion; not easily drawn into conversation, but of kindly nature and pleasant in his manner with children' (Dymond, 443). He died, unmarried, on 30 September 1837, at his home in Teignmouth, and was buried in West Teignmouth churchyard. He left estate of nearly £14,000, including Luny House, other local property, and his Mark Lane house, which he had retained. Most went to his niece, Mrs Elizabeth Haswell (*née* Wallace), who was his nearest surviving relative. At the end of his life he is said to have engaged Moses Gompertz (*c.*1813–1893), better known as a diorama painter, as an assistant and after his death either Gompertz or one of his niece's six sons, or both, spent some months completing a large number of unfinished works for sale. This and the fact that a talented amateur pupil, Captain Hulme of Exeter, is said to have 'caught his style' (Dymond, 447) can produce attribution problems. The National Maritime Museum, Greenwich, has forty oils, mostly of naval scenes, and sketchbooks. The Royal Albert Memorial Museum, Exeter, also has a collection and while many museums also hold examples of his work, most are probably still in private hands given their regular appearance on the market. Two large pictures of the bombardment of Algiers (1816), which Luny painted in 1819 for the commander there, Admiral Lord Exmouth, remained at the latter's home, Canonteign House, until sold in 1992. PIETER VAN DER MERWE

Sources C. J. Baker, *Thomas Luny* (1982) [exhibition catalogue, Royal Albert Memorial Museum, Exeter] · R. Dymond, 'Thomas Luny: marine painter', *Report and Transactions of the Devonshire Association*, 18 (1886), 442–9; 19 (1887), 107–90 [incl. list of works] · Graves, *RA exhibitors* · Graves, *Brit. Inst.* · Graves, *Soc. Artists* · Thomas Luny picture list, 1807–35, NMM [photocopy] · E. H. H. Archibald, *The dictionary of sea painters of Europe and America*, 3rd edn (2000) · *British paintings* (1992) [sale catalogue, Sothebys, 15 July

1992] • *Maritime and naval battles* (2000) [sale catalogue, Christies, 9 Nov 2000] • D. Messum, *The Devonshire scene: works by John White Abbott, James Leakey, Thomas Luny* (1973) [exhibition catalogue, David Messum Gallery, Beaconsfield] • H. J. Powell, *Poole's Myriorama! A story of travelling panorama showmen* (2002)

Likenesses T. Luny, self-portrait, c.1770–1775, Teignmouth council, Devon

Wealth at death under £14,000

Lupo, Thomas (*bap.* 1571?, *d.* 1627/8?), violinist and composer, son of Joseph Lupo (*d.* 1616), violinist, and his wife, Laura Bassano (*d.* in or before 1596), was probably the 'Thomas s[on] [of] Basanew' baptized at St Olave, Hart Street, London, on 7 August 1571. Laura's brother Augustine *Bassano [*see under* Bassano, Alvise] lived in the same house, hence the ambiguous entry in the baptismal register. Both the Lupo and Bassano families had been recruited to the court of Henry VIII from Venice in 1540, the former among a group of string players and the latter as wind instrumentalists and instrument makers. Some, if not all, were Jewish; Lupo (also styled Wolf and Lopez) was a surname frequently adopted by Jews in gentile society. Among the Lupo family who arrived in 1540 were Ambrose (*d.* 1591), Alexander (who served at least until 1544), and Romano (*d.* 1542), all titled 'da Milano'. Two sons born to Ambrose before he left Venice were Peter and Joseph. They may have come to England with their father, but in the 1550s both joined the musicians' guild in Antwerp. Joseph became a member of the string consort at the English court from Michaelmas 1563, and Peter (*d.* 1608) followed at Lady day 1567. By privy seal of 13 January 1601 Joseph received a £200 gift from the queen for his 'long and faithful service'. He was buried at Richmond on 23 April 1616. In 1607 Peter received £20 for his service 'and for relief of his present necessitye', suggesting that he may have been in poor health then. Two sons of Joseph—Thomas and Horatio (*bap.* 1583, *d.* 1626)—and one son of Peter—also Thomas [*see below*]—in turn joined the group. Horatio was baptized at St Olave, Hart Street, on 5 November 1583. In 1607–8 he was one of ten musicians serving Thomas Sackville, earl of Dorset, and he was a court violinist from Christmas 1611.

The elder Thomas Lupo, the subject of this article, was admitted among the violins at court on 26 January 1588. Augustine Bassano bequeathed him 'Twoe of my beste Lutes … and alsoe all my musicke bookes and other bookes' (LMA, DL/C/359, fols. 301–2). During James I's reign he participated in the composition and performance of music for a number of masques; the third of five songs printed for *Lord Hay's Masque* (6 January 1607) was by him. For Jonson's *Oberon* (1 January 1611) and *Love Freed from Ignorance and Folly* (3 February 1611) he was paid £5 for setting the dances, and he later received a further £10, perhaps for the corresponding work in Campion's *Lord's Masque* (14 February 1613).

Lupo was among the group of musicians appointed to serve Henry, prince of Wales, from Christmas 1610, but they were disbanded following the prince's death on 7 November 1612. Eventually the remaining musicians, including Lupo, were reappointed to serve Charles as prince of Wales from 1617. On 10 May 1619 Lupo resigned his post as violinist, but from Christmas 1620 he became 'Composer for our violins, that they may be the better furnished with variety and choise for our delight and pleasure in that kind'. So far as is known, all music attributed to 'Thomas Lupo' is by this man. On 8 February 1622 £20 was ordered to be paid to 'Thomas Lupo, one of the [prince's] Musicons, for a Booke by him presented' (PRO, SC 6/Jas. I/1685).

This present may be one indication of Lupo's new status as an official composer at court; it was among the musicians of Charles, prince of Wales, that the most innovative work was done by Lupo, Orlando Gibbons, John Coprario, and Robert Johnson. Together with his colleague Alfonso Ferrabosco (*d.* 1628), Lupo had already supplied a substantial body of music for viol consort. Lupo, although less strict in using imitative devices than was customary, rather explored a lively instrumental style, with changes of tempo, metre, and groupings within the ensemble. This variety continued in later years, but in company with Orlando Gibbons and Coprario, Lupo turned to smaller groups, writing treble parts apt for violin rather than viol. Some pieces are lightweight, similar to masque dances, while others introduce rapid passage work. Contrasts of instrumental colour—violin, viol, and organ—are a feature of much music emanating from Charles's musicians in the 1620s.

Lupo lived at Greenwich for some years, and four of his children were buried there between 1616 and 1620. He may have moved to Gillingham, Kent, later; from there on 26 July 1627 he appointed a deputy to receive £106 13*s.* 4*d.* from his arrears, but 'before he could subscribe his wife by violence kept him of[f], & would not p[er]mitt him' (PRO, E 406/45, fol. 239*v*). His wife, Lidia, was probably the 'Mrs Lupoe' buried at Greenwich on 10 April 1651. Lupo seems to have died about the end of 1627, since on 16 February 1628 he was replaced as court violinist by his son Theophilus. On 6 June 1629 Theophilus wrote a letter from Cooling, Kent (which is within the manor of Gillingham), assigning arrears to pay debts. In 1631 he was named as one of two players of the contratenor violin in the court band. He played in the inns of court masque *The Triumph of Peace* in February 1634. Sixteen two-part airs composed by him are known. He was buried at St Giles Cripplegate on 29 July 1650.

Thomas Lupo (*bap.* 1577, *d.* in or after 1647), violinist, son of Peter Lupo (*d.* 1608) and his second wife, Katherine Wickers, was baptized at St Botolph, Aldgate, London, on 7 June 1577. He began service in the court violin band at midsummer 1598 at the age of twenty-one and served until the breakup of the court music in 1642. Until the death of the elder Thomas Lupo [*see above*] he was usually called 'the younger' or 'junior' in the records, but some references are ambiguous. Evidently he played the tenor violin: he is named as one of two 'low tenors' in a list dated 12 April 1631, and was paid £6 for supplying a tenor violin by warrant of 21 July 1632. He too played in *The Triumph of Peace* in February 1634, and he was one of the Corporation of Musick in Westminster named in its charter of 15 July 1635. The last known reference to him is dated 5 April

1647, when he signed an acquittance for £6 13*s.* 4*d.* from Cromwell's committee of the revenue (responsible for paying some maintenance to former court servants).

ANDREW ASHBEE

Sources J. Jennings, 'The viol music of Thomas Lupo', MMus diss., Sydney, 1967 · G. Dodd, *Thematic index of music for viols* (1980–) · A. Ashbee, ed., *Records of English court music*, 9 vols. (1986–96), vols. 3–8 · P. Holman, *Four and twenty fiddlers: the violin at the English court, 1540–1690*, new edn (1993) · D. Lasocki and R. Prior, *The Bassanos: Venetian musicians and instrument makers in England, 1531–1665* (1995) · P. Walls, *Music in the English courtly masque, 1604–1640* (1996) · A. Ashbee and D. Lasocki, eds., *A biographical dictionary of English court musicians, 1485–1714*, 2 vols. (1998) · LMA, DL/C/359, fols. 301–2 · PRO, SC 6/Jas. I/1685 · PRO, E 406/45, fol. 239v

Lupo, Thomas (*bap.* **1577**, *d.* in or after **1647**). *See under* Lupo, Thomas (*bap.* 1571?, *d.* 1627/8?).

Lupset, Thomas (*c.*1495–1530), ecclesiastic and scholar, was the son of Thomas Lupset, member of the Company of Goldsmiths and moneylender, and his wife, Alice, and was born probably in St Mildred's parish, London. Before 1508 he entered John Colet's household. On 24 October 1508 he received from the king the chapel of St Margaret, Hilborough, Norfolk, probably on Colet's recommendation. Lupset studied Greek and Latin under William Lily, probably at St Paul's School. By mid-1513 he was at Cambridge, probably in Pembroke College, when he assisted Erasmus in editing the New Testament. Despite this early prominence, Lupset disappears until three years later when he was in London, enmeshed in difficulties with Erasmus over his revelation of the alleged authorship of *Julius exclusus* (now thought not to be by Erasmus), a manuscript (apparently autograph) of which Lupset had in his possession. By the same time he had come to know Thomas More, to whom he passed this manuscript and several others written by Erasmus.

In early 1517 Lupset went to Paris in order to see through the press Thomas Linacre's translation of Galen's *De sanitate tuenda*. He sought Guillaume Budé's criticism of the manuscript, and after its printing Erasmus repeatedly asked Lupset to send him a copy. Having produced Linacre's book, Lupset also saw More's *Utopia* into print. Among the prefatory material was a letter from Budé to Lupset. Another such letter prefaced the 1519 Paris edition of Galen's *Methodus medendi*. In addition to men of the stature of More and Budé, Lupset was already known to Richard Pace, the king's secretary. During a quick visit to Louvain, Lupset met Edward Lee, then deeply embroiled in an attack on Erasmus's New Testament, a text which Lupset vehemently supported. Lupset tried to talk Lee out of publishing his most intemperate criticisms by telling him that a young man (Lee) should not contend with an old one (Erasmus). In December 1519 Erasmus wrote Lupset a long letter defending his work. Early the following year, Lupset contributed three of his own letters, and two of More's, to *Epistolae aliquot eruditorum, nunquam antehac excusae* (published by Thierry Martens in December 1519 and by Froben in 1520) which attacked Lee. Lupset responded to Lee's charge that he was largely responsible for the 'tragedy', although it is unknown what may have lain behind Lee's criticism. The sum of Lupset's sometimes thinly supported argument fell on Lee's lack of principles and his poor scholarship, although Lupset's letter to Wilhelm Nesen made some points in detail, along with the accusation that Lee was insane. The *Epistolae* went through three editions, helping to make Lupset's reputation.

Lupset returned to England by late 1519 or early 1520. Shortly before that Colet had died, leaving books to Lupset. Erasmus asked Lupset for information about Colet in order to write a remembrance which became his letter to Justus Jonas of 13 June 1521, but Lupset apparently did not provide very much material—at least Erasmus's text contains little concrete biographical detail. In early 1520 Lupset took up residence in Corpus Christi College, Oxford, when he was identified as BA (Emden says of Paris, Gee of Oxford), and was made lecturer in rhetoric and humanity by Cardinal Wolsey's appointment. More, Lupset's first biographer George Lily, and the University of Oxford all highly praised Lupset's efforts. He had among his students the subsequently prominent translator Gentian Hervet, but Hervet's chronology is sufficiently confused to make it difficult to say when. Lupset incepted as MA on 9 July 1521. Lily's statement that Lupset left Oxford because he could not compete with his successor as lecturer, Juan Luis Vives, may be disproved by chronology: Lupset had left Oxford before Vives's appointment.

Italy On 31 January 1522 Lupset received a royal grant of a pension from the abbot of St Mary's, York, and a little later the living of Ashton, Derbyshire. By March 1523 he had vacated the rectory of Claypole, Lincolnshire, and on the 24th of that month became chaplain of St Nicholas's Chapel in the parish of Stanford-le-Hope, Essex (until death). Probably already before these last transactions, Lupset had left Oxford for Padua, very likely in company with Thomas Starkey. He carried recommendations to Niccolò Leonico Tomeo from William Latimer and Cuthbert Tunstall. Once arrived, Lupset immediately encountered Reginald Pole, whom he may have known from Oxford and in whose household he probably lived. With Pole he shared instruction from Leonico, and Leonico asked both to look over the preface to his *Dialogi* published in 1524. In early 1525 Lupset was in Venice, whence he kept Leonico minutely informed about the campaign leading to the battle of Pavia, sending him a map. Later that year Lupset introduced Pole to Erasmus in a long epistolary encomium dated 23 August 1525. He provided Erasmus with manuscripts, among them one of Chrysostom, perhaps of his commentary on Acts. Possibly through Pole's patronage Lupset received the rectory of Great Mongeham, Kent, on 21 April 1526 (vacated by July 1530; it went next to Pole's client Starkey). At the same time he became rector of Snargate, Kent, and St Martin Ludgate on 3 July 1526 (until death).

While in Italy, Lupset became close to Pace, ambassador to Venice, with whom he spent much time both there and in Padua, although he probably did not act as Pace's secretary as Anthony Wood thought. Lupset was among four Englishmen who received special credit for preparing the Aldine edition of Galen which appeared in five volumes in

1525. In early 1526 Lupset went to Paris for unknown reasons, returning to Padua whence he set out for England with Pole in the autumn, making another stop in Paris which probably extended into 1527. On his return to England, Lupset hoped to devote himself to sacred literature, especially Chrysostom, but Wolsey appointed him tutor to his illegitimate son Thomas Winter, who was being sent to Paris. Lupset arrived there before 28 February 1528, the date of his first letter thence. Either before or after this episode, Lupset tutored Edmund Withypoll, son of Paul Withypoll, an alderman of London, along with Christopher Smith. He may also have been close to John Leland, who addressed three poems to Lupset. Lupset ended his tutelage of Winter in 1529, and Wolsey apparently recalled him, perhaps intending to employ him in his new college in Oxford.

A burst of writing That summer, in Wolsey's palace of the More, Lupset wrote his *Exhortacion to Young Men*, addressed to Withypoll and printed by 24 August 1529. It began with a complaint about Lupset's enforced attendance on Wolsey, and urged Withypoll to attend to his soul first, his body next, and worldly possessions only last. Lupset offered Withypoll a short list of essential reading, beginning with the New Testament, to be read according to the church's interpretation, which Lupset seems to have thought meant Chrysostom and Jerome, a less than orthodox pairing. He added Aristotle's *Ethics*, Plato, Cicero, Seneca (who appears in all three works), Erasmus's *Enchiridion*, Galen, and lastly Aristotle's *Politics*. The *Exhortacion* has been called the most polished piece of English prose written to this time. It was likely at more or less the same moment that Lupset produced *A Treatise of Charitie*, first published in 1533 and intended for the use of a nun. It begins with a definition of charity which Lupset made equivalent to all of Christianity, and argued the Stoic point that tranquillity of mind was its 'chief effect' (Gee, 228). Towards the end of the work, Lupset criticized William Tyndale's translation of the Latin *charitas* as 'love' in his New Testament, just as More had done. Lupset also argued the somewhat peculiar point that faith led to fear of God which issued in works of charity. Charity meant unconditional love of one's neighbour for God's sake, and Lupset concluded that 'both God is charity and charity is God' (Gee, 231). In this treatise, as in all his other writings, Lupset stressed the necessity of contempt of the body and of this life. All three also have an anti-clerical edge.

In the summer of 1529 Lupset may have visited Pole at his mother's house at Bisham, an occasion which could have given rise to Starkey's *Dialogue between Pole and Lupset*, a work nurtured when Starkey and Lupset were together in Paris immediately afterwards. It is possible that the efforts of Lupset, the character in the *Dialogue*, to induce Pole actively to serve the commonwealth were undertaken on behalf of the king. The real Lupset certainly expected great things of Pole, as the praise of him towards the end of *A Compendious Treatise of … Dieyng Well* manifests by stressing England's hopes for Pole. The work's point is simple and in line with Lupset's other two original compositions: a good death required contempt of this life. It opened with a lengthy treatment of the Roman Canius who laughed at a death sentence from Emperor Caligula, and included a much briefer list of Christian martyrs. Lupset admitted that he could not do the job on the subject that a Carthusian might, and his stress on the 'paynims' confirms his judgment.

Whatever his thoughts on the future life, for the moment Lupset attached his career prospects to Pole in preference to Wolsey. In October 1529 Pole left England for Paris, allegedly to continue his studies, but this was a pretence to cover his mission on Henry's behalf to the theologians and lawyers of the University of Paris. Lily repeated the pretence but also correctly observed that Lupset had joined Pole at a time when he stood in 'the king's high favor' (Hirsh, 16). Lupset almost certainly accompanied Pole on the evidence both of a list of instructions from Pole to him concerning a trip to Paris, and the fact that Lupset's last work, *Dieyng Well*, directed to Pole's servant John Walker, was finished in Paris by 10 January of what must be 1530. In any case, Lupset certainly took part in Pole's procuring of a favourable opinion on the king's divorce from both faculties. In the later stages of the negotiations he acted as messenger to and from Pole. At the end of April he received 100 crowns from the king and in May another £10 'by way of reward' (Gee, 139), as well as the rectory of Cheriton, Hampshire, on 1 August 1530, and a canonry of Salisbury and the prebend of Ruscombe Southbury five days later, very likely through royal (or at least Wolsey's) patronage.

Like Pole himself, Lupset was able to compartmentalize his attitude to royal service and to royal policy. At nearly the same time as he performed well in Paris, he also wrote his neo-Stoic works, and translated Chrysostom (and according to Lily wrote imitations of his sermons), as well as a work, now lost, criticizing the formulation of policy during drunken spells in the royal palace, which may have owed something to Pseudo-Dionysius's *Celestial Hierarchies*, and must certainly have been meant as criticism of Henry VIII. Its only manuscript was burnt in 1538 during the investigation of the Courtenay conspiracy. Lupset also claimed in the *Exhortacion* to have retranslated Xenophon's *Oeconomia* since 'Raphael's' translation was so poor, but the only new version known appeared under Hervet's name from Berthelet's press in 1532. Lupset also intended to English Simplicius's commentary on Epictetus's *Enchiridion*.

Lupset probably accompanied Pole back to England in late summer 1530, but died in his mother's house of tuberculosis on 27 December. He was buried in St Alfege Cripplegate, under the inscription 'Hic situs est Thomas Lupsetus vir Graece et Latine, atque in sacris literis eruditissimus' ('here lies Thomas Lupset, a man most learned in Greek and Latin, as well as in theology'). Some of his manuscripts passed to Pole. Lily correctly summarized Lupset's position at his death as much in Henry's eye. The first collected edition of Lupset's works appeared in 1546 and was reprinted in 1560. In addition, he translated one of Chrysostom's sermons and probably Colet's convocation sermon. T. F. MAYER

Sources G. Lily, 'Virorum aliquot in Britannia qui nostro seculo eruditione [et] doctrina clari, memorabilesque fuerunt elogia', in P. Giovio, *Descriptio Britanniae, Scotiae, Hyberniae et Orchadum* (Venice, 1548); edn in E. L. Hirsh, 'The life and works of George Lily', PhD diss., Yale U., 1935 • J. A. Gee, *The life and works of Thomas Lupset with a critical text of the original treatises and the letters* (1928) • *Gentiani Herveti Aurelii quaedam opuscula* (1541), 45 • Biblioteca Apostolica Vaticana, Vatican City, Rossianus 997, fols. 22v–24r, 37v–38v, 39v–40r, 40v–41r, 41r–42r, 42r–v, 43r–v • Emden, *Oxf.*, vol. 4 • T. F. Mayer, *Thomas Starkey and the commonweal: humanist politics and religion in the reign of Henry VIII* (1989), 33, 47–8 • *Opus epistolarum Des. Erasmi Roterodami*, ed. P. S. Allen and others, 12 vols. (1906–58), nos. 1053, 1595; vol. 6, p. 186 • PRO, SP 1/57, fols. 248r–249v • *LP Henry VIII*, 4/3, no. 6505; 5, no. 1799 (p. 749); 13/2, no. 829 (p. 339) • I. Hutter, 'Cardinal Pole's Greek manuscripts in Oxford', *Manuscripts in Oxford: an exhibition in memory of Richard William Hunt (1908–1979)*, ed. A. C. de la Mare and B. C. Barker-Benfield (1980), 108–14 [exhibition catalogue, Bodl. Oxf.]

Lupton, Donald (*d.* **1676**), clergyman and writer, was born of unknown parents. The place of his education is unknown, but he took an MA degree and presumably was ordained by 1627, when he served as a chaplain with the English troops in Germany. He was with the force commanded by Sir Charles Morgan that landed in April 1627 and subsequently with the garrison of Stade until its surrender in April 1628. He later wrote that he had many years' experience abroad. Lupton was in London by 1632, when he published *London and the Countrey Carbonadoed and Quartred into Severall Characters*, which is a characterization of aspects of life and places in the city and the provinces. Dedicated to Lord Goring, this is largely light-hearted and witty in tone, but contains some critical comments, such as those concerning animal baiting. In 1636 Lupton's *Emblems of Rarities* was published—a wide-ranging selection of brief items covering history, topography, social customs, and natural history, interspersed with legends and fantastic tales.

Lupton's first publication on spiritual matters was *Objectorum reductio, or, Daily Imployment for the Soule* (1634), consisting of a set of fifty-nine homilies on both biblical and everyday topics. It was followed by *The History of the Moderne Protestant Divines* (1637), covering the lives and beliefs of prominent continental and English scholars, and *The Glory of their Times, or, The Lives of the Primitive Fathers* (1640), which has accounts of leading scholars down to Thomas Aquinas. In March 1642 the House of Commons was told of 'dangerous Words' spoken by Mr Lupton, a clergyman, and the case was referred to the committee for scandalous ministers. There is, however, no evidence that it was Donald Lupton who was reported.

Lupton's later books were less substantial. With the outbreak of civil war he drew on his earlier experiences in writing *A Warre-Like Treatise of the Pike* (1642), dedicated to the earl of Essex, the parliamentarian lord general. In it he argued against the continued use of the pike and in favour of the musket and short pike, and included an examination of the morality of the soldier's profession, acknowledging the deleterious effects of warfare.

By 1652 Lupton was no longer living in London, but his observations during a visit prompted *The Freedom of Preaching, or, Spiritual Gifts Defended*. He considered that laymen from any background who were so gifted should be permitted to preach, and was critical of the presbyterian clergy for their restrictiveness. But his pleas for greater toleration did not extend to the Quakers, whom he castigated in *The Quacking Mountebanck, or, The Jesuite Turn'd Quaker* (1655). Lupton was also critical of the clergy and lay impropriators in two pamphlets against tithes, *The Tythe-Takers Cart Overthrown, or, The Downfall of Tythes* and *The Two Main questions Resolved … if Tythes be Put Down*, both dated 1652. He condemned the existing system and suggested that the clergy could be maintained by a fixed levy.

State affairs attracted Lupton's attention during the wars with the United Provinces and Spain. In *England's Command on the Seas, or, The English Seas Guarded* (1653) he justified the government's policy of upholding England's maritime rights. His *Flanders, or, An Exact and Compendious Description of the Fair, Great, and Fat Countrey of Flanders* (1658) was prompted by the English army's campaign there and includes a description of Dunkirk, recently ceded to England, and an account of the battle of Nieuwpoort in 1600. On 27 March 1663 Lupton was appointed by the dean and chapter of St Paul's as vicar of Sunbury, Middlesex. He died in 1676 and was buried at Sunbury on 8 March. STEPHEN PORTER

Sources *JHC*, 2 (1640–42), 502 • *DNB* • parish register, Sunbury, Middlesex, 8 March 1676 [burial]

Likenesses portrait (of Lupton?), repro. in D. Lupton, *The history of the moderne protestant divines* (1637), title-page

Lupton [*née* Greenhow], **Frances Elizabeth** (**1821–1892**), educationist, was born in Newcastle upon Tyne, the eldest of the four children of Thomas Michael Greenhow (1792–1881), surgeon, sanitary reformer, and founder of the Newcastle school of medicine and surgery, and his first wife, Elizabeth, daughter of Thomas Martineau. Frances Greenhow was educated first at her aunt Rachel Martineau's school in Liverpool and later at Miss Turner's school in Nottingham. She saw much of her aunt Harriet Martineau when at home in Newcastle and maintained a close friendship with her. In the course of her later journeys between Nottingham and Newcastle she stayed with the Luptons in Leeds and on 1 July 1847 married Francis Lupton (1813–1884), a woollen merchant, with whom she had five sons. They settled first at Potternewton Hall, near Leeds, moving to Beechwood, Roundhay, Leeds, in 1860. The Unitarian Luptons were members of a group of professional and business families in Leeds that was much involved in educational and social endeavour. Francis Lupton was one of the founders of the Yorkshire College (later the University of Leeds) and chairman of its finance committee from the beginning.

From childhood Frances Lupton had been part of, and influenced by, the Unitarian tradition. The strong set of liberal and social attitudes which this kindled expressed itself most obviously in her pioneering work for the promotion of the education of women. In 1865 the Yorkshire board of education established a ladies honorary council which subsequently became the Yorkshire Ladies' Council of Education. As its general honorary secretary from

1871 to 1885 she was the powerful driving force of the organization. Existing alongside this body for some years was the Leeds Ladies' Educational Association, in which she was also very active, chairing many of its committee meetings. Both organizations were anxious to facilitate the taking of university local examinations by girls, and the Leeds Association organized Cambridge local examinations in the city. Concerned at girls' poor results Frances Lupton persuaded the Yorkshire Ladies Council to set up a library committee which opened a students' library in 1871.

But above all, more and better schools were needed for girls, and a standing committee was set up by the Ladies Council to find ways and means of directing endowments to serve the needs of girls' education. Resistance by entrenched local interests to any use of charitable funds in Leeds for girls' education led to a meeting of representatives from the Leeds Association and the Ladies Council presided over by Frances Lupton, which formed a committee to raise funds through a joint-stock company to found a girls' high school. Funds were raised, premises rented, and head and staff appointed, and the Leeds Girls' High School began life in 1876. Mrs Lupton remained vice-president of the high school council until 1891 and her business management was vital to its firm establishment.

The keen social and educational awareness of Frances Lupton and the Ladies Council showed itself particularly in the provision of lecture courses for women on health and nursing. In 1873 she wrote to Sir Henry Cole of the Department of Science and Art asking for assistance in organizing cooking classes in Leeds. Although no help was then forthcoming, she found strong support among other members of the Ladies Council and a school of cookery was established in 1874. This expanded and also began to teach 'instructresses' of cookery. The demand for such teachers by the school boards in the 1880s led to the Yorkshire Training School of Cookery developing regular teacher training courses. These were handed over to the local authority in 1907, eventually to become part of Leeds Polytechnic, subsequently the Leeds Metropolitan University. Frances Lupton died of diabetes at Beechwood, Roundhay, Leeds, on 9 March 1892 and was buried in the family tomb at Roundhay churchyard.

PETER GOSDEN

Sources C. A. Lupton, *The Lupton family in Leeds* (1966) • *The Inquirer* (18 March 1892) • I. Jenkins, 'The Yorkshire Ladies Council of Education, 1871–91', *Thoresby Society Miscellany*, 17 (1978), 27–71 • *Annual Reports* [Yorkshire Ladies' Council of Education] • *Annual Reports* [Leeds Ladies' Educational Association] • M. H. Webster, *The early years of the Yorkshire Ladies' Council of Education* (1972) • G. Kitson Clark, 'The Leeds elite', *University of Leeds Review*, 17/2 (1974) • E. C. Kitson, *Sanitary lessons to working women in Leeds* (1873) • H. M. Jewell, *A school of unusual excellence: Leeds Girls' High School, 1876–1976* (1976) • m. cert. • d. cert.

Archives Leeds City Archives, Yorkshire Ladies Council of Education, minute books and papers

Likenesses J. Gilbert, portrait, 1858, priv. coll.

Wealth at death £335 12s. 8d.: administration, 28 April 1892, *CGPLA Eng. & Wales*

Lupton, Joseph Hirst (1836–1905), scholar and schoolmaster, was born in Wakefield on 15 January 1836. He was second son of Joseph Lupton, headmaster of the Greencoat School at Wakefield, Yorkshire, and his wife, Mary Hirst, a writer of verse, some of which is included in *Poems of Three Generations* (1910). In the cathedral at Wakefield Lupton placed a stained glass window, by C. E. Kempe, in memory of his parents.

Educated first at Queen Elizabeth's Grammar School, Wakefield, and then at Giggleswick School, Lupton was admitted in 1854 to a sizarship at St John's College, Cambridge. In 1858 he graduated BA being bracketed fifth in the first class in the classical tripos, and was awarded one of the members' prizes for a Latin essay.

After assisting the headmaster of Queen Elizabeth's, Wakefield, Lupton was appointed, in 1859, second classical master in the City of London School, then in Milk Street, Cheapside. Ordained deacon in 1859 and priest in 1860, he served as curate in two London parishes. Proceeding MA in 1861, he succeeded to a fellowship at St John's College, Cambridge. On 30 August 1864 he married Mary Ann, daughter of Thomas St Clair MacDougal, a colleague at the City of London School. They had three sons and two daughters. She died on 4 October 1879. On 26 August 1884 he married Alice, daughter of Thomas Lea of Highgate; she died on 20 February 1902.

In 1864 Lupton was appointed sur-master and second mathematical master in St Paul's School, London, where he remained for thirty-five years. From 1876 he was the school's librarian, restoring and cataloguing a collection which had been in a poor state.

Lupton, who had published in 1864 *Wakefield Worthies*, an account of the town and its chief inhabitants, subsequently devoted his leisure to researches into the life and works of Dean Colet, the founder of St Paul's School. He published for the first time several works of Colet, in most cases with a translation and an erudite introduction. In 1887 his chief original work. *The Life of Dean Colet*, gave a scholarly presentation of Colet's aims and career.

Lupton was Hulsean lecturer at Cambridge in 1887, became preacher to Gray's Inn in 1890, and won the Seatonian prize for a sacred poem at Cambridge in 1897. He proceeded BD in 1893 with the thesis *The Influence of Dean Colet upon the Reformation of the English Church*, and DD in 1896 with a dissertation on Archbishop Wake's *Project of Union between the Gallican and Anglican Churches* (1717–20). Lupton died at 7 Earl's Terrace, Kensington, on 15 December 1905, and was buried in Hammersmith cemetery.

In memory of his first wife Lupton erected a drinking fountain at Brook Green and founded the Mary Lupton prizes for French and German at St Paul's School for Girls. In memory of his second wife he founded the Alice Lupton prizes for music at St Paul's School for Girls, and for scripture and church history at the North London Collegiate School for Girls.

Besides the works already mentioned, Lupton published a life of St John of Damascus, introductions to Latin verse composition, and a *Commentary on the First and Second Books of Esdras in the Apocrypha*. He also edited More's *Utopia* in Latin and in English as well as editing and translating works of Erasmus. He was a contributor to the *Dictionary of National Biography*, to Smith and Wace's *Dictionary of Christian Biography*, to Hasting's *Dictionary of the Bible*, and to *Notes and Queries*.

FOSTER WATSON, *rev.* C. A. CREFFIELD

Sources J. Lupton, *The Eagle*, 27 (1906), 238–52 · *The Pauline* [magazine of St Paul's School, London], 17 (1899), 95–7 · *The Pauline* [magazine of St Paul's School, London], 24 (1906), 12–19 · R. B. Gardiner and J. Lupton, *Res Paulinae* (1911) · *The Paulina* [St Pauls (Girls) School Magazine] (March 1906) · private information (1912) · Venn, *Alum. Cant.*

Wealth at death £14,328 7*s*. 10*d*.: probate, 1 Feb 1906, *CGPLA Eng. & Wales*

Lupton, Roger (1456–1540), college head and founder of Sedbergh School, was born in July 1456 in the parish of Sedbergh, Yorkshire, possibly the son of Thomas Lupton. He was at King's College, Cambridge, from 1479 until at least 1484; he was admitted BCnL in 1484 and in DCnL in 1504. He was probably employed in the court of chancery. One Ralph Lupton, who attended Eton College and King's College, Cambridge, and who graduated BA in 1510, was also from Sedbergh; and he became a doctor of canon and civil law and is recorded as a member of Doctors' Commons on 8 October 1518, aged about forty.

Roger Lupton's earliest known appointment was on 15 September 1484, when he was presented by Richard III to the rectory of Harlton, Cambridgeshire. By 24 November 1500, when he was nominated a canon of Windsor, Lupton was already a chaplain to Henry VII. In this capacity he attended the king's funeral in 1509 and was one of those charged with distributing to the poor of the capital the royal bounty of £400 which Henry's will provided. Lupton continued in high standing in the first years of the next reign. He was clerk of the hanaper of chancery between 27 July 1509 and October 1514 at £40 per annum, served on the commission of the peace for Buckinghamshire in 1512, and acted as receiver of petitions from Gascony during the parliamentary session which opened in February 1515.

Lupton also acquired several ecclesiastical benefices. By December 1496 he was installed as a canon and prebendary of St Mary's College, Warwick; on 29 November 1498 he was appointed prebendary of St Michael in the same college. On 16 November 1503 he was presented to the rectory of Brancepeth, co. Durham, and on 26 October 1506, by royal grant, he was collated to the prebend of Shipton in the diocese of Salisbury, holding both benefices until his death. Admitted on 22 August 1487 to the vicarage of Cropredy, Oxfordshire, he is reported to have vacated it in October 1519. Yet some connection was maintained, for he bequeathed to this parish £6 13*s*. 4*d*. 'for keeping the clock at Cropredy and ringing daily both winter and summer the curfew and day bell there'.

But it is for his connections with the schools of Eton and Sedbergh that Lupton is chiefly remembered. He was admitted as a fellow of Eton College in February 1504, a formal prerequisite of his election as provost a few days later. Lupton is known to have entertained the countess of Richmond at the provost's lodge in 1504 or 1505, and Henry VII himself dined in the hall in October 1505. Lupton changed the face of Eton. He caused a chantry to be built in the college, completed in 1515, which still stands, and erected Lupton's tower, 'the great tower with double turrets, that is perhaps the most characteristic feature of Eton, leading from Schoolyard to Cloisters' (Benson, 23). On 4 July 1515 Lupton bought from Richard Dycons the manor of Pirton in Hertfordshire for the sum of £500. Through licences secured in April 1516 and a deed of 1518, he arranged for the manor to pass to his successors in the provostship. He also donated to the college several rare books and manuscripts.

Lupton also founded a chantry at Sedbergh, first mentioned in a deed of 23 July 1523. The earliest evidence that a school was attached to it appears in a decree of 24 March 1525, issued by the archdeacon of Richmond, concerning a lady chapel in Sedbergh church where 'fitting place shall be kept free for the chaplain and scholars celebrating Mass and anthem'; on 12 August 1527 the abbey of Coverham granted to Lupton 'one small close called school house Garth, on which a school house has been erected to found a free school' (Wilson, 3–4). The foundation deed, signed by Lupton on 9 March 1528, provides for a priest, who shall be 'good, honest and of laudable conversation, be able to teach a grammar school' but also be of 'sufficient wit and worldly policy' to manage its property; he was to have a month's holiday yearly, but should provide for an able scholar to deputize in such absences. The school was to admit 'in especial my kinsmen, and them of Sedber, Dent and Garstall, and then all other' (ibid., 5), and its first known master was Henry Blomer, whose will was signed on 5 November 1543. A survey of dissolved institutions recorded on 20 February 1551 that there was at Sedbergh a chantry 'called Lupton chantry, founded for a schole and so contynued … founded by Dr Lupton to pray for his sowle and to kepe a free schole'; the school was refounded by a charter dated 14 May 1552 (Leach, 2. 303).

In May 1527 Lupton began an association between his new school and Cambridge University, founding six scholarships at St John's College, to be offered first to natives of Sedbergh, Dent, and Garstall. He retained the right to elect the scholars during his lifetime, entrusting the task to the college thereafter. In this period he added further to his own substantial revenues. By 1526 he had vacated the rectory of Great Haseley, Oxfordshire, but took a pension of £30 per annum. On 4 June 1525 he was collated to the prebend of Centum Solidorum in Lincoln Cathedral; installed on 9 November that year, he had resigned by 18 July 1528, the date of his installation as prebendary of Caistor in the same diocese. On 11 July 1529 he was named to a commission for the administration of the chancery during the absence of Cardinal Wolsey, and in November he was a member of the conference advising on the marriage of Henry VIII to Katherine of Aragon.

It seems that Lupton accepted the legality of the divorce. On 14 July 1534 the provost and fellows of Eton signed unanimously a repudiation of the authority of the pope in England, and acknowledged the royal supremacy.

But in 1531 Henry had forced the college to surrender valuable properties in Westminster in exchange for lesser estates elsewhere; the event is remembered to this day in the rhyme

Rex Henricus Octavus
Took from us more than he gave us.

The fellows may have feared that Eton would be dissolved altogether, which would explain their support for moves to depose Lupton from the provostship in 1535. By this time government policy was in a radical phase, and Lupton may have been thought insufficiently enthusiastic in the cause of change; it has been suggested that the immediate cause of his removal was a statement of his regret at the execution of John Fisher on 22 June 1535. The fellows of Eton were anxious to co-operate; it is clear that they were engaged in selecting his successor without Lupton's knowledge. In March 1536 Lupton resigned. The very next day the fellows met, arranged to inform the bishop of Lincoln (under whose jurisdiction Eton then was) of the news, and proceeded immediately to elect a successor.

Lupton cannot have been fundamentally opposed to the breach with Rome; he held on to his several benefices, including the canonry of Windsor. When, just before his death, he complained to Thomas Cromwell, it was in the voice of a wronged servant, not of an opponent: 'I have lived eighty three and a half years, and have been taken for an honest man, and now a sort of light men inform you to the contrary' (Clarke and Weech, 10). In his last will, dated 23 February 1540, he bequeathed 'my soul to the Holy Trinity, trusting by my faith that I have in the passion of Cryst to be saved', a formulation which bears the marks of the Reformation. Lupton died, unmarried, at Windsor on 26 February 1540 and was buried the following day in his chapel at Eton, 'where a monumental brass represents him vested in the distinctive cope then worn by the canons of Windsor' (Lyte, 116). STEPHEN WRIGHT

Sources Emden, *Cam.* • H. L. Clarke and W. N. Weech, eds., *History of Sedbergh School, 1525–1925* (1925) • B. Wilson, ed., *The Sedbergh School register, 1546–1909* (1909) • H. C. M. Lyte, *A history of Eton College* (1911) • A. Benson, *Fasti Etonienses, a biographical history of Eton* (1899) • Venn, *Alum. Cant.* • A. F. Leach, *English schools at the Reformation, 1546–8* (1896) • W. Sterry, ed., *The Eton College register, 1441–1698* (1943) • *Fasti Angl., 1300–1541*, [Lincoln] • C. Hollis, *Eton: a history* (1960) • R. Clutterbuck, ed., *The history and antiquities of the county of Hertford*, 3 vols. (1815–27) • A. Platt, *The history of the parish and grammar school of Sedbergh* (1876) • G. D. Squibb, *Doctors' Commons: a history of the College of Advocates and Doctors of Law* (1977) • will, PRO, PROB 11/28, sig. 4

Likenesses monumental brass, Eton, chapel

Lupton, Thomas (*fl.* 1572–1584), political and religious controversialist, does not appear in the historical record except as the author of six or seven books and some incidental compositions. Yet his *œuvre* gives a good sense of a real individual. His moralistic nationalism and abhorrence of a money economy is already evident in his earliest-known composition—two poems in fourteeners written in commendation of John Jones's medical treatises on the benefits of the waters of Bath and Buxton (*A Brief Discourse*, 1572, 1574), where he argues that English sores should be treated not in foreign spas but by cheaper and better English waters. The same attitudes appear in a more serious vein in his prefatory poem to Barnaby Rich's *Alarm to England* (1578). There he joins such soldier-poets as Barnabe Googe and Thomas Churchyard in urging immediate action against England's enemies.

The twenty-nine folios of closely written manuscript that Lupton addressed to the queen cannot be dated, but clearly they come earlier than his *A Persuasion from Papistry* (1581), where he reminds Elizabeth of his earlier proposal for 'a thing that is necessary, reasonable and commodious to many and hurtful to none, which was by your Grace only to be authorised for the great relief and succour of your subjects'. The 'thing' proposed in the manuscript was nothing less than a scheme of national insurance which would lead not only to the repair of broken bridges and coastal defences but also require the rich and noble to pay annual sums for the support of the indigent and sickly.

The attitude behind such proposals has its most conventionally literary expression in the morality play *All for Money* of 1578. In a series of tableaux or dialogues money is shown to destroy all possibility of moral conduct in learning, law, marriage, and priesthood. The section on learning is probably the most interesting: the character Learning With Money hopes to be both wealthy and learned, but he is soon put right by the properly penniless scholar Learning Without Money; Money Without Learning and Neither Money Nor Learning are, of course, doomed to damnation, the latter because 'God hath hardened his heart'. The book culminates in the archetypal oppositions of Jesus against Judas and Lazarus against Dives. The eternal suffering of these money-sinners provides a warning for everyone.

Dives and Lazarus appear again in Lupton's last printed work, *A Dream of the Devil and Dives* (1584, republished 1615). Once again money is the issue. Lupton, on the premise that dreams are revelations of God's truth, describes how the dream of a dialogue between the devil and Dives reveals God's judgment of an England where the rich will not help the poor, lawyers cheat their clients, landlords rack rents, judges accept bribes, and soldiers kill their neighbours. The work ends with a vision of the apocalypse forecast by Regiomontanus for 1588.

Lupton's two contributions to religious controversy, *A Persuasion from Papistry* and *The Christian Against the Jesuit* (both 1581), belong to a central denominational controversy of the time. After two years as 'the Pope's Scholar' in the Jesuit-controlled English College in Rome, John Nichols, a lapsed protestant clergyman, returned to England in 1581. Imprisoned in the Tower of London, he was persuaded to return to protestantism, and before the end of the year published a series of works proclaiming the errors and horrors of Rome. These writings were immediately contradicted and ridiculed by Father Robert Persons in *A Discovery of J. Nichols Minister Misrepresented a Jesuit*, incidentally dismissing Lupton's *Persuasion from Papistry* as a tissue of ignorant irrelevancies. Lupton's theological treatise does not, on the face of it, deal with the Nichols controversy, but its concern for a national church as the basis for a purified moral estate implies the correctness of Nichols's choice. In the manner of the time Lupton immediately countered Persons's attack in *The Christian Against the Jesuit*, narrowing his focus and sharpening the tone.

Lupton's concern for a national control of morals appears again in *Siuqila, Too Good to be True* (1580, 1581) but in a more secular mode, following the lead of More's *Utopia*. An ideal community called Mauqsun (*nusquam*, nowhere) is described by one Omen (*nemo*, nobody) and contrasted with Ailgna (Anglia, England). In Mauqsun godliness is preserved by unrelenting surveillance and drastic punishment, so that English tolerance of backsliding is avoided. The second part or 'knitting up' of *Siuqila* is sometimes cited as a possible source for Shakespeare's *Measure for Measure*.

A Thousand Notable Things of Sundry Sorts (1579)—a heterogeneous collection of folk remedies and witty sayings largely drawn from Renaissance encyclopaedias—is Lupton's least moralistic work, and also his most popular one; it was kept continuously in print until the nineteenth century. G. K. HUNTER

Sources Bodl. Oxf., MS Jones 16, summary catalogue 8924 · M. Lascelles, *Shakespeare's 'Measure for measure'* (1953) · E. Rose, 'Thomas Lupton's golden rule', *Tudor rule and revolution: essays for G. R. Elton* (1982)

Lupton, Thomas Goff (1791–1873), landscape, portrait, and subject engraver, was born in Clerkenwell, London, on 3 September 1791, the son of William Lupton, a goldsmith, and his wife, Mary, *née* Clarkson. Lupton was apprenticed to the mezzotint engraver and portrait and historical painter George Clint in 1805. He exhibited portrait drawings at the Royal Academy between 1811 and 1820. On 30 May 1818 Lupton married Susannah Oliver (*b.* 1800?), and they had six sons and one daughter. Clint had engraved two plates for J. M. W. Turner's *Liber Studiorum* (*c.*1806–19), and after Lupton completed his apprenticeship, he engraved, under Turner's close supervision, his first mezzotint plate for the series, *Solway Moss* (1816; original watercolour untraced), which as Lupton later claimed 'placed me at once among my brother scrapers, an artist' (Pye and Roget, 65). Lupton also engraved for the *Liber Studiorum* the published plates of *Dumblain Abbey, Scotland* (1816, original watercolour, *c.*1806–7, Tate collection), *Water Cress Gatherers* (1819; original watercolour untraced), and *Ben Arthur, Scotland* (1819; original watercolour untraced), as well as the unpublished subjects *Dumbarton* (1820s; original watercolour untraced) and *Ploughing Eton* (1820s; original watercolour, Tate collection), and may have also worked on *Stonehenge* (1820s; original watercolour, Museum of Fine Arts, Boston) although this plate is traditionally attributed to Turner. He continued to work with Turner, with whom he became especially friendly, and who valued highly Lupton's expertise and sensitivity. After Turner's death in 1851 Lupton provided important anecdotal information to early commentators on the artist including John Ruskin, John Pye, and Walter Thornbury.

Lupton played a significant role in the evolution of the use of steel plates for engraving, an important issue, since

Thomas Goff Lupton (1791–1873), by George Clint

copper plates were unable to produce large numbers of impressions and were consequently uneconomic. William Say had successfully engraved a soft steel plate in 1820, but found the medium unsympathetic, and abandoned his investigations. Lupton experimented, first with nickel and the Chinese alloy tutenag, and subsequently with steel. In 1822 he successfully engraved Clint's portrait of the actor John Shepherd Munden (original painting untraced) in mezzotint on steel, for which he was awarded the Society of Arts' Isis gold medal on 30 May 1822. Lupton used steel for the remainder of his career. His early engravings on steel include the *Infant Samuel* (original painting untraced) of 1822, after Sir Joshua Reynolds, the *Passage Boat*, and *A Group of Cattle* after Cuyp published by W. B. Cooke in 1824, and five plates after Turner's designs for the *Rivers of England* (1823–7) in the 1820s. In 1826 Lupton collaborated with Turner on the *Ports of England* (1826–8), acting as engraver and publisher, but by 1828 only six mezzotints of the proposed twelve had been published, and the remaining six did not appear until 1856, after Turner's death, when the complete series was published by Ernest Gambart as the *Harbours of England* with a commentary by John Ruskin. Lupton also collaborated with Turner on single large mezzotint plates of *Calais Pier* (original painting, exh. 1803, National Gallery, London) and *Folkestone* (original watercolour untraced), but they remained unpublished in his lifetime. *Calais Pier* was abandoned because of the excessive alterations demanded by Turner, but was eventually published in 1892 by Henry Graves on behalf of the Artists' General Benevolent Institution. Between 1858 and 1864 Lupton re-engraved fifteen of the *Liber Studiorum* subjects on steel for a projected series to be published by Colnaghi and dedicated to John Ruskin, but the plates were never issued.

Lupton was a highly regarded, versatile, and prolific engraver. In addition to his accomplished work for Turner, he also engraved numerous portraits after artists such as Henry Perronet Briggs, George Clint, Thomas Lawrence, and Joshua Reynolds, as well as illustrations for *Gems of Art* (1823), *Beauties of Claude Lorrain* (1825), and Lady Charlotte Bury's *Three Great Sanctuaries of Tuscany* (1833). His finest single plates include *Wellington Surveying the Field of Waterloo* after Benjamin Robert Haydon (1841; original painting, 1839, NPG); *Lord Byron* after Thomas Phillips (1824; original painting, 1814, Gov. Art Coll., British embassy, Athens); and *The Eddystone Lighthouse* (1824; original watercolour untraced) and *Sunrise, Whiting Fishing at Margate* (1825; original watercolour untraced) after Turner. Lupton became friendly with John Ruskin in the 1850s, and engraved a number of plates for his publications, notably the *Stones of Venice* (1851–3). Lupton taught Ruskin's protégé George Allen, who subsequently made engravings for Ruskin's books. Lupton also took on William Oakley Burgess as his pupil in the late 1830s. An active supporter of the Artists' Annuity Fund, Lupton was president between 1836 and 1838. Lupton died on 18 May 1873 at his home at 4 Keppel Street, Russell Square, London, where he had lived for thirty-six years. His youngest son, Nevil Oliver Lupton (*b.* 1828), became a landscape painter; he was awarded the first Turner medal at the Royal Academy in 1857, and exhibited landscapes regularly there until 1857.

GILLIAN FORRESTER

Sources *DNB* • *The Athenaeum* (31 May 1873), 702 • *Art Journal* (1873), 208 • T. Lupton, 'Paper in the polite arts: engraving in mezzotinto on steel', *Transactions of the Society Instituted at London, for the Encouragement of Arts, Manufactures and Commerce*, 60 (1823), 41–3 [letter] • D. Alexander, 'Lupton, Thomas Goff', *The dictionary of art*, ed. J. Turner (1996), 806 • B. Hunnisett, *Engraved on steel: the history of picture production using steel plates* (1998), 64, 66, 68, 70, 80, 95 • R. K. Engen, *Dictionary of Victorian engravers, print publishers and their works* (1979), 130–31 • *The collected correspondence of J. M. W. Turner*, ed. J. Gage (1980), 266–7 • G. Forrester, *Turner's 'drawing book': the Liber Studiorum* (1996) [exhibition catalogue, Tate Gallery, 20 Feb – 2 June, 1996] • G. Forrester, 'Thomas Goff Lupton', *The Oxford companion to J. M. W. Turner*, ed. E. Joll, M. Butlin, and L. Herrmann (2001), 180–81 • J. Pye and J. L. Roget, *Notes and memoranda respecting the 'Liber Studiorum' of J. M. W. Turner, R.A.* (1879) • C. Wax, *The mezzotint: history and technique* (1990), 102, 118, 120 • R. Ormond, *Early Victorian portraits*, 2 vols. (1973), 277 • G. Ashton, *Pictures in the Garrick Club: a catalogue of the paintings, drawings, watercolours and sculpture* (1997), 198–9 • J. Pye, *Patronage of British art* (1845), 392 • W. Thornbury, *The life of J. M. W. Turner R.A.* (1904), 196–8 • private information (2004) [family] • *IGI* • *CGPLA Eng. & Wales* (1873)

Likenesses G. Clint, group portrait, oils, 1820 (*A new way to pay old debts*), Garr. Club • G. Clint, oils, NPG [*see illus.*] • S. Clint, plaster • N. O. Lupton, pen and ink (after plaster bust by S. Clint), BM

Wealth at death under £1500: probate, 18 Aug 1873, *CGPLA Eng. & Wales*

Lupton, William (1676–1726), Church of England clergyman, was born on 1 June 1676 at Bentham, Yorkshire, the son of Thomas Lupton, who served as rector there for fifty years. William matriculated at Queen's College, Oxford, on 30 March 1694, and graduated BA in 1697, MA in 1700, BD on 14 February 1709, and DD on 15 February 1712. He was elected a fellow of Lincoln College in 1698, and briefly served as curate to George Bull at Avening, Gloucestershire. It was probably through Bull's influence that he became rector of Richmond, Yorkshire, in 1705. He resigned this position in the following year and was appointed lecturer of St Dunstan-in-the-West, London; and in 1714 he became preacher of Lincoln's Inn and afternoon preacher at the Temple. On 13 September 1715 he was presented to the ninth prebendal stall in Durham Cathedral.

Described as a 'violent partizan of the high church' (Noble, 3.110), Lupton was known to be a good preacher. Robert Nelson spoke of his sermons as 'a fit model for the preachers of the rising generation' (Allibone, *Dict.*, 1.1144). His reputation led to his selection as the preacher for the fiftieth anniversary of the episcopal consecration of Nathaniel Crew, and to his delivery of the Lady Moyer's lectures at St Paul's, London. He published several of his sermons separately, and a collection of sermons was published posthumously in 1729.

Although he claimed in his farewell sermon at St Dunstan's that his sermons had been focused on the 'practical duties of religion' (Lupton, *Christian Conversation*, 40–41), they did at times have political implications. He was notable for his championship of the doctrine of eternal punishment, and upheld the orthodox view of this doctrine in a sermon preached before the University of Oxford on 24 November 1706, entitled *The Eternity of Future Punishment Proved and Vindicated* (1708). In this sermon, which was one of several attacks by high-churchmen on John Tillotson's sermon preached before Queen Mary on 7 March 1690, Lupton claimed that the reflections of Tillotson's sermon were 'not only precarious, but plainly false' (Lupton, *Eternity*, 9). Another address with political overtones came on 30 January 1724, when he preached before the House of Commons an anniversary sermon for the martyrdom of Charles I entitled *National Sins Fatal to Prince and People* (1724). In it he suggested that the wickedness of the people led to the downfall and sufferings of the king, an event allowed by God so that the rebellious might 'fall into the pit'. Lupton complained of attempts during his lifetime to 'demolish [Charles's] virtues, and improve his infirmities scarce separable from man, into vices of the first magnitude' (Lupton, *National Sins*, 28–9).

Lupton died at Tunbridge Wells, Kent, on 13 December 1726, and was buried there.

ROBERT D. CORNWALL

Sources Foster, *Alum. Oxon.* • *A biographical history of England, from the revolution to the end of George I's reign: being a continuation of the Rev. J. Granger's work*, ed. M. Noble, 3 (1806), 109–10 • T. Birch, *The life of the Most Reverend Dr John Tillotson, lord archbishop of Canterbury* (1752) • Allibone, *Dict.* • *IGI* • *Fasti Angl.* (Hardy), 3.317 • *The occasional paper* (1718) • T. Swinden, *Enquiry into the nature and place of hell* (1727) • W. Lupton, *Christian conversation: a farewell sermon* (1726) • W. Lupton, *National sins fatal to prince and people* (1724) • W. Lupton, *The eternity of future punishment proved and vindicated* (1708)

Likenesses G. Vertue, line engraving, 1727, BM, NPG; repro. in *Twelve sermons preach'd on several occasions* (1729)

Lurting, Thomas (1628x32–1713), sailor and religious writer, was pressed into the navy in 1646 at the age of about fourteen according to his later account. After fighting in Ireland for two years he served in the Dutch and Spanish wars. In time he rose in his profession until he became boatswain's mate in the frigate *Bristol* commanding 200 men.

In 1657 Lurting was at Santa Cruz in the Canaries with General Blake and gives a vivid account of the fighting and of his deliverance from harm. It was here that a great change began in his life. A soldier, put on board ship for a short time, had been at a Quaker meeting in Scotland and talked to two young crew members about it. Some time after he left his influence became apparent when the two began to meet in silence together and refused to hear the ship's priest or take off their hats to the captain. At first Lurting was one of those who persecuted the two violently but, as they were joined by others, Lurting eventually felt that his violence was wrong. He struggled against his sympathy for them, but talked with one of them, Roger Dennis, and spent time alone feeling the influence of God doing 'heart work' within him (Lurting, 13). After more than six months' inner turmoil Lurting identified himself as a Quaker by joining in silent meetings with Roger Dennis and four others, much to the anger of the priest and the captain. The Quakers' influence on the ship grew during the next six months and so did their number, to twelve men and two boys.

The ship was next ordered to Barcelona on a raid against the Spanish and the fledgeling Quakers acquitted themselves bravely in the fighting, being ignorant that Quakers in general refused to bear arms. However, according to his later account, Lurting was stunned in the midst of the battle by the realization that God was forbidding him to fight or kill. On a later occasion, with the support of the other Quakers in the ship, Lurting refused to fight; the captain threatened to kill him but Lurting stood staring at him silently until he backed down.

Lurting left the navy and worked as a merchant seaman with the help of other Quakers in London. Several attempts were made to press him into naval service again but he escaped. His adventures were not over, however, for in 1663 his ship was captured by Turkish slavers near Majorca. Lurting and another Quaker, George Pattison, overcame their captors by trickery alone, then joined forces with them to flee their mutual enemy the Spanish, and finally put the Turks ashore in Algiers unharmed without a gun being fired. This exploit brought Lurting a measure of fame and he wrote an account of it for George Fox, published in 1680, as *To the Great Turk*.

In later years Lurting left the sea and settled with his wife, Elinor (1643/4–1709), in Rotherhithe. He took time to reflect on his life and expanded what he had written into a fuller account, published in 1710 as *The Fighting Sailor Turn'd Peaceable Christian*. Elinor died aged sixty-five on 13 March 1709 and was buried in the Quaker burial-ground in Long Lane, Bermondsey; four years later, on 30 March 1713, apparently aged eighty-four, Lurting died of a fever at Stepney and was buried on the same day in the same burial-ground as his wife. GIL SKIDMORE

Sources T. Lurting, *The fighting sailor turn'd peaceable Christian* (1710) • 'Dictionary of Quaker biography', RS Friends, Lond. [card index] • W. M. White, *Six weeks meeting, 1671–1971* (1971) • J. Smith, *A descriptive catalogue of Friends' books*, 2 vols. (1867) • Quaker digest registers, RS Friends, Lond.

Luscombe, Matthew Henry Thornhill (*bap.* 1775, *d.* 1846), missionary bishop, baptized on 16 April 1775 at St Paul's, Exeter, was the son of Samuel Luscombe, physician at Exeter, and his wife, Jane a collateral descendant of Sir James Thornhill. He was educated at Exeter grammar school and admitted pensioner at Trinity College, Cambridge, on 22 May 1793. He migrated to St Catharine's, Cambridge, on 27 December 1793, where he graduated BA 1798 and MA 1805. He was ordained to the curacy of Clewer, Windsor. From 1806 to 1819 he was master of the East India Company's school at Haileybury, Hertford, and held the curacy of St Andrew's in that town. Walter Farquhar Hook was one of his pupils at Hertford, and became a close friend. On 20 January 1810 he was incorporated MA of Oxford University, joining Exeter College, and proceeding BCL and DCL in February 1810.

In 1819 Luscombe moved to Caen, and subsequently to Paris. In 1824 George Canning looked to appoint Luscombe embassy chaplain at Paris, and, in recognition of the need for supervision of Anglicans overseas, general superintendent of the English congregations on the continent. However, he soon afterwards agreed to a proposal made originally by Luscombe's former pupil Hook, that the bishops of the Scottish Episcopal church should consecrate Luscombe to a continental bishopric, with the status of a missionary bishop, giving him jurisdiction over people rather than territory. On 20 March 1825 Luscombe was consecrated at Stirling by Bishop Jolly of Moray. Hook attended as chaplain to preach the sermon on the Catholicism of the Anglican church. In the course of the same year Luscombe assumed the office of chaplain at Paris. In lieu of the room at the embassy or the French protestant Oratoire in which the services had been held, he erected in 1834, and partly paid for, a church in the rue d'Aguesseau. He officiated at Thackeray's marriage in Paris in 1836. Luscombe met immediate difficulties arising from the lack of clarity regarding his authority, and the extent to which he had government backing. One congregation at Boulogne refused to recognize his authority, and there were complaints that he was attempting to exercise jurisdiction rather than influence over the clergy in Belgium. Luscombe's right to ordain was questioned, and in 1840 was restricted to confirmation, thus calling into question the status of clergy he had previously ordained.

Luscombe married the only daughter of Henry Harmood, commissioner of the navy. They had a son, Henry, who died in 1833, and two daughters, Susan and Frances. Luscombe held high-church principles. He was one of the founders in 1841 of the *Christian Remembrancer*. He also published sermons and *The Church of Rome compared with the Bible, the fathers of the church, and the Church of England*

(1839). He dedicated an anonymously published poem 'Pleasures of Society' to Canning. Luscombe also interested himself in fine arts, both as a collector and as an artist.

Luscombe died suddenly of heart disease at Lausanne on 24 August 1846, and was buried at La Sallaz cemetery. No attempt was made to appoint a successor as missionary bishop. He left a bequest for divinity scholarships at Glenalmond College, Perthshire.

J. G. ALGER, *rev.* ELLIE CLEWLOW

Sources Venn, *Alum. Cant.* • J. Pinnington, 'Bishop Luscombe and Anglican order in continental Europe', *Historical Magazine of the Protestant Episcopal Church*, 38 (1969) • Foster, *Alum. Oxon.* • *GM*, 2nd ser., 26 (1846), 539–40 • W. R. W. Stephens, *The life and letters of Walter Farquhar Hook*, 2 vols. (1878) • *Galignani's Messenger* (1 Sept 1846) • parish registers, Lausanne, 24 Aug 1846 • *IGI*
Archives LPL, Fulham MSS

Lush, Sir (Charles) Montague (1853–1930), judge, was born at Balmoral House, Upper Avenue Road, Hampstead, Middlesex, on 7 December 1853, the fourth son of Sir Robert *Lush (1807–1881), lord justice of appeal, and his wife, Elizabeth Ann (*d.* 1881), daughter of the Revd Christopher Woollacott, a London Baptist minister. He was educated at Westminster School and at Trinity Hall, Cambridge, where he obtained a first class in the classical tripos of 1876. He was called to the bar by Gray's Inn in 1879, and joined the north-eastern circuit. After the Married Women's Property Act (1882) was passed, he wrote *The Law of Husband and Wife*, which was the standard work for many years.

Lush's career progressed slowly at first, but he gradually acquired a leading position at the common-law bar in London, and in 1902 he became queen's counsel. On 27 December 1893 he married Margaret Abbie (1871/2–December 1925), the daughter of Sir Charles Brodie Locock, second baronet; they had four sons and two daughters. He became a bencher of Gray's Inn, and in 1911 was made an honorary fellow of Trinity Hall, Cambridge.

Lush began to be widely recognized as a sound lawyer. His small stature and gentle tones seemed to disqualify him for a jury practice, but he developed unsuspected gifts of advocacy, and for eight years was in great demand, for jury actions in particular. Lush held his own among such leaders as Edward Carson, Rufus Isaacs, H. E. Duke, and John Lawson Walton. His often emotive eloquence, combined with an appearance of complete simplicity and candour, often secured unexpected verdicts. He was just as successful in the Court of Appeal, appearing in such notable actions as *Paquin Ltd* v. *Beauclerk* (1906, husband's liability for goods supplied to his wife) and *Hulton & Co.* v. *Jones* (1910, liability for unintentional defamation).

In October 1910 Lush was appointed a judge of the King's Bench Division under the Additional Judges Act and received a knighthood. The bar approved; he seemed to possess all the qualifications for a great judicial career. But he did not live up to expectations. Courageous to a fault as a barrister, he lacked confidence as a judge. In his anxiety to do justice, he hesitated to make a decision and detected difficulties in cases which seemed simple to others. Sometimes he allowed his feelings to master his judgement, as in *Harnett* v. *Bond* (1925), where his sympathy with the plaintiff, who alleged that he had been wrongly detained as a lunatic, resulted in a verdict for £25,000 damages against the two defendants. The Court of Appeal's order for a new trial was affirmed by the House of Lords.

Lush sat occasionally as a temporary member of the Court of Appeal, and in 1915 he was appointed president of the railway and canal commission. Increasing deafness compelled him to retire in 1925. Although he was sworn of the privy council in the same year, he never sat as a member of the judicial committee. Lush died on 22 June 1930 at his home, Tanglewood, Stanmore, Middlesex.

THEOBALD MATHEW, *rev.* HUGH MOONEY

Sources *The Times* (23 June 1930) • *The Times* (28 Dec 1881) • b. cert. • m. cert. • personal knowledge (1937)
Likenesses Ape Junior, caricature, Henschel-colourtype, NPG; repro. in *VF* (18 Jan 1911)
Wealth at death £47,267 6*s.* 8*d.*: resworn probate, 30 Aug 1930, *CGPLA Eng. & Wales*

Lush, Sir Robert (1807–1881), judge, was born at Shaftesbury, Dorset, on 25 October 1807, the eldest son of Robert Lush of Shaftesbury, and his wife, Lucy, daughter of Joseph Foote of Tollard, Wiltshire. He was educated at a school in Shaftesbury and afterwards spent several years in a solicitor's office. In 1836 he entered himself as a student at Gray's Inn. He published several law books before he was called to the bar. *The Act for the Abolition of Arrest on Mesne Process* appeared in 1838, together with a treatise on the Wills Act. In October 1840 *The practice of the superior courts of common law at Westminster in actions and proceedings over which they have a common jurisdiction* was published; it became a standard work on common-law practice and ran to several editions. The editor of the third edition (1855) was James Stephen, the eminent professor of jurisprudence at King's College, London.

In 1839 Lush married Elizabeth Ann (*d.* 1881), daughter of the Revd Christopher Woollacott of London. They had several children, including at least four sons. Two of these became prominent lawyers: Herbert W. Lush, KC and judge, and Sir (Charles) Montague *Lush QC. Another, suffering from delirium, committed suicide, and the fourth died suddenly and unexpectedly.

Having practised for a short time as a special pleader, Lush was called to the bar by Gray's Inn on 18 November 1840, and joined the home circuit. Until 1857, when he became a queen's counsel and a bencher of Gray's Inn, he was a busy junior. In 1842 he edited the common-law portion of *Chitty's General Practice of the Law*. Although he was small and unassuming, his learning and clarity of expression gave him instant success in commercial practice. He attached himself to the court of common pleas, and shared with Sir William Bovill the lead of the home circuit. He never sat in parliament. He was, as Lord Westbury wrote of him, 'a very learned and distinguished man', who, 'so far as I know, has no politics at all' (Nash, 69).

On 30 October 1865 Lush succeeded Mr Justice Crompton in the court of queen's bench. He was one of the three judges who tried the Tichborne claimant. When the Judicature Acts came into force in November 1875, he sat in chambers for many weeks drafting the rules of practice with Sir George *Jessel. Lush was a member of the judicature commission and of the commission on the penal code in 1878. Afterwards, in May 1879, while still a puisne judge, he was appointed a member of the privy council by Lord Beaconsfield. In October 1880 he succeeded Lord Justice Thesiger in the Court of Appeal, but his health soon failed, and on 27 December 1881 he died at his home, 60 Avenue Road, Regent's Park, London.

J. A. Hamilton, *rev.* Hugh Mooney

Sources *The Times* (28 Dec 1881) · *Solicitors' Journal*, 26 (1881–2), 142 · *Law Journal* (31 Dec 1881), 630–31 · *Law Times* (31 Dec 1881), 158–9 · E. Foss, *Biographia juridica: a biographical dictionary of the judges of England … 1066–1870* (1870) · T. A. Nash, *The life of Richard, Lord Westbury*, 2 (1888), 69 · W. Ballantine, *Some experiences of a barrister's life*, 7th edn (1883), 57 · J. D. Woodruff, *The Tichborne claimant: a Victorian mystery* (1957), 392 · *CGPLA Eng. & Wales* (1881)

Likenesses Lock & Whitfield, woodburytype photograph, NPG; repro. in T. Cooper, *Men of mark: a gallery of contemporary portraits* (1881) · Maull & Polyblank, photograph, carte-de-visite, NPG · Spy [L. Ward], caricature, watercolour study, NPG; repro. in *VF* (31 May 1873) · chromolithograph caricature, NPG · oils, Gray's Inn, London · wood-engraving (after photograph by J. & C. Watkins), NPG; repro. in *ILN* (25 Nov 1865)

Wealth at death £28,837 13*s*. 10*d*.: resworn probate, May 1882, *CGPLA Eng. & Wales* (1881)

Lushington, Charles (1785–1866). *See under* Lushington, Stephen (1782–1873).

Lushington, Edmund Law (1811–1893), classical scholar, was born on 10 January 1811 at Prestwich, Lancashire, the son of Edmund Henry Lushington (1766–1839), chief commissioner of the colonial board of audit and master of the crown office, and his second wife, Sophia (*c*.1780–1841), daughter of Thomas Philips of Sedgeley, near Manchester. He spent his childhood at Hanwell, Middlesex, and was educated at Charterhouse School (1823–8) where he became head of the school while still young and not very robust and found the exacting duties of captain somewhat irksome. Thackeray was one of his contemporaries there and was also with him for a time at Cambridge. Entering Trinity College, Cambridge, in 1828, Lushington was two years Tennyson's junior and with him, Arthur Hallam, Trench, and others, was associated in the select club of twelve called the Apostles (commemorated in *In Memoriam*, lxxxvii). He was made a scholar in 1830.

In 1832 Lushington was senior classic and senior chancellor's medallist. The year was a specially brilliant one, Henry Alford, Richard Shilleto, and William Hepworth Thompson, afterwards master of Trinity, also being in the list. In *The Virginians* (vol. 1, chap. 41) Thackeray makes a covert though sufficiently obvious allusion to the brilliant scholarship of Thompson and Lushington. Lushington was elected a fellow in 1834 and became an assistant tutor in 1835.

In 1838 Lushington succeeded Sir Daniel Keyte Sandford as professor of Greek at Glasgow, gaining the appointment over Robert Lowe (Lord Sherbrooke), after Archibald Campbell Tait, subsequently archbishop of Canterbury, had withdrawn his candidature. On 14 October 1842 Lushington married Cecilia Tennyson, sister of Alfred, Lord Tennyson. The marriage ceremony was performed by Charles Tennyson Turner, Lushington's marriage with his sister being celebrated by Tennyson in the epilogue to *In Memoriam*.

Lushington's colleague as professor of humanity was William Ramsay. C. J. Fordyce, a more recent occupant of Ramsay's chair, described them as 'a pair of professors who not only outshone all their predecessors but vastly outshone their contemporaries in the other [Scottish] universities'. Their pupils included a number of men who later became prominent classical scholars: W. Y. Sellar, L. Campbell, D. B. Monro, and J. Frazer. Nevertheless, Lushington's abilities were not as well suited as Ramsay's to the teaching of large elementary classes which constituted much of their work. His wife disliked Glasgow and preferred to remain in England during the university term. In 1875 he resigned his chair, the university conferring on him the honorary degree of LLD. He settled at Park House, Maidstone, the residence described in the prologue to *The Princess*, which is dedicated to his brother Henry. In 1884 he was elected lord rector of Glasgow University, and the principal, John Caird, welcomed him with a fitting eulogy when he delivered the customary rectorial address. He died at Park House on 13 July 1893. He was survived by his wife and his daughter Cecilia.

Although believed to have written anonymously for some of the reviews, Lushington made few acknowledged contributions to literature. He translated into Greek Tennyson's *Oenone* and *Crossing the Bar*, the version of the latter giving the poet especial satisfaction. He contributed interesting reminiscences to volume 1 of H. Tennyson's memoir of his father, Lord Tennyson. He collaborated with Sir Alexander Grant in editing in 1866 (2nd edn, 1875) the *Philosophical Works* of James Frederick Ferrier, prefixing to the volume of *Philosophical Remains* a thoughtful memoir and appreciation. He published the Glasgow rectorial address in 1885.

T. W. Bayne, *rev.* Richard Smail

Sources J. O. Waller, *A circle of friends: the Tennysons and the Lushingtons of Park House* (1986) · C. J. Fordyce, 'Classics', *Fortuna domus: a series of lectures delivered in the University of Glasgow in commemoration of the fifth centenary of its foundation*, ed. [J. B. Neilson] (1952), 21–40 · H. Craik, 'Tennyson and Lushington', *Tennyson and his friends*, ed. H. Tennyson (1911), 89–97 · *The Times* (14 July 1893) · *Glasgow Herald* (14 July 1893) · *The Athenaeum* (22 July 1893), 132–3 · *Classical Review*, 7 (1893), 425–8, 476 · H. Tennyson, *Alfred Lord Tennyson: a memoir by his son*, 2 vols. (1897) · Venn, *Alum. Cant.*

Likenesses photograph, *c*.1865, repro. in Waller, *A circle of friends*, 82 · T. Woolner, bust, exh. RA 1877, U. Glas.; copy, Maidstone Museum

Wealth at death £70,045 0*s*. 8*d*.: resworn probate, May 1894, *CGPLA Eng. & Wales* (1893)

Lushington, Sir Godfrey (1832–1907), civil servant, was born at Westminster on 8 March 1832, the fifth son of Stephen *Lushington (1782–1873), Admiralty judge and MP, and his wife, Sarah Grace Carr (*d*. 1837). He had four brothers, including a twin, Vernon *Lushington, and five sisters, two of whom, Alice and Fanny, later ran a school.

His was a whig–Liberal family, strongly represented at the bar and in the public service.

Educated at Rugby School, Lushington entered Balliol College, Oxford, in 1850, where he obtained a first in *literae humaniores* and a fourth in mathematics (1854). He was president of the Oxford Union Society in 1854. Elected, as his father had been, to a fellowship of All Souls College (1854) Lushington, as a young turk in sympathy with the Oxford University reform movement, embarrassed many of the older fellows of the college by challenging the restrictive basis on which college fellowships were awarded. With two other former Balliol men, W. H. Fremantle and A. G. Watson, he took the case to the college visitor in 1859 and then to the court of queen's bench, before finally carrying the point in 1864. In 1858 he had been called to the bar at the Inner Temple.

Lushington's reforming instincts were encouraged by his participation in Richard Congreve's Oxford coterie of followers of Auguste Comte, which included E. S. Beesly, J. H. Bridges, and Frederic Harrison. One of the earliest English converts to the religion of humanity, he wrote for the Positivist Society, to which he gave extensive financial support, in the 1860s and 1870s. He was latterly regarded by other positivists as a conservative figure, and he withdrew his subscription from the London Positivist Society in 1899 following a breach over the Dreyfus affair, on which Lushington had written at length in *The Times*.

One of the earliest teachers at the Working Men's College in London, founded in 1854, Lushington provided help for the embryonic labour movement as it struggled to make its case. He was a member of the Social Science Association's committee on trade societies and strikes, whose influential report was published in 1860. He contributed an essay, 'Workmen and trade unions', to the 1867 manifesto of academic liberalism, *Questions for a Reformed Parliament*. Sharing his father's abhorrence of slavery, he was a member of the Emancipation Society, which in 1862 backed the North in the American Civil War. Always ready to challenge misguided authority, he was an active member of the Jamaica committee, established in 1866 to prosecute Governor Eyre for his handling of the Morant Bay rebellion; in 1867, using his expertise in prize law, he attacked what he perceived as the bullying of Spain in the case of the cargo ship *Tornado*.

On 3 June 1865 Lushington married Beatrice Anne Shore, daughter of Samuel Smith of Combe House, Surrey, and sister-in-law of A. H. Clough. They had no children. Between 1866 and 1869 he was secretary to the pollution of rivers commission and the digest of the law commission, and in 1868 unsuccessfully stood as Liberal candidate for Abingdon. In 1869 he was appointed by H. A. Bruce legal adviser at the Home Office. In 1876 he became legal assistant under-secretary and in 1885 permanent under-secretary.

Lushington's legal expertise, zealous application, and high-mindedness made him an ideal support for successive home secretaries. His balanced advice during the preparation of legislation was set out in detailed, closely argued memoranda, written in a tiny, regular hand. His masters found the resource of what H. H. Asquith called 'a subtle and many-sided mind, and of a wide and generous culture' (letter to Henry Cunynghame, 3 Jan 1895, PRO, HO 45/9892/B17626/26) invaluable during a turbulent period when poverty, unemployment, and a lack of effective management within the Metropolitan Police exposed successive governments to major public-order crises in the capital and raised key issues about freedom of speech and of association. Despite this invaluable support Lord Salisbury's suspicion of his former 'socialist' leanings blocked several strong recommendations from Henry Matthews (home secretary 1886–92) for Lushington to be awarded the customary honours. He was finally made KCB in 1892 and GCMG in 1899.

Yet, reformer that he was in his youth, Lushington did not always take advantage of the process of change inspired by Northcote and Trevelyan that swept through the civil service after 1870. While able young officials, recruited through open competition, were on their way up the hierarchy, Lushington found it difficult to delegate work and was against promoting them over the heads of their pedestrian seniors. A much-needed shake-up in the administration of factory and mining legislation was prevented by Lushington's conservative emphasis on the law and order aspect of the work, and led to a crisis in Home Office administration in the early 1890s.

Lushington's retirement from the Home Office in 1895 provoked exceptionally warm tributes, especially from his Home Office colleagues who had appreciated Lushington's personal kindness and well understood that a certain austerity and lack of bonhomie were part of his impeccable standards and high moral principle. He thereafter took an active part in public life, serving as an alderman of the London county council until 1898. In 1903 he was appointed a member of the royal commission on trade disputes. Lushington died unexpectedly on 5 February 1907 at his London home, 34 Old Queen Street, Westminster, and was buried at St Katharine's Church, Savernake Forest. His wife survived him. JILL PELLEW

Sources *The Times* (6 Feb 1907) · *The Times* (11 Feb 1907) · E. S. Beesly, *Positivist Review*, 15 (1907), 70–71 · J. Pellew, *The home office, 1848–1914* (1982) · home office papers, PRO · R. Harrison, *Before the socialists: studies in labour and politics, 1861–1881* (1965) · C. Harvie, *The lights of liberalism* (1976) · M. S. Vogeler, *Frederic Harrison: the vocations of a positivist* (1984) · W. R. Ward, *Victorian Oxford* (1965) · *WWW*
Archives All Souls Oxf., letters to Sir William Anson · Bodl. Oxf., corresp. with Sir Edward Du Cane · Bodl. Oxf., corresp. with Sir William Harcourt · UCL, E. S. Beesly MSS · UCL, corresp. with Sir Edwin Chadwick
Likenesses pen drawing, Gov. Art Coll.
Wealth at death £57,060 7*s*. 1*d*.: probate, 22 March 1907, *CGPLA Eng. & Wales*

Lushington, Henry (1812–1855), colonial administrator, was born at Singleton, Lancashire, on 13 April 1812, the second son of Edmund Henry Lushington (1766–1839), of Park House, Maidstone, chief commissioner of the colonial audit board, and his second wife, Sophia, *née* Philips (*c*.1780–1841). He was educated from 1823 to 1828 at

Charterhouse School, where he was head boy at the age of fifteen, and became a student of Trinity College, Cambridge, in October 1829. Despite ill health, which became chronic, he won the Porson university prize for Greek iambics twice—in 1832 and again in 1833—and graduated senior optime with a first class in the classical tripos. He graduated BA in 1834, was elected fellow in 1836, and proceeded MA in 1837. Although he was called to the bar at the Inner Temple on 20 November 1840, he lacked the constitution and interest to build a law practice, and his skills as a writer and interest in political affairs made him more successful as a pamphleteer.

Lushington was an admirer and later favourite adviser and critic of Tennyson's work; in 1839 he met the poet for the first time, and they became friends. In 1847 Tennyson dedicated *The Princess* to him. Lushington's elder brother, Edmund, married Tennyson's sister Cecilia.

In 1847 Lushington was unexpectedly appointed chief secretary to the government of Malta by Lord Grey. This was a demanding post, since the first civil and Catholic governor had just been appointed and constitutional reform was being proposed. In 1849 Lushington brought forward the proposed code of laws before the newly elected legislative council and became deeply involved in debates, in which he supported full religious equality before the law. Although in weak health, he remained at his post until 1855.

Lushington's interests were literary and political. He wrote verse and commentary, and published *Joint Compositions* with George Stovin Venables in 1840 and *'La Nation Boutiquière' and other Poems* with his brother Frank in 1855. His first political pamphlet was *Fellow Commoners and Honorary Degrees* (1837), an indictment of title and privilege, and this was followed by other criticisms of contentious political decisions, such as Britain's invasion of Afghanistan (*A Great Country's Little Wars, or, England, Afghanistan and Sinde*, 1844) and the imposition of the railways at home (*The Broad and Narrow Gauge* and *Fallacies of the Broken Gauge*, both 1846). In 1851 he published *A Detailed Exposure of the Apology put forth by the Neapolitan Government in reply to the Charges of Mr Gladstone*, and in 1853 *The Double Government, the Civil Service, and the Indian Reform Agitation*.

In 1855 Lushington's health became poor enough for him to decide to leave Malta to visit England. He died on the way home, while staying in Paris, on 11 August 1855. He was buried in Boxley, Kent.

G. C. BOASE, *rev.* LYNN MILNE

Sources J. O. Waller, *A circle of friends: the Tennysons and the Lushingtons of Park House* (1986) • *GM*, 2nd ser., 44 (1855), 441
Archives National Archives of Malta, corresp. relating to work in Malta • priv. coll. | NL Wales, Venables MSS
Likenesses E. U. Eddis, chalk drawing, Courtauld Inst.

Lushington, Sir James Law (1779–1859). *See under* Lushington, Stephen Rumbold (1776–1868).

Lushington, Stephen (1782–1873), judge, was born in London on 14 January 1782, the second of five children of Sir Stephen Lushington (1744–1807) of South Hill Park, Berkshire, a director and later chairman of the East India Company, and his wife, Hester (*d.* 1830), daughter of John Boldero of Aspenden Hall, Hertfordshire. His father was created a baronet in 1791, the title passing to his older brother, Henry, in 1807.

Stephen Lushington (1782–1873), by William Holman Hunt, 1862

Lushington was educated at Eton College and at Christ Church, Oxford, where he took degrees in civil law. He matriculated in 1797, at fifteen, and graduated BA in 1802, MA in 1806, BCL in 1807, and DCL in 1808. He was elected a fellow of All Souls College in 1801 and held the fellowship until 1821, resigning it on his marriage as was then required. His marriage, on 8 August that year, was to Sarah Grace (*b.* 1794), daughter of Thomas William Carr (1770–1829) of Frognal, Hampstead, Middlesex. She died in 1837 after a harrowing illness, by which Lushington was deeply moved. There were ten children, of whom one, Edward Harbord Lushington (1822–1904), became a senior Indian civil servant, another, Vernon *Lushington (1832–1912), a county court judge, and another, Godfrey *Lushington (1832–1907), Vernon's twin, permanent under-secretary in the Home Office.

Lushington was called to the bar in 1806 (Inner Temple), and in 1808 he was admitted as a member of Doctors' Commons, the society of civil lawyers who, until 1858, constituted an independent branch of the English legal profession. The civilians had a monopoly in the practice of Admiralty law and of ecclesiastical law, which then included matrimonial disputes and the probate of wills.

Lushington had a distinguished career as a civilian, becoming judge of the most important diocesan court (the consistory court of London) in 1828, judge of the high court of Admiralty in 1838, and judge of the court of arches (the court of appeal for the ecclesiastical province of Canterbury) in 1858. As dean of the arches (as the judge was called) Lushington was also president of Doctors' Commons, attaining that office, however, only to preside over the dissolution of Doctors' Commons, because the law reforms of 1857, transferring jurisdiction over matrimonial cases and over the probate of wills to secular courts, effectively put an end to the separate profession of civil law. As Admiralty court judge he became a member of the judicial committee of the privy council, which was the final court of appeal from the English civilian courts, and from colonial courts throughout the British empire.

Lushington was a member of parliament in 1806–8, and in 1820–41 (with a short absence in 1830–31). After the Reform Act of 1832 he sat for the populous London borough of Tower Hamlets until his retirement from parliament in 1841. He was a consistent supporter of the whigs and described himself at the close of his parliamentary career as still a party man and strongly attached to party principles. However, Lushington voted independently where whig policy on sugar duties conflicted with his anti-slavery sentiments, and he did not hesitate to praise political opponents when he considered that they had embraced sound policies, as, for example, Peel on Catholic emancipation. He was described by a contemporary observer as a reformer, between the categories of whig and radical reformer. He was a forceful and effective speaker, who had the ear of the House of Commons. Lushington supported most of the liberal reforms of his era, including parliamentary reform, Catholic emancipation, full civil rights for Jews and dissenters, and reform of the criminal law. He favoured the secret ballot, and triennial parliaments, but not universal suffrage—not even universal adult male suffrage. He was one of the founders of the Society for the Diffusion of Useful Knowledge, and spoke at the laying of the foundation stone of London University. Above all else he was constantly active, in and out of parliament, in the cause of anti-slavery.

The anti-slavery campaign was directed first at the abolition of the slave trade, which was achieved in 1807, and only later at the prohibition of slavery itself, which occurred in 1833. Lushington spoke and voted for the abolition of the slave trade in 1807. He was chiefly responsible for an act of 1824 to abolish the transfer of slaves between British colonies, a kind of intercolonial slave trade. He was extremely active in securing the emancipation act of 1833, working very closely with T. F. Buxton, Wilberforce's successor as leader of the anti-slavery movement. Buxton admired Lushington's diligence and judgement and relied on him heavily: Buxton's son, Charles, wrote that 'every idea, and every plan, was originated and arranged between them' (C. Buxton, *Memorials of Sir Thomas Fowell Buxton*, 1850, 133). On the monument to emancipation erected in 1866 by Charles Buxton, Lushington's is one of the six names inscribed (the others being Buxton, Wilberforce, Clarkson, Macaulay, and Brougham). For many years after 1833 the slave trade was carried on under the flags of other nations, and Lushington played an active and important role in the campaign to suppress this trade, presiding over a committee in 1842 to draw up a code of instructions for British naval officers, and negotiating a treaty with France on this question in 1845.

The reason for Lushington's retirement from parliament in 1841 was a statute (the Admiralty Court Act) disqualifying the judge of the high court of Admiralty from membership of the House of Commons. Lushington himself saw no incompatibility in the two roles. Ten years later he was offered an opportunity to re-enter parliament as a life peer. There was an urgent need at the time for reform of the House of Lords in its role as a supreme judicial court. One solution canvassed was that distinguished judges might be appointed as life peers. The suggestion, however, was controversial because it altered the political balance between the government and the House of Lords, and, in the end, the idea was abandoned. Lushington was offered a life peerage in 1851, and the offer was repeated in 1856, but he, accurately foreseeing the political controversy that would ensue, declined both offers.

Lushington had a successful practice in Doctors' Commons until his appointment as Admiralty court judge. In 1816, as adviser to Lady Byron, he was largely instrumental in securing for her a separation from Lord Byron, the poet, a result for which Lady Byron was grateful throughout her life. In 1820 there occurred an enormous political sensation when a bill was introduced in the House of Lords to deprive the queen (Caroline of Brunswick) of her title and to dissolve her marriage with the king (George IV) on the ground of the queen's alleged adultery. The proceedings in the House of Lords were conducted as a trial, and Lushington was one of the counsel for the queen. He spoke in her defence forcefully, and, according to contemporary accounts, effectively. The defence was successful, and the bill (though it passed by a narrow margin) was dropped by the government. Lushington kept in close touch with the queen, who made him an executor of her will. He was present at her death, and accompanied her body for burial in Brunswick.

Lushington's judicial philosophy preceded the scientific school of thought that flourished in the second half of the nineteenth century. The traditions of Doctors' Commons, where law reports only came into use at the beginning of the century, did not lend themselves to a theory that every point of law was objectively determinable. Nor did Lushington lean towards such a view: his decisions in the consistory court and in the Admiralty court show his determination to retain a large measure of flexibility, even at the cost of certainty and predictability. He gives the impression of a judge who has selected his own destination. The style of his judgments is confident, forceful, and persuasive, with frequent references to general considerations of justice. In matrimonial cases he showed himself very sympathetic to the interests of women, not because he favoured political rights for women (he did not) but because he thought that the wife was the weaker party and required the protection of the court for that reason. In the prize cases that came before him during the

Crimean War, which he himself described as 'political' cases, he showed himself very sympathetic to the interests of the British crown, and most impatient with technical arguments in the opposite direction. His judgments in instance (non-prize) cases in the Admiralty court were highly respected and widely influential, and continue to be cited throughout the English speaking world, well over a century after Lushington's death.

The mid-nineteenth century was a period of high controversy in the Church of England, and Lushington was at the centre of several disputes. One of the most politically controversial questions of the time was that of church rates, which were taxes levied on the whole population of a parish to support the fabric of the parish church. Rates were vigorously opposed by many of those who dissented from the Church of England. Lushington was pulled in two directions on this question. Politically his sympathies were with the dissenters, and he had spoken in parliament against church rates. But as an ecclesiastical court judge it was his duty to enforce the law, and in that capacity he caused the committal to prison of a conscientious objector to church rates, John Thorogood. In a case on a crucial legal point (the Braintree case) Lushington decided against the validity of the rate.

Other controversial ecclesiastical cases arose out of the revival of Catholic doctrine and ritual in the Church of England, and out of the beginning of a critical study of the scriptures. On these issues Lushington's decisions show him to be as conservative in theology as he was liberal in politics. He was himself a loyal churchman, and an attender at services in the parish church at Ockham, where he occupied the principal pew as one aspect of his role as conscientious and generous village squire. He had no sympathy whatever with the changes in church furnishings associated with the Gothic revival, nor with the introduction into the Church of England of what he saw as alien Catholic doctrines and practices. On the other hand he was not an evangelical, and his friends in the anti-slavery movement regretted that he was not 'truly religious'. On the question of critical study of scripture Lushington had to judge an important book of essays published in 1860 (*Essays and Reviews*). He condemned two of the essayists, who, however, subsequently appealed successfully to the privy council.

After an illness in 1867, at the age of eighty-five, Lushington resigned his judicial offices but retained the administrative office of master of the faculties until his death in 1873, hearing disputed cases at his house in his ninety-first year. In December 1872 he travelled from Ockham in Surrey to Oxford in order to vote for A. P. Stanley in a controversial election for the office of select preacher. He returned the same day, fell ill, and died four weeks later, at his home, Ockham Park, Surrey, on 19 January 1873, just after his ninety-first birthday. A. P. Stanley was the generally acknowledged leader of the broad church party, who had been invited to contribute to *Essays and Reviews*, and whose views Lushington might be said to have condemned in his judgment, which Stanley had reviewed in a courteous, but critical, article. The journey to Oxford and back therefore suggests a gesture, and it was so perceived at the time. Stanley reciprocated by officiating at Lushington's funeral in Ockham church, and at his burial in the churchyard, on 20 January. Two weeks later Stanley paid handsome tribute to Lushington, describing him as:

> the venerable judge whose career was fired from first to last by a generous sympathy with human suffering, by noble indignation against wrong, [and] by a firm persuasion of the indissoluble bond between what was highest in religion and what was greatest in morality. (Waddams, 347)

Lushington's younger brother, **Charles Lushington** (1785–1866), born in London on 14 April 1785, East India Company servant, was secretary to the government of Bengal, 1823–7. On returning to England he was elected to parliament for Ashburton, 1835–41, and then for Westminster, 1847–52. He was a reformer, favouring the ballot, triennial parliaments, and the extension of the suffrage. He opposed all religious privileges, and published three works on religious questions. He married, first, in 1805, Sarah (*d.* 1839), daughter of General Joseph Gascoigne, and second, in 1844, Julia Jane, widow of Thomas Teed of Stanmore, Middlesex, who died in February 1866. Charles Lushington died at 118 Marine Parade, Brighton, Sussex, on 23 September 1866. S.M. WADDAMS

Sources S. M. Waddams, *Law, politics and the Church of England: the career of Stephen Lushington, 1782–1873* (1992) • Holdsworth, *Eng. law*, vol. 16 • O. Chadwick, *The Victorian church* (1966–70) • HoP, *Commons, 1790–1820*, 4.470–71 • J. M. Collinge, *Officials of royal commissions of enquiry, 1815–1870* (1984) • memorial, Ockham church, Surrey • family tree, descendants of Thomas William Carr [privately printed]

Archives Bodl. Oxf., corresp. and papers • NRA, priv. coll., political and family corresp. | BL, corresp. with Lord Aberdeen • BL, corresp., mainly with the second earl of Liverpool • Bodl. RH, corresp. with T. F. Buxton

Likenesses T. Wright, stipple, pubd 1821, NPG • W. Holl, engraving, 1824 (after A. Wivell), BM • H. B. Burlowe, plaster bust, 1833, All Souls Oxf. • W. Walker, mezzotint, 1834 (after W. J. Newton), BM, NPG • W. H. Hunt, oils, 1862, NPG [*see illus.*] • G. F. Watts, oils, 1867, Trinity House, London • B. R. Haydon, group portrait, oils (*The Anti-Slavery Society Convention, 1840*), NPG • G. Hayter, group portrait, oils (*The trial of Queen Caroline, 1820*), NPG • W. H. Hunt, chalk drawing (study for oil painting), repro. in *Pre-Raphaelitism and the Pre-Raphaelite Brotherhood* (1905), 220 • Maull and Polyblank, carte-de-visite • R. B. E. Taylor, print, repro. in *ILN*, 62 (1 Feb 1873), 96 • albumen photograph, NPG

Wealth at death under £100,000: probate, 22 Feb 1873, *CGPLA Eng. & Wales* • £60,000—Charles Lushington: probate, 1866, *CGPLA Eng. & Wales*

Lushington, Sir Stephen (1803–1877), naval officer, second son of Sir Henry Lushington, second baronet (1775–1863), who was consul-general at Naples, 1815–32, and his wife, Fanny Maria (*d.* 26 May 1862), eldest daughter of Matthew Lewis, under-secretary at war, was born at Bedford Square, London, on 12 December 1803. Dr Stephen Lushington (1782–1873) was his uncle. He entered the navy in October 1816 on the frigate *Tagus* (Captain James Whitley Deans Dundas) in the Mediterranean. From 1817 to 1821 he was with the Hon. Robert Cavendish Spencer in the *Ganymede* and *Owen Glendower* on the Mediterranean and South American stations. He was afterwards in the *Hind*, also in the Mediterranean, with the Hon. Henry John Rous, and in her boats was employed in suppressing piracy in the Greek archipelago until promoted lieutenant on 13 July 1824. In 1825 he was lieutenant of the sloop *Zebra*, and in 1826–7 of the frigate *Cambrian*, in which he was present at the battle of Navarino on 20 October 1827. Three days later he was moved by Sir Edward Codrington into his flagship, the *Asia*, from which, on 13 May 1828, he was promoted to command the bomb-vessel *Aetna*. In her he had a distinguished part in the capture of Kastro Morea on 30 October 1828, for which he was especially complimented by the French admiral in command and was nominated a knight of the orders of St Louis and the Redeemer of Greece.

On 28 October 1829 Lushington was promoted captain, but had no employment until 19 January 1839, when he was appointed to the *Cleopatra* (26 guns), fitting for the West Indies. His health broke down, and after a long illness he was invalided home in November 1840. He married in 1841 Henrietta (*d*. 22 Sept 1875), eldest daughter of Rear-Admiral Henry Prescott; they had two daughters. In 1845–6 Lushington commanded the steam frigate *Retribution* on the home station, and in 1847–8 the *Vengeance* (84 guns) on the home station and in the Mediterranean. From November 1848 to March 1852 he was superintendent of the Indian navy. In July 1852 he commissioned the *Albion* for service in the Mediterranean, and was still in her when the Crimean War broke out in 1854.

At the beginning of the siege of Sevastopol, Lushington was landed in command of the naval brigade, with the services of which his name was throughout most closely associated. He was promoted rear-admiral on 4 July 1855, was nominated a KCB the following day, was made an officer and a commander of the Légion d'honneur, and was awarded the order of the Mejidiye (second class). From May 1862 to December 1865 he was lieutenant-governor of the Royal Naval Hospital, Greenwich. On resigning he was promoted vice-admiral (1 October 1865), placed on the list according to his original seniority, between April and October 1862. On 2 December 1865 he was made admiral, and on 13 March 1867 a GCB. He died at Oak Lodge, Thornton Heath, Surrey, on 28 May 1877.

J. K. LAUGHTON, *rev.* ROGER MORRISS

Sources J. Marshall, *Royal naval biography*, 3/2 (1832), 88 · O'Byrne, *Naval biog. dict.* · *The Times* (31 May 1877) · *Army and Navy Gazette* (2 June 1877) · Boase, *Mod. Eng. biog.* · Burke, *Peerage*
Archives NMM, logbook | BL, letters to Sir Charles Napier, Add. MSS 40033, 40042
Wealth at death under £16,000: probate, 16 June 1877, *CGPLA Eng. & Wales*

Lushington, Stephen Rumbold (1776–1868), politician and administrator in India, was born at Bottisham, Cambridgeshire, on 6 May 1776. He was the fourth son of James Stephen Lushington of Rodmersham, Kent, vicar of Newcastle upon Tyne and prebendary of Carlisle, and second son of his father's second wife, Mary, daughter of the Revd Humphrey Christian of Docking, Norfolk.

Lushington was educated at Rugby School and the Linton Academy, Cambridgeshire, and in 1791 obtained a writership in the East India Company's Madras service. In 1792 he was appointed assistant in the military, political, and secret department; in 1794, deputy Persian translator to the government; in 1796, deputy secretary to the board of revenue; and in 1798, secretary and Persian translator to the board of revenue. From 1795 to 1799 he was private secretary to General George *Harris (afterwards first Baron Harris), commander-in-chief of Madras and conqueror of Mysore, and in 1797 married Harris's eldest daughter, Anne Elizabeth (*d*. 1856), with whom he had six sons and two daughters.

In January 1803, after four years as a district collector in Ramnad and Tinnevelly, Lushington was appointed registrar of the *sadr* and *faujdari adalat*. Later that year, however, he returned to England and settled on an estate in Kent procured for him by General Harris. In 1807 Harris propelled him into parliament as the conservative member for Rye, a seat purchased with Lord Wellesley's aid on the understanding that Lushington would use his parliamentary privilege to champion Wellesley and Harris's record of conquest in India. In 1812 he was returned for Canterbury, which seat he continued to hold until 1830. He was chairman of the committee of ways and means from 1810 until 1813, and, under Lord Liverpool's administration, joint secretary of the Treasury from 1814 until 1827. In 1827 he became a privy councillor and was appointed governor of Madras.

Lushington's predecessor in Madras had been Sir Thomas Munro (1767–1827) and Lushington soon quarrelled with Munro's acolytes, notably Henry Sullivan Graeme and David Hill. Schooled in the Cornwallis tradition of permanent settlement, he disliked Munro's famous ryotwari settlement and also his proposal for criminal trials by Indian juries. His tussle with Munro's supporters, however, was not essentially one of principle, but an attempt to stamp his own authority on an entrenched administrative cadre. He was accused, with justification, of jobbery and nepotism, instances of which stood out all the more against the background of stringent economies he introduced in order to reduce Madras's deficit before the company's charter came up for renewal in 1833.

Lushington returned to England in 1832 at the end of his five-year term. Having refused to surrender his Canterbury seat on his appointment to Madras, he had lost it in the general election of 1830. He regained it in 1835 but retired from parliament at the dissolution of 1837. He was created an honorary DCL of Oxford in 1839 and in 1840 published a biography of his father-in-law, *The Life and Services of General Lord Harris*. His first wife died in 1856, after which he married, in 1858, Marianne, daughter of James Hearne of Great Portland Street, London. There were no children of this marriage and Marianne died in 1864. Lushington himself died at his residence, Norton Court, Norton, near Faversham, Kent, on 5 August 1868, aged ninety-two.

Lushington's younger brother **Sir James Law Lushington** (1779–1859) obtained a cadetship in the Madras army in 1796 and was promoted to colonel, 3rd Madras light cavalry, in 1829 and general in 1854. Elected a director of the East India Company in 1827, he served as vice-chairman of the court of directors in 1837–8, 1841–2, and 1847–8, and chairman in 1838–9, 1842–3, and 1848–9. He was created CB in 1829, KCB in 1837, and GCB in 1838. A tory, he represented in succession Petersfield (1825–6), Hastings (1826–7), and Carlisle (1827–31) in the House of Commons. In 1836 he married Rosetta Sophia Costen; the marriage produced no children. He died at his residence in London, 26 Dorset Square, on 29 May 1859, and was survived by his wife. KATHERINE PRIOR

Sources HoP, *Commons, 1790–1820* • B. Stein, *Thomas Munro: the origins of the colonial state and his vision of empire* (1989) • *WWBMP*, vol. 1 • *The correspondence of Lord William Cavendish Bentinck, governor-general of India, 1828–1835*, ed. C. H. Philips, 2 vols. (1977) • S. R. Lushington, *The life and services of General Lord Harris* (1840) • BL OIOC, Haileybury MSS • *ILN* (15 Aug 1868), 163 • G. A. Solly, ed., *Rugby School register*, rev. edn, 1: *April 1675 – October 1857* (1933) • Burke, *Gen. GB* (1894) • W. W. Bean, *The parliamentary representation of the six northern counties of England* (1890) • *GM*, 3rd ser., 7 (1859), 91 [James Law Lushington] • *East-India Register and Directory* (1827–54) [James Law Lushington] • *A list of the officers of the army … serving under the presidency of Fort St George* (1835) [James Law Lushington] • G. P. Judd, *Members of parliament, 1734–1832* (1955); repr. (1972) [James Law Lushington] • *DNB* [James Law Lushington]

Archives BL, corresp., Add. MSS 29472–29474 • BL, letter-book, Add. MS 50137 | BL, corresp. with John Charles Herries, Add. MS 57374 • BL, corresp. with Lord Liverpool, Add. MSS 38266–38323, 38411, 38458, *passim* • BL, corresp. with Sir Robert Peel, Add. MSS 40204–40594 • BL, Broughton MSS [James Law Lushington] • BL, letters to Sir J. C. Hobhouse, Add. MSS 36469, 36479 [James Law Lushington] • BL OIOC, letters to Sir G. A. Robinson, MS Eur. F 142 • BL OIOC, Broughton MSS [James Law Lushington] • BL OIOC, letters to Lord Tweeddale, MS Eur. F 96 [James Law Lushington] • CKS, letters to George Harris • Derbys. RO, corresp. with Sir R. J. Wilmot-Horton • U. Nott. L., letters to Lord William Bentinck

Likenesses M. O'Connor, lithograph, BM • J. Penell, oils, Corporation of the City of Canterbury

Wealth at death under £20,000: probate, 1868/72, resworn • under £12,000—James Law Lushington: probate, 1859

Lushington, Thomas (1590–1661), author and theologian, was born at Sandwich, Kent, and baptized at Hawkinge, near Folkestone, on 2 September 1590, one of four children of Ingram Lushington (Lussyngtoun) and his wife, Agnes. He matriculated at Broadgates Hall, Oxford, on 15 March 1607, and graduated BA in 1616 from Lincoln College. In the interval he held some public employment. He proceeded MA at Lincoln College in May 1618, and afterwards returned to Broadgates Hall to study theology. Sir Thomas Browne, author of *Religio medici*, was his pupil there.

Audacious in the pulpit and unconventional out of it Lushington made his mark preaching at St Mary's, Oxford, on Easter Monday 1624, when he denounced the popular desire for war with Spain, and spoke contemptuously of the House of Commons—'the peasant' who 'under pretence of his privilege in parliament … would dispose of kings and commonwealths' (*Hist. U. Oxf.* 4: *17th-cent. Oxf.*, 583). His sermon, delivered with wit and gusto, gratified some of his hearers, who interrupted with cheers, but not the authorities. The vice-chancellor reprimanded him and insisted on a recantation of his views the following Sunday. The edition of the two sermons by Edward Hyde, earl of Clarendon, *The Resurrection of our Saviour Vindicated* (1741), claimed that they had been 'formerly published under the feign'd name of Robert Jones D.D.', but no firm evidence of seventeenth-century English editions has come to light.

In the altered circumstances of the later 1620s Lushington's views were no bar to preferment. He proceeded BD in July 1627 and DD in June 1632, and became the friend and chaplain of Richard Corbet, dean of Christ Church and then from 1628 bishop of Oxford. On 10 June 1631 he was presented by Bishop William Laud to the prebend of Beminster Secunda in Salisbury, in succession to Corbet, and in 1632 he accompanied Corbet on his translation to Norwich. In 1633 he became vicar of Barton Turf and of Neateshead, Norfolk, and in 1636 of Felixstowe and Walton, Suffolk. In 1639 he was presented by the king to the rectory of Burnham Westgate, Norfolk, and in 1640 he became rector of Burnham St Mary, Burnham St Margaret, and Burnham All Saints.

During the civil war Lushington lost all these livings and turned to writing. At some time he had begun to study Socinian works, which had been circulating in England for the first time from about the 1620s. In 1646 he published, as G. M., *Expiation of a Sinner*, a translation of a commentary on the epistle to the Hebrews by Johannes Crellius and Jonas Schlictingius, the Socinian exegetes, and a notable innovation in English divinity. *The Justification of a Sinner* (1650) was a similar translation, this time of the epistle to the Galatians, like its predecessor not verbatim, but rather a free paraphrase with considerable additions by the author. At every point Lushington followed his Socinian authorities. Christ is subordinate to God the Father, and far from being a substitute for the sins of humanity, Jesus is the bringer in of good news and forgiveness, the exemplar of God's love for mankind. This moral doctrine of the atonement appealed to Lushington and marked him out as an exceptional theologian. His writings were vigorously attacked by Edmund Porter in *God Incarnate* (1665), and Lushington's refusal to acknowledge the Pauline authorship of Hebrews greatly annoyed his critic, but New Testament scholarship has since vindicated the conclusion that the epistle is non-Pauline.

Two more of Lushington's works appeared in 1650. A treatise on the theology of Proclus survives in manuscript and his *Logica analytica*, edited by Nicholas Bacon, the first of what was intended to be a two-part work, was published. Noteworthy is the author's use of the phrase 'Right Reason', which was to be characteristic of both Oxford and Cambridge latitudinarians.

In 1660 the surviving bishops sought to warn the returning Charles II against accepting Lushington's services as a chaplain until his suspect opinions could be investigated. While he apparently regained his livings he declined further preferment. He died at Sittingbourne, Kent, on 22 December 1661, and was buried four days later in the south chancel of the church. No trace remains of the monument erected in his memory by his kinsman and heir, Thomas Lushington of Sittingbourne, with its eulogy of the character and learning of this high-church 'heretic'. H. J. MCLACHLAN

Sources H. J. McLachlan, *Socinianism in seventeenth-century England* (1951), 108–17 • A. Wood, *Historia et antiquitates universitatis Oxoniensis*, trans. R. Peers and R. Reeve, 2 vols. (1674), vol. 2, p. 335 • Wood, *Ath. Oxon.*, new edn, 2.262 • T. Lushington, *The resurrection of our saviour vindicated … in a sermon preach'd at St Mary's in Oxford*, ed. E. Hyde (1741) • T. Lushington, 'Commentary on Galatians', Christ Church Oxf. • BL, Harley MS 4162 • BL, Add. MS 1858 • CCC Oxf., MS 301, fols. 186, 205 • Bodl. Oxf., MSS Rawl. E. 21, E. 95 • R. Wallace, *Antitrinitarian biography*, 3 (1850), 170–73 • *DNB* • *Hist. U. Oxf.* 4: *17th-cent. Oxf.* • Foster, *Alum. Oxon.*

Archives BL, sermons, Add. MS 1858 • BL, sermons, Harley MS 4162 • Bodl. Oxf., sermons, MSS Rawl. E21, E95 • CCC Oxf., sermons, MS ccci, fols. 186, 205 • Christ Church Oxf., commentary on Galatians

Lushington, Vernon (1832–1912), lawyer and positivist, was born on 8 March 1832 in London, the fourth son of Stephen *Lushington (1782–1873) and his wife, Sarah Grace, *née* Carr, and twin to Sir Godfrey *Lushington, whom he closely resembled in appearance, abilities, and temperament. After their mother's death in 1837, the twins were brought up by a maternal aunt at their father's seat in Ockham Park, Ripley, Surrey, and spent a year at Cheam School. Vernon served for three years in the Royal Navy, studied at the East India College, Haileybury, and in 1852 matriculated at Trinity College, Cambridge, where he took a first class in civil law in 1854–5, LLB in 1859, and LLM in 1885. Admitted to the Inner Temple in 1852, he was called to the bar in 1857.

Early expressions of Lushington's social conscience were a pamphlet of 1855 defending the Crimean War as 'a fight for justice', journalism supporting trade union legislation, and relief efforts for unemployed factory operatives. He also taught at the Working Men's College, founded by his father's friend F. D. Maurice, and published in its magazine. His genial spirits were much admired by his colleagues, including Dante Gabriel Rossetti, whose fateful introduction to Edward Burne-Jones Lushington arranged. In the *Oxford and Cambridge Magazine* (1856), founded by Burne-Jones and William Morris, Lushington wrote on paintings by Rossetti and Ford Madox Brown and a series on Thomas Carlyle.

Lushington's legal career progressed steadily. In 1864 and 1868 he published reports of Admiralty court cases during the years of his father's eminence as an Admiralty judge. In 1868 he took silk and the next year became a bencher. From 1864 to 1869 he was deputy judge-advocate-general, and in 1869 he became secretary to the Admiralty. Upon his retirement in 1877 he was named a county court judge for Surrey and Berkshire, and served until 1900. Independently, he monitored abuses of martial law.

Both Lushington twins adopted Auguste Comte's positivism in the 1870s, and participated in the joint translation of Comte's four-volume *Positive Polity* (1875–7) under Richard Congreve. A few years later they joined Frederic Harrison and others and broke with Congreve to found a new positivist centre, Newton Hall, which in their affluence they supported generously. Vernon lectured there on the religion of humanity, science, and the arts; arranged musical programmes; led cultural pilgrimages; and wrote hymns, sonnets, and forty-nine entries for *The New Calendar of Great Men*, the positivists' biographical dictionary. He also had other verse printed privately.

Lushington had a happy family life. On 28 February 1865 he married Jane (1834–1884), daughter of Francis Mowatt, a former MP. After her death he found consolation with their daughters, Katherine, Margaret, and Susan, all talented musicians. Kitty, who married Leopold Maxse, was the model for Mrs Dalloway in the novel by her friend Virginia Woolf; Susan, who remained single, was made an MBE for her work with amateur musicians. Lushington's London house was in Kensington Square, and his country residences were in Surrey, first at Pyrford, then at Cobham. He died of bronchitis at 36 Kensington Square on 24 January 1912 and was buried in Pyrford churchyard.

MARTHA S. VOGELER

Sources *WWW* • J. Foster, *Men-at-the-bar: a biographical hand-list of the members of the various inns of court*, 2nd edn (1885) • *The Times* (25 Jan 1912) • *The Times* (29 Jan 1912) [funeral] • *Law Journal* (24 Jan 1912) • *The Athenaeum* (3 Feb 1912), 132 • E. S. Beesly, memorial address, *Positivist Review*, 20 (1912), 65–6 • F. Harrison, memorial address, *Positivist Review*, 20 (April 1912), 92–3 [incl. bibliography by P. Descours of Lushington's positivist publications, pp. 93–4] • Venn, *Alum. Cant.* • J. L. Davies, ed., *The Working-Men's College, 1854–1904* (1904) • M. S. Vogeler, *Frederic Harrison: the vocations of a positivist* (1984) • H. W. McCready, 'Elizabeth Gaskell and the cotton famine in Manchester: some unpublished letters', *Transactions of the Historic Society of Lancashire and Cheshire*, 123 (1971), 144–50 • D. Hudson, *Munby, man of two worlds: the life and diaries of Arthur J. Munby, 1828–1910* (1972)

Archives priv. coll. | BL, Positivist Society MSS • BLPES, Frederic Harrison MSS • BLPES, London Positivist Society MSS • Bodl. Oxf., Congreve MSS • UCL, Francis Galton MSS

Likenesses E. Walker, photograph, 1858 (after photograph), NPG • photograph (after photograph), NPG

Wealth at death £19,798 16*s*. 1*d*.: resworn probate, 5 March 1912, *CGPLA Eng. & Wales*

Lusignan, Alice de. *See* Alice, *suo jure* countess of Eu (*d.* 1246).

Lusignan [Valence], **Aymer de** (*c.*1228–1260), bishop of Winchester, was one of the younger sons of Hugues (X), count of La Marche, and his wife, *Isabella of Angoulême (*d.* 1246), the widow of King John.

The king's half-brother Aymer de Lusignan was born in Poitou, probably at the family stronghold of Valence near Angoulême, and in 1242 was promised the lordship of Couhé, a small portion of his family's Poitevin estate. As a younger son he may already have been destined for a career in the church. As early as July 1242, when he can have been no more than fifteen years old, his half-brother *Henry III attempted to present him to the church of Northfleet in Kent. In June 1246 he was successfully presented to the church of Tisbury in Wiltshire by the king, and in the summer of 1247 he took up residence in England together with his brothers Guy, Geoffrey, and William de *Valence. Through royal favour he received a rich haul of benefices, including the churches of Wearmouth and Chester-le-Street in the diocese of Durham, Kirkham in Lancashire, Blakeney in Norfolk, Deddington in Oxfordshire, and St Helen, Abingdon, the prebends of Holme in York Minster and Oxgate in St Paul's Cathedral,

London, and pensions of 10 marks a year from the abbeys of Crowland and St Albans. The chroniclers allege that the king demanded a pension for Lusignan from every abbey and priory in England. From July 1247 until at least the following September he was in residence at the schools of Oxford, supported there by the king and studying under a tutor named Master Vincent, canon and later archbishop of Tours. At much the same time the Paris grammarian Master John Garland composed a commentary, intended to instruct Lusignan in the rudiments of grammar.

Aymer de Lusignan's residence at Oxford was marred by the murder of one of his servants, leading to the suspension of the city's privileges by the crown between November 1247 and January 1248. In 1247 the king attempted unsuccessfully to have Lusignan promoted as provost of Beverley Minster, and in 1249 the monks of Durham rejected a proposal that he be elected their bishop. During these same years he continued to spend time in Poitou. In August 1248 he was appointed one of the executors of his father, and in March 1249 he did homage to the abbot of St Maixent for his estate at Couhé. Following the death on 1 September 1250 of William of Raleigh, bishop of Winchester, in the following November the king commanded the monks of St Swithun's Priory to elect Lusignan as their bishop, and preached a lengthy sermon in Winchester Cathedral, reminding the monks of their special obligation to the crown. Although reluctant to elect a candidate who was manifestly lacking in age or experience, the monks capitulated and Lusignan was elected on 4 November. After special lobbying by the king, his election was confirmed by the pope in January 1251 and shortly afterwards he was provided with papal dispensation, allowing him to remain unconsecrated as bishop and to continue to enjoy the income from his other ecclesiastical benefices, estimated by the chronicler Matthew Paris, an inveterate critic of Lusignan, as being in excess of 1000 marks a year. He returned to England in June 1251 and on 23 July was received at Winchester with a splendid feast, being provided with a set of costly vestments and chapel furnishings by the king.

Quarrels and controversies Aymer de Lusignan's years as bishop-elect were to be marked by violent controversy. Soon after his return, in September 1251, he became involved in a dispute with the merchants of Southampton over their refusal to suspend trading during the period of the great Winchester fair, a dispute which was to be protracted until 1254. More seriously, in November 1252, following attacks by the official of the archbishop of Canterbury on the prior of St Thomas's Hospital, Southwark, Lusignan incited various of his supporters, including his brother William de Valence, to make a violent raid upon the archbishop's houses at Lambeth and Maidstone and to carry off the archbishop's official to imprisonment at Farnham Castle. The official was later released, but the archbishop, Boniface of Savoy (*d.* 1270), issued a sentence of excommunication against Lusignan and his supporters, which was not lifted until January 1253 following interventions by the king and an appeal to the papacy. Later that same year Lusignan became embroiled in an equally fierce dispute with the monks of his cathedral convent at Winchester, inspired by his claims to supervise the appointment of the prior of St Swithun's, to nominate his own candidates to subsidiary offices within the priory, and by his insistence that the monastic obedientiaries render accounts for their offices before the episcopal exchequer at Wolvesey Palace. The monks, led by their prior, William of Taunton, appealed against Lusignan to the pope, leading to the temporary imprisonment of various members of the convent, and the exile of various of Lusignan's opponents to other English Benedictine houses.

In June 1256 the dispute was temporarily healed, following mediation by Pope Alexander IV and the English Franciscan Adam Marsh (*d.* 1259). However, the hostility between monks and bishops was by no means resolved. To fund their appeal the monks had been forced to borrow heavily from Italian merchants, so that in return for repaying some of these debts, Lusignan persuaded the monks to sell him the Isle of Portland with the manors of Weymouth and Wyke in Dorset. Throughout these years he continued to receive a stream of gifts, wine, venison, and timber, from Henry III. His profits from the Winchester fair were boosted by royal trading privileges, and new markets were awarded by the king to at least three of Lusignan's episcopal estates. Lusignan himself speculated in the lucrative market in Jewish debt, and obtained the king's permission to purchase land at Woolwich and Greenwich from the monks of St Jean-d'Angély in his native Poitou. Through royal favour he was able to marry his niece Alice to Gilbert de Clare (*d.* 1295), son of the earl of Gloucester, and for several years in succession he was granted exemption from hunting offences in the king's forests. In 1255 the king lobbied unsuccessfully to have him promoted archbishop of York.

The penalties of favouritism Lusignan was not entirely subservient to the royal court. In April 1253, for example, he supported the other English bishops in their resistance to a demand for taxation, an action for which he is said to have been bitterly rebuked by the king. Perhaps as a result of this, and in the aftermath of his dispute with Archbishop Boniface, by July 1253 Lusignan's enemies had persuaded the pope to rescind the earlier licence by which he had been allowed to retain the ecclesiastical rents and benefices he held in addition to his income from Winchester. At a time of ever mounting financial crisis, the promotion of Aymer and his Lusignan brothers was widely resented in England. His dispute with Archbishop Boniface demonstrates the extent to which the Lusignans were also at odds with the king's supporters and kinsmen from Savoy, including not only Boniface himself, but also Boniface's niece, Queen Eleanor, Henry III's wife. Aymer de Lusignan and his brothers were widely criticized as Poitevin outsiders, an image enhanced by their continuing contacts with France and Poitou. Many of the clerks and knights in Lusignan's episcopal household were drawn from Poitou, and he himself spent long periods overseas—between January and September 1257 on a visit to his homeland, in January 1257 as ambassador sent to negotiate a truce with Louis IX, and in January 1258 as an envoy to request the restoration of Henry III's lands in France.

The outcry against Lusignan reached its climax during a parliament summoned to Oxford in June 1258. Two months earlier his men had been involved in a violent clash with the followers of John Fitzgeoffrey (*d.* 1258), lord of Shere in Surrey, in which one of Fitzgeoffrey's men was killed. Henry III had refused to give a hearing to Fitzgeoffrey's complaints, fuelling an armed resistance to the crown headed by the English barons. In the ensuing turmoil Lusignan was appointed one of the twelve royalists sent to negotiate with the baronial opposition, but shortly afterwards, at the end of June 1258, he and his brothers fled from the Oxford parliament to Winchester. The barons pursued them there, and threatened to lay siege to Lusignan's castle at Wolvesey. He was accused of homicide, following the death of Fitzgeoffrey's servant, and dark rumours circulated of a poison plot against various of the English barons. Offered the choice between remaining in England, in baronial custody, and accepting exile overseas, Lusignan chose exile, so that he and his brothers set sail from Dover on 14 July. He was permitted to carry away with him only 3000 marks of his vast accumulated treasure; the remainder was spent by the barons over the next two years, partly in attempts to persuade the pope to remove Lusignan from his office as bishop of Winchester.

Last years, death, and reputation Initially Lusignan intended to reside at the schools of Paris, but he was refused permission by the French king, Louis IX, brother-in-law of Henry III's wife, Eleanor of Provence. Instead he travelled to the papal court. There he obtained a favourable hearing, and in January 1259 the papal penitentiary Velascus was dispatched to persuade Henry III to restore Lusignan to his see. Prompted by the barons the king replied that the bishop's exile had been justified, and that Lusignan had done much to sour relations between Henry, Queen Eleanor, and their son, the Lord Edward. Meanwhile, in January 1259, the Winchester monks had been persuaded to elect Henry of Wingham (*d.* 1262) as bishop in Lusignan's place. The Winchester estates were plundered by the barons, and Lusignan's appointees ejected from their offices in the cathedral by the monks of St Swithun's. In January 1260 Henry III wrote again to the pope, asking that Lusignan might be translated to another bishopric, outside England. Despite this, having reached the canonical age of thirty, on 29 May 1260 Lusignan was ordained priest by the pope, and on the following day was consecrated bishop of Winchester. He then set out for England, accompanied by Velascus and by his former tutor, Vincent, archbishop of Tours, who was empowered to declare a papal sentence of interdict and excommunication until the Winchester estates should be restored. However, at Paris Lusignan became ill, and died at the abbey of Ste Geneviève on 4 December 1260. On receiving news of his death King Henry ordered that special masses be said, and feasts celebrated in his honour at Winchester and Oxford. Two years later, no longer constrained by the baronial council, Henry commissioned a further series of feasts and prayers to mark the burial of Lusignan's heart at Winchester Cathedral, on 20 March 1262.

In his lifetime Aymer de Lusignan was heavily criticized by the English chroniclers, for his foreign birth, his greed, his lack of learning, and his encouragement of violence. The dispute with St Swithun's Priory, which first erupted in 1254, was to continue to plague his successors at Winchester for many years to come, resulting in a financial crisis for both bishops and monks. However, despite this, and despite the fact that for much of his time as bishop-elect Lusignan was an absentee from Winchester, his episcopal administration appears to have operated with considerable efficiency. He or his officials issued numerous charters, ordaining vicarages, settling tithe disputes, encouraging gifts to the Winchester hospital of St Cross, and ending a dispute over jurisdiction with the archdeacon of Surrey. The Winchester account rolls demonstrate a high level of alms-giving to the poor during his years as bishop-elect. Despite his supposed lack of learning Lusignan was still able to serve as one of the judges in the literary contest between the poets Henry d'Avranches and Michael of Cornwall. Through his speculations in the land market he obtained possession of Portland in Dorset and an estate at Woolwich in Kent, originally intended to augment the revenues of the see of Winchester, but in the event seized by Lusignan's baronial opponents following his exile. Most remarkably of all, his heart tomb at Winchester, decorated with the arms of Lusignan, of Henry III, and of Henry's brother, Richard, earl of Cornwall, king of Germany (*d.* 1272), appears to have been venerated as a shrine. Miracles are said to have occurred there in the immediate aftermath of his heart's burial in 1262, and money, presumably votive offerings, was still being collected from the tomb more than a decade later.

NICHOLAS VINCENT

Sources *Chancery records* • H. W. Ridgeway, 'The ecclesiastical career of Aymer de Lusignan, bishop-elect of Winchester 1250–60', *The cloister and the world*, ed. J. Blair and B. Golding (1996) • Paris, *Chron.* • *Ann. mon.* • A. Teulet and others, eds., *Layettes du trésor des chartes*, 5 vols. (Paris, 1863–1909) • M. A. Richard, ed., *Chartes et documents pour servir a l'histoire de l'abbaye de Saint-Maixent*, 2 (Poitiers, 1886), no. 452 • *Registrum Johannis de Pontissara, episcopi Wyntoniensis AD MCCLXXXII–MCCCIV*, ed. C. Deedes, 2 vols., CYS, 19, 30 (1915–24) • letter-book, BL, Cotton MS Julius A. ix, fol. 170r–v • PRO, assize rolls, eyre rolls, etc., JUST 1/1187 m.1 • H. S. Snellgrove, *The Lusignans in England, 1247–1258* (1950) • *The shorter Latin poems of Master Henry of Avranches relating to England*, ed. J. C. Russell and J. P. Heironimus (1935) • *Fasti Angl., 1066–1300*, [Monastic cathedrals]

Archives BL, Cotton MS Julius Aix, fols. 170r–170v

Likenesses seal • tomb effigy, Winchester Cathedral

Lusignan, William de. *See* Valence, William de, earl of Pembroke (*d.* 1296).

Lusk, Sir Andrew, baronet (1810–1909), banker and politician, was born on 18 September 1810 at Pinmore, in the parish of Barr, Ayrshire, the son of John Lusk, a small farmer and a strict Presbyterian, and his wife, Margaret, daughter of John Earl, of Knockdolian, Ayrshire. Brought up at home in strong religious principles, Lusk was educated at Barr parish school. At twenty-five he left home with his brother Robert to start a small wholesale grocery business in Greenock, where he gained some experience in journalism. The business prospered, helped by the rapidly expanding sugar trade of Greenock, and Andrew, leaving it in his brother's charge, went to London. In 1840 he opened premises at 63 Fenchurch Street as a dealer, first in groceries for export, and afterwards in ships' stores. A wide connection was soon built up, and the firm continued after his lifetime under the style of Andrew Lusk & Co. He married on 24 October 1848 Elizabeth (*d.* 1910), daughter of James Potter of Grahamstown, Falkirk, and his wife, Jane, daughter of John Wilson of Falkirk. There were no children.

Lusk was the founder of the Imperial Bank in Lothbury in the City of London, and was its chairman from its establishment in 1862 until its incorporation with the London Joint Stock Bank in 1893, when he moved onto that board. He was for many years chairman of the General Life Insurance Company, which he joined at a critical moment in its existence, steering it to prosperity.

In 1857 Lusk was elected common councilman for Aldgate ward, and on 8 October 1863 alderman of that ward; he removed to the ward of Bridge Without on 12 February 1892 as a preliminary to retirement as alderman in 1895. In 1860–61 he served as sheriff, and on Michaelmas day, 29 September 1873, was chosen lord mayor. During his mayoralty he raised a fund of £150,000 for the relief of the Bengal famine; entertained Sir Garnet Wolseley at the Mansion House on his return from the Second Anglo-Asante War; presided at the banquet given by the corporation at Guildhall on 18 May 1874 for Tsar Alexander II, after his daughter's marriage with the duke of Edinburgh; and on 4 August 1874 he received a baronetcy. As a City magistrate he was shrewd and genial. He was a prominent member of the Fishmongers' Company, then a stronghold of City Liberalism, and served as prime warden in 1887. He was twice master of the Spectacle Makers' Company, in 1869–70 and 1870–71. He was also JP for Middlesex.

On 13 July 1865 Lusk was elected Liberal MP for Finsbury, then one of the largest constituencies in London. He retained the seat until the division of the constituency in November 1885, when he retired as MP. Lusk was a useful member of committees and a critic of the estimates, but took little part in the debates. He was a staunch friend of Lord Beaconsfield, although they were opposed in the house. After the Liberal split on the home-rule question in 1886 he became a Liberal Unionist.

Lusk, who resigned his alderman's gown on 24 September 1895, died in his ninety-ninth year at his residence, 15 Sussex Square, Hyde Park, on 21 June 1909, and was buried in Kensal Green cemetery. He was survived by his wife. The baronetcy became extinct on his death. He left over £15,000—one-sixth of his estate—to charitable institutions.

CHARLES WELCH, *rev.* ANITA MCCONNELL

Sources *City Press* (26 June 1909), 4e–f • *ILN* (26 June 1909), 924 • *The Times* (19 Sept 1895), 3f • *The Times* (25 Sept 1895), 3e • A. B. Beaven, ed., *The aldermen of the City of London, temp. Henry III–[1912]*, 2 vols. (1908–13) • *Dod's Parliamentary Companion* (1884) • 'Biographies and portraits: Sir Andrew Lusk', *Bankers' Magazine*, 47 (1887), 1111–14 • *The Times* (22 June 1909) • *The Times* (25 June 1909) • *The Times* (5 Aug 1909) • personal information (1912)

Archives Mitchell L., Glas., Glasgow City Archives, papers • Strathclyde Regional Archives

Likenesses T. McKinlay, oils, 1862, Scot. NPG • MacKinky, portrait, 1868, priv. coll. • Faustin, chromolithograph caricature, NPG, V&A • Maull & Co., photograph, carte-de-visite, NPG • H. McCarthy, marble bust; in Guildhall council chamber in 1912 • Russell, photograph, repro. in *ILN*, 134 (26 June 1909) • Spy [L. Ward], caricature, chromolithograph, NPG; repro. in *VF* (7 Oct 1871) • portrait, repro. in 'Biographies and portraits' • wood-engraving (after photograph by Disderi), NPG; repro. in *ILN* (15 Nov 1873)

Wealth at death £96,659 13*s*. 1*d*.: probate, 4 Aug 1909, *CGPLA Eng. & Wales*

Lustgarten, Edgar Marcus (1907–1978), broadcaster and author, was born on 3 May 1907 in the Broughton Park district of Manchester, the only child of Joseph Lustgarten, a Latvian-born Jewish barrister, and his wife, Sara Finklestone. From Manchester grammar school, where he shone as a debater, he went up to St John's College, Oxford, in 1926; in his final year, 1930, before graduating BA, he was president of the Oxford Union. Called to the bar, he joined his father on the northern circuit, practising from chambers at 48 King Street, Manchester, and was soon recognized as an astute cross-examiner; he enjoyed working before juries because, as he afterwards said, 'they were susceptible to an emotional appeal' (*Sunday Times Magazine*, 21 Sept 1975). On 6 September 1932 he married Joyce Goldstone (*d.* 1972), a member of a Manchester family that had become wealthy from the manufacture and marketing of electrical gadgets.

Rarely burdened with legal work, Lustgarten began writing articles on diverse subjects. Encouraged by acceptance of some of them by the BBC North Region, based in Manchester, he concentrated on the writing of radio scripts—to such effect that, by the mid-1930s, the total fees he received for broadcast material sometimes exceeded the total of the fees marked on his briefs. A devotee of variety entertainment, he turned his hand to revue sketches and lyrics for songs; he also pseudonymously presented as well as devised radio programmes, including compilations of jazz records (thereby becoming a disc jockey before that term was coined).

At the outbreak of the Second World War in 1939 Lustgarten was turned down for military service because he had 'grade 2' feet; his diminutive stature may have contributed to the rejection. Recruited by the BBC as a counter-propaganda radio broadcaster, he moved with his wife to London, eventually to reside in the H1 set of chambers in Albany, next to the Royal Academy of Arts in Piccadilly. Reusing the pseudonym of Brent Wood so as to hide his Jewishness, he broadcast to foreign countries virtually nightly throughout the war, often rebutting Nazi propaganda disseminated from Germany a few hours earlier by William Joyce (Lord Haw-Haw)—whom he respected, though only as 'a great broadcaster'. After the war he remained with the BBC, producing both radio and television programmes.

Lustgarten's first book, the crime novel *A Case to Answer*

Edgar Marcus Lustgarten (1907–1978), by Count Zichy for Baron Studios, 1955

(1947), sold well and was made into a film entitled *The Long Dark Hall* (1951), starring Rex Harrison and Lilli Palmer. In 1949 he published *Verdict in Dispute*, a collection of accounts of notable trials, and followed this with a similar volume, *Defender's Triumph*, in 1951; these titles are generally considered to comprise the best of his true-crime essays, stylishly written and focused upon turning-points in the proceedings.

It was in the autumn of 1952 when he—or rather, his voice—became famous, with the transmission on the Light Programme of the six-part series *Prisoner at the Bar* in which, displaying his gift for mimicry, he played all the parts, ranging from timorous spinster to crusty judge, in reconstructions of murder trials. Between the first broadcast and the sixth, the estimated listenership rose from 2 million to 6 million, one of the steepest increases ever. There were rave reviews, the one in the *Sunday Chronicle* describing Lustgarten as 'a spellbinder and a wizard with words … a natural microphone genius', and ending: 'Let's hear more of him' (5 Oct 1952). Almost every year for the next two decades or so, the BBC presented similar series starring 'the one-man repertory company'. Also during that time, there were spin-offs from the radio success: he wrote many series of articles on true crimes for national newspapers; he received commissions from book publishers; he amended some of his radio scripts for a series of audio cassettes; and, in a studio decorated and furnished in resemblance of his own study, he introduced and spoke the tailpiece to short films of fictional crime stories that pretended to be factual.

In 1954 Lustgarten, who for the past four years had worked on a freelance basis for the BBC, switched to the newly formed independent company Associated Television (ATV) as a producer, and sometimes chairman, of current-affairs discussion programmes. He was an expert chairman, for though his hooded eyes gave him the appearance of a tired lizard, he had the lawyer's ability to think on his feet, and, having prepared meticulously, he could make illuminating comments in addition to asking probing questions. The most successful of his programmes were *Free Speech*, 1955–61, and *Fair Play*, which ran from 1962 until 1965, when he rejoined the BBC for three years, chiefly as a narrator of factual programmes.

Lustgarten's wife died from cancer in 1972. During the latter years of their marriage his undoubted love for her had been tested by her addiction to gambling, hers for him by gossip she heard of his frequenting night-clubs and fashionable restaurants in the company of flashily dressed young women, rarely the same one twice.

In 1978, by which time Lustgarten was living in a flat, 138 Clarence Gate Gardens, near Regent's Park, he published his fifth crime novel. It was entitled *Turn the Light out as you Go*. On Friday 15 December he visited the reference department of Marylebone Public Library. No one knows what he hoped to learn. While seated at a reading desk, he suffered a heart attack. He was taken by ambulance to St Mary's Hospital, Paddington, but was pronounced dead on arrival. JONATHAN GOODMAN

Sources J. Goodman, 'Edgar Lustgarten: the murder man', *Radio lives*, BBC Radio 4, 20 Aug 1992, BBC WAC · 'Lustgarten, Edgar (Marcus) 1907–1978', *Contemporary Authors*, new revn ser., 22 (1988), 286–7 · private information (2004) [J. Goodman; G. Singh] · *Sunday Times Magazine* (21 Sept 1975), 5–7 · *Sunday Chronicle* (5 Oct 1952)

Archives FILM BFI NFTVA, performance footage | SOUND BL NSA, documentary recording · BL NSA, performance recording

Likenesses Count Zichy for Baron Studios, photograph, 1955, NPG [*see illus.*]

Wealth at death £8762: probate, 12 April 1979, *CGPLA Eng. & Wales*

Luthuli, Albert John (1898?–1967), human rights campaigner and president-general of the African National Congress, was born—according to his own calculations, in 1898—in Southern Rhodesia, the second surviving son of John Bunyan Luthuli, an evangelist and interpreter at a Seventh Day Adventist mission at Solusi near Bulawayo, and his wife, Mtonya. His family came from the strongly Congregationalist Zulu community, mainly of small farmers, of Groutville near the coast in northern Natal. Luthuli's mother had come with her mother from the royal kraal of Cetshwayo to Groutville where she became a Christian and learned to read, though not to write. After his father's death in Rhodesia, Luthuli's mother eventually returned to Groutville, where his uncle Martin Luthuli had now been elected chief. To keep her son at school she grew vegetables, and laundered for white people in the nearest town, Stanger. Teaching was almost the only career open to an educated African so Luthuli

Albert John Luthuli (1898?–1967), by Neville Lewis, 1962

went from the local school to the Ohlange Institute, then to the Methodist Institution at Edenvale to qualify as a teacher. In 1918 he was appointed to a one-teacher country school. There, living with a deeply Christian family, he took stock of his own upbringing, was confirmed in the local Methodist church, and became a lay preacher.

A bursary in 1920 took Luthuli to Adams College, a Congregational foundation near Durban, where he stayed on to train teachers in his turn. He founded the Zulu Language and Cultural Society, and became a lifelong soccer fan. His interest in the organization of African and interracial sport continued throughout his life. The subjects he taught were Zulu, school organization, and music. Singing was a particular strength in his life: he sang well and his voice was part of his charisma. He could inspire hope in situations which might have been marked only by bitterness and frustration. He himself drew courage from hearing 'Nkosi sikelel' iAfrika' ('God save Africa'), the anthem of African determination, hope, and endurance. Profoundly influenced by the Christian outlook he found at Adams, Luthuli saw that Christianity was relevant to the problems of society, a recognition he expressed through political action.

In 1927 Luthuli married Nokukhanya Bhengu, granddaughter of a hereditary Zulu chief; they had seven children. Their home was at Groutville but Luthuli continued to work at Adams. After insistent requests from the Groutville tribal elders Luthuli agreed to stand for election as chief of the Umvoti mission reserve. Unwilling to leave the life of teaching, he yet felt an obligation to serve his own community. When he became chief in 1936, in contrast to the orderly life at Adams College, he found himself confronted daily with the besetting problems of poverty and land hunger, and with the destruction of families resulting from migratory labour and the pass system. He founded with some success the Natal and Zululand Bantu Cane Growers' Association to assist the small-scale growers, and when an advisory board to the South African Sugar Association was set up Luthuli served on it until 1953. As the city of Durban expanded there came the problem of land rights. With the future Bishop Zulu, Luthuli revived the Mission Reserve Association and assisted the Umlazi mission reserve in negotiations with the Durban corporation and the native affairs department. Such work brought Luthuli into public affairs and some associations brought him into touch with white people, notably the Natal Missionary Conference affiliated to the Christian Council of South Africa. He served as a Natal delegate and later as an executive member. In 1938 he was a delegate to the International Missionary Conference in Madras. This, and a lecture tour in the United States on missions in 1948, gave him opportunities of seeing South Africa in a wider perspective.

In 1945 Luthuli was elected to the executive of the African National Congress (ANC) in Natal and became steadily more involved in national questions. This hitherto moderate body was taking new shape, partly because of disillusionment with the ineffectual Native Representative Council, called a 'toy telephone', which had been established by J. B. M. Hertzog in 1936 and to which Luthuli was elected in 1946. The end of the Second World War and the four freedoms of the Atlantic charter brought a more militant attitude; young militants set up a youth league of the ANC. With the return of the white Nationalist Party to power in 1948 came a succession of measures to implement the blueprint of apartheid, to control all forms of organized protest, and to silence individual dissenters. Natal leadership of the ANC was not rising to the occasion and in 1951 Luthuli, supported by the young militants, became president of Congress in Natal. Defiance of unjust segregation laws by non-violent, passive resistance had already been centrally planned and in 1952 Luthuli brought Natal into the defiance campaign and into close co-operation with the Indian National Congress. This marked a momentous personal decision for Luthuli, whose past approach had been that of 'knocking in vain, patiently, moderately and modestly at a closed and barred door' (Luthuli, 235). He himself did not defy, but organized and inspired. Summoned to Pretoria, he was told that he must choose between the ANC and his chieftainship. His decision was to resign from neither. The government deposed him, but both the title and the standing of chief continued to be accorded him by his people. In a statement after his deposition he concluded 'the road to freedom is via the Cross' (Paton, 265).

At the end of 1952 Luthuli was elected president-general of the ANC. In 1953 he was banned, in terms of the Riotous

Assemblies Act and the Criminal Law Amendment Act, from the major cities and from attending public gatherings. A second banning order was imposed in 1954 when this had expired and he was about to lead a massed protest against the enforced removal of Africans from Sophiatown and elsewhere. It ran for two years and confined him to the magisterial district of Stanger in which Groutville lay. In early 1955, after a stroke, permission had to be obtained to allow him to be moved to a hospital in Durban.

Luthuli was debarred from attending the Congress of the People held at Kliptown near Johannesburg in June 1955. The freedom charter which it adopted brought ANC policy into question and put Luthuli into a defensive position over the extent of control exercised in ANC affairs by communist members of the Indian National Congress and the White Congress of Democrats. Luthuli's vision of a democratic multiracial South Africa and his immediate aim of mustering non-violent opposition to apartheid made him place great importance on the interracial Congress alliance. The ANC itself did not have a clear policy so much as a bundle of aspirations. Luthuli was no theorist, was little concerned with the political colour of his allies, and tended to shelve some problems. Moreover he led a loosely knit movement in which spirit outshone organization. He realized the difficulties of organizing a national campaign to oppose the Bantu Education Act of 1953 which transferred control of African education to the native affairs department. Many would choose a bad education rather than none at all. Nevertheless he supported the principle of mass opposition to this new threat and although the campaign of 1955 was not successful it left its mark by giving centrality to the issue, showing publicly the strength of African rejection.

Luthuli's second ban ended in 1956 and he was able to deliver his presidential address to Congress in person, his theme: the struggle must go on. But on 5 December he was one of 156 people arrested on a charge of high treason. Another was Z. K. Matthews, a former colleague at Adams College, and author of the freedom charter. Luthuli was eventually released on bail and, at the end of 1957, with some sixty others, discharged. The trial continued until March 1961 when the remaining accused were acquitted of conspiring to overthrow the state by violence. In this period Luthuli's dignified bearing, authority, and gravity, as well as his sense of humour, became well known. He was a guest at the houses of prominent white people in Johannesburg and he warmed to the concern of Bishop Ambrose Reeves, who took charge of the Treason Trial Defence Fund. Luthuli had often regretted the lack of involvement by white Christians in the sufferings of black Christians and warned that black people would come to reject the white man's God and the paternalism of white Christians.

In 1958 the Africanist wing of the ANC withdrew from Congress to form the Pan-African Congress, a lack of African unity which was a bitter blow to Luthuli. He now toured the larger cities speaking to white and multiracial audiences as well as from Congress platforms. At a meeting in Pretoria in 1959 he was assaulted by young white men who objected to an African addressing a white study group. His restraint and dignity on this occasion increased his personal renown. The sincerity and urgency of his speeches made a strong impression: his opposition to apartheid and to racialism was in the cause of peace.

In December 1958 Luthuli was again able to attend the annual conference of Congress in Durban at which it was decided to intensify the campaign against the pass system. In May 1959 a third banning order was served on Luthuli, lasting for five years. In 1960 he called for a national day of mourning after the shootings at Sharpeville in Transvaal and at Langa in the Cape at the start of the anti-pass campaign called by the Pan-African Congress. The ANC in its turn now called for the burning of passes and Luthuli, in Pretoria for the treason trial, ceremoniously burnt his passbook. The government declared a state of emergency and outlawed both the ANC and the Pan-African Congress. Luthuli was arrested. His health was declining and the next five months were spent mainly in the prison hospital. His prison sentence suspended on health grounds, he returned to Groutville and to banishment. When South Africa's continued membership of the Commonwealth was debated in March 1961 Luthuli cabled *The Times* advocating South Africa's expulsion. At Groutville in 1961 he learned that he had been awarded the Nobel peace prize for 1960. He was allowed to travel to Oslo to receive it and in his address spoke of the paradox that such an award should be made to a man from a country where 'the brotherhood of man is an illegal doctrine' (Callan, 58). From Oslo he returned to banishment.

In 1964 the last and severest ban was imposed, forbidding access even to the neighbouring town of Stanger. Now virtually under house arrest, as far as his health allowed Luthuli worked on the land or in his small shop. He had few visitors but in 1965 Senator Robert Kennedy went to see him. On 21 July 1967 Luthuli was struck down by a freight train while crossing a narrow railroad bridge near his home. He was buried in the graveyard of the Groutville Congregational Church. Some 7000 Africans, some wearing the uniform of the banned ANC, and a few hundred white people, many of them diplomats, gathered to pay tribute to him. His old friend Alan Paton gave the address but was forbidden by law to quote anything that Luthuli had ever said or written. 'The great story of his life', Paton said, 'is the story of his fortitude' (Paton, 267). In 1968 Luthuli was awarded the United Nations human rights prize. Luthuli spoke for his people, voicing both anguish and aspiration; he succeeded too in focusing world attention on the destructive effects of the apartheid system which debased personality, destroyed relationships, and threatened peace. ANNE YATES, *rev.*

Sources A. Luthuli, *Let my people go* (1962) • M. Benson, *Chief Albert Lutuli of South Africa* (1963) • M. Benson, *South Africa: the struggle for a birthright* (1966) • A. Paton, *The long view* (1968) • E. Callan, *Albert John Luthuli and the South African race conflict* (1962) • personal knowledge (1981)

Likenesses N. Lewis, portrait, 1962, priv. coll. [*see illus.*] · photographs, Hult. Arch.

Luton, Simon of (*d.* 1279), abbot of Bury St Edmunds, was probably a relative of Sir Robert of Hoo, a knight of St Edmunds and holder of extensive estates including The Hyde, near Luton in Bedfordshire, from which Simon derived his name. Some time before the mid-thirteenth century Luton became a monk of St Edmunds. Having held the offices of almoner and sacrist in succession, he was elected prior in 1252: a fellow monk describes him as 'very prudent and circumspect' and well deserving this promotion (Arnold, 2.294). He was elected abbot on 14 January 1257, a fortnight after the death of Abbot Edmund of Walpole. Pope Alexander IV insisted that Luton went to Rome for confirmation of his election—the first English abbot to do so. According to the contemporary Bury chronicler the journey cost £2000. Luton received the papal blessing at Viterbo on 22 October. He arrived home before 12 January 1258, on which date Henry III granted him his temporalities.

The abbey was already involved in litigation with Richard de Clare, earl of Gloucester, who claimed the abbey's rich manor of Mildenhall. Agreement was reached only in 1259 when the earl abandoned his claim in return for the grant of a number of St Edmunds properties. Luton, at his succession, was also faced by conflict with the Friars Minor. During the abbatial vacancy they had violated the abbey's spiritual monopoly within the town, but had been expelled. The king then forcibly established the friars in the town in 1258, but in 1263 Pope Urban IV upheld the monks' appeal against this violation of their privilege. The monks gave the friars an alternative site at Babwell, outside Bury's north gate.

The barons' war and its aftermath had serious repercussions on St Edmunds. The town became the scene of disorder: rebels sheltered there and townsmen revolted against the abbey's authority. Once restored to power, Henry took retributive action against the abbey and town. He twice took the liberty of St Edmunds into his hands (in 1265 and 1266); Luton had to pay heavy fines to regain both it and royal favour. Nevertheless, Luton himself was loyal to the king. Clearly Henry trusted him: Luton was sent on an embassy to Paris in 1259, to procure ratification of the treaty of Paris on Henry's behalf; he was summoned with his knights to serve the king in 1260 and 1261 (leaders of the baronial opposition were not summoned on either occasion); and in 1267, when Henry was investing London against Gilbert de Clare, earl of Gloucester, Luton and his knights were with the royal army at Stratford Langthorne.

Throughout his abbacy Luton was dogged by indebtedness, owing to the cost of litigation, of papal and royal taxation, and of other impositions. He and the convent resorted to the common expedient of borrowing, mainly from Italian merchant bankers. The chronicler estimated that the debts amounted to 5000 marks in 1260, divided equally between abbot and convent. Even Henry was concerned at the abbey's 'intolerable burden of debt' (BL, Harley MS 645, fol. 253) and recommended specific domestic economies. To reduce his own expenditure, Luton obtained a royal licence on 19 June 1268 to live abroad until Christmas 'with a moderate household, for the relief of himself and his church' (*CPR, 1266–77*, 238). Presumably to save domestic expenses and raise cash, he leased some time before 1272 his commodious residence in Aldgate in London, and similarly, in 1278, his residence at Stapleford Abbots in Essex.

Despite his worldly difficulties Luton has to his credit two notable achievements. In the mid-thirteenth century the prior had founded St John's Hospital, the Domus Dei, in Bury for the temporary relief of begging, but healthy, poor, putting the almoner, who at that time was Luton himself, in charge. But the site, in Southgate Street within the town walls, was cramped and inconvenient, and Luton when abbot erected a larger building on a spacious and convenient site on the royal road just outside the town's south gate. The cost of the new Domus Dei was probably met at least in part by gifts from benefactors. Luton also had built a large and splendid lady chapel, the last major addition to the abbey church, which was paid for by his own friends and relatives. Simon of Luton died on his manor of Melford, Suffolk, on 9 April 1279, and was buried in the lady chapel, having bequeathed £100 to the convent.

His successor, **John of Northwold** (*d.* 1301), abbot of Bury St Edmunds, derived his name from the village of Northwold, near Thetford in Norfolk. He was interior guest-master when elected abbot, on 5 May 1279. He received papal confirmation in Rome and on 5 November Edward I granted him his temporalities. He arrived back at St Edmunds on 28 December: the Bury chronicler estimates that the journey to Rome had cost over 1675 marks.

The abbey's finances had suffered badly during the six months' vacancy of the abbacy. Edward had taken over not only the abbatial property (to which he was entitled) but also the convent's property—'neither prayer nor price could wring it from his grasp' (*Chronicle of Bury St Edmunds*, 68). He allowed the convent maintenance but enjoyed the profits of its estates himself. To prevent this happening again Northwold procured, in 1281, royal confirmation of the division of property between abbot and convent, for which he paid 1000 marks.

St Edmunds continued to suffer from oppressive taxation. So severe was the assessment of the papal tenth granted by Nicholas IV to Edward in 1291 that Northwold produced detailed complaints of the over-assessment of this and the convent's properties. The abbey also suffered from Edward's *quo warranto* campaign, which challenged the claims of liberty holders to jurisdictional rights and consequently to profits of justice. Northwold was a leader in parliament in 1290 of the liberty holders' opposition. The parliament rolls record that 'the abbot of Fécamp, the abbot of St Edmunds and others' petitioned the king. In response Edward conceded that liberties recognized by Henry III in 1234 or earlier should be recognized in future (*RotP*, 1.35). A contemporary story enlarges on Northwold's part in obtaining this important concession. It relates that

Northwold produced the abbey's charters of privilege and accused Edward of revoking liberties granted by his predecessors. He concluded: 'I am broken by age and exhausted by my labours to recover these privileges; I can do no more, but commit to the Supreme Judge the case between the martyred Edmund and his church, and you, my Lord King'. Northwold went sadly home, but that night Edward was so terrified by a vision of a revengeful St Edmund that next day he agreed to hear liberty holders' claims: '"St Edmund", he said, "had raised his banner for them all"' (Arnold, 2.365).

Northwold evidently had considerable administrative ability. In 1300, when Edward was at odds with the magnates over their military obligations, Northwold commissioned a detailed survey of the knights' fees of St Edmunds. He was also a reformer. In 1280 he issued statutes in chapter to eradicate abuses in the abbey's domestic economy, and in 1294 he drastically reformed St Saviour's Hospital. The latter had been founded by Abbot Samson for the care of poor and sick men and women, but had lapsed from its original ideal. Northwold legislated to restore its charitable function, though in future women were not to be admitted and it was to include seven priests among its inmates, to celebrate mass daily.

Despite the abbey's financial difficulties Northwold was a builder. He had the choir of the abbey church rebuilt and ornamented with paintings 'by a certain of his monks, John de Wodecroft [and] a certain painter of the Lord king's' (kitchener's register, fol. 9). He built a chapel dedicated to St Botwulf, abutting the south transept, which was, however, appreciably smaller than Abbot Simon's lady chapel. He also founded the (still surviving) Chapel of the Charnel in the cemetery adjoining the abbey, where lay inhabitants of Bury were buried. Northwold had been distressed at the sight of bones, which had been disinterred to make room for new graves, left scattered about. He provided for two chaplains to celebrate masses for the dead in the chapel, and for bones to be placed in its crypt.

Northwold died on 29 October 1301 and was buried on Sunday 12 November 'before the altar' in the choir (kitchener's register, fol. 9). He bequeathed 165 marks to the convent, besides 20*s.* to it and 20*s.* to the poor on his anniversary. ANTONIA GRANSDEN

Sources A. Gransden, ed. and trans., *The chronicle of Bury St Edmunds, 1212–1301* [1964] • T. Arnold, ed., *Memorials of St Edmund's Abbey*, 3 vols., Rolls Series, 96 (1890–96) • A. Gransden, 'The abbey of Bury St Edmunds and national politics in the reigns of King John and Henry III', *Monastic Studies*, 2 (1991), 73–86 • C. Harper-Bill, ed., *Charters of the medieval hospitals of Bury St Edmunds*, Suffolk RS, Suffolk Charters, 14 (1994) • A. Gransden, 'John de Northwold, abbot of Bury St Edmunds (1279–1301) and his defence of its liberties', *Thirteenth century England: proceedings of the Newcastle upon Tyne conference* [Newcastle upon Tyne 1989], ed. P. R. Coss and S. D. Lloyd, 3 (1991), 91–112 • *CClR, 1256–68* • *CPR, 1258–1301* • *RotP*, 1.35 • W. E. Lunt, *Financial relations of the papacy with England to 1327* (1939) • W. E. Lunt, *Papal revenues in the middle ages*, 2 vols. (1934) • F. Hervey, ed., *The Pinchbeck Register*, 2 vols. (1925) • 'Liber albus', BL, Harley MS 1005 • Werketone register, BL, Harley MS 638 • Kempe register, BL, Harley MS 645 • pittancer's register, BL, Harley MS 27 • kitchener's register, Bibliothèque Municipale, Douai, MS 553

Lutterell, John (*d.* 1335), theologian, is of unknown origins. He was ordained a priest before 1304, having received a papal dispensation for illegitimacy, and he was later granted dispensations of non-residency to permit him to enjoy the income from his benefices while in residence in Oxford. By 1317 he held the degree of DTh. In July of that year, probably in response to a university supplication, he was made a canon at Lichfield with expectation of a prebend, and in December 1319 he was made canon of Salisbury with the prebend of Axford. On 10 October 1317 he was elected chancellor of the university, and soon afterwards travelled to the Roman curia at Avignon in order to pursue the university's case against the Dominicans at Oxford. The friars were contesting an award made by arbitrators in 1313, on a dispute between the Dominicans and the university, over the latter's control of admission to the degree of bachelor of theology. Lutterell returned to England in 1318, where he was one of the two representatives of the university to argue their side of the case before Cardinal Gaucelin, which was decided largely in favour of the university.

Lutterell had become involved in a dispute with other masters and scholars at Oxford by the summer of 1322. Despite many statements to the contrary, there is no evidence that this matter concerned either his philosophical or theological views, or his opposition to William Ockham's teaching, and its causes remain obscure. The opposing masters appealed to the bishop of Lincoln, who removed Lutterell from office before the beginning of August. They also appealed to the king, who on 12 August blocked Lutterell's attempt to take the matter abroad to Avignon, either in person or in writing. Lutterell and a delegation from the university presumably appeared before the king at York in October, as ordered, although mandates for royal letters of introduction to the pope on Lutterell's behalf had been issued on 30 August 1322.

Lutterell left for Avignon soon after 20 August 1323 to present his case to the pope. He was summoned to return to England by Edward II in May 1325, but by that time he was serving on a papal commission to examine the orthodoxy of the *Questions on the 'Sentences'* of Ockham, who had been called to the papal curia in the summer of 1324. John XXII intervened to permit Lutterell to remain at Avignon. Lutterell extracted fifty-six propositions from Ockham's work and wrote a treatise quoting and attacking these 'errors'. The commission on which Lutterell served dismissed twenty-three items, either because the majority on the commission did not believe they were false, or because they concerned philosophical as opposed to theological issues. In the end, two lists of fifty-one erroneous propositions were drawn up in 1326, but no official condemnation emerged. After a year or two back in England, Lutterell returned to Avignon early in 1329 with letters of commendation from John Grandison, bishop of Exeter. By October 1329 he had returned to England, and in May of the following year Grandison recommended Lutterell to the dean and chapter at Salisbury as a candidate for that vacant see. Nevertheless he was unsuccessful. In April

1334 Lutterell was made a canon at York, with the prebends of Bickhill and Knaresborough. He returned to Avignon in 1330, 1332, and 1333, and served alongside Walter Chatton on the commission to investigate the views of Durand de St Pourçain and Thomas Waleys regarding the beatific vision in the summer of 1333. He died in Avignon on 17 July 1335.

In theological terms Lutterell was a realist, and in his *Libellus contra Ockham* relied frequently on the positions of Thomas Aquinas. He also wrote a letter, *Epistula de visione beata*, in support of John XXII's views on the beatific vision. Apart from references to his *In vesperiis magistrorum*, nothing has remained from his teaching at Oxford. W. J. COURTENAY

Sources *CClR*, 1318–23, 413; 1323–7, 373 • *CPR*, 1321–4, 336 • H. E. Salter, ed., *Mediaeval archives of the University of Oxford*, 1, OHS, 70 (1920), 105–6, 285 • H. E. Salter, W. A. Pantin, and H. G. Richardson, eds., *Formularies which bear on the history of Oxford*, 1, OHS, new ser., 4 (1942), 4–5, 14–16, 37, 39, 71–9 • *Snappe's formulary and other records*, ed. H. E. Salter, OHS, 80 (1924), 70–71, 303–5, 325 • Emden, *Oxf.*, 2.1181–2 • F. Hoffmann, *Die erste Kritik des Ockhamismus durch den Oxforder Kanzler Johannes Lutterell*, Breslauer Studien zur Historischen Theologie, new ser., 9 (1941) • F. Hoffmann, *Die Schriften des Oxforder Kanzlers Iohannes Lutterell*, Erfurter Theologische Studien, 6 (1959) • J. Koch, 'Neue Aktenstücke zu dem gegen Wilhelm Ockham in Avignon geführten Prozess', *Recherches de Théologie Ancienne et Médiévale*, 7 (1935), 350–80; 8 (1936), 79–93, 168–97 • A. Pelzer, 'Les 51 articles de Guillaume Occam censurés, en Avignon, en 1326', *Revue d'Histoire Ecclésiastique*, 18 (1922), 240–70 • C. Trottmann, *La vision béatifique: des disputes scolastiques à sa définition par Benoît XII*, Bibliothèque des Écoles Françaises d'Athènes et de Rome, 289 (1995), 537–43

Luttichuys, Isaack (*bap.* 1616, *d.* 1673). *See under* Luttichuys, Simon (*bap.* 1610, *d.* 1661).

Luttichuys, Simon (*bap.* 1610, *d.* 1661), painter, son of Barent Luttichuys, was born in London and baptized at the Dutch church, Austin Friars, London, on 6 March 1610. His parents presumably returned to the Netherlands when he was young; his brother Isaack's first dated portrait betrays a Dutch training. Simon, however, is not recorded in the Netherlands until 1649, when he and his sick wife, Anneke van Peene, made a joint will at Amsterdam. In 1655 he was married at Amsterdam for a second time, to Johanna Cocks of 'Naerfick' in England. He worked mainly as a still-life painter, and influenced the celebrated Willem Kalf, who finished one of Luttichuys's pictures after his death. In 1660 at Breda he painted portraits of Charles II, James, duke of York, and Henry, duke of Gloucester, which were engraved by Cornelis van Dalem. He died in Amsterdam, where he was buried on 16 November 1661 NS. An inventory of his effects was drawn up in January 1662.

Luttichuys's younger brother, **Isaack Luttichuys** (*bap.* 1616, *d.* 1673), painter, was baptized at the Dutch church, Austin Friars, on 25 February 1616. In 1638 he signed and dated a portrait of Anne Blaeu, mother of the Dutch poet P. C. Hooft, and a resident of Amsterdam. In 1643 he married Elisabeth Winck at Amsterdam, but she soon died, bequeathing their baby daughter 1000 guilders in October 1645. He had remarried by 21 January 1647 NS; his second wife was Sara Gribert (or Grabey or Grelant). Isaack was principally a portraitist, though he occasionally made still lifes. He seems to have encountered financial difficulties in his last years; in 1668 he had to pawn twenty-one paintings and some household effects to honour a debt of 793 guilders. He was buried in the Westerkerk at Amsterdam on 6 March 1673 NS. L. H. CUST, *rev.* PAUL TAYLOR

Sources F. Meijer, ed., *Catalogue of the Ward collection, Ashmolean Museum, Oxford* [forthcoming] • A. Bredius, ed., *Künstler-Inventare*, 8 vols. (The Hague, 1915–22), vol. 4 • Thieme & Becker, *Allgemeines Lexikon*

Wealth at death paintings in his house in Amsterdam were valued after his death at 165 guilders: Bredius, *Künstler-Inventare*, vol. 4, pp. 1288–91

Lutton, Anne (1791–1881), Wesleyan Methodist preacher, was born on 16 December 1791 in Moira, co. Down, the youngest of the eleven surviving children of Ralph Lutton (1751–1828), classical scholar and linguist, and Anne Lutton (1751–1816), his wife and cousin. Anne had no regular systematic education, though she could read and write from an early age. She was taught arithmetic and needlework at home, and at seventeen attended a Moravian school for instruction in satin stitch and embroidery, English grammar, and geography. At twenty-two she embarked on the study of Latin and Greek, and went on to master several European languages as well as Hebrew, Samaritan, Syriac, Arabic, and Persian. Anne's parents were members of the established Church of Ireland, into which she was baptized as an infant, and belonged also to the local Methodist society. Her upbringing was both respectable and religious, and her accounts of fluctuating periods of religious conviction during adolescence reflect Anne's solemn and pious nature rather than any serious doubts. From the age of twenty her religious anxieties intensified, and on 14 April 1815, following a Methodist class meeting, she underwent a classic religious conversion.

Seeing no conflict between her Anglican faith and upbringing and her attachment to Wesleyan Methodism, Anne Lutton maintained loyalty to both throughout her life. In 1820, when she was confirmed into the Church of Ireland, she was already a Methodist class leader and preacher. Although the propriety of female public preaching was disputed among Wesleyan Methodists, many supported the view that the individual who was compelled by God had no choice but to obey. Anne Lutton took care that her meetings never clashed with church services, and, in accordance with the Methodist ruling of 1803, addressed only groups of women. As a result, her work seems to have won general acceptance, although one Anglican minister in Dromore did speak out against such activities. Between 1818 and 1831 she presided over 159 meetings in twenty-seven locations throughout the north of Ireland. Large crowds gathered to hear her, and she was credited by contemporaries as being responsible for individual conversions and contributing towards local revivalist fervour. Reports of men dressing as women in attempts to hear her reflect the novelty aspect of female preaching. In 1830 she spent six months in Dublin, holding weekly lectures for women and visiting the poor, the sick, and the imprisoned.

From 1832 she spent much of her time on visits to Methodist friends in Bristol, becoming permanently resident there in 1837. Although continuing to be active in religious circles and undertaking evangelistic visits to Ireland, she was best known during this period of her life as a 'great class leader', at one time presiding over six classes a week. She was a prolific writer of both poetry and prose, and a selection of her verse, several religious tracts, and contributions to religious journals were published during her lifetime. Her life was one of deep piety, strict religious discipline, and self-denial, the last frequently leading to prolonged periods of ill health. She declined at least one offer of marriage, fearing distraction from her religious vocation, but had a wide circle of Methodist and evangelical friends. She was blind from 1863, and died at her home, Llanberris Villa, 12 Cotham Road, Bristol, on 22 August 1881. She was buried on the 27th in Arnos Vale cemetery.

While her contemporary reputation, like her writings, must be seen in the context of a particularly pious religious tradition, Anne Lutton's life is a fascinating record of that brief period of female public activism within the Methodist movement, perhaps more unusual in Ireland than in England. Her letters to family and friends, spanning a fifty-year period, provide rare insight into female piety and local religious practice in nineteenth-century Ireland. MYRTLE HILL

Sources *Memorials of a consecrated life: compiled from the autobiography, letters, and diaries of Anne Lutton* (1882) • C. H. Crookshank, *History of Methodism in Ireland*, 2–3 (1886–8) • A. Lutton, *Traits of a Christian character* [n.d.] • d. cert.

Archives priv. coll.

Likenesses A. Lutton, photograph, repro. in *Memorials of a consecrated life*, frontispiece

Wealth at death £968 15*s*. 8*d*.: probate, 22 Nov 1881, *CGPLA Eng. & Wales*

Lutton, Elizabeth (*b. c.*1498, *d.* in or before 1553), Benedictine nun, was the daughter of Stephen Lutton (*d. c.*1526), son and heir of William Lutton, a landowner in the village of Knapton. She may well have been sent for her education to Yedingham Priory nearby, where about 1512 at the age of fourteen she was veiled as a nun in the presence of the abbot of Rievaulx and two of his monks, a canon of Bridlington, the prioress of Wykeham, the Yedingham community, and divers lay people. There for a dozen years or more she followed the rule of St Benedict, though not without complaint: a senior nun later recalled that she was much given to light conversation, and often asserted to her fellows, but not to the prioress, that she had been professed against her will. Then early in 1526, soon after Agnes Brayerdricke had succeeded Dame Elizabeth White as head of the house, Elizabeth Lutton became pregnant. Forbidding her to consort with her sisters, the new prioress segregated her from the rest of the community in a house outside the cloister until after the baby's birth when at the intercession of her confessor, Dom John Francis, a Scarborough grey friars, she received her back into the convent after correction.

Stephen Lutton died about the time of the scandal, leaving Elizabeth Lutton as his sole heir, and to avoid the inheritance problems this might cause her grandfather created a trust to divert his estates to his younger son Thomas and his descendants. At this juncture Sir Robert Constable of Flamborough, who had visited the priory at the time of the nun's disgrace, realized that he might be able to turn the situation to his own advantage, and he supported a scheme for Thomas Scaseby, who may have been the father of her child, to abduct Elizabeth from the priory. This he did late in 1531 or early the following year, subsequently marrying her 'contrary to the laws of God and Holly Church, and to the detestable and pernycyous example of all other lyke offendors, and to the ruyn and decay of holly relygyon' (Brown, *Yorkshire Star Chamber Proceedings*: 1, 188).

The ensuing territorial dispute between two factions of the local gentry and their tenantry led to petitions and counter-petitions to the Star Chamber and to an investigation in 1532 into the circumstances of Elizabeth Lutton's profession by the ecclesiastical authorities at York. This apparently resulted in the annulment of the marriage, and Thomas Lutton regained the family lands, his niece being forced to resume the habit for the second time. If, as seems more than probable, Elizabeth Lutton can be identified with Elizabeth Sutton, one of the eight nuns who together with the prioress surrendered the house to the crown in August 1539, she received a pension of 26*s*. 8*d*. at the dissolution. Nothing survives about her life after this date, but she had apparently died before February 1553 when her name was omitted from the list of pensions being paid to former Yedingham nuns.

CLAIRE CROSS

Sources ecclesiastical cause MSS concerning Elizabeth Lutton's profession as a nun some twenty years earlier, 1532, Borth. Inst., CP G216 • W. Brown, ed., *Yorkshire Star Chamber proceedings*, 1, Yorkshire Archaeological Society, 41 (1909), 186–8 • H. B. McCall, ed., *Yorkshire Star Chamber proceedings*, 2, Yorkshire Archaeological Society, 45 (1911), 140–42 • W. Brown, ed., *Yorkshire Star Chamber proceedings*, 3, Yorkshire Archaeological Society, 51 (1914), 110–13 • J. W. Clay, ed., *Yorkshire monasteries: suppression papers*, Yorkshire Archaeological Society, 48 (1912), 170–71 • G. W. O. Woodward, *The dissolution of the monasteries* (1966), 42–5 • C. Cross and N. Vickers, eds., *Monks, friars and nuns in sixteenth century Yorkshire*, Yorkshire Archaeological Society, 150 (1995), 550–51 • F. D. Logan, *Runaway religious in medieval England, c.1240–1540*, Cambridge Studies in Medieval Life and Thought, 4th ser., 32 (1996), 89–96 • *VCH Yorkshire*, 3.127–9 • king's remembrancer: accounts various, PRO, exchequer MSS, E 101/76/24 [Yedingham pensions list Feb 1552/3]

Archives Borth. Inst., ecclesiastical cause MSS, CP G216

Luttrell [Lutterell] **family** (*per. c.*1200–1428), gentry, first put down roots in Yorkshire and Lincolnshire, with their main residence at Irnham in the latter county, but later developed a second, and still surviving, branch in Somerset. Typical substantial gentry in their military exploits and social connections, they probably originated in Normandy, and established themselves in the east midlands in the later twelfth century. **Sir Geoffrey Luttrell** (*d.* 1216/17), a loyal adherent of John both as count and king, married Frethesant, one of the two coheirs of the *Paynel family, which had estates in Yorkshire and elsewhere. Their son, **Andrew Luttrell** (*d.* 1265), was successfully to claim land in Lincolnshire and Somerset from another branch of the Paynel family. Andrew, who was principally resident at Irnham, served as sheriff of Lincolnshire in 1251, and followed his ancestors as patron of religious houses at Roche, Drax, Nostell, and Bristol.

Sir Geoffrey Luttrell (*d.* 1269/70), son and heir of Andrew, was settled at Hooton Pagnell, Yorkshire, by 1253, and was founder of the senior branch of the family which retained most of the Paynel as well as the Luttrell lands. He later followed his father at Irnham. His son **Robert Luttrell**, Lord Luttrell (*d.* 1297), who served in Wales in 1277, was summoned to other campaigns in 1282, 1287, and 1291, to a council in 1287, and by writ (twice) to parliament in 1295; he was thus the only member of his family to rank as a peer (he had also been described as a baron in 1285). Robert's son Sir Geoffrey *Luttrell (1276–1345) accompanied the king's sister-in-law Blanche of Lancaster to Paris in 1298, was regularly summoned to fight against the Scots between 1297 and 1319, and was also called upon to attend a council at Westminster in 1325. He was allied by his own marriage to the Sutton family, and to the Scropes by the marriages of two of his sons, and these alliances, involving complicated legal transactions, together with his own religious and family predilections as expressed in his comprehensive will, seem to have provided much of the inspiration for the creation of the famous Luttrell psalter, perhaps made in the late 1330s (BL, Add. MS 42130).

Sir Andrew Luttrell (*d.* 1390), who fought in France over a period of twenty years, maintained his father's Lancastrian links by serving Henry, later duke of Lancaster, in Gascony in 1345 and helped to found a chantry at Croxton Abbey, Leicestershire, at which Henry was commemorated. **Sir Geoffrey Luttrell** (*d.* 1419), the son of Sir Andrew's son, another Sir Andrew Luttrell (*d.* 1397), was the last male of his line and died on 3 January 1419 at the siege of Rouen, fighting under his distant cousin Sir Hugh Luttrell of Dunster, Somerset. Geoffrey's only child, Hawise Luttrell (*d.* 1422), took any remaining claims to a barony to the Belesby and Hilton families.

Sir Alexander Luttrell (*d.* in or before 1273), younger son of the first Andrew Luttrell (*d.* 1265) of Irnham, acquired from his father the former Paynel manor of East Quantoxhead in Somerset, thereby establishing a branch of his family in that county. He probably died abroad while on the crusade led by the Lord Edward in 1270–72. His son **Sir Andrew Luttrell** (*d.* in or before 1324) was summoned to fight against the Scots in respect of land in Devon. He had probably acquired this through his marriage into the Ralegh family, which was the beginning of the process which made the Luttrells of Somerset a family of importance in the west country. **Sir Alexander Luttrell** (*d.* 1354), Andrew's son and heir, married into the Mandeville family, served on but one royal commission, and was murdered at Watchet, near East Quantoxhead. His grandson, the son of Alexander's son Thomas (*d. c.*1366), **Sir John Luttrell** (*d.* 1403), was, like his distant cousin Sir Andrew (*d.* 1390), a servant of the house of Lancaster. He received an annuity of £10 from John of Gaunt, and this was increased by Henry IV, who created him knight of the Bath at his coronation. In 1401–2 he served as sheriff of Somerset and Dorset, and in 1403 fought for the king at Shrewsbury against the Percys and Owain Glyn Dŵr.

Sir John died without legitimate children. His heir, **Sir Hugh Luttrell** (*d.* 1428), was the grandson of another Sir John Luttrell, younger brother of the murdered Alexander, whose Devon connections had brought him election as MP for the county in 1360 and 1363. But more important was the marriage in 1359 of Sir John's son, Sir Andrew Luttrell (*d.* 1378), to Elizabeth [**Elizabeth Luttrell** (*d.* 1395)], daughter of Hugh Courtenay, tenth earl of Devon, and Margaret, daughter of Humphrey (VII) de Bohun, earl of Hereford and Essex. Elizabeth, rewarded with her husband (until his death in 1378) with a crown annuity of £200 for services to Edward, the Black Prince, and his wife, vastly increased what came to be the Luttrell family holding in Somerset by her purchase in 1376 of the reversion of the Mohun family's castle at Dunster and three adjoining manors for the sum of 5000 marks.

Meanwhile Andrew's surviving son Sir Hugh, who was heir only to a small estate in Devon, was making his way first in the service of John of Gaunt and later of Richard II, whom he accompanied to Ireland in 1394 and again in 1399. He was confirmed in office and annuities by Henry IV, who employed him on diplomatic missions to France and Flanders. He held office as lieutenant of Calais (1402–3) and mayor of Bordeaux (1404), and in 1404 was elected MP for Somerset. In 1395 the death of his mother brought Sir Hugh land in Norfolk and Suffolk, to which the death of Sir John Luttrell in 1403 added East Quantoxhead and other lands in Somerset. The death of Lady Mohun in 1404 made his fortune, although a formidable legal challenge by the Mohun heirs was only defeated with the help of pressure exerted by the House of Commons, of which Sir Hugh was then a member. From that time until his death in 1428 Sir Hugh lived at Dunster Castle, which he substantially strengthened, and which served as a base for his operations against Owain Glyn Dŵr in 1405. He was twice elected MP for Devon (1406, 1407) and three times more for Somerset (twice in 1414, 1415), and remained active in support of the crown, serving as steward of the household of Queen Joan by 1410. On Henry V's second campaign to France, Luttrell was lieutenant of Harfleur (1417–21), and for eighteen months from July 1419 he was seneschal of Normandy. He died on 24 March 1428, leaving lands in Somerset, Dorset, Devon, Wiltshire, and Suffolk, and successors who were to continue, to their cost, to support the house of Lancaster.

The Luttrell arms were azure a bend between 6 martlets argent.

ROBERT W. DUNNING

Sources H. C. Maxwell Lyte, *A history of Dunster* (1909), 1 • GEC, *Peerage* • J. Backhouse, *The Luttrell psalter* (1989) • E. G. Millar, *The Luttrell psalter* (1932) • R. W. Dunning and L. S. Woodger, 'Luttrell, Sir Hugh', HoP, *Commons, 1386–1421*, 3.655–60 • *VCH Somerset*, 5.122
Archives Som. ARS, Luttrell of Dunster deposit, DD/L
Likenesses manuscript illumination, BL, Add. MS 42130, fol. 202v; *see illus. in* Luttrell, Sir Geoffrey (1276–1345)

Luttrell, Sir Alexander (*d.* in or before **1273**). *See under* Luttrell family (*per. c.*1200–1428).

Luttrell, Sir Alexander (*d.* **1354**). *See under* Luttrell family (*per. c.*1200–1428).

Luttrell, Andrew (*d.* **1265**). *See under* Luttrell family (*per. c.*1200–1428).

Luttrell, Sir Andrew (*d.* in or before **1324**). *See under* Luttrell family (*per. c.*1200–1428).

Luttrell, Sir Andrew (*d.* **1390**). *See under* Luttrell family (*per. c.*1200–1428).

Luttrell, Edward (*fl.* **1680–1724**), crayon portrait painter and engraver, may have been born in Ireland, possibly in Luttrellstown or Dublin. No details of his birth and parentage have been traced, but evidence from Edward Luttrell himself links him to the Luttrell family of Saunton Court, north Devon (see Noon). In 1683 the artist dedicated his manuscript treatise 'An epitome of painting' to his 'much Honored … Kinswoman Maddam Dorothy Luttrell'; a member of the Saunton Court family, she was the aunt of the diarist Narcissus Luttrell (1657–1732), of whom Edward Luttrell was thus a kinsman (and, probably, a near contemporary).

Luttrell began, possibly about 1670, as a law student at New Inn, London, meanwhile 'drawing by practice for his Pleasure', with 'no instructor or regular teaching from a Master' (Vertue, *Note books*, 1.42). 'Drawing by practice' presumably prompted Luttrell's crayon adaptations (BM) of etchings by Rembrandt and after other masters. He then gave up law study and became a pupil of the crayon and pastel portrait painter Edmund Ashfield.

Luttrell had the urge to experiment: in Vertue's phrase, he had 'a mechanical head'. Buckeridge credits him with 'multiplying' the range of crayon colours used by Ashfield; more innovatively, Luttrell 'found out a method, unknown before, to draw with those chalks or crayons, on copper-plates' (Buckeridge, 355). This method, indirectly derived (according to Vertue's sardonic account) through Luttrell's printseller friend Floyd from an assistant to the Dutch engraver Abraham Blootling (1640–1690), consisted of roughening a copperplate with a rocker (or engraving tool), giving its surface a 'tooth' to retain chalks or crayons whose powdery substance had previously demanded fixatives (prone to discolour).

Luttrell's manuscript manual 'An epitome of painting, containing breife directions for drawing painting limning and cryoons, wth the choicest receipts for preparing the colours for limning and cryoons, likewise directions for painting on glass, as tis now in use amongst all persons of quality: and lastly, how to lay the ground, and work in mezzo tinto, all by Edward Luttrell, 1683' (34 numbered pages; Yale U. CBA) was compiled for and dedicated to his 'Kinswoman' Dorothy Luttrell. Experimentally, Luttrell sometimes added watercolour or gouache to his own crayon portraits.

Luttrell's work in crayon or pastel is uneven in quality. His finest works include a tender portrait of a woman (unidentified, but evidently known to Luttrell) in olive-green headdress and low décolletage, signed in monogram (BM), and a portrait of an unknown man, possibly an artist (Huntington Art Gallery, San Marino, California). Luttrell's flesh tones range from cream, rose, and ginger to light red. His best-known sitter was Samuel Butler, the author of *Hudibras* (three versions: on oak panel, *c.*1680, NPG; Bodl. Oxf.; and Yale U. CBA). Luttrell's portraits are almost all of single sitters, bust length; but in 1694 John Evelyn recorded admiration for a group portrait of his cousin George Evelyn's ten children, 'all painted … in one piece very well by Mr. Lutterell in Crayons upon copper and seeming to be as finely painted as the best Miniature' (Evelyn, *Diary*, 5.187). At the other extreme, Vertue mentions 'one head as big as life' (Vertue, *Note books*, 3.12), but this has not been traced. Luttrell's facility for working quickly—'very quick', according to Vertue (ibid., 1.43)—produced some scratchy works, perhaps survivals of the 'many heads' drawn for the engraver Isaac Becket 'to finish & polish them up' (ibid.).

Mezzotint portraits solely by and after Luttrell (few dated) include only two of clerics (Bishop Gilbert Burnet and Francis Higgins, the allegedly seditious archdeacon of Cashel), although such commissions usually provided a steady livelihood for engravers. Less well-known sitters—among them the naval physician Robert Cony, Mrs Marie Helyot (*d.* 1682), and the amateur draughtsman Francis Le Piper (probably Luttrell's friend as well as his associate in work for Becket)—suggest that Luttrell could afford to select subjects for their appeal to him. Vertue records that 'Mr. Luttrell thinks his Best head of his doing is Mr. Le Piper' (Vertue, *Note books*, 1.43). Luttrell engraved two portraits (*Lord Shaftesbury* and *Lord William Russell*) after Kneller, and drew various (mostly imaginary) royal portraits for John Vanderbank to engrave for Bishop White Kennett's *Compleat History of England* (1706).

Luttrell appears to have lived and worked chiefly in Westminster, London. In 1711 he is listed as one of the twelve directors of Kneller's academy in Great Queen Street. The date of his death is not known, but presumably was after 1723, the year in which Vertue lists him among 'Living painters of Note in London' (Vertue, *Note books*, 3.12).

JUDY EGERTON

Sources [B. Buckeridge], 'An essay towards an English school of painters', in R. de Piles, *The art of painting, and the lives of the painters* (1706), 398–480, esp. 355 • Vertue, *Note books*, 1.42–3; 3.12 • P. J. Noon, *English portrait drawings and miniatures* (New Haven, CT, 1979), 11–2 [exhibition catalogue, Yale U. CBA, 5 Dec 1979 – 17 Feb 1980] • E. Croft-Murray and P. H. Hulton, eds., *Catalogue of British drawings*, 1 (1960), 434–8 • E. Waterhouse, *Painting in Britain, 1530–1790*, 2nd edn (1962), 232 • E. K. Waterhouse, *The dictionary of British 16th and 17th century painters* (1988), 184–5

Luttrell, Elizabeth (*d.* 1395). *See under* Luttrell family (*per. c.*1200–1428).

Luttrell, Lady Elizabeth (*d.* 1799). *See under* Henry Frederick, Prince, duke of Cumberland and Strathearn (1745–1790).

Luttrell, Sir Geoffrey (*d.* 1216/17). *See under* Luttrell family (*per. c.*1200–1428).

Luttrell, Sir Geoffrey (*d.* 1269/70). *See under* Luttrell family (*per. c.*1200–1428).

Luttrell, Sir Geoffrey (1276–1345), landowner and patron of the Luttrell psalter, lord of Irnham, Lincolnshire, was the son of Sir Robert Luttrell of Irnham (*c.*1255–1297) and his wife, Joan. Her parentage is unknown; she was still living in June 1320. Luttrell was born on 23 May 1276 at Irnham and baptized on the following day, Whit Sunday, in the parish church. Two younger brothers and four sisters, two of whom were later nuns at Hampole, are recorded. On his father's death in 1297 he inherited the manors of Irnham and of Hooton Pagnell, Yorkshire. He also had smaller holdings at Gamston and Bridgford, Nottinghamshire, and at Saltby, Leicestershire. His chief concern for the rest of his life was the administration of his estates. In 1318 he obtained a royal licence to grant his lands to his brother Guy in return for a life interest, with remainder to his two eldest sons, and in 1331 he sought a papal dispensation to remain in his marriage in spite of remotely possible impediments of consanguinity. Both moves seem to have been undertaken specifically to safeguard the interests of his heirs. In 1312 and again in 1320 he was involved in property disputes with neighbours, one of them the prior of Sempringham, to which his uncle Robert, rector of Irnham (*d.* 1315), had been a substantial benefactor.

Sir Geoffrey was not particularly prominent in a wider public context, though in 1298 he had been one of ten gentlemen travelling with the widowed countess of Lancaster, Blanche, former queen of Navarre, on her return to France. On some thirteen occasions between 1297 and 1319 he was called for military service and fought in the Scottish border wars. In 1324 he was included on a list of forty knights of the region summoned by the sheriff to attend a council at Westminster, though there is no record that he did so. In December 1325 he was named commissioner of array for Kesteven, though a deputy was soon appointed on account of his ill health.

Luttrell married, probably about 1297, Agnes, daughter of Sir Richard Sutton of Sutton-on-Trent, Nottinghamshire, a great-nephew of Oliver *Sutton, bishop of Lincoln (1280–99). She died on 12 June 1340. The couple had four sons and two daughters. The eldest son, Robert, was dead by February 1320 when Andrew (born in 1313 and ultimately his father's heir) and Geoffrey were married to the two infant daughters of Geoffrey *Scrope (*d.* 1340), a rising lawyer who became chief justice of king's bench in 1324. A younger Robert appears in his father's will as a hospitaller. Elizabeth, probably the first child, married the heir of Sir Walter of Gloucester, escheator south of Trent, and Isabella took the veil at Sempringham.

Sir Geoffrey Luttrell (1276–1345), drawing [with his wife, Agnes Sutton, and his daughter-in-law, Beatrice Scrope]

Luttrell is chiefly remembered as the patron for whom the magnificent psalter which bears his name was written and illuminated in the second quarter of the fourteenth century. The book, quite clearly intended as a visual statement of family status, includes a miniature portraying him armed and on horseback, offered helmet, lance, and shield by his wife and daughter-in-law. All three are identified by their armorials. The work of the Luttrell psalter's principal illuminator, known only from this single manuscript, has a vigour and a sureness of characterization that sets it apart from the work of his contemporaries. His famous marginal illustrations of contemporary everyday life have been constantly reproduced for more than a century.

Luttrell died on 23 May 1345, his sixty-ninth birthday, at Irnham, where he was buried. A copy of his will, dated 3 April 1345, is preserved in the register of Bishop Thomas (II) Bek at Lincoln. Alongside the predictable and lavish arrangements for the welfare of his soul, which include bequests to ten different religious communities near his various estates, there are legacies to no less than sixteen family members. There are also bequests, both in money and in goods, to named servants whose roles are specified, suggesting a very close-knit household community.

JANET BACKHOUSE

Sources GEC, *Peerage* · E. G. Millar, *The Luttrell Psalter* (1932) · J. Backhouse, *The Luttrell Psalter* (1989)

Likenesses manuscript illumination, BL, Add. MS 42130, fol. 202*v* [*see illus.*]

Wealth at death approx. £450—specific sums and possessions, excl. lands: will, Bishop Bek's registers at Lincoln, fols. 100–01

Luttrell, Sir Geoffrey (*d.* 1419). *See under* Luttrell family (*per. c.*1200–1428).

Luttrell, Henry (1653/4–1717), army officer, was a son of Thomas Luttrell (*d.* 1673) of Luttrellstown, co. Dublin, and of Barbara Sedgrave, and a younger brother of Simon *Luttrell (*c.*1643–1698). As a young man he served in the French army, but after the accession of James II in 1685 he was commissioned as a captain in Princess Anne of

Denmark's regiment of foot. In 1686 he was given command of the 4th troop of Horse Grenadier Guards, whom he led in a skirmish with Prince William's troops at Wincanton on 20 November 1688. At the revolution he went back to France, from where he sailed with the fleet that brought King James to Ireland on 12 March 1689. He represented Carlow in the Dublin parliament of May 1689 and was given a regiment of cavalry. In July 1689 he took part in the duke of Berwick's raid on Enniskillen and distinguished himself by chasing the Williamite horse back into the town. In October that year he played an important part in Patrick Sarsfield's capture of Sligo by scattering a larger force of Williamite cavalry at Ballysadare. Luttrell was made governor of the town, which he then fortified.

After the battle of the Boyne (1 July 1690) the Jacobite government moved to Limerick, and Luttrell, then a brigadier, 'was perpetually speaking ill of Tyrconnell', the Jacobite lord lieutenant, 'and inflaming everybody against him' in favour of 'his intimate friend' Sarsfield (Fitzjames, 80). Berwick acknowledged Luttrell to have 'a great share of sense, a great share of address, a great share of courage, and was a good officer; capable of anything to accomplish his ends' (ibid., 97) but referred to him as 'a most dangerous incendiary' (ibid., 82).

In September 1690 Tyrconnell sailed to France. In his absence Luttrell, Sarsfield, and the other 'caballing gentlemen' (Gilbert, 111) forced Berwick to send a delegation to France to urge King James to replace Tyrconnell as viceroy. The two Luttrell brothers were chosen as delegates, as was Brigadier Thomas Maxwell, who had instructions from Berwick to tell James not to allow Luttrell back to Ireland. He correctly guessed Maxwell's mission and had to be restrained by his brother and the bishop of Cork from throwing him over the side of the ship. At St Germain James received both Maxwell and a desperate letter from Tyrconnell stating that he would be able to control Sarsfield so long as Luttrell was kept away, but by the time Luttrell's delegation was permitted to address James, Tyrconnell had left the country for France. Luttrell returned to Ireland after convincing James that if he were detained the Irish would take their revenge on Berwick. On 19 May 1691 he arrived in Limerick with the new French commander, St Ruth, and resumed his campaign against Tyrconnell, now also returned to Ireland.

At the battle of Aughrim Luttrell commanded the brigade of dragoons that formed the first line on the left wing. The battle ended in disaster for the Irish army, the remnants of which made for Limerick. The failure of his troops, and those of his immediate superior, Dominic Sheldon, to halt the Williamite advance was crucial to the latter's victory, and he was subsequently accused of cowardice or of treachery. But there was no immediate clamour against him, and he was dispatched with a cavalry force to disrupt Ginckel's siege of Galway, though held off at Kilcolgan Bridge. When Galway surrendered, he provided the escort that brought the garrison back to Limerick. During the handover the commander of the Williamite escort party asked Luttrell whether the Irish were ready to treat. He replied that 'such a thing might well be if General Ginckel had a sufficient power' (Gilbert, 149) to grant terms. A few days later a messenger from the English camp was caught bringing a letter to Luttrell to let him know that Ginckel did have that authority. He was arrested by Sarsfield and on Tyrconnell's orders was tried by court martial for corresponding with the enemy. His defence was that he had merely spoken to the letter's author during a ceasefire. The tribunal acquitted him by nineteen votes to five. Lord Westmeath, who watched the tribunal, wrote that 'it was impossible that he could be found guilty by men that had either honesty or honour' (Harris, appx 75). Nevertheless, Tyrconnell, who had cast his vote against him, kept him locked up in Limerick Castle, where he remained until after the treaty.

There is no other evidence or contemporary suggestion that Luttrell was a traitor to the Jacobite cause up until the treaty of Limerick (3 October 1691), but the resentment generated by his harsh treatment by his comrades drove him firmly into the arms of the Williamites. Under the terms of the treaty the Irish troops were given the choice of going to France to serve King James, of joining King William's army, or of laying down their arms. Luttrell harangued his men and, as he later claimed,

> not only did bring to his Majestie's service the Regiment of Horse he formerly had commanded, but by himself and his friends did perswade many of the Irish to do the like and prevented 8,000 of them from goeing into France to serve against his Majestie. (McNeill, 80)

He was awarded £500 per annum and succeeded to the family estates at Luttrellstown, his brother having been outlawed.

Luttrell travelled to the continent for each of King William's campaigns for the rest of the Nine Years' War, but, although he was chosen to command a proposed Irish brigade which was to serve in the Venetian service against the Turks, he was never given another post. In 1699 his brother's widow sued him for her jointure on Luttrellstown. He initially defended the action by having her arrested for returning from France without a licence. The case was finally decided against him in 1709.

Luttrell married, in 1704, Elizabeth, daughter of Henry Jones of Halkyn in Flint; they had two sons. He was shot dead in his sedan chair near his Dublin house on 3 November 1717 and was buried at Luttrellstown. It was at first feared that he had been assassinated in revenge for his actions in 1691, and a £1000 reward was offered to secure the murderer. It was later generally believed that the motive behind his killing had more to do with his adultery than his politics.

Luttrell's second son, Simon Luttrell (1713–1787), was in 1768 raised to the peerage as Baron Irnham, and later as viscount (1781) and earl (1785) of Carhampton. He was the father of General Henry Lawes *Luttrell, second earl of Carhampton (1737–1821); of John Luttrell-*Olmius, third earl (*d.* 1829) [*see under* Luttrell, James]; of James *Luttrell (*c.*1751–1788); and of Temple Simon *Luttrell (1738?–1803) [*see under* Luttrell, Henry Lawes]. PIERS WAUCHOPE

Sources F. E. Ball, *A history of the county Dublin*, 6 vols. (1902–20), vol. 4, pp. 1–19 • *Calendar of the manuscripts of the marquess of Ormonde*, new ser., 8 vols., HMC, 36 (1902–20), vol. 8 • C. McNeill, 'Reports on the Rawlinson collection', *Analecta Hibernica*, 1 (1930), 12–178, esp. 79–84 • J. Fitzjames [Duke of Berwick], *Memoirs of the marshal duke of Berwick*, 1 (1779) • W. King, *The state of the protestants of Ireland under the late King James's government*, another edn (1692) • *CSP dom.*, 1673–5; 1686–90 • P. Wauchope, *Patrick Sarsfield and the Williamite war* (1992) • *The manuscripts of the House of Lords*, new ser., 12 vols. (1900–77), vol. 8, pp. 313–15 • J. T. Gilbert, ed., *A Jacobite narrative of the war in Ireland, 1688–1691* (1892); facs. edn (1971) • W. Harris, *The history of the life and reign of William-Henry* (1749) • C. Dalton, ed., *English army lists and commission registers, 1661–1714*, 6 vols. (1892–1904) • GEC, *Peerage*, new edn, vol. 3 • *A geneological account of the family of Luttrell, Lotterel or Lutterell* (1774)

Likenesses P. Lely, oils, priv. coll.; in possession of Lady Du Cane, 1893 • engraving, repro. in Ball, *History of the county Dublin*

Wealth at death 4000 acres in co. Dublin, co. Kildare, and co. Meath

Luttrell [*formerly* King], **Henry** (**1768–1851**), wit and poet, an illegitimate son of Henry Lawes *Luttrell, second earl of Carhampton (1737–1821), was born on 14 May 1768. His mother was rumoured to be a gardener's daughter from Woodstock named Harman; under the surname King he attended Charterhouse School between 1778 and 1783, before proceeding to Trinity College, Dublin, where he graduated BA in 1790 and LLB in 1791, in which year he was called to the Irish bar. He took the name Luttrell, and through his father's influence he obtained a seat for Clonmines, co. Wexford, in the last Irish parliament (1798), and a post in the Irish government, which he subsequently commuted for a pension. He was sent to the West Indies about 1802 to manage his father's estates there, but soon returned, and obtained an introduction to London society through the duchess of Devonshire. Although always financially insecure, he was socially successful and was looked upon as one of the most agreeable, accomplished, and entertaining men of his day.

In 1819 Luttrell published some graceful, if rather colourless, elegiacs entitled *Lines Written at Ampthill Park in the Autumn of 1818*, and dedicated to Henry, Lord Holland. On an altogether different plane was *Advice to Julia, a Letter in Rhyme*, published early in 1820. Influenced by Horace, the poem was a 'society epic', offering vignettes of London life. Tom Moore, who was to some extent its literary sponsor, described the volume as 'full of well-bred facetiousness and sparkle'; it was greatly improved in the third edition of 1822 (when the title was slightly altered to *Letters to Julia, in Rhyme*), and 'is now', said Christopher North, writing in the following year, 'quite, quite a bijou'. Luttrell's only other printed volume was his *Crockford House* (1827), a satire on gambling which did not enhance his reputation.

Luttrell travelled much in Europe, and kept a diary, but his real greatness was as a talker and diner-out. Moore took counsel with him before destroying the manuscript memoirs which Byron had entrusted to his discretion. He was 'always bracketed with Rogers', compared with whom he is described as 'less caustic, but more good-natured', and the two were 'seldom apart, and always hating, abusing, and ridiculing each other'. No one, according to Rogers, 'could slide in a brilliant thing with greater readiness'. He was a frequent guest at Holland House, where many of his best *mots* were uttered. Despite his great reputation as a wit, and his contemporaries' taste for recording his epigrams, they did not withstand translation into written form. He appears in many volumes of recollections of the period. He did not lack a serious side: Greville described him as 'a philosopher in all things, but especially in religion'.

Luttrell survived most of his contemporaries, and was described by Raikes in 1843 as visiting Paris 'pour chasser l'ennui, though without effect' (*Portion of the Journal*, 4.269). In 1850 he married Ann Springer, daughter of John Cutler of Clapton. It is possible that he had been married previously. He died at his house, 31 Brompton Square, London, on 19 December 1851.

THOMAS SECCOMBE, *rev.* K. D. REYNOLDS

Sources Burtchaell & Sadleir, *Alum. Dubl.* • R. L. Arrowsmith, ed., *Charterhouse register, 1769–1872* (1974) • *The Greville memoirs, 1814–1860*, ed. L. Strachey and R. Fulford, 8 vols. (1938), vol. 2, pp. 425–6 • *A portion of the journal of Thomas Raikes from 1831 to 1847: comprising reminiscences of social and political life in London and Paris during that period*, 4 (1858), 269 • P. W. Clayden, *Rogers and his contemporaries*, 2 vols. (1889) • *Memoirs, journal and correspondence of Thomas Moore*, ed. J. Russell, 8 vols. (1853–6) • *N&Q*, 2nd ser., 11 (1861), 70 • A. Dobson, 'A forgotten poet of society', *St James's Magazine and Empire Review*, 33 (1878), 43–52 • Boase, *Mod. Eng. biog.*

Archives BL, letters to Lord Holland and Lady Holland, Add. MS 51594

Luttrell, Henry Lawes, second earl of Carhampton (**1737–1821**), army officer and politician, was born at Cranford, Middlesex, on 7 August 1737, the eldest son of Simon Luttrell, first earl of Carhampton (1713–1787), landowner and politician, of Castlehaven, co. Cork, and Judith Maria (*d.* 1798), daughter of Sir Nicholas Lawes and Elizabeth Cotton. Educated at Westminster School and Christ Church, Oxford, Luttrell began his military career in 1757 as ensign in the 48th foot, rising in 1759 to lieutenant in the 34th foot and captain of the 16th light dragoons. In April 1762 he became a major and was made deputy adjutant-general of the British forces in Portugal; he received the local rank of lieutenant-colonel in October 1762 and in February 1765 was made lieutenant-colonel of the 1st regiment of horse.

In 1768 Luttrell entered politics as member for the Cornish borough of Bossiney. Thereafter Luttrell embarked on something of a personal crusade against John Wilkes, whom he attacked in his maiden speech. In 1769, after Wilkes's election for Middlesex had been declared void for the third time, Luttrell offered to stand if the government would ensure his return on petition. Although heavily defeated in the election on 13 April 1769 by 1143 votes to 296, the House of Commons carried a motion by 197 to 143 declaring Luttrell elected, which sparked popular outrage. Horace Walpole reported that Luttrell was hissed out of the theatre, assaulted as he left the house, and for several months 'did not dare appear in the streets or scarce quit his lodgings' (Walpole, 3.359). Luttrell was frequently attacked in print, particularly by the political satirist Junius who, representing the views of anti-court whigs, disparaged his election as an 'arbitrary appointment [which] invades the foundation of the laws themselves' (*Letters of Junius*, 83, letter 15, to the duke of Grafton, 8 July 1769). Luttrell's personal unpopularity was compounded by his family's scandalous reputation. Junius compared his 'unnatural union' with Middlesex to the clandestine marriage of Luttrell's sister, Anne Horton, to the duke of Cumberland (ibid., 316, letter 68, to Lord Chief Justice Mansfield, 21 Jan 1772). Nevertheless, as reward for opposing Wilkes, Luttrell sought and received the position of adjutant-general in Ireland. In 1774 he resumed his former seat for Bossiney which he held until 1784. On 25 June 1776 he married Jane (*d.* 1831), daughter of George Boyd and Anne Hamilton of Dublin. He received a marriage settlement of £20,000.

Luttrell's military career meanwhile had advanced apace: he became colonel (brevet) in August 1777 and major-general in November 1782. As adjutant-general in Ireland he displayed the same thrusting ambition and contempt for public opinion that he had in England. In 1779 he proposed a highly unpopular and unsuccessful scheme to bring the Irish Volunteers under government control. He was also active in Irish politics and sat for the borough of Old Leighlin from 1783 to 1787. During 1786 he was tasked with subduing agrarian Rightboy protesters in Munster, and went on a whirlwind tour with a special commission and 2000 soldiers. He attempted pacification both by a show of military force and by the negotiation of mutually acceptable levels of clerical tithe. The mission failed amid recriminations. His proposals for lower tithes were construed as sanctioning protests and the clergy complained that his failure to follow up his threats provoked a renewal of the disturbances. Nevertheless, he became colonel of the 6th dragoons in 1788, and in 1789 lieutenant-general of the ordnance in Ireland.

On the death of his father in January 1787 Luttrell, who had earlier quarrelled acrimoniously with his father over the settlement of Luttrellstown, co. Dublin, succeeded to the family titles and estates. In 1790 he re-entered the Westminster parliament for Plympton Erle and held that seat until 1794; thereafter the dangers of Irish insurrection and possible invasion occupied his attention. In March 1795 he advocated that armed loyalist associations should hold Dublin if its garrison moved against an invader. In May that year he was given unlimited authority to tackle the Defenders in Connaught. Here he encouraged magistrates to arrest men on suspicion, many of whom (estimates vary between 1300 and 200) were sent to serve on the fleet. Although brutally effective, his impetuous methods alarmed the viceroy, Lord Camden, who vetoed his plans for armed anti-Defender loyalist associations in October 1795. Camden later admitted that Carhampton had exceeded the laws in Connaught, and an indemnity act was passed early in 1796. When establishment of an Irish yeomanry was being canvassed in the summer of 1796, Carhampton toured various parts of Ireland to enlist support but, typically, portrayed the dangers in such lurid terms that he caused agricultural prices to plummet and actually encouraged disaffection. In October 1796 he became Irish commander-in-chief by default, the first choice to succeed General Cunninghame, Sir Charles Grey, having declined on health grounds. Carhampton zealously set about improving Ireland's defences but was overtaken by events when a French invasion fleet appeared at Bantry Bay in late December 1796. His handling of this crisis was subjected to heavy criticism, particularly the decision to abandon Cork. Afterwards Edward Cooke summed him up as 'quick, but flighty', and noted that: 'It is unfortunate but true that Lord Carhampton has different ideas about the defence of Ireland from every officer in the whole army' (PRO NIre., Sneyd MSS, T3229/2/22, Cooke to Auckland, 9 Feb 1797; BL, Add. MS 33103, fol. 130, Cooke to Pelham, 3 Feb 1797). The northern commander, General Knox, criticized Carhampton for refusing to believe that republicans had infiltrated the militia. Knox also deplored Carhampton's impetuous behaviour, highlighting an undignified fracas in a Newry public house in April 1797 when he tore a green handkerchief from a United Irishman's neck. His reputation made him a target for the disaffected and there was a plot to assassinate him in May 1797, for which two men were executed, one the blacksmith on his own Luttrellstown estate. By now Camden was considering replacing him, telling the home secretary: 'with all the merit he possesses, there is certainly a degree of indiscretion in his character, that makes him unfit for the chief command of the army' (PRO, Home Office 100/68, fols. 233–4, Camden to Portland, 28 April 1797). As a suitably experienced successor was again unavailable, Carhampton remained in command until November 1797 when he was replaced by Sir Ralph Abercromby; he was compensated with the master-generalship of the ordnance and was made a full general in January 1798.

Carhampton had opposed the union of Britain and Ireland when it was first mooted but by June 1799 Cornwallis reported that: 'he has sold Luttrellstown, and means to vote for the Union which he so loudly and indecently reprobated' (*Correspondence of … Cornwallis*, 3.112). He later had second thoughts about the sale of Luttrellstown and tried unsuccessfully to renege on the agreement with the purchaser, the wealthy Dublin bookseller Luke White (T. Kemmis to Carhampton, 11 May 1802, PRO NIre., T 3404/37). Having purchased an estate at Painshill, near Cobham, Surrey, Carhampton re-entered parliament in June 1817 as MP for Ludgershall and held the seat until his death. He died at his home in Bruton Street, London, on 25 April 1821, survived by his wife and his only known child, a natural son, Henry *Luttrell (1768–1851). The title passed to his brother John Luttrell-*Olmius (*d.* 1829) [*see under* Luttrell, James]; his two other brothers, James *Luttrell (*c.*1751–1788) and **Temple Simon Luttrell** (1738?–1803), politician, had predeceased him. Temple Simon Luttrell, probably born on 8 September 1738, had been educated with Henry at Westminster and on 26 April 1778 married Elizabeth Gould (*d.* 1803), daughter of Sir Henry *Gould (1710–1794), judge. He sat as MP for Milborne Port from 1774 to 1780, and gained some notoriety during the war against America for his attacks on the Admiralty and for campaigning against the press gang. The violence of his speeches against Lord North, however, lost him his seat. He was arrested at Boulogne on 18 September 1793 and when his captors realized that his sister, Anne, had been married to the duke of Cumberland, they triumphantly announced him to be the king of England's brother. He was released on 14 February 1795 and died in Paris on 14 January 1803, leaving no children; his widow died in Kensington three months later on 21 May.

A. F. Blackstock

Sources PRO, Home Office 100 series, vols. 18, 57, 67–9 • BL, Pelham MSS, Add. MSS 33102, 33103 [1796–7] • *The letters of Junius*, ed. J. Cannon (1978) • H. Walpole, *Memoirs of the reign of King George the Third*, ed. G. F. R. Barker, 4 vols. (1894) • *The manuscripts of J. B. Fortescue*, 10 vols., HMC, 30 (1892–1927) • *The manuscripts of the duke of Beaufort … the earl of Donoughmore*, HMC, 27 (1891) • *Report on the manuscripts of the marquess of Lothian*, HMC, 62 (1905) • *Correspondence of Charles, first Marquis Cornwallis*, ed. C. Ross, 3 vols. (1859), vol. 3, pp. 35, 112 • Sneyd MSS, 9 Feb 1797, PRO NIre., T 3229/2/22 • PRO NIre., Shannon MSS, D 2707/A3 • *GM*, 1st ser., 7 (1737), 514 • *GM*, 1st ser., 13 (1743), 51 • *GM*, 1st ser., 8 (1738), 490 • *GM*, 1st ser., 73 (1803), 92, 487 • *GM*, 1st ser., 91/1 (1821), 468 • J. Brooke, 'Luttrell, Hon. Henry Lawes', HoP, *Commons* • D. F. Fisher, 'Luttrell, Hon. Henry Lawes', HoP, *Commons* • GEC, *Peerage* • J. Lodge, *The peerage of Ireland*, rev. M. Archdall, rev. edn, 7 vols. (1789) • Burke, *Peerage* (1830) • CKS, Pratt papers, U840/0181/5 • BL, Egerton MSS, Add. MS 3260, fols. 82–3 • *Brown's reports of House of Lords appeals, 1701–1800*, vol. 7, pp. 388–96

Archives BL, corresp. with second earl of Chichester, etc., Add. MSS 33102–33103, 33118 • CKS, corresp. with first Marquess Camden, relating to Ireland • NAM, Nugent MSS • PRO NIre., Annaly–Clifden MSS

Likenesses H. D. Hamilton, pastel miniature, NG Ire. • J. Petrie, engraving (after drawing by P. Maguire), repro. in *Hibernian Magazine* (1797)

Wealth at death under £60,000 personal property within province of Canterbury sworn: *GM* 1st ser., 91/1

Luttrell, Sir Hugh (*d.* 1428). *See under* Luttrell family (*per.* c.1200–1428).

Luttrell, James (*c.*1751–1788), naval officer and politician, was born at Four Oaks, Warwickshire, the fourth and youngest son of Simon Luttrell, first earl of Carhampton (1713–1787), of Castlehaven, co. Cork, and his wife, Judith Maria, *née* Lawes (*d.* 1798). His elder brothers were Henry Lawes *Luttrell, later second earl of Carhampton, Temple Simon *Luttrell [*see under* Luttrell, Henry Lawes], and John, later third earl [*see below*]. James entered the Royal Navy in the mid-1760s and was promoted lieutenant on 2 February 1770.

In December 1775 Luttrell was elected MP for Stockbridge in Hampshire. Prior to this he had spent time in America. In parliament he attacked the North administration's policy towards the War of Independence, describing the British campaign as 'unjust, rash and savage' (Brooke, HoP, *Commons, 1754–90*, 3.66). With his brothers John and Temple Simon, he also spoke out against the naval policy of the earl of Sandwich. Luttrell remained an active critic of the North government until 1780 when he was encouraged to modify his views with the offer of a command at sea as part of negotiations between Luttrell and the court's spokesman, Lord Irnham. In late July 1780 he was promoted first lieutenant of the *Belliqueux* and became captain on 23 February 1781. In the following year he took command of the *Mediator* in which, in December, he achieved some celebrity for his actions against the French navy. On 12 December the *Mediator* was patrolling off Ferrol when an American ship and four French vessels attempted to break out. Luttrell was able to break through the allied line and one French ship, the *Alexandre*, surrendered. Luttrell chased and captured another, the *Menagerie*, later that day. Next morning, the *Mediator* spotted two more of the vessels. However, in view of the fact that Luttrell's ship already carried 300 prisoners and a crew of only 190 he decided not to pursue them. This may have been as well, since during the night the French officers attempted to seize the British ship. Luttrell brought his prizes back to Britain: the action was commemorated by several paintings and led the king to write that Luttrell's 'skill as well as bravery … deserve much approbation' (ibid.).

In 1783 Luttrell was appointed to command the ship of the line *Ganges* but his naval career was nearing its end. He stayed with this ship for only six months before resigning, probably on the grounds of ill health, to become surveyor-general of the ordnance in March 1784. In April he was elected MP for Dover. He remained at the ordnance until his death, unmarried, from tuberculosis on 23 December 1788.

Luttrell's brother, **John Luttrell-Olmius** [*formerly* Luttrell], third earl of Carhampton (*c.*1740–1829), naval officer and politician, was the first earl's third son. He entered the navy in the mid-1750s, being promoted lieutenant in October 1758. In 1762 he became captain of the *Mars* and of the *Achilles*, the Portsmouth guardship, three years later. On 13 June 1765 he married Elizabeth (*d.* 1797), daughter of John Olmius, first Baron Waltham; they had three children, two of whom died in infancy. In 1774 he was elected MP for Stockbridge but vacated the seat in the following December for his brother James. With James and Temple Simon, John attacked the policies of Lord Sandwich whom he accused of selling naval offices, a charge refuted during a celebrated trial in 1773.

John Luttrell's next naval appointment was as captain of the *Charon* in which he sailed for the West Indies in March 1779. In October he led a squadron and captured the Spanish stronghold of St Fernando del Omoa, and seized bullion worth some $3 million. In 1780 he was returned as MP for Stockbridge after which, in line with his brother, he shifted his position in favour of the court and against the American War of Independence. He was disqualified from holding the seat when, in 1784, he became a commissioner for managing excise. Luttrell took the additional name of Olmius after his wife became heir to Lord Waltham's estate in April 1787. Following her death he married (on 16 July 1798) Maria Anne (1776/7–1857), daughter of John Morgan; the couple had one daughter. Luttrell-Olmius became third earl of Carhampton on the death of his brother Henry in 1821. He himself died on 17 March 1829 at Devonshire Place, Middlesex, whereupon the title became extinct.

Michael Partridge

Sources *DNB* • 'Anecdotes of the Hon. Capt. James Luttrell', *European Magazine and London Review*, 3 (1783), 5–6 • *Steel's Original and Correct List of the Royal Navy* (1790–92) • *Memoirs of Rear Admiral Sir Michael Seymour, Bart, KCB*, ed. R. Seymour (1878) • GEC, *Peerage*, new edn, vol. 3 • *GM*, 1st ser., 58 (1788), 1131 • R. Beatson, *Naval and military memoirs of Great Britain*, 2nd edn, 4 (1804), 474–83 • J. Brooke, 'Luttrell, James', HoP, *Commons, 1754–90* • J. Brooke, 'Luttrell, John', HoP, *Commons, 1754–90*

Likenesses J. Pell, engraving, 1783 (after R. Dodd), NMM • W. Argus, line engraving (after J. Millar), BM, NPG; repro. in *European Magazine and London Review* • R. Dodd, oils • J. Millar, oils

Luttrell, Sir John (*d.* 1403). *See under* Luttrell family (*per.* c.1200–1428).

Luttrell, Narcissus (1657–1732), annalist and book collector, was born on 12 August 1657 in Holborn, London, the third but eldest surviving son of Francis Luttrell (1613–1677) of Gray's Inn (a cadet of the Luttrells of Staunton Court, Devon) and Catherine Mapowder (*d.* 1685), daughter and coheir of Narcissus Mapowder of Holsworthy, Devon.

Luttrell was educated at Sheen School and entered a fellow commoner of St John's, Cambridge, in February 1674. He received an MA by royal mandate in 1675, but even before his matriculation at Cambridge he was admitted in August 1673 to his father's inn. Luttrell succeeded his father in April 1677. He was called to the bar in 1680, and though he appears to have abandoned practice early in life, he was subsequently elected as bencher in 1702 and ancient in 1706.

Luttrell did, however, put his legal training to use, serving actively as a Middlesex JP for three decades from 1693. On various occasions he also served as a deputy lieutenant, a commissioner of oyer and terminer, and a commissioner of land-tax assessment. He was also twice elected to the House of Commons, sitting for Bossiney (Cornwall) in the second Exclusion Parliament (1679–80) and then in the parliament of 1690–95 for Saltash (Cornwall) upon being returned at a by-election in October 1691.

Luttrell does not appear to have been a frequent speaker in the Commons, and what is known or may be surmised of his political views is not altogether consistent. On the one hand, his obituarist in the *London Evening Journal* (6–8 July 1732) characterized him as an exclusionist and a staunch whig, while suggesting that it was Sir Robert Walpole who was responsible for his ouster from the Middlesex commission of the peace in 1723. On the other hand, Luttrell was on good enough terms with Robert Harley, a fellow MP in the 1690–95 parliament and also an avid collector, to solicit (unsuccessfully) a place for his son, Francis ('bred a scholar' and called to the bar), from him as head of the Treasury in 1712, invoking the names of such staunch tories as Francis Gwyn and Sir William Drake as 'compurgators' for the rightness of his son's political views (Luttrell to earl of Oxford, 23 Jan 1712, BL, Add. MS 70247; Luttrell to earl of Oxford, 12 Aug 1712, *Portland MSS*, 5.210). It may also be significant that his tenure as a Middlesex deputy lieutenant began under the Harley ministry and that it was not renewed by George I's first ministry. Suffice it, then, to say that his scholarly and collecting activities brought him into contact with a political cross-section that also included Jacob Tonson and Thomas Hearne.

Luttrell's chief contributions were as annalist and collector. Since Macaulay drew attention to them, his chronicles (compiled from newsletters and newspapers) of contemporary events, *A Brief Historical Relation of State Affairs from September 1678 to April 1714* (1857), have been frequently cited by students of the period. Even more valuable, as a firsthand account, is the parliamentary diary he kept assiduously during his second term of service in the Commons; the diary is preserved—as are the materials for the *Historical Relation*—in the Codrington Library of All Souls College, Oxford. Although the diary (published in 1972 by Clarendon Press) is almost wholly devoid of personal references, it provides a very full account of the debates of the 1691–2 and 1692–3 sessions. Given Luttrell's habits and the survival of much other parliamentary material among his manuscripts in the Codrington Library, it seems quite likely that he kept a similar diary for the final two sessions of that parliament, but its whereabouts, if extant, are unknown. In addition, there survives a brief diary of his service as a deputy lieutenant during 1713–14 (LMA, ACC 619). There is also his private diary for 1722–5 in the British Library; written in Greek characters, its contents have been extracted by P. Dixon in *Notes and Queries* (207, 1962, 388ff.).

In addition to his public service, Luttrell accumulated a valuable collection of contemporary publications, including both political (some listed in his Popish Plot catalogues) and poetical works. After more than three decades of acquisitions (beginning in his student days), he calculated in 1706 that he had laid out over £1500 on such purchases; unfortunately, his wish that his library pass intact to some 'public' institution such as Gray's Inn was not wholly heeded by his descendants. So while a substantial number of the printed works from his library were eventually acquired by the British Library, many (often bearing his colophon) have found resting places elsewhere; dated items are listed in *The Luttrell File*, compiled by Stephen Parks with Earle Havens (1999). Meanwhile, a large number of his manuscripts found their way by the gift of Luttrell Wynne (grandson of his sister Dorothy Wynne, and a fellow of All Souls College) to the Codrington Library in 1786. More recently, Professor James Osborn donated many items he acquired (at Sotheby sales in 1936 and 1957) in the course of his researches on Luttrell to the Beinecke Library of Yale University. Still others are dispersed and some are not now traceable.

Luttrell made many of his purchases while residing at a house in Holborn (opposite the Three Cups tavern) that he inherited from his mother in 1685. He also inherited other realty worth over £200 p.a., including property at Tregony and Launceston, Cornwall, from his parents (Luttrell MS C65). He married in February 1682 Sarah, daughter of Daniel Baker (a prosperous London merchant), and their only child, a son, Francis, was born that December.

From 1710 onwards, Luttrell resided in a newly purchased residence (acquired from the third earl of Shaftesbury for £1200) in Chelsea. After Sarah's death in July 1722, he married in May 1725 Mary, daughter of John Bearsley of Wolverhampton. A son was born to them in 1727 but did not survive. Luttrell died at Little Chelsea, after a long illness, on 27 June 1732, leaving his widow, Mary (*d.* 1745), and his only surviving child, Francis, by his first wife. He was buried at Chelsea. At Francis's death in 1749 the Luttrell library passed to his Wynne kin, eventually to be dispersed by sale and gift. HENRY HORWITZ

Sources F. E. Ball, 'Narcissus Luttrell', *N&Q*, 152 (1927), 111 • P. Dixon, 'Narcissus Luttrell's private diary', *N&Q*, 207 (1962), 388–92, 411–15, 452–4 • F. C. Francis, introduction, *Narcissus Luttrell's Popish Plot catalogues* (1956) • H. C. M. Lyte, *A history of Dunster and of the families of Mohun and Luttrell*, 2 vols. (1909) • J. Osborn, 'Reflections on Narcissus Lutrell, 1657–1732', *Book Collector*, 6 (1957), 15–27 • *The parliamentary diary of Narcissus Luttrell, 1691–1693*, ed. H. Horwitz (1972) • BL, Add. MS 70247 • *The manuscripts of his grace the duke of Portland*, 10 vols., HMC, 29 (1891–1931) • Yale U., Beinecke L., Luttrell papers, C65 Osborn shelves • S. Parks and E. Havens, eds., 'The Luttrell file: Narcissus Luttrell's dates on contemporary pamphlets, 1678–1730', *Yale University Library Gazette*, occasional suppl., 3 (1999) [whole issue]

Archives All Souls Oxf., papers • BL, diary, Add. MS 10447 • BL, unfoliated Harley papers, Add. MSS 70201, 70247 • LMA, diary • Yale U., Beinecke L., corresp., notebooks, and annotated library

Wealth at death see will, PRO, PROB 11/653, sig. 210

Luttrell, Robert, **Lord Luttrell** (*d.* **1297**). *See under* Luttrell family (*per. c.*1200–1428).

Luttrell, Simon (*c.*1643–1698), army officer, was the eldest son of Thomas Luttrell (*d.* 1673) of Luttrellstown, co. Dublin, and his wife, Barbara Sedgrave, a daughter of Henry Sedgrave of Cabra, co. Dublin. Henry *Luttrell (1653/4–1717), also subsequently a Jacobite officer, was his brother. He married in 1672 Katherine Newcomen (*d.* 1704), a daughter of Sir Thomas Newcomen, bt, of co. Dublin, and of Frances, a sister of Richard Talbot, earl of Tyrconnell. The marriage was consecrated twice, firstly by a Church of Ireland divine because his wife was a protestant, and secondly by one of his wife's Catholic uncles, Peter Talbot, the archbishop of Dublin, who refused to recognize the first ceremony. In 1673 Luttrell succeeded to an estate of over 4000 acres in the counties of Dublin, Kildare, and Meath.

Luttrell's religion excluded him from any military position until the accession of James II in 1685, when he was granted a captain's commission in Richard Hamilton's regiment of dragoons. When Tyrconnell became the lord deputy of Ireland in January 1687, Luttrell was promoted to the lieutenant-colonelcy of his father-in-law's regiment and made a privy councillor of Ireland. Trapped in England at the time of the revolution, he wrote on Christmas eve 1688 a pathetic letter to the duke of Ormond begging for a pass to leave the country: 'I have been sick these two years. I am now paralytic … If God gives me my health, and if your Grace promises me leave, I will go and serve the Emperor' (Ball, *Manuscripts*, 11). He was allowed to go to France, and within three months he sailed with the exiled King James to Ireland, where he was made a colonel of dragoons.

In May 1689 Luttrell sat as a member for the county of Dublin in the Irish parliament, and in September was appointed the governor of the city. He was responsible for Dublin's security at a time when raids by English men-of-war, armed risings by the protestants, and shortages of essentials were feared and expected. He 'chained up the streets and made breastworks at the entrance into each, to secure that naked place' (*CSP dom.*, *1686–7*, 279). He gave orders prohibiting protestants from carrying arms, assembling in groups of more than five, or going out at night, and issued a proclamation that those who traded in goods at inflated prices 'should be punished with death and hanged at their own doors' (Ball, *Manuscripts*, 382).

Luttrell left Dublin shortly before the arrival of King William's victorious troops after the battle of the Boyne (1 July 1690) and travelled to Limerick. In November 1690 he was part of the delegation sent to France to get King James to remove Tyrconnell as lord lieutenant. The duke of Berwick, who described him as being 'of an obliging disposition' and 'a man of honour' (Berwick, 82), included him in the mission as a moderating influence on his brother (whom Simon had to restrain from throwing Brigadier Maxwell over the side before their ship had left Galway). The mission to France was unsuccessful in that Tyrconnell was not replaced, but Luttrell stayed on in France to urge the French to send more supplies to Ireland.

Despite Luttrell's efforts, the supply fleet he sailed with only reached Ireland on 20 October 1691, almost three weeks after the treaty of Limerick had been signed. Under its terms he was entitled to recover his estates if he submitted to the new government. He instead returned to France and was outlawed in Ireland for high treason. His estate was confiscated and given to his brother Henry. He remained with the exiled Jacobites as colonel of the Queen's regiment in the Irish brigade, with whom he served in Italy and Spain. He was promoted to brigadier in the French army in January 1696, and died in France on 6 September 1698 aged about fifty-five. He was buried in Crest in southern France. He left no children. His wife erected a memorial to his memory in the chapel of the Irish College in Paris before returning to Ireland, where she sued Henry Luttrell for her jointure on the estate. She died in 1704. Her case was taken to the House of Lords by her second husband, Thomas Amory, who emerged triumphant in 1709. J. T. GILBERT, *rev.* PIERS WAUCHOPE

Sources F. E. Ball, *A history of the county Dublin*, 6 vols. (1902–20), vol. 4, pp. 1–19 • *Calendar of the manuscripts of the marquess of Ormonde*, new ser., 8 vols., HMC, 36 (1902–20), vol. 8 • *The manuscripts of the House of Lords*, new ser., 12 vols. (1900–77), vol. 8, pp. 313–15 • C. McNeill, 'Reports on the Rawlinson collection', *Analecta Hibernica*, 1 (1930), 12–178, esp. 79–84 • J. Fitzjames [Duke of Berwick], *Memoirs of the marshal duke of Berwick*, 1 (1779) • W. King, *The state of the protestants of Ireland under the late King James's government*, another edn (1692) • *CSP dom.*, *1673–5*; *1686–90* • J. C. O'Callaghan, *History of the Irish brigades in the service of France*, [new edn] (1870) • P. Wauchope, *Patrick Sarsfield and the Williamite war* (1992) • M. Sandrea, 'The death of Brigadier Simon Luttrell', *Irish Sword*, 20 (1996–7), 184

Luttrell, Temple Simon (**1738?–1803**). *See under* Luttrell, Henry Lawes, second earl of Carhampton (1737–1821).

Lutwyche, Sir Edward (**1634–1709**), judge and politician, was born on 6 September 1634, the only son of William

Lutwyche (*b. c.*1601) of Lutwyche Hall, Shropshire, and Elizabeth, daughter of Richard Lister of Rowton Castle, Shropshire. In 1644 he entered Shrewsbury School, and he was admitted to Gray's Inn on 12 May 1652 and to Lincoln's Inn on 26 May 1652. He evidently chose Gray's Inn, being called to the bar there on 1 June 1660. By this date he had married Anne (*d.* 1722), daughter of Sir Timothy Tourneur of Bold, Shropshire. They had two sons and seven daughters. In January 1684 Lutwyche was made a serjeant-at-law; he was made a king's serjeant on 4 November 1684 and knighted ten days later. Under Chester's new charter of 1684, Lutwyche was named recorder. Following the accession of James II he was made chief justice of Chester in October 1685, and returned to the House of Commons in a by-election for Ludlow on 14 November 1685. He resigned from both positions when elevated to the bench as a justice of common pleas on 21 April 1686. In his new position Lutwyche upheld the dispensing power, although not in ecclesiastical cases, and thus retained his seat on the bench until the revolution of 1688.

Lutwyche's stance on the dispensing power ensured that he was exempted from the Act of Indemnity of 1690. He returned to private practice and was fined 40*s.* for refusing the oaths at York assizes in April 1693. He was still practising in 1704. Lutwyche's death was reported by Luttrell on 11 June 1709 and he was buried in St Bride's, Fleet Street. The main beneficiary of his will was his son Thomas *Lutwyche, an important tory lawyer, who received his father's books, chambers, and 'the manuscripts by me prepared as an abridgement of the Common Law', which was to 'be printed and published at and by the care and inspection and collation of my son Thomas'. This was the work published in 1718 in both folio and octavo editions. STUART HANDLEY

Sources HoP, *Commons, 1660–90*, 2.783 • Sainty, *Judges*, 78 • Baker, *Serjeants*, 448, 524 • Sainty, *King's counsel*, 22 • R. Tresswell and A. Vincent, *The visitation of Shropshire, taken in the year 1623*, ed. G. Grazebrook and J. P. Rylands, 2, Harleian Society, 29 (1889), 346–7 • will, PRO, PROB 11/527, sig. 95 • will, PRO, PROB 11/585, sig. 241 [Anne Lutwyche] • *Le Neve's Pedigrees of the knights*, ed. G. W. Marshall, Harleian Society, 8 (1873), 391 • J. Foster, *The register of admissions to Gray's Inn, 1521–1889, together with the register of marriages in Gray's Inn chapel, 1695–1754* (privately printed, London, 1889), 261 • W. P. Baildon, ed., *The records of the Honorable Society of Lincoln's Inn: admissions*, 1 (1896), 265 • R. J. Fletcher, ed., *The pension book of Gray's Inn*, 1 (1901), 430 • N. Luttrell, *A brief historical relation of state affairs from September 1678 to April 1714*, 6 (1857), 452 • A. Boyer, *The political state of Great Britain*, 24 (1722), 656 • Foss, *Judges*, 7.254

Likenesses R. White, line engraving, 1703 (after T. Murray), BM, NPG; repro. in *Reports* (1704) • print (after T. Murray), Serjeant's Inn

Lutwyche, Thomas (*bap.* **1674**, *d.* **1734**), lawyer, was baptized on 21 September 1674, the first surviving son of Sir Edward *Lutwyche (1634–1709), justice of the common pleas, and his wife, Anne (*d.* 1722), daughter of Sir Timothy Tourneur. Lutwyche was a king's scholar at Westminster School, and was elected to Christ Church, Oxford, where he matriculated on 4 July 1692, but took no degree. He was called to the bar at the Inner Temple in 1697, was reader there in 1715, and treasurer of the inn in 1722. Lutwyche was made QC towards the end of Queen Anne's reign, and was an able lawyer. He was married to Elizabeth, daughter of William Bagnall of Bretforton, Worcestershire; they had two sons and three daughters.

A member of the October Club, Lutwyche was returned as MP for Appleby by Lord Thanet in 1710, and held the seat until 1722. He was MP for Callington, Cornwall, between 1722 and 1727, and for Agmondesham, Buckinghamshire, from 1728 to his death. A high tory, Lutwyche delivered, on 6 November 1723, a strong speech in parliament against the bill for laying a tax upon papists. In 1725 he was one of the organizers of the trial of Lord Chancellor Macclesfield; and he was said to have refused the post of attorney-general in succession to Sir Robert Raymond.

Lutwyche died on 13 November 1734 and was buried at the Inner Temple Church. Among his papers were some manuscript reports of 'select cases, arguments and pleadings' in the queen's bench in the reign of Queen Anne. These were first published in 1781 as a supplement to the authoritative *Modern Reports* of cases since the accession of Charles II. J. M. RIGG, *rev.* ROBERT BROWN

Sources HoP, *Commons* • Foster, *Alum. Oxon.* • *Old Westminsters*

Lutyens, Sir Edwin Landseer (1869–1944), architect, was born on 29 March 1869 at 16 Onslow Square, London, the ninth son and tenth of the thirteen surviving children of Captain Charles Henry Augustus Lutyens (1829–1915), soldier and painter, the great-grandson of Nicolaus Lütkens, a merchant of Dutch origins who moved from Hamburg to London in the 1730s. Captain Lutyens, the son of Charles Lutyens, deputy commissary-general of the British army, served in the 20th regiment of foot in Montreal, Canada, where, in 1852, he married Mary Theresa Gallwey (1832/3–1906) from Killarney, the daughter of a major in the Royal Irish Constabulary, who had abandoned her Roman Catholic faith and become a devout evangelical protestant. On returning to England, Charles Lutyens had invented the stadiometer, a range-finder for artillery, before leaving the army to become an animal painter. He became a close friend of Sir Edwin Landseer, who wanted to adopt the future architect; but his mother, who disapproved of the artist's morals, would not part with him.

Education and marriage Ned (as Edwin was known) Lutyens had rheumatic fever when young and was considered too delicate to go to public school (although he attended Sutherland House, a boarding-school in Wandsworth, for about two years). He later told Osbert Sitwell,

> Any talent I may have had … was due to a long illness as a boy, which afforded me time to think, and to subsequent ill-health, because I was not allowed to play games, and so had to teach myself, for my enjoyment, to use my eyes instead of my feet. My brothers hadn't the same advantage.
> (O. Sitwell, *The Scarlet Tree*, 1946, 266)

In 1876 Lutyens's mother acquired The Cottage at Thursley, near Godalming, as a second home, and the family then spent half the year in the country. This enabled Lutyens to experience rural Surrey; he would roam the countryside and visit the local carpenter or the builder's yard in Godalming and so acquired a profound knowledge of

Sir Edwin Landseer Lutyens (1869–1944), by Meredith Frampton, 1935

traditional building craftsmanship. He also drew the outline of cottages and barns on a sheet of glass with pieces of soap, thereby developing the acute comprehension of three-dimensional form in terms of wall and roof planes which characterized his architecture.

Possibly on the advice of the artist Randolph Caldecott, a neighbour in Thursley, Lutyens was enrolled in 1885 at the National Art Training School in South Kensington, close to his London home. He left after two years without finishing the course. Lutyens then became an articled pupil in the office of Ernest George and Peto in London. He would later disparage George's love of sketching, but it was in this office that Lutyens learned how to draw. It was also here that he met the architect Herbert Baker, who later recalled how Lutyens,

> though joking through his short pupillage, quickly absorbed all that was best worth learning: he puzzled us at first, but we soon found that he seemed to know by intuition some great truths of our art which were not to be learned there. ('Architecture and personalities', *Country Life*, 1944, 15)

Lutyens stayed with George for only a year before setting up on his own early in 1889 at the age of nineteen, having received a commission from a family friend, Arthur Chapman, to design Crooksbury, a house near Farnham, Surrey. The first phase of this house and Lutyens's other early buildings are not particularly remarkable. They reflect the influence of Ernest George in the use of the vernacular manner of the home counties of England, whose revival had been the basis of modern domestic architecture for several decades. Lutyens greatly admired the houses of Richard Norman Shaw, in whose office he would have preferred to study, and those of Philip Webb, on whom he published an obituary article in 1915, recalling that:

> The freshness and originality which Webb maintained in all his work I, in my ignorance, attributed to youth. I did not recognise it then to be the eternal youth of genius, though it was conjoined with another attribute of genius—thoroughness. (Lutyens, 'Webb')

Lutyens first met his principal mentor, Gertrude Jekyll, in 1889. Her interest in the young architect combined with her knowledge of the traditional building crafts of Surrey became crucial to his development and she became his constant and indispensable collaborator in designing the gardens of his houses. Aunt Bumps, as he called her, became hugely important to Lutyens and introduced him, directly or indirectly, to many of his future clients—not least Edward Hudson, the editor of the magazine *Country Life*, whose patronage and publicity greatly helped to advance his career. As Lawrence Weaver wrote, 'it would be difficult to exaggerate the importance of her influence' (Weaver, xviii).

Munstead Wood, a new house near Godalming for Miss Jekyll, was built in 1895–7 after several years of discussion with her young architect friend. Built of local stone and oak timbers by local builders, it was Lutyens's first sophisticated essay in reinterpreting the domestic vernacular of Surrey, and his client was pleased to find that 'there is nothing sham-old about it; it is not trumped-up with any specious or fashionable devices of spurious antiquity' (G. Jekyll, *Home and Garden*, 1900, 1). Munstead Wood was much visited and admired, and it led to other commissions. The solicitor William Chance and his wife, having seen the house nearing completion, immediately decided to change architects for Orchards, their proposed new house near by, thereby launching Lutyens's reputation of being somewhat over-anxious to obtain work.

This success coincided with his marriage, in August 1897, to Lady Emily Bulwer-Lytton (1874–1964) [*see* Lutyens, Lady Emily], daughter of the late Edward Bulwer-*Lytton, first earl of Lytton (1831–1891), viceroy of India, whose wife, Edith Bulwer-*Lytton, *née* Villiers (1841–1936) [*see under* Lytton, Edward Bulwer-], the dowager countess of Lytton, initially opposed the match. Lutyens was and remained much in love with Lady Emily, and his regular and expansive correspondence with her when they were apart is a principal source of documentation for his life. It was, nevertheless, a union of two strong-willed individuals with little in common; Lady Emily's withdrawal from the physical side of marriage after the birth of their five children combined with her serious involvement with theosophy and infatuation with Krishnamurti eventually led to near-estrangement, as has been described by their youngest daughter, Mary (*Edwin Lutyens by his Daughter*). Before their official engagement Lutyens presented Emily with an exquisite casket containing, among other items, the drawings for an ideal 'little White House' in the country. In the event, the family always lived in Georgian houses in London—first at 29 Bloomsbury

Square until 1914, then at 31 Bedford Square until 1919, and then at 13 Mansfield Street.

Houses and gardens Marriage had an immediate impact on Lutyens's career by increasing the need to secure more work. To satisfy the Lytton family he had been obliged to take out a life insurance policy for £11,000 and this contributed to the financial difficulties, incompetently managed, which worried him for the rest of his life. Marriage to the daughter of an earl did not, however, lead to aristocratic commissions, although it certainly provoked the jealousy of his architect contemporaries. It may have given the shy young architect greater social confidence but, as Mary Lutyens concluded:

> he met nearly all his clients directly or indirectly through the Jekylls. Apart from the house he built for his mother-in-law [Homewood, 1900–01] and St Martin's Church, both at Knebworth, the commissions he did get through his wife might equally well have come if he had never met her. (M. Lutyens, *Edwin Lutyens*, 62)

Lutyens became accomplished at finding wealthy 'patrons' (as he preferred to call them), and keeping them. Oswald P. Milne noted that 'He had a wonderful way with clients. He was marvellous not only in dealing with materials but in dealing with human beings. He always got them to spend what he wanted them to spend' ('Reminiscences on Sir Edwin Lutyens', 232). Lutyens seldom worked for the landed aristocracy, and although he did not secure any South African tycoons, most of his clients were self-made or second-generation rich—bankers, solicitors, shipowners, publishers, stockbrokers—together with a few of the cultivated imperialist bullies who set the tone of the Edwardian period. Some were rather dubious, like Willie James, the half-American crony of Edward VII. Typical, perhaps, was Julius Drew, the founder of Home and Colonial Stores, who would add an 'e' to his name and ask Lutyens to build him an ancestral castle in Devon.

In 1897 Lutyens was busy with twenty-five jobs, including five new houses: Fulbrook, Berry Down, Orchards, Sullingstead, and The Pleasaunce at Overstrand. Over the next few years followed a series of romantic houses designed in a vernacular manner reinterpreted with unusual wit and control; these confirmed his reputation and led to his being described in Hermann Muthesius's study *Das englische Haus* (1904) as 'a young man who of recent years has come increasingly to the forefront of domestic architects and who may soon become the accepted leader among English builders of houses, like Norman Shaw in the past' (Muthesius, *The English House*, ed. D. Sharp, translated J. Seligman, 1979, 55).

Such houses included Overstrand Hall (1898–9); Tigbourne Court (1899–1901); Goddards (1899)—in fact, a 'home of rest' for 'ladies of small means'—and Marsh Court (1901–4), a *tour de force* in brick, flint, and chalk. Perhaps the most representative of these early houses was the Deanery Garden at Sonning (1899–1901) for Edward Hudson of *Country Life*, described by Lutyens's biographer, Christopher Hussey, as 'a perfect architectural sonnet, compounded of brick and tile and timber forms' (Hussey, *Life*, 95). Here—as elsewhere—the architecture of the house was integrated with the formally composed gardens by the projection of visual axes and solid walls. Thinking of these early houses, Lutyens's great American contemporary, Frank Lloyd Wright, wrote in 1951 how 'To him the English chimney, the Gable, the Gatepost monumentalized in good brickwork and cut-stone were motifs to be dramatized with great skill' (Wright, 260).

There were, however, several rather more eccentric houses designed by Lutyens which were influenced by the art nouveau as well as by the work of C. F. A. Voysey; deliberately excluded from the pages of *Country Life*, these remain less well known. One was The Ferry inn at Rosneath, Argyll (1897–8), commissioned by Princess Louise, and it was on the way there that Lutyens encountered the Glasgow tea-room interiors designed by his contemporary Charles Rennie Mackintosh. The most notable of these inventive designs, which indicate the possibility that Lutyens might have followed a very different course of development, is Le Bois des Moutiers at Varengeville-sur-Mer designed for the Anglophile banker Guillaume Mallet, whom he met on his first visit to Paris in 1898 in the course of designing the British pavilion for the Paris Exhibition of 1900.

Heathcote, a large villa at Ilkley designed in 1905, represented a very different approach. Inspired by the work of Michele Sanmicheli at Verona, it is an inventive essay in mannerism which revealed that Lutyens was seeking to engage in a more challenging language of form. 'In architecture Palladio is the game!! It is so big—few appreciate it now, and it requires training to value and to realise it,' he had written to Herbert Baker in 1903 (Hussey, *Life*, 121), and, eight years later, in a celebrated letter of January 1911, describing Heathcote to Herbert Baker, he wrote of:

> that time-worn doric order … You can't copy it. To be right you have to take it and design it … It means hard labour, hard thinking, over every line in all three dimensions and in every joint, and no stone can be allowed to slide. (ibid., 133)

But if Heathcote represents a profound change in Lutyens's thinking, he did not repeat the experiment. What would be used again were such personal mannerisms as the pilaster which 'disappeared' into the rustication between base and capital. 'Architecture is building with wit,' Lutyens remarked (ibid., 164), although for many such persistent visual jokes eventually palled.

In later Edwardian houses, such as the Salutation at Sandwich (1911) and Great Maytham (1907–9), Lutyens used a simpler classical manner—what he described as the 'Wrennaissance' style. Middlefield, near Cambridge (1908–9), in its austere simplicity and masterly handling of roof planes and chimneys, suggests that a distinctive modern English domestic architecture could have evolved out of Lutyens's abstraction of the Georgian tradition. Nor was Lutyens's domestic work a simple progression from the vernacular to the classical, from the picturesque to the axial and symmetrical, as some commentators have insisted, for he had been using classical elements—and playing games with them—almost from the beginning.

Grey Walls, Gullane (1900–02), fused the vernacular

with the classical through insistent geometry; at Little Thakeham (1902–3), an Elizabethan exterior contains a baroque great hall and at Papillon Hall (1903–4) Palladian elements were combined with half-timbering on the fashionable Edwardian 'butterfly' plan. Lutyens's delight in paradox is perhaps supremely demonstrated at Folly Farm, Sulhampstead, where the original building of 1906 was designed in the William and Mary manner but was enlarged six years later by a brick wing with huge sweeping roofs of tile which Lutyens called his 'cowsheds'. This is a work which exemplifies his claim that 'There is wit and may be humour in the use of material. The unexpected, where it is logical, is fun' (Lutyens, talk at Architectural Association, 56).

Very few of these buildings were country houses in the traditional sense. Most are best described as 'villas'—that is, comparatively small and tightly planned residences for the wealthy which were essentially adjuncts to cities and were intended for entertaining at weekends. In such houses Lutyens displayed a mastery of domestic planning, separating functions and making the visitor perform an often circuitous route from entry to principal room. Lutyens was generous with circulation spaces and Sir Nikolaus Pevsner noted that 'England has never been particularly keen on ingenious or monumental stairs, and Lutyens's are among the finest she has produced' (Pevsner, 225). Comparisons have been made between the plans of Lutyens's houses and the contemporary work of Frank Lloyd Wright in the United States, and although neither architect influenced the other, the American admired the Englishman because, as the South African-born architect Allan Greenberg has written, 'in Lutyens he found a great mind grappling with related problems, and using similar organizational principles' (Greenberg, 147).

A further category of Lutyens's houses are those in which he developed an abstracted language of form seemingly derived from military architecture. In 1903 he had restored and altered Lindisfarne Castle for Edward Hudson but he had already tried the style in the brick Red House at Godalming (1899), a brilliant design on a spiral plan placed on the side of a steep hill. Similar austere abstraction would be employed at Abbey House at Barrow in Furness (1913–14), a guest house for Messrs Vickers, and in the additions to Penheale Manor, but the masterpiece in this manner is Castle Drogo in Devon (1912–30), an essay in the sculptural handling of planes of granite in which the grand corridors and staircases seem much more impressive than the principal rooms. What survives today is less than half of what was originally proposed for Julius Drewe in 1910 but it confirms Pevsner's opinion that 'Sir Edwin Lutyens was without doubt the greatest folly builder England has ever seen. Castle Drogo beats Fonthill' (Pevsner, 219). Lutyens was an expensive architect to employ, yet he wrote of his client: 'Only I do wish he didn't want a Castle, but just a delicious loveable house with plenty of good large rooms in it' (Lutyens to Lady Emily Lutyens, 3 Aug 1910, *Letters*).

Imperial architect Lutyens's achievement in domestic architecture was celebrated by Lawrence Weaver in the illustrated book *Houses and Gardens by E. L. Lutyens*, published in 1913 at a time when his career had changed direction dramatically. The first drawings for Castle Drogo were made *en route* for South Africa, where he was to build the Johannesburg Art Gallery (1911–40) and where his old friend Herbert Baker was working on the Union Buildings for the government at Pretoria. Lutyens had already designed the premises for *Country Life* in the manner of Wren at Hampton Court in 1904, and for some time had been hoping to secure a 'big work'. He had been bitterly disappointed by his failure in the competition for the county hall in London in 1908 but was invited to design the two churches and other buildings in the centre of Hampstead Garden Suburb that same year; this was his first foray into town planning and showed that his vision was now much more formal than that of Raymond Unwin. Lutyens paid homage to Wren in the design for the British Pavilion at the international exhibition in Rome in 1911 (subsequently rebuilt as the British School in Rome) but the opportunity he had been hoping for eventually came in another continent.

In January 1912 Lutyens was asked to join the commission of experts to advise the government of India on the site and planning of the new capital, whose transfer from Calcutta to Delhi had been announced the previous year. On the understanding that he would be given the central buildings to design, he set out with Captain Swinton, chairman-elect of the London county council, who understood the politics of town planning, and John A. Brodie, city engineer of Liverpool. Eventually Lutyens left a dominant imprint on the new city and designed Viceroy's House (now Rashtrapati Bhavan), his supreme masterpiece, at its heart; an impeccable and inventive statement in his personal, monumental classicism, it is arguably one of the finest buildings in the world. In the long and complicated history of this project, what is impressive is how Lutyens succeeded in realizing his aesthetic ideals despite the vacillations of the viceroy, Lord Hardinge of Penshurst, together with conflicting political opinions over the style of the government buildings, the machinations of other, jealous architects, and the compromising deliberations of civil servants.

Lutyens's appointment as architect was confirmed only in January 1913, along with that of Herbert Baker who, at his suggestion, was brought in to design the secretariat buildings. The political imperative, that such important structures should reflect oriental as well as Western values, was energetically resisted by Lutyens, who argued against the use of the Mughal pointed arch by claiming that 'One cannot tinker with the round arch. God did not make the Eastern rainbow pointed to show his wide sympathies' (letter to Baker, 29 Aug 1913, Hussey, *Life*, 296). Lutyens was at first disparaging about the indigenous architecture of the subcontinent, writing that, 'There is no trace of any Wren. Is there an Isaac Newton? I doubt it. Without the one you cannot have the other' (ibid., 277). In the event, however, Lutyens fused Indian elements, both Mughal and Hindu, into his architectural language while he wrapped the Buddhist railing from the stupa at Sanchi around the central imperious dome of Viceroy's House.

Lutyens later observed:

> East and West can and do meet, with mutual respect and affection … There are two ways of building in India, one to parade your building in fancy dress … or to build as an Englishman dressed for the climate, conscious only that your tailor is of Agra or Benares, and not of Savile Row or Petticoat Lane. ('Sir Edwin Lutyens at the A.A.')

He was obliged to scale down the design over the winter of 1913–14 while retaining the precise geometry and coherence of the concept, Herbert Baker recording in 1931: 'I watched silently and with admiration Lutyens's tenacity in his fight with the Viceroy and the Government' (Hussey, *Life*, 321). Viceroy's House is larger and finer than Versailles; as the American historian Henry-Russell Hitchcock observed:

> Towards the designing of such a major monument generations of Frenchmen and others who had studied at the Beaux-Arts had been prepared; there is a certain irony that the opportunity came to an Englishman, trained in the most private and individualistic English way. (*Architecture: 19th & 20th Centuries*, 1968, 407)

It was Baker's idea, to which Lutyens acceded, that all the government buildings should be raised up on a single acropolis—Raisina Hill, to the south-west of the old walled city of Delhi. Owing to illness and overwork, it was only later that Lutyens fully appreciated that the gradient of the axial approach between the secretariat buildings must obscure the view of the portico of Viceroy's House from the Great Place below Raisina Hill. This became a cause of bitter dissension between the two architects and, despite the support of the king, Lutyens was defeated on this issue in 1916. He never forgave his former friend for this apparent surrender to expediency over what he regarded as a transcendent aesthetic issue; Lutyens had met, as he characteristically put it, his 'Bakerloo'.

Originally it had been planned that New Delhi would be completed by 1918 but owing to the First World War—which resulted in the temporary cessation of the architects' annual winter visits to India—and then to subsequent political uncertainty, it took much longer. Viceroy's House was not occupied until 1929 and the city was inaugurated only in 1931. Many other architects were involved in its creation, most of them under the inspiration of Lutyens rather than Baker, such as Robert Tor Russell, responsible for many of the houses and bungalows; Henry Medd, who designed the two churches, now cathedrals, in New Delhi; and Arthur Shoosmith, Lutyens's permanent representative in India who designed the remarkable St Martin's garrison church. In January 1931 Lutyens and his wife travelled out to India for the official opening of the new capital together with Edward Hudson; Lady Emily Lutyens wrote home that Hudson was 'so moved that he can hardly keep from tears. He said to me yesterday "Poor old Christopher Wren could never have done this!"' (Hussey, *Life*, 522). Hudson was surely right.

War memorials Lutyens was knighted in the new year honours in 1918 for his work at Delhi and for his unpaid advice to the Imperial War Graves Commission. His role in commemorating the British dead of the First World War was responsible for his becoming a national figure. In July 1919 the prime minister, Lloyd George, asked Lutyens to design a temporary 'catafalque' in Whitehall for the planned peace celebrations, to which the architect replied, 'not a catafalque but a Cenotaph' (Hussey, *Life*, 392). The design was apparently completed that same day. So perfectly did the tall, slim pylon with its alternate set-backs supporting a symbolic sarcophagus express the grief of a mourning nation that the popular demand arose that it should be re-erected in stone. Seemingly simple, the permanent Cenotaph, unveiled on armistice day 1920, is a monument of extraordinary subtlety, all its surfaces being curved according to calculations based on the *entasis* or optical corrections of the Parthenon. Other war memorials included those at Dublin, Leicester, and Rochdale, and Lutyens was responsible for the mercantile marine memorial on Tower Hill, London.

An abstracted monumental classicism—what Christopher Hussey called his 'Elemental Mode'—also characterized Lutyens's work for the Imperial War Graves Commission. He had been approached by Fabian Ware, the creator of the commission, in July 1917 to visit France and to advise on the design of the proposed permanent war cemeteries. He was deeply moved by the experience, writing how:

> the battlefields—the obliteration of all human endeavour, achievement, and the human achievement of destruction, is bettered by the poppies and wild flowers—that are as friendly to an unexploded shell as they are to the leg of a garden seat in Surrey [and how] the only monument can be one in which the endeavour is sincere to make such a monument permanent—a solid ball of bronze! (Lutyens to Lady Emily Lutyens, 12 July 1917, *Letters*)

In the event Lutyens's recommendations had a dominant influence on the work of the commission. Humanist rather than conventionally Anglican in outlook, he was in favour of a uniform, secular headstone and strongly opposed to placing a Christian cross in every cemetery (whose advocate was, typically, Herbert Baker), proposing instead that each should have 'one great fair stone of fine proportions … raised upon three steps' (Hussey, *Life*, 374), a sort of altar which became his Stone of Remembrance, modelled with pronounced *entasis*. As one of the three (later four) principal architects to the commission for France and Belgium, Lutyens was responsible for 126 of the war cemeteries, usually working with one of the several assistant architects, who were strongly influenced by his conception of a resonant monumentality combined with the use of careful planting of shrubs and trees (on which Gertude Jekyll advised). The largest and best-known was that at Étaples, where twin cenotaphs on arched pylons stand above the graves, each with the still, stone flags which Lutyens wanted to have in Whitehall..

With half of the million British empire war dead buried, there yet remained the problem of those casualties whose bodies were never found or identified. It was the commission's policy to erect memorials to the missing on which their names were to be carved. Lutyens designed that in the faubourg d'Amiens cemetery at Arras (1927–32). He also designed the Australian memorial at Villers-Bretonneux (1936–8), unaccountably superseding the winner of a competition for the memorial, William Lucas. But the largest and most impressive was the memorial to the missing of the Somme at Thiepval (1927–32). This was the culmination of an interest in the triumphal arch form which began with the Rand regiments' memorial in Johannesburg (1911–12) and the realization of a novel conception of an arched structure—first proposed for an unexecuted memorial at St Quentin—in which a hierarchy of arched tunnels pierced the structure on two axes while the cubic masses of masonry stepped back on alternate planes according to Lutyens's personal sensibility. This exercise in precise geometry and proportion created enough wall space on which to carve the names of 73,357 men missing from the Somme offensive of 1916. An awesome exercise in intellectual formal control, the Thiepval Arch is the defining monument of the British experience of the First World War as well, arguably, as the finest monumental structure raised by a British architect in the twentieth century.

Late work A harmonic hierarchy of arches on two axes also governed the design of the interior of the Metropolitan (Roman Catholic) Cathedral in Liverpool, which was commissioned by Archbishop Richard Downey in 1929. Lutyens's proposal, which was for a cathedral twice as large as St Paul's in London and with a dome wider than that of St Peter's in Rome, expressed his admiration for Wren but also, in the visual integration between exterior elevations and the vaulted interior spaces, revealed a continuing concern with truthful expression which perhaps derived from the Gothic revival. The design was a conception of the highest intellectual and mathematical sophistication in which the resolution of nave and aisles with the central domed space resolved problems which had defeated Michelangelo and Wren. The design was exhibited at the Royal Academy in 1934 in the form of a colossal wooden model made by Messrs John B. Thorp (now at the Walker Art Gallery, Liverpool). Work began in 1933 but by the time the Second World War effectively put an end to the project, only a portion of the crypt had been built. Nevertheless, wrote Sir John Summerson, 'It will survive as an architectural creation of the highest order, perhaps as the latest and supreme attempt to embrace Rome, Byzantium, the Romanesque and the Renaissance in one triumphal and triumphant synthesis' ('Arches of triumph', *Lutyens: the Work of … Sir Edwin Lutyens*, 52).

Lutyens designed comparatively few country houses in the 1920s and 1930s. Gledstone Hall, Yorkshire (1923–6, with Richard Jaques), was his most formal, classical design, considered by A. S. G. Butler, who compiled the Lutyens Memorial volumes, as 'a work of art worthy of being listed, one day, as a national monument' (Butler, 1.55), although later generations have found it less admirable than the architect's earlier houses. The British embassy in Washington, DC (1927–30), was designed in a similar domestic manner, but in brick. Middleton Park, Oxfordshire, for Lord Jersey (1935–8), was Lutyens's last house and the only one built for a member of the old landed aristocracy. It was designed in collaboration with Lutyens's only son, Robert, from whom he had earlier been estranged.

The application of a chequer-board pattern to the elevations of the blocks of council flats in Page Street for Westminster city council (1929–30) was a novel essay in abstraction but it was an unfortunate commission partly because Lutyens had no particular interest in this building type but also because he created controversy by taking on the job from another architect. Benson Court for Magdalene College, Cambridge (1928–32), and Campion Hall for the Jesuits in Oxford (1935–42) were more sympathetic works while The Drum inn at Cockington, Devon (1934–6), showed that Lutyens, even in his sixties, would still devote care to a commission which interested him and that he had not lost his love of the sweet vernacular of southern England despite his mature concern with proportional systems and extending the language of classicism.

Much of Lutyens's work between the world wars was the result of acting as consultant for the exterior design of commercial buildings. One former pupil suggested that in this 'big business epoch … something in the subject was not quite appropriate to his special talent' (J. M[urray] E[aston], *Architectural Association Journal*, 59, Jan 1944, 48) and Lutyens would probably not wish to be remembered by his commissions on the Grosvenor estate in London. More deserving of respect is Britannic House in Finsbury Circus for the Anglo-Iranian Oil Co. (1920–24), a magnificent if flawed attempt to apply the language of Palladio to a seven-storey steel-framed structure. The façades Lutyens designed for buildings of the Midland Bank, owing to his friendship with Reginald McKenna, chairman of the bank, are more inventive and more successful. For the head office in Poultry in the City of London (with Gotch and Saunders, 1924–39), a grand classical building in a canyon-like street, he experimented with unusual combinations of forms and with intimidatingly precise optical corrections and dimensions. The Midland Bank in Manchester (1933–5) is an austere miniature skyscraper modelled with the architect's acute sculptural feeling.

During these years Lutyens indulged in the contemporary enthusiasm for replanning London for modern conditions and he worked with Sir Charles Bressey on the highway development survey, published in 1938 as the Bressey–Lutyens report. In 1930 criticism of his role as adviser to the London county council over the bill for rebuilding the Charing Cross Bridge provoked his resignation from the Royal Institute of British Architects—an institution with which his relations had often been cool (afterwards he became president of the Incorporated Association of Architects and Surveyors but rejoined the institute in 1939). He was a member of the Royal Fine Arts Commission at its foundation in 1924. Although an established knighted architect, Lutyens never lost the respect of the younger generation who warmed to his wit and irreverence, as well as appreciating his genius. This continuing admiration was shown by Robert Byron's eulogy in the special January 1931 number of the *Architectural Review* which celebrated the completion of New Delhi and vicariously settled old scores by damning the contributions of Sir Herbert Baker.

As for the new architecture being imported from continental Europe, 'These adventurous young men thrill me tremendously and all my sympathies are with them,' Lutyens insisted in 1931 in one of his very few published writings; 'But good architecture needs more than bright ideas, and by my traditional standards most modern buildings seem to me to lack style and cohesion, besides being unfriendly and crude' (Lutyens, 'What I think of modern architecture', 777). However, in his interest in abstraction and geometry, and in his intuitive and inventive comprehension of form in three dimensions, Lutyens's architecture was not as far removed from that of Le Corbusier as has often been supposed. He remained, however, concerned with the texture and colour of traditional building materials. 'My generation is—perhaps I ought to say was—a humanist generation,' Lutyens explained.

> We believed that the measure of man's architecture was man, and that the rhythm of a building should correspond to the rhythms familiar in human life. All architecture must have rhythms, that affect the eye as music does the ear, producing vibrations in the brain. (ibid., 775)

The office and family As his career flourished, Lutyens inspired devotion from his young assistants, who were not well paid but were treated kindly and with respect. He demanded high standards and often complained that 'They never realize that a working drawing is merely a letter to a builder telling him precisely what is required of him—and not a picture wherewith to charm an idiotic client' (Lutyens to Lady Emily Lutyens, 5 Feb 1897, *Letters*). Oswald P. Milne worked for Lutyens in 1902–5 when the office was on the ground floor of the house in Bloomsbury Square 'and was a fairly domestic affair', and he recalled that:

> Lutyens occupied the front room, and the large back room was the drawing office, with perhaps three pupils and three or four draughtsmen. There was also a little office by the stairs where the secretary worked. I believe that the telephone had just been introduced … He was a great worker. If not visiting a job, he stood working at his drawing-board in the front office—I do not remember him ever sitting down—legs apart and usually smoking a pipe. He spoke somewhat incoherently; he never explained himself; his wonderful fund of ideas and invention were expressed not in speech but at the end of his pencil. If we were in difficulties we would invite him to come over and help us out. He would put a piece of tracing-paper over the drawing, and in a minute or two he had sketched half-a-dozen solutions to the problem. He then put a ring round the one he preferred and left us to carry it out. He never gave explanations or talked about the work, but somehow we managed to pick up what he wanted. ('Reminiscences on Sir Edwin Lutyens', 232)

Lutyens first opened an office at 6 Gray's Inn Square. In 1910 the office was transferred from the family house in Bloomsbury Square to 17 Queen Anne's Gate, moving to 5 Eaton Gate in 1931, while in 1913 a separate office for the New Delhi drawings was opened at 7 Apple Tree Yard, Westminster, moving to 17 Bolton Street in 1924. Lutyens's informal partnership with E. Baynes Badcock proved highly unsatisfactory and ended after three years in 1901. He was succeeded as office manager by A. J. Thomas, who ran the office during Lutyens's absences and finally left in 1935. Lutyens was afterwards assisted by his son Robert. Edward Hall and George Stewart were both long-serving assistants upon whom Lutyens relied. In addition to the New Delhi representatives, assistants and pupils who later achieved eminence on their own included J. J. Joass, J. D. Coleridge, Milne, H. L. North, J. Murray Easton, Sir Hubert Worthington, and Sir Basil Spence.

When the office was in Bloomsbury Square there was a rigid demarcation between the office and the domestic areas of the house. Here Lutyens's five children were born: Barbara (1898–1981), who married Euan Wallace and, after his death in 1941, Herbert Agar; Robert (1901–1972); Ursula (1904–1967), who married Viscount Ridley; (Agnes) Elisabeth *Lutyens (1906–1983), the composer; and (Edith Penelope) Mary *Lutyens (1908–1999), the novelist and biographer, who later observed that 'I suppose we were lucky in that none of us was called Gertrude' (M. Lutyens, *Edwin Lutyens*, 61).

By the 1920s, when the family had moved to Mansfield Street, Lutyens's relations with his wife were at their most strained owing to her infatuation with Krishnamurti as well as her potentially embarrassing sympathy for Indian nationalism. With her knowledge and approval, however, he found compensation with Lady Sackville, whom he had first met in 1916 in Lady Cunard's box at Covent Garden. They became very close for a while and 'Lady MacSack' provided 'McNed' (as he called them) with his first car, a Rolls Royce, and helped him financially. Josephine Victoria Sackville-West (1862–1936), mother of Vita, was half-Spanish, the illegitimate daughter of one Lord Sackville and the estranged wife of another; she was very possessive and emotionally unbalanced, and by 1932 was writing to the president of the RIBA accusing Lutyens of malpractice over work he had done for her. At this time Lady Emily Lutyens was becoming reconciled with her husband, and later recalled that:

> If it had not been for [his] extraordinary understanding and patience, and his great love, there would long ago have been a complete break-up of my home … He seemed to understand without words all I was going through and welcomed me back without a single reproach or reminder of how much of our lives together I had wasted. In the last years of his life I like to think that we were closer to each other than we had ever been before. (*Candles in the Sun*, 1957, 186)

By this time Lutyens had become a popular social figure, much in demand for lunch and dinner parties because of his flippant unorthodoxy and humour. Many examples of Lutyens's huge fund of puns and jokes have been recorded; he was also an inspired caricaturist and cartoonist. His comprehension was visual and emotional rather than verbal, and his often inspired inarticulateness seems to have been a defence of an essentially shy man against the world. 'Lutyens's public appearances are few. If he has to make a speech he reads it very badly, in an undertone, like a sulky child made to play charades,' John Summerson recorded (anonymously) in 1937. 'But if a discussion interests him volleys of devastating wit come popping out all the time' (Summerson, 'Architect laureate'). Behind all the jokes, however, Lutyens was a profoundly serious artist, intolerant of any compromise which might undermine the pure integrity of his architectural conceptions.

Sir Osbert Sitwell wrote that: 'One had never seen before, and will never see again, anyone who resembled this singular and delightful man. An expression of mischievous benevolence was his distinguishing mark' (O. Sitwell, *Great Morning*, 1948, 19). Most of his clients were very happy with their architect, often returning for more, and many became loyal friends. Other close friends included the artist Sir William Nicholson and the author and playwright Sir James Barrie, for whom Lutyens designed the stage sets for *Quality Street* in 1902. He was also a witty and resourceful designer of furniture and retained a taste for unusual ideas for interior decoration such as black walls and green-dragged floors.

The idea of building an elaborate doll's house to present to Queen Mary emerged at a dinner party given in 1920 by Sir Herbert Morgan at which Lutyens, Princess Marie Louise, and E. V. Lucas were present. Lutyens designed this giant miniature building and co-ordinated the various artists and craftsmen involved in its creation. It was assembled in Lutyens's house in Mansfield Street before being exhibited at the British Empire Exhibition at Wembley in 1924, and is now on display in Windsor Castle. The ingratiating whimsy of the conception reflected the concerns of a disorientated nation recovering from a world war as well as compensating for Lutyens's frustration over the slow progress at New Delhi at the time; as a design it was the most pompous and least interesting of his creations.

Lutyens was of above average height with unusually long legs; John Summerson recorded that he was:

> a rather big man with a phenomenally round, bald head fixed with wonderful precision on his shoulders. He has small, very blue, provocatively innocent eyes, curiously set; vaguely like portraits of Inigo Jones. He wears a steep butterfly collar and a neat, ordinary tie, and moves with a certain critical, half-humorous deliberation, by no means unimpressive. He smokes absurd little pipes, specially made for him … You rarely see him but in the company of a pack of fans, sniggering at his cracks and wondering what the great Lut will say or do next. Bores all over the Empire hoard his doodles, do their damndest to collect and recollect some encounter, some passage of wit, wherein they stood irradiated for a moment in the sunshine of authentic Genius. (Summerson, 'Architect laureate')

Last years Lutyens's last years were undermined by the cessation of building work after the outbreak of the Second World War and by bouts of pneumonia and the development of cancer of the lung. Increasing infirmity may justify distancing him from the academic sterility of the Royal Academy plan for London published in 1942 and produced by a committee of architects of which he was chairman—mainly to give him something to do. Lutyens had been elected president of the Royal Academy in 1938 and devoted much of his time to its affairs almost until the end of his life. He was touched that his son, Robert, published a book about his work in 1942, *Sir Edwin Lutyens: an Appreciation in Perspective*. Lutyens died of bronchial sarcoma on 1 January 1944, at home in Mansfield Street surrounded by some of the drawings of his unbuilt cathedral. The funeral service took place in Westminster Abbey on 6 January and his ashes were later placed in the crypt of St Paul's Cathedral in an urn designed by his son. He left £42,271, a figure which included the value of the Mansfield Street house and its contents and £10,000 for the Liverpool cathedral design, a fee which, ever fearful of tax debt, he had arranged with Archbishop Downey to be paid after his death.

'He was a magician, a spell-binder, and few of us have not been in thrall to him,' wrote H. S. Goodhart-Rendel in an obituary.

> He seems to leave behind him a grey world, full of grim architectural Puritans on the one hand and gentleman-like architects who do the done thing on the other. He took Shaw's place, but who is to take his? (Goodhart-Rendel, 'Lutyensian appreciation', 52)

Lutyens's architectural career spanned dramatic social and technical changes and somehow, owing to both good fortune and assiduity in cultivating clients, he managed to rise above the revolution in architectural thinking which transformed the nature of practice after his death. He succeeded in becoming a national figure like no other architect apart from his hero, Wren, while continuing to produce a stream of buildings which were remarkable for their humanity as well as for their originality, sophistication, and sense of control. For many his architecture seems to manifest eternal truths about form and material; as Lutyens himself put it, 'everything should have an air of inevitability' (Hussey, *Life*, 164). Once, when asked by a student, 'What is proportion?', Lutyens replied, 'God' (*Architectural Association Journal*, 36, 1920, 56), suggesting that his approach was as much intuitive as based on system. Lutyens's personal motto was *Metiendo vivendum*: 'By measure we must live' (Hussey, *Life*, 589).

Six years after Lutyens's death, the continuing relevance of his achievement was asserted by the publication of the Lutyens Memorial: three large illustrated volumes by A. S. G. Butler and the biography by Christopher Hussey, who argued that:

> the Thiepval Memorial, the Poultry bank, and the designs for Liverpool Cathedral … constitute forward bases, of great cogency, established by Lutyens's genius as starting points for the advance of the Humanist tradition into the questionable future. They embody in architectural language his 'true spirit', his faith in accumulated knowledge, his insistence on unity based on reality, and his humanity. (Hussey, *Life*, 589)

Hussey began by stating: 'In his lifetime he was widely held to be our greatest architect since Wren if not, as many maintained, his superior' (Hussey, *Life*, xvii). In the event, however, Lutyens's reputation declined in the changed architectural and social climate of the post-war decades, although Le Corbusier, when planning his own new Indian capital at Chandigarh, could write that New Delhi

> was built by Lutyens over thirty years ago with extreme care, with great talent, with true success. The critics may rant as

much as they like, but to have done such a thing demands respect (at least it demands my respect). (W. Boesiger, ed., *Le Corbusier: Œuvre complète, 1952–1957*, Zürich, 1957, 50)

Only, perhaps, since the exhibition of his work held at the Hayward Gallery in London in 1981–2 has it been possible to evaluate his achievement more objectively and dispassionately. It is nevertheless significant that Lutyens's life and work have inspired the finest collection of writing in English ever devoted to an architect.

Sir Edwin Lutyens was awarded the royal gold medal for architecture in 1921 and in 1942 became the first architect on whom the Order of Merit was conferred. He became a fellow of the Royal Institute of British Architects in 1906 and was elected an associate of the Royal Academy in 1913 and an academician in 1920. Knighted in 1918, he was created KCIE in 1930. In 1924 the American Institute of Architects awarded Lutyens its gold medal and in 1932 he was made an officer of the Légion d'honneur.

GAVIN STAMP

Sources J. Brown, *Lutyens and the Edwardians: an English architect and his clients* (1996) • A. S. G. Butler, *The domestic architecture of Sir Edwin Lutyens* (1950); repr. (1989) [facs. repr. 1984] • R. Byron, 'New Delhi', *ArchR*, 69 (1931) • D. Gebhard, 'The master builders: 13', *Sunday Times Magazine* (14 May 1972), 18–30 [Viceroy's House] • H. S. Goodhart-Rendel, 'Sir Edwin Lutyens, OM, PRA', *RIBA Journal*, 3rd ser., 51 (1943–4), 51–2 • H. S. Goodhart-Rendel, 'The work of the late Sir Edwin Lutyens, OM', *RIBA Journal*, 3rd ser., 52 (1944–5) • R. Gradidge, *Edwin Lutyens: architect laureate* (1981) • A. Greenberg, 'Lutyens' architecture restudied', *Perspecta XII* (1969) • A. Hopkins and G. Stamp, eds., *Lutyens abroad* (2002) • C. Hussey, *The life of Sir Edwin Lutyens* (1950); repr. (1989) • [P. Inskip], 'Edwin Lutyens', *Architectural Monographs*, 6 (1979) [repr. 1986] • R. G. Irving, *Indian Summer: Lutyens, Baker and imperial Delhi* (1981) • E. Lutyens, 'The work of the late Philip Webb', *Country Life* (8 May 1915), 618 • E. Lutyens, informal talk at Architectural Association ordinary general meeting, 25 Oct 1920, *Architectural Association Journal*, 36/405 (Nov 1920), 55–7 • E. Lutyens, 'What I think of modern architecture', *Country Life* (20 June 1931), 775–7 • 'Sir Edwin Lutyens at the A. A.', *Architectural Association Journal*, 48/546 (Aug 1932), 63–7 [informal meeting 2 June 1932] • M. Lutyens, *Edwin Lutyens by his daughter* (1980) • R. Lutyens, *Sir Edwin Lutyens: an appreciation in perspective* (1942) • R. Lutyens, *Notes on Sir Edwin Lutyens* (1970) • *Lutyens: the work of the English architect Sir Edwin Lutyens (1869–1944)* (1981) [incl. C. Amery 'Introduction', M. Lutyens, 'Sir Edwin Lutyens', J. Brown, 'Gertrude Jekyll and the pattern of partnership', J. Cornforth, 'Lutyens and *Country Life*: 81 not out', G. Stamp, 'New Delhi', J. Summerson, 'Arches of triumph: the design for Liverpool Cathedral', and catalogue entries by C. Amery, J. Brown, J. Edwards, R. Gradidge, M. Lutyens, M. Richardson, G. Stamp, and S. Williams] • *The letters of Edwin Lutyens to his wife, Lady Emily*, ed. C. Percy and J. Ridley (1985) • N. Pevsner, 'Building with wit: the architecture of Sir Edwin Lutyens', *ArchR*, 111 (1951) • 'Reminiscences on Sir Edwin Lutyens', *Architectural Association Journal*, 74 (March 1959) [with contributions by J. Brandon-Jones, C. Hussey, H. Bagenal, R. Furneaux Jordan, H. Farquharson, O. P. Milne, N. Hannen, H. Worthington, W. Curtis Green, A. G. Shoosmith, H. A. N. Medd, H. Austen Hall, and A. S. G. Butler] • J. Ridley, *The architect and his wife: a life of Edwin Lutyens* (2002) • M. Richardson, *Sketches by Edwin Lutyens* (1994) • [J. Summerson], 'Daniel (in the lion's den)', *Night and Day* (28 Oct 1937) ['Architect laureate' (unsigned); repr. in *Night and Day*, ed. C. Hawtree, 1985, 195–7] • J. Summerson, 'As I knew him: Sir Edwin Lutyens', transcript, June 1951, BBC WAC • L. Weaver, *Houses and gardens by E. L. Lutyens* (1913) [repr. 1914 and 1925 as *Houses and gardens by Sir Edwin Lutyens*; facs. of 1913 edn 1981; repr. 1985, 1987, and 1988] • F. L. Wright, 'Sir Edwyn Lutyens', *Building* (July 1951) • personal knowledge (2004)

Archives CKS, letters and plans • RIBA BAL, corresp. and papers | Bodl. Oxf., caricatures, sketches, letters to Lewis family • Commonwealth War Graves Commission, Maidenhead, corresp. and papers relating to work for Imperial War Graves Commission • CUL, letters to Lord Hardinge • Cumbria AS, Carlisle, letters to Lord Howard of Penrith • NA Scot., letters to Lord Lothian • NRA, priv. coll., corresp. with Nathaniel Lloyd relating to construction of Great Dixter • RIBA BAL, letters to S. A. Alexander • Tate collection, corresp. with Lord Clark • TCD, corresp. with Thomas Bodkin | SOUND BBC WAC • BL NSA, documentary recordings

Likenesses photograph, *c*.1920, NPG • E. Dulac, drawing, 1922, priv. coll. • W. Rothenstein, sanguine, black and white chalk drawing, 1922, NPG • W. Stoneman, two photographs, 1924–34, NPG • B. Partridge, pencil drawing, 1927, NPG • B. Partridge, pencil, pen, and ink drawing, *c*.1927, NPG • A. John, oils, *c*.1928, Castle Drogo, Devon • W. R. Dick, bronze bust, 1932, Government House, New Delhi; copy, RIBA • M. Frampton, oils, 1935, Art Workers' Guild, London [*see illus.*] • H. Coster, photographs, 1942, NPG • bronze cast of death mask, 1944, NPG • R. Lutyens, oils, 1959, NPG • A. John, oils, priv. coll.

Wealth at death £42,271 0s. 8*d*.: probate, 17 April 1944, *CGPLA Eng. & Wales*

Lutyens, (Agnes) Elisabeth (1906–1983), composer, was born at 29 Bloomsbury Square, London, on 9 July 1906, the fourth of five children and third of four daughters of Sir Edwin Landseer *Lutyens (1869–1944), architect, and his wife, Lady Emily *Lutyens (1874–1964), daughter of (Edward) Robert Bulwer-*Lytton, first earl of Lytton, statesman. She was educated at Worcester Park School, Westgate-on-Sea. She turned to music at an early age, not because of any conspicuous talent for it, but 'as another form of my need for privacy' (Lutyens, 10). The family's reaction to her musical aims was at first more one of apathy than of outright opposition, and, after a period of private piano and violin lessons, in January 1922 she was permitted at fifteen to study at the École Normale in Paris. In 1926 she entered the Royal College of Music, London, becoming a pupil of Harold Darke for composition and of Ernest Tomlinson for the viola. She had cause to be grateful to Darke, who managed to arrange for almost everything she composed at this time to be performed. This was most unusual for the Royal College of Music, where Brahms was the god of 'new' music. Lutyens was emphatically not sympathetic to Brahmsian ideals, yet working in this style for exercises enabled her to develop a powerful compositional technique. Among her friends from this time were Anne Macnaghton, the violinist, and Iris Lemare, and together they founded the Macnaghton–Lemare concerts, which began in 1931 at the Mercury Theatre, Notting Hill Gate. The main aim of the concerts, which continued until 1994, was to 'discover and encourage composers of British nationality by having their works performed'.

On 11 February 1933 Elisabeth Lutyens married Ian Herbert Campbell Glennie, who had also been a Royal College of Music student. He was the son of William Bourne Glennie, a minor canon of Hereford. They had a son and twin daughters. They were divorced in 1940, and in 1942 Elisabeth Lutyens married Edward Clark (1888–1962), a tireless champion of new music, who had previously worked for the BBC in Newcastle upon Tyne and London. He was the

(Agnes) **Elisabeth Lutyens** (1906–1983), by John Vere Brown, 1963

son of James Bowness Clark, coal exporter, of Newcastle. They had one son.

For much of her life Elisabeth Lutyens endured relative poverty (with occasional help from her family over such things as housing and children's education), a considerable amount of ill health, physical and mental, and widespread lack of recognition of her originality and achievements. None the less, she never ceased to compose, her opus numbers extending to at least 135, in addition to which there are a hundred film scores from 1944 to 1969 and about the same number of musical commissions for radio. She admitted that the continual steady drinking involved in discussing the radio projects turned her into an alcoholic. Most of her life, apart from moves to Northumberland and other areas during the Second World War, was spent in and around London.

Lutyens was a prolific and versatile composer, one for whom neglect may have been discouraging but made no essential difference to her development and productiveness. From the outset she veered away from what Constant Lambert termed 'the cowpat school of English music' and described integrity as 'not a virtue [but] a necessity for an artist' (Harries, 53). She was the outstanding pioneer of serial music in England, and while she would have liked more performances of her works, her fulfilment lay in composing them. Her first work to become known through performance was a setting for a ballet, *The Birthday of the Infanta* (1932), after Oscar Wilde. This was given at a Royal College of Music Patrons' Fund concert while she was still a student (the score has since been withdrawn). The main work of the pre-war years was the chamber concerto, op. 8 no. 1 (1939), for nine instruments, which antedated by several years any knowledge of Webern's concerto for a similar ensemble. The first work to be performed abroad was the string quartet no. 2, op. 5 no. 5, given at the International Society for Contemporary Music festival at Cracow in 1939. Possibly her best-known work is *O saisons, o châteaux!*, op. 13 (1946), for soprano and strings, to a poem by Rimbaud. Many of her later works make use of words, some written by herself, and others by an enormous range of writers, among them Stevie Smith and Dylan Thomas, with whom she was personally acquainted. At a relatively late stage she turned to dramatic music, and her opera 'charade' *Time Off? Not a Ghost of a Chance!*, op. 68 (1967–8), to her own libretto, was staged at Sadler's Wells theatre, London, in 1972.

Lutyens relished company and good talk and could be provocative and outrageous, as when ringing up a Jewish pupil at 1 a.m., saying 'the PLO's all right' (private information). Her sitting-room was very welcoming to a new pupil, with a large pot of steaming tea on the table, a standard lamp created from a French horn bell, and the work-desk with its stopwatches and slanting architect's board; the sense of excitement and joy in the act of composing this generated in a young composer can be imagined. She had various rather unsatisfactory arrangements with publishing firms, and eventually formed her own, the Olivan Press, which in the 1960s and 1970s published many more works than all the other publishers had managed over her entire career. In 1969 she was appointed CBE and awarded the City of London Midsummer prize. York University awarded her an honorary DMus (1977). She died in Hampstead, London, on 14 April 1983.

JAMES DALTON, *rev.*

Sources E. Lutyens, *A goldfish bowl* (1972) · M. S. Harries, *A pilgrim soul: the life and work of Elisabeth Lutyens* (1989) · private information (1990) [Robert Saxton] · *CGPLA Eng. & Wales* (1983) · A. Payne, 'Lutyens, (Agnes) Elisabeth', *New Grove* · Burke, *Peerage* (1967)
Archives FILM BFI NFTVA, 'Mothers by daughters', 14 June 1983 | SOUND BL NSA, documentary recording · BL NSA, 'A goldfish bowl', Feb 1973, M4702R, M4846R, M4744R BD7 · BL NSA, oral history interviews · BL NSA, performance recordings · BL NSA, *Talking about music*, 1LP020024652 BD2 · BL NSA, *Talking about music*, 161, 1LP020041751 BD2 BBC TRANSC · BL NSA, *Talking about music*, 201, 1LP020196131 BD3 BBC TRANSC
Likenesses J. V. Brown, photograph, 1963, NPG [*see illus.*]
Wealth at death £51,870: probate, 20 July 1983, *CGPLA Eng. & Wales*

Lutyens [*née* Bulwer-Lytton], **Lady Emily** (1874–1964), theosophist, was born on 26 December 1874 in Paris, the third surviving child among the five children of (Edward) Robert Bulwer-*Lytton, first earl of Lytton (1831–1891), a diplomatist and poet, and his wife, Edith Bulwer-*Lytton (1841–1936) [*see under* Lytton, (Edward) Robert Bulwer-], daughter of Edward Villiers and his wife, Elizabeth Liddell, and a lady-in-waiting to Queen Victoria. Emily Lytton was brought up in Lisbon, where her father was British minister, and then in India (1876–80), where her father was viceroy. After leaving India the family returned to Knebworth, where she was educated by governesses, whom she despised. A voracious reader, she devoured her father's library of Walter Scott and Bulwer Lytton; reading aloud was a lifelong passion.

In December 1887 Lord Lytton was appointed ambassador in Paris, and the thirteen-year-old Emily went to live in the embassy. She began an intimate correspondence with a 71-year-old clergyman, the Revd Whitwell Elwin. Throughout her life she wrote letters almost daily; her letters to various correspondents, especially her husband,

Lady Emily Lutyens (1874–1964), by F. A. Swaine, 1913

form an extraordinarily complete record of her life. She published the correspondence with Elwin as *A Blessed Girl* (1953). Robert Lytton died in November 1891, and Emily returned to England with her family. She did not formally 'come out', but her sister Betty, who was married to Gerald Balfour, introduced her to the circle of 'Souls'. Disapproving and priggish but also a rebel, Emily became infatuated with the 53-year-old Wilfrid Blunt, a friend of her father. This flirtation is candidly described in *A Blessed Girl*.

Soon after she broke with Blunt, the 21-year-old Emily, who by now considered herself 'on the shelf', met the architect Edwin Landseer *Lutyens (1869–1944), who, though a coming man, was very much outside her social class. They were married in August 1897 and lived at 29 Bloomsbury Square, London. The house was also Lutyens's office and the centre of his successful country-house practice. Emily and Edwin Lutyens had five children, born between 1898 and 1908: Barbara, Robert, Ursula, Mary, and Elisabeth. Mary *Lutyens (1908–1999) became a writer of some note and Elisabeth *Lutyens (1906–1983) became a distinguished composer. Emily, who disliked entertaining, was unfulfilled by her role as architect's wife. She was drawn to the women's movement, joining first the Moral Education League, which campaigned for prostitutes suffering from venereal disease, and then the Women's Social and Political Union. She introduced to the movement her sister Lady Constance Georgina Bulwer-*Lytton (1869–1923), who became a prominent suffragette and hunger-striker, but Emily disliked militancy and resigned from the union in 1909.

Emily Lutyens discovered the new religion of theosophy through the Mallets, French clients of her husband who lived at Le Bois des Moutiers, Varengeville. Theosophy is an eclectic mix of Hinduism and Christianity, and Emily was converted by Annie Besant, the charismatic leader of the movement. In 1911 Mrs Besant brought to England a sixteen-year-old Indian boy, Krishnamurti, the future world teacher whose remarkable aura the clairvoyant theosophist C. W. Leadbeater had noticed on the beach at Adyar, near Madras. Waiting with the crowd of theosophists at Charing Cross station, Emily wrote, 'I had eyes for none but Krishna', an odd figure with long black hair wearing a Norfolk jacket (Lutyens, *Candles in the Sun*, 30). Emily was promoted by Mrs Besant to the esoteric section of the Theosophical Society and appointed English representative of the Order of the Star in the East. She travelled the country lecturing, acted as editor of the theosophist journal *Herald of the Star*, and introduced wealthy converts, including the American heiress Miss Mabel Dodge, whose generosity financed the society.

Emily became a strict vegetarian, and relations with her husband grew strained. She later admitted that only her overwhelming personal love for Krishnamurti bound her to theosophy. Some questioned her emotional involvement, but her support helped to protect Krishna and his brother Nitya, who were smuggled to England in 1912 pending a lawsuit brought against Mrs Besant by their father, who alleged immoral acts by C. W. Leadbeater. In 1916 Emily established an all-India home rule movement, holding meetings in her London drawing-room. This was perhaps tactless, as her husband was then designing an imperial capital at New Delhi, but Emily was annoyed to receive a letter from Edward Hudson, editor of *Country Life*, telling her that she had a genius in her care and that looking after him should be her sole concern.

Theosophy was very fashionable in the 1920s. Krishna, with his film-star looks, mesmerized audiences in India, California, Australia, and the Netherlands. Emily travelled the world with him, becoming convinced that he was indeed the Messiah. In 1925 Emily formed the League of Motherhood, but by now the Theosophical Society was swept by hysteria and divided over Krishna's claims to be the world teacher. Emily supported Krishna when he tried to dissolve the society, and in 1930 she followed him in resigning from theosophy.

Emily Lutyens was in many ways ahead of her time. A fearless and outspoken critic of the casual racism of the British in India, she was a feminist, a vegetarian, and a socialist. She was twice asked to stand as a Labour candidate. Her unconventional marriage is prolifically documented in the letters she wrote to her husband, 5000 of which survive. She played little part in actively promoting his work, but in times of crisis her advice was good. Sir Edwin Lutyens died in 1944. In 1953 Lady Emily published *A Blessed Girl*, a vivid and sharply observed account of an upper-class girl growing up in late Victorian England. In 1957 followed *Candles in the Sun*, the absorbing story of her theosophical years. Written with the collaboration of her daughter Mary, this is still the best account of the movement. She also published *The Birth of Rowland* (1956), a collection of her parents' letters. Lady Emily died at her home, 2 Hyde Park Street, Paddington, London, on 3 January 1964. JANE RIDLEY

Sources E. Lutyens, *A blessed girl* (1953) • E. Lutyens, *Candles in the sun* (1957) • M. Lutyens, *Edwin Lutyens* (1980) • J. Ridley, *The architect and his wife: a life of Edwin Lutyens* (2002) • *The letters of Edwin Lutyens to his wife Lady Emily*, ed. C. Percy and J. Ridley (1985) • d. cert.
Archives RIBA, MSS
Likenesses F. A. Swaine, photograph, 1913, Mary Evans Picture Library, London [*see illus.*]
Wealth at death £13,926: probate, 5 Feb 1964, *CGPLA Eng. & Wales*

Lutyens, (Edith Penelope) Mary (1908–1999), writer, was born on 31 July 1908 at 29 Bloomsbury Square, London, the youngest of the five children of Sir Edwin Landseer *Lutyens (1869–1944), architect, and his wife, Lady Emily *Lutyens (1874–1964), daughter of Robert, first earl of Lytton, and his wife, Edith Villiers. Mary Lutyens had a comfortable but unconventional Edwardian childhood. Edwin Lutyens was preoccupied by his work, which often took him away from home, and he played little part in his children's lives. Emily Lutyens converted to theosophy in 1910, and her obsessive devotion both to the cult and to the young Krishnamurti (known familiarly as 'Krishna'), hailed as the New Messiah, sometimes left little time for her children. Mary was summoned each morning to her mother's meditation room to recite: 'I am in a link in a golden chain of happiness which stretches round the world and I promise to keep my link bright and strong' (Lutyens, *To be Young*, 16), but the most important figure in her childhood was Nanny, her nurse. (When Lady Emily laughed aloud one day her children were terrified and ran out of the room thinking she had gone mad; they had never heard her laugh before.)

Mary was educated by governesses and from the age of eleven at Queen's College, Harley Street, London. (She was not amused when, after she had been there for three years, her father asked her which school she was at.) Her mother removed her from school at fifteen and took her to India; while her father supervised the building of Britain's new imperial capital at New Delhi, her mother escaped to the theosophical compound at Adyar, near Madras, to be with Mrs Besant and Krishna. Mary's sympathies at this time were firmly with her mother. Aged sixteen, she experienced a spiritual awakening; her exaltation was linked to her growing infatuation with Nitya, younger brother of Krishnamurti. The story of this relationship is touchingly told in her memoir *To be Young* (1959).

Nitya died of tuberculosis in 1925 and Mary fleetingly transferred her affections to Krishna, but she seems to have sensed that theosophy was a dead end for her. She had always wanted to be a writer—as a child she lived in the stories of her imagination—and now, summoned by her father to Claridges to meet Sir Roderick Jones, chairman of Reuters, she began a new life. Encouraged by Jones (with whom she had an *amitié amoureuse*) and also by his wife, Enid Bagnold, she began to write, breaking with theosophy.

In 1930 Mary married Anthony Sewell (*b.* 1904/5), a stockbroker. She had one daughter, Amanda, born in 1932, but the marriage was not happy. Mary had a series of love affairs, and the marriage was dissolved in 1945. In 1933 she published her first book, *Forthcoming Marriages*, an uneven collection of short stories, some closely related to her own experiences. Encouraged by the book's success, she began to make a career as a novelist. Needing money, she wrote for women's magazines; in the late 1930s she contributed prolifically to *Women's Weekly* and *Women at Home* under the pseudonym of Esther Wyndham. Esther Wyndham's stories were later published by Mills and Boon. With novels such as *Perchance to Dream* (1935) or *Family Colouring* (1940) she 'combined her ability to view emotional situations close up with a gift for conveying a strong sense of the sort of society in which she had grown up' (*The Times*). Between 1939 and 1943 she published one novel a year.

In 1945 Mary married the furrier and art historian Joseph Gluckstein Links (1904–1997), known as Joe. After a rackety youth, her life became more settled; she used to say 'Joe made me nice again' (*The Independent*). She still published fiction, but she broadened her range. She wrote each morning in bed, using pencil in an exercise book; Joe often typed her work. In 1959 appeared an autobiography, *To be Young*, which told the story of her childhood in theosophy. She also moved into biography. As with all her work, the catalyst was personal. Ever since their honeymoon, Joe and Mary Links had paid regular visits to Venice. Not only did Venice inspire Joe Links's important research work on Canaletto and his guidebook *Venice for Pleasure*, but Joe also discovered a trove of letters between Ruskin and his wife, Effie, at the time of their Venice honeymoon. These gave Mary a new project. She published three volumes on the Ruskins and their milieu—*Effie in Venice* (1965), *Millais and the Ruskins* (1967), and *The Ruskins and the Grays* (1972). Mary Lutyens's informal but meticulous commentary skilfully wove contemporary letters to form an absorbing narrative; dealing frankly with the failure of the Ruskin marriage, the trilogy broke new ground, bringing literary success. Mary Lutyens was elected to the Royal Society of Literature in 1976.

The revival of interest in Edwin Lutyens's work, signalled by a major exhibition at the Hayward Gallery, prompted Mary Lutyens to read the vast correspondence exchanged between her parents. The result was *Edwin Lutyens: a Memoir* (1980)—an intimate and affectionate portrait of her parents' extraordinary marriage. Mary Lutyens used to say that she wrote the book to vindicate her mother, and she was surprised and dismayed to find that readers sympathized with her father, the victim of her mother's obsessive love for Krishnamurti. Furthering her father's reputation as an architect became a major preoccupation with the formation of the Lutyens Trust, in which she played a leading part.

Mary Lutyens published several works of family history, including *Lady Lytton's Court Diary* (1961), the diary of her grandmother as lady-in-waiting to Queen Victoria. *The Lyttons in India* (1979) told the story of her grandfather, the first earl of Lytton, viceroy of India, who ordered the invasion of Afghanistan. Mary Lutyens was a world authority on theosophy. She remained on affectionate terms with Krishnamurti, whom she saw whenever he came to London, and she wrote his biography in three volumes. *Krishnamurti: the Years of Awakening* (1975) is a definitive account of the theosophical movement. She died on 9 April 1999 at her home, 8 Elizabeth Close, Westminster.

Mary Lutyens was elegant and metropolitan. She could be disarmingly direct. She was a fluent and prolific letter writer. She was meticulous about facts and a stickler for accuracy; but perhaps her greatest gift as a writer was her ability to apply the insights and narrative skills of a novelist to non-fiction. JANE RIDLEY

Sources M. Lutyens, *To be young* (1959) • M. Lutyens, *Edwin Lutyens: a memoir* (1980) • *The Times* (13 April 1999) • *The Independent* (13 April 1999) • *Daily Telegraph* (April 1999) • private information (2004) • M. Lutyens, *Forthcoming marriages* (1933) • M. Lutyens, *Millais and the Ruskins* (1967) • *The Guardian* (13 Oct 1997) [obituary of J. G. Links] • m. certs. • d. cert.

Wealth at death £630,821: probate, 28 July 1999, *CGPLA Eng. & Wales*

Lutz, (Wilhelm) Meyer (1829–1903), conductor and composer, was born on 19 May 1829 at Münnerstadt, near Kissingen, Germany, the son of a music professor, Joseph Lutz (1801–1879), and his wife, Magdalena (1809–1862). His elder brother later became Baron Johann Lutz, prime minister of Bavaria, under 'mad' King Ludwig. Lutz studied with his father, then in Würzburg, and he first visited Britain, as a pianist, in 1846. He returned in 1848 to settle, and worked as a church organist and a theatrical conductor, notably, from 1850 to 1855, at London's Surrey Theatre. His first original stage composition, the one-act *The Charmed Harp*, was produced there in 1852.

For many years Lutz conducted provincial concerts and touring opera troupes, several headed by the tenor Eliot Galer, who was in 1859 responsible for mounting, at Liverpool, Lutz's opera *Zaida, or, The Pearl of Granada*, composed to a libretto by the company's bass, Oliver Summers. Galer also produced Lutz's *Blonde or Brunette* (1862), *Cousin Kate* (1863), and *Felix* (1865) in London, where the striving musician ('a graceful composer in the school of Auber'; *The Era*, 1865) was also represented by the cantatas *Herne the Hunter* (Crystal Palace, 1862) and *King Christmas* (Oxford music hall, 1863), and material for the Christy Minstrels.

In February 1869 Lutz was appointed music director at the recently opened Gaiety Theatre, and there, over the next quarter of a century, the plump, bearded, and bespectacled musician, 'always delightful and mostly disagreeable' (*Evening News*, Sydney, 1903), established himself as a personality in the British theatre, conducting the operas, operettas, *opéras bouffes*, and burlesques mounted under John Hollingshead's management and simultaneously compiling the scores for the Gaiety's pasticcio entertainments. These scores occasionally included some original melodies, but Lutz's rather politely academic stage music was heard mostly on the occasions of his own Gaiety benefit programmes. In 1881 his operatic version of *Black-Eyed Susan, All in the Downs*, was given such a performance. Lutz continued to attempt lofty themes and strains—Christine Nilsson performed his scena *Xenia the Sclavonian Maiden* (1869), and his cantata *The Legend of the Lys* was sung at the Covent Garden Promenade Concerts in 1873—but he had altogether more success with the light, dancing melodies for a couple of little shows, *On Condition* (1882) and *Posterity* (1884), performed by Lila Clay's all-ladies troupe, and with such ditties as Alice Atherton's popular 'Eyes of English Blue'.

In 1885, when George Edwardes took over the management of the Gaiety, pasticcio burlesque there gave way to shows with new songs—songs written in a light, danceable, 'popular' style. Lutz at first assembled these scores piecemeal from various local songwriters, but he soon switched to providing virtually all the required music himself. Between 1886 and 1893 he composed for *Monte Cristo Jr*, *Miss Esmeralda*, *Frankenstein*, *Faust-up-to-Date*, *Ruy Blas and the Blasé Roué*, *Carmen up-to-Date*, *Cinder-Ellen up-too-Late*, and *Don Juan* a body of efficient, tulle-weight tunes and songs which served prettily to illustrate the comic high-jinks and girlie antics of the 'new burlesque' genre. Most of the most successful songs heard in these shows were interpolated numbers, but perhaps the biggest hit of the new burlesque era was actually composed by Lutz. The 'Pas de quatre', a jolly barn-dance tune written for *Faust-up-to-Date*, was still popular fifty years later.

Lutz was connected, by his marriage on 19 July 1856 to Elizabeth Cook (*b.* 1835), to several important British theatrical families. Elizabeth's brothers, the bass Thomas Aynsley Cook (1833–1894) and the baritone John Furneaux Cook (1839?–1903), and her unmarried sister, Alice Aynsley Cook (1850?–1938), had high-profile careers in English opera and musical theatre. Aynsley Cook married Harriet Farrell Payne (1830–1880), an operatic contralto and a daughter of the famous Payne family of pantomimists, and their daughter, Annie, became Mrs Eugene Goossens jun. After Elizabeth Cook's death, Lutz married, on Jersey, to avoid the prohibition against marrying a deceased wife's sister, Emily Cook (*b.* 1847?).

After his retirement from the Gaiety in 1894, Lutz continued to conduct and write songs intermittently, and he had a song featured in Edwardes's production of *The Girl from Kay's* just weeks before his death, at his home, 115 Edith Road, Kensington, on 31 January 1903. He was buried in St Mary's, Kensal Green. He was survived by his wife. KURT GÄNZL

Sources K. Gänzl, *The encyclopedia of the musical theatre*, 2 vols. (1994) • K. Gänzl, *The British musical theatre*, 2 vols. (1986) • *The Era* (12 Aug 1899), 13 • *CGPLA Eng. & Wales* (1903) • J. Hollingshead, *Gaiety chronicles* (1898) • will • m. cert., 19 July 1856 • Joslin collection, Lutz MSS

Likenesses photograph, repro. in Hollingshead, *Gaiety chronicles*

Wealth at death £575 7*s*. 10*d*.: probate, 12 March 1903, *CGPLA Eng. & Wales*

Luwum, Janani (1922–1977), archbishop in the Anglican Church of Uganda and martyr, was born in 1922 at Pajong, near Mucwini in east Acholi, Uganda, to Eliya Okello, a peasant farmer, and his wife, early converts to Christianity in this remote area of northern Uganda. Like many others of his generation, he gained his education piecemeal. After Gulu high school he attended Boroboro Teacher Training College and taught at Puranga primary school. In 1947 he married Mary Lawil; they had four sons and four daughters, and his wife survived him. In 1948, under the influence of the east African revival movement, Luwum experienced a radical Christian conversion, and was selected to train as a lay reader at Buwalasi Theological College. Here his potential was spotted, and in 1953 he returned to train for ordination, being made a deacon in 1955 and a priest in 1956. After two years' parish work at Lira Palwo he spent 1958 at St Augustine's College, Canterbury, returning to be vice-principal of Buwalasi before attending the London College of Divinity from 1963 to 1965. After only a year as principal of Buwalasi, in 1966 he was appointed provincial secretary of the Church of Uganda, a very responsible position at a difficult period in the church's development as it adjusted to becoming an autonomous province of the Anglican communion.

In 1969 Luwum returned to northern Uganda as its bishop. It was a sign of the times that President Milton Obote and his Uganda Peoples' Congress virtually hijacked the consecration service, insisting that it be held in Pece stadium rather than in the church, and packing it with party followers. Less than two years later Obote was ousted from power by General Idi Amin, who turned on the people of Lango and Acholi, most of whom had supported Obote. Luwum comforted those whose husbands, sons, and brothers had been killed or detained, and tried to track down those who had disappeared. In 1974 he was elected archbishop of Uganda, Rwanda, Burundi, and Boga-Zaïre. Although an Acholi, he established good lines of communication with Amin and used his entrée on behalf of people in need.

In 1976 matters reached crisis in Uganda as violence escalated. In August Catholic, Anglican, and Muslim leaders met under Luwum's chairmanship to discuss the deteriorating situation. Amin, furious that he had not been told about the meeting, and afraid because Muslims as well as Christians were involved, demanded the minutes, which Luwum as chairman had signed. Amin's security men who attended the consecration of a bishop in western Uganda heard an outspoken sermon against the random violence which was destroying the country. Christmas was 'abolished' and the archbishop's Christmas sermon was abruptly taken off the air. Plans to celebrate the centenaries of both Anglican and Catholic churches seemed endangered.

Early in February 1977 Amin's security service learned of an Acholi plot against the regime. In the early hours of 6 February soldiers raided the archbishop's house at gunpoint, accusing him of secreting arms, but finding none. A day later they raided Bishop Okoth's house with the same result. Luwum possibly knew of the plot, but few would seriously suggest he was involved. On 8 February the Anglican bishops met to discuss the growing threat, and drafted a letter to Amin: 'The gun whose muzzle has been pressed against the Archbishop's stomach … is a gun which is being pointed at every Christian in the Church,' they wrote.

On 16 February Amin called the press, diplomatic corps, officials, and church leaders together. Captured weapons were paraded, and wild accusations made against the church. When the parade was finally dismissed, Luwum alone was detained. He was murdered some time that night. No one believed the official story that he and two others had been killed in a car crash. On Sunday 20 February thousands poured up the hill to Namirembe Cathedral where a grave had been prepared, and the funeral was to be held, but there was no body and so no funeral service. Eventually the tension was dispelled as the crowds began singing the Uganda martyrs' hymn, and the retired Archbishop Sabiti spoke of an empty grave and the risen Christ. By then Luwum had already been buried. Soldiers had taken his body back to Acholi where it was buried on 18/19 February by Mucwini church. While the soldiers dug the grave, relatives opened the coffin to confirm that the body was that of Luwum, and gunshot wounds in the head, mouth, and stomach were noted. The grave is marked simply 'Janani Luwum'.

In 1998 a statue of Luwum carved by Neil Simmons was placed on the west front of Westminster Abbey, together with nine other martyrs of modern times. Luwum is also commemorated in Canterbury Cathedral, and in the Church of England calendar on 17 February. Uganda has found his memory more problematic. His only memorial there is the Archbishop Luwum Theological College at Gulu. Amin's overthrow did not bring an end to violence, and continuing ethnopolitical factionalism has postponed reconsideration by the Church of Uganda of Luwum's significance for Ugandan Christianity.

M. LOUISE PIROUET

Sources M. Ford, *Janani: the making of a martyr* (1978) • K. Ward, 'Archbishop Janani Luwum: the dilemmas of loyalty, opposition and witness in Amin's Uganda', *Christianity and the African imagination: essays in honour of Adrian Hastings*, ed. D. Maxwell and I. Lawrie (2002) • J. Sentamu, 'Tribalism, religion and despotism in Uganda: Archbishop Janani Luwum', *The terrible alternative: Christian martyrdom in the twentieth century*, ed. A. Chandler (1998) • M. L. Pirouet, 'Religion in Uganda under Amin', *Journal of Religion in Africa*, 11 (1980), 13–29 • *WWW, 1971–80* • K. Ward, 'The Church of Uganda amidst conflict', *Religion and politics in east Africa*, ed. H. B. Hansen and M. Twaddle (1995), 72–105 • A. Chandler, *Christian martyrs of the twentieth century: ten new statues on the west front of Westminster Abbey* (1998) • Consecration Committee, *Consecration of Bishop Janani Luwum, 25 Jan, 1969* (1969) [souvenir containing biographical note] • *Voice of Uganda* [Kampala] (17 Feb 1977) • *The Standard* [Nairobi] (18–24 Feb 1977) • *Daily Nation* [Nairobi] (18–24 Feb 1977) • *Sunday Nation* [Nairobi] (20 Feb 1977); (27 Feb 1977)

Archives Church of Uganda, Namirembe, Kampala, provincial offices, corresp.

Likenesses photograph, repro. in Sentamu, 'Tribalism, religion and despotism in Uganda'

Luxborough. For this title name *see* Knight, Henrietta, Lady Luxborough (1699–1756).

Luxford, George (1807–1854), botanist and printer, was born on 7 April 1807 at Sutton in Surrey, from where the family subsequently moved to nearby Reigate. At the age of eleven he was apprenticed to a printer and in the sixteen years he remained with him made up for his truncated schooling by extensive reading and acquiring a knowledge of French, Latin, and Greek. He also developed a fondness for field botany and entomology, and spent his leisure hours in combing the district in search of plants. *A Flora of the Neighbourhood of Reigate* (1838), which he printed himself, was the eventual product of that.

After three years in Birmingham (1834–7), Luxford returned south and set up on his own as a printer in London. Within a few months Longmans had switched to him the contract for printing Loudon's *Magazine of Natural History*, perhaps at the instance of his fellow Surrey naturalist, Edward Newman (1801–1876), who was at that point one of its chief contributors. Newman had become convinced that separate magazines catering for the respective subcommunities of natural history were a commercial proposition and was then looking for a vehicle through which to prove that belief. Luxford's business seemed ideal, and, after first being taken on as a partner, Newman was allowed to buy it outright in 1841. That June a botanical monthly, *The Phytologist*, made its appearance from this stable, with Luxford named as editor. That this was no mere trade convenience was quickly shown by the frequent learned contributions made by the editor to the earlier numbers. Luxford's appointment in 1846 as lecturer in botany at St Thomas's Hospital and his election in 1848 to the council of the Botanical Society of London (of which *The Phytologist* had effectively become the publishing outlet) came as added credentials.

Luxford remained editor of *The Phytologist* until 1851, but, even after his retirement from business, continued to act as compositor and reader. *The Phytologist* was, however, never a financial success and was kept in print for as long as thirteen years only by cross-subsidies from Newman's more profitable ventures. On Luxford's death, on 12 June 1854 at 10 Victoria Place, Hill Street, Walworth, publication of the journal ceased; this seems to confirm the supposition that Newman had kept it going only out of loyalty to his former partner, although letters provide evidence that Newman subsequently sought in vain to recruit other leading botanists to take Luxford's place. Luxford had proved himself irreplaceable.

D. E. Allen

Sources *Proceedings of the Linnean Society of London*, 2 (1848–55), 426–7 • T. P. Newman, *Memoir of the life and works of Edward Newman* (1876), 20 • D. E. Allen, 'The struggle for specialist journals: natural history in the British periodicals market in the first half of the nineteenth century', *Archives of Natural History*, 23 (1996), 107–23 • D. E. Allen, *The botanists: a history of the Botanical Society of the British Isles through a hundred and fifty years*, St Paul's Bibliographies (1986), 22, 214 • *The Phytologist* (1841–54) • C. E. Salmon, *Flora of Surrey*, ed. W. H. Pearsall (1931), 51 • d. cert. • *DNB*

Luxmoore, Charles Scott (1792?–1854). *See under* Luxmoore, John (1756–1830).

Luxmoore, Sir (Arthur) Fairfax Charles Coryndon (1876–1944), judge, was born on 27 February 1876 at Kilburn, London, the eldest son of Arthur Coryndon Hansler Luxmoore, artist, of Danescliffe, St Lawrence in the Isle of Thanet, and his wife, Katherine Frances Jane, daughter of Richard Martin, of the Irish bar. Although related to an ancient Devon family, he was, as Archbishop Lang described him, 'in every fibre of his being a man of Kent' (*Canterbury Cathedral Chronicle*, 2). From the King's School, Canterbury, he entered Jesus College, Cambridge, in 1894, and represented it in almost every sport. He was a good wicket-keeper, but in rugby football he excelled as a hard-working, thrusting forward, and played against Oxford in 1896 and 1897. But as he often ruefully admitted, his studies were neglected and he passed his examinations without distinction (he graduated with a pass degree in 1900), something that surprised those who knew him only later in life.

Called to the bar by Lincoln's Inn in 1899, Luxmoore had the good fortune to become a pupil in the busy chambers of George Cave. But his athletic career had still not reached its climax. He played for England against Scotland in 1900 and in the following year against Wales. Then he turned all of his great energy and determination to his profession. His practice at the bar grew rapidly and he shared to the full the prosperity at 4 New Square. Early to bed and up again at dawn, he thrust forward through the day. The unwieldy glazed doors of the fine set of Chippendale bookcases which adorned his chambers were always flung open, and reports piled upon textbooks lay about the floor. Somehow he would steer a course between them as he paced up and down dictating drafts and opinions. On 31 July 1907 he married Dorothea Tunder, the daughter of Thomas Popplewell Royle, of Chester; they had three daughters and two sons.

In 1919 Luxmoore applied for silk, and quickly won a commanding position in the court of Sir J. M. Astbury, to which he attached himself. On Luxmoore's motion, Astbury delivered his famous judgment in May 1926 that the general strike was illegal. Luxmoore's mature style of advocacy seemed to have been modelled on his forward play: restless, eager, forceful, but never unfair. His Cambridge contemporary Thomas Inskip, later first Viscount Caldecote, whom he first met on the football field, thought that 'the secret of his rather surprising success … was his capacity for thoroughness and hard work', as well as high natural intelligence (*The Cantuarian*, 11). In 1922 Luxmoore became a bencher of Lincoln's Inn. Four years later he captained the Bar Golfing Society and revived the match between the English and Scottish bench and bar, which had fallen into abeyance.

Luxmoore was appointed a judge of the Chancery Division with the honour of knighthood in February 1929. He had an instinct for the point, and an astonishing memory for cases which guided him to wider principles, but the same qualities that had assured his success as an advocate counted against him as a judge: 'he was inclined to indicate too soon the way in which his mind was working and he could not always resist the temptation to argue instead of listening to argument' (*Law Journal*, 313). He did not plumb the depths of equity or explore the foundations of the legal system, and he would not have claimed great learning. But by careful analysis, clear exposition, and shrewd judgement, he embellished English law. Of the earlier actions which he tried, *Vanderpant* v. *Mayfair Hotel Company, Limited* (1930), which related to nuisance by noise, was of more than local interest; *In re Ross* (1930) was an important decision on the elusive doctrine of 'renvoi'; and *Spyer* v. *Phillipson* (1931) clarified the law of tenant's fixtures. In *In re Caus* (1934), he upheld the validity of a bequest for masses.

Luxmoore's promotion to the Court of Appeal in October 1938, with the rank of privy councillor, met with universal approval. There he participated in many important decisions. He was a courageous judge, and his dissenting judgments in several instances paved the way for successful appeals. One illustration of this arose out of rivalry between two trade marks for stockings, Rysta and Aristoc. In the House of Lords ([1945] A.C 68), tribute was paid to his formulation of the problem (*Law Reports, Appeal Cases*, 1945, 68), and he had an unrivalled knowledge of trade mark and patent law. Another illustration is the case of *In re Grosvenor* (1944), which related to *'commorientes'*; there his minority judgment was converted into a majority decision in the House of Lords of three to two. A third illustration may be found in the case of the *'Liteblue' Diary* (*G. A. Cramp & Sons, Ltd* v. *Frank Smythson, Ltd*; 1944). As he did not normally preside in the Court of Appeal or deliver the leading judgment, his extended dissenting judgments are apt to attract notice. But more often he was the powerful ally of the majority, and he played a very full part in the court's deliberations.

Luxmoore bought Bilsington Priory near Ashford, Kent, for his home. In 1924 he stood as a Liberal for the Thanet division, but without success. He was mayor of New Romney (1920–26) and speaker of the Cinque Ports. From 1931 to 1940 he chaired the East Kent quarter sessions, and from 1929 to 1940 the East Kent rating appeal committee. He also chaired a committee which reported in 1943 on post-war agricultural education; almost all its recommendations later passed into law. He was president of the Kent County Cricket Club and always remained deeply devoted to the county.

The death of his sons, Charles and Coryndon, on active service in November 1939 and June 1940, and the delayed reaction of overwork, finally broke Luxmoore's health. In March 1944 he was taken ill in court. He returned to work with vigour but without illusion. On 25 September 1944 he sat for the last time, and died the same evening in the West London Hospital in Hammersmith after a heart attack. He was buried at Bilsington. He was survived by his wife and three daughters.

Death cut Luxmoore off from the law's highest honours. But few judges have won such distinction in so many fields. To his love of Kent, his school, and the cathedral must be added his devotion to Jesus College, of which he was elected an honorary fellow in 1938; to Lincoln's Inn, which he served as treasurer in the difficult days of 1943; and to every phase of the administration of justice.

R. F. Roxburgh, *rev.* Mark Pottle

Sources *The Cantuarian*, 20/1 (Dec 1944), 9–15 · *Canterbury Cathedral Chronicle*, 40 (Oct 1944) · *The Times* (26 Sept 1944), 7e · *Law Journal*, 94/4107 (30 Sept 1944), 313 · *Annual Report* [Jesus College, Cambridge] (1945) · Venn, *Alum. Cant.* · personal knowledge (1959) · private information (1959)

Likenesses W. Stoneman, photograph, 1935, NPG · J. Bateman, oils, King's School, Canterbury

Wealth at death £27,784 5*s*.: administration, 1 Jan 1945, *CGPLA Eng. & Wales*

Luxmoore, John (1756–1830), bishop of St Asaph, was born at Okehampton, Devon, the son of John Luxmoore and his wife, Mary Cunningham. He was educated at Ottery St Mary School and at Eton College, whence he passed as a scholar in 1776 to King's College, Cambridge; he graduated BA in 1780, and proceeded MA in 1783. On 30 June 1795 he was created DD at Lambeth by Archbishop Moore. He became fellow of his college, having been tutor to the earl of Dalkeith (later the duke of Buccleuch). Backed by the duke's influence, he obtained a series of preferments: he became rector of St George the Martyr, Queen Square, London, in 1782, prebendary of Canterbury in 1793, dean of Gloucester in 1799, and rector of Taynton, Gloucestershire, in 1800. In 1806 he exchanged St George the Martyr for St Andrew's, Holborn. In 1807 he became bishop of Bristol and in 1808 he was translated to Hereford, and in 1815 to St Asaph. In 1808 he resigned the deanery of Gloucester, and in 1815 the benefice of St Andrew's, Holborn. On 6 April 1786 he married Elizabeth Barnard, the niece of Edward Barnard, provost of Eton. The couple had a large family.

Luxmoore published little, other than visitation articles and several sermons. He gained a reputation less for his intellect than as an example of eighteenth-century episcopal avarice. To D. R. Thomas, the historian of St Asaph diocese, Luxmoore was, quite simply, the worst offender in the matter of nepotism and plurality in its annals. He held, as was usual, the archdeaconry of St Asaph at the same time as the bishopric, but also held many other preferments besides. His family, moreover, were treated with similar liberality, and it has been estimated that he and they at one time absorbed as much as £27,000 per annum of church income in the two dioceses of St Asaph and Hereford; even after the bishop's death, his family continued to enjoy £7000 from the diocese of St Asaph alone.

Luxmoore died at the bishop's palace, St Asaph, on 21 January 1830. His eldest son, **Charles Scott Luxmoore** (1792?–1854), attended Eton College and distinguished himself as a classical scholar while at St John's College, Cambridge, where he completed his degrees with great reputation. He graduated BA in 1815, and proceeded MA in 1818. He married on 10 September 1829 Catherine (*d.* 1830), the youngest daughter of the Rt Revd Sir John Nicholl.

Following in his father's footsteps, and owing his early advancement to him, Charles Luxmoore became a noted pluralist. Ordained deacon and priest in 1815, he became rector of Bromyard, and also the following year of Cradley and of Darowen, Montgomeryshire. In addition he held a prebend at Hereford from 1819, as well as being at St Asaph the dean (1826–54) and also the chancellor of the

John Luxmoore (1756–1830), by unknown artist, *c.*1820

diocese. He died at Cradley, Herefordshire, on 27 April 1854. 'The death of the Dean of St Asaph removes another gigantic pluralist' noted the *Clerical Journal* (Venn, *Alum. Cant.*). He was buried in the cathedral at St Asaph.

MATTHEW CRAGOE

Sources D. R. Thomas, *Esgobaeth Llanelwy: the history of the diocese of St Asaph*, rev. edn, 3 vols. (1908–13) • [J. Watkins and F. Shoberl], *A biographical dictionary of the living authors of Great Britain and Ireland* (1816) • R. A. Austen-Leigh, ed., *The Eton College register, 1753–1790* (1921) • *GM*, 1st ser., 56 (1786), 351 • *GM*, 1st ser., 100/1 (1830), 272 • *GM*, 1st ser., 100/2 (1830), 649 • *GM*, 2nd ser., 41 (1854), 663 • Venn, *Alum. Cant.* • *DNB*

Likenesses portrait, *c.*1820, St Asaph Cathedral Library [*see illus.*] • G. Hayter, group portrait, oils (*The trial of Queen Caroline, 1820*), NPG • oils, Eton

Luyt, Sir Richard Edmonds (1915–1994), colonial governor and educational administrator, was born on 8 November 1915 in Breda Street, Cape Town, South Africa, the second of the three children of Richard Robbins Luyt (1886–1967), broker, and his wife, Roberta Wilhemina Frances, *née* Edmonds (1891–1943). His forebears were Cape farmers and traders of Afrikaner stock, and Dick (as he was always known) grew up as 'a little bilingual boy' (*UCT 200 Club Newsletter*). Both sides of his family had strong associations with the University of Cape Town and it was hardly surprising, therefore, that after schooling at Diocesan College, Rondebosch (Bishops), he should follow in his father's footsteps to the University of Cape Town in 1933, where he studied economics and gained his BA. This was followed by 'three wonderful years' (ibid.) as a Rhodes scholar at Trinity College, Oxford, where among other things he won a rugby blue and captained the university cricket team. According to his own account he learned more of Africa at Oxford than he had done in his homeland, and 'fired with the excitement of opportunity and service' (ibid.) he joined the British colonial service.

Following the outbreak of the Second World War, Luyt tried to volunteer for the army, but in 1940 he was sent out instead by the colonial service to Northern Rhodesia. From there it was not long before his wish to be released for military service was fulfilled, and he was posted as a sergeant to a 600-strong Ethiopian guerrilla unit in the campaign led by Orde Wingate to liberate Ethiopia from the Italians. In March 1941 he displayed magnificent leadership of his platoon against numerically superior Italian forces at the River Charaka action. More generally, he gave outstanding service throughout the campaign and in 1942 was awarded the DCM for his 'great coolness and courage' (*London Gazette*). Almost simultaneously he was commissioned in the field. After the defeat of the Italians, Wingate gave him a prominent place in the parade on the occasion of Emperor Haile Selassie's triumphal return to Addis Ababa. He spent the rest of the war with the British military mission in Ethiopia. Early in 1945 he was demobilized with the rank of lieutenant-colonel, and by the middle of the year was back in Northern Rhodesia.

In 1947 Luyt returned to Oxford briefly to study trade unionism and industrial relations in Africa. On his return to Northern Rhodesia he spent the next six years, first as a district officer, then as a senior labour officer, in the copperbelt. On 24 April 1948 he married Jean Mary Wilder (1916/17–1951), daughter of John Robert Wilder, company director, of Tettenhall, Staffordshire; they had one daughter. In 1953 Luyt was posted to Kenya and served as labour commissioner from 1954 to 1957, and later as permanent secretary in various ministries, and as secretary to the cabinet. In these capacities he established a reputation as a shrewd and determined negotiator and a firm administrator. Friends from that time recall his ability to get on with people at all levels and from any number of backgrounds, particularly Africans. The good relationship he established with Tom Mboya, the trade union leader and emerging politician, was an important example. Meanwhile, his first wife having died, tragically, in 1951, Luyt married, in 1956, (Eileen) Betty Reid (*d.* 1999), daughter of Mervyn and Rosa Reid; they had two sons.

A further spell in Northern Rhodesia, this time as chief secretary, followed from 1962 to 1964. During this time Luyt became a close friend of Kenneth Kaunda. When Zambia received its independence in 1964 Luyt moved to pastures new, as governor of British Guiana. When he arrived racial tension between the East Indian and African communities was already at breaking point and it was not long before vicious rioting flared up, with serious loss of life. Reacting with calm but decisive authority, Luyt suspended the constitution and assumed full emergency powers himself. Prominent trouble makers were imprisoned, including the deputy prime minister, and Luyt was soon at loggerheads with the prime minister himself. But order was restored and elections followed.

When Guyana became independent in 1966 Luyt stayed on for a few months as governor-general.

In 1967 Luyt returned to South Africa and the following year embarked on a new career as vice-chancellor of his alma mater, the University of Cape Town. These too were troublesome times, of a different kind but calling for the same qualities of courage, firmness of purpose, and integrity that he had displayed before. He was forthright in his condemnation of the policies of the government, and strongly opposed to apartheid. He resolutely resisted pressures from the authorities over the enrolment of black students, the imprisonment of staff and students without trial, and the use of riot police to suppress student demonstrations. Outside the university he was active in the End Conscription Campaign and the Civil Rights League. When he retired in 1980 the *Cape Times* said in an editorial that:

> he carried out the duties of his office with dignity and tolerance, often in difficult and provocative circumstances. On taking leave of the university, he may look back on thirteen years of outstanding service which had its roots in a total commitment to the cause of basic human rights and the preservation of academic freedom. (private information, S. Saunders)

Luyt was a good-looking man with rugged features, a wiry physique, and an engaging smile. Throughout his life, and however elevated his station, he never lost the common touch. He was, for example, a keen gardener who, when permanent secretary in Nairobi, was known to leave bags of home-grown vegetables outside the doors of colleagues' quarters. He was also an enthusiastic and talented sportsman and when on tour in British Guiana, where cricket is so popular, he was sometimes to be seen keeping wicket in a local match, to the delight of the onlookers. He was appointed CMG in 1960, KCMG in 1964, GCMG in 1966, and KCVO in 1966. Most of all he treasured the DCM he won in 1942, although he did not talk about it. He died at his home, Allandale, 64 Alma Road, Rosebank, Cape Province, South Africa, on 12 February 1994. He was survived by his second wife, the daughter of his first marriage, and one of the two sons of his second marriage.

JOHN LEAHY

Sources D. Shirreff, *Bare feet and bandoliers: Wingate, Sandford, the patriots and the part they played in the liberation of Ethiopia* (1995), 66–278 • A. Clayton and D. C. Savage, *Government and labour in Kenya, 1895–1963* (1974, [1975]), 321–429 • R. Luyt, 'Cape Town over the years', *UCT 200 Club Newsletter* (April 1994) • *WWW, 1991–5* • *The Times* (15 Feb 1994) • *Daily Telegraph* (10 March 1994) • personal knowledge (2004) • private information (2004) [Lady Luyt, S. Saunders, other friends and colleagues] • m. cert.

Archives priv. coll., Gojjam diary • University of Cape Town Library, MSS

Likenesses photograph, repro. in Luyt, 'Cape Town over the years'

Lyall. *See also* Lyell, Lyle.

Lyall, Alfred (1796–1865), philosopher, was born at Findon, Sussex, on 6 February 1796, the youngest son of John Lyall (1752–1805), of Findon, who was engaged in shipping, and his wife, Jane Camming or Comyn (*d.* 1867), of Newcastle upon Tyne. George *Lyall, MP, and William Rowe *Lyall, DD, dean of Canterbury, were his brothers. He was educated at Eton College and at Trinity College, Cambridge, where he matriculated as a pensioner in 1813, and graduated BA in 1818.

After spending some time in Frankfurt and Geneva, Lyall settled in a small house of his own at Findon with his widowed mother, to whom he was devoted. While at Findon he edited the *Annual Register* from 1822 to about 1827. The winter of 1825–6 he passed with an invalid sister in Madeira, and on his return he published in 1827 an anonymous narrative entitled *Rambles in Madeira and Portugal*. The book was accompanied by a folio volume of lithographic sketches by Lyall's friend and fellow-traveller James Bulwer (*d.* 1879), later rector of Stody, Norfolk.

Subsequently Lyall returned to Findon and applied himself to philosophy. He produced, anonymously, a thin volume entitled *Principles of Necessary and Contingent Truth* (1830), which was intended as an introduction to a larger work that was never executed. In 1829 Lyall took holy orders, as curate to his old friend John Hind (*c.*1757–1832), vicar of Findon.

In December 1830 Lyall married Mary Drummond (*c.*1812–1878), the daughter of James T. Broadwood. They had eleven children, including Sir Alfred Comyn *Lyall, lieutenant-governor of the North-Western Provinces of India, and Sir James Broadwood Lyall (1838–1916), lieutenant-governor of the Punjab.

The winter of 1833–4 Lyall passed at Rome, where he kept a journal. In 1837 he was appointed vicar of Godmersham, Kent, and resumed the editorship of the *Annual Register*, at the request of Rivingtons, the proprietors. A serious illness soon forced him to give up the editorship, and, although a careful and charitable pastor and a good neighbour, he became unable to write much. In 1848 he became rector of Harbledown, near Canterbury.

In 1856, under the title *Agonistes, or philosophical strictures, by the author of the 'Principles of necessary and contingent truth'*, Lyall published his maturer views, which resembled those of Sir William Hamilton. About a third of the book consists of a very close and generally adverse discussion of the philosophical theories of John Stuart Mill. Lyall also contributed to the 'History of the mediaeval church' in volume 11 of the *Encyclopedia metropolitana*. He died at Llangollen, Denbighshire, on 11 September 1865, and was buried at Harbledown.

H. M. CHICHESTER, *rev.* C. A. CREFFIELD

Sources Boase, *Mod. Eng. biog.* • Venn, *Alum. Cant.* • Burke, *Gen. GB* • H. M. Durand, *Life of … Sir Alfred Comyn Lyall* (1913) • private information (1893) • *CGPLA Eng. & Wales* (1865)

Wealth at death under £7000: probate, 10 Nov 1865, *CGPLA Eng. & Wales*

Lyall, Sir Alfred Comyn (1835–1911), administrator in India and writer, was born on 4 January 1835 at Coulsdon in Surrey, second son of the seven sons and four daughters of Alfred *Lyall (1796–1865), philosopher and rector of Harbledown, Kent, and his wife, Mary Drummond (*c.*1812–1878), daughter of James Broadwood of Lyne, Sussex. Both families were originally from the Scottish border, though his mother's family had Swiss and highland links. The

Sir Alfred Comyn Lyall (1835–1911), by Eveleen Myers

family moved in elevated social and business circles, a circumstance which added charm and self-confidence to the natural elegance of Lyall's tall, slender frame. One paternal uncle, George *Lyall, was chairman of the East India Company and twice MP for the City of London; another, William Rowe *Lyall, was dean of Canterbury. A younger brother, Sir James Broadwood Lyall, was to become lieutenant-governor of the Punjab.

After a childhood at Godmersham and Harbledown in Kent, Lyall attended Eton College as a foundation scholar from 1845 to 1852. In 1853 his uncle George secured him a writership in the East India Company, and Lyall joined the last intake of patronage boys into the company's college, Haileybury. As with Eton, he did not find it the most stimulating of environments—'one well-organized humbug', according to his biographer (Durand, 21)—but in his occasional humorous and poetical contributions to the *Haileybury Observer* he began a habit of literary jottings which was never to leave him.

The mutiny Lyall arrived at Calcutta in January 1856 and in May was appointed assistant magistrate of Bulandshahr district. It was an opportune posting for a young man of adventurous spirits, for shortly afterwards Lyall found himself in the thick of the great rebellion of 1857. He lost all his possessions, including a carefully hoarded supply of books, but for a time the exhilarating life of an irregular cavalryman was wonderful compensation. On 21 May 1857, under fire from hostile villagers, he fled his burning bungalow at Bulandshahr and rode through the night to Meerut. There he joined a corps of volunteer horse and plunged enthusiastically into skirmishes, including an encounter in a cane-field which saw his horse killed under him. In late September he joined Colonel Greathed's column charged with clearing the road to Agra; then he fought under the command of Frederick Roberts to regain control of Bulandshahr, afterwards remaining behind to reimpose civil authority on his old district. He was willing to hang captured rebels but he did not relish it, and soon he was hankering after a less grotesque occupation and lamenting his lost books. In 1858 he joined mopping-up actions in Rohilkhand, and subsequently received the mutiny medal for his services.

Lyall's reading of the rebellion stayed with him all his life, turning him into, in Eric Stokes's words, a 'liberal authoritarian'—a liberal who believed in the power of the sword and gave a wide berth to social and political reform. Convinced that Muslims had started the rebellion, Lyall henceforth insisted that they had to be conciliated and shielded from the disruption of modernization if they were not to rise up again. Such a perspective was to have a profound impact on Britain's devolution of power to India. The rebellion also made Lyall doubt that the British could long hold on to India peaceably, but his resulting pessimism was not of an especially gloomy cast. He had a sharp sense of humour, and often saw the funny or absurd side of Britain's position in India.

In 1861 Lyall returned home on leave and while there met Cornelia Arnoldina (Cora) Cloete, a young, handsome woman of a Dutch Cape family who, like Lyall, had lived through the Indian turmoil of 1857. In spite of his parents' perpetual misgivings about his financial management, Lyall insisted on marrying Cora on 12 November 1862, in time to take her back with him to his new post as assistant magistrate of Agra. Cora was a resilient, active woman, and outdid her husband in sports, but it was a strength he did not resent—especially as it enabled her to join him on his cold-weather tours about the district. Throughout their married life Cora's pragmatism and adaptability were a necessary complement to Lyall's restless, easily bored spirit.

West Berar and essays on religion In 1864 Lyall was transferred to the Central Provinces, and in 1867 he was made commissioner of West Berar, a territory recently annexed from the nizam of Hyderabad. Berar should have been a challenging appointment but Lyall was uncomfortable with the energetic reformism of his chief, Sir Richard Temple, and withdrew instead into private study. In 1870 he published the *Statistical Account or Gazetteer of Berar*, which was hailed as a model of its kind and signalled a new trend in European interpretations of Indian religious behaviour. In it Lyall argued that Hinduism was a living organism, capable of daily change and development, not the fossilized religion of long-dead Brahmans, the view currently being propagated by Professor Max Müller. He developed his argument in several essays, doing for Indian religion what Sir Henry Maine, a former distinguished legal member of the viceroy's council, had already done for Indian law, privileging customary law over textual precepts. Maine quickly recognized in Lyall a kindred spirit, and arranged to have his essays published in the *Fortnightly Review*, a literary introduction which bore fruit in a lifelong friendship between Lyall and the *Review*'s editor, John Morley.

Lyall's essays had clear administrative implications. The British had to recognize, he argued, that the introduction of Western education and technology was creating a spiritual interregnum in India in which people's loss of faith in the old ways was in danger of boiling over into rebellion against the one stable presence in the country—the foreign government. The British were bound therefore to move cautiously in dealing with old institutions and habits. These early essays on religion were also intensely personal, and marked for Lyall the loss of his own faith and entry into what he only half-jokingly called 'the dreary desert of scepticism' (Durand, 109).

Lyall's writings brought him attention in Calcutta, the British capital in India. In 1873 the viceroy, Lord Northbrook, appointed him home secretary, and then, in 1874, governor-general's agent in Rajputana. Northbrook intended that this latter post should be an apprenticeship for Lyall to become foreign secretary, but after the viceroy's resignation in 1876 the understanding lapsed and Lyall mouldered away in Ajmer. Disappointed by the long wait, he buried himself in researching and editing a Rajputana gazetteer along the lines of his earlier Berar work.

Lytton and the Anglo-Afghan War In 1878 Lord Lytton, the viceroy chosen by Disraeli, finally summoned Lyall to Calcutta as foreign secretary. Their shared literary interests were expected to make them congenial working partners, but it was known that Lyall had his doubts about Lytton's recent attempts to evict a Russian mission from Afghanistan. To safeguard against Lyall's contacts with Liberals like John Morley, Lytton forbade him to correspond with friends on matters of policy unless he guaranteed to back the official line to the hilt. These were hard terms for someone who was used to employing his voluminous correspondence as a means of reflection, and Lyall inevitably found himself isolated from friends and harried by Lytton's rapid-fire instructions. Sir Henry Daly's view from the political agency at Indore was that Lyall, 'with the brains of a genius, has not the backbone of a mole when necessary to oppose the viceroy' (Chew, 57).

Lyall was foreign secretary throughout the Second Anglo-Afghan War, from April 1878 until September 1881. Initially he tried to temper Lytton's enthusiasm for forward action in Afghanistan, arguing for a lasting Anglo-Russian agreement instead of a volatile Anglo-Afghan one, but his advice fell on stoppered ears. When in September 1878 Lytton overreacted to the amir's repulsion of a British mission, Lyall supported his decision to dismember Afghanistan. The country was duly invaded and partitioned, with Yakub Ali placed on the throne in Kabul and a British puppet, the Wali Sher Ali, on that in Kandahar. For his role in these proceedings Lyall received the CB.

Only when this disastrous policy was shown to have failed, with the murder in September 1879 of the resident in Kabul, Sir Louis Cavagnari, did Lyall break free of Lytton's old thinking. By May 1880, with Gladstone's appointee, Lord Ripon, on his way out to replace Lytton, Lyall was fully in favour of retreat and of handing over the whole country to Abdur Rahman, who, though a former Russian pensioner, was the strongest contender for the position of amir. On a mission to Kandahar in the autumn of 1880 Lyall charmed the Wali Sher Ali into resigning his throne, thus removing one source of embarrassment. He also helped convince Ripon of the wisdom of sticking with Abdur Rahman and of retaining for defensive purposes the frontier districts of Quetta, Sibi, and Pishin. When in 1881 Abdur Rahman proved strong enough to see off a rival, Britain heaved a sigh of relief and celebrated with a new round of honours: this time Lyall picked up a KCB. It was no small irony that an administrator who was legendary among his colleagues for his irritating ability to see both sides of a question should have been twice decorated for pursuing contradictory policies.

Lieutenant-governorship In 1881 Ripon appointed Lyall lieutenant-governor of the North-Western Provinces and chief commissioner of Oudh, a prestigious post but something of a disappointment after the drama of the previous years. Lyall was ill suited to the cultural backwaters of Allahabad and Naini Tal. Unlike the governors of Bengal and the Punjab, the North-Western Provinces and Oudh chief never shared a residence at either Calcutta or Simla with the government of India authorities, an isolation which exacerbated Lyall's pessimism about the shaky foundations of British rule and spurred him to call for his own legislative advisers. In January 1887 the first legislative council of the North-Western Provinces and Oudh met; it was composed very largely of officials, together with a few, hand-picked landholders and lawyers. Lyall had no desire for a more radical body; he wanted simply to widen the consultative base for local legislation, co-opting a handful of 'respectable native gentlemen' into the governing process, while at the same time loosening Calcutta's stranglehold on provincial administration.

Tetchy relations with Calcutta were further soured by Lyall's tardiness in implementing Ripon's local self-government rules. Although he declared himself in favour of Ripon's ideals, he distrusted the electoral principle and in legislating for the rural district boards he insisted on the government's right to nominate the electorate from which the members would be chosen. The same cautious respect for traditional elements in society underpinned his approach to tenancy reform in Oudh. Ripon urged him on with reform, but Lyall would agree only to measures which had the support of the talukdars or large landlords, in accordance with the post-mutiny policy of propping up the landlords to ensure their loyalty to the raj. The Tenancy Act of 1886 did offer tenants longer, more secure leases, but Lyall's primary purpose in framing it was to head off the possibility of a peasant uprising against the talukdars.

Lyall's educational reforms were similarly double-edged. The liberal in him would not allow him to withhold Western education from Indians, but he was determined to control its delivery. A new local university, cut off from the pernicious influence of Calcutta, was the solution: Allahabad University was opened in 1887 as an examining institution only, with a loose federal structure designed to prevent it from affording cover to an anti-government clique.

Lyall's paralysing cautiousness meant that Ripon left India disappointed in the man he had hoped would be a great reformer. The tensions inherent in Lyall's liberalism were more quickly grasped by an outsider. Visiting him in 1884, Wilfrid Scawen Blunt observed: 'Lyall, as a man, is everything that is charming and sympathetic; as an official he has graduated in a thoroughly bad school' (Blunt, 149).

Retirement and writing In 1887 Lyall retired from the Indian service and returned home to England. He served on the Council of India for an unusually long term of fifteen years, during which he was largely concerned to moderate the pace of reform in India and to push for an Anglo-Russian agreement on Afghanistan. Upon his retirement in 1902 he was made a privy counsellor; he had been made KCIE in 1887 and GCIE in 1896. He hoped to be chosen viceroy after Lord Lansdowne, and in the interim rejected the governorship of Cape Colony in 1889 and that of New Zealand in 1892; but when John Morley put forward his name to Lord Kimberley the latter dismissed him instantly as 'too wavering'.

Although disappointed, Lyall had ample compensation in England, having settled comfortably into the world of the literary and cultural élite. His essays won him a clutch of honorary degrees—an Oxford DCL in 1889, a Cambridge LLD in 1891, and, in 1893, the first honorary fellowship of King's College, Cambridge—and he was a member of numerous clubs, including Grillion's, the Literary Society, Grant Duff's Breakfast Club, and the Athenaeum. He was one of the founding fellows of the British Academy in 1902, chairman of the governors of Dulwich College in 1907, and a trustee of the British Museum in 1911. Few of his acquaintances could resist commenting on his charm and irony, and the latter, which had been one of his greatest undoings as an effective administrator, won him admirers ranging from Alfred Lord Tennyson to Sir Spencer Walpole and Leslie Stephen. Nor did his well-known opposition to women's suffrage noticeably limit his circle of female friends, among whom he counted Gertrude Bell, Lady Lyttelton, and his cousin, the writer Countess Martinengo di Cesaresco. In constant demand by society hostesses, had he so desired he need never have dined at home again.

Amid the socializing and speaking engagements, Lyall continued to write. In 1882 he published *Asiatic Studies*, a collection of his articles, and in 1889 he followed this with a second volume. The essay was his preferred medium, and he wrote frequently for the *Edinburgh Review* as well as contributing to the Cambridge Modern History and the *Encyclopaedia Britannica*. A popular collection of poetry, *Verses Written in India* (1889), entered its sixth edition in 1905. He wrote several longer works, including a sympathetic study of Warren Hastings (1889), a volume on Lord Tennyson in the English Men of Letters series (1902), and an authorized biography of Lord Dufferin (2 vols., 1905). His historical magnum opus, *The Rise and Expansion of the British Dominion in India*, began life as an Oxford lecture in 1891 and expanded into a full-length work in its fifth edition of 1910. In it he challenged Sir John Seeley's account in the *Expansion of England* of Britain's conquest of India as fortuitous, arguing instead that there was an overwhelming logic and natural purpose to the forces which had brought East and West together in India. He was ultimately a believer in the civilizing mission of the West, but his debilitating fear of too rapid change rendered his liberalism largely theoretical. As late as 1909, when John Morley consulted him on Indian electoral reform, Lyall persuaded him of the necessity of introducing separate, communally based electorates. India had not yet made the shift from status to contract, Lyall warned, and traditional interest groups, such as the Muslims and large landlords, still needed to be conciliated if the British were not to be tossed out of India by a revolution of their own making.

Lyall's last years were dogged by heart disease. He died suddenly on 10 April 1911 on a visit to Lord Tennyson, son of the poet laureate, at Farringford House, Freshwater, Isle of Wight, and was buried on 14 April at his childhood home of Harbledown, near Canterbury in Kent. He was survived by his wife, Cora, and two sons, Frances Alfred and Robert Adolphus (Indian army), and two daughters, Sophia Magdalene and Mary Evelina, who married Sir John Ontario Miller of the Indian Civil Service. Shortly after his death, Lyall's family commissioned an official life by Sir Mortimer Durand. Durand deliberately focused on Lyall's literary career and friendships, skipping over the substance of his official work. This was a misreading of where Lyall's influence lay: his poems and other literary writings soon faded from view, but his articulation of liberal authoritarianism lived on in the peculiar 'castes and communities' nature of Britain's seminal experiments in Indian electoral responsibility. KATHERINE PRIOR

Sources E. C. T. Chew, 'Sir Alfred Comyn Lyall: a study of the Anglo-Indian official mind', PhD diss., U. Cam., 1970 • H. M. Durand, *Life of … Sir Alfred Comyn Lyall* (1913) • C. A. Bayly, *The local roots of Indian politics: Allahabad, 1880–1920* (1975) • F. Robinson, *Separatism among Indian Muslims: the politics of the United Provinces' Muslims, 1860–1923* (1974) • W. S. Blunt, *India under Ripon: a private diary* (1909) • E. Stokes, *The English utilitarians and India* (1959) • E. S. Stokes, 'The administrators and historical writing on India', *Historians of India, Pakistan and Ceylon*, ed. C. H. Philips (1961), 385–403 • *The Times* (11 April 1911) • *DNB*

Archives BL OIOC, corresp. and papers, MS Eur. F 132 | BL, corresp. with Lord Ripon, Add. MSS 43602–43603 • BL OIOC, corresp. with Sir Henry Durand, MS Eur. D 727 • BL OIOC, letters to John Morley, MS Eur. D 573 • NAM, letters to Earl Roberts • Queen Mary College, London, letters to Lady Lyttelton • Surrey HC, letters to Bertha Broadwood • W. Sussex RO, letters to Wilfrid Scawen Blunt

Likenesses J. J. Shannon, oils, 1890, University of Allahabad, India • Violet, duchess of Rutland, lithograph, 1892, NPG • C. Williams, oils, 1908, Dulwich College, London • H. J. Hudson, oils (after oil painting by J. J. Shannon), NPG • E. Myers, photograph, NPG [*see illus.*] • J. J. Shannon, etching (after C. W. Sherborn), NPG • C. W. Sherborn, etching (Grillion's Club series; after J. J. Shannon), BM • photographs, repro. in Durand, *Life of Sir Alfred Comyn Lyall*

Wealth at death £56,141 11*s.* 5*d.*: resworn probate, 15 May 1911, *CGPLA Eng. & Wales*

Lyall [*née* Rostron], **Dame Beatrix Margaret** (1873–1948), social worker and local politician, was born on 27 October 1873 in Beddington Lane, Beddington, Surrey, the third of eight children of Simpson Rostron, barrister, and his wife, Christina Jane Riley. Educated at home, her parents' Christian faith, as expressed through various political and philanthropic activities, formed her as a 'Christian citizen' (Lyall MS DD/289/3/1). Her father was a churchwarden, magistrate, and the chairman of the local Conservative Party. Her mother ministered to the poor. As a child she readily helped with mothers' meetings and taught at Sunday school.

On 15 June 1899 Beatrix married a childhood friend, George Henry Hudson Pile (1872–1938), a solicitor. He assumed his mother's name, Lyall, by deed poll in 1914. They settled in Chelsea, London. Desiring to be of public service but considered too young for great responsibilities, she visited workhouse inmates and the penurious lonely and sick. While feeling diffident about public life, her competence and growing faith in her vocation of Christian service led her first to become a local leader of the Mothers' Union and then to establish a reputation as a forceful public speaker, especially on the subject of infant welfare.

During the First World War, Beatrix Lyall's gift of oratory was used by government departments to raise civilian morale. Her addresses to miners and munitions workers during night breaks were published by the British Women's Patriotic League. She was a member of the War Savings Committee from the end of the war to the committee's dissolution in 1921, and served as the only woman on the London appeal tribunal under the Profiteering Act. Her high public profile after the war led her local Conservative Party to ask her to stand as a candidate for the London county council (LCC). In 1919 she was elected councillor for East Fulham. In 1920 she became a magistrate and was made a CBE. In 1924 she was created DBE.

When Beatrix Lyall first entered the LCC women had to be content as back-benchers but her political career illustrates how far attitudes to women in public life changed after 1918. She served on several committees, and was chair of the parliamentary committee before being elected the first female vice-chairman of the LCC in 1932. During her years on the council she was 'a hard fighter' (*Fulham Chronicle*, 21 May 1948, 6) not only in representing her constituents' interests but also in espousing her own strongly held views. She was a member of the national council for the Conservative and Unionist Association, and of the executive of the Primrose League.

Running parallel to her political career was Lyall's work for the Mothers' Union both as the diocesan president for London from 1921 to 1936 and as a member of the Mothers' Union's central council. A central vice-president for eleven years, she was granted the honour in 1937 of being made a life vice-president. She was a speaker much in demand because she left the impression 'of a vital personality which had its springs in a sure and certain faith in God' (*Workers' Paper*, July 1948, 103). Through numerous newspaper articles and pamphlets she promoted the organization's view of Christian marriage and its condemnation of divorce. She played a constructive role on committees, although her enthusiasm for a cause made her sometimes too impulsive. Her undoubted talents and energy meant that she was twice nominated central president, an honour which she felt she could not accept because of domestic and other work commitments.

Despite the great sorrow of the deaths of her daughter and husband within a year of each other in the late 1930s, Lyall continued to be 'a tireless social worker' (*The Times*, 11 May 1948). During the Second World War she was the head of hospital supplies for south London, and sat on the executive of the National Council of Women. Latterly she lived at the Prince of Wales Hotel, De Vere Gardens, Kensington, London, where she died on 8 May 1948 having suffered a series of heart attacks. The bishop of Kensington officiated at her funeral, following which she was cremated at Golders Green, Middlesex.

CORDELIA MOYSE

Sources Hammersmith and Fulham archives, Lyall MSS, DD/289/3/1–3c · *The Times* (11 May 1948) · *WWW* · *Workers' Paper* (July 1948), 103 · *Fulham Chronicle* (15 Feb 1924) · *Fulham Chronicle* (21 May 1948), 2, 6 · *West London and Fulham Gazette* (3 June 1938), 4 · b. cert. · m. cert. · d. cert.

Archives Hammersmith and Fulham archives, London, MSS | LMA, London Mothers' Union MSS · Mothers' Union, Mary Sumner House, London, MSS

Likenesses photograph, 1930–39, Hammersmith and Fulham archives · two photographs, 1930–39, LMA

Wealth at death £20,379 3*s.* 9*d.*: probate, 14 Sept 1948, *CGPLA Eng. & Wales*

Lyall, Sir Charles James (1845–1920), administrator in India and orientalist, was born in London on 9 March 1845, the eldest son of Charles Lyall, banker, of Stoke Green, near Slough, and his wife, Harriet, daughter of John Matheson of Attadale, Ross-shire. He was educated in London at King's College School and King's College and afterwards at Balliol College, Oxford, graduating BA in 1867. In 1865 he came first in the open competition for the Indian Civil Service; two years later he took up the first of several district and secretariat appointments in the North-Western Provinces. In 1870 he married Florence, elder daughter of Captain Henry Fraser of Calcutta, with whom he was to have two sons and five daughters.

Lyall was under-secretary to the revenue, agriculture, and commerce department of the government of India from 1873 until 1879. From 1880 until 1889 he was principally engaged as secretary to the chief commissioner of Assam. In August 1889 he was summoned to Calcutta to officiate as home secretary to the supreme government, in which post he was confirmed in 1890. In 1894 he returned briefly to Assam as acting chief commissioner and then in December 1895, after a year's furlough, took up the post of chief commissioner in the Central Provinces, where he remained until his retirement from the service in July 1898. He had been gazetted KCSI twelve months before.

Upon his return to England, Lyall joined the India Office

as judicial and public secretary, serving in that capacity for twelve years until his retirement in 1910. Growing nationalist agitation in India, and the attempt to appease it with the introduction of the Morley–Minto reforms, made Lyall's period of service an unusually full one.

Remarkably, notwithstanding his formidable official duties, Lyall also established himself as one of Britain's foremost scholars of Eastern languages. At Balliol he had distinguished himself as a student of Hebrew, and from there he moved on to Arabic, Persian, and Hindustani. While in India he published a *Sketch of the Hindostani Language* (1880), *Translations of Ancient Arabic Poetry* (1885), and a *Guide to the Transliteration of Hindu and Muhammadan Names* (1885). In 1907–8 he wrote introductions to two ethnographical monographs on Assam and edited a third, *The Mikirs*, by the late Edward Stack, for which he taught himself the rudiments of the Mikirs' language in order to translate into English some folktales collected by Stack. His chief devotion, however, was to the early, pre-Islamic, literature of the Arabs, and on this subject he published a number of works: *Ten Ancient Arabic Poems* (1891–4), *The Diwans of ʿAbid ibn al-Abras and ʿAmir ibn al-Tufail* (1913), *The Poems of ʾAmr Son of Qamiʾah* (1919), and his masterpiece, a two-volume edition of *The Mufaddaliyat: an Anthology of Ancient Arabian Odes Compiled by al-Mufaddal, Son of Muhammad* (1919–21). His translations were particularly successful in combining an accurate rendering with a poetical diction which imitated more or less the metres of the originals, although usually without any attempt at rhyme.

The merit of Lyall's literary work was recognized throughout Europe and honorary degrees were conferred upon him by the universities of Oxford, Edinburgh, and Strasbourg. He was elected a fellow of the British Academy and King's College, London, and a vice-president of the Royal Asiatic Society, of which he was a prominent member. He helped found the London School of Oriental Studies and represented the government of India at oriental congresses in Rome (1899), Hamburg (1902), Algiers (1905), and Copenhagen (1908).

Lyall died at his home, 82 Cornwall Gardens, London, on 1 September 1920 and was buried at Putney Vale cemetery five days later.

William Foster, *rev.* Katherine Prior

Sources 'Obituary notices: Sir Charles James Lyall', *Journal and Proceedings of the Asiatic Society of Bengal*, 2nd ser., 16 (1920) • E. Hilliard, ed., *The Balliol College register, 1832–1914* (privately printed, Oxford, 1914) • R. A. Nicholson, 'Sir C. J. Lyall, 1845–1920', *PBA*, [9] (1919–20), 492–6 • F. R. Miles, ed., *King's College School: a register of pupils in the school … 1831–1866* (1974) • *The Times* (4 Sept 1920), 1 • *CGPLA Eng. & Wales* (1920)

Archives Somerville College, Oxford, corresp. | Bodl. Oxf., MacDonnell MSS • NAM, letters to Earl Roberts • NL Wales, Rendel MSS

Wealth at death £44,214 19s. 2d.: probate, 26 Oct 1920, *CGPLA Eng. & Wales*

Lyall, David. *See* Swan, Annie Shepherd (1859–1943).

Lyall, Edna. *See* Bayly, Ada Ellen (1857–1903).

Lyall, George (1778/9–1853), shipowner and merchant, was the eldest son of John Lyall (1752–1805), a merchant and shipowner of London and Findon, Sussex, and his wife, Jane Camming or Comyn (*d.* 1867). On his father's death in 1805, he took over the business. Lyall married, and he and his wife, Margaret Ann, had two sons and two daughters.

The peace of 1815 brought a deep and long depression. Lyall believed that reforms were needed if prosperity was to return, and supported the 'liberal' wing of the tory (later Conservative) persuasion. In 1821 he was elected a member of the newly formed Political Economy Club, a discussion society made up of eminent economists and select businessmen, who regarded Adam Smith's *The Wealth of Nations* as the starting point of their discourse. Lyall questioned the usefulness of the Navigation Acts. These were imposed in the seventeenth century to protect trade and shipping; but by the 1820s they seemed to Lyall, and a coterie of like-minded people, detrimental to British enterprise. His commercial experience, and broad outlook, enabled him to give valued advice to William Huskisson who, as president of the Board of Trade (1823–7), made the first dent in the Navigation Acts by negotiating reciprocity treaties with European states and reducing duties on imports.

The 1832 Reform Act promised further change, and Lyall sought a place in parliament to be part of it. Unsuccessful at first, he filled a vacancy in 1833 for the City of London but, defeated in 1835, he did not stand again until 1841. By this time, free trade had become a hotly contested topic. By bringing it to a select committee in 1844, Lyall hoped that his views would prevail. Though he chose its members and briefed witnesses, the committee ended without a report because there was no consensus between free traders and protectionists. Two years later, in 1846, however, the repeal of the corn laws (of which Lyall approved) paved the way for the repeal of the Navigation Acts in 1849. Illness prevented his seeing his work come to fruition; he retired from public life in 1846. During his active years, in and out of parliament, he sat on a variety of select committees: foreign trade (1820, 1824), wrecks (1843), joint stock companies (1844), and the merchant seamen's fund (1845).

In 1823 Lyall, as chairman of the Shipowners' Society (1823–5), presided over a meeting at The London tavern to press for reform in Lloyd's system of registering ships, because it was inefficient and corrupt. No progress could be made before 1833 when he and his colleague George Palmer (1772–1853) formed a provisional committee to bring together the various interests, and in 1834 the New Lloyd's Register of Shipping came to life under strict rules and supervision of a permanent committee, of which Lyall was an original member. He promoted the important Marine Indemnity Company at Lloyd's, and the London Docks and Guardian Insurance companies. In 1830 he was elected a director of the East India Company, and was chairman in 1841–3 and 1844–6.

Again, in 1833, and in conjunction with Palmer, Lyall was a founder member of the General London Ship Owners' Society. It replaced the earlier society, and was much more effective as a lobby for the shipping interest, though many members were staunch protectionists and did not agree with Lyall's views.

Lyall had a sharp mind but he was a poor speaker. With his shy and unobtrusive habits, it was perhaps surprising that Lyall occupied so many important posts. Through his sound judgement, high principles and clear objectives, however, he exercised great influence, and, on occasion, could speak very winningly: in 1834, he persuaded the house to repeal statutes that taxed merchant seamen, and deprived their widows, and orphans, of their tiny pensions; he argued that the maintenance of the Greenwich Hospital, the object of the tax, was the responsibility of the nation.

An honourable man, grave in manner and gentle in temperament, Lyall was respected in the public sphere and loved by his friends. Nutwood Lodge in Reigate, Surrey, was his country retreat. He died at his London home, 17 Park Crescent, Portland Place, Regent's Park, on 1 September 1853. J. A. HAMILTON, *rev.* FREDA HARCOURT

Sources *GM*, 1st ser., 75 (1805), 1179 • S. Palmer, *Politics, shipping and the repeal of navigation laws* (1990) • *The Political Economy Club*, 6 (1921), v • Lloyd's Register of Shipping, minutes 1833–4; and 'A brief outline of the origin ... and history ...', Lloyd's Archive, 71 Fenchurch Street, London • General London Ship Owners' Society, minutes, 1833–4, 12 Carthusian Street, London • BL, Add. MSS 38748, fol. 217 • PRO, PROB 11/2178, sig. 678, fols. 222–7 • *Hansard* 3 (1834), 23.1145–57 • 'Select committee on ... British shipping', *Parl. papers* (1844), vol. 8, no. 545 • 'Select committee on ... foreign trade', *Parl. papers* (1820), 2.365, no. 300 • *Annual Register* (1853), 252–3 • *WWBMP* • d. cert.

Archives BL, corresp. with Sir Robert Peel, Add. MSS 40486–40592, *passim* | Chamber of Shipping, London • Lloyd's Archive, 71 Fenchurch Street, London, Lloyd's Register of Shipping MSS

Likenesses Philips, line engraving, NPG, MacDonnell collection, 34, 304

Wealth at death £50,000—stocks and shares: will, PRO, PROB 11/2178, sig. 678, fols. 222–7

Lyall, Robert (1789–1831), botanist and traveller, was born in Abbey parish, Paisley, on 26 November 1789, the son of William and Janet (*née* Tassie or Tassin) Lyall. Probably educated at Paisley grammar school, he served an apprenticeship before matriculating in medicine at Edinburgh University (1807–10). In September 1808 he bought a house in Paisley High Street but almost immediately went to Manchester, where he spent a year as house surgeon to the Manchester Royal Infirmary, specializing in burns and ophthalmia.

A letter read at the Linnean Society in February 1811 and six papers on plant irritability in Nicholson's *Journal* (1809–11) reveal Lyall's talent for botany. At Manchester he made lasting friendships with Dr Peter Roget, the chemist Thomas Henry, and John Dalton, the natural philosopher; they all held senior positions with the Manchester Literary and Philosophical Society to which Lyall was elected a corresponding member in January 1810, on his return to Paisley where he practised as a surgeon. He was a member of the Royal Physical Society of Edinburgh in 1809–10, became a licentiate of the Royal College of Surgeons of Edinburgh on 22 March 1810, and was appointed medical practitioner to the Paisley Town Hospital in 1811 or 1812. He sold his High Street property in 1813, and published a

Robert Lyall (1789–1831), by Maxim Gauci

competent *Essay on the Chemical and Medicinal Qualities of the Candren Well in Renfrewshire* in 1814.

During 1815 Lyall went to Russia as physician to a St Petersburg nobleman, accompanied Dmitry Poltoratsky, a progressive agriculturalist, to his Kaluga and Oryol estates, and became Countess Orlov-Chesmenska's house doctor, a position which he held four years. In May 1816 he graduated as a doctor and surgeon at the Imperial Medico-Surgical Academy, St Petersburg, with a thesis on staphyloma. As a foreign member of Edinburgh's Wernerian Natural History Society at Moscow in January 1817, Lyall joined the select Imperial Agricultural, Natural History, and Physico-Medical societies.

Some time before 1819 Lyall married. Little is known about his wife, Mary (Mariya); possibly she was Russian. In 1819 the couple visited England and Lyall conveyed numerous seeds to the Royal Botanic Gardens at Kew and discussed plans for a book on Moscow with publishers. From March 1820 he acted as General Nashchokin's physician at Semenovskoye, near Moscow. Between April and August 1822 he escorted a Marchese Pucci, Count Salazar and Edward Penrhyn to the southern Russian provinces. He returned to London with his family in August 1823.

In 1823 Lyall published his *Character of the Russians and a Detailed History of Moscow* (from the middle ages to 1820 and its rebuilding after the 1812 fire). Attractively illustrated, it included noteworthy descriptions of scientific societies, Moscow plants, edible mushrooms, Russian baths, and architecture. His outspoken criticisms of the nobility and the peasantry had precipitated his departure from Russia, and the book's dedication to Tsar Alexander was disavowed by the Russian vice-consul. Lyall replied to a particularly biased critique of his work, which appeared in the *Quarterly Review* of 30 December 1824, challenging the anonymous writer—John Barrow (1764–1848)—one of the founders of the Royal Geographical Society to a duel in February 1826.

On Tsar Alexander's death Lyall wrote three very frank articles in the *New Monthly Magazine and Literary Journal* (January–March 1826) about the tsar (reproduced in *The Times*), Grand Duke Constantine, and Tsar Nicholas, stressing their despotism and the inquisitorial police state. Further anecdotes of Nicholas and publication of Lyall's memoirs of Alexander's reign, advertised in 1826, never materialized. The two volumes of Lyall's informative *Travels in Russia, the Krimea, the Caucasus, and Georgia* appeared in 1825. Critical as ever, his targets included Russian civil and military hospitals, the Orlov family, and Count Razumovsky's famous Gorenky Botanical Garden, near Moscow. Lyall's brief *Account of the Organization, Administration, and Present State of the Military Colonies in Russia* (1824) resulted from these journeys and was translated into German and French. His annotated pamphlet, *Medical Evidence Relating to the Duration of Human Pregnancy*, in the Gardner peerage cause at the House of Lords, reached two editions (1826 and 1827), gaining him recognition in *The Lancet*, which also printed his letter on the difficulties of determining pregnancy (19 Aug 1826).

Lyall, a member of the Royal Asiatic (1823–7) and Linnean (1824–7) societies, succeeded James Hastie as British resident agent for Madagascar (1826), and was elected one of the Zoological Society's first corresponding members in May 1827 (from when his lithograph portrait by Gauci may date). According to his official journal he disembarked with his large family at Port Louis, Mauritius, on 2 October 1827 and sailed to Tamatave in Madagascar, where he met the island's King Radama I, before returning to Mauritius to await the travelling season. He arrived at Tamatave for his next visit in the following June, to be informed of Radama's serious illness; he hastened in July to the capital, Tananarivo, in the island's interior, which he reached on 31 August after the king's death. Queen Ranavalona refused to receive him as an agent of the British government in November 1828, but as the weather was unsuitable for travelling Lyall spent time at the capital, botanizing, and collecting natural history specimens. On 29 March 1829 he was arrested for 'sorcery'—offending the gods by collecting plants and reptiles. He was banished from the island and he and his family returned to Tamatave on 22 April and sailed back to Mauritius.

The *Journal of the Royal Institution* for 1831 reproduces Lyall's recordings of the Madagascan capital's weather between January and 25 March 1829, made with Adie's sympiesometer, Rutherford's thermometer, and Daniell's hygrometer. In a letter from Port Louis, dated 1 September 1829, to William Jackson Hooker, professor of botany at Glasgow University, Lyall bitterly regretted his disrupted plans to advance science, especially natural history, in Madagascar. Nevertheless, he shipped 450 Madagascan plants to Hooker and others to the Linnean, Wernerian, and Medico-Botanical societies and to his friend, Sir Alexander Crichton, in London. Two surviving catalogues describe Lyall's plants, which were incorporated with Hooker's collections in the herbarium of the Royal Botanic Gardens at Kew after Hooker's death in 1865. Other Madagascan plants collected by Lyall are at Edinburgh, New York, and in Mauritius; specimens from Mauritius are also at Kew, while some from St Helena are preserved in Berlin. Altogether fourteen species of Madagascan plants have been named after Lyall. In April 1830 he sent a box of untraced Madagascan minerals, with an extant catalogue, to Professor William Buckland (1784–1856) for the Geological Society of London. Lyall had prepared an account for the press from his private journal about his experiences at the Madagascan capital, but died on 23 May 1831 at Port Louis, Mauritius. His death certificate gives the cause as a malarial fever, contracted in Madagascar during 1828. JOHN H. APPLEBY

Sources *Index Kewensis*, Royal Collection · review, *QR*, 31 (1824–5), 146–66 · S. P. Oliver, 'Dr Robert Lyall', *Gardeners' Chronicle*, 3rd ser., 11 (1892), 519–21 · *DNB* · U. Edin. L., MS La II/647, fols. 258–262 · RBG Kew, directors' correspondence, vols. 52–3 · review, *Edinburgh Medical and Surgical Journal*, 6 (1810), 67–75 · *Edinburgh Medical and Surgical Journal*, 7 (1811), 6–13, 313–16, 382–3 · R. Lyall, 'Example of congenital amanrosis as a family disease', *Edinburgh Medical and Surgical Journal*, 13 (1817), 132 · A. Lasègue, *Musée botanique de M. Benjamin Delessert* (1845) · R. Lyall, *An answer to the observations on 'The character of the Russians' in the Quarterly Review* (1825) · P. K. Holmgren and others, *The herbaria of the world*, 6th edn (1974), pt 1 of *Index herbariorum*, ed. F. A. Stafleu · A. J. Clark, ed., *Book catalogue of the Royal Society*, 5 vols. (1982), vol. 3, p. 589 · 'A collection of several hundred dried plants from Madagascar', *Transactions of the Linnean Society of London*, 16 (1833), 794 · *Paisley Advertiser* (25 Feb 1826) · *Paisley Directory* (1813) · parish register (birth), Abbey parish, Paisley, 28 Nov 1789 · d. cert.

Archives BL, journal, Add. MS 34408 · Linn. Soc., papers · NHM, department of botany | BM, MS GEO a–i · U. Edin., Laing MS ii/647

Likenesses M. Gauci, lithograph, BM, Wellcome L. [*see illus.*]

Lyall, William Rowe (1788–1857), dean of Canterbury, born in London on 11 February 1788, was the second son and fourth child of John Lyall (1752–1805) of Findon, Sussex, a Scottish merchant and shipowner in the city of London, and his wife, Jane Camming or Comyn (*d.* 1867). His elder brother, George *Lyall (1778/9–1853), was MP for the City of London and chairman of the East India Company. William Lyall was educated at Fulham Park School, and in 1805 entered Trinity College, Cambridge, where he graduated BA in 1810 and MA in 1816. In 1817 he married Catharine, youngest daughter of Joseph Brandreth, physician, of Hall Green, Liverpool. There were no children of the marriage.

Lyall was curate of Fawley, Hampshire, from 1812 to 1815, when he moved to London. He was appointed chaplain to St Thomas's Hospital in 1817, and soon afterwards assistant preacher at Lincoln's Inn. In 1822 he became examining chaplain to William Howley, bishop of London, his patron, by whom he was appointed rector of Weeley, Essex, in 1823 and archdeacon of Colchester in 1824. He was Warburtonian lecturer at Lincoln's Inn in 1826, when his subject was 'The prophetical evidences of Christianity'. In 1827 he became rector of Fairsted, Essex, and in 1833 exchanged this living and that of Weeley for the cure of Hadleigh, Essex, where he carried out a notable revival of the parish. In June 1841 Howley, now archbishop of Canterbury, appointed him to the archdeaconry of Maidstone and to a prebendal stall at Canterbury, and the following year he became rector of Great Chart, near Ashford. In November 1845 he accepted Sir Robert Peel's offer of the deanery of Canterbury. Earlier he had been one of the founders of St Augustine's College, Canterbury, and as dean he did much for the restoration of the cathedral.

Lyall made his name as a young man with two articles in the *Quarterly Review* (6, 1811, 1–37; 12, 1814, 281–317) challenging the metaphysical system of Dugald Stewart and proving that an Anglican theologian could match the Scottish Enlightenment on its own ground. He was editor of the *British Critic* in 1816–17, and in 1820 was entrusted by Archbishop Howley with the editorship of the *Encyclopaedia metropolitana*, intended to act as a Christian counterweight to the secular *Britannica*. His contributors, enlisted from all tendencies, included the future adversaries R. D. Hampden and J. H. Newman. The latter wrote the articles on Cicero and Apollonius of Tyana—his first published work. From 1832 to 1846 Lyall was co-editor with H. J. Rose of the *Theological Library*, which ran to fourteen volumes. The conference he and Rose organized at Rose's rectory at Hadleigh, Suffolk, in 1833 is generally regarded as marking the inauguration of the Oxford Movement, though Lyall himself stood aside from the movement. His increasing interest in biblical scholarship bore fruit in 1840 in his major work, *Propaedia prophetica: a View of the Use and Design of the Old Testament*, which made his reputation as an interpreter of Jewish religion and society. Though he appointed his brother, four nephews, and three nephews-in-law to livings at his disposal, he took pains to match the appointee with the appointment, and demanded high standards from his clergy. Cheerful and courteous in manner, he was eirenic in his churchmanship and inherited from his father a sound instinct for business which served him well as an organizer of church building in Essex and cathedral restoration in Canterbury.

Lyall suffered a stroke in 1852 from which he never recovered; he died at the deanery, Canterbury, on 17 February 1857, and was buried in Harbledown churchyard on 26 February. G. Martin Murphy

Sources C. Dewey, *The passing of Barchester* (1991) • Venn, *Alum. Cant.* • *GM*, 3rd ser., 2 (1857), 491–2 • B. Harrison, *Charity never failing: a sermon preached in Canterbury Cathedral on the occasion of the death of the Very Revd W. R. Lyall* (1857) • G. Pearson, editor's notice, in W. R. Lyall, *Propaedeia prophetica, or, the use and design of the Old Testament examined*, ed. G. Pearson, 3rd edn (1885)

Archives BL, letters to Philip Bliss and others

Likenesses T. H. Maguire, lithograph, pubd 1857 (after W. Buckler), BM; NPG • oils, the deanery, Canterbury, Kent • recumbent effigy, Canterbury Cathedral

Lydford, John (*c.*1337–1407), canon lawyer, was born in the diocese of Exeter, probably at Lydford in Devon, about 1337—he was known to be almost seventy in 1406. He was probably educated at Stapledon Hall (later Exeter College) in Oxford; after his death his executors gave some of his books to the college. His brother Robert was also a student there. Lydford's will mentioned Robert Hereward, archdeacon of Taunton, as one of his early benefactors, and he asked to be buried in Exeter Cathedral at the feet of a canon of the same name. Most of our knowledge of his career is taken from his memorandum book or formulary, which has survived among the Exeter diocesan records. Gaps in the diocesan registers make the date and place of his ordination uncertain, but by 1361 he had been presented by the crown, during the vacancy of the abbey of Abingdon, to the benefice of Lockinge in Berkshire, and entries in the memorandum book suggest that at this time he was gaining experience as a proctor in the Salisbury ecclesiastical courts. Perhaps the most important step in his career was his exchange of Lockinge for a prebend in the free chapel of Bosham in Sussex. Here, with the approval of Bishop Grandisson of Exeter (*d.* 1369), the patron, he joined a distinguished group of west-country canonists, John Shillingford, Ralph Tregrisiou, and Robert and Nicholas Braybrooke, who were closely attached to the rising west-country churchman, William Courtenay (*d.* 1396), the future archbishop of Canterbury. He also encountered the Arundel family, who were later to employ his services in Avignon. In 1368 Courtenay went to Oxford as chancellor of the university and was accompanied by Lydford as his clerk. When in 1369 Courtenay became bishop of Hereford, Lydford went too, and was soon dispatched by his master to act as his proctor at the papal court at Avignon. He was resident there for long periods between 1370 and 1376, and acquired much expertise and professional knowledge which made many clients and friends for him to the end of his life.

By 1370 Lydford seems to have proceeded *doctor utrius legis* and had become an advocate in the court of arches. More importantly for his career, however, he was taken up by William Wykeham, first as a proctor in Avignon and then, from 1377 to 1394, as his diocesan official. He had already played an important part, in 1376, in persuading the pope to intercede with Edward III to restore Wykeham to royal favour, and it seems likely that he also advised Wykeham on the acquisition of the bull which authorized the foundation of New College, Oxford. During his tenure of the officiality Lydford was certainly occupied with the endowment of the college, but his memorandum book shows him as also busy in the details of diocesan visitation and with a number of difficult law cases affecting episcopal authority. The household records of the bishop's establishment show him also to have been a regular and frequent guest of the bishop on occasions unconnected with diocesan business. At the same time he maintained his links with Courtenay and his fellow canonists. This was the peak period of Wyclif's activity and of Lollard agitation, and Courtenay was deeply involved. When in 1382 Courtenay convened the so-called Earthquake Council at Blackfriars in London, Lydford appeared as one of the canonist assessors and helped to draw up the condemnation of Wyclif's doctrines. Even after the end of his official employment by Wykeham and Courtenay, Lydford maintained his concern with heretical doctrines, and the memorandum book includes copies of such important documents as the appeal of the Lollard Nicholas Hereford to Rome, and the articles drawn up by Baldwin Shillingford in 1395 against William Thorpe's heretical preaching in the diocese of London. It seems certain that Lydford had become a Lollard expert. By 1385 the centre of Lydford's interests had shifted back to Exeter. He had been a cathedral canon from at least 1376 and in 1385 became archdeacon of Totnes; from this time until his death in December 1407 his principal residence was in Exeter. There are regular signs in the Exeter chapter books of his activities there, and the episcopal registers of Bishop Brantingham and Bishop Stafford, as well as his own memoranda, show that he was regularly employed as adviser and administrator by the bishops and the chapter officials.

Lydford's true importance was as an experienced canonist, whose opinion was sought by ecclesiastics and laymen at all levels. He was not particularly learned, but his memoranda reveal him as an intelligent and adaptable administrator whose activities touched the church and also the state at a good many points. It is known that he borrowed, and presumably read, the chapter manuscript of 'Speculum historiale'. He took pride in the 'good letters' he wrote, and he carefully enumerated in his will his beautiful, large, noted breviary, a fair *legenda sanctorum*, a long crimson robe furred, and the black maple cup from which he had drunk much good wine.

DOROTHY M. OWEN

Sources J. Dahmus, *William Courtenay, archbishop of Canterbury, 1381–1396* (1966) • Emden, *Oxf.*, vol. 2 • F. C. Hingeston-Randolph, ed., *The register of Edmund Stafford, 1395–1419* (1886), 389 • F. C. Hingeston-Randolph, ed., *The register of John de Grandisson, bishop of Exeter*, 3 vols. (1894–9) • F. C. Hingeston-Randolph, ed., *The register of Thomas de Brantyngham, bishop of Exeter*, 2 vols. (1901–6) • *Fasti Angl., 1300–1541*, [Exeter] • *John Lydford's book*, ed. D. M. Owen, Devon and Cornwall RS, new ser., 20 (1974) • D. M. Owen, 'The Practising Canonist', *Proceedings of the fourth international congress of medieval canon law* (1976), 45–51 • [T. Netter], *Fasciculi zizaniorum magistri Johannis Wyclif cum tritico*, ed. W. W. Shirley, Rolls Series, 5 (1858) • D. Wilkins, ed., *Concilia Magnae Britanniae et Hiberniae*, 4 vols. (1737)

Archives Archivio Vaticano, Vatican City • Exeter College, Oxford, muniments • Winchester College, muniments | Devon RO, Exeter diocesan records, Exeter chapter muniments • LPL, archiepiscopal registers, Hereford chapter muniments

Lydgate, John (*c.*1370–1449/50?), poet and prior of Hatfield Regis, was born at Lidgate in Suffolk, 'wher Bachus licour doth ful scarsli flete' (*The Fall of Princes*, bk 8, l. 194), a few miles south-west of Bury St Edmunds where he was to spend most of his life, and where, presumably, there was a better supply of wine to refresh his 'drie soule'. Later in the poem he refers to his village, at the time of the slaying of St Edmund at Hoxne, with some pride as:

> be olde tyme a famous castel toun;
> In Danys tyme it was bete doun.
> (ibid., bk 9, ll. 3431–5)

Elsewhere, in his *Isopes fabules*, an apology for his lack of rhetorical skill leads him to remark wryly:

> Have me excusyd: I was born in Lydgate;
> Of Tullius gardeyn I passyd nat the gate.
> (*Minor Poems*, 567)

The date of his birth can be estimated from two references in his works: in the prologue to *The Siege of Thebes* (1420–

John Lydgate (*c.*1370–1449/50?), manuscript illumination [kneeling left, with Henry V]

22?) he says he is 'nygh fyfty yere of age' (*Siege of Thebes*, l. 93), and in *The Fall of Princes* (completed in 1438 or 1439) he speaks of his 'mor than thre score yeeris' (*Fall of Princes*, bk 8, l. 191)—and of his 'pallid age' and 'tremblyng joyntes'.

Youth and education In his *Testament*, a penitential poem which contains some apparently autobiographical material, Lydgate describes his conversion from a sinful life through the sight of a crucifix with the inscription *vide* ('Behold my mekenesse, O child, and leve thy pryde') depicted on the wall of a cloister in the monastery. This event occurred when he was 'wythinne xv' years of age (*Minor Poems*, 356), after he had 'entered religion'. The poem, probably in traditional manner, somewhat heightens its portrayal of his 'myspent tyme' (Lydgate says that he 'ran into gardyns' to steal apples—just as St Augustine robbed a pear tree), but there is no reason to doubt the general truth of its biographical details. Lydgate presents himself as a feckless child:

> loth to lerne, loved no besynesse,
> Save pley or merth, straunge to spelle or rede

who did not want to go to school and was:

> redier cheristones for to telle
> Than gon to chirche, or here the sacryng belle.
> (*Minor Poems*, 352–3)

He was a jester and a scoffer, who went to bed late and got up late, did not wash for dinner, and hated rebukes or correction—in short, 'a chyld resemblyng which was not lyke to thryve', 'like a truant'. Even in the monastery, where he made his profession 'a yere complete', he was at first ill-disciplined and riotous (preferring 'good wyne that was clere' to contemplation and 'holy histories') until his life was changed. The recollection of the word *vide* causes him, now in his 'last age', to take up his pen and compose a 'litel dite'—which is an eloquent lament from the crucified Christ to sinful man.

Lydgate's literary career clearly owes much to his

monastic upbringing. The majority of his poems bear the mark of a pious and learned mind. He is often referred to simply as the Monk of Bury—by others and by himself (*Siege of Thebes*, l. 93), and that rich and powerful abbey provided him with one of the finest libraries in England, and, probably, with valuable connections to sources of literary patronage. At some stage he studied at Oxford, probably at Gloucester College, the Benedictine hall, although the surviving evidence is thin. John Shirley, the fifteenth-century scribe who seems to have had a fairly close connection with him, and who provides much valuable and generally trustworthy information in his rubrics to his poems, says in his copy of the version of the Aesopic fable of the dog and the cheese (Bodl. Oxf., MS Ashmole 59, second half of the fifteenth century) that Lydgate made it 'in Oxenford' (*Minor Poems*, 598). That Lydgate is probably to be identified with 'notre treschier en dieu Dan J. L. vostre commoigne [your fellow monk]' for whom Prince Henry wrote to the abbot of Bury, between 1406 and 1408, for the 'continuance in the study of divinity or canon law at Oxford' on the recommendation of the chancellor of the university, Richard Courtenay (Legge, 411–12), may indicate that he returned to Oxford later for a period of further study. It has been suggested by J. Norton-Smith (*Poems*, 195) that during his time at Oxford he made the acquaintance of the prince of Wales (who was probably at Queen's College *c*.1398), his future patron, and of Edmund Lacy of University College, who went on to become dean of the royal chapel at Windsor and (from 1420) the bishop of Exeter for whom Lydgate translated *Gloriosa dicta sunt de te* (*Minor Poems*, 315–23). Bale's claim that he also studied at Cambridge does not seem to be supported by any evidence—that Lydgate wrote a set of verses on the foundation of that university (ibid., 652–5) need not be significant. Bale also says that after returning from travelling in France and Italy, Lydgate opened a school for the sons of noblemen. This too is unproven, though some lines in *God is myn Helpere* may, if they are genuinely autobiographical, support the idea of travel (and, perhaps, some adventure):

> I have been offte in dyvers londys
> And in many dyvers regiouns,
> Have eskapyd fro my foois bondys
> In citees, castellys, and in touns;
> Among folk of sundry naciouns
> Wente ay forth.
> (ibid., 28)

Early works and patronage By the end of the fourteenth century Lydgate was well advanced on his ecclesiastical career. He was ordained acolyte on 13 March 1389, and subdeacon on 17 November or December of that year. He became deacon on 31 May 1393, and four years later priest, on 7 April 1397. The earlier stages of his literary career are less clear. Apart from Shirley's not very informative note on the Aesop, there is nothing to fix the dates of many poems in the early years before *c*.1412. It is often assumed that his poems concerned with love are from this period, but this is simply conjecture. There are a number of these without any indication of date, like the *Ballade of her that hath All Virtues* (*Minor Poems*, 379), written 'at the request of a squyer that served in loves court'. One might guess that this kind of commission is likely to have come his way after he had already become known as a poet. His very 'Chaucerian' poems *The Complaint of the Black Knight* (alternatively known as *A Complaynt of a Loveres Lyfe*) and *The Flour of Curtesye* are often thought to have been written at the very beginning of the fifteenth century, as imitations of and perhaps acts of homage to the recently dead poet whom Lydgate admired and always refers to as his 'master'. His indebtedness to Chaucer can hardly be exaggerated: his poetry is full of Chaucerian topics, themes, and verbal echoes. He praises Chaucer again and again for his eloquence and for the way that he has 'illumined' the English language, but does not claim to have met him. He was, however, a friend of the poet's son Thomas Chaucer (*d*. 1434), for whom he wrote an elegant poem on the occasion of his departure on a journey (perhaps as part of an embassy to Burgundy in 1414). Thomas Chaucer seems to have had a circle of friends with literary interests. His daughter Alice (*d*. 1475) married (as her second husband) Thomas Montagu, earl of Salisbury (*d*. 1428), and after his death William de la Pole, earl of Suffolk (*d*. 1450), both men with some literary tastes. Lydgate's *Virtues of the Mass* (*Minor Poems*, 87–115) is said in a rubric in one manuscript to have been done at the request of the countess of Suffolk.

Lydgate seems to have begun enjoying literary patronage at the beginning of the fifteenth century. *The Temple of Glass*, an ambitious Chaucerian dream poem, is usually regarded as an early work: the manuscripts indicate a process of extensive revision. The poem was very popular in the fifteenth century. It is, according to Shirley, written 'à la request d'un amoureux'—if so, he cannot be identified. In the final version a motto which the dreamer sees on the lady's garment reads *de mieulx en mieulx*: this is one that was used by the Pastons, but it also appears in earlier French poetry, so that the suggestion that it has some connection with them—and in particular with the marriage of William Paston and Agnes Berry in 1420—cannot be accepted with certainty. In the temple of Venus the dreamer overhears the lament of a beautiful lady who is bound to one whom she does not love, and later that of the knight her lover. Venus urges patience and faithfulness and consoles them with the hope that their future joy is fated. From this period probably comes *Resoun and Sensuallyte* (*c*.1408?), which is attributed to Lydgate by the sixteenth-century antiquary Stow: it is based on the first part of a French allegorical poem *Les échecs amoureux* expanded into a learned and encyclopaedic work (containing, for example, extensive information on mythology).

First mature works *The Troy Book* is the first of Lydgate's major poems that can be precisely dated. It was commissioned by Prince Henry on 31 October 1412, and, after eight years, the completed work was presented to him, now Henry V, in 1420. The prince, says Lydgate in the prologue, wished to have recalled the ancient worthiness of 'verray knyghthod' and 'the prowesse of olde chivalrie' (*Troy Book*, prologue, ll. 75–8) and to have the 'noble story' made available in English (ibid., ll. 111–15). Lydgate's main source is the thirteenth-century Latin *Historia destructionis Troiae* of Guido delle Colonne (a copy of which was in the library at Bury) which itself is a version of Benoît de Ste Maure's *Roman de Troie*. In five books containing over 30,000 lines in couplets Lydgate records the whole story from the Argonauts, the founding and destruction of old Troy, to Priam and the building of the new city, Paris and Helen, the outbreak of war, the battles, and the fates of the heroes. The story has an episodic structure, and is elaborated with rhetorical laments, descriptions, and speeches. These often have an impressive eloquence—some of the natural descriptions (of dawns, for example), some of the laments for the dead heroes, or the lament of Troilus and Criseyde at their parting, or the lament for Troy (*Troy Book*, bk 4, ll. 7036ff.), for instance. Lydgate demonstrates here already his skill at constructing scenes of pathos. He works into the narrative a mass of encyclopaedic material relating to history and mythology (for example, the descriptions of the attributes of the goddesses in the judgement of Paris, or of the ancient theatre and the performance of tragedies). *The Troy Book* presents a 'mirror for princes', both in particular episodes marked by sententious comments:

> late Priam alwey your merour ben,
> Hasty errour be tymes to correcte
> (*Troy Book*, bk 2, ll. 1898–9)

and as a whole, emphasizing a number of major themes including the dangers of political discord and war:

> Lo what meschef lyth in variaunce
> Amonge lordis, whan thei nat accorde
> (ibid., bk 3, ll. 2342–3)

as well as the power of Fortune, the transitoriness of earthly things, and the impermanence of human ambition.

The Siege of Thebes (1420?–22), probably based on a French prose version of the *Roman de Thèbes*, is not a commissioned work. No doubt intended as a companion piece to *The Troy Book*, it may also be a compliment to Chaucer (though hardly an attempt to improve on him, as has been suggested). In the prologue Lydgate imagines himself joining the Canterbury pilgrims on their return journey from Canterbury, and is persuaded by the Host to tell the first tale. The fiction is kept up throughout by a number of comments, and a reference to *The Knight's Tale* when Theseus appears. In three parts, amounting to only 4716 lines, it is notably shorter than *The Troy Book*, and, while not exactly brisk, it is less encyclopaedic. It contains some vivid descriptive passages and some fine pathetic scenes, but Lydgate is, as usual, concerned to underline the significance of the material, and again to offer a 'mirror for princes'. A king should be generous and liberal, and free from 'doubleness'—'trouthe shulde longe to a kyng' (*Siege of Thebes*, l. 1722)—and Lydgate warns of the dangers of falsehood and discord. In the opposing views of Jocasta, who urges negotiation rather than war (ibid., l. 3655ff.), and the council of Adrastus, which argues that to give up 'the hegh emprise' would be an act of cowardice and dishonour, and would betray their glorious ancestors, 'that whilom [formerly] wern so manly conquerours' (ibid., l. 4117ff.), Lydgate is presenting a contemporary English dilemma. The poem ends with a denunciation of the destructiveness of war (springing from pride, covetousness, and false ambition) and a vision of peace when the sword and spear of Mars will no longer menace, but 'love and pees in hertys shal awake' and bring between countries 'pees and quyet, concord and unyte'—words that seem to be echoing the phrasing of the treaty of Troyes (1420) which (for a time) brought peace between England and France.

Perhaps from this period comes an impressive religious poem of some 6000 lines, *The Life of Our Lady*. It is impossible to be sure of its date, but a rubric in one manuscript says that it was compiled 'at the excitation and styrryng of our worshipful prince, kyng Harry the fifthe'. If this is correct, it would support the date of 1421–2 given to it by its modern editors, but it is strange that there is no reference to Henry in the text itself. Possibly he suggested the work but died before it was completed.

The death of Henry V on 31 August 1422 did not cause any interruption in Lydgate's Lancastrian patronage. Since the heir to the throne was only nine months old, the effective government was in the hands of a regency council, and it may be that an awareness of the tensions within this and of the potential dangers led Lydgate to compose his only known prose work, *The Serpent of Division*. A date of December 1422 has been suggested, but has not been universally accepted, nor has the suggested identification of the 'most worshipful master' at whose request it was written with Humphrey, duke of Gloucester, the protector of England. It is a tract on the horrors of civil war as exemplified in the life of Julius Caesar. The material comes from Lucan's *Pharsalia*, a French version of that, and the *Speculum historiale* of Vincent of Beauvais. Whatever the precise date of *The Serpent of Division*, the topic was relevant and the moral direct: 'all prudent prynces whiche have governaunce in provynces and regions schulde take ensample what harme and damage is and how finall a destruccion is to bene devyded amonge hemselfe' (*The Serpent of Division*, 58). Duke Humphrey was later certainly an important patron of Lydgate, and the poem that Lydgate wrote (1422–3) for his approaching marriage with Jacqueline of Hainault (*Minor Poems*, 601–8) suggests an already close relationship. A poem entitled a *Complaint for my Lady of Gloucester and Holland* (ibid., 608–13), which expresses warm sympathy for Jacqueline after her abandonment by Humphrey, carries the annotation 'Lidegate daun Iohan' in Bodl. Oxf., MS Ashmole 59, a late Shirley manuscript, but Shirley's rubric attributes it to 'a chapellayne of my lordes of Gloucestre'.

In 1423 Lydgate was elected prior of Hatfield Regis, Essex, a small alien priory appropriated to Bury, an office that he held until 8 April 1434, although he was probably not resident throughout that period (in 1426 he was at Paris, and at other times at London or Bury). It is usually thought that perhaps *c*.1425 he wrote his version of the story of *Guy of Warwick* (*Minor Poems*, 516–38), based on chronicle rather than romance sources, for Margaret, the eldest daughter of Richard Beauchamp, earl of Warwick, and his first wife, Elizabeth, though the rubric recording her request gives her later title countess of Shrewsbury and Lady Talbot, and, if it is not simply an indication of the date of the copying, could support a later date (she married John Talbot in 1433, and became countess of Shrewsbury in 1442). Lydgate, however, certainly had connections with Beauchamp in the period 1425–6, and his *The Fyfftene Joyes of Oure Lady* (ibid., 260–67) is said in one rubric to have been done at the instance of his second wife, Isabella, the daughter of Thomas, Lord Despenser.

Paris: translations from French It was perhaps in the service of the earl of Warwick, then acting regent of France during Bedford's absence, that Lydgate went to Paris in 1426. In July of that year at Warwick's request he wrote a verse account (from the French of Laurence Calot) of *The Title and Pedigree of Henry VI* designed to prove the king's claim to the French throne (*Minor Poems*, 621–8). *The Pilgrimage of the Life of Man*, a verse translation of Guillaume de Deguileville's *Pèlerinage de la vie humaine* done for Warwick's deputy Thomas Montagu, earl of Salisbury, and his wife, Alice Chaucer, was begun in 1426 and was finished by 3 November 1428, the date of Montagu's death from a wound received at the siege of Orléans—unless 'we assume that the abruptness of the end, and the lack of the usual dedicatory epilogue, indicate that the patron was already dead' (Pearsall, 173). Unusually, Lydgate does not record his authorship in the text, and it has been questioned. The illustration often reproduced as showing Lydgate and a pilgrim presenting the book to Montagu is in fact pasted in as a title-page in BL, Harley MS 4826, which includes a copy of Lydgate's *St Edmund* but not the *Pilgrimage*. The work is attributed to Lydgate by Stow, but it has been suggested that this rests on a misunderstanding of an ambiguous remark by Shirley in a versified list of contents to one of his manuscripts, in which he mentions a prose translation of the 'humayne pilgrymage' and then about ten lines later refers to Lydgate's translation 'of this booke and of other mo'. The question is whether the 'book' is the Middle English prose translation (not, it seems, by Lydgate) or the French original. If it is not the latter, it would seem that here lies the origin of a misattribution. There would perhaps be more urgency in solving the problem if the verse translation were more distinguished.

Poems for illustrations and pageants It is, however, certain that Lydgate translated the French *Danse macabre* ('The Dance of Death'), which he says he saw on a wall in Paris (it had been painted in the cemetery of the Innocents in 1424–5). This is a good translation and it was used to accompany a painting of the dance in the cloister of the Pardon churchyard on the north side of St Paul's Cathedral in London, where it survived until 1549. It is one of a number of poems which are intended to, or could be made to, accompany illustrations, whether in manuscripts or in the form of wall-paintings or painted cloths. His *Bycorne and Chichevache* (*Minor Poems*, 433–8) on the monsters that eat, respectively, patient husbands and patient wives, is a 'devise of a peynted or desteyned clothe for an halle a parlour or a chaumbre', and provides (at the request of a worthy citizen of London) what is apparently a text to accompany a series of images. Religious poems of this kind include *The Dolerous Pyte of Crystes Passioun* (ibid., 250–52), which seems designed to be used with the *imago pietatis* of the wounded Christ ('looke on this fygure', 'my bloody woundis, set here in picture', and so on). Similarly, *On the Image of Pity* (ibid., 297–9) is to accompany an image of a *pietà*. 'Beholde and se this glorious fygure', begins *The Image of Our Lady* (ibid., 290–91), which is apparently to accompany a copy of the painting of the Virgin by St Luke in Rome. Stanzas from Lydgate's *Lamentation of Mary Magdalen* and his *Testament* were painted in the Clopton chapel of the Holy Trinity at Long Melford, Suffolk (a church that belonged to Bury), in the later fifteenth century.

These poems are sometimes close to pageants or mummings. *The Legend of St George* (*Minor Poems*, 145–54) was, according to Shirley's rubric, 'the devyse of a steyned [painted] halle … ymagyned by Daun Johan the Monk of Bury Lydegate, and made with the balades' for the London Guild of Armourers (St George 'roode in steel armed bright'). The note in the manuscript 'the poete first declarethe' suggests that the verses were read out when the paintings were first presented or installed. However, they may also have been painted on the walls with them. A number of Lydgate's semi-dramatic mummings or disguisings survive. Some of these are for royal occasions—Christmas celebrations at Eltham or Windsor—some for city guilds or civic occasions—for the mercers (Epiphany 1429), the goldsmiths (Candlemas 1429), the sheriffs of London at Bishopswood (May day). They are sometimes simply the verses to be spoken by a presenter before the giving of gifts, sometimes introducing or accompanying processions or the entry of characters (as perhaps Fortune and the four cardinal Virtues in the London mumming for 'the great estates') or mimed actions (as perhaps in the *Mumming at Hertford*, a rather lively piece described by Shirley as 'a disguysing of the rude upplandisshe [rustic] people compleyning on hir wyves, with the boystous aunswere of hir wyves').

Henry VI's coronation (at the age of seven) in London in 1429, and later in Paris, is celebrated in a *Roundel for the Coronation* (*Minor Poems*, 622) and other poems. There is also a verse description of the pageants that greeted the young king on his return and entry into London in 1432 after his coronation in Paris (ibid., 630–48). A number of courtly occasional poems probably come from this time, as for instance the *Balade on a New Year's Gift of an Eagle* (ibid., 649–51), which according to Shirley was presented to the king and his mother, Queen Catherine, on new year's day at the castle of Hertford. In 1433 the king spent Christmas at Bury. He was received with great splendour, and remained until Easter 1434, when he became a member of the abbey's confraternity (which included a number of powerful nobles and their wives, some of whom were Lydgate's patrons). At the request of the abbot, William Curteys (*d.* 1446), Lydgate wrote for the king the legend of the patron saint of the abbey and the region, St Edmund, and of St Fremund, the martyr's nephew. In the *Legend of SS Edmund and Fremund*, Lydgate brings to the saint's life the epic quality already attempted in *The Life of Our Lady*. Its 3700 lines, divided into three books, tells the traditional story of his martyrdom at the hands of the Danes in a fluent narrative with some excellent dialogue and dramatic scenes. The king, presented as both hero and martyr, lion and lamb, is presented as the protector of and the exemplar for the young 'sixth Harry'. His three crowns, expounded in the prologue as those of the kingdom, martyrdom, and chastity, correspond to Henry's English, French, and heavenly crowns. Lydgate wrote a number of other saints' legends, not all of which can be dated—those, for instance, of St Margaret (ibid., 173) for Lady March, or the *Legend of SS Alban and Amphibel* (in 1439 at the request of Whethamstede, the abbot of St Albans), in 4700 lines treating the 'prothomartyr of Brutis Albion' in a rather grand manner.

The fall of princes Lydgate was now already embarked on his most ambitious work. *The Fall of Princes* was begun *c.*1431 at the request of Humphrey, duke of Gloucester, and completed in 1438 or 1439. It is based on Laurent de Premierfait's French version of Boccaccio's *De casibus virorum illustrium*, and runs to 36,365 lines in nine books. The long task weighed heavily even on Lydgate, who makes a number of semi-comic references to it, and at some point wrote a begging poem, the *Letter to Gloucester* (*Minor Poems*, 665–7), a witty request for funds. If Humphrey was niggardly with money, he was less so with advice and encouragement, suggesting, for instance, the inclusion of envoys (which summarize, comment, present 'remedies' of Fortune, and instruct princes), or the use of Coluccio Salutati's *Declamation of Lucretia*, which he lent to Lydgate. The poem follows the pattern familiar to English readers from Chaucer's *Monk's Tale* of a succession of 'tragedies' ranging chronologically from Adam to King Jean of France, captured at Poitiers in 1356. The fallen princes pass in front of the author, Bochas, in his study, lament, tell their stories, or urge him to do so. Lydgate's strong sense of pathos is evident in some of his expansions, for example of the lament of Canacee. His sententious envoys sometimes become sombre choric laments for heroes (such as that on Alcibiades), and he can achieve moments of melancholy grandeur, as in the envoy on Rome at the end of the second book. There is much evidence of his wide reading and of a sympathy for the stories of the ancient world. He urges the traditional doctrines of moderation, the avoidance of pride, and the pursuit of virtue, and demonstrates the horror of discord and strife between kinsfolk. This advice, though couched in general terms, was highly relevant to contemporary princes. *The Fall of Princes* was very popular in the fifteenth century: more than thirty manuscripts survive, some of them finely illustrated, and it was quarried for excerpts. It goes into sixteenth-century printed editions, and is a model for *The Mirror for Magistrates*.

Later poems and death Lydgate was at Bury, it seems, from 1434 until his death. He was awarded a royal annuity of 10 marks (22 April 1439), the last grant of which was made at Michaelmas 1449. From this period comes *The Debate between the Horse, Goose and Sheep* (*Minor Poems*, 539–66), which contains an allusion to Philip of Burgundy's attack on Calais in 1436. During the last years of his life Lydgate wrote some verses on the marriage of Henry VI and Margaret of Anjou and the pageants for her entry into London in 1445. What seems to be his last long poem, *The Secrees of Philisoffres*, a translation of the *Secreta secretorum* then attributed to Aristotle was left unfinished, and was completed by his disciple Benedict Burgh. That Lydgate's final line (1491) with the words 'deth al consumyth' is followed by the note 'here dyed this translator, and nobil poete: and the yonge folowere gan his prologe on this wyse' makes a very dramatic story.

The actual date of Lydgate's death is not certain, but is probably 1449 or 1450. The suggested later date of 1451 depends on a remark by Bishop Alcock that Lydgate wrote a poem on the occasion of the final loss of France and Gascony, but the fact that his royal grant ceases after 29 September 1449 suggests that Lydgate died between that date and Michaelmas of the following year. This seems to be confirmed by the description of him as 'sumtyme monke of Byry' in John Metham's *Amoryus and Cleopes*, written in the twenty-seventh year of the sixth King Henry, by which he may mean 1449. He was buried at Bury abbey, and a three-line epitaph (according to Tanner) described him as one 'qui fuit quondam celebris Brittaniae fama Poesis' ('who was once renowned poet of famous Britain').

Assessment and reputation Much of Lydgate's vast output is impossible to date, and the range of topics that he treats (outside those listed above) is very large: religious lyrics, translations of Latin hymns, verse prayers, poems of moral advice, didactic poems, fables, satires, instructional poems on table manners, rules of health, or in praise of the nine properties of wine, and so on. In the course of the fifteenth century many anonymous works were attributed to him: modern scholarship denies him the authorship of, for instance, *The Assembly of the Gods*, *The Court of Sapience*, and *London Lickpenny*. It has also been tentatively suggested that he may have had some hand in *The Libel of English Policy*, but there is no external evidence to support this. Equally impressive is the list of his patrons, beginning with two kings and continuing with royal dukes and noblemen and their wives to the lesser gentry in what is a veritable roll-call of the great and good in late medieval England. Add to this the London merchants and the guilds, and the justice of Thomas Warton's remark can be comprehended: 'his muse was of universal access; and he was not only the poet of his monastery, but of the world in general' (Warton, 1774–81, repr., 350).

Lydgate's reputation was at its height in the fifteenth century: he is praised again and again, and his name is regularly linked with those of Chaucer and Gower as one of the masters of English poetry. His fame continued through the sixteenth century, but gradually faded. In the eighteenth, interest was rekindled and he received a judicious account in Warton's *History of English Poetry* and enthusiastic praise from Thomas Gray (*Some Remarks on the Poems of John Lydgate*, 1760). This very sympathetic and thoughtful treatment of his compassion for suffering and his skill in creating scenes of pathos has been eclipsed by the vituperative denunciation of Lydgate by Joseph Ritson in 1802 as 'this voluminous, prosaick, and driveling monk', whose works 'by no means deserve the name of poetry' (Ritson, 87ff.). Scholarly interest in the nineteenth and twentieth centuries in Germany and England has produced edited texts of his works, and provided more material for understanding the literary culture that moulded him and which he helped to mould. This undoubtedly voluminous and often uneven poet will probably never recover his contemporary reputation, but at his best he can produce impressive moments and scenes, and is certainly a poet worthy of the name. DOUGLAS GRAY

Sources D. Pearsall, *John Lydgate* (1970) • W. F. Schirmer, *John Lydgate: a study in the culture of the XVth century*, trans. A. E. Keep (1961) • *Poems: John Lydgate*, ed. J. Norton-Smith (1966) • Emden, *Oxf.* • M. D. Legge, ed., *Anglo-Norman letters and petitions from All Souls MS 182*, Anglo-Norman Texts, 3 (1941) • K. Walls, 'Did Lydgate translate the *Pèlerinage de la vie humaine*?', *N&Q*, 222 (1977), 103–5 • J. Lydgate, *The fall of princes*, ed. H. Bergen, EETS, extra ser., 121–4 (1924–7) • J. Lydgate, *Lydgate's Troy book: AD 1412–20*, ed. H. Bergen, 4 vols., EETS, extra ser., 97, 103, 106, 126 (1906–35) • J. Lydgate, *Siege of Thebes*, ed. A. Erdmann and E. Ekwall, EETS, extra ser., 108, 125 (1911–20) • J. Lydgate, *Minor poems*, ed. H. N. McCracken, EETS, extra ser., 107; old ser., 192 (1910–34) • J. Lydgate, *The life of our Lady*, ed. J. A. Lauritis, R. A. Klinefeller, and V. F. Gallagher, Duquesne Studies, Philological series, 2 (1961) • J. Lydgate, *The serpent of division*, ed. H. N. McCracken (1911) • [J. Lydgate], *The dance of death*, ed. F. Warren and B. White, EETS, 181 (1931) • T. Warton, *The history of English poetry*, 4 vols. (1774–81) • J. Ritson, *Biographica poetica* (1802)

Archives BL, Cotton MSS [copies] • BL, Harley MS 4826 • Bodl. Oxf., Ashmole MS 59 • Venerable English College, fifteenth-century collection of poems

Likenesses manuscript illumination, BL, Royal 18 D.ii; repro. in Pearsall, *John Lydgate*, frontispiece • manuscript illumination, BL, Harley MS 2278, fol. 9; repro. in Pearsall, *John Lydgate*, pl. 3 • manuscript illumination, BL, Arundel MS 119, fol. 1 • manuscript illumination, BL, Cotton Augustus A.1.v • manuscript illumination, BL, Harley MS 1766, fol. 3 • manuscript illumination, Bodl. Oxf., MS Digby 232, fol. 1 [*see illus.*] • tinted drawing, BL, Harley MS 4826, fol. 1* [paste-in]; *see illus. in* Montagu, Thomas, fourth earl of Salisbury (1388–1428)

Lydiat, Thomas (1572–1646), chronologist, was baptized on 4 April 1572 at Alkerton, Oxfordshire, one of several children of Christopher Lydiat (*d.* 1613/14), citizen of London and, since 1567, lord of Alkerton manor. He entered Winchester College about 1584, and matriculated from New College, Oxford, on 28 January 1592. He became a full fellow in 1593, graduated BA on 3 May 1595, and proceeded MA on 5 February 1599. He contributed poems to the memorial collections *Oxoniensium stenagmos, sive, Carmina ab Oxoniensibus Conscripta in obitum illustrissimi herois, D. Christopheri Hattoni militis* (1592) for Christopher Hatton, and *Oxoniensis academiae funebre officium* (1603) for Queen Elizabeth.

Lydiat relinquished his fellowship in 1603 rather than study divinity, owing to 'a great defect in his memory and utterance, of which he often complained' (Wood, *Ath. Oxon.*, 3.185). He pursued instead his key interests in astronomy and chronology, subsisting on private means. Lectures on these subjects delivered in 1599 were published as *Tractatus de variis annorum formis*, together with his *Praelectio astronomica de natura coeli et conditionibus elementorum* and *Disquisitio physiologica de origine fontium*, in London in 1605. These were a significant contribution to burgeoning scientific and theological debates on the nature of the cosmos and the structure of the calendar. Lydiat's use of physics supported the developing belief in a fluid universe, and, like Kepler, he abandoned the established astronomical principle of circularity in the face of empirical observation. He was one of the first to state that the sun 'describes a segment, not of a circle, but of an oval line' (*Praelectio astronomica*, cap. 7, p. 64). He remained harnessed to scripture, however, arguing that creation, while fluid, was finite, being ultimately contained within a sphere surrounded by water and controlled by God. Lydiat's early work simultaneously defined the 'octodesexcentenarian' period, by which he managed to reconcile solar and lunar months in a complex annual calendar on a 592-year cycle.

These multiple claims launched Lydiat into protracted arguments with the continental scholars Kepler and Scaliger. The latter called Lydiat 'the greatest monster that ever England produced' and 'the veryest fool in the whole world' (Plot, 223), comparing him to travelling troupes of English actors. Among other matters, Lydiat challenged Scaliger's dating of both creation and the birth of Christ; his ideas were in turn refuted in Scaliger's *Isagogici canones chronologiae* (1606). Lydiat defended himself in his *Defensio tractatus de variis annorum formis … contra J. Scaligeri obtrectationem una cum examen ejus canonum chronologiae isagogicorum* (1607), and the *Recensio et explicatio argumentorum … insertis brevibus confutationibus opinionum Scaligeranae … atque Johannis Keppleri* (1613).

Lydiat's growing reputation led to his appointment as chronographer and cosmographer to Henry, prince of Wales, who made him a member of his household on an annual pension of 40 marks. In return Lydiat dedicated to Prince Henry his key work on chronology, *Emendatio temporum ab initio mundi … contra Scaligerum et alios* (London, 1609). He was introduced to James Ussher, through whose influence he moved to Ireland; he was admitted as a fellow of Trinity College, Dublin, and graduated MA from that institution in 1609. Ussher attempted to procure him the mastership of a school in Armagh with an annual income of £50, but by August 1611 Lydiat had returned to England. Ussher later built on Lydiat's research in constructing his famous protestant chronology of world history, and the two remained lifelong friends. Suggestions that Lydiat was Ussher's brother-in-law are without foundation, and there is no evidence that he ever married.

In 1612, perhaps as a result of the death of the prince of Wales, Lydiat became rector of Alkerton, his family parish. He remained based here for the rest of his life, rebuilding the rectory in 1625 and remodelling the chancel about the same time. He continued to engage in scholarly pursuits, producing over 600 sermons and harmonies of the gospels in English, Hebrew, and Greek together with other works. In the 1620s Lydiat published three astronomical and chronological works: *Solis et lunae periodus seu annus magnus* (1620), *De annis solaris mensura epistola astronomica ad Hen. Savilium* (1620), and *Numerus aureus melioribus lapillis insignatus* (1621). These reiterated his rejection of the Gregorian calendar and attempted a more pragmatic version of his octodesexcentenarian one. His later manuscript works established rules for chronological enquiries, and eventually proposed a new solar calendar with the year beginning on 1 March and the Christian era with Christ's baptism, formerly dated to AD 29. Such efforts argued for the supremacy of reformed over Catholic religion, but Lydiat rejected any alignment with millenarian interests in dating Christ's second coming.

In 1625 Lydiat's brother Richard fell into debt, a circumstance leading to the mortgage of Alkerton manor, and its sale in 1630. Thomas Lydiat incurred grave financial difficulties, and was imprisoned for debt continuously between 1627 and 1633 in Oxford and Southwark. An incomplete form of bail from Southwark prison for £700 dated 8 July 1630 is suggestive of the extent of his woes (Bodl. Oxf., Bodley MS 313, fol. 44). Financial relief and personal freedom were eventually obtained through the efforts of several scholars, including most notably Ussher and Laud, but also Sir William Boswell and Robert Pink, the warden of New College. According to Wood, John Selden declined to contribute to the cause because Lydiat had contradicted his 'Marmora Arundeliana' (Wood, *Ath. Oxon.*, 3.186). Lydiat's interest in ancient chronologies led him to petition the king during the 1630s for permission to travel to Turkey, Armenia, and Abyssinia but, unsurprisingly, given his credit history, these efforts met with no success.

Lydiat was opposed to some of Laud's reforms, writing manuscripts on altars, bowing at the name of Jesus, and incense from prison in 1633 (BL, Harley MS 2405). He nevertheless counted many puritans among his friends and neighbours, including John Dod and Robert Cleaver, the ministers of Hanwell and Drayton, Oxfordshire, and Sir Anthony Cope, to whom he had dedicated his *Defensio* in 1607. During the 1640s Lydiat sided with the royalists and continued to speak out in favour of episcopacy. In 1644 he wrote to Sir William Compton, governor of Banbury Castle, complaining that his house had been pillaged four times by parliamentary forces to the value of £70, and that he was twice carried off by soldiers, once to Warwick and once to Banbury; he signed himself the 'old and weak minister' of Alkerton (Bodl. Oxf., Bodley MS 313, fol. 82). His sufferings in the civil war and his passion for scholarship to the exclusion of his physical needs led Samuel Johnson to recall him in the verse:

> If dreams yet flatter, once again attend;
> Hear Lydiat's life and Galileo's end
> (*The Vanity of Human Wishes*, 1749, ll. 163–4)

Lydiat died at Alkerton on 3 April 1646, possibly as a result of an assault by soldiers. He was buried the following day in the chancel of Alkerton church, near his parents. His will left goods valued at £169. In 1669 the fellows of New College erected a monument over his grave, as well as a memorial in the college chapel.

Lydiat's nephew Timothy Lydiat (1618–1663), also rector of Alkerton, may have inherited some of his manuscripts. By the 1670s they were in the possession of John Lamphire, and a part of this collection was published as *Canones chronologici* (1675). Lamphire's nephew Dr William Coward presented fifteen manuscripts to the Bodleian in 1695. A manuscript of his treatise on the Arundel marbles survives at Trinity College, Dublin, and was published as 'Marmoreum chronicon Arundelianum cum annotationibus' in Humphrey Prideaux's *Marmora Oxoniensia* (1676). Lydiat was described in his own century as 'the happy Inventor of a more accurat period' (Plot, 224) but soon faded into obscurity. Nevertheless, he represents both the breadth and integration of Renaissance scholarship and the peculiar focus of protestant polemic, for he drew together astronomical and chronological research with textual criticism, mathematical advances, and theological debate in order to comprehend time and space.

PETER SHERLOCK

Sources R. Poole, *Time's alteration: calendar reform in early modern England* (1998) · R. Plot, *The natural history of Oxfordshire* (1677) · W. Donahue, *The dissolution of the celestial spheres* (1981) · *VCH Oxfordshire*, 9.44–53 · Wood, *Ath. Oxon.*, new edn, 3.185–9 · Foster, *Alum. Oxon.*, 1500–1714, 2.953 · parish register, Alkerton, 4 April 1572, Oxon. RO [baptism] · A. Gratton, *Joseph Scaliger: a study in the history of classical scholarship*, 2 vols. (1983–93), vol. 2 · monument, Alkerton church, Oxfordshire · Bodl. Oxf., MS Bodley 313, fol. 44 · A. J. Apt, 'The reception of Kepler's astronomy in England: 1609–1650', DPhil diss., U. Oxf., 1982 · J. Simmons, *Parish and empire: studies and sketches* (1952), 107–14

Archives Bodl. Oxf., corresp. and papers · Bodl. Oxf., sermons, MSS Rawl. E 75–76 · TCD, papers · TCD, two theological treatises and MS of 'Annotationes ad chronicon marmoreum' | BL, Thomas Lydyat's 'Answer to Altare Christianum' and 'Two little treatises', 1633, Harley MS 2405

Wealth at death £169: will and probate, 1646, *VCH Oxfordshire*, 9.50

Lye, Edward (*bap.* **1694**, *d.* **1767**), Anglo-Saxon and Gothic scholar, was baptized at St Mary's, Totnes, Devon, on 6 September 1694, the ninth of twelve children of Thomas Lye (*bap.* 1655, *d.* 1710/11), vicar of Broadhempston (instituted 4 May 1705) and schoolmaster of Totnes grammar school, and his wife, Katherine Johnson (*b. c.*1660, *d.* in or after 1736). He described his father to Thomas Percy as 'a good Classical Scholar … yet an indolent Schoolmaster' (Percy, fol. 258*r*) who left his family poorly off. He first attended his father's school, but received little tuition there; later he attended a grammar school at Crewkerne, in Somerset, where he had family and where the master was a man of good reputation named Leaves. Although he suffered ill health during these years and was forced to spend some time at home his studies proceeded more surely than they had at Totnes. He was admitted a servitor of Hart Hall, Oxford, and matriculated from the university on 28 March 1713. He graduated BA on 19 October 1716 and MA on 6 July 1722, and was incorporated at Cambridge University in 1724. While at Hart Hall he won the friendship and patronage of the principal, Dr Richard Newton, and the vice-principal, his tutor John Davys, who was also,

Edward Lye (*bap.* 1694, *d.* 1767), by Frances Reynolds

from 1719 to 1740, rector of Castle Ashby, Northamptonshire, seat of the earl of Northampton and one of the closest parishes to Little Houghton and Yardley Hastings, where Lye held successive livings.

Lye was ordained deacon at St Margaret's, Westminster, on 17 March 1716 by Edmund Gibson, bishop of Lincoln and a noted Anglo-Saxonist, and priest on 20 September 1719 at Peterborough by White Kennett, another Saxonist. He spent a short time as a curate at Melchborne, in Bedfordshire, and was nearly a year in a second curacy at Orlingbury, Northamptonshire, before being presented to the vicarage of Little Houghton in the same county by a wealthy local patron, William Ward (instituted 13 October and inducted 3 December 1720). He resigned this position in 1749. On 6 October 1737 he was presented to the more lucrative rectory of Yardley Hastings by James, earl of Northampton, and inducted on 10 October. He never married and remained rector of Yardley Hastings for the rest of his life. Though based in rural Northamptonshire he had a wide circle of friends and acquaintances, comprising fellow scholars in Britain and Europe (especially in Sweden), fellow clergymen, and members of the nobility who were patrons of learning. From 1756 until his death he was mentor and friend of Thomas Percy, vicar of the neighbouring parish of Easton Maudit, and helped him with several of his publications, including *Reliques of Ancient English Poetry* (1765).

Between about 1730 and his first published work, an edition of Franciscus Junius's manuscript etymological dictionary of the English language, *Etymologicum Anglicanum* (1743), Lye set himself the task of learning Old English and Gothic, together with something of the other early Germanic languages, and, he confided to Thomas Hearne in a letter of 1732, 'I have a mind to turn Editor' (E. Lye to T. Hearne, 9 June 1732, Bodl. Oxf., MS Rawl. lett. 7, fol. 320*r*). This he did, adding material of his own and a short Old English grammar to Junius's Bodleian manuscript dictionary. This handsome publication was supported by James Compton, fifth earl of Northampton, and printed at the Sheldonian Theatre, Oxford. Lye also turned his attention to Gothic and by late 1732 he had 'read over the Gothick Gospels … and drawn up a Grammar of that Language', as he tells Hearne (Lye to Hearne, n.d. [1732], Bodl. Oxf., MS Rawl. lett. 7, fol. 321*r*). Thus when in the late 1730s the Swedish Archbishop Eric Benzelius the younger (1675–1743) was seeking someone to complete and publish his edition of the *Codex Argenteus* of the Gothic gospels in Uppsala University Library his English contacts, including Sir Hans Sloane and Lord Granville, informed him that Lye was the natural choice. Benzelius's edition, with preface, additions, and a Gothic grammar by Lye, was published by the University of Oxford in 1750. In January of the same year Lye was elected fellow of the Society of Antiquaries.

Lye died at the rectory, Yardley Hastings, of gout, from which he had suffered for many years, on 19 August 1767, aged seventy-three. He was buried on 21 August 1767 in St Andrew's, the parish church, where there is a plain grave slab to his memory in the chancel floor, to the right of the altar, with a memorial inscription composed by his friend Thomas Hunt, professor of Hebrew at Oxford. It speaks of his character as a man of simplicity, openness, and probity, yet one of great erudition and outstanding knowledge in the fields of Northern languages and antiquities.

Lye's reputation as a scholar of Anglo-Saxon and Gothic was high in his own day, both in Britain and in Europe, but became obscured by early nineteenth-century philologists like J. M. Kemble and Joseph Bosworth, who were keen to make a distinction between their own, German-influenced scholarship and that of their predecessors. Yet after the high point in Anglo-Saxon scholarship established by George Hickes, Humfrey Wanley, and their colleagues in the early eighteenth century Lye was the only significant scholar in this field before the nineteenth-century philologists, and they used his work as the basis for their own. This is particularly true in the area of lexicography: Lye's posthumously published *Dictionarium Saxonico et Gothico-Latinum* (1772), which was completed by his friend Owen Manning, was the material basis upon which Bosworth constructed his Anglo-Saxon dictionary (1838), and this formed the foundation for T. Northcote Toller's enlarged *Anglo-Saxon Dictionary* of 1898. Lye and Manning added significantly to the vocabulary of Old English prose and poetry, and their work greatly assisted early nineteenth-century editors. One poetic project that Lye worked on with Oxford colleagues, but which was never published for lack of funding, was an edition, with illustrations and a Latin translation (Lye's contribution), of the Junius manuscript of Old English poetry (Bodl. Oxf., MS

Junius 11). Lye's translation was inherited after his death by Thomas Percy and burnt in a fire at Northumberland House in 1780.

MARGARET CLUNIES ROSS and AMANDA J. COLLINS

Sources T. Percy, 'Memorandum of the life of the Revd. Edward Lye', [n.d.], BL, Add. MS 32325, fols. 257–67 [c.1769–1771] • 'Literary correspondence of Edward Lyle, 1729–1767', BL, Add. MS 32325 • parish register, Totnes, St Mary, Devon RO, 6 Sept 1694 [baptism] • parish register, Broadhempston, Devon RO, 6 Jan 1711 [burial: Thomas Lye] • parish registers, Yardley Hastings, Northants. RO, 1737–67 • will, PRO, PROB 10/2467 • 'Minutes of the Society of Antiquarians taken by Mr. Ames their secretary', vol. 2, 1741–51, BL, MS Egerton 1042, fol. 132v • H. I. Longden, *Northamptonshire and Rutland clergy from 1500*, ed. P. I. King and others, 16 vols. in 6, Northamptonshire RS (1938–52) • Foster, *Alum. Oxon.* • *GM*, 1st ser., 37 (1767), 430 • *Northampton Mercury* (24 Aug 1767) • Maurice Shelton, letter to Edward Lye, 10 Nov 1736, Queen's University, Belfast, Thomas Percy collection • *IGI* • M. Clunies Ross, 'Revaluing the work of Edward Lye, an eighteenth-century septentrional scholar', *Studies in Medievalism*, 9 (1999), 66–79 • R. Frank, 'When lexicography met the Exeter book', *Words and works: studies in medieval English language and literature in honour of Fred C. Robinson*, ed. P. S. Baker and N. Howe (1998), 207–21 • T. A. Birrell, 'The Society of Antiquaries and the taste for Old English, 1705–1840', *Neophilologus*, 50 (1966), 107–17 • J. A. W. Bennett, 'The history of Old English and Old Norse studies in England from the time of Francis Junius till the end of the eighteenth century', DPhil diss., U. Oxf., 1938 • Nichols, *Lit. anecdotes*, 9.752 • *Letters of Samuel Johnson*, ed. G. B. Hill, 2 vols. (1892), 121–2 • letters to Thomas Hearne, Bodl. Oxf., MS Rawl. letters 7

Archives BL, papers, literary corresp., Add. MS 32325 • Bodl. Oxf., autographs, MS Autog. d. 21 • Queen's University, Belfast, collection • S. Antiquaries, Lond., *Caedmonis Monachi Paraphrasis poetica*, ed. F. Junius (Amsterdam, 1655), with handwritten annotations and translations by Edward Lye and Owen Manning, MS 823/2 | BL, Add. MS 28167 • BL, corresp. with C. Lyttelton, vol. 3, Stowe MS 756 • BL, letters to Sir Hans Sloane, vol. 20, Sloane MS 4055 • BL, extracts relating to the crown jewels, Stowe MS 560 • BL, corresp. with C. Wetstein, etc., vol. 5, Add. MS 32418 • Bodl. Oxf., letters to Thomas Hearne I–M, MS Rawl. lett. 27 • Bodl. Oxf., letters to Thomas Hearne, vol. 7, MS Rawl. lett. 7 • Bodl. Oxf., Thomas Percy papers, MS Percy c. 11 • Bodl. Oxf., Thomas Percy papers, MS Percy d. 3 • Bodl. Oxf., Rawlinson's continuation of Wood's *Athenæ Oxonienses*, MS Rawl. J., fols. 3, 4 • Castle Ashby, Northamptonshire, Compton archives • Kungl. Svenska Vetenskapsakadamiens Bibliotek, Frascati (Centre for the history of science), Stockholm • Stifts och Landsbiblioteket, Linköping, Sweden, Bref till A. B. Eric Benzelius den Yngre XVI, Br. 10: 16; XVII, Br. 10: 17 • Stifts och Landsbiblioteket, Linköping, Sweden, Brev. till C. J. Benzelius, Br. 13a • Stifts och Landsbiblioteket, Linköping, Sweden, Brev till C. J. Benzelius II, Br. 13b • Uppsala University, Handskriftsavdelningen, Samling af Bref till Johan Hinric Lidén, vol. 4, G. 151: C • Yale U., Osborn MS 12482

Likenesses T. Burke, engraving, pubd 1784 (after F. Reynolds), NPG • T. Burke, stipple and line engraving (after his earlier work; after F. Reynolds), NPG • F. Reynolds, oils, Bodl. Oxf. [*see illus.*]

Wealth at death £1030—at least; plus interest on shares in Wellingborough turnpike road; 1 horse; 1 piece of meadow; 1 piece of freehold meadow at Grendon, Northamptonshire; collection of silver plate and household goods and furniture; extensive library of printed books [left to Owen Manning and sold in 1773]; intellectual property, subscriptions, and materials for publication of *Dictionarium Saxonico et Gothico-Latinum* [left to Owen Manning]: will, PRO, PROB/10/2467

Lye [Leigh], **Thomas** (1621–1684), nonconformist minister, was born on 25 March 1621, the son of Thomas Leigh of Chard in Somerset. He matriculated from Wadham College, Oxford, on 4 November 1636, was elected scholar on 6 October 1637, and graduated BA on 25 May 1641. He then migrated to Emmanuel College, Cambridge, where he was elected fellow and proceeded MA in 1646. He was headmaster of Bury St Edmunds School for a short time in 1647, and was incorporated MA of Oxford on 8 May 1649. He appears not to have been chaplain of Wadham College, as Wood claims, but was vicar of Chard when signing the attestation of Somerset ministers in 1648.

In 1651 Lye ran into trouble at the hands of Colonel John Pyne (1600–1678), a powerful man in Somerset. On 4 August the council of state wrote requiring that Lye be required to take the engagement to the Commonwealth or face banishment from the town and its surrounding area and debarment from preaching in Somerset; on 24 August, apparently resigned to his fate, he preached a farewell sermon to his parishioners. But on 18 November the council, 'being now satisfied of Mr Lye, takes off their said order, and leaves Lye at liberty to preach at Chard or any other place' ordering that 'this be signified to Colonel Pyne' (*CSP dom.*, *1651–2*, 21). In 1654 Lye's official rehabilitation was complete: he was named as an assistant to the Somerset commission for the ejection of scandalous ministers. In 1658 he was invited by the parishioners to the charge of All Hallows, Lombard Street, London, and was admitted on 27 October. He was named as a commissioner for the approbation of ministers under the act of 14 March 1660. Lye married twice. His first wife, Rebecca, in her will, left property at Bury St Edmunds, Suffolk; the will was proved on 16 February 1658. His second wife, Sarah, was buried at Clapham on 28 September 1678.

In November 1660 Lye and other London ministers wrote thanking the king for his gracious concessions concerning ecclesiastical affairs, but he was ejected from All Hallows in 1662 by the Act of Uniformity. It was reported in 1665 that, though lately in Scotland, he now kept a school at Clapham in Surrey. In 1669 he was said to be preaching at Morgan's Lane, Southwark. Wood recorded that 'he usually held forth in conventicles with Dr Henry Wilkinson … and William Bridge' of Yarmouth (Wood, *Ath. Oxon.*, 4.134). On 30 April 1672 Lye was licensed as a presbyterian teacher at his house in Clapham, where he continued to teach children for many years. In this role he is said to have been popular and successful, and issued his *Plain and familiar method of instructing the younger sort according to the lesser catechism of the assembly of divines* in 1673. Edmund Calamy the younger was taken to Dyers' Hall (aged about four) by his mother to be catechized by 'good old Mr. Thomas Lye … she having been herself catechised by him in her younger years' (Calamy, *Historical Account*, 1.73). On 1 January 1678 Ralph Thoresby, then in London, was 'At the Fast all day. Mr Lye prayed and preached very well … showing that examination is everyone's duty' (*Diary*, 1.9). On 18 April 1683 Lye was presented at the Guildhall for holding conventicles, and may have been imprisoned. One of his former pupils recalled in a lawsuit, *Attorney-General* v. *Hewer* (1700), that Lye often attended service at the parish church before preaching in his own house, that he gave up schoolteaching after being imprisoned in the Marshalsea, and that he used to go to town on Saturday nights in order to preach at a conventicle the following day. This was probably the congregation Lye had gathered which met at Dyers' Hall, Thames Street. He died at Bethnal Green on 7 June 1684, and was buried four days later at Clapham; two unmarried daughters, Sarah and Mary, survived him.

BERTHA PORTER, *rev.* STEPHEN WRIGHT

Sources *Calamy rev.* • Wood, *Ath. Oxon.*, new edn, vol. 4 • Venn, *Alum. Cant.* • Foster, *Alum. Oxon.* • *CSP dom.*, 1651–2 • E. Calamy, *An historical account of my own life, with some reflections on the times I have lived in, 1671–1731*, ed. J. T. Rutt, 2 vols. (1829), vol. 1 • Wood, *Ath. Oxon.: Fasti* • will, PRO, PROB 11/376, fol. 233 • *The diary of Ralph Thoresby*, 2 vols. (1830)

Likenesses line engraving, pubd 1814, BM, NPG; repro. in *Farewell sermons of ejected ministers* (1662)

Wealth at death see will, PRO, PROB 11/376, fol. 233

Lyell, Charles (1769–1849), botanist and literary scholar, was born on 7 March 1769 at Southampton Buildings, Holborn, London, the eldest son of Charles Lyell (1734–1796), naval officer, and Mary Beale (*d.* 1813). After attending St Paul's School, London, he was educated at St Andrews University and at Peterhouse, Cambridge. Destined for a legal career, he was entered at Lincoln's Inn in 1788 but did not go there before taking his Cambridge degree in 1791 (he proceeded MA in 1794). His legal studies were interspersed with continental travel until 1796 when he abandoned the law on inheriting the Scottish estate of Kinnordy, Kirriemuir, Forfarshire. In the same year on 4 October he married Frances Smith (1773/4–1850), with whom he raised three sons and seven daughters.

In 1798 Lyell leased Bartley Lodge in the New Forest, which became the family home until 1826. Here he developed an interest in cryptogamic botany, collecting lichens and mosses in particular, and corresponding with leading botanists. He did not publish, but many of his finds were described in James Sowerby and James Edward Smith's *English Botany* as well as in specialist monographs. Several species bear his name, besides the genus *Lyellia* of Robert Brown.

In 1813 he became a fellow of the Linnean Society. From 1826 he lived permanently at Kinnordy House, and, in addition to botany, began to study Dante's poetry, eventually publishing some translations, initially at his own expense. He built up an impressive herbarium and a valuable library.

Lyell took great interest in the intellectual development of his eldest son, Charles *Lyell (1797–1875), but, as a staunch tory for whom science was a gentlemanly attainment, was initially alarmed by his son's wish to abandon law in favour of establishing a career in science. More conventionally, his younger sons, Henry and Thomas, entered the army and navy respectively. Lyell died from influenza at Kinnordy House on 8 November 1849, while serving as vice-lieutenant of Forfarshire. He left the debt-ridden estate of Kinnordy in trust to his eight surviving children, thus disinheriting Charles as principal heir and new laird of Kinnordy.

ANNE SECORD

Sources L. G. Wilson, *Charles Lyell, the years to 1841: the revolution in geology* (1972) • J. A. Secord, introduction, in C. Lyell, *Principles of geology*, abridged edn (1997), xi–xiii • L. G. Wilson, *Lyell in America: transatlantic geology, 1841–1853* (1998), 311–13 • *Gardeners' Chronicle* (17 Nov 1849), 727 • Venn, *Alum. Cant.* • 'The cryptogamic herbarium of Charles Lyell', *Journal of Botany, British and Foreign*, 37 (1899), 143–4 • W. J. Hooker, *British Jungermanniae: being a history and description, with colored figures, of each species of the genus, and microscopical analyses of the parts* (1816)

Archives priv. coll. | Linn. Soc., J. E. Smith letters • NHM, herbarium • NHM, letters to members of Sowerby family • RBG Kew, directors' corresp. • Trinity Cam., Dawson Turner letters • U. Edin. L., letters to David Laing

Likenesses silhouette, repro. in Wilson, *Charles Lyell*, fig. 3

Wealth at death Kinnordy House and entire estate of Kinnordy; trust established for eight surviving children: Wilson, *Lyell in America*

Lyell, Sir Charles, first baronet (1797–1875), geologist, was born at Kinnordy House, Kirriemuir, Forfarshire, on 14 November 1797, the eldest son of Charles *Lyell (1769–1849) and Frances Smith (1733/4–1850). A few months later his parents left the family estate and moved to the south of England, renting Bartley Lodge near Lyndhurst, Hampshire.

Education and early research Lyell was educated at private schools, latterly in Midhurst, Sussex. As a boy living in the New Forest, he developed an enthusiasm for natural history; as an undergraduate at Oxford, those interests focused on geology. He entered Exeter College as a fellow-commoner in 1816, and attended the lectures on mineralogy and geology by William Buckland in three successive years. Geology, in his father's opinion, was at least 'rational and gentlemanlike' (Wilson, *Charles Lyell*, 44), even if it distracted his son from more serious studies. However, Lyell graduated BA in 1819 with a respectable second class in classical honours (MA in 1821), and entered Lincoln's Inn to prepare for a legal career. As an aspiring young man of science he also joined the Geological and Linnean societies; Buckland was one of those who proposed him for the former.

While still an undergraduate Lyell had begun to look at the world with a geologist's eyes, but his serious research dates from 1821, after he met Gideon Mantell. Lyell worked on correlating Mantell's 'Secondary' formations in Sussex with those further west. He also studied in Hampshire the still younger 'Tertiary' formations, above the distinctive Chalk: Thomas Webster had claimed that those in the Isle of Wight were similar to those that Georges Cuvier (1769–1832) and Alexandre Brongniart (1770–1847) had famously described around Paris. In short, Lyell worked on the kind of geology (later termed stratigraphy) on which the leading members of the Geological Society were then engaged.

Lyell was called to the bar in 1822, but geology was becoming more important to him than the law. In 1823 he was elected a secretary of the Geological Society of London, and he spent that summer in Paris, making himself known in scientific circles and improving his command of the then premier language of science. He met established figures such as Cuvier and Brongniart, and the latter's former student Constant Prévost (1787–1856) showed him the formations of the Paris basin. Conversely, Lyell explained to the French geologists the field evidence for

Sir Charles Lyell, first baronet (1797–1875), by Lowes Cato Dickinson, 1883 [replica; original, *c.*1870]

the sudden 'geological deluge' that Buckland, following Cuvier, had recently invoked to account for the puzzling 'diluvial' deposits in England.

However, Prévost convinced Lyell that the Parisian formations could have been deposited under conditions similar to those in present seas and lakes, and that Cuvier and Brongniart had been too quick to dismiss such close analogies: the rocks might be due to 'actual' or 'modern causes', or processes observably active in the present world. In the summer of 1824, after taking Prévost on a tour of southern England, Lyell followed his lead. Staying at Kinnordy, he studied the sediments deposited in a small lake that had recently been drained. In his first scientific paper, read at the Geological Society that winter, he claimed that those modern lake deposits were closely similar to some of the Parisian rocks, so that there was no sharp contrast between the 'former world' and the present. This paper was the model for all Lyell's later work in geology: modern causes were, he claimed, adequate to explain all the traces of the remote past.

By 1825 Lyell's father was evidently displeased at his son's failure to establish himself in a successful legal career, and in 1826 Lyell did spend more time on legal work in London and in the west of England; however, it was in that year that his parents moved back to Kinnordy, so that the paternal presence became more remote. Lyell resigned as secretary of the Geological Society, but was promptly appointed foreign secretary instead; he was also elected a fellow of the Royal Society. Having joined the new Athenaeum in 1824, he was becoming known in intellectual circles well beyond those of the geologists. In 1825 John Murray invited him to write for the tory *Quarterly Review*, despite his known whig sympathies; this offered Lyell a much-needed new source of income to supplement his modest allowance. He used his essays with gentlemanly tact to advocate among leading tories the cause of moderate reform: he criticized the lack of government support for the sciences, and the unreformed state of the ancient universities; in particular, he criticized the clerical domination of higher education in England.

Origins of the *Principles of Geology* In 1826 an essay in the *Quarterly Review* on the Geological Society's publications enabled Lyell to promote his favourite science, and he praised the society for having replaced the earlier vogue for speculative theorizing with an emphasis on careful observation. Lyell accepted the common view that more complex living organisms had appeared on earth in the course of time, as the earth had slowly cooled, but he also argued that modern causes might account for far more than most geologists allowed; in this respect his views were now diverging from those of Buckland and others at the Geological Society. He began to plan an introductory book that would expound his emerging conception of the science: geology would only become scientific, he believed, if it were based on modern causes, because they alone could be witnessed directly and therefore be known to be 'true causes' ('verae causae').

In 1827, while working as a barrister on the western circuit, Lyell read and was fascinated by the evolutionary speculations of Jean Baptiste de Lamarck (1744–1829), realizing that the mutability of species—if established—would affect geology as much as the sciences of life. But Lyell recoiled from the implications of Lamarck's ideas for the dignity of man, and he saw that the fossil evidence for progression in the history of life could easily be turned into an argument for evolution. He began to claim by contrast that the fossil record was by its nature too imperfect to support that notion, and that the physical world was a stable balanced system like that advocated earlier by James Hutton and John Playfair.

Lyell's essays for the *Quarterly* culminated in 1827 in a long review of a new book on French geology by his friend George Scrope. Lyell agreed with Scrope that 'Time! Time! Time!' was needed in geological explanation, and that there had been no abrupt catastrophe in the geologically recent past; the book suggested to him that the 'lost links in the great chain that unites the present with the past' (*Quarterly Review*, 36, 1827, 443) might still be preserved in Auvergne. In 1828 he joined Roderick Murchison for a fieldwork tour on the continent, and after discussions with Prévost and other Parisians they went straight to Auvergne. Lyell was duly impressed by Scrope's evidence and agreed with his conclusions. Later, in Italy, Lyell developed a rough timescale for the most recent era of the earth's history, as represented by the Tertiary formations. He used the expertise of local naturalists to count the number of fossil species that were known to be still living in present seas, inferring that the percentage would be inversely proportional to the age of each formation. This assumed that new species had somehow appeared, and older ones become extinct, at roughly constant rates, uninterrupted by any catastrophic events. The probabilistic basis of this idea is likely to have been derived from contemporary debates in political economy; certainly Lyell expounded it later in terms of an analogy with changing human populations.

As he travelled alone through Italy into Sicily (Murchison and his wife had returned to England), Lyell believed his hypothesis was confirmed. In the vicinity of active volcanoes such as Vesuvius and Etna, he found putatively recent formations (with a high percentage of extant species) far above sea level, just as he expected if crustal elevation were causally linked to volcanic activity. In Sicily thick formations of this kind underlay the huge cone of Etna, which in turn appeared to be extremely ancient in relation to human records of its more recent eruptions. In effect, Etna and the recent formations beneath it linked Lyell's geological timescale to the timescale of human history, confirming Scrope's inference about the vast time available for modern causes to have had their effects. After leaving Sicily early in 1829 Lyell reported to Murchison how his forthcoming book would expound the true principles of geology: modern causes, acting at their present intensities, were adequate to explain all the observed traces of the remote past. In Paris, on his way back to England, he found that Gerard Deshayes (1797–1875), an expert on fossil molluscs, had pre-empted his ideas on the Tertiary formations; but Lyell turned this to his advantage by paying Deshayes to identify all his fossils and to integrate the results into Deshayes's much wider survey. Back in London, Lyell expounded his views at the Geological Society, and revised his earlier drafts into a far more ambitious publication.

Publication and first reactions The first volume of Lyell's *Principles of Geology* was published by Murray in July 1830. Its ambitions were clear from the title—'Principles' still recalled Isaac Newton's *Principia*—and the subtitle stated clearly that it was 'an attempt to explain the former changes of the earth's surface, by reference to causes now in operation'. Surprisingly for a work on geology, the volume was devoted not to the remote past but wholly to the present world. Lyell gave a systematic description of modern causes such as volcanoes and earthquakes, sedimentation and erosion, culled from a wide range of sources, including many accounts of voyages and expeditions to remote parts of the globe; however, his main source was the great compilation of the physical and topographical changes recorded within human history, published in 1822–4 by Karl von Hoff (1771–1837)—Lyell had learned German specifically in order to read it. He used Hoff's data to illustrate his own view of the earth as a system of balanced antagonistic processes: erosion balanced by sedimentation, for example, and crustal elevation by crustal subsidence. A preliminary section of the book presented a 'grand new theory of climate' (Lyell, *Life*, 1.261), which interpreted long-term climatic changes as the products of an ever-changing physical geography: this neatly undercut what Lyell himself had earlier regarded as conclusive evidence for a slowly cooling earth.

The volume began, however, with a forceful criticism of other geologists, thinly disguised as a history of geology itself. Lyell presented the history of the science as a long battle between views similar to his own, and those that arbitrarily invoked catastrophes at every turn; his own emphasis on the 'uniformity' of nature was treated as synonymous with being truly scientific. Furthermore, Lyell virtually equated his opponents with the many authors who were claiming scriptural authority for limiting the timescale of the earth's history to a few thousand years. In effect, geologists such as Buckland, who did indeed identify the 'geological deluge' as the biblical flood, but who assumed unlimited time for the still earlier history of the earth, were treated by Lyell as no better than the 'scriptural' writers—despite the fact that it was Buckland who had urged Lyell to use his review of Scrope as an opportunity to attack the literalists.

In effect, Lyell was fighting on two fronts: against most other geologists, who doubted the total adequacy of modern causes for understanding the past; and against much wider social groups, who still treated the biblical narratives of creation and the flood as literal history, untouched by the biblical criticism taken for granted on the continent. Lyell wanted not only to make geology truly scientific, but also, as he put it privately, 'to free the science from Moses' (Lyell, *Life*, 1.268). That wider aim accounts for the great interest and attention that the *Principles* received immediately, at least in Britain, not only among men of science but also among the general educated public. The more scientific reviews were mixed: Lyell's claim that the power of modern causes had been underestimated was found important and even persuasive, but his criticisms of other geologists were regarded as grossly unfair; above all, his scepticism about organic progression was considered utterly unconvincing.

In 1831 Lyell was appointed professor of geology at the new King's College in London. Among the clergymen on its governing body, Edward Copleston was worried by Lyell's opinions on the creation of man and the flood, but the rest were not. Lyell lectured at King's in 1832 and 1833; in the latter year he gave similar lectures at the Royal Institution, to which women were admitted, thus swelling his audience and his fees. But Lyell found this work brought him too little income to justify the distraction from his writing, and he resigned from King's and gave no further courses at the Royal Institution.

Lyell had spent the summer of 1831 on fieldwork in Germany; while there he had met the 23-year-old Mary Horner, eldest daughter of the whig reformer and geologist Leonard *Horner. They were married in Bonn on 12 July 1832; after a geological honeymoon, they settled in Hart Street, Bloomsbury, close to the British Museum and to the Geological Society's premises in Somerset House.

Mary was well educated, and fluent in French and German, and was soon helping Lyell with translation, and offsetting his handicap of poor eyesight for reading. However, she seems to have been somewhat excluded from the scientific conversation at their dinner parties. A few years later, after one such occasion, Charles Darwin—himself soon to be married—commented tartly, 'I want *practice* in ill treating the female sex—I did not observe Lyell had any compunction' (*Correspondence*, 2.166). When, a little later, Emma Darwin gave their first dinner party, she recorded that 'Mr Lyell is enough to flatten a party, as he never speaks above his breath, so that everybody keeps lowering their tone to his' (Wilson, *Charles Lyell*, 459). There were no children of the Lyells' marriage.

The second volume of the *Principles* appeared in 1832; it dealt with modern causes in the organic realm, and particularly with the relation between organisms and their environments. Lyell rejected Lamarck's theory of the incessant mutability of species, arguing instead that they were real stable entities, and that they appeared and became extinct in a piecemeal manner in time and space. Extinctions were attributed not to sudden catastrophes but to gradual changes in the environment, as expounded in the first volume; the origins of species were attributed implicitly to some equally natural process as yet unknown. In an incisive review of this volume, William Whewell coined the terms 'uniformitarian' and 'catastrophist' for two opposing sects among geologists, but at the time there were few if any full-blooded uniformitarians apart from Lyell himself.

Lyell's concept of the stability of individual species validated his timescale for the Tertiary era, which formed a cornerstone of the third and culminating volume of the *Principles* (1833). His review of modern causes, both inorganic and organic, had merely provided the 'alphabet and grammar' of geology (*Principles of Geology*, 3.7); they were the means by which nature's historical records could be deciphered, in order to reconstruct the course of earth history. Lyell used Deshayes's massive lists of fossil species to arrange the Tertiary formations in inferred chronological order. Based on the increasing proportions of 'recent' species, Whewell proposed to Lyell the Greek-based names 'Eocene', 'Miocene', and 'Pliocene'; Lyell split the last into 'Older' and 'Newer' parts, thus defining four successive periods of Tertiary time. He reviewed the evidence for the state of the earth during each period in turn, beginning nearest to the directly observable present and working backwards into the more obscure past. He claimed that the whole Tertiary era of earth history proved the earth's essential uniformity through time; the still older formations were discussed much more briefly. The alleged evidence for radically different conditions in the earliest era of all was eliminated by Lyell's concept of 'metamorphism'—deep burial in the earth's crust had altered the oldest rocks beyond recognition and destroyed their fossils, and they were not really 'Primary' at all. Lyell therefore concluded that Hutton had been right to argue that the earth showed no signs of a beginning or an end to its stability, although he denied that this implied that the natural world was eternal or uncreated.

Criticism and further editions By the time the last volume of *Principles* was published, Lyell had already produced second editions of the first two. Cheaper editions of the whole work followed in 1834, 1835, and 1837, each revising his argument in the light of critical reviews and new publications. In 1834 Lyell travelled in Scandinavia, and became convinced that the land around the Baltic had indeed risen insensibly slowly and without earthquakes, even within recorded history. He presented this work—a fine example of his claims about modern causes—as his Bakerian lecture at the Royal Society later in 1834; at the same time he was awarded the society's royal medal, but explicitly for his work on modern causes and their application to the Tertiary formations, rather than for his more controversial claims. The citation reflected the balance of opinion among leading geologists; even Prévost and Scrope, Lyell's strong supporters on the power of modern causes and the redundancy of catastrophes, criticized their friend's rejection of a broadly directional history for the earth. Other critics pointed to Lyell's apparent inconsistency, in conceding that the human species was very recent while denying all other signs of organic progression. So when Darwin, who had read the *Principles* on his voyage round the world, settled in London in 1836 and proved to have closely similar geological ideas, Lyell soon treated his younger colleague as his closest ally.

Lyell served as president of the Geological Society in 1835–7, and used his anniversary addresses to evaluate current research in the light of his own approach to the science. His emphasis on modern causes made steady headway among geologists, but other aspects of his work did not. His percentage timescale, for example, was criticized by those with more expert knowledge of Tertiary fossils: the names for the Tertiary periods survived, but Lyell was forced to weaken their statistical basis, until his use of fossils was almost indistinguishable from that of other geologists. The mixed reception of his ideas was reflected in his decision to divide his work into two distinct parts: from the sixth edition (1840) onwards, the *Principles* became purely a treatise on modern causes and their balanced interactions. Lyell planned a separate book on the use of fossil molluscs in Tertiary geology, but such a work never appeared.

Lyell did return to his original plan for a book that would explain his conception of geology at an introductory level, and thereby propagate it more widely. *Elements of Geology* (1838) reviewed the whole stratigraphical record, from the most recent formations back to the most ancient, interpreting it in terms of the 'uniformity' of terrestrial processes through time. The second edition (1841) was greatly expanded, incorporating the treatment of the Tertiary formations that had now been excised from the *Principles*. Both *Elements* and *Principles* were successful and popular works, as their publishing history shows. Appropriately for a barrister, Lyell wrote stylishly and persuasively, and explained technicalities clearly; his books reached a wide audience of the educated public, far beyond those who were actively engaged in geology. French and German translations, and American editions, made his approach well known throughout the scientific world.

Later geological work In 1841–2 Lyell was invited to the United States and gave the Lowell lectures to a vast audience in Boston. He and his wife also travelled widely, and two volumes of *Travels in North America* (1845) recorded not only his geological observations, but also their opinions on the country's social and political problems: those opinions were liberal in respect to education, less so in the matter of slavery. They revisited America in 1845–6 and he gave the Lowell lectures again; two further volumes about their travels appeared in 1849. In 1846, on their return from America, they moved to a grander house in Harley Street. By this time Lyell had become a prominent man of science, an adviser to government on scientific issues, and an associate of Prince Albert. He was knighted in 1848, and served on the Royal Commission for the Exhibition of 1851. He made two further visits to America in 1852 and 1853, on the latter occasion representing the 1851 commissioners at the Industrial Exhibition in New York.

The successive editions of Lyell's books were kept up to date with the latest research, but their underlying ideas changed little. When he served a second term as president of the Geological Society in 1849–51 he again criticized the supposed fossil evidence for organic progression and still defended his earlier interpretation of the earth's history, although both positions had become increasingly implausible to other geologists. Lyell's last major research project was related to the resurgent theory of 'craters of elevation', by which the largest volcanic cones were attributed to sudden crustal elevation rather than to the slow accumulation of volcanic materials in successive eruptions. During the winter of 1853–4 he countered this serious challenge with field observations on Madeira and the Canary Islands; in 1857 and 1858 he went to look again at Etna; and he persuaded Scrope to return to geology and support his case with evidence from Auvergne.

Lyell and evolution The Canaries and Madeira also brought the puzzles of endemic island faunas and floras back to Lyell's attention, and in private he wrestled once more with the possibility of an evolutionary mechanism for the origin of species. When in 1856 Darwin told him about his theory, Lyell urged him to publish it without delay, and then struggled with its implications not only for his geology but also for his view of human life. By this time he had almost abandoned his earlier nominal allegiance to the liberal wing of the Church of England; he had become *de facto* a Unitarian after seeing the role of that denomination in America. But even unitarian theology left him with acute problems about the dignity of man, if the human species had evolved from primates.

Two events in 1859 led to Lyell's last major publication, *Antiquity of Man* (1863). One was the research by other geologists that finally established that early human beings had lived alongside the mammoths and other extinct mammals of the glacial period, known by this time by Lyell's name, 'Pleistocene' (formerly his 'Newer' Pliocene). This locked the human species firmly into earth history, by extending human history far beyond the reach of textual records into a prehistory recorded only in fossil bones and stone artefacts. The bulk of Lyell's book was devoted to a rather derivative account of this research. The other event in 1859 was Darwin's publication of his *Origin of Species*. Lyell reviewed the evidence for evolution quite favourably—in a section added awkwardly on to his book on prehistory—but Darwin was disappointed that his old mentor failed to announce clearly his own acceptance of the theory. Only in the next (tenth) edition of the *Principles* (1867–8) did Lyell give qualified approval to evolution as the true mechanism for the origin of new species, which he had left so vague thirty years earlier; the book was enlarged and recast to accommodate the change. But Lyell also had to alter his entire perspective on the history of life, finally conceding that successively higher forms of life had been formed in the course of time. He even allowed that the human species was no exception, at least in its physical aspects; but he remained sceptical about the adequacy of Darwin's theory to account for the origin of the mental and moral aspects that were most distinctively human.

Last years Lyell had been active in the British Association since its early years, and at the meeting in Bath in 1864 he served as its president. He was created a baronet the same year, and in 1866 he received—belatedly—the Wollaston medal, the Geological Society's highest award. The *Elements* reached in effect its eighth edition in 1873 (it had been called a *Manual* since 1851, and the last two editions were called *Student's Elements*); the *Principles* was published, just posthumously, in a twelfth edition in 1875. Mary Lyell died on 24 April 1873, and Lyell himself less than two years later, on 22 February 1875, at their London home at 73 Harley Street. Like other leading Victorian men of science, he was buried in Westminster Abbey.

MARTIN RUDWICK

Sources *Life, letters, and journals of Sir Charles Lyell*, ed. Mrs Lyell, 2 vols. (1881) · *Sir Charles Lyell's scientific journals on the species question*, ed. L. G. Wilson (1970) · L. G. Wilson, *Charles Lyell, the years to 1841: the revolution in geology* (1972) · L. G. Wilson, 'Lyell, Charles', *DSB* · C. Lyell, *The geological evidences of the antiquity of man*, 1st–4th edns (1863–73) · C. Lyell, *Travels in North America*, 2 vols. (1845) · C. Lyell, *A second visit to the United States of North America*, 2 vols. (1849) · M. J. S. Rudwick, 'Lyell and the *Principles of geology*', *Geological Society, London, Special Publications*, 143 (1998), 3–15 · M. J. S. Rudwick, introduction and bibliography of Lyell's sources, in C. Lyell, *Principles of geology*, 1 (1990), i–lviii; 3 (1993), 113–60 · J. A. Secord, introduction, in C. Lyell, *Principles of geology*, abridged edn (1997) · S. J. Gould, *Time's arrow, time's cycle* (1987) · R. Porter, 'Charles Lyell and the principles of the history of geology', *British Journal for the History of Science*, 9 (1976), 91–103 · M. J. S. Rudwick, 'Charles Lyell's dream of a statistical palaeontology', *Palaeontology*, 21 (1978), 225–44 · M. Bartholomew, 'Lyell and evolution', *British Journal for the History of Science*, 6 (1972–3), 261–303 · M. Bartholomew, 'The singularity of Lyell', *History of Science*, 17 (1979), 276–93 · D. Ospovat, 'Lyell's theory of climate', *Journal of the History of Biology*, 10 (1977), 317–39 · W. F. Bynum, 'Charles Lyell's *Antiquity of man* and its critics', *Journal of the History of Biology*, 17 (1984), 153–87 · J. B. Morrell, 'London institutions and Lyell's career, 1820–41', *British Journal for the History of Science*, 9 (1976), 132–46 · R. Laudan, 'The role of methodology in Lyell's science', *Studies in the History and Philosophy of Science*, 13

(1982), 215–49 • R. H. Dott, 'Lyell in America', *Earth Sciences History*, 15 (1997), 101–40 • *The correspondence of Charles Darwin*, ed. F. Burkhardt and S. Smith, 2 (1986) • bap. reg. Scot.

Archives American Philosophical Society, Philadelphia, corresp. • Kinnordy House, Kirriemuir, family MSS • NRA, priv. coll., corresp., journals and MSS • U. Edin. L., MSS | BL, letters to Charles Babbage, Add MSS 37183–37200 • CUL, Darwin MSS • GS Lond., letters to Roderick Impey Murchison • ICL, corresp. with Thomas Huxley • NL NZ, Turnbull L., corresp. with G. A. Mantell • Royal Institution of Great Britain, London, letters to W. R. Grove • RS, corresp. with Sir John Herschel

Likenesses J. M. Wright, print, 1836, NPG; repro. in Wilson, *Charles Lyell* • G. Richmond, chalk drawing, *c.*1853, NPG • L. C. Dickinson, oils, 1883 (after his portrait, *c.*1870), NPG [*see illus.*] • Elliott & Fry, carte-de-visite, NPG • T. H. Maguire, lithograph, BM; repro. in T. H. Maguire, *Portraits of honorary members of the Ipswich Museum* (1852) • Mayall, carte-de-visite, NPG • W. Theed, bust, Westminster Abbey, London • W. Theed, bust, RS • albumen print, NPG • oils, GS Lond.

Wealth at death under £30,000: proved, 9 March 1875, *CGPLA Eng. & Wales*

Lyell, James Patrick Ronaldson (1871–1948), book collector, was born on 1 September 1871 at 50 South Hill Park, Hampstead, London, the son of John Ronaldson Lyell, solicitor and chief clerk of the Thames police court, and his wife, Martha Elizabeth Groom. He was educated at Merchant Taylors' School and at University College, London, and was admitted solicitor in April 1894. He eventually became senior partner of Gard, Lyell & Co. He was a member of the Metropolitan Water Board (1910–26) and in 1900 contested East Marylebone unsuccessfully as a Liberal. He served as an elder in the Presbyterian church at Hampstead, where he was also a justice of the peace and for many years chairman of the magistrates' bench.

Lyell was moderately well off but not rich. He married on 17 April 1901 Agnes Stuart (1863/4–1949), daughter of James Stuart Balmer, civil servant, and they had one daughter, Agnes, who predeceased her parents. He began to collect books as early as 1889, and from 1891 to 1911 was especially interested in acquiring incunabula. In 1914 he began to take an interest in early Spanish books, and it was the lucky purchase, for only £4, of a copy of the great Complutensian polyglot Bible (Alcalá de Henares, 1514–17) which inspired him to write and publish in 1917 his first book, a life of Cardinal Francisco Jimenez de Cisneros, archbishop of Toledo (*d.* November 1517), followed in 1926 by his best-known work, *Early Book Illustration in Spain*. The preparation of this book caused him to visit Spain several times and to learn Spanish. A new translation, with up-to-date notes, entitled *La ilustración del libro antiguo en España*, edited by J. Martín Abad, was published in Madrid in 1997. These two books on Spanish subjects are still standard works in their field. Lyell's Spanish and Armada collections are both now in America, mainly in Harvard University Library. He also collected Greek and oriental manuscripts, as well as English books printed abroad. While living in Hampstead he made a small collection of local topography and gave it to the public library there when he decided in 1927 to move to Oxford. He seems to have had little direct contact with the British Museum, except that in November 1943 he presented one French incunable to the museum, the library having bought three of his Italian incunables as early as 1920; but he was so devoted to the Bodleian that he made Oxford his headquarters and in 1932, at the age of sixty-one, having become a member of New College, he took the degree of BLitt for a thesis 'based on my collection of books relating to the Spanish Armada'. About 1936 he changed his taste in collecting, and began to acquire medieval manuscripts, eventually accumulating about 250, of which in his will he bequeathed a choice of 100 to the Bodleian. These became the subject of the detailed catalogue published by A. C. de la Mare in 1971.

Lyell and his wife moved to Abingdon at some time before 1940. He died at the Warneford Hospital in Oxford on 23 December 1948, and his wife died a short time later. He was cremated and his ashes interred at Hampstead cemetery. Under the terms of his will, a Lyell readership in bibliography was established in Oxford, and the first lectures were delivered by his friend Neil R. Ker, university reader in palaeography and fellow of Magdalen College. In a paper which Lyell read to a society at Radley College in 1939, he remarked: 'I have written numerous articles and brochures on other books of mine'; and 'I am at present engaged in the preparation of an annotated catalogue of some of my remaining manuscripts and books' (Lyell, 281). Lyell's personal and bibliographical papers, including his own miscellaneous notes on his manuscripts and their acquisition, were bequeathed to the Bodleian Library. As R. W. Hunt of the Bodleian noted in 1951: 'Lyell was never a social success, and made no attempt to ingratiate himself with anyone … His complete indifference to the ordinary standards of success may explain why his name is not even mentioned in books of reference' (Hunt, 69). Nevertheless, he was a self-taught bibliophile and scholar of extraordinary enthusiasm and discrimination, and one who deserves to be remembered not only by Oxford but by the whole bibliographical world. DENNIS E. RHODES

Sources R. W. Hunt, 'The Lyell bequest', *Bodleian Library Record*, 3 (1950–51), 68–72 • J. P. R. Lyell, 'Books and book collecting', *Bodleian Library Record*, 3 (1950–51), 278–281 • D. J. McKitterick, *The Sandars and Lyell lectures* (1983) • A. C. de la Mare, introduction, *Catalogue of the collection of medieval manuscripts bequeathed to the Bodleian Library, Oxford, by James P. R. Lyell* (1971) • Mrs E. P. Hart, ed., *Merchant Taylors' School register, 1561–1934*, 2 (1936) • b. cert. • m. cert. • d. cert.

Wealth at death £39,250 0s. 1d.: probate, 10 May 1949, *CGPLA Eng. & Wales*

Lyfing [Living, Ælfstan, Æthelstan] (*d.* **1020**), archbishop of Canterbury, was abbot of Chertsey from about 989 until either 998 or 999 and then bishop of Wells until 1013. He was also known as Ælfstan or Æthelstan. In 1013 he succeeded the murdered Ælfheah at Canterbury while England faced the devastating Danish invasion. Understandably there was a delay before he was able to obtain his pallium, so that Ælfwig was consecrated bishop of London by Archbishop Wulfstan at York in February 1014. Lyfing is said by Gervase to have consecrated both Edmund Ironside and also Cnut, in 1016. The inference would be that the former ceremony, at least, was performed before the archbishop was granted his pallium, because, when he returned from Rome, he brought with him a letter from

Pope Benedict VIII, addressed to Cnut. Evidently this urged the king 'to exalt God's praise everywhere; to suppress wrong and to establish full security' (Lawson, 129), an indication that Lyfing had reported to Rome the prevalence of apostasy and lawlessness resulting from the recent warfare. Lyfing was said to be very prudent, and to give very firm advice, whether in matters of church or state. He obtained from Cnut a solemn confirmation of the liberties of Christ Church, Canterbury, as a defence against predatory royal officials, and also grants of land for his church. He donated fine ornaments to the cathedral and restored its roof. Lyfing died on 12 June 1020. He was buried in Christ Church, Canterbury, on the left side of the altar of St Martin. EMMA MASON

Sources D. Knowles, C. N. L. Brooke, and V. C. M. London, eds., *The heads of religious houses, England and Wales*, 1: 940–1216 (1972) • S. Keynes, *The diplomas of King Æthelred 'The Unready' (978–1016): a study in their use as historical evidence*, Cambridge Studies in Medieval Life and Thought, 3rd ser., 13 (1980) • John of Worcester, *Chron.* • M. K. Lawson, *Cnut: the Danes in England in the early eleventh century* (1993) • *The historical works of Gervase of Canterbury*, ed. W. Stubbs, 2 vols., Rolls Series, 73 (1879–80) • *Willelmi Malmesbiriensis monachi de gestis pontificum Anglorum libri quinque*, ed. N. E. S. A. Hamilton, Rolls Series, 52 (1870) • E. B. Fryde and others, eds., *Handbook of British chronology*, 3rd edn, Royal Historical Society Guides and Handbooks, 2 (1986)

Lyfing [Living] (*d.* **1046**), abbot of Tavistock and bishop of Worcester, was an ambitious monk who prospered in the disturbed political conditions between the death of Æthelred II in 1016 and the accession of Edward the Confessor in 1042. He was a member of an ecclesiastical dynasty, a monk of Glastonbury or Winchester, abbot of Tavistock before 1027, and was probably a protégé of Earl Godwine, a favourite of King Cnut. In 1027 he accompanied the king on his visit to Rome, and, after his return with Cnut's admonitory letter to the English church, was appointed to succeed Eadnoth, bishop of Crediton, who had died on the journey. At about the same time, he followed his uncle, Brihtwold, as bishop of Cornwall, a union of dioceses which was to last until 1877. After Cnut's death Lyfing backed Harold I in 1035–6 and in 1038 or 1039 was rewarded with the rich bishopric of Worcester. But his supposed implication in the murder of Edward the Confessor's younger brother, Alfred, in 1036 caused the next king, Harthacnut, temporarily to deprive him of Worcester (1040–1). However, Lyfing's support of Edward in 1041–2 left him in peaceful possession of the three dioceses.

Clearly a 'vicar of Bray' figure, Lyfing received no favourable notices from either contemporaries or later historians. William of Malmesbury, writing in the different climate of the 1120s, thought him, 'shamefully ambitious, an invincible, it is said, perverter [*tyrannus*] of the ecclesiastical laws, who valued nothing unless it entirely served his purpose' (*De gestis pontificum*, 2.94). But, to be fair, the churches of Crediton and, particularly, Cornwall were poorly endowed; and Worcester, coveted by similarly indigent York, provided an important royal counsellor with a suitable income. The pluralism was also part of a general centralizing tendency of the time. Lyfing seems to have made proper provision for Worcester's spiritual needs by employing Ealdred, abbot of Tavistock and his successor in that see, as his suffragan. One book owned by Lyfing, the Lanalet [St Germans] pontifical, may have been copied for Tavistock, of which he was a great benefactor. And it may be that he left his successor in the West-Saxon dioceses, the important reformer, Leofric, with foundations on which to build. Lyfing died between 20 and 25 March 1046 and was buried in Tavistock Abbey.

FRANK BARLOW

Sources *ASC*, s.a. 1038, 1044, 1045 [texts C, E] • *Florentii Wigorniensis monachi chronicon ex chronicis*, ed. B. Thorpe, 2 vols., EHS, 10 (1848–9) • *Willelmi Malmesbiriensis monachi de gestis pontificum Anglorum libri quinque*, ed. N. E. S. A. Hamilton, Rolls Series, 52 (1870) • G. H. Doble, ed., *Pontificale Lanaletense*, HBS, 74 (1937) • F. Barlow, *The English church, 1000–1066: a history of the later Anglo-Saxon church*, 2nd edn (1979) • H. P. R. Finberg, *Tavistock Abbey*, 2nd edn (1969) • P. W. Conner, *Anglo-Saxon Exeter: a tenth-century cultural history* (1993)

Lyford, William (1597?–1653), Church of England clergyman and author, was born at Peasemore, near Newbury, Berkshire, one of at least five children of William Lyford (*d.* 1631/2), the rector there. He matriculated from Magdalen Hall, Oxford, on 28 April 1615, aged seventeen, became a demy of Magdalen College in 1617, and graduated BA on 15 December 1618. A fellow from 1620, he proceeded MA on 14 June 1621, was ordained, and in 1624 also became a fellow of Pembroke College.

In 1630 Lyford published, as *The Tryall of a Christians Syncere Love unto Christ*, a posthumous edition of sermons by his Magdalen contemporary William Pinke (*c.*1599–1629), a trenchantly anti-Catholic work which he dedicated to Pinke's former student George Digby. Having obtained his BD degree on 12 May 1631, on 5 July he supplicated for a licence to preach. In 1632, following the death of his father, Lyford became rector of his home parish of Peasemore (a living occupied by 1637 by his younger brother Edward (*b.* 1605/6)); however, it seems to have been his institution in 1631 or 1632 to the Dorset vicarage of Sherborne, on the presentation of the king and at the suggestion of George Digby's father, John Digby, earl of Bristol, that led him in 1633 to resign his Magdalen fellowship. Soon afterwards he married his wife, Elizabeth, who outlived him.

Lyford published in 1642 the first edition of his *Principles of Faith and Good Conscience*, a catechism designed as a three-year course of preparation for communion, with a chapter for each week and some repetition 'of purpose better to root those main points in weak understandings' (A4); this was subsequently abridged for young people (1649, 1656). On 23 October the following year he was cited by the House of Commons to attend the Westminster assembly, of which he was nominally a member, but he did not sit. According to Richard Baxter, he believed that parliamentarians had acted unlawfully in going to war against the king, and John Walker assumed he was a royalist, but there is no evidence that Lyford attracted parliament's disapproval: he received an augmentation of his stipend from the county committee and in 1647 was one of the committee of triers of ministers. On 12 December that year he preached at St Mary's, Oxford, a traditional Calvinist exposition of the regeneration and sanctification of the elect, published as *The Translation of the Sinner from Death to Life* (1648).

From 1647, according to his own later account, in the wake of *The Testimonie of the London Ministers*, Lyford became involved in the controversy over toleration, drawing up 'exercises' to encourage his 'people' not to 'condemn all things in the Lump, but bee able to discern things that differ' (Lyford, dedication). In a sermon preached before the sheriff, Sir Gerard Napper, at Dorchester assizes on 17 July 1651 and published posthumously as *The matching of the magistrates authority and the Christians true liberty in matters of religion* (1654), Lyford steered what he hoped was a moderate and sober course between the magistrate's duty to promote preaching and restrain idolatry and the people's liberty not to be forced into a particular act of worship. He also eschewed extremes in *An Apologie for our Publick Ministerie and Infant Baptism* (1652), dedicated to John Raymond, and in his last *Three Sermons Preached at Sherborne* (1654), but despite acknowledging the roles of faithful 'private Christians' and even of unordained preachers in being 'a just rebuke to a rotten, formal, dead Clergie' (ibid., 22), both works are trenchant defences of an ordained and publicly maintained ministry.

Lyford died at Sherborne on 3 October 1653 and was buried in the chancel of his church. An address given by 'W. H.' at his funeral was reproduced in an edition of his *The Plain Mans Senses Exercised* (1655), a lengthy further contribution to the toleration controversy. By his will dated 2 September 1653 Lyford left money and land in Dorset, Berkshire, and Hampshire to his son William and seven daughters, and £120 for an exhibition for a poor scholar at Magdalen College, 'by way of thankfullnes for [God's] mercy to me in that Colledge, and in way of Restitution for a summ of money which according to the corrupt custome of those daies I did receave for the Resignation of my fellowship' (PRO, PROB 11/239, fol. 385). William Lyford the younger (*d.* 1678) had matriculated at Magdalen the previous November, and it was in his study there that on 22 October 1653 he wrote the dedication to his father's *The Matching of the Magistrate's Authority*.

VIVIENNE LARMINIE

Sources Foster, *Alum. Oxon.* • Wood, *Ath. Oxon.*, new edn, 3.345–6 • J. Hutchins, *The history and antiquities of the county of Dorset*, 3rd edn, ed. W. Shipp and J. W. Hodson, 4 (1874), 250, 264 • B. Brook, *The lives of the puritans*, 3 (1813), 161 • PRO, PROB 11/239, fol. 385 • *Walker rev.*, 135 • I. Green, *The Christian's ABC: catechisms and catechising in England, c.1530–1740* (1996) • W. Lyford, *An apologie for our publick ministerie and infant baptism* (1652) • *STC, 1475–1640* • Wing, *STC* • [W. Lyford], *The plain mans senses exercised* (1655)

Lygon, Frederick, sixth Earl Beauchamp (1830–1891), Church of England layman and politician, was born on 10 November 1830, the third son of Henry, fourth Earl Beauchamp (1784–1863), and Lady Susan Caroline Eliot (1801–1835), daughter of William, second earl of St Germans.

Frederick Lygon, sixth Earl Beauchamp (1830–1891), by John Watkins, *c.*1866–8

The Lygon family was settled at Madresfield, Worcestershire, from the mid-fifteenth century, and was connected with the Beauchamp family through Richard Lygon, who married Anne, daughter of Richard Beauchamp, second and last Baron Beauchamp of Powick (*d.* 1503). William Lygon, seventh in descent from Anne, died in 1720, leaving a daughter Margaret, who married as her first husband Reginald Pyndar, and by him was mother of Reginald Pyndar, who assumed the surname of Lygon. He died in 1788, having married Susannah, daughter of William Hanmer, and was father of **William Lygon**, first Earl Beauchamp (1747–1816). The first earl, born on 25 July 1747, matriculated at Christ Church, Oxford, on 2 May 1764. He represented the county of Worcester in parliament from 1775, as a follower of Pitt from 1783 until 1806, when he was created Baron Beauchamp of Powyk, Worcestershire. At his father's death in 1788 he had succeeded to estates in Worcestershire, Warwickshire, Derbyshire, and Gloucestershire. These were the patrimony of no more than a well-to-do squire, but in 1798 he inherited part of the vast personal wealth of William Jennens, a kinsman of his mother, enabling him considerably to increase his Worcestershire property and influence. On 1 December 1815 he was made Viscount Elmley and Earl Beauchamp. He died suddenly at his house in St James's

Square, London, on 21 October 1816. He had married, on 1 November 1780, Catharine, daughter of James Denn, and their children included William Beauchamp, John Reginald, and Henry Beauchamp, successively second, third, and fourth earls. His widow, a formidable businesswoman and a discriminating collector, survived until 1844, outliving her eldest son, who died in 1823.

Frederick Lygon was educated at Eton College (1844–7), and matriculated at Christ Church, Oxford, on 15 December 1848. He graduated BA in 1852 and was a fellow of All Souls College during 1852–66. As an undergraduate he adopted Tractarian views and formed a lifelong friendship with Henry Parry Liddon. He resisted an attempt by Edward Howard to convert him to the Roman church, but hoped for some kind of inter-communion between Rome and Canterbury. He did not take Anglican orders, but instead became 'the ecclesiastical layman par excellence' (Chadwick, 2.365), representing the high-church party on committees and commissions, and contributing assiduously to journals and newspapers. As a religious author his most influential work was 'The day hours of the Church of England, newly transcribed and arranged according to the prayer book and the Authorised Version of the Bible', published anonymously in 1858. It was generally adopted as an office book by the Anglican communities, and remained in widespread use until recent years (private information).

From 1857 Lygon also developed a parliamentary career, speaking frequently in the Commons and later in the Lords, although he was always a churchman first and a politician second. From March 1857 to April 1863 he sat as a Conservative for Tewkesbury, briefly holding office as a lord of the Admiralty in March 1859. In 1863, on the death of his father, he succeeded his elder brother Henry as MP for West Worcestershire, a seat he held until he himself became sixth Earl Beauchamp in March 1866. Like his brother before him he was a friend of Benjamin Disraeli, for whom he wrote speeches on church questions and whose second administration he joined, as lord steward, in 1874. Later he served under Salisbury as paymaster of the forces from June 1885 until January 1886, and again from August 1886 until July 1887.

On inheriting the Beauchamp estates in 1866 one of his first tasks had been to complete the reconstruction of Madresfield Court begun by the fifth earl, including the provision of a chapel (the remarkable decoration of which was to be the work of the next generation). In February 1868 he married Lady Mary Catherine Stanhope (*b.* 1844), daughter of Philip Henry *Stanhope, fifth Earl Stanhope (1805–1875), who died in 1876 having had five children, the eldest of whom, William *Lygon (1872–1938), was to become the seventh Earl Beauchamp. Two years later, on 24 September 1878, he married Lady Emily Annora Charlotte Pierrepont (1853–1935), daughter of the third Earl Manvers, with whom he had a further four children. His role as a conscientious Victorian landlord, combined with his enthusiasm for education and ecclesiastical architecture, resulted in the building of schools and chapels on his properties. He was involved locally in the foundation of Malvern College and the Alice Ottley School for Girls, Worcester, and at Oxford in the early years of Keble College and later in the establishment of Pusey House. He was made lord lieutenant of Worcestershire in 1876.

Born to a somewhat elderly father, and losing his mother at the age of five, Frederick was perhaps a rather reserved and lonely figure as a young man. Later he acquired a more worldly exterior, being remembered by Archbishop Benson as 'brusque' and 'a very smart, bright man' (GEC, *Peerage*). He had a love of music, and was a founder member of the St Cecilia Society: an early publication was a hymnal for Madresfield church in 1853. He was an FSA and a member of the Roxburghe Club, for which he edited the *Liber regalis* in 1870. He died on 19 February 1891 at Madresfield Court and was buried at Madresfield, characteristically leaving instructions that no tomb or monument was to be erected in his memory.

R. J. Olney

Sources Madresfield Court, Malvern, Worcestershire, Beauchamp MSS · private information (2004) [D. E. Williams] · *DNB* · GEC, *Peerage* · *Principal family and estate collections: family names L–W*, HMC (1999) · J. de la Cour, *Madresfield Court* (privately printed, [n.d.]) · O. Chadwick, *The Victorian church*, 2nd edn, 2 vols. (1970–72) · HoP, *Commons*, *1754–90* · *GM*, 1st ser., 86/2 (1816), 381 · *The Times* (20 Feb 1891) · Foster, *Alum. Oxon.*

Archives NRA priv. coll., corresp. and papers | BL, corresp. with Benjamin Disraeli, Add. MS 61892 · Bodl. Oxf., corresp. with Benjamin Disraeli · CKS, letters to Lord Stanhope and Lady Stanhope · LPL, corresp. with E. W. Benson · LPL, corresp. with A. C. Tait

Likenesses J. Watkins, carte-de-visite, *c.*1866–1868, NPG [*see illus.*] · R. Lehman, oils, 1878, Madresfield Court, Worcestershire · T. H. Maguire, lithograph (after G. Richmond), NPG

Wealth at death £114,741: GEC, *Peerage*

Lygon, William, first Earl Beauchamp (1747–1816). *See under* Lygon, Frederick, sixth Earl Beauchamp (1830–1891).

Lygon, William, seventh Earl Beauchamp (1872–1938), politician, was born on 20 February 1872, probably at 13 Belgrave Square, London, eldest son of Frederick *Lygon, sixth Earl Beauchamp (1830–1891), and his first wife, Lady Mary Catherine (1844–1876), only daughter of the historian Philip Henry *Stanhope, fifth Earl Stanhope. He was styled Viscount Elmley until he succeeded to his father's earldom in 1891. He was educated at Eton College (1885–90) and at Christ Church, Oxford; like his father he was elected president of the Oxford Union Society (1893). He was sent down from Christ Church in May 1894 by the dean, Francis Paget, for putting up notices criticizing the college authorities for the expulsions which followed a commotion involving members of the Bullingdon Club. This 'good looking, smooth faced young man' (Blunt, 2.29) made a precocious entry into public life as mayor of Worcester (1895–6) and as member for Finsbury on the London school board (1897–9). He made a 'display' of independent thinking in reaction to his 'Papa', who was described by two fellow earls as 'the most straitlaced and pompous old prig' and as 'a bigoted and rather bitter High Churchman: of narrow sympathies, and not more than moderate

William Lygon, seventh Earl Beauchamp (1872–1938), by George Charles Beresford, 1910

understanding' with 'a stiff manner and touchy disposition' (Vincent, 159; Lpool RO, earl of Derby diary, 21 Feb 1891).

As a Progressive in London politics Beauchamp was surprised to be nominated by Joseph Chamberlain as governor of New South Wales. He was installed on 18 May 1899, but went on leave on half pay in October 1900 and never returned to Australia before his retirement on 2 November 1901. Tactless remarks about convict history and the Dreyfus case, coupled with a correct sense of the dignity of his office, made Beauchamp unpopular with some colonialists at a time of increasing nationalism and radicalism. However, his deft exercise of his limited political prerogatives, his sympathy for bushmen and assiduity in visiting rural areas, his innovative luncheon for suburban mayors, his efficiency during an outbreak of bubonic plague, and his supervision of negotiations for the Pacific cable belied his reputation as an inept placeling.

On 26 July 1902 Beauchamp married Lady Lettice Mary Elizabeth Grosvenor (1876–1936), younger daughter of Victor Alexander Grosvenor, Earl Grosvenor, and sister of Hugh Grosvenor, the second duke of Westminster. She had 'an attractive manner and pretty gestures, with an evident desire to please that is very winning' (FitzRoy, 187). This marriage brought him material and social advantages: he was sincerely devoted to his wife, who sat as a magistrate. They had three sons and four daughters.

Like other repatriated proconsuls Beauchamp felt neglected on his return. Protectionism so repelled him that he allied himself with the Liberals: his great Belgravia house became a London power-house for that party. On Campbell-Bannerman coming into office Beauchamp's expectations were such that his valet declared: 'We shall 'ave Hindia or Hireland, but we don't know which' (Wilson, 431). Instead he was made captain of the Honourable Corps of Gentlemen-at-Arms (20 December 1905), sworn of the privy council (8 January 1906) and appointed lord steward of the royal household (1 August 1907 to 21 June 1910). Asquith brought him into the cabinet as lord president of the council (21 June 1910 to 7 November 1910) and first commissioner of works (8 November 1910 to 6 August 1914). 'Interesting and erudite', judged an official with whom he had regular dealings, 'he has great quickness in making up his mind, and his judgment is as a rule sound; he has, moreover, considerable resolution' (FitzRoy, 421, 440). As a radical Beauchamp was 'very strong' against high naval expenditure (*Political Diaries of C. P. Scott*, 78), and tendered his resignation on 3 August 1914, the day before the declaration of war. He was reconciled by the German invasion of Belgium, and on 5 August resumed the lord presidency, which he retained until the cabinet reconstruction on 26 May 1915. He represented the government at Buckingham Palace when George V signed the declaration of war. A cabinet colleague described him in 1915 as 'a nonentity of pleasant manners, a good deal of courage, and a man of principle, but with no power of expression' (*Inside Asquith's Cabinet*, 229).

Beauchamp strove to conciliate the Liberal Party during the Lloyd George schism, and was influential in the party's counsels during the 1920s. As Liberal leader in the House of Lords from 1924, he strenuously asserted that his followers should occupy the opposition front bench in the House of Lords, and was aggrieved when in 1925 Marquess Curzon of Kedleston, as leader of the house, pronounced in favour of Labour. Among other public honours he bore the sword of state at the coronation of George V (1911), became lord lieutenant of Gloucestershire (1912) and lord warden of the Cinque Ports (1913). He was chancellor of the University of London from 1929, and an ecclesiastical commissioner. He was created KCMG (16 February 1899) and KG (22 June 1914), and received honorary degrees from Glasgow (1901), London (1929), and Cambridge (1930). But he was obliged by a scandal in 1931 to resign from the royal household as well as to relinquish the lord lieutenancy, chancellorship, party leadership, and other offices including (in 1932) the lord wardenship.

As early as 1901 Lord Mersey had described Beauchamp's house-party for forty guests at Madresfield: 'Everything was done in great style: minstrels in the gallery at dinner, numbers of footmen in powder and breeches and a groom of the chambers worthy of Disraeli's novels' (Mersey, 190). Beauchamp's menservants gradually became more conspicuous. He behaved indiscreetly with young men at Walmer Castle, where he entertained such flamboyant friends as Ernest Thesiger. Though he was podgy in appearance and ponderous in manner, he enjoyed the gaiety of others. By 1927 Lord Lee of Fareham 'was painfully cognisant of B.'s unsavoury moral reputation', and protested when he presented the prizes at a school speech day (*Good Innings*, 282). Hugh Walpole visiting 'the Baths at the Elephant & Castle … saw Ld Carisbrooke naked: saw Ld Beauchamp in the act with a boy' (*Diary of Virginia Woolf*, 211).

Beauchamp's ruin was accomplished by his brother-in-law the duke of Westminster, who was jealous of his public offices and domestic happiness. During 1931 Westminster denounced Beauchamp's homosexuality to George V, who reportedly said, 'Why, I thought people like that always shot themselves' (Lees-Milne, 52). He informed his sister of her husband's irregularities with such brutality that her sanity was endangered. He tried to suborn Beauchamp's daughters into testifying against their father, and took away his youngest son to live on a Grosvenor property. Beauchamp was dissuaded from suicide by his second son, but Westminster's insistence on a warrant being issued for his arrest drove him into exile. Arthur Ponsonby on 16 July confided to Hugh Dalton 'the sad case of Lord Beauchamp, who had a persistent weakness for footmen, and has been finally persuaded by Simon and Buckmaster to sign an undertaking not to return to England' (*Political Diary*, 148–9). From 1931 he travelled in Germany, Italy, and France, and revisited Australia in 1932, 1934, and 1938. Robert Bernays, who stayed with Beauchamp in Paris shortly after George V's death, reported that he was 'still vainly hoping that with the change of monarchs he will be allowed to return' (*Diaries and Letters*, 257). When his wife died later in 1936 he travelled from Venice for her funeral, but was prevented from leaving his ship at Dover by friends who believed that Westminster would ensure his arrest. The warrant was nevertheless suspended some months later to enable him to attend the funeral of his second son. Afterwards it was annulled by his former colleague Sir John Simon.

Beauchamp (who retained the devotion of his children) died of cancer on 14 November 1938 at the Waldorf Astoria Hotel, New York city. On 25 November he was buried in Madresfield churchyard. His family misfortunes inspired Evelyn Waugh's novel *Brideshead Revisited* (1945), in which Lord Marchmain is based on Beauchamp. He was succeeded by his eldest son, William Lygon, eighth (and last) Earl Beauchamp (1903–1979).

RICHARD DAVENPORT-HINES

Sources GEC, *Peerage* • *DNB* • *AusDB* • C. Sykes, *Evelyn Waugh* (1975) • S. Hastings, *Evelyn Waugh* (1994) • A. Fitzroy, *Memoirs* (1927) • W. S. Blunt, *My diaries: being a personal narrative of events, 1888–1914*, 2 (1921) • *The Crawford papers: the journals of David Lindsay, twenty-seventh earl of Crawford … 1892–1940*, ed. J. Vincent (1984) • Fifteenth earl of Derby, diary, 21 Feb 1891, Lpool RO • J. Wilson, *C. B.: a life of Sir Henry Campbell-Bannerman* (1973) • *The political diaries of C. P. Scott, 1911–1928*, ed. T. Wilson (1970) • *Inside Asquith's cabinet: from the diaries of Charles Hobhouse*, ed. E. David (1977) • *A good innings: the private papers of Viscount Lee of Fareham*, ed. A. Clark (1974) • *The diary of Virginia Woolf*, ed. A. O. Bell and A. McNeillie, 5 (1984), 211 • J. Lees-Milne, *Prophesying peace* (1977) • Viscount Mersey [C. C. Bigham], *A picture of life* (1941) • Christabel, Lady Aberconway, *A wiser woman?* (1966), 127 • *The political diary of Hugh Dalton, 1918–1940, 1945–1960*, ed. B. Pimlott (1986) • *The diaries and letters of Robert Bernays, 1932–1939*, ed. N. Smart (1996)

Archives Glos. RO, corresp. and papers as lord-lieutenant of Gloucestershire • Madresfield Court, Worcestershire, corresp., scrapbook • Mitchell L., NSW, corresp., diary, and papers • NRA, priv. coll. • Worcs. RO, papers as lord warden of the Cinque Ports | BL OIOC, letters to Lord Reading, MSS Eur. E 238, F 118 • Bodl. Oxf., letters to Herbert Asquith • CAC Cam., Churchill MSS • HLRO, letters to David Lloyd George • Nuffield Oxf., corresp. with Lord Emmott | FILM BFI NFTVA, news footage

Likenesses G. C. Beresford, photograph, 1910, NPG [*see illus.*] • W. Stoneman, photograph, *c.*1917, NPG • Bassano, photograph, *c.*1926, repro. in Fitzroy, *Memoirs*, facing p. 554 • W. Stoneman, photograph, 1930, NPG • photograph, 1930, repro. in N. Harte, *The University of London, 1836–1986* (1986), 218 • T. Cottrell, cigarette card, NPG • C. Gere, watercolour drawing, NPG • Spy [L. Ward], caricature, lithograph, NPG; repro. in *VF* (20 July 1899)

Wealth at death £140,993 4*s.* 7*d.*: probate, 27 Jan 1939, *CGPLA Eng. & Wales*

Lyhert, Walter (*d.* 1472), bishop of Norwich, was from Lanteglos by Fowey in Cornwall. His only known kinsman (*cognatus*) is John Lyhert, who predeceased him and was a co-beneficiary of the bishop's own chantry. Once Lyhert became a bishop, he always acted as proctor in parliament for Edmund Lacy, bishop of Exeter, for many years an invalid. A hospital in Plymouth, Devon, received 10 marks (£6 13*s.* 4*d.*) in Lyhert's will. There is no evidence of any kinship with the Norwich family of his name.

Lyhert was admitted as sophist and fellow to Exeter College, Oxford, *c.*1420, and had graduated BA from there by 1425. Equally important, he formed an association there with John Halse of Kenedon, Devon, with whom he remained friends until death. Lyhert was a fellow of Oriel College from 1425 to 1427. Having achieved the degree of MA he received that of BTh in 1441, but was awarded the degree of DTh only after his episcopal promotion. On 1 June 1435 he was elected provost of Oriel, and retained the office until 1446, when Halse succeeded him.

Lyhert had been ordained subdeacon in April 1427, deacon in July, and priest on 20 September, doubtless in connection with his admission to the rectory of Lamarsh, Essex, on 7 October that year. A series of exchanges of benefice followed. On 24 February 1441 he was presented by the crown to the rectory of Bradwell-on-Sea, Essex, perhaps showing that he had begun to attract influential notice. It remains a mystery none the less exactly how he secured the patronage he now did. On 10 February 1444, as a 'king's clerk and chaplain', he was granted the wardenship of St Anthony's Hospital in London, a significant preferment. And by 1445 he had become chaplain to William de la Pole, earl of Suffolk, then the major figure around the king, and on 24 January 1446, still a 'king's clerk', he was papally provided to the see of Norwich, on Suffolk's petition and in supersession of Henry VI's initial nomination of his own confessor, John Stanbury. Custody of the temporalities had already been granted to him on 10 January 1446 and they were formally restored on 26 February. Lyhert was consecrated at Lambeth on 27 February 1446 and enthroned on 3 April. He made an extensive primary visitation between June and August 1448, but otherwise was no more than a periodic guest in his diocese before 1450.

It was a startling advance to a first-rank see for a man of

Lyhert's background, but the fact that it brought yet further major resources and patronage in East Anglia under Suffolk's control inevitably made Lyhert highly vulnerable. Accordingly, his position (undoubtedly to Suffolk's satisfaction) as confessor to Queen Margaret of Anjou was noted by his irascible Oxford contemporary, Thomas Gascoigne, and confirmed as fact, in 1447 at least, in parliament. John Halse had become her long-term chaplain. In that year too, Lyhert was rendered open to further criticism by his friendship with the increasingly notorious Bishop Reginald Pecock, who gave him a copy of his latest, highly controversial, sermon.

On 16 August 1447 Lyhert was appointed as one of five principals in a delegation to seek peace but, more specifically, collaboration with the French in securing unity in the church; leaving London on 24 August, they achieved an extension of the truce, moved on to Lyons in late October and on 8 November were in Geneva seeking to persuade the antipope, Felix V, to resign. Returning to London on 14 January 1448 Lyhert had a personal interview with the king at Windsor the next day. Remaining in London around the court, he witnessed some council writs but was doubtless primarily in personal attendance on the queen and a reassuring presence to Suffolk. Unsurprisingly, he attracted abuse and lampoons at the time of the latter's fall from grace and subsequent murder in 1450 and was threatened directly by a mob in his diocese, to which he retreated, but he escaped physical harm then and political condemnation in parliament afterwards. He was not seen as an evil influence.

Lyhert spent the early 1450s very much as a resident diocesan. However, when the king fell ill, he was one of the six leading bishops who on 5 December 1453, alongside six equally tentative lay peers, announced formally their reluctant consent to maintain the burden of governance while the king was incapacitated. Five months later, on 3 April 1454, when the duke of York became protector, Lyhert followed other bishops in saying he was ready to attend the council when his colleagues required, but asked 'that he have lycens among other to attend to his ayre and to vyeset his diosses as hit aperteneth unto hym' (Griffiths, 'King's council', 80). Clearly he recognized that his connections with the queen and court forbade him to lend credibility as a councillor to York's regime. Lyhert stayed until July, but did not return to London until November, and remained thereafter when the king recovered. He did, however, go back to his diocese before politics suddenly erupted into battle in the spring of 1455. This did not leave him free of the consequences. It was reported in the aftermath of the first battle of St Albans that John (I) Paston, a bitter local opponent of the late duke of Suffolk's regime in East Anglia, intended to seize this chance to denounce the bishop and two other leading henchmen in parliament. Paston hastily denied this.

As the queen reasserted factional control in the following years, Lyhert became increasingly a resident diocesan. However, he did resume long-term residence in London in late 1459, presumably to bolster the Lancastrian court after it had driven its enemies into exile by war but had to expect their invasion. Hence, some time about October 1460, when these rivals appeared to have gained a decisive upper hand militarily, at least in the south, he felt the need to sue out a permanent exemption from parliaments and councils, in consideration of his age, long service at home and abroad, and 'his desire to follow things divine' (*CPR, 1452–61*, 642). This was an obvious ploy to avoid involuntary collaboration with the new regime, and, in fact, Lyhert did not miss a single parliament under any dynasty or regime until the day he died. When Henry VI was restored briefly to the throne in September 1470, Lyhert, like other veterans, rallied to him in London and stayed there over the winter, but suffered no consequences when Edward IV won his throne back in the spring.

Edward IV, of course, had had no public role for Lyhert to fill after 1461, which left him free to give his entire attention to his diocese, where his conscientiousness on visitations, in particular, made a considerable impression. According to the Paston family (with whom he now became very friendly), he took pains with his clergy, seeking to alleviate those in financial straits. However, he failed totally to break apart the scandalous (to the Pastons) betrothal of Margery Paston and their steward, Richard Calle, although he tried hard.

Lyhert was a considerable benefactor to Norwich Cathedral, promoting the building of a spire that might remain upright and of the rood-screen, with his delightful three-pun rebus (a hart lying in water) sculpted freely round the church. He inherited a perennial jurisdictional feud between the bishop and the cathedral on the one side and the city on the other, which had several times turned violent and in 1442 had led to a major and damaging riot across the cathedral enclave. Lyhert more than held his own, in Norwich and also in Wymondham, where he responded with similar vigour to defiance against his jurisdiction in 1448. In a confrontation with the earl of Oxford in 1462 'my lorde dyde quyte hym als curageousely as ever I wist man do' (*Paston Letters*, 2, 269). His register built up into by far the most immaculate and neat record of its kind in the whole of later medieval England, a massive calligraphic gem. This does not, in itself, prove pastoral zeal or spiritual sensitivity, but as a theologian by training (if not an original author) and with no external distractions, Lyhert's full-time residence and steady touring of his diocese suggest a mind concentrated on its work. Nevertheless, he delegated ordination ceremonies to suffragans almost throughout his episcopacy.

Lyhert's final 'testament' was made at Hoxne, Suffolk, always his favourite residence, on 13 May 1472. His 'will', mainly dealing with his chantry, had been made on 31 March 1471. The testament had a clear direction. The funeral expenses were not to be 'superfluous and excessive', but 'in moderation', without 'solace for the rich and well-founded' but rather for 'the sick and needy', with 2*d.* for every pauper at the funeral and again at the trental. There were to be three months' wages and board for all his servants, with handsome bonuses for each of them besides. No less than £100 was to be distributed to his poor tenants. One deceased servant, Richard Hedge, was to be a specified beneficiary within the bishop's own chantry, where the priest was to preach to the laity weekly through Advent and Lent. He bequeathed liturgical items to Exeter, Oriel, and All Souls colleges at Oxford, and 100s. each to Gonville Hall and Trinity Hall, Cambridge. The residue of his estate was to be used for impoverished scholars in Oxford and Cambridge. His funeral and other bequests make it no surprise to find him bequeathing a copy of the distinctive *Sermones dominicales* of Philip Repingdon, bishop of Lincoln, celebrated moralist and nominally repentant Wycliffite, to Mr John Wilton of Cambridge. Lyhert died at Hoxne on 24 May. He was buried, as he wished, before the door of the rood-screen he had built, in Norwich Cathedral. It was probably when the tombstone was later moved to the eastern door of the south choir aisle that his brass was discarded. R. J. SCHOECK

Sources *Chancery records* • Emden, *Oxf.*, 2.1187–8 • N. Davis, ed., *Paston letters and papers of the fifteenth century*, 2 vols. (1971–6) • T. Gascoigne, *Loci e libro veritatum*, ed. J. E. Thorold Rogers (1881) • C. W. Boase, ed., *Registrum Collegii Exoniensis*, new edn, OHS, 27 (1894) • C. L. Shadwell and H. E. Salter, *Oriel College records*, OHS, 85 (1926) • will, PRO, PROB 11/6, sig. 7 • *RotP*, vol. 5 • R. A. Griffiths, *The reign of King Henry VI: the exercise of royal authority, 1422–1461* (1981) • I. Atherton and others, eds., *Norwich Cathedral: church, city and diocese, 1096–1996* (1996) • R. A. Griffiths, 'The king's council and the first protectorate of the duke of York, 1453–1454', *EngHR*, 99 (1984), 67–82 • N. H. Nicolas, ed., *Proceedings and ordinances of the privy council of England*, 7 vols., RC, 26 (1834–7), vol. 6

Lyle [Lile], **Agnes** (*fl.* **1825**), ballad singer, was the daughter of a 'customary' weaver from Locherlip who was born *c.*1731 and died *c.*1811, and from whom she learned her songs. She was residing in Kilbarchan, 5½ miles east of Paisley, Renfrewshire, in 1825.

Firsthand knowledge of Agnes Lyle comes from manuscript sources made by William Motherwell (1797–1835), poet, journalist, writer, and ballad collector and editor. In the early 1820s he entered into a collaborative project, which soon became his alone, to produce a book titled *Minstrelsy: Ancient and Modern* (published in fascicles whose parts were gathered together in 1827). He read books, corresponded with experts, and engaged in field collecting. And he seems to have had particular success collecting materials from women and even identified in a manuscript notebook (Harvard U., Houghton L., MS 25242.16) a group designated 'old singing women'. Agnes Lyle, or Lile, as he sometimes wrote her name, was one of these women. She was probably then in her fifties, he in his twenties, so she seemed old to him, as did her Kilbarchan neighbours whose songs he also recorded: Mrs King, Mrs Thomson, Nancy Holmes, and Agnes Laird.

Motherwell's collecting notebook (Harvard U., Houghton L., MS 25242.16, copy made for Francis James Child), where he wrote reminders and notes to himself, and the manuscript which offers fair copies of materials gathered by collecting and correspondence (University of Glasgow, Murray MS 501) suggest that he made three visits to Agnes Lyle, probably in the late summer and autumn of 1825. In total, he may have collected as many as thirty-two items of which twenty-one are full texts; he paid her for her help. He mentioned her in a letter to C. K. Sharpe (Harvard U., Houghton L., MS 25241.56F), commenting that she wept in the process of singing 'Sheath and Knife', a tale of incest and death. In addition to locating the source of her repertoire—her father—Motherwell also includes comments made by Lyle:

> I was informed by A. Lile that she has heard a longer set of the ballad ['Lord Jamie Douglas'] in which while Lady Douglas is continuing her lament she observes a troop of gentlemen coming to her father's and she expresses a wish that these should be sent by her lord to bring her home. They happen to be sent for that purpose and she accompanies them. On her meeting however with her lord … her heart breaks and she drops down dead-at-his feet.

Francis James Child, the great nineteenth-century American editor of balladry, recovered Motherwell's manuscripts and printed texts in his five-volume work (*English and Scottish Popular Ballads*, 1882–98); most of Lyle's full texts are given there and attributed to her. That publication brought Agnes Lyle's name to public view and set the stage for an analysis of her repertory (McCarthy).

In the introduction to his *Minstrelsy*, Motherwell had described a method of generating texts built on commonplaces which suggests something like oral formulaic composition (Lord). It may be that this was a technique he observed in the singing and song production of Agnes Lyle, a technique analysed from internal textual evidence alone by McCarthy who also suggests that her repertoire represents her radical political leanings resulting from the depressed situation for the weaving community in the early part of the nineteenth century. Yet her songs also present an array of strong, active women, who love despite all the obstacles. This may well reflect her own hopes. MARY ELLEN BROWN

Sources W. Motherwell, ballads, U. Glas., Murray MS 501 • W. Motherwell, ballad notebook, Harvard U., Houghton L., MS 25242.16 • W. Motherwell, letter to C. K. Sharpe, Harvard U., Houghton L., MS 25241.56F • F. J. Child, ed., *The English and Scottish popular ballads*, 5 vols. (1882–98) • W. B. McCarthy, *The ballad matrix* (1990) • A. Lord, *The singer of tales* (1960) • M. E. Brown, 'Old singing women and the canons of Scottish balladry and song', *A history of Scottish women's writing*, ed. D. Gifford and D. McMillan (1997), 44–57 • M. E. Brown, 'The mechanism of the ancient ballad: William Motherwell's explanation', *Oral Tradition*, 11 (1996), 175–89 • C. P. Lyle, ed., *Poems and ballads of Kilbarchan*, 2nd ser. (1931)

Lyle, David (*fl.* **1755–1762**), maker of mathematical instruments and stenographer, was the author of a treatise entitled *The art of short hand improved, being an universal character adapted to the English language, whereby every kind of subject may be expressed or taken down in a very easy, compendious, and legible manner* (1762). He describes himself on the title-page as a master of arts, having graduated at Glasgow in 1755. Nothing is known of the circumstances of his birth, or of his death.

In the dedication of the work to the earl of Bute, Lyle states that it was by his lordship's good offices that he was enabled to bring his new mathematical instruments to great perfection, and that, at his desire, he had completed a set of them for the king. This set comprises four silver volute compasses, now in the King George III collection in the Science Museum, London, all similar in design and, according to the inscription on the largest and most complex, made in 1760. The compasses were designed to draw spirals of different types according to a changeable drum attached to the instrument. Few examples of this style of compass survive because they were not widely used owing to their limited field of application and the difficulty in manipulating them, and Lyle's has been described as one of the less successful bids to gain royal patronage. Other instruments by him are not known, and none was in the large collection of his patron, the earl of Bute, when it was sold in 1793.

The introduction to Lyle's method of stenography, which he calls the other production of his younger days, contains a detailed essay on the theory of the art and criticism of the systems of Weston, Macaulay, and Annet. He was not successful, however, in reducing his theory to practice, for although his beautifully engraved tables of words and sentences are elegant and concise, a close examination reveals that their shortness is produced, in the majority of instances, by omitting words or syllables necessary to the sense. His vowel scheme, on a phonetic basis, was more extensive than any previously attempted, but the merits of the system are purely theoretical.

THOMPSON COOPER, *rev.* PHILIP N. GROVER

Sources A. Q. Morton and J. A. Wess, *Public and private science: the King George III collection* (1993) • J. H. Lewis, *An historical account of the rise and progress of short hand* (privately printed, London, c.1825) • *The theory of David Lyle's phonetic shorthand, with notes by Edward Pocknell* (1882) • J. A. Chaldecott, *Handbook of the King George III collection of scientific instruments* (1951) • E. G. R. Taylor, *The mathematical practitioners of Hanoverian England, 1714–1840* (1966) • E. H. Butler, *The story of British shorthand* (1951) • G. Clifton, *Directory of British scientific instrument makers, 1550–1851*, ed. G. L'E. Turner (1995) • G. Adams, *Geometrical and graphical essays*, 4th edn (1813) • G. L'E. Turner, 'The auction sales of the earl of Bute's instruments, 1793', *Annals of Science*, 23 (1967), 213–42 • K. W. Schweizer, ed., *Lord Bute: essays in re-interpretation* (1988) • W. I. Addison, *A roll of graduates of the University of Glasgow from 31st December 1727 to 31st December 1897* (1898), 344

Archives Sci. Mus., King George III collection

Lyle, (Charles Ernest) Leonard, first Baron Lyle of Westbourne (1882–1954), sugar refiner and politician, was born at Highgate in London on 22 July 1882, the only son of Charles Lyle and his wife, Mary, *née* Brown. The Lyles were a family of shipowners active in Greenock. Leonard Lyle was educated at Harrow School and Trinity Hall, Cambridge. In 1903 he joined the family sugar-refining firm of Abram Lyle & Sons, becoming a director on the retirement of his father in 1909. In 1904 Leonard married Edith Louise (*d.* 1942), daughter of John Levy. They had two daughters and one son, Charles John Leonard (*b.* 1905), who also entered the family firm, becoming a member of the board in 1929.

During the First World War, Leonard Lyle served as a captain in the Royal Army Service Corps, and in the British Red Cross Society. His political career began in 1918, when he was elected coalition Unionist MP for the Stratford division of West Ham, London; he subsequently served as parliamentary private secretary to Charles McCurdy, the food controller. He was defeated in 1922, and did not stand for Stratford again. In 1923 he was elected as a Unionist for Epping, which he represented for only one year before making way for Winston Churchill. He was knighted in 1923 and created a baronet in 1932. Lyle did not seek re-election for parliament until 1940, when he was elected, unopposed, as Conservative member for Bournemouth, where he had made his home, and where for some time he served as a JP. He stood for the seat again in 1945, and received the largest majority of any Conservative candidate at that election. He did not take his seat, however, for within a matter of weeks he made way for Brendan Bracken, a close colleague of Churchill, the second time Lyle had sacrificed his seat for his party. As a reward, Lyle was raised to the peerage as Baron Lyle of Westbourne in Churchill's resignation honours list.

Lyle's industrial interests were almost exclusively concerned with the sugar business, though he was also a director of Lloyds Bank. In 1921 Abram Lyle & Sons amalgamated with Henry Tate & Sons to form Tate and Lyle. A director of the new firm, Lyle became its chairman in 1928, continuing in that office until he was made president in 1937. During the years of his chairmanship he saw Tate and Lyle become the largest sugar refiner in the UK. This was achieved largely through the takeover of smaller concerns, but also because the company had moved into beet sugar production in the 1920s. In 1936 the British Sugar Corporation was established to exercise a monopoly in beet sugar production, and Tate and Lyle sought alternative sources of supply of raw sugar. In 1938, following Lyle's commercial initiative, the company bought cane estates and refineries in the West Indies. Lyle became chairman of a subsidiary, the West Indies Sugar Company. His interests in the West Indies, and Jamaica in particular, were said by contemporaries to extend beyond the merely commercial. He enjoyed good relations with Alexander Bustamante, the trade union leader, and later chief minister of Jamaica. Indeed, Bustamante supported Tate and Lyle in their anti-nationalization drive in the late 1940s.

Lyle is best remembered for his organization of opposition to the idea of nationalizing the sugar refining industry by post-war Labour administrations. By 1949 Tate and Lyle had a virtual monopoly in the production of refined sugar from cane, and a dominant position in all sugar refining in Britain. Not surprisingly, the fear of nationalization led the company to the forefront of resistance. In this it had the help of the organization Aims of Industry, a leader of the free enterprise lobby. Lyle was to become a director of this organization in 1950. From somewhere (it is unclear whether it was Tate and Lyle or Aims of Industry) came the idea for the cartoon character Mr Cube to represent the company. It became a symbol of anti-nationalization. The image first appeared in the press in July 1949, and on sugar wrappers in October of that year.

Lyle worked tirelessly to defend his business; he was robust and forthright, without being discourteous. The success of the campaign is debatable, however. Any intention to nationalize sugar refining was abandoned with the defeat of the Labour government in 1951. But the nationalization of Tate and Lyle was never formally proposed; the king's speech in 1950 included a proposal to nationalize the British [beet] Sugar Corporation only. Mr Cube thereafter remained an advertising symbol.

An accomplished athlete, Lyle represented England at lawn tennis, was a well-known figure at Wimbledon, and became chairman of the Lawn Tennis Association in 1932, and later honorary vice-president. He was the first chairman of the International Lawn Tennis Club from 1924 to 1927, and president of the Professional Golfers' Association from 1952 to 1954. He was a keen yachtsman and was elected a member of the Royal Yacht Squadron in 1952. Even in later life he gave the appearance of one who had only recently ceased to be an active sportsman. He also became deputy president of Queen Mary's Hospital for the East End (of London). Lyle died at his home, Greystoke, Marlborough Road, Canford Cliffs, Bournemouth, on 6 March 1954. His son succeeded to the title.

ROGER MUNTING

Sources P. Chalmin, *The making of a sugar giant: Tate and Lyle, 1859–1989*, trans. E. Long-Michalke (1990) [Fr. orig., *Tate and Lyle, géant du sucre* (1983)] • *The Times* (8 March 1954) • *The Times* (27 July 1945), election suppl. • P. Chalmin, 'Lyle, Charles Ernest Leonard', *DBB* • A. Hugill, *Sugar and all that: a history of Tate and Lyle* (1978) • *WWW* • C. E. Lysaght, *Brendan Bracken* (1979) • *DNB*

Likenesses B. Dunstan, oils (posthumous), Tate and Lyle, London

Wealth at death £664,910 2*s*. 6*d*.: probate, 24 May 1954, *CGPLA Eng. & Wales*

Lyle, Robert, first Lord Lyle (*d.* *c.*1470), nobleman, came of the family of Lyle of Duchal in Renfrewshire. The family's rise to prominence in national politics had been begun by Robert's father (also Robert), who served as a hostage for James I in 1424, when the value of the Lyle estates was assessed at £200 Scots per year. The younger Robert Lyle harboured ambitions, in alliance with his brother-in-law Robert, Lord Erskine, to half the lands of the earldom of Mar, by right of his descent from a younger coheir of Isabel, countess of Mar; he pursued this claim, albeit unsuccessfully, in the 1440s, during the turmoil of James II's minority. It is not clear when Lyle succeeded his father, but he had done so by 1445, when he was styled lord of Duchal.

Lyle married a daughter of Andrew, Lord Gray, and it was probably through Gray's influence that he achieved a rise in status, which resulted in his being elevated to the peerage in 1452. His promotion certainly seems bound up with the king's conflict with the Black Douglases, since Gray is named as one of the men who took part, alongside James II, in the killing of the eighth earl of Douglas on 22 February in that year and he may have recommended Lyle as a loyal man in the potentially troublesome south-west of Scotland. That Lyle was with the king's army in the field on 18 July 1452, during the summer campaign waged against Douglas supporters, would have emphasized his loyalty. His career thereafter is rather more obscure, but he is a frequent witness to royal charters in James III's minority. He died *c.*1470.

Robert Lyle, second Lord Lyle (*d.* 1497), was the son of the first Lord Lyle and his second wife, Margaret Wallace. He succeeded his father even though he appears to have had an older brother, Alexander, who was described as the son and heir of Robert, Lord Lyle, in a bond made by Robert, Lord Boyd, in January 1466; Alexander must have predeceased the first Lord Lyle. By March 1472 the younger Robert Lyle had been appointed an ambassador to England. He may have established contact with the exiled James, ninth earl of Douglas, for on 22 March 1482 he went on trial before a parliamentary assize, charged with treasonably corresponding with the outlawed earl. Lyle was acquitted, no doubt owing to the king's influence. The importance of the trial of a notably loyal supporter of James III on remarkably insubstantial charges (Douglas did not even accompany the invading English army later in 1482) lies in the evidence it provides for opposition to James III and his more powerful supporters at this time.

Lyle resumed his diplomatic career almost immediately, taking part in several embassies to the English court, one of which, in 1484, was to conclude a treaty whereby a marriage was arranged between Prince James and Anne de la Pole, daughter of the duke of Suffolk and niece of Richard III. Although the marriage never took place, owing to the death of Richard III at Bosworth in 1485, the treaty may indicate the position of influence which Lyle had built up with the English king.

Lyle's hopes for advancement in the late 1480s were blocked by the return from exile before 1488 of the earl of Buchan. When Buchan was outlawed in 1485, Lyle acquired some of the earl's Angus lands, and probably hoped to secure further rewards for his loyal service. Buchan's reinstatement in favour with James III may have been instrumental in turning Lyle from loyal king's man to rebel. In 1488 he was at the January parliament held in Edinburgh, where he was proposed as a royal justiciar, but in April he was appointed to negotiate with the king on behalf of the Scottish nobles who were now in rebellion against James III. Lyle was named in the proposed settlement, known as the Aberdeen articles, as one of those commissioned by Prince James to negotiate with the king for the rebels, and Lyle's grievances against Buchan are mentioned specifically.

Lyle was almost certainly present at the battle of Sauchieburn on 11 June 1488, when James III was killed, and he was at Edinburgh a few days later, involved in drawing up an inventory of the royal treasure. On 23 June, the day before James IV's coronation at Scone, Lyle was at work there drafting another inventory, and he secured the position of justiciar of Bute and Arran in July 1488. He was one of those who sat in judgement on Buchan when the latter was tried for treason on 8 October 1488, although he cannot have been happy about the pardon granted to his old adversary. In the same parliament he received extensive powers in criminal jurisdiction in his home area of Renfrewshire, along with John Stewart, earl of Lennox, and Stewart's brother, Matthew, and it was with these men that Lyle was to go into open revolt against the government in the summer of 1489.

Lyle probably resented his exclusion from a government which was now dominated by the Hepburns and the choice of Lord Drummond, in preference to himself, as royal justiciar for the justice ayre in the south-west in February and March 1489; he may also have had suspicions concerning the apparent disappearance of part of the royal treasure for which he had prepared inventories in June 1488. The Lyle–Lennox alliance held the castles of Duchal, Crookston, and Dumbarton, and it was the alleged abuse of their judicial powers, particularly towards the Semples in Renfrewshire, that precipitated a response from the government, fearful that the rebellion would spread. Some of Lyle's Angus lands were granted to the earl of Buchan even before Lyle's forfeiture in July 1489, and a reward of £40 Scots in land was offered for Lyle's apprehension.

On 11 October 1489 the rebels were defeated at the battle of the Field of the Moss, but James IV was nevertheless compelled to consult with the three estates and to reach a settlement with the rebels. The parliament held in February 1490 proceeded to annul the forfeitures passed the previous summer against the Lennox Stewarts and Lyle, who were present to hear the king declare their forfeitures null and void and order the original processes to be removed from the parliamentary records. Lyle resumed his position as justiciar, was appointed ambassador to the Spanish court on 26 February 1491, and was one of the auditors of the exchequer in 1492. He died in 1497. He was married to Margaret Houston, and their son, Robert, became third Lord Lyle. C. A. McGladdery

Sources *CDS*, vol. 4 • Rymer, *Foedera*, vol. 11 • J. M. Thomson and others, eds., *Registrum magni sigilli regum Scotorum / The register of the great seal of Scotland*, 11 vols. (1882–1914), vol. 2 • *APS*, *1424–1567* • *Scots peerage*, vol. 5 • N. Macdougall, *James III: a political study* (1982) • N. Macdougall, *James IV* (1989)

Lyle, Robert, **second Lord Lyle** (*d.* **1497**). *See under* Lyle, Robert, first Lord Lyle (*d. c.*1470).

Lyle, Thomas (**1792–1859**), physician and poet, the son of Robert Lyle and his wife, Mary, *née* Cochrane, was born in Paisley on 10 September 1792, and was educated at Paisley grammar school. He attended medical classes at Glasgow University. About 1815 he set up as a druggist in the High Street of Glasgow, and in 1817 he was licensed as a surgeon by the Faculty of Physicians and Surgeons of Glasgow. He practised in Glasgow for ten years before moving to Airth, near Falkirk, Stirlingshire. In 1853 he returned to Glasgow, where he found employment as surgeon to the Barony district parochial board during the cholera epidemic of 1853–4. He seems not to have enjoyed much success as a doctor. He was of a retiring disposition, happiest on botanical excursions, collecting old ballads, or writing verse for his own amusement.

Lyle is remembered solely for the still popular song 'Let us haste to Kelvin Grove, bonnie lassie', written in 1819 and first published in the *Harp of Renfrewshire* (1820). Some controversy arose as to the authorship, owing to the ascription of the song, by an editor of the *Harp*, to John Sim. The story is told by Hugh Macdonald in *Rambles Round Glasgow* (2nd edn, 1856):

> Mr. Sim, who had contributed largely to the work … left Paisley before its completion for the West Indies, where he shortly afterwards died. In the meantime the song became a general favourite, when Mr. Lyle laid claim to it as his own production, and brought forward evidence of the most convincing nature (including letters from Sim himself) to that effect. (pp. 283–4)

It appeared that Sim had transcribed the song in his own hand and his executors concluded that it was Sim's. To the end of his life Lyle felt some bitterness at the mistake that had compelled him to prove authorship of his own work. The 1872 reprint of the *Harp* still attributed 'Kelvin Grove' to Sim. Lyle contributed to R. A. Smith's *Irish Minstrel*, and edited *Ancient Ballads and Songs* (1827). The latter work contains his own poems and songs, including a revised version of 'Kelvin Grove' and a section of *Miscellaneous Poems, by Sir William Mure, Knight of Rowallan*. His own poems reflect his private interests, being filled with botanical references or modelled on old songs, with a romantic morbid cast over all. Lyle died of typhus fever, at his house, 61 Duke Street, Glasgow, on 19 April 1859, and was buried in the cemetery of the West Relief Church, Paisley, on 23 April. He was described as a widower on his death certificate, but nothing is known about his wife.

J. C. Hadden, *rev.* Hamish Whyte

Sources C. Rogers, *The modern Scottish minstrel, or, The songs of Scotland of the past half-century*, 4 (1857), 261–3 • G. Eyre-Todd, ed., *The Glasgow poets: their lives and poems*, 2nd edn (1906), 209–10 • R. Brown, *Paisley poets: with brief memoirs of them and selections from their poetry*, 2 vols. (1889–90), vol. 1, pp. 269–70 • H. Macdonald, *Rambles round Glasgow*, 2nd edn (1856), 283–4 • J. G. Wilson, ed., *The poets and poetry of Scotland*, 2 (1877), 129 • W. Harvey, *The harp of Stirlingshire* (1897), 113 • J. Ross, ed., *The book of Scottish poems: ancient and modern* (1878), 743 • C. Rogers, *A century of Scottish life* (1871), 219 • correspondence, *Glasgow Herald* (March–April 1895) • A. Duncan, *Memorials of the Faculty of Physicians and Surgeons of Glasgow* (1896), 100 • d. cert. • *The Post Office directory of Glasgow*

Lyly, John (**1554–1606**), writer and playwright, was the eldest of eight children of Peter Lyly (*d.* 1569) and his wife, Jane Burgh (or Brough), of Burgh Hall in the North Riding of Yorkshire. He may have been born in Rochester, where his father is mentioned as a 'notary public' at the installation ceremonies for John Ponet in 1550, or perhaps in Canterbury, where the births of his younger siblings are registered between 1562 and 1568.

Early years and family connections Lyly inherited a family name already notable in the annals of literary scholarship. His grandfather, William *Lily, was a leading member of the generation of scholars that brought Italian humanism to England, a colleague of More, Colet, and Erasmus in the founding of St Paul's School, the first humanistic grammar school in the country. Lily was high master there from 1509 until his death in 1522 or 1523, when he was succeeded by his son-in-law John Rightwise. Lily's fame as a grammarian was carried into succeeding generations by the name attached to the standard Latin grammar book (generally known as Lily's grammar though it was the result of collaboration with Colet and Erasmus). Interestingly enough, its dry scholastic forms, asserting a necessary relationship between stylistic purity and moral rectitude, teaching 'pure' Latinity by means of model sentences inculcating virtue, can be seen to foreshadow the mode of Lyly's later fictions, where the connections his grandfather established are put to question.

The family's scholarly inheritance was carried forward by William's eldest son, George *Lily, who, like his father, travelled to Italy in pursuit of the sources of humanist knowledge; but there, appointed as secretary to Reginald Pole, he was soon caught up in the religious battle between Pole and his kinsman Henry VIII. When, in the reign of Mary, Cardinal Pole became archbishop of Canterbury, George Lily became a canon of Canterbury Cathedral, establishing the family's connection with that part of the country. Fortunately for the family, both Pole and George Lily died about the same time as Elizabeth came to the throne, so that the surviving members were able to distance themselves from the tradition of Catholic loyalty. John Lyly's father, Peter, had in 1554 been given, no doubt by his brother's influence, the reversion of a canon's stall in Canterbury Cathedral, but the reversion never fell due, and he navigated the troubled religious situation at Elizabeth's accession without penalty, and went on to serve the protestant Archbishop Matthew Parker as a minor ecclesiastical functionary, a 'registrar'.

Lyly's family on his mother's side belonged to a tightly-knit group of landowners in the area around Richmond, Yorkshire—Hauxwell, Middleton Tyas, East Harsley, Gilling West, Caterick. The intermarriages between members of these families is very complex, but it is known that in the mid-sixteenth century Sir Ralph Rokeby had married a daughter of the Burgh family and also that Lyly's mother, Jane Burgh, possessed lands that had earlier belonged to the family of Rokeby. The connections forged by this marriage were reinforced when, on 22 November 1583, John Lyly married the heiress Beatrice (Betteris) Browne (whose mother was a Rokeby). For the career of John Lyly perhaps the most important point about these family ties was that they intersected at various points with the family of William Cecil, Lord Burghley, whose aunt, Joan Cecil, had married a member of the Browne family. The humanistically inclined Burghley must also have known George Lily from the time when he accompanied Cardinal Pole on his mission to England.

It seems probable that John Lyly was educated at the King's School in Canterbury, his two younger brothers being named in the school register. In 1569 he entered Magdalen College, Oxford, following in the footsteps of his grandfather and uncle. Anthony Wood reports that Lyly:

> was always averse to the crabbed studies of logic and philosophy [the staples of the curriculum]. For so it was that his genie being naturally bent to the pleasant paths of poetry (as if Apollo had given him a wreath of his own bays, without snatching or struggling) did in a manner neglect his academical studies. (Wood, *Ath. Oxon.*, 1.676, paraphrasing Blount's dedicatory epistle to his *Six Court Comedies* (1632))

In spite of these disadvantages he passed through the grades of BA (1573) and MA (1575). In 1574 he had besought Lord Burghley as chancellor of the university ('patronus suus colendissimus') to obtain letters appointing him to a fellowship at Magdalen. The proposal was not taken up, but Burghley remains so constant a factor in Lyly's life that it seems possible that Lyly was trying to exploit the family loyalty that Burghley certainly displays in his relation to Beatrice's cousin, the separatist, Robert Browne, bailing him from prison, reinstating him in his parish, and overriding the laws of the land to do so. It is clear that Lyly continued to cherish the family connection even after Burghley's death, giving his eldest son the name of Robert Browne Lyly (and repeating the name for his second son when the first died) and marrying his daughter Frances to William Browne of Tolthorpe, the separatist's nephew.

Given his academic disappointments, Lyly seems to have taken refuge, like others since his time, in a belief that London would support the ambitions that Oxford had denied. He is next heard of living in the Savoy in the Strand. This institution had been founded in the reign of Henry VIII as a hospice for the indigent and the enfeebled, but by the time Lyly resided there it had come to serve as a London address for noblemen and their servants. The master of the Savoy at this point was William Absolon (appointed in 1576), another native of Canterbury, who had taught in the King's School between 1564 and 1566 when Lyly was of age to be a pupil there. It was in the Savoy, Gabriel Harvey records, that 'young Euphues hatched the eggs his elder friends laid' (*Works of Gabriel Harvey*, 2.124).

Euphues *Euphues, the Anatomy of Wit: Very Pleasant for All Gentlemen to Read* was published in 1578, and immediately made Lyly the most fashionable author in England. The book is, as Harvey's gibe indicates, a mosaic composed of scraps of humanist wisdom and gossipy classical quotations (mostly from Plutarch and Pliny) and much of this material is indeed copied out of the encyclopaedias compiled by the greatest of the 'elder friends', Erasmus. His *Adagia*, *Similia*, *Apophthegmata*, and *Colloquia* are continually drawn on.

Under the incrustation of these classical ornaments *Euphues* tells a simple story, recording what might be regarded as the basic humanist legend: a young man 'of more wit than wealth, and yet of more wealth than wisdom' (*Works*, 1.184) supposes he can succeed in the world by mere gifts of nature without worldly experience, and armed only with theoretical knowledge and literary precepts. The history of the *euphues* thus provides a scholastic variation on the story of the prodigal son. The name comes from Roger Ascham's educational treatise, *The Scholemaster* (1570), which states that *euphues*:

> is he that is apt by goodness of wit and appliable by readiness of will to learning, having all other qualities of the mind and parts of the body that must another day serve learning. But commonly the fairest bodies are bestowed on the foulest purposes. (*The Scholemaster*, ed. E. Arber, 1870, 38)

The moral purpose of the tale is to anatomize or open up this quality of untrained natural capacity so that the reader can understand the route that eventually leads from wit to wisdom. But where the prodigal son learns his lesson in a pigsty, Lyly's Euphues learns it in terms of a linguistic bravura that invites not only censure but also admiration (and imitation), so that it highlights a basic contradiction between the moral and the narrative. There is also, as contemporaries noticed, an implicit claim that the brilliantly endowed Euphues should be recognized as a version of the brilliantly endowed John Lyly (an early example of the man of letters setting himself up as a 'personality'). Euphues (like Lyly) leaves Athens (Oxford) and travels to Naples (London) where his conversation dazzles the beautiful heiress Lucilla, at the same time as her sophisticated poise and social charm dazzle him. But love leads to betrayal and Euphues, disillusioned by the amoral superficiality of the smart set, returns to 'Athens' and spends his time there writing letters of moral advice stressing the danger of leaving young men free to choose their own way of life. Becoming a 'public reader in the University' (*Works*, 1.286.26), he busies himself with 'searching out the secrets of nature and the hidden mysteries of philosophy' (ibid., 1.286.28–9). But after ten years of this he feels the need to make a further move away from society and turns from philosophy to divinity and now advises his correspondents to abandon worldly life.

As early as 1579, in the second edition of *The Anatomy of Wit*, Lyly is beginning to compromise this moral pattern in preparation for a sequel that must return his hero to the ways of the world. He now writes to 'my very good friends, the gentlemen scholars of Oxford' (*Works*, 1.324) and promises that in the next volume 'Euphues at his arrival [in England] I am assured will view Oxford, where he will either recant his sayings or renew his complaints' (ibid., 1.325.15–16). In the event, when *Euphues and his England* was published in 1580, this forecast, like many others, was not fulfilled. It is clear that the intention to expand the Euphues saga was difficult to achieve. Lyly had created an effect so distinctive in its combination of humanist gravity in matter with self-conscious frivolity in manner that he was more or less obliged to repeat the book if he was to repeat the success. It was a success that had allowed him to hold the attention of a notoriously fickle world of fashion to such a degree that, as Edward Blount, his first editor, reported, 'all our ladies were then his scholars, and that beauty at court which could not parley Euphuism was as little regarded as she which now there [1632] speaks not French' (ibid., 3.3). But such success has to renew itself if it is to survive.

Lyly's dedication to his new patron, Edward de Vere, seventeenth earl of Oxford, indicates a second ambition for the book: he describes the new *Euphues* as 'containing the estate of England … the conditions of the English court and the majesty of our dread Sovereign' (*Works*, 2.7.15–19). This is a more directly political agenda than had appeared in the earlier volume. No doubt his social success so far was encouraging him to aim his hopes for patronage at the highest in the land.

The new narrative tells how Euphues and his companion Philautus leave Italy and sail to England and then travel from Southampton to the court in London, accumulating as they go many moral observations about Englishness. The substance of the work is not, however, in the narrative but in the episodes by the way, the letters to and fro, the discussions of love and virtue, the *sic et non* of scholastic disputation. The book culminates in rhapsodic praise of the queen. No doubt as part of the effort to win her favour, it begins with a dedication to 'the ladies and gentlewomen of England', and with that in mind he makes a somewhat less than flattering effort to stress its frivolity, telling the readers that 'Euphues would rather lie shut in a lady's casket than open in a scholar's study' (*Works*, 2.9.4–5).

Secretary to the earl of Oxford and early plays at Blackfriars In his relationship to the earl of Oxford, Lyly seems once again to have been caught in the paradoxical overlap between wit and wisdom, court and college, Italianism (as that was understood) and Christian humanist values. Certainly, as secretary to the 'Italianate' earl, he was still very much under the gaze of the *patronus* to whom he had pledged lifelong allegiance, the humanist Lord Burghley, Oxford's father-in-law. A surviving letter from Oxford to Burghley, dated 30 October 1584, shows the difficulty of the situation he had acquired. Burghley had summoned Amis (another Oxford retainer) or Lyly to come to him, presumably to report on the earl's affairs. Oxford is in high dudgeon:

> I pray, my lord, leave that course, for I mean not to be yowre ward nor yowre chyld … and scorne to be offred that injurie to thinke I am so weake of government as to be ruled by servants, or not able to govern my self. (Feuillerat, 533)

An earlier letter from Lyly to Burghley shows the other side of the same situation: Lyly is in disgrace with his master and looks to Burghley to shield him, pledging loyalty to the lord treasurer and his daughter, the countess of Oxford. The whole situation suggests that Lyly's pleas for support had been answered by Burghley with a post of honour (made palatable to the earl by exploiting his well-known interest in literature and men of letters), that was as much to Burghley's advantage as to Lyly's.

As a member of Oxford's household Lyly must have had something of the role of a literary middleman. His prefatory letter to Thomas Watson's *Hekatompathia* of 1582 (dedicated to Oxford) shows him deploying his Euphuistic style as a mode of self-advertisement. Oxford's service also brought Lyly tantalizingly close to the goal of his career, the court. Given the vexed relations between the queen and the earl, the connection was, however, a perilous one at best. Oxford was excluded from court in 1580 and was not readmitted until 1583. In 1583 and 1584 there were performances at court by a new acting troupe called Oxford's Boys (in reality, apparently, a nonce group composed, as title-pages state, of 'the Children of her Majesty's Chapel and the Boys of [St] Paul's [Cathedral]'). This group performed at court on 'Newyear's Day at Night' 1583 and Shrove Tuesday 1584. Lyly was paid £10 on 25 November 1584 for a play before the queen 'on shrovetuesdaie at nighte' and the same warrant mentions another play performed 'upon newyeresdaie at nighte' by 'the Earl of Oxford his servants', John Lyly being the payee. It seems clear that these payments refer to Lyly's first two plays, *Campaspe* and *Sappho and Phao*. The evidence suggests that Oxford and Lyly had found a mutually advantageous situation: Lyly could display his literary talents before the queen, and Oxford could ingratiate himself with his recently offended sovereign by procuring for her a uniquely elegant entertainment, offering a blend of courtly compliment, classical learning, songs, and witty dialogue.

The printed prologues and epilogues of these two plays record that they were performed not only at court but also in the small 'private' playhouse located in the former Blackfriars monastery, where choirboys had for many years performed (euphemistically 'rehearsed') plays before select audiences that were happy, no doubt, to participate in a court occasion, even if only at second hand, and willing to pay an entrance fee larger than that for the public playhouses. The division of the Blackfriars into a warren of tenements, to be used for dwelling spaces or for business purposes, created, however, a tangle of leases and sub-leases almost impenetrable to the modern mind. Lyly's use of the Blackfriars as an apparently essential part of his playwriting enterprise had been achieved by legalistic chicanery that had deprived the landlord of his rights and transferred the property to the earl of Oxford, who passed it to Lyly. This created, of course, an inherently unstable situation, and some time after the performance of *Sappho and Phao* the landlord secured a court order that restored the property to his possession. As a consequence, there were to be no more plays in the Blackfriars for sixteen years. The performance of *Gallathea*, written by Lyly as his third play for the court, had to be shelved. In 1584 and again in 1589 Lyly disposed of the quite ample spaces in the Blackfriars he had leased for himself and his family. He was once again a man on the move, in more senses than one.

Plays for the Paul's Boys Lyly's career as a court dramatist had suffered a reverse but not a fatal blow. In the period 1587–91 he is found in the parish of St Martin Ludgate, where four of his children were baptized. This brought him close to St Paul's, whose choirboys eventually took *Gallathea* to court in 1588, and also performed it in their private playhouse in the St Paul's precinct. The Paul's Boys then brought to court two more of his plays, *Endymion* in 1588 and *Midas* in 1589. But the Paul's Boys playhouse was in its turn closed down in 1590. What was left of the courtly enterprise had to be rescued by the printing press. A prefatory note to *Endymion* (1591) announced that 'Since the plays in Paul's were dissolved, there are certain comedies come to my hands by chance which were presented before her Majesty at several [i.e. different] times by the Children of Paul's' (*Works*, 3.sig. civ). A printed version of *Midas* (by the same publisher, who seems to have entertained the possibility of an edition of the collected plays) followed in 1592.

Three plays by Lyly remain unaccounted for in this tally: *Mother Bombie* (1594), *The Woman in the Moon* (1597), and *Love's Metamorphosis* (1601). This is a body of work of uncertain provenance. The title-pages of the first two state that they were played by the Children of Paul's, but no mention is made of the court, and indeed, as far as *Mother Bombie* is concerned, Lyly seems to have given up the courtly vein of classical allegory and returned to an earlier mode of classically organized scholastic comedy. The title-page of *The Woman in the Moon* says 'As it was presented before her Highness' (*Works*, 3.239) but gives no indication of the acting company. It is Lyly's only play in verse:

> the first he had in Phoebus' holy bower
> But not the last, unless the first displease
> (*Works*, 3.241)

which suggests that the author was looking forward to a new court career, perhaps with an adult company—adult companies continued to perform while both children's troupes were silenced. But it seems that his first offering in verse did displease, for no more is heard of Lyly's ambitions as a playwright. By the last decade of the century Lylian dramaturgy must have been seen as incurably old-fashioned.

Reputation Lyly had made his name by inventing a new style, but the style had come to be identified with a bygone age and the writer identified with it was now no longer fashionable. *Euphues* continued to be reprinted (twenty editions of the two parts were printed before the end of the century), but its admirers were no longer at the top of the social scale. More avant-garde writers condemned its mechanistic rhetoric and its self-consciously bizarre similes from natural history. The same process appears when the reputation of the plays is considered. When the dainty pastoral fantasy, *Love's Metamorphosis*, was printed in 1601, its title-page carried the legend, 'first played by the Children of Paul's and now by the Children of the Chapel' (*Works*, 3.299). In 1601 a mention of the Chapel Children must refer to the new company of that name, revived in 1599 or 1600 under a new system of entrepreneurship. It is natural to suppose that the company should have begun with material like *Love's Metamorphosis*, already on its books, but the revival of such plays was greeted with scorn by new dramatists like Marston, Jonson, and Chapman who were taking over the boys' companies for their own satiric purposes. These new men derided plays like Lyly's as 'musty fopperies', 'mouldy dry fictions', 'ghosts … of plays departed a dozen years since', and the actors seem to have accepted the new focus as the one most likely to attract their new target audiences from the inns of court.

Open hostility to Lyly's mode of writing was of course merely a passing phase promoted by those who were hoping to replace him. Caroline nostalgia for the supposed national unity of Elizabethan times restored his reputation to some degree, though not in terms that bear any relation to the facts of his life or the purposes of his art. Edward Blount's 1632 collected edition of the plays (*Six Court Comedies*) presented him as a quaint figure from the past, 'the witty, comical, facetiously-quick and unparalleled John Lyly', 'a rare and excellent poet whose tunes alighted in the ears of a great and ever-famous Queen', and 'whom Queen Elizabeth then heard, graced and rewarded' (*Works*, 3.2). He has become 'old John Lyly who will be merry with thee in thy chamber' (ibid., 3.3).

Final years The same process of slippage can be seen in Lyly's personal life. Burghley's daughter, the countess of Oxford, died in 1588, so that any position that Lyly occupied between Burghley and de Vere would be less important. The ever volatile earl seems to have found new interests (including a self-pleasing military posture in the defence of England against the Spanish Armada), and in any case he had been given a pension by Elizabeth in 1586, and there was nothing more he could hope from her. Lyly, none the less, could still think of himself as a man with prospects. In 1589 he was favoured with a seat in parliament, and he continued to find patrons willing to nominate him as an MP for the next three sessions, though, like other carpet-baggers, he had to move his district from one end of the country to the other. That at least secured him some social status, not to mention the standard rate of 2*s*. a day, but it can hardly have satisfied his ambition.

Lyly was made an esquire of the body, but without stipend. In 1594 he was admitted as a member of Gray's Inn, but only as part of a Christmas revel. In 1588 the queen seems to have promised him something more substantial than these merely titular honours. She apparently told him that he should 'aim all [his] courses at the Revels'—that is, 'think of himself as in line for appointment as Master of the Revels, or at least chosen for the post in reversion' (Hunter, 356). This was a promise that haunted Lyly for the rest of his life. He clung to it as if to a lifeline, but as a verbal promise it lacked substance, and some political factors made it improbable. As a man associated with the earl of Oxford, Lyly must have been regarded as an enemy by the powerful faction of the Howards. The Howards' client Edmund Tilney was already in possession of the revels' post, and another client, Sir George Buc, was soon afterwards assured of the reversion. Elizabeth was not one to allow personal contact to overcome political expediency.

Lyly himself may have unwittingly contributed to his own misfortunes. Some time in 1588 or 1589, ever anxious to please those in authority, he volunteered or accepted an invitation to join Thomas Nashe in a series of pamphlets counter-attacking those being written by the anti-episcopal Martin Marprelate. He was, of course, a well-known writer, but for this purpose he was an unfortunate choice; anyone less suited to the cut and thrust of political satire can hardly be imagined. Perhaps the bishops thought that the lively satirical dialogues of the servant boys in the sub-plots of the plays provided a model he could draw on when attacking their enemies. But the effect in the plays is controlled by highly artificial, almost geometrical structures, quite opposite to the freewheeling inventiveness of Martin or Nashe.

It may, however, have been less Lyly's skill as a comic writer than his theatrical expertise that attracted the invitation to defend the bishops. Gabriel Harvey says that Lyly and Nashe 'have the stage at commandment, and can furnish-out Vices and Divels at their pleasure' (*Works of Gabriel Harvey*, 2.213), but in *Pappe with an Hatchet*, the one pamphlet that is undoubtedly his, Lyly speaks as if the licensing authorities would not permit anti-Martinist plays to be performed: 'would those comedies might be allowed to be plaid that are pend, and then I am sure he [Martin] would be decyphered and so perhaps discouraged' (*Works*, 3.408.18–20). In voicing such an ambition Lyly was, of course, running against a primary factor in Elizabethan control of the stage—that matters ecclesiastical should not be represented there. He may, however, have been imprudent enough in his zeal for the establishment cause to defy the ban and employ the Paul's Boys he had at his 'commandment' in the anti-Martin campaign. If so, this may be a reason why the Paul's Boys were shut down in 1590, bringing Lyly's career as a writer to an absolute end.

The only expression of Lyly's literary talent in the last sixteen years of his life appears in the begging letters he wrote to Elizabeth and to the Cecils, works treasured in various manuscript collections for their stylistic brilliance but ineffective in securing the income and status he believed he deserved. He reminded the queen of her promise; he hoped to be given a grant out of the confiscated estates of the Essex conspirators, but more important suitors were there before him (thus the estates of Sir Charles Danvers were given to Oxford—though they never in fact reached him). He begged, in vain, for a post in the office of tents and toils (which supplied scenery for royal entertainments). In 1592 he left London and lived on his wife's lands in Mexborough, but in 1595 he is back in London, where he is found in a very modest property (valued at £3) in the grounds of St Bartholomew's Hospital.

Even after the death of Elizabeth, Lyly seems to have persisted in his pleas for support. A letter from Toby Mathew, bishop of Durham, to 'his very loving cousin' Sir Julius Caesar, King James's master of requests (dated 9 February 1604), asks Caesar to intercede with the king 'in regard of [Lyly's] yeres fast growing on, & his insupportable charge of many children all unbestowed, besides the debt wherein he standeth, which I greatly feare will lye heavy upon him to his & their utter undoing' (Austin, 146–7). It is not known if this proposal had any more effect than its predecessors. Lyly's last two children were baptized in St Bartholomew-the-Less in 1603 and in 1604 or 1605, and he himself was buried in the same parish on 30 November 1606. G. K. Hunter

Sources *The complete works of John Lyly*, ed. R. W. Bond, 3 vols. (1902) • A. Feuillerat, *John Lyly: contribution à l'histoire de la renaissance en Angleterre* (1910) • G. K. Hunter, *John Lyly: the humanist as courtier* (1962) • M. Eccles, *Brief lives: Tudor and Stuart authors* (1982) • J. Foster, ed., *Pedigrees of the county families of Yorkshire*, 3 vols. (1874) • *VCH Yorkshire North Riding*, 2.292 • J. Dover Wilson, 'John Lyly's relations by marriage', *Modern Language Review*, 5 (1910), 495–7 • Wood, *Ath. Oxon.*, new edn, 1.676 • 'Browne, Robert (1550?–1633?)', *DNB* • *The works of Gabriel Harvey*, ed. A. B. Grosart, 3 vols. (1884–5) • E. K. Chambers, *The Elizabethan stage*, 4 vols. (1923) • J. Lyly, *'Campaspe' and 'Sappho and Phao'*, ed. G. K. Hunter and D. Bevington (1991) • R. West, letter, *TLS* (11 June 1976), 706 • D. Jones, 'Much ado about washing: John Lyly at St Bartholomew's', *Thomas Lodge and other Elizabethans*, ed. C. J. Sisson (1933) • W. B. Austin, 'John Lyly and Queen Elizabeth', *N&Q*, 176 (1939), 146–7 • parish register, London,

St Clement Danes, 22 Nov 1583 [marriage] • parish register, London, St Bartholomew-the-Less, 30 Nov 1606 [burial] • parish register, London, St Martin Ludgate [baptisms] • parish register, London, St Bartholomew-the-Less [baptisms]

Archives NRA, letters and literary MSS | BL, Lansdowne MSS, letters to Burghley

Lynam, Charles Cotterill (1858–1938), headmaster, was born on 15 June 1858 in Stoke-on-Trent, the eldest of fourteen children, ten sons and four daughters, of Charles Lynam (1829–1921), architect, and his wife, Lucy Emma, daughter of Robert Garner MD FRCS. He was educated at King William's College, Isle of Man, described by his brother A. E. Lynam as 'a romantic place in those days with few of the traditions or restrictions of the modern public school' (Sidgwick, 5–6). Here he first developed his love for the sea, which influenced so much of his later life.

After leaving school Lynam spent a short time in his father's office. In 1879 he won a mathematics scholarship to Hertford College, Oxford, and was awarded a second in mathematical moderations (1880) and a third class in mathematics (1882). He was a radical and something of an agnostic, and read a long paper on the evils of war at the Union Society at a time when such views were certainly not popular. Meanwhile his passion for sailing was developing by cruising and sailing on the inland waters of the Thames. His chief activity, however, was rugby football. He played for the university for three years, being a three-quarter in the renowned fifteen captained by Harry (Jugs) Vassall. Unfortunately he suffered damage to a knee which left him with a permanent slight limp.

In 1882 Lynam was appointed assistant master at the Oxford preparatory school in Crick Road, founded as a day school in 1877. In 1886 he became headmaster and in 1895 moved the school into premises designed by his father in Bardwell Road, where it became known as the Dragon School, starting the long Lynam tradition which continued with his brother Hum and nephew Joc. Affectionately known as The Skipper, in the preparatory school world Lynam became renowned for his 'advanced' views. In 1893 he was a founder member of the Association of Preparatory Schools (IAPS) and first editor of the *Preparatory Schools Review*. As chairman of the IAPS in 1908, and again in 1921, he made an inspired plea for a wider cultivation of a liberal humanism by all teachers of youth, actively encouraging originality in boys and affording them every opportunity to discover and develop their own interest and genius. He was also a strong supporter of co-education, and his daughter was the first girl to enter the school.

As a yachtsman Lynam had a touch of genius. His cruises in *Blue Dragon I*, *II*, and *III* up the west coast of Scotland and across the North Sea to Norway and the North Cape became legendary. In recognition of the latter, a distance of 1387 miles, he was awarded the challenge cup of the Royal Cruising Club.

In 1885 Lynam married Catherine Alice (1865–1957), daughter of James Hall of Kynsal Lodge, Audlem, Cheshire. They had one son and one daughter. After his retirement in 1920 he continued his travels around the world, and on board the MV *Alcinous*, bound for Australia, he died on 27 October 1938, and was buried at sea (lat. 37° 13′ N, long. 11° 107′ E). LESLIE PLUMMER, *rev.*

Sources C. H. Jaques, *A Dragon century, 1877–1977* (1977) • *The Draconian* [also known as the *Draconian Register*] • F. Sidgwick, *The Skipper: a memoir of C. C. Lynam* (1940) • *Blue Dragon*, logs, Dragon School library

Likenesses C. C. Lynam, self-portrait, oils, repro. in Jaques, *Dragon century*, 142 • photographs, repro. in Jaques, *Dragon century*

Wealth at death £2343 2*s*. 4*d*.: probate, 23 March 1939, *CGPLA Eng. & Wales*

Lynam, Robert (1796–1845), schoolmaster and literary editor, was born in London on 14 April 1796, the son of Charles Lynam, spectacle maker, of the parish of St Alphage, London Wall. Lynam was admitted to Christ's Hospital in March 1806, where he passed as a Grecian in 1814. He graduated BA from Trinity College, Cambridge, in 1818 and proceeded MA in 1821. In 1818 he was appointed assistant mathematical master at Christ's Hospital, and was promoted to fourth grammar master in 1820. Having previously taken orders, he resigned the post in 1832 for that of assistant chaplain and secretary to the Magdalen Hospital. It is not known when Lynam married but in 1828 his wife gave birth to a daughter.

Lynam is chiefly remembered as an editor. While working at Christ's Hospital he edited Charles Rollin's *Ancient History* (1823), *The Complete Works of … Philip Skelton* (1824), *The Complete Works of William Payley* (1825), and *The Works of Samuel Johnson* (1825). Lynam's career as a writer includes a collection of sermons and the succinct *History of England during the Reign of George III* (1825), but his most significant work was *The History of the Roman Emperors, from Augustus to the Death of Marcus Antonius* (1850). His self-confessed purpose was to fill a gap left by Hooke and Gibbon 'with the object of connecting the History of the Roman Republic with the History of the Decline and fall of the Roman Empire' (preface, *History of Roman Emperors*). *The History* was praised by the editor, the Revd John T. White of Corpus Christi College, Oxford, who claimed that Lynam's 'depth of reflection satisfies the most acute and penetrating reader, and at the same time the pomp and harmony of his language gives pleasure to the most critical ear, and the most refined taste' (ibid.). However, it attracted little critical attention when it was published posthumously, perhaps because it had the misfortune to appear almost simultaneously with Merivale's *Romans under the Empire*.

Lynam remained active in the church. He was made St Matthew's day preacher at Christ's Hospital in 1821 and 1835. He was subsequently curate and lecturer of St Giles Cripplegate until his death. He died from lung and liver disease on 12 October 1845 at 4 Bridgewater Square, St Giles Cripplegate, London. He was survived by his wife and nine children. LAURA E. ROMAN

Sources *GM*, 1st ser., 98/2 (1828), 637; 2nd ser., 24 (1845), 542 • R. Lynam, *The history of the Roman emperors* (1850) • *The complete works of the late Rev. Philip Skelton, to which is prefixed Burdy's life of the author*, ed. R. Lynam, 6 vols. (1824) • *The works of Samuel Johnson*, ed. R. Lynam (1825) • J. Lechlot, *Christ's Hospital exhibitioners* (1885), 40 • *DNB* • d. cert.

Likenesses H. Adlard, stipple and line engraving (after Hervé), NPG · Hervé, portrait · portrait, repro. in Lynam, *History of the Roman emperors*

Lynam, William Francis (1832/3–1894), writer, was born in Galway, co. Galway, Ireland. Very little is known about his early life, except that he had a brother, James, but by 1863 he was living at Churchtown House, Dundrum, co. Dublin. He was commissioned in the 5th Royal Lancashire militia in 1867 and retired in 1881 with the rank of lieutenant-colonel. In 1887 he moved to Clontarf, co. Dublin. He was editor of *The Shamrock*, a weekly paper originally owned by Richard Pigott and later by William O'Brien. He also contributed to the *Irish Emerald* and the *Weekly Freeman*. He was best known, however, as the author of the 'Mick McQuaid' stories, which appeared in *The Shamrock*. They comprised conversations between the optimistic McQuaid and the pessimistic Perry Garrity. The stories lightheartedly criticized the methods and manners of the growing class of rural dealers, land agents, and lawyers, and their control and use of local institutions. The first story, 'Mick McQuaid's Conversion', began to appear on 19 January 1867. Other stories included 'Mick McQuaid, Under Agent' (1869–70), 'Mick McQuaid, MP' (1872–3), 'Mick McQuaid's Spa' (1876–8), and 'Mick McQuaid Alderman' (1879–80). Many Mick McQuaid stories were reproduced as penny numbers and the first three series were issued as a quarto volume of nearly 600 pages, *The Adventures of Mick McQuaid*, in 1875. *Darby the Dodger*, a stage comedy in which a rural trader is given his come-uppance by his long-suffering neighbours, followed in 1877. William O'Brien, in particular, attempted to do away with McQuaid but this damaged sales and he was restored to the paper. Other Lynam characters in *Shamrock* serials included Dan O'Donovan, Corney Cluskey, and Sir Timothy Mulligan but none achieved anywhere near the popularity of Mick. Lynam's writings were so well known that Carrolls used the name of Mick McQuaid for one of its brands of pipe tobacco. Mick had himself smoked Carrolls' tobacco during his philosophical debates with Garrity. For one of Carrolls' designs in the 1920s, it is said that the artist drew on the facial features of David Lloyd George, H. H. Asquith, and Horatio Bottomley for a caricature of Mick.

William Francis Lynam died of liver failure on 17 August 1894 at his home, 2 Warrenpoint, Clontarf, co. Dublin, aged sixty-one. He was a Roman Catholic and is said to have been 'a man of much piety' and to have 'lived a very retired life' (Brown, 178). He never married. Unusually for the ephemeral world of serial fiction, Mick McQuaid stories were frequently republished and, indeed, were still being reprinted twenty-five years after their author's death. MIHAIL DAFYDD EVANS

Sources D. J. O'Donaghue, 'The author of "Mick McQuaid"', *The Irish Book Lover*, 3 (1911), 4–7 · S. Brown, *Ireland in fiction* (1919) · J. Sutherland, *The Longman companion to Victorian fiction* (1988) · Boase, *Mod. Eng. biog.* · d. cert. · www.pjcarroll.ie/story/1889.html, 24 Sept 2001

Lynch, Arthur Alfred (1861–1934), Irish nationalist, was born on 16 October 1861 in Smythesdale, on the Victorian goldfields, Australia, the fourth of fourteen children of John Lynch (1828–1906), a mining surveyor and civil engineer from Teermaclane, co. Clare, and his wife, Isabella, daughter of Peter McGregor from Perth, Scotland. Arthur's father, a liberal-minded unbeliever prominent in the diggers' insurrection of 1853, the Eureka stockade, eventually became a magistrate and chairman of his local council. In *My Life Story* (1924) Lynch depicts himself as a precocious genius performing prodigies of both body and mind, equally enthralled by athletics and the differential calculus. When reading Locke's *Essay Concerning Human Understanding* as a schoolboy in Melbourne's public library, Lynch reportedly experienced 'undulations' such as those 'a musician might feel when listening to a Beethoven sonata' (Lynch, 50).

Having found fault with numerous schools including Grenville and Ballarat colleges, Lynch entered the University of Melbourne in 1878. The outcome of his protracted education was a second-class certificate in civil engineering (1882) and a third-class degree in philosophy (1886). He proceeded to Germany and France in search of worthier mentors, studying physics, physiology, and psychology at the University of Berlin, and medicine at the Hôpital Beaujon in Paris. Curious, versatile, opinionated, and plausible, he found his métier in journalism, scraping a living around Fleet Street between 1889 and 1895 before covering the Asante expedition for the *Evening News* (1896), and working as Paris correspondent for the *Daily Mail* (1896–9). He also composed unreadable Byronic and Keatsian verses, along with withering critiques of his more distinguished contemporaries, in *Modern Authors* (1891) and the satiric *Our Poets!* (1895). Alfred Harmsworth regarded him as 'a very able journalist, but … a most unpractical person otherwise' (Redmond MS, 15202).

Little is known of the influences that transformed the Australian dilettante into an Irish rebel and politician. Lynch's loneliness as an Australian student in Berlin had been interrupted in 1888 by 'two extraordinarily pretty Irish girls', daughters of John Donor Powell. Powell had just died after thirty-six itinerant years as a Methodist minister, culminating in his election to presidency of the Irish conference while serving in Belfast in 1887. Marriage to Annie Powell (*b.* 1865/6) followed after a decent interval (seven years) on 14 September 1895, beginning a lifelong alliance that generated no children and few traces, Lynch professing 'reticence about entering into domestic matters' in *My Life Story* (pp. 79–80). The extended courtship presumably required visits to Ireland, reinvigorating Lynch's childhood sense of Irishness and his admiration for Parnell—enhanced by the manner of Parnell's downfall in 1891. By July 1892 Lynch was sufficiently active in Irish affairs to become Parnellite parliamentary candidate for Galway City, using his demagogic flair to gain selection despite disapproval from the 'bosses'. Lynch's oratory and his father's money did not prevail against the influence of Father Peter Dooley PP, and the anti-Parnellite John Pinkerton was returned at the general election by a majority of 644 votes to 593.

Like many frustrated Parnellites, Lynch began to dabble

in revolutionary conspiracies, not only in Ireland but also in Britain, America, and France. This element is missing from *My Life Story*; but the police kept careful track of his involvement in the commemoration of republican martyrs, reporting his many contacts with the Irish Republican Brotherhood and its London-based Parnellite splinter, Dr Mark Ryan's Irish National Alliance. In 1894 he succeeded Ryan as president of the Parnellite version of the Irish National League of Great Britain. Lynch allied himself with the most bellicose fragment of the murderously divided American Clan na Gael (whose camps he inspected for the home organization in 1893), allegedly becoming a 'paid tool' of the Brooklyn contractor William Lyman (CBS 27098/S). In Paris he dined and designed with modish 'exiles' such as Maud Gonne, as well as cultivating every accessible great man from Rodin and Zola to Anatole France and Clemenceau. He fitted easily into the roving band of cosmopolitan, more or less Irish intellectuals for whom Ireland represented right against the British empire's might.

For Lynch and his circle the war against the Boers represented the same issue of principle. Equipped with a Kodak camera Lynch left Paris for the Transvaal, ostensibly as a war correspondent for newspapers in Paris, London, and America. After reaching Pretoria in January 1900 he immediately affirmed allegiance to the South African Republic and declared his willingness to take up arms in its defence. Upon meeting General Louis Botha in Johannesburg he was invited to command a new troop initially drawn from Afrikaners of Irish origin, which became known as the 2nd Irish brigade. President Paul Kruger flattered him with the title of colonel, but the council of war declined Lynch's offer to lead 10,000 men to Cape Town to overthrow the government and establish a United States of South Africa. Lynch urged his potential recruits to 'remember that Irishmen who fall in this war will be joined in Irish memories for ever with Sarsfield, with Wolfe Tone, and with Robert Emmet' (DPP 4/36). The brigade's seventy members played a modest part between March and May 1900 in the retreat through Natal and in the prelude to the fall of Pretoria. Lynch and his men seldom came under fire, apart from a minor sally at Sunday River Bridge near Elandslaagte in Natal, and his command was tarnished by allegations that he had sold horses back to his army suppliers for personal gain. He returned to America and France to publicize the faltering Boer cause and his own celebrity as a warrior.

By August 1900 Lynch was already importuning John Redmond to field him in the forthcoming general election, while modestly not desiring 'to make a point of my action in the Boer War' (Redmond MS 15202). In October 1901 he was nominated as a candidate for Galway at a by-election, having been recommended by William Redmond as 'a sincere, honest Irish Nationalist, an able and upright Irish gentleman' (CBS 27098/S). Lynch reassured the electors that he did 'not think armed force can accomplish the liberation of Ireland'; lingered in Paris while 'low fiends of women and children' cursed and howled at his opponent in Galway; and duly trounced the Unionist reformer Horace Plunkett by 1247 votes to 472 (DPP 4/36; Trevor West, *Horace Plunkett*, 1986, 58). After much prevarication Lynch informed *The Times* of his intention to return from Paris to enter parliament, and was arrested (June 1902), charged with high treason, prosecuted with judicious but lethal elegance by Sir Edward Carson, sentenced to death, imprisoned for life after commutation, and deprived of his seat (January 1903). In Brixton prison he studied Hamilton's *Quaternions*, thus anticipating Eamon de Valera's choice of diversion when interned at Arbour Hill in 1924. Released on a ticket-of-leave after a year of petitioning and agitation Lynch settled in Paris until pardoned in July 1907. After release he renewed his medical studies, graduated from the University of London in Paddington as MRCS and LRCP in 1908, and took up general practice in Haverstock Hill, near Hampstead Heath.

In 1909 Lynch at last entered parliament after narrowly securing the nationalist nomination for an uncontested by-election in West Clare, despite reiterated discouragement from John Redmond and opposition from the Catholic clergy. He had gained local applause seven years earlier by offering to surrender his interest in a tiny estate, near Quilty, to the tenants. Since the twenty-four tenants had paid no rent for several years, and since Lynch's acquisition of the 100 acre estate in 1896 was of dubious legality, the self-sacrifice was purely theatrical (CBS 27098/S). During his nine-year tenure Lynch seldom visited the constituency, but was recurrently embroiled in rhetorical tussles with the clergy and the *Clare Champion* because of his anti-clerical views and admiration for Oliver Cromwell, encapsulated in *Ireland: Vital Hour* (1915). Clerical distrust had doubtless been intensified by his 'mixed marriage' to a Methodist. He was an ineffectual but assiduous parliamentarian, voting in all 233 divisions arising from the Government of Ireland Bill in 1912. Though excluded from most major debates by the nationalist whips, understandably ill disposed towards an unruly and unpredictable member, Lynch used the midnight hours to address emptying benches on a multitude of topics ranging from sight tests and suffrage to swine fever and race suicide.

Having advocated Irish support for the empire in any war against Germany six months before August 1914, he was equally precipitate in chastising Asquith, Grey, and Kitchener for their inept wartime leadership. By 1916 he was generally dismissed as a colourful maverick, receiving scant credit from Sinn Féin for his invocation of the Easter rebels as 'heroes and martyrs' (August 1916), or for his invitation to de Valera and all factions of constitutionalists to work with him 'in one general movement' (March 1918). Disappointed in such overtures he offered to form and lead an Irish brigade in the service of the allies, an offer which Lloyd George found 'difficult to agree and difficult to refuse' in October 1916, given Lynch's exhibition of 'fine soldierly qualities' in South Africa (Fitzpatrick, 95–8, 258). Astonishingly the cabinet eventually induced the War Office to commission Lynch as a colonel on special service in association with the Irish Recruiting Council (27 June 1918), despite a staff officer's acid observation that 'Mr. Lynch has no military training whatsoever, certainly not as regards methods now employed in the British army' (WO 374/43377). By 8 September Lynch's expensive and energetic campaign, systematically subverted by Harry Boland's Sinn Féin, had realized but four recruits for the 10th (service) battalion, Royal Munster Fusiliers. The kilted pipers were silent, and the patriotic green headdress, with its wolfhound badge, remained unworn. 'Lynch's brigade' was disbanded on 25 January 1919, three months before the colonel relinquished his second commission.

While still nominally a member of the Irish Parliamentary Party, Lynch had embraced socialism and joined the Independent Labour Party. In the 'coupon election' of December 1918 he stood for Labour in South Battersea, securing only one vote in seven. Lynch's subsequent career was divided between general practice and authorship of ever more idiosyncratically ambitious works such as *Ethics* (1922) and *The Case Against Einstein* (1932), which Lynch considered his crowning intellectual achievement. It thus surpassed even his *Principles of Psychology* (1923), which he had deemed 'destined to be a lamp to the feet of men when the British Empire itself is forgotten' (Lynch, 134). Other works included the melodramatic *Moments of Genius* (1919); *O'Rourke the Great* (1921), an unflattering fictional portrait of the Irish party that had cold-shouldered him for so long; and *The Rosy Fingers* (1929), which called for a 'Concord of Free Republics' embracing Europe, America, and a reformed British Commonwealth. Lynch believed himself to be a genius, greater than almost all the great men against whom he had measured himself in body and mind, and whose defects were painstakingly recorded in his autobiography. For all their charm, wit, colour, and erudition, his writings convey more of the charlatan than the genius. Yet Lynch was also an intellectual cosmopolitan, who found no inconsistency in declaring himself 'an Irishman' while also seeking both French and South African citizenship (DPP 4/36). His deepest loyalty was perhaps to an Australia that he seems never to have revisited, 'whose greater destiny I behold as in a vision, and whose children of the new dawn I salute' (*The Rosy Fingers*, 304).

On 25 March 1934, following two operations prompted by ptomaine poisoning, Lynch died in St Mary's, the Paddington hospital where he had trained as a doctor. His death was marked by guarded and sadly inaccurate obituaries in *The Times* and the *Irish Times*. Veteran republicans perhaps recalled the black-haired, brown-moustached warrior, with his long thin nose, 'gentlemanly' appearance, and 'good English accent' (CBS 27098/S), who had once ridden across the veldt in pursuit of glory and the mantle of Sarsfield. He was survived by his wife.

DAVID FITZPATRICK

Sources A. A. Lynch, *My life story* (1924) • G. Serle, 'Lynch, Arthur Alfred', *AusDB*, vol. 10 • *DNB* • *The Times* (26 March 1934) • *The Times* (28 April 1934) • *Irish Times* (26 March 1934) • PRO, DPP 4/36 • PRO, WO 374/43377 • PRO, CO 904/18 • NA Ire., CBS 27098/S • *Hansard 5C* (1913–18) • D. Fitzpatrick, *Politics and Irish life, 1913–1921: provincial experience of war and revolution* (1998) • NL Ire., Redmond MSS, MS 15202 • m. cert. • d. cert.

Archives NA Ire., crime special branch, Royal Irish Constabulary, reports on Lynch, CBS 27098/S • NL Ire., corresp. with Redmond • PRO, register of suspects, CO 904/18 • PRO, transcript of Lynch's treason trial, 1903, DPP 4/36 • PRO, Lynch's officer file, 1918–19, WO 374/43377

Likenesses photograph, repro. in A. A. Lynch, *Ireland: vital hour* (1915), frontispiece • photograph, repro. in Lynch, *My life story*, frontispiece

Lynch, Benjamin (1913–1946), boxer, was born on 2 April 1913 at 17 Florence Street in the Hutchesontown district of Glasgow, the second son (his elder brother died when he was a child) of John Lynch (*d.* in or after 1946), railwayman, and his wife, Elizabeth Alexander (*d.* in or before 1946). Lynch began to box as a schoolboy, first at a Catholic church club, then with an amateur boxing club called LMS Rovers. He never worked long at another job and slipped easily between amateur and professional at boxing saloons in the Gorbals. His fine balance in the ring was spotted by his future manager, Samuel Wilson, who ran a 6*d*.-a-week gymnasium. Wilson, who was still in his early thirties, was an astute trainer who sparred with his boxers. It was customary for boxers to box frequently, and Lynch had twenty-five contests in his twentieth year, by which time he was acknowledged to be the best 'wee' man in Glasgow. In May 1934 he won the Scottish flyweight championship narrowly on points over fifteen rounds. The local man who promoted this match was George Dingley, an entrepreneur and referee, who, with Wilson and Lynch, developed great enthusiasm for boxing among people on the Clyde. When the return match was fought six weeks later, more than 10,000 spectators watched the same result at Third Lanark Football Club's ground. When Lynch beat Jackie Brown (of Collyhurst) at Belle Vue, Manchester, overwhelmingly in two rounds in September 1935, it was only his third contest outside Scotland in five years of professional boxing.

Lynch thus became Scotland's first world boxing champion. He successfully defended the world flyweight title three times in three years against worthy contenders, an achievement unsurpassed by British boxers before. Lynch moved the headquarters of boxing in Scotland from Edinburgh to Glasgow, and made practicable the use of football stadiums for open-air boxing shows. He was a fine orthodox boxer, fiercely determined in the ring, with a strong punch.

On 13 February 1935 Lynch married a Glasgow girl, Annie Lynch McGuckian (*b.* 1914/15), a coat maker and the daughter of Robert McGuckian, a dock labourer, at Headless Cross, Gretna. They had at least one son, who died in 1970, but the marriage broke up in 1939.

Lynch ungraciously dropped Wilson early in 1936 before losing his first fight in two and a half years, a non-title match in Belfast. In theory he was his own manager, although Dingley had organized his serious bouts. The initial defence of his title was the first world championship held in Scotland. It brought 40,000 people to Clyde Football Club's ground, where Lynch won comfortably. His third defence (the second was in London) packed this south-side football stadium again, and the gate money

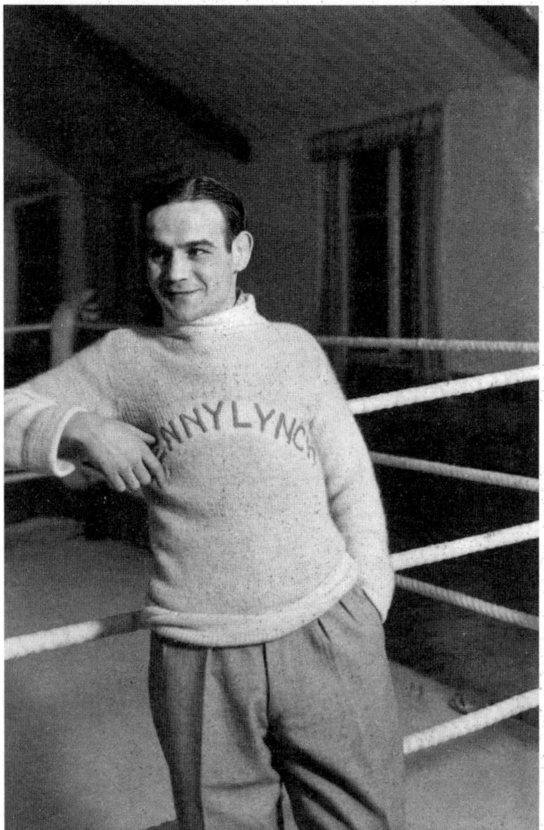

Benjamin Lynch (1913–1946), by unknown photographer, 1937

was reputed to exceed £12,000. Lynch knocked out Peter Kane of Golborne in the thirteenth round, and it was generally agreed that this had been one of the finest contests between flyweight boxers. It also turned out to be Lynch's last world championship fight.

Boxing almost fortnightly demanded minimum training and Lynch thrived with this pattern of exercise. World champions took matches much less frequently and in between Lynch liked to drink. He did not relish training, though the flyweight limit was 8 stones. At his height (5 feet 3 inches) he would undoubtedly soon have naturally outgrown the division. For his fourth defence, in June 1938, Lynch was 6 pounds overweight and he was stripped of his title. He had two more contests in the autumn, losing both, by which time the little man who had so recently been Scotland's pride was an alcoholic. Cures were tried twice without effect, and his licence to box was refused on medical grounds in September 1939. The Gorbals produced flyweight boxers and hard drinkers in profusion in the 1930s, and Lynch died there, at 1301 Govan Road, on 6 August 1946, of cardiac failure and chronic alcoholism. He was buried at St Kentigern's cemetery, Lambhill, Glasgow. STAN SHIPLEY

Sources P. McInnes, *Ten and out! a biography of Benny Lynch* (1990) • B. Donald, *The fight game in Scotland* (1988) • W. Barrington Dalby, *Come in Barry!* (1961) • G. E. Odd, *Ring battles of the century* (1948) • *Boxing* (1937) • b. cert. • m. cert. • d. cert.

Archives British Boxing Board of Control, 1 Calverts Building, London

Likenesses photograph, 1937, Hult. Arch. [*see illus.*] • photographs, Hult. Arch. • portrait, repro. in *Boxing* (13 Oct 1937), front cover

Wealth at death £55: confirmation, 26 April 1948, *CCI*

Lynch, Dominic (1622–1697), Dominican theologian, was born in co. Galway on 4 August 1622, the son of Peter Lynch of Shrule and his wife, Mary Skerret. He was professed as a Dominican friar at St Mary's Priory, Galway, and was ordained subdeacon at St Nicholas, Galway, on 23 February 1644. Shortly afterwards he was sent by his superiors to Seville, where he studied philosophy and theology at the friary of San Pablo. He graduated DD at the Dominican Colegio de Santo Tomás in Seville on 19 September 1665 and was elected regent there on 8 May 1674. Before he could be inaugurated a commissioner had to travel to Galway to check his pedigree for purity of blood. The commissioner's report was printed in the *Miscellany of the Irish Archaeological Society* in 1846. Lynch was elected by his brethren of the province of Andalusia to attend the congregation of the order held at Rome in 1686, over which he presided as moderator. Lynch published a four-volume *Summa* of Thomist philosophy (Paris, 1666–86). He was regent at the Colegio de Santo Tomás for eighteen years, and died there on 11 December 1697. He was buried at the college in the same year.

THOMPSON COOPER, *rev.* G. MARTIN MURPHY

Sources J. Hardiman, 'The pedigree of Doctor Domnick Lynch … 1674', *Miscellany of the Irish Archaeological Society*, 1 (1846), 44–90 • T. S. Flynn, *The Irish Dominicans, 1536–1641* (1993), 106 • D. de Góngora, *Historia del Colegio Mayor de Sto. Tomás de Sevilla*, 2 (1890), 200–09

Lynch, Hannah (1859–1904), novelist and journalist, was born in Dublin on 25 March 1859. Her father was a committed, non-violent Fenian who died during Lynch's childhood. It was a predominantly female environment, her mother's two marriages having produced eleven daughters. In *Twenty Five Years: Reminiscences*, Katherine Tynan recalled that the Lynch–Cantwell girls were brought up by a mother 'of spirit and cleverness', 'very bookish', and 'full of personality' (Tynan, 78), and 'among the writers, thinkers, orators, politicians, conspirators of their day' (ibid., 77). She described Lynch herself as 'one of the few people I have known who eat, drink, and dream books' (ibid., 76–7). Lynch received a convent education in England, after which she was employed as a governess on the continent. During this period she made her first acquaintance with France, a country which became her permanent home and provided her with much material for her writing.

After an upbringing that strongly united literature, politics, and the interests of women, Lynch once back in Ireland gravitated towards Anna Parnell and the Ladies' Land League. She became its secretary, and put her name to the league's first address to the women of Ireland on 4 February 1881. When the paper *United Ireland* was banned, Lynch took the type over to Paris and used her familiarity with the city to have it printed there. By 1885 she had published her first novel, *Through Troubled Waters*, a tale exploring the complexities of Irish familial and political life. She also maintained a lively presence in the periodical press, writing for *Macmillan's Magazine* under the pseudonym E. Enticknappe. In January 1888 the Dublin *Evening Telegraph* carried her amusingly deflating account of the cult surrounding the young W. B. Yeats.

Lynch's literary career accelerated in the early 1890s. *The Prince of the Glades* was completed in 1890 in Paris, and was dedicated to Anna Parnell. *Rosni Harvey* appeared in 1891, the same year in which Lynch published a pioneering study of George Meredith. In 1892 she produced the satirical *Daughters of Men*, set in the international community of Athens. Her early familiarity with France and Spain also enabled her to publish several full-length translations. She remained unmarried and childless, travelled extensively in Europe, and became Paris correspondent for *The Academy*.

By late 1894 the strain of her itinerant lifestyle and constant literary work was taking its toll on Lynch's health. In the following year she returned to Britain and was treated in a Margate hospital. In February 1895 she approached the Royal Literary Fund for a grant, explaining that illness had significantly reduced her earnings, in addition to which she was suffering from severe eye strain and writer's cramp. An award of £25 was made, and by 1896 her health had significantly improved.

After 1896 Lynch placed greater emphasis on the already apparent feminist element of her fiction. She openly satirized masculine *fin de siècle* culture in 'Dr Vermont's Fantasy' (1896), and drew attention to the moral dilemmas facing passionate, nonconformist women in novels such as *Jinny Blake* (1897) and *An Odd Experiment* (1897). The serial publication of *Autobiography of a Child* in *Blackwood's Magazine* between 1898 and 1899 stirred considerable interest, particularly for its descriptions of the brutality and deprivation suffered by a rebellious Irish girl in an English convent school. It was alleged that the narrative had been dictated to Lynch by a Dublin girl, but many suspected that the book was an account of Lynch's own experiences. A further novel, a study of French culture, and another translation were published between 1900 and 1903.

Yet despite her consistent output and growing reputation, Lynch was dogged by financial worries that both resulted from, and exacerbated, her worsening health. In 1902 an overseas trip intended to provide rest and generate income had the opposite effect, and she subsequently developed a debilitating stomach complaint which prevented her from working. In April 1903 she applied to the Royal Literary Fund once again, from her Paris address at 60 avenue de Breteuil. Help was forthcoming, but by December 1903 her condition had deteriorated, and she died in Paris in the following month, probably on 15 January.

FAITH BINCKES

Sources J. Sutherland, *The Longman companion to Victorian fiction* (1988) • R. C. Alston, *A checklist of women writers, 1801–1900: fiction; verse: drama* (1990) • K. Tynan, *Twenty-five years: reminiscences* (1913) • J. M. Côté, *Fanny and Anna Parnell: Ireland's patriot sisters* (1991) • A. Brady and B. Cleeve, *A biographical dictionary of Irish writers* (New York, 1985) • *WWW, 1897–1915* • G. Krishnamurti, *Women writers of the 1890s* (1991) [catalogue for book dealer Henry Sotheran] • Allibone, *Dict.* • J. S. Crone, *A concise dictionary of Irish biography* (1928) • K. Tynan and C. Read, *The cabinet of Irish literature*, vol. 4 (1904) • R. F. Foster, *The apprentice mage, 1865–1914* (1997), vol. 1 of *W. B. Yeats: a life* • S. J. Brown, *Ireland in fiction* (1916) • K. O'Ceirin and C. O'Ceirin, *Women of Ireland: a biographic dictionary* (1996) • *CGPLA Eng. & Wales* (1904)

Archives BL, Royal Literary Fund, letters • U. Leeds, Brotherton L., letters to Edmund Gosse

Wealth at death £126 17*s*. 1*d*.: probate, 18 April 1904, *CGPLA Eng. & Wales*

Lynch, Henry Blosse (1807–1873), explorer in Mesopotamia, born on 24 November 1807, was one of the eleven sons of Major Henry Blosse Lynch (*d*. 1845) of Partry House, Ballinrobe, co. Mayo, and Elizabeth, daughter of Robert Finnis of Hythe, Kent. Among his brothers were Thomas Kerr *Lynch and Patrick Edward *Lynch. Henry Blosse joined the Indian navy as a volunteer, under the name of Henry Lynch, in 1823, and was rated as midshipman on 27 March the same year. He was employed for several years on the survey of the Persian Gulf. He had a talent for languages, and made a close study of Persian and Arabic. On his promotion to lieutenant in 1829 he was appointed Persian and Arabic interpreter to the Gulf squadron, a post he held until 1832. During that time he was repeatedly employed in negotiations with the sheikhs of the Arab peoples of the gulf. He obtained leave from India in 1832 and was shipwrecked in the HEICS brig *Nautilus* in the Red Sea; after leaving his shipmates, he crossed the Nubian Desert north of Abyssinia, descended the Nile to Egypt, and thence shipped home.

In 1834, owing to his great local knowledge and general abilities, Lynch was selected as second in command of the expedition under Colonel Francis Rawdon Chesney to explore the Euphrates route to India, as well as to extend British political and commercial influences in the area. Lynch made preparations for the landing of the expedition in the Bay of Antioch, and chose a site near Bir or Birecik, on the Euphrates, for slips, in which the two steam vessels sent out from England in pieces were put together. He was constantly employed in delicate negotiations with neighbouring sheikhs, displaying much tact and judgement. When the two steamers were launched, Lynch received command of the *Tigris*, and surveyed over 500 miles along the River Euphrates. On 21 May 1836 the *Tigris* foundered in a hurricane, with the loss of twenty lives, including Lynch's brother Richard Blosse, lieutenant in the 21st Bengal native infantry. This episode underlined the difficulty of riverine transport and suggested that sea-going steamships were still the best means of communication with India. After Chesney's return to England in 1837, Lynch was given command of the expedition, and ascended the Tigris to a higher point than had ever before been reached, carried out extensive surveys, and completed the Tigris map in 1839. He was a useful source of intelligence to the British government during a politically tense period.

Lynch was promoted commander on 1 July 1839. The court of directors of the East India Company, anticipating important results from the navigation of the rivers of

Mesopotamia, sent out that year, round the Cape, in pieces, under charge of Michael Lynch, Henry Blosse's brother and a lieutenant in the Indian navy, three river-steamers. They were specially constructed by McGregor Laird, whose company had provided Chesney's steamers and was to develop close ties with the Royal Geographical Society and government. The steamers were put together at Basrah, near the delta, and in 1840 four steamers were regularly sailing between Baghdad in the interior and Basrah. During Lynch's absence in 1841 two of his party steamed up the River Euphrates as far as Beles. Lynch resumed command at Beles in the autumn of 1841, when a base-line for the Mesopotamian survey was measured on the plain between Beles and Jiber, and connected by chronometric measurements with the Mediterranean. Ironically, the result of the two Euphrates surveys was to reveal the superiority of the sea compared with the river route to India. Lynch proceeded to Baghdad, and remained there in charge of the postal service between Baghdad and Damascus until late in 1842. He continued to advocate the importance of the riverine link and, writing to the Royal Geographical Society and Admiralty, pointed out the strategic and political advantages which would accrue to Britain if she exerted her influence in the area.

Lynch commanded a flotilla off the mouth of the Indus in 1843, keeping open communication with Sir Charles James Napier's army in Sind. From that time until 1851 he was employed as assistant to the superintendent of the Indian navy, and a member of the oriental examination committee at Bombay, where he was a very active member of the Bombay Geographical Society. He became captain on 13 September 1847, and was appointed master attendant in Bombay dockyard in 1849. In 1851–3, as commodore, he commanded a small squadron of vessels of the Indian navy, which served with the Royal Navy during the Second Anglo-Burmese War, at the conclusion of which he was made CB. He returned to Britain, and on 13 April 1856 retired from the service.

Lynch established himself in Paris. At the end of the Anglo-Persian War of 1856–7 he was delegated by Lord Palmerston to conduct the negotiations with the Persian plenipotentiary, which resulted in the treaty of Paris of 4 March 1857. The shah, in recognition of his services, nominated him to the highest class of the Lion and Sun. Henry was probably the brother with whom Thomas Kerr Lynch founded the Euphrates and Tigris Steam Navigation Company, which operated under the protection of the Foreign Office, in 1862. Lynch should not be confused with Captain William Francis Lynch, United States navy, whose surveys of the Jordan and Dead Sea were made a few years later, and were, like Lynch's, reported in the *Journal of the Royal Geographical Society*. Lynch died at his home at 6 rue Royale, Faubourg St Honoré, Paris, on 14 April 1873. He left a widow, Caroline Ann, whom he had married in August 1838, daughter of Colonel Taylor, at one time political resident at Baghdad.

H. M. CHICHESTER, *rev.* ELIZABETH BAIGENT

Sources Burke, *Gen. Ire.* • R. A. Stafford, *Scientist of empire: Sir Roderick Murchison, scientific exploration and Victorian imperialism* (1989) • F. R. Chesney, *The expedition for the survey of the rivers Euphrates and Tigris*, 2 vols. (1850) • C. R. Markham, *A memoir on the Indian surveys*, 2nd edn (1878) • *Galignani's Messenger* (19 April 1873) • *CGPLA Eng. & Wales* (1873) • J. B. Kelly, *Britain and the Persian Gulf, 1795–1880* (1968)

Archives BL, Hobhouse MSS

Wealth at death under £45,000: probate, 9 May 1873, *CGPLA Eng. & Wales*

Lynch, James (1626–1713), Roman Catholic archbishop of Tuam, was a native of Galway city and a member of an influential local family. He received his early education from the Irish Jesuits and in 1651 entered the Jesuit run Irish College at Seville. Illness forced him home in 1653 but he later returned to Spain and took a doctorate in theology at the University of Salamanca. He taught in Compostela. In 1659 he was shipwrecked off San Sebastian. By 1668 he was parish priest of Galway and attached to the collegiate church. A noted preacher and administrator, he managed to remain popular with seculars and regulars alike, something of a feat in seventeenth-century Ireland. Thanks to his family connections he had the support of influential Catholic laity in rebuilding the local church.

Lynch's pastoral success brought him to the attention of Propaganda which, since the death of John de Burgo in 1666, was searching to fill the vacant see of Tuam. Lynch was an attractive candidate, especially as he had avoided any involvement with or sympathy for Peter Walsh's *Remonstrance*, which had sought to distinguish unqualified temporal loyalty to Charles II from spiritual allegiance to Rome. Backed by the local clergy and gentry and enjoying the support of several members of the hierarchy he was appointed to Tuam in 1669 and consecrated at Ghent later in the year. His early correspondence to Rome summarizes the main problems in his archdiocese: authority disputes with regular clergy, a badly educated secular clergy, a dispirited local gentry, and a general ignorance of religion and morality among the laity. While these problems were unremarkable for a seventeenth-century Irish diocese they were exacerbated by the virtual breakdown in the machinery of ecclesiastical government following the Cromwellian wars. Lynch set himself a rebuilding programme. Despite authority disputes with the regulars, he requested that the Irish Capuchins be allowed to establish houses in his diocese. He asserted his authority over suffragan dioceses even when it brought him into conflict with Propaganda. Roman firmness did not deter him from trying to adapt church law, especially that concerning marriage, to local circumstances.

His activities attracted the unwanted attentions of the civil administration and during his early career he endured sporadic harassment. Disaffected Catholics took advantage of anti-Catholic legislation to put pressure on Lynch. In 1671 a Galway based Augustinian, Martin French, brought him before the civil courts in Galway to face the charge of exercising foreign jurisdiction. When he was found guilty of *praemunire* Lynch appealed his case to Dublin where it collapsed. However, in 1674 French again brought charges and this time Lynch was imprisoned prior to transportation to Spain, where he spent many years. While absent in Spain he was named as a ringleader of the Popish Plot in 1678 and was lucky to escape the fate of his archiepiscopal colleagues Oliver Plunket of Armagh and Peter Talbot of Dublin. Between 1682 and 1684 he exercised episcopal functions in Seville. At the accession of James II he returned to Tuam and worked in relative freedom until the Jacobite defeat.

During the 1690s Lynch led a nomadic existence, living on the continent but frequently visiting his diocese, as in 1698, to oversee appointments. While abroad he governed through vicars, one of them his nephew Dominic Lynch. The ageing archbishop remained active in Irish ecclesiastical affairs. In 1704 he was in communication with Queen Mary concerning the filling of the vacant see of Elphin. After 1707 he settled permanently in France and enjoyed a pension from the French king. Solicitous of his own family's fortunes, in 1710 he unsuccessfully applied for the appointment as coadjutor of Tuam for his nephew Dominic. He died at the Collège des Lombards, Paris, on 29 October 1713, leaving a substantial bourse for Galway students in the Irish College there. He was buried at St Paul's Church, Paris. THOMAS O'CONNOR

Sources C. Giblin, ed., 'Catalogue of material of Irish interest in the collection *Nunziatura di Fiandra*, Vatican archives [pt 1]', *Collectanea Hibernica*, 1 (1958), 7–134 • C. Giblin, ed., 'Catalogue of material of Irish interest in the collection *Nunziatura di Fiandra*, Vatican archives [pt 2]', *Collectanea Hibernica*, 3 (1960), 7–144 • C. Giblin, ed., 'Catalogue of material of Irish interest in the collection *Nunziatura di Fiandra*, Vatican archives [pt 3]', *Collectanea Hibernica*, 4 (1961), 7–137 • C. Giblin, ed., 'Catalogue of material of Irish interest in the collection *Nunziatura di Fiandra*, Vatican archives [pt 4]', *Collectanea Hibernica*, 5 (1962), 7–130 • C. Giblin, ed., 'Catalogue of material of Irish interest in the collection *Nunziatura di Fiandra*, Vatican archives [pt 6]', *Collectanea Hibernica*, 10 (1967), 72–138 • C. Giblin, ed., 'Catalogue of material of Irish interest in the collection *Nunziatura di Fiandra*, Vatican archives [pt 7]', *Collectanea Hibernica*, 11 (1968), 53–90 • C. Giblin, ed., 'Catalogue of material of Irish interest in the collection *Nunziatura di Fiandra*, Vatican archives [pt 8]', *Collectanea Hibernica*, 12 (1969), 62–101 • C. Giblin, ed., 'Catalogue of material of Irish interest in the collection *Nunziatura di Fiandra*, Vatican archives [pt 9]', *Collectanea Hibernica*, 13 (1970), 61–99 • C. Giblin, ed., 'Catalogue of material of Irish interest in the collection *Nunziatura di Fiandra*, Vatican archives [pt 10]', *Collectanea Hibernica*, 14 (1971), 36–81 • C. Giblin, ed., 'Catalogue of material of Irish interest in the collection *Nunziatura di Fiandra*, Vatican archives [pt 11]', *Collectanea Hibernica*, 15 (1972), 7–55 • B. Millett, ed., 'Calendar of volume 1 (1625–68) of the collection *Scritture riferite nei congressi, Irlanda* in Propaganda archives', *Collectanea Hibernica*, 6–7 (1963–4), 18–211 • B. Millett, ed., 'Catalogue of volume 294 of the *Scritture riferite nei congressi, Irlanda* in Propaganda archives [pt 2]', *Collectanea Hibernica*, 8 (1965), 7–37 • B. Millett, ed., 'Calendar of the collection *Scritture riferite nei congressi, Irlanda* in Propaganda archives [pt 3]', *Collectanea Hibernica*, 9 (1966), 7–70 • B. Millett, ed., 'Catalogue of Irish material in fourteen volumes of the *Scritture originale riferite nelle congregazione generali* in Propaganda archives', *Collectanea Hibernica*, 10 (1967), 7–59 • B. Millett, ed., 'Catalogue of Irish material in vols. 129–131 of the *Scritture originale riferite nelle congregazione generali* in Propaganda archives', *Collectanea Hibernica*, 11 (1968), 7–18 • B. Millett, ed., 'Catalogue of Irish material in vols. 132–139 of the *Scritture originale riferite nelle congregazione generali* in Propaganda archives', *Collectanea Hibernica*, 12 (1969), 7–44 • B. Millett, ed., 'Catalogue of Irish material in vols. 140–143 of the *Scritture originale riferite nelle congregazione generali* in Propaganda archives', *Collectanea Hibernica*, 13 (1970), 21–60 • B. Millett, ed., 'Calendar of volume 2 (1669–71) of the *Scritture riferite nei congressi, Irlanda* in Propaganda archives [pt 1]', *Collectanea Hibernica*, 16 (1973), 7–47 • B. Millett, ed., 'Calendar of volume 2 (1669–71) of the *Scritture riferite nei congressi, Irlanda* in Propaganda archives [pt 2]', *Collectanea Hibernica*, 17 (1975), 17–68 • B. Millett, ed., 'Catalogue of Irish material in vols. 370 and 371 of the *Scritture riferite originali nelle congregazioni generali* in Propaganda archives', *Collectanea Hibernica*, 27–8 (1985–6), 44–85 • 'Irish ecclesiastical colleges since the Reformation', *Irish Ecclesiastical Record*, [new ser.], 9 (1872–3), 208–21 • E. A. D'Alton, *History of the archdiocese of Tuam*, 2 vols. (1928) • W. P. Burke, *The Irish priests in the penal times, 1660–1760* (1914) • *Archivium Hibernicum* • *Analecta Hibernica* • *Gazette* [Paris] (4 Nov 1713)

Archives Propaganda Archives, Rome, letters

Wealth at death will, 15 March 1711, *Collectanea Hibernica*, 36–37 (1994–5), 92 • donated 6000 livres to Collège de Lombards, 1707, *Collectanea Hibernica*, 34–5 (1992–3), 85

Lynch, John (*d.* in or after **1677**), historian, was born in Galway to an ancient family of the city. Neither his father's nor his mother's name is known; the often-stated suggestion that his father was the Alexander Lynch who had a school in Galway in 1608 has been shown to have no basis. Having received part of his early tuition from the Jesuits, he was sent to France in 1618 to further his education. Apparently bound for Rouen, he was persuaded by fellow Galwayman Francis Kirwan (who may also have been related to him) to go instead to the Jesuit college of Dieppe where Kirwan was a professor. He later spent a period in the Jesuit college of Douai before moving to Rouen, where he stayed from 1621 to 1624. During his time in France his fellow students included men who were later to be leading members of the Irish hierarchy.

On his return to Ireland, Lynch was ordained priest early in 1625 and within a couple of years was appointed chaplain to Sir Richard Blake, who was mayor of Galway in 1627–8. In or about 1630 he was appointed archdeacon of Tuam. There remain only some minor details from his own hand of his ecclesiastical activities over the following decade or so, but his intellectual interests are reflected in his commissioning in 1643 of the Irish scholar and scribe Dubhaltach Mac Fhirbhisigh to copy a fragmentary collection of early Irish annals from a manuscript belonging to the learned family of MacEgan.

Lynch attained a degree of prominence and even notoriety during the tumultuous decade which followed the outbreak of the Irish rising of autumn 1641. He and his old mentor, Francis Kirwan, now bishop of Killala, as firm supporters of the leading Galway Catholic magnate, Ulick Bourke, marquess of Clanricarde, were closely identified with the Old English party. This brought them into direct conflict with the Italian papal nuncio, Giovanni Battista Rinuccini, archbishop of Fermo. The latter's machinations during his sojourn in Ireland in 1645–9 split the Catholic confederate camp and the Irish hierarchy. When in summer 1651 Galway city was invested by the Cromwellian army of Sir Charles Coote, Lynch was one of a small minority of the clergy which favoured surrendering on terms; and his few like-minded colleagues were consequently reviled as 'anti divines and pseudo preachers' (J. T. Gilbert, *Contemporary History of Affairs in Ireland*, 2, 1879, 71). After a nine-month siege and with famine looming, the city was suddenly surrendered. Although the terms were quite generous, little leniency was shown to the Catholic clergy: they were obliged to leave Ireland within six months. Even a moderate such as Lynch was not spared and before the end of 1652 he went into exile in France. He appears to have settled in or near the town of St Malo in Brittany, and there he spent the remainder of his life.

Lynch was far from idle during his exile. He spent several years researching and writing a number of major works, some of which appeared in print during his lifetime. The best-known of these was *Cambrensis eversus*, which was largely written in the 1650s and published under the *nom de plume* Gratianus Lucius in 1662, probably at St Malo. This learned refutation of the perceived anti-Irish slanders of the twelfth-century Cambro-Norman ecclesiastic and propagandist Gerald of Wales (Giraldus Cambrensis) is combined with a cleverly persuasive defence of the Old English cause in the wars of the mid-seventeenth century. It also contains much evidence of Gaelic learning—particularly in relation to genealogical material, some of which was probably supplied by Dubhaltach Mac Fhirbhisigh. The next work of Lynch's to appear was *Alithinologia, sive, Veridica responsio ad invectivam* which was issued under the *nom de plume* Eudoxius Alithinologus in 1664, probably at St Omer. This book, together with a further volume entitled *Supplementum alithinologiae*, published in 1667, powerfully and skilfully argues the Old English case against the pro-Rinuccini faction in Rome. The only other work of Lynch's to appear in print during his lifetime was a life of his friend and former teacher Kirwan, who had died in Rennes in 1661; this little book, entitled *Pii antistitis icon*, was published in 1669.

Lynch's most ambitious work, his voluminous history of the Irish bishops, *De praesulibus Hiberniae*, arranged on a diocesan basis and filling 1081 manuscript pages, was completed towards the end of 1672. Marshalling as it does an impressive array of source material, in both Irish and Latin, it must have taken several years of painstaking and onerous research work to compile. Lynch says that he wrote for relevant information to the person in charge of each Irish diocese, with very mixed results. He did not, however, live to see the work in print; it was finally published in 1944 in two large volumes. Another work of his which did not appear in his lifetime (it was published in 1846) was a Latin poem dating from 1667 in which he explains that he cannot return to his native land while a certain person (probably Charles Coote, president of Connaught) was still in power. A letter which he wrote about 1664 to a French scholar, M. du Boulay, correcting his linking of the terms 'Scotia' and 'Scoti' to medieval Scotland rather than to Ireland, was printed by Charles O'Conor as an appendix to his edition of Roderic O'Flaherty's *Ogygia Vindicated* (1775). One other work of Lynch's which has never appeared in print is a translation into 'elegant Latin' of Geoffrey Keating's history of Ireland (*Foras feasa ar Éirinn*). It has been suggested that this was completed before Lynch left Ireland in 1652.

The date of Lynch's death is uncertain. Most authorities suggest that he died in either 1673 or 1674, but evidence has been adduced that he was still alive in 1677. While it has been suggested that he may have spent his final years in Paris, it seems more likely that he passed away in St Malo, where he had lived for a quarter of a century.

Nollaig Ó Muraíle

Sources N. Ó Muraíle, 'Aspects of the intellectual life of seventeenth century Galway', *Galway history and society: interdisciplinary essays on the history of an Irish county*, ed. G. Moran and R. Gillespie (1996), 149–211, esp. 155–65, nn. 31–118 • *DNB*
Archives Mazarin Library, Paris, annotated copy of 'De praesulibus Hiberniae'

Lynch, John (1697–1760), dean of Canterbury and pluralist, was born on 5 December 1697 at Staple-next-Wingham, Kent, one of two surviving sons of John Lynch (*d.* 1733) and his wife, Sarah, daughter of Francis Head esquire of Rochester. His father, whose family had been settled at Staple for many generations, was a colonel of militia and deputy lieutenant who served as high sheriff for Kent in 1714. After education at King's School, Canterbury, under Mr Smith, Lynch matriculated at St John's College, Cambridge, on 24 June 1714, where he proceeded BA in 1718, MA in 1721, and DD in 1728. Following ordination in December 1721, he quickly attracted the patronage of William Wake, the archbishop of Canterbury, by whom in 1723 he was appointed prebend of the fourth stall in Canterbury Cathedral and rector of All Hallow's, Bread Street, London, which he exchanged for All Hallows-the-Great in 1730. The rectory of Sundridge, Kent, was added in 1725. Further preferment followed his marriage to the archbishop's youngest daughter, Mary, in 1728: the mastership of St Cross Hospital, Winchester, and, in 1731, the valuable rectories of Ickham and Bishopsbourne, and the sinecure rectory of Aynesford. At this point Lynch relinquished Sundridge and his London living. On 18 January 1734 he was installed as dean of Canterbury, succeeding Elias Sydall, and in 1735 he became treasurer of Salisbury. During this time he resided principally at Lambeth Palace, attending to the affairs of his father-in-law, the archbishop. After Wake's death in January 1737, Lynch divided his time between the deanery at Canterbury and his family home at Staple, 8 miles away.

Lynch's accumulation of preferment attracted critical notice, even in an age accustomed to such practices. His conduct inspired at least one satirical print, *An Ass Loaded with Preferments* (BM 2269; Stephens, vol. 3, pt 1), published in February 1737, and by this time it was generally believed that his 'taking advantage of his father-in-law, the Archbishop of Canterbury's weak condition, and presenting himself to all that falls in the Archbishop's gift … was … very scandalous' (*Egmont Diary*, 2.263). This charge was forcefully repeated in *The Life of Dean L—nch*, an anonymous work of 1748, which alleged that ambition alone had caused Lynch to marry a wife who was 'exceeding plain in Person and much deformed' (*Life*, 8) and that his selfishness had led him to neglect his brothers and aged father, and driven a younger sister to despair. The same work also charged Lynch with rapacious behaviour towards the tenantry on the cathedral estates, maintaining that 'Yeomen and Farmers he rated as his Dogs' (ibid., 29).

The accuracy of these claims may be doubted. Lynch and his wife (who outlived him by several years) had a large family: five daughters and two sons, one of whom, Sir William Lynch, served King George III as envoy to the court of Turin. Friends pointed out that some of his appointments, notably the mastership of the hospitals of St Nicholas, Harbledown, and St John, Canterbury, brought no emoluments and much trouble, and that, elsewhere, his generosity was commensurate with his wealth. He was said to have expended above £3000 of his own money on repairs to his prebendal houses and deanery, and to have been a liberal and hospitable supporter of a wide range of public charities. The high reputation of the King's School at this time was also credited, in part, to his interest and encouragement. As a clergyman he was respected. In 1747 he was nominated prolocutor of the lower house of convocation, and he was considered a good preacher, although no remarkable qualities are evident in his only published sermon, delivered before the Society for the Propagation of the Gospel in 1735. In 1757 Lynch suffered a paralytic stroke and was granted a royal dispensation, excusing him from all duty. He made a partial recovery, and continued to entertain at the deanery, but his faculties began to leave him some months before his death, which took place at Canterbury on 25 May 1760. He was buried in the church at Staple. RICHARD SHARP

Sources E. Hasted, *The history and topographical survey of the county of Kent*, 2nd edn, 9 (1800), 187ff.; 12 (1801), 41–4 • H. J. Todd, *Some account of the deans of Canterbury* (1793), 211–19 • J. M. Cowper, *The lives of the deans of Canterbury* (1900), 165–73 • *The life of Dean L–nch, by a yeoman of Kent* (1748) • N. Sykes, *William Wake, archbishop of Canterbury*, 1 (1957), 242; 2 (1957), 256 • *Manuscripts of the earl of Egmont: diary of Viscount Percival, afterwards first earl of Egmont*, 3 vols., HMC, 63 (1920–23), vol. 2, p. 263 • F. G. Stephens and M. D. George, eds., *Catalogue of prints and drawings in the British Museum, division 1: political and personal satires*, 3 (1877) • Venn, *Alum. Cant.*
Archives BL, Letters to Samuel Pegge, Add. MSS 42619–20
Likenesses engraving, 1737, BM • portrait, deanery, Canterbury; repro. in Cowper, *Lives of the deans*, facing p. 165
Wealth at death see Venn, *Alum. Cant.*, 3.120

Lynch [*married name* Fox], **Patricia Nora** (*c*.**1894–1972**), children's writer and journalist, was born in Cork on 4 June about 1894. (There is some uncertainty as to the year of her birth.) Her mother, Nora, had been reared by a story-teller from Bantry and Patricia grew up in an atmosphere of folklore and story-telling. The family lived in Sunday's Well and the Fair Hill areas of Cork city. Her father died when she was young and her mother moved with Patricia and her brother to London. She was educated in Ireland, England, and Bruges in Belgium.

Lynch noted in later life that 'I was brought up to think that the best thing I could ever do would be to die for "the cause"' (cutting from *Irish Press*, 1957, NL Ire., Fox–Lynch MSS) and she remained an Irish nationalist throughout her life. In London she became a friend of Sylvia Pankhurst and was a supporter of the suffrage movement, and it was Pankhurst who sent Lynch to Dublin in the aftermath of the 1916 Easter rising to report on the event for the *Worker's Dreadnought*. She travelled alone to Dublin and wrote the first eyewitness account of the rising from an Irish viewpoint. Her piece in the *Worker's Dreadnought* was later reprinted as part of a pamphlet entitled *Rebel Ireland* published by the Workers' Socialist Federation.

On the 4 October 1922 Lynch married the journalist and writer Richard Michael Fox (1891–1969). Fox had been born in Leeds and had been a conscientious objector during the First World War, spending three years in prison for his stance. The couple, who had no children, lived for a short time in Tottenham but soon moved to Dublin, where they resided in Glasnevin. In Ireland they became involved in the Irish labour and nationalist movements and were ardent theatregoers. They held regular get-togethers on Wednesdays at their home, attended by literary and other figures, and became friends with such people as Sean O'Casey, Peadar O'Donnell, Liam O'Flaherty and Maud Gonne MacBride. Fox, who became an Irish citizen, worked as a sub-editor for the *Irish Press* for a number of years and Lynch also worked for the same paper.

Lynch's first children's book, *The Cobbler's Apprentice* (1933), won the prestigious Tailteann medal. She was a prolific author and published over fifty books and two hundred stories, many of which were translated into other languages. Her work appeared under her maiden name, and almost all of it was for children, although also appreciated by adults—one example of her ability to cross audiences in this way can be seen in her account of her early years, *A Storyteller's Childhood* (1947), which reads very much like a fairy tale. Her stories generally are simple, mingling fact and fantasy, and containing elements of Irish folklore, such as fairies, leprechauns, and talking animals. They were illustrated by artists such as Sean Keating, Jack B. Yeats and George Altendorf. Among the most famous were *The Turf Cutter's Donkey* (1934), which was chosen as a Junior Book Club Selection, and *The Grey Goose of Kilnevin* (1939), which was selected by the Cardinal Hayes literature committee in America as one of the best one hundred books published there in 1941. Other honours included the Irish Women Writers' Club award for *Fiddler's Quest* (1941), and the Eugene Field Society of America certificate of service to literature. In 1967 Lynch was elected to the Irish Academy of Letters, and a number of her books were adapted for Radio Telefis Éireann, the Irish national radio station.

Lynch and her husband were extremely close, and after his death in 1969, unable to manage alone, she lived with the family of Eugene Lambert, the puppeteer. Lynch died on 1 September 1972 in a nursing home in Monkstown, Dublin, and she was buried with her husband in Glasnevin cemetery, Dublin. MARIA LUDDY

Sources *Irish Press* (2 Sept 1972) • *Irish Times* (2 Sept 1972) • accession list for Fox–Lynch MSS, NL Ire.
Archives NL Ire., corresp., literary, other MSS [consists of forty archival file boxes]
Likenesses photographs, NL Ire.

Lynch, Patrick Edward (**1810–1884**), army officer, was one of the eleven sons of Major Henry Blosse Lynch, 73rd foot (*d.* 1845), of Partry House, Ballinrobe, co. Mayo, and his wife, Elizabeth, daughter of Robert Finnis of Hythe, Kent. Henry Blosse *Lynch and Thomas Kerr *Lynch were his brothers. He received a cadetship in 1826, and on 16 February 1827 was posted as ensign to the 16th Bombay native infantry, in which he obtained his subsequent promotions. He was one of the detachment of eight British officers and fourteen NCOs sent to Persia (as part of the British policy to ensure Persia as a buffer against Russia) to support Abbas Mirza. They reached Bushehr in November 1833 and Tehran in March 1834, and were employed under Sir Henry Lindesay Bethune. Lynch commanded a corps at Kisir Chur and the defeat of the Shiraz princes, for which he received the thanks of the shah, the decoration of the Lion and Sun, and the British local rank of major in Persia. The British detachment was withdrawn from service in 1836 to 1837.

Following the British–Indian invasion of Afghanistan (1839) and the restoration of Shah Shuja, in summer 1840 Lieutenant Lynch was appointed political agent in the Ghilzai area of eastern Afghanistan. Apparently ambitious and wanting to increase his own power, he was not an independent arbiter above tribal politics but became involved in them. Following Ghilzai discontent he initiated, without authorization, an aggressive and provocative policy. On 30 April 1841 he attacked a fort 7 miles from Kalat and killed almost all its inhabitants; later, attempting to justify this, he produced stories, apparently unfounded, of conspiracies. According to M. E. Yapp 'the evidence suggests that Lynch was deliberately trying to cow the Ghilzays by a demonstration of ruthless force and determination' (Yapp, 323). He alienated support and in an uprising was besieged at Kalat-i-Ghilzai, and decided to resign. Sir William Macnaghten had already ordered his replacement, and wrote that Lynch was not only imprudent 'but a very dangerous character' (ibid.). He was replaced and his policy reversed.

During the Indian mutiny Lynch served at Belgaum. In 1858 he commanded his regiment with the forces from Aden which captured the stronghold of Sheik Othman, and was mentioned in dispatches. He commanded at Aden and Assurghur, and was brigadier-general at Ahmednagar and Deesa. He became major-general in 1872, and retired with the rank of lieutenant-general in 1878. Lynch married Emily Elizabeth (*d.* 1 May 1902), daughter of Captain Sturton of Ersland House, Reigate. They had one son, Colonel Henry Blosse Lynch, Dorset regiment (1856–1936), and five daughters. Lynch died at his seat, Partry House, Ballinrobe, Mayo, on 23 May 1884.

H. M. CHICHESTER, *rev.* ROGER T. STEARN

Sources *East-India Register* • Burke, *Gen. Ire.* • Kelly, *Handbk* • M. E. Yapp, *Strategies of British India: Britain, Iran and Afghanistan, 1798–1850* (1980) • D. Gillard, *The struggle for Asia, 1828–1914: a study in British and Russian imperialism* (1977) • J. B. Kelly, *Britain and the Persian Gulf, 1795–1880* (1968) • P. Macrory, *Signal catastrophe: the story of a disastrous retreat from Kabul, 1842* (1966); repr. as *Kabul catastrophe* (1986) • C. Hibbert, *The great mutiny, India, 1857* (1978); repr. (1980)
Wealth at death £2493 9s. 5d.: probate, 25 Oct 1884, *CGPLA Ire.*

Lynch, Richard (1610–1676), Jesuit and theologian, was born at Galway on 15 November 1610, and came of a leading family of that town. He was a student at the Irish College at Santiago de Compostela in Spain before entering the Society of Jesus there on 14 September 1626. Having graduated DD he taught theology for many years at Valladolid and at Salamanca, where he enjoyed a high reputation. He published a three-volume compendium of scholastic philosophy (Lyon, 1654), and a two-volume treatise *De Deo ultimo fine* (Salamanca, 1671). He died at Salamanca on 18 March 1676. He is not to be confused with another Richard Lynch (1611–1647) who entered the Andalusian province of the Society of Jesus at Seville in 1632 and was rector of the Irish College at Seville from 1644 until his death in 1647.

THOMPSON COOPER, *rev.* G. MARTIN MURPHY

Sources A. de Backer and others, *Bibliothèque de la Compagnie de Jésus*, new edn, 5, ed. C. Sommervogel (Brussels, 1894) • F. Finegan, 'Irish rectors at Seville, 1619–1687', *Irish Ecclesiastical Record*, 5th ser., 106 (1966), 45–63 • A. Astrain, *Historia de la Compañía de Jesús en … España*, 6 (1920), 99

Lynch [*née* Foulks], **Theodora Elizabeth** (1812–1885), poet and novelist, was born at Dale Park, Sussex, the daughter of Arthur Foulks and his wife, Mary Ann McKenzie. Her father, of Redland House, Bristol, ran the Lodge estate sugar plantation in St Dorothy's parish (near Old Harbour, in modern St Catherine parish), Jamaica. Little is known of Theodora's early life. On 28 December 1835 she married Henry Mark Lynch at her father's plantation. Her husband was born in Kingston, Jamaica, on 29 October 1814, the second son of John Lynch of Kingston. He was admitted as a student of the Middle Temple on 31 May 1837, called to the bar on 12 June 1840, and returned to Jamaica to practise law. He was nominated to become a judge in the colony, but died of yellow fever on 15 July 1845 before taking up the post. He was buried at Halfway Tree church, St Andrew, Jamaica, on 16 July 1845.

Following her husband's death Theodora returned to England and began her writing career. Her first publication was a book of poetry: *Lays of the Sea, and other Poems* (1846; 2nd edn, 1850). The following year she turned to prose in *The Cotton-Tree, or, Emily, the Little West Indian: a Tale for Young People* (1847; 2nd edn, 1853; 3rd edn, 1854). She continued her prose work in *The Family Sepulchre: a Tale of Jamaica* (1848), which aimed 'to instruct the young mind how to meet the "last enemy" with true Christian fortitude and composure'. Her stories were often set in the West Indies and were well laced with catechistic didacticism. Drawing on her own experiences of her youth in Jamaica, they offer intriguing insights into Jamaican society in the last years of slavery and the early years following emancipation. For example, she refers in *The Family Sepulchre* to a white child as a 'buckra piccaninni', African terms for 'white' and 'child', respectively. She published another thirteen volumes of stories and novels, including *Maude Effingham: a Tale of Jamaica* (1849); *The Little Teacher* (2nd edn, 1851); *The Mountain Pastor* (1852; 3rd edn, 1853); *The Red Brick House* (1855); *The Wonders of the West Indies* (two editions, 1856); *The Story of my Girlhood* (1857); *The Exodus of the Children of Israel, and their Wanderings in the Desert* (1857); *Songs of the Evening Land, and other Poems* (1861); *Rose and her Mission, a Tale of the West Indies* (1863); *The Sabbaths of the Year,*

Hymns for Children (1864), and *Years Ago: a Tale of West Indian Domestic Life of the Eighteenth Century* (1865). Theodora Lynch died at 81 St John's Wood Terrace, London, on 27 June 1885, and was described in her *Times* obituary as 'a poet of considerable merit'. THOMAS W. KRISE

Sources *DNB* · *The Standard* (2 July 1885), 1 · *The Times* (9 July 1885), 6b · d. cert.

Lynch, Sir Thomas (*d.* 1684), colonial governor, was the son of Theophilus Lynch (*b.* 1603) and his wife, Judith, eldest daughter of John Aylmer, bishop of London. Nothing is known of Lynch's early life and education before he went out to Jamaica in the army of General Robert Venables in 1655. He had returned to England by 1660 when, as a captain, he petitioned the government for a passage back to Jamaica in one of the king's ships. While in England he secured for himself the lucrative appointment of provost marshal of Jamaica for life.

Sir Thomas Lynch was one of most successful settlers in early Jamaica, serving as governor of the island between 1671 and 1676 and between 1681 and 1684. He distinguished himself as a strong advocate for the future development of the island and as a devoted representative of planter interests against the interests of buccaneers. Along with his great rival Sir Thomas Modyford, Lynch was a principal founding father of Jamaica in a crucial stage of its early development.

By 1664 Lynch possessed the most promising plantation in Port Morant. He worked this 1000 acre tract with a labour force of five white servants and thirty-seven slaves. By his departure for England in 1665 he had planted 45 acres, had erected a splendid sugar works, and built a well-furnished two-storey plantation house, suggesting an investment of at least £3000. He had also established himself as a person of political importance. In December 1662 he was lieutenant-colonel of the militia; in April 1663 he was sworn in as a member of the council; and in April 1664 he became president of the council. He remained a councillor when Sir Thomas Modyford became governor in June 1664 but appears to have fallen out with Modyford by February 1665. He wrote to Lord Arlington on 12 February 1665 that Modyford had discharged him from the council without giving any public reason. This falling out may have encouraged him to leave for England in 1665 instead of staying in Jamaica, where he had intended to 'marry, send for his relations and make this his England' (PRO, CO 1/19/31).

On 3 December 1670 Lynch was knighted at Whitehall and in 1671 was revenged on Modyford when he was appointed in Modyford's stead as lieutenant-governor of Jamaica. He returned to a colony plunged into factional strife: buccaneers versus planters. Lynch was on the side of the planters, reminding Whitehall officials that 'if Jamaica have easy government, be defended from enemies, and supplied with negroes and servants, and have no privateering, in six years it may produce as much sugars as Barbadoes' (*CSP col.*, 7.477). He opened up the Jamaican frontier to settlement, issuing 1200 patents for planting, mostly in unsettled parishes. He maintained good relations with the island's assembly, raising the republican and civilian part of the colonial constitution towards equality with its authoritarian and military foundations. He fostered trade, encouraging Jewish merchants and other religious minorities to engage in clandestine trade, in which he himself also participated. He was less successful in rooting out buccaneering and in implementing the treaty of Madrid of 1670. He tried to establish open trade with Spanish America but the Spanish were not prepared to buy 'so much as an emerald' from the British because they believed Lynch had breached the treaty by encouraging logwood cutting in Spanish territory and because they did not accept his boastful claims that he had eliminated privateering (Zahedieh, 'The merchants of Port Royal', 575). Although privateering did diminish in the early 1670s, it did not disappear but stabilized at lower levels. Lynch's attempt to lure privateers into planting by promising them grants of 35 acres if they gave up their way of life was seldom taken up. His arrest and execution of Peter Johnson, a privateer with a string of murders to his account, led to popular unrest in Port Royal, where Johnson was mourned 'as if he had been as pious and innocent as one of the primitive martyrs' (PRO, CO 1/30/67–8). More importantly, Lynch's contacts in England were less powerful than those of the buccaneers and, to Lynch's disgust, Sir Henry *Morgan, 'Admirall of the Pryvateers' sent back to England in disgrace in 1672, was appointed lieutenant-governor in late 1674 and returned to Jamaica in triumph in 1675.

Lynch went back to England. Probably at about this time he married Vere, daughter of Sir George Herbert. Their only child, Philadelphia, was baptized on 4 June 1676 at St Martin-in-the-Fields and later married Sir Thomas Cotton, bt. It is unclear when Lynch married his second wife, Mary, daughter of Thomas Temple of Warwickshire, who subsequently married Colonel Hender Molesworth, governor of Jamaica, 1684–7. They had no children. Lynch was reappointed governor of Jamaica in 1681. Although he considered that 'Arguing with Assemblys is like philosophising with a Mule', he secured a twenty-one-year revenue act that guaranteed regular fiscal income to the royal government (Dunn, 159). His second governorship was marked by conflicts with Sir Henry Morgan's pro-buccaneering faction but buccaneering was declining as planting began to prosper, much to Lynch's satisfaction. In 1682 he claimed that planting and trade were flourishing so much 'that within 15 months every man's freehold … is almost risen in value from 50 to 200 percent' (Claypole, 173). Highlights of his governorship included the publication of the first compilation of Jamaican laws and the first detailed map of settlement in the island. He died in 1684 and was buried in the cathedral at St Jago de la Vega. At his death he was the principal planter in Jamaica, owning 21,438 acres and a mansion of thirteen rooms. He left a lavish inventory, which included furnishings of £1236, silver worth £361, a coach, chariot and thirteen horses, and 100 books, as well as slaves and sugar-making utensils. His nephew Peter Beckford, whom Lynch appointed as captain of forts, succeeded him as the leading and wealthiest planter in Jamaica. TREVOR BURNARD

Sources *CSP col.*, vols. 1, 5 • PRO, CO 138/1–4 • R. S. Dunn, *Sugar and slaves* (1972) • S. S. Webb, *The governors general* (Chapel Hill, NC, 1979) • A. P. Thornton, *West India policy under the Restoration* (1955) • A. Whitson, *The constitutional development of Jamaica* (1929) • N. Zahedieh, 'The merchants of Port Royal, Jamaica', *William and Mary Quarterly*, 43 (1986), 570–93 • N. Zahedieh, 'A frugal, prudential, and hopeful trade', *Journal of Imperial and Commonwealth History*, 18 (1990), 145–68 • PRO, CO 1/19; CO 1/30 • W. Claypole, 'The merchants of Port Royal, 1655–1700', PhD diss., University of the West Indies, 1974 • *DNB* • *IGI*
Archives PRO, CO 138/1
Wealth at death over £10,000: inventories of Jamaica; Dunn, *Sugar and slaves*, 269

Lynch, Thomas Kerr (1818–1891), explorer in Mesopotamia, was the son of Major Henry Blosse Lynch (*d.* 1845) of Partry House, Ballinrobe, co. Mayo, and Elizabeth Lynch, *née* Finnis, of Hythe, Kent. He was the younger brother of Henry Blosse *Lynch and Patrick Edward *Lynch. His early years were spent at Partry, after which he entered Trinity College, Dublin. On leaving college he joined his brother Henry on the second Euphrates expedition of 1837–42, with the aim of establishing steam communication with the areas drained by the Euphrates and Tigris and the Persian Gulf. Ironically, the difficulties which he encountered proved the unattractiveness of the river compared with the sea route to India: but Lynch, with a brother, probably Henry, set up the Euphrates and Tigris Steam Navigation Company in 1862. Its steamers regularly plied the rivers and, because it was the only formal representation of British interests in the area, it received protection from the Foreign Office. Lynch travelled extensively in Mesopotamia and Persia. After his return home he was for some years consul-general for Persia in London. He was made knight of the Lion and Sun by the shah of Persia. Lynch died at his home at 33 Pont Street, London, on 23 December 1891, leaving a son and daughter from his marriage to Harriet. He was the author of *A Visit to the Suez Canal*, with ten illustrations (1866). ELIZABETH BAIGENT

Sources Burke, *Gen. Ire.* • *The Times* (29 Dec 1891) • *CGPLA Eng. & Wales* (1892) • R. A. Stafford, *Scientist of empire: Sir Roderick Murchison, scientific exploration and Victorian imperialism* (1989) • J. B. Kelly, *Britain and the Persian Gulf, 1795–1880* (1968)
Wealth at death £52,909 6*s.* 10*d.*: resworn probate, 5 Feb 1892, *CGPLA Eng. & Wales*

Lynch, Thomas Toke (1818–1871), hymn writer and composer, was born at Dunmow, Essex, on 5 July 1818, the son of John Burke Lynch, a surgeon. He was educated at a school in Islington, London, where he was afterwards an usher. In 1841 he became a Sunday school teacher and district visitor, occasionally preaching and giving lectures on sight-singing and temperance. In 1843 he entered Highbury (Independent) college, but shortly withdrew, mainly from ill health. He was pastor of Highgate Independent Church 1847–9, and then until 1852 of a congregation in Mortimer Street, which moved to Grafton Street, Fitzroy Square. In September 1849 he married Sarah, daughter of the Revd Edward Porter of Highgate, and in 1852 delivered a course of lectures on literature at the Royal Institution, Manchester. Ill health, from which he constantly suffered, prevented him from preaching for some years. He resumed in 1860 in Gower Street, pending the opening of Mornington Church in the Hampstead Road (pulled down in 1888 for the expansion of Euston Station), where he worked until his death on 9 May 1871 at his home, 76 Arlington Street, Regent's Park.

Lynch's congregations were always small, and he was not a popular preacher. His *Hymns for Heart and Voice: the Rivulet*, a book of a hundred poems and hymns published in 1855, gave rise to a bitter controversy which deeply affected the nonconformist churches in England, particularly the Congregationalists and Baptists. Lynch's aim was to unite his appreciation of God's work in nature and history with a firm grasp of Christian truth, but his naturalistic imagery provoked a series of vituperative reviews from Calvinists in the religious press, in which the verses were described as pantheistic and theologically unsound. The so-called Rivulet controversy almost resulted in the dissolution of the assembly of the Congregational Union of England and Wales. Lynch himself replied to his opponents, under the pseudonym Silent Long, in *The Ethics of quotation*, and in a pamphlet of doggerel verse entitled *Songs Controversial* (1856). The dispute was eventually settled by the intervention of Thomas Binney. Lynch's most notable hymns are 'Lift up your heads, rejoice', 'All faded is the glowing light', and 'Where is thy God, my soul?' He was also a composer, and set twenty-five of his own tunes to his hymns; these were published posthumously.

J. C. HADDEN, *rev.* LEON LITVACK

Sources W. White, *Memoir of Thomas Toke Lynch* (1874) • *A critical and descriptive notice of the Rev. T. T. Lynch, reprinted, with additions, from the Marylebone Mercury* (1859) • J. Julian, ed., *A dictionary of hymnology*, rev. edn (1907) • E. Routley, *An English-speaking hymnal guide* (1979) • D. Campbell, *Hymns and hymn makers*, 5th edn (1912) • J. I. Jones and others, *The Baptist hymn book companion*, ed. H. Martin (1962) • J. Moffatt and M. Patrick, eds., *Handbook to the church hymnary, with supplement*, 2nd edn (1935) • K. L. Parry, ed., *Companion to 'Congregational praise'* (1953) • S. Cox, *Divine sympathy and help: a funeral sermon preached for the Rev. T. T. Lynch* (1871) • *CGPLA Eng. & Wales* (1871)
Wealth at death under £1500: probate, 10 Nov 1871, *CGPLA Eng. & Wales*

Lynch, William Fanaghan [Liam] (1893–1923), clerk and Irish revolutionary, was born on 9 November 1893 in Barnagurraha, co. Limerick, the fifth of seven children of Jeremiah Lynch (1845–1914) and his wife, Mary Kelly, on their farm. Liam, as he was familiarly known, attended school in nearby Anglesboro until 1909 and always remained deeply attached to his family and home. In 1910, however, he began an apprenticeship in a hardware store in Mitchelstown, in north Cork. After completing his three years he found permanent employment as a clerk in Fermoy.

Lynch was an ardent partisan of the Irish party and joined the Ancient Order of Hibernians and the Irish National Volunteers. His patriotism was romantic in nature—as expressed in his membership of the Gaelic League—and charged with a sense of historical grievance.

This passionate nationalism overwhelmed his party allegiance in May 1916 when aroused by the sight of the rebel Kent brothers being marched through Fermoy as prisoners in the wake of the Easter rising. Lynch then embraced the republican cause with the love of a religious convert. He helped reorganize the Irish Volunteers (IRA) in Fermoy in 1917 and was elected as an officer of the company. Tall, bespectacled, and very shy, Lynch had a 'priestly' manner and was by no means a natural leader: he made himself one through the force of his own convictions. He became the adjutant of the Fermoy battalion later in 1917, spent much of 1918 as a full-time organizer, and was elected the first commander of the 2nd (North) Cork brigade in January 1919.

Although eager for direct action Lynch dutifully waited for permission from the Dublin general headquarters to launch his first attack. This came in September 1919 when he led an ambush of a military party in Fermoy. The guerrillas succeeded in capturing the vital rifles but Lynch was wounded in the shoulder. Forced to go on the run while recuperating, he left his job behind for good.

At this point Lynch declared an Irish republic to be eighteen months away, revealing an optimism which sustained his efforts until the end. Most of his time was spent in a succession of farmhouse headquarters, punctuated by visits home and to Dublin. Here he came to know Sean Treacy, Michael Collins, and other leaders of the revolution. Lynch turned down the job of deputy chief of staff to return in March 1920 to Cork, where he became the *de facto* governor of his brigade area, dealing with crime, labour, and trade disputes. He also took part in a series of famous episodes, including the kidnapping of General Lucas, his British opposite number, in June. After October 1920 his fighting career took second place to organizational work. The inter-brigade conferences he hosted helped pave the way for the establishment in April 1921 of the 1st southern division, incorporating co. Cork, co. Kerry, co. Waterford, and part of co. Limerick. Lynch was its founding commander, thereby trading a position of active authority for one with vague duties and almost no staff.

The truce of July 1921 allowed Lynch to create a proper divisional apparatus—the most powerful in Ireland. The Anglo-Irish treaty of 6 December gave it a new political purpose. He opposed the agreement but he was equally committed to republican reconciliation. Thus, after rejecting the authority of the pro-treaty general headquarters in January 1922, he spent the following months negotiating with all factions to preserve a united front and stave off civil war.

The object of Lynch's efforts was an IRA convention, which would consider anti-treaty resolutions. The new provisional government ultimately banned the meeting. The republicans met regardless, voted Lynch to the top of the executive slate, and appointed him chief of staff.

Lynch had already defused a local crisis in Limerick, and now set about mending the split in IRA ranks. After much haggling he was able to strike a deal for shared authority within an effectively independent army. This new constitution was overtaken by events, however—chiefly the general election, which produced a large pro-treaty majority—and was defeated in convention in June 1922. Lynch found himself in a minority within a divided IRA.

Republican unity came with the provisional government's attack on the IRA executive's Dublin stronghold on 28 June. Lynch returned to Munster to establish a war headquarters. He continued to seek peace through negotiation, but the opposing national army had seized the initiative and pressed home its advantage. By August 1922 the IRA had been forced underground once again.

Once his own efforts had failed Lynch forbade any further attempts at a truce and warded off Eamon de Valera's attempts at political guidance. He remained firm in his belief in ultimate victory, even while his forces were decimated over the winter of 1922–3. His hopes increasingly relied on secret schemes which came to nothing, and he came under mounting pressure to convene a meeting of the army executive. He had moved his headquarters to Dublin in November 1922, but returned to Cork in February 1923 to meet the dissidents in his old division. The long-postponed executive conclave was finally held on 23 March, and Lynch found himself once again in a minority. Before the 'peace' issue could be resolved, Lynch's Tipperary hideout was discovered by free state troops on 10 April 1923. He was shot in a firefight as he tried to escape, and died that day in captivity in Clonmel. He was buried in Kilcrumper graveyard, outside Mitchelstown, on 15 April.

PETER HART

Sources F. O'Donoghue, *No other law* (1954) • P. Hart, *The I.R.A. and its enemies* (1998) • NL Ire., Florence O'Donoghue MSS • University College, Dublin, Richard Mulcahy MSS • University College, Dublin, Ernie O'Malley MSS • private information (2004) • S. Lankford, *The hope and the sadness* (1980) • Irish Military Archives, Dublin, Michael Collins MSS • M. Hopkinson, *Green against green: the Irish civil war* (1988) • C. S. Andrews, *Dublin made me* (1979) • M. Ryan, *Liam Lynch: the real chief* (1986)

Archives Irish Military Archives, Dublin, Michael Collins MSS • NL Ire., Florence O'Donoghue MSS • University College, Dublin, Richard Mulcahy MSS • University College, Dublin, Ernie O'Malley MSS

Likenesses photograph, *c.*1918, NL Ire. • group portrait, photograph, 1922, repro. in G. Morrison, *The Irish Civil War* (1981) • Sheehan, oils, NG Ire.

Wealth at death £309 5*s.* 7*d.*: administration, 1923, *CGPLA Éire*

Lynd, Robert Wilson (1879–1949), journalist and essayist, was born in Belfast on 20 April 1879, the second of the seven children of a Presbyterian minister, the Revd Robert John Lynd and his wife, Sarah Rentoul, who was the daughter of the Revd John Rentoul of Ballymoney, Antrim, who ran a private school for girls in Knock, Belfast. There were Presbyterian ministers among his ancestors on both sides, one of these, a great-grandfather, having emigrated from Scotland to Ireland. Lynd was educated at the Royal Belfast Academical Institution (1890–96), and at Queen's College (later Queen's University) where he graduated in 1899 and from which he received the honorary degree of DLitt in 1946. It was here that his nationalism, socialism, and love for sport were forged.

In 1900 Lynd worked at Manchester for three months on

the *Daily Dispatch*, and then moved to London where he believed he could make a career in literature. Sharing a studio in Kensington with an artist from Ulster, Paul Henry, he lived hungrily on freelance journalism and the conversation of his friends from 1901 to 1908. His first regular job was on the staff of the twopenny weekly *To-Day*, where he was paid 30s. a week for writing essays, dramatic criticism, book reviews, and gossip, a salary which was raised to 2 guineas when he also contributed short stories. A little later he added to his earnings by writing book reviews for *Black and White*.

In 1908 Lynd joined the *Daily News*, at first as assistant literary editor under R. A. Scott-James. He became literary editor towards the end of 1912 and remained on the paper (which became the *News Chronicle* in 1930) until near the end of his life. Although the space allotted to reviews dwindled, he added distinction to his paper with signed essays and characteristic descriptive accounts of football and cricket matches and other public events. But the best of his journalistic work appeared in weekly papers, first in *The Nation* and then, from 1913 until the end of the Second World War, in the *New Statesman*. For more than three decades many thousands of readers turned to the *New Statesman* to read his genial, witty essays, signed Y. Y. Collected volumes of his essays appeared at frequent intervals. In 1906–7 he wrote for *The Republic*, the organ of the Irish Republican Brotherhood, and maintained close connections with the Gaelic League in London. In 1905 he contributed 'A plea for extremism' to *Uladh* under the pseudonym Riobard ua Floinn, calling for support of all aspects of Irish culture. His *Rambles in Ireland* was published in 1912, with illustrations by Jack B. Yeats. And in 1917, he published *If the Germans Conquered England*, an ironic pamphlet responding to the executions that took place during the Easter rising. *Ireland a Nation* (1919) was Lynd's most specifically political book, which he described as 'a cold blooded appeal to reason on behalf of Irish nationalism'. In the 1920s he continued to plead Ireland's case in the *New Statesman* and the *Daily News*, though he separated from Sinn Féin. His other books include *The Art of Letters* (1920) and the very successful *Dr. Johnson and Company* (1927).

Lynd was a romantic personality and a Romanticist in temperament. His broad brow and wavy hair, lustrous dark eyes, and regular nose and chin made up a face which was arresting and genial. Devotion to Ireland and Irish nationalism gave a background to his interests, which in the main were humanistic and literary. He was at his best as a light essayist and he wrote innumerable essays on trifling everyday topics, half-serious, half-whimsical, witty, gracious, engaging—delightful because they are the quintessence of an almost Elian personality.

On 21 April 1909 Lynd married Sylvia Dryhurst (*c*.1888–1952), daughter of Albert Robert Dryhurst, assistant secretary at the British Museum. She was a journalist and became a novelist and poet and a leading member of the Book Society committee. Their home in Hampstead was the resort of those in literary circles. They had two daughters. Enjoying conviviality in all its forms, a good talker and a good listener, generous, gentle, humorous, and modest, Lynd had a host of friends. In 1942 he was knocked down by a motor cycle and suffered several broken ribs. In consequence he suffered much pain, but went on writing. He died at his home, 5 Keats Grove, Hampstead, London, on 6 October 1949 of emphysema and was buried in Belfast city cemetery. In 1990 a selection of his Irish writings was edited by Sean McMahon as *Galway of the Races: Selected Essays*.

R. A. SCOTT-JAMES, *rev.* SAYONI BASU

Sources S. McMahon, 'Introduction', in R. W. Lynd, *Galway of the races: selected essays*, ed. S. McMahon (1990) · *The Times* (7 Oct 1949) · D. MacCarthy, 'Introduction', in R. W. Lynd, *Essays on life and literature* (1951) · *John O'London's Weekly* (1 April 1949) · R. Welch, ed., *The Oxford companion to Irish literature* (1996) · *CGPLA Eng. & Wales* (1950)
Archives BL, letters from Rebecca West, RP3186
Likenesses photograph, *c*.1913–1914, NPG · photograph, 1917, repro. in R. Lynd, *Books and writers* (1952), frontispiece · Trefusis, sketch, 1925, repro. in R. W. Lynd, *Galway of the races: selected essays*, ed. S. McMahon (1990) · D. Low, pencil cartoon, *c*.1926, NPG · photogravure, pubd 1926 (after D. Low), NPG · H. Coster, photographs, 1933, NPG · H. Lamb, chalk drawing, *c*.1950, NG Ire., NPG · Lady Kennet, bronze bust, Queen's University, Belfast
Wealth at death £1991 4s. 3d.: administration, 7 March 1950, *CGPLA Eng. & Wales*

Lynde, Sir Humphrey (*bap*. **1579**, *d*. **1636**), religious controversialist, was baptized on 24 August 1579 at St Margaret's, Westminster, London, the eldest of four sons and two daughters of Cuthbert Lynde (*d*. 1608), latterly a prominent member of the Grocers' Company and citizen of London, and his wife, Margery, *née* Baylie (*d*. in or after 1608). He was educated at Westminster School, being a queen's scholar and victor, and at Christ Church, Oxford, where he matriculated in 1597 and graduated in 1600. He began his MA, being one of the two bachelors chosen for the influential university post of collectors, who divided the determining bachelors into classes and organized their disputations. According to Anthony Wood he continued no further because a relative left him an estate. In June 1601 he was admitted to the Middle Temple, London. His father's death in 1608 brought him appreciable wealth.

By young manhood Lynde had come to a very strong protestant faith, and he became increasingly widely read in theology. On 31 January 1610 he married at St Martin-in-the-Fields, London, Elizabeth, daughter of Sir Alexander Brett (*d*. 1609) of Whitestaunton, Somerset, and his wife, Anne Gifford. The family was a recusant one, but Lynde evidently claimed Elizabeth for protestantism. Daniel Featley described this as a match

> made in heaven before it was consummate on earth, for he affianced his Spouse to Christ before he contracted her to himselfe … and by thus uniting her to himselfe by spirituall as well as carnall bonds, he had her heart knit unto him to his last breath: and in the Kalendar which hee made of all Gods blessings, … he put her as the chiefest. (Featley, 215)

They had three surviving sons and six daughters.

On 11 November 1613 Lynde was knighted at Royston by James I, according to John Chamberlain on payment of £500. By 1614 he and his wife owned the manor of Clapham, Surrey, which they sold. He may then have leased a house at Twickenham, Middlesex, where several children were born between 1618 and 1626. He inherited or bought land in Cobham, Surrey, which became his country home, and became a JP and commissioner in the shire. His close friendship with Richard Chamberlain, clerk of the wards on the court of wards and liveries, and with Sir Walter Pye, king's attorney there, make it possible that they were once colleagues. He became MP for Brecknockshire in 1626, when Sir Walter decided to sit for Herefordshire after being elected for both. He was active on committees connected with religion, such as that considering if Bishop Richard Mountagu's books were harmful, and one on excommunication, besides those on local and general issues, but in 1628 apparently stood down in favour of Sir Walter's son.

Lynde could have held higher office, but preferred to devote much of his time to theology. His views caused him to become friends with the earls of Lincoln and Warwick, Sir Henry Hastings, Thomas Gataker, Daniel Featley (chaplain to Archbishop George Abbot), and probably others in his circle. He always accepted the doctrine and discipline of the Church of England, and wanted to receive communion kneeling when mortally ill, praying, 'O Lord, accept the will for the deed: I bow the knees of my heart unto thee, though I cannot of my body' (Featley, 217).

In 1623 his cousin Edward Bugges sought Lynde's help, when conversion to Roman Catholicism was pressed on him on the grounds that there was no protestant church before Luther, and no salvation apart from Rome. Ultimately, finding Bugges with the Jesuit John Fisher, Lynde debated these questions with him. Later he invited Dr Featley and Dr Francis White, dean of Carlisle, to his London house in Sheer Lane for an after-dinner debate with Fisher and others in the presence of his family, friends, and Bugges, with carefully minuted proceedings. After four hours Fisher refused to answer. The king was pleased, and ordered Featley to publish *The Roman Fisher Caught* (1624), but forbade further debate.

That year Lynde began contributing to the wider controversy about whether the Roman church was a true one by publishing material defending Anglican theology, starting with *The Book of Bertram the Priest* (1623), a translation of a Carolingian work which maintained that the eucharist gave spiritual food, but denied transubstantiation. This was followed in 1625 by his first original work, *Antient Characters of the Visible Church*. In 1628 these arguments were developed in *Via tuta, or, The Safe Way*, dedicated to the religious and well-affected gentry of the realm, and were argued very lucidly and succinctly in short chapters. Lynde attacked Roman Catholicism for deviating from the faith and practice of the early church, and, by the Council of Trent, for making articles such as the papal supremacy, which he argued was contrary to scripture and early church history, an essential part of Roman faith. He contended that from the seventh century the Roman church had deviated gradually from apostolic faith over such matters as vernacular service and 'worship' of images, whereas the Anglican church was now true to original Christian doctrine, and was therefore the safe way to salvation. Lynde followed this in 1630 with *Via devia* in a similar format. This was dedicated to the 'ingenuous' and moderate Romanists of the kingdom, offering to accept a heretic's punishment if he did not prove the faith he professed ancient and catholic. He attacked Rome's inconsistency in stating its faith was scriptural, yet preventing the laity from reading the Bible, and suggested its real motivation was to stop people discovering how their doctrine was contradicted by scripture. He contended that most erroneous Roman Catholic doctrine was based on tradition and lacked antiquity and universality, and that the most substantial part of Roman teaching did not derive from the primitive church and was not accepted by the early fathers and councils. Since it had not been called by the emperor, and was neither general nor free, the Council of Trent was invalid.

These two works constituted almost a new genre, written by a cultivated gentleman for his peers, and enjoyed wide and lasting fame and influence. Sir Francis Herris mentions *Via tuta* as having brought about his conversion in 1628. Both books were translated into French in 1645, and were much reprinted in Britain, including a nineteenth-century edition to stem conversions from Anglo-Catholicism to Roman Catholicism. *Via tuta* was also contemporaneously translated into Dutch and Latin. In response to Lynde, John Floyd, sometimes identified with the Jesuit Robert Jenison, published *A Pair of Spectacles for Sir Humphrey Linde to See his Way Withal* (1631), arguing that he had failed to show where the Anglican church was before Luther. Lynde replied with *A Case for the Spectacles*, published posthumously as Laud refused to license it earlier, allegedly because he was a layman, but probably because he disagreed with its theology. John Heigham contributed with *Via vere tuta* (1631), largely invective which does not seriously answer Lynde's arguments; and other similar works followed. After his death Featley contributed to the debate with *Stricture in Lyndomastigem*, defending his friend's views and strengthening the anti-popery and anti-Arminian arguments of the time.

Lynde suffered violent fits and terrifying pains in his last illness, possibly as a result of prostate and brain cancer, but remained lucid. He made a final public profession of faith to prevent any rumours that he had been reconciled to Rome. He reported to his wife and Featley that he had seen a vision of himself presented before God in a shining damask robe. He died at Cobham on 8 June 1636, and was buried in the chancel of the parish church on 14 June, survived by his wife. ELIZABETH ALLEN

Sources W. B. Bidwell and M. Jansson, eds., *Proceedings in parliament, 1626*, 2: *House of Commons* (1992), 19, 205–6, 305, 340–41, 374; 3: *House of Commons* (1992), 97, 180, 189–90, 340, 405, 444 · D. Featley, *A sermon preached at the funerall of the Right Worshipfull Sir Humphrey Lynd, knight* (1638), 215–19 · *DNB* · Wood, *Ath. Oxon.*, 1st edn, 1.513–14 · *VCH Surrey*, 4.39 · PRO, PROB/11/112, fols. 82v, 83r · parish register, Westminster, St Margaret's, 13 Dec 1577, City Westm. AC [marriage] · parish register, Westminster, St Margaret's, 24 Aug 1579, 4 Aug 1580, 15 Aug 1581, 17 Oct 1581, 31 Jan 1586, City Westm. AC [baptisms] · W. A. Shaw, *The knights of England*, 2 (1906), 153 · T. Mason, ed., *A register of baptisms, marriages, and burials in the parish of St Martin in the Fields ... from 1550 to 1619*, Harleian Society, register section, 25 (1898), 92 · [T. Birch and R. F. Williams], eds., *The court and times of James the First*, 2 (1848), 408–9 · will, PRO, PROB/11/171, fols. 220v, 221r, 221v · A. Searle, ed., *Barrington family letters, 1628–*

1632, CS, 4th ser., 28 (1983), 42 • E. Poole, *The illustrated history and biography of Brecknockshire* (1886), 394–5 • *The letters of John Chamberlain*, ed. N. E. McClure, 1 (1939), 484 • Foster, *Alum. Oxon.* • H. A. C. Sturgess, ed., *Register of admissions to the Honourable Society of the Middle Temple, from the fifteenth century to the year 1944*, 1 (1949), 78 • *VCH Somerset*, 4.232–3, 237–8 • F. Brown, 'The Brett family', *Proceedings of the Somersetshire Archaeological and Natural History Society*, 28/2 (1882), 79–88, esp. 83–4

Wealth at death exact sum unknown; all lands, chattels, tenements, and leases to wife and Richard Chamberlain: will, PRO, PROB/11/171, fols. 220*v*–221*v*

Lyndhurst. For this title name *see* Copley, John Singleton, Baron Lyndhurst (1772–1863).

Lyndsay [Lindsay], **Sir David** (*c.*1486–1555), writer and herald, was the eldest son of David Lyndsay (*d.* in or before 1524), who held lands in the Mount, located just outside Cupar in Fife, and in Garleton, near Haddington in East Lothian. The identity of his mother is unknown. He had four brothers: John, Alexander, Patrick, and another David.

Early life and education Little is known of Lyndsay's early life and education. He was probably born in Fife and most likely received schooling either privately within his father's household or at the grammar schools of Cupar or Haddington. That he did receive at least a grammar school level education is borne out by the knowledge of Latin that he displays in his writings. It is not clear whether he attended a university. In 1508–9 one 'Da. Lindsay' is listed among the students of St Salvator's College at St Andrews University. However, Lyndsay is rarely referred to as 'maister' by contemporaries. This suggests that if he did attend university he never completed his degree. At what point he entered into service at the court of James IV is also obscure. A mention of a Lyndesay as having been employed in the service of the short-lived infant Prince James in 1508 may well be a reference to the poet. About this time Lyndsay also appears to have been granted the rights to the Garleton property previously held by his grandfather (also David Lyndsay) who died in 1503. This may suggest that he was at this point setting out on an independent career. In 1511 a pension of £40 was awarded to a David Lyndsay who was probably the writer. Later that same year payment was made to David Lyndsay for a play coat for a dramatic piece performed before James IV and Queen Margaret Tudor at Holyrood Abbey. Lyndsay's later involvement in court pageantry makes it very probable that this was indeed he.

Lyndsay's own account in 'The Complaynt of Schir David Lindesay' makes it clear that he was appointed usher to James V shortly after James's birth on 12 April 1512. He received an annual payment of £40 for this post and held it until 1522. In 1517 he is referred to as master of the household. While it is unlikely that Lyndsay actually held this prestigious position, which was in 1516 held by the duke of Argyll, it is possible that he was carrying out the duties of the post in the duke's absence. Lyndsay also appears to have been present at an alleged incident in Linlithgow in 1513, shortly before the battle of Flodden, when a robed figure appeared to James IV in St Michael's Church and warned him of the dangers of going to war. George Buchanan claims to have heard the story from Lyndsay himself, but it is unclear whether it is based on an actual incident or is an invention after the fact.

Career at court, 1522–1542 About 1522 Lyndsay married Janet Douglas (*d.* 1542x55). Little is known of her background, but the fact that Lyndsay incorporated the heart which was the heraldic emblem of the Douglases into his own family coat of arms suggests that she was well born. In 1524, presumably consequent on the death of his father, Lyndsay inherited the estate of the Mount in Fife. Also in 1524 the twelve-year-old James V was declared to be of age and Margaret Tudor, the king's mother, began to rule in his name. This resulted in Lyndsay's losing the post of master usher as Margaret set about filling the court with her own allies and associates. This would appear to have been merely a matter of political expediency rather than personal animosity, however, as his pension continued to be paid throughout the mid-1520s and he seems to have remained associated with the court, albeit in a more marginal position than previously. Lyndsay's diminished role at court continued through the period 1525–8 when Archibald Douglas, earl of Angus, seized custody of the king and took over the reins of government. He was only restored to favour after James escaped from the Douglases in 1528.

The period 1528–30 saw a considerable degree of literary activity from Lyndsay, all of which was produced in the environment of James V's court. It was probably about 1528 that Lyndsay's first extant poetic composition 'The Dreme of Schir David Lyndesay of the Mount, Familiar Servitour to our Soverane Lord King James the Fyft' was completed, though the text may be a revision of material composed in 1526. The poem, in which the narrator is led by Dame Remembraunce through hell, purgatory, heaven, and earth, includes a reminder to the king of his childhood closeness to Lyndsay (ll. 8–13). This may be a covert appeal for Lyndsay to be restored to a prominence befitting his intimacy with the monarch. In 1530 he produced 'The Complaynt of Schir David Lindesay', an overt petition to the king for advancement at court. In December 1530 Lyndsay completed his most significant work of this period, 'The Testament and Complaynt of our Soverane Lordis Papyngo'. In this poem the tale of the death of a parrot serves as a moral exemplum which leads to the delivery of advice on how James should govern, how the courtiers should conduct themselves, and how the clergy should be reformed. These poems demonstrate a socially engaged attitude which characterizes all of Lyndsay's writings, emphasizing the injustice which results if monarch, nobility, or clergy fail to recognize their social responsibilities. The poems also feature Lyndsay's earliest engagement with ideas of religious reform. At this stage in his career, while he certainly advocates reform, it is not evident that he is much influenced by specifically protestant thinking. His emphasis is predominantly on the clergy's social abuses and the need for the secular authorities to take action to rectify matters. This position does not necessarily involve opposition to

Roman Catholicism, focusing as it does on the conduct of the clergy rather than on the constitution or doctrine of the church. Nevertheless, some elements of the poems may indicate the influence of protestant ideas. 'The Dreme' expresses some hesitancy as to the doctrine of purgatory (ll. 344–50). 'The Testament' urges that the clergy should be permitted to wed 'with lycence of the Pape' (l. 1055), a proviso which seems merely sarcastic given the papacy's intransigence on the question of clerical celibacy. But while these aspects of the poems indicate that Lyndsay may have been to some degree influenced by protestant thought, it is the need for less radical reforms in order to counteract the clergy's exploitation of the populace that Lyndsay chooses to emphasize most heavily. 'The Testament' also provides a list of great English and Scottish writers that indicates in Lyndsay a strong interest in the value of vernacular writing, another theme which recurs in his work.

In 1530 Lyndsay was appointed Snowdon herald, for which he received livery and an annual fee of £40. He is referred to twice in the 1530s as Lyon king of arms, the chief heraldic post in Scotland: once on an embassy to England and once in his involvement in the funeral of James V's first wife. Since the title of Lyon king was held until 1542 by Thomas Pettigrew, it is probable that Lyndsay was asked to step into the role for important state occasions when Pettigrew was for some reason incapable of serving. As a herald, Lyndsay's duties entailed serving as a messenger for the king, assisting in royal ceremonies, pageantry, and festivities, and administration of matters of noble lineage and heraldry. The role involved Lyndsay in a considerable degree of foreign travel. In the summer of 1531 he was dispatched to Flanders in order to negotiate a continuing trade agreement and seek recompense for acts of piracy against Scottish ships. He also corresponded with James V, giving information on the social and political situation in the Netherlands. In addition, he carried a portrait of Dorothea of Denmark back to the king as a preliminary step in marriage negotiation. Lyndsay's involvement in James's marriage negotiations was stepped up in 1532 when he travelled to France via England as part of an embassy sent to seek the ratification of the 1517 treaty of Rouen, which promised a marriage alliance between James V and a French princess. Lyndsay's role was probably less to take an active part in the negotiations and more to keep James in touch with their progress. He left France before the embassy was concluded and returned to Scotland, when he reported back to James. Lyndsay was very shortly sent back to France to present a letter from James to François I of France, before returning to Scotland in November 1532. Lyndsay returned to France in 1534 to assist in furthering negotiations for James's marriage to Princess Madelaine of France, and probably returned to Scotland towards the end of that year. On 23 August 1535 he was in attendance at the English court with Lord Erskine, who received the Order of the Garter in James V's name. Erskine left England for France shortly afterwards but it is not known whether Lyndsay accompanied him or returned to Scotland. In any case Lyndsay was certainly again in France in 1536 in preparation for the royal marriage between James and Madelaine, which occurred on new year's day 1537. A short time after the wedding Lyndsay was granted 20 crowns to return to Scotland ahead of the king and his new bride. This suggests that he was being dispatched to assist in preparing the festivities for the return of James and Madelaine, though, as it transpired, the preparations turned out to be for the new queen's funeral.

Lyndsay seems to have played little part in the negotiations of James V's second marriage, to Mary of Guise-Lorraine, and from this point until the king's death his duties were exclusively carried out within Scotland. He was involved, however, in organizing Mary's reception in Scotland in 1538. He played important roles in the pageantry on her arrival at St Andrews, where she appears to have been publicly welcomed by him with advice on wifely obedience. He was also heavily involved in arranging the festivities on her entry into Edinburgh, where Lyndsay again played a role in greeting her and was involved in composing a poem of welcome. In 1540 he helped entertain the English envoy Sir Ralph Sadler, who had come to seek to persuade James to institute religious reforms in line with those instituted by Henry VIII in England. Lyndsay's pro-reform beliefs may have made him seem to James to be a most appropriate candidate for such a task. In 1540 Lyndsay was also involved in the arrest of Sir James Hamilton of Finnart, master of works, formerly a favourite of the king. Lyndsay's involvement was in his capacity as Lyon king of arms and he was not involved in engineering the arrest. Robert Lindesay of Pitscottie claimed that Hamilton's fall was engineered by supporters of religious reform who feared that the master of works had been recruited by the clergy as part of a campaign to persecute nobles suspected of heresy. If this was indeed the case, the incident indicates the heightening tensions between Catholic and reforming factions at court and underlines the fact that Lyndsay's own sympathies towards the reformers placed him at risk from an increasingly hardline clergy.

There are five surviving poems from Lyndsay written between 1530 and 1542. 'The Answer quhilk Schir David Lindesay Maid to the Kingis Flyting' was composed some time before 1537 and, in the tradition of flyting verse, abuses the king, attacking him for his promiscuity. Lyndsay, however, gives the flyting a moral twist, transforming it from gratuitous insult into moral exhortation against sensuality. The poem demonstrates Lyndsay's participation in court entertainment as well as his ongoing concern that monarch and court retain their dignity. 'The Complaint and Public Confessioun of the Kingis Auld Hound, callit Bagsche' can only be dated from some time in the 1530s. A mock complaint from the mouth of a dog, this poem sees Lyndsay continuing his concern over the conduct of the court, warning courtiers of the dangers of excessive ambition. 'The Deploration of the Deith of Quene Magdalene' was composed shortly after Madelaine's death in July 1537 and is an ornate piece, based on French models, which ceremoniously honours the dead queen. 'Ane Suplication Directit frome Schir David Lyndesay, Knycht, to the Kyngis Grace, in Contemptioun of Syde Tallis' was composed some time between 1537 and 1542, and is a comic moralizing complaint against the pride taken in new fashions. The poem is evidently written for the entertainment of the court. 'The Justing betwix James Watsoun and Jhone Barbour' was composed some time between 1538 and 1540. This comic poem describes a mock tournament between two inappropriate combatants, and was again clearly written as a piece of courtly entertainment. A striking feature of Lyndsay's writings in this period is that, unlike his earlier writings, it focuses almost exclusively on courtly issues, with little attention paid to the problems of clerical corruption. This no doubt reflects the extent to which Lyndsay was at this time immersed in the business of court. It also perhaps suggests that, with James V firmly installed in power, Lyndsay considered the conduct of the monarch and his nobility as being of primary importance in influencing Scottish society, and turned his attention there accordingly. One further poem from this period sometimes attributed to Lyndsay does deal with religious reform: 'Kitteis Confessioun', a satire on the Roman Catholic sacrament of confession. If the poem is indeed by Lyndsay, it is clear evidence of his being directly influenced in this early stage of his writing career by protestant critique of Catholic doctrine, despite his focus on courtly issues. Confession, however, is not a topic which Lyndsay devotes much attention to elsewhere in his writings, and the attribution seems doubtful.

In early 1540 Lyndsay was probably involved in the production of a dramatic entertainment played before the king and some English visitors at Linlithgow Palace, and he may in fact have been the author of the piece. Only a description of the play survives: it featured a poor man presenting a complaint to parliament with the proceedings being supervised by a king, and contained considerable anti-clerical comment. The structural parallels with the second half of *Ane satire of the thrie estaitis* has led some critics to argue that this was in fact the first version of Lyndsay's most famous work. The parallels, however, are not extensive. It thus seems more likely that Lyndsay incorporated material from this earlier piece when later composing the more extensive *Ane satire*, just as he incorporated material from his other earlier works, such as 'The Testament [of the] Papyngo' and 'The Tragedie of the Cardinale'.

In October 1542 Lyndsay was officially appointed Lyon king of arms and received his knighthood. Lyndsay's completion of a register of coats of arms in 1542 may have been related to his official promotion to the post of chief heraldic officer. Strikingly, the text of the armorial register is almost entirely composed in the vernacular, indicating a strong commitment on Lyndsay's part to championing the authority of his mother tongue even for such an official and ceremonial purpose. The death of Lyndsay's wife, Janet Douglas, probably occurred about this time as she is not mentioned in any records after 1542 until 1555, when she is cited as being dead.

Retirement from court After the death of James V in December 1542, Lyndsay became closely involved with the new government of the regent, James Hamilton, second earl of Arran. Arran initially instituted a policy of toleration towards reformers and sought rapprochement with protestant England, and Lyndsay found himself once again involved in diplomatic duties. In the spring of 1543 he was sent to England to return James's Order of the Garter, and possibly travelled with an embassy sent to negotiate a marriage between the infant Mary, queen of Scots, and Prince Edward of England. Henry VIII commented in a letter to the earl of Arran that 'the said Lord Lyon used himself right Discretelye and much to our contentacioun' (*Works*, 4.269). That Lyndsay should have been sent to England at a time of such delicate negotiations is a sign of the high regard with which Arran viewed him and also that his sympathies were perceived to be in line with Arran's new policies. However, Lyndsay's time of prominence was brief, as by the end of 1543 Cardinal David Beaton had strengthened his grip on the reins of government, so that the policies of rapprochement with England and toleration of religious reformers soon lay in tatters. Lyndsay's position was made precarious by these developments. Accordingly, he retired from the court to his estate in Cupar in October 1543, and was still based there in March 1544. From then until the end of his life he was much less involved with the court than previously, though he did attend parliament in November 1544 and October 1545. In 1543 he received only part payment of his pension, and after this it was all but stopped entirely.

Lyndsay's retirement from the centre of government coincided with an intense heightening of religious tensions throughout the country and put him much more in touch with popular reforming sentiment. When Cardinal David Beaton was murdered at St Andrews Castle on 29 May 1546, the killers were known to Lyndsay as neighbouring landowners. Six months into the ensuing siege of the castle (which lasted fourteen months) the earl of Arran summoned Lyndsay to act, in the role of Lyon king, as an intermediary between the government forces and Beaton's killers to arrange a parley. The choice of Lyndsay for such a task indicates his status as both a trusted servant of the state and one known for reforming views, which would make his approach more palatable to those in the besieged group (as well as his being known personally by them). Lyndsay may have remained in contact with the group after his official task was finished. John Knox noted that, when the besieged band were debating whether they should invite him (Knox) to preach, Lyndsay was among them, though he was certainly not with them when St Andrews Castle finally fell.

It was probably no earlier than the beginning of 1547 that Lyndsay produced his poem 'The Tragedie of the Cardinale'. In this poem he depicts the ghost of the murdered Beaton condemning himself out of his own mouth as he narrates his life story while berating his own sinfulness. The poem is vituperative in its attack on the corruption of the Catholic clergy, reviling Beaton's pursuit of secular interests and interference in affairs of state as a neglect of his spiritual duties and misuse of his religious authority. The poem proposes a model of clerical behaviour that, in restricting the clergy to the pastoral care of their congregation's souls, would deprive the church of almost all influence in political decision making. Lyndsay's discussion of Beaton's murder is couched in terms which, in ascribing his death to the divine will, avoid condemning the deed and may even suggest approval of the murderers' actions. As with the attacks on the clergy in Lyndsay's earlier works, the criticism of Beaton is directed not towards doctrine but towards the cardinal's moral corruption and the social ills it brings about. This poem, though, is addressed to a wider audience than his earlier courtly works, suggesting that Lyndsay, by focusing on concrete practical effects ascribed to Beaton's malignity, is tapping directly into and seeking to inflame popular dissatisfactions over the role and conduct of the Catholic clergy. The poem, then, sees Lyndsay's reforming sentiments developing into a much more populist and outspoken mode of criticism than had been seen in his earlier attacks on the church. According to Lindesay of Pitscottie, the Dominican provincial council condemned and burned 'The Tragedie of the Cardinale' in 1549, though there is no extant documentation of this elsewhere.

Towards the end of 1548 Lyndsay was recalled to diplomatic duties when the earl of Arran sent him to Denmark to complain about acts of piracy against Scottish vessels and to seek military aid against the English, whose aggression against Scotland had increased after their victory at the battle of Pinkie. The Danes refused to send a fleet to aid in fighting the English, but were accommodating with regard to the piracy. Lyndsay also managed to arrange permission for Scots to trade arms in Denmark. His attempted return to Scotland in February 1549 was delayed when his ship was wrecked not long after setting out, giving him a close brush with death. He finally returned to Scotland in the spring of 1549, and does not appear to have travelled abroad after this. He was still involved in the administrative duties of his role as Lyon king of arms, and in 1550 he presided over a case between two gentlemen, both of the name Burnet, who were in dispute over which coats of arms they should bear.

In 1550 Lyndsay composed 'The Testament of ane Nobil and Wailyeand Squyer, William Meldrum'. The poem is a eulogy to William Meldrum, a friend and neighbour of Lyndsay in Fife. It takes the form of a chivalric romance, glorifying Meldrum's life by comparing him to other great heroes of romance. Lyndsay's treatment of the romance genre, however, raises questions about the propriety of Meldrum's amorous attachments. These are not couched in such a way as to satirize his friend, but they do suggest that Lyndsay entertained serious doubts about the courtly love ethos which was so closely associated with the chivalric ideal.

Final years Lyndsay's most famed literary achievements were reserved for his final years. *Ane satire of the thrie estaitis* was performed on Castle Hill at Cupar, Fife, in June 1552. The play is the only extant morality drama from Scotland, but that the genre was highly evolved is clear from Lyndsay's masterful and flexible handling of it, as he incorporates elements of other genres, such as the French *sotie*, and stresses the political as well as moral dimensions of the drama. Indeed, Lyndsay's play is one of the finest examples of the tradition in Britain. The play maintains, even after ten years of minority rule by an infant queen, a vision of society that is strongly focused on the king as the central figure, and it continues Lyndsay's long-standing concern with the proper ordering of the court as necessary for a healthy society. The play's criticisms of the clergy are much more openly influenced by protestant reformers than any of Lyndsay's previous works. For instance, it satirizes the Catholic clergy's claims that translation of the Bible is heresy, and the character of Veritie, who urges the dissemination of such translations, is overtly described as a Lutheran. In other respects the play continues Lyndsay's customary stresses on the social ills caused by a corrupt clergy, and on the need for the secular authorities to take the church in hand and impose reform on it. *Ane satire* is divided into two parts, the first dealing with the moral reform of the monarch and the court, the second addressing the reform of society in general through legislation enacted by the parliament. This structure suggests a significant tension in Lyndsay's attitudes. The first part ascribes central importance to the role of the monarch. In the second part, however, the king is almost totally passive and merely supervises the actions of the parliament, whose legislative powers are assigned the dominant role in producing reform. The second part, then, may suggest that Lyndsay experienced some dissatisfaction with a monarch-centred system which had led to twenty-five years of unstable minority rule between 1513 and 1552. The imbalance between the two parts suggests that while Lyndsay is unwilling or unable to radically remodel his conception of the monarch's role as the head of government, he simultaneously feels a desire for political authority to be more thoroughly invested in parliament. That the play was successful and memorable is indicated by its being performed two years later, on 12 August 1554, on Calton Hill in Edinburgh before an audience that included the regent, Queen Mary of Guise-Lorraine.

The year 1554 also saw the publication of what may be Lyndsay's most ambitious work, *Ane dialoge betuix experience and ane courteour*, also referred to as *The monarche*. This long poem of 6338 lines takes the form of a world history from the fall of Adam and Eve to the day of judgement. The poem's reforming emphasis is very strong: Lyndsay condemns, among other things, pilgrimages and the veneration of saints, the papacy, and the doctrine of purgatory. Moreover, in setting these issues within the framework of an eschatological history, Lyndsay presents the drive towards reform not just as necessary for the correction of social ills but sanctions it as an integral part of God's plan for humanity and the Scottish nation. Unsurprisingly, after the Reformation took effect in Scotland in 1560 *Ane dialoge* became Lyndsay's most popular work, being used to present the establishment of the kirk as the realization of a divinely appointed mission. *Ane dialoge* also contains a lengthy disquisition on the value of the vernacular, which Lyndsay praises for its utility in making important matters accessible to the populace as a whole and not just a narrow educated élite. This represents the clearest statement of the populist vision of reforming literature that Lyndsay developed in his later life.

Lyndsay was still acting as Lyon king of arms in 1554–5, though service at important state occasions had been passed on to up-and-coming heralds. At this time Lyndsay presided over a hearing at which a messenger, William Crawford, was accused of various abuses of his post. This is Lyndsay's last known act in his role as chief herald. He died in 1555, some time before 13 March, leaving no offspring.

David Lyndsay's reputation as a writer increased in the two centuries after his death, with his name becoming a byword for authoritative information. Since then, he has been overshadowed by the reputation of other Scottish writers, and while *Ane satire* has received widespread critical recognition in modern times, Lyndsay's poetry has been neglected until very recently. Yet while Lyndsay certainly never set out to be a virtuoso literary technician, his flexible command of literary forms, his appealing concern over social injustices, and his gift for the witty expression of serious ideas make the study of his writing highly rewarding. Recent criticism, notably the work of Janet Hadley Williams and Carol Edington, suggests that Lyndsay may again be coming to receive due recognition as a gifted artist as well as one of the most popular and eloquent voices of the Scottish Reformation.

J. K. McGinley

Sources J. B. Paul, ed., *Compota thesaurariorum regum Scotorum / Accounts of the lord high treasurer of Scotland*, 5 (1903), 196, 431; 6 (1905), 232, 423, 455–6; 7 (1907), 16; 8 (1908), 275, 403; 9 (1911), 259, 347 · *LP Henry VIII*, 9.151, 165; 15.248; 18/1.37 · G. Burnett and others, eds., *The exchequer rolls of Scotland*, 23 vols. (1878–1908), vol. 15, pp. 116, 229; vol. 16, p. 12 · *The works of Sir David Lindsay*, ed. D. Hamer, 4 vols., STS, 3rd ser., 1–2, 6, 8 (1931–6), vol. 2, pp. 2–6; vol. 4, pp. 255, 269 · J. M. Thomson and others, eds., *Registrum magni sigilli regum Scotorum / The register of the great seal of Scotland*, 11 vols. (1882–1914), vol. 2, p. 1633; vol. 3, pp. 2529, 2748; vol. 4, p. 1006 · *Facsimile of an ancient heraldic manuscript emblazoned by Sir David Lyndsay of the Mount, Lyon king of arms, 1542* (1822) · *The poetical works of Sir David Lyndsay of the Mount*, ed. G. Chalmers, 3 vols. (1806), vol. 1, p. 39 · R. Lindesay of Pitscottie, *The history & chronicle of Scotland*, ed. A. J. G. Mackay, 3 vols. (1928–34), vol. 1, pp. 244, 379 · G. Buchanan, *The history of Scotland from the earliest point of the regency of the earl of Moray*, ed. and trans. J. Aikman, 6 vols. (1845), vol. 2, p. 190 · M. Livingstone and others, eds., *Registrum secreti sigilli regum Scotorum*, 8 vols. (1908–), vol. 2, p. 4910 · *The works of John Knox*, ed. D. Laing, 6 vols., Wodrow Society, 12 (1846–64), vol. 1, p. 186 · *APS, 1424–1567*, 429, 438, 441 · A. Clifford, ed., *State papers of Sir Ralph Sadler*, 3 vols. (1809), vol. 1, p. 47 · *LP Henry VIII*, 4.581–2 · 'Instruction to David Lyndsay, 1548', NA Scot., RH 2/7/6, fol. 142 · J. D. Marwick, ed., *Extracts from the records of the burgh of Glasgow*, 2, Scottish Burgh RS, 12 (1881), 89, 196–7 · *City of Edinburgh old accounts*, 2 vols. (1899), vol. 1, p. 110 · C. Edington, *Court and culture in Renaissance Scotland: Sir David Lindsay of the Mount* (1994) · *Sir David Lyndsay: selected poems*, ed. J. Hadley Williams (2000) · J. Hadley Williams, 'David Lyndsay and the making of King James V', *Stewart style, 1513–1542: essays on the court of James V*, ed. J. Hadley Williams (1996), 201–26 · D. Lyndsay, *Ane satyre of the thrie estaitis*, ed. R. J. Lyall (1989)

Lyndwood, William (*c.*1375–1446), administrator, ecclesiastical lawyer, and bishop of St David's, was born in Linwood, near Market Rasen, Lincolnshire. One of the seven children of John Lyndwood (*d.* 1419), a successful woolman, and his wife, Alice, William Lyndwood is depicted as a child, but dressed precociously in the robes of a doctor of laws, on his father's monumental brass in Linwood parish church.

Education and early career The first step in Lyndwood's education that can be traced was as a commoner at Gonville Hall, Cambridge; an inscription by a window in the old library of Gonville and Caius College enjoined viewers to offer prayers on his behalf. However, only the outlines of his subsequent academic career are visible. He is reported to have become a fellow at Pembroke College, and at some point during these early years he moved to Oxford, where, according to Thomas Fuller, he 'proceeded doctor of laws (probably rather by incorporation than constant education' (Fuller, *Worthies*, 2.10). He was at any rate BCL by 1403 and DCnL and DCL by 1407, and Lyndwood himself referred to his having lectured on the canon law. He also took holy orders at about the same time; he was made deacon on 15 February 1404, and priest on 12 March 1407.

Only a little more than a year after receipt of his doctorate, Robert Hallum, bishop of Salisbury, commissioned Lyndwood to serve as official of his consistory court at Salisbury, the first step in a judicial career that led remarkably quickly to the highest judicial offices in the English church. In 1414 Archbishop Henry Chichele, with whom Lyndwood had been associated at Oxford, and to whom he later dedicated the *Provinciale*, nominated him as chancellor and auditor of causes in his court of audience. Three years later Lyndwood became the official principal of the court of arches in London. Court documents issued in his name have been preserved in contemporary formularies. Besides handling the ecclesiastical litigation routinely dealt with in these courts, he was delegated from time to time to judge a number of maritime cases, and he also took part in some of the prosecutions of Lollards that occurred during these years. Lyndwood served as prelocutor for the lower clergy at provincial convocations in 1419, 1421, 1424, 1425, and 1426, and in January 1431 he acted in the place of an indisposed Archbishop John Kemp of York, to deliver a sermon devoted to the blessings of unity within the realm at the opening of parliament.

Such an administrative and judicial career was not then thought incompatible with the holding of ecclesiastical benefices, at least if obtained with the proper dispensations, and Lyndwood accumulated a considerable number over the course of his career. In a purely economic sense, they were the base of that career, providing him with a stream of income without requiring performance of the duties associated with the cure of souls. The first recorded benefice came to him even before he had been ordained deacon. On 30 November 1396, through royal patronage he was preferred to the wardenship of St Nicholas's Hospital, Scarborough. To this benefice, he added the wardenship of St Mary's Chapel in Scarborough Castle on 25 January 1399. In November 1403 he became rector of Walton on the Wolds, Leicestershire. He had surrendered this rectory by March 1410, when he was collated to the benefice of Winfrith Newburgh, Dorset, a benefice he later surrendered in exchange for the parish of St Mary in Romney Marsh, Kent, in March 1417. In September 1411 he had received a papal dispensation allowing him to hold an additional incompatible benefice with or without cure of souls for seven years, a dispensation that was made perpetual in 1421. Following this grant, he became rector of Shoreham in Kent with the dependent chapel of Otford in October 1415 (vacated by August 1425), rector of All Hallows, Bread Street, London (vacant by August 1433, when he became rector of Wimbledon), and in 1424 rector of Tring in Hertfordshire (occupied until he became a bishop), a parish he remembered with the gift of a book in his will. In addition to these benefices, Lyndwood held prebends in what now seems an astonishingly large number of England's cathedral churches: Exeter, where he was canon and prebendary from 1419 to 1442; Hereford, where after a dispute with Thomas Berkeley in the 1420s he occupied the prebend of Hunderton until 1442; Lincoln, where he was archdeacon of Stow between 1434 and 1442; St David's, where he was canon and prebendary of Llanwrthwl from 1421 to 1442; Salisbury, where he held the prebend of Ruscombe Southbury from 1412 to 1424, and that of Bishopstone from 1424 to 1434; and Bath and Wells, where he was prebendary of Taunton from 1419 until 1433.

Diplomat and bishop As with many prominent civilians, Lyndwood's talents found an outlet in diplomacy. Already in July 1417 he had accompanied Henry Ware, keeper of the privy seal, to Calais to negotiate the extension of the truce with the duke of Burgundy. In 1422 he was sent to Portugal to help negotiate a treaty with that country, and in the following year he accompanied John Kemp on a diplomatic mission in France. In 1431 he was chosen to be a member of the retinue that attended the coronation of Henry VI as king of France on 16 December, and when he returned to England early the following year, he was appointed keeper of the privy seal. Subsequently he was involved in negotiations leading up to the Congress of Arras in 1435, and also in the formulation of several agreements with the Hanseatic League and other German interests, various commercial treaties in the Low Countries, and in 1438 a truce with the Scots.

Besides the continuing and active part he took in convocation, Lyndwood was called upon to give articulate voice to English interests at the Council of Basel (1431–2). He played a part in the foundation of Eton College, and was also appointed one of the commissioners responsible for drafting the statutes of King's College, Cambridge. Finally, and rather late in life for so prominent an ecclesiastic, he was given the Welsh bishopric of St David's after the death of Thomas Rodeburne in 1442. He was provided by the pope to the see on 27 June, received the temporalities on 14 August, and was consecrated on 26 August. He held the see until his death, which occurred on either 21 or 22 October 1446. His will was proved on 26 November 1446, and his body was buried in St Stephen's Chapel in the palace of Westminster, following the desires expressed in the will. The later history of the burial spot is uncertain, but in 1852 a body with a crosier thought to be Lyndwood's was discovered in the crypt. It was reinterred in Westminster Abbey in the north wall of the north cloister, a short distance from the east entrance door. The black marble ledger, under which it rests, is unfortunately now invisible because of construction carried out at a later date around the cloister door.

The *Provinciale*: its purpose and principal features Lyndwood's enduring reputation rests not on his career, successful though that was. It rests on the compilation of a single work, the *Provinciale*, which he had begun by 1422, while he was serving as judge in the court of arches, and which he had completed by January 1434. Although early references exist to two other works by Lyndwood, the one his lectures on the *Decretum Gratiani*, the other a commentary on a portion of the Psalms, the *Provinciale* alone has survived. It is a collection of the most important ecclesiastical legislation enacted within the province of Canterbury between the Council of Oxford in 1222 and Chichele's archiepiscopate. To these statutes, or constitutions as they were more properly called, Lyndwood added two royal responses to clerical demands made in the constitutions: the writ *Circumspecte agatis* (1286) and part of the *Articuli cleri* (1316). The completed *Provinciale* was accompanied by a comprehensive subject matter index, bearing a Latinized form of his name (Gulielmus de Tylia Nemore) and, more importantly, by his own extensive marginal gloss. In the fashion of the European *ius commune* (as the amalgam of Roman and canon law taught in continental universities was known), the gloss clarified the meaning of the constitutions, related them to the general law of the church, raised legal points of doubt and controversy, and commented upon their observance in the English spiritual courts.

The *Provinciale* belongs firmly within continental legal traditions. This is so not simply because the authorities Lyndwood cited were the treatises of continental jurists. It is also a fair assessment because, in so far as his great work has a theme, that theme is the harmonization of the English provincial constitutions with the law of the Western church. He organized his work into five books, each divided into separate titles, thereby following exactly the model of the basic canonical text, the *Decretales Gregorii IX* (1234), rather than the chronological order of the constitutions. Similarly, the work's first title is *De summa trinitate et de fide catholica*, just as it is in the *Decretals* and the Roman law codex. In it, Lyndwood placed a constitution from the Council of Lambeth (1281) designed 'for the information of simple priests' in the rudiments of the Christian faith (*Councils & Synods*, vol. 2, ed. F. M. Powicke and C. R. Cheney, 2 vols., 1964, 2.900).

It must be admitted that, despite Lyndwood's best

efforts, the fit between his project and the canonical texts of the Western church was far from perfect. Lyndwood was obliged by the material at his disposal to omit some of the titles that appeared in the *Decretals*. There is no heading *De rescriptis*, for instance. Papal rescripts of justice were not a subject treated by the English provincial constitutions. Moreover, local conditions required that some subjects be treated at greater length than is found in the *Decretals*. For example, Lyndwood's title *De testamentis* occupies a proportionally larger share than that same title does in the Gregorian *Decretals*—one result of the English church's more expansive jurisdiction over testamentary succession compared to that of most continental churches. Conversely, Lyndwood's title *De jure patronatus* occupies a lesser share of his treatment. The English royal courts kept spiritual jurisdiction over patronage questions within narrower limits compared to most places across the channel. Lyndwood was also obliged to put the law of defamation under the title *De sententia excommunicationis*, rather than the title *De iniuriis*, where a continental jurist would have thought it more apt, because defamation was incorporated into the decrees of the Council of Oxford (1222) excommunicating several kinds of violators of the church's laws.

Impact of the *Provinciale* Lyndwood's *Provinciale* filled a real need. The constitutions it collected and upon which its gloss commented were of immediate importance in the work of the English spiritual courts, and no other source dealt with them so directly. Lyndwood himself evidently held a high opinion of the value of his work. His will provided that it should be chained and kept in St Stephen's Chapel in Westminster Abbey, so that recourse could be had to it 'for the correction of other books to be copied from the same treatise' (Hunter, 419). The fate of this volume, or that of the other copy Lyndwood mentioned with particular approbation in his will, cannot now be discovered. It seems unlikely that a single archetype can be found, given the variations in the text and glosses in the fifty-five or so manuscripts that have survived to the present day.

By modern editing standards, Lyndwood's method of compiling the constitutions seems quite inadequate. He was guilty of false attributions and he transcribed some of the texts incorrectly. He seems to have deliberately changed the wording in a few instances. However, Lyndwood's goal was not to produce a historically accurate transcription. It was to produce a serviceable collection of texts and commentary, suitable for use in the everyday study and practice of ecclesiastical law in England. Subsequent experience shows that he did not miss the mark. That it was considered an economic proposition to reprint Lyndwood's work so many times is a tribute to its success. The constitutions around which it was built controlled the character of much of the litigation heard in the consistory courts, and Lyndwood's gloss is the best guide to that character. English parochial clergy, academics, and professional ecclesiastical lawyers all owned and used copies of this book.

The Reformation did not curtail its currency in England. Because the scope of ecclesiastical jurisdiction in England was not fundamentally changed during the sixteenth century, ecclesiastical lawyers continued to use the *Provinciale*. Its influence has been quite long-lasting. Edmund Gibson testified to its influence upon later generations in his *Codex juris ecclesiastici Anglicani* (1713), and in the twentieth century it was used in the draft revision of English canon law of 1947 produced by the Vaisey Commission. The relevance of its treatment of English ecclesiastical practice recommended it even to English common lawyers. Their citation of the glosses of the *Provinciale* when questions of ecclesiastical law arose in the royal courts is a continuing feature in sixteenth- and seventeenth-century reports.

Publications of the *Provinciale* Whatever the problems of textual transmission, the later history of the *Provinciale* amply confirms the high opinion Lyndwood and his contemporaries had of the work. It appeared in thirteen pre-1640 editions listed in the *Short-Title Catalogue*. The earliest was printed in Oxford, probably in 1483, under the imprint of Thomas Rood. An impressive volume of some 350 folios, it was not only larger than any book printed there for the next hundred years, it was also one of the first law books to be printed in England. An octavo edition, without the gloss, was published with Caxton's cipher at Westminster in 1496. This text was itself reprinted by the same editor with minor variations and abridgements in 1499, and also twice in that year by Richard Pynson. Other London editions appeared in 1517, 1529, and 1557. An English translation without the gloss was published by Robert Redman in 1534. Continental publishers also took it up. Folio editions of the work, including the entire gloss and supplements from the constitutions of cardinals Otto and Ottobuono (papal legates to England during the reign of Henry III), were published in Paris in 1501, 1504, and 1505, and an edition also appeared at Antwerp in 1525.

Thereafter the demand for it lessened, perhaps because of the extent of printing that had already occurred and the uncertainty about the future of the canon law in England that was caused by the Reformation. However, a later version, edited and abridged by Robert Sharrock of New College, Oxford, was printed there in 1664 under the title *Provinciale vetus provinciae cantuariensis*. This edition was followed quickly by what has become the standard edition, the *Provinciale (seu Constitutiones Angliae)* printed at Oxford in 1679. It includes Lyndwood's full gloss, the constitutions of Otto and Ottobuono, together with the gloss on them written about 1340 by John Atton (or Acton). Its reprinting in 1968 stands as a reminder that it deserves the accolade once conferred upon it by Thomas Fuller. He described it as a work 'highly esteemed by foreign lawyers', and as one that would 'be valued by the judicious whilst learning and civility have a being' (Fuller, *Church History*, 1.500). R. H. Helmholz

Sources B. E. Ferme, *Canon law in late medieval England: a study of William Lyndwood's 'Provinciale' with particular reference to testamentary law* (1996) • J. Hunter, 'A few notices respecting William Lynwode, judge of the arches, keeper of the privy seal, and bishop of St. David's', *Archaeologia*, 34 (1852), 403–5 • A. C. Reeves, 'The careers of William Lyndwood', *Documenting the past: essays in medieval history presented to George Peddy Cuttino*, ed. J. S. Hamilton and P. J. Bradley (1989), 197–216 • Emden, *Cam.*, 379–81 • J. H. Baker, 'Famous English canon lawyers: IV William Lyndwood, LL.D. (†1446) bishop of St David's', *Ecclesiastical Law Journal*, 2 (1992), 268–72 • F. W. Maitland, 'William Lyndwood', *Canon law in the Church of England* (1898), 1–50 • 'Precedent book, court of arches', CKS, DRb Pa o 10, fol. 192 • *Fasti Angl., 1300–1541*, [Lincoln] • *Fasti Angl., 1300–1541*, [Exeter] • *Fasti Angl., 1300–1541*, [Hereford] • *Fasti Angl., 1300–1541*, [Salisbury] • *Fasti Angl., 1300–1541*, [Bath and Wells] • *Fasti Angl., 1300–1541*, [Welsh dioceses] • C. R. Cheney, 'William Lyndwood's *Provinciale*', *Medieval texts and studies* (1973), 158–84 • E. F. Jacob, ed., *The register of Henry Chichele, archbishop of Canterbury, 1414–1443*, 4 vols., CYS, 42, 45–7 (1937–47) • T. Fuller, *The church history of Britain*, ed. J. Nichols, 3rd edn, 3 vols. (1842) • Fuller, *Worthies* (1811)

Likenesses monumental brass, Linwood church, Lincolnshire • woodcut, repro. in W. Lyndwood, *Provinciale seu, costitutiones Anglie* (*c.*1480), fol. lv

Lyne, Joseph Leycester [*known as* Father Ignatius] (**1837–1908**), Church of England monk and preacher, was born on 23 November 1837 at Trinity Square, London, the second of seven children and the second son of Francis Lyne (1801–1888), a merchant in the City of London, and Louisa Genevieve Leycester (1815–1877), daughter of George Hanmer Leycester of White Place, Berkshire, a descendant of the Leycester de Tabley family. Lyne was baptized at All Hallow's, Barking, on 29 December 1837. The church register was left in arrears for a month, and because this caused him some doubt about the validity of the sacrament, he was conditionally rebaptized in 1860. In 1844 Lyne went to Manor House, Holloway, a preparatory school, and three years later he entered St Paul's School, London, then under the headship of Herbert Kynaston. Regarded as a dreamer, an eccentric, and pious, he was also fascinated by Judaism. An incident of corporal punishment caused a nervous breakdown, and his parents removed him from the school in 1852. Lyne eventually finished his education at private schools at Spalding and Worcester, where his interest in religion and the clerical state increased.

On his mother's suggestion, Lyne wrote to a relative, Robert *Eden, the Episcopalian bishop of Moray, Ross, and Caithness. The bishop procured his entrance into Trinity College, Glenalmond, Perthshire, where he studied theology from 1856 to 1858. Lyne also began to dream about establishing an order of Anglican monks. The warden, John Hannah, commented on his piety and moral character, but academic worries brought about another breakdown. Lyne then found employment as a catechist in Inverness and Glen Urquhart, but his Roman Catholic teachings brought him into conflict with Bishop Eden and the parishioners.

On 23 December 1860 Lyne was ordained deacon for the diocese of Exeter by the bishop of Bath and Wells, Lord Auckland, on condition that he remain a deacon for three years and abstain from preaching in the diocese of Exeter during that time. He soon became an unpaid curate under George Rundle Prynne, the Tractarian incumbent of St Peter's in Plymouth. Lyne's fascination with monasticism continued, and he founded the Society of the Love of Jesus, based on monastic principles, and called himself Brother Joseph. At Plymouth he received encouragement in his monastic dreams from Priscilla Lydia Sellon, the founder of a community of nuns, and Edward Bouverie Pusey. But the young idealist fell ill again and went to Belgium to recuperate. There he visited Roman Catholic monasteries and convents and studied their rules. While on the continent he adopted a monastic habit sent by Pusey and Sellon.

In 1861 Lyne replaced A. H. Mackonochie at St George-in-the-East, London, and took charge of a mission church, St Saviour's. He refused to abandon his Benedictine habit as requested by his vicar, Charles Lowder, and resigned. He now called himself Father Ignatius, and in 1862 tried to establish a monastic community at Claydon, near Ipswich. Threatened by angry protesters and refused a licence to preach by the bishop of Norwich, John Thomas Pelham, he moved his small community to Elm Hill near Norwich in 1863. Problems continued with the bishop, and this forced Father Ignatius to appeal to the bishop of Oxford, Samuel Wilberforce, who urged submission to Pelham. Father Ignatius even took his crusade to the floor of the Bristol church congress in 1863, but failed to win support. He continued to promote the revival of Anglican monasticism, and received some encouragement from interested Roman Catholics. In 1865 he asked the archbishop of Canterbury, Charles Thomas Longley, to ordain him a priest, but refused to abandon his association with Benedictinism and his monastic habit, two conditions demanded by Longley. Internal problems and financial difficulties marked his stay in Norwich; in 1866 he was dispossessed of his property and the community dispersed.

While Father Ignatius searched for a permanent home for his brotherhood, he established a community of Anglican nuns at Feltham, and preached in a number of London churches until 1868, when the bishop of London, Archibald Campbell Tait, prohibited him from preaching in the diocese. Supported by a wealthy benefactor, in 1869 Father Ignatius purchased a property at Capel-y-ffin in the Black Mountains, south Wales, and built Llanthony Abbey. He sought funds for his project by preaching engagements and by appealing to wealthy benefactors. As abbot he adopted monastic customs in an eclectic manner. There were even reports of miracles and heavenly visions. Because of his erratic personality, his frequent absences from the monastery, including a trip to Canada and America in 1890–91, and his questionable status within the Anglican church, this venture did not succeed. His convictions also brought some notoriety: in 1872 he publicly confronted Charles Bradlaugh; in the following year vice-chancellor Sir Richard Malins ordered Father Ignatius to release a young man, a ward in chancery, from the monastery; religious differences with his father resulted in public denunciations; and he attacked the theological views of Charles Gore at the Birmingham church congress in 1889.

Unable to receive orders in his own church, Father Ignatius was ordained a priest on 27 July 1898 by Joseph René

Vilatte, also known as Mar Timotheos, a Syrian archbishop and metropolitan for the Old Catholic church in America. For a time he dreamed of establishing a British Old Catholic church. Toward the end of his life he channelled his enthusiasm into the revival of Welsh culture; he also became a Zionist, British Israelite, and a believer in the flat-earth theory. Following a stroke, Father Ignatius died on 16 October 1908 at his sister's home at Darjeeling Castle Road, Camberley, Surrey, and was buried at his monastery in Wales on 23 October. This property passed into the hands of the Anglican Benedictines of Caldey island, south Wales, in 1911. According to the Revd Francis Kilvert's diary, Father Ignatius's 'face is a very saintly one and the eyes extremely beautiful, earnest and expressive, a dark soft brown. When excited they seem absolutely to flame' (*Kilvert's Diary*, 2 Sept 1870). A charismatic preacher and flamboyant individual, Father Ignatius published collections of sermons, tracts, hymns, and novels about monastic life. RENE KOLLAR

Sources A. Calder-Marshall, *The enthusiast* (1962) · Baroness de Bertouch, *The life of Father Ignatius O.S.B., the monk of Llanthony* (1904) · D. Attwater, *Father Ignatius: a Victorian* (1931) · *The Times* (17 Oct 1908) · P. F. Anson, *The call of the cloister: religious communities and kindred bodies in the Anglican communion*, 4th edn (1964) · R. Kollar, 'Dr Pusey and Fr Ignatius of Llanthony', *The Journal of Welsh Religious History*, 2 (1985), 27–40 · A. Drummond, 'Father Ignatius', *Church Quarterly Review*, 151 (1951), 63–86 · B. Palmer, *Reverend rebels: five Victorian clerics and their fight against authority* (1993) · *Kilvert's diary: selections from the diary of the Rev. Francis Kilvert*, ed. W. Plomer, new edn, 1 (1960) · Father Michael [M. David], *Father Ignatius in America* (1893)

Archives Norfolk RO, papers, incl. autobiography | LPL, Benson MSS · LPL, letters to C. T. Longley, and related papers · LPL, corresp. with A. C. Tait, and related papers

Likenesses watercolour drawing, 1867, NPG · photograph, 1890–91, repro. in Palmer, *Reverend rebels* · pencil drawing, 1897, NPG · Ape [C. Pellegrini], chromolithograph caricature, NPG; repro. in *VF* (9 April 1887) · W. & D. Downey, woodburytype photograph, NPG; repro. in W. Downey and D. Downey, *The cabinet portrait gallery*, 2 (1891) · Mason & Co., two cartes-de-visite, NPG · S. A. Walker, carte-de-visite, NPG · photographs, repro. in Calder-Marshall, *The enthusiast* · photographs, repro. in Baroness de Bertouch, *Life of Father Ignatius* · photographs, repro. in Attwater, *Father Ignatius*

Wealth at death £2510 11s.: probate, 11 Dec 1908, *CGPLA Eng. & Wales* · £1200—stocks: Calder-Marshall, *The enthusiast*

Lyne, Richard (*fl. c.*1570–*c.*1600), painter and engraver, was one of the earliest English artists whose works have been preserved. Vertue noted that he was one of the engravers employed by Matthew Parker, archbishop of Canterbury, and worked for him, in company with Remigius Hogenberg, at Cambridge and at Lambeth Palace. John Ingamells considered that the portrait of Parker at Lambeth, of which a small engraving on copper was made by Hogenberg, is:

> more likely to derive from the print which was intended for Parker's *De Antiquitate Britannicae ecclesiæ* 1572, which was based on the miniature portrait stuck in the Corpus Christi 'Black Book of Corpus Christi College' (MS 582, the Parker Library, Corpus Christi College, Cambridge). (Ingamells, 317)

Lyne drew and engraved at Parker's expense a very interesting map of the University of Cambridge for John Caius's *Historia Cantabrigiensis* (1574). He also painted and engraved in that year a large genealogical chart of the history of Great Britain ('of this Hogenberg. is graved. a small. plate' (Vertue, *Note books*, 2.71) which appeared in Alexander Neville's *De furoribus Norfolciensium Ketto duce* (1575). Vertue noted further that the original was 'done in wood, but very plain & well. to which the name is set. "Richardus Lyne' servus D. Matths. Archp Cant. Sculpsit 1574"' (ibid., 71–2). Lyne is mentioned by Francis Meres in his *Palladis tamia* (1598) as among the leading painters of the time. L. H. CUST, *rev.* ANNETTE PEACH

Sources Vertue, *Note books*, 2.71–2 · J. Ingamells, *The English episcopal portrait, 1559–1835: a catalogue* (privately printed, London, 1981), 317 · E. K. Waterhouse, *The dictionary of British 16th and 17th century painters* (1988)

Archives CCC Cam., Parker collection

Lyne, Sir William John (1844–1913), politician in Australia, was born on 6 April 1844 at Great Swan Port, Van Diemen's Land, the eldest son of John Lyne, a farmer, and his wife, Lillias Cross Carmichael, *née* Hume. Educated privately and at Horton College, Ross, Tasmania, he spent some time pioneering in western Queensland and as a municipal official in Tasmania, where on 29 June 1870 he married Martha Coates Shaw (*d.* 1903). They had three daughters and a son. In 1875 Lyne took up land at Albury, on the New South Wales border with Victoria, where, as Big Bill, bluff and plain-spoken bushman, he became very well liked. In 1880 he was elected to the New South Wales legislative assembly.

Originally an advocate of the small settlers and a supporter of free trade, Lyne later became sympathetic to the interests of larger landholders and a committed protectionist. But despite this, and despite moving to Sydney in 1887, he remained a popular local member: he retained his seat until federation, when he was elected to represent the area in the commonwealth house of representatives.

In the assembly Lyne aligned himself with the opponents of the Free-Trade leader Sir Henry Parkes, and in the political turmoil which marked the period held office in three short-lived administrations under Sir Patrick Jennings (1885) and George Dibbs (1886–7 and 1889). He was secretary for public works in the Dibbs government from October 1891 until August 1894. In 1895 he became leader of the opposition. Outclassed in debate by the Free-Trade premier George Reid, he nevertheless kept his Protectionist Party together, and worked to convince the Labor members, on whom Reid was forced to rely for his majority after 1898, that his party was sympathetic to their social policies.

Though he represented a border constituency where support for the federation movement, which complicated politics throughout the 1890s, was stronger than elsewhere, Lyne was far from enthusiastic about it. He was elected to the convention of 1897–8; but, convinced that the constitution it drafted was not in the best interests of the colony, he opposed acceptance at referendums in 1898 and 1899. In the circumstances subsequent events were ironic. He became premier in September 1899 as a result of subterranean intrigues with committed federalists, who distrusted Reid, and the Labor Party, which distrusted the federalist leader Edmund Barton. Labor supported him as he put through a budget of bills promised to it, and in December 1900, as premier of the largest colony, he was commissioned by the governor-general to form a federal ministry. But he was deserted by the federalists who had used him to oust Reid, and had to return his commission. He was rewarded by the portfolio of home affairs in the cabinet subsequently formed by Barton. He became minister for trade and customs in August 1903 and retained this office under Alfred Deakin, who succeeded Barton, until the government fell twelve months later.

Lyne was unwilling to give the Reid–McLean coalition (August 1904 – July 1905) even the equivocal support accorded it by Deakin. When Labor rejected a proposal for a coalition with Protectionists under his leadership, he returned to trade and customs in the second Deakin ministry, transferring to the treasury two years later and becoming responsible for putting through the first thoroughly protectionist tariff.

In the increasingly unstable situation caused by the existence in parliament of three almost equal parties, Lyne favoured an alliance with Labor. This proved impossible, and when Deakin withdrew his support of a short-lived Labor government and accepted the alternative of fusion with the supporters of Reid, Lyne parted with him on angry terms. Though he never joined the Labor Party he continued to support it until 1913, when, isolated and ill, he lost his seat for the only time. He died three months later, on 3 August, at his home at Double Bay, Sydney, and was buried with Anglican rites at South Head cemetery on 6 August. He was survived by his second wife, Sarah Jane, *née* Olden (1869–1961), whom he married probably in 1905, their daughter, and the children of his first marriage. He had been appointed KCMG in 1900.

Despite a certain political ineptitude and a tendency to bluster in the face of criticism (both demonstrated at the 1907 London conference on merchant shipping, where he tried to insist that British vessels trading to Australia should conform to Australian manning scales and pay rates), Lyne was an efficient departmental minister.

W. G. McMinn

Sources C. Cunnerin, 'Lyne, Sir William John', *AusDB*, vol. 10 • J. A. La Nauze, *Alfred Deakin: a biography*, 2 vols. (1965) • A. Deakin, *The federal story: the inner history of the federal cause*, ed. J. A. La Nauze, 2nd edn (1963) • B. Nairn, *Civilising capitalism* (1973) • L. Nyman, *The Lyne family history* (1976) • NL Aus., Lyne papers • d. cert.

Archives NL Aus. | NL Aus., Deakin MSS

Likenesses T. Cowan, bust, marble, Parliament House, Canberra, Australia • W. H. Gocher, portrait, oils, NL Aus.

Wealth at death £17,862: probate, *AusDB*

Lynedoch. For this title name *see* Graham, Thomas, Baron Lynedoch (1748–1843).

Lynegar, Charles [Cormac Ó Luinín] (*fl.* **1708–1731**), Irish-language scholar and antiquary, was probably born in co. Fermanagh, Ireland, the son of Matha Bán Ó Luinín. The self-styled *ardollamh Éireann* ('chief master of bardic learning in Ireland'), he belonged to the last generation of *seanchaidhe* ('shanachies' or antiquaries), hereditary keepers of the genealogies and legendary history of the Irish chiefs in medieval and early modern times. The medieval Uí Luinín, like many others of their profession, were also hereditary erenaghs, or stewards of church lands, in the parish of Derryvullen, co. Fermanagh. An Ó Luinín took part in transcribing the annals of Ulster, which record individuals of this surname as scholars and churchmen from the late fourteenth century onwards. Even after the Ulster plantation a Giollaphádraig, or Patrick Ó Luinín (*fl.* 1638–1641), was employed as scribe and genealogist by the nobleman Brian Mag Uidhir of Tempo. The protestant Reformation resulted in erenagh families becoming simply tenants of Anglican bishops in the relevant dioceses, and many converted to Anglicanism, perhaps including Charles's grandfather, Matha Ó Luinín. He changed his name to Matthew Lynegar and translated the name of the family estate, Ard Uí Luinín, to 'Mount Lynegar' and his hereditary profession of *seanchaidh* to 'chief antiquary and king-at-arms of Ireland', in which character he drew up pedigrees for many English planter families as well as the descendants of Irish chieftains.

Charles Lynegar appears to have inherited some of his grandfather's manuscripts, but not Mount Lynegar. The collector Charles O'Conor of Belanagare (1710–1790) styled him Cormac ('of the Cúl'), son of Matha ('the White') Ó Luinín, suggesting an association with the half-barony of Coole, co. Fermanagh, rather than the barony of Tirkennedy in which Mount Lynegar itself lay. Army lists of the period have been searched in vain for a commission justifying his use of the title Captain Lynegar. The earliest definite information known is his employment by the fellows of Trinity College, Dublin, in 1708 to teach Irish to the divinity students there, not as a permanent member of staff, but paid by voluntary contributions collected among the fellows themselves. He used the title 'Professor of Irish at Trinity College Dublin' thenceforth to 1731, when his teaching was interrupted by a sojourn in the city's Marshalsea prison for debtors. Nothing further is known of his career.

During these years Lynegar supplemented his meagre salary by drawing up pedigrees for the Anglo-Irish and Gaelic aristocracy and assisting John Richardson in translating the Book of Common Prayer into Irish (published in 1712). As well as acting as scribe for John Hall, vice-provost of Trinity, he addressed an Irish eulogy to him in 1709, composed in a faulty version of the bardic metre *deibhidhe*. He was later to reuse some of the verses in a similar eulogy addressed to Lord St George, vice-admiral of Connaught (1727–35). Lynegar formed one of the circle of Irish scribes and men of letters that gathered in Dublin around the leading figures of Tadhg and Seán Ó Neachtain, though he was not apparently popular with them. A satire in Irish accuses him not only of protestantism, but of falsifying genealogies to flatter the patrons who paid him. It is these

Irish-speaking colleagues who sometimes refer to him as Cathal, the more usual Irish-language equivalent for the name Charles. KATHARINE SIMMS

Sources M. H. Risk, 'Charles Lynegar, professor of the Irish language, 1712', *Hermathena*, 102 (1966), 16–25 • C. Quin, 'A manuscript written in 1709 by Charles Lynegar for John Hall vice-provost of Trinity College Dublin', *Hermathena*, 53 (1939), 127–37 • D. O'Sullivan, 'A courtly poem for Sir Richard Cox (Cormac an Chúil mac Mathabhain Uí Luinín cc.)', *Éigse*, 4 (1943–4), 284–6 • D. Greene, 'A dedication and poem by Charles Lynegar', *Éigse*, 5 (1945–7), 4–7 • B. Ó Cuív, 'Sgiathlúithreach an Choxaigh', *Éigse*, 5 (1945–7), 136–8 • F. Carroll, 'Captain Charles Linegar, professor of the Irish language', *Irish Book Lover*, 32 (1952–7), 42 • P. Ó Conchubhair, *Éigse*, 4 (1943–4), 154 • T. O'Rahilly and others, *Catalogue of Irish manuscripts in the Royal Irish Academy*, 30 vols. (Dublin, 1926–70) • R. J. Hayes, ed., *Manuscript sources for the history of Irish civilisation*, 11 vols. (1965) • K. Simms, 'Charles Lynegar, the Ó Luinín family and the study of Seanchas', in T. Barnard, D. Ó. Cróinín, and K. Simms, *A miracle of learning* (1998), 266–83
Archives NL Ire., genealogies, MSS 94, 516 • NL Ire., genealogies, MSS 5, 326; 11, 069; G 709 • Royal Irish Acad., autographs, MSS 997, 1035

Lynford, Thomas (*bap.* **1650**, *d.* **1724**), Church of England clergyman, was baptized at St Benedict's, Cambridge, on 30 October 1650, the son of Samuel Lynford (1609–1657?), prebend of Exeter. Lynford's father was ejected from his living and died before the Restoration. Lynford was educated under Mr Leeds at Newark and then at Bury St Edmunds grammar school before being admitted sizar at Christ's College, Cambridge, on 16 July 1666. He graduated BA in 1670–71 and proceeded MA in 1674. He was ordained in March 1674 and that year became curate at Fen Drayton, Cambridgeshire. The following year he became vicar of Great Ellingham, Norfolk, which he resigned in 1676. Lynford was now a tutor in Cambridge, one of his pupils being Robert Perceval, a nephew of Sir Robert Southwell, whom Lynford took pains to impress as a possible future patron. In July 1675 Lynford was made a fellow of Christ's College, although there appears to have been some initial opposition to his election. He was incorporated at Oxford in July 1676. By 1679 he had made sufficient contacts in London to preach a sermon before the lord mayor. In December 1685 Lynford became rector of St Edmund the King, Lombard Street, in the City of London and consequently resigned his fellowship in 1686. During James II's reign he wrote the *Ninth Note of the Church Examined*, which was republished by Bishop Edmund Gibson in *Preservative Against Popery* (1738), and published several other anti-popish tracts.

In October 1689 Lynford was created DD during William III's visit to Cambridge. He was licensed on 25 November to marry Elizabeth Dillingham (1666/7–1744?) of St Giles-in-the-Fields, London. They had no children. In 1695 he was living in the parish of St Gregory by Paul's. After presentation by the king, in April 1700 Lynford was installed as a prebend of Westminster. The founding charter of the Society for the Propagation of the Gospel in June 1701 described Lynford as a chaplain-in-ordinary to the king. In September 1709 he was collated as archdeacon of Barnstaple. Lynford was an opponent of Francis Atterbury, dean of Westminster and bishop of Rochester, in his attempt to build a new dormitory for Westminster School, which involved him in the resulting cases in chancery and before the House of Lords. Lynford served as subdean of Westminster in 1723. He died on 11 August 1724.

As chaplain to William III, Queen Anne, and George I, Lynford published a few sermons, but evidently had no great opinion of his own literary merit for his will, written in April 1724, instructed his nephew, Dr William Herring, not to publish anything he found after his death 'because I am sure nothing deserves it' (will, fol. 69*v*). This self-effacement continued with his funeral instructions which ordered burial in St Edmund's, Lombard Street, at midnight 'without Sermon, without Escutcheons, without any Bearers but the Common Bearers of the Parish' (will, fol. 68*v*). His books were divided among his wife, Christ's College, Sion College, the deans and chapters of Westminster and Exeter, and Herring. Most of his estate was left to his wife, whose will was proved in 1744.

STUART HANDLEY

Sources Venn, *Alum. Cant.* • will, PRO, PROB 11/599, sig. 194, fols. 68*v*–69 • *Fasti Angl., 1541–1857*, [Ely], 87 • *Fasti Angl.* (Hardy), 1.408 • J. L. Chester and J. Foster, eds., *London marriage licences, 1521–1869* (1887), 872 • R. Newcourt, *Repertorium ecclesiasticum parochiale Londinense*, 1 (1708), 344 • D. V. Glass, introduction, *London inhabitants within the walls, 1695*, ed. D. V. Glass, London RS, 2 (1966), 186 • *The life and times of Anthony Wood*, ed. A. Clark, 5 vols., OHS, 19, 21, 26, 30, 40 (1891–1900), 3.312 • BL, Add. MSS 46951B–46952; 22910, fol. 229 • *CSP dom.*, *1700–02*, 358 • S. H. A. H. [S. H. A. Hervey], *Biographical list of boys educated at King Edward VI Free Grammar School, Bury St Edmunds, from 1550 to 1900* (1908), 244 • C. Jones, 'Jacobites under the beds: Bishop Francis Atterbury, the earl of Sunderland, and the Westminster School dormitory case of 1721', *British Library Journal*, 25 (1999), 35–54 • *IGI*
Archives BL, letters to Southwell, Add. MSS 46951B–46952
Likenesses oils, Christ's College, Cambridge

Lynn, Alan (**1347/8–1432**), Carmelite friar and theologian, was born in Bishop's Lynn in Norfolk. Nothing is known of his family. He joined the Carmelite convent in the town and undertook his studies at Cambridge University where he incepted as DTh some time after 1407. He continued to lecture at Cambridge on the scriptures, and was noted for his familiarity with the works of the church fathers. In 1407 (when he was fifty-nine years old) he was listed as lector in theology at the Carmelite house in Norwich and was one of two Carmelites who swore to having seen the arms of the Hastings family painted in the priory at Bishop's Lynn forty years previously. It is likely that at this time he was lecturing to the Carmelite students there. He later returned to Bishop's Lynn, where he became a close friend and spiritual guide of Margery Kempe, who mentions his name on numerous occasions and had a great appreciation of his wise advice. He was still alive when she dictated the first draft of her book in 1432, but he probably died shortly afterwards. An inveterate classifier, Lynn composed few original works: a tract on the four senses of scripture (of which John Bale preserves a few lines), a collection of sermons, and lectures on theology and Aristotle. His major output was a series of indices to the works of the church fathers and theologians of his day. These covered the books of Aquinas, Augustine, Alcuin, and others, up to John Baconthorpe (*d*. 1346), another Carmelite, and John Lathbury (*d*. 1406). At least two of these survive, as *tabulae* for *Reductorium morale Bibliae* and *In revelationes Brigittae*, both by Pierre Bersuire (BL, Royal MS 3 D.iii, fols. 1–44; Oxford, Lincoln College, MS Lat. 69, fols. 197–234). John Bale saw all these works in Norwich where Alan Lynn compiled them, probably to help with his teaching there, and they give an interesting insight into the breadth of reading current in his day.

RICHARD COPSEY

Sources J. Bale, Bodl. Oxf., MS Bodley 73 (SC 27635), fols. 2, 40, 119, 139, 197*v*, 200*v*, 201*v*, 204*v*–205, 208 · *The book of Margery Kempe*, ed. W. Butler-Bowdon (1944), 15, 124, 137–8, 153, 154–5, 197, 198 · J. Bale, Bodl. Oxf., MS Selden supra 41, fol. 175*v* · J. Bale, BL, Harley MS 3838, fols. 92–92*v*, 201*v*–202*v* · Bale, *Cat.*, 1.551–3 · Emden, *Cam.*, 381–2 · J. Cox, 'Carmelites of King's Lynn: a newly discovered chartulary', *Memorials of old Norfolk*, ed. H. Astley (1908), 134 · P. Jean-Marie de l'Enfant Jésus, 'Alain de Lynn', *Dictionnaire de spiritualité ascétique et mystique: doctrine et histoire*, ed. M. Viller and others (1937–95) · *Commentarii de scriptoribus Britannicis, auctore Joanne Lelando*, ed. A. Hall, 2 (1709), 434 · J. Bale, *Illustrium Maioris Britannie scriptorum … summarium* (1548), fols. 185–6

Archives BL, Royal MS 3 D.iii, fols. 1–44 · Lincoln College, Oxford, MS Lat. 69, fols. 197–234

Lynn, George, the elder (1676–1742), astronomer and antiquary, was born at Southwick House, near Oundle, Northamptonshire, the second son of George Lynn (1647/8–1682), lord of the manor of Southwick, and his wife, Mary (*d*. 1722), the eldest daughter of Walter Johnson of Spalding. His younger brother Walter *Lynn (1677/8–1763) became a medical writer. George Lynn married Elizabeth (*d*. 1742), the daughter of Humphrey Bellamy of London; they had two daughters, who died unmarried, and a son, also George Lynn [*see below*].

Lynn possessed a 13 foot telescope, with which he made a variety of astronomical observations. Those of the eclipses of Jupiter's satellites, made in 1724–6 and 1730–35, he sent to the Royal Society. He also sent to the society his account of the aurora borealis of 8 October 1726 and his meteorological register covering the fourteen years up to 1740.

Lynn became in 1719 a member of the Spalding Gentlemen's Society, to which he gave an extensive table of logarithms which he had compiled. With the noted antiquary William Stukeley, he was in 1745 one of the founders of the Brazen-Nose Society, so named after a famous 'university' at Stamford, on whose site they met weekly. About this time a ploughman at Cotterstock, a mile from Lynn's house, uncovered a Roman tessellated pavement, of which Lynn and his son prepared a drawing which Vertue engraved for the Society of Antiquaries. Lynn died on 28 June 1742 and was buried at Southwick on 5 July. His son, **George Lynn the younger** (1707–1758), antiquary, was born in London. After attending school in Spalding he entered St John's College, Cambridge, and was in 1723 admitted to the Inner Temple; he was called to the bar in 1729. He joined the Spalding Gentlemen's Society in 1723 and the Society of Antiquaries in 1726. He married in 1734 Anne (*d*. 1767), the eldest daughter of Sir Edward Bellamy of Frinton Hall, Essex, lord mayor of London in 1735, and through her inherited the manor of Frinton. Lynn died childless on 16 May 1758; a handsome monument by Roubilac was erected to him in Southwick parish church.

A. M. CLERKE, *rev.* ANITA MCCONNELL

Sources Venn, *Alum. Cant.* · J. Bridges, *The history and antiquities of Northamptonshire*, ed. P. Whalley, 2 (1791), 469, 472 · Nichols, *Lit. anecdotes*, 6.72, 116 · R. Wolf, *Geschichte der Astronomie* (Munich, 1877), 699 · W. Whellan, *History and gazetteer of Northamptonshire* (1849), 743 · E. Green, 'Pedigree of the family of Lynne of Southwick, co. Northampton', *The Genealogist*, 1 (1877), 345–54, esp. 353–4 · *An account of the Gentlemen's Society at Spalding, being an introduction to the Reliquiae Galeanae* (1784), no. 20 [3/1] of *Bibliotheca topographica Britannica*, ed. J. Nichols (1780–1800)

Lynn, George, the younger (1707–1758). *See under* Lynn, George, the elder (1676–1742).

Lynn, Kathleen (1874–1955), physician and political activist, was born on 28 January 1874 at Mullafarry, near Killala, co. Mayo, Ireland, the second of four children of Robert Lynn (*d*. 1923), an Anglican clergyman, and his wife, Katharine Wynne (*d*. 1915). By 1886 the family had moved to Cong, co. Mayo, where Robert Lynn became the rector. In 1891 Kathleen Lynn went as a boarder to Alexandra College, Dublin, from where she matriculated in 1893 from the Royal University of Ireland. From October 1897 Lynn took classes at the Catholic University's school of medicine in Cecilia Street, Dublin, and in the Royal College of Surgeons of Ireland. In 1898 she won the Barker anatomical prize awarded by the college. She graduated MB BCh BAO from the Royal University of Ireland in 1899. Lynn conducted her internships at Holles Street Hospital (1897–9), the Rotunda Hospital (1899), the Royal Victoria Eye and Ear Hospital (1899), and at the Richmond Lunatic Asylum. In 1898 Lynn was appointed the first woman resident doctor at Dublin's Adelaide Hospital, but staff opposition to her appointment meant she did not take up the post. She completed postgraduate work in the United States in the early 1900s before working as a duty doctor at hospitals in the city of Dublin as part of her wider general practice based at her home at 9 Belgrave Road, Rathmines, Dublin. Lynn became a fellow of the Royal College of Physicians in Ireland in 1909, and was promoted to clinical assistant in the Royal Victoria Eye and Ear Hospital in the same year.

Lynn was a supporter of women's suffrage and a member of the Irish Women's Suffrage and Local Government Association and the militant Women's Social and Political Union. She tended gaoled and hunger-striking suffragettes in 1912. Her work among the poor of Dublin also led her strongly to support socialism. Lynn supported the Irish Women Worker's Union and became its vice-president in 1917. She joined the Irish Citizen Army on the invitation of its founder, James Connolly, and acted as a medical officer during the 1913 lock-out. With the outbreak of the Easter rising in 1916 she acted as medical officer to the insurgents at the College of Surgeons on Stephens Green. Along with others she was arrested and imprisoned in Kilmainham gaol. Her father had no sympathy for her nationalist ideas and was shocked at her involvement in the rising. He later disinherited her. Lynn was deported to England but was not imprisoned, spending time instead with a doctor near Bath. She was allowed to return to Ireland in August 1916 but was arrested again in October 1918 for her political activities. On this occasion the intervention of the lord mayor of Dublin helped her to avoid deportation. She nevertheless found it impossible to find employment in any hospital on her release from prison.

Lynn, along with four other women, was co-opted onto the executive of Sinn Féin in 1917 and campaigned for her friend Constance Markievicz in the general election of 1918. Lynn was also a close friend of the activist Hanna Sheehy Skeffington. Lynn was also a committee member of Cumann na dTeachaire (League of Women Delegates), formed in 1917. Members of Cumann na dTeachaire were interested in the health of women and children and they expressed immediate concern at the possible spread of venereal diseases once the war ended. The committee began to investigate the possibility of establishing a hospital to care for infants suffering from VD-related illnesses. With the outbreak of the influenza epidemic Lynn opened a temporary hospital in 37 Charlemont Street, Dublin, in November 1918. From this venture, with her companion Madeleine ffrench-*Mullen (1880–1944), and the support of members of Cumann na dTeachaire, she opened St Ultan's Hospital for Infants in 1919. The hospital was staffed by women and catered for babies up to two years of age, with children up to five being treated in an out-patients department. Lynn used her influential contacts to secure funding for the hospital and she and ffrench-Mullen undertook their first fund-raising tour in the USA in 1925.

Lynn opposed the Anglo-Irish treaty of 1921 as it was not, she noted in her diary for 7 December 1921, 'what Connolly and Malin and countless others died for'. Elected to the Dáil in August 1923 as a republican candidate, she followed an abstentionist policy; she lost her seat in the general election of 1927. Lynn had been elected to Rathmines urban district council in 1921 and remained in municipal politics until the amalgamation of the council with Dublin corporation in 1930. Public health, housing, and working conditions were her primary concerns as an elected politician. Lynn became disillusioned with Sinn Féin's failure to embrace social reform, and after 1926 concentrated her energies on her medical practice and on the hospital.

St Ultan's proved to be a pioneering research hospital. Dorothy Stopford-Price, who introduced the BCG tuberculosis vaccine to Ireland, worked in the hospital from 1923. By December 1936 Stopford-Price had vaccinated thirty-five children in St Ultan's with the new vaccine, and the national BCG committee operated from the hospital from 1949. In the 1930s it was suggested that St Ultan's should amalgamate with the National Children's Hospital, Harcourt Street, Dublin. Lynn believed that the new hospital would be non-sectarian. However, there was a concerted effort by Catholic clerics and medical men to establish a Catholic children's hospital in Crumlin, a project which secured funding in 1939. As a result the proposed amalgamation came to nothing.

Lynn was also involved with An Óige (a youth hostelling organization), and her cottage at Glenmalure in co. Wicklow was given to them after her death. She was a co-founder of the Irish Paediatric Association in 1933. An enthusiastic supporter of the Irish language, Lynn was also a member of Cumann Gaelach na hÉaglaise. In the aftermath of the Second World War she acted as vice-president to a Save the Children committee which brought refugee German children to Ireland. Kathleen Lynn died on 14 September 1955 in St Mary's Nursing Home, Ballsbridge, Dublin. She was buried in Dean's Grange cemetery with full military honours.

MARIA LUDDY

Sources K. Lynn, diaries, 1916–55, Royal College of Physicians of Ireland, Kildare Street, Dublin 2, Ireland · H. P. Smyth, 'Kathleen Lynn', *Dublin Historical Record*, 30/2 (1976–7), 51–7 · M. Ruane, 'Kathleen Lynn', *Ten Dublin women* (Dublin, 1991), 61–7 · K. E. Murphy, *Journal of the Irish Medical Association*, 37 (1955), 321 · K. Lynn, typescript statement to the Irish military history bureau, Allen Library, Richmond Street, Dublin · M. Ruane, 'Kathleen Lynn (1874–1955)', *Female activists: Irish women and change, 1900–1960*, ed. M. Cullen and M. Luddy (Dublin, 2001), 61–88

Archives Allen Library, Richmond Street, Dublin, papers · Royal College of Physicians of Ireland, Dublin, diaries | Royal College of Physicians of Ireland, Dublin, St Ultan's hospital records

Likenesses photographs, Royal College of Physicians of Ireland, Dublin, St Ultan's hospital records

Lynn, Nicholas (*fl.* 1386–1411), Carmelite friar and astronomer, presumably came from Bishop's Lynn in Norfolk. By his own account he was a friar and a member of the order of the Blessed Mary Mother of God of Mount Carmel, and during the late fourteenth century he became a lecturer in theology at Oxford. John Bale described him as 'philosophus, cosmographus et astronomus inter omnes sui temporis celeberrimus' ('the most celebrated philosopher, cosmographer, and astronomer among all of his time'; BL, Harley MS 3838, fols. 72*v*–73).

In 1386 Lynn composed, at the request of John of Gaunt, a *Kalendarium* designed for the years from 1387 to 1462. Succeeding a similar work by Walter Elvedene, Lynn's *Kalendarium* is designed for the latitude and longitude of Oxford and includes a daily calendar with saints' days, the daily position of the sun in the zodiac, the lengths of artificial and vulgar days, times of new and full moons, hourly shadow lengths depending on the altitude of the sun, dates and times of solar and lunar eclipses, and daily ascensions of the signs of the zodiac, as well as charts of solar and lunar eclipses, tables to determine the celestial houses, a table to show what time of day or night a given planet reigns, a means of discovering the dates of movable feasts, and other tables concerned with the motion of the sun and the moon. At the end of the *Kalendarium* is a series of explanatory canons, some of which show the most propitious times for phlebotomy (bloodletting as a medical treatment), a matter of interest so important to physicians that long after the *Kalendarium* had expired scribes still copied them. Lynn's *Kalendarium* survives in whole or in part in more than sixteen manuscripts and in one printed edition. Geoffrey Chaucer referred to it in his *Treatise on the Astrolabe*.

Richard Hakluyt in his 1589 *Voyages* identified Nicholas Lynn as a Franciscan friar said to have sailed in 1360 from Norfolk to the polar regions, and to have written an account (now lost) of his adventures, entitled *Inventio fortunata*, which he presented to Edward III. Hakluyt's information was originally derived from the Dutch cartographer Gerardus Mercator. In 1569 Mercator published a map of the Arctic regions bearing a legend stating that, according to the Dutch explorer Jacobus Cnoyen of 's-Hertogenbosch, an English priest in 1364 reported to the king of Norway that four years earlier an unnamed Franciscan mathematician from Oxford had visited the Arctic region and measured the height of mountains with an astrolabe. John Dee read Mercator's published report and asked for more details. Mercator said in reply that the friar was the author of the *Inventio fortunata*, which he had presented to the king of England. Dee then assigned the Oxford Franciscan to the haven of Bishop's Lynn in Norfolk, and added that he took his name from this port. Dee did not, however, mention the forename of the friar. It was Hakluyt, who read and quoted both Mercator and Dee, who was the first to state that the Franciscan mathematician and Arctic explorer from Oxford was Nicholas Lynn. Although the voyage from Bishop's Lynn to the Arctic attributed to the Franciscan may well have occurred, as many such voyages did, and although the *Inventio fortunata* may well have been written, since it was cited by the mapmaker John Ruysch in 1508, there is no surviving evidence to identify the Carmelite Nicholas Lynn with the Franciscan explorer of 1360.

Towards the end of his life Lynn resided in the Carmelite convent at Cambridge, where, according to Emden, he became a subdeacon in 1410 and a deacon in 1411. The date of his death is not known. SIGMUND EISNER

Sources *The Kalendarium of Nicholas of Lynn*, trans. G. MacEoin, ed. and trans. S. Eisner (1980) • J. D. North, *Chaucer's universe* (1988), 92 • M. P. Kuczynski, 'A new manuscript of Nicholas of Lynn's *Kalendarium*: Chapel Hill MS 522, fols. 159*r*–202*r*', *Traditio*, 43 (1987), 299–319 • Emden, *Cam.*, 370 • Emden, *Oxf.*, 2.1194 • R. Hakluyt, *Voyages*, 1 (1962), 99–101 • E. G. R. Taylor, 'A letter dated 1577 from Mercator to John Dee', *Imago Mundi*, 13 (1956), 56–68 • A. Diller, 'The mysterious Arctic traveller of 1360: Nicholas of Lynn', *Isis*, 30 (1939), 277–8 • G. Sarton, 'The mysterious Arctic traveller of 1360, Nicholas of Lynn?', *Isis*, 29 (1938), 98–9 • D. M. Smith, *Guide to bishops' registers of England and Wales: a survey from the middle ages to the abolition of the episcopacy in 1646*, Royal Historical Society Guides and Handbooks, 11 (1981) • M. C. Seymour, *The metrical version of Mandeville's travels* (1973), 126 • E. F. Jacob, ed., *The register of Henry Chichele, archbishop of Canterbury, 1414–1443*, 4 vols., CYS, 42, 45–7 (1937–47) • BL, Harley MS 3838, fols. 72*v*–73 • BL, Cotton MS Vitellius C.vii, fols. 264–9

Lynn, Ralph Clifford (1882–1962), actor, was born on 18 March 1882 in Broughton, Salford, Lancashire, the son of Gordon James Lynn, insurance manager, and his wife, Janet Thomas. He was a grand-nephew of the Victorian novelist Eliza Lynn Linton. He made his first stage appearance as an actor at Wigan in *The King of Terrors* in 1900, and played in many small productions and roles before first performing in the West End, at the Empire Theatre in October 1914 in *By Jingo if we do*, a revue by A. Wimperis and H. Carrick, with music by H. Finck.

In these early roles it was said that Lynn 'typified the contemporary monocled "nut"' (Travers, 88), and was essentially playing 'stock' parts. The turning point in his career came in 1922, when Leslie Henson and Tom Walls cast him in *Tons of Money*, a sparkling farce by W. Evans and V. Shaftesbury which ran for two years at the Shaftesbury Theatre. Also in that cast was a young John Robertson Hare, and the team of Walls, Hare, and Lynn was thus created, one which was to stay together for the next eleven years. With their subsequent production *It Pays to Advertise* (1924), by R. C. Megrue and W. Hackett, they moved to the Aldwych Theatre, where they were joined in 1925 by the playwright Ben Travers, who later described Lynn as an 'ideal farce actor … I have never seen or heard of any actor in any field with such an instinctive and unerring gift of timing' (Travers, 91). Over the next decade a succession of 'Aldwych farces' would run for at least 200 performances each, and some for many more: *A Cuckoo in the Nest* (1925), *Rookery Nook* (1926), *Thark* (1928), and *Plunder* (1928), all by Ben Travers, alone occupied the years from 1925 to 1929, and to them all Lynn brought his own unique brand of wistful stooging, specializing in the '"silly ass" roles' (*The Times*, 10 Aug 1962, 11). But Lynn was remembered as 'always painstaking about his work. Nobody ever appreciated so well as Ralph how intensely serious is the job of being funny' (Travers, 94). In 1920 Lynn married Gladys Miles. They had a son and a daughter.

Lynn appeared in at least twenty motion pictures between 1929 and 1937, beginning with the short *Peace and Quiet* in 1929 and *Rookery Nook* in 1930, at least five productions in 1933 alone, and ending with *For Valour* in 1937. But his only real home was in Aldwych farces as part of the Travers team which ran triumphantly into the 1930s. He contributed a good deal to the success of the farces, both through his performances and through his ability always to see 'the ridiculous side of things'. A number of lines in the farces were added on the basis that they were 'exactly the sort of thing Ralph himself would have said in the circumstances' (Travers, 91–3).

With the Second World War came one more hit, *Is your Honeymoon Really Necessary?* by E. Vivian Tidmarsh (1944), which Lynn produced and played for more than two years at the Duke of York's Theatre and a further two years on tour. After the war he rejoined Robertson Hare for two more Ben Travers farces, *Outrageous Fortune* (1947) and *Wild Horses* (1952). Lynn continued with sustained regional tours right through his seventies, playing similar roles. He made his last London appearance in 1958. He died on 8 August 1962 and was cremated at the south London crematorium, Streatham Vale, on 14 August.

SHERIDAN MORLEY, *rev.*

Sources *The Times* (10 Aug 1962) • *The Times* (15 Aug 1962) • B. Travers, *A-sitting on a gate* (1978) • P. Hartnoll, ed., *The Oxford companion to the theatre*, 4th edn (1983) • E. M. Truitt, *Who was who on screen*, 3rd edn (1983) • personal knowledge (1993) • *CGPLA Eng. & Wales* (1962) • b. cert. • F. Gaye, ed., *Who's who in the theatre*, 14th edn (1967)

Archives FILM BFI NFTVA, performance footage

Likenesses L. F. W. Daniels, bromide print, 1932, NPG · photograph, repro. in *The Times* (10 Aug 1962) · photographs, Hult. Arch.
Wealth at death £4981 16s.: probate, 19 Nov 1962, *CGPLA Eng. & Wales*

Lynn, Samuel Ferris (1836–1876), sculptor, was born at Fethard, co. Wexford, the son of Henry Johnston Lynn, lieutenant in the Royal Navy, and his wife, Margaretta Ferris. He studied modelling at the Belfast School of Design, and architecture with his elder brother, William Henry *Lynn, who established a highly successful architectural practice. He moved to London in 1854 and enrolled as a pupil at the Royal Academy Schools, where he achieved early success as an exhibitor, being awarded a silver medal in 1857 for a model from life and a gold medal in 1859 for the best historical composition, *Lycoan Imploring Achilles to Spare his Life*. His group *Procris and Cephalus* won for him the academy's travelling studentship. He remained a frequent exhibitor at the Royal Academy throughout his life, while he participated in the Royal Hibernian Academy exhibitions in Dublin on only four occasions. His first exhibited work in Dublin (1864) was a subject piece, *Evangeline* (plaster), previously exhibited at the Royal Academy in 1858 and at the International Exhibition in London in 1862. This sad and reflective figure, representing the heroine of Longfellow's poem of the same title, was illustrated and discussed in the *Art Journal* in 1865. Lynn lived most of his working life in London, where he was engaged in the early 1860s as assistant to Patrick MacDowell and later to John Henry Foley, both of whom were also Irish sculptors and whose influence remains evident in his work. His wide range of expression in his ideal works, from the violent and vigorous to the gentle and sensitive, echoes the range of MacDowell. Foley was engaged on work for the Albert Memorial in Kensington Gardens when Lynn was working in his studio and his portrait style reveals itself in Lynn's monumental portrait work.

Like most Victorian sculptors, Lynn executed a considerable number of imaginative works while making his career as a portrait sculptor. Among his monumental portrait sculptures, most of which are in Northern Ireland, the marble statue of Lord Farnham in Cavan, co. Cavan, executed in 1871, was described in the *Irish Builder* as 'evincing great artistic learning, diligent study and marked ability'. Farnham is shown in the robes of the Order of St Patrick. Shortly before this work Lynn received the commission to execute the statue of Prince Albert for W. J. Barre's Albert memorial clock tower in Belfast, completed in 1869. Surely influenced by Foley's many statues of the prince, Lynn's portrait, executed in Portland stone, was described as 'noble and commanding' (*ILN*, 5 Feb 1870, 153). In 1873 his bronze statue of the marquess of Downshire, less formally grand and more casual in appearance, was unveiled on his estate at Hillsborough, co. Down. A further statue in Belfast (and one of Lynn's last works), commemorating the Revd Dr Henry Cooke, erected in College Square in 1876, replaced a statue of the earl of Belfast by Patrick MacDowell which was removed indoors. The MacDowell statue, executed in bronze, had been labelled 'the Black Man', a name which transferred to the bronze Lynn portrait. A tomb monument by Lynn commemorating Joseph Makesy (1868), taking the form of an angel uncovering a medallion portrait of the deceased, is in Waterford Cathedral. Lynn was also engaged to carry out architectural sculpture, examples of which are at the Lancashire Insurance office in Manchester (1861) and the Provincial Bank (now the Allied Irish Bank) in College Street, Dublin (1864). The pediment of the bank building shows a representation of Commerce and Agriculture by Lynn.

Lynn had a short but full career; he died on 5 April 1876, at the age of forty, at his home in Crumlin Terrace, Belfast. While he failed to be elected to the Royal Academy in his lifetime, he did become a member of the Institute of Sculptors in London in 1861 and was elected an associate of the Royal Hibernian Academy in 1872. On the presentation of two of Lynn's statuettes to the Belfast Municipal Art Gallery in 1907, Thomas Drew, president of the Royal Hibernian Academy, described 'the grace of pose and dignity' in his monumental sculpture and drew attention to his mastery of drapery (*Belfast Municipal Art Gallery and Museum Quarterly*, 6). His obituary describes a 'man whom to know was to love; a kinder and better friend it was impossible to meet' (*Belfast News-Letter*, 7 April 1876). This is further supported by the words of a contemporary and friend, Dr Kyle Knox, who wrote about Lynn in 1916 on the occasion of a joint exhibition of the works of the Lynn brothers in the Belfast Municipal Art Gallery. Knox described a 'bright, happy and pleasant companion, … always ready for jokes' (Knox, 11).

L. H. CUST, *rev.* PAULA MURPHY

Sources W. G. Strickland, *A dictionary of Irish artists*, 2 vols. (1913); facs. edn with introduction by T. J. Snoddy (1969) · M. Anglesea, 'The Lynn brothers, architect and sculptor', *GPA Irish Arts Review Yearbook*, 6 (1989–90), 254–62 · K. Knox, 'S. F. Lynn', *Belfast Municipal Art Gallery and Museum Quarterly*, 32 (1916), 11 · *Belfast Municipal Art Gallery and Museum Quarterly*, 6 (1907), 6 · '*Evangeline*, from the statue by S. F. Lynn', *Art Journal*, 27 (1865), 372 · *ILN* (7 Jan 1860), 17 · *ILN* (29 Sept 1866), 312 · *ILN* (5 Feb 1870), 153 · *ILN* (9 Aug 1873), 127, 129 · *ILN* (10 July 1875), 45–6 · *Belfast News-Letter* (7 April 1876) · 'The Farnham statue', *Irish Builder*, 14 (1 Jan 1872), 12 · *Irish Builder*, 18 (15 April 1876), 102 · *Irish Builder*, 18 (1 May 1876), 122

Lynn, Thomas (1774–1847), naval officer in the East India Company and teacher of navigation, was born on 2 January 1774 at Woodbridge, Suffolk, one of at least two sons of James Lynn, a medical practitioner, and his wife, Elizabeth. In order to be accepted into the navy of the East India Company, Thomas and his brother John were provided with fraudulent baptismal certificates indicating that they were three years older than they actually were; Thomas was only eleven when he was taken on the books of HEIC *Valentine* as captain's servant in 1785. In due course he rose through the ranks, and made several voyages to the West Indies, then to the East Indies and China. He was serving as first mate by 1798, and his last voyage was to China as captain of the *Barkworth*, in 1816–17.

Lynn was then appointed examiner in nautical astronomy to the East India Company's officers. He was based at 34 Trinity Square, Tower Hill, where he may have resided with his daughter, Mary Emma (probably born soon after he settled in London), and at 148 Leadenhall Street, in the City of London, the latter being well known to mariners as it was adjacent to East India House and occupied by a succession of scientific and nautical instrument makers. Lynn also advertised that he would instruct Royal Navy officers and supply instruments and chronometers. He published sets of star tables and pamphlets on telegraphic communication and practical navigation, and contributed a detailed chapter on the various routes to and from Chinese ports to the three-volume work on China in the Edinburgh Cabinet Library series issued in 1836.

By 1836, however, Lynn's income was inadequate and he was obliged to dispose of his publications and sell his copyrights. He and Mary Emma moved to 1 Marine Terrace, East Cliff, Dover, where he died on 2 May 1847. Mary Emma inherited less than £300; her appeal to the East India Company for a portion of her father's pension was refused. A. M. CLERKE, *rev.* ANITA MCCONNELL

Sources W. T. Lynn, 'Capt. Thomas Lynn', *N&Q*, 7th ser., 1 (1886), 268 • BL OIOC, B/74, 961; B/214, 961 L/MAR/C/652–666; L/MAR/C/669, certificate 383 • PRO, PROB 11/2063, sig. 787 [will] • IR 26/1779 [death duty register] • census returns, 1841, PRO, HO 107/494 • personal knowledge (1893) • *GM*, 2nd ser., 27 (1847), 676 • d. cert.
Archives BL OIOC
Wealth at death under £300: PRO, death duty registers, IR 26/1779

Lynn, Walter (1677/8–1763), physician and inventor of a fire engine, was born at Southwick House, near Oundle, Northamptonshire, the third son of George Lynn (1647/8–1682), and Mary (*d.* 1722), eldest daughter of Walter Johnson, of Spalding, Lincolnshire. He had a twin sister, and was the younger brother of the astronomer George *Lynn. He went to school at Spalding, and then to Peterhouse, Cambridge, in 1695 (BA 1699, MB 1704). He was in York in 1710, and published *An Essay towards a More Easie and Safe Method of Cure in the Small Pox* (1714), in which he described his own case of the disease. He produced a further work on smallpox in 1715. Lynn lodged for a time in Daker Street, Westminster, and said he had a sincere intention to serve the public, particularly ladies and the gentry, but found this impossible, partly because of his poor constitution. In addition, he had no licence to practise physic in London and, although advised by John Mapletoft to get a licence, did not feel fit to do so.

Lynn therefore diverted himself with mechanics and the performance of music. In 1712 he was elected an extra regular member of the Gentlemen's Society at Spalding. He wrote a satire *Nyktopsia, or, The Use and Abuse of Snuffers* (1726), and in the same year printed *The case of Walter Lynn, M.B., in relation to divers undertakings of his, particularly for the improvement of an engine to raise water by fire*. This was to be an improvement on Captain Thomas Savory's engine, and Lynn hoped for but did not get a reward from parliament. *The Case* does not say what the improvements were. Lynn had submitted his invention to Isaac Newton, Christopher Wren, Wren's son, and Brook Taylor. Despite the backing of Christopher Wren, among others, Lynn was disappointed in his hope that the Royal Society would try out his engine. He denied that if his engine lessened the expense of fuel, Newcastle trade would be less, and seamen's employment diminished.

Lynn said others found him 'morose, lazy, discontented and melancholy' (Axon, 241). He died in March 1763, apparently aged eighty-five, and was buried on 19 March at Grantham, Lincolnshire.

R. B. PROSSER, *rev.* JEAN LOUDON

Sources W. E. A. Axon, 'Walter Lynn', *N&Q*, 7th ser., 7 (1889), 241–3 [repr. of *The case*] • E. Green, 'Pedigree of the family of Lynne of Southwick, co. Northampton', *The Genealogist*, 1 (1877), 345–54 • Venn, *Alum. Cant.* • Nichols, *Lit. anecdotes*, 6.72

Lynn, William (1792–1870), hotelier and sports promoter, was born in 1792 at East Grinstead, but nothing else is known about his early life. He first ventured into the catering trade in London before moving to Liverpool, where in the 1820s he leased the Waterloo Hotel in Ranelagh Street in the suburb of Aintree. He was renowned for the excellence of his seafood—for over forty years he supervised the city's municipal banquets—but his efforts as a sports promoter led to the establishment of the Waterloo cup, hare-coursing's premier event, and the Grand National, the world's most famous steeplechase. Nevertheless, like many publicans and hoteliers of the time, it is probable that he provided sports events as an adjunct to his hotel trade, anticipating that customers would be attracted by the entertainment.

Lynn's first race promotion was in 1828 when he provided the Waterloo Gold Cup, value £100, for a flat race at the Maghull racecourse's second recognized meeting. The next year he leased the adjoining Aintree course, erected a grandstand, and ran a flat-race meeting. Soon he was organizing three meetings there a year and in October 1835 he devoted one of them to hurdle events. Captain Martin Beecher (after whom Aintree's Beecher's Brook fence is named) rode two winners, both with the same horse, Vivian, and in an ensuing conversation remarked on the success which his friend Tom Coleman had had with the Great St Albans Steeplechase. This tempted Lynn to announce the running of a steeplechase at Aintree for 29 February 1836, appropriately leap year day. The event proved popular with spectators as, unlike most steeplechase courses, which were point-to-point across country, this involved two circuits of a 2 mile course, most of which was visible from the grandstand. In 1839, however, Lynn's name was missing from the Aintree card. The traditional story is that ill health forced him to withdraw from the project, but, given his longevity, this may have been a diplomatic excuse to cover his precarious financial position. He continued to act as secretary to the Aintree Racing Company until 1843 but was declared bankrupt in June 1844.

Lynn has certainly been treated unfairly in sports history: not only does the official history of the Grand National fail to mention his name, but, somewhat illogically, turf historians have always regarded the 1839 race as the first Grand National, despite the earlier races. The title of the race remained the Grand Liverpool until 1843, when it became the Liverpool and National; the more famous name was adopted only in 1847.

Lynn's other sporting achievement was the founding of the Waterloo cup for hare-coursing in 1836. Melanie, a dog nominated by Lynn, won the event, though its owner was Lord Molyneux, eldest son of the earl of Sefton on whose Altcar land the contest was run. The prize at the inaugural meeting was a silver snuff-box and 16 sovereigns—the stake money from the eight participants.

Little is known about Lynn's activities from 1843. He continued as a hotelier until August 1870 when the Waterloo was acquired by a railway company in order to construct a station. He died two months later in the early hours of 11 October 1870 at his home, Norwood Lodge, Norwood Grove, West Derby, Liverpool. He was buried in the grounds of Liverpool Cathedral. His obituary in the *Liverpool Mercury* makes no mention of wife or children.

WRAY VAMPLEW

Sources R. Green, *A race apart: the history of the Grand National* (1989) • M. Seth-Smith and others, *The history of steeplechasing*, [2nd edn] (1969) • *Liverpool Mercury* (12 Oct 1870) • H. Cox and C. Richardson, *Coursing* (1899) • J. Pinfold, 'Where the champion horses run: the origins of the Aintree racecourse and the Grand National', *International Journal of the History of Sport*, 15 (1998) • R. Longrigg, *The history of horse racing* (1972) • d. cert. • *CGPLA Eng. & Wales* (1870)

Wealth at death under £1000: probate, 18 Nov 1870, *CGPLA Eng. & Wales*

Lynn, William Henry (1829–1915), architect, was born on 27 December 1829 at St John's Point, co. Down, the elder son of Lieutenant Henry Johnston Lynn of the Irish coastguard service and his wife, Margaretta, daughter of Samuel Ferris MD of Larne, co. Antrim. He was the brother of the sculptor Samuel Ferris *Lynn. He was educated at Dr Newland's private grammar school at Bannow, co. Wexford, before being articled at the age of seventeen to the architect and engineer Charles Lanyon (1813–1889) in Belfast, and serving as clerk of works on the Queen's College (now the Queen's University), Belfast (1846–9), and the county court house, Belfast (1848–50). He was taken into partnership by Lanyon in 1854 and remained with him until 1872, when the firm of Lanyon, Lynn, and Lanyon (as it had become with the addition of Lanyon's son John in 1860) was dissolved. Thereafter, Lynn practised on his own until his death.

Lynn was a prolific designer who worked in a wide range of historic styles and normally displayed an eclectic taste. His work was at first mainly medieval revivalist but later was also classical in inspiration. Early works include the Belfast (now Northern) banks at Newtownards, co. Down (1854), and Dungannon, co. Tyrone (1855), which are among the earliest examples of Venetian Gothic detailing in Ireland. He designed a number of linen warehouses in Belfast, his most conspicuous being that built for Richardson, Sons, and Owden (1865–9), and he also designed many churches throughout Ireland for various protestant denominations. Among his most notable churches are the former St Andrew's Church of Ireland Church of 1860 in Dublin and Carlisle Memorial Methodist Church of 1874–5 in Belfast.

Lynn was very successful in competitions both at home and abroad, although some of his prize-winning designs were not built. The most important competition successes in his time with Lanyon were the unexecuted design for the New South Wales parliament building in Sydney, Australia (1861), a multi-towered Gothic composition, followed by his Italian Gothic design for Chester town hall (1863), which was built and opened in 1869. Competition successes in his later independent practice included Paisley town hall (1875–82), designed in a classical manner, and Barrow in Furness town hall (1877–87), designed in a Gothic style. He was also considered to have supplied the best design in the competition for Birmingham council house (1871), but was disqualified for a minor infringement of the rules.

Lynn was recognized in his time for his planning abilities, and Alfred Waterhouse, the assessor for both the Birmingham and Barrow in Furness competitions and himself a great planner, once told Aston Webb that 'there was nothing he would better like to do than to sit behind Lynn and look over his shoulder while he pinned an antiquarian sheet to his board and laid out a large plan' (Webb, 91).

Most of Lynn's important later work is in Belfast, where he designed the public library (1883–8), the harbour office extension (1891–5), and Campbell College (1891–4). From 1910 to 1915 he was architect of St Anne's Church of Ireland Cathedral in Belfast, begun by his former pupil Thomas Drew (1838–1910), where he provided the design for the baptistery in 1915 (erected in 1922–4). Beyond the British Isles Lynn was responsible for civic improvements at Quebec, and the chapel at the British embassy in Constantinople, both commissioned by the marquess of Dufferin and Ava.

Lynn's honours included the gold medal for architectural drawing at the Paris Universal Exhibition in 1867, presidency of the Royal Institute of Architects of Ireland in 1885–9, and nomination for the royal gold medal of the Royal Institute of British Architects in 1911. Unlike his long-time partner Charles Lanyon he had no interest in public life but was entirely devoted to his career, and in the opinion of Aston Webb he was 'the greatest Irish architect of his century' (Webb, 91).

Lynn died of pneumonia on 12 September 1915 at his home, Ardavon, 250 Antrim Road, Belfast, and was buried in the city cemetery. He was unmarried.

PAUL LARMOUR

Sources H. Dixon, 'William Henry Lynn', *Quarterly Bulletin of the Irish Georgian Society*, 17 (1974), 25–30 • A. Webb, 'Leaves from the life of the late W. H. Lynn', *RIBA Journal*, 24 (1916–17), 91–2 • 'Exhibition of works by W. H. Lynn, R. H. A., and S. F. Lynn, A. R. H. A., with notes by Dr Kyle Knox', *Quarterly Notes of the Belfast Municipal Art Gallery and Museum*, 32 (spring 1916), 1–10 • *Belfast News-Letter* (13 Sept 1915) • *Northern Whig* (13 Sept 1915) • *The Builder*, 109 (1915), 219 • R. M. Young, 'William Henry Lynn', *RIBA Journal*, 22 (1914–15), 506 • P. Larmour, 'An architect of genius', *Perspective*, 2/6 (July/Aug 1994), 35–6 • P. Larmour, *Belfast: an illustrated architectural guide* (1987) • C. E. B. Brett, *Buildings of Belfast, 1700–1914*, rev. edn (1985) • 'Contemporary British architects', *Building News* (17 Jan 1890), 115 • P. Larmour, 'Lynn, William Henry', *The dictionary of art*, ed. J. Turner (1996) • M. Anglesea, 'The Lynn brothers, architect and sculptor',

GPA Irish Arts Review Yearbook, 6 (1989–90), 254–62 • *CGPLA Ire.* (1915)

Archives RIBA BAL, corresp. and drawings

Likenesses photograph, *c.*1886, repro. in *Irish Builder and Engineer* (9 Oct 1915) • Abernethy, photograph, repro. in 'Exhibition of works by W. H. Lynn' • Magill, photograph, repro. in 'Contemporary British architects'

Wealth at death £68,681 12*s.* 11*d.*: probate, 22 Oct 1915, *CGPLA Ire.*

Lynne, Walter (*d.* in or before **1571**), publisher and translator, was a native of Antwerp, and seems to have been active as a publisher in the Netherlands. A Wouter van Lin is known to have issued in Antwerp two editions of Gassar's *Cronycke* in 1533 and 1534, and of Erasmus's *Bereydinghe tot der doot* in the latter year. About 1540 he moved to London, where he quickly established a comfortable prosperity. Having settled in Billingsgate, he was assessed on goods of a value of 20*s.* in 1541; by 1549 this had risen to £10, placing Lynne among the most substantial members of the alien community. Lynne is not known to have worked in the book trade during the reign of Henry VIII, but he was quick to appreciate the new opportunities that opened with the accession of Edward VI. The new reign brought a large increase in the volume of books printed in England, mostly vernacular protestant works, and Lynne soon established a place in the forefront of this trade. On 1 December 1547 he was granted a seven-year patent for the sole printing of *The Beginning and Endynge of All Popery*, which he had Englished from a German translation of *Vaticinia, sive, Prophetiae*, by Joachimus, abbot of Fiore. Between 1548 and 1550 at least twenty-one books were published under Lynne's imprint. He was a publisher rather than a printer, employing the presses of a variety of colleagues in the expanding printing industry, most prominently two fellow Dutch immigrants, Nicolas Hill (Van den Berghe) and Steven Mierdman. Many of the books published for Lynne bear his distinctive mark, a ram and goat with the initials W. L. He also ran his own bookshop in St Paul's Churchyard, the centre of the London trade.

Lynne's special area of expertise was the publication in English of books by the continental reformers. Among his editions were popular works of Luther, Bullinger, Bernardine Ochino, and Urbanus Rhegius. Many were his own translations—others were contributed by prominent English protestants such as John Poynet and Thomas Norton. In his translation of Carion's *Chronicles* Lynne indeed described himself as 'one that spendeth all his tyme in the setting forth of books in the English tongue'. Lynne had been generously treated by leading members of the Edwardian protestant élite, and these debts were acknowledged in the gracious letters of dedication with which he prefaced several of his works. Carion's *Chronicles* was one of two books dedicated to Edward VI, and there were dedications to the king's sister, Elizabeth, and three (the largest number) to Anne, duchess of Somerset. In *The True Belief in Christ and his Sacraments*, dedicated to the duchess, Lynne expressed the wish that all men would read it:

> not as they have been heretofore accustomed to read the fained stories of Robin Hood, Clem of the clough with such like … but to put away their new errors (grounded upon the Romish rock) by the knowledge of the old faith that is builded upon the foundations of the prophets and apostles.

In his translation of Bullinger's sermon on magistracy Lynne presented his work as a direct acknowledgement of the gracious reception he had received in England. He told Edward VI:

> Considering what great benefits I have receyved of thys your majesties realm of England which hath so many years nourished and succoured my poorlife hitherto. I thought myself no less bound of very duty by to show some office of recompension thereto.

Other, less happy, personal experience might also inform these dedications, such as the bereavement which he says prompted him to publish *A brief collecion of all such texts of the scripture as do declare the most blessed and happy estate of them that are visited with sickness.* To what is here referred is unclear. Lynne and his wife, Anna (*d.* in or after 1571), joined the Dutch church in 1550. A daughter, Katherine, attended catechism class in the Dutch church; perhaps it was the death of a sibling which sent Lynne in search of consolation literature.

Lynne clearly enjoyed a measure of patronage from the Edwardian regime, since two editions of Cranmer's *Catechism* are numbered among his publications. He was also expanding his business enterprises to other forms of trade, such as the import of wine and hops. In June 1549 he received a licence to import 800 tuns of Gascon wine. With his other ventures prospering, Lynne was by 1550 able to withdraw from publishing, and after this year no books were published with his sponsorship. On the death of Edward VI he reconciled himself to the change in regime and remained in England. This was unsurprising—although Lynne had joined the new Dutch church in 1550, he was not close to the church hierarchy, in contrast to his Dutch printing colleagues Hill and Van der Erve, who both served as elders. Not surprisingly therefore it was Hill and Mierdman who were rewarded with the official commissions of the foreign churches, whereas the most assimilated Lynne was overlooked. This probably concerned Lynne little, since by this stage his time as a publisher was drawing to a close. He lived on in Billingsgate ward until his death some time before 1571, when his wife, Anna, described as a widow, was assessed for taxation. Although his period of activity in the London printing industry was relatively short, Lynne was nevertheless an important figure, not least for the part he played in the injection of capital and expertise from the more sophisticated continental centres of publishing, particularly Antwerp, during this critical period, when the London printing industry entered a new phase of its sixteenth-century development. ANDREW PETTEGREE

Sources E. G. Duff, *A century of the English book trade* (1905); repr. (1948) • A. Pettegree, *Foreign protestant communities in sixteenth-century London* (1986), 86–92 • E. J. Worman, *Alien members of the book-trade during the Tudor period* (1906) • R. E. G. Kirk and E. F. Kirk, eds., *Returns of aliens dwelling in the city and suburbs of London, from the reign of Henry VIII to that of James I*, Huguenot Society of London, 10/1 (1900), 25, 61, 85, 134, 161, 202, 209–10, 214, 331, 443; 10/2 (1902), 70 • *CPR*, 1547–8, 61 • PRO, E/122/81/32A, mm 16r, 17r, 18d

Lynott, Philip Parris [Phil] (**1949–1986**), singer and guitarist, was born at Hallam Hospital, West Bromwich, Birmingham, on 20 August 1949, the illegitimate son of a black Brazilian father, Cecil Parris (to whom he subsequently dedicated his 1974 book of poetry, *Songs for while I'm Away*), and an Irish mother, Philomena Lynott (*b.* 1930). He was raised by his grandmother in Dublin, and the circumstances of his birth were kept secret. As a mixed-race, illegitimate child, Lynott initially encountered prejudice from neighbours, but despite the difficulties he was generally popular and confident. By the age of eleven he had joined his first band, the Black Eagles, with Brian Downey and other boys from the Crumlin area of the city. Thin Lizzy was formed in December 1969, and after a year playing in Ireland, was signed by Decca Records. The band, consisting of Lynott (vocals and bass), Downey (drums), and Eric Bell (guitar), arrived in London in March 1971. Their first single to make the charts was a rock version of the traditional Irish song 'Whisky in a Jar', which reached number six in the British charts. The album *Nightlife* was cut in 1974 and *Fighting* in 1975.

Membership of Thin Lizzy underwent several transformations; it had a succession of notable guitarists (including Gary Moore, Scott Gorham, Brian Robertson, John Sykes, and Snowy White), but Lynott was always the central attraction. Influenced by Elvis Presley, Jimi Hendrix, and the early Van Morrison, he wrote the majority of the band's material. As a singer, his boisterous delivery and blues-tinged phrasing was ideally suited to hard rock, but he was equally capable of delivering a more soulful and melancholic inflection. His most important achievements, however, lay in the innovations he brought to hard rock or heavy metal (a term coined to describe rock music characterized by an overdriven/heavily distorted electric guitar attack, the absence of keyboards, and the use of the blues-based pentatonic scale). Lynott emulated the twin guitar attack of the 1960s band the Yardbirds, but his use of overdrive produced the harder edge more characteristic of heavy metal, as, for example, in 'Chinatown' (1980). His collaboration with Geddy Lee of Rush also helped to promote the bass guitar as a lead instrument, as in the 1976 single 'Dancing in the Moonlight'; that record is also notable for the prominent role taken by the saxophone, in evidence of Lynott's love of experimentation. It was, however, the Celtic influence and the feel for narrative that most distinguished Lynott's contribution to heavy metal. The songs 'Johnny', 'Black Rose', 'Emerald', and 'Warrior', for example, bring story-telling to metal lyrics and a sensitivity to imagery which is easy to overlook in comparison with Lynott's aggressively macho stance.

In 1976 Thin Lizzy shot to headline status with the transatlantic hit single 'The Boys are Back in Town', a Lynott song from the album *Jailbreak*, which was acclaimed as the single of the year by the *New Musical Express*. The band's second album of 1976, *Johnny the Fox*, was less successful, but in 1977 Lynott and the band toured the United States as the guests of the glam-rock band Queen, headlined at the Reading Festival in August, and released their eighth

Philip Parris Lynott (1949–1986), by unknown photographer, *c.*1975

album, *Bad Reputation*. The year ended with another successful tour of the USA, this time as top attraction, supported by Graham Parker and the Rumour. In 1978 a double album *Live and Dangerous* reached number two in the charts. In early 1979 the album *Black Rose* was cut in Paris and followed by a major tour of the United States and Britain.

It was at this time that Lynott first became dependent upon heroin, and although Thin Lizzy toured Japan and organized a scratch band, the Greedy Bastards, his behaviour became increasingly unpredictable. Lynott's first solo single, 'Dear Miss Lonely Hearts', reached number thirty-two in the British charts and was followed in April 1980 by the album *Solo in Soho*, and the next Thin Lizzy album, *Chinatown* (1980). On 14 February 1980 Lynott married Caroline Crowther, daughter of the entertainer Leslie Crowther, with whom he had two daughters. Described by his wife as 'a romantic idealist who believed in myths and legends' (*The Rocker*), he became increasingly reliant on heroin and his numerous sexual escapades finally led to the breakdown of the marriage, and they separated in 1983. Lynott continued to tour with Thin Lizzy throughout 1981, visiting the USA, Australia, the Bahamas, and Europe, as well as gigging in Britain. At the end of the year the band released another album, *Renegade*. In the mean time, Lynott had two more notable solo successes, with 'King's Call' (a tribute to Elvis Presley) and 'Yellow Peril' (1982), which was used as the theme tune for the BBC television show *Top of the Pops*. In the summer of 1983 Thin Lizzy split up, after playing a last concert at Nuremburg. Lynott then formed a new group, Grand Slam, but it failed to develop, and his subsequent solo, 'Nineteen', did not sell. On Christmas day 1985 Lynott collapsed from a drug overdose at his home, 184 Kew Road, Richmond, Surrey. He died ten days later, on 4 January 1986, at Clouds Clinic, East Knoyle, near Salisbury, from heart failure and pneumonia. His funeral mass was celebrated on 9 January at St Elizabeth of Portugal Church, Richmond, and he was buried in St Fintan's cemetery, in Sutton, Dublin. SHEILA WHITELEY

Sources P. Lynott, *My boy: the Phil Lynott story* (1995) • C. Larkin, ed., *The Guinness encyclopedia of popular music*, concise edn (1993) • BBC 2, *The rocker: a portrait of Phil Lynott*, 12 July 1996 • B. K. Friesen and J. S. Epstein, 'Rock 'n' roll aint noise pollution: artistic conventions and tensions in the major subgenres of heavy metal music', *Popular Music and Society*, 18/3 (autumn 1994), 1–18 • J. S. Epstein, *Adolescents and their music: if it's too loud, you're too old* (1994) • D. Weinstein, *Heavy metal: a cultural sociology* (1991) • b. cert. • Róisín Dubh, 'The electronic Thin Lizzy magazine', www.cs.may.ie/~adamw/BlackRose.html, 20 May 1999

Archives FILM BFI NFTVA, 'The rocker: a portrait of Phil Lynott', BBC2, 12 Jan 1996 • BFI NFTVA, performance footage | SOUND BL NSA, oral history interview • BL NSA, performance recordings

Likenesses photograph, *c*.1975, Hult. Arch. [*see illus.*] • photographs, Hult. Arch.

Wealth at death £322,744: administration, 1986

Lynskey, Sir George Justin (1888–1957), judge, was born on 5 February 1888 at 26 Thomas Lane, Knotty Ash, Liverpool, the eldest of four sons and two daughters of George Jeremy Lynskey (1861–1921), who had been born in the west of Ireland and who later became a prominent solicitor and Irish National League alderman in the city of Liverpool, and his wife, Honora Mary, *née* Kearney. He was educated locally at St Francis Xavier's College, and at the University of Liverpool, where he graduated LLB (1907), LLM (1908), and where he later received the honorary degree of LLD (1951). He entered his father's firm, qualified as a solicitor in 1910 with first-class honours, and was awarded the Rupert Bremner gold medal of the Law Society.

Lynskey then joined his father in practice, and on 24 September 1913 married Eileen Mary, daughter of John Edward Prendiville of Liverpool; they had two daughters. In 1920 he was called to the bar by the Inner Temple, and joined the northern circuit, taking silk in 1930. It was said that he acquired one of the largest practices of his day at the provincial bar; one of his pupils was David Maxwell Fyfe, who, as Lord Kilmuir, was later lord chancellor. 'Genial, friendly, rubicund, with an inherited love of hospitality and conviviality, he was extremely popular with his brethren on the Northern Circuit' (*Law Times*). He was made a bencher of the Inner Temple in 1938 and judge of the Salford court of record from 1937 to 1944.

But the next stage was not quite automatic. In 1944 some judicial vacancies arose, and there was natural speculation as to the likely appointees. Lynskey, locally schooled and from a redbrick university, with a large practice but almost exclusively in Lancashire and very rarely appearing in the law courts in London and not generally known there, did not have the background of normal High Court appointments at that time. Also, many of the High Court judges dealt with cases in specialized subjects heard exclusively in London. So there was reportedly some surprise when Lynskey was appointed to the King's Bench Division by Lord Simon, the lord chancellor, with the customary knighthood.

Lynskey's very substantial experience of criminal cases was very useful on assize, where he proved an outstanding judge. He was constantly absent from London trying cases in all parts of the country. Contemporaries admired his breadth of knowledge, 'his clear and quick mind' which enabled him rapidly to see the essentials of a case; those who appeared before him respected his 'unfailing courtesy and patience' (*DNB*; *The Times*). He possessed 'an especial talent for finding a short way to torpedo ingenious but bad points' (*Law Times*).

Lynskey came to national prominence as a result of the famous tribunal which he chaired in 1948 to investigate allegations of corruption involving ministers and civil servants at the Board of Trade. On 9 October 1948 the prime minister's office issued a statement that irregularities had been alleged and an inquiry was set up, the home secretary, Chuter Ede, appointing Lynskey as chairman, assisted by two KCs, Godfrey Vick and Gerald Upjohn, their terms of reference being to investigate whether there was any justification for allegations that payments or rewards had been given to ministers or civil servants. The context for the Lynskey tribunal lay in the shortages in post-war Britain and the necessity for licences, rations, and clothing coupons. In the period of austerity the public regarded offences against these regulations as not only a crime but morally wrong, and the Attlee government's immediate and stern response to the allegations of wrongdoing by public servants was in keeping with the public mood.

The Lynskey tribunal sat for twenty-six days and heard many witnesses. Such was the importance of the issues that the attorney-general, Sir Hartley Shawcross, lately prosecutor of war crimes, was recalled from UN duties to represent the government. The principal allegations concerned the activities of Sydney Stanley, an immigrant undischarged bankrupt from Poland, a man of great charm and style who lived in one of London's most fashionable addresses and who, in return for bribes or favours, was alleged to be able to arrange almost anything at top governmental level. Those said to have sought his influence included the Sherman brothers, owners of a football pools firm; and those accused of having received favours included John Belcher, a Labour MP and parliamentary secretary at the Board of Trade, and George Gibson, a director of the Bank of England.

As there was no actual defendant, the normal rules of evidence did not apply, and the inquiry allowed the wildest allegations to be made, and to be publicized. It was a 'field day' for the press. Among those caught up in the accusations was the former chancellor of the exchequer, Hugh Dalton, who was exonerated. Although there is no easy simplification of the tangled web, the chief allegations concerned Stanley's offers to use his contacts to assist Sherman's football pools of Cardiff, who wanted a licence for a larger paper allocation than they had been allowed, who wished to have a prosecution against them for a breach of the paper regulations dropped, and who needed the consent of the Capital Issues Committee for their proposals to become a public company. Stanley was also alleged to have taken bribes from an importer of pintables for amusement arcades to obtain the necessary import licences. To secure favours Stanley was alleged to have made small gifts to Belcher and Gibson, including having suits made for them by a West End tailor, for which Stanley paid the bill and supplied the clothing coupons.

Church House, Westminster was packed with lawyers, press, and public for the daily hearings of the tribunal, the star of which was Sydney Stanley, dressed immaculately and answering with great charm the direct accusations of bribery and corruption. The inquiry closed just before Christmas 1948, and on 28 January 1949 its report was issued. It laid some blame on John Belcher and George Gibson who resigned their offices. The civil service was completely cleared. Stanley was described as one who continually uttered lies, and who held himself out as one who could influence the ministries in return for favours. *The Times* stated that the report laid bare Stanley's manoeuvres with devastating lucidity, but when the report was presented to the House of Commons on 3 February Shawcross announced that there would be no prosecutions. Members complained that the guilty had gone free, the innocent had been ruined, and that Stanley had become a national hero. Lynskey received well-earned congratulations from Chuter Ede, and there the matter ended. It has been observed that 'The Inquiry was a most difficult one to conduct and to keep within reasonable bounds. It was generally agreed that Lynskey's handling of it was a masterly combination of firmness and fairness' (*The Times*). Lynskey himself remarked at one point in the proceedings that what the tribunal had to decide was what was 'legitimate business' (J. Gross, 274).

Lynskey declined promotion to the Court of Appeal when it was proposed to him by Lord Jowitt, lord chancellor in Attlee's government. In December 1957 he had just completed the assize list at Manchester assizes when he was suddenly taken ill with a coronary thrombosis. He died in the Manchester Royal Infirmary on 21 December 1957. He had kept the Roman Catholic faith, and Archbishop Godfrey gave the absolution at the requiem mass at Farm Street, London, followed by interment at Brooklands cemetery, Weybridge, on 31 December. Lynskey was survived by his wife and their two daughters.

GRAEME BRYSON

Sources *DNB* · *WWW* · *The Times* (23 Dec 1957) · *Law Times* (3 Jan 1958) · *St Francis Xavier's College Magazine* (1957) [with photo] · *Gore's Liverpool Directories* (1889) [home, solicitors and barristers' chambers] · *Gore's Liverpool Directories* (1917) [home, solicitors and barristers' chambers] · *Gore's Liverpool Directories* (1922) [home, solicitors and barristers' chambers] · *Gore's Liverpool Directories* (1928) [home, solicitors and barristers' chambers] · H. T. F. Rhodes, *The Lynskey tribunal* (1949) · J. Gross, 'The Lynskey tribunal', *Age of austerity*, ed. M. Sissons and P. French (1963), 255–75 · S. W. Baron, *The story of Sidney Stanley and the Lynskey tribunal* (1966) · K. O. Morgan, *Labour in power, 1945–1951* (1985) · personal knowledge (2004) · private information (2004) [Mrs Noreen Wightman-Smith, daughter] · P. J. Waller, *Democracy and sectarianism: a political and social history of Liverpool, 1868–1939* (1981) [on George Jeremy Lynskey] · *The political diary of Hugh Dalton, 1918–1940, 1945–1960*, ed. B. Pimlott (1986)

Archives FILM BFI NFTVA, news footage

Likenesses photograph, repro. in *St Francis Xavier's College Magazine*

Wealth at death £16,584 17*s*. 10*d*.: probate, 28 April 1958, *CGPLA Eng. & Wales*

Lyon [*née* L'Amy or Lammie], **Agnes** (**1762–1840**), poet, eldest daughter of John Ramsay L'Amy (or Lammie) of Dunkenny, Forfarshire, and his wife, Agnes Hamilton, was born at Dundee early in 1762. On 25 January 1786 she married the Revd Dr James Lyon of Glamis, Forfarshire, with whom she had ten children.

Agnes Lyon wrote humorous poetry, mostly on domestic subjects, for her own pleasure and that of her family. She claimed that she rarely made corrections or allowed her writing to interfere with the running of her household: 'She ne'er neglected house affair,/Nor put her little babes aside,/To take on Pegasus a ride' (Rogers, 2.85). She directed at her death that her manuscripts should remain unprinted, unless the family needed pecuniary assistance. She has chiefly been remembered for the song beginning 'You've surely heard of famous Niel', written at the request of Niel Gow for his air, 'Farewell to Whisky'. She died on 14 September 1840.

J. C. HADDEN, *rev.* SARAH COUPER

Sources C. Rogers, *The modern Scottish minstrel, or, The songs of Scotland of the past half-century*, 2 (1856), 84–95 · P. R. Drummond, *Perthshire in bygone days* (1879) · Irving, *Scots.* · *IGI*

Lyon, Alexander, **second Lord Glamis** (*c.***1430–1486**?). *See under* Lyon, Patrick, first Lord Glamis (*c.*1400–1460).

Lyon, Alexander Ward [Alex] (**1931–1993**), politician, was born on 15 October 1931 at 60 Osmondthorpe Lane, Osmondthorpe, Leeds, the son of Alexander Pirie Lyon, master fish fryer and grocer, and his wife, Doris, *née* Ward. Both parents were devout Methodists. Rejected by Leeds grammar school, he attended West Leeds High School, from where he gained entrance to the law department of University College, London. While still a student he married, on 7 July 1951, Hilda Arandall (*b.* 1928/9), dress designer, and daughter of John Arandall, of Leeds; they had two sons and a daughter. He was called to the bar by the Inner Temple in 1954, and became a prominent figure on the north-east circuit. He later became chairman of the Society of Labour Lawyers.

Lyon contested York for the Labour Party in October 1964, and in March 1966 succeeded in defeating the personally popular Conservative MP Charles Longbottom. He held the seat until 1983. In assiduously nursing the constituency, he displayed a foretaste of those very qualities—tenacity, to the point of occasional obduracy, and a high-minded sense of principle—which in subsequent years were to irritate senior colleagues. Once in parliament he became immersed in the long-running Rhodesian crisis, and was conspicuously brave in making clear to Harold Wilson that many in the Labour Party

Alexander Ward Lyon (1931–1993), by unknown photographer

would not support him in moves which looked as if they were giving in to Ian Smith and racism. But the event which made a seminal contribution to his political perceptions was the *cause célèbre* of the Kenyan Asians. The number of immigrants from Kenya rose steadily each month throughout the winter of 1967–8. Some 13,000 arrived in Britain in the first two months of 1968, twice as many as in the whole of 1965. The tabloid press exaggerated the extent to which they were drawing bountiful assistance from the social services, and carried endless stories of boatloads of illegal immigrants being smuggled ashore on isolated beaches on the south coast of England. In April 1968 Enoch Powell—Lyon's *bête noire*—made his notorious 'rivers of blood' speech and dockers marched to the House of Commons to support him. Lyon was prominent in the opposition to Powell's views, and acted as a focal point for resistance to harsh treatment of east African Asians. He voted against the government on the Commonwealth Immigrants Act of 1968.

In 1969 Lyon became an additional parliamentary private secretary at the Treasury, then parliamentary private secretary to the paymaster-general, Harold Lever. Following Labour's defeat in the general election of 1970 he became an opposition spokesman first on African affairs, then on home affairs. He supported Britain's entry into the EEC, and voted with the Conservative government in the crucial vote on 28 October 1971. He again defied a three-line whip on the Housing Finance Bill of 1972 and was consequently dismissed from the Labour front bench. Nevertheless, following Labour's narrow victory in the election of February 1974, he was appointed by Harold Wilson minister of state at the Home Office, responsible for race relations and immigration issues. He was at this time considered by many contemporaries as a possible future leader of the Labour Party. Nevertheless, his eighteen months as minister of state were controversial, and were marked in particular by disputes between him and his senior officials over the application of the immigration rules. When James Callaghan succeeded Wilson as prime minister in April 1976, he dismissed Lyon, and divided responsibility for immigration and race relations between several other ministers. There was significant, and by no means ephemeral, public discussion of whether, by this act, Callaghan was showing himself illiberal over race and immigration, or whether Lyon had been too zealous in helping immigrants. Lyon's friends pointed out that, unlike many of his predecessors in this difficult ministerial berth, who had simply sat in their sepulchral room in the Home Office, he had at least ventured forth to India, Pakistan, and Bangladesh, applying his razor-sharp QC's mind to the cause of delays in granting certificates of entry into Britain for dependants of people already settled. His critics—in an age of Powellite rhetoric—crudely, and almost certainly in error, thought that Lyon could single-handedly lose Labour a general election.

Following his return to the back benches, Lyon was appointed, in 1978, chairman of the UK Immigrants Advisory Service, in succession to Lord Foot. He was a member of the select committee on home affairs and chairman of the Parliamentary Labour Party home affairs group, both from 1979 to 1983. After his first marriage ended in divorce, he married, on 19 February 1982, Clare Margaret Short (*b.* 1946), daughter of Francis Gerard Short, headteacher. She was at that point director of Youth Aid and the Unemployment Unit, but in June 1983 was elected Labour MP for Birmingham Ladywood. At the same election Lyon lost his own seat. Shortly afterwards he was diagnosed as suffering from spinal muscular dystrophy. He resigned as chairman of the UK Immigrants Advisory Service in 1984. He bore a long illness with characteristic courage, and with enormous support from his wife, Clare. He died at the Westbury Nursing Home, Newport Pagnell, Buckinghamshire, on 30 September 1993; he was survived by his wife and by the three children of his first marriage.

TAM DALYELL

Sources *The Independent* (1 Oct 1993) • *The Times* (1 Oct 1993) • *WWW, 1991–5* • personal knowledge (2004) • private information (2004) • b. cert. • m. certs. • d. cert.

Likenesses photograph, repro. in *The Independent* • photograph, News International Syndication, London; repro. in *The Times* [*see illus.*]

Wealth at death under £125,000: administration, 11 Jan 1994, *CGPLA Eng. & Wales*

Lyon, Claude George Bowes-, fourteenth earl of Strathmore and Kinghorne in the peerage of Scotland, and first earl of Strathmore and Kinghorne in the peerage

of the United Kingdom (**1855–1944**), landowner, was born in Lowndes Square, London, on 14 March 1855, the eldest son of Claude Bowes-Lyon, thirteenth earl of Strathmore and Kinghorne (1824–1904), and his wife, Frances Dora (1832–1922), daughter of Oswald Smith, of Blendon Hall, Kent. He succeeded as fourteenth earl on 16 February 1904. He was educated at Eton College, and was given a commission in the 2nd Life Guards, which he resigned in 1882. On 16 July 1881 he married Nina Cecilia (1862–1938), daughter of the Revd Charles William Frederick Cavendish-Bentinck. They had four daughters and six sons. On 26 April 1923 the youngest daughter, Elizabeth Angela Marguerite, married Prince Albert Frederick Arthur George, duke of York, afterwards George VI, and consequently became queen consort.

Lord Strathmore was of a retiring disposition, but took a strong personal interest in the welfare of his tenantry and in the management of his estates. He encouraged small-holdings as a form of tenancy, and probably had more small-holding tenants than any other proprietor in the district south and east of Aberdeenshire and Argyll. Interest in forestry led him to take an active part in the development of his plantations, especially of larch, and he was one of the first to rear larch from seed, which he brought over from Norway. In 1904 he was appointed lord lieutenant of Angus (Forfarshire) in succession to his father, but he resigned in 1936; he was also president of the Territorial Association of the county. On 1 June 1937 he was created earl of Strathmore and Kinghorne in the peerage of the United Kingdom by his son-in-law King George VI. He died at his residence, Glamis Castle, on 7 November 1944.

F. J. Grant, *rev.* K. D. Reynolds

Sources Burke, *Peerage* · personal knowledge (1944) · *WWW* · GEC, *Peerage*

Archives Durham RO, corresp.

Likenesses W. Stoneman, photograph, 1928, NPG

Wealth at death £75,955 6*s*. 0*d*.: confirmation, 17 July 1945, *CCI*

Lyon, Elizabeth [*nicknamed* Edgware Bess] (*fl.* **1722–1726**), prostitute and thief, was born at Edgware, Middlesex, from which her alias was derived. Nothing is known of her parentage or early life, not even whether Lyon was a maiden or married name. She may, however, have been the Elizabeth Miller, alias Lyon, convicted at the Old Bailey and branded in the hand in October 1721 for stealing a piece of silk and 5 yards of cambric from the house of John Davenport, where she lodged, in the parish of St Peter Westcheap, London. Lyon acquired contemporary notoriety as the mistress of the celebrated criminal John (Jack) *Sheppard (1702–1724). They met at the Black Lion alehouse in Lewkenor's Lane, St Giles-in-the-Fields, London, in 1722 or 1723, when Sheppard was an apprentice, and it was Lyon who first induced him to steal. She became a confederate in many of his robberies and escapes. On 25 May 1724 they escaped together out of New prison in Clerkenwell, and on 31 August she assisted him to escape from the condemned hold in Newgate.

After Sheppard's execution on 16 November 1724 Lyon exercised a similarly profound influence over other youths. In March 1725 she was committed to the Westminster house of correction, Tothill Fields, for 'seducing a shopkeeper's son to go a thieving with her' (*Parker's London News*, 31 March 1725). In the following summer she was cohabiting with a young painter named James Little (1708–1725). Lyon is said to have 'hurried him headlong to his destruction' (Guthrie, 4), but he had already turned to crime before their relationship. On 29 August, after robbing Lionel Mills, a button seller, in a field near Montague House, Little was arrested in Lyon's house off Lewkenor's Lane. He was convicted at the Old Bailey in October and executed at Tyburn on 3 November 1725. In March 1726 Lyon was herself indicted at the Old Bailey for robbing the house of Edward Bury, a butcher, in Allen Street, Clerkenwell. The principal witness was her accomplice, John Smith, an employee of Bury. 'She persuaded me to rob my master's house', he told the court, 'and said she'd go with me, and put me in the way, for I was a mere ignoramus at such sort of business' (*Select Trials*, 1.469).

Lyon was convicted of felony and sentenced to seven years' transportation. She was transported on the *Loyal Margaret* (Captain John Wheaton) and a landing certificate, dated 1 October 1726, records her safe arrival at Annapolis in Maryland. Her subsequent career is unknown. A 1732 account described her as 'a large masculine woman' (Hayward, 182), but the little we know of her suggests a beguiling as well as a forceful personality. 'A more wicked, deceitful and lascivious wretch there is not living in England', Sheppard allegedly said of her after they had quarrelled (*Narrative*, 14). A woman of loose morals she undoubtedly was, but Lyon sometimes placed herself at personal risk to assist Sheppard to escape from captivity. As a figure in romances such as William Harrison Ainsworth's *Jack Sheppard* (1839), the anonymous *Edgeworth Bess, or, Shephard in Danger* (1867), and Joseph Hatton's *When Rogues Fall Out* (1899), as well as in numerous Sheppard stage plays, Lyon acquired some fame in the Victorian period.

Philip Sugden

Sources *The history of the remarkable life of John Sheppard* (1724) · *A narrative of all the robberies, escapes, &c. of John Sheppard* (1724) · J. Guthrie, *The ordinary of Newgate: his account of the behaviour, confession, and dying words of the malefactors who were executed on Wednesday the 3rd of November last at Tyburn* (1725) · *The proceedings on the king's commission of the peace* (1720–21) [Old Bailey sessions papers, 11–14 Oct 1721] · *The proceedings on the king's commission of the peace* (1723–4) [Old Bailey sessions papers, 8–10 July, 12–14 Aug 1724]; (1724–5) [13–15 Oct 1725]; (1725–6) [2–7 March 1726] · Middlesex gaol delivery rolls, LMA, esp. MJ/GSR 2427, 2429 and 2459 · *Select trials … at the sessions house in the Old Bailey*, 1 (1734), 435–49, 469–70 · landing certificate, CLRO, misc. MSS, box 57, no. 8/26 · A. L. Hayward, ed., *The lives of the most remarkable criminals* (1927), 181–9, 286–8, 470–73 · H. Bleackley and S. M. Ellis, *Jack Sheppard* (1933) · *London newspapers* (1724–6) · P. Rawlings, *Drunks, whores and idle apprentices: criminal biographies of the eighteenth century* (1992), 39–75

Archives LMA, Middlesex and Westminster sessions of the peace and gaol delivery rolls

Lyon, Emma. *See* Hamilton, Emma, Lady Hamilton (*bap.* 1765, *d.* 1815).

Lyon, George Francis [*alias* Said-ben-Abdallah] (**1795–1832**), naval officer and explorer, son of a colonel in the

George Francis Lyon (1795–1832), by John Jackson

army, was born at Chichester, Sussex. Around 1805 he was educated at Dr Burney's naval academy, Gosport, Hampshire, and entered the navy in 1808, had the commission of lieutenant confirmed in 1814, and saw much action.

Lyon was at Malta in September 1818 when Joseph Ritchie, secretary to the consul in Paris, arrived there on his way to Tripoli to begin his attempt to reach central Africa from the north. Captain Frederick Marryat, who was to accompany Ritchie, proved unable to do so, and Lyon volunteered to take his place, by his own admission purely from a wish to rise in his profession. In November Lyon joined Ritchie at Tripoli. He already had some knowledge of Arabic, and for the next four months studied the language and religious and social customs of the Arabs, adopting the alias Said-ben-Abdallah. After long delays at Tripoli and a short expedition to the Gharian Mountains, they and a servant, transparently disguised as Muslims, left Tripoli for Murzuq, the capital of Fezzan, the bey of which supported the expedition. Lyon suffered from dysentery and the extreme heat, and on 20 November 1819 Ritchie died. Lyon, in poor health and the victim of Ritchie's mismanagement of the whole expedition, pushed on to Tajarhi, and thence managed to reach Tripoli in March 1820, and London in July 1820. The account of his and Ritchie's journey was published as *A Narrative of Travels in North Africa* (1821), illustrated from Lyon's own drawings.

Lyon was promoted commander in 1821, and appointed to the *Hecla* under the orders of Captain William Edward Parry in the *Fury*. The expedition, Parry's second in the search for the north-west passage, sailed on 8 May 1821, entered the Arctic region through Hudson Strait, examined Repulse Bay and the neighbouring coast of Melville peninsula, and wintered at a small island to the eastward of the Frozen Strait. The next summer they went further north and entered Fury and Hecla Strait, but the season being then far advanced they turned back, wintered at Igloolik (lat. 69°21′ N, long. 81°44′ W), and came home in autumn 1823, as signs of scurvy among the crew made it inadvisable to stay. On 13 November Lyon was promoted captain, and the following year he published *The private journal of Captain G. F. Lyon … during the recent voyage of discovery under Captain Parry* (1824). In January 1824 he was appointed to the *Griper*, which had been on Parry's first voyage of 1819. Lyon's instructions were to reach Repulse Bay by whatever route he judged best, and from it to examine the coast of the mainland westward to the point where John Franklin's voyage had ended its survey. He sailed on 6 June, but the season proved unfavourable, and he returned to England in November, to publish *A brief narrative of an unsuccessful attempt to reach Repulse bay through Sir Thomas Rowe's Welcome* (1825).

In June 1825 the University of Oxford conferred on Lyon an honorary DCL; and on 5 September he married Lucy Louisa (*d.* *c.*September 1826), elder daughter of Lord Edward *Fitzgerald. Shortly afterwards he went to Mexico as one of the commissioners of the English Compánia de Real del Monte, which mined silver there. On the voyage home his ship was wrecked at Holyhead on 14 January 1827. Most of Lyon's papers and mineral specimens were lost, as he mentions in his *Journal of a Residence and Tour in … Mexico* (2 vols., 1828). When he landed he received news of the death of his wife four months earlier. He afterwards went to South America on mining business, but finding his sight rapidly failing—the result apparently of an attack of ophthalmia in Africa—he set out for England to obtain medical advice. He died on board the *Emulous*, sailing from Buenos Aires, on 8 October 1832.

ELIZABETH BAIGENT

Sources J. Marshall, *Royal naval biography*, 3/1 (1831), 100–24 • A. Adu Boahen, *Britain, the Sahara and the western Sudan, 1788–1861* (1964) • Foster, *Alum. Oxon.* • *GM*, 1st ser., 103/1 (1833), 372–4 • Burke, *Peerage* • *DNB*

Archives Derbys. RO, Gell MSS, reports about his journeys in polar seas by John Franklin • Som. ARS, letters to Sir Henry Bayntun

Likenesses M. Ganci, lithograph (after E. Allingham), BM • J. Jackson, portrait; Christies, 25 Sept 2001, lot 4 [*see illus.*] • R. J. Lane, lithograph (after his earlier work), NPG

Lyon, Hart [Hirsch Lewin or Loebel] (**1721–1800**), rabbi, was born in Rzeszow, Poland, the son of Rabbi Aryeh Loeb ben Saul (1690–1755), a man of distinguished rabbinical lineage who was sometimes known by the surname Loewenstamm, and his wife, Miriam (*d.* 1753), daughter of Rabbi Zevi Hirsch ben Jacob, surnamed Ashkenazi (1660–1718). The latter, known as Hakham ('Sage') Zevi, was a renowned authority on Jewish law who, as rabbi of Altona and later of Amsterdam, was consulted by the Great Synagogue in Duke's Place, London, on controversial points during its formative years and visited London in 1714. Having attended a *yeshivah* (rabbinical academy) between about 1736 and 1745 in Glogau, where his father had been rabbi before moving to Amsterdam, Hirsch Loebel (as he

Hart Lyon (1721–1800), by Edward Fisher (after James Turner)

was then called) devoted himself to the full-time study of traditional Jewish texts and, unusually for the time, Hebrew grammar. In 1751, when the celebrated theological dispute between Jacob Emden and Jonathan Eybeschütz had begun, he issued a pamphlet supporting the position of Emden, who was Hakham Zevi's son.

Hirsch Loebel's reputation as a Talmudist, together with the congregation's well-remembered association with his much respected grandfather, persuaded the Great Synagogue in 1756 to appoint him to its pulpit following the death in office of Rabbi Aaron Hart. He assumed his duties early in 1757, and while serving the congregation was known as Hart Lyon, the literal translations of his forename and patronymic. His appointment heralded a period of co-operation between London's two Ashkenazi congregations, for the Hambro Synagogue agreed to pay £100 of his annual salary of £250 and looked to him for guidance on matters affected by Jewish law. Similarly, a group of Jews who—to the consternation of the Great Synagogue authorities—founded a third Ashkenazi congregation in the capital in 1761, recognized Lyon's authority on such issues, and sought his approval of the man they chose to be their rabbi. Lyon thus enjoyed a status which foreshadowed the position of chief rabbi, created later in the century.

However, Lyon was deeply unhappy with the state of Jewish observance and education in London and with British Jewry's acculturationist impulse. In sermon after sermon, often characterized by some ninety minutes' discussion of the Talmud augmented by a homily of comparable duration, he admonished his congregants for their religious laxity and eagerness to imitate the habits and fashions of gentile society. Tensions between Lyon and the Great Synagogue's lay leaders were perhaps evident in their extraordinary denial of his request to be allowed publicly to refute allegations made by Jacob Kimchi, a pious Jewish peddler from Turkey. In a pamphlet published at Altona in 1760 Kimchi accused the officials who, under Lyon's jurisdiction, supervised ritual slaughtering arrangements in London, of disregarding the letter of Jewish law. The Great Synagogue's decision rankled, and, frustrated by his congregants' indifference towards Jewish learning, Lyon set up a continental-style *bet midrash* (house of study) in his home and spent an increasing amount of his time there. His accomplishments as a scholar were better appreciated on the continent, and he possibly regretted taking the London offer in preference to a slightly earlier one from Dubno in Poland.

In 1763, thoroughly disillusioned with London Jewry, Lyon accepted a call to be rabbi of Halberstadt, and left the Great Synagogue in the spring of the following year. Lyon's cousin, Israel Meshullam Zalman Emden, hoped to succeed him, but had to be satisfied instead with the pulpit of the Hambro Synagogue, where he was called Meshullam Solomon. In 1770 Lyon, known as Hirsch Lewin, became rabbi of Mannheim, and in 1773 of Berlin, where he remained for the rest of his life. Although opposed to the more extreme manifestations of Jewish enlightenment thought which were circulating among Berlin's Jews, he collaborated with Moses Mendelssohn in preparing a book on aspects of Jewish law which appeared in 1778 as *Ritualgesetze der Juden*. His commentary on the classic Jewish text *Pirke Avot* ('Chapters of the fathers') was published posthumously in 1834. He also wrote Hebrew poems, some of which were printed.

Lyon and his wife, Golde (*fl.* 1720–1800), daughter of David Tevele Cohen, a leader of the Jewish community in Glogau, had six children: the controversial scholar Rabbi Saul Berliner, who died in London on 19 June 1790 after fleeing Berlin accused of forging rabbinical texts; Chief Rabbi Solomon *Hirschell; Abraham David Tevele Berliner, a merchant; and daughters Sarah, Reisel, and Beilah, whose knowledge of the Talmud and attainments in Hebrew testify to her father's enlightened attitude towards the religious education of girls. Lyon died in Berlin in 1800 and was buried there.

During his ministry at the Great Synagogue Lyon sat for his portrait in oils by James Turner; it was subsequently engraved by Edward Fisher and sold as a print at Cornhill under the title *The most Learned High Priest Hart Lyon, Rabbi London*. The department of prints and drawings at the British Museum has an impression of Fisher's mezzotint, but Turner's painting, which used to hang in the Great Synagogue, is believed to have been destroyed in the blitz. HILARY L. RUBINSTEIN

Sources C. Duschinsky, *The rabbinate of the Great Synagogue, 1756–1842* (1921) • C. Roth, *The Great Synagogue, London, 1690–1940* (1950) • sermons, Jewish Theological Seminary, New York, Adler papers • D. Kaufmann, 'Rabbi Zevi Ashkenazi and his family in London', *Transactions of the Jewish Historical Society of England*, 3 (1896–8), 102–25

Archives Jewish Theological Seminary, New York, Adler papers

Likenesses E. Fisher, mezzotint (after J. Turner), AM Oxf., BM [*see illus.*] • J. Turner, oils

Lyon, Sir James Frederick (1775–1842), army officer, a descendant of the Lyons, lords Glamis, was son of Captain James Lyon (*d.* 1775), 35th foot, and his wife Mary (later Mrs George Coke), daughter of James Hamilton of Ballencrieff, East Lothian, and great-great-grandson of Sir Patrick Lyon of Carse (1637–1694). He was born on board a transport ship homeward bound from America after the battle of Bunker Hill, where his father had been killed. On 4 August 1791 he was appointed ensign, 25th foot (later King's Own Scottish Borderers). He became lieutenant on 26 April 1793, captain on 5 April 1795, major on 21 February 1799, brevet-colonel in 1811, major-general in 1814, and lieutenant-general in 1830.

Lyon served with detachments of the 25th as marines on board the *Gibraltar* (80 guns, Captain Mackenzie) and the *Marlborough* (74 guns, Captain Hon. George Berkeley) in the Channel Fleet under Earl Howe. He was present at the actions of 27 and 29 May, and the great victory of 1 June 1794. He afterwards served with his regiment in the island of Grenada during the reign of terror there, when Governor Home and all the principal white inhabitants were massacred by the slaves. He was on Lord George Lennox's staff at Plymouth in 1797–8, and was subsequently aide-de-camp to the Hon. Sir Charles Steuart at Minorca. In 1799 he was appointed to a foreign corps, originally known as 'Stuart's', or the Minorca regiment, raised in that island by Sir John Stuart (afterwards count of Maida), with Lyon and Nicholas Trant as majors. The corps was successively known as the Queen's German regiment and the 97th (Queen's), and was disbanded as the 96th (Queen's) in 1818. Lyon was with it in 1801 in Egypt, where it was engaged with Bonaparte's 'invincibles' at the battle of 21 March 1801, and was highly distinguished. Lyon subsequently commanded the regiment in the Peninsula from 1808 to 1811 at Vimeiro, Talavera, Busaco, and the first siege of Badajoz. In June 1813 he was sent to Germany to assist in organizing the new Hanoverian levies (distinct from the King's German Legion), and he was present at the operations in the north of Germany in 1813–14, under the prince royal of Sweden. He led a division of Hanoverians at the battle of Göhrde in Hanover, on 13 September 1813, and afterwards was in charge of a mixed force of Russians, Hanoverians, and Hanseatics, under Count von Benningsen, which blockaded Hamburg. He commanded the 6th Hanoverian brigade during the Waterloo campaign and the advance to Paris. The brigade was with the reserve near Hal on 18 June, and did not engage. Lyon commanded the inland district in 1817, and he led the troops in the Windward and Leeward islands, with headquarters at Barbados, in 1828–33. He was promised the governorship of Gibraltar, but was disappointed. Lyon was a KCB and KCH (1815), GCH (1817), and had the orders of the Sword in Sweden and Maximilian Joseph of Bavaria, with gold medals for Egypt, Vimeiro and Talavera, and the Hanoverian and Waterloo medals. He was colonel of the 24th foot, and equerry to the duke of Cambridge.

Lyon married Anne, daughter of Edward Coxe of Hampstead, and niece of the Revd George Coxe (his stepfather), Peter Coxe (1753?–1844), and Archdeacon William Coxe (1748–1828), the historian. Lyon lived latterly at Grosvenor Lodge, Tunbridge Wells, Kent, and died at Brighton on 16 October 1842.

H. M. Chichester, *rev.* Roger T. Stearn

Sources *Dod's Peerage* (1842) • *Army List* • J. Philippart, ed., *The royal military calendar*, 3rd edn, 3 (1820) • R. T. Wilson, *Narrative of the campaign in Egypt* (1802) • *The dispatches of … the duke of Wellington … from 1799 to 1818*, ed. J. Gurwood, new edn, 3: *India, 1794–1805* (1837) • marquess of Londonderry [C. S. H. Vane-Tempest-Stewart], *Narrative of the war in Germany and France, in 1813 and 1814* (1830) • N. L. Beamish, *History of the king's German legion*, 2 (1837) • *Naval and Military Gazette* (22 Oct 1842) • A. J. Guy, ed., *The road to Waterloo: the British army and the struggle against revolutionary and Napoleonic France, 1793–1815* (1990) • T. C. W. Blanning, *The French revolutionary wars, 1787–1802* (1996) • R. Muir, *Britain and the defeat of Napoleon, 1807–1815* (1996) • *GM*, 2nd ser., 19 (1843) • Burke, *Peerage* (1999)

Likenesses plaster bust, Barbados

Lyon, Sir John, lord of Glamis (*d.* 1382), administrator and landowner, is of obscure origins. Chroniclers writing early in the sixteenth century deliberately emphasized his supposed lowly origins and claimed that he had originally been called John Myll and had received the surname Lyon from Robert II as an indication of, and reward for, his service to that monarch. An origin in the north-east of the kingdom, perhaps Angus, may be indicated by his steady accumulation of territorial interests in this area. He emerges into the light of historical record on 9 July 1368, when he had a grant of lands in the lordship of the Garioch from David II. It seems likely that Lyon had already entered royal service by the date of this grant. In April 1369 King David gave him a lifetime right to receive 10 merks from every justice ayre north of the Forth. In the same year Lyon was paid for his expenses in undertaking a diplomatic mission to London, where he was identified as the keeper of the king's privy seal. In January 1370 he was acting as an auditor of exchequer and by February of the following year he was serving as King David's secretary, an office which probably also included the keepership of the privy seal. Quite clearly, he was a highly literate and well-educated layman.

After the death of his royal patron on 22 February 1371 Lyon retained an important role in the administration of the new king, Robert II. He was confirmed as keeper of the privy seal by 3 May 1371 and continued in that office until 1377. Similarly, the flow of direct royal patronage to him was unaffected by the change in regime. One of the most significant honours occurred in March 1372, when he was granted the royal thanage of Glamis by King Robert in free barony. Thereafter John was occasionally styled lord of Glamis. He was also the beneficiary of grants from a number of other noblemen, probably a reflection of his ability and his influence in royal government.

Lyon's steady progression through the royal administration became a meteoric social and political rise during 1377. By 2 October 1377 he had married Johanna Stewart, daughter of Robert II and widow of Sir John Keith, son of Sir William Keith, the marischal, who had died shortly before 27 December 1375. The couple received the royal thanage of Tannadice through the marriage settlement. Perhaps as part of his elevation to the status of a royal son-in-law, Lyon was knighted, on a date between 27 June 1376 and 2 October 1377. Finally, on 20 October 1377, he was appointed chamberlain (the chief royal financial officer) in succession to Walter Biggar (*d.* 1376) and John Mercer, who had acted as a temporary collector and receiver of royal revenues in the immediate aftermath of Biggar's death. Lyon's domination of key royal posts was further extended before February 1380 to include the sheriffdom of Edinburgh with custody of the castle, offices for which he was given a fee specially augmented by his royal father-in-law.

Lyon's rapid rise to a privileged and influential position at the heart of royal government and his personal territorial aggrandizement seem to have aroused considerable resentment. The circumstances of his marriage to the king's daughter, in particular, may have given cause for concern. Certainly, on 10 May 1378 Robert II was required to issue a remission to his 'beloved son' John Lyon and his daughter for their clandestine marriage, a concession ratified by Johanna's brothers John, earl of Carrick (the future Robert III), Robert, earl of Fife, and Alexander, lord of Badenoch. The idea that Lyon's marriage to Johanna and his subsequent social elevation were not universally popular resurfaced in later tales surrounding his death.

Lyon was assassinated on 4 November 1382 by another prominent royal councillor, Sir James Lindsay, lord of Crawford, whose family had experienced a number of political setbacks during 1382, and who may well have held the influential Lyon responsible for the direction of royal policy. Lyon's role in the creation of Robert II's son Alexander as earl of Buchan in 1382, a title to which Lindsay also had a claim, may have been crucial, although the steady territorial build-up of Lyon's interests in Angus, an area dominated by Crawford's Lindsay kinsmen, perhaps also played a part. Sixteenth-century chroniclers suggest that Lindsay's assassination of Lyon arose from Sir John's ingratitude to Lindsay after the latter, a close friend, had secured a place for Lyon in Robert II's government and protected the chamberlain from the king's wrath after Lyon had been seduced by Princess Johanna.

Lyon is said to have been buried in Scone Abbey, a traditional site for the coronation and burial of Scottish monarchs; if this is correct, it gives some indication of the regard in which he was held by his royal father-in-law. After his death his widow went on to marry, between 20 November 1384 and 24 May 1385, Sir James Sandilands of Calder. The last reference to her occurs in 1404, when she was styled lady of Glamis. She is reputed to have been buried at Scone. Lyon and Johanna had one son, also John, whose son Patrick *Lyon was created Lord Glamis in 1445.

S. I. BOARDMAN

Sources G. Burnett and others, eds., *The exchequer rolls of Scotland*, 2–3 (1878–80) • J. M. Thomson and others, eds., *Registrum magni sigilli regum Scotorum / The register of the great seal of Scotland*, 2nd edn, 1, ed. T. Thomson (1912) • W. Bower, *Scotichronicon*, ed. D. E. R. Watt and others, new edn, 9 vols. (1987–98), vols. 7–8 • G. W. S. Barrow and others, eds., *Regesta regum Scottorum*, 6, ed. B. Webster (1982) • W. Stewart, *The buik of the croniclis of Scotland*, ed. W. B. Turnbull, 3 vols., Rolls Series, 6 (1858) • *CDS*, vol. 4 • W. Fraser, ed., *The Red Book of Menteith*, 2 vols. (1880) • S. I. Boardman, *The early Stewart kings: Robert II and Robert III, 1371–1406* (1996) • R. Nicholson, *Scotland: the later middle ages* (1974), vol. 2 of *The Edinburgh history of Scotland*, ed. G. Donaldson (1965–75)

Lyon, John, third Lord Glamis (*c.*1432–1497). *See under* Lyon, Patrick, first Lord Glamis (*c.*1400–1460).

Lyon, John (1514?–1592), founder of Harrow School, was the son of John Lyon (*d.* 1534) and his wife, Joan; the family owned land in Preston near Harrow. A man of substance, by 1562 John Lyon had the largest rental in Harrow. He had a long-standing interest in education, having for many years spent 20 marks a year on the education of thirty poor children. In February 1572 he obtained a royal charter for the foundation of a free grammar school for boys at Harrow. He bought lands in Marylebone to be held by himself, his wife, and the governors of his school, the rents to be applied to road repairs on the Harrow and Edgware roads. In 1579 it was proposed that Lyon should pay £50 as a loan to the state but the attorney-general, Sir Gilbert Gerard (a trustee and governor), intervened, arguing that paying would involve selling lands that would otherwise have been used to maintain the school. No buildings were erected until after the death of Lyon's widow, Joan, in 1608 when money was made available according to his instructions.

In 1591 Lyon drew up statutes for the future conduct of the school. The governors were to appoint the master and usher who were to be paid £20 and £10 per annum. They had to behave themselves well and neither was permitted to marry. £300 was to be set aside to construct a building for the school and to house the schoolmasters; additional funds were provided for heating. Thirty good and learned sermons were to be preached annually at the rate of 6*s.* 8*d.* per sermon, £20 per annum was to be distributed annually among the poorest families, and £20 given to four poor scholars to enable them to study at Oxford and Cambridge. To be admitted to the second form boys had to be able to write out sentences before they could learn how to translate English into Latin. The statutes laid down in detail the curriculum to be taught over five years, which consisted of mainly Latin authors with some Greek for the fifth form, together with the catechism, Lord's prayer, ten commandments, and the articles of faith. The schoolmaster was to be responsible for the conduct of his charges, severely punishing lying, stealing, fighting, and filthiness, although the rod was only to be used moderately. Play was permitted on Thursdays and occasionally on Sundays, and archery was encouraged. The governors were to provide all the library books needed, but the parents were to supply paper, ink, pens, books, and candles for the winter.

Building began after Joan Lyon's death but the cost was more than double that envisaged in the statutes and took until 1615 to complete. The first scholar was elected to university in 1617. At first the value of John Lyon's funds were barely sufficient to cover the cost of maintaining the school, but subsequent changes in land values altered the situation entirely. The development of Harrow from a free grammar school into a public school was made possible by a clause in the statutes which permitted the master to admit boys from outside the parish if there was space and the governors agreed. By the beginning of the nineteenth century it was considered that there were so many 'foreigners' that parishioners were deterred from sending their own children. Following the report of the Clarendon commission in 1864 and the Public School Act of 1868 the Harrow School governors in 1874 created the lower school of John Lyon which by the early twentieth century had become autonomous. The fund originally intended for road maintenance was handed over for other charitable purposes in 1991 and in 1999 was still actively supporting education. John Lyon died on 3 October 1592, and was buried in Harrow church, where a brass memorial tablet was later erected to both him and his wife.

Caroline M. K. Bowden

Sources N. Carlisle, *A concise description of the endowed grammar schools in England and Wales*, 2 (1818), 125–38 · *Charter orders and rules to be observed and kept by the governors of the free grammar school at Harrow* (1853) · P. M. Thornton, *Harrow School and its surroundings* (1885) · E. J. L. Scott, *Records of the grammar school, Harrow* (1886) · E. W. Howson, G. T. Warner, and others, eds., *Harrow School* (1898) · accounts, 1608–1709, Harrow School, MS 17.891

Likenesses brass effigy, Harrow on the Hill church

Lyon, John, seventh Lord Glamis (*b. c.*1521, *d.* in or before 1559), nobleman, was the son of John Lyon, sixth Lord Glamis (*d.* 1528), and his wife, Janet Douglas (*d.* 1537), second daughter of George Douglas, master of Angus, and sister of Archibald Douglas, sixth earl of Angus. The seventh lord was still a minor when he succeeded his father in 1528.

In July 1537 Lyon and his mother, who had married as her second husband Archibald Campbell of Skipness, and Lyon's brother George and several others were apprehended on charges of conspiring to poison James V. These charges against Lady Glamis and her family probably originated in the family's close connection to the Douglases. In addition a long-standing dispute over the ward of the earldom of Erroll, sold by the sixth Lord Glamis to George Leslie, fourth earl of Rothes, in 1527, and over the ward of the lordship of Glamis itself, purchased by Rothes in the following year, may have created enmity between the latter and the Lyons, and encouraged Rothes to conspire against Lady Glamis and her family, not only to vindicate a reputation which was under shadow at court, but also to end the dispute in his favour and to his own financial gain. Lady Glamis was tried, convicted of treason, and publicly executed. Lyon was himself tried on 18 July 1537 on a charge of concealing his mother's conspiracy and was condemned to death, but since he was a minor, aged sixteen, his execution was deferred, and he remained a prisoner in Edinburgh Castle at the crown's expense. He later claimed that he had been misled into making a confession on the understanding that his lands would not be forfeit.

Lyon's estates were forfeited, however, and annexed to the crown on 3 December 1540. The king had been distributing the Glamis lands among his friends from September 1537 and continued the grants until 1542. Lyon was released from prison following James's death on 14 December that year, and his lands and title were restored to him by act of parliament on 15 March 1543. On 6 February 1544 he married Janet Keith, daughter of Robert, Lord Keith, and sister of the fourth Earl Marischal; they had two sons, John *Lyon, who became eighth Lord Glamis, and Thomas *Lyon, who was master of Glamis for much of his life, and also one daughter, Margaret. It took several years to recover all the Glamis lands, most notably those in the barony of Kinghorn, gifted to James Kirkcaldy of Grange and not recovered until after William Kirkcaldy's forfeiture in September 1548 for his part in the murder of Cardinal Beaton.

In the early years of Queen Mary's minority Glamis was most closely associated with the opponents of the queen mother, Mary of Guise, and the cardinal. He supported the earl of Arran's flirtation with protestant preaching in 1543 and allowed the former Dominican friar John Rough to preach at Glamis kirk. Mary of Guise anticipated a reconciliation with Glamis in 1544, but it appears that he remained in opposition to the pro-French orientation of the regime for another two years. Between 1546 and 1547 he sat on the privy council on four occasions, and in November 1547 he was present at the siege of Broughty Castle, then occupied by English forces.

Thereafter Glamis disappears from public life. There is a charter to him dated at Glamis on 4 October 1548, and he was served heir to his grandmother, Elizabeth Gray, countess of Huntly, in 1549. On 17 April 1550 his eldest son was infeft in the family estates, reserving a liferent to the parents. He 'spent his latter years abroad, where having contracted a sickness he came home' (*Scots peerage*, 8.283). He had died before 18 September 1559, when John Stewart, fourth earl of Atholl, had a gift of the ward.

Mary Black Verschuur

Sources R. Pitcairn, ed., *Ancient criminal trials in Scotland*, 1, Bannatyne Club, 42 (1833) · J. M. Thomson and others, eds., *Registrum magni sigilli regum Scotorum / The register of the great seal of Scotland*, 11 vols. (1882–1914), vols. 3–4 · *Reg. PCS*, 1st ser., vol. 1 · *CSP Scot.*, 1547–63 · J. Bain, ed., *The Hamilton papers: letters and papers illustrating the political relations of England and Scotland in the XVIth century*, 2 vols., Scottish RO, 12 (1890–92) · *Scots peerage*, 8.278–88 · *The Scottish correspondence of Mary of Lorraine*, ed. A. I. Cameron, Scottish History Society, 3rd ser., 10 (1927) · G. Burnett and others, eds., *The exchequer rolls of Scotland*, 17 (1897) · J. Cameron, *James V: the personal rule, 1528–1542*, ed. N. Macdougall (1998) · M. H. B. Sanderson, *Cardinal of Scotland: David Beaton, c.1494–1546* (1986) · G. Donaldson, *Scotland: James V to James VII* (1965), vol. 3 of *The Edinburgh history of Scotland* (1965–75)

Archives NRA Scotland, inventory of Glamis charters

Lyon, John, eighth Lord Glamis (*c.*1544–1578), nobleman and administrator, was the eldest son of John *Lyon, seventh Lord Glamis (*b. c.*1521, *d.* in or before 1559), and Janet, daughter of Robert Keith, Lord Keith, and sister of the fourth Earl Marischal. He succeeded to the lordship on the death of his father in 1558, inheriting with it the extensive possessions acquired by successive generations of the Glamis family. These territories were largely concentrated in Angus (Forfarshire), where by the sixteenth century they had been erected into a burgh of barony, giving their lords widespread power and influence in that county. In 1561 Glamis married Elizabeth (*d. c.*1581), daughter of William Abernethy, fifth Lord Saltoun. They had four children, a son, Patrick, who became ninth Lord Glamis, and three daughters: Elizabeth, who married Patrick, sixth Lord Gray and, after divorcing him, William Ker, son of the redoubtable Sir Thomas Ker of Ferniehurst; Jean, who married successively Robert Douglas the younger of Lochleven, Archibald Douglas, eighth earl of Angus, and Alexander Lindsay, first Lord Spynie; and Sibilla, who appears to have remained unmarried.

Glamis was certainly a participant in the tortuous and violent events of the 1560s, if in a mainly unspectacular way. Thus in 1565 he supported Mary's marriage to Darnley, but shortly afterwards showed his approval of the earl of Moray's subversive actions against the queen by taking part in the so-called chaseabout raid against her in August of that year. In February 1567 he was in Edinburgh at the time of Darnley's murder, but there has never been any suggestion that he was involved in that affair. Thereafter, he was initially in favour of Bothwell marrying Mary and was present at their wedding. But like many other noblemen he became disillusioned with Bothwell, and after Mary's forcible abdication in 1567 he became a member of the king's party. Its leader, Moray, now appointed him a privy councillor, and for the next decade he was seldom missing from the council's meetings.

Following Moray's assassination in January 1570 Glamis was a pallbearer at his funeral in St Giles's, Edinburgh. He received further promotion when the new regent, the earl of Lennox, appointed him an extraordinary lord of session. However, it was to be during the regency of his distant kinsman, James Douglas, fourth earl of Morton (they were first cousins, once removed), that the career of Glamis really took off. He had had experience of Morton in 1571 when the pair of them had acted as commissioners in talks between the Scottish and English governments held at Berwick, and when Morton was installed as regent in November 1572 Glamis quickly emerged as a key figure in his government. Thus, in February 1573, following the regent's settlement with the Hamilton and Gordon families known as the pacification of Perth, Glamis became one of the three officials responsible for mediating in any disputes which arose north of the River Tay. Later that year he reached the pinnacle of his career when, on the death of the fifth earl of Argyll, he became chancellor, on 12 October 1573. He was notably active the following year, when in August 1574 he accompanied Morton to the north-east of Scotland in an expedition designed for 'the establishment of justice and punishment of disordouris and enormittis attemptit aganis our Soverane Lordis authoritie' (*Reg. PCS*, 2.388).

Glamis was also closely involved in executing the regent's ecclesiastical policy. Here, the return from abroad of the fiery Andrew Melville posed a distinct challenge to Morton, who in March 1575 appointed the chancellor to head a committee responsible for drafting an acceptable church settlement. In an attempt at finding a solution to this question, in 1576 Glamis contacted Theodore Beza, Calvin's successor at Geneva. However the latter's reply, attacking bishops and emphasizing the separate authority of the kirk, was not one likely to have appealed either to the regent or to his commissioner.

March 1578 was a climactic month for Glamis. On the 10th Morton's resignation as regent was confirmed by a royal proclamation at Stirling, while exactly one week later, on 17 March 1578, the chancellor himself was killed in a street brawl in the same town. The role played by Glamis in the temporary overthrow of Morton is debatable. On the one hand Calderwood and Hume of Godscroft claim that the chancellor joined Morton's opponents as soon as the crisis occurred. Certainly there is some evidence that Sir Thomas Lyon of Baldukie, the brother of Glamis, was involved in the negotiations for the regent's dismissal. On the other hand, on the day before Glamis was killed Morton wrote to him confidentially, asking him to use his influence with the boy king on his behalf. And on hearing of the death of Glamis, the ex-regent commented that it was 'an unhappy chance quhilk no doubt is to my great greif' (Thomson, Macdonald, and Innes, 1.105). Certainly, there is nothing here to suggest that Morton felt aggrieved at, or betrayed by, Glamis in 1578. Glamis's death came as a result of a scuffle between his own followers and those of David Lindsay, eleventh earl of Crawford, as they passed each other in the narrow streets of Stirling. Glamis was shot through the head, possibly, as Hume of Godscroft suggests, because he was 'a tall man of stature and higher than the rest' (Hume, 2.255).

A somewhat elusive figure in modern eyes, Glamis was undoubtedly highly regarded by contemporaries and by seventeenth-century historians. Thus Andrew Melville composed a Latin epigram to his memory, while the English ambassador observed that he was 'very wise and discreet but of no party or favour' (*CSP Scot.*, 1574–81, 253). In the following century David Calderwood described Glamis as 'a learned, godly and wise man' (Calderwood, 3.397), but the best obituary notice is perhaps that of Bishop John Spottiswoode, who commented that 'the death of the chancellor was much lamented falling out in the time when the king and country stood in most need of his service' (*History of the Church*, 2.283). G. R. HEWITT

Sources *Scots peerage* • G. Brunton and D. Haig, *An historical account of the senators of the college of justice, from its institution in MDXXXII* (1832) • *Reg. PCS*, 1st ser., vol. 2 • *CSP Scot.*, 1571–81 • D. Calderwood, *The history of the Kirk of Scotland*, ed. T. Thomson and D. Laing, 8 vols., Wodrow Society, 7 (1842–9), vol. 3 • J. Spottiswood, *The history of the Church of Scotland*, ed. M. Napier and M. Russell, 2, Bannatyne Club, 93 (1850) • *The autobiography and diary of Mr James Melvill*, ed. R. Pitcairn, Wodrow Society (1842) • D. Hume of Godscroft, *The history of the house and race of Douglas and Angus*, 2 (1743) • T. Thomson, A. Macdonald, and C. Innes, eds., *Registrum honoris de Morton*, 2 vols., Bannatyne Club, 94 (1853) • G. Donaldson, 'Lord Chancellor Glamis and Theodore Beza', *Miscellany … VIII*, Scottish History Society, 3rd ser., 43 (1951), 89–113 • G. R. Hewitt, *Scotland under Morton, 1572–80* (1982)

Lyon [Lyoun], **John, of Auldbar** (*fl.* 1608–1649), poet, was the eldest son of Sir Thomas Lyon of Auldbar and his first wife, Agnes (1540?–1586?), daughter of Patrick, Lord Gray, and widow of Sir Robert Logan of Restalrig, and Alexander, fifth Lord Home. He was declared heir to his father on 6 August 1608. Subsequently he was frequently imprisoned for debt. On 16 February 1611, he married Eupham, a daughter of George Gladstanes, archbishop of St Andrews, but died childless. He is last mentioned in 1649, in the records of the commissary court of Brechin, as a citizen there; the date of his death is unknown.

Lyon has been identified with the author of 'Teares for the Death of Alexander, Earle of Dunfermeling', a poem of about 250 lines, printed by Andro Hart in 1622, and reprinted by the Bannatyne Club in 1823. The one copy of the original print known to exist is held in the Huntington Library. In the dedication to Lady Beatrix Ruthven, Lady Cowdenknowes, daughter of the first earl of Gowrie, the poet states that he is related to her by 'band of blood', and signs himself 'your Ladiships Cousen, most humblie devoted to serue you, John Lyoun.' This may be explained by the relationship between the lady's husband, Home of Cowdenknowes, and Lyon of Auldbar's mother, by her marriage to Lord Home.

T. F. HENDERSON, *rev.* J. K. McGINLEY

Sources *Scots peerage*, 8.287 · G. Crawfurd, *The lives and characters, of the officers of the crown, and of the state in Scotland* (1726) · *Reg. PCS*, 1st ser., vols. 8–10 · J. Lyoun, *Teares for the death of Alexander* (1823)

Lyon, John (1710–1790), Church of Ireland clergyman and antiquary, was the son of John Lyon, a blacksmith or ironmonger, and his wife, Sarah; who lived at the poorer end of Stephen Street in Dublin; he was probably born and was baptized on 5 October 1710 at St Bride's. Admitted to Trinity College, Dublin, in 1724, as a pensioner, he was elected scholar in 1727, received his BA in 1729, his MA in 1732, and his DD eventually in 1751. His modesty and discretion gained him the patronage of Swift, who prized such qualities in young clergymen, as early as 1736. With Swift's help Lyon became a curate at St Bride's (October 1737) and a minor canon at St Patrick's Cathedral (July 1740). By this time, at Swift's request, Lyon had moved into the deanery to keep Swift's accounts, serve as his almoner and amanuensis, and generally 'to have an Eye upon him and his Affairs on Account of his departing Memory' (Lyon, 'Materials', facing p. 124). From Swift or his executors he received a large portion of Swift's private papers. In 1743 he also inherited the papers of Rebecca Dingley, the companion of Esther Johnson and co-recipient of the letters from Swift published as the *Journal to Stella*. Eventually Lyon disposed of most of his Swift letters, including those from the *Journal*, for publication in additional volumes of John Hawkesworth's edition of Swift's works (1766). Some of the remaining manuscripts later passed to Sir Walter Scott for use in his own Swift edition (1814). In 1765, for George Faulkner's projected quarto edition of Swift, which was never published, Lyon wrote his 'Materials for a life of Dr. Swift', arguably the most reliable of all early accounts of the dean, comprising extensive additions and corrections entered in a loosely interleaved copy of an earlier life by Hawkesworth. This volume next passed to the London editor John Nichols, who, without knowing its author or title, published Lyon's work in his 1779 supplementary volume to the Hawkesworth edition of Swift. By then a quarter of Lyon's original interleaved pages were missing, and several more were lost before the volume finally came into the possession of the Victoria and Albert Museum. The missing sections were published after the discovery in 1997 of a near complete early transcript.

Lyon passed most of his later career at the two Dublin churches where he began. St Bride's he served as incumbent after 1764, and at St Patrick's he was successively prebendary of Rathmichael (1751–64), Tassagard (1771–87), and Mulhuddart (1787–90). From its inception in 1746 he served as secretary to the governors of St Patrick's Hospital, founded under Swift's will, and was elected a governor in 1773. A gifted antiquary, he built up an extensive archive of notes relating to Irish church history, using records that have since been largely destroyed. Much of his collection was later dispersed. 'Although Dr. Lyon did not, himself, publish any work on the subject of Irish antiquities,' William Monck Mason remarked in 1819, 'there is no one to whom the Irish antiquarian is more indebted; to his diligence we chiefly owe the preservation of whatever remains of the ecclesiastical antiquities of Dublin' (Mason, lxiii). At St Mary's, Dublin, on 12 January 1754, Lyon married Sarah Hatfield (*d.* February 1790), who apparently brought him a modest fortune and some connections in the church hierarchy. He died, without surviving issue, in Dublin in June 1790 and was buried on the 12th in St Patrick's churchyard.

A. C. ELIAS JR.

Sources A. C. Elias, Jr, 'John Lyon's "Materials for a life of Dr. Swift", 1765', *Swift Studies*, 13 (1998) · W. G. Carroll, *Succession of clergy in the parishes of S. Bride, S. Michael le Pole, and S. Stephen, Dublin* (1884), 23–6 · *The account books of Jonathan Swift*, ed. P. V. Thompson and D. J. Thompson (1984), ix–xi · [J. Lyon], 'Biographical anecdotes of Dean Swift: in addition to the life by Dr. Hawkesworth', *A supplement to Dr. Swift's works*, ed. J. Nichols, 2 (1779) · [J. Lyon], 'Materials for a life of Dr. Swift', University of Pennsylvania · Burtchaell & Sadleir, *Alum. Dubl.*, 2nd edn, 519; addenda, 141 · J. B. Leslie, list of succession of Church of Ireland clergy in the diocese of Dublin, Representative Church Body, Dublin, MS 61 · J. B. Leslie, *Armagh clergy and parishes* (1911), 331 · parish register, Dublin, St Bride's, TCD, MSS 1478–1480 · W. C. M. Mason, *Hibernia antiqua et hodierna: being a topographical account of Ireland, and a history of all the establishments in that kingdom, ecclesiastical, civil, and monastick* (1819), lxiii · *The works of Jonathan Swift*, ed. W. Scott, 1 (1814), vii–viii · parish register, St Mary's, Dublin, Representative Church Body, Dublin, MS 277.1.1 · *DNB*

Archives Abbotsford House, Abbotsford, Borders, catalogue of books with an accounting of the books' sale after Swift's death · NL Ire., notebooks on Irish church history, MSS 100–101, 103–105 · V&A NAL, Forster collection, no. 579

Wealth at death approx. £3000; five residential leaseholds in Dublin: Carroll, *Succession of clergy*

Lyon, John (1734–1817), Church of England clergyman and antiquary, was born on 1 September 1734 at St Nicholas in the Isle of Thanet, the son of the village blacksmith. Early on he exhibited a determination to improve his mind, taking a slate and books with him when minding cattle at St Nicholas Court Farm, before being apprenticed to Mr

Coleman, an intelligent shoemaker in the village who was also the local doctor. About 1760 he was engaged as an assistant at a school in Margate owned by Michael Trapps (*d.* 1766), whom he succeeded as principal in 1766. Lyon compiled the first guidebook to the Isle of Thanet, *A Description of the Isle of Thanet, and Particularly of the Town of Margate*, published in 1763, when Margate had been a pioneering seaside resort for less than thirty years. In introducing prospective holiday-makers to the facilities and interesting places in the locality he provided a valuable source for the early history of the seaside resort.

Lyon learned Greek and Latin from the vicar of St Peter's, Thanet, who assisted his admission to holy orders in 1770. He combined the curacy of Minster in Thanet with his school until 1772, when he was elected by the parishioners to the perpetual curacy of St Mary's, Dover. His studies also embraced electricity, antiquities, and botany. He never married and lived frugally, wedded to his writing desk and his electrical experiments. His principal work was *The history of the town and port of Dover, and of Dover Castle: with a short account of the Cinque Ports* (2 vols., 1813–14). Although there were earlier specific studies of the castle and harbour, Lyon produced the most comprehensive history of Dover to date, having already researched and published a history of the castle in 1787. In devoting 264 out of a total of 756 pages to the castle, plus original engravings and plans, he provided a unique piece of scholarship, especially as subsequent Dover historians bemoaned the loss or destruction of the castle records. One such historian, John Bavington Jones, wrote that he had been forced 'to follow the track of earlier historians' (Jones, preface).

Lyon, who was elected a fellow of the Society of Antiquaries, submitted two papers to the society: the first in 1775 described a Roman bath discovered in Dover (*Archaeologia*, 5, 325–34), and the second in 1792 contained observations of the site of the ancient Portus Iccius (*Archaeologia*, 10, 1–16). A letter to John Nichols in 1785 on the history of St Radigund's, or Bradsole Abbey, was printed in *Bibliotheca Topographica Britannica*, and his account of William Tothall FSA, which he communicated to his fellow antiquary Andrew Coltee Ducarel, found its way into print in Nichols's *Biographical Anecdotes of William Hogarth*. The Kentish historian Edward Hasted acknowledged his debt to Lyon for much information relating to Dover and its neighbourhood. Indeed in a letter of 6 April 1799 Lyon updated information supplied in 1791 and 1792 on the eve of publication of the fourth volume of the first folio edition of Hasted's *The History and Topographical Survey of the County of Kent*. Lyon also published four works on electricity, including one on the effects of lightning, and submitted to the Royal Society a notice 'Of a subsidence of the ground near Folkstone, on the coast of Kent' in 1786 (*Philosophical Transactions*, 16.91).

Much disabled by a fall in 1806, Lyon was voted an assistant by his parishioners. He suffered a gradual decay, a paralytic affliction that deprived him of movement and speech. He died in Dover on 30 June 1817 and was buried in July in the churchyard of his native parish of St Nicholas, Thanet. He left an estate reputedly worth £10,000 to his two sisters and five nephews and nieces. As requested, his executors destroyed his manuscripts and correspondence, but his collection of books, shells, insects, and minerals was sold by auction in November 1817.

GORDON GOODWIN, *rev.* JOHN WHYMAN

Sources *Thanet Magazine* (July 1817), 57–65 · J. B. Jones, *Annals of Dover*, 2nd edn (1938), 239 · E. Hasted, *The history and topographical survey of the county of Kent*, 2nd edn, 4 (1798), v, 24, 59–60, 65, 67, 86, 117–18 · E. Hasted, *The history and topographical survey of the county of Kent*, 2nd edn, 9 (1800), 490–91, 506, 546 · A. Macdonald, 'Plans of Dover harbour in the sixteenth century', *Archaeologia Cantiana*, 49 (1937), 108–26, esp. 108, 120, 126 · J. Boyle, 'Some discoveries about Edward Hasted and his *History of Kent*', *Archaeologia Cantiana*, 97 (1981), 235–59, esp. 241–2 · J. Boyle, 'Hasted in perspective', *Archaeologia Cantiana*, 100 (1984), 295–304, esp. 298 · J. Boyle, *In quest of Hasted* (1984), 11–12, 21, 24, 127 · *GM*, 1st ser., 87/1 (1817), 641–2

Wealth at death approx. £10,000: *Thanet Magazine*, 65

Lyon, John, ninth earl of Strathmore and Kinghorne (1737–1776). *See under* Bowes, Mary Eleanor, countess of Strathmore and Kinghorne (1749–1800).

Lyon, Patrick, first Lord Glamis (*c.*1400–1460), courtier, was the son of Sir John Lyon of Glamis (*c.*1377–*c.*1435), son of Sir John *Lyon (*d.* 1382), whose marriage in 1376 to Princess Joanna Stewart, daughter of Robert II, was probably the making of his family. The younger Sir John appears infrequently on record, but is stated to have married his first cousin once removed Elizabeth Graham, younger daughter of Euphemia, countess palatine of Strathearn, and Sir Patrick Graham of Dundaff and Kincardine; as her parents are considered to have married *c.*1406, however, this is unlikely, unless it was a second marriage. Patrick Lyon, the eldest of Sir John's three sons, was a hostage for the ransom demanded for James I and remained in England between 1424 and 1427. He was knighted by 1440 and in 1445, being among the richest barons in the land, assumed one of the new peerage styles, which (after some typical early variants) was settled as Patrick, Lord Glamis. Following the collapse in the autumn of 1449 of the Livingston faction which had so dominated court politics since especially the mid-1440s, Glamis rose to prominence. From late 1449 he regularly witnessed crown charters, indicating that he was a fixed member of the king's daily council. His arrival at court was sealed by the marriage in early 1450 of his son and heir, Alexander, to Agnes, daughter of William, Lord Crichton, who was effectively now the power behind the throne. His royalist stance was probably influenced by an old feud between the Lyons and the Lindsays, earls of Crawford, the leading allies of the Douglases and the dominant family in Angus—James Lindsay of Crawford had murdered Patrick Lyon's grandfather.

Glamis was master of the king's household from at the latest April 1450 until the end of 1451 and again from late 1454 to the middle of 1455. In the mid-1450s the king began to rely on his loyalty to assist in the exploitation of the crown's interests in the north. He acted as commissioner when crown lands were leased and was appointed keeper of the castles of Kildrummy and Kindrochit, both in Aberdeenshire, and Balvenie, Banffshire, for which he received fees. The family's main estates were in Angus, but Lord Glamis also possessed land in Stirlingshire, Perthshire, Aberdeenshire, Berwickshire, and Fife. He ceased to witness crown charters at the end of 1458, perhaps because of his activities in the north.

Glamis married Isabel (*c.*1410–1485), daughter of Sir Walter *Ogilvy of Lintrathen, about 1428; they had four sons and one daughter. He died on 21 March 1460 and was buried in Glamis kirk. His widow then married Gilbert, first Lord Kennedy (*d. c.*1479). She is credited with finishing the building of the old castle at Glamis, as well as two stone bridges in the area and the aisle of the kirk where her first husband lay, and where she herself was buried after her death on 12 January 1485.

The eldest son of Patrick and Isabella, **Alexander Lyon**, second Lord Glamis (*c.*1430–1486?), did not have as active a public life as his father. He succeeded to the keeperships of Kildrummy and Kindrochit castles, but was removed from office *c.*1462. He was a frequent auditor of causes in parliament (1468–71, 1479–85) and occasionally a lord of the king's council in judicial matters (1480–84). He is said to have died in 1486. His marriage to Agnes Crichton was apparently childless. She married Walter Ker of Cessford (*d.* 1501) after October 1487 and died after July 1501. Alexander was succeeded by his brother **John Lyon**, third Lord Glamis (*c.*1432–1497), who had already acted as an auditor of causes and lord of council in judicial matters. He was an unusual member of the nobility in being a graduate (possibly of the University of Paris). After the death of James III at Sauchieburn in 1488 John quickly established himself with the new administration; he was a constant witness of crown charters from 1489 to 1495 and also justiciar north of Forth, a regular auditor of causes, and lord of council. By April 1479 he married Elizabeth Scrymgeour (supposedly daughter of John Scrymgeour of Dudhope, constable of Dundee), who died before 20 October 1492. Glamis died on 1 April 1497 and was buried in Glamis kirk. Among their four sons and seven daughters was John, fourth Lord Glamis (*d.* 1500); his three brothers were killed at the battle of Flodden. ALAN R. BORTHWICK

Sources Glamis Castle, Forfarshire, Strathmore muniments • J. M. Thomson and others, eds., *Registrum magni sigilli regum Scotorum / The register of the great seal of Scotland*, 11 vols. (1882–1914), vol. 2 • *APS*, *1424–1567* • G. Burnett and others, eds., *The exchequer rolls of Scotland*, 23 vols. (1878–1908) • *CDS*, vol. 4 • various collections of manuscript estate and other papers in archives offices and in private hands in Scotland and England, priv. colls. • [T. Thomson], ed., *The acts of the lords auditors of causes and complaints, AD 1466–AD 1494*, RC, 40 (1839) • [T. Thomson] and others, eds., *The acts of the lords of council in civil causes, 1478–1503*, 3 vols. (1839–1993) • *Scots peerage*, vol. 8 • tombstone, Glamis kirk, Glamis
Archives Glamis Castle, Angus, Strathmore muniments • priv. coll.

Lyon, Sir Patrick, of Carse, Lord Carse (1637–1694), judge, was the son of Patrick Lyon of Carse and second cousin of Patrick Lyon, third earl of Strathmore and Kinghorne. He was admitted a member of the Faculty of Advocates on 11 July 1671, having previously been a professor of philosophy at the University of St Andrews. A resident of Dundee, he has been credited with the erection of a sculptured stone to commemorate the Restoration, outside his home in Whitehall Close. He was appointed admiral-depute in November 1674, and on the death of Lord Nairn was nominated an ordinary lord of session, taking his seat, with the title Lord Carse, on 10 November 1683. On 20 February 1684 he succeeded Sir James Foulis of Colinton as one of the lords of justiciary, but was removed from his offices in 1688, apparently because of Jacobite sympathies. He acted as a commissioner of supply for Forfarshire in 1689 and 1690, as he had in 1685. He is said to have compiled a collection of the decisions of the court of session between 1682 and 1687, no longer identifiable, and a collection of genealogies, held by the National Library of Scotland, and used by Sir George Mackenzie in his work on the subject. He married, after 1684, Elizabeth, sister of William Gray of Invereightie and widow of Patrick Lyon of Brigton. Carse died on 4 January 1694, and in October 1695 his son Magister Patrick Lyon of Carse was declared his heir.

A. H. MILLAR, *rev.* DEREK JOHN PATRICK

Sources G. Brunton and D. Haig, *An historical account of the senators of the college of justice, from its institution in MDXXXII* (1832) • *The book of record: a diary written by Patrick first earl of Strathmore and other documents relating to Glamis Castle, 1684–9*, ed. A. H. Millar, Scottish History Society, 9 (1890) • *APS*, *1670–86*; *1689–95* • D. M. Walker, *The Scottish jurists* (1985) • F. J. Grant, ed., *The Faculty of Advocates in Scotland, 1532–1943*, Scottish RS, 145 (1944) • *Journals of Sir John Lauder*, ed. D. Crawford, Scottish History Society, 36 (1900)
Archives NL Scot., genealogical collections
Likenesses J. de Wet, portrait, *c.*1688; known to be at Glamis Castle in 1893 • R. White, line engraving, BM, NPG

Lyon, Patrick, third earl of Strathmore and Kinghorne (1643?–1695), nobleman, was probably born on 29 May 1643 (possibly 1642), the only son of John Lyon, second earl of Kinghorne (1596–1647?), and his second wife, Lady Elizabeth Maule (*d.* 1659), only daughter of Patrick *Maule, first earl of Panmure (1585–1661). He succeeded to the title of earl of Kinghorne at the age of four on the death of his father on 12 May 1647 (sometimes given as 1646). The late earl had spent a fortune engaging the covenanters' cause under Montrose; despite an act of parliament passed in his favour on 27 March 1647, this expense and a fine of £1000 imposed in 1654 by the Act of Grace left the estate in serious financial trouble. The earl's widow had married George *Livingston, third earl of Linlithgow, on 30 July 1650, and this eventually brought even greater difficulties. Nine years later, on the death of Lady Elizabeth, Linlithgow brought successful claims against the estate, which reduced Kinghorne to relative poverty.

The loss of so much seems to have galvanized Kinghorne into regaining his family's position. Having completed his studies at the University of St Andrews, the young earl returned to his estate in 1660 and took stock. What he found were two large, empty houses whose entire contents had been sold off to satisfy creditors, chiefly the earl of Linlithgow. What could not be carried off was burdened with debt. Embarking on a strict regime of household control, Kinghorne paid off his father's debts within seven years. On 23 August 1662 he married Lady Helen Middleton (*d.* 1708), second daughter of John

Patrick Lyon, third earl of Strathmore and Kinghorne (1643?–1695), by Sir Godfrey Kneller, 1686

*Middleton, first earl of Middleton (*c.*1608–1674); Archbishop James Sharp performed the wedding ceremony in Holyrood Abbey. The couple moved into Castle Lyon (later known as Castle Huntly) in the Carse of Gowrie, and the earl quickly followed the current trend among the nobility for domestic modernization.

A spectacular example of the craze for 'reforming' old houses was later provided in the rebuilding of Castle Glamis, to which the earl was able to move in 1670. From the mid-1670s Kinghorne was an ally of John Maitland, duke of Lauderdale, and, like him, was typical of the royalist aristocracy in his apparently conflicting emotions about his castellated home. These emotions are expressed in his *Book of Record*, together with careful details of the extensive building operations which employed him until 1689. On the one hand, he insisted 'that everie man who hes such houses would reform them, for who can delight to live in his house as in a prisone' (Lyon, earl of Strathmore, 33). Indeed, there was 'no man more against these old fashions of tours and castles than I am' (ibid., 19). Yet he was 'inflam'd stronglie with a great desyre to continue the memorie of my familie' by retaining 'my old Great Hall, which is a room that I ever loved'. His solution involved reorientating and extending the castle into a symmetrical V-plan, by adding a new western wing: both wings were given gables and the roofs were heightened to enhance an already 'romantic' profile. An entrance was set at the centre, and a new diagonally aligned series of courts was created. A quite ordinary tower house was thereby transformed into a composition of overpowering baroque dynamism—a startling and (for Scotland) unprecedented solution. Of his design the earl wrote that 'tho it be an old house and consequentlie was the more difficult to reduce the place to any uniformitie yet I did covet extremely to order my building so that my frontispiece might have a resemblance on both syds' (ibid., 41). Internally, a new great apartment was formed in the expanded shell of the castle, and the 'old Great Hall' was converted into a drawing-room. Kinghorne designed the whole scheme himself, having decided not to 'call in … Public Architecturs' (ibid., 42). He was the last of the great self-taught noble architects, and his house is a fascinating expression of his character, romantic yet practical. A magnificent portrait (1683) by Jacob de Witt of the earl and his family reveals as much as any written account could. The luxuriantly wigged earl is pictured in Roman dress within a severely classical setting. His children are gathered round, with sleek hunting hounds in attendance. The earl raises his hand in the style of Marcus Aurelius to gesture at his house in the middle distance, and the viewer's gaze is drawn to Glamis in all its gemlike glory. The complementary cults of house, family, learning, and manliness are all proudly displayed.

The basis of all Kinghorne's endeavours seems to have been the regaining of lost dignity. His title as third earl was a relatively new one (1606), limited to male heirs, and on 30 May 1672 he obtained a new charter enabling him to nominate a successor in the absence of male issue. On 1 July 1677 he managed to procure another charter giving his heirs and successors the titles of earls of Strathmore and Kinghorne, viscounts Lyon, and barons Glamis, Tannadyce, Sidlaw, and Strathdichtie. Strathmore's achievements were family-orientated, rather than on a national scale. After the Restoration he made a minor contribution to public affairs, and on 10 January 1682 he was sworn into the privy council. After the uprising of 1685 he provided stores for the army and carried out various other ancillary duties. He was rewarded with lands in Kintyre but these were soon taken back by the crown, and he obtained instead the post of extraordinary lord of session (27 March 1686) with a pension of £300. In 1688 he resisted his instinct to deny the claim of the prince of Orange, but thereafter he was suspected of Jacobite leanings, and in 1689 he was relieved of his office as lord of session. On 25 April 1690 Strathmore swore allegiance to King William, but this was the end of a relatively uneventful public life. He died at Castle Huntly (Castle Lyon) on 15 May 1695 and was buried in the family lair at his own fantastic creation, Glamis. He left three sons and two daughters; John Lyon, second earl of Strathmore and Kinghorne (1663–1712), was a tory and an opponent of the treaty of union, who only escaped arrest as a suspected Jacobite because illness confined him to Glamis. The third earl, also John Lyon, took part in the 1715 uprising and was killed at Sheriffmuir.

RANALD MACINNES

Sources GEC, *Peerage* · P. Lyon, earl of Strathmore, *The book of record*, ed. A. H. Millar (1890) · R. Innes Smith, *Glamis Castle* (1993) · R. MacInnes, '"Rubblemania": ethic and aesthetic in Scottish architecture', *Journal of Design History*, 9/3, 137–51 · D. McGibbon and T. Ross, *The castellated and domestic architecture of Scotland*, 5 vols. (1887–9), 2.113–25

Archives NL Scot., genealogical collections

Likenesses J. de Wit, group portrait, 1683 (with family) · G. Kneller, portrait, 1686, Glamis Castle, Forfarshire [*see illus.*]

Lyon, Sir Thomas, of Auldbar, master of Glamis (*c.*1546–1608), nobleman and administrator, was the second son of John *Lyon, seventh Lord Glamis (*b. c.*1521, *d.* in or before 1559), and his wife, Jean, daughter of Robert Keith, master of Marischal; he was perhaps two years younger than his elder brother, John *Lyon, later eighth Lord Glamis (*c.*1544–1578). The Lyon family held substantial lands in Aberdeenshire, Perthshire, and Fife, but their power base and main estates lay in Forfarshire. Descended from Robert II through the marriage of the latter's daughter Johanna to Sir John Lyon (*d.* 1382), and closely linked through marriage and geographical proximity to the comital families of Angus, Argyll, Atholl, Huntly, and Rothes, the Lyon family was prominent in local and national politics from the 1360s onwards—though not always in favour with the monarch. Thomas's father had been declared a traitor in 1537 and was forfeit until 1544. His brother John, Lord Glamis, backed Regent Moray against Mary, queen of Scots, from 1567, and was consistently loyal to the protestant regencies of Moray, Lennox, and Morton; on 8 October 1573 he was appointed chancellor of the kingdom in the name of James VI. These loyalties undoubtedly helped secure for Thomas Lyon, while he was still a young man, the post of attendant upon the infant James VI in Stirling Castle. Also around this period Thomas was slowly establishing a position for himself within his family's sphere of influence: in March 1567 he was presented by his elder brother to the Forfarshire chaplainry of Baikie (valued at under £10 a year), and in 1571 Glamis allowed him to purchase the estate of Scrogerfield (Thomas was a committed protestant who drew revenue from the chaplainry until at least 1576).

On the violent death of the eighth lord on 17 March 1578 Thomas Lyon became responsible for the tutelage and upbringing of his nephew Patrick, ninth Lord Glamis (1575–1615), a position he held until 1596. Through traditional family influence, religious conviction, and individual force of personality, the master of Glamis (as he was called from his being his nephew's heir presumptive) was soon able to draw on long-established Lyon alliances in and around Forfarshire. He also used his considerable political abilities to manipulate his nephew's lordship so as to acquire significant additional estates and to expand his personal sphere of influence within Forfarshire (in December 1579 he had to lodge a security for £5000 that he would not impinge on the estates belonging to his sister-in-law and her daughter). Some time before 1575 he married Agnes (*d.* 1580x86), daughter of Patrick Gray of Buttergask and sister of Patrick, fifth Lord Gray (and widow successively of Robert Logan of Restalrig and Alexander, fifth Lord Home). The marriage, which produced two daughters, caused an acrimonious dispute between the master and the family of his wife's previous husband, the Homes. Although Lyon was granted the right to act as keeper of Home Castle for the crown in November 1578, he was relieved of the post a month later, as Andrew Kerr, commendator of Jedburgh, had obtained possession and was unwilling to surrender.

Building upon his local influence, Lyon expanded his involvement in the national arena: in March 1578—at the time when his elder brother was killed—he was involved in the negotiations which secured the resignation of James Douglas, fourth earl of Morton, as regent; and in 1582 he was one of the most prominent of the Ruthven raiders who undertook a palace coup against the regime of Esmé Stewart, duke of Lennox, and James Stewart, earl of Arran. A little before dawn on 23 August 1582, Lyon, with William Ruthven, first earl of Gowrie, and John Erskine, second earl of Mar, accompanied by 1000 troops, surrounded Ruthven Castle (Huntingtower) in Perthshire and announced to the king that he was under their control. While the other malcontents placed before their monarch a supplication detailing the wrongs committed by Lennox and his supporters, the master suggested to the king that instead of preparing to hunt in the fields he should return to his playroom and his hobby horse. After the raiders had returned the king to his boyhood residence of Stirling, the master again confronted the king when the latter wanted to visit his capital. When James burst into tears on being refused permission to visit Edinburgh, Lyon, who had blocked the way by placing his leg across an open doorway, responded with the comment that 'better bairns should weep than bearded men' (*History of the Church*, 2.290). During the period of the Ruthven regime, the master appeared at first in the sederunts of the privy council, but he exercised his influence mostly in close counsels with the earls of Angus and Mar.

On James's 'escape' from the Ruthven regime to St Andrews in June 1583, Lyon was ordered to ward in Dumbarton Castle (within three days) and was instructed to surrender his houses of Glamis, Auldbar, Baikie, and Dod. Instead he fled from Scotland, taking refuge first in Ireland and then in England. On 31 January 1584 he was charged to leave Scotland, England, and Ireland, under pain of treason. Within three months, however, he was back in Scotland (along with Angus and Mar), in an attempt to overthrow the politically dominant earl of Arran by seizing Stirling Castle (on 17 April 1584) and holding it against the king's government. The rebellion was short-lived and the master, along with his companions, again fled, faced by King James at the head of an army said to number 12,000. He took up residence in Westminster and secretly corresponded with the English government. In Scotland, parliament passed an act of forfeiture on 22 August 1584 against him, along with Angus, Mar, and their supporters.

In October 1585 Lyon secretly returned to Scotland and met with other discontented lords at the residence in Kelso of Francis Stewart, first earl of Bothwell. By 2 November the lords were before Stirling Castle seeking Arran's removal from authority and their own pardon. Arran fled through the castle postern, and on 4 November Lyon and other conspirators were pardoned. Three days later Lyon was officially admitted to the privy council, and he also replaced Arran as captain and commander of the king's guard. Shortly afterwards, on 2 December, he was appointed treasurer (in succession to the third earl of Montrose), with a salary of £1000 Scots a year. Although he never achieved the office he coveted most—that of chancellor (like his late brother)—in December his estates were restored in parliament, and on 9 February 1586 he was created an extraordinary lord of session, again replacing Montrose. It was unusual for so prominent a nobleman to take on the onerous and regular duties of the session, but such a position had been held by Lyon's brother between 1570 and 1573, and the master may have owed his promotion more to heritage than to legal knowledge.

His first wife having died, on 9 February 1586 Lyon married Eupheme, daughter of William Douglas, fifth earl of Morton; they had two sons and a daughter. His influence within the Angus homelands of the Lyons led to his becoming involved in his family's long-running feud with the Lindsay earls of Crawford (recently aggravated by the eleventh earl of Crawford's alleged responsibility for the death of the eighth Lord Glamis). In November 1579, in an attempt to settle the feud, Crawford was obliged to give assurance that he would not harm the master of Glamis and would seek licence to travel to the continent (on surety of £10,000), but this action was unsuccessful and the feud continued, with bloodshed on both sides, throughout the early 1580s (while Crawford supported the Lennox and Arran regimes, and the master strongly opposed them). On 14 December 1586, however, as senior representative of the Lyons, the master of Glamis exchanged assurances with Crawford to settle their differences, and six months later, following a reconciliation banquet given by the king, Thomas Lyon and the earl walked arm in arm along the High Street of Edinburgh to parliament.

In January 1587 Lyon was appointed a commissioner for grants from crown lands, but his influence waned somewhat towards the end of the 1580s, partly because of his difficulties in dealing with the chancellor, John Maitland of Thirlestane. He lost the captaincy of the guard to two of the king's favourites, firstly to Alexander Lindsay (later first Lord Spynie and the earl of Crawford's uncle—an action which renewed the feud), and then on 28 November 1588 to George Gordon, sixth earl of Huntly. Strongly protestant and an Anglophile, the master was usually an opponent of the conservative Huntly, making him an obvious target for attack when the earl and his supporters rose against the king in 1589. The master attempted to oppose the rebels, but was surprised and cornered in his house at Kirkhill by Huntly's lieutenant, Sir Patrick Gordon of Auchindoun. On his failing to surrender, the house was burned around him and he was captured and taken north to Auchindoun; he was released only when the king took to the field and marched to oppose Huntly.

Lyon was knighted at the coronation of Queen Anna on 17 May 1590, but continuing difficulties with Thirlestane and suspicions of involvement with the renegade earl of Bothwell (with whom previously he had been at odds) led to his being imprisoned in Blackness Castle for a short period in November 1591, and then being warded north of the River Dee (his ward, Lord Glamis, was also placed in protective custody as a result of the master's links with Bothwell). Lyon also briefly lost his seat on the session (restored to the earl of Montrose) but recovered it in March 1593 on the promotion of John Cockburn of Ormiston. In May 1593 he was advanced to be an ordinary lord of session, following the death of Lord President Provand. The master's involvement with Bothwell was short-lived; indeed, he was exiled from court during the earl's brief recovery of favour in the autumn of 1593. Reconciliation with Thirlestane followed and the two men returned to court following Bothwell's fall. In April 1594 the master led 400 royal troops into a confrontation with Bothwell during the latter's 'raid' on Leith, but after the king's vanguard under Lord Home had been scattered, Lyon's troops also dispersed, having done little fighting.

Lyon's position became significantly weaker during 1596. In that year a group of eight commissioners, the Octavians, took over responsibility for management of the royal finances. The master initially refused to demit the office of treasurer, but the Octavians established that large sums of money were due to the exchequer from him, and in return for his leaving office these debts were cancelled. On 6 March the master of Glamis was replaced as treasurer by Walter Stewart, Lord Blantyre, after receiving a gift of £6000. Also in 1596 the master's nephew Patrick, ninth Lord Glamis, came of age, and his wife gave birth to a son and heir, John (later tenth Lord Glamis and second earl of Kinghorne). No longer master of Glamis, Sir Thomas Lyon of Auldbar (as he was thereafter usually known) and his nephew initially came to an amicable agreement regarding the former's acquisition of estates during Glamis's minority. Shortly afterwards, however, the pair fell out over a transaction concerning Tannadyce (the estate was subsequently held by James Lyon, an illegitimate son of Sir Thomas's), and Auldbar entered litigation against his nephew (which he lost). During 1598 Auldbar removed himself from public life and was permitted to remain away from court 'in respect of his greet deseis' (Brunton and Haig, 205). He also demitted his place on the session. Thereafter he lived quietly on his estates, for long enough to see his nephew elevated to comital status as earl of Kinghorne, Lord Lyon, and Glamis, in July 1606. Sir Thomas Lyon died in Forfarshire on 18 February 1608.

ROB MACPHERSON

Sources *CSP Scot.*, *1547–1603* • G. Brunton and D. Haig, *An historical account of the senators of the college of justice, from its institution in MDXXXII* (1832) • G. Crawford, *The lives and characters of the officers of the crown and of the state in Scotland from the reign of King David I to the Union of the two kingdoms* (1726) • *Scots peerage*, 8.281–8 • [T. Thomson], ed., *The historie and life of King James the Sext*, Bannatyne Club, 13 (1825) • *Reg. PCS*, 2nd ser. • *Reg. PCS*, 1st ser. • *APS*, 1567–1625 • T. Thomson, ed., *Acts and proceedings of the general assemblies of the Kirk of Scotland*, 3 pts, Bannatyne Club, 81 (1839–45) • D. Calderwood, *The history of the Kirk of Scotland*, ed. T. Thomson and D. Laing, 8 vols., Wodrow Society, 7 (1842–9) • J. Spottiswood, *The history of the Church of Scotland*, ed. M. Napier and M. Russell, 3 vols., Bannatyne Club, 93 (1850) • C. T. McInnes, ed., *Compota thesaurariorum regum Scotorum / Accounts of the lord high treasurer of Scotland*, 12–13 (1970–

78) • M. Livingstone, D. Hay Fleming, and others, eds., *Registrum secreti sigilli regum Scotorum / The register of the privy seal of Scotland*, 5–8 (1957–82), vols. 5–8 • G. Burnett and others, eds., *The exchequer rolls of Scotland*, 23 vols. (1878–1908), vols. 20–23 • J. M. Thomson and others, eds., *Registrum magni sigilli regum Scotorum / The register of the great seal of Scotland*, 11 vols. (1882–1914), 1546–1608, vols. 4–6

Lyon, William (*d.* 1617), Church of Ireland bishop of Cork, was born in Chester; little is known about his early career. He may have been educated at Oxford University, though Justice Saxey said that he had been 'some time a tapster [innkeeper] by London way' (PRO, SP 63/216/59), while yet another source stated that he had been a seafarer in his youth. In 1595 he claimed to have been in Ireland for twenty-five years, suggesting that he had arrived in 1570. On 6 November 1573 he was presented to the vicarage of Naas (co. Kildare), to which he added Bodenstown (co. Kildare) on 23 July 1580; but it is not clear whether he was always resident, since on 24 November 1577 he had received permission to hold two Irish benefices while living in England. By the early 1580s he was certainly in Ireland, serving as chaplain to Lord Deputy Grey, and accepting in 1582 the impoverished southern see of Ross (nominated 30 March, letters patent 12 May). By August 1582 Grey had granted Lyon the profits of the neighbouring see of Cork, and the mayor of Cork soon petitioned for Lyon to be made bishop. As early as April 1583 he was termed bishop of Ross and Cork. In November 1583 he was granted Cork *in commendam*, and finally on 24 March 1586 the queen ordered that it be annexed to Ross, along with the adjacent see of Cloyne. His wife was called Elizabeth; they had a son, William, and two daughters, Mary and Elizabeth.

Lyon was that rarity in late-sixteenth century Ireland, an active, resident English bishop. He played his part to the full as a local official: he served on the commissions for ecclesiastical causes in Munster of 1583 and 1594, on the national commission of 1602, and on the civil commission for the government of Munster during the 1590s, and he reported regularly to Dublin and London about political and religious affairs in the province. But his long episcopate was far from easy. The first part was punctuated by wars and upheavals: the Desmond rising of 1579–83, followed by the Munster plantation, and then by the Nine Years' War (1594–1603), which reached its devastating climax in Munster. Moreover, these military struggles became intertwined with the fierce contest between Reformation and Counter-Reformation for the religious loyalty of the people. As if this was not enough Lyon also struggled with a serious financial crisis as his Irish predecessors, seeing little future for themselves in the Church of Ireland, had leased out episcopal endowments. Cork and Ross were worth only £70 p.a. when he became bishop, Cloyne even less, his predecessor having granted it away in fee farm for a rent of only £3 6*s.* 8*d.* p.a., leaving Lyon without even a residence there.

Initially Lyon made progress in establishing conformity, if not protestantism. He himself contributed to the building of a see house (at a cost of £300), a church, a free school, and even a bridge, in Ross, and provided new testaments and prayer and schoolbooks (albeit in English and Latin). By 1589 he had, according to Lord Deputy Fitzwilliam,

> reformed so many people, which at his coming unto these parts are most wild and disordered, by informing them in the principles of religion, as they are not only become thereby so obedient to law … but also are so forward to have the word of God preached, and to communicate, as it is wonderful … that one age, much less one man, not learned in their own language, in so short a time, could have wrought them to like perfection. (PRO, SP 63/142/9)

But it was always an uphill task. Visitations of his dioceses from the early 1590s reveal serious problems. Though a core of local Irish and Anglo-Irish clergy remained, lay invasion of church property, rampant pluralism, and the large number of vacant and impropriate benefices without cure, suggested that the Church of Ireland was struggling pastorally. In all there were about thirty clergy in Cloyne, nearly all reading ministers, serving 125 benefices, fifty-five of which were vacant.

Lyon confirmed the general picture of decline. In 1595 he wrote to Burghley complaining that because of the suspension of the laws against recusancy and the activities of the Catholic clergy, the supply of clergy and parishioners had dried up. Existing ministers were leaving to become 'massing priests'; replacements, especially Irish born preachers, were impossible to find. The people, heeding the warnings of the priests that the Church of Ireland liturgy was the 'devil's service', were refusing to come to church. 'Within these two years … where I have had a thousand or more in a church at sermon, I now have not five' (PRO, SP 63/183/47). In 1598 his house at Ross was destroyed by a local chieftain. In 1604 Lyon reported again. He found the mere 'face of a church', 'torn and rent', and 'overwhelmed with the palpable darkness of idolatry', with 'few qualified incumbents'. Throughout his dioceses 'no marriages, christenings, &c' had been done 'but by Papist priests this seven years' (PRO, SP 63/221/35A). Lyon's reports are, it is true, not devoid of special pleading. Convinced that Roman Catholicism was inherently antichristian and disloyal, he believed that missionary activity needed to be backed up by firm civil measures to enforce conformity, something which the politic Burghley was unwilling to do after the outbreak of the Nine Years' War.

In fact, the shift in religious attitudes was much too deep to be changed by official coercion, as became evident when Lyon set about rebuilding the church after the coming of peace in 1603. Under the aggressive lord president, Sir Henry Brouncker, a religious experiment was conducted in Munster. Brouncker used his powers to the full to force recusants to come to church, while Lyon sought to create a fresh ministry to accommodate the new parishioners. The impact of fines and imprisonment did produce a temporary increase in conformists, at least in the cities where there were preachers, but the Catholic leaders proved defiant, and the disruption caused to the civil life of the province by the harsh enforcement measures led the English privy council to order the suspension of the campaign.

The future for the Church of Ireland in Munster lay with the growing community of English colonists. Lyon attracted university educated clergy from England by uniting five or six benefices. By 1615 the ministry was very different from the 1590s. The old local clergy had almost disappeared, replaced by émigrés. In Cloyne there were thirty-five resident clergy, of whom fifteen were now preachers. The quality of the ministry had thus improved, but its coverage was mostly limited to the areas of English settlement. Underpinning the changes in ministry were improvements in the church's finances. Lyon spent a considerable amount of time during the second part of his episcopate in seeking to recover church property. He compiled a terrier for Cloyne, in preparation for a lengthy, though unsuccessful, battle in the courts and parliament to recover the see lands. He built a palace at Cork at a cost of over £1000, and managed to raise his overall income by 1615 to £200 p.a.

Lyon died on 4 October 1617. In 1849 his tomb (built, rather pessimistically, in 1597) was discovered near the see house in Cork, and his remains removed to the cathedral. As with his background, there are conflicting accounts of Lyon's abilities. Saxey thought him 'utterly unlearned' (SP 63/216/59), but he impressed Brouncker as a man 'whose piety, courage and honesty I cannot commend sufficiently' (SP 63/219/134). Brouncker was of course Lyon's ally, and Saxey was notably dismissive of Irish clerics. The truth probably lies in between—certainly the evidence of the visitations and his surviving correspondence suggests a competent and dedicated administrator struggling with a difficult task. ALAN FORD

Sources *The whole works of Sir James Ware concerning Ireland*, ed. and trans. W. Harris, 1 (1739), 365 · W. M. Brady, *Clerical and parochial records of Cork, Cloyne, and Ross*, 1 (1863), 49–52 · PRO, SP 63 · visitations of Cork, Cloyne and Ross, Bodl. Oxf., MS Carte 55, fols. 580v–585r · visitations of Cork, Cloyne and Ross, TCD, MS 566, fols. 146r–169v · visitations of Cork, Cloyne and Ross, BL, MS 19836, fols. 61r–76v · M. A. Murphy, ed., 'The royal visitation of Cork, Cloyne, Ross, and the College of Yougha', *Archivium Hibernicum*, 2 (1913), 173–215 · *The Irish fiants of the Tudor sovereigns*, 4 vols. (1994) · A. Ford, *The protestant Reformation in Ireland, 1590–1641*, 2nd edn (1997) · A. Ford, 'Reforming the holy isle: Parr Lane and the conversion of the Irish', *'A miracle of learning': studies in manuscripts and Irish learning*, ed. T. C. Barnard, D. Ó Cróinín, and K. Simms (1998), 137–63 · *CSP Ire., 1574–1614* · Cloyne terrier, 1605, NL Ire., MS 13901
Archives NL Ire., MS 13901 · PRO, state papers Ireland
Likenesses oils, 1800–40, Bishop's Palace, Cork

Lyons, Sir Algernon McLennan (1833–1908), naval officer, born at Bombay on 30 August 1833, was the second son of Lieutenant-General Humphrey Lyons (1802–1873), officer in the Indian army, and his first wife, Eliza, daughter of Henry Bennett. Admiral Sir Edmund *Lyons was his uncle. After education at a private school at Twickenham, Middlesex, he entered the navy in 1847. His first service was in the frigate *Cambrian* bearing the broad pennant of Commodore James Hanway Plumridge on the East Indies and China station, and on the return of the ship to England in November 1850 Lyons joined the *Albion* (90 guns) in the Mediterranean. In October 1853 he was promoted mate, and on 28 June 1854 was transferred, as acting lieutenant, to the paddle frigate *Firebrand* (Captain Hyde Parker).

The Crimean War was in progress, and Parker, with the *Vesuvius* and a gunboat, had for some weeks been blockading the mouths of the Danube; on 27 June 1854 he had destroyed the Sulineh batteries. He now decided to try to destroy the guardhouses and signal stations higher up the river, through which communication was maintained with all the Russian forts, and on 8 July he entered the Danube with the ship's boats, one division of which was commanded by Lyons. The first station reached was defended by a stockade and battery, and the banks were lined by Cossacks, who maintained a heavy fire. Parker was fatally wounded, and the command of the *Firebrand*'s boats devolved on Lyons. The attack was successful, five signal stations being destroyed and the Cossacks dispersed. Lyons was mentioned in dispatches and, his promotion to lieutenant having already been confirmed, he was noted for future consideration. On 17 October the *Firebrand* took an important part in the bombardment of Sevastopol, towing into action the *Albion*, flagship of his uncle, Sir Edmund Lyons. The *Albion* was set on fire by the batteries and was for some time in a dangerous position; the *Firebrand* had a difficult task to tow her off. In December 1854 Sir Edmund Lyons became commander-in-chief and chose his nephew to be his flag lieutenant. Lyons shared in further operations in the Black Sea, especially at Kerch and Kinburn, and was promoted commander on 9 August 1858 in his uncle's hauling-down vacancy.

In 1861–2 Lyons commanded the *Racer* on the North American station during the American Civil War, a duty which called for the exercise of tact in the protection of British interests. On 1 December 1862 he was promoted captain, and after waiting for employment, as was then customary, was appointed in January 1867 to command the *Charybdis* in the Pacific, where he remained until 1871. In October 1872 he was appointed to the frigate *Immortalité* and acted as second in command of the detached squadron. From 1875 he was for three years commodore-in-charge at Jamaica, and in April 1878 took command of the *Monarch* on the Mediterranean station, where he served until promoted rear-admiral on 26 September of that year.

In 1879 Lyons married Louisa Jane (*bap.* 1853), daughter and heir of Thomas Penrice of Kilvrough Park, Glamorgan; they had two sons and two daughters. In December 1881 he was appointed commander-in-chief in the Pacific, on 27 October 1884 became vice-admiral, and in September 1886 assumed command of the North America and West Indies station, whence he was recalled home by promotion to admiral on 15 December 1888. From June 1893 he was for three years commander-in-chief at Plymouth, became admiral of the fleet on 23 August 1897, and reached retirement age on 30 August 1903. He was made KCB in 1889 and GCB in June 1897. In February 1895 he was appointed first and principal naval aide-de-camp to Queen

Victoria. He died on 8 February 1908 at Kilvrough, Glamorgan, of which county he was a deputy lieutenant and a JP. He was survived by his wife.

L. G. C. LAUGHTON, *rev.* ROGER MORRISS

Sources *The Times* (10 Feb 1908) • G. S. Graham, *The China station: war and diplomacy, 1830–1860* (1978) • A. D. Lambert, *The Crimean War: British grand strategy, 1853–56* (1990) • Kelly, *Handbk* • Boase, *Mod. Eng. biog.* • Burke, *Peerage* • *CGPLA Eng. & Wales* (1908) • *IGI*

Wealth at death £14,043 8*s.* 6*d.*: probate, 22 April 1908, *CGPLA Eng. & Wales*

Lyons, Edmund, first Baron Lyons (1790–1858), naval officer and diplomatist, the fourth son of John Lyons of Antigua and St Austen's, Lymington, in Hampshire, was born on 29 November 1790 at Burton, Christchurch, Hampshire. Vice Admiral John Lyons (*d.* 1872), for many years in the Egyptian service, was his elder brother. Lyons went to sea with his godfather, a friend of his father's, Admiral Sir Richard Hussey Bickerton, in the *Terrible* in 1798; after this he attended Hyde Abbey School near Winchester until 1803, when he joined the frigate *Active*, commanded by Bickerton's cousin, Captain Richard Hussey Moubray. He remained in her for four years, serving at the passage of the Dardanelles by Sir John Duckworth in February 1807. Shortly afterwards Lyons went to the East Indies; he was appointed acting lieutenant in the following year, and commissioned on 22 November 1809. On 9 August 1810 he took a notable part in the capture of Banda Neira, principal island in the Banda group, west of New Guinea. Lyons then served as flag lieutenant to Rear-Admiral Drury aboard the *Minden* (74 guns). In 1811 the fleet was preparing to capture the heavily fortified port of Marrack, south west of Batavia, but a boat attack was postponed on receipt of intelligence that additional Dutch troops had arrived. On 25 July 1811 Lyons was sent to land Dutch prisoners; on his way back to the fleet, having had a clear sight of the defences, he decided to attack the fort by surprise. On 30 July, shortly before midnight, he landed with only thirty-four men under the embrasures of the fort. This small force stormed and captured the battery, and then Lyons led a charge that dispersed the garrison. When the Dutch troops returned they were driven off by two heavy guns. Lyons then dismantled the fort, spiked the guns and withdrew his men. His actions were highly praised, and although Commodore *Broughton's dispatch did not lead to a promotion he was noted at the Admiralty for early elevation to the rank of commander. This action was widely regarded as the most outstanding example of individual bravery in the wars which followed the French Revolution, and lived in the memory of the service for decades.

Lyons continued off Java, commanding captured gunboats and serving ashore until his health broke down and he returned to Britain. He was promoted commander on 21 March 1812. In 1813 he commanded the brig *Rinaldo* in the channel, and on 7 June 1814 he was posted captain. In the same year he married Augusta Louisa, daughter of Captain Josias *Rogers RN; they had two sons and two daughters. He remained unemployed until 1828, when he

Edmund Lyons, first Baron Lyons (1790–1858), by George Frederic Watts, 1856–7

commanded the frigate *Blonde* in the Mediterranean, during the closing stages of the Greek war of independence, co-operating with French troops at the capture of Kastro Morea, in the Peloponnese, for which he was awarded French and Greek orders. In 1829, while attending the British ambassador in Constantinople, the *Blonde* cruised around the Black Sea, and became the first British warship to visit Sevastopol, the Caucasus, and Odessa. Twenty-five years later Lyons was to be the only senior officer with experience of this sea. In 1831 Lyons moved into the *Madagascar*, and in 1833 he escorted the new King Otho from Trieste to Athens. On paying off in January 1835 he was made KCH and appointed minister and plenipotentiary at Athens, where he remained for almost fifteen years. He proved less satisfactory as an ambassador than as a naval officer, lacking subtlety and often resorting to hectoring and overbearing methods. On 29 July 1840 he was created baronet, and in July 1844 he was made a civil GCB. Between 1849 and 1851 he was minister to the Swiss confederation; he then moved to Stockholm, where his wife died. Lyons, who remained on the navy list, had reached the rank of rear-admiral on 14 January 1850. In November 1853 he was appointed second in command of the Mediterranean Fleet, with his flag aboard the new screw steam battleship *Agamemnon* (91 guns).

Lyons's appointment was well calculated for coalition warfare, particularly where the command was shared by four senior officers. His linguistic skills and diplomatic experience added a new dimension to the planning of the allied forces. In addition Lyons's character and energy were in marked contrast to the calm, measured approach of the commander-in-chief, Vice-Admiral Sir James Dundas. Lyons was in direct personal correspondence with the first lord of the Admiralty, Sir James Graham, who relied on him to push through his plans for an amphibious assault on Sevastopol. This he did at a series of allied councils of war in July and August 1854, in opposition to the views of Dundas. Lyons relished his position, and soon began to differ from his admiral, allowing his asides to be recorded by a party from *The Times*, including John Delane, Austen Henry Layard, and William Howard Russell, who relayed his views to the public, and cabinet ministers. The correspondence with Graham was improper and indiscreet, and Dundas recognized the want of trust in him it implied.

Lyons, with his white hair and slight physique, always fancied that he resembled Nelson, and consciously attempted to model his conduct accordingly. However, he lacked the sustained intellectual power that was such a feature of Nelson's approach to warfare. Lyons was aggressive, dynamic and forceful, but he did not originate a single major operational or strategic movement, being the executor of other men's plans. Dundas, recognizing his subordinate's talents, delegated to him the organization of the transports for the invasion of the Crimea, and Lyons promptly handed the task on to his flag captain William Mends. Mends's plan proved highly successful, much to Lyons's credit. Lyons quickly struck up a rapport with Lord Raglan which greatly assisted inter-service co-operation in the subsequent campaign. Dundas left inshore operations and liaison to Lyons, remaining afloat with the main fleet.

Lyons captured Balaklava, and advised Lord Raglan to adopt it as the base of the British army, a decision that was to have unfortunate consequences when the army had to winter in the Crimea. Lyons led the inshore squadron in the diversionary attack on Sevastopol on 17 October 1854, and ignoring Dundas's orders closed in to engage the fortifications. While this demonstrated his personal bravery, the ships were damaged and unnecessary casualties were sustained. Afterwards Lyons accepted that Dundas had been correct. The failure of the raid on Sevastopol led the government to seek a scapegoat, and Dundas was chosen. Lyons succeeded to the command in January 1855. Working closely with Lord Raglan he improved supply arrangements in the Bosphorus, where Rear-Admiral Frederick Grey took command, and at Balaklava. His most important contribution to the war lay in securing French consent to the capture of Kerch and occupation of the Sea of Azov in May. This operation, long urged by Graham, destroyed the logistic support of the Russian army in the Crimea, determining the outcome of the campaign. As the direction of the Crimean campaign increasingly fell under French control, reflecting the relative sizes of the two armies, Lyons found that opportunities for wide-ranging operations declined. In June 1855 he suffered a double blow, losing his son, Captain Edmund Lyons RN (1819–1855), who had been severely wounded in a night attack on Sevastopol, and his close friend and colleague Raglan. After the fall of Sevastopol he led an expedition to capture Kinburn on 17 October 1855, an enterprise notable for the first operational use of armoured warships. This opened up the Bug and Dnieper rivers for allied operations. In July 1855 he was nominated a military GCB.

In January 1856 Lyons attended the allied council of war in Paris, where he pressed for a more energetic prosecution of the war. After the peace of Paris he completed his term as commander-in-chief in the Mediterranean. He was promoted to the peerage as Baron Lyons of Christchurch on 23 June 1856. On 19 March 1857 he became a vice-admiral, and from December he held the temporary rank of admiral. Already a sick man, Lyons returned to Britain in early 1858 and, after commanding the squadron that escorted the queen to Cherbourg in August, he went ashore. He died on 23 November 1858 at Arundel Castle, the seat of his son-in-law, Henry Granville Fitzalan *Howard, fourteenth duke of Norfolk. He was buried in the vault of Arundel Castle. Lyons's elder son, Richard Bickerton Pemell *Lyons, followed his father into the diplomatic service, where he had a distinguished career.

Lyons was distinguished for his bravery, spirit and commitment. His service as a diplomat in the minor European posts was a worthwhile alternative to long periods on half pay, and provided him with skills and insights that he put to good use in the Crimea. Like his inspiration, Nelson, he was as lavish with his praise of others as he was anxious to be praised by his superiors, and his energy and determination earned him the commitment of those under his command. Nevertheless he was limited by his character and intellect. A balanced assessment of him was provided by Lord Clarendon, the foreign secretary, in 1856: 'tho' he has some ability & considerable firmness I think him singularly deficient in judgement, he is moreover irritable & one of the vainest men I ever knew' (Lambert, 329).

Lyons's contribution to the Crimean campaign was immense, from the allied council of war that decided to attempt the operation, through the transport of the British army, the provision of naval support afloat and ashore, providing advice and support for Lord Raglan, and carrying out the critical Kerch operation. Without him the operation might never have been attempted. His enthusiasm, energy, and leadership made him an outstanding fleet commander, but his limited grasp of strategic issues denied him true greatness.

ANDREW LAMBERT

Sources S. M. Eardley-Wilmot, *Life of Vice-Admiral Edmund, Lord Lyons* (1898) • A. D. Lambert, *The Crimean War: British grand strategy, 1853–56* (1990) • J. W. D. Dundas and C. Napier, *Russian war, 1854, Baltic and Black Sea: official correspondence*, ed. D. Bonner-Smith and A. C. Dewar, Navy RS, 83 (1943) • A. C. Dewar, ed., *Russian war, 1855, Black Sea: official correspondence*, Navy RS, 85 (1945) • *CGPLA Eng. & Wales* (1859) • W. Sussex RO, Lyons papers • BL, Wood MSS • Cumbria AS, Graham MSS • NMM, Dundas MSS • NAM, Raglan MSS • U. Southampton L., Broadlands MSS • private information (1893)

Archives W. Sussex RO | BL, Wood MSS • BL, correspondence Lord Aberdeen, Add. MSS 43135–7, 43166 • Cumbria AS, Graham MSS • NAM, Raglan MSS • NAM, Codrington MSS • NL Scot., correspondence Sir George Brown • NMM, Dundas MSS • PRO, Canning MSS • PRO, Leveson-Gower MS • SUL, Broadlands MSS

Likenesses J. H. Lynch, lithograph, pubd 1854, BM, NPG • G. Zobel, mezzotint, pubd 1854 (after R. Buckner), BM, NPG •

L. Dickinson, oils, 1855, Arundel Castle, West Sussex • M. Noble, marble bust, 1856, Arundel Castle, West Sussex • G. F. Watts, oils, 1856–7, NPG [*see illus.*] • M. Noble, marble statue, 1860, St Paul's Cathedral, London • D. J. Pound, stipple and line engraving (after photograph by Kilburn), NPG • M. Thomas, oils, Admiralty House, Portsmouth • enamel miniature, Arundel Castle, West Sussex • engraving, repro. in Eardley-Wilmot, *Life of Vice-Admiral Lord Lyons*, frontispiece

Wealth at death £45,000: probate, 28 March 1859, *CGPLA Eng. & Wales*

Lyons, Eric Alfred (1912–1980), architect and town planner, was born on 2 October 1912 in Highbury, London, the eldest of the three children of Benjamin Wolff Lyons (1877–1946), soft-toy manufacturer, and his wife, Caroline, *née* Emanuel (1887–1974). During the First World War, while Lyons's father was on active duty in France and Belgium, the family lived in Brighton, but returned to London at the close of hostilities to live in Balham. Lyons attended Rae Central School, Clapham. His father's shock at the horrors of war seriously shook his religious faith, and thus Eric Lyons was raised as a non-practising Jew.

In 1929 Lyons began his architectural career articled to the architect J. Stanley Beard in Baker Street, London, also studying part-time at the Regent Street Polytechnic. Lyons rose to become an assistant to Beard and then, from 1933, went on to work for a variety of architects, including W. E. Trent, Leslie Kemp, and Andrew Mather. Lyons's period as an assistant to the early English modernist E. Maxwell Fry and his short-term German partner Walter Gropius, the founder of the Bauhaus, then escaping Nazi persecution, put Lyons in touch with the most advanced architectural thinking of the period. In 1938, an inauspicious year for architects as the impending war began to dry up commissions, Lyons commenced architectural practice with Geoffrey Paulson Townsend, whom he had met at the polytechnic.

With the outbreak of the Second World War in 1939 Lyons registered as a conscientious objector. Nevertheless, he served by working for the cinema architect Harry Weedon, creating factories and hostels. During the war he met, and married on 18 March 1944 a schoolteacher, Catherine Joyce Townsend (*b.* 1922); no relation to his partner. They had four children: Richard, Jane, Antony, and Naomi. In the year they married the Lyonses first rented then went on to purchase a large Victorian house, Mill House, Bridge Road, East Molesey, near Hampton Court, to which Lyons made an addition, also building his studio office in the garden.

In 1948, upon re-establishing private practice with Geoffrey Townsend, Lyons began to design furniture in the Tetra range for Packet Furniture Ltd. In the same year he also built Oaklands, a block of twenty-four flats, on a site obtained by Townsend in Twickenham, Middlesex. This scheme was to be the first of about sixty speculative housing developments which made Lyons's architectural reputation as a sensitive designer of quality buildings integrated with fine landscaping. As their practice grew in the mid-1950s, Townsend took on the role of developer and was thus forced to resign his membership of the Royal Institute of British Architects, as at that time it was considered a conflict of interest for registered architects to engage in 'nonprofessional' business. Lyons's partnership with Townsend then acquired the registered company name of Span Developments Ltd.

It was the large estate of Parkleys, Ham Common, London, completed in 1956, with 169 flats and a row of six shops, which brought Lyons to prominence as an architect of the new gentle style of post-war modernism which humanized the rigours of the modernist movement by lessons learned from Scandinavian design and the quadrangles and courts of Oxbridge colleges. The flats were small, but well planned, and the rows of buildings set out around courtyards, with flat roofs, principally elevated in brick and tile-hanging, with ribbon windows and cross-wall construction. Parkleys, like most of Span housing, attracted residents who were middle income, and often architects and designers themselves. The fine planting at Parkleys induced the architectural photographer John Donat to comment of the estate: 'It is like walking through a salad' (*Building*, 6 July 1976).

The following year saw the completion in Blackheath, a green suburb of south London, of the first of nineteen Span developments of various sizes in the area, two of which were erected after Lyons's death, but to his designs. Many of these were built within the large gardens of once prosperous villas, thus affording Lyons and his team a good foundation for their landscape designs. Leslie Bilsby, a local builder and developer with a sharp taste for modernism, joined Span Developments at the time and, with Lyons, frequently had to fight the local authorities and residents, who did not take kindly to their modern insertions.

An appreciable asset to Eric Lyons's practice, and his friendship, was Ivor Cunningham, who joined the firm in 1955 and became a partner in 1963, creating the Eric Lyons Cunningham Partnership (which Lyons's son Richard joined as a partner in 1972). Cunningham was responsible for much landscape design and the detailing of plant layout.

Over the decades Eric Lyons developed the Span style of housing, moving to higher and sharper building outlines, sloping roofs, and differing window patterns. But the initial ideology remained: private dwellings conceived as part of the landscape and designed on the basis of a variety of standardized modules. This was a concept which, as Lyons had hoped, successfully encouraged community spirit, engendering a collective purpose while maintaining the privacy of the family and individual. Residents were encouraged to preserve a tight control on any proposed changes.

Other concentrations of Span housing around London were in Twickenham, Putney, and Weybridge, with further examples scattered in such towns as Cambridge, Cheltenham, and Oxford. However, Lyons's most ambitious Span work was the creation of a whole new village in Kent, New Ash Green, where, beginning in 1966, he created over 500 dwellings and a town centre with fifty-seven shops. Lyons was forced to withdraw from the scheme in

1969, due to financial problems, a most distressing situation for him. He won an international competition for the central area of the new resort of Vilamoura in the Algarve, Portugal, begun in 1973.

Lyons's principles of social commitment in architecture permeated his commissions outside Span, most noticeably in his designs for schools and public housing. Two notable schemes were Castle House, a fourteen-storey council block (1961–3) that towers over the centre of Southampton, and the World's End estate for Chelsea borough council, completed in 1977. Built in collaboration with the architect H. T. Cadbury-Brown, World's End comprises a series of high-rise towers of polygonal-shaped flats that form a distinctive skyline on the River Thames. Lyons called World's End 'a metropolitan village'.

Eric Lyons was outspoken on his architectural views and fought many planning battles with local authorities on issues of anti-modernism and the density of his developments. He was widely admired because of his enormous commercial success in getting his ideas built. Very active in the politics of the Royal Institute of British Architects, he was a popular choice as president between 1975 and 1977, receiving numerous awards and medals for his housing and town planning. He was honoured as an honorary fellow by the American Institute of Architects, made a member of the Académie d'Architecture, France, and appointed OBE in 1979. Eric Lyons died at home on 22 February 1980 of motor neurone disease and was cremated.

NEIL BINGHAM

Sources private information (2004) [I. Cunningham, C. Lyons, R. Kaye] • office records, Eric Lyons Cunningham Metcalfe, architects • A. L. Morgan and C. Naylor, eds., *Contemporary architects*, 2nd edn (1987) • *Woman's hour*, BBC Radio 4, 1978, BL NSA • *Building* (6 July 1976)

Archives SOUND BL NSA, *Woman's Hour*, S. McGregor interviewer, BBC Radio 4, 1978

Likenesses K. Vaughan, bronze bust, RIBA • W. Woodington, oils, RIBA

Wealth at death £421,351: probate, 16 April 1980, *CGPLA Eng. & Wales*

Lyons, Sir Henry George (1864–1944), geologist and museum director, was born in London on 11 October 1864, the son of Thomas Casey Lyons, and his wife, Helen, daughter of George Young, of Apsley Towers, Ryde, Isle of Wight. His father, who was of Irish descent, had retired from the army with the rank of general after being governor of Bermuda.

Lyons was educated at Wellington College (1878–82), where he was a scholar and showed early interest in geology; he was elected to the Geological Society at the age of eighteen. From the Royal Military Academy, Woolwich (1882–4) he proceeded, as lieutenant, Royal Engineers, to Chatham for a course of military engineering (1884–6). Posted to Gibraltar in 1886, he explored its caves and sent specimens to the British Museum. A report made at the age of twenty-three while he was at Aldershot, on the water supply from the Bagshot Sand was his first scientific publication (1887).

In 1890 Lyons was posted to a company of the Royal Engineers at Cairo where he found time for research in geology and Egyptology. In 1895 he was sent to Aswan to report on the stability and provide for the strengthening of the temples on the islet of Philae, which were due to be submerged for most of each year on the completion of the Aswan Dam; his report to the public works ministry, *The Island and Temples of Philae*, established his reputation among engineers, administrators, and archaeologists, as he discovered the remains of some Christian churches. He was transferred in 1896 to organize a geological survey of Egypt under the Egyptian ministry of public works. In London on 6 July 1896 he married Helen Julia, elder daughter of Philip Charles Hardwick, architect, of London, granddaughter of Philip Hardwick. They had one son and one daughter.

In 1898 Lord Cromer recommended that Lyons head the cadastral (revenue) survey of Egypt. Its purpose was to register plots and their boundaries, simplify methods of land tenure and rate land for a land tax which was to provide an increasing share of tax revenue. Lyons thus retired from the British army and from 1901 took permanent service under the Egyptian government to build up a joint geological and cadastral survey department. His geological survey also covered aspects of geodesy, meteorology, and hydrology, and he published the respected *Physiography of the River Nile* (Cairo, 1906), which incorporated much original research. He was also able to complete in eight years the *Cadastral Survey of Egypt* (Cairo, 1908), which took the survey beyond its original fiscal aims to provide a detailed and thorough inventory of agricultural resources. By this time he had begun an observatory and a meteorological office. He appears to have been the first to explore the upper atmosphere by use of instrument-carrying kites. He made the arrangements for British, American, and Russian expeditions to observe a solar eclipse at Aswan in 1905, and for a wider visit to Egypt by members of the British Association. The survey and scientific departments he established continued his work after he retired from them. In 1906 he was elected FRS, being proposed by Herbert Hall and George Darwin. This was a particular distinction for a man whose formal scientific education was confined to that of a military engineer. Retiring from Egypt in 1909 he received the grand cordon of the Mejidiye order.

Two years as university lecturer in geography at Glasgow failed to give Lyons the opportunities for leisure and research which he had hoped for, and in 1911 he was appointed secretary to the advisory council and assistant to the director of the Science Museum, South Kensington. He became the keeper of a department in the museum in 1914 but, when war broke out, he was recalled to organize recruiting for the Royal Engineers, and later, as commandant in London, to create a special meteorological service for the Royal Engineers. He then became successively administrator and director of the Meteorological Office freeing the former director, Sir Napier Shaw to train the meteorologists urgently needed during the war.

The relationship between Lyons and Shaw was uneasy, perhaps not least because of their very different visions of the future of the Meteorological Office whose incorporation into the RAF Lyons favoured.

In 1919, with the retiring rank of colonel, Lyons returned to the Science Museum, where he became director in 1920. The museum's fine collections were then very poorly housed. A new building, begun in 1914, and brought progressively into use from 1922, enabled him completely to reorganize the museum. He introduced working models which visitors could operate, exhibited new developments such as the aeroplane, cinema, radio, and gramophone, and, with the help of his family, designed the children's gallery. Attendance figures practically tripled during his directorship. He was knighted in 1926 and he retired in 1933.

Meanwhile recognition and opportunity had come to Lyons in a wider scientific community. In 1919 he had become secretary-general of the International Union of Geodesy and Geophysics, and in 1928 became general secretary of the International Research Council, later the International Council of Scientific Unions. He was foreign secretary of the Royal Society (1928–9) and treasurer (1929–39), reorganizing everything from its publications to its plumbing. He was largely responsible for the edition of the Royal Society's *Record* published in 1940, and for the issue of the Society's *Notes and Records*. In 1940, although displaced from his house and library by bombing and increasingly crippled by arthritis, Lyons began his book *The Royal Society, 1660–1940: a History of its Administration under its Charters*, which was published posthumously in 1944.

Lyons served his fellow scientists in a number of other directions, as honorary secretary of the Royal Geographical Society, president of the Royal Meteorological Society, and member of the councils of the Geological and the Royal Astronomical societies; while as chairman of the Athenaeum's executive committee he transformed the club as he had the Royal Society. He acted as chairman of a committee appointed in 1935 by the Ministry of Health and the secretary of state for Scotland to advise on the inland water survey of Great Britain. He received the Victoria medal of the Royal Geographical Society (1911), the Symons gold medal of the Royal Meteorological Society (1922), and the honorary degrees of DSc (Oxford, 1906) and ScD (Dublin, 1908). His success in so wide a variety of fields stemmed from his great energy, enthusiasm, and administrative skill which all underlay his easy-going and cheerful nature.

Lyons died at his home, Picketts Field, Great Missenden, Buckinghamshire, on 10 August 1944, being survived by his wife, son, and daughter. ELIZABETH BAIGENT

Sources D. Follett, *The rise of the Science Museum under Henry Lyons* (1978) • H. H. Dale, *Obits. FRS*, 4 (1942–4), 795–809 • *Nature*, 154 (1944), 328–9 • *WWW* • R. J. P. Kain and E. Baigent, *The cadastral map in the service of the state: a history of property mapping* (1992) • J. Burton, 'Pen portraits of presidents: Sir Henry George Lyons', *Weather*, 53 (1998), 90–92 • *DNB*

Archives Sci. Mus., journal, incl. corresp. and papers | CAC Cam., corresp. with A. V. Hill | FILM BFI NFTVA, documentary footage

Likenesses W. Stoneman, photograph, 1917, NPG • photograph, National Meteorological Library; repro. in Burton, 'Pen portraits of presidents', 91

Wealth at death £4545 6*s*. 9*d*.: probate, 5 Jan 1945, *CGPLA Eng. & Wales*

Lyons, Israel, the elder (*d.* **1770**), Hebrew scholar and teacher, was born into a Polish Jewish family. He settled at Cambridge where he resided for nearly forty years, earning his livelihood by keeping a silversmith's shop, and giving instruction in the Hebrew language to members of the university. The Cambridge antiquary William Cole notes that in 1732 Lyons lived in a lane at the Great Bridge Foot, called the Pond Yards, but afterwards removed to a house in St John's Lane, near the corner of Green Street. In 1769 he was occupying the corner house of the Regent Walk. According to the same source Lyons and his son Israel *Lyons, mathematician, and his daughter Judith were often found fighting together, and were considered unorthodox by other members of the Jewish community in Cambridge. In 1735 he published *The Scholar's Instructor* (4th edn, 1823); followed by *A Hebrew Grammar* (1763) and *Observations Relating to Various Parts of Scripture History* (1768). Lyons died in Cambridge on 19 August 1770. According to Cole he was buried, at his own request, in the churchyard of Great St Mary's, Cambridge. John Bowtell states that his daughter Judith was a sensible and ingenious woman, but took to fortune-telling, and died a pauper in All Saints' parish, Cambridge, where she was buried on 21 April 1795. THOMPSON COOPER, *rev.* PHILIP CARTER

Sources C. H. Cooper, *Annals of Cambridge*, 4 (1852), 381 • Nichols, *Lit. anecdotes*

Lyons, Israel, the younger (**1739–1775**), mathematician and botanist, was born at Cambridge, the son of Israel *Lyons the elder (*d.* 1770). He was something of a prodigy, especially in mathematics, and Robert Smith, master of Trinity College, paid for him to attend school; however, after a few days Lyons left, saying that he could learn more on his own in an hour than at school in a day. Presumably he continued to educate himself with his father's help. He became proficient in French, Latin, and medieval English history. It is not known if Lyons remained of the Jewish faith, which would account for his not entering the university. In any event, he probably coached students privately, like his father.

In 1758, before he was twenty, Lyons published a 270 page *Treatise of Fluxions*, dedicated to his patron, Smith. Such was his standing that the subscription list has 266 names, nearly all from the university; it includes eleven masters or presidents of colleges, one of them the vice-chancellor, seven professors, and six college libraries, besides the provost of Oriel College, Oxford. With his friend Michael Tyson he had been studying the local flora, resulting in his 1763 *Fasciculus plantarum circa Cantabrigiam nascentium*, of 106 plants unknown to John Ray, thirty of them also unremarked by Thomas Martyn in his *Plantae Cantabrigienses* of the same year. On the strength of his reputation Lyons was taken to Oxford in 1764 by Joseph Banks, then an Oxford undergraduate, to lecture there on botany.

On 13 June 1765 Lyons was engaged, together with George Witchell, to compute the tables for the first half of 1767 for the first issue of the *Nautical Almanac*. Lyons also laid down rules and computed tables for correcting astronomical observations for the effects of refraction and parallax; these were published in 1766 in *Tables Requisite to be used with the* [*Nautical Almanac*]. An extended version of his tables, calculated with Thomas Parkinson and [Richard?] Williams, both of Christ's College, was edited by Anthony Shepherd and published in 1772. Further short calculations by Lyons appeared in the *Almanacs* for 1774, 1776, and 1778. Lyons's survey of Cambridgeshire, which in 1770 he proposed to publish by subscription, seems to have found insufficient support.

In June 1773 an expedition sailed towards the north pole under C. J. Phipps. Appointed by the board of longitude as official astronomer, Lyons was to test chronometers by L. Kendall and J. Arnold, which he did to their satisfaction. His observations and calculations were published by Phipps in 1774. Some of his unattributed calculations were found to be in error.

On his return, Lyons married, in March 1774, Phoebe Pearson, daughter of Newman Pearson of Over, Cambridgeshire, and settled in Rathbone Place, London. There he died of measles on 1 May 1775, while preparing a complete edition of Halley's works sponsored by the Royal Society. His paper on spherical trigonometry, read posthumously to the society, was printed in the 1775 *Philosophical Transactions*. Other papers appeared as the astronomical section of J. Seally's *Geographical Dictionary* (1787). According to the *Gentleman's Magazine*, Lyons was known for his extraordinary genius and extensive knowledge. Charles Hutton described him as a very extraordinary young man for parts and ingenuity, though a less favourable report described him as very debauched. His short scientific career was remarkably varied and relatively successful. RUTH WALLIS

Sources C. Hutton, *A mathematical and philosophical dictionary*, 2 vols. (1795–6) • C. J. Phipps, *Voyage towards the north pole* (1774) • D. Howse, *Nevil Maskelyne: the seaman's astronomer* (1989), 86, 91, 127 • R. V. Wallis and P. J. Wallis, eds., *Biobibliography of British mathematics and its applications*, 2 (1986), 432 • G. C. Gorham and T. Martyn, *Memoirs of John Martyn … and of Thomas Martyn* (1830), 122 • *GM*, 1st ser., 45 (1775), 254–5 • S. Horsley, *Remarks on the observations made in the late voyage* (1774) • *DNB*
Archives CUL, papers • Linn. Soc., annotated copy of *Flora Anglica* • Suffolk RO, Bury St Edmunds, botanical notes

Lyons, John Charles (1792–1874), horticulturist and antiquary, was born on 22 August 1792, the only child of Charles John Lyons (1766–1796), captain of the 12th light dragoons, and his wife, Mary Anne (*d.* 1855), daughter of Sir Richard Levinge. His grandfather, who survived his father, was John Lyons (*d.* 1803), a landed proprietor, of Ledestown, Mullingar, co. Westmeath. John Charles succeeded to his grandfather's estate in 1803. He attended Reading School and matriculated at Pembroke College, Oxford, on 21 May 1810, but took no degree. He served as a magistrate and was high sheriff for co. Westmeath in 1816. On 14 March 1820 he married Penelope Melesina, only daughter of Hugh Tuite of Sonna; they had a son and a daughter. After her death in February 1855, he married, on 12 November 1856, Frances Ellen, third daughter of Thomas Walsh of Belleview, co. Westmeath, with whom he had two sons and two daughters.

Lyons is best-known for his studies on the cultivation of orchids, of which he had a large collection at Ledestown. The failure of his first collection of orchids from Mexico led to his discovery that there was no authority on their cultivation. His *Remarks on the Management of Orchidaceous Plants, with a Catalogue* (1843) was produced on a printing press at Ledestown. It received the gold medal of the Royal Horticultural Society of Ireland. Lyons was a practical man, who engraved the illustrations for his books, designed and constructed his printing presses and greenhouses, and also built clocks. Besides contributing to horticultural journals, he wrote several antiquarian works, printed on his own press, including *A book of surveys and distribution of the estates forfeited in the county of Westmeath in the year 1641* (1852) and *The Grand Juries of Westmeath from 1727 to 1853* (1853).

Lyons died on 3 September 1874 at Ledestown, and was buried in the family grave at All Saints' Church, Mullingar, Westmeath. MARIE-LOUISE LEGG

Sources E. C. Nelson, *John Lyons and his orchid manual* (1983) [incl. repr. of manual (1843)] • G. Wilson, 'J. C. Lyons and his orchid manual', *Journal of the Royal Horticultural Society*, 68 (1943), 175–8 • *Westmeath Guardian* (11 Sept 1874) • Foster, *Alum. Oxon.* • Desmond, *Botanists*, 401 • Burke, *Gen. Ire.* (1912)
Archives RBG Kew, Herbarium collections, corresp. with William Hooker
Likenesses photograph (of two portraits), repro. in Nelson, *John Lyons and his orchid manual*
Wealth at death under £5000: probate, 7 Oct 1874, *CGPLA Ire.*

Lyons, Joseph Aloysius (1879–1939), prime minister of Australia, was born on 15 September 1879 at Stanley, Tasmania, the fourth son of Michael Henry Lyons (1845–1929), a descendant of Irish Catholic immigrants and a storekeeper who later owned a butchery and bakery in Ulverstone, and his wife, Ellen (1847–1913), the daughter of John and Catherine Carroll from co. Kildare. Michael Lyons prospered in business until he lost all his savings betting on the 1887 Melbourne cup. Soon afterwards his health deteriorated and he was unable to support his family. When he was nine, young Joe was sent to work as a messenger in a drapery and later as a 'printer's devil' for the *Coastal News* at Ulverstone. At twelve, he was cutting scrub when his unmarried aunts took over his care and sent him back to school. Lyons eventually became a pupil teacher and from the age of seventeen taught in a succession of remote rural schools. He often clashed with the authorities over the extremely poor conditions teachers then experienced. In 1907 he upgraded his qualifications at the Hobart teachers' college.

Posted next to Launceston, Lyons became active in the Workers' Political League (later the Labor Party), in particular with his attacks on the inequities of education department policy. Tasmania's non-Labor government

Joseph Aloysius Lyons (1879–1939), by Howard Coster, 1935

tried to silence him with a motion in parliament, which it lost by one vote. This boosted Lyons's reputation in Labor networks, even more so when many of his recommendations on education policy were upheld by a royal commission report. In 1909 he resigned as a teacher to contest the seat of Wilmot in the Tasmanian state elections.

Lyons appealed to ordinary constituents. He claimed loyalty to socialist ideals but was not ideological. He attended his first Labor conference in the state in 1909 and quickly gained the confidence of the influential state unions. In 1912 he was elected president of the Tasmania branch of the Labor Party. When Labor formed a government in Tasmania in April 1914, Lyons served as treasurer, minister of education, and minister of railways.

On 28 April 1915, at the age of thirty-five, Lyons married Enid Muriel Burnell (1897–1981) at St Brigid's Catholic Church, Wynyard. Enid had just completed her teacher training. The courtship had begun when she was fifteen. Lyons was accused in private of cradle-snatching, and their marriage, a few months before Enid turned eighteen, reflected worry at a possible political scandal. Enid, a Methodist, converted to Catholicism before marrying. Their union, however, proved a lasting partnership, with Lyons tutoring his wife in the art of political life. In 1943 Enid Lyons became the first woman elected to Australia's house of representatives. In spite of being told they might never have children, the couple had six sons and six daughters. Their sixth child, Garnett, died aged sixteen months in 1925; their last child, Janice, was born in 1933 while Lyons was prime minister.

During the divisive conscription debates (1916–17), Lyons strongly opposed conscription, which advanced his profile with Labor. He also supported home rule for Ireland and condemned the executions of the Easter rising rebels in Dublin. In the state election of 1916, however, the Nationalists (conservatives) campaigned by saying Labor favoured the enemy, Germany. Labor lost. In November 1916 Lyons was elected opposition leader, and in 1923, when Labor took office as a minority government, he became premier of Tasmania.

As premier, Lyons—who also held the treasury, education, and railways portfolios—began cautiously and maintained amiable relations with his opponents. This consensus style was a hallmark of his political career. His reform of Tasmania's financial structure helped Labor retain government in 1925. Lyons's time as premier was possibly the happiest and most fruitful of his career.

Labor lost the state election of 1928. Lyons became restless with state politics and accepted the invitation of the prime minister, James Scullin, to contest the federal seat of Wilmot, which he won in October 1929. Lyons was immediately given a senior cabinet position, as postmaster-general. However, he did not find the shift to Labor federal politics easy. The party factionalism of the much larger trades halls of Sydney and Melbourne wore him down. He approached his portfolio extremely conventionally—opposing debt and stressing balanced budgets as unemployment worsened with the economic crisis after the stock market crash of 1929. His lack of radicalism irked some of his caucus colleagues.

In August 1930 the treasurer, Ted Theodore, stood aside pending an inquiry. Lyons became acting treasurer and attended the meetings that adopted the 'Melbourne plan'. Sir Otto Niemeyer, of the Bank of England, had recommended adjustments to Australia's economy to cope with the depression. Budgets must be cut. This caused uproar from caucus radicals, who included Theodore. Caucus voted to postpone repayment of a £28 million overseas loan, and Lyons launched a nationwide appeal to raise the money to convert the loan. It was a triumph, and Lyons expected Scullin would now back him for the treasury portfolio. However, Theodore was reinstated in January 1931 to appease the unions.

During the loan conversion Lyons had worked closely with several business figures. A 'group of six' had secretly acknowledged his political skills and popularity. They were the Victorian Nationalist MP Robert Menzies (later prime minister) and five Melbourne businessmen headed by the stockbroker Stanliforth Ricketson, who had known Lyons in Tasmania. Lyons, they believed, stood out as the only politician who could lead a revived conservative force and win government at the next election. Australians were alienated by the two major political parties, and populist citizens' groups were growing. Late in January 1931 Lyons resigned from cabinet with his colleague James Fenton; in March he held discussions with the group; in April he and Enid were mobbed as heroes in Adelaide at the Citizens' Leagues conference. The Murdoch newspapers (then owned by Keith Murdoch), in Melbourne and Adelaide, campaigned for them as well. By May, Lyons was parliamentary leader of a new conservative (anti-Labor) party, the United Australia Party.

Labor suffered a crushing defeat in the federal election of December 1931. Lyons had broken Labor's stranglehold on the Catholic vote at a time when sectarianism divided communities—around a quarter of Australians being descended from Irish Catholics and most of the remainder from Anglo-protestant backgrounds. In 100 years of federation, Lyons was the only Catholic non-Labor Australian prime minister and one of the few, before 1972, not a freemason.

Early Lyons budgets were conservative, holding firmly against any temptation to solve unemployment by spending. Financial responsibility was the order of the day. There was some relief for farmers, and costs were trimmed by lowering pensions and public-service salaries. By 1934 there were signs of economic recovery. After the Ottawa agreement at the 1932 Imperial Economic Conference, which asked the dominions to lower tariffs, Lyons refused to drop tariff levels below those prevailing during Scullin's period of office. Some vestiges of Lyons's Labor past, it seemed, remained. His conservative colleague and leader of the Country Party, Earle Page, complained that Lyons was protecting failing industries.

Lyons won the 1934 and 1937 federal elections convincingly. His record of three successive terms was matched only by First World War prime minister William (Billie) Hughes. The United Australia Party won an overall majority in 1931, but after 1934 it was forced to govern in coalition with the Country Party. The Lyons family, meanwhile, had won the hearts of a nation as ordinary Australian folk. Life was a constant juggle in private, since they maintained their family house, Home Hill, in Devonport, Tasmania. However, the frequent presence of 'Honest Joe' Lyons with Enid and children in the prime minister's residence in Canberra was a unifying symbol in hard times. Lyons also took advantage of air travel, covering tens of thousands of kilometres meeting voters; in the 1937 election he covered 9600 km to attend forty-three meetings in forty-three days. He used radio to great effect, and both he and Enid were excellent communicators.

While the Lyons era brought stable and improving times, most legislation from the period had little lasting effect. One exception was the creation of the Commonwealth Grants Commission in 1934. Joe and Enid Lyons made two official trips abroad in 1935 and 1937 to Europe and the United States, requiring long absences from home. Lyons, however, enjoyed being away from the tensions of cabinet. Both he and his wife were empire loyalists. When in 1936 the dominions were consulted on a proposal for legislation permitting Edward VIII a morganatic marriage to Wallace Simpson, Lyons, without consulting cabinet, refused consent. The couple attended the coronation of George VI in 1937, on a visit where Enid was made a dame grand cross of the order of the British empire and Lyons was awarded an honorary doctor of laws at Cambridge University.

Lyons was a gifted administrator. His management style served well in economic crisis. Rivals, though, underestimated his strengths and jockeyed for his position behind the scenes. By 1938 a change of approach was needed, but Lyons had lost direction. His last months were miserable. Stress took its toll. After collapsing from heart failure, he died in office on Good Friday, 7 April 1939, in St Vincent's Private Hospital, Sydney, with Enid at his bedside. A nation mourned his death, and he was given a state funeral in Sydney on Tuesday 11 April. His body was taken by navy vessel to Devonport, Tasmania, where a large crowd saw him buried on 13 April at the Catholic Church courtyard. His remains were transferred in January 1969 to Devonport Lawn cemetery. ANNE HENDERSON

Sources *AusDB* • K. White, *A political love story* (1986) • M. Grattan, ed., *Australian prime ministers* (New Holland, 2000) • P. Hart, 'J. A. Lyons: a political biography', PhD diss., Australian National University, 1967 • E. Lyons, *So we take comfort* (1965) • Lyons papers, NL Aus. • A. W. Martin and P. Hardy, *Robert Menzies: a life*, 2 vols. (1993–9) • F. Green, *The servant of the house* (1969) • M. Hogan, *The sectarian strand* (1987) • E. Lyons, *Among the carrion crows* (Rigby, Adelaide, 1977) • *DNB*

Archives National Archives of Australia, official papers • NL Aus., papers | NL Aus., Dame Enid Lyons' personal papers | FILM BFI NFTVA, documentary footage

Likenesses H. Coster, photograph, 1935, NPG [*see illus.*] • W. McInnes, portrait, 1936, King's Hall, Old Parliament House, Canberra; on loan to NPG; official portrait

Wealth at death £344: *AusDB*

Lyons, Sir Joseph Nathaniel (1847–1917), caterer, was born on 29 December 1847 in Kennington, London, the son of Nathaniel Lyons, an itinerant vendor of watches and cheap jewellery, and his wife, Hannah Cohen. He was educated at the Borough Jewish school in the East End of London. He began as an optician's apprentice, exhibited watercolour paintings at the Royal Institution, and wrote simple novelettes. He also had a mechanical bent, and designed quick-selling gadgets, which he used his showmanship to promote at the many regional and metropolitan exhibitions being organized in the last quarter of the nineteenth century.

In 1887 Lyons ran a stall at the Liverpool Exhibition, selling for a shilling a combined microscope-binocular-compass which he had invented. At this time the Salmon and Gluckstein families, successful tobacco merchants, were turning their attention to catering, seeing the need for good, cheap, clean places to get a cup of tea. They decided to operate a pilot scheme at exhibitions, needed someone to run it and act as 'front man', and turned to Lyons, who was a distant relative of Isidore Gluckstein's fiancée. Lyons agreed to run a tea pavilion at the Newcastle Jubilee Exhibition of 1887, and to use his name, because it was felt to be beneath the dignity of the Salmon and Gluckstein families to go into catering.

The Newcastle pavilion was so successful that in 1887 a private company was formed to develop the families' catering interests. The firm organized catering at the Glasgow exhibition and the 1889 Paris Exhibition, and then took over the catering at Olympia and the Crystal Palace.

In 1894 a public company, J. Lyons & Co. Ltd, was formed. The first teashop opened in 1894 in Piccadilly, London, and during the next few years a chain of teashops was opened in the capital.

Lyons was made chairman for life. His extrovert personality made him the ideal host at the company's restaurants. There is some evidence that he was involved in the negotiations for property, and he certainly became associated publicly with the great success of the firm. But there is no doubt that the real organizational flair, the risk taking, and the shrewd perception of the profit opportunities in catering belonged to members of the Salmon and Gluckstein families, and the real power in the company lay with them. Lyons married Psyche, daughter of Isaac Cohen, manager of the Pavilion Theatre, Whitechapel Road. They had no children.

Lyons was a deputy lieutenant for the county of London. He was actively involved in the Territorial Army and was responsible for the introduction of athletics into the training programme. He contributed to several charities, notably the Little Sisters of the Poor in Hammersmith and the Music Hall Benevolent Fund. He was knighted for his public services in 1911. Lyons died at the Hyde Park Hotel, Knightsbridge, on 22 June 1917 and was buried at the cemetery of the United Synagogue, Willesden.

D. J. Richardson, *rev.* Christine Clark

Sources D. J. Richardson, 'Lyons, Sir Joseph Nathaniel', *DBB* • D. J. Richardson, 'The history of the catering industry, with special reference to the development of J. Lyons and Co. Ltd. to 1939', PhD diss., University of Kent, 1970 • T. C. Bridges and H. H. Tiltman, *Kings of commerce* [1928] • S. Aris, *The Jews in business* (1970) • A. C. B. Menzies, *Modern men of mark* (1921) • d. cert.

Likenesses portrait, repro. in Bridges and Tiltman, *Kings of commerce* • portrait, repro. in Menzies, *Modern men of mark*

Wealth at death £58,967 15*s*. 11*d*.: resworn probate, 21 Aug 1917, *CGPLA Eng. & Wales*

Lyons, (Francis Stewart) Leland (1923–1983), historian, was born on 11 November 1923 in Londonderry, the elder son (there were no daughters) of Stewart Lyons, bank manager, and his wife, (Florence) May, *née* Leland. He was educated at Dover College in Kent and Trinity College, Dublin, which he entered in 1941. Two years later he was elected a foundation scholar, and in 1945 took an outstanding first with a gold medal in modern history and political science. In 1947 he completed his doctoral thesis on the Irish Parliamentary Party, and was appointed lecturer in history at Hull University. He returned to Dublin in 1951, and held a fellowship at Trinity College until 1964. In 1954 he married Jennifer Ann Stuart, daughter of Lieutenant-Colonel Archibald Donald Cameron McAlister, of the 11th hussars and Cheshire regiment; they had two sons.

Lyons's principal scholarly mentor in the 1950s and afterwards was T. W. Moody, who pioneered a new objectivity and scientific precision in the writing of Irish history. The readiness to depart from comfortable orthodoxy led to what may justly be called a renaissance in Irish historical study. The embattled and embittered recent past of

(Francis Stewart) Leland Lyons (1923–1983), by Derek Hill, 1980

the Irish national movement rendered such 'revisionism' doubly difficult, yet by the same token doubly valuable. Well into the post-war years, Irish historiography remained bound up with politics, to the impoverishment of both. Separation of the two was to be of incalculable importance not only in the establishment of a clearer-headed sense of Irish national identity, but also in the liberation of political activity from historical shackles. The work of Leland Lyons represents a decisive phase in this process. His view of revisionism, as he was to express it in his candid W. B. Rankin memorial lecture given in Belfast in 1978, and published as *The Burden of our History*, was that it was 'proper' only in so far as it was 'a response to new evidence which, after being duly tested, brings us nearer to a truth independent of the wishes and aspirations of those for whom truth consists solely of what happens to coincide with those wishes and aspirations'.

Lyons, of Presbyterian and Church of Ireland stock, brought to the study of history the best of Anglo-Irish—though not Ascendancy—qualities. Sharp-sighted yet temperate in judgement, formidable in mastery of detail yet elegant in synthesis, he became by general consent the foremost Irish historian of his day. His work *The Irish Parliamentary Party, 1890–1910* was published in 1951, and his striking treatment of a single critical year, 1890–91, *The Fall of Parnell*, in 1960. On a very different canvas he wrote *Internationalism in Europe, 1815–1914* (1963) for the Council of Europe.

Lyons returned to England in 1964 as the first professor of modern history in the University of Kent at Canterbury.

In so doing he went back to the county of his early schooling, which was now to benefit from his accomplishments in the establishment of its new university. He served as master of Eliot College at the University of Kent from 1969, and published two major works: *John Dillon* (1968), which won the Heinemann award of the Royal Society of Literature, and *Ireland since the Famine* (1971). The former, a relentlessly detailed account of the doomed parliamentarian nationalist, showed the capacity of biography to approach the complexity of total history. The latter was the first attempt at a true total history of modern Ireland, demonstrating the extent of the historical revision so far achieved.

In 1974 Lyons returned once more to Trinity, as provost. In an outward sense this was the pinnacle of a brilliant academic career. Inwardly, however, it may be thought that the most significant event of that year was his appointment as official biographer of W. B. Yeats. Yeats was the ultimate subject for the Anglo-Irish historian, and (to use his own word) came to engross his intellectual energies. In 1977 he published a second large-scale biography, *Charles Stewart Parnell*. What might for many a scholar have been his final masterpiece became a preparatory exercise for the daunting work on Yeats. By this time, Lyons's writing displayed such harmonious style, subtlety of argument, and understated judgement that careless readers could miss much of his reinterpretation of Parnell. But the real earnestness of his future performance came with the Ford lectures which he gave in Oxford in 1977–8, which were published as *Culture and Anarchy in Ireland, 1890–1939* (1979), winning the Wolfson history award in 1980. They challenged those who argued the 'essential unity' of Ireland to accept the 'essential diversity' of its cultures and to build on their strength.

In 1981 Lyons resigned his office as provost of Trinity; his unstinting devotion of energy to the public role of a university head in times of stress and change had come into serious conflict with his overriding determination to pursue his work on Yeats. That work, so impressive even to those entrenched in the bastions of literary criticism, came to an end with awful suddenness when Lyons succumbed to acute pancreatitis in August 1983. He died in the Adelaide Hospital, Dublin, on 21 September 1983.

In 1962 Lyons was elected a member of the Royal Irish Academy and in 1974 a fellow of the British Academy. He was FRHistS and FRSL. He was elected an honorary fellow of Oriel College, Oxford, in 1975, and was awarded honorary doctorates by the universities of Pennsylvania in 1975, Hull, Kent, and Queen's, Belfast, in 1978, Ulster in 1980, and St Andrews in 1981. Known as Lee, Lyons was a graceful and reserved man. He added to his academic achievements formidable gifts as a squash player.

CHARLES TOWNSHEND, *rev.*

Sources R. F. Foster, 'Francis Stewart Leland Lyons, 1923–1983', *PBA*, 70 (1984), 463–80 · *The Times* (24 Sept 1983) · *WWW* · *CGPLA Eng. & Wales* (1984)

Likenesses D. Hill, portrait, 1980, TCD [*see illus.*]

Wealth at death £44,160—in England and Wales: probate, 10 Feb 1984, *CGPLA Eng. & Wales*

Lyons, Lewis (1862–1918), trade unionist, was born on 20 November 1862, at 20 Fashion Street, Whitechapel, London, of German-Jewish parents, Moses Lyons, a journeyman tailor, and his wife, Hannah Goldsmith. Educated at the Jews' Free School, Bell Lane, Spitalfields, from about 1869 to 1873, he left at eleven to start work as a tailor's machinist in one of the many small workshops in the East End of London. Of strong socialist convictions, he soon became acutely aware of the iniquities of the trade—low wages and long hours of work (up to eighteen hours a day) in unhealthy conditions. This, he believed, was caused largely by the prevailing system, commonly known as 'sweating'. Labour was subdivided, each worker being involved in making only a small part of each garment, with no apprenticeship available that would enable him or her to become a skilled tailor earning higher wages.

Lyons campaigned for the licensing, under strict conditions, of all workshops, improved physical conditions, a four-year apprenticeship, higher wages, and a shortened working day, with penal procedures to enforce compliance. Handsome and charismatic, Lyons speedily emerged despite his youth as the principal figure in London's Jewish tailoring trade unions, being involved, usually as secretary, in running no fewer than nine unions between 1885 and 1912. His constant agitation at his workplace, the poor pay his union employers could afford, and his behaviour at public demonstrations led to frequent dismissal, regular visits to his home by bailiffs, fines, and on two occasions short spells of imprisonment. He met his wife, Fanny, whom he married in 1887, while linking arms against the police at a Trafalgar Square protest meeting. The couple had two daughters. His constant shortage of funds, and the time he had to spend attending to his financial private affairs, may to some extent have obstructed his work.

To promote his ideals Lyons wrote widely in the local and national press, including articles in the *East London Observer*, *Jewish World*, the *Tailor and Cutter*, *The Briton*, and *Reynolds*, often under pseudonyms. The culmination of this activity was the production of his own penny monthly journal, *The Anti-Sweater*, that ran for eight editions from July 1886 to February 1887. He wrote, edited, and published the paper while working full time as a machinist. Invited to give evidence to the House of Lords select committee on the sweating system (1888) Lyons made an impressive wide-ranging survey of the state of the tailoring sweating industry, and detailed suggestions (though to some extent impractical) for improvement.

The following year was pivotal for London's immigrant tailors, and for Lyons's career. Public meetings of three tailoring unions resolved on a call for a strike to secure a twelve-hour working day and other improvements in working conditions. As chairman of the elected strike committee Lyons was its driving force. The strike, which began on 29 August 1889, was settled following the mediation of Lord Rothschild and Samuel Montagu. Though initially apparently successful, Lyons said later that within weeks the employers ignored the concessions they had made.

The 1890s was a difficult decade for unions because of a trade depression, and during this time Lyons fell foul of many of his socialist colleagues and earned their distrust. He became convinced that employees had interests similar to those of their immediate employers, who were themselves sub-contractors earning little more than their employees. Lyons believed they should combine forces and present a united front against the superior employers. This led to attacks upon him by trade unionists and anarchists for what were perceived to be capitalist leanings. He was accused of misappropriating funds of the Tailors', Machinists' and Pressers' Union without the members' sanction, though this remained unproven. 'How long', wrote the (Yiddish) *Arbiter Fraint*, 'will you allow yourselves and your union to come to such shame, by letting this man lead you by the nose? … Do you want a union which will be strong enough to press your interests? Then get rid of Lyons' (10 July 1891).

Shortly afterwards Lyons settled with his family in Bristol, where he ran a tobacconist shop selling rolled cigars made by his wife; but by the turn of the century they had returned to London. He once again became involved in union affairs and in April 1911 was elected to sit on the tailoring trade board, but ill health forced his early retirement.

Lyons made an important contribution to developing trade unions, particularly among newly arrived Jewish immigrant workers. Completely independent of thought, he was not fazed by the eminence of his opponents, crossing swords with the chief rabbi, Hermann Adler, and speaking out fearlessly in favour of immigrants when giving evidence in 1903 to the royal commission on alien immigration. He told the commission that the 1901 census had revealed that there were 80,074 tailors and tailoresses in London alone; and when the chairman asked him to 'Call it 80,000', he replied 'No, my Lord, we will call it 80,100; we will not make it less than it is' (*Royal Commission*, q.14073).

Lewis Lyons died on 7 July 1918 at his home, 255 Franciscan Road, Tooting, Surrey, as impecunious as he had been throughout his life. He was a compassionate man, but did not truly appreciate when to subjugate his ideals to the reality of what could be achieved. In its obituary the *Jewish World* (24 July 1918) said that he was guided by a sense of the wrong the poor had to endure, and by the conviction that much of their suffering was avoidable. His work brought him no material advantage, a fact that marked him as one 'in whom was the spirit of service to his fellows'. GERRY BLACK

Sources *The Anti-Sweater* (1886–7) • A. J. Kershen, *Uniting the tailors* (1995) • W. J. Fishman, *East End Jewish radicals, 1875–1914* (1975) • W. J. Fishman, *East End, 1888* (1988) • *Jewish World* (24 July 1918), 7 • L. P. Gartner, *The Jewish immigrant in England, 1870–1914* (1960) • H. Pollins, *Economic history of the Jews of England* (1982) • D. Feldman, *Englishmen and Jews: social relations and political culture, 1840–1914* (1944) • *Arbiter Fraint* (10 July 1891) • 'Royal commission on alien immigration', *Parl. papers* (1903), 9.1, Cd 1741; 9.61, Cd 1742; 9.935, Cd 1741-1; 9.1041, Cd 1743 • *CGPLA Eng. & Wales* (1918) • b. cert. • d. cert.

Wealth at death £15 6*s*.: administration, 26 July 1918, *CGPLA Eng. & Wales*

Lyons, Richard (*d.* 1381), merchant and financier, was of unknown origins, though it is possible that he was a Fleming who settled in London. It is likely that he was also illegitimate, and this may help explain alike the lack of family information, his apparent failure to marry into an established London family, and his slow acceptance into the ranks of the ruling classes of London. There appear to have been no children of his marriage to Isabella Pledour, from whom he was divorced in 1363.

Lyons had by then become a very wealthy vintner and shipowner. At the time of his divorce his property, revenues, and goods in London alone were valued at £2443, and his wife claimed 5000 marks (£3333. 6*s*. 8*d*.) as her share of his total wealth. Lyons dealt in wine, wool, cloth, iron, and lead. Not surprisingly, with an apparently Flemish background, he had considerable business interests in Flanders and was heavily involved in overseas trade, travelling abroad with three servants in 1368. Although probably resident in London from the 1340s, it was not until 1359 that he first purchased property in the city. Similarly, although an active London tradesman in the 1340s, it was not until the later 1350s that he became accepted into the London merchant community. After 1359 Lyons emerged as a leading city merchant and became increasingly involved in city politics and government, though it was not until 1374 that he was appointed both alderman (of Broad Street ward) and sheriff. Like many other fourteenth-century London merchants Lyons sought wealth in the city but gentry status in the countryside by purchasing property outside London. In 1364 he bought his first extra-mural property, in Essex, and his assumption of gentry status and a decline of interest in London gradually followed. In 1380 he represented Essex in parliament, and during the peasants' revolt in 1381 his manor of Overhall at Liston in Suffolk was a target for attack. At his death he held lands in Essex, Kent, Suffolk, Surrey, Sussex, Middlesex, and Hertfordshire, as well as London property which included a large house adjoining the Guildhall of the merchants of the Hanse of Germany in Thames Street, and other property situated in Cosyn Lane in the Ropery.

Lyons was closely involved with John Pecche (*d.* 1380) and Adam Bury, both leading London merchants, engaged in the exercise of the sweet wine monopoly. The latter was granted to Pecche by the crown in November 1373, when Bury was mayor of London. Under this monopoly only three taverns in London were allowed to sell sweet wines; all of them had been leased by Lyons from the city during Bury's first mayoralty in 1365. In 1376 all three Londoners were impeached on various charges of corruption by the Good Parliament, which also brought a number of other accusations against Lyons alone, including the misuse of his position as collector of the wool subsidy and member of the king's council to avoid exporting his wool via the staple at Calais; the appropriation for himself of customs duties that had not been sanctioned by parliament; the charging of usurious levels of interest on loans to the crown; and the purchase of royal debts owed to others at a fraction of their worth but obtaining full repayment of them at the exchequer. He was found guilty of these charges and imprisoned, his property was seized in June, and he was dismissed from his aldermanry in August. Although he was pardoned by the crown in March 1377, he was never restored to office in London.

Lyons had been closely linked to the crown as a financier and adviser. He lent sums to the crown himself, but mainly acted as a middleman on behalf of the crown during the 1370s to arrange loans from denizen and alien merchants in London and to secure the payment of royal debts. Undoubtedly his involvement with the crown gave him influence; in June 1375, for example, he obtained the king's consent to the release of Thomas Gisors, a London merchant, from prison, together with royal protection against his creditors while he was conducting his business, so as to enable Gisors to raise money to repay his debts. Lyons held a number of royal appointments, including a commission to investigate an attack on three Portuguese merchant ships in 1371. He was keeper of the king's moneys at the Tower of London in 1375, and collector of the petty customs in 1373 and of customs and subsidies in 1375.

Lyons was killed in Cheapside during the peasants' revolt on 14 June 1381. Froissart suggests that Lyons was killed as an act of revenge for some much earlier slight to Wat Tyler, the leader of the rebels, who had been his servant or apprentice. But the chronicler Knighton, perhaps more plausibly, connects Lyons's death with his lasting unpopularity from the days when he had been convicted of extortion and fraud. Lyons was buried in the church of St Martin Vintry, London, where according to Stow there was an impressive effigy of him.

ROGER L. AXWORTHY

Sources A. R. Myers, 'The wealth of Richard Lyons', *Essays in medieval history presented to Bertie Wilkinson*, ed. T. A. Sandquist and M. R. Powicke (1969), 301–29 · G. Holmes, *The Good Parliament* (1975) · *Chancery records* · exchequer documents, PRO · R. R. Sharpe, ed., *Calendar of letter-books preserved in the archives of the corporation of the City of London*, [12 vols.] (1899–1912), vols. G–H · *RotP*, vol. 2 · J. Stow, *A survay of London*, rev. edn (1603); repr. with introduction by C. L. Kingsford as *A survey of London*, 2 vols. (1908); repr. with addns (1971) · *Chronicon Henrici Knighton, vel Cnitthon, monachi Leycestrensis*, ed. J. R. Lumby, 2 vols., Rolls Series, 92 (1889–95) · J. Gairdner, ed., *The historical collections of a citizen of London in the fifteenth century*, CS, new ser., 17 (1876) · R. Bird, *The turbulent London of Richard II* (1949) · A. H. Thomas and P. E. Jones, eds., *Calendar of plea and memoranda rolls preserved among the archives of the corporation of the City of London at the Guildhall*, 6 vols. (1926–61) · *Chroniques de J. Froissart*, ed. S. Luce and others, 15 vols. (Paris, 1869–1975) · R. R. Sharpe, ed., *Calendar of wills proved and enrolled in the court of husting, London*, AD *1258* – AD *1688*, 2 vols. (1889–90)

Lyons, Richard Bickerton Pemell, Earl Lyons (**1817–1887**), diplomatist, was born on 26 April 1817 at Lymington, Hampshire, the elder son of Edmund *Lyons, first Baron Lyons (1790–1858), naval officer and diplomatist, and his wife, Augusta Louisa, *née* Rogers (*d.* 1852). After attending Winchester College, he went to Christ Church, Oxford, where he graduated BA in 1838 and MA in 1843. He

Richard Bickerton Pemell Lyons, Earl Lyons (1817–1887), by unknown engraver, pubd 1878 (after Maull & Co.)

entered the diplomatic service in 1839 as an unpaid attaché at his father's legation in Athens. In 1844 he was made a paid attaché and transferred to Dresden and then Florence. His first major appointment came in December 1858 when he succeeded Lord Napier as British envoy in Washington.

Lyons reached Washington on the eve of the civil war and, like many observers, believed that the dissolution of the United States was a strong possibility. He feared that American politicians might try to divert public opinion from domestic problems by increasing their attacks against foreign powers, especially Britain, and was particularly suspicious of William Henry Seward, the secretary of state in the Lincoln administration. As the civil war unfolded, Lyons had to deal with numerous problems. Among them were the defence of Canada, which he believed would be the first target of a possible attack from the northern states, and the question of cotton supply to Britain from the southern states after Lincoln's decision to order the blockade of the southern coast. It was, however, the *Trent* affair that established Lyons's lasting reputation. In the autumn of 1861 the southern states had sent two of their leading politicians to Europe to try to secure formal recognition for the Confederacy. They embarked on the (neutral) British mail steamer, the *Trent*, which was later intercepted by a vessel of the northern states. Public excitement over the affair grew so intense that war between Britain and America seemed for a time unavoidable. Through tact and firmness Lyons was largely responsible for the avoidance of confrontation between the two countries.

In the spring of 1865 poor health brought about by physical exhaustion forced Lyons to resign his post in Washington; a few months later he went to Constantinople to replace Sir Henry Bulwer. He stayed there less than two years and in October 1867, after the resignation of Earl Cowley, was moved to Paris, where he represented Britain for a continuous period of twenty years, which made him one of the longest-serving British ambassadors in Paris in modern times. The presence of such a reliable and conciliatory man in the most sensitive and important post in Europe gave both Liberal and Conservative British governments an essential guarantee that their instructions would always be carried out according to the terms determined in London. His efforts on behalf of various governments were rewarded with a viscountcy (1881) and an earldom (1887).

The twenty years Lyons spent in Paris were of momentous importance in French history: the last years of the Second Empire, its fall and the Franco-Prussian War, the Paris commune, the establishment of the third republic, and the start of the Boulanger crisis, which threatened to engulf the basis of the new republican settlement. Lord Lyons had decided views on the evolving situation in France. Because he did not consider a working and orderly parliamentary democracy possible in France, he constantly favoured strong men, such as Napoleon III and later the republican leader Léon Gambetta, to lead the country. He believed that only they could pacify France, heal the political and social divisions within French society, and, no less importantly, maintain a strong attachment to the entente with Britain and a commitment to free-trade policy.

These two decades were no less fraught with major international problems: the rise of Prussia and the consequences for the European order arising out of the Franco-Prussian War; the Eastern question; the French invasion of Tunisia and the start of French colonial expansion; and the Egyptian question. On all these issues Lyons favoured a close understanding between France and Britain in order to avoid a new confrontation between France and Germany which would, he believed, destroy the entire European system. Following British action in Egypt in the summer of 1882 and the formal end of dual control of that country, Lyons found himself at the receiving end of a bitter confrontation between Britain and France which lasted until 1904: the last five years of his embassy must rank as the worst time he spent in Paris. Unlike some in London he accepted the responsibilities facing Britain in Egypt and believed that, having decisively established its authority over Egypt, Britain should not withdraw from the task it had entered upon. He therefore advocated the best possible arrangements both for securing Egypt's finances and for respecting French financial rights there. During this difficult period Lyons contributed greatly, by his conciliatory manner, in preventing the lack of cordiality between France and Britain from producing any irremediable estrangement.

By the time Lyons relinquished his post at the end of October 1887 he was an exhausted man who, after nearly fifty years of official duties, longed for some rest. On the formation of the second Salisbury administration in 1886, the new prime minister had offered him the Foreign Office, but he declined on the grounds of ill health and age. His last days at the embassy were very trying, but in accordance with Salisbury's wish he stayed on a few more months, though not without considerable misgivings. The earl of Lytton, who had served under Lyons as chargé d'affaires, succeeded him.

In November 1887 Lyons converted to Roman Catholicism. Later the same month, while staying at Norfolk House, St James's Square, London, with his nephew the duke of Norfolk, he suffered a stroke which paralysed him. He died there on 5 December and was buried at Arundel on the 10th. All his titles became extinct.

BERNARD SASSO

Sources Lord Newton [T. W. L. Newton], *Lord Lyons: a record of British diplomacy*, 2 vols. (1913) • B. Sasso, 'The embassy of Lord Lyons in Paris, 1867–1887', PhD diss., U. Wales, 1991 • S. Gallas, 'Lord Lyons and the civil war: a British perspective', PhD diss., University of Illinois, 1982 • L. Williams, 'The career of Sir Edward Malet, British diplomat, 1837–1908', PhD diss., U. Wales, 1982 • B. Willson, *The Paris Embassy: a narrative of Franco-British diplomatic relations, 1814–1920* (1927) • *The political correspondence of Mr Gladstone and Lord Granville, 1868–1876*, ed. A. Ramm, 2 vols., CS, 3rd ser., 81–2 (1952) • *The political correspondence of Mr Gladstone and Lord Granville, 1876–1886*, ed. A. Ramm, 2 vols. (1962)

Archives W. Sussex RO, corresp. and papers | BL, letters to W. E. Gladstone, Add. MSS 44407–44501, *passim* • BL, corresp. with Sir Austen Layard, Add. MSS 38961–39134, *passim* • BL, corresp. with Sir Augustus Paget, Add. MS 51231 • BL, corresp. with Sir Charles Wentworth Dilke, Add. MS 43883 • Duke U., Perkins L., corresp. with Edmund Molyneux • Emory University, Atlanta, Georgia, Savannah consulate corresp. • Herts. ALS, letters to earl of Lytton • Lpool RO, corresp. with fifteenth earl of Derby • National Archives of Malta, corresp. with Sir William Reid • NL Ire., letters to Lord Monck • NL Scot., letters to Sir Henry Elliot • NMM, letters to Sir Alexander Milne • NRA, priv. coll., letters to Lord Hammond • PRO, corresp. with second Earl Granville, PRO 30/29 • PRO, letters to Lord Hammond, FO 391 • PRO, corresp. with Lord John Russell, PRO 30/22 • PRO, corresp. with Odo Russell, FO 918 • U. Nott. L., letters to duke of Newcastle

Likenesses Ape [C. Pellegrini], caricature, watercolour study, NPG; repro. in *VF* (6 April 1878) • lithograph, NPG; repro. in *Whitehall Review* (23 March 1878) • wood-engraving (after photograph by Maull & Co.), NPG; repro. in *ILN* (18 May 1878) [*see illus.*]

Wealth at death £114,278 1s. 10d.: probate, 15 March 1888, *CGPLA Eng. & Wales*

Lyons, Robert Spencer Dyer (1826–1886), physician, was born at Glanmire, Cork, the second son of Sir William Lyons (1794–1858), a merchant of the city who was mayor in 1848 and 1849 and was knighted by the queen on her visit to Cork on 3 August 1849. His mother was Harriet, daughter of Robert Spencer Dyer of Kinsale. Robert was educated at Hamblin and Porter's Grammar School, Cork, and at Trinity College, Dublin, where he graduated MB in 1848. He became a licentiate of the Royal College of Surgeons in Ireland in 1849. In 1855 he was appointed pathologist-in-chief to the army in the Crimea, where he reported on the disease then prevalent in the trenches before Sevastopol (*Report on the Pathology of the Diseases of the Army in the East*, 1856). On 8 September 1855 he was awarded the Crimean and Turkish medals and clasps for

Sevastopol. Lyons was professor of medicine and pathology in the Catholic University medical school in Dublin, and in 1857 he undertook a voluntary mission to Lisbon to investigate the pathological anatomy of the yellow fever which was raging there, and for his report on that subject received from Dom Pedro V the cross and insignia of the ancient order of Christ. He soon returned to Ireland and joined St George's Hospital, Dublin, where he took an active share in the education of the army medical staff. Lyons was also a senator of the Royal University in 1880, crown nominee for Ireland in the General Medical Council of the United Kingdom on 29 November 1881, physician to the House of Industry hospitals, and visiting physician to St Patrick's College, Maynooth. In 1870 he was invited by Gladstone's government to act on a commission of inquiry into the treatment of Irish treason-felony prisoners in English gaols, and in connection with this inquiry he visited many French prisons and reported on the discipline exercised in that country. He enthusiastically recommended the reafforesting of Ireland, and with the agreement of the government collected information on forests from foreign countries, which was embodied in an article in the *Journal of Forestry and Estate Management* in 1883. He sat in the House of Commons for the city of Dublin as a Liberal from April 1880 to the general election in 1885, and spoke on the Parliamentary Oaths Act in May 1883. Lyons wrote widely on subjects in medicine, education, and forestry, publishing a number of essays and monographs between 1850 and 1885. Of these *A handbook of hospital practice, or, An introduction to the practical study of medicine at the bedside* (1859), *Intellectual resources of Ireland: supply and demand for an enlarged system of Irish university education* (1873), and *Forest Areas in Europe and America, and Probable Future Timber Supplies* (1884) are of particular interest. In 1856 Lyons married Marie, daughter of David Richard Pigot, lord chief baron of the exchequer in Ireland. He died on 19 December 1886 at 89 Merrion Square, Dublin, and was survived by his wife.

G. C. Boase, *rev.* Jeffrey S. Reznick

Sources *The Times* (21 Dec 1886) • *Freeman's Journal* [Dublin] (20 Dec 1886) • *Midland Medical Miscellany* (1 Feb 1884), 33–5 • J. B. Lyons, 'A Dublin observer of the Lisbon yellow fever epidemic', *Vesalius*, 1/1 (June 1995), 8–12 • *WWBMP* • Boase, *Mod. Eng. biog.*

Archives Bodl. Oxf., Wodehouse MSS

Likenesses woodcut, 1836, repro. in R. Burgess, *Portraits of doctors and scientists in the Wellcome Institute of the history of medicine* (1973) • portrait, 1884, repro. in *Midland Medical Miscellany*

Wealth at death £2844 8*s*. 8*d*.: administration, 22 March 1887, *CGPLA Ire.*

Lyons, Sir William (1901–1985), motor vehicle manufacturer, was born on 4 September 1901 at 26 Oxford Road, Blackpool, the only son of William Lyons, an Irish music seller and musician, and his wife, Mary Jane (Minnie) Bancroft, from Lancashire. Educated at Poulton-le-Fylde grammar school and Arnold House, the young Lyons preferred sport to academic subjects, excelling at running. At his father's instigation, he became a trainee with Crossley Motors Ltd, but soon developed a desire to start his own business.

The road to self-employment began when Lyons became

Sir William Lyons (1901–1985), by unknown photographer

junior salesman for Jackson Brothers, who held the local Sunbeam franchise, thereby gaining some insights into marketing methods. Lyons's penchant for speed led him to become a motor cycle enthusiast; this brought him into contact with William Walmsley, who had started a business by acquiring ex-war department motor cycles and producing highly stylized side-cars named the 'Swallow'. Lyons immediately saw their commercial potential and, with the financial backing of both firms, a partnership to produce them was formed in 1922, the Swallow Sidecar Company. Lyons's dedication, his instinct for selecting the right staff, and his bank manager's willingness to tolerate the breaking of overdraft limits, brought some success. This was despite stiff competition from cheap all-weather motor cars, not least the Bullnose Morris. In 1924 he married Greta (*d.* 1986), daughter of Alfred Jenour Brown, a schoolmaster, of Cuddington, near Thame; they had two daughters and a son, who was killed while driving a Jaguar to Le Mans in 1956.

Lyons's ambitions soon expanded into the motor car coachbuilding field after he purchased an Austin Seven and saw scope to improve its stark appearance. A larger factory was leased in Cocker Street, Blackpool, and the firm's expanding activities were symbolized by its name change to the Swallow Sidecar and Coachbuilding Company. Lyons recruited skilled workers from the midlands, the most significant being Cyril Holland, a creative bodymaker who could interpret the ideas of his employers and bring them to the manufacturing stage. Special bodies were fitted to Austin Seven chassis, with the coachwork featuring long-lasting aluminium panels, the bodies being painted in bright attractive colours rather than the conventional stark black. By giving a very basic car the veneer of a luxury model, and selling it at a reasonable price, Lyons had found a winning formula. He secured orders from several distributors, the biggest being from Henlys, which boasted car distribution agencies nationwide, and wanted 500 units.

This was a crucial breakthrough but also provided a major headache, with Austin chassis accumulating at Blackpool railway station, reflecting the fact that Swallow's existing capacity could not cope with demand. Lyons decided to relocate the firm to the midlands where the lines of communication with Austin would be much shorter and the right kind of premises, labour, and materials were in abundant supply. In 1928 Lyons secured the lease to a 13 acre site in Coventry where a former shell-filling factory was situated. Chassis from Austin now came by road and there was ample storage space at the rear of the factory.

The relationship with Austin soured and Swallow turned increasingly to other firms to manufacture chassis to which they added Swallow coachwork. At this time Lyons developed a close working relationship with John Paul Black (1895–1965) managing director of Standard Motor Company, which led to Black's agreeing to provide Swallow with chassis and engines, a crucial step towards the production of the latter's own motor car. A Lyons sketch gave birth to the long, low, rakish look which was to become famous; the SS 1 sports car which resulted was an immense success, so much so that by 1933 the company had discontinued its other body-making activities. Sidecar production was increasingly marginalized, being wound up finally in 1944. The sleek and distinctive look of the SS 1, together with its highly competitive price and sound marketing, brought success. As a sports car *per se*, however, it left much to be desired, not least a competitive engine. The SS 1's saloon engine provided by Standard delivered poor performance against competitors and produced the jibe 'more slow than go'.

Lyons recognized that he needed to address this weakness by developing in-house tailor-made engines. A subsidiary, SS Cars Ltd, was formed in October 1933 and two years later was floated successfully on the stock market. Lyons retained a 50 per cent holding and later acquired additional shares to ensure he had a majority interest. At this point Walmsley, increasingly uninterested in the business, retired, leaving Lyons at the helm to develop SS Cars Ltd as he wanted. In April 1935 Lyons established an engineering department, appointing as chief engineer the capable William Heynes, who quickly showed his worth by upgrading the performance of Standard engines. Lyons selected the name 'Jaguar' to launch his new saloon, which was unveiled with a fanfare of publicity at London's Mayfair Hotel. The change in emphasis towards saloons was completely vindicated by sales—for the rest of the 1930s these cars made up the greater part of profits.

The war interrupted progress, with SS Cars forced by circumstances to play a supporting role to larger firms by manufacturing and repairing parts for bomber and fighter aircraft. Lyons used the breathing space thus provided to his advantage by expanding production facilities and, more significantly, by developing with his designers a new post-war engine—the famous XK. Lyons took advantage of the mercurial Black's offer to sell him the original tooling from which the Jaguar engines had evolved. At the end of the war, symbolizing Lyons's new-found independence, Jaguar Cars Ltd was born.

Lyons's post-war strategy was built on generating overseas sales, especially to the United States. The XK 120 sports car, later seen by Lyons as marking the real beginning of his company's success, was launched in 1948. As its name suggested, it was capable of speeds in excess of 120 m.p.h. This performance was due to the remarkable XK engine, the world's first mass-produced car engine with twin overhead camshafts and hemispherical combustion chambers. At Lyons's instigation the model was entered for Le Mans, winning the gruelling 24-hour race no fewer than four times between 1953 and 1957, thereby establishing Jaguar's racing pedigree beyond doubt. Export success, especially in the United States and Australia, led to Lyons being knighted in 1956.

Lyons took the opportunity to acquire the former Daimler shadow factory in Browns Lane, Coventry, which boasted 1 million square feet of production space. This provided a sound base from which to produce a succession of highly successful sports and saloon models, based on variants of the XK engine, including the E-Type Jaguar two-seater sports car and the XJ 6 saloon, which came closest to Lyons's ideal of the perfect car.

In the early 1960s Lyons embarked on a policy of expansion and diversification, acquiring Daimler (1960), Guy Motors (1961), and Coventry Climax Engines Ltd (1963), which gave him an entry into the field of commercial vehicles, fire-engines, and fork-lift trucks. Such moves did not guarantee Jaguar's independence and when the British Motor Corporation acquired Pressed Steel, Jaguar's main body suppliers, Lyons felt compelled to submit to a takeover by the Longbridge giant in July 1966. Two years later, Jaguar became part of the Leyland group. Lyons was unhappy at the association and did his best to ensure that Jaguar retained its distinctive identity. It was a losing battle, with Jaguar's reputation being dragged down by the overall managerial deficiencies of British Leyland. Lyons opted to retire from his executive positions at Jaguar in 1972, but continued to take an active interest in the company as its honorary president. He was immensely pleased when Jaguar, under Sir John Egan, began to regain its reputation, finally returning to private ownership in 1984.

Lyons's awards and honours were considerable. He undertook many distinctive positions in the motor industry, including a period as president of the Society of Motor Manufacturers and Traders (1950–51). As Jaguar's fame grew so did Lyons's personal recognition. In 1954 he was appointed a royal designer for industry and in 1969 received an honorary doctorate of technology from Loughborough University, but he was denied the accolade of the freedom of Coventry. He died on 8 February 1985 at Wappenbury Hall, Leamington Spa, his Warwickshire home. STEVEN MOREWOOD

Sources S. Morewood, 'Sir William Lyons', *Pioneers and inheritors: top management in the Coventry motor industry, 1896–1972* (1990) · A. Whyte, *Jaguar: the definitive history of a great British car*, 2nd edn (1985) · A. Whyte, *Jaguar XJ40: evolution of the species* (1987) · P. Porter, *Jaguar: the complete illustrated history*, 2nd edn (1990) · K. Clayton, *Jaguar: rebirth of a legend* (1988) · b. cert. · Coventry Evening Telegraph Library · private information · *The Times* (9 Feb 1985) · d. cert.
Archives Jaguar Cars Ltd, Brams Lane, Coventry | SOUND University of Coventry, Interview with Sir William Lyons (tape recording)
Likenesses photograph, NPG [*see illus.*]
Wealth at death £3,417,111: probate, 29 April 1985, *CGPLA Eng. & Wales*

Lysaght, Edward (1763–1811), poet and wit, was born on 21 December 1763, the son of John Lysaght of Brickhill, co. Clare, a protestant gentleman, and Jane Eyre, daughter of Edward Dalton of Deerpark in the same county. He was educated at Dr Patrick Hare's school at Cashel, and at Trinity College, Dublin, where he graduated BA. His degree was incorporated at Oxford in 1787, and a year later he proceeded MA from St Edmund Hall, Oxford.

Lysaght complemented his academic work with legal study. In 1784 he became a student at the Middle Temple in London, and also at the King's Inns in Dublin. He was called to the English bar during the Easter term in 1788, and joined the profession in Ireland later that year. Initially, he practised English law, being employed as counsel in many election petitions, including, in 1784, the petition arising out of the celebrated Westminster contest with Charles James Fox.

Lysaght's legal career in London did not prosper, however, and he therefore decided in 1797–8 to return to Ireland to become a member of the Munster circuit, where, for a time, he enjoyed a considerable practice, being appointed a commissioner of bankruptcy, and, later, a police magistrate for Dublin.

In Dublin, Lysaght also increasingly became a notable society figure, particularly in literary and theatrical circles, where he achieved a considerable reputation as a *bon vivant*, satiric wit, and improvisatore. At the time of the Act of Union, he hired himself out as a political squib writer and pamphleteer, whose Swiftian anti-English satires in *The Lantern* made him enemies determined to blacken his name. Jonah Barrington, for example, states without authority in his *Personal Sketches* (1827–32) that, although posing as an opponent of the Union, Lysaght in reality took money from Castlereagh to write in the government interest.

Lysaght did not, however, manage his money well, and his social popularity did not prevent him from dying impoverished in 1811. His collected poems were published in the year of his death, prefaced by a memoir. A subscription raised by the bench and bar of Ireland for the benefit of his widow and two daughters raised over £2000. His patriotic ballads and often sentimental and bawdy love songs were also recalled with affection in Ireland throughout the nineteenth century, and were continually anthologized. Lysaght's wit was also not soon forgotten. In 1829, in Sydney Owenson's popular novel *The O'Briens and the O'Flahertys*, a flirtatious woman is informed that her behaviour warrants an epigram in the *Freeman's Journal* 'from Curran or Lysaght' (Deane, 2.870). Lysaght's most famous poem, 'The Man who Led the Van of the Irish Volunteers', appeared in *The Field Day Anthology of Irish Writing*. C. L. FALKINER, *rev.* JASON EDWARDS

Sources R. Hogan and others, eds., *The Macmillan dictionary of Irish literature* (1980), 733–4 · R. Welch, ed., *The Oxford companion to Irish literature* (1996), 321 · S. Deane, A. Carpenter, and J. Williams, eds., *The Field Day anthology of Irish writing*, 1 (1991), 484, 492, 496; 2 (1991), 870 · W. J. Fitzpatrick, *Irish wits and worthies* (1873) · Foster, *Alum. Oxon.* · E. Lysaght, *Poems*, ed. H. Griffin (1811) [incl. a biographical memoir] · J. Barrington, *Personal sketches of his own times*, 3 vols. (1827–32)

Lysaght, John (1832–1895), manufacturer of sheet iron, was born in the parish of Mallow, co. Cork, Ireland, in March 1832, one of several children of William Lysaght, farmer, and his wife, Frances Atkins. After receiving his early education in Ireland, in his late teens he was sent to Birmingham and Bristol where he trained in civil engineering and, perhaps more crucially, established a friendship with Robert Clarke, whose father had a number of business interests. One of these, in Bristol, specialized in 'zincing' iron buckets and, on his father's death in 1857, Clarke made a present of it to Lysaght. Not long after, in 1858, the latter married Ellen Moss (*d.* 1882). They had at least two children.

Over the succeeding decades, the business expanded substantially. By 1860 galvanized and corrugated sheet iron were being produced, alongside a widening range of galvanized products destined mainly for the agricultural industry. In 1869 the business was moved across Bristol to St Vincent's where, in contrast to the six men and a boy employed in 1857, 400 men were employed in 1878. John had also started, in 1876, a constructional department for the production of structural ironwork at nearby Netham.

Expansion created openings within the business for several of Lysaght's relatives; these included his eldest surviving son, Frederick Percy, and nephew, Sydney Royse Lysaght, who on his death became respectively chairman and managing director of John Lysaght Ltd. Sydney's brother, **William Royse Lysaght** (1858–1945), steel manufacturer, also played a prominent part in the company's development. Born on 23 July 1858, one of several children of Thomas Royse Lysaght, John's elder brother, and Emily Moss (sister of Ellen), in 1874 William Royse was sent by John to the Gospel Oak Company's works at Tipton, Staffordshire, to learn the business of producing sheet iron. When, in 1878, Lysaght, in order to provide a regular supply of puddled iron, acquired the Swan Garden ironworks at Wolverhampton, William Royse was brought from Gospel Oak to run the plant.

John Lysaght's business interests were incorporated in 1880 under the title John Lysaght Ltd, with a registered nominal capital of £162,000. Despite this, however, Lysaght remained clearly in charge of the company's development, and it is recorded that he had a strong aversion to committees. He also did not approve of the contract labour system which operated in the west midlands, a factor which undoubtedly contributed to several conflicts with the labour force there. At Bristol, however, where labour organization was quite different, Lysaght operated a humanitarian system which, in the 1880s, included the provision of a factory canteen, a large meeting hall and recreation centre, a well-stocked library, and a sick and medical club for the workforce.

Growth during the 1880s, based largely on exports, especially to Australia (in 1885, 90 per cent of the firm's output was exported, with the bulk, around 70 per cent, going to Australia), led to the purchase of other works. When the Osier Bed ironworks was acquired in 1885, William Royse also became responsible for its management. By the early 1890s, however, it was clear that Staffordshire was doomed as a sheet-producing region, so Lysaght, together with William Royse, planned the development of a new sheet-rolling complex on a coastal site at Newport, south Wales. The Orb Works, as the complex was called reflecting the 'Orb' brand name which Lysaght had adopted for his products in 1857, commenced production in 1897, but he did not live to see it. He died on 1 October 1895, from a neck tumour, at his home at Springford Stoke Bishop, Gloucestershire. At that time his business employed nearly 3000 workers in Bristol and Wolverhampton. A Conservative in his political sympathies, Lysaght had not been particularly attracted to public life, though he had been a magistrate in Bristol and its high sheriff in 1882.

In 1901, having overseen the movement of sheet production from Wolverhampton to south Wales, William Royse Lysaght took over management of the Orb Works which, by 1913, alone employed 3000 workers. He was subsequently responsible for the decision to build the Normanby Park Steelworks at Scunthorpe, which was designed to supply the Orb Works with steel. The experience gained by William Royse and his brother Sydney from the development of the Orb and Normanby works played an invaluable role in subsequent developments in Australia. Following the interruption of supplies from Britain during the First World War, the company decided to establish a production plant at Newport, New South Wales. This plant, which came into production in April 1921, was to help make Lysaght's Galvanised Iron Proprietary Ltd one of the largest steel producers in Australia. Before completion of this project, the Lysaght business interests were sold to H. Seymour Berry and, in 1920, amalgamated with those of Guest, Keen, and Nettlefolds Ltd.

William Royse Lysaght married Effie Elizabeth Stavern Gladstone in 1890; they had three children. A member of the Iron and Steel Institute since 1888, William Royse was elected to its council in 1915 and became a vice-president in 1924 and its president in 1933–5. His role as spelter adviser to the Ministry of Munitions during the First World War led to his appointment as CBE in 1918. He was also a deputy lieutenant and justice of the peace for Monmouthshire, and the county's high sheriff in 1915. He died on 27 April 1945 at his home in Castleford, Tidenham, near Chepstow, Monmouthshire. TREVOR BOYNS

Sources C. Baber and T. Boyns, 'Lysaght, John', *DBB* • E. Jones, 'Lysaght, William Royse', *DBB* • *The Lysaght century, 1857–1957* (1957) • *Western Daily Press* (2 Oct 1895) • *Bristol Mercury* (2 Oct 1895) • *Bristol Times and Mirror* (2 Oct 1895) • *Midland Evening News* (2 Oct 1895) • K. Warren, *The British iron and sheet steel industry since 1840: an economic geography* (1970) • d. cert. [William Royse Lysaght]
Likenesses photograph (William Royse Lysaght), GKN archives; repro. in Jones, 'Lysaght, William Royse'
Wealth at death £424,214: probate, 25 March 1896, *CGPLA Eng. & Wales* • £277,367 17s. 8d.—William Royse Lysaght: probate, 29 Oct 1945, *CGPLA Eng. & Wales*

Lysaght, William Royse (1858–1945). *See under* Lysaght, John (1832–1895).

Lysons, Daniel (1727–1800), physician, was born on 21 March 1727, the eldest son of Daniel Lysons of Hempsted Court, Gloucestershire, and Elizabeth, daughter of Samuel Mee of Gloucester. He matriculated at Oxford as a gentleman commoner of Magdalen College on 2 March 1745, graduated BA in 1750 and MA in 1751, and was elected fellow of All Souls College, where he proceeded BCL in 1755. On 5 July 1756 he was licensed to practise medicine, and in 1759 he became DCL. This degree was commuted to MD on 24 October 1769. He practised for a few years at Gloucester, and was the physician to the infirmary there. About 1770 he settled at Bath, and in 1780 was elected one of the physicians to the Bath General Hospital. He married Mary, daughter of Richard Rogers of Dowdeswell, on 6 December 1768; there were no children. Under the then statutes his marriage inevitably led to the resignation of his fellowship, but he evidently was not a man who bore grudges: three years later, in 1772, he presented the All Souls Library with its finest manuscript—the mid-thirteenth century Amesbury psalter.

Lysons published several works on fevers and their treatment. He died at Bath on 20 March 1800, leaving his considerable fortune to his nephew, Daniel *Lysons (1762–1834), the topographer.

GORDON GOODWIN, *rev.* CLAIRE L. NUTT

Sources Foster, *Alum. Oxon.* • *GM*, 1st ser., 70 (1800), 392, 483 • Burke, *Gen. GB* • private information (2004) [J. S. G. Simmons]
Likenesses T. Kettle, oils, Courtauld Inst.
Wealth at death left a 'considerable fortune'

Lysons, Daniel (1762–1834), antiquary, was born on 28 April 1762, probably at Rodmarton rectory, Gloucestershire, the elder son of Samuel Lysons (1730–1804), rector of Rodmarton and Cherrington, and his wife, Mary (1734–1791), daughter of Samuel Peach of Chalford in the same county. He had a brother, Samuel *Lysons (*bap.* 1763, *d.* 1819), antiquary and archaeologist, and a sister, Mary (1765–1848).

After attending Bath grammar school Lysons went to Oxford, matriculating from St Mary Hall on 26 March 1779. He graduated BA in 1782 and proceeded MA in 1785. He was ordained and served as assistant curate of Mortlake from 1784 to 1789 and curate of Putney from 1789 to

1800. At this time he began work for his *Environs of London* (4 vols., 1792–6), a topographical account of the parishes within 12 miles of London. A contemporary recounted that Lysons 'spent seven hours up to his knees in water in the vaults of Stepney Church copying epitaphs' (Fleming, 49) and he extended this industry and meticulousness to all his work. He treats Surrey parishes in the first volume, which includes notable demographic sections compiled from primary sources. This volume was only partly superseded by *The History and Antiquities of Surrey* of Owen Manning and William Bray (3 vols., 1804–14). The second and third volumes cover Middlesex parishes and are a great advance on previous works. The sections on Essex parishes draw quite heavily on *The History and Antiquities of the County of Essex* (2 vols., 1762–8) of Philip Morant but their range is greater, covering births and baptisms and agriculture. The work was supplemented by *A Historical Account of those Parishes in … Middlesex … not Described in the 'Environs'* (1800), and in 1811 by a second edition of and a supplement to the *Environs*. Many of the illustrations were drawn and etched by Lysons and his brother Samuel and the whole represented a very considerable antiquarian achievement.

The *Environs* was dedicated to Horace Walpole, a close friend of the two brothers and their keen correspondent. Walpole nicknamed Daniel 'Stumpity' or 'Stumpety Stump', perhaps a reference to a limp, or to his incessant toil and travels. He talks of 'the two Lysons, and their strong legs and activity and perseverance. Of their being so absorbed by their pursuits as to believe those who they speak to are equally interested with themselves' (Lewis, 15.334). Despite the gentle mockery Walpole was obviously fond of the two and had earlier appointed Daniel Lysons his 'chaplain'. The brothers had other well-placed friends and connections; their correspondence with Thomas Lawrence, who painted them both, and Mrs Piozzi survives.

On the death of his uncle, the physician Daniel *Lysons (1727–1800), Lysons inherited Hempsted Court and the family estates in Gloucestershire. On 12 May 1801 he married, at Bath, Sarah (1779/80–1808), eldest daughter of Lieutenant-Colonel Thomas Carteret Hardy of the York fusiliers. They had two daughters, Sarah (1802–1833) and Charlotte (1807–1848), and two sons, Daniel (1804–1814) and the antiquary Samuel *Lysons (1806–1877). In 1804 Lysons succeeded to the family living of Rodmarton.

The two Lysons brothers collaborated on *Magna Britannia, being a concise topographical account of the several counties of Great Britain*. It was intended to fill the gap between large-scale county histories and Camden's *Britannia*, and was even more ambitious than the *Beauties of England and Wales*, on which work had recently begun. The brothers made personal visits to collect material and still more was collected, following established practice, by circulating printed questionnaires to local worthies, the post office exceptionally allowing replies by clergymen to be sent free of charge. The first volume of *Magna Britannia*, covering Bedfordshire, Berkshire, and Buckinghamshire, appeared in 1806; Cambridgeshire, Cheshire, Cornwall, Cumberland, Derbyshire, and Devon had also been published by 1822, when the work ended. The decision to curtail the project was taken on the death of Samuel Lysons in 1819; Daniel, who was extremely fond of him as well as dependent on his expert archaeological skills, declared: 'I cannot go on with[out] my fellow labourer. Our lives wd not have sufficed to the completion had they been protracted even to old age. It is as well to give up now' (Steer, 49). The papers amassed in compiling the work are at BL Add. MSS 9408–9471.

Unsurprisingly there are parts of *Magna Britannia*, such as that on Buckinghamshire, where the Lysons brothers seem on weaker ground than Daniel Lysons did in Middlesex, but overall the standard of the work is extremely high. Although their emphasis on church and manor was traditional, they included new material on such topics as commerce, population, and manufacture, and were far less preoccupied than many antiquaries with arms and pedigrees, and far less concerned than local topographers to rehearse the glories of the county.

On 2 July 1813 Lysons married Josepha Catherine Susanna (1780/81–1868), daughter of John Gilbert Cooper of Thurgarton Priory, Nottinghamshire; they had one child, Daniel *Lysons (1816–1898). Lysons was a fellow of the Society of Antiquaries (1790) and of the Royal (1797) and Linnean societies. In addition to his antiquarian writings he published several religious works and collected cuttings from newspapers which were subsequently deposited at the British Museum. His *History of the origin and progress of the meeting of the three choirs of Gloucester, Worcester, and Hereford* (1812) remains a standard work of reference on that festival. He died at Hempsted Court on 3 January 1834 and was buried at Rodmarton.

Lysons was one of many clergyman–topographers but he had the advantage of ample means, an excellent collaborator in his brother, and very considerable scholarly and artistic talent. His work stands out for his ability to organize and present clearly a mass of material, for the emphasis he laid on primary sources such as parish records, deeds, and censuses, and for his scrupulous citing of sources. His documented accounts corrected those of earlier antiquaries who had relied on folk memories, and set the standard for successors, including the Victoria History of the Counties of England. The contents of his books were more widely copied than his methods, and the volumes remain of value nearly 200 years after their publication. ELIZABETH BAIGENT

Sources C. R. J. Currie and C. P. Lewis, eds., *English county histories: a guide* (1994) · Walpole, *Corr.* · Burke, *Gen. GB* · Foster, *Alum. Oxon.* · Redgrave, *Artists* · *Gloucestershire Notes and Queries*, 2 (1884), 535 · *GM*, 2nd ser., 1 (1834), 558–9 · *GM*, 1st ser., 78 (1808), 94 · F. W. Steer, ed., *The letters of John Hawkins and Samuel and Daniel Lysons, 1812–1830* (1966) · L. Fleming, *Memoir and select letters of Samuel Lysons* (1934) · D. E. Williams, *The life and correspondence of Sir Thomas Lawrence*, 2 vols. (1831) · *DNB*

Archives BL, corresp., collections, drawings, Add. MSS 9408–9471 · S. Antiquaries, Lond., commonplace books · Warks. CRO, letters · Yale U., Beinecke L., corresp. and papers | BL, letters to Joseph Hunter, Add. MS 24870 · Bodl. Oxf., letters to William

Nicholls · Cornwall RO, corresp. with John Hawkins · Cornwall RO, letters to John Hawkins · Cornwall RO, letters to F. V. Jago · JRL, letters to Hester Piozzi · JRL, letters to Davenport family · W. Sussex RO, Hawkins MSS

Likenesses G. Dance, pencil drawing, 1793, BM · T. Lawrence, oils, repro. in Fleming, *Memoir and select letters*, facing p. 36 · engraving, repro. in Steer, ed., *Letters of John Hawkins and Samuel and Daniel Lysons*, facing p. 49

Lysons, Sir Daniel (1816–1898), army officer, born on 1 August 1816 at Rodmarton, near Tetbury, Gloucestershire, was second son of the Revd Daniel *Lysons (1762–1834), the topographer, and his second wife, Josepha Catherine Susanna (1780/81–1868), daughter of John Gilbert Cooper of Thurgarton Priory, Nottinghamshire. He was educated at the Revd Harvey Marryat's school at Bath and at Shrewsbury School (1829–32), where he twice saved boys from drowning. He spent two years (1832–3) with M. Frossard at Nîmes to learn French. On 26 December 1834 he obtained by purchase a commission as ensign in the 1st Royals, joined the regiment at Athlone in February 1835, and went with it to Canada in the following year.

Lysons became lieutenant on 23 August 1837, and, owing to his skill as a draughtsman, he was employed on the staff of the deputy quartermaster-general, Colonel Charles Gore, during the Canadian uprising. He was present at the action of St Denis (November 1837), was mentioned in dispatches, and was at the capture of St Eustache (December 1837). He was deputy assistant quartermaster-general from 1 December 1837 to 12 July 1841, and with the assistance of officers of the line he surveyed much of the frontier. A keen hunter, he portrayed his Canadian life, and especially moose hunting, in his *Early Reminiscences* (1896).

On 29 October 1843 the right wing of the Royals left Quebec for the West Indies in the transport *Premier*, which was wrecked six days afterwards in Chatte Bay, on the right bank of the St Lawrence. Lysons was active in saving those on board and, being sent back to Quebec for help, he made in four and a half days what was reckoned an eight days' journey of 300 miles. His exertions were praised in general orders, and he was rewarded by a company in the 3rd West India regiment on 29 December (captain by purchase). He went from England to the West Indies in spring 1844, and was given command of the troops in Tobago; but on 24 May he was transferred to the 23rd Welch fusiliers, then stationed in Barbados. He was brigade major there from 3 November 1845 to 15 March 1847, when he accompanied his regiment to Halifax, Nova Scotia.

Lysons returned with his regiment to England in the autumn of 1848. He was town major at Portsmouth from 18 June to 21 August in 1849, and drew up a system of camping and cooking there. Promoted major (by purchase) on 3 August, he rejoined his regiment at Winchester, and served with it during the next five years at Plymouth, Liverpool, Chester, and Parkhurst. In April 1854 he embarked with it for Turkey, and was the first man to land in the Crimea in September. The 23rd formed part of the 1st brigade of the light division. At the Alma it lost over 200 officers and men, including its commanding officer. Just before the battle Lysons joined the 2nd division as assistant adjutant-general, but succeeding to the lieutenant-colonelcy of his regiment on 21 September, he returned to take command of it. He was present at Inkerman, though suffering from fever.

In the assault of 18 June 1855 Lysons commanded the supports of the column furnished by his brigade. He was wounded in the knee, but brought the brigade out of action, and had command of it for a time. In the second assault, on 8 September, he led an attack on the right flank of the Redan, and was severely wounded in the thigh. On 25 October he was given command of the 2nd brigade of the light division, and retained it until the end of the war. He had been mentioned in dispatches, was made brevet colonel on 17 July 1855 and CB (5 July), and received the Légion d'honneur (fourth class) and Mejidiye (third class).

Lysons returned to England in July 1856, and resumed command of the 23rd. On 16 January 1857 he exchanged to the 25th foot, and on 24 November went on half pay, having been appointed on 5 November assistant adjutant-general at headquarters. In this office he was employed on the revision of the infantry drill-book and its adaptation to the needs of the volunteers. He also prepared *Instructions for Mounted Rifle Volunteers* (1860). On 6 December 1861 he was sent to Canada in connection with the *Trent* crisis, and he was deputy quartermaster-general from 27 August 1862 until 30 September 1867. This gave him an opportunity of extending the frontier surveys on which he had worked as a subaltern. He was a member, representing imperial concerns, of the 1862 commission on Canadian defence, which reported (March 1862) in favour of the old sedentary militia system, from which an effective defensive force could be trained.

Promoted major-general on 27 December 1868, Lysons commanded brigades at Malta (July 1868 to March 1869) and Aldershot (April 1869 to June 1872), then commanded in the northern district (July 1872 to June 1874). A system of his devising was issued by authority in 1875 as *Infantry Piquets*. From 1 April 1876 to 30 June 1880 he was quartermaster-general at headquarters. He became lieutenant-general and was made KCB on 2 June 1877. On 25 August he became colonel of the Derbyshire regiment, and on 14 July 1879 a general. He was also honorary colonel of the 1st volunteer battalion, Royal Fusiliers. From 1 July 1880 to 1 August 1883 he commanded the Aldershot division, and he was then placed on the retired list, having reached the age of sixty-seven. On 29 May 1886 he received the GCB, and on 4 March 1890 he was made constable of the Tower.

In 1856 Lysons married Harriet Sophia, daughter of Charles Bridges of Court House, Overton. She died in 1864, and in 1865 he married Anna Sophia Biscoe, daughter of the Revd Robert Tritton of Morden, Surrey; she survived her husband. With his first wife he had four sons, of whom the second, Henry, won the Victoria Cross at Hlobane in the Anglo-Zulu War of 1879, when a lieutenant in the Scottish Rifles and Colonel Evelyn Wood's orderly.

Lysons died at his residence, 22 Warwick Square, Belgravia, London, on 29 January 1898, and was buried at Rodmarton. Vigorous to the last, he had been writing on army reform a month before (*The Times*, 17 December 1897).

E. M. LLOYD, *rev.* ROGER T. STEARN

Sources D. Lysons, *The Crimean War from first to last* (1895) • D. Lysons, *Early reminiscences* (1896) • *The Times* (31 Jan 1898) • R. Broughton-Mainwaring and R. Cannon, eds., *Historical record of the Royal Welch fusiliers, late the twenty-third regiment, or, Royal Welsh fusiliers … in continuation of the compilation … by R. Cannon* (1889) • A. D. Lambert, *The Crimean War: British grand strategy, 1853–56* (1990) • C. Hibbert, *The destruction of Lord Raglan* [1961] • I. Knight, *Brave men's blood: the epic of the Zulu War, 1879* (1990) • J. E. Auden, ed., *Shrewsbury School register, 1734–1908* (1909) • J. Monet, 'Campbell, Thomas Edmund', *DCB*, vol. 10 • Kelly, *Handbk* • *Hart's Army List* (1891) • Boase, *Mod. Eng. biog.* • Burke, *Peerage* • *CGPLA Eng. & Wales* (1898)

Likenesses Lock & Whitfield, woodburytype photograph, NPG; repro. in T. Cooper, *Men of mark: a gallery of contemporary portraits* (1882) • R. T., wood-engraving (after photograph by Done and Ball), NPG; repro. in *ILN* (15 March 1890) • Spy [L. Ward], chromolithograph caricature, NPG; repro. in *VF* (13 April 1878)

Wealth at death £6158 8*s.* 10*d.*: probate, 23 March 1898, *CGPLA Eng. & Wales*

Lysons, Samuel (*bap.* **1763**, *d.* **1819**), antiquary, was baptized at Rodmarton, Gloucestershire, on 17 May 1763, the second son of Samuel Lysons (1730–1804), rector of Rodmarton and Cherrington, Gloucestershire, and his wife, Mary (1734–1791), daughter of Samuel Peach of Chalford in the same county. Daniel *Lysons (1762–1834), historical topographer, was his brother. His nephew Samuel Lysons (1806–1877) was also an antiquary. After attending Bath grammar school Lysons was placed in June 1780 with a Bath solicitor named Jeffries. In October 1784 he went to London, having been previously entered at the Inner Temple, and began studying law under a Mr Walton. For several years he practised as a special pleader, and was therefore not called to the bar until June 1798, when he chose the Oxford circuit. In July 1796 he was introduced by Sir Joseph Banks to George III and the royal family, with whom he became a favourite. He was an excitable, vigorous, and ambitious man, with a loud voice and a penetrating eye. His friends included many leading personalities, such as Horace Walpole and Mrs Piozzi. Samuel Johnson met him and was impressed by him. In December 1803 he was appointed keeper of the records in the Tower of London and ceased practising law. Under his rule the staff was increased from one to six, and he did a considerable amount towards arranging the archives. He held the post until his death.

In November 1786 Lysons became a fellow of the Society of Antiquaries. In November 1812 he was nominated one of the vice-presidents of the society, and from 1798 to 1809 he held the honorary office of director. He was elected fellow of the Royal Society in February 1797, and was appointed vice-president and treasurer of the society in 1810.

Lysons was an artist of some skill, and between 1785 and 1796 was an occasional exhibitor at the Royal Academy of views of old buildings. He also contributed numerous etchings to his brother Daniel's *Environs of London*.

A field archaeologist much ahead of his time is revealed by the reports of the sites upon which Lysons worked, such as the Woodchester Roman pavement and other Roman sites, including Horkstow in Lincolnshire, Frampton in Dorset, Bignor in Sussex, and Bath. He was able to illustrate these reports quite lavishly. His greatest publication was the *Reliquiae Britannico-Romanae* (2 vols., 1801–17), which was a survey of sites and finds in Roman Britain. He collaborated with his brother Daniel in producing *Magna Britannia*. In 1818, when the honorary office of antiquary professor was revived in the Royal Academy, Lysons was chosen to fill it. He died, unmarried, of heart failure on 29 June 1819, at Cirencester, Gloucestershire, and was buried on 5 July at Hempsted, for long the home of the Lysons family.

GORDON GOODWIN, *rev.* BRIAN FRITH

Sources L. Fleming, *Memoir and select letters of Samuel Lysons* (1934) • *GM*, 1st ser., 89/2 (1819), 90, 273–5 • J. Evans, *A history of the Society of Antiquaries* (1956) • review of *Etchings and views and antiquities in the county of Gloucestershire* and other works, *Gloucestershire Notes and Queries*, 2 (1884), 169–70 • parish register (baptism), Rodmarton, Gloucestershire, 17 May 1763 • parish registers (death), Hempsted, Gloucestershire, 29 June 1819 • E. Evans, *Catalogue of a collection of engraved portraits*, 2 vols. [1836–53] • Burke, *Gen. GB* • Redgrave, *Artists*

Archives BL, corresp. and papers, Add. MSS 9408–9471 • Glos. RO, drawings and papers • Gloucester Public Library • S. Antiquaries, Lond., drawings, corresp. and papers • Yale U., Beinecke L., corresp. and papers | Bodl. Oxf., corresp. with William Nicholls • Cornwall RO, corresp. with John Hawkins • JRL, letters to Hester Piozzi • W. Sussex RO, Hawkins MSS

Likenesses T. Lawrence, pencil drawing, 1790–99, NPG • G. Dance, pencil drawing, 1793, BM • S. W. Reynolds, mezzotint, pubd 1804 (after T. Lawrence) • W. Bond, stipple, pubd 1823 (after W. J. Newton), BM, NPG • W. J. Newton, stipple, pubd 1823, BM, NPG • Daniell, engraving (after G. Dance) • Robinson, engraving (after T. Lawrence) • portrait, priv. coll.; in possession of the Revd Samuel Lysons, 1868

Lysons, Samuel (**1806–1877**), Church of England clergyman and antiquary, born at Rodmarton, Gloucestershire, on 17 March 1806, was the eldest surviving son of the Revd Daniel *Lysons (1762–1834) of Hempsted Court, Gloucestershire, and Sarah (1779/80–1808), eldest daughter of Lieutenant-Colonel Thomas Carteret Hardy of the York fusiliers. He matriculated at Oxford from Exeter College on 24 November 1826, graduated BA in 1830 with third-class honours in classics, and proceeded MA in 1836. He was ordained deacon in 1830 and priest the following year. In 1833 he succeeded his father as rector of Rodmarton, Gloucestershire, a living in the gift of the family. On 1 January 1834 he married Eliza Sophia Theresa Henrietta (*d.* 1846), eldest daughter of Major-General Sir Lorenzo Moore; they had four sons and two daughters. Two days after his marriage his father died and he succeeded to the family estates, which comprised Hempsted Court and other lands in Gloucestershire. When in 1838 he took up his residence at Hempsted Court he found the adjoining suburb of Gloucester, known as High Orchard, in a state of neglect, particularly the area known as Sudbrook, where there was very poor housing by the canal. Lysons built a church there (consecrated as St Luke's on 21 April 1841), furnished it with an endowment of £1000, and officiated in it himself without a stipend. Schools were erected, charitable clubs organized, and a scripture reader provided at his expense. Altogether he spent between £5000 and £6000 for the benefit of the district, which rapidly improved. His first wife having died the previous year, on 11 March 1847 he married Lucy (*d.* 1872), daughter of the Revd John Adey Curtis-Hayward. In 1866 old age led him to resign his duties at St Luke's and, having presented a successor to the living, to resign its patronage to the bishop of the diocese. From November 1865 to February 1876 he was rural dean of Gloucester, and on 24 December 1867 he was installed as honorary canon of Gloucester Cathedral. In 1872 he married Gertrude Savery, second daughter of Simon Adams Beck of Cheam, Surrey.

Lysons contributed frequently to the local press and occasionally lectured at local literary and scientific societies. He also published eight books. His preferred, although not his only, subjects were the topography and archaeology of Gloucestershire. He was elected FSA, but is a very minor figure among antiquaries compared with his father and uncle, whose monumental work he did not attempt to finish. He died at Hempsted Court on 27 March 1877, being survived by his widow, two children from his third marriage, and five from his first. He was buried in Rodmarton churchyard. His library was sold at Sothebys on 12 July 1880.

GORDON GOODWIN, *rev.* ELIZABETH BAIGENT

Sources Burke, *Gen. GB* • Foster, *Alum. Oxon.* • *CGPLA Eng. & Wales* (1877) • C. R. J. Currie and C. P. Lewis, eds., *English county histories: a guide* (1994) • J. Stratford, *Gloucestershire biographical notes* (1887) • *Gloucestershire Notes and Queries*, 2 (1884), 514–16, 533 • Crockford (1833–66) • L. Fleming, *Memoir and select letters of Samuel Lysons, 1763–1819* (1934)

Archives S. Antiquaries, Lond., diaries and cash accounts | Bodl. Oxf., corresp. with Sir Thomas Phillipps

Wealth at death under £25,000: probate, 25 April 1877, *CGPLA Eng. & Wales*

Lyster, Anthony George (1852–1920). *See under* Lyster, George Fosbery (1821–1899).

Lyster, George Fosbery (1821–1899), civil engineer, was born on 7 September 1821 at Mount Talbot, co. Roscommon, the son of Colonel Anthony Lyster and his wife, Jane Fosbery. His father was a substantial Irish landowner with an aristocratic lineage traceable to the reign of Elizabeth I; of his mother little is known. Lyster was educated privately and at King William's College in the Isle of Man, before becoming a pupil of James Meadows Rendel. He then worked on various harbour and railway projects, mostly under Rendel's patronage, and on Rendel's death succeeded him as engineer-in-chief at St Peter Port, Guernsey. In 1861 he was appointed engineer-in-chief to the Mersey Docks and Harbour Board, the best-paid salaried engineering post in the country. He completed the works of John Bernard Hartley in correcting errors Rendel had made at the previously independent port of Birkenhead, by then part of the port of Liverpool.

Lyster's works were often marred by delay and overspending, but they far exceeded in scale, cost, and complexity any previously undertaken by a single port authority. He constructed or reconstructed almost 200 acres of docks, spending an estimated £19 million. Lyster married in 1841 Martha Eliza Sanderson, daughter of the speaker of the house of assembly of Antigua, and they had four children. She died about 1889, and on 21 June 1898 Lyster married Blanche Emily Isabella, daughter of Captain Francis Maude RN, in a society wedding.

Lyster's greatest single project was also the largest by a dock engineer to date, namely the works under the Dock Act of 1873, to the value of £4.1 million. The strategic layout was sound, as was the practical execution, but failures in the middle stages of design meant that much had to be re-worked by his son within a few years. Possibly his greatest success was his two-storey transit sheds, against which must be set a fundamental, and persistent, failure to provide sufficient depth of water and the repeated construction of silt-sluicing systems which did not work.

Although Lyster inherited a system under which far more work was done 'in-house' than in other ports, one positive consequence of the scale of his work was that large numbers of young dock engineers received their training in Liverpool. They then moved on, spreading Liverpool techniques around the world. By 1889 his powers seem to have been failing and in 1891 he went formally into semi-retirement.

The appointment of his son, pupil, and assistant, **Anthony George Lyster** (1852–1920), civil engineer, as 'heir apparent' caused dissension within the Mersey Docks and Harbour Board, to the point where the chairman, Alfred Holt, himself an engineer, resigned. Born on 5 April 1852 at Porth y Felin, Holyhead, Anglesey, Wales, A. G. Lyster did indeed succeed on his father's eventual retirement in 1897, but, with a fine irony, proved to be the better engineer. He had been involved in some pioneering developments early in his career, including electric site lighting, and became a significant authority in such 'high-tech' fields as ferroconcrete construction and sand-pump dredging. A. G. Lyster directed enormous works under successive acts of parliament, which transformed his father's efforts into an effective modern dock system, most of which continued to serve the port well until the container revolution changed the ground rules. Above all, he provided the basic designs of the Gladstone Dock system (completed 1927) which, for the first time in half a century, anticipated changes in shipping instead of reacting to them.

A proposed reorganization within the Mersey Docks and Harbour Board in 1912 threatened A. G. Lyster, by then one of the country's most distinguished engineers and president-elect of the Institution of Civil Engineers, with reporting not to a standing committee of the board, but to the general manager. He took this as such a professional affront that he resigned without further ado. He retained a consultancy, and became a partner in Sir John Wolfe Barry & Partners, undertaking work for other ports, including Bombay.

Little is known of the personal characteristics of either G. F. or A. G. Lyster. Neither is recorded as having any hobby apart from volunteer soldiering. They contrast markedly with their craft-based predecessors: G. F. Lyster was a proprietor in Liverpool's most exclusive club. He owned a town house in fashionable Princes Park, a country estate, Plas Isaf, near Ruthin, and a flat in Cadogan Gardens, London. He was an urbane charmer of committees and inspired listeners with great (albeit sometimes misplaced) confidence in the soundness of his judgement. On 11 May 1899 G. F. Lyster died at 97 Cadogan Gardens, London, of pneumonia. He was survived by his second wife. He was buried on 16 May in the family vault at Llangynhafal, Plas Isaf, near Ruthin, Denbighshire.

Lyster's son was less socially accomplished, suffering some awkward moments with the board and its committees. He also kept a lower public profile but seems to have been respected by his peers. On 3 December 1892 A. G. Lyster married Frances Laura Arabella de Windt (formerly Long), sister of Viscount Long of Wraxhall. There were no children from the marriage. Lyster died at 10 Gloucester Gate, Regent's Park, London, on 17 March 1920. He was buried at Braden Lane, near High Wycombe, Buckinghamshire. His estate was left in trust for a nephew, subject to the lifetime interest of his widow. ADRIAN JARVIS

Sources B. G. Orchard, *Liverpool's legion of honour* (1893) • *PICE*, 139 (1899–1900), 357–66 • *PICE*, 217 (1923–4), 447–9 [obit. of Anthony George Lyster] • Newscuttings file, Merseyside Maritime Museum, Mersey Docks and Harbour Board Archive, II A2J • A. Jarvis, *The Liverpool dock engineers* (1996) • 'Anthony George Lyster: a biographical sketch', *Ferro-Concrete*, 4 (1912), 5–10 • m. certs. • b. cert. [A. G. Lyster] • d. certs. • *CGPLA Eng. & Wales* (1899) • *CGPLA Eng. & Wales* (1920) [Anthony George Lyster] • *Liverpool Mercury* (17 May 1899)

Archives Inst. CE, notebook relating to harbour works • Merseyside Maritime Museum, Liverpool, Mersey Docks and Harbour Board Archive

Likenesses C. W. Walton, engraving, Inst. CE • double portraits, lithographs (with Anthony George Lyster), repro. in Orchard, *Liverpool's legion of honour*

Wealth at death £10,146 3*s*. 8*d*.: probate, 5 Aug 1899, *CGPLA Eng. & Wales* • £16,705 9*s*. 5*d*.—Anthony George Lyster: probate, 7 June 1920, *CGPLA Eng. & Wales*

Lyster, Sir Richard (*c*.1480–1553), judge, was the son of John Lyster of Wakefield, Yorkshire, and his wife, who was one of the Beaumont family of Whitley. His grandfather Thomas had settled in that town in the reign of Henry VI, and a Thomas Lyster of Wakefield was an attorney of the common pleas from the 1470s until at least 1501. A Richard Lyster was sued for dues by Clement's Inn in 1487–8, but this can hardly have been the present subject and may have been the namesake who was at Gray's Inn in 1508. The future lord chief justice became a member of the Middle Temple about 1500, and is so described in 1502 when he acted as an attorney in the court of requests. He is mentioned as an arbitrator in London in 1503. He owned (and probably wrote) a manuscript account of the serjeants' feast of that year, perhaps as part of a private notebook of reports. After a year's respite on grounds of ill health, he became a bencher of the Middle Temple and gave his first reading in 1516, followed by a second reading in 1522, and served as treasurer from 1522 to 1524.

Lyster came to public prominence in 1521 when he was appointed solicitor-general, from which position he was promoted to attorney-general on 4 September 1525. On 12 May 1529 he was appointed chief baron of the exchequer, was sworn in by Wolsey on 3 June, and knighted. As chief baron he supported Audley and Cromwell in pressing the judges to decide *Lord Dacre's case* (1535) in favour of the crown, thereby enabling the Statute of Uses to be passed. After presiding over the exchequer for sixteen years he was made chief justice of the king's bench on 9 November 1545. Since he was not already a serjeant-at-law this necessitated a private coifing on the same day, only the second creation of its kind to be recorded. His speech to the new serjeants in 1547 was described by a contemporary as 'a godly, thowghe sumwhat prolixe and long declaration of their duties' (Dugdale, 118). By this time Lyster had moved from Yorkshire to Southampton, where he lived in a house in St Michael's parish which Leland praised as 'very fair'.

Lyster married first Jane, daughter of Sir Ralph Shirley, and widow of Sir John Dawtrey, whose portrait by Holbein is in the Royal Collection, and second Elizabeth Stoke, with whom he had a son, Sir Michael Lyster (*d*. 1551), and a daughter, Elizabeth, wife of Sir Richard Blount. Lyster resigned from the office of chief justice in the first half of 1552 and died on 16 March the following year. He was buried the next day at St Michael's Church, Southampton. To his eldest son, Richard, he left all his lands in the south, and to his younger son Charles all his lands in Wakefield and elsewhere in Yorkshire. His grandson Richard was obliged to bring a slander action in 1557 to challenge an assertion that he was Sir Michael's illegitimate son by Maud Vane, whereas he claimed to be the son of Sir Michael's wife, Elizabeth. In 1567 the chief justice's widow caused a monument to be erected in St Michael's Church, with his effigy in judicial robes and collar of SS.

J. H. BAKER

Sources Foss, *Judges*, 5.305–7 • H. L. L. Denny, *Memorials of an ancient house* (1913) • F. Madden, 'Remarks on the monument of Sir Richard Lyster in St Michael's Church, Southampton' (1845) • C. H. Hopwood, ed., *Middle Temple records*, 1: *1501–1603* (1904) • Sainty, *Judges*, 9.94 • Baker, *Serjeants*, 113, 169, 524 • *The reports of Sir John Spelman*, ed. J. H. Baker, 2 vols., SeldS, 93–4 (1977–8) • PRO, PROB 11/36, sig. 30 [will] • PRO, REQ 1/3, fol. 6*v* • PRO, CP 40/902; 40/966; 40/983; 40/1171 • W. Dugdale, *Origines juridiciales, or, Historical memorials of the English laws*, 3rd edn (1680) • inquisition post mortem, PRO, C/142/102/67

Likenesses effigy on monument, 1567, St Michael's Church, Southampton

Lyster, Thomas William (1855–1922), librarian and literary scholar, was born on 17 December 1855 in Kilkenny, the elder son of Thomas Lyster of Rathdowney and Jane Smith of Roscrea. Lyster's father died early, leaving him as the main support of the family. Friends and colleagues were later to ascribe his strength of character and determination to this single event. He was educated at Wesleyan School, Dublin, and later at Trinity College, Dublin, where he graduated with MA senior moderatorship in English and German. He married Jane Robinson Campbell, daughter of James Campbell of Galway.

Early in his career Lyster acquired a reputation for scholarship, publishing books and articles on German and English literature. He translated Heinrich Düntzer's life of Goethe (1883) and contributed many publications to the

Thomas William Lyster (1855–1922), by John Butler Yeats

English Goethe Society. He also published many critical editions of Milton, wrote articles on Shakespeare and Jane Austen, and edited Hall's *History of English Literature*. He was elected a member of the Royal Irish Academy in 1913.

Lyster was appointed assistant librarian at the National Library of Ireland in 1878 at the relatively young age of twenty-three, and served there until his retirement some forty-two years later. He succeeded William Archer as librarian in 1895, remaining in that post for twenty-five years. In 1880 he was appointed as examiner in English under the intermediate education board, and in subsequent years he produced several textbooks which were adopted by the board, which ran to many editions.

It was as librarian of the National Library that Lyster truly left his mark. He embraced librarianship enthusiastically, and became an advocate of the radical modern movement, actively encouraging the application of the Dewey decimal classification system, supporting the formation of Cumann na Leabharlann (the Library Association of Ireland), emphasizing the importance of local newspapers and ephemera, and suggesting a subject index to periodicals. He was a tireless lecturer on library topics, promoting the development of the public library system in Ireland, defending the rights of ordinary citizens of access to books and information. He was elected vice-president of the Library Association (UK) in 1899, and in a paper to the annual conference of that association in 1902 entitled 'The idea of a great public library: an essay in the philosophy of libraries' showed himself to be both a follower of Panizzi and an admirer of Newman. In the concluding pages of this paper, he argued against censorship:

> in a great library all things, good and evil, fall into their places, are seen in the just light, and proportion, and the *totality* of the record of human thought and feeling is a witness for what is wholesome, true and good.

Despite this liberal and even-handed approach, Lyster found himself under attack on more than one occasion, and by different divides—the nationalist newspaper *The Leader* attacking him, a non-Catholic, for daring to lecture to a Catholic body, while the *Irish Protestant* complained that the National Library failed to acquire some notable anti-Catholic polemic. His greatest legacy is having suggested a British index of periodicals in a paper to the Library Association in 1913. The first subject lists appeared in *The Athenaeum* two years later, and signalled the way for the *Subject Index to Periodicals* which in turn was a forerunner of the *British Humanities Index*.

In his relations with the public and the staff of the library, Lyster was always fair and genial. More than any other librarian he generated a corpus of affectionate folklore. His sheer physical bulk and kindliness towards young students and readers made him a larger-than-life figure. Among the recorded lore is one memory from a long-serving staff member of Lyster walking around the bookstacks, keys in hand, calling 'I'm coming, I'm coming', to avoid surprising the unwary at something they should not have been doing. He is immortalized in Joyce's *Ulysses* in the famous library scene where, unnamed, he is referred to as the Quaker librarian.

Lyster retired in 1920. Two years later, on 12 December 1922, he died at his home, 10 Harcourt Terrace, Dublin. His wife survived him. Such was his impact that in 1926, four years after his death, a memorial plaque was erected in his memory—the only such tribute to a librarian of the National Library of Ireland since its establishment in 1877. The list of subscribers who contributed to and organized the bronze and silver table reads like a who's who of Irish society of the day. The poet W. B. Yeats, a lifelong friend, who also delivered the oration, conducted the unveiling ceremony. PATRICIA DONLON

Sources *The Times* (27 Dec 1922) · *Thom's Irish who's who* (1923) · A. Maclochlainn, 'The National Library of Ireland, 1877–1977', *Irish University Review: A Journal of Irish Studies*, 7/2 (1977), 157–67 · D. Foley, 'Librarians as authors: an uncritical review', *An Leabharlann*, 18/4 (1960), 103–17 · *WWW* · W. A. Munford, *Who was who in British librarianship, 1800–1985* (1987) · documents of the T. W. Lyster Memorial Committee, NL Ire., MS 10541 · T. W. Lyster, *An essay in the philosophy of libraries* (1903) · *CGPLA Eng. & Wales* (1923) · d. cert.

Archives NL Ire., documents of the T. W. Lyster Memorial Committee · NL Ire., author's corrected copy of 'The idea of a great public library'

Likenesses J. B. Yeats, drawing, NL Ire. [*see illus.*] · photograph, NL Ire.

Wealth at death £406 17*s.* 6*d.*: sealed probate, 17 Feb 1923, *CGPLA Eng. & Wales*

Lyte, Henry (1529?–1607), botanist and antiquary, was born at Lyte's Cary, Somerset, the eleventh, in direct descent, of his name settled at that place. He was the second and eldest surviving son of John Lyte (*d.* 1576) and his first wife, Edith Horsey (*d.* 1556). Lyte became a student at Oxford about 1546 but it is unlikely that he took a degree. Anthony Wood wrote of him:

> After he had spent some years in logic and philosophy, and in other good learning, he travelled into foreign countries, and at length retired to his patrimony, where, by the advantage of a good foundation of literature made in the university and abroad, he became a most excellent scholar in several sorts of learning. (Wood)

His son recorded that he 'was admitted of Clyffordes Inne'. From 1559 Lyte seems to have managed his father's Somerset estate until the latter's death in 1576, when his stepmother, who had already sown discord between him and his father, brought a writ of dower against him. Lyte seems to have served as sheriff, or perhaps only as under-sheriff, of Somerset during the reign of Mary, and perhaps until the second year of Elizabeth. He captained one of the Somerset trained bands formed to fight the Spanish invasion, and was serving at Tilbury at the time of the armada.

Lyte was married three times: in September 1546 to Agnes, daughter and heir of John Kelloway of Collumpton, Devon, who died in 1564 and with whom he had five daughters; in July 1565 to Frances, daughter of John Tiptoft, citizen of London, who died in 1589 and with whom he had three sons and two daughters; and in 1591 to Dorothy, daughter of John Gover of Somerton, Somerset, with whom he had two sons and a daughter.

Lyte was a distant connection of Aubrey, who speaks of his 'deare grandfather Lyte' and of a 'cos. Lyte of Lytes-Cary', and says that Henry Lyte 'had a pretty good collection of plants for that age'. The garden at Lyte's Cary was well known in its day for having all possible kinds of fruit including ninety varieties of pear; a description survives in an extant list in the handwriting of Lyte's second son, Thomas.

Lyte's first and most important work was his careful translation of the *Cruydeboeck*, or herbal, of Rembert Dodoens (Antwerp, 1554), taken from the French edition of De l'Escluse (1557) and augmented clearly, in a different typeface, by his own notes. His only additional matter concerned the habitats of some Somerset plants. His working copy, annotated in Latin and English in his neat handwriting, endorsed 'Henry Lyte taught me to speake English', is in the British Library. It was printed in folio at Antwerp, in order to secure the woodcuts of the original. A dedication to Queen Elizabeth, written from Lyte's Cary, states Lyte's wish to contribute something to the welfare and renown of his country as well as to the health of its people. Other editions, without woodcuts, were published in 1586, 1595, and 1619; an abridged version appeared in 1606.

Lyte was interested in genealogy of a fanciful kind and spent much time in seeking to show how the British were of Trojan descent, as set out in his second work, *The Light of Britayne: a Recorde of the Honorable Originall and Antiquitie of Britaine* (1588), which was also dedicated to Elizabeth, and which contained her portrait. Lyte presented a copy of this work to the queen on 24 November 1588, when she went in state to St Paul's to return thanks for the defeat of the armada. Two small works on the same subject, written in 1592, were never printed. Lyte also drew up *A table whereby it is supposed that Lyte of Lytescarie sprange of the race and stocke of Leitus … and that his ancestors came to Englande first with Brute*, now in the British Library, and wrote a poem entitled 'A description of the swannes of Carie that came first under mightie Brute's protection from Caria in Asia to Carie in Britain', later printed in *Notes and Queries* (6th ser., 8, 1883, 109–10). Lyte died in the house in which he was born, on 15 October 1607, and was buried at the north end of the transept of Charlton Mackrell church.

Lyte's second son, who succeeded him, was Thomas *Lyte (1568–1638), genealogist. His third son, Henry (*b.* 1573), was one of the earliest users of decimal fractions, and published in 1619 *The Art of Tens and Decimall Arithmetike*, dedicated to Charles, prince of Wales, and based mainly on the French work *La disme*, published in 1590. He is described as a teacher of arithmetic in London. G. S. Boulger, *rev.* Anita McConnell

Sources R. H. Jeffers, *The friends of John Gerard, 1545–1612* (1967), 23–5 • H. Downes, 'A relic of Henry Lyte's library', *Proceedings of the Linnean Society of London*, 134th session (1921–2), 19–20 • P. Elliott, 'Some ancestors of Elizabeth Leigh who married Thomas Joliffe at Kingston, Isle of Wight, 1660', typescript, 1981, Society of Genealogists, London, Family Tracts, vol. 106 • C. E. Raven, *English naturalists from Neckam to Ray: a study of the making of the modern world* (1947) • *N&Q*, 7 (1853), 570–71 • Wood, *Ath. Oxon.* • R. Pulteney, *Historical and biographical sketches of the progress of botany in England*, 1 (1790), 88–95

Lyte, Sir Henry Churchill Maxwell (1848–1940), archivist and historian, was born at 1 Hyde Park Place, London, on 29 May 1848, the only son of John Walker Maxwell Lyte (1825–1848), of Berry Head, near Brixham, and his wife, Emily Jeannette, daughter of Colonel John Craigie, of the East India Company. He was the grandson of the hymn writer Henry Francis *Lyte (1793–1847), and through his mother was descended from Charles Churchill (1656–1714), the elder brother of the great duke of Marlborough. After preparatory school at Geddington, Northamptonshire, he was educated at Eton College (1861–6) and Christ Church, Oxford (1866–70), where he graduated in the school of law and modern history in 1870.

In 1875 Lyte published his first book, *A History of Eton College, 1440–1875*, and in 1886 *A History of the University of Oxford from the Earliest Times to the Year 1530*, works which still retain some value. He served as an inspector for the Historical Manuscripts Commission between 1879 and 1886, and wrote a number of reports, including those on the muniments of the dean and chapter of St Paul's Cathedral, and the duke of Rutland's manuscripts at Belvoir Castle. In 1886, when he was still only thirty-seven, he was appointed, at a critical moment, to the deputy keepership of the public records, a post which he held with distinction for forty years.

By this time the initial momentum of the 1838 foundation of the Public Record Office had been checked. The plans of Sir Francis Palgrave (1788–1861) and Sir Thomas Duffus Hardy (1804–1878) to publish records *in extenso* had broken down: the department was ineffective and divided by personal jealousies. Lyte infused fresh energy into the office: the buildings were extended; a vast accumulation of documents was sorted; and the chief classes were made available for reference in a new series of lists and indexes. Above all, he instituted and carried far towards completion the invaluable series of calendars of the chancery rolls (1891–1986).

Lyte's best work was done by 1914, although he maintained his authority to the end of his career. He was dissatisfied with the outcome of the royal commission on public records (1910–18), which left him at odds with Hubert Hall (1857–1944), and it seems that he stayed in office partly to preclude Hall's appointment as his successor. After the war he directed the publication of the exchequer texts known as the *Book of Fees* (1920–23), and assembled *Historical Notes on the Use of the Great Seal* (1926), a baffling compendium, but one still not superseded at the end of the twentieth century.

In 1926 Lyte resigned, at the age of seventy-eight. His great accomplishment had been to make the Public Record Office a vigorous and efficient department which was also a notable centre of scholarship. An able staff, including C. G. Crump (1862–1935), C. H. Jenkinson (1882–1961), and Charles Johnson (1870–1961), co-operated in a long series of publications which both assisted and profoundly influenced the development of historical research. Official recognition of his services came early. He was appointed CB in 1889 and KCB in 1897; he was an original fellow of the British Academy, and in 1929 he received the honorary degree of LittD from the University of Oxford.

Lyte married on 3 January 1871 Frances Fownes (*d.* 1925), elder daughter of James Curtis Somerville JP, of Dinder House, Dinder, Wells, Somerset; they had three sons and three daughters. Lyte retained his good health and zeal for study to the last, keenly interested in genealogy, and cultivating an informed taste for photography. He died after a short illness at Dinder House on 28 October 1940 and was buried in Dinder. His life's work was the creation of a new tradition in the Public Record Office, which has endured as his monument.

V. H. Galbraith, *rev.* G. H. Martin

Sources C. Johnson, 'Sir Henry Churchill Maxwell-Lyte, 1848–1940', *PBA*, 26 (1940), 361–79 • J. D. Cantwell, *The Public Record Office, 1838–1958* (1991) • R. W. Southern, 'Vivian Hunter Galbraith, 1889–1976', *PBA*, 64 (1978), 397–425 • personal knowledge (1949) • m. cert. • *WW*

Archives English Heritage, Swindon, National Monuments Record, topographical and architectural photographs • PRO, corresp. as an HMC inspector | BL, corresp. with Macmillans, Add. MS 55076 • King's Cam., letters to Oscar Browning • LUL, letters to J. H. Round

Likenesses S. M. Fisher, portrait, *c.*1929, PRO • W. Stoneman, photograph, 1930, NPG • S. M. Fisher, oils, 1933, NPG

Wealth at death £54,294 9*s.* 1*d.*: probate, 29 Jan 1941, *CGPLA Eng. & Wales*

Lyte, Henry Francis (1793–1847), hymn writer, was born on 1 June 1793 at The Cottage, Ednam, near Kelso, Roxburghshire, the second son of Captain Thomas Lyte (*d.* 1850) and Anna Maria Oliver, and a descendant of the botanist Henry *Lyte and the genealogist Thomas *Lyte. His parents appear never to have been married, though Anna Maria was always referred to as Mrs Lyte. Thomas Lyte's military career necessitated frequent moves, and the family followed him to Edinburgh, Newmarket, Manchester, and Liverpool, before settling in Ireland in 1797. They first resided at Ballyshannon, and then in Dunmore, co. Galway. When the couple separated in 1801 Henry stayed with his father and his brother Thomas, and was then sent to Portora Royal School, Enniskillen, in October 1803. He missed his mother greatly, and rarely saw his father, who was away for long periods on military duty. Because he spent both the terms and the holidays at the school, he developed a close relationship with Dr Burrowes, the headmaster, who became a surrogate father to the boy, taking over his financial responsibilities and eventually becoming his guardian. It was while at Portora that Lyte began to compose poetry.

Lyte entered Trinity College, Dublin, in 1811, and distinguished himself academically by winning a university scholarship in 1813, and the chancellor's prize for English verse in three successive years. He graduated BA in February 1814, and considered a career in medicine; this course of study was soon abandoned in favour of holy orders, and he was ordained deacon on 18 December 1814. His first curacy was in Taghmon, co. Wexford, where he stayed for eighteen months, but his frequent attacks of asthma led him to resign this post. He then travelled through France on horseback from September 1816 to summer 1817. After his return to England, Lyte was moved from one curacy to another before eventually being given a position at the chapel of ease in Marazion, Cornwall, on 24 June 1817. On 21 January 1818 he married Anne, daughter and eventual heir of the Revd W. Maxwell of Falkland, co. Monaghan. The couple lived at Nevada House, Fore Street, where on 29 September 1818 Anne gave birth to their first son, Henry William. It was while at Marazion that Lyte underwent a spiritual experience at the deathbed of a neighbouring clergyman, Abraham Swanne. Lyte claimed that this encounter altered his whole view of life: he emerged with a deeper faith, and preached with a new vitality.

In January 1820 the family left for Sway (near Lymington), Hampshire, to live in temporary retirement; it was here that Lyte produced many of his poems. The couple's first daughter, Ann Maria, was born in January 1821, but died a month later. Early in 1822 the family moved to Bramble Torr, a house near Dittisham, Devon; here a second daughter, Anna Maria, was born on 20 April. Lyte held no full-time position at Dittisham, but while there he was asked to do temporary duty at the chapel of ease at Lower Brixham. In May 1822 he was invited by the trustees of the chapel to remain at Brixham permanently. He refused, and went instead to Charleton, where he became curate on 6 July 1822. He stayed for almost two years, before moving back to Brixham in April 1824.

Henry Francis Lyte (1793–1847), by George Henry Phillips (after John King, *c.*1831)

Lyte began by ministering in two churches, St Mary's Church, Brixham, and the new district church of Lower Brixham. He joined the schools committee, and by June 1824 had become its chairman. He took a keen interest in the development of education, and in addition to conducting annual school examinations he established the first Sunday school in the Torbay area; he also undertook to teach in his recently established Sailors' Sunday School. A second son, John Walker, was born on 2 January 1826. On 13 July 1826 Lyte was instituted as the first incumbent of Lower Brixham, and the family moved to Burton House in Burton Street. A third son, Farnham, was born on 10 January 1828. Early in 1833 the Lytes moved from Burton House to Berry Head House. Henry added to his income by taking resident pupils, who were tutored alongside his own children. He also published *Poems, Chiefly Religious* (1833; 2nd edn, 1841), which contained some of his early hymns, notable for their scriptural emphasis. In 1834 his *Spirit of the Psalms* was published, which contained one of his best-known hymns, 'Praise, my soul, the king of heaven'. By this time Lyte's health was deteriorating, along with his chances of obtaining any preferment; in 1835 he sought appointment as the vicar of Crediton, but was turned down on account of his increasingly debilitating asthma and bronchitis.

During the 1840s Lyte spent increasing periods abroad. First he holidayed in Norway in the summer of 1842. He then decided to spend the winter of 1844 in Naples, but his progress was hampered by illness, and he spent considerably more time abroad than he had wished; finally he returned to England in May 1846. By August he was off to the continent again, intending to winter in Rome; he ended up staying until May 1847, and returned to England in June, in very poor health. He spent the summer at Berry Head, where he wrote his most famous hymn, 'Abide with me'. He left for the continent again on 1 October 1847. By 5 November he had reached Nice, where he was seized by influenza and dysentery. He died at the Hôtel de la Pension Anglaise on 20 November, ministered to by Henry Manning (later archbishop of Westminster), and was buried in the grounds of the Anglican chapel in the old cemetery, Nice. In 1848 his extensive library, chiefly theology and old English poetry, was sold in London over seventeen days. A volume of *Remains*, consisting of poems, sermons, and letters, was published in 1850; it included 'Abide with me', which was first sung (to his own tune) at his memorial service in Brixham in 1847. Though his poetic energies were directed at scripturally and evangelically minded audiences, his lyric gift was universally appreciated. The example of 'Abide with me' is instructive: intensely personal and contemplative, yet nationally popular—even being sung (always, after its publication in 1861, to W. H. Monk's tune, 'Eventide') on secular occasions such as at football matches, and especially, since 1927, at the English cup final. A memorial tablet to Lyte was placed in Westminster Abbey in 1947. LEON LITVACK

Sources B. G. Skinner, *Henry Francis Lyte: Brixham's poet and priest* (1974) · A. M. M. Hogg, *Remains of the late Henry Francis Lyte* (1850) · J. Appleyard, *Henry Francis Lyte* (1939) · H. J. Garland, *Henry Francis Lyte and the story of 'Abide with me'*, ed. L. Melling (1956) · T. W. E. Drury, *Henry Francis Lyte: a memorial discourse* (1948) · W. Maxwell-Lyte, 'Henry Francis Lyte', *Hymn Society Bulletin*, 41 (Oct 1947), 5–6 · J. Julian, ed., *A dictionary of hymnology*, rev. edn (1907) · E. Routley, *An English-speaking hymnal guide* (1979) · J. Moffatt and M. Patrick, eds., *Handbook to the church hymnary, with supplement*, 2nd edn (1935) · M. Frost, ed., *Historical companion to 'Hymns ancient and modern'* (1962) · E. Routley, *A panorama of Christian hymnody* (1979) · parish register (baptism), 13 June 1793, Ednam parish, NA Scot.

Archives priv. coll., travel journals · priv. coll., papers, incl. manuscript poems | Portora Royal School, Enniskillen, Northern Ireland, archives

Likenesses miniature, 1826, priv. coll. · oils, 1840, Montclair Art Museum, New Jersey · J. King, oils, Portora Royal School, Enniskillen, Northern Ireland · G. H. Phillips, mezzotint (after J. King, *c.*1831), BM [*see illus.*]

Lyte, Thomas (1568–1638), genealogist, was born on 17 April 1568, the son and heir of Henry *Lyte (1529?–1607), botanist and antiquary of Lyte's Cary, Charlton Mackrell, Somerset, and his second wife, Frances (*d.* 1589), daughter of John Tiptoft of London. His commonplace book records that he was educated at Sherborne School, Clifford's Inn, and the Middle Temple. Wood claims he spent 'several years in academicals' at Oxford without taking a degree (Wood, *Ath. Oxon.*, 3rd edn, 1815, 2.649). He was twice married: on 2 February 1592 he married Frances (*d.* 1615), daughter of Henry Worth of Worth, Devon; and about 1620 Constance, daughter of George Huntley of Boxwell, Gloucester, and widow of Nicholas Baskerville and Sir John Sidney, became his second wife. His marriages resulted in seven sons and six daughters. The family lived at Lyte's Cary, where Lyte repaired the chapel in 1631, adding heraldry and tablets describing his extensive pedigree. He was active in Somerset politics from 1628 until his death, primarily as a justice of the peace.

Lyte was a devotee of British antiquities, particularly genealogy, and was admired by Camden (*Britannia*, 1695, col. 61). Some of his manuscripts are published in the Harleian Society volume *Wiltshire Visitation Pedigrees* (1954). In 1605 he wrote 'Britaines monarchie', a manuscript dedicated to King James whose ancestry it traced. It begins with the 'Brittish genealogies and the historie of Brute', this mythological inclusion justified as the 'order which Antiquitie hath left and we by tradition have received' (BL, Add. MS 59741, fol. 8). The king's descent then continues through the Romans, Saxons, Danes, Normans, Scots, and Picts.

Lyte's principal work was an illustrated copy of the royal genealogy, presented to the king at Whitehall on 12 July 1610. The chart, 'contayning the bredth and circumference of twenty large sheets of Paper', was hung at court 'in an especiall place of eminence' (A. Mundy, *Briefe Chronicle*, 1611, 477–8) and engraved in copper for better preservation. It has disappeared, although Lyte's ink copy survives. It assures James of his 'most rightfull inheritance' (BL, Add. MS 48343) by comparisons with Henry VII; the controversial figure of Mary, queen of Scots, is barely mentioned. The king rewarded Lyte with the extravagant gift of a miniature royal portrait set in gold and diamonds, preserved in the British Museum. It is described as 'the finest Jacobean jewel in existence' (H. C. Smith, *Jewellery*, 1908, 303–4). Lyte died at Lyte's Cary on 18 September 1638 and was buried the next day at Charlton Mackrell among his forebears. PETER SHERLOCK

Sources H. C. M. Lyte, 'The Lytes of Lytescary', *Proceedings of the Somersetshire Archaeological and Natural History Society*, 38 (1892), 1–110 • H. C. M. Lyte, 'The Lytes of Lytescary: supplement', *Proceedings of the Somersetshire Archaeological and Natural History Society*, 77 (1931), 115–35 • A. W. Vivian-Neal, 'Thomas Lyte and the Lyte jewel', *Proceedings of the Somersetshire Archaeological and Natural History Society*, 104 (1959–60), 124–5 • Bodl. Oxf., MS Rawl. D. 810, fols. 3–5 • Bodl. Oxf., MS Rawl. D. 859, fol. 76 • parish register, Charlton Mackrell [burial], 19 Sept 1638 • T. Lyte, family pedigrees, Som. ARS • inquisition post mortem, PRO, C 142/730, fol. 74 • T. Lyte, commonplace book, Som. ARS

Archives Salisbury and South Wiltshire Museum, Salisbury, Wiltshire pedigrees • Som. ARS, commonplace book • Som. ARS, family pedigrees | BL, pedigree of James I and 'Britaines monarchie', Add. MSS 48343, 59741

Likenesses oil on oak panel, 1611, Somerset County Museum, Taunton; repro. in Vivian-Neal, 'Thomas Lyte and the Lyte jewel', pl. 6

Wealth at death see PRO, C 142/730, fol. 74

Lythe, Robert (*d.* in or after **1574**), surveyor and map maker, is first recorded in 1556, as engaged in mapping the English pale at Calais on the instructions of the royal auditor, John Chaloner. Eleven years later, perhaps on Chaloner's recommendation, Lythe entered the service of the queen's deputy in Dublin, Sir Henry Sidney, at a time when disorders in Ireland were creating a demand for new maps of the country, and especially of Ulster. He began work in September 1567 at Carrickfergus, which Sidney intended to fortify, but bad weather and the danger of violence prevented his mapping more than a small part of the surrounding countryside and he soon returned to England. When he returned to Ulster the following year the same difficulties caused the same lack of success, surveying activity being confined to the south-east of the province. This time, however, Lythe remained in Ireland. Early in 1569 Sidney directed him to the country's three southern provinces, and by the autumn of 1570 Lythe had mapped parts of Ulster, and almost the whole of Ireland south of a line from Killary harbour to Strangford Lough.

Lythe was paid 4*s*. a day for his survey, increased to 8*s*. while he was travelling. There is no contemporary account of his methods, except that he surveyed several stretches of coastline from a boat. Some of his material came from local informants rather than personal observation, but in general his maps are impressively accurate, in spite of the speed with which they were produced, and much more detailed than anything previously available for most parts of Ireland. His output included one large general map of Ireland (now lost), and a smaller general map whose coverage of the north was probably copied from earlier cartographers. He also made a separate map of the area he had surveyed himself, several regional maps, two town plans (Carrickfergus and Newry), and a plan of the fort of Corkbeg, co. Cork, his only signed work.

By the 1580s Lythe's survey of Ireland was being copied by other artists in simplified form, and after 1590 the substance of it began to appear in print, though never with any acknowledgement to its originator, who was, indeed, probably almost unknown outside official circles. None the less, it was eventually Lythe, by way of John Speed's *Theatre of the Empire of Great Britaine* (1612), who provided several generations of British and foreign map users with their image of central and southern Ireland, entitling him to be ranked in terms of cartographic influence alongside the later but better-known Elizabethan map-makers Christopher Saxton and Timothy Pont. Lythe left Ireland in poor health in November 1571, and is unlikely to have returned, although there were still hopes two years later of employing him in Ulster as an engineer. He mapped the Isle of Sheppey and a proposed fort at Swaleness, Kent, in 1574, but after that there is no record of him.

J. H. ANDREWS, *rev.*

Sources J. H. Andrews, 'The Irish surveys of Robert Lythe', *Imago Mundi*, 19 (1965), 22–31 • J. H. Andrews, 'Robert Lythe's petitions, 1571', *Analecta Hibernica*, 24 (1967), 232–41 • J. H. Andrews, *Shapes of Ireland: maps and their makers, 1564–1839* (1997)

Lytlington, Thomas (*fl.* **1390–1401**). *See under* Prince, Gilbert (*d.* 1396).

Lyttelton, Alfred (**1857–1913**), sportsman and politician, was born on 7 February 1857 at Hagley Hall, Worcestershire. He was the eighth son and youngest of the twelve children of George William *Lyttelton, fourth Baron Lyttelton (1817–1876), and his wife, Mary Glynne (1813–1857) (W. E. Gladstone's sister-in-law). Arthur Temple *Lyttelton and Edward *Lyttelton were his brothers. His mother,

Alfred Lyttelton (1857–1913), by H. Walter Barnett, 1903

exhausted by child bearing, died six months after his birth. Despite this and his father's melancholia, Alfred Lyttelton had a serene and sunny disposition that was noticed by all. Brought up in a sporting and especially a cricketing family (which could field an eleven composed only of Lytteltons), he went to a preparatory school in Brighton and then to Eton College (Evans's house) in January 1868, where he was tutored by W. Johnson Cory, who encouraged him to study history. At Eton he was known as a supreme all-round sportsman. Curzon, his friend there, later wrote that 'no athlete was ever quite such an athlete, and no boyish hero was ever quite such a hero as was Alfred Lyttelton'. The rest of his life, Lyttelton felt, was to an extent an anticlimax. In 1875 he went to Trinity College, Cambridge, where he was an Apostle as well as the leading cricketer of his day. He was disappointed with a second class in history, but played cricket for Cambridge from 1876 until 1879, when he captained an undefeated team. He took up royal tennis at Cambridge, and held the amateur championship from 1882 until 1896, while continuing to play cricket. With little family money available, he was called to the bar in 1881 and made a steady income. From 1882 to 1885 he was legal private secretary to Sir Henry James, the attorney-general. He resisted Gladstone's attempts—intense after 1886—to persuade him to stand as a Liberal, preferring instead the social life of the Souls, though he was untainted by their decadence. In that context he met (Octavia) Laura Tennant [*see below*], whom he married in May 1885. She died following childbirth eleven months later, leaving a son who died from tubercular meningitis in 1888. Their romance and her early death added to Alfred Lyttelton's reputation as a man apart. On 18 April 1892 he married Edith Sophy Balfour [*see* Lyttelton, Dame Edith Sophy (1865–1948)], also a Soul and daughter of Archibald Balfour, a London businessman. They had two sons and a daughter, one of the sons dying in infancy. The surviving son, Oliver *Lyttelton, was a member of Churchill's war cabinet. Her memoir of her husband shows a dispassionate and shrewd mind.

Unwilling to buck the family tradition during Gladstone's political lifetime, Lyttelton waited until 1894 overtly to declare his Liberal Unionism. He was Liberal Unionist MP for Warwick and Leamington from 1895 to 1906. He also increased his standing at the bar, being recorder of Hereford, 1893–4, and of Oxford, 1894–1903, and taking silk in 1900. In that year Joseph Chamberlain rather surprisingly sent him to South Africa as chairman of the Transvaal concessions commission to plan post-war reconstruction, his elder brother Neville *Lyttelton becoming commander-in-chief at almost the same time. Alfred Lyttelton impressed Milner, who suggested to Chamberlain that he should succeed him as high commissioner.

On Chamberlain's resignation in September 1903, Lyttelton was appointed colonial secretary, a dramatic elevation and one for which he felt himself unprepared and unsuited. He accepted, against the advice of his officials, demands from Milner and the mine owners for indentured labour to solve the labour shortage in South Africa; the Chinese Labour Ordinance of 12 March 1904 led to the outcry over 'Chinese slavery' and 50,000 Chinese on the Rand, an important factor in the 1906 election, though the Liberals, once in office, were unable immediately to cancel the ordinance. He also, by letters patent of 31 March 1905, granted representative government to the Transvaal, a constitution abrogated by his Liberal successor on 8 February 1906. In April 1905 Lyttelton sent a dispatch advocating what he hoped would become a permanent 'imperial council'; the Unionist government fell before this body met and the Liberals used the traditional term 'colonial conference', and abandoned Lyttelton's proposal for a permanent secretariat. As in all his major initiatives as colonial secretary, Lyttelton acted against the advice of his officials.

Lyttelton lost his seat in the 1906 general election, but was unopposed for St George's, Hanover Square, at a by-election in June 1906. He held the seat easily in 1910. He did not return to the bar but was a director of the London and Westminster Bank and other companies. He opposed Welsh disestablishment, advocated housing and town-planning reform, and supported women's suffrage and the government's Trade Boards Bill to improve conditions in sweated industries. He was an active supporter of the university settlement movement.

In 1913 Lyttelton and his family took a holiday in east Africa, but he was unable to throw off lassitude, though continuing his duties. While scoring 89 in a cricket match at Bethnal Green he was struck in the stomach and developed an abscess, from which he died on 5 July 1913 at 3 Devonshire Terrace, London, a nursing home. He was buried in Hagley churchyard. The Oxford–Cambridge cricket match was briefly stopped to mark his passing and H. H. Asquith gave a memorable tribute to the Commons on 8 July. If Lyttelton's pre-eminence was that of the cricketer, his colonial secretaryship was bolder and more coherent in its imperial objectives—unpopular though they were—than might have been expected from one often regarded as a charming, Corinthian dilettante. Like a hero in a Buchan novel, he touched a nerve in his contemporaries, prompting Asquith, his political opponent, to say of him that 'he, perhaps of all men of this generation, came nearest to the mould and ideal of manhood, which every English father would like to see his son aspire to, and if possible to attain'.

(Octavia) Laura Lyttelton (1862–1886) was the daughter of Sir Charles *Tennant and his first wife, Emma Winsloe. She was a prominent Soul and led an emancipated, flirtatious life, smoothly moving from the manufacturing background of her family into the odd mixture of liberation and snobbery which constituted the Souls. Adolphus Liddell and Gerald Balfour were two of her conquests. She seems to have selected Alfred Lyttelton in a search for stability and security. She was ambivalent about her engagement ('the fact is marriage is a lower form of life—a happier, I am sure, but a more egotistical'; Jalland, 108) but successfully projected with her husband the image of a perfect couple. Her early death, on 24 April 1886, eight days after childbirth and possibly weakened by tuberculosis, shocked society and created an enduring legend. H. C. G. Matthew

Sources E. Lyttelton, *Alfred Lyttelton: an account of his life* (1917) • R. Hyam, *Elgin and Churchill at the colonial office, 1905–1908* (1968) • G. H. L. Le May, *British supremacy in South Africa, 1899–1907* (1965) • E. T. Raymond, *Portraits of the new century* (1928) • P. Jalland, *Women, marriage and politics, 1860–1914* (1986) • *DNB* • E. Lodge, *Peerage, baronetage, knightage and companionage of the British empire*, 81st edn, 3 vols. (1912)

Archives CAC Cam., corresp. and papers | BL, corresp. with Arthur James Balfour, Add. MS 49775 • BL, corresp. with Mary Gladstone, Add. MSS 46233–46234 • BL OIOC, letters to Lord Curzon, MSS Eur. F 111–112 • Bodl. Oxf., corresp. with Margot Asquith • Bodl. Oxf., corresp. with Lord Selborne • CAC Cam., Chandos MSS • CAC Cam., corresp. with Lord Esher • Herts. ALS, letters to Lady Desborough • HLRO, corresp. with Andrew Bonar Law • HLRO, letters to Herbert Samuel • King's AC Cam., letters to Oscar Browning • Nationaal Archief, The Hague, letters to Fanny Reay-Hasler • NL Aus., corresp. with Alfred Deakin • U. Birm., Chamberlain MSS

Likenesses H. W. Barnett, photograph, 1903, NPG [*see illus.*] • B. Stone, photograph, 1904, NPG • M. Beerbohm, caricature drawing, 1908, AM Oxf. • W. G. John, marble tablet, exh. RA 1915, St Margaret's Church, Westminster, London • W. Allingham, stipple and line engraving (after photograph by Smartt & Sons), NPG; repro. in *Baily's Magazine* (1898) • Ape [C. Pellegrini], chromolithograph caricature, NPG; repro. in *VF* (20 Sept 1884), pl. 314 • Elliott & Fry, photograph, NPG; repro. in *Our conservative and unionist statesmen*, 1 (1897) • P. A. de Laszlo, oils, Eton • double portrait, photograph (with Laura Lyttelton), repro. in Lyttelton, *Alfred Lyttelton*

Wealth at death £49,099 13*s*. 8*d*.: administration with will, 9 Oct 1913, *CGPLA Eng. & Wales*

Lyttelton, Arthur Temple (1852–1903), bishop-suffragan of Southampton and writer, was born in London on 7 January 1852, the fifth son and one of the twelve children of George William *Lyttelton, fourth Baron Lyttelton of Frankley of the second creation (1817–1876), and his first wife, Mary (1813–1857), second daughter of Sir Stephen Richard Glynne. Among his brothers were Alfred *Lyttelton, Sir Neville *Lyttelton, and Edward *Lyttelton. He was at Eton College from 1865 to 1870, in which year he proceeded to Trinity College, Cambridge, where he was a pupil of Henry Sidgwick (1838–1900). Placed in the first class of the moral science tripos in 1873, he graduated BA in 1874, proceeding MA in 1877 and DD in 1898. After a year at Cuddesdon Theological College near Oxford he was ordained deacon in 1876 and priest in 1877. From 1876 to 1879 he served as curate of St Mary's, Reading. Having then accepted appointment as master designate of Selwyn College, Cambridge, he spent three years (1879–82) as tutor of Keble College, Oxford, learning the art of mastership from its first warden, Edward Talbot (1844–1934), his mother's brother-in-law. On 3 August 1880 Lyttelton married Mary Kathleen (1856–1907) [*see* Lyttelton, Mary Kathleen], daughter of George Clive of Perrystone Court, Herefordshire, who had been an MP; they had two sons and a daughter.

Aged only thirty, Lyttelton was installed as the first master of Selwyn on 10 October 1882, taking on the additional duties of dean and tutor. The new foundation prospered under his leadership, soon acquiring an *esprit de corps* which owed much to his character. He combined moderate high-churchmanship with political Liberalism, being linked by close family ties with W. E. Gladstone, whose wife was his maternal aunt. True to these principles he was instrumental in drawing up a declaration on disestablishment signed by Liberal members of the Cambridge senate.

Lyttelton was Hulsean lecturer at Cambridge in 1891 but two years later resigned his mastership, feeling the need to exchange academic for pastoral work, and took up the post of vicar of Eccles, Lancashire. There he was able to put into practice some of the reforms he had previously advocated in theory. While at Eccles he served as rural dean and in 1895 was elected proctor for the clergy in York convocation. The following year he was appointed a chaplain-in-ordinary to Queen Victoria. In 1898 the bishop of Winchester, Randall Davidson, invited Lyttelton to become his suffragan, and he was consecrated bishop of Southampton on 30 November 1898. In the same year he was made provost of St Nicholas's College, Lancing, becoming responsible for the southern group of the Woodard schools, and in 1900 he was appointed archdeacon of Winchester. Lyttelton seemed destined for the highest office in the church, but in 1902 he fell ill with cancer. He died at his home, Castle House, Petersfield, Hampshire, on 19 February 1903, and was buried at Hagley, Worcestershire.

Noble in bearing and austere in his style of life, Lyttelton combined firm faith with a strong sense of social obligation. Like his friend Henry Scott Holland and his uncle

Edward Talbot he was a contributor to *Lux mundi* (1889). His broad literary interests are displayed in his posthumous *Modern Poets of Faith, Doubt and Paganism, and other Essays* (1904), to which Edward Talbot contributed a personal memoir. G. MARTIN MURPHY

Sources W. R. Brock and P. H. M. Cooper, *Selwyn College: a history* (1994) • E. S. Talbot, 'Memoir', in A. T. Lyttelton, *Modern poets of faith, doubt and paganism, and other essays* (1904) • B. Askwith, *The Lytteltons: a family chronicle of the nineteenth century* (1975) • Venn, *Alum. Cant.* • H. E. C. Stapylton, *Second series of Eton school lists … 1853–1892* (1900) • *The Times* (21 Feb 1903) • *Church Times* (27 Feb 1903) • *CGPLA Eng. & Wales* (1903)
Archives BL, letters to Mary Gladstone, Add. MS 46235 • CAC Cam., corresp. with Lord Esher • King's AC Cam., letters to Oscar Browning • Lancing College, letters to E. C. Lowe • Worcs. RO, corresp. and papers relating to marriage settlement
Likenesses photograph, NPG • portrait, repro. in A. T. Lyttelton, *Modern poets of faith, doubt and paganism, and other essays* (1904)
Wealth at death £538 5*s*. 0*d*.: probate, 1 April 1903, *CGPLA Eng. & Wales*

Lyttelton [Littelton], **Sir Charles, third baronet** (**1629–1716**), colonial governor and politician, was born in Frankley, Worcestershire, a younger son of Sir Thomas *Lyttelton, first baronet (1595/6–1650), royalist officer and politician, and Catherine Crompton (*d*. 1666). As a member of a substantial county family which by the next century had developed into 'a powerful Whig cousinhood' (Montgomery-Massingberd, 92), Lyttelton committed himself wholeheartedly to the royalist cause; he served in the royalist forces at Colchester in 1648, and after their defeat escaped to France, where in 1650 he was appointed cupbearer to the exiled Charles II. He appears to have served as a messenger between the king and his English supporters during the late 1650s, and after the Restoration Charles II recognized his services by knighting him in 1662. That same year Lyttelton and Katherine Fairfax (*d*. 1663), whom he had married in 1661, departed for Jamaica, where Lyttelton was to serve as lieutenant-governor to Thomas Windsor, seventh Baron Windsor. In the course of the voyage Katherine gave birth to the couple's first child, a son, but neither mother nor infant survived for long; both died in January 1663 and were interred in the cathedral at Spanish Town, Jamaica.

By that time Lyttelton had succeeded to the governorship of Jamaica, Windsor having turned the office over to him on 20 October 1662, a mere ten weeks after the two men's arrival on the island. Lyttelton immediately set to work on the project of developing a full civil government for encouraging English settlement of the colony, which England had acquired from Spain in 1655. He was instrumental in the creation of an island assembly, a body which was 'fairly and indifferently drawn by the votes of all the inhabitants' (*DNB*), and which was responsible for dealing with the colony's financial and legal needs. The assembly passed legislation regarding taxation, hunting, and planting, and set up religious and judicial authorities throughout the island, creating an infrastructure upon which the following decades' prosperity was based. Lyttelton also made Jamaica's internal and external security a priority, granting letters of marque to English privateers,

Sir Charles Lyttelton, third baronet (**1629–1716**), attrib. John Closterman, 1690s

with the intent that they serve as a striking force against potential Spanish and Dutch attacks. He entered into negotiations with the Maroons, African slaves who had run away from Spanish plantations and frequently attacked English settlements, granting them landholdings and promising them 'the same state and freedom as the English enjoy' (Dunn, 242) provided that they cease their raids. Not all Maroons were willing to accept the offer, but enough did so that the threat they posed diminished sufficiently for planters to become more willing to settle in remote areas of the island. Lyttelton's other activities as governor included establishing a town and fortifications at Port Royal, erecting Fort Charles, and repairing St Katherine's Church, in Spanish Town.

In Lyttelton's opinion, the English settlers were 'generally easy to be governed, yet rather by persuasion then severity' (Cundall, *The Governors of Jamaica*, 19), and local residents asserted that under his administration Jamaica was peaceful, healthy, and prosperous. None the less, on 13 February 1664 the king recalled Lyttelton and issued a warrant for Sir Thomas Modyford to assume the office of governor. On 2 May of that year Lyttelton sailed for England, where he was commissioned as major and subsequently lieutenant-colonel of the lord admiral's regiment, precursor to the Royal Marines. He served as governor of Harwich and Landguard Fort, and then of Sheerness, and after 1682 he and Sir William Beeston acceded to the request of the governor and council of Jamaica that they serve as the London agents for the colony. On 12 May 1685 he entered parliament as member for

Bewdley, Worcestershire, a seat he retained until the revolution of 1688, at which time he resigned all of his appointments rather than subscribe to the oaths mandated by William and Mary. In 1693 Lyttelton's elder brother Henry died, allowing him to succeed to the family's title and estates. At this time Lyttelton, his second wife, Anne Temple (*d.* 1718), and their children settled at Hagley, Worcestershire, where Lyttelton spent the remainder of his life. He died at Hagley on 2 May 1716, and was buried with Anne in the vault at Over-Areley, Staffordshire. NATALIE ZACEK

Sources F. G. Spurdle, *Early West Indian government* [1962] • S. A. G. Taylor, *The western design: an account of Cromwell's expedition to the Caribbean* (1965) • F. Cundall, *The governors of Jamaica in the seventeenth century* (1936) • R. S. Dunn, *Sugar and slaves: the rise of the planter class in the English West Indies, 1624–1713* (1972) • W. J. Gardner, *A history of Jamaica* (1873) • F. Cundall, *Historic Jamaica* (1915) • E. Long, *The history of Jamaica* (1774) • H. Montgomery-Massingberd, *Debrett's great British families* (1988) • *DNB*

Archives BL, letters to Lord Hatton, Add. MSS 29577–29579

Likenesses attrib. J. Closterman, portrait, 1690–99, Hagley Hall, Worcestershire [*see illus.*] • P. W. Tomkins, stipple, BM, NPG; repro. in A. Hamilton, *Memoirs of Count Grammont* • P. W. Tomkinson, engraving (after drawing by S. Harding), repro. in Cundall, *Governors* • portrait, Institute of Jamaica, Spanish Town

Lyttelton, Charles (1714–1768), bishop of Carlisle and antiquary, was born in Hagley, Worcestershire, the third son of the twelve children of Sir Thomas Lyttelton, fourth baronet (1685–1751), MP, and Christian Temple (1688–1759), daughter of Sir Richard Temple of Stowe, Buckinghamshire, and maid of honour to Queen Anne. At least between 1725 and 1728 he was educated at Eton College, where he was a member of Horace Walpole's 'triumvirate' with George Montagu. He was admitted a student at the Middle Temple in 1731, but the following year matriculated from University College, Oxford. However, he returned to the law without taking his degree; he resided in lodgings at the Inner Temple and was called to the bar at the Middle Temple on 26 January 1739. He suffered from a severe respiratory illness at this time, taking the waters at Bath in 1739 after four months' poor health, and complained frequently afterwards of a constant cough and winter catarrh. He took annual summer tours on horseback of parts of Great Britain for the sake of his health as well as for interest.

In 1740 Lyttelton gave up the law for the less strenuous demands of the church, continuing his studies at University College and graduating DCL in 1745. In 1742 he was ordained by the elderly John Hough, bishop of Worcester, and the same year was instituted to the rectory of Alvechurch, Worcestershire. He was ambitious for preferment in the Church of England and had strong family connections with those in government, especially through his brother George *Lyttelton, Lord Lyttelton, and his cousin George Grenville. Influence brought him appointment as chaplain-in-ordinary to George II in 1747, with the duty of waiting at court each December, and as dean of Exeter Cathedral in 1748, a position which was worth £500 a year. He was disappointed of a bishopric when vacancies arose in 1756 and 1758, but Grenville helped him secure the

Charles Lyttelton (1714–1768), by James Watson, pubd 1770 (after Francis Cotes, *c.*1765)

bishopric of Carlisle in 1762, worth £1300 a year, and he vacated Alvechurch and Exeter. His means were further increased by a bequest of over 2000 guineas from Lord Angelsea in 1761. Lyttelton had found Exeter remote from London, but in the few months of each year that he was there he began a scheme of restoration and refurbishment in the cathedral, starting in 1751 with reglazing the great east window. He was the first person to recognize the significance of the cathedral muniments and to try to arrange them. He found Carlisle even more remote, the weather disagreeable, the cathedral poorly furnished, and his residence at Rose Castle neglected and stripped by his predecessor. His restoration of the interior of the choir, carried out in collaboration with his amateur architect nephew, Thomas Pitt, Lord Camelford, was probably essential but was condemned as 'barbarous' by R. W. Billings and the new woodwork was removed in 1853–6. His substantial repairs to the Strickland Tower at Rose Castle have also not survived. A sermon on libel preached before the House of Lords in 1765 was his only published religious work; his chief interest in church matters was historical and particularly focused on medieval ecclesiastical architecture.

Lyttelton's earliest research, from at least 1731, was into Worcestershire history, and in 1738 he purchased the Revd William Thomas's important collection of the papers of Thomas Habington, the seventeenth-century county historian. Lyttelton added further notes on parishes with family connections, and wrote unpublished histories of Alvechurch, Hagley, and Frankley. His collections were used extensively by Dr Treadway Nash for his

History of Worcestershire and his account of the fabric of Worcester Cathedral is inserted into Valentine Green's *History of … Worcester* (1796). He was elected fellow of the Society of Antiquaries of London in 1740, and his interests developed with a pioneering study of English Romanesque architecture, which was then called Saxon. He attempted to define its distinctive features by an analysis of detail, discussing his findings with other antiquaries from about 1742. With his friend Smart Lethieullier, he collected drawings of Saxon churches, and exhibited them at meetings of the Society of Antiquaries; A. C. Ducarel dedicated his *Anglo-Norman Antiquities* (1767) to Lyttelton for first interesting him in the subject. Lyttelton's essay, 'Some account of the cathedral church of Exeter', written in 1754 but not published until 1797 by the society, was the first history of the building. The society had no journal for publishing articles until *Archaeologia* started in 1770, after his death. However, several of Lyttelton's papers were printed in the first three volumes, and demonstrated the breadth of his antiquarian interests, notably 'A dissertation on the antiquity of brick building in England' and a perceptive paper recognizing that stone axes were made before the use of metal. He was elected fellow of the Royal Society in 1743, but his scientific concerns were limited to the study of fossils, on which he wrote two short papers published in the *Philosophical Transactions* for 1748 and 1750. While publishing very little himself, Lyttelton used his knowledge and influence to assist other scholars. The Cornish historian William Borlase in particular acknowledged his help and wrote *Observations on … Scilly* in the form of a letter to Lyttelton.

Lyttelton had assisted the Society of Antiquaries in obtaining its royal charter in 1751, and served as president from 1765 until his death. He was a painstaking and methodical researcher, and his successor as president, Dean Milles, paid tribute to his knowledge of English history, retentive memory, affable temper, and willingness to receive and communicate information on points of antiquity. He was a prolific and informative letter writer, and before his death seems to have intended publishing accounts of his annual tours sent to friends, especially Sanderson Miller. He died, unmarried, at his house in Clifford Street, Westminster, on 22 December 1768, and was buried in the family vault in Hagley church. His estate amounted to £6715 and he bequeathed many of his books and manuscripts, including the thirteenth-century Lindsey psalter, to the Society of Antiquaries. The rest of his letters were subsequently dispersed with other Lyttelton papers by Sothebys at a sale on 12 December 1978, and his accounts at a sale on 20 July 1989. BERNARD NURSE

Sources Nichols, *Lit. anecdotes*, 5.378–81 • M. Wyndham, *Chronicles of the eighteenth century*, 2 vols. (1924) • T. Cocke and C. R. Dodwell, 'Rediscovery of the romanesque', *English romanesque art, 1066–1200*, ed. G. Zarnecki, J. Holt, and T. Holland (1984), 360–90 [exhibition catalogue, Hayward Gallery, London, 5 April–8 July 1984] • P. A. S. Pool, *William Borlase* (1986) • L. Dickins and M. Stanton, *An eighteenth century correspondence being the letters … to Sanderson Miller* (1910) • W. Gibson, 'The finances and legatees of Charles Lyttelton (1714–1768), bishop of Carlisle', *Transactions of the Cumberland and Westmorland Antiquarian and Archaeological Society*, [new ser.,] 96 (1996), 187–93 • J. Evans, *A history of the Society of Antiquaries* (1956) • C. Brooks, *The great east window of Exeter Cathedral* (1988) • D. W. V. Weston, *Carlisle Cathedral history* (2000) • C. Lyttelton, letters to William Mytton, BL, Add. MS 30315 • H. A. C. Sturgess, ed., *Register of admissions to the Honourable Society of the Middle Temple, from the fifteenth century to the year 1944*, 3 vols. (1949) • R. A. Austen-Leigh, ed., *The Eton College register, 1698–1752* (1927) • Walpole, *Corr.*, vol. 40 • *IGI* • Foster, *Alum. Oxon.* • *DNB*

Archives BL, corresp., Stowe MSS 752–754 • BL, church notes and notes on Aubrey's *Natural history of Wiltshire*, Add. MSS 69373, art 9, 69375A • Hagley Hall, Worcestershire, antiquarian history of Hagley • S. Antiquaries, Lond., antiquarian and personal corresp. and papers | BL, corresp. with Thomas Birch, Add. MS 4312, fols. 270–328 • BL, letters to William Mytton, Add. MS 30315 • BL, letters to Jeremiah Milles, Add. MS 32123 • Bodl. Oxf., letters to George Ballard • Bodl. Oxf., letters to Francis Drake • Bodl. Oxf., letters to A. C. Ducarel • Bodl. Oxf., letters to Richard Gough • Bodl. Oxf., letters to Jeremiah Milles • Hunt. L., letters to Elizabeth Montagu • Penzance Library, Morrab Gardens, Penzance, Borlase MSS • Staffs. RO, letters to Sir Edward Littleton • Warks. CRO, Sanderson Miller MSS

Likenesses A. Ramsay, oils, *c.*1763, Hagley Hall, Worcestershire; repro. in A. Smart, *Allan Ramsay: a complete catalogue of his paintings*, ed. J. Ingamells (1999), fig. 557 • J. Watson, mezzotint, pubd 1770 (after F. Cotes, *c.*1765), BM, NPG [*see illus.*] • P. Audinet, engraving (after F. Cotes), repro. in Nichols, *Illustrations*, 3.313

Wealth at death £6715: Gibson, 'The finances and legatees of Charles Lyttelton'

Lyttelton [*née* Balfour], **Dame Edith Sophy** (**1865–1948**), public servant and author, was born in St Petersburg, Russia, the elder of two daughters (there were also five sons) of Archibald Balfour, a prosperous merchant in Russia, and his wife, Sophia. She was educated privately and made her mark on London society in the 1880s as an intelligent, quick-witted, and attractive young woman, who moved in the aristocratic circle of friends known as the Souls, which included A. J. Balfour, George Curzon, Margot Tennant (later Asquith), and Alfred *Lyttelton (1857–1913), her future husband. Lyttelton, a famous amateur athlete and cricketer, and a nephew of Gladstone, was the eighth son of the fourth Baron Lyttelton and his wife, Mary, *née* Glynne. He had first married, in 1885, Laura, *née* Tennant (the elder sister of Margot), who died in 1886. Edith Balfour became his second wife on 18 April 1892 when they were married at Bordighera on the Italian riviera, and together they had two surviving children, a daughter, Mary Frances, who married Sir George Lillie Craik, second baronet, and a son, Oliver *Lyttelton (1893–1972), who became first Viscount Chandos and, like his father, colonial secretary.

Alfred Lyttelton's first marriage to Laura Tennant had been extremely popular and her premature death, after having given birth to a baby son who survived her by only two years, was deeply mourned. His second marriage, though, was to prove no less popular, and Beatrice Webb, who met the Lytteltons in September 1892, thought them 'a charming pair … graceful, modest, intelligent and with the exquisite deference and ease which constitutes good breeding' (*Diary*, 2.22). After Alfred Lyttelton became Liberal Unionist MP for Leamington in 1895 Edith, or D. D. as she was commonly known, played successfully the role of the political wife, entertaining at their home in Great College Street, Westminster. She also exercised a significant influence on her husband's career. He habitually looked to her for advice and it was their joint decision that he should concentrate on politics rather than the bar after their marriage. She afterwards assisted him at elections, on occasion even speaking on his behalf, and as a convinced supporter of women's suffrage she encouraged his grudging acceptance of the cause. When in 1900 he was appointed chairman of a government committee to investigate monopolies in the Transvaal, she accompanied him; the experience better equipped her to support him when, as colonial secretary from 1903 to 1905, he had to defend the controversial use of Chinese labour in the Rand.

Their marriage was a genuine partnership, based upon strong mutual attraction and complementary ambitions, and after Alfred Lyttelton's sudden death on 5 July 1913 his wife published, in March 1917, a reverential biography. This was favourably reviewed in *The Times* as an 'intimate portrait' of a universally beloved man (*The Times*, 19 March 1917). It did not, though, meet with the approval of Virginia Woolf, to whom Edith Lyttelton had been held up in youth as an exemplar of 'charm and interest'. Woolf was appalled by the emotionalism of the biography and imagined that it was the author and not the subject who hungered for worldly success: 'Poor man! I suppose she drove him on to be a celebrity and a politician, which wasn't his line. However, all his sins are paid for by this sort of monument' (*Letters of Virginia Woolf*, 2.153). Whatever the merits of this assessment, Edith Lyttelton had a range of activities and interests to match those of her husband, and it is ironic that he was continually urging her, before his own untimely death, to reduce her engagements in the interests of her health.

One of Edith Lyttelton's chief interests, imperialism, was nurtured during her visit to South Africa in 1900. There she met, and developed a high regard for, Alfred, Viscount Milner, and discussed with him at length his political views. She returned to London determined to promote the imperial vision that they shared, and in Violet Markham and Violet Cecil, both of whom had also been to South Africa and had contact with Milner, she found like-minded partners. The three women were central figures behind the Victoria League, which was established in 1901 amid a wave of pro-imperial sentiment generated by the Second South African War. The league brought together high-ranking women from both sides of the political divide on the common ground of empire. It disseminated information, established an 'imperial library', raised funds for the relief of refugees and the tending of war graves, and provided hospitality for imperial visitors to England. Edith Lyttelton helped to found the movement and served as honorary secretary until she retired owing to ill health. She also supported the related cause of imperial preference, through the Women's Tariff Reform Association.

Lyttelton's strong philanthropic instincts, which were shared by her husband, also found outlets nearer home. She was involved in particular in the Edwardian campaign against 'sweated' labour and this subject was the inspiration for two of her many plays. Her dramatic efforts were encouraged by her close friendship with George Bernard Shaw and Mrs Patrick Campbell, and the latter played the lead in *Warp and Woof*, Edith Lyttelton's first production, which opened at the Criterion in June 1904. The play dealt with the hardships experienced by women working in the London fashion industry and it was the subject matter, rather than the drama itself, that generated the most interest. Lyttelton's depiction of working women was dismissed by one society critic as unconvincing—'frank factory girls, speculating in broad cockney dialect as to what they would do if they were "lydies"' (*The Times*, 4 July 1904; Frances Balfour to the editor, 30 June 1904). But the accuracy of Lyttelton's portrayal of their exploitation could not be so easily dismissed, and was in fact vigorously defended in the correspondence columns of *The Times*.

Lyttelton returned to the theme in December 1912 with a study of the '"sweating" system' in *The Thumbscrew*, which had a single showing at the Little Theatre under the auspices of the Pioneer Players. In all she wrote seven plays, and a translation of Edmond Rostand's *Les deux pierrots*, but none ran for more than a few weeks and the last, an adaptation of Disraeli's *Tancred*, was condemned as 'unhappily tedious' by *The Times* and 'intolerably tedious' by Virginia Woolf (*The Times*, 17 July 1923; *Diary of Virginia Woolf*, 2.258). It closed after a short run at the Kingsway Theatre in July 1923, but Lyttelton's love for the theatre remained unabated. She also wrote a novel, *The Sinclair Family* (1926), and *Travelling Days* (1933), an account of her travels in the Far East and India.

It is as a versatile public administrator, rather than an author, that Edith Lyttelton is to be remembered. She was particularly active in advancing the interests of working women and served on the first executive of the National Union of Women Workers, which was founded in 1895. She was also chairwoman of the Personal Service Association, established in London in 1908 to co-ordinate the efforts of well-to-do women who sought to alleviate distress arising from unemployment in the capital. At the outbreak of war Lyttelton was a founder of the war refugees committee, for which she was honoured with the médaille de la reine Élisabeth by the king of Belgium in June 1918. She was made deputy director of the women's branch of the Ministry of Agriculture in 1917, served on the central committee of women's employment from 1916 to 1925, and was vice-chairman of the Waste Reclamation Trade Board from 1924 to 1931. After the war she devoted herself to the League of Nations and was the British substitute delegate in Geneva (1923, 1926–8, and 1931), where her interests focused on the opium trade and the 'white slave' traffic. She was made a DBE in 1917 and a GBE in 1929 in recognition of her many public services.

After the death of her husband Edith Lyttelton became increasingly interested in spiritualism and was a member of the council of the Society for Psychical Research, serving as president in 1933–4. She brought to this difficult subject an independent mind, and her calm reasoning convinced her of the existence of what she termed the 'superconscious'—a spiritually elevated version of the subconscious, which she believed enabled the properly receptive mind to foretell events and realize communion with the dead. She lectured on the subject and wrote many books, including *The Faculty of Communion* (1925), *Our Superconscious Mind* (1931), and *Some Cases of Prediction* (1937), and it also inspired her 1926 biography of her friend Florence Upton, the painter and creator of the 'golliwog' character, who turned to spiritualism towards the end of her life.

Edith Lyttelton also devoted herself after 1918 to the foundation of a national theatre in London. This, she believed, should be 'a theatre where the prices of the seats should be within the reach of all; a true people's theatre dedicated to the highest expression of dramatic art' (*The Times*, 20 May 1924, Chandos to the editor). She was an effective member on the executive committee of the Shakespeare Memorial National Theatre, and her efforts in this direction were consciously carried forward by her son, who was the first chairman of the National Theatre (1962–71). He remembered his mother as a woman 'catholic in her tastes and interests' (Chandos, xiv), and she combined the instincts of a Victorian imperialist and philanthropist with those of an Edwardian suffragist and social reformer, the imagination of a dramatist with the practical bent of a public administrator. She died at her home, 18 Great College Street, Westminster, London, on 2 September 1948. MARK POTTLE

Sources *The Times* (11 June 1904) • *The Times* (8 July 1904) • *The Times* (4 July 1904) • *The Times* (18 May 1912) • *The Times* (16 Dec 1912) • *The Times* (4 June 1913) • *The Times* (19 March 1917) • *The Times* (29 June 1918) • *The Times* (20 Dec 1918) • *The Times* (17 July 1923) • *The Times* (8 May 1924) • *The Times* (20 May 1924) • *The Times* (4 March 1925) • *The Times* (1 March 1929) • *The Times* (3 Sept 1948) • *WWW* • Burke, *Peerage* (1939) [Cobham] • census returns, 1881 • J. Bush, *Edwardian ladies and imperial power* (2000) • *The diary of Beatrice Webb*, ed. N. MacKenzie and J. MacKenzie, 4 vols. (1982–5), vol. 2 • Lord Chandos [O. Lyttleton, first Viscount Chandos], *The memoirs of Lord Chandos: an unexpected view from the summit* (1962) • *The diary of Virginia Woolf*, ed. A. O. Bell and A. McNeillie, 2 (1978) • *Collected letters: Bernard Shaw*, ed. D. H. Laurence, 4 vols. (1965–88), vols. 2–4 • *The letters of Virginia Woolf*, ed. N. Nicolson, 2 (1976) • *The letters of Virginia Woolf*, ed. N. Nicolson, 4 (1978) • *Lantern slides: the diaries and letters of Violet Bonham Carter, 1904–1914*, ed. M. Bonham Carter and M. Pottle (1996) • d. cert.

Archives CAC Cam., corresp. and papers | BL, corresp. with Lord Gladstone, Add. MS 46046 • BL, letters to Mary Gladstone, Add. MS 46234 • BL, corresp. with League of Dramatists, Add. MS 63411 • BL, corresp. with Society of Authors, Add. MS 56741 • Society for Psychical Research, London, corresp. with Sir Oliver Lodge • W. Sussex RO, letters to L. J. Maxse

Likenesses photograph, repro. in *The Times* (1 March 1929), 20

Wealth at death £8713 1s. 10d.: probate, 28 Feb 1949, *CGPLA Eng. & Wales*

Lyttelton, Edward (1855–1942), schoolmaster, Church of England clergyman, and cricketer, was born at Hagley, Worcestershire, 23 July 1855, the seventh of eight sons of George William *Lyttelton, fourth Baron Lyttelton (1817–1876), and his first wife, Mary (1813–1857), daughter of Sir Stephen Richard Glynne, eighth baronet, and sister-in-law of W. E. Gladstone. Neville Gerald *Lyttelton, Arthur Temple *Lyttelton, and Alfred *Lyttelton were his brothers. After attending a dame-school in Brighton, Lyttelton went to Eton College in 1868. The family's sporting prowess, especially in cricket, was quickly made manifest and in his last year at the school, 1874, he was captain of the Eton eleven. He went up to Trinity College, Cambridge, in 1874 and captained the university side that beat the Australian touring team in 1878; he also played county cricket for Middlesex. He played association football for England against Scotland in 1878. He left Cambridge with a second class in the classical tripos, graduating BA, 1878, MA, 1881, BD, 1907, and DD, 1912.

After touring France and Germany, Lyttelton was appointed as assistant master at Wellington College in 1880, staying until 1882, when a vacancy arose at Eton. An important experience was his residence at Cuddesdon College in 1883 and 1884 in preparation for taking holy orders. Already imbued with a deep sense of religion from his father, he was ordained in 1886. At the age of thirty-five, he was appointed master of Haileybury, where he introduced a number of educational experiments, taking a special interest in music and also health and hygiene. Boys were divided into two groups for classics, those who were to pursue the study further and those for whom it was training for the reasoning faculty. Lyttelton also introduced handicraft for the less gifted linguists. His reforms met with some opposition from staff and parents, though he was popular with all who came into contact with him. He was assisted in his work by his wife, Caroline Amy (*d.* 1919), daughter of the Very Revd John West, dean of St Patrick's, Dublin, whom he had married in 1888. They had two daughters. Recognition of his concern for education came in 1893 with his appointment as a member of the royal commission on secondary education under James Bryce. Its report recommended a central authority under a minister of education. Lyttelton was also a member of the consultative committee on education, established in 1900 to advise the new president of the board on any matters referred to it.

On the retirement of Edmond Warre as headmaster of Eton College in 1905, Lyttelton succeeded to the post. Warre had begun to introduce changes in the school's curriculum and organization and Lyttelton lost no time in imposing his own ideas on the existing regime. In 1906 he introduced two important changes: Greek was no longer required of boys entering the school, and under certain conditions boys might do no classical work at all, specializing in mathematics, modern languages, science, or history. His enthusiasm was not matched by his organizing abilities or financial acumen and his experiments were not always successful. The last years of his headmastership were made difficult by the outbreak of the First World War. He preached a sermon at St Margaret's, Westminster, in March 1915, suggesting that it was wrong to condemn the German nation and that the allied politicians should act generously in the peace settlement. This led to a public storm of protest.

Lyttelton resigned his post in 1916, having undergone a spiritual crisis. This took the form of the need for self-discovery through a study of religious works. His career now took a different turn. In 1917 he became a curate to the Revd Richard (Dick) Sheppard at St Martin-in-the-Fields and from 1918 to 1920 he was rector of the small parish of Sidestrand in Norfolk. He was invited to become dean of Whitelands College, Chelsea, a teacher training college for women, in 1920. The post was a combination of chaplain and lecturer on the Bible. He remained there until 1929 when he retired after a serious operation. He moved to Norwich, where he was honorary canon, 1931–41. Near the end of his life, at the age of eighty-six, he was invited to Lincoln, where he became honorary canon, taking temporary charge of one of the city's churches. He died at his home, the Old Palace, Lincoln, on 26 January 1942. PETER GORDON

Sources E. Lyttelton, *Memories and hopes* (1925) • C. Allington, *Edward Lyttelton: an appreciation* (1943) • T. Card, *Eton renewed: a history from 1860 to the present day* (1994) • L. S. R. Byrne and E. L. Churchill, *Changing Eton* (1937) • *CGPLA Eng. & Wales* (1942)

Archives BL, letters to Mary Gladstone, Add. MS 46235 • BL OIOC, letters to Curzon, MSS Eur. F 111–112 • Bodl. Oxf., corresp. with Gilbert Murray • King's AC Cam., letters to O. Browning

Likenesses H. H. Brown, oils, 1905, Haileybury College, Hertfordshire • W. Rothenstein, sanguine drawing, 1923, NPG • T. B. Gibbs, oils, Lady Margaret School, Parsons Green, London • W. Rothenstein, drawing, Eton • J. Russell & Sons, photograph, NPG • Spy [L. Ward], chromolithograph caricature, NPG; repro. in *VF* (9 May 1901)

Wealth at death £2734 17*s*. 1*d*.: probate, 21 April 1942, *CGPLA Eng. & Wales*

Lyttelton, George, first Baron Lyttelton (1709–1773), politician and writer, was the eldest son of Sir Thomas Lyttelton, fourth baronet (1685–1751), landowner and politician, of Hagley, Worcestershire, and his wife, Christian (1688–1759), the daughter of Sir Richard *Temple (1634–1697) and the sister of Richard Temple, first Viscount Cobham (1675–1749). He was born on 17 January 1709, probably two months premature, and baptized the same day at St James's, Westminster. He remained frail in appearance throughout his adult life—his tall, thin frame, pale face, and lanky gait frequently caricatured by political satirists. Lyttelton was educated at Eton College and at Christ Church, Oxford, where he matriculated on 11 February 1726, but did not take a degree. He was a talented scholar with strong literary ambitions, whose first poem, *Blenheim*, a patriotic paean to the Churchill family, was published in March 1728, about the time he departed for the grand tour. While in Italy, Lyttelton wrote the outspoken poem *An Epistle to Mr Pope, from a Young Gentleman at Rome* (published 1730), prompted by the recent appearance of Pope's *The Dunciad*. Lyttelton depicts Virgil's ghost reprimanding Pope for wasting his talents on 'meaner satire': instead, he should aspire to epic verse and 'join the PATRIOT's to the POET's praise' (Lyttelton, *Epistle*, 5–6).

Lyttelton and the patriot opposition Patriotism and poetry were the twin themes which came to dominate and define Lyttelton's own life. The most significant single event in his early political career was Robert Walpole's dismissal in 1733 of his uncle Richard Temple, Viscount Cobham, from both his ministerial place and his regiment, part of a government purge meted out on former whig stalwarts who

George Lyttelton, first Baron Lyttelton (1709–1773), by Benjamin West, 1773

had criticized the ministry for suppressing an investigation into the affairs of the South Sea Company. Cobham retired to his family seat at Stowe in Buckinghamshire and built up a formidable array of opposition support among his cohort of young nephews, using his vast wealth to secure some of them parliamentary seats. Lyttelton may have assisted his father, a loyal Walpole whig, in the campaign that same year to defend Walpole's Excise Bill, but by 1735 he had been won over to his uncle's politics, though his father did not (as the press reported) threaten to disinherit him as a result. At a by-election in 1735 Lyttelton was returned for the Pitt family borough, Okehampton in Devon, joining his cousin Thomas Pitt in representing the town. This political group, which included Lyttelton, Thomas Pitt, William Pitt, and Richard Grenville and George Grenville ('the cousinhood'), as well as Viscount Cornbury and William Murray, were known as Cobham's Cubs or the Boy Patriots (all were under thirty in 1735). A new force on the political scene, they attracted praise for their apparently disinterested patriotism as well as ridicule for the Ciceronian rhetoric which distinguished their political speeches. In April 1736 Lyttelton, Pitt, and Richard Grenville provoked controversy with their daring attacks on George II and Walpole in speeches congratulating Frederick, prince of Wales, on his marriage to Augusta of Saxe-Gotha. Lyttelton had first been introduced to Frederick in 1732 by Bubb Dodington, and he soon became a close confidant. In 1735 Lyttelton was appointed Frederick's equerry and in 1737 his secretary, promotions widely read as a public declaration of the prince's affiliation with the opposition.

The friction between the Cobham circle and the group

of opposition whigs led by Pulteney and Carteret emerged in rivalry over management of Frederick: it was Lyttelton who warned the prince that Pulteney's parliamentary motion pressing for an increase in the prince's civil-list allowance would damage his popularity. The motion, which Lyttelton in the event supported, was defeated in February 1737. When in late 1737 Frederick finally broke with his parents and established his separate 'court' in Norfolk House, a centre of opposition activity, he came to rely increasingly on Lyttelton for advice: he was, in Pope's words:

> the Man, so near
> His Prince, that writes in Verse, and has his Ear.
> (A. Pope, *Epilogue to the Satires*, 1.45–6)

Lyttelton shared Frederick's cultural interests and was widely perceived as the 'Maecenas' who brought deserving poets to his royal notice. In practice only a handful of poets—Richard Glover, James Thomson, and David Mallet—received financial reward, but Lyttelton undoubtedly helped use Frederick's influence to inspire and mobilize a campaign of patriot writing in the late 1730s. On 14 April 1737 the ministerial *Daily Gazetteer* satirized him as Littledone, a troublemaker who has urged the playwrights of his acquaintance to 'put into their Plays all the strong things they can think of against Courts and Ministers, and Places and Pensions'. Lyttelton's extravagant puff in the opposition journal *Common Sense* for Glover's patriot epic *Leonidas* was clearly designed as a hit against the ministry, as well as to incite Pope (whose poetry is compared unfavourably to Glover's) to turn his pen to loftier themes.

The relationship between Pope and Lyttelton was complex and significant, hinging on shared literary and aesthetic interests. Their extensive correspondence in the period between 1738 and 1741 reveals Lyttelton's efforts to persuade Pope to produce his own 'Moral Song' for the nation, and to act as moral and literary supporter to the prince, to be 'as much with him as you can, Animate him to Virtue' (*Correspondence of Alexander Pope*, 4.138). Lyttelton came the closest to achieving this aim during 1738, the year in which Pope was heavily involved with the patriots, editing their stage plays and becoming involved in details of the new broad-bottom coalition within the opposition. Pope twice compliments Lyttelton by name in his two dialogues of the *Epilogue to the Satires* of that year. It is perhaps significant that, even after Pope's disillusionment with patriot politics set about 1740, Lyttelton's name is absent from Pope's unpublished satiric fragment 'One Thousand Seven Hundred and Forty' indicting other members of the group.

As a writer himself Lyttelton contributed substantially to the opposition campaign. Although he began his published career as a poet, his 'Observations on the life and reign of Queen Elizabeth', written in 1733 but never published (Hagley MSS), reveals the impact of Bolingbroke's recent *Remarks on the History of England* in its concern with the politics of Elizabeth's reign. The essay, an imagined conversation between Walter Ralegh, Henry Wotton, and Sir Francis Bacon, is rich in historical parallels with the Walpole era. Two years later Lyttelton's *Letters from a Persian in England to his Friend at Ispahan* (1735), a series of fictional letters commenting on the manners and mores of Walpolian England, made a significant impact on the literary-political world. Their lively, humorous style coupled with their pointed attacks on the government made them one of the most widely read opposition works, and they went through several editions within the space of a year. Lyttelton also contributed to one of the most important opposition journals, *Common Sense, or, The Englishman's Journal*, started in February 1737 after the demise of *The Craftsman*, taking up that journal's campaign for a unified country opposition. In 1739 he also published, anonymously, *Considerations upon the Present State of our Affairs at Home and Abroad*, one of many warmongering pamphlets of that year, which echoed his own parliamentary speech of February 1739 attacking the convention with Spain.

The fall of Walpole and the middle years In the general election of May 1741 Lyttelton unsuccessfully challenged his tory rival Edmund Lechmere for a seat after an attempt by opposition whigs and tories to share the representation of the two Worcestershire seats had broken down. This quarrel occasioned Sir Charles Hanbury Williams's *Political Eclogue*, a much-cited political satire with a famous caricature of a lofty Lyttelton inappropriately citing Roman precedent to the blunt squire Lechmere. Three months earlier the disunity which dogged opposition attempts to oust Walpole had made itself apparent in Samuel Sandys's unsuccessful motion of 13 February 1741, supported by Lyttelton, to remove Walpole 'from the king's counsels and presence for ever'. The subsequent satirical print series *The Motion* shows various opposition leaders, including Pulteney, Marchmont, and the unmistakably emaciated figure of Lyttelton, lagging behind a Whitehall-bound stagecoach exclaiming, 'Lost it!', or, 'Oh, my place!'. Walpole was forced to resign office in February 1742. Cobham's cohorts were excluded from the new Pulteneyite administration drawn up in March. Pulteney's later justification for his own desertion of patriotism included the accusation that Lyttelton, Pitt, and the Grenvilles had also entered negotiations with the ministry before February, a charge substantiated by the Ayscough diaries, which showed that Lyttelton, acting with Frederick's approval, had (unsuccessfully) negotiated Walpole's 'Security and Protection' from impeachment in return for ministerial places.

After Walpole's fall Lyttelton and Pitt remained in the reconstructed broad-bottom opposition, retaining an ambiguous position as members of the household of Frederick, who had become reconciled with his father and the new Pulteney administration. During the next two years Pitt effectively displaced Lyttelton as leader of the Cobham circle: certainly Lyttelton shared little of Pitt's violent anti-Hanoverianism. After the death of Wilmington, Lyttelton was one of a junto of nine then controlling opposition policy who favoured a coalition with the Pelhams to overthrow Carteret. On Carteret's downfall, Lyttelton was appointed a lord of the Treasury in the new broad-bottom administration in December 1744 and was subsequently dismissed from Frederick's household. With the rest of the group he joined Pitt, who was still out of place, in harassing the government: but on Pitt's admission to office in February 1746 he once again became a staunch defender of the administration.

When his former master Prince Frederick launched the new Leicester House opposition in 1747, Lyttelton, now a staunch ministerialist, was deeply embarrassed by the publication of Bolingbroke's *The Idea of a Patriot King*, an untimely reminder of his former patriot allegiances, and refused Bolingbroke permission publicly to dedicate the work to him, as it had been in its manuscript form in 1738: 'Mr Lyttelton sent him word, that he begged nothing might be inscribed to him that was to reflect on Lord Orford, for that he was now leagued with all Lord Orford's friends' (Walpole, *Corr.*, 20.59). In fact in 1747 Lyttelton himself redeployed for ministerial purposes the same broad-bottom tactics as the new Leicester House opposition in a rival bid to gain tory support for the ministry. In the anonymously published pamphlet *A Letter to the Tories* (1747), he posed as a non-Jacobite tory in order to exhort the tories to an alliance with the ministerial whigs. His disguise was soon seen through in Horace Walpole's *Three Letters to the Whigs, Occasion'd by the Letter to the Tories* (1748), but his friend the writer Edward Moore defended him from this attack in *The Trial of Selim the Persian for Divers High Crimes and Misdemeanours* (also 1748). In the months before Frederick's death in 1751 it appears that Lyttelton, Pitt, and others from the cousinhood had attempted to renew their connections with him: according to Horace Walpole, rumour circulated that after Frederick's death Lyttelton had written a letter to his father lamenting the loss of this new arrangement and that the letter had inadvertently fallen into the wrong hands and been drawn to George II's attention. Egmont noted that no one knew how far this negotiation had really proceeded except the prince, and 'the secret is buried with him in his grave' (Sedgwick, 1.60).

On the death of his father in September 1751 Lyttelton succeeded to the baronetcy and took over the running of Hagley Hall. In political terms the most significant event of the 1750s was the rift which occurred between himself and other members of the cousinhood, a quarrel which was to last for several years. On Henry Pelham's death in March 1754 Lyttelton resigned his seat on the Treasury board and accepted the post of cofferer in the duke of Newcastle's administration. He refused to join Pitt in opposing Newcastle after the other cousins were turned out, but in November 1755 'on the contrary was made Chancellor of the Exchequer in the room of Legge, which was resented with the greatest acrimony by the whole Cousinhood' (*Memoirs and Speeches of … Waldegrave*, 174). Lyttelton was widely regarded as being personally unsuited to the role of chancellor, lacking the financial acuity to master the office. When Newcastle resigned in November 1756 in the face of popular opposition, Lyttelton retired from office, and on 18 November 1756 he was created Baron Lyttelton of Frankley.

Hagley, marriages, and personal life In his personal life during these years Lyttelton experienced the extremes of brief happiness and prolonged unhappiness. Numerous accounts suggest that his personal manner, perhaps as a consequence of shyness, could be awkward and aloof, particularly in his dealings with women. He was fortunate in his first marriage, on 15 June 1742, to Lucy Fortescue (1717/18–1747), the 24-year-old daughter of Hugh Fortescue of Filleigh, Devon, and his wife, Lucy Aylmer. Lyttelton was devoted to her, and Thomson depicts him and his 'lov'd Lucinda' as a latter-day Adam and Eve in the Edenic setting of Hagley in a passage added to *Spring* (1744). The marriage produced three children, Thomas *Lyttelton (1744–1779), Lucy, and Mary. His wife's early death, on 19 January 1747 at the age of twenty-nine, while giving birth to Mary, was a tremendous blow. Lyttelton's *Monody* to her (probably his most famous poem, later parodied by Smollett) has a simple directness which transcends its literary conventionality. Lyttelton's remarriage two years later, on 10 August 1749, to Elizabeth (1716–1795), the daughter of Sir Robert *Rich, fourth baronet (1685–1768), and Elizabeth Griffith, proved a mistake. There seems to have been little warmth between them. The children from his first marriage went to live with their grandmother at Ebrington in Gloucestershire. Lyttelton would arrange for his daughter Lucy to spend time with him at Radway, the home of his friend the architect Sanderson Miller, but her stepmother was never of the party. The marriage became acutely strained in 1756 when 'scandalous reports' (Dickins and Stanton, 346) circulated widely about her affair with George Durant. It reached a crisis in the spring of 1759 when, according to Lyttelton, she made herself the 'talk of the town' (Wyndham, 2.279–80) by writing love letters to an Italian opera singer, Signor Tenduchi, an episode which led to Lyttelton's formal separation from his wife after granting her a separate maintenance equal to her jointure. Yet there were also other consolations during these years. One of these was spiritual. As a young man Lyttelton may well have imbibed some of his uncle Cobham's anti-clericalism, if not atheism. But in 1747 he emerged as a devout Christian, producing, under the influence of his cousin the poet and cleric Gilbert West, his *Observations on the Conversion and Apostleship of St Paul*, a work to which, Dr Johnson conceded, 'infidelity has never been able to fabricate a specious answer' (Johnson, 3.450).

Long before he inherited Hagley Hall from his father in 1751, Lyttelton had embarked on the ambitious gardening programme which would make Hagley Park one of the most admired landscape gardens of the eighteenth century. Work was well in hand by July 1739, when Pope made his first visit, and by 1745 he had created a place which rivalled his uncle Cobham's estate at Stowe and was recognized as a distinct advance in garden art. The park enjoyed a spectacular natural situation, and was 'improved' by Lyttelton, who was in part inspired by Pope's ideas. It acquired an Ionic rotunda, a Palladian bridge, a grotto, and a hermitage; on Whichbury Hill within the park the ruins of a Roman camp were 'cut out into ridings … [to afford] many romantic and beautiful scenes' (Brownell, 223). In 1748 Sanderson Miller, doyen of the Gothic, supplied a 'ruined' quasi-medieval tower for the grounds. But the new Hagley Hall designed by Miller and erected between 1756 and 1760 was designed in the fashionable Palladian style, plans for a Gothic building having been rejected. Lyttelton's interest during these years in 'romantick' landscapes pervades his *Account of a Journey into Wales*, written in 1756 though not printed until 1774, one of the earliest Romantic tourist accounts of Wales, containing a notable description of Mount Snowdon's sublimity.

Lyttelton as friend and patron Lyttelton's historical significance derives as much, if not more, from his extensive activities as a friend and patron of writers as it does from his political career. Although in the late 1730s some of these activities were driven by a political agenda, Lyttelton was also capable of a more disinterested patronage. He genuinely enjoyed the company of writers and took pleasure in involving himself in their literary careers. His friendship with Pope transcended party politics, as did his friendship with James Thomson. Thomson was a frequent visitor at Hagley. It was here that he revised *The Seasons* in the summer of 1743. The interleaved copy of the first volume of his 1738 *Works*, on which Thomson wrote his revisions, also contains many revisions in Lyttelton's own hand. Lyttelton, in his posthumous edition of Thomson's poems, was responsible for revising and shortening *Liberty* (1735–6), imbuing its patriotism with a slightly more optimistic slant, as befitted a then supporter of the ministry. It was Lyttelton who arranged the posthumous performance of Thomson's tragedy *Coriolanus* at Covent Garden in January 1749 for his family's benefit. Thomson included an affectionate tribute to Lyttelton in his *Castle of Indolence* (1748), 'serene yet warm, humane yet firm his mind', a man whose active nature made him a reluctant inhabitant of Thomson's palace of pleasure.

Lyttelton's friendship with the dramatist and novelist Henry Fielding dated from their schooldays at Eton. The verse epistle that Fielding composed about 1731–2 defending his cousin Lady Mary Wortley Montagu from Pope's recent attack on her was dedicated to Lyttelton. It has been argued by Thomas Cleary that Fielding's political sympathies closely followed those of Lyttelton and other members of the cousinhood, both in and out of government. It was to Lyttelton that Fielding dedicated *Tom Jones* (1749), a novel which he had read in manuscript and had done much to promote. It has been suggested that Lyttelton, sometimes known as the Good Lord Lyttelton (in recognition of his moral character, but partly to distinguish him from his reprobate son the 'wicked' Lord Lyttelton), may have helped inspire *Tom Jones*'s Squire Allworthy. Other literary friends were Richard Glover, David Mallet, the love poet James Hammond, Richard Shenstone, who engraved a tribute to him at the Leasowes, Edward Moore (whom he helped to found the paper *The World* in 1753), and Voltaire, with whom he corresponded. Yet Lyttelton probably received sharper and more lasting criticism from his role as literary patron than he did from his years as an opposition MP. From the early portrait of the propaganda master Littledone in the late 1730s, to the attacks on him for using his herd of 'placemen and pensionaries' to tout *Tom Jones* in the coffee houses, through to Smollett's cruel caricature in *Peregrine Pickle* (1751) of the naïve but vain Sir Gosling Scragg, fed with the 'soft pap of dedication', Lyttelton was accused of using his wealth to gratify his vanity and unfairly sway literary opinion. Other writers, notably Lord Hervey and especially Horace Walpole, delighted in ridiculing his unco-ordinated movements, ungainly appearance, and general air of unworldliness.

Late years Upon his accession to the House of Lords in November 1756 Lyttelton continued to play a vigorous role in political debate, but during the years of political controversy and instability which marked the eight successive ministries between 1757 and 1770 he declined to take office when offered to him, preferring a back-seat role. His rift with the Pitt–Grenville cousinhood lasted for at least eight years. During the debates on the Prussian treaty and the bill for the extension of habeas corpus in 1758 Lyttelton was violently attacked by Temple: both peers were compelled by the house to agree not to take the matter any further. Horace Walpole reported in April 1764 that Lyttelton, Pitt, and Temple had once again become reconciled: that year they attempted to form a party against Lord Bute, and Lyttelton spoke on 30 April 1765 in a debate on the Regency Bill arguing that the regent should be nominated by the king in conjunction with parliament in an effort to curtail Bute's influence. During the efforts to create a new administration in the summer of 1765 Lyttelton refused the offer of the Treasury made by the duke of Cumberland, George III's uncle and intermediary and Pitt's old enemy. Lyttelton once again remained loyal to the cousinhood when he refused Cumberland's offer of a cabinet seat in the new Rockingham administration. He was one of the few peers to protest Rockingham's repeal of the Stamp Act in 1766, an unpopular stance 'delivering down an attestation of their tyrannic principles to posterity' (Walpole, *Corr.*, 22.410)—incompatible, some thought, with the libertarian principles of Lyttelton's former patriot youth. When it was widely rumoured in September 1767 that Pitt was about to resign, Lyttelton sent Grenville, one of the chief contenders for office, plans for an unlikely coalition ministry between the Grenvillians, Rockinghams, and Bedfords, with himself as 'cabinet councillor extraordinary'. In his last years he joined in the cousinhood's support for Wilkes, in January 1770 openly condemning the proceedings of the Commons against him.

Much of the energy that Lyttelton had directed at politics in his early years was in his later years channelled into his writing—two large projects in particular, the *Dialogues of the Dead*, first published anonymously in 1760, and the *History of the Life of Henry the Second*, finally published in 1767. The *Dialogues of the Dead*, three of which, nos. 26–8, were written by the bluestocking writer Elizabeth Montagu, with whom Lyttelton forged a close friendship in his later years, were very well received, going through three editions within three months, the first selling out on the day it appeared, 17 May. Lyttelton published four more new dialogues in 1765, which were added to the rest in a fourth edition that year. The dialogues were frequently reprinted in periodicals and anthologies. Subsequent criticism has been less favourable, much in the vein of Horace Walpole's scathing inversion '*Dead* dialogues' (Walpole, *Corr.*, 21.407). Certainly Lyttelton's *Dialogues* lack the humour and playfulness of their Lucianic model: the dialogue between Addison and Swift in particular betrays Lyttelton's dislike of satire. Many of the dialogues deal with politics ancient and modern, and here Lyttelton is cautious to avoid offence, offering a balanced moderation between speakers which can seem bland. The most thought-provoking is perhaps that between William Penn and Cortez, a dialogue which seems to undermine the hollowness of Penn's piety and which gives the last word to Cortez. The *History of the Life of Henry the Second* was Lyttelton's labour of love, a work on which he was engaged intermittently over a period of some thirty years. Lyttelton first mentioned it in a letter to Pope of 13 June 1741, then intending it as a 'Work of some Instruction and Pleasure to my Countrymen, and I hope to the Prince my Master, for whose service I chiefly design it' (*Correspondence of Alexander Pope*, 4.348). Frederick was long since dead when the first two volumes and an unnumbered volume of notes were published in 1767, the third volume with notes in December 1771. Lyttelton had clearly been obsessed by the inaccuracy of his printers: Dr Johnson claimed that the work had been printed 'twice over', some parts three or four times, and that this 'ambitious accuracy' cost him at least £1000. Critical opinion was mixed, but many concurred with Walpole that it was a laborious read.

Lyttelton died at Hagley Hall on 22 August 1773, aged sixty-four. He was buried in the parish church, where he had requested that an inscription to his memory be engraved on his first wife's monument. The account of his death given by his physician appended to Johnson's life of Lyttelton (1774) implies that he may have died of hepatitis. Johnson prints this account in full in his brief biography of Lyttelton to 'spare me the task of his moral character' (Johnson, 3.454). Johnson's apparent distaste for the task in hand may have sprung less from personal dislike of Lyttelton than from his particular suspicion of the two dominant areas of Lyttelton's life, his engagement in the patriot politics of the 1730s (a cause to which the young Johnson had once himself subscribed) and his claims to literary patronage, a Johnsonian *bête noire*. Ironically, it is precisely to these two areas that more recent accounts of Lyttelton's life and work have paid especial attention.

CHRISTINE GERRARD

Sources *Memoirs and correspondence of George, Lord Lyttelton, from 1734 to 1773*, ed. R. Phillimore, 2 vols. (1845) • R. M. Davis, *The good Lord Lyttelton* (Bethlehem, Pa., 1939) • L. M. Wiggin, *The faction of cousins: a political account of the Grenvilles, 1733–1763* (New Haven, Conn., 1958) • C. Gerrard, *The patriot opposition to Walpole: politics, poetry, and national myth, 1725–1742* (1994) • L. Dickins and M. Stanton, *An eighteenth century correspondence being the letters … to Sanderson Miller* (1910) • Walpole, *Corr.* • H. Walpole, *Memoirs of the reign of King George the Second*, ed. Lord Holland, 2nd edn, 3 vols. (1846) • *The correspondence of Alexander Pope*, ed. G. Sherburn, 5 vols. (1956) • S. Johnson, *Lives of the English poets*, ed. G. B. Hill, [new edn], 3 vols. (1905) • M. Wyndham, *Chronicles of the eighteenth century: founded on the correspondence of Sir Thomas Lyttelton and his family*, 2 vols. (1924) • M. R. Brownell, *Alexander Pope and the arts of Georgian England* (1978), 219–23 • Nichols, *Lit. anecdotes* • T. Nash, *Collections for the history of Worcestershire*, 2 vols. (1781–2) • John, Lord Hervey, *Some materials towards memoirs of the reign of King George II*, ed. R. Sedgwick, 3 vols. (1931) • M. McCarthy, 'The building of Hagley Hall', *Burlington Magazine* (April 1976), 214–25 • R. Harris, ed., 'A Leicester House political diary, 1742–3', *Camden miscellany, XXXI*, CS, 4th ser., 44 (1992), 375–411 • *The memoirs and speeches of James, 2nd Earl Waldegrave, 1742–1763*, ed. J. C. D. Clark (1988) • T. R. Cleary, *Henry Fielding: political writer* (Waterloo, Ont., 1984) • R. R. Sedgwick, 'Lyttelton, George', HoP, *Commons, 1715–54* • J. Brooke, 'Lyttelton, Sir George', HoP, *Commons, 1754–90* • R. Graves, *Recollection of some particulars in the life of the late William Shenstone Esq.* (1788) • GEC, *Peerage* • Hagley Hall, Worcestershire, Hagley MSS

Archives Hagley Hall, Worcestershire, corresp. and papers • NL Wales, travel journal in Wales • Worcs. RO, legal documents, corresp. and papers | BL, corresp. with Philip Doddridge, RP 1778 [copies] • BL, corresp. with earls of Hardwicke, Add. MSS 35591–35611 • BL, letters to duchess of Marlborough, Add. MS 61467 • BL, corresp. with William Julius Mickle, RP 272 [copies] • BL, corresp. with Elizabeth Montagu and others, RP 2377 [copies] • BL, corresp. with duke of Newcastle, Add. MSS 32707–33068 • BL, letters to Mrs Stephen Poyntz • Hunt. L., letters to Elizabeth Montagu • PRO, letters to first earl of Chatham, PRO 30/8 • U. Leeds, Brotherton L., letters to Alexander Pope • Yale U., Beinecke L., corresp. with Philip Doddridge; corresp. with William Julius Mickle

Likenesses B. West, portrait, 1773, Hagley Hall, Worcestershire [*see illus.*] • R. Dunkarton, mezzotint, pubd 1774 (after B. West, 1773), BM • G. H. Every, mezzotint (after J. Reynolds), BM, NPG • G. Townsend, caricature, NPG • oils, NPG • political print, repro. in F. G. Stephens, *Catalogue of prints and drawings in the British Museum: division I, political and personal satires*, 3/1 (1877), pp. 369–72

Lyttelton, George William, **fourth Baron Lyttelton and fourth Baron Westcote (1817–1876)**, educationist, eldest of the three sons of William Henry *Lyttelton, third Baron Lyttelton of Frankley and third Baron Westcote of Ballymore (1782–1837), and his wife, Sarah *Lyttelton (1787–1870), daughter of George John *Spencer, second Earl Spencer, was born in London on 31 March 1817. William Henry *Lyttelton (1820–1884) was his younger brother. He was educated at Eton College, 1827–33, and entered Trinity College, Cambridge, the following year. His intellectual qualities were rapidly recognized. He was a Newcastle scholar, a medallist (1834), and graduated BA, MA, and joint senior classic in 1838.

While still at Cambridge, Lyttelton succeeded to the peerage in 1837 on the death of his father. Many of his activities were directed towards the west midlands, where the family home, Hagley Hall, was situated. He was lord lieutenant of Worcestershire from 1839 to the end of his life. He formed an early interest in education, promoting night schools and working men's institutes. He became principal of Queen's College, Birmingham, in 1845, the first president of the Birmingham and Midland Institute in 1853, and he took an active interest in promoting the Oxford and Cambridge local examinations in the midlands. He was one of the founders (1852) of Saltley Training College, Birmingham, a Church of England institution, and taught in the Sunday school at Hagley for many years. Lyttelton's high-church outlook was formed mainly at Cambridge and pervaded his whole life. He took a close

George William Lyttelton, fourth Baron Lyttelton and fourth Baron Westcote (1817–1876), by Ernest Edwards, pubd 1865

interest in episcopal matters and was critical of many aspects of the church. When the Association for Promoting the Reform of Convocation was formed in 1869, he became its first president.

Lyttelton had become acquainted with Mary Glynne (1813–1857), daughter of Sir Stephen Glynne, eighth baronet, of Hawarden, when he was eighteen. Mary was a year younger than her sister, Catherine, and they were devoted to each other. A double wedding took place at Hawarden in July 1839, between Mary and Lyttelton, and Catherine and William Gladstone. Gladstone admired his new brother-in-law for his brilliant scholarship and his wit. In 1861 the two men published a volume of translations into Greek of part of Milton's *Comus* and Tennyson's *Lotos-Eaters* and into Latin of Goldsmith's *The Deserted Village* and Gray's *Ode to Adversity* (work on the volume was intended by Gladstone to be a distraction for Lyttelton following the death of his wife). The Glynnes had evolved a private language, Glynnese, which an outsider would not readily have understood. Lyttelton compiled a *Glossary of the Glynne Language*, which was privately printed in 1851.

Gladstone wrote of Lyttelton's character after his death, 'It was in the highest degree child-like and in the highest degree manly: a manner occasionally blunt veiled a temper of remarkable sweetness' (*Brief Memorials*, 47). He possessed a high moral character and held sincerely to his beliefs, often in the face of opposition. Lacking in tact, he gained the reputation of an eccentric. When he was under-secretary of state for the colonies in Peel's administration (January–July 1846) his chief, Gladstone, was obliged to rebuke him for amending the minutes of senior civil servants. Of a manic-depressive temperament, he found the strains of office very great and suffered from depression as a result. He held no further political office.

Lyttelton's interest in colonial affairs now took a different form. In 1847 Edward Gibbon Wakefield, an expert on colonial settlement, and John Robert Hadley, the son of an Anglo-Irish landowner, established the Canterbury Association, a Church of England corporation, which founded the province of Canterbury in New Zealand in 1850. Its aim was to buy up land from the Maori and resell it to settlers. The profits were to be used mainly in founding a cathedral, schools, and a university. The association soon ran into financial problems and Lyttelton, who was never wealthy, as its chairman was called on to assist in clearing the debts. The work of the association occupied much of his time. The port of Lyttelton, near Christchurch, commemorates his connection with the scheme. A new constitution provided for the establishment of six provinces in New Zealand in 1852, and the Canterbury Association was dissolved. Lyttelton visited the colony in 1867–8, and recorded his experiences in two lectures given in 1869.

From the 1850s there was a revival of public interest in the problems of public education. In an address, *Thoughts on National Education*, delivered in 1855, Lyttelton declared himself in favour of compulsory elementary schooling on a nationwide basis, supported by public funds or rates, though he deprecated attempts to exclude religion from school education. He was a supporter of the National Association for the Promotion of Social Science, which provided a forum for discussion of educational questions. He was one of the seven members of the royal commission, appointed in 1861, under the chairmanship of the fourth earl of Clarendon, to investigate the state of the nine great public schools. In 1864 another royal commission was instituted, chaired by the first Baron Taunton, to inquire into the 3000 endowed private and proprietary schools not covered by Clarendon. Lyttelton was once more called upon to serve. Although by background an élitist, he believed that intellectual ability should be recognized regardless of class, and favoured scholarships for poor boys. He was also convinced that educational provision for the daughters of the middle classes was inadequate. In 1867 he was responsible for drafting the chapter for the Taunton report which advocated more schools for girls and the training of suitably qualified women to teach them. He surprised many colleagues by changing his views on the question of the conscience clause, now supporting the right of parents to withdraw their children from religious instruction in schools.

The Taunton commission report, published in 1868, revealed the muddled state of the endowments and their application, and recommended that a new central authority should oversee the administration of education by provincial boards. This recommendation was received with hostility by Conservative politicians, headmasters, and governors. Instead, an Endowed Schools Act the following year empowered a commission to carry out much needed reforms. Gladstone, now prime minister, appointed Lyttelton as head of the endowed school commission, assisted by two other commissioners, to redistribute charitable endowments, reform governing bodies and trustees, and ensure that schools were financially efficient. He confronted well-established institutions in a somewhat quixotic manner and without public support. When the Conservatives came to power in 1874, the commission's work was transferred to the Charity Commission and Lyttelton lost his post.

Lyttelton's wife, Mary, died in 1857, exhausted by childbearing and leaving eight sons and four daughters. The third son, Neville Gerald *Lyttelton, had a military career; the fifth son, Arthur Temple *Lyttelton, was a bishop; the eighth son, Alfred *Lyttelton, became colonial secretary; and the seventh son, Edward *Lyttelton, was a schoolmaster and a cricketer. The second daughter, Lucy Caroline [*see* Cavendish, Lucy Caroline, *under* Cavendish, Lord Frederick Charles], was a churchwoman and promoter of women's education, as was the third daughter, Lavinia [*see* Talbot, Lavinia]. On occasion, the family fielded a full cricket eleven of Lytteltons.

In 1869 Lyttelton married Sybella Harriet, widow of Humphrey Francis Mildmay MP. They had three daughters. He requested Gladstone to grant him an earldom in November 1873 as he disliked the possibility of inheriting the title of Viscount Cobham from his distant cousin, the duke of Buckingham and Chandos, but this was refused. Lyttelton became increasingly subject to fits of depression and in 1876 he was accompanied by his family to Italy. On his return to London, he was placed under close medical supervision but on Easter Tuesday, 19 April, he managed to elude his attendant and threw himself over the balusters of the staircase in the family house, 18 Park Crescent, Portman Place, London. He died the same day and was buried on 22 April 1876 at Hagley. PETER GORDON

Sources J. F. Mackarness, ed., *Brief memorials of Lord Lyttelton* (1876) • G. W. Lyttelton, *Ephemera*, 2 vols. (1865–72) • B. Askwith, *The Lytteltons: a family chronicle of the nineteenth century* (1975) • P. Gordon, *Selection for secondary education* (1980) • D. I. Allsobrook, *Schools for the shires: the reform of middle-class education in mid-Victorian England* (1986) • Gladstone, *Diaries* • GEC, *Peerage*

Archives CAC Cam., family corresp. and papers • Canterbury Museum, corresp., diaries, and papers | BL, corresp. with W. E. Gladstone, Add. MSS 44238–44240 • Bodl. Oxf., corresp. with Lord Kimberley • Bodl. Oxf., corresp. with Sir T. Phillipps • Bodl. Oxf., Wilberforce MSS • Canterbury Museum, corresp. with J. R. Godley • Devon RO, letters to Sir Thomas Dyke Acland • LPL, corresp. with A. C. Tait • NL Wales, corresp. with earl of Powis • St Deiniol's Library, Hawarden, letters to Glynne and Gladstone families and duke of Newcastle • Trinity Cam., letters to J. W. Blakesley • Trinity Cam., corresp. with W. Whewell • U. Durham, Grey of Howick MSS • Hagley, Worcestershire, Hagley Hall MSS

Likenesses E. Edwards, photograph, pubd 1865, NPG [*see illus.*] • J. Forsyth, statue on tomb, 1888, Worcester Cathedral • G. Richmond, portrait, Hagley Hall, Worcestershire

Wealth at death under £12,000: probate, 6 Sept 1876, *CGPLA Eng. & Wales*

Lyttelton, Sir Henry, second baronet (1623/4–1693). *See under* Lyttelton, Sir Thomas, first baronet (1595/6–1650).

Lyttelton, (Octavia) Laura (1862–1886). *See under* Lyttelton, Alfred (1857–1913).

Lyttelton [*née* Clive], **Mary Kathleen (1856–1907)**, women's activist, was the second daughter of George Clive (1805–1880) of Ballycrog, co. Mayo, and Perrystone Court, Herefordshire, and his wife, Ann Sybella Martha (*d.* 1907), second daughter of Sir Thomas Harvie Farquhar. Mary's father was for many years chairman of Herefordshire quarter sessions, a Metropolitan Police magistrate, and, from 1852 to 1862, under-secretary of state for the Home Office.

On 3 August 1880 Mary married the Revd Arthur Temple *Lyttelton (1852–1903), then tutor at Keble College, Oxford. In 1882, when her husband was appointed master of Selwyn College, they moved to Cambridge, where 'the early generations of Selwyn men were conscious of Mrs Lyttelton's influence as the hostess at the lodge' (*The Times*). Lyttelton later became bishop of Southampton (1898).

Mary Lyttelton devoted much of her life to fighting for the improvement of women's lives in general, and for the extension of the suffrage to women in particular. Three years after the formation of the National Union of Women Workers (NUWW) in 1895 she was among the vice-presidents; she also served on the executive committee before taking over the post of president of the NUWW. Believing firmly that 'the withholding of the franchise is very prejudicial to the right development of women, and that the education given by the vote is essential to their true progress' (Mrs A. T. Lyttelton, *Women and their Work*, 1901, 10), Mrs Lyttelton also sat on the executive committee of the Central Society for Women's Suffrage, formed in 1888 when the women's movement split over its relationship with the main political parties, before it reformed in 1897 as the National Union of Women's Suffrage Societies.

Mrs Lyttelton's views were succinctly set out in her book *Women and their Work*, which she published in 1901. Including chapters on 'the family', 'the household', and 'philanthropic and social work', the book was a manual advising women on modes of behaviour, duties, and goals. She believed that such a manual was required because, at the beginning of the twentieth century, society, and particularly the position of women in society, was in a state of transition and 'it is with women at this moment that the power to advance and the power to convince lies' (*Women and their Work*, 11). *Women and their Work* was permeated with her deep religious beliefs: she held that each sex should strive for the 'Christian ideal' of 'preserving its own special characteristics' while attempting 'to acquire the highest qualities of the other' (ibid., 25). A woman, she argued, would never be able to advise or be useful to men unless the 'inspiring motive' of her life was 'to glorify God, and to enjoy Him for ever' (ibid., 4).

Mary Lyttelton's approach to social activism was a practical one. She had spent three years as a poor-law guardian and had found the experience invaluable: 'The value of knowing that you are working so to speak, before the public, and that if you make a mistake it will be known, is immense' (Hollis, 17). She was an impressive and intelligent public speaker: her obituary writer in the *Englishwoman's Review* opined that 'Few who heard it will forget the brilliant paper, touched with delightful humour, which she read so recently as last October at the Women's Suffrage meetings of the NUWW at Tunbridge Wells.' 'A considerable student of literature' (*The Times*, 15 Jan 1907), she worked for many years as a journalist, writing reviews and eventually becoming editor of the women's section of the high-church paper, *The Guardian*. She died on 13 January 1907 at Perrystone Court, Herefordshire, from influenza and weakness of the heart, and was survived by a daughter and two sons. SERENA KELLY

Sources *The Times* (15 Jan 1907) • *Englishwoman's Review*, 38 (1907), 72 • P. Hollis, *Ladies elect: women in English local government, 1865–1914* (1987), 16–17 • Burke, *Gen. GB* (1914)

Wealth at death £1562 2*s*. 3*d*.: administration, 24 Feb 1907, *CGPLA Eng. & Wales*

Lyttelton, Sir Neville Gerald (1845–1931), army officer, was born at Hagley, Worcestershire, on 28 October 1845, the third of the eight sons of George William *Lyttelton, fourth Baron Lyttelton (1817–1876), educationist, and his first wife, Mary (1813–1857), second daughter of Sir Stephen Richard Glynne, eighth baronet, and sister of Mrs W. E. Gladstone. Gladstone was both Lyttelton's uncle and his godfather, and Lyttelton felled trees with him. The brother of Arthur Temple *Lyttelton, Edward *Lyttelton, and Alfred *Lyttelton, Neville (Nevy to his family) was allegedly the least able of the Lyttelton brothers. From a devoutly Anglican home, he attended the Revd W. M. Church's small but aristocratic private school at Geddington, near Kettering, Northamptonshire, from September 1854 to December 1857. At Eton College from 1858 to 1864, he was president of Pop in 1863—'something like king of the school' (Lyttelton, 26)—house captain, commandant of the Volunteer corps, and in the Eton eleven (1862–4). In 1864, without a crammer, he passed the army examination, and in January 1865 was commissioned ensign (by purchase) into the rifle brigade, a regiment much favoured by Etonians, and went to Canada where he helped defeat the 1866 Fenian invasion. In 1867 he acted as secretary to the Oregon boundary commission. In July 1869 he became, by purchase, lieutenant. He was promoted captain in October 1877 and major in February 1882.

After various posts in England, Ireland, and India (where he shot big game and served in the expedition of 1877–8 against the Jowaki Afridis), Lyttelton became, probably because of his relationship to Gladstone, private secretary to H. C. E. Childers, secretary of state for war in Gladstone's 1880 ministry. In 1882 he took part in the Egyptian campaign, including the battle of Tell al-Kebir (mentioned in dispatches, brevet lieutenant-colonel), as aide-de-camp to Sir John Miller Adye to whom, as governor of Gibraltar, he was military secretary from 1883 to 1885. He married, on 1 October 1883, a second cousin, Katharine Sarah (*d.* 27

Sir Neville Gerald Lyttelton (1845–1931), by Lafayette, 1905

March 1943), youngest daughter of James Archibald Stuart-*Wortley [*see under* Wortley, James Archibald Stuart- (1776–1845)].

From 1885 to 1890 Lyttelton was military secretary to Donald Mackay, eleventh Lord Reay, governor of Bombay, and after joining the 3rd battalion of his regiment at Jullundur as second in command he returned to England in 1893, having shortly before been promoted to command the 1st battalion. He then commanded the 2nd battalion in Ireland.

A junior member of the Wolseley ring, Lyttelton was, through Buller, from December 1894 assistant adjutant-general in AG7 department (responsible for updating mobilization planning) at the War Office, and also from 1895 secretary of the new army board. From October 1897 he was assistant military secretary. In 1897 he was made CB.

Recommended by Sir Francis Grenfell for the appointment, in 1898, under Kitchener in the Sudan, Lyttelton took command of the 2nd British brigade, including at the battle of Omdurman; he was promoted major-general. In 1899 he commanded the 2nd infantry brigade at Aldershot.

In the Second South African War (1899–1902) Lyttelton commanded in Natal under Buller the 4th brigade, and successively the 2nd and 4th divisions. He was considered one of the few senior officers who emerged with an enhanced reputation from the war, gaining credit for his handling of his troops at Spion Kop, Vaal Krantz, and the relief of Ladysmith. He later contrasted Omdurman, where '50,000 fanatics streamed across the open regardless of cover to certain death', with Colenso, 'where I never saw a Boer all day … and it was our men who were the victims' (Lyttelton, 212). Charming, ambitious, and trusted by Buller, he became Buller's leading covert detractor, criticizing him to other officers and Bron Herbert, the *Times* correspondent. According to Henry Rawlinson, Lyttelton was 'full of abuse of Buller' (Pakenham, 368). He commanded in the eastern Transvaal, in the operations against General C. R. De Wet, and in Natal again. He was promoted lieutenant-general and made KCB (1902). After the war, he was commander-in-chief in South Africa from June 1902 to January 1904, and he and his wife tried to reconcile British and Boers. He and General Louis Botha discussed the conduct of the war with great interest.

Following the recommendations of the War Office (reconstitution) committee (the Esher committee), in 1904 the War Office was reorganized. Apparently the most important phase of Lyttelton's career was as chief of the general staff—though initially there was no such staff—and first military member of the new army council from February 1904 to 1908, when he was involved with the army reforms under first Balfour and Arnold-Forster and then Haldane. However, Lyttelton's contribution was less than his position suggested.

Apparently Edward VII initially suggested Lyttelton for his posts, but from the first defence insiders were doubtful and critical. Fisher considered him 'the dullest dog I'd ever met! We Don't want dull dogs for this new scheme' (Gooch, 48). Esher wanted French, whom the king vetoed. Balfour, a friend of the Lyttelton family, favoured Lyttelton's appointment. He was apparently appointed largely because he was an establishment, safe, compliant man. His brother Alfred considered him not 'intellectually up to the post' (Fraser, 152). Repington warned Esher that Lyttelton knew almost nothing of the problems of imperial defence and strategy. Lacking administrative and strategic capacity, he was incompetent and inactive. Arnold-Forster (secretary of state for war, 1903–5) wrote that Lyttelton was 'becoming a scandal … the Army laughs at him … the work of the department is getting into a hopeless mess' (ibid., 152) and wanted him sacked. Balfour, advised by Esher of the lack of any viable replacement, refused. In February 1906 Sir George Clarke wrote that Lyttelton 'has been a disastrous first C.G.S.' (Gooch, 100).

Haldane, secretary of state for war from December 1905, reduced the army council to a largely executive role. He did not have a high opinion of Lyttelton, whom he considered did not support him effectively. According to E. M. Spiers, Lyttelton was feckless, malleable, and failed to lead the army council. In August 1906, following the report of the royal commission on war stores in South Africa, which criticized the military administration in South Africa while Lyttelton was commander-in-chief—though exonerating him from personal involvement in the waste and corruption—Lyttelton offered to resign. Haldane refused to accept his resignation, preferring to retain 'an indebted and amenable Chief of the General Staff' (Spiers, *Haldane*, 123). Both the initiative and the detailed planning of Haldane's reforms were by men other than Lyttelton, who was doubtful about Haldane's special reserve and Territorial Force proposals, preferring a militia scheme he himself drafted. According to Sir James Edmonds he favoured rifle brigade officers for promotion. His limitations were shown by his suggestion, at a committee of imperial defence meeting on 6 June 1906, that a land attack on Egypt across the Sinai peninsula could be defeated by ships in the Suez Canal. He was concerned with the training of the staff and the formation of the Officers' Training Corps. In this and in two other matters, events were to justify him: in a dispute with Arnold-Forster over the introduction of the 18-pounder field gun, on which he and his military colleagues succeeded, and in his criticism of the changes in staff organization inaugurated by Kitchener in India, of which he strongly disapproved and to which he later attributed the disasters in Mesopotamia during the First World War.

In 1908 Lyttelton, promoted full general in 1906, went to Ireland as commander-in-chief. From 1912 until his death he was governor of the Royal Hospital, Chelsea. During the First World War he was a member of several committees and of the commission on the war in Mesopotamia. He was appointed GCB in 1907 and GCVO in 1911, and he was sworn of the Irish privy council in 1908. He was a keen tennis player and cricketer: a member of MCC and I Zingari, he scored eight centuries. He published his memoirs, *Eighty Years* (1927), in which he was critical of Buller and Arnold-Forster, and misleading on his own role as chief of the general staff. Following family tradition, he supported the Liberals.

Lyttelton died at the Governor's House, the Royal Hospital, Chelsea, London, on 6 July 1931, survived by his wife and their three daughters, the eldest of whom, Lucy Blanche, married C. F. G. Masterman, and the youngest, Mary Hermione, married W. L. Hichens. An aristocrat whose career was facilitated by his aristocratic and political connections, Lyttelton was a brave and competent field commander, but a failure as chief of the general staff and member of the army council. ROGER T. STEARN

Sources *The Times* (7 July 1931) • N. Lyttelton, *Eighty years* (1927) • personal knowledge (1949) [*DNB*] • E. M. Spiers, *Haldane: an army reformer* (1980) • J. Gooch, *The plans of war: the general staff and British military strategy, c.1900–1916* (1974) • T. Pakenham, *The Boer War* (1979) • P. Magnus, *Kitchener: portrait of an imperialist* (1958) • T. Travers, *The killing ground* (1987) • P. Fraser, *Lord Esher* (1973) • E. M. Spiers, *The late Victorian army, 1868–1902* (1992) • G. R. Searle, *Corruption in British politics, 1895–1930* (1987) • *WWW* • Kelly, *Handbk* • *Hart's Army List* (1891) • Burke, *Peerage* • H. E. C. Stapylton, *Second series of Eton school lists … 1853–1892* (1900) • GEC, *Peerage* • J. P. Trevelyan, *The life of Mrs Humphry Ward* (1923?) • S. Fletcher, *Victorian girls: Lord Lyttelton's daughters* (1997) • Gladstone, *Diaries* • *CGPLA Eng. & Wales* (1931) • *DNB*

Archives Bodl. Oxf., diaries • King's Lond., Liddell Hart C., letters and copies of letters to his family • Queen Mary College, London, corresp. • Worcs. RO, corresp. and papers | BL OIOC, letters to governor of Bombay, MS Eur. F 102 • NRA, priv. coll., letters to Sir J. S. Ewart • St Deiniol's Library, Hawarden, letters to Henry Gladstone • U. Birm. L., letters to his daughter, Lucy Masterman

Likenesses two photographs, 1865–*c*.1890, repro. in Lyttelton, *Eighty years*, 48, 144 • A. Stuart-Wortley, oils, 1893, Royal Hospital, Chelsea, London • Lafayette, photograph, 1905, V&A [*see illus.*] • H. H. Brown, oils, *c*.1912–1913, Royal Hospital, Chelsea, London •

H. H. Brown, oils, Hagley Hall, Worcestershire • H. Browne, portrait, repro. in Lyttelton, *Eighty years*, frontispiece • Spy [L. Ward], cartoon, NPG; repro. in *VF* (5 Sept 1901)
Wealth at death £1575 1s. 11d.: probate, 25 Sept 1931, *CGPLA Eng. & Wales*

Lyttelton, Oliver, first Viscount Chandos (1893–1972), businessman and politician, was born on 15 March 1893, the only son (another died in infancy) and elder child of Alfred *Lyttelton (1857–1913), politician, and his second wife, Edith Sophy *Lyttelton (1865–1948), daughter of Archibald Balfour. He was educated at Eton College (where his uncle Edward *Lyttelton was headmaster) and Trinity College, Cambridge. His university career was cut short after just two years by the outbreak of the First World War. He immediately volunteered. Initially commissioned in the 4th battalion, Bedfordshire regiment, he was transferred to the Grenadier Guards, where he eventually rose to the rank of brigade major. He served in France continuously from early in 1915 to April 1918, when he was wounded in a gas attack. He was mentioned in dispatches on three occasions and won the DSO and the MC. Among the most important and enduring friendships he made during these years was that with Winston Churchill, whom he met in the trenches in 1915 after the latter had joined the guards in the wake of the Dardanelles disaster.

Lyttelton returned to Britain in February 1919 and shortly afterwards joined the banking firm of Brown Shipley & Co. In January 1920 he married Lady Moira Godolphin Osborne (1891–1976), daughter of George Godolphin Osborne, tenth duke of Leeds, and his wife, Lady Katherine Frances Lambton. They had a daughter and three sons, one of whom, Julian, was killed on active service in October 1944. In August 1920 Lyttelton was invited to join the British Metal Corporation, a firm established at the instigation of the British government with the long-term strategic objective of undermining Germany's domination of the metal trade and making the British empire self-supporting in non-ferrous metals. After a brief apprenticeship Lyttelton served as general manager of the corporation and subsequently as managing director. He also became chairman of the London Tin Corporation and joined the boards of a number of foreign companies, including that of the German firm Metallgesellschaft. He became one of a small group of individuals who through their multiple, interlocking directorships, effectively controlled the global metal trade. With only slight exaggeration, Lyttelton once joked, *'l'étain, c'est moi!'*. On the outbreak of war in September 1939 he was appointed controller of non-ferrous metals. He set about exploiting his extensive network of personal contacts and his intimate knowledge of the mining industry in order to secure for Britain vital supplies of metals at highly advantageous rates. His unconventional methods caused some anxiety at the Treasury, but over the course of the war they saved Britain a substantial amount of money.

Churchill's war cabinet After becoming prime minister in May 1940, Churchill sought to bring his old friend into his administration. His first step was to attach Lyttelton to his

Oliver Lyttelton, first Viscount Chandos (1893–1972), by Elliott & Fry, 1941

defence office as supply co-ordinator. In the reshuffle announced early in October, Lyttelton became president of the Board of Trade. The prime minister encouraged him to find a parliamentary seat and gave him his enthusiastic backing. Lyttelton discovered, however, that an endorsement from Churchill was still regarded as a handicap by Conservative Party managers. The elevation to the Lords of the sitting member eventually freed the Aldershot division of Hampshire. Lyttelton held the seat from 1940 until 1954. One of his most important decisions while at the Board of Trade was to introduce clothes rationing. As he correctly predicted, this met with public support despite Churchill's warnings to the contrary.

At the end of June 1941 Churchill sent Lyttelton to Cairo as minister of state and member of the war cabinet. He wished to relieve Britain's military commanders of some of the sensitive political and diplomatic problems raised by the conflict in the Middle Eastern theatre. These included liaison with General De Gaulle and the Free French, and the close supervision of Britain's client regimes in the region. Controversially, and against the initial advice of the military, Lyttelton accepted the view of the British ambassador in Cairo that the security of the British base in Egypt depended on the creation there of a government with greater public support. On 4 February 1942 British tanks surrounded the royal palace and King Farouk was obliged to appoint as his new prime minister the Wafdist leader Mustafa al-Nahhas. The spectacle of Britain using force to install the head of an avowedly anti-

British movement in the name of greater democracy must have appealed to Lyttelton's sense of the absurd.

At the end of February 1942 Lyttelton was recalled to London to succeed Lord Beaverbrook in the recently created post of minister of production. He paid particular attention to the vital task of co-ordinating production with the United States government. At the time of his appointment to the post, his standing among Conservative back-benchers was probably at its height. He was identified by Churchill—and by more objective observers—as a potential rival to Anthony Eden for the future leadership of the party. Yet although the challenge of power excited him, Lyttelton was not conventionally politically ambitious. He remained most at home in the City, and he tended to trust the judgements of fellow businessmen more than those of party politicians or civil servants. When presented as a minister with what he regarded as a particularly patronizing or obtuse piece of advice, he would sometimes reply with the stark minute 'O.L., born 1893'. He certainly brought to his various ministerial posts valuable business acumen which few officials shared. It is difficult to believe, for example, that the government would have experienced the problems it did with the Colonial Development Corporation had Lyttelton entered the Colonial Office in 1945 rather than 1951. Yet he was sometimes unduly dismissive of the views of talented and astute subordinates. One of his principal recreations was poking fun at the pretensions of government and its agents. Lyttelton's sharp wit and talent for mimicry (inherited from his father) delighted his friends. Yet, although lacking real malice, his peculiarly black sense of humour struck some as cynical or even callous. His most serious political shortcoming, however, was his failure ever to master fully the art of parliamentary debate. A particularly poor performance responding for the government to John Wardlaw-Milne's motion of no confidence in July 1942 undoubtedly harmed his prospects for promotion.

Colonial secretary Lyttelton remained minister of production during Churchill's caretaker government of May to July 1945, combining this with his old job as president of the Board of Trade. After the Conservatives' defeat in the 1945 general election, he became chairman of Associated Electrical Industries (AEI). He retained his parliamentary seat and acted as a prominent member of Churchill's front-bench team. As chairman of the Conservative backbench trade and industry committee, he led opposition in the Commons to the government's proposals to nationalize the steel industry. In 1950, with the death of Oliver Stanley, he became chairman of the party's finance committee. Churchill, however, pointedly refused to confirm that the chancellorship would automatically be his in any future Conservative administration. When the Conservatives were returned to power in October 1951, a number of factors persuaded Churchill to make R. A. Butler chancellor of the exchequer in preference to Lyttelton. Lyttelton's weakness in debate was an important one. Furthermore, Churchill was warned by Eden that Lyttelton's close association with the City was likely to antagonize the Labour opposition. Indeed, it was feared that Lyttelton's reputation as a 'City shark' (Butler's own phrase) might even undermine business confidence in the new government.

Instead, after Lyttelton had expressed disappointment in the offer of the Ministry of Materials, Churchill sent him to the Colonial Office as secretary of state, a post that had been occupied by his father in Balfour's administration. Lyttelton carried unusual weight in cabinet for a colonial secretary, and he deployed this to considerable effect. His first priority was Malaya, where the recent assassination of the high commissioner, Sir Henry Gurney, had severely undermined British confidence in their ability to defeat a communist guerrilla movement. Lyttelton quickly recognized the need to combine the responsibilities of high commissioner and commander-in-chief. He selected Sir Gerald Templer for the task and provided him with the necessary authority both to undertake sweeping counter-insurgency measures and to promote rapid constitutional change. In October 1952 the newly appointed governor, Sir Evelyn Baring, declared a state of emergency, presenting Lyttelton with another major military operation to oversee. In its initial stages the British response to unrest in Kenya was poorly formulated and may actually have exacerbated the problem of armed resistance. Only with the appointment as commander-in-chief of General Sir George Erskine in June 1953 did the campaign against the Mau Mau begin to turn in the Kenya government's favour.

Lyttelton had few qualms about the sometimes brutal measures employed against those identified as terrorist suspects or sympathizers. He regarded the increasingly vocal minority of Labour MPs who questioned this approach as at best sentimental and at worst disloyal. The evident embarrassment and division produced on the opposition benches by the government's decision in 1953 to remove Cheddi Jagan's radical administration in British Guiana caused Lyttelton some satisfaction. Yet the overall direction of British colonial policy underwent little significant change during his time as secretary of state. Shortly after assuming office, Lyttelton had, at the suggestion of his senior officials, publicly reaffirmed the government's commitment to leading the colonies to 'self-government within the British Commonwealth'. He was prepared to pursue that policy not only in Malaya, where he was fairly optimistic about the long-term political prospects, but also in west Africa, where he decidedly was not. In February 1952 he recommended to his colleagues 'with great reluctance but without any doubt or hesitation', that the Gold Coast be granted the formal trappings of cabinet government, and that the colony's radical nationalist leader, Kwame Nkrumah, be given the title of prime minister (cabinet memorandum, 9 Feb 1952, C(52) 28, PRO CAB 129/49). At constitutional conferences in London in July and August 1953 and in Lagos in January 1954 Lyttelton constructed a new, federal constitution for Nigeria and prepared the ground for the achievement of internal self-government for Nigeria's eastern and western regions in 1956. In his *Memoirs* (published four years before Nigeria's collapse into civil war) he rated these negotiations the most successful of his time at the Colonial Office.

Lyttelton vigorously promoted plans, inherited from the Attlee government, for a federation of Northern and Southern Rhodesia and Nyasaland, a scheme that commanded the active support of his former colleagues in the mining industry and the almost overwhelming opposition of the African populations of the two northern territories. He was attracted by the notion that a similar federation might be attempted in east Africa. When, however, he publicly expressed tentative support for such a scheme in June 1953, he provoked a constitutional crisis. The traditional ruler of Uganda's largest and most important province, Edward Mutesa, kabaka of Buganda, used the widespread outrage over the suggestion as a pretext to defy the modernizing programme of Uganda's new governor, Sir Andrew Cohen, and to assert Buganda's autonomy. When the kabaka refused to co-operate, Cohen insisted that he be exiled to London and Lyttelton reluctantly agreed.

Later years In December 1953 Lyttelton warned Churchill that his various financial commitments would soon force him to seek more remunerative employment. He estimated that his ministerial salary represented an annual loss of some £10,000–12,000 on his potential earnings as a captain of industry. He wished to take up the chairmanship of his old firm, AEI, which was about to fall vacant. Fearing a further erosion of the Conservatives' slender parliamentary majority, Churchill summoned the directors of AEI to Downing Street and urged them not to press for Lyttelton's early resignation. Lyttelton was persuaded to remain at the Colonial Office until the end of July 1954. He was subsequently (9 September 1954) elevated to the House of Lords as Viscount Chandos of Aldershot.

Chandos resumed his business career with the same energy and enthusiasm as before, although with considerably less success. He undertook an ambitious programme of expansion and development at AEI. Yet profits declined, and only four years after his retirement in 1963, the company was absorbed by its rival the General Electric Company. During his second term as chairman of AEI, Chandos also served as president of the Institute of Directors. In addition, he sat on the boards of ICI and Alliance Assurance Co. Ltd. His extra-political interests had always ranged far beyond the business world to embrace modern and classical literature and the performing arts.

In retirement Chandos devoted a considerable amount of time to the National Theatre. He served as chairman of its board from 1962 to 1971, and then as president until the time of his death. This was something of a labour of love: his mother, to whom he was devoted, had long campaigned for the establishment of such a theatre. The Lyttelton Theatre, part of the National's complex of buildings opened on London's South Bank in 1976, serves as a fitting tribute to his efforts in this field. Yet he found himself increasingly out of sympathy with the prevailing artistic climate and, in particular, with the approach of the National's flamboyant literary manager, Kenneth Tynan. He came close to resignation from the board over plans to stage Rolf Hochhuth's play *Soldiers*, a work set during the Second World War, which both attacked Churchill over the saturation bombing of German cities and implied that the British secret service had been responsible for the death of Sikorski, head of the Polish government-in-exile. Chandos's elegantly written *Memoirs* appeared in 1962 to warm reviews, and they were followed six years later by *From Peace to War: a Study in Contrast, 1857–1918*.

Chandos died in a London hospital on 21 January 1972. He was buried on 29 January in Hagley, Worcestershire, the Lytteltons' ancestral home. He was succeeded as second viscount by his eldest son, Anthony Alfred (1920–1980).

PHILIP MURPHY

Sources CAC Cam., Chandos MSS · interview for the Oxford Colonial Records Project, Bodl. RH · PRO · Lord Chandos [O. Lyttleton, first Viscount Chandos], *The memoirs of Lord Chandos: an unexpected view from the summit* (1962) · D. Goldsworthy, ed., *The conservative government and the end of empire, 1951–1957*, 3 vols. (1994) · H. Pelling, *Churchill's peacetime ministry, 1951–55* (1997) · A. Seldon, *Churchill's Indian summer: the conservative government, 1951–55* (1981) · *The Times* (22 Jan 1972) · *The Times* (27 Jan 1972) · private information [Sir Peter Smithers] · *The Times* (22 May 1976), 16 · Burke, *Peerage* (1999)

Archives CAC Cam., corresp. and papers · PRO, corresp. and papers, CO 967/239–276 | Bodl. RH, Oxford Colonial Records Project, interview with Lord Chandos on his political career, 1970 · Bodl. RH, corresp. with R. R. Welensky · CAC Cam., Churchill MSS · CAC Cam., corresp. with E. L. Spears, incl. corresp. relating to Chandos Literary Trust · Nuffield Oxf., corresp. with Lord Cherwell · U. Hull, Brynmor Jones L., letters to Irene Forbes Adam | FILM BFI NFTVA, news footage · BFI NFTVA, propaganda film footage · IWM FVA, actuality footage | SOUND BL NSA, oral history interview · Bodl. RH, recordings of Oxford Colonial Records Project interview · IWM SA, oral history interview

Likenesses Elliott & Fry, photograph, 1941, NPG [*see illus.*] · W. Bird, photograph, 1962, NPG · D. Low, two pencil caricatures, NPG · F. Topolski, lithograph, NPG; repro. in *Topolski's Chronicle*, 8 (1960)

Wealth at death £78,637: probate, 1 May 1972, *CGPLA Eng. & Wales*

Lyttelton [*née* Spencer], **Sarah, Lady Lyttelton** (**1787–1870**), courtier, was born at Althorp, Northamptonshire, on 29 July 1787, the eldest daughter of George John *Spencer, second Earl Spencer (1758–1834), and his wife, Lavinia Bingham (1762–1831), daughter of the first Earl Lucan. Her youth was happy, if uneventful, spent among a large circle of family and friends. At Althorp she engaged in good works, teaching the village girls, and at Spencer House in London her family held a prominent place among the whig aristocracy, although she did not care greatly for the amusements of society. Her looks were described no more fulsomely than as 'pleasing' and throughout her life she was shy, the result of her mother's sharply snubbing manner. A deeply religious evangelical, her warm and sympathetic nature made her the confidante of her family. On 3 March 1813 she married the Hon. William Henry *Lyttelton (1782–1837): Creevey described them as 'the happiest couple in the world' (GEC, *Peerage*). They had three sons and two daughters, whose upbringing was Lady Sarah's main preoccupation. On 12 November 1828, William Lyttelton succeeded his half-brother as third Baron Lyttelton, and Hagley Hall, near Stourbridge, in Worcestershire, became Lady Lyttelton's home. Lord Lyttelton's death on

Sarah Lyttelton, Lady Lyttelton (1787–1870), by George Salisbury Shury, pubd 1864 (after Henry Weigall)

30 April 1837 after a decade of ill health left her a widow, and the approaching marriage of her eldest son, George William *Lyttelton, to Mary Glynne, made her feel it appropriate to leave Hagley.

In 1837, Lady Lyttelton was offered the position of lady of the bedchamber to the young Queen Victoria, and, her mourning for her husband over, she went into waiting for the first time on 2 October 1838, attending the queen at her marriage in 1840. Her sympathetic disposition made her a favourite at court, although she felt that she 'blundered and boggled as usual' (*Correspondence*, 279) in her tasks of handing the queen her shawl, her bouquet, bag, or opera glasses. In 1842 Prince Albert reorganized the royal household, and the nursery in particular, and Lady Lyttelton was appointed governess. She took up her position, which was no sinecure, in April 1842, taking charge of the preliminary education of the princess royal and the prince of Wales, who nicknamed her 'Laddle'. She found her position agreeable, despite difficulties with the prince of Wales, about whom she remarked 'my heavy burden [is] increased to a crushing weight when I think of that child' (*Correspondence*, 362). She enjoyed the full confidence of both Victoria and Albert, except perhaps on questions of religion; but was, nevertheless, diffident about her competence.

In October 1850 her youngest daughter, Lavinia, died, leaving four young daughters, and Lady Lyttelton resigned her appointment in the following month. She returned to Hagley, where, after 1857, she transferred her talents to the education of the twelve motherless children of her eldest son: one of them recalled her as 'a stately, benevolent figure full of kindness and dignified humour, and of steadfast old-fashioned piety' (Lyttelton, 10). It was at Hagley that Lady Lyttelton died, on 13 April 1870, and she was buried there in the family vault.

VIRGINIA SURTEES

Sources *Correspondence of Sarah Spencer, Lady Lyttelton, 1787–1870*, ed. Mrs H. Wyndham (1912) • B. Askwith, *The Lytteltons: a family chronicle of the nineteenth century* (1975) • GEC, *Peerage* • E. Lyttelton, *Alfred Lyttelton: an account of his life* (1917)

Archives Hagley Hall, Worcestershire | Royal Arch., papers relating to employment as governess

Likenesses J. R. Swinton, portrait, 1850, Hagley Hall, Worcestershire • G. S. Shury, engraving, pubd 1864 (after H. Weigall) [*see illus.*] • G. Hayter, portrait, Hagley Hall, Worcestershire • J. Jackson, portrait, Hagley Hall, Worcestershire • H. Weigall, portrait, Hagley Hall, Worcestershire

Wealth at death under £10,000: probate, 20 May 1870, *CGPLA Eng. & Wales*

Lyttelton, Sir Thomas, first baronet (1595/6–1650), royalist army officer and politician, was the eldest son of John Lyttelton MP (1561–1601) of Hagley, Worcestershire, and Muriel (*d.* 1630), daughter of Sir Thomas Bromley, lord chancellor. His father was implicated in Essex's rising (February 1601), and, after being convicted of high treason, died in prison. Thomas matriculated at Balliol College, Oxford, on 22 June 1610, but was a member of Broadgates Hall when he supplicated for the BA degree (2 July 1614). In 1613 he became a student of the Inner Temple. Lyttelton was both knighted and created a baronet in July 1618. He married Catherine (*d.* 1666), daughter and heir of Sir Thomas Crompton of Driffield, Yorkshire, and Hounslow, Middlesex; they had twelve sons and four daughters. He represented Worcestershire in the parliaments of 1621–2, 1624–5, 1625, 1626, and April–May 1640, and in 1640 he served as high sheriff for the county.

On the outbreak of the civil war Lyttelton offered to raise a regiment of foot and a troop of horse for the king. Charles I consulted him at Shrewsbury in September 1642 about troop movements, and appointed him colonel of the Worcestershire horse and foot (3 September 1642), praising his 'approved fidelity, wisdom, valour and circumspection' (*Diary of Henry Townshend*, 2.86). By the beginning of 1643 he was governor of Bewdley, but the county's royalists lacked supplies and failed to overcome their neighbours' indifference. In May 1644 Bewdley, poorly fortified, was taken by a parliamentary force masquerading as stragglers from Prince Rupert's army, and Lyttelton was captured in bed at Tickenhill by Colonel 'Tinker' Fox. He was sent to the Tower of London, and though released on bail, was recommitted (29 November 1644), by parliament, fearful of his influence in Worcestershire. His house at Frankley was burnt to the ground by Prince Rupert to make it unavailable to the parliamentary troops. On 6 March 1645 parliament fined him £4000 for his delinquency, and he was still a prisoner in June 1646. He died at Newcastle House, Clerkenwell, Middlesex, on 22 February 1650, and was buried in Worcester Cathedral.

Lyttelton's fifth but eldest surviving son, **Sir Henry Lyttelton**, second baronet (1623/4–1693), royalist politician, succeeded to the baronetcy on his father's death. He matriculated from Balliol College, Oxford, on 12 September 1640. His first marriage was to Philadelphia (*d.* 2 Aug 1663), daughter of the Hon. Thomas Carey, groom of the bedchamber to Charles I. She was maid of honour to Queen Catherine of Braganza. Secondly he married, on 2 November 1665, at Wroxeter, Shropshire, Lady Elizabeth Newport (*d.* 7 March 1724), daughter of Francis Newport, first earl of Bradford. A royalist, he was taken prisoner at the battle of Worcester (3 September 1651), and was imprisoned in the Tower until April 1653 on a charge of providing arms without licence to the Scottish army.

On his release Lyttelton joined the action party of royalist conspirators in the midlands, and, as high sheriff of Worcestershire (1654–5), he was able to purchase arms. Although he took no part in Penruddock's rising (1655)—he may have been deterred from this by the arrest of his brother Charles—he was implicated, with two of his brothers, in Booth's insurrection (1659) and was again committed to the Tower, where, treated with great respect, he appears to have remained until the Restoration. Charles II wrote to him from Brussels, full of appreciation for his sacrifices and promising future rewards.

Described by his brother Charles (16 August 1664) as 'dry, illiberal' and 'troubled with his fits of the spleen' (Thompson, 1.36), Lyttelton refused in 1661 both a peerage and an invitation to stand as MP for Worcestershire. He preferred to live on his estates at Upper Arley, Staffordshire (now in Worcestershire), where his vineyards produced light wines pronounced indistinguishable from those of France. At a by-election (21 February 1678) he became MP for Lichfield, but he served on no committees and made no speeches. He retained his seat (March–July 1679) but became totally inactive in parliament, and was even absent at the division on the Exclusion Bill. Indeed he refused all further invitations to stand as MP for Worcestershire and for Lichfield. He was a JP for Worcestershire and Shropshire, deputy lieutenant for Worcestershire and Staffordshire, a freeman of Worcester and an alderman of Bewdley. He died, without children, at Upper Arley on 24 June 1693, and was buried in the local church, where a monument to his memory was erected. He was succeeded in the baronetcy by his brother Charles *Lyttelton (1629–1716). BASIL MORGAN

Sources HoP, *Commons, 1660–90* (1983) • W. R. Williams, *The parliamentary history of the county of Worcester* (privately printed, Hereford, 1897) • GEC, *Peerage* • J. W. W. Bund, *The civil war in Worcestershire, 1642–1646* (1905) • M. Atkin, *The civil war in Worcestershire* (1995) • J. R. Burton, *History of Bewdley* (1883) • *Diary of Henry Townshend of Elmley Lovett*, ed. J. W. Willis Bund, 4 pts in 2 vols., Worcestershire Historical Society (1915–20) • R. Hutton, *The royalist war effort, 1642–1646* (1982) • *JHC*, 1–4 (1547–1646) • Foster, *Alum. Oxon.* • *VCH Worcestershire* • T. Nash, *Collections for the history of Worcestershire*, 2nd edn, 2 vols. (1799) • E. M. Thompson, ed., *Correspondence of the family of Hatton*, 2 vols., CS, new ser., 22–3 (1878) • H. R. Mayo, ed., *The registers of Over Areley … 1564–1812*, Worcestershire Parish Register Society (1916) • *DNB*

Archives Bodl. Oxf., financial papers • S. Antiquaries, Lond., corresp. and papers

Lyttelton, Thomas, **second Baron Lyttelton** (1744–1779), libertine and politician, was born at Hagley, Worcestershire, on 30 January 1744, the son of George *Lyttelton, first Baron Lyttelton of Frankley (1709–1773), and Lucy (1717/18–1747), daughter of Hugh Fortescue of Filleigh, Devon. The dissolute son of a pious father, Lyttelton attracted fascinated, and horrified, attention in life and death.

Youth He was educated at Marylebone boarding-school between 1756 and 1758 before proceeding to Eton College. He was a precocious boy, and his father had praised him at fifteen for his charm and intelligence, but added: 'my only fear is that he may please the ladies too well' (*Elizabeth Montagu*, 140): George begged his friend Elizabeth Montagu to instil the prudent advice that 'no charms are truly amiable but those that are under the government of wisdom and virtue' (ibid., 140–41). By the time Tom was sixteen, doubts were multiplying. At the grand opening of the new Hagley Hall in 1760 he was commissioned, according to Charles Townshend, 'to have opened the ball with the first person of the first class, mutinied, and would dance only with a smart girl he had brought in the morning from a neighbouring village' (*Lothian MSS*, 242). In November 1761 he went to Christ Church, Oxford, where he received a long letter of advice from Mrs Montagu, explaining that 'the morning of life, like the morning of day, should be dedicated to business' (*Elizabeth Montagu*, 253), and advising him to study history.

In 1763 Lyttelton's father began to negotiate a marriage for him with Anne, daughter of Lieutenant-General Warburton of Winnington, Cheshire. Since the arrangements could not be legalized until he was of age, it was decided to send him on the grand tour to mark time, with expenses paid by his wealthy uncle, Sir Richard Lyttleton. This was a mistake. His companions included the Damer brothers, also Etonians, and scarcely calculated to encourage sobriety. George Damer became involved in a scandal with an Italian coachman, whose family had to be bought off; in 1776 John Damer at the age of thirty-two shot himself in a brothel in Covent Garden in the company of three prostitutes and a blind fiddler. Within a few months Lyttelton had run up heavy gambling debts and had fought two duels. Edward Gibbon, who did devote himself to history, met Lyttelton in Rome and complained that he monopolized the conversation 'avec une volubilité étonnante' (Gibbon, 121). Further acquaintance confirmed 'beaucoup de gasconade' (ibid., 143) and Lyttelton shocked the future historian of the Roman empire by insisting that one could do Rome in twenty days. Nor was Sir Horace Mann, the diplomat, more impressed: 'a very odd young man … his contradictory temper makes it impossible for him to agree with anybody, and his behaviour in general disobliges and offends so that he is shunned both by the English and Italians' (Walpole, *Corr.*, 22.251). A further consequence of his conduct, soon reported home, was that Miss Warburton began to have second thoughts: 'she is trying to find someone she can like better' explained Mrs Montagu (Blunt, 53). The match was called off.

On returning home in 1765, Lyttelton soon quarrelled

with his father and went abroad again, spending some time in prison in Paris after a scuffle in a brothel. Mrs Montagu amiably attributed his misfortunes to 'inexperience' (Blunt, 70), but conceded that 'Mr Lyttelton has so many times acted out the same indiscretions that to assist him again would only be to encourage him' (ibid.). Extricated once more, he stood for Bewdley, a single-seat borough disputed between the Winnington and Lyttelton families, and, after a singularly rowdy election, was returned at the general election of 1768. In a maiden speech in May 1768 he warned of trouble ahead in America, and in November spoke in favour of hearing John Wilkes's complaints. But in January 1769 he was unseated on petition. Looking back on his stay in the Commons, Lyttelton regretted it had been so brief: 'I was possessed of that ready faculty of speech which would have enabled me to make some little figure in the Senate … I mingled in public debate, and received the most flattering testimonies of applause' (Blunt, 80–81). Immediately after his expulsion from the house, Lyttelton resumed his continental travels, mainly in Italy and the Low Countries. John Gray, the historian, journeyed with him from Venice to Milan in the spring of 1771, and commented that he gambled 'like a madman' (Melville, 244). He was also susceptible to gross flattery and 'should others be silent, he will trumpet forth his own excellencies' (ibid., 245).

Baulked for the time being of a political career, Lyttelton embarked on matrimony. On 26 June 1772, at Halesowen, Staffordshire, he married Apphia (1743–1840), widow of Joseph Peach, governor of Calcutta, and daughter of Broome Witts, of Chipping Norton, Oxfordshire. 'Lord Lyttelton's son', wrote Mrs Boscawen, 'has persuaded a very rich (and very worthy) East Indian widow … to take him with all his faults; it is to be hoped she will help him to amend them, for tis so great a work that he will want assistance' (Delany, 2nd ser., 1.443). To the dismay of his father, who seems to have admired his prospective daughter-in-law more than her fiancé did, Lyttelton brought forward the marriage, less from ardour than because he needed the £20,000 dowry rather urgently. The experiment failed, and the following year—as told in the broadside *The Rape of Pomona*—he absconded to Paris with a barmaid from Bolton's Inn at Hockerill. He was back in time to take part in another drunken brawl in July 1773 over the actress Elizabeth Hartley, an event celebrated in another pamphlet, *The Vauxhall Affray*. From these fresh predicaments he was rescued in August 1773 by the death of his father, which enabled him to resume his parliamentary career.

Lyttelton in the Lords Provided with a new audience, Lyttelton took up his role in the Lords with some enthusiasm. On 22 February 1774 he spoke on the issue of literary property, in favour of authors' rights. He followed in June by supporting the Quebec Bill, insisting that the French Canadians had proved their loyalty and were entitled to toleration: 'the gloomy reign of persecution and priestcraft were now at an end' (Cobbett, *Parl. hist.*, 17, 1773–4, 1405). Throughout 1774 and most of 1775, despite his admiration for the former prime minister William Pitt, earl of Chatham, Lyttelton supported the government's attempts to bring the Americans into submission, insisting that there was no distinction between legislation and taxation. On 20 January 1775, when Chatham moved that troops be withdrawn from Boston, Lyttelton asserted his independent support for the administration: 'now, therefore [is] the time to assert the authority of Great Britain' (ibid., 18, 1775–6, 163). Horace Walpole thought highly of his eloquence, and his reported speeches are far from foolish. On 12 May 1775, in a long speech, he moved the second reading of a bill to allow a playhouse in Manchester, remarking that recreation was particularly necessary in new industrial towns and that 'the sixpence spent at a theatre is much better laid out than at an ale-house' (ibid., 635). He had a dislike for the former lord chancellor Charles Pratt, first Baron Camden, whom he attacked on 7 February, and again on 17 May when Camden moved to repeal the Quebec Act. Lyttelton defended it as an excellent bill, based upon the principle of toleration, and insisted that Camden's intentions were to raise a storm and distress ministers. He was sufficiently pleased with his speech to have it printed and circulated.

But when in the course of the summer his exertions went unrewarded, Lyttelton demonstrated that he could bite. When the new session began in October 1775 he changed sides abruptly and became a savage critic of those whom he had once courted. On 26 October he defended Chatham in his absence, declared that ministers were not to be trusted, and demanded that all acts regarded by the Americans as grievances should be rescinded. On this occasion Lyttelton struck lucky, catching Lord North in one of his moments of despondency. William Nassau de Zuylestein, fourth earl of Rochford, one of the secretaries of state, was unwell and anxious to resign, and Augustus Henry Fitzroy, third duke of Grafton, the lord privy seal, was so dissatisfied that the king urged his dismissal. On 7 November, North warned the king that the ministry was in danger of dissolution. On the same day he minuted that 'Lord Lyttelton has this morning agreed to give a constant support to administration upon condition that he may expect before the end of the session a Privy Council office of the value of £1500 a year' (*Correspondence of George III*, 3.280). The outcome was Lyttelton's appointment to the lucrative sinecure of chief justice in eyre, north of Trent, and a second volte-face. On 10 November he attacked 'the audacious, insidious rebels' in America and was warmly congratulated by the first lord of the Admiralty, John Montagu, fourth earl of Sandwich, on 'the finest [speech] ever delivered within these walls' (Cobbett, *Parl. hist.*, 18, 1775–6, 927, 931). 'This hopeful young man', commented Walpole:

> who on being refused a place spoke *for* the Americans, and in two days, on getting one, *against* them, being reproached with such precipitate changes, said that with his fortune nobody could expect he thought of the value of the salary. (Walpole, *Corr.*, 24.151)

For most of the rest of his life Lyttelton supported the government, playing a useful, if subsidiary, role. On 14

March 1776 he opposed Grafton's motion for conciliation, saying it would make Britain a laughing-stock; after Saratoga he said that Britain should not give up because of one set-back (5 December 1777), and on 7 December 1778 that the Americans were to blame for the savagery of the contest. But during 1779 he, like others, began to despair. In April he stood aside while Sandwich was attacked, admitting that America could not be regained. According to Walpole he had turned against the court on not being given the seals as secretary of state on the death of Henry Howard, twelfth earl of Suffolk. In June 1779 the king, in a memorandum on a change of government, noted: 'Lord Lyttelton to be removed, his place offered to Lord Beauchamp' (*Correspondence of George III*, 4.352). On 27 September 1779 he wrote to North to remove Lyttelton, 'whose private character makes him no credit to my service' (ibid., 4.451). Rather than walk the plank, Lyttelton jumped. On 25 November he launched a violent attack upon the ministers: the war was now a madness and the government 'a rope of sand, crumbling away day by day' (Cobbett, *Parl. hist.*, 20, 1778–9, 1041). This would presumably have done the trick and secured Lyttelton's dismissal had he not died, two days afterwards, at his Surrey home, Pitt Place, Epsom, at the age of thirty-five. He was buried at Hagley.

Life after death Even after his death Lyttelton continued to astonish the world. Within days rumours were circulating of supernatural happenings, and as a ghost Lyttelton stalked throughout much of the nineteenth century. There were two separate accounts. The first, attested by William Henry *Lyttelton, first Baron Westcote, Lyttelton's uncle and successor in the Hagley estate, was that before his death Lyttelton had told his friends that a woman had appeared to him, first in the guise of a robin, and prophesied his death within three days. The irrepressible Walpole thought it must be the first time that any female had found difficulty in obtaining entry to Lyttelton's bedchamber. On the third evening Lyttelton had joked that they had 'bilked the ghost', but soon after he retired to bed his manservant found him dead. In view of the life he had led it would be idle to speculate on what illness had carried him off, though 'cramp in his stomach' was suggested (*Eighth Report*, HMC, 1.206). The second story was that, at the very moment of his death, his figure had appeared to a friend 30 miles away. The purpose of neither visit was closely identified but Lyttelton would have been pleased to know that he died as he had lived, much talked about.

Lyttelton is credited with two works, neither proven with certainty. *Poems by a Young Nobleman Lately Deceased* appeared in 1780, and in a second edition the author was identified as Lyttelton. The *Monthly Review* thought the poems 'poor, contemptible, and vulgar' (*Monthly Review*, 62, 1780, 131), and the *Gentleman's Magazine* regretted that they had ever been printed. *Letters by the Late Thomas Lord Lyttelton*, distinctly wordy, also appeared in 1780. They were later claimed by William Combe, author of *Dr Syntax*, but his role may have been that of an enthusiastic editor. The suggestion, briefly canvassed, that Lyttelton was the author of the *Letters of Junius* is preposterous, since he is known to have been on the continent for almost all the time that the letters were appearing. JOHN CANNON

Sources J. Brooke, 'Lyttelton, Hon. Thomas', HoP, *Commons, 1754–90* · R. Blunt, *Thomas, Lord Lyttelton* (1936) · Cobbett, *Parl. hist.*, 17.1002, 1404–5; 18.163–4, 276, 634–7, 664–6, 713–14, 927–31, 1272–4; 19.491–5; 20.21–4, 455–63, 1038–45 · GEC, *Peerage* · T. Frost, *Life of Thomas, Lord Lyttelton* (1876) · Walpole, *Corr.* · *Elizabeth Montagu, the queen of the blue-stockings: her correspondence from 1720 to 1761*, ed. E. J. Climenson, 2 vols. (1906) · *The correspondence of King George the Third from 1760 to December 1783*, ed. J. Fortescue, 6 vols. (1927–8) · *N&Q*, 8 (1853), 31 · *N&Q*, 2nd ser., 1 (1856), 198 · H. Walpole, *Memoirs of the reign of King George the Third*, ed. G. F. R. Barker, 4 vols. (1894) · *The historical and the posthumous memoirs of Sir Nathaniel William Wraxall, 1772–1784*, ed. H. B. Wheatley, 5 vols. (1884) · *Thraliana: the diary of Mrs. Hester Lynch Thrale (later Mrs. Piozzi), 1776–1809*, ed. K. C. Balderston, 2 vols. (1942) · *Calendar of the manuscripts of the marquis of Bath preserved at Longleat, Wiltshire*, 5 vols., HMC, 58 (1904–80) · *Report on the manuscripts of the marquess of Lothian*, HMC, 62 (1905) · *Second report*, HMC, 1/2 (1871); repr. (1874) · *Eighth report*, 3 vols. in 5, HMC, 7 (1881–1910) · *QR*, 90 (1851–2), 91–163 · Boswell, *Life* · *Correspondence of William Pitt, earl of Chatham*, ed. W. S. Taylor and J. H. Pringle, 4 vols. (1838–40) · *Memoirs and correspondence of George, Lord Lyttelton, from 1734 to 1773*, ed. R. Phillimore, 2 vols. (1845) · L. Dickins and M. Stanton, *An eighteenth century correspondence being the letters … to Sanderson Miller* (1910) · M. Wyndham, *Chronicles of the eighteenth century*, 2 vols. (1924) · *GM* · *The autobiography and correspondence of Mary Granville, Mrs Delany*, ed. Lady Llanover, 1st ser., 3 vols. (1861); 2nd ser., 3 vols. (1862) · *Memoirs of William Hickey*, ed. A. Spencer, 4 vols. (1913–25) · *The letters of David Garrick*, ed. D. M. Little and G. M. Kahrl, 3 vols. (1963) · *Letters of Tobias Smollett*, ed. L. M. Knapp (1970) · E. Gibbon, *Journey from Geneva to Rome*, ed. G. Bonnard (1961) · H. Walpole, *Journal of the reign of King George the Third*, ed. Dr Doran, 2 vols. (1859) · *The rape of Pomona* (1773) · *The Vauxhall affray* (1773) · F. G. Stephens and M. D. George, eds., *Catalogue of political and personal satires preserved … in the British Museum*, 6 (1938) · *State trials*, vol. 20 · L. Melville, *The life and letters of Tobias Smollett* (1926) · *JHL*

Archives BL, notebook with draft letters and poems, Add. MS 19428 · Worcs. RO, legal documents | PRO, Chatham MSS

Likenesses Battoni, portrait, 1764, repro. in Blunt, *Thomas, Lord Lyttelton* · C. Townley, mezzotint, pubd 1781 (after R. Cosway), BM · R. Brompton, portrait, repro. in Blunt, *Thomas, Lord Lyttelton* · Cosway, portrait (*Vision*), repro. in Blunt, *Thomas, Lord Lyttelton* · T. Gainsborough, oils, NPG · P. Hoare, oils, Stourhead, Wiltshire · caricature, repro. in George, ed., *Catalogue* · miniature, repro. in Wheatley, ed., *Historical and posthumous memoirs* (1884) · oils (after T. Gainsborough), NPG · stipple, BM, NPG; repro. in H. Walpole, *A cataloge of the royal and noble authors of England, Scotland and Ireland*, ed. Parks (1806)

Wealth at death though a libertine, seemingly managed estates better than pious father; supposedly left £40,000 ready money (unlikely); bequests to various ladies: *Public Advertiser* (7 Dec 1779)

Lyttelton, William Henry, first Baron Lyttelton and first Baron Westcote (1724–1808), colonial governor and diplomat, was born on 24 December 1724 in London, the sixth son of Sir Thomas Lyttelton, fourth baronet (1685–1751), and of his wife, Christian (1688–1759), daughter of Sir Richard Temple. He was at school at Eton College before going to Oxford, where he matriculated at St Mary Hall on 22 June 1742. He entered the Middle Temple on 1 November 1743 and was called to the bar in 1748. Rather than practising the law, however, he went into politics with the encouragement of his kinsman William Pitt, being returned to the House of Commons for his father's borough of Bewdley in 1748. Pitt seems to have been instrumental in his obtaining the governorship of the colony of South Carolina in 1755.

After being captured at sea and briefly confined in France, Lyttelton reached South Carolina on 1 June 1756. The colony was very rich, exporting great quantities of rice and indigo, but its small white population, heavily outnumbered by African slaves, made it very vulnerable to attack either by the French or by the Native American peoples of the interior. Lyttelton was successful in persuading the fractious assembly that represented the white community to vote money for the colony's defence and to accept policies aimed at conciliating the native peoples. However, relations with the most powerful of them, the Cherokees, remained tense. When in 1759 approximately twenty-four Englishmen were murdered on the Cherokee frontier Lyttelton rejected the credentials of a Cherokee peace delegation and led an armed incursion into Cherokee territory in order to force his own uncompromising terms on the Cherokees. Lyttelton demanded that twenty-four Cherokees be surrendered for execution and that the Cherokees should also kill any French emissaries. Lyttelton's actions provoked a long and costly war, but initially it was widely supported both in South Carolina and in Britain.

Lyttelton learned in February 1760 that on the strength of his apparent success he had been promoted to the governorship of Jamaica. His friend and political ally, George Montagu Dunk, earl of Halifax, president of the Board of Trade, told him that although the people of South Carolina were losing 'the best governor they ever had', he was getting 'the best government his Majesty has to bestow' (letter of 15 Nov 1759, Lyttelton MSS). Lyttelton left South Carolina for Britain on 4 June 1760. Before leaving Britain for Jamaica he married on 2 June 1761 Mary, daughter of James Macartney of Longford in Ireland. They had two sons and a daughter. She died in Jamaica on 28 May 1765.

Jamaica, with its great sugar plantations, was the most valued of all British colonies. It too, however, had acute problems of defence and of an assertive white population, often at loggerheads with the governor through their assembly. In December 1764 Lyttelton was drawn into a long and bitter dispute with the assembly over members' claims to the privilege of judicial immunity. Lyttelton believed that such claims were both 'destructive of the just Influence of His Majesty's Prerogative' and contrary to 'Publick Justice' and to the rights of individuals (Greene, 30). In the hope of avoiding conflict while maintaining his position Lyttelton dissolved the assembly three times, but each new assembly—meeting from March to June 1765, in August 1765, and May 1766—continued to assert the privilege of judicial immunity. Lyttelton's threat to seek new powers from the British parliament was at first supported by the Grenville ministry, but the Rockingham administration preferred that he pursue compromise. Unwilling to change his policy Lyttelton left Jamaica on 2 June 1766, leaving his lieutenant-governor, Roger Hope Elletson, to follow the path of conciliation.

Lyttelton served as ambassador to Portugal from 1767 to 1770, when he left on leave, resigning when required to return. In Britain he married his second wife, Caroline (1745/6–1809), daughter of John Bristowe of Quidenham, Norfolk, on 19 February 1774. They had a son and a daughter. Lyttelton was returned for parliament again for Bewdley in 1774, holding the seat until 1790. He consistently supported the government of Lord North, serving as a lord of the Treasury from 1777 to 1782. In 1776 he was given the Irish title of Baron Westcote of Ballymore. He inherited in 1779 the estates of his nephew Thomas Lyttelton, including the new house at Hagley in Worcestershire, which became his seat. In his few recorded Commons speeches, no doubt influenced by his experiences as a governor, Lyttelton insisted on enforcing the rights of Britain over the colonies by coercion and war, if need be. He went into opposition with North after 1783, but left him to adhere to the Pitt administration in 1787. In 1794 he was given a British peerage as Baron Lyttelton of Frankley.

Lyttelton shared some of his brother George *Lyttelton's ambitions as a poet and man of letters, privately publishing a volume entitled *Trifles in Verse* in 1803. In his youth he went on the grand tour of Europe with Henry Thrale, and through Thrale's wife, Hester, became acquainted with Samuel Johnson, who dismissed him as having 'more chaff than grain in him' (Balderston, 1.300). Oxford University made him an honorary DCL in 1781.

Lyttelton died on 14 September 1808 at Hagley, and was buried there. He was survived by his second wife, Caroline, who died on 19 September 1809 at Castle Fraser, Aberdeenshire; by his eldest son with his first wife, George Fulke (1763–1828), who succeeded as second Baron Lyttelton and Westcote; and by his children with his second wife, William Henry *Lyttelton, later third Baron Lyttelton and Westcote (1782–1837), and Caroline Anne (*d.* 1833), who married Reginald Pole-Carew (1753–1835), MP. He was predeceased by the other children from his first marriage, Charles (*d.* 1781) and Hester (*d.* 1785), who had married Sir Richard Colt Hoare. P. J. Marshall

Sources M. M. Drummond, 'Lyttelton, William Henry', HoP, *Commons, 1754–90* • J. B. Lawson, 'Lyttelton, William Henry', HoP, *Commons, 1715–54* • GEC, *Peerage* • U. Mich., Clements L., Lyttelton MSS • J. P. Greene, 'The Jamaica privilege controversy, 1764–66: an episode in the process of constitutional definition in the early modern British empire', *Journal of Imperial and Commonwealth History*, 22 (1994), 16–53 • J. Oliphant, *Peace and war on the Anglo-Cherokee frontier, 1756–1763* (2000) • *Thraliana: the diary of Mrs. Hester Lynch Thrale (later Mrs. Piozzi), 1776–1809*, ed. K. C. Balderston, 2nd edn, 2 vols. (1951) • will, PRO, PROB 11/1494, fols. 212–13 • *A descriptive list of the state papers Portugal, 1661–1780*, 3 (1983) • *Report on manuscripts in various collections*, 8 vols., HMC, 55 (1901–14), vol. 6 • Burke, *Peerage* (1967) • W. Stitt Robinson, 'Lyttelton, William Henry', *ANB* • H. A. C. Sturgess, ed., *Register of admissions to the Honourable Society of the Middle Temple, from the fifteenth century to the year 1944*, 1 (1949), 333

Archives BL, papers and corresp. relating to his embassy, Add. MS 20847 • Duke U., Perkins L., letter-book • Hagley Hall, Worcestershire, corresp. and papers as governor of Jamaica and papers • U. Mich., Clements L., corresp. • Worcs. RO, letter-books and accounts while governor of Jamaica and South Carolina [copies] • Yale U., Beinecke L., letter-books as governor of South Carolina | Bucks. RLSS, letters to Scrope Bernard • Hunt. L., letters to James Abercromby • PRO, Jamaica corresp., CO 137 • PRO, Portugal corresp., SP 89/63–70 · PRO, South Carolina corresp., CO 5 · U. Mich., Clements L., corresp. with William Knox · Yale U., Beinecke L., corresp. with P. Doddridge

Likenesses J. Reynolds, oils · B. Wilson, oils, Antony, Cornwall; repro. in A. J. O'Shaughnessy, *An empire divided: the American revolution in the British Caribbean* (2000)

Wealth at death under £40,000; freehold in manors of Hagley, Frankley, Churchill, Great Cradley, and Rowley in Worcestershire, Shropshire, and Staffordshire: PRO, death duty registers, IR 26/145; will, PRO, PROB 11/1494, fols. 212–13

Lyttelton, William Henry, third Baron Lyttelton and third Baron Westcote (1782–1837), politician, was born on 3 April 1782 in Berners Street, London, the son of William Henry *Lyttelton, first Baron Lyttelton of Frankley and first Baron Westcote of Ballymore (1724–1808), and his second wife, Caroline (1745/6–1809), daughter of John Bristowe of Quidenham, Norfolk. Lyttelton matriculated at Christ Church, Oxford, on 24 October 1798, graduated BA on 17 June 1802, and MA on 13 December 1805, and was student from December 1800 until 1812. He was a considerable Greek scholar and a favourite of Cyril Jackson, the dean. On 5 July 1810 he was created DCL on the occasion of Lord Grenville's installation as chancellor (he had played some part in the election). He unsuccessfully contested Worcestershire in a by-election in February 1806, but was elected the next year, and represented the county until 1820 as a zealous member of the whig party.

Lyttelton's maiden speech was made on 27 February 1807 in favour of the rejection of the Westminster petition; and on 16 March he brought forward a motion (rejected by forty-six votes) expressing regret at the substitution of the duke of Portland's administration for Lord Grenville's. He attacked the new ministers, especially Spencer Perceval, for raising a cry about 'religion' and 'awakening the furies of bigotry and fanaticism to the manifest injury of all true religion' (Cobbett, 9.434). In opposition to most members of his party he supported the expedition to Copenhagen, but he voted with them on Whitbread's motion for the production of papers relative to it. Lyttelton felt strongly the old whig jealousy of the influence of the crown and court. In supporting Curwen's bill for the prevention of the sale of seats, he suggested that the duke of York, the late commander-in-chief, had to some degree corrupted members of parliament; and in speaking on the budget resolutions of 1808 he declared that 'the influence of the prerogative had increased fourfold to what it was in former times' (ibid., 11.22). Again, on 4 May 1812, in a debate on the Royal Sinecure Offices Bill, he asserted that 'it was notorious that the regent was surrounded with favourites, and as it were hemmed in by minions', and he strongly opposed a clause in the Royal Household Bill (19 March 1819), which awarded an extra grant of £10,000 a year to the duke of York. Nevertheless, Lyttelton in 1819 thought that 'the revolutionary faction of the radicals ought to be opposed'. In the same session, on 2 December 1819, he made a weighty speech in favour of the second reading of the Seditious Meetings Prevention Bill, although he blamed ministers for having made the measure necessary by want of conciliation, and thought an inquiry needful into the Peterloo massacre of

William Henry Lyttelton, third Baron Lyttelton and third Baron Westcote (1782–1837), by Sir George Hayter, 1810s

1819. Between 1816 and 1819 he actively opposed state lotteries, three times introducing unsuccessful motions against them.

Lyttelton interested himself also in naval and military questions, and succeeded in obtaining an important modification of the order which deprived officers in the army of their half pay if they were unable to make affidavit that they had no other emolument or employment under the crown, and were not in possession of a certain private income. He also advocated ending the employment of child chimney sweeps, and he was a strong opponent of the property tax. He supported Sheridan's motion of 6 February 1810 against the standing order for the exclusion of strangers from the house. In the same session, on 16 February, he opposed the voting of an annuity to Wellington, whose merits he considered to be far short of those of Nelson. He spoke strongly against the Aliens Bill in 1816 and 1818. In 1820, short of money both for the election and for normal expenditure, he did not stand again. On the death of his half-brother, George Fulke, second baron, on 12 November 1828, he succeeded to the titles. He did not take much part in the debates of the House of Lords, but on 6 December 1831 he made a strong speech in favour of the Reform Bill in the debate on the address. He was appointed lord lieutenant of Worcestershire on 29 May 1833.

On 3 March 1813, Lyttelton married Lady Sarah Spencer (1787–1870), eldest daughter of George John, second Earl Spencer, who was a lady of the bedchamber (1838–42) and governess to Victoria's children (1842–50) [*see* Lyttelton,

Sarah]. With her he had three sons: George William *Lyttelton, who succeeded to the title (and was Gladstone's brother-in-law), Spencer Lyttelton (1818–1882), who became marshal of the ceremonies to the royal household, and William Henry *Lyttelton, canon of Gloucester; and two daughters, Caroline (*b.* 1816), who died unmarried, and Lavinia (1821–1850), wife of Henry Glynne, rector of Hawarden. His wife died, aged eighty-two, at Hagley on 13 April 1870; her *Correspondence*, edited by Mrs Hugh Wyndham, was published in 1912.

Besides his accomplishments as a Greek scholar, Lyttelton enjoyed a great reputation as a wit: for a time the *Letters of Peter Plymley* were ascribed to him before Sydney Smith's authorship of them was known. In August 1815, through his friendship with the captain, he obtained a passage on board the *Northumberland* from Portsmouth to Plymouth, and privately printed fifty-two copies of *An account of Napoleon Buonaparte's coming on board H.M.S. Northumberland, 7 Aug. 1815; with notes of two conversations held with him*; he also printed a *Catalogue of Pictures at Hagley*. He also published *Private Devotions for School Boys*; another edition, revised and corrected by his eldest son, appeared in 1869, and further editions until 1885. Lyttelton was a staunch whig, a bad speaker, and a good conversationalist. He died on 30 April 1837 at his brother-in-law's house, Spencer Park in London.

G. Le G. Norgate, *rev.* H. C. G. Matthew

Sources HoP, *Commons* • GEC, *Peerage* • *GM*, 2nd ser., 8 (1837), 83 • W. Cobbett, ed., *Parliamentary debates, 1803–20*, 41 vols. (1812–20)
Archives Hagley Hall, Worcestershire, diaries | BL, letters to second Earl Spencer • Devon RO, letters to E. Copleston • W. Sussex RO, letters to duke of Richmond
Likenesses G. Hayter, drawing, 1810–19, NPG [*see illus.*]
Wealth at death under £10,000: GEC, *Peerage*

Lyttelton, William Henry (1820–1884), Church of England clergyman, the second of the three sons of William Henry *Lyttelton, third Baron Lyttelton (1782–1837), and his wife, Lady Sarah *Lyttelton (1787–1870), eldest daughter of George John *Spencer, second Earl Spencer, was born on 3 April 1820. After education at Winchester College he matriculated at Trinity College, Cambridge, in Michaelmas term 1838 and graduated MA in 1841. Ordained priest in 1844, he held the curacy of Kettering, Northamptonshire, from 1843 to 1845, but for reasons of poor health spent much of this period travelling in Germany, where he came under the influence of a liberal and evangelical theology somewhat at variance with his family's high-churchmanship. In 1847, however, he was appointed by his brother, George William *Lyttelton, fourth Baron Lyttelton (1817–1876), to the rectory of Hagley, Worcestershire, where he remained until his death. He was appointed an honorary canon of Worcester in 1850, and a canon of Gloucester in 1880.

Lyttelton married, on 28 September 1854, Emily, youngest daughter of Henry *Pepys (1783–1860), bishop of Worcester. After her death on 12 September 1877, he married, on 5 February 1880, Constance Ellen, youngest daughter of the Hon. Grantham Yorke, dean of Worcester, who survived him. There were no children of either marriage.

Besides contributing a chapter on the physical geography and geology of the Clent district to William Harris's *Clentine Rambles* (1868), Lyttelton published some minor works of apologetics. He died at Great Malvern, Worcestershire, on 24 July 1884 and was buried at Hagley.

J. M. Rigg, *rev.* G. Martin Murphy

Sources B. Askwith, *The Lytteltons: a family chronicle of the nineteenth century* (1975) • Venn, *Alum. Cant.* • *The Times* (25 July 1884) • *CGPLA Eng. & Wales* (1884)
Archives BL, letters to W. E. Gladstone, Add. MSS 44376–44449
Likenesses J. Jackson, oils, *c.*1826, Althorp, Northamptonshire • A. R. Venables, oils (as a child), Hagley Hall, Worcestershire
Wealth at death £7234 1*s.* 6*d.*: probate, 29 Oct 1884, *CGPLA Eng. & Wales*

Lyttleton, Raymond Arthur [Ray] (1911–1995), astronomer, was born on 7 May 1911 in Warley Woods, near Birmingham, the only son and youngest of three children of William John Lyttleton and his wife, Agnes, *née* Kelly. Both parents were Irish, but as his father came from a protestant family and his wife from a Catholic one, they found life in Ireland difficult and moved to England some years before Ray was born. His father worked in the Post Office, where he eventually attained a senior position.

Lyttleton (who grew up in Harborne, near Birmingham) showed his abilities early, and he shone at King Edward's School, Birmingham (1924–30). His outstanding mathematical abilities were immediately recognized by staff and fellow students, but he also won numerous prizes in other subjects. He disliked Latin and religion and anything connected with these subjects then and throughout his life. He was enthusiastic about cricket and this, too, lasted all his life. He played to a good standard until he was forty, and became very knowledgeable in its laws. He applied physics to account for the trajectories of swinging balls. The school also developed his lifelong passion for clear and precise English.

In 1930 Lyttleton entered Clare College, Cambridge, where he read mathematics and performed outstandingly to gain first-class honours in both parts of the mathematical tripos. On graduating in 1933 he was awarded a graduate studentship, rare in those days, and started research in dynamical astronomy under William Marshall Smart; soon he had published his first paper. Throughout his long, distinguished, and varied research career he retained a special liking for this subject, which deals with the motion of massive bodies under their mutual gravitational attraction. His demonstrated ability led to his being awarded an Eliza Procter fellowship to research at Princeton University under Professor Henry Norris Russell. There he made important contributions to the difficult subject of the origin of the solar system. (One of his later contributions in this field was that Pluto may be an escaped satellite of Neptune.) After two fruitful years in Princeton he was appointed assistant lecturer in mathematics at Cambridge, and was elected to a fellowship at St John's College in 1937; he also received his Cambridge PhD. In early 1939 Lyttleton met Fred Hoyle. Together they produced a series of influential papers, some on the internal constitution of stars and others on the gravitational accretion of inter-stellar matter by stars. These papers pioneered the study of the two-way interaction between stars and the inter-stellar medium.

In spring 1939 Lyttleton met Meave Marguerite Hobden (*d.* 2001), daughter of F. Hobden, formerly of Shanghai. They were married on 9 August 1939. Lyttleton's father lent them his car for their honeymoon in the south of France. A nerve-racking return journey got them back to Britain on the day war was declared (3 September 1939). In 1940 Lyttleton joined the Ministry of Supply as an experimental officer, first at Christchurch, then at Shoeburyness. From 1943 to 1945 he was technical assistant to the scientific adviser at the War Office.

Lyttleton returned to Cambridge in 1945 to become lecturer in mathematics. On the strength of his research and his immaculate teaching he became Stokes lecturer in 1954, reader in 1959, and professor of theoretical astronomy in 1969. (He became emeritus professor on retirement in 1978.) He was a member of Cambridge's Institute of Astronomy from 1967. Though his original fellowship at St John's College had expired in 1940, he was again elected in 1949 and remained a fellow there until his death. He was awarded the Hopkins prize of the Cambridge Philosophical Society in 1951. In 1955 he was elected a fellow of the Royal Society and he received the society's royal medal in 1965. He was also closely associated with the Royal Astronomical Society, as a fellow from 1934, as geophysical secretary from 1949 to 1960, and as a member of council from 1950 to 1961 and 1969 to 1972. He received the society's gold medal in 1959.

Lyttleton was an active researcher all his life. He particularly enjoyed finding gaps in the foundations of accepted hypotheses and elaborating the contrary view. It was healthy for science that his colleagues had to plug these gaps, but he tended to adhere to his heterodox views for longer than was justified. This, together with his brilliant, but caustic wit, made him less popular with the generality of his colleagues, but also gave him a few close friends. His interests widened to include geophysics, a field in which he made a number of contributions, some of them at odds with received wisdom, such as his arguments (based on his dynamical astronomy) for a slowly shrinking earth, which he linked with mountain building. His originality, the mark of a major scientist, never left him; nor did his meticulous analysis or his precision in expression.

Lyttleton's lectures were always a model of logical structure and clarity. He was visiting professor at Brandeis (1965–6) and Brown (1967–8) universities. His special subject of dynamical astronomy became of great importance in the space age. Thus he became a frequent visitor to NASA's jet propulsion laboratory in California, where he spent a few months every summer. He was much interested in explaining his fields of science to a wider public through his BBC lectures, through his Halley (1970) and Milne (1978) lectures at Oxford, and through his semi-popular books. These included *The Comets and their Origin* (1953), *The Modern Universe* (1956), a brilliant description of the then state of astronomy, and *The Earth and its Mountains* (1982), a beautifully argued presentation of his rather heterodox views. Lyttleton remained active in his later years, even when his health troubled him. He died at his home, 48 St Albans Road, Cambridge, on 16 May 1995, of emphysema. His body was cremated eight days later at the Cambridge crematorium. He was survived by his wife, Meave. There were no children of the marriage.

HERMANN BONDI

Sources H. Bondi, *Memoirs FRS*, 43 (1997), 305–19 · *WWW, 1991–5* · *The Times* (19 May 1995) · *The Independent* (22 June 1995) · personal knowledge (2004) · private information (2004)
Archives RS, MSS · St John Cam., MSS
Likenesses photograph, repro. in *The Times* · photograph, repro. in *The Independent*
Wealth at death £243,760: administration with will, 25 July 1995, *CGPLA Eng. & Wales*

Lyttleton, Thomas. *See* Littleton, Sir Thomas (*b.* before 1417, *d.* 1481).

Lytton, Lady Constance Georgina Bulwer- (1869–1923), suffragette, was born on 12 February 1869 in Vienna, the second daughter and third child in the family of four sons and three daughters of Edward Robert Bulwer-*Lytton, first earl of Lytton (1831–1891), diplomat and poet, and his wife, Edith Bulwer-*Lytton (1841–1936) [*see under* Lytton, Edward Robert Bulwer-], daughter of the Hon. Edward Villiers and niece of George Villiers, fourth earl of Clarendon. She was the great-granddaughter of the early nineteenth-century feminist Anna Wheeler. Her paternal grandfather, Edward, first Baron Lytton, was a prominent Victorian man of letters. Her childhood was spent in Vienna, Paris, Lisbon, and India, and at the family seat at Knebworth, Hertfordshire. She was taught by a governess, and acquired a permanent love of music and art from a visiting Austrian music teacher, Fräulein Oser. She was connected by kinship and marriage to a wide range of aristocratic, artistic, and literary circles; one sister married Gerald Balfour (later second earl of Balfour), brother of the future prime minister, and another married the architect Sir Edwin Lutyens.

From 1887 to 1891 Lady Constance lived in Paris, where her father was ambassador. In 1892 she went with her mother on a visit to South Africa, where she met the feminist Olive Schreiner and fell traumatically in love with an unmarriageable man. She never married. From an early age she had a strong dislike for conventional aristocratic 'society'. After the death of her father in 1891 she withdrew entirely into private life, devoting herself almost obsessively to the care of her mother, even though the latter soon came out of retirement to become a lady-in-waiting to the queen. For many years her life was almost a caricature of the daily round of the Victorian upper-class spinster. She arranged flowers, polished brasses, and lavished her affections on dogs. But the regime was self-imposed: for all her withdrawn and self-effacing outward personality, her correspondence reveals a woman of decisive and original views about art, literature, politics, and religion. Her family and friends made many attempts to draw her into public life, including offering the sub-

Lady Constance Georgina Bulwer-Lytton (1869–1923), by Bassano, 1911

editorship of a literary magazine, but these were all rejected. John Morley described her as 'cultivated and original, and witty and talented, and [yet] she considered herself quite giftless' (Raymond, 308).

Lady Constance's life changed dramatically in 1905 when her godmother and great-aunt Georgiana, Lady Bloomfield, left her a legacy of £1000, which she donated to the revival of morris dancing. Mary Neal, a leading protagonist of the folk-dance movement, was also the organizer of the Esperance Guild for working girls, which she had founded jointly with Emmeline Pethick-Lawrence, who was treasurer of the Women's Social and Political Union (WSPU). Lady Constance visited some suffragettes imprisoned in Holloway gaol, and this experience transformed her into a public figure with a single-minded burning cause. She joined the WSPU in 1909 and thereafter she lobbied parliament, travelled the country addressing mass meetings, and mobilized her influential contacts on behalf of the suffrage campaign.

Lady Constance's protest activities led to her being imprisoned in Holloway in early 1909, but she was treated leniently on the grounds of having heart trouble, after the authorities became aware of her powerful connections. Later in the year she was again arrested for throwing stones at a ministerial car during a political meeting in Newcastle, and again released quickly. In early 1910 she decided to test the existence of class differences in the treatment of suffragist prisoners, and assumed the dress and name of a working woman, Miss Jane Warton, for a further protest in Liverpool. She was imprisoned in Walton gaol, went on hunger strike, and was this time force-fed eight times before her release, with no medical examination. Her account of her imprisonment, delivered to a mass meeting at the Queen's Hall on 31 January 1910, did much to bring the practice of force-feeding to an end. Some months later she became a paid organizer for the WSPU, and moved into a worker's tenement in the Euston Road.

However, the strain of Lady Constance's ordeal proved permanently to have undermined her health. In August 1910 she suffered a heart attack, and two years later she had a stroke which left her paralysed. With her left hand she wrote *Prison and Prisoners* (1914), an account of her suffragette experiences and an indictment of conditions in prisons. She died on 22 May 1923 in London and was buried at Knebworth on 26 May. Her letters, published after her death, are a moving monument to an unpretentious, spiritual, and quintessentially private woman, whose life was almost accidentally invaded by a great public cause.

JOSE HARRIS, *rev.*

Sources *The Times* (23 May 1923) · *The Times* (25 May 1923) · E. N. Raymond, *Victorian viceroy: the life of Robert, the first earl of Lytton* (1980) · Burke, *Peerage* · *Letters of Constance Lytton*, ed. B. Balfour (1925) · C. Lytton, *Prison and prisoners* (1914) · *WWW* · A. Dejey, *The Europa biographical dictionary of British women* (1983) · J. Purvis, 'The prison experiences of the suffragettes in Edwardian Britain', *Women's History Review*, 4 (1995), 103–33

Archives Museum of London, corresp. and papers, incl. MS account of prison experiences | BL, corresp. with Arthur James Balfour, Add. MS 49793, *passim* · Women's Library, London, letters to Alice Ker; letters to Elizabeth Robins | FILM BFI NFTVA, *Shoulder to shoulder*, BBC 2, 17 April 1974

Likenesses Bassano, photograph, 1911, NPG [*see illus.*] · N. S. Lytton, drawing, 1911, repro. in Balfour, ed., *Letters of Constance Lytton*, frontispiece · photograph (aged seventeen), repro. in Balfour, ed., *Letters of Constance Lytton*, facing p. 2 · photograph (aged thirty-nine), repro. in Balfour, ed., *Letters of Constance Lytton*, facing p. 128

Lytton, Edith Bulwer-, countess of Lytton (1841–1936). *See under* Lytton, Edward Robert Bulwer-, first earl of Lytton (1831–1891).

Lytton, Edward George Earle Lytton Bulwer [*formerly* Edward George Earle Lytton Bulwer], **first Baron Lytton (1803–1873)**, writer and politician, was born on 25 May 1803 at 31 Baker Street, London, the third and youngest son of Colonel (later General) William Earle Bulwer (1757–1807) of Heydon and Wood Dalling, Norfolk, and Elizabeth Barbara Lytton (1773–1843) of Knebworth, Hertfordshire. His elder brothers were William Earle Lytton Bulwer (1799–1877), who inherited the Bulwer family estates in north Norfolk, and (William) Henry Lytton Earle *Bulwer (1801–1872), who was knighted in 1848 and raised to the peerage as Baron Dalling and Bulwer in 1871. His daunting array of names is a source of frequent confusion. His forenames were Edward George Earle Lytton (the last of them being his mother's maiden name). For the first forty years of his life his surname was Bulwer though out of respect for his mother's family, to whose estates he was heir, he often styled himself Edward Lytton Bulwer. When his mother died in 1843 and he came into his inheritance, he

Edward George Earle Lytton Bulwer Lytton, first Baron Lytton (1803–1873), by unknown photographer

changed his surname by royal licence to Bulwer Lytton (without a hyphen, though others sometimes supplied one), thus becoming Edward George Earle Lytton Bulwer Lytton. He was created Baron Lytton of Knebworth in 1866. For consistency, and concision, he is referred to below simply as Bulwer, the name by which he was longest known.

Both sides of Bulwer's family were of ancient descent. Turold Bölver, who appears as one of William the Conqueror's retainers in Bulwer's novel *Harold* (1848), was assigned the manor of Wood Dalling in Norfolk as part of the Norman settlement. The Bulwers prospered, but established themselves among the county's most prominent landed gentry only in the mid-eighteenth century, when they married into the wealthy Earle family, owners of the neighbouring Heydon Hall. Bulwer's father, William Earle Bulwer, who inherited both estates, was enrolled at Pembroke College, Cambridge; more inclined, in his son's words, to Bacchus than Minerva, he left without taking a degree and embarked on a military career. The Lyttons were of similarly ancient lineage, having given their name to the village of Lytton (now Litton) in the Peak District of Derbyshire, where they settled soon after the conquest. (In *Harold* another of William's guard at Hastings is named de Littain.) Their seat at Knebworth in Hertfordshire was purchased in 1490 by Sir Robert de Lytton, who had fought alongside Henry Tudor at Bosworth, and who, predictably, appears in Bulwer's novel *The Last of the Barons* (1843). In the mid-eighteenth century Knebworth descended to Bulwer's maternal grandfather Richard Warburton Lytton, an accomplished but eccentric scholar of classics and oriental languages who separated from his wife soon after the birth of their only child Elizabeth in 1773. Shuttled back and forth between her estranged parents, Elizabeth Lytton grew into a young woman of uncommon intellectual accomplishment and considerable social hauteur. In 1798, after a brief courtship, she married William Bulwer, colonel of the 106th regiment, the Norfolk rangers. It proved an ill-starred union. An energetic and ambitious soldier, Colonel Bulwer was also self-willed, short-tempered, and chronically subject to gout. He had little time for his children, least of all for the infant Edward, on whom his unhappy wife lavished maternal affection in proportion to her husband's brusque indifference. In 1804, having raised two regiments at his own expense, he was promoted to the rank of general and entrusted with the defence of the north-west of England in the anticipated event of a French invasion. He was expecting a peerage from a grateful government when, in July 1807, he died from a stroke.

Early life, 1807–1827 Left comfortably off, the widowed Mrs Bulwer moved to London. The two elder boys were sent away to school, and Edward was effectively brought up as an only child. Under his mother's devoted tutelage he was reading by the age of four and writing verse at seven. The most significant event of these early years followed the death of Richard Warburton Lytton in December 1810, when his grandfather's vast library was transferred to London. For the next twelve months, before his mother sold the collection that had all but taken over her house, Edward explored his grandfather's books, delighting especially in chivalric romances but dipping also into all manner of scholarly tomes and obscure treatises, thus acquiring a taste for both romantic legend and antiquarian enquiry that he was never to lose. Already precocious, he was stirred by this voracious browsing to new levels of intellectual pretension, and when, aged eight or nine, he is reported to have asked 'Pray, Mamma, are you not sometimes overcome by the sense of your own identity?' (Lytton, 1.36), his mother decided it was time he was sent to school.

Over the next two years Bulwer attended three separate establishments, but learned little and failed to make a single friend. Then, at eleven, he was enrolled at Dr Hooker's fashionable academy at Rottingdean, where boys were prepared for entry to Eton College and Harrow School. There at last he drew inspiration from his teachers and found comradeship among his peers. He discovered Scott and Byron, wrote poetry for the school magazine, and excelled at boxing. Four years later, in September 1818, Dr Hooker confessed to Mrs Bulwer Lytton (who had thus changed her name after inheriting the Lytton estates from her father) that there was no more he could realistically offer her son, and recommended that he be sent to a public school. In the event, following an interview with Dr Keate at Eton, the fifteen-year-old Bulwer persuaded his mother that he was altogether too grown-up to continue in formal education, and that he should be allowed to 'leap at once from Master into Mister, from the big boy into the young man' (Lytton, 1.46). Tall and athletically proportioned, already sporting whiskers and a moustache, at fifteen Bulwer carried himself with a self-assurance verging on arrogance. The outward air of confidence, however, masked a nature which at heart was acutely self-conscious and deeply insecure. It was a contradiction that increased with the passage of time.

From 1819 to 1821 Bulwer studied with a private tutor, the Revd Charles Wallington at Ealing, under whose enlightened care he came to love the classics, and was taught swordsmanship by Byron's fencing-master Henry Angelo. While at Ealing he fell in love with a girl a year or two older than himself, but the romance was abruptly severed when her father took her away without warning and forced her to marry against her wishes. Bulwer was heartbroken, and for several months was plunged into a desperate melancholy. He dramatized the experience in several of his stories, most strikingly, fully fifty years later, in the Lily Mordaunt episode in his novel *Kenelm Chillingly* (1873). The other major event of his time at Ealing was the publication of his first volume of poetry, the Byronic *Ismael: an Oriental Tale*, which was issued by Hatchards at his mother's expense in April 1820.

Bulwer went up to Cambridge in January 1822 aged eighteen and a half. After a term at Trinity, which he found stiffly academic, he transferred to Trinity Hall. As a fellow-commoner there he read widely in philosophy, political economy, and social history. His closest friend was Alexander Cockburn, later lord chief justice, who introduced him to the union. After a nervous start Bulwer developed into a regular and not unsuccessful speaker, and served successively as the society's secretary, treasurer, and president. He also maintained a steady literary output during his time as an undergraduate. In 1823 the Cambridge firm of Carpenter & Son published his second volume of rather undistinguished imitative verse, *Delmour, or, The Tale of a Sylphid*, and later that year he was invited by W. M. Praed to write for the newly launched *Knight's Quarterly Magazine*, to which he contributed both poetry and prose under the pseudonym of Edmund Bruce. In the long vacation of 1824 he made a pilgrimage to Ullswater, to visit the grave of the girl he had loved and lost at Ealing, who had written to him on her deathbed. Having passed an overnight vigil on her tomb, he spent several weeks in the Lake District immersed in a self-conscious philosophical solitude similar to that of Erasmus Falkland, the hero of his first novel, which he was drafting at the time. On his return home, in September he renewed an earlier acquaintance with Lady Caroline Lamb, whose house at Brocket Park was just a few miles from Knebworth, and who was recovering from the news of the death of her former lover Lord Byron. Dazzled by her talk of Byron, and intoxicated by the idea of taking his place at her side, the 21-year-old Bulwer, eighteen years her junior, was readily enslaved and rapidly seduced. Throughout the Michaelmas term at Cambridge they exchanged intimate letters, but soon after he came down for the Christmas vacation she cast him off for a new admirer.

Vain and hypersensitive, Bulwer was deeply offended by the malicious gossip that had attended this liaison, and soon after he left Cambridge in summer 1825 (though it was not until the following year that he proceeded to his ordinary degree) he took himself indignantly off to France. In the Paris of the restored monarchy he indulged for a while in the conventional dissipations of a monied young blood. For all his dandification and exquisite airs, however, Bulwer was too intellectually inclined and too subject to melancholy reflection to be satisfied for long by mere pleasure seeking. After a few months in Paris he moved to the romantic solitude of Versailles, where he read Rousseau and Mill, and completed a new volume of Byronic and satirical verse (*Weeds and Wild Flowers*, privately printed later in 1825). The day he returned to London, on 25 April 1826, a week before his twenty-third birthday, he attended a soirée and there met the woman who became his wife. Beautiful, headstrong, and extravagant, Rosina Anne Doyle Wheeler [*see* Lytton, Rosina Anne Doyle Bulwer (1802–1882)] was the youngest child of Francis Massy Wheeler, who had inherited a crumbling house and impoverished estate in co. Tipperary, where he lounged by day and drank by night, and Anna Doyle *Wheeler, an Owenite socialist and advocate of women's rights. Rosina's parents separated when she was nine. After a tempestuous upbringing with her mother in Guernsey and France, in 1825 she was introduced into London society by her great-uncle Sir John Doyle. Mrs Bulwer Lytton disapproved strongly of her son's liaison, which cut across her plans for him to make a brilliant marriage as a stepping-stone to a public career. She regarded Rosina as a vulgar Irish adventuress, and did all in her power to prevent the relationship from developing. Bulwer's genuine desire not to upset his mother was reinforced by a prudent assessment of the practical consequences of marrying against her wishes. By the provisions of his father's will his independent income was barely £200 per annum; that he was living at ten times this level was due solely to his mother's generous allowance. In the event, and though Rosina's private income was less than half his own, the courtship continued and they were finally married on 29 August 1827. Obdurate to the last, Mrs Bulwer Lytton refused to attend the ceremony, and for a full year thereafter would neither receive her son nor answer his repeated and anguished letters. She also terminated his allowance. The couple set up home in the country, at Woodcot House in Oxfordshire, 6 miles from Reading, an imposing residence whose rent and upkeep accounted for virtually their entire combined income. With his allowance suspended and a luxurious lifestyle to support, Bulwer immediately set about earning money by the only means that seemed appropriate—namely by writing. During the next decade he published a dozen novels, two dozen short stories, five plays, two volumes of poetry, a history of Athens, a sociological survey of English life, and at least a hundred periodical essays and reviews. By 1834, barely ten years after Bulwer the undergraduate was awarded the chancellor's medal for English verse at Cambridge, Bulwer the literary lion and best-seller was hailed by the *American Quarterly Review* as 'without doubt, the most popular writer now living' (16.507).

Literary career, 1827–1840 Bulwer's professional literary career began modestly, when Henry Colburn issued his first novel, *Falkland*, in March 1827. A lurid tale of adultery and gloomy philosophical posturing, it attracted little attention and sold poorly. Despite this, Colburn recognized the potential of his new recruit and offered £500 for another novel. Utterly different in character, *Pelham, or, The Adventures of a Gentleman*, published in May 1828, became a huge best-seller (George IV is reported to have ordered several copies to ensure that it would be available in each of his residences). Henry Pelham is the most consummate dandy in the canon of 'silver fork' fiction, his affectation of wearing black for dinner setting a fashion for evening dress that has persisted to the present day. Significantly, however, he is unsatisfied by the empty extravagances which he has elevated to an art form, and his tireless exertion to clear a friend of a charge of murder measures his transformation from self-indulgent fop to productive citizen. This pattern of growth from egotism to an awareness of social obligation marks the beginning of a moral agenda that was to dominate several of Bulwer's novels over the following decade. In the first of these, *The Disowned* (December 1828), which replicated the formula of social satire intermixed with sensational incident, the hero is a soberly contemplative scholar who learns that self-fulfilment proceeds from philanthropic action rather than solitary thought. Less didactic in its conception, *Devereux* (1829) is a rambling tale of political intrigue and Gothic melodrama set in the early eighteenth century, whose chief interest lies in its portrayal of the good and the great of the period: Swift and Pope, Bolingbroke and Voltaire, Louis XIV and Peter the Great. It is notable also for the rhetorical excesses of its apostrophic style: 'Wild brooklet … Fortune freights not your channels with her hoarded stores, and Pleasure ventures not her silken sails upon your tide' (1.63). This mannered floridity of diction, accompanied by the persistent capitalization of abstract nouns, was to become a distinguishing and disfiguring feature of Bulwer's prose.

Paul Clifford (1830) represented a radical new departure. Its eponymous hero was a highwayman, and its leading aim was to expose the pointless barbarity of the penal code of the day. The book's guiding moral was neatly expressed in its final sentence: 'The very worst use to which you can put a man is to hang him'; though more recently, and far less seriously (such being Bulwer's late-twentieth-century fate), attention has focused rather on its opening words—'It was a dark and stormy night.' In *Eugene Aram* (1832) Bulwer took Newgate fiction into unprecedented territory by fashioning a hero out of a notorious murderer. The historic Aram was an itinerant provincial schoolmaster (he had briefly been tutor to Bulwer's aunts in Norfolk) who was hanged for murder in 1759. In the novel he is presented as a high-minded philosopher who, ground down by poverty, had been induced to take part in a robbery which turned to murder. Wracked for years by guilt, he is subsequently redeemed by love, only to be arrested on the day of his wedding. Predictably, the book gave rise to a storm of indignant protest, even as it ran through numerous editions. Bulwer's condescending aristocratic manner and air of intellectual superiority had already provoked the hostility of reviewers such as Lockhart, Maginn, and Thackeray, who had mounted a barrage of vituperative attacks on him in the *Quarterly Review* and *Fraser's Magazine*. Now the entire tribe of London literary journals rose almost as one to condemn the immorality of the book and the hypocrisy of its author. Smarting from this experience, Bulwer issued his next novel (*Godolphin*, 1833) anonymously. The tactic backfired. Without the talismanic name of Bulwer to commend it, the story of Percy Godolphin's progress from intellectual self-absorption to the altruistic vision of a great and gifted soul proved a rare commercial failure, despite the blood-curdling catastrophes that crowded its pages. The reviews, at least, were merely lukewarm—even, deliberately so, that in the *New Monthly Magazine*, which was written by Bulwer himself. He had been editing the journal since November 1831, responsible for regular features such as the 'Monthly commentary' and 'The politician', as well as for numerous individual essays and reviews, some of which were later collected in *Asmodeus at Large* (1833) and *The Student* (1835).

In summer 1833 the strain of incessant work led to a breakdown in Bulwer's health. In August he resigned the editorship of the *New Monthly*, and in September he set out with Rosina on a recuperative visit to Italy. That same month saw the publication of his most original work of non-fiction, *England and the English*: a survey of the current state of politics, society, and manners; education, morality, and religion; art, literature, and science. Few of his contemporaries could have attempted so ambitious an account of the national character; still fewer could have carried it off with such consistent *élan*. On his return from Italy in February 1834 he brought with him the near-completed manuscript of what became his single most successful book, *The Last Days of Pompeii*. Published in July 1834, it rapidly achieved classic status and remained a best-seller for the rest of the century; it was translated into at least ten languages (no fewer than sixteen French impressions had been issued by 1864), was frequently dramatized, and twice adapted as an opera. Two years after the death of Scott, Bulwer's epic tale of Roman indulgence, Christian martyrdom, and the cataclysmic eruption of Vesuvius established him as the most popular historical novelist of the day. This standing was confirmed by *Rienzi, Last of the Tribunes* (1835), about the rise and fall of the demagogue who briefly seized power from the warring baronial factions of late-fourteenth-century Rome. Gibbon had dismissed Rienzi as a mixture of the knave and the madman; for Bulwer he is a hero and visionary, whose fanatical pursuit of popular liberty is fired by the inner strength of his aspiring spirit. An amalgam of careful scholarship and wilful invention, of political allegory, philosophical idealism, and extreme melodrama, the novel was the direct inspiration of Wagner's opera of the same name.

As already indicated, Bulwer's literary output during this period was not restricted to novels. His other major publications included the narrative poem *O'Neill, or, The Rebel* (1827) and the verse satire *The Siamese Twins* (1831); a loosely connected set of short stories entitled *The Pilgrims of the Rhine* (1834); the historical study *Athens: its Rise and Fall* (1837); and the illustrated novella *Leila, or, The Siege of Granada* (1838). Between 1836 and 1840 he wrote five plays for his friend the actor–manager William Macready. Two of these, *The Duchess de la Vallière* (1836) and *The Sea-Captain* (1839), were merely successful; the melodrama *The Lady of Lyons* (1838) and the comedy of manners *Money* (1840) proved among the most resilient stage works of the Victorian era; while the historical verse drama *Richelieu* (1839) contains the most famous words he ever wrote:

> Beneath the rule of men entirely great
> The pen is mightier than the sword.
> (II.ii)

After parting company with the *New Monthly* he continued his journalistic career by contributing regularly to the *Edinburgh Review* and, from March to October 1838, by editing the short-lived *Monthly Chronicle*. It was in the latter that he published his long essay 'On art in fiction', a pioneering account of the theory and practice of the genre which marked his most significant contribution to the literature of the 1830s. This contribution was appropriately crowned by *Ernest Maltravers* (1837) and its sequel *Alice, or, The Mysteries* (1838), whose 2000 pages are filled to overflowing with the grand passions, romantic adventures, and philosophical disquisitions that had come to characterize Bulwer's fiction. The most exemplary and programmatic of his *Bildungsromane*, the story of Maltravers's six-volume apprenticeship to politics, literature, and love examines (in the capitalized words of the preface) the effect of worldly experience on 'those great principles by which alone we can work out the Science of Life—a desire for the Good, a passion for the Honest, a yearning after the True'. Time and again, it was the intellectual content of Bulwer's fiction which his contemporaries singled out as its main distinguishing feature. Whether anatomizing the social causes of crime, exhuming representative episodes in history, or analysing the dynamics of spiritual aspiration, his novels were habitually grounded in a rigorous examination of moral, political, and philosophical issues. Each in its own way was designed as much to educate as to entertain; by 1837 he had become 'the metaphysician-novelist of England' (*Monthly Magazine*, 24.541).

Private and political life, 1827–1841 After two years at Woodcot, where their daughter Emily was born in June 1828, the Bulwers moved to London. Effeminately handsome and languidly aristocratic, with his long auburn hair in ringlets and his six-foot frame resplendent in the latest fashions, the author of *Pelham* was fêted to a degree which must have gratified even his vanity. He had been paid £900 for *The Disowned* and a princely £1500 for *Devereux*, all of which and more he laid out in late 1829 on the purchase and extravagant furnishing of 36 Hertford Street, just off Park Lane. There, neglecting his wife and child, he devoted himself to political networking and literary endeavour. He worked incessantly, like a man possessed. Exhausted and explosively irritable, he was described by a family friend as seeming 'like a man who has been flayed, and is sore all over' (Lytton, 1.249). The domestic quarrels that inevitably ensued were exacerbated by the restoration of more cordial relations between Bulwer and his mother (who had finally agreed to receive him soon after the publication of his significantly titled novel *The Disowned*). Already jealous of his fashionable friends such as the young Disraeli and Lady Blessington, and excluded from his career aspirations, Rosina now felt increasingly supplanted in his emotions by her domineering mother-in-law. It was in this inauspicious context of literary drudgery, mounting debts, and marital friction that Bulwer embarked on his political career.

In April 1831 Bulwer was elected MP for St Ives in Huntingdonshire, as an independent radical. His maiden speech on 5 July was in support of the second reading of the Reform Bill, one result of whose passage in the following year was to sweep away his own constituency. At the general election of December 1832 he successfully stood for Lincoln, which he represented until 1841. As a backbencher he promoted legislation on issues of literary, intellectual, and libertarian interest. His bill to establish dramatic copyright was enacted in 1833; his campaign against the monopoly of London's patent theatres (Covent Garden and Drury Lane) led to the abolition of the royal patent in 1843; his persistent call for the reduction of stamp duty on newspapers (the so-called 'taxes on knowledge') finally bore fruit in 1855, when the duty was repealed. Only in the boldest of these initiatives was he frustrated: first mounted in 1832, his impassioned challenge of the crown's right to censor plays, through the office of the lord chamberlain, remained unrealized for well over a century. (By a nice irony, the last lord chamberlain to exercise this power before its abolition in 1968 was the husband of Bulwer's great-granddaughter.) As a speaker Bulwer was unimpressive: his voice was weak, high-pitched, and betrayed the occasional stammer; his style of delivery was self-conscious and oratorically mannered. Appropriately, it was the power of his pen that marked the most influential moment of his political career. When the king dismissed Lord Melbourne's ministry in November 1834 and invited the duke of Wellington to form a government, Bulwer wrote a pamphlet in support of the whigs (whom, as a radical, he disliked rather less than the tories) entitled *A Letter to a Late Cabinet Minister on the Current Crisis*. Within six weeks it had run through twenty-one editions, sold 30,000 copies, and was widely believed to have influenced the result of the ensuing election. In recognition the victorious Melbourne offered Bulwer a junior lordship of the admiralty, which he declined—presumably as insufficient inducement to change his party affiliation. By the late 1830s, however, Bulwer's opposition to household suffrage and the repeal of the corn laws signalled a break with the mainstream radicals. In July 1838 Lord Melbourne recommended him for a baronetcy (ostensibly for services to literature) in

Queen Victoria's coronation honours, but at the general election of 1841 he lost his seat to a tory. He did not return to parliament until 1852.

The demands of Bulwer's political career placed further strain on a marriage which had rapidly ceased to be as romantic as the courtship that preceded it. His neglect of his wife and family was unchecked by the birth of a son, Edward Robert Bulwer-*Lytton (1831–1891), in November 1831, and his ostentatious philandering with the society beauty Mrs Robert Stanhope in 1833 threatened to break the marriage apart. Later that year, hoping to rekindle their relationship, the Bulwers left the children with a governess and travelled to Italy. The trip was a disaster. He was fascinated by the country, she detested it. In Rome, which she described as 'dirty, barbarous and dismal' (Lytton, 1.266), Bulwer left Rosina to her own devices and threw himself into work on *Rienzi*; in Naples, while he studied with the archaeologist Sir William Gell, she flirted outrageously with a Neapolitan prince. They quarrelled violently and returned to England. There, by degrees embittered, recriminatory, and hysterical, they decided on a trial separation, whereupon he promptly embarked on another affair (with a Miss Laura Deacon, who remained his clandestine partner for many years and by whom he had three children). Extremely provoked, in February 1836 Rosina raided his apartments at the Albany and publicly accused him of entertaining his mistress there. The die was now irrevocably cast. On 19 April 1836 they signed a formal deed of separation, citing 'incompatibility of temper'.

Literary career, 1841–1873 Bulwer's creative energy remained undiminished, despite increasing problems with his health, and in the early 1840s he published three major novels in quick succession. The sensational melodrama *Night and Morning* (1841) turns on the moral distinction between socially induced criminality and socially respectable vice. *Zanoni* (1842), arguably his most original work of fiction, is set during the French Revolution and steeped in the occult lore of which he had become a serious student. The eponymous hero is a Rosicrucian sage who has mastered the secret of immortality but relinquishes this gift to save the life of the woman he loves. The spectacular dénouement, in which he dies in her place on the guillotine, clearly anticipates that of *A Tale of Two Cities* almost twenty years later. In *The Last of the Barons* (1843), which follows the career of Warwick 'the Kingmaker' in the Wars of the Roses, Bulwer portrays the eclipse of baronial power in the late fifteenth century as prefiguring that of the landowning aristocracy in the nineteenth—in each case by middle-class commercial interests. His poetic output in the 1840s was similarly wide-ranging. The miscellaneous collection headed *Eva, a True Story of Light and Darkness* (1842) was followed by a translation, *The Poems and Ballads of Schiller* (1844), prefaced by a long biographical essay; then by *The New Timon* (1846), a discursive romance of contemporary London in heroic couplets; and finally by *King Arthur* (1848–9), a gargantuan epic in twelve books which proved an embarrassing failure. After a hiatus of almost four years, in December 1846 he returned to prose fiction with *Lucretia, or, The Children of Night*, another sensational tale of criminal low life (based on the true story of the forger Thomas Wainewright) which prompted another round of indignant critical attacks, to which Bulwer responded in his pamphlet *A Word to the Public* (1847). *Harold, the Last of the Saxon Kings* (1848) addressed less contentious ground; the novelistic product of painstaking research, its account of the Norman invasion exemplified the heavily footnoted, scholarly antiquarian style which Bulwer had made his own. In a distinctly lighter vein, and scaling new heights of popular success, *The Caxtons* (1849) chronicles the domestic life of an amiably eccentric family, focusing in particular on the youthful experiences of the outlandishly named Pisistratus Caxton, who eventually emigrates to Australia to retrieve the family's fortunes.

With the renewal of his political career, Bulwer's literary activity in the 1850s was restricted to just one play, two novels, and a handful of essays and stories. The comic drama *Not so Bad as we Seem* was written to raise funds for the Guild of Literature and Art which he and Dickens had established to support impoverished authors. It was first produced at a gala performance before the queen and Prince Albert at Devonshire House in May 1851; besides Dickens himself, the amateur cast included Wilkie Collins, Douglas Jerrold, John Forster, Mark Lemon, John Tenniel, and Augustus Egg. The sprawling four-volume sagas of English provincial life *'My Novel'* (1853) and *What Will he Do with it?* (1859), each billed as 'by Pisistratus Caxton', sought to extend the winning formula of *The Caxtons*, but their invention was less spontaneous and their humour more laboured. Though his new publications were few, the commercial value of Bulwer's backlist was growing in proportion to the ever greater demand for cheap fiction from an ever larger reading public. In 1853 George Routledge paid the unprecedented sum of £20,000 for a ten-year lease of the copyrights to his nineteen existing novels. Of the various cheap formats in which these were then reissued, the 1*s.* 6*d.* Railway Library proved the most successful, and in 1857 W. H. Smith reported that Bulwer was the most requested author at his station bookstalls.

Bulwer's next novel, *A Strange Story* (1862), was commissioned by Dickens—for many years past a personal friend and literary admirer—for the weekly magazine *All the Year Round*. A powerful tale of murder and madness, of magic and the *elixir vitae*, its underlying aim was to reveal the inability of natural science to explain supernatural phenomena. It is better known today, however, for providing Bulwer with the opportunity of persuading Dickens to alter the ending of *Great Expectations* (as a *quid pro quo* for Dickens's editorial advice on the conclusion to *A Strange Story*). Characteristically, the novel was underpinned by voracious reading in the relevant scientific and philosophical literature, much of which is more explicitly manifest in his essay collection *Caxtoniana* (1863). Further volumes of verse, *St Stephens* (1860), *The Boatman* (1864), *Poems* (1865), and *The Lost Tales of Miletus* (1866), were followed by two plays, *The Rightful Heir* (1868) and *Walpole* (1869), and then by a translation, *The Odes and Epodes of Horace* (1869). His short novel *The Coming Race* (published anonymously in 1871), a dystopian satire on evolutionary theory and the emancipation of women, is one of the earliest English examples of science fiction. An American mining engineer descends into the centre of the earth and encounters a subterranean people whose extraordinary technological and telekinetic power derives from their control of a mysterious energy called vril. The book proved so popular (it ran through eight editions in eighteen months) that the word vril briefly entered the language, signifying a strength-giving elixir: the name of the famous beef extract product Bovril is a composite of 'bovine' and 'vril'. *Kenelm Chillingly*, a throwback to Bulwer's philosophical *Bildungsromane* of the 1830s, was issued just days after his death in January 1873; its first impression of 3150 three-volume sets sold out on the day of publication. *The Parisians* (1873), a tale of politics and society set during the last days of the second French empire, and the unfinished novel of ancient Greece *Pausanias the Spartan* (1876) were both published posthumously, thus bringing to a close a career that had spanned six decades at the forefront of English letters.

Very few of Bulwer's contemporaries were as prolific, and none was as successful in so many genres. During his lifetime he was outsold only by Dickens, and only Dickens was more widely translated. For thirty years after his death he remained a pillar of the literary establishment; besides innumerable cheap reprints, no fewer than twenty-five multi-volume collections of his complete novels were issued in Britain and America between 1875 and 1900. The twentieth century, however, witnessed a sharp decline in Bulwer's popularity. The reasons for this eclipse are closely bound up with those for his earlier success. Bulwer's great gift was to anticipate and define contemporary taste. With his ornately rhetorical style and lofty moralizing manner he was pre-eminently a writer for his own time, and as that time passed so did his special appeal. In certain quarters he had been roundly condemned for both tendencies from the outset: no other Victorian writer of note attracted such consistent critical animosity or was more cruelly parodied. As Ruskin noted in 1840, 'Everybody has a spite at Bulwer because the public think him clever, and they don't' (*The Diaries of John Ruskin*, ed. J. Evans and J. H. Whitehouse, 3 vols., 1956–9, 1.82). When he ceased to appeal to the common reader his reputation sank almost without trace. Nevertheless, his historical significance was immense, for he epitomized that category of writers who, in his own words:

> form a link in the great chain of a nation's authors, which may be afterwards forgotten by the superficial, but without which the chain would be incomplete. And thus if not first-rate for all time, they have been first-rate in their own day. (*Ernest Maltravers*, 1.286)

Public and private life, 1839–1873 When they separated in 1836 the Bulwers were both thirty-three. Nine turbulent years of marriage now gave way to nearly forty of unrelenting misery. Rosina exacted a furious revenge for being cast off by her husband, and being denied access to her children, doing all in her power to blacken his name and poison his happiness. Whatever the merits of her case, her remorseless litany of abuse struck home, and to the end of his days Bulwer was humiliated and embittered by the spectre of scandal. By the deed of separation Rosina was granted an annuity of £400, a sum she considered grossly inadequate to her needs and expectations. Like Bulwer himself ten years earlier, she turned to literature to supplement her income, and in novels such as *Cheveley, or, The Man of Honour* (1839) and *The Budget of the Bubble Family* (1840) she ridiculed thinly veiled representations of her estranged husband and his pretentious family. Acutely embarrassed at thus being held up to public derision, Bulwer grew ever closer to his mother, whom he had come to venerate as his one constant support against the malice of the world. When she died in December 1843 he was overcome by grief. 'All that I have ever met in the world of sympathy, generosity, and faithful friendship', he wrote to a friend, 'is identified with the name of Mother. The thought of that loss seems to me like the taking away of the candle from a child who is terrified at the dark' (Lytton, 2.21). Four years later his daughter Emily died of typhus fever at the age of nineteen. Rosina, recently returned from a nine-year exile on the continent, accused him of precipitating her death by wilful neglect. Painfully aware that he had done little to secure Emily's happiness by consigning her to a succession of governesses, Bulwer was doubly distraught. The trauma of his daughter's death encouraged him to cultivate the affection of his son (who was later to become viceroy of India and first earl of Lytton) and for the remainder of his life he derived great satisfaction from their intimacy. Meanwhile Rosina intensified her campaign of abuse. On the occasion of the royal première of *Not so Bad as we Seem* in 1851 she wrote to Prince Albert threatening to pelt the queen with rotten eggs for supporting the work of a scoundrel. She also had playbills pasted up around Devonshire House advertising *Even Worse than we Seem* by 'Sir Liar-Coward Bulwer Lytton, who has translated his poor daughter into Heaven, and nobly leaves his wife to live on public charity'. Six years later, with his political career in the ascendant, she further embarrassed him by issuing a pamphlet entitled *Lady Bulwer Lytton's Appeal to the Justice and Charity of the English Public* (1857). Worse was to follow. At the parliamentary election at Hertford on 8 June 1858 (which was to confirm him in the recently offered post of colonial secretary), in the midst of his address from the hustings Rosina pushed her way through the crowd and denounced him as a monster who should himself have been transported to the colonies long ago for mistreating his wife and murdering his daughter. Deeply humiliated and sorely provoked, he reacted by having her committed to a private asylum. He had, however, underestimated the influence of her friends, and of his enemies: mobilizing the anti-government press on her behalf, she was released within the month, whereupon Bulwer felt obliged to increase her settlement and pay off her debts. Despite this concession, in 1864 she embarked on another round of public attacks, addressing spiteful letters to his political colleagues and literary friends (to Wilkie Collins, for example, she insisted that Count Fosco in *The Woman in White* was a poor representative of villainy when compared to her husband). Rosina died in obscurity in March 1882, still obsessed by her ill treatment at his hands. Each of them the product of an unhappy union, their own marriage proved among the most publicly acrimonious of the century.

After losing his seat in parliament, during the early 1840s Bulwer showed little interest in party politics, but towards the end of the decade his renewed friendship with Disraeli and his growing sympathy for Disraeli's brand of toryism rekindled his ambitions. In spring 1851 he published another influential pamphlet, *Letters to John Bull*, which criticized the notion of free trade as a universal panacea for social and economic ills. In thus attacking both the whig administration and its radical supporters, he had little option but to align himself formally with the Conservative opposition. The electors of his home county of Hertfordshire invited him to stand as their representative, and at the general election of July 1852 he re-entered parliament as a tory. Despite the deafness which inhibited his performance in debates, he soon became a front-bench spokesman, notably in his bellicose advocacy of the army's cause in the Crimean War. In 1858 Lord Derby offered him the post of secretary of state for the colonies in the new tory government. Though cut short by illness, his brief period of office was marked by two notable achievements: the establishment in 1858 of the new colony of British Columbia, and the separation from New South Wales in 1859 of the new colony of Queensland (there are towns named Lytton in all three territories). Ill health forced him to resign his office in December 1859 but he retained his seat until 1866, when Lord Derby offered him the peerage he had long coveted in recognition of the public distinction of the Lytton family as well as of his own political service. In the event, isolated and increasingly infirm, he never spoke in the Lords.

Bulwer's health had never been robust. From the age of sixteen he had suffered from an irritation of the middle ear which caused severe pain and progressively impaired his hearing, while the pressure of incessant work and the nervous tension engendered by his domestic troubles took a heavy toll on an already fragile constitution. Frustrated at the ineffectiveness of the drugs, purgatives, and bleeding recommended by his physicians, in the early 1840s he began to read widely in medical and quasi-medical literature. When, in January 1844, he suffered another complete collapse in the wake of his mother's death, against all professional advice he turned to Dr Wilson's hydropathic establishment at Malvern. He recorded his appreciation of hydrotherapy in the pamphlet *Confessions and Observations of a Water Patient* (1845), and for the rest of his life he maintained a keen interest in 'alternative' medicine, particularly as concerned the diagnosis and treatment of nervous disorders. When the vogue for spiritualism crossed the Atlantic in the early 1850s, he attended séances by the prominent mediums D. D. Home, Alexis Didier, and Charles H. Forster. In 1853 he confided to his son that 'there are wonderful phenomena in our being all unknown to existing philosophy' (Lytton, 2.44), and though sceptical of fashionable clairvoyants he was convinced that agencies of spiritual communication known to the magi of old were still recoverable if one could but penetrate their mysteries. He attended experiments conducted by the hypnotist James Braid, the phrenologist John Ashburner, and the mesmerist John Elliottson, seizing on them as a potential key to a 'scientific' understanding of the hidden life of the spirit, which he had earlier sought through exhaustive research into the hermetic tradition of the ancients and the occult arts of the middle ages.

To the end Bulwer remained a bundle of contradictions: at once hugely ambitious and painfully shy, generous of spirit but haughty in manner, profoundly intellectual yet regularly dismissed as superficial. Though craving recognition, he hid behind a protective mask of lofty self-assurance and aristocratic superiority which provoked exactly the opposite response. Over the course of a long career he made the acquaintance of most of the leading writers and politicians of the day, but he had very few close friends (most notably Disraeli and Dickens, Lady Blessington and John Forster). He received his share of public honours—baronetcy and peerage, knight grand cross of St Michael and St George, honorary doctorates at both Oxford and Cambridge—but in his private life he became an increasingly retiring and lonely figure, whose chief satisfaction derived from solitary study rather than from social intercourse. From the 1840s onwards he spent long periods abroad, most often in Germany and the south of France. Though he kept up a London residence (taking a succession of houses in Mayfair and Park Lane), he was always happiest out of the public gaze at his ancestral home of Knebworth, which in the mid-1850s he gothicized with turrets, domes, and gargoyles. He was equally solicitous of his personal appearance, dyeing his hair and resorting to corsets and make-up to disguise the ageing process. In 1874, when describing Charles Greville as the vainest man who had ever lived, Disraeli added 'and I don't forget Cicero and Lytton Bulwer' (W. F. Monypenny and G. E. Buckle, *The Life of Benjamin Disraeli*, 1910–20, 5.348). Bulwer died at Argyll Hall, Torquay, on 18 January 1873, probably from a cerebral abscess brought on by the middle ear complaint which had afflicted him throughout his adult life. He was buried in Westminster Abbey, and obituaries marked the passing of England's foremost man of letters. Fifty years later G. K. Chesterton provided a more cautious epitaph when he remarked that, quite simply, 'you could not have the Victorian Age without him' (*The Victorian Age in Literature*, 1916, 1925 edn., p. 136).

ANDREW BROWN

Sources V. A. Lytton, *The life of Edward Bulwer, first Lord Lytton*, 2 vols. (1913) • E. R. Bulwer-Lytton, first Earl Lytton, *The life, letters and literary remains of Edward Bulwer, Lord Lytton*, 2 vols. (1883) • T. H. S. Escott, *Edward Bulwer, first Baron Lytton of Knebworth: a social, personal, and political monograph* (1910) • M. Sadleir, *Bulwer: a panorama*, 1: *Edward and Rosina, 1803–1836* (1931) • C. W. Snyder, *Liberty and morality: a political biography of Edward Bulwer-Lytton* (1995) • A. C. Christensen, *Edward Bulwer-Lytton: the fiction of new regions* (1976) •

J. A. Sutherland, *Victorian novelists and publishers* (1976) • J. L. Campbell, *Edward Bulwer-Lytton* (1986) • d. cert. • R. L. Woolf, *Strange stories and other explorations in Victorian fiction* (1971)

Archives BL, corresp., Add. MS 33964, fols. 278–88 • Boston PL, letters • Herts. ALS, corresp. and papers • Hunt. L., letters, literary MSS • Indiana University, Bloomington, letters • Knebworth House, Hertfordshire, corresp. and literary papers • Princeton University, New Jersey, corresp. and literary MSS | Baylor University, Waco, Texas, letters to Robert Browning • BL, corresp. with Lord Carnarvon, Add. MSS 60780, 60783 • BL, corresp. with W. E. Gladstone, Add. MS 44241 • BL, letters to M. Napier, Add. MSS 34614–34621, *passim* • BL, letters, as sponsor, to the Royal Literary Fund, loan no. 96 • BL, corresp. with Anna Steele, Add. MS 59662 • Bodl. Oxf., letters to Richard Bentley • Bodl. Oxf., corresp. with Disraeli family • Bodl. Oxf., letters to William Jerdan • Bodl. Oxf., letters to George Henry Lewes • CKS, letters to duke of Cleveland and duchess of Cleveland • CKS, letters to Lord Stanhope • CKS, letters to Lady Harry Vane • CUL, letters • Herts. ALS, letters • Herts. ALS, corresp. with Emily Mary Dunston concerning a lease • Herts. ALS, letters to Charles Garrard and Mrs Drake Garrard • Lincs. Arch., letters to Charles Tennyson d'Eyncourt; letters to Tennyson d'Eyncourt family • Lpool RO, letters to fourteenth earl of Derby • NL Scot., corresp. with Blackwoods and literary MSS • NL Wales, letters to Johnes family • Norfolk RO, corresp. with Sir Henry Lytton Bulwer • Trinity Cam., letters to Lord Houghton • U. Nott. L., corresp. with Sir W. Denison • UCL, letters, mostly to Lord Brougham • UCL, corresp. with Sir Edwin Chadwick

Likenesses A. E. Chalon, watercolour drawing, 1828, Knebworth, Hertfordshire • H. W. Pickersgill, oils, *c*.1831, NPG • F. Bromley, group portrait, etching, pubd 1835 (*The Reform Banquet, 1832*; after B. R. Haydon), NPG • Count D'Orsay, lithograph, 1837, NPG • J. Doyle, pencil caricature, *c*.1839, BM • E. Landseer, with Count D'Orsay and Lady Blessington, lithograph, 1840, Royal Collection • Count D'Orsay, lithograph, 1845, NPG • G. Cook, stipple, pubd 1848 (after R. J. Lane), NPG • D. Maclise, oils, 1850, Knebworth, Hertfordshire; copies, Trinity Cam.; Hughenden Manor, Buckinghamshire • E. M. Ward, oils, 1851, Knebworth, Hertfordshire • L. Ward & T. Mercquoid, watercolour drawing, 1873, Knebworth, Hertfordshire • Ape [C. Pellegrini], chromolithograph caricature, NPG; repro. in *VF* (29 Oct 1870) • M. B. Foster, pencil drawing, V&A • T. M. von Holst, oils (as a youth), Knebworth, Hertfordshire • F. Léquire, Parian-ware bust, Knebworth, Hertfordshire • C. G. Lewis, group portrait, mixed engraving (after T. J. Barker; *The intellect and valour of Great Britain*), NPG • D. Maclise, ink drawing, V&A • D. Maclise, print, BM, NPG; repro. in *Fraser's Magazine* (1832) • Mayall, three cartes-de-visite, NPG • J. Phillip, group portrait, oils (*The House of Commons, 1860*), Palace of Westminster, London • J. Thomson, stipple (after F. R. Say), BM, NPG; repro. in *New Monthly Magazine* (1831) • marble medallion, Knebworth, Hertfordshire • photograph, NPG [*see illus.*]

Wealth at death under £70,000: resworn probate, Sept 1874, *CGPLA Eng. & Wales* (1873)

Lytton, Edward Robert Bulwer-, first earl of Lytton [*pseud.* Owen Meredith] (**1831–1891**), viceroy of India and poet, was the only son of Edward George Earle Lytton Bulwer *Lytton, first Baron Lytton (1803–1873), and his wife, Rosina, *née* Wheeler (1802–1882) [*see* Lytton, Rosina Anne Doyle Bulwer]. He was born in London on 8 November 1831 and educated first privately, then at Harrow School and at Bonn, where he specialized in modern languages. He began composing poetry early and showed a precocious talent. Although not published until 1855, most of the poems in his first volume, *Clytemnestra, The Earl's Return and other Poems* (which went under the pseudonym Owen Meredith), were written before 1849. This was followed in 1857 by *The Wanderer*, a volume of lyrical

Edward Robert Bulwer-Lytton, first earl of Lytton (1831–1891), by George Frederic Watts, 1884

poems. Both were fairly well received by literary audiences, particularly for their poetic diction, vivid description and strokes of imagination. Reviews such as those in the *Edinburgh Review* and the London *Spectator* were guarded, however, speaking largely of the poet's youth and promise, and his need to develop his powers. In form, the poems were widely held to be too imitative of Browning. Lytton's interests in poetry at this time brought him into contact with London literary circles where he developed friendships with Charles Dickens and John Forster. He was especially close to Forster, conducting a voluminous correspondence with him, and acting as one of his executors at Forster's death in 1876.

Diplomacy and literature Lytton was at the same time pursuing a diplomatic career. In 1849 he went to Washington as private secretary to the ambassador, his uncle (William) Henry Lytton Earle *Bulwer, Baron Dalling. He acted in the same capacity when Dalling was moved to Florence before becoming paid attaché to the embassies at The Hague and then Vienna. From Vienna he went to Belgrade as acting consul-general and collected commercial intelligence. In 1862 he was appointed second secretary at Vienna, and in 1863 was made secretary of legation at Copenhagen at the time of the marriage of Princess Alexandra of Denmark with the prince of Wales. Lytton himself married, in 1864, Edith Villiers [*see below*]. In the same year he served at Athens and in the following year at Lisbon, where he negotiated an important commercial treaty. At both of these courts he also acted as chargé d'affaires.

Meanwhile, Lytton's literary reputation was further enhanced by the publication in 1860 of *Lucile*, a novel in verse, which some reviewers objected would have been as well cast in prose. It was a poem with which later he was to become disenchanted. It represented the first of a series of experiments in which he attempted to reproduce in the English language the rhythms and diction of continental prose and verse. In *Lucile* he drew heavily on George Sand's *Lavinia* and sought to catch, in rhyming anapaestic couplets, the sensibilities of the French novel. The next year, in conjunction with his friend Julian Fane, he wrote *Tannhauser* (published under the pseudonyms Neville Temple and Edward Trevor). In the same year he published *Serbski pesme*, based upon Serbian national songs. These works had a very mixed reception. His *Tannhauser* was thought a pallid imitation of Tennyson and his *Serbski pesme* was subjected to a severe attack by Lord Strangford in the pages of the *Saturday Review*.

None the less, Lytton persevered, and reproduced his Serb-derived poems in the appendix to *Orval, or, The Fool in Time* (1869). *Orval* was a paraphrase of Count Sigismund Krasinski's *Infernal Comedy* and was heavily influenced by the Polish school of mystical poetry which had arisen out of the loss of Polish independence. Lytton became closely associated with the count, and was attracted to the idea of writing heroic social drama. In 1868 he had published *Chronicles and Characters*, which consisted of poetic imitations of great men at the time of great events, from the era of Greek mythology to the days of Richelieu. However, it was compared unfavourably to Victor Hugo's *Légend des siècles*. Lytton had to wait until the publication of *Fables in Song* (1874) to establish his full poetic reputation. *Fables in Song* expressed his own voice much more directly and was credited with gracefulness and luminosity. The next year he privately circulated among friends *King Poppy*, which he came to regard as his finest achievement. However, he was unable to revise it for publication until shortly before his death, and it appeared only posthumously, in 1892.

During these years Lytton also continued his diplomatic career, being successively employed from 1868 to 1872 at Madrid and then at Vienna, where he had a large share in the negotiation of another commercial treaty. From 1872 to 1874 he was secretary to the embassy at Paris; in November 1874 he was promoted to be British minister at Lisbon. In January 1873 he succeeded as second Baron Lytton on the death of his father, to whom he was deeply attached. A two-volume biography of his father which he published in 1883 dealt extensively with the latter's early literary and political career. However, it drew to a close before 1836, the year in which his father and mother began the acrimonious separation proceedings which—in law courts, on theatrical stages, and in literary works—were to scandalize polite society for the next thirty years. Lytton's loyalties were clear, and one commentator observed that the biography was 'only too complete on the unhappy relations between his father and mother' (*Chambers*, 638).

Viceroy of India The most significant phase of Lytton's public life began in January 1876 when, a year after Lytton had declined the governorship of Madras, Disraeli offered him the viceroyalty of India in succession to Lord Northbrook. The appointment, which was usually reserved for politicians rather than men of letters, caused general astonishment. But Disraeli, a literary man himself, was insistent. It may have been that he saw in Lytton's highly developed romantic sensibility the perfect instrument for one of his own most favoured projects—the proclamation of Queen Victoria as queen empress of India and the construction around her of a new system of imperial monarchy. These were to represent the first, and visually the most stunning, of Britain's many contributions to the culture of the new imperialism which was rising in Europe at this time.

Lytton arrived in India, and was installed as viceroy on 12 April 1876. He immediately threw himself into the task of organizing a great durbar, or pageant, to celebrate the proclamation; this took place on 1 January 1877. The key feature of the durbar, which attempted to hark back to the rituals of the Mughal empire, was the ceremonial display of loyalty and fealty to the queen empress expressed by India's own princes and maharajas. Since the Indian Mutiny of 1857 British policy had turned away from seeking to expand direct rule and to transform and Westernize Indian society. A new respect had been found for the remaining indigenous princes, who still held a third of the sub-continent's territory and on whose 'traditional authority' the British now hoped to build the pillars of their raj. Lytton's durbar publicly symbolized their closer association with the crown as well as the new ethos of conservatism which marked the era. Critics, both at the time and since, have mocked the garishness of the durbar's displays and its blatant invention of oriental traditions, devised to suit melodramatic European tastes rather than faithfully to recreate the Mughal past. But the durbar's rituals were to set a public style of rulership which henceforth characterized the British raj, and provided inspiration for the new ceremonials of imperial monarchy which were subsequently developed in Britain to celebrate coronations and royal weddings and jubilees. In India, the new alliance with the princes held firm until the very last decade of British rule.

In a variety of other ways too, Lytton's viceroyalty served the ends of the new imperialism and the growing assertiveness of British power in the world. But they were ways which provoked high levels of controversy and revealed deepening contradictions in Britain's imperial project. Lytton's term of office was one of the most turbulent in viceregal history, ending in widespread public outcry, the defeat of Lord Beaconsfield's government, and the near bankruptcy of the government of India.

On the one hand, and in sharp contrast to a rhetoric aimed at evoking India's medieval princely past, Lytton pushed hard to advance British economic interests, even at the expense of the revenues and economy of India itself. Much influenced during his diplomatic career by the ideology of free trade, he enacted in India the repeal of the duties on cotton imports against the advice and votes of virtually his entire executive council. This emboldened him to pursue a radical reform of the whole customs and excise system which was to make India one of the most advanced free-trading economies in the world. In his last year in office he also gave his fervent support to a plan greatly to improve India's internal systems of transport and communication, most notably by vastly expanding the railways. How a supposedly traditional and princely India might have survived the large-scale onslaught of modern technology—any more than of free-market economics—is not clear, but the India Office quashed most of the plan for reasons of financial stringency.

The Second Anglo-Afghan War On the other hand, Lytton's sympathies for India's princes also conflicted with his attitudes towards the traditional rulers just beyond its borders. In what was to become the *cause celèbre* of his viceroyalty, he adopted a very 'forward' policy towards Afghanistan and provoked the Second Anglo-Afghan War. Ostensibly, his actions in Afghanistan were a defensive response to Russian expansion towards Turkmenistan and Samarkand which threatened the neutrality of Kabul. This was the more the case because failures by the British in 1873 to provide guarantees of protection to the Afghan amir, Sher Ali, had alienated him from their cause and opened the way for increasing Russian influence. However, there is much in Lytton's conduct to suggest that Beaconsfield's government had long decided on a policy aimed at bringing Afghanistan directly under the control of British Indian authority. The idea that it should be in relations with Calcutta, which secured for India a 'scientific frontier', was included in the treaty of Gandamak, signed with the puppet Amir Yakub in 1879. And Lytton clung to the notion of extending the Indian railway system to Kandahar in order to anchor the kingdom permanently to the sub-continent to its south.

The Afghan imbroglio began shortly after Lytton's installation as viceroy. He immediately dispatched an emissary to Sher Ali requesting treaty discussions. When the amir refused even to admit the emissary, Lytton was provoked to the celebrated remark that Afghanistan was merely 'an earthern pipkin between two metal pots'. Other problems delayed the crushing of the pipkin for a further two years. Then, in 1878, Lytton launched an invasion across the Khyber and Bolan passes which initially met with considerable success. Sher Ali was forced to flee Kabul, dying in exile the next year, and a new amir, the British client Yakub, was imposed in his stead. A permanent residency was also established under the direction of Major Louis Cavagnari, a notorious member of the 'forward' school who had little regard for or sensitivity towards indigenous peoples. Cavagnari cabled regular reports stressing the popular 'support' which the invasion was receiving and the 'calm' which it had restored to Afghan society. On 2 September 1879 he informed Lytton, 'All well'. The next day Cavagnari, his staff, and their entire escort were massacred inside the residency at the start of a large-scale uprising which had been brewing for many months. Lytton responded by unleashing a new conquest force; this met with bitter resistance and made only slow progress. British soldiers matched Afghan brutality measure for measure until stories of atrocities began to circulate back in England. The escalating costs of the war also caused widespread concern, although their full extent was not known until afterwards. In February 1880 Lytton even managed to post a budget showing a surplus of £400,000; however, due to peculiarities in the system of military accounting, this was later revealed to conceal a deficit in excess of £4 million. The total cost of the war was £17,490,000 against Lytton's own estimate of £5,750,000. In addition, £5 million was spent on constructing railways at the frontier.

In Britain, the Second Anglo-Afghan War became a major issue at the general election of March 1880, where Beaconsfield's Conservative government was soundly beaten by W. E. Gladstone's Liberals. Lytton promptly tendered his resignation, which was handed to the queen at the same time as Lord Beaconsfield's own. The Gladstone government appointed Lord Ripon as viceroy and dispatched him with the first task of extracting the army from Afghanistan, ending the war, and terminating the 'forward' policy.

Assessment of Lytton's viceroyalty Yet if the controversy surrounding the Anglo-Afghan War represented the highest point of contention in Lytton's viceroyalty, it cannot be said to have been an isolated peak. From the very beginning his term of office was conflictual, especially in relation to two other issues. First, he came to alienate the rising class of Western-educated Indians, who were then starting to express their own political voice, and then to play an inadvertent role in stimulating Indian nationalism. In 1878, to silence vociferous criticism of his Afghan adventure, he passed the Vernacular Press Act, which singled out newspapers published in Indian languages and subjected them to procedures of censorship. This was widely regarded in India as a tacit form of racial discrimination and a sign of the hollowness of the promise in the queen empress's proclamation that all her subjects within the empire were to be accorded equal rights. At the time of the proclamation the promise had been baited with the offer to open immediately one-sixth of the vacancies in the Indian Civil Service to native-born Indians. Its emptiness may be judged from the fact that it took another forty years for this goal to be achieved. Lytton's viceroyalty highlighted that contradiction between the words and the actions of British imperialism which was to provide the animus behind the eventual foundation of the Indian National Congress in 1885.

The second issue also had a bearing on Indian nationalism, although it was scarcely less important for provoking anti-imperial sentiment in Britain. Shortly after Lytton took up office, one of the worst famines in British Indian history broke in the south and the west. The severe loss of life which followed in its wake contrasted sharply with imperial propaganda which had long emphasized the benefits bestowed on India by British rule. There were even suggestions that British misrule had been a primary cause of the famine, an accusation brought to the attention of the British public by the activities of the journalist William Digby and the businessman Dadabhai Naoroji, a British resident, who was a Liberal member of parliament and later three times a president of the Indian National Congress. Lytton sought to have the charges repudiated in

Britain while, in India, he reformed the procedures of famine administration so drastically as to hint that there may have been substance to them. The nature of his reforms remains controversial. Convinced of the efficacy of free trade, he staunchly supported the policies of Sir John Strachey and Sir Richard Temple which eschewed direct intervention in the grain market but instead offered money for work. However, the policy may have underestimated the weakness at that time of the infrastructure supporting a system of market distribution. Large areas of the country were poorly served by railways and roads and as many as 5 million people died of starvation during the famine.

None the less, the long-term effects of the establishment of the new famine code were undoubtedly beneficial and mark the most significant—and perhaps the only—achievement of Lytton's viceroyalty. Market infrastructure was much improved by roads built under the money-for-work programme. In addition, procedures for monitoring drought and price levels were put in place in order to detect and take preventive measures against potential famine ahead of time. A royal commission on famine in India (1880) explored the conditions behind the original disaster and gave its approval to the new famine code, which served (and continues to serve) India down to the end of the twentieth century. After 1876–8, no subsequent famine was to cause remotely so much devastation and loss of life, and between 1901 and 1943 India was safeguarded from famine entirely.

Resignation, and the French embassy Following his resignation Lytton returned to England; he was created earl of Lytton on 28 April 1880. He made one speech in the House of Lords in defence of his Afghanistan policy but then withdrew from public life for several years, during which time he concentrated on his writings, producing the two-volume biography of his father and several other works. He had high hopes of *Glenaveril*, a narrative poem in six books published in 1885, but it was not well received. However, his *After Paradise* (1887), which returned to the spirit of *Fables in Song*, drew more positive critical acclaim. In 1887 he was elected lord rector of Glasgow University and then, amid characteristic controversy and voluble opposition, was appointed ambassador to France.

Lytton was not at all in sympathy with the politics of the Third Republic. He did, however, have an extensive knowledge of French literature and culture which was to stand him in good stead. He converted the British embassy into a literary salon regularly attended by the cream of Parisian intellectual society in which French politicians of different parties could also meet and converse. His role became that of influencing discussion rather than leading and directing it. In consequence, he drew praise from all sides and can be credited with having preserved and developed friendly relations with France during a period of repeated political irritations. He did not accept his belated acclaim gracefully, once remarking: 'I devoted my life to India and everybody abused me. I come here, do nothing and am praised to the skies' (*DNB*). He continued to write poetry. *The Ring of Amasis* (1890), which he reworked from an earlier romance, was a disappointment. But his *Marah*, which drew on Heine, and *King Poppy* (published posthumously in 1891 and 1892 respectively) were among his most distinguished efforts. Lytton died very suddenly at the British embassy, 39 faubourg St Honoré, Paris, on 24 November 1891, and was buried at his family's country seat at Knebworth, Hertfordshire. He was survived by his wife, **Edith Bulwer-Lytton** [*née* Villiers], countess of Lytton (1841–1936), the second daughter of the Hon. Edward Villiers and the niece of George Villiers, fourth earl of Clarendon. They had married on 4 October 1864 after a courtship complicated by his penury. She brought him £6000 a year and bore him four sons and three daughters, including Elizabeth *Balfour, later countess of Balfour (1867–1942), Lady Constance Georgina Bulwer-*Lytton, who was later to earn notoriety as a suffragette, Victor Alexander George Robert Bulwer-*Lytton, who succeeded to the earldom and served as governor of Bengal and acting viceroy of India, and Neville Stephen *Lytton. Lady Lytton was devoted to her husband and strongly supported his diplomatic career as companion and hostess. However, it was as vicereine of India that she came into her own. Finding the viceregal court 'very dull and coarse' compared to the glittering palaces of Europe, she set out to transform its style. She and her daughters became particularly distinguished for their displays of high fashion, sustained by regular supplies from the couturiers and milliners of Paris. She also became a noted benefactress of the cause of female education, especially with regard to the zenanas of the Indian princes.

After Lytton's death Lady Lytton faced straitened financial circumstances. Her husband had been a particular favourite of the queen, who had even permitted him the rare distinction, while viceroy, of addressing her in the first person. She responded to Lady Lytton's plight by inviting her—in a letter also written in the first person—to attend court as a lady-in-waiting. This role Lady Lytton performed from 1895 to 1905, serving also Queen Alexandra. During the first four years of her service she kept a diary, parts of which were published many years after her death. It records the daily comings and goings and the gossip of the court during Queen Victoria's last years. In 1905 she withdrew from court to a long retirement spent quietly in a house built for her on the Knebworth estate. The house maintained her connections with India for it was designed by her son-in-law Sir Edwin Lutyens, who was the principal architect of the last British imperial capital at New Delhi. She died in her ninety-sixth year, on 17 September 1936, and was buried beside her husband at Knebworth.

Both during his lifetime and afterwards, Lord Lytton was compared to the ideal 'Renaissance man'. Certainly his talents—as poet, linguist, diplomat, and statesman—were many and varied. However, his greatest achievements came in those areas for which he had only limited regard. His bearing, interest in culture, and knowledge of European languages made him highly successful at moving in the diplomatic circles of aristocratic Europe, and also at introducing to English audiences the genius of the continental Romantic movement. But his own poetry and statesmanship were marked by over-ambition. With the exception of two or three works, his poetry lacked originality and rarely rose above the level of pastiche. In addition, the elaboration of the famine code apart, his viceroyalty in India was a many-sided failure which helped to set the British raj on the path to its eventual extinction. His disaster in Afghanistan broke the spell of British invincibility and encouraged other European powers then rising to challenge for colonial possessions and a share of world dominance. His policies of discriminating between the rights of British and of Indian subjects within the empire and of favouring the traditions of the princes over the modernities represented by the Western-educated classes contributed to the deepening isolation and ossification of the imperial state. As imperial rituals and display became ever grander, the British raj alienated ever broader sections of Indian public opinion and doomed itself to fall among the first victims to anti-colonial nationalism in the twentieth century. DAVID WASHBROOK

Sources A. B. Haslan, *Owen Meredith* (1946) • E. Balfour, *The history of Lord Lytton's Indian administration, 1876–80* (1899) • A. Forbes, *The Afghan wars, 1839–42 and 1878–80* (1892) • W. Digby, *The famine campaign in southern India* (1878) • J. Strachey, *India* (1888) • M. Lutyens, *The Lyttons in India* (1979) • *Lady Lytton's court diary, 1895–99*, ed. M. Lutyens (1961) • G. Hamilton, *Parliamentary reminiscences and reflections*, 1: *1868–1885* (1916); repr. (1917) • *The Times* (25 Nov 1891) • *The Times* (26 Nov 1891) • D. Patrick, ed., *Chambers's Cyclopedia of English literature*, new edn, 3 vols. (1901–3) • GEC, *Peerage* • *DNB* • *CGPLA Eng. & Wales* (1892) • Boase, *Mod. Eng. biog.*

Archives BL, corresp. and papers, Add. MSS 44873, 59611–59613 • BL OIOC, corresp. and papers mainly relating to India, MS Eur. E 218 • Herts. ALS, corresp., papers, and literary MSS • Hunt. L., letters • Knebworth House, Hertfordshire, corresp. and papers • priv. coll. • Ransom HRC, papers • U. Cal., Berkeley, papers • V&A • V&A NAL, inventory of papers preserved at his home • V&A NAL, letters and papers | Balliol Oxf., corresp. with Sir Robert Morier • Baylor University, Waco, Texas, letters to Robert Browning • BL, letters to Lord Carnarvon, Add. MS 60797 • BL, letters to T. H. S. Escott, Add. MS 58776 • BL, letters to W. E. Gladstone, Add. MSS 44398–44507 • BL, letters to Lady Holland, Add. MS 52121 • BL, letters to Lord Iddesleigh, Add. MS 50027 • BL, corresp. with Sir Austen Layard, Add. MSS 38969–39164 • BL, corresp. with Sir Augustus Paget, Add. MS 51231 • BL, letters to Royal Literary Fund, loan 96 • BL, corresp. with Anna Steele, Add. MS 59662 • BL OIOC, letters to Sir Owen Tudor Burne, MS Eur. D 951 • BL OIOC, letters to Sir Mountstuart Grant-Duff, MS Eur. F 234 • BL OIOC, corresp. with Sir Alfred Lyall, MS Eur. F 132 • BL OIOC, letters to Lady Strachey, MS Eur. F 127 • BL OIOC, corresp. with Sir Richard Temple, MS Eur. F 86 • BL OIOC, corresp. with Sir Philip Wodehouse, MS Eur. D 726 • Bodl. Oxf., letters to George Bentley • Bodl. Oxf., letters to Richard Bentley • Bodl. Oxf., letters to Sir John Crampton • Bodl. Oxf., corresp. with Benjamin Disraeli • Bodl. Oxf., corresp. with Sir William Harcourt • Bodl. Oxf., corresp. with Sir Henry Taylor • CAC Cam., corresp. with Lord Randolph Churchill • Ches. & Chester ALSS, letters to Rhoda Broughton • CKS, letters to Julian Fane • CKS, letters to Edward Stanhope • CUL, corresp. with Sir J. F. Stephen • Hatfield House, Hertfordshire, corresp. with Lord Salisbury and others • Herts. ALS, letters to Priscilla Fane relating to memoir of Julian Fane • Herts. ALS, letters to Charles Kent • Hove Central Library, Sussex, letters to Lord Wolseley • King's AC Cam., letters to Oscar Browning • Lpool RO, letters to Lord Derby • NA Scot., letters to Sir H. B. Loch • NAM, corresp. with Sir Frederick Haines • NAM, letters to Earl Roberts • NL Scot., corresp. with Blackwoods • NL Wales, letters to Betha Johnes and Augusta Hall • Norfolk RO, corresp. with Lord Dalling and Bulwer • NRA, priv. coll., letters to Sir Edward Clive Bayley • PRO, letters to Lord Ampthill, FO 918/53 • PRO, corresp. with Lord Carnarvon, PRO 30/6/15 • PRO, corresp. with Lord John Russell, PRO 30/22 • PRO, letters to Odo Russell, FO 918 • PRO NIre., Perceval MSS • Royal Institution of Great Britain, London, letters to John Tyndall and Louisa Tyndall • Som. ARS, letters to Sir William Jolliffe • Suffolk RO, Ipswich, letters to Lord Cranbrook • Trinity Cam., letters to Lord Houghton • U. Leeds, Brotherton L., letters to Sir Edmund Gosse • U. St Andr. L., letters to Wilfrid Ward

Likenesses J. E. Millais, portrait, 1876, V&A • G. F. Watts, oils, 1884, NPG [*see illus.*] • J. Brown, stipple (after Legrange), NPG • H. Furniss, pen-and-ink caricature, NPG • A. Gilbert, marble roundel, Knebworth, Hertfordshire • Lock & Whitfield, woodburytype, repro. in T. Cooper, *Men of mark: a gallery of contemporary portraits*, 1 • G. Pilotell, drypoint print, BM • E. Stodart, stipple and line engraving (after photograph by Bassano), NPG • G. F. Watts, sketch, Knebworth, Hertfordshire • miniature, Knebworth, Hertfordshire • woodburytype, NPG

Wealth at death £79,721 14*s*. 9*d*.: probate, 29 Feb 1892, *CGPLA Eng. & Wales*

Lytton, Elizabeth Edith. *See* Balfour, Elizabeth Edith, countess of Balfour (1867–1942).

Lytton, Sir Henry Alfred [*real name* Henry Alfred Jones] (**1865–1936**), actor, was born in Kensington, London, on 3 January 1865 (he always gave the date erroneously as 3 January 1867), the only son of Henry Jones, jeweller, and his second wife, Martha Lavinia Harris. He was educated at St Mark's School, Chelsea, where he took part in amateur theatrical performances and from where he ran away in an unsuccessful endeavour to become a professional actor. A few years later, in 1882, Jones made his first appearance on the professional stage at the Philharmonic Theatre, Islington, in *The Obstinate Bretons*, in the cast of which was his future wife, Louie (1862/3–1947), daughter of William Webber of London, whom he married in 1884. Through her influence he secured an engagement with the D'Oyly Carte Company and he made his first appearance at the Royalty Theatre, Glasgow, in February 1884 in the chorus of *Princess Ida*. He appeared under the name H. A. Henri, his wife's stage name being Louie Henri. He remained with the D'Oyly Carte Company only a short time before joining another touring company, the London Comedy and Operetta Company.

Early in 1887 Jones was engaged by Richard D'Oyly Carte at the Savoy Theatre, London, as understudy to George Grossmith the elder. Fortune smiled on him almost immediately, for in January 1887, a week after the production of *Ruddigore*, by W. S. Gilbert and Sir Arthur Sullivan, his principal fell ill, and Jones made a great success in Grossmith's part of Robin Oakapple. It was after this success that, at the suggestion of Gilbert, he adopted the name Lytton. He then toured with the D'Oyly Carte Company for several years, and it was not until April 1897 that he again appeared in London when, at the Savoy Theatre, he succeeded George Grossmith as Ferdinand the Fifth in *His Majesty*. From 1897 to 1899 he appeared at the Savoy in revivals of *The Yeomen of the Guard*, *The Grand Duchess*, *The Gondoliers*, *Trial by Jury*, and *HMS Pinafore*, increasing his reputation very considerably.

In July 1899 Lytton undertook the management of the Criterion Theatre, London, producing a farcical comedy, *The Wild Rabbit* by George Arliss, which, however, was unsuccessful. He returned to the Savoy in the same year and he remained there until 1903, playing leading parts in *The Rose of Persia* (1899), *The Pirates of Penzance* (1900), *Patience* (1900), *The Emerald Isle* (1901), *Iolanthe* (1901), *Merrie England* (1902), and *A Princess of Kensington* (1903). During the next six years Lytton was seen at various London theatres in *The Earl and the Girl* (Adelphi, 1903), *The Talk of the Town* (Adelphi, 1905), *The White Chrysanthemum* (Criterion, 1905), *The Spring Chicken* (Gaiety, 1906), *The Little Michus* (Daly's, 1906), and *My Darling* (Hicks, 1907).

Lytton returned to the Savoy in April 1908 to appear for the first time at that theatre in *The Mikado*. From that date until his retirement in 1934 he played exclusively in the D'Oyly Carte Gilbert and Sullivan repertory in London and on tour. He played no fewer than thirty characters in these operas during his career, and he appeared in all of his famous parts during the seasons at the Prince's Theatre in 1919, 1921, 1924, and 1926, and again at the Savoy in 1929–30 and 1932–3. His performances as John Wellington Wells in *The Sorcerer*, Sir Joseph Porter in *HMS Pinafore*, Major-General Stanley in *The Pirates of Penzance*, Reginald Bunthorne in *Patience*, the Lord Chancellor in *Iolanthe*, Ko-Ko in *The Mikado*, Robin Oakapple in *Ruddigore*, Jack Point in *The Yeomen of the Guard*, and the duke of Plaza-Toro in *The Gondoliers* were unexcelled either by his predecessors or his successors. It is remarkable that he was not the original exponent of any of these parts, but his popularity in them was extraordinary. Undoubtedly his best impersonation and his own favourite part was his Jack Point, which was full of intensely human appeal, romance, and pathos. He made his last appearance with the D'Oyly Carte Company at the Gaiety Theatre, Dublin, in June 1934. For twenty-six years Lytton was the mainstay of the company, and in 1930, when he was knighted, he was entertained at luncheon by 500 men and women representative of the stage, literature, art, politics, the law, and commerce. After the celebration of his stage jubilee he received a national testimonial, and among the signatories of the album that accompanied the gift were the prime minister, Ramsay MacDonald, Stanley Baldwin, and Lloyd George, the presentation being made by the last-named. At Christmas 1934 he entered on his last engagement when, at the Prince of Wales's Theatre, Birmingham, he acted as the emperor in the pantomime *Aladdin*, his first and only part in pantomime.

According to his own confession Lytton could not read a line of music and all of his songs were taught to him by his wife, who played them over and over again until he had mastered them. He possessed a light, pleasant voice with crystal-clear diction, a high sense of comedy, and a remarkably keen sense of timing, which gave poise and distinction to every part that he undertook, and his acting always appeared to be perfectly spontaneous. Lytton died at his home, 54 Barkston Gardens, Earls Court, London, on 15 August 1936; he was survived by his wife and his two sons and two daughters. A son was killed in February 1918 while serving in the Royal Flying Corps; two others died in infancy. He was the author of two books, *The Secrets of a Savoyard* (1922) and *A Wandering Minstrel* (1933).

J. PARKER, *rev.* K. D. REYNOLDS

Sources *The Times* (17 Aug 1936) · *Daily Telegraph* (17 Aug 1936) · J. Parker, ed., *Who's who in the theatre*, 8th edn (1936) · H. A. Lytton, *The secrets of a Savoyard* (1922) · H. A. Lytton, *A wandering minstrel* (1933) · personal knowledge (1949) · private information (1949) · *CGPLA Eng. & Wales* (1936)

Likenesses F. W. Burford, photograph, NPG · H. Coster, photographs, NPG · H. L. Oakley, silhouette, NPG

Wealth at death £14,877 4s. 7d.: probate, 27 Nov 1936, *CGPLA Eng. & Wales*

Lytton, Neville Stephen Bulwer-, third earl of Lytton (1879–1951), artist and army officer, was born on 6 February 1879 in Calcutta, the fourth son and youngest of seven children of Edward Robert Bulwer-*Lytton, second Baron Lytton (1831–1891), who was created earl of Lytton in 1880, and his wife, Edith, *née* Villiers (1841–1936). At the time of Neville's birth his father was serving as viceroy of India. Neville Lytton was educated at Eton College (1891–6), and at the École des Beaux-Arts of the Sorbonne in Paris (1896–9).

As a younger son who had apparently little chance of succeeding to the title (although two of his brothers died before his birth), Lytton was able to develop his wide artistic talents. Fluent in French and an ardent Francophile throughout his life, he fell under the influence of the poet Wilfrid Scawen *Blunt while studying art in Paris. He also developed an interest in folk art and the arts and crafts movement. On 2 February 1899 Lytton married Blunt's only child, Judith Anne Dorothea (1873–1957), who succeeded as Baroness Wentworth in her own right in 1917. They had one son, Noel Anthony Scawen, born in 1900, and two daughters. Alternating between Paris, London, and his family home at Balcombe in Sussex, Lytton established a reputation as a society painter; he had his first one-man exhibition at the Carfax gallery in 1904, and gave a paper to the Art Workers' Guild in London in 1907, subsequently published in 1911 as *Water-Colour* with a dedication to Blunt, in which he expressed strong opposition to modernism in all its forms. He also owned an ivory flute which he played well, was an accomplished Morris dancer, and won the tennis international amateur cup in Paris three years running (1911–13).

Lytton's main contribution to public life came quite unexpectedly in the First World War. In 1914, with the rank of captain (he became major in January 1915), he helped raise the 11th (Southdown) battalion of the Royal Sussex regiment ('Lowther's lambs'), part of 116th brigade, 39th division. He served with the battalion on the western front in early 1916 before being slightly wounded, and with the brigade staff during the battle of the Somme. In autumn 1916 he was selected for a general staff appointment with section I (d) of general headquarters of the British army in France, as a press liaison and censorship officer. His outspoken war memoirs, *The Press and the General Staff*, published in 1920 and illustrated with his own drawings, are an invaluable source on the British

Neville Stephen Bulwer-Lytton, third earl of Lytton (1879–1951), self-portrait, 1938

army's attitude towards the press and propaganda during the war. He finished the war with four mentions in dispatches and the OBE.

Following the war Lytton settled once more in Sussex. His wartime experience with the press led him to pursue an occasional career as a journalist as well as resuming life as a painter. His discursive and semi-autobiographical book *The English Country Gentleman*, published in 1925, includes commemorative essays on Blunt, who had died in 1922, and on his own sister, Lady Constance Bulwer-*Lytton, the suffragette, who had died in 1923. Examples of Lytton's art appear in this book, including the Balcombe frescoes which he completed in 1923. He also edited the volume in the Lonsdale Library series dealing with *Winter Sports* in 1930.

In 1923 Lytton's first wife obtained a divorce, and in 1924 he married Rosa Alexandrine (Sandra) Fortel of St Rambert-en-Bugey, near Lyon. The couple had one daughter. They settled in France, where Bulwer-Lytton became a Sociétère of the Société Nationale des Beaux Arts as well as a regular contributor to all major exhibitions in France and Britain. In 1936 he exhibited a portrait of his brother Victor in his robes as second earl of Lytton.

On the outbreak of the Second World War, Lytton was employed by the French foreign office to make propaganda radio broadcasts to the United States. After the French defeat in 1940 he and his wife retired to her home town, which was in Vichy France. In autumn 1941 they obtained permission to leave for Portugal and so returned to Britain, circumstances recounted by Lytton in a series of propaganda articles expanded in 1942 into the book *Life in Unoccupied France*.

After the war Lytton and his wife settled in France once more. In 1947 he succeeded his brother as third earl of Lytton, but took no part in public life. He died at home in Paris, 8 rue du Val de Grace, of old age on 9 February 1951. His funeral took place at the British embassy church in Paris on 13 February, and he was buried on the same day at Valmondois, Seine et Oise. The son of his first marriage succeeded as fourth earl. STEPHEN BADSEY

Sources N. Lytton, *The press and the general staff* (1920) • N. Lytton, *Water-colour* (1911) • N. Lytton, *The English country gentleman* (1925) • N. Lytton, *Life in unoccupied France* (1942) • *The Times* (12 Feb 1951) • *The Times* (10 Feb 1951) • *The Times* (14 Feb 1951) • *The Times* (19 Feb 1951) • *Debrett's Peerage* • G. D. Martineau, *A history of the royal Sussex regiment* [1953] • *WWW* • *Army List* • Burke, *Peerage* • *CGPLA Eng. & Wales* (1951)

Archives FILM IWM FVA, actuality footage

Likenesses W. Rothenstein, sanguine, 1906, NPG • N. Lytton, self-portrait, oils, 1938, Russell-Cotes Art Gallery and Museum, Bournemouth [*see illus.*] • N. Lytton, self-portrait, oils, Knebworth House, Hertfordshire • photographs, repro. in Lytton, *English country gentleman*

Wealth at death £13,690 13*s*. 8*d*. in England: probate, 26 June 1951, *CGPLA Eng. & Wales*

Lytton, Rosina Anne Doyle Bulwer [*née* Rosina Anne Doyle Wheeler], **Lady Lytton** (**1802–1882**), novelist, was born on 4 November 1802 in co. Limerick, Ireland, the younger of the two surviving children of Francis Massy Wheeler (1781–1820), grandson of Hugh, first Baron Massy of Duntrileague, and his wife, Anna *Wheeler (1785?–1848x50), advocate for women's rights and daughter of Nicholas Doyle, protestant archbishop of Cashel. Rosina Wheeler was brought up with her sister Henrietta (1801–1826) at the Wheeler family home, Ballywife, Kilross, on the border of the counties of Limerick and Tipperary. In August 1812 her mother deserted her father and, assisted by her brother John, left Ireland with her sister Bessie and two daughters. The fugitives embarked on a voyage to Guernsey aboard the *Ocean Pearl*, which belonged to Anna Wheeler's uncle General Sir John Doyle, who presided as governor of this Channel Island. Here Rosina entered into a more affluent lifestyle, developing her wit and talent for mimicry, and mingling with aristocrats who had fled the French Revolution. Between 1816 and 1820 she received an inadequate education at a private school in Kensington in London, which is dramatized as Miss James's school for young ladies in her fictional autobiography: *Miriam Sedley, or, The Tares and the Wheat: a Tale of Real Life* (1851).

As a dark-haired beauty with cupid-bow lips, Rosina entered into society, where she attracted the attentions of Edward George Earle Lytton Bulwer *Lytton (1803–1873), who, in April 1826, proposed marriage. Edward's mother opposed the match, and when the wedding went ahead on 29 August 1827 carried out her threat of putting a stop to

Rosina Anne Doyle Bulwer Lytton, Lady Lytton (1802–1882), by John Jewel Penstone (after Alfred Edward Chalon, 1852)

her son's income. Since this forced him to support his wife by writing novels, a considerable pressure was placed on the marriage. Tensions arising from financial strains and Edward's marital infidelities even erupted into domestic violence against Rosina. Not one placidly to accept this situation, Rosina on a trip to Naples retaliated against her husband's adultery by flirting with a Neapolitan prince. Her action prompted Bulwer Lytton, in 1836, after nine years of marriage, to draw up an agreement to separate. The most painful repercussion was that Rosina was parted from her children. Except for four months in 1858, she never saw her son Edward Robert from 1838 to the time of her death in 1882. She was also denied access to her daughter Emily, and had to be granted a special dispensation by her husband in order to visit Emily, who was then dying of typhoid fever, in 1848.

The annuity of £400 that Rosina received as a separated wife from Bulwer Lytton was inadequate for her needs. This reduced income forced her to leave the metropolis for less expensive parts of the country such as Llangollen in north Wales and then Taunton in the west country. Pursued by creditors, she supplemented her income by publishing novels, and also used her writing to exact revenge on her husband for his desertion. Many of her works set out to attack him, as did the satiric best-seller *Cheveley, or, The Man of Honour* (1839) and *The Budget of the Bubble Family* (1840), the latter of which ridiculed Bulwer Lytton's family and their ancestral seat, Knebworth House in Hertfordshire. Other fictional exposés of her marriage and the plight of separated wives include: *The School for Husbands, or, Molière's Life and Times* (1852), *Behind the Scenes: a Novel* (1854), and *The World and his Wife, or, A Person of Consequence: a Photographic Novel* (1858). Even novels more removed in setting, such as *Bianca Cappello: an Historical Romance* (1843), contain fierce polemical passages protesting the ill treatment of women by their husbands. Other novels containing unconventional heroines include: *The Peer's Daughters: a Novel* (1849) and *Very Successful!* (1856), the latter of which was particularly well received.

Rosina drew attention to her reduced state in the newspapers and even made an appeal for funds from the public in her *Appeal to the Justice and Charity of the English Public* (1857). The sparring between husband and wife became more intense when Rosina launched a public and vicious verbal attack on Bulwer Lytton from the hustings while, as colonial secretary in Lord Derby's administration, he was canvassing in Hertford for re-election as a tory MP. The result was that her husband, angry and mortified by this very public humiliation, had Rosina confined in a private lunatic asylum in Inverness Lodge in Brentford. As a result of the public protest spearheaded by her women friends, she won her freedom after three weeks.

A scandalous autobiographical revelation of Rosina's ill treatment at the hands of her husband written in 1866 appeared in book form in 1880 entitled *A Blighted Life*. Bulwer Lytton had died in 1873, but the memoir aroused the disapproval of their son, Edward Robert Bulwer-*Lytton (1831–1891), who had remained loyal to his father's memory. Rosina denied that she had intended it for publication, and wrote the appropriately entitled pamphlet: *Refutation of an audacious forgery of the Dowager Lady Lytton's name to a book of the publication of which she was totally ignorant* (1880).

Towards the end of her life Rosina adopted the pseudonym of George Gordon Scott for her historical novel *Clumber Chase, or, Love's Riddle Solved by a Royal Sphinx: a Tale of the Restoration* (1871). Under her own name she published a collection of essays called *Shells from the Sands of Time* (1876). Retaining vestiges of her legendary beauty in old age, she died at her home, Glenômera, 77 Longton Grove, Upper Sydenham, Kent, on 12 March 1882, plagued by physical pain, sorrow, and debt. She was buried in the churchyard of St John the Evangelist at Shirley in Surrey, but her grave was unmarked until 12 March 1995, when her great-great-grandson David Lytton Cobbold, second Baron Cobbold of Knebworth, arranged for a tombstone to be erected on her grave with the inscription she had requested: 'The Lord will give thee rest from thy sorrow, and from thy fear, and from the hard bondage wherein thou wast made to serve.'

Rosina had brought about her 'hard bondage' through her refusal to conform to the duties of a Victorian wife, which required women to 'suffer and be silent'. By drawing attention to the plight of married women and separated wives through her novels, pamphlets, and journalism, Rosina contributed towards the mounting pressure that eventually brought about legislation designed to protect the interests of women. Rosina Bulwer Lytton represents far more than a case history of a hysteric or an unorthodox minor Victorian novelist. For her undoubted talent and extraordinary courage in speaking out against injustice she deserves a permanent place in women's history, as she has provided an often unrecognized source of inspiration to those who have followed. Her most immediate legacy was passed to her granddaughter Lady Constance Georgina Bulwer-*Lytton (1869–1923), who became one of the heroines of the Edwardian women's suffrage movement. MARIE MULVEY-ROBERTS

Sources L. Devey, *Life of Rosina, Lady Lytton* (1887) • M. Sadleir, *Bulwer: a panorama*, 1: *Edward and Rosina, 1803–1836* (1931); new edn as *Bulwer and his wife: a panorama, 1803–1836* (1833) • *Letters of the late Edward Bulwer, Lord Lytton, to his wife*, ed. L. Devey (1884) • *Unpublished letters of Lady Bulwer Lytton to A. E. Challon, R.A.*, ed. S. M. Ellis (1914) • H. Small, *Love's madness: medicine, the novel, and female insanity* (1996) • d. cert. • E. R. Bulwer-Lytton, first Earl Lytton, *The life, letters and literary remains of Edward Bulwer, Lord Lytton*, 2 vols. (1883)

Archives Herts. ALS, corresp. and papers • Hunt. L., letters and literary MSS • Knebworth House, Hertfordshire, papers | Bodl. Oxf., letters to Mary Anne Disraeli • Lpool RO, corresp. with earl of Derby

Likenesses miniature, 1830–34 • A. E. Chalon, drawing, 1852 • J. Jewel Penstone, stipple engraving (after drawing by A. E. Chalon, 1852), NPG [*see illus.*] • ivory miniature • miniature, Knebworth, Hertfordshire

Wealth at death £405 10s. 0d.: probate, 28 May 1882, *CGPLA Eng. & Wales*

Lytton, Victor Alexander George Robert Bulwer-, second earl of Lytton (1876–1947), politician and colonial administrator, was born at Peterhof, the viceregal residence at Simla, India, on 9 August 1876, the third but first surviving son and sixth of seven children of Edward Robert Bulwer-*Lytton, first earl of Lytton (1831–1891), diplomat and viceroy of India, and his wife, Edith Bulwer-*Lytton, *née* Villiers (1841–1936) [*see under* Lytton, Edward Robert Bulwer-], niece of the fourth earl of Clarendon.

Victor, named after his godmother, the queen, went to England in 1880 as Viscount Knebworth. In November 1891, while a schoolboy at Eton, he inherited his earldom, barony, and 600 acre estate of Knebworth in Hertfordshire. He would never need to work for a living, though the loss of a large sum in bad investments in 1893 compelled him to let Knebworth House more frequently than he liked.

Lytton recalled himself as a morbidly self-centred youth—testimony to the moral earnestness which characterized him as an adult. Inspired by the writings of Emerson and R. L. Stevenson, his view of life as a quest for truth evolved during three years at Trinity College, Cambridge (where he took a second in history in 1898), and three years of continental travel. There was a hint of knight-errantry about the wiry young man who began his career in 1901, as assistant private secretary to George Wyndham, chief secretary for Ireland, after failing the Foreign Office entrance examinations. His long narrow clean-shaven face looked gravely handsome; his manners were extremely dignified. The family motto, *Hoc opus virtutis* ('This is the work of valour'), meant a good deal to him: the proper role of the aristocrat was to lead and pioneer.

On 3 April 1902 Lytton married Pamela Frances Audrey Chichele-Plowden (1873/4–1971), a society beauty, previously wooed by Winston Churchill. They were sharply different personalities: he rather unworldly, essentially shy, and prone to absorption in thought; she more spontaneous, gregarious, and ambitious, and not at all interested in theorizing. Having lost his own father early, the earl deliberately sought to be a friend to their four children, while remaining close to his wider family. Gerald Balfour and Edwin Lutyens were his brothers-in-law.

Lytton had taken his seat in the House of Lords as a Conservative in January 1902. Temperance and labour legislation were not usual interests for a tory peer, however, and his firm support for free trade alienated him from the party mainstream after tariff reform became a major issue in 1903. He refused to vote against the 1909 budget and he voted in favour of the Parliament Act in 1911. With his habitual rectitude, liberal imperialism, and love for fishing and ornithology, he reminded journalists of a youthful Sir Edward Grey, and many wondered why he was not a Liberal. Lytton latterly explained that he had never succeeded in finding more liberalism in the Liberal Party than in the Conservative Party. He was best-known before 1914 as an advocate of female suffrage. Affected by the courage of his sister Lady Constance Bulwer-*Lytton (1869–1923), an active suffragette, the earl chaired the all-party 'conciliation committee' that drafted the Parliamentary Franchise (Women) Bill in 1910. His readiness to sympathize with the Women's Social and Political Union, even without condoning its militancy, angered party leaders, but unpopularity would never deter him from supporting any cause that he believed to be right (although he may have been a philanthropist more at ease with ideas than with people).

Isolated at Westminster, Lytton involved himself with the Men's League for Women's Suffrage, the International Association for Labour Legislation, the Eugenics Society, the Hertfordshire and Essex Public House Trust, the garden cities movement, and boys' clubs. After chairing a royal commission on the Brussels, Rome, and Turin exhibitions (1910–11), he joined the advisory council of the Victoria and Albert Museum and wrote a biography of his grandfather, the novelist Bulwer Lytton. *Mens sana in corpore sano* ('a healthy mind in a healthy body') being another of his precepts, he roller-skated and cycled around London and often went skiing at Mürren, Switzerland. The Alexander technique was one of many unorthodox cures and diets that featured in his faddish pursuit of relief from headaches and occasional bouts of despondency.

In 1913 Lytton met the controversial American educationist and psychotherapist Homer Lane (1875–1925), who enlisted his support for the Little Commonwealth community for delinquent children and offered to give him private counselling. The earl became an eager disciple of Lane, developing his ideas into a personal philosophy called 'creative love'. This synthesis of the teachings of Christ and Freud suggested eliminating morality (as commonly understood) and restoring belief in the original virtue of all human desires. Conventional theology harmed mankind with its emphasis on sin and redemption. Happiness was the goal. These notions were expounded by Lytton in *New Treasure* (1934) and other writings on the Bible and sex education.

The wartime coalition gave Lytton the chance to hold government office. He was civil lord of the Admiralty under Balfour from 26 July to 10 December 1916, and additional parliamentary secretary to the Admiralty from 7 February 1917. Directing routine aspects of the blockade, he showed himself as diligent in administration as he was effective in debate. After three months as the British commissioner for propaganda in France (September–December 1918) he returned to the civil lordship on 27 January 1919 and helped establish the Ministry of Transport. He was sworn of the privy council in August 1919.

Lytton became parliamentary under-secretary of state for India on 22 September 1920. He worked to persuade British universities to admit more Indian students and strongly seconded Edwin Montagu's liberal approach to Indian constitutional reform. Montagu, after failing to secure him the viceroyalty, talked Lytton into taking the governorship of the Bengal presidency in 1922. Though averse to abandoning his cabinet ambitions, the earl genuinely believed in preparing India for responsible government within the British empire. Honoured with a knighthood, he arrived in Calcutta on 28 March with high hopes of making Bengal a model of the new system of provincial dyarchy. His plans went awry when the nationalists of the Swaraj party won the Bengal elections in November 1923 on an obstructionist platform. Their leader, C. R. Das, who would not take ministerial office himself, repeatedly used his majority to block the appointment of anyone else. In 1924 Lytton reassumed full powers and governed without ministers until the last days of his term. A spate of political murders, linked to revolutionary conspiracies, drove him to introduce detention without trial.

From 10 April to 9 August 1925 Lytton was acting viceroy while Lord Reading went on leave. His own (delayed) mid-term break came in June to September 1926. Calcutta suffered outbursts of communal rioting in 1926 and 1927, as Muslims objected to Hindus playing music outside mosques. Critics argued that Lytton spent too much time at Darjeeling, pondering on the glory, mischief, and pity of it all. He did love the mountains, but work was not neglected. His priorities were to combat corruption and change the language of instruction in secondary schools from English to the vernacular. It shook him to realize that Indian nationalists did not want a sympathetic governor. What could be done with people who lacked any sense of social service? He left their sad land with relief on 28 March 1927.

Lord Lytton headed the Indian delegation to the League of Nations assembly at Geneva in autumn 1927 and 1928. In 1931 he was there as a British representative. Failing a ministerial career, he put himself forward as a peace campaigner, and, once on the executive of the League of Nations Union, he was frequently mentioned in the same breath as Viscount Cecil (1864–1958), its other tory luminary.

When, in December 1931, the League of Nations instituted a five-man commission of inquiry into the outbreak of war in Manchuria, the British government proposed Lytton as a member, and his four colleagues elected him chairman. The Lytton commission covered thousands of miles between 29 February and 20 July 1932, harried by spies and propagandists, while it collected evidence in Tokyo, Shanghai, Nanking (Nanjing), Mukden (Shenyang), and Harbin, before settling in Peking (Beijing) to write up its findings. Fever stopped Lytton drafting the full text himself, yet he managed to reach a compromise with Claudel, the French member, who shrank from rebuking Japan. The 148 page report was signed on 4 September 1932 and published in October.

Thorough and fair, the Lytton report admitted the legitimacy of Japanese grievances against China but strongly criticized Japan for resorting to military action. It said that Manchuria should be autonomous under Chinese sovereignty—a proposal that stood no chance of being implemented, as the Japanese had won the war and created the puppet state of Manchukuo. On 24 February 1933 the League of Nations adopted the report; Japan then announced its withdrawal from the league. Nothing more was done.

To the dismay of some league enthusiasts, Lytton, who was world famous in 1932–3, firmly opposed economic or military sanctions against Japan. Believing that opposition merely strengthened and stimulated wrongdoers, he predicted that Japanese public opinion would turn against the militarists, if Japan were left alone, disgraced yet unchallenged, to reflect on its aggression. This was entirely in accordance with 'creative love'—and badly mistaken.

Awarded the Order of the Garter in 1933, Lytton was desolated by the death in a flying accident of his elder son, Viscount Knebworth MP (1903–1933). His memorial volume, *Antony: a Record of Youth* (1935), made a deep impression on readers in its day. By dint of his industry, integrity, eloquence, and title, the earl played a prominent part in many public bodies, such as the Royal Society of Literature, the Old Vic Association, and the Town and Country Planning Association. He carried on supporting reform in India (albeit with reservations) and, as chairman of Palestine Potash Ltd, urged adherence to the Balfour declaration: Jews and Arabs could work together in unpartitioned Palestine. Above all, as vice-chairman (1935–8) and chairman (1938–45) of the League of Nations Union, he exhorted the British government to defend international law and pursue collective security through the League of Nations—even after loyalty to internationalist ideals threatened to distance him from political reality. He admitted the need for rearmament, though, and backed Churchill's 'Focus in defence of freedom and peace'. Pacifists in the League of Nations Union disapproved of Lytton's moderation, which failed in its tactical aim—which was to win back tories to the pressure group and thus increase its influence *vis-à-vis* the National Government. The Munich agreement appalled him; his capacity for moral indignation never waned.

From 1940 to 1941 Lytton chaired the Council of Aliens, which advised the Foreign Office on internment, but he resigned in protest at interference by MI5. As chairman of the Entertainments National Service Committee (1942–5) he supervised deferment of military duties for actors. His younger son, John (1910–1942), was killed in action. Co-president of the United Nations Association from 1945, he advocated a nuclear strike force under UN control. He opposed nationalizing electricity, having held chairmanships in the industry. Lytton died at Knebworth House on 25 October 1947 and was buried at Knebworth on 30 October. He was succeeded in his titles by his brother Neville Stephen Bulwer-*Lytton.

Contemporaries hailed Victor, earl of Lytton, as a great British nobleman who might have attained the highest public offices, had he only been slightly less idealistic about free trade, or votes for women, or India, or collective security. Such fame was never likely to outlive him. The Lytton report on Manchuria alone kept his name familiar to students of international relations between the world wars. JASON TOMES

Sources *Hansard 4* · *Hansard 5L* · Lord Lytton, *Pundits and elephants: being the experiences of five years as governor of an Indian province* (1942) · Lord Lytton, *New treasure: a study of the psychology of love* (1934) · *Documents on British foreign policy, 1919–1939*, 2nd ser., ix–xi (1965–70) · C. Thorne, *The limits of foreign policy: the West, the League and the Far Eastern crisis of 1931–1933* (1972) · D. S. Birn, *The League of Nations Union, 1918–1945* (1981) · Lord Lytton, *Antony: a record of youth* (1935) · W. D. Wills, *Homer Lane* (1964) · *The Times* (27 Oct 1947) · E. Marsh, *A number of people* (1939) · *League of Nations: appeal by the Chinese government: report of the commission of enquiry* (1932) · Lord Lytton, *Can we survive the atomic bomb?* (1946) · private information (2004) · *DNB* · M. Lutyens, *The Lyttons in India* (1980) · *WW* · Burke, *Peerage* · *CGPLA Eng. & Wales* (1948)

Archives BL OIOC, corresp. and papers relating to work as governor of Bengal, MS Eur. F 160 · Bodl. Oxf., file relating to work as councillor on Society for the Protection of Science and Learning · Knebworth House, Hertfordshire, corresp. and papers · U. Glas. L., letters | BL, corresp. with Lord Cecil, Add. MS 51139 · BL, corresp. with Lord Gladstone, Add. MSS 46068–46082 · BL OIOC, corresp. with F. M. Bailey, MS Eur. F 157 · BL OIOC, letters to Lord Reading, MSS Eur. E 238, F 118 · Bodl. Oxf., corresp. with Gilbert Murray · PRO, admiralty files, 1916–1920 · U. Glas. L., letters to D. S. MacColl · U. Leeds, Brotherton L., letters to Edmund Gosse

Likenesses E. Mills, photograph, *c*.1911, NPG · W. Stoneman, two photographs, 1920–43, NPG · photograph, *c*.1925, NPG · O. Whiting, bronze head, *c*.1937, Knebworth House, Hertfordshire · P. Vincze, bronze plaque, *c*.1947, Knebworth House, Hertfordshire · N. Bulwer-Lytton, two portraits, Knebworth House, Hertfordshire · Spy [L. Ward], caricature, lithograph, NPG; repro. in *VF* (19 Sept 1906)

Wealth at death £77,947 10*s*. 8*d*.—excluding settled land; £22,500—limited to settled land: probate, 1948, *CGPLA Eng. & Wales*

Lyveden. For this title name *see* Vernon, Robert, first Baron Lyveden (1800–1873).

Lyzard, Nicholas (*d*. 1571), painter, was born in France to unknown parents. He entered the service of Henry VIII in the late 1520s or early 1530s, and is possibly identical with the 'Master Nykolas' who worked with Hans Holbein the younger at Greenwich Palace in 1527, or with Nicholas Lasora, one of the painters working in 1531 on the 'Coronation' picture for Whitehall Palace. The painter is first securely referred to in a list of foreigners resident in Westminster in 1540 when he was assessed at £30 in goods. Lyzard successively worked for Henry VIII, Edward VI, Mary I, and Elizabeth I, and acted as assistant to the serjeant painter Anthony Toto, to whose post he succeeded on 1 November 1554. His salary, however, seems to have fallen into arrears and a document of 10 April 1556 restates his position at court and awards him outstanding back pay. Lyzard seems to have been primarily a decorative painter, in 1550 producing costumes and visors for women in masques, and between 1556 and 1571 painting and gilding beds, banners, a carriage, and a barge for the royal wardrobe. He also worked on revels at court between 1544 and 1568 and is documented as producing heraldic painting for the obsequies of María of Portugal, queen of Spain, in 1555; for John III of Portugal in 1557; for Emperor Charles V in 1558; Henry II of France in 1559; and for Emperor Ferdinand I in 1564. On special occasions Lyzard also produced religious art, as is shown by his new year's gifts to Mary I and Elizabeth I respectively of a 'table painted with the Maundy' (Auerbach, 146) in 1556, and 'a table painted of the history of Ahasuerus' (Nichols, 45) in 1558. In this last year he worked on the funeral effigy of Mary I, and in 1559 he contributed to the decorations for the coronation of Elizabeth I. Between 1564 and 1568 he also worked on architectural painting at Whitehall and Strand palaces. With his wife, Margaret, he had five sons, four of whom were decorative painters employed by the office of revels, and four daughters. From 1540 or earlier Lyzard was a parishioner of St Martin-in-the-Fields, London, and was buried there on 5 April 1571.

P. G. MATTHEWS

Sources E. Auerbach, *Tudor artists* (1954), 51–2, 59, 91–4, 107, 111–12, 116–18, 145–6, 174–5 · M. Edmond, 'Limners and picturemakers', *Walpole Society*, 47 (1978–80), 60–242, esp. 178–9, 212 · E. Croft-Murray, *Decorative painting in England, 1537–1837*, 1 (1962), 26–7, 182 · R. Strong, 'More Tudor artists', *Burlington Magazine*, 108 (1966), 83–5 · A. Feuillerat, ed., *Documents relating to the revels at court in the time of King Edward VI and Queen Mary* (1914) · A. Feuillerat, ed., *Documents relating to the office of the revels in the time of Queen Elizabeth* (1908), 122 · J. G. Nichols, 'Notices of the contemporaries and successors of Holbein', *Archaeologia*, 39 (1863), 19–46, esp. 45 · will, PRO, PROB 11/53, fols. 132*v*–133*r*

Wealth at death left wife £80 in ready money and £20 in household goods: will, PRO, PROB 11/53, fols. 132*v*–133*r*

M'. Names starting M'— are alphabetized as though they started Mac—.

Maas, Jeremy Stephen (1928–1997), art dealer and historian, was born on 31 August 1928 in Penang, Malaya, the son of Oscar Henry Maas (1884–1957), a Dutchman who owned a rubber plantation in Malaya, and his American wife, Marjorie Turner, *née* Pope (1893–1988). Maas spent much of his youth travelling through Europe with his mother before being educated at Sherborne School, Dorset, and, after national service, Pembroke College, Oxford, from where he graduated with a third-class degree in English in 1952. While at Oxford he read William Gaunt's *Aesthetic*

Adventure (1949), which first kindled his interest in the highly unfashionable subject of Victorian painting. He worked briefly in advertising and for the printing firm Balding and Mansell, before joining Bonham's, the London auctioneers, where he started the company's watercolour and drawings department. On 10 November 1956 he married Antonia Armstrong (Toni) Willis (*b.* 1932), a noted equestrian and artist, and like Maas (who was 6 feet 4 inches) strikingly tall. They had two sons and a daughter. In December 1960 Maas opened his own small gallery at 15a Clifford Street, Mayfair, just off Bond Street, London. From the start he specialized in Victorian paintings, watercolours, and drawings, especially the Pre-Raphaelites. Through his gallery and its exhibitions, and through his books, he was one of the pioneers of the Victorian revival. During the 1960s and 1970s many great Victorian pictures passed through his hands, notably Lord Leighton's *Flaming June*, which he bought from another dealer for £1000, and sold for £2000 to Luis Ferré of the Ponce Museum, Puerto Rico. Many other museums purchased from him, as well as the leading collectors of the day, including Paul Mellon, Sir David Scott, Barry Humphries, and Andrew Lloyd-Webber. Maas also exhibited some contemporary artists, one of whom, John Ward, became a close friend and confidant, and painted Maas in a characteristic pose in his gallery in 1965.

Maas's first book was *Victorian Painters* (1969), at that time the best and most comprehensive survey of the subject. It was to remain in print for many years, and appropriately Leighton's *Flaming June* adorned its cover. His other books included *Gambart, Prince of the Victorian Art World* (1975), a biography of the great Victorian dealer; and *Holman Hunt and the Light of the World* (1984). Maas also amassed a remarkable collection of photographic portraits and cartes-de-visites of artists, which became the basis for *The Victorian Art World in Photographs* (1984). One aspect of Victorian art that particularly fascinated him was fairy painting; the exhibition on the subject held at the Royal Academy not long after his death was a fitting memorial. Maas also helped to found the perennially popular watercolour and drawings fair in 1986.

The shambling, pipe-smoking, at times brusque Maas was an awesome figure, but much loved by his friends and fellow-dealers in the art world. He was also intensely shy, never at ease in large gatherings, or with strangers. Like many shy men he had a surprising penchant for loud ties. Thus he generally hid downstairs in his very small gallery, and left it to his genial and sociable partner Henry Ford to cope with the clients. They formed a remarkable team, and those fortunate or interested enough would be conducted down the narrow staircase to meet the great man. Once the barrier of reserve was penetrated, they would find in Maas not only a huge reservoir of knowledge and enthusiasm, but also a wonderfully laconic wit. No one seemed to know more about the sexual and other peccadilloes of Victorian artists. 'Did you know', he would say, excitedly puffing on his pipe, 'that Mulready would never paint a model unless he had slept with her?' His books were similarly scholarly and entertaining at the same time, and full of insights. He was also generous to other dealers and historians working in the field, never holding back his own huge store of information and photographs. He was one of that very rare breed—a scholar–dealer; he also had an outstandingly good eye for quality, in spite of affecting to being mildly colour-blind. He died of renal failure and arterial disease at his home, Martins, Amberley, Arundel, Sussex, on 23 January 1997, and was buried on 29 January at St Michael's Church, Amberley. He was survived by his wife and three children; the elder son, Rupert, succeeded him in owning and running the gallery. CHRISTOPHER WOOD

Sources *The Times* (1 Feb 1997) • *Daily Telegraph* (28 Jan 1997) • *The Independent* (31 Jan 1997) • *The Guardian* (3 Feb 1997) • personal knowledge (2004) • private information (2004) • *CGPLA Eng. & Wales* (1997)

Archives priv. coll.

Likenesses J. Ward, portrait, 1965, Maas Gallery • photograph, repro. in *Daily Telegraph* • photograph, repro. in *The Times* • photograph, repro. in *The Guardian*

Wealth at death £208,095: probate, 20 Oct 1997, *CGPLA Eng. & Wales*

Maas, Joseph (1847–1886), singer, was born on 30 January 1847 at Dartford, Kent, the son of Joseph Maas, descended from an old Dutch family. At the age of ten he became a chorister at Rochester Cathedral, and was soloist there for five years. He studied with the cathedral organist, and with a Mrs Galton, eldest sister of Louisa Bodda-Pyne, who engaged him to sing as a boy treble at her concerts in the provinces. When he left the cathedral he became a clerk in Chatham Dockyard, but continued his musical studies with Louisa Bodda-Pyne in London. In 1869, financed by a Mr Wood of Rochester, he went to Milan, where he had singing lessons for two years under San Giovanni.

In February 1871 Maas replaced Sims Reeves at a concert given by Henry Leslie's choir at London's St James's Hall with great success, and on 29 August 1872 made his stage début at Covent Garden as Prince Babil in Dion Boucicault's *Babil and Bijou*. In 1872 he went to the United States as a member of Clara Kellogg's English Opera Company. He returned to England in 1877, and the following year sang Gontrau in the first English performance of Ignaz Brüll's *The Golden Cross* at the Adelphi Theatre under Carl Rosa. As a result of this he was engaged as principal tenor in the Carl Rosa company. During the three seasons 1878–80 his main roles were the title part in Wagner's *Rienzi*, Wilhelm Meister in Ambroise Thomas's *Mignon*, and Radames in Verdi's *Aida*, all of these being performed in English for the first time. Maas also sang for the Italian Opera at Her Majesty's Theatre in 1880, and in 1883 he made a memorable appearance in Wagner's *Lohengrin* at Covent Garden. At the 1884 Norwich festival he performed *Apollo's Invocation*, written for him by Massenet, and in May 1885 he created the part of the Chevalier des Grieux in the first London performance of Massenet's *Manon* at Drury Lane. He was an indifferent actor, but he had a pure tenor voice, of considerable power and compass, which he managed with ease and feeling.

Maas was popular in the concert room as well as on the stage, and in Handel's oratorios and in English ballads he was almost without a rival. His first oratorio appearance was at the Sacred Harmonic Society in *Messiah* on 4 April 1879. He had many engagements in London and the provinces and sang in Paris in 1884 and in Brussels at the Bach and Handel festival in 1885. His last important performance was at the Birmingham festival in 1885, where he sang in the first English performances of Dvořák's *The Spectre's Bride* and Stanford's *Three Holy Children*.

Maas married Catherine, daughter of J. H. Ball JP, of Stroud, Gloucestershire. They had one daughter. He died of a rheumatic affliction at his home, 21 Marlborough Hill, St John's Wood, London, on 16 January 1886, and was buried at Child's Hill cemetery, West Hampstead. His grave is marked by a marble monument with a carved portrait. A Maas memorial prize was founded in 1887 for the encouragement of tenor singers and is competed for annually at one of the British music colleges in turn.

J. C. HADDEN, *rev.* ANNE PIMLOTT BAKER

Sources G. Hanger, 'Joseph Maas: a centenary memoir', *Opera*, 37 (1986), 136–41 • Grove, *Dict. mus.* • *New Grove* • Brown & Stratton, *Brit. mus.* • Boase, *Mod. Eng. biog.* • *MT*, 27 (1886), 93–4 • *The Athenaeum* (23 Jan 1886), 145 • *CGPLA Eng. & Wales* (1886)

Likenesses marble carving on grave monument, 1886, Child's Hill cemetery, West Hampstead, London • photograph (as Phassilis in *Babil and Bijou*), repro. in Hanger, 'Joseph Maas', 137 • two prints, Harvard TC • wood-engraving, NPG; repro. in *ILN*, 88 (6 Feb 1886), 128

Wealth at death £8236 10*s*. 9*d*.: resworn administration, Feb 1888, *CGPLA Eng. & Wales* (1886)

Mab, James. *See* Mabbe, James (1571/2–1642?).

Mabb [Mab], **John** (*c*.**1515–1582**), goldsmith, was the eldest son of John Mabb of Clayton in Sussex and Joane Goble. He was apprenticed to Thomas Jones and became free of the Goldsmiths' Company in April 1539. From 1558 (and probably from 1540) he resided in Goldsmiths' Row in the parish of St Matthew, Friday Street, where he practised as a goldsmith. He followed a conventional company career, entering the livery in 1552, serving as renter in 1561–2, as warden in 1563–4, 1567–8, and 1571–2, and as prime warden in 1577–8. In parallel with his ascent of the company hierarchy he served the *cursus honorum* in parish and ward: he was churchwarden of St Matthew's, Friday Street, in 1559–60, and common councillor for the ward of Farringdon Within from 1560 to 1577. He was briefly a governor of Christ's Hospital in 1560–62, but seems to have been more engaged with Bridewell Hospital, of which he was a governor from 1570 to 1577, becoming associated with the determined and controversial moralism of the regime of Robert Winch, the treasurer from 1576.

Mabb never scaled the heights of the city plutocracy, but his subsidy assessments in the 1570s (£120) place him among the top 5 per cent of the citizenry. His financial acumen was widely appreciated—he had served as the treasurer of Bridewell in 1572–3 and as a city auditor in 1574—and on the dismissal of George Heaton he was elected on 13 December 1577 to the highly demanding position of chamberlain of the city. His skill was sufficient to see off a challenge from Matthew Colclough, a candidate backed by Sir Christopher Hatton, in August 1579, and he retained the office until his death in 1582. Mabb's civic activism was characteristic of a man who adopted a forward protestant position. Leaving money for twelve sermons after his death, he requested his favoured preachers: Toby Matthew, then vice-chancellor of Oxford University, Edwin Sandys, archbishop of York, John Aylmer, bishop of London, Alexander Nowell, dean of St Paul's, Adam Squire, archdeacon of Essex, and Richard Lewes. All were conformist, but all were noted for their commitment to preaching.

Mabb was the author of the

> Remembrances faithfullie printed out of his own hand writing; the true copie whereof was found carefullie wrapped up with his last will and testament, and other writings of great weight; and by himself thus entituled, A declaration of my Faithe; mine opinion of religion; a thanksgiving to God for all his benefits; an exhortation to my children, wherein all such are to learn a good lesson, as the Lord hath crowned with any kind of blessing and especially with bodily issue. (Arber, *Regs. Stationers*, 3.418)

He was doubtless thinking of the blessings of his own marriage to Isabella, daughter of Richard Colley of Shropshire, for there were five sons and three daughters alive when he drew up his will in 1578, of whom three of the boys and two of the girls had reached majority. His will carefully divided the moveable goods among them and provided for his widow according to the custom of London. His properties in Hertfordshire, Sussex, Southwark, and London were to go to his widow during her life, and then were to be divided among the five sons. The pattern of his charitable giving was conventional, but spread widely: there were bequests to the poor in the London parishes, for poor maidens' marriages, among the goldsmiths, and in his birthplace, to the London prisons, to Christ's Hospital, for highway repair in Sussex, and for poor scholars studying theology at the universities. But in the spirit of the civic moralism with which he had been associated, he was careful to ensure that 'no notorious swearer, adulterer, or drunckerd shall have annye parte of this my legacie in annye wise' (PRO, PROB 11/65, fol. 7). He died in 1582 and was buried on 28 December in the parish church of St Matthew, Friday Street.

IAN W. ARCHER

Sources court minutes, Goldsmiths' Company, London • journals, CLRO, court of common council • repertories of the court of aldermen, CLRO • will, PRO, PROB 11/65, fol. 7 • Arber, *Regs. Stationers* • D. Mills, 'Aspects of tenure in the Goldsmiths' Row in Cheapside, Elizabeth to James I', diploma in local history diss., London, 1982 [deposited at Goldsmiths' Hall] • M. Benbow, 'Index of London citizens involved in city government, 1558–1603', U. Lond., Institute of Historical Research, Centre for Metropolitan History • J. J. Howard and G. J. Armytage, eds., *The visitation of London in the year 1568*, Harleian Society, 1 (1869) • A. M. B. Bannerman, ed., *The register of St Matthew, Friday Street, London, 1538–1812, and the united parishes of St Matthew and St Peter Cheap*, Harleian Society, register section, 63 (1933)

Wealth at death one third in 1578 amounted to approx. £400; so perhaps estate of at least £1200: will, PRO, PROB 11/65, fols. 6–7

Mabbe [Mab], **James** (**1571/2–1642?**), translator, was born in Surrey, in the diocese of Winchester, the son of John Mabbe and Martha, daughter of William Denham of London. His grandfather, also named John Mabbe, was a well-known member of the Goldsmiths' Company who served as chamberlain of London in 1577. Mabbe matriculated aged sixteen at Magdalen College, Oxford, on 9 February 1588, received his BA on 8 February 1594, was elected to a perpetual fellowship in 1595, and received his MA on 17 October 1598. He was a scholar of the Goldsmiths' Company, but in August 1602 the company voted to turn Mabbe's scholarship over to someone else. Mabbe had already been granted leave the previous April to spend a year in France, and presumably he took the opportunity to travel before embarking on the study of civil law in 1603.

To this period belong Mabbe's first modest literary efforts. In 1598 he dedicated a treatise entitled *The Dyet of Healthe* (now lost) to the Goldsmiths' Company, and in 1600 he wrote a Latin commendation for fellow Magdalen scholar Charles Butler's *Rhetoricae libri duo*. He contributed one Latin and one Italian poem to Oxford's volume in honour of James I, *Academiae Oxoniensis pietas* (1603); in 1605 he presented a Latin oration when the royal family visited Magdalen; and in 1611 he wrote an anagram and Latin verses for John Florio's *Queen Anna's New World of Wordes*. An autograph poem addressed by Mabbe to 'Sir G. T. K.' (probably Sir George Trenchard, knight) survives in the Bodleian Library (MS Add. 29419, fols. 56*v*–57). Meanwhile, he served as junior proctor of Oxford in 1606, senior dean of arts in 1606–7, and junior dean of arts in 1609–10.

On 4 July 1609 Mabbe supplicated for the degree of doctor of civil law, but his thirst for travel soon led him in a different direction. In April 1611 he accompanied his former Magdalen classmate Sir John Digby on a mission to Madrid to negotiate a marriage between Prince Henry and Ana, daughter of Philip III. According to Wood, Mabbe spent several years as Digby's secretary in Spain, improving himself 'in various sorts of learning, and in the customs and manners of that and other countries' (Wood, *Ath. Oxon.*, 3.53), a statement confirmed by a letter Mabbe wrote from Madrid in 1612 describing various Spanish wonders. In 1613 he was made prebendary of Wanstrow, Wells, but he was absent in July 1615, perhaps travelling again. About this time he sent a copy of the 1613 edition of Lope de Vega's *Rimas* (now Balliol 700 a.14) to his Oxford friend Will Baker via fellow Hispanist Leonard Digges, who wrote an inscription on the flyleaf comparing Lope de Vega to Shakespeare.

For about the next fifteen years Mabbe taught at Magdalen (where he served as bursar six times between 1617 and 1630), suffered from gout, occasionally travelled to the continent, and translated various Spanish works. In 1622 his close friend Edward Blount published an elaborate folio edition of *The Rogue*, Mabbe's translation of Matheo Aleman's picaresque novel *Guzman de Alfarache*. This translation, made partly from Barezzo Barezzi's Italian version and partly from the original Spanish, was popular and influential enough to go through four editions by 1656; Mabbe's modern editor calls it a 'triumph' which 'might very well pass for a piece of masterly English prose' (Fitzmaurice-Kelly, xxiii). Mabbe dedicated the volume to his friend Sir John Strangeways of Dorset, and included many marginal notes explaining Spanish customs. In 1623, under the initials I. M., Mabbe contributed a short poem to the Shakespeare first folio, of which Blount was co-publisher; two other poems in the volume were by Ben Jonson and Leonard Digges, both of whom had commended Mabbe's book the year before.

Mabbe's next translations were of a religious nature. His folio manuscript *Advertisements Touching Festivall Dayes* (BL, Harleian MS 5077) is dated 27 December 1626. In the dedication to his 'worthy friend' John Browne of Frampton Court, Dorset, Mabbe says that this translation (the original of which is unknown) has been delayed by illness, and is an appendix to an earlier work. Secord tentatively suggests that this earlier work may have been Cristobal de Fonseca's *Devout Contemplations*, of which Mabbe published his translation in 1629, dedicated to Strangeways and Sir Lewis Dyves and their wives. Secord also demonstrates that Mabbe was the translator of *Christian Policie, or, The Christian Common-Wealth*, from the Spanish of Juan de Santa Maria, first printed in 1632 with a dedication to James Hay, earl of Carlisle, and mistakenly attributed by earlier commentators to Edward Blount.

In 1631, under the pseudonym Don Diego Puede-ser (James May-be), Mabbe published *The Spanish Bawd*, a lively and thorough translation of Fernando de Rojas's well-known play *La celestina* (partly via Alfonso Ordonez's Italian translation and Jacques de Lavardin's French version). He had originally done the translation many years earlier, in a manuscript dedicated to his old patron Strangeways (now Alnwick Castle, MS 510), but the printed version, considerably revised, was dedicated to Sir Thomas Richardson, newly appointed chief justice of the king's bench. *The Spanish Bawd* was considerably less successful than *The Rogue* in its day, but it has similarly impressed modern critics with its fluency and verbal inventiveness.

In 1633 Mabbe left Oxford and eventually went to live with Strangeways at Abbotsbury, Dorset. There he did his last translation (again as Don Diego Puede-ser), consisting of six novellas of Cervantes printed in 1640 under the title *Exemplarie Novells*, with a dedication to Susanna Strangeways, daughter-in-law of Sir John. A second edition, published in 1654 under the title *Delight in Severall Shapes*, omits Mabbe's name and his original dedication, and a third edition in 1742 wrongly ascribes the translation to Thomas Shelton. Mabbe was succeeded as prebendary of Wanstrow on 7 December 1642, and presumably died that year. Although the relevant records are lost, Wood says that he was buried at Abbotsbury. He never married.

DAVID KATHMAN

Sources G. M. Lacalle, 'An English Hispanist: James Mabbe', in [F. de Rojas], *Celestine, or, The tragick comedie of Calisto and Melibea*, trans. J. Mabbe (1972), 7–31 • A. W. Secord, 'I. M. of the first folio Shakespeare and other Mabbe problems', *Journal of English and Germanic Philology*, 47 (1948), 374–81 • G. M. Lacalle, 'A manuscript version of Mabbe's *Celestina*', *Revue de Littérature Comparée*, 39 (1965), 78–91 • Wood, *Ath. Oxon.*, new edn, 3.53–4 • Foster, *Alum. Oxon.*, 1500–1714, 3.956 • J. Fitzmaurice-Kelly, introduction, in [M. Aleman], *The rogue, or, The life of Guzman de Alfarache*, trans. J. Mabbe, 4 vols. (1924), ix–xxxvi • H. W. Allen, introduction, in [F. de Rojas], *Celestina, or, The tragicomedy of Calisto and Melibea*, ed. H. W. Allen, trans. J. Mabbe [1923], lxxvii–lxxxiv • P. E. Russell, 'A

Stuart Hispanist: James Mabbe', *Bulletin of Hispanic Studies*, 30 (1953), 75–84

Mabbott, Gilbert (*bap.* **1622**, *d.* in or after **1670**), parliamentary official and newsletter writer, was baptized at St Mary's, Nottingham, on 8 September 1622, the son of Edward Mabbott, probably a cordwainer, of Nottingham. His mother was possibly Margaret Watson. As an assistant in early 1643 to John Rushworth, clerk-assistant of the House of Commons, Mabbott became connected with the parliamentary army secretariat and subsequently acted as London agent for the army during the English civil war and interregnum. His importance lies in his combined roles of army agent, official correspondent, and parliamentary licenser of newsbooks and pamphlets.

Throughout the 1640s and 1650s Mabbott was a prolific and energetic professional newsletter writer. Apart from keeping army commanders in both England and Scotland informed about domestic and foreign affairs, he wrote regularly to individual correspondents: for example to Ferdinando, second Baron Fairfax of Cameron, during the civil war, and from September 1658 to Henry Cromwell, lord lieutenant of Ireland. Mabbott also supplied news to the borough of Hull from 1652 to 1656 during and after the first Anglo-Dutch war. Surviving examples of his newsletters show that they were often produced in multiple copies, with additions or omissions as appropriate to the recipient. He also kept in constant touch with his brother-in-law the army secretary Sir William Clarke. During the 1650s Mabbott was official agent for the town of Leith.

From March 1645, when he became deputy licenser to Rushworth, until March 1647, when both men were dismissed, presumably for political reasons, Mabbott's name appears regularly in the Stationers' Company register. He was reinstated as licenser on 30 September 1647 at the express request of the commander-in-chief of the parliamentary army, Sir Thomas Fairfax (later third Baron Fairfax of Cameron). From then until his resignation (or dismissal) in May 1649, Mabbott was progressively less successful in controlling the press, his imprimatur often appearing without permission. As 'agent of the army' his name reappeared on the Stationers' Company register from 1653 to 1655, when he entered the *Perfect Diurnall* and several pamphlets.

Dubious contemporary claims that Mabbott was editor or co-editor of the *London Post* and its continuations (1644–7) and *Mercurius Brittanicus* (1649) are unsubstantiated, although he may have had a hand in the *Perfect Diurnall* (1642–55), edited by Samuel Pecke. Mabbott's reputation as a Leveller, which rests solely on his alleged editorship of the radical newsbook *The Moderate*, is open to question. It is possible that he contributed to early issues of this newsbook, but there is no evidence that he was responsible for editing it, and nothing in his career or conduct to link him directly to the Levellers.

After the restoration of Charles II, Mabbott petitioned successfully for the lucrative office of manager for licences of wine and strong waters in Ireland for himself and his eldest surviving son, Kympton, then aged seven. Letters patent were granted in January 1661 and Mabbott moved to Dublin during the following summer, and by April 1663 was living in George's Lane there. In July 1663 members of the Holy Trinity Guild in Dublin complained about his aggressive behaviour in enforcing licences to retail wine (Gilbert MS 78, 137) and he surrendered the office to the crown in June 1664 for £4800. In December 1670 he was named in an Irish chancery decree. No more is heard of him after this, although Kympton was acting as agent for the commissioners of the sick and wounded at Plymouth in 1703.

Mabbott married Martha, daughter of Thomas Hilyard of Hampshire, and sister of Dorothy, wife of the army secretary William Clarke. They had at least two daughters and five sons. On 20 February 1656 Mabbott was named in a court case for adultery, but the defendant was acquitted (Jeaffreson, 3.292). FRANCES HENDERSON

Sources Mabbott corresp., Hull City RO • parish registers, protestation returns, St Mary's, Notts. Arch. • A. N. B. Cotton, 'London newsbooks in the civil war: their political attitudes and sources of information', DPhil diss., U. Oxf., 1972 • *The Clarke papers*, ed. C. H. Firth, 4 vols., CS, new ser., 49, 54, 61–2 (1891–1901) • F. M. S. Henderson, 'New material from the Clarke manuscripts: political and official correspondence and news sent and received by the army headquarters in Scotland, 1651–60', DPhil diss., U. Oxf., 1998 • J. Frank, *The beginnings of the English newspaper, 1620–1660* (1961) • *JHC*, 5 (1646–8) • *JHL*, 10 (1647–8) • C. Nelson and M. Seccombe, eds., *British newspapers and periodicals, 1641–1700: a short-title catalogue of serials printed in England, Scotland, Ireland, and British America* (1987) • BL, Lansdowne MS 823 • G. E. B. Eyre, ed., *A transcript of the registers of the Worshipful Company of Stationers from 1640 to 1708*, 3 vols. (1913–14), vol. 1 • *CSP dom.*, *1643–61* • Pearse Street Public Library, Dublin, Gilbert MS 78 • J. C. Jeaffreson, ed., *Middlesex county records*, 4 vols. (1886–92), vol. 3 • F. S. Siebert, *Freedom of the press in England, 1476–1776* (1952); repr. (1965) • Clarke MSS, Worcester College, Oxford • BL, Egerton MS 2551 • BL, Add. MS 21417 • C. H. Firth, ed., *Scotland and the Commonwealth: letters and papers relating to the military government of Scotland, from August 1651 to December 1653*, Scottish History Society, 18 (1895) • *The Moderate* • *Perfect Diurnall* • *London Post/Weekly Post-master* • *Mercurius Brittanicus* • *Mercurius Pragmaticus* (15 May 1649) [for King Charles II; Thomason tract E 555(13)] • *Mercurius Elencticus*, 44 (20–27 Sept 1648) • *Man in the Moon*, 26 (17–24 Oct 1649) • Hunt. L., Hastings MSS, Irish papers, box 17, HA14196
Archives Hull City RO, corresp. | BL, Lansdowne MS 823 • Worcester College, Oxford, Clarke MSS

Mabbott, John David (1898–1988), philosopher, was born on 18 November 1898 at Duns, Berwickshire, the home town of Duns Scotus and of David Hume. He was the eldest of the four children of Walter John Mabbott and his wife, Elizabeth (Bessie) Davies. His father had recently become headmaster of the Berwickshire high school at Duns. His mother, daughter of a Welsh monumental mason, David Davies, who had practised as a sculptor in London, was also a teacher, and just before her marriage had been a housemistress at St Leonard's School, St Andrews. John Mabbott was educated at a village school near Duns, and then at his father's school. He always warmly acknowledged his debt to his happy upbringing, to his mother's love of music, and to his father's scientific and intellectual curiosity. He went up to Edinburgh University in 1915, specialized in classics after his first year, and was called up in 1917 and commissioned in the Royal Garrison

John David Mabbott (1898–1988), by Lafayette, 1926

Artillery, serving until the end of the war in coastal defence in the Forth area.

On his return from military service Mabbott consulted one of his Greek teachers at Edinburgh, A. W. Mair, about where to continue his studies. The latter was a sensitive, distinguished, and somewhat eccentric Hellenist, whom Mabbott greatly admired. Mair, having observed his philosophical interests and ability, advised Oxford. He was elected to an exhibition at St John's College in 1919, and took a first class in *literae humaniores* in 1921. His tutors were J. L. Stocks and the young H. M. Last. He then took the unusual (in those days) step of reading for a BLitt, and completed his thesis on the development of Plato's theory of ideas in 1923, R. G. Collingwood being one of his examiners. This was the only form of graduate course then available; Mabbott's dissatisfaction with it as a training for a philosopher was to motivate him later in promoting important reforms. In 1922 he also spent some time in Ireland, and saw something of the troubles. This (like a later visit to Romania in 1928) left a deep impression, discernible in his later political thinking.

No academic post in philosophy being immediately available, Mabbott was appointed in 1922 to a lectureship in classics at Reading. Here he first encountered E. R. Dodds, with whom he had many interests in common, who in his own memoirs, *Missing Persons* (1977) describes the young Mabbott as one destined to be 'the genial head of a great Oxford College'. A year at Reading was followed by a year's philosophy teaching at Bangor (1923–4), after which he was brought back to Oxford to succeed J. L. Stocks at St John's. From then until the Second World War he devoted himself largely to teaching and to college affairs. He did however develop his interests in moral philosophy, and the article 'Punishment', published in *Mind* in 1939, was powerful and original, and became very well known. Already in 1926 he was influential in mobilizing the younger philosophers of the time in a regular discussion group—the 'wee teas', a breakaway from the philosophers' teas of the older generation of H. W. B. Joseph and H. A. Prichard. Founder members included Gilbert Ryle, H. H. Price, W. F. R. Hardie, and C. S. Lewis; among later recruits were W. C. Kneale, Oliver Franks, and H. M. Cox.

On 30 June 1934 Mabbott married (Sheila) Doreen (Keith) Roach (1905/6–1975), daughter of Thomas Haynes Roach, accountant, of Cheam, Surrey; it was a happy, but unfortunately childless, marriage. At the beginning of the war he was recruited by M. J. Paton into the research department of the Foreign Office, then under Arnold Toynbee in Oxford, but soon moved to London. His responsibilities at first related to future peace settlements in central Europe, and especially Romania; but from 1942 he was deputy director, responsible for internal administration of the department. He was appointed CMG (1946) for his services.

The post-war years were eventful; pupils now included the philosophers A. N. Flew, J. L. Ackrill, and Colin Strang. Mabbott was now completing his most influential work, *The State and the Citizen* (1948). Lucid and jargon-free, this deservedly had a long life as an 'introduction to political theory'. Mabbott owed much to T. H. Green and Bosanquet, but was often critical of them. He writes, of course, with the range of reference of the thirties and forties, and the book now has considerable historical interest. But it also has intrinsic and lasting value, in its closely argued discussions of the limits and purposes of the state, and particularly perhaps in its incisive critiques of terminology: the 'seven senses of "common good"', or the perils inherent in the word 'society'. In style and form it is characteristic, and shows the cast of his mind very well.

In 1947 Mabbott was narrowly defeated in an election for the presidency of St John's, but he continued to play an active part both in the college and in the university. It was in these years that he collaborated with Gilbert Ryle (always a close friend) in the establishment of the graduate degree of bachelor of philosophy, a decisive innovation which made Oxford a magnet for young philosophers from many countries, especially the USA, and produced one of the leading philosophy graduate schools in the world.

Mabbott's ambition to forward the development of professional philosophers was always complemented by his concern to train pupils for responsibility in public life. He felt strongly that moral and political philosophy, and the exact thinking that they demanded, were not activities to be confined to the lecture room and the tutorial. The daily work of decision and discipline, in college and elsewhere, put principles into practice and afforded examples to illustrate them. In St John's he held almost every office except that of bursar, and as president (1963–9) tactfully handled such student excesses as there were. Among his many contributions to university affairs, the chief was perhaps his chairmanship of the Oxford colleges admissions office, which endeavoured to put some order into the diversity of systems which colleges had been using to select undergraduates. Outside Oxford he was a pillar of the centre for the study of social and moral issues established in 1947 at Cumberland Lodge in Windsor Great Park by the Christian Foundation of St Catherine. In his later years also he was active in the Council for the Protection of Rural England, and fought hard and successfully to defend Otmoor against the extension of the M40 motorway. Enthusiast for responsible authority as he was, he had a strain of anti-authoritarianism; a zealous trespasser when he thought there was a right of way, he had a gleeful sort of sympathy for the rebellious and the troublesome, so long as their rebelliousness was of a kind he approved.

Mabbott retired from the presidency of St John's in 1969, and lived for the rest of his life at Islip, near Oxford, much involved in local affairs. In 1973 he published his last philosophical book, *John Locke*. His wife died in 1975, and he solaced his loneliness partly by public work, but also by writing *Oxford Memories* (1986), where much of his early life is recorded. He remained at Islip until a few days before his death, when he was persuaded to move into St John's, where he died on 26 January 1988. A memorial service was held for him at St Mary's on 30 April 1988.

Mabbott was a brisk, active man, and he always retained the upright carriage and vigorous movement of his youth. His direct, unpretentious writing style well reflects the man. His personal contribution to philosophy was considerable, but not as significant as the stimulus he gave to others at an important juncture in the history of British philosophy. D. A. RUSSELL

Sources J. Mabbott, *Oxford memories* (1986) · St John's College, Oxford, records · personal knowledge (2004) · m. cert. · d. cert. · *WWW*

Archives SOUND BL NSA, oral history interview

Likenesses Lafayette, photograph, 1926, NPG [*see illus.*] · P. Wardle, drawing, 1969, St John's College, Oxford

Wealth at death £371,858: probate, 25 April 1988, *CGPLA Eng. & Wales*

Maberly, Catherine Charlotte (1805–1875). *See under* Maberly, William Leader (1798–1885).

Maberly, Frederick Herbert (1781–1860), politician and Church of England clergyman, born on 18 April 1781, was the son of Stephen Maberly of Reading and London. Educated at Westminster School, he entered Trinity College, Cambridge, on 23 April 1802, graduating BA in 1806 and MA in 1809. He was ordained to the curacy of Bourn, near Caxton, and in 1807 married, at Bourn, Ann Kimpton. He soon began to display the eccentricity for which he later became notorious. At Chesterton, near Cambridge, he erected, for no declared reason and at great expense, a large dwelling, of which all the rooms were on one floor. In politics he was at this time a whig, but his anti-popish zeal was so fanatical that he resisted the movement for Catholic emancipation with the utmost determination, and increasingly represented ultra-tory views. About 1812 he travelled all over England in a van distributing tons of protestant tracts. His pamphlet *The Melancholy and Awful Death of Lawrence Dundas, Esq., an Undergraduate of Trinity College* (1818) was hyperbolic in tone and denounced the Fitzwilliam Museum for exhibiting 'disgraceful and licentious pictures' which would lead undergraduates 'to the commission of fornication'. None the less, it called attention to the lax supervision of undergraduates in lodgings in the town of Cambridge, and led to the introduction of a system of licences on 27 March 1818.

In 1826 Maberly took an active part in the opposition to Lord John Russell's re-election for the county of Huntingdon. In 1829, when the sheriff of Cambridgeshire declined a requisition to call a meeting to oppose the Catholic Relief Bill, Maberly issued a manifesto, dated 2 April (Cooper, 4.560), declaring that on 11 April, the occasion of the execution of a criminal then under sentence of death, he would address the crowd and move a resolution in favour of a petition for the impeachment of Wellington and Peel. Under pressure from the county magistracy he abandoned his intention on 9 April, but he subsequently appeared at the bar of the House of Lords to impeach the duke of Wellington and was summarily ejected. In 1834 he strenuously opposed the Poor Law Amendment Act, and on 11 June 1836 assembled a large meeting of labourers, principally from outlying villages, on Parker's Piece in Cambridge, to protest against the act and the way it was being implemented. On 26 July 1837 he was charged with assaulting a constable. In the meantime, during the brief tory government of 1834–5, he received from the bishop of Ely the rectory of Finborough in Suffolk, effectively a reward for his staunch support of the tory party. There his political activities diminished and he gave away much of his salary to the poor, so that when he died at Stowmarket on 24 January 1860 he left his family much impoverished.

J. A. HAMILTON, *rev.* H. C. G. MATTHEW

Sources *GM*, 3rd ser., 8 (1860), 511–12 · Venn, *Alum. Cant.* · C. H. Cooper and J. W. Cooper, *Annals of Cambridge*, 5 vols. (1842–1908) · *Cambridge Review* (17 Nov 1945)

Maberly, William Leader (1798–1885), army officer and civil servant, was born on 7 May 1798, probably at Shirley House, Surrey, the son of John Maberly (*d. c.*1832) and Mary Rose, daughter of William Leader, coachmaker to the prince of Wales. His father was a manufacturer and army contractor, and also MP for Rye in 1816–18, and for Abingdon in 1818–32. Educated at Eton College and at Brasenose College, Oxford, on 11 November 1830 Maberly married Catherine, who was the elder daughter of the Hon. Francis Prittie of Corville, co. Tipperary. **Catherine Charlotte Maberly** (1805–1875) was herself an author, who between

1840 and 1856 published nine novels and works of non-fiction, including *The Present State of Ireland and its Remedy*.

Like many men of his social background, Maberly found positions and advancement in government service. In the army he entered the 7th dragoons as a lieutenant in 1815, and subsequently served in the 9th dragoons in 1817–18. He was a captain from 1818 to 1825 in the 100th foot and the 84th foot, a major in the 72nd highlanders in 1825–6, a lieutenant-colonel in the 96th foot in 1826–7, and in the 76th foot from 1827 to 1832, when he went on half-pay. He did not retire from the army until 1881. In the House of Commons, Maberly was MP for Westbury, 1819–20, Northampton, 1820–30, Shaftesbury, 1831–2, and Chatham, 1832–4. Maberly's parliamentary career was characterized by a tendency to follow his father's political outlook (the elder Maberly turned against the tories in 1819), and by an oratorical style which was said to be indefatigable but ineffective.

Yet it was as a senior civil servant that Maberly came to occupy a position of public prominence. After serving as surveyor-general of the ordnance in 1831–2, clerk of the ordnance in 1833–4, and commissioner of customs in 1834–6, Maberly became secretary of the Post Office in 1836. There he quickly encountered challenges, and some difficulty because of three complicating situations. The first arose from the fact that he had succeeded an extremely able administrator, Sir Francis Freeling, who had led the Post Office with distinction for thirty-eight years. The second was the result of the changing economic environment in which the department was functioning in the mid-nineteenth century. Increasing demands for service from the business community, and complex questions involving the new contractual relationships with railways and steamships, increased the strain on the Post Office and Maberly. The third, and most vexing, entanglement grew out of the campaign of Rowland Hill (1795–1879) for postal reform, launched in 1837. Hill criticized the Post Office on a number of levels, but his most important claim was that a simplified system of postage prepaid on the basis of weight would not only better serve the public, but would within five years regain the net revenue (profit) levels achieved earlier under a system which had put the taxing function of the Post Office before its social and economic functions. Hill's proposal bore fruit in 1840 with the implementation of the penny post.

For the rest of Maberly's career at the Post Office he contended with Hill and his reforms. Hill later claimed that any difficulties and shortcomings of penny post (it was not until 1873 that revenue recovered to maintain consistently pre-reform levels) were the responsibility of time-serving insiders such as Maberly. Such a judgement does not do justice to the complexity of the situation. Maberly did at times evidence a relaxed approach to administration, as his attention was often focused on the management of family land in Ireland. But he was not incompetent. He had a clearer understanding of the economics of the postal service, and a better grasp of the nuances of administering a large bureaucracy, than did Hill. Maberly also worked harder to implement penny post than Hill recognized.

It was to no avail. After Hill was installed in 1846 as secretary to the postmaster general to promote his ideas from within, friction between the two increased. Hill emerged the victor, when, in 1854, he replaced Maberly as the senior civil servant in the Post Office. Maberly was transferred to the board of audit, where he served until 1866. Catherine Maberly died on 7 February 1875. Enjoying a pension of over £1700 per year, Maberly lived in retirement until 6 February 1885, when he died at his home, 23 Gloucester Place, London. C. R. PERRY

Sources M. J. Daunton, *Royal Mail: the Post Office since 1840* (1985) • C. R. Perry, *The Victorian Post Office: the growth of a bureaucracy*, Royal Historical Society Studies in History, 64 (1992) • HoP, *Commons* • d. cert. [Maberley, William Leader] • d. cert. [Maberley, Catherine Charlotte] • *CGPLA Eng. & Wales* (1885)

Archives Post Office Records, post 30, postmaster general minutes and memoranda | BL, corresp. with Sir Robert Peel, Add. MSS 40496–40570 • W. Sussex RO, letters to the duke of Portland; letters to the duke of Richmond

Likenesses portrait, repro. in Daunton, *Royal Mail*

Wealth at death £56,915 9s. 3d.: resworn probate, April 1886, *CGPLA Eng. & Wales* (1885)

Macadam, Elizabeth (1871–1948), social worker, was born on 10 October 1871, in the village of Chryston outside Glasgow, to the Revd Thomas Macadam, a minister of the Free Church of Scotland, and his wife, Elizabeth Whyte. Her girlhood was spent partly in Canada, where her father was first minister of St Andrew's Presbyterian Church in Strathroy, Ontario, and then professor of political philosophy at Morrin College, a small Presbyterian college in Quebec City. She was educated at Strathroy high school and attended classes at Morrin College. Their mother having died and their father having retired to Toronto, Elizabeth and her sister Margaret returned to Scotland as young women, and lived for a time in the household of their maternal uncle, the Revd Alexander *Whyte, then minister of St George's Free Church in Edinburgh.

It is not known how Elizabeth Macadam came to decide upon a career in social work, or to move to London, but in 1898, having acquired some experience of kindergarten work in Germany and having lived for a time at the women's settlement in Canning Town, she was awarded one of the newly endowed Pfeiffer scholarships to train in social work at the Women's University Settlement in Southwark. She remained at the settlement for four years, taking part in district visiting and other programmes developed by the settlement, and running an evening school for about a hundred 'rough' adolescent boys and girls, for which work she was paid a salary by the local school board.

Elizabeth Macadam's chance to make an original contribution to the development of social work as a practice and a profession came in 1902, when she was hired to take over the wardenship of the Victoria Women's Settlement in Liverpool, a position she held until 1910. Assisted by Emily Oliver Jones, who had also trained at the Women's University Settlement, and by Eleanor Rathbone, she not only improved the settlement's organization and finances but also altered its philosophy and direction. First, she began to transform the settlement into, in her words, 'a laboratory for experiments in social reform'—and indeed the dispensaries, clinics, clubs, and classes for disabled children pioneered by the settlement both stimulated demand for and served as the core of later statutory municipal services. Second, her horror of the 'uncertain, hap-hazard efforts' of private benevolence led her to place great importance on the development of social work as a profession. In 1904 the settlement launched a training programme for social workers that combined lectures on poverty, child welfare, and civic administration with a course of practical work undertaken in collaboration with municipal and voluntary associations. In 1910 Liverpool University absorbed this programme and appointed Elizabeth Macadam as the first lecturer on the methods and practice of social work; by the outbreak of the First World War, this course had more than a hundred students.

Having established a modest but solid reputation as an innovator in the field of social work, Elizabeth Macadam was asked by the wartime Ministry of Munitions to help devise training courses for welfare workers; she also served on the women's advisory committee to the liquor traffic control board. This work took her increasingly to London, and at the end of the war she and Eleanor Rathbone (who had become a close friend and companion) bought a house there together. From 1919 Elizabeth Macadam acted as secretary to a new Joint Universities Council for Social Science, which had been established to co-ordinate the training of social workers. She also wrote several significant works on the development of this new field, publishing an authoritative study of the evolution of training for social work in 1925 (*The Equipment of the Social Worker*), an intelligent survey of the complex and evolving relations between state and voluntary efforts in 1934 (*The New Philanthropy*), and a revised edition of the first book in 1945.

Elizabeth Macadam assumed that the end of the First World War would inaugurate a new partnership between the state and the voluntary sector, and that trained social workers like herself would be called upon to help plan the work of reconstruction. Yet new opportunities were slow to develop, and during the last twenty-five years of her life she spent much of her time supporting Eleanor Rathbone's expanding and complex political career. Macadam's public commitments increasingly came to mirror those of Rathbone: thus, after Rathbone became president of the National Union of Societies for Equal Citizenship (NUSEC) in 1919, Macadam became a NUSEC officer and an editor of its paper, the *Woman's Leader*; likewise, Macadam helped to run the campaign for family endowment (family allowances) which Rathbone spearheaded. Rathbone was the stronger intellect of the two and was often in the public eye, yet archival records show that the two friends collaborated closely; certainly some portion of Rathbone's considerable public achievement was aided by Macadam's steady support and careful organization of both Rathbone's parliamentary campaigns and their joint life. This relationship is hard to capture, for both women were reserved about their private lives and maintained officially separate public careers. Yet their personalities, dissimilar as they were, were complementary, and the two were extremely close. Elizabeth—practical, organized, demanding, and even somewhat bossy—kept the more abstracted and emotionally diffident Eleanor on track, and was probably the only person with whom Eleanor felt entirely comfortable. The two friends continued to share a house in London until Rathbone's sudden death in January 1946. Having never ceased to regard herself as a Scotswoman, Elizabeth Macadam returned to Edinburgh for the last two years of her life. She died of cancer at her home, 7 Nile Grove, on 25 October 1948.

SUSAN PEDERSEN

Sources M. D. Stocks, *Eleanor Rathbone: a biography* (1949) · G. F. Barbour, *The life of Alexander Whyte, D.D.* (1923) · Victoria Settlement MSS, U. Lpool · M. Simey, *Charitable effort in Liverpool in the nineteenth century* (1951) · private information (2004) · b. cert. · d. cert.
Archives priv. coll., B. L. Rathbone · U. Lpool, Rathbone MSS · U. Lpool, Victoria Settlement MSS
Likenesses photographs, priv. coll.
Wealth at death £22,000 19*s*. 2*d*.: confirmation, 24 Dec 1948, *CCI*

McAdam, John (1806–1883), reformer and campaigner for Italian unity, was born on 5 August 1806 at Port Dundas, Glasgow, the second son of James (or Thomas) McAdam (*d. c.*1821), carter, and his wife, Helen Baxter, both originally from rural Stirlingshire. His education, partly in an overcrowded school in Glasgow's Cowcaddens, included Latin, but its effects were overwhelmed by his family's poverty and his father's death. McAdam helped the family out by driving carts and from 1822 to 1828 he was a 'weary' apprentice shoemaker (*Autobiography*, 3). Despite working long hours, which aggravated an asthmatic condition caused by an earlier accident with gas, McAdam continued his education through membership of a book club. From 1828 he was self-employed.

McAdam first came to prominence during the Reform Bill agitation of 1832, when he was appointed a delegate to the Trades Committee, created to establish a newspaper to give the Glasgow working classes a voice. He was also appointed to the Vigilance Committee, which was given a watching brief after the defeat of the Reform Bill in the House of Lords in May 1832. In this capacity he was a leading organizer of the Black Flags demonstration held in Glasgow on 12 May 1832 in protest at this and at the resignation of the Grey ministry. At the general election of 1832 McAdam was himself put up as a radical candidate for Glasgow, but did not go to a poll.

McAdam's political activities appear to have led some of his customers to take their business elsewhere. Partly for this reason he emigrated to Canada in the summer of 1833, hoping to take up farming. The following fourteen years did not realize his ambitions. He worked as a shoemaker and trader and travelled throughout North America, during which time he encountered the ideas of the Italian patriot Giuseppe Mazzini (1805–1872). In the later

1830s McAdam defended Mazzini at a meeting in Vicksburg, Mississippi, and also supported his ideas in the newspapers. These included a united and republican Italy and the essential unity of all struggles for civil and religious liberty.

On his return to Glasgow about 1847, McAdam joined his brother William in his successful pottery business. McAdam saw his brother's support as essential in allowing him time for political and fund-raising activities in the following years. In December 1851 McAdam married Mary McIntyre. They had a daughter and seven sons who survived infancy. McAdam was soon politically active again. The reformers and Chartists in Glasgow were split between the 'moral suasionists', who were willing to co-operate with others less advanced, and the more extreme 'irreconcileables' (*Autobiography*, 16). McAdam tried, as in 1832, to encourage co-operation. He helped to form the Glasgow committee to the National Parliamentary and Financial Reform Association, which by late 1849 was holding meetings across Scotland and demonstrating the effectiveness of getting middle- and working-class reformers to co-operate. McAdam was also active in the Glasgow Parliamentary Reform Association, founded in 1852 and revived at various times thereafter, which attempted to unite reformers of all shades in the city. A highlight was the visit of John Bright to Glasgow in December 1858, when McAdam was part of the welcoming and platform party. Although strongly favouring manhood suffrage, McAdam was willing to accept Bright's proposal for household suffrage as the most liberal reform that could be obtained. He was a prominent member of the election committees of Glasgow Liberal MPs such as Robert Dalglish and George Anderson both before and after the 1868 Reform Act, and chaired the city's twelfth ward Liberal committee for a time.

The most important element in McAdam's political activity was his pivotal position between various European nationalist and freedom movements and Scottish reformers. He saw this work as an integral part of the 'political education and action' (*Autobiography*, 92) of working men during a period when he believed they were too concerned with trade-union matters. In retrospect McAdam can be seen as one of the leaders who helped to bridge the years between Chartism and the revived parliamentary reform agitation of the later 1860s.

McAdam's efforts took various forms. He was a prominent member of various Glasgow organizations set up to support freedom movements—above all in Italy, but also in Hungary and Poland. These included the Society of Friends of Italy, active in the late 1850s, and the Glasgow Committee for the Emancipation of Italy, established in 1857, of which McAdam was secretary. This committee raised money for the unsuccessful expedition led by Carlo Pisacane to incite rebellion in Calabria in 1857 and thereafter for the defence of two British engineers, Henry Watt and Charles Park, who had been imprisoned on complicity charges in Naples. On the outbreak of war in Italy in 1859 three organizations, all under McAdam's auspices, were active in raising funds. These were the Glasgow Garibaldi Italian Fund, the Ladies' Garibaldi Benevolent Association, and the Glasgow Working Men's Fund for Garibaldi. The last reflected McAdam's belief in separate working-class organizations.

McAdam was himself a tireless fund-raiser who made use of contacts with wealthy Liberals such as the Tennants, owners of the St Rollox chemical works, and the Coats, thread manufacturers in Paisley. He also used his own resources. On his mission to Italy for the Glasgow Garibaldi Italian Fund in 1860–61, for example, he purchased clothing for over 500 British Garibaldian volunteers. His reputation as an ardent Mazzinian does not appear to have hampered his activities, but it did lead him to take a less prominent role. In 1859 he suggested Robert McTear as secretary of the Glasgow Garibaldi Italian Fund, so as not to lose Garibaldi support from those who suspected Mazzini's aims. Though particularly good at raising money from 'those who shuddered at the very idea of Italian Unity' (*Autobiography*, 138), he also restrained Scottish volunteers from going to Italy, especially after it became apparent that they were not needed. Third, McAdam became the personal and proud friend of the leaders of these European movements. He corresponded with and met Mazzini between 1857 and 1871 and the Hungarian nationalist Lajos Kossuth from 1854 to 1880. McAdam acted as an intermediary between these two when, for example—in the tense situation of 1859–60, caused especially by the part taken by Hungarian troops under Austrian command in Italy—he tried to ensure that they used no other Scottish contact. Most memorable for McAdam was his visit to Garibaldi on Caprera at the close of 1860. McAdam was responsible for publicizing the activities and ideas of these leaders through the Glasgow press. Offprints were passed back to him for distribution to other, including London, papers. He also produced a stream of his own letters to newspapers and, in 1857, a pamphlet, *Mazzini Vindicated by a Sketch of his Eventful Life: and the Struggle for Italian Liberty*.

After 1860 McAdam, though still active, was less successful. This was partly owing to the public perception that further Italian unification was a matter for the Italians themselves. In 1861 he organized the Garibaldi Italian Unity Committee in Scotland, which carried on fund-raising. He also continued to act as an intermediary, for instance in the difference of opinion between Mazzini and Garibaldi over the priority of liberating Venetia or Rome. In 1864 Garibaldi, a fellow freemason, asked McAdam to be his guide in Scotland. When the planned visit appeared in jeopardy, McAdam was sent to London by the working men's reception committee to try to persuade Garibaldi to carry out his plans. McAdam's opponents accused him of trying to politicize the visit into a fund-raising event for nationalist causes. In non-Italian causes he arranged the lectures given by the French socialist Louis Blanc in Glasgow in October 1860 and helped organize the lecture given by Karl Blind and a subscription in Scotland, both in support of the Polish uprising in April 1863. He also helped publicize Blind's views on the

Schleswig-Holstein question and, later, on the republic declared in Spain in 1874.

Although McAdam's correspondence was increasingly about subjects such as agricultural implements with Garibaldi and family matters with Kossuth, there was one public cause in which McAdam very successfully managed to involve many European activists. This was the revival in 1865 of the movement first started in 1856 to erect a monument to Sir William Wallace on the Abbey Craig at Stirling. McAdam was active in forming a Glasgow committee to raise subscriptions and also persuaded Kossuth, Mazzini, Garibaldi, Blind, and Blanc to contribute. Their support was expressive of the link between European revolutionary movements and the struggle for reform at home. McAdam was one of those who saw themselves as exporting the freedoms they already enjoyed, a symbol of which was the cult surrounding Wallace. This essentially protestant and republican form of civil and religious liberty found its antithesis in the Austrian, French, and papal forces it helped to combat.

In June 1873 McAdam was given a presentation by Glasgow citizens in recognition of his services to reform. During the last ten years of his life he was in failing health. Involvement in his brother's property speculations, as a result of which William McAdam emigrated to New Zealand in 1879, left him penniless. He admitted that he had perhaps neglected his family in supporting the exiles who came to him for help, but justified this by its effect on the condition of Europe and the pleasure it had given him. John McAdam died at his home, 175 Berkeley Street, Glasgow, on 18 November 1883. His wife survived him.

GORDON F. MILLAR

Sources *Autobiography of John McAdam*, ed. J. Fyfe (1980) • *The Scotsman* (20 Nov 1883) • *Glasgow Herald* (20 Nov 1883) • *North British Daily Mail* (20 Nov 1883) • *Glasgow Herald* (19 Nov 1883) [death notice] • J. Fyfe, 'McAdam, John', *BDMBR*, vol. 2 • J. Fyfe, 'Scottish volunteers with Garibaldi', *SHR*, 57 (1978), 168–81 • J. Fyfe, 'Aid to Garibaldi from John McAdam and the city of Glasgow', *Pages from the Garibaldian epic*, ed. A. P. Campanella (Sarasota, 1984), 71–88 • J. F. McCaffrey, *Scotland in the nineteenth century* (1998), 60 • A. Wilson, *The chartist movement in Scotland* (1970) • *IGI* • private information (2004) [J. Fyfe] • m. reg. Scot. • d. cert. • J. Ridley, *Garibaldi* (1974)

Archives Durham RO, letters | Hungarian National Archives, letters to L. Kossuth; letters to F. Pulszky • Museo del Risorgimento, Milan, letters to Mazzini • National Library of Hungary, letters to S. Vukovics • University of South Carolina, Columbia, A. P. Campanella collection of G. Garibaldi, letters to Garibaldi

Macadam, John (1827–1865), chemist and politician in Australia, was born at Northbank, near Glasgow, in May 1827, the second son of William Macadam and his wife, Helen Stevenson. After being privately educated in Glasgow, he studied chemistry at the Andersonian Institution (1842–5) and became assistant to Frederick Penny. After two years of advanced study with William Gregory at the University of Edinburgh, he became a medical student at the University of Glasgow in 1848, and graduated MD in 1854.

In 1855 Macadam went to Melbourne to fill the post of lecturer on chemistry and natural science at the Scotch College, and on 18 September of the following year he married Elizabeth Clark; they had one son, Kirkland Macadam, who later became the first professor of chemistry of the University of Melbourne. Macadam was one of the earliest members of the Philosophical Institute (from 1859 the Royal Society) of Victoria. He edited the first five volumes of the society's *Transactions*, and held the post of secretary from 1857 until his election as vice-president in 1863.

Macadam was active in Australian public affairs. He was elected to the legislative assembly of Victoria in 1859, representing the district of Castlemaine, and he served as secretary of the exploration committee of the Burke and Wills expedition. As an MP he was instrumental in the passing of laws on medical practitioners and adulteration of food in 1862 and 1863, but resigned his seat in 1864.

Macadam was appointed lecturer in theoretical and practical chemistry at the University of Melbourne in 1862, and also held the posts of government analytical chemist (1858–65) and health officer to the city of Melbourne (1860–65). In May 1865 he fractured his ribs and then developed pleurisy, but sailed in the autumn for New Zealand, to give evidence at a murder trial. Severe weather aggravated his condition, and he died on board the *Alhambra* on 2 September 1865. He was buried in Melbourne general cemetery on 28 September 1865.

Macadam was a talented analytical chemist, and published his work in Glasgow and Melbourne. He contributed two papers to the Royal Society, Victoria: 'On kerosene' (*Transactions*, 6, 1914), and 'On Dalton's atomic theory' (not printed). He wrote several reports, including one on the resources of the colony of Victoria, presented to the Royal Society of Victoria in 1860.

P. J. HARTOG, *rev.* K. D. WATSON

Sources *AusDB* • *GM*, 4th ser., 1 (1866), 141 • Boase, *Mod. Eng. biog.*

McAdam, John Loudon (1756–1836), builder and administrator of roads, was born in the west-coast town of Ayr, at 22 Sandgate, on 21 September 1756, the youngest child and second son of James McAdam of Waterhead (*c*.1718–1770), and his wife, Susannah Cochrane (*b. c*.1717). His father was a minor laird and his mother a niece of the seventh earl of Dundonald, while his middle name records his paternal great-grandmother's links with the Loudoun family; but despite these advantages McAdam's early life was unsettled. Ancestral lands at Waterhead were sold off, the family's home in the parish of Carsphairn was destroyed by fire, and they were obliged to move to a rented house, Blairquhan near Straiton. This misfortune was compounded by an ill-advised investment in a bank in Ayr which failed two years after James McAdam's death in 1770. The family was left straitened but not impoverished, and in this difficult situation the fourteen-year-old John Loudon had to find a way to make a living. His origins and background had prepared him well for this task: he had benefited from the Scottish parish school system, having attended classes in Maybole where he is reputed to have made a model cross-section of the nearby road; as part of the Scottish diaspora he had relatives overseas to whom

John Loudon McAdam (1756–1836), by unknown artist, *c.*1830

he could look for openings; and he had an instinctive belief in his own worth as a gentleman.

Early business ventures In 1770 the young McAdam left home for New York, where his father's brother William had already established himself in trade and society as a prosperous merchant with a well-connected wife. McAdam was taken into the home of this childless couple and came to work closely with his uncle in ventures such as the sale of naval prizes. The antagonism of the American colonies to British rule, leading to the outbreak of hostilities in 1775, created difficulties for the McAdams as it did for other 'loyalists', but while his uncle retired to the country John Loudon continued in business. By 1778 he was sufficiently well established to propose marriage to Gloriana Margaretta Nicoll (*d.* 1825), the daughter of a wealthy lawyer whose family had long held positions of responsibility in the colony. When in 1783 the former colonies achieved independence, McAdam and his wife sailed from America with their two children, Ann and William, and such fortune as they had been able to secure. This proved sufficient for the purchase of a house and estate at Sauchrie, between Ayr and Maybole.

John Loudon McAdam's enforced return propelled his career into its second phase, as a Scottish country gentleman and business entrepreneur. He became a magistrate; a trustee of the Ayrshire turnpike roads; deputy lieutenant of the county; and the officer in charge of a volunteer artillery corps when in 1794 a French invasion seemed imminent. His business interests came to prejudice this settled life, for the Sauchrie estate had to be sold when bankruptcy threatened as a result of his association with the British Tar Company, established in Muirkirk in 1782 by his kinsman Archibald Cochrane, ninth earl of Dundonald. McAdam realized the importance of this pioneering venture, the first to produce commercially profitable coal tar, and from the mid-1780s he was successively agent, manager, and owner of the rights to the patent and the works. However, difficulties in establishing sales of coal tar for the bottoming of ships, and in maintaining supplies of coke of the right quality and quantity for the nearby Muirkirk Iron Works, led to severe legal and financial problems which were only resolved in the later 1790s by the sale of McAdam's estate and his second departure from Scotland. Despite these upheavals he retained an interest in the company and associated coalworks, and his eldest son William became manager there. For many years McAdam received an income from this source which provided some degree of financial independence, and in 1931 a cairn was built in his honour, to mark 'the site of his tar kilns 1786–1827'.

In 1798 the family moved south, spending a few months in Kingsdown, Bristol, where a fourth son (their seventh child) was born. He was named John Loudon junior, and like his surviving brothers William and James he was to become a road surveyor. Further sisters Gloriana and Georgina had been born in Scotland in the late 1780s. They moved on to Falmouth where McAdam found work as a prize master, a role that had proved profitable in wartime New York, but when the peace of Amiens of 1801 put an end to the taking of prize ships the family was again adrift. They returned to Bristol, but although this was to be a more permanent move the city's directories suggest a reluctance to settle, for between 1802 and 1826 they rented five houses on the slopes of Brandon Hill—two in Park Street, two in Berkeley Square, and one in Dowry Parade, all genteel dwellings which would have offered comfort rather than the grandeur of the houses of the merchant princes in Clifton.

Improver of roads The reasons for settling in Bristol have never been explained, except in terms of the opportunities provided by this second city and major port. Entries in the directories from 1807 for 'McAdam, James & Co., Manufacturers of Lampblack, Mineral Paints, Oils etc, near the Glass-house, Limekiln Lane', suggest that Bristol may have offered McAdam a chance to resume his interest in the chemical industry through his second son, James, while maintaining the connection with the British Tar Company. McAdam established himself in Bristol civic life as successfully as he had in his native Ayrshire. The incorrect 'Lowdin' was replaced by 'Loudon' in the directories and 'Esq.' was added as a sign of status. McAdam never attained membership of the select Society of Merchant Venturers, but he was made a freeman of the city by the common council in 1805. In 1811 he helped to establish the Bristol Commercial Rooms, becoming the first president, and between 1815 and 1820 he played a leading part in the campaign for a new gaol in the city. Such activities were peripheral to his main interest, however—the improvement of the roads that were so vital for the growing economy—and it was to this end that he became a trustee of the large and important Bristol Turnpike Trust.

By the early nineteenth century the fact that the methods of road construction were haphazard, and the surveyors largely untrained and of low esteem, was causing official as well as private concern. Sir John Sinclair, chairman of the board of agriculture, supported a series of parliamentary committees which reported regularly from 1806. Evidence was invited, and in 1810 Sir John received an impressive memorandum from McAdam which was edited and published as an appendix to a report of the following year ('Select committee on … turnpike roads and highways', *Parl. papers*, 1810–11, 3). Extracts were included in McAdam's first book, *Remarks on the Present System of Road Making* (1816), which was so influential that it had reached nine editions by 1827. McAdam's views were based on a study of the conditions found on extensive travels, covering, he claimed, 30,000 miles between 1798 and 1814 ('Select committee on … turnpike roads and highways', *Parl. papers*, 1820, 2). These led him to conclude that the main legislative efforts of the time were misdirected, for they were concerned with the regulation of traffic (especially in respect to wheels and weights) in order to preserve the roads, rather than with methods of construction that would accommodate the traffic.

McAdam's recommended system of road construction involved the careful preparation of a well-drained subsoil, levelled, but with a slight fall from the centre of 1 inch to the yard. The roadstone was to be broken by seated workers with small-handled hammers into rough pieces weighing no more than 6 oz that would fit into the mouth. McAdam had observed that large stones were likely to be cracked by passing vehicles and sent flying, but that smaller, angular ones, applied to a depth of 10 inches and compressed by workmen, were consolidated by traffic to produce a resilient and impermeable surface which improved over time. These techniques were simple, effective, and economical. The substantial foundations which were such a feature of the roads built by his contemporary Thomas Telford, often at government cost, played no part of McAdam's system, and further economies came from the fact that the roads were no longer to be overburdened with stone, and that much of that already heaped upon them could be stripped off, reworked, and reused.

Organizer of roads McAdam's advice extended to the organization of roads, which were to be controlled by the trustees with the assistance of an 'executive officer'—preferably a trained surveyor of good social standing in receipt of a salary which would place him beyond corruption. In December 1815 McAdam was offered the chance to put his theories into practice by his fellow Bristol Turnpike trustees, who invited him to become their general surveyor of roads at a salary of £400 per year. The challenge was accepted and over the following years the Bristol Trust was managed with great skill and economy. By 1819 it controlled 178 miles, and McAdam's salary had risen to £500 per annum, out of which he supported his office and family, and kept a carriage, horses, and servants. His work on the road from Bristol towards Shepton Mallet was noted by Sir John Coxe Hippisley, whose recommendation to the postmaster-general provided McAdam with further opportunities for public activity, since good roads were vital to the speedy delivery of mail.

As his reputation grew McAdam was able to extend his influence further by becoming, with the support of his family, a surveyor or consultant to other trusts. By 1819 he, James, and William worked for twenty-five trusts, and over the whole period to the death of his grandson in 1861 the family were surveyors to almost 150 trusts (Reader, appendix 1). The support of the Post Office and the board of agriculture remained firm, and parliamentary committees continued to provide a platform for McAdam's views. His claim for financial compensation for the country-wide work undertaken on behalf of the road system, mostly at his own cost, was recognized, and between 1820 and 1825 McAdam received £6000 from public funds ('Select committee on the petition'). However, his fame on the national stage produced little joy in Bristol, where the turnpike trustees felt themselves neglected, despite the appointment in April 1824 of McAdam's son John Loudon jun. as joint general surveyor. McAdam's absences provoked a vote of censure and he chose to resign; nevertheless, he agreed to return on his own terms when invited to do so, perhaps because the surveyorship of the adjoining Bath Trust was then in view, offering the chance of managing the two important trusts side by side. McAdam was appointed to the Bath roads in 1826 and maintained his connection with both until his death in 1836. He conducted the business of the Bristol Trust with his son John Loudon, and that of the Bath Trust with his grandson William.

At the same time as his difficulties with the Bristol trustees, McAdam's links with the city were further weakened by the death of his wife in 1825. Two years later he moved to Hoddesdon in the Hertfordshire countryside and married her younger relative, Anne Charlotte Delancey (1786–1862), who was born in Bath but who had American connections. They lived amiably, with summer visits to Scotland where McAdam delighted in places connected with his boyhood. His surveyorships increased at this time, perhaps in association with these journeys, for they came to include seven in northern England and six in Scotland. Most were held until his death, and it was while returning from a visit to Scotland in 1836 that the eighty-year-old McAdam died on 26 November in Moffat, the former home of his grandmother in whose grave he was buried on 2 December. The tombstone still stands, but an attempt by his son James to raise a public monument failed and the fund was closed in 1849. It had been supported by many eminent people, but the public who had so recently shown great enthusiasm for the 'macadamizing' of the roads had failed to respond, perhaps reflecting the downturn in the fortunes of the roads in the face of railway competition.

Significance The first systematic builder and administrator of roads in Britain since Roman times, McAdam was one of that select band whose achievements have led to their names becoming part of the common language.

From the 1820s the term 'macadam' or 'macadamized' came to mean a good road surface, achieved by the judicious use of stone over which horse-drawn vehicles could travel quickly and smoothly within a well-planned and organized network which approached something of a national system. The survival of the term was ensured by the arrival of the motor car with its accompanying clouds of dust, for the control of this nuisance by the application of tar to road surfaces gave rise to its evolution into 'tarmacadam' and 'tarmac'.

McAdam deserves to be remembered for his ability to create and seize opportunities, and to overcome failure. His greatest achievement lay in devising a simple and economical system of construction which brought speed, efficiency, and comfort to the roads. With his strong sense of his own worth he conferred distinction upon the work of the road surveyor, elevating into a profession what had previously been considered a humble task. He was not an engineer on a grand scale like his rival Thomas Telford or the early railway builders, but by his tireless advocacy of the cause of good roads he effected great changes in the transport system of the country. His emphasis on good management inspired the wish to consolidate the trusts into fewer but larger ones, with higher and less variable standards. This aspiration was never given legislative reality, but because McAdam's three sons and four grandsons followed him into the profession he came close to achieving this aim through his family connections. The warmth of feeling within this circle is shown by surviving letters and accounts, which recall McAdam's 'eyes of remarkable brightness' (Devereux, 146). McAdam may have refused the knighthood later accepted by his son James (Webb and Webb, 184), but he could not deny the immortality gained by having his name pass into the language.

BRENDA J. BUCHANAN

Sources W. J. Reader, *Macadam: the McAdam family and the turnpike roads, 1798–1861* (1980) • R. H. Spiro jun., 'John Loudon McAdam, colossus of roads', PhD diss., U. Edin., 1950 • R. Pember [R. Devereux], *John Loudon McAdam: chapters in the history of highways* (1936) • W. Albert, *The turnpike road system in England, 1663–1840* (1972) • J. L. McAdam, *Remarks on the present system of road making* (1816) [and later edns] • J. L. McAdam, *Narrative of affairs of the Bristol district of roads* (1825) • J. L. McAdam, *Observations on the management of trusts for the care of turnpike roads* (1825) • J. R. Hume and J. Butt, 'Muirkirk, 1786–1802: the creation of a Scottish industrial community', *SHR*, 45 (1966), 160–83 • B. J. Buchanan, 'The Great Bath Road, 1700–1830', *Bath History*, 4 (1992), 71–94 • S. Webb and B. Webb, *The story of the king's highway* (1913) [repr. 1963] • W. T. Jackman, *The development of transportation in modern England*, 1 (1916) • T. Codrington, *The maintenance of macadamised roads* (1879) • *Dumfries & Galloway Courier* (30 Nov 1836) • *DNB* • *Ayr Advertiser* (15 Dec 1988) • 'Select committee on … turnpike roads and highways', *Parl. papers* (1810–11), 3.855, no. 240; (1820), 2.301, no. 301 • 'Select committee on the petition of Mr. McAdam', *Parl. papers* (1823), 5.53, no. 476

Archives Man. CL, Manchester Archives and Local Studies, observations on his life and work • Museum of the City of New York, papers | BL, letters to Lord Grenville • NA Scot., Seaforth muniments • NA Scot., corresp. with J. A. Stewart-Mackenzie and Keith Stewart • Post Office Archives and Record Centre, London, corresp. • University of Strathclyde, Glasgow, Muirkirk papers

Likenesses C. Turner, mezzotint, pubd 1825, BM, NPG • A. Edouart, silhouette, 1827, Scot. NPG • oils, *c.*1830, NPG [*see illus.*]

Wealth at death £1500: R. H. Spiro jun., 'John Loudon McAdam, colossus of roads', PhD diss., U. Edin., 1950, appx H, pp. 488a–b and pp. 458–61

McAdoo, Henry Robert (1916–1998), Church of Ireland archbishop of Dublin, was born at 13 The Crescent, Cork, on 10 January 1916, the eldest son of James Arthur McAdoo (1876–1948), a company director, and his wife, Susan Good (1885–1971), a governess, both of Cork. Henry was educated at Cork grammar school and Mountjoy School, Dublin. He then had a distinguished academic career at Trinity College, Dublin, where he was a foundation scholar in modern languages (1936), held a moderatorship in French and Irish with gold medal (1938), took his PhD in 1940 and DD in 1949. He was ordained deacon in 1939 and priest in 1940. On 1 February 1940 he married Lesley Dalziel Weir (*b.* 1918), daughter of James Arthur and Ethel Lynthorne Weir of Dalkey, co. Dublin, and they had one son and two daughters. Following a curacy at Christ Church Cathedral, Waterford, and incumbencies in the dioceses of Cork and Ross, he was appointed dean of Cork in 1952. He was elected bishop of Ossory, Ferns, and Leighlin on 11 March 1962, and elected archbishop of Dublin and bishop of Glendalough in 1977.

McAdoo's preaching, like his lecturing and writing, was crystal-clear, somewhat didactic yet entertaining. His strong pastoral instincts were exemplified by such slim publications as *No New Church* (1946), in which he sought to build up the confidence of the members of the Church of Ireland by an examination of their place in the newly emergent independent Ireland. Likewise, *Where do Anglicans Stand?* (1970) and *Being an Anglican* (1977) were expositions of the Anglican method of doing theology, as he saw it, endeavouring to prepare Anglicans, and most particularly members of his own church, for ecumenical dialogue by equipping them with a sound understanding of their faith.

With the publication of *The Structure of Caroline Moral Theology* in 1949 McAdoo established his reputation as a scholar of considerable stature in his chosen field of Caroline divinity and piety. Indeed at the time of his death he was still regarded by some as 'foremost of Caroline scholars' (Carroll, *Wisdom and Wasteland*, 13). His wide reading in the works of Jeremy Taylor and his contemporaries convinced him of their importance for the present day, not least because of 'their repeated admonition that piety becomes a meaningless burden of rules unless we go first to the heart of the matter, the life of God in the soul of man' (*Structure*, xii). *The Spirit of Anglicanism* appeared in 1965. Here he contended that Anglicanism was not a theological system, the absence of an official theology in Anglicanism being 'something deliberate which belongs to its essential nature' (*Spirit*, v). The great divines of the Caroline period, according to McAdoo, stated a method in theology, rather than outlining a system.

From 1967 McAdoo was a member of the joint preparatory commission of the Anglican–Roman Catholic International Commission (ARCIC), appointed by Pope Paul VI and the archbishop of Canterbury, Michael Ramsey. From 1969 to 1981 he was co-chairman of the commission

(ARCIC I), which laid the foundations for a new approach to Anglican–Roman Catholic relations. He gave himself unstintingly to the task, and his hand is evident in the commission's statements on eucharistic doctrine, ministry and ordination, and authority, culminating in the final report presented to the churches of the Anglican communion and the Roman Catholic church in 1982. While participation in ARCIC brought him little gratitude in some parts of his own church, it earned him the Canterbury cross for services to the Anglican communion. In later life he made no secret of his disappointment that the ecumenical opportunities presented by the work of both ARCIC I and ARCIC II were not more urgently addressed by the ecclesiastical authorities. He might well have agreed with the political maxim that 'all politics are local politics', when he considered the suspicion with which his participation in ARCIC was viewed by some members of the Church of Ireland, and indeed the somewhat cool reception—some would have described it as cautious—accorded to its statements at home. That he did not proceed from Dublin to Armagh is at least partially explained by a comment of his own that he had no intention of exchanging a milieu in which he was relatively acceptable for one in which, in his own view, he would be quite unacceptable. Father Michael Hurley SJ, doyen of Irish ecumenists and founder of the Irish School of Ecumenics, has claimed that ARCIC I's *Final Report* (1982) was the greatest of Bishop McAdoo's many great achievements, crediting him and his Roman Catholic co-chairman, Bishop Alan Clark, with an ecumenical breakthrough in emphasizing that church union was to be achieved, not by acceptance of an elaborate plan, but by 'stage by stage' reconciliation and convergence (Hurley, 350).

McAdoo contributed greatly to the work of ARCIC while at the same time benefiting hugely from the opportunities that the commission afforded him for discourse with other scholars. His perspective gradually moved from that of a philosopher (albeit one with strong pastoral instincts) to that of a theologian, and as major theological themes appeared on the commission's agenda he came more and more to discern the theological, even sacramental, dimension to the work of the Caroline divines. Though never unaware of their piety (he revered, indeed shared, the spirituality of Taylor's *Holy Living and Holy Dying*), McAdoo's *The Eucharistic Theology of Jeremy Taylor* (1988) shows more appreciation of the sacramental content of Taylor's theology than he had noted previously. *Anglican Heritage: Theology and Spirituality* (1991) was a reminder that, since heritage has in large measure made us as individuals what we are, so the process of corporate recollection is for the church an essential element in self-understanding, not least of our spirituality.

McAdoo kept up his reading and writing in retirement, publishing, with Kenneth Stevenson, *The Mystery of the Eucharist in the Anglican Tradition* (1995), a comprehensive and detailed synthesis of Anglican eucharistic tradition, inevitably informed by his ARCIC experience. His last book, *Anglicans and Tradition and the Ordination of Women* (1997), presented the case for ordaining women to the priesthood at a time when the matter was still controversial, though he offered his book, not in a controversial spirit, but as a positive expression of the Anglican method. His academic achievements were recognized by the awarding of an honorary degree by Seabury-Western College in the United States (1962) and election to honorary fellowship by Trinity College, Dublin, in 1990.

Nor did McAdoo's academic and international commitments render him neglectful of his diocesan obligations in either Ossory or Dublin. A firm believer in the denominational school system (at least in the Irish context), schools and their teachers were of particular concern to him. While persistent in his demands on government on behalf of the Church of Ireland's educational interests, he was listened to because at the same time he could see that many aspects of state policy, including the frequently unpopular amalgamation of small schools, were ultimately for the good of the children, and so he was prepared to incur local opprobrium, however uncongenial to him, in support of such proposals. His appreciation and use of the Irish language also stood him in good stead in political circles, though an early interest and competence in Celtic studies fell by the wayside as pastoral, administrative, and ARCIC affairs made increasing claims on his time and energy. He retired in 1985 and died in St Vincent's Hospital, Dublin, on 10 December 1998, survived by his wife. He was buried in the churchyard of St Canice's Cathedral, Kilkenny, on 14 December 1998. KENNETH MILNE

Sources T. K. Carroll, 'Henry Robert McAdoo', *The Furrow*, 1/5 (May 1999), 304–8 · M. Hurley, 'Henry Robert McAdoo', *Doctrine and Life*, 49/6 (July–Aug 1999), 350–55 · W. J. R. Wallace, ed., *Clergy of Dublin and Glendalough* (2001) · *The final report of the Anglican–Roman Catholic international commission* (1982) · T. K. Carroll, *Wisdom and wasteland: Jeremy Taylor in his prose and preaching today* (2001) · personal knowledge (2004) · private information (2004) · b. cert. · m. cert. · d. cert. · *The Times* (15 Dec 1998) · *The Guardian* (17 Dec 1998) · *Daily Telegraph* (15 Dec 1998) · *The Independent* (12 Dec 1998)

Archives Representative Church Body Library, Dublin | SOUND Representative Church Body Library, Dublin, interview with Dr McAdoo in his retirement

Likenesses A. Festing, oils, 1985; photographic copy, Chapter House, Christ Church Cathedral, Dublin

Mac Aedh, Malachy (*d.* 1348), archbishop of Tuam, was a canon of Elphin and in 1307 was elected bishop of that see by one party of the canons. The remaining canons chose Cathal Ó Conchobhair, abbot of Lough Cé, who obtained possession of the bishopric and was consecrated by the archbishop of Armagh. Malachy was supported by the metropolitan, William Bermingham, archbishop of Tuam; he therefore went to Rome, where, after three years, the pope decided in his favour, annulling the election of Cathal. On 22 June 1310 Malachy received consecration from Nicholas, bishop of Ostia and Velletri, and the papal decision was confirmed by the king, Edward II, on 7 December 1310. In 1312 Malachy was elected archbishop of Tuam; the king issued a commendatory letter to the pope on 24 August and on 19 December the archbishop received consecration. The temporalities were restored on 1 April 1313. As archbishop, Malachy pursued his predecessors' aim of assimilating the diocese of Annaghdown within the diocese of Tuam. In 1325 Gilbert, bishop of Annaghdown, complained that he had been deprived of his see by Malachy. On 31 July 1327 Pope John XXII, on the petition of the archbishop, sanctioned the union of the three dioceses of Annaghdown, Killala, and Achonry with Tuam. Edward III opposed the proposal claiming that the rule of an Irish bishop was being substituted for that of an English one, but on a vacancy to Annaghdown in 1330 the bull took effect so far as that see was concerned. Malachy died in Tuam on 10 August 1348, and was buried in Tuam Cathedral. According to Thomas Tanner, he wrote, *inter alia*, an Irish list of the kings of Ireland from Niall Noígiallach to Ruaidrí ó Conchobair.

C. L. KINGSFORD, *rev.* MARGARET MURPHY

Sources *CEPR letters* • *CPR, 1307–13* • J. A. Watt, *The church and the two nations in medieval Ireland* (1970) • Tanner, *Bibl. Brit.-Hib.* • W. M. Hennessy, ed. and trans., *The annals of Loch Cé: a chronicle of Irish affairs from AD 1014 to AD 1590*, 2 vols., Rolls Series, 54 (1871) • *AFM*, 2nd edn

Macalister, Arthur (1818–1883), politician in Australia, was born in Glasgow, the son of John Macalister, a cabinet-maker, and his wife, Mary, *née* Scoullar. Trained as a solicitor, in 1839 he emigrated to Australia with his newly wed wife, Elizabeth Wallace Tassie. After holding a couple of minor government posts and running a Sydney store, he began working for a solicitor in Sydney and in 1850 was admitted to practice. He then moved to Ipswich (near Brisbane) and soon entered local politics. He twice failed to win a seat in the New South Wales parliament, but he was a supporter of the separation of Queensland from New South Wales and when this was effected he was elected for Ipswich in the first Queensland parliament in 1860, and quickly became one of the most prominent public men in the colony.

Appointed secretary for lands and works in Robert Herbert's government in 1862, in February 1866 Macalister succeeded Herbert as premier. During the next ten years he held various ministerial positions, was twice premier (1866–7 and 1874–6) and speaker in 1870–71. In 1863 he was largely responsible for establishing the narrow gauge (3 feet 6 inches) for Queensland's railways, with the construction of the line to Toowoomba. He always backed railway extension, but his land policy was more variable. His land act of 1863 allowed pastoralists longer leases on easier terms but, when he was premier in 1875, his ministry's land act restricted pastoral leases in settled areas and encouraged agricultural settlement by resuming much pastoral land. As a liberal, he was critical of cheap imported labour, supporting measures to control both Pacific islanders and Asians. As a Presbyterian, a mason, and chairman of the Board of Education from 1862 to 1867, he opposed sectarian schools, his ministry being responsible for introducing the 'secular' State Education Act in 1875.

Meanwhile Macalister's health was failing and, after an 'apoplectic' (or 'epileptic') fit in 1875, he visited England, ostensibly to enquire into the selection of immigrants. While there he was appointed CMG, but in June 1876, three months after his return to Queensland, he resigned as premier. He was then appointed agent-general, based in London, acting as Queensland commissioner at the Philadelphia International Exhibition on the way over. He resigned this post in November 1881 and returned to the neighbourhood of Glasgow where he died, bankrupt, on 23 March 1883. Known as Slippery Mac, he often broke his promises and changed his attitudes and allegiances, but he was an able administrator as well as an astute politician and his tergiversations were no greater than those of many others. His wife died in Brisbane on 14 September 1894, survived by two sons and three daughters out of their nine children.

A. G. L. SHAW

Sources *AusDB* • C. A. Bernays, *Queensland politics during sixty years, 1859–1919* [1919] • *Queenslander* (18 March 1876) • B. R. Kingston, 'Land legislation and administration in Queensland, 1859–1876', PhD diss., Monash University, 1983 • P. D. Wilson, 'The political career of the Honourable Arthur Macalister CMG', BA diss., University of Queensland, 1969 • P. Wilson, 'Arthur Macalister: "Slippery Mac"', *Queensland political portraits, 1859–1952*, ed. D. J. Murphy and R. B. Joyce (1978), 45–69 • T. A. Coghlan, *Labour and industry in Australia, from the first settlement in 1788 to the establishment of the commonwealth in 1901*, 2–3 (1918) • *DNB*

Wealth at death bankrupt in Scotland: *AusDB*

MacAlister, Sir Donald, first baronet (1854–1934), physician and medical administrator, was born at Earls Dykes East, Perth, on 17 May 1854, the second of the ten children (six boys and four girls) of Donald or Daniel MacAlister (1825–1881), and his wife, Euphemia (*d.* 1905), second daughter of Angus Kennedy, of Bowmore, Islay. He was baptized Daniel on 23 June 1854, though later he adopted Donald as his first name.

The 'Tarbert MacAlisters' had long been settled on Lochfyneside as landholders and later as crofters and fisherman, but MacAlister's father had become a publishers' agent, living successively in Glasgow, Perth, Aberdeen, and, from 1864 until 1881, in Liverpool, where he was employed by Blackie & Son. He had a large family and narrow means, so that Donald, the eldest son (Duncan, the first-born, had died in infancy), had not only to provide for his own education but also, in his early manhood, to bear the greater part of the maintenance and education of his brothers and sisters. Donald's younger brother Sir John MacAlister (1856–1925), who had intended to follow a medical career but was diverted into librarianship and journalism after a breakdown in health, also became a medical administrator (as secretary of the Royal Society of Medicine).

Donald MacAlister's education began in Charlotte Street, Aberdeen, with the inspirational William Rattray. His learning of the shorter catechism there was a memory he always carried with him. In 1866, this 'fine bright lad of twelve' went to the Liverpool Institute, then under the direction of the Revd John Sephton, to whose teaching and guidance MacAlister owed much (E. F. B. MacAlister, 7). There he won the Royal Geographical Society's gold medal, a prize which indicated his academic prowess and through which he came to the notice of Francis Galton. In 1873 he entered St John's College, Cambridge, on a scholarship. His expressed intention was to read medicine but he was advised to read mathematics, in the Cambridge

Sir Donald MacAlister, first baronet (1854–1934), by Olive Edis

conviction that this subject was the true basis for a liberal education. He was a member of the Cambridge Apostles from 1876 to 1882. In 1877 he emerged as senior wrangler of his year and first Smith's prizeman. He was elected fellow of his college and retained his membership for life. He taught at Harrow for a term and contemplated a career in mathematics. In this he was encouraged by Galton to apply for the chair at Glasgow University left vacant by Hugh Blackburn's retirement as professor. Under Galton's patronage he published a technical paper on the mathematical distribution of the geometric mean in the *Proceedings of the Royal Society*.

MacAlister decided against a mathematical career and instead turned to his original intention of studying medicine: first at Cambridge, then in 1879 at St Bartholomew's Hospital, London, and finally for a brief spell under Carl Ludwig at Leipzig. In 1881 MacAlister settled in Cambridge, where he was appointed Linacre lecturer and deputy to the regius professor of physic, Sir George Paget. In 1884, when he graduated MD, he became consultant physician at Addenbrooke's Hospital. He won wide recognition and in 1886 was elected fellow of the Royal College of Physicians. He gave the Goulstonian lecture entitled 'The nature of fever' and delivered the Croonian lecture. He was co-editor of *The Practitioner* from 1886 to 1895 and prepared an English edition of E. Ziegler's *Textbook of Pathological Anatomy and Pathogenesis* (1883). MacAlister's main energies were already being drawn to organization and administration. At Cambridge he took an active part in college and university affairs and was regularly re-elected to the council of the university senate.

On 19 March 1895 MacAlister married a distant relative, Edith Florence Boyle Macalister (1873–1950), daughter of Alexander Macalister (1844–1919), professor of anatomy at Cambridge, and his wife, Elizabeth Stewart (1843/4–1901). From 1893 until 1904 MacAlister was senior tutor at St John's College, and at their home, Barrmore, he and his wife entertained tutorial pupils for Sunday lunch (where on principle wine was not served, though Mrs MacAlister made a point of passing around the cigarettes). There were no children of the marriage.

A decisive event for MacAlister was his election in 1889 as the representative of Cambridge University on the General Medical Council (GMC), when he defeated the Downing professor of medicine, Peter Latham (1832–1923) by 194 votes to 140. The GMC became one of MacAlister's chief fields of activity, and he was a member for forty-four years. At the age of fifty he was unanimously elected as president and he took office on 29 November 1904. MacAlister inaugurated his own reforms: in 1905, for instance, he brought in a notice directed against advertising and canvassing, a practice he regarded on a par with infamous conduct. He never ceased to emphasize that the council existed for the good of the public and not for the protection of the medical profession. MacAlister effectively controlled the gateway to the profession by regarding it the duty of the GMC 'first, to prevent the unfit from gaining access to the Register, and, secondly, to remove the unworthy from it' (W. Pyke Lees, *Centenary of the General Medical Council, 1858–1958*, 1958, 12). In 1907 he signalled his approach to educational reform—to training in midwifery. However, he cajoled the council: 'we must be content to hasten slowly' (London, Great Portland Street, General Medical Council, GMC minutes, vol. 65, 1928, 442). MacAlister set out a forward-looking agenda in his address 'On the General Medical Council, its powers and its work' in 1906.

MacAlister ruled the GMC with a rod of iron. He made himself expert on such diverse business matters as preliminary and postgraduate education, the registration of nurses and midwives, Indian medical education, and the National Insurance Act. In the council chamber he displayed an uncanny memory, while his command of precedent and procedure coupled with a native ability of reconciling divergent views enabled him to streamline GMC business.

In 1907 MacAlister was nominated for appointment by the crown as principal of Glasgow University. When he claimed he knew Cambridge but not Glasgow, the prime minister, Henry Campbell-Bannerman, himself a Glaswegian, persuaded him: 'I love them both, but with a difference; Cambridge is bright, but Glasgow is warm' (*The Times*, 16 Jan 1934). The university was on the verge of a great period of growth, and MacAlister gained the confidence of city and university alike. While his health was never completely reliable, he did not shirk hard work. The expansion of the arts faculty claimed his first attention, and inevitably the faculty of medicine followed shortly afterwards; a chair in medical education was established in 1910. Departmental lectures were to be open to both men and women, and in effect Glasgow put down its marker as a centre for medical study and research, a move which gained early success and attracted students from all over the world.

The expansion of the university continued after the First World War. MacAlister pressed on with the establishment of endowed chairs and during his time at Glasgow more than twenty were created, several through the Carnegie United Kingdom trusts of which he was vice-chairman. There were, for instance, chairs in Italian, Spanish, and a faculty of engineering which was established in 1923. The ambitious building programme continued. A long overdue arts faculty building was completed in 1928 and the erection of the beautiful war memorial chapel, a project dear to MacAlister's heart, was completed; one of his last acts as principal was to see it dedicated. The social and athletic side of Glasgow student life was not neglected, this being a project both MacAlister and his wife could enter together. They saw it as their duty to furnish the needs of students in their leisure hours.

MacAlister's genius with minutiae did not blinker his perspective. He took a leading part in the general university business of the country. He was one of the founders of the Universities Bureau of the British Empire, and was for many years chairman of the standing Committee of Vice-Chancellors and Principals of the British universities. He served on the Treasury committee of 1908 on the University of Wales, the commission on the Queen's University, Belfast, and the royal commission on the civil service (1912–15). He was chairman of the medical consultative committee of the Scottish board of health and had a long and active association with the development of the Highlands and Islands Medical Service Board.

MacAlister was fond of travel and acquired languages with astonishing ease. In his widely known *Echoes* (1907), he translated Spanish, Italian, and Russian verse into English; Greek and German verse into Russian; Provençal into Scots; and quatrains from ʿUmar Khayyam into Romani. At a dinner party he once replied to a toast in seven languages (of his reputed fourteen in which he could summon sentences), including Japanese and a dialect of Chinese. He had a special interest in Russian and Romani, and, in 1915, he was president of the Gypsy Lore Society.

MacAlister held honorary doctorates from thirteen universities in Britain and overseas. He was appointed KCB in 1908 and created a baronet in 1924. In the latter year he received the freedom of the city of Glasgow, and after his resignation as principal in 1929 he was elected chancellor of the university.

On 24 November 1931, after an unbroken twenty-seven years in office, MacAlister stood down from the presidency of the GMC on the grounds of ill health. He appeared reluctant to sever all ties and at the same meeting as his resignation he was elected to the examinations committee, which he had first joined in 1892. He also retained his chairmanship of the pharmacopoeia committee and oversaw the new edition of the *Pharmacopoeia* that replaced his own enormously successful edition of 1914.

Motivated by strong principles and unwavering Presbyterian beliefs, MacAlister carried through organizational change with remarkable skill, bringing Glasgow University and the GMC into the twentieth century. In August 1933 he suffered a stroke, and he died of acute appendicitis on 15 January 1934 at his home, Barrmore, Lady Margaret Road, in Cambridge, where he was buried at St Giles's cemetery. A. J. CRILLY

Sources *DNB* • E. F. B. MacAlister, *Sir Donald MacAlister of Tarbert* (1935) • personal knowledge (1949) [*DNB*] • personal knowledge (2004) • *The Lancet* (20 Jan 1934) • *BMJ* (20 Jan 1934), 125–7 • S. Godbolt and W. A. Munford, *The incomparable Mac* (1983) • Blackie & Son, *A short history of the firm A. A. C. Blackie, Edinburgh* (1959) • J. Y. W. MacAlister, *A memorial to his family and friends* (1926) • R. G. Smith, *Medical discipline: the professional conduct jurisdiction of the General Medical Council, 1858–1990* (1994) • H. D. Rolleston, *The Cambridge medical school: a biographical history* (1932) • *WWW* • Munk, *Roll* • Venn, *Alum. Cant.* • parish register, Perth, Earls Dykes East [birth], 17 May 1854 • m. cert. • d. cert. • *WWW, 1916–28* [Alexander Macalister] • gravestone [wife]

Archives CUL, corresp. • U. Glas., corresp. | CUL, letters to Sir George Stokes • King's AC Cam., letters to Oscar Browning • NL Scot., corresp. incl. Sir Patrick Geddes • St John Cam., letters to Sir Joseph Larmor • U. Lpool L., letters to John Sampson

Likenesses M. Greiffenhagen, portrait, 1924, General Medical Council, London • E. Walker, photograph, 1924, repro. in MacAlister, *Sir Donald*, frontispiece • Bassano, photograph, repro. in *The Lancet* • O. Edis, photograph, NPG [*see illus.*] • G. Henry, portrait, U. Glas. • Kilpatrick, photograph, Wellcome L. • Montminy and Cie, photograph, Wellcome L. • G. Paulin, bust • Russell, photograph, repro. in *BMJ*

Wealth at death £61,575 13*s.* 6*d.*: probate, 22 May 1934, *CGPLA Eng. & Wales*

MacAlister, Sir (George) Ian (1878–1957), architectural administrator, secretary of the Royal Institute of British Architects, was born in Liverpool on 1 April 1878, the younger son of Sir John Young Walker MacAlister (*b.* 1856), a librarian and later secretary of the Royal Society of Medicine, and his wife, Elizabeth Batley. He was a nephew of Sir Donald MacAlister (1878–1957), chancellor of Glasgow University. He was educated at St Paul's School and at Merton College, Oxford, where he obtained second classes in honour moderations (1899) and *literae humaniores* (1901). In 1902–4 he was aide-de-camp and secretary to the earl of Dundonald, general officer commanding the Canadian army. After leaving Canada and before becoming secretary of the Royal Institute of British Architects in 1908, MacAlister was a freelance journalist, particularly interested in the empire and in naval and military history. In the First World War he was a lieutenant in the Royal Defence Corps.

MacAlister's long tenure of office until his retirement in 1943 saw remarkable changes in the Royal Institute of British Architects for which he was in a large measure responsible. Until the early part of the century the institute was very much a London society: its members in the provinces and overseas had little influence in its government. MacAlister was determined to alter this, and he encouraged and helped to organize the foundation of allied societies in the provinces and the Commonwealth.

He was particularly keen on ensuring closer links with the members in the dominions and the allied societies overseas. Similarly he was anxious to secure friendly relations with the American Institute of Architects, of which he was elected an honorary member in 1936.

The membership of the institute increased greatly during MacAlister's secretaryship; at the same time standards of qualification were raised. He worked enthusiastically for architectural education, especially in the expansion of the board of architectural education, which was responsible for maintaining standards and encouraging the growth of the recognized schools of architecture. Perhaps his greatest triumph was in securing the passing of the Architects Registration Acts of 1931 and 1938. He advised his council on the policy to be followed when the government decided that the institute would not be the registering authority, aiming to ensure that standards would not suffer. He was largely successful in achieving the aims and objectives which he and the council had so much at heart—the greater unity of the profession and the competence of its members.

In 1934, the centenary year of the institute and the year in which he was knighted, MacAlister organized its move from Conduit Street to new headquarters in Portland Place.

MacAlister is remembered as an attractive personality. He was good-looking with blue eyes, a high colour, and a winning smile which added charm to the warmth of his greeting. He was also a persuasive speaker with a scholarly choice of phrase. His letters—and he was a tireless writer of letters and memoranda on a wide variety of subjects—were models of clarity and concision, free of jargon and full of shrewd and witty comments. Shortly after his retirement he was knocked down by a motor cycle dispatch rider in the City and, after many months in hospital, remained a semi-invalid for the rest of his life. He moved from Hampstead to Tonbridge, where he enjoyed coaching some pupils from Tonbridge School and, when his health allowed, he was a regular spectator at the school cricket and rugby matches.

On 7 January 1909 MacAlister married Frances Dorothy (*b*. 1886/7), elder daughter of Robert Cooper Seaton, barrister, and later classical master at St Paul's School. They had four daughters and three sons, of whom the two elder lost their lives while serving with the Royal Air Force in the early part of the Second World War. MacAlister died at Tonbridge on 10 June 1957. His wife survived him.

C. D. Spragg, *rev.* Catherine Gordon

Sources *The Builder*, 192 (1957), 1080 • *Architect and Building News* (20 June 1957), 800 • *RIBA Journal*, 64 (1956–7), 388 • *Architects' Journal* (20 June 1957), 910 • *The Times* (11 June 1957) • m. cert. • *CGPLA Eng. & Wales* (1957)

Archives King's Lond., Liddell Hart C., corresp. with Sir B. H. Liddell Hart • RIBA BAL, corresp. with Harry Goodhart-Rendel • RIBA BAL, RIBA nomination MSS

Likenesses H. Knight, oils, *c*.1936, RIBA

Wealth at death £241 7*s*. 8*d*.: probate, 25 July 1957, *CGPLA Eng. & Wales*

MacAlister, Sir John Young Walker (1856–1925), librarian, was born on 10 May 1856 in Perth, the second of the surviving three sons and three daughters of Donald MacAlister (1825–1881), publisher's agent, and his wife, Euphemia Kennedy (*fl*. 1826–1905). Educated at Liverpool high school, MacAlister gave up his medical studies at Edinburgh University because of pulmonary tuberculosis, or phthisis, which dogged his life and work. However, though plans for a medical career were abandoned, this time was productive. MacAlister's medical knowledge became useful in his career as a librarian and it was at Edinburgh that he met and, on 7 January 1875, married Elizabeth (*b*. 1854/5), daughter of George Batley, an architect; they had two sons, Donald and Ian. According to the marriage certificate, MacAlister was then employed as a commercial traveller.

MacAlister's professional career began in 1877 with his appointment as sub-librarian at Liverpool Library. He became librarian of Leeds Library in 1880. A move to London in 1887 was significant for his career, for librarianship, and for medicine. He applied successfully for the new post of librarian at the Gladstone Library of the National Liberal Club. On arrival in London he found he had also been successful in another application for a much better-paid post: librarian to the Royal Medical and Chirurgical Society. The Gladstone Library released him to accept the latter position, but MacAlister nevertheless worked for six months on a voluntary basis to organize its library.

Once established at the Royal Medical and Chirurgical Society, MacAlister began to make an impression on the wider library community. At the Library Association's conference in 1887 he gave a much discussed paper on the nature of librarianship. Tapping into fears about the status of the emerging profession and the tendency of committees to award senior posts to those without experience of librarianship, the paper caused him to be proclaimed 'a leader' (Godbolt and Munford, 28), a voice for the profession when one was sorely needed. The same conference elected him its joint honorary secretary, and between 1890 and 1898 he occupied the post alone. As honorary secretary he was involved in many consequential projects. In 1889 MacAlister edited (he later also published) the new Library Association journal *The Library*, which debated practical library management as well as literary issues and made its editor well-known among librarians. The journal discussed the contentious subject of public libraries and open access, and in 1895 this led to MacAlister's being a co-defendant in a libel case brought successfully by the indicator-advocate Charles Goss. The determination to develop librarianship demonstrated in his role as editor also prompted MacAlister to offer prizes to librarianship students and to support the establishment of the first library school at University College, London, in 1919.

The early 1890s saw MacAlister's involvement with library legislation which culminated in the 1892 Public Libraries Act. The act regularized aspects of public library provision and provided a clear definition of the term 'library authority'. MacAlister performed one further outstanding service to librarianship by initiating plans for chartered status for the Library Association in 1895. After some difficulties the royal charter was granted in 1898, thus establishing a legal identity for the association. Rather belatedly MacAlister's work was acknowledged by the association with his election as vice-president, in 1905; he was also wartime president between 1915 and 1919.

MacAlister's powers of persuasion were also exercised on behalf of the medical community. His employer, the Royal Medical and Chirurgical Society, was one of many medical societies and MacAlister had long advocated amalgamation. These hopes were revived in 1905, with a plan backed first by Sir William Osler, regius professor of medicine at Oxford, and later by Sir William Church. A meeting at the Royal College of Physicians supported the idea of a single medical society, and MacAlister was instrumental in eventually establishing the Royal Society of Medicine in 1907 as a result of the amalgamation of fifteen societies.

Despite periodic ill health MacAlister injected a dose of élan into the library profession and the medical societies. He initiated and invigorated projects in both arenas and yet has attracted little historical attention. Occasionally his extensive social acquaintances, cultivated through membership of the Savage and other London men's clubs, were drawn upon to augment his professional activities, such as during the second international library conference in London in 1897. Although *Who's Who* cites 'sleeping' as his recreation, his other activities included establishing the University of London Press Ltd in 1910. During the First World War he was organizer for the Emergency Surgical Aid Corps for the Admiralty, the War Office, and the Metropolitan Police, and was honorary secretary of the surgical advisory committee to the War Office. He was knighted in 1919. MacAlister died from heart failure on 1 December 1925 at his home, 33 Finchley Road, London, a few months after resigning from the Royal Society of Medicine. His ashes were interred at Tarbert, Loch Fyne, Argyll, on 5 December. EVELYN KERSLAKE

Sources S. Godbolt and W. A. Munford, *The incomparable Mac: a biographical study of Sir John Young Walker MacAlister (1856–1925)* (1983) • S. Godbolt, 'Sir John Young Walker MacAlister (1856–1925): a biography', FLA diss., Library Association, 1975 • *WWW* • [J. D. Brown (?)], 'Workers in the library field: J. Y. W. MacAlister, F.S.A.', *Library World*, 1/10 (April 1899), 192–8 • *The Times* (3 Dec 1925) • *Library Association Record*, new ser., 4 (1926), 1–4 • W. A. Munford, *Who was who in British librarianship, 1800–1985* (1987) • L. S. Jast, 'The Pseudonyms', *Library Review*, 5/33 (1935–6), 8–14 • E. A. Savage, *A librarian's memories: portraits and reflections* (1952) • J. Minto, *A history of the public library movement in Great Britain and Ireland* (1932) • m. cert. • d. cert.

Archives Library Association, London | Royal Society of Medicine, London, corresp. files

Likenesses E. Kennington, oils, Royal Society of Medicine, London

Wealth at death £12,974 11s. 10d.: probate, 1926, *CGPLA Eng. & Wales*

McAlister [*née* McMackin], **Mary Agnes Josephine** (**1896–1976**), politician, was born in co. Donegal, Ireland, on 26 April 1896, the eldest daughter of Charles McMackin, publican, and his wife, Winifred Deeney. The family moved permanently to Glasgow in 1903 and settled in the Camlachie district, to the east of the city, and then in Tradeston, a dock area to the south of the River Clyde. She was educated at the Franciscan Convent of the Immaculate Conception, Charlotte Street, in Calton, a Roman Catholic girls' school with a strong academic reputation. After the First World War she embarked on a nursing career, training at Knightswood Hospital, which specialized in the treatment of tuberculosis. This professional commitment was carried into McAlister's political career, as throughout her life health and welfare were her chief campaigning concerns.

On 24 November 1927 she married (Joseph) Alexander McAlister (*b*. 1892/3), who was also of Irish origins. He ran a small window-cleaning company in Glasgow. From 1932 the couple settled in the city's Anderston district, where they reared four daughters. Anderston was then an industrial community of long standing, and contained the main dockland area to the north of the Clyde. Of mixed residential profile, its riverside tenement housing was among the most decayed and overcrowded in Glasgow, and the process of slum clearance had already commenced by the 1930s. It is uncertain when McAlister joined the Labour Party, but in the first post-war municipal election of 1945 she was elected to Glasgow corporation for the Anderston ward with a substantial majority. She subsequently took a high profile in civic affairs, becoming a bailie (magistrate) in 1947 and serving as convener of the health and welfare committee between 1952 and 1955. She also maintained a professional interest in health, serving with the Civil Nursing Reserve during the war and later as honorary president of the Glasgow branch of the Royal College of Nursing.

McAlister's local knowledge and municipal experience meant that she was a likely candidate for the Kelvingrove parliamentary constituency, although Labour's prospects of success were by no means good. Walter Elliot, one of Scotland's most distinguished Conservative and Unionist politicians, held the seat. Elliot's base of support was traditionally to the north of the constituency, in the Victorian terraces and substantial tenements of the Park district. Yet by the 1950s there were signs that Park was changing in character, to the electoral benefit of the Labour Party. It was becoming less residential, as properties were converted into commercial premises. There was also a growing proliferation of hotels, lodging-houses, and rented dwellings. At the same time Labour's working-class base was eroding, as slum clearance precipitated a sharp decline in Anderston's population. In the midst of Kelvingrove's unpredictable social transformation, Elliot died suddenly on 8 January 1958. His widow, Katharine Elliot, a leading Unionist activist in her own right, was chosen to stand in the by-election, set for 13 March 1958. McAlister was selected as her Labour opponent.

For all the perpetuation of the Elliot charisma, McAlister found herself in an unusual position of advantage. The Conservative government was unpopular, and only weeks previously had suffered a chastening by-election loss when Labour had won at Rochdale. Overwhelmingly, McAlister emphasized economic issues in the Kelvingrove campaign, especially Scotland's growing unemployment levels, pensions, and, above all, the 1957 Rent Act. The partial removal of rent controls was an attempt to encourage landlords to improve properties that had not been cost effective, but critics such as McAlister claimed that this was causing hardship and anxiety over the threat of eviction. The Rent Act had particular resonance for Kelvingrove's private tenants, and placed the Unionists uncomfortably on the defensive. The controversy also deflected attention away from damaging splits within Labour's ranks, notably over nuclear disarmament, even though McAlister unswervingly toed the party line on the issue. Her loyalty to Labour's leadership prompted the pro-Unionist press to dismiss her as the insubstantial product of 'machine politics' (*Glasgow Herald*, 14 March 1958), bolstered by the weight of an efficiently organized Labour campaign.

A novelty of the by-election, first pioneered in Rochdale, was the televised live 'forum', where all the candidates were given the opportunity to state their views. McAlister came across well in broadcasts, largely because the two minority candidates, standing for the Independent Labour Party and on an 'independent liberal home rule' platform, concentrated their attack on the Unionists. The focus of media attention may have helped McAlister to win Kelvingrove by a majority of 1360 votes, but the surprisingly low poll of 60 per cent indicated that there were many Unionist abstentions. Her parliamentary career thereafter was brief, and over the eighteen months that she served as MP her relatively few contributions to Commons debate were on her favoured topics of health and housing. By the time of the general election in 1959 the government's fortunes had revived, with an economic upturn and easing of the rents controversy. After a more subdued campaign in Kelvingrove, albeit marred by sectarian references to McAlister's religion, the new Unionist candidate regained the seat by a majority of 1101, although the turnout was high and Labour's vote increased.

While McAlister did not return to electoral politics after her Kelvingrove defeat, she continued to take an interest in welfare issues. She served as a member of the National Assistance Board from 1961 to 1966, and on the Supplementary Benefits Commission up to 1967. The following year, after her retirement from public life, she was awarded the CBE for services to health and welfare in Scotland. She died of a heart attack on 26 February 1976 in Gartnavel General Hospital, Glasgow, and was buried on 1 March at St Kentigern's cemetery, Lambhill. Small, slight, and sharp-featured, McAlister was a dedicated community and health campaigner, whose fleeting success in Kelvingrove obscured the fact that she was one of Glasgow's most prominent female politicians of the 1950s.

IRENE MAVER

Sources *Scottish Catholic Observer* (12 March 1976) · *WWW* · *WWBMP* · m. cert. · d. cert. · *Daily Record* (14 Feb 1958) · *Daily Record* (27 Feb 1958) · *Daily Record* (14 March 1958) · *Evening Times* (5 March 1958) · *Evening Times* (14 March 1958) · *Forward* (21 March 1958) · *Glasgow Herald* (4 March 1958) · *Glasgow Herald* (6 March 1958) · *Glasgow Herald* (10–14 March 1958) · *Manchester Guardian* (14 March 1958) · *The Scotsman* (26 Feb 1958) · *The Scotsman* (5 March 1958) · *The Scotsman* (8 March 1958) · *The Scotsman* (12–15 March 1958) · *The Scotsman* (27–8 March 1958) · *The Times* (14 March 1958) · *Glasgow Herald* (7 Nov 1945) · *Glasgow Herald* (9 Oct 1959) · *Glasgow Herald* (8 June 1968) · *Glasgow Herald* (1 March 1976) · *Glasgow Observer* (16 Oct 1959) · *Hansard 5C* (1959), 601.1549–51; 609.502–6 · D. Dow and M. Moss, *Glasgow's gain: the Anderston story* (1986) · J. Cunnison and J. B. S. Gilfillan, eds., *The third statistical account of Scotland: Glasgow* (1958) · T. Gallagher, *Glasgow, the uneasy peace: religious tension in modern Scotland* (1987) · NA Scot., SC 36/48/1378, pp. 346–9 · NA Scot., SC 36/51/586, p. 428

Likenesses photograph, repro. in *Glasgow Herald* · photograph, repro. in *Manchester Guardian* · photograph, repro. in *The Times* · photograph, repro. in *The Scotsman* · photograph, repro. in *The Scotsman* (26 Feb 1958) · photograph, repro. in *The Scotsman* (12 March 1958) · photograph, repro. in *The Scotsman* (14 March 1958) · photograph, repro. in *Manchester Guardian* (14 March 1958) · photograph, repro. in *Glasgow Herald* (4 March 1958) · photograph, repro. in *Glasgow Herald* (11 March 1958) · photograph, repro. in *Glasgow Herald* (14 March 1958) · photograph, repro. in *The Times* (14 March 1958)

Wealth at death £3457 2*s.* 3*d.*—divided estate between four daughters: NA Scot., SC 36/48/1378, pp. 346–9; will, NA Scot., SC 36/51/586, p. 428

Macalister, Robert Alexander Stewart (1870–1950), archaeologist, was born at 19 Leinster Road, Rathmines, Dublin, on 8 July 1870, the son of Alexander Macalister (1844–1919), professor of anatomy at Trinity College, Dublin, and then, from 1883, at Cambridge University, and his wife, Elizabeth (*d.* 1901), daughter of James Stewart of Perth. He was educated at Rathmines school, Dublin, and the Perse School, Cambridge, before entering St John's College, Cambridge, in 1889, graduating BA in 1892 having been ranked fourteenth junior optime in the mathematical tripos. He went on to study geology and developed an early interest in both European prehistory and the archaeology of Palestine. While engaged in geological research in the Sedgwick Museum of Geology at Cambridge early in his career, he taught the first courses in prehistoric archaeology at the university, before a faculty of anthropology and archaeology came into being. He was, in a real sense, one of the founders of archaeology at Cambridge.

Between 1900 and 1909 Macalister was active in the Near East. He was director of excavations for the Palestine Exploration Fund, excavating notably at Gezer, publishing *Excavations in Palestine* (2 vols., with the Revd F. J. Bliss, 1902) and *Bible Sidelights from the Mound of Gezer* (1906). He was to remain associated with the Palestine Exploration Fund for many years and was again director of excavations in 1923–4. His widely read *History of Civilization in Palestine* (1912) went into a second edition in 1921, while the three-volume *The Excavation of Gezer* (1912) established his reputation as an archaeologist of the first order. He also published *The Philistines: their History and Civilization* (1913) and *A Grammar of the Nuri Language* a year later.

Macalister's other interest was Celtic archaeology and epigraphy, in which he remained active throughout his long career. While working in Palestine, he was already studying early Irish literature, his three-volume *Studies in Irish Epigraphy* (1897–1907) establishing his credentials as a Celtic specialist. In 1909 he was appointed professor of Celtic archaeology at University College, Dublin, holding the chair until 1943. He rapidly became prominent in Irish scholarly circles, serving as chairman of the ancient monuments advisory board of the Irish Free State, and as president of the Royal Society of Antiquaries of Ireland (1925–8). He also served as president of the Royal Irish Academy (1926–31) and of the Cambrian Archaeological Association (1932–3).

In addition to his Irish and Near Eastern interests, Macalister maintained an active interest in European prehistory and taught courses in the subject at Dublin. He wrote a survey of the field for his students. *A Textbook of European Archaeology* (1921) served as a standard text in inter-war university classes on both sides of the Atlantic, until superseded by the works of Vere Gordon Childe. He also extended his skills of synthesis to Celtic and Irish archaeology, publishing *Ireland in Pre-Celtic Times* in 1921. Like his European volume, this became a standard text. His syntheses were broad-brush accounts of prehistoric societies that were still little known, even to the narrow coterie of European and Irish prehistorians of the day. As such, they formed an important corpus for a new generation of students who were to bring more scientific methods to bear on prehistory.

Celtic archaeology and history occupied much of Macalister's later career, although he still published on Palestine, notably on the Hill of Ophel in Jerusalem (1925). *A Century of Excavation in Palestine* (1925) summarized early fieldwork in the region and merited a second edition five years later. Increasingly, however, his attention shifted to Irish prehistory, and he duly wrote the *Archaeology of Ireland* (1925; 2nd edn, 1944), again a standard work. During the 1920s and 1930s Macalister published some distinguished contributions to Celtic studies, which focused both on epigraphy and on archaeology. *The Excavation of Uiseach* (1929, with R. L. Praeger) and *Tara: a Pagan Sanctuary of Ancient Ireland* (1931) are still regarded as significant monographs. Macalister was a prolific and versatile writer, writing *A History of Western Europe* for schools (1928), in which he melded archaeology and history into a single narrative. During his later years he spent much time working on basic records of Irish history, among them *The Book of the Taking of Ireland* (4 vols., 1938–41). *Corpus inscriptionum insularum Celticarum* (vol. 1, 1943) represented an attempt to edit all the extant texts of Celtic inscriptions in the British Isles, a project he never finished.

Macalister enjoyed a distinguished career and was honoured with LittD degrees from Cambridge, Dublin, and the University of Wales. Glasgow University awarded him an honorary degree of LLD. A renaissance scholar of a now vanished style, his academic interests were far wider and more eclectic than those of today's more specialized archaeologists. Macalister was also a talented musician who composed and published a suite in D minor for piano and violin in 1927. He was organist and choirmaster of Adelaide Road church in Dublin from 1920 to 1927. Upon retiring from the Dublin chair, he lived in Cambridge, and died at his home there, Barrymore, Lady Margaret Road, on 26 April 1950. He never married. BRIAN FAGAN

Sources *The Times* (27 April 1950) · *WW* (1949) · G. Clark, *Prehistory at Cambridge and beyond* (1989) · b. cert. · d. cert. · Venn, *Alum. Cant.*

Archives Palestine Exploration Fund, London, corresp., notebooks and papers relating to excavations in Palestine · Royal Anthropological Institute of Great Britain and Ireland, London, papers relating to Palestine | Bodl. Oxf., corresp. with J. L. Myres · U. Lpool L., letters to D. E. Yates and papers relating to *Secret languages of Liverpool*

Wealth at death £8589 0s. 10*d*.: probate, 8 June 1950, *CGPLA Eng. & Wales*

McAll, Robert Stephens (1792–1838), Congregational minister, the eldest son of the Revd Robert McAll and his wife, Jane, *née* Lea, was born at Plymouth on 4 August 1792 and received his earliest education in Gloucester and Cornwall. He was sent at the age of thirteen to the Congregational academy at Axminster, then to Hordle's academy at Harwich, and finally to Hoxton Academy in 1809. Here his liveliness, independence of spirit, and 'over-due propensity to disputation' led to his expulsion. He lived for eighteen months with Dr W. B. Collyer, and then studied medicine at Edinburgh University. His undergraduate career was outstanding and in his second year he was offered, but declined, the office of president of the Royal Medical Society. In 1814 he was appointed chaplain of the Undenominational Sunday School at Macclesfield, Cheshire, and in 1823 St George's Chapel, Sutton, Macclesfield, was built for him. He stayed there until 1827, when he accepted the pastorate of Mosley Street Independent Chapel, Manchester. McAll's preaching was of a florid, prolix nature, but gripped his hearers; sometimes his addresses lasted for nearly two hours. Contemporaries were fascinated by him: to Dr Raffles he was 'wonderful', to Robert Hall 'miraculous', and to Dr Collyer 'a seraphic spirit'. Aberdeen conferred on him an LLD. In Manchester he was a prominent force within the powerful evangelical leadership of the town. He served on the committee of the Naval and Military Bible Society, the Manchester Female Penitentiary, and the Manchester branch of the Anti-Slavery Society. He produced a number of printed sermons and poems, as well as *Discourses on Special Occasions*, published in 1840 with a memoir by Dr Ralph Wardlaw. Another collection, with a preface by 'T. H.', appeared in 1843. McAll died on 27 July 1838 at Swinton and was buried in Rochdale Road cemetery, Manchester. His only daughter predeceased him; his son, Dr R. W. McAll (1821–1893), promoted in 1872 the Independent Protestant Mission in Paris. C. W. SUTTON, *rev.* IAN SELLERS

Sources R. Wardlaw, 'Memoir', in R. S. McAll, *Discourses on special occasions* (1840) · T. Raffle and others, *Funeral addresses occasioned by the … death of … R. S. McAll* (1838) · *Evangelical Magazine and Missionary Chronicle*, new ser., 16 (1838), 435–7 · newspaper cuttings, Man. CL

Likenesses W. Ward, mezzotint, pubd 1837 (after J. Bostock), NPG · Woolnoth, stipple (after H. Bostock), NPG

McAllister, Anne Hutchison (1892–1983), speech therapist and teacher, the daughter of Robert Dempster McAllister, apothecary, and his wife, Anne Hutchison Macnee, was born at Main Street, Biggar, on 29 November 1892. She graduated MA (1917) and BEd (1924) from Glasgow University, and after teaching in a Glasgow school studied phonetics in order to apply its script to the teaching of reading. She became a lecturer in phonetics at Stow College, Glasgow, in 1919, and later at the city's teacher training college at Jordanhill. After being invited by Matthew White, a paediatric surgeon, to investigate and treat the speech problems of children with cleft palates which White had repaired, Anne McAllister in 1929 established a speech clinic attached to Glasgow's Sick Children's Hospital, with helpers recruited from among psychologists, phoneticians, and teachers. By the early 1930s a practical training course had been established, supplemented by lectures on psychology, phonetics, and the anatomy and physiology of the speech organs. The course led to the foundation of the Glasgow School of Speech Therapy in 1935, of which McAllister was principal until her retirement in 1964.

McAllister carried out research on the speech rhythms of over 21,000 Dunbartonshire schoolchildren and found that many were suffering from speech defects; she published her findings in *Clinical Studies in Speech Therapy* (1937). Between 1935 and 1940 she broadcast courses on speech training to Scottish schools and in 1938 she published *A Year's Course in Speech Training*; this was followed in 1941 by *The Primary Teacher's Guide to Speech Training*. During the Second World War McAllister was recruited by John Gaylor, neurologist at the Killearn Hospital, to assist in studying the speech and language problems of servicemen who had suffered head injuries. This led her to start studying neuroanatomy and neurology in order to help her to understand different types of aphasia and dysarthria.

During the course of her work McAllister had come into contact with many other speech therapists and in 1945, with the help of medical specialists and others, she played a key role in the establishment of the College of Speech Therapists, which organized the profession's training, examination, and registration. McAllister was one of the college's twelve founder fellows. She was appointed OBE in 1953.

McAllister was at heart a teacher. Her therapy was a form of remedial education and her interests extended from speech therapy to physical disabilities and learning difficulties. She became national president of the Special Schools Association in 1961. McAllister was extremely shrewd and could be trenchant in her criticism of the indolent and sloppy, but was kindly, firm, and resourceful with her patients. She never married and with regard to spinsterhood she said, 'Once you get over the disgrace, it's the best life!' She died at her home, 31 Rowallan Gardens, Glasgow, on 5 April 1983. CATHERINE E. RENFREW

Sources C. Renfrew, *British Journal of Disorders of Communication*, 18 (1983) • H. Wood, 'Anne McAllister, OBE', *College of Speech Therapists Bulletin*, 374 (1983), 2–3 • *CCI* (1983) • b. cert. • d. cert.

Wealth at death £74,846.77: confirmation, 4 July 1983, *CCI*

Macallum, Hamilton (1841–1896), landscape painter, was born at Kames, Argyll, on 21 May 1841, the second son of John Macallum JP, proprietor of the Kames gunpowder works, and his wife, Janet Hamilton. He was christened John Thomas but elected to use his mother's maiden name instead. As a boy he showed an interest in art, but this was opposed by his father who insisted on his entering a merchant's office in Glasgow, in preparation for a commercial career in India. Eventually, *c*.1864, with his father's permission, he travelled to London and entered the Royal Academy Schools. He first exhibited at the Royal Academy in 1869 and remained a regular exhibitor there and elsewhere in London for the rest of his life. Throughout his career, Hamilton Macallum divided his life between London and his various painting grounds. For some years he had a base at Loch Fyne, Argyll, with fellow painters of the sea Colin Hunter and William McTaggart. He also sailed extensively around the edges of the western highlands of Scotland in his yacht, visited Heligoland, toured south Italy and visited Capri in 1887, and also worked extensively in south Devon from his studio at Beer.

Macallum enjoyed working in full daylight either in the open air or in the glass studio he erected at his home on Haverstock Hill, Hampstead. Seascapes and other water- or light-filled landscapes were his favourite subjects, for example *Haymaking in the Highlands* (1878; Glasgow Art Gallery and Museum). He made a particular study of the effect of sunlight on water and achieved an extraordinary luminosity. However, his contemporaries criticized his colour as false or metallic, and at times his paintings suffered from weaknesses of composition and drawing and Macallum's overtly sentimental treatment of his figures. In 1896 Macallum exhibited *The Crofter's Team* (Tate collection) at the Royal Academy and it was acquired for the nation through the Chantrey bequest. Hamilton Macallum died suddenly of heart disease at Beer in Devon on 23 June 1896. He was survived by his widow, Euphemia Hill, daughter of John Stewart of Glasgow, and one son. She subsequently (13 March 1900) received a civil-list pension of £100 per annum in consideration of her husband's merits as an artist.

WALTER ARMSTRONG, *rev.* JOANNA SODEN

Sources P. J. M. McEwan, *Dictionary of Scottish art and architecture* (1994), 342 • J. L. Caw, *Scottish painting past and present, 1620–1908* (1908), 327–8 • Bryan, *Painters* (1903–5) • Graves, *RA exhibitors* • W. Armstrong, *Scottish painters* (1888), 77–8 • b. cert. • d. cert. • *CGPLA Eng. & Wales* (1896)

Wealth at death £1567: probate, 10 Aug 1896, *CGPLA Eng. & Wales*

McAlpine family (*per. c.*1870–1967), civil engineering contractors, came to prominence with **Sir Robert McAlpine**, first baronet (1847–1934). He was born on 13 February 1847 in Newarthill, Lanarkshire, the second of four children and elder son of Robert McAlpine (1816–1853), a colliery manager, and Ann Paterson (1823–*c*.1900), a weaver's daughter. Because of his father's early death Robert left the local parish school at the age of ten in order to contribute to the family income by working as a trapper in a local coalmine. In July 1858 his mother married Thomas Reid Malcolm; they had eight sons. By 1862 Robert was working at the coalface, but left two years later to become an apprentice bricklayer in Coltness. In 1868 he went into

Sir Robert McAlpine, first baronet (1847–1934), by H. Walter Barnett, *c.*1932

business as a jobbing brickbuilder, and on 12 June married Agnes Hepburn (*d.* 1888), the daughter of a master shoemaker from the Lanarkshire village of Forth. They had six sons and four daughters.

Robert McAlpine worked on small building and repair jobs in Lanarkshire until 1872, when he won his first major contract, to build 100 miners' cottages at Stonefield near Hamilton. The profits from the contract enabled him to expand the business; by 1877 he regularly employed over one hundred men (including, for a brief period, the blacklisted Lanarkshire miner and later Labour politician, James Keir Hardie), and his annual turnover exceeded £100,000. In 1875 he began to invest in property, building tenement houses and villas to let in Hamilton, Stonefield, and Motherwell. He leased three brickworks to provide him with the raw materials required for the business, but he also experimented with the use of concrete to make lintels and doorsteps, and by 1876 was building house walls of rubble concrete blocks. The use of concrete was rare in the Scottish building industry at this time, and Robert's activities earned him the nickname Concrete Bob.

Like most rising businessmen in central Lanarkshire, Robert's political sympathies lay with the Liberal Party. In 1878 he was elected to Hamilton town council to represent the Burnbank ward, in which he built most of his houses. He did not seek re-election in 1881, owing to a dramatic change in his personal fortunes. Robert's house-building ventures collapsed in 1880, in the midst of a severe economic recession. It became increasingly difficult to let his properties, and he was therefore unable to gather sufficient sums in rent to meet interest payments on loans and mortgages raised to acquire land and build houses, and which were secured on the property. With debts of about £90,000, and assets which were almost all in the form of unwanted property, he was forced to petition for the sequestration of his estate.

In January 1880, with financial ruin looming, Robert took his cashier, William Richmond, into partnership in his contracting business. By the terms of the agreement, Richmond became sole partner when Robert became bankrupt. This manoeuvre prevented the business from falling into the hands of Robert's creditors, and he was able to continue to win contracts, albeit nominally as an employee of the firm, until he was discharged from bankruptcy in August 1881. In the summer of the following year the firm won a contract worth over £300,000 to build what was believed to be the largest factory in Europe, for the Singer Manufacturing Company, at Kilbowie, Dunbartonshire. The successful progress of the contract enabled Robert, in January 1883, to dissolve the partnership with Richmond and regain sole ownership of his business.

In 1884 Robert won the contract to build the Barrhead to Ardrossan section of the Lanarkshire and Ayrshire Railway—his first major public works contract. As on previous contracts, he employed his two brothers-in-law, his brother William, and five of his half-brothers, the Malcolms, as site managers and foremen. He also brought his eldest sons, Robert junior and William, into the business, which became known as Robert McAlpine & Sons. **Sir Robert McAlpine**, second baronet (1868–1934), born at Forth, Lanarkshire, on 17 October 1868, studied mathematics and chemistry at the University of Glasgow in 1886–7; he continued into 1888, studying civil engineering, but left before the end of the academic year. Robert proved to have an aptitude for engineering and site management. His brother **William Hepburn McAlpine** (1871–1950), born on 31 October 1871 at Daffanbank, Merry Street, Motherwell, proved an efficient administrator in the firm's head office in Glasgow. In April 1893 Robert and William became their father's partners. Between 1884 and 1904, Robert McAlpine & Sons built nearly 150 miles of railway in Scotland and Ireland, pioneering the use of mass concrete in railway works. The firm's most famous contract was for the construction of the 40 mile Mallaig extension to the West Highland Railway in 1897–1901, which included the impressive 21 arch Glenfinnan Viaduct, and the Borrodale Viaduct, which featured the longest concrete bridge span (127 ft 6 in.) ever to have been built. McAlpine's third son, **Sir (Thomas) Malcolm McAlpine** (1877–1967), who was born on 19 June 1877 at Hamilton, Lanarkshire, began work for the firm on the Mallaig contract, but in 1898 was struck by flying debris while supervising blasting operations. He was rushed to Glasgow and his injuries attended to by the famous surgeon, Sir William Macewen. His place on the contract was taken by his younger brother, **Sir Alfred David McAlpine** (1881–1944), who was born at Bothwell Street, Hamilton, on 6 November 1881. Malcolm returned to work with the firm in 1899, and became a partner that year. Alfred became a partner in 1902. Granville McAlpine (1883–1928), Robert's youngest surviving son by his first marriage, became a partner in 1905 but left in 1910; he worked only periodically for the firm thereafter, as a salaried agent and, after 1924, as a junior partner.

Agnes McAlpine died in childbirth in April 1888. On 21 August of the following year, Robert married Florence Margaret (*d.* 1910), the daughter of William Palmer, a doctor of Roxburgh, Newtonhamilton; they had three children. On 22 December 1896 Robert McAlpine junior married Lillias Cooper Bishop (1876–1948), daughter of Thomas G. Bishop, the founder of Cooper & Co. They had one son and two daughters. William McAlpine married Lillias's younger sister, Margaret Donnison Bishop (*d.* 1970) on 6 April 1898; they had three sons and two daughters. Malcolm McAlpine married Maud, daughter of James Gibson Dees of Whitehaven, on 2 September 1903; the couple had three sons. Alfred McAlpine married Ethel May (*d.* 1961), daughter of James Williams, in 1907; they had one son, Alfred James (Jimmie) *McAlpine (1908–1991), and two daughters.

Robert McAlpine senior ceased to take charge of individual contracts after 1898, and after 1906 he delegated the task of making up tenders for major contracts to his sons and their staff. He continued to be involved in the firm, however, negotiating with clients and touring worksites. He became particularly interested in the concept of garden cities, and he ensured that many of the ideas of the movement were adopted in the development of the Holy City, a large tenement housing estate which the firm built during 1904–10 in Radnor Park, near the Singer factory in Kilbowie. The estate was devastated during a German bombing raid in 1941, and was acquired from McAlpines by Clydebank burgh council after the war.

In 1900 McAlpines won its first contract in England, for the construction of a graving dock at Hebburn, on the Tyne. In 1905 Malcolm McAlpine set up the Victoria Agency in London as part of a plan to win contracts for the firm in England, and by 1914 McAlpines had worked successfully on a number of reservoir and railway contracts south of the border. The volume of work in England increased dramatically during the First World War, when the firm was engaged to build army camps, munitions factories, and aerodromes.

Malcolm McAlpine moved his family home to Northwood in 1909, and in 1917 bought Fairmile Court in Cobham, Surrey. His father moved to Hertfordshire in 1912, and then to Knott Park, in Oxshott, Surrey, in 1916. The head office was transferred to London in 1916, and Robert junior (in 1917), and finally William (in 1920), settled in England shortly afterwards. In 1918 Alfred, who had lived in Wales since 1911, settled at Marchwiel Hall, near Wrexham in Wales.

Robert McAlpine's political sympathies switched from the Liberals to the Conservative Party at some time in the early 1900s, but he had no objection when, in April 1918, his daughter Roberta (*b.* 1898) married Richard Lloyd George, eldest son of the prime minister. In June that year McAlpine was created a baronet. He celebrated the honour by donating £15,000 to help set up the Institute of Agricultural Botany at Cambridge. In 1921 Malcolm McAlpine was made KBE for services rendered to the Ministry of Munitions—largely for his role in ensuring completion of the controversial motor transport depot at Slough in 1919. Alfred, who was chairman of the Wrexham division of the Conservative Party in 1921–8, became high sheriff of Denbighshire in 1923, and a life governor of Wrexham War Memorial Infirmary. He was knighted in 1932 in recognition of his public service.

During the 1920s McAlpines built many new council house estates, such as Bellingham for London county council and Wilbraham for Manchester corporation; won road contracts such as those for the construction of the Birmingham to Wolverhampton road and the reconstruction of a section of Watling Street; and was engaged by the crown agents for the colonies to build Takoradi harbour on the Gold Coast. The company's reputation as a pioneer of concrete construction techniques was instrumental in winning its most prestigious contract of the decade, for the construction of Wembley stadium and the British Empire Exhibition buildings. The chief architects, John Simpson and Maxwell Ayrton, and the consulting engineer Evan Owen Williams (1890–1969), were determined to use ferroconcrete extensively in the work, because of its relative cheapness as a building material, and in order to dispel a common belief that concrete was an ugly material which should be hidden away behind facing bricks, stone cladding, or some other disguise. Wembley stadium was begun in 1922 and completed in time to host the Football Association cup final on 28 April 1923. The massive palaces of industry and engineering, and the other exhibition buildings, were completed at the end of the year. Sir Robert McAlpine senior believed that the exhibition buildings offered final proof that a British dislike and suspicion of concrete construction was finally being overcome, and he proclaimed to a reporter from the *Glasgow Herald* that 'we have now definitely entered the concrete age' (12 Nov 1923).

McAlpines followed up its success at Wembley by building the critically acclaimed Black Cat factory in Camden and the Firestone Tyre and Rubber Company's factory at Brentford. In 1929 the firm began work on the Dorchester Hotel in London's Park Lane, and the hotel opened in 1931. McAlpines, which was a member of the syndicate that financed the venture, bought out the sole remaining partner in 1937 and the Dorchester was run by the McAlpine family, through Dorchester Hotel Ltd, until 1976.

In 1925 the McAlpines became involved in the sugar-beet industry, building a factory at Wissington for British Sugar Manufacturers and subsequently building others at Peterborough, Selby, Bardney, and Brigg. William McAlpine was convinced by optimistic forecasts about the industry's future, and the firm accepted shares and debenture stock in British Sugar and the Central Sugar, Lincolnshire Beet Sugar, Second Lincolnshire Beet Sugar, and Yorkshire Sugar companies, after building factories in partnership with the Dyer Company of Cleveland, Ohio.

After the First World War, the semi-retired Sir Robert continued in his role of elder statesman of the firm, touring sites and offering advice to his sons and interviews to the press, when they were sought. Robert junior, too, took a back seat during the 1920s, leaving William in charge of central financial and administrative matters. Sir Malcolm and Alfred, with an army of trusted managers, remained in charge of important sites and project management, although William was sometimes called upon to return to site management—most notably when he took charge of contracts, each worth over £2 million, for the enlargement of Tilbury docks, 1926–9, and Southampton docks, 1927–35. The three brothers shared the responsibility for the strategic direction of the business.

Sir Robert McAlpine died at his home, Knott Park, Oxshott, on 3 November 1934. Robert junior inherited his title, but died just thirteen days later, on 16 November, during a sea voyage en route for Cape Town. His son, (Alfred) Robert, inherited the baronetcy from his father, but he took no part in the affairs of the firm, and William was made chairman of McAlpines. William died on 20 February 1950 at his home, Badgemore House, Badgemore, Henley-on-Thames, and was succeeded at the head of the company by Sir Malcolm.

During the late 1920s and early 1930s McAlpines created a number of limited companies to complete large contracts, or take responsibility for contracts undertaken in a geographical area—Sir Robert McAlpine (London) Ltd, for example, was engaged on major dock construction and extension contracts in London during the late 1920s. McAlpine (Midland) was set up in 1930, and in 1934 the other partners agreed that the subsidiary should be run by Sir Alfred alone, as his own business. In 1940 Sir Alfred and his son Jimmie formed a new company, Sir Alfred McAlpine & Son, to acquire the business of McAlpine (Midland), thus ending their formal ties with McAlpines.

The McAlpines were a family of keen sportsmen. Sir Robert and Robert junior were enthusiastic sailors, and the latter regularly participated in Cowes week in his schooner *Suzanne*. The four eldest sons owned racehorses, and Sir Malcolm (who set up his own stable with Pat Hartigan in 1913) achieved the greatest successes in 1921, when Shaun Spadah won the Grand National, and in 1952, when Zabara won the Thousand Guineas at Newmarket. Sir Alfred was active in promoting county cricket in north Wales, serving as president of the North Wales Cricket Association, and he was also an enthusiastic supporter of both Manchester City and Wrexham football clubs. Sir Alfred died at Marchwiel Hall on 25 May 1944.

Sir Malcolm, who had served as chairman of the home ores committee during the First World War, and as chairman and then vice-president of the Federation of Civil Engineering Contractors during the 1930s, became chairman of the Committee of Engineers and Contractors and of the Opencast Coal Technical Advisory Organisation during the Second World War. He was most proud of his role in designing the concrete breakwaters built by McAlpines and other firms for the Mulberry harbours, deployed in France after D-day in 1944. McAlpines continued to rank as one of Britain's leading firms of contractors after 1945. William's and Sir Malcolm's sons, who had begun working for McAlpines in the 1920s and 1930s, played an increasingly active role in the firm's activities after the war, and ensured that it remained a family firm. Sir Malcolm died at North Foreland Hall, Cliff Road, Broadstairs, Kent, on 12 April 1967.

From the First World War, Sir Robert McAlpine & Sons was recognized as one of Britain's leading public works contractors. Significantly, the most famous British folksong celebrating the life of the itinerant construction site worker, or 'navvy', written during the early 1950s by Dominic Behan, was entitled 'McAlpine's Fusiliers'. The company, trading in the early twenty-first century as Sir Robert McAlpine, remains a leading building and civil engineering contractor in the UK. IAIN F. RUSSELL

Sources I. Russell, *Sir Robert McAlpine and sons: the early years* (1986) • I. Russell and G. Dixon, 'McAlpine, Sir Robert', *DSBB* • I. Russell, 'McAlpine, William', *DSBB* • T. Gray, *The road to success: Alfred McAlpine, 1935–85* (1987) • *Glasgow Herald* (12 Nov 1923) • *The Times* (13 Feb 1967) [Sir (Thomas) Malcolm McAlpine] • *Glasgow Herald* (13 April 1967) [Sir (Thomas) Malcolm McAlpine] • *Helensburgh and Gareloch Times* (21 Nov 1934) [Sir Robert McAlpine junior] • *The Times* (5 Nov 1934) [Sir Robert McAlpine senior]

Archives U. Glas., Archives and Business Records Centre, Sir Robert McAlpine & Sons archive

Likenesses H. W. Barnett, photograph, *c*.1932 (Sir Robert McAlpine), NPG [*see illus.*] • photographs, McAlpine archive • portrait (Sir Robert McAlpine junior), repro. in *The Bailie* (14 Sept 1904), 3

Wealth at death £205,794 9*s*. 7*d*.—Sir Robert McAlpine senior: probate, 4 Feb 1935, *CGPLA Eng. & Wales* • £373,413 10*s*. 8*d*.—Sir Robert Alpine junior: confirmation, 19 Feb 1935, *CCI* • £141,351 2*s*. 2*d*.—William Hepburn McAlpine: probate, 4 July 1951, *CGPLA Eng. & Wales* • £151,799—Sir (Thomas) Malcolm McAlpine: probate, 12 Dec 1967, *CGPLA Eng. & Wales* • £345,460 3*s*. 5*d*.—Sir Alfred David McAlpine: probate, 26 Oct 1944, *CGPLA Eng. & Wales*

McAlpine, Sir Alfred David (**1881–1944**). *See under* McAlpine family (*per. c*.1870–1967).

McAlpine, Alfred James [Jimmie] (**1908–1991**), contractor and businessman, was born on 15 June 1908 at Lindisfarne, Lundin Links, Fife, the eldest of three children of Sir Alfred David *McAlpine (1881–1944) [*see under* McAlpine family], contractor, and his wife, Ethel May Williams (1887–1961), daughter of James Williams of Aboyne, Aberdeen. His father was the fourth son of Sir Robert *McAlpine (1847–1934) [*see under* McAlpine family], the founder of Sir Robert McAlpine & Sons; Alfred David McAlpine was a partner in the firm. The family moved from Scotland in 1911 and took up residence in Glan Ceirw, Cerrigydrudion (Merioneth), after the birth of the second child, Gladys Gwendoline (1910–1978); McAlpine's father had been made partner in charge of the construction of the Alwen dam and reservoir in north Wales. The third child, Ethel Mary (1915–1989), was born at Glan Ceirw, and in 1918 the McAlpines moved again, to Marchwiel Hall, near Wrexham. Sir Alfred and Lady McAlpine eventually bought the property, and lived there until their deaths; it was then inherited by Ethel Mary, who lived there with her husband, Peter Henry Bell (1911–1977).

McAlpine was educated at Sandroyd preparatory school

(1919–22) in Cobham, Surrey, and then at Repton School (1922–6). There he was a member of Orchard House and a keen cricketer, playing for the first eleven in 1926. He then enrolled at Pembroke College, Cambridge, but did not graduate, and in 1928 he took up employment with Sir Robert McAlpines at its site on the Great West Road at Brentford, Middlesex—the Firestone Tyre and Rubber Co. Ltd. He was employed as a timekeeper. It was quite normal for the young members of the McAlpine family at that time, and subsequently, to take up very junior positions on company construction sites, which reflected the founder's view that potential partners needed the knowledge that site works gave them so that they had an improved understanding of their ultimate management roles within the company. McAlpine worked on a number of sites during the late 1920s and 1930s, when there were financial difficulties within the construction industry brought on by the depression. There was a general lack of work even though the company managed to secure contracts in the north-west and midlands, where his father was mostly involved, but in 1930 the company established a subsidiary company and opened offices in Manchester. McAlpine's father was made chairman of this company, which was styled Sir Robert McAlpine & Sons (Midlands) Ltd and secured work for, among others, Bowater and the Manchester Ship Canal Company, and its largest contract was the construction of the Birkenhead section of the Mersey Tunnel.

After the death of Sir Robert McAlpine in 1934 and the death of his eldest son in the same year, owing to the continued worldwide depression the partners decided to close their midland subsidiary and invited Sir Alfred (knighted in 1931) and his son, Jimmie, to move to the south-east, where it was considered there were better work opportunities. This offer was refused, for by now the McAlpine family were settled in north Wales and had become important members of the social, political, and sporting communities. Father and son therefore decided to take their chances with their subsidiary business and gave up all interests in the parent company. This severance took place in 1935, and in 1940 the 'Midlands' name was transferred back to the parent company and the new company of Sir Alfred McAlpine & Son was formed, with Jimmie McAlpine as vice-chairman. He became chairman on the death of his father in 1944 and held this position until retirement in 1985, when he became life president and when his surviving son, Robert James McAlpine, became chairman.

McAlpine married five times. He first married, on 24 June 1931, Peggy Barbara Sanders (1910/11–1986), daughter of John Ernest Sanders, an exporter. There were two sons: Robert James (*b.* 1932) and Alfred William (1935–1962). McAlpine's second marriage was to Mary Kinder Read (1916–1993), daughter of Frank Hargrave Read, manager of a shipping company, on 1 April 1940. There was one daughter, Valerie Anne (*b.* 1942). McAlpine married thirdly Rosemary Lavery (1913–1983), divorced wife of James Harold Lavery, and daughter of Charles Hugh Gregory-Hood, army officer, on 17 September 1951. Again there was one daughter, Sally Dorothy (*b.* 1952). McAlpine's fourth marriage, on 27 October 1959, was to Eleanor Margaret Wallace (*b.* 1932/3), daughter of John Nicholson Wallace, merchant. There were no children of this marriage, which, like its three predecessors, ended in divorce. McAlpine married finally, on 31 October 1979, Cynthia Greenaway (*b.* 1941), daughter of Harry Whitney, a master baker. McAlpine's residence from 1931 to 1939 was at Barnfelde, Burton Road, Rossett, near Wrexham; next he moved to Tickwood Hall, Much Wenlock, Shropshire. From 1958 until his death he lived at Gerwyn Hall, Marchwiel, near Wrexham.

McAlpine often remarked that it was the war that had put the company onto a firm financial footing and that he had been lucky to have taken over when he did. He was, however, also quick to acknowledge that the senior staff he took with him when the companies split were an important, if not the most important, factor in the successful growth of the company. McAlpine's lack of technical training and the fact that his father ran the business autocratically could easily have isolated him from his senior staff, but he performed his role as chairman with a light hand on the tiller, suiting his temperament and training. All but one of the managers who transferred to the new firm with McAlpine remained with him until their retirement, which provides some indication of the loyalty engendered by McAlpine and the family name.

Post-war construction—airfields, opencast coal production, power stations, industrial building—kept the company busy during the 1950s. At the end of the decade, motorways—which were to carry the company through until McAlpine's death—were just beginning to feature; the company built these first in the Belfast region, and then, in 1961, it constructed 26 miles of the M6 between Warrington and Preston, Lancashire. McAlpine had distinct reservations about tackling a job of this size and it is well recorded that he worried that this contract, almost equal in value to the annual turnover of the company at that time, was a risk which could prove, in the business sense, fatal. His early work experience during the depression had made him extremely cautious and throughout his forty years as chairman he insisted that the company maintain a high level of liquidity, having substantial cash reserves and minimum borrowings. Fortunately the job was successful and this gave McAlpine confidence to allow the company to develop further motorway teams. Indeed, within his lifetime McAlpine saw the company become the country's leading motorway builder. His love of large civil-engineering projects was never in doubt, as was his rather dismissive attitude to other sectors of the construction industry. He was fortunate that while he was chairman sufficient civil-engineering work became available for the company, keeping the business not only viable but also highly successful.

Since leaving school McAlpine had maintained his interest in all sports and in particular cricket. During the seasons of 1930 and 1931 he captained Denbighshire County Cricket Club, then a member of the Minor Counties League, and he also played for the Free Foresters. He was a lifelong supporter of the game, a member of the I Zingari and the Northern Nomads, and, most importantly, an enthusiastic sponsor of his local village team, Marchwiel, and of the many cricket festivals organized at Marchwiel Hall. He was a lover of the five-day game and liked nothing better than watching Geoff Boycott craft—albeit sometimes slowly—one of his many centuries. He expressed the view that one-day cricket was well and good but that 'proper cricket' was the game he most enjoyed. He was a keen golfer all his life, though he regarded golf as a mere game.

McAlpine was part of an industry which was well known for its characters and he was undoubtedly one of them, but throughout his working life he kept very much out of the industry limelight and was little known outside the company. He was a shy man who shunned publicity except within his own company, where he was known by everyone by the slightly feudal title of Mr Jimmie. It was part of the received wisdom within the company that he was able to pick the right person for the job, but indeed it is more likely that he had a complete trust in the abilities of his senior managers to engage competent staff. He did, however, have the skill to engender an almost childlike loyalty to him, as the clan leader, and to the company. This loyalty extended to his workforce, whom he insisted on talking to and encouraging every time he visited the sites, which he did regularly until a short time before his death. He was aware that this patriarchal role was one which he could do with ease and which was of substantial importance: his actions bound together his directors, staff, and workers in a way which was, even then, quite unusual for a chairman of a multi-million pound business. He was always relaxed and very much at ease with his staff and was genuinely pleased to share their leisure time. He talked to them in language they understood and in ways that made them feel valued, praising their qualities rather than criticizing their faults, and taking a broad and tolerant view of their mistakes.

McAlpine died of heart failure at Macelor Hospital, Wrexham, on 6 November 1991, and was buried later in the month in St Garmon's churchyard, Llanarmon Dyffryn Ceiriog, an area he loved and where for many years he had enjoyed shooting. His grave is alongside that of his younger son, who was killed in a car crash in 1962. He was survived by his fourth and fifth wives, and by three of his children. HOWARD J. STEVENS

Sources I. F. Russell, *Sir Robert McAlpine & Sons: the early years* (1988) • A. Gray, *The road to success: Alfred McAlpine, 1935–1985* (1987) • J. Slinn, 'McAlpine, Sir Alfred David', *DBB* • *The Times* (13 Nov 1991) • *The Independent* (4 Jan 1992) • b. cert. • m. certs. • d. cert. • private information (2004) • personal knowledge (2004)

Likenesses photograph, repro. in *The Times* • photograph, repro. in *The Independent*

Wealth at death £1,107,788: probate, 14 Feb 1992, *CGPLA Eng. & Wales*

McAlpine, (Archibald) Douglas (1890–1981), neurologist, was born in Garscadden, Glasgow, on 19 August 1890, the eldest of three children and only son of the marriage of Sir Robert *McAlpine, first baronet (1847–1934) [*see under* McAlpine family (*per. c.*1870–1967)], civil engineering contractor and founder of the firm of Sir Robert McAlpine & Sons, and his second wife, Florence Margaret Palmer (*d.* 1910). There were five sons and three daughters of his father's first marriage. He was educated in Edinburgh at Kirton College, at Cheltenham, and later at Glasgow University, where he qualified with distinction MB ChB in 1913. He joined the Royal Army Medical Corps in August 1914, was posted to the 13th Field Ambulance in France, and later became a regimental medical officer with the King's Own Scottish Borderers. In 1915 he joined a hospital ship and then transferred to the Royal Navy. He served in HMS *Falmouth* at the battle of Jutland and was aboard in August 1916 when she was sunk off Flamborough Head. Subsequently in Scapa Flow he boxed and played rugby for the squadron. He was mentioned in dispatches.

In March 1918 McAlpine moved to the RN sick quarters in Plymouth and treated nervous ailments with hypnosis. Soon after demobilization in November 1918 he decided on a career in neurology and worked on post-encephalitic Parkinsonism with J. G. Greenfield at the National Hospital, Queen Square, London. He became MRCP in 1921 (FRCP, 1932) and MD in 1923. After a short period spent with Lhermitte at the Salpetrière in Paris, he was appointed in February 1924 as physician for nervous diseases at the Middlesex Hospital and assistant physician and pathologist at Maida Vale.

At the Middlesex, McAlpine was an out-patient physician without beds, but in 1930 a neurological unit was created through a gift from his family firm, which made it possible to convert a derelict group of small rooms into two pleasant wards holding twenty-four patients; neurosurgical beds were added later. There he taught and practised with such enthusiasm and firm but gentle discipline that he inspired many of his juniors to practise neurology.

In the Second World War, McAlpine was successively adviser in neurology in the Middle East, in India command, and in south-east Asia. During the battle of El Alamein, when over 200 head-injured casualties were admitted to a mobile neurosurgical unit within a week, he assisted, even though a brigadier, in examining and treating them. He was again mentioned in dispatches.

McAlpine's major interest was the study of multiple sclerosis. The massive clinical data he collected were analysed in his book *Multiple Sclerosis* (1955). In 1951 he initiated the formation of the Multiple Sclerosis Society of Great Britain (finally established in 1953). He recruited the first medical panel and the medical advisory research committee, of which he was the first chairman. His enthusiasm initiated and nurtured research programmes and encouraged many others to work in the field. In 1969 he became the first recipient of the Charcot award of the International Federation of Multiple Sclerosis Societies.

McAlpine was sometimes thought to be shy and at times abrupt, but those who knew him well appreciated his kindness, generosity, and above all his empathy. He was an avid sportsman, an expert fly-fisherman, and also interested in shooting, golf, skiing, photography, and ornithology.

In 1917 McAlpine married Elizabeth (Meg; *d.* 1941), daughter of Isaac Sidebottom, textile merchant. They had a son and a daughter. He married, second, in 1945 Diana Christina Dunscombe (*d.* 1981), daughter of Bertram Plummer, a solicitor, of Leicester. They had one son. He died in his sleep at his home, Lovells Mill, Marnhull, Dorset, on 4 February 1981; his wife died a few days later.

John Walton, *rev.*

Sources Munk, *Roll* • *BMJ* (7 March 1981), 827 • personal knowledge (1990) • private information (1990) • *CGPLA Eng. & Wales* (1981)

Wealth at death £42,471: probate, 17 Aug 1981, *CGPLA Eng. & Wales*

McAlpine, (Robert) Edwin, Baron McAlpine of Moffat (1907–1990), engineer, was born on 23 April 1907 at Ravenscourt, Thorntonhall, near Glasgow, the second of three sons and fourth of five children of William Hepburn *McAlpine (1871–1950) [*see under* McAlpine family (*per.* *c.*1870–1967)], engineer, and his wife, Margaret, daughter of Thomas Bishop, founder of the grocery chain Cooper & Co. His father was the second son of Sir Robert ('Concrete Bob') *McAlpine (1847–1934) [*see under* McAlpine family (*per.* *c.*1870–1967)], founder of Sir Robert McAlpine & Sons, builders and public works contractors. Sir Robert's male grandchildren were expected to follow their fathers and join the family firm, and McAlpine, his elder brother, Tom, and younger brother, Malcolm, were no exception. McAlpine was educated at Oundle School, leaving at eighteen years of age in 1925 to work for Sir Robert McAlpine & Sons in its London office as a junior clerk. He became a partner in the firm in 1928, and took charge of a number of prestigious contracts. During the 1950s, however, he succeeded his uncle Sir Malcolm McAlpine as the partner primarily responsible for the firm's relations with its clients, and for winning new business.

Sir Robert McAlpine & Sons had built the fashionable Dorchester Hotel on Park Lane in 1929–31, and the family retained control through a private company, Development Securities Ltd, until the mid-1970s. McAlpine made the hotel a hub of the construction industry, hosting official events such as the dinner of the Federation of Civil Engineering Contractors; informal gatherings of fellow contractors (including the so-called 'Dorchester group') to review matters relating to the industry; and impressive lunches and dinners at which McAlpine entertained and discussed business with existing or prospective clients. Prominent politicians and civil servants were among those who attended industry functions at the Dorchester, and one rival contractor noted that McAlpine became 'the very personification of the construction industry in many people's eyes' (Morrell, 26). The last of the firm's famous Christmas lunches was held in 1978, but McAlpine continued to host important business and social functions at the Inter-Continental, one of many of London's most famous hotels which were built by Sir Robert McAlpine & Sons. In 1978 Sir Robert McAlpine & Sons formed Newarthill plc, a holding company which controlled a number of the family's companies, and which was set up largely to obtain a valuation for the businesses. The McAlpine family remained the controlling shareholders in Newarthill, and McAlpine served on the board. The company was taken back into the family shareholders' hands in 1990.

In 1955 Sir Robert McAlpine & Sons joined the Nuclear Power Plant Co., one of the British consortia formed by contractors, consulting engineers, and other specialist firms to tender for the design and construction of nuclear power stations. McAlpine was the partner chosen to represent and promote the firm's business in this potentially lucrative field, and he became deputy chairman of the Nuclear Power Plant Co. in 1955, and chairman four years later. In 1960, when the group joined with the AEI–John Thompson Nuclear Energy Co. to form the Nuclear Power Group, McAlpine became deputy chairman, and succeeded the chairman, Sir John Chandos, in 1966. On behalf of the Nuclear Power Plant Co. and then the Nuclear Power Group, Sir Robert McAlpine & Sons were civil engineering contractors for seven nuclear power stations, including those at Bradwell and Torness. In 1973 McAlpine became vice-chairman of British Nuclear Associates, a partner in the National Nuclear Corporation. As an advocate of European co-operation in the development of nuclear power, and a believer in superiority of the advanced gas-cooled reactor over the pressurized water reactor, he was an implacable opponent of Arnold Weinstock of GEC, the Conservative government's favoured candidate to lead the British nuclear industry. But McAlpine was also interested in the potential of alternative forms of energy to nuclear power, and Sir Robert McAlpine & Sons became involved in the development of wind farms and tidal barrages.

On 8 December 1930 McAlpine married Ella Mary Gardner Garnett (*d.* 1987), the daughter of James Gardner Garnett, schoolmaster, of North Vancouver, Canada. They set up home at Lyttle Hall, near Redhill, Surrey, and, when the house was requisitioned in 1941, moved to Benhams, Fawley Green, Henley-on-Thames, Oxfordshire. They had four children: Patricia (*b.* 1932), William (*b.* 1936), (Robert) Alistair (*b.* 1942), and David (*b.* 1946), and the boys joined the family firm. McAlpine was a staunch conservative but did not become active in party politics, whereas his second son, Alistair, was treasurer of the Conservative Party from 1975 to 1990 and deputy chairman from 1979 to 1983. McAlpine was knighted in 1963. In 1979 he was made a life peer, and took the title Baron McAlpine of Moffat. He inherited the family baronetcy in 1983, on the death of his elder brother, Tom. When Alistair took his place in the House of Lords in 1984, the two McAlpines were said to be the first father and son to sit there together each in his own right. Following Ella's death in 1987 McAlpine married her sister, Nancy Whitaker Hooper (*b.* 1906/7), herself a widow, on 15 January 1988.

McAlpine enjoyed the theatre and the company of theatre people, and was a member of the Garrick Club. He was an enthusiastic breeder of racehorses for both the flat and steeplechasing, and owned his own stud near his home in Henley-on-Thames. Although he won no classics he won the Racehorse Owners award in 1978 for the success of his two-year-old filly Devon Ditty. He was a member of the Jockey Club, and chairman of Sandown and of the British Racing School. One of his favourite forms of recreation was to gamble on horse races and, when abroad, at the casino. He was a discerning cigar smoker and he possessed many thousands, stored with cigar merchants around London. The *Annual Obituary* (1990) referred to McAlpine as 'one of nature's salesmen, instinctively sniffing out an opportunity, speedily turning the opportunity into a deal, but then, as the deal became a project, becoming impatient to move on to the next prospect' (*Annual Obituary*, 51). The obituarist captured something of McAlpine's restless energy and entrepreneurship, but not the widely noticed friendliness and charm of a man who genuinely loved meeting and entertaining people. He died at the Chiltern Hospital, Great Missenden, Buckinghamshire, on 7 January 1990, of gastrointestinal haemorrhage and cancer of the pancreas. He was succeeded as sixth baronet by his eldest son, William.

IAIN F. RUSSELL

Sources A. McAlpine, *Once a jolly bagman* (1997) • 'Lord McAlpine of Moffat, British industrialist', *Annual Obituary* (1990), 51–3 • I. F. Russell, *Sir Robert McAlpine & Sons: the early years* (1988) • D. Morrell, *Indictment: power and politics in the construction industry* (1987) • *The Times* (8 Jan 1990) • Burke, *Peerage* • *WWW, 1981–90* • m. cert. [Nancy Hooper] • d. cert.

Likenesses photograph, repro. in McAlpine, *Once a jolly bagman* • photograph, repro. in *The Times* • photographs, priv. coll.

Wealth at death £6,326,450: probate, 27 Feb 1990, *CGPLA Eng. & Wales*

Macalpine, John (*d.* 1557), Dominican friar and protestant reformer, also known as John Machabeus, was born in Scotland of well-to-do parents according to John Bale. After studying at the University of Cologne he was licensed as BTh by the Dominican order in 1525. At Cologne he had been a classmate of John McDowell and possibly Henry Balnaves. Macalpine served as prior of the Dominican convent at Perth from 1532 to 1534. By August in the latter year he had adopted protestant tenets, and was cited with others to appear at Holyrood by James Hay, bishop of Ross, acting as a commissioner for Archbishop James Beaton of St Andrews. Instead of complying Macalpine fled to England, prompting the tribunal to condemn him in his absence. In England Macalpine was befriended by Nicholas Shaxton, the evangelical bishop of Salisbury, whose chaplain he had become by May 1535, and who on 12 July 1538 collated him to the prebend of Bishopstone in Salisbury Cathedral. Macalpine married Agnes Matthewson (or Macheson), another Scottish exile, whose sister Elizabeth wed Miles Coverdale about 1540.

By 1540 Macalpine had left England for Saxony, where he matriculated at the University of Wittenberg and associated closely with Philip Melanchthon. With Luther presiding, Macalpine engaged in a scholastic disputation at Wittenberg in 1541. Inclined toward the humanists, Macalpine (who Latinized his own name as Machabeus) was widely read in patristics and scholastics as well as in canon law and the proceedings of church councils. After receiving his DTh degree at Wittenberg, in 1542 Macalpine became professor of theology at the University of Copenhagen, which he served as chancellor in 1544 and 1549, and also chaplain to King Christian III (*r.* 1534–59). At Copenhagen, Macalpine initiated the Melanchthonian tradition in Danish theology which reached its zenith in his younger contemporary Niels Hemmingsen. Macalpine also found time to assist Scottish students who came to Denmark, including James Erskine of Dun, whose tutor Richard Melville of Baldovie brought Erskine to Copenhagen to study with Macalpine. The latter maintained his contacts with Melanchthon, recommending one James (possibly James Balfour, who would soon join John Knox), to both Melanchthon and Alesius. After Sir David Lindsay visited Macalpine at Copenhagen in 1548, the latter reportedly provided funds for the publication of Lindsay's *Ane Dialog Betuix Experience and ane Courteour* (1553); the claim is made on the title-page, but is probably spurious. While visiting Denmark as an ambassador in the spring of 1550, the earl of Rothes took some documents to Macalpine. The same year saw the publication of a folio edition of the Bible in Danish, translated from Luther's German version, a project to which Macalpine contributed.

Although Macalpine was a Lutheran, his outlook toward Calvinists was eirenic. This was evident in 1553 when John a Lasco brought a group of Calvinist exiles to Denmark in search of refuge, only to be denied. Whereas Peder Palladius, superintendent of Zealand, opposed their request for asylum, Macalpine refused to follow suit. The following year Macalpine twice prevailed on Christian III to intervene with Mary Tudor on behalf of Coverdale, whom she finally permitted to go into exile in February 1555. Macalpine wrote a commentary on Deuteronomy, which was published posthumously, and a treatise, *De conjugio sacerdotum*, which Archbishop Matthew Parker subsequently bequeathed to Corpus Christi College, Cambridge. Following Macalpine's death in Copenhagen on 5 December 1557, his body was buried there, in Our Lady's Church, with Christian III in attendance at the funeral. Macalpine's son, Christian Machabaeus (1541–1598), a professor at Copenhagen from 1565 to 1567 and a friend of Hemmingsen, went on two embassies to Russia and was ennobled in 1580.

RICHARD L. GREAVES

Sources A. Ross, 'Some notes on the religious orders in pre-Reformation Scotland', *Essays on the Scottish Reformation, 1513–1625*, ed. D. McRoberts (1962), 185–244 • J. Spottiswood, *The history of the Church of Scotland*, ed. M. Napier and M. Russell, 1, Bannatyne Club, 93 (1850), 130–31 • *The acts and monuments of John Foxe*, new edn, ed. G. Townsend, 8 vols. (1843–9); facs. edn (1965), vol. 6, pp. 705–7 • T. L. Christensen, 'Scots in Denmark in the sixteenth century', *SHR*, 49 (1970), 125–45, esp. 137–8 • J. Durkan, 'The cultural background in sixteenth-century Scotland', *Essays on the Scottish Reformation, 1513–1625*, ed. D. McRoberts (1962), 274–331 • J. Durkan, 'Some local heretics', *Transactions of the Dumfriesshire and Galloway Natural History and Antiquarian Society*, 3rd ser., 36 (1959), 67–77 • M. A. F. B. Petersen, 'Dr Johannes Macchabeus: Scotland's contribution to the Reformation in Denmark', PhD diss., U. Edin., 1935 • G. Donaldson, *Scottish church history* (1985) • *The autobiography and diary of Mr James Melvill*, ed. R. Pitcairn, Wodrow Society (1842) •

T. McCrie, *Life of John Knox*, [another edn] (1898) • M. H. B. Sanderson, *Cardinal of Scotland: David Beaton, c.1494–1546* (1986) • J. Kirk, *Patterns of reform: continuity and change in the Reformation kirk* (1989)

McAlpine, Sir (Thomas) Malcolm (1877–1967). *See under* McAlpine family (*per. c.*1870–1967).

MacAlpine [McAlpine], **Neil** (1786–1867), lexicographer, was born in Kilchoman, island of Islay, the son of Dugald McAlpine, a house carpenter, and his wife, Betsy, *née* McAlpine. After attending university and theological college (probably in Edinburgh) he spent much of his life as a parochial schoolmaster at Kilmeny in Islay, having failed to secure a charge either before or after the Disruption of 1843. During the famine of 1846 he arranged for a boat-load of food to be brought to Islay, and thereby incurred the wrath of the landlord, John Ramsay; as a consequence he lost his teaching post, and had to survive on a salary of £5 a year as registrar of his parish, and latterly on parochial benefit. MacAlpine died, unmarried, on 14 December 1867 at Kilmeny. John F. Campbell, the Islay folklore collector, described him in 1860 as 'a clever eccentric man' (Mackechnie, 1.53).

MacAlpine is remembered for his Gaelic–English dictionary, entitled *The Argyleshire Pronouncing Gaelic Dictionary*, which was first published in Edinburgh in 1832 and was still in print in the 1970s. It was intended for use in schools (the Gaelic schools network, begun in 1811, had expanded greatly by the middle years of the century). It is an intelligent culling of existing works, such as Armstrong's 1825 dictionary and the *Highland Society Dictionary* (1828), with new input especially from Islay usage, but also from other sources, notably from Allan Ross, a Lewis colleague who worked for a time in Islay. MacAlpine quotes Skye, Lochaber, Harris, and Perthshire usages, and specific printed sources, gives imitated pronunciations throughout in a fairly consistent way, and provides a good range of examples of usage. An English–Gaelic section was compiled about 1845 by John Mackenzie, who was unduly critical of MacAlpine, but who justifiably remarks that MacAlpine's work 'has the merit of being the first to present a Dictionary divested of antiquated Irishisms' (preface to *Dictionary*, 1934 edn, x).

Derick S. Thomson

Sources J. Mackenzie, preface, in N. MacAlpine, *Pronouncing Gaelic dictionary*, new edn (1934) • J. Mackenzie, preface, in N. MacAlpine, *An English-Gaelic dictionary: being part second of the pronouncing Gaelic dictionary* (1853) • J. Mackechnie, ed., *Catalogue of Gaelic manuscripts in selected libraries in Great Britain and Ireland*, 1 (1973), 34, 53 • d. cert.

McAlpine, Sir Robert, first baronet (1847–1934). *See under* McAlpine family (*per. c.*1870–1967).

McAlpine, Sir Robert, second baronet (1868–1934). *See under* McAlpine family (*per. c.*1870–1967).

McAlpine, William Hepburn (1871–1950). *See under* McAlpine family (*per. c.*1870–1967).

PICTURE CREDITS

Liston, John (*c.*1776–1846)—Garrick Club / the art archive

Litchfield, Harriett (1777–1854)—Garrick Club / the art archive

Little, Alicia Ellen Neve (1845–1926)—© National Portrait Gallery, London

Little, Andrew George (1863–1945)—© National Portrait Gallery, London

Little, William John (1810–1894)—Wellcome Library, London

Littlejohn, Sir Henry Duncan (1826–1914)—Scottish National Portrait Gallery

Littleton, Edward, Baron Littleton (1589–1645)—© National Portrait Gallery, London

Littleton, Edward John, first Baron Hatherton (1791–1863)—© National Portrait Gallery, London

Liveing, George Downing (1827–1924)—private collection; photograph National Portrait Gallery, London

Liversidge, Archibald (1846–1927)—© National Portrait Gallery, London

Livingston, James, first earl of Callendar (*d.* 1674)—© National Portrait Gallery, London

Livingston, William (1723–1790)—Sons of the Revolution in the State of New York, Inc. / Fraunces Tavern ® Museum, New York City

Livingstone, Dame Adelaide Lord (*c.*1881–1970)—© Science & Society Picture Library; photograph National Portrait Gallery, London

Livingstone, Charles (1821–1873)—David Livingstone Centre, Blantyre / National Trust for Scotland

Livingstone, David (1813–1873)—Scottish National Portrait Gallery

Llewelyn, John Dillwyn (1810–1882)—by courtesy of the National Library of Wales

Lloyd, Albert Bushnell (1871–1946)—© National Portrait Gallery, London

Lloyd, Bartholomew (1772–1837)—by kind permission of the Board of Trinity College Dublin

Lloyd, Charles (1784–1829)—© National Portrait Gallery, London

Lloyd, George Ambrose, first Baron Lloyd (1879–1941)—© Cecil Beaton Archive, Sotheby's; collection National Portrait Gallery, London

Lloyd, Marie (1870–1922)—© National Portrait Gallery, London

Lloyd, Richard Dafydd Vivian Llewellyn (1906–1983)—© National Portrait Gallery, London

Lloyd, (John) Selwyn Brooke, Baron Selwyn-Lloyd (1904–1978)—© National Portrait Gallery, London

Lloyd, William (1627–1717)—His Grace the Archbishop of Canterbury / The Church Commissioners for England; photograph National Portrait Gallery, London

Llwyd, Humphrey (1527–1568)—by courtesy of the National Library of Wales

Llywelyn ab Iorwerth (*c.*1173–1240)—Master and Fellows of Corpus Christi College, Cambridge

Lo, Kenneth Hsiao Chien (1913–1995)—Getty Images – Graham Wood

Loch, Sir Charles Stewart (1849–1923)—Family Welfare Association; photograph National Portrait Gallery, London

Loch, Henry Brougham, first Baron Loch of Drylaw (1827–1900)—© National Portrait Gallery, London

Loch, James (1780–1855)—© National Portrait Gallery, London

Lock, (Graham) Anthony Richard [Tony] (1929–1995)—Getty Images – J. A. Hampton

Lock, Walter (1846–1933)—© National Portrait Gallery, London

Locke, John (1632–1704)—© National Portrait Gallery, London

Locke, Matthew (*c.*1622–1677)—Faculty of Music, University of Oxford

Lockey, Thomas (1602?–1679)—© Bodleian Library, University of Oxford

Lockhart, Sir George, of Carnwath, Lord Carnwath (*c.*1630–1689)—in the collection of the Faculty of Advocates; photograph courtesy the Scottish National Portrait Gallery

Lockhart, George, of Carnwath (1681?–1731)—in a private Scottish collection; photograph courtesy the Scottish National Portrait Gallery

Lockhart, Sir James, of Lee, Lord Lee (1588/1599–1674)—in a private Scottish collection; photograph courtesy the Scottish National Portrait Gallery

Lockhart, John Gibson (1794–1854)—Scottish National Portrait Gallery

Lockhart, John Macgregor Bruce (1914–1995)—© reserved / News International Newspapers Ltd

Lockhart, Sir Robert Hamilton Bruce (1887–1970)—Christie's Images Ltd. (2004)

Lockhart, William (1621?–1675)—Scottish National Portrait Gallery

Lockhart, Sir William Stephen Alexander (1841–1900)—© National Portrait Gallery, London

Lockwood, Sir Frank (1846–1897)—The Honourable Society of Lincoln's Inn. Photograph: Photographic Survey, Courtauld Institute of Art, London

Lockwood, Margaret Mary (1916–1990)—© Kenneth Hughes / National Portrait Gallery, London

Lockyer, Sir Joseph Norman (1836–1920)—© National Portrait Gallery, London

Lockyer, Nicholas (1611–1685)—© National Portrait Gallery, London

Loddiges, George (1786–1846)—Royal Horticultural Society, Lindley Library

Lodge, Sir Edmund (1756–1839)—© National Portrait Gallery, London

Lodge, Eleanor Constance (1869–1936)—© reserved; Queen Mary & Westfield College, University of London

Lodge, Sir Oliver Joseph (1851–1940)—© National Portrait Gallery, London

Lodge, Sir Richard (1855–1936)—© reserved / courtesy of the University of Edinburgh's Collections

Lofft, Capel (1751–1824)—© National Portrait Gallery, London

Loftie, William John (1839–1911)—© National Portrait Gallery, London

Loftus, Adam (1533/4–1605)—by kind permission of the Board of Trinity College Dublin

Loftus, Adam, first Viscount Loftus of Ely (1568–1643)—National Gallery of Ireland

Loftus, Lord Augustus William Frederick Spencer (1817–1904)—© National Portrait Gallery, London

Logan, James (1674–1751)—courtesy of the Historical Society of Pennsylvania Collection, Atwater Kent Museum of Philadelphia

Logan, Sir William Edmond (1798–1875)—© National Portrait Gallery, London

Logier, Johann Bernhard (1777–1846)—© National Portrait Gallery, London

Logue, Michael (1840–1924)—© National Portrait Gallery, London

Lolme, John Louis de (1741–1806)—© National Portrait Gallery, London

Lombard, Peter (*c.*1554–1625)—National Gallery of Ireland

Long, Charles, Baron Farnborough (1760–1838)—© National Portrait Gallery, London

Long, George (1800–1879)—© reserved; courtesy of Brighton College

Long, John St John (1798–1834)—© National Portrait Gallery, London

Long, Walter Hume, first Viscount Long (1854–1924)—© National Portrait Gallery, London

Longespée, William (I), third earl of Salisbury (*b.* in or before 1167, *d.* 1226)—© English Heritage. NMR

Longespée, Sir William (II) (*c.*1209–1250)—© English Heritage. NMR

Longhurst, Henry Carpenter (1909–1978)—Getty Images – Hulton Archive

Longley, Charles Thomas (1794–1868)—© National Portrait Gallery, London

Longstaff, Tom George (1875–1964)—Alpine Club Photo Library, London

Longworth, Maria Theresa (1833–1881)—© National Portrait Gallery, London

Lonsdale, (Lionel) Frederick (1881–1954)—© National Portrait Gallery, London

Lonsdale, John (1788–1867)—© National Portrait Gallery, London

Lonsdale, Dame Kathleen (1903–1971)—Getty Images – Charles Hewitt

Lopes, Sir Lopes Massey, third baronet (1818–1908)—© National Portrait Gallery, London

Lopez, Roderigo (*c.*1517–1594)—The British Library

Lopokova, Lydia Vasilievna (1892–1981)—© 1978, Estate of Duncan Grant

Loraine, Robert (1876–1935)—© National Portrait Gallery, London

Lord, Cyril (1911–1984)—© National Portrait Gallery, London

Lord, Percival Barton (1808–1840)—© National Portrait Gallery, London

Lord, Thomas (1755–1832)—Marylebone Cricket Club, London / Bridgeman Art Library

Lorimer, James (1818–1890)—Scottish National Portrait Gallery

Lorimer, Sir Robert Stodart (1864–1929)—Scottish National Portrait Gallery

Loring, Sir Neil (*c.*1315–1386)—The British Library

Lort, Michael (1724/5–1790)—© Fitzwilliam Museum, University of Cambridge

Losey, Joseph Walton (1909–1984)—© reserved; collection National Portrait Gallery, London

Losh, Sara (*bap.* 1786, *d.* 1853)—© National Portrait Gallery, London

Loss, Joshua Alexander [Joe] (1909–1990)—Getty Images – Hulton Archive

Loudon, Jane (1807–1858)—© reserved

Loudon, John Claudius (1783–1843)—by permission of the Linnean Society of London

Lough, Ernest Arthur (1911–2000)—© News International Newspapers Ltd

Loughlin, Dame Anne (1894–1979)—© National Portrait Gallery, London

Louis, Alfred Hyman (1829–1915)—© National Portrait Gallery, London

Louisa [Louisa Stuart], styled countess of Albany (1752–1824)—Galleria degli Uffizi, Florence, Italy / Bridgeman Art Library

Louise, Princess, duchess of Argyll (1848–1939)—© National Portrait Gallery, London

Love, Christopher (1618–1651)—© National Portrait Gallery, London

Love, Geoffrey (1917–1991)—© Derek Allen; collection National Portrait Gallery, London

Lovelace, John, third Baron Lovelace (*c.*1640–1693)—Wadham College, Oxford

Lovelace, Richard (1618–1657)—by permission of the Trustees of Dulwich Picture Gallery

Lovell, George William (1804–1878)—© National Portrait Gallery, London

Lovell, Sir Thomas (*c.*1449–1524)—© Dean and Chapter of Westminster

Lovelock, John Edward (1910–1949)—Alexander Turnbull Library, National Library of New Zealand, Te Puna Matauranga o Aotearoa (F-51288-1/2)

Lovett, William (1800–1877)—© National Portrait Gallery, London

Low, Sir David Alexander Cecil (1891–1963)—© Karsh / Camera Press; collection National Portrait Gallery, London

Lowe, Arthur (1915–1982)—Getty Images – Hulton Archive

Lowe, Sir Drury Curzon Drury- (1830–1908)—© National Portrait Gallery, London

Lowe, Elias Avery (1879–1969)—© Tate, London, 2004; collection The Metropolitan Museum of Art, Gift of Joseph Lowe, 1956. (65.232) All rights reserved, The Metropolitan Museum of Art

Lowe, Eveline Mary (1869–1956)—© reserved; collection Guildhall Art Gallery, Corporation of London

Lowe, Sir Hudson (1769–1844)—© National Portrait Gallery, London

Lowe, Robert, Viscount Sherbrooke (1811–1892)—© National Portrait Gallery, London

Lowin, John (*bap.* 1576, *d.* 1653)—Ashmolean Museum, Oxford

Lowndes, William (1652–1724)—© Crown copyright in photograph: UK Government Art Collection

Lowry, Laurence Stephen (1887–1976)—© National Portrait Gallery, London

Lowry, (Clarence) Malcolm (1909–1957)—Rare Books and Special Collections, University of British Columbia Library, Malcolm Lowry Collection

Lowry, Robert Lynd Erskine, Baron Lowry of Crossgar (1919–1999)—© reserved; News International Syndication; photograph National Portrait Gallery, London

Lowth, Robert (1710–1787)—© National Portrait Gallery, London

Lowther, Hugh Cecil, fifth earl of Lonsdale (1857–1944)—by courtesy of Felix Rosenstiel's Widow & Son Ltd., London, on behalf of the Estate of Sir John Lavery; collection National Portrait Gallery, London

Lowther, Sir James, fourth baronet (*bap.* 1673, *d.* 1755)—The Lord Cavendish of Furness, D.L. Photograph: Photographic Survey, Courtauld Institute of Art, London

Lowther, James, earl of Lonsdale (1736–1802)—private collection

Lowther, James (1840–1904)—© National Portrait Gallery, London

Lowther, James William, first Viscount Ullswater (1855–1949)—The de László Foundation; Witt Library, Courtauld Institute of Art, London

Lowther, Sir John, of Lowther, first baronet (1606–1675)—private collection

Lowther, Sir John, second baronet (*bap.* 1642, *d.* 1706)—© National Portrait Gallery, London

Lowther, John, first Viscount Lonsdale (1655–1700)—reproduced by permission of the Marquess of Bath, Longleat House, Warminster, Wiltshire, Great Britain

Loyd, Samuel Jones, Baron Overstone (1796–1883)—The Loyd Collection. Photograph: Photographic Survey, Courtauld Institute of Art, London

Luard, (David) Evan Trant (1926–1991)—© National Portrait Gallery, London

Luard, Henry Richards (1825–1891)—The Master and Fellows, Trinity College, Cambridge

Lubbock, John, first Baron Avebury (1834–1913)—© National Portrait Gallery, London

Lubbock, Sir John William, third baronet (1803–1865)—University of London, Senate House

Lubetkin, Berthold Romanovich (1901–1990)—made available by courtesy of John Allan

Lucan, Arthur (1885–1954)—photograph with permission of Lucan and McShane family for OMRALAS (Old Mother Riley, Arthur Lucan Appreciation Society)

Lucas, Sir Charles (1612/13–1648)—private collection

Lucas, Charles (1713–1771)—© National Portrait Gallery, London

Lucas, Sir Charles Prestwood (1853–1931)—© National Portrait Gallery, London

Lucas, David (1802–1881)—© National Portrait Gallery, London

Lucas, Edward Verrall (1868–1938)—© National Portrait Gallery, London

Lucas, John (1807–1874)—© National Portrait Gallery, London

Luce, Sir (John) David (1906–1971)—© National Portrait Gallery, London

Lucy, Charles (1814–1873)—© National Portrait Gallery, London

Lucy, Godfrey de (*d.* 1204)—The British Library

Lucy, Sir Henry William (1843–1924)—© National Portrait Gallery, London

Ludlow, Edmund (1616/17–1692)—Yale Center for British Art, Paul Mellon Collection

Ludlow, John Malcolm Forbes (1821–1911)—© National Portrait Gallery, London

Lugard, Dame Flora Louise, Lady Lugard (1852–1929)—© National Portrait Gallery, London

Lugard, Frederick John Dealtry, Baron Lugard (1858–1945)—© National Portrait Gallery, London

Lumisden, Andrew (1720–1801)—Scottish National Portrait Gallery

Lumley, Benjamin (1811/12–1875)—© National Portrait Gallery, London

Lumley, John, first Baron Lumley (*c.*1533–1609)—© National Portrait Gallery, London

Lumley, Lawrence Roger, eleventh earl of Scarbrough (1896–1969)—© National Portrait Gallery, London

Lumsden, Sir James, of Innergellie (*fl.* 1629–1651)—in a private collection; photograph courtesy the Scottish National Portrait Gallery

Lumsden, Dame Louisa Innes (1840–1935)—© National Portrait Gallery, London

Lunardi, Vincenzo (1759–1806)—© National Portrait Gallery, London

Lunn, Sir Henry Simpson (1859–1939)—© National Portrait Gallery, London

Lunsford, Sir Thomas (*b. c.*1610, *d.* in or before 1656)—by permission of Lord Braybrooke / Photograph © English Heritage Photo Library

Lupton, Thomas Goff (1791–1873)—© National Portrait Gallery, London

Lushington, Stephen (1782–1873)—© National Portrait Gallery, London

Lustgarten, Edgar Marcus (1907–1978)—© National Portrait Gallery, London

Luthuli, Albert John (1898?–1967)—© reserved; private collection; photograph National Portrait Gallery, London

Luttrell, Sir Geoffrey (1276–1345)—The British Library

Lutyens, Sir Edwin Landseer (1869–1944)—Art Workers' Guild

Lutyens, (Agnes) Elisabeth (1906–1983)—© John Vere Brown; collection National Portrait Gallery, London

Lutyens, Lady Emily (1874–1964)—© Mary Evans Picture Library

Luxmoore, John (1756–1830)—by kind permission of St Asaph Cathedral library

Lyall, Sir Alfred Comyn (1835–1911)—© National Portrait Gallery, London

Lyall, Robert (1789–1831)—© National Portrait Gallery, London

Lydgate, John (*c.*1370–1449/50?)—© The Bodleian Library, University of Oxford

Lye, Edward (*bap.* 1694, *d.* 1767)—© Bodleian Library, University of Oxford

Lyell, Sir Charles, first baronet (1797–1875)—© National Portrait Gallery, London

Lygon, Frederick, sixth Earl Beauchamp (1830–1891)—© National Portrait Gallery, London

Lygon, William, seventh Earl Beauchamp (1872–1938)—© National Portrait Gallery, London

Lynch, Benjamin (1913–1946)—Getty Images – Hulton Archive

Lynott, Philip Parris (1949–1986)—Getty Images – Hulton Archive

Lyon, Alexander Ward (1931–1993)—© News International Newspapers Ltd

Lyon, George Francis (1795–1832)—Christie's Images Ltd. (2004)

Lyon, Hart (1721–1800)—Ashmolean Museum, Oxford

Lyon, Patrick, third earl of Strathmore and Kinghorne (1643?–1695)—in the collection of the Strathmore Estates; photograph courtesy the Scottish National Portrait Gallery

Lyons, Edmund, first Baron Lyons (1790–1858)—© National Portrait Gallery, London

Lyons, Joseph Aloysius (1879–1939)—© National Portrait Gallery, London

Lyons, (Francis Stewart) Leland (1923–1983)—© reserved; by kind permission of the Board of Trinity College Dublin

Lyons, Richard Bickerton Pemell, Earl Lyons (1817–1887)—© National Portrait Gallery, London

Lyons, Sir William (1901–1985)—© National Portrait Gallery, London

Lyster, Thomas William (1855–1922)—courtesy of the National Library of Ireland

Lyte, Henry Francis (1793–1847)—© Copyright The British Museum

Lyttelton, Alfred (1857–1913)—© National Portrait Gallery, London

Lyttelton, Sir Charles, third baronet (1629–1716)—by kind permission of the Viscount Cobham, Hagley Hall. Photograph: Photographic Survey, Courtauld Institute of Art, London

Lyttelton, Charles (1714–1768)—© National Portrait Gallery, London

Lyttelton, George, first Baron Lyttelton (1709–1773)—by kind permission of the Viscount Cobham, Hagley Hall. Photograph: Photographic Survey, Courtauld Institute of Art, London

Lyttelton, George William, fourth Baron Lyttelton and fourth Baron Westcote (1817–1876)—© National Portrait Gallery, London

Lyttelton, Sir Neville Gerald (1845–1931)—V&A Images, The Victoria and Albert Museum

Lyttelton, Oliver, first Viscount Chandos (1893–1972)—© National Portrait Gallery, London

Lyttelton, Sarah, Lady Lyttelton (1787–1870)—© National Portrait Gallery, London

Lyttelton, William Henry, third Baron Lyttelton and third Baron Westcote (1782–1837)—© National Portrait Gallery, London

Lytton, Lady Constance Georgina Bulwer- (1869–1923)—© National Portrait Gallery, London

Lytton, Edward George Earle Lytton Bulwer, first Baron Lytton (1803–1873)—© National Portrait Gallery, London

Lytton, Edward Robert Bulwer-, first earl of Lytton (1831–1891)—© National Portrait Gallery, London

Lytton, Neville Stephen Bulwer-, third earl of Lytton (1879–1951)—Russell-Cotes Art Gallery and Museum, Bournemouth, England

Lytton, Rosina Anne Doyle Bulwer, Lady Lytton (1802–1882)—© National Portrait Gallery, London

Mabbott, John David (1898–1988)—© National Portrait Gallery, London

McAdam, John Loudon (1756–1836)—© National Portrait Gallery, London

MacAlister, Sir Donald, first baronet (1854–1934)—© National Portrait Gallery, London

McAlpine family (*per. c.*1870–1967) [Sir Robert McAlpine, first baronet (1847–1934)]—© National Portrait Gallery, London